A Tapestry of Thoughts

A TAPESTRY OF THOUGHTS

The National Library of Poetry

Nicole Walstrum, Editor

A Tapestry of Thoughts

Copyright © 1996 by The National Library of Poetry
as a compilation.

Rights to individual poems reside with the artists themselves.
This collection of poetry contains works submitted to the Publisher by individual authors who confirm that the work is their original creation. Based upon the authors' confirmations and to the Publisher's actual knowledge, these poems were written by the listed poets. The National Library of Poetry does not guarantee or assume responsibility for verifying the authorship of each work.

All rights reserved under International and Pan-American copyright conventions. No part of this book may be reproduced, stored in a retrieval system or transmitted in any form, electronic, mechanical, or by other means, without written permission of the publisher. Address all inquiries to Jeffrey Franz, Publisher, P.O. Box 704, Owings Mills, MD 21117.

Library of Congress
Cataloging in Publication Data

ISBN 1-57553-064-3

Manufactured in The United States of America by
Watermark Press
One Poetry Plaza
11419 Cronridge Dr., Suite 10
Owings Mills, MD 21117

Editor's Note

This anthology contains a wealth of poetry describing the richness of life in its many forms. Through many of these poems, readers experience events possibly never encountered in their own lives. This quality illustrates writing's wonderful capacity for entertaining, sharing, and making us more compassionate toward others. Yet some writers also use poetry's vicarious nature to empower the reader. In such cases, poetry becomes a tool indicating ways to live one's own life more fully.

"The Lady of Shalott," a classic poem by Alfred, Lord Tennyson (1809-92), exemplifies this application. This verse tells the tale of an artist who lives second-hand, through a mirror's images, and then intricately weaves these life experiences into a beautiful tapestry. However, it is evident that the Lady of Shalott is fearful of abandoning her art to explore the outside world herself. This fear manifests itself in a fabricated curse, which she believes will strike if she leaves her loom or even looks directly out the window. Initially, the Lady of Shalott's art is fulfilling enough for her, as shown in lines 37-45:

> *There she weaves by night and day*
> *A magic web with colours gay.*
> *She has heard a whisper say,*
> *A curse is on her if she stay*
>   *To look down to Camelot.*
> *She knows not what the curse may be,*
> *And so she weaveth steadily,*
> *And little other care hath she,*
>   *The Lady of Shalott.*

Yet later in the poem, the mirror's intriguing reflections lead to the Lady's growing awareness of her stifling condition: "'I am half sick of shadows,'" she declares in line 71. Once prompted to examine her limited life, the Lady ventures outside but soon dies, fearing her curse's consequences.

Tennyson's poem aptly portrays the predicament of many people in any society. Loneliness, anger, and fear of failure or of being hurt lead many people to fixate on certain aspects of their lives. "The Lady of Shalott" illustrates how even art, with its liberating power to describe and share, can be constricting. Poetry, in particular, with its potent style, can be overwhelming. Poets may be caught within their art, unable to reach beyond its boundaries.

Not unlike the Lady of Shalott, Emily Dickinson often wrote about nature and the world yet actually spent little time beyond the confines of her home. Kenneth H. Brown's "Emily Dickinson" (p. 127) discusses the life of that famous recluse poet, immediately noting the artist's limited life:

> *Long before your body died*
>   *you locked it in the garden and the house.*
> *Made your announcement in poems to yourself.*

Here, Brown addresses the conception that Dickinson did not experience much life first-hand, nor did she share much of her poetry with others. Had she done so, perhaps her life would appear less closed to the outside world. Nevertheless, Kenneth Brown's poem is a sensitive painting of Dickinson's existence; there is a sense of sadness rather than one of condemnation toward the manner in which she chose to live her life. This twinge of sadness is most evident by the poem's concluding assessment that, although Dickinson has endured due to her celebrated poetry, the art itself could not compensate for the perceived lack of full living she did while alive:

> *It [death] did not stop your mouthful of poems*
> *nor the moss that crept on the stone*
> *toward your engravèd name.*

Joe Dowell's impressive "For The Love Of Nature" (p. 258) also addresses the risks of remaining tightly wound in poetry, dwelling on its specifics rather than experiencing what verse represents. Dowell's work beseeches the reader to value nature for its own worth, not for what can be written about it. He immediately states, "For the love of Nature, leave your words behind. / You insult the earth by thinking it looks better lined." Nevertheless, countless writers over time have attempted to capture nature's majesty, working and reworking their poetry to make it perfect. Dowell warns that such activity is a precious waste of time; Nature is never capturable: "Not even the verses bequeathed us by Blake / Are fair to the wonder of stars on a lake."

Dowell also cautions that for too long we have tried to make nature fit into a category of human-devised beauty, thus detracting from its truly sublime character. This point is evident when he says, "Look at the world before human word / Inked it and left it linguistically blurred." Dowell's skillful use of rhythm and a constrained rhyme scheme give his poem a certain momentum which supports the sense of urgency imparted by such words.

Yet Dowell's talent as a poet reaches beyond his technical skill. He confesses his awareness of what is beyond his own writing. While intent on disclosing his message to the reader, he hints that he is conscious of the possible downfall in his own poem: readers may become caught up in his own invariably limited descriptions of nature. This awareness is manifest in the following passage: "For the love of Nature, look away from these words. / Your eyes must be free to soar off with the birds."

Nature is also prominent in William Neville Chemnick's "The Misogynist's Wife" (p. 24). The author uses nature to address a familiar topic in a fresh manner -- the suppression of women. More specifically, this poem adroitly examines the decline of ancient female goddess religions during the rise of today's prominent religions.

The poem's title alone alerts the reader of woman's overall oppressed condition, as a misogynist is one who hates women. Its first stanza adeptly continues this tone:

> *Pariah, asleep among the reeds*
> *The wind has learned your lullaby*
> *You speak the language of the trees*
> *The seed has been planted in the garden of Gaia . . . .*

Gaia (or Gaea) was an earth-goddess in ancient mythology who was considered the mother of everything and an advisor to both gods and humans. A goddess of such power gave a certain status to women, and invariably connected woman's power to nature. This notion is embodied by the fact that, for centuries, women often were the village healers, with a knowledge of herbs and plants at their disposal. Nevertheless, all of the power imparted to women in the above lines is counteracted by the initial reference to woman as "Pariah," or detested outcast.

When did this oppressive attitude appear? The speaker maintains that the growth of traditionally male-dominated religions such as Christianity eventually overshadowed the goddess religions. He states: "Your mythology, forgotten by the serpent's daughter / Disappears like the mist off the holy lake." The serpent's daughter refers to Eve, whose actions in the Garden of Eden set the precedent for a view of woman as inherently weak and sinful. Over time, then, the nature-related authority of many women became suspect; it seemed that power in the hands of an innately evil being could only lead to more evil. This view erupted into witch hunts, whose first victims often were the once-revered healers. Using the image of female goddess religions as a dying flower and that of woman as its petals, the speaker describes the act of burning alledged witches as, "Petals broken from a dying flower / Burned at the stake for their seductive color." Yet witch hunts could not eliminate woman's potential, as after the burnings "only ashes smell of roses." Therefore, the speaker predicts a resurrection of woman's power.

Of course, this optimistic outcome cannot be without first eradicating the harmful view of woman as being intrinsically wicked. First, a conscious effort to establish true equality is necessary. Then, armed with nature's power, woman has the ability to discard and surpass the long-living conception of evil woman:

> *Where there is light there is ebony*
> *A perfect balance, tipped by the stars*
> *A mystic's potion of hemlock and rose hips*
> *Will stop the curse of a hated woman, doomed to live forever* . . . .

Rose hips, the fleshy part of a rose, have a history of medicinal use. One property rose hips are believed to possess is a revitalizing power. This information suggests that woman, previously referred to as rose petals, has the power to rise from her repressed position. Furthermore, the addition of rose hips to hemlock, a poison, does indeed imply the work of a "mystic's potion": if rose hips could restore life taken by hemlock, perhaps woman's strength can be restored after this poisoning period of repression. In addition, it is important to remember that hemlock poison comes from a tree of the same name, and woman can "speak the language of the trees." Is it not possible, then, that woman knows the poison's antidote and simply needs to apply it? The beautiful, enchanting language in "The Misogynist's Wife" delivers a solid message of hope to women: by being their true, natural selves, they too have the power to "tip the balance" in their favor.

Other poems in *A Tapestry of Thoughts* deftly exemplify psychological ways in which people stifle themselves. For example, Brett P. Michael's untitled piece (p. 472) examines the constraints that guilt can place on one's life. The speaker in this intense poem has committed an immense transgression toward his partner. The words "searing red hands / that have traced another's sin" imply the act in question is adultery. The sin, however, is immaterial in terms of the persona's grave sense of shame, implied heavily throughout this work by the author's superb use of numerous religious images: "The church of guilt chants / Its hymn for the beggar son"; "the pit bull of denial / eats me for its last supper"; and "the satiated savior / spits at my life." That final image particularly shows the depth of the speaker's guilt; he feels unworthy of even the ultimate forgiver's forgiveness.

While wrapped in his shame, the speaker makes a feeble attempt to reach beyond his world of guilt. He tries to make contact with the reader when he pleads, "Join me in my self-denigration." Unfortunately, it is obvious that the speaker has limited ability to forge this connection; not only does the character say "join me" rather than "help me," he also directly returns his attention to his "self-denigration." Obviously, his sense of sin no longer allows him to relate to others.

Although self-absorbed with guilt, the speaker does display a degree of awareness of his partner. It seems that the speaker previously has committed other sinful acts toward his companion but none as devastating. He laments that this act is the last straw for his partner, finally surpassing the limits of her forgiving nature:

>*I linger in the sieve of forgiveness*
>*too substantial to pass*
>*between its generous perforations*
>*lying with the other filth*
>*in the gutter of your malaise . . . .*

Perhaps the essence of this poem is best presented in an all-encompassing religious image used to depict the speaker's behavior: "hedonism my heaven and hell." These words aptly describe the persona's selfishness yet they also portray his sense of despair, as he feels he has no choices left. This hopelessness, in turn, causes a feeling of empathy to develop in the reader. Thus, while this poem stresses the risks of being consumed with guilt, the sense of empathy it imparts also warns the reader how easy it is to become similarly self-absorbed.

Robert DeRose's highly original "The Lonely Bookkeeper" (p. 3) remarkably depicts the possible outcome of being too wrapped up in one's occupation. The author cleverly uses his title to render his character's "business" highly applicable: the persona literally may be a bookkeeper by trade, a librarian, or a book lover or student who constantly keeps books at hand via "my backpack." As a result, DeRose effortlessly pulls us into the bookkeeper's world, showing how easily his situation could be applied to anyone's life. This relevancy, as well as the poem's complex images, resulted in its being awarded the Grand Prize.

Whether the bookkeeper's love of his work pushed other things out of his life or his concentration on the work serves to fulfill what's lacking in his life is unimportant. We simply know that he values his occupation more than anything. Like any person obsessed, the persona is so immersed in his business that normal activities like eating become secondary. Probably from working through a meal, the bookkeeper is ravenous and, rather than enjoying his food, he eats like an animal:

> *I stab the carrion through its belly*
> *and give it mouth to mouth.*
> *The waitress returns while I mock chipmunk dining. . . .*

An intriguing bounty of food imagery fills this poem, supporting the theme behind DeRose's words. As food is a main source of sustenance for most creatures, these images illustrate how work has become the bookkeeper's only nourishment. Yet this deficient sustenance does not have a very pleasing or healthy effect on the bookkeeper, whose "posture / is lumpy oatmeal."

Eating imagery serves yet another duty in this verse. The bookkeeper has made work his source of sustenance but the work itself paradoxically eats up the rest of his life's possibilities. The line "the book eats light from my eyes" literally refers to the ruination of his eyesight by the tedious attention to detail his occupation requires. However, this passage also implies that the more wrapped up he becomes in his work, the less he can see of the wider world. Ironically, the persona is aware of this consumption but seems inclined to change nothing: "my spectacles serve as thick reminders / that what you love kills you off." Here, he concedes that his dense eyeglass lenses, a by-product of his "love," are further distancing him from the above-mentioned light of the outside world. The bookkeeper knows that this devotion devours his time -- in essence, his life -- but, perhaps fearing change from his safe routine, acknowledges no other possibilities for his life.

Despite the mild manner of this poem, the result of the bookkeeper's situation is alarming. To begin with, his identity in the "real world" is becoming less substantial. This point is shown by the speaker's brief interaction with another person, a waitress. The waitress demonstrates disinterest in the persona by being "a deliberate blur to somewhere else" who does not talk directly to him: "she asks the painting behind me how it feels." The persona's response of "Muft Feachy" is perhaps the most revealing. With his mouth full of food, he jumbles his intended words, presumably "just peachy." Symbolically, however, the man's garbled speech indicates that he is losing his ability to speak humankind's language and, thus, his capacity for relating to others. This seemingly simple closing remark lingers long after the poem closes. How many times have we, in the midst of despair or anger, kept busy to suppress our feelings and told ourselves that everything is "just peachy"?

Regrettably, I do not have the time and space to critique the many other fine poems in *A Tapestry of Thoughts*. I still wish to express my appreciation of all of the poets who contributed their work to this anthology. In addition, I would like to thank the editors, assistant editors, and office personnel who have helped make this publication possible.

Nicole Walstrum, Editor

Cover Art: Tracy Hetzel

Winners of the North American Open Poetry Contest

Grand Prize Winner

Robert DeRose / Savannah, GA

Second Prize Winners

Cicely d'A. Angleton / Arlington, VA
Kenneth H. Brown / Chico, CA
Melissa Caldwell / Boston, MA
William Neville Chemnick / Seattle, WA
Cliff Clark / Farmington, NM
Pamela Cohn / Santa Monica, CA
Joe Dowell / Bloomington, IL
Karen A. Gitzen / Ontario, OR
Brett P. Michael / State College, PA
Kathleen Rampton / Santa Rosa, CA

Third Prize Winners

Slade Anderson / Roslindale, MA
Elizabeth Angelone / Wallingford, CT
Carol Willette Bachofner / Victorville, CA
Leann L. Baldwin / Laconia, NH
Elizabeth Barb / Mercer Island, WA
Erek L. Barron / Silver Spring, MD
Jonathan Michael Bitz / Durango, CO
Elise Bochinski / Weston, CT
James S. Bouchie / APO New York, NY
Shannon Bush / Los Angeles, CA
Kristen Corning / Seattle, WA
James R. Cravens / Ottawa, KS
George A. Crawford / Knoxville, TN
C. Borden Davis / Agoura Hills, CA
Patrick Du Long / San Jose, CA
Gary Eckman / Van Nuys, CA
Emma Mai Ewing / Nashville, TN
Cheryl A. Fazenbaker / Akron, OH
Florence Wallach Freed / Lincoln, MA
Alexander Galahad / West Trenton, NJ
Ginny Garrett / La Porte, TX
Grace Roberson Hicks / Corsicana, TX
Mustafa Jahich / Etobicoke, ON, Canada
John C. Johnston / San Diego, CA
George T. Jones / White Plains, NY
David Kennedy / Albuquerque, NM
D. J. Knoll / Washburn, MO
Dr. Edward R. Krivda / Scottdale, PA
Kay E. Kuter / North Hollywood, CA
Mary R. Lewis / Odessa, FL
Jeremy Mathews / Pasadena, CA
Edward R. McGrath / Altadena, CA
Marjorie Millison / La Conner, WA
Bryan Moore / Cartersville, GA
Isabel Mueller / Glendale, CA
Peg Nelson / Virginia Beach, VA
Roger Owens / Laguna Beach, CA
Derenz M. Perez / Kearns, UT
Vellene Peterson / Reno, NV
D. J. Ray / Carolina Beach, NC
Robert V. Rhodes / Pasadena, CA
Daniel Richards / Fort Bragg, CA
Andrew Robbins / Dickinson, ND
Gladys H. Robinson / Denver, CO
H. Rogers / Vinton, IA
Mae Sallila / Sweet Home, OR
Mara Schramm / Frazier Park, CA
Gary A. Schuler / Marion, KS
Judith Townsend Seime / Danbury, CT
Jennifer Sheldon / Valparaiso, IN
Daphne Sparrow / Somers Point, NJ
Carol J. Stratman / Omaha, NE
Doris Toppen / North Bend, WA
Brant J. Wardner / Dickinson, ND
Emma Warnock / Muncie, IN
Miles B. Wells / Houston, TX
Nicola Wickl / Scappoose, OR
Barbara Vecchione Yablansky / East Meadow, NY
Aaron Zaritzky / Chapel Hill, NC

Congratulations also to all semi-finalists.

Grand Prize Winner

The Lonely Bookkeeper
Rainbow Pencils
Worming through their paces,
noting err and quality
as the book eats light from my eyes.
My posture
is lumpy oatmeal,
my backpack
an unkempt beard
my spectacles serve as thick reminders
that what you love kills you off.

The door scoffs cold up my shirt,
a woman, a deliberate blur to somewhere else,
drops off my five-dollar feast
of cheese-embalmed bread
and turns around before I can look up.
I stab the carrion through its belly
and give it mouth to mouth.
The waitress returns while I mock chipmunk dining,
she asks the painting behind me how it feels.
"Muft Feachy."
   Robert DeRose

My Dad

Dad, our years together have swiftly gone by,
your death came so quickly and I don't understand why.
It just seems like yesterday I was Daddy's Little Girl,
when it came to being a father you were very thorough.
You taught me to read when I was only four,
it is memories like these I will always adore.
As the years went by and adolescence approached,
you were always there to be my coach.
We struggled through it, it wasn't always fun,
But I suppose a father's work is never quite done.
You taught me the difference between right and wrong,
to be independent and always stay strong.
When the time finally came and I was out on my own,
I always knew I was welcome, to come visit your home.
When my son was born, and I became a new mother,
you were a wonderful grandfather, I would have chosen no other.
At times I feel I could do nothing but cry,
But your love will always remain brightly through my dark sky.
Changes occur and things on earth all come to an end,
but I will always love you my father and friend.

Tracey A. Jackson

The Last Goodbye

My love, I stand beside you now,
Yearning to go to that "special place"
But I cannot leave you yet, my dear,
As I dry tears from your beautiful face;
For I feel you are not ready,
To open your heart for me,
So I can go on to my heavenly home
With no regrets when your heart sets me free.
I know it takes great courage my love,
To "let go" as I walk "through the light,"
But I promise I'll always be with you,
Until it's your time to walk through the light.
And there, my darling, we shall meet again,
Without tears, for there's no need to cry!
And I'll always remember that beautiful day,
When you smiled and said goodbye,
For you finally understood I could not go,
Until you released me, and let me "come home."
And one day we shall both walk together,
In "Eternity", our Heavenly Home.

Sharon Warner

The Children....

For all the children who will never
    write, walk, or talk like all the other children
    I give you my heart and soul.
You seem not to notice what each day
    brings upon these children.
The world is so small compared to
    the large piles of pain each day
    brings to these special children.
What can we do but be a caring friend.
For every time these children need to cry,
    stand beside them and tell them how
    much you really care.
Please never stare but please put a hand
    out to show you care.
Take each step carefully and watch
    the children and help them understand.
It will be so hard, but watch them
    grow full of grace and into beautiful
    people who can teach the world
    to be as one!

Rebecca Davis

Imagine

Would you like to ride on a rainbow?
Would you like to sleep on a cloud?
Would you like to step into the looking glass?
Come with me, I'll show you how!

Would you like to dance with the unicorns?
Or meet a wish granting gnome?
Would you like to find a magic lamp
With a genie all your own?

Step into my magic world,
I'll show you what to do.
And when I'm done, you won't need me,
You'll have a magic world too!

It's a world of sunshine and happiness.
A world where tears never fall.
A world of wishes and dreams come true.
It's constructed by you, after all.

Just close your eyes, I'll guide the way
to candy cane trees and soda pop days.
Nothing's impossible; you'll have limitless fun,
all you need to find this place is...imagination!

Wendy Lee Ketterer

Badge Of Infirmity

The Badge,
Worn proudly —
A badge, only time could pin to his stature —
Caused demeaning, furtive glances cast by,
Yet, misunderstanding youth,
Youth, afraid of revealing a derisive inner thought
Lurking at the corner of lips.
Lips, revealing judgements, yet,
Knowing only of the present,
The immediate.
Proud of a lithe, young, shirtless, tan body,
The world at his finger-tips,
His badge is yet to be formed
In the crucible of life.
Each of us, passing through mortality,
Must mold his own "Stone Face"
Formed from the materials
Of his own creation.

Russell B. Cornelius

The Lonely Bookkeeper

Rainbow Pencils
Worming through their paces,
noting err and quality
as the book eats light from my eyes.
My posture
is lumpy oatmeal,
my backpack
an unkempt beard
my spectacles serve as thick reminders
that what you love kills you off.

The door scoffs cold up my shirt,
a woman, a deliberate blur to somewhere else,
drops off my five-dollar feast
of cheese-embalmed bread
and turns around before I can look up.
I stab the carrion through its belly
and give it mouth to mouth.
The waitress returns while I mock chipmunk dining,
she asks the painting behind me how it feels.
"Muft Feachy."

Robert DeRose

The Rose

A thousand breaths of life I see
withering, crying, surrendering beauty.
Each petal so soft and tender and pure,
alone a bloom in spring, it's heart will not sing.

A given death, a tattered soul
robbed of your precious rainbow glow,
when such an effortless gift of love
could have given you the wings of a graceful dove.
    Dara Smith

Meadow

Walking down a dirt road
With towering pines on each side,
The sun is blocked, causing a cool darkness,
When suddenly you burst forth into a brilliant golden glow,
A huge meadow filled with wildflowers as far as the eye can see.
Under a brilliant blue sky and blazing sun,
It is a sight to take your breath away.
Run through the meadow, feel the freedom,
Spin and dance among the wildly hued flowers,
See the birds darting here and there
As hundreds of butterflies soar.
The meadow gives you acres of beauty to enjoy.
Gather your arms full of flowers
To take home to add sunshine to every room.
Beautiful meadow, so brilliant, so very peaceful and quiet,
Hidden down a dark dirt road.
    Ruth Cooke-Zimmermann

Ring Tale

The ring of life expands
With possibilities beyond our imaginations.
And, then it contracts
When actualities confine our realizations.

Our ring intersects others with whom
We share moments of our life's journey.
And, whether alone or with another
The ring is continuously turning.

Through our lives we each discover
Our own and separate pace.
Yet, don't we all eventually
Find ourselves at the same place?

A part of me wants very much
To now find that question out.
Yet, in my heart I already know
That's what life is all about.
    Tim Smith

The Widow

There she stands silently crying,
With only a hint of a tear in her eye.
Surrounded by strangers all with sad faces
But they're speaking of someone she knows.
A hero they call him, they're singing his praises,
Above and beyond what he had to do.
He fought for his country with honor and valor,
Doing what he knew he had to do.
And she has his letters all filled with sweet memories,
The promise that he would be coming home soon.
She shivers just slightly, though the hot sun burns brightly,
She can't help but sob softly as she thinks of it all.
Yes they have their hero, but she lost her darling,
That fateful day when he gave his life,
She lost her best friend and she gained a new title
A widow they call her, a dead hero's wife.
    Patricia V. Blair

To Try

Though life is fraught with highs and lows
  With no one path sublime,
You draw from strength within your soul
  To rise, to reach, and to climb.

We suffer our losses and frustrations deep
  Through years of giving to gain;
Our lives enriched by learning to leap
  The chasms that brought us our pain.

So take to wing, your fate to find,
  Let not your fears override
The greatest gifts of those who try:
  A brave heart, a sound mind, and your pride.
    M. G. Mason

IN HIS LOVE

  Life is a long and winding road
    with many twists and turns
  Sometimes the path we may choose
    Offers no hope only struggles
    with which we must cope
In these times of indecision and self doubt
There is someone in whom we can place our trust
  Someone to guide us thru those difficult times
    For in his love we shall find
    The light to lead us from the dark
    The wisdom to search our souls
  To reflect and to heal the conflict that haunts our being
    and release the demons buried inside us
    Remember
      to show his love for us
      He died on the cross for our sins
      And in his death
    WE ARE BORN AGAIN
    Salvatore A. Canazzi

This Miracle Is Mine

God, you created hands that have touched me
  with love, warmth and art.
Through a smile - the wonder of you -
  Love has filled my heart.
My eyes have opened wide to see
  their hope for an eternity
My nose has known the scent of
  beautiful flowers
My lips have wished for more precious hours
My feet have the ability to do a dance
My heart knows the joy of real romance
My hands have been given the gift to write
My soul is filled with mysterious delight

Miracle, miracle, here you are!
You came to me like a shooting star!
    Ruth J. Lebans

A Soldier's Resolve

Hey Soldier who marches with heavy feet
Your cadence or heart is your beat
Someone's hot death is gripped in your hands
Your own life is gripped in another's command

Shelling, shrapnel and smoking rounds
Piercing bullets sent enemy bound
Fire erupting from the ground

When will this be over?
One resolve alone
Say again soldier
I will come home!
    S. J. Vick

Caring For Someone

Caring is something, that we should all do
With love in our hearts, that is always true
You help a small child, to all they shall see
All the beauty in life, that will always be
You help the elderly, with soft tender care
The hope that you give, is sometimes so rare
You care for the people, that have lost their way
You bring back the dreams, of their yesterday
You wish for peace, and all to be free
A world of happiness, just could be the key
Caring for someone, is something we feel
We all should share, for one's heart to heal
So don't look away, and say life's unfair
For in all of us, is a heart that can care
So caring for someone, is a very small thing
But it's a big part of the love it will bring

Vincent Cea

The Love Of A Lifetime

You can feel it grow, so strong yet so mild
With love in her eyes, a smile in his heart
Their love so strong, they'll never part
Soon comes the news, with a terrible blow
With tears in her eyes, she cries please don't go
It can start so slow, or it can go so fast
But when life's so real, you want it to last
She wants the answers, so she looks to the sky
But the only thought in her mind, is why?
The pain is getting stronger as time goes on
She knows soon one day her husband will be gone
Just rest at peace, when he sees the light
God's made his choice, so it's got to be right
He waves goodbye, and you see him grin
She thinks to herself, he didn't win..
But in reality, they both have won
Because they've already had, the love of a lifetime...

Shellie Siebel

Serenity

A new morning brisk with dew on the grass,
with loon's on the lakes,
echo on glass.

At the head of a mighty river that flows through this land,
walleye's dance in water,
a site which is quite grand.

With the changing of the guard, bold colors turn placid white,
the leaves now are gone,
where cold air fills the night.

These days spent outdoors with a sport we play untamed,
in the small town of Eveleth,
you'll find it's hall of fame.

Season's pass, the landscape turns, turning like a top,
for those who choose to stay indoors,
the biggest of Mall's is here to shop.

This place called home, just east of the Dakotas',
God can only smile and say,
I like this Minnesota.

Tony Schmidt

Caged

You are locked up in a world where only your thoughts tell the truth.
You do what others tell you do,
You say what others want you to say.
I am on the inside of the bars,
I am the one who is free.

Rachel Caverly

Spaceship Earth

What is happening to our Spaceship Earth worldwide?
With hurricanes, earthquakes and volcanic eruptions plied;
Fires, floods, droughts and tsunamis pernicious,
To say nothing of winds and rains so vicious.
Tornadoes, cyclones, blizzards, monsoons and typhoons to name a few
It seems as though our world has gone askew!

Of all the natural violence to our Spaceship Earth so fair
To health problems of AIDS, Ebola and Drug Abuse none can compare.
Is Mother Nature trying to give us timely warning
To change man's negative destructive ways so alarming?
Hate crimes, terrorists' acts, domestic, gang and gun violence are the rule —
Including bombings, land mines, poison gas, and arson so cruel.

Child abuse, drive-by shooting, hijacking and killings so gory;
Cults, corruption, political cheating and graffiti — each has its story.
The irrational plundering of Earth's natural resources is man's game;
Fouling in every way his Spaceship nest is man's blame.
Such is the deplorably sorry condition of our time!
Can the trend be reversed to assure our Spaceship Earth a happier clime?

Sophie E. Schnitter

The War Is Over

The war is over! I'm free!

At last, I can abandon these cold, muddy trenches.
With heavy heart, I shall leave my dead comrades behind.

I want to forget the confusing din of battle,
Even more, that consuming fear of dying.

I want to erase the haunting cries of the wounded
And the wearisome toil of gathering the dead.

How often have I dreamed of returning home again.
Though the road may be long, I shall not tire.

I want to run and shout through the streets of my village,
"I'm back! I'm here! I'm alive!"

I want to sing and dance with the children.
I want to joke and laugh with my friends.

I will shed tears of joy with my family.
I will whisper tender words to my love.

The war is over! I'm free!

Thomas Stufflebeam

"Eternal Diamond Sun"

The river and the meadow are alive
With geese and gulls and with the cows and corn,
And in the grassy glen 'neath honey's hive,
A love, a love like none before, is born.

How precious is the moment we have here!
A pair of lovers, young and full of life,
And full of those ideals they hold so dear;
He holds her close, asks "Will you be my wife?"

Her eyes begin to brim with joyous tears,
As she beholds the ring he offers her;
They'll now be wed, together for all years;
No love before has ever been so sure.

Eternity is but a speck in time,
For theirs is love as timeless as is rhyme.

Patricia Noyes

Old Age Is

Plunging in the vortex of a whirlpool
With ever increasing speed
Descending into the abyss of nothingness
Flailing arms to escape
the inexorable erasure of being
Being sucked up in the funnel of a cyclone,
Tossed back and forth helplessly
and spewed forth into oblivion.

Is the unpeeling of layers of dissimilation
with which we maneuvered our way to this time.

Is the confrontation of what we are.
The eternal flame of feeling
is masked appropriately.

Yet, can they see?
Do they care?

Age is a test of love.
Rosemary Pittman

Memories

There was a time that I could see,
With closed eyes see my personal history.
Pages of the past, one by one,
Places I've seen and the things I've done,
A treasure to have the kind of joy
Like a toddler receiving a first new toy.
My mind somehow has taken its toll,
Some people say it's just getting old.
It's sad to relinquish this part of being,
Especially when you enjoy this type of seeing.
A creature of nature with not much voice,
to say I want a different choice.
Now and then I compare the two,
After all that would be all of you.
Accepting life this point in time
Makes sense, is logical, Youth be left behind.
Ralph Manginelli

Say Your Grace America

First of all, thank You GOD for a brand new day
With another chance to open doors of opportunity my way
Thank YOU for this home of freedom and choice
Where one human can make a difference by use of a voice

We worry; not about famine and for this we give thanks
Nor about slaughtering shells from mortars and tanks
Thank You for the right to vote and decide
In that big White. House who it'll be to reside

Having a variety of privileges and not putting them to use
While nations of less fortune suffer from countless abuse
Due to these reasons, each night we should pray
For He has opened many doors of opportunity our way
Darrell Strong

Sunshine

I watch sunshine rise to greet the day,
  with a warmth and glow that you just can't say.
The feeling surrounds you like never before,
  each day can't compare to the one before.
Weather it's cloudy or bright it doesn't matter you see,
  sunshine's warmth is deep inside me.
With a smile and hug what can I say,
  my sunshine knows how to warm my day.
Patty Leko

Down Is Not Far

It's not our place to judge why that man is stooping there
With an outstretched hand, his head and feet bare
Repeating the same plea over and over, his eyes a blank stare
And, it doesn't matter who you "think" you are
Or, what you "think" you represent
It may be hard to fathom, but down is not far.

How difficult it must be for him to "get up" and try to save face
When we know it's hard to "stay with the program" at this ungodly pace
To what do we attribute his addiction, restriction, or misguided
    prediction?
Hopes dashed, dreams trashed, a door in the mind left slightly ajar?
Whatever the rhyme, whatever the reason
Folks need to be mindful that down is not far.

I think of "them" most often on long, wintry nights
And pray daily some semblance of hope and rays of sunlight
Will reach those who are hurting and hungry and homeless
Who long ago lost all faith in reaching that star
In passing, don't question the man or the reason
Share your blessings and remember that down is not far.
Sarah A. Browner

Never Forgotten
Dedicated To The One I Love (Pete)
Now that you're gone I feel so lonely
With all of my heart, I long for you only.
I miss your warm embrace, your tender touch
Oh my darling, I love you so much.
My life was so full when I was with you
and now you're gone, I am so lonely and blue.
Now that I have to say good-bye
every minute of every day I ask myself why.
You were my Love, my Friend, my Life,
I loved so much, being your wife
so, until we meet again,
I'll live the rest of my life with memories of you
in my heart and NEVER FORGOTTEN.
R. Scauzillo

Vengeance

My love I come to you
with all my heart
I come to you
For death will never do us apart.
In the madness of the night
I come before you with a pale sight.
To your surprise at the break of sunrise
your mind contends to the wicked lies.
In the mist of the hour, I lay before you, my deathly power.
For with my life, I surely paid but with my soul I surely stayed.
And yet is seems, like nothing more but memorable dreams
dreams that haunt you in the night
dreams that make you wish for the next morning's light.
So white became my corpse of life.
So brown became my blood from your wicked knife.
Cold is all that I feel; now it's your soul that I must steal.
Vengeance is what I've come to take killing me was your own mistake.
Now it's time to pay for your vicious crime.
Now that you'll never wonder
what it is like to be placed six feet under.
Gloria

A Snowy Day Memory

As I sit looking out my window on this snowy winter's day.

I smile to myself, for a fond rush of childhood memories come rushing back my way.

There I see a little child all bundled up from the cold; as I look closer to that child I see that child is me.

Oh how I loved those snowy days; the memories fade and I turn to look down and watch the children play.

For today I understand why the children love to play on this snowy day, for there won't be any school on this snowy day.
Sylvia DiNunzio

"The Ocean Needs Our Help"

Treat it with kindness and it
  will give in return;
Treat it with harshness and you
  will get burned.
The life within it is dying quick;
  some people's ignorance of it makes me sick.
Dumping continues more each year;
Many shed a heartfelt tear.
Some people are trying to help the ocean,
But the excessive pollution sends
  that help in backward motion.
Maybe it will all get better soon;
Or is this just the wishful thinking
  of a hopeful loon?
Patricia Tarantino

Working Man's Lament

Don't let a butterfly come in and clutter my world.
Why should a willow tree reach out and bother me, girl?
I'm such a busy man, with all the work I can do;
No time for silly things, no time for children or you.

No time to sing, no time for pleasure;
No time to search for hidden treasure.
No time to love——no time to live—no time to give!

Why does a robin sing, why are clouds drifting above?
Why do you follow me, why do you long for my love?
I'm just a weary man, whose days are hurried and few;
Too late for happiness, too late to find it with you.

Don't let a butterfly come into my world!
A. Roberta Wiatt

Help Love

I am you and you are me,
Why is that a mystery,
Love was here but now its gone,
There is no love to carry on,
Loving caring all for you,
But in your life there is no room for two,
Why you don't like me I don't understand,
If you learn to try I'll give you a helping hand,
I love you with all my heart,
Hoping we will never part,
Give us a try,
And I won't start to cry.
Sandra Franklin

Untitled

What brings a man to kill another man; is it jealousy or hate?
Why does it take murder to wake us; are we blind to the violence?
There is too much hate and anger in the lives...the lives of children.
Gangsters, thugs, punks and the like;
they strap their guns like stuffed animals.
Innocence is lost when a child is neglected,
never shown love these children will never know love,
nor will they know peace or happiness.
Gangs are replacing the family in our society,
drug use brings on drug use; which leads to gun use.
We do not reach out for the lost children, we save only the "good kids."
Without attention a fire will burn out of control, so will the children.
Without emotion kids are killing kids, saying they are men;
they're only little boys with big guns.
They gangbang, street hustle, dope deal, and they even kill!!
For what is a man who hasn't killed another man?
Spinning their wheels trying to be men...trying to stand tall,
yet told by society they will only fall.
How will this hatred end; when will men quit killing men?
Sean Thompson

Afterthoughts Of Terrorist Attack

God, you have millions of children on Earth,
Who know they're responsible for their behaviour since birth.
But there are those who have hearts of pure sin,
And do evil deeds with no remorse within
So God, please send your Son before the next bout
Of evil so deadly we are tempted to shout,
"Please Jesus come to relieve all our pain
From having disaster strike again and again!"

The world is filled with greed, lies and wrong,
We've looked down on those who've rebelled for so long;
That we did not think it could happen to us -
Rock throwing, poison gas, and all of that fuss.
But sin comes home to roost like chickens at night
So we're all in this mess, come what may, come what might.
"God, please send your son to relieve all our pain
From having disaster strike again and again.!"
Velma Ruppel Gish

Prothalamium
October 27, 1995

In that dark silence of the stellar deep
Whither my soul, at last freed, its lost
  mate shall seek,
Without aid of accustomed sense for guide,
Lost, lonesome, incomplete, wand'ring,
  searching
Endless rooms of endless eternities,

Til, surely, Oh my Love, at last love
  shall be drawn
To its lost love again: two souls made one.

And all the promise of that first sweet promise
  Shall be kept.
Robert F. Schmidt

"The Oldies Have Got A Hold On Me"

Some days the things I would like to see happen, but haven't yet, or things I would like to see come true, but probably never will, for the "Oldies have got hold on me." I haven't kicked the bucket "Yet", and until I do I'll keep trying to make my dreams to come true.
Veneta Jones

My Small Happiness

Is this the end of it?
While I was not aware of it,
it has become my joy to hear your voice.
Once in a while, can you let me hear your voice?
At least
could you leave that small happiness to me?

Is this the last chance to see you?
While I was not aware of it,
it has developed throbbing of my heart to see you.
Once in a while, can I have a chance to see you?
At least
could you leave that small happiness to me?

Is this SAYONARA?
While I was not aware of,
I must have grown in my love for you.
Always, I will be praying for your happiness.
Always
I shall cherish this small happiness preciously.

Toshiko Honda

Will To Survive

I feel my fellow trees push to survive,
   while gazing at the neighborhood
   mummified beehive.

I wallow in the rhythm of the land's heartbeat.
   I realize now, our spirits will always meet.

I hear the land scream with infuriating blame.
   I understand now, will and hope is the same.

Tandy Lenore Watson

The Birthday

The silver framed mirrors of her soul gaze at the maps
which the years have drawn upon her face.
The colors and shapes of the kaleidoscope that was her life
seem a little less vibrant.
The memory of the faces are fading fast.
The voices of the past grow silent now with the passage of the years.
Astonished, she pulls away from the reflection.
Today she is fifty!

Sylvia M. Pommier

The Mermaid - Imagination Or Reality?

I see an image escape from beneath,
Which is human from head to waist
With shimmering fins of a tropical fish,
Deposit herself on an emerging rock,
And absorb the spellbinding scenery.

As she views the luscious landscape
And the frothy white floating pillows,
I realize she is not of mine own world.
Her metallic wet hair glistens in the sunlight
As it caresses her voluptuous firm breasts.

Then, with an extended arm, like mine own,
She produces a majestic conch from beneath,
Where she herself had just emerged.
And raising it to her moistened red lips,
Sounds thrice, then returns it to the deep.

With her searching crystal blue eyes,
The hue of the vast surrounding sea,
She peers into my sheltering lagoon.
When her inquisitive eyes cross mine,
She vanishes under the sparkling mirror.

T. Steven Swager

The Search

Times have change since days gone by.
Where we live isn't necessarily where we die.
No longer are we fixed to where we grew.
We are constantly searching for different or new.

A hometown is just an imaginary place.
We don't recognize our neighbor by his face.
A handshake is not enough for a pact.
We allow television strangers to tell us how to act.

Friendship rarely linger; somehow they disappear.
We are left alone to cope with our anguish and fear.
Though we've been told repeatedly, two or more must pray.
We push and shove each other while looking for our way.

We refuse to love and mary the friend next door.
Our hungering for far out fantasies leave us wanting more.
In this world of lonely seekers most will never find
The serenity of memories they chose to leave behind.

Dianna Christy Holler

"Thirst For Love"

Thirsting for love in a hostile world,
where dreams are often shattered.
Where the path to happiness takes a southern curl,
and a heart lay languid and battered.
Searching for love in the darkest shadows.
End of the hunt, the final stop?
Combing the beaches, the brightest meadows,
thirsting for love without a single drop.

Looking for love through teardrop eyes,
gives only a blurred illusion.
This loneliness is what I most despise.
There is no escape, no solution.
Again someone has stolen my heart.
Again there is pain as love is spilled.
Thirsting for love, a brand new start,
yet my cup remains unfilled.

Stafford A. Nelson

Children

Children are God's greatest gift
When your feeling down who gives you a lift?
Some things they do you say, oh that kid
But then you think, the same things you did.
You'll see how you've done as they grow
By the teenage years you'll really know
Just by their actions and respectful voice
Then you'll feel the way you've raised them a good choice.
The years you've spent conforming them to your mold
Now take a look who's watching over you
As the tides turn and you're growing old.

Dewayne Thompson

Passage Of Time

Remembering the past when the yard was in bloom
You and I there our respect till noon - with mother
And dad waiting, work to resume
There in that yard when it was all in bloom
Now evening has come with its shadowy past as rose
Petals fall guess nothing good last
Twilight creeps in as the night birds call -
Soon to remember the echoes of fall
There in that garden while it's all in bloom
Now the blooms have all faded and the yard grows bare
But oh how sweet to have been there
There in that yard when it was all in bloom

Patricia Coffey McDonald

Mysterious Journey

I Loved your Eyes,
   when they searched and found...Mine.
I Adored your Face
   when in the crowd you first looked back at me
   and held me with a Smile that embraced me,
With each smile more enchanting than the last -
I Cherished your Voice
   when you first softly spoke...My name.

A simple thing called Love
   is still the Great Unknown, isn't it -
   a mysterious fascinating venture.
Come, take my hand and walk with me...
   talk with me and let us explore
This, the mysterious Journey at its beginning...
   a prelude to Life's yearning for Itself.
   R. Dean Moudy

Warm Breath That Blows

He is the warm breath that blows
when the candle cries her tear-like wax.
He subsides the burning pain when it attacks
her body so frail and when her suffering shows.

He is the flower that steadily grows
when the earth so dry is full of cracks.
He is the warm breath that blows
when the candle cries her tear-like wax.

He is the flame and when inside she knows
there is nothing she lacks.
She melts with sweat that covers her back.
Her light glows.
He is the warm breath that blows.
   M. K. Hill

Not Guilty By Unanimous Decision

It was a beautiful summer day with family and friends around
When suddenly from the sky God's trumpet gave a sound
Then a great white light appeared The Creator came about
Stating "court's now in session" my time was here no doubt

No question I was ready and gladly I admitted
Because Jesus is my lawyer, I'm sure to be acquitted
Now the courtroom resembled churches and surprisingly in the pew
Were John, Paul, and Peter just to name a few

An ultimate experience being there on judgement day
Seeing all my Biblical Buddies supporting me all the way
Now it was Satan turn to testify and what great lies he told
Trying to recruit me how could he be so bold

Objection your honor!!!!! Jesus shouted with dignity and pride
My client lived a righteous life because he walked right by my side
Now after giving my testimony from the heart with great precision
I was found NOT GUILTY BY UNANIMOUS DECISION
   Paul L. Tabron

The Seasons Of Love

Summer comes in fiery fashion
   with hearts that float in fields of passion,

Then Autumn comes to settle all
   as doubts arise and spirits fall.

Soon Winter finds a way to start
   and making icy cold the heart,

The Spring it melts the ice and snow
   for with the Spring a new love grows.
   Teresa Nicole Ross

"ONE"

You came to me in the springtime
When love was fresh and new,
Filled with all the hopes and dreams of the morning dew,
Blooming flowers and life were everywhere around us,
Moment of our blossoming love.
Our red, rose could not survive,
A western wind came and blew it far away,
Killed it before it had a chance to thrive.
Many cold, cold winters have passed since Springtime,
I still remember your shining face and angelic eyes,
   And no other rose can bloom in my heart,
   No other soul can preside,
   In the deep recesses of my heart,
   Where only You reside.
   Won J. Hah

My Baby's Mamma

Young parenthood is such a soul-changing thing.
When innocence is lost, it complicates the pain.

Long days ahead meeting my child's needs,
I'll do this alone, or so it seems.
Now I have to take control,
I've changed my priorities, dreams, and goals.

My heart is no longer open and warm,
It's now hard and cold to protect it from harm.
My love and compassion meant nothing to you,
My time, my commitment, my relationship is through.

You know, it never occurred to me,
After all this time, I would only be -
"My baby's Mamma" is what you said,
I play those words over and over in my head.

A term so simple that means so much,
A phrase more cutting than the sharpest touch.
I call those words "the kiss of death,"
When you hear those words - there's nothing left.
   Shelia Redmon

My Heaven

My heaven's a place where I can go
When I'm feeling alone, sad and low.
I don't have to die to go to this place
Just close my eyes and look into space.

My palace is large with big gold gates
Loving arms come out with warm embrace.
I feel so good with these comforting lights
They take me away from life's wrongs and rights.

My heaven's my place for no one else
I can get away and be by myself.
A place you can talk with someone unseen
the voice answers questions asked only by me.

Heaven's so calm and I make it my own
It's a place everyone goes when they feel so alone.
Enjoyable sounds make my heart patter
The sounds have the power to make me matter.

I'm never alone when I go to this place
I just close my eyes and look into space.
   Robert James Owen

Summer Days

I remember hot, muggy afternoons
When I tried to catch fireflies in the yard
And watched the clouds roll in.

I remember throwing cicadas at friends,
Pine cones at neighborhood brats,
From the protection of garbage cans

I remember tennis courts that rocked with noise
From the banging and clinging of the fence.
Baseball fields full of kids
Trying to organize a game.
I would leave when I became bored,
Sitting in the shaded woods listening to the fanfare
Wishing life wood go slower and school would start latter.
   Peter Mallow

Untitled

In the darkness of the night; it just seems long
When I look out the window waiting for dawn.
Up in the sky; stars, planets-what ever may be
Go on shimmering endlessly;
The heavens look so free.
So I'll close my eyes, shut them up tight
Think about soaring, I shall take flight!
Spread my wings no walls do I see
Freedom flight in the dark of the night.
Away from the pain - just for awhile
Up with the angels - to dance in the clouds
See all the rainbows, one, two, and three.
Then - touching my hand
I see the Lord, Jesus and he's saying to me
It will be alright - for you are with me
Go back now - for it's the sun you shall see!
Down thru the clouds and back to my bed
Close my eyes, shut them up tight
Back from the heavens to sleep thru the night
   Patricia A. Harris

"Lord Jesus"

Lord Jesus, I need thee!
When I arise to greet the day,
Lord Jesus, I need thee
When I start on my way
Every way is filled with the unknown
So Lord you must be my guide, I'm no good alone
Lord Jesus I need you, when my trails have been crushed
Lord Jesus I need you, more than to be bossed
No other, no one can be so wise and caring
Lord Jesus I need you at sunset
Lord Jesus I need you at dark time bearing
Lord Jesus I need thee at prayer time at night
And when I go to sleep I need to watch over your we mite
Lord Jesus I need thee each day!
Lord Jesus I need thee in the every way!
   Will Mae Nalis

Reality

The sky is blue or so it seems, or is this only in our dreams?
What is true and what is real? Is it all we see and all we feel?
Or is this real?
And if it is only a dream, Is not a dream, the reality to the dreamer?
Just as to some, it might only be a dream which has not yet ended?
Find the time to look about, Seek the truth and know the dream is real.
See yourself and know the truth, love and light of thy Father.
Bathe in the reality of the dream and become one with all!
   Sharron Bartlett

Winter

The winter seems so cold
  When I am without you.
    I feel alone and unwanted,
      As if no one knows I'm alive.
        But when you are with me
          The whole world changes.
      I have no worries, no fears,
        And I feel no sorrow.
          When you are around
            All hate disappears
              And everything around me seems perfect.
        The winter seems to melt away
          When I feel the warmth of your arms around me
        But when you leave
          I am alone again and I miss you.
            The cold feeling inside of me returns
        And all I can think of
          Is when you return to me
            And winter is over
              In my heart once again.
   Rebecca Hranj

A Family Is A Precious Gift

The holiday season comes once a year
   When everyone is filled with laughter and good cheer
Everywhere you look, people are rushing and on the go
   It's the only time of year total strangers will say hello
So we continue on our way, with a smile on our face
   Not wanting to lose any time, or fall out of the race
The race that seems to consume us, the whole season through
   Never stopping to enjoy it with those who are closest to you
A family is a precious gift given to us the day we are born
   Not a big shiny box waiting to be opened on Christmas morn
To have our attention for a few hours at a time
   Being together on birthdays, holidays and when everything is fine
But to be there for each other day in and day out
   Because truly isn't that what a family is all about
Or have we become a "Family" in namesake only
   If that is the case - our lives will certainly be lonely
I consider myself lucky in an odd sort of way
   I have celebrated many holidays like they were just another day
So everyday I count my blessings, for no matter how far you roam
   No phrase could be more perfect: "THERE'S NO PLACE LIKE HOME"
   Theresa Brown

Through A Child's Eyes

When do kids succumb to the pressures of their peers?
When does innocence and honesty become sarcasm and jeers
When is a person who is over-weight...
just a big kid...not a blimp?
And a kid who has MS is still just a kid...
with a little limp?
And any other kid with a handicap at birth....
is still treated just like all the rest,
with value and with worth.
A limp, a pair of glass's, a hearing aid, a lisp,
through the innocence of a child,
they pay not attention to any of this.
They're all a rainbow of children,
with no thought to criticize.
They're lucky to view the world....
and each other,
through a child's eyes.
   Sandra Jeanne Pina

Time To Ponder

Oh, that elusive, so civilized a thing called time.
When did it once commence to be?
How did this time beget its birth and then begin?
For sure, it did when once the universe began.
What then they were, those many moments;
Way long before such time was here?
"Oh my," I marvelled up within my thinking self.
"Time must have been a thing so very strong and real;
For marking long ago's before the universe began."
"Hmmm? Was I an 'AM' before the universe began?"
A quizzer's voice inquires inside my dazzled thought,
"When will our time be coming to an awful end?"
"Why, of course," I quickly cried.
"Time will end when thence our universe does end!"
"What then will be the name of eons long;
That surely must exist from there and on, and on, and on?"
"My, oh my," this time I wailed aloud and long.
"There'll be more time, and time; and time again.
Will it never ever come unto a fiery end?"
"Or is our time a nuisance precept far away from real?"
　　E. Lewis Frasier

Is My Purpose, Of Past To Present, To Give An Option To Those Willing?

I came from a society that was not very violent.
What did happen was love, peace, and an occasional uproar.
So as I grew, I learned from what was offered to me.

As I learned to live with love, peace, and happiness...
Others learned to be smart among the streets of their city.
These people grew up in a world full of violence.

The path of life I choose, led me to the streets of the violent.
Here I lived only to gain knowledge, that was not yet offered to me.
I experienced the streets, just long enough to live through it.
I discovered that the violence, lead only to the death of those
Caught in its trap.

With this knowledge, I'm ready to leave.
I cannot just stay here, watching those around me wither away.
So, I leave here to live, giving those willing,
an option not to die in the violence.
　　Shelly Stinson

"Our Father" Who Lives In Washington

You serve as the father of America, and we as a nation elected you to be the head of our household. You were chosen by the children of democracy. In your words, we listen for guidance and authority. In your actions we seek consistency, we search for truth, laughter and love.

We learn from both your examples and from your mistakes. We understand that you are but one, whom many depend on for security — well-being of our family. Keeping in mind that every family includes more than one member, whether it is the boy and his dog, a mother and her child, a friend and a friend, you are right-we're all God's children.

American is currently dysfunctional. And you, the leader of our family has spoken, "family matters!" It's time for responsibility, Accountability, and family counseling. The problem areas America's family face today are real: Unemployment, race relations, education, safety, morality, ethics, crime, security, and health.

So Father of America, I hear your call. And as a member of you family, I answer, I'm here to help! I SHARE WHY FAMILIES MATTER.
　　Sherry L. Wyatt

Good-Bye

O Father, my father! How do I say good-bye?
We've been together so long, you and I.

I don't believe I can face the days upon days and night upon night without the comfort of your warm embrace.

How shall I see you again? The glint in your eye, the sweet and loving smile?
How can I be without you, even for a while?

I turn and I look and what should I see?
In my children's faces - part of you, part of me!

I see you in myself and in my sisters, too!
Little looks and small movements, and there - it is you!

For now to me it is so clear
You will always be with me - always be near!

For although, for now, our ways must part,
You will always be here...in my soul, in my heart.

I have just but to think of you, and you will return;
The love between us will again start to burn.

You may even appear in a Heavenly light
To assist me in times when day seems as night.

O Father, my Father, I will miss you so! And yet what a comfort it is to know you are with me always, wherever I go!
　　Terry L. Miles

A Memorable Flight

As we waited in the fog-shrouded airport,
We wondered if our flight might be cancelled.
Since it wasn't, we reluctantly boarded the plane.
After the usual announcements,
We taxied down the runway,
And soon were airborne.
Suddenly we burst into
A veritable fairy land.
We seemed to be floating on a sea of blue
With white caps bobbing up and down
As they chased each other.
White-covered mountains were everywhere.
While the golden rays of the sun
Brought everything into focus.
Then brown and green patches appeared below us
With the tiny houses, people and cars,
We were returning to earth;
The fantasy was over.
　　Theophane Guilfoyle

Love Was Forever

Love was still here
we were in still and quiet air.
Flowers and leaves all around
but not a breeze to be found.
Look out at the stars all around
this place where we live is round.
Where do you think the place is bound
straight to the bottom if a cure isn't found.
Our young ladies and men
will have to begin again.
The planet was meant for the love of all.
Now you and I are gone.
But all the time you knew
I loved you forever was written on a stone
where it stands alone.
　　William A. Emmrich Jr.

A Moment Of Silence United

A moment of silence, let today be the day
We unite as one and all shall say:

"United we stand divided we fall"
In peace on earth for one and all.

United in love so there will be no more hate
Today, not tomorrow for it may be too late.

United let's sing like the angels above
In peace, harmony, kindness and love.

United in harmony is a wonderful thing
We can make this a reality and not just a dream.

United today in our heart and soul
Today we can make this a common goal.

United our goal is to live in peace
So our children can grow and play at ease.

United no fear, no hatred, no violence
Let's do this today in a moment of silence.

Let us all unite today and become one
And God will say, "My children, well done."
Rosetta E. Ross

Not To Worry

I had a long talk today with one who is close to me
We talked about what has been and wondered about what might be
I told him I had found a beauty unlike any other I have ever known
Then I asked him how to keep from losing her touch and being alone
He told me not to worry friendship is all it would take
Give her love along with heart
And this piece of her you will never break
I told him I reached the age when my life was ready to begin
I believe he felt my fright when I wished to be five again
He told me not to worry, success and happiness would come to me
And he said if I would always believe
Then a child at heart I will always be
For the advice, I thanked him
He replied, "It was nothing at all."
Then I stepped away from the mirror
And took off down the hall.
Tim Jurischk

Ad For 2555 AD On The Uni-Communicator (The U-C)

New: Moonbeam elevators and rainbow escalators,
   We stock stardust chariots and nebulators.
The astral vehiculators, reliable at all locations;
   Your "GALAXY SERVICE", for celestial innovations.
We have meteor cycles and sunburst surries;
   The best in angel packs, to loose your worries.
Come and browse 'til your hearts' content;
   Accessories available by Philos Portent.
For your local recreation, or travel to the stars;
   Visit Jupiter, Uranus, Saturn's moons or Mars.
Get going and see the "worlds," beyond your sun,
   Travel consultants available, to plan your fun.
S. Brownlee-Cobb

Forsaken Moments

A glimmer of hope was all we had.
Time had extolled its final ray of chance upon us.
We cried mercilessly begging for just another moment.

So many times we had charged that an abundance of
opportunities would be there. The swelling hour of eternity
fell upon us as we embraced one another for our sorrowful actions.
Yvette R. Blair

A Real Dram

I just had a dream of you and I,
We put on our wings and began to fly;
Where we were going I did not care,
Cause you stayed in my arms, all the way there.

Upon our arrival, I heard a loud voice;
It said, "you are here by spiritual choice;
We engaged in a kiss, and fell to the ground,
We made love together, with a classical sound.

Moaning and groaning, giving all we got;
Kissing and hugging while passion is hot.
Oh no! You're facing, no please don't go...
Stay with me always, and let our love grow.

As I slowly awake, with love I still feel,
Somehow I believe that my dream, was REAL!
LuAnn Cremo

Thanksgiving Day

Thanksgiving Day is lots of fun
We meet, we eat, we play, and run
We eat pies, cakes and food that's great
Until we get a stomach-ache.
We laugh, we love, we sigh, we cry
Until it's time to say goodbye.
God gives us families, food and health
And to some of us, He also gives wealth.
God shows His love to us in so many ways
That we should honor Him especially on Thanksgiving Day.
Steven Sorrows

Past

I was the eldest among us four.
We lost our Dad when I was five.
Till then, I always asked:
"How was it, to have a Dad?"

Mom gave us our need, except for love.
She's beside me, but it seems we're miles apart
Nobody lead our way, nobody cared.
We're the lost sheep in the desert.

Yesterday, path of thorns that led to grief.
Today, deep scars that make me weep.
Bitter memories of sorrow and pain,
Shadows that hunt me every now and then.

Those trials of life made me strong.
The best foundation to carry on.
Now that I have my very own,
I have to lead the right direction.
"Little One" Gloria

Happy Holidays

'Tis the changing of a season as winter nears,
  we know that Christmas will soon be here.
We find ourselves occupied and busy as bees,
  outside we see the leaves have fallen from the trees.
We think of our friends and loved ones we hold dear,
  that makes life worthwhile throughout the year.
It's time to thank them and show them how we feel,
  phone calls, gifts and cards we show we are real.
Good wishes with caring and love we must show,
  so that through the year hearts will know.
When people care it makes life worth living,
  let us all rejoice in this season of giving.
Before we sit down for the holiday feast,
  did we send good tidings for those who have the least?
Think back to summer when you heard the cooing Dove,
  open your heart and display that special gift, love.
Robert M. Rampani

My Best Friend
Dedicated to Stephanie Masters
Her name is Stephanie Masters, she used to come and play
We had a lot of fun until she moved away
Her brother was just little, sometimes we got in fights
But other times he'd hang with us late on Friday nights
One day her dad decided that they would leave this town
I wasn't really happy, I was pretty much down

One night she came over to tell me good-bye
Neither of us could help it, we just had to cry
Now all I have is memories of her when she was here
I really really miss her, I wish that she was near
We sometimes call each other but we mostly just write
I wish I could see her again on just one more Friday night
Ronda Cole

A Daddy Yearns For His Daughter
Who can doubt a Daddy's love,
We are truly blessed from God above;
A daughter is innocent, playful and sweet,
The love she shares just can't be beat.

Her mother moved out and took the baby too,
But Daddy's Faith in God carried him through;
The visitation with his daughter is not enough,
and life, at times, can be very tough.

God sent him a friend who became his wife,
He granted him a new perspective on life;
God blessed them with another child,
She's playful, sweet and very mild.

There's a pain you feel when you miss her dearly,
The Judge granted us 60 days yearly;
The Judge mandates Daddy's first born live with her mother,
Now we find that's not the case, she resides with another.

Where's the justice, it just doesn't seem fair,
We are a family and have so much to share;
Oh Lord help us and guide us in knowing what to do,
We pray for God's will and we give it all to You.
Tammy Kilmurray

The Homeless Prayer
Christmas came, Christmas went
We are cold and hungry in our little tent.
We have no wood to keep us warm,
How can we make it through another storm?
   The rich people say we are not too smart
   Because the only thing we got is a shopping cart.
   We try to tell them that we try so hard
   Things were so bad we could not start.
Our children are hungry and very cold
That's why this story has to be told.
Do people care about our plea?
Think, some day you could be like me.

   When we are dead we are all the same
   Why can you help us, you got no shame?
   God gave you plenty, but gave us not
   You gave us nothing, and that's a lot.

Please give us food, clothes, not just a dime
That's all we hope for Christmas time,
When God call us and ring that bell
We paid for our sins already in this living hell.
Gene Delmenico

My Pride And My Joy, My Son
Let me abide in life persevering in your goals, my son.
Waste not your strength in untoward conduct.
Respect the General Welfare won
That our lives might reap peace and product.

Abuse not your sound body, my son
By consuming ingredients which distress
So you must beg from those who may already be in want
Because of their inabilities and meager resources.

Your physical body ought to encourage cheerfulness, my son
To promote unfailing success for our community,
Thereby consummating fruitful goals begun
Which advance the General Welfare in perpetuity.

At last the world seems right, my son
Because the pain I once felt has vanished.
Once again I enjoy perfect consolation,
For my tears, previously so voluntary, have been banished!
Theodore R. Reich

"In Orbit With My Thoughts"
The first time I fell in love, I recall,
was with myself on one of those rainy mornings,
drinking hot chocolate and swinging on my parent's porch swing.
The one place I never wanted to leave.
The one time I never wanted to end.
I loved myself for being one who could see the passion
of the ripples in the puddle created
by the constant drip from our rusted gutter.
I loved myself for being one who had the ability
to see through the clouds and onwards to the sun.
The sphere in my head that thinks the world revolves around it,
thinks that it is the brightest in the universe
or more so; believes it is a flame for eternity.
Above all, I loved myself for being one who could handle himself
not moving for half an hour, sipping cold cocoa,
and imagining the depth to the puddle I would've cried by now
if I was stationary.
Shawn David Hendricks

No Promise For Tomorrow
Laughing, smiling, talking, crying. That
was all his time was buying.
I remember the phone call saying
he didn't make it.
I remember the pain, and I still
can't take it.
They say it was his time to go;
that's a fact I don't want to know.
I would do all that I could
to get his life back;
It's his gorgeous smile, that we all lack.
I miss his glowing, and happy face,
One that no one can replace.
I feel bad, you're probably wondering
why, this just that I never got to say goodbye.
His death has left us all in deep sorrow,
but we've got to realize there's not promise for tomorrow.
Peggy Trimby

"Doing A Little Bathroom Dance"
I gotta go, I gotta go, hurry, hurry
What am I gonna do...?
First I sat and then I stood, what else could do?
Then I jiggled and did a little dance!!!
I went to the bathroom, look what I did
Pee my pants!!!
Tiffany Milligan

In A Whisper Of Time

An icy frost touches her fiery bloom,
Waning exquisite petals into certain doom.
Powerless to bask in the warmth of the sun,
Her beauty grows pale, her passion is done.

A wailing wind plucks and swirls her leaves,
Scattering each recklessly, yet she cleaves.
The meadows were canopies of her gold and red;
Now she stands silent and cold, instead.

Ice clutches tightly to the banks of the river,
Bridling the energy that made the earth quiver.
The stream flows ever cautiously into the deep,
Through woodlands and valleys in endless sleep.

Shifting winds whisper of breezes ever gentle;
Sweet lights of sun caress the earth's mantle.
Cloudy skies spill over with soft, stroking rain,
Creating a new beginning, erasing all the pain.

Reach into the depths of your heart, don't fear;
Time is a fleeting glance through life's mirror.
Changing one's destiny to the beautiful, the sublime,
Lies steadfast in the spirit in a whisper of time.
   Pauline M. Bembenek

The Potato Experience

There we sat, all in a row,
Waiting for the potatoes to grow
From tiny little eyes, that could not see,
To nice big green plants way up to the knee.

All through the summer we ho-ed and water did lug,
Always on watch for the fearful potato bug.
When tiny white blossoms on the branches did appear,
We knew that potato dishes on the table would soon appear.

Good old boiled potatoes with my fork I would mash,
Then add salt and pepper, it makes my lips smack,
Potato soup so hale and hearty,
Is delicious enough for any party.

Potato pancakes, french fries, and has browns so brown,
Are served by the best restaurant in town.
The possibilities are endless for this treat without fat,
You can eat them easily wherever you're at.
   Pat Schwappach

The Score

We were Holy Grails to each other once.
Visions too sacred to be touched;
we were the objects of such fiery longings
that satisfaction was only a dream.

Now, we're too human, our problems too real
to be wished away with light-tight eyes
when it would be healthier
for us to let go than to ache.

There's an apology lurking here, I suppose,
for abandoning the starched promises
we made when our newborn feelings
strove to stand on wobbly legs.

But my sorries stick unsounded,
because if we tally our overdue account,
contracts broken and pledges kept,
between us, the scales hang fairly balanced.
   Peg Nelson

The Pioneers

The trail we walk on is worn from its use, for although it is new to us, it has forever been used. We walk side by side our hearts filled with joy, for the beautiful feelings our surroundings employ. Our paths have hidden dangers of which we ignore, for our hearts drive us forward to endure and explore. We fell upon the trail that led us to here, now we look upon the mountain with an eager fear. To climb to the top is easy they say, but a fall to the bottom is the price so many must pay. Our hearts are our guide to see us unto this trail we walk until forever is through. There will be hardship for sure to cause us great pain, but if together we fight it there will always be gain. The ground may be rocky, the trail quite steep, but with patience and understanding at the top we will meet. When our journey has ended and forever draws near, we will look back upon our trail of memories held dear. We think of our children on the paths they have taken, hoping their choices will not be forsaken. For they follow a trail of which we once took, a trail of love of which all hope to look. We yearn for the feeling as it whispers our name, it's the frontier of love which we all hope to tame.
   Ronald J. Hanson

Mario

A man with hopes, a man with dreams;
Until drugs and alcohol tore him at the seams.

A caring man with two children in tow,
wondering where their futures will go.

A woman who loved him with all her heart,
couldn't take the pressure and decided to part.

The yelling, the screaming, the chaotic nights,
lead her to heartache and endless fights.

Will he remember when the dawn breaks
what the family endured and all their heartaches.

Where is that kind and thoughtful man we once knew,
Please come back to me; I'll always wait for you.
   Susan Silva

Metaphor

Like a thief she slipped in.
Unaware of my presence,
With a smile,
She took all that I had.
My feelings of self worth,
My reason for laughter,
All my dreams.
Gracefully she took all I had.
I stood in silence,
The tears welling hot in my eyes,
The lump swelling in my throat.
I must remain silent,
And gracefully accept my loss.
Any attempt to try to save it would be vain.
To utter a word would cause others to scorn me.
I have to let go,
And let bygones be bygones.
   Rebecca Zimmerman

The Island

I am a man on an island surrounded by tears.
Unable to swim, and full of fear.
Is life so dismal that one can't enjoy.
With my heart full, or is it just a toy.
I won't look down or turn my head.
When one day the word is finally said.
One day soon I'll break the fear.
I'll leave my lonely island in the sea of tears.
   Robert E. Perkins

Untitled

To look down the street, to look down the corner.
Trying to find something that I don't know what.
I walked to the corner, I walked to the store.
I looked in the corridor and peered through the door.
It seemed I was lost or I had lost something or someone.
I had been left behind or so it seemed.
I knew where I was going and where I belonged.
A feeling I had was oh, so strong.
No matter where I was or the time had been,
I was growing tired and my hopes becoming slim.
I felt pain, yet I had no wounds.
So if I feel this way,
and there is nothing left to lose,
why am I so scared?
Why does my heart feel bruised?
Scott Nickell

Young People

Young people living in the streets.
Trying to beat crime but can't succeed.

Looking for money here and there.
Killing up each other like they don't care.

Is this world to tough for them.
They don't realize how much they've sinned.

What can we do to help our kids?
Pray for an answer that God will give.

It's sad to see them put behind bars.
Looking at the blood from the wounds and scars.

Realizing inside of them, how troubled they must be.
Yet, trying to figure out away to live in society.

Life's not a game that you can play.
If there's something you need, God will find away.

So turn to God, instead of those guns.
He's more powerful and you won't have to run.

You can be someone special in your life.
Just believe in yourself and keep your pride.

No matter what color or race you are.
Just always believe what's in your heart.
Shara Larry

Barefoot In The Shadows

I walk barefoot through the pebbles of life,
trying to be a good mother and wife.
I often hit on a step, smooth and nice,
and wonder why I question the price.
Just when I'm expecting another smooth step,
I feel the pain of that next Jacquard step.

As I walk along the babbling brook,
enjoying each angel and hidden crook,
I question my presence in this universe.
A voice then says, "Don't go in reverse.
Just walk on those pebbles, sharp or smooth;
think of the pleasures that wait for you move
and walk barefoot not questioning why.
Never look back on things that lie."

The master will soften even those worst pains;
he promises wonders for those who honor his name.
Just have faith as you walk barefoot
alone in the shadows of life's pebbled brook.
Alma Showalter

The Spoken Word

Listening to the daily news on television, I sit comfortably rocking
Truly want comes to my ears is quite shocking,
First, I had better explain and clearly set the stage
I'm a widowed taxpayer advancing into old age.
I know changes or allowances in oral worlds are quite numerous
Not long ago laughing was a "no no" at "shady" talk even if humorous.
Announcers abided by regulations set in communication
"Pregnancy," "Abortion," "Condoms" were
    "no no's" in relaying their information.
Time changes; what to my ears, in the winter of 1994, did I surprisingly hear!
The subject of "Teaching Masturbation" in schools did appear.
Permissible in this age are of conversations being frank
In view of various citizens ideas, are they questioned or are they blank?
Will limitations ever be on discussions in talk shows or "so called" news?
Will listeners, regardless of age, become mislead or eventually "blow a fuse?"
Should my devious mind change and simply adjust
Accepting "Freedom of Speech" and toleration showing no disgust?
Should more privacy be placed on subject so absolute
Open-mindedly thinking that no minds will it pollute?
In this good "old" United States on progress and growth we depend
As a good American, do I approve the language and merely follow the trend?
E. Pearl Roberts

Unknown

I sit alone at night, wondering if all my hopes and dreams will come true.
I ask God for forgiveness of my sins, praying that he forgives a few.

I ponder all the questions of life, and what it has in store.
Never knowing when my time will end and death will be at my door.

Painful memories haunt me, but what over powers them are the good.
I wake up each morning, wondering if I should...

I dream my dreams alone inside my mind.
Longing for someone to share them with, waiting for the perfect kind.

I'm waiting for the day that life has something worth meaning to give.
I wonder why I am here and my reason to live.

I love myself, but no one else seems to care.
Not knowing if I am right, this goes down as one of God's unanswered
    prayers.

I'm longing for the time when hurt will set me free.
I'm asking God to give me someone special, to live out my greatest fantasy.

I have my whole life to live and shouldn't be feeling this way.
It all seems so real, and only time will make it go away.
Tiffany Hartford

Entangled Rose

A sad little rose entangled with weeds,
tried vainly to lift it's weary head,
won't someone please rescue me,
while my petals are still soft and red?

Spring and summer have passed and gone,
autumn is saying goodbye,
winter will come with a blanket of snow
and cover me when I die.

Where have my cousins of roses gone?
Where are the hands that tended our needs?
Why was I left to die all alone,
in this garden entangled with weeds?

Once more let me feel a ray from the sun.
Let my petals be kissed by the sweet morning dew.
Then I'll drift away on the cold winter wind
and scatter my fragrance for you.
Willa Hamrick

Oregon

Oregon, land of tall majestic pines.
Trees so tall, they seem to reach the heavens.
Mist from the night torrential rain
Rises ever slowly, and makes the treetops
Ever so more beautiful, as they seem to pierce the clouds.

Oregon, land of rain and sunshine.
Though water we have plenty, the sun is always ready,
To bathe the land of Oregon, with the warming rays
That God has surely sent us.

Oregon, land of majestic mountains and volcanos.
Dressed in green with beautiful trees,
The snowy tops, all seems free.

Oregon, land of farms, both big and small.
With green and amber that waves so tall.
Which consist of strawberries, grain, corn and all.

Our land is blessed with each of these.
Truly the hand of God has set this feast.
Now it is but for us to enjoy.
This beautiful land, we all call
OREGON.

Santos F. Garcia

The Times Of Fear

The times of fear, the waking up, hearing noises, voices the
Total fear when no one's here. The absence of everyone within
The house the waking up at 11 until dawn, the calling out of
Names wishing some one would answer.
The hurting, the pain, the moments of fear, I lay here wondering,
Thinking when the calls will come again, hoping, wishing, the
calls and crying would all stop.
The times of fear when no one's here sometimes when I'm
Alone walking in every room even in the halls I wonder
Will anyone come soon? Waking up in my empty room, looking
around hoping nothing moves,
I toss and turn as I close my eyes hoping no one finds
me dead; I try to forget the past which has come and gone,
But I sometimes find myself, wondering will any of this ever
stop, my times of fear when no one's here in my empty shell
I drop a tear!! As I move on, and leave my past, and all these
memories, my times of fear, I sometimes dream he's here with me
hurting me, holding me, saying you're my dear; I hear myself screaming
in my empty room. But no one's here; the times of fear when no
   one's here.

Teresa Brown

Missing You

I stand on the ground, and look
To the sky, and the splendor
Before me, resembles your eyes.
I see once again, the beauty
You hold. And as the day passes
Your memory unfolds. With the
Pass of a cloud, the cry of a bird.
I cherish the songs of your voice I once heard.
The warmth of your breath,
As gently we kissed, with the
Passing of time are the pleasures I miss.
And the songs of our lives, in memory preserved.
Are like beautiful notes, of a song I once heard.
Yet with the absence, alone we must stand.
So while lost in the skies,
Love, please hold my hand.

Tyler Richard Johnston

The Other Side

We all want to get to the other side,
to that proverbial "greener pasture" illusory in nature,
where we tell ourselves it will be different.
A fresh set of circumstance with which to deal,
will rejuvenate us and restore our sense of purpose,
a new love, a new life, if only then.

The challenge lies in inner space,
the journey through the intricate nuances of self,
the inner voice that cascades down into caverns
of phantom images unmistakably your own.
You...who have seen the truth an returned, unscathed.
You...who have now been released unto your own destiny
and bring a quiet dignity to surface,
where before there was none.

The opiate of the mind,
what a joy to have discovered it
at the source of life and feeling.
The other side...
has been here all along.

Carol Chapman

"He Called Me Jim"

One year ago today when they came for my loving son,
To take him away, to war, a battle to be won.
I made a vow to my son, as they took him away,
I'll be here waiting, for his return home to stay.

It's one minute after midnight, one year has already gone,
I guess my son is still fighting, and I am still alone.
I'll get a good night sleep, and keep my son in mind,
While tomorrow lingers on, my son I might find.

I can see a tall man walking down that dusty road,
Maybe it's my son, all tired from wagging his heavy load.
I'll run half way down to meet him, and hold him so tight,
I just pray that it's my son, coming back home tonight.

The man is getting closer, please dear God, I pray,
Open my eyes a little better, just enough to see today.
The man opened his arms, and held me close to him,
I'm just your son's best friend, "He called me Jim."

The tall man took my hand, for there is something he had to say,
Forgive me precious one, but they buried your son today.
I made a vow to wait here, But I will see him up there,
So I will close my eyes now, for I have lived my life's share.

Wilma Faye Cummings

A Bowl Of Cherries

"You think life is just a bowl of cherries!"
You said that to me when I was eighteen years old.
I laughed, but thought what you said was quite cold.
I soon found out that you were right,
When you uttered to me one night,
"I won't be seeing you anymore."
At that time I believed that I had complete control of my life,
And that I would someday be your wife.

Then, I learned to cope; to live with hope.
And today I am glad that you married another,
Because when I look at my husband, our daughter and three sons,
I know that life is loving and sharing the good times and the bad
   with each other.
I hope you and your wife have also loved and shared the good and the bad.

However, I still laugh when I remember the words said by you.
"You think life is just a bowl of cherries,"
Because at times I still do.

Theresa Luppowitz

Being

Do you ever just feel like staying in pajamas the whole day?
To sweat and not want to bathe.
To itch and scratch and not ask, "Why do I itch?"
Not comb hair.
Not brush teeth, and just be.
To feel completely comfortable in oneself just the way you are,
And be thankful in it.
Today, I didn't have to wake.
I could have gone on to my father's house, but God said not so, today.
Today, I have no regret of how God made me, especially if this is in his will.
I am, what I am.
I love me, cause God created me.
It's so good just to be.
To not care what anyone says or even thinks.
But, being free to be.
To be disobedient, to be foolish,
God loves me anyhow.
Accept yourself completely for who you are.
Before asking someone to accept you, accept yourself in the fullness of God.
Let self go and enjoy just being.
Tiffany Ann Williams

Pages

There, when all else fails, is where to look.
To read, the expressionless page.
From lifeless vellum, it moves, the book.
Stirrings from within, the long dead sage.
To be heard, and heard again.
Thought to be new, an old refrain.
To live, to learn, to re-learn.
For that which is there, why yearn?
To lift, lift the heavy, heady lid, lid of the tome.
And I will bring my sage home.
I bring home my tome, my book.
When all else fails, this is where I look.
William Scott

If Time Permits

If time permits a look-back just before I die,
 to ponder the condition and performance of my life,
What then shall be the thoughts upon my heart and mind,
 that will be of great concern at this sacred time?
Shall priorities quickly change within each gasping breath,
 and those urgent things that seemed so great now be put to death?
Will I fear my passing soul that's filled with discontent,
 and cry out for one more day to correct time misspent?
No not I for I still live and time is on my side,
 to do those important things that urgent things deny.
And at death's door I shall smile and my soul will rest in peace,
 for I shall have accomplished what time permitted me.
Robert R. Anderson

God

Hear the word which utters no sound.
Touch the body which has no flesh.

Climb the walls that protect you from your past.
Raise up your life unto the heavens.
Open blind eyes and see the truth.
Break the chains that bind the flesh.
Scream praise to him above.
Whisper not your love,
Release your soul,
Embrace your soul,
Embrace faith.
Witness,
God.
ISIL

Questioning The World

Have you ever been on the brink of insanity?
To live in today's world it maybe required,
"How could this be true?" you say,
Read on and you shall see.

In a world where the innocent lay dead
And the guilty walk the street
Their voices scream for vengeance from beyond the grave,
But who will answer their cries?

The police? Trust them as you would an enemy,
Their badges used to be symbols of justice
Now they are nothing but hunks of metal.
Then, who else can we trust in?

Justice? One can still believe in this,
It is the ones who uphold it you cannot.
Some say justice is blind
This is because someone has stolen her eyes.

Who is left, who can be an idol for our children?
Today, children worship a singer who kills himself
as if he were a god.
Now I ask you, "Whom can we trust in this world?"
Paul Pikutis

"New Found Love"

I long to hold Death in an impassioned embrace,
To kiss her sweet, full lips,
To caress the curve of her face,
To know a love that no other could eclipse.

The love I felt for Life has faded,
With her, everything has become dull and mundane,
All that we shared is now painful, jaded,
To try to stay together would only be in vain.

Too much has changed for things to stay as they are,
The past is gone, the future will never happen, and the present is left up to me,
Dreams and desire can only go so far,
To ask for anything more is to risk insanity.

All my pain, my new love can mend,
For my new found love will never end.
William M. Mahaffey

Thoughts Of Yesterday

The phone call came, on a Sunday night
To inform us she hadn't been home
It wasn't her absence that cause us fright
T'was the fear that she wasn't alone

A week passed us by and our hopes never were
For her to walk through the door
She'd been gone many times, but always returned
Could it be, she'd return never more

But as iron turns to rust and hope pales to fear
The phone rang, she had been found
She was murdered and put in the trunk of her car
In an area outside of town.

Not a trace of her movements were made after three
And no one showed us the way
Please help us, come forth, if you saw her that morn,
Don't show us a crime that pays.

Her last living night is a jumble, a maze
A dreadful state of confusion
We need all your help, and with God's Shining light.
It may help us to find the conclusion.
Shirley Davis

Thanksgiving Day Reflections

This is the time of year for reflections...
   To give thanks for the things that we have.
Knowing, no matter the weather,
   We survive times, both good and bad.

Looking upon this time of year...
   In decay, we find beauty so deep.
The colours of fall, turned to winter...
   Brings us pictures to eternally keep.

Although my dreams, seem like the fall...
   Decay and darkness surrounded my bones...
Your love, like a breath of spring sunshine,
   In your heart, I'm making my home.

My hopes and dreams, they go to the Lord.
   My faith in Him will always ring true.
Just as the fall brings with it Thanksgiving....
   In my darkness...He brought me to you.
     N. Y. Faux

Always Near

I walked out into the crisp November air,
To find you had already been there.
You said you would always be around.
I find your love, everywhere, does abound.

You and I loved this time of year.
It's almost as if you were physically here.
You went to your Heavenly Home...but
I have never really felt alone.

Is it possible to be in two places?
I think maybe...yes.
We were always together and you were my protector.
I feel you are still my director.

Our love was so strong...neither could do wrong.
When the end came, we didn't say...so long.
You went on to wait,
Until I meet you at the Gate.
   Pauline Young

"Knowest Thou This Child Of God?"

She was cute and courteous, always very sweet.
To be with her made life seem such a treat.
She wasn't always perfect, though mistakes were very few,
But grow by trial and error, did she; every day or two.

As school daze came and school days went, so did boys and love.
Yet of these three, not all would stay, though some fit like a glove.
Soon a new life she would lead, leaving far behind
The little girl of younger years, now a woman with her own mind.

The family years are trying years and hers were different not.
Each child she had, she happily bore, such a wonderful lot.
But children demand attention with restrictions placed on each
For they're too young to understand, the world's not all a beach.

A month goes by, and then a year, then 5, then 10, then more.
She looks around in disbelief, no more feet across the floor.
Again they are two, her 'boyfriend' and she, centers of the core.
Undeniable proof is the never-previously-open bathroom door.

Knowest thou this child of God? Who is she? What's her name?
She's changed a little, year by year, and grown from wild to tame.
A rose is a rose by any name; but of her, there simply is no other;
From first she was—and ere shall be, the miracle known as mother.
   S. N. Eddy

The Nightingale

From Silver Lining of a cloud, came the Radiant Nightingale,
To appear in arbored garden, like a fascinating fairy tale.
Aspiring quest of wonderments and mysteries of newfound lands,
The nightingale placed its Gentle Crest and Trust upon my hands.
A Special Bond from henceforth molded, in Shield of Ivory Case,
With understanding Unity when, together, we came face to face.

Unique, The Gracious Nightingale, among the flocks of songbirds,
Its brilliant Crescendo of Melodies, surpassing mortal words!
A Giving Heart, soft and natural, as its smooth plume of feathers,
And Spirit strong and stout, withstanding each storm that it weathers!
With Angelic Songbird upon my shoulder, clearly I can see
The beginning of enduring friendship, truly meant to be.

Among beauty of the nightingale, whence unfurls its Inspiring Wings,
Is the "Message" of a songbird...Unconditional Love it brings!
For, these trusting harmonies make the world a better place,
The Seraphic Song...among creatures of Earth's breadth and face.
   R. Sarah Farrar

Let Us Rejoice And Be Glad

In the beginning, God created Earth;
To animals, plants, and mankind gave birth.

When God saw His people were going astray,
He sent His prophets to show them the way.

   Let us rejoice and be glad!

God showed us true love by giving His Son;
Through Jesus He taught us to love everyone.

All through the years God has proven His love,
By sending His spirit from Heaven above.

   Let us rejoice and be glad!

Though life may be gloomy, and it may be grey,
Jesus will guide us along the right way.

And when days are all sunny and cheery and bright,
We must remember that God made it so right.

   Let us rejoice and be glad!

When suffering an illness is getting us down,
We'll remember it's less than a thorn-laden crown!

We'll give thanks for the blessings of families and health;
They make us richer than money or wealth.

   Let us rejoice and be glad!
   Dixie Lee Lene Kethley

Untitled

If you look into her eyes,
You will see she often cries.

She is not like any other child,
She has already seen the wild.

She holds a pain that's strong and true,
But there is nothing you can do.

I would like the power to change the past,
That is something she would ask.

She hides her tears long out of sight,
And lets them flow freely in the night.

I never see happiness in her eyes it seems,
Maybe that's something she finds in her dreams.

What she really needs is a friend,
Being lonely is now way for a life to begin.
   Robin Kills-A-Hundred

Felicity

Sailing
To a distant shore, beyond and
Through the stones and seas
There's got to be more than ordinary
Life can offer
Breathing fire
I can braid the shattered mirrors
And the bloodstanding wings
In time will move right through the wind and learn again to fly

  Flecity
    Reaching, searching, hoping to find
    All that can be

Soaring
Through the winter clouds
It's all the will of Heaven
When the first flake falls
And the staring eyes
That always seem to linger
In the early sun
Nothing fades the flowered beauty that opens to the sky...
    Sylvia Tosun

Going For Two

I gather my thoughts and compose this rhyme, for the NLP for a second time. You published my first despite my complaint, railing 'gainst your twenty line restraint. You were nice as could be (you said it was swell), but this one could flop, I realize full well. So judge you now these lines of verse, consigned to your hands for better or worse, But mind you I repeat my beef - that damnable rule about keeping it brief! Twenty lines or less to craft a poem leaves precious little room to roam, Giving birth to lines of thought so flimsy, as to allow for little more than whimsy. Where art thou, O elusive Muse? What subject to choose- what meter to use? Lament a long-dead love affair? Been there, done that - had my share, but none of them, I must confess, would fit in twenty lines or less. Poets have used up more lines than this, just getting past love's first passionate kiss. So toss we out affairs d'amour - there's more to life than that, for sure. Indeed so many things, like sailing ships and sealing wax, and cabbage and kings, of note to a bard of an earlier day, but beyond my scope, to my dismay, because you decreed that I not exceed a number of lines far less than I need. 'Tis oft been said, and I do agree, that the soul of wit is brevity. Here now the fruits of brevity - this sad attempt at levity .
    Ray Smith

The Snow....

Pure and white are the specks in flight as we peer through the cracks in the blinds.

So powerful it seems are those tiny white beams that invoke pleasant thoughts in our minds.

As children we braved many cold winter days just to play in the billowy ice.

Boisterous, but creative, our appetites were sated, as we burrowed in the snow just like mice!

The moon puts on a show, as the world sparkles in its glow, We are witness to this miracle once more.

For as we watch the snow flurry, we are released from all worry, until the creditors find us, and break down the door!
    Sandra L. Oshetsky

An Attempt To Explain

Thoughts swirling, circling, interweaving...
Thoughts confusing, fleeting.
Nerves twisting, jumping, cringing —
Struggling to focus, to keep from sinking.

Body and mind-numb-functioning only to get by,
To get by all of those around.
Plodding, drudging, through the day...
Bearing the awful night.

Dark, oppressive gloom, surrounding the heart and mind,
and the soul - floating out there - somewhere else..,
Worthlessness, hopelessness weighing heavier -
Blocking out the could be, should be, and
used-to-be joyful things.
A dark tunnel in which there is no light,
no end, and no change.
Overwhelming sickening pain in which only you
can bear - because no one else can feel it.
How can this be explained to others, when
one can't explain it to their self?
    Susan Leppert

To Pray

  Our Father Who Art In Heaven.
Those smooth soothing words, which began the answer
To a question asked of our Lord. How should we pray?
In homage, with head bowed to show our humbleness.
From deep within our hearts, grateful for the kindness.
With pride in our saviour, who suffered for the unworthy.
With shame in ourselves, for we know that we are guilty.
To love, with love for all that has been given.
In determination, to cleanse, and mend, and never again be riven.
With tears in our eyes, the sorrow of past transgressions.
Yet smile beaming, from the comfort of confessions.
In the sinking of spirit, because of the stain.
To the lifting of hope, for the end of the pain.
Through darkness we learn, the price that life costs.
Through light we will know, at last were not lost.
For in the end as our LORD began,
Thine is the kingdom, the power, the glory, forever...AMEN.
    Steven James

November Mourn

It seems just yesterday
Those leaves were green and orange and red.
Full of life and beauty,
Soft and moist,
Swaying rhythmically to the music
of a gentle breeze.

But today those same leaves are brown,
Stiff and dry.
They rustle desperately on the branches,
Stubbornly resisting the challenge of the autumn wind,
A wind that in the end must prevail.

And so we, too, lose our softness and color,
Our youthful grace replaced
by clumsy determination,
As we steadfastly struggle to endure
Against the inevitable adversary
Death, who in the end, must prevail.
    Susan F. Mallow

A Loss

We planned our dreams for the future.
Those five and a half months we were together were the best months of
  my life.
Then I pushed you away. Why, I don't know.
You cheated and lied and it's all my fault.
You were the best thing that ever happened to me.
But because I acted dumb, you left me.
The pain is none I have ever encountered before.
I feel like this is a nightmare - so when will I awake?
Only a few weeks ago we were so happy holding each other arm in arm.
Everyone keeps saying it'll work out,
But I don't think you want to try.
I don't blame you if you hate me, I already do.
I acted stupid and now I am suffering.
I am sorry for all the pain I have caused.
The one thing I wish most is for you to be mine once again,
Because I love you more than anything on this earth.
I hope you will never forget me, for I will always remember you.
The love we shared was very special to me.
But now I am left crying and all alone.
  Victoria Deloian

You Are Your Daddy's Little Girl

Dedicated to Brianna Jenee Riley
In loving memory of her daddy, Jamey

That blonde hair,
Those eyes so blue,
That little stature looks just like, you know who.

That beautiful smile
That laugh he loved so sweet.
Are all parts of your daddy, in you made so complete.

It's like looking into a mirror at the child he used to be.

You are your daddy's little girl, you were the apple
Of his eye.
No daddy loved a little girl more, for his precious
Little girl he worshiped and adored.

Reflections of your daddy will live on in you, and in the
Children you will one day have.
You'll look into their eyes one day and time will take
You back to days gone by, to precious memories of a loving
Daddy and his little girl.
  Renee Riley

HAPPY BIRTHDAY BONNIE!!!

Seventy years young, I'm told you are
  Tho' you never look it or act it, by far;
Five kids have never slowed you down,
  Or kept you from enjoying a Western Hoe-down!

A Waltz — a Schottische — a Two-Step — and
  Your feet fairly fly to the beat of the band!
Whether pairs, or round, or line dance, too,
  Not even the young can keep up with you!

As 'round and 'round the floor you go,
  My hat's off to you, I want you to know
For being warm-hearted, and caring and giving,
  And enjoying the life that you are living!

Each new step in life like the ones on a floor,
  You've taken in stride — and ready for more
With laughing blue eyes and oh, so petite
  Happy Birthday, Bonnie — with the dancing feet!
  Sunny Martin

Desert Brown

It's just so brown.
This scorched desert.
But for the harsh,
Orange-Yellow fireball,
And Blue sky, and White clouds.
The eagle's White neck circling;
hunting for bright Red, Black, Yellow, coral snake dinner.
The occasional Green of cactus, and pine, on higher ground.
And the snow capped mountains where
Silver rivers run over slick Gray rocks,
hiding pastels of Blue, Green, and Pink on rainbow trout.
Sunset brings Yellow, Gold, Orange, Scarlet, and Red,
of a dying sun.
Then cools to Purple evening.
Red scorpion menacing,
after the Black night has fallen.
Shimmering stars,
more than in the city.
It's just so brown,
this scorched desert.
  Steven S. Perkins

Reflections

Axiomatic as the loop of the sun or the sequence of tides on the beach,
this old world can jolt with fear or stun with stars beyond reach. We
take the blessings with standard conceit and resent when the trials
come to bother. Yet the richness of one is diminished in scope if
we're not often honed by the other.

Precious is beauty in the flutter of air as the butterfly caresses the
rose, or the leaves of the trees play tag with the bees in an active
sort of repose. When hawks and sparrows and chickadees swim in
drafting cylindrical splendor, our child within yearns to soar to a
realm where reality's more sturdy and tender.

Fresh cut grass and the fragrance of earth when light summer rains
come through, quicken the spirit of hope and dreams like the rush of
love when it's new. And in those moments the soul extracts the value
of life extant, and embraces humanity, one and all, with a charity extravagant.

But the pearl of a sphere we treasure and trash does intrude with
crackling reminders, that we're not in charge of this awesome domain,
lest we thicken our spiritual blinders. The delicate thread between
here and there can be snapped at the whim of our Master. And our
terminus once thought conventionally slow soon veers perniciously faster.

While 'midst the poles from beginning to end make the time for keen
introspection of all that you are and want to be with finite judgment
and circumspection. And lavish the gift of friendship true and the
riches of love profound, for on that path lie treasures untold and
joys that can only astound.
  Roberta I. Teague

Annie's Song

This life was meant for living, not watching through the glass.
This life was meant for loving the people that we pass.

For in the circle of our lives a million days abound,
and in our hearts a rhythm beats until it forms a sound.

I hope your sound is a love song that plays throughout your days,
for all we leave when we are gone are notes upon the breeze.

These notes will pass from place to place, a melody from within,
an image of another time filled with all that we had been.

An opera of a life once lived to come and sing again.
  Sandra Salute

Track Of Fools

They play by no set of rules
This dog track of fools
They hurry and scurry to and fro
But no one can they call bro
Because it's one for one
And it's not long they will all be done
This track of fools

Although different they still are clones
Always searching for a riches unknown
They long for that day to grab that one rose
As their worlds come to a crashing close
This track of fools

Young and old they hope and wait for that date
In their hearts they know their terminal fate
As they leave one last time to turn and wave
To die and be put in a pauper's grave
This track of fools

W. E. Grimsley

A Special Happy Birthday For Our Christmas Gift In 1965

God gave you to us to cherish on this earth
Thirty years ago on this December day
Twenty-seven years, 7 months, 27 days from birth
For whatever reason, God chose to take you away

We brought you home on that Christmas Eve night
Brother, sister, dad and mother to love you
You were so pretty; we held you so very tight
Amazed that you were so small and so new

Through the years you grew in strength and stature
To deal with whatever seemed to come your way
You left behind an almost true and exact picture
For whom we thank God we have each and every day

Our memories, some glad and some sad, come forward
As we remember the joy you brought in your own way
And even though we cannot see you, our every word
Says to you, through God's ears, Happy Birthday

Wilma Frauenberger

Planet Star

I glanced at the sky and found myself gazing
Thinking to myself if there is life up above in the stars
We are floating in the same atmosphere
Shining lights everywhere - lights on
On that particular planet or should I say star
Just imagine looking down among the planet Earth
From one of those stars
How the street lights and car lights would
all look combined
This planet star we call Earth would look
just like another shining star...

Robin L. Tremblay

War

   Boys walk off the plane with bags on their backs not knowing what to expect, or exactly what to do.
   They scope and scan diligently for the prey.
The problem is, the predator may become the prey.
   The bushes shake and rustle as the prey is flushed out. Bullets fly and whiz through the air, there is a scream, a groan, and then a thud....
   Often with war the irony is, boys with bags on their backs, become men on their backs, in bags.
   War is hell and worse at that.

Russell Larson

The Last Unicorn

The Last Unicorn slowly raised his sleepy head,
Thinking of the youth he once had,
Running through the lush forests,
Eating apples and cotton candy off of the tall trees
and tasting the cool streams.

The Last Unicorn shed a tear,
A tear of happiness,
A tear of sorrow,
A tear that tells his whole life story,
A final tear for untold glory.

The Last Unicorn lowered his sleepy head,
Then raised it once more,
He looked at the sky and saw the pretty, white fluffy clouds,
Moving this way and that without sound.

The Last Unicorn lowered his head for the last time,
and remembered his last memories,
for the last time...

Tiffany Amorella

A Saintly Father

Dear Daughter of a saintly Father,
Thinking about my Grandpa makes me bother
To translate my feelings into writing.
Because within me there has begun fighting,
Fighting that, urges me to respect his life.
To correct my own, so that I can avoid eternal strife.
To us, on the surface of faith, it seems small,
But that's due to our own inability to live tall.
It is not so easy, for to live tall in the eyes
of God has a great demand.
For within himself is the war between Satan and God,
Of which God must command.
Human weaknesses are plentiful and vast
And I feel that the best means to please Him is to begin today.
To place in our hearts what the Bible and great men say:
"There is an Arm that never tires when human strength gives way
There is a love that never fails when earthly loves decay."

Terry Smith

My Child

Look my child and you will see,
things you thought could never be.
Dream little one and you'll realize,
the future is right before your inquiring eyes.
And remember when someone does you wrong.
Don't give up on others; your friends are not gone.
You see sometimes you must turn the other cheek.
Believe me child, it doesn't mean your weak.

There's lessons to be learned, pleasures to behold.
Songs to be sung and stories to be told.
Search for what is right, avoid all that's wrong.
Happiness is waiting and you can have it for your own.
And when you come to the mountains, don't go around.
There's a lesson to be learned from what is found.
Some things can be changed, others cannot.
Take heart my child, make the best of what you've got.

Vickie K. Wingo

Waves Of Humanity

They wave hell, they wave goodbye.
They're born, they grow and then they die.

Some are quite impressive with their steep and shining face.
Some are unintrusive and barely make a splash.

Some will take your breath away with beauty, form and grace.
Some come thundering in with a roar and then a crash.

Some are very powerful, they'll sweep you off your feet,
They'll drag you in their undertow and strip you of your dreams.

Others will caress you and make your life complete.
They can be so refreshing, actually be just what they seem.

They take away, they leave behind, their legacy remains.
This planet's well aware of them, it daily feels the strains,

As they wave hello and wave goodbye,
Oblivious to what remains.
Dan Avery

1986 World Series

The outlook wasn't brilliant for the New York nine that day,
They trailed by five to three in the last inning of play.
And when Backman flied out harmlessly,
And Hernandez did the same,
A sickly silence fell upon the patrons of old Shea.

Then Carter ripped a single to the happiness of all,
And the rookie Kevin Mitchell tore the cover off the ball.
And when the dust had settled and fans saw what had occurred,
Two Mets had staved off defeat, Ray Knight became the third.

Then from 50,000 throats there rose a rusty yell
It rumbled through the valley, it rattled through the dell.
It knocked upon the mountain and recoiled upon the flat
For Mookie, the mascot of the Mets was standing at the bat.

Oh somewhere in this favored land the sun is shining bright,
The band is playing somewhere and somewhere hearts are light.
And somewhere men are laughing and somewhere children shout,
That somewhere is New York City, the Mets have lucked it out.
R. Giordano Jr.

Common Sense Stew

Some people foolishly made nonsense stew.
They stood and squabbled about what to do.
Intellectualism, wasted stock.
Justification, split the chopping block.
Disagreement rose, and tongues for tasting,
now were used for special interest wasting.
Added legalese prolonged the slow cook.
The pompous with their pride finished the gook.
Mulligan tasted it and got profane.
He stumbled outside into the rain.

We put together a COMMON SENSE stew
with just basic ideas on what to do.
We took priority, it was our base,
then with necessity, we filled the space.
We put in the reasoning, just a bit
and calmly sat back when the time was fit.
Working together made it a fun chore.
The aroma brought a knock to the door.
Mulligan wanted to taste and have plain
common sense. He came in out of the rain.
C. Borden Davis

Mountain Memories

Mountains call my name as no one can.
They seek me out of hiding with their call.
Memories of a long forgotten plan.
The sights, the sounds, the beauty of it all.
Like magnets with the power to draw me near.
The air is crisper, thinner as I go.
Lowly plains behind, the peaks appear.
They glisten with the kiss of newborn snow.
Icy roads soon curl and wind away.
The mountain stream my constant roadside friend.
Fir trees dressed in white to greet the day.
Perhaps a sign this time will have no end.
Alas, the setting sun to hide this sight,
Too quickly shuts down mountain memories for the night.
V. Wilson

For Our Children's Sake

We see our children running scared.
They have no more dreams to spare.
Let's wipe away their tears; don't let them cry.
Let's take them by the hand, and reach for the sky.
Let's fulfill their dreams, once again -
Let's guide them through the promised land.
Don't we see and hear their cry for help?
Or do we not know how to take that step?
We can make a difference for our children now -
So why not take the time, while time is allowed.
Teresa G. Whitaker

Jenny's Memories

Jenny's memories are old now.
They fade with the dawn, to return only with the coming darkness.
They are memories of a long time past.
Of happiness, and life, and love.
Memories of a better time.

Jenny's memories are cold now.
They flee with the warmth of returning spring, and hide in
　　shadows until winter.
They are memories of yesterday.
Of laughter, and smiles, and love.
Memories of a kinder time.

Jenny's memories are just that now - memories.
Nothing more or less.
The bad times of all the yesterdays fade and are lost.
The good times sharpen in focus until they are unrecognizable
　　for what they really were.
All is gone, still, quiet.
And all that is left
Are Jenny's memories.
Sharon A. Viljoen

Of Times Past, Of Times To Come

How suddenly we do forget the loved ones we have known,
Through death we diminish the love we was once shown,
Our memories just seem to fade into a misty blur,
How and why they do is just so unsure,
Her face is just acknowledgment of someone we once knew,
How sad it is that we must face this undeniable truth,
As years go by with only thoughts of one so dear to heart,
I wonder if in heaven she thinks I've done my part,
to live by standards she held high while in this earthly place,
That someday I might live with her if I only keep the faith,
so Mother while you live with the one who is able to keep us all,
Please keep a place in heaven till one day we hear our call.
Paige Morgan

Untitled

Emotions are strange things we are feeling.
They are a part of everything we deal in.
There are good and bad, happy and sad.
But the worst emotions are the one's we try to hide.
By keeping them locked away inside.
When I look into your eyes, I sadly see.
Those hiding emotions, that totally confuse me.
What are you thinking? Please let me in,
I'm here to listen. I'm more than a friend.
I can feel your whispers, I can hear your tears.
Reach out to me. I'm one who cares.
What are these doubts, that are in your heart.
Those lonely thoughts that are tearing you apart.
Your sadness is a lock. Let me be your key.
I give to you my full devotion.
And together we will end, those mixed emotions.
Sadia Abdul

"There's Something In The Stars"

   The skies are dark, the moon is on,
There's light upon the ground.
   The waters; slapping upon the shore,
The sand is smooth, and there's a chill, set all around.

   There's a melody flowing in the air,
Making the Mocking Birds sing.
   There's a wonderful glow upon the earth;
All the churches are hence rejoicing.

   The stars are shining; millions at once,
Lighting up the sky.
   For every child looking up,
There's a dream within their eyes.

   There's something in the stars,
Which brings wonder, joy, and gleam.
   There's something in the stars,
In which we've never seen.

   It's a hope, a wish, a wonder,
Floating all about.
   But it's something in the stars,
In which we can only dream about.
Wendy Britt

Love

   My love for you is strong,
therefore I am writing you a song.
   My love for you is true,
even though you may not have a clue,
   My love is just for you.

   Every time I see you,
I forget what to say, what to do,
   When you hold me with all your might
in your arms so sweet and tight.

   Sometimes, I drift off to a far away land
with music and dancing, us hand and hand.
   Hoping the night would never end.

   When it's time for me to say good-bye,
I feel I want to cry...
   Cause in the few hours I spent with you
I didn't get to say what I wanted to.
   Yea, I hugged and kissed you.
but, did I say, "Be careful and watch what you do."

   And I want you to know...
I'll always love you!
Sara Coakley

Valley—Hay

There is a valley beyond the peak,
there trees the land the streams I seek.
How soon can I go when will it be, a blade of grass an old oak tree.
Maybe the wind will guide me there, light as feather a human hair.
Could be a pebble a stone away, this place I call Valley—Hay.
We all have a valley within our heart,
some of us find some of us part.

Look far enough deep into the breeze,
close your eyes beneath the trees.

The wind the crickets the pebbles will say,
welcome my love to Valley—Hay.

Is that a stream that sparkles so, can't be sand diamonds glow.
Could that be a tree trunk of gold,
branches of rubies I was told.

Blades of grass beneath my heel,
so tender so tender they make me feel.

Can this be heaven my Valley—Hay
a tree a branch a stream away.

Beyond the peak thee old oak tree,
there was a valley meant for me.
Joseph T. Wyatt

Everyone's Best Friend

Whenever I'm lonely, sad, and blue,
There is only one friend I feel close to,
I can talk to him anytime through the day or night,
He will listen to me and not put up a fight,
He will get me through trouble, sorrow, and pain,
I can tell all to Him and not feel any shame,
His light shines in my heart, He's always on my mind,
He's the closest friend you'll ever need; the best you'll ever find,
When you walk through the valley where you must go alone,
It will give you such comfort to know you've received the light He has shown,
So open up your heart and receive His love today,
It's the greatest gift you'll ever get for the price He had to pay,
If you ever need someone like you've never needed before,
Just listen a little harder, He is knocking on your door,
So open up your heart before this day is done,
And you'll find everyone's best friend,
God's only Son.
Leona Babcoe

Desperation

I have no friend, my pain won't mend,
There is no reason I should attend this life of mine,
Now it must end!

I've found myself here by the shore, hoping for an open door,
Asking God to take me in, "Please forgive me for my sin!"
God refused to answer me, I'm alone here by the Sea.

It's beauty makes me question why, do I truly want to die?
Can there be a life for me, or shall I walk into the sea?

The sun is like a bouncing ball, upon the water I watch if fall,
The Ocean plays a splendid game of color and motion,
It tries in vain, to keep it's friend a moment longer,
But the sun is so much stronger, it vanishes within the sea,
A sudden chill comes over me.

The water reaches for my feet, the ocean breezes smell so sweet,
The sand is cool, the air is warm, above my head the sea gulls swarm.

God has made this wondrous place,
I think there's something I must face,
I'm not alone here anymore, God has led me to the shore,
To show me that my destiny, is not to die down in the sea.
Sharon L. Solimine

I Thought You Knew

When work scope changes, and only you know,
There is a good chance, that something will blow.

With all not knowing what changes are pending,
You're more exposed than if you're lending.
The time it takes for a tailboard meeting,
Is well advised, and the crews best greeting.

We are all exposed to info new,
And assume the job with a change in crew.

"I didn't know of the change you speak,"
Is nothing to hear, after you've crossed the creek!

Ron L. Heckenberg

A Penny

There are times it seems we treat life as a penny
there are a lot of good things and blessings are many
we forget of the times when we laugh and we play
we forget how to smile and we forget how to pray
our memory returns when we treat others kind
our heart remains calm as we gain peace of mind

How simple it seems when we gain simple sight
to show one love we forget how to fight
remember a penny is still only one cent
but if you are in need it can be spent
it will help pay for the purchase of what you wish to buy
so let not the penny be simply a piece of the pie
all of the good things we forget to have cheer
remember a penny when you look in the mirror
a smile today will warm some ones heart
and this smile today is only a penny apart

Yollanda L. Garretson

"No Angels Only Devils"

I don't have no angels in my world
There all devils dancin' to and fro
They bring the hurt
The teardrops, the emptiness
Oh it covers me like a blanket of
Snow that quickly melts away from the heat
Oh I'm burning up 'cause my love for you will and
Always is in my soul
Every hour, every minute, every second of every day that
Passes me by without you to say
Hey or slap in the side is a day of emptiness
A day the devils took away
A day I was burnin' up with love
For seein' you once again and forever
'Cause I just can't help but love you
No angels only devils carryin' me away

Roxana Bellavia

The Real You

When I look at you, I do not see the kind of shoes
you wear, the color of your face, your dress, the
color of your hair.

No, these things are not important, what you wear,
how you dress, the pigment of your skin. I look
farther than your face, I try to look within.

I look for you, the person that you really are
or what you dare to be. I look farther than your
dress, I look for the warmth buried in your heart,
the part that's hard to see at first glance, but
is surely there if anyone should care to guess.

Rose Ashleman

"Tomorrow"

Some day the clouds will vanish and the heavens will be blue
Then we will be together and I'll make it up to you.

I will be gathering all the stars and giving you the dawn
For all the shadows of today will be forever gone.

For every tear of loneliness your heart may cry tonight
I promise you a dozen smiles to make your hours bright.

For every moment you must wait with memories and tears
There will be months of happiness extending into years.

There will be nothing ever to remind you of the past
But your desires and your dreams when I fulfill, at last.

Think not of some tomorrow when the clouds may hide the sky
Or of the possibility that we may say goodbye.

Just let me hold you in my arms and draw you close to me
Then I shall touch the pinnacle of perfect ecstasy.

The past can never come again, the future is not here
But we possess the present when we are together, dear.

So let us be content to put our other thoughts away
And let us live in happiness, the hours of today.

Rachel Eskew

First Lady In Dallas

Oh, No! Her cry ... and Jackie's lips breathed in
Their greatest gasp!
She never heard the "crack!" and "zing!"
Nor mortal rasp in metal's onslaught!

Oh, No! Shrieks absurd and people-shouts were lost
Amid the din of a dread behemoth
Crashing through her thought,
What her eyes could see, but she could not!

Oh, No! And then he fell ... her gentle husband ...
Freedom's chief, lay shattered in her lap ... flowing,
As: Resolved to be ripp'd from such humanity ...
Streaming over the pink she wore ...
A fluent nation's muted roar!

Oh, No! The stop-gap of her tears and love
And frantic, futile fingers, weren't enough
To hand us back what we were only lent:
A young - but mortal - President

W. L. Drew

The Misogynist's Wife

Pariah, asleep among the reeds
The wind has learned your lullaby
You speak the language of the trees
The seed has been planted in the garden of Gaia

Petals broken from a dying flower
Burned at the stake for their seductive color
Now only ashes smell of roses
In the garden where your lost soul was found

Your mythology, forgotten by the serpent's daughter
Disappears like the mist off the holy lake
Yet, I will find you buried alive
For I still believe in magic

Juggle the planets with your thoughts
Touchstones from the dark side of the moon
I will summon the last of the fireflies
And weave them into the sun

Where there is light there is ebony
A perfect balance, tipped by the stars
A mystic's potion of hemlock and rose hips
Will stop the curse of a hated woman, doomed to live forever

William Neville Chemnick

The Night Before

While walking out onto the sand-filled road from the hotel,
The wind blew the tumble weed and sand behind me.
I saw a young cowboy on his horse, lavished in leather,
chaps and a brown ten gallon hat fit for a lady.
"Howdy Miss," he said as he lifted his hat and gave me a
wink of the eye. He rode as whistling wind blew him by.
My cowboy boots with spurs caught the shining sun and
glared my view towards the saloon, where I had left my
horse the night before. My eyes dried from the sand and
my throat parched. I could only taste what was waiting
for me. It felt as if it were a mile down the road, only
next door, as I strolled. As I shuffled towards the door,
my horse let out a call. I looked at him and said,
"Just one more for the winding road."
He smiled as I entered through the shudder doors, bellied
up to the bar for one more. I slammed my empty glass
against the bar and left without a word. Jumped onto my
saddled up horse and road into the sunset while riding to
my small cabin where the cactus roamed.
  Patricia Bowker

The Key

Behold a door, too narrow for two,
the way to happiness, you must pass through.
You can't enter selfishly, proud, or alone,
for your passage thereafter reflects a love that has grown.

The secret to enter is simple — so kind,
not one going forward or the other behind;
with his arms he will hold her as she wraps herself 'round,
two souls looking forward as they step from the ground.

The once narrow opening is now warming its way
toward embracing the love that it feels on this day.
And having passed through they're amazed at the view,
not the garden of eden, or heavens of blue,

But halls upon hallways of passageways and doors,
all waiting to open to reveal what's in store.
The key to the maze is that as long as there's two,
there'll never be a door that won't open for you.
  Paul E. Rivet

Just One Little Kiss

Just one little kiss, can mean so much
the way to express, such a passionate touch
Just one little kiss, from you to me
keeps my world, in harmony
Just one little kiss, from me to you
creates the warming, perspective view
Just one little kiss, can erect a smile
with tenderness and meaning that lasts awhile
Just one little kiss, we'll here's the sun
vibrant feelings, happy and young.
Just one little kiss, it warms the heart
no better way, for any day to start
Just one little kiss, may bring out a cheerful tear
with what a way to look back at every year
As we grow older and reminisce
warm days that began with
Just one little kiss
  Robert Charles Keraghan

A Recipe For The Day

Take the beauty of the day,
  the warmth of the sun,
  the coolness of the gentle breeze,
  the surprising of a rainbow,
Along with a cheerful song of the heart,
  the kindness of a stranger and
  the hug of a friend,
Mix altogether with the laughter of good times,
  the remembrance of yesterday,
  the joy of today,
  and the promise of tomorrow
  and you will have a recipe of the day
  to help carry you along the way.
  Richard D. Clark

The Eye...

The eye...
The truth...a window...
Look...deep...the truth...it's real.
Experience the journey.
Dare to explore.
Accept the challenge.

The eye...
Blinking...pleading innocently...welcoming uncomfortably.

The eye...
A pathway to the soul.
A glimpse...an image...a reflection of the truth...
Who you are.
Genuine...delicate...pure...
A light unto darkness.
The unknown...but real.

The eye...
A tear drops...then another...gently.
An outlet...ointment for the heart...the healing begins.

The eye...
Full of truth.
  B. Renee Wright

The Little Things

It's the little things that matter the most.
The things you take with you, coast to coast.
It's Christmas morning in a child's eyes.
It's the tears that come with many good-byes.
It's picking out flowers for Mom and Grandma.
It's getting the card for Dad and Grandpa.
It's choosing the gift for that special day.
It's knowing that he'll always stay.
It's Thanksgiving day with all the trimmings.
It's birthdays shared and all the gift-givings.
It's Easter Day and togetherness.
It's a little boy and his cleverness.
It's the time you take just for yourself.
It's knowing when to take the cookies off the shelf.
It's knowing that you've done your best.
It's realizing when you've been blessed.
It's losing someone and feeling the pain.
It's sharing that pain and getting up again.
It's taking the time to say "I love you".
And it's hearing in return "I love you, too".
  Shelley Hewes

Heath

What can I say, my son, to make you understand,
The things I want for you when you become a man.

I know you're only a little boy, but now's the time to start,
For there are so many things I want to say that are within my heart.

I want you to know God as a very special friend,
To pray and have faith, and repent of all your sins.

To be hard-working and ambitions, to set yourself a goal,
But to God's world hand His people, don't ever be cold.

Take life in your hands, and make it what you will,
But don't ever be afraid to love, or to feel.

To be your own man is what I want for you, son,
But to be sensitive enough to share it with someone.
   Trisha Truelove

The Symphony

A walk thru the park presents thoughts of you
The sweet songs of the birds excite me
The silent rush of the wind arouses me
The deep drop of the waterfall thrills me
Together, like you and I, they are in harmony.

In unison they compose a never ending symphony
The birds vocalize, leading in bass and soprano
The sweet sensation of their song heard far and near
A flock's overhead leading in a soft song of love
A flock's in the background singing a chorus in rhapsody.

The constant flow of the waterfall drops in the lake below
The infinite cascade is never deafening and never domineering
The tune that is created is monotonous and always in the grove
The melody heard is rhythmic with a good swaying cadence
The end result is mesmerizing and soothing to the soul.

A gust of the wind rustles through colorful leaves in the trees
The sudden rush demanding the spotlight and immediate attention
It carries the mixture of pleasurable melodies all around
The pleasantry of the symphony is overwhelming and heavenly
Rivaled only by thoughts and joys of being wrapped in your arms.
   Roger D. Bendolph

The Promise Of A New Day

When I find life's turmoil overwhelming
the sweet somnolent wings of peaceful slumber
erect a citadel from the myriad web of each day's existence
putting to order the bewildering chaos of today's measure—
softly, quietly the robe of sleep curves round me—
suspending the taunt-tensioned nerves beyond my slumber
giving me strength to face the challenge of tomorrow
clearing my mind and my heart and my soul of hesitancy
steeling my nerves...
Helping to smooth the way where I may find certitude of purpose,
   of plan, of future's road stretched out before me..
and the gentle world of a life with you, O my Beloved.

As my dreams turn quietly over one by one
filling my sleep with hope and the sweet music of our love
making me joyful and strong and smoothing my mind
of all the uncertainty of life's cloudy by ways...
then I awaken doubt-freed and with firmness and purpose
step out into the golden light,
   the promise of a new day.
   Wray Christine Stewart Jones

Call My Name

It seems like every time I call your name
The sun lights up the sky
And it seems like every time I call your name
I never have any reasons to say goodbye
It seems like every time I call your name
My love for you grows even more
And it seems like every time I call your name
My heart melts like never before
It just seems that whenever I call your name
Sometimes you're not anymore there
And that's about all I can bear
Since you're no longer here with me
My world will never ever be the same
So I'll keep calling your name
   Robert Lee Elliott II

Night Sky Magic

The moon shed dripping silver o'er my room,
The stars brought faraway thoughts to my heart,
I gazed with my arms outstretched to the world;
I remembered the hopes and dreams of my youth,
Love, success and happiness - could they still be mine?
The magic of the night enchanted every fibre of my being,
It brought me close to the divine power in the universe,
The strength within my soul.
Feasting on the beauty of this splendid night sky,
I reveled in the joy, the excitement of life —
Life with its challenges, its strange mysteries
And its high hopes!
   Ruth Stewart

Imagination

I am floating above a stormy sea
The spray from choppy waves wets my skin
Salt is on my tongue

Through the blackness
I see a yellow light slicing the night
Closer it comes until I can almost feel its heat
In its wake, cold waves drench me in a watery embrace
The light fades slowly
All is quiet once more
Just the gurgle of the sea
and
The sound of stars twinkling are with me
   Zilla Martin

"J.W." Forever In Our Hearts

If you looked through his window
You could be sure he was playing Nintendo
Adults could surely get a clue
Prejudice of color he never knew
Up one street and down the other
He had so many friend there's not time to cover
Though his years were only ten
He could make you laugh again and again
At breakfast he loved to eat Pop-Tarts
Remembering pictures taken with your heart
The stories he told were many
If you lacked imagination he had plenty
At Christmas he always made a list
You can rest assured he will always be missed
His family will always wonder why
The pain gets easier as days go by
For someday we'll all be together
But for now he lives in our hearts
FOREVER
   Regina Wilson

Untitled

A cold sweat,
   the sound of fingernails scratching pavement.
A weak voice crying out.
He was there.

All around, a hellish arena of reds
   brick, blood, sun.
Grasping innocence with one hand, knuckles whitened from the strain.
Relief—
   letting go to embrace the darkness.

He feels it wash over his body
   the certainty, the strength,
     a living, breathing cold.

Standing alone, a small shiver shudders through his frame.

No hesitation then, mars his actions, his sense of direction.
None to offer solace - the family, friends, victim
   they had all deserted him not a moment before.

So as he must,
   he runs west, toward the darkness, as fast as he can,
all his divergent worlds calling helplessly to him
   from the void.
   Wesley Gamble

Nature's Wonders

Behold the beauty around us
The sky so beautiful, so blue
The rising sun, so bright, beaming with pride
Dawning the start of a new day.

Mountains, valleys and hills, all laced with marvels
Golden daffodils, flowering trees swaying with the breeze
Chirping birds, buzzing bees, murmuring brooks
Where pure and gentle water flows.

Look at the setting sun
As daylight ends
Watch the moonlight on the sea
And the brightness of the stars above.

Enjoy the beauty of the spring
As the winter breaks away
The azure blue of summer skies
And the golden leaves of fall.

What a feeling of ecstasy
Enjoying all these things of awesome beauty
Simple, treasured and everlasting gifts
Which God created for you and me!
   Sam Querubin

Family To You I Say

My dear family,
You said I would live to be one hundred three,
But guess what this is the end of me.
I died in tears, I died in dread, I died in love,
But I'm still dead.
I was coming home from a party, you see,
Then he kissed me.
I told him to keep his eyes on the road.
He told me I was a beauty to behold.
I pushed him away and said, look out.
And he did look all about.
We hit a truck on the first of July,
And that's the day that we died.
He went through the window, so did I.
We lied dead on the ground and died.
To my Mom don't cry,
To my Dad be brave,
To my brother take care,
My soul has been saved.
   T. M. Montgomery

A Week's Worth

Another week has just begun.
The sky is cloudy, there is no sun.
The birds still sing, the dogs bark.
The gulls are crying. Do you hear a lark?

The ocean's waves are hitting the rocks.
The water's foamy but it's not hot.
The sound of thunder breaks the quiet.
The lightning flashes through the night.

The rain starts off with a pitter-patter.
With each drop falling the people scatter.
The umbrellas go up, the ponchos go on
And little people are putting galoshes on.

The ducks on the pond are enjoying the rain,
Though most people think the rain is a pain.
After the rain and the wind decide to stop,
Most of the clouds have given up.

There's a rainbow out with its beautiful hue.
The earth's freshly washed and smells all anew.
The birds are singing, the dogs barks.
The gulls are crying Hush! Hear the lark?
   Patricia A. Heverly

Love And Rain

This dry and lonely season may never end I fear,
The skies are drained and love is gone as well,
Memories and dust are all that's present here,
I long for cooling breezes and spring's eternal spell.

We often walked together beneath a blessed shower,
and brushed away the raindrops with tender loving hands,
There is no substance left to nourish our love's flower
and rains that use to come, now visit other lands.

Yesterday has passed into forgotten memory,
today is more important, hope dawns in every sun,
If God can still remember to end this misery,
Perhaps the curse will end before today is done.

Must I weather these dead times and persevere till then,
Till love returns and raindrops fall to start my life again.
   H. L. Williamson

Hard To Hold

Hard to hold
The simplest dreams when Love is a challenge
So warm, then so cold
It seems your heart is refusing to balance

I'm not blind to the strain because I've been lost in the pain
But I know that passion like ours should not be hard to hold

When we touch, it's easy to see
Why Love has drawn us together
I may dream too much, but I believe
These feelings will last forever

Spurn me and turn me black-eyed cold
Maybe you think you don't burn me, but Love is the scar you scold
And I know that passion like ours should not be hard to hold

Hard to hold
And harder to reach you through the stormy confusion
At Love's threshold
You're forcing me closer to that bitter conclusion

I'm not blind to the strain
And I can't go back to the pain
Of a heart ripped open by passion far too hard to hold
   R. Minicozzi

Through The Sea Of You

In the coal of night, my mind plows like a ship through
The sea of you.
I still feel your warm embrace,
I wish you still felt the closeness too,
Our bodies used to trace.

In the coal of night, my mind plows like a ship through
The sea of you.

Inside me, you carved an unknown piece of art,
We are the wood, fate is sharp as a knife,
That cuts away every piece of my heart.

In the coal of night, my mind plows like a ship through
The sea of you.

Though there is nothing left of us today,
The memory of us as we once were,
Is burned in my soul, and is here to stay.

In the coal of night, my mind plows like a ship through
The sea of you.

Ashley Vaughan

Social Insecurity

Words can't convey the pain that I feel,
The result of a small mistake.
Several weeks later the condition persists,
Though it took only seconds to make.

Social Security is a wonderful thing,
But it sometimes goes awry.
When I reported the death of my beloved wife,
They declared the decedent was I.

They stopped sending my monthly checks,
While new payments were sent to my wife.
She also received a new Medicare card -
Further proof of the loss of my "life."

After personal visits and many phone calls,
And countless words having been said,
I've been told that "progress is being made."
We now are both shown as "dead."

William L. Cregar

Ode To The Rocky Mountains

I've this melancholy calling to see Her Majesty, My Queen,
the Regal Rocky Mountains, garbed in Her robe of green;
The snowy cap, so white, so pure, that She wears for a crown;
The veins of gold and silver, that She wears as a gown.

Oh, humble homage I shall pay, when She looks down from above,
And sees me roam in Her domain, of flower, fawn and dove.
And lets me rest my weary bones, 'neath Her stately pines.
Envy, I, the clouds that bow to kiss Her spired shrines.

Again Her valleys call to me, my heart says I must go.
I need feel Her balmy breezes; need touch Her rain and snow.
Then wade across Her babbling brooks, and repose in Her lap,
Of flora, rock, and lake and tree, that She wears for a wrap.

There's but one place on earth, that I know was Heaven lent.
I know this place, for it's a place, I've many hours spent.
And, like those before me, I must one day quit Her scene.
But, She'll be wooed by those who follow, Her Majesty, My Queen.

Richard Beougher

You

The words you deliver to me from a breeze
The profound sensation you let me experience at your proximity
The refined figure you make me hallucinate at your remoteness

You put me in a state of euphoria
You intensely liberate me so high
You deprive me of ecstasy when you are a remote image in the horizon

I embrace myself when my attention meditates of you
I neglect myself when your ambiguity doesn't permeate in my garden
I elate myself when your reflection glows as divine epic

The vivid caress that electrifies me
The fascination that makes me impatient
The rapture of exhilaration that animates me

All the expressions I cannot begin to translate
All the desires I have not confessed
All the love that cannot be denoted

Patricia I. Torres

Untitled

Nothing which we are to perceive in this world—
  The power of your intense fragility;
Whose texture compels me with the
  color of its countries, rending me
  with each breath.

I do not know what it is about you
  that closes and opens; only something
  in me understands the voice of
  your eyes is deeper than all.

Somewhere I have never traveled, gladly
  beyond any experience, your eyes
  have their silence; In your most
  frail gestures are things which
  enclose me, which I cannot touch
  because they are too near.

Your slightest look easily encloses me,
Though I have closed myself like fingers,
You always open each, petal by petal
Slowly and mysteriously giving way
  to all that is within.

Philip J. Davis

Down The Path

Of course I am a grandmother but does this say: I am walking down the path of old age.

Sure, I found a few more gray hairs this morning, as I looked in the mirror.

My bones ache a little more, a few faltered steps, an occasional memory loss; nothing to be alarmed about.

As for my figure, just a small thickening in the middle, hips a tad more padded, biceps a fraction too limp: happens to everyone, sooner or later.

Come to think of it, I am a little wiser now; realize the danger of my foolish youth, try to instill this to my sons, doesn't take effect

Inevitably, I gave up riding my Harley, couldn't stand hanging low in the curves.

Try to slow the hands of time; appreciate God's gifts a little more, mediate more on the hereafter. Still not quite the signs one would expect to see down the path.

When my gentlemen friend calls tonight, I will feel the familiar stirring of love awakening, eyes twinkling, heart fluttering.
I shall smile, for I have not traveled so far down the path of old age; maybe just halfway.

Wilma Duncan

An Invitation

I'm gonna go to Heaven, I'd like you to show up too.
The path is straight and narrow, but there's lots of things to do.
We can run and play among the clouds, and never have a care.
Or We can join the Angel band and play our music there.
We can sit at Jesus' feet and listen to him talk, about
how He healed the sick, and how let the crippled walk.
We can have a big reunion with our friends up in the sky.
We'll never have a worry, and we never more will cry.
There is no pain in Heaven, and there is no sadness there.
There's only joy and happiness for all of us to share.
Please come.
Vivian Jaynes

Jaded Moon

Drowning in an ocean of blue,
The only light is green, shining from the pale moon.
He pulls me out and takes me to shore.
My naked body rests upon the midnight floor.

Engulfed by the light that forsakes my destiny,
I am lost in his shelter,
Away from reality.
I climb the jaded mountain.

Warmth covers the nightly shore
Tightly wrapping his arms around my body,
I collapse into his world,
Drowning in daffodils and cotton tails.

I reached the top of the mountain.
I can touch the light.
But he moves away,
Faintly in sight.

I dangle alone in a world of blue.
My only existence comes from the warmth
Of the green, nightly moon.
Zazy Ivonne Lopez

Noises Of My Past

I lie in bed and think of the noises of my past,
The ones I always have and the ones that never last.

I remember my old choo-choo train that went round and round,
I remember the noisy rain that fell quickly to the ground.

I lie here in my bed and think of my noise past,
My life flies by and time just does not last.

My wooden bed grow cold as I grow slightly dead,
The only noise repeating is the silence in my head.
Stacy Getsinger

Farewell, Brother

Now that you've crossed the river, brother,
There's peace in my heart you see.
Your life was bound with suffering,
God has released the bonds and set you free!

You desired to leave us, and all your trials,
Your heartaches, disappointments and despair.
Deep down you were searching for answers
But they seemed elusive everywhere!

Good-bye and farewell, dear brother,
As you are ushered into pure light.
Words escape me as I lift you in prayer.
Godspeed! As you behold the beautiful light!
Sarah Graber

My New Daddy's Face

Sometimes I find myself still searching for those words,
the ones a daddy says to his little girl.

Opportunities have come and gone with only disappointment left.
Does he even notice this incredible theft?

Does it matter enough to search all of my life?
Can one person's indifference touch my soul like a knife?

I've searched and searched and thought I'd found
my daddy's love all around.

But the replica faded as the morning crept up,
and I wondered what happened as I gazed into my cup.

So what do I do in all my dismay?
They say forgive and go on - that's the only way.

But how, I say. I don't know how.
Then at the feet of Jesus I bow.

He puts His hands upon my face and says
"Come with me. I'll help you run the race."

So I take His hand as I look into His eyes,
and He kisses my forehead and wipes my tears dry.

Little by little as I walk in grace,
I'm starting to trust my new daddy's face.
Sharon Paro

Time

Time is a-tickin' and two clocks there be,
The one for the young seems to tick....to slow you see.

While the clock of the older, ticks way too fast,
We hear them exclaim, just seems like only yesterday, too quickly they pass.

Often the younger are heard to state, my birthday never seems to get there and, I can't wait,

While from those older as they do exclaim....I just had one,
I'll skip this one without hesitate.

Seems a real fear of passing thirty, for it's often been said
I have spent half my life now, and so few more's our dread.

For you see...tis not always the dying, ahhh...but yet on the mind,
Tis of things not yet done, and....the feeling were time behind.
Paul A. Still

Satisfaction

I sit in the well kept kitchen of mine.
The oak sashed window frames my two story view.
I like to sit with a glass of wine
in that hour before dinner when the tree
by the garden casts its long shadow.
I watch the stove for any signs of trouble.
Canning vegetables is such a slow
process. My tomato crop is double
what it has been the last few years. At last,
my plot is safe from its chronic disease,
a fat ground hog who could always sneak past
my best defense and eat my zucchinis
that was until I caught the brown devil
and beat his head flat with a steel shovel.
Sean McFeely

Harken

"Harken, my soul. Who goes there?"
"The nurse, my friend. I've come to make my rounds."
"Treat me kindly - as I know you will."
"And that I will. It's what I'm trained to do."

"Harken, my soul. Who goes there?"
"The doctor, my friend. I've come to make my rounds."
"How am I doing? I know you will tell."
"You are doing well. I'll see you tomorrow."

"Harken my soul. who goes there?"
"The night nurse, my friend. Are you comfortable?"
"What time is it? I'm very tired."
"Past your bedtime. Now take your rest."

"Harken, my soul. Who goes there?"
"An angel, my friend. Are you ready?"
"Am I awake, or am I dreaming?"
"Come with me. Your journey has been approved."
Thos M. Lybbert

Awesome Goodby

When the sunshine goes, the woods are dreary
The mood of the birds and the flowers is sad,
Bedecked, all for naught, in their varying gay raiment
No shimmering sheen, gloriously behead
Through the thick-leafed boughs of green
No sky of blue is beholden
Gone, too, the magical network of lace
Woven by nature with beauty and grace
Ah, yesterday! What a day to remember
The woods, the hills, and the fields overall,
Had surrendered, whole-soul, to the giving of beauty
Through sunshine displaying the farewell of fall.
One ponders, in wonder, this magical power
Which annually fanfares such awesome good-byes
But then after waiting a long, restful period
Earth causes more grandeur to spring back alive.
Ruth Pearson

Going Home

Going home has such a sweet sound
The memories flow so easy, they're all around
To be in the place of my childhood
To be back on the mountain, deep in the woods
Where as a child I ran and played
From daylight to dark that's where I stayed
To hear my dad drive up in the yard
Coming home from work all dirty and tired
With mom in the kitchen busy as a bee
Serving up the taters and the soup beans
Taking turns doing the dishes
And all the other chores
Knowing when we finished these
There would always be one more
So many things have changed over the years
To think back brings me joy and tears
I now have a family of my own to raise
Now it's their turn to make memories
Of their childhood days
Sheila Dietz

The Ultimate Judge For OJ

I hope we never lose sight of the real issue here:
The loss of two lives, their families left behind to dry the tears.
From a violent past, to bloody shoe prints and gloves,
Many suggest the jury was too quick to judge.
It's hard not to lose faith in our judicial system,
When you believe he walked in part due to his wealth and position,
For the victim's families there was no justice,
In large part because of the jury's decision to rush this.
Cochran dealt the racial card from the bottom of the stack,
In hopes that the jury would help "end racial injustice" for the blacks.
OJ was not made to answer to the public for now;
But deep in my heart, I know he will someday, somehow.
He will have to answer to his own conscience for the death of his
    ex-wife and friend,
And then to the Ultimate Judge when his own life comes to an end.
Sharon Walters

Growing Up

The suitcase starts out empty all new and fresh and clean
The load is not a burden, the bearer skipping happily
But piece by piece it becomes full as minutes turn to hours
Until what needs to go inside is a pile that nearly towers
It starts our very slowly, on piece here, one piece there
The burden becomes larger - though still not too much to bear
But there comes a point in all our lives as minutes turn to years
Where the load just gets so heavy it can drive you close to tears
Things packed in so quickly it fills up to the top
Yet more and more keeps coming - Will it ever stop?
The bag is barely liftable so heavy it's become
You roll your eyes to heaven saying: Can't I take out some?
But God will never give us more than our suitcase can hold
And He in His true wisdom makes us wise as we grow old
The experience and knowledge of the older folks is real
It's only then we finally learn to put our load on wheels.
Paula Eiden

Full Circle

I've come full circle, it's quiet a relief,
The last seven years were encompassed in grief.

I've come full circle, my fantasies are at rest,
The illusions created were mere figments at best.

I've come full circle, I delight in my life,
I no longer carry the burden of strife.

I've come full circle, I'm at peace with myself,
Those familiar uncertainties have been put on the shelf.

I've come full circle, feeling anger no more,
At parents who tried, but just couldn't keep score.

I've come full circle, I forgive and forget,
I feel quiet accomplished, my needs have been met.

I've come full circle, I can fly on my own,
I feel comfort around me, I am finally home.
Sheryl Milman

The Chosen

The angel walks down from the heavens holding out her hand to the one she chose. The chosen falls deep into a sleep, a sleep of love and passion, not knowing what lies ahead, the chosen continues in his sleep.

The chosen dreams of when he may return to the heavens with his angel. Sadly he awakens with the reality that the angel is for now and not forever.

In all reality the chosen would not change a thing if he could. Even if he knew at the beginning, nothing would change.
Shaun Klein

Not Out Catching Fireflies

I feel soft pillows about me as I run through the lawn at
The house I grew up in, albeit not young anymore. Not
Waiting for father to end his commute, not out catching fireflies...
I rescue this dream on broad shoulders of fantasy, from the
Untimeliness of waking time, with curt denial of morning
Breath and an end to smile.
The grass is moist still where the sprinkler was set. The
Leg of lamb calls forth suppertime; would it be able to whet
The appetite changed by time and place, my body drawn tighter
Stronger lines line my face?
An eye opens the conscious like a door to a vault where
Pillows are like prickly blades of grass finding fantasy
At fault.
As if Castor has lost his Pollux to the vast Gemini sky,
The awakening before me bleeds a tear from my eye.
   Timothy P. Sullivan

The Sacrifice

The day was dark and dreary, the sun hid behind the clouds,
the heavens cried tears upon the earth, as He made His way through
   the crowds.

He wore beads of sweat, a tattered robe, and a crown of thorns on
   His head,
and the jeering crowd began to yell, "We want Jesus dead!"

A heavy stake He carried, but never once complained,
for He knew His fate that was to be, that the prophets had proclaimed.

As Jesus Christ was crucified, and mocked the "King of the Jews",
He prayed to God. "Forgive them, they know not what they do.

His heavenly Father turned away, He could not bear to see,
His beloved Son take all our sins, and die on Calvary.

His body had been beaten, His throat was parched with thirst,
and vinegar was given Him to drink, the crowds they cheered and
   cursed,

And Mary stood by and sadly watched, as they crucified her son,
and finally when the ghost was gave up, the prophecy was done.

For Jesus shed His blood for us, so that we may be born again,
and be rebirthed unto the Lord and be forgiven for our sins.

Just kneel and pray and thank Him, for the sacrifice He made,
the ultimate act of love and the enormous price He paid.
   Sharon Reisch Cherry

Marching Band

Parents are packed into the stands
The greatest bands are in demand
All in step they step onto the field
And suddenly everything seems real
The drum major gets them ready to begin
As they prepare to perform once again
Then the show starts and the crowd is hushed
The tempo moves fast and is almost rushed
Then everything decrescendos down very soft
And the slow looming solo is suddenly caught
The difficult moves, the changes in tempo
But somehow they make it seem very simple
When the show is done and the crowd explodes
Even the judges think it was a really great show
Nobody can deny the work they've put in
The hours of practice has come to an end
The final show now come and gone
A new reputation leading them on
   Sara Monk

The Sound Of Loneliness

No longer can I take it: Off goes the TV;
the furnace is crackling; its fan is blowing; cars drive by
I must look out: No, no one for me.

The refrigerator hums — every now and then
More cars go by my window. Still no visitors —

Minutes and even hours just....drag...right on by!
There's never total silence — even lights make noise
I'm feeling sort of lost, and empty inside

Then, suddenly I realize: All that I hear is the sound of loneliness

I strain to listen:
my new watch — it really ticks!
And my telephone — YES, I HEAR! — it does not ring.
   Sandra McCormick

"Midnight"

The night is dark, the moon is full
The fog is rolling in
The sea is high and by and by
A man is climbing in

At first you think, its but a dream
But then to your surprise
You hear him at your bedroom door
And see his shinning eyes

"Don't be afraid my dear" you hear him calmly say
"For at the stroke of midnight you shall die this very day"
You hear a clock striking twelve, the clock across the way
He's coming closer with a knife, your life you'll have to pay.

The next morning, there are policemen, standing all around
And on the ground a body lay, with blood all around.
Don't be afraid, my dear" you hear him calmly say
For at the stroke of midnight you shall die this very day.
   Alexandria Williams

The Change

The leaves are falling, it's a beautiful fall,
The fire is burning, to hear the warmth call,
The air is colder, as the days linger on,
The wind is boulder, from dusk until dawn

And this will all change, after twelve long weeks,
Then people will be sliding, on ice covered creeks,
About the time we're all tired of being all bundled up,
Winter goes away, like a streak of our good luck

Then it turns to spring, the air all fresh and clean,
The flowers bloom, the birds sing, it's time to change again,
From winter coats and jackets, to a cooler kind of dress,
Washing windows, painting, to clean our winter mess.

Day by day the heat gets stronger,
As time goes by the days get longer,
The sun beats down, the crops grow fast,
Ah! Yes! It's summer at last.

The changes we must make for each season,
Certainly there must be a reason,
but it's hard for us to understand,
The changes required by man.
   Paula Cole

Life

What a wonder.
The feelings and adventures, the love and the excitement,
It is just a part of our life.
The joy of being here, in this place called Earth.
The buzz of the bees, the whistle of the wind,
The warmth of the sun, all give me that feeling,
That feeling, of life.

You see, without life, there would be silence,
All alone in a deep, black hole.
Screaming and yelling for someone to help-but it is no use,
Because there is no life.
Life is a gift you see, the best gift of all.
Life, should be treated in a way in which the end is near.

Tomorrow. Is there a tomorrow?
Life is a mystery, a mystery that will never be solved.
So, as I put it in words of these

Please live your life to the fullest.
Be caring, be loving, but most of all, be thankful.
For as we know it, there will never be a better experience,
or beauty than-our short, short....life.

Ryan Lee McClelland

Shooting Star

As the moon spills over the sun,
the echoes of days sink into the horizon.
The sugar cane swallows the light,
and the sun is stolen by the palms of the earth.
A day of hard work and toil comes to a close,
as strokes of purple and pink paint the sky.
The crescent moon and single star watch over the fields,
as midnight prepares her beauty.
A blanket of stars then embraces the sky.
It is strange,
that although our lives are headed in different directions,
our paths are lightened by the same moon.
In ideas and thoughts we are worlds apart,
yet together we smile at the same sunset,
and together we have wished upon the same star.
Our laughter may never again be united,
but our memories will forever light my soul.
With each shooting star I wish only the best for you.

Shannon Byrnes Ortiz

Where?

The dry leaves blew under the swings,
  the chains spotted red and brown with rust.
The rain dripped slowly down the tree limbs onto
  the rust spotted slide.
I watched as the wind stirred the leaves under the
  slide and wondered where the children were?
Why the rust and the dead leaves and the silence on the
  play ground?
A squeak from the merry-go-round startled me as the
  breeze tried to turn it.
And I wondered where are the children?

The Jungle Jim looked bare and unused, rusted and
  neglected, you could almost hear it call out
    "Children come play on me, come climb on me and
    have fun with me."
There were no children playing or running in the yard,
  no children laughing or yelling,
    no children any where.
Where, where are the children?

G. W. Climie

Nowhere In The World

Nowhere in the world is seen
The beautiful quiet, Christ can bring
To a heart that is torn, shattered, and bruised.
He is with us everywhere.

Darkness fills the lonely soul.
Turmoil holds us from our goals
Of lifted hands, of heaven's songs,
And of pouring out our hearts in prayer.

Many turn in times like these
To devices used by some to ease,
The agony of loneliness and pain of total emptiness,
To rid the grief of life's despair.

Reaching out for help, we find,
At times, that which numbs the mind
Or ending life not ours to take.
But then we ask, "Who cares?"

"Lord help us understand and see,
Nowhere in the world will be
Refuge, solace, and Salem's peace,
Found only in your presence here."

G. Stuart McCain

Torment Of The Night

Now I lay me down to sleep;
  the beast within starts to creep.
From the deepest recesses where I hide my fright;
  the creature, undaunted, returns night after night.
In the darkness, no sight or sounds;
  unfettered, its terror abounds.
Haunted by this hellish power;
  forced awake I count each hour.
This alien has made my body its lair;
  it feeds on my hate, my anger, my despair.
Regurgitating cruelties I've long since repressed;
  a nocturnal vigil to those whose lives I've transgressed.
My life's defects are magnified and inspected;
  no detail too small, no aspect is neglected.
Anguished, I twist and turn and writhe in bed;
  naked to the thoughts that siege my head
And at first light, the monster retreats;
  like a vampire after evening feasts.
Its victims, overtime, sucked of their being;
  The break of dawn sends the night's torment fleeing.

Richard H. Lashoones

"Yours Till Eternity"

Pain stalks in the blunders
The anguish puts us sunder
Torment in the shadows
Cast against the consciousness
To seek the heavenly splendor
Will it ever be accessible
To taste the wine of life from all omissions
Until ones love
The rejoiner so delectable
No matter where you wander
Or what you'll achieve
Your love will never be interminable
For the righteous one
True to be
Yours till eternity...

Sandy Engler

Prison Song

On the road to recovery.
That's where I'm gonna go.
I'm ready for it now.
My heart tells me so.

Changing with the days, and growing spiritually,
Brings joy to my life, it will set me free.
Learning about myself, is part of this too.
My inner voice will help, to guide me thru.

Each step I take
will be done with care.
And in each moment,
I'm fully aware.

People in my path,
will look different to me.
When I start reaching out,
helping them to see...

That life doesn't end,
when they put you away.
It's time to recover.
Where's your will? Here is the way!
Pamela S. Mansfield

Who I Am With You

I am strong, truthful and most of all happy.
That's face not truth, they're all lies.
Every day I live, I give you not me, not, who I am
I pretend to be someone, something different.
Something you would picture in a fairy tale,
your fairy-tale, not,
my fairy-tale would be to give you truth.
Truth is all of me good, or, bad, sinner, or
witness, pretty or ugly.
I would love to give you who I am, but,
not now, not ever.
Why? You would give her up, throw her away,
you would no longer be proud.
In your fairy-tale, I excel at everything.
In truth, I excel at almost everything except,
opening up, who I am with you,
a saint and have nothing but, sacred thoughts.
Behind you, a saint but, with devilish thoughts.
That makes me who I am.
Who I am with you and behind you.
K. C. Colom

Bean Of Beans

Round, firm, and fully packed
Yellow and smiling
The sturdy soybean
High in protein
Deplete in cholesterol
Non-nitrated
Maybe even organically grown
Age old nutrient of the Orient

You should soak them, boil them, and summer them.
Then you can season them
Toss them into a salad,
Bake them into a loaf,
Drop them into soup,
Make them into tofu,
Drain them into milk,
Saute them, refry them.
Buy them, try them!
Pat Cooney-Cummings

Welcome Home

I never thought the time would come so soon,
that we would have to say good-bye.

I never thought in a thousand years,
that you would be the first to die.

I never knew the days would go so fast,
when we were just getting real close.

I never thought that I would love you so much.
I never wanted to let go.

To the hopes, the dreams and the possibility,
that we would start all over again.

To love each other, to know each other,
for me to be your true friend.

The clouds decided to open up,
The heavens decided to move apart
To welcome you home today, but in my heart, mind and soul,
is where my daddy will always stay.

I'll never forget our last moments together, we became closer than we
ever could, to see a side of my daddy, that I thought I never would.

From my heart and soul, I wanted you to know,
that I loved you more than words can express.

For I never knew, that the time would come so soon,
for my daddy to be laid to rest.
Anita L. Chatman

Summer Of '93

In the summer of '93, my son came to work for me.
That was the summer that dreams came true,
The time I became close to you.
I'm the Father, you're the son
Without an example of what was to be done.
My Father was cold and distant, never a kind word to say.
I never had a pattern, to show me the way.
Years went by, the game was all wrong,
I felt the need to be forceful and strong.
The force was met with rebellion, the strength pain.
Following a path in which no one would gain.
Mom said to be patient, she said to be kind,
If you expect the light of love to shine.
The summer was here, it was '93, my son was 12.
And came to work with me.
I showed patience, encouragement and pride,
As he worked at my side, I saw a glimmer of light,
In his eyes.
The summer is over, the best of my life,
When it ended, the light was bright.
Ronnie Lindler

Untitled

It's been said, "In the beginning God created
The heavens and the earth."
But when he created "Man",
Both these things lost all worth.
For man's ability to create
Exceeds his ability to judge
He has created things like
Holes in the atmosphere, acid-rain, and toxic sludge.
As much as we love our world,
Not many are trying to save it.
Mankind has become a world of "Indian-givers,"
But God's the one that gave it.
Patrick L. Pierce

Changing Seasons

The winter sun had us perceiving
that the season is short, but it's deceiving.
It conceals the frigid air that's waiting
and makes us think the cold's abating.

Springtime was warm, drifts disappeared.
Then more snow came, as some of us feared.
It took a while for early flowers.
'til warm sun showed its magic powers.

The hot days of summers we took in stride.
Some like cool weather so they stayed inside.
But if the body can absorb the heat and sun rays,
it should keep us warm through the cold winter days.

In autumn we noticed the leaves start to fall.
They flutter and circle with each little squall.
The northern lights changing lit up the sky.
Then we knew that the summer was saying goodbye.

We made a full circle, winter is back.
We'll read about next year in the new almanac.
In the meantime we're ready with shovel and scoop
We'll bolster our forces with some hot chicken soup.

Rose J. Chambers

What Is Music

Music is a lullaby,
That soothes and makes a child so sleepy.
A piano, a harp, an organ or violin,
Reaches and holds us all so deeply.

The star-spangled banner, our national anthem,
Makes us stand and sing with pride.
Music is the universal language
Understood by everyone worldwide.

In church we sing our hymns and anthems
As David sang his psalms to God.
And singing Handel's great "Messiah"
Makes us feel so close to God.

The scriptures say the morning stars sang
And rejoiced when God created the earth.
And Moses sang his song of praise,
When the nation of Israel received its birth.

The bible tells us God will sing
O'er his creation and rejoice.
So what is music? God is love
And music is his voice.

Vivian Higgie

I Am A Girl Who Can't Hear

I am a girl who can't hear and believes
That one day I will be able to hear.
I wonder if I'll ever hear rain falling from the sky
I hear a well built boy calling my name.
I'd like to be able to hear the animals making noises.
I am a girl who can't hear.
I pretend that I can actually hear the world.
I feel the ocean waves splashing.
I touch a vibration of sound out of no where.
I worry that I will never be able to hear.
I cry when someone gets make fun of.
I am a girl who can't hear.
I understand that being deaf is something special.
I say that the deaf can do anything anyone else can do.
I dream that one day every deaf person will able to hear.
I try my best to understand people when they speak.
I hope that one day God will let me hear
the ocean waves splashing.
I am a girl who can't hear.

Tacey Ann Brock

Verdant Leaves, Idle Creature

Thy lacking moisture, verdant leaves
That in which I, inhaled
Produced to my life, a bee
Within the bounds of times, that I desired

I didn't heed to be me
Yet, to be he, as well as free
He mayest, been negative
Yet, so loved, as well respected

Farther aft, I, soared' afresh
Yet, this time, was not the same.
What I crave for, now its me, for Aye!
Wert art I? Ay!? I is gone!
Nevertheless that which is dead wilt ne'er come!

Ultimately now, I perceive
'Tis me, who I desire to be
But likewise late, now I am he,
Yet, It is thee! Who I wish I save!

I'm only a idle creature, now! Aye! Ay!?
Aye! = Always, Ever
Ay! = O! Oh! Ah! An expression of sorrow

Sergio Hernandez

Jesus

There's someone in my life,
that I will always keep in touch.
Because I love him very much.
He's with me every day
in my work and play
when I'm hungry he makes sure I'm fed
he tucks me into bed
when I'm cold he holds me in his arm
until I'm warm
when there's hurt and sorrows
eh says don't worry there are bright tomorrows
he's someone every body knows of
so full of love
he died for all to be free
the best thing that ever happen to me
some believe he's coming back
I'm not one to attack
to me he never depart
he's here right in my heart
Jesus is his name none other is the same.

Betty James

He Inspired Me

He inspired me...
That frightened, lonely, troubled teen.
He had made bad choices; joined a gang.
It took courage to admit the wrongs he had done.
He shared it all with viewers via the TV screen.
He inspired me...
He had written a prayer asking God to help him turn his life around.
It took courage to read this in front of strangers and peers.
He did it while I sat listening, tears streaming down my cheeks.
He inspired me...
I wanted to embrace him; to show him that I care.
I wanted him to know that his actions to change
were signs that God was already reacting to his plea for help.
I wanted to encourage him to remain hopeful and strong.
I wanted him to know he was becoming a positive role model
for others to follow.
But I did nothing.
I became the frightened, lonely, troubled adult.
We were united yet separated via the TV screen.

Suzanne C. Totsch

Remembering D.D. 1994

You see waves
That flow toward the shore
You hear the music of the waves
As the tides flow and the sands reach for more

You hear songs
Of gulls that are screeching
You smell the sweet scents
From the tides and the sands that are reaching

I see red waves,
Carrying the blood of the wounded and dead
I hear the blasts of the guns
From ships behind and guns ahead

I hear the moans
of the wounded that I dread
It smell the death
of the bodies floating and stacks of dead

Those who were there remember
As thoughts blast through their minds
And bring tears
That is impossible to leave behind.

Robert E. P. Moranda

Bonds Unbroken

In our lives we often find,
that bonds are often broken;
   Promises forgotten words go left unspoken.
  I know of one bonds in my life,
That has stood the test of time,
   The bond that you and I have shared,
That's only yours and mine.
   All these years and together,
From childhood up till now.
   Through many kinds of weather,
We made it through somehow.
   And here we stand at present, with children
of our own, and sharing all this wisdom,
   From times that we have known.
Often times I've wondered, just what did God
   Intend, when he crossed our paths together
   And gave to me a friend. Whatever was his
Reason, it never need be spoken,
   for you and I will always share,
   A bond forever unbroken.

Tanya S. Parmalee

The Hand

She cringes in a corner faraway from her comfy bed,
terrified of the hand above her head.
Many times before that hand has hurt her,
as if it were,
a slap for a mistake that she had once made
and before this had not been paid.
She tries to find someone who does care,
but right then it seems there's no one there.
Her screams shatter the still night air,
reaching out to someone who might care.
She tries to hold back the tears
that would shaw she fears
the hand above.
And to think this was the man she did once love.
The tears come to her eyes
because of the man she now does despise.
She has no strength left to fight,
she prays for someone in the night,
but all that's there
are screams in the shattered air.

Tonya Loewen

"Woman"

When he holds you think of me, I will hold you more
tenderly, when he smiles, see my face, pretend his arms
are my embrace, and when he loves you speak my name,
remember I always been the same.

   And when you come home, neon signs will
stop their blinking, stately philosophers will stop their
thinking, the city no longer hustle and bustle, it will
forget its hustle, babes in arms, will turn from their
mother's breast and get their rest, children will be
forsaken by their dandy's and forget their candies, when you
come home.

Tom Gray

Who Cares

Who cares anymore about the lost innocence, the
tears of a child, that cries for help in the
cold lonely nights
-NOT MANY-
Who says that they, care, cries when a child's life
is wasted and tries to stop the lost innocence
of a child
-JUST A FEW-
Who talks about a change, how a child's life is
a precious thing, unreplaceable and
does nothing, but talk
-A LOT-
Who wishes that a world full of wealth would just stop,
take the time to care and stop the
crying of a child
-AGAIN, JUST A FEW-
Who hopes for changes, tries to make a difference,
and hope maybe one day others will take
the time to care
-I DO, AND SO SHOULD YOU-

Vilath Keoviengxay

The Prayers Of Jesus

Jesus went to a place of old they called Gethsemane,
Taking with him Peter, and the sons of Zebedee.
He commanded that they stay with him to pray,
To keep the watch, as daylight slipped away,
For He knew soon, within a tomb of death He'd lay.
He had to pray, so on from them He wandered,
To fall again upon his knees and to beseech his God—
If this cup could be removed from destiny—
Let it be!
And once again He prayed. This prayerful plea He made;
Father, not my will, but Thine be done on earth this day.
But Abba, Father—I ask if there's a way
To have this cup taken away, for fearful and distressed
This day am I.
But not my will, my Lord! I have to save a sinful world
That they might be with you—as I shall be, after my agony.
And then they took my Lord away.

Robert E. Morgan

The Rose

I doubt the rose that blooms on the windowsill.
The sound of the crashing waves feel too strong.
As the salty white granules begin to eat away the flesh,
buoyancy; the key to the world, struggles to be found.

The petals appear to be falling, like a rock from the sky.
Slaloming in and out to prevent total darkness,
the natural light seeps through.
As this blind man attempts to see, "Is the rose really red"?

William Momary

Generations

Reality and thoughts of things like this,
takes time and much more.
We want to be human first, which we must.
We can win prizes, become famous
there can be romantic interludes,
and careers, and successes in life.
But what was out of place, seemingly
was already in the order of things.
In retrospect, validating other lives, our lives
are about lessons learned,
lessons to yet to be lived and learned.
Socially we are not immune,
we are not totally alone, individuals only,
we must become more responsible
to ourselves, to our families, to society,
to mankind, and the great qualities that lie ahead
in the comprehension of the total reality of all things
to work out the universalisms that gather to surround us
as we grow and age along.
How certain the times, the ways, and generations go by.

Wayne Rogers

Summer Solstice

On June 21st, the south direction sent
Summer to the Western Hemisphere.
The east direction sent gifts of light, wisdom.
A wind from the north cleansed the
Hearts and souls of mankind.

Sun dancers attached to a sacred pole
Danced, prayed, endured, dreamed.
Relentlessly, they offered praise and
Thanksgiving to the Great Spirit!
Spirit ancestors danced alongside, giving strength.
"All life is Sacred! Sacred! Sacred!
Sacred!" Sang throughout the Plains.

At 3:00 p.m., four sun dancers broke loose.
Jesus, too, broke loose from the sacred pole.
Hatred, misunderstanding, indifference
Broke loose from the world.
All mankind broke into songs of joy!

In a reddish-peach sunset, forgiveness,
Hope, generosity, and peace formed a
Sacred Circle, bringing sweetness upon the earth!

Paula Sailer

Till Paper Meets Light

Pen, paper, sword, light
Strike through, cut clean
Reveal the soft and silvery night
Beneath the jagged shores that dream.

The roar rises higher in once fat fields
The dark descends earlier in the morbid lake
And all the gasping city machines
Creep along their filthy way
Seeking cave light under tar and rock
Shutting away the hordes behind a rising gate.

Later, the silken lizards slide
Around corners, into alleyways
Slip down to the murky waterside
To blow flutes and amorously play.

While light flickers behind closed blinds,
A mind sits silently at penside
Dreaming of a sword sharp enough to cut
A city block, to carve it into a field
And turn the earth till rock meets rock
Till paper meets light.

Roger Owens

Call Of The Angels

How many more Darkened Days? Too many blinded by the Light, like deer standing dazed and confused, yet marveling at its ESSENCE! We Hear the Call. We See the Light. We Seek the Truth. Be true to self - if you hide behind a veil of your own Weave, you can NEVER see the Light of Truth. Is it too blurred; too confusing? DROP YOUR VEIL! All is waiting to be known to the ones open to TRUTH in Heart and Mind. Seek and you WILL find! The only thing to fear is fear itself. Do NOT fear the Light, for it is You! Through devolution of flesh's material desires, all that is left is pure, brilliant, electric Light! It is You-look in the mirror, see the Angel, who is truly the self, PATIENTLY waiting for the chance to Shine, when ALL Angels are freed of material weights and chains then may Heaven truly manifest on Earth! LISTEN to the cries of your Angel! No one can free the Angel but you who imprisoned. So patient, ready and willing to show the way! All you MUST do is put away your EGO through willingness to surrender to Truth. REMEMBER THIS: the Truth is profound, compelling and deep-be willing to seek or stop halfway in fear of the unknown. To let go of old habits, ways, and thoughts is a painful process. To he who bears the pain and sorrow of letting go. LET THE TRUTH BE KNOWN, for they are the True Seekers! Seek and Awaken the time is at hand. All know the Path-so few REMEMBER!

Patti Jean Nelson

The Strongest Woman I Know

The strongest woman I know has a heart of gold and a never dying
  spirit.
The strongest woman I know is a fighter, never gives up and always
  hopes for the best.
The strongest woman I know is an angel, loved by everyone and touches
  each life she meets.
The strongest woman I know is fighting, fighting something that can't
  be fought or cured.
The strongest woman I know loves life and that shouldn't be taken away
  from her so soon.
Everyone says, God works in mysterious ways,
but that shouldn't mean taking an angel from earth just so she can be
  an angel in Heaven.
The lives she has touched will never forget the gentleness of her touch,
  the sweetness of her voice and her warm, loving smile.
The strongest woman I know will live on in each one of our hearts.
The strongest woman I know may be called wife, mother, sister, aunt,
  or friend but I will always call her
  NANA!

Stacey Lynn Holsey

Until Tomorrow

Sitting here alone listening to the
sound of rain, like a rhythmless drum
over and over.

It's late in the night laying here
thinking about tomorrow, wishing
the night would end.

Everyday is different with new words
to be spoken, hoping never to be bad.

Just sitting here, thinking of you,
wishing you were here for eternity.

I speak with new words, some not knowing the meaning.
How can I be here alone? Wish you were here.

Every night seems like no morning ever to come.
The rain has stopped, no more music, the night is quiet.
Sweet dreams to you, until tomorrow.

Tacha Renee Olson

Challenger's Last Flight

America and the world are quiet right now.
Sorrow and pain are profoundly intense today.
People are reeling with astonishment;
Families are crying in anguish and dismay.

A "major malfunction" the disaster was called
For lack of better words at the moment.
Seven souls met their Heavenly Father.
That won't change, no matter what term they invent.

In six days in the Beginning
God created the Earth and the Heaven,
And now, in literally the twinkle of an eye,
He's recalled the souls of these courageous Seven.

They had no fear and felt no pain.
This is something of which I feel sure.
They were living their dreams, reaching for stars.
Instead they found Jesus-so gentle, strong, and pure.

Vicky L. Bishop

Sunshine And Rain

Our lives are like the weather
Sometimes sunshine, sometimes rain.
We can have wonderful days, then we can
Have bad days and can hardly stand the pain.
God has made it this way, he wants us
To enjoy the good days, and learn from the bad.
Sometimes it's hard to understand how good
It can be, and others make us feel so sad.
Life is like going to school - we all have a lot
To learn, and it really never ends.
Sometimes we can only learn with pain
So we have to be our own best friend.
God is there for us no matter what.
He wants to see us with a happy face.
Even when we are in pain it will end
Because God is always there with his grace.
I pray that everyone will realize with
The Lord you can only gain.
He will be sure you will have more sunshine
And not have so much rain.

Sandy Truncellito

Untitled

If I lived a hundred years
somethings I find will change.
The attitude and behaviours through our eyes will rearrange
surrounding will be different, what's important now will be gone.
Our desires and dreams of forever, we'll sing in
our wishful songs.
10 thousands of people thru the years we've met
understandings of differences will shape the
standards we'll set
Of all the places and faces we've met and will
continue to see.
The one I'm truly amazed with is the one
I call me.

Penny Allen

Northern Star

O, Northern star, tonight you seem alone;
The vastness of the darkening sky above
Reveals a splendid glory all your own.
You've spent your years in sending rays of love
To many who, as day is closing in
Cast lingering glances toward the velvet sky.
O, Northern star, you know not greed or sin;
No wonder! For you dwell near God on high.

Lorraine O. Schultz

Will He Ever Come Home?

I can feel it in my bones.
   Something is wrong.
I can feel the dark shadow coming over me.
   For a few minutes now.
Mixed emotions.
   Fear, anger, loneliness, anxiety, nervousness.
8 o'clock. No calls.
   Faithful caller every night.
Ten minutes past the hour. Tick Tock.
   No calls.
Twenty minutes past the hour. Tick Tock.
   No calls.
Thirty minutes past the hour. Tick.
   Rrrring Rrrring.
I knew it. That's him!
   Hope, joy, happiness, big smile.
"Hello honey"
   ....Silence.

Claudine Jones

A Silent Lament

Like tortoises, they carry their homes with them.
Some are well organized, some disheveled.
Some on rolling shopping carts, or baggage carryalls.
Some you push, some you pull.
Some are jerrybuilt mini caravans.

    No home
    No silverware drawer
    No closet
    No stove
    No refrigerator
    No knickknacks
    No antimacassars
    No love

With catastrophic cruelty, the finger of fate pointed
At the hearts and homes of these weary souls,
Leaving only echoes from deaf ears,
Darkness from blinded eyes,
Crumbs from callous hearts.
They gaze into the face of futility at the edge of life.

Vonda Angel   1995

Castaway

Adrift within a dream on the ocean of the night,
Solid footing abandoned, tossed by waves of doubt;
Waves like snowflakes, different but alike;
Unique in their individualistic sameness;
Motionless motion, to or from oblivion.
Thirst and hunger pressing upon me,
Slowly moving toward the edge of infinity
Surrounded by an endless horizon;
A cloudless sky with searing sun;
A water covered desert of desolation,
The perfect camouflage.
I view, with parched lips, the albatross,
A harbinger of the future.
Constantly confronted by a mirage of safety,
Of a place and time illusionary,
A vision of what was not to be.
The rapture of savoring love's first kiss,
Kept alive within a lingering fantasy.
Castaway, I join the lost souls
In a struggle to be born again - to love.

Philip A. Eckerle

A Plea

O! Muse of Poetry speak to me
Softly I hear your aeolian harp
Sitting beneath the olive tree
Musing if I can write-inspired

When I hear the sound of Chi'ng
A piece of hollowed sonorous stone
That singular echo; that singular tone
My heart relaxes as

On the second strike music emits
Harmony composes my heart sings

All sixteen pieces are ringing
A melody they are singing
My heart reposes

Five chromatic notes make not symphonic grace
Nonetheless, emotions rise to enjoin
The joy on a Chinese face

Learn from thy sister Muse
The breast of beasts music does soothe
Teach me not to loathe to write-poetry
As thou hadst Homer muse and indelibly left us, Odyssey!

Richard J. Lee

Untitled

Cathy,
Soft, graceful touches pierce the heat of her body's passion;
Warm, soulful kisses; eyes shut, the mind wanders,
To whom do I feel these heart-felt emotions?
Cathy, Oh, Sweet Cathy.

Her smile, her eyes; both rival for a sparkle,
The first catches your attention; the other melts your heart.
Lips that press softly and speak of her love,
Glances so sincere when she's close to her love.
To whom have I found these depths of sweet love?
Cathy, Oh, Sweet Cathy.

Skin that is flawless; soft in all spots,
Muscles sensitive to all her loves' nearness.
To touch her is to feel her; become her, imbibe her.
To feel her is a rhapsody; soft and harmonious as symphonies sound.
To whom do I sense that love is about?
Cathy, Oh, Sweet Cathy, my wife.

Sportshots Randy Lefko

Untitled

Your skin was darker than mine,
society would never accept us as two of a kind.
Together at home the loving was great,
why are people determined to hate?
You were black and I was white,
Why did others feel the need to fight?
Did prejudice have to show its ugly face,
just because we are of a different race,
It was impossible for us to enjoy our time together,
because of all the storms we had to weather.
The hatred grew worse day after day,
they were determined to stand in our way.
At first they were easy to ignore,
but then we grew tired and could not take anymore.
The relationship was over before it ever really started,
the demands of others made sure we parted.
When society learns to judge people not on color or race
the world would be a much happier place.

Patricia George-Demotte

Voyage On A Tramp Steamer

Under the endless and brilliant skies of the
Society Islands - in a disturbed, ill-mannered sea —
I found myself, as a curious and at first reluctant
passenger on a so-called tramp steamer named the
Vaeanu (Tahitian for the big sea), enjoying the surreal
fantasy of an escapist. Occasional, brief rains
fell from the dark clouds which drifted past the
myriad stars and a sliver of the Moon, suggesting
that the mythical Selene was with Endymion.

The water around us shimmered, and I surveyed
the silhouettes of long dormant volcanoes.
At some precise moment long after midnight,
I acutely felt the tension/the balance between
complete, pure and unfettered freedom and
the horrid, suffocating chains of constraint.
As robust breezes and sea sprays became
my companions on deck, I relished the
vistas and hoped that the liberation and
freedom from space and time that I
perceived could be mine.

Wayne Bell

Islands

   Land man or man's mind
    Tides and oceans against them
   The isolation

Scattered shacks and concrete buildings/sardined between dead-rock beaches
Fancy hat houses top jungle clothed mountains
    Sea and Ocean all around
    Idle ship with coral anchor

Comedy's eyes on carbon copy faces
Take toy taxis to unspeakable places
Where they pay play money to wear a worm's rag
And sit like the lotus to eat raw fish
While a painted white face
Plays a stretched snake and sings

In a castle neighborhood of tiny temples
Jeweled mad dogs guard my fault
    That ogre concrete turtle gorged with ashes bones and vases
    The battles and dead of a wounded sun remembered
Nothing personal but Donne
Okinawa does not want US and I am made an island

Vellene Peterson

Oh Wreched Animal

Pay head to my words oh wreched animal:
You who build only to destroy.
You who give life only to kill.
You who love only to hate.
You who console only to mock.

To your former talents I pray tribute.
For it is these that give me hope.
These are the ones that give you mastery of the world.
It is only though them that you will take your rightful
Place in the BIG PICTURE.

To your later...those shadows that mask your potential.
Those that make you the most Vial and Evil of the UNIVERSE denizens.
It is to those masks that you must strive to enfold upon themselves.
So that only the warmth of enlightenment will
Be left to show the way to eternal inner peace which will radiate to
the universe.
If not it will be through your own inflexibility.
Oh wreched animal that the universe will -
MOCK YOU, HATE YOU
KILL YOU, DESTROY YOU!!

A. J. Christian Lucard

Sugar For The Cancer

The tension can be seen like the steam over pot
the places in between can get pretty hot
what to be
what not to be allowed
if you bow to be free
then you crush to be proud
crush the truth of your shame
all who know
you disdain
and of reminding affairs
those with venerated years
speak wis-dumb
for your ears only hear
rationalizations of sugar for the cancer
Vaughn Benjamin

Progress

Then:
   Spring reigned as Queen in my hometown park.
   Her lavish regal robe had an elegance rare:
   Lilac lace, pansy buttons on soft moss velvet
   With butterfly jewels sparkling here and there.

Now:
   Success reigns supreme in our park Plaza Mall.
   Its wash-and-wear royal robe of concrete gray
   Has escalator seams and cash register pockets,
   With plastic snap-on butterflies to tell us its May.
Dorothy Hubbard Roth

Caution

Achievements you so admire,
   To the appearance of your own desire.

Fulfillment you did not have,
   Satisfaction you did not pleasure.

Life as you knew it,
   Pertained only to you at your own measure.

To all that you have,
   You still have a hart of hollow sounds.

Power is to whom you belong,
   And the cry of the weak, sings your favorite song.
Steve Robert Edwards

Hypnos

You hypnotize me, you mesmerize me;
you turn my bones to jelly; and I am nothing but a nellie.
You're five foot seven at the core,
reduces my six foot four to the floor.
When I am in your presence, my mind becomes a menace.
When your eyes direct their fire, I am nothing but a mire.
Your voice but does command, that I am but a man.
With your head held so high, I can neither breathe nor sigh.
You smile like a vixen, and I am but a nixon.
Your lips so red, I am neither alive nor dead.
You thrust your breasts so large and white and I am but a neophyte.
You're round and curved sex like bait - draws my
manhood toward its gate, and if thou will it open
I will plunge and plunge till molten, my seed
that spills within your hill.
For only then will I have reached the zenith,
with love for you only you my queenth.
Robert P. Martin

A Voyage Apart

This last night together, my long-distance love, I hope will often yield
A warming thought in the frost to come as you walk alone the fields.
Near crystal-glassed water and bare china plates we rest in padded cherry
And browse our padded menu books atop the still Queen Mary.

We'd come aboard just moments ago past black and white photo displays
And I saw in them an expression or two of a lover in dismay.
Their inward young faces looked so much like mine as we climbed a ladderway
And just as back then this liner again will witness a parting this day.

The creased-crossed cloth of tender beige held large white floral plates
While silver arrayed in a symmetrical way gave off a gleaming grace.
The glassware rose up to meet the red bloom of single budding flower
In dim candle glow I avoided your eyes while I pointed out far city towers.

I don't now recall a subject at all we talked about that evening
For your beauty was wine and your voice was a song and the next day
   you'd be leaving.
The ship had held the two of us within her charm that dinner
And helped us know the love we had would stay strong through the winter.

With coffee sipped up and diets smashed down into pieces by tiramisu
We left the enchantment of our window table to walk the deck in pea soup.
We slowly trod the teakwood decks as lovers used to do
But this time we would set our sails and split ourselves in two.
Robert Bero

Untitled

The thought of the man, tremble my hand, yet empowers me to keep
writing the sound of his voice, renders no choice, in the line the
pied-piper I follow for I hear fine, delicious as wine, these are
the songs of the swallow. Princely in stature, my body moves with
him, slowly brings me to rapture hard as a boulder, his almighty
sword, more power than 100 soldiers.
His kingdom of cement, this is where you will find him, a ruler
without an election come day or come night, there's always a fight
Take heed and bring your protection.
Their will be no song, there will be no dance, their will be no court
jester miming no jousts or beheading, yet plenty of weddings of he
and the words he is rhyming.
Wanted by many, they try to bewitch him, in hopes that his beauty is
catching pity them so, how their ugliness holds them prisoners like
words on an etching.
Friends he has many, foes he has more, who try to steal his title
Try as they may, let them steal it away, for he knows it is not
everlasting from when he is gone, only Gods realm will live on,
but for now he is my only King.
Colleen Hampton

To The Turkey Family On Thanksgiving

You shouldn't worry about suffering ill fate,
you're going to end up on a clean dinner plate.
You're going to be loving that nice warm oven,
scented with rare spices and wine.
No human gets treated that fine.

When it's all put together
you won't have a feather
to clean or grain to peck
and there'll be warm gravy all round your neck.

You'll end up in a belly with cranberry jelly
and potatoes and gravy and wine.
Though you don't have a feather
you'll stay warm together with all that food and spice
and you've made someone happy, 'cause you're nice.

When dinner is over you'll hear someone say,
that's the best damned turkey ever had, today.
So ruffle your feathers and stick out your neck,
That axe will make someone happy, so what the heck.
Walton V. Bailey

To Our Son Richard Paul Leone III

Your tiny body inside of me, a gift from up above,
   was created in your Mommy and Daddy's love.
The ups and downs of pregnancy - the closeness that I felt,
   now your death, is what we were dealt.
We never thought the time would come, when we must say goodbye,
   we wanted you very much, so pardon if we cry.
For all the special offers and free samples too,
   that special parents-to-be club membership, now leaves us out and blue.
We never got to hold you, but you're real just the same,
   and that's why today, you're given a special name.
For all the plans we had for you, and all the things to do,
   we now must realize that God wanted you too.
Perhaps God tires of calling the aged to go,
   and so he picks a flower just before it can grow.
So now that you are not with us, we who are left behind,
   must realize, God loves children - angels are hard to find.
As all the words of wisdom come our way,
   we know no replacement, can ever take your day.
For every little outfit, fun toys and diapers too,
   we'll never have the thrill to share this all with you.

To Mommy and Daddy, you are very dear,
   for in our hearts, soul and mind, you are always near.
Our hearts are ripped and torn,
   the day you died was the day you were born.
But you're a part of our family, a part of our love,
   and for now you just rest with God up above.
Our special little boy, remember we love you and how much you're missed
   until we meet again, we send up a kiss.
   Susan A. Leone

"'Tis The Season"

It's that time of the year, when Christmas is near,
   yet something is not right today.
Spouses are shouting, children are pouting,
   the prevalent mood is dismay.

Though the stockings are hung, and Christmas songs sung,
   and even the tree has been trimmed.
We've had such hectic nights, someone even stole our lights!
   And that holiday feeling has dimmed.

We've more shopping to do, and our dollars are few,
   will we ever get everything ready?
We've got baking to do, for parties and school,
   we must keep at it quite steady.

We've put the cards in the mail, bought gift wrap without fail,
   only ten days left to prepare.
Tension is building, tempers unyielding,
   it's easy to drift into despair.

But hold it right there — 'tis the season to care.
   Oh Lord, won't you please fill my heart?
Bless us with peace, so that anger may cease,
   and good will to each other may start.

You are the reason we celebrate the season —
   may we honor you with our love.
Focus our attention on your will, not our tension.
   May your blessings descend from above.

Let me feel like a child, all tender and mild,
   like I did so many years ago.
May I enjoy the preparation, and wait in anticipation,
   with eyes bright as a candle light's glow.
   Stephanie L. Armstrong

The Love Of A Friend

A smile in the sunshine,
A breath of fresh air,
A handshake, a hug
To show that they care.

The wind in the sky
Blowing black clouds away,
A big four-leaf clover
Bidding fortune to stay.

A tear shared together,
A shoulder when in need,
An encouraging word
That you are loved indeed.

When life throws this fortune
In abundance your way,
Take care to enjoy it
Every minute, every day.

You'll see it so clearly
Your joy has no end!
What better gift in life
Than the love of a friend?
   P. Andrew Cumbo

Our Harbor Queen

Proud and tall she stands.
A beacon in her hand.
To welcome those oppressed
to freedom in this land.
A symbol for all to see,
that here in America you can truly be free.
To think - to work - to dream
To be all that you can glean.
In a land that allows you freedom to choose.
Our lady is a symbol to people,
That here they can not lose!
   Thelma Rafle

Light

Which left the Pleiades
2,000 years ago
arrived just when
a Mayan's eye
peered upwards
through the stone shaft
of the Temple of the Jaguar Sun.

Other rays

Began their earthward journey
before I even existed
to meet my eye
in the expanse of desert sky
after Vigils.

Grace

Sets out from God
before I need it
rushes light-years toward me
meets me at the very moment I fall.

When it arrives
I am there.
   Sheryl Frances Chen, O.C.S.O.

A Pause For Love

Alone at a bar, my life ... an empty cup;
My search for love and truth yet unresolved;
Tormented by doubt that won't ease up,
I pour me wine and drink to feel absolved,
My emptiness settles on lees unsolved.
High, neath lamps that part a lonely mist,
A beauty dances by, I get involved.
She wants me, I wish, unable to resist,
Hoping to kiss this sweet lady of mist.
Do I see what I feel, mutual energy?
Man, for a dog's life in Eden kissed;
It just once I could know such synergy,
I'd dance upon a rainbow's arch and swoop
Down on Mount Baldy for a double scoop.
Ralph F. Lopez-Urbina

Sands of Time

The body is laden with hidden chains.
    The thorns of pain are deep.
The spirit within, yearns to be free while
    the sands of time pass slowly.
But the soul is determined to endure,
    for there is Hope.
Just when the heart has all but stopped,
    a spear of light pierces the gloom and
    a pool of warmth springs forth.
The icy veins begin to thaw and
    life itself, once again flows.
Robert J. Schmucki

I Love You

Mother and Father I want to say
you're the best. I am happy you
gave me a life. You had problems with
my oldest brothers and sisters before.
You raised me to respect and
honor my elders. Taught me not to
hate or fight. Others say you
made good examples of parenthood.
They don't understand what goes on in
the house, to them we are the family
they wish they had. To us, we wish we
never had problems with drugs or
alcohol. Although our father will teach
us again and take our sins away this
is the time I want to say,
"I love you very much."
Thank you for being
there when I needed you the most.
Sandra Tunuchuk

Time

The world has so much to offer,
    Yet it has nothing.
Life is hard,
    Yet it is easy.
The good things keep you going,
    Yet the bad things slow you down.
The reason "Why we are here?"
    No living thing really knows.
For one day we shall have it all.
    But until then we must survive.
Ruby Bonner

Untitled

Mother dear O, mother dear
    you're close in every way
I feel your presence in my life
    throughout each passing day.

The times I feel like giving up
    your presence makes me sure
That even though life's hard to bear
    I really should endure.

You used to always tell me
    that a person has one mother
And once she passes on
    there'd never be another

In spite of all our ups and downs
    I thought it was a crime
To be the one to make amends
    therefore, I didn't take time

I know that all your efforts
    were meant to do me good
And even though I wanted to
    I still misunderstood.
Wilma J. Barclay

The Affair

Thoughts of you consume my life.
Your soft, sensual lips inviting mine.
Your smooth, sensitive skin perspiring,
aglow with sexuality.
Our bodies entwined in deep passion.
The scent of Oscar de La Renta
seducing my entire existence.

Drowning in a tidal wave of pain,
will I ever be myself?
Can I ever be myself again?
The only hope I have is to reach out.
Nothing's there.
Still, the memories remain.
Tim Hart

Even Though Your Gone..

Even though your gone
Your not so far away
My dreams and memories of you
Are with me everyday

Even though your gone
I'll always have you near
I'll always think of you as mine
And wishing you were here

Even though your gone
In my heart you'll always stay
The memory of your smile
And your loving ways

Even though your gone
And I'll never see your smile
I'll always have the thought
I had you for awhile!
Toni R. West

Thru The Sky

Nowadays all things come to pass
your never knowing what will last
Don't count on anything to stay
    Everything goes away
One thing that will never die
is my love for you
    It's growing thru the sky
The harmony from the inside
is something that we just can't hide
forever we'll be together
    being here or
    being wherever we go
One thing that will never die
is my love for you
    It's growing right thru the sky.
Rudolph Gornati

A Memory Away

You'll often hear him calling you,
you'll see him walking by.
You'll feel his presence near you,
and at times, you'll hear him cry.

For never will he leave you,
the man you loved so dear.
His presence always with you
his love forever near.

This man who brought you many things
that others might not see.
This man who's deep within your heart
where no one else can be.

A place reserved for only him
until your final day
Forever in your thoughts and hearts;
A memory away.
Anderson

Wretched Heart

As you crawled on your slummy belly,
You slithered toward me.
Lisping words too beautiful to be true,
Emotions too fierce to be real.
Tightening, coiling, suffocating.
You lurked.
You sharpened your teeth on me,
Always muting my pleas for help.
I offered no resistance.
And you demanded my surrender.
Randi L. Fujimoto

My Special Rainbow

Red is for the rose
You send with love.
Blue is for the color
of the sky above.
Green is for the tree
We sit under and talk.
Yellow is for the sun
Which underneath we walk.
These colors remind me
of — how I love you so
for you are my special rainbow.
Patricia A. Williams

Infinity

On the scorched shoreline
You run
Bare foot
A breath of wind kisses
Your face
You turn back
Smiling
The waves lapping my motionless body
On the sand.
To you, as we are one,
I give infinity.

Renza Moscatelli Baker

The Heartache Of Love

You taught me how to love again
You opened up my heart
It's hard for me to let you go
Now that we're apart

I want to feel the love inside
My heart, which now just pains
I want my eyes to feel the sunshine
and not to feel the rain

I know as time passes by
The rain will go away
The sunshine will come back again
To start another day

A day in which the pain I feel
Will gradually subside
A day in which my love for you
Will not make me want to hide

A day in which to you I'll say
I love you as a friend
Our love is in the past
My heart is now amend

Tammy L. Buck

Your Heart

When you open your heart to someone,
you open your arms to a life of love.
I myself haven't really been "In love."
You think I don't know enough,
well you're wrong because when
someone does fall "In love" with me
they won't know what hit them and
when they do find out, I may throw
them back.

Virginia Cordoza

Untitled

Dear People,
You may think the world is flat,
Or just a piece of lint,
Upon a young chap's hat.
Once you have realized what
Mistakes you've caused,
"A undividing censory,"
Will cause you to think and pause.
Once you have accepted the Lord
Into your heart,
You'll realize that you
and the heavens are not so far apart.
So once you start believing in thy father,
"The ruler of thy earth,"
When you die you'll have
The chance to feel again,
"The enchantment of rebirth!"

Singinn Lawson

"When Love Passes You By"

Dedicated to Sarah

If love should pass you by,
You may not know it right away.
You may not feel it or even cry,
But you'll need it back one day.
If you hurt the one you love yearly,
Why should they come back to you?
To be hurt again would cost them dearly,
But to be loved by you would be new.
New in the sense that it is finally true,
No more loneliness or illusion.
New in the sense that it is finally you,
Only happiness and good confusion.
So if this poem applies to your life,
I say go out and try...
To find that someone for your wife,
Because it's terrible when love passes you by.

Robby Lohr

"Lillian"

Lillian you're wonderful
You make life worth while
I will kiss your sweet sweet lips
Every time you smile
You give me love and devotion
My heart is full of emotion
Our happiness is here to stay
Your love for me I'll never betray
We plan our future come what may
We'll have a lovely wedding day
Our fate has come our way
Darling we found paradise
Since we're man and wife
No more stress and no more strife
We'll have a wonderful life

Paul Salerno

Fantasy

When I win the lottery
You know what I will do
I'll take a trip to Mexico
And buy a yacht or two

I'll give a call to all my friends
And throw the biggest bash
It will be quite a thrill for me
To pay for it in cash

I'll gather up a hundred bums
And give them carte blank
Can you believe the sight we'll make
On entering the bank

When I spend all of it
And end up without a dime
Don't shed a tear for me my dear
I had a real good time.

Patricia Cox

Memories

Joys of children we are told,
Will lighten our hearts
When we are old.
They laugh and play and always run.
They are a treasure to everyone.
You see they are as precious as gold.
The children we always remember,
When we are old.

Theresa C. Allen

You

I once was lost in guilt and sin
you helped me find my love, again.

You held my hand for many long, years,
each day you'd wipe my tears.

Each morning I'd hear you say,
"Be strong and you'll make it, today",

I'm forever saved because of you,
how I would pray and sing, the day
through.

When judgement day finally had came,
how I rejoiced and praised your name.

Everything, was so starry and bright,
I was a Christian and that was right.

We held hands and walked each day,
we would sit together and sweetly pray.

I'm lonely no more because of you.
You'll always be my friend,
each heavenly day through.

Rhanda Hopper

My Favorite Teacher

I looked up to you
You conversed with me
Your walk was so proud
Full of dignity.

You were so kind
To this young kid
Stimulated my mind
To go on, never quit.

Words wise and smart
You looked intense
So you reached my heart
There was no pretense.

I remember you
My teacher guide
Being thankful to you
For your guiding light.

Importance of teaching
So omnipotent
Into the future reaching
Your professional trend.

Ursula Hrouda

Today, Tomorrow And Always

Today, tomorrow and always
  You are and will be
    On my mind and in my heart.

Days will come and they will go,
  But you will always remain
    A part of my fondest memories.

Your laughter, your warm smiles,
  The many unspoken words,
    Your warm tender embrace,
      The twinkle in your eyes.

You are and always will be
  A very, very special friend;

One who will not,
  And cannot
    Ever be replaced.

Susy Valenzuela

You And I

We're friends,
You and I know that,
If one of us has a problem,
We help each other solve it,
We both share and admit,
The things we did,
If one of us got in trouble,
We both stand up together,
And tell the truth,
Why should we lied,
'Cause we got nothing to hide,
We believe that one day,
Our friendship will last,
If we stay together,
And never betrayed each other,
I believe we will be best friend.
And hope we won't forget.
That we will be friend always thru the end.

Sovonn Pov

"He Says He Truly Loves Me"

He says he truly loves me —
  Yet, I rarely feel his touch,
Or hear him say those tender words
  I yearn for oh so much!

He says he truly loves me —
  Though, his eyes no longer shine
With "love-light" that he claims he has
  Reflecting into mine.

He says he truly loves me —
  But, he leaves me all alone
To wander through this darkened house
  Where love has darker grown.

He says he truly loves me —
  Though, my heart's a crumpled shape.
I'm drowning in a Sea of Tears
  From which there's no escape!

A smile ...a touch...one gentle word,
  Is that too much to ask?
He says he truly loves me —-
  But...it seems too hard a task!

Yvonne Dieffenbacher

Fall Morn

Yea awake,
Yea rise,
Peer out the window,
Terrain blanketed with frozen dew,
Canopy of evergreen 'tis covered
  with a veil of lacework
Sun shooting out beams of
  iridescent light,
All's aglow on this fall morn,
Diligently we prepare,
Our day has commenced.

Sharleen C. Hutchins

Name, Yesterday

Yesterday you said you loved me,
you said you really cared,
I'll never forget the times we shared,
with tears in my eyes,
Now's the time for one last goodbye,

Regina Herndon

Untitled

What a mother
would not give
For a trouble
free child to
love
Regardless
what we do
In this world
we see

Trouble free
they will never
be
No matter how
much we love
them.

Penny Hook

Void

Blackened time that passes on
World stands still, the days are gone
Nothing is left to fall back on
  The void is silent.

I have seen the April Showers
I have dreamed the end of ours
I have felt the atom's power
  Fill the void of Silence.

Ancient ruins that have crumbled
They once stood but now they're humbled
Wave of light, cleansing rumble
  The void is silent.

Things that mattered, matter not
Things that were, now they're not
Time stands still, time stands still
  The void is silent.

Dismal fate, the world turns on
big mistake, the Earth has gone
Time progresses on, and on, and on,
  But still, the void is silent.

William Swartz

Days Of Dreaming

Day by day I seem to drift away,
wondering about my dreams.
  How things should be.
Only as it seems.

Because day by day I dream of dreams.
And hoping they never slip away.

Sitting alone hours of the day.
By myself just drifting away.
Hoping that someday my
dreams come true.
That's what I do day by day.

Penny Temple

"On Security"

Now all you thieves watch out.
You better play it cool.
Watch what you say and do.
Because the security guard
is watching you.

Ted Franklin

Spirit Song

  Like the song of a spirit, the
wolf's cry rises and echoes across
valley and plain.
  Like the thunder of storms, the
buffalo run, a remembrance of
ancient times.
  Like the music of flutes, the
eagle soars, forever free and proud.
  Like the evening shadows, the
cougar prowls, guardians of the
dark canyons and forests.
  Like the majestic mountains, the
bears stands, mighty, unbeaten king.

Tiffany Ann Voyles

Sad Boy

So sad for the boy
without a best friend.
So sad for the boy
who use to laugh with no end.
So sad for the boy
who now sits alone, memories in his head.
So sad for the boy
who is my friend.
So sad for the boy
who cried with no end
So sad for the boy
who looked so dazed.
So sad for the boy
who stood there and prayed.
So sad for the boy
whose hurt won't go away.

Tonya Higginbotham

A Revelation

Love's encounter to be revealed
with years of feelings forever sealed.
A grand illusion after all,
a place for lovers to rise and fall.

The yes you mays, the no I wont's,
the endless days of do's and don'ts.
At last you either compromise,
or finally breach between the ties.

Questions forever, answers never,
loves great game of pain and pleasure.
So little to gain, so much to lose,
and no time left to pick and choose.

Our love's too strong to turn away,
the time has come to kneel and pray,
to smell the roses along the way,
and turn to fight another day.

To be as one forever more,
and keep the ties, forget the score!

Tammy A. Weeks

My Fondest Treasure

A rose will bloom and wither
With winter's first cold bite

My love for you keeps growing
Every day and every night

We've shared life's fondest feelings
And all its joys and pleasures

But the love that you have brought me,
will be my fondest treasure

Vicki L. Ray

Source

Imagination base and creator of man's all
With unseen fires a candle lights
And puts possible in impossible sights
Builds the low, median and tall.

Some call it dreams with open eye
A thing of nothing vapor of soul
Yet creator of solids as plans unfold,
Maker of the stamp man "made by."

Form nothing to all-quite a step!
A thought began as basic need
Or one from necessity-sown seed
It grows, flourishes then opens as a tulip

Energy impregnated with imagination
Giving birth to all- bad and good
Rising to is where nature only stood
And flying spaceward, Each generation.

B. Thornton

At A Wedding

My Laurel Tree
With thee I dance
I made a wish
This is my chance

To be with you
At lofty height
So now I wish
There was no night

To pass between
To cut our tie
To make us say
Our last good-bye

So here this is
Our last romance
My Laurel Tree
With thee I dance
My Laurel Tree
With thee I dance

Robert D. Thayne

Colors Of The Wind

You can dream of the wind you can paint
with the wind colors of the wind with the
wind you see the colors of the wind.
See the morning, noon, afternoon and
night and midnight. They all are
colors, morning can be so bright
noon can be so blue, afternoon
can brown, night can be dark,
goodnight. Midnight can be darker
then a marker.

Tina Sabessar

"Dreamer"

Are you a dreamer, or a
wish maker, or a keeper of hidden
secrets?

If so come to my shop
of boxes, and bags wrap them
and keep them put away!

So no one can harm your
dreams, so you can cherish them
for always.

Elisabeth A. Scouten

Fall

On a dark and dreary day,
with the wind blowing fast,
the trees were swaying happily,
As the leaves fell at last.

Autumn is here,
the leaves change their colors,
not a single one,
looks like another.

From green, to red,
to yellow, to gold,
brings back memories,
of times of old.

I watch and I wait,
as the season unfolds,
dreaming into the future,
to see what it holds.

The beauty of nature,
comes from above,
bringing forth all the blessings,
of His love.

William M. Besenhofer

White Wings

Gentle things
With soft fragile wings
Slender white fingers
To shudder and shake
With a cool blue touch
Shake away cold grasp of night
To turn gentle faces
To the soft growing light
Then to speak on soft gentle tones
To beg the light to grow
Gentle breath to blow on your face
Teasing you to sing
Open your voice
To others far away
Sing until wind and word
Now do not exist

Shannon Shay Casey

"Moonlight Queen"

She's trapped in the ocean
with love as release
she walks the beach
in hope of peace.

She walks the beach in search of him
her love to find, his heart to win.
Her heart is lonely and hollow inside
the moonlight is her only guide.

Only one can find the way
only one in the light of day.

She walks the beach
with tears in her eyes,
for she only walks
in the blackest of skies.

She walks and searches
for a love to be seen
her walk is eternal
as the "Moonlight Queen."

Tammy Monaco

To A Friend

The road to hell is paved, they say,
With good intentions on the way.
The road to life, if that were so,
Is where no one could ever go.

Each good intention of the spirit,
Is a step to those who hear it.
Tiny bits of wisdom gained,
Add up to knowledge when it's trained.

Don't worry, friend, go on and walk.
You fell, and so the people talk
And laugh at you, but friend, don't fret.
You've built more road than they have yet.

Though you do wrong, your heart wants right.
And though you stumble through the night,
Each time another fell, you tried
To help him up. Let Wisdom guide.

Sally Clark

Joy In Retirement

Don't enter your retirement years
with dread, apprehension and fears

You worked hard and gave them your all
You were always at their beck and call

You survived the fast pace and rat race
Now you have come to a stopping place

No more rushing deadlines to meet
No more tired, worn-out, sore feet

No more time clocks to punch
No more having to miss lunch

Even if all time is now your own
Do not just sit around and moan

Look around and you will find plenty to do
Volunteering can be a real blessing to you

Life ahead will be such a breeze
Just relax and do as you please.

Rose Brickle

The Mistress

I love my husband dearly
with all my heart and soul
but he has a mistress
one that I can't control

She occupies his mind
every night and day
she often comes between us
when all I want is play

She's long, back and sleek
a beauty in her rights
but she gets on my nerves
and she puts up quite a fight

Thru the years of marriage
I've just learned to cope
with this beauty of the sea
and her periscope

So you see - she's not a woman
but a nuclear submarine
she's my husbands way of life
but I'm the woman of his dreams

P. J. Taylor

A Country Night

On a clear blue evening
With a red dusk sky
The silver stars twinkle
As the night passes by

As the cool night breeze
Blows gently on my face
How beautiful it is
This peaceful place.

The outline of the tall pine trees
Let's your mind wonder
What secrets they keep.

As the whip-poor-will sings
In a far off field
The Hoot Owl hoots
To let you know he's near.

The sounds of rippling water
In the near by stream
Dances with moonbeams
As it flows to the sea.

Shelia Owens

Blue Skies

A bird, far away and dark,
Wings its way straight across the skies
...the blue sky of Arizona.
Upon the tips of leaves sunshine rests,
Cloudless skies
...the blue sky of Arizona.

It's morning time,
The sky is clear and warm,
There's a stillness.
Silence rests heavy upon the earth
Pleasant breezes await in solitude
As northern clouds form
Around distant mountain peaks.

Rachel A. Frehren

For Christina

I for you
will bid the earth succumb
bountiful harvest for your spread
warm comfort for your bed.

I for you
the heavens will implore
all you desire
all you deserve.

For you are I-
and I are you-
my precious piece of eternity-
I wish these things for we.

Theresa Thompson

Wind Song

The breeze from afar
whispers softly to its brother
With a sense of compassion;
with a yearning to run free
It's words are strong, yet the message,
wildly innocent
A desperate cry to be heard
for only a moment-
Before the world sleeps,
and the wind sings no more.

Victoria N. Gaulrapp

Understanding Why

Please let me understand
Why You took this gentle man.

A man so sweet, a man so kind,
Who lost his life, so young in time.
I miss him so, I cannot say,
I pray for him most every day.

Because we are so far apart
Please, Dear Lord, heal our hearts.

I miss him so, words cannot say.
Dear Lord, I miss him so much each day.

I miss his smile, I miss his touch
I miss this loving man so much.

I will try to understand
Why you took this gentle man.

Tell him everything is fine.
Tell him we will meet in time.

Patricia Filkohazi

The Storm

What makes the day so dull and gray?
Why do the clouds move on this way?
Could it be a storm in view,
To cast a shadow on the new?
Will it last long on land and sea?
Oh! tell us Lord what can it be;
What can it be that you will send
That seems this day to never end?
Alas! the sky turns black as ink;
Perhaps the ships at sea may sink.
Would not the sun come shining through,
To dry the tears and rain?
And tell us that a storm
Like this will never come again.

Samantha Smith

Ode To A 'Possom

Mr. 'Possum, Mr. 'Possum,
Why did you move so slow?
There's danger on the highways
As cars fly to and fro!

Mr. 'Possum, Mr. 'Possum,
You just can't move that way,
If you eat left and right of center,
'Twill be your dying day!

Mr. 'Possum, oh, Mr. 'Possum,
It may be too late for you,
But if you're ever on the road again:
Grab your lunch, run, run,..
Then chew, chew, chew!

Ruby Nelle Harrison-Ballard

Unknown

Who am I? Where am I going?
When will this ride end?
Will I see another tomorrow?
Will I live again?
Is there a God in heaven?
Is there a Satan's ghost?
Time takes me forward.
To where is yet unknown.

Sharon Carr

The Left Hand Of God

Oh Lord, I cried despairingly,
Why did you give then take away
The shining robes of divinity
That were mine at dawn of day,
For soft and warm they covered me,
And now my clothes are old and grey.

Then I beheld with wonderment
The pierced left hand of God on high,
Flung across the firmament
Where galaxies were wheeling by,
And oh my soul, how eloquent
This symbol was of whence and why.

Unknown, unlearned, and unworthy,
I had dined one night with you
On crumbs of immortality
And drops divine of crimson hue.
On ponder well this mystery
So old and yet forever new!

Edward E. Abbott

The Day Before

If today has come and gone,
Why can't we see tomorrow?
If yesterday is only tomorrow,
Why is there so much sorrow?
If you can see what tomorrow may bring,
Would you change your style?
Would you face each day with a smile?
For when you're gone,
It'll be for a long, long while.
If tomorrow was the day before,
Would you sacrifice and give a little more?
Would you spend your time wisely,
While on the earth you will stay.
Could you give a little more?
Help the ones in need,
Instead of living in your own greed.
Would you sacrifice your wants,
To give in to someone's pain,
Or would you think of only what you have to gain?
If tomorrow was the day before.

Ruthie Gratz

The Language Of Children

You are a child, I am a child.
Why can't we embrace like
grown-ups' clasped hands?
Precisely touching tightly to
remember the child's touch when it
was pure and simple and full of love.

You are a child, I am a child.
For the heart cannot grow old
and only in the heart can silent
rooms contradict the absence of speech.

You are a child, I am a child.
Why can't we understand our unheard
utterances sitting in new found lofts
making us grander than lovers,
grander than ourselves.

Vicente S. Froilan

Autumn Friend

I wish I had an autumn friend
Who too may be alone.
We'd talk about the summers
And the springs that we have known.

Oh how we'd laugh, and cry and sing!
Share stories of the past!
The good, the bad, the hopes, the plans
The dreams that didn't last.

If we could watch the autumn leaves
Together quietly
We wouldn't dread the winter storms
That soon were sure to be.

Nor would we even notice
How cool the day had grown.
Instead we'd be remembering
The warm days we have known.

Oh, I'll find this special friend.
Somehow, somewhere, you'll see.
How I wish I had an autumn friend
To share this day with me.

Virginia Cravanas

But Did You Tell Him

I met someone the other day
Who told me her Dad had passed away
And oh how she missed him
Looking at her I wanted to cry
But instead I did reply
But did you ever tell him
She looked at me with great surprise
And I could see it in her eyes
But he knew how I felt and yet
And I replied as before
But did you ever tell him?
Oh sure we know how you feel
But sometimes can't you make it real
Say the words - show your mind
Not when we're gone and you're left behind
We're here today, we see and feel.
For all of you out there now
Speak from your hearts - tell of your love
We're here now and not up above
But did you tell us!

Pauline Boxer

My Hope, My Prayer

My Lord, my life
who guides me by night,
by day and way
endless love of to say.

A wish, a gift
holiness to lift
His love from above
like wings of a dove.

A hope, a dream
to all that have seen
His tower and power
and works of an hour.

My want, my prayer
for all those to care,
to share and raise
our Lord in their praise.

L. P. Edwards

God Made A Wonderful Mother

Who is the woman who gave me life?
Who bore all the pain and the strife?
Who hushed me in her arms to rest,
And on my cheek sweet kisses pressed?
Who was it singing sweet lullabies,
And rocked me so I would not cry?
Who ran to help me when I fell,
And kissed the part to make it well?
How many buttons are missing today,
How many toys were in her way?
Who was there through my troubled teens,
And gave me a shoulder on which I could lean?
    God gave me a wonderful mother
A mother who never grows old.
He made her smile of the sunshine,
And he molded her heart of pure gold.
In her eyes he placed bright stars,
In her cheeks fair roses you see.
    God made a wonderful mother,
And he gave that dear mother to me.

Susan L. Miller

To My Father

You were our voice,
who better expressed
the storm and the rose
the time and the impossible.

How can I accept
that you ran out of words,
that I have already read
your last verse?

Forgive me if I make
this poem for you:
You are the poet.

Lina G. Del Prado

Untitled

Sunset shadows,
Whispering wind,
Mists of spring rain,
A warmth from within.

The moon above,
Casts amber light,
As distant waters,
Surrender to night.

A bottle of wine,
On a beach alone,
Two lonely hearts,
Have found a home.

Terry J. McComb

Insanity

Among life's cobwebs we dwell
While the soul's aflame in hell...
Striving endlessly amid the torment
We mute our minds to their discontent
And wander deeper among the strands
To inevitable journeys on this land
Where creatures prey upon our mind,
As closer is spun the web that binds
Til the spider is conqueror of our mind.

Peggy L. Nuckols

Untitled

Something you know
Which you hold
you were meant to share with me,
causing no anxiety.
Our strengths would bring us close -
So close I think I fear you
and what you show to me
This time I can't close inside of me,
And crest away in denial
But enter blindly
In distant hope
Of endeavors I won't betray.
Think of this
Sweet creature of the wild
Kiss away the tear of
this resistant child.

Sarah Present

The Awakening

You've awakened something in me
which I thought had ceased to be.
Your velvet voice, your tender touch
aroused the need in me

I had built a wall around my heart
so safe, secure and strong.
It locked out all attempts at love
until you came along.

You weakened my defenses,
my heart's door, you opened wide,
and then you sealed it back again
with all your love inside.

You've made my life so wonderful
with love so warm and true,
and this feeling you've awakened is
THE LOVE I FEEL FOR YOU.

Woodrow W. Edwards Jr.

Your Place Or Mine?

This world is full of myriad things
Which bop and beep
And clang and ping
And crash and bump
And clatter about...
Seemingly in pointless absurdity.

Unless, like me, one feels the need
To participate and communicate
And sate one's senses with
Audio moods and video scenes,
Joyfully aware of
Persons, places and things.

For only then do the
Bops and beeps, et cetera,
Become the beat of vibrant lives
Reaching for goals,
Intent in their purpose,
As the world goes 'round ... and 'round...

Ruth Phares Goldman

A Way Of Life

There is a way of living life
   Which at times is difficult
For the present it's demanding
   But it brings a great result.

Though it never will allow us
   To live in our own way,
For it makes demands upon us
   Which make life really pay.

For it says, "Love your neighbor!"
   Don't be selfish, always share.
If we try to keep, we lose it
   For others we must care.

When we see a need before us,
   We'll always lend a hand.
But this way of life is trying
   For others oft' misunderstand.

This way of life is Christlike
And we can't afford to hate,
It often is demanding,
But the Pension Plan is great.

Raymond W. Knowles

Say...

Where you gonna sleep?
Where you gonna stay?
You're nuts, you're crazy,
Don't run away!
That's what They say.

I say...
Where am I gonna sleep
If I don't run away?
In my father's bed.
He says that's the only way.
Social worker tells me
Help is on the way,
But I can't wait no more.
Pain and shame.

That's what I say!

Pam Thielen

A Light for Stephanie

*Dedicated in memory
of Stephanie Kuhen.*
A light shines,
where there once was none.
A little girl lost,
No more fun.
It shouldn't have happened,
there was no reason.
When will it end,
the killing season.

Valerie Peak

"Life Lines"

Yesterday is over
today is moving fast
tomorrow is the future
created by the past

Yesterday you cannot change
today is where you start
tomorrow can be better
if you live it from the heart.

Tom Tyler

Untitled

Dear Jesus I keep wondering
Where my child might be
I know he is afraid and helpless
And probably thinking of me

The days pass by with anger
My courage comes and goes
If only you could tell me Lord
You are the only one who knows

I anticipate good news
When the ring of my phone I hear
But every time I pick it up
I put it down shedding a tear

So please keep him safe dear Jesus
To you this is my prayer
And someday when I open my door
Let it be my child standing there

Dennis Vannoy

Sanctuary

A little place
Where love and warmth will greet my friends,
And I can serve as God intends;
Where those who enter seeking peace
Will find a needed short release
From all the trying, daily things
That living life so often brings.

A little place
Where books and music feed the mind
Of loved ones who are so inclined;
Where those who came will want to stay,
And gladly come again some day;
Where everyone who comes will find
(Though they're not ever richly dined)
What e'er specific help they need
New strength, new hope, new life, mind freed!

A little place
Where it is warm,
And folks may shelter
From life's storm!

Verna Smith

Amidst A Time Of Racial War

Amidst a time of racial war
Where injured hearts have grown too sore
Where words of hatred have been thrust
Upon each other, with disgust
Where legal force has been misused
To victimize and to abuse
Where children have been taught to hate
With prejudice, their fellow mates
Where humans have been bound in chains
And looked upon with cruel disdain
Where venom flowing through our veins
Make us indifferent to this pain
Where battered souls with vengeful spite
Cannot forgive the color White
Where those oppressing Blacks so long
Cannot admit that they were wrong
We cannot seem to understand
That within different colored hands
We're all the same in flesh and bone
Composed of blood and dust alone.

Rayza Leon

Treasure

Everything is lost treasure
When you're eight years old
Curiosity and imagination
Are set off
By the cloth sack
In the pond
Out of reach
Under a foot of water
By building a bridge
From stones and logs
We got to it
Inside the sack
Were stones
And the forty-five lives
Of five kittens

Terence Osmond

Courage

To be able to laugh
When your world falls apart-
To keep your tears held inside
When fear clutches your heart-

To bravely walk onward
Where lesser men can not-
To stand above all other men
Where fearsome wars are fought -

To set the good example
When, inside you want to run -
These are the signs of courage
That stand out when your life is done.

Virginia Kirby

Death Of A Race, Birth Of An Age

In the bottomless realm of death.
When we meet our final rest.
Before us lies the unknown.
Lost in time forever we roam.
Beckoning dreams to reappear.
Familiar sounds for us to hear.
Entangled in our own despair.
Not remembering or how to care.
As machines we now become.
Trapped in metal technology won.
Put together as better beings.
Perfect in all as lifeless machines.
Behind the door beyond our time.
Deep in the earth buried in rhyme.
Existed once as feeling forms.
Forever lost forever me.

Kristin Hansen

Foxhole Religion

The final day has come at last
When all the happy dreams I've known,
Yes, all of them must pass
Into dark oblivion.
Oh, I pray that they would never end,
But go on and on into eternity,
That fate could never send
Me back to stark reality.
But a pattern has been cast
To which we all must bow,
To live our lives, then die at last,
I fear, for me that time is now.

Robert J. M. Unger

Run Away

Someday the time is going to come.
   When we get sick of the fighting.
     We start to run.
It's been a day and now a night.
   Hold on heart, hold on tight.
After all we've been through
   and all we've shared
     will we stop running
        and realize what's there?
We have to stop now
   before that day.
We've built too much
   to throw away.
Do you understand
   what I'm trying to say?
I'm starting to run,
   run away!

Tina Morales

Rose Petals

Have you ever seen a rose bud
when the petals are tightly closed,
Just waiting for the coming hours
to release the power it holds?
The anticipation of its wakening
catches the eyes of all,
Stirring the imagination of the soul
no matter how small.
When at last the petals bloom
and the fullness is revealed,
A sadness starts to unfold
for the petal's fate is sealed.
The color starts to darken
the ends begin to dry,
A petal starts to fall
as a gentle breeze goes by.
At last the rose is broken
gone its gentle shell,
But its memory has been given
and in love it will dwell.

Victoria Gibson

Wings Of Love

Wings to some are freedom
When like an eagle they can fly
Wings to some are given
When loved ones say goodbye

Then wings of life are tears
for a lonely heart to cry
But wings of friends are made of love
With these we truly fly.

So fly dear one on wings of flight
that are not strong enough for two
see the world taste its delights
Let's see what wings will do.

When you wish your wings to rest
or stay forever more
Fly on wings made of love
and knock upon my door

Vivian Holmer

Mom

I never thought I'd see the day
When I'd have to let go from you,
Your tender voice, your comforting smile
I wish it wasn't true.
But that day has come and you are gone,
Forever I will be blue,
It's a dream no more
It's reality
God has taken you.
I can't explain the pain inside
That hurts from day to day,
It can't be healed
No medicine will do,
Forever it will stay.
So I sit in my room and look for things
That make me think of you
But all I see are three red roses
And death has struck them too.

Louis Daigneault

Emily

You touched your sock and then you smiled
When I said "sock" today
We're starting to communicate
In such a subtle way

My most enchanting moment was
When I gave birth to you
Your father witnessed everything
So magical and new

And now you're running, climbing and
You laugh with dancing eyes
You're such a little innocent
Yet bright and fun and wise

You look like such an angel when
You're sleeping in your bed
The Lord made you His gift to us
Soon after we were wed

A sweeter little treasure, I
don't think we'll ever see
My dear, we're yours forever - and
We're called a family.

Teresa M. Mosteller

Forever Friend

You are my friend,
When I hurt you stretch out your hand,
and your heart.
You cover and protect me with your arms,
You are always there.

When I wondered if I would die,
Physically or emotionally,
You smiled at me and loved me,
And I knew I would again find the
strength to live on.

You are my forever friend.
You love me with your heart, and
Your body and your soul.

Patti Montoya

Untitled

It is so hard to be alone
When everything around is bright,
When people smile all day long
And you pretend you are alright.

You go home with you dream
That there'll be someone somewhere soon
And hug your pillow instead of him,
Wipe tears and look at sky and moon.

You try to find your happy star,
But there are so many up there,
You ask when happiness will start...
Argue with silence you won't dare.

With pain inside your heart and cry
You won't even notice him.
He's here, he's just a little shy,
Your date, a person of your dream.

Why do we have to wait so long
Before two hearts will meet each other?
With tender touch and gentle tone
They'll say the sweetest words, I LOVE YOU!

Yelena Gorodetskaya

Passing Seasons

Good old barn when you were new,
when all the work on you was through
How nude you must have felt
without your weathered coat and stain.
No rust upon your weather vain.
No tilt to wall, or missing board;
no owls or webs or hay bales stored.
No lovers, yet, within your loft,
with scattered straw on skin so soft.
No secrets yet. No tales to tell.
No birth of foal. No leather smell.
But passing seasons, wind and rain,
have weathered wood and weather vain.
And owls and lovers, foals and straw;
missing boards and leaning walls;
have come to you, as life's unfurled,
melding you into your world.
So now, in classic state you hold,
the life worn beauty of the old.

Robert V. Rhodes

Night Wind

Ah, moan of Night Wind through the trees,
What seek you there but wanton lust
Of naked limbs laid bare of leaf
And trembling in your whirl-wind dust?

Cry not beneath my cottage eaves,
Nor beat with fingers on my pane;
Ten thousand souls in torment weep
For entry....but in vain!

Go seek the wide, the open space,
The loneliness of distant moors;
Or throw your voice upon the sea
Who loves your wild, discordant roars!

Oh, sighing Night Wind, God has made,
I am alone ... I am afraid!

Ruby Zundell Wilson

Eternal Love

I can't understand
what is inside you
your heart is cold
I think heart blazing
it is confused
Don't leave life
go on beside me
I want to make you
Regret the loss
of true love
when it is so loud
and nothing can
destroy it is strong
Please don't live in the past
I can offer you happiness
and my life eternally
for you love forever
Just you can choose
for this eternal love

Virginia Maria Reece

Will I Regret Tomorrow

Will I regret tomorrow
   What I have done today
An unkind word I've spoken
   A smile I've turned away

Will I relieve those hours
   With sadness and disgrace
Because my word I've broken
   And him I cannot face

Will I withdraw into myself
   And cower in a corner there
Since pride did hurt another
   or I said I did not care

Or will I hear my master
   his voice so warm and kind
Listen, walk and pray with him
   And walk the narrow line

To do kind deeds for others
   Not for me, myself
But to show my love of God
   My brethren, friends, and self

Walter R. Soulages

If A Dog Could Talk

If a dog could talk I wonder
what he'd say. Take me for
a walk but you wear the
collar! I don't want a bone,
give me a soft pretzel instead!
This dog food has got to go.
How about that roast instead!
How about some soda with my roast?
You sleep on the rug
and I'll take the bed!
Let me drive the truck and
you sit in the back.
Yes it sure would be wild if
dogs could talk!

Ray Mancini

Life

What does it mean?
What does it suggest?
What is its purpose?
What is its quest?

Does it mean to explore,
To love or to hate?
Does it suggest to build,
To overcome or to make?

Is its purpose to learn,
To change or to grow?
Is its quest something that we
Are never to know?

I think so...

Paivi Haapanen

Can You Hear The Music?

When the wind blows softly
What do you hear?
Can you hear the music
soft and low?

When the snow glistens in the tree tops
What do you hear?
Can you hear the music
faraway, yet so near?

When a child looks up and offers a smile
Is your heart so touched
the music soars within?

Music is there for all to hear
At all times of life, at birth and death
In summer or winter
Let your thoughts wonder,
Let the music appear

Sandi Adams

Along The Old Yangtze

'Twas all along the old Yangtze.
What did not all those sailors see.
The bursting shell and screaming plane.
A town of houses burst in flame.

The boom across the river thrown.
The Chinese dying all alone.
Dropping bombs in cities streets.
Looking on as a sunless mother weeps.

War is a terrible thing to see.
There is a lot of places I'd rather be.
I'd rather be looking from afar.
At the hell of this damn war.

Robert V. Fields

The Day My Sister Changed Her Name

Over the past twenty-five years
We've shared the laughs and the tears

Sometimes good, sometimes bad
Sometimes happy, sometimes sad

As we grew and made our way
I knew we'd say good-bye someday

You would marry or maybe I
Either way we'd say good-bye

So on this day a brother I gain
The day my sister changed her name.

David A. Lamothe

The Place

A place for news, good or bad;
Were thoughts unscramble,
And wounds mend.

A place for laughter;
Where memories abound,
The mind ponders; past,
Present, a future unknown.

A place for lessons,
As elders expound
Of experiences learned along hard roads.

A place to soothe the tender spirit;
To touch the place within,
That part so deep,
So much you.

A place for family,
business, togetherness.
and solitude.
The kitchen table.

G. D. Wabschall

Mountain Of Glory

Gently once the mountain mist,
Went softly as a virgin's kiss.
The fading bugle of an elk,
Nature's concert being dealt.

Echoes through the valley too,
Stories of the mountain's doom.
Man's material infatuation,
Of future and past generations.

Daniel Timothy Pope

Animal Instinct
(Just Fantasy?)

Animal Instinct (Just Fantasy?)
We were fantasizing, weren't we?
Never found one to be so good.
You nearly drove me to insanity
Doing things I never would.

Each time we made love was different
It's hard to point out the best.
You never owned my love, you rented it
Each time you put our fire to rest.

The wood in the fire is still burning
But the flames are almost gone.
You should have read what you're signing
Don't break the lease; can't live on my own.

I need time to find another tenant,
One who his rent on time would pay.
One who wouldn't take me for granted,
Someone who would not run away.

Sandra Regina Mendes

Baby Smiles

Have you ever watched as babies sleep
They must be in an angel's keep
The way they giggle and smile
It makes you stop and watch awhile
Soft spoken words from above
Telling them of God's mercy and love
If you have a heart like that of a child
You too can hear the words so soft and mild

Tim Bass

My Idea Of A Perfect Day

People ask how our day goes,
We say it was a perfect day,
People didn't get on our nerves,
And nothing wrong came our way.

But my perfect day would be,
When the world would be in harmony,
They would help one another,
They would be one big happy family.

My idea of a perfect day,
Is when we all can say,
I love everyone on the universe,
In every possible way.

My idea of a perfect day,
Is when there would be no fear,
No killers, no stealers, no destroyers,
And losing the one that is so dear.

So now you know what my perfect day is,
A day without stress,
A day without all the violence,
And everybody is at their best.

Tamika Brown

Ship Of Life

Life is like a ship
  we sail
Plotting its course
  in calm and gale.
Piloted by hope,
Propelled by love,
Sustained by faith
  In God above,
And when its voyage
  finally ends;
Enriched by kindness
  of wonderful friends.

Ray Combs

No One

We sulk, but no one sympathizes.
We lose, but no one encourages.
We cry, but no one notices.
So we complain, but no one listens.

We run away, but no one runs after us.
We return, but no one rejoices.
We wonder,
Will no one ever notice?
Will no one ever care?

Suzy Mosher

From The Heart

Wrapped in each others arms,
We lay still.
Our hearts beating,
Our bodies one.
Your touch is gentle;
Your lips, are soft;
I am afraid
My feelings are strong,
My heart is opened.
But there it was,
Your honesty was overwhelming,
You felt the same way.

Tina M. Busch

On The Eve Of Another Year

We have come a long, long way,
We have stumbled again and again,
We have struggled hard every day;
But all in all we have made gains.

We have learned by trial and error,
And hope to profit by our mistakes,
So, on this eve of a new tomorrow;
Let's keep the resolutions we make.

We are about to turn another page of time,
And give out with a hearty cheer,
When we hear the strains of Auld Lang Syne;
Announcing the dawn of another year.

Yes, another year goes own in History,
Recorded for us by Father Time,
Who has brought peace and prosperity;
To the homes of mankind.

The pendulum sways, time is fleeting,
Soon you'll hear that old refrain,
That brings that old, but new greeting;
Of, "Happy New Year", to you again.

Pauline Pickering

Remembrance

These are the same steep sun rocks
We climbed down together
Tucked our shoes and things
  in shadowy crevice
And slipped into the sea
Which held us together
Yet not close enough
But for a while

And the waves and current
Were too strong for us to fight
So we swam to nearby beach
Where we climbed back up
To the top and continued on
Only salt sweet air between us
And all dried off we drove home

Robert J. Fabiano

In God's Power

In God's power
We can fulfill,
Not the lust of our flesh
But only His will.

In God's power
We can choose this day,
To serve only Him
And walk in His way

In God's power
We can totally depend,
On the precious Holy spirit,
Our guidance and friend.

In God's power
We can live our life,
Free from selfishness,
And strife.

In God's power
We can be grateful today,
For whatever He sends
Is His will and His way.

Rachel Ligon

The Coming Autumn

Summer's gone, it's autumn now
We can feel it in the air
As we watch the squirrels, gather food
For their oncoming winter's care

We've made it through the summer's heat
And now the colors fill the air
The trees have changed their summer gowns
For the Autumn coats they'll wear

The earth will yield its harvest
For the farmer's labors, he'll share
It's easy to see watching all this
Why this is my favorite time of year

The days, they seem to get shorter
Though the advance of winter, we fear
Each passing morning seems, darker
As the approaching winter is near

R. C. Stamper

Sympathy

God has written a symphony for our lives,
We are born, we grow, we live, we multiply,
And when our song is ended we die,
But the tune lives on,
In our children
In our grand children
In our great-grandchildren;
The song, has words of joy and gladness,
Of pain and sadness, this too shall pass;
But the tune lives on,
So let us sing a happy tune,
As we pass along this way,
That our children, and their children,
Will take courage, as they live day by day,
Knowing the writer of the Symphony,
And the tune lives on!

Pauline Good Zielke

Daddy's Shadow

Working out in the yard
Watering down all the trees
Here comes Daddy's shadow
So happy and so free

Following each step he makes
As he move from tree to tree
She stays close behind
By tugging at his knee

She smiles and she laughs
For she thinks her Dad is best
As she helps in her own way
By being a tag-along guest

She runs to keep his pace
For she thinks it's kind of fun
Staying close to Dad
'Til all his work is done

So as he works within the yard
Through the heat of the day
He can rest assured
His shadow is there to stay!

Pamela Wadkins

Pension

On the verge of tears I wait
watching and listening to the rain
as it continues to pelt the window
where I stand

Shivering with cold, and completely alone
I shrink even further
into the damp, musty blanket
I have wrapped around me

Hungrily my fingers poke out
in their never ending search
for tiny crumbs of food
which may have escaped them yesterday

The few people passing by
do not notice me at all
and in my embarrassment
I cannot call out my needs to them

Trembling all over with hunger and cold
I can only wait patiently and hope
that this will be the day
my small check is finally delivered
Sarah Elizabeth Rose

Brand New

God takes me, God takes you,
washes us clean, just like brand new.

Our world lies
in material waste,
not our spirits
when there is
faith.

First we crawl,
then we walk...
Stumble, and we
fall.

Do not worry,
God picks us up.
Not just some,
or just a few.
But all of us
yes me and you.

For there with him we will be,
brand new for eternity.
Rene Conley

My Flag

I love my flag
Want her proud of me
Lift it high, never drag
She will always keep me free.

I'll fight for my flag
She represents every race
I never want to be a brag
Or ever let her lose face.

I'll die for my flag
Never let them tear her down
Keep my faith and never lag
She is our country's shining crown.
Ida Brodsky

Revel In It

Wallow in misery,
Wallow in Joy.
Nag, complain, laugh, pity.
You like to dwell on all of it,
never letting anything go
Because I know
you like to revel in it.

You look at those pictures
Over and over again.
They're worn at the edges
Gazed upon too much.
Afraid to let go?
You sit here
turning through the past,
Bringing up old feelings.
Stop! Look to the future
Alas no, you like to revel in it.
Edgar Hernandez

Solitude

How amazingly peaceful it can be
   Walking along the shore.
Silence being broken by a cry of a gull,
   And the sound of the ocean roar.
Oh to lose oneself in that peacefulness,
   Never having again to return,
To face once more the problems of life
   Knowing there's no other place I can turn.
It's there by the water I like to sit,
   And quietly reminisce,
And let the outgoing tide wash away,
   All of my loneliness.
Rose C. Devine

Perspective

Perspective is a
   vibrant prism

Tones and colors changing
   as days innumerable
     pass by.

Memories
Desire
mix and blend
their blues and purples
fiery reds and yellows.

Regrets
black and grey
give way to diamond brightness
   in time.

Hope shines through
in summer's green.

Flashes of insight
   move us
In life's spin
   of love and pain.
Pamela J. Haley

Blending

Compare life's conflicts to a boiling pot
With bubbles rising to the top.
As each one bursts, tis soon forgot.
But each one helps to blend the lot.
Sue Sandberg

"I Need You"

Here I am all alone.
Very sad, very blue,
Where are you, when I need you,
Of all times, someone to share.
When times get rough, and hard to bare.
This time, I wish to share with you.
That special love, I need you.
Oh how can I convince you,
That my love for you is real, is true.

Here I am all alone, very sad, very blue,
wish you were here, honestly, I need you,
All these day's and nights,
Are to long, to many tears.
This bond we have, the many years,
A feeling of sadness, oh is it really true,
The love I want, is really you.
Ronald G. Spinelli

Wave Of Sorrow

O wave that caused distress to bear;
Upon the breast of those who care
Beneath the angry raging storm;
A dear beloved is gone.

As the soldier aims his gun;
Upon another woman's son,
The bugler plays his song of sorrow;
To a long and empty tomorrow.

Whose form can fill the empty space;
Rest forever, that lonely place,
Within a sad heart its pain reside;
Finds peace with time - as evening tide.

In the garden that has lost its luster;
Where life begins an endless summer,
And the sun has set upon its dreams;
As dried up brooks and silent streams.

Embrace the thought that life goes on;
Sad or happy in whatever form,
And grasp each moment as a prize;
For in the schedule of time, life dies.
Sylvia Tonge

I Played All Day

I played all day from dawn to dusk
Until the white moon rose
A silver knife, a gleaming tusk.
From where? Nobody knows.

It fills the night with cold white light
And spreads across the land.
Black shadows rise and play all night
Till day reveals its hand.

The moon and sun; the night and day.
A never ending game.
Repeating in the same old way,
But really not the same.
Wade Tokumine

Untitled

Like Humpty Dumpty falling from the wall.
Words come tumbling from my brain.
I merely reassemble them...and lo.
The birth of my latest Quatrain.
Robert Sherman

My Undying Love

I will love you
Until forever comes
Or until death has
Conquered me
But even then
If I can't love
You physically
I will always love
You spiritually
And if the time does come
God forbid it does
That I shall roam the earth no longer
Just know I will
Always watch over you
Even if you find another love
Because you know that
All I want for you
Is happiness even if
It can't be
With me

Shannon Senteio

Deeply Ingrained

Way down deep, dark and old,
Unreached by human hand,
Deeply embedded in the grain,
The very soul of man

Lies dormant, lies sleeping.
The beliefs of all mankind,
Not of this world beliefs,
But of holy divine!

Unchanging patterns,
As ancient as the night,
Premise as old as mankind,
What's right is right!

Look not to mankind,
For guidance and rules,
For God, in his wisdom,
Already gave us the tools!

Thelma Moore

Untitled

The key to the door
Unlocks the way
To a brighter future
To a brighter day

The key to the door
Holds hope for tomorrow
No more crying, no more tears
No more grief, no more sorrow

The key to the door
Leads to beauty and love
From the green grasslands
To the blue sky above

The key to the door
Contains promises for you and me
Through good and bad
Whenever we disagree or agree

The key to the door
Unlocks my heart
My love and care goes everywhere
Whether close together or far apart

Shaunquetta Johnson

The Reunion

Our hands
United as though you never left
Welcome home
A kiss
The beauty of a rainbow
And the fury of a storm
As one
The embrace
Refusing to let go
But no longer mine to hold
Out of reach
The goodbye
Hopes again established
And promises remaining
Broken
Love
Replaced by hate
Replaced by love

Pamela Friedman

Untitled

As I sail the bay
Under the deep blue sky
  With view of the golden gate
As clouds scud by
  My heart is full
Of song and dance
  When I think of you
And our great romance
  You are so wonderful
My very best friend
  Our feelings are strong
That it will never end
  I could send you flowers
And candy too
  But nothing lasts longer
Than a friend like you.

Richard Close

In A World Of Mine

In a world where feelings go
un-noticed and sanity is lost.

Dreams only come true in your sleep
and reality is a nightmare.

Man's only strive is power,
not happiness within.

When one stands up for what
they believe, the other falls in fear

The hand that reaches out with
love, only waves good-bye.

In a world of mine.

Taryn Tramel

Look Inside Not Outside

  You need a friend to talk too.
To love you and to care? Well,
Don't look at the color of my skin
Look in my heart instead.

  There's too much hate
Not enough love in the universe
We see. Don't look at the
Color of my skin, look in
My heart instead

Shirley A. Whaley

The Fall Of Autumn

Fall waif fallen leaf
Tumbling clouds shout disbelief
In a crackling wind
The trailing gold
Stiffly...spilling out
Flying - like pagan garlands strung
From moss covered towers
Freed from high above
The spinning tykes
All knitted caps and flailing laces
Falling turning
Upward faces
Dizzying...their ruddy cheeks
And watery eyes
In the cold laden air
Spry and un compromised
Prancing along
Kicking fiery leaves high
To a silent earthen song

L. J. Donahue

The Little Child

A little child roams the street
Trying hard to find something to eat.
He doesn't have much of a home
They just leave him all alone.

The child eats out of the garbage can,
There on his tiny legs he can hardly stand.

His clothes are all torn,
He probably wonders why he was born.
We wonder how he gets by
And if he will live or die.
He never saw a pair of shoes.
It seems like he is the one that will lose.
He doesn't even know his parents name
All the people look the same.
This little guy is kind of sick
Maybe someone will adopt him pretty quick.

A childless couple would take him today
And start him on a new life right away

Let's all do what we can
And let him grow up to be a man.

Bud Farrell

Afar

In the distance,
Train whistles echo,
Someone going somewhere,
In the distance,
A tree stump,
A deserted spider web,
In the breeze, weeds dance.
Gazing toward the sky,
Balloons fly away,
In the distance,
Laughter of children at play

Jacqueline Johnson

Untitled

It's a nice feeling
When you're filling a need
And the need you're filling
Is the feeling you need

Chris E. Kuehn

Intentions

Reeds, slowly whispering,
Touching, touching, to reconcile,
Those trampled, youthful, and
Fragile tendrils.

Unthoughtfulness, without design.

Reeds, slowly down,
With each aligned.
Broken forgiveness;
Trials time.

Reeds,
Tender thoughts by elders
That honor display,
Will hold the day.

Too many reeds are broken.
Misleading observations reign.
Roswita B. Davis

"Touch Me"

Lord:
   Touch me when things go wrong
   Touch me when I sing your songs
Lord: Touch me when I kneel to pray
   Touch me, teach me, what to say
   Touch me with your eternal love
Lord: Touch me from up above
   Touch me as I live this day
   Touch me so I live it in a Godly way
Lord: Touch me when the day is done
   Touch me and make today a victory won
   Touch me when I go to sleep
Lord: Just touch me, my soul to keep
Paul B. Mansberry

No Time

How oft have I passed on by
Too busy to hear another's cry?

No time, I said, as on I rushed,
Not noticing a heart was crushed.

"These things I must do," I thought.
These things — I've now forgotten what.

Surely they were extolled
For all my time they stole.

I have learned at last
I hope before all time is past,

To pause along this winding road
To help with another's heavy load.

This is what my precious Lord
Has done, while hanging unadored.

He paused upon Calvary's tree,
To rescue the likes of me.
Vera Caldwell

Untitled

The door of love open
the pain of sadness was their
When the door of love open
love was gone
Someone new walk in
the door of love was open
Rose Carrozza

From South Of The Border

There came a boy from Mexico
to work and learn and grow.
He was very young indeed
searching for something he did need.
A richer life is what he was told
full of promises and the dreams you hold.
He thought his dream was meant to be,
when he raised a family with me.
Many problems came about
which he gladly figured out.
So while fighting drugs and guns and wars
the American dream, my dear is yours.
Peggy Zavala

To Kill A Soul

The angels looked down,
To where he played,
Knowing what prices,
The child would pay.

The times he laughed,
The times he tried,
The way he lived.
It was all a lie.

Through years of abuse,
And times of pain.
The little child grew,
So lost and afraid.

Looking to the wrong,
Thinking it was right.
The mind couldn't tell.
What was black, what was white.

The day was getting near,
The day the angels cried.
The little boy's fear,
Died when he died.
Stephen B. McGraw II

Some Thoughts

It is not wise
To try to smell with the eyes.
And so it goes
To see with the nose.

And to speak with the ear,
Now, that's the job for the mouth.
And the lips don't hear.
No. It's all turned about.

Yet the mind can touch just like the hand,
And carry farther than the legs over land.
The stomach is emptied, but filled again,
While the mind is insatiable to the end.
Christopher Murphy

High Notes

I am playing my music
The notes are high notes
The princesses dance to my tunes
And hug me at the end of each sound
I'm excited about my guests
Regal princesses are my gifts
Some one of them will marry me
Echo it loud, the notes are high notes.
Wycliffe E. Tyson

Untitled

Frendz bring the beauty
To the world
But only
When they let you be you
Liking you for who you are
And not for what they can gain
By changing you
Into another
And frendz let you grow
With your own
Beliefs
Helping to add strength
To every weakness
You hold
As you do with them
For frendz make the world turn
Cause without frendz
It would not be as beautiful
Without the laughter, joy, or love
Frendz bring to your hearts.
Teri Ann Oho

Inner Universe

Where we run, where we hide
To that place we go in our mind.
Where we reach inside ourselves,
To find the soul, who there does dwell.

Who it is and how it forms
A mystery, yet so many are born.
They search there path from inside,
They listen to there inner guide.

The higher self that no one sees,
The one who tells us what we need.
The one who's right, listen or not,
Our inner soul who lights our thoughts.

The outer body it will decay,
The inner soul will fly away.
Out to the stars, up to the heavens,
Back to the universe from which all things
are given.
P. J. Lewis

Forty Acres And A Swimming Pool

A new generation of blacks have aroused
  to take over where the previous left off.
Discarding old slogans such as
  "40 acres and a mule."
"Where the hell can I park a mule in this
  city?" they ask.

No more expecting others to give them what
  they need.
No more expecting reparations for
  four hundred years of torture.

This new generation of blacks will
  go out and get what they want.
They will rise to the top and
  excel in all they do.

They will maintain all calm and cool-
  when they change their subtle slogan,
to "40 acres and a swimming pool."
Warren A. Allen

Dusty Soap

I went into the shower,
To take a nice hot bath.
But once inside, I changed my mind,
And took another path.

I looked upon the shower,
The soap hung on a rope.
I got undressed and climbed inside,
To get real clean, I hope.

As the nice hot water splashed my face,
It felt so good to me.
And as the soap hung on the rope,
T'was a knot, I could not see.

Now, as I struggled, and I pulled,
The rope would not come free!
But with a final tug, it gave,
I went, I fell you see.

My elbow started bleeding,
My head was sore and hurt.
And then I had to climb back out,
....Still covered with my dirt!

Robert D. Wright

To Daddy, With Love

I wish I knew the words
To say that you mean to me,
You warm my heart and soul
Sometimes it's difficult to see.

The feelings are happy ones
They bring joy through and through,
When I think of our family
I can't imagine it without you.

You've taught me morals and values
Sometimes I've strayed away,
But now that I'm getting older
The lessons are here to stay.

You give so much of yourself
I know you don't think it's enough,
With all the materials things you share
There's nothing better than your touch.

You've always stood by me
Though the good times and the bad,
I can't think of anything more special
Then to have you for my dad.

Susan Roubal

Artists And Poets

An artist uses brush and palette
To produce a painted art;
A poet uses pen and paper
To create a picture from the heart.

An artist employees vivid colors
Brushed on a taut linen frame;
The poet uses words of imagery
Trying to visualize the same.

An artist's work is arranged
In galleries for public view;
A poet's work is hidden in books
And found by very few.

A picture painted by an artist
Can be purchased for a price;
The poem is read and then forgotten
Unless it merits reading twice.

William R. Reilly

"Enemy Is Silence"

Silence came boldly
to our gathering one day
As usual, uninvited
not an audible word to say
As minutes wove among us
like a predator on the prowl
Ill at ease was our wary party
of what was left unsaid just now
Darting eyes, adjusted collars
Deep breaths and knuckles clutched
Time stood still for just a moment
and lifted its head as a lion would such
to test the air for the scent of a prey
then disappeared as quickly
as the brief time it had stayed

Rhonda Ann Kubosh

Cuddled Up To God

What a wonderful feeling
To know I can be
Cuddled up to God
Feel his arms around me.

Are you tired- discourage -
Fell hopeless and blue?
His everlasting arms
He will put around you.

He isn't so distant -
He isn't very far.
He's waiting for you
Right where you are.

He's loving Father,
His grace is matchless too.
So cuddle up to God
And feel His arms around you.

Why don't you try it,
See what it can do,
When you cuddle up to God
And He puts His arms around you?

Roberta A. Black

"God, I Love You"

How thankful I am
to have a father like you,
To walk beside me
my whole life through.

To love me, to guide me
to show me the way,
How to live more victoriously
day by day.

God, I'm so blessed
that you've chosen me,
Your grace, your forgiveness,
your mercy to see.

It comforts my heart
to know that you care,
It matters, you listen
and answer my prayers.

God, I love you.

Angela Bernal

"The Dream"

We had a dream of a baby boy
to fill our hearts full of joy.
We waited nine months to see
what sex our child would be.
And finally the day came
to give our child his full name.
But sorrow follows after delivery
for God has called our little baby.
It's no ones fault our baby died;
for not joy but sorrow we cried.
He's in the best place we know,
but it hurts to let Christopher go.
Now we have to live life on
even if our beautiful son is gone.
We'll try again for another boy
to fill our hearts full of joy.
We'll never replace our little son
but God will bless us with one.
That one dream maybe gone
but at least our dreams are still strong

Linnie Renee Hillger

Daughter

The wind blows hard the snow starts
to fall and as it grows colder I
think of you, you left me for a warmer
place, almost hard to believe, I am
your daughter, I thought you would
always be here but now that you're gone
I have nothing to do, I feel
lifeless and overwhelmed with my
thoughts. There is nothing here for me,
why wouldn't they let me go with you,
my mother. I feel all alone so far
from home, I miss you even if you
have hurt me and left me here.

Reanne Williams

God's Greatest Gift

My father sent me into this world
To cleanse it of its sin
I talked to glory, love, power, and life
Was crucified then rose again

I am what waits for those who seek
The answer to all who ask
The living spirit of my father
So to you I impart my earthly task

Spread the news of the living savior
That the kingdom of God may be know
The cross which I was raised upon
Shall be your cornerstone

If you ever believe the price too high
For things which I may ask of you
Remember, I've already paid you debt
When I shed my blood and died for you.

Steven P. Miller

Cover Up

Some ask me why I wear a hat,
The bottom line to this is that -
My hair "alone" is quite a mess -
Which causes lots and lots of stress.
But with a hat upon my head
Strangers "smile" at me instead -
Of looking at my zippered neck,
Which helps to heal this aging wreck

C. G. Pulse

I Was A Slave

I broke the rocks
To build the roads,
Used as an ox
For heavy loads,
I worked the fields
In the blazing sun,
I crawled, and kneeled
Wanting to run.
Shackled and chained
To God, I cried
"How much pain,
Before I die?"
This new land was not for me
With folded hands
I begged to be free
Then, violence was torn
In smoke filled air
A nation was born,
God answered my
   Prayer.

William J. Nagel

The Secret Of My Song

I breathe, I blow
to Bach and Brahms
with delicious moans,
caros and *mios*.

Like a javelin,
like a drill,
like Donald Duck,
mellow and shrill,
I hoot, I howl, and glissand
with studied ease.
So many notes
to find simplicity.

I take the bravas as my due
for 30 years of may-mee-mah-moe-moo.
While the wolf, the wind, *die nachtigall*
all know the secret of my song:
I breathe, and then I blow.

Susanna Ralli

Budding Soul

My mind drifts hazily back
to a smooth sail upon a still
narrow river that swirled
sinuously and widened slowly
before spilling into the sea

Reminiscing with beating
heart of a change in tide
when waters became rough
and rolling as my ship met
with murky, grey seas and

I was fatefully tossed upon
coral lined shores to be beaten
by rain, kissed by sun, and caressed
by the winds that carried silent
secrets of moons to come.

Serene T. Marshall

The Price

The price we pay to live each day
The things we say to pass each day
Until the day we pass away
At least we can say we had a chance to stay

Quinn Lin

Born To Boil

Battalions clang
thunder angrily claps
innermost conspiracy thrashes
train whistles and teapots scream
chugging turmoil spews out
splashing, scalding exposed flesh
blisters with the sun
trapping expedition stops short
the headquarters of physical control
in a frying pan fizzling tissue
internal mutiny
contorting, thrashing, shredding organs
systems fail to operate
insanity is a hard won ally

Sara E. Pratte

Winding My Way Back Home

The plane knifed upward
through the white murk
on its short flight
from Raleigh-Durham to
Newark
later on, in clearer visibility
we could spot
David Byrne's baseball diamond
the black stewardess's
copious tresses
cascaded over the
back of her white shirt
as she hurried to the
front of the plane
which descended upon
Christmas in August

Walter De Las Casas

The Wind

How do you hear the wind blow?
Through the rustling of the leaves.
The leaves that once were silent now
sing out on a breeze.

How do you hear the wind blow?
Through the music of the chimes.
They play us a tune, a sweet melody,
a rhyme.

How do you hear the wind blow?
Through the limbs as they swing and
sway.
How do you hear the wind blow?
On the wings of a bird as she fly's away.

Susie Wolf

Elegant Expressions Of Love

Each time we stop to love and ponder
   through life's ups and downs,
I gaze with fondness and wonder
   upon your lovely crown.

Your endless love and prayers you see
   sends my love "forevermore,"
Fondness and splendor from thee
   in faith, trust, and hints of folklore.

Forgiveness and kindness shall be
   always willing, and in learning,
   must in triumph be
You and I forever yearning...
   ...for God's eternity

Roy Edgerton

Evil

Evil thoughts consume my mind
thoughts of love
I will never find
Death so soon to come for you
Without warning you are to die
Though I know it waits for me,
I just don't want to know why.
Do you feel its dead
Breath upon your skin?
And somehow you know,
you just can't win.
But yet you wonder why
there is so much hate
and the answer is,
this is our fate
we brought evil
among the human race
now we all are to be
put in our place

Shannon Ouellette

Our House

There you stood with your arms open
Though you'd already closed the door
Into your heart and you knew it
As you held me you closed it again
So hard that the windows to your soul
Shattered and the shards that rolled
Down your cheek cut into mine

I looked through those broken panes
And saw that you had let someone else
Paint over the walls inside . . .
And she didn't even bother to read
Any of the writing on them

We said our goodbyes after lunch
I had to catch the last train back
Back to the life that had taken me
So far away from you

I waved goodbye from across the street
And somewhere
Somewhere inside of me
I felt a roof cave in

M. Concepcion G. Hiponia

A Desert Succulent

A desert succulent is become my heart,
Though broad and deep of root,
Can only store what you impart;
So scarce it bears no fruit.

Environed in this desert earth,
Semi-arid, too, your season;
Wind-blown, you are, of dusty worth
With prickliness for reason.

Leaf-reduced to stem am I
Adjust to foreign soil;
Your water in such short supply
That thirst demand I toil.

Until my heart, brief desert bloom,
Explodes in glory; withers soon.

Sandra Solomon Pridgen

Rainy Days

How I cherish rainy days
Those warm and cleansing showers,
Falling gently upon the land
My spirit and soul it empowers.

There's something about a rainy day
That makes you feel cozy inside,
Yet, how glorious to run outdoors
It's delicate freshness to imbibe.

Rainy days are meant for thinking
About things past and present,
To snuggle with a good book
The time perfect and quiescent.

Just to sit and watch the clouds
As they roll across the sky,
Says the best will never change
What promises they do imply.

When some days become a burden
And seem so full of strife,
Remember the blessing of the pain
For this is what gives us life.

Shirley Bragg

Untitled

So long as we can say
this is the worst,
we can't comprehend placid challenge

So long as we know simple minds
serendipity can't be understood, and desire
of complexity will not grow. Moments seem
but trivial, salted water, time drifts
to an endless shineless finish.

So long as we make sense
our sense can not be complicated,
and contradiction of ordinary canon
rests in a lump of wet gun power
futile in a feudal ditch.

So long as we can say not possible
Impossibility can not be challenged.
Directions lead to a wall, hiding
forgotten doors under broken bricks
and ivy twisted hinges.

So long as we can say this is the worst,
we can't comprehend a future.

Summers McKay Newell

Flash

I had a fish
  who splashed
    and splashed
He swam like lightning,
  so I named
    him Flash.

At first he was scared,
  a tiny
    bit mad.
But after he saw me;
  he was not
    a bit sad.

Sarah Loreman

Indifference

This is not happiness,
This is a hunger of the soul.
Such a painful yearning
You should never know.

When I confronted you
I burnt my ships behind me.
I was lost in your apathy
You could not care to find me.

I hate myself for loving you still.

I curse the fate
That chains me to you
In my bitter frustration
I drink a cup of humiliation.

A toast to you
On bended knee.
Throw down your glass
Turn away from me.

I hate myself for loving you still.

Tony A. Lynch

The Walls

The walls are all built,
this castle is my home,
I don't need anybody,
I'd rather be alone.

I didn't mean to build this place,
It's taken a long time,
life handed me the hammer,
and helped me draw the lines.

The walls are strong like iron,
the windows there are none,
It's dark in here and very cold,
will I ever see the sun?

I try to open up the door,
but life pushes me back in,
there's too much hatred in the world,
I'm afraid to come out again.

So I stay here in this lonely place,
this castle in my mind,
where I can be just who I am,
and the walls don't seem to mind.

Sally L. Szatkowski

Heartbroken

I'm in love because when I met
this boy we had everything in common.
He said he loved me, he said he cared,
he said he would always be there.
We even went out to the movies
and he sang to me out of harmony.
Until that Wednesday night I thought
he was right. Then he hit me and
we began to fight. When I got home
that night I was in fear because
all his untruthful words made me
break down into tears. I fastened
the doors and windows. Since I couldn't
go to sleep I had a little bit of something
to eat. I couldn't believe
it, but it wasn't a dream because
he made me scream.

Sandra Marie Husser

Sometimes

  Sometimes when, I'm alone I
think of the times when being happy
was all that was on my mind!

  Sometimes I wonder, sometimes
I fade, yet I always seem to be in
the same space, a space of my own
so far away, where dreams are swept,
and memories kept away!

  Sometimes in life I fall
asleep awake in a world dead on
my feet. The meanings are clear my
minds full of fear, I'm alone with
my thoughts I don't want to be here.

  Sometimes I feel a change
come about, I then revive all
life and hope to forget any ridden doubts.

  Yet sometimes I believe
that somehow sometimes in between
all this I'm only sometimes ME!!

Shelly L. Rouse

Love And Memories

Love and memories are two of a kind,
They both last forever,
In the heart and the mind.

No matter how far away you maybe,
Just one thought can bring you to me.

It feel's so good being next to you,
That sometimes I think your to good
To be true.

I may not say it reach and every time,
But I hope you know that I will always
Love you until the end of time!!

Joanna M. James

Friends

Their names are Bessie and Smokie
They are my pride and joy
When I'm sad they show their affection
When I'm asleep in bed they warm my feet
People ask why I'm so protective
I won't let them out the door
They may think I'm being selfish
They say they'd be all right
But if they were hurt I couldn't bear it
My feline friends for life

Sarah Ryan

Gratitude

Flowers and trees are in full bloom,
The night is full of fragrance.
The sky has weaved its web of light,
Its glories we behold.

In the expanse of all this beauty,
how can we even consider the
difficulties of life? Can it all
be an oversight as we struggle from
Rags - to the oh so desirable riches?

Perhaps if we ponder these things
through, we will - at last - realize we
have already attained more than the
richest man could afford.

Regenia Skinner

The Eyes Have Seen

Look into my eyes. What do you see?
They are a mirror - a reflection of me
Throughout my life, they have held
Every feeling - every memory

From the day of my very first breath
Like a camera rolling, always rolling
So much they have seen
So much - so much

The early years of violence, abuse and pain
The fear and the tears
The struggle to survive, all hidden
Hidden there, there within my eyes

The middle years, raising a son
The efforts to protect him
From the pains I had known
The joy that he gave; the one moment of sunshine

The later days as I finally learned who
Who I was, and what I could be
The peace that it gives in this time of life
Lies there - there within my eyes
Sandra M. Ward Gursky

Love Story

When I called you that very first time,
There was only one thing on my mind:
I wanted you to be my friend,
I never imagined how it would end.

It didn't take too long for me to realize
There was something more in your eyes.
I never thought you'd really care
Enough to say you would always be there.

When you said that, I was so surprised
I felt tears form in my eyes.
Then I fell in love with you
And there was nothing I wouldn't do.

Suddenly, everything fell apart
And I felt a terrible pain in my heart.
I didn't think I could make it through
Without being there with you.

So far, I have done all right,
But I still think of you in the night.
Maybe we could try again someday,
If not, I'll still love you anyway.
Roxanne L. Hobbs

The Poem Of Life

I have walked upon this earth
The desert sands call me
The forests whisper to me
The rivers and streams cleanse me
The ocean overwhelms me
The sky opens out to me

All is harmony around me
I feel the life in the earth
It is sacred to me
I am one with the earth

Listen do you hear
Do you see the winds
Keep in touch with your self
Do not deny the way
If ever you close the door
It will forever be locked
Rajandra Littlewolf

My Lady

The moment our eyes met
 there was a feeling of joy
 within my heart.

The happiness I feel
 when I hear her voice.

Her laughter is the sound of
 her love of life.

Her embrace is the comfort of
 a summer night.

Her touch is that of a butterfly,
 so delicate and gentle.
Her eyes will bewitch,
 those eyes that tell so much
 about her and yet hold a mystery
 of a secret place within her soul.
She awakens all my senses,
 to the joys of life, and touches
 my soul.

This is my Lady.
Paul T. Tholl

Millennium

As we close the millennium,
there is an undertow of dread.
Mystics bring a state of terror,
they see the world come to an end.

Is humankind destined for death?
Are we just leaves blown by the wind?
Or do we control our epitaph?
And our future, can we rescind?

An ecological crises,
World resources are depleted.
Frustration and anger arises,
racism precipitated.

Our youth involved with gangs and crime.
No father figure in the home.
Politics deal with the sublime.
A government catacomb.

When all this has been said and done.
All these things we have caused, my friend.
Ahead a new millennium.
We can put chaos to an end.
Rambaldo Mendoza Jr.

"On A Cold Winter Morning"

The snow falls
Striking the frozen earth
Another life is gone another friend is dead
We are all like the snowflakes
Cold and bitter, yet soft and delicate
All of us different
And all of us the same
Tears flow like a rushing river
A hollow sensation invades
The wind now blows in their memory
Calling our names
Our heads hang low in grief
And the snow falls on a cold winter morning
Sara A. Erly

Magic

Magic—children
The words flow together.
They mingle and tweet.
Our curiosity peaks.

We ask—
Adults smash.
Killing dreams
We no longer can have.

We grow up.
Authority rules.
Time lines-dead lines and taxes.
We have lost the magic.
We wish for it again.
It does not come.
We grow old.
Bitter and gray
We remember the magic,
Wishing for it again.
We die.
And the magic we resume.
William Michael Ruprecht Jr.

Relive

In the still of the night
the unsurpassed lives in its
fullest bloom for I render
no offense as it renovate
the mind it occupies by
the elude found here within

The impact rejoices universal
by every nerve that answers
to its reframe tragedy recreated
as the scene relives it focuses
to the finest reach of the
after past behind the distant
days gone by

In the still of the night
I bare and again I bare the
plastered pity on a relived
tragedy subjugated to its wish
In the still of the night
Raymond A. Heywood Sr.

Peace Of Mind

He lifted up and high his chin
to better smell and taste the sea,
and freedom clear, pure as the wind
was present here eternally.
He watched the waves forcefully crash
against rocks uncompromising
standing forbidding, grey as ash,
outlined by autumn's sun rising
far in the east, from the ocean,
seen only at first as a glow,
transforming all in slow motion -
nature's so magnificent show.

He now felt his pain and despair,
fragments of anger subsiding
on cushions of water and air
his spirit as sea gulls gliding
in layers of conscious forgiving,
no longer anyone blaming,
no longer the past reliving,
pure feelings of peace remaining.
Tom Bergmann

As I Sit Here

As I sit here thinking of all
   the things we use to do.

I think of the way you use
   to laugh and smile.
I think you were to live all
   you life because you were the good man.

Your son will treasure all the
   memories he had with you.
For Daddy has gone to heaven
   with the angels in the sky-above.

Junior though your not here
   to make us laugh.
Your here to protect and
   guide us.

The way you made fun of all
   of us we still keep in our hearts.
We still waits for you to show
   your face again.

But, I guess that really
   was the end.

Rest In peace

Presilla Garcia

Peace

Don't laugh, don't point don't make fun of
The things I do to seek the dove

When your pools of blood mean victory
You kill the heart, destroy it's seed

On scattered winds may angels fly
And seek the truth from all your eyes

Upon these winds the dead will fall
To haunt the weary souls of all

When they laugh, point and make fun of
All you do and all you love

Look to the sky, the first bird you'll see
A snow white dove, remember me?

Shannon Mathis

Dreams

In my dreams
the sun shines bright.
In my dreams
there's a moon at night.

In my dreams
you're always there.
In my dreams
you always care.

In my dreams
there's a rainbow high.
In my dreams
there are clouds in the sky.

In my dreams
flowers grow.
In my dreams
the rivers glow.

In my dreams
that's where I'll be.
My dreams, my special dreams,
mean the world to me.

Shana Axton

Amazonas

The river is my life and soul
The stream my transport
The water my source, my energy
The heavens my spirit
The land my home.

My life flows like the river
   sometimes kind
   sometimes cruel.
It floods my firma
   I move higher — waiting the ebb
   I always return — as it falls low!

I am the river. The river am I.
There are millions of us.
We have no country
   only the river.
I am the river. The river am I.

Richard H. Stork

Through The Window

Through the window
The sounds of creatures
The sight of nature

The wind rustles gently
Through the boughs of trees
Like man's desire to be free

The rain softly falls
The smell, the taste
Rolling down the skin, like a baste

The grass grows tall
In the summer turns green
Pleasing to the eyes, as seen

The sun gives life
To those from the soul
To you we are loyal

S. Baker

Untitled

I shall not make a poem.
The softness of the clouds
the stillness of the blue horizon
the sweetness of the salt air
I shall not write a poem
For the editor will print it
In microscopic size
And all is lost, lost
For I shall not make a poem
To be lost.

Pauline Sorgen

Space

Space is so alive and fine
That I wish it could all be mine.

The comets and meteors are bright and gay;
They put on such a wonderful play.

The sun and planets are rotating;
To see them it would be so fascinating.

I would like to see the stars;
I know I can't because they're so far.

I would like to be an astronaut someday,
But for now I will just run and play.

Priya Nandapurkar

Untitled

Giving up is not a choice.
"The show must go on"
It doesn't matter what we think,
Things must happen.
The world laughs when we are down,
But we must get up,
and we will.

Giving up is not a choice.
Life is an on going battle, and
we are all soldiers.
We all die eventually.
So let us prepare for our future,
Let us fight the world's ways with
our knowledge,
and let the world know that we
are prepared, willing, and smart,
and that we do not intend to
give up.

Laura Stuart

Test

Red hand goes round and round the clock;
The seconds go by fast.
The long and short hand tell the time;
I know this time won't last.

The classroom clock ticks all the time;
Just now I realize it.
The loud sounds of the ticking clock
Annoy me just a bit.

"The time is up," my teacher says.
I know I did my best.
Cross my fingers for good luck;
I need to pass this test.

Poppy Major

Love, Crucified!

With hands held wide by painful stings
The Savior proves the love he brings.
Pricked of thorns, the life grows dim.
With tears the Father mourns him.
There he drowns in echoes of humanity.
Drops of blood respond to man's brutality.
Under the darkness of death he sleeps,
But in this agony love still keeps
The stars shining in lofty skies,
And awakes the pulsing sunrise.
The rosebud opens to breath anew
As teardrops sparkle like morning dew.
Fresh scent gathers remembrance,
So testifies the fragrance:
In mysterious action,
Wounded love bled compassion.

Peter Rolny

The Circle Theory

A stream-its water flows as Life's current;
The rocks-Life's events-past, present, future.
Leaves fall into the fray to be swept away
As people, they are swept away by Time.

The murmur of the stream-Life argues Time;
She does not want to yield to His will;
She battles Him, though Time has forever,
As Death shall conquer one for the other.

Shay T. Harding

"Awakening"

It only happens when you see the lights
The pages of the book will turn,
And from the dark unfolding nights
The young and tender learn...
That greens and blues come everyday
But how that yellow shoots
Its golden arrows on their way
To feed the hungry roots.
And growing is the lonely joy
That time alone commands
For with its clay constructs a boy
And fires it into man.
Then through the passage of the years
The soul like sand, is sifted.
Far past the time for no more tears
'Til all the pains are lifted.
M. Harrison

Where Have You Been?

Superficial prayers
the ones nighty said,
the message is there
but from the heart it's not shed.

Customary words, become blurs
just words from the head.
Only when in need
does prayer pull a thread.

So busy in life
to feel what we pray,
moving so absently through,
day after day.

When the path starts to crumble
and we fumble to sustain.
We reach out in desperation
and in the Lords name.

Forgive me, oh Lord,
forgive me my sins.
How desperately I need you
Where have you been?
Sharon Rekett

My Dream

My dream of life is just to be
the mother of a child
so sweet, so cute, so loving
so meek and yet so mild

To have a little daughter
dressed in pink and lace
with charming little hands
and a very lovely face

Who'll grow into a woman
beautiful as can be,
eyes of blue that sparkle
with a twinkle just for me.

I'll try to help her learn to be
a woman wise and true,
to raise her children as I did
the best that I could do.
Sarah Balkam

The Child Inside

As years go by I cannot count
the lessons I have learned.
I finally got, then cast aside,
the "things" for which I yearned.

I started young and foolish,
wishing I were old and wise.
Now I can see just what I sought
in every child's eyes.

If only I can keep alive
the treasures that youth held:
The feeling of a summer's morn',
the way the flowers smelled,

The wonder of a rainbow,
the joy of each new quest,
knowing that I was the first
to find a fairy's nest.

I WILL not lose that innocence,
for I've come to realize
there is no point to life at all
if the child inside me dies.
Sali Sheppard-Wolford

Autumn

'Tis autumn again
The leaves are falling from the trees
Their myriad colors so glorious to see
Thousands of acorns falling to the ground
And pine needles making carpets all around.
'Tis autumn again

There's a smell of apples in the air
Jugs of cider being sold everywhere
In the country, road stands
display their harvest wares
Churches and homes invite all to
their wonderful fairs.

Ah! 'Tis autumn again
What a wonderful time of the year
God, the master painter, thru nature
shows He's near
Let us enjoy this season, day by day
drink in the beauty about us as
we go our way.
Shirley Campbell Horton

Brother

Colors can be smelled,
Sounds can be seen.
Voices can be heard,
A never ending dream.

A quantum leap of choice,
By an experimenting child.
Too many questions must be solved,
The thoughts are racing wild.

A visit by an angel,
On a trip to paradise.
Life became a gamble,
Just one roll of this kid's dice.

Have you ever looked at the sunset,
Through eyes that have never seen?
Discover your faith in the ones you love,
And you'll never wake up from that dream.
Tyler Krebs

Winter Night

Dark, cold and forbidding
The lake's gaping hole.
Its movement frozen solid
By winter's blowing soul.

The night is filled with silence.
There are no sounds at all,
Except the hooting of an owl
Who sings his lonely call.

The darkness of the evening sky
Is lit by lunar light.
The full moon shines upon the lake
With moon beams of the night.

The sleeping trees surround the lake.
They dance their winter dance,
As gale winds blow right through their boughs
Without a passing glance.

And then the clouds begin to form,
And with them comes the snow.
Dropping crystal, frosty flakes
On every naked bough.
Sheila B. Roark

Anger

GOD: Today I felt my anger strike
The feelings in me I did not like
I could not begin to understand why
People could not see with my eye
Why they would not say or do
As I would for them too
But when I speak in angry voice
I virtually give them no choice
But to respond with more anger still
And let me know their ill will
For words of criticism and hate
No matter how just my debate
Only increases their frustration
And leads me to alienation
So God next time I choose to speak
Let my words be strong, but meek.
    Amen
Thomas H. Greene Jr.

The Drummer Boy Loves All

Tall - heavy - skinny - small
The drummer boy loves all.
Play his music, turn his key
The drummer boy will dance with glee.

He is happy to hear you call
"Hey drummer boy beat your drum for all."

His drum beats the message of love for you,
For he wants you to be happy too.

Now the music stops
He is still on the floor
His drum is silent—it beats no more,

But the message is there if you call
"Hey drummer boy beat your drum for all."

Tall - heavy - skinny - small
The drummer boy loves all.
Richard Fritz Adamson

Anniversary

A year gone by
The daily walk hard and then
Memories we have
With emptiness its been
Time has a way
Of slipping on so fast
No matter the time
Your always part of the past
A town you loved
Friends you'll always keep
We'll and meet again
Around Jesus feet

Shirley Frederick

Untitled

Charts and passage
The boundaries
The brave and foolish
Discovery
The doubting.

A sign from the stars
The veins of space
Wisdom of a map
secret connections
small secret channel

Madness comes, with fever
Moonlight cackle
The hiss of ocean devils
The sea growls,

Beneath her mask, an
open world of fantasy
and horror and there is
a strange sun rising
from her womb.

Tom Denzel

Fields

Like coarse ground pepper
   the blackbirds spice
     the shorn and golden hayfields,

More here, less there,
   ever changing the flavor and color
     of the noontide fields.

Now they line the wire fences
   like the beads upon an abacus,
     counting the passage of the seasons.

Veronica Callister

My Autumn Years

These I count the sweetest days
the autumn of my years,
It seems they pass so rapidly
Or so it appears.
I've counted all the skies of gray,
And I have counted blessings
Through my life and have come my way.
All the worries I've put aside,
I have tried to see the good,
My life it flows near even tides
or in that neighborhood.
And I shall spend my pining years
As life has me addressed,
And I can say throughout my years
That I've been truly blessed.

Tom Tibbs

Worry...Free

The sky is blue, like it usually is
The air seems fresh like spring
Drier today is my face from tears
From some distant worry thing

The sun is bright, like it normally is
The air seems to smell like spring
Bad times and relationship over years
Lifting, leaving me able to sing

It's the Fall of the year and AAHH
How nice it is to be free
From things that happened in the past, far
From the present things that be

My body even feels light
As if removed from a load
I danced some tonight
Welcoming my life's new road

The sky is blue, like it usually is
The air is fresh, through it's fall
Tucked away, for now, are my fears
From those worries yet to call

Sheila D. Ford

Shared

We shared everything
that was his or mine
We shared our love
when it was time

The things we had
the times we shared
No one else
could've compared

We shared so much
in so little time
I wonder where is
that love of mine

Maybe he's gone
cause we shared too much
Maybe I shouldn't have
loved him as such

Maybe I should've changed
before the final day
I just might have not
chased my love away

Masala

Wind Whispers

I heard the wind today whisper to me,
That he world is not all we
presume it to be;

In the lightness of day we believe
what we see,
But in the darkness of night our
souls fly free;

Is it our fear of our freedom flight.
That dissolves the remembrances of
our minds sight;

Come soar with me today,
We can teach our minds to obey;

To open up and see,
What it is to be free.

Troyce L. Turner

The Cries Of A Lonely Heart

Oh, the long and lonely hours
  that stretches into weeks,
Then on they stretch to months and years,
  but still she prays and weeps.

The world is full of people
  but no one seems to care
If her days are full of heartache
  for they have no time to spare.

They don't know the awful heartache
  of growing old and weak
And having no loving family there
  some living words to speak.

She cries and cries as she lives alone
  and prays for strength to know
What she can do to help herself
  so her life won't be so slow.

She tries so hard to help herself
  she wasn't born a quitter,
But it's being alone day after day
  that sets her heart to quiver.

Pearl Blank

Word

Love is but a word
That someone has made
The meaning is never clear
But can always be explained

If ever the word love
Could mean what we think
Then life would be a paradise
Only as a dream

Rhonda Crews

Where Are Your Eyes

...Am I the vendor
That sold my daughter
  This boy of anger?

Mama's into T.V. screen
  Daddy he is never seen
I'll color my hair yellow and pink
  Where are your eyes?
Why aren't you watching me?

Aliston Crawford

What Is Nature?

Flowers cover the grassy field
that separates mankind from animal, beasts.
Houses cover the places
animals are and used to be.
Trees cover the animals or
beasts that hide natures true beauty.
Nature is everything.
We have nature as a handful,
we can't give out everything around us.
Nature is trees, plants, animals,
houses, even our own clothing is nature.
What you are reading now is nature.
It's like when flowers bloom after winter,
they look like they've never bloomed
before.
Nothing can stop nature, from the fastest,
hawk to the slowest slug can't
stop nature, because that's what they are.

Tara Ann Mackey

From Men To Gods

In Time, in there, I'll find,
That path that once was lost.
Direction for the soul, for mine,
That leads me throughout time.
To have, to hold, to grasp and to know
Of all the things which be.
To make and to give
Of all the good thou brings.
Still I'm sure that somewhere there,
The things that I have heard,
- the things that thou hast said,
Are just forgotten, yea not lost,
Dormant in mine head.
But surely I know,
As thou didst tell,
That this knowledge rent,
Will, in time spent,
Be mine to wield.
But for now, my faith will be my shield.

Richard Zeller

Tranquility

See the butterfly
That passes over my eyes
A breeze without wind.

The forest singing
A quieting melody
While I think and tire.

There is but nothing:
No sound, no noise; yet I hear
A calm lake's ripple.

Why do I ponder?
A soothing and silent day
Answers my question.

The tall blades of grass
Nestle under my body.
I feel sedated.

The sun sinks slowly
Behind the horizon's edge
As we slip away.

On me looks the sky, stars, moon, cool night air.
I Dream the butterfly.

Eduardo M. Solozabal

"A Mother's Love"

A mother's love is something
that no one can explain
it's deep and it's devoted,
whether life brings joy or pain
it believes beyond believing
and it never would condemn
and it's filled with all the beauty
of the largest, brightest gem
it's far beyond defining
it defies all explanation
and it still remains a secret
like the mysteries of creation
a many splendor miracle
we cannot understand,
and another wondrous evidence
of God's tender guiding hand.

Robert Wayne Hoffman

A Whisper In The Wind

A whisper in the wind,
That never seems to end.
A whisper in the wind.
That tells us spring is again.
A whisper in the wind.
That tells us when summer will steam again.
A whisper in the wind
That tells us fall will fall again,
A whisper in the wind.
That tells us winter will snow again
A whisper in the wind.
That never seems to end.
A whisper in the wind.
That will never end.

Regina A. Myers

"Of The Love For You"

There once was a light
that lived in the night.
Like the love for you
in my heart.
The light grew strong
as the night went on.
Like the love for you
in my heart.

The light grew so,
there were no place to go.
But to reach for
the blissful skies.
Like the love for you
in my eyes.

So there's stars in the skies.
To remind you each night.
"Of the love for you in my heart"

Shelia Harris

"Memories"

A photo of your face
that I can never replace.
Yet we shall part; we know it,
and know why.
We know our pain and pleasures
you'll always be in my heart,
There is a quality of pain
that burnishes my heart,
Love is an abrasive
It's touch we dare endure.
When all the scars are fused,
The pain in my heart acquires
only from being used.

Kurstin Alu

Broken Glass

Broken glass, on the front door
step, caught my eye as I passed
the home of people unknown, and
I begin to visualize. Hearing the
sounds of sorrow coming from
within. Man brutalizes woman
with child at her side and I
feel the pair and terror while
I sympathize. The vision resembles
my past like the broken family
resembles the glass

Whitney Jaye Goetzinger

Love

Love is just a word
that has no meaning
to certain people
they believe love
is the greatest word
in the eyes of the beholder
Know one really understands love
till everyone realizes
what the true word
love means from the
heart and soul of the human being
alive inside both
people and ourselves
if your lover and you
believe in true love
Till the end
keep on dreaming
for the real love
finds yourself before
love comes and hurts you forever and ever

Phillip Quintela

Love

I have this love inside my heart,
That beats for only you.
I've felt it from the very start,
And I hope you felt it too.

When I look into your eyes,
it makes me realize,
That the love I have for you,
will always be true.

And your smile,
what a perfect sight,
leaves me speechless,
and dreaming at night.

I glance once, and then once more,
I feel my heart drop to the floor,
and then wonder, will I have to wait anymore
Or is this the love I've been waiting for?

Ruth Mosseri

When I Stand Alone

When I stand alone I have more faith
than all the world can hold.
You give me strength and courage,
You make me strong and bold.
When there's no-one with whom to share,
My life feels darkened with despair,
It's through those times you've taught me
Just who is always there.
Through all my hurt and all my fears
You brought me through and dried my tears.
On bended knees I do recall,
You've been there for me through it all.
Thank you Lord who reigns supreme,
My life, my Savior, and my King.

Vida Trujillo

Snow Flake

The winter's beauty with
the white snow. The peace
that is in the air.
The snowflakes falling
silently.

Vicky Paliouras

The Angel

And the Lord God observed the angel Gloria
tending him
Toiling long hours to calm and soothe
the man
The Lord God paused longer to watch
the angel Gloria pick the man up
and
With great effort carry him to a
Wonderful place of quiet and rest
It was then the Lord spoke and
said
My angel Gloria has truly done my work
and through me
has already been rewarded
For her brother is now in my care
Robert B. Weiss

Fresh Wind

Sea breeze wrapped in salten mist
Tempest tossed to twist
The gulls wings sing thru
Slicing the air with care

Stirring the sea to froth
Spirit this wind is to be
Sailing the flying fish free
Tis a joy to me

Greeting the cliffs so strong
Giving the sand a place to belong
Shells wash to meet again
Their cycle of life
A crabs true friend

The moon silver in the night
Jewels the shore as once before
Shimmering the darkness of waves end
Sending it's blanket of energy white
Frothing across in delight
On this we can depend
This wind a wave it will send
Peter Chatto

Teach Me

Teach me compassion
Teach me love
Teach me how it stems
From above

Show me mercy
Show me truth
Show me how to
Bear much fruit

Discipline me quickly
Do it in love
Discipline me regular
And show me God's love

Correct me when I'm angry
Correct me in my wrath
Leading in the direction
Of God's holy path

Let me see Jesus
Living in you
So I may learn how
He can live in me too
Paula M. Megginson

Some Things Should Be Remembered

Young love, first love
  Sweet ecstasy divine,
Such was our young love
  Yours and mine.

The light in your eyes
  As you gazed at me
Bespoke a deep and fiery flame.
  The thrill was much the same for me,
When gently you would speak my name.

The bliss of a kiss...
  is fondly remembered.
The glory as you held me in your arms,
  The splendor of beauty...
Our love had it all!
  First love! Yours and mine!

Young love, first love...
  Sweet ecstasy divine!
Some things should be remembered
  Your love...and mine!
Vonda L. Fletcher

The Blue Jewel

Our planet Earth
Sweet cradle of our life,
Earth that was alive,
Like a blue jewel in the sky.
With waters blue surrounding
Large ancient borders
Of traveling plates,
Floating on the ocean of fire
For aeons of time.
Ocean of fire pulsating yet
Like a warm heart,
Deep in the chest of a deserted Earth,
Who fed, nurtured,
Carried and endured,
The crazed burden of life,
Gone now.
Life that had destroyed,
All that good Earth could provide.
Silvia Radulescu

Eternity

Silence echoes through the trees
sun-caught leaves burning gold,
while upon the ground shadows weave
an ancient history of this forest old.
Faded memories linger here;
the teeth of time leave them still.
For many thousand, endless years
they remain and always will.
Though life is short and time forever...
to eternity are souls are called.
We shall always be together
for time remembers and keeps us all.
Scott Patton

Untitled

Sit down have a talk with me
tell me where I'm goin'
and how it's gonna be.
Tell me the story about
how this thought survived.
How man turned livin'
into who's supposed to die.
Ruth Nix

The Prophet

The prophet fills my head
His teachings of my salvation
  Suffocate my soul
While ease of same
  gives me breath.

To change is to live
To live is happiness.

His eyes saw through
  to my deepest emotions
His hand reached out
  to destroy my fears
  yet fear was the cause of my retreat.

Once in a dream
I fell to my death
While trying to touch my destiny.
Tara T. Santini

Deal Gently

He who checks a child with terror,
  Stops it's play and stills it's song,
Not alone commits an error,
  But a grievous moral wrong.

Give it play and never fear it,
  Active life is no defect.
Never, never break it's spirit,
  Curb it only to direct.

Would you stop a flowing river,
  Thinking it would stop to flow?
Onward it must flow forever,
  Better teach it where to go.
Richard N. Hathaway Jr.

Untitled

In the blue frosty heavens
Stars are shining bright;
As Pagette lies sleeping
Comes the first glow of light,
Then the bells are ringing
The music playing clear,
The guests are awaiting
For the bride to appear,
And standing at the alter
The groom sheds a tear,
For standing there before him
The one he holds so dear,
And as they leave together
To begin as Man and Wife,
We all ask God's Blessings,
For the rest of their life.
Thelma Catalani

Feathers

Dogga claims a beautiful
  soft pillow
Calling Catkin and Grey to
  come and play
Barking, "It's sleeting outside;
  let's make our own fun."
Dopes, I hadn't meant to
  cover you.
Now something is happening;
  it's raining fathers!
Where is my soft pillow now?
Only the skin is left
Ruth E. Pearson

Langkawi

Crunchy sand, scrunchy sand
Squiggles through your toes.
Wispy wind, crispy wind
Brushing on your nose.
Baking sun, flaking sun
Warming on your skin.
Chinking ice, twice as nice
Slices of lime in gin.
Hasty eats, spicy treats
Fire on your tongue.
Water warm, tropical storm
Sweating in the sun.
Insects call, coconuts fall
Buffaloes slowly browsing.
Birds sing, hammocks swing
At noon people drowsing.
Music chimes, gentle rhymes
Set your mind to dreaming.
Jet skis, palm trees
Life's slow and breezing.

Sarah Spanoghe

Planet—Earth

Words of love, I've heard
Sound of joy from bird to bird;
Smells of pleasure by a range of cuisine,
Moves from a gentle breeze unseen,
Touches so delicate before an embrace;
Seen an ancient starlight from space.

Words of hate, I've heard
Sounds of pain as cat killed bird;
Smells of disgust at some cuisine,
Moves so fierce by gales unseen,
Touches that roughly freed an ugly embrace;
Seen death in a challenge for space.

If words were never heard
No sounds from the songbird;
To smell nothing, a universal cuisine,
In a vacuum of stationary air unseen,
So touch reachingly and look to embrace
What's seen all around our planet in space.

Phillip Kallonas

Untitled

A mis-fit of
Sorts
I see the patches
and the dirt
A floppy hat
is dead weight
on her head
Pushing on through the night
Preferring to ignore
the lights and sounds
of the city
Distracted momentarily
by a stray cat
She reaches out to touch it
I see the patches
and the dirt
and the love that
is dead weight
on her heart.

Shana C. Sloan

Flow Chickahominy

Still water on the beaver pond
Songbirds tune to the trumpeter swan
Willow waves like a maestros wand
Ol chickahominy sings her song

Big ol bullfrog singing bass
Cricket playing fiddle on the Queen Anne's Lace
White water weaving her melody
Flow chickahominy

Crawdads dancing the doe see doe
Eagle cries like an indians soul
Water from heaven sets you free
Flow chickahominy

Grandpa beaver slaps his tail
Warns his babies of the coyotes wail
Coyotes singing in the key of C
Gray fox picking up the harmony

Come on flow chickahominy
To the river to the sea
Sweet water symphony
Flow chickahominy

Ted Sipkowski

Simplicity

Simplicity - does not exist anymore
Somewhere, back in my past
a closed door...
locked out simplicity...forever more.
Before the knowledge
of right and wrong.
The days were short
and the nights long.
There was simplicity...but never more.
NOW!
There is only...
rational decisions, complex dilemmas,
and logical reasoning.
Joy does not come
as easy as before,
because...simplicity just does not exist
anymore.

Tammy Kirkland

"Pieces Of A Dream"

In our quest of life
Sometimes hard it may seem
But we must hold on
To our pieces of a dream.
Keep striving - keep hoping
Even if society becomes mean
There is always hope - always a chance
Of achieving your wondrous dream.
Dr. Martin Luther King, Jr. often said
'I HAVE A DREAM'
It never died - it still lives on
In out true Black King.
He fought hard for his quest
He marched and preached so long
Now his promise is coming through
His dream still lives on.
His main objective was to be
In perfect harmony for you and me
Black and White for all to see
To get along in Unity.

Sheila Noel Johnson

Untitled

I must find something to wear,
Something to wear
To hide myself
From the way I am
From how I've become
Over the years
Worn
Soiled
Before Death finds me
Naked,
Alone
I must find something to wear.

Jim Beakey

"Good News"

"God news, good news is
Something that every one want
to get good news can bring joy smile
Good news can more pain what good
News can bring to you.
With good news you may want to do
Something good for yourself good news
Can bring peace to your mine what
good news can do for you. Good news
can bright up your day. Good news
Have you got cry good news with good
news you will want to do something
for other, with good new you will want
To talk right do night good news may
take affect on your life it may change
your life you may be able to do thing
you all ways want to. Good news what
Good news can bring to you. God news
Can stop you from doing something bad.
Good news can keep you from hurting
good news.

Mary Frances Yaroslawski

A Woman's Lot

We raise our kids the best we can,
Some of us without a man.
We do it all, we do too much;
And try to keep our woman's touch.

Waiting for "At last, I'm free,"
Wanting: "All that I can be."

But before we can break loose,
Around our neck's another noose.
For now, our parents need our care;
Without us, just how would they fare?

Another load's upon our backs
As down the road, we make more tracks.

Will we ever reach that "promised land";
That is, while we still can stand
And dance, and laugh, and love, and sing?
Oh, how we covet everything
We'd like to think we're put here for.

Perhaps the next life offers more.

Vivian Carlsson

Tepee

Like an arrow
Soaring up to the sky
Reaching for our ancestors
Smoke swirling in my eyes

Silhouetted peaks
Animate the horizon
All in a circle
They surround me

Buffalo have passed this way
So have the elk
The wolves howl at my door
I still stand firm

Drums beating
Echo in the wind
Fire flickering in my pit
Keeps the warmth within

Summer, fall, winter, spring
Seasons of my soul
History has been my friend
The ages I behold.

Raymond J. Cuminale

I Need You

I know I'll never have you
So why do I cry
I know you'll never care
So why do I try
I'm going to try to forget you
I'll tell myself this lie
I know I'll love and need you
Till the day I die.

Paula Boudreaux

"The Great American Flag"

Not just a piece of colored cloth
so much more than stars and stripes
but the blood shed
the murder
and the complete dedication of so many
lives
this represents life
and victory in death
the great American soldiers die for us
do not disrespect!

Fires have burned
in the sky
people murdered
families cry
one lost life effects so many
so please
I beg you
honor your country
honor your flag

Steven A. Jarosz

God

God is the Almighty King,
The Universe, his Kingdom.
He rules with a gentle hand
So that we have our freedom.
He asks nothing in return
For the many things He gives,
Except that we would trust Him
And acknowledge that He lives.

Rebecca Cunningham

"Messy House....Happy Hearts!"

Eat over the plate,
  so the crumbs don't fall.
Please wash your hands,
  before touching the walls.
My floors were just swept,
  so wipe your feet good!
I work hard all day...
  is that understood?
So, now they're all grown,
  with lives of their own.
Don't see those kids much,
  though sometimes they phone.
My house, yes it's neat, hardly ever needs cleaning,
  no marks on the walls,
  if you know what I mean.
But, now it's too late... to toss them a ball,
  help them to bake, or dress up a doll.
  For I made my choice to keep my house clean,
Should have put my kids first,
  how quick they're eighteen.

Sharon Potton

Untitled

I looked up and saw it there,
So perfect, hanging without a care.
The oval shape glistening brightly,
it was really quite sightly.
laced in gold
it had a story that couldn't be told,
it was new, but really it was old,
rocking back and forth gently.
No one knew what tit meant to me.
I reached out to it,
only thing the rim and tipping it over.
Down down, down it fell till it reached the ground,
Down, down, down I fell till I reached the ground.
I grabbed it quickly and put it to my chest,
as to put it to rest.
I pulled off its price,
and did not think twice.
I placed it upon my head,
and that was enough said.

Rachael Owings

A Love Poem

With a buds secret yet unknown until it opens and is shown,
  so my love for you still grows...

As the sun begins to rise and its brilliant glow covers the sky,
  so do you light my life...

The soft dance of the leaves as they are caressed by a gentle breeze,
  so are your hands touching me...

As the morning clouds drift brushing the grass with a light mist,
  so is your kiss on my lips...

Just as a rivers path will lead on a course to find the sea,
  so does your love follow me...

As the rain replenishes the earth and quenches natures thirst,
  so has my heart ended its search...

In the mirror of your soul I believe the reflection of love I see,
  so your heart also belongs to me...

Our bud of love has broken and two hearts have at last spoken,
  so that our flower of love has opened...

Theresa Dischinger

Petals Of Love

As soft petals extend from a flowers bud,
So intimacy extends from love.

The gift of this union is not to abuse.
It is to enhance, to complete, to set our
souls free.

Marriage is that union in which God said
"Be one".
When we are with God in Heaven, He will be our
flower, and with him we are one.

But as we are yet earth-bound,
we need that
encounter, that substitute
for a celestial hug.

We need those succulent
petals of love.
  Susan T. Garner

Utterances Et. Al.

My thoughts are fragile
so I share them with a book of pages empty
that I may see how they stand alone

In the distance is seen the largeness of mountains
some new, some humbled by time,
wind and rain and sun and more,
now small and worn but wise
from the passing of days
and the forgiveness of pain,
eager to be, again, a canvas
for the new born sun.

My thoughts for you cannot be shared
with ears deafened by years
and times, now gone.
They can be but songs of longing
pressed between the leaves of books
as a pebble cast
in the midst of mountains
for know one to seek
but someone to find
  Richard M. Hughes Jr.

River Rock

I plunge with you immersed deep in a dream
Smooth river rocks silver in dappled streams
Swirling cascades of diamonds and gold —
I am sunburned, and dazzling, and old.
I am river rock. Liquid stone. Not him.
Do not touch. Do not dry. I am not gold,
Am I? Not some diamond hunter's gem?
I am river rock. But am I what I seem?
Let us swim now deep inside and fly —
Cascading soaring dazzling gleams.
Let us do what we want. This is our dream.
Ah, the alabaster rock, the gilded stone —
This rock is more precious when left alone.

Dreams free us from prisons we cannot unlock.
I am river rock. I am river rock. I am river rock.
  Richard J. Sides

Autumn

Crisp morning air edges in with a chill,
Smokey haze pokes tendrils around that old hill.
Shiny onyx crows tarry along barbed-wire fences,
Color intensely shatters upon the sight senses.
Foliage of faded crimson, old gold, russet, soft wine,
Brassy ochre, dulled bronze, cinnamon, scarlet divine
Are accented by tree trunks of light coffee, grey-brown.
Muted, dying leaves over the ground are laid down.
Sparkling azure skies glimmer with airy light,
Supporting the honking sounds of wild geese in flight.
Ruby-red tomatoes shyly hide in rusting vines;
Chrysanthemums burst forth in glory all sublime.
In the breeze, garnet, wheat-tan grasses sway,
Fire-fly lanterns bob through the fields at end of day.
The smell of wood fires drifts languidly on the air
And down by the barn comes the nicker of the mare.
Along by the hedges, deep amethyst shadows stealing,
Aided by the hoot of an owl stirs a shivery feeling!
The coyote trills his mournful, lonesome call
As upon the land glides the rich essence of fall.
  D. J. Knoll

My Children

My children, my children I call them ... but I am only one
small part of their lives. They are only temporarily mine until
God gives them their purpose and meaning in life.
I am one stepping stone in their great journey of life. But ...
while they are with me, I will love them with al of my heart and
I will try to protect them from all harm and suffering.

When the time comes to let go ... I know it will be very painful
... pain that I can now only imagine ... and life goes on, but
never the same again. You will have your own life, your own
love, and hopefully your own children ... and life goes on.

If this cycle is somehow broken and things fall apart for you,
you know you will always have a place in my home and in my heart.
For I will listen, I will understand, and I will have compassion.
Together we will make things right and I will help you start all
over again ... for life must go on ... but never the same again.
We will all learn from our mistakes and my hope for you will be
strong. I will be praying for your happiness and that whatever
you do will not be wrong ... because life must go on ... even if
never the same again.
  Ursula Weiss

Journey

If someone would have told me
six months is all we would share,
I would have cried, how can it be? it's just not fair,
for you see I've waited for what seems like
eternity for our paths to cross.

My heart is heavy as you take your
leave this day, I want to scream
no, you can't go! I've just begun to
learn and you can't leave me this way.

Comforting to me is the light that now
burns so bright within me. I can see now
that you have work to do, more who need
to learn through you.

I wear my brave smile today,
and as I take that final walk with
you and I give you a hug and say farewell
it is not good-bye,
for I know that before this journey's end
somehow, somewhere our paths will
cross once again.
  Robin L. Berry

"The Wind"

The wind blows gracefully through the trees
Silent, yet softly
A poetic dance
They bow their leaves down and touch the ground
Or sway them to and fro high to kiss the sky
And then the birds
With their morning song sing
Like a conductor with a symphony
Perfectly sing
Nature is in harmony with man
She sings a song like a nobody can
The first dawn's light
They gather together
The sunbeam dances through my window
As light as a feather
"It is morning!" As the world sings out
Bless this day Lord!
Let us give praise and shout!

Patricia Schlosser

Cadaverous

There they lie, so cold...of the racks
Sightless, immobile, on their backs
Staring eyes, only fuzz for hair grows
Grotesque, stiffened fingers and toes

Trembling, we lift scalpels with trepidation
Poised for that moment of desecration
When we violate that precious barrier to what lies within
And forever mar the beauty of all that unbroken skin...

The first cut made, curiosity replaces repugnance and fear
We marvel at the incredible design and the skill of the engineer
Delving with renewed passion, we go deeper, yet deeper
Uncovering terrible secrets with our blunt seeker

Did this slippery, convoluted brain
Once house every motion from delight to pain?
We breathe a silent thank you for this ultimate gift...
Was that our imagination, or did those lips briefly twitch?

Into a smile which understands, forgives and condones
A smile that transforms that mere collection of flesh and bones
Then, exhausted, yet satisfied that we have performed well
We are greeted at home by the comment "You smell!"

Lally Russell

Incandescent

Emotional ripples like waves in the sea
Shudder my body with enchanting power
Conceived at the instant the beauty is seen
Through the non-existent atmosphere surrounding me
Undressing her with invisible hands
Casually moving mentally towards her soul
Yearning and burning to see the light
Which will pour from her pores in a conscious waterfall
The knowledge of her magic like an endless book
Having more pages than can be mortally read
Words of an ancient language long forgotten
Known only to her and the one she chooses to teach
Breaking through my shell with self-assurance
Stepping upon her path in hopes of being lifted
To the space where her light fills all
Where her soul brings ultimate euphoria

Stewart J. Murr

Untitled

A grey fog swirls around naked trees,
  Shown in the pale moonlight.
    A restless heart looks and waits,
      For sleep to come, yet none tonight.
What beasts do wander within the fog,
  That cause the change of heart and mind.
    Its fear's own hand which reaches out,
      Which tears his heart in pale moonlight.
Is it ghosts or memories which surround his head,
  Never seen in night's own light.
    A minute can tick and will not wait,
      The ticking stabs without a knife.
Grey fog swirls around night's trees,
  It soon leaves with morning's light.
    I did not sleep and yet I dreamed,
      Of yesterday, like grey fog night.

Thomas Baird

Laurie

My heart fell to I don't know where.
Shock, numbness as I found you lying there
With blood all around.
I held you, I cradled you snugly in my arms.
I could not protect you from this insidious harm.
I longed to hear you make a sound.

I stroked and smoothed back your long dark hair,
Your deep brown eyes and your skin so fair.
You looked at me and I looked at you
And silently we both knew
That our time together was nearly through
And you softly said, "I love you."

I laid my lips upon your brow and then
I knew that God was ready for you now.
I knew that an angel had kissed you too.
I whispered, "God will take care of you."
No mother's love could have been more deep,
And I am so thankful that I was able
To rock you to sleep.

Violet F. Gaudet

Conversations With My Aunt

My aunt would sit in her easy chair
She would look right through me into my soul
She called me Bobby
I asked her questions
She would close her eyes and tell me about past generations
About life as it was lived
The red bearded Irishman who delivered milk
The gentle mid-wife who was murdered at dawn on her way to help deliver a baby
I sat and listened
Treasures of experience were being offered
She would say thank you when I left
My aunt with a terminal illness
died
but I learned

Robert Alan

Untitled

A woman aged with time sits and rocks,
Rocks she does with the wind that whispers,
Whispers songs of travel and romance of country sides,
Countries of far off places and scenic sights,
Sights of hilltops, babbling brooks and changing skies,
Skies of color changing over looking growth of lives,
Lives that age with time...

Sabrina Young

"Ginger"

My best friend "Ginger" was bought in a store,
She was just a pup, the kind I adore!
Her coat was soft and her tummy was round,
Her tail was bobbed and her ears turned down;
Her paws were big and her eyes just danced
As she shook an old sock and started to prance,
Now she's grown; and getting quite old
I often wonder how she could of been old.

No friends do I have as faithful and true,
To cheer me up when I feel blue,
To keep me company when I am alone,
To always greet me when I came home,
Always happy, and never words unkind,
A dearer friend I will never find.

Peggy Ann Davis

Triple By-Pass

Mom
She aged ten years in less than twenty-four hours
The life sucked from her
Like the sun sucks the earth dry
Plastic tubes protruded from her neck
IV arm bruised
Eyes open yet empty as a barren field
Sickening sweet get-well flowers
Combined with hospital disinfectant
Rubber soles squeaking through the halls
I fight the tears
To smile.

Valerie MacKenzie

Slow Dancing With My Soul Sister

Carefully, my chest against hers.
Shallow, my breathing of her fragrance.
It would be incest wouldn't it?

The melody lifts our feet,
Turning within themselves, intricate, intimate,
not touching.

Swirling downward, gliding
beneath the shallow ceiling of the sea,
amidst glittering silver slivers of thought,

Deeper, where a surviving moonbeam
shines upon a pearl...

To the blackness of the ocean floor
where, arms folded about our knees, we sit and chat
on the soft furled brow of God.

The music stops,
always too abruptly it seems. I bow
and return to my side of the room.

Alone again, I glance up amidst the dull
inextinguishable murmuring and I see our subtle bodies
still slow dancing at the center of the floor.

Robert Ritchie

Why There Is Color In The Clouds

Right after the rain is done falling
Over the land, the Dragonlord Vib'g'yor
Yawns, opens his golden eyes to see the sun, and stretches his
Gigantic silver/white wings to loosen the muscles
Before he begins his trek across the sky.
Into the sky he jumps, and falls not down but up, and
Vibrant colors from scarlet to lavender dance on his wings,

Raining an insuperable, nirvanic barrage of wonder.

Thomas Charles Niemeyer

Morning

The aromatic fragrance of freshly cut grass
Sends my senses reeling into a frenzy of sweet pleasure
As it wafts in through my open bedroom window.
The whistled song of morning sung by a sparrow
perched in the fig tree at the corner of my room,
lifts my mind from a melancholy dream of days of old.
As I open my eyes I see the first rays of golden sunlight.
The light drifts through my room and settles on the wall opposite me.
I watch the shadows of oak leaves dance on my wall,
As a cool spring breeze stirs outside.
It occasionally sends a taste of the clean, fresh air to my beside.
The call of nature to re-begin life has woken me.

Wayne Barnett

For Grown Up Kids

Children like:
Sandy beaches and wishing on a star,
To roll down a hill or climb a Box Car,
Swinging on branches and verses that rhyme,
Running through rain and stories at bedtime.
To be the captain of the ship - to wonder, to explore,
To be general of an army, to go through an open door.
Secret hideouts and mudpuddles and dolls,
Dogs and cats and balls and bats. But most of all,
As grown ups want to be needed
Children need to be wanted.

Vivian Gleeson

'Sea Dreams'

I pause to wrestle with my emotions on a slow ship asea,
   sailing the oceans
Surface ripples, harmonious sways
Slicing through the water as a knife to a cake
For ages her face has not hanged, nor majestic posture been rearranged
Become hypnotized as I watch her dance
Eternal mistress whom whispers enhance
My soul rattles the cage while mind is asleep
Flickering dreams that are murky and deep
Blurry images flip as a page
Forever constant night and day
When I awake it won't make sense
Locked in the dream by a glass fence
Enchanting you are ole mystic sea
With stories of what was and shall be

Still dreaming am I, caught in your wake
You do not want me to escape
Yet I smash through the glass of my restless slumber
Conscious, alert and wrought with wonder.

Steven Terry

Still A Rose

Is not a rose, still a rose, when it is with Blemish and flaws?

Is not a rose, still a rose, when its petals have browned
or been attacked with mold or pest?

Is not a rose, still a rose, when it is not the perfect rose?
Its color not so bright, its bloom not so full and oh!
Just right?

Is not a rose, still a rose, when it is cut from the bush to
be displayed and admired? Yes! I suppose, a rose is still a rose!

Patrice Crawley

A Garden Of Beauty

A garden of beauty, a field of love
Row upon row I see sent from above
To be admired, but never touched, each with its own beauty
None are the same, but all are one
To love them all impossible, to love just one a waste of my soul
Oh, to be able to hold each
Even the special few, which seem beyond my reach
To love a rose today, a lily tomorrow
To bring each joy, and never know their sorrow
I could never choose one above the some
I would never feel content, knowing there are still so many yet to hold
The fault must lie within me, perhaps I need more love than a single flower can give
I fear all the love I have would blot out the sun and suffocate the one,
So filled with this unenviable fate of not having one
for fear of losing the whole
I may become as the bee, going from flower to flower
to satisfy that unquenchable part of me
Or I may end as the gardener,
Alone in the midst of all this beauty
Stephen Therrien

Life

As I walk the path of life, I learn the difference between wrong and right.
  I learn the difference between day and night.
  But I never understood some of the people who cared.

At times I felt I'd known them for years,
  At times I felt they were total strangers.
  But when you break it down to the last drop you do.
  But who knew.

Between being hurt and being loved, you have to learn something.
  People don't always like you.
  And they don't always hate you.

In life there are ups and downs.
  You have to learn to live with the downs like you live with the ups.
Sometimes downs get the best of you,
  but in the end of all this hurt, love, and confusion
  something magnificent will come of it...
A person who cares for you and wants to be with you,
  And an almost perfect life if you go the right way.
  Perfect doesn't mean being rich,
  it means having friends, family, and a spouse who care for you.
Samantha Griffin

"Facing The Dragon"

The inner battle rages, old defenses are breached.
Retreat on a path of melting illusions, the dragon
awakens from its sleep.

The warrior prepares for the intimate dance, the
conflict begins. No blows are exchanged but painful
familiar wounds are felt by both.

The warrior faces the dragon with his shield, as it
spits out white, how, fire at him.

He deflects it back at the dragon, loud painful sounds
are heard, the stench of burning flesh fills the air.

The dragon falls and rolls into a nearby hole dying,
dying, dead...

The warrior buried it and into marks the spot with his
sword.

He frequently visits the spot, as time passes, and sees
something beautiful growing, in the spot fertilized by
the dragons remains.

Perhaps a new way...
Richard Miller

Strawberry Tree In The Courtyard

Such prestigious visitors alight on you:
Red-breasted robins, sparrows, hummingbirds and doves.
Such an oasis in the Civic Center.

The other day, a hummingbird sat on a branch.
How honored I felt,
that my presence was accepted as an equal.
She remained so still.

The young red-breasted robins,
so goofy looking.
With baby fuzz and black spots on their pale breasts.
Such innocence.

How these winged lovelies enjoy the strawberries.
I have never seen them tipsy though.
They handle the brew well.
Although, not all partake.

The hummingbird was totally nonchalant.
Perhaps, a respite from activity was all that she desired.
She did not need the strawberries.

Such a lady!
Veronica Espada

Dancing With The Butterflies

He stood on the bridge,
  Ready to take the plunge.
Life had lost all meaning,
  He felt so useless and worthless.

The record spun mercilessly in his head,
  "Kill yourself! Kill yourself!"
You no good son of a gun
  Its better if you were never born.

His abusive and alcoholic father's words.
  for nineteen years and more,
This was all the love he knew.
  Now, he was hopelessly lost in Co-Dependency.

But wait, what's that flicker of light?
  Where did it come from?
Oh! Its mother dead long ago
  And she's saying "Don't!"

Suddenly, everything's bright and gay.
  Gladness wells up in his human heart.
The sun is shining brightly in his garden again.
  And the little boy inside is dancing with the butterflies.
Deodath Ragoonanan

The Perch's Fin

The pond is glass again ... water has come in ...
Rain didn't do it, though the gathering wind
Says that could be the next way; it's better now
The willows at the edge bend and bow
To see themselves, and the little current
Has the upstream bridge's railing telling where it went ...
Neon descending and rising out of itself
Along the whole length of side-board betrays the water's stealthy...
Summer nearly won ... it drew the corners in
Like an old man's mouth, and the perch's fin
Broke the surface; yet it's full again
And color in its face; it's been
Like that sometimes for ponds and for those of us
Who last, though nothing must
Gerald Garbarini

Forget Not There Is Another Day

Forget not there is another day
Rage may surge at the middle of the night
Then endure life and interlude the play

Worry if pain is felt along the way
Otherwise, hardships maybe tough to fight
Forget not there is another day

Think, good people, that you are made of clay
Alike a bird purposely shot in flight
Then endure life and interlude the play

Some people just dream their lives away
Aimless and thoughtless like a dope in flight
Forget not there is another day

Mostly elders, some youngsters, fear the day
The day, wondering what they do is right
Then endure life and interlude the play

You, my friend, looking forward to Monday
Do not forget this may be your last night
Forget no there is another day
Then endure life and interlude the play

Hasan A. Qureshi

"I Love You"

When I stare at night into the sky I feel your
presence pass me by.
I turn to look and all I see is the empty space
by my side.
When I think of you, I can't help but think of your eyes so true.
Whenever I think of those eyes I feel a longing
for you to be by my side.
I stand there by myself and I have to think of
your love and tenderness.
I stand there and think of you and of how much
I love you.

Shelley D. Munn

The Mug Of A Thug

That face you love so well, that of a three year old.
Pondering the facts of hell, sometimes defiant, but basically bold.
At first glance, you see the scratch,
of his sibling sister's, long dangerous fingernail.

His smidgen of a nose protruding, from his face being alluding.
The stream of snot flowing from both of his nostrils.
It flows from his nose, unable to stop
Like the tidal surf, slamming the eroding rock.

Then you kiss that tiny lip, tasting the nasty drip
upon your tongue, right on the very tip.
The smirk upon his lips, the glimmer in his eye,
trying to scheme a way, to soar above the sky.

Those eyes they are so gray, reminded of a dreary day, but then you
wonder, where is the thunder, erupting from a three year old.
Look deeply into those eyes, and see the storm brewing
that makes you wish, you'd already said your goodbyes.

His curly hair a flow, that would make most girls glow,
waving through the air, so fine and very fair.
That's a three year old's face, so dainty and very proud,
only the devil knows, three year olds are worthy foes.

D. Wilcox

Hands

Little dimpled hands, so brown from the sun
Playing in mud pies, where they have so much fun
Patting each cake, till it's just the right size
Hardening almost, before your eyes.

Small lovely hands, wearing a ring
A wedding band, betrothed in the spring.
The same hands that just a few years ago
Made the mud pies that lay in a row.

Small lovely hands with a trace of wear
Caressing a babe with loving care.
And dreaming if these chubby hands too
Would make mud pies as she used to do.

Worn weathered hands from tail and pain
Never to make mud pies again.
Folded and laying across the breast
Worn, weathered hands at last at rest.

Zelma K. Smith

Gift Giving

If I could give a gift to the world it would be
peace and harmony between you and me.
No heart would be filled with anger or hate.
No one would care what was on your slate.
The streets wouldn't be filled with crime.
Homeless wouldn't need that last dime.
Drugs and alcohol wouldn't claim lives.
People wouldn't have to buy guns and knives.
People wouldn't have to clutch their blanket at night.
Everything wouldn't have to end in a fight.
Everyone's hearts would be filled with love.
Everyone would get their guidance from above.
The air would be something we could breathe.
This is something we desperately need.
The water in the world would be pure,
Of that you can be definitely sure.
Every creature would have his own place.
Life would not be a high speed chase.
If I could give a gift to the world it would be
To live without worry, oh to be that free!

Tonya Faught

A World At Peace

There, after the lake of tears, beyond the valley of pain,
pass the forest of wounds and graves,
make your way through the bloody rain,
you can even see this place clearly through your sight.
It will happen only if you stop to fight,
there's a better world for you to live.
Just come and see then you'll believe...

When you'll come there, a child of tomorrow will be your guide.
The dove of peace will give you a ride.
The smell of love will fill the air,
and then we all will know you really care.

Until the day you'll find this place,
the day there will be no meaning to race,
You will have to overcome all wars, to give-up something of yours,
then there will be no worries at all,
then you'll know you reached your goal.

A day without violence, a world at peace.
Where instead of hurting people you give a friendly kiss.
Where the rainbow's shining over all the shaking hands,
and your enemies will finally become your friends.

Ron Brosh

"Lost"

Lost in the universe in search of a force
Out of control in an abyss of space
Adrift my soul relinquished of hope
An entity of piano, no love to abide
Reaching! Reaching! Higher and higher
On to the peak of eternity, soaring my soul
Searching my place in time, my essence of life

Open the door! Open the door! My Creator, my God
Life is mine to claim
Energy flowing electrifying, consuming, positive light surrounds me
A voice! A voice! Energizing my soul
Calling my name, lifting my spirit, this energy divine
an aurora of light and love
Calling! Calling! Calling my name, come back,
Come back, I love you
A soul of desire, passionately in search of mine
Called me back, to my place in time
Communion of souls, the force of love
My destiny, my love, my life

Mary Ann Wear

The View From Palomar

Who can conceive our boundless universe?
Our infinity of stars,
The endless horizons,
And the neighborliness of our solar system.
The moon that keeps one face always to earth,
A mere two forty-three thousand miles away!
Mercury dancing about our sun
In its perpetual heat and cold.
The planet Mars in our ken!

And the science man restlessly and resolutely
   pierces the void,
Leaving our God on his pinnacle of ice and snow
For some intuitive beauty in the heart of things —
The inevitability of galaxy meeting galaxy,
If so ordained, in this free-wheeling universe,
Or so it seems to be.

The light years meet our delighted and watchful eye
Our difficulties with God are resolved —
As we reduce our complexity of what makes the world go around -
To a simple what.

Romayne Waye

The Circle

We come to the circle, angry, hurt, confused.
Our emotions naked as a child just born.
Grief is our common thread.
Grief that sometimes flows like a gentle rain,
And other times breaks in torrents of agony.

Our pain washes the circle like waves washing on the shore
And then returns to us, warmed by compassion,
Enriched by the understanding of the group,
And guided to our hearts by the wisdom of the leaders.

This is our group, our circle of care.
We are strangers, entrusting our thoughts to each other,
Strangers who become friends by the magic of the circle.
The circle that focuses our caring to heal our hurt.
Nothing can match the circle, unbroken, everlasting.

Paul L. Smith

In Praise Of You

Tis comfort you are, as are warm days
Or rains, soft and gentle.

A morning mistcover you are, obscuring faults from
Strange eyes.

A reflecting moon you are, lighting hidden paths
For me to choose.

A seamstress you are, stitching us together
With small kind acts.

A lifebuilder you are, creating a pastel world
Of soft excitement.

Do not warm days and soft, gentle rains
Bring the beauty of flowers?

Do not faults misted make strengths
Show stronger?

In finding hidden paths for me to choose
Do I not walk straighter?

Are not the small stitches stronger than tragic rips
That come uninvited?

Soft pastel excitement lovestitched by you
Makes life full.

Robert E. Allen

True Love

   Love can be a strong emotion
or love could mean zero.
   Love can burn in your heart
or love could be your hero
   Love means patience and understanding
honesty, trust and sharing
   Love always sees two sides
and love never stop caring
   Questions in love are always clue
that the love your in just isn't true.
   To be in love it takes a lot, from
both sides, everything you've got.
   All decisions in life are very tough,
but in love you can never get enough.
   The decision is hard but before you start...
Know that to find true love you must
   follow you heart.

Tara Rohe

Clay Town

Quiet and expectantly solemn
Perfectly arranged identifiable columns
Drooping flowers and weather beaten wreaths
Expressions of honorable time earned grief

Minds etched with memories to mourn
As Biblical clay returns where born
A bidding of farewells against a blacken sky
No understanding why life must die

No life left standing as night swallows day
Selected occupants brought here to stay
They lay as rigid as their blankets of stone
Except for the scavengers that rattle the bones

Mysteries undiscovered by those with breath
No answers granted to those of wealth
A minority claimed to have journeyed back to tell
That Clay town has a tunnel that leads to heaven or hell

Mona Lisa Bass

Manifestation Of Love

If poetry could be expressed without words
Only to be seen not read or heard
Believe me when I say it's true
it would manifest itself in the beauty of you

If the stars and moon were taken from the sky
they would manifest themselves through your eyes
though missing from above they would not be gone
For I can't think of anything better than your eyes for which to gaze upon

If the wind, always moving, never still
were to stop blowing at nature's windowsill
it would manifest as your feelings
and if direction and speed of your feelings change
my heart will serve as the weather vane
to see if it will be gentle breezes in my hair
or violent storms that fill the air

If our love for each other were to exist as something else
it would be as the body and soul
for without the other neither is truly whole

Steve Ausmus

"Shine Sweet Souls"

To rest, we see the shine of tomorrow,
Only to be busied with tedious tasks.
If only, only the sun would but shine longer!
If only, only the moon would gleam stronger and the stars brighter!
O, glorious day will come, when all is not lost.....
No more fuss, confusion, worries.
But then there will be no shine,
There will be no gleam, but do not fret, my dear sweet souls,
For eternal rest waits beyond the stars.
There, all souls greet one another, a joyful embrace from breathing bias.
No prejudice, no bitterness, no remorse.
All gone are they, only to be respun...like new cloth...clean and fresh.
Tales say there is a light...true, there is a light, some bright, some dim.
Sweet souls, you must make you're own shine, and never loose your
  luster.
But if by chance you should fade, well, look out, beware, make
  yourself shine.
Never loose hope, for in life, you can help, and teach, and love.
So make yourselves shine, sweet souls!
Shine for all eternity! Shine for those to come....

Susan Zimmerman

Out Of Sight

   I have dreams of monsters in my sleep
only I'm awake and the monsters are real
they come into my head with a rage so strong
I pray to God that they won't prolong
they control what I think, what I say, and what I do
They control my life in this hell bent zoo
Except with a sword that is all my own
Which cuts through the wind and separates the clouds
Although that is where my head is and reality is dim
Yet the light helps me see while I sleep
While I'm dreaming in this true yet fanciful land
Maybe when I awake the monsters will part
For I will slay them with a sword from my heart
And then a dimension will come into view
Of something so real and a feeling so new
A feeling of flying above the clouds
Yet I'm down to earth and my love is so proud
How can I explain this feeling so real
When all that is gone, has been concealed and then when I go to sleep
at night the love that goes through me is out of sight

Brian Franklin

My Husband

We promised to love and be faithful
One to the other until parted by death.
We shared these sacred vows before God
On the special day we were wed.
You are my husband.

I feel safe and secure in your strength and wisdom
And in the presence of your being.
I depend on you.
You are my protector.

I share my innermost thoughts and deepest emotions with you
And as we bind our hearts and minds together
I feel your comfort.
You are my soul mate - my very special friend.

As we share the ultimate gift of love
That needs no words and we become one
In body and soul -
You are my lover.

Paula R. Spells

A Rascal Called Time

Time, you rascal, you're moving too fast,
One second you're now; next instant, the past!
Slow down and grant us more moments of joys,
Like sunsets and rainbows; and grandkids with toys!

At one time you crept like a snail in reverse
When we were just kids and dared not to curse.
Bewildered by watches, we just waited and yearned
For what seemed like, forever, before Christmas returned!

So listen, you rascal, take your foot off the gas;
Narrow the neck in your main hour glass;
Turn back each clock, muzzle Big Ben;
And let us be kids awaiting Santa again!

Walt Anderson

A Tangled Web

As man navigates through vast centuries,
one must look at the domicile he has created.
For one could say it is much like the spider's, or is it?
The spider, an oft feared creature by all mankind
because of his ravenous appearance and venomous bite.
Yet man, well thought of by himself, intelligent and enchanting.
The spider worries not about war and despair,
but only of the next fly that entangles in his web.
Man creates war, prejudice, and hate
which has poisoned souls throughout known existence.
The spider has no politics, and only cares about being preyed
while man is politically correct and to the Lord does not pray.
The spider, content and handsome in his silken luxury,
and man, always searching for a new, sometimes fatal, destiny.
Oh, maybe we need look at it again, for indeed
it is true, what a tangled web we weave.

Robert T. Pinson

The Messenger

Rhiannon on a horse so white,
Prances through the sky in mist of flight,
To deliver a message to the God's inscriptive in gold,
With all importance on a scroll,
Opens the Heavens for a lady so fair,
As she delivers a message with such great care,
In their hand she lays it within,
As the winds start to spin,
Rhiannon and her horse are back on earth,
And in your dreams the answers rebirth.

Sarah McBride

The Song Of The Sparrow
(The Sweet Sounds Of Life Are Wonderful!)

The smell of the sweet Honey Suckle Tree
On the ridge above me.
Colours of beauty surround my soul.
My heart is open, for all to see!

The song of the sparrow
You can hear for miles.
It brings love, peace, joy
and tranquility!

Open skies, open the world
To a whole new reality,
For its the Sparrow who sings a
song of hope and honesty!

I've opened that special window
To a new beginning.
My door welcomes all who want to enter.
For it is that door which is giving me a
new ending!

My path through life as been dark and narrow
But the light of sweetness came close
   When I heard...The song of the Sparrow!
   Terri S. Cockriel

To The Love Of My Life

More and more, the thoughts of you keep coming to my mind.
On the highway, then all through my day, it is happening to me all the time.

I know I am very blessed, loved and made complete
By you, my lady, my woman the very best.
This is why I sat here thinking, talking about you to myself,
Knowing that our love will endure all life's test.

When I hold you in my arms, sweet you are baby, sexy and warm,
From your taste to your touch, I love you very much.

You provide me such love and concern, that I wonder sometimes
Am I enough to make you happy?
Then that look comes to your eyes girl, and all that you do, tells me
That I am your special kind of Daddy.

So this is why very moment, I sat in though of you in many
Wonderful and fulfilling ways.
I need for you to know you are my baby, and that in my future
I foresee, loving you the rest of my days.

Thank you baby for loving me as your man, as I will close now
With my thoughts of you, well in hand.
I WILL FOREVER LOVE YOU!
   Raymond Beasley

New Years Keep Coming

Forever the earth around the sun does wend
On continuous orbit that's without end;
And when it reaches the spot it started from,
Old years will depart and new years will come.
As old years deeds become things of the past,
The lessons taught become a memory
To be kept, for great feats of history last,
And help shapen the course of destiny.
But it is the actions we take today,
Guided by the acts taken yesterday,
Which set the course for history to flow
As it rambles on to make tomorrow.
Thus, actions performed this year become
Footsteps that help guide the new years to come.
   Ralph Lehman

Dreams Of Yesterday

Innocent child, you are a spark of freshness.
On a glowing autumn morning
You met an enchanting stranger,
A unique man,
with stars burning in his eyes.
Together you strolled through his mysterious world,
Teaching you lessons, giving his love,
His touch transformed you.
Soon autumn shifted to a dead winter,
And rapidly you matured and grew old
But you were delighted,
content to stay by his comforting side...

...I open my eyes to a fresh morning.
Memories linger, they still follow
Never distant from my thoughts.
An image of yesterday, a child and the man she once loved
They continue to walk in my dreams,
Visiting me on dark nights.
   Sarah Thomas

Through Clouds Of Love

I gazed at the clouds in the sky one day
Oh! What a glorious sight!
They seemed to be sitting on the mountain top
Majestic and billowy white.

My thoughts strayed freely as I drove down the road
To the day Christ ascended above,
He stretched out His hand through the billowing clouds
And offered everlasting love.

It was the most precious gift He could possibly give
And He didn't ask much in return,
Just love one another and follow His ways,
Be faithful and willing to learn.

As the clouds started moving and fading away
I thought of God's heavenly plan
And of the day I'll ascend in the clouds
And He will be waiting to take my hand.
   Peggy Ogle

Seeds For Thought

Ever vigilant am I, to learn and to change and to grow
Oh to be better, Oh to do better, and to know

For life is a series of opportunities and leads
And opportunities are: an open invitation to succeed

Search for wisdom, do I, search for knowledge and intuition inside
For knowledge is information, but wisdom: Is knowledge applied

In the desire to live fully, to live honestly, and kind
To have faithfully, and diligently revered my mind

Ever watchful, am I, for I can improve by being intentional
And believing in our creator, that we are all born most exceptional

As we are all capable: If we are willing to have grown
For our lives bear the fruit, from the seeds of thought we have sown.
   Pam Jennings Spencer

A Dying Breed

The mourning ceased abruptly. One large jagged rock bounce
Off the casket with a scream; I swore I felt his motions!
Three stately figures in swaddling robes seeped through, wearing
barbed wired hats as protection from acerbic stares, precipitating
sulfur and drizzling pain.

All that was visible after the songs were the leaves in the wind
Down-spiralling, agitated, meandering from forest to shore While
Father and I stood trembling in the bone chilling breeze; waiting,
Waiting for the word, an open door; perhaps a light, a cure, or
something more.

Morning rose quickly after a hard lumbering night of drifts and lows.
Enfleshings bled all over my balking brow - Dripping, draining into
encrusted sores, like corpulent broken-down drummers Playing
euphonious arrangements on skins for the embalmed and the bereaved.

Flying red flowers all caught up in the wires of thought.
Political prisoners cuffed in fear, robbed of craft and spirit,
Placed under fire and ice by their estranged friends. Here, interred,
is one who warns of the sign on the door - post clear -
"Leave Babylon Tonight!" - and harness your despair.

Robert T. Lewis

Flight To Heaven's Golden Dawn

Golden honey bees gather nectar from bouquets
of wild blossoms, and the essence of the green
greets me with the fragrant perfume of aspen,
oak, cedar, and pine. Blankets upon beds of
vivacious sunflowers, violets, and dove-white daisies
dance gleefully in the breath of summer's radiance.

Song birds of all feathers sing angelic
ballads of poetry from the swaying emerald
canopies that have been warmed by Heaven's grace;
And the rainbow's spectrum flows into an effervescent stream
Where salmon of the pinkest virtue school among the champagne falls
And from there the water foams like sweet ale flooding a frosty stein
I close my eyes and spread my wings; for I am home....

Sean H. Cardones

Heart

Love engenders wisdom, discovers dimension
of the stirring ineffable emotions of the
heart and soul long to be, as my soul cries
out to say, how can this be, buried with in me
so deep, as my heart and soul speak.

May you be enkindled that will enlace you
with new beginnings and no end of love,
discover dimension of emotions, as my
heart and soul speak gently to smooth the way.

As life lingers on to express the giving
and sharing, I have, as life beacons on.

Shirley L. Davis

The Balloon

Whither away, elusive balloon.
Sailing along this bright afternoon.
Where did you come from, where will you go?

Who is watching you from far, far below?
Did you slip from the hand of a tiny boy
Who had just been given you as a bright new toy?

Is his mournful cry heard though the crowd
As he sees you float away to a fluffy white cloud?
Or did you just break free from a bunch of balloons
Moored on a stick to be sold to tycoons?

Wanda Anderson Paul

The Funeral

When I Observe the presence
of the somber
procession, creeping forward
slowly, but willingly,
tires are rotating ever so carefully.
The motorcade, finally motionless,
arranges in a haphazard manner.
When the casket is unloaded from
the black car with laced windows,
I feel a sadden sense of sadness and sorrow, for
when it is carried
and passes from hand to hand
making its journey tediously, but anxiously,
seeking with desire its home of
fresh upturned dirt,
I realize my true friend is gone.
The casket now creaking,
as it is lowered into its plot
is relaying a message; like a
voice calling its friend for the last time.

Walter Lee Stark

March On

We gasp, we smile, we feel the heat
of the Million-Man March that was on Oct. 16th
March On, March On.

Society's played with our heads and put us down,
but now we showed them we ain't playing around.

They raped our women, they poisoned our souls
but we're here to let you know we are on a roll
March On, March On.

Togetherness brings happiness to the heart
And the dawn of a new day is about to start
March On, March On.

No more encapturing of the mind, no more brothers in bind.
We've put all that behind.
March On, March On.

We'll bring encouragement to our children and smiles to our presence
and all faith is being restored in the Blacks Man's Essence
March On, March On.

We're all children in God's name. We're throwing away
the knives and the guns. We are family, We are one.
March On, March On.

Shamekka B. Mitchell

Truth

When staring into the eyes of time,
Nothing seems to fit or rhyme.
Yet when you ask if you are doing right,
There is a simple nod with no worry or fright.

We wonder through our memories
Thinking of morals with simple stories,
To tell the children with eager eyes,
That not everything starts in a bed of lies,
That, even today, truth really does exist.
Though it's hard to see within this mist.

It reigns of justice and all that is good,
Even to those who have not understood.
Because the truth always prevails,
Leaving no secret, hidden trails.

Christy Keele

Divorce

Thru ages eternal, men have dreamed of heights, of power,
of new world conquered, even a woman's kiss.

And for their dreams have become stronger, braver, even immortal.

And little girls have dreamed quieter, more practical, sweet dreams
that hide under their heart and grow like a tiny embryo
and make women out of frightened children.

Oh yes, dreams fulfilled are the end of waiting, nighttime waking,
handling and planning, then placed back into the secret hiding place.

But what can replace a dream that dies like a aborted embryo,
a part of the soul that turns to scar?

Wait! Whose dying dream is that? No, It cannot be!
I warmed it with my body, fed it with my love, I will not let it go;
and yet, it flies away to find abode with a new life.

I cry, I hurt, I cannot heal. I hang my head and walk away thru life,
I dare not look to that secret place of my golden dream lest my pain
turns to death.

And yet, I ask of life, of God, can there be a dream to compare with
this? Nay I say...I shall not dream again.

Yvonne Wood

All Alone

He's drawing a picture,
Of how he feels.
There's a child,
Standing all alone.
No one even looks his way.
Why do they stay so far away.
Is there something wrong with him.
Of course not.
Their just afraid of something new and different.

Shannon Hatalla

The Incomparable Breezeman

L is for the Lady or man in your life, which God gives;
O is for the Order of each step takin' at the beginning of the
   relationship, which god directs;
V is for the Vigorous vibes felt, which brings two humans closer
   together, which God perceives;
E is for the Everlasting, understanding of the relationships' love,
   joy and happiness, because God is love; that's what love is.

Frederick C. B. Swanson Sr.

Affinity

The never-ending love affair betwixt the sea and shore
Now tender, now docile, sweetly caressing, gently prodding
Enticing, beguiling, alluring in warmth
Conversely tempestuous, growling, angry, defiant, cold, austere
Lashing away in conception of miniscules, corroding majestic
Metamorphosing in time eternal
Oh awesome creation, yet creative
Suspending in a watery domain manifestations without number
God's omnipotence to project
Hues of blue, green, gray, gold, silver
Challenges of white, black bespeaking temperaments in rage unlimited
Provocative, inspiring, inviting, tempting, gay, playful
Fearsome, monstrous, disrupting, engulfing
Inducing humility, respect, philosophy, peace
Emotional vicissitudes of attachment, ad infinitum
Sea and Shore, Man and God
One

Solveig Johansen

Poem In Time

Poetry always fascinated me, yet I always despised tests;
Now in my old age I realize; Yep! I'm quite a feisty mess.
My mother, husband and friends look at me with sadden eyes;
For the sound of Poetry is only for strange guys.
My children look at me saying "Mom, it's been a lot of years;
I felt it should have been they, who shed a million tears.
So I took a chance for later years and wrote them down;
I filed them away but NOT with a frown.
Then God gave me Grand-daughters named Brandy and Heidi.
"C'mon Grandma, your writing isn't flighty, "IT'S MIGHTY";
You gave us love and courage, to aim our goals high, night after night;
So go for it Grandma, "GET IN THERE AND FIGHT."

Shirley Mae Morgan

In Loving Memory

Love flowed from my dad like a bottomless well
Nourishes a barren, dry land.
Gave me guidance and love, purpose and strength,
always there when I needed a hand.

He was there when I called, there when I cried
There when I needed to talk.
Dependable, strong, loving and stern
Held my hand when I first learned to walk.

In my life I made choices, some good and some bad
Still he loved me and stayed by my side.
Shared my joy when I laughed, hugged me tight when I cried
And he always looked at me with pride.

He set standards and lived them, rules and obeyed them,
Gave us values we'll never regret.
He was one in a million, a true gift my life
And his goodness I'll never forget.

Polly Harrison

The Barbarian

Nothing here but sky and sea
Nothing here but wind and me
Nothing here but him
He has sandstone thighs and granite eyes
He has a chrome-planted smile
He leaves no fingerprints
He leaves no marks at all
At least not where they can be seen
Nothing here but earth and sea
Nothing here but me ... and him
I make a mad dash
Through the dark unknown
From safety zone to safety zone
He drifts like a blue wolf through the white emptiness
And he is there, in the shadows
Waiting for me
He tells me "I AM the light"
Nothing here but sky and earth
Nothing here that does not hurt

S. L. Reay

Why Oh Why........

My leaves are pale green, with a touch of rich crimson,
My petals rejoice in the light from above,
My flowers vibrantly show off, their beautiful colors,
Tints and hues that reflect a garden, created with love.

I glory in this splendor, of grace and of beauty,
But somehow it seems, I should be feeling fantastic,
Why oh why is it, that I don't have more sensitive feelings?
Maybe it's because... I'm just made of plastic.

Silvio John Tringali

Pumpkin, Pie And Spice...Of Plenty

Oh, wow, jump-up, get tough, and shout like a fool -
not trying to be coolly reaching out or about me,
it's you I am stark, raving mad about, now.

Where winter's chill has yet to come, all the warmth of
colored leaves, with sunshine bouncing down, awakes me.
Leave me, or take me to some winter wonderland,
and cool, or best, this red tempest running through me.

I can't quiet this drive from within, when the crunch of
crackly leaves conceives a steady din that, says in me,
Go, go, go, go, go - go hard or soft ground can stop me.
No planes, trains, or other traffic can pull reins on me.

Shout, if you will, but watch-out if you see me, when siblings
turn orange in the field and cornstalks grow yellow with age -
When sage and berry-bushes are trimmed with autumn winds,
and ev'ning shadows grow longer, earlier everyday,

I can't stay still, nor will I try; but lie before me and
I'll catch you up in arms quick as smooth, round, brown stones
can roll down hill over dry grass; and you can bet
hot sassafras, your sweet, fresh pumpkins will be mine.

It's time, toot, toot, toot, make way for the Autumn Horn...
   m. l. farahay

What Is Race?

If all to offer adorns an empty coffer.
Not to adulate nor down. Profaned, profound often bound.
Ambassador to individuality not conformity.
Worst secluded best shuffled.
Drawn away love won't stray.

Confines consciences, culture, and class.
Moreover must matter last
Primordial purpose exist beyond bliss.
Pompous liaison between soul and sort.
Malign, bestowed beware hate will port.

Purpose, pond or function.
When all's equal an aesthetic conjunction.
Apparent alias that echo nature absent manufacture.
Prejudged, perplex perhaps non native to perverse.
Tried by circumstance mimics a curse.

Organic ingredient in a crucible called earth.
Distinguished, distanced, and dissolved at birth.
Opposite apostasy foible flanked by fallacy.
Shadows the resume of character oh irony and strife.
That taints the template of life.

   Carl Singleton

God's Promise

   I called upon the Lord today. He answered
my prayers without a delay. I told him of
my troubles and dreams. He said" things are
not as bad as they seem." Come with me, take
my hand, I will lead you into the promised
land. I will wipe the tears from your
face and fill your heart with loving embrace.

   You will never be alone as long as you
trust and believe in me. Someday soon in
the heavenly kingdom is where you shall
be. Where trumpets shall sound and angels
shall sing. Praises of glory to the almighty
king. Do not let the devil tempt you to
give in. We will fight the battle together
and we shall win.

   Shirley Jager

Truth?

I have become
not one
but all the things I dread
Images conjured up
from deep inside my head.
Deception, lies, distortions of the truth
reality twisted, promises broken
I alone am scared
and the pain I suffer is all now that I have to call my own.

My heart is heavy, my head is light
My body is numbed by eternal pain
My heart sinks inside myself
Inside to the place that I go to hide from
   the evils of the world
Sinking deep and slowly into all consuming darkness
I feel I am drowning
Submerged into a sea of melted hopes and long
   forgotten dreams
I am all that I swore I would never become
Others may be fooled, but in the end the truth
   reveals itself to one.
   Jade Buitenkant

The Joy Of Adversity

Never rebel when trials come our way
Nor embittered and cynical
When trouble seems here to stay.

Just let patience have her perfect work
And let our faith prove its greatest worth.
When we are tested we're brought closer
To Our Lord,

We gain new Vistas we have never seen before,
We draw from new sources of power more and more,

We strengthen our Values when stress
Knocks at the door, yes, joy can come from
Adversity, and also a crown of life for all
Eternity.
   Elsie D. Morris

This "Love" I Give To You

"Love" is not listed in any book of knowledge
nor can any amount of coins purchase it.

"Love" for you is deep into my heart and soul,
way beyond the point of entry.

This "Love" is hearing your words and seeing that smile
of approval upon your face.

Love is never by any means a word of just four mixed
letters, put into correct order.

This "Love" I give to you and "You" only because you have the gift,
but perhaps never knew that is the gift that looks deep
into my heart and soul forever true.

This "Love" I give to you because it is a gift no coins or
other people could ever, ever begin to touch.

This "Love" I give to you because without your gift to me,
my heart and soul would no longer be.

This "Love" I give to "you" heart and soul for the touch by you
   Rene Mallory

Kiss Of Death

Obscured by the her blue eyes that pierced my soul,
No words could make their way to my stunned lips.
Love sent to me from her could make me whole.
Yes, with one kiss my helpless heart she grips.

To live without her love would be to die.
Risk life and limb I would to hold her near,
Until I'm hers my empty heart will cry.
Embraced by her, I'll need not shed one tear.

Love's gun did shoot me when she took my hand,
Oh, how her touch did make me lose my breath.
Veracious was her smile, now understand,
Entombed I was by her sweet kiss of death.

Killed by a kiss was once, for me, no thought,
But now I know how, thus, death can be wrought.
   Troy D. Montes

Time In A Bottle

Who is God
No, who am I
Am I my own Lord and Master
If so
with all of my power
why can't I control time
Time you see is the currency
The price we pay for living
Now that the haze of my addiction has lifted
I realize I can't spend my time
On pain misery and self pity
I can only use what I have left
on living
Again
Who is God
Do I really need to know
If so I'll just ask
Because I know now
Time well spent
Will tell
   John G. Fontaine

Baseball's Delayed

There was no baseball to watch tonight.
No super pitches or catches in right.
No home run hits or double plays.
It's the middle of August, and Baseball's Delayed.

Delayed they say until owners and players agree
About money and such, but what about me?
A fan like many who just loves the game
Played by little leaguers, minors and those in the Hall of Fame.

What happened to the players like Ruth, Aaron and Mays?
What has happen to those good old days?
When baseball was ran and played with a respect for the game,
Those people really deserved to be in the Hall of Fame.

Though I am only a kid and a fan of one,
I hope you all get your acts together and bring back the fun.
For I feel everyone is being well overpaid
Except for the fans, because Baseball's Delayed.
   Zachary Wrightsil

Joy

Joy is like daisies spreading across an open field
It is the sound of laughter at a town's fair
Or the taste of cool refreshing water in the summer
It's the smell of money after you cashed a check
It is a person's smile
Or a touch of a trophy after winning.
   Wesley Chandler Davis

The Back Seat

Rosa Parks, for the front seat she did fight
No sitting in the back we've won that right.
But still we black folks go to the back seat

We don't have to get up for the white man if we sit in front,
We can sit wherever we want.
But still we go to the back seat.

Rosa Parks, for the front seat she went to jail,
But you black folks don't care, you say forget R.P. she
can go to hell.

Why did R.P. fight for the front seat?
When it's the black man that the black man is trying to defeat,
And till this day black folks STILL go to the back seat!!!
   Thurayyah Anisha Pitts

The Gift

There was no cause for the gift you gave to me,
no rhyme or reason, no special occasion,
and still you gave it to me anyway.

It was one of the most intimate gifts I have ever been given
and yet your name does not linger in my mind or pass by my lips.

By giving it to me its value become infinite,
but had you choose to keep it, its value would have been nothing.
By giving it to me it became us,
but had you choose to keep it, it would have died and there would be no us.

I can't touch it, BUT it touched me.
I can't hold it, BUT my heart can and does.
I can't understand it, but yet I do.
I don't own it, BUT it is now a part of me.

Today as you passed me you looked into my eyes,
connected into my soul and ever so gently SMILED to me.
For that brief moment there was total serenity and acceptance.

We did not exchange names and probably never will,
but we did connect on a most profound and often forgotten level,
the human level.
Thank you for this, and for your gift, the SMILE.
A gift that I too choose to give away.
   Robyn Wager DeNise

Within

I fall down and cry out in pain
No one hears my screams
Tears pour down my face like the rain
I wish these were only dreams
I can't get up off the hard ground
No longer am I strong: I feel so weak
Like a clock left unwound
I can't wake up to the happiness I seek
I look around at all the faces
At all the people who have lied
That's when I know I've been looking in the wrong places
That's when I turn to look inside
   Shelly Jozwiak

Tomorrow's Man

The child that was once nestled safely in his mother's arms
Leans boldly against the sunset of an era.
In him, as in all others, the future begins.
Cluttered with uncertainties, seeded with hope
He is driven by destiny and protected by faith.
Hopes, dreams and worlds to be conquered are before him.
As he turns to walk into the sunrise of tomorrow,
His mother smiles.
   Paula J. Ander

A Realm Out Of Time

Once the wind stopped in a place where no birds flew,
No footprints in the sand,
No early morning drops of dew,
No thoughts in this universe,
No words ever spoken,
It was what it was,
A dimension without dimensions,
Where nothing could be broken

Once the wind stopped in a place where no flowers grew,
No love,
No hate,
No war,
No crime,
No measurement of antiquity,
A realm out of time

Once the wind stopped, but nobody knew,
Not physically, but in a sense of heart and soul,
Where lost and weary travelers go,
A place your heart may come to know.
   Rebecca M. Thomas

Blinders Of Love

   Running on the edge of madness...I can see only her.
Never noticing the ledge that falls away at my feet every time
I slow. The jagged rocks cut deep into my flesh, yet still
I keep chasing. Impervious to the pain and the gait winged
reptiles of the night that fly all about me. They swoop down
attacking, slicing my belly open. As my insides spill out
upon the ground my only thoughts are of her. While the cold
grasp of death pulls me into the eternal black void of damnation,
my body falls. Yet as the last breath passes from my physical
body, my spirit will chase on, loving her for all eternity.
   Robert E. Adams

Changes

Distant eyes suddenly become mine, as my life will change forever,
My mind drifts from time to time, getting away from it all,
The heaviness worry of what could be, makes me try to assure safety,
Everyday things become harsher reality, trying to achieve financial
   security,
Realizing the fate that was handed to me, though I can't help to
   worry, and I try my best,
Sometime in September, I'll be put to the test,
A miracle is entering my life, an entity of many dreams, the
   responsibility is staggering,
And a true test no doubt, what will they become, as guardians we must
   clear a rout,
The task that lies in front of us, is one many have taken, for us its
   the first,
We pray night and day, for everything to be OK,
Ten fingers and toes and healthy, learning and smiling day to day,
We want the best, but sometimes it doesn't work out that way,
We live our life together, handling whatever come our way,
Career moves taken, affect our child's future, so we're careful about
   the choices we make,
For all that has been given, and for all we have received, we are
   thankful to the Lord,
We are about to be blessed, the greatest blessing of all, the birth of
   a life is handed to us,
And we shall do our very best not to fall,
So to put it all in perspective about what has been read,
I'm going to be a father, enough said.
   J. Scott Brown

"The Genuine Feeling"

You're a genuine feeling that ignites my heart.
My love for you has grown stronger since the very start.
When I first saw you, I was feeling blue.
But you filled another's place made me feel brand new.
Your eyes carried a look that blazed through me.
Devotion, loyalty, and unity was all I could see.
The loving memory of your stare, starting to haunt me everywhere.
A cut or mark I can't erase.
The facts of love that I'm ready to face.
These feelings of affection, I'm experiencing desire.
My love for you is a burning fire.
A reluctant lover is what you are,
   teasing and pleasing, moving like a jaguar.
Mystical and passionate is the way we act.
When we are both together, of time I lose track.
Sensitive and cool minded, you're so special to me.
You're the genuine emotion of harmony
   like no one else could ever be.
   Wayne D. Sams

My Life With You

My life has been with you
My life will always be with you
But now as it draw to its close, release me.

I have loved with you.
I have travelled with you
Where life took me —
but now release me.

My life belongs with you
But now as it draws to its close
Release me.

Return me to my beginnings
To the moors — the wildness
in my soul

Let me wander wild forever more on cold bleak mountains
Let me wander where I may — released, wild, free.
Until at last I am returned to you. Forever.
   Peggy Beal

A Twisted Stick

As I sat with my eyes to the west,
My life was full of strife and turmoil.
But I felt I had given my very best.
My tears began falling on the soil.

My tears could only express my pain.
I felt hopeless and gripped with fear,
I thought for a moment I was going insane.
Then a twisted stick I saw so clear.

I heard an audible voice in my ear,
the lesson I would learn from the twisted stick,
would help me gain strength and remove my fears.
Because of love and nurturing I would not remain sick.

It takes years for a tree to root and stand tall.
Without proper care, love, and preparation,
you too like the twisted stick will fall.
And find yourself alone in separation.

For once like you, the stick in your hand
was so straight, full of life, and part of a mighty tree,
The stick has become twisted and part of a bigger plan.
With love, care and nurturing you can live and be free.
   Pete Cunningham

"My Get Up And Go Went"

When young I often heard older people say...
"My get up and go has got up and went"...
I didn't understand until now I'm there...
And I want to know, is where does it go?...

It was here only last year and I did a lot...
But now I do little and then I just plop...
If someone can come up with a pill for that...
They would make a mint and then they could go...

Places like Monte Carlo and Morocco...
Or San Francisco and San Diego...
Or to see the works of Michelangelo...
Or any place else they would like to go...

I know we all would be flocking to their door...
But that is not to be in my lifetime...
So I have to be content with what I can do...
And some of the other things just forego...

But I'll not just sit or give up or let go...
What I do undertake I'll do with gusto...
Even if some tries will be a fiasco...
And I hope all of you will say, "Ditto"...

Ruth I. Mason

The Golden Years

My hear is gray, my back is bent
My get up and go "has got up and went".
I remember when I was full of vim and vigor;
Back in the days when I still had a figure.
Now my hips and waist are about the same size
I look in the mirror, I can't believe my eyes,
I walk by park benches, looking for a man
One took a look at me and got up and ran.
(His can is still lying there)
It's what to expect when you hit the golden years,
You can live with your memories,
Or cry in your beer.

Billie Runbeck Percy

"Path Of Yesterday As Tomorrow"

Today holds yesterday's memories as tomorrow's plan
My eternal path yet taken, lead by nail-scarred hands
My savior guides me thru this weary land
As many temptations around me stand
He gave comfort to my aching heart and trembling hands
As I parted with loved ones to me so grand
Then I knew the souls once they held, was in his hands
When we placed these bodies, beneath the sand
As one day before him everyone will stand
For this part we all have, in our master's plan
I will await his call, to gladly take his hand
As I have been no stronger to pain or heartache in this land
for to carry my pain and sorrow, to only him I can.

Willie M. Jordan

Moon Dreams

Across silver skies stars give light to guide great things.
Most dramatic of all could only be our moon made of cheese.
Its creamy colors and craters deep where unknown creep.
The man on the moon watches over us.
He catches our midnight dreams and stores them in clouds
  passing by on midnight walks.
One by one, each and every one, dreams are tucked away.
With moon dust and shiny moon rays, our moon is there to
  keep our dreams safe.

Windy Wicklund

"Dedicated To My Dad"

I looked up to the sky today, and what did I see?
My daddy standing tall and proud over me.

I stretched my arms upward, as far as I could.
But I knew trying to touch him would do me no good.

I miss you dad, and wish you were here,
I'd feel much better knowing you were near.

You had so much more warmth and love to give,
And I just don't understand, why couldn't you live?

It's gets so much harder as life goes on,
Trying to realize that you really are gone.

I want you to know Dad, that I really love you,
And I also know that you love me too.

I go to sleep at night, dreaming of you,
Looking so happy in all that you do.

There are so many things I want to say,
They all seem to add up, day by day.

I want to tell you what's going on in my life,
And knowing you aren't here cuts like a knife.

I don't understand why life is so unfair,
But I know I will see you again...somewhere.

Shamara Glenn

"My Son"

Oh, to walk in a dream and touch the softness again that means so
  much to me.
Swaying to a haunting melody, weaving like a swan as it glides on the
  black lake
In a dance on the wind, because there is no place to run!
Crying, only because there is no laughter, no more, to gladden my
  heart.
A pain in my throat, swells with each thought of you
As you ran to greet me at the door.
You do not run to me now.
You cannot run to me now.
You are the dream that wanders so softly in my mind,
That I hold and cherish, still warm in my heart.
So small, only two, but a man eager with life, just growing up...
Then you were gone!
We cried, your mother and I...
We lifted you from the street...and we cried...
I love you more because I could not love you enough in two years...

Oh, to walk in dream and touch the softness again,
And wake, and find you here, my son.

Roy Russell

"The Beauty Of You"

The cool, brief breeze of time rolls by,
Mountains seem ablaze as the sun rises high.
A beauty abounds from all living things,
Bathed in the warmth that each new dawn brings.
Find in this moment, all that should be.
All living things in gentle harmony.
Now, to gaze in amazement could not be so rare
So much has been given us for all things to share.
Yet with all this beauty it still feels so new
For I find myself captured by the beauty of you.

Tommy Hahn

California Paradise

There's a "Nature style revue" in California
Mother Natures's dressed in colors just for you,
With a paradise to view
On the hills and mountains, too,
In the verdant forests green
So much beauty can be seen
Reaching toward the skies of blue
Mixed bouquets of myriad hue
In the valleys—in the deserts
In the leas of California
Floral beauties on display
Pastel shades and colors gay
There are rainbow hues on earth
In CALIFORNIA.

Vivian A. Thompson

The Power Of Prayer

When my path becomes rocky, all uphill,
More than ever I need to seek God's will.
Striving to learn, reach His ultimate goal.
My life is in God's hands, His to control.
Through humble prayer, The Lord's presence is felt.
Doubts and uncertainties just seem to melt.
With The Lord's power, the frustrations cease.
I can find solace, have an inner peace.
Seek His guidance with quiet devotions,
Through The Holy Spirit, not emotions.
If I listen with my heart and obey,
He will take my hand and show me the way.
Have faith, trust in The Lord, He'll do the rest.
Never doubt His love, for He knows what's best.

Robin A. Brown

Moms

Moms; They're sweet, kind and easy to love.
Moms; They're the people who take care of
  you when you're sick and even when
  you're well.
Moms; They're the ones who make you brush
  and floss your teeth, wash your
  face, and go to the bathroom before
  you go to bed.
Moms; They're the ones who can annoy you the most.
And even when they annoy you the most
that they can, and think you hate them
at the time, that's really the time when
you love them the most.

Stacey Kittle

Day-Dream

Holly of the river dances through my mind
Meeting my memories, leaving footprints behind
Stepping gingerly from spot to spot
Dangling feet in the river of thought.
Stopping presently on the beach of a scheme
And building a sand castle out of a dream
She looks through a forest that experience made
And then to the clouds of fantasies played.
And as she leaves, from the tracks of her toes
Out of the ground springs a soft, red rose.

Scott Michael Perrine

Poletic Poletic

Mister chairman,
May I have the floor.
I want to implore.
That we explore,
The suggestion of Mr. Gore,
With regard to balancing the budget;
To which the Republican think, it has already merit
But the president think, its not quiet correct,
And will veto it,
Even it will lead to his defeat, to his presidential seat.

But as for me, I am already too old
For all these Bolshevist.
Why can't we all set, and work together
As associate,
And use our knowledge in technology,
To produce all our life necessity,
For our bright future destiny.
"OK".

Stanley B. Garibay

He

He walks slowly and carefully down the street as if he
may fall off of an invisible cliff...

He smells the air and for a moment he thinks he
smells something familiar from long ago...

He looks at the stars and then at his feet...He
realizes his shoes are tattered and torn.

He listens to the silence of the night. He realizes
he's not the high school rebel he once was.

He has no money, just a bottle of bourbon in
his hand as he wonders what happened to his life...

He sits on a park bench and wonders again...where
all the years went he wasn't looking ...
at eighty-six years old.

He laid down on the bench .....fell into sleep...dreamless,
forever sleep.

Tawna Duvall

The Long Walk Home

Many miles were covered before I returned.
Many hearts broken, many souls lost.
I traveled to find peace in my heart and soul.
My heart and soul was lost till my long walk home.

I met many old and clever faces for wisdom.
I saw numerous great lands but never enjoyed them.
I searched for peace and strength to live.
My heart and soul was lost till my long walk home to you.

I am home and finally at peace.
I came back to you to give you my love.
The long journey home gave me peace and experience of others.
And now I can share my long walk home with you.

Sara E. McCarty

A Place Called Quiet

With a touch of bright yellow, you lit the moon.
Motioned me to follow, our time is coming soon.
In my steps, you sensed my fear
So you grasped my arms and pulled me near.
Took the trembles of doubt from my hand
With faith, you smiled...we will make our stand.
Of our love for each other, some will find cause to riot.
If we fall...we will enter, with God, a place called quiet.

Philip Matosich

This Mirror Of The Past

Oh brass framed mirror, how did you after all these years
manage to still look so fine.
Not a scratch or a crack, after two hundred years of time.

How many people have you seen, fixing there hair just right.
And how many did you see pass you in the middle of night.

Your beautiful old mirror, the stories you could tell me, if
only you could talk.
The echo's of the past, and the journeys I would walk.

I wish that I could go back in time, and see what you have seen.
All I can do is wonder, as I stare at you and dream.

As I sit here in front of you, in this old wooden chair.
I can sense a presence, for I feel a brush of cold air.

Could this be a spirit, that lived here at one time.
Maybe it's your owner, that stay's and keeps your shine.

It's strange how everything is all covered in webs and dust.
Except you that looks so new, as everything else is rust.

You must of been a special gift, to some one that was loved.
That some one may still be here or with our God above.

Wanda Dee Sullman

The Golden Ring

*For Trung Tran and troubled Vietnamese-American youth like him,
wherever they may be.*

Here within the Golden Ring, Yang and Yin
Male and female, stiffness and tenderness, heat and cold.
Here within the Golden Ring, two tear drops;
   tears of human joy and suffering.
Here within the Golden Ring, two fish;
   their bodies a harmony.

Let me be a fish in living water;
A lotus white as the breast of a snowy egret;
A yellow flower singing to the sun from a pond's murky water,
   spreading an intoxicating perfume;
An autumn leaf sliding down invisible air into a stream,
   dreamward.

Let me be a living book of perfect symmetry;
A scroll unfurling words of love that
   bind me to humanity.

Patrick Du Long

Bicential Blues

Now, there aren't no men that want to be sold,
Makes no difference the quality of his clothes.
To get on a boat against your will
I believe it would give me a chill.
To be sold down the river away from your wife
Would make a black look, get his knife.
She'd be unhappy away from her man.
If he had to die he'll pay with his life.
It makes no difference the color of skin
The person with love will surely win
Cause killing anyone is a great big sin.

Wanda Argatha Hamilton Merchant

Autumn Fall

Leaf foliage, colors blend vivid bright allure
Leafy leaves, shed, rescind.
Falling - blow in the wispy wind
Varying pallet-red-yellow-orange-brown galore.

Falling - blow in the wispy wind
Blow, leaf foliage, descend.

Ruby Edmund

"See That Old House..."

See that old house perched upon the hill.
Majestically sullen, quiet and still.
Once it rang with the sounds of laughter and joy.
Its walls with yellowed wallpaper...
   echoed with the running and
   playing of two little girls, and five little boys.
The smells of cooking and baking filled
   the rooms with the aromas of love.
The lilt of joyous singing billowed to the sky above.
Now the house lays barren, vacantly
   quiet and empty of need.
The children are all grown and gone on their way.
No longer does the house ring with joy,
   and laughter, for love is gone...
   it has no master.
All that is left are the stories told
   by the trees, in the whispering,
   whistling sound of the breeze.

Dedicated to all of my brothers:
Floyd, David, Wayne, Buford, and Zendall Greene,
<Body>and to my sister: Omega Greene
...All of whom I love very much,
and I'm happy each of you are part of my life!
Vernieca (Squeaky)

Vernieca G. Weaver

Memory Bouquet

Memories created from two united,
loving hearts, is a gift to truly treasure.
From each shared moment, precious memories
blossom, bestowing perfect pleasure.
Each cherished memory is like a flower blooming,
among the thorns and thistles of life.
The flowers must be cultivated by communion of
body and soul, watered by tears of joy and strife.
The blooms must be daily nurtured, with
warmth of love, laughter and compassion.
And daily maintained, with distant dreams
and pleasant, passing passions.
So collect every unique, beautiful, fantastic,
flower, through all the happy years.
Create a memory bouquet that will comfort,
when sorrow gives birth to tears.

Patricia Stone Guynn

Love Is

Love is sharing all the smiles and the frowns.
Love is being together for the ups, and staying for the downs.
Love is holding an umbrella for her in the rain.
Love is being partners in joy and partners in pain.
Love is shown by a few thoughtful, well-chosen words.
Love is looking thru a window with her at a nest of baby birds.
Love is as simple as rubbing a back that is hurt.
Love is an ego builder, when not feeling worth.
Love is the birth of a son, who in life has turned out to be best.
Love is remembering the good times, and forgetting the rest.
Love is flexibility, adjusting to moods, able to bend.
Love is saying, "You are truly my best friend."
Love is letting her pick the movie out, not always getting your way.
Love is being with her, forever and a day.

Paul Kubaszak

Love

Love is this feeling I have for you
Love is a heartbeat that beats for you
Love is a feeling that makes you blue
Well, that's what I used to think
Cause after I met you, I started to sink
I drowned in a potion, a potion of love
And when I am with you, I feel like a dove
I feel like I'm soaring above in the sky
But if I ever lost you I'd fall down and die.
Now that I have you, my heart feels a change
You erased all the memories that caused me much pain
My gratitude exceeds far from eyes that see
Like a rose that loses its petals
I shall also die for thee.
   Yalit Martinez

My Very Special One

When our life together first begun, how I treasured in your
love, and considered you a gift from above.
Years passed by, our marriage was blessed with a baby, so
pink and fair.
She had my nose and your hair.

Then arrived the second baby girl.
We had her such a short while. Our Father in heaven chose
this little one not to live in this world.
Together we stood as she was placed in foreign sod.
Never to hear her tiny feet trod.

Next came another and another tiny, beautiful baby girl.
The years flash past, our lives were in a whirl!
You making a living, me making cookies, and prom dresses,
While they combed and curled their tresses.
We stand in awe at all the gifts as God blesses.

Well, the girls are gone now, they have husbands, children
and homes of their own, but we are not alone.
Our lives are full of God's grace, love and fun,
We share it all together, you and me, My Very Special One.
   Theda D. Yager

Happier Place

Love thy neighbor, love each other
Love all people as if a sister or brother
Love thy mate, love thy child
Embrace all people, tame or wild
Love all colors, love all races
Embrace different people in all the
World's places
Embrace all knowledge, culture and views
Love the less fortunate, our help they can use.
If all people on earth would love and embrace
This world would become a much happier place.
   Bill O.

I'm Finally Free!

We've been friends for years
lots of laughter sometimes tears
one dark day I thought I could end it all
give it up take the final fall
our friendship somehow changed that day
you saved me - and showed me the way
to face all my fears
and sometimes with tears
to accept the good with the bad
because of you - in no longer SAD
don't you see I'm living, laughing and loving
again just being me!
Because of you - I'm finally free!
   Roberta Rondeau

The Baby

Betrayal
Loss
Rejection
Where's the baby?

Faded yellow past;
the archway to secret closet
safeguards polyester pants, brown leather shoes
matronly memories.

Rejection slices numbness
sticks on flypaper in my heart.
He said; "It's good."
and

Love trickled drop by drop
out;
world vanished in a poof of smoke.

Reliving his face
I triedItriedItried
ItriedItried.

He never loved me all the years.
What about the baby asleep in the corner?
   J. P. Sweeny

On Visiting Harriet Tubman's Birthplace

Sign says "Turn Right" so we drive and drive down Old
Bucktown Road
looking for some sacred plot, some tourist sign, some thing.
Past mobile homes, farms, and narrow fields,
past sloping skylines, piercing skies, ready-to-harvest golden corn,
We slow at every marker.
One time we see her walking along the road
but it is only shadows.
Then we spot her in the fields
but it is only dust.

So we're turning again and again onto another back road
searching and searching
until there is nothing there to see.
And we know why there isn't any tour.
So we wait for the heroine, the Female Moses,
to come and take away our shame
but only the air and the landscape and a little white post remain.
   Sheree Van Vreede

Thunder And Lightning

Have you ever sat and watched a thunder storm?
Looked deep into the cloud to see where the lightening is
coming from, but never really found the source?

To me, I see myself as the thick heavy thunder clouds.
You are the lightening.
You are the thunder rumbling from my soul.

The lightening is you sparks my soul to life.
My soul answers with the strong proud sound of thunder.

Lightening and thunder.
You and I together.

You can not have a good thunder storm with one or the other
missing. You can't have one without the other.

Without you there is no spark of lightening to light my soul to life.
And without that spark my soul will never answer with
the loud proud of thunder.

We are the thunder storm.
Inseparable, together, forever.

You can't have one without the other!!!
   Lorrie Sue McClary

Untitled

Who am I, why am I here, why this solace existence
living in a world of such beauty but just living
eating, working and sleeping, looking in the mirror
each morning seeing myself grow older, wondering
why am I here, who am I, is this all that I am.
Scared of dying, thinking about death, so very very
scared of dying, who am I, why am I here.
Looking into space thinking when I'm gone, is this
all that I am, is this all that I'll ever be.
Who am I, why am I here, looking into space thinking
is this all that I'll ever be. When I die, all that
I am will be gone, my thoughts my dreams, all that
makes me, me, gone, gone forever, is this all that I
am. Who am I, why am I here, scared so scared of dying,
why is it so hard to understand who I am and why I'm
here. This body that I have grows older and weaker
but in my mind I'm still a boy. Young at heart yet
filled with so much pain. Why, why, why. Is there
no answer to my question. Will I have to die to
get an answer. Will no one answer who am I and why am I here.

Rajendra Dwarka

Acorn

I am only a small acorn
Living among the leaves who are my kin
Families and more families are the branches from sea to sea
With each city we build a strong tree
Whose roots are buried deep in our nation

I wonder what my role on the tree should be
Will I be something to drop off
Maybe I'll bloom into a beautiful flower
Or I might just be here to help someone survive
But, someday I hope to blow away with leaves of my own.

As the nation we have felt our roots tremble
In our cities the trees have bent but not broken
Each branch has embraced others firmly
As we lost some beautiful leaves, others are here to remember
Those small tiny acorns who never had a chance.

Tammy James

The Deficiency Child

It saddens my heart to see you,
Little child of woe.
So early in life, you suffered pain
And the scars there will still remain.

What hope lies for you?
Is there something I can do?
I'll try.
Don't you give up hope.
Fight on, little child of woe.

We can all make a difference!
1. We can support the world-wide project.
2. We can help others understand.
3. Make a personal contribution.
4. Join the Kiwanis mission to virtually eliminate iodine
   deficiency around the world by the year 2000.
5. Learn more about Iodine Deficiency Discover.

Teach me to feel another's woe
To hide the fault I see.
That mercy I to others show
That mercy show to me.

Vaudaline Thomas

I Am The Rouge

I hid in shadows and behind closed doors
Listen to the creaking of the floor boards
   I am the rouge
Walking down dark and lonely roads seeking nothing but wanting
   something
Run but can't hide the, end of the proverbial line
Cops shoot so I should die
Fly on wings to the after realm
Don't know the deal
All I did was steal
And what I got was killed
Laying in some grassy field I see the stars shining overhead
Why must I end up dead
It will be answered in either heaven or hell
Modern medicine
Thomas Edison
Why me why now
So close to go now
Flatline
Time to die.

Robert Mercer

Beauty

Beauty is found in many forms
Like a beautiful rose crested with thorns,
Like the setting sun on a warm summer's eve,
Or the beautiful sound of the wind in the leaves.

Like the glory of the beautiful sky at dawn,
Or a gentle doe with her newborn fawn,
Like the brilliant colors of a bright autumn day,
Or a glistening dewdrop caught in the sun's golden ray.

But in a world where such beautiful things abound,
I've seen the most beautiful thing to be found.
This beauty that I speak so highly of,
Is the beautiful woman that I love.

She is indeed a beauty to behold,
And by far, the most beautiful woman I know.
Her face seems to glow, just like the sunshine,
And her soft, sweet lips are so very fine.

And if I searched each country, from shore to shore,
I could never find a beauty that I'd savor more,
Than the beauty I see each and every time,
I look into the eyes of this sweetheart of mine.

Robert McKibben

Unborn Love

Somewhere down, deep within my soul
Lies an unborn song, my heart will know,
When at last I meet, with my destiny,
My heart will sing and the music will be.

At times my heart leaps and it starts to race,
Then I find there's——just a handsome face,
So till the moment comes and I meet my fate,
Be still my heart, the music must wait.

Someday soon, God will open the door
And my heart will find, what it's searching for
When he opens my eyes, I'll find Mr. Right,
And realize-that it's love at first sight.

Now when my heart leaps and it starts to race,
I'll recognize-the love in his face,
And know the moment has come for my heart to sing,
My love will fly, for my heart has wings.

Patricia Volkmann

Then And Now

Pieces of dreams once believed to be real
lie in the back of my mind with the hope of rebirth.
Shards of illusions of the way life was and should be
slice at my veins as I walk this earth.

Imprints of deeds appear on the beach of my soul
as the wave of youth recedes from the sands of time.
All promises proved lies be it to others or self,
dreams dangle like lures over this wave of brine.

How different it was in a younger man's clothes
when the light meant day, and the darkness night.
Such a contrast indeed to the way it is now,
that the boundaries of each are being consumed by twilight.

Many battles were fought to get to this point
with battalions of hopes whose files do not cease.
And the one truth to hold and never let go
is that winning the war does not entail winning the peace.
Robert L. Harpool

Imaginary Trace

I gaze at the map for hours
Let my finger wander
along imaginary routes

Finger mazes winding intricately like a snail shell

Our lives wind together so closely parallel
that they blend into one line
traced by my index finger on the chart

You have traveled through cities, countries, continents,
to break the unity, to place barriers between us

If I could follow my finger across that map
to touch you,
grope for a tangency of you,

to trace the elusive lines of your body,
compare it to the memory I hold of it,

to unite our borders, erase the boundaries that isolate us

to retain you there
no longer an evanescent imaginary trace
on my brain

but how to do it
Viviane Carson

Peace At Last

The time has come
my mother's pain is gone.
She stayed so strong
for so long.
Never once has she succumbed to defeat.
She fought year after year, week after week.
My mother may be far away
but her children will think of her each and every day.
I've never felt so much pride;
my mother never had to hide.
She has reached climatic bliss;
for eternity she will be missed.
The best has yet to come
for our lives will be done
then I will feel again her caress
to soothe away the despair that's held within my chest.
Not one existing word cold justify my mother,
but I know that there is no other.
To the bravest woman I have known
your spirit's free and free to come home.
Ralicia Gugliotaa

Untitled

Here I am
laying here
underneath this big oak tree
Turtles, sailboats pass me by
all the while I lay here
underneath this big oak tree
They seem to be passing by
slower to the naked eye
But up there in that big blue land
they are moving faster than I can clap my hands
Have you ever wondered why
Jack really went up in that sky, besides wanting to be rich?
Um...well...while I lay sit and sigh
I cannot help but wonder why
Why I see so many things that are slower to the naked eye
but faster in that big blue sky
When here in realities eyes my life's passing ME by
All the while I sit and sigh
and all the while I lay here
underneath this big oak tree
Tatina Elizabeth Kearse

The Diary

Years and years of memories
Laid here before me
A glimpse of the past
   With a flip of a page
The nice even strokes of life
The years gone by
   The words tell a story
     So smooth
     So rough
The life you had, the dreams you wanted
All laid out in notes
   Like soft strange songs from the Heavens
Unable to grasp or - to hold on to
   Like a distant planet dancing in the moonlight
You see the images so clearly,
   But they're gone, in the past
But always there
   Like a destination along an empty road
Susan Heidmann

Black History Month

B Is for the beauty we find in each other,
L Is for the love we share with one another.
A Is for ability, black folks have a lot
C Is creativity: mosaic, melting pot.
K Is for the killings that took place in the south
H Is for the harmony we seek to bring about.
I Is for importance, this month has its own.
S For satisfaction we get with justice sown.
T Is for talented, Carver and Drew to name but two,
O Is for oppression, our forefathers struggled through.
R For restoration of peace, of love, of hope.
Y Is for the youth just grappling to cope.
M For Martin Luther; he fought for civil rights.
O For opportunity; seize it, forget the fights!
N Is for a nation outsprung from immigration.
T Is for the tapestry each ethnic thread does weave.
H is for the happiness we seek behind to leave.
Phyllis M. Mitchell

My Best Friend!

I pulled into the driveway and my excitement grew,
Knowing that our friendship would be made anew.
My heal was aching from memories of you,
Of times I hurt you and made you feel blue.
I know that's in the past and I should let go,
Forgive and forget it all that you know.
I don't want to hurt you or make you afraid,
I just want to be near you to comfort and aid.
I want to share in you world like no other one,
To brighten your life like the early morning sun.
As I open the door and I see you smile
I'm comforted in know you'll let me stay for awhile.
I hope you will trust to share,
A special thought that shows you still care.
A gentle stare or a loving touch,
Will one day remove all that is rough.
Life may be hard and we'll have to sigh,
But as true friends, I know we'll survive.
From the beginning I've always known,
I'd give my life to save your own.
   Ruth A. McNaughton

Satan's Den

Suicide is not a good thing
Just because of the constant ring
in your ears, telling you that you're worthless
when all you need is some rest.
So, as you kill yourself
Lay a note on the shelves
That way they'll know
The feelings you never showed,
Although they may commit suicide,
You watching, while they sigh,
You'd have friends in bad health,
You shouldn't have killed yourself,
Now you and your friends
are condemned to Satan's Den.
   Ryan Sentz

Nightsense

Listen to the moon next time it sings.
Join the chorus of the stars.
Hum the tune of the pitted orb in cheesy harmony
   as it pulls you into the blue of night.

Feel the breath of rocks as they sigh.
Let your heart beat with the rhythm of growing grass
   and your blood flow smoothly in sync with night jasmine.
Dance in the quiet of night's concerto.

Touch the sound of the cricket's serenade.
Feel the heat of the firefly's ballet.
Let your eyes listen to the nightingale's trill
   and your ears see the whoosh-womp flight of owls.
Drown in the music of the night.
   Patricia Hotop

Harpy Eagle

Harpy eagle flying through the sky,
looking for something to run by.
He sees a mouse running around,
and he swoops down hard for his delectable meal.
He catches the mouse and takes it home,
and the eagle eats it all alone.
   Sarah Brady

CENSORED

Are you a fervent believer in

Creamy tea and toast mornings,
Jasmine afternoons,
Rosemary dusks,
Olive evenings, and
Pomegranate nights?

   Do you savor the sun when it gets so hot,
      Like being smothered in ointment,
      And all you can see is

Blueberry haze
Strawberry waves, and
Whipped cream clouds of desire?

      Oh wild intoxication! Empty delirium!

And now you whisper in my ear
   - 'Be quiet!'
and I sigh and say
   - 'Oh, all right.'
   Robin D. Clements

Twilight

The sun is going down, I fear, the moon is shining bright.
I've survived another day to spend another night
Alone within my dreams, all those dreams that can't come true.
The sun is going upon the days I spent with you.

In the darkness of the night, I comfort myself.
I go get the album from its altar on the shelf.
I sit flipping pages of a past I left behind.
Then I stop and realize, the times were in my mind.

There was a time when we were close and I remember well,
The only thought I entertained was feeling Cupid's spell.
A time of joy, and love, and light. A time of no more pain.
As with day, the sun must go, and darkness comes again.

Perhaps there was a time when I could work things out with you.
But Arthur's reign has ended and the Golden Age is through.
Darkness has descended on the land within my head,
And I fear perhaps the Once and Future King is dead.

To hallowed walls I soon return. I know you'll be there too.
Since you moved and went away, I've heard no more from you.
The twilight now almost complete, the darkness all around.
I close my eyes and feel the warmth fade as the sun goes down.
   Phillip G. Bunce

Sailing In The Bay

On one blustery Autumn day,
My friend and I,
were to go sailing in the bay;

His ship was a real beaut',
it was red and yellow,
and still very much brand-new too;

The sails were also very bright and colorful too,
as they skid skyward fast along the mast,
Yes, it seemed as though this was just the sort of day,
that was simply made,
to just last and last;

For this was the day I had long awaited,
this was the day,
the weather was great,
and we sailed all day,
about the bay;
   Russell D. Nolen

When Shane Was 3

To the sweetest little angel who ever walked the Earth
I've loved you since I've known you - only since your birth

Your curiosity excites me
Your cleverness astounds
I love the person you've become
You've grown by leaps and bounds

The wonder that you hold inside becomes my inspiration
The love I feel becomes the blocks that strengthen our foundation

I look at you with wonderment
You look the same at me
We're both amazed by who you are
and who we hope you'll be

If hope inside you blossoms
If honesty prevails
Your wings will surely carry you
The wind will fill your sails

You'll fly to heights I've never know
You'll see sights yet unseen
You'll go to places I would love
For you this is my dream
   Paula O'Brien

In My Own Words

I know a hundred poems, a thousand lines.
   I've lived the images of others but created none.
   Yet I must choose my own words if this is to be done—
My stuttering, inarticulate heart redefines
Humbly with hopeless inadequacy a feeling that shines
   Too brightly to be emulated by some poet's lesser sun;
   Means too much to be cast in the glibness of anyone
Else's eloquence, or trusted to another's designs.

Petrarch, Shakespeare, Rossetti have said it better
   Than I ever shall. But it was their profession.
Perhaps their feelings were as intense as mine for you;
   It matters not. I make to you not a debtor
To them, owing my own heart mostly, this confession:
   Infinitely, eternally, desperately, I love you, I love you.
   Richard Edward Cain

"The Beauty Of A Storm"

Have you ever stood at a window to watch a storm?
It's such a beautiful sight to see.
Dark clouds make the sky appear angry.
Or is God upset with the world today
   And is releasing His anger on you and me?

The wind is blowing hard, bending the trees.
It's as though the leaves wave to me —
Reassuring me that everything is alright.
Rain falls hard and I become scared
   But it's only God watering His creativity.

God's powers are wonderful.
And He is the creator of all.
He made it possible for us
To enjoy these things
   No matter how big or small.

No matter how bad or great things are,
There's a purpose which God brings.
It's up to us to use it for all mankind.
We should get on our knees and thank God
   For letting us enjoy these things.
   Pamela Sue Brown

Warning

Stop, look and listen for all the world to hear;
It's not to late to change things when the warning signs are here.

It's a time to pull together, reunite us one and all;
To give a helping hand, no matter how big or small.

O' planet earth, we've abused you that is true;
Our ozone, air, water, land and sometimes even food.

There's too much hunger, hate, violence, wars and crime;
Innocent people even children in the cross fire line.

We must all work together, toward peace and happiness;
Which means give and take with love, understanding and kindness.

So now's the time for us to act, your gut instincts are the best;
But seek the help that's needed, let the experts do the rest.
   Sharon Corley

Wisdom Done Gone

Just as a cat, it comes, it goes,
it's here, it's there, prowling always.
Beneath the sun, beneath the moon,
beneath this, beneath that, roving everywhere.

All know of its' presence, it's always about them.
No one cares though, surprising not it's presence is.
It has always been there, they think.
Yet I ask? "Has the cat always been?"
I would think not.

Running amuck at dusk, at dawn,
during the coldest of Winters, the warmest of Summers
Springs as green as green itself, the most beautiful Falls.
This I speak of is the most precious commodity of all.
Time I speaketh of.
   Rodney Lynn Ruble

Thinking of Marie

Marie, when often I say, I'm thinking of you...
It's because I can see deep into your heart, and that's all I can do.

If the real treasures in life, are ever to be known
Well, they just cannot be found, when you are alone.

I'm looking for a life partner, so caring and true
Oh Marie, Marie, if it could only be you.

For the first time in my life, I can see inside
And when I'm with you, there is nothing to hide.

There was such a warm and content feeling, within my space
When one night I dreamt that, well...I touched your face.

My Selfish Love wants to know more about you every single day
My Unselfish Love says to stay away, she has her own life, I'd just
   be in her way.

Shall I dare ask her to go on a 'window-shopping' spree?
If I don't, I will have to be content, just Thinking of Marie.

I know Life would be good with my Marie...we'd have a ball
Then I could leave this world knowing, I've done it all.

If I ever want her to know, how much I really care
Well, to win a woman's love, is worth at least one dare.

So I'll send in my poem, for all the world to see
And then she'll know it's me, who's Thinking of Marie...
   T. R. Chauvin

Nature's Way

Back in the spring of '94 as the season began to break
It was our habit to wake up early,
Sip our coffee and watch nature come awake.

We heard ecstatic chirping- what a happy bird it must be;
We looked out at the feeder and "Baldy" we did see.

Now, we knew was a cardinal by his red beak and his feathers;
His eyes were big and black and round, he acted like the others.

But where was his beautiful crest- to cast him as majestic?
It was my guess that he was young- but boy, he looked pathetic.

His head was small, and round and bare- not one feather on his pate.
But he flit around without a care, so resigned was he to his fate.

It's been a year, now '95- and our habits have not changed.
What joy we felt when we looked out
To see "Baldy" back, not much rearranged.

His feathers had turned a brilliant red- maybe compensated by nature;
But what he lacked upon his head- could never diminish his stature.

He still flit and chirped so happily- knowing where to come for food.
But this time he brought his family- he had more reason to be in a good mood.

And so if you think you're not handsome-
Just remember "Baldy" and his part;
In nature it's not how you look- but surely what you feel in your heart.

Patricia A. Ruckman

"Stranger Danger"

The way the world is now, you just can't blame her.
It was late, she needed gas, and I happened to have been there.
A friendly smile and wave, just like my father would have done,
And I felt her abject terror, as if I'd fired a gun.

I had to shut my eyes against this blast of trepidation;
She was terrified, and I, aghast, at causing this sensation.
I quickly staunched my first response - to tell her who I am.
On a lonely night, on a Texas road, I knew I was just "a man."

As sad as this event has made me, greater truths unfold:
No other response is possible, in a world that's grown this cold.
She can never teach her daughter to try and spare my feelings,
Nor would I ever ask her to believe the world is healing.

I could tell her that I would not allow the weak to come to harm,
That when I'm near she's safer than some girls in their Daddy's arms.
But every time I hear about the dangers in this world,
I weep, for there is no solace for a frightened little girl.

Tony Barker

I Can't Swim

I never knew such sensuous idiocy
more intimate pain than this self-discovery
as close as lids when they are firmly closed
yet such distance us when eyes are wide, open and staring...
through the fiery curtain and on out into the echo stomach of space
when I swallow I watch the spit land
clumsily like a scavenger bird on one leg
"Are you ready to feast?"
Feast on this soul's morsel
clung to it's cage of bones
at last! I never knew and will continue to know not still
this naive sense of each other.
I've been such a stone
and you the rippling water
so dash me into your lake!
And together we will watch our circles
spread
forever outwards further to places
we will touch but never know.

Wong Ji

Reunion

I just stood there, transfixed—unable to move or speak...
It was as if time had slowed nearly to a stop.
My breath caught in my throat and I could hear—could feel
  the pounding of my lifeblood as it rushed, raced, screamed
  through my entire body!
Bright lights surrounded us as they handed you into my arms— wrapped
  now in those soft, pink blankets when, only moments before you were
  clothed, bathed, nourished by the warmth of your mother's womb.
Time, then, vanished and in it's place was formed the moment when I
  saw you.
NO! I mean I SAW you! In that instant I recognized you!
Crystal-clear, huge, profound eyes of blue (a blue not of this earth)
  gazed into mine and then, like an arrow of light,
  pierced through the shields and armor right into my living soul!
You touched my heart in a way no one has ever done before.
Somewhere inside my memories, cloaked by the veils of forgetfulness in
  time, a spark shot out of the darkness...I REMEMBER YOU!
Loving spirits - friends throughout eternity together...
The time is now for your arrival in that beautiful little body.
I have waited for you so long! (all my life...)
He has sent you to me-finally and the joy I feel knows no boundaries!
You have come to light my way to remind me once again that I am here
  merely to love.

Sara Toni Lashley

Lingering Haze

It was never supposed to be for us.
It was an accident in nature that we met.
An illusion witnessed only by dreamers.
  A shooting star, pounding of the heart,
the bold flash of lightning. A whirlpool of
emotions with no rescue or lifeline.
Rushing the mind, and flooding the soul.
  The closing of eyes, the catching of breath,
the controlling of senses. To glance again.
  The star, fallen, has disappeared. The
heartbeat slowed to silence. The whirlpool
has been washed away by the wisdom of tears.
  It was never supposed to be for us,
and lightning never strikes twice.

Rosalee E. Gill

My House

As I looked upon the large old house, with its weather beaten sides,
it was all my mind could do to keep tears from flowing from my eyes.
For I remembered at one time roses there had grown, and along the walk
(which now was bare) had been lined with cobblestone.

As I stepped upon the large old porch, my heart began to pound, for I
thought for a moment I heard the familiar sound. The sound of talk
and laughter which had always taken place, on this old porch, which
was now adorned with patterns of cobweb lace.

I opened the door and went inside, and looked at the tattered walls.
Could this be that big bright yellow room where I had sat and played
with dolls? Was the fireplace (now filled with trash) the one I had
loved to see, the one that contained the dancing frames that had once
so fascinated me?

Then I looked to the staircase, how much bigger it seemed back then,
but I saw there weren't that many steps, perhaps eight, or maybe even ten.
I walked to the top of the creaking stairs and saw in front of me a door.
A door which seemed to say to me "Come in, come see, there's more."

I entered the room quite slowly, unaware of the tears on my face, for
this was the room of my childhood, where all of my dreams took place.
I realized then I could never remove this house from within my mind,
For this house contained the memories I loved. This house which had
  been so kind.

Susan Hodges Coren

Loneliness Undone

My heart once denied the love it longed to feel;
It was afraid because it might not be real.

I confined my heart to world of its own;
So I had to face the world all alone.

Then you came to me like the sun through the clouds;
And the love that I couldn't feel was somehow allowed.

You showed me that it's alright to let love inside of my heart;
And if I let my guard down I won't fall apart.

The words 'I love you' just don't seem to say enough;
You made me see that loving someone isn't that tough.

Now I feel lost when I'm not by your side;
Without your love I feel empty inside.

I'll never leave you with doubts of whether or not my love is true;
Because the love that we share, no one could ever undo.

Shannon M. Haywood

A Year Ago Today...

It was a year ago today that we first met,
It was a year ago today that our futures together were set.
The day we met, we sat and talked for hours...
A few days later you were bringing me flowers.

A year ago today, holding hands beneath a starry sky,
You tenderly proclaimed your unwavering love for me.
I, so impulsive, and caught off-guard, meekly stammered this reply
 O.K.—well—let's just wait and see
Although I was not that easy to convince....
I'm happy to say we've been together since..
I love you tremendously; of this you can be sure;
I loved you a year ago today - and I'll love you forever more.

Sandra Franklin

Life....

A Flower Garden is a vision of beauty
It touches the heart,
It is food for the soul,
It is a joy to behold
And a stroll in the Garden invites solitude.

It erases the furrowed brow
It fosters a smile instead of a frown
And quiets the aching heart.
It brings a measure of peace and contentment
And a fragrant flower Garden will be a blessing for all.

Wilma W. Ferguson

Love

The strong fragrance of love is found in the hearts of many.
It shines through the eyes of lovers,
Whose passion is too vast for boundaries.
It glimmers from the smiles of admirers,
Whose fondness is shown through shy gestures.
It reeks in the kinship of family,
Whose togetherness is their sign of affection.
It speaks through the language of chums,
Whose lives sustain on their loyal friendship.
It glares from the acts of complete strangers,
Whose selfless deeds are done warmly in a way to help another.
It lives in the souls of people,
Whose relations become fruitful from the seed of this tenderness.
It comes from our creator, God,
Who is the home of love, from which we grow and
nurture ourselves by the pleasures of its passion.

Melissa Anne Gomez

Christmas Time

Christmas time spreads love for all, sharing, giving, standing tall. It seems these days reveal our best. Did God choose Christmas as our test? He hopes our heart will open wide. He prays we remember that His son died. To give us life and live as He would, He prides himself on all our good. We were made in His image, and from day to day, we plan our lives to go the right way. The road we choose may falter or bend, but remembering in God, we have a friend. At Christmas Time we seem to think more of all we should be, and of all things before. When Christmas Time comes around each year, know who came to us, and whose message is so clear. Wait not til His birthday to praise, to love and to give. Each day of your life, just be thankful you live.

Sandra M. Barthlein

Crossroads

As broken family ties are for sure,
  it seems almost too much to endure.
Times spent struggling to understand,
  are broken only by a new dealt hand.
Crosswords, Yatzee and cards are a real way,
  to find escape from the pain and start another day.
Feelings felt for a loved one's broken heart,
  as mom or dad set off for a new start.
The meaning of a promise taken so lightly,
  can leave a little girl's thoughts so unsightly.
The turmoil within only a matter of time,
  a new beginning at 6:00 am as old grandfather chimes.
A soft voice says, "Hurry along, or you'll be left aside,"
  the yellow school bus has arrived outside.
Crosswords, Yatzee, and cards are a real way,
  to find escape from the pain and start another day.

-Tana Vogel

The Baby Cries

As I gaze into the crystal clear pond
It saddens me, for all that's dear to me is gone
Reflections of shadows that were once happy
Now laid buried and can only be recalled in memory
The smiling faces coupled with children's laughter
All doomed, dead bodies of human agony—piled in slaughter
I look up towards God, with feelings stirring in remorse
Instead I find, God—oh God—he died at the cross
What should I do—I feel darkness closing in on me
Hopelessness and uncertainty is in my future-I see
How can just me save something as vast a humanity
I guess I can start by loving others—yes with sincerity
And show the Angel of death—we see all of his lies
For love will nurture contentment and the baby—
  Will Not Need to Cry!

Wayne A. Paglinawan

Images

I've walked along the beach and felt my feet upon the sand.
I've felt a touch upon my face and imagined it was your hand.
I've thought of you in dreams, in hours of day and night, and I find
That hard as I try there is no way to expel you from my mind.

I feel a warmth within my body and I feel you near.
I think of loving you with all my heart, and I feel fear.
I feel the wind caress my being, and the rain gently embrace my face,
And I think of times we've had as I close my eyes and trace,

Every precious moment we've spent together, every pleasure so real,
Every time we've had to the past now fallen, I can feel.
Any maybe someday a time will come to be.
When with me you can finally feel free.

Patti McGonigle

Today

Today as I look at the things around me
It makes me sad at what my eyes see

Factory and office jobs are on the decline
At the unemployment office, men and women wait in line

In the USA, most people go to sleep in a nice warm bed
But as each day passes, on sidewalks more blankets are spread

Children are going to bed with empty tummies
While lying next to them are their crying mommies

Years ago parents worried about cigarettes and beer
Now drugs are their greatest fear

For measles and mumps there is a vaccination
Now for AIDS for sure we have an obligation

Higher ups say there is a slight recession
But ask those families, they'll say this is a depression

Just look around and open those eyes
Too long now we've been told little white lies

Please don't let these sad and terrible things happen to me
I love the USA, the land of the free

This is a country like no other
Let's all join together and help our sister and brother
   Sandra J. LaCount

Nature's Way

Nature has its own little way, and unlike you and me.
It knows just when the rain will fall, and when to grow a tree.

It takes our world, and breaks it down, into four little parts (seasons).
It knows just when the snow will fall, and when the summer starts.

It knows just when the sun will shine, and when the moon will glow.
It knows just when the air is calm, and when the wind will blow.

And when you see the flowers bloom, in spring time of the year.
And when you feel so good inside, you want to shout and cheer.

And when you turn your head up high, and see the stars above.
Its beauty seems to always fill your head and heart with love.

But when I see the clouds float by, like cotton in the air.
They seem so calm, and in control, without the slightest care.

What makes the clouds up in the sky, and winds that make them blow.
The snow, the rain, the plants, the sun, the rivers that will flow.

Have you ever watched a flock of birds, so swift, so light, and sure.
Like the birth of a new day come to life, so sweet, so fresh, and pure.

For all these things that make the world, they come from up above.
God make them up, for you and me, and filled them up with love.
   Tyrone Faulkner

I'll Never Give Up

Though the hills of success, may be a hazard to climb
I'll never give up, I've made up my mind
Though on the wrong road I may stray
I'll never give up until I find the right way
If a flood washes me out to the sea, I can't swim,
But by determination from the water I'll be set free
If I am doubted among a few, who are they to ridicule
If my love is taken advantage of in some way, still
My hope I won't give away
Some challenges in life are smooth, and others are rough
From the beginning to the end, I'll never give up!
   Faye O. Shilling

Villanelle

Please ask forgiveness on this brand new day
It is not too late to lift the burden.
Cry, cry tears and all your sorrow away.

Though knowing deep down it is not your way.
The heavy hearth you carry is leaden.
Please ask forgiveness on this brand new day.

Adversity sneaks in without much say
But a teacher of soul, it can heighten.
Cry, cry tears and all your sorrow away.

Do not fight the strength that lies close today;
Grasp in full spirit, let your soul brighten.
Please ask forgiveness on this brand new day.

Like golden rays that upon us will play,
See the shining light once not forgotten.
Cry, cry tears an all your sorrow away.

Carry your journey and plead it to say
In love's stark duel; the pain will hearten.
Please ask forgiveness on this brand new day.
Cry, cry tears and all your sorrow away.
   Traces T. Haney

What Is Love?

It is not something you can hold in the palm of your hand.
It is not something you can smell or taste.
It is something that hits you like a tidal wave and leaves
you immersed in it forevermore.

It is the feeling I get when she holds my hand, or gently
presses her lips to mine.
It is a constant yearning for the smell of her perfume;
it is the heartache of sleeping in an empty bed.

I hold back the tears as I think of her time and again,
keeping my pain wrapped up inside.
It tears me apart when I wake up and realize that it has
not gone away, that it will not go away, because something
has overcome me that will be with me forever.
   Ray Gutowski

Finding The Way

What is it that has come upon me?
It is difficult to just try and see.
For certain something is in the air
And to me it appears to be something quite rare.
Most of the time it certainly seems
That my head is filled with ongoing dreams
Of being, sharing, doing things together
With this person whom I'll always remember.
I wish God gave me nerves of steel
So I could easily say what I really feel.
Indeed I have kept my feelings locked up inside,
I don't know how much longer they can hide.
If this opportunity somehow slips away
Will I ever wake up the next day?
Hopefully I'd have done my part
If ever I find my way into her heart.
   Scott Atkinson

WithoutEnd

Have**you**ever**wondered**why**words**end**where**they**do**?
If**a**thought**can**go**on**forever**or**a**story**be**told**over
and**over**a**hundred**times**by**a**hundred**people**in**many
ways**then**why**do**words**have**this**limitness**to**them.
These**endings**and**beginnings.   I**would**think**that
words**should**run**together**and**go**on**forever**and**ever
withoutend.
   P. K. Baldwin

Universal Language Of Love

Love is the universal language all over the world
It has been around since the beginning of time
Although, there are other emotions we share
Love is something very precious and rare

We have all kinds of love
Love of parents for their child
Love of one's family and friends
And love of a man and woman

During a person lifetime
We will encounter all types of love
Knowing how to handle it
Comes with age and maturity
And love can sometime still be misguided

There is no condition on loving some one
It is the only thing that is natural and free
With no strings attached
People not knowing the real meaning of love
Will try to put a price on it
No matter who or what you are
The greatest gift of all is your love of God
   Sarah Everton

Loneliness Is An Ugly Word

Loneliness is an ugly word; a terror in disguise.
it causes sages to lose their wits, so fools become the wise.
And women weep with silent tears
filled with the frustration and the fears.
That crowd the passing of their years.

Loneliness is an ugly word, a mirror to all souls.
a panacea to explain the dimming of one's goals.
How strangely stilled become their pleas,
hidden from a world that sees
their strength - and not their trembling knees.

Loneliness is an ugly word; a villainous task master.
Upon rearing its nasty head, courts nothing but disaster.
Then crowded rooms become silent tombs,
and empty nights - mean barren wombs;
as love, once rejected, no longer blooms.

Loneliness - is an ugly word!
   Stanley S. Kroen

The Plumber

When you are in a hurry, and company is due
is when things fail to operate, and you don't know what to do.
The faucet forms a steady drip, and the pump just never stops,
and you test each thought that comes to mind as the drip turns into drops.

You dial the plumbers number and pray that he will come
as you get a busy signal; so relieved there's someone home.
Then try again in a few minutes as time goes fleeting by,
to find that no one answers no matter how you try.

Now the sink becomes a problem for the water won't run down,
and no one cares to know you when the plumbers out of town.
The furnace gadgets get fowled up as your friends knock at the door;
why do these things torment me, and what else could be in store?

You think up a few excuses for all the works that are to blame,
and somewhere behind the story, there pops up the plumbers name.
But the worst embarrassing nightmare when one feels one wants to cuss,
is when guests want to use the bath room, and the toilet will not flush!
   Ruth V. Shillito

Besides Get Those Done By Five

A verse or two
Is what thing I will do
During the time that I am up to this time alive -

It is slightly not easy to write a verse or two
To you also you
At the time which I am old moreover
Can't see alive
Just mentioned verse or two
To make it easier to get through
During the time that I up to this time thrive.

I have unsuitable spectacles on to easily get through
Just mentioned verse or two
Thing I've at all times desired to do
Besides get those done by 5:00.
   Rosa Leonora Galfano

John William

One of the greatest wonders of our incredible earth
Is the mystical event of a new baby's birth.
Now that all the long waiting has past
Dear little John has been born at last.
O' how precious is this delicate little child.
So meek, content and beautifully mild
He warms your heart when at his attentive parents he smiles.
Like the swift shimmering wings of a gleaming white dove.
Little John was certainly a gift from our Father above.
Now when he is older and wants to proclaim
He'll call out with a loud clear voice.
JOHN WILLIAM's my name!
   Ruth Kinzie Giebler

Sometimes

Sometimes I wonder of life
is it worth the time of
endless motion, as long
as we wait - out the
adventure, survival and commotion,
Sometimes I wonder if
Christ has come during our nightmares and forgotten;
Or perhaps just not looking
we fail at the dream that we are grasping.
Are we all remote and far away in our dreams.
And his special touches are softly spoken.
Sometimes I wonder, is the zest of life broken?
No, I wonder of his love, was it meant for you and I?
I just wonder sometimes when I am alone;
Is he here tonight as am I dreaming?
I just haven't woke.
I just wonder sometimes.
He has said, "I am with you always," it seems like
just yesterday that he kindly spoke; as I wait for him
on the morrow, will I still wonder of his presence?
   Shannon Stanford

Life's Seasons

My life is like a tornado, like thunder when I cry.
If snowflakes were my happiness,
Then winter would fly by.
People are like teardrops, that glisten in the night.
We are but only mirrors, breaking in the light.
If our souls could shine, and tell all that we feel.
Then mirrors would be windows for our words to heal.
   Tiffany Marie Tague

Raindrops Upon The Pane

Soft whispers of the wind
   inviting the cooler season in
Where you will hear my gentle change
   as the drops ebb upon the pane.

Idle summers forthwith shall pass
   and you will mutter a sweet alas
And I will waltz as the graceful crane
   as the drops ebb upon the pane.

Secret shadows past the moon
   send flickered memories across your room
Sweet treasures veiled in the rain
   as the drops ebb upon the pane.

There I shall visit you my friend
   where the inherent journey shall know no end
For I am the flowing vein
   as the drops ebb upon the pane.

Patricia Ann Mayorga

"Excuse Me, Sir..."

Grinning, I turn to playfully participate with a close friend.
Instead, I confront an unfamiliar face.
My cheeks quickly ripen into deep crimson.
Flesh feels feverish and my body swells up in complete...
Don't you know what this does to me?

I review my entire physical appearance in seconds...
Crew neck sweatshirt, blue jeans, and black hightops.
No mascara, no earrings, no fancy jewelry or fancy hair.
No sway, wiggle or flirt.

I scrutinize my personal identification...
My older brother and I playing combat and cowboys.
No purse, no skirt, no ruffles or pink.
Parents fretting about their "young lady."

I compare my economic position of 36 years...
No meaningful career, no lives saved, or awards on the mantle.
No 30 year mortgage, luxury car or exotic travels.
I'm tired of washing my clothes at the stinking laundromat.
You really don't know what this does to me!

I shift my weight to one foot, shove my hand in my pocket.
And just look at you.

Virginia E. Moore

Hang In There

I created the old and the new.
In your mother's womb created I you.
Yes, I created all; in Heaven and in Earth.
Also, the oceans and the seas.
The evidence is there even in the morning dew.

Centuries upon centuries I have been faithful to you.
You can stand like the trees, — tall.
No need to worry about the fall.
Behold, I hold the sky, the moon and the stars.
Just take me by the hand — and stand!

The fire wheels are turning, as time marches on.
The days and nights are sometimes cold.
But remember what was told.
The sun is still burning.
I created the old and the new.
Always, great is my faithfulness unto you!

Stephanie C. Jenkins

Tribute To A Dear Mother

With the holidays come joy and sadness.
In times like these just remember the gladness,
For a mother was taken who was ever so dear.
Just trust in the Lord and keep her memories near.

Right now it does not seem right.
Answers are wanted, a little insight.
But deep in your heart you must certainly know
That it was the Lord who said it was her time to go.

He will be with her every step of the way;
Knowing this mother, every now and then stopping to pray.
She always prayed for other people's problems
Hoping the Lord would help her to solve them.

She never stopped living; she only switched places
To a land above all of familiar faces.
She is gone now forever to be with her maker.
In this happy land no one will ever forsake her.

Phillip L. Morgan Sr.

The U.N. Needs You

Fellow constituents, once again it is time to participate
in the UNITED WAY CAMPAIGN.

Whether your contribution be a dollar or a dime,
I rest assure you it will be right on time
for someone who needs clean clothes to put on
or someone who is desperate to have a home.

But most important it will help some child
and possibly could purchase you a smile
for giving comes from the heart even if
it's only just a small part.

So fellow constituents dig into your pockets
and see what monies you can sock it
right into the United Way Campaign,
They will be most grateful to receive it
once again!

Rosemary Wells

Lost Dream

I will find you
in the harmony of loving hearts,
When the earth and the sun embrace,
and the hearts are not for malice,
but only for loving.
In which moment, we can see love flowing
in the earth's translucent veins,
and we can hear the beat of blossom's pulse
in orchards.
In which moment, each drop of water is an ocean,
And the sky is overflowing with bright stars,
And the earth is only for living.
When the rainbow of poems falls on our hearts,
and there is not any between hearts.
When the earth is a red apple
hanging from the green branch of the galaxy,
free of any greedy teeth in pursuit.
In those green moments,
there won't be any lover's heart lonely.
And I will find you my lost dream!

Rohollah Piryaei

Today And Forever

Today and forever you'll walk hand in hand;
In the church you gave each other golden wedding bands.
May God bless today and for the rest of your life
All the vows you made as you became husband and wife.
Nearest to your heart is the bond you both have shared,
Down the aisle arm in arm to begin your married years.
Sincerest wishes from friends and family as you both go past
Hoping the happiness you share today will forever last.
As the years go flying by, if you ever grow apart,
Remember the day you said, I do, and let the feelings fill your hearts.
Only to each other are the words you both have told;
Never let another come between your bands of gold.
Remember every moment of this your wedding day;
Always keep it close to heart in each and every way.
Friends are how you two became one together;
Forgiving and forgetting is insurance for forever.
Every minute you get is precious, so thank the Lord above.
Remember on this sacred day, He blessed you both with love.
To have, to hold, to honor and trust, until death do us part;
You vowed this to each other, so keep it close in heart.

Paula J. Masaitis

Meekness

A meek and quiet spirit within you
In sight of God is considered pure
A submissive attitude to want to learn
It brings you to God's Will to discern

Obedience to leading to search God's Will
In Holy Book which teaches us still
All things work, together, for good
When we find the knack looking for it's food

At end we find we are polished gold
For we belong to the Master's true fold
Now slow in speaking, not given to wrath
Remember you were washed in baptismal bath

You are more than Conqueror in God's Peace
Serve Him in beauty of meekness with increase
In Holiness and Grace as you dwell in His Love
Perfected you'll gain a Crown in Heaven above

Susan Essler

Piscean Pleasure

Forever swimming as we do
In separate waters are we two

Gill to Gill
yet, out of reach
I LOVE YOU STILL

Your mind and mine are intertwined
Always, till the END OF TIME

If Fate should be cruel and keep us apart
The Stars will demand your place in my heart

Silently, have I loved you so,
eternity may pass, I will not let you go

Sister and brother
my Souls only true lover

So much unsaid still remains
as once again the tide has changed

If for now, the currents pull you toward the MOON
Always and Forever will I be waiting on NEPTUNE

Sabrina Parker

Grief

A tragic event occurred this past Wednesday
in Oklahoma City,
A day, starting out for most like any other
ended in utter tragedy.

Self-proclaimed patriots
by means of anarchy,
Decimated the lives of many
By their ruthless act of inanity.

A somber veil of gloom
enshrouds this nation,
Whose very soul was rocked
from its foundation.

The bewildered masses cry-out
in disbelief,
"How could this happen?...
This is not the Mid-East!!"

Emotion laden rescuers remove
those who remain,
While all of us cope
with this National shame.

Thomas R. Schatz

Spider The Fat

One day I was sitting
in my web. When I felt something hitting
me. It was my stomach. I saw
a girl come and sat on Miss
Tuffet. She had food, and since
it was my tuffet I winced
at the thought of her
sitting there. A fur
would be the price she had
to pay. When I called from above she got mad
and said, "Go away." So I
thought about what my
dad would do. He would go
and ask for food. So slowly,
I lowered myself down to
sit by her. Yelling like a Moo
Cow she ran. Leaving her bowl
of food, so I ate filling up the hole
that was in my stomach. That
is the end of my story told by Spider the Fat.

Samantha Armstrong

Untitled

Nine months have passed to wait for you
   You'll day know how special
A moment never to forget
   We've named you Angle Gabriel

How foolish are my fears someday
   A thorn will pick your finger
Or that the ground may scrape your knee
   I'm mother, I remember

And proud I'll be to hear you talk
   The first time you say "daddy"
You'll graduate in no time now
   Your present,...a new Caddy

Till when my son you'll understand
   We hope you'll always know
A love so great that in your hearts
   Our love will overflow

In these three months you've been awake
   Alive with kicks and cues
My son, we ask you grow old
   May God always be with you

Sandra Ivonne Delgadillo

Mamas

When children cry, their tears they hide
  in Mama's loving arms,
And though she says, "This world's not blessed!"
  Her love will keep us warm.

Through bikes and planes and broken trains,
  she stands guard at the door,
And dries our tears, and kills of our fears,
  and says, "There's so much more."

Through years we grow, our pain she knows,
  she swears, "It's not that bad
We've had good food, clean warm beds
  more love than most have had!"

She's done her best, we'll find the rest,
  It's true-we're older now.
Her time is done, we're on our own
  She's done all she knows how.

But when Mamas cry, their tears they hide
  in no one's loving arms,
And we say, "Yes-our lives are blessed!"
  But who keeps Mamas warm?

    Shawne Penwell

Worth-While

If I can make a mark
In life as I walk
Then I'll feel my life has been worth while
If I can make someone smile
And replace a tear with a smile
Then I'll feel my life has been worth while
If I can lend a hand
To a fellow man
If I can comfort a lost child
If I can help someone to see
How much God means to me
Then I'll feel my life has been worth while
And then when time has come
And my life on earth is done
And God welcomes me home with a smile
Then I'll know my life on earth
Had been worth while

    Sandra Bird

Stuck In The Round

(This poem is dedicated to the many concerned and patient students
in English 305 who pulled me through, emotionally and physically,
the hairy trauma of cutting the plastic spokes -
one by one - of a round brush stuck in my hair.)

Help! I'm so wound up in myself - and I fear
there's no hope of straightening out now.
Somehow I'll survive, with just stubs for limbs
and with whatever God will allow.

Ouch! How embarrassing to be severed from my home,
my friends and the place of my birth.
Who are these long, stick-like appendages
untangling my length and my girth?

I once dreamed of becoming a river,
long and sweeping, waving gently, flowing strong.
Painful, impending amputation -
clip, snip, clip, nip - it won't be long.

Brushed out clumps of hair lay in bewilderment -
dead ends without blood, lacking life;
could it be possible to grow new limbs?
The scissors sliced like a knife.

    Sally L. Spiro

Untitled

The Black and Brown and Brass,
In a blanket of fresh flowers.
The sun streaks cleanly through the cloudless sky.
Tears blur my vision;
I blink in disbelief.
A gust of wind flaps the canopy;
My mind drifts to moments past.
A thousand laughs and stories,
As only he could tell.
An ice cold draft raised in song,
And now SILENCE...
Untangling my anger, grief, sorrow and sadness...
For what could have been.
JUSTICE VIOLATED.
Lost is the smile, the wit, the wisdom.
And now,
The Black and Brown and Brass,
In a blanket of fresh flowers
Lies within the tomb,
Bill my friend

    Randolph B. Cook

Little Things

Little things raping my mind
Imagining demons tearing my eyes blind
I can't stand the things ripping at my insides
Until the clock ticks and time abides
My sanity slowly torn from me
Limb from limb you'll soon see
Anger eating away at my soul
Confusion making me feel unwhole
Silence echoing loudly throughout my head
Burning rapidly just like they said
Lights flashing before my eyes
Darkness growing and diminishing in size
Enveloping the world that I live in
Torturing me because its immersed in sin
And maybe all the questions trapped inside my brain
Are the only things that keep me sane.

    Zhenus Wahidi

"15"

I wish that I was 21 instead of just 15
I'm ready to get out and see the world
I think I'm ready to be seen

I wish I had my driver's license instead of hitchin' rides
I'm ready to get my own set of wheels
And move to the driver's side

I wish that I was out of school instead of the 9th grade
Forget the diploma—I'm getting a job
'Cause see I've got to get paid

I wish I had a good payin' job instead of this 3.65
This minimum wage has got to go
How else am I gonna survive

I wish I had my own place instead of livin' at home
I need to be out and doing some things
I need to be on my own

But to get my place I'll need a job—for a job I'll need my schoolin'
I guess I'll quit wishin' and just be 15
'Cause who in the world am I foolin'

    Rhonda H. Lowe

No, I'm Not God

No, I'm not God.
I'm not even an angel.
All I am is a human being doing my best to understand.
Doing my best to make sense out of chaos,
  to live with the inconceivable,
  to try to stay at peace within myself.
Doing my best to keep sane,
  to hold onto my beliefs,
  and to trust that no man knows God's mind,
  and that my thoughts are just as right,
  just as true,
  and just as real as the next man's.
Susan Scott

What Is A Friend

I know I've never told you so
I'm glad to have you as my friend
When I call and need to chat
You're always near as the phone
Hello, hello, are you there!
You say I've been busy doing this and that
But never too busy to chat and listen to my many concerns
I know sometimes I burden you down with the cares of the day
But you're never too busy to lend a listening ear
Although our visits are far and in between
And our telephone conversations are many
You're always there to be a friend
Whenever things go wrong for you
I'm always there to listen to you
When the cares of life gets all bogged down
Together we can conquer them all
I thank you for being my friend
Sylvia D. Howard

My Husband

All these years of searching
I'm free
The joy I have now, its because of you
You took away the pain, filled it with love

My heart was so cold
And the hurting of memories
I have no longer

Every time I hear your voice
I feel so warm inside
When I see your smile
I'm falling in love and over again

I thank you for the dreams of today
and tomorrow
I just wanted to say
I love you.
Robin Haflin

Questions?

Love makes me wonder why it hurts? And why it has so many perts?
I know love is a very strong emotion from within.
We grow up learning it and passing it on to our next of kin.
Love even has the power to make people sin.
When love hurts it also makes me wonder how it got started.
Was it when the first two parted?
Love is suppose to be a joyful feeling inside, something you
want and have with pride.
And if you make that commitment it should always be side by side.
Teresa Eiter

Here I Am

I traveled down many a road,
I'm a loner but I'm never alone.
Place's that I've been, people that I know,
Some passed away, other's moved on.
Here I am, I'm playing you, my song.

My father was a master, in carving wood.
His spirit still linger's, in mysterious ways.
Time's have changed, things no longer the same,
I know today, where I once went wrong.
Here I am, I'm playing you, my song.

On that full - moon night, underneath the moon.
Next to the flowing stream.
A gust of energy, carried us away.
Wondering where you are,
Wishing, on a shooting star.
Here I am, I'm playing you, my song.
Gary Vachon

His Nail-Pierced Hands

One day in heaven with Jesus I'll stand,
I'll get to touch his nail-pierced hands.
To see the one who suffered for me;
Oh, the agony and pain of Calvary.
To look into his loving eyes,
And to know that it was for me he cried
They know not hat they are doing, Father please forgive,
I must give my life that they might live.
He freely gave all for me that day,
His glorious blood washed all my sins away.
Praise, glory, and honor for His amazing grace;
For he suffered and died and took my place.
Death He overcame and victory was won,
By God's loving gift - Jesus, His Son.
One day in heaven, when Jesus I see,
I'll thank Him and praise Him on bended knee.
One day in heaven with Jesus I'll stand,
I'll get to touch His nail-pierced hands.
Camela Walker

Love Is In The Sky

My love, your love is like the sky to me. But
if your love should fade into darkness. I should
cry till dawn, then laugh, with the sound of joy
in my heart, because you're here once more, and
my heart is healed once again.

But if darkness should stay forever, I will cry till
I die and if you would come straight down from the
sky to stand by me I would not care if it were skylight
or night dark.

You could look uglier than ugly or cuter than cute.
But I would always love you. Stand by me and love me
more than ever and I should never cry again.
Talana Caine

"Ode To A Rubber Duck"

Oh little yellow Duckie, floating in my bath,
I know you well, as we are friends and travel the same path.
You swim with me, and play and splash — great comfort you do bring;
You sit and bob on water warm, and listen to me sing.
I use you when I bathe at home, and take you on the road,
A weary day - a sudsy soak - you help to lift my load.
So I sing your praise, oh rubber fowl, and keep you ever near,
We shall not part, not you and I, of that I'm surely clear!
H. Winfield Wyatt

It

It is not any place; it is everywhere.
If you look for it, it is you who is lost!
It is faster than light, yet stiller than death.
It has a thousand names, but none that apply.
It is older than time, and newer than now.

Yet some put a face on it, and call it God.
Some sense the wind in it, and call it Spirit.
Some feel emotion from it, and call it Love.
Some see the color of it, and call it Light.
And some say its fragrance is ethereal.

With all the words, I cannot convey to you
what I taste of the cool spring rain on my face,
what I smell in the roses, and citrus blooms,
what I feel for the new lovers at midnight,
what music I hear in the children's laughter,
or what beauty I see in my baby's face.

I'm a dumb creature in wonder of it all.
   Susan Folger Quezada

Where Does Time Go?

Is time Heaven sent?
If you are a schemer or a dreamer is it only lent
Today is the first of May, the Spring of your youth.
Tomorrow is the last of September, Autumn of truth?
Where does time go?
Is there someone who keeps it for awhile?
Then after every life season, when we want our time back,
Does the time keeper say, "that is a skill which I lack"?
August or December, value each day, bask in the sun, roll in the hay.
A life ill spent, a youth well meant, what has the time keeper lent?
Some days in the sun, some love and some fun, a night of pure fear,
When you know the end's near.
Now is the time to shed a few tears.
We all pass this way, enjoy it now,
For even our last day is dear.
   H. H. Hunter

Destiny Cries

I sit and analyze life and wonder
   if people see what I see,
I cry over a painful past and think about
   what is my destiny.
Did I have to go through all those hurtful days
   to get to a future,
One that still might not be so bright
   with surroundings so impure?
Mutual trust degrades as silent wrongdoings
   unleash onto blind hearts,
When bridges are crossed the gullible realize
   that pain has many parts.
Strong beliefs are broken down
   with unfair deceit.
Can we conquer the battles of life and love
   or do we continually retreat?
   Shelia Henderson

Flying Fish

I once saw a flying fish,
I hope it won't be served on someone's dish.

Out of the water I saw it rise,
Boy, what an amazing surprise!

Out of the water and into the air,
I was so frightened, what a scare!

It was back in the water in the blink of an eye,
I didn't even have a chance to say goodbye!
   Talia Wohlgelernter

It's Summer Time Again

This scorching weather is not for me
I'd rather shiver in my undies somewhere
   in Alaska maybe
The starch escapes from my blouse
The curl in my hair vanishes and my slip
   clings to my legs, it's a decent thing
These short skirts, why I might have
Tripped and fallen a dozen times
   the problem is getting to where you must go
From where you live and back again
It doesn't matter how disheveled you look
Opening the locks on your door after your
   days work is over because New York is so exciting
In spite of the hundred degree temperature
And is does get cooler as the sun goes down.
So much stupendous entertainment
So much to see. Even though this scorching
Weather is not for me, New York is.
   Pamela Rankin-Smith

Through Your Eyes

If I could be anywhere,
I'd be with you
We would walk, and maybe talk,
then I sit by your side.
I wish you could see, how heavenly
you look through my eyes.
Now if I only how you feel,
I'd know what to do.
Mystery surrounds how you'll look,
what you'll say or do,
but I can imagine how you'll feel towards me.
I've told you what I've done and said before,
how I feel, and that I'm a fool.
Yet you don't reply, and I wonder why.
For I can only see my mirror image,
and know the illusion of my face,
But my soul longs to know
how I look through your eyes.
   Richard S. Fifoot

I Am

I am a happy guy who enjoys peanuts
I wonder what they pack styrofoam in when it's being shipped
I hear the sneezing of people in the pollinated world
I see a colorful cow walking to market
I want a year's supply of animal crackers
I am a happy guy who enjoys peanuts.

I pretend I am the game show host on Wheel of Fortune
I feel as clean as Diana Ross when I step out of the shower
I tough the morning smog with my toenails
I wonder if I'll get a good grade on this poem
I cry when Ward argues with the Beaver
I am a happy guy who enjoys peanuts.

I understand Gumby is made of clay
I say without the sun it would probably be dark
I Dream of Jeannie
I try to do good on my poems
I hope Gumby never joins the skinheads
I am a happy guy who enjoys peanuts.
   Travis Lewis

To Understand

I just don't understand anymore.
I wish I could be a bird and soar.
I'd glide across white clouds and though trees
Forgetting the awful times,
Just sitting back and enjoying the breeze.
Without a doubt,
I'd let my feelings come flowing out.
I'd take the time to think things through
So I could bring my life to anew.
I'd want the whole world to see
That I'd found a way to believe again, as it should be.
If I could soar like a bird,
I could find many answers I need to know
So my life could easily flow.

Tia Spence

I Will...

As the years gather round me like grandchildren
I will wear my wrinkles proudly and with style
Knowing full well that I've earned them.
I'll let my hair go gray and curl if it wants to.
I'll put flowers in it and wear long dresses
With silvery scarves and earrings that don't match.
I'll crawl into the tub at night with a book
And not come out till the next day.
I'll sing out loud and perhaps off key.
I'll write poems in coffee houses and on buses
And late at night when I can't sleep.
I'll learn to play with toys again.
I'll bake more cakes and gain a little weight
And cook dinner when I want and if I want.
At restaurants, I'll embarrass my children
Sending back food when it's not hot enough.
I'll talk to myself out loud and give good audience
And I'll remember always to talk to strangers
Until the years pile up and cover me
and my grandchildren are gathered round my grave.

Tamar Fagin

To My Brother

On this your 35th birthday I wanted to give you something just from me,
I wanted to let you know how I feel about you this February 19, 1993.

A poem that I composed myself seems just the right way,
To let you know how much I love you now and every day.

I remember when you were born, you had no hair and was very tiny.
I thought he must not like us, for you were always whiny.

As you grew, I always looked upon you as more than just my brother,
I fed you, changed you, protected you as if I were your mother.

I thought by ignoring and even helping you out of Jams,
That you would be alright, but we both know that was just a scam.

I didn't always like you or the things you said and did,
But I always loved you for you seemed to be just a lost kid.

Up until three years ago, a family unit we were not,
There was a lot of wasted time, lies, love and who knows what.

So many things and people have changed,
God it seems, our lives are to be rearranged.

No longer are you lost and alone but are loved by us,
We are a family, together, forever, bound by love and in the Lord
We must trust.

Sandra Anderson

"Myself"

I have to live with myself, and so
I want to be fit for myself to know:

I want to be able as days go by,
Always to look myself straight in the eye:

I don't want to stand with the setting sun
And hate myself for the things I've done.

I want to go out with my head erect
And be proud of myself with all respect:

But here in this struggle for fame and pride,
I try to walk tall with no shame to hide:

But I never can hide myself from me
I simply see what others are able to see:

So whatever happens, I want you to see
The new person I am respectful and self conscience free!

Richard David Diaz

Untitled

   I touch my head,
   I touch my chin,
Then I do touch my skin, for there is where I feel sin.
   I touch my ears,
   I touch my eyes,
For now there are tears, were once there were lies.

Roy Olsen

I Too, Once Was A Child

Once upon a time...
I too, was a child
My face small and mild...
My cheeks so rosy..
And my little hands, holding a big chocolate chip cookie...
Mom looked so big, as I looked up at her...
As she smiled, as she wiped my little face..
I thought, this will be wonderful
If this was always the case..
But, one day it came to be...
That I was not no longer, that little child
Who's mind would ponder...
Now, I'm all grown up, and still deep down inside..
I still remember being a child
With a sincere smile...
Holding true to my big heart...
Even thou the world is cold and cruel
I still hold true
That sweet little child, deep inside my heart...

Saundra Diamante

Thoughts...of You

I thought about you the other day
in a sort of melancholy way.
I wonder if you think of me too
in the same way I think of you?

Often, I look around at the faces that I see
Are you somewhere out there
also looking for me?
How does one go about searching for a face
from yesterdays time and space?
I never thought I would be haunted
by such a memory
one that has seemingly lasted for eternity.
What would I do
If ever I should run in to you?

Pamela D. Faulkner

Emergence

Thru all the ages of time
I tarry not on the worries of a world
For there are places and times not available to all
I fear not the unknown
For it is the substance of which we all come and when we leave
We have lived for a purpose
A purpose for which we may now be blessedly ignorant
I stand on a mountain
Before me I watch the clouds go by
Yet are they the ignorant who chose to forget
Was there nothing back there worth remembering knowledge
Knowledge, that love is the strongest force in the universe
In all the vast blackness that is far, far
More complicated than wishing upon a star
On choosing to ignore that which eludes us for now
To the hawk high in the tree
And the majestic eagle
To the winds I send my spirit
Carry me home, for I am tired enlighten my soul
Lift me up take me home.
Patricia Patterson

"The Path He Paved"

I've touched the place where Christ was born, I've visited the tomb.
I sometimes wonder what Mary thought, when Christ was in her womb.
I've seen his crucifixion place, way up on a hill.
Mother Mary watched her son die, my tears begin to well.
To think this man has died for me, to ensure me lifelong dignity.
If I follow the path he's paved, not in vane, my life be saved.
When I pass through to the next dimension, may I be so strong.
To confess my sins to God almighty, the many things that I've done wrong.
God will know of all my sins, well before I speak.
May I speak with purity, to God my heart so meek.
Thank you God for being there, with all your warmth and grace.
May someday I be so blessed, that I may touch your face.
Susan L. Kline

"Within The Ancient Walls"

Walking down the alleyways
I sense a history that has come before me.
The Jerusalem stones are filled with glory;
Her houses tell the unknown stories.

Winding through the streets of old,
I can hear the sound of children playing
While women sneak behind the walls
And men are wrapped in fringes, praying.

So many miracles have come to be
Inside this city of divided unity.
And yet, there is still a missing link
Which cannot be found among the rubble and stink.

We have not yet travelled as a pair
To find our way together down the ancient thoroughfares
And experience the wonders that are told
Within the gates of Jerusalem of Gold.

Until the day when we shall find
Our love among the city's art,
I'll have to hold you close to me
And place a kiss upon your heart.
William Robert Bronstein

Hidden Beauty

As I look upon the stars at night,
I see your twinkling eyes.

As I gaze at the morning sun,
I see the brightness of your face.

As I listen to your voice,
I hear a sweet melody.

For, your beauty, character, purity
Is a precious gift from God that you cannot hide—
As you are only showing your true nature.

Yes, you possess all these qualities —
And I feel privileged to understand them
And impart it to you personally.

So, go my fair lady, and continue to shower
Your graces, for I will forever be thankful...
Samuel G. Balocating

Souls

In Dreams,
    I see your eyes, and through them, your soul.
It tempts me.
    It draws me close to you.
Deep, inside of you.
    Gently, I let go, and you wrap me tenderly
Into your being.
    Feelings overwhelm me in a rapid, rush of passion.
I breathe deeply inside of you, giving you all
    Of myself, as we breathe as one.
Softly, slowly, we hold each others souls,
    And speak intimately with our hearts.
We gather strength and compassion and love
    From each other and give it freely for the
world to see.
    In reality,
I look into your eyes, and you look into mine.
    And our Souls touch.
And our dreams come true.
Tina M. Poston

Different Eyes

As I sit here, wishing to be different,
I see the world in all of it's different shapes and colors.
I see myself sitting in all of these confusions,
Wishing to be different.
Then I see the homeless, sitting there on the street,
Also wishing to be different.
They sit there wondering.
Not wondering if they should buy that dress in the store window,
But wondering if they are going to eat a meal that day.
Now I am haunted with a vision of death.
A vision of children who have died young,
Children who died because of parents who have made mistakes.
I once again see myself,
Though I am not wishing to be different.
I am wishing for them to be different,
For them to have everything I have.
Parents, a house, food, and health.
I will never again wish to be different.
For I already am.
Stephanie Hampton

Appreciating Not Understanding

Walking down the mountain,
I see the river. It shines.
Reflecting its memories
onto my skin.
I try to listen to its conversation,
but I cannot listen cannot comprehend.
I look to the stars blinking vigorously
like they are speaking in code.
Sending messages which are thousands
of years old.
But I don't understand!
I hear the wind blowing.
It travels into my ears
screaming about what's happening in the world
and telling me where it's been.
But my ears are not friends with the wind.
They can't comprehend.
I was not supposed to understand!
But to enjoy them as friends!
Robert L. Pepper

Doorway To Immortality

She grasps my hand so tightly
I see her veins
The pale skin stretched taught over dry bones
She's crying
Her head slumps and she rests her shoulders
Not so grand a finale
I Reach for my sweater and look around
I should leave
It's cold here, I shiver
I'm all alone, but for the lingering essence
Of one who's left before me
In the silence of the stillness a tear falls
A crystal plummeting slowly, now quickly
To meet the cold death of my leg
The door closes.
Rebecca Lee

Just For You

Here I am. I'm walking in the garden.
I see a pretty rose.
Should I pick it for my baby?
Will she kiss me? Who knows?
I walk over to it.
Should I pick it? Well I might.
Just looking at it brings chills
It is such a beautiful sight.
If I don't pick it- with the daisies it will live.
Such peace and meaning it will give.

I think I'll pick it. It means so much.
It means I love you and your so soft to touch.
This flower is so special, I should know.
I watched it climb. I watched it grow.
There is not that many flowers, like this one.
There are just a few.
It is so very special,
That is why I picked it.
Baby, this rose is just for you!
A. James Lewis

Where Did They Come From?

I see a bird, and a sheep herd. Where did they come from?
I see a cat, it's holding a rat! Where did they come from?

Have you ever heard of God. Glad to see you nod.
He is the creator, the originator.

I see a man jog, everyday with his dog. Where did they come from?
I see a flower, up high in a tower. Where did they comes from?

Do you see God? Is he holding a rod?
He has a son, and only one.

I see a hog, it's chasing a frog! Where did they come from?
I see a boy, playing with a toy. Where did they come from?

Jesus is the name that brought Him his fame.
He died on the cross for everyone's sins.
It was a great loss but now there are hymns.

I see a bee, it's headed for me! Where did it come from?
I see a snake! Oh, it's only a fake. Where did it come from?

The question is "Where did everything come from?"
Not from a crumb not even a drum.
God has made everything big and small. So where did they come from?
From God and that's all!
Swati Vyas

The Sailor's Tale

As I was looking across the sea,
I saw someone staring back at me.
Her hair was that of a fireball,
how tall she was I can't say at all.
From the distance I could see,
her eyes so deep staring back at me.
Big golden shells she wore for a shirt,
and a long silvery tail made due for a skirt.
She sang out across the waves,
a deadly song so the old sailors say,
"Come to me from the land above,
to my world below of undying love.
Come with me to the bottom of the sea,
and make passionate love to me."
Shall I go with her to the depths below?
My answer to that my friend is,
"No."
For I am not a love sick nave,
nor do I want a watery grave.
Dawn Henderson

Immortalized

D—deeply and dearly loved by many
I—immaculate, immeasurable, immersed in grace
A—articulate, ascendent, not having to be ashamed
N—not lacking in character, memorable in all ways
E—eager, enthusiastic, earthy and easy in mannerism
M—melanotic mentor, married in a beautiful ceremony
I—illuminating idol, impelled to speak out
C—constructive, considerate with congenital love
H—happy and hasty like Helios driving the 4 horse chariot
E—epitomize her not
L—lamenting is good for the soul, but let her go
E—embalm her now, for she remain in memory
D—deceased from this physical life
U—unbridled from heavens greetings
N—nightmarish terror no more
C—cleansed from litter and impurities
A—amidst the heavenly clouds and rays of sun
N—nearer and dearer to the Creator above
Trilbia D. Coe

The King Is Coming

I saw a horse up in the sky, and it was walking down.
I saw a man upon the horse, and he wore a golden crown.
I heard a man rushing in, on "his" head was not a crown.
He looked like the man upon the horse, but his toe nails made me frown.

The people clamored, it's the Lord, the Lord.
I told them this is not true.'
The Lord doesn't have dirty toe nails,
It's Satan...He's trying to fool you...

His toe nails were long and dirty, and on his head there was no crown.
But all the people loved him, and to his feet they all bowed down.
I said, "The Lord's still coming", REPENT, REJOICE, BELIEVE.
This isn't Jesus, but Satan, he's here only to deceive.

If you think you see Jesus coming, look him over head to toe.
If he has no crown and dirty toe nails, with "him" do not go.
He'll try to snare you in his trap, but escape is yours today.
Kneel down and ask forgiveness, REPENT, when you pray.

Be ready for his coming,
Watch both night and day.
Because the Lord is coming...
It's time...PREPARE THE WAY

Peter T. Van Bysteren

In The Safety Of The Night

As my love lays curled in my arms, wrapped safe within the night
  I run my fingers through her hair and let her know I'm there.
We hold each other close and there, under the covers in the night
  there is love so fair.
No strangers; no danger; no threat of loneliness.
  Just love and sweet caress as sleep calls with tenderness.
We slip to dreams of yesterday, eager for tomorrow
  to wake again in love as friends,
  to share our joys and sorrows.
Peace...Peace as I sleep,
  the love so my life curled close in my arms.
My heart; my love; my life; safe from harm.

Anton P. Orth

Four Leafs

I once found a four leafed clover - and that day I met you.
I realize now what a wondrous day that was
What possessed you to find me still eludes me.
What keeps you there for me, I couldn't say.
But I marvel everyday -
You caught me by surprise.
Wasn't looking, but was found.
By something twinkling, sparkling and bouncy.
I know that someday I'll find myself,
Questioning how I could have possibly let you slip away,
And knowing I'm a fool for life.
Or having you there with me, and not recalling what a remarkable gift
I've been blessed with.
But I'll always thank my maker,
for the brilliant light you brought into my life.
Into the future I cannot see -
But as long as I breathe, I'll forever know,
that four leaf clovers are rare, and that I love you.

F. R. Grant

To The Men And Women Of Desert Storm

I'm sorry you had to leave right away.
I pray God keep you all safe,
Each and every day.
For you're the United States best,
Who have come to the call.
You stand for pride and integrity,
You represent us all.
You do your best we know you can,
Even if you do have to deal with Saddam.
May your stay there be short and your pride stand tall,
For our prayers are with you one and all.
Our flags will hang and our yellow ribbons too
Just to show you that we are in support of you.
We won't take them down, till you all come home
Just to show you that you don't stand alone.

Sandra A. Epps   Harper, KS

Softly He Speaks, Tenderly He Listens

Softly He speaks, it comforts my soul
I pray for His strength, He helps me to grow
The pain and the sorrow will desert me and then
My heart shall be filled with happiness again
His love drowns the hurt
I must trust and be true
It is then in His mercy shall I live my life through
He shares His spirit with all who believe in His name
Tenderly He listens to thoughts of joy and of shame
Forgiveness shines eternal and ever flows His love
His caring eyes can see all creation from above
Patient in His wisdom He waits and guides our days
Father, we give our souls to You with everlasting praise
My fear has now gone, now beyond darkness there is light
I feel hope and understanding
My spirit shall take flight
May I feel You in my life
I open my heart to Thee
Let me feel Your presence, Lord
For then I shall be free....

Rhonda Jo Springer

Untitled

The decision was very easy for me,
I only hope that you will see.

Does it matter that I knew the hour, the who, the why, the when
Or that I didn't bother to stop and pick up the pen?

I couldn't leave without letting you know,
I really did love you so.

I wanted to give you joy all through your life,
But I only made you sad by being your wife.

It is of no consequences how we leave this earth,
But to look at your soul to see what you're worth.

It will not be I who will sit lonesome through the night,
It will not be I who will cry till dawn's light.

Although I'm willing to take the blame,
I can see now it was all just a game.

Goodbye my love, let your life go on,
Only my physical body will be gone.

I will miss you I think, in my after-life,
Because for so long I was your wife.

I hope that you will live a full life,
And maybe someday you'll get a new wife.

Patricia A. Eich

Why?
In Memory of "Grandpa" Bennet Ballestad
Why did you leave me when I wasn't ready to let you go?
I needed you here or didn't you know?
For I was young and didn't understand,
But you and me made a two man band.
The pictures of you and I
Are now reflection in my eye.
When you died you left me here.
Why when you know I love you so dear?
You made me laugh; you made me cry
And when I think about you tears come to my eye.
If only I could see you I'd hold so you couldn't go,
But why is it angels don't fly this low?
The stories you told me and the way you would hold me
Are carved in my heart and the next time we meet we'll never depart.
I love you!
  Timothy Eric Schultz

My Beautiful Birds
What in the world are the birds chirping about
I must get up and find out
Aha it's the rain, hurray hurray
We have been praying for it in vain:
At last now it makes everything smell so sweet.
That high pitch sound the birds are making
Is for the joy they find in the rain,
Yesterday they were all lined up on the telephone lines,
Looking and searching for just a breeze
Now they have all flown into the trees,
Enjoying the rain on the leaves,
I used to feed them on my porch;
They were fun to watch as they hopped about.
But I had to stop: My neighbors complained.
Do you think birds are stupid
Not so: They won't dirty where they eat.
But I miss watching them, with their antics
And hopping on their little feet.
  Carolyn M. Warner

I Was....
I was there to rock you to sleep,
I made sure you had enough to eat.
I was there to kiss your toes,
I was there to wipe your nose.
I was there to give you a hug,
I was there when you caught your first bug.
I was there when you were sick,
I was there to be strong for you like a brick.
I was there when you fell off of your bike,
I was there to tell you, you were alright.
I was there when you drove your first go-cart,
I was there when you got your first broken heart.
I was there when you picked your first flower,
I was there when you built your first tower.
I was there through think or thin,
It doesn't make a difference if you lose or win.
I knew you were smart and clever,
I will love you forever.
  Robin Moore

My Legacy To Uncle
There was a man whom I admired oh how
I loved him so; He told me I'd be a painter,
that was so many years ago.

He taught me to play the Harmonica, and called
me his little tee-tot; he's been gone for six years
now and those memories are all I got.

I'm all grown up now, Uncle, I've learned to love
a man; I know I want to be an artist but I
acquire you're poetic hand.

I remember a poem you wrote for my mother
on mothers day; I've kept it all those years, and
in my heart it will always stay.

Well up there in the clouds, it must get lonely
Sometimes; but I think about you often and remember
that you will always be by my side.
  Shandra Carlson

Vanp I
Betrayal shoots through every fiber of my being.
I loved and my beloved just took
   what I offered
But I failed to enjoy it
and spit it out and withered me.
Oh God! Lord Jesus!
How can I face myself with
   What I've done to us, with us?
I am nothing more than an emptiness,
A bottle with a few bitter drops
   of regret and sorrow
For the loss of my innocence,
My self-respect,
and myself.

To you who bears this guilt, I feel.
I empathize. 'Twill hurt, and I
   can offer you no remedy except
Understanding
Oftener a bitterer pill to swallow
   Than the Original Guilt.
  Susan Cates

Untitled
   Sitting on my front which I do everyday,
I look up at the Heavens, the stars, the milky way,
A bright light came down and flashed quickly before my eyes,
then moving much slower, then stopping, not wanting to pass by.

   The light drew near so bright, such warmth U was receiving,
nothing on earth ever compared to this great feeling.
Staring into me right thru my soul, yet with no eyes,
A smile we shared as it slowly floated deeper inside.

   I felt it dance so happily in me.
We laughed with such love, so careless and free.
I knew what it was right from the start,
For only an angel from God could touch me in my hurt.

   It whispered these words is sincere loving and kind.....
"I love you my child go seek and find, many others who need
me who are lost and blind.
   Tell them of your new sight, even if only a few,
and I also will love them,
as I do you".
  Deborah McDevitt

A Time Of Solitude

Upon the beach on a mound of sand,
I look at the clouds, the face of God
Where the sea meets the land.
Sitting a top a beautiful sand dune, I listen
To the soft breezes that whisper a harmonious tune.
I feel so relaxed, not even a care;
I watch crabs wash ashore and in a second, they disappear.
I wonder while listening, and thinking how I can hear;
The huge, ominous waves crashing on the cliffs that lie near.
And while enjoying that quiet, seashore peace,
I realize that my problems drift into the sky and soon cease.
God made all this beauty—this is His turf,
The bellowing clouds that drift high, and the gulls that comb the surf.
If you are ever down, lack hope and feel despair,
You can lie on dune and discover tranquility and solace there.
As for me, I shall lie on this beautiful mound of sand,
And enjoy God's beauty, where the sea meets the land.
Paula Ann Landrum

A Place Called Home

I want to go home and sleep in my bed,
I long to forget the pain and loss.

During my life I've been called son,
Brother, husband and father.

As a young man I left the home with my parents
And made a life with my friend, my wife.

For 50 years I supported our family by working in the mill
And together we survived the depression and the wars.

As the years passed my children married and moved away,
Having their own families to raise.

Tragedy struck and my wife passed away,
My life was shattered, but still I went on.

I gave up my home to live with my son,
But fate was cruel and took him from me.

Oh, the tragedy. Oh, the grief. It's too much to bear,
But once again I made it through.

Into my daughter's house I moved next
Until Alzheimer's stole my life.

Now I live here, in a rest home for the elderly,
Endlessly pacing, waiting, searching, for a place called home.
Tracy L. Smith

The Color Is Gray

The color is gray even though the sun shines
I live life day to day, and lost all that is mine
There is nothing but death, and chaos, and gloom,
So why is this horror allowed to resume
Words have lost meaning, feelings don't show
They say run, so we run enduring blows as we go
I once had a family, but now they're just thoughts
I've seen men speak of faith, but have faith I cannot
My cares and concerns were for everyone else
In these camps of corrosion my concern is myself
My God was my savior, but what the truth brings
Is that God has stepped down and now Satan is king
I believe in one thing, I have to move on
The sun remains shining, but the light is far gone
Russell Bustamante

The Lord Holds My Hand

The Lord is my shepherd my hand he holds
I knew he is with me where ever I may go
The roads I have traveled have been so long and dark
He has always been with me he never left my heart
He has lead me to people who were his true friends
He has shown me his love time and time again
Through laughter and tears he has always been near
He has taken my hand walked me through all my fears
There is no one other who can hold me so tight
For the Lord is my shepherd through the darkest of night
There is nothing I have that the Lord hasn't given me
The very air I breath the flowers and the trees
This world is so crowded it's people are so cruel and cold
Lord where would I be if my hand you didn't hold.
Shirley A. Bascko

The Game

As I walked out on the field and looked in the stands
I heard the great roar of the crowd as they threw up their hands.
The only thing I could do was stand there and stare
As emotion, intensity and nervousness ran through the air.

I was so filled with fear and excitement that I started to cry
But the tears soon turned to adrenaline as the coach slowly walked by.
To get us all focused, we counted to ten
Together we would fight, and together we would win.

But if we lost, we'd still have our pride
We would never depart from each other's side.
Together we win, and together we lose
A team we will be, that's what we choose.
Shawn R. Barrett

Sounds In The Night

As I lie awake, in my bed at night.
I hear the leaves blowing through the night
The thunder crashing,
The wind is howling,
I wonder if it will be all night
I pull the covers above my head.
To hide my tears, and to hide my fears.
I hear my mother walking down the hall
My father sounds like crickets running through the walls.
They open the door turning on the light.
They're telling me every thing's alright.
As I fall asleep as the hold me near
I have no tears, and I have no fears
As I hear the sounds drifting through the night
I do know now it will be alright.
Charlayne Oram

Abuse Across This Nation

There is abuse across this nation.
I hear it all the time on the tube in the news.
You know what I mean, you hear it too. I know you do..
..There are abuse children in shelters or on the
street, living of fear and harsh realities.
..There are abused seniors whose cries are seldom heard
or mistaken for the casualties often plagued by the elderly.
Why must our glorious nation be have in such a manner?
..The child did not ask to be born nor did he bid you
to manhandle him in such a way.
He only implores you to love him unequivocally.
..The senior did nothing to warrant such disparage,
for she raised you and nourished you
in your years of young.
So I say unto this nation, break the shackles of
abuse and rise above it into the palms of protection
and savor the bounty.
Sharel Williams

Untitled

I have seen hatred in his eyes,
I have felt it in his hands as they trembled with
  abomination for me.
Let me run free,
Take the chains that bind my swollen purple wrists.
I have to breathe,
And I want to live for the happiness of your love.
As I reach out to you, unlock me from his chains.
So I can feel my blood circulating,
My arms moving with freedom.
But Still...
I can feel his presence in my soul.
As I shake my head from the fear in which I feel,
I realize that he is in me, until you take me in your arms,
And show me the light,
For the darkness was too much,
And I have forgotten how to love.
   Rosemary Masters

I Have Been

I have been the rain and I have been the snow...
I have been a stone on a mountain and the stream that slides past
   the meadows...
I have been the hill that has no end...
I have been the highway that leads nowhere...
I have been the sky with clouds and the storm that nourishes the
   innocent and homeless...
I have been the tree that hovers amongst the forest animals and the
   flowers that die during certain seasons...
I have been the grass that gives cushion and the mud that causes
   confusion...
I have been the ocean that crashes on the rocks and cliffs that
   block its paths...
I have been the eagle and the cry it gives...
I have been the deer that stands in silence and the prey it conquers...
I have been the mountains with open views and the caves they hide...
I have been the friend of many and the need of one...
I have been the celebration of today and the achievement of tomorrow...
But mostly I have been the one God's hands made and in His power
   I survive and belong...
   Teresa Rogers

The Price Of A Chicken

What is the price of a chicken?
I guess it depends on how much a man is willing to pay
people buy, and sell, they buy and sell all the live long day.
How come there is no tally on the price of a human soul.
Could it be they have become like a chicken,
quickly bought and quickly sold.
And who is left to keep the tally of the price of a human soul.

Is there no one to speak for those who's blood cry out from the ground?
Where are all the counselors and all the judges, can no one at all be found.

No! cried a voice from the past we don't have time for tears;
these things are nothing new, they have been going on for
hundreds and thousands of years.

You see a chicken is very important a belly it will fill,
and him who does the selling, it will help fill his till.

You see the dead don't do nothing, they don't make money, buy,
sell or build. And the dead or soon forgotten under the burden
of tomorrow's bills.
   Sharlene Ruffin

"Lost To The Sea"

Below the waters churn upon stones, lands of time washed in and out
   with the tides
The cliffs still green with spring, stand firm refusing to be swept
I feel the wind from behind, tossing my hair in front of my face
The tendrils and curls lick my cheeks like mad waves
Carefully, I shift and peer into the roaring depths beneath
All that was left had been taken by the sea
Orphan to the world and hills, I watched the sails cross the horizon
Soon the sun would set, and darkness would fall over the isle
Darkness always seem to follow these moments
The saline air tinges my throat as I lean closer to hear the pounding waves
Like demons they hiss and spit, crashing as if lightening upon the shore
What power must lurk behind the wispy foam and gentle pools
Power enough to kill and drown, to hide treasures deep and scatter
   families wide
All that is lost to the sea is beaten into the shore one grain at a time
"Father!" I cried out to the sea "I'm not afraid of this green beast!"
Learning further, the wind thrust me dangerously forward
Suddenly, the waves burst upon the cliffs and paralyzed my sight
Reaching to wipe the salt from my burning eyes, I realize my mistake
   too late
Falling, I feel the currents crying out to consume me, a hungry beast
Churning me against the rocks, until I am returned from whence I came
   Wendy Lazenby

The Horns Of Dilemma

How solemn does the moon stare from above
when the sky bleeds dew for the morning flowers?
Where is time when there is no Love?
When chance is adrift caution lingers for hours.
What about life and its lack of security?
What about perfection and the realm of impurity?

Shadows of doubt are subject to change the world:
an epilogue of fate, all records of logic
are governed about in eternity's swirl.

Endless uncertainty, artificial regulations, unaccepted society proves
   to be hip;
Life is full of expectations, when nothing is something and something's
   a trip.
My classic treasure of parallel thoughts
show signs of acceptance but still has it's faults.
In this season of mists and mellow blindness,
a medium of certainty, a flower of time;
far greater than all is pure loving kindness.

The horns of dilemma, on the horns of dilemma, crashing the skies with
   mulberry highs,
uncertainty spaces the mastering races.
Suspended judgement collects haziness;
a darting motion streaks over the ocean and I'm riding with time, on
   the horns of dilemma.
   J. Jerry Stup

Reconciliation

As each new day weaves patterns in our lives, both gain and loss,
We find ourselves somewhere between Christ's manger and His cross.
The beauty of the angels' song as they proclaim His birth,
Falls silent in His borrowed tomb that ends His life on earth.
Can we always view the manger surrounded by its peace?
Or does living sometimes weave in a pain that will not cease?
If we accept the Christmas child and in His love abide,
We also can confront the cross, for Christ walks by our side.
We do not fear the darkest night, instead we see His star.
It tells us that our Savior lives, and those we love not far.
The manger beckons. Come, let's kneel. We know not what's in store.
With certainty and praise rejoice! We live forevermore!
   Marjorie W. Lyon

It's Only Beginning

Rain in my eyes,
snow on the mountains,
simple good-byes,
and it's only beginning.

Strengthened encouragement,
camouflaged secrets,
Fortunes withheld,
and it's only beginning.

Outraged remarks,
captured illusions,
disregarded consideration,
and it's only beginning.

Rain in my eyes,
snow on the mountains,
simple good-byes,
and it's only beginning.

Tanya Bamber

Love Senses ... Lost

I've seen the sight of love,
smelled the scent of love,
tasted the flavor of love,
felt the touch of love,
and heard the voice of love.

But...
I haven't seen the sight of love
since the last time I saw you,
smelled the scent of love
since the last time I smelled your scent,
tasted the flavor of love
since the last time I tasted your kiss,
felt the touch of love
since the last time I felt your touch,
nor have I heard the voice of love
since that last time I heard your voice.

I fear that I shall never
see, smell, taste, feel, or hear love again;
now that you are gone.

Veronica Davis

The Inhumanity Of Traffic

Many stand,
sit,
wait on the side of the road,
staring at the traffic
racing,
rushing,
speeding by,
never stopping
for the person
standing,
sitting,
waiting on the side of the road
for the despair,
the courage
to step into
the racing,
rushing,
speeding
traffic.

Rocquel Lynn Hejtmanek

Our Fathers Have Gone To Rest

It has been a week,
Since you have lain with empty arms.
Life devoid of all its charms.
Heroes of the skies,
Now with God lies.
Metal is torn,
Life so forlorn,
A flying machine.
You are told to look ahead,
Though the days are bleak and cold.
Just waiting for someone to hold.
Little lives are past.
A time to grow up,
Too fast.
Pain untold,
Grief so bold,
Just waiting for someone to hold.
A land and people scarred,
Need much time to heal.

Shelly Anderson

Untitled

Window
sill
silent
still

Drapes
draw
lines

Night
contains
cement
consent

You're
so
pretty
in
the
dark
he repents

Marje Schiller

Little Child In Darkness

Little child in darkness,
Shh...do not tremble anymore.
Take this time to rest,
It is you who I've come for.

Place your tiny hand in mine,
Together, we shall rise,
And leave this madness all behind,
This world, I should despise.

I shall wipe away your blood-stained tears,
And protect you from the rain,
Come, into my arms, yes, I am here,
To kiss away your pain.

Stop crying now my little one,
For it is on this glorious night,
All your human days are done,
   You are now,
   My Child of Light.

Linda Lee Douglas

The New Grandbaby

You should see our new grandbaby,
She's a love, the dear,
She's soft and sweet, the cuddly kind.
And we're so glad she's here.

She has hair of the loveliest brown,
And eyes of heavens own blue,
And the sweetest smile, but then,
I guess most babies do.

She is pert as a starlit summer night,
Fresh as a rain dripped dawn,
Sweet as a flower, petal fresh,
Gentle as a new born fawn.

You ask, "What's so special about this one?"
Well, I thought on that for awhile,
And I guess it's just because you see,
She is our first grandchild.

Vera L. Purkey

Simple Love

He liked green
She liked blue

He liked football
She liked movies

He liked steak
She liked chicken

"Let's go camping"
"I don't like roughing it"
"Let's eat out"
"I like your cooking better"

And thus they lived
Happy as could be

He loved that woman
With eyes of green

She loved that man
With eyes so blue

Rebecca Cole Erni

Spirit

If you could only see her the way I do
   She is warmer than the sun rays,
   Brighter than the milky way
   Softer than a petal of a rose,
   More caring than all of those.

If you could only see her the way I do
   A real woman of the world
   No others could ever compare with her
   Strong in the body and spirit
   More beautiful than the center of a rose
   A real woman deserving of only the
   purist of loves

If you see her the way I do,
   Understand the way I love her,
   Why I love her
   For she is woman and I am man.

Robert C. Litviak

Memories Of Christmas

When Mother Nature comes,
she blows her cool breath of life.
And our days once long,
move closer to our nights.

The bayou now full,
with her sweet summer tears.
She brings back to us,
memories of tranquil years.

Christmas bells begin to ring,
filling our lives with love and laughter.
To our life's book we add,
another Christmas chapter.

Christmas is the time to be,
with family and friends.
To create memories that will soon be,
Set free on southern winds.
Shannon E. Bonton

Am I Dreaming

Here I sit in this world of unknown
Set me free from this casual misery
In my heart I want to speak
The mind has control so I creep
By...by the thousands of people
Seeing...yet not seeing
What is it? Where am I?
Do I know?
Or can it be just in my mind
Maybe I'll awake
Finding this to be a lifeless nightmare
Like before, I relive it all
Does it not stop?
Someone tell me where does it end
RoShawn Hardin

Showers

They
send dirt swirling
down the drain
steamy oblivion
drowns all sounds
rids us of our guilt
and pain
and doubt
along with
undreamt dreams
and
silent screams
of tortures
that remain
unknown....
Guaranteed
to leave us
clean
Rebecca Ferguson

Alive

I can't feel any longer
I can't think any more
My eyes are dark with tears
I can't smile any more
and there are no more words
I can say.
Just hold me and make me live again.
Patricia M. Corrales

Love: Quest Or Question

Do you think love is overrated?
Seems that way once you've dated.
Do you think that sex is bait?
There are many who don't wait.
Have you met a couple losers?
Perhaps even a few boozers.
Are you waiting for prince charming?
How long you wait can be alarming.
Have you prayed on your knees
To be immune from all STDs?
Do you think the end is near,
Causing you to live in fear?
Love, was that the question?
Starting a major chain reaction.
Can the nineties be this painfully sour?
Why don't we leave it to our higher-
power?
Rachel Kia

A Passing

I had a call the other day
Seems a friend had passed away.
I know the Lord up above
Took a soul, a wife did love.

Its very hard for us to know
Why its someone's time to go.
Our tears run in complete despair
Wishing this loved one could still be there.

Keep in mind that what ever we feel
Say a prayer on our knees, we kneel.
He has not died, just gone away
We'll meet again another day.

So hold your head up high
Dry your tears and say not he died.
We'll meet again along the way
God's promise, each and every day.
Sheri Adams

The Language Fallacy

The emotion dies as it reaches the lips,
sealed forever in its silentness.
No words be speak the things we feel....
These words are something much less real.
No thoughts can find their utterances,
just foul sounds and utter un-sense.

The meaning shifts—the meaning changes.
The speaking of the world estranges
the very purpose from its conclusion.
We speak all fiction, fantasy, delusion....
  We SPEAK.
Jenny P. Jaus

Colorado

Where 'er the rivers roar,

Endless beauty,
  shore to shore;

Throughout the mountain tops,
  their beauties never stop.

Now we humans have destroyed,
  this wondrous country,
    still and void.
Jennifer Toles

Colors In Chaos

There are colors in Chaos.
  Sand sifts swiftly through the web
    Which covers all the grey
      As life comes to its ebb.

The day is far gone.
  The night comes swiftly on.
    Music jars the frame of being
      Which gently takes us home.

Echoes of the mind defer
  The sounds of silence still.
    There are notes we cannot hear
      Which speak and alter human will.

The Source of Being waits for all
  To answer faith with total grace.
    The others leer with unsuspecting gall
      While truth encapsulates our inner space.
J. Philip Klinger

Wing-Burst

The beach, in barren Arctic whiteness,
(Sand piles soft as fresh snow drifts),
Is stretched in yearning to the ocean,
Awaiting only summer's kiss.

Sea gulls stiff as frozen statues
watch the tides through narrow eyes,
Till an unseen vision bids them
SOAR IN WING-BURST
toward the skies.

The promise that's unveiled in nature,
In the birds and sand and sea.
Is that in stillness stirs the changing,
From what is, to what can be.
Mara Davis

unabashed in-

separable cheeky
ruddiness and involuntary
blushes rush to
fuel the true red of
sugar maple conflagrations
race quicker than all
cars across the hills
fire the panic of
the heart caught for life
in exorbitant red
contractions leaping
to your throat with
every palpitating falling
sumac leaf
Radka Donnell

Dark Angel

Play your hard for me my friend
  Pluck my heart strings till the end

Brush my cheeks with feathers of gold
  Help me wash away the cold

On a cloud I wish to sleep
  Lined with silver do not weep

Nourished by the milky way
  Float away I shall to stay
Sharon Cordero

Constantine

Your bridges valse with the wind
Rocked by "Caleches" in my memory
Your mornings on red mountains
Shining like fires
In the deepness of the sea
On your foggy holes
Like a branch I bent on my knees
In a prayer of pain and thankfulness
I feel breezy
I feel deezy
With tears and smile I turn
I keep your breath
Your heart is here
Around my head
Around the universe
You fill my loneliness
You are the most faithful love
Thank you to be you

Bariza Laib

Haunted By The Mud

I am haunted by the mud of earth the
rock that use it as a grave the root
that depths its soul so brave and
shoots the stem of strength to birth.

I walk upon the mud of day ragged wood
and stone of clay I hear a whisper soft
so sweet come near my dear and hear me
greet the thunder of water that fall as
snow of yesterday winter call.

Oh sweet grass of sugar that grow so
female cow can cud to let you know a
milk of milk of many blade of nourish
young so afraid creeping walking un-afraid.

So into age I do depart that which
nourished my sweet heart oh mud of earth
I improve give me peace which I adore
sleep well sleep well among the rock and
root their home as haunted mud I do dwell
oh dwell farewell farewell.

Helen Sherwin

Wind Chimes

Be still, and listen to the sound,
Ringing in the air, and all around.
Tubular in sound and in it's shape,
It's echoing voice you cannot escape.
Lay to sleep, and rest your weary mind,
It will sing to you, with music so kind.
Listen and cherish, the beauty of her song,
It sounds so gentle, and never wrong.
Each pitch, so different,... from the rest,
I hope the neighbors, won't protest.
Unless of course, they hate music and rhyme,
Relax and enjoy, the sound of wind chimes.

Joel Galindo

Halloween

Halloween is fun.
On Halloween you go trick-or-treating.
On Halloween you go to people's houses.
On Halloween you dress up.
On Halloween you get bags of candy.
On Halloween you always say, "Boo!!"

Randy Pierce

The Twilight Horseman

Powerful steed beneath his heel
riding night with arms of steel
with the moon's angelic embrace,
and the helm upon his face
he knows bravery and songs of deed
in battle he will always lead
and lo!
He leaves with the dawn,
to reappear with weapons drawn.

Ryan Mitchell

The Four Horseman

Ride on four men of evil fame
ride on your destiny acclaim
wish heavy heart
we share our fate
reluctantly
we seek our date
with evil lurking everywhere
no nation has this horseman's spared
the second one is also there
anguish sorrow and despair
the third
though stealthier than the rest
will reap a greater harvest yet
but the last
surveys the carnage bold
and from the body takes the soul

Robert J. Franciskovich

Machinery Of Weathered Pine

Defining the marvel of tears,
residing in the hollow
of a frown, upon the cliff,
standing in the midst of beauty,
twisting off the husks,
there, the lawn was eroded
by surf, the flames of winter.
Tight patience of standing
within the doorway without
needing to evade or run from
storms of claws,
this adventure was the center
of their practice. A decent
matter, the occupation of
gathering or of hunting for
the proper time and the
quietude of an abstract place
made a file of references.

Baron Joseph A. Uphoff Jr.

A Woman I Know

Her soulful eyes
Paralyzed our unarmed hearts
Dazing us like a motionless breeze

Her lingering lips
Captured our master minds
Confusing us with an addictive charm

Her vocal innocence
Seized our thoughtful wonders
Healing us like sun rising winters

Her affinial beauty
Frees my suspended soul
Bestowing eternal euphoria

Sun-Ki Cnoi

Lonely

Weeping eyes tears lost love
Reminiscing brilliance a morning dream
Sorrow filling a lonely void
Caressing thoughts of yesterday

Sunshine weeping grass glittering dew
Days passing to shattered tomorrows
Moon shadowing a starless sky
Time moving thru nature's tomb

Death whispering on silent winds
Burial clouds strolling in black space
Mind demented by suffering sorrow
Bloodshot visions of Dante's hell

Velvety hills of tortured jade
Mourning soul silently dying
Virgin veils of new white lace
Love sleeping in eternal peace

R. C. Perez

My Garden

There are flowers in my garden,
red and yellow, black and white.
Some are hiding in the shadows.
Others striving to be in sight.

Children are like all these blossoms.
Some are bright and very gay.
Others are shy, like the violet.
Each I tend throughout my day.

Shirley J. Hammil

Distance Between Life And Reality

The distance between
Reality and fantasy...
Is the difference between
Life and death

You can't be real
and still live in a dream...
Other's living, won't notice
the difference between...
Your life and their death

Slipping between the
cracks of truth
I realize, that I'm not free.

That my actions...
causes reactions...from others
leaving them in a space

Too large to fill
with just one thought
Therefore, your constant thought
will be rewarded, by my knowledge.

Daniel Koontz

"Youth"

And there lies the
Picture of Youth;
Under a tree,
Her long hair a
Myriad glistening pool.
Gazing up at the boughs that
reach to be near her innocence
As, knees spread, the wind
comes and
kills.

Stanci J. Cloud

"Melodic Magic"

A musical masterpiece
rang through my ears
denying bad thoughts
ignoring all fears,
entranced by this tune
and its hard driving beat
A thought crossed my mind
as I sat tapping feet,
the person who wrote this
A genius for sure,
has grasped a great feeling
but for me so much more!

Robert J. Coffey III

Dandelion

Dandelion, rowdy fellow,
Prodigal in blatant yellow,
Banned from garden, scorned, indicted,
Unconcerned as if invited,
You return with poise undaunted.
By your vigor I am taunted.
As my roses loved and pampered,
Watered, sprayed, lest growth be hampered,
Daily grow more weak and sickly,
You continue spreading thickly.
I give up; I am defeated.
All my patience is depleted.
Dandelion, lusty fellow,
I'll have to learn to love your yellow.

Virginia Jotter

"We Are All Alone"

Don't make me go to sleep.
Please I won't go and complete.
I can't care to obtain fortune and fame.
Is their someone to blame?
Can this be one persons shame?
I am afraid to live.
Others are afraid to die.
Someone please take my hand.
Someone please show me where to stand.

Jason P. Stoughton

All My Happy Things

My tricycle, my wooden swing,
Piggyback rides with brother Jim,
A birthday gift from a boy named Nick,
All my happy things.

My senior prom, a proud Dad and Mom,
A special beau, who I loved so,
Then wedding bells, gosh it was swell,
All my happy things.

Soon came Jill, then came Bill,
In my heart, I hear them still,
I'm lonely now, and days are long,
Cause all my happy things are gone.

Rosalie Cartwright

The Flag

Flag flapping in the wind.
Swaying back and forth.
Flag flying freely.

Tara Larivee

Halloween

Halloween, what a night!
People screaming in a fright.

Halloween, what a sight!
With evil sorcerers and courageous knights.

Hey, what's that scream?
Someone meet a ghoulish team?

There are witches all around
Seeking victims on the ground.

Draculas roaming here and there
Drinking blood everywhere.

Humans running to hiding places
To get away from frightful faces.

Maam? Sir? You don't need to fear,
It's that spooking time of year.

Kids are eating candy,
Princesses are looking dandy.

Fugitives are on the run.
Grab a costume and have some fun.

Get yourself a monstrous fleet
And lets go "Trick or Treat!"

Sokhoeun Nhoung

Letters

Scripting the feelings
Pen racing through the soul
Embracing words. Phrases
Moods charted in neat lines
Flowing out. Forward as signs
Expressing the designs of the mind
Face to face is better
Then the text of the letter
Or idle telephone chatter
You cannot read the eyes
Expressions or body inflection
Words on re-constituted wood
Not understood as they should
They cannot reach out
Shout the pain

William Cibbarelli

As A Seraph

Here I am sir,
One and only.
Your servant,
And a slave,
but now in spirit.

Here I am boss,
I hope and believe,
you remember me,
though now out of flesh.

Hey Mr! Why you running?
Didn't you call me?
Here I am, sir,
The one you sworn,
for his departure and no return,
but now in great flames.

Here I am once again;
Bringing you a message,
from one above your powers,
but now as a seraph
to tell you that; "Your days are numbered."

Godfrey M. Kgaphola

Pass It On

If you receive a welcome smile,
  pass it on to keep it in style.

If you receive a word of praise
  pass it on to insure it stays.

If you receive a pat on the back,
  pass it on to those who lack.

If you receive a hug from a friend
  pass it on helping others mend.

If you receive a financial lift,
  pass it on share your gift.

If you receive a faith that's strong,
  pass it on to those who long.

If you receive a message of hope,
  pass it on so others may cope.

If you receive an abundance of love,
  pass it on praising God above.

If you receive an answer to a prayer,
  pass it on, your blessings share.

If you receive God's blessings today,
  pass them on without delay.

Patricia Rivers

The Flower

The men have poured cement
Over the river bank.
They say, "We have conquered
Nature. We have locked it
Under a smooth even surface."
But I smile.
Yesterday I saw
A flower growing
Through a crack. Breaking out
Of the concrete cage.

Sherry Sung

Constantly

Constantly you are on my mind.
Our memories together
Can only be described
As one of a kind.
Constantly I wish you were here.
I would do anything,
For your body to be near.
Constantly I am dreaming of you,
And wishing at least one dream
Would come true.
Constantly thoughts of you
Appear in my head,
But it only wish for you to appear
next to me in bed.
Constantly I search for your love,
But I can never be found.
Constantly I cry,
Because without you
I feel like I will die.
Constantly you are on my mind,
Maybe one day your love I will find.

Tonia Bagby

Our Christmas Tree

In the spirit of this year,
our home has the smell
of Noble Fir.

With branches green and strong,
they bare the ornaments of
our family lore.

The little sombrero, the little shamrock,
and many more.

Some are old, some are new,
but most important,
they tell our family story.

You can look at each, and everyone,
but in our mind, we know
the story.

Our center piece this year
a white shiny bulb with golden trim
of two encircling hands holding a heart and
crown

THE CLADDAGH RING—FRIENDSHIP,
LOYALTY and MOST OF ALL
LOVE.
Tony C. Munoz

The Prey

Startled from his feeding ground,
or from his place of rest.
He's fallen prey to the predator,
must give this run his best.
Racing thoughts, running feet
to what safety zone?
Pounding heart, panting lungs,
this race cannot be long.
If he escapes he may live
to see another day.
If He's caught he's just a meal
served upon a tray.
Determination becomes the force.
Hunger is the drive.
But fate will be the only one
to take or save a life.
Stan Harris

To Whom It May Concern:

Cry for me a river
one that flows to the west.
See that it is strong enough
to race with the best.
Let it be beautiful
one with waterfalls of rage.
Let it have time enough
to play the angels games.
Let it be crystal clear,
Let it be free.
May there never be a dam to trap it.
May it someday reach the sea.
But let it see the world
and join where others flow.
Let it gather bits and pieces,
but always know its home.
And from whose tears this River begins
Let the eyes be mine
for each tear that falls
is an experience called growth inside.
Tanya Frazer

Love And Reality

Oh! Love, glorious love
One seen from far and near
Shining and sparkling in all corners
Like a lively star

In their minds.
Yet you abandon them
As a disloyal lover
In the face of reality;

Their minds winding in uncertainty
Fools and fighters, they are
In he end.

But yearning for you, they do,
With all their minds, with no wind,
In this spell nothing stops them,
Not even the gloomy gleam of reality
In their minds.
Okokon Sam Udosen

Patience

Prevailing in
one place

Conceiving
a spinning
wheel

Flourishing
from within

Im
per
cep
ti
ble

Met
a
mor
pho
sis
J. Sandler

Let Me See

Oh Father, how it grieves me,
Once the deed is done,
That I have said some thoughtless thing,
That may have hurt someone.

I truly want to be your child
To let you shine through me,
It's not my will, but thin O Lord
That sets the captives free.

I see faults, were you see wounds,
To be healed with balm of love.
With soothing words and arms that hold,
As gentle as a dove.

Please let me see with your eyes and ears,
My brothers cares and woes,
That my days, can sing your praise,
From now to evermore.
Sharie D. Clark

Paradise

"Paradise," now, lost or found,
On the long, winding road,
Approaching, "The fork in the sand,"
Hearing, in the distant, sound,
"A songbird's delight," with,

Fertile earth," A babbling brook, aglow,"
Among the ferns, and fragrant flowers,
Not, a cloud, "a pure blue heavenly sky,"

A slight breeze, "A symphony of angels,"
"A celebration of life, now,"

Now, fate, "destiny," so to avoid,
The loss, of "paradise," found,
For only, a short way more,
Lies, the telltale "fork in the sand,"
Beyond, awaits "greeds" menacing, "scorn."
Sofia Mary Ann Notariänni

Niagara Falls

I came to Niagara
On the boarder of Canada
As wild as Alaska
And pretty as ancient Ankara
Falls pull down her white hair
On the shoulder of the lair...

Niagara, like a giant we kiss,
I silently hearkened her
Falling...
With deep heart in a dreaming world
I knew she's attracted my soul!

I stood next to her
Feeling warmly
Like smelling water from Niagara
Like seeing her in the real dream
I was insane...!

Good-bye Niagara!
  See you one day not far away
As if you showed me your bright hair...
  ...heavenly-fair...
Paul Cao

The Marker

There's a granite headstone
  on my father's grave
  in a city
    near the sea

There is no marker
  where my mother lies
  no chiseled litany

My father left
  a huge stone house
  high on a harboured hill

My mother left a space
  in my heart
  that years of tears
  cannot fill...
Rhoza W. Bailey

Dreams

Into the night
On dragons wings they fly,
towards a dawning light
that over centuries lie.
Tis not a careless flight
upon a cursed breed,
But that of a mystic sight
upon a stealthy steed.
They go to a place in the future
Where dreams are borne to live.
There, fantasy becomes a reality
and nothing is there to forgive.
Only the pure of heart can enter
And children are that we know,
With dreams as their mentor
Quickly, quietly they must go
Into the night
on dragons wings they fly.
Teresa DeGreek Contreras

Edelweiss

We see her as a mountain flower
On a ledge so very high
Her face a glow in the autumn sun
A whisper of days gone by,

A love so cherished
By my wife and me,
A fragrance that will grow
Through all eternity,

So blessed are we
To have been a part,
Of this majestic flower
We hold in our heart,

Our tears that fall are ones of joy
Refreshing as a morning dew,
Slowly trickling down upon the flower
A new life, created for you.
Ray Montgomery

Thoughts of You

Your eyes that rival the ocean
on a clear summer day,
stir in my soul
like a light summer breeze
will fan the aspen's leaf.
I sit and watch
as drip by sunwarmed drip
the pine boughs reach upward for the sky.
The dreams of the unfulfilled
desires never forgotten
the silent stars
the standing trees
the breathless dawn anew
I sit and watch
where the sky loves the sea
the first light slices the blue
I sit and watch
and think of you.
Timothy Billings

Baseball in the Middle Ages

Sunset is blues'd with fire.
Old bones are iced.
Eye black runs down sweating faces.
We didn't win
when looking at the score.

We did by our pride, and joy
never loses.
Timothy E. Williams

Life Is A Song

Don't sing, you say?
Oh, yes,
You do.
You sing a song of Life

You sing a song of Love or hate
A song of joy or sadness.
A song that's loud and strong
Or weak and barely heard.

A song that soars to heaven
or sinks beneath the earth.
A song so sweet, so lovely
that Angels gather round.

You see, it's you, this song.
The notes, the words and rhythm
Are choices given freely by
God's great gift of Life.

Instead of singing solo
Let's sing our songs together
Become a mighty choir and
make a joyful sound.
Patty Rachel McClatchy

Love Thee

I hold thee
Oh I need thee
I comfort thee
Oh I lean on thee
I talk to thee
Oh I believe in thee.
I trust thee
Oh I kiss thee
I hug thee
Oh I touch thee
I love thee
Boyd

Eyes Of The Beholder

"What is a grandson", someone said
  Oh, a little boy with cheeks of red,
A freckled face and lots of noise,
  What else can be said of little boys?

"What is a grandson", Now I fear
  The words sound different to my ear.
Why, it's the wonderment of birth,
  The dearest treasure found on earth.

It's peace, it's hope, it's every joy
  All wrapped up in one little boy,
For the wonder of a grandson lies
  Within the fond beholder's eyes.
E. Lucille Revill

The Gang-Way

The people do not know around,
Of what goes on inside the town;
Or even what is going down
In the gang-way.

It's easy to label them as fools,
Misguided and born to break the rules,
But ignorance is their primary fuel
In the gang-way.

The life they choose, not always their own
Choice of face will but by peers and homes.
Until there is a line of drones
In the gang-way.

Black as soot or white as day,
There is no color that cannot play.
Children innocently lead astray
In the gang-way.
Robin Duerr

The Dreams of Others

Standing here at the edge
Of the sea I can hear
The yellow rose like
The sun beaming down on the dew
Each Sunday morning.
My heart is filled
With sadness as I sit here
And watch my father
Sail to a land
Of wonder
The boat whistles
Like a man dying
In crumpled sheets
And a new man
Is being born
From the waves
Which thrash against
The rocks and
Swallow the dreams of
others.
Rebecca Rinker

Brush Of Time

  Time is the painter
of the memories we share;
  Of the people we love,
and the people that care.

  And time paints the memories
of all that we try;
  Times that we laugh,
and times that we cry.

  Time paints the memories
of what used to be;
  Of love that was shared
between you and me.

  The paintings undone
no work will go on;
  'Cause the Time that we waste
is Time that is gone.
Rock Mullenix

Kissing the Shadows

I still blow kisses at the window,
of the house, where once you lived.
Climb imaginary ladders to reach
your bedroom ledge.
Fight for balance with your memory,
Love restrains accusing winds.
I watch you through a pane of glass
pull the covers from your bed.
kneel in silence, head bowed,
Prayers and Dreams untangled, said.
Off to sleep now darling one,
I'll be the blanket you tuck in.
I still blow kisses at the window,
as your eyes reflect my lips.
Hold time a prisoner chained and still,
with you alone to spend.
And though the house now dark and cold,
Without your warmth within,
Daily, I blow kisses at the window,
Where my heart, and you, still live.
   Robert C. Larkin

Relic

This was the forge
of the first
rainbow man

Once he extracted
a rainbow of dreams
from a charred witness

From the firewall
of a dying heart,
a pulsing morning star

And hammered out
a new world
long since gone
   Rob Meci

The Jack "O" Lantern

The spark of a candle, the spark
of bright in color of green, yellow
and red and a funny face indeed is the
Jack "O" Lantern.
The time of autumn with the
yellow of pumpkin.
The mellow of pie yes, pumpkin pie
but, the smell of the pumpkin yes,
indeed is the face of the lantern
true indeed, the turn of a knife
an eye to the left and one to the right
a triangle for a nose, a mouth of
a crescent with pegs for the teeth
a cut round the top, and off comes the top.
Inside a light of a candle.
Back with the top. In the gloom of the night
on a post of a fence. "Wow" what a
funny face the
face of the lantern, a Jack "O" Lantern.
   Raymond Draghi

Our Family

A family is made up
Of a mother and a dad
Sometimes they are happy
Sometimes they are sad.

A family is made up
Of children in the home
This is to assure us
That we won't be all alone.

A family is made up
Of our loved ones all around
One happy reunion
When they all come down.

Down on the farm is where we'll be
Praying and working so patiently
For our family a labor of love
Is our mission from above.

To train up a child in the way he should go
So others in this world will know
Our family is comprised of not only us
But JES plus-us.
   Terry Beagle

Sunset Over New Jersey

From the 39th floor
of a Manhattan skyscraper
just east of the Hudson River,
the periphery of planet earth
all along the horizon
over New Jersey
is enveloped in orange color.

In the sky
massive and dusky clouds border
the fire-like sunset
and press down the orange glow
submerging it below
earth's curvature.

As earth tilts and rotates
the interim between sunlight
and darkness decreases.

For a moment, I envision myself
floating weightless in space
watching this phenomenon
as if I am not from earth.
   Minos Milonas

By The Sea

As we leisurely walk
O'er the warm sand,
Soft is the touch
Of your gentle hand.

Like the timeless waves
Rolling ceaselessly ashore,
So shall I love you
Till time is no more.

As the warm trade winds
Softly caress the sea,
So shall I hold
Your love within me.

Let us walk together
By the shimmering sea.
Throughout all our days
And into eternity.
   William O. Anderson

The Nut Tree

I had a little
nut-tree, nothing
would it bear, but
a silver nutmeg, and
a golden pear. The
King of Spain's
daughter came to visit
me, and all was
because of my little
nut-tree. I skipped
over water, I
danced over sea, and
all the birds in the
air could not catch me.
   Sarah Scott

Skyride

Blue allows red to flirt with gold,
Now that its time for the sun to go.

So wide,
So high,
So glorious is the sky.
An abundance of colors
Entertain my eyes.
While observing as far as I can see,
I've forgotten what was troubling me.

Fluffy white figures float on by,
Providing room for the twinkle of night.

To glide,
To fly,
To be up in the sky,
I would ride on the clouds
And leave my worries behind.
While letting my troubled mind run free,
I've found beauty, tranquility and peace.
   Tara Miller

New Year

A new day is dawning
Not a cloud in the sky,
We must change our way of living
It will be hard but we must try;
There are fences to be mended.
There are gates that must be closed,
If we succeed in this universe
We must wake up and never doze;
We must look for all the good things
And forget about the bad,
Just smile and be happy
And this day will be the best
   You've ever had.
   Vivian Hooks

Loving You

   Love is such a lonely feeling,
no one knows this as much as me.
   As you don't love me,
I must suffer all alone.
   I never imagined being in love,
could be as painful as it is
until I fell in love with you.
   I do not fully understand,
why something so beautiful could,
hurt so much at the same time.
   The sweetest pain I'll ever,
know is loving you.
   Paula S. Ewing

The Truth Hurts

His eyes and hair are dark,
Not a blemish on his perfect face
His muscular arms and legs will
   never be mine to touch.

He's sweet and caring,
Considerate and understanding,
But none of these will he express
   towards me.

I meet his eyes in the hallway,
But his eyes shift to someone else.
She has stolen his heart.

My mind says I'll never receive his love,
But my heart says to wait forever.
Someday my heart will realize
   that the truth hurts.
   Shelley Hinton

Little Child Sittin' On The Corner

Little child sittin' on the corner,
No one to turn to,
No one to love you,
Your world seems so hopeless,
Sittin' on the corner,
Your heart is broken,
Dreams are shattered forever.
Little child,
Your world is gray and blue,
Where has life gone wrong
No one knows,
No one cares,
No one to turn to,
No one to love you,
What lies ahead for you,
Little Child,
No one knows!
   Sherry Trees

Confused And Bewildered

Look around and wander why,
No one sees our tears
or hears our cries,
the old are lonely
the young confused,
the bewildered are the middle,
filled with the blues.

We all struggle to understand,
who we are, what were about
Should we continue
or just stop and shout?

How do we stop this
merry-go-round,
or are we all
hell bound?
   Teena Tate

Untitled

I could wonder
of time
I could wonder
of here
I could think
of now
I could shed
A tear
   Gary Dale Pogue

Too Many Thoughts

I sit in my bedroom all alone
No one else here, no one home.
I sit here thinking of many things,
As a piano from my cassette player sings.
What am I thinking of I ask?
I do not know.

My thoughts, all jumbled up in my brain
Of joy, sadness, fear and pain.
They collide in my head
Turning to something I dread.
I just sit here, no longer knowing
Exactly what my brain is doing.

What am I thinking of I ask?
I do not know.
Am I insane?
This is profane.
I do not know what it is I'm thinking.
Please help me for fear I am sinking.
   T. Kipper

Shadows

No rest for the wicked
No help for the poor
Throw salt in my wounds
to settle the score

I'm backed in a corner
and willing to fight
A dog which is wounded
is likely to bite

So rest with the wicked
Give help to the poor
Feel guilt for the dying
Outside of your door

Don't do it to please me
for I'm not the one
Who lurks in the shadows
with my head to your guns
   Scott E. Behrends

What Will We Do?

A way of life is no longer.
No freedoms, no life.
Empty eyes look to question,
But no answers come.

What will we do?

Hope is no longer.
Children crying from hunger.
No home, nowhere to go.
Nothing.

What will we do?

A way of life is no longer.
No hope, no future.
Emptiness, loneliness,
No love.

What will we do?
   Rhonda Carrell

To

To know what was
Never known.

To feel what was
Never felt.

To emerge into a world
Of intertwining vitalities.

Brought together by a mere
Touch of fate.

Two souls
Destine to venture together.

Two identities
Forever becoming one.
   Blundon

Good-Bye

For six years I've keep hidden
My weeping and my pain.
I only cried but once back then
And now I cry again.

A hundred sobs of sadness,
A hundred years of sorrow
Afraid of what the future holds
Afraid to face tomorrow.

I miss you more than tongues can tell
And much more than I thought,
I miss the way you'd talk to me
And all the love you brought.

It hurt to know you left me.
It hurt to see you die.
But most of all it hurt me so
To have to say good-bye.
   Sarah Martindale

My Time Has Come

My time has come
   My time has passed
I believe all good things aren't
   meant to last.
      Things will come
      Things will end.
I am just wondering how my broken
   heart will mend?
      This pain I feel
      Tears me apart inside...
I hope he sees the tears in my eyes
   because today I will cry
   but tomorrow I shall die.
   Sarah McFarland

The Mate

The one that I do marry
must possess those traits,
which sprout from the soul,
that make the perfect mate.
Now what this is does differ,
depending on point of view;
but, I feel that I have found them
in no other but you.
It would sadden my heart
if you did not agree,
so I'm glad that you
do feel the same towards me.
   Susan G. Kimball

Where Did You Go

Where did you go
My own dear Lord?
What did you do?

Did you climb again
The hill of CALVARY?
(It was too dark to see
The blood stains on the rocks.)
Did you look down at the sleeping city
And laugh for joy
For what you had accomplished?

Or did you go
With speed of light
Back to beloved Galilee
To walk along the shore
While the stars winked out,
To remember, to remember
To whisper softly
"Follow me ... Follow me ... Follow me."

Thomas Manus

My Lord, My God

My Lord, God almighty
My mind could never know
My eyes could never see
All your splendor and majesty
For you are so great and
I am so small
My mind could never comprehend it all
All I can do is bow down to my knee
And worship thee
For that sacrifice you made out of love
That special gift that came from above
All the pain you bore at Calvary
Severe suffering and agony
You did it all just for me
And all my life, I could never repay
What you did for me in a single day
For you are so great and I am so small
The master creator of it all

Tena Glover

In My Loneliness

Where are you my love;
My love by the sea.

Where are you my love;
My love, can't you see.

My soul cries out for you;
Oh how I want you with me.

Open my heart and come to me;
On the wind once again.

Kiss my lips and touch my face,
You have filled me with so much grace.

Are you there, anywhere;
My love, can't you see.

Are you only in my dreams my love,
Or are you out there, searching for me.

Come to me my love,
Let me hold you close to my heart.

In my loneliness only
Will we ever be apart.

Peggy Heathman

Thank You

Before you came into my heart
My life was like rapids, dangerous,
Unpredictable, and deadly,

Since you have been here, my life
Is a calm cool brook with the water
Trickling down ever so slow, and sure,

Instead of seeing all of the dark clouds
   Explode with lightning, and hearing the
  Roar of thunder of what my heart
   Was once like, before you taught me to
  Notice how soothing the rain felt;
On my face when I lifted my eyes
  To the sky to see a never ending
rainbow.
The symbol of peace, and tranquility
  You call it.

That is what YOU have brought
  Into my heart, and my life
   Thank you...

Tiffany Ann Hunter

Just Say No

I wish there was a way -
My heart to control.
For the frequent breaking
Is talking it's toll.

It seems, every time,
That I open up my heart -
It doesn't take long
Before it's torn apart.

I give them the chance
To simply refuse me.
Instead they wait,
And let silence confuse me.

It hurts all the more,
And makes it harder to cope -
When a lack of denial
Creates a false sense of hope.

It would be much kinder,
And easier on my heart -
If they simply said no
Right from the start.

Ronald DeMille

"To My Darling Tomorrow"

To my darling tomorrow,
My heart fills with cheer and sorrow;
Knowing that yesterday is gone,
And today will be you tomorrow.
Sometimes I wish you would come right away,
Sometimes I wish you would just go away.
To my darling tomorrow,
I will never see you; I know that.
I wish I could change that horrible fact.
All day long you make me wonder,
It's a great spell you've put me under.
To my darling tomorrow,
Never will I know what you hold,
For life is unpredictable and cold.
To my darling tomorrow,
Your life will go on forever,
Mine will soon be gone, however,
To my darling tomorrow.

Susan Hoy

He Is Alfa, He Is Omega

My father makes the sun to shine
My father makes the seasons of time
My father makes the rain to fall
My father makes the tree grow tall

My father makes the wind to blow
My father makes the flower to grow
My father makes the bird to sing
My father, well, he makes everything

His name is Alfa
His name is Omega
He is God
He is my creator

Susan Donnelly

Rebecca's Dream

My guardian angel says, "Follow your dream!"
My family says, "No!"
My best friend says, "Go for it!"
My heart just doesn't know.

My dream is somewhere out there.
My life is there, too.
My soul wants to follow.
Oh God, what do I do?

I want so much in my life.
It's there for me to find.
I hope for luck and happiness,
But do I cross that line?

I have to take the first step.
I'll never know unless I try.
I'm going in blind and in the dark,
But my dream will never die.

If I fail, and no one is there
And I can't go any longer,
I know I tried and followed my heart.
I'll know it all made me stronger.

Samantha Jimenez

My Dear Lover

Oh Lover
My dear lover
Why did you leave me?
Why did you lie?
Why did you hide your face
When you wanted to cry?
Why did you leave without saying goodbye?
Oh lover
My dear lover come back to me
tell me how you feel,
I don't want anymore lies
I don't really mind if you wanna cry
just tell me you're not scared
to love and have just one
Oh lover
My dear lover
Please come back to me
I am down on my knees and begging you please
Oh please my Dear Lover
Just come back to me.....

Tara Lawbaugh

No More Tears

You've beaten down my self esteem,
My confidence is gone.
You've filled me with such hatred,
Now my tears are pure poison.

You've strangled my emotions,
I've tried to reason why.
You battered and abused my love,
Now my tears have all run dry.

You carried things, oh much too far,
For oh, so many years;
But now it's you who's broken hearted,
Now there's no more tears.

Ray Favichia

Enchantress

You are my Helen, my Juliet,
  My Cleopatra, my Sheban Queen,
    My Ezmeralda, and my Dulcinea;

All the most poignant,
  Most beautiful loves,
    That the ages have to offer;

And if I made love to you
  Each moment, of each day
    Until the end of time,
      It would not be enough...

Never will I be sated
  With your beauty,
    For you always leave me
      Wanting more
        Needing more, of you....

You are my beloved,
  My torment, my salvation,
    You fill my senses,
      Crowding out all
        That is not you...

Tienne

2 A.M.

Old rag doll
Moth eaten, button eyes
Threadbare and torn seams
She, like a lover's quarrel at 2 a.m.
hurts my heart
Empty void into this back alleyway
Kicking cans and broken glass
Revolving around the dim candle
Alone
A parade of the horribles
singing trashcan sonnets
and burnt out memories
The rain never does come down
Still, I'm afraid to go upstairs
Those broken locks and pale walls
murmuring lies and screaming death
So I dance with the rats
to the sound of far off sirens
and wonder
Were you really ever there?

Slade Anderson

A Skier's Creed

I ski so free from care and strife-
More than a sport-my 'way of life.'
To pit oneself 'gainst hill and clime;
To breath clean air; to feel sublime!
It is such fun, such joy, such wealth.
The wind and sun aid one's good health.
Snow covered trees are quite a sight-
Give urge to ski with all my might.
Exuberate and shout "whoopee."
Sometimes it seems just God and me.
To scan from high - far hills and sky.
I pray to ski - until I die!

Ray C. Campana

My Moment

In the solitude of my mind,
morals speak with great passion,
judgment is profound,
truth exists if I am willing.

I am not where I want to be.
Dreams travel into reality,
life seems but an instance in time.
Like a river flowing,
has my moment flowed by?

But yet, I reach out,
surrounded by hope,
encouraged by a smile.

Fearful of the unknown,
confident of my being,
I run along the river of life,
ahead of the flow,
ready to fill my cup,
with my moment.

Robert E. Perhach

Remember

When life's in a turmoil, deep despair
Marriage broke, needs repair,
Everyone against you, it's not fair
  Remember, Jesus is there.

Things are happening, out of luck
Out of control, running amuck,
All life's cares, you want to chuck.
  Remember, Jesus is there.

Nightmares, you can't sleep
Worries, cares, into your mind creep
No money, dirty clothes in a heap
  Remember, Jesus is there.

Jesus will help you through, somehow.
Pray to Him!! Pray right now.
Before His altar humbly bow
  Remember, HE IS THERE!!!

C. LaReeve Glover

Hamel The Camel

Hamel the camel
Livid on an oasis
Instead of two humps
He had two faces

He had a mind to go west
Had a mind to go east
Because of indecision
There's nothing left of the beast.

Sherry Sitzlar

In Search Of

Across the roads of
many places,
I search the soul
among the faces,
the Spark of Light
that is my flame.

Instead, a structure of
earth creations,
I find with heart
among the nations,
a place of Peace
that is its name.

The wandering pilgrim of
weary bones,
I rest the mind
among the tomes,
a word of wisdom
that is so tame.

"Traveling Pilgrim, you find a home;
When Temple, Heart, Soul, is the same."

Donald L. Carrier

"Race"

My race is different from others
many people hate me for it
the points
the stares
and even the glares
make me feel sad
sometimes makes me feel like
why did God give me this color
but then I know I'm like no other
the person in side is like no other
which I try to hide
I don't get why people make fun of my race
and say it to my face
they say my race is no good
I wish they could see the real me
not my color
if it weren't for that
I'd be glad instead of sad

Nicole Bergh

The Hiding Place

Deep within life's stormy sea,
Man seeks and finds a hiding place.
Once there, withdraws unto himself,
Seeking rest and inner peace.

Reason demands he break the bonds,
Of struggle that has mapped his course.
But first he must explore his mind,
To find the key that unlocks the door.

Traveling the roads within the mind,
He finds success alive inside.
Bound by chains forged by his thoughts,
Links built slowly one at a time.

The mind must change its thinking,
Negative thoughts gagged and tied.
The "culprit" is alive and healthy,
Built by man's daily way of life.

The chains that bind must be broken,
For success to be released and thrive.
The mind finds each link was forged,
By thinking, "I'm afraid — I will not try."

Sandra J. Starks

Upside Down

Blades of grass fall from above
making not a sound,
while leaves from trees grow slowly
down upon the ground,
and clouds break loud upon the rocks
searching for the shore,
while seas float gently through the sky
high above Earth's floor,
and cats chase cars and mailmen
barking oh so loud,
while dogs chase birds and rodents
stealthy, quick and proud,
and people run and drive and curse
thinking they are right,
while Nature's turning upside down
we ignore her plight.
Timothy J. Bennett

The Thought Of You

The subtle things you do,
make me fall in love with you.
The expressions on your face,
wanting to share a long embrace.
The things I feel from your eyes,
I hate our partings and good-byes.
The gentle tones of your voice,
they make me need you, I have no choice.
The soft touch of your strong hand,
it takes me away, into another land.
The sweet feeling of your smile,
sets me free like a little child.
I'll never be happy, but always blue,
if I can't ever be next to you.
Sarrah Jane Hiller

The Power Of Your Tongue

When you speak in one's behalf,
Make him smile or make him laugh.
If you don't, you'll cause him grief,
His joy is gone, you are the thief.
He tried his best to be accepted,
But now he hurts, and feels rejected.
His joy of life has gone astray,
He hopes it comes to him someday.
Till it comes, he'll play the part,
But it won't be, from his heart.
Snide remarks, you did make,
Are like a bite and can cause hate.
Things you said so long ago,
Hurt him deep, he can't let go.
When he does his very best,
Failure is his success.
So be careful when you speak,
So no havoc, may you wreak,
Or the message you may send,
Could make him take his life, the end.
Tom Dorr

Childhood Memories

Blue dreams through the sky,
Light feathered breeze.
Senses of vanilla.
Sights of tall plentiful flowers.
Lively frolic grass,
Swaying in the wind.
Young children skipping in,
Their hair floating in the air.
Rick Davis

Mirrored Faces

Something's out there
Lurking in the darkness
Sneaking through the blackness
Hiding from those who care

Distant planets in a row
In my head the shadows grow
What is right and what is wrong
There are those who know no different

Cosmic forces pushing down
On he who wears the crown
The battle continues in my head
Which is good and which is bad

Life is strange for those who know
The brilliance of the plan
Put your life in retrospect
Scrutinize to get respect

Who's that lurking in the darkness
Mirrors of our true reflection
Look into the darkened eyes
To find there he who cares
Robert S. Farris

Night

Hurry anointed obscure friend
Lure me toward tranquil worship
Motionlessly suspended we will lie
Stroked by a velvet touch of silence

Come dark silken lover
I shall unfold the tenderness of heart
That hides itself amid watches and words
Conceal me within your quiet whisper

Release secure serene pleasure
In an unhurried healing embrace
Embalm me in the fluid fragrance of solace
Where deeply and finally I can be at peace.
Shannon James

The Dark Embrace

Night falls,
Luminating with darkness;
Artist's brush strokes on canvas
Emulate the welcoming embrace.
Stars like glitter, or glitter like stars;
Who can say?
The closing eye reflects torchlight,
Reducing it,
Disturbing not the essence of rest,
Of cessation, of finality.
The mortal eye sees not
What the soul's eye perceives;
A mother's dark embrace.
Comfort is offered, but rarely taken.
Darkness is not given her proper due.
Sarah B. Douglas

A Clam I Am

A clam is what I am
Inside is where I hide...

But now I need to come out!
I dare ye to come out!
Dare ye not, for who are you?

I will come out and when I do
I'll tell my story that's what I'll do!
Gina Pizzano

Key Word Of Christianity

Key word of Christianity is Love!
Love others!
Help others!
Love is Jesus order!

Key word of Christianity is Love!
Respect others!
Honor others!
Love is Jesus policy!

Key word of Christianity is Love!
Be sincere!
Be honest!
Be modest!
Love is Jesus teaching from Gospels!
Joy

"Love"

Love is pure, love is divine!
Love is like, a - - song
Which pleases the river of time,
Leading directly to the mind!!
It travels through, the deepest depths.
The darkest nights, even to —-
The "wilds of the wilder-ness"!!
It can never be, sur-pressed,
Oh no! "Never"! For it lies —
In the safe-test and "most scared"
of all place: Embed-ed with-in
"The pure in heart"! Never ending,
always true, ever loving, me,
and you! For the love alone,
shall survive, in simpli-city?
Sinceri-ty, the humble,: —
servant, Meek and mild, gentle —
As a "Little Child"....
Umoja I. Kuumba

Love

Love is as precious as rubies.
Love is an everlasting trip which
Brings two together.
Love is a family or just a friend.
    Where does love come from?
    Maybe...
The sun could shine it across the sky,
The sky could spread it across the clouds,
The clouds could rain it upon the earth,
The earth could feed it to the trees,
The trees could scatter it into the rivers
The rivers could quench the thirst of birds,
The bird could sing it to the animals.
But I know that love grows in the heart.
Rayna Michelle Birdsall

Reflect

Come with me across the span of time,
Look upon the Universe as your teacher
Savor the abundance of knowledge
Contained within the delicate creature -
   the butterfly.
Oh, informed man, tremble at the
dynamic energy displayed by the sun -
Are you still boasting of all that
You've done?
Reflect for a moment on your gain.
Has it resulted in a world free
   from pain?
Sarah L. Campbell

Mr. Whimsy

Surely he knew the reason why.
Lincoln laughed so he wouldn't cry.
The cares he knew were grey 'n blue
boys of our farmland broad 'n true.
Sons who so often fell to grape
that flew from cannon on landscape.

His own tragedy in a son
whose fragile life hardly begun.
It flickered and then was no more,
tearing the Lincolns to the core.
His zest for living would return,
a united nation he did yearn.

So keen he'd often entertain
those who came for personal gain.
Larger than life at six foot four,
just imagine his laughter roar!
He knew something that is enshrined:
subtle humor can soothe one's mind.
William F. Greene

Our Destiny

Our love burns eternal
Like the light of the heavens
It will never die

Our souls are connected
Like the land to the sea
They can never be separated

Our hearts beat as one
Like the waves beat the shore
They will never cease

Our lives will lead us
Like the stars guide the traveler
They have mapped our destiny
B. L. Mattox

I Am

I am fat,
like a hat.
I am round,
like a mound.
I am a dragon,
the size of a wagon.
I am a butterfly,
bigger than earth and sky.
I am a flea,
bigger than a tree.
I am a whale,
smaller than a quail.
I am a mouse,
bigger than a house.
I am a clown,
that has a frown.
I am a bat,
that has a hat.
I am a teacher,
that has a preacher.
Tiffany Richardson

Siesta

Furred chin turned skyward
Mystic smile hides her secret —
Tabby in repose.
J. H. Buckner

"The Storm"

Thunder roars.
Lightning flashes.
Eyes burn red
beneath their lashes.
The storm attacks
the inner cage
which holds a beast,
the beast called Rage.
Walls grow holes
and chairs take flight
as Rage lets loose
with all its might.
Like a hunter's arrow
slays a beast,
my rage falls dead
at Sense's feet.
Calming winds
put out the flame
but, Rage's mark
will still remain.
Richard A. Wallander

Come, Let Us Reason

As I walk toward the evening,
　Light gathering images,
Pass through the reasoning,
　Of what was the day.

Reflections of the light,
　Dance upon my memory,
Awaking in my night,
　The dreams of reality.

As I walk toward the morning,
　The reasons are yet dreams,
The sun gathers the imagery,
　Of what was the night.

Pure and clean are the thoughts of the light,
　Of what was the day,
Of what was the night,
　Without the reason there is none.
Wayman C. Hart

Look Up

When you're at the bottom of a deep well.
Lift up your head.
Look up!

See the light way up there.
It's coming your way.
And it wants to stay.

When you're outside all alone at night,
Lift up your head
Look up!

See the light beams way up there.
Close your eyes.
Reach up.
Touch a star.
In your mind, it's really not that far.

Life is good.
Life is sweet.
Look up!

There is a guiding light,
Shining bright,
Bringing comfort to your soul.
Thomas Berntsen

Day Dreamed

Out of the corner of my eye
life seemed

like passing me by...its fleeting,
aglow, dimly seen.

Peripheral experience sprightly
streamed

away. I turned - no light, no you!
Who had dreamed?
Paul Edward Gingell

Eternal Love

Life can be happy
Life can be sad
People live and people die
They may be friends
They may be family
But in our hearts
And in our Souls
Their memories will never die
Ronald J. Lewis

Bridges

From the oldest to the youngest
lies a span of many years

From July to late September
just a summer flying fast

Let the days we spend together
and the memory of the past

Be the bridge we build together
with memories that will last
Sara A. Earner

Listen

Listen to me you see
Let your mind be free
Listen to my heart
not to love it won't stop

Listen to me you see
life is a new meaning
to reach for you dreams
as typical life may seem

listen to me you see
the little love me a lot
that I take to my heart
will never be apart

Listen to me you see
open to God you learn
what you have to cherish
in life you do parish

Listen to me you see
I'm happy to be alive
to be with the one you love
floating away like a dove.
Shannon Davis

A Plea With The Devil

I plead with you master,
Let my soul be free.
My senses are dying,
There's nothing left of me.

I sit by myself crying,
Yet the tears don't swell.
Why am I living,
When I'm committed to hell?

"Satan Rules the World,"
I used to say in fun.
Now he has my soul,
Time on earth almost done.

About to face eternity,
More than a lifetime in pain.
I sold my soul to the Devil,
There's nothing for me to gain.

So I plead with you master,
Let my soul be free.
Let me rest in peace,
Before there's nothing left of me.

Tanya Taylor

Circle

I taste your sweet tears,
let me drink your pain away.
Hazy dreams of days gone by.
Lazy days beneath cloud filled skies,
you always have a home in my heart.
Staring through tear-filled eyes,
your soft hair waved in the breeze.
Waved as you walk the broken
path of life without me.
Bleak is life when no one cares.
Cold air rattles bones where no one's
there to hold you tight.
Condemned to failed lovers,
contemplating your big mistake,
the broken path circles around
to my front door.
You now see, in this big world,
no one can love you more.
Pain in over, love's gone full circle,
our paths stray shall no more.

Robert Mesen

Moms

How do I love thee
Let me count the ways

There's faith - hope - charity
On any given day.

Though the kids grow older
And wiser - so they say.

It's mom or mother
There she is - to help you
Through the day.

Sometimes those days seem
Awfully long and the years,
They just slip away!

But in your heart, your mom
Is near, she never fades away

You see her eyes, you smell her
Scent - from which your soul there
Lies and so it goes her love unfolds
Before your loving eyes.

Sher Sequeira

Failing The Fall

Gentle winds flutter down
Leaves of red, yellow and brown;
Earthly ground growing old
Drying, dying from the cold.

The color of life is blue and gray
When memories yearn a younger day;
A time to sit to stroll the past
Knowing your next could be the last.

Innocence driving, diving to a trust
Grabbing and groping towards a lust;
Like a star streaking to a virgin land
Time can't stop the grains of sand.

Your soul aches from longing love
The heart plummets and impales from above;
Scarcity of scars can't even show
Your heart's death from sinking so low.

Combining, controlling all 2 the same
When you start to play this thoughtful game;
Your innocent, autumn stands 2 tall
As your hearts, life fails the fall.

Todd A. Raasch

Untitled

Clouded visions of love
   lead to tears of despair
   and hearts of stone.

Loneliness trembles in the darkness,
   touched by the silence
   echoing in the corners of your soul.

Tyson Worrell

Battered Wife

Whispering traces almost unseen
Laughing lover calling his queen
Retracing memories of years gone by
Sheltered lives shattering after a cry
Battered and beaten down to a bruise
She gets right back up not wanting to lose
Resenting and hating his woman's good heart
He tells her he hates her to tear her apart
Taking a breath to help hold back the tears
Refusing to leave him despite all her fears
Realizing mistakes he starts to cry
Saying he's sorry like other days gone by
Believing him again, forgive and forget
Somehow she knows it's not over yet
Although she knows it's a terrible crime
She'll let it happen "just one more time"

T. L. McCarthy

Tale Of The Shy One

So incredibly Shy
It made her Cry
Oh no! Oh please, no!!!
I don't want to read today!
She was pleading
Hands now trembling
With a look of fear in her eyes
I often wondered why?
But to read her papers
She has, oh! So much to say
So take her to the Dance,
All she needs is a Chance
A little Understanding,
Can go a, Long, Long Way.

Robert A. Morch

Phrase Dance

Constel   lation
     of
        recol
lections,
              move
      ments
          re-enact
  ed.
          Form
to
     arouse,
         acqui
sition
           of
    your
at
        ten
  tion!

J. D. Fallahee

My Pillow's Fancy

I talked to my pillow...
Last night,
kissed and caressed her in deranged frenzy.
And that I loved her verily,
I assured her...eternally.

In crazy murmurs...to her I mentioned,
about my childhood pillow fantasies...
about ethereal angels from the world of eros.
And in my delusion...I could hear her say
I will love you always.

How beautiful
It is to exalt our dreams
to sidereal realms, and how sad it is
to find reality...
on a wrinkled...kiss-moist...pillow case!!!

Vladimir Vega Jr.

Glitter

Exercises in futility;
Large oceans of energy
fly the flying field,
Friends laugh together,
others must yield.

Certain arches sting toes blue,
skies lost redemption
Echoes untrue?

Inside my Dream she lives on -
Forgotten sorrow sleeps
beside the Dawn.

Ancient beams crawl upon faces,
wounding and burning
suspect strangers traces -

Watered by-ways dreams to gold
Summed up few and short
Have souls been sold?

Lost cause left unknown
Amber rains fall alone
The Currents Choice beyond sanity.

Vincent Osborne

Stepping Stones To Jesus

Count it all joy when trials come
Just call them stepping stones
Climb each one that's in your way
You won't have to climb alone

Stepping stones to get to Jesus
Let us climb higher each day
Each burden and each heartache
Will get us closer if we pray

Deception is the devil's tool
He'll throw stumbling blocks your way
He'll tell you, you can bear no more
Climb on the Rock and stay

He knows that we have a hedge
That Jesus stands in the center
All he can do is walk around
He knows that he can't enter

A stairway to Heaven
Is what we're traveling on
Let's stand our ground and not look back
Just climb those stepping stones

Willie Mae Case

I Saw Into The Future

Some sad divination,
just a hellbound train
not returning to the station.
In my body felt a dying
reverberation.
Then my fears became their very
realization.
So I screamed for an investigation
A reason for this lost destination.
But you sent me an abandoned invitation,
To our unions separation.
I felt the chill of firsthand desperation,
As you laid blame for my damnation.
We dreamed the damage of preset detonation,
our empty faces and ending spaces -
foretold our obliteration.
And my mind could not know its own
mesmerization -
but in a trance I waited,
for your train never returning to the station.

Tom Harwell

Between The Raindrops

All my life
I've written my feelings
upon paper
Straight from the heart
and always on the line
Hoping someone other than love
would see my words
for all their worth
For twenty some odd years
they've gone unheard
while screaming silently to be seen
until a broken heart
lead me to find a silent victory
between the raindrops...

Richart Drake Lewis

Dreamlover

In all the years I've lived
I've wondered who you are.
You're always in my dreams
Yet you always seem so far.
Your body I can see so clear
So muscular and strong.
I admire your good qualities
But to see your face I long.
Are you real or just an image
Inside a young girls head.
A young girl sleeping peacefully
In the warmth of her own bed.
If you're real send a sign
If not just go away.
My sleep will not be bothered
In any sort of way.

Pamela Palardy

The Face Of Love

I've looked into the eyes of love.
I've felt it's warm embrace.
I've held in my arms.
I've touched its beautiful face.

I never thought I'd have it.
I never really cared.
I never thought I'd feel it.
But suddenly it's there.

He's given me this beautiful gift.
No one has given me before.
He had the key to my heart.
And tenderly unlocked the door.

This love that he's shown to me
Surely must be it.
It's in every breath I take
It's underneath my skin.

Each morning when I wake
I thank the Lord above.
For without him I'd be blind
To the face of love.

Tracy A. Blaine

Too Long

I've been too long outside in the storm
I've been too long outside looking in
I've been too long just hanging around

Why do I feel so sad and forlorn
Why am I waiting for life to begin
Got to keep my feet on the ground

If I keep living it up, living it up
Then I long to be on the outside
Please, Please take me on in

I long to drink from your cup
Forgive my foolish pride
I'm tired of living in sin

So look down upon me one more time
I'll rise my hands to the night time sky
And I'll call out your name

Look at my heart and soul, and my mind
Watch over me till the day I die.
I'm not asking for fortune or fame

But, I've, just, been too long on the outside.

William Addison

Musings Of A 73 Year Old

Have you ever pondered the mysteries of time,
 Its wonders and its why's?
Why when you're young, it creeps along
 And when you're old it flies.
When you're a child awaiting Christmas
 It seems to take so long.
But summer passed so quickly
 Like a short and lilting song.
Where does time go, I wonder?
 The months and years go by.
You're young - then middle age - then old,
 You've hardly time to sigh.
You'd like to slow time a bit
 And make the good times last,
But it rushes you along though life
 It seems to go so fast.
You've realized that life is short
 As you're rushing toward its end.
Time use to be such fun, but now
 you know that time's no friend.

Peg Briscoe

The Happy Light

A siren cuts through quiet streets,
It's woeful duty known
to one, a waiting soul,
The final rest alone.

And in the loneliness of night,
his weary mind awaits.
In eager wonderment,
it's deeds to celebrate.

Where went the children's song,
The simple promised dream;
Like clouds in sunset skies,
Not really what they seem.

The plain and silent chores
of life - the greatest joy;
The best of years not known,
till all the years employ.

The heroes of the night,
their wailing sound is near.
Too late - the journey ends;
The happy Light is here.

Robert M. Scudder

Camouflage

The look of death is all around
it's stench is in the air
we, as they, hide in the night
afraid of the death we seek

If morning comes but brings no light
it casts no shadow to kill
why are they here
better yet, why are we

Wet, dirty, cold and hungry
no longer what I was at the start
willing but not wanting to die at the start
wanting but not willing to now

I live out of spite of their land and mine
for there's little else for me to live for
abandoned by those I thought cared
and hatred by others I do not know

If peace comes tomorrow I have not won
because a soldier has no peace after war
just a battle of another kind

Robert W. Ferrier

Daughters

God gave me daughters
It's so amazing how he knew
that my live would be enriched
by everything they do.

Beautiful from their hair to their toes
life is full of leotards and bows.
Daughters are so charming and sweet
although they are not always so neat!

I rely on the Lord
to help me make sure
my daughters know they're adored
and can feel secure.

Through Him, I tell them,
we are all loved and cared for.
He knows what we need, you see,
that's why He sent daughters to me.

Robbi Richardson

The One You Love

You only hurt the one you love, so

Handle my heart with care
It's fragile deep, down there
Why let love bust
To love is to trust.

Life is full of joys and sorrows
Sometimes it's grief and pain
Laughter and tears must go hand 'n hand
'Til two become one again, then

You only hurt the one you love

Love isn't love 'til
Together we've shared whatever comes
Intimacy after infancy
Infancy we'll overcome
Maturity produces one.
Yet we fail, feeling dumb; the cycle,

You only hurt the one you love.

Sandra Hennager

The Prince Of Peace

We live in world of violence and hate,
it's a never ending pain.
But there is a light ahead of us
when Jesus comes again.

He'll take away our sorrows,
and wipe away our tears,
We'll walk with Him in Heaven
and live eternal years.

We have a future ahead of us,
and many things to do.
We won't be staying on this earth,
we're pilgrims passing through.

A place awaits us in the sky,
A mansions where we will live.
With beauty for each of us to see,
One more gift that God will give.

So keep looking for that special day,
When we'll see the heavens release,
and army of angels coming down
with our Lord, the Prince of Peace.

Tammy Bovee

To Crystal

I'm in love, but it's not an ordinary love,
It's a love of friends,
A love worth more than any other love,
A love that shows I care, I'll
share and will always be there.
A love of never forgetting good
times or bad times,
Even times that weren't time at all,
This is love is so true,
It's worth more than the
world can give and more,
But it's not worth more than you.

Patricia Foss

She's Not A Baby Anymore!

She's not a baby anymore
It's a happy kind of sad,
When baby girl turns to daughter
And 'Da-Da' turns to Dad.

She's not a baby anymore
When her highchair becomes a stool,
The car seat, walker, crib and stroller
Find her heading off to school.

She's not a baby anymore
As her baby talk fades away,
And she reads, and writes, and reasons
While she plans her wedding day.

She's not a baby anymore
But there's something she doesn't know,
She'll always be my baby
Because her daddy loves her so!

Will Means

Love

Love is an ecstasy...
It soars you high
To the very realms of the sky
In its hue
You see naught
The whites and blacks of life
It is a fantasy ...
Which fades
Touching the earth
It is a blossom of blind
It disappears to open eyes
It is a predicament of sentiments
Forgotten to the worldly sane....

Roma Singh

To My Teenage Son

Today as I write this poem to you,
  it seems to be quite a task to do.
For as your mother who loves you so,
  I also must find a way to let go.
It wouldn't be right to hold on tight,
  you need to go out and experience life.
But fears from molehills to mountains can grow,
  soon you'll be on your own, you know.
Now that you are in your teens,
  I must remember the fun that means.
And hope we taught you the very best,
  for on your own you learn the rest.

Robin D. Wurzer

A Mother's Love

A mother's love runs deep and strong
it never goes away,
every time I hold you close
I love you more each day.

You look up at me with that beautiful face
and a smile that melts my heart,
to me you're a very special child
and you were right from the start.

As the years go by and you grow so fast
there's nothing you can't do,
just put your tiny hand in mine
and I'll be there to guide you through.

For now, just enjoy your life
go run and play and have fun,
because no matter what you do
you will always be my son.

Paula Brenneman

America

America means freedom.
It means the freedom to think and pray,
To choose what to do each and every day.
The freedom of speech and
The freedom to teach.

American means liberty and justice for all.
It means a fair trial and
Protection for the small.

America means a chance at life to
Have an education and learn.
To have hope in the future
And pride in the past.

America means pride in what this country is.
Pride in those that died
And were willing to give.

Rebecca King

My Guiding Light

Sometimes the world seems to envelop me.
It makes me feel so alone and scared.
   Then, the touch of a tiny hand and the
words, "I love you mom," make me realize
I am never alone.
   The laughter of a child is the most
beautiful song in the universe.
   What can make us feel more important
than the trusting smile of a child?
   When I begin to weaken, I think of the
role I play in these young lives
and it gives me strength.
   Yes, I can be strong, because they
are strong for me when I need them.
   They are my sunshine in a storm...
My rainbow when it's through...and
my guiding light when I feel left alone.

Sally Dyer

My Pen

My pen is frozen with anger and mourning.
I wish only to set the tip to paper.
I only want a word a letter to begin.
I need my pen to pick up my hand and
  sway forth to feeling.
I need my fingers to create new language.
My pen is my mind, body, and spirit.
My pen is dry.

Tracy B. Swisher

Time

Take time to work
  It is the price of success.
  Take time to think
It is the source of power.
  Take time to play
It is the secret of perpetual youth.
  Take time to read
It is the fountain of wisdom.
  Take time to be friendly,
It is the road to happiness.
  Take time to dream
It is hitching your wagon to a star.
  Take time to love and be loved
It is one of life's glories.
  Take time to laugh
It is the music of the soul.
Phil Sikora

Expressions

It is given, it is taken away
It is real and deeply cherished

It is withdrawn and sadly missed
It can heal, it can cause pain

It is open and honest
It is vague and confusing

It can be in the palm of one's hand
Still it can be beyond one's grasp

It is a feeling
  sometimes difficult to express

It is strong, but can be easily destroyed
It needs nurturing to grow or it will be lost

It is beauty in its purest form

It is love
Vicky Pryor

Trampled Flower

Don't stomp on that flower,
It is but a victim of pain,
As it sparkles in the April shower.

There it shivers in a cower,
And no one cares that it is slain,
Don't stomp on that flower.

Will it even notice the prowler,
For it has nothing to gain,
As it sparkles in the April shower.

The intruder nears with footsteps louder,
Tromp, tromp is his refrain,
Don't stomp on that flower.

Awe surrounds the little flower,
Yet it is trampled with disdain,
As it sparkles in the April shower.

If we were to mimic the flower's cower,
Everything would be overcome by rain,
Don't stomp on that flower,
As it sparkles in the April shower.
Susannah Kirby

It Is Another Beginning

It is a bright new morning.
It is another beginning.
Jesus is always at our sides.
Jesus is Lord of heaven and earth.

He will always answer prayers.
Jesus, we love you as a father.
Please be compassionate to us.
We will sing and glorify your name.

He is calling us for a special mission.
He is a very awesome God, bless him.
Open the gates of doubt and let him in.
He will never, ever forsake his people.

"Come to me," says the savior, "Follow me."
"I want to be your friend," says he.
"I will give you rest and peace."
"How I love you," says Jesus.
Mary F. Guilmette

Obsession...

The fire has consumed me,
  it has taken control.
The heat is engulfing,
  it is taking its toll.

The crackling embers
  burn through each tier,
bequeathing upon me
  the soot of its sear.

The only appeasement
  to squelch the flame,
is the gratification,
  of possessing my claim.
Stacy Minor Roth

Cancer Rules

Angry and cruel
It has no mercy
Breaks all the rules
Takes the one who wants to live
One whom has so much to give
Robs his dreams and life's desires
For all he gives, to all inspired
Cancer rules, yet cannot spoil
What's been planted in my soul
A lifetime in my soul
A lifetime in my soul...
Donna Ruby

Morning Hour

The most precious time of every day
is in the early morning hour
when the very first sun ray
awakens the sleeping flower
and the night creatures start hiding away
from the sun's golden flow
as the day begins to grow
and your loved ones while yet sleeping
their heartbeats are still keeping
their rhythm with hope and love
thus you raise your face above
in worship for the gifts He gave
'cause once again all have survived
to prosper in a rich full life
and therefore then you touch your heart
and say a jillion times, I thank you God.
Ute Dahmen

"Friends"

Just because I have a beau,
it doesn't mean friends have to go.
Both guys and gals are precious to me,
friends forever can't you see.
Just because I have a beau,
it doesn't mean friends have to go.
Sometimes guys will ask my advice,
on how to date a girl that's nice.
Just because I have a beau,
it doesn't mean friends have to go.
Girls in friendship should closer be,
to support one another, don't you agree.
Just because I have a beau,
it doesn't mean friends have to go.
As a teen, life is hard enough;
without a friend it could be rough.
Just because I have a beau,
it doesn't mean friends have to go.
Why, oh why can't you see,
friends forever we all could be.
Thressa J. Wengland

The Light

To expect something of someone
is to invite disappointment
to accept someone as they are
is to invite friendship
as our lives entwine
our friendship through out time
grows ever stronger
like the twist of a vine
as it reaches for the light
the light of truth
the light of friends
the light that grows from deep within
though opposite
as day and night
I love the light
you have brought into my life
and on this day
and all others too
when I think of friend
I will think of you
William Leddrew Youngblood Jr.

All I Want

All I want,
  Is to be loved by you,
To be in your arms,
  To feel the softness of your lips
  To hear you whisper 'I love you.'
All I want,
  Is to be loved by you,
To be able to call you,
  In the middle of the night,
  And talk about us.
All I want,
  Is to be loved by you,
To tell you how much I care,
  To write letters of love.
All I want,
  Is to be loved by you,
But most of all,
  To be with you.
Sandy Corcoran

Baby Smile

Do I look, or should I not?
Is there something behind
That contented face,
As we look at up turn lines?

Should it be a moment
Savoured from just one time.

A second! So swift, so sudden
As here and gone.

So short, but truly meant for all.

From the shallowness
of its mind,
Expressing everything we love

Sincere enough to move you,
It's the dribbling smile
Of a baby's face.

So innocent and so sweet,
Looking out from its little space
It warms our hearts

William Lewis Perry

Mommie

This dark place I'm living in
Is loud and hollow just like tin.

And when there's banging on the door,
The pain and hurt seem evermore.
I look to you for love and care,
My longings are too much to bear.

I hope for loving touches mommie,
Value and worth don't take them from me.

Each day I try to do what's right,
Only to look at your face with fright.

Because again I've failed to please,
Thunder and lighting strike with ease.

I hide my head and try to run,
But there's no escape until it's done.

It's quiet now in this dark place,
Loneliness and terror came face to face.

I feel so sick down deep inside
Gentleness and love escape and hide.

I love you Mommie, please stop the aching.
Mommie please, my heart is breaking.

Toni Hartnett

"Night Of Day"

The night of day
is plain and simply
something people don't see
they think shadows can hide
easier at night
only because it's dark
but during the night of day
shadows are allowed.
They mimic everything
make them look bigger or smaller
thinner or fatter, but
during the dark of night
the shadows do not hide
but in fact, they dominate
'tis during the night of day
where they become sneaky, deceitful
It is not night you should fear
for fear lies in the night of day.

Terri Wallow

A Maturing Child

A poem when first conceived,
is like a diamond in the rough.
It cries for attention
and receives it.
At all hours of the night,
and in the early morn.

It is shaped by all the senses,
discipline it is given.
At times unruly and rebellious,
testing breaking rules.

It may not get a polished edge,
now as it demands.
Falling by the wayside
for awhile or forever.

But with patience, love, and understanding,
it eventually matures.
Reaching its potential,
in a very trying world.

by Phillip Bedolla

Moon

In a big black sky there is one glow.
Is it a star? The answer is no.
What is this thing 12 hours from noon?
Its light in the dark, it is a moon.
Every night it shows its white face,
seen by all countries, cultures, or race.
It's the eye of God, looking over the earth.
It's there when we die and at our birth.
So look out your door some night soon,
and take a long look at the moon.

Zach Spaulding

I Call

I call and you answer
Is anyone really there?
I can say the words
Do you even listen?
Does the voice have a mind,
Or the Mind have a voice
Speak up, I can not hear you
Silence is a slow death.
Can tear warm a cold heart?
Words of tenderness melt away the ice.
A steady hand will lift me up
Walking beside me gives me courage.
A smile took away the loneliness
A confidant can take away the emptiness.

Rene S. Reindenbach

Searching

I have looked for you
   in the fields...
I have sought you
   among the cities...
My cries have been heard
   in the heavens,
   the wilderness,
   the waters of
Oceans, rivers, lakes, ponds and creeks...
The crying out for the soul mate
   one forever seeks.

V. Joy Haag-Smith

Screaming Eagle

The eagle cries as he flies
Into the heart of the son
Together through their lives
They become one

Connected by lifeforce
As we grow
Seen as sunlight
The eyes of the eagle

Patterns interweave and entwine
Elders reading the signs
Joining in song
Of the eagles and beyond

William R. Kelley

The Garden

Uplifting my spirit,
Inner peace,
Joy,
At one with my soul
   In the garden.

I cannot change the world,
But can still find beauty.
I can make a difference somewhere,
If nowhere but
   In the garden.

Peace and serenity
Knowing that I tried
Maybe— just maybe— I touched someone
And they blossomed like the flowers
   In the garden.

Renee Gorham Bennett

Good Advice

I wish you the best of luck
in your future endeavors.
Make your career a successful one,
and keep your head above the clouds.
Don't ever take advantage of anyone,
and keep an open mind.

Take compliments with a smile,
and bad remarks with a grain of salt.
You only pass this way but once.
Watch your back and protect your assets.

Don't lie to your heart,
but don't deny the truth.
Broaden your horizons,
but don't leave a tattered trail.

Good friends are hard to find,
associates are a dime a dozen.
Kill your enemies with kindness,
it's the sweetest revenge.

Good advice works if followed,
don't wander from your inner thoughts too far.

P. E. Mullick

Oh My Papa

Jesus wept.
In the end he cried out.
Then he rose up,
To hold His hand.

William Darryl Jackson

Come Walk With Me

Come walk with me
In warm spring days
with life anew

Come walk with me
In long summer days
with life so full

Come walk with me
In cool fall days
with life so brief

Come walk with me
In cold winter days
with life almost finished

Come walk with me
For soon I will have
to walk alone

Ruth Cambridge

On Earth As It Is In Heaven

You are the only one
in this lifetime I loved
with all my mind, body, and soul
and knew what that meant.

Even though you aren't here
you will always be with me
for when we loved
we loved together
and I will forever miss you.

We found the deeper connection
of two lost souls
that is rarely found
and even rarer to hold
not easily recognized by most
and felt by few
and I will always love you.

Pamela Oakes

The Net

I finally got caught
in the World Wide Web
Now my brains are being sucked
right out of my head.

There's more here than
I really wanted to know
but at least now
I'm part of the show.

Chat lines and forums
filled with judgement and hate
any wisdom stuck in
seems to dissipate

To a lonely,
seldom-visited place
somewhere dark and cold,
deep in cyberspace.

Are computers the tools
to set us free,
or a time-wasting distraction
sucking brains out of me?

Paul Nelson

Stormy Oceans

Stormy oceans in stormy skies
in the starless winter night
echo the pounding of my heart
as whitecaps spray my upturned face....
The wind caresses my loosened hair
as if to say, "Come dance with me
and be a partner to the sea
and we shall move eternally
to the song of wailing seabirds
to the melody of rhythmic waves."

Someone it there who like stormy seas
clings to my mind, calls to me
like windswept seafoam pounding surf
making me dance to his unwritten song
echoing the rhythm of oceans, seabirds,
harmonizing in dynamic symphony
with internal waves of thought
I thought belonged alone to me...

Terri K. Coppa

The Meeting

I can't help but wonder,
in the realm of time and space,
if things would be different
in a different place.

Under different circumstances,
in a different light-
would it all seem wrong,
but still feel right?

Eyes are the windows
that betray what's inside.
What we don't want to known,
but can't seem to hide.

Betraying our passions
that lie deep within.
Tempting our lust
with original sin.

Roxanne L. Precht

Death

Death is all of us,
   in the future of our lives.
Long, soft, subtle cries.

Age makes it happen,
   or accidents to many.
What's death without fear?

We live through our life,
   some never want to leave it.
'Til death do us part.

Neither light nor night,
Can stop it from happening.
No way it won't pass.

Life is really sweet,
   to those who will accept it.
Others use suicide.

Don't think of future,
Think present, and live while you can.
Cause when death comes,
You'll never live again.

Paul M. Howell

The Blood Of The Lamb

Red, white
in the fountain,
I can see the light.
Giving me the hope,
the strength to carry on,
I see it with both eyes.
But never measure it in size.

The great day that he comes
it will be in my forehead
and that evil Satan will be dead.
Victory, Victory to us.
Everyone will see,
it will end the curse
and bring salvation to you and me.

Robin Lynn Moffett

A Postscript

Our love was like a taper, lit
In the early evening,
Which brighter glows each passing hour
To illumine every moment.
We nurtured it with tender care -
Watching over it with prayer;
We cast out every doubt or fear -
Which might have caused a shadow.
Near fifty years our candle flamed
It's glory unabated
The light it gave was e'er the same
As when it first was lighted.

Verda Fausett Pfaff

Untitled

Life is full of ups and downs
In the city and in small towns.
Going through it day by day,
Struggling through it along the way.
If you are in a happy time,
It won't last long with all the crime.
If people would just keep to themselves,
And put their hate up on the shelf,
What a wonderful place this earth would be,
We'd leave it for our kids to see.
For there is only just one race,
That is of course, the human race.

Wendy Ottosen

Easter Rain

The rain drummed out your name
In my heart and my brain
Then paused by a distant well
And tossed a coin
For a magic spell.

It played colors with the sun
Counting out rhythm for fun
While music on a wet stone
Played a dream
That won't leave me alone.

Vernon M. Sikorski

"God's Wonders"

My eyes have seen God's wonders
In many different ways
My eyes have seen Gods wonders
In every passing day
In the splendor of the trees
With there beautiful fall leaves
In the sweetness of a birds song
All through summer days long
In the mountain so tall
To the pebble so small
With the sky so blue
And in me an you
To the whiteness of the snow
These are some of God's wonders
For all to know

Roseann Bieth

Untitled

I still love you
In confusion and illusion,
I will always love you.
You disobey and not behave,
I will always love you.
You cursed me and hurt me,
I will always love you.
In the mist of the all you do,
I will always love you.

Pamela Lawrence

Did You Know You Were My Hero?

Somewhere in the past
in another place and time -
Our souls must have crossed
and yours was linked to mine -

For on the day we met
it seemed time stood still -
I couldn't think or move
my heart raced against its will -

But soon my mind awoke
to the reality of it all -
For when your hand touched mine
I knew my soul had heard your call -

And your love had never wavered
through all the years you searched -
It stayed as solid as the rock
in which Jesus built his church -

That's why you're my hero
and I give praise to the Lord above -
for my search too is over
and I thank you for our love -

Rebecca Casey

Love

Love is but a four
    letter word.

Love has no boundaries
    challenges or cares.

Words that are spoken
    or words that are not

Tells me my friend
    if you love me or not.

Patricia Muldoon

Bears

Prancing and pawing,
In a nice cool spring breeze,
The little cubs are playing,
In a graceful like ease.

Eating sweet honey,
Licking their chomps,
Getting bigger and bigger,
While in the grass,
They will romp.

Almost grown-up,
But still just not quite,
A teenager? Yes,
Seeming to grow-up,
Even faster than light.

Tony Misiano II

My Treasure

I have a trove of treasure
Impossible to measure.
Unguarded by a garrison
Gold tarnishes in comparison.
My treasure feeds no greed,
But rather fulfillment breeds.
My trove cannot be worn
Yet everything and place adorns.
Gems falling as a shower,
Hour after hour and hour,
Would be only noisome litter
Near my treasure's glitter.
And every added season
Adds interest, and reason
That a prize from any quarry
Is a sorry sort of glory.
Anyone who can true be
To diamond, emerald, or ruby,
Silver, gold, or precious pearls,
Has never held my little girl.

Steve Krause

My School (TTU)

My school since 1940
imperfect though it be!
God told me He would start it
in a true vision of prophecy.

He said it would be ready
when I was ready too!
In His plan for the future
He told me what to do.

I asked a logical question
would I later head its track,
He said, that in their sight
I would always be a "Quack"!

There was a mystery time-span
that would be a long delay!
Before that I would graduate
To the true vision of the way.

The Master's will is now unfolded
In God's school of nuts and bolts!
But like the prophet Daniel
His message gave me many jolts.

Newell A. Hawkins

Insidious Eyes

Please don't put your trust in me
I'm liable to implode
This island is sinking rapidly
Farewell to my abode

Sour truths are flowing from this heart
And crowding out my mind
But their purpose is self-destructive
I'm sure they will find

People do not realize
They can foment such pain
Pleading blissful ignorance
Bright shadows of their thoughts I feign

If I could channel out this beast
Pregnant in my soul
I know that it would make
A young recipient grow old

So tick tick tick away
Time-bomb of insanity
I challenge you to a duel:
The winner gets longevity...

Robert Berg

Jail

Jail
I'm here.
The clock ran out.
Now, I'm lock up, trapped up,
I tripped.
I thought I had you fooled.
I got fooled.
The clock ran out.
I'm here.
Jail.

Ronald Alston

Best Friends Forever

Best friends forever is truly what we are
I'll never leave you for you are my star
When we first met I knew from the start
I'd always want you close to my heart
Best friends forever means love is ever near
That there is someone who will always care
And this is a treasure worth more than gold
This true devotion that comes from the soul
Best friends forever is so beautiful to be
To know that you are a part of me
No matter what I do or where I may go
Because I will forever love you so.

Robert Barwick Jr.

You

   Look out, you dark night,
I'll join your name,
   My soul, will follow too,
The heart I have, has no will,
   I have, the lovers shame,
Now alone, in this silent night,
   I hear the sounds of you,
Drifting slowly, off to the side,
   Your love, obscured from view,
Never again, will daylight bring,
   The warmth, that made me new,
Gone now forever, in that distant sky,
   Is all I loved, yes you.

Warren Littman

What Mama Said

Johnny Brown hit me.
I'd like to kick him dead,
"But a good girl wouldn't kick him."
That's what Mama said.

Next he pulled my ponytails.
I wanna hit him in the head.
"No, no, don't hit him!"
That's what Mama said.

He got me in trouble with Teacher.
I wanna stick him with my pencil lead.
"Goodness Child, don't stick him."
That's what Mama said.

Worst of all he tried to kiss me,
And I yelled good and loud.
Then I punched and kicked him hard,
And I socked him in the mouth.

Mama didn't say 'bout kissin',
But I knew she'd see red.
So I said, "Let's be friends."
That's what Mama would have said.

Sonya Brown

Untitled

Had I never fallen in love with you,
I'd be okay right now.

My heart would not be broken,
My eyes would not be swelled.

My days would be filled with laughs,
My body filled with joy.

Instead I'm filled with sad memories,
And my soul still aches for you.

Had I never fallen in love with you,
I wouldn't be so scared.

So scared of being hurt again,
And left in misery.

But had I never fallen in love with you,
I wouldn't know to look,

To look for truth and honesty,
To look for someone new.

Sarah Colene Miller

Dream Of The Prodigy

You must be good
I would ask if I could

I am curious to know
How far will I go?

The night has come about
My success I doubt

I am now attempting to come
Sure that I will be there for some

But why am I now stalling?
When in my mind you are obliviously calling

If I miss it all
My life will surely take a fall

Troy J. Stone

Untitled

What's happening
 I will tell you
We don't have any roses
But we have another moses.

What's happening
More power in the word
This I have heard.

What's happening
Pastor C. Glover can teach
any place and any where
 What's happening
 Don't be still
 Move in God's will.
What's happening
Don't you know
Pastor C. Glover is getting
 Better and better
  now you know

Praise God
Ruth Wade

The Bridge

I want so to know you,
I want to be your friend.
But there's a wall between us,
The color of our skin.

We cannot be friends,
Your too black and I'm too white.
How can we bridge the gap,
That history's made so wide.

If I could only know you,
See and feel your pain,
Not as a casual observer,
But as a friend who's here to stay.

But I'm not a person,
I'm a color that can't be trusted.
It makes me sad and angry,
The distance that's between us.

The bridge must be started
Let it be by us.
I don't see any colors,
All I see is us.

Paula Matli

Your Choice

I see you standing there
I want so bad to come say "Hi"
To hear your voice, to see your smile
If only - I could have been your choice
To have you as mine
And me be yours
If only - I could have been your choice
You and me, touching, holding, loving
Always making something of nothing
If only - I could have been your choice
To me there was no other
Only you and me, forever and ever
If only - I could have been your choice
But - today it is my choice
My turn to chose
And today my love
It is you that will lose
If only - I would have been your choice.

Terri J. Burdick

The Warmth In My Heart Is You

I sleep and I see you.
I wake and you're there.
I smile and I see your smile.
I touch and I feel your embrace.
The warmth in my heart is you.
I walk and you walk with me.
My mind plays games of unity.
You're with me each breath I take,
each step I make.
I'm you and You're me,
a part only we can see.
The warmth in my heart is you.
I love you.

Peggy Turner

Rotation

The start of new day
I truly shine on the bay.

I rise with great power
An truly devour,
The coldness and darkness,
I rise with great power.

I give life to the new
I give light to the few
I illuminate with such courage,
I rise with great power.

I say an revoir
All within hours
I shine on no more towers

I fall far from east
I RISE WITH GREAT POWER

Michael Esquivel

"As The Days Go By"

I remember the day like it was yesterday
I thought to myself why not
 give it a try.
From day one you were kind of shy
 But as the days went by
 we came to know each other.
I must say I never expected what
 came to be for I saw before
 me the most beautiful
 relationship blossom like a rose.
As the days went by we became
 so close you were like an
 angel sent from the heavens.
More time has passed and we
 have learned so much.
What I have learned is that love
 is too strong to hold inside.
It is plain to see something so pure
was made to be shared between you and me.

Shannon Marie Hamilton

"Truth"

A poet
Is a know it all.
Who rhymes with words
And we should fall.
For phrases so
Beyond us all.
They leave us feeling
Dumb and small!

Valene Goudie

Companion

As each day goes by
I think how lucky am I
To have someone who cares,
And my dreams to share.
For my tears and fears
He is always there.
For my pain and sorrow
His shoulder to lean on I can borrow.
After all these years together
And lots of stormy weather
He's my lover, companion and friend
But the best of it is
He is my husband.

Wanda Sullivan

"Too Late"

As I look out our front door,
I see them carry you away.
You passed away in your sleep last night.
I never took time to say,
I love you and I need you;
I never told you so.
You were married to my father,
so many years ago.
Yet! As I stand here
I hear my father cry,
"We'll all be with you,
when it's our time to die!"
I look away in shame.
I never said I love you
until you went away.

Robert D. Martin

Thoughts of a Birdwatcher

As I sit here rocking in my chair
I rock and rock while I comb my hair
The trees are alive with leaves so green
The birds on the fence all sit and preen
The big gray cat behind the fence
Sits and waits, for the birds to relax
And become fair bait
The birds know the cat's about
They squawk and holler and also shout
It scares the cat and he scampers out
The birds now know that he has gone
They rush to safety and give the alarm
That all is well and free from harm
The sun now starts to sink and set
Shadows lengthen and darkness sets
The day is over the night begins
And tomorrow will start again

I. Stewart DeWitt

My High Spirits

High spirits in a lofty place,
I rise above the air, thinking of laughter.
How happy it is to see the earth,
Down, down below me, right on the ground.
And as I rise higher,
I see light blue, just waiting to greet me.
Chirping birds twittering supreme noise.
The sun winks and sneers at me, and guides me
   higher up.
Every tree is now an ant.
And every man out of sight.
Then I begin to drowse.
And as I grow sleepier, I think
That dawn is the first step home.

Wai-Ping Chim

Untitled

When I'm alone
I reflect on all the yesterdays.

The whys and cries
And those who never
Bothered to understand.

And then I think of you
And I wonder how I could
Ever have been happy
Without you.

Paula Ann Lemaster

Wedding Vow

In the day of eternal waiting
I poured a cup of hope for two.
Hope deferred makes the heart sick,
So God brought me to you.

Since God has finally answered
The prayer of my longing heart.
I promise to love and nurture you
Forever and from the start.

I promise to walk beside you
In the valley and on the peak.
When the world seems to be against us
I promise to turn the other cheek.

I promise to follow Jesus
Because He is our Lord and King.
And I promise to hold you Martha
As long as you wear this ring.

Sean Tucker

FPrivate Tears

Time has withered the fragile rose
I nourish still with private tears
That lay gentle on photographs
Frozen moments of your spent year s

I hear your voice ride a warm breeze
I hear you then calling to me
But echoes are sounds of silence
As I feel it filter thru me

I feel the pain that pierces my chest
Like shards of glass will ease with time
As dreams are lost to dawns embrace
Reality is not as kind

Sue Blackwood

Joe

There's a little boy living
   in our house,
That's very plain to see.
   His toys are scattered from
      room to room,
Home ain't what it used to be.

I'm still the boss in this mansion
   and what I say still goes.
But what can I do, when
   two eyes of blue
Laugh at me with his finger in
   his nose?
He has the energy of a rocket,
   and the drive of a passing jet.
   He's also a part time monster
But he's still the family pet.

Peggy Pruitt

Capitals

When I was liTtLe,
I NevEr UndErStoOd
WhY ThE capItAl lEtTerS
NeVer weNt wHerE I THougHt ThEy shOulD.

mY tEAcHeR uSed tO TelL mE
oVeR aNd OveR TiLL I wAs sIck
bUt I dIdn't UndErsTand
Why ThEy Can'T Go WhEre I pIck.

AlWaYs iN nAmeS anD plAceS,
bUt nEveR aNY plAce riGhT.
It sEemEd wHeRevEr I USed 'em
ThEy nEvEr lOokEd jUsT rIghT.

WhEn I gOt olDer I UseD TheM finE,
bUt PEoplE sTill tEll mE aLL thE timE
ThAt I STill mAkE a Few mIStaKes,
bUt ThAt's JuSt a HaBit oF mINe.

Now thAt I'm GrOwEd uP,
I NotIceD soMeTiN' NuW,
I Awso hAv a ProBlUm
wIT my SPEwIN' TwO.

Randi Stephensen

'I Know A Person'

I know a person, a person
I miss. A person with love and
wonderful bliss.
A person with a heart and
a person with a mind. A person to
hold and a person that's kind.
This person is fun in more ways
than one. This person is wonderful
and too much fun.
This person shows happiness
everywhere they go. This person expresses
happiness and is not afraid to show.
This person has friendship
in ways that are true.
I know a person and
that person is you.

Paula Green

My Pisces Love

I love your name.
   I love your face.
I love your smile,
   and your warm embrace.

I love the way you talk,
   your gentle teasing way.
I love the way you walk;
   you excite more each day.

I love the way you speak my name,
   the way you hold my hand.
I love all the great things
   that we've done and planned.

I love you in the morning
   and in the nighttime too;
But MOST of all my Dorann -
   I'm really in love with you!

Thomas G. Leavy

Untitled

As I sit here,
I look around.
I see the land,
the land is me.
Peaceful am I,
just as the clouds,
floating above the earth,
no worries.
I grow with the land.
I am a tree.
Arms as branches,
reaching towards the heavens.
Hoping,
Dreaming,
that soon I shall return.

Angie Otto

Moon Face

I set to sail end of summer.
I left a lot behind.
But time and sea and things that happen,
to people when they're apart.
Has made me remember one,
Moon Face,
That's what she called herself.......
As I put time and distance behind me,
She was in front of me.
She was alongside of me.
Moon Face, she called herself once,
lives inside of me.
I love her now,
I loved her then, even before I knew her.
I'll love her soon, my Moon Face.
The time and distance so long since past
is here close again.
I love her and she is mine,
and this time I'll leave the sails behind.

W. A. Courter Jr.

For Buckwheat

Grateful to have shared life with you-
I know you loved me too.
Knew you couldn't stay forever,
Still you had to go too soon.
Did all I could to save you, Wheat
But money wouldn't do
And would've traded places, Buck
But GOD didn't want me to.

Some might say "He's just a Cat"
And for them that might be true-
But I loved you as I love myself;
I'd have done anything for you.
So your space beside me's empty now,
This house has empty rooms.
And though the hurt has drained my heart
I keep it full with thoughts of you.
Farewell dear friend.

Robert Simon

utile Efforts

I sang a song for you to hear,
I painted a picture for you to see,
I grew a rose for you to smell, and I
planted grass for you to touch; But
you did no hear my song, you did
not see my picture, you did not smell
my rose, and you did not touch my grass.

Tracy Nichols

Untitled

Upon my little tree, so deep.
I heard a bird with a little peep.

His peeps were filled with love.
Now he's a lovely dove.

He sings his song every day.
I'm afraid he might fly away.

He's been in my tree since he was a baby.
So if he goes where nobody knows.
We will miss his songs.

We hope he finds a female bird.
So he can make his own little flock.
So they can sing around the clock.

Shari Johnson

The Walk Through The Garden

As I walk through the garden
I hear a voice say, "Pardon."
I look around and nothing is there,
Soon something moves my hair.
I turned around and an Angel stares,
For I could not compare to its beauty.
I felt a warmth through my body,
For it was the touch of an Angel.
So I cannot swear;
I know it was there
Though it never spoke to me.
I know it did through its beauty.
If I hear a "Pardon" again,
I'll remember that walk through the garden.

Tiffany Leigh Daniels

"It's Only A Dream"

As I write this poem
I have news to share,
To my family and friends
Just because they care.

I'm getting released
Yes, it's true,
So there's really no reason,
For feeling so blue.

I'm coming home,
Tomorrow's the day,
And this I promise,
I'm sure going to stay.

As I approach the house,
I hear but just a scream.
At this time I open my eyes
Just to realize it's only a dream.

Raul M. Federico

Reflections

I am a mirror of memories past,
I am a mirror of reflective glass.
I am a mirror that sees love and strife,
I am a mirror that reflects mortal life,
I am a mirror of records and schemes,
I am a mirror of hungry and fiery dreams,
   And I am the mirror
      you hold in your hand.

Shari Land

Planting Flowers In The Rain

Digging in the squishy Earth
I find a worm squiggling
to get under the mud.
The purple pansy slides out of its
basket with one pull and
I spread the roots.

I look at the area,
big rocks, small tree.
Where should I place the
pansies?

Small splashes of rain
hit my head and shoulders.
I study the area again
and dig ten holes for the pansies
that perfectly offset the
rocks and tree.
A pleasing arrangement.

Satisfied, I clean up.
It has been a good, rainy,
day of work.

Kathleen D. Mangan

First Love

For the first time
I fell in love
I cannot describe
The feeling inside
It's a special feeling
One like no other
It is so great
That it rules out hate
Your first love
Only comes once
So treasure it forever
Cause you won't have another

Tahnee Higgins

Healing Grief

Your presence surrounds me.
I feel you in your chair.
I hear you walk across the floor,
But know that you're not there
And yet it's comforting to know
Our spirits still communicate
From there to here below.

Physically, no longer here
Your face I cannot touch
And deep within the inner depths
I miss you, oh so much!
And yet it's comforting to know
Our spirits still communicate
From there to here below.

Ruth Scofield

The Pope

Brought
Hope
To a nation
Troubled by
Strife and woe
The message is
Peace
The meaning is
Love

M. I. Gowen

What Can I Do

I can't bear the sight;
I feel the pain,
The suffering of the world,
This weight on my shoulders.
What can I do?
To the point of insanity,
I strive to know goodness,
When all I see is murder;
There is no innocence anymore,
What can I do?
I see the news on television,
As tears stream down my face,
Pain and suffering throughout the world.
Where are we going?
Where have we been?
All dreams are shattered with a bullet,
Love is lost,
All that's left is hatred,
What can I do?
Robert Moore

Fire/Ice

Fire
I feel on fire
Heat
Burning desire
The need is strong

ice
numb
embracing the cold
without need
time to go inside
alone.
Renee Prewitt

Consummation

Holding, gripping.
I feel his warmth all over me.

Grasping, pulling.
I felt his struggle of passion.

Grabbing, hugging.
I feel his strength below me.

Touching, stroking.
I calm his fears and confusion.

Shifting, rocking.
We rise above reality on a cloud.

Pounding, galloping.
We discover a world of release.

Slowing, quieting.
We are one, my horse and I.
Molly Black

Untitled

To grandma
Roses are red
Violets are blue
Everything meant to
me
Is you
Shawn McCullough

Untitled

Ever since I was a little girl
I dreamt of that one true love
and of this day I'd share with you
in the presence of God above.

It all started with that first dance,
or was it the walk in the sand;
was it the spell woven by the moonlight,
or the way you held my hand?

You made me think, you made me laugh,
and then you made me love
all the world surrounding us,
the sky and stars above.

And thinking of our life together
I cannot hide my smile
from the warmth of friend and family
as I walk down the aisle.

As I say I'll marry you
my mind rests assured
our hearts have joined together,
laughing at the wonder of it all.
Tracy Noffsinger Conder

Homage

"Dear are you there?
I can't see you anymore."
"Oh my, look at his little eyes,
He has Mommy's eyes for sure."
"Where have you all gone?
I can't hear you at all."
"Look at the little precious,
hands and feet like a doll."
"My heart feels so heavy,
It pounds like a drum."
"Watch his little mouth,
No teeth yet, just gums."
"Hold my hand dear, please,
Tell me, am I dying?"
"Oh you sweet little baby,
Now why are you crying?"
R. E. Tekavec

Forever Love

My heart is as tender as yours
    I can no longer take the hurting

I tried to be courageous
    but my heart could not sustain the blow

We are not together today
    because of our misunderstanding

A beautiful dream died
    before it had a chance to grow

I won't fight with or explain to you
    anymore

My admiration, respect, and love to you
    is always and forevermore
Susan Y. Chen

"I Can Overcome Any Circumstance"

My mind is like a pearl
I can do anything in the world
If you can see it come true,
There's nothing you can't do.

Who was it that said,
"When it rains, it pours"?
When you close one window
He opens many more doors.

Just because it rains
doesn't mean I have to drown
So hold your head up
And stop feeling down.

But how will I make it?
What is my chance?
I've come to realize
"I can overcome any circumstance."
Patricia F. E. Richardson

When Love Is Gone

You can't get in touch with me because...
I am nowhere
Eking out a meager existence on nothing
Loving only the utter emptiness of my life

It is a dismal place I am
Will a light ever break this dark, gloomy
barrier that has enclosed me?
Will not some precious ray glimmer fourth
and shatter this spell of darkness?

Enveloping walls of darkness
Cold and foreboding
It seeps thru my skin
Thru flesh, to the very center of my soul

Oh sweet light please shine,
Warm this coldness from my bones
Oh sweet light give me love
Take me home
Victor A. Bradley

Looking Back

Born to a world of peace
i am immortal
Free to experience
Living for the passion of the moment
Dreaming of tomorrow
Looking back on yesterday
Watching what i have become
Seeing what i could have been
Searching deep inside myself
But never satisfied

Born to a world of war
i am mortal
Yet i shall live forever
Flying through the dreams of those
Who live to carry on
And in the essence of my soul
That which is mine for eternity
i see my life in but a glance
And for once perhaps i am
(Will be) Satisfied
C. Regan Robertson

Goodbye To Love

Where do I go from here,
  I am empty I am cold.
Just leave me be,
  and don't come near.

Let me walk alone,
  it is lonely, but safe.
I must be strong,
  and on my own.

I am detached,
  and I do not belong.
I loved and took the risk,
  but something went wrong.

No joy and no pain,
  feelings no more.
And what is left,
  is less than before.

Simone Rini

Childhood

Voices in the dark, yelling, screaming
Hug your teddy bear, tears streaming.
Life's real scary for a kid at night
When your mom and dad just fight.

They don't stop to think of how you feel
They don't even care if you're real.
You just lie in your bed and shake
And listen to the dishes break.

You wonder if it will ever end
If Mom and Dad can be friends.
Why can't the fighting cease
So you can all live in peace.

Wes Taylor

To A Deceased Loved One

'Tis often I remember,
How you touched my life with love;
The times we spent, before you went
To join the Lord above.

Although it's been a while,
Since from your life you did depart;
Your memory is still embedded
Deep within my heart.

Time has a way of mending
Broken hearts, and drying tears;
Instead, it leaves fond memories
Of you throughout the years.

It comforts me to know
That you are now within God's care;
In addition, I feel blessed
For the time that we did share.

I see death as a journey
To God's kingdom, free from sin;
Someday I too, will take that trip
And be with you again.

Salena L. Ware

Soulful

Overwhelms me
How the hills talk.
Shiny rays of sun,
Every corner
When they walk.

The endless sky
Lies all above me.
Playful enough,
It peeks again
In the blue blue sea.

Cliffs grew taller
And waves hugged
Again those rocks.
Real became unreal
Or unreal it is not.

My mind leaped
Into the sky.
It leaped before me.
I adore this oneness
With the nature thee.

Shamal Patki

Retirement

Oh sweet moment
How oft I've thought of thee
when carefree as in days of youth
Once more my heart will be

Oh sweet moment
Thou long awaited friend
renew the fire inside of me
That I might burn again

Oh sweet moment
From hence comes time to share
The pleasures of the golden years
With those for whom I care

W. D. Hay

"To All My Lost Loved Ones"

Lost.
No one to care for.
No one to care for you.

Lost in memories.
Trapped in present time,
and the future.

Lost in love,
consumed by hate.
Waiting to die,
confined by pain.

Hopelessness,
Hoping to just drift away.

Afraid to go,
but you know,
peace and happiness will follow,
and loved ones will guide you on
your journey to nowhere.

Finally you will be found.

ReAnna Liermann

God Needs Me

God needs me, Mommy.
He's calling from above.

He brought me into this world,
Not entirely right.

To show that he can love us,
In each a different light.

God needs me, Mommy.
He's calling from above.

Don't cry Mommy,
I'm very, very, loved.

Jody Reichel

Untitled

You have no faith, you don't believe
I bust my butt until I grieve
From the pain you have caused within me
Your destructive trust
Is a bit like lust
Something that is quick and wanton
It only leaves me open
For more of that hateful stress
I wish it was more a soft caress
Of words that show you know
My work is more than a simple blow
Into the wind, and ends up in my face
But it seems my pace
Is not worthy of your grace.

Terance Ormond

To Woman

Stand a little closer to the wall
Out here where I stand tall
There is no room for you and me
And that's the way it's meant to be

If I am to be all that I am
If I am to climb as high as I can
I cannot be smothered by too much love
My spirit free must soar above
All earthly things that tend to bind
You see I'm not the anchored kind

So, if you are content to tag along
There's part of me that must belong
And that part to you I truly give
If me and myself are to fully live
So stand a little closer to the wall
And use its strength to hold me lest I fall

Will Solo

Saving Grace

It seems as though someone or something
is blowing in my ear; I turn to see
what it is and see a loving, courageous,
and glorious man who wishes to introduce me
to someone. The wind I felt in my ear
was the breath of life, the breath of God
(The Holy Spirit) that delivers God's grace
to me. The man upon whom I turn is
Jesus Christ (my Salvation); the bridge to
eternal life. He introduces me to God
Almighty (my maker). Upon understanding
and believing in this, I am saved.

T. Greg Hill

Love

Yesterday you called me from miles away,
Your voice was so sweet
It was like music to my ears,
You were so calm and warm
My body relaxed and felt content.

I wanted to reach out and touch you,
When I remembered you were far away.
It is so easy for us to love each other
Even when we are far apart.

Now my heart is filled with love
I am convinced that you are the one for me.
Let us hold on to each other and never let go.
Before we know it, our 50th will be here.

Lucy Springer

Heirloom Treasure

Many years ago, when you were just a lad,
Your Mom and Dad received a gift, from your Daddy's Dad.

It was a rocking chair, from your Grandpa Ed,
to help you get to sleep at night and rest your weary head.

If you were tired or maybe feeling sad, whether it be night or morning,
you woke up Mom and Dad, always without warning.

And as they awoke to see the hour on the clock,
it didn't seem to matter much, for with you it was time to rock.

As time went on and you began to grow,
The hours they spent rocking you, were not as many as you know.

And so the time may come, when you also shall be blessed,
with children to call your own, at which time you'll get no rest.

But always know the special times with them you shall spend,
will create a loving bond, for which there is no end.

And when your children are grown, and you wish they were still there,
oh the special memories you will have, as you rock in this rocking chair.

Mary VanDenbussche

Searching

You say you love me, but I know it isn't so.
Your love for me changes as the wind blows.
In your mind you want to love me.
But, in your heart you really don't.
Because you're still in love with her.
You've spent years searching for someone like her.
But, you've never found anyone who comes close.
You know why.
Because there is only one person like her on this earth.
You tell me you love me just because I'm here.
When, the truth is, you're lonely and missing her.
If you can't let her go, then let me go so I can find
someone who loves me even when the wind blows.

Kathe R. Neuman

Your Loyal Friend

The Lord gave life to a hungry stray kitten -
You gave her a home warm as a mitten -
You answered her prayer with compassion and love,
From that animal friend far up above.

Vivisectors mutilate, blind and burn,
Little kittens with nowhere to turn -
You rescued her from the vivisector's den -
She will always be your loyal friend.

Larry Hicks

Do Not Let Me Go

You lay here beside me, holding me close
Your hands caressing my body, sweetly, gently.
You guide me through the glorious night
Your lips breathing life into my soul. Awake. Alive.
You open up and share with me
Your eyes are windows to your soul.
I know not what tomorrow holds
So tonight my lover, do not let me go.

Tomorrow is only hours away
I dare not open my eyes.
I'm afraid to see you there
I'm afraid you'll be gone.
Today was a good day, but night is upon us now
so tonight my lover, do not let me go.
For tomorrow is a new day
and only hours a way.

Melissa Lettre

My Friend

Your soul is the mirror of my endeavors
Your body is my guide
That you awaken in me the path that is right
Arouses my living with pride
The state of being, in every man
Holds mysteries known only to one
Why, remains the answer to him
But how, is for man to get done
Your heart beats strong, the goodness of life
Your heart speaks truths of peoples fears
While no man can honestly claim perfection
You've proven commitment over the years
I feel I've been blessed with an angel
You've guided my soul to greater heights
The days are gone of questioning
What needs done, is what is right

Melanie Harris

The Hawk And The Raven

Your thoughts and words overwhelm me
Your actions and deeds astound me
I think of you and my heart increases
I hear from you and my problem ceases
You look upon me and see straight through
Your eyes follow me in all that I do
In your eyes I am wanted, loved and cherished
In your presence my insecure self has perished
I look upon you and my future brightens
Your arms surround me and my heart tightens
You call me lass and you call me love
When with you my heart soars like a dove
You call yourself hawk, I'll call myself raven
My soul I give to you as your own safe haven
My feelings I will share, my thoughts and my needs
All I ask of you is truth in word and deed
For the raven and the hawk they soar in the sky
The spirit of the two together they fly
Their wings almost touching, they're never apart
Connected at the soul, entwined by the heart

Michelle Wolfe

You

You will never understand how I feel about you.
You taught me things I didn't know were possible.
You helped me through some tough times.
You were hard to get to know.
You are all that I ever really wanted.
You have moved on and are now out of my reach.
You have forgotten how I used to laugh at your jokes,
   and cheer you up when you were down.
You didn't remember to call when you promised that you would.
You used to care, but now have forgotten.
You don't realize how many times I've defended you and I still do.
You don't know how many times I've cried over losing you.
You will never be mine, but I still love you anyway.
You are my best friend and will always be close to my heart.
   Laura Watson

Mother Earth

Mother Earth,
You stand tall amongst the many
gladiators of the universe.
You are a sentry protecting life,
filled with wonders
Like the Mojave and the Grand Canyon.
An aviary, a hangar for life.
Mankind is your helmsman,
but we are all rookies
compared to the vast knowledge
that you hold.
Experience etched into your very soul,
yet man handles you like a malleable piece of steel,
unaware of the pain they are causing.
Yet you survive through it all,
and give life to a new day.
   Norma A. Cervantes

For Ian

Your love was the seed
you planted in the bounteous folds of my soul
Carefully, I allowed this rapturous being forth
to find a home there,
Now, your body is no longer here,
but your love lingers still and warms me
like the sun on a May morning
I will never feel in anyone else
the nurturing I received from your love, your devotion
And I long for the day
we are together for all of eternity,
again...
   Maureen Holland Harris

Sad Summer

I suspect you mischievous little boy
You peeked behind the door and saw the glory.
Although Daddy provided for all your needs
And Mommie gave you sustenance
There was a light behind the door
Where you found so much more.
T'was hard to leave
brother Gabriel and sister Tanya.
But it was your time to say good-bye.
And so you did.
We all reach out to wish you well.
You know how much we love you now.
We'll see you one by one
When each life is done.
Help us hold your hand in ours
Until united we become
And make again our summer fun.
   Mary Alice Harrington

Emily Dickinson

Long before your body died
   you locked it in the garden and the house.
Made your announcement in poems to yourself.
   When the expected carriage came
You doubtless welcomed it. The bier
   was laid behind the liveried driver,
The horses charged the road whose hooves
   clopped crazy consonants
      without their vowels.
Atmosphere of autumn afternoon
pressed the grave like a blanket of iron.
It did not stop your mouthful of poems
nor the moss that crept on the stone
toward your engravèd name.
   Kenneth H. Brown

"Love"

I was feeling so low and wanted to be alone.
You know — how a dog feels when he wants to bury a bone.
A walking I went, not seeing a thing,
When suddenly a man stood before my being.
With a look in my eyes and a soul I could see
He told me to tell Him all my troubles to be.
Then I was done and with a caress to my cheek —
He said, "Troubles there are, but troubles are not Me.
Open your eyes and enjoy what you see, life is a
challenge, it was meant to be.
Love is the key, it will open all doors, and when
you have love you will always find more.
Trust in Me, for I am your friend — we have been so
from beginning all the way to the end.
I will see you soon and show you much more,
for Heaven is mine — love's key to the door —
For all those who love and trust Me on My shores."
My life is now showered in all that I love, and
Soon I will join my friend that I
Love, Trust, and Adore.
   Lelia Patterson

A Mom's Secret

When you get married is there a transpired transformation?
You ask yourself is it you, is it him, is it the children?
You feel as though you are in a dream that belongs to night.
What happened to the girl you were? Where did you go?
What game did they play on you, whose in collaboration?

It seemed as though one day you woke up and realized something
had changed, you were no longer you.
The role you've been playing has been exemplary,
You just can't figure out where you lost yourself.
The sun comes up and you look in the mirror and what you see
   you have no clue.

You look for yourself everywhere, but you can't be found.
Is this what life is once you've left that safe nest, once the egg is broken?
Do we continue to pick up the shells, while we take care of children
who now call you mom.
As the children grow, who we were seems to be fade further away
that person leaving, not knowing were she's bound.

Maybe one day we'll meet again on a quiet summers night.
Or maybe one day I'll wake up and be her all over again.
But for now I must be what I am for everyone around me.
And when she comes I will welcome her, there will be no fight.
   Linda Detamore

One Final Try

I'm standing here looking into your eyes.
You ask me to listen to your love filled outcries.
I think and I wonder on what I should do.
Then my heart tells me I need to be with you.
But now things have turned and again you're changing your mind.
So all I can say is "Have you gone blind?"
You couldn't have possibly missed all the times I have cried.
Or overlooked our bond that once tied.
So I'm begging and pleading this one final time.
To the heart of my young love to come stand next to mine.

Nathaniel Ray McAtee

Dying Soul

When I'm around you I feel unwanted
you are the hunter and I am the hunted
I feel this way because of love
I've lost everything I've dreamed of
My broken heart is all that remains
I will never be able to get rid of the pain
You are not just a memory
But you are and always will be my everything
My heart is broken because of you
but you don't realize what you do
I can't hurt you the way you hurt me
Please come rescue me from the misery
Why can't you see what I'm going through
You don't even realize I'm hurt cause of you
You don't understand the problems you've made
but my thoughts of you will never fade
I have no ways to express my pain
Why does love hurt, can someone explain
My heart is crying while my soul is dying
but somehow I have the strength to keep on trying

Kiffany Wunderlich

Daydreaming

Daydream, oh daydream, oh wondrous thing
You are the castle of which I am king.
You are the warm sandy beach where I play.
You are the wall that will keep tears away.
You are the cloud with the soft velvet lining.
You are the place where the sun is always shining.

Daydream, oh daydream, oh now I must go.
But before leaving I want you to know,
If it were possible here I would stay,
But reality chases my daydreams away.

   What is a day dream? It's a strange question
but think about it. I've thought about it for awhile
and came to a conclusion. Daydream is a place where
one can go to get away from the unpleasant things
life can hold. It's a place where one has strength
and powers that one usually doesn't have. It's a
place where one can create beautiful things and
escape for a little while. It's not a place one can stay.

Melodee King

"The Crossroads Of Life"

   When we start the great journey which is life, we come to a path which is dark and blank. But in the distance we can see the roads which are the crossroads of life. It really doesn't matter which road you take, but what we make of the road we take. There are many twists and turns. You can make it right or you can make it wrong. You can make something of yourself or you can make nothing of yourself. You have a chance sometime in life to correct your mistakes before you get to the end of the crossroads which is the end of life.

Nick Camara

A Long Wait

   "Tick-tock," the clock sounds. Days are shorter now than before. Yet last minutes, last seconds; seem like an eternity! Eager to go home, that is so comforting. After whips are slashed by the slave drivers. Children we are, slaves it seems. Teachers are they, whips they lash, it seems! Rumors fly between each group. Some the high others the low. Rumors hurt people's feelings, yes they do. She likes him, while he likes her. "She" her tears flow waiting to soak her pillow. As soon as the bell rings. While, "Her," waits to gossip about "She" and "Him." As soon as the bell rings. "He," a troublemaker he is. Waits to cause all kinds of trouble. As soon as the bell rings. "One" waits for football practice. Not bright either! He thinks a scholarship will definitely be awarded. "Another" makes sure all her books and supplies are with her in order to study. A scholarship will definitely be awarded! So many thoughts roaring for the bell. Others gossip while eyes swell. The bell rings. For one moment for such a confusing day, the same emotion for all. JOY!

Megan Milliken

one last good-bye

one last good-bye
      yes, i owe you that
one last good-bye from these forsaken lips.
i owe you one last
      good-bye —
but not a word will i utter.
One last kiss
      yes, you needed that
one last kiss from this broken soul.
i owe you one last
      kiss —
but not a hair will i touch.
one last farewell
      from deep within my heart
one last farewell from a forlorn child
yes, all these i owe you —
      but you owe me more.

and not a word will we utter.

Lorrie Serrao

"Thoughts"

I was there with you last night, even though you ignored me.
Yes, I can feel the pain you're going through.
You see, when you hurt, I hurt too.
I held out my hand, you didn't want it.
I looked deep into your eyes, but you could not see.
I opened my heart, but you did not enter.
I held out my arms, but we did not embrace.
I spoke, but you did not listen.
I know you are frightened, for I am frightened also.
I have been hurt for too long, to hurt.
I have felt hatred for so long, that I cannot hate.
I have felt pain for so long, that I cannot induce pain.
I have been someone else for so long, it's hard to be me.
I've been so weak, it's hard to be strong.
Let us be ourselves, so that we may always walk together in
  perfect harmony.

Nancy Luchene

Love

Love is nothing but a tear in the sky.
When it turns dark and gloomy, you start to cry.

When the sun comes out again, you swear this love you feel
  could never end—it could never die.
You just caught yourself in another lie.

Again, we all know every day, like love, has its end.

Lacee Ginger

Oh, For A Dove

Amid the violence of our century,
Wracked by millions of dead around the globe,
Some have a dream.

We yearn for a peaceful place
Where religions are calm
Where states love their neighbors
Where armies cease to fight
Where families twine lovingly with one
   another.

Must it be a dream?

Our world has enough problems.
   The ozone hole is enlarging.
   All waters are polluted.
   Continents teem with pressure from people.
Beauty is disappearing.

Yet, we the people, have power.
We can create our own force
And keep this small planet a good home.
We must.
   Margaret Gaffney

Views

If the world was full of views, would the love of one subside?
Would we testify of honor with a fearless noble pride?

Would we criticize the different? Would people have no worth?
Would we understand our questions, if our hearts ruled the earth?

Can you contemplate the changes? Our thoughts have led the way,
To a sorrow filled resort and a challenged world each day.

We can grow a hatred friendship, give our brains a chance to lurk,
People get insulted when our minds go to work.

We see hollow halls of darkness, an endless bitter pain,
A place where we experience a taste of sour rain.

We find our home in anguish. We don't know where to start.
We can't control our anger, when our mind controls our heart.

But the brighter side is better. A warming sun is seen.
We hear a gentle laughter and a thought that's whole and clean.

If we want to know the answers, there is one thing we must find.
It's the power we possess to let our heart control our mind.
   Mike Addams

Solitude...A Portrait of Alaska

Charcoal sky star sprinkled, log cabin nestles peacefully
Woodsy fragrance fills crisp night air, lone wolf howls
Answering moon's amber glow...
Peeping through spruce trees pointing heavenward
Branches heavily laden with new fallen snow
Warm chinook blows gently from the south...

Dancing lights through the treetops, weaving, trailing
Away into air...
Snow disappears, radiant sun melts Ice...
Droplets form gullies, slowly seeping into thirsty ground
Dainty flowers poke tiny heads
Serenely through bare spaces of earth...

Icicles dripping as sun rays beam down...
With regal might and power
Today...
Damp, soggy earth
Warmed with hope
Tomorrow...
Promise of rebirth, life to wilderness...
Spring!
   Laurie Ostrem

A New Life Begins

In the morning you can hear them fight,
wondering if this has gone on all night.
She opens the door and walks outside,
screaming at him, "You're out of your mind!"
He comes after her with his fists held high,
she just stands there and begins to cry.
Stopping him in his tracks,
she finally realizes all of the things he lacks.
She finally becomes stronger,
as she walks out the door.
Knowing now that he'll never hit her anymore.
She's moved on with her life,
found someone new and became a good wife.
The past with all the pain is buried and gone,
Never to be brought up again.
With her new life she's moved on.
   Kristen Kinsella

A Dream For The Ode

Now wake from your slumber my sweet one; revealing cool jeweled eyes of
wonder, eyes of reflecting rivers. You my child, you are the center.
Wake up... We laughed like soft naked children, held up in the warm
forgiving arms of innocence. A quest through eyes of grandeur.
Visions are new black prisms, unbound. Lost in beauty's eyes, sweet
words of comfort ride on your breath. I seek to know you.

Awake, shake lies of shady legion, once given to dance in a ring of
silence. Now given as true, my child my sweet, to dance in a ring of
fire. Dance for the day and mourn for the night, dance to forgive and
dream for the ode. Now night and day become as one, rough waters
swim out to the moon, who among you will run with the tide...
let's embrace the night love, it's our turn to try.
   Michael Matsinger

Untitled

Once we could fly high in the sky
With words and love and touch
We've been places no one else has been
I love you so much.

As we fly together high and low
The colours glow so bright
You are the one to soar with
And I know I'm right.

When sight turns to touch which in turn sends vibrations
All through our bodies new sensations
Vibes, a beat, an electric shock
Uncontrollably riding through space, face to face

This beauty is so mystical
Your touch, like the air is light
I'm drifting away with you
For a long and silky night
   Margot Conway

Self

Ofttimes people try to be
What they think they thought they ought to see,

When through broken mirror scrutinized
Every fault at double size,
And wondered what another's eyes
Would see without the ugly guise
Of smiles and laughs and petty lies.
   Nathan Walton

Moments Of Wonder

I run along the sandy beach side, and watch the sea roll in and out with the tide.
I see the sea gulls in graceful flight, and watch them as they slip from sight.
I gather the pretty sea shells as they roll in from the sea, and have the strangest feeling they are meant just for me.
I see the seaweed like golden strands of hair, as the waves come in and toss them in the air.
The little sandpiper runs along with me, and I wonder at his luxury to be free.
I watch the children building sand castle in the sand, and wish it could as peaceful across the land.
The waves come in with long white fingers and erase my footprints from the sand, and the wind blows the sea spray across my face and hand.
I know that I shall come again another day, and watch the wonders of the sea at play.
Marjorie E. Place

The Chill Of Unrequited Love

The morning yawned and stretched
With the opening of my eyes.
Dewy dampness sent a chill
Through the marrow of my soul,
Even as the glow of a warmth slowly radiated.
It was a hard to tell the toll
Of last night's torturing sighs
By the wetness on my window sill.
Whether it was just the day that dawned
Or that a transition had taken place
That made the love so subtly cold to me.
This salty, breeze change penetrated
The soft, still, warm glow of sunrises before.
As the morning lifted the shade of dimness
To the light of a full-pledged day,
I glanced at the fading, doubtful dark
That would be covered by a blanket of brightness.
And only the chill of dew could bring to me
The tears of the night's death.
Michele M. Lopez

"This Is Free"

Have you ever walked down a country lane
With the moon shinning high
Hearing the whippoorwill's mournful refrain
So lonely, you could cry?

Have you ever sat on an old stone wall
Counting toadstools on the trees
Down an old well did you call
Your voice echoing in the breeze?

Have you ever waded a country stream
With water most to your knees?
If you have missed this, you can dream
Then you can go wherever you please.

I hope you will see a country fall
With colors oh so bright
You can sit on that old wall
Watching the colorful sight.

With geese heading toward the south
Their flight pattern, you will see
So amazed, you will open your mouth
And all of this is free.
Mary Emily Evans

The Armour Of God

When planning to go out in the world,
   with the evil and temptation,
Don't go alone - take the LORD.

If you need to choose between right and wrong,
   Put on the Breastplate of Righteousness.
That will separate you from the throng.

So many times we fail.
   Carry the Shield of Faith,
And let the LORD prevail.

There is no need worrying about death
   If you wear the Helmet of Salvation.
With this your mind can rest.

To pierce the spiritual cobwebs away,
   Use the sword: The word of GOD.
And see if your spirit doesn't sway.
Kristie F. Baity

Let Me Die With A Little Dignity

I want a barbarian's funeral — to share my crypt
With pottery, jewelry, and pages of my poetry.
You can leave my hair uncombed, my nails unscrubbed and please
Don't paint my parchment face with a moth white thick paste
Or dot my cheeks with the circles of an imbecile.

When the night explodes into pieces as dark as a
Bull's form, don't tell my friends I was a good
Daughter or a willing workaholic — that the
Accuracy of my columnar sheets was so
Sacred to me that I worked like a sulky, solemn
Ill-tempered scrooge on many a withered Xmas eve.

Tell my friends I was a creature of the night, talking to
Unseen spirits under many a full moon — living
For visions, lines, and cockeyed connections
And I loved every fretted minute of my madness.

When the squeaky gate motions me to my final rest
I hope someone will honor my crazy ragged quest
Kiss my brow, recite a few of my favorite lines to me
Lie me down softly on pages of my poetry
And let me die with a little dignity.
Kathleen Rampton

Green Is The Color Of Faith

Faith blossoms silently in early spring
With new green leaves beginning to appear
To hide the worms for which the robins sing
When perfect lawns bring happiness and cheer.

Faith then renewed is welcomed by bright green,
And daffodils with smiling faces—gold—
As with the rising sun whose lovely sheen
Alerts the world its wonders to behold

Awakes the sheltered birds and feeds the world.
So many green things are alive today,
In quiet places from which hate is hurled
Can rest the soul while chasing stress away.

Green mountains rise to bless the eye, explore
A better view of heaven than before.
Mary Hamilton Neary

Hugs

If I could erase all the hurts of man,
With just a touch from this human hand.

I'd reach out and hold all that I see.
To ease each heart and set each and mind free.

For because of these times of push and shove,
We forget to hand out just a small pinch of love.

We do not purposefully seem so cold,
But it feels so strange, others to hold.

If we could but learn to kiss and to hug,
Our burdens would not be so heavy to lug.

For only with love is the spirit set free,
So I wish for a hug, for you and for me.
Melody L. Richardson

Romance

The whisper of two lovers' voices,
with bloom of heart upon their faces.
Aroma she lures them in,
enticing lonely hearts within.

A gentle touch, with eyes of longing
urge on soft spoken words of love,
"I'll love you until...your eyes...your lips..."
and offerings, of flower bouquets with Baby's Breath.

Alluring images of pleasures and promises.
Lover's dreams and lover's schemes
are sealed with a kiss!
Maxine Louis

My Neighbor

My next door neighbor's a likeable chap,
With a grin on his face and his cap pushed back.

He looks on life with a great big smile,
To meet him and know him is really worthwhile.

When you're grouchy, or gloomy, or down and out,
And you meet this fellow, you're sure to shout

That things aren't really as bad as they seem,
Though the clouds are dark, there's always a gleam.

The sun is shining just over the hill,
And will shine for you if you have the will

To look for others with troubles too,
And give them a hand and see them through.

In doing this you will always find
That your own small troubles are left behind.
Mel Bunch

Mom

Mom, all my years of being with you,
You have helped me make my dreams come true.

We sit and talk until day turns to night.
And by the end, I know what I'll do is right.

I listen to what you say and do,
So, when I grow up, I'll be just like you.

It's special to know that you are there,
And all you do for me is care.

I'm so glad that you are you,
Because no one else but you would do!
Kimberly Ann Townsend

On Maui's Haleakala, I...

...Journeyed through darkness up volcanic-coned mountain,
   winding ever upward on dark macadam ribbon,
    with edging plants unseen and domed sky unlighted.

...Stood upon the brim of its immense-darkened caldron
   searching for crater hidden by sunken banks of clouds,
    the mists swirling about me as I shivered in the cold.

...Suspended and awed by its gigantic-cloud canvas
   awakening to morning glow with clouds surface tinted,
    rim edge highlighted by molten band of gold.

...Freed from space 'n time by scene-scape vibrant
   floating in spiritual awe beyond this dimension,
    saw God's fingers extend skyward, earthward, left 'n right.

And at that instant
...wished that my self-made filters
   diversity, separation, disharmony would resolve!

I could walk away into the pale, pastel morn
   with brothers and sisters united in spiritual love
    and together create a safe, harmonious place.

...Knew my wish included us all.
Jimi James

The Distortions Of The Socially Elite

What will become of me?
Will I cease to exist through the eyes of the socially elite?
Because they just happen to have selective blindness and can't see?
Or will they finally accept my presence and offer me a seat?

Maybe they'll drive me crazy with their ignorance
Then the elite doctors shoot me up with drugs and reality settles in soon
The Pompous Upper Class say I'm insane just by one glance
This misfit kid is surely no crazy loon.

They tell me to adjust my attitude
Or I'll be one more statistic
Heading down a road due for servitude
Or will I save my ass with one more trick?

"Born a misfit, die a misfit," that's what they always say
But let's turn the looking glass upside down.
I say those "God-complexed freaks" will pay some day
I just hope I'm around when the war goes 'round.
Michael Tubosnick

Remembrance

After I'm gone and my name comes to mind
will I be remembered as a man who was kind
Loved ones left behind to work and play awhile
will they recall a warm spirit
will they remember my smile
After I'm gone my ashes in the air
will I be remembered as a man who cared
Will soft breezes blowing and the melodic chimes ring
invoke lucid memories of how I enjoyed such things
Will brilliant sunsets and big harvest moons,
birds in flight and the ocean blue
cause friends to warmly reflect
that I valued these wonders, too
After I'm gone and on the tribunal day
will filled glasses be raised
and a warmhearted toast made
"Here's to you old friend.
May you rest in peace.
You're remembered fondly
so let your troubles cease."
Keith Allen Groover

A Family Of Strangers

I see others with their families, and it always makes me cry
Why does it seem that a happy life, has all but passed me by
Oh yes, I've had acquaintances, these never lasted long
The bottle was my only friend, in its eyes, I did no wrong

To know that someone cares for you, is a very special feeling
But I would turn to alcohol, and just stare at the ceiling
"My life is over, just get drunk," I'd say from time to time
And feel sorry for myself, when I didn't have a dime

A fellowship of strangers, has made me again feel wanted
And put perspective back in a life, that alcohol had stunted
They don't care what I give to them, at this I stop to think
The one thing they do care about, is my desire not to drink

I've been alone for most my life, ever wary to the danger
Of close and personal contact, especially with strangers
Now I don't have to hide my face, no need to pull a scam
For this family of strangers, has accepted me for who I am

Matthew A. Hasemeier

Untitled

Oh troubled heart and wondering mind,
Why do you seek what you'll never find?
If skies are blue, or it should rain,
We still must prepare for the last refrain.

If the troubled heart would look to the sky,
Good thoughts may linger and the rest would die.
While the wandering mind can go round and round,
True feeling could pass and then never be found.

For passing through in life, time, and love,
Can keep hope down if you can't rise above.
Sometimes what is there is already the best,
Just keeping good thoughts and forsaking the rest.

There are not always answers to all questions we raise.
Things look so clearly, but the mind is a haze.
So why should we worry, everything is all right,
Living is simple, take it calmly, don't fight.

Happiness is love, so there's no need to cry,
But love doesn't seem real, till it's about to die.
Poems and songs tell these stories, you know,
Life just moves on, but thoughts come and go.

Linda G. Bradshaw

Love Yourself

Why are you feeling loneliness?
Why do you reach, but no one's there?
Why must clouds cover your sunshine?
Why must problems be intolerant to bear?

Why must you depend on others,
To help see your problems through?
For they are bared down heavily,
Having problems upon them too!

Now stop! Let us take a minute,
To acknowledge what is true.
The self-love and strength within yourself,
Can help you see things through.

So, love yourself and devote yourself,
For the happiness you seek to find.
And once you feel content within,
You will find your peace of mind.

If you find yourself reliving these questions,
As you go along life's way.
Remember...you must seek deep within,
To bring forth your most pleasurable days.

Mary M. Cherrington

Wild Horses

I need help, but I want to look tough.
Why do I act the way I do? Please
somebody show me the answer; I want
to roam like wild horses. I want to
run in open fields knowing no one will
capture us. They run free letting the
wind blow their problems away, letting the
sweet smell of wild flowers, fresh spring air.
They go day by day with no worries.
They don't care what the next day will
bring, they're unselfish always there for
each other. They depend on each other.
No worries could tear them down,
no broken hearts. Hearts just filled
with love and the eagerness to run
free and wild in those fields.
I want to have no worries. I want to run free.
I want to run in the fields with those horses.
But in a world as crazy as this world is,
the closest to freedom you'll have is in Heaven.

Kendra Bartholomew

My Old Tabby Cat Pete

Rolled up in a ball on my window seat is my old tabby cat
　whose name is Pete,
an odd name you say, but you're far from wrong,
he was named for exhaustion, as Pete is forever asleep.

I try to entice him with catnip or yarn,
　even a succulent tidbit or two,
but although he seems to purr with delight,
he just sighs, turns away and closes his eyes.

I never had a companion such as he that I can yell, laugh and cry
or tell my troubles to with no reply.
He just looks at me with those soulful eyes, not saying a word
(as cats can't talk), in a masked disguise.

A loyal friend who soothes me when in distressful strife,
as he never talks back (as I say cat's can't talk)
　or tries giving advice.
He's always there to comfort me, my tabby cat Pete,
　the light of my life.

The sun shining through the windowpane gives his gloriously
bright colored coat a look of ripe golden corn at harvest time,
which reflected beauty that fills my heart with hope.

I love to hug my tabby cat as he's so soft and warm,
a tonic to my soul, this precious little ball of fur,
a place within my heart he holds.

Marolyn E. Baker

Untitled

This is the story of the maiden Mel,
Whose friends dared her to go with them to hell.
She agreed to go with them and find out,
What true pain, death, and sorrow were about.
Her friends saw through her act of bravery
And the truth of how she felt they could see.
Alone, afraid, beset with fears of hell,
But never would her thoughts to them she tell.
Her hair she always wore in the same part
Though plain she looked kindness was in her heart.
Her heart was sad when she saw people suffer,
Since before hers she put the needs of others.
The sight of people burning in the flames
Made her weep though she did not know their names.
Everyone could see it there on her face,
Her eternal home was not in this place.

Melody A. Black

To Always Remember

I went to the wall today, to see the names of the heroes who's faces I've never seen. I can't know what they knew, and I'll never feel the things they felt. The fear of an enemy unknown. The joy of their family and friends.

The crushing sorrow of having a buddy die in their arms with the unanswerable "why me?" on their lips. I won't ever hear the stories they shared or the songs they sang. I won't ever see the beautiful sunsets they saw or smell the things they smelled.

The only thing I can do is help those who are here, and weep with them for those who are not. To keep alive their memory, and never forget the cost.

Oh yes I've been to the wall today.

Have you?

Marlena A. Crotsenburg

"What Is A Friend"

A friend is one you can always trust,
Who will stand by you every day.
One who will be there to lift you up,
When you've fallen along the way.

He will be your strength when you are weak,
You're grateful for his listening ear.
He possesses a heart that is full of love,
And he is there to wipe your tear.

A friend will also correct you,
When in love he knows you are wrong.
He will do all that he possibly can,
To put back in your heart a song.

He will praise you too, when the time is right,
When he knows you have done your best.
And you've truly given your all,
Even though you were put to the test.

And best of all, he will show you love,
As he remembers you daily in prayer.
Your friend will ask God to bless you,
And keep you in His care.

Myrtis Allen

Untitled

There once was a newt named Arnie
Who was in no relation to Barney,
Through he was green with a purple tint
Even some orange if you really squint.
Happily he wiggled each and every day
Never from his homeland did he stray.
That is, never until that fateful morn
When Arnie's little sister was born.
Oh, how that brat did wail,
Enough to make boats bring in anchor and sail.
Arnie got fed up and decided to leave.
He decided to go on Saturday's eve.
No one noticed that he was missing,
Except those cats who won't stop hissing.
Depressed, Arnie wandered into the street.
He just stood there looking at his feet.
The big truck was speeding, the drivers yelled "seat."
But poor Arnie just went SPLAT!!

Katie Moore

Is It?

Is it really God,
  who makes the sun's brilliant colors welcome dawn to each
  new day?
Is it God,
  who makes a young girl, with golden curls cry because her
  virtue has been stolen, by a man she thought she knew?
Is it God,
  who makes the smell of burning leaves during a New England
  autumn bring warm memories to all who smell it?
Is it God,
  who causes a mother in South Central, LA to scream while
  her baby dies of gunshot wounds he didn't deserve?
Is it God,
  who created love between a man and a woman, passionate
  and unyielding?
Is it God,
  who allowed the still moving mothers and fathers and
  children to be buried in Germany simply because of their name?
Is it God?

Leann L. Baldwin

On Reaching 80

Happy Birthday to a handsome hunk
Who (like God) doesn't like junk
A listener who can get musically drunk
Listening to concerts a cut above funk
He claims the French deserve a big chunk
of praise for gourmet cuisine
'Tis true, that's no bunk
He knows he'd feel digestively punk
If he dined on bagels and doughnuts "to dunk."
In sports news and markets the eyes are oft sunk
Who's winning? Who's losing? What's gaining? What's shrunk?
His aesthetic commitment would fill a large trunk
He tends to like artists who show some real spunk
Many times all his cares are unloaded, KERPLUNK!
As he heads for the outdoors and like a good monk
Meditates on the joy of being alive.

Kathryn J. Potter

A Vision Passing

Death is not an easy thing; it tears our heart, it hurts and stings; who could have ever told us though, of the pain and sorrow of "Letting Go."

We live at present in a loved ones eyes; as years go by we too must die.
We lift our head, to face the sky; too often ask, the question why?
We think perhaps, but who am I?
and cherish memories we can't deny.

The circle ends, with hopes in mind; your love and goodness, we look to find. In the legacy you leave behind. Gives strength to fight our fears, sometimes; so lost in grief, confusion follows; when hearts are heavy, our sole seems hollow.

LOOK FOR ME, IN A FACE A GLOW! How great love is! When letting go. I'll carry you across the land, to help you learn and understand; my very presence, you can only know, I leave with you my heart and soul. As my love reflects, in child's laughter; is this not what you are searching after?

As I lift my head to face the sky, you need not ask more questions why. We meet with love, leave in peace; I'll remove your burdens, heartache and grief. A kiss good-bye, a quick look at life, hold close the memories, my way of life; in all your anguish, hurt and sorrows, I LIVE through you, I plan your tomorrows.

Michele Wade

Untitled

To contemplate my father's death
while, yet, within him lies the breath of life,
the softly spoken word,
the nodded head, the common bond,
the oft said dreams, now barely heard,
that still persist through troubled mind
a lifetime-long, short moment shared,
of present tense and future blind,
of all the chance and hope we dared
to stare the odds down till we find
the answers, every parents' child sought
to stave off destiny we fought
and have a few more moments caught
between the kiss and the caress,
the peace of mind and the duress,
of laughter's tear and heart's embrace,
eternal dance and finite race,
until we catch the star and ride the wind
and then, with dreams fulfilled, relent,
to finally leave, without a trace.
   Mark Lawrence Stevens

Sorrow

There's no such thing as sweet sorrow,
  which brings sadness on tomorrow.
There may be tears,
  but some may be cheers.
Sadness can come and go,
  from a hug, a smile, or just plain hello!

A touch of love, here and there,
  or a little kindness everywhere.
Maybe a phone call to give a cheery lift;
  or even a little surprise gift.
A get - together for a walk,
  or even cry a little, or talk.

A whisper in your ear
  "remember, I'm always here."
Or to tell you those three little words, "I LOVE YOU"!
  Things like that to help you through.
But remember it's all up to you
  to return your feelings too.
   Laura VeOla Dudding

Country Living

I love the country side,
Where peace and quiet doth abide,
Far from the city noise and rush,
And night time settles with a hush.

In the lush green alfalfa fields,
There are singing meadowlarks and whippoorwills,
While leaves rustle in the trees,
From a soft evening breeze.

We have wide open spaces,
And beautiful sunsets that tint our faces.
With sunset comes the sound of crickets,
Nestled in the brush and thickets.

Dawn comes with a burst of light.
O' hear the mockingbird's song so bright.
Another day is born,
On this great sunshiny morn.
   Lajuana D. Burton

Where Will Frogs Sit?

Gone is the watering spring,
Where horses and cows bent to drink,
Now gone - they have widened the road.

Sometimes on an evening in May,
At the edge of the spring on a rock,
I sat - enwrapped in the stillness of evening.

From the opposite side and so still
A frog with veiled eyes stared at me.
We sat - in the fragrance of twilight.

When bull-dozers bludgeon all springs,
Rip up the moss edging of brooks,
Where, oh where will green frogs find a rock
To sit - just to sit in the evenings?
   Lura Martin Swig

The Loss

DEAR GOD, What Went Wrong...
Where has my gray-haired lover gone?

What has happened to the sun that had swept across his face?
It has gone and found a new place.

What has happened to the fate of my soul mate?
Has he gone or disappeared or just walked off to contemplate.

Will he stay or will he go?
I really don't know.

Maybe, only time will tell.
Hurry Up! My time is all gone and my future has taken a sail
BOY, this sure seems like HELL!!
   Leisa A. Wascher

Passage

The time has come for the journey
Where God and I must walk,
Hand in hand we will cross the bridge
Where the youthful road turns into maturity ridge,

Naivet'e and girlish wonder,
Nature has transformed with eternal power,
Destiny holds court in woman's honorable hour,

Humbled, wombless, refined,
Faithful and thankful to God for this passage sublime,
Why does this passage seem tearful and sad?

The miracle of birth did not passed through me,
God graced a different path for my destiny,

This magnificent emergence to freedom and choice,
Has filled my new world with many new blessings,
So, I say without doubt,

Stand proud mature women,
Hold your head high,
Be a proud child of God,

Take flight...enjoy passage!
Sing as birds fly
   Leslie Maxwell Cook

Smile

Sunshine perpetuates the feeling of your smile
warm against my heart
penetrating through my eyes to melt smoothly down the pathway
to my soul
illuminating me inside and out
I smile back at you.
   Kimberly D. Wonson

Dare To Discover

Dare to discover a world with no pain,
Where even the losers stand to gain
A world where someone raises a voice
And doesn't get hit, while a mother and
Child quietly sit. Where time and age have
No opinion and color no dominion.

Dare to discover a world with no shame
How everything is accepted and no one is
To blame, while violence is a thing of the past
As peace is a part of the future.
Now close your eyes and imagine it fast
In a flutter of an eye "I love you" is spoken
Another life saved another heart unbroken
Where hate becomes a word said almost never.

Dare to discover a world with peace lasting forever.
Meredeth Shellnutt

Seasoned Soul

River of peace why do you rush on so?
Where did you leave your quiet peaceful ways?
The fallen leaves of autumn leaves me cold.
While children love the leaves of purest gold.
The golden sun of autumn gives one hope.
While the cool breeze of night destroys them all.
Life that looked so bright begins to die.
Oh, autumn world you do affect the soul.

The blossoms of purest white open up their eyes.
The cool breeze blows gently through the trees.
River of peace returns to peaceful ways.
As birds above sing their song of praise.
And you feel like a thousand twinkling stars.
As the autumn affected soul returns to life.

Kay Chartre

Oh, Paint Me A Land

Oh, paint me a land where dreams will come true,
where birds in the air will always be blue.
Where the sky up above us will always be bright,
where people stay home during the night.
Oh, paint me a land where children are educated,
where they don't waste their time becoming vegetated.
Where we will no longer be afraid to open doors,
where different countries will no longer be in wars.
Oh, paint me a land where the children will play,
where there won't be any crimes in which you pay.
Where there will be no guns or weapons or any hate,
where people can follow all of their many fates.
Oh, paint me a land where we will all be free,
where generations find the truth they seek.
Where we won't worry about money, power or wealth,
where we will worry only about our own health.
Oh, where is this wondrous land, so great,
it is in our minds, waiting for the paint.

Megan VanderVort

Christmas

People think Christmas is something that it's not.
They say it's because of opening presents,
   that's what they thought.
But it's really because of Jesus' birth.
That's why we have Christmas on earth.
We ought to thank Jesus because if he wasn't born
There wouldn't be a Christmas morn!

Katie Totdahl

For All The Father Forgotten Children....

Father Father Father
Where are you
I am here waiting
Waiting for you

Daddy daddy
do you know me
recognize me

Or am I a sliver from by-gone days
Not to be revisited
I don't want to be
a father forgotten child

Where are all the daddies - where have you gone

We wait in the hope, in the light of day
at night as we dream
to be remembered, to be loved

You held me once
I have a photograph
Tender eyes gazing upon your new baby
remember me daddy, please remember me

Lynn Thomas

"My Gentle Friend"

My gentle friend, is what you are
when you're close, or afar
a love we share that could only be
between close friends, as you and me
when God made you, He had only goodness in mind
Thank God you were in His line, to be filled
with goodness, understanding, and grace
to pull me thru the hard times I've faced
you're my gentle friend, I'll always love
sent to me from Heaven above. You've walked with me
when my trials were hard, you've stood for me
when my world was chard. Thru all the pain, I carried around
you've made me smile, when I had nothing but a frown.

My gentle friend is who you are, your friendship I'll
treasure no matter how far.

Mary Jane Settle

People

Life is funny, for people make a difference in your Life.
When your young you want to be older.
When your older you want to be young.
In your life its who you are and who you become.
When your older you have memories of your life.
Some of these memories are both good and bad.
There are people who hurt you and people who care.
I've felt love from family, friends and support
from those who cared.
I've been hurt and felt pain and learned from it.
I've been shaped by those around me and by my own self.
Each of us walks different walks in life.
We say words that makes sense to only us.
We share our feelings and emotions, others may not understand.
We all have our own agenda in life to fulfill.
   Thank God for People

Mary Ellen Elmer

In My Mind's Eye

In my mind's eye, I can see a place frozen in time.
  When we were together and everything was fine.

In my mind's eye, I can look into your eyes,
  so bright and loving, that tear up when I say good-bye.

In my mind's eye, I can feel your soft skin,
  skin so soft it was like a sin.

In my mind's eye, I can see our touching lips,
  lips so soft and full that I will always miss.

In my mind's eye, I can hold you in my arms so tight,
  arms holding and loving long into the night.

In my mind's eye, your face I can see,
  you will always be a special person to me.

In my mind's eye, I can see us together happy and true,
  as the rainbow loves the rain, and how much I love you.

In my mind's eye, you can see all this and more,
  just by closing your eyes and open your mind's door.

Michael Allan Tafoya

Mid-Night

In the wee hours
when the sun is still dreaming
of the man in the moon, I stir

My eyes focus on the speck of light
that glints through the venetians
from the lone lamppost outside my bedroom window, still stirring

My thoughts wander to the events of the past day
and wonders what the new day will offer
In full stir

I turn on my right side, brushing the hair
of my pillow and yawn body tired,
mind awake, stirring less

I place my arm around the other pillow
remembering a time when someone was there
as a sad smile forms on my lips, I close my eyes
letting old memories flood my vision, hardly a stir

My breathing is deep and heavy
My heartbeat is soothing in my ears
somewhere, a dog is barking, I think
I am still

Madeline C. Ercolano

To A Waterfall

I sat at your feet and in wonder and awe
  I listened to the symphony of sound.
   And watched your joyful leaps...your quiet falls.
Dimensions multiplied by wider terrain
  Of granite-resisting and yielding
    To thy persistent fall.

A small quiet stream...
  Suddenly catapulted downward over a shelf of hard rock
   Over many shelves...into many pools
     Had found freedom...expansion...many exciting leaps
Individuality...expression...excitement.
  A quickened pulse of life...pushing, pulling, demanding
    And the silent flow had found a voice!

I looked down...at the narrowing, converging path.
  To tame?...to contain?...all this wild energy?
    One last wild embrace...one last joyful leap.
And the undisciplined, aimless flow
  Had found the quiet depths of a pool...
    And the silent, small stream was once again
Ready to flow gently and joyfully down the valley.

M. Englestad

Another Day

Oh come with me to another day
When our country was just on its way
When brave men chose liberty or death
For love of country was on their breath

When seeing a war-torn flag at dawn
Inspired an anthem sung on and on
When failure was endured for success
And strong men prayed this land God would bless

When families and friends were torn apart
So that our nation could get a start
When hatred was for an unjust cause
And unity emerged without pause

Where is the love of country today?
It's buried in causes gone astray
It's lost in hate and words to avenge
But there is no progress in revenge

So come with me to another day
When bigotry has faded away
When love for our country reigns again
Uniting, healing the hearts of men

Kay Bryant

Their Auntie's Love

I never will forget the day...
when my sister called me "Auntie" for the very first time.
I looked through the window of the nursery...
and without anyone showing me; I knew the baby nephew which was mine.

He was screaming and yelling...
which showed that he had inherited our family's wit.
When the nurse brought him to the window...
I knew that he possessed my heart... all of it.

I never knew I was capable of loving one so much.
I was there for his first words, steps and teeth.
His smile, his laughter, and his walking about the house....
His very existence has brought so much joy to this family.

The day came when my sister gave me another...
now my wonderful nephew has a precious little brother.
These two little guys make my world seem as peaceful as a dove.
One thing is for certain, my nephews will always have their auntie's love.

Lori D. Williams

Moses

Pharaoh was a mighty man in days of long ago,
When Moses came before him saying, "Let my people go."
Pharaoh didn't see the need to listen or obey,
So he replied to Moses, "No, these people stay."

What Pharaoh didn't realize and Moses surely knew,
Was that Moses' God had spoken, and His word's always true.
So Pharaoh had to learn about the pestilence and hail,
The fire and frogs and first-born death and pests that did assail.

"I've had enough!" the Pharaoh said, "Find Moses; bring him here.
I somehow feel he knows about this death and grief and fear.
Take your people, Moses, their valuables in tow,
Leave Egypt far behind you; please hurry now and go!".

But mighty Pharaoh soon forgot, how black the darkness was,
Of rivers running crimson red, what cattle murrain does.
So Pharaoh told his army, "I need them here to work,
To tend my kine and make my bricks; go after them; don't shirk."

A wide sea lay ahead of them, mighty army in the rear,
It seemed destruction was at hand, with capture drawing near.
But God above had planned a route, unknown to mortal mind,
Dry passage through the vast red sea with Egypt left behind.

Linda S. Nicholson

Grandma

Oh grandma,
When I was young, you sang me to sleep,
When I was young, you held me tight,
When I was young, you pushed me to and fro,
Oh grandma,
When I am old, you listen to my songs,
When I am old, you need me to hold you,
When I am old, you let me push you to and fro,
Oh grandma,
How times have changed.
Oh grandma,
If you will listen to my lullaby,
If you will be held tight,
If you will be pushed to and fro,
I will be old forever.
Oh grandma,
Don't leave me grandma.

Kristen McElduff

The Wind In The Trees

I miss the days before they were grown,
When I had no time to call my own.
Now I sit and listen to the wind in the trees
And I have nothing to do, no others to please.

My mind wanders back to another day,
When all my time was spent a different way.
To a place in time, when my children needed so much.
They wanted my love, my attention and such.

Time didn't seem to go quickly then,
Still I cherished each moment I spent with them.
I loved watching them learn and grow and play.
I wouldn't have spent my time any other way.

No matter what else there was to do,
Or if I was tired or busy they knew
That I would always be there for them;
That I always wanted to be with them.

Did I know then that today would come?
After all those years that I spent on the run
Now I have nothing to do, no others to please,
So I can sit and listen to the wind in the trees.

Lynn D. Mintz

Our Love

Like it was just one day age,
When I first met you, though.
Nothing expected in either of our eyes,
And now you think, oh what a surprise.

It seemed to be only as friends,
Now it seems our love will never end.
With this love that has been given,
It's sure to say our hope has risen.

Now the question's how long we'll stay,
With all the love that's given each day.
But with all the hope that lies deep in our hearts,
Hoping and praying we'll never be apart.

The real thing is, is that we're together,
Giving love that will be forever.
And to you my love, who I'll never forsake,
Is all the more love that I will take!

Lisa Zakrzewski

Colors

When I am born I am pink,
When I am scared I am white,
When I am cold I am blue,
When I am sick I am green,

I am colored, many colors,

Why when someone is born they are black,
When they are scared they are black,
And when they are sick they are black,
And they still call them colored,

We are all colored,

Our bodies, on the inside of our heart all change color,
Like the house of changing color in *Wizard of Oz*,
We change like the skin of a chameleon,
But we all have differences on the inside,
All unique,
All special,
All great,
All smart,
But in different ways.

Kate Fettis

The Garden

When the snow flakes are gently falling;
When children are playing and snow-balling;
I will think of you, and of the summer sun;
And the garden will be on my mind.

When the cold and harsh winds blow;
When the birds are leaving in droves;
Your memories in my heart glow;
And the garden will be on my mind.

When days are short, nights are long;
I will listen to music and sing a song;
A song about happiness, about love, about you;
And the garden will be on my mind.

When I am in a faraway place;
Somewhere on the earth searching for a trace;
I will see your eyes, your smile, your face;
And the garden will be on my mind.

When the dark clouds cover sun's face;
I will imagine the sunny days that I always praise;
I will be full of feelings that I could not phrase:
AND THE GARDEN WILL BE ON MY MIND.

Nabil Cyrus Fani

Look To The Top Of A Tree

Look at the top of a tree and you will see,
What God in his love now has given to you and to me.
New branches and tender green leaves, turning ever to God,
Looking and worshiping, drawing from life-giving sod.
So we in out lives, now can also look upward and see,
His love and his helping if we will but quiet be.
Kind thoughts and kind feelings, God's love, is beginning to grow,
From the tinniest seed of a thought, which at first he did sow.
Stronger and bigger we steadily grow in our place,
Knowledge and wisdom, enlightenment, show in our face,
Achieving the highest of life for us here on this earth,
Assembling all of those things, our life now has a new birth.
Striving and working to concentrate - faltering never,
Through love, we will dwell in the House of our Lord, for ever!

Lawrence Wilson Smith

Golden Years

Golden years and golden tears of days gone by.
We're looking through the hour glass at you and I.

I know you've always kept me inside your mind,
and I know you would never ever leave me behind,
I know you've always loved me, never put anyone above me,
and I know we will never part.

Fifty years have past us by never once wondered why,
Fifty more could come through the door,
and it would still be you and I.

Golden years and golden tears of time gone by.
We're looking through the hour glass at you and I.

No one will ever replace you inside my heart,
and I hope you know I've loved you right from the start.
No one will ever take you, and I will never forsake you,
and I'll always keep you in my heart.

Fifty years have past us by never once wondered why.
Fifty more could come through the door,
and it would still be you and I.

Golden years and golden tears the years flew by.
We're looking through the hour glass at you and I.
   Loren T. Jeffries

Los Indios

O, if the wind could speak.
   We'd hear of legends long time lost.
Legends of "Indios" in my part of the world.
   The valley.

Karankawas, coahuilticans, tejones,
   Pintos and narices.
Tribes long forgotten gone forever.
Enslaved by white man,
   Los Espanioles, conquistadores.

If one listens closely to the whispering wind.
You'd hear laughter, crying and suffering of my people
   Los Indios.

Who as colonization progressed in my part of
The world the valley,
We grew extinct, like my brother the coyote.
We joined other tribes to survive.
My brother lost his racial identity by mixing
His blood with others, to become
   Los Mexicanos Americanos.
   Oralia Cortez Garcia

Graduation Poem

In the beginning of this class
We found ourselves in doubt
As the time passed by, it became
More real
We put forth our ability as the
School year passed

We learned how to communicate with each other
In more ways than one
The most important part was understanding and that's what took
   us further

Through situations and circumstances
We never got upset
Thanks to our parents and teachers
You're someone we'll never forget

If someone should hinder me of my goal
After teaching us all these things
We find comfort in knowing
After graduation our hearts will gladly sing
   Lindell Sledge

Social Tapestries

The fabric of society is divided,
weaved on separate looms,
into cultural time tapestries;
prejudicial borders edge the taut hems.
Fibers of emotion become enmeshed,
on the viscous web of time,
stuck in the universal fibers of the heartbeat.

Ancient rotations restrain the sagacity,
the axis turns, the wisdom is trapped
in heirlooms of opinionated control.
The cycle continues, handed down
from one generation to the next,
fortified in antique chests of the soul,
until naked emotion is catapulted
through the barriers of the tapestry of time.

The translucent edges of the heart's darkness
unthread; man becomes an enlightened sage,
viewing the Earth through kaleidoscope lenses,
weaving a symmetrical, social tapestry of harmony,
woven of threads from one interdependent loom.
   Lorraine Millings

In The Chapel

In the chapel, each Sunday night,
   We think and pray by candle-light.
Each head is just a silhouette,
   With minds as close to God as they can get;
IN THE CHAPEL WE KNOW SO WELL.

The evening through we sing and pray,
   And for a bit we even play.
But comes the call at nine o'clock,
   We all slow down to a calm, quiet walk;
TO THE CHAPEL WE KNOW SO WELL.

How many times have we talked there,
   Just you and I, and the One who cares?
Many thoughts and dreams have been unwound,
   And many, many solutions found;
IN THE CHAPEL WE KNOW SO WELL.

God is present, we all know,
   In each pew and candle-glow.
No other place would I rather be,
   Than there in the Chapel, to pray with thee;
THE CHAPEL WE LOVE SO WELL.
   Nancy Kildow

My One Penny

Treasures of the heart, are the memories
we make. Whether you are happy or sad, it
involves emotion.
My pleasure, is to tell you about a memory
that continues still today.
I may not have a lot of since but, I always's
have one Penny. You see the difference between
my penny and the one you may have, is my
Penny is a dear friend.
I guess, some people have good luck charm's
but, it's one penny I don't think I'll ever choose
to loose. For you see my Penny has been
there for me since, I was thirteen. I'd say
that takes a lot of devotion to stick around that
many years. I'm rich with my one Penny,
because a true friend, you just can't buy.
No matter how hard you look or try,
pennies aren't for sale. True friends you just
cannot buy.
   Mary Christine Lucas

Mrs. Tate And Mrs. O'Shea

Of General Hospital, Room three-thirty-eight,
we have the opinion of one Mrs. Tate:
The walls are mold green, the room is too small
and crowded and stuffy. There's noise in the hall.
The food is repugnant, the nurses neglectful,
the workers so bad that she can't be respectful.
The chair isn't soft; it pinches her butt.
Prison would be better, she feels in her gut.
Hallelujah! Mrs. Tate went home yesterday.

Room three-thirty-eight welcomes Mrs. O'Shea.
She's tired of cooking; she likes the food here,
especially breakfast, it's good, hearty fare.
"The French toast and pancakes are tasty," she said,
"and I love to be served my breakfast in bed."
The temperature's perfect, the walls a cool green.
The chair is quite comfy, the floor is mopped clean.
The room's a nice size. The nurses are kind.
This type of attention, at home, you don't find.

The room had been lousy, but now it is cherry.
It must be the work of the good bedpan fairy.

Lois Conway

Before Man

We once roamed the forests, proud, lean, and tall;
We frolicked in the meadows, unafraid of most all.

We adapted to the seasons, our herds grew in size;
We thank mother nature for our protective disguise.

We battled the elements, including fire, and flood;
The sense for survival was instilled in our blood.

Nature provides, but also takes away,
As we fall victim to our own natural prey.

As cities and tall buildings and populations grew,
We went deep into the woods, we hid, we withdrew.

First came the arrows, followed by guns;
Are we forever to be on the run?

A shot is fired, I stumble and fall;
Was it my destiny to end up a trophy on your wall?

Lora L. Ommondson

Help

You're not alone in this world that we live
We face many problems, with nothing to give
There's a pain in all of us which gives us grief
When the pain is over, we take a sigh of relief

How many times have you stopped to think,
Of the hungry and homeless that sit on the street
The pain that's within them never is done
Some of them die of murder by gun
More of them die from nothing to eat

The rich ones that are there look on and walk by
With money to spend and none they'll give on.
Help the homeless they are all human too,
And take out a blanket and give it to whom?

Give it to him the freezing old man
The one in the corner with his face in his hands

Help them all out, they'd do the same for you,
If you had to live with the pain too.

Lyndsey M. Eymann

Days End

The wind blows listlessly across the beach
waves bounding toward the shore with boundless energy
warm sand falling gently between my toes
The sun blazes down upon my head.
Children's laughter heard in the distance
Sea gulls flying high above unconcerned
Sailboats dotting the horizon in brilliant colors
Water slapping at my ankles
Sea spray hitting my face
A sense of calm settles in.
The wind turns slightly cool as an array of hues
cover the sky
The softened sun meet the vast ocean
Another day has gone.

Kelly Steepleton

Fairies

There are fairies near by
   watching you and I.
Their mischievous eyes are upon us.
These little dears with elfish ears
   can hear the lovers sigh.

The fairies know not sadness
   though troubles there may be.
Their hearts are pure and joyful
   and full of tranquility.

They follow the weary wanderer
   and put his mind at ease.
They flit unseen around us
   high in the great old trees
Up the grassy hillsides, down to the gray, green seas.

Wherever a saddened lover
   or tender heart may be.
Know that they are not alone, with life's inequities.

Natalie Sands

The Dock Rat Society - The Legend Of Benny Schwartz

He fought in the Spanish American War.
Was a recognized expert on Indian lore.
With the circus he traveled near and far.
Sailing Lake Michigan he was a star!

The founder of Dock Rats, that prestigious society,
He was a man of experience and sobriety.
His stories insured a devoted congregation.
The kids hung around for most of their vacation.

Dock Rats were much admired.
At the age of twelve I so aspired.
Initiation was strict he stressed!
It was to be thrown in the water completely dressed.

And so one day it happened to me.
Soaking wet and full of glee,
Home I came with joyful look,
"I've got my name in the Dock Rat book!"

Nancy Groth

Free

I believe everyone's mind and soul are free
We have the power to make it soar, live, and love
We wish upon stars and wait for magic to appear
I believe the only way to be free
Is not to wish upon stars
But to take control.
Reach for your goals
And allow your spirit to soar
Like a bird...free..free at last

Leeah Borner

Security

Sun drenched feet
Warm smiling hands
Make the whole world happy
When the sun goes to sleep
The moon wakes up
Nothing really seems friendly anymore
Creeping, crawling
Dark and dreary when you are
Supposed to be in bed, but cannot go to sleep
Because your socks make you cozy
The darkness will not hurt
And the sun is coming around the bend
She peeks over the treetops to scare away
The creepies
Everything is good
With sun drenched feet
And warm smiling hands
The whole world is happy

Katie Whitteker

"Thinking Of You"

Lying here in my bed, with many thoughts of you,
Wanting to see your face, even a phone call will do.
Alone here in my room, feeling sad and blue,
Darling I never meant those unkind words
that I said to you.
Outside the wind is howling, snow and rain
are falling upon the windowpane.
All the world looks dark and dreary,
Oh how I wish that I was in your arms again.

Lena Faulkner

The Abyss

I'm in a place where no one goes. It's dark here. There are no walls, no floors. There's no space, nor time. It's black. But I'm here, and I'm alone.

It's a place where no one goes ... and I feel nothing.

I've been here before, briefly. There's a sense of permanence this time. It's not cold. It's not hot. It's nothing. They see me, and they think I'm real. It looks right. They touch my hand, or my arm, when they speak to me, and they feel warmth.

I'm in a place where no one goes ... and I feel nothing.

I don't always hear the words they speak. I nod, or say something superfluous, and that suffices. I want them to touch more, so I could feel. I don't want them to touch at all.

I'm in a place where they can't be ... and I feel nothing.

I should cry. I should scream. There are no tears. It's more distant than a voice. I'm at the depth of the ocean where there are no sounds, and if I scream I'll die, and it's just me.

I'm in a place where they can't be...
and I feel nothing.

Lori L. Greenan

Exempt From Vengeance

Moss, leaves, and bark involve the multitude of sight,
while hidden in a pine tree an owl is silent due to light.
Mercy is not visible here among predator to the feeble prey,
but revenge will never traverse the thoughts,
from the living that are kin of the dust.
Once an act of killing has passed
in the territory of unseen noise,
another death will not occur unless it simply must.

Kenneth W. Wood Jr.

I Must Die

The old Tree stood silently by the mill,
Waiting, watching, slumbering still,
Awakened by nightly dreams that kill,
The deadly sting of winter's hail.

"Spring! Spring!" The old Tree wailed,
"Send down your caressing, velvet gale,
My heart is worn and just may fail,
Within the sight of winter's tail.

Spring answered the Tree with ferocious might.
There was a mighty, spectacular fight,
Lightening swords danced through the night,
Morning dawned on a frozen sight.

Laughter rang from the old Tree's core,
"Spring is a flighty, adolescent girl,
She knocks and flirt at nature's door,
Then retreats for another lure."

The laughter died in a mournful sigh,
Snow birds heard his one last cry,
Spreading their wings, attempting to fly,
From that whisper, "I MUST die."

Mary S. Cook

A Father's Challenge

As I lie awake in bed tonight,
Waiting silently for time to pass,
My thoughts drifted and took a flight
On tomorrow's herculean task.

Far away, a thousand miles
A son, a daughter and a wife;
Full of dreams in their eyes,
Hoping for a better life.

In this glorious land of the free,
Fate's elusive, faith's the key.
I seek my golden opportunity,
To work and be what I can be.

Life's a river, flowing into the sea
Fear not the valleys, I'll find a way.
Hold on to the dreams of my family
Soon I'll be there, to reach the bay.

Miguel Mojado Jr.

Funeral

We gather at the entrance into grace
waiting for the service of the dead to begin.

Talk and warmth are exchanged
as we slowly fill the room save one corner

Where the open pink and white museum stands.
Inside, a waxen memory is revealed.

Death lies in that corner.
Tho some of us view what remains, none stay long.

Only a pedestaled Jesus with its large
gold medallion and red top-knot remains there.

As the service begins,
a new life is wheeled in peering thru blankets.

Her tiny smile greets us.

Lianne Kinsella Tolman

Radiance Dance

Delicately spirited, unique.
Vividly crisp!
Straining innately,
Virgin vines grasp, ripe and elated.

A miraculous treasure.
Absorbing His sparkling trance of power.
Selfish — unknowing;
Desire's thirst burning but oblivious.

Tempestuous spells dam fluidity,
The intensity uprooting buried weakness.
Given the grace — surviving!
To blossom to Her perennial cadence — righteously beholden.

Awarded with the significance to prevail;
A journey, one's own.
Rootbound in darkness,

Unaware — alone

Hungered destiny comes — and ends,
Then Beauty is one's own.
Immortal radiance illuminating value,
After the inevitable wilting of precious petals.

Laine Souza

Alone!!!

Alone, I am all by myself; like a porcelain doll
   upon a shelf.
No one knows what I'm thinking; no one care's what
   I'm feeling.
On a shelf so fragile and pretty; never showing
   any pity.
I think I'm real; I can see; I can feel.
I always cry, though my face remains dry.
No tears are shown; though I'm so alone.
Someone finally takes me down; now I have a
   smile, not a frown.
Slowly, my smile disappears, as my glass ears' hear.
"Since she's so little, we shall put her in the middle."
I'm put in place, on a shelf of black lace.
Here comes the tears, as the lady disappears.
As the shelf doors slam; I realize, a porcelain
   doll is all I am.

Kristy Lynch

Anchor Of The Soul

We wonder what the future holds
Tossed about in the sea of life.
Where will I go or what shall I be
When the world creates winds of strife?
It is to easy to get off course
And be rocked and swayed by the things of this world,
To be tempted by the Enemy's hand,
Our ship into a storm is hurled.
As the storm approaches winds begin to howl
The boat could seem to fall apart,
Yet a guidance from within the hull
Reminds us who is the owner of our heart.
For within my lifeboat I know I'll find
An anchor that always gives me hope.
A whisper that comes from within,
The spirit reminds, "Hush. Be still and know."
The anchor of my soul provides
A peace that calms the storm within,
And provides an inner sanctuary
To again focus my trust and hope in Him.

Michele Lee Botts

Peace

Children hungry in the streets, men fight on as women weep
Untold, countless, faceless foes, fight for What? No one knows.
Shoot to kill - not just stop! Man - woman - child - a too young cop!
Faces in jails we cannot see, living better than you and me
Little children tossed from home to home, others simply left to roam
Emergency rooms filled with self-induced wounds, this has to stop!
It must stop soon!
We coddle the criminal and let the child die, we pay for organs to sustain our lives.
We run in fear from malls and stores to hide in our homes with locks on the doors.
The color of skin guides the paths we choose - Wrong color, too bad, guess you lose.
Places in college, at work, on a jury, chosen by color, it just causes fury.
Not the person, the soul inside, guides the choices, it's just not right.
Too many possessions. Not enough money. Credit far above any salary.
It's not funny.
Where are we going? When will it stop? Peace is the answer and must start at the top.
Nation with nation, not against. Friend helping friend, not money spent.
People taking a stand on what is right. Educate the children so they don't have to fight.
Feed one another as best you can. Reach out your hand to your fellow man.
Give of yourself, don't just take. Pity the man who drops out of the race.
Make the guilty responsible for their sins and give the real victims their true amends
Peace is the answer, without and victim
When our souls chose the pathway, then peace can begin!

Marlee Payne Shaw

War

Too many times they've gone to war,
trying to settle the unkept score.

Two different teams with two different dreams,
both trying to make them come true.

To conquer the other, they must slay each other,
both trying not to lose.

Too many bodies in the trenches we dug,
open grave sites for those we have loved.

Two teams heading home, weary from war,
one found glory, the other wounded and sore.

To think or to say, what have we lost, what have we gained,
nothing. Why do we keep playing this game?

Melissa Zemann

Will They Remember When I'm Gone

A sweltering jungle,
tropical rain,
exotic insects, alien chirps.

The acrid odor of cordite, putrid death scents.
Maimed, unwanted bastard children
crowd orphanages.

A comrade falls,
his eyes fade
while his life seeps through my fingers.

The challenge of Southeast Asia.
We failed,
and the plantations prospered.

We battled the communist blight,
and died for a noble cause
black markets sprouted capitalist wealth.

We failed,
with empty promises
and false hope.

Linn Booth

Why God Made Little Girls

God made the world with its huge
towering trees and majestic mountains and restless
seas. Then paused and said "it needs one more
important thing... Someone to laugh and dance and
sing to walk in the woods and gather flowers
to commune with nature in quiet hours. So
God created little girls. With laughing eyes
and bouncing curls with joyful hearts and infectious
smiles. And with enchanting and feminine ways.
And when he'd completed the task he'd
begun he was pleased and proud of the job
he'd done for the world when seen through
a little girl's eyes and greatly resembles paradise.
   Lisa Cregger

Tonight Could Be So Beautiful

Tonight could be so beautiful if only we would speak
Tonight could be so beautiful if only we wouldn't weep
When things get tense I don't understand why it has to be this way
And then I realize that we don't have to make it this way
If only we would try
Things could be better things would be better
Things would be better
If only we would try
Tonight could be so beautiful if only we would try
   Melanie Myers

"A Salute To Mother On Mother's Day"

Happy Mother's Day!
Today is special because it's for you.

I can't be there in person but everyone knows
That a few words of prose will travel a long way
on this special day.

Although you may think that your job is done,
The children are raised, the work is diminished.
We need mothers all year through, to talk to, to listen
And to heal our sorrows...we're never finished!....

Some of us are lucky we have mom for years
Others are cut short and sadly I fear.
Never knowing or loving their aging faces,
listening to their learned advice, and sharing God's graces.

So this day we salute you for a job well done!
You have taught us well the value a mother holds.
Some of us young and some of us old.
Our love only increases as time unfolds...

A salute to my mother a world away...
May your heart not be too lonely on this Mother's Day.
   Lynne Drummond

The Unprofitable Servant

Abba, Father, not that slothful and faithless tree
To which you came year by year, seeking fruit
And found it proud and careless, yet barren
Cursed in righteous fury, perished,
Withered and dried up at its roots

Oh! I pray you instead, that other fig
Which your faithful husband man tended
Long suffering and determined, dug about and dunged
By your grace and loving kindness, perchance
One season yet to heal my sore remiss

(Mark 11:12-14; Luke 13:6-9)
   Murl Ming

A Special Time

From the time I awake at dawn
To the time I retire at dust,
This is a special time.
To enjoy life in all its splendor,
To feel the breezes and see the trees,
Oh! I'm so glad to be alive today.
This is a special time.
To walk thru the day into the night,
To see the sky darken and the stars shine bright,
They glisten and gleam and give me time to dream,
This is a special time.
Hoping it's not too late to have a special someone,
To have and to hold for the rest of my life,
This will be a special time.
The greatest time of my life
To enjoy love, music and the simple things in life,
I have the time now for that special time.
   Mary Patricia Hickey

The Adamant Irish

A true son of Ireland defends his ideals
To the fullest extent of his might.
Depending on decency, honor, and truth
And the armor of justice and right.

Beware of the Irish when you and your cohorts
An evil connivance have hatched.
When you've counted the cost at the end of the fray
You'll find you were overmatched.

Your briars and barbs and brambles and thorns
May bloody and scar my skin.
When you've given your all in your effort to beat me
I still won't have given in.

You'll never succeed in your plan to dislodge me
From the ramparts I choose to defend.
Your deceit and decay will provoke your destruction
And I'll surely prevail in the end.

The soul of an Irishman never submits
To the cruelties men can apply.
When the tormentor tires of his senseless attacks
Undefeated, unyielding, undaunted stand I.
   Otis Lee Earley

A Pond Of Peace

An excursion to a Pond of Peace
To stillness and seclusion
To reflect, recharge soul and body.
To ponder the meaning of one's existence within
A milieu where chaos wrests order, strength, and purpose
From the course of daily survival.
I seek refuge, though temporal and visionary.

A hanging branchlet, funnels collected dew.
Crystalline droplets, timed with perfection,
Kiss the glass-like surface — assimilate and disappear.
But they leave their watermarks
Of continuous ripples radiating in concentricity
To mesmerize and comfort
As voices heard,
As feeling felt.
Undiminished, undistorted, unobstructed,
The calmative patterns of peace widen.
It is my voice that speaks,
It is my heart that feels,
Silently, steadily spreading across my Pond of Peace.
   Kazu Maruoka

"Destiny Divine"

The road is too bumpy, too windy too vast,
to know where I'm going this far in advance.
I could hope, I could strive, I could plan to the tee,
but where my path leads me I have yet to see.
It's a mystery to me.

I'll know where I'm going when I get there, and I'll
get there in time.

I'll know where I'm going when I get there, only then
will I know my Destiny Divine.

My goals have changed, have developed, have grown,
but which path I should take is still somewhat unknown -
'cause constant distractions backtrack me in time-
will I ever find my Destiny Divine?
It's a mystery to me.
Maria Calabro

The Only Question!

   Our lives before we arrive in Heaven are a 'treaty'!
To get to heavens open gate, I must treat you as I would that you treat me!
   Has not...this been the Heavenly Compact which our Father has asked of us?
We know our Father treats us with Mercy, can we do I likewise?
   High Shepherd of the River
A promise recalls...
   the return of mercy
I look up, I see
   Living water cross the sky;
Flowing on, night lights to Day...
   NEW CITY of GOD!
Gladness reigned.
   Tombs go empty, yet again!
All the Prophets LIVE!
   "So will you!"
Nicky Van Nav

Home, Far Away

When thinking of a poem to write, my thoughts just seem to stray,
   To family, friends and countryside, in a land so far away.
The land is green, it's forty shades, breathtaking from the air,
   It's Ireland that I speak of, referred sometimes as, Eire.
In dreams when I revisit, their faces seem so clear,
   The darling Irish children, so well loved and so dear.
I see the lakes and mountains, bay of Dingle and Tralee,
   The beauty of its seashore, keeps calling back to me.
Traveling down their narrow roads, thru fields of green for miles,
   Each one we passed, on bike or foot,
   Would wave hello with a smile.
In song it's called "fair city," it's history so renowned,
   The churches and the streets of old, busy, thriving Dublin town.
Words can't express my feeling, for that country 'cross the miles,
   It calls and beckons, next time, please try to stay awhile.
Nancy L. Espisito

Life In Paradise

A time and place where no one dies
Where only joy and laughter multiplies.
A time when choruses of praise continue to rise
To honor our Creator living beyond the skies.
A time when there will be so much happiness
because all our efforts, He will bless.
A time when the earth won't be a terrible mess
because in beauty and splendor it will be dressed.
A time when our dead loved ones will arise
That will be life in God's promised paradise!
Mary E. Lang

"Let Me Be Me"

As a kid, I should be free
To express myself in the many ways that are me

Who are you as my parent to decree
That I can't be me?

Am I to become a monument to a history
Whose intent-I can't even began to understand...?

Yet to please you
I would do all of these things...

Become a me...I don't know
Even though it hurts me so...to show you
The depths of my love...For you...
My Mother, my creator, my being...
...My first love...who is able...to confuse, even use
Cruel and undue punishment...such as...the past mistakes...

Mistakes are apart of this game called life...
No one knows better than you
How many times did you say you've been a wife...?

So mother please be gentle, love and forgive me
Remember only by your example...can I land on my two feet
And become the man you've always wanted me to be.
Kathy Wooden

Storms

As the bright orange sun meets the horizon
to end a warm summers day
The waves slowly reach the shore
As the evening sky rolls in
The hidden stars illuminate the darkening sky
as the moon appears from out of no where
the sea glimmers as the waves become stronger
and harder, the dark clouds rolled in.
The crashing of thunder,
woke all that was around
The lightening lit up the sky
as if it were day
The waves crashed fiercely
as the rain pounded down onto the shore
As the sun rose.
all returned to normal
As if nothing every happened.
Melissa A. Bifano

Doodles And Dabbles

When I doodle, I doodle thus, and when I dabble, I try
To create a doodle that looks like a dabble to fool the untrained eye.
I doodle the center of all life—clear essence that owns no gray,
But then I dabble a smudge or two to smear it all away.

I guess I won't look at a center, can't focus on the spot,
So I dabble away the doodle to make it what it's not.
Some say I avoid all nuclei—the part that exposure brings clear,
So I dabble a cloud on my doodle, a pall to cover my fear.

I sketch in confusion and dabble in guilt and smear in a crisis or prank
And watch as my doodle is dabbled to death—to emptiness, darkness, a blank.
So, what is the meaning of this strange art, the doodles I dabble awry?
It must be fear, my terrible fear, to look God in the eye.
Mary R. Lewis

"Away From The Hill"

Moving away was hard for me to do,
to be true my soul was empty and blue.
All that I could think about for a year,
was my youth to make you seem close and near.
Winter was definitely no problem,
the snow was not in my thoughts of longin'.
spring was new with life but it came and went,
the memories flowed about times well spent.
Summer was when I longed for you the most,
trying to catch a glimpse of an Ozark ghost.
falls is when I dare say it happened,
I left them dry desert caverns.
when I entered the hills at last I knew,
that you would take care of me through and through.
Markeeta McGehee

Change The World...

Centuries ago, the Great Floods were cast,
To balance the evildoers of the past,
Today, Life's Famine, the Battles of AIDS,
The Great Master's sign of shame laid.

Truth must stand trial,
For treasons to lie,
About the real feelings to love,
Given one more chance from above.

Build a strength for the World dome,
Share a message of love from home,
Love unconditionally and forgive pain's worth,
The happiness of an enemy comes first,
Care to offer a helping hand,
Treat a stranger like a friend,
As the heart's goodness shines true,
Lessons of kindness learned by so few.

Watch the ways of the world change,
Through the reflections of a loving heart,
Honestly, openly and willingly to start,
The seeds of the Great Master's love reins.
Lourdes P. Stein

Your Precious Face

As I'm working today my mind is wandering
To a beautiful time and place.
And in these thoughts my mind sees an image.
None other than your Precious Face.

The brow is furrowed, the mouth has a smile,
The eyes twinkle with love.
And I can't help but love deeply this face,
That was molded by the Lord up above.

And I see in this face the love that I need.
And all that my heart desires.
And the eyes reflect the love in your heart.
And it lights my inward fires.

So take care of that face, that Precious Face.
Keep it healthy and gay.
I will love it always with a deep rooted love,
Until the end of my days.
Luella L. Lawrence

Live With Laughter!

You can't live your life without laughter.
'Tis an impossible thing to do.
If you're 'round those who are drudgerous
You find it rubs off on you.

Sometimes there's born in this world
A person, whose color is gray.
They dim the sunshine for everyone 'round
And put darkened clouds in their way.

They walk in a room, spreading their gloom
Their hopelessness hangs in the air
To dampen your dreams; drain your life's blood,
And you find that you no longer care.

But when you're around someone happy,
Your spirits soar high to the air
With a vengeance, skirting the stars,
And your worries are easy to bear.

So if you find you're a gray person,
It's still not too late to repent,
'Fore wretches who have to be near you
Are old, and wrinkled and bent!
Marie Matthews Hackney

"A Day In The Life"

I awoke refreshed;
Tingling shower reviving my spirit, caressing my flesh.
A new adventure, another day to celebrate life.

When arranged, fled the captive walls
To delight in the chill of winter;
Nipping cold teasing my cheeks, pinching my nose.

I am a part of today;
A voice in the expanse of life.
I feel fulfilled in my perceptions of existence.

Each experience, whether painful or pleasant,
belong to me.
My daily gifts from the Giver of all life.

May I always, as long as I return anew
With the freshness of morning,
Never neglect to rejoice

With the unfathomable ecstasy
of awareness;
Of experiencing the act of living.
Marsha E. Scholes

Our Yesterdays

I'm looking over my shoulder to a
time that was yesterday.

And the years just fade away and once more
familiar places and familiar faces I see. And
as they pass in review, Beautiful moment's
spent with you.

They are memories to share and keep
Perhaps one day again we'll meet. Alas, somewhere,
long the way.

Our hair has turned to gray, beautiful
memories still remain of a time when we were
young. Back to a day when our friends began

Who can remember when or where I just know
you have always been a special friend
Leoma Cardwell Allen

Our Family

From the dawning of life at the birth of a babe,
'Til suddenly it seems you've reached middle age,
Until death takes its toll on the sick or the old
A family will stand together.

Molded and bonded by generations of love,
Strengthened and guided by grace from above.
Welded by faith, compassion, and trust
Giving one to the other that which is just
A family will stand together.

From the roots of our beginning, to each twig on our tree,
This love is unshaken through eternity.
Nothing can break us or tear us apart,
For each to the other we've given our heart
And our family will stand together.
Kathy Sellers

From Eden To The Crossing

Life, I find you in this crossing where I stand,
Through which the red sea nourishes that tree,
Onto that vine, I wrap about my hand,
And take from it a fruit, and set me free
Into chaotic worlds, I find myself
In Anger, hating everything I've done,
And anger is the world in which I dwell
To live my life a virtuous man, a son
Is I who does return to crossing roads;
Here I find you twice for nourishment,
To gain my soul and walk along these roads,
Of which one path brings voices heaven sent,
The other bridges worlds, return is made
By me a son to bear more fruitful works,
And make his offer to or sinful trade,
For fall, it gives the season of our births;
Take from this the map of life I give,
To live my life as this, I long to dwell,
Learn of me, my vows I seek to live,
And if I should fail, Damn me to Hell.
Newton Tak

The Necessity of Obedience

The future of God is promise I will receive,
this is the message which came to me.

The Spirit of God is my power,
He is my friend who sees for me.

I love to greet him in the morning,
when I am awaken, I humble myself and
kneel down and pray to thank him for the gift he
have given once more, another day.

It's protection, shelter, clothes, and food to eat.
Alone with all that he gave me good friends,
and peace in my heart, too.

Strength that will supply me for the day.
But, yet I sometime become afraid.
He just whisper, "I am beside you."
It's just you and me, peace be still.

Thy pardoning, oh Lord let me hear.
Praise I will sing forever and ever more.
Leotha Womble

The Message

Step back and take a good look,
  this education requires no book.
Existing once - love, honor, kindness,
  rapidly diminished now left behind us.
Deadly sins reside at the campfires of our very souls,
  succumbed by their venomous smoke, burned by malignant coals.
We're maliciously knighted daily, on bended knees,
  held captive by dark and unyielding forces.
Helpless and awaiting our sentence or rescue.
  Which will it be?
Mindy Marshall

Birthday Sixty Five

Now, that you are sixty five
Think of those good years that have gone by.
Don't worry about that grey in your hair,
Just be thankful you got Medicare.

And even tho your get up and go,
got up and went,
Thank the good Lord
For the blessings He sent.
Then, whatever span of life God
permits to you,
Keep in good faith day by day,
Until the good Lord calls you away.
Mildred Turkington

Untitled

  Time passes and I regret
  Things happen and I regret
  People change and I regret
  Memories die and I regret
  Feelings change and I regret
  Time passes and I regret
Happenings happen, some I could have delayed,
  some I didn't.
Sorrow surrounds, Time has passed..Sorrow surrounds,
  hesitation...why...confusion...why

I couldn't have known - no way of knowing;
  I'm growing, so are you;
And still, time passes, time passes.
Looking back - "No, let's not." Painful decisions.

Fate has taken it's toll...Do you think
  I do, often too much.
Depressing suggestions, thoughts, ideas,
feelings, images, lyrics, words....
That have been written
  And will never be erased.
Meredyth Biggs

In A MUD (Virtual Reality)

Oh, "EdeNet Gardens" are dandy and fine,
Where souls have pleasure to meet,
Where one can imagine a bottle of wine,
Another - some bread or some meat.
And souls would drink from the bottle at once,
With no collision of lips,
And souls would circle and jump in a dance,
The dance, which provokes and tips...
Meanwhile, their bodies, in front of the screens,
With fingers a - glued to keyboards,
Enjoying the freedom of souls and sins,
Would wiggle like power cords.
Konstantin Berdichevsky

Depressed And Confused

Confusion is everywhere: So many choices, so little time
They say, "These are the best years of your life"
Well if they are, kill me now
"Friendship is forever," or so they'll tell you
But who can you really trust
Everyone has betrayed you and if they haven't, they will
People say, "Be happy ... you're so young,"
but then they force you to do things you don't want to do
What can you do?
Is there something to take away the pain
You can't run from life or can you
You're screwed!
There are too many restrictions, too many rules
who wants to be ordinary and average ... they do
But why? There is so much here so much to experience
I want to be someone, not just anyone, someone special,
someone that makes a difference
Life is such a confusing state

Karen Ann Kniffin

The Stars

I watch the stars shine on me. They twinkle and they glow.
They like me, I think.
They are faithful, if unrecognizable, and they make no sound.
They like me, I think.
They do not argue, give no hassle, have no worries.
They like me, I think.
The sky is dark behind their beauty. It only adds to their loveliness.
They like me, I think.
They do not yell, do not control, indeed they want nothing.
They like me, I think.
I think of them in their bright glory and a tear touches my cheek.
I think of them so majestic and free
and am awed to think that they like me.

Myra Middleton

Memories

Sweet memories are like the choicest wines,
They grow more sweet and mellow through the years.
The heart will keep them as within a shrine,
And time will ever soothe the sting of tears.
The tender memories of perfect hours
Remain in all their beauty in the heart,
The past in soon serene within their powers,
While sorrow and despair will soon depart.
Each day must bring its lot of joy or care,
And though perhaps the balance seems to show
That troubles come in far too large a share,
It still is very comforting to know
That life is like old wines, sweet memories stay;
The bitterness is lost along the way.

Larry Miller

Losing Someone

Sometimes it is very hard to understand that someone has past away. they are in heaven and happy as can be. When you are experiencing a death in the family you feel bad. When you walk into the funeral home and see someone that was close to home it makes you feel sad. But they're in heaven now in that never ending light so happy and so bright. They will have a special spot in your heart forever. You will never forget them. When you say your last good-byes it seems forever. When the work is all over, He will call you home and you will meet again.

Matt Anderson

The Song Of Joe

"Don't worry. It's ok."
These familiar words will live on in the Song of Joe.

If ever there is a time of doubt or sorrow,
These words will comfort you more than you know because
They are in the Song of Joe.

Every time I wash my breakfast dishes,
Or ever grab a hamburger for lunch,
Or maybe prepare pasta for dinner I will hear those
words and his singing in the Song of Joe.

Every time I tread upon the path that he has taken or,
Every time I see a chair he has been in or a cup of coffee,
Even every time I order eggs made in a special way that he
always made,
I will hear his words and remember the Song of Joe.

To some he was the great protector,
And to others he was wisdom incarnate,
To me he was all of that and much more,
But he will always be Joe,
In this Song of Joe.

Matthew Nguyen

My People

Men litter the streets, waiting for a low paying job.
These...are my people.
Men pushing lawn mowers to clean your beautiful yards,
These...are my people.
Women cleaning your houses and cooking your meals,
These...are my people.
Street vendors selling little trinkets to earn money,
These...are my people.
Somehow, someday tired of your indifference, weary of all
the hard work, they will rise up to change,
These...are my people.

Karina Escalante

The Poem Sculptor

In every flower, bird or tree
There lies a line of poetry —
One thought, expressed in rhyme and meter, hides.
In every strain of melody
A lyric struggles to be free —
A verse, yet raw and unrefined, abides.

Before the story can be told,
Before poetic lines unfold,
The writer's mind and hand must first be wed.
He sets the thought's parameter,
Employs trochee tetrameter,
And beautifies the story to be said.

Owen E. Humphrey

Barren

The cold wind blows bringing my hair to my face
There isn't a sight of anything any place
As if I'm snowbound on a winter's day
Alone in the world in every way
Like a little island all alone in the sea
No one can hear, see, or speak of me
I am invisible to the whole world
Except when needed to be ridiculed
The whole world is my enemy including myself
Hatred is silent and deadly like a stealth
It's hard to be alone in a room of thirty
Everyone is clean but my soul is all dirty
In my head and in my soul it is barren

Nicole Lutton

Crackers

Animals are so delicious.
There are only two grams of fat per herd;
this makes them nutritious.
Cats, dogs, lions, birds...

When I crunch it is so tantalizing.
The power I have over these faceless creatures.
Selecting:
Which is first to meet the annihilator.

Now the bird's tail, then it's feet.
Next the head.
That was its last peep.
Dead.

Kathryn Erickson

Prostitution

I never knew much about prostitution
Then one day I ended up in this institution

Some girls said they only did it for the kicks,
Some girls said they only did it cuz they needed a fix.

A "Lady of the Night" she called herself,
Wasn't picky about those gents.

The only importance to her acts
Was for the money that they spent.

It's a sad situation, this thing called prostitution...
Then one day I ended up in this institution....

Kathleen Anita Fritz

Untitled

Think a while of the brightest smile,
then hold it in your heart a while.
Think of stardust on new fallen snow,
By the light of the moon, then you'll know
what it was like to know her name,
and why things will never be the same.

She was morning dew, and the first sun beam
she was as bright as a child's first dream.
We hold her in our hearts, so dear
and wish we could still hold her near
but, we know, in heaven she will fly
while we ponder and try to reason...why?

Yet she knows the answers, I guess I will too,
God called her name and away she flew,
on the wings of an Angel sent to Earth,
as it was when she arrived at birth.

Michelle Lynn Argo

My Destiny

This is how I spend my time:
   Trying to write little poems that rhyme.
I prayed for something new to do
   Again you came to my rescue.
You have given me this new direction
   Although, I know, it's not always perfection.
With your guidance, I'll try to do my part.
   For it all comes from a grateful heart.
I thank you, Dear God, for the
   Inspiration you have given me.
I never dreamed writing poetry
   Would be my destiny at eighty-three.

Margaret Starkey

Forever Friends

Friends listen, they share their minds,
their love withstands the test of time.

Friends give, they are always there,
they live to always care.

Friends understand, oh yes indeed,
you can count on a friend to know what you need.

Friends love to help you when you are feeling down,
they'll give you support, they'll be your clown.
Friends make you laugh which gives you the strength,
to go through any trial, no matter what the length.

Friends lift you up, they hold your hand,
they are there to help you stand.

Friends don't give up and walk away,
they stay with you every step of the way.

Friends can survive as long as they are together,
as they continue to walk through all kinds of weather.

I have a friend who is very close,
there is a special bond we share,

My friend and I,
We are friends forever.

Lorraine Roberts

"Love's Many Ways"

"Love is a feeling we feel many ways...
   The words that are spoken, the deeds that are done,
And the true feeling of devotion that never betrays."

"It's something that turns into blue, skies that were
   Gray, love brightens many a gloomy, dark day.
Love is a smile, a touch, or just being there when you
   Are needed so much."

"Sometimes love can be a painful thing, but it's worth
   Any hurt, for the wonderful joy it can bring.
He who has not loved and been loved by someone, leaves
   One of life's greatest joys left undone. How sad,
To have denied yourself something you could have had."

"It's never too late to discover love out there...
   To find someone special with whom your feelings you
Can share. We all need and want to know, that in this
   World, that someone does love us and truly does care."

"Sometimes looking for love, you need not start...
   For most times it's already been there, in a special
Spot in your heart. It begins before you even realize
   It's already of you a part."

Mileah J. Rector

Love

Love is such a little word
To describe such a big feeling.
Because of love
People have drawn a sword
And sent countries reeling.
Because of love, babies are born,
And people go to meet anywhere-everywhere.
Love comes to the tired and worn,
The young and the old, the ugly and the fair.
Love is indescribably wonderful and true.
Without love — life is so dull, so sad.
Love is you,
And I am glad.

Michael G. Martini

Open Letter To Summer

At the towers by the lake
the wind scampers over my bare chest.
I am reminded of darker days:
Of a glove abandoned in solitude,
amid endless land of white
and tree of ice, contorted in
an accusatory pose.

My soul thanks the heavens
for its remedy: One part summer, the other love.
They warm this body better
than the sun itself, with its
merciless beating pattern of heat;
so do they serve to cool the
aforementioned overkill.

I am lulled as a baby by
a mother's mellifluous song at twilight,
My mind oblivious to harm.
The water is calm, the chair
is convincingly hospitable.
Summer is in season and I am in love.
  Kevin McCracken

Observations Of Nature

A mild day near the end of October, off I go to the woods again.
The wind is rustling the dried leaves and branches.
A clump of red leaves hang on a stalk, stirred by the wind.
Cattails abound. Crickets chirp signs of spring,
even though it's fall. The smell of fallen leaves is great.
A tree lies across the path. My feet rustle leaves as I walk.
The geese are honking to each other out on the shimmering lake.
A garter snake just slithered in front of me, then hid.
Coming up to a stand of pines, the smell changes
from Autumn leaves to pine needles.
Each one of these trails puts me in a different mood and feeling.
So many of the big trees lay broken from the wind's force.
A peaceful brook runs silently under a foot bridge.
On another trail, my mood changes, and the quiet is all consuming.
My feet slide on the damp leaves, and I head for the end of the trail.
  Kathleen Mae DePalma

Leaving

We started down the road together.
  The wind at our backs, our faces to the sun.
Hands entwined, we walked looking forward.
  No longer as two, now we were one.

So many things came between us
  Causing hurt and pain within our hearts.
We stayed together and faced the world.
  Our spirits roamed, we drifted apart.

Words were left unspoken.
  Finally there was nothing left to say.
We could not take back the spoken words.
  Somehow we had lost our way.

One dwelling held us; we traveled different roads.
  Out hearts gave out a sad and lonely cry.
My heart had left you long ago.
  I did not have to walk away to say goodbye.
  Mary S. Rogers

My Beloved Brother

Words cannot express
The way we felt that day
When a spur of the moment
Your life was taken away

We must cope with losing you
But it just seem so hard
When they took you away
It just tore us all apart

Everyone must travel the road of death
But only God has the right to choose
So to the ones that done that to you
Are the ones who is going to lose

We may have lost you in this life,
But at the end of the road there is a happy ending
You can be for sure our dear love one
That they will soon turn in to surrender

We haven't forgot about you
We never will
For vengeance is mine saith the Lord
And peace shall be still
  La'Tesha Vinson-Akins

Face Like Flint

What's it like to just merely exist? It's not walking in holiness, the way the Lord intended you to live. Just a great void within You that no man can fill.

You will look to sex, and that doesn't fulfill. You look to people, and they let you down. If you go to church, and you don't walk in holiness, you are missing the blessings God intended for your life, because God said, "Be ye holy as I am holy."

When you listen to the wrong people, and music, you are headed for a fall because you have made satan your master here on earth. If you don't repent of your sins, he will be master of your spirit for eternity, when you are thrown into the lake of fire.

One must walk in the spirit, so you will not fulfill the lusts of The flesh. We are all made in the image of God, but who do we serve? Jesus walked a holy life because he walked in the spirit, and not in the flesh, so he didn't sin.

What is it going to take for humanity to see the light? Jesus said, "I am the way, the truth and the life, no man comes unto the Father but by me." The only way is believing in my heart that Jesus died for my sins. Repent of my sins, and ask Jesus to come into my heart. So I can live with Jesus for eternity.
  Linda Zuolenski

Mother's Stories

A kingdom I would give
To hear the stories, at my mother's knee
of places far away, of wonders great and free

In awe I would wait, as each story would unfold.
Of secret gardens, as flowers would unfold.
Each story so exciting and so bold.
Of carriages of silver and gold.

I'd hold my breath in anticipation
As each prince would ride in without inhibition.
To save some maiden fair
From some horror, she was unaware.

Not like today, when all is so very cold.
No imagination can you use
When all is put so ugly and so bold.

So listen dear as I repeat
The stories told to me, I thought so neat!
  Linda M. Nacoff

Winter's Coming On

The bright sun isn't out today
The warmth from the air is gone
The chill and the mist and the clouds gather 'round
Winter's coming on

The leaves are falling from the trees
The grass has turned to brown
In the wind you can feel a certain chill
And soon snow will cover the ground

There'll be Thanksgiving and Christmas and New Years too
It won't be very long
Because it is you see
That winter's coming on

It is a time when the family is close
And brings joy to the heart
There isn't much going on outside
And there's laughter 'round the hearth

Summer's over with swimming and fun
The beautiful glow of the setting sun
Over the swimming hole is gone
Because it is you see, that winter's coming on
   Mary Motl

A Prayer

Dear God, a prayer to calm the mind,
The thoughts, emotions one can find inside a restless soul.
So vulnerable to words and deeds
of others with their special needs, to reach a final goal.

What is our purpose here on earth
if not to live life after birth with love for all creation.
What joy is found in nature's art,
Perfection in the smallest part, such total stimulation.

So deeply can the soul explore
and then discover always more, in those with special feelings.
The softness, scent, the gentle touch
Arouse the senses, say so much, a multitude of meanings.

How happy those who share a part,
of beauty so formed through the art, of God's unique creation,
Intensely feeling every word
Unspoken, yet so clearly heard, with mutual adoration.

How few can feel and therefore share
Such cosmic power between a pair that trigger deep emotions,
How few can give and therefore find
a deeper love - one of a kind, eternal as the oceans.
   Michael Jay

Eggshell

Love can be as fragile as an eggshell,
The trust can be broken at the ring of a bell,
When one must have secrets and quiet conversations,
It can lead to love's devastation.

When two people are truly in love,
They are true to one another as with the dove,
Open and honest with hearts full of caring,
Understanding the strengths and weakness of one another will
Keep them sharing.

If feelings start getting rough and talking is needed,
It doesn't matter how the plant was seeded,
Always willing to lend a shoulder to one another,
Never turning a deaf ear to their significant other.

So if you feel love has found a place,
Be sure not to make it a disgrace.
Always keep the lines of communication open,
And love like the eggshell won't be broken.
   Lisa A. Cross-Livingstone

Untitled

Mourning...
The sunset once loved me.
Then it set and the simplistic figures of life became shadows,
We talked somber tones a few seconds
They left unburdened with contradictions they left me.
Walking
Feeling for the way,
No light aides.
The horrible reality of what totally
    consumes
My will to be leads me to an angry place.
I am alone
As I have been since the sky changed from a red, purple
To a deep sullen black I am so close to.
But I am not welcome.
Depictions of sincere faces are staring at me
I choose not to accept.
Destruction
Of myself has been accomplished
Mourning.....
   Laurie Salgado

What Is Ebony?

Ebony is the flame and smoke in the sky,
The time of departure as we say good bye.

Ebony is the hair of Hiawatha just after it rains,
And the wind against the tall swaying crane.

Ebony is the massive wingspan of a red-necked vulture,
Slaves who were hung in shackles because of their culture.

Ebony is obscure when the stars are out and bright,
I wish I may, I wish I might, have this wish I wish tonight.

Ebony is the scent of the rose, its fragrance so bold and strong,
Astronauts on the moon, their distance ever so long.

Ebony is mournful, the depressed emotion of agony,
Now you know my opinion of what in the world is EBONY!
   Layron Livingston

Nature's Harmony

The music, the flowers,
The sun and the showers,
They are there for a while
And then gone.
I see them, I feel them,
Their harmony is sweet.
The beauty will meet in a song.
Whatever the way, by night or by day,
I walk along feeling the glow.
The flowers and music adorn the scene,
The moon enhances the flow.
All nature is ours - the earth, sky, the seas,
A gift from the Lord,
From the lake to the trees.
We'll care and preserve it
In true accord.
   Mary Becker

Creation And Curse

I often sit and wonder how the world came to pass,
The story goes of how Adam and Eve went through their phase,
How Noah loaded the Ark with two of everything.
Moses climbed the mountain to learn of how law and order should start,
But what puzzles me the most is why, why, why, God put us on this great big planet,
Nothing seems to be going right,
There is crime and violence running through the streets like fire,
So much damage is done to nature and the wild things,
Even families hurt each other,
It should be to where we would do anything for our brothers.
A lot has to change before we are able to see a calm through the lands once again,
That is why I don't understand why God made this big world that we all live in.

Lorie Walters

Carousel

This carousel of life is always turning, always moving
The same speed it keeps while it is moving, always spinning
We were born on the same carousel and on it we will die
It doesn't change when we hurt and it doesn't stop if we cry
We were all born as equal, and equal we will remain
No matter what all we have or dreams left to sustain
If you're born the richest you can die a lowly shell
Go from rags to riches overnight if you're character you can sell
Money isn't everything and power lies in the soul
You can always be the greatest, no matter how young or old
The day you were born you were given a name
You should live up to it for it will always be the same
Time is passing on and days are going by
You only have one chance to live and then it's time to die
If you make the best out of life; give a lot of caring and love
This carousel you have lived will be better for those to come

Melanie Browning

"Growth"

Tho my human love goes unreciprocated,
The power of God is unequated!

Many times I tried and fell,
Yet somehow I know the future will tell,

Through sorrows and trials my heartaches will bring,
Truth, unsurpassed joy, and that beautiful thing
Called love.

For my soul now has profound adoration,
For Him and all His miraculous creation!

Today I am grateful.

Maureen K. McGivern

Daydreams

Often I find myself lost in a daydream,
Staring out of a window, at a place where time stands still.
I see many things that remind me of you.
For it is you who brought sunlight into my days and
warmth into my nights.

I see a delicate bud blooming into a beautiful flower,
I see me, when I'm with you.
I see a rainbow spanning across the clear blue sky,
I see how you've colored my world and made it brighter.
I see a brook, bubbling with enthusiasm,
I see the excitement you've brought into my life.
For it is you who awakened my emotions
and made me realize that all the beauty
in the world comes first from the heart.

Kimaree Estes

"The Cop"

His job has always been to protect and serve.
The pay is far less then he deserves.
He patrols the streets eight hours a day.
His back-up is still ten minutes away.
He's the nicest man that you've ever met.
Some people thank him, but many forget.
"Why does he do this?" Many will ask.
No silver bullets. He wears no mask.
Decent pay and a little respect.
Is it too much for him to expect?
Some nights he worries and is unable to sleep.
With layoffs and lawsuits, seven days a week.
But he keeps on fighting the war in the streets.
Answering calls and patrolling his beat.
Considered lucky, because he's still alive.
Collecting a pension at age fifty-five.
To those who have fallen, doing their job,
At domestic disputes or stores being robbed.
I ask your family and all of your friends,
"How can we stop the violence . . . WHEN WILL IT END?"

Marc Haiungs Sr.

Was I That Woman

Was I that woman at the top of the stairs?
The one you were marveling at?
She had styled her hair, and put on a smile;
But still felt slightly fat.

Was I that woman, you garnered so close;
As she danced the night into day?
She laughed, and joked, and held your attention
With every word she would say.

Was I that woman, warmed with your coat;
While you whispered in her ear?
She, surely, must have thought she was dreaming;
As you swept away all of her fear.

Was I that woman you tenderly kissed;
While refusing to say "Good-bye"?
The woman you asked to see again;
As you wiped a tear from her eye.

I really can't swear that it happened.
Although, it all seemed so right.
Was I, indeed, that woman, my dear?
Was I that woman, that night?

Linda Davis

Soul Song

Only think of you, and my heart proclaims exquisite poetry.
Simply embrace you, and my senses compose stirring music.
Merely be with you, and my soul resonates with an impassioned song.
Swaying softly with you, I become a symphony:
My fingers acres tender melodies
    Along your arm,
My hands impress enchanting notes
    Across your back,
My heart provides a substantial rhythm
    Against your breast.
Moving gently with you, I become a choir:
My mouth kisses sensuous verses
    Along your skin,
My breath whispers a loving euphony
    Across your cheek,
My tongue darts a delightful chorus
    Against your lips.
Dancing close with you
I share the song you make me feel.

Kevin M. Zachery

Pound My Brain Numb

Others merely catch a glimpse from their cheap seats
the nose bleed section of the auditorium surrounding my heart
you had front row

And although the crinkle around your eyes when you smile
still can bring me to my knees - catch my breath - leave me in bed
for hours with a ball of fire in my gut
the thought that I used to be "the distraction" does the same

The snowball pattern continues you say,
and now there's someone new (poor girl) spread the pain
as thick as your sloppy kisses which started in dark and ended
with light

My heart is Used Tattered Torn
and the short film of our short intersection replays horribly damaged images
faded colors - washed out emotion - a spliced story line which
jumps skips and snags

I'm the main attraction in your world of distractions,
but your journey back to the candy counter for something sweeter
has left your seat empty
and the show continues
without you.

Kristen Corning

In The Eyes Of A Child

I look into the eyes of a child, and suddenly see
   The mystery of all life, gazing back at me.
Though the child is young, the mystery is old,
   And harbors knowledge, that's as yet untold.

The child knows fear not at all, of a world so large and vast,
   And fetters not, over the role it has been cast.
But in accepting each challenge, with full joy,
   Makes their own world itself, their aim and toy.

As those eyes pulled me deep within, I seemed to take a dive,
   And saw long forgotten memories, come alive.
If we could go back, to our own childhood days,
   We'd see more clear, and quickly change our ways.

Things that we take for granted, to them are such a treasure,
   The simplest of things, can bring them so much pleasure.
Ever eager to help—giving total love,
   Showing us—Heaven's HERE—not up above.

Their eyes sparkling and shining with faith, that all love will last,
   Grabbing each moment, for they sense, it soon will pass.
Just one fleet instant, in the gaze from that child,
   But for me? I just went ten thousand miles.

Opal Gibson

God's Choice

Our Grandmother was a wonderful hen
She was survived by loving children, all ten
when she was a fighter
her days got brighter
even when her days were dull
she still loved us all
but all in the end
we must look around the bend
for we must be happy
for she is with Pappy
she would want us to be strong
for she has said so long
Grammy had a wonderful life
It was so thick, it could not be cut with a knife
for now we must rejoice
for it was God's choice

Linette M. Gehris

"God's Love"

Over the hills came the sound of a bird,
The most beautiful song I ever heard,
Like the song of the beautiful Meadow Lark,
Or the "hoot" of an Owl, in the deep dark,
Or one from an old pine tree.
Though you might not agree,
The "hoot" of an Owl is music to me.
Down in the valley, far below,
Wild poppies, and Roses sway to and fro!
Tall, wild Delphinium and bright Fireweed,
Drop their seed on the ground for birds to feed.
White, blossomed, wild Cherry Trees
Sway in the gentle breeze,
As do tops of tall Fir and tall Pine trees,
Under white puffy clouds, in skies so blue.
God's gift of love, like him, so pure, so true.
His blessings on us, here below,
Life, spring, summer, fall, and winter snow.
I was inspired to write all this because I heard
The beautiful song of a far away bird.

Marjorie H. Lockwood

He Was There...All The Time

The dewdrops lay on the grass...like sheathes,
The mist would rise...and blow gently as the breeze.

The butterfly searched...and found...a rose
The bee searched nature...his nectar to bestow.

The wind blew gently...like a soft subtle spirit,
It languished and listeth...with breathtaking ease.

Thus, relaxed and soothed...by an unnatural calm,
I allowed my mind...to luxuriously roam.

To the lowest of valleys...and to higher heights,
I climbed life's literal mountains, to find...

A Supernatural Saviour, Who was there...All the time.
I rushed to greet him, as if a brand new friend...

But I remembered...I had seen him in Nature, in the beauty
of a Rose, patiently awaiting to be magnified...and praised.

My void was filled...I no longer pined...
for joyfully, I found...

He was there...all the time.

Lillian H. Williams

The Vanishing

The majestic trees reach up to the sky
The chain saws simultaneously groan
Looking at this picture I wonder why
All this beauty cannot be left alone

The shade of broad leaves, the chirping of birds
Yet, can it be a place of destruction?
The animals die, it's more than just words
Mother Earth cries against the abduction

So many species in one surrounding
Best source for medical technology
Long-awaited cures they are now finding
Recent advances in Biology

Nature's vanishing treasure, we lament
Disappearing every waking moment

Lisa Dillon

The Magnificent Queen

As the sun sets to show the end of the day,
The magnificent queen comes out, but not long to stay;

She hovers over the world low and high,
Moving over the land, water, and the sky;

She shows off her loveliness, her elegance and grace,
As people watch her from all over the place;

As she moves over the land, the world seems to cease,
For the creatures below are then silently at peace;

For her long and sweet songs and the splendor of her beauty,
Calm down the world as though it is her duty;

What does she look like? Well, it is as plain as can be,
We all see her often, both you and both me;

Her eyes are the stars glowing brilliant in sight,
The sky is her gown growing still at the light;

The moon is her spirit, showing off the bright glow,
Of the love that she has for the world far below.

Have you guessed who she is?
Do you know the name right,
Of the magnificent queen,
For her sweet name it NIGHT.

Kristie McPherson

Love? It's A Hurting Game

There is a story to be told how love first gets it's start
The hurt, the pain, one beholds their feelings to impart
Somehow, someway it must be told to show the feeling of the heart

This thing they call a hurting game is played with hearts to feel the pain
A pain that never can be spoken only to a heart that has been broken
Feeling that you'll go insane if you lose this hurting game

There comes a time within your life your heart must take a fall
There is no one that you can blame it's not a game of ball
It only affects the players of two and the game is played with you

Then comes the time to count the score to see who wins this hurting game
Your heart is tense and your pulse will soar and this game of hurt
  for you is no more
Then when the final score is read the tears will flow and you'll wish
  you were dead
Love? It's A Hurting Game

Lee A. Parker

Longing For The Dream

Last night I dreamed you lay next to me.
The heat from your sleeping body kept me warm.
Awareness of your presence helped me to sleep soundly,
secure in the knowledge your love would protect me from harm.

As I awoke, I sensed the void where I dreamed that you had lain.
Cold reality worked its way slowly through me.
Another day without you, revives the ebbing pain;
and I long for the return of the dream,
for that's where I want to be.

Only in my dreams can I touch and hold you.
The sweet memory of your kisses again become real.
Your arms gently pull me close to you,
and it's your heart beating that I feel.

It's because of your love that I desire to live.
It's the sound of your voice that carries me through each day;
but it's in my dreams we share all the love I have to give.
So while you are apart from me,
it's in my dreams I long to stay.

Kathlene Lilly-Antis

Birthdays Birthdays

Celebration; excuses. Time for fun! Reassures of
the heart flow forth from within without,
to points of no return. Yet, if you could, would
you? We play hard for the things we see
in our mind, as what we want them to be. Do
we remain young? Possibly. Growing old only
to others, in their minds, in their minds
eye. Seeing us, so loosely playing/holding
on to the ground we walk on, one can only
wonder how we evade the responsibility
of being in control.
Suddenly, carelessly in control!
Celebrating to the winds of time.
forever...

Leanne Faux-Fakis

It's Sunday And Joe's Making Breakfast

The morning sun reaches through the trailer window, touching the formica table where I sit, reading the paper. It's Sunday and Joe's making breakfast.

"Hey, Joe—some coffee!" Joe, in his pajamas, scratches the gray whiskers on his two day unshaved face and winces, the many years of life streaming into wrinkles around his eyes.

He grumbles under his breath, "Spoiled rotten". I giggle. He grins, "Just like a twenty year old." Joe likes my laugh—says it sounds like twinkling bells.

He sets the mug of coffee down on the formica table with a thud. I glance into the mug. "Not enough milk," I say, reproachfully. "Last time I'm making you breakfast," he says and sticks out his tongue.

"I love it when you make those faces at me." He grins and I think to myself, 'this is my life—breakfast in a silver trailer serve by a scruffy man in pajamas.'

Joe sets a plate of burnt toast and a bottle of strawberry jam on the table next to the mug of coffee.

"Your breakfast, my Queen."

Lisa McLaughlin

Inside Feelings

I sit and wonder how does life revolve,
The every day problems how they solve,
A night put under with laughs and fun,
In everyone's life what's done is done.

Love is put forth with reaction and force,
When growing up just has to take its course,
Grasping for the good times of the past,
When knowing the good times roll on so fast.

Having an opened mind to what life has to offer,
Even the back street evils seem to speak softer,
People in this fast-pace world seem to wonder,
Why some lovers drift away and go down under.

In a relationship or friendship once in time,
We look upon fantasy as a mountain to climb,
I don't know why it is some people forget,
That everyone needs friends and love in the same kit.

They want to scream out and say "hey" in here,
Sometimes their backed to the wall with fear,
It's nice to know that life has so many choices,
With different expressions in their voices.

Lorrie Ericson

"An Anguished Soul"

Dedicated in loving memory to Pius Braun

Deep in our soul cries the voice we seek,
the earth shall be inherited by the mild and meek.
Can the awaited answer that comes within,
be buried much deeper inside our kin?
The whispers at night come and go,
but can you hear what you need to know?
Such lies the answer in our true spirit,
not by our own selfish merit.
Let it go, this anguish unspent,
for it is not worth our purposeful intend!

Monica Braun-Hille

The Demon Anger

Anger is the demon unseen,
the destructive force we must avoid.
It has the power to demean,
the force to make one's life null and void.

Harsh words, raised fists, uncontrolled feelings,
these are all anger's trumpets.
The dark side of life keeps us reeling,
only self control serves as one of our safety nets.

Unreasonable beings become a danger,
their loss of control can cost a life.
We can find ourselves to be a total stranger,
unknown to others as if cut off by the sharpness of a knife.

How to take back what one has lost?
The search must start from within.
Negative thoughts and feelings must be tossed,
the healing of heart and soul will begin.

The seeds of anger must be undone,
replaced by positive thoughts and actions.
Peace of the soul, a sense of life's fun,
these must be present in all human functions.

Margaret C. Collier

Funeral Home

The organ music falls quietly on the mourners.
The deceased wore navy, the widow wore black.
A rosary encircles his hands as the widow weeps quietly
over the satin lined coffin.
A cold metal casket is draped with stars and stripes,
which reminds me of his days in World War II.
Fragrant flowers abundantly surrounds,
family and friends with painful frowns.
Tears rolling down sad faces, like uncontrollable waterfalls.
His children are mourning, their hearts are broken.
Sisters and brothers gather in clusters, remembering good times
spent with their brother.
Emptiness, loneliness, sorrow and grief.
Bibles, priests, crosses and prayers.
Clutched tissues catching our tears,
All for the one we love so dear.

Nancy R. Rodriguez

Stolen Moments

On such a day there will come a stolen moment for us!
The precious time to cherish and feelings will be just!
We will bare our souls unto each other and become one —
as we lay soul to soul, flesh to flesh, and
heart to heart till the day is done.
And until we have another stolen moment,
we have the best memories to keep.
There certainly will come more moments because our
spirits connect so deep.
So here and now I will be true to no one else but you!

Kathy Barr

Disposable Dreams

Rice paper wings touch down to scoop the yellow powder
The bee dances swiftly like an angel from flower to flower,
Golden glow against a clear blue sky, carefree and alive
The bee heads home, seeking warmth from his cozy bee hive.

Greeted by his lovely wife, who scurried home from work like he,
They hustle and bustle to co-create their baby's sweet honey
Through all seasons, buzzing magic with co-workers' creation
Then suddenly the bee is in suspended animation.

For a boy has grabbed its' wings like an evil scientist at play
The bee awaits his fate, which may indeed unfold today
Paralyzed with fear, his body like an iron rod, stiffens
His stinger plunges like a needle dipped in poisonous venom.

Powerless over his instinct, he stings the boy's taunting friend
Who had stunted the boy's growing pride which is now on the mend
As he wickedly whines, "See, it does so hurt!" the bully asserts
And carelessly tosses the bee's corpse away like an old used t-shirt.

Nancy J. Pratt

The World Of A Child

How to measure the glory of these days?
The beauty of our children's ways?

Watch how they move about in their own little space
Gliding through time at their own unique pace

Children explore their world in ways that only they understand
Moment by moment, for their time is unplanned

They run and climb and jump in flight
Their day is a blank canvas, which they paint with delight

Their energy really knows no bounds
As they savor every sight and smell and sound

They're read to, and read to, and completely immersed
For a child, the tenth time is as great as the first

Does anything compare to the look in their eyes
As you hold them close and sing sweet lullabies?

Listen to the sounds from their beds as they move in the night
And their soft-spoken requests for "a little more light"

Yes, the world of a child is a world to behold
With the countless blessings and joys that unfold.

Michele Maszk Murney

"If I Could Just..."

Is there a way to explain
The beauty I see in you?
It goes beyond my imagination
it superseded my expectations
and I even wonder, Is it true?

It has been a while since the last time I saw you,
but I really don't care how long it has been
a mental picture that talks about you
is shining my days that used to be blue
and seeing you again is now my dream.

If you could just hear the things I tell the stars
It seems like I'm living in a fantasy world
a place where your hair holds hands with the wind,
a place where your hopes make friends with my dreams
a magical place, a paradise, fantasy girl.

If I could just be with you
If I could just see you again
If I could just taste your smile
and just for a little while
If I could just hold your hand.

Mario Hernandez

I Am

I am a child of the heavens, a fair haired girl given life in
the Americas.

I am a citizen of the earth, a product of love born into
inequality by the standards set much before the coming of my
time.

I am Irish, from many generations, given into the hands of society.
The luck of my ancestors has instilled itself in me.
Deep within is found the stubborn determination of my father
and the gentle hope of my mother.

I am not many things, alas what I am I know. My ties are not
to the earth, although of it I am an inhabitant.

I am a new creation, my old self laid aside. I am from history,
yet by my very existence, I also create history.

I am me.
Kellie J. Hales

Untitled

Little bits and pieces —
   that's all they've left behind
A sweater, a ring, a picture or two, whatever we can find
To hang onto these treasures is like having of them around me in my
   busy life to share special moments when
I long to call and say "hello - how are you doing today?"
That's when I realize these little bits and pieces, however small they
   small they seem, are all that's left of these people I loved —
   now all I can do is dream.
I don't want to ever forget the things they've done for me, the home
   they shared, childhood memories,
   and all the times they cared.
I miss you both so much these days — it helps to remember you and
   hang on to my bits and pieces and shed a tear or two.
Kristy Ellis Workman

Through The Eyes Of A Child

You can only see God through childish eyes,
That wonder up at star-filled skies,
Only children know what the heavens hold,
For only they can see what the eyes don't behold,
Their innocence keeps their faith ever strong,
Not yet understanding right from wrong,
You will only see God through the eyes of a child,
The eyes that are loving, tender, and mild,
Children truly know that way and set the best example,
For childhood seems to be the only heavenly sample.
Marie Broderick

No Regrets

Life is a path we carelessly travel;
The mistakes we make leave knots to unravel.
Had we been blessed with special sight;
We may have been guided by the poet's light.

But no regrets...since we learn from the knots.

Taking apart and reworking those threads
Gives us time to clear the doubts from our heads.
We can learn to feel and learn to hear;
Loving the closeness of those who are near.

But no regrets..since we learn from the knots.
Maria E. Wale

"Our Daily Visit"

When you see the sun inch slowly away
That will be me having one last look at your day

When you see a star fall out of the skies
That will be a tear leaving my eyes

When you see a petal from a rose as it doth part
That will be me when I broke your heart

When the early morning breezes fill your air
That will be me rearranging your hair

When you are watching the ripples across your lake
That will be me searching for your face

When the wind dips forth and grasps the sand
That will be me holding your hand

When you see a little squirrel and speak with it
And it stops dead still to listen
That will be me when you said "Good bye"
And I died in that one second

When our little bird starts singing
But he is not there......

That will be me
LaWanda Parks

Please Make It So

Are the people today so poor and so blind
That we have no compassion for our fellow mankind?

If you can't share a fortune of silver and gold
Then share the vast treasures you already hold.

Treasures so boundless that try as you may
You will never run out though you give it away.

So give to the rich, the homeless, and poor.
Give us your blessings. You can always give more.

Give us your hand as I shall give mine
Extended in friendship for now and all time.

Then give it again whenever there is need
For hands that give help almost always succeed.

Give us a smile whenever we meet
And the smiles we return will be smiles you can keep.

Give us a hug at a time of great sorrow.
It shall be returned. Perhaps even tomorrow.

Give us assurance that you mean what you say
So we may give trust that lasts day after day.

Then finally give love for it is then we shall know
That the world will be safe. PLEASE HELP MAKE IT SO.
Leslie A. Cole

AIDS

   AIDS is a disease are we all know.
That takes away our children's life so they can't grow.
And so many people have grown so cold are to
give it to another that will never
know what it's like to grow old.
For kid's these days who think it's
a joke end up with AIDS, and
then they croak. And so many
people still don't understand how this
disease started or how to make it end.
For to give it to people or babies
and then turn your heads and walk away.
To me it just doesn't seem
to be the human way.
THINK ABOUT IT AIDS
Linda Farr

Dreams

Dreams are the ideas
that have brought throughout the years
the laughter
the tears and the things we hold dear

Dreams are the feelings
that inspire the few
who admire the flowers with their accent of dew
to take pencil and paper
and describe them for you

Dreams are the hopes
of people like me
to see one world, one planet, one nation
one planet, one nation
and everyone free

Dreams are the seeds
that when planted with care
can grow oh! So fair
and their fruit is our love

Dreams
Dreams are made of magic
and magic is made of Dreams

Max Rieken

Dancing Ladies

Admiring my dancing Ladies, while they
Swirl and sway. Makes me realize I've
made a difference in our World Today.

   God's Creation, through my gentle hands.
Has added Beauty to our Lands.

   When a Breeze blows and the leaves twirl,
Causing a melody. I silently hope the
pleasure of this event is appreciated, not only by me.
A winters Storm is the ultimate test to
show the strength of a struggle, then: The
   Reward of A Rest.
Nature being like man, so neatly tied
into GOD's plan.

Martha Wells

Untitled

Life's war rages on
survival battles fought on individual fronts
the society rejects stand at the corner
alone with their companion voices
deep deep inside
voices that we buried deep deep in them
voices that turn their dreams
into nightmares
voices that assassinated ambition and bury hope
in empty beer bottles on our side walks
voices sending them to the land fills
of our times trash dump
the internal debate rages on and on
debating the reality of reality
the living hopelessness
we pass them by
and shake our heads in disbelief
we turn away
mocking as we pass
brothers sliding into human land fills.

Osita Okpaleke

Alone

My soul cries because I'm alone.
Surrounded constantly by people, places, things;
But nonetheless, alone.
Empty feelings, sad.
A longing to be held, touched, loved.
Look, my hands are real.
They can reach out and support.
Guide, wipe away pain, give strength.
Or just be there when needed.
My shoulders are here to lean on;
To help carry your burdens.
My legs can be your strength.
My eyes can be your guide.
You need only ask and it will be given to you.
I'm patient, I'll wait.
For one day you'll come.
But I'm human. I still feel the pain of being alone.
Someday soon I'll be whole.
Complete with you by my side.
But for now, alone.

Lisa Morris

The Bet

A dark cloud drifts across the moon,
Strengthening my feeling of impending doom.
Climbing the worn down front steps one by one,
I remind myself there's a bet to be won!
I open the door and tip-toe inside
And try not to think about the night old Mr. Weaver died.
I creep through the living room and down the hall
Trying to ignore the shadows lurking on the wall.
As I walk along the creaking floor,
In the distance I hear a slamming door.
I jump and turn and start to run,
But then I remember there's a bet to be won!
I mount the stairs up to the old north tower,
To shine my flashlight every hour.
As I am overcome with fright
I wonder how I'll last 'til midnight.
A tree branch scrapes and scratches the windows,
And I hear ghostly noises as the wind blows.
How I wish I could turn and run,
But again I remind myself there's a bet to be won!

Larisa Durrenberger

Oh Heart Of Mine

Oh heart of mine, what time has done
Stolen our hopes, our dreams unsung
Oh heart of mine, where lives the tears of years unkind
The ones we earned, the ones we hide
Oh heart of mine, quiet the echoes of our past
Ones unsettled, and the fears that last
Oh heart of mine, rich like the kingdoms of the dead
So much to put behind, still so much that lies ahead
Oh heart of mine, let us see what we recall
Each love we stumbled over, each painful time we'd fall
Oh heart of mine, tell me the things from which I hide
Of laughter that we passed on, the hand we never touched
The dream we failed to follow
For in its time it seemed too much
Oh heart of mine

Marlena Marie Hyslop

Meeting Between Gargoyle And Man

A grim face meeting flesh. Sweat dripping down each.
Steadily, one unsheathes his sword. The other remains still.

"What is he up to?
Has he no protection?"

Hot, steamy breath.
Claws long sharpened.

"What use is his sword,
What use is his bravery?"

Muscles flexed,
Knuckles white.

Fangs clenched,
Legs tense.

A slash of the sword,
A victorious cry!

"I won!
Yet why am I so frightened?"

The beast's eye flickers.
A claw cuts the air.

Silence.
Death.
    Marissa Buschow

Night Sounds

Crickets sing a song with wings, chirping through the night...
   soothing as a soft summers breeze.

With them comes the faint whistle of a train,
   scuttling along the tracks with a pitter patter;
   like rain on the sill of my window.

Not far in the distance, you can hear the busy traffic.
In the night on the lonely road, cars and trucks
   race against time.

They can never know the serenity of such
   soothing music, as that of...night sounds.
    Kathy L. Kovach

"The Darkness Of Reality"

Outside in the darkness by myself, all alone
Sometimes when I look so deep it deals like a home
Your imagination becomes reality or so it seems
The pressures are gone, you get lost in your dreams
An occasional star flickers, the moon it shines
Your peak of existence, no more need to climb
As your vision broadens for only your eyes to see
You get to make all thing's as you want them to be
It doesn't last long, the darkness soon ends
Reality is returned as the light comes in
It was for awhile as the darkness leaves
The sun hurts your eyes as you fall your knees
You stand up and prepare fro the day ahead
The pressures return as the darkness is dead
Why doesn't it last forever you after think
As your dreams fade, thoughts vanish and everything sinks
You must wait and be patience, don't be deceived
For darkness returns the reality, I must believe
    Lonnie Lynn

Brokenhearted

Sometimes I wonder why I even bother,
Sometimes I wonder why I even try.
Because no matter whatever goes right,
you will always think that I lie.
I could cry in front of you,
but the tears wouldn't touch your face.
Because you wold find evidence of deception,
in the most ridiculous places.
I could tell you that I love you,
I could tell you that I care.
But no matter what I say to you,
you will always feel malice there.
Well this time, I refuse to grovel,
I refuse to show how weak I am without you.
Because you would just use my weakness against me,
and punish me for all that I do.
    Kim Anderson

"Unborn"

You were just a little egg, a little seed to me,
something that was not planned, something I could not see.
Then I noticed, you were more than and egg,
More than a seed, you were a little person that soon depend on me
You were something new to me, more like a shock,
Then I thought it to be beautiful, that you were pure luck.
Your Daddy to be was only a teen,
I was already a woman, but my years were nineteen.
Although I could not see you, and you could not be heard
My wish was to conceive you, and have a little girl.
Nine months have passed since, and you are in my arms,
You are a beautiful baby, and you have your mother's eyes.
Now I know, I really understand,
What it's like to be needed, and be a guiding hand.
You will always be in my heart, and no matter where
You go and what you do, you will always have me sweetheart,
And the life I gave to you...
    Maria Jimenez

He's Innocent

On a dark night in June,
Something sinister appeared
And two lives ended too soon.

The grief would be unbearable.
In minutes, many hearts would be broken
That only God could heal, many prayers must be spoken.

A rush to judgment was made in haste
Laws of man were in question, many hours in waste.
Whispers began a football hero was arrested.

There was silence as she began to speak.
The truth that everyone wanted to seek
Came out in a shout, he's innocent!

There were tears in his eyes
And a smile on his face
As he left from this dreadful place. He's innocent!

Some believe that justice was not done
But it is over, it is through
And his life he can redo. He's innocent!
    Orie Thomas

A Surrogate's Cry

You're someone else's treasure
Someone else's girl for good.
And when our relationship started
It was this I understood.

But knowing that I'll never
see your face again
causes my heart such tremendous grief
from which I may never mend.

So little, so tiny and you know not a thing
of all the love I feel inside;
I would gladly take you as my own
But the laws would never abide.

For all of my life I will remember that day
when I watched you go away
to a world I know so little about,
No, the tears wouldn't stop that day.

Dear Lord, dear Lord, I pray so much
that You'll bless this precious, sweet one.
Maybe one day she'll know about me
and just what it was I've done.
Kelly Bowser

Dementia's Edge

Never having known the warmth of love against her cherub cheeks.
The soft surprise of her golden gaze, the senseless suspense of her
passion pen, I can almost cry...but only from behind the gaze of
cold stone dead eyes.

And never can I ever recall the Peridot skies she put me to, back
where I caught her swirling eyes on the glimpse of a hooligan's plight.

Yes the path of love is the path to hell, and a bleeding laugh in the
fist of a sinister hand...the hand of her's pushing me back to before
the beginning, The desolate Dust of this of potent past, this of the
now for all I am now is a grain of Speckled dust upon an unkept floor,
as seen as the wind.

And the winding of the scene dragging to a stall of stale passion into
a fermented Crawl upon the dusk, into the dawn, and the jar of argent
lethe I pour into my Reeling head, dementia's edge: What is the
love that's lost?
Michael Black

Where Is The I In Ecology

Devastation in this nation of our air, earth and sea
Should be clearly plain by now, yet still we fail to act somehow
Why can't we let it be!
Refrain from abuse, many ask what's the use, there is no I in
ecology

Save the whales, wolverines, manatees and others,
Where is the future air for our sons and daughters?
Depletion of the ozone layer,
Does the future hold a prayer?

It's up to you my friend, indeed, involve yourself in ecology
A blinded eye shall never see
Health and spirit will abide,
Only if we smooth out the ride

The road is always distant and unsure
Yet the journey yields the cure
Time travelers we all must be
For the future holds our destiny

There should be no hesitation,
Now's the time for preservation
With these thoughts and current action
We'll bring forth solution and satisfaction
Kim Ogilvie

A Difference

What's happening to this world today?
So many souls have gone astray

Life's not the same anymore
Everyone's turned; the rich and the poor

Gangs and violence have scared us numb
How could we have been so dumb

We let our children out on the street
Knowing exactly what kind of people they'll meet

Drugs and power corrupt our mind
Which leaves all our hopes behind

Death happens every day
But just a fraction chips away

That fraction may not seem like a lot
But it's bigger than we all thought

What's going to happen in a few years?
The thought in my mind brings me to tears

This violence has to come to an end
So speak out to a friend

Let them know the meaning of interference
We're the only ones that can make a difference
Leigh Grant

Necessary Dreams

Please let the pain of today...fade away.
Slip my body into death...be refreshed.
Quiet heart, spirit and my mind...just unwind.
Leave me now, this conscious state...lay I wait.

The heavy load - it won't unfold
The wind is gone - can't carry on
To burdens light - take into flight

Pray Lord that time of solitude...lifted mood.
Break right now and swiftly come...justly numb.
I see to count, no fence, no sheep...would I leap?
To clouds upon the other side...there I'd hide.

My muscles ache my soul to take
Do dry my tears - relieve my fears
My lover sleeps - and here I weep

Morning there's no burden tow...we both know
So why delay, what's the wait...at the gate?
I think I see, now understand...by Your hand.
The answer is no dream escape...but to face.

I wanted flight - I needed fight
The choice You give - is mine to live
I know my quest - not lasting rest
Nancy Cardone

Spring Is Coming

Spring is coming and flowers bloom.
The grass is green.
The trees are too!
The wind blows softly on the ground.
The grass leans to and fro!
Your hair is blowing in your face.
You're playing with your friends all day.
The sun is shining all day long.
You'll wear shorts and dresses instead of pants.
You're having fun all spring long.
Spring is coming soon!
Madison Leigh Wance

Haunted House Of Horror

I got in my cart as the clouds closed in
Slam! The door shut, as a room filled with blackness
Then out stretched two arms
   Two long arms
And then a light flashed
   A very dim light
As the room became cold
   Freezing cold
I shut my eyes tight
Just screaming with terror
To be scared is to die
   Die inside
I wanted to find a place to hide
   Far
   Far away
Then the cart came to a stop
   A dead
   Dead stop
I sat in shock, scared and alone....
   Lacey Lozier

Sisters

Understanding, thoughtful, the same but different
   sisters...

Happy, sad, angry or serene
   sisters...

No disguises, no need to be fake-we know each other best
   sisters...

Trusting, caring, always open and honest
   sisters...

Laughing, crying, singing together
   sisters...

Always there to lend support no matter where we go
   near or far...

Best of friends for a lifetime
   sisters...

   You and me!
   Lee Ann Spina

Choices

The complexity of our lives can be likened to both
the leaf afloat on the surface of the twisting stream
and the salmon fighting its way upstream to spawn.

Gone are the days when the majority of our children
were nestled in the womb of the family, guided
through their choices in early day-to-day life and
taught right from wrong in the eyes of the family,
society and God.

Choices are the essence of our existence.

Like the leaf afloat on the surface of a twisting
stream, the ambiguous are tossed from circumstance
to circumstance through the highs and lows of life at
the mercy of their environment.

But the resolve of the salmon, in its single
mindedness of purpose and inflexibility of choice, is
a testimony of indomitable will.

This wide latitude of extremes best explains our
dilemma in steering a wide course of choices through
life's intricate maze.

   Lois Beck

It's A Difficult Period, Indeed

My little girl is growing older, it's a difficult period, indeed.
She's twenty-one in her esteem, but only three to me.
Couldn't we compromise a little since she's really seventeen?

My little girl is growing older, it's a difficult period, indeed.
She wants to be independent which means she wants her way.
I know the strings must be lengthened, but can't Dad ever have
   his say?

My little girl is growing older, it's difficult period, indeed.
She really knows what she wants and that's great I'm told.
But how do I get her to want what I want, without me being bold?

My little girl is growing older, it's a difficult period, indeed.
She's a one way communicator; at sending she's just great.
I'm not bad at that myself, it's at receiving we don't rate.

My little girl is growing older, it's a difficult period, indeed.
My little girl is has moved away, spanking was not her cup of tea.
It was hard to grasp, but now I know she is no longer three.

My little girl is growing older, it's a difficult period, indeed.
I miss my little girl of three who now no longer is.
I'll always love her and her older she, for they're both a part of me.
We have both grown older and it was a difficult period, indeed.
   Monte Elchoness

Grandma's Retired

Grandma's retired or so people say
   She's sixty five and stays home all day
Changing diapers, bathing the baby
   Picking up toys, working without pay

She runs to the store, cleans the house too
   Peels potatoes and carrots to put in the stew
Cause Grandpa is hungry and so are the kids
   Her feet are aching, but what else can she do

Dinner is over, the dishes are done
   The kids have gave home one by one
But Grandma's too tired to have any fun
   Because she's just worked from sun to sun

She sets down and wonders where did the time go
   Is she retired or just to tired to go
On those cruises and fishing trips too
   That she planned to go on with you

Grandpa just smiles and says it's alright
   Cause the 49'ers are playing the Cowboys tonight
Tomorrow will go eat or do something fun
   If were not too tired when the work is all done
   Margaret Pugmire

The Chair

The old woman sat in her chair.
She was a faded and gray.
She reads awhile and gazes at the sky
Maybe she will bake a cake by and by.
The soft winds blow her hair as she sits alone in her chair.

Today she is growing old, and the old woman sits in her chair.
The day is cold but fair.
There is no one there to talk to her or to care.
The sun rises and the sun sets.
Maybe you will come along, and sit and rock with her.
Will you be the one to care, about the old woman in the chair.
   Neda Hinson

Linda, You Were There

(You were there, it was September, 1956.
There were so many things different than what we'd been used to).

The campus was huge and the teachers were many,
There was so much to do, that's what made us so skinny!
You were there for Little Deuce Coupes, El Caminos, Corvettes, Flames and Fins,
for Waterfalls, French Twists, Flat Tops, Page Boys, and Bobby Pins.
You were there for Full Petticoats, Dyed-To-Match, Ivy League and
Chemise, for cruising The A&W, Harvey's, The Clock and Hody's.
You were there for the Bop, the Bunny Hop, the Shag and the Stroll,
for Elvis, Buddy Holly, the Coasters and the beginning of Rock'n Roll.
You were there for Senior Square, Sophomore Week and wearing Red and White,
for Assembly, the Sweethearts Ball and the Junior/Senior Prom Night.
You were there for Gidget, Love Me Tender, Giant and A Summer Place
for Beach Parties, Grunion Hunting, Surfing and an occasional Submarine Race!
You were there for Football Games, Drill Team and wearing Maroon and Gold,
for Sock Hops, Modern Dance and Leotards...Gee, weren't YOU Bold!
You were there for The Blade, The Buccaneers, Sadie Hawkins and the
Treasure Chest, for Ditch Day, the All Night Party, Graduation and all the rest.
But no matter what you did, no matter what you'd see,
When You Were There, So Were We!!

Marilou Vernon McCullough

On a Street Corner

On a street corner is no place to live. People should care, people
should give. Sleep on a park bench, on a grate, on a stair. People
should help, people should care. Dirty and hungry and always on the road.
People should stop and help carry their load. Caring and
sharing is what life is about. People, people, don't just take
another route. Feeding the hungry and housing the poor. People,
people we have to do more. A smile, a touch would mean so much. A
kind word, a helping hand People, people, is that too much to demand?
The sneers and the jeers Bring these people to tears. Humanity is
crying. Look! Look! People are dying! They are hurting and hurting
and hurting some more. Why people, don't you open the door? Greed and
violence are setting us apart. People, people let's have a heart.
A child is cold and hungry out there.
But no one is listening, there's no one to hear.
We've got to slow down and open our hearts.
There are people out there who need new starts.
A father lost his job and can't make ends meet.
Now there's another family on the streets.
On a street corner is no place to live.
People should care, people should give!

Debbie White

Why The Children?

Shadows cross the broken wall.
Shots ring throughout the crowded hall.
Blood spills onto the floor, as fear locks another door.

Screams
Replace precious dreams.
A gun hangs from the hand of an angry child.
Allowed to run free and go wild.
A mother cries, as her child dies.
Tormented by pain too deep to bare.
Some show concern, but others do not dare.

Love has turned into hate, and a solution is needed before it's
too late.
This disease is quickly covering our land
Like a wildfire growing out of hand.
We must search for a way
To make it stop before tomorrow is today.

Kay Smith

Untitled

Baby girl is born unto thee,
her life is gone and never shall be seen.
I'll always love her precious life
even though you wish everything in strife.

I yearn to see her face and cuddle her body,
but I'll always know her as a somebody.
If in all dream, baby girl, I'd care,
but with family I shouldn't dare.

I'll always wonder of your growing years,
and of each thought, I'll shed many tears.
I'll love you daily as each passes
and continue in prayer unto womanhood.

I love you little niece,
a lost one of ends love.
Your mother is good and special child,
but as she was, was only a child.

Sandra Wrigglesworth

A Call To Arms

Stand with me!
Help till this here land
Though parched and dry the
land maybe
Not far down I smell sweet sand.

Stand with me!
Help make this seed sown.
Hard and different it maybe
It is still one of our own.

See the seed sprout
Like a fist through stone.
Braced for life's hard bout
Knowing it won't be alone.

See the tree grow
Breaking new ground.
Others like it will grow
'Cause now it's a softer ground.

Uko-Bendi Udo

If Looks Could Kill

If looks could kill
   he'd be dead.

Claws tearing
Teeth chewing
Paws scratching
Swipe of the claw
   and it's torn.

Eyes piercing
Nostrils flaring
Tongue cursing
Slam of the door
   and he's gone.

Time passing
Door opening
Fur flying
Feline caught but just one.

Tempers cooling
Ways mending
Cat living
All is quiet at home.

Pamela R. McQuary

God Needed An Angel In Heaven

He planted the seed
He watched Her grow
Then felt the need
To let Her go.

He saved Her from sin
And the evils of this earth
He took her with him
From the moment of birth.

So hold Her close to your heart
And she'll never die
She's safe with our Lord
Somewhere in the sky.

We can't understand why
But when all is said and done
God needed an angel in Heaven
And He chose the best one.

Robin Fusco

God's Tears

The ocean is God's tears
He shed for you and me
When He died on the cross
at the place called Calvary
When his heart get so heavy
It makes the ocean over flow
Because we don't accept the love
He wants so much to show.

If you just take a minute
To let him know you care
and go down to the ocean
you can find Him everywhere
in the sound of the sea gulls
on the rushing mighty wind
in the shells that lie scattered
upon the salty sand.
For each thing he has a reason
and a place for it to be,
And the promise that up in Heaven
there'll be no more tears for you and me.

Roxan D. Crosby

"Daddy's Girl"

The day she was born,
he kissed her rosy cheek.
She gleamed as if to know him
although she could not speak.

Each day she grew and so his love,
Heaven's little angel sent from God above.

He taught her about the Bible,
and she was quick to learn.
He said, "Do good things in life
and good things will return."

And still today in every way,
She's the center of his world
So cry your eyes out Mama
but she's Daddy's little girl!

Randy Bell

A Place Of My Own

Where do you go when you
have no home,
No place to call your own.
You walk the streets as long
as it's light
But when it gets dark you
start feeling the fright.
Where will I go to keep warm tonight?
Where will I go so I'm out of sight?
Out of sight of people and such,
So I can sleep and not get
kicked or punched.
There's a cardboard box in the alleyway.
Well, tonight I have a place to stay.
I fall asleep as I'm thinking
Tomorrow will be a better day.
Maybe, just maybe,
I'll find a place to stay,
Some place to call my own.

Wesley Palm

The Miracles Of Life

The Miracles of Life
   Happen to us every day;
Sometimes we don't take notice,
   As we rush along our way.

The Miracles of Life
   Can be at any turn;
They just appear, like angels;
   They help us all to learn.

The Miracles of Life
   Are like a child's toy;
Sometimes they are forgotten;
   When found, they bring lost joy.

The Miracles of Life
   Show up when least expected;
The answers that they give us
   Are better than projected.

The Miracles of life
   Can help us climb each hill;
They're not within our power;
   From God, they shine at will.

Tom Blaisse

Warning

In a world where
handsome princes
and pretty maidens
lived happily ever after;

Baby's bottle
was always full
and diapers
never needed;

Ken never left
the unwrinkled,
always perfect
Barbie;

Guns made noise
but never hurt
and G.I. Joe
never died.

How could I
have been prepared
for the real life
I would meet?

Renee Olive

Forgotten Tears

A baby born long ago
Had hardly a chance we know
She lived longer than expected
But even when protected

A plague came sweeping
The red death seeping
The fever burns, the whole world turns

People in black create a procession
There is a mother in deep depression
Her child lies and suffers no more.

Tara Lynn Burgason

Bridge To Past Love

Between two distant points a bridge
Had been built, a bridge since untrodden.
Memories recalled had bridged
A self who dare not be forgotten.

She asked herself why
The bridge had been suspended in time,
The bridge from which love's shy
Timeworn passion had become timeless.

Why had love's yearnings outlived death?
The bridge between two distant points,
The bridge had reunited loss and death,
An abyss of love had the bridge pointed.

Patricia Urroz Rapold

Marine

Very dark and foliage green,
guns ablaze and people scream.
The sounds of death where people stay,
planes with napalm drop today.
My mind cold, racing with fear,
to run or stand with death so near.
With strength and courage I shall stay,
my life's with God this very day.
The answer comes from men so free,
we're here to fight my brother and me.
With blood dropping upon the ground,
a soldier lie smiling, not a frown.
His belief held with-in his hand,
a cross of silver "THE STRENGTH OF MAN!"

Sonny

Cucumbers

Tiny pale-green tendrils,
groping,
curling, twirling,
climbing,
hoisting, moisting
rain-spattered
canopies,
splayed leaves
dancing,
tittering, prancing.
Underneath,
yellow butter blossoms
unfurl,
and soon
long, dark-green shadowy tubes,
hiding, hanging, heavily
dangling.
Pluck.
Seed-sliced, cut, crisp-cool
crunch!

Wendy Caldwell Maloney

Great Thing For Thee

Great things for thee
Great things for thee,
With feeble hands and trembling knees?

Great things for thee
Great things for thee,
Lord!, take me further than my eyes can see!

Great things for thee
Great things for thee,
As you hang from Calvary's tree
with no self-sufficiency??

Yes Lord! Great things for thee,
 great things for thee!
For thee God, make my life to be...
 "GREAT THINGS FOR THEE!!"

Richard C. Fuller

"Life Is A Garden"

Life is a garden,
 Good friends are the flowers.
And time spent together,
 life's happiest hours;
And friendship, like flowers,
 Blooms ever more fair,
When carefully tended,
 By dear friends who care;
And life's lovely garden
 would be sweeter by far.
If all who passed through it,
 were as nice as you are!

Paul Jay Crow

The Rose And The Butterfly

The good nectar of the rose
Gives yet another day
To the wary butterfly
That feeds along its way.

Just so, she has touched my life;
her praise was needed dole.
She gave me new direction,
And spurred my listless soul.

Oh, I'd like to say to her,
"I love you, and I care";
But what my need for grieving,
When she denies despair?

Now, she pales, as the cold winds
Blow death - she cannot stay.
I'll weep, as the butterfly,
When the rose fades away.

Pauline Parker

Prejudice

Why are we mistaken
for what we cannot help,
why can't people understand
we cannot change ourselves

Why can't people realize
we cannot change our race,
all we truly need to do
is let everyone be embraced.

Why are we so prejudiced
when we simply cannot see,
the person being picked on
could have been you or me.

Shannon Duncan

Untitled

Just like the wind
gently touching my hair
a breeze so fresh

A silky wave brushing my skin
a tingling with a touch
to let you know there is only a person
with a power as such

To move your heart
and create in your mind
the loveliest of settings
and a place so kind

That you will relax and worries flee
and realize just how beautiful
life really can be
just like the wind my wife refreshes me

Steven Longmire

To Lisa

It wasn't your time to go
gentle, loving spirit
it was a mistake
caretaker of the soul
take me instead
cried the hurt and pain inside
you don't deserve it
I don't deserve it
we don't deserve it
to leave so suddenly
at the beginning of life
with all doors open
a heart overflowing with love
a body bursting with vitality
a soul searching for answers
and finding them within yourself
to give to others
in your long life's path
cut short so hard and fast
it hurts
no, it was a mistake
it wasn't your time to go

Susan Guttzeit

Through The Eyes Of A Child

The world is full of many things
From wind blown clouds to angels wings,
Bright flowers blooming all around
And glistening snow upon the ground.

The most exciting sights are seen
Not by a poet or reigning queen,
But through the eyes so undefiled
Of an honest innocent little child.

The seed of a thistle on the breeze
And the new born birds in spring time trees,
A fuzzy insect so beguiled
All fill the eyes of a little child.

An ocean wave upon the sand
The gentle touch of a father's hand,
A tiny deer out in the wild
Are very special to a child.

But the thing all children want to see
Is not a bluebird or a bee,
Or the graceful flight of a peaceful dove
But the tender warmth of a mother's love.

Robert Dean Olson Sr.

A Dew Drop

A dew drop fell before me,
From the Tree of Life.
In falling no one saw it,
Concerned with their own strife.

I saw it for a moment,
Before the ground it met.
The pitiful little cry it gave
Fell 'pon ears that were deaf.

And so a little goodness,
A little bit of hope,
Is vanquished for eternity,
Yet no one else doth mope.

Scott Hartman

Deliverance

Notes sang out as light dances
From snow-capped peaks,
And glinted to the eternal void,
Filling full the barren waste.

And a vap'rous whisper floats past,
Trilling playfully the beaten ears,
Weathered and old,
Breathed anew a vivant spirit.

Hope wafting from its glacial grave
To the fired heaven's bliss,
And the chill, frozen sigh
A heaved, stuttered pant.

Fall! Fall! Fall! the brazened leaves
Of Autumn that count the counted breaths,
For now happiness reigns -
Joyous in life's limited perpetuity.

In one contains the wondered skies,
And all to mine own greedy palms
The flaxen goddess, sleeping lay,
Awaiting the Bell's dawn.

G. Egan Wheeler

Special Gift

I've been given a special mission in life
From my higher power above...
He gave to me a beautiful child
Who needs special care and love.

There is a reason why God chose me
To mother this needy child...
I believe He knew He could count on me
Whether the problems are severe or mild.

I feel that I've taught Jamie a lot
But I know he's taught me more...
He's shown me that life's worth living
No matter what it has in store.

He needs patience and understanding
And he requires lots of care....
I do my best to provide these things
And assure him that I am there.

I don't regret for one moment
The job that I've been given...
Each time I look at him I'm reminded
That he's my special gift from heaven.

Sandy K. Kracht

Yitzhak Rabin

Gold and crimson leaves falling
From an azure blue sky,
To the desert floor,
Where they would wither
And live no more!
All this beauty makes me
Wonder why?
Why this beauty had to die.

Could it be,
That in their lying there,
They built some soil
For a flower to grow
And spread throughout the land
So Israel's story yet untold,
Would blossom and unfold!

Philip E. Davis

She And I

She and I, as one of two.
Forever, it's true
We can never be blue,
Just she and I
We live and die.
So true and sure
We live in our own world
By our own words
How can it be?
We now can see.
She and I

Bill Stamper

A Love Confession

Ah! Fair damsel of delight,
For you I live, laugh, and fight.
To come to you my homeward way,
And know my love will never sway.
To be among the trees and grass,
With you my fair and bonnie lass.
To you I pledge my heart and soul;
With love my everlasting goal.

Quentin Quick

"Mt. Calvary"

Mt. Calvary is where Jesus died
for you and me
He took away our sins when He hung
on that tree
He did not know us but
yet He cared
and because of Him our lives
were spared
Jesus loved us then and His love is
still the same
He is always listening, just call upon
His name
He is there to comfort you in times of
pain and despair
Yes He is a true friend because He
is always there

Tara Clemmons

World War II Poem

Off to war we go
For what, I don't know
Fighting the German planes
On the American plains
Also the Japanese
Who bombed Pearl Harbor
Seeing men get killed
By the Jewish killer, Hitler
Oh, off to war we go
But I don't want to go
And all of the killing,
Filling all of the graves
I don't really want to go
But since I am American, off to war I go.

Cory Dellenbach

I'm Sorry!

I write to say I'm sorry, I'm sorry
for what I did. I caused pain in your
heart, pain I didn't mean.
I was stupid and selfish, didn't know
what to say. When you told me you
loved me, I felt nothing had changed.
So why? Why now that you're gone,
do I feel this way? I feel lonely with
fear, there are tears in my face.
Is it love? Is it pity? Will it vanish
away? This feeling I have doesn't seem
to go away.
In the years to come, will it still
be here? Will it be in my heart?
Will it disappear?
I guess time will tell, there's
nothing to fear, if it's still in
my heart, it was meant to be here.

Valerie Cortes-DeJorge

Life Is Test

Life is a test of many things,
For we know not how steep the path,
Or how rough the terrain,
But we're sure He's there 'til the last.

My mind pictures a steep mountain,
Topped off by a golden crest,
With its craggy sunlit summit,
And I'm anxious to attempt the test.

It takes the form of a citadel,
So majestic, so regal and so strong,
I know not how to begin my climb,
But He is there to help me along.

So long as I have the humility,
To ask my most faithful Guide,
He'll provide me with the footholds,
With trust and courage to abide.

Our faith and trust must be in Him,
For He has all the needed power,
And the strength for us to succeed,
Shall render us to Him in solemn prayer.

Rachael Johnson

Fifty Years Gone

Fifty years gone
For those who lived free,
Still going on
In those who did see.

Never ever over;
Sanity they sacrifice;
For those who lived through,
The fire and the ice.

Fire did burn
Those they did love.
Hearts of ice stole their souls,
As if a caged dove.

Liberation and hope
Was all the free could send,
But soon it too dwindled,
For it could never end.

Fifty years gone
For those who lived free,
The screams and the shouts
Still in those who did see.

Rachel Heck

Human Scorns

Ended the day
for the new one to go away
deeply sadden by my tears
face with throughout the years

Emotional torn by human scorns
what should I do
there out to get me
and not live my misery

They must be crazy
It's just not that easy
What should I do
Where can I go

No place to hide
It's spiritual felt inside
Tell me should I cry

Rochelle Britton

If You Came Back From Heaven

If you came back from heaven
For only just one day
I would hold close and hold you tight
And pray that you could stay

If you came back from heaven
For only just one day
I would want to hear you love me
And I would tell you the same

If you came back from heaven
For only just one day
I would want to hear about Jesus
And Peter, Paul, and James

If you came back from heaven
For only just one day
We would sit and talk all day long
And I would hear your sweet voice say

When you come home to Heaven
It won't be for just one day
For there we will spend eternity
In heaven is where we will stay

Dana Dunn

Untitled

Oh dear Lord I hope your near
For I have something for you to hear
I can't rely on only you
To try to help me make it through
My problem is I'm not too strong
To face all problems that come along
But since I'm here and since your there
My dreams are your for us to share
I wish I was open, I wish I was free
Like a big green field or restless sea
But since I'm tight, and all boxed in
There's no way it seems that I could win
So when I cry and shed my tear
It proves that life is what I fear
Susan Manweiler

"My Calling"

I will suffer no more!!
For I have opened God's door
The bright light and faces I know
This was my calling to go.

I have not left my loved ones behind
For I know I'll be on their mind.

When your calling day is due
I'll be waiting at God's door
For you!!!
Shirley M. Calmes

"Blank Tale"

And so he made the final strokes of the pen,
for he was finished.
He had fired off another
perfect
blank page.
He had worked so hard on it.
So complex in its emptiness.
So loud in its silent statement.
In marvelous, exhaustive order.
And oh so good the feeling
of spilling out the words
the
end
yet again, across the clear white page.
The story was brilliant.
But no one else would ever know it.
T. L. Closson Jr.

The Garden

A garden for young and old to see
Flowers grown from a single seed
Lush and plenty its boundaries hold
Roses and hostas with lily folds

Obscure pathways lined with petals
A place to rest, spirits to settle
Daffodils, tulips so brilliant yellow
White pines flow weeping willows mellow

Daisies and hyacinths on summer morn
Bamboo and bonsai their branches adorn
Japanese bridges, a garden for tea
Nature's theatre, beautiful and free

Oaks straight and tall saluting the sun
Mirrored lakes, a grand illusion
Alive and fertile the ground will bear
Happiness and pleasure that must be shared
Terry Warnecke

My Sister Elnora

My sister knew she would soon leave,
for God had called on her one day.
He would be beside her in her trials,
and hold her close as she passed away.

As God took my sis away from me,
and held her head in restful sleep.
I saw the clouds in the sky cry,
and heard those weeping willows weep.

I wasn't there when she went away,
she didn't hear the words I wanted to say.
Too late as I bid her a final farewell,
and sent her on her journey that July day.

My heart was sore that she was gone,
she was now free of that terrible pain.
As sure as there is a God above,
we will be together some day again.

I could only hurt and cry for my loss,
as they placed her beneath that prairie loam.
The flowers will bloom and sun always shine,
there in that place she now calls home.
Wheeler Laymon

Thoughts Of Summer

This is my favorite time of year
For baseball seasons almost here
I love the picnics in the park
Playing hide-and-seek till dark
Riding bikes with best friend
Coming home at the days end
Building cabins in secret places
High in trees-no signs, no traces
Counting day's until school will be out
So I can go fishing for bluegill and trout
I'll go to the pool and swim all day
Then I'll come home, too tired to play
I'll stay up at night and sleep until late
Hurry up, summer, I just can't wait!
Steven Przybylowski

Release

Searching all through my life
For an existence that was meant to be
Grasping at my dying faith
This blackness will not set me free
Feeling nothing seeing nothing
Shadows thrive within my heart
I know now I cannot run
From something which of me is part
Withering each moment
That I am forced to live
Undying death embrace me now
I've nothing more to give
I shall become eternal
Once I've passed from this plane
The other world will welcome me
I'll know no more sorrow
And feel no more pain.
Roseann Zamora

Mother's Day

There comes a day
For all to say
In their own special way
How much one love's their own Mother

When you think back to simpler times
Nursery rhymes and innocent minds
Fear was near but real unclear
Making you wish you could just disappear

Mommy came with the light
To make everything alright
She brought the water you thought you needed
And words of advice in which you heeded

Never will there be any other way
To say what you have to say
In your own special way on any other day
To the one who always made everything OK!
Reid Douglas Monroe

Shalimar

Brightly sparkling waters playing
Foaming, bubbling stone to stone,
Double rows of poplars watching
From their hilltop mountain home...

Red leaves of giant chenar trees
Once sewn by Persian kings,
Fall into the pond and swim
In pools of water rings...

Stepping stones a pathway make
Like lily pads afloat the lake,
From edge to brim we step between
Fresh cascade and bright sunbeam...

Fountains leap-frog to the lake
Where Himalayan peaks forsake
The heavens to reside... and
There... behind the ripples hide...

Breaking to fragmented floats
In wake of small shikara boats..
While Shankracharya's bells above
Tell of sacred...... timeless love...
Tobi Kumar

Angelic Friends

You and I are kindred spirits
Flying side by side.
We travel far and yet stay close
With love to see us through.
It is the love that leads us here
Into each others arms.
Together we must travel on
And not let fear invade us.

Stay open to your love, dear one,
It's special flowing style.
Your spirit flies with ours tonight
And you must not deny it.
Kindred spirits know the way
Into your open heart.
Stay open then and let them in
The joy will surely follow.
Sue Ellen Roberts

Before The Dawn

Long, blonde, wavy hair
Flashing in the sun, tan legs, strong
Calves,
She sets the volleyball for me -
I spike it.
"Score!" we yell as one.
I give her a high five,
She gives me one, too.
"Stay awhile longer," she says,
Swimming to cool off.
Hand in hand
We walk towards the sunset,
Her name, I never knew.
Who cares?
Waiting for the green flash before the
Sun goes down...
"Scott! It's time for school. You're
Going to be late!"
Gosh, darn it!
A dream

Scott Gordon

Midnight 727

Night bird,
Flap your wings and roar.
You have swallowed us all
and now you soar,
To great heights
and new events.

Night bird,
With your wings of steel.
You carry emotions
disguised as people;
To new places,
leaving behind,
memories.

Robert Benton Hille

Urban Scrawl

Shattering glass in the night;
First thought; whose car's getting boosted?
Just a kid breaking bottles, turns out.
Still, I drive a wreck for a reason

Knock on my door in the noontime;
Is it money of my souls they want?
Crack fix or time for Jehovah?
Or a nut? Check for the pistol.

Finding needles in a haystack's hard?
Not if you look in my yard.
Who want's to walk barefoot anyway?
Shoes are cheap, comparatively.

I've grown used to the sound of gun fire.
Sirens sing me to sleep.
God, I love this city!
I've a bridge for sale here, too.

William Eichelberger

Remember Me

ONE DAY, when along you came,
 Forgotten was my dream of fame,
You succeeded me to tame,
 But now you are gone, and I'll
  Never be the same.

Margaret B. Young

"Ode To The Workaholic"

Fill my day with industry
 Fill the extant void
With lack of thought and apathy
 With shards of dreams destroyed
But why complacent? Lost? Bereft?
 When there's still work to do
Only seven Mondays left
 And then my week is through
No desire for sympathy
 This trap is my design
What a great dichotomy
 The happy heart and mine:
One the heart I long to find
 The other in my chest
Obsolete becomes my mind
 And useless without rest
Ecclesiastic vision, I;
 "Vain" personified
But my, oh my, the time flies by
 The Sabbath crucified.

Benjamin Frandsen

Ray And Fay

Ray dear we are old and gray
Fifty years since our wedding day
shadows and sun for every one as
the years roll on; ray dear, when the
word went wry, hard and sorrowful
was I! Ray how you cheered me then

Things will be better sweet wife again!
Always the same Ray my dear
never fear, but my heart was wild
until you whispered "Heaven know best"
then my heart found rest
Ray, dear, t'was your loving hand that
showed the way to a better hand.
Dear, as you kissed each tear, life grew
better, and Heaven more dear.

Hand in hand when our life was may,
Hand in hand when our hair is gray,
Shadow and sun for every one, as the
years roll on, hand in hand when the long
night tide gently covers us side by side

Julia Ottice Simkins

Vanishing Child

An innocent and precious life
Fell victim to the pain of strife
A child is gone
Vanishing child

Instead of joy and happiness
A little child is laid to rest
We look upon
A vanishing smile

This vanishing is deja vu
The next child might belong to you
It's time to do
Something yesterday

They vanished but no magic
To their untimely demise
And the tragic consequences
Come as no great surprise

For we've allowed the madness
To go on to victimize
Another innocent child
Vanishing child

Paul E. Collins

What Is Love

 Love is that special
feeling shared between
two people, that's grown
over the years, stronger and
stronger.

 Love is a special
bonding between best
friends, as well as mother
and daughter relationships.

 Love is not just a
feeling you have inside
but, and emotion you feel
when that special someone
is near.

Ruth Rodriguez

Summer Is Over

Summer is over.
Fall has just begun.
Leaves will turn colors in the sun.
When the witches and goblins
have all settled down,
leaves will be falling
 to the ground.
Thanksgiving, then Christmas
 soon will be here.
Then we will be wishing
 each other a Happy New Year!

Phyllis Colucci

My Father's Aging

Today, I looked at my father's
face and saw more than a
face, more than a man.
I read the lines across his brow,
the pain in his eyes, the lines
that time had made.
A hand that's not so strong anymore,
a body that won't let him do
the things he wants to.
I cried as I looked in his eyes
I saw his heart pleading to
stop the pain. I saw his hair had
turned white, I never noticed before.
So as the seasons pass, he waits
for the reasons, and pleads to
God, I want to run once more!

Roberta Holland/Hetterick

The Cat

Mystery in fur, enigma with a purr.
Explosive action when not napping,
In the lap when nothing's happening.
A friendly nudge, nip or touch,
we respond with a stroke or praise,
Aloof, maybe, but the cat remains
the lord of all that it surveys.

Paul A. Koceski

Salome Of The Mists

Tossing her gay veils of spray
Every which every other way...
She flings herself to the sky
And prances and dances away...

The patter of splashes like rain
When her veils fall back again...
Seems to step up her pace while
Catching her shadow's refrain...

How can anyone dare to feel sad...
When this lady so lively and glad
Puts on a wild show that rivals...
The best belly dancers of Baghdad.

All day long she soaks up the sun
Golden rays reflect one by one...
And at night when she dances she
Stirs up romances with great abandon.

Little boys gather round midnight
From all over town just to see..
The first Avenue fountain, 'stepping high',
This mysterious... bubbling... Salome....

Tobi Kumar

Will You Think Of Me

Every time you look at the morning sunlight
every time you see the moon so bright
every time you see the sea
will you think of me

As each rain drop fall from the sky
as each fluffy white cloud goes by
and spring time blossoms in the trees
will you think of me

For when you look into a child's eyes
and with the unconditional love you surmise
where only true innocence can still be
will you think of me

In each day and in each night
holding onto that love with all your might
and not wanting to let it be
will you think of me

For all things that matter still
not one can control my will
as each though I tell you true
For I will always think of you

Terry Steffey

Ocean Whisper

Star is born from candle light:
Days gone by stars are bright
Light days bring morning song
from the ocean's blue swells
Let the sea gulls fly free because
they were meant to be. So fly
free in the deep blue sea.
The ocean whispering through
will help days go by
When a star is born everything
will come true by the ocean's
Deepest blue sea that the
sea gulls will have to be free.
Wouldn't that be wonderful in
our deepest blue part of the sea.

Patty

"I Am Me"

Here and now I am me.
Ever present for all to see
  the me I am inside.
I have nothing to hide.
  Sitting here in my solitude,
I am content with my attitude.
  For I am me! The one and only!
No longer shall I be lonely.
  I am not weak!
No more shall I be meek!
  For I am very strong.
I know now where I belong.
  I now enjoy being me!
I accept the me I turned out to be.
  I am quite pleased.
I am now at ease.
  I am empowered!
I have been love showered.
  Because I am me,
There is so much that I can be!

Tamara Lee Hagen

Yet She Still Stands "America"

Oh America blessed by God
Ever Great ever free
oh sweet land of opportunity
that blended the greatest and the
best of hell as and imperial rome
of every conceivable culture from
the farthest corners of the world,
you whom gave us our prized and
cherished liberty from our founding
fathers to Martin Luther King.
that marvelous woman Amelia Earhart
you whom amazed and gave
us the wizard of Menlo park.
You whom destroyed that evil
leader of Nazi Germany,
you whom sent the first man
in space where old glory still
stands up on the lunar surface
America, you are still the envy
of the free world, when the walls of Berlin
came down

Michael Garcia

Reflections In The Pool

You are always on my mind,
even when my eyes are closed.
I see your face as you were
many years ago.

It is true my love was strong,
when we were young and new.
but love has rode the many years,
to test the time of day.
And my love is still as strong,
as the sun and moon
that passes over on its way.

I look for tomorrow to tell her
I adore. Until the day should come,
I'm not able any more. My eyes
will remember forevermore,
the love I found, so many years ago
when love knocked at my door!

Richard Duffy

LOST BENGAL OF RUNTHAMBOR

Within the forest
dwells magnificent splendour
of savage beauty;

She stalks silently
with powerful padded feet,
cautious and alert.

Runthambor beckons
this great prehistoric beast,
huge fanged denizen....

THE TIGER!

Sharron Verlinda

"Walls Of Tears"

No love or guidance given you
during your young years;
went to school, worked and, all alone,
came home to "WALLS OF TEARS"!

Your basic needs and nurturing
were never given you.
It's a miracle that you survived...
After all that you've been through!

You didn't get involved in
drugs, gangs or violence.
When you saw some good out there,
you chose the path to take...in silence.

No one knew the strength you had
or virtues you possessed,
until someone cried "WALLS OF TEARS"
and their rescue you addressed.

Robbed of your own childhood,
held on to your dreams for years,
your identity and self-esteem...
your escape from "WALLS OF TEARS"!

Patricia A. Wessel

Hail Timbuktu

  Man and many sunk
Down and thru' these savanna archives
  Jalis hail your *Zas* and *Sunnis*
Cascading on generations unwind
Subduing me in relapsing love
  But where sunk you?

Crenelated roof campuses rent
  verdant steppes bald
  your remains ruined
shoving forth new shades
Of the tired and traumatized
Blistered by the Hamattan grits
Asking if you were mythical.

Hail Timbuktu! Rain Timbuktu!
  Thus when the animated sun
Spruces up The Niger-bend
  Like an autumn ballroom,
Tell me tales of a distant-near
  Themes of my elusive past
My heart shall throb — Hail Timbuktu.

Saihou Omar Gigo

Don't

Don't pretend to understand
Don't pretend to care.
There's nothing you can say or do
To break this glassy stare.

Don't try to make it better,
Don't try to lick my wounds.
Even if someone could help
It surely isn't you.

Don't stroke my hair and smile,
Don't shout at me and curse.
Do not come any closer
Just fix your own life first.

Don't find your way inside me,
Don't pray apart my heart.
There's nothing real inside me
Except a bitter dart.

Don't try to see it my way,
Don't lay your hand to heal.
You'd like to make things better
And cheapen what I feel.

Philip Dahlstrom

Night Visions

Are you lonely at night?
Does time ache your soul and
dreams never come to your bed?
Like a soft sigh upon the moon's thrust.
Does your wish come ever near?
Soon the pools of quicksilver will
run fast upon your breast and
forever virtue will live.
Is today the day ... or is it
tomorrow that I will be King?
Here we play and fight
on the sands of forever!

Richard Edward Miller

The Descent Of Intercourse

Words and sex
Divided
Never to meet?
Hovering in the air,
Hanging out
Somewhere -
A link?
A strand?
Remains, to be found
Lying dead in a crypt (or a crib)
Imperative, perhaps
You slither down deep
Way, way
Under the ground
To wait - hope - wait
For something to come
Some creature or God
To utter
Some new, strange
Meaningful sound

Sandra Ortez

Untitled

Embrace the strength
Dismiss your length
Realize all
Especially for the fall
Savour the flashing flow
Prepare for the climax of the show
Can't help this, I'll try to fight this
Treason
Pure perjury
Unknown...early days so soon to
Memorize
Must sympathize
Baby steps
I leap back, mother may I?
Oh, what corruption
has been smothered
Touched without admittance
Scratched

Rosalyn Payen

Conflict

I harshly judge those who
   desire others like themselves.
To me 'tis vile and cannibalistic
   to crave flesh of one's own kind.

Preachers, politicians and polymaths
   call for equal rights
and brotherly love for those who
   triumphantly slipped past
their closet door.

I condemn at a distance,
   but when face to face with Mary,
the pansy queen, I chat of
   shallow things and slip
hypocritically behind my own closed door.

Shirley R. Whittington

The Passing

Going forward, you gone back
desert sun stops in its track
rain must follow and not fall
flowers too will heed their call.

Today is you as today is gaze
night hesitates before the dawn,
a kiss, a touch, a long hello,
from where we stand, we take the blow.

Eyes to stars we chant inquire
this simple task to prayer desired,
stilled souls you ripple chance
for we sleep in the arms of fortune's dance.

Carew Papritz

My Room

It's like a jewel cave,
filled with treasures.
If you look long enough,
you'll find one.
You must be alert
while passing through;
otherwise you could get hurt.
My parents say it's a mess
but to me
it's a treasure chest.

Sara Conrad

Yesterday

A rising from one aspiration
denied by your hesitation
fueled by emotional starvation
my rage becomes mundane.

Don't coy with alteration
or attempt petty manipulation
I'm on to your temptation
of causing me pain.

All I wanted was to share with you
equal equality, to be fair to you.

What makes you run from me?
Pretending your done with me?
Why are you so defending me?
Purposefully offending me.

I was ready to try with you
run and hide and cry with you,
but you've pushed me too far away
maybe testing to see if I'd stay...
   but I won't...

Now together is just yesterday.

Daniel Kaminsky

Separation

Awake, sleeping Angel
Daytime begins
Time for Sadness to fill
your eyes-
Warmth won't be present
Separated we will be.

Home, food, clothes are
all Necessities with a
Tearful Price of Sacrifice-
Aged Wisdom, Opened Eyes
One day you too will
See as I.

Sloppy wet kisses,
Choking hugs, we begin
our hours of separation,
Patiently waiting
Yearning for each others comfort
wrapped in arms
Singing childish songs.

Suzanne Guinn Knoll

End 'O' Earth

The earth stops spinning
Day turns to night
The sun turns to ice
The summers turn to winters
The wind becomes colder
The air becomes older
Earth starts to fade away
Mankind becomes no more
So it ends
The earth's life
Can it be gone
Can it regain its beauty
With mankind gone
The cycle begins a new.

Shawn O'Connor

Ruled By Ignorance

A premonition illuminated by the
darkness of ignorance
A blanket of hate and hypocrisy
sheltering the world
Step by step, Day by day
We seem to grow stronger
We seem to gain knowledge
But blinded by simplicity
We are forced into exile
Safe within the innocence of
our own beginning
Safe as we will ever be in a
world ruled by ignorance.
Saffron LeBlanc

Mirrored

Water drizzles.
Darkness falls.
Lightning strikes.
Thunder calls.

Tears pour.
Blackness worn.
Sadness stuns.
Hearts torn.

Blue sky,
Sun shines.
Clouds fade.
Nature signs.

Smile spreads.
Face lights.
Eyes sparkle.
Laughter writes.

Rain storms.
Death glooms.
Day clears.
Life blooms.
Victoria Elizabeth Seawright

The Stranger's Shelter

The nightsong of the blackbird
Cuts through the misty air
I wander through the darkness
Hibiscus in my hair

Its melody is eerie
Across the glistening lake
And violet clouds are nearing
The sky is theirs to take

The first few drops of rainfall
Rest gently 'pon my cheek
And in the nearby distance
I hear a soft voice speak

The storm that's now approaching
Shall pass and fade away
'Til then my tent is peaceful
Together let us stay.
Susan Burghart

Battling Skies

Desolate wind
Cuts through like knives on a lake
Of slowly forming darkness

An abyss of night
Shrouds itself in nothing
As the forlorn passing of time
Mourns a setting sun

The sun leaks out
Punctured by mountains
Crowning itself
With a bloody legacy of clouds
On the vanishing horizon

Here
Surrounded in solitude
Strangled by memories
Of the petals
   of a lily white moon
Tiphanie M. Henningsen

What Is Beauty?

Beauty is a drop of rain,
Crystal clear.
Beauty may be far away;
Beauty may be near.
Beauty is the ocean waves,
Rolling in sky high!
Beauty is a flash of lightning;
How lovely, how sublime!
Beauty can be anything,
Even something small.
Either you see beauty everywhere
Or don't see it at all.
Shayna Lavin

Lost Child

A lost child,
   crying out for help,
   yet never receiving.
To be alone,
   lost in this cruel world,
   with nobody to love.
Lost,
   trying to find her way,
   yet getting forced back more each day.

His temper went wild,
   she cried for help,
   but nobody was believing.
Alone,
   on her bed she lays curled,
   praying for help from above.
Was it worth the cost,
   a lost child every day,
   because he got drunk one day.
Veronica Vigil

Poem Of The Morning

Swiftly blows the Breath of God.
Crisp, autumn breezes
Swirling painted leaves.
Warning of the chill to come
Suggests a close embracing of myself.
Stir the coals of love
Within my heart, O God
Lest I fear the cold
And close the door.
Nelma Hyde

Why?

Why did God put me on this earth?
Couldn't he have had a different birth?

My life is just one big mess,
If I weren't here it would be a bless.

Why have I spent my life crying?
When inside my heart is dying?

One by one a piece of me is falling.
Maybe soon death will be a calling.

Why do you treat me this way?
When one day you know you will pay.

My life is a mess, yes that's true,
That's why I've decided the hell with you!
Sarah Kreycik

The Search

My Father God, you seem so far away.
Confusion overwhelms my simple mind.
"Be still and know that I am God," You say.

But where shall I discover You, I pray.
Your presence is beyond what I can find.
My father God, You seem so far away.

"Am I not here each moment of the day?
Do I not teach you when you free your mind?
Be still and know that I am God," You say.

But doubt has mired my peace in slow decay.
I feel ensnared by the passage of time.
My father God, You seem so far away.

"If you listen, I will show you the way.
Follow me and you will not be denied.
Be still and know that I am God," You say.

I will follow You to a brighter day,
But allow me to walk a path well tried.
My father God, You seem so far away.
"Be still and know that I am God," You say.
Vanessa L. Clemens

Columbia You Were Terrific

Although the launch they had to delay
Columbia you proved yourself today
Although you lost a few tile
Your success should make us all smile
You withstood re-entry with all that heat
And watching you glide was really neat
Almost everything turned out fine
And touchdown was right on time
The flight was really great
And that landing was first rate
Or to be a little more specific
Columbia you were terrific
So Columbia now your first flight is done
Rockwell has proved its self to everyone
And whether your part was big or small
Now I think all of us here can stand very tall
William "Shortfellow" Koss

Life

River flowing to the sea
Color changes blue, white, brown
giving along the way sustenance
to deer, squirrel, tree, people.

Banks guide it's path
Gravity its onward speed
Colored by the things it touches
by motion purified

Leaves ride on waters top
Slow, fast, smooth, rough
Sun, shade, dark, moon
Die with death live anew.

Baby born into the world
Life cord from mother cut
Without food dies
Without love wilts
Moving a long
Changing with age
We are leaves
In the river of life.

Stanley Williams

Self Declaration

Place a
Chariot
at My
Feet

While a
Fire
Burns inside
Me

Let all
the Stars
Extinguish
in My
Grip

And Hear
 My
Laughter
Echo in
the Night

Samantha Crawford

On Hearing Maya Angelou

The Rock——she stands
carved from dark stone
Her blood warmed by the molten
core of Earth where beats
the never-ending pulse-drum
Her eyes split open the central
grain wherein hides the spark of life

The River — she stands
dripping from her dive in
waters racing sea-ward mingling
her blood once more with life-source
Ever more clear of eye
She sees behind all shadows
She senses all scents wind-blown

The Tree—— alone she stands
swaying with the rising of her song
She sings — the birds take flight
Her song tells all she sees
She sings "Good Morning" and
dances into the New Day

Paula Loomis

Mother And Daughter

The mother who long ago
Carried the jeweled crown
Of youth with the dignity
And composure of a queen,
Now recalls being then unaware
Of youth's similarity
To the rose whose petals
In short time wilt
Then fall to the ground.

With sigh and tearful eye
She observes her daughter
Carrying the jeweled crown of youth
With the grace of royalty—-
Unaware of youth's sudden
Unfoldment, brief stay,
And hasty departure—-
Oblivious to its impermanence
That will one day sadden her being.

Sara Lee Skydell

An Anniversary Poem To Mom And Dad

Thank you for helping me through the years
Caring for me and calming my fears.
Putting up with me when I made it rough
Thank you for not making things too tough.

Nothing I could ever say would make up
For what you do for me each day
You made me laugh when things went wrong
And helped me to be a little more strong.

You watched me grow throughout the years
Helped me through school and dried my tears
Even though I screamed, I yelled and whined
You would listen all the time.

I made things harder than they needed to be
But you still sat and listened to me
I want you to know I'm thankful for the
Thoughtful things you do
And please don't forget that I'll
Always love you.

Serena Masetta

Me

Do I look the way I feel?
  Can you tell
  Am I real?

See my smile
  Is it real
  Does it tell
  How I feel?

Only a few
  Know me well
  Others see
  But they can't tell.

Those feelings - ME
  Way deep inside
  Keeping ME safe
  With them I hide.

ME ... I share
  With oh - so few
  The real ME
Is it known by you?

Shirley J. Koelling

Nothing Ever Gets Lost

From bitter trials conceived at worse
Can life spring forth without a curse.
Where forests fires once did rage,
Pine trees and flowers now take stage.

From violent thrashing of the wind
Some seeds from certain grains descend.
From painful work by grains of sand,
A lustrous pearl on shore may land.

The moths, their wings renewed for flight,
Must struggle with cocoons at night.
The rain and snow to earth may fall,
But from the moisture, trees grow tall.

The mighty oak begins as seed
A drop of water fills the oceans need.
In fall the leaves cover the earth,
So that each spring the flowers give birth.

'Twas on a tree that He gave all,
And died for man, from God did fall.
Worthless man - how great the cost!
But nothing ever does get lost.

Virchel E. Wood

B-47E 53-2123

Lifted as a feather,
By the hand of God.
She soared majestically,
To protect our sod.

Throughout the Cold War,
She flexed her might.
And in the end,
Never had to fight.

Her glory lay,
Not in damage done.
But greater yet,
In the peace she won.

She is gone now,
Bye and bye.
Deep in my heart,
She still soars high.

Ralph W. Bleiler

Lady Of The Northern Lights

Once on the cusp of winter's cruel crust,
 By the fringe of the far north sea,
There lived one lady too loving for lust,
 Mistress of the last frontier was she.

Out of the night clothed only in light,
 Like a garment of golden graces,
She danced a devotion of divine delight,
 For the fraternity of frozen faces.

They cast off coats of shivers and sins,
 As her vision veiled virtue from vice,
And winter subsided like spring begins,
 Liberating their lives from the ice.

Now some in this grand but lonely land,
 When northern lights swirl in the sky,
Say the lady is dancing at God's command,
 To soothe sourdough souls from on high.

Philip M. Wright

The Loving Touch

I am a bud, picked too soon,
But touch me, and I shall bloom.

I am a raging, rambling stream,
But touch me, I will be calm and serene.

I am a hill, unnoticed and small,
But touch me, I will be a mountain tall.

I am a bitter grape on the vine,
But touch me, I will become sweet wine.

I am a gloomy shadow of night,
But touch me, I will show you the light.

I am a lonesome drop of rain,
But touch me, I'll be a fountain again.

I am a hurricane out to destroy,
But touch me, I'll be a breeze of joy.

I am a bird with a broken wing,
But touch me, for you I will sing.

I am a feeble broken twig,
But touch me, I'll grow into a tree so big.

I am not what I want to be,
But I can, if you just touch me.

Sabine Landry

In Love

At the present time it's raining
But there's sunshine in my home,
And though there's no one near me
I do not feel alone.

Some irksome things have happened
But their weight rolled off of me -
They cannot change my way of thinking
And I'll still sing cheerfully.

The world has lots of problems
And there's sadness all around,
But I know it's not for always,
So my spirit can't be bound.

And storms of every nature
May oftentimes be rife,
So why am I so happy?
I am still IN LOVE WITH LIFE.

Rachel Hartnett

Soul Of Pain

Heart so true
Filled with sorrow
Love that is true
But heart is hollow
Storm and cloud follow deep
Tortured soul set aside to weep
Pain follows through and through
Running hard nothing to do
Voice of resin calling near
But fear inside away you steer
Pain of soul keeps you strong
Breathing hard still going on
Deep tonight
Still soul has fright
Where to turn you do not know
Hiding close to darkness though
Passion of fear still does burn
To end this life your body earn
But the love of all you know
Still toward life you know to go.

Ron Pollard

A Teardrop

There are many kinds of teardrops
But the one I love the best
Is the one which flows from heaven
And falls upon they breast

It is a happy teardrops
As it flows down both your cheeks
It shows you love dear Jesus
As the love for Him you seek

You can hear a preacher, preaching
As the Holy Spirit comes within
And a tear will flow from Heaven
As he seeks many souls to win

And you can hear someone a singing
A beautiful Gospel hymn
And a tear will flow from Heaven
As a blessing flows deep within

Oh I do love those teardrops
And the blessing they do bring
It is like a flowing river
As the Angels begin to sing

Ethel C. Kauffman

Someone That Knew

We thought it wouldn't happen,
but someone knew it would.

No one knew who had to go,
but someone knew who could.

No one knew when one got hurt,
but someone knew when one would die.

No one knew who would die,
but someone knew who would cry.

No one knew this many would die,
but someone knows where they all lie.

Stephen Watts

Perfection

I'd like it to be perfect
But nothing ever is
From little chores to big chores
What I thought would be a whiz
Takes twice as long, looks half as good
And try hard, as I may
I'm never really satisfied
When things don't go my way
I must learn not to mind
And know I've done my best
Then look for sunshine to enjoy
And fill my life with zest.
For we're always really climbing
And striving to succeed
And if it was too easy
There would be no need
For us to say our prayers
Or ask for guidance from above
And help with all our cares
Or know his perfect love.

Tessa E. Downing

Lining

The lines are our friends—
But not really.
Make friends with the lines,
But know that they are your restrictions,
Your limits,
Your boundaries,
If your will is strong,
Your curiosity uncontrollable,
You will draw your own lines,
Erase them at will,
And have the courage to really live.

Talia Page

"The Forgotten"

The song with so much feeling,
  but never really heard.
The book with so much knowledge,
  but never really learned.
The art with all its beauty,
  but never looked upon.
The kiss of endless love,
  but never truly felt.
The person with so much to give,
  but with nobody, who cares.
All these precious things have come
  to exist in the world of the forgotten.
Our hearts and in our minds.

Sharon L. Popovich

"Love"

Love, seems a Hollywood cop-out
But love's not a fleeting emotion,
It's a sharing of life's deepest meaning,
As deep and as wide as the oceans.

Real love is a gift from our Father,
Who loves us when we're not at our best,
And keeps loving in spite of,
The tempters real trying to test.

Love selflessly given
To all, deserving or not.
Is what God really expects of us,
Even though that's expecting a lot.

Love is not self gratification,
Love is not easy to give.
God's help makes it all start to happen,
As long as He gives us to live.

Robert W. Ross

Untitled

God bless this home
But I've known in my heart
God has blessed it all along
Right from the very start
From the mantle, each window
Each and every door
It was planned by angels
With blessings galore.
And so, from the basement
To the very tip top dome
Thanks, Jesus, for blessing
Our home sweet home.

Phyllis Compton

Ship...Don't Sail

I'm not trying to hold onto you forever.
But, I need more time to share with you
today.

Time to
do
with you,
be
with you,
see
with you.

You came...a light;
a guiding light in the forest.
a deep, dark, insensitive forest.

I cling to you
as do leaves to a tree.
Until the season comes to let go.
Trembling leaves...
drifting to the ground,
becoming strong sailing ships
against the wind.

Please don't leave.
Gina Osher

Absent Eyes

All eyes
burnish
Their own life

Both eyes
Decipher
Their own gift

Some eyes
Furnish
Their own gift

But,
At the end

No eyes
Will see
Their own truth!
Ramina S. Yesaeil

Bubbles Floating Over Me

Bubbles Bubbles over here,
Bubbles Bubbles over there.
Look around you and see,
Bubbles floating over me.

They are floating can't you see?
Floating over through the tree.
Look closely and you will see,
Bubbles floating over me.

Don't try to catch one with your hand,
They break easier than a castle made of sand.
But watch carefully and you will see,
Bubbles floating over me.
Sheena R. Williams

Nightmares

Scary, horrible
chilling, thrilling, frightening
monster, screams, angels, sunsets
relaxing, imagining, drifting
beautiful, peaceful
dreams
Peter Benjamin Fortin

Wondering

My heart awaits to be
broken or born.
Day-by-day it is sadly torn.
What kind of heart hath
this man?
I have yet to understand,
how do I appear in your
critical eye?
Day-by-day are you living a lie?
Is what I felt just fantasy?
Are all my dreams from yesterday?
If we are destined not to be
and all your thoughts
are far away,
go gather them all
and say goodbye to me.
Rhonda Amador

"Life"

What is life, day after day?
   Breath on the river,
So beautiful and gay.
   Moving with great current,
with what you have chose.
   with motion of life,
Always be on your toes.
   the grace of time,
is happiness you see.
   But don't forget,
He made the reason in me.
   The glitter of sparkler,
the smile of time.
   Makes you wonder,
how long will life be mine!
   Life moves by spirit,
don't ever forget.
   God is the one;
who put it here,
   that's it!
Shirley Jean Willey

Sunrise

Through my window
Breaks dawns early hour,
Ray by ray...
The sun
Pokes through the
Edge of night;
Ignites the sky in
Fiery blaze,
Meadows, trees, blush
And glow, embraced by
Dawns encircling light!
Walter E. Anderson

In Time

Time will take away the pain,
but the memories will always
remain, like a painting in
a picture or a part in a play
you took my breath away.
Devastated by your departure
but facing the reality
Reaching out for happiness
hoping it will find me.
Sydney O'Neil

The Beauty Of Spring

Lovely little flowers
Blooming in spring
Lovely little birdies
Come out to sing.

Lovely little grass
On which upon it I stand
It seems to be holding
Hand by hand

Lovely gleaming sunshine
That shines all the day
And the lovely breeze
Which cools you at play.
Roberta Cross

Blessed Are We

Blessed are we He's among us
Blessed are we for He's there
Blessed are we He's among us
Blessed are for He cares

He's there to watch us
He's there to guide us
He's there to answer each prayer
He's there to walk with us
He's there to talk with us
He's there to lighten the shadows each day
He's there and cares for us
He's there and bared for us
He's there for all he shame we have known
He's there to walk with us
He's there to talk with us
He's there to lighten the shadows each day
Sally Anne Sugiura

Shadow

Dark, silent creeping silhouette
Blankly carving defined height,
Shade-maker, dimming earth's palette,
Cloud obscured, consumed by night.

A victim, vanished from the sphere,
Awaits moon and sun for sight.
Again, sharp angled shapes appear,
Darkness that depends on light!
Rhea T. Pullen

The Old Water Mill

You stayed far behind me,
Between two times, between two burdens.
On a steep bank, far away.
On the other side of the world.
I know that you are a remnant of centuries,
With two gratings of erosion,
With two boundaries of dying,
And with one river flowing away.
Under your hard stones
I, too, used to grind my bones
And make my bread of them.
O good old water mill!
Now you are grinding the rib of time,
Under your cracked stones.
And you take autographs from passers-by
In order not to remain nameless and alone.
I have been erased from your memory
Like a circle drawn on sand.
I, who used to grind a hard living with you.
Mustafa Jahich

Auschwitz

Ye realms of ghosts that linger here
Beneath the Polish sky,
These rails once carried cargo trains
That brought you here to die.
Your silent shades behind the wire
Still beg for mercy with your eyes,
While chimneys belch their human smoke
Into indifferent skies.
You lift your tattooed arms to God
He does not hear your prayers,
And marching boots and children's screams
Resound about the towers.
Ye phantom throngs, depart this place,
The brutal blows you feel
The savage guards and vicious dogs
Are no longer real.
Though work did never make you free
All mankind grieves your fate,
And we have heard your desperate cries
But many years too late...

Rosemary Muntz Yasparro

The Rose And The Thorn

Whether day or night or in the morn,
Beneath every rose there is a thorn,
Some sweet talk and a smiling face,
Can be the beginning of utter disgrace.

You have to make sure that you are right,
When you do anything in the day or night.
Your friends encourage you in joys unknown,
When there's a problem, you are all alone.

Make the best of all you can,
Be a friend to every man.
Don't have anyone at your beck and call,
And you'll be pleasing to one and all.

Remember the thorn beneath the rose,
You'll have all friends and no foes,
Think with your head, not your heart,
From your friends you'll never part.

Ramsundar Persad

First Born Son

Dedicated to Andrew Thomas Hansen
Love and enjoy him while he's small,
before you know it he's six feet tall.
No more snails and puppy dog tails,
his devotion to family and home life pales.

He's off to find out what life's all about,
his determination makes him stout.
He tries to make it on his own,
dreading having to come home.

Life's demands can take a toll,
sometimes it's like hitting a pole.
Success is sweet and life is good,
he always knew if he tried, he could.

Girlfriends come and girlfriends go,
his heart breaks and tears flow.
I always knew he deserved better than that,
finally he decided on a dog and a cat.

Someday he will take a wife
and be off to make a new life.
But in my heart he will always be,
the most important thing to me.

Pam Montag

The Epitaph

Death came
    before it will ultimately come
I died today
    when you left with him
I was silent
    in my casket of hurt
and could not stop
    the sound of your steps going away
the dirt of many memories
    is thrown on me
And only a cold epitaph remains
    to tell of us together

Paul White Eagle

Menu

What to eat, what to eat.
    Beef, chicken, or pig's feet
Your eyes say one thing,
    Your mouth another
Your stomach says whoa!

Some people live to eat,
    Some eat to live,
And never the twain to meet
    What to have for dinner
That will make you thinner!

What to eat, what to eat,
    Breakfast, lunch, or supper...
Think this, think that,
    It's got me beat!

When the stomach growls,
    Breakfast, lunch, or dinner,
Beef, lamb, fish, or fowl
    Whatever, you're a winner!

Virginia J. Brady

Reasons To Join Scouting

We joined the scouting program,
Because of the values they have,
I thought my son might need them,
Since life sometimes is bad.

There are so many avenues,
And kids have to make decisions,
Hopefully it will help him choose,
But that is only one of the reasons.

Kids of today live stressful lives,
There is evil on every block,
Scouting helps combat that problem,
But who know what it will unlock.

There could be an Eagle inside,
Just waiting to get out,
With the right guiding force,
Imagine what could come about!

Pat Sharp

Rain Castles

The raindrops live in castles
Built of pure white light,
They swell to fill the turrets,
Calling to the wind to cross the drawbridge,
Inviting the thunder in
To sing an ancient song
Of weeping skies.

Janet Redmon

"Dear Diary"

Three innocent lives taken so brutally,
because of a choice I made so cruelly,

I live everyday with sadness in every
breath, because they couldn't choose
their own life or death.

How can I laugh, knowing they never
had that chance.

Seven years later, still hurts everyday,
wishing now, that then I had found
the right way.

It will haunt me forever,
hearing them begging me to
choose for the better.

Please God, forgive me for
what I have done,
for it should not be me,
but them who gets to wake
and see the sun.

Paulanne Heide

God's Plan

I am part of heaven
    Because I am part family

What went before is
    The cause of my being

I am a mixture of many things
    Blended into the family of man

I am free yet bound
    By the threads of the past

Some of me is in heaven
    Some of me does not yet exist

I am as those before me
    A part of what is
    A part of what was
    A part of what will be

I am eternal
    I am God's plan

Simon J. Burttschell

Joy

The rain,
beating on my windowpane.
The wind,
With words that have no end.
The sun,
tempting beaches and fun
God's love,
from above.
His son, merciful and kind.
A true friend we find.
A love so deep and rare.
We know.
We are always in his care.

Sandra Yokeley

Before The Memory Fades

Pause with me one moment
Before the hands of time
Wipe clean
The slate.

Ruth Gretchen Head

"Memories"

No matter where life takes us
Be it near or far away
It's good to know there is a place
That calls us back one day
If only in our memory
And for just a little while
It's always there within our heart
And gives us cause to smile
A memory is space and time
A golden thread with love to bind
To bring me home lest I stray
To warm my heart ...To light my way

Wanda Wiles

Dance

Letting go
Be free of worries
Showing what you want
Who you are
How you feel.

Going nuts
Freaking out
Spastic motion
Spotlight, greenlight
On you.

All wet
in pain
High on life
Flippin' out
Havin' fun
Livin' it up
Dancing...

Sabra Lynn Garrity

O, The Folly Of It All!

It happened at the Mardi Gras
Azaleas filled my heart with awe
Romantic music swelled the air
I wore a red rose in my hair.

A dashing sheik I met perchance
And pronto he asked me to dance
Enchanted with his mystic masque
I did not think his name to ask.

We glided 'neath a desert sky
I prayed this bliss would never die
But when his face he did reveal
I thought (oh no, this can't be real!)

Where is my Sheik of Arabie?
Dear dear, what fools we mortals be!
My castles tumbled to the ground
I had not my Prince Charming found.

Rita R. Barrett

What Do You Think?

Do you think I'm stupid,
do you think I'm dumb?
Do you think I'm an old, lazy bum?
My Mom says you shouldn't care
what other people think;
but I always have,
what do you think?

Ryan Cameron

Imaginings

Imagine an iridescent sun rising.
Awakening many fields of iris,
As sonnetta birds sing,
And opulent rivers mill and weave.

Imagine a scarlet zenith at its peak.
The infinite spaces filled with treasures.
Reticent beings gathered amidst the knolls,
And rain the sweetness thereof.

Imagine concealment of the heart's desires.
Gold threads of light and longing.
Luminous in it's tide and flowing...
    Actually breathing.
As the intricacies reveal themselves.
And...after doing so,
Perceive the sun as one thing true.
The heart and mind, another.
For deep within the absolute...
    Lies the secret to one's omnipresence.

Renee Le Grand

The Bountiful

I who have nothing
Awake each day in splendor,
I who have nothing
Hear the birds sing against
    The blue, clear sky.
I who have nothing
See the trees of green,
    Butterflies and morning glories.
I who have nothing
Taste the dew on my lips as I
    Stroll during the early morn.
I who have nothing
Feel the serenity in my soul,
I who have!

Sharon B. Evans

Imagine, If You Can

When you look
at my picture,

Can you see
the endless, sleepless
nights of worry
wearing thin upon my face?

Can you see
the desperation and
loss of hope
within my vacant eyes?

Then,
when you close
your eyes at night,
Imagine, if you can,
my tears
within your heart.

G. Noreen Dillon

The Birds Are Going Away

The birds are going away
Away they go today
Oh over the hill
They go, they will
The birds are going away
Today

Rebecca Wuest

The Greatest Is Love

In her cold grave she is lying,
    Asleep, to wake never again;
When past are her smiles, love and sighings,
    Oh! Why do her memories remain?
Sunshine and spring have lightened,
    The red roses placed upon her grave;
Though the roses have brightened,
    Autumn now covers them with leaves;
Winter has wildly destroyed them,
    With her cold wind as sad as a knell;
The shroud of the wreath has veiled them,
    Still deep in my heart she dwells!
The shadow and sunshine have vanished,
    The clouds and day light flee away;
But from my heart will not banish,
    The thoughts of my wife are to stay.
My love for her is still shining,
    Because GOD'S promises are still bright;
While her body in dust is reclining,
    Her soul lives in GLORY and LIGHT.

William O. Shepherd

The Dance Of Life

It begins quickly
As we're abruptly thrown into the light
Our movements faster
as we learn each new step

Moving towards each other
we find our way around the circle
we laugh, we cry,
we lose, we win

We move from one love to another
hoping for perfection
accepting only one,
and then leaving it behind

Our movements begin to slow
as we create new steps to follow ours
and we look back
to see if we missed a few

Did we learn enough?
Did we find that smile?
It no long matters
as the dance comes to a close.

Sue A. Garner

Dark Friend

Death, cloak of darkness,
Enfold us all.

Eraser of pain and worry,
Remove the wall.

Allow all light to enter,
forevermore.

Rosamond C. Martin

With Someone You Love

With someone you love,
Embrace a special bond
Because you don't know what you've got
Until it's gone

With someone you love,
Hold tight to and treasure
Because take it from me,
They won't be around forever

Tara Warner

"A Beauty So Adored"

All alone a rose does strain
As the wind slaps it around;
As clouds wring out rain
It seems no hope can be found.

Petaled arms tightly held
Closely to chilled core,
Until the storm finally quelled
And hovered no more.

Rays of gold peek through,
Allowing the rose to dry.
It opened petals anew
Seeming to release a sigh...

Up it arched, to be warm
Opening more by the minute.
The rose forgot the storm,
And all the struggle with it.

Now the rose reveals
All the beauty it stored
No longer it conceals
A beauty so adored...

Stephanie Alayne Garcia

Lost

I am lost in this moment of silence
as the wind gently moves through the trees
as my sky turns to burning blue powder
I long for more moments like these

The sun now hangs over the meadow
and the strawgrass has all turned to gold
I think of you now in this moment
and wonder what the future may hold

I am lost in this moment of beauty
when all the world seems to be new
and I pray there is no one to find me
for I'm lost in the memory of you.

D. Michael Withrow

Ruthless Affection

I killed her with kindness,
As the saying goes.
I treated her
As an expensive rose.
I watered her daily
With a shower of smiles.
Just to see her
I walked many miles

Then one day
She began to fade,
And she looked ever worse
At each effort I made.
The weaker she looked,
The harder I tried,
And just like that
Our love had died.

Love is a fiend
As he does his part:
Intoxicating minds
While destroying the heart.

Sean Murphy

To Live By Faith Is Love

As the flower in the field grows
As the birds in their nest provide
As the leaves of the trees,
so secure against the wind
So is my Love for you.

Who is to say what shall we eat
or what we shall wear?
Is it not the flower's care!
What about the birds,
so high they soar?
To return to their nest,
safely and secure!
The tree stands so high,
its leaves angels touch,
But they fall so gently to the arms
of the one that holds its trunk

So as the trees, and the birds,
and the flowers fair,
So is my love for you,
is always there.

Timothy J. Booy

Portia's Love Oath

I hope to be your only love,
As sweet and elegant as a dove.
Not one that you should worry about
But one that will arouse no doubt
I ever another should cross my path
He'll find my faith is in your behalf.
I'll never leave your binding net,
A net of love and tender care,
A net too precious to even share.

Portia Crawford

Untitled

I said goodbye to a friend last night
As she lay in her hospital bed.
I said goodbye to a friend last night
But she never heard a word I said.

I said goodbye to a friend last night
As machines clicked and whirred
I said goodbye to a friend last night
But my friend never stirred.

And as I sat and watched my friend
Who always had charm and grace,
The sight of those cold, unfeeling machines
Made tears stream down my face.

I said goodbye to a friend last night
Then did what machines cannot do.
I took her hand, caressed her cheek,
And whispered, "I'll always love you."

Susan Clark

Untitled

Once I was a Debutante
And now I am a Dilehaunte
I dibble and dabble
at everything -
And I'm not very good
at anything

Rosalind E. Taylor

Feathered Friends

Did you see the feather fall,
As it took off from the nest.
To flutter over buildings tall,
First to east and then to west.

Did it cause your heart to stall,
As higher and higher still it went.
To become a dot so small,
Before it made its swift descent.

Did it hear a special call,
As if to God its soul it lent.
And go up to a hidden wall,
And glide with it to full extent.

Does it know the secret hall,
Thru which all our souls some day are sent.
Or does it only teach us all,
That feathered friends to us are lent.

Hilda Ann Ezzat

"Letters"

Just sitting here thinking
As I picked up paper and pen
There's not a soul to write to,
Like I did way back when.

So many have gone their separate ways
Work and family filling their days
Only to be heard from
Maybe, now and then.

But to me the saddest of
It all, my friend
Are the ones that are gone forever
Never to be heard from again.

Ruth E. Baker

Life With Love

I wake up with the morning doves
As I look to the one I love
I kiss him gently and whisper in his ear
"I thank God for you, you are so dear.
You are my love and my best friend
We'll be together to the end!"

We gave our hearts to one another
We planned a happy life together
We laughed and cried through work and play
We know our love is here to stay.

When Jesus says it's time to go
We'll know we've tried our best.
Life was full, it's time to let go,
We'll now go to rest!

Life goes on when we are gone,
Now our children carry on
Joy and sorrow come with life
We'll meet one day beyond the light.

E. L. Orosz

The Samurai

The Samurai waits,
As the Shogun commands him,
He knows he must fight.

Cymud Moghadassi

The Immortal Road

'Twas all but death in life, I said
As greeted by night and day
I turned my back to the sun
And cast my shadow cross the land
All covered by my darkness
Withered in my soul
I cast my eyes toward heaven
Only to see the door was closed
All fell to dust around me
The door stood solid still
Life in death or death in life?
The choice I had was gone
Upon my weary way I went
Without a glance behind
'Twas death in life, I said again
The end shall never come
Suzanne T. Suter

Bliss

Each night as the sun goes down
As evening shadows draw near,
Beckoned by the waning warmth
Chaotic thoughts begin to clear.
The jumbled patterns of the day,
Take shape, fall in line, one by one.
Plans become dreamy, then coherent
Trouble and sorrow separate from fun.
Life that is lived each day
A separate entity in itself alone,
Related from one to the next
Yet immovable to each as stone.
Castles are built and occupied
Beauty and splendor reign,
Heroics and courage are the order
Respect, Admiration, and prestige attained.
Is carried through by the happy bliss
of the dreamer who is unaware,
The dreamer who waits for the 'morrow
With ne'er a thought for it's care.
Robert M. Costle

Enough!

As free as nothing
As concrete as something
Ride your pride
Trust your lust
Until it becomes dust.
Rebirth thru weather,
Raindrops I plot
I had enough!
Rick Wojtala

Winter's Fury

Wind twirls
Around me
Little white angels
Dance towards the earth
Blades of coldness
Pierce my skin
They slay my warmth
And hope
Leaving me
A lump of despair
As cold
Death approaches
I lift my head
"No!"
Yael Miller

Daughter, Arise

Why are sitting there with your arms folded, pondering? Don't you know it's dangerous to let your mind go wondering?
You're saying, who am I? What can I do? There are many lost souls out there, they need you.
Daughter arise, you're not alone. Jesus Christ is there with you to give you strength to go on.
Stephanie Jackson

The Guys!

The guys at school
are really cool,
They're not a fool,
They're really cool,
But just don't droll,
Or you'll look like a fool,
But just don't stare,
But they don't really care!
MacKenzie Carruth

Untitled

Now the Catalogs I receive
Are quite abundant,
And even some I receive
Are really redundant.
By that I mean
I usually get two
Of the same kind.
What's a Gal to do?
Now some fashions are lovely,
But most I don't need,
Especially those Gowns
With feathers down to your knees.
So all you designers
Please give us a break;
We'd all love to be young,
But 17 we ain't.
Roselyn Carter

Life's Ups And Downs

The ups and downs in life
Are placed on a staff of time,
To exist, some only a moment
Others, a more lengthy prime.

These ups and downs in life
Cause the pulse of our heart
To create the rhythm and tempo;
Our music's magical start.

The events of our lives
Paint a pictures of words,
Used with this music,
Create the songs to be heard.

Some live their "Ups and downs"
Repeatedly singing the chorus.
While others sing their musical lives
Adding a melody to all of us.
Samantha Rose

Sisters

We four sisters
are all that's left
of the nine that were
of the Babcock nest.
Five brothers, all gone
to our Father above,
we remember them dearly
with all of our love.
With crutches and canes,
poor eyesight and hearing,
our hearts overflow
with this great meeting.
We're all in our eighties
and have had a full life,
with children and friends
and being a good wife.
"I love you" said one.
"I've missed you" said another.
And we'll always remember
this day we're together.
Ruth Cowan

(i didnt couldnt wouldnt ask you why)
april
just perchance i saw in your soul
(cleverly disguised as a woman)
and heard in your laugh
april
(poorly masquerading as a girl)
and i recognized and knew
you are april

i know that now
just as i now know why
ive loved you and why
i love you

(and if only you did could would)
rex d. savage

Promise

Another leaf has fallen
Another soul has gone
But still we have God's promise
In every Robin's song.

For he is in his Heaven
And though he takes away
He always leaves to mortals
The bright sun's kindly ray.

He leaves the fragrant blossoms
And leaves the forest green
And gives us new found comfort
When we on Him will lean.
Wilma L. Roades

Another Day

Thank you God for each new day
Another one to work and pray

Were it not for each day granted
Each of us may stone cold be planted

Or, we could in ill health lay
Most would rather work and play

Thank you God for each day of health
And thank you God for each blessed self
Linda M. Larsen

The Silent Student

What words have roamed behind that face
And wormed about that hidden place
As thoughts that never were expressed
Yet grooved deep trails by their impress?

What light poured through that darkened eye
To spread its visions — probe and pry —
Feeding ideas that move inside
And bore their paths to deep reside?

Or, were the worms of thought
  a silent foe,
Who dug their paths to no avail
  and die instead of grow?
From dead cocoons no butterfly
  nor dragon born;
And nothing's done
  by words unformed.

Robert L. Herrick

Untitled

Tell me about love
And when you do
Let the words drip from your
  Tongue like the
    Juices from
      Sweet cherries
When you think about love
Do you think about:
  Pain
    A death
      And the loss of love?
Love is fragile
Love is sacred
And love
For those who use it
  Will last
    Forever.

Shad Allerheiligen

The Sea Of Life

Here we are, on the sea of life
  and we often feel we are alone,
Steering our boat across the deep
  blindly, seeking our way home.

Storm clouds, keep on moving in
  and darker clouds are drifting near,
But somehow, we are in His hands
  He, who does comfort, doubt and fear.

We are forging forward, hour by hour
  still holding firmly to the wheel,
Is how we know our course is right
  and it's His nearness, we can feel.

Then we know, there's One on board
  to point us safely, o'er the way,
One, who will protect and watch beyond
  and steer us gently into bay.

Pauline Day

Haiku

What a joy to see
Ballerinas in the air
Dandelion seeds

Yoshiyuki Otoshi

A Tribute To Rabin

We come from a faraway land
and we are engaged in a common
goal for peace.

We are deeply saddened, but strongly united
no matter how long the struggle last we
will fight for it.

Rabin is but the fight has just begun
is real unite and let peace go on

We must have one goal, only one mind
victoriously we shall go on with the
example of dedication you left behind.

Israel the united, oh Israel the free
stand up for your Motherland and
fight for peace.

Trocy Phillips

Untitled

Have you ever lain flat on the ground,
And watched the clouds float all around?
Seeing different things in each cloud form,
First a bear, then a castle with a dorm.
Maybe a dragon happens by,
Or even a plane pulled by a fly.
A whale just floated into view,
There's so many things to see and do,
As you watch the clouds dance about,
It makes you want to jump up and shout.
There goes a dog, then a cat, a pirate ship,
A house, a pile of snow on which to slip.
All these things, you may see someday,
While on the lawn you chance to lay.

Vivian C. Summerall

Baby Love

I sit in front of you,
And watch you till dawn,
You are in my dreams,
You are my everything.

You don't know when I come,
or when I leave,
I am always there,
because I really do care.

You are a child,
And I am a mother,
I'll do everything I can,
To protect you.

Tara Marcincuk

Parenting

Pure love and joy
Always be there for your child
Remember, a child is a gift from God
Embrace him into your world
Nurture his talents and abilities
Trust yourselves and trust your child
Inspire him to be great
Nothing you will ever do in your lives
  will be as important
Give of yourselves willingly, the rewards
  will be who your child becomes because
  you both cared.

Paula Nelson

Thunder Calls

As I sit upon my windowsill
and watch the stars above me
I fade into my favorite dream
and watch the world pass by me.
As I rise above the mountain tops
and pass the bright lights below
I scream and yell as loud as I can
to see how far my screams will go.
It stretches farther than my reach
and is taken from my control
If I stand upright and listen close
I can hear the thunder roll.
Lightning strikes the hills with power
smashing to the ground
with heavy rain my call is answered
and thunder is the sounds
lightning forks around me
as my favorite dream begins to fall.
I soar down slowly to where I wait
for my lightning volts and thunder calls.

Stacy Fox

Marriage....Hearts And Minds Together

So shall we live,
And though the first sweet,
sting of love be past
There shall succeed
a faithful peace.
Beautiful friendship tried,
by sun and wind,
Durable from the daily dust of life;
and though with sadder,
still with kinder eyes,
We shall behold
all frailties;
We shall haste
  to pardon and with mellowing,
minds to bless.

Roberto V. Alada

Heaven

My time is drawing near
And this I am aware
So there's no need to worry
Because God will meet me there

I'll meet a lot of friends in heaven
So I will not be alone
We'll all be one big family
In "Heaven" our Happy Home

So I want you to be happy
And don't shed a lot of tears
Let not your heart be troubled
Just cherish the golden years

I know we'll meet again
And what a joy that day will be
To have you by my side
The way you used to be

Yasmin N. Kearse

Hard To Witness

The butterfly is dying,
And there is nothing we can do.
It fluttered so so softly,
Only moments ago in plain view.
I saw it there above the porch,
All alive, absorbed in flight.
Now it lies upon the floor,
Without a sign of life.

There are no fancy gadgets
To let its heart regain a beat,
Or tubes to fill with medicine
And wounds that we could treat.
Its yellow wings are folded,
While it lies there in this heat.
How hard it is to witness,
Such a beauty in defeat!

Sharon L. Bosch

A Prayer For My Boys

God thank you for the day I live
and the meaning of the word forgive.

God give me eyes to see the best
and let my doubts be laid to rest.

God show me how to make a friend
and see how hope will never end.

God help me trust my fellow man
and do the very best I can.

Amen

Sharilyn Penhall

What He Is To Me

The gentleness in his hands,
And the love within his eyes;
His caring touch,
And his soft goodbyes.

He's all I think about
Day and night.
He's the light of my life,
And the eyes of my sight.

His caring soul,
And his loving heart,
Fill my life with joy,
Even when we're a apart.

Only his touch
Can heal my pain,
And his true love
Is my only gain.

Theresa A. King

The River

The river whispers to the child,
Come swim in my water,
So cool and refreshing,
So clear and sparkly and smooth.
I'll take you around bends,
Through the forest and trees,
Where the deer lay and the birds fly so high.
Oh, come swim in my water,
So clean and refreshing,
Oh what is your answer child?
The child leans forward,
and whispers softly back,
I can't, I forgot my swimming suit!

Tess Honquest

Untitled

I pull the covers tightly
  and talk with him
    then sleep.
Horror visions
  almost nightly
I close my eyes
  and in they creep.
Like a movie inside me
  starts whirring, spinning
    when I rest my head
Images played on my eyelids
  from the beginning
    Hell's inception in my bed.
Try to cheer and think
  a happy thought
It lasts only a minute
My bough of freedom
  broke in my loft
Still on fire as I lay in it.

T. A. Wind

A Message From Jesus

You awakened this morning
And started on your way.

You said you had much to do;
You didn't stop to pray.

I had hoped you'd take some time
To seek after me

And see how I could help you
In being the best you could be.

Today you were in my presence
As you are everyday,

But you will only find me
When you read My Word and pray.

Sharen Pinkett Pannell

Untitled

Come, let us fly away together
  and start our lives anew on Mars.
We'll cast aside or earthly tether
  and dance among the glittering stars.

From dusk till dawn me will sashay
Up and down the Milky Way.

Enthroned within our diamond palace,
We'll watch the Aurora Borealis.

Instead of baths we'll don our flippers
And swim the Big and Little Dippers.

We'll waltz around with Scorpius
to Music played by Orpheus.

Weary of flitting here and there,
We'll rest in Cassiopeia's chair
And clap while Perseus saves Almeeter
From the monster that would eat her.

We've lost our joy in earthly treasures;
  their gold has turned to dross.
We'll sample now celestial pleasures
  beneath the Southern Cross.

Walter S. Liggett

My Slippers

They're green, soft, cuddly, and warm;
And snuggle beneath my bed-
'Till early morn.

Often they hide from me
When I'm in desperate need;
Early morning chills attack me,
And I shiver to my knees.

These cuddly friends save me
From the cold linoleum floor,
And help me make it to the carpet
Just beyond my door!

T. L. Wilbur

Nature's Promise

When wing the birds to northern clime
And snowdrifts dwindle to dark pools,
Then who can stop the poet's rhyme?

And so come forth the lines below—
The poet's voice will not be still
Tho words be not enough, I know.

In Mother Nature's seasoned year
No moment is so joyous, free,
As when Spring's first green blades appear.

For great though Mother Nature be
Nothing excels, of all her gifts,
Her promise of Eternity.

Ruth F. Smith

To Be Free

I wish I could come out in the open
And say what I have to say
leave all my problems behind
and do anything, any day.

But I'm just a timid child
That doesn't understand
How or when to be free
Or how to lend a hand

I wish I could leave this world
This God-forsaken place
Not to follow any instructions
Not to see a single face

I don't know how it feels
Or how it is to be
Me owning myself
Me being so free

I would walk a thousand miles
Or wait hours until I see
A place where I'd be left without problems
Oh how I'd love to be so free

Rebecca Velazquez

The Beauty Of You!!

I've gazed upon the desert
and saw it's beauty there.

I've seen the rolling farm land,
the quiet village square.

I've gazed upon the meadows
their flowers kissed with dew.

But never have I seen one
as beautiful as you.

Raymond A. Brown

Untitled

It's ripen time
And pickin' time
In summer time
For berries and melons
On a vine
And canning time
For jellies
And jams
And mother dear
I wished you
So I could whisper
In your ear
Your jellies and jams
at canning time
Were the best in all your years.

E. Russell Gray

Somebody Up There Likes Us

Without a radio
  and no television
We are the product
  of our parents' great vision

With God's helping hand
  from way up in heaven
The family he loves
  ended up with eleven

We were poor as could be
  but who the hell cared
Cause we had enough love
  that everyone shared

The shack that we lived in
  was something to behold
The wind blew through the walls
  and it was so cold

It had only four rooms
  but we did not live in squalor
A kitchen, two bedrooms
  and of course the parlor

Stephen J. Kostoulakos

When Seas Run Wild

When seas run wild
And Nature's fury is unleashed
Thrilling is the seascape
Of phosphorescence spuming on the beach!

Thrilling - aye, awesome too,
For flesh gooses up
As the thundering surf
Disgorges from its bloated maw -
Seakelp, fish, crustaceans and at times
The killer whale itself....

Random prey ingested and inhaled
By the omnivorous surf - and then
Coughed up on hostile, fatal sands!

When seas run wild
And Nature's potent fury is unleashed
Thrilling - and awesome - is the seascape....

Thomas P. Ulmer

Raison D'Etre

Carved in stone as statues sleep
And lasting to the eye
We in life have to seek
Or dance on celestial sky

Evasive to my hands or heart
I wonder who you are
As the sprites who dance or part
Encased by celestial stars

As your loving hands caress
Or morning cups the sun
The fool on the hill unharassed
By the runner whose mile is run

For as life's wisps we shall bring
The shine to the morning star
All are born to live and sing
Before night proclaims we were.

L. M. Gasrel Black

My Judge And Jailer

I've locked myself in a dungeon
And I've thrown away the key,
I made myself forget where
So I am never to be free.

The walls are built of sorrow
The ceiling made of pain,
The floor laid out in darkness
While the door is sealed with hate.

Tho' you still can see me
And talk to me as well,
On the outside I show laughter
But inside's a living hell.

Solitude surrounds me
As my heart slowly turns to stone,
I've done my crime, and now serve my time,
My sentence - is alone.

I have nothing to reach out to
Only the ghosts only I can see,
For I am my Judge and Jailer
Who is never to be free.

Robert Christiano

The Final Answer

When I was a child, I saw death,
and it frightened me.

But, when I grew older
I came to see

Death is a friend
Who sets you free.

J. Eileen Copeland

Everlasting Tears

My love for you is real,
and in my heart it is sealed.

I thought I'd always be with you,
now I have to live without you.

But without your love,
I can not rise above

And face all my fears,
So my eyes are filled with everlasting tears.

Sara Van Nostern

The Bus Ride

He looked at my face
And I smiled at him
He turned round to face me
And I removed my goggles to see him
He winced and I blinked
He wrinkled and I flushed
The sun made his forehead to crease
And the wind made my hair to fluff
He was uneasy
And I felt uncomfortable
He opened his mouth without a word
And I chuckled without a response
We both understood, we both knew
It was all so beautiful
I'd never forget the bus ride

A. Odi Bosah

Chris

I know this Babe named Chris
and I say, not to be remiss
that she is sweet as Jewish
apple cake
And as serious as lean corned beef
She is tall, blonde and brown eyed
quite witty too!!!

She can't recall sometimes
but she's no one's fool!
She maybe mind someday, I dream
but until then
She is my friend
My queen!

Robert J. DiGennaro

Untitled

I know you love,
  And I love you too!
But what can I say,
  I don't know what to do.
I gave you my heart,
  and that's a good start.
I'd do anything that I could
  and believe me I would
You say you love me,
  and I know that it's true.
Just take me seriously
  when I say, I love you!

Angela D. Brooks

Momma

I went to church the other day,
and I found it so hard to kneel and pray.
Dear God:
I'm troubled and I don't know what to say,
Except: Why did you take my mother away!
She wiped my tears and filled my heart,
now that she's gone I'm falling apart.
I stared at the cross a very long time,
then I heard a voice and it was not mine.
My child I'm sorry I thought you knew,
I did it to save her, not to hurt you.
I beckoned her soul to come with me,
to no longer be in pain but rather at peace.
Come pray with we now and try to see,
your mother is happy and content as can be.
I've made her an angel and put you in her care,
So no matter where you go,
you'll always know she is there.

Peggy Johnson

Passage

SuAn, an old and long-time friend, a cat,
   and I amble the grounds,

Embraced, each, by his own thought.

But we share the hushed rush of autumn
   that hails us from cross the creek,

And this is a moment of grand awareness.

We pause, then, each, as one, to touch,
   to exchange our signals of love.

Ted G. Miller

Life

   As I stop and think of Jesus,
and his dying on the cross.
Then I blame it on the Jews,
for how his life was lost.

   I wonder, is that judging,
with a plank in my own eye?
For what is there I would have done,
if I'd been standing by?

   When I look a little farther,
I start to shift the blame.
Then I start to hang my head,
just burning with the shame.

   As I think of my free living past,
my life so full of sin.
I start to wonder which of his hands,
they drove my first nail in.

   The prophets in the old books say,
that Christ was born to die.
But, I wonder whose the most guilty,
the Pharisee's or I........?

Rick Buoy

Sea Of Life

Once I stood on lonely shore
And gazed upon the sea.
There I beheld a sailing ship
Swift and sure and free.
Borne from swell to swell,
And traveling to and fro,
With only wind to take her
Wherever she must go.

How oft our lives are like a ship
Pushed by fickle wind,
Set sail upon the sea of life
With no port at journey's end.
So as I gazed on foamy sea
And thought of land I'd trod,
I knew my soul was led, not by fate,
But by the hand of God.

Phillip Mike Lokey

Can It Be True

Beneath the apple tree - where we
always use to be.
When I gazed into your eyes.
Twas like looking at the skies.
They seemed to say.
Can I be true
That I am really in love with you.

Uno I. Alongo

Barbie, Ken, And G.I. Joe

They had Barbie dreams and Ken hopes
and G.I. Joe who'd search and scope
the lay of the land and always keep
them safe awake and safe asleep.

But Barbie dreams did not include
raising kids without much food,
or working money solely spent
on paying bills and paying rent.

Ken hopes were not meant to mean
lonely meals before the screen,
with no one pressed against him tight
in the hollow-soul hours of the night.

G.I. Joe tried hard to reach
each and every war-torn beach,
but the rules changed some war-red day...
and no one listened anyway.

Barbie, Ken and G.I. Joe
lived a world they couldn't know,
dreamed of dreams that couldn't be
in a time of plastic unreality.

Susan E. Nolan

Autumn Allegory

It's time...

For air conditioners to be covered
and fans unplugged and stored,

For fresh wood to be chopped and
piled up in cords outside the door,

For breezy summer attire to be
replaced by clothes of sturdier stuff,

For summer bed linens to be topped
by comforters filled with puff,

For tree leaves to turn from greens
to harvest yellows, browns and red,

For brittle leaves to magically disappear,
leaving the branches lonely and sad.

Yes, now is the time
of change from Summer to Fall.

But, I won't miss it,
because I love Autumn best of all.

Ralph Haworth

Just One Kiss

Of all I've ever wanted,
   and all I'll ever need.
I can only think of one thing,
   for which I'd surely bleed.

Of all I've ever had,
   and all I'm sure to gain.
I'd give them all to you,
   in return for just one thing.

So tonight before you lie down,
   please think of me and smile.
Barefoot on a road of glass,
   for you I'd walk a mile.

Of all I've ever wanted,
   one thing I can't resist
I'd give you anything,
   all I have for just One Kiss.

Thomas W. Navarro II

Why

Why why I asked
And all I heard was silence
Only the wind was blowing
Whispering
Remember
Remember me
And me and me and
Six million voices I heard
And I remembered

I close my eyes so I can see
And I remember
With every breath of life I take
I do I do I do remember
Six million and
My Papa too
And many more I do remember
But I survived
Why
Me
To live I must I must remember

Paia Reisch

Love In Motion

Love is a covering
And a current flowing
Many rivers mingling,
Needing, wanting.

Love is the yearning protection
For a mother's child.
And the yearning affection
For a lover's side.

Love is creation in motion,
Passion in stride.
A deep filling process
Of unity applied.

What lays in a heart
To pull through the blood,
Power of life enfold
By faith understood.

Stephen Hays

Mat Of Many Colors

I am the white one,
Am I not the black one?
No wait! I am the red one.
I am all.

Red, white, black
Am I not my own choice?
No wait! I have my own voice.
I am all.

If I am that or any other?
Does it matter?
Will I become any fatter,
If I am one or all?

Voices, choices
who will listen when I call.
Can I become all of
Any other?
   You decide.

Violet Speta

Life

Life has its hard times
along with it good
things don't always work out
the way that it should
there is all kind of sorrows
and so many woes
As we go down life's weary road
there is so many problems
that we must endure
so many heartaches
of this I am sure
but things will get better
If we just hold on
and keep on remembering
life is just like a song
Suzanne Reitenauer

Hold Me Close

Hold me close but never too close
Allow me my space to breathe
Be there with than a helping hand
Show me and help me succeed.

Be there when the morning comes
And the world is asleep
Be there through the good and bad
And hold me when I weep.

Be then when at last it is night
So that with someone I can share
Be there always so that in return
I can have someone about whom to care.

Be there for me to love through life
Through all the mornings, days, and nights.
Be there for me to hold through life
So with another to share the sights

Hold me close but never too close
Just allow me my space to breathe
Be there with an outstretched hand
Help me to fulfill my needs.
Richard A. Fox

'All Pity Not Known'

All pity is not unknown to me
All sorrow and all bliss
My eyes not blind, not stricken wary
Nor lips unfettered to foolish kiss.

This the harbor my heart knows well
From sky to shore alike,
The passing of all waking smell
From orchard breath and like.

For before the earth is air
For that, the seeming sky,
And neither here nor there
Is that last goodbye.

For that no longer
I've wept till morn,
And presently that, now grown stronger
Is that last voice to forlorn.

And if we not feel the sun again
Until our days are over,
And not the silence heard of man,
And not my eyes to stir.
Rebecca Leigh Nelson

December Light

The morning has come
All misty and gray
The birds have flown south
Their songs gone away

But ever in stillness
The morning is pure
The sacred light dawning
So bright and so sure

Make this day worthy
Of history's page
Memorable moments
That never shall age

At good deed remembered
Gives hope to the ones
Who've yet to encounter
The love of God's sons.

My children, don't waste it
This light is for you
Who can enter the Garden
To lead others in too.
Noelle Juliet

Question

Why is it that we fight
Against things that aren't right
And then turn around
And do these things ourselves

We all take our turn
But we never seem to learn
From the mistakes
That everyone must have

Those people who excel
Must be under some spell
To understand
This world in which we live

It's really kind of strange
That nothing has a change
But then again
Nothing can be the same
Tanya Brown

Untitled

Restless quiver-
A serpent slithers
Gliding along-
A sin dune river
Searing echo-
A mind unleashed
Caverns untamed-
Desire to be reached
Envelope a realm of illusion-
An eclipse of surreality
Reverberate within brittle logic
Carelessly shattering moon beams
I am the conductor-
Of endless dreams
Richard James Welch

The Godless Race

What do we really know
about another's race?

We do know it's not polite
to be BASE,
About another's RACE.

So, what can we do, to improve
this CASE?

I truly hope, we'll be able to use
MORE TASTE,

When discussing another's RACE.

To MANY, it may be more
important to SAVE FACE,

Rather than using GRACE,
When discussing another's RACE.

What a waste to only DEBASE,
Without any taste,
Another's RACE, in OUR OWN RAT RACE.
Richard Connors

Retirement

Retirement is an exciting word
a word mixed with emotion
One works many years
to achieve this well earned reward
The time is actually here
a new outlook is in view
Why do I feel so funny inside?
It may be Excitement and Apprehension
with my work set aside
Whatever it may be
Happiness or Anticipation
I'm looking forward to
Retirement ... A long vacation
Sandra Baker

Loving Robert

I met a man..
A very fine man was he
He played with the children,
and enchanted me
a fine man was he.
I met a man...
An adventurous man was he.
He climbed every mountain
Just for me.
A fine man was he.
I met a man...
A cultured man was he.
He went to the shores, 'theatres' and more
to see the sights with me.
A fine man was he.
I met a man...
A loving man was he.
He showed us love,
and married me.
A very fine man was he.
Susan Ryan

"Illusion"

Upon your face, an illuminating smile,
A twinkle still shines in your eyes.
Well practiced in your verse,
Proficient in a well guarded disguise.

You are not what you appear to be,
You have cast an illusion.
I see not what is before me,
A dark soul still casts a shadow.

Partially illuminated by a facade,
The darkness still sets apart;
Your reality and illusion now as one,
Visible only by a compassionate heart.
Shari L. McCabe

Alone Again

A look
A tear
You left
I'm here

Alone again
Many nights
Dark room
Without lights

Bright moon
Soft sheets
Lonely nights
Certain needs

Waking up
Gentle rain
Missing you
Alone again
Sebastian

"The Arrow"

A tender touch...
A sweet caress...
The aura that surrounds you...
In gentleness...
The glow of the moon...
The light of day...
Things you enhance...
In your own special way...
You give me hope...
And inspiration...
With a touch of love...
A sweet sensation...
Yes you make my heartbeat...
With the rhythm of the sea...
Playing out a special song...
Deep inside of me...
Tis a song of love...
For you and you alone...
Tis a song of love...
Like you've never known...
Terry Lee Taylor

Wild Geese

I heard wild geese flying over,
A strange whirring sound,
Sailing to a warmer climate
Away from frozen ground.

Wild geese — free on the wing,
Seeking the sunshine warm.
Above my head send their cry,
They are a graceful swarm!

But oft-time: If I were a wild goose
I'd bear me with wings brave
Away from frozen life,
To a land for which I crave!

And they — they fly over
To new haunts year after year,
And I — I am a human
Remaining in my sphere!
Ceils B. Flenniken

Tomorrow

There's a tone in the wind
A sorrow in the wind
For Tomorrow

For People's lives that evil's undone
And days to come for everyone
For powerful machines that churn the land
Stealing life from soil and future man

For animals extinct and lakes gone dead
And for children to come a living dread

Too much worry about money made from trees
Too much care for things of ease
Too little time for the creator of all
Too much care for things that fall

Too much faith in the glory of man
Too much pride in the things from our hand

There's a crying in the wind
A sighing in the wind
For things wrought by hands of men
That will not mend
Robert Rogers

An Ode To Second Baptist

A haven in the midst of troubles,
A refuge from the cold,
A solace to the lonely heart,
A place where we can be made whole.

A joyous place as we sing our praises
And lift our eyes in prayer.
We hear the words from times untold
As we worship with our loved ones there.

From past, to present, to future
We all will have left our mark
On a place we know as Second Baptist,
A place so dear to our hearts.
Veronie Holloway

Our Love

It was instant attraction
A rapid ascension to love
With an overpowering satisfaction
A heavenly flight like a dove

For decades, our love has endured
We cannot bear to be apart
Of our love, we are assured
We share one heart

Our souls are tethered
Ecstasy, we obtain
All woes, we've weathered
Our love will never wane
Pat Killinger

Luminescent Love

Luminescent as a pearl,
A priceless work of art,
Beauty far beyond compare,
Strikes the bleeding heart.

Expectantly I waited,
Knowing you would come,
Tearing down my fortress,
Vowing not to run.

Vulnerable as a child,
Crying for someone,
Caring not the price,
Paid for battles won.

Is it worth the bounty,
The soul grudgingly pays,
For a timeless moment,
Where dreams now lay.

We cannot live without,
This blessing from above,
Wrapped in ghostly riches
Is the gift of love.
Vivian Clark

"Bird Of Thanks"

We're thankful for the Eagle's Club,
  A place to congregate.
    We're thankful for its members,
      To whom we can relate!

We're thankful for the happy times,
  Spent here with friends so dear.
    We're thankful for the memories,
      That we accumulated here!

We're thankful for the kindness,
  Extended from the heart.
    We're thankful for the courtesy,
      Shown from the very start!

We're thankful for the turkey,
  A tasty bird to eat.
    We're thankful for the eagle,
      A bird that takes no back seat!

We're thankful for Thanksgiving,
  A time for us to stress,
    Our feeling for the Eagles,
      The 'bird for thankfulness!'
Richard E. Nickel

A Scented Room

A scented room, a candle lit,
A picture hanging near,
All take me back to long ago
When love was living here.

Our life was such a perfect one,
At least I thought it so.
But then you said we lived a lie
And it was time to go.

I'll never give my heart again.
I couldn't stand the pain,
Of holding on to someone dear
And have them leave, again.

So I'll just sit here, in this room
With the scent of rose in bloom,
And wait until the candle dies
And the picture hangs in gloom.

Sandra DeBlanc

Songs

The needle is sharp
A pain-staking poke between the toes.
What isn't dreamed?

You can't call up from the desk
Room 103,
Hotel Rector.

The night is cooled by weather.
Rain echoes,
A constant tapping.
Spilling down the roof gutter
Flooding the pavement below.

It must be a different view from the hills,
Overlooking insanity.
And you can't smell the fresh blood spill.
Death is so permanent
Never accepted
By the fashion conscious.
Never changed.

The radio fills the air.
Words not remembered.

Sam Hamid

A Time To Die

The morning mist begins to rise
A never ending wonder to my eyes
I watch as life begins to stir,
A new day dawning so beautiful to see
But will this be the lost for me.
How time has flown, not always kind
So many things I'll have behind.
My days are few and filled with pain.
Have all the sorrows been in vain
I close my eyes and I can hear
The by-gone sounds of children dear.
Their loving smiles and happy ways
Sustain me through these days
So blessed was I, to have their love
The greatest present from above
As darkness creeps across my room
A peaceful sleep I pray for soon
I'll take God's hand held out to me
And know at last that I am free.

Dorothy Beddal

The Cycle Of Rain

The darkening clouds cover
a naked earth.
Slowly the mists caress
earth's trees and grass.
The rain develops a rhythm
with the land,
The muffled roll of distant thunder
warns animals to take cover,
The flash of lightning binds
those in awe,
The heavy claps of thunder create
magic to those unknowing.
The rains lighten to signal retreat.
The sun peaks through the clouds
to see that all walks of life
are in one comfortable doze.

E. Lynn K. Clements

Untitled

I often wish that I could see
A million stars at night
Like those I saw from my front porch
And thought a lovely sight.
Then I would wish upon a star
And felt it would come true.
Now that I am a shut-in
It's something I can't do.
Then, too, I wish that I could see
The change that time has brought
Upon the town I've always loved
I've heard that time has wrought.
I'd like to visit Granddad's woods,
Talk to my favorite tree
Where I, so innocent, played house;
It would mean so much to me.
My memories buried deep within
Will never go away.
I'll hold them in my secret heart
Forever and a day.

Pauline Pilkenton

Old Friend

I hear a song
A melody of days long gone,
And I miss you.
It's just knowing
You are no longer
A part of my world
I long so to tell you
How much you meant to me.
Not as a lover,
But as a friend.
So many times
You helped me through
difficult times.
And now you are beyond my reach.
Perhaps - perhaps
In God's own time
We shall meet again.
Until that time
I will cherish the memories.
I miss you old friend.

Elsie S. Dillon

"Gramps"

A boisterous man once walked this earth
A man who called the Pines his own
He laughed at coarse, crude words of mirth
This man whose spirit lived alone
I say alone, because you see
I knew him well - he lives in me.

When trouble comes and brings its grief
I hear his voice so loud and clear,
I recall his strength - it brings relief;
His memory discards my fear.
I speak in praise of this old man
Above all things he loved God's land.

Someday we'll meet and laugh again
When time is done and the last leaves fall
I pray he'll smile and take my hand
And walk with me in heaven's hall.

Rembert G. Rollison

The Unknown

I, alone in this world,
A lonely being:
It strikes a cord,
in my already pained heart.
It impels me to think,
the reason for living
for, eventually, you are left alone.
It always happens,
as time passes by;
and years fly
one reaches out
towards the unknown.
There lies the fear of death,
of the tortures of hell,
what lies ahead,
one may never know.
Until, one is sunk,
deep into the dark waters,
from where there is no return.

Roohi Vora

Turning Pages In A Woman's Life

Today I walk from my mother's house
A little girl
Tomorrow I awake
In a grown-up world
Faces change and places change
Turning pages in a woman's life.

Today I walk down the aisle
Another by my side
Faces change and places change
Turning pages in a woman's life.

Today I hear a soft cry
I feel a warm breath
I see a new life
Turning pages in a woman's life.

Many faces change and places too
With life anew
Today I hear "Grandmother, come here"
Turning pages in a woman's life.

Sally Dauphin

Untitled

In a moments time
A kiss still lingering
A hug of such depth
A jewel of rarest kind,
Sparkled in lights
in a moments time,
A life time of seeking, finally,
Capturing of one so caring
Thank you, for that time
Of a new beginning
Sharing, in a time of knowing
someone cared,
To look deep inside
　In a moments time
　　F. R. Senato

The War Against Us

A struggle against life,
A fist fight for justice,
A degrade of our manhood,
To keep the government above us.

The hatred of our color,
The spell that has been spinned,
They watch us and laugh,
When our troubles begin.

They live off our tears,
Their souls grow off their glory,
As we weaken and shatter,
They write their own story.

Of how they excelled,
Using hatred and lust,
It's a never ending battle,
When the War's Against Us.
　　Joie Jordan

Games

I'll play your game and play it well,
A feast before you greed.
With smiles and sighs,
Then well placed cries,
I'll satisfy your needs.
Then when you think you've had your fill,
And you plan to go,
I'll smile and merely nod my head,
And say, "Let it be so."
For I know more of men than you,
Freedom is my chain,
I have nothing left to lose,
While you have all to gain.
　　Ruth Lewis

Untitled

Mrs. Kisses does the dishes,
and then she goes to sleep.
When she wakes up
she hears a noise
it's the boys
playing with the toys.
　　Zachary Brewer

The Cask Of Amontillado

Rage and insult provoked
a deed of madness.
The perfect revenge camouflaged
beneath a clever smile.

Deep within a hidden grave
lies a threat fulfilled.
Stone cold eyes gazed with satisfaction
as tears fell from the midnight sky.

The wine taster's plight,
disturbed nevermore.
A punishment in silence,
alone forevermore.

An underestimation of an adversary,
an overlooked disadvantage,
buried alive,
attacked with insularity.
May he rest in peace.

(Based on a short story
by Edgar Allan Poe)
　　Wendy Fernandez

Bill

The lane leads to an old house
A broken fence on either side
Insects eating and mating
Heat the big oak hides
Cows chew their cuds
While swatting at flies
The earth is serene
As bees do their chore
The old woman comes once more
To gather mail or wave a hand
At strangers who stare and travel the land
Slowly she turns
Walks down the lane
To a house where memories remain
Of one loved dearly many years before
Then came flu and fever
She looks out the door
At a grave on the hill
Where she goes daily
His name was Bill
　　Wayne Henderson

Untitled

Shy and yet hopeful, a tentative smile
A flicker of light reflects in their eyes
Apprehension and wanting, urges on hold.
Feelings known.

Thoughts of emotion, feelings untold.
Expressions hollow, empty, cold.
Questions unanswered, never asked.
Feelings gone.

Pain and rejection always one step away.
Wondering how life could be so cruel.
What was said, what was done, always lost.
Forever alone.
　　Patricia A. Rex

'A Man Of A Kind'

I try to describe
a man of a kind
who flirts with his eyes
and shows you a smile.

The best of the friends
the lover, the fake
who's nice and smart
but plays with your heart.

You think and believe
his endless love is
but one day you see
he's killed all your dreams.
　　Veronica Ruiz

Santa Fe Clouds

Santa Fe clouds waltz gracefully
Across the sunsetting horizon
Ever moving, ever changing
Violet, amber and rose-colored clouds

Animated visions of life
Challenge and inspire
All who choose to open wide
Their eyes
And their mind
To see the pictures in the sky
　　M. Elise Solloway

My Mind

A painted face,
A plastered smile.
A battered heart,
An open wound.
A screwed up life,
Graffiti walls.
Broken mirrors,
Abandoned halls.
Left or right?
Right or wrong?
Mangled bodies,
Sirens song.
Kiss and tell,
Seek and find.
Runaway.
Please read my mind.
　　Shelley Ziehms

Untitled

Circular stars all aligned
and connected,
vast deep space,
black at the farthest point,
deceived in sight.
The mind's eye visualizes
　"reality,"
spinning, spinning,
circular continuum.
　　J. J. Kilcran

Beachcomber's Meditation

My only responsibility is to cherish my existence.
I gently caress the earth, tiny grain of sand by tiny grain of sand.
I celebrate the sun by basking in its warmth.
I live hand to mouth, knowing my Lord has prepared for me a path.
And that paving this path are the answers to all my question and the
    fulfillment of every need.
The sea gulls sing to me of life, death, and life begun again.
The pattern they weave through the skies is the blanket I wear at
night to comfort me as the wind make its presence known.
The fish frolic about me, as I refresh myself in the cool water, the
cycle of the sun has been strong.

My art is my breath. As it enters me, so do the sights and sounds
around me. As it leaves me, it takes all that I am and sets if free
to mingle with the vibrancy around it. My sense tingle as the purpose
of life unfolds. I am here to be one with this fluid planet. To
filter, through my existence each grain of sand, blade of grass, and
drop of water, and take from it its very soul - only to return to it
my own spirit. Blended together, soul and spirit multiply their
intensity and in a quiet, yet earth shattering blast, they unfold into
a psychedelic experience of life.

Stefanie A. Olivares

What Happened When I Began To Dream as I Dozed off Listening to the Exuberantly Beautiful Melodies of Mozart's "Eine Kleine Nachtmusik"

I awaken from the conscious state,
I flutter into the drifts of imagination, the dreams.
I am enveloped in a massive blanket of fictional truth,
Reverberations of ecstatic pleasure race along the warmth of the marrow
Concealed inside the wall of euphoria encasing my bones.
I tear apart from the weakening clutches of the conscious state.
My journey is directed into the thorough vaults of creativity,
Which rest upon a smooth stone in the center of my
    personal, imaginary sea of brilliant diamonds.
The nectar of my imagination,
Seeps from the open crater of the volcano,
Standing upon the reinforced foundations of the vast vaults of
    complete creativity.

J. Patrick Pace

The Mask

　　As I sit here gazing into this face,
I feel uncomfortable and out of place!
　　As I stare, I see two sides.
I can't help but wander what it hides!
　　The eyes are coal-black, the smile is fake.
What measures of deceit will it take?

　　One side is open, honest, and believing.
The other is cold, dark, and deceiving!
　　I feel I have looked in these eyes many times before.
Because of breath-taking fear, I closed the door!

　　On one side I see love and happiness show.
On the other, I see painful secrets that make tears flow!
　　Most of humanity have two sides.
Few like this, have deep dark evil that it hides!
　　Not many can read both sides of it's face.
There's still a few in the human race.

　　There are no lines to separate the love from the hate!
Unlike most faces, it gives a sense of knowledge of its own fate!
I HAVE DECIDED, IT'S TOO MUCH OF A TASK,
TO FIND WHAT EVIL LURKS BEHIND THE MASK!

E. R. Harris

I Love You

I sit under the stars and think of you.
I feel so cold, so alone.
Why did you leave me to drown in sorrow.
Not having you here to talk with.
Not having you here to hold.
Not having you here to comb Mikael's hair.
The son that still calls your name at night when he is frightened.
Why didn't I go that night?
Why did you insist?
You said you'd be with me forever.
That was all I hoped for.
I'm sorry I don't mean to blame you.
He was drunk.
He should have died.
God I wish you could see your son.
He looks just like you.
Now here I sit under the stars thinking of you.
I love you.

Reuben Pratt

Bleeding Memories

I'm awakened by a cry in the wind,
I drift outside,
leaves are blowing through my hair,
why am I here.

I listen for those desperate cries,
I wonder who is crying,
It reminds me of a certain child,
A child who woke up and cried in the middle of the night,
A child frightened to death of being alone,

A child who held future or promise
A child who's dreams were shattered,
A child who's beauty was hidden by rags and bruises
that child was me,

I was a child who had love to give
A child who could have been more,
A child who was scared to be alone
that child still lives in me

　　Were those my cries
　　Let out inside me
　　or were they memories?

Rita Greene

Deceitful Honesty

I love you, and I love me, its the mystery of deceitful honesty
I don't know you, and I don't know me, is there truly a dedicated need
It is so easy to say the lie, that makes the pain flee our sides
Yet when the lie is no longer told, the leftover is much to toll
My hatred for you shouldn't stagger you
With its deeds of raping, killing, and even uneducating.
Which isn't to defeat you.
It is mere donated expressions of my love's pending worth.
An obese oppression given as an epic gift
Which cannot even be lifted, with a thousand platinum folk-lifts
However do I love you, do I even love me
Perhaps it is too profound a quest for me to self seek
I'd rather lay down on hazed ground, and close my eyes
To then simply reply I love you...I love you...I love you
Than to see an acrimonious reality
For reason that just maybe, just maybe I do not love either of us
Tale of the deceitful truth

Zora Shenete Le-Sueur

Apple Season

As my mind wanders back in time,
I detect the scent of apples in the air
and the smiling face of my Mother so kind,
You couldn't match this memory anywhere;

After rushing home from school,
There in the kitchen she would stand,
With a fresh-baked apple pie in her hand;

Many years and memories have come and gone
since I left that old farm home,
But I still long, you see,
Just to sit, once again, beneath that old apple tree;

Whether eating apples in a pie, under a tree, or by an open fire,
These simple joys of life we do not tire;

The old home seems so near today as I stand in a
kitchen like my Mother once stood,
Now my family comes rushing in to say,
"Grandma, apple pie, it smells so good!"

Today, it's Autumn, the scent is again in the air,
and for a very good reason,
I'm excited, because it's APPLE SEASON!

Sharon L. Coleman

Echoes Of Your Memory

My tears they fall since now you're gone
I close my eyes, my heart can see
Echoes of your memory

A touch, a smell, a word, a thought
Bring back such memories of things once forgot,
Or so I thought

Such visions of love, of caring and sharing,
So many things that caress my heart
Like arms they envelope me

I close my eyes, my heart can see
Echoes of your memory

Nor can I hold you, or touch you no more,
For you are gone, taken from me
You were mine for a short while,
My love, My child

And now what I have, are beautiful
Echoes of your memory

M. Elaine Crawford

The Iron Horse

The trains immortal sounds of past,
Haunt the rails that no longer last.
The hills and towns along it's way,
Could tell some tails of yesterday.
Those eerie whistles that broke the night,
Would make you sit up with fright.
The steam would make a swishing and puffing sound,
As it blew from the stack and all around.
The black smoke would roll out across the plain,
And trail on back through the train.
As one stood along the track,
You would feel the vibrations go up your back.
You'd get the smell of hot ashes and steam that would last,
The big wheels made heavy sounds as they past.
As the train went clickety clack out of sight,
You knew it would be back the following night.
It's legend lives through books and of course,
The old timers knew it as the iron horse.

R. L. Samuelson

Where The Roses Sing

I live in a land where the roses sing!
I caught them at it in early spring.
Thought I was hearing the kids from school,
Out back, cross the way at the swimming pool.

Out I went to the bank of the water so blue
Not a child was in sight, I'm tellin' you true!
So I hurry along still following sound
And on to a garden and 'twas this I found

An Arbor of Roses I'd seen oft before
From my kitchen window, O, the hours I'd adored!
Now, tiny pink rose buds, barely opening their eyes
Were trilling Soprano, and another surprise

Shyly, they turned happy faces to me.
"We sing," they spoke soft, "to your neighbor Marie
"For she, long ago, a great sadness has known.
"We bring her good cheer and great comfort from Home.

"We sing on in secret our melodic LAY.
"For she alone knows what it is that we say.
"Heaven holds all her heart to beguile!
"She will travel the Way with a song and a smile!"

Theresa A. Trout

Too Late?

Stop!
I can't though I want to.
Turn back!
It's too late to turn.

It happened so fast,
Happening even before it seemed to have been a thought.
Too fast to think twice,
Too fast to take thought.

Like a vacuum
Sucking in anything near it.
Pulling, drawing
Now a victim.

Beginning in innocence,
Now ending in deception.
How did it happen?
Why didn't I stop it?

I long to change it,
I can't, it's already past.
No changing the past,
Only the future.

Robert Christian Kuhn

Funny Face, I Need You

Funny face, I need you,
Funny face want you go through
 this World with me,
Funny face don't hold back,
Funny face hope you got a
 loving heart,
Funny face don't look back
 yesterday,
Funny face look above see
 what will happen,
Funny face guiding me through,
Funny face theirs will be
 better days ahead,
Funny face, I need you for eternal,
 through-out this Universe, on that some bright day.

Tommy Parrish

Writers

At times I read from one who touches me.
I bleed or laugh or cry or ponder.
'Cause such new thoughts, presented prime,
reach deep in memory of mine.
Those writers glimpse from of their own
what I have missed, skipped merrily by,
or sadly put aside, too powerful with which to ply.
An untapped pot, searching for its spout,
with buried seeds to grow to know the how or why.

Like the camel's nose beneath the tent,
ever satisfaction seeking,
those who write invite
lost memories' awaking.
Seeds wait to be reborn,
to celebrate those moments past
that make for memories to last.
Writers write because of need.
Readers read to grasp such feed
to nurture memories' survival.

William R. Nelson

I Led Him Into Battle

He was so young, he could have been my son, and I led him into battle
I asked, "Where are you from, what made you come," he said "I'm
from Seattle, and I've never smoked before, but see'n what's in store,
there's not much harm in try'n." "I'm not scared of death and war,
I saw it all to get ashore, but I'm awful scared of die'n." "It hurts
a lot you know, I don't mean to let it show, I just can't stop the
pain." "I don't wanna go, is death a friend or foe, do you think it's
all insane." I held his hand in mine, I tried to pass the time, but I
couldn't stop my tears. I talked of folks back home, of the woods I
used to roam, but I couldn't stop his fears. He asked me, "Could
you pray, maybe help me on my way, and tell my mom I love her."
"Dear God in heaven, I said, help the wounded and the dead and remember
wives and mothers." He expired at my side, and my heart was filled with
pride, I dried my tears again. "Follow me," I cried to the young men
at my side, and I knew right there and then that they would serve me
well, to escape this living hell, as I led them into battle. Many
more would die, and I would hear the wounded cry, from New York
to Seattle. Your mothers love you too.

Paul R. Postal

"With All My Love," On Valentine's Day

Each morning when I awake,
I anticipate your caressing embrace;
Just to be held close in your masculine arms,
Enticing me with all your charms;
Your love surrounds me like an endless sea,
That continues on throughout an eternity

On occasions when I encounter,
A day filled with sorrow;
You've given me the courage,
To look ahead to a brighter tomorrow

The things you do and say,
Touch me in a very special way;
With each passing day,
My love for you,
Grows stronger in endless ways

You'll always have a special place in my heart
Because I'll always love you,
Until Death do us part;
My Darling, I love you,
Happy Valentine's Day!!

Stephanie Nago

The Great Willow

I am a tree.
I am free.
Whatever man will make of me, I will be.

I give clean air.
I have cool shade.
I am big.
I am beautiful.

When other trees see me they think of what man will make of me.
Some trees think I will be a sturdy boat to float in the sea.
Others might think of me as a strong house for a cold winter's stay.

As a tree I will provide cool shade for a small boy.
I will give some nice clean air to all humans in need.
My roots will protect the soil from rain and wind.

While I am a tree come enjoy me;
For someday I will be what man makes of me.

Steven Trimmell

Hello Old Friend

Hello old friend
How's it going?
The scars from past years
they're a showing
and the pain inside
it's a growing.

So stay for awhile and I'll hold you like my child
and we will be one in time, let it be.

Your eyes, they look dark
but they're glowing
And the smile on your face
is all knowing
but the tears in my eyes
they're a flowing.

My health, well babe
it's a slowing
and my mind, inside,
it's a blowing
but to you this is all
I've been owing.

T. Lynette Warburton

Poppa

I never told you how dear you were to me,
How much your approval meant...
Now you are gone, yet still I feel you near.

Your arms were strong and sure
When I would run down the street
To meet you in childish exuberance.
Even as tired as you were... you would
Swing me up into the air... I shrieked happily!

Later, when life and love were sometimes painful,
It was you who held me when I wept
And told me that this was part of living,
And that living demanded courage and grit.

You were kind, proud, giving,
Honest and trustworthy.
With nobility
Poppa, you showed me how to live
By example... never by lecture.

Now that death has claimed you, there is an emptiness
That cannot be filled. That special bond between
Father and daughter is sadly missed. Oh, Poppa!

Shirley A. Weston

Salvation

The promise of heaven is too big to be true
How do we get it and what can we do

God made it so simple for the young and the old
To accept him, heaven on earth you can hold

When the world gets unbearable and nothing seems true
The God in the bible is as real as me and you

So begin with a prayer and invite him in
To a heart that is open is where you begin

After you tell him what's on your mind
When you are finished, a new life you will find

Dianne Sykes

To Hear You Tell It?

To hear you tell it, our skin is unattractive, yet you spend many hours in the sun to look like us.

To hear you tell it, we were weak - however, we were the only people strong enough to withstand the abuse, degradation and diseases that were heaped upon us as we were thrown into bondage, yet we emerged victorious.

To hear you tell it, we could not be educated, yet from our people came doctors, lawyers, professors, scientists and teachers.

To hear you tell it, we could not be creative, in spite of that we aspired to be writers, poets, artists, composers and spokespersons.

To hear you tell it, we would not be productive, but we are bankers, executives, business persons and technical workers.

You sought to keep us in bondage, bust just as God delivered the children of Israel by the hand of Moses, from our people emerged great freedom fighters constructive in helping us obtain our freedom.

Regardless of the image that you have of us, I am here to tell you that we are attractive, proud, strong, educated, creative, productive and free; BUT NOT TO HEAR YOU TELL IT!

Juanita E. Moore

Change

Summer ends and leaves turn gold, reminding us of things of old.
Hot cider by the fireplace, the smell of burning leaves.
Then comes the snow and the cold as so boldly we venture into
Mother Nature's wonderland of white.
Wrapped in her overcoat of crystals the earth rests, readying it's self for the next season.
The friendly loneliness encompasses us, telling us to rest and rejuvenate, prepare to grow again.
Lo, the earth rests. Preparing itself for the spring.
While under a mantle of white, God's creatures rebirth.
Amber leaves have fallen and flora and fauna sleeps.
The beauty of the frozen woodland, and the song of the wind.
Reminds us of the new world that awaits us tomorrow.

Ray Sofield

Lost Cause

Just another lost cause, another reason to pause and think of what I fight for.
Trying to be light only to be blown off never to burn bright.
Why must this go on, why must history always repeat itself day after day night after night.
And as they will never see my own way they will also never see the part of me that dies with every effort put down, every dream that sinks in the bay of my heart.
Just another lost cause, another reason to pause.

Sarah Factor

Toft

Toft - the sweetest little hamlet, where home lives in my heart.
Home - the loveliest place on earth where memory imparts.
Thoughts - the treasured book of child and girlhood years.
Love - the cherished days with parents so fondly endears.

Fields - enriched with trees and hedgerows shade the blackberry and wild rose.
Lanes - enhanced by brightness which the buttercup bestows.
Birds - encircling in the freshness of the morning dew.
Bees - enchanted by the clover and wild flower hue.

Bells - softly pealing o'er the fields inviting us to church.
Owls - shrilly hooting in the spinney, timid prey to search.
Cows - quietly grazing in the grassland 'neath the shady trees.
Sheep - calmly chewing and lambs skipping frisky in the breeze.

Home - spacious rooms where we enjoyed many happy hours.
Orchards, gardens, bright with myriads of sweet spring flowers.
Tennis - played 'neath summer skies, friends came from far and wide.
Walks, strolling along contentedly in the lovely countryside.

Thanks - grateful ones to God, on bended knees I give this day.
Blessings - he bestowed on me, as I pass along life's way.
Whatever task befalls me, however far we roam.
May we took with joy and love to this our happy home.

D. M. Maynard

Come, My Son

Come, my son, it is time to sleep,
his voice was gentle, low and deep.
I am afraid, I said, I don't want to go,
there is no pain, he said, nor fear below.
There is so much yet I want to do, and be,
Take joy, my son, in what you have done and been.
But I don't want to leave those I love, so dear;
All those you love, he said, will come, like you, here.
The beauty, the fun, the tears, now spent.
This splendid repast, like any feast, must end.
I come, old man. My father, I must follow you,
All is now......

Sheldon Wolf

"What Do Ye Loosing The Colt?"

"What do ye, loosing the colt?" saith the man standing by....
"His spirit is subdued, his attitude renewed, his body is imbued,
Because the Lord hath need of him!"

"What do ye, loosing my husband?" asked a weeping wife, all ragged and wan...
"He is made a loving husband, a compassionate father, a worthy son,
Because the Lord hath need of him!"

"What do ye, loosing our mother?" cried tattered and hungry children, faces pinched by the wind...
"Look at mother now! She's clean and free of drugs, tobacco and discontent!
Because the Lord hath need of her!"

"What do ye, loosing America?" shouted the nations, straining at their chains...
"Restoring her foundation-stones, strengthening her family ties, nurturing her young...
Because the Lord hath need of her!"

Fern E. Rains

Longevity

The grass is thin high up here, like the hair upon his head,
His horse is hobbled for the night, as he lay down to bed.
He gazes curiously at the stars of the midnight sky,
And wonders softly to himself, all of the reasons why.
Why he managed to live so long, during perilous times out west,
How come others fell so short, when he put them to the test.

Trouble comes when you least expect, it doesn't matter why,
You choose to fight or run away, most often words aren't tried.
Then leather slaps and bullets fly, and someone sometimes dies,
These are harsh times way out west, the stories told aren't lies.

The Red Man, White Man, and Outlaw too, have put each to the test,
And in the end one man stands, the other tried his best.
'Tis this night these questions asked, the answers short to come,
All players stay in this game of life, until their days are done.

And who's to say why one man lives, while others meet their day,
The Boss up in the sky above, will always have his way.
So rest your mind of troubling thoughts, let stars fade from sight,
Cover up and hunker down, goodnight old friend, goodnight!

Timothy L. Smith

A Children's Hell

Look at the frown on the child's face,
his eyes... they are filled with tears.
Watch how that child stares into space,
with a look of terror and fear.

Look at that child look down at the ground,
with sad eyes of being scared and alone.
See how he jumps at the littlest sound,
why is he afraid to go home?

Wow... those look like marks on his back,
is it possible that he could have fell?
Or will his name be just another one stacked
with all the other kids living in hell?

Why must some children, face life afraid,
of everyone and their brother.
Why is it, some children must pay,
because God gave them that father or mother.

When a child is abused or physically marred,
not only do those battered wounds swell,
but their spirits are also intensely scarred!
For children like this... Life is hell!

Glen G. Ohnstad

Do It Yourself!

Do it yourself! Do it myself?
How can I ever put up a shelf?
Yards of lumber—tons of nails.
He who hesitates always fails!

Get with it, boy start the hammering
Quit your wailing and your yammering
Tow the line - straighten the end
This is the "do-it-yourself" trend!

Ouch - there goes my best thumb!
How can anyone be so dumb?
Nail the wood, my fine feathered friend
Use your head - it's the "do-it-yourself" trend!

Bang! I'll act as if I really know how
Crack! What do you suppose happened now?
Oh, well, two shelves are better'n one
At least, the job is finally done.

Up go the records and the books
Say, did you see how it looks?
To you, O mighty hammer, I do bend!
I'm with it, boy! The "do-it-yourself" trend.

Ruth Grossman

Wallstreet Warriors

Daylight's vision fades away, with the closing hammer falling.
Hindsight rules: yet again the predictions proved appalling!

As the quiet shroud of night converges,
back from the hereafter the eternal optimist emerges.

In stealth this guru feeds a nameless beast,
gaining wisdom through the random droppings from its feast.

Visionless, of course, but never refuted.
Tomorrow's picks will again go undisputed.

Never a predictor of pending doom;
always a horizon where profits loom.

Loath to say "sell," always claiming to know best,
just how to guide we victims in our relentless quest.

Senseless advice? An obvious no-brainer?
For us, it's an insider's tip on a sure-thing gainer.

Consider the source, consider the inference.
Senseless advice? Would we really know the difference?

We must pursue, we must prevail...an endless lust for greed.
Alas, for it is upon US that the mindless brokers feed.

J. J. Russell

September 1st

I watch the young readied for school;
High school and college, these kids are no fools.
I wish I could, just one more time,
Walk the campus, know a schedule, stand in line.
Carry books, and gossip and go to class
With computers and Shakespeare, both hard to pass.
Meet people in my section and lab,
Purchase equipment, supplies and run a tab.
Find teachers and students, surrounding all new;
Sit near a boy, have feelings of youth, when love is due.
Borrow a pencil I don't need, pretend to be busy so I read.
To dream again of this boy, a picnic a walk, just us two.
School would lend me all of this,
Memories and dreams feelings of bliss.
If I were a teen just one more time,
I would collect my honors, stand in line.
Be a good student. Make them proud.
No drugs, no babies, no sleeping around,
To be perfect as I vowed.

Ruby Stewart

My Tree Stand

Once upon a time, with my bow in my hand,
High in a tree, in a deer hunting stand,
Twelve point bucks I was told there would be,
But where had they gone? Where could they be?

Then all of a sudden there was a 'crack,'
The sound of a twig that had just been snapped.
I looked all around and right under my tree,
Was the buck, right there, where Dad said he would be.

I drew back my bow and he looked up at me,
Sitting up there in my deer hunting tree...
Not a thought did he think, not a word did he say.
He didn't say bye, he just ran away.

I was sad but not discouraged,
'Cause one day there will be,
A deer that won't run,
From my deer hunting tree.

Terry Roehrman

Guadalupe

Young, lonely and so beautiful
Hidden tears filled with sadness
When the new day came
The tears would have ended
A flower blooms and then it fades away
Laughter hides your tears inside
Sorry that the winds of happiness has passed you by
A new day return
The book I close
The story remains to be untold
I hope you found the happiness
You were looking for
Rest my love
The time has come
For pain to fly away
Good bye my friend
Dry your eyes
My Dear Guadalupe
Maria W. Wade

Guardian Angels I See

Some people believe Guardian Angels exist, they are sent here by God to protect and assist.

For me there is no doubt in my mind, their help and assistance, go beyond being kind.

These Guardian Angels I'm so lucky to see, I am fortunate to know them, all personally.

They're my friends and family who helped me survive, they came to my rescue, and kept me alive.

When I was not well, and full of despair, I need only look up, to see one standing there.

When help was required, there was no need to ask, they all seem to know their own special task.

I could name them by name, if ever need be, these beautiful "Guardian Angels" I see.
Patricia Hoglund

A Drink With Death

I wake and drink a toast to the dancing stars
Heralding the arrival of the moon
They battle through brightness, their boasting thunders
How they pale in comparison to the reflection of the one
Hidden from me as night fills my soul
Even Selene blushes in the embrace of night
As she racer her chariot through the sky
Befriended by death, I drink to the night's debauchery
Liquid fears pour down my throat, quenching my burning heart
Death is thankful I've stopped living
We walk together, though he is only visible through my eyes
I lose track of the twinkling demons
And wonder how were so alone
Death and night continue laughing and I drink again
And again 'til the morning dawn plagues the horizon
Threatening a new day
Night races to safety, suddenly ashamed
Death is left with me
But I have chosen this friend and he is faithful
We go inside and drink again
Steven Craig

She

She will run to you
Her warmth will greet you
She will never betray your deepest thoughts
You will have great respect for her.

If she is enraged though,
Her warmth she will take with her
And leave you with a chill as cold as ice.
If she is angered
She becomes violent and sometimes hurtful and damaging
Still she will comfort you in your joy and sorrow.

Her love is vast, her temper unpredictable
But she will always let you dream
And dream with you.
SHE is the Ocean!
G. Kelly

Untitled

Today you'll carry her home, walking with
her in a peaceful roam.
Never thinking it could happen to a loved one,
or even someone we know, it will hurt so deep inside to let her go.
None of us, as mothers never understood,
how can she be robbed of her motherhood?
Thinking about how everyone takes life for granted,
really not knowing what tomorrow will bring,
our only wish is that God will take her under his wing.
She was a good person as her friends, and
loved ones, as anyone could see, we all wonder,
how could this be, why did she have to get HIV?
Her life was a normal one, she hasn't did
anything, someone else hasn't done.
With her being put in the ground, and all
the flowers laid over her in a mound everyone
that attends can hear nothing but hearts pound,
with all the sorrow that lingers around.
This is for my sister who had HIV, you'll never understand
how much you mean to me.
Somehow I know, you're in a much better place and when
its my time, we will once meet again face to face!
Ruth Ann Keffer

Monsters In The 90's

"Hush baby, there are no monsters under your bed," said a mother to her child. Then she remembers when she was young, and she asked her mother if there were monsters under her bed, and her mother said, "Hush baby there are no monsters under your bed." But the mother has no idea what it's like growing up in the 90's:

    With the fear of being shot while getting the mail, with the fear of getting high just to "fit in," with the fear of joining gangs to feel loved and needed, with the tears from crying yourself to sleep over divorced parents.

The child lies in the dark and thinks to herself, "Good, mom fell for the lie. She actually thinks I still believe in monsters under the bed. Now she thinks I'm so scared that she'll let me stay up longer. Then "BANG" a loud noise rips through the silence down the street. "DRIVE-BY, get under the bed!" the mother cries. Ten minutes later, mother and child are sitting on the bed holding each other. "There are monsters, aren't there?" the child asks. The mother replies, "Yes honey, there are monsters, but not under the bed."
Toni Clevenstine

"Together"

The drainage of thy water
  Heavenly flows through thy soil
    Seeping into a world of its own
      Each water droplet bonded
        Together.

The petals of thy flower
  Enclosing the rich center
    Protecting thy soul
      Each bright petal linked
        Together.

The rainbow of thy colors
  A spectrum of rays of light
    Glistening through the reflections of time
      Each ribbon of color tied
        Together.

The human race of thy earth
  Speckled with love and hate
    Woven into an intense body and soul
      All in need to stand
        Together.
   Stacy Lena Spawn

My Love Is Near

My love is gone. He left today.
  He walks with God and some will say,
I must be happy for him now, though I confess I know not how
  To bridge the gap and find my way.
He smoothed my path most every day, counseling encouragingly.
  We laughed at troubles dwindling so,
They never seemed unsurmountable.
  His strengths erased my fears in life,
And as his wife, I knew no strife.
  Just family to crowd my time with endless friends, both his and mine
To fill those fifty years sublime.
He speaks to me, "Dear one, don't pine,
Enjoy our dividends divine, our home, our children fine,
  All nature's bounty, ever free, then you alone will never be
While sharing life's sweet memory. You'll see.
  God's heaven holds us close, our key,
Invisible it's true, but solidly. Trust me."
  Awake, my heart. Dost feel him near, still quieting my every fear?
Dost wonder why I hold him dear?
   Tede Adrienne Allmon

A Trip Back In Time

The old horse looked so majestic and free,
he stood quite alone on a mountain top peak.
His black, satin coat showed many a scar,
from brave battles fought both near and afar.
A high pitched neigh came up from his throat,
it pierced the night air with its challenging note.
He seemed to be telling the world he was king;
telling all listening he still reigned supreme.
His gently sway back told of his years,
hollows above his eyes spoke of past fears.
If horses could talk on the stories he'd tell,
of adventures and journeys of sickness and health.
To go back in time; what a grand thought,
to a time when he was younger, a time when he fought....
The young horse looked so majestic and free,
he stood quite content on a mountain top peak.
Surrounded by stars and fresh, midnight air;
by trees and by grass and dozens of mares.
He gave a loud whinny; from this place he'd not roam,
this was where his heart was; this was home.
   Paige McCorkle

He Is There

God is everywhere.
He shows his beauty in the quiet sunsets.
The birds seem to sing out his praise
Deep in the depths He is there.
The fish in the sea displays His creativity and splendor.
Like the air we breathe, He is there.
Never far, always near.
Like a parent watching their sleeping child,
So our Father watches over us,
Longing to draw near.
   Tamara Edmiston

A Tiny Hand . . .

A tiny hand reaches out for Daddy.
He sees the world through your eyes,
For he has not yet experienced life.
You are his vision of times to come.
He praises you in his own little way.
His love for you, unconditional.
He longs to be acknowledged, loved.
Expecting to be cared for, nourished . . .
Body and soul.
For a moment in time, he is sheltered
From the world around him.
If only childhood were to be perpetual,
  . . . happiness unending!
   Teresa M. Kelly

The Big Game

He walked up to the plate with the bat in his hand
he pulled down his cap and spit in the sand.
A practice swing as he stared down the center
hoping his hit would make the bat splinter.
He glanced at the bases and then at The Man
who told him to hit it as hard as he can.
On the mound stood the pitcher with sweat in his eye
going through motions to let the ball fly.
The score was tied up, eight to eight
and he was hoping the batter was going to swing late.
He let the ball fly with a grunt and a groan
as he aimed that ball right across home.
But the batter was ready and knew what to do
he gritted his teeth and dug in his shoe.
He felt the bat shudder as he hit that fast ball
then he saw it fly up and over the wall.
Through the roar of the crowd and at a dead run
He heard his Mom shout, "Way to go, Son!"
He ran all the bases without looking up
deciding where to put his Little League Cup.
   Penny L. Todd

I Do Not Know

If you should call and no one answers the incessant phone
I am adrift and all alone
The shadowy recess of my mind comes to life
Causing, oh, such strife
As I cling to the last strands of my stratagem
No one can see my desperate fall into oblivion
The blues lured me darker and deeper
I must now embrace my Keeper
Laughter or pain?
I do not know
The constant tearing renders me insane
   Tra Vu

The Fool

The fool is one who never thinks.
He or she glides along on a happy song.
Good natured and compatible;
Morals questionable and aids a possibility.
   A fool is somebody's tool.
That person doesn't know the facts.
He or she just does what is necessary
To get along without trouble or work.
Progress and knowledge — what are they?
   Don't know and don't care.
A tragedy happens, the world is changed.
Now, the fool wakes up and takes notice.
He or she has no religious faith for support
So it is rough, hurtful with no solutions.
   Time to change.
The moves are made as the future looms.
With proper guidance, the one is one longer a fool.
That one has new understanding and new morals.
Can make a lot of difference for all to see.
   The Lord Jesus would help.

Ruth Partridge

Jesus Is Our Saviour!

Jesus is our Saviour,
He lets us know He needs no favor
He gives us his holy words with perfect flavor.

Jesus sits high and above,
He sends us his heavenly dove,
to bring us lots of love.

Jesus protects us with His perfect hands,
and projects his Holy Spirit throughout the land.

Jesus gives us his mighty grace,
He will help us to run his pace,
to defeat Satan in this last race.

So remember...Jesus is our Saviour
He blessed us with his heavenly touch,
our love for him can never be to much!

Ricky Clemons

My Hero

My dad in my eyes, no one is better
He is my hero, a real go getter.
He worked hard all his life,
Working for him self, his daughters and wife.
The pain I feel, so sad and blue
Just because I'm losing you.
The stab of pain, the ache so strong,
Knowing full well you'll soon be gone.
The pain I feel of love I will miss,
I can't begin to make a list
My Dad, my Dad, always so tough,
Growing so weak, his voice so rough.
He's the man I looked up to in life,
I now say goodbye with pain for his wife.
The crack in my voice, the break in my heart,
Knowing full well of pain that will start.
His memory will live with us all,
Day to day we'll all recall.
How strong he was, so rough and tough.
Goodbye to Dad, I'll miss you so much!

Robin J. Kubitza

Bubo Makes The Army

When our boy reached eighteen and his draft day neared,
He got so impatient he went and volunteered.
I tried to talk him out of it, but he'd only say;
'I know it's hard but I've got to learn that way'.

Soon he got a letter from our president,
It was important, for greetings he had sent.
Bubo was so happy, he spent the entire day,
Showing it to friends and bragging I'm 1A'

Soon the day came to go for his exam,
The requirements are high to work for Uncle Sam.
'All keep your fingers crossed,' he said' on every hand,
For I go to try to fool the best doc's in the land.'

'If I haven't got a cold my asthma doesn't show
And I can breathe, I think, so he will never know'.
So Mama tuck me in and pin my covers tight,
For I know my goose is cooked it I take cold tonight.

When I saw him coming I knew that he was in,
I could tell by his walk and funny little grin.
He said, 'Add a star our your flag for me,
For we've got another soldier in our family.'

Wilma Wilkie

License To Love

It all started with a test drive.
He fell in love with my shiny exterior.
Once polished and waxed,
I was taken for a short ride to be shown off.
All I was good for was getting from place to place.
He said how fast and where we were going.
My rear view mirrors showed traces of fire,
Like my heart beating with intense desire.
Unfortunately, I was driven too fast.
Materialistic memories were distorted by gas fumes.
Now sitting with a fine coat of dust,
My many parts extracted,
And all that is left is an empty shell.
It's still a mystery to me,
Why you need a license to drive and not to love.

Tracy Schmierer

A Day At Work

Guy in traffic - oh what a jerk!
He cut me off on my way to work.

Cop pulled me over - 'cause of my speed
Pointed to the sign, said "Can't You Read?"

Gotta hurry to work, just can't be late!
Or else the boss will be irate!

My computer's so slow - takin' so much time,
Every minute I wait, wish I had a dime.

My printer's got problems, it won't print -
Don't know what's wrong - not even a hint!

I got people wantin' this, and people wantin' that,
That's one good way to get rid of body fat!

I got papers to file, papers to fax,
Much more to do, no time to relax.

I can't find your file - where could it be?
I got people on the phone screaming at me!

Work extra hours - don't get a dime!
'Cause the boss said "No overtime!"

My phone - it just rings and rings,
Guess the day ain't over - till the fat lady sings!

Robert Allison

"Why"

I'm five years old, I live with my Dad
He beats me so, though I've done nothing bad
He comes home late when I'm asleep
He pulls down my pants and begins to beat

I try to run and try to hide
But all I can do is curl up and cry
It happens when he's drunk, even when he's not
Is it for fun, I'm all he's got

I love my Dad though he beats me so
I could never leave, where would I go?
I wonder sometimes, if I'll ever die
One of these nights instead of just cry

Every night this goes on
And every night I cry
And all I can do
Is just ask WHY?

Peter Dottore

10-30-95

I look to find the shiny faces that
   have always been there to guide me,
   but they are not there.

I can only see darkness.

Why aren't the glowing guiding lights
   burning; burning in celebration, in mourning?

Are they, too, lost and can't find their way?

Does my face glow? Can it be seen, or does it
   disappear in the midnight sky?

I want to be a bright and shiny star that everyone can see.
I want to be real.

Jack-o-lanterns flicker in the wind but one crisp autumn evening
Stars shine forever...

Paula K. Linn

Ready

I am ready to go to that city my Lord
has gone to prepare, but first I must tell
others about Jesus, so they can meet Him there.
I must witness to others about His wonderful
saving grace; so someday with me they
too may see His glorious shining face.
When I think of His wonderful mercy and
this world so full of sin; I think of those
who will be left untold, when the Lord
says this is the end.
I pray that the Lord will give me
the power to make the lost understand;
that salvation is knocking at their hearts
door, but death may take the upper hand.

Sarah L. Heath

Poetry Under The Pines

ETERNITY - a perfect moment,
smiles and laughter, brilliant colors absorb
the sunshine, a warm loving feeling flows between us;
taste the gentle breeze, as it sweeps
through your mind, scattering thoughts
into patterns, never to exist again.

Kathleen McNeil

Chew, Swallow, And Stick

Chiclets, gumballs, Bazooka Joe,
Gums that squirt, gums that blow,
Green apple bubble was my fave.
For days and days I would save.
That wad of green chewy goo
blew better bubbles old than new.
Blowing perfect bubbles was an art,
and it was sad when time to part
with the rubbery, blubbery hunk of gum.
Dad always said, "Don't be so dumb!"
Because we always swallowed it.
Dad would jump around and throw a fit.
"It doesn't matter the kind of weather
If you swallow your gum, your butt will stick together!"

Teresa L. Sample

Green

I am a verdant lush bright-dark green
Greeeeeenne
I believe in life
I support life
I call to life and shimmers up a response.
I spring to life
I feel like moss on the feet to eyes that see me.
I coooool rage.
Spring is my time of year
the season when I reign.
I am a royal green.
Not even white can reign over me.
"Winter never fails to turn into spring".
Yes. Oh, yes. I am ever green.

Kathleen Perez Dewey

Wooden Teeth

Kaleidoscope flash of blurred standing forms...
   grab the brass ring...reach out!
The dizzying pace of the faux steeplechase,
   of painted fillies in an unending race,
again, please...again! I am no fanatic; more!
   the rise and fall, hold tight, don't slip
and guess when the calliope shall fade, or
   why my mount would sport green lips?
an enameled grimace to invisible spurs
   so frozen, in absolute horror
wide eyed...wild eyed, let us gallop beyond
   and find some magic, I wish, I...
believe, straight up in your stirrups I stand
   and snap the reins to let you know
it is time for us to go, to break the bonds
   of this carousel life, and fly

G. Fred Logan

Memories Of The Past

Memories of the past
Good or bad are always to think day in and day out
As the years pass
Per sunrise awaken
Our lives are more than what we can say
Thou year after year a smile or a glum shall all come near
Thou I shall avoid bad for good
But for what comes I shall take to
My awake
Thou memories are special good or bad
Nor far or near
I shall always accept what is to be my destiny

Tony Sousa

The Tomb

The undisturbed stillness of the dark's fear,
glistening upon the bleak and dreary atmosphere,
carrying over the questionable shadows, cast
by the mocking expressions of the moon.

Embedded deep beneath the flesh of the soul,
lies the treachery and hatred years old,
as the every decaying trust from within,
as to commit itself to each moral sin,
filters ever-steadily throughout each pore.

Behind the eyes of an ice cold heart,
welcomes the putrid stench of death's mark,
where life was once open and flourishing,
now lies discreet and cast down upon.

Don't deny the unrelenting bombardment,
of the cold tortured inhibitions within us,
lying under the crimson layered emotion,
we all yearn to achieve in its highest state,
only to fall prey to the infinite tomb.
   Wayne Brown

Blessings From An Angel Lost

A gentle soul and soaring spirit sands of sunsets sunrises with love
Gifts of love gifts from the heart
Words spoken wise and true words of hope to me and you
Tides of life recede and come life ends and life has begun
Tireless devotion many don't know teacher of lessons so many will grow
Angels are rare and they don't stay long so listen closely soon
   they'll gone
Pockets overflowing of unaware knowing innocently unknowingly knowing
Too deep to measure
Who could compare to our treasured angel they are so very rare
So we thank the heavens for our friendly guest and weep to see him leave
Heaven has called him back from us really we shouldn't grieve
Tears shed are for ourselves for we will miss our angel
And treasures be gave and the things be knows
Goodbye dearest one it's time once again to be free
From the prison that bound you so others could see
Death and rebirth are transcendental and so to home you soar
As for me I am certain with all my heart that heaven is richer
And earth is poorer
   Gwen Harris

Growth

I've search the heavens and the earth
   from the time of my birth.
On life's never ending quest
   continuously wandering without rest

I've search the Alps, the Himalayas and more
I've crawled around searching the desert floor
I've search the sphinx, the pyramids and other things
I've traveled to Mecca to embrace the King.

I have studied Confucius, Plato and Socrates
No truths they revealed, only hypocrisies
The church did not provide a solution
while the Good Book only added to my confusion

Having search endlessly
I finally looked deep inside of me
And to my surprise I found
It was with me all the time.
   C. Thomas Capers

100% Dad

I don't need much, just love and time.
From the day I was born, I thought you were mine.
As time went by, I came to see
There was another, someone other than me.
You made many promises, you knew you wouldn't keep.
You hurt mom many times.
I heard it in my sleep.
The pain in her eyes, the hurt on her face,
The one that was always there,
You wanted to replace.
Now she's gone, and everything's sad;
I wish you could have been a 100% Dad.
   Theresa Ann Deeds

Dream For The Year Of The Child

I dreamed the earth star, exploited and strife torn,
From its universe orbit fell into the forever of nowhere.

Statesmen in a multitude of tongues
Debated, argued, and considered
The purposes and the where about
Of an appropriate international congress.

Scientist consulted multi-lingual computers,
Only to report that planet earth was indeed doomed,
As they had so often forewarned.

Skeptics nervously scoffed that it was but a minor aberration
And urged life continue accordingly.

Philosophers pondered and at length concluded
That what was to have been had been written in the stars
From the very beginning of time.

And poets rushed to compose the final epitaph.

Suddenly, from the mist and despair of helplessness,
Children everywhere joined hands
And together hoisted the net of peace and brotherhood;
And just as earth touched the brink of forever nowhere
The children caught the falling star.
   Fred G. Burke

Hope

Shades of night cast a shadow on the meadow pond,
Frogs croak ever so rhythmically on the waters edge.
One lone stranger with pad and pen, writing a farewell
letter to "Whosoever cares."

Then just as he was ready to plunge, a sound out of no
where with such a gentle voice; "Don't be so foolish, I
care most". He turned to see who it could be.

The gentle voice kept speaking, "I have sought you
through the night, please don't continue your plight.
For it was long ago I gave my life for yours".

Then he fell on his knees; Oh what an awesome sight,
In his mind's eye he saw the cross that night.
Blood stains of crimson red, a crown of thorns upon his
head, a bruised and battered body, a spear driven side.

Then he looked upon that face of love: tender mercies,
grace and hope filled his empty soul. With new faith
He took hold of life's most precious gift.
   Ruth Atkins

Leave Your Dreams Behind

Killer of the heart
friends who talk versus enemies that walk
you can find your voice, if you just
repeat your choice, it is only fair
stay away from the heat, and the lions' lair

Hurt and pain fill your brain
Eye of the mind and of life
are both still alive
Redeem yourself tighten your belt
and begin to fly

Fly away from the tears, leaving the years.
Behind. Unlock the memory of the love and the
blood still flows over the fingers and onto the
black night rose.

Open the door and turn on the lights
watch forever, stare into the darkness
of your dreams. Live and die why bother
To cry if you can't believe
in immortality.
  Heidi Kunz

My Brown Eyed Baby Boy

From the time the Doctor said, "It's a boy!" My joy knew no bounds.
Friends asked, "Who does he look like?" My answer was quick and proud.
"He's in a class of his own. Just look at those shining brown eyes."
The color was not all important, but the way he used them was.
The first few days of his life, his eyes expressed wonder and
amazement in such commanding ways. He seemed to know they
were tools of learning and he was anxious to learn.
As days grew into weeks, however, the brown eyes sparkled with joy.
He made himself understood in many audible ways, but the brown
eyes of my baby spoke volumes, before ever a word was said.

His changes in moods and emotions were often too rapid to follow.
In the same moment, those eyes could show anger, hunger, hope and pain,
All mingled with anxiety and shining through crystal tears.
But only seconds later, a bottle of warm milk in hand,
Tears vanished and eyes were aglow with happy gratitude.
At play time, my baby's eyes mastered hundreds of fairy dances,
With grace and charms that excelled Snow White or Peter Pan.
Even with growth into teen years, the characteristic talking eyes
Lost no intensity of expression. For eyes are windows to
Personality, and mirrors of the soul.
  Raymond C. Barr Sr.

Poem Of Advice "Mother To Daughter"

Be careful my daughter
For what the world has in store
Not all dreams come true
And you can't open every door
Stay as smart, beautiful and wonderful as you are
Don't let anyone deny that you are a superstar
As a women you are strong
And always will belong
Lawyer, Doctor, Construction if you choose
Intelligence is always the weapon to use
Be open minded and trusted
Be loved, not lusted
These are few words of advice
Make the right choices, I can't always supervise
This is to let you know that I'll be there
I'll never stop loving, and I'll always care
  Shauntay Dunbar White

The Old Manhattan Bridges

The long and dark road of which I roam,
For those buildings arch up height,
are taller than me as I take a stroll along side,
out by down the nearer path of the
old Manhattan bridges
One lonely, old but
wise man whom told
of himself, gave
a helping hand in
to build that bridge,
that stands of
where I roam,
no one knows
for only a spot
of sun light
shines against the
shadows behind
me picture a tiny
figure of the
upper part of my body
  Zelda Marie Conner

I Live For Now And Not Before

I live for now and not before
for the past is heartache and very sure
The nights I couldn't sleep on my back
Because of that hard undeserving smack
The painful memories I try to hide
But it's so hard, they are still inside
I try to forget and not be to sad
But I still feel it, it hurts so bad
These feelings I have are down so deep
Please God help me hear my weep
Well I have a family now and things are better
Except for those hard times that I remember
But now my life is happy and worth
So much more
Because this is now and not before
  Sandra Petrillo

"Special Delivery"

I thank God everyday for the miracle sent to me.
For the nine months I carried you,
The reality I could not see...
I never thought it was possible to love someone so much,
And I always wondered what it would be like the first
time we'd touch.
When I'd heard that cry,
And saw that beautiful face,
When they laid my first born in my arms,
I knew no one could take your place.
You are my "little angel" which I will always love,
Sent "special delivery" from the Lord up above.
  Sara Seymour

The Beauty Of Colored People

Brown like the earth braised with the sun
For superior complexion colorful and fun
Plum brushed lips raised cheek bones
And dark colored eyes complete the tones
Bright woven garments and jewelry to match
Give a vision of beauty so precious to catch
All across the land their spirits soar free
Standing tall and proud in complete autonomy
Under the moon they dance to celebrate life
And soon will retire waking at morrows daylight
  Robert Wright Jr.

The Mirror

Looking in the mirror used to be a pleasure
For she saw one steady and sure,
As life got harder, she dimmed the lights
Her illusion kept intact,
Days spent sleeping,
Nights of self destruction
An afternoon in a courtroom
Loss of one loved
Self pity, self destruction.....

Sunlight shining as she looks in the mirror
Hollow face, dull eyes, skin and bones,
She cries for the scars on her arms as well as her heart,
The mirror shows her the truth
Wasted time, wasted life,
Broken mirror in a thousand pieces.

Changes from within her soul
A new mirror, a new story to tell
Ten years passed
Looking in the mirror is again a pleasure,
She has learned, her own self-worth......................
    K. Renee Grizzle

Jack In The Box

Jack in the Box is a very nice place
for eating when busy while out on the go.
But jacks are not always a tool for some car
or toys for a child to play with.

Nor is a name like McDonald's,
you most truly and surely must know,
always for farms with the some mooing milk cows
in a barn with a dog and a blacksmith.
    Terry Roberts

Silent Meditation

We thank Thee for love and life,
For awareness of the beauty of creation — Yours and ours,
For being able to experience fulfillment.

We turn to Thee when we are lonely or afraid.
We pray to strengthen our will and to ease our countless fears,
For being able to hope, to dream, and to take care of
   others so we can seek peace.

When the wind chills you, I will ask the sun to warm you.
When your mood overtakes you, I will ask lovebirds to serenade you.

Seek wisdom and you will find true life.
Cherish it and it will keep you happy.
    A. P. Alpert

The Demon

As I shoot out into the wind toward the open sea, the storm dies
Gasping for breath I see a translucent face rise out of a dark cloud
   before me
Rushing away from the cloud I desperately manage to escape
I plunge into a sheer wall of darkness
As I am cradled by the same dark cloud, I start to die
Changing shape as it moves towards the shallows, the human
   mind combined with evil terrify my almost lifeless body
Barely able to stay ahead of the collapsing tunnel, a shape comes
   ghosting towards me
I try to escape but the trail I must follow steepens as I go
As I look back on the detail of the surroundings I was engulfed in,
   the demon sacrifices my soul
    Sarah Howard

I Am Your Son

He drops to his knees, in a garden at night.
Folds his hands together, holding them tight.

Let me speaks to you father, there are things to be said.
Things I'm frightened of father, things that I dread.

I've taught all your sheep, through words and deed.
I've cured the sick, some souls I've freed

Strong words I've used, against your enemies here.
I was never afraid father, you were always near.

I love my friends father, I hold them so dear.
To continue your works, is all that they care.

But you say my journeys over, with one task left to be done.
With my life that is given, the battle will be won.

But I'm afraid of death father, the crucifixion I fear.
At the hands of these people, that you hold so dear.

So I plead with you father, pass this cup from my hand.
And find another solution, to your wonderful plan.

But you are my father, and I am your son.
So not my will father, But your will be done.
    Tony Meli

"What Kind Of Love Is There?"

My love she's like crystal springs that
flow from the mountaintops to cup in
my hands; to obtain in my lips; it
just leaks through my fingertips.

My love she's like a spring breeze that
blows all the beautiful fragrances to my nose;
that I can never hold.

My love she's like a beautiful snowflake
that floats from heaven; most intricate
beauty; once landing on my fingertips;
just melts away.

I said, "my love, what kind of love do
you have for me? Is it like ice cream,
once taken out of the freezer, it just melts away?"

"Or like hair spray; once you go out
into the mist, it just dissolves?"

"What kind of love do you have for me?"
    Steve Trueay

My Dad

I can't believe it's fifteen years, since last I saw your smiling face.
Fifteen years of tumultuous past, and you not here for a trace.
You have guided me and mine, even though you were no here,
Because through it all, I asked your help and low and behold, you
   steered.
Through birth and death, marriage and divorce, your love was always felt.
When times were tough or going great, you stood behind me, so I
   couldn't melt.
Even now you keep your vigil, giving me my strength,
Because your love is often felt when I am out at length.
I love you, Dad and I'm sure you know, how much I miss your person,
But until it's time for me to part this world which we rehearse in,
I promise to pass on to ours, the love and strength and character,
Which you have given and continue to give throughout your life and after.
    Sandy Mann

The Gift

There is no greater bonding, than a mother and her child.
Feeling loved so deeply, so strong, but yet so mild.

That special, gentle moment as he's pulled toward the breast.
The nurturing, the loving, is felt with his caress.

The first time I heard it - the beating of his heart.
I couldn't stop from crying. I nearly fell apart.

To bring a child into this world, is a blessing from above.
Because there is no greater gift, than to give a child your love.

All the wondrous moments, I think I could have missed.
If God had not given me, this truly miraculous gift.

Not planning on a baby, is not the same as a mistake.
It's realizing that when given, you willing must take.

For nothing else now matters, except the happiness of my son.
And realizing how blessed, my life has now become.
Randee K. Slings

Unforgotten Promises

I'd walk for miles to hear your voice,
Feel your touch and see you rejoice.
I'd climb a mountain as high as the sky,
Just to see the beauty in your eyes.
I'd do anything to make you see,
I still have the love for you that you once had for me.
I never knew our love would end like this,
Oh how much your love I miss.
One day you were here the next day gone,
I'll never hear your voice over the phone.
I'll never see you smiling back at me,
The way your smiles use to be.
I'll never hear your footsteps walking by my side,
For when you see me pass, you always run and hide.
I'll never feel your strong arms squeezing me tight,
The way you used to hold me every single night.
I pray one day you will realize your pride isn't as important
To others as your love is to me. I'll thank God for the day I see,
You pass by and smile or blink your eye, then I'll know you still
Remember me and I still exist.
Rebecca Cook

The Love

Watching the fan blades revolve on my bracelet is mesmerizing
fear anger jealousy.
My fingers move so quickly I cannot keep track of them
betrayal pain hurt
Hearing the beat effects me too well, I make no sound
back again to exhaustion
I go on, and on, and on, and on, and on
wear me out please
I don't want to think anymore
I don't want to cry anymore
I don't want to feel anymore
I can't!
Traci R. Dishman

Hope

Imagine a tree, strong and tall, this is your father,
he is your strength
Imagine a stream running along side it, this is your mother,
she is your love,
Imagine yourself with the one you love leaning against
the tree, and the grass all around it, those are your friends,
and look at the beautiful view beyond, this is the world.
Shawn D. Overholser

Untitled

A struggle with images,
fashion images.
Fashion images surrounded me,
engulfed me,
ensnared me.
Tormented by the female deity,
the goddess of cyan, yellow, magenta and black.
She harassed me.
Delicate bone structure,
graceful curves,
her retouched figure digested and tempted me.
Does a woman choose to fast or eat?
Fast to become a female deity,
because musculature = masculinity.
I digested her philosophy:
Sandy creams of taffeta and chiffon.
"Golden goddess of beauty,
I have finally abandoned thee and thy retouched color realm,
defeated but sane."
Roberta Marino

Reaching For You

Reaching out through the darkness
Far beyond the misty way
A time appears, no hopes, just shadows
Leaving it a total gray
No hopes, no dreams, no creation to make
No love, no hate, no feelings
It's the voice of the past behind us
Slowly are memories are fading
Reach out and hold it with your tightest grip
Don't let it slip away
Our memories are a part inside us
Remember the past each day
Love and hate are just illusions
Time does not exist
There's something foggy in the distance
Covered fully with the mist
Forgetting is the mist inside us
Taking all our dreams away
Memories are the things that guide us
And keep going day by day
Patricia Ford

Peaceful Compassion

From somewhere in the dark a child's voice called out
  faintly without fear or want.

He saw the fox glide unerringly across his path, sleek
  in its way, with tail trailing in regal splendor
  raised silver, to and fro'.

From darkness to light, incandescence, to shadow, to
  darkness once again.

An echo of haunting laughter and voices burned into memory,
  with fleeting visions of past remembrances makes the
  silver creature surreal.

Frozen in time, the fox stopped at the edge of darkness
  before disappearing forever, turned its head and
  looked back over its shoulder, then continued on into
  darkness, knowing its way.

From a short distance one can make them out in the mist
  of a forgotten time.

The child sits in a moonlit meadow, upon an old stump of
  a tree that was once tall and majestic, stroking a
  silver fox, asleep in his lap...
Ronald Jay Hernandez

"Lovers Obsessed"

Eyes of forest green gazing loving into,
Eyes of mystical blue.
Nature scarcely seems to notice,
As they sit there among the grass and flowers.
They truly look as if they belong there.
Soft breezes blowing gently
Through their hair.
If they stood in the Barren Desert,
It would still be the same.
There's love and emotion there,
Between these two lovers
That only they can feel.
Silently they touch,
And gently they kiss
Eyes only for each other.
They're hoping this day will never end.
And in their hearts
And in their memory
It never will.
Wanda Jones

Carlee's Angel

Hair as golden as the sun,
Eyes as deep as sea,
Brought to Earth to be my son,
Heavenly Father entrusted you to me.
Loved and cosseted in the womb,
I waited anxiously to hold you to my breast.
Alas, when the time arrived,
God saw fit to recall you to his service.
Oh, what a warrior you must be,
To be taken from me like this!
I am comforted with the knowledge
That you are home with your Eternal Father.
In years to come, when the moment arrives,
What a great and glorious reunion we shall have!
I will know your golden hair and deep-sea yes,
Know the divine opportunity of holding you,
In my arms,
Knowing you are and will always be mine—
Carlee's angel.
Suzanne I. Parker

Untitled

Vision is a better scholar and more willing than the ability to hear;
Expert advice is often uncertain, but examples are always clear;
And the highest of all those in the service of God are the men who live by their belief,
For to see the good in action is what all of us seek for relief.
I can promptly learn how to do the task, if you'll let me perceive it done;
I can observe your fingers in action, but your lips too fast may run;
And the instructions you deliver may be of great wisdom and true,
But I'd rather get my exercise by observing what you do.
For I may not deduce your persona and the exalted advice you produce,
But there's no disagreement how you dance and how you seduce.
Sam Stuart Snyder

"Horse Praise"

He moves like a show horse trots along so proud
He performs perfectly, as if there were a crowd
He would be a winner if he entered the race,
He would receive much applause for his beauty as well as his grace
Bonnie Ruth Shaulis

Verbs

Maneuver my mind to think all and any of your wishes.
Evoke my interests, ideals and dreams.
Escape through me, live within me, exist for me.
Manipulate language to control me, perplex me,
Delight me, anger me, assuage me.
Dilate my mind to accept your thoughts,
Adapt your language to my being, adopt your intricacies.
Ply my senses with rationale.
Educate me to what is within you, around you, of you.
Tease my reasoning with your motives; captivate me with expression.
Motivate me to feel, to think, to live!
Extricate me from within the prison of my body.
Heighten me to the vastness of my soul.
Deliver me from my earthly bonds.
Patricia J. Carlsen

Babies Crying

I knew that nothing was foolproof.
Everyone must take that chance.

Some say "life" is the only right, regardless of circumstance,
No matter how dark the night. Are they with me during these times
Of weariness, of fright... of bitterness, of despair?

Have they the right to judge me, when they were never there?
They snort and say that I've made my bed and in it, I must lie.
I go to bed with that taint and every night I cry.

Immediately, I silence my tears, for someone else is crying too.
I am the one responsible for her. What am I to do?
Doesn't she deserve a real home surrounded by family?
Not scraping through the gutter in Welfare's company.

They have prescribed what I must do: Abandon her to strangers, if my love is true. Should I do a deed so cruel? Just pass the buck and go back to school. I could not concentrate! Does she wear clean clothes and have good food on her plate? Does someone read her a story, a nursery rhyme and send her to school on time?

The only "life" for her and me: Painful existence — no other way to be. She is denied her childhood; I, my youth. No education. No career. No home. I have a new baby with me now; why do I feel more alone?
Stella Schreiber

The Day

Everyone standing not looking around
Every head bowed, thoughts toward the ground
Memories pass as the lonely groom cries
As he walks toward the casket
Tears in his eyes

His father comes for comfort
His Mother steps back
As more people follow
All dressed in black

The young man looks at his young wife to be
How could this happen, at least why to me
He slips on her ring and draws very near
And whispers "I love you" in her cold ear

The preacher and service watched so close
As the brave man rose and spoke
I never thought that this is how it would be
To see the day
Me without her, her without me
Teresa Morris

Untitled

When I look into your eyes, I see a love that burns like an
   ever-glowing candle,
Unwavering, very certain of its destiny; not even the strongest
   wind could extinguish it.

When I look into your eyes, I see our life together,
   I see the past and all the wonderful memories it holds,
   I also see the future, and all the memories it will create.

I will never find a love greater than my love for you; you alone
   fill my heart with complete happiness.
Nothing in this world could give more pleasure than spending
   eternity with you.

My heart is aching to hold you, and see the love so strong
   in your eyes.
I long to be near you, caressing you, and loving you.

The hours go slowly, and the days seem like an eternity,
   but soon all we hope for and we long for, will become a
   wonderful reality.

Sandra Blok

"My Mighty God"

My precious Yeshua, my mighty God, I love you so
Even as the storm winds blow
And I find myself surrounded by many foes
I will look upon Your face
I will draw from your infinite grace
For who is greater than you
Who is able to perform the miracles that you do
I know that there is none more magnificent, there
is none greater, none more brilliant and true
No! There is no one who will ever love me as You do
Carry me away on the wings of the wind
Breath new life into me and let's begin again
I want to walk with you and only you this very day
May your Holy Spirit always stay
Within the reach of my mind and heart
May your precious love for me never depart
Please use this vessel to show others how to receive
A brand new start for you are mine and I am yours
You are my gracious Lord you met me right where I was at
Saddened and grieved all alone where I quietly sat!

Rebekah S. Geneva

This Love Is Meant For Me And You

I'll be there when you need a friend, I'll be there with you until the end
I'll be there when you need someone, I'll be there until the feeling is done

Though we are so far apart, I can feel it in my heart
The days that we have spent together, will last in my memory forever
Yes it's true, this love is meant for me and you

I'd be the one to tell you something, I'd be the one to let you know
I'd be the one to tell you nothing, I'd be the one to let you go

Though it's hard for me to say, I know there is no way
For us to stay apart, can't you feel it in your heart
Yes it's true, this love is meant for me and you

I'll be there in times of sorrow, I'll be there throughout tomorrow
I'll be there until the end of time, I'll be there when you say you're mine

Though I thought it could not be, the two of us, just you and me
The way love should be from the start, bonding us heart to heart
Yes it's true, this love is meant for me and you

Robert Opat

Death

A cloud has settled all around,
   encompassing the earth.
Resting on the edge of reality.
Cold winds emanate from its boundaries,
   as rivers of blood run to its sides.
What is this strange thing called death
that rips at our hearts and minds.
How often have we felt the Reaper's blade,
   as it slowly passes us by, smooth as silk,
but in the same motion strikes someone down.
What evil force guides his hand
that he may choose who's next to go.
Is it Satan, or merely the deeds of man
come back to haunt his mortal soul.
This cloud, this Angel of Death,
   it's all around us now.
Resting, lying in wait for us.
There is no escape from this creature of the night.
One can only hope that tonight it will pass you by.

Rob Sizer

The Journey

The journey begins with two individual souls.
Each person with their own agenda and goals.

They spent years searching for the perfect one.
Finally finding each other and knowing their heart had been won.

Each very discriminating about the choice of a mate.
When finding each other they knew it was fate.

They have shared joy, laughter, and fears.
Knowing their friendship and love will last through the years.

The decision was made to become man and wife.
Becoming one as they continue through life.

And so the journey begins.
Hand in hand, best friends!

Regina Holton-Muller

The Five Sided Mirror

A five-sided mirror, each side with a different face
Each face with a different voice, each voice wanting something different
All voices talking continuously, there is mass hysteria in my head
Five different puzzle pieces that fit no puzzle
I used to feel somewhat whole, I don't know who "I" is anymore
I am a piece to a puzzle that doesn't fit anywhere
Afraid, scared, panic, fear, differentness
Death means peace, peace from this insanity
This is a bad dream, a nightmare, when will I wake up
No acceptance of the bizarreness and no where to turn
Devastation! Who is it that remembers the trauma? The devastation
I am an erupting volcano, my pieces being scattered in places
I will never know, gone forever
I wish I could have known them
My eyes are but windows, I'm inside looking out
I can see what I have no control over, I don't feel safe anymore
I wonder when this nightmare will end

Sabrina Scribner

Beautiful

B ecause of you, my mind, spirit, body and soul feel beauty.
E very time you call me **beautiful**, I feel like I have won the pageant.
  Crown me! I'll be your queen.
A lways ready to share your throne,
U nder any and all circumstances,
T o the end of time.
I would like to make a promise, an oath, a vow,
F riends, forever, in a royal union, dignified, loyal and proud.
U nmoving, undaunted, under your spell.
L iving a twentieth century fairy tale, right here, right now.

Shawna Collette Haney Evans

Reflections

You and I lead similar lives,
  Dying to live, living to die:
Not to change the face of earth,
  Just to fill our own life's worth.
To do our part and do it well,
  To one day have a tale to tell:
And though our lives be somewhat the same,
  Mine is filled with sun, while yours with rain.

Entwined so close and yet so far,
  Grasping at the nearest star:
To find, to have, to hold, to keep.
  To strengthen us when we grow weak
You never grab! You grasp at what?
  I have gold while you have dust:
And though our lives be somewhat the same,
  My smile is relaxed, while yours is strained.

No comfort, no laughter, not even a peep.
  To find, to have, to hold, to keep.
I'm engulfed by heart, while you the brain;
  While our lives stay still, somewhat the same.

Thomas B. Trotter

How The Spider Came To Be

In a mystical land in a far away place,
dwelled a splendid weaver with fingers of grace.

Although her work was exceptional great,
little did she know her arrogance would influence her fate.

One day she boasted to a women in disguise,
and the wrath of a goddess flamed into her eyes.

She made a bold challenge with a foolish heart,
and suffered as her tapestry was torn apart.

In shame and sorrow she dashed from that place,
and took her last breath as she hung with a sad face.

Athena had mercy and chose to revive her,
so now you see, we know Arachne as the weaving spider.

Shastyn Grills

The Barrel

It was as if I never realized he was alive until I saw him dropping
dropping
dropping.
My heart was pumping faster every second going faster
faster
faster.
It was as he was dropping out of my life.
I just wanted to jump in with him.
After I thought that he was gone far away from me.
I finally realized he's gone.

Perrie Schad

Glass Dancers

When they took to the slippery surface of reality
dreams hovered loosely in the halls
where they were split so each could find room
sounds that hung on the tongue
were pushed out briefly
as bright bodies of shells
the words of children
who poured their forces
into elbows and fingers
that felt like riddles
at the center
spines melted into movement
with birth a turn at their back
how could they simply
faint into the grave
so they danced a dance
that felt like glass

Finding what was brief before them

Phil Algosino

Dreams

Dreams can vary in size.
Dreams are your one and only prize.
When you dream it will come true.
Even though you will think that it won't come through.
A special dream is one not to lose,
But one of the many to choose.
Your dreams are unique,
And you make them complete.
So dream many more dreams and you will become pleased.

Tiffany Murray

Mysterious Answers

Roses are black which means death
Don't turn your back or you'll lay to rest
Out in a grave all cold and dark
Cold like a cave where you'll see no spark of life
Just that of the living dead
So with a knife right through your head
Walk with me through the streets of the living dead

We walk through the streets all cold and wet
We walked to find life but your vision was set
Your vision was set on one single black rose
The rose seemed oddly familiar
Familiar in a way that no one else knows
I try to keep walking but you are still watching
Watching for an answer you know will never come
The thought crossed your mind to just get up and leave
But as you stared into the petals of that single black rose
You found that answer no one else knows
But you also found out it can never be told

Shannon Rozum

"Romancing"

Never stop romancing her, this I tell to thee,
For your love for her should flow like the river, wild!
Furiously passing over any obstacles in your way,
and that is just how it should be, every single day.
For then her love will never shy away.
Never stop romancing her,
Your ravishing beauty,
Your beloved miss,
And then you will forever live,
In complete and total bliss.

Scott J. S. Edgar

Within

Don't look at a figure and be so quick to judge
Don't laugh at a figure that hurts
Don't look at a figure by its color — as we are all one
Look within——look within

A body that's clothed is what we see
We sometimes forget what's within
A heart — a soul — that's filled with love
Look within——look within

There is no tomorrow or yesterday
For the end of the tunnel is here today
We can't say "we should have done it yesterday"
As yesterday is gone and we only have today
See it today — within — within

Sylvia Ishizaka

Inside

Don't deny the feelings that are coming from inside.
Don't deny them spirit, don't deny them pride.

The pain may seem unbearable, the light may seem so dim.
But look into your heart and soul, the answer is within.

And when you're feeling discouraged, and in your time of need,
Look within yourself for the power to succeed.

If you want something bad enough, your heart won't let it go.
And if it's meant to be, then your heart will let you know.

When you get those feelings that are coming from inside,
Give them all your spirit, give them all your pride.

And trust in knowing that your heart will guide you through the way.
Meant to be or not, never lock your dreams away.

Shannon Smith

Room By The Sea

I have a room by the sea.
Don't ask me why. I guess it was to be.
I needed a place to help me feel free,
A place I could think, a place to be ME.

Somewhere to relax and hide from the world.
There's too much to take, then we're caught in a swirl.

One has to escape, once in awhile
To stop, reflect and perhaps play like a child.

So to really feel free,
Once in awhile, we need a "Room by the sea."

Bunny S. McLean

"Does Anybody Care"

Does anybody care... If I can't see the sun, does it shine my way?
Does anybody care... No surroundings, my head full of heavy
  burdens. No place to lay.
Does anybody care... When a heart beats no more. Due to
ignorance,
  and unwilled fear.
Does anybody care... That my sorrows are so deep, only the rain
  and thunder can represent my tears.
Does anybody care... That my world is really cruel.
Does anybody care... About this knot that curls in me, (known as
  pain) from going days without no food.
Does anybody care... Leftover drinks, uneaten foods are my meals.
Does anybody care... The pressured eyes of souls on me, the only
  remorse I feel.
Does anybody care... So lonely, without a overseer, very cold in
  this dark and heartless night.
Does anybody care... Tell me! Really care about my life.
If it's really just the caring... Then I don't think anybody does.

Veronica Hatcher

Faces

When you look at their flat faces,
do you see the beauty of their graces?
Or instead when gazing into their almond eyes,
do you feel compelled to exorcise?

Do you believe their knowledge of life and love,
emits effervescent light like that of a dove?
Do you recognize the purity of their hearts and souls?
Or do you see their fate strewn with pigeon-holes?

Do you believe they are true perfection,
as transcended as Emily Dickinson?
Can you comprehend, we are greatly unenvolved
and our eternal conflicts remain unresolved?

Why do we so boldly insist they conform,
when our hearts, souls and minds require reform?
Can you see them from their heightened perspective?
They are progressive; and us, we are oppressive.

Victoria Kaloss

Mothers Questions

What happens when your family is grown and gone?
Do you have time to think of the great beyond?
Oh no! You think to yourself,
I cannot be put upon a shelf.

So you take life with the biggest grin
and start out to do it over again.

This one, without babies and dirty hands
Giving to life one of its greatest fans.

Your life you may feel is finished,
But to your kids you will never be diminished.

Virgie Burchfield

What Is Reality?

What is reality?
Do you face reality?
Do you escape from reality?
Or, do you create your own reality?

Your own reality can be as simple
or as complex as you want.
Your own reality can place you in the center.
Your own reality can even blow bubbles in your face.

But do you always want to live in your own reality?
What if others' realities conflict?
You'll have to adapt to theirs.

Or, see a reality as it is.

Rebecca Barton

Father

Father can you teach me to walk
Father can you teach me to talk
Father can you teach me to tie my shoes
Father can you teach me not to abuse
Father can you teach me to fly a kite
Father can you teach me to ride a bike
Father can you teach me to be strong and wise
Father can you teach me what you know of life
Father can you teach me to be faithful
Father can you teach me how to raise a son
Father can you do these things I ask if so...
Why weren't they done?

Tiffen B. Pickering

Do You Whisper?

Do you whisper in the night, to the lover laying next to you?
Do you ever hold her tight, and try to see her through?

When the raindrops turn to tears,
do you try to comfort her fears?
- And chase away the darkness,
with the turning of the years?

Secrets buried with a solid notion, that you must have created -
but when her cries turn to screams,
Do you keep her satiated?

Demons cast a backwards glance, at the host that they once knew.
But after time buries the loss, does she get closer to you?

Do you whisper in the dark,
about a time you once remembered -
trying to make her see the light,
or why her soul's dismembered?

For all the confusion and honest pain,
that she endures is real.
So keep her softly close to you,
and tell her how you feel.

Renee Hartman

Enlightenment

Possessions, possess me not!
Do not bind me...
Let me go empty handed
When in my turn to go
Up to the Almighty.

Just let me take along
The scent and colors of the flowers
The songs of birds, the smile of children,
The melancholic memories of dusk,
The lights of a sunrise.

The beauty of a clear stream cascading
From a mountain, the colours of October leaves,
The falling of the rain on tin roof.
The shining of the stars on a dark night...
The joy of old friendships...
My love for life, for all mankind.
And please, give me no promises
But those of plowed fields and ripe vineyards!

Emilia Cordova de Sicard

Such Is Life

Mem'rable moments whirl carousel like
Distorted by motion and time.
Droplets of pain from spiritless eyes
Release all the mis'ry that's mine.

Endless it seems is this font with its dreams
Springing boundless from fragmented heart.
Remembrances mine evolvements of time
Events without end without start.

Humbled by woe beaten down by the foe
Eyes upward in quiet lament.
Heavily burdened I heavenly cry
In answer, destiny's silent.

Mem'rable moments far echoes of yore
Cherished yet hurtful are rife.
Tears come and go as memories flow
As it was, so it is, such is life.

C. Edwin Gray

Beyond The Cries Of Life

With love's splendor, hope blooms farther anew,
  dimmed by man's flattering lips and boastful tongue undue.
Earnestly cherished winsome and tender moments shared in place,
  amidst afflictions, heartaches, and disgrace.
Loving more dearly through thick and thin,
  along life's struggles that never seem to slim.
Love leaves no mar of doubt, deceit, and distrust,
  through all the years, life's ups and downs entrust.
Moving onwards to make life's very best,
  the paths of the seas we swim to quiet rest.
Of abundant humility of heart and serenity of treats,
  clothed with gladness and mantled with good feats.
Rock of refuge is Him, the hope and the light,
  the torrents of lose heart and desolation shall turn bright.
Ever rescuing and raising the spirit of compassion,
  overwhelmed by unending love and devotion.

Remedios H. Badiang

Light Beyond The Mountain

Search the Light beyond the Mountain
  Diligence, bravely beyond tall tales.
    Seeker surfaces on the rim for a faithful abode
    Longing for a beauty and magnificent glow
      of the Light beyond the Mountain; Light
      of solid hues and enchanting features
        Honestly displayed
Stretching into the skies like arms outreached
  The Light as a figure of the Lamb so True
    The Lamb Jesus Christ as a Smiling View.
      The Light so Bold beyond the Mountain near
        With songs of Salvation heard from afar,
        The Bright and Morning Star.
Search the Light which sprays beyond the Mountain.
  Search the Light which soars beyond the Mountain.
    And all be heard!

  Praise to the Lamb of Hosts!
  Salvation I to He!

Vaughn Brent Smith

Learn To Mend

Today he's small and fragile, his hands can hold no weight.
Destined for the heavens, to open up their gate.
His life has been so lonely, his fears have caused him pain.
The webs have been so tangled, we question if he's sane.
His words are quick forgotten, his sentences half done.
Asleep before his finish, his fight he has not won.
So many promises broken, too many lies untold
Too many tears have fallen, no time left to be bold
His mind has grown so lonely, the pain too much to bare.
With them he'll show no mercy, he has no time to care.
Fold your arms upon your chest, so tired you can't see.
It's time to rest, just let it go, with God is where you'll be.
To live a life eternal, no sickness shall you grieve.
The weight has lifted, stand up tall, in truth you must believe.
Our love for you we cherish, never to forget
One time we were a family, and you our sturdy net.
Up there you will be safer, protected from the fight
And as we look into the stars, our prayers will fill the night.
Someday we'll be together, a family once again
Then maybe we can all forget, with God we'll learn to mend.

Tammy Lee Bradley

Lost In Early July

Lost in early July; my soul confused;
Deep in worries, lonely thoughts bring emptiness;
No path to comfort; once whole Heart, abused;
Need to run, be free, escape loneliness.

Reaching for dreams, no trails that lead to hope;
Now is a trap; now shows darkness always.
Cries for refreshing relief ask to cope.
Falling Heart, left broken, feels sunless days.

Silent prayers, whispers for strength to get through.
Cries in my wintered world left unheard.
Shivering for a warm touch; love from you;
Close my eyes, hold us close; Heart beats the words.

Found in August; my prayers heard from above.
Hope brought you, Sweetness; Heart relieved with love.

Wendy Waddell

Little Boy Of Mine

How peaceful you look, little boy of mine
Deep in sleep, unaware of my stare
So very secure, without much of a care
You know you are safe, little boy of mine.

How sweetly you smile, little boy of mine
Are you dreaming? Is it a sweet dream?
Do angels talk to you? (Or maybe they sing.)
You know you are watched over, little boy of mine

How sweetly you sigh, little boy of mine
Still fast asleep, you move ever so slightly
As I tough your beautiful face, just lightly
You know you are wanted, little boy of mine.

How sweetly you smile, little boy of mine
With your arms outstretched, and your eyes open wide
Waiting to be cuddled, (your love you don't hide)
You know you are loved, little boy of mine

Tabatha Rodriguez

Remember Us

As much as it hurts, wipe the tears we've wept.
Deep in our hearts ADELIA's kept.
Safe from the world of man made pain.
The wisdom of all, to what remains.
what has been and will be, our beloved shall be.
Who has been and will be family.
Overseeing all we say and do.
We only want to say we love you.
Tears are wiped but still fall from the eyes.
That only wanted to say goodbye.
But there's no goodbye, 'cause we'll see you soon.
Just remember us, when we enter the room.

Tramell L. Collins

Early Autumn

    The kiss of autumn came as quietly as early sleep. One day it was summer, then a soft breeze began to blow ever so lightly. A few gray clouds appeared and a kitten soft mist began to fall. Summer had departed, autumn was born. It was harvest time.

    I looked upon the land pleased and happy inside at what I saw. Man's labors had born so many rewards. I looked into the heavens. The huge white billowing clouds sailed peacefully from horizon to horizon. I felt the cool breeze upon my face and I know there is a God and today, in this place, He is smiling.

A. Ford

The New Man

I am the new man
Dark as the moon that glows beneath the stars.
I am the new source of life,
Shining like the gleam of new gold bars.
I am the future for what life may become.
I am the ultimate, the father and the son.
I am the new man with a great purpose in life,
No values, no lust, no material things I strive.
I am the new man.
I am black and I am African.

Steven James Ward

Memory

I walked by the ocean, and the high-flung spray
Dampened my cheeks and on my lips lay.
I stood on a mountain, between earth and sky
And the wind caught my breath as it went sweeping by.
I lay in a meadow and watched the clouds pass —
Shadows gliding darkly over sunny grass.

Or was it tears by the ocean, and not the blown spray —
Laughter on the mountain that took my breath away?
And in the meadow was it memory, drifting past an inner eye,
Shadows of the mind, like clouds in the sky?

Ruth Allion Kelley

Shadowed Brilliance

Twenty years ago I first saw his smiling face amidst a shadowed
Crowd...
To this day, our closeness and friendship have made me
Very proud.
For, to know this wonderful person whose vision will
Always remain with me...
Is to love for showing and teaching me everything
That life could be...

Sally Daly Tucker

Christmas Morning

A subtle breeze winds through the trees
Crisp is the air, frost clings to leaves
Stars fade to bring a sky so clear
Night's magic past brings Christmas here

Throughout the night, children can't sleep
Christmas joy is theirs to keep
Night dreams come true, the magic kind
Feelings to last their whole lifetime

Then that voice so long to hear:
"Time to get up, it's time for cheer"
As little feet now hit the floor
for the tree they run, their waits no more

Young eyes stare wide, they have it all
The magic gift, for those so small
Night's magic pst, brought Christmas here
And children's joy has brought the cheer

Night dreams come true, the magic kind
To be a child, at Christmas time
Forever young, I'll always be
On Christmas morn, next to the tree...

Stephen Edward Molcsan

Untitled

Summer is the season of hills
covered in green velvet, and
watermelon juice dripping from your chin, and
it's the season of lying in the clover
looking at the lethargic clouds
dreaming of what creature
the lacy mass looks like.

Summer is the season of breeze
and sitting in the shade of an oak, and
drinking lemonade so cold that
it gives you an ice cream-headache.

It's the season of swinging
in a hammock while dragging your feet
in the cool dirt, wondering why
nature allows winter to creep in.
   Sally Reed

Change

It rides upon the winds ever out of reach.
Controlled, planned, unforeseen, but never forsaken.
Like the tide that crashes blindly at the rocks.
It's timeless and unyielding.
I've seen it in life, waiting for death bringing madness then peace.
Some hope for it, others despise it neither can stop it.
I feel it there in the back of my mind, yet I know not what it brings.
Seasons never come but within it winter lies.
Nothing and yet everything begins or ends at its horizon.
Surely, you must feel it coming are you ready look out!
There it goes, everything does and yet nothing.
Have I come full circle or has everything remained the same.
I thought and was wrong, searched for understanding and found none.
Listen for it rides upon the winds always there all around,
Like the sign of the times.
I have you have they have, we all have and will again and again.
If you are she, many times might your mind, it's your nature.
Anything and nothing brings the winds.
I welcome it for without them we will have no hope and all will be lost.
   Royce L. Lathrop

An Angel By Thy Side

   An angel is by thy side. There he will always be; to
comfort, encourage and strengthen Thee. So, as you travel down
those lonely roads, I say be not afraid and be of good cheer for
the Angel is there by Thy side. So go, go, I say and leave it
all to me. For I've sent one of my Angels to help protect Thee.
To see you through your valleys and to see you over your
mountaintops.

   In the past, I've tried speaking with you, to let you know
of my Angel I've sent to be with you and at that time you would
question me, saying, "No this can't be GOD'S choice, an Angel
sent for me by the sound of his voice?" But now the time has
come for you to heed and listen to the gentle voice inside your
head. Child I say, Listen, Listen, Listen, for I've sent this
Angel to help watch over you.
   Sharon Griffin Burke

Prayer For Leaders

Lord, please give them the power to make command decisions best
   suitable for the people they lead.
Help them to act as responsible representatives of their congregation.
Give them the power to guide their people out of any darkness that may
   overcome them.
Please give them the sensibility many leaders have held before.
To you, Holy Lord, I humbly request that you give them the compassion
   needed to judge their followers.
Amen
   L. J. Milone III

Animal Logic

Andrea sat in front of me, alphabetically placed,
collecting pencil shavings for a pretend mouse
she kept in her desk and fed at lunch.
We were eight — teeth not fully in,
limbs too long for our bodies.
Every Thursday we won the spelling bee,
walked the path back to her house,
went by way of the basement to avoid her father,
with his constant drooling grin from tumbler
after tumbler of gin. We'd watch her sister
pull some boy to her new breasts and kiss him,
and when her older brother and his friends
wanted to see us swim naked in their pool,
we'd go to the kitchen in a rush, hear her deaf mother half-speak,
half-sign to the construction workers who seemed always there,
   rebuilding something.
We'd slide into the bottom of an unused refrigerator,
sip sweet soda and whisper poems from even younger childhood.
In June of that year we were promoted to our own reading group.
We read a story about a fox so fantastic, he disguised himself,
slipped into another animal's skin and never came out.
   Pamela Cohn

December

Beautiful snowflakes falling from the sky.
Cold winter winds blow them high
Ice and sleet are all around.
Just look at the snowmen all wearing their crowns.
December, December the best time of the year.
Wonderful December will soon be here.
   Sarah Shay

Fall

BANG hammer   construction
CLANGing
against the breeze
that carries Autumn's leaves
      the dust from a workman's shoes
      a young woman's perfume

   that carries infants away to the time before Time

      And they GIGGLE   And they LAUGH
      shaking comet filled RATTLES
      secure in their knowing
      the point is pointless
      in regretting what's past
   d j ray

Memorial Day Tribute

General John A. Logan in the year of 1868,
Civil War Vet's graves he did decorate
Today the stars and stripes so gently waves
also flowers on the graves.
As solemnly we stand with heads bowed low
And humbly pray, we will show
To the loved ones laid to rest here and beyond
The Heavenly Father has called them, home.
He placed in our hands the unfinished tasks
Our Divine Savior, He does ask.
To consecrate, uphold and defend
Remember death is not the end.
Now follow our footsteps and pass along
A moment to pay tribute by word and by song.
Aim the guns forever high
Fire them loudly towards the sky....
Taps from afar can be heard -
Our flag so gently unfurled.
   Ruth M. Edwardson

God's Grace

Open my eyes Lord, that I may see,
 Cast away the demons, that pressures me.
Open my ears Lord, that I may hear,
 So that I may keep your word always near.

Open my mind Lord, so I can understand,
 The plan of salvation, from the son of Man.
Open my arms Lord, so that I may hold,
 To keep someone warm, so they won't get cold.

Open me up Lord, so that I may share,
 To show people I do love them, and I care.
Open the door Lord, for those to get in,
 So they may confess of their sin.

Open my feelings Lord, so people can see,
 What your loving grace, has done for me.
Let the doors of your love, always be open wide,
 So in their heart's Lord, you can reside.

Thank you God, for your beloved son,
 What power of giving, you have done.
If happiness you seek on this very day,
 Open yourself to Jesus, the truth and the way.
   Ronald A. Matrisch Sr.

Changing Places

Once a walking-talking tree
Came up and said to me,
"Would you like to trade places with me?"
"Sure" I said, "I'll trade places with you,
But you've got to do what I tell you to.
I live in that house down the street;
Don't be surprised when my mother you meet.
You'll usually have to do the dishes, sweep the floor,
And other boring chores."
The tree said, "I don't want to change places
Any more.
It's fun just standing here, just watching
The eagles soar."
I said, "That's just fine with me,
I'm happy with who I be."
So we said good-bye and walked away,
Willing to talk another day
Maybe I'll trade in a century,
But for now, I'm happy being me.
   Stormy Richardson

Untitled

   Your eyes, peering into mine, the wind
calms to a slow cool breeze, the rain turns
to a mist, that cools our bodies, cools the heat
when we touch. Your lips, full of colors, showing
signs of luscious taste. When we kiss, the oceans
begin to roar. Your body, more beautiful than
a summer sunset on the Rockies, yearning
to be caressed.
   My head spins when I think of these
things. My body aching to be next to yours;
to feel the silky smoothness of your skin, to feel
your body against mine. First to tremble in
my arms, then to feel the calmness of your
temple, hearing only our hearts beat at a
rhythmic pace.
   Our love, enough to diminish all
hatred, and strong enough to last an eternity.
We'll fill the earth with colour, fill the
universe with a rainbow of love. Our hearts,
forever beating as one.
   Steven D. Brown

Oh How I Wish

In a moment's thought, I'm swept away
 by visions of you that fill my day
At night is when I touch your face the only place we can embrace
I bring your hands up to my lips
 where I may plant a soft, tender kiss
It was love at first sight in my heart we belong
 it's there in my heart I feel it so strong
Call it fate or destiny whatever it is we were meant to be
Like a nursery rhyme you say at night
 about a star so shiny and bright
I wish I may I wish I might
 Oh how I wish we could last through daylight
The night has come and the night has gone pretty soon it will be dawn
Will you be there in the morning
 after my alarm clock blares out its warning
Will you be there when I rise when I finally have to open my eyes
Alone I wake with thoughts of you
 another nights wish that didn't come true
A heavy sigh to start my day
 I'll see you tonight where again I'll pray.
   Steven Fischer

The Creator's Loving Trick

Who isn't smitten
By a baby, puppy or a kitten?

Who doesn't smile?
Who isn't beguiled?

   This must be God's way
   So we invite them to stay!

When they are held dearly
Who can think clearly

Of teenagers, cars and hats!
Of a pup grown up, and cats!

   But God knows what He is doing
   Even if it is our undoing!

Who isn't smitten
By a baby, puppy or a kitten?
   Robert Keenan

My Best Friend Is Dead To Me

I still remember him, I still know his name
But without him, nothing is the same
I didn't see him before I left my old home
I never said good-bye, I felt him alone

I remember all the times we spent together
But shattered and scattered in my mind
I won't remember them forever
Laughing and playing I still remember the silly things he said
But now I'll never see him again
As if he were dead

I wish I could go back in time
To meet him again
To change a penny to a dime
I told him, "I'll call you when I reach my new home"
I told him, "I'll write you, I won't leave you alone"
But I lost his number, I lost his address
He probably thinks I forgot him, I feel so depressed

I'll always remember what he said
"We're best friends to the end....."
But to me, he is dead.
   Peter A. O'Connell

Time

"Time heals all things," my Mother used to say,
But when a heart is broken, the pain doesn't go away.

The sadness, hurt and sorrow somehow seem to stay,
Hidden under the surface waiting to display,
The feelings that we try to hide from people day to day.

But when a heart is happy, the healing will begin,
The days are not as long, and you realize you might win.

The sadness slowly drifts away, the hurt begins to fade,
The sorrow is replaced with peace, great progress has been made.

So if you'll "heed these words," as Mother used to say,
Sadness, hurt and sorrow have now given way,

To a heart that's happy filled with hope, and a brighter future brings,
If we'll just believe in, "Time heals all things."
Ruth E. Drowne

Young Tornado

Distance through the wind he will take
but to the valley he will break
with his shape it is evermore from the sea to upon
the shore round and round he goes creating a path that know
one knows but only he the one so bright the one with out fear
or fright so with all his might he reaches for the sky till
it is night but wait to a surprise someone stands on a hill
nearby watching with joy not fright who is this person who
stands with no fear or fright watching someone so mighty then
they who is it is but one person it is a mother watching as her
son rolled slowly in the sand below.
Terry R. Pennington Jr.

Looking Into A Dream

Do you have a dream? It could come true!
But to make it happen is all up to you.
It could be reality, so does it seem,
Tomorrow reality, but today just a dream.

You could be wealthy, rich, a star!
But dreams in your head could seem so very far.
You could be an astronaut, and fly to the moon!
But you think, "Me be a space man? You must be a loon!"

You could be the President of the U.S. of A.
If you believe in your dreams it could happen any day.
You could be a doctor and help those who are sick,
But you think, "Boy, this guy is really off his stick!"

But you could really be one, this is no lie.
You could really be one, but it is you who must try.
It could be reality, so does it seem,
Tomorrow reality, but today just a dream.
J. C. Ballard

Simply Stripes

Instead of those stripes, if a zebra wore dots,
Do you think he'd go crazy looking at spots?

If given a choice, would a zebra wear plaid?
If he matched at the seam, he'd really look rad!

If a zebra took off his black and white hide,
Do you think he'd discover a rainbow inside?

Well, a zebra is glad he has what he has.
He's got black and white stripes: such basic pizzazz!
Terri R. Wilson

My Mystery

There is me, and there is you
But there is nothing for us to do.
You tell me that you see the sunset in my eyes
But that is not true, so I tell you that they're lies.
Then you wonder how come I don't believe you
Cause nothing you've told me has ever been true.
I've always believed you'd be there for me
But when I was blind, it was you I could not see.

Now I've gone to a place I'd only dreamt of going
One night you invited me there—the danger unknowing.
It was to be for only a short time
Now the memory of you is locked into my mind.
At night I wonder if the feelings will ever end
Or is it that now you're my lover, and no longer my friend?

The doors of time have locked us up in a dream
Wishing of being only where we cannot be.
There is no way to prove that this is love
Since loving you was only something I've dreamed of.
How am I to believe if you're really thinking of me
If it's true, then we are, equal partners in a mystery.
Stacey Geneczko

Autumn

Autumn is my favorite time,
but only if I know it rhymes.
The leaves are brown not blue or green
and I hope my sister is not mean.

Autumn makes me think of Halloween,
the witches and ghost are so very mean.
I like pumpkins and black cats;
jack-o-lanterns and crazy bats.

Autumn makes me think of Thanksgiving,
and the pilgrims who had hard living.
The Thanksgiving meals are so very big,
and my favorite trees look just like twigs.

The autumn air can grow so cold,
and the harvest moon that's bright and gold
The cornstalks stand so straight,
and the pumpkin pie is on my plate.

Autumn is my favorite time!
Rebecca J. Grewe

November

The days have grown shorter - the nights cool and long.
But old Mother Nature never goes wrong.
Now Indian Summer with colors to spare
Holds wondrous beauties for all to share.

The wild geese flying over with their shrill cry
Are in perfect formation up in the gray sky.
They seem to be carrying summer away
And tell us that winter is coming to stay.

The leaves are a riot of red and gold
Silently falling the grass to enfold.
The trees seem to spread their branches so bare
Standing as sentinels, weary with care.

The nuts are falling with a thumping sound
Among the leaves upon the ground.
Golden pumpkins are gathered and stored away
The corn is harvested and so is the hay.

Now Thanksgiving comes - that glorious day
When the pilgrims gave thanks in their most humble way
Let us, too, give thanks in earnest prayer
To our Great Creator for his watchful care.
Jimmie Ruth Cohen

"Ode To An Unborn Child"

Today we celebrate the Baby Jesus' birth.
But, now you're just an embryo.
You're with us in our thoughts today,
We're watching and waiting the weeks away.
So just be patient little one and we will too
For soon you'll be a part of us and we a part of you.
You'll come to us as Jesus did,
Your birth will be a special day.
The love and joy that you will bring
Will not compare with anything,
You don't know now just what's in store
But God will open wide the door.
So now we await your arrival dear;
We know that time is drawing near,
You'll soon be here with us on earth
With each passing year you too will celebrate His Birth.
   Phyllis J. Rider

Values

It used to be, a penny bought more than a penny's worth;
But now it cost more than that just to make it.
It used to be, a pregnancy was carried through to birth;
But now some women let their doctors "take" it.

It used to be, we earned the salary our bosses paid us;
But now it all depends on who we are not what we do.
It used to be, the innocence of childhood lasted longer;
But now our children know much more than we would like them to.

It used to be, you did the crime, you did time in prison;
But now we set the guilty free, through courts of indecision.
It used to be, that marriage meant you joined as one forever;
But now it only lasts as long as there's no "stormy weather".

It used to be, that we held dear, our faith in GOD above;
But now we're not allowed to pray at schooltime anymore.
It used to be, that we believed in words like trust and love;
But now they don't appear to mean as much as one before.

What happened to the values that our grandparents possessed?
Where did we so far astray to let our morals waste away?
We've let our values slip into decay and such unrest;
That we will have to pay a price, in souls, come judgement day.
   Stephen L. Birks

War

Another argument has started in the world
but nothing is resolved unless there is a fight
A fight for honor and peace
A fight for their country and a fight for victory
Men in black and white carrying pride with them
Guns, swords, and attitudes
An argument starts and they cannot resolve the problem
So they die for just a problem, just a word
Risking their own lives and leaving loved ones behind them
Cemeteries scheduled for over ten thousand deaths
Deaths of many nationalities and religions
Deaths of people who just had a problem
People who just said a word
An unnecessary matter called war
Many deaths caused from this matter
To stop it, you have to make it's enemy larger and stronger
Everybody knows what War's enemy is .... PEACE
   Ted Gomez

"An Angel Of My Own"

I'll cover you with all the shadow
  but not until your time will I show you the light.

I'll cover you with all the glory
  but not all the fright.

I'll cover you with all the power,
  but not all the weakness.

Who would give all of this so freely to me?

You silly, can't you see,
  its my guardian angel that GOD
  has sent to walk with me.

This is the greatest gift from GOD,
  for this only means you have been
  Blessed by thee!
   Sharee Raphael Schnoebelen

The Best Of The Assortment

All mothers come in different shapes and sizes
But none can compare to the one I call minezes,
Helping when she can and wherever she may
Mother always comes to save the day.
You've been around a little while,
And I think you're the best, this side of the Nile.
These words can't begin to explain
The love that I feel for my great dame.
She's a wonderful Mother, so that you see,
Mother, Dear, you're the best that can be.
   Toby L. Houtz

Haven '92

Not so much the scent of smoke,
But more, the pungent near-taste of having been burned
Marks the somber bouquet that attends a frail breeze
Lifting lightly now the delicate curtain that alone separates me
From an anguished, bleeding city.

Mere days earlier
Tree trimmers tidied our quiet street
Bright sunlight dappled the new leaves
Cascading into gutters
Out of which crouching guardsmen now sprout
Their grotesque camouflage ironically failing them,
Identifying them in the leaves absence.
They smoke in watchful protectiveness
Of our quiet street, our lucky store,
Spared by looters
But plundered by marauding neighbors
Whose bewildered faces and heavy footfalls
Echo a panic that can only find comfort
In the embrace of the last roll of toilet paper,
The last can of tuna.
   Steven Fowler

It's Him

It's him,
I can feel his presence.
Like a silent alarm that only my ears can depict.
Anxiously looking and extremely alert, I look through the crowd;
hoping to see his face.
I see him, there he is.
One of a thousand, but everyone seems to fade, till I can see only him.
   Sarah Champine

One Dream At A Time

Everyone knows to LIVE one day at a time,
But living with you, every day is a dream come true,
And LIFE was never so fine.

One day and one dream at a time.
No worries about what tomorrow may bring,
LIVE to the fullest each moment sublime,
Knowing full well death has no sting.

HAPPINESS is only a state of mind,
We find it not thru fortune and fame,
But rather thru following our dreams, one dream at a time,
And finding this is "The Name of the Game."

Always set your dreams as high as you can.
Then "hitch your wagon to a star."
Keep your eyes on HIM not man,
And HE will guide you from afar.

LIVE one day and one dream at a time.
William Forrester O'Brien Sr.

"The Daughters Of Friends That Live Down The Street"

I know it sounds like an old cliche',
but it seems like just the other day,
they ran around in diapers and tiny bare feet,
the daughters of friends that live down the street.

To see them today it's hard to recall,
they ever were babies, they look grown after all,
but they haven't quite got there, but soon they will be,
turned loose on this town for everyone to see.

What a sight this release will surely cause,
boys hearts will tremble and make them pause,
The evident beauty, the style and grace,
It's easy to see by one look at their face.

But there's a deeper glow seen only by some,
the friends and family, maybe a special someone,
the manners and respect so important to all,
should make their parents, stand proud and tall.

Know this as truth, my dearest of friends,
you've done a great job from beginning to ends;
It's a privilege to know you, a real special treat,
my friends and their daughters that live down the street
Ronnie C. Mayes

"Is Love Blind?"

Some people say that true love is blind.
But, I think that they are most unkind!
With love's eyes I can more clearly see,
What's deep inside the one so dear to me!

The barriers are down and I've looked inside,
Seen what to others my loved one may hide.
You didn't see the many tears he shed,
As he sat long hours at his mother's death bed...

Nor seen him take the hand of his little child,
And help her into bed; to read quite awhile.
These things don't happen just occasionally,
But they happen more often in front of me.

You can ridicule me for having this love,
But, I know it comes from heaven above!
I wish I could share it with you someday...
To help you have more happiness along your way.

No! Love is not blind, I think love has 20/20!
When we look for good, we can see plenty.
It's those who don't care who are really blind,
They look for things of a much different kind.
F. Daphne Phillips

What You've Done To Me

The abusive words you've said to me have really made me cry
But I didn't think it'd matter so I shrugged it off and sighed
When you said it to my face, I thought how could you friend
Or so that is what I thought "Friends forever 'Till the End"
Both of you had teamed up, both of you had said, "I do not
like you anymore, you are not my friend."
I thought you would be joking
I thought it's make believe
'Till I had run into you I knew I was deceived
I thought how could you
How could you be my friends
I thought we'd stay together, best friends were 'till the end
But now I can control it, I'm not hurt anymore
'Cause the past is the past and that was way before
I have found some better friends who do not treat me bad
They always make me happy, they never make me sad
They treat me like a real friend, they're there through thick and thin
That is what a real friend does and you're not one of them.
Sheena Paguia

What Goes Around

What goes around, comes around, is saying we all know
but, did you ever stop to think, just how the concept goes.
Perhaps, when we were younger, we were spiteful, mean or cruel
to an unsuspecting person, at home, or work, or school.
Then when our turn comes around, to endure a crushing blow,
we're aghast, forgot the past, undeserving, don't you know!
So, if you have a feeling, a vengeful, binge attack,
I'd caution that endeavor, cause, someday, you'll get it back.
Susan Ingram

Devil's Wind

The wind blew strong, though not for long
but destruction it hath wrought;
turning whitecapped swells into Devil's tails
smashing ships upon the rocks.

Cursed wind why so angry
casting sailors in the sea?
Your howls so cold and chilling
causing pain and misery.

Damn you to a Devil's end,
what caused your destructive spree?
For ships have been your loyal friend
and sailors your company.

Now wander 'round the earth alone
no place to hide your head;
for you have lost your only friend
and turned blues seas to red.

Condemn you to the depths below
no solace in your tomb.
Seeds of destruction no longer sow,
return you to the Devil's womb.
William Henry Jones

Sparrow

A sparrow flies on tiny wings
Can see so many heavenly things.
To and fro to build a nest
So she and he can settle and rest.
And soon will come their offspring
To celebrate they chirp and sing.
Into the world they have bring
They miracle of life, another song to be sung.
William A. Rhyan

At Work Call

We gather today to work like before,
but among the sounds, the people I see
something is different
but what is missing?
    The shriek of the saw has not lost its voice.
The hammer pounds further, the drill still hums...
Every tool I have heard continues to speak,
but my ears still insist
a sound is missing.
    So I glance at the faces silent at work
while others are smiling, laughing, or talking.
"Everyone is accounted for,"
I keep thinking.
Nevertheless,
a voice is missing.
    The question lingers and toys with my mind.
Still wondering, and not answering,
all sounds become one
forever echoing,
"Someone is missing..."

Tamara DeAnn Yolo

Brothers And Sisters

Why is it to be you can't walk the streets?
Brothers killing brothers every time they meet
Sisters on their back to buy that pack
Babies on I.V's because Mother's got HIV

What's wrong with us are we blind?
This disease is killing our own kind
We don't have to let this problem be
Let's join together as a unity

Black, white, Vietnamese Puerto Rican if you please
It doesn't even matter what race or creed

What will our children say as they get older
No one ever showed us as how to be a soldier
Teach our children that's coming up today
that education is the only way

Brothers and Sisters the time is at hand
Do it now make that stand!!!!!

Sondra R. Santos

Love The Little Children

Little children eyes, some blue some brown, some black.
Bright shining, as the stars up in the sky.

Little children ears are ready to hear, all that is
being told to them.
Little children imagination is superb, they tell all
Thoughts all secrets, in their little minds.
Little children fold their little hands in prayer,
And tell the Lord their needs and wishes too.
These little children, how I love them so.
My little friends there little children, that I teach.
Little children, they never change, they never fret.
Little children always smile, and always laugh with,
with everyone.
Little children never tire, they are so full of energy.
Little children are a blessing in my life.
Little children I love you so.

Josie G. Nodal

Light

Light? Which light to follow?
Bright and dark tomorrow.
Paths are not justified... Paths will be crucified.
Was there light? Show me.
Chills... frozen memories slowly tick away.
Old, wrinkled pages are in the wind... blowing around.
Ferociousness, forgetfulness, forgiveness...my emotions.
Light? Where? I see nothing.
Furry afterwards, after thoughts...away with them!
On one side, yes. On one side, no.
Which way to go? Which way to go?
Which path to follow? What light?
Numb, dumb, spinning...my inner self I'm throwing.
Where is the war? Fight!
Shrinking...growing...exploding...
Falling a step up to reach you...
Falling a step down to avoid you...
Light? Which light to follow?
Who cares if there's tomorrow?

Sal Licata

Leaves On One Green Bough (Phyllis: "One Green Bough")

Truth forces me to own that I have seen
Blue eyes that once my Phyllis's outshone.
There have been girls more beautiful of mien,
But them and all their tribe I've now outgrown.
There once was one whose charming Southern speech
Could momentarily rescind my strength of will;
And there was one who'd "gladly learn and teach" —
But when I taught, the course was all uphill.
I thought Adele was pretty, I admit,
And Peggy was "divinely tall and fair."
Some lissome were, and others had some wit;
Both Gods and men were awed by Helen's hair.
But Phyllis shines alone in these poor lines,
For she the best these qualities combines.

Ted Johnson

Sailor Jack

Sailor Jack was a man of the sea,
  Big as any man would want to be,
Narrow of hips and shoulders wide as a door,
  With little effort he'd drop men to the floor.

Sailor Jack is a myth that was born,
  By a cabin boy sailing round the horn,
A lad in his teens and a yearning to go,
  Whenever the four winds might blow.

Sailor Jack was this cabin boys name,
  One taste of the sea and there he'd remain,
He grew to a man and learned to trim sail,
  He fought rough seas and many a gale.

Sailor Jack fought his way to the top,
  Once he started he could not be stopped,
Soon he was Captain of his ship,
  A fair minded man that wanted no lip.

Sailor Jack has now retired from the sea,
  And tells the small boys what they could be,
He tells of the sunsets, storms and the rides,
  But goes away with the outgoing tide.

Ray E. Payne

Hourglass

Deny me air or sun or song
Before subjecting this soul
To an instant spent in absence of her.
All these and more is she is these eyes;
So infinitely much more.
For as certainly as a rose
Denied the caress of the light of day will not grow,
So would this body grow cold and withered without her near.
See her, fire and water,
And know the weightlessness of inspiration.
See her, velvet and diamonds,
And know sincerest devotion.
Just like childhood evenings
Chasing fireflies under summer moons
Are our ecstasies over too soon.
They are satin, the days we share;
Each of them another ray of gold,
Lancing the clouds that follow me;
Another jewel to a treasury
Whose worth devalues the riches of any emperor.
   Anthony Beal

Blond Fields

Blond fields stretch and wave
beckoning these leaden feet
to spring unleashed
to grab their feathery fingers
and sway among their sunny trails
falling into golden arms
I feel the pulse of warm earth
as flesh and clay reunite
home content
nestling deep within this untamed heart
where I can walk unclothed and know
that though the grass may not be often green
and barren trees yearn quietly
Its my field to plough
my weeds to battle
my hands firmly grasp the work they were created for
and sweat pour down to quench my thirst
sleep comes sweet from a task well done
and your smile is all I need
returning from the fields
   Sherry Sturges

Why?

Why?
Because I asked why!
Do you know why?
Oh, you do.
Well then, answer this.
Why do we have racial tension goin' on?
Why do we have gang fights at a game, after school,
   during school, or during a nice cool jam?
Why do we have blind justice?
Why do we have black on black crime?
Why do I have a hole in my ceiling where the mice
   and rats have torn up and the landlord sits on
   his tired behind and doesn't fix it?
Why do we have prostitutes on the streets when they
   can be three-piece suit wearin', money-makin' women?
Why do we have nice, intelligent, young girls
   havin' babies and plenty mo'?

You can't answer that, can you? Well answer this:
Why am I askin' you why and you don't even know who I am!?
   Tamika C. Le Deoux

Clouds

I'm drifting. The clouds are not.
Beautiful, beyond description"
Yellow, peach, orange effervescent
with gray, red and purple
and bright, so very, very bright
where the sun pushes through the darkness
to bring fire to the sky.

I feel that I know these clouds.
Maybe I've dance on their brilliant tops.
Maybe I've floated through their downy soft centers.
Maybe they've held me in their arms of light.

I only know that someday I'll dance on them once again
and feel their softness carry me upon the wind.
   Carol S. Pate

Ode For Thought

Concentrated thought in action creates the moves one makes
be they moves of wisdom or moves creating serious mistakes

Concentrated thought is powerful energy that one directs
forming future events and feelings for all the thought effects

Thinking at its best includes the results before any action new
to not latter be sorry from thoughts results coming back askew

Thought is one's inner power, thought is one's driving force
be they thoughts of goodness or thoughts of deep remorse

Concentrated thought is one's creating who he/she will become
if thoughts are of the passions in time from self one will run

Concentrated constructive thoughts brings life's best over time
they build self worth for a life fulfilling, friendly and fine

Thoughts of passion's lust, vanity, anger, attachment and/or Greed
invites unbalanced painful negative results coming back with speed

Thinking about harmonious principles while planning a higher goal
invites highest good balanced living for one's mind, body and soul

Allowing only positive, caring thoughts to always stay in one's mind
builds harmony and balance at its fullest the wise thinker will find

Thought's journey on life's middle road while to one's self one is true
Brings an intuitive knowingness as to which thoughts should stick like glue
   F. W. Gaines

"Just For You"

Are you coming back to see me soon my darling
— Be my angel, be my honey, be all mine —
Don't you know I need you, need you, darling,
— Make two hearts one a-beating, yours and mine —
   I am lonely, I am blue,
   I am longing now for you.
Bring your charms into my arms, my love divine.
With my lips on your a-pressing
And your pretty hair caressing,
— It's like golden bells a-ringing, sweet and clear,
With your lovely eyes a-bringing
— To my heart the joy of singing —
Tell me you'll be mine forever, forever, dear.
Far across the lonely miles I reach you, darling.
— In your hand I print a message just for you —
Can't you feel I love you, love you, love you, darling
— That I'm waiting, watching, longing just for you —
   Oh my darling, don't you see
   Heaven's gift you are to me
Gift of life — my darling wife, a sweetheart true.
   Herbert M. Ortman

There Is Power In The Grave Of The Saints

My best friend had passed
away and I felt so sad, although
the Lord would come to me
and make my heart feel glad; still,
there was this feeling,
I just could not feel free, I cried out to God and
said Lord, Lord, Lord,
let mama speak to me, as I made my way to the grave yard,
with his presence so real that day,
I went up to the grave, where daddy and mama lay,
then I talked to my mama as in days we once knew.
I said, mama, I enjoyed all those good old times I had with you.
Then the spirit spoke through me like waves from a mighty sea,
there is power in the grave, of the saints that's been set free.
Pauline Bramblett

A Part of Me

Standing behind the door
Awaiting the moment to come into sight
Entering stages of different past live's
Holding onto memories that were just right
Closing out pain of earlier days
Awaiting the moment of escape
Challenging the spirits of evil
Dwelling on thoughts of true lust
Wondering out of my mind and into my internal soul
Balancing them until I am whole
Wrestling sacreds of the unknown
Watching childhood dreams be thrown
Fascination is not a dream
Forget I will not
It's all a part of me
Toni A. Rihn

The World At Peace

Sitting on a rock gazing out
at the masterpiece
that lays spread out upon the land.
The ripples in the unforgotten.
mass of water appear magically.
Light outstretches from
outrageous rays being reflected from the sun ahead.
Paths of light are found
drifting on the water.
The sun is hung over the brilliant blue puddle.
Purple and pink hues tint the evening sky.
Small golden rays emerge
from the giant mass of light.
As I sit and stare out at the
vivid images, peace settles
in my soul.
Paved in my mind is tranquility.
Rebecca VanMarter

Spirit

Soaring in your heart like an eagle in the sky.
Catching an updraft to rest in God's hands.
Then plummeting earth bound in search of sustenance through
earthly means.
Always searching for just that morsel, which will feed the hunger.
Not knowing, that if he'd pause and gaze at the sights
Around him, below, above, inside
It's there
Within
The heart
of all.
Find yours and let it soar.
Patty Meiners

Untitled

At the end of the rainbow there's a pot of gold
At least that's what I've been told.
As a child we open our eyes up wide
Yes we're looking for the other side.
Do we really grow up in this day and age
Still having that thought in mind?
I guess there's still hope
In this world of poverty, war and dope.
Our children are different
They don't play as we did, now they have computers
That they think can I teach them to live.
My days as a child, I can see clear
I played outside...with no fear
My mind was my computer, it learned and grew as I did
I was happy back then...being a kid.
The children today, I'm sad to say
Haven't really learned the way.
Someday can they look back and say
At the end of the rainbow there's a pot of gold
At least that's what I've been told.
Debra Steigerwalt

Grandma

My dear Sweet Grandmother now you're gone,
At first I wondered if life could go on.
I sat long nights at the side of your bed
And listened so carefully to each word you said.
"I'm so afraid to go," you cried. "I am too, I cannot lie."
"For if you go surely part of me shall die."
""Will you come back for me?" I sighed.
"When you reach the light, I'll be just inside."
Then as you dozed, I studied your face,
And with finger each line I would trace.
"I'll burn in my mind each memory of you."
"The ones there, in your heart will do."
"Never forget me Grandma," I cried,
And I held her hand as she peacefully died.
"Just one more question, just one more look,
Just one more kiss and we'll close this book."
"Don't leave me Grandma, here all alone."
"I must leave you my child, it's time to go home."
"But what shall I do without you here?"
"Just reach in your soul, for I've taught you that dear!"
Patricia Marriott

A Sonnet To Sight

A kitten cuddling near its mother's side
At birth is blind- but such a searching stare!
Exploring sightless, eager to confide,
As if a heaven undiscerned were there.

There is no groping from human child.
He lies reclined with lustrous limpid eyes,
By sight of earth, not hidden heaven, beguiled
He looks at colors, shapes-the worldly guise.

Both babe and kitten see with equal sight
When covering eyelids lift their shades.
A spool of twirling twine or swinging light
Can busy both with eyeball escapades.

But kitten grown to cat still claws at twine,
While man from babe can reach a sight divine.
Keith Rice

Living Death, Death Living

One cold, still August night
Asking for Death was I...
But Death did not answer I

Then realizing Death had no answer
I talked to Death, did I
And like an early evening dawn...
The warmth and softness of Death was I feeling,
So I embraced Death, and Death embraced I

Realizing...I asked Death to come and go
Like an old Friend...
Until one night, I could finally stand no more

I asked Death when could Friendship return I?
Death looked at I, and finally answered
After a long while...
When Earth, Eternity, and I
See one another eye to eye

Now long asked I?
Death, he looked me in the eye...
And with a sigh, only said
Aye!!

Roger Plessen II

Holocaust

For those in doubt the Holocaust began,
Ask those whose loved ones lives came to end,
First books then people fueled
pillars of flame to the sky,
As justice to those accused was denied,
Scores of people were gathered day and night,
The choice of freedom no longer casting a light,
Resettlement of Jews was the big lie,
The truth known to world leaders later denied,
When accused asked what have I done wrong,
The answer nothing,
Only in our new world order,
Undesirable don't belong,
Only a few were tattooed to be kept,
Brutality and starvation the order of the day,
For those tattooed left,
Today is prejudge and racial hate
designated to a world past,
Did lessons learned yesterday last.

Willie C. Williams

Bedford Interlude (Marie's Discovery)

You can know you don't belong,
As you know those guys were wrong;
　See the visions as your heart begins to race.
In a room, once for the lonely,
Came the boys, now as then only;
　Deliver me, to my former state of grace.

As a voice forever taunting,
As their lives will go on haunting;
　Rescue me not, for I really have no fear.
Though the spirits may be leery,
Send a note, for I am weary;
　Welcome all, for I promise I'll be here.

Of the folks who came to wonder,
You can't tear their hopes asunder;
　Feeling passes, and then comes back in a while.
Not a day can you affect them,
Even when your deeds neglect them;
　And for this, I save a tear and a smile.

Thomas Porky McDonald

A Seasoned Journey

As a star falls, so does my heart
As the sun rises, so does my hope
As freely as the river flows, so does my love
As sudden as a storm is my anger
As a tree grows, so does my respect
And as it branches out, so does my knowledge
Lost between innocence and maturity,
An adolescent flower yet to bloom

Tobra Spoonmore

Fall Colors The World

Fall prepares the world for the storms of winter.
As the crisp breeze blows,
　Leaves of all colors fall from the trees.
The oak stands tall and strong
　Majestically holding its branches heavenward.
Green pines stand out strong
　Among the leafless branches of the maple.
Pine cones are scattered across the ground
　Among the colored leaves and broken branches.
The goldenrod shines with a golden luster
　As the sun makes brilliant the colors of fall.
The sun-ripened apples
　Cast the tree in a crimson red.
Purple, yellow and red mums spot the landscape
　Coloring where the leaves have not touched.
The time for winter is coming.
Change is in the air.
Fall colors the world.

Tina L. Curtis

Deth's Mourning

Deth comes riding on a pale, pale horse
As people's lives end their course
Her eyes, like deep green moss,
Always search for souls that are lost
But who's to know, who's to say
Who's to die, who's to stay
The Dark Lady knows not herself
Who will be remembered by momentos on a shelf
All she knows is the sadness and grief of others,
Who have lost fathers, daughters, sons, and mothers
She has no family, she's always alone,
Over the millennia while others become bone
She rides on, filled with remorse
Accompanied by her only friend, a pale, pale horse

Sharon Cunningham

Restlessness

Staring out upon the ocean
　as if it were a mirror to reflect my thoughts;
Wanting to play in its waters
　but being content to sit and ponder;
There is so much I want to do,
　a feeling of restlessness wells up inside.
Is it possible to chase my rainbows?
　Can I glide like a sea gull above the waves?
The sun, blazing orange, slowly sinks over the horizon.
　The cool breeze sends its shivering message.
Fear of the unknown must be overcome
　for the journey to reach its highest peak.
A dream of standing upon the cornice
　not knowing but the very next step;
Of pushing off into the unknown territory
　to discover the realms of a life uninhibited.

Tom Neth

"Time Walks By"

Minute by minute, hour by hour, day by day
  As I see myself die
No one around me to relieve my loneliness
  No one around me who really cares
Each day that passes, the pain and emptiness
  Always seems stronger
I see nothing but conflicts
  No meaning to life
Yet no meaning to death
I'm like a rope in a tug-of-war
  Always being pulled upon
Constant anger, constant pain and constant fear
  But all inside
As I see myself die
Never anymore happiness
  Only hopelessness and helplessness
Shall the day arrive soon
  Or shall I survive
How can I live a constant lie
  For... she must die
    Vickie J. Lauzon

Why Me, Woman?

Why, why did God put the blame on me?
As I read the words of Genesis, I ask
What is God trying to teach me?
That psychology was used, a truth unmasked.

He is a God of love, he has all learnings
We know He could have placed the apple tree
At another place where it was not tempting
Fact, not fiction, He's sowing the learning seeds.

If two people are called into court for a crime
Brought before a judge and jury and asked why;
And the older one puts the blame on the younger, saying
He talked me into it; sarcastic laughter is the replay.

When some say life had not learning in the beginning
God tells us they had the use of psychology
They had the learning to take a little bit of earth
And make the body's of man and woman; Biology.

Now I have the answer of why God blamed me
Woman, some call the weaker sex
He wanted to teach me survival in a world of reality
The answer is love, a love that lasts.
    T. M. Hatfield

Daddy

Where are the memories of you and me,
As a little girl on your shoulders, so she could see;
The bedtime stories you read while I sat on your knee,
Days at the park, you pushing me on a swing,
Silly stories you'd tell and songs we would sing,
A day at the zoo, so many animals to see,
A kite that we flew that got caught in a tree,
Birthday parties with balloons and a cake,
The doll that you gave me, I'd remember with the photos you'd take,
The boys that you questioned that came to the door,
Sleepless nights waiting up and pacing the floor.
A tear in your eye, a smile on your face,
A flowing white dress all made in lace.
Where are the memories of you and I,
We'd barely said "Hello" and there was never a "Goodbye."
    Terri Anderson

Next Time I'll Get Off

You have my love on a carousel, up and down.
Around and around; the same carnival sound,
The same tinkling song bearing me along.
You have my love on a carousel, up and down.
Around and around; the same carnival clown,
The same tiny bell that lured me to the carousel spell.

It's a fun ride going nowhere, trapping time in a snare;
And time to you is a cotton candy moment,
Not meant for care, that you casually share.
The music will stop.

The song will go away and I will not pay
the cost of one more ride to stay near your side another day.
No longer can I hide my tears behind a smile;
No longer can I lay aside my hurting pride for awhile;
No longer can I disclaim the pain wrapped around my heart
Like a vise; no longer can alibis disguise the lies I tell myself.
The music will stop.

The tiny bell will hush; into the night I'll rush
and cry my tears on the run, and dry my tears in tomorrow's sun.
The music will stop. Next time I'll get off.
    Renee E. Williams

November Musings

The trees are so barren, the night air so cold —
Are these things more noticeable as I grow old?
Yet a granddaughter's arms encircling my neck
Serve to remind God's not finished with me yet.

Leaves curled and dry, mingling with snow,
Stir memories of Montana winters years ago.
We dressed in as many layers as we could
And stoked the old stoves with coal or wood.

No forecasts of weather, no choices of food;
We ate whatever we had, and knew life was good —
Parents who loved us and were always there
To share joys and sorrows, let us know they cared.

Now my thoughts leap forward, wondering how long
It will be before joining that heavenly throng,
When I can forget about supper, the endless dishes,
Unwashed curtains and Christmas card wishes.

Life is a paradox, always wanting less or more
Of whatever we're given from life's bountiful store.
Life is a puzzle to solve (if we could)
But of one thing I'm sure - my life has been good.
    Ruth M. Clark

Lonely Tears

  Cry the tears of lost loves; lost lives.
Bleed the blood of the ones who are no longer lonely and isolated,
Smile the unhappy smiles of our lonely nights; our lonely tears,
Plant the seed from which nothing but the unwanted unneeded
truth can grow, and the reality of pain and suffering becomes
a familiar part of our hearts; our minds.
There's an endless hole of emptiness and its felt deep within
where it lingers upon all happiness; until there's no more.
  Knocking on the door, but the emptiness echoes in our ears,
as does the pain and harsh attempts to reach whatever it
is we long to know or to see.
Words are insignificant coming from the tongues of those who
know not of pain, or truth, or life; words are only words.
  There's only love, but it's lost; life is lost, now only tears.
We bleed in our lonely and isolated grief,
We smile our unhappy smiles in our lonely nights, with our lonely tears.
    Tara Wood

Elegy For A Pup

O' Man!
Another living creature died today.
A small nameless puppy passed away.

Two young girls stroked its trembling body
And showered tears upon its fur
As they learned the painful lessons of reality.

Death does not come soft and silent in the night.
It comes in ugly forms of fleas that bite
And worms that suck the bowels.
It comes with desperate moans and howls.

The pup was not theirs to love and own.
They found it dying and brought it home.
They dared to steal it from the litter
Where they were hired to play the sitter.

The owners,
Beings deemed intelligent,
Of small creature needs were sadly negligent.

They had to go away.
They had important things to do and say.
The pups were only toys with which their children played.
   Peg Muszynski

Lost Love

Your youth and charms will soon fade away
and you'll look back on the love thrown away.
It's so sad now and you're all alone
An empty house cannot be a home.
There's no love left to stand by your side, with
whom you have laughed with and with whom you have cried.
You can't reminisce with someone not there
For dreams were meant for lovers to share.
Ah, but you thought you had it all
Never to wait for true love to call
Just kept moving from one to another
Running and searching for the perfect lover.
That's all gone now as you sit and cry and dwell
on all the love gone by. How heartless and selfish
you've been thru the years, causing hurt and pain and endless tears.

You wish you could start life over again, for now you see
how foolish you've been. True love is not a one night stand,
It's something you build with your love hand in hand,
And when it's done right as the years pass by
You won't have to sit alone and cry.
   Paul F. Hartnett Sr.

The Stranger

I see in your eyes, dear stranger, the sorrow
And the frozen tears of an eternity void of Love
And I'm sorry.

I see in your eyes the intense fears
That breed the beast of rage
And I'm fearful.

I see in your eyes the deepest emptiness
I've ever known, and such loneliness
And I feel so alone.

I see in your eyes the saddest soul
Masked by lost faith, broken dreams and lost hopes
And I understand.

I see in your eyes a child — lost
From the ancient wisdom and love so craved
By a searching young heart
A child lost in the eternal night.
And I feel my heart — break.
   Suzanne C. Lee

The Guardian

When the mist floats gently over the tops of your shoes,
And you stop to watch in fascination;
I will be watching from the woods.
You will not see me.

As you take each unsteady step toward home,
And the mist drifts upwards around your knees;
I will follow in the shadows. You will feel me there,
But you will not see me.

When you can barely see the familiar homes of your neighborhood
And the mist covers you like a soft cool blanket;
I shall be near to feel your fears.
You will not see me.

As you run up the front stairs of the most familiar home,
The chill you felt will soon be out of mind.
I will wait and watch and follow you,
But you will not see me.

When the mist turns to a fog so thick you cannot see,
I will come close to you, to take your hand and guide you.
Don't be afraid; for I am your Guardian Angel.
You will not see me.
   Rinda L. Webber

Navajo Nation

I stand amidst the ruins, broken pottery in my hand,
and wonder who held this vessel whole, what woman, or what man;
I know what lies before me, shattered on the ground,
bespoke a whole tribes history, lying in shards around.

For like this shattered vessel, this tribe too, was whole,
and one day was scattered; how? No one will know!
I feel a sadness creeping, a crying in my soul,
for I know the day is over, for the mighty Navajo.
   Robert Forrest Stauffacher

"Hope That Will Never Die"

   Hope is something that we all have a need for
and when it flourishes, it opens many a doors.
It helps us to see what we are worth
and the purpose for our birth.
   Hope is something that grows deep within
and as long as we have it, we will not bend
from our dreams and desires,
but hope will strengthen us through life's fires.
   Although we face many challenge as we go
with hope inside us we must know
that in order to be successful and have a piece
of the 'pie'
we must have hope that will never die!
   Georgia Lacefield

Robin

The time of year the robin builds her nest
And when dead grass, or twig or string do show
From dawn to dusk she works without a rest
To make a bed uphill or down below.
An egg a day is laid by her, save four
The father comes to watch and take a count
Is that enough, or should she lay some more?
That's fine, my dear, you laid the right amount.
Upon the nest she sat for days and days
And took time out to hunt for her own food.
Then switching with her mate to work out ways
To make the cycle whole for their own brood.
When all are hatched and take their wings to flight
This time next year this brood will make its plight.
   L. Blanche Dinsmore

You Touched My Life

You came into my life one gloomy day,
   And touched it in a special way,
     Like no one ever has before.

You calmed my anger and empty pain,
   With a blinding smile that chased the rain,
     Like no one ever has before.

You laughed your way into my heart,
   Lifted my spirits for a life's fresh start
     Like no one ever has before.

You touched my body, snuggled close to me,
   Consumed me with passion and set me free,
     Like no one ever has before.

You touched my life in a special way,
   And now that you have gone I can only say
     Thanks.

B. Staton

An Embrace

As we shun goodbyes, we say so long,
   and time marches on.
With it the sun will shine,
   bringing forth joys of another kind.
Love we may have known, together, slipped by,
   escaping from our grasp with a sigh.
To forget is beyond our reach too,
   for we will always remember the me and you.
Though time comes between us, a new day
   descends upon us in a free sort of way.
Treasured memories are just that,
   neither I nor you can bring them back.
So as we part with a kiss or embrace,
   the future seems less hard to face.

Terry A. Johnson

Ship Of Time

I've been on this ship all of my life, through joy and sorrow, grief and strife. As a young woman the joy was there, with husband and children for which to care. There were ups and downs and the ship was tossed upon the waves until love was lost. For years the job of captain was mine, and I tried to steer a straight line. With children to raise and bills to pay, I stayed at the helm hoping one day to find someone strong, praying that fate would send a new captain and I could be mate. Fate answered my prayers and sent him my way, but again after some time he went away. Again as captain I did my best, working during the day and at night to rest, knowing that somewhere there had to be the man of my dreams, a captain for me. Then like a bold of lightning out of the blue, he came along—good, strong and true. Now my life is complete with happiness and love—all the things I had prayed for from God above. Now my ship is on an even course with no more sorrow and no more divorce. For the rest of my time, in my golden years, I have someone to share my happiness and fears. We have time to play and grandchildren to love and once again I thank God above. Yes, you ride the ship of time for years on end, till you reach the safe harbour of God's arms 'round the bend.

Thelma R. Jones

Untitled

When I was a little girl, I used to dream of my knight in shining armor riding in to rescue me on his great white steed.

Since I've grown up, I've learned that knights are imaginary, and the only white steeds left haven't yet been captured or tamed. I do know one thing, however:

If knights still existed, you would be mine. And the white steed? That would be your faithfulness, caring, understanding and undying love.

Pamela Brinar

Goodbye, Erato

Oh, I have swigged an icy mountain pool
And stolen swatches from a morning sky.
I've carried saintly wisdom home from school
And caught a mountain range in either eye.

I've heard the godly music of the spheres
And smelled a lilac Heaven in the spring.
The tintinnabulations in my ears
Are more melodious than anything.

When I appropriated all these things,
I had a feeling I was out of line.
But now, I know that my redemption brings
The knowledge that they were already mine.

Goodbye, Erato; you are now dismissed,
For I have now received the Holy Muse
And as my master, He may now insist
On what I say and kiss what words I use.

Lewis Harrison

Vanity

Her birthday was in the dark part of winter
and, smiling, he would give her Mardi Gras beads
because she could wear them with class.
Other women looked gaudy
or cheap in that synthetic sparkle,
but she had a warm vitality
that could make plastics real.
There were green teardrop beads one year,
dark and swollen to match her eyes,
and then huge round blue beads,
neatly and precisely positioned,
"...for all the shades of love," he said.
He gave her pear-shaped yellow beads
in case she ever needed sunlight,
and tiny plastic seed necklaces for her dreams.
She kissed him and said,
"Love never thinks of authenticity."
And he knew that a string of faceted red beads
had more fire around her neck
than any hissing diamond.

Vanessa McLean

The Next Time

When first it was called justice, they built a rugged cross
and scourged a man of honor whose life through sin was lost.
A purple robe, a crown of thorns, and insults without cease
were deemed a fitting tribute for the "King," God's Prince of Peace.

When next they named it justice, it beat a tender lad
who stole a rich man's morsel to feed his dying dad.
The cane marks laid a bloody path, from head to grimy heel
because a "toff" begrudged a peasant man his final meal.

And once more claiming justice, they coiled a hempen rope
and looped it tight around the necks of men who'd lost all hope.
Whose only crime the colored skin that separates their race
from one himself called master, because of his white face.

Then in the name of justice, they walked with measured tread
upon the backs of zealots; six million honored dead.
And goose-stepped down the avenues in ranks of forest green
to idolize a monster like the world had never seen.

When I imagine justice, it holds a helping hand
stretched out toward the homeless, the lost, downtrodden man,
it battles crime and poverty, gives workers all they're due
The next time I see justice, I hope it looks like you.

Teena Shields

Here On This Mountain

Here on this mountain where the maples burn
And scarlet flowers storm the meadow glade
Each year I spend a day among the fern
Until the sun sets and the twilight fades.

This quiet nook was once my secret room
This patch of mossy rock served as a bed
I lay here many a summer afternoon
And watched the swallows flying overhead.

Where are they now, those dreams of yesterday
Lost as the dreamer, when the dream is done
A few that mattered, saw the light of day
But most of them would perish, one by one.

Now I must leave, go back the way I came
Back to the city noise, and grime, and smell
Leave my beginnings to the wind and rain
Leave —almost—all I need and love as well.
   Wayne E. Vitatoe

A Heavenly Hinterland

Come walk along Presilla Road in April or in May
And revel in God's handiwork at the dawning of the day;
Then rest awhile on this miracle mile for an enchanting view
Of Ventura's fragrant flora infiligreed with dew.

Or come at noon when things are in tune as they were meant to be
And the midday sun is beaming down on tussock and on tree,
Imparting to all creatures the warmth of its rays
So to insure they will endure the colder winter days.

But I urge you to come in the evening just after the sun has set,
For a view of this heavenly hinterland you never will forget;
For the skyline then dominates the scene and engenders a strange
   presence
And your heart will pound as you gaze around upon such magnificence
   Great Grandpa Moran

First I Must Conquer The Mountains

First I must conquer the mountains, closest to God.
And prepare for the avalanches, of spiritual falls.
The margin for error, is as deep as his calling.
For every step, breathes him closer to me.

His supply depot, is my sense of purpose.
A shelter, unspotted from this world.
For I grip, the cliffs that bind.
And hide myself in thee.

For he stills my fears, and calms my heart.
He steadiest my feet, and guideth my hands.
To move these mountains, through faith I can.
Which have been willed to us all, by one touch of the master's hand.

As my breath today, could be tomorrow's last.
But today, has brought me closer to thee.
If my body fails, and gives no more.
For tomorrow, I shall rise above them all.
For I have conquered myself through God.
   Sarah S. Peterson

My Son

He's so very small
And not very tall
Not as long as my arm
Oh! But, what a charm
Big smiles, and little giggles
He loves to just wiggle
What a surprise he came to be
But, he I would not have seen
I too young and he so small
I hope he grows very tall
He will stand up straight and strong
For I will be there to help, that he does none wrong
We will grow up together, he and I
Together we will grow and sometimes cry
He is mine you see, not yours or theirs
The love of my life-line, that will never break
At times we may both grow weak
But to be together we'll make it, alright, you will see
Isn't love the greatest test of all
For here he is with me.
   Ruby B. Dobrick

Shut In

Looks like the snow has arrived
And its only November of ninety five
The snow is coming down ever so hard
I can't see my own little yard
If it wasn't for the trees ever so tall
I'd think I was standing in an all white hall
The wind is pushing the snow so hard
And there's still no sound within my yard
The snow is falling and its freezing outside
Now I have to sit in my room as thought to hide
I hate the winter and all it's cold
I hate the freezing and all its snow
I hate the things that lock me up
If only I were young and my legs were fine
I'd play in the snow and forget the rhymes
   Robert R. Duwe

Life

My relationship began with a slap
And it was painful
But I was willing to go until the end
Because you never Know...

The pain continued but I'm not a sap
I just Believe that from bad there will be good
And that's when we really begin
Because you never know...

As we grew together a little pleasure began to enter
And along with pleasure came distraction
That took me all around her curves and up and down her hills
I didn't give up because you never Know...

My relationship with her is over she ended it
Now that I'm in this cold dark place
alone I reflect on the ups and downs we went through
It wasn't that bad and I'm glad I didn't end it sooner
Because you never know...

She might just be worth it
   Timothy Vincent

The Pump

It does give a hoot, and it does give a care.
And it does have feelings as it just stands there.

Little tin cup and wrought iron rust,
It'll stand there forever, it has to it must.

It sees people come, and it sees people go.
It sees spring green grass, and white winter snow.

This pump has feelings, and only I know it,
For no one else can see the unique way it shows it.

It stands in the spring, and it stands in the fall.
And it always gives its cup and water to all.

This little pump means a lot to me,
And maybe someday, someone will see.

It does give a hoot, and it does give a care.
And it's not just something that only stands there.

Wendy A. T. Schlosser

The Other Woman

Everyone said it would happen eventually - another woman.
And it did.

Now, he spends most of all his time with her.
He always made me feel like I was the prettiest and smartest woman he knew.
Now, she's the one who catches his eye and stirs his thoughts.

All this time I've known about her, I've had to wonder what she is like.
Does she think he's got the greatest brown eyes in the world like I do?
Or has she seen plenty of brown eyes?
Maybe it really annoys her the way he throws his coat on the floor.
Or... maybe she doesn't mind.

Long at last, my wait is over.
The day has come - to meet her.
To put to rest all my fears of her... or confirm them.

I must remember that he loved me first.
I must be brave and strong,
When I meet his Kindergarten Teacher.

Tina Dannemiller

The Dream

Last night I had a dream,
And I woke up with a scream
It was scary and very frightening,
Outside it was raining and lightning.

I dreamt that everybody was against each other,
And they even disrespected their own mothers.
Little girls were selling their bodies,
Instead of playing with cute little dollies.

The boys were selling crack,
So they can put clothes on their families' back.
This is not how the world should be;
I wish people could only see.

People are either shot, raped or dead,
People only care for their own lives instead.
Nobody should take away others lives;
And if they get caught, they have to pay the price.

I thought everyone was supposed to be kind;
And try to use their own minds.
What is today and tomorrow supposed to mean?
For me this is reality, but to others, it's just a silly dream.

Yusheria Chopane

Today

We drove past a grave yard today
And I felt some sorrow
For all those people who had died
And not lived to see tomorrow
They lay there in peace in their place all alone
For in all the misery
A tear was never shown
Now I look at my life
What do I live for
When I look at my riches such as love, family and friends
I know I'm not poor
For what will happen to me in the future
I should live with lots of happiness and little sorrow
Cause what I know is what I'll say
Live today for today and tomorrow for tomorrow

Sena Koleepkv Harjo

Gone Appetite

I just caught me a little trout
  and he's all tuckered out
    from splashing about

I thought about having the little
  bugger for my dinner
    but now for some reason as I unhook my spinner
  just the thought of it all
makes me feel like a sinner

So swim away little trout
  to your little troutie wife
    I'm sure not eating you is
    no detriment to my life

And tonight as you dine
with your honey on bugs
I'll return home to mine
in a shower of hugs.

Tim Boadway

Forgiveness

Have you ever been worried and unhappy as hell?
And had no one, your problems to tell
And you sat and you looked at a clock or a sign,
And wanted to write a letter but couldn't write a line.
Have you ever been lonesome and really blue?
And you just didn't know what to do
Have you ever thought back at the things you have done?
And wondered why you didn't fight, instead of run
Have you ever believed there is a God in the sky?
And suddenly disbelieved and wondered why...
Have you ever accomplished all the things you desired?
And suddenly found your whole life and body tired.
Have you ever mistrusted the people you love?
And prayed at night for forgiveness above.
Have you ever swore to God you'd change your ways?
Only to be misled in just a few days.
Have you ever had any of these happen to you?
Ask God to forgive and this he will do...

Everett Jack Monroe

Standing Among Many

Standing among many, I feel the tears fall from my face
And gather a feeling of displace.

Standing among many, I feel the blood pump through my veins
As emotions like these drive me insane.

Standing among many, I feel the pain in my feet
And I can hear a distant faint heartbeat.

Standing among many, I feel the sorrow of a thousand souls
And I see the body that has taken the tolls.

Standing among many, I feel no greater, nor no less
But I do seem different than the rest.

Standing among many, I feel content
Wishing my soul was pure one hundred percent.

Standing among many, I think of my sins present and past
Asking are they forgiven so that I may last

Standing among many, I feel my breath heavy and worn
As I look to the hill and see the three bodies ragged and torn.

Standing among many, I feel a cold death inside
Because that day, I saw Christ die.
Rachel E. Freeman

Whistling

I've been whistling ever since I learned,
And for me many comments it has earned;
Wherever I go I whistle on my way,
Whether I'm at work or play.

I have no desire to myself call attention,
So of my whistling I seldom make mention;
Mostly I whistle a joyous sacred song,
That elates my spirits and helps me along.

When my life here is over and done,
Then my final victory will have been won;
I've been wondering if there in Heaven's land,
There'll be somewhere a whistling band?

If there are whistlers there in glory,
I want to share with them my story;
For this habit has brought me much joy,
Ever since I learned it as a boy.

I want to go on whistling as long as I live,
For in this way praise to my Lord I give;
If my whistling makes your burdens lighter,
Then surely your road will be a little brighter.
Will H. Havens

The Break Of Dawn

It creeps up like a cougar after its prey.
And then it towers over us, and devours us,
soaking us up with the strands of its long
golden fingers.
We are death under the heat of its fangs
against our flesh.
And yet...
When it awakens us,
Streaming in on us,
We see nothing, we feel nothing,
but warmth, and the fantasy in the light of...
A New Day.
Shanna Zitting

Ka ua

Ka ua falls and strikes the roof
And far above the clouds aloof
Drift and float just where they will,
Then anchored boats let water spill.

At first steam rises and wisps away
From the kettle sloshed on stove-hot pavement;
Then keikis slip and slide and play,
Or with wide mouths catch a droplet of intoxicant.

Ka ua bathes the world and sprinkles coolness all around
On roads and trees, cars and seas as it washes all the ground;
Ka ua pits and grooves and sculpts the white beach sand,
But white sand turtles dig until they hide themselves again.

Ka ua sews with silvery threads as if an artist seamster,
Wet webs woven like the work of a granddaddy-long leg spider;
Ka ua fills the streams that flow and bid farewell to mountains
But promises to return again when she fills again the ocean.

Ka ua beats outside like the practiced drummer of a band,
Who timely strikes his cymbals on a rhythmic rubbish can;
Inside the muffled sounds make cozy beds for old and newly weds
And softly drum sweet reflections in mellow, sleepy heads.
Keoni Aloha

An Observation

There is terror riding in the streets today
And every day, and every night
It is more horrible than anything I've seen
It teaches Violence, Fear,
All things that should not be here
Those that speak against it
Speak!
Bravely speak
They do not hear
Because that monster in the streets...whispers
rejoice in distortion
The monster preaches
Covers with its cloak
Just one word it says
Its name
Ignorance
Repeated over
Ignorance
its name is Ignorance
Shall we be rid of thee?
Polina Vinnik

"I Will Mourn For Them"

The deadened leaves drift past the windowpane
and drop to the ground as if shot by a bullet.
I will mourn for them.
A few short weeks ago they adorned the tall trees
with stunning colors of red, orange, gold and yellow.
I will mourn for them.
They shimmered, they shone in the bright Autumn sun
as the green Summer leaves transformed with the season.
I will mourn for them.
The trees soon will be bare as the Winter takes hold,
but as sure as God's in His heaven, the Spring buds will return.
I will mourn them no longer.
C. J. Pool

Dare To Discover

To discover is to try little things when you are young,
And do many larger things when you are older.

When I was young:
I discovered that I could walk - if I tried hard enough.
I discovered that I could swim - if I tried.
I also discovered that I could dance beautifully - if I tried and tried

I am not always able to do things right the first time,
But I work at them until I can.

As I grow older:
I want to keep on discovering
And help the Earth to be better so we can live in a happier place
And our children can live in a better world.

When I'm old and have gray hair,
I still will be discovering things that I have never discovered before.
And when you are old and have gray hair,
Remember, you're never to young or old to discover new things in life.

Samantha L. Middleton

Desolation

I asked for you to stop for a moment
   and comprehend emptiness...
    the mere product of a shattered soul,
   left only to ponder
   what it is that brings a laugh
   or draws a tear,
   searching for that spark of life
   that I find only in you.
For like life and color being restored
   to a desolate wasteland,
   so your mere presence
   penetrates the walls of my calloused heart,
   reminding me what it was once like
   to feel.

Ryan Bengard

Until We Meet Again...

Last night as I was sleeping, someone took me by the hand,
And as I woke this morning, I was in the promised land,
There was singing and rejoicing, as they met me at the gate,
They said my name was in His book upon this very date.

The beauty of His Kingdom, the peace that filled the air,
He had lifted all my burdens, no more worries, no more cares.
It's just as He had promised, no pain, no tears, no sin,
And then that's when I realized God had made me whole again.

They shouted "Hallelujah," trumpets blowing, I heard bells ring,
And then they said "It's time my friend, for you to meet the King,"
As I gazed throughout the Heavens, my eyes seen such a sight,
Our Lord descending from the clouds in the midst of a glorious light,

As I trembled standing before Him, upon my judgment day,
He wretch for me and said "Dear child, you trusted and obeyed,
You see I took you from a world, so full of hate and strife,
And because you believed and kept my word you'll have everlasting life,"

So please don't cry, don't grieve for me, for I am not alone,
I am up here with my Father, I have finally been called home.

Pam Browning

Sonnet: An Illusion

Oh, my love, problems are great and many
And any solutions; too small and few
It cannot be that our love is ending
Come what may, I want to stay beside you
You cannot forget all the times we had
Nor all the laughter, and the nights we shared
If you'll remember, it wasn't always bad
There was a time when we both really cared
But, of course, that all is now in the past
Happy times are over for you and I
It was an illusion our love could last
Now is the time for us to say good-bye
  In a world such as this, love can't survive
  Better not to fight it, just let it lie.

Wendy J. Ballard

Love Is Like Water

Love is like water
although it is as transparent as the wind.

Love can be as deep as an ocean
while at the same time light as a rain drop.

Love can be powerful like a tidal wave
or gentle as a stream.

Love can be turbulent like a raging rapid
or easy as a flowing river that's always moving.

Love is like water seeking it's own level
filling each erase, every crevice.

Love is like water when you try to control it
or dam it up it goes in the opposite direction.

Love is like water when you try to hold it
it slips through your fingers, try to contain it
it turns stagnant.

Love is like water free
the way God intended for it to be.

Pamela R. Barlow

"Two Great Fathers"

I have one that's great
also one that's never late
I have one with a mind on a steep incline
Also one that's simply divine
I have one that dots the i and crosses that t
Also one that parted the Red Sea
I have one that will give me his last bite
Also one that will give me everlasting light
I have one that knows the way
Also one I seek each day

These two great fathers in which I speak
They both contain their own unique
A father that's here
In the earth's atmosphere
A father that's there
And at the same time everywhere
The one that's here with me
We both await the day to see
Our Father which is in heaven
That rested on day number seven.

Roderick F. Evans

Grandmothers Views

Sisters and sisters, brothers and brothers,
All this brings a gleam to the eye of the mother's mother.
When she sees a baby play with some toys,
Her diary is filled with words describing joys.
As long as the family is kind,
There are no problems a grandmother can find.
And as long as grandmothers are glad,
Nothing in the world can go bad
So just remember, mom, dad, sister, and brother
You all are nothing but trash without each other.
   Wolfgang

America Hear My Cry

Each day I awaken to live another day of my life
All of them different, but all of them nice

Living is like a treasure, knowing I can gain
Storing what it teaches me, creating my domain

Today I'm a victim, of another man's pain
My life to him worthless, my life to him shame

I lay here helpless, a piece of rubble from a blast
My life is now leaving me, but it's leaving me too fast

Weakened I start crying, crying for their fame
Help me Mommy and Daddy I know only your name

My parents can now hold me, but they can't feel my pain
As I leave I'm just a memory, they will bury my remains

From my parents who ask why, to the men who carried me bye
I leave you with a thought!
   Warren A. Robertson

The Grand Old Oak Tree

I saw a grand old oak tree, standing alone,
All of the other trees, once there, was now gone.
Cut down by man, or blown down by the wind,
But, somehow or other, this old oak was spared,
No doubt by now the others were fuel for a fire!
Then as I looked at the grand old tree, seems I saw its history.
Seems, I visioned this tree with pretty green leaves!
Turning to red or golden brown in autumn, such a sight to see!
Then the pretty leaves falling softly to the ground.
And little wild animals playing in them, running round and round!
And, I visioned pretty birds building a nest in the limbs.
Then teaching their young to fly from this very old tree.
Seems, I thought about all the cows, rabbits and deer
That no doubt has walked here and taken shelter under this tree.
Now although soon, this old oak to will be gone,
But, I hope in a way, it can live on and on.
By the words, I try to write in this poem.
Oh! It was such a pretty sight to see.
The very old, grand "old oak tree!"
   Rosia Horton

Rejuvenation

Visions of your beauty rejuvenate my soul
As if angels descended just to cleanse the old
An invasion of dreamlike images conquer me night and day
But also healing me with renewed strengths to guide my way
Lifetimes are spent and wasted with emotions locked inside their hearts
Never realizing that expressing them might grant a new start
Each passing day without as much as a glance of you seems an eternity
Goddesses of fate please hear my effusion and shine on my destiny
   Ron Blaylock

And The Clock Of The Universe Began To Tick

In the beginning there was total darkness,
all material was compressed in a tiny sphere,
and it contained a sense of hidden past, immersed in an eternal dream.

No, in the beginning was the force,
which compressed the gigantic universe into a tiny mass of clay
and turned the day of a living world into a never ending Night,
and hidden in the clay of atoms was a tremendous energy ready to explode.

No, it can't be, in the beginning was an eternal Painter,
who had a tiny soul, which he planted out of shear love
in the heart of the unliving world,
and suddenly the ball of clay began to rotate.

Yes, this was the beginning of life in the womb of clay,
it was yet engulfed with the darkness of a never ending night.
When the ball of clay could not contain the gigantic soul,
the whole mass exploded and the day and sun were born out of night.

The day was a tiny quantum of light, which encircled its mother;
and tears of joy flew from the dark eyes of its mother Night.
Suddenly planets and moons were born from those tears,
and the clock of the universe began to tick.
   Vishnu P. Joshi

A Wonderful Surprise

Weep no more, my Dear
All hard times do disappear
Growing on makes you spark
You can be as happy as a lark
Go for a walk, look at the people
Meditate on the tall church steeple
Stare, look and view the life
Forget about all the tangled strife
Life is one big gigantic maze
Stand tall, look them straight in the eye
To all the weaklings, giving in, say good-bye
You're an amazing and powerful being
Self-confidence and poise is what I'm seeing
It's a wonderful surprise
So hold your head up high, cause
You're gonna prosper, by and by
Take courage for the whole day
Dry all of those tears away
You make the whole world a grandstand
With your peace and love stand
   Velma Jean Bennett

Final Good-Bye

I kiss you, and kiss you - My love - my life...
Ah, how I shall miss you.
I arise and go now, as if in slow motion.
The sadness - beyond all words
To be hid in my heart,
The clouds - I gaze at their journey above
Dropping like veils of the morning.
All I have is thoughts of you - And I
Slowly read - dream of every soft look...
Your eyes had once filled my gaze.
The beauty of our love ... so true.

And bending down to me, knowing, shortly
I would be gone.
The sorrows of your changing face
Murmur, saddened, how love fled.
And paced, and hid your face - in your hands
I am haunted by good-byes.
Awakening, in our hearts, my beloved, a sadness
that may not die - will not die
For our love was more beautiful than first love.
   Tiona J. Kline

Who's The Criminal

I believed you when you said you loved me
After how you hurt me can I be blamed for hating you
You took something away I'll never have again
I said no but you did only what you wanted to
I asked you not to, I kept begging you to stop
After trying to force you to stop you started hitting me
Though at first I blamed myself I told you no
That's not at all how I dreamed making love would be
I've been violated yet some look at me like I'm the criminal
Let them believe what they will we know who's to blame
I'll probably spend my life in prison for what I'm going to do
You're going to die so you never make another woman feel the same.

Shawn M. Arey

Granny's Boys

Each night as you sleep, I stand by your beds;
Adjusting the covers and softly touching your heads.

Sometimes I get angry when things don't go right,
But you always forgive me and hug me so tight.

Summer is fun - we swim in our pool,
But before we know it, you'll be back in school.

Now school is starting —your jeans are too small;
Guess we'll have to make a trip to the mall.

Homework every night and study for a test;
I know you don't like it, but granny knows best.

New clothes for easter, toys under the tree;
Santa and the bunny —you knew it was me.

Ball practice each day, even though I'm so tired,
But for the sake of your teams, I'll do what's required.

Your bikes on the driveway and games on the floor;
"We'll pick them up", you promise once more.

Your room's disaster —I just want to cry;
"We'll clean it up later, or at least we'll try."

I tuck you in bed and hold your hands while you pray,
And I think all is well as we end this day.

Sue Davis

Until We Meet Again

When summer winds blow and cool breezes ring the chimes from above, I will imagine the sound of your voice, the touch of your hand and the warmth of your arms wrapped about me.

As snowflakes fall covering the ground and building eves, I will see us in the snow in shorts and a funny hat having a snowball fight. I will peer into your eyes and feel your love around me.

Walking through bright spring flowers, standing in front of a fresh water fall feeling the fine mist on my face. The leaves on the trees begin to change color, I will look above the branches and know that you are watching.

Memories of the joy, the laughter, and the love you brought into my life are forever in my heart. As the weeks go by and the seasons change my joy is forgotten, my laughter is silent and my love waits to be with you. Until we meet again.

Victoria Stonaker

Twice A Month Dad

Although I am half of them, I wonder how they feel
    about their twice a month dad.
I wonder if they will share with me the first bike
    ride they ever had.
I wonder if they think of me when they lay down every night,
    'cause to me they are always here, come darkness or light.
I wonder if I'm too strict on the weekends they are here,
    but I want them to know wrong from right, be it ever so clear.
I wonder if they know the hurt of being called the wrong name.
    Or hearing, "Oh It's just Daddy," the feeling is just the same.
When my time comes I want them to know the love I have
    for my daughter and my lads.
That no matter what went on in life, they were loved
    by their twice a month dad.

Wyndom Wix

"Life"

I have learned ... I must keep learning.
About other people:
Their personalities and motives.
About myself: Examine my motives...
Of words and thoughts.
Am I gaining bits of insights,
Or am I judging with criticism?
Even tho' these things may not become words,
If only in my thoughts ...I must deal with all of these.
Is this being prepared for my next phase of life,
Or is this a daily battle I must fight?
I can not go through life without thinking,
I must measure my steps as I go.
I cannot prevent every pit fall...
Only if I am willing to keep learning..
With much prayer...
God will help me through them all!

Sophia Simmons Borger

The Laughter

   The laughter, indeed it shades my tears...
about as much as I wish for the long lost years.

   In a society within a society, with its own set of rules...
of yes indeed, I've paid my dues.

   Conforming to my new home with the resiliency of a child...
my smile is an effective mask - for a while.

   Taking on what seems a hedonistic view...
for long-term goals just won't do.

   Not in this world, this society of mine...
where laughter shades tears, and smiles don't reach eyes.

   Oh, I have a few acquaintances, but not many friends...
not in this world where change never ends;

   Where death is quite common, and so is disaster;
but man, you can't tell with all this damn laughter.

   Patrick Lane Davis

Isolation

Loneliness isn't in being alone so much
As in the realization: "All that I have inside
Will never find a voice and, so, must hide."
It's reaching out - with no one there to touch.

Pat O'Malley

A Family Connected

We are all intertwined together
A woven link combined of common threads.
We become united in crises
   a concrete union of strength.
Although we are all individuals
We are simultaneously a tribe of people
   Who have a kinship of love and caring.
One by one or on our own..
We shall stand proud and announce
   That deep in our hearts we are family.
We are each a blend of our parents...
   Our brothers and our sisters...
   Grandparents, aunts and uncles and cousins.
We are a family...
   Although we may sway and become apart
   Our heart will remind us of that link we share.
   That unbreakable bond we all know.
When all is said and done...
   After all there is only one thing
   On the entire earth that will matter...That is family
   Ruth Shoemate

From Fog

As I looked across the field and woods,
a wall, it seemed, there stood.
'Twas gray and thick
beyond the trees,
a curtain of God there stood.

The grass is green, and thick and lush,
and the flowers in bud, outward push.
The trees with leaves still yet as feathers,
with bark so wet and dark.

There will be a morning, as I've seen before,
when the curtain will be lifted.
But only after a kiss of the sun
sends fingers of light,
to paint the earth in it's riches.

The light will explode to touch all in it's path,
and dance life into wet, soft, moist earth.
The outstretched branches, with the feather like fingers,
and flowers with buds that give one last effort,
will dissolve God's curtain of fog.
   Penny Coy

A Shot In The Night

A place just any place.
A time just any time.
What place and time just doesn't matter.
A shot in the night, where is the damn back-up!
Too long, just took them to damn long.
"4 to PD., 4 to PD!
"P.D. to cars received report of shooting on the block."
"4 to P.D. I need the ambulance. I'm already here.
I need back-up."
Where's the damn back-up?
"Damn man, why didn't you throw the
gun down, why?"
Gun got to find the gun, found it, got to
hold onto it.
Where the Hell is the back-up?
Just any place.
Just any time.
A shot in the night.
   Rickey Paul Miller

A Lonely Tear

It's like a river in slow motion,
a symbol of stirred emotions.

Slowly falling to my chin from my cheek,
it is love from you I seek.

From my eye it is a tear,
not of joy or sadness, but fear.

Fear of losing the one I'm always thinking of.

Afraid to let go of the one I truly love.
   Rubi M. Garcia

The Joy In Simple Things

I find so much joy in simple things.
A squirrel that scampers
A bird that sings

A lovely sunset that ends the day
A moons so bright it lights the way

Stars that twinkle up in the sky
White clouds that make pictures while drifting by

Budding trees so regal and tall
A blooming rose that's spreading over a wall

A stream that gurgles as it wends its way
A pair of kittens as they romp and play

The rain as it patterns on the grassy lawn
The sparkling dew in the early dawn

A bobbing robin bringing a message of spring
The honeysuckle blooming and the sweet essence it brings

The rustling of leaves stirred by the wind
A beautiful rainbow with it colors that blend

All these things and much, much more; so simple and free
Are the rich blessings God had given
For my eyes to see.
   Rachel I. Parker

A Change Is Near

A change is near and its quite clear
   a song has got to be sung.
Before this can happen a major shift with my self
   has got to be done.
Evaluate, investigate, propagate, rejuvenate,
   examine, explore, speculate, coagulate, negate
The old, build up the new feelings inside me
Go for it baby it's all for me and can be for you.
Keep calm be cool, use your mind, you'll be
   surprised at what you find.
It's all right here for the sake of my being.
Open your eyes don't miss what I'm seeing.
Happiness health and wisdom too, a world
of great that's just for you.
And only you can make it all happen.
Think thoughts out to the hundredth degree
Go for it baby and you will see
   Take my word
   Believe in me.
   J. P. McCarthy

The Only Child

Mary, I have an only child too
A son that I'm raising, just like you
And I wish that somehow there could be a way
That I could ask you about the day

When you were a mother raising one child.
Did you give him firm guidance, or let him run wild?
Did he learn on his own, your miracle son?
Did he suffer from being your only one?

Mother Mary please, will you calm my fears
And tell me the story of the coming years
Where a good and true son made his way on the path
He shed many tears but enjoyed a good laugh

And loved his parents and made some mistakes
But lived life to the fullest - and when he awakes
In the kingdom of heaven at the end of the road
Ready to rest and lighten his load

There will be no question of the place he has earned
For his mother taught him and he had well learned
That the way and the light forever have shone
From the Son of Mary, who also traveled alone.

Terry Zerfas

The Guest Who Came And Blessed Our Home

She came out of nowhere; or so it seemed
   A ray of light; a radiant beam.
A quiet and unassuming face,
   A treasure of beauty, elegance and grace.

She was soft-spoken and patient, yet strong and deep,
   Offering to earn her board and keep.
A fountain overflowing with "living word."
   Abounding in wisdom, seldom heard.

There was no idle gossip; no folded hands,
   A person of compassion who understands.
She was a tranquil soul with a healing touch,
   So very few are made of such.

It was not so much what was said, or what was done,
   Just a matter of being such a special one
Who, in passing along a certain way,
   Could smooth someone's path, or brighten their day.

And thus she has come and now is gone,
   But her angel spirit lingers on.
And so, because of her presence, she has become,
   The guest who came and blessed our home.

Raphael B. Jones

Jesus

On this day so long ago
   A child was born so the story goes,
     This special child sent from above,
       Came down to teach of his Fathers love.

He gave his life, though willingly,
   To dictators who refused to believe,
     Yet through the years his fame did grow,
       Until the day he met a formidable foe.

This mystical man with the jolly face,
   Dressed up in red and took his place,
     And now when Christmas comes around,
       The name of "Jesus" can't be found.

This man who's name is Santa Claus,
   Takes all the credit for the cause,
     With his prancing reindeer and fancy sleigh,
       He moved right in and shoved Jesus away.

Vickie E. Tracy

Happy Birthday Ramona

In Little Rock Arkansas, August, nineteen thirty-five
a new United States Citizen of America did arrive.
A little girl with raven hair and big brown eyes
said, "Hello world, I'm here to see what I can do
about the things happening in you."

I'll sing and laugh and cook and sew,
bask in the sunshine and play in the snow.
I'll swim in your oceans, your mountains climb;
in your posh restaurants I'll love to dine,
look at your flowers and also your squirrels.
I'll have three sons and by them some girls,
wear diamond rings and also pearls.

I will conquer your towns with work and a will,
I will worship my God and his will fulfill.
With happiness I will live my life
with love for others, and even some strife,
but I'll be ok! So smile and say,
"Welcome Little Girl,
I'm glad you came to stay."

Ruth McNeely

Halloween

There are ghosts in the corner; there are goblins everywhere.
A mood of haunted horror pervades the crisp night air.

And somewhere in the darkness,
Beneath a full moon's glow,
A werewolf howls,
A black cat prowls,
A witch flies to and fro.

So terrified and trembling, we wait with bated breath,
As spooky sights and scary sounds frighten us to death.

Come crouch beside a gravestone,
And listen to the dead...
The mournful wails,
The gruesome tales,
Throughout the landscape spread.

Let us exorcise the demons that we know so well,
Drive them out and send them down the River Styx to Hell!

Now don the masks and beg for treats,
And wander wicked down the streets.
What rough beast slouching in the sun
Proclaims the devil's work be done?

Sandra R. Kovach Cheshire, CT

Eyes Open

As a babe, safe in the arms of mommy and daddy
A message that is instilled in me
"She can grow up to be, whatever it is she wants to be."

As a child, my life still so carefree
This important lesson is lost on me.

In my youth, my eyes wrongly see
That happiness comes only with money.

But as I age, a world opens in front of me
Where lives are dictated by men of history
Countries battle war and atrocity
Families torn apart by savagery
Tales of pain and slavery
All at once, almost unnoticed by me,
I realize I have grown up to be
Exactly what I wanted to be.

Free.

Sabine D. Bryttegard

Yesterday, Today And Tomorrow

The mirrored reflection of what used to be,
A longing inside for the strength of a tree.
Whimsical memories to be set free!
Daily reminders of the pain in me.

Older by far than I care to say,
My body, my mind, Oh what a price to pay!
Memories so vivid never fade away,
Constant reminders of a bright yesterday.

The mirror reflects an age old sight,
My body, my soul are losing their light.
Once again I'll spend such a long lonely night.
But one day soon my spirit will take flight.

Above and beyond all the woes I've known,
Soaring higher and higher, but never alone.
Renewed and refreshed from Spirit to bone.
With joy unspeakable I reach my heavenly home.

With outstretched arms I will be welcomed in.
The light so bright it glows from their skin.
An ocean of faces without a hint of sin,
"Jesus is Lord" they sing in praise of Him!

Sandra Frame

Life Is A Circle

The old man knew the end was near
A long, winding path did bring him here
His mind ventured back in time
When life was peaceful and sublime
When youth was like the glistening dew
Begging for the day to ensue
When laughter and joy filled the air
And nothing could break a lover's stare

But life, like a day, must always set
So mankind does regret
As seasons fade from green to brown
A schoolboy's grin becomes a man's frown

But through the darkness is a flicker of light
Youth may be hiding, just out of sight
For life is a circle that will never break
And youth will return for you to take

The old man knew the end was near
Yet he welcomed it without sadness or fear
For the old man sensed youth within his grasp
So with a smile, he breathed his last

Patrick Carlson

Gift Of Love

A gift that was meant to be
a life of love inside of me.
A miracle that has just begun
two hearts beating together as one.
That moment I bowed down to pray,
God would protect you as you were on the way.
Even though you were a baby I didn't know,
my heart filled with love that continued to grow.
That day came for you to come to earth,
God gave me strength while giving birth.
As you were born, I could finally see
God's precious gift given to Daddy and me.
As I prayed God listened from above,
He sent an angel to watch over the gift of love.
Now each day you're awake, each breath that you shall take
and when you go to sleep at night may she shine you with her guiding light.
Thank you God for his new life that has living,
God's most precious gift that could ever be given...
...the gift of love.

Stacey Martinez

The Miracle

Late last night in the warmth of my bed
A light so bright filled my head.
This sudden light as bright as the sun
Revealed a miracle, a child, my daughter, a woman now.

A child so innocent, so perfect, with love for me
All lost on a young mother too blind to see
Work, chores, errands, rules filled my mind
No time spent holding and loving this beautiful child.

This child struggles and fights to find her own way
Falling and stumbling but what do I say
No words of encouragement, no words of love
Just words of impatience and words of fear, judging her every move.

She fought her battle and now she has own
She came through the cold storm to the warmth of the sun
She laughs, she loves, she forgives and forgets
Her heart filled with compassion and fairness to all.

But how has she succeeded and who should she credit
Only this miracle, herself
This child, my daughter, a woman now.

S. D. Grissett

The Ice Princess

Long ago and far away upon a snow banked hill
a kingdom made of ice still sits within the winter chill,

I have been there many times and always seem to find
the quiet valley far below a vision in my mind,

A crystal pond of solid ice shimmers sun-filled rays
as a girl comes out to skate each and every day,

Her hair is pulled behind her head up on it sits a crown
her gloves fit over each small hand she wears an ivory gown,

I have only seen this girl this princess on the ice
in my dreams I've seen her there not just once but twice

The first time was a year ago when I dreamt up this place
how graceful she had looked back then the smile on her face,

The second time I saw this girl was not too long ago
I closed my eyes and traveled to the valley in the snow,

But by then the crystal pond had melted into glass
and with her skates tucked in her arms the princess left at last,

Returning to her castle that still sits up on the hill
in my sleep I'll wait for her when winter brings a chill

And thought I've been back many times since then I have not seen
the princess skate up on the ice the girl within my dreams.

C. Patrick Hawley

Human Kind

As depression descends and darkness begins
A dormant memory filled with confusion
Like a cavity the depth of deterioration from within
Judgement as an identity a deficiency of the mind

The precision of time as infinite as the beginning of time
With the presumption of life eternal dashed
An end to blinded want an unfulfilled meaning of truth
Laden chains which bind a heart with passion

An never ending circle of denial that leads to anguish
Unable to reclaim what now is lost with time
The winds of future hope surround the death of human kind

Gary K. Roussel

For David... On The Occasion Of Our 10th Anniversary

I know I've told you this a hundred different times...
   a hundred different ways...in the past ten years.
I just wanted to tell you one more time.

To me, you are so very beautiful, and sexy, and fun to be with.
I love the way you look, the way you laugh, the sound of your voice..
   the way your mind works.

I love the way you feel, and the way you make me feel...
   younger than I am, and important, and female.

It's astonishing to me that you don't know, all the time, that you are
   wonderful. So fine!

If I get to live another hundred years,
   and do everything you can do in a lifetime...

Like go to the moon in a spaceship... and spend some time on the
   floor of the sea....

Knowing you will still have been one of the most amazing...and
   exciting... and valuable experiences of my life.

And, even if I never see you again...

I will love you every day of that hundred years.
   Patricia Ann Riley

Gittin' Ready

A golden leaf flutters down to stomp the earth.
A heavy seed loaded stem sags with all its worth,
Flocks of birds noisily tear through walls of coolin' air.
In orchard the peace is torn by color of apple an' of pear.

Tall majestic green corn leaves hang, turnin' golden brown.
Orange pumpkins peek 'neath wilted leaf from frosty ground.
Smooth water wrinkles in designed crystals of ice.
A wasp defends territory, angered by death's comin' price.

Rich green alfalfa darkens, touched by frosty brush.
Pausin' ducks an' geese call from water an' from rush.
Cud chewin' cows choose sunshine in which to lay.
Sun drifts south an' thereby shortens every day.

Day time temperature may still go high.
But a chill on the breeze says it's nigh.
The cowboy scurries ta git done afore the call.
'Cause he knows, winter follows this thing called fall.
   Pete Davis

Children Seeking

Children seeking something, they yet not know
A child runs through the kitchen bare...
Chasing after a ball, He hits a chair.
Soon to stumble and fall,
Unlike most adults who fear change, would not try again at all.
The child who's little hands, wipe the tears from his eyes
Gets up sees the ball and again he tries.
He's tired lame and limp
Gets the ball in his hand and looks in amazement.
What can he really see?
This is a goal, so young achieved.
To us all it is...is a ball.
But in this child's heart, even so short, makes him feel so tall.
Only if this thrill to seek a goal could stay with us all.
Like a young child that was sure to fall
Got back up to chase the bouncing ball.
The ball is the ups and downs in life we all must learn to face...
But if we could only keep that smile on the young child's face.
   Raymond K. Baker

Black Velvet Nights, Etc

I miss like-souled companions:
A cat's tail stroking my leg,
A dog's mysterious, spine-tingling howl,
Mourning doves lined up in wait at a bird bath,
A wren shrieking me away from her nest,
A bee infatuated with my perfume.

But mostly I miss black velvet nights:
Secret, silver-scalloped clouds scudding in front of the moon,
Damp, dew-drenched air splitting my lungs,
A bouncy, thirsty turf beneath my feet,
The wild unfettering of my intellect and will
Expanding into the universe of its Creator.

In the garden of life
I ended up a potted plant.
   H. Rogers

Rachel

A mother, a child, never apart
A birth, a time, never forgot
A dream, a hope, not far beyond a touch
The child, my life, forever, day by day
I love her from places in the heart never touched
I would die for her, if I must

My baby so precious and new
Every turn, every look, something new
I used to take for granted my time with her,
Not anymore, the colors are brighter
The tilt of her head, trying to learn something new
That little girl, my daughter

I will always have time for "Mama, come look" and there before
My eyes, she is cradling her baby dolls
She sings them a lullaby, just like mama
The smile, the need to show, she too, can love and care
And take time out to sing to her babies, everyone

For my daughter Lord, I thank you
Please let me enjoy my time with her
Today, tomorrow, and yesterday too.
I love her, I do
   Theresa Mousseaux

The Dry Season

We left the highway an hour ago, crossed the threshold between smooth
pavement, billboards, thoughts of home, and where we are now—
the brush
stands tall and straight, stretching for rain, stalks still green, but
the leaves fading to a dull brown
the color of high deserts
the color of plateaus.

We stop where the ground is flat in between scattered mesas and get
out to touch the earth, to soil our shoes and gulp dusty air. We came
here to heal, to let the wind caress the pain from us, to purge the
smog and tension in great sighs to be swept up by dust-devils, to
discover the place where water hides in the summer, where the burros
rear their young, where the bubbles of hot springs sing and echo
between the water-reeds.

There is a small cave ahead, where a falcon leaps into the sky and
glides leaf-like toward the flatland. I would very much like to climb
up there, to sit at the mouth and look at the valley.
Maybe, I will crack open sandstone and find a fire opal for her.
Maybe, she will catch her breath and weave a thundercloud for me
   Thomas Andrew Sepulveda

Night Goddess

A purple shadow whispers to the moon,
Swims in the rose misted dusk.
With hair of sweet rusted honey
Her gown is a sea of tiny dew-kissed petals.
She robs the beauty of the smooth pink sky.

Milky white skin of silver light,
Cool bare feet
Beat lightly the rhythms of sundown,
Dancing, brushing soft toes over drowsy earth,
Chanting a luscious symphony
For lazy sleeping forests and the flooding spring.

She plays untouched behind night's teasing bed
of time and bitter need,
Revels in the splendors of the last dying rays,
Drunk from the light of a melting sun.

Rachel Coff

The True Meaning Of Christmas

When I go outside in December I feel the cool breezes around me.
I watch as snow settles on the ground and I even catch
some on my tongue.
It sends shivers up and down my spine.
As night falls, all the Christmas lights come to life;
red, blue, orange, an white.
I stare with all my might for I know that soon I will go to bed,
but when I wake up there are gifts everywhere.
When I go to look in my stocking I remember that the true
meaning of Christmas is not stockings filled with candy or
packages filled with toys, but it is the joy in a family for
being able to be together that counts.
So, before I go to my stocking, I glance at the nativity scene
and thank God for such a good family.
Then it is present time!

Sally Schwartz

Bio-Techno-Logica

sunny future
hobble space telescope photos
wide field planetary camera 2
age of the Universe
galaxies conflict in the cosmic zoo
elliptical age of sudden light
cross-sectional planetary maps
prototype planetarium bionic being
cerebral robotics revolution's total recall
terrarium and aquarium biosphere 3 paradigm
astronomy universal logarithms in experimental asteroid science
black-hole space vacuum
psychopathic scientists team
Earth pollution breath
ozone destruction space-watch
cocoon space life in a colonial nuclear crypt
ether dream in a Milky Way
radioactive waste station
interplanetary raped ghosts voyage
quantum hell-paradise leap theory expectations

Rafael Franco-Cuevas

Only God Knows

I guess I missed my star, as it came whistling through.
It must have been so bright, I couldn't see what to do.
But as I am reflecting, I see the things undone.
Somewhere there is an answer — only God knows!

I missed my children growing, through their adolescent years.
When marriages are broken, more than two shed tears.
Wishes cannot take me back, to undo things I've done.
Somewhere there is an answer — only God knows!

I guess I miss my dad, though we fought hard at times.
When stubborn faces selfish, it's a battle of the minds.
But fishing; hunting; memories; shall make it worth the wait,
for a never changing season — only God knows!

Randy Capen

The Negro Man

History was faced with a task in the midst of the past that has now
    formed into the ugly face
of racism in the present. Is it because of fear, memories, and tears,
Is it because of the attitudes we adhere. Does it make leaders of
America lie? Behind closed doors can you hear the negro man cry? Did
you know his heart still weeps? While his past continues to get
thrown at his bronze-colored feet.
In his workplace, no signs of the negro man in sight,
Being drawn out of his world will be his plight.
Not recognizing how he has been changed,
Through trying to survive in America's game.
Then on the tenth month, 16th day, of the ninety-fifth year,
A beautiful moment came into view, the day of atonement for the negro
    man came true.
A day where the want of turmoil filled the skies,
A day when your unknown brother gently wiped your tears from your eyes.
A day that allowed no separation of color-depth, educational-level, or
economical background, A day where the negro man came together
negro men that came to share.
So if you are a person that is confused, lost, or unobjectively bound,
This event was beautiful and needed for all races if they are ever to
    to be mentally found.
For one day we will all be one race pure and true,
Learn from your history, or the negro man will be you.

Phillip Tolar

A Final Farewell

The news came to us, one rainy June,
And we weren't prepared to lose you so soon.
Your time with us, would be just a while,
Time to witness your strength, memorize your smile.

The Lord was standing, outside his gate,
The time was near, and He could not wait.
His job for you, was special, I'm sure,
And through His love, we would endure.

You suffered enough, to let us know,
That it was time for us to let you go.
Towards the end, when we were alone,
You spoke so often, of going home.

You were my mother and my very best friend,
With a love and devotion, I'll not know again.
You're with me always, deep in my heart,
So strongly placed, we're never apart.

I hope someday, to see you again,
So our love and friendship, anew, can begin.
It sometimes takes a lot, to face a new day,
But I can get through it, in my mother's way.

Radie M. Larzelier

Mermaids

She skims the water, and believes in herself.
And never under estimates her worth.
She is one with the tides, where she remains,
Only to emerge in the ocean's turbulent sure.

The days come and go, but she will remain.
She is part of an endless cycle that never stays the same.
For she is a mermaid, and happiness she brings.
Just one smile is so sweet, that it makes
the entire world sing.
   MacKenzie Straub

"We Were Ten"

   We were ten, then nine, now eight, so we are what we are.
Aundrie an invalid could laugh and cry, miraculous spirit none could buy.
   Jean is too nice and so very sweet, Thernest quite smart and so discreet.
   As for Robbie you never knew, there was no clue to what she would do. Joyce was the spitfire of our charade, Connelly the romantic thinks he's a jade.
Melba wore a yellow dress with a bow in her hair, children
Like her, they come very rare. Then comes Elliot Mr. Dynamite
Who could make you laugh in spite.
   Marva and Margo two of a kind, the big surprise and the end of the line.
   Thernest and Senora the top of the stack, put all of us together as a matter of fact.
   ("My Father Said")
   When trouble comes be at ease, bow down on bended knees. The unseen angel most holy and divine, overcomes darkness and a fearful mind. When trouble comes be at ease.
   The greatest blessing of all men is to have a family like we ten.
   Robbie J. Thornes

Daughters

Cuddly and sweet in the arms of your mother,
A rose bud unfolding to the promise of life.
It's hard to believe that one day you'll be
A mother yourself and somebody's wife.
I look at you now with your dimples and smiles
Your teeth like small pearls, your hand like a star.
And I nestle you close as I think to myself
What wonderful miracles baby girls are.
   William Marquis Sr.

Untitled

My wings are black and broken.
My heart is hard and brown.
The love I once had for you crashed to an evil frown.
My soul doesn't smile anymore,
and it cries when you walk by.
You used to say you love me,
but now you say good-bye.
I cry with the sun.
At night when I'm alone.
Because you left my heart lonely and cold.
People tell me to smile, but I forgot how.
I can try to remember when you're not around.
   Sarah Sharp

Roots

From the bleak moon horizons, a resplendent blue planet rises sublime
But a speckle in the vastness of space, a glimmer in a stretch of time;
So alluring an earthrise, *deja vu* strikes in this moonwalking earth creature
Who, unraveling deep secrets of the past, sees this past in his future.

Venerable Earth, four and half billion year refuge, yet uncertain,
Her destiny forged by forces without, wrought by convulsions within,
Oasis in a system of barren, hostile worlds of benevolent Sun
Nurturing all creatures, predators and prey alike, from virus to man.

Threat of mass extinction in this planet gone deranged, depleted, dying,
Grim consequence of foolish man's greed, turf wars and reckless tinkering;
Generations pass, common sense remains, ever vigilant the wise
That generations come well planed and wars mere tantrums to compromise.

Whirling this galactic span, chance collision should Earth disintegrate,
Or freeze dry in a dwindling sun, or in a red giant incinerate;
So much in so short a time in the cosmic calendar can man achieve,
Perish not like dinosaurs, he can pre-empt stellar exodus and live.

Thence he travels with speed of light, transcends what he's capable of knowing,
And he seeds the stars with his kind, this legacy is his purpose of being;
Mortality bonds him closer with his God, redeemer, mollifier
As he finds in another star his roots. Mightier than he. Godlier.
   Wilmo C. Orejola

"Of Life—Of Time"

It's so amazing as a youngster Time doesn't matter at all. You don't have a care in the world, just a ball.
Life is so amazing, there is so much ahead, so much TIME, to do kid stuff complain and whine.
Your parents or guardian are indeed the world, so powerful, so loved so much TIME to enjoy it.
You find out that as TIME ticks so does age, and that youngster has to turn the page, Of Life.
Those precious ticks bring with them responsibility, the future and your visions as well as such tough-
tough decisions. Battling the world by yourself seems like such a chore. This thing called TIME has
made all decisions mine not a parents or guardians anymore. This world and thing that we call TIME,
makes Life seem somewhat scary, parents and guardians are happy but weary. With TIME comes age,
and again you must turn another page. You look for guidance, but TIME has made you the one, who gives
helpful advice and does what needs to be done! Your parents or guardians have since retired or have passed on, and that has passed the torch on to you. Its your TIME to make a way in life whether happy or blue. I'm very thankful, I had so much love and guidance with my TIME. My teachers are the one's that have passed me the torch as well as planted their seed! I only ask this thing called TIME to grant me all the TIME with my teachers, that I need!
   Vincent Shawn Reavis

My Love For Thee

Take this kiss upon thy cheek,
And in separation of thee I shall avow;

The visions which are within a dream of the heart which is pure.
Your eyes which have the sparkle of the moon reflecting off the ocean,
Giving me a breathless reaction of disbelief.

It feels as if I'm in a dream,
And so I bend over and grab a handful of sand,
But yet how few.
O, God, can I not grab so tight that it slips through my grasp!
Which is reality of life, or is it just my confusion?
   Shawn Eugene Norris

The Little Fat Gorilla

The little fat gorilla
Came through the stage door left.
Her white gloved fingers
Brushed
The glossed mahogany floor.
She came from no cream essence
She should have never left her cage.
But for ten long years she curtsied
Memorizing each and every page.
The thin blonde ladies laughing
Let her read a line or two.
Her fat, brown fingers trembling
Her voice rang clear and true.
Her last words barely spoken
As she walked back to the truck.
Where they drove her on to
Auschwitz
With a butterfly and a duck.
   Jean Brooks

The Answer: Suicide

I wonder as I wander out under the sky
Why I can't help myself to cry
I wonder as I wander out under the sky
Why, oh why did he have to lie
I wonder as I wander out under the sky
Now a big thing that was once a little lie
I wonder as I wander out under the sky
How can I go on living this life
I wonder as I wander out under the sky
What should I do knowing it's all a lie
I wonder as I wander out under the sky
Telling myself, I didn't even try
I wonder as I wander out under the sky
I can't believe this, how could he lie
I wonder as I wander out under the sky
How could he lie to me right through my eyes
I wonder as I wander out under the sky
What do I do next, now should I die
I wonder as I wonder out under the sky
Is my only answer suicide?
   Kristen Alberre

T L C

The patient's been toasted and milked and souped.
She's bright and smiling but her helper is pooped.
I've smoothed her sheets and tugged her covers
And read her stories of ships and lovers.
I'm bushed, exhausted, and out of whack.
If only her nurse would hurry back!

My "Rise and Shine" has lost its snap.
Hours have passed since I had a nap.
Please spare me the list of things to do
And your offer of coffee to see me through.
Don't bring me tonics or stimulants
Just hang me on the clothesline by the a** of my pants.
   Garold W. Curo

Sexual Collision

We're a sexual collision
on a California highway.
We're a 30 car pileup
on a foggy afternoon.
We're a bumping and a grinding
in the middle of the night.
You're looking at me.
I'm thinking of you,
I think therefore you are.
I will I know you do.
I'm addicted to you, I'm stuck, I'm trapped.
Can't think of a better place,
Couldn't pick a better time.
Wouldn't want it any other way.
Shouldn't go away.
Shoulda been today.
We're a sexual collision
on a California highway.
   Jack Mandile

Oh My Child

I'm lying here trying hard to fall asleep
I've tried everything even counting sheep
But this fear and ache I hide is keeping me awake
The house is very quiet, only for awhile
He comes up to my room, on his face he wears a smile
How can he do this? Doesn't he think it's wrong?
Doesn't he feel any guilt all day long?
He leaves after filling his need
Deep inside I bleed. Bleed with the anger and want to tell
What did I do to deserve this living HELL?
These awful thoughts stick out in my mind
I wish they would fade away and go blind
He treats me like royalty, just so I won't speak
I'm only a child, I make it seem unreal
Doesn't he know how I feel? Does he think that I enjoy this?
Does he think I like that kiss? He asks for my forgiveness
Why, does he think that he'll go sinless?
I hate that awful man, no one knows exactly why
They all just think I'm mad. They say,
"You've gotta love that guy, he's your one and only DAD."
   Nicole Castillo

Schism

Animosity breeds, fed by the press.
Hate consumes, racism looms
while the media
feeds the masses.
White on black
has gone from
black to white
like day into night.
It's not just a white thing anymore.
TV and newspapers shovel their sh**
of the man holding people down.
We should all
realize we're all
human beings and have
common ground.
Mankind - the species above all others,
but we can't get along
because of race and color.
   Chris Powell

Friends

Friends are the very best
Even if they're sometimes a pest
Friends will right you when you're wrong
When you're sad they'll sing you a song

People have written many rhymes
About a lot of good times
Although sometimes it may seem
Life is not just peaches and cream

Friends are there to pull you through
The b*t*h called life too
It would be nice if people cared
Whether you died or were spared

Well listen up to you hear
Most people live in fear
Of having the wrong kids for friends
Upon their peers their judgment depends

Neal Piché

The Rape

He touches her tenderly
And says don't worry
He locks the door
And shuts the shade
She knows this is wrong,
But what is she to do
He covers her mouth
She yells
But they are unheard
The tears roll from her eyes
And her heart beats faster
Her cries scream of agony
Her mind races
With immortal thoughts
And the virgin child is no more.

Melissa Brasil

Lactations Of A Paining Generation

Flow thickly from the breast
Choking novice throats to insanity
and wantonness.

Some are fed by bottle pumped
or even by straw
Milkshake blood slows us down to the
impeccable ghetto crawl.

Us, bruised sucklings
on the breast swollen from beatings
Follow each other in zombie procession
jetting out bile's hope
That yearns to coat the reasons

By which we should love.

Sometimes sour milk
will wind up in some cheese

A solid

Giving up no liberties
For refreshment and mind-ease.

Shannon Bush

Football

Rice and Young standing on a field,
A lady sang the anthem and they both kneeled
First came the pass, then came the run
They got near the end-zone and this starts the fun
L.T. and Long busted through the line
To the running backs this was one big stop sign
Young saw the dust and that huge mass
Then pulled down his pants and showed them his @$$
This got L.T. and Long really fired up
And everyone thought that they were going to erupt
Long came from one side and L.T. from another
They crunched Young for talking about their mother
Even though the ball had already been thrown
Steve Young lay there in a pile of blood and bone
But L.T. wasn't finished and neither was Long
And young now realizes that he was really wrong!

Kent Moran

Ntwadumela

The world is still the spider sucking my life from within
leaving my body dry, hanging on this web
despite of my struggles I'm still weighted down to the bottom
while you surface to the top, still being harassed
won't let me smoke my crops, I am like an eagle without its eyes
a fly with no wings, a bee without its sting
my mind is as powerful as our rotation around the sun
my heart as strong as the force that keeps it
but yet you rather save the trees that grow, then my soul
and you wonder why the poison seeps from the earth
and you wonder why the Gods piss on your towns
and you wonder why the children murder
the beast is heard from sea to shining sea
- doomed to self destruction
but I will not be saddened by your treatment
revenge is the taste in my mouth
I will return on a flaming horse
with a legion of death beside me
you will swallowed by a sea of men
who scream out my name, Ntwadumela... the revolution is near.

Ruben Rodriguez

Truth Becomes Her

Do I eat and drink a diet of illusion?
To sustain and nourish me...
drain and ravage me?
I starve for truth, yet gorge on lies,
craving pretense others despise

Am I binging and purging on lies?
Drink in deceit, such a relief!
Piss out toxins — they were my belief
I am cleansed and purified
I am soiled and terrified

My name is Anne...I am a "pretendaholic"
Shadow figure, mysteriously serene
Lies become my cloak, truth the dagger
to protect my self, yet I stab at truth

My game is bluff...more "The Fool" am I
Thinning shadow figure, layered with fake fat
With trump card played
and cloak out of closet,
again I stab at the truth
Tell me, which way is the dagger pointed now?

Jacqueline Anne Texier

Second Chances

As I drift off to years gone by; quite often I might add;
  comes into focus big brown eyes and blond hair of a cheerful lad,
A boy who's home was rich with love, homemade bread and chocolate pie;
  a boy who's life was a fairy tale, which he would learn as years went by.

He loved to play toy soldiers, hide from his dog, and catch a bug;
  he loved the endless days of summer, ice cream, and a mother's hug
He loved the fall the best by far, cool weather and pumpkins and
  pine straw; then came turkey, cold breezes and Christmas, the
  sounds of a lonely saw.

But as time went by his interests changed, he began to grow his wings;
  for now he was into cars and parties, and hadn't time for those
  childish things.
Books and class, new friends, new jobs, new problems and things of
  concern; political science, to vote on new issues, global warming,
  and flags that would burn.

And it slowly began to dawn on the boy, as he pondered with a
  regretful sigh; that he had casually taken every day for granted,
  that his childhood had passed him by.
And the more he thought what a fool he had been, the bluer that he
  became; in knowing that no matter how hard he tried, things could
  just never be the same.

So listen, dear children, how I do plea, don't wish and count time to
  be grown; for the one that I speak of, whose memories I share, are
  none other than those of my own.
But in closing this tale there's a happy note, for I'm going back to
  my childhood, you see; for the Lord has blessed me with two little
  boys who will spend their childhood with me.
  Stephen C. Huggins

"Racial Democracy"

Lincoln's democracy of the people for the people.
Racial democracy for the Blacks, for the Whites.
Strange things, they are history creators and destroyers.

Pope Paul says "This s a colorful land"
Of hospitality and greatness in sand.
This sand embraces all the immigrants
who greet this magnificent land.

Offered equal opportunities to all beyond
Colour, Creed and Race, the main principles
of the leader of democracy, The Great America.

Blacks are the heart of America, Whites are the brain,
Asians are the legs and others are the frame.
This is called the "American Gentleman."
How can this Gentleman be a Racist?

Let us join, Chain our hands together
To fight racism, preserve Unity of land together,
To maintain Peace, Brotherhood and Advancement of land.
United we fight Evils, join mains streams of land.

"O'h Media - Don't call as Black or White Americans anymore,
We are Americans of America and are Americans only".
  Narinder Nath Chawla

The Wonders Of God!

The wind did blow. Branches swaying, leaves singing in
their own way. The sound was different when the wind blew
the fongs of a palm tree, Knocking against each other,
crackling as the wind continued to blow. The rain
caused a bit of a fog at a distance. We didn't get the
rain, only the blow. Music to my ears. Sight to the
eyes. The wonders of GOD.
  Charlotte M. Ryan

Miracles

If you never saw a miracle
you're not looking very hard.
They're happening all the time - you see,
right in your back yard.

Flowers from a tiny seed,
babies from the womb,
night then light, water and ice,
birds flight, songs in tune.

Where did air come from, water too,
why are clouds white in a sky of blue?
How did the cell divide to be me?
How is the pollen found by the bee?

You never saw a miracle?
Just look and you will see,
they're all around, put here by God,
two are you and me.
  Larry R. Buss

You

You always tell me
you're not like the rest.
You say you won't hurt me,
my fears, you repress.
Each night on the phone
you are gentle and kind.
And during the day
it's you on my mind.
But if it seems like
I don't really care,
please know that I do
and I'll always be there.
It's just my little way
of protecting myself
I don't think you'll hurt me,
but it's my heart on the shelf.
So if you are thinking
about you and I,
just know that I need you
to stay by my side
  Melissa Scuccimarri

'Tis My Heart Will Always Know'

How much I love you
  You'll never know

'Tis my heart will
  always know

Cause forever is what
  my heart desires

'Tis my heart will
  always know

You and me
  Me and you

Is what will
  always be

Always and forever
  for Eternity!
  Kristin Ernst

Untitled

They say that when you fall in love
you'll know it's a gift from God above.
The most precious gift is when you can
give of yourself, one woman, one man;
it's much more than just a love affair,
so much more than only saying "I care."
It's holding on when you can't let go
And times get tough, and you want to grow;
please take my heart, my love, my hand
and together we'll build from grains of sand.
Our dreams will soar on wings of doves
let's open this precious gift of love.

Lisa Belmonte

Please Join

Welcome to the club
You'll be paying out your dues
Monies are not collected
We all stand to lose

There is no discrimination
Men and women of varied races
All the children range in ages
And come from numerous places

The local chapters are endless
National headquarters are out of town
It's whereabouts are in question
The president is unknown

Members compare case histories
The plots vary in degree and length
They are all different and yet the same
Contrasting weaknesses and strengths

In the end it doesn't matter
The losses are all the same
In this club of unhappy endings
A fraternity house to share our pain

Margery Mulberg Tuckman

"The Waiting Game"

Little birdies in a cage,
you look down at that cat with rage.
The cat looks up at two plump,
   flittering feather balls with a
   slavering mouth;
He's hoping the cage will fall.
Dreaming it will happen, the cat
   waits and waits prepared to pounce,
   play and maul
A dream of feathers flying everywhere,
   these now screaming, bald tidbits
   look ready to eat.
The cat hears the tune of a can opener
   in the house,
He awakens from his dream and heads for
   the music he hears.
Oh well! the cat meows, after lunch,
I'll nap and then, catch that tricky
   little mouse!

Lillian C. White

Heaven's Little Stars

Oh little stars gleaming in the night
You light the sky for angels flight
You sparkle and shine
So heaven can be found

Sometimes you're still
Sometimes you fall to the ground

So we watch and study
With a telescopic eye

And in our amazement
We don't know why

You shine so brightly in the sky

Miranda Skriba

Daniel

Blonde and so precious
You laugh with your eyes
They sparkle like stars
As blue as the skies.

Quick and mischievous
Both told by your grin
Your cute little giggles
Mask the trouble you're in.

Fat little cheeks
Mama's favorite to kiss
And gentle bear hugs
A grandmas pure bliss

The stories you tell
With words so few
Are priceless to her
And I'll always love you.

Marilyn Nelson

Legacy Of Love

Blind and cold and cancer ridden,
You held your head so high!
You took all that life threw at you
And never questioned why!

We tried to be as brave as you
But knew we could not be.
So, we cried out to our Lord above
To hear our earnest plea.

Then, he wrapped you in His loving arms
And carried you Home on High.
Now, we no longer see the pain you felt
Or hear your muffled cry.

We only love you more each day
For your blessed legacy.
For you taught us of Love and Hope
And Patience and Charity!

Michelle Lanier Herrin

Darling

Popped in at lunch
You were asleep,
Watched you dreaming
without a peep
Grabbed a bite
Without a sound
Love you so much
Please stay around.

Kerry A. Burke

Attitudes

You fuss, shout and yell,
You are pure venom,
   And you make peoples lives
An utterly, living hell.

If this is the way you live,
Then why do you live at all?
   Are you happy and content,
When you make others look small?

This life is full of stress,
And an awful lot of sorrow.
   Why can't you be kind to others
And look forward to tomorrow?

Kathleen Williams Flores

Alone

In so many ways I feel alone.
Yet I know I'm not, because
I have an everlasting friend
right in my soul.
He shines a lot of light
and has an everlasting love.
One that will never end.
He has faith and almighty strength.
No one else has. He brings hope
and happiness even in the simplest
ways. He brings goodness and he
fills an empty soul with the
love and strength it needs
to know you're not alone.
God is that special friend
Who will take care of you
And bring you his love and
happiness to share with you

Manuela Dague

Forever . . .

The water flows over the same dam
   year after year
Over and over again
   through the sun, rain
Winter, Summer
   over the stones made smooth and worn.

Where does it go to -
   never to be seen again,
Never to return to the same place
   but yet it goes . . .
Without anticipation of the unknown,
Without expectations of glory.

Mary Lou Faitoute

Way Up There

When you see the world, the
World from high above, it is
Better than any aphrodisiac.
The feeling you share with the
Clouds: Your heart feels as pure
As the air and the moon, a place
Where no violence can take
Place, a calm, quiet place warm
And gentle. Happy, no worries or scares.
Just you and the air.

Nicole Christine Catlin

God Sent

Her solid rough hands
   worked to the bone,

Her tiny pale face
   only from which love is shown,

She leaves the world untouched,
   Sprinkling it with sunshine.

She's fragile and loved
   very much

To everyone who surrounds her,
   she touches with her gentle heart.

Her title she holds,
   she plays the best part.

She walk with God
   leading her way,

She's my Grandma,
   and I'm proud to say

A place in my heart,
   for her there will always be,

For I'm most thankful,
   that she was a God Sent gift to me.

Kriston B. Wood

The First Day Of Our Last Year

My little son and I
work outside,
Digging the earth
Till there's room enough,
To plant a small pine,
A small pine,
Our first Christmas tree.

So hard, it is to believe
That so soon, already we'll leave.

But today, in sunshine and crisp air,
The first day of our last year,
We work hard to replace
What was once lost in a storm,
Leaving behind us, - a tree,
Hopefully to live on-

In memory of our time,
We've spent in this home.

Mary Morimoto

Untitled

"Who is that woman?"
"Why Dad, she's your wife!
The woman you have lived with
Most of your life!"
His eyes seemed dazed,
He couldn't comprehend,
So I tried to explain,
Started over again.
"Dad, she's my mother,
Now, don't you see?"
He turned and then said,
"She's purty, ain't she."

Marian A. Hufnagel

One Voice

O nations of shame
Words so untame
Casting the blame
O nations of shame.

Of memories in sorrow
Words cannot hallow
Yesterday's tomorrow
Of memories in sorrow.

Children do play
Learning to say
This is the way
Children do play.

Of memories in sorrow
Words cannot hallow
Yesterday's tomorrow
Of memories in sorrow.

O nations of shame
Words so untame
Casting the blame
O nations of shame.

Marvin Blevins

Untitled

You darling, my
Wonderful work of art -
So many fine lines I
So long to caress -
But you are not
Present -
You are suspended
High above the earth
Leaving the laws of
life below -
I reach out to you
Always my wonderful
Work of art -

Nikki Burchett

These Three Things

The great outdoors I do explore
With wonder and delight
To catch the breath of life!
Yet, books are living things to me
Through them I live vicariously
To gain an insight into life.
Friends are people that I know
Who set a little spark aglow
And add the zest to life.

Lila Ruth Stokes Matthys

Chic

Chic is a unique creature
with many little features.
He has a brown and green eye,
but he thinks he's sly.
Chic has black and white fur,
and he loves to purr.
He likes to swim,
and climb tree limbs.
Chic likes to eat cheese,
but he gets nervous when he sees bees.
Chic likes the color green,
but he doesn't like to eat beans.
Chic is afraid of bats
because Chic is a cat.

Olla Najah Al-Shalchi

I Love The Trees

I love the trees in winter
   with lofty limbs upraised
I love the trees in springtime
   with tender buds arrayed
I love the trees in summer
   with glossy leaves of shade
I love the trees in fall
   with colors on parade.

Marguerite Keltz Edwards

Tapestry

My life has been a tapestry,
With little bits and threads of "me."
Woven by the master's care,
There's little pieces everywhere!

But all the bits and all the parts
Come from the depths of my own heart.
God alone has seen them all
And woven Life from my downfall.

Do well to ponder your own life;
The good, the bad, the toil, the strife —
And wonder when the weaving's through,
What tale will your life tell of you?

When little threads: hopes and fears,
Sorrows, joys, dreams and tears,
All are place in God's own hand
He waves a tapestry that stands.

Kristin Downer

"Serenity"

The high, jagged mountains,
   with frosty-white peaks...
A bright colored sky,
   with soft cloudy streaks...
The birds in the air,
   who glide with such ease...
A caressing, cool wind,
   which blows thru the trees...
The path, thru a meadow,
   which winds to a stream...
A soft, grassy knoll,
   where you sit back and dream...
The old willow tree,
   near the top of the hill...
Are places that time
   just seems to stand still.

Lauri L. Parnella

God Is Real

When I see a baby smile
with a love glowing from the eyes.
Or see a flock of geese
flying across warm blue skies.
When my eyes look on autumn colors
painted on a hill of trees,
or see a field of wild flowers
and many flying buzzing bees.
Or see an old grey haired man
holding hands with a loving wife,
and I know that all is well
for it's such a lovely life.
I know that God is real
I feel joy both day and night.
For only God's great love
could make so much so right.

Larry L. LaPean

Epiphany January 6

One night in a stable, Jesus was born,
   Wise men were led by a star,
Herod was out-witted and Jesus would grow
   to save all sinners near and afar.

2000 years have passed since then
   and now we all live to see
year after year we all celebrate
   January 6, Epiphany.

If we come to HIM in humility
   and let Him know we're contrite
He will forgive us all our sins,
   He is the Way, the Truth and the Light.

Lillian T. Johnson

"Be In"

Summer days are growing short,
winter is upon us.
The coolness that descends each day,
a blanket of reminders.
"Be in, be in" the twilight screams,
the sun exhausts itself.
Shadows roam and darkness sings,
pouncing like a lion.
The stars are crying out to night,
please give peace a chance.
Your cover is embracing
death and violence.
The dawn is stretching out a hand,
shining with an eloquence,
encouraging humanity
to rise above the ignorance.

Marlene J. Griffin

If

If I cry into your shoulder,
Will you take away my pain?
If I hold onto your hand,
Will you lead me through the rain?

If I gently close my eyes,
Will you guard me from all danger?
If I find I'm by myself,
Will you never be a stranger?

If I ever lose my balance,
Will you come to catch my fall?
If I suddenly can't find you,
Will you come answer my call?

If I want to reach the sky,
Will you help me fly my kite?
If I find myself in darkness,
Will you help me find the light?

If there's something I can't reach,
Will you get it from above?
If you see my heart is empty,
Will you fill it with your love?

Karen Sautter

Sunset And Sand

Remember the days of sunsets and sand
sitting on the life guard stand?
Surrounded by an orange sky,
we were only silhouettes, you and I
we were only silhouettes, you and I.

Lori Richardson

The Winged Seed

Even the barren sand
Will receive the winged seed
To search its depths
For the level where
It will electrify into clusters
Of joyful, wild grass
As life's continuity.

So, too, I've watched the dying
Cling to life
While a mysterious growth
Was being seeded
In some other perpetuity.

Lillian L. Unanue

"The Pain Will Cease"

Although at times your pain feels it
will never cease to end.
Always remember I'm here,
I'll be your friend.

The days ahead may seem blue
or clouded with gray.
I am here to push the
storms away.

When your feeling lonely or sad
I'm here to ease your mind
Help you forget your troubles
make them both yours and mine.

I know whatever happens
it was simply meant to be,
although you can't believe it
things will get better, you'll see.

So I will leave this paper now
but I will never leave you out of my heart.
Don't forget I'm here for you,
even when we're apart.

Melissa Krauss

My Love Will

The love I have for you,
Will endure throughout the years,
Growing stronger every day,
Fed by your laughter and tears,

It will stand the test of time,
Weathering each new storm,
Protected by your presence,
Where it's kept safe and warm.

My love will always be,
A beacon in the night,
To guide and give you comfort,
An ever shining light.

My love will give you courage,
To start each brand new day,
It will give you joy and hope,
Down life's uncertain way.

Forever my love will last,
For there will never be,
Someone with a greater love,
Than the love you have from me.

Linda Rincon

A Circle Of Love

Hold the circle of your love around me
Wide enough to let me roam.
Give me space to have a sense of freedom,
Circle close enough to keep me home.

Love me just enough to let me go
That I may bring to you my heart,
And in willing love submit my all
So love's circle will never part.

Let me circle you with love -
That love which sets you free,
Gives you room to change and grow,
Allows you to be whom you must be.

Then to each other will our love bind us
With cords that always stretch and grow,
Enfolding gently, firmly, for all time
This wondrous love we share and know.

Martha M. Rogers

Is This True?

Why do I feel the way I do
Why do I always think about you
Why does my love grow more and more
With each passing day
Why does my mind seem to wander
so far away

Am I really as special as you say I am
Do you love me as much as I do you
With all these questions I wonder why
Someone as great as you didn't just
pass me by

I guess what I'm trying to say is
Thanks for loving me the way you do
Also, thanks for choosing me to be with you.

Maegan Michelus

My Friend

I have a friend
Who's more than a friend you see
And all the neighbors agree.

She stands nice and tall
And is always on call, so it seems.
We all watch and keep track,
And try to pay back, some good deeds.

She's always so busy,
Goes so fast - makes us dizzy,
We try but we can't keep up.
To fast even, for her Pup.

She drops by for a minute,
And we hope she'll sit and visit,
But she talks while she waters your plants.
She goes from room to room pushing the vacuum,

And then looks around saying, "What else?"
If she ever takes off
It's not to play golf,
She's to busy a bee.
My friend, BEVERLY.

Mae C. Reed

Quest For Perfection

To the beauty that lives within my soul,
who's being elusive brings,
me exploring all of my broken paths,
and innermost secret things.

I've looked so deep inside of me,
searching for the key,
that will never fit the secret lock,
lost inside of me.

Through books and brain I seek to gain,
a meaning that's confined,
in my soul, within my shell,
and etched across my mind.

Through all who know this spiritual art,
to all the feeling in my heart,
To learn my soul and truly be,
the beautiful soul inside of me.

Laurie Jo Baumle

Buffy

I have a little furry friend
Who lives with me.
Her name is Buffy.
She's soft and fluffy
And good as a dog can be.
She takes me for walks
And almost talks
And brings me safely home.
Whatever the weather
We're happy together
And have no desire to roam.

Lucile H. Steele

Friendship

A friend is someone who stands by you
   who knows your every way
who doesn't look at you, as an old shoe
   and watches you grow each and every day.

They do not judge your every fault,
   nor judge your broken fences
instead they can look within your garden
   and help to mend the fences.

They can look beyond the dust,
   the dirt and all the hurt
They can love you till you bust
   and says it's just a silly quirk.

A friend is always there
   through the think and the thin
for when they too will turn around
   you too will be a friend.

Linda Cole

To My Husband

You're warm, you're passionate,
You are very dear.
I love you and I want
You all the year.
It's been along time,
Since we first met, and
I'm here to say, with
That warm smile, and
Those dimples, you stole
My heart away.

Margaret Hahn

Untitled

Red
White
And Blue
Three buttons
Looking at them
A man
Frenzied
In alarm
Which one?
Blue of calm everlasting skies
White of infinite peace
The red
He lays his finger
On the red
And
In a defining roar
He is
No more.

Loni Kuberka

Treasures

Treasures, not such an easy word to define,
While I know the meaning of all of mine,
Some I have sort of tucked away in store,
And seldom ever look at them any more,
Some make me sad, others make me smile,
Still I get them all out once in a while,
None were ever precious stones or gold,
Nor could any of them have been sold,
The old quilt always on Granny's bed,
Someday it would be mine she said,
Pappy's watch told the time each day,
Was handed to me when he went away,
A wooden rolling pin made by my dad,
It was the only one Mother ever had,
Her pretty china so delicate and fair,
A lock she saved from my baby hair,
There are other treasures only I can see,
For they are locked away in my memory,
But the treasures held dearest to me,
Are all clearly defined as "My Family."

Mary Kline

Autumn Years

In the Autumn of my life...
while fog-filled memories whirl
inside my mind...
like parchment leaves of reds
and browns...
aloft on gusty puffs of wind...
I view my life and weep for that
which might have been.

MaryAnn Maddux

"The Four Seasons"

Winter, Spring, Summer and Fall,
Which one do you like best of all?
In the Winter, it is cold,
And the wind is very bold,
In the Spring, flowers grow,
And everything is aglow,
In the Summer, it's time for fun,
We swim and sit in the sun,
In the Fall, the leaves come down,
Reds, yellows and golden brown.

Madeline DeMoro

Why??? Darkest

The Sun Sets slowly on this summer day
Which makes my pain so hard to go away
I wait for the moon to show a sign
So I can hide my sorrows and try to unwind

I find it hard to live through the day
Without looking for a dark hole to stay
I ask myself WHY DARKEST seem to be
My only sign of release

I try to hide behind the clouded shades
That makes the world seem old in age
The blue jays sings it tunes
That makes my day even harder to consume

All alone in the day
Only darkest seems to share my forte
Climbing every mountain valley and stream
But the light seems to still follow me
I look for that hole that big dark hole
Where I can rest my head peacefully.

Nikisha Thornhill

Lost and Found

Have you ever looked back and wondered;
Where's the you you used to be?
I was lost for so long
Then I found you
And in finding you, I found me.

Kathy L. Carleton

Christmas In The Heart

There is a secret place
Where joy begins to start —
An anticipated, serene retreat,
Called Christmas in the Heart

Jeweled in radiant splendour
With Golden memories as its art —
Silver thoughts linger on its walls
When Christmas is in the Heart

Perfumed in fragrant aroma
To invigorate and exhort —
Ambitions soar and goals arise
If Christmas is in the Heart

Illuminated with kindness
To resist the enemy's fiery dart —
A spark glows in loving wonder,
Where there's Christmas in the Heart

A dwelling with many chambers,
Whose miracles will never depart —
Its gifts keep on returning;
Everyday can be Christmas in the Heart!

Mary Livingston Stenhouse

Untitled

Loppy Doppy
Big jaloppy
Chimichonga
Walkie Talkie
Coffee Toffee
China Cho
Frappy Jap
Arapaho

Matt R. Garcia

Big Empty

I feel low
where is the glow...
I don't know......
I am empty
like a dark hole
nothing within
I long for things
things for filling
I want to be full
I am in the middle
the middle of nothing
it is Wednesday
the middle of the week
so to speak
days are no difference
to me...how long is the wait
how much will it take
I have little
little left for it...
this big empty.

Nina D.

Untitled

Moms are there to pick you up
When you've fallen down.
Dads are there to catch the ball
And toss the frisbee 'round.
Moms are there to hug and kiss,
Oh, and Dads are too.
They tuck you in to bed at night
And say "sweet dreams" to you.
A better pair, no one could find,
So sweet and full of love.
Since the day you brought me home,
I've thanked the One above.

Laura Beth McDonnell

In All Your Splendor

I saw you for a fleeting moment
When you let your guard come down

I saw that you were softly crying
As your tears fell to the ground

I saw the sadness in your eyes
When you saw the hunger on their face

I heard compassion in your voice
I knew you would gladly trade your place

I saw you as a humble person
Who one day would wear a crown

I saw you in all your splendor
When you let your guard come down.

Kenneth J. Hashbarger

Hurricane

Hurry away, don't come back,
Until it's safe and sound.
Run from me, hide from me.
Reckless paths, I am bound.
I'm ruthless, I'm trouble
Coastal storms, I'm the worst.
And if I'm at my toughest,
Now prepare to feel the burst.
Escape me if you can.

Marci Smith

To My Husband Of 22 Years

I was alone, and oh so lonely,
When you came into my life.
You filled my heart with joy,
When you ask me to be your wife.

Our years have been a blessing,
Sent from God above.
It's been a pleasure knowing you,
And sharing with you my love.

Your kind and patient ways,
Have been my strength and light.
Just knowing that you love me,
Fills my heart with delight.

Louise Holzman

Mother And Son

There was fun in the old days
When we could be wild,
But then too many years in between
Without a child

It's not too long ago
I seem to recall,
He was only a prayer
For us one and all

Now things have changed
For the better of course,
And our family has grown
Thanks to you, Ei, the force

Your determination and courage
Is an inspiration to everyone,
Whose life is yet to be filled
With the joys of their own new son

Eric is as special
As they come in life,
And I thank God every day
That you are a loving mother and beautiful wife

Kevin T. Corlett

Take Thou This Life

I have braved the darkest night
When the storm raged at its height;
I have watched and stood my ground
When despair stalked all around;

I have reached a helping hand
To guide the ship-wrecked to the land
And as a lighthouse beacon strong,
God placed me here where I belong,
Shining forth His powerful light
Impassive, strong, throughout the night.

Now, Father, hear my thankful prayer
Placed humbly on Your Golden Stair;
No credit mine, that You should choose
This mortal me, this life, to use.

Mary Wales

Untitled

With hope and desperation
we all must try,
stopping the tears
from our loved one's eyes.
Unwrap yourself
from your cloak of vain,
for you are not long
from your brother's pain.

Misty Dawn Grogan

Promises Of Heaven

Oh, to be in Arkansas
when the leaves begin to fall
and to be at mother's folks
where we went to pay a call
on her sisters, only two,
and brothers, there were seven.

Oh, to be in old Ashdown
when the pears turn in the fall
and to once more see the steam
curling up the kitchen wall
while Grandma coddles breakfast eggs
and fashions rolls plumped with leaven.

To sit in the front room
and hear Aunt Helen play
"Shall We Gather at the River"
on the Baldwin one more day
while the daylight falls away
would be most promising of heaven.

Mary Franklin Friesz

Vietnam Sky

Once there was a time
When the doves could fly
Wherever they liked
In the clear, blue sky.

Then there was a time
When they could only fly
At the risk of their life
'cause bullets tore the sky.

Now though it's peace time
They still cannot fly:
Trapped in the barbed wires
Strewn by past hatred and strife.

Khiem Vinh Thai

Time Spiral

There are times -
When our anger over powers us.

There are times -
When rage surrounds us.

There are times -
When mental abuse belittles us.

There are times -
When physical fatigue reduces us.

There are times -
When our survival depends on us.

- - -

Time is there -
When our understanding empowers us.

Time is there -
When love surrounds us.

Time is there -
When kind words improve us.

Time is there -
When hope strengthens us.

Time is there -
When our actions unite us.

Lynda Jean Bryant

"I Wonder"

I wonder if he thinks of me
when it's quiet and he's alone
I wonder if he remembers my
number when he looks at the phone
I wonder if he hurts inside
when they play our song
I wonder if he yearns for me
when a couple strolls along
I wonder if the memories
keep him awake at night
I wonder if he wishes that
we never had that fight
I wonder and question until
my wonders run out
But most of all - I wonder,
if he wonders, what I'm wondering about.

Keri-Ann McCarthy

Speaking Of Touch

Where I touch, is the mind of men
When I touch, I let them in
How I touch, is very gentle
What I touch, is very mental
Why I touch, is like the quiet sea
Knowing how peaceful it can be
Watching him sneak from
behind the waves—
I wonder why he put
my heart in a grave.

Latrice Banks

A Son-net To My Son John Thomas

John was a batten' son of-a-gun
When ever he got to bat, you could
hear the bat go crack.

From the top of the stands to the
bottom of the rack -
And everyone would sing out
Out of the park 'o' John, you
batten' son of-a-gun -

And the pitchers were alarmed,
As they about threw off their arms

Out of the Park "O" John

Mick Chatterton

Life

When one dreams of yesterday,
What does it mean to say;
I've lived my life.
How about you?
Have you fulfilled your life's desire?
To dream of the land afar
What does it mean, when you say,
was it really a dream?
Now we know it was real
As you see; you can feel.
And make your dreams reality
It is not pity one feels for others,
We want to think of them as brothers!
Remember to live your life to the fullest
That's all there is to give...
One's remarkable intelligence.

Marie Christman

In My Mirror

In my mirror
What do I see?
A strong Black Woman
What is my destiny?
In my mirror
I see two eyes
So full of hate
And so full of pride.
In my mirror
I'm so full of pain
So many troubles
Will I ever be whole again?
In my mirror
I do see hope
With strength and determination
I am not a joke
In my mirror
I do see love
I feel God's love surround me
Like an angel from above.

Mary Bannister

God's Cry

Last night, it was thundering and lightning.
What a beautiful sight and yet, frightening.
I wonder, was God showing his anger?
Was this a warning? Are we in danger?
During this out cry the winds were strong,
lightning bolts many, bright and long.
Can still hear the thundering in my mind,
like loud yelling from someone unkind.
Raindrops pounded against the wall.
God loves me so but he loves us all.
Love so strong he allowed many to sleep.
Were those raindrops or did I hear God weep?

Leisa Bunkley

Rainbow Of Love

We're a rainbow of many children
We're a force made of love
Those of our prejudice neighbors
Will never rise above.

I was raised with loving values
My mama said to me one day,
Never judge a person's colors
Judge their hearts and what they say.

There will come a time on earth
When all men shall live in peace
All our colors will not matter,
And we'll tame that prejudice beast.

Then we'll live as God said,
In a world where there's no hate
Where love and peace come together
We'll seal our destiny, seal our fate.

So I tell you, all my brothers
Let's make a chain, that spreads around,
Let's come together for all the children
Finally, rejoicing in the love we've found.

Karen Brown

The Testimony

Tears of blood fall from my weak, weary eyes
Welling up from a heart that has suffered so
    much pain.
If they fall to the barren ground will they
    be swallowed up and forgotten?
Or, if they fall into those hands that mean
    so much
Will they be gathered up, protected, and
    loved for what they really are?
Feelings of one who is incapable of doing
    any different

Lynn E. Wilkinson

An Affair In July

The fourth of July...
We patiently awaited its arrival,
arrangements are made with anticipation
that this day will be celebrated in Glory.

The events of the day are carefully planned
to meet at a designated place,
the day goes by
filled with laughter and joy

The flicker; a tiny little flare
ignites the wick to form a spark;
building... building... its energy
through the streamline

Then suddenly,
as if night became day
the skies are lit up
with explosions of color

As quickly as it came
the day ended in exhilaration,
and when we left,
our Hearts stayed behind.

Lydia B. Henderson

It's Too Late...

In our quest for what awaits us
    we leave things behind,
And some of what is left
    are those people we seldom find.

Those who love us the most,
    and are keen on what we need.
Those who we treat austere,
    who are few and far between.

When we realize what has passed
    reflect upon our actions and ways.
How we treated those who love us.
    It's too late... they're on their way.

Kandice Dawn Taylor

Dreams

Dreams are wonderful in many
ways...
    There what you can keep forever and
always...
    They move with you through your life,
don't ever let them go...
    For if you let them leave your side
then you'll never know...
    what could have been!

Morning Star Gray

Water Windows

Silent, silver skipping minnows
Walking on the water windows

Mirrors of a world below
Where the fish and coral grow

World unknown - world to explore
Water world of yesteryore

Liquid beauty flowing wild
Mighty mother nature's child

Tiny diamonds sparkle there
Created by the sun in the air

Oh! What wondrous beauty lies
Hidden from the human eyes

Circles wider ever spreading
Where the wily fish are treading

Just beyond the angler's reach
As he fishes from the beach

Water wonder smooth as ice
Does the weary soul entice

Come and spend some time with me
And I will set your spirit free
Moline Hogg

Untitled

What mystery before my eye,
Vivid colors across the sky.
While still the rain comes down around me,
Suddenly, the sun has found me.
A thing of beauty fills my view
And dazzles me with every hue.
Where once the day was dark as night,
Now is bathed in blinding light.
My soul renewed, I'm filled with joy,
The man inside yields to the boy.
And yet the joy is bittersweet,
The experience is incomplete.
For the rainbow's essence is only such
That I may gaze but never touch.
Lawrence M. Shelton

Sad: We Are Born, Grow And Die

Sad is when life between our fingers
vanishes away, and
each day knowing that little by little we die,
with fingernails and teeth,
the more we cling to life.

We are born, grow and die;
everyone shares the same destiny.

If soon, I would die,
these things I would ask:
a good death and he who loves me,
my ashes spread over the sea.

We are born, grow and die;
everyone shares the same destiny.

If my dreams do not materialize,
if my life was to be left unchanged,
if he who loves me would abandon me,
then, my death in vain would be.
Without history,
nobody would remember me.

We are born, we grow, we die...
Karmen D. Santos-Prior

Unending Glory (Ode To Jean)

A family is a treasured glory,
Valued more with every story.
Every member has a place,
Holding it with style and grace,
Adding to its loving face.

Through the years it stays together,
Championing every kind of weather.
Guided by a loving spirit,
Felt by all, and all can hear it,
One need only to be near it,
'Cause love will light the way.

We hold so dear the glorious Mother,
Whose love will bind them like no other.
Who taught them to know right from wrong,
And showed the way to make them strong,
With shining light and tender song.

As years pass by the love still grows,
Continuing on, as unending prose,
As the flickering flame of a candle glows,
'Cause love will light the way.
Linda Northrop

Raining Inside

My finger engraves circles in my window
Upon the security of glass,
Winter mist melts magically into water
Under my touch,
Crowding in from the crisp air
Blanketing the entire area.

Conglomerating as stagnant droplets
Of thoughts in my mind.
They grow together. Drawing pools.
Drip-drip
Painfully they fall away. Lost.

Rain. Cold
Will you leave and take this fog around me?
I long to rub my hand over my window
And leave it dry.
But, I cannot.

I am raining inside.
Laura Winckler

Let Your Head Rest

Let your head rest
Upon my breasts
And let your tears
Fall freely upon
My thirsty flesh.

Hold my hand tightly,
Let me feel
The pain unbearably
Life has brought you.

Let me love you
With love in all
Its entirety,
That I may reign
In your heart for all
Eternity.
Olivia S. Snead

Seeking True Love

Life isn't Happy, it is actually Sad;
Until you have Found
 Someone to Love!!
Love's just Good and Good for you.
E'en when you're All Alone,
 It will gladly Hold your Hand.

When the Sun is Shining,
 And the Weather of your Life Warm,
You can easily find Burning Passion
 But rarely True Love!
Love is Free, Forever Free and Priceless!
Yet, True Love is Difficult to Find
 BUT Stop Not Thy Search!!

Seek another's Love, I SAY
 When the Weather of your Life is Cold.
And Seek another whose Life is Bitterly
Lonely, Too
 BUT Most Important, Humbly Pray for Love!!
Then it will Certainly Happen and Never Leave!!
True Love will Live On and On
 And Never END!!!
Linda G. Walker

Untitled

Pain
Unfurnished,
Raw and empty.
Blinding lights,
Contractions of
A labouring heart;
Stillborn emptiness,
Stiff and sore.
Crawling to warming
Escapes,
To sleep and never to awaken.
Buried in a cold box
In frozen ground.
A single tear
Sliding down a lonely cheek
In mourning.

As I painfully rise,
As I painfully smile,
I fall to my death.
Mary Jill Eppley

To Calvary

If I should forget that you
understand and that you're there.
That you see my tears when they
fall, and hear my every call.
If I should tend to stray from
the path your love has chosen me to go.
 If I forget of your word, and
promises, and my faith grows
weak and my heart loses hope.
Help me to lift my eyes to you,
 and to remember your love for me.
 And lest I forget, lead me back
 to Calvary.
Lisa Hernandez

The Lady And The Moon

There is a young lady,
under the moonlight.
She is searching for some miracle.
But there is no miracle
except the moon.
The moon is too far,
far away.
She wishes she could
reach the moon.
And if she could,
maybe she would
become famous.

Muoi Chung

Wonderful Amazing Grace

Wonderful, marvelous, amazing grace!
T'was amazing grace that cleansed my soul,
Amazing grace that made me whole.
Amazing that His grace set free,
Once sin blind eyes now glory see.
Lame, undone, poor and alone;
That blood for sinners did a tone.
Amazing grace that Christ our King,
Would cause our broken hearts to sing.
It shall forever be my song.
Till one day midst that heavenly throng,
I cast myself before His feet,
To thank Him for that grace so sweet.

Wonderful, Marvelous, amazing grace!

Leslie Jordan

Silence

The wind blows north and east
Trees shiver and no one speaks
We all hold hands and bow our heads
Waiting for the fire to rise again
As we wait, the clouds turn black,
But still no one said a word, at least not yet
The leaves fell gently to the ground,
But blew away faster than sound
As I walked through the forest, I
didn't hear a thing, not even me
It's like I'm trapped in a box with no way out
That's when I realized, the fire will never rise
And there will be silence for the rest
of our future lives

Lauren V. Puccio

Quiet Strategy

I wore his favorite color,
Touched perfume to my wrists;
A sweet gardenia in my hair
Just in case we kissed.

I lured with steak and salad
Soft candlelight and wine.
Played music low and sensual
In this scheme to make him mine.

I learned to share his manly sports,
Went fishing on the strand;
Pursued with quiet strategy
Until he won my hand.

Katherine Murphy

Identity

I am a part of something big,
Too big to fully understand,
As each small leaf upon a twig
Is part of more than just its sprig.

I stretch to meet the vital thought,
The sacred impulse, the new life,
The ancient promise I was taught,
The inspiration to be caught.

I am a part of something true,
Infinite and awesome.
My insight is a tiny clue
To deeper vision, larger view,

And I rejoice to be upon the twig!

Margaret Brenton

We're Proud Of You Today, Our Son

We're proud of you today, our son!
To your bride we give our greatest gift
Filled with love, and pride, and joy.
It's the greatest gift a parent has
It's you, our son, our boy!

We're proud of you today, our son!
We've said these words so many times
On all your special days.
You've always filled our hearts with pride
In so many cherished ways.

We've proud of you today, our son!
We see the boy who always came
To share with us his life.
And today we give that son we love
To his love, his precious wife.

We're proud of you today, our son!
May your new life be filled
With love, and peace, and joy
For you'll always be a part of us
Our son, our little boy.

Leslie Liakos

Non - The Last Plane

Turning back the hands of time
To when I first began,
Turning back the hands of time
To avoid the eternal plan.

Ending all emotion,
Ending all my fear,
No time for joyous romance,
Time's non-existent here.

Drifting through oblivion
I saw the dawn of man,
Discovering keys of knowledge
Which unlock the cryptic plan.

Unveiling the infinite Spirit
To find that I am God,
And yet I cannot rest here
Within this land of Nod.

Well before the soul that was,
Now changed forever is me,
The essence I've discovered
To finally set me free.

Mary Helen Wallachy

Four Angels In The Sky

I put them on a plane today,
to there father far away,
Then I saw my Angels cry,
as they kissed me goodbye.
Tears I fought to hold back,
as I felt my heart would crack.
Then I heard the roaring plane,
"Oh" Dear God I'm going insane.
Four Angels in the sky.
Four Angels riding high.
Four Angels roaring by.
Plane don't crash,
I'll surely die.

Katheryn McCormick

Comes The Weeping Wind

Up from the house
to the standing cliff
walking along the edge of shadows,
listening for drums,
rattle of gourds,
eyes searching the prairie
for protruding rocks in a circle
where lodges once stood,
comes the weeping wind
wrapping around my soul.

Karen Schafer

This I Know

He gives me faith
To struggle and preserve even though
There are storms in life
His hands take mine
And it holds it tight
I cling to Him.

He alone can help me cope
He alone can give me hope
There is no one else
So strong and kind as He.

For He strengthens me,
Whenever storms and trials
Are being encountered by me
He gives support.
When rough winds blow
God is always there.
This I know.

Mendiola Feliciano

"Thinking Out Loud"

Oh, the wonders of youth!
To see things as they are
And not to dissect or mar.
For what do you gain
If all is in vain;
This life is much, much more.
Living and dying cannot be measured
With all our worldly items
We have so sincerely treasured.
But we must say to ourselves,
"What part do I play in the
Scheme of life?" For this, you
May have to ask of yourselves.

Mamie A. Ferguson

The Remodel

Here I am to redesign
   to reconstruct.
  Need to tear out a wall here,
   paint, scrape, sweat,
    rewire, wallpaper (pre-pasted please)
  put in new plumbing
   change the locks
  I can rearrange the furniture
    hang pictures
I want
  to know the woman
   I am not yet
    I have not seen
only felt
  a shadow
   passing
silently
  waiting

Kathleen Jones

"Mind At Ease"

A soft caress from a gentle hand,
To raise the spirit of weary man.

With mind, soul spirit uplifted grandly,
To feel a part of this human family.

No bitter tear shed from hardened eyes.
No lifeless heart, silent deep inside.

Only joyous life filled with harmony and peace
And a heart full of love, with mind at ease.

Mark Hester

Think Of The Men

Crushed leaves used as camouflage
To make the person seem a mirage.
And when the enemy doesn't see,
That's when our men set prisoners free.
America owes so much to them.
First and foremost, think of the men.

Battle grounds are the set of their play.
But, for our men, it's not time to play.
For when the bombs are laid to rest,
That's when our men try their every best.
America owes so much to them.
First and foremost, think of the men.

Some men are back from their military stay
In countries that are far far away.
But some were not so lucky, it seems.
For we can only remember them in our dreams.
America owes so much to them.
First and foremost, think of the men.

Michelle L. Slotke

Quest

I seek to find a perfect time
To lay my head to rest
Upon the pillow of my thoughts
To seek a dream
That lets me go
Beyond the boundaries of this world
To find a voice within
my soul
That speaks to me and lets
me find
The question and an answer

Lu Wrede

The Culprit

I invented grief and fear
To keep me from remaining here;
I created war and strife
To make me seek a better life.

It this were a pleasant place,
I might settle down to waste
Futile efforts to revive
Things that only seem alive.

Was there ever any doubt
How this drama came about?
Each atrocity I see
Had its origin in me.

All this treachery and greed
Are the pestilence I breed
Trying to befoul my nest
Til it offer me no rest.

Only then will I decide
To begin the search inside
For the presence I detect
Watching me....in retrospect.

Magill Echols

Our Flag

Wave high oh flag of America
To guide each growing youth
Your colors shining there on high
Gives them courage faith and truth

No other flag in any land
Is half as fair or strong
Because you stand for America
To which we all belong

Your colors fill our hearts with pride
As you wave above our land
For you we'll fight the world to save
And keep peace in our great land

So people of America
Display your flag with pride
Keep old glory waving high
And let her be your guide

Olive Obney

Nostalgia

I want to go home
To gentle people, soft voices
Ladies and gentlemen.

Evening clothes
Gloves and hats.

I want to sit again
By the fireplace
With the drapes spread open,
And watch the snow
Fall softly and silently.

I want to Christmas shop again,
Clothed in fur coat
And boots and gloves
Scarf and fur hat.

And know again that
most speak the truth,
When they say,
They love me and miss me,
Even as I love them,
And miss them.

Margie Davis Zeller

The Reaper

Here comes the reaper
to come and get me
to take me away
and let me do my deed

The Reaper came
as I saw and
took his hand
I walked with him
as I grasped his bony hand

We walked through
the fiery pits of hell
as I could see
spirits everywhere

The Reaper came for me
not for you, not for them
as you can see
I'm the living of the dead

Lisa Brock

In Passing

Life to one, fate decrees,
to be short or long.
This sacred ground, a mother's arms,
will receive, neither,
seed nor egg, to grow,
but to replace, in soil disturbed.
A name, from dust to...
In this,
earthen plot, a hole, a beginning,
an end.
A marker, monument, to an existence.
Here lies, an epithet, forgotten.
Life enjoyed, endured,
to conclude.
Standing, isolated.
Friends, relatives, sons and daughters,
pass. Tears, why?
Words of guilt, life changed.
Their time in destiny, to arrive alone,
will exit the same.

Marshall Fazzone

There's No War

Have you ever tried to explain
  to a girl or a boy
Why their daddy's not writing
  any more letters of joy
Or why they'll never see their
  daddy again
Because of a telegram the War
  Department did send
"We regret to inform you" was
  how it begun
"But your little ones' daddy's
  work here is now done"
Of course we all know there
  isn't a war
But try to explain this to the
  little ones who will
  see their daddies no more.

Marion Kraft

Of Space And Time

To paraphrase a famous song
Time does go by
Like the whisper of a memory
In the twinkling of an eye

We occupy a space in time
And pray no one disturb us
We hesitate to let them in
For fear they will perturb us

The space we need is not measured
And something we adjust to
To give our world the room to grow
Is something that we must do

The time that we spend worrying
About some meager possession
The space we need to keep it in
Can lead to great depression

So we sit and meditate
In our own little niche
When our bones start to disintegrate
We won't know what from which

Lee Ferber

Untitled

Once more to be little, happy, and gay
Tie up my shoes and run off to play
Running and jumping through the
Grass and the weeds
Climbing the hills and climbing the trees
Fall to the ground and look
To the sky
Pretend I'm an airplane
Way up - oh so high!

Now it is night time
And no time to play
Pick up the toys
And tuck them away
Off now to dreamland
My dear little child
Time for the sandman
To play for a while.

Kandy Conley

Home Sweet Home

Of all the places I have been
    throughout the U.S.A.,
There's one place that I like the best,
    and it's there I want to stay.
The people there are folks I know,
    they call me by my name.
I never seem a stranger there,
    and others are the same.
My neighbors wait to greet me
    when I come home each day.
The kids call, "Hi," as they ride by
    or when they're out at play.
The flowers there smell sweeter,
    their fragrance fills the air,
The birds sing far into the night,
    and there's beauty everywhere.
The skies are even bluer,
    The snow much whiter, too.
There's just no place like Home-Sweet-Home
    When your wandering days are through.

Mary E. Stokes

Life

What is life but a simple journey
    through time?
What are we but actors and
    actresses, with no rehearsed lines?
Is death but the end of life's
    career?
Who am I to question its meaning
    year after year?
And yet, it is, that death is but life's
    fair toll.
And hell is but just treatment
    for the lies that we've told.
Life, forever complex, due to
    its simplicity.
Embrace the knowledge of
    such simple ways,
And then, only then, shall
    you be, forever free...

Katherine M. Watters

Leap Year, Birthday Greetings

To you my dear,
This day comes every year.
Earlier on three,
We will agree.
Just makes you special, you see,
Everyone will agree.
Sending you this fax is an idea new,
Hopefully it will do.
Progress rings out,
Love it brings about.
News of you is good to shout,
But we'd love to have you near,
Cause you're thought of special all year.
Yes we think of you often it's true,
Wishing you health and happiness too.
Simply across the miles,
Thoughts of you bring us smiles.
Yes, it's your birthday and don't you know,
We all dearly love you so.

Larry V. Brooksher

Thirty Seconds

All I ever asked for was
    thirty seconds of your time.
I didn't think it was too
    much to ask for, at the time.

A simple hug, or a small embrace
    would have brightened up my face.
But, most often, you were too busy
    on overdrive, going full speed ahead,
Leaving me feeling lifeless, near dead.

All I ever asked for was thirty seconds
    of your time...
Was that too much, at the time?
Perhaps, now I should only ask for
    fifteen seconds of your time.
Would that be too much to ask for,
    at this time?

Karl T. Bergeron

Tears

Some tears are like rain,
    they just go by.
Some tears help the pain,
    and turns to a smile.
Some tears are like stains,
    which fade with time
But stay with you can't
    really say why.

Mary Catherine Bell

Time's Race

Your senior year has come and gone,
They dedicated the yearbook to you.
Crystal wrote a poem, an unsung song,
Which made me weep anew.

The Wisdom of the Ages
We do not hold,
Nor are our memories always
Silver and gold.

I am haunted by the "what ifs..."
If only, I had done.
Would I still have been too late
And your life still lost instead of won?

Or would the past be written differently,
Would the sands of time still run,
If only I had done...?

It's best not to wonder,
Nor too deeply ponder,
What a few seconds time could have undone.
For the sands of time, their race have run.

Linda K. Lilienthal

That's Life!

When writers pen biographies
They choose their subjects well,
The object of their research
A book that's sure to sell.
They haunt newspaper archives,
Hunt through the library shelves
For bits of information
To educate themselves.
But why, I often wonder
Do they choose losers or winners,
Or characters who tend to be
Either saints or sinners?

Kathleen Hunter

My Secret Wish!

God grant me a wish
to show what I can do,
If you'll just plant the seed
I'll raise your child for you.

I'll hear its every cry
I'll wipe away its tears,
and I'll give it love and morals
for its up and coming years.

I'll teach it all I know
and help as it learns more,
for you know this precious life
of yours I would adore.

I'll love it and protect it
and keep it safe with me,
For I know inside my heart
I'll be raising it for thee.

Laura E. Falor

Women

Women are the fruits of our lives.
They are the mothers and wives.
No one is more valuable,
No one is more loved,
No one is more treasured,
Than she who's being thought of.

You can see it's in their nature.
It's in their beauty.
It's in the way they make sure
You're taken cared of properly.

No, it's not that they're better.
It's their uniqueness, their charm.
It's their tender loving care.

Never take for granted their independence, too.
They are people just like me and you.
So use your common sense
And love each one near to you.
Make sure you always do!
Melody Padilla

Words Of Wit

When I write my words of wit
They are more than a little bit
Listen when I say
You had better pray
Tidings of good joy
Are better than poy
Tis that time of year
To drink a good beer
Buy your tree
Make it me
I stand tall
Above them all
I won't giggle
I do wiggle
Decorate me well
I won't tell
I am your tree
It is me
I Love You
Merry Christmas
Michael A. Martin

A Gift For The World

It's a world without a future
There's so much that is wrong.
If we don't do something now
This world may soon be gone.

It's the children without morals
Breaking all the laws.
Corrupted at their birth
They know not of their flaws.

It's a teenager who's pregnant
She made a big mistake.
She's concerned about her future
Not the life she's gonna take.

It's a hate that shows no mercy
The colors black and white.
One of them steals the day
While the other takes the night.

My life that seems so simple
But the fighting does not cease.
For the struggle I have fought for
I would give the gift of PEACE.
Kimberly Metz

"In A Picture Frame"

You're not extinct in my heart,
There's just a little part that's missing.
It's been a long time no see,
But I still love you, though.

You're everything I'd like to be,
From my heart below.
I wake up in the morning and I see,
Your picture below in a picture frame.

It is such a shame,
That all I can see of you,
Is in a memory, instead of in front of me,
It's in a picture frame.
Kristina Sojka

My Love

On my head I had a bounty.
Therefore I was arrested in Latah County
It crossed my mind that I should run
I did not, as the Sheriff had a gun

By running I had nothing to gain
In two weeks I left Moscow on the chain
Now here I go around and around
Someday I'll land feet on the ground

If you happen to look for me in your sleep
Believe me baby in my dreams you I keep
So please pray for me and sing your songs
My love for you can do no wrongs
Lonnie Williams

Untitled

I close my eyes and dream
There you hear no yells not even a scream.

My mind wanders to a joyous place
A land where a smile is on every face.

Everyone is happy and full of cheer.
Their heart is no longer covered with fear.

No more cries through out the night
Not one disagreement, argument or fight.

No hatred and lies
Only beautiful land and gorgeous skies.

You are not criticized for who you are
your pain is healed without a bloody scar.

I am cut free, yes free
No more pretending I can be me.

A land which disregards my sex and race
Oh, Lord I wonder is there such a place.
Kelley Wilkins

In My Life

In my life
there is someone who cares,
someone who knows.
This person is there
each time I go forth,
to help with the pain
that's deep within;
to show me the way
through life's obstacles.
Nika M. Macias

Going Home

I wandered far from home one day,
Then realized I was lost.
I turned around in circles then,
Trying to find the Way.
I ran up to a Stranger,
My eyes full of tears.
"Do you know the Way?" I cried,
Tugging on His garments.
He turned and looked upon me,
And smiled a gentle smile.
Reaching out, He took my hand,
Guiding me as we went.
"I'll show you the Way to safety,"
He spoke as we went along.
"The road is straight and narrow,
With nary a turn or crook.
If you'll follow as I lead you,
I'll shelter you from harm."
Now I'm following His every footstep,
And finally headed Home!
Marsha G. Reason

I Had No Idea

I thought nothing
Then I found out
At the same exact moment - You!
Ah, so there is something else
I suspect - I know
Yes, I know, I really know

It's like a dark tunnel - the past
But I didn't know
Incredible light and joy and pain
It's OK - God! to even get a glimpse
It's OK It's OK. No matter what

I had no idea. How could that be
I think I suspected
But not for me
Not in this life
But.....
Madelyn Boyce Mikkelsen

"The Chicken"

Their bones are used for jewelry
Their body used for meat
Their feathers for a pillow
For breakfast their eggs we eat.

They wake us at the crack of dawn
And will be a loving pet
For your garden give fertilizer
Or to hatch others eggs....will set.

And if you dare to gamble
Will fight until the end
Will take the name of "coward"
But could we have a better friend?
Nedra Thompson

Who I Love

For who I love is a choice,
the one I love, I trust, I care
about. The person I love is
a secret, but I hope he loves
me too. He is a friend, a
playmate and he is the
greatest person I've ever met.
Michelle Smith

My Brother

I have a brother, a younger brother,
the youngest of us four.
He talks, listens and comforts,
but then there's so much more.

He has his own style, you see,
and when they simply look
most folks disagree.

He understands me when others don't
and is always there to help.
I often wonder what he does
when his world begins to melt.

The pain he feels he rarely speaks
but I can hear it in his voice.
And when I call I often wonder
how long have his eyes been moist?

You must be true at heart
and understand a friend to see
my brother, my younger brother,
who means so much to me.

Kanda LuAnn Force

Now

A lead in.
The years take time.
Anything will not abstain.
Substance in process breaks reigns.
That late in the day it rains.
Missing circles close in on answers.
Slam it back down.
Kick the drain underground.
A fling corked sits backwards.
That sign is inside a card.
Chase it toward the back yard.
Escaped pressure sparks residue.
Take it back, I don't like it new.
Lay down and throw sheets up in the air.
An exit will cause stupidity and flare.
A change in venue resorts to numbness.
Direct blending finds a way out.
Crack it open and observe.

Laurie Christenson

From A Teenager's Eyes

From a teenager's eyes
the world is a lie.
The secrets unfold
and reveals fool's gold.
Confusion strikes them
and to them it's all dim.
The future to all is unknown
but nobody wants any one to know.
The wants and needs change like the tide.
Thoughts and beliefs in time all die.
Conformists are the enemy
and the only belief is anarchy.
These are the thoughts of a teenager gone
looking back to the anger's dawn.

Mike Norris

The God Called "Video Games"

Through the winds of change
The violent children came
Trained to kill and maim
By the God called -
 "Video Games"

Traveling merchants bear the blame
Selling intelligence games
Aboard an academic train
For the God called -
 "Video Games"

In a world where no peace reigns
Numbers substitute for names
Men live and die in pain
With the God called -
 "Video Games"

Civilization goes up in flames
Among the barren brains
Deceived by the great fame
Of the God called -
 "Video Games"

Martha Margaret Rockwood

Lucky Star

Your friends may lie,
The truth can't come from strangers,
If I knew why,
We wouldn't be in this danger,
I'm just wishing on another lucky star.

Life is hard,
It is not made to measure,
We will go on,
It's the same in pain and pleasure,
Wondering how we ever got this far.

The world is cold.
A heart gets torn and tattered,
The one you hold,
It can be dropped and shattered,
I'm just wishing on another lucky star.

Life goes on,
As sure as the sky,
Has come and gone,
In the wink of an eye,
I'll wish on another lucky star.

Leigh Anne Karanfilian

The Real World

 While we look upon this world, we see the things that should not be seen. The terror the horror the fear and the hate.
 We dream of a fantasy world full of love, peace, wealth and life. But we don't live our dream. We live in a world of suicides, murders, and homicides. Although we run and hide we cant escape death on the other side. We destroy our young ones we destroy our old ones. We watch those in pain and suffering, and yet we wonder
 "Can this happen to me?"
If this is how the real world is........
Then none of us have come prepared.

Krystal Garcia

Alone

I sit here and I think about
The things that could have been,
The walks in the park,
The love in the dark,
Do you think of way back then?

My smile used to make you laugh,
Your touch, it made me melt.
Do you remember?
Please say you do.
In the beginning how we felt.

So now I sit here all alone
Though your memory is here to stay
One day you'll come back
This loneliness I will lack
But now my heart's meandering away.

Marni L. Fuqua

Homing

In the first hour after dawn
The sun lights the
Blue western hills.
Far below in the valley
Someone releases the pigeons.

They circle, wheeling higher.
All their white breasts gleam.
Now for a moment I've lost them,
A hundred at least.
But no. There they are,
Dark-winged, reappeared.

Exalted, turning together
Breasting east, vanishing west
Against the morning mountains.

How like joy that flashes,
Or suddenly remembered loss,
Or hope that sustains
Is the flight of homing pigeons.

In the last hour before twilight
I watch for them again.

Lucie C. Hagens

Eye To Eye

We're older now
The summer's gone
Two different schools
and don't see eye to eye
I'm not sorry to say this will make me cry
I think it's time to say good-bye
Good-bye my love I'll never forget you.
The way you cried that night
The way you held me tight
Good-bye my love good-bye
I'm sorry we don't see eye to eye

Kendra Bristol

Conclusions

Some dreams lay dormant.
They arise with challenges
 as old beliefs die.

Michelle M. Lindsay

A Dance With Daddy

The crackle of an old record
The start of a new song
A tug on a pig-tail
A dance to follow along.

The plant of my foot
on yours twice the size
I follow the beat
with enchanted-like eyes.

Forward
   One-Two-Three
Back
   Two-Three-Four
In every dance with Daddy
I learn a little bit more.

Karen L. West

As His Hands Are Gently Folded In Death

As his hands are gently folded in death,
The sounds of weeping
Circles the room.
A river of tears
Washes his soul away.
Angels' wings come and take him
Into the light
His soul is released,
As his closed eyes
Fall into a peaceful sleep for ever.

Melissa Miller

A Letter To My Friend

I see
the sorrow in your face,
worn with worry,
filled with pain.
I grieve with you.
I know your loss of
husband, confidante and friend
who's now become your child.
No longer does he share your days,
thought he's still there you're
so alone. And he, who once was
strong, is so confused and lost.
This gentle man must now be told
such things as how to dress and
when to go to bed. Your life which
once was ordered and secure, is
now in disarray.

I'm here, my long-time friend,
and if you need me,
I will come.

Macelle Beveridge

Night Lights

As I gaze into the starry night,
Stars twinkle so, with such delight!
That as I think mine every thought,
I know the answers must be sought,
By those twinkling stars above,
That seem to speak
Sweet words of love,
To comfort all who care to gaze,
Upon their misty, moonlit haze.

Kathleen Daugherty

Dark Clouds

Dark clouds are not just in
the sky above.
Dark clouds are also on the
earth below.
Dark clouds have many faces.
Dark clouds display the faces
of jealousy.
Dark clouds display the faces
of evil people.
Dark clouds display the many
faces of hatred and racism.
Dark clouds are people
who don't have a good
word to say to you or
about you.
Dark clouds do not have any
light behind them, only darkness.

Katie Watts

"The Sick Child"

Strong and brave as you may be,
   the sick children will be the bravest
   you will ever see.

Growing up and being sick,
   the unlucky one who has been picked.

Tough as it may seem,
   but can lead you towards
   your dreams.

Appreciating life more,
   In the wind,
   Up so high you will soar.

Pain and struggling sick kids go through,
   but the most courageous you can prove.

Nichole Leigh Villa

I Believe

I believe that we should help
the sick and poor,
and lecture those with money,
yet yearn for more.

I believe that you can set
a goal and accomplish it,
but you won't achieve anything
if you decide to quit.

I believe that we are all equal,
each brown, black, and white,
and we shouldn't let racism
begin any kind of fight.

I believe that we should
always love each other,
including your father, mother,
sister, and brother.

I believe that love
is a unique, building block,
and if we all work together
we can create a very special rock.

Misty Nicole Melton

"The Sea Still Lives"

The wind blows soft and easy.
The sand sinks into the sea.
The fish are having babies
And the sea falls fast asleep.
For the sea still lives,
For the sea still lives.
For the sea I know still lives.
For the sea that you know, it may live.
But the sea I know, I know it lives.
In you or me the sea lives
between you and me let's see.
The sea lives for no one, it lives for itself
It doesn't belong to me or you.
The sea belongs to itself, for the sea I know
it needs me for the sea you know, it needs you.
The sea knows who it needs,
for the sea knows its needs,
And the sea still lives in me and you.
For the sea still lives!

Lisa A. Jones

The Robin

I'd like so much to go to her aid,
The robin in my yard with a broken leg.
But, if I extended my hand one length,
She would fly.
For I could not pass to her my intentions;
So desperately she struggles with the worm.
She totters— almost falls.
Her head turns, seeking direction,
To where young mouths wait,
Wings lift.
In her triumph,
My heart sings.

Kenneth Risinger

Call My Name

The house was quiet and still,
The radio was playing a gentle refrain.
I felt someone was with me
Then I heard your voice call my name.

The sun was setting in the west,
Fleecy clouds made a lovely frame.
My heart seemed to stand still
And I heard your voice call my name.

Memories crowd into my senses
As softly as gentle falling rain.
I soon wore your engagement ring
Loving your special way of calling my name.

Now I'm not hallucinating or dreaming
Or trying to analyze my brain.
It was simply love and memories
Made me wish you'd call my name.

The days will pass by in a rush.
Time on earth is like a small grain.
Someday I'll see you again
And hear you call my name.

Lorraine Schlesselman

"Mother"

If only somewhere I could find...
The perfect words to say,
How very much I love you Mom...
On this your special day.
But words can simply not express...
The love I feel for you,
The way your always by my side...
Those days I feel so blue.
And as I begin to reminisce...
Of the happy times we share,
I get this feeling deep inside my heart...
How very much you care.
Perhaps as much for me mother...
As I do care for you,
And now I hope you understand...
Just how much I love you too.
Cause even though my love for you...
Mere words could not express,
I hope that deep inside your heart...
Mom...you know I've tried my best!!!

Linda D. Potter

Opossums

The opossum eats slugs.
The opossum eats bugs.

The opossum looks like a rat.
But is the size of a big house cat.

50 chompers!
50 whompers!

They have a pouch like a kangaroo.
As all marsupials do.

The opossum has a long hairless tail.
And is a mammal like a whale.

They don't carry rabies.
She does carry babies.

They've been around for millions of years.
They also have millions fears.

They survive by playing 'possum.
And I think they're totally awesome.

Nicholas Rothweiler

Thy Rib Of A Man

Taken from a rib of a man,
The Lord saw that life shall expand,
He then created a new life,
He created for a man a wife,
They then called her woman,
Which was taken from a man,
And they shall be one flesh,
So they shall together cherish.
Therefore in time of need,
They shall help one another see,
That they shall be together,
And thou shalt be forever,
Woman wasn't made from thy head,
So she shall never go up above a man it
  was said.
Nor was thou made from thy feet,
So she shall not be stepped upon nor beat,
They shall walk side by side,
And forever shall they look upon
  each other and forever confide.

Melissa Ann Soliz

The Lion And The Mouse

A mouse ran up a lion
The lion was awaken,
Before the mouse could run
The lion had him taken.
The mouse wanted to be spared
He wanted to be freed,
The lion was reasonable
And finally agreed.

While the lion was walking
He got caught in a hunter's net
He was very scared and puzzled
Not knowing what he'd get.
The lion struggled and struggled
He wouldn't ever stop,
Until his fellow friend the mouse
Made the trap drop.

This is the lesson,
You should learn to do.
If someone does a good deed for you,
Do a good deed for them too.

Kate Tyson

Family Circle

As time ends for a loved one
the last breath they did breathe,
will send life to the babe
on the new family tree.

Life is pure, and good, and clean
the road to death an uncertainty,
but we will all travel
through life's ups and downs
for this is the road
that we have all found.

With the passing of time
we shall find
that life is a circle
that shall never die!

Linda Joedicke

King Midas

King Midas, King Midas
The hummingbird
He sits on his perch and guards his word
If anything comes upon his way
He picks up his courage and fights it away

If it's a rainy day
Much to his dismay
He can not sit upon his perch
And has to go away.

Nicole Murdoch

Oblivion

Empty, it is
void

Seeking, it is
tired

Longing, it has
yearned

Far too much

Far too long

Resignation.

Lori G. Libutaque

Mother

I am yours you are mine.
The good times the bad,
we love each other still.
I've needed you - you've needed me..
mother and child - Sand and Sea.
The waves and the mighty waters crash
against the soft warm sand.
What would the sand be without the
waves and the water's movement?
Lifeless, silent, desert hot and Brittle.
What would the water be without the Sand?
- Bored, Lonely and Still -
Together Sand and Water...beautiful
Raging, smooth, sparkling crest of waves...
Smashing, colliding...
- Loving the sand, loving the sea -
Never ending, everlasting Love
between you and I - My mother - Your child.

Laura Starr Perkins

Chances

We've seen each other through
the good times and the bad
and well we can recall
the joys and tears we've had.

We've been here for each other
no matter what the price
and still we each accepted
the tossing of the dice.

And through the years I've loved you
in all the ways I can
and watched you change forever
from where you once began.

And though we seem familiar
with all that we have known
unspoken we've decided
to reap what we have sown.

May never come the time
when loves and friendships end
and gone are all the chances
for friends to love again.

Lisalynn Sabine

Apathy

Hello, my dear
The day is grey
Stilled within a naked thought
Not unknown the stagnant place
Where once I was and am again.

Come in, my dear
The door is open
Viewed from eyes of hollowed glance
No life remembered fills this space
Where once I was and now am taken.

Yes, my dear
The time to leave
Stayed the fallen autumn voice
Never silenced ghost of grace
Here vacant now and vacant still.

Leah Nunez

School In 1995

The school bell rings!
The children scatter
To find their place
In the educational ladder.
The computer clicks
  Math, Science, Biology
    appear,
Your personal file is complete!
It can reach across the world
  with the internet!
Math is now in,
Spelling bees are out,
You wonder how long
This age will last!
Martha L. Yinger

A Beautiful Day

We look above to see
the bright blue sky,
then we look below
to see green grass grow.

We see sun shining,
all around
it brightens,
our surround.

Birds chirping all around,
day and night we hear,
loving relaxing sounds.

Animals roaming, go burrowing,
in the ground,
looking for shelter, and food,
they find a happier life, too.
Laura S. Brackett

When? - A Soldier's Lament

Now dead am I, my voice is mute
the battle quiet to my ears

Why was I sent to die this day
in streaming jungle and mud

Why was I sent to die this day
when manhood was but a bud

And here I lie on a battlefield
what remains of twenty years

Grandfather died on a battlefield
in a war to end them all

Father died as young as I
to make the Third Reich fall

My brother's death on the battlefield
was yet another transaction

That wasn't a 'war' was what they said,
only a 'Policing Action'

Now here I lie, on a battlefield
all life's blood did I lend.

Oh, merciful God in heaven
when will it ever end?
Kenneth R. Bellemare

Sundown

I'll look for you at sundown
That's where our dreams are born,
Where all those bright tomorrows
Await each coming dawn.

And with it comes a feeling
That I've never known before,
Doubts and fears that mattered once
Don't mean much anymore.

Love that's born at sundown
They say will never die,
Like a flower made in heaven
Adorns the evening sky.

So I'll look for you at sundown
And I won't feel alone,
We'll dream of bright tomorrows
Like those we've never known.
Larry A. Berger

Keep Her On A String

She don't leave me alone;
That's not the only thing
She calls me on the phone;
I keep her on a string
  She don't take me to the next level,
    intellectually
  She don't take me to the next level,
    where I want to be
I don't want her around;
when sex the only thing
I don't want her around;
I keep her on a string
  She don't take me to the next level,
    never fulfilling me
  She don't take me to the next level,
    But I keep her on a string
She's the one thing I despise,
  The one thing I demise,
  The one thing I realize,
I keep her on a string.
Michael Radoslovich

Uninvited Companion

There's a spider in my Kitchen
That's as welcome as can be
'Cause this tiny little spiders came
  To share my home with me.

'Till it crawled into the picture
I was livin' all alone
Now - it's oh so very obvious
  It also calls it home.

It scampers 'round the kitchen
On the floors, the walls and sink
And, Nena Eva Bathers
  To ask, what do you think?

Well! I'm worried little spider
Wish you'd stay up off the floor
'Cause, if I step upon you, sweetie, Squash
  You'll simply be no more.

So, stay up high you little darlin'
On the ceiling, walls and sink
And, don't you care or ever worry 'bout
  What anybody thinks. So there.
Lucille Gossett Bingham

A Sister

A sister is a friend
that you will always need,
a sister is a friend
that you will always have.

Although you go through
fights at times
and you both act
like sour limes

One of you turns
around and makes up
then surprises you
with a token of love

We just have to remember
she'll always love you
and that, you know,
will always be true.

Friends will come
and friends will go
But you're forever,
this I know.
Kristin M. Menswar

Love Is Wonderful

Love is a feeling
That you have inside
To some people this feeling
Is something they cannot hide
There is a certain kind of love
Called agape love
It comes from our heavenly father
up above, oh what a wonderful love
Love is wonderful
Yes it's wonderful
To some people love is something
To others it's nothing
I love to be loved
It something I can't hide
It makes me feel so good inside
Marlena Brown

Sunday Mornings

How do you paint the joy
That Sunday morning brings?
What color will sing a song
To music played on heart strings?

How do you paint the peace
You feel surrounding you?
What color would be pretty?
Is it red, or is it blue?

How do you paint the wonder
Of a Sunday morning's face
Whose smile is made of sunshine
In a frame of green grass lace?

How do you paint the gift
Of God's redeeming love?
What bright color would portray
Such blessings from above?

How do you paint the beauty
That Sunday morning brings?
Mix your paints with lovely thoughts
And brush with angel's wings.
Merle H. Prosser

New Year

There is something I hear
That rings in my ear,
It tells me something is near,
It must New Year!
New Year is full of tons
Of games and fun.
Each happy boy and girl
wait for the countdown to start,
Some people keep playing darts.
10,9,8,7,6,5,4,3,2,1...
New Year has come
With all its fun!
It comes with joys
And some toys.
It brings laughter and happiness,
For each person.
But then nothing rings in my ear,
I'm full of fear...
It's just that there is no more New Year.

Kent Lee

My Dream

A struggle of life
that never ends
seemingly brightened
but only darkened
by those who
call themselves friends
in a distance
a light shines
ever so brilliantly
casting shadows
on broken promises
which seem to lay
beyond my reach
yet I hold
their visions
in the palm of my hands
my dream, my light
guide me through
the darkness
of this evil world

Nicholas J. Strazzulla

Mojo Risin'

Walking into a room
That may be filled with doom
A feeling of numbness
Seeing the strange
Hearing the unusual
A fire of pain, that will always gain
Could you hold,
Something bold
The beast sat down to the feast
Wanting,
Waiting,
Longing,
Louring
Who will love
The lonely dove
Could you soar above the sky
Or,
Just die?

Nyki Sebby

"Little Ones"

Thank God for all those little ones
   that laugh and play, sing and run,
The joy and heartaches they give us all
   With all the ups and downs that fall,
And all the love and joy they bring
   They make your heart rejoice and sing,
They make you happy when you're sad
   Even if they're all you have,
They're a gift of love from above
   Who entrusted you to give your love,
When they get you down and you think
   You're done....
Remember you once were a little one.

Mike McClain Sr.

Fantasy

Was that a little fairy sprite
That I saw on our lawn last night
Dancing in the pale moonlight
To the fountain's tinkle tine?
But I'm too old for fairy lore
It must have been the girl next door
Whose father owns the grocery store
She hates to sell but long before
Told me that she likes nothing more
Than when a silver moon's a-soar
To sneak out her back kitchen door
And dance beneath our sycamore
A hymn of worship to the moon.

Lydia Caplan

Ode To The Hunter

There's really something mighty queer
That hunting season falls each year,
Precisely when the leaves pile up,
And winter's chores again erupt.
Storm windows wait for weeks and weeks,
The late tomatoes and the leeks.
Toward dusk the hunter staggers home
Too tired to talk, too tired to roam,
But rest he must for on the morn
Another hunting day is born.
So loved ones wait with bated breath
For some poor pheasant's timely death.
While somewhere in you cozy glen
A happy hunter missed again.

Lois Fitzpatrick

I Thank You Because...

You are the strings
That hold my heart in place

You are the tissue
That wipes away my tears

Yours are the arms
That keep me safe

You are the weapons
That fight away my fears

Yours are the eyes
That I get lost in

You are the one
Who can fill this emptiness...
In my heart.

Kat Slater

"Love Bytes"

Computer technology has changed our lives
Tearing husbands away from homes and wives.
Bulletin Boards and Cyber-Sex
Invade our homes, families wreck.

Clandestine scheming on the Internet
Laid secret plans, they finally met.
"Harmless fun" many users say
Ask survivors how spouses stray.
Traditional marriages collapse and decay
Promises break, love slips away.

Within minutes all vows can shatter
Their spouse and home no longer matter.
Deserting their spouse of twenty-five years,
Broken, alone, and so full of fears.

Compu-Serve tears lives apart
Bitter resentment will never depart.
Four years later the loss still lingers,
Dreams for the future slipped through her fingers.

Just how far has the world progressed
To have love in marriage forever suppressed?

Linda M. Schaefer

Moss

I cannot be a flower...
Tear it from its roots and
its beauty, life and rigor wither

I cannot be a tree...
Although its roots run long, deep and strong
it is immovable

I have always been partial to the moss...
It is rooted, yet delicately
and once severed from its grounding
it can flourish again with the warm
air and earth...whatever it can
craftily use to be whole again.

Michele Beard

On Photographers

Photographers are a special breed
Taking pictures is their creed
For shutterbugs there is no cure
They love what they do
You can be sure
So many subjects from which to choose
People, animals and gorgeous views
A camera is a useful tool
For snapping pictures around the pool
A word of warning to the wise
At a crucial moment you'll need supplies
Check your film and batteries, too
Don't run out or you'll feel blue
When opportunity and light are right
The picture you capture
Can be an elegant delight
Even though you're an amateur
Photography can hold an extraordinary allure.

Marian L. Anderson

Advice

Read deeply the innuendos;
Take them to your heart and mind.
Live and give with real abandon
In brief and sacred times you find.

If, indeed, you must accept
That there are promises to be kept,
And that other obligations bind
In the culture of our time

Deal constructively with reality.

Let compassion warm your competence
But not destroy your soul.

Marjorie Holaday

The Sequence

The Lady holds her Son
Surrounded by gold leaf.
Gifts of pearls, amber, and silver
Placed in gratitude,
  In painful sorrow,
    And in promises fulfilled.

Faint whispers uttered
Breaking the holy silence.
Memories of a distant anguish linger.
Feel the hurt,
  Feel the misery,
    Feel the heart beat
As the souls cry out
From behind the barbed wire fence.

A demon once stalked.
Evil has been entombed.
The prayer of the people
Of the Church of the Holy Rood
Ignite the flame
  For eternal peace.

Mary E. Rocco

Brown

Bear our
superior
spirit guide
symbol

Victim

Alaska
Canada
Yellowstone

Nowhere

Will we
miss anything?
Replace anything?

Learn anything?

We
dream it
hope it

And doubt it

Destruction is
our legacy

Our epitaph

Kary J. Worthington

Living

In the morning of my life
  Sunlight glaring in my eyes
    I want to be cuddled.
Showers in the Springtime
  Shooting bulbs and blooming buds
    I see colors arrive.
Summer's afire with hope
  Working and adventuring
    I want to be helping.
Gathering together in Fall
  Morsels and messages
    I want to preserve.
Freezing rain ushers Winter
  Shortened days to fill
    I huddle against the cold.
Evening's lamp is turned to low
  Making final touches
    I hear my Maker's call.

Mary Ann

Emotions

You're unaware!
Suddenly they're there.
Does anyone care?

They're black.
They're blue.
Sometimes called moods.

You laugh.
You cry.
Even wonder why?

Then without notice,
Like a roaring Ocean
You realize, it's only Emotions!

Nora L. Thacker

Untitled

Here I am
Stuck in a thought
Wondering what to do

Here I am
With this gut feeling
Waiting for the phone to ring

Here I am
Wishing for my dreams to come true
I am not going to sit here and become blue

Go out and search
is what I am going to do
and say to myself "Why Not?"

Merrilee I. Bruegger

Chained

Limitations — prisoner's lair —
Stronger chains I've never known.
Just when I have broken free
Brutal walls then hinder me.

Calling out — someone to hear —
No sound, no voice, no one responds.
Or maybe — yes — a sound is heard —
Or is it hope disguised as word?

Try a different door — again —
And limitation blocks the path.
Close my eyes to dream — or flee
The cobwebs of my destiny.

Mary Mason

The Swimmer

The swimmer
strong and powerful
dives

The racer
bold yet graceful
flies

The contender
dashing yet elegant
sprints

The winner
euphoric and proud
triumphs

Kyle Mckown

Au Revoir Noel

Knowing love's course - to our soul,
Still - I dare not scale, the —
Glass mountain, where you hide.
The varied beauty in our lives,
Perceived alone, turns sad, as -
Below, I wait in vain.
No one should part in December
November will always come,
This Christmas, will be, but once.

Hear the echo of the "Angelus" - falter
Pink cheek carolers send, our
"Agnus Dei," across a white moonlit alter
-
Trailing "Hallelujah", and -
Our Christmas pain.

A golden star, a sprig of holly,
Your worn-out "Teddy bear", keep vigil.
Kneeling at my tomb, remembered warmth-
I let, upon the snow drifting vast,
Here, I will wait - if - only to borrow,
Love, from every Christmas past!

Lilia

Step Upon Spring

The chilling thrill of
Spring's first grass
beneath my feet,

Bare as I step
into worlds
newly unknown,

Upon seeds silently sown,
slowly stirring from slumber
cold,

Life reaching green
towards
newfound warmth
in sun and sky.

Bold cycle of earth
felt
wet and soft
under heels and toes.

Kimberly Greene Angle

"A Chorus Line At Sea"

I'm singing in a Chorus Line
Spreading joy
Like a quiet trumpet rumor.
Visions of life
Looking towards heaven.

I wake up.
My head is spinning.
The tides rolls out —
Out of my eyes, out to sea
As the dream fades.

I will relive it again...
As I sleep.

Kerri Elizabeth Pierce

41, 40, 39

Damn orange numbers
Spray-painted on huge backs
Of dying animals
Arrogant penknives
Claim small plugs of flesh
Only to expose
Half-digested meals

Hammer hands
Saw jaws
Cut poke touch take
Smooth white cylinder teeth
From lost beasts stranded
Alongside the wet depths
They call home

Beautiful chaste mouths
Gleam like wishful bridal satins
Waiting as dark eyes rage
Sudden whooshing breaths
Ask for nothing more
Than silence

Karen Oftelie

   Sitting here listening to the
sounds of harmony, the harmony
   of souls.
Souls reaching, looking searching for
that piece that was skipped in the
   last beat.
Beat your hands to the sound of your,
Walking, waking dreams. Dream of
the destruction that could would,
and will end. To end is the last,
to stop...
   And that's why in the
heart of hurt, and pain always
   Ends
in pieces...

Lauren Block

Could I Find A Quiet Place

Could I find a quiet place,
Somewhere in my heart full of grace.
Could I find a quiet place,
Somewhere to rest my soul.

Could I find a quiet place,
Where the waking hours have no haste.
Could I find a quiet place,
Somewhere to rest my soul.

MaryAnn White

My Sister

I have only one hero,
sometimes she hates me though,
she's my very best friend,
and our friendship will never end.
I've always idolized her,
she's always been real mature.
She doesn't know how I feel,
but in the last year our friendships
gone uphill.
This is someone I'll always remember,
and this someone is my sister.

Mandie Jo Parks

Hope

One day, I found somebody.
Something special happened.
I saw rainbows and stars,
hearts and diamonds,
rubies and fuchsia and scarlet and magenta,
The world was going great.
I felt happy, lucky, and cheerful.
Until,
She moved on.
Before I knew it, my heart broke.
I felt depressed.
I saw night and dark,
I cried,
I cried like the hole in the Titanic.
I saw black, white, emerald and gray...
But Hope, there is always you.
Always hope that I will get that love back.

Michael Libby

SOME GUYS!

Some guys are rough,
Some guys are tough,
Some guys are true and
Some guys like royal blue,
Some guys say be mine,
Some guys say she's mine,
Some guys are liars and
Some guys are drug buyers,
So pick a guy that's right for you.
Do you like a guy rough
or tough or a true blue, or a
guy that says
be mine or she's mine or a
liar and a drug buyer?

Nicole McCormick

Here Comes The Sun

Here comes the sun
So shiny and light
Here comes a day
So cheery and bright
Here comes the blossoms
Blooming in May
Chasing all gloom and cares away
Here comes the time
For kites in the sky
Here comes a time
For living on high
Here comes the time
For children at play
Here comes a
Lovely beautiful day

Martha Berlin

Untitled

Between you and me,
So pure is the love,
That I'm flying free,
Like a snow white dove.
Our love is so strong,
It can't be denied,
With you I belong,
Our hearts side by side.

Marty Witt

Forgotten Space

I enter the place where I was begotten
So long ago, I must have forgotten.
I enter that place of the Divine
Where I sit; and gaze and become refined.

There in this unfamiliar place
I acquaint myself with its inner space.
Its openness and apparent emptiness
Fills me with curiosity and completeness.

I explore the space once more.
I climb into its inner core.
I find a burning fire
Within the embers of each new desire.

The secrets waiting my arrival
Are unlocked.
Behold their beauty is unrivaled
As along this labyrinth I travel.

The searching, the centering,
The entering-in begins.

Mary Elizabeth Henaughan

Our Past!

We were so good,
So happy.
When we were together
But that was only in the past!

You seem to be happy
With the girl you're dating,
But I suffer everyday
Just because of our past!

I see a dream
Then get up
Start to feel sorry,
Because it was just a dream!

I love you a lot
But don't think you love me back,
What can I do
To get your love?

Can't you see
That I'm falling apart,
Because you left me

Lyudmila Maronyan

Premises Of The Heart

I see a weeping willow tree.
So beautifully it flows
In the wind, the sunshine,
On a pretty day,
As I walk by so disclosed.
I said to myself of the willow tree,
I know your beauty shows,
But no one knows of the willow tree
That weeps within my soul.

Nancy L. Brown

Like A Rose

Your eyes like a rose,
So beautiful aloft.
Your skin like a rose,
So gentle and soft.
Your body like a rose,
So sturdy and strong.
Your arms like a rose,
So they hold me long.
Your kiss like a rose,
So the smell so sweet.
Your love like a rose,
So I've fallen your feet.
For you are my rose,
So beautiful and loving.
For you are my rose,
So I await your coming.
My beautiful beautiful rose.
Nina K. Dear

Pine Grove

A little white country church
Sits nestled in a grove of pines

The bells ring out on Sunday morning
Across the river, across the fields of corn

Cross over the swinging bridge
Cross over and join the song

Gentle country people welcome you
With love and caring hearts

Make haste to worship in the pines
Make haste and join the throng

Gather by the swollen river
For the baptizing of the saved

Warm summer winds are blowing
Come eat dinner on the grounds
Lois Deal Bressler

Springsong

The jaunty birds are in the trees
Singing harmony with bees
While puffy pillows in the skies
Change their forms for wond'ring eyes

Squirrels walk their tightrope wires
Strutting 'round like country squires
Houses rise high in the air
As though a giant placed them there

Children playing on the walks
Writing in the street with chalks
Dusk is falling slowly down
Dropping nighttime all around

A backdrop now of midnight blue
Showing off the glowing moon
Stars there wink like shining treats
High above the city streets
Karen Mshar

Just For You Mom

If I measured my love for you with
stars it would take them all from the sky.
If I measured it with water, it would
drain the oceans dry.
But I can say it better with four words
so true - MOM I LOVE YOU.
Marie R. White

Salute To A Wife

I guess it's been said before
Since much is said in life
But just in case you missed it
Here's tribute to a wife.

Much fun is made of marriage
Detractors never rest
When love survives the years
Real brides must be the best.

Mother, planner, boss of home
Counselor to the young
Doctor Mom she's called
Let's ensure that praise is sung.

Along comes grandma's role
It fits her like a glove
Who best deserves blue ribbons
From the power who dwells above.

Fifty years slip by
Much too fast it's true
Here's one who well remembers
The lucky day she said "I do."
Leonard F. Rathbun

Open Line

Orchestra of music
silently reads the note
Answers with a letter
to forefill the hope.

Yesterdays of tomorrow
sight of wild streams
flowing words of activities
into life's beam.

Doors open at different threshold
the messenger linked to three
body, soul and mind
In effort to pleasing thee.
Nancy M. Musca

"Beauty Is Born"

At the rise of the golden sun
 she's born.
All her glow is present.
Her single, gold, sane shaped
 horn is alive.
Her air light wings dancing
 free in the wind.
She is one of a kind great
 and magnificent.
As she gallops and plays
 her mane dances.
Though as the sun sets,
 her glow starts to fade.
Her gold, sane shaped, horn
 fades to nothing.
Her wings are still.
She is gone, yet still magical.
Megan O'Neill

Untitled

How sad it would be
To have a brain
That could not see
Kerry Coffman

A Rose For Mary

Citizen of Ireland
She visited
While in the Glenn
From Ireland.
She walks among us.

Mary's Family Story
Ely-Ealy
Bennett-Colby-City
Garrett-McCarthy
Full of Glory.

Citizen of Ireland
Came by Sea.
Her love will keep eternally.
Tranquility restored in her sleep.
She walks among us.

Never forgotten
Written on stone.
Always visited.
Never alone.
A rose for Mary.
Nathan A. Ely

A Mother's First Hunt

Her night gone, but first light here
She steeled herself, because of her fear
I'm going now, I've come to say
I understand, that was her way.

The door closed, her concern was cold
She called him once, and that was old
You will call if you can
He smiled at her and then he ran.

Her day was long, so very long
She busied herself, that too her way
Slowly night came, that very day.
Her son came home, safe and gay.

The mother older, also the son
Trust and courage, both had won
A boy in the woods, the mother agrees
In a peaceful forest among the trees.
Kathleen C. Sottile

"Now"

It is about time
She looks into a mirror
And realized he made no error

She looks now deep within
At her natural born inner skin

She view herself very unique
This tremendous step is for keeps

Where land flows with dignity
She drinks from rivers titled courtesy

For one's self and body
Entertained with honor as a lady

Not as the streets mire
But one who wears Queen attire

It is about time

She saw beyond folk eyes
And realized he created no disguise

She saw finally a flower
Standing tall on self-esteem high tower

O' it is about time
Marcina P. Beasley

"Shear Delight"

Our dog is smiling ear to ear
She knows she looks just grand
I could never do this by myself
It takes a professional hand

Her coat is trimmed to such perfection
She knows she's quite a sight
The way she struts to show it off
Her pose, a photographers delight

Her ears are plucked, her nails done too
She looks so prim and proper
She'll probably ask to go out tonight
To a show, or perhaps the opera

In just a few short weeks from now
She'll know its time again
To have her groomer fuss over her
Shear delight, can't wait till then!

Michael A. Ciullo

She Is

She is my wife to be.
She is my best friend.
I pray to God we have a long, happy life
that will never end.

Sometimes we disagree,
like every couple does,
But I could never walk away.
Because I am truly in love.

She is the most beautiful woman
Inside and out,
I was the lucky one to be chosen
So I could find out.

I thank God every night for the
woman in my life.
To show him my happiness
I want her to be my wife.

Lorin Myers

Solitude

The lake, like green glass,
shattered, as I dropped
my canoe on its clear stillness.
It trembled, as my oars
dipped in and out, silently, coaxing me
further down stream.
Trees reached their feeble
limbs to one another like a canvas
blocking out the distant sun.
Birds screeched, crickets murmured,
as solitude settled heavily
around me.

Kim Turner

The Mysterious Horseman

The mysterious horseman
rides in the dark.
With his armor and his silver horse.
Blends into the dark
like a star in the sky.
Fighting for his village.
So brave so strong.

Michael McLaughlin

My Angel

God from heaven above,
sent an Angel for me to love.

I was ready to give up
when my Angel appeared
whispering words of
encouragement in my ear.

He talked with me, and laughed with me,
and cried with me too, as he listened
to what I had been through.

Then with words of encouragement and love,
he showed me the road to
joy, happiness, life, and love.

My Angel has stuck by me
through thick and thin, and
I love that man more than anything.

So if your troubled and full of woe,
or just looking for a special someone,
maybe you too, will be sent an Angel to know,
but don't expect him to be as great as mine,
for there is only one of that kind.

Linda Wilbraham

Approaching Home

Her liquid blue eyes
Seep onto the rotting floor of the boxcar
As it passes through life
Breathing
With no regard for her
So blue
Memory dances in her mind's eye
No control
Kaleidoscope spinning
Too fast
Familiar streets
Strange steps
She leaps into the blue
Unable to run
To feel
To SCREAM!
She floats toward safety
Someone follows

Laura Allan

Brutally Raped

I clinch my hands and shut my eyes,
Scared of what is hear.
I gasp for air and hum a song,
Just so I won't hear.

Footsteps getting closer,
To the bed in which I lay.
I fight back, but he is strong,
For my life is what I pray.

So as I lay here naked,
Stripped of all my clothes,
I wonder what will happen next,
But he's the only one who knows.

My thoughts are interrupted,
By a gun held near my back,
And when he pulls the trigger I know,
I'm an innocent victim of a brutal
  rape attack.

Norell Spiler

Strangers

Wind whipped the cold, stone wall
scaling the sidewalk's edge.
Silently towering, shadowing, daunting
the courage of a heart of spring.

An approaching footstep, a sidelong glance
quickly retreats to the concrete floor
where all risky ventures are squelched
by endless trompings of the crowd.

The castle bricks moan in anticipation,
breathing a waning objection of dismay
in hopes to dishearten this living heart,
ignorant of cruel conventions.

A second, involuntary look
answered by the cracking of lips
and the revelation of a smile
bringing a breath of spring warmth

and the crumpling of the castle wall.
This breach of cold, indifferent protocol;
the simple action of a smile - returned,
leaving strangers not so strange.

Mindy Moodie

African Sunrise

Red, yellow, orange,
Rushing together like little ants
Running from their enemy.
Like a fox, deer, or duck
Running from a hunter.

Sunrise turning into purple,
As the colors rush together.
Looking like paint
On paper blending together.

The African people may cherish this sunrise,
But then again they may not.
For they may see it again
Before their time passes,
Or perhaps their heavenly spirits may.

Red, yellow, orange,
Running together like animals
Running from a forest fire.
Trying to escape,
Trying to survive,

Noreen L. Lyell

A Rose

Into the beauty of a flower
Our Master Gardener
Breathes His divine love
Into the bud of a Rose.

In the heavens above
Our Master Gardener
Graces His spiritual love
Into the petals of a Rose.

In the wonder of His being
Our Master Gardener
All seeing is believing
Into the touch of a Rose.

Like His hands there is no other
Our Master Gardener
Fashioned from love a fragrance
Into the beauty of a Rose.

Milan

Hymn Remembered At Sugar Hollow, Virginia

Blue Ridge Mountain trout stream
rolls, flows down over mossy rock
in a miniature waterfall;
sun shades, shadows
my pen-in-hand on paper.

Thanks to trout, watermountain.
"Lest we ne'er forget
of rocks and trees
and skies and seas,
God is the ruler yet!

Sun sparkles down thru
cumulus cloud,
down to mint rivulet,
falls over snapping
turtle shell rock.

"And to my listening ears
all nature sings
and round me rings
the music of the spheres."

Lucky Jacobs

Remembering You

The blue of your eyes
remind me of the sky as
I cherish the days I have
not with you.

As the seasons be done
one by one everyday was a
splendid one, as I remember
you.

If only I could hold you,
talk of the seasons that had
begun, so many seasons ago.

I do not cry of thinking
of you, nor the seasons that
left us with fun.
I have only the skies to remind me
of the eyes that came from my
love one.

Melissa Marshall

Remember Me!

To everyone who loved me
Remember, and I shall be
The brightest star, the reddest rose,
The bluest part of the sea.

Remember the good things
My laugh, my touch, my smile
Cause I have not left you,
I'm just gone for a while.

There can't be sorrow
There must be no tears
For now I'm in Heaven
Where there are no fears.

So remember me, my friend.
And we will meet again
In that great land of Peace
Where Angels, God does send.

Marilyn Hawkins

Winter Revelation

Leaves
Rejected by branches
Crushed
Under heaviness of snowflakes
Are forgotten
While etchings of black limbs
Using sky as background
Demand and receive
Admiration

Melva Y. Blair

The Dance

Fleeting gazes lock
recognition begins
Each mind can imagine
what may lie within.

A fluttering heart
the attraction is true
and nothing compares
to his feeling so new.

With a hesitant step
and a tentative smile
the drama unfolds
without pretense or guile.

A heightened awareness
and a tingling of senses
acknowledge no doubt as
anticipation commences.

And with one breathless sigh
your souls take a chance
and skip lightly away
on their choreographed dance.

Nancy Kammer

"Dreams"

A dream is a dream, but...is
reality truly different?
A thought is a moment, a moment
a memory...
Look around what do you see?
the past...the present...
what do you think about?
The future...is it scary...
beautiful...
You can dream...you dream,
think, imagine what your
reality is to be, you dream
dreams can come true...
Dreams are reality
Different for me and to you...

Melanie Zolcienski

He Can't Love Me...

Fear drapes this man.
Steered clear of a loving hand.
Does her being seem wrong?
Or was he doubtful all along?
Feelings are stifled from past regret,
Wondering if he can feel again.
Memories are vivid, but make him alone.
He searches for comfort, it's safe at home.
Will he stop before he's done?
Love can't take place, until it's begun.

Kellie Kontis

Spoken Silence

There's fire in my eyes,
Rage in my stomach,
Power in my hands,
Words in my mouth.

Speaking out to the world
Without making a sound.
My personality,
Cries aloud.

I can show off my hate,
My love and my fear.
Display my sadness,
By just shedding a tear.

You see, the best things,
Go unsaid.
My body is the words,
That just need to be read!

Nicholas Burns

The Hardest Words

Love, they say, it will abide,
Pushing pride down deep inside.

A hurting heart makes one so meek,
A level of pain it tries to seek.

But there are words so hard to say,
Games that people always play.

Emotions can't be put on display,
Logic always gets in the way.

But in my dreams late at night,
That's the time I'll hold you tight.

In my head when I'm all alone,
That's the place I'll make it known.

In my thoughts each and every day,
That's the only way I'll say,

I love you, I love you,
I love you, I love you.

Michael G. Lang

Death

Through the perilous struggles to
Pursue respect from our eldest,
We are denied by the natural
Passing of their life.
The naiveness of childhood is
Gradually outgrown as the length
Of their breath slowly dithers.
After the passing, you regret
The things you've done, you want
To outshine the past with even
More wonderful memories.
You want the time back while
Still in the present time.
You cannot enter the past.
Therefore you are afraid
Of the future.
Eventually, the sadness hardens
Becomes a great memory in
Which you seek to remind
You of the times you did have.

Nathan Bennett

Release Your Burdens, And With Me Walk

O great man of orthodox mind,
pondering others' thoughts, torn from direction.
Rid Yourself of such trivial burdens.

Release Your soul to the higher plain,
Whereupon few have tread
Taste the new life to which You are reborn!

Free Your inner-being and learn to walk.
Lean upon me to steady Your step.
Grasp my hand to guide You.

Gaze upon me,
Your guard,
Thine pools of blue!

Krystal Lynn Larmay

The Pearl

As I was walking by the sea
Pondering God's will for me,
A rocky shell there caught my eye
It beckoned me to not pass by.

I picked it up and peered inside
And found within a gem did hide,
A perfect pearl was tucked within
I was reminded of where it had been

A tiny bit of sand you see
Like a tiny test of God to me,
Built itself a shelter from harm
Like I am sheltered by God's arm.

Not once, or twice, but many times more
The sand washed in and was sheltered o'er,
Until one day this pearl was made
Beautiful and perfect there it laid.

Life's problems open our eyes to see
Our pearl is constantly growing to be,
A beautiful life, free and victorious
Formed by God's own hand and glorious.

Kathi Day

Glass Heart

I give to you this heart of glass
please take good care of it;
For when you do, this heart will last
it's love will never quit.
Because it's glass, in it you'll see
the love it holds for you.
The colors of love will never fade
This glass heart will keep them true.

Because it's glass, it's strong enough
to cut through those times of tears.
And in it, we'll store precious memories
that we'll acquire through the years.

Because this heart is made of glass
These few words I have spoken.
Remember them... please cherish them
for glass hearts are easily broken.

Lori Bitoushana

Word's To My Children

Hold fast, my children, to your youth.
Please don't grow so fast.
Make each tomorrow better than today,
And make the good times last.

Reach out to love, and you'll be loved
Experience new things each day.
Sing and laugh, and be carefree,
For your youth is slipping away.

There's so little time for me to say
All that I'd like you to know.
So listen, my children and never cease
To allow your mind and body to grow.

Linda Roth

The Voice

Somewhere inside, there is a voice, a face
  pleading begging
    let me see,
    let me speak

But wisdom is short lived
  as reason and unreason,
    speak louder

Still insistent voice remains,
  a whisper

At times a face smiles,
  unexpected

Uncertainty prevails, long standing
  has earned it's right to rank supreme
    unfaltering

The strong survives
  wins the battle

But there is no war,
  only love

How could this be,
  there is no one there, only me

Laura Mueller

Urban Development

Warm rays shine in patches,
permeating the green canopy.
Heavy black boots crunch
broken twigs, marking long trails
winding through cold dawn darkness
in the middle of nowhere.
Chained monsters buzz and grumble
loud enough to wake the sleeping owls,
disturbing serene beauty
as each pine, each oak,
falls to the ground,
crying in splintery pain.
Sticky sap covers new green leaves
like life blood running
down the severed trunk.
Spotted hunters and field mice alike
flee from once peaceful homes.
Where will they go?

Michelle Kurisu

Silver Linings

When the shadows of your sorrows
  overwhelm you from within,
And the dreams inside you crumble
  disappear or just wear thin.
Look beyond the gray of sorrow
  to the promise of the sky,
Where it's dark clouds are illumined
  with a glorious silver line.
Our lives may not be happy,
  and may only bring us pain,
So look unto the heavens where
  God's love is made more plain.
Life's sorrows, trials and triumphs
  may all seem too much a cost,
But in the silver linings
  is the truth not all is lost.
Friend, look unto the heavens
  and let your spirits soar.
For within each pain we suffer
  is the promise, God will restore.

Laurel J. Wilbur

The Sea

I sit on a cliff
Overlooking the sea
Thinking of love,
Pondering the mystery.

Must the past overshadow today,
Preventing us from the delight
Of what is near, of what is now?
Instead of alone, in the night

Being overtaken by fear and doubt?
The ocean hides its abundance below
A turbulent surface, whipped by
The wind, pulled by the moon's glow.

Sweeping away yesterday's footsteps
Leaving behind a new shell,
Some broken seaweed, an anemone.
What a story she could tell.

My life is reflected there.
I see my confusion, my history.
I see the life and the death
Left by the indiscriminate sea.

LouEllen Campbell

Handful Of Stars

Walk softly my love
Only once we pass this way
Talk softly my love
You may influence someone today

Laugh softly my love
Yours in beauty flames
Sleep softly my love
Moonbeams are dancing on frosted panes

Run softly my love
Catch each moment and treasure
Time is so swift and fleeting
A blink of the eye and its over

Fling me a handful of stars my love
Ere I enter the long night of sleeping
Cast your magic spell my love
And home I shall go without weeping

Lillian Smith

My Son

Although this day you take a wife,
Our son you'll be all of our life.
We hope that happiness you'll find,
And to each other, please be kind.

Strength, integrity and character,
Yours these are now and forever.
So stable and strong are you,
May your love also be true.

As to your sister I did say,
These words I say again today.
Ne'er will our vigil fail,
Our help you may avail.

Although we are so far apart,
You always are in both our hearts.
Ne're once will mom and I not care,
Not just for you, but also Claire.

Now that you have a life anew,
To share between the two of you,
We wish you all the happiness,
Also your marriage, may God bless.

Maurice J. Brouillette

Building Our Queen A Kingdom

We are building our queen a kingdom
Our queen is a puppy you see.
She is a half a dog
high and two dogs long
and cute as she can be.

Our neighbor gave us a puppy
All black with little brown feet
As she grew we learned to love her,
but, we couldn't keep her from the street.

By now she was queen of the house
and the yard she wanted to rule
keeping her there was a problem
with the children going to school
So we called the fence company out.
And they set the poles today
we are building our queen a kingdom
So our queen can go out and play.

Mary Anita Kirby

"One"

There's only one chance for every mistake;
One expectation.
Time spins rapidly, as you race with it.
You try to erase your mistake,
To fix the broken heart;
To gain an understanding.
Moments begin to pass you by,
You realize that life is precious;
Past is never too far.
You might lose yourself, but gain a second;
A second of understanding who we are.
We only get one chance.
One chance for life,
And one for love.
There's one for death,
And one for growth;
But one chance to renew your one dream.
Only one chance.

Nicole Necci

Discover Life

What do you see of the Earth?
Or life
Or anything around you.
Just open your eyes
And see the glory of life.
Open your eyes
See the land
And the sky.
Watch a bird fly slowly by.
See a smile, hear a laugh
Feel the sunlight warm your back.
Just open your eyes
And you shall eyes
That life is full of many things:
Like love, and peace
Friends, and foes.
So many things
To see and do
To experience life;
Just open your eyes and see.

Larry Mahler

Cement

Off of the rooftop
onto the concrete
a drastic fall,
a dying cause.
The cement scrapes
my flesh
the blood that
seeps
an ending pain
The feeling that each
measure of pain
is complete.

Lanette F. Latting

"Love Is A Rose"

Lasting deep roots of truth.
Only with strong bonds of
Virtues, faith, and hope.
Everlasting nourishments
Of beauty,

Instilled in the sunshine of warmth and
Soils of growth and prosperity.

Always inlaid with delicate, lustful

Rose petals of passion,
On the continuing cycle
Stem of life. Uplifting and
Ending with plentiful leaves of success.

LaTricia M. Quan

Name

Swimming motionless
Pair of sandals on an empty
Beach
drowning heart
The matches burned down the house
Danny was only six
left home alone again by mommy
accident
now Daddy's lost his name
who are we without each other
how can we dance alone

Michelle Sien

Metamorphosis

We cannot change on our own,
only with God can we do this.
Like a Butterfly, can our beauty unfold.
A caterpillar is seen spending its
time in a cocoon,
So do we spend time in Sin, wrong doing
and being unloving.
In time the butterfly emerges, with
beautiful colors and is set free.
With God and His Son's love,
when we go to Him in prayer
and ask for help, He changes us and
sets us free to be the kind of person
we really should be, and all those
around us see the metamorphosis.

Margaret S. Matyok

Dear Gene

You were just a dream
One that come true
What have you done
I've fallen in love with you
You make me feel great
Just like our first date
All my dreams are true
And it's because of you
My love is true
Like the sky is blue
So don't turn your back
Or my love will turn black
Please hold my heart
So very tight
While I dream of you
All through the night.

Kimberly Gay

Ode To My Mother

No masterpiece you painted
  One ceiling high in Rome,
But both your girls and son remember
  You lived one in your home.
You panned no epic poem
  That critics might call art,
But with a grander vision,
  You wrote one in you heart.
You craved no Parian marble
  In sculptured greek design,
But with you God Blessed loving fingers,
  You shaped this life of mine.
You built no white cathedral
  By echoed footsteps trod,
But in simple faith you made
  Our home a house of God.
Not the hand of Raphael,
  Or Michelangelo,
Could paint my Mother as she is -
  Only her children know.

Mary V. Prisock

Through The Eye Of A Lie (Of Love)

One sees the other as a thing of
possession to the other sees in the eyes
deception and knows the pain ahead.
But the other wants no passion.
So from the other that wants it
over to find another like no other.

Michael J. Saulis

A Senior's Reflection On Getting Old

As one sits and reminisces about past years
One also sheds a few more tears
Some years were good some were bad
Some made you happy some made you sad.

As time is getting short for me
I wonder next year where I will be
I've accomplished my goal on what
I wanted to be
A sea going sailor who loved the sea.

I've sailed the Atlantic ocean.
The Pacific and Indian too
I have sailed from Newport to Timbuktu
Rio was my city and Cape Town too
Rome, Beirut and Athens to name a few.

As I now reminisce you know I am getting old
Once I was cocky, once I was bold
Oh, the memories I now remember
Are now all smoke, ashes and a small ember
These memories will always live in my heart
Some of these memories have also torn me apart.

Louis G. Tashash

Bare

A garden
once bathed in sunlight,
nourished by rain
exotic and rare, exquisite colors
and fragrance divine, that
bloomed freely and flourished
until....
you came along and tore apart
each blossoming petal and ripped
the stems, screaming in pain,
from their luring roots,
laughing all the while
until it was bare
and when you were finished said:
"I thought you always knew,
they were already dead!"
I've replanted my garden
far away from the likes of you;
It will grow and flourish again,
but will you?!

Mona Bari

A Single Candle

Today we come together here
On this, a special day,
To honor those whom we hold dear —
The friends who've passed away.

Although they're gone, each memory
Is strong within us yet
And we, their Aggie family,
Will pledge not to forget.

We burn for them this single light,
A sign to show we care —
A single candle burning bright
To let them know we're there.

So let us take a solemn vow
With those who've mustered here
That should indeed the fates allow,
We'll meet again next year!

Lynnette A. Cardenas

Christmas

When the snow has gently fallen
On the trees and on the ground
We look ahead to Christmas
And the joyous ringing sound.

With the bells that line the city streets
And the holly here and there
You cannot help but sense somehow
The "Christmas" in the air

When the long glad day is over
And night has softly come
We say good night to all we love
With "MERRY CHRISTMAS EVERYONE"

Lorraine Morgan

Relished

We have felt the cool fresh night air
  on our bodies
and relished in the touch of our caresses

I try to remember this, when distance
  has taken over
as time has once again driven
  a wedge into my side
and I lean back and remember summer
  the warmth and laughter
in your face...

Yes, your face, strength and gentleness
  all molded into one
your eyes deep withholding distance
  but sparkling
We have felt the cool fresh night air
  on our bodies
and relished in the touch of our caresses

But the quietness of summer ends
  and we two part...

Linda J. Smith

Forever Has An End

The words we whispered
On a moonlit night
The promise that we lived by
Which seemed so right
Everything has been displaced
The love has been upset
And yet there's a painful yearnin'
It seems I can't forget
The plans we made are all erased
No more dreams of us together
And now that we're apart
Tell me...
What happened to forever

Natashia M. Jones

The Sun Shines

The sun always shines
on a leaf or a flower

Which splendor will bloom
within the day's hour

Whose beauty is wondrous
for all eyes to see

Which lasts a short time
just for you and for me.

Naomi Reed

Garden Of Dreams

I dance amongst the flowers
Of your days
Swaying in and out
Trying to grab hold
Of anything certain
Waiting for a time
When I flourish
Within your core
Basking in the essence
Of your juice
Before the blight comes
Eating at the roots
Of our love
Wilting away our passion
Dead amongst the weeds
Never to grow again

Marcia Herr

"Love From Two"

I rock these tiny bundles
of pink and blue
a little longer than
most other grandmas do.

I play much harder,
to share their carefree fun
"hiding and seeking"
always on the run.

When we tea for three
there's cups of four;
Our "pretend" guest
is here once more.

I double their hugs,
kiss away each tear
hold them extra tight
to erase every fear.

I'll tell them someday
why so much love comes their way
It's from the "other" grandma too
who had to "go away"............

Maxine Haddox

The Gift Of Giving

This time of year our hearts are full
of peace good will
toward man.

So often our time is spent
in frantic search
for that perfect
gift.

The real gift is not in money spent,
but in the brotherhood
of man.

Gifts will tarnish and turn to dust.
Food lasts only a day.
But the real gift
of love and friendship,
lasts forever and a day.

A gift given from the heart,
can never rust or fade.
For a gift given from the heart
is a little bit of heaven!

Nancy C. Rasey

Untitled

My clearest angel
  of devotion
Came to my eyes
  at dream time

It's there in copper-lidded
  breathless horror
"Being" gathers back its meaning

And only there
the foreign tongue
Will reign for me
Dusk to dust.
Mike Latham

Target

A heap
of crumpled feathers.
Black tipped wings
Spread
in stifled flight.
Suppliant little head
Forever bowed
In mute protest
Of a beebe shot.
Madeline Shelvey

My Four Stages Of Life

When I stop and think
Of any little co-inky-dink
I find sometimes it takes over my life.
Then what I realize is,
That is has begun!
With all the fun
Irony comes.
I don't let life scare me
I embrace it.
Knowing a surprise will come.
After all,
The co-inky-dink transforms into...
The coincidence of having,
The fate of loving,
The irony of hearing,
And the destiny to know.
Lisa Reddick-Langford

Reflections

Feeling sad and feeling glad
Of all the things we did not do
And many things that drove us to
Who we are today.
Is there time to do it all
Can we be proud when we fall
Ups and downs make us strong
Doing our best all day long.
Do we help those in need or
Are we too obsessed with speed
Racing through each day
Not caring who is in our way.
It is time to search your heart
Where are we going, did we do our part
It is never too late to pave the way
A little change will make us say
Hey, we did our best to save the day.
Karen Little

Santa's Coming, Maybe

Hear ye, hear ye,
Now listen to this,
Susie, Ricky,
Mary, and Chris.

You better be good
Little girls and boys,
Or Santa might not,
Bring any goodies or toys.

While you're waiting,
For his Ho, Ho, Ho'ing,
He might just keep on,
Go, go, going!
Lovey Baldwin

Money Can't Buy Me Love!

There was a time I traveled the high road
Nothing was out of my reach
Material things were mine
Life was a real peach!

But suddenly I realized
I didn't really have it all
My life was missing love and great passion
I was heading for a fall.

One morning as I woke
The words appeared in my mind
"Is this all there is?"
I'm in a real bind!

Then suddenly into my life
A dark man just appeared
Offering his attention and compassion,
Undying love, which at first I feared!

I gave up the material things
And went for the love
Now I *do* have it all
And I'm thanking God up above!
Marva J. Daniels

Lackluster Love

All we play are games.
Nothing left is real.
No one cares for love,
Or what you're supposed to feel.

All we're told are lies-
Prisoners of deception,
And all our disbeliefs,
Are all our misconceptions.

We're locked up in a cage,
Due to all their fears.
We're drowning in a pool,
Of lovers' quarrels tears.

We all are filled with history,
That haunts us like a ghost.
And so we continue to hurt,
The ones we love the most.
Michelle Belsky

Race

It is not black,
  Not white,
    Not brown or red.
It is not the best,
  Not the worst.
It hates and wounds,
  And it frowns.
It loves and glows,
  Grows and discovers.
It makes mistakes, and miracles,
  Inequality, and bonds.
It knows torture,
  And exquisite pain.
It is rainbow bright and beautiful,
It is a race,
  Not black, not white,
    Not brown nor red.
It is just one human race!

  We all must rise above
    The hate.
Karen Scott

Contentment

I want to live
Not just exist
To feel, experience and grow
To meet each day with open arms
And learn along the way

There is an aching in my soul
A loneliness to be filled
A need to make a difference
To make a brighter day

To ease a sorrow, wipe a tear
To lend a helping hand
To see my children doing well
Content then I will be
Kay Belvin

Star Scorched

Not from the galaxy
not from the heavens
but here on earth
a star was born.

In the quiet of our dawn
in a shelter by design,
but, alas, with a taunt,
that stirred the wrath of fate.

A light amidst the darkness
a weightless strength
conceived by a passion
that only heaven knows.

This world could not accept
such a celestial flame
but, this itself, served only
to fan the blaze ignited.

Its brilliance burned brightly
Its space in time was brief
climaxed in a deafening silence
scorching souls when flickered out.
Linda Quintero

Healed

Disease no way my hand you'll hold.
Nor possess my life in your control.
I take a stand against your name.
My life this date, is not the same.

Disease you come in many forms.
You twist our life, create a storm.
Try as you may, my life is spared.
Because my Creator, His Son he shared.

Disease you try to knock me down.
I will not fall into your plans.
My mind has better things to do.
Then waste it on the likes of you.

Disease no matter what you're called.
You can't have me, your power is stalled.
So no matter how sick or bad I feel.
By Jesus stripes, I am totally healed.

Mary L. Want

Treasures

No need for canvas
Nor artists pots,
Just think of painting
With your thoughts.

White cloud ships sailing
Thru summer skies,
The heavenly blue
Of a kitten's eyes.

The pure sweet notes
A robin sings.
The glint of sunlight
On a cardinal's wings.

A treasure of paintings
That can't be bought.
Safely stored away
In your private thoughts.

Just pick out a brush
And paint what you see
Of all of the Treasures
The Lord gave to thee.

Olive F. Anderson

Nothing Has Changed

We are here to-day and gone tomorrow,
None so big to demand great sorrow.
None so powerful to be missed tomorrow,
The world was here before we came.

The Sun appears in the East at morn,
The Weather, man still does scorn,
What makes Man so forlorn?
Seasons come and Seasons go,

Trees and Mountains do survive,
Bees and Birds are kept alive,
They worry not of struggle and strife.
Why then, for Man such a troubled life?
Man first must learn how to exist.

Animals and Plants for us co-exist,
Let's take a lesson from their bliss,
Love thy Neighbor and head the list.
Who cares more for Man's fate
Than Man Himself?

Mary Baker Roden

So Late At Night

I have no one to love me,
No one to hold me tight.
That's why I'm always whistling
So very late at night.
I have no one to love me,
No one to treat me right.
That's why I'm always whistling,
So very late at night.
With a heavy heart I sit in my window,
I whistle a tune.
In my heart I hope for a miracle from
The magic in the moon.
For one that'll treat me right,
And love me so late at night.

Luegenia Van Buskirk

Alone?

I am yet again on my own
   no more promises and nothing to show
I gave it all away
   to a man who never cared
I am alone again
   or am I really?
I still have my wisdom
   that will remind me of my doings
I still have my strength
   that helps me in what I do
And best of all
I still have the memories
   that are everlasting through
This thing we call life.

Marie Ann Morgan

You Travel Alone

No matter where you travel
No matter what you do
No matter who your companions are
Be they many or few
You never seem to be happy
You keep looking for something new
Of you are looking for happiness that lasts,
Take God along with you,
Or you travel alone.

Lyda R. Wilson

No Greater Joy for US Than Life

Joy is for US
No greater joy for you
No greater joy for me
Can ever exist without Love
There must be Trust

Joy is for US
No greater joy for us
No greater joy for me
Can ever exist without Peace
The Feeling must come from the Heart

Joy is for US
No greater joy for you
No greater joy for me
Can ever exist without Hope
The tears WE shed must be for each other

Joy is for US
No greater joy for you
No greater joy for me
Can ever exist without Life
We must live every moment to its fullest

Lgfowler

You Didn't Know

You never saw the goose-step you
never heard THE HEIL

You didn't think twice about
the draft waving your
bravest smile

You didn't see British air raid shelters
strangers huddled
as one when faced with deadly
danger valiantly made
it fun

You didn't see gas chambers
hear the screams
smell the smoke

You didn't see our victory sweet
or glimpse Germany's grim defeat

You didn't see naked half-dead Jews
staring at us one
by one
You didn't see your dad
come home
you were my youngest son

Mimi Eagan

A Song For Me

I was touched by his dynamic presence.
My attention was grabbed.

His demeanor was intoxicating.
I knew he was THE ONE.

Intrigued, was I, while I watched.
Mesmerized, also, while I listened.

I sat in awe while the melodies flowed
from his heart, through his lips, like
cascading water -
Freely -
Naturally -

Something inside, that laid dormant
for so long, had awakened.
I never met him, but I knew him;
I knew him well.

I wait with anticipation for our next
one-sided encounter, and dream of the
day when his song will be:
A SONG FOR ME.

Lynn M. Scannapieco

Ode To My Black 501's

Trotting through the
mountains on horseback
hiking up the steep hillsides
climbing over rocks and
fences
My black 501's
now a faded grey

Laurie Ann Tarvin

"Good Morning America" -ABC

"I can't change the direction
of the wind, but I can adjust
my sails to always reach my destination."

Martha Lynn Joiner

Falling Dreams

I have watched
my dreams fall
endlessly from the sky
not landing in my lap
but falling under my feet
with each dream I have,
fall below me
I have many of tears
I feel now as if I
could just stop it all,
stop dreaming
so I don't have to watch
them fall stop all hope
So I won't end up disappointed
and heartbroken
I want to catch them
put them back in the sky
to cure my disappointment
and also
to mend my broken heart.
   Maria Rotchford

Chrissy

There once was a girl
named Chrissy
who was so very very prissy
she fell down the hill
and took a big pill
and proved she was no sissy.
   Monica Mosteirin

"Taking Time"

As I sit and watch the sunset,
My mind wanders away.
As my mind wanders do things I can't forget,
It becomes the ending of another day.

I wander to dreams, hopes, and wishes
And I wonder if they'll ever come true
But I know it all takes time
If they did, what will I do?

At this time I am very lonely,
That is why I am in the crack.
And I get a funny feeling,
Its a cold shiver going up my back.

Maybe I'm not lonely,
Could it be that I'm depressed.
I could be sick and tired,
Maybe the way out is death.

Many different things happen to me,
That is why I write my thoughts down.
I always write my feelings and thoughts.
And they appear different from what they sound.
   Michelle Davis

A Perfect Rose

A perfect rose is nature's eternal gift.
   See how the petals caress each other
In total communion!
   And the deep crimson enchants
      the eye.
   Michael Garfield

This Realm Of Mine

Oh what a world! What a beautiful world!
My world of thoughts and desire
To some I s'pose it's a dreamer's world
But dreams are aflame with fire!

I can go where I like, do what I please
In this lovely realm of mine
With no interruptions 'tis a life of ease
Confusion and chaos go sailing by.

It's always so lovely, so cool and so calm
The people I meet are mine
I like that deep inner part of myself
It's like wine when you're thirsty for wine

So let people come, and let people go
Let nations and countries hold sway
I always know where my kingdom begins
At the dawn and the dusk of each day!
   Karen Ely Thiele

Nature Man

Raped by the constraints of society,
nature man forgets his morality.
Common decency turns to propriety,
void of individuality and personality,
rediscovering nature through piety.

Nature man has to conform —
there goes any sense of self-will.
Natural instincts repressed by the norm,
sanity begins to distil to nil;
government creates the storm.

"When will there be an insurrection?"
asks the man without freedom;
his thoughts and beliefs are regurgitation
(the prevailing drum from Christendom).
Nature man awaits his resurrection.

Civilization is raw corruption;
it sucks the spirit clean out.
Ambition replaces traditional gumption,
human pawns fill the drought with grout —
society is nature man's interruption.
   Mark Comfort

The Dance

Through the crowd,
Our eyes meet.
The music begins
And we are in each other's arms.
Your touch is so gentle,
As if I were glass.
We are swept away
In a sweet, romantic dance.
All we see is each other
As we are pulled closer together;
And then our lips almost touch,
And...
The music box stopped,
And she began it again.
   Kimberly Massey

Release: Future Found In Past

The Bible says we cannot enter the "Kingdom of Heaven" in our present bodies, they have to be changed, and "faith is the substance of things hoped for, the evidence of things not seen." What else are human eyes limited to seeing, senses perceiving? Suspicions of other dimensions soon coming to light. Human faith now believes heaven is another dimension only perceived by the substance of souls. Not unrealistic. Before the present generation passes, the concept of multiple dimensions may soon be proven fact. Parallel universes could conceivably answer great, unfathomable questions. One major, being scientifically pondered: space travel via molecular-restructuring; only theory, or a 3-dimensional-provable-concept?———LOOK FOR ANSWERS SOON!

S. Brownlee-Cobb

To My Son On His College Graduation

How very proud I am tonight....
You've studied hard-fought the fight.
After all the times of pain and doubt,
The time is here - what it's all been about.

How long ago, when you first began...
To take those steps in becoming a man.
Twenty-some years - where has time gone,
When a lullaby was our special song?

Grade school was hard enough you cried...
High School required strength from inside.
You resisted pressure and taunts from peers,
And made me proud through-out all those years.

Then college looked you straight in the face...
"Dear Lord," I cried, "Help him finish the race."
So many prayers I've said for you, Son....
How proud I am for the race you have won!

You hold in your hands your degree tonight,
And I think of how hard you fought the fight.
As you stand up there-the battle won,
With pride I can say, "That Man? He's my Son!"

Becky Hickok

An Ode To You

The summer of your life came and passed, without the carefree, youthful world of fantasy—
And boyhood skirmishes didn't fit into your world of grim responsibility.
As years went by the pattern held and pulled you like a boggled weight
From dawn to dusk you struggled on, bound by the tiring hand of fate.
Your body and your soul grew tired, and worn from never-ending strife,
You didn't find in work-filled hours the child you couldn't be in early life.
As darkness came in those last days you couldn't feel your human worth,
And in your painful solitude, your journeyed from this home on earth.
To soaring heights of joy and rest, above the clamorous cry of humankind;
God grant your soul eternal bliss—a happy spirit and sweet peace of mind.
Unknown to those you left behind in this earthly home of our abode,
But we'll reunite again someday, and walk together on that tranquil road.
Where pain and death will come to us no more, and love flows freely like a babbling stream
With joyful noise and restful quiet, we find fulfillment of life's dream.

Diane Bridges

Forgive

Forgive, because God has forgiven you.
Your sins are no longer scarlet but washed white as snow.
Jesus came for you.
You may never die as horribly,
as Christ paid the price of salvation
For you and me so we can live eternally with Him.
You will be among Angels if you forgive.
If your life is in tangles,
you don't have to live at angles.
You don't have to be afraid, or try to hide.
God knows our problems; He'll listen,
He'll tell us if we try to listen.
We shouldn't mess around; we could get knocked to the ground.
Don't get up to fight back; forgive them.
Life is so short, so precious.
God loves you, and it will break His heart
if we fight back or don't forgive.
Don't waste your precious life on an enemy;
forgive them instead.
God will bless you, and He will be happy, too.

Jessica Bartholomew

Untitled

From the very moment when they called and said she's here,
Your new adopted baby girl you'd soon be holding near.
You didn't have to take me in, you could have walked away,
Instead you held and fed and loved me more and more each day.

Those tender years - the teaching, caring, wiping all the tears,
The photos, each new step I took, a loving mother's fears.
It never crossed your mind that birth you didn't give to me,
For anyone can have a child, but mother still not be.

Birthday parties came and went - I grew before your eyes,
The Christmas trees, the dolls the dresses - my how fast time flies.
It wasn't always easy - as I grew I caused you pain,
The sunny days grew cloudy, but you withstood all the rain.

You never gave up when most would - you didn't walk away,
You stood by your commitment, "From this child I'll never stray."
A mother's love they say is there when first she holds her child,
But yours decision from the start of all those long walked miles.

There is no way to thank you for the years you've given me,
But I can tell you that I love you and my "Mom" you'll always be.
I hope if that chance comes in life for me as did for you,
That I can give just half as much as you did and still do.

Jill E. Jordan

One's Inner Fire

In the still of the night as you lay there alone;
  your mind will reminisce over the day's work that's been done.
Was it eventful or not; did you finish all before deciding to stop;
  could you have done more; or is it merely an afterthought?
If there were a change made in your daily routine would your
  accomplishments be greater; that is yet to be seen.
The clock of life has its limits as we are all aware;
  death can sometimes knock before any of us are ready or prepared.
Each day should be filled with your inner most desires and goals;
  living life and dreaming a dream which only you possess and hold.
Only you can spark that inner fire which will enlighten your life;
  may it burn bright, never losing sight, allow this inner fire to
  shine throughout the day and night.

Donna L. Swanson

Our Little Secret

Five years is a long time to admire, wouldn't you say?
Your lips lingered on more than just my lips that day.

Your eyes are sinfully brown, your hair devil black.
Words are sweet with manipulation, but I see through
   your beautiful peaches and cream complexion.

A solid wall surrounds the heart and soul.
I know I am one of many who think they can break it.

I'm not afraid of who you are; just what you are.
With every heart break, a layer of plaster covers yours.
I won't let you crack mine, but you come closer.
I let you embrace me once. I thought that was forgotten long ago.
   But you embrace me again, your eyes danced with delight,
   anticipation.
As I lay under a weight of sin, you kiss my forehead tenderly.
I know all will be forgiven or forgotten.

We meet again on friendly grounds. I say my goodbyes.
You say you love me, with your eyes. I know it won't be long
   before I forget, until I see you again.
   Alyson Nicole Krawchuk

Thoughts Of You

As I contemplate your image in my mind...
Your face, your smile, your personality so kind;
Time is irrelevant, time is still,
But my heart palpitates for you with a jubilant feel.

After a short time apart, I reminisce.
Seconds later I realize it's your kiss I long for and miss.
These thoughts of you rule my space,
They are thoughts free of ire.
They are thoughts of friendship, love and desire.

I reminisce of a woman, to me, so dear.
I reminisce of a woman beautiful and sincere,
As my thoughts of you are simple and pure.
Like the symbol of Peace and Love,
The white dove,
My thoughts of you matriculate from the Heavens above.
   John Woodley

Daddy's Love...

If you're a girl you'll understand what I'm trying to say
your daddy is the one who's there to lead you on your way
he's the one who teaches you what's right what's wrong
without knowing he's the one,
who teaches you all along
with his love he protects you under lock and key
with his support he stands by you
in what you want to be
a daddy's love is the love that's tender and so true
a daddy's love a real love
and one that sees you through...
   Christine A. Lennox

Listen

Listen if you can to a singing bird, and
you will suddenly understand.
There can be beauty and sound but it has to be found
and you can find it anywhere in the land.
Listen if you can to the falling rain,
and you will suddenly realize.
That everywhere you look there's a wide open book,
which you could read without using your eyes.
   Julie Moetzinger

Memory

Today, you know that you are hurting and your heart's about to break.
You wish that this was all a dream from which you would awake.

The dark, cold reality, a loved one dear has died.
His time had come to meet his king; you couldn't keep him...though
   you tried.

No longer is he suffering, nor is his body racked with pain.
No more striving for each breath in hopes that he might gain....

One more precious moment to complete tasks left undone.
But God said, "Your work is finished. You must come home, my son.

Your loved ones will miss you, and in pain, I know they'll grieve.
But I have left them ways of healing if only they would believe."

All through life, there are special moments that at the time we do not see.
Until a loved one is called home, then we walk the road of memory.

So remember all the good times and the laughter that you shared.
Live each day in Godly peace in knowing...Mr. Greathouse knew you
   cared.
   Jamie A. Haag

Untitled

Last night, while I slept, I dreamed of you.
You were under the stars, under the night, under Heaven itself.
I saw God look down upon you.
He smiled and shined His light.
I heard the Angels sing, the Moon whisper, the Twilights twinkle.
You gazed about, then laughed and danced.
You spoke to God and the Angels,
you spoke to the Stars, the Moon, the Earth and to Heaven.
You seemed so happy, so joyous.
I started to wonder what made you this way.
I was jealous at not sharing in the joy.
I stepped closer to you and asked,
"What makes you Dance and Laugh so? Why are you so joyous?"
You looked at me with innocent, yet knowing eyes.
And carefully, clearly, with a smile sweet as honey,
you whispered,
"I, too, am dreaming of you."
   Heather Dawn Wolfe

The Eagle

I remember when you came home from school;
You were in the second grade.
You shook your head with long brown braids
   hanging in loops over your shoulders.
"Today the teacher asked us all to be animals,"
   you proclaimed.
"Oh, and what animal were you?" We asked.
"An eagle, of course" was your reply,
   as if to say how could we not know.
Years later I saw you lying in a hospital bed.
You had taken pills and drowned them with a bottle of wine.
You could hardly talk due to the soreness left by the tubes
   that had recently been taken from your throat.
Your stomach had been pumped and you were a pasty white
   and you looked scared and harassed.
As I watched you with tears in my eyes
   and worry in my heart, I wondered
   "What happened to the eagle?"
   Carolyn Elaine Cliver

Tears Of Joy

You picked me up from the mire so deep
You washed me clean, over this I weep.
For the joy you've brought me frees my heart
The bondage is broken, the chains fell apart.

You've freed me! You've freed me! To Love as you do,
to spend eternity forever with you.
To reach out and touch a dying world,
And bring to repentance those through your spirit upheld.

Your forgiveness of Sin works beauty untold,
The fruit will be sampled by those who are bold.
Forgiveness of sin brings peace in my heart
And assurance that my Lord and my God will not part.

Thank you, my Lord, for your dying grace
And the will to keep sharing despite what I face.
  Dawn Thomas

Dream Of You

When the night is round it holds out its hand
You take hold
Leading you into the night
The night is full of surprises
Invites you in
Passion ignites
Stars shine
Music in your heart sings
Dawn comes
You open your eyes
Looking forward to another night
  David Wright

Gambler

You're a gambler, a high dollar bet
You roll the dice every chance you get
You play me like your money games,
You're not after my love, but you're after the fame,
——of my heart
You laid out the Kings, and you laid down the Jack
GAMBLER ready for attack
I'm the one, the one in charge, I won't let you play
—with my heart
Now I am the gambler, now I place the bets
I roll the dice, so you get what you get
So take it
  Take it like a man
Don't walk away with your face in your hands
  Reflected,
The games in your face—
It's my time, my heart, and my place
So busted
That's what you are
GAMBLER
  Beverly Macklin

Memories

When your loved one is gone,
you only have memories to live on;
Remember the laughter, the smiles, and tears;
Remember the love that lasted through the years.

God blessed us with a love that was true;
I'm so glad He gave me you;
In my heart you'll always be;
because you are a part of me.
  Edna Alu

A Quiet Strength

You give me strength, standing quietly by
You listen, you advise, your support you freely give.
Without you to lean on, I'd be an eagle with one wing.

We go together, you and I
We understand each other without talking
When we're down, we reach out to each other
When we soar, there's no one higher.

We are a book and cover
With a beginning but no end
We are two that make one
We are love, complete and done.
  Diane Curley

A Broken Heart

You left me so suddenly, right out of the blue,
You just turned and left, you gave me no clue.
How could you do that, didn't even say goodbye,
Yet you sneered and laughed, when I started to cry.
I sat in my room, all sad and alone,
Just after you told me, right over the phone.
With my head hung low, and my eyes shut tight,
I tried not to cry, with all of my might.
As I sat by the window, a tear dropped my eye.
I sadly whispered, "I want to die."
  Gil Quijada Jr.

For The Love Of Nature

For the love of Nature, leave your words behind.
You insult earth by thinking it looks better lined.
Look at the world before human word
Inked it and left it linguistically blurred.
For the sake of the Real, leave your books in the city;
Nature will flee from the words of the witty.
No alphabet cluster has ever been made
That captures the green of a leaf-gabled glade.
You won't ever find in the form of a book
The silver-blue dance of the moon on a brook.
Not even the verses bequeathed us by Blake
Are fair to the wonder of stars on a lake.
For the love of Nature, look away from these words.
Your eyes must be free to soar off with the birds.
To follow those clouds laughing over the sky,
The last thing you need is a word in your eye.
These twenty-six faces of Nature "on line"
Unconsciously throw primal vision "in sign."
This ink-blackened wordweb has moved in between
Your earth-cradled mind and that natural scene.
  Joe Dowell

Possession

"Thoughts of you are invading my mind, dreams of
you has taken over my sleep, my life does not belong
to me. Loving you has become an obsession, wanting
to possess you has become a fantasy"

Wanting to see you is all I live for
having you want me is a dream come true!
When we are together I cannot even think. You
are part of everyday, every night, every second that I exist!

Your face is there for me to miss, if only we had ever
kissed! My soul would be forever bliss! For you have
invaded my mind and I will love you till the end of time!
  Jeanette Jackson Jones

A Friend Like You...

A friend like you has touched my mind with your wisdom
You have touched my body with yours and
You have touched my soul with so much passion but most of all,
You have touched my heart with the most precious gift you have to
  give.....
Your friendship, a friendship that is forever.

Somehow we found a place in each other's lives and
We made a place in each other's hearts
It blows my mind that we have created the unbreakable bond
We are connected by choice
We have created our very own unique memories,
Therefore, everything which is now behind us shall never be forgotten
We have shared precious moments in time
And what we have today I only pray will grow stronger tomorrow.

In my times of need your voice has been my encouragement
Your laughter has been my light in the darkness and
Your smile has been my shining star
In my times of need these qualities of yours
You have so graciously shared with me
Have given me the ability to realize I am strong and I have value
What would I do without a friend like you.

Angela Adriatico

"From My Heart"

A voice keeps saying to me from the back of my mind,
"You have a message to share with all of mankind.
It's the Good News of Jesus and His saving grace;
Now is the hour and now is the place."
How shall I do this and where do I start?
I know I must be gentle and speak from my heart.
Jesus taught His twelve for nearly three years,
And still His Word fell on many deaf ears.
Such a challenge this message puts to me,
For some will listen and many may flee.
If only one will hear me it's all worthwhile;
To change their life and to give them a smile.
With Christ by my side, I know I can do this;
Listen for needs, no opportunity miss.
Then tell how the Good News took over my life;
Took away all the sorrow, the anger and strife.
My own witness is the best place to start.
I will be gentle and will speak from my heart.

Jeanne Sha

Grandparents

Grandparents are special, they hold you when
  you cry
Even with a letter they can wipe a tear from
  your eye
When you are small, they tell you stories; you
  keep them all your life.
You cherish them and hold them dear
You don't want them to ever go away
But then your grown and life doesn't seem
  to be the same as they told you it would someday
You wish you were a little girl so you could
  climb back on there knee
You'd start life over once again and make
  them proud of thee
So when there time on earth is through they
  will know
They were the most important thing in life
  you've ever known

Bonnie Jean West

Soar Love

I never thought love could be so agonizing.
You could suck the blood from my body,
the blood feels as though it no longer flows.
You could incise my wrist,
it could bleed no more then my heart.
I could become blind but love is not blind...
Love could only see as clear as an eye.
It is such sorrow...that my eye couldn't see as clear as I desire.
Love is like life...it has its good and evil.
It lasts for awhile then it begins to diminish until.
DEATH comes.
I don't know why my love had to escape,
There are times on cloudy days that I see soar love floating
high above me.
It has no way of returning...
It remains with its veins strangling my heart.
Why did you leave me when I was a small child?

Julie Silva

A Special Place

Did you ever have a place,
you could call you very own?
A place where when you felt troubled,
you could go and be alone.
Maybe this place is a meadow of daisies,
or a tree house in the woods.
But it doesn't really matter,
where this place is found.
What does matter is that when no one else listens,
or comforts you when you're down,
Your special place will bring you up again,
and will turn your frown the other way around.

Andrea Mae Stricker

You Can See It In Their Eyes...

It is a place of darkness, confusion, anxiety.
  You can see it in their eyes, clouded.
  In their shoulders, tense.
  In the way they speak,
    too much, too fast
    or too little, too softly.
Then we sit together.
  I listen.
  We discuss.
  They discover.
They lead me as far as they can.
When they stop, I point out the different roads we can take,
  and we start again.
Eventually, we walk into a clearing
  of light
  of knowledge,
  of calm.
You can see it in their eyes, sparkling.

Cathie Jean Culver

Shores Of Life

My dear tonight, as we walk in the shadows of the moonlight.
With the clasp hands of our love,
With the cooing of the doves around about us,
In the cool of the evening.
With life so wonderful,
as our hearts are entwined with the beauty of our love,
and in our togetherness we walk the shores of life.

Edwin Lyle Kinkead

"That Warrior Boy Of Mine"
"That Warrior Boy For Christ"

That warrior boy of mine, that warrior boy for Christ,
You can find him winning souls out in the high school play yard.

That warrior boy of mine, that warrior boy for Christ,
The one with the tube socks, crew socks, and pins,
He loves our Christ anyway, even though he lost his father at ten.

That warrior boy of mine, that warrior boy for Christ,
Out playing in the field with friends,
Even though a young man now, remains so painfully thin.

That warrior boy of mine, that warrior boy for Christ, Was guarded by
God's angels, when the enemy's bullet tried to slay him.

I've tried to raise him not to live his life in fear,
Nor to depend too much on men. I told him it was his
Father up in heaven who was with him even then.

I have wept at the things this old world has done to him; But he keeps
on going any ways, with his textbooks, trombones, and hymns.

I don't just love him because he is my flesh and blood,
I don't just love him because his suffering soul refused to shod,
I also love him because Christ made such an impact on his life
That he will probably go wherever God chooses to send him,
Even, I imagine, where only angels may sometimes dare to trod.

Cynthia Austin-Thorn

Will You Be There?

Every time I close my eyes
  you are there.
Every time I dream
  you are there.
Every time I open my eyes to see if we're for real,
  you are there.
Every time the wind blows
  you are there.
Every time I feel you're gone
  you are there.
And every time I think I don't believe
  you are there.

When I give up and I can't stand,
  will you be there?
When the light is dim and I can't see
  will you be there?
When my breath is dying and I wish for death
  will you be there?
When nobody is there
  will you be there?

Julie Spahr

Dear Dad

   Dear Dad my heart is aching, because
you've left this place, and I can never on this
earth see your familiar face or hear your voice or see
your smile. Yet, dear Daddy I see you everywhere.
I see you in faded overalls and the cap your used.
to wear. I see you in the redbud and every fragrant
rose, the tall and stately Iris and the wildflower
that grows. I see you in my brothers from
Dickie to Tom. I see you in the tired eyes
of our lovely Mom. I see you in my sisters
for their hearts are aching too.
We're sadly waiting Daddy till we can
be with you.

Eldora Andrea Beasley

The Song Of Longing, The Melody Of Desire

You are the dark song of the morning.
You are the unquenchable thirst of longing.
You are the prickling heat of desire.
You stand, basking the rest of the world with your aura,
Shining bright, driving some to madness.
Yet, you do not know it.
I stand, observing all that you do,
Hoping, yearning, pleading, begging,
For a glance, one small display of recognition. No more.
However, you avoid my adoring looks.
The song moves to a second verse.
Your beauty is not evident to some.
Your allure, blurred by the tainted eyes of sin,
Is as clear to me as fresh snow on a midwinter's day.
The song crescendos and reaches denouement.
Surely, you are aware of my love,
You must certainly know my dedication.
Why do others see, while you, with the beauty and grace of a
Goddess, the brilliance of a lone candle in a sea of darkness,
Are blind?

Howard S. Han Jr.

In Honor Of Her

Wow, what a singer
Yolanda killed her when she pulled the trigger
She was married to a 16 year old boy
Which I think should still be playing
with toys.

They're still having the trial in court
But I think this time it will be short
Yolanda now has 90 years
For all Selena's family tears.

We don't know how far she could have gone
We don't know how good she could have been
But we do know we missed a chance
All because of a stupid sin.

Selena now will rest in peace
As Yolanda waits for the jury to speak
We all want Yolanda to die
So give her the chair and don't let
This devil slide!!!!

Cynthia Clemente

Wings

We sail through life upon fragile dragon wings,
Yet we are but human beings.
We eat, we breathe, we work and play,
With goals we fill our day.
But do you ever stop and think,
That we might be teetering on the brink?
We strive to reach the goal,
To climb out from the hole.
Dreaming the impossible dream,
That we endeavor to achieve,
Somehow.
But why achieve the impossible dream?
What could reaching it possibly mean?
Accomplish the goal, look around,
And wonder what others can be found.
And then you die, well, what then?
Your children begin the journey again.
But what does it matter to you? You're dead.
With all this spinning 'round your head,
You have to wonder,
Why?

Jessica Stewart

Country And Self

My native tongue was taken
yet I speak.

My name was discarded
yet I have an identity for which I am very proud.

After being whipped, branded, beaten, bought and sold
I survive.

Despite being labeled as inhuman
I have a productive mind.

I fought and defended the values of America, even when
I was denied the freedoms associated with being an American.

My religious beliefs were altered
yet I pray.

Regardless of all the pain, hardship, and struggle
I remain proud of my country, proud of myself.

Beverly Taylor

Blood Stained Wood

I remember when He created me,
Yet I did not recognize it was He.
Thorns placed upon His head,
Head to toe He was covered in liquid red.
Upon his back I was placed.
Sad and broken was He,
I feeling disgraced.
Up to a hill I was carried upon someone else's back,
For He was too frail,
His body so dreadfully pale.
Upon the hill I was placed higher than a tree,
Nails were driven through Him and into me.
Then I realized it was the Master who was hanging upon me,
Doing this to set the world free.
Death came upon Him as His head fell low,
Leaving me full of sorrow.
Three days past and the resurrection came,
And this blood stained wood was forgiven,
And forever will I glorify His name.

John Porter

As We Walk, Today

As we walk, today hand in hand, my little one, I think back to
yesterday, when you said your first real sentence.
Oh I am so proud!
My child I would love to be around, always to hear every new
word and thought. To kiss away all the hurts and fears of
your young life.
I wish I could hold your hand forever, and guide you swiftly
across life's ups and downs.
As we walk and talk, I'll show you the beauty of God's great earth.
I will teach you the names of all the pretty flowers, and trees.
We'll look at the grace of birds in flight. I will teach you
to love yourself and the world around you.
Oh my little one, I wish for you a good life, because
someday, you will walk alone. But you will take with you, all
of my love, and teachings.
All the best to you my child, today, and always, as we walk.

Doris C. Terry

For A Brother

They lowered his body into the cold hard clay
Yes they buried my youngest brother today
I stared at the gravesite until I cried
Nothing I could do although I'd tried
I prayed and prayed and still he died
Watched him die slowly and also tearfully
He passed away finally but not gracefully
The disease doesn't care if you're poor or rich
It kills by wasting your body inch by inch
You're dead without a chance to really fight back
The resources to battle the dreaded disease they lack
Its so expensive and so hopeless you think
And then you get sicker and its over in a blink
AIDS you know something you really stink
I don't know who you're supposed to be an aid to
But at the mention of your awful name I boo
May you claim your last victim and soon
And all the doctors will declare its high noon

David Meadows

Dear Mother I Remember When You Were Mommy

I don't say that with hate, or to imply that you have done something
wrong, but there was a time when no other word would fit my feelings
   for you.
I wrote a poem once, about a woman whose lover had cheated on her,
and though I knew little of the subject,
the words flowed easily.
There is a line, hidden in the middle,
between the cries of love and the joke set in the last few words.
This is where the true message hides.
It says, "We share a passion for running from reality,
but you can't run from shared lies."
We are lying to ourselves mother.
And the answers are not hiding in a pill,
given to us by a faceless doctor.
Or waiting to be uncovered in the pages of a book.
If the sitcoms are not lying,
they are inside of us.
Please help me look.
I need to love you.

Dianna Anglin

Surprise Visit

If Jesus knocked on your front door and asked to stay awhile;
Would you gladly let him in, or would you ponder for awhile?
Could you look into his eyes or would you be staring at the floor?
If Jesus came to your house, would he be welcome inside your door?

Would you set an extra place for him and invite him to seep with you;
Or would you make excuses and find too much work to do?
Would you hide those certain magazines under the pillow in the chair
Or would you smile and invite him in to show you love and care?

So if we feed the hungry, tend the sick and visit elders too
Well be extending a helping hand, while serving our savior too.
If we do all these things, in Jesus name I pray
We'll show others by our actions, his love for them each day

He should always share our bounty, and love and serve the poor
Because he always loves us, he proved this by our shame he bore
He gave his life on the cross that day for all who invite him in,
Then we'll be blessed beyond measure when we go to live with him

Audrey M. Nelson

My Perfect School

My perfect school...
would have a swimming pool, and use water gun
power by every other hour.
My perfect school...
would be fun in the sun on the run.
My perfect school...
would talk about girl talk, and we'd take a mile long walk.
My perfect school...
would have lunch for two hours, and call the boys cowards.
My perfect school...
the teachers would be taught how to be cool.
My perfect school...
the teachers would teach us how to swim in the pool.
My perfect school.

Anina Lindsay

A New Day

Last night I wanted to lay down and die and leave all of my cares and worries in this world behind.

Last night I wanted to be free, free from all of my pain and suffering.

I no longer wanted to be bothered with the thoughts that lie heavily on my mind.

So last night I put them all to bed. I laid down on my pillow and rested my head.

Last night I fell into a deep sleep leaving behind all of my problems for that particular moment in time.

Today is a new day. It is a day that was not promised to me.

Today is the day that I will find the strength to have peace in my heart, soul, body, and mind.

Today I will dance in the sunlight and sing in the wind.

Today I will rejoice in all of the beauties in this life, because a new day is about to begin.

Angelique Williams

Dedicated

One day he woke up, looked up at the sky,
wondering how long he had till he'd die.
It was then when it hit him, not knowing where it came,
to teach us all about it, this disease without a name.
He would dedicate his life, no matter what it would take,
to educate us toward a decision we would make.
You wonder now what this disease may be,
it's a disease we call H.I.V.
Because of something as common as protection,
he lost his life with no intention.
And for this guy who cared so much,
I'd like him to know our hearts have been touched.

Barbara Mercedes Moro

Untitled

I miss you more every day that goes by
Without you here to tell me why
Why things are the way they are
Without you saying you've come so far
It seems as though - no matter how hard I try
I still can't figure out why???
Sometimes I still talk to you
And ask for direction in my life
I know for sure you hear me
Because things always turn out right
The little signs that give me faith
They make me smile and feel really great
They prove to me your always here
Through my life's trials, tribulations, heartache, and fear...

Carrie Clugston

A Legacy

Memory is a legacy we leave when we depart this life, but if left without a reminder, it too will wither and die. The sunlight's reflections on the Grecian Urn containing the essence of what you were, of what you are and of what you will be, proclaim to the world that the Sun is the diffuser of your memories.

By breasting the currents of life, you have become one with nature.

The slanting rays of a setting Sun create a misty shroud of magenta one pond flanked by weeping willows and covered with water lilies.

The sparkling ripples from a summer stream murmur tranquilly to trysters nearby. And the distant call of a whippoorwill signals the coming night when young hearts will meet to see if they are meant for each other. These are but a few of your memories conveyed by those forces of nature essential to life.

Oh, though you have bowed-out on that tropistic journey to your ultimate destiny you will emerge again—perhaps on some foreign and unfamiliar shore; and if we happen to meet, we will not recognize one another, but silent whisper in the wind will stir the chemistry that unites us.

We are one after all.

Jacky R. Whitehead

The Young And The Restless

Are you Young and Restless, Searching for Tomorrow?
With your lives already filled with pain and sorrow.

You may also feel that you're Bold and Beautiful,
And that life has a lot to offer you.

Don't be deceived, God is not mocked,
The devil is waiting to knock you off your block.

For he has come to rob and to kill,
Too see you buried on Blue Berry Hill.

Listen All My Children this is what I'm trying to say,
Don't let Satan lead you astray.

Please, stop gambling with your life.
For you'll lose your soul too Satan for the price.

In Conclusion:
Listen All My Children, don't stand at The Edge of Night,
Searching for Tomorrow watching As The World Turns.
If you've listen carefully there's a lesson to be learned.

You may be Young and Restless, Bold and Beautiful thinking life has a lot to offer you,
But you only have One Life to Live so let Jesus be your Guiding Light and you'll be blessed All the Days of your Lives.

Joan Draine

This is my black poem...

All cries to soothe you,
With words to cool you,
And thoughts to fool you.

Windy when they blow
And silent when they go,
Muffled whimpers are all it is.
Life is never shining in grand bliss.

My woman beautiful I dare
For the dearly beloved to spare
But in the end it's all cold
The anguish being more than threefold.

Senseless prayers I send in despair,
Takes a strong shoulder to support the new heir.

...This is my black story.

Anne Klein

Home

Home is a place with open doors
   with warm smiles and hugs on the house
It lets the warm in and kicks the cold out
The fire welcomes free spirits and loving hearts
   so curl up beside it in an old country blanket

Home is an oven filled with pies
   and potatoes with watchful eyes
Cookie dough to be cooked
   and ginger bread houses in fancy styles

Home is a place with open minds
   and caring lives
We'll open our doors, will you open yours?
   Emily Lockard

The Miracles Of God

The Miracles of God are as numerous as the stars
With the stroke of a brush He puts the rainbow in the sky
He adds color to the petals of the rose and lets the tiny sparrow fly

He bathes the Morning Glory with drops of dew
Glistening like sparkling diamonds in the early morning sun

He covers the meadows with a carpet of velvet green
   dotted with flaming red of the Indian Paint Brush

He makes the warm summer rain, giving life to the hundreds of
   seedlings lying dormant in the ground

And as Fall approaches, the trees take on their brown, red and
   golds producing a blaze of glory against the autumn sky

Then the snows of winter come covering every tree and shrub,
   turning the landscape into a winter wonderland
And it seems that the whole world is at peace

But the greatest miracle of all is when He takes the soul of
   wayward man, cleanses it in His blood and transforms
   him into a new creature

All The Angels in Heaven Rejoice!
   Judy Grosso

To Michael

I leave you today, trying not to look back
with sadness my voice is about to crack
but my eyes are trained to search for your face
no matter the time, no matter the place

I leave you today, counting minutes until tomorrow
waiting days to see you, holding deep my sorrow
I'll wait forever, to be with you, you know
the longer I wait, the more love will grow

I leave you today, traveling far from your side
but look up at the sky so big and wide
the moon and stars that you see above
are in the same sky that I see my love

I leave you today, my bags packed tightly
I'll think of you often, daily and nightly
and when I return to your arms again
I'll hold you as tightly as I possibly can

I love you today, tomorrow, next week
I'll be there to support you in whatever you seek
be careful, my love, for you are my breath
without you beside me my life is like death
   Alison Determan

The Struggling Mom

Have you ever seen a struggling mom
with one baby in a stroller and two in her arms?
She has to buy groceries, more and more.
If you were a struggling mom, you'd buy out the whole store.

She has to teach them right from wrong.
She has to teach them how to get along.
She has to teach them how to walk.
She has to teach them how to talk.

Then the struggling mom goes into her room thinking she's about to die
But instead she sat on the bed and just cried.
Her son, Big Blue, came into say
"You're going to give me credit one day."

Big blue put all three babies in their baby chairs
got out a comb and brush and whipped up their hair.
The struggling mom came out of her room and said,
"Thank God," finally I get to go to bed!

She gave her son a big hug and kiss.
She said, "you're one son I'm going to miss."
When you grow up to be a man,
You're the number one son I'm going to recommended.
   Christina F. Y. Rowe

Celebration

Now yesterday has come and gone
With its hopes, dreams and songs
In its place is left only memories.
Heed well the lessons you have learned
As another page in life you now turn
And even regrets will yield a soothing peace.

It is yet to be seen what tomorrow will bring,
New mountains to climb, new songs to sing.
The future is something we're not meant to know.
It may be a breeze you can handle with ease
As you sail on life's ever changing seas
Or tempestuous, contrary winds may blow.

Ah, but today, you hold in your hands
With life's sweet fulfillment oh so grand
As two become one, meeting their destiny...
A celebration of life at its very best,
Two hearts united, may your union be blest.
May this day live forever, a precious memory.
   Jamilah D. Pasha

Untitled

I am a Cobweb,
With dew laced in my intricate pattern
So that the beauty of my sight will lure the
unsuspecting into my trap.

I am the fly caught in my own web.
Together the wind sweeps us away.
The web is fragile, the fly not so brave,
We soar to the ocean, the sea.

My love trapped in his own misery lies in the
foaming mystical sea.
Drawn together forever, we will wash up on
beaches where children play,
As once we did.
Our names will be forgotten,
But we will know.
   Elaine L. Schulz

Thanks To A Friend
Dedicated to a former student and Vietnam survivor
Day in and day out we walk in the rain and in the dark.
With cries and screams that blend in the night. We walk with our
guns held very tight.
Gunshots and bombs fill the air. How I wish that I wasn't scared.
A warning was given that the enemy was near. I stood and
prayed that they would disappear.
Five in our company out on patrol yet some how I was left all alone.
A gun was shot with fire a blaze. My thoughts returned me to home,
where I want to stay.
Peace and courage was given to me from a young soldier that set men free.
This soldier had just saved me. I turned to say thanks but he was gone.
I thought it strange for I know all of the men of this company.
This was the only time that this happen to me.
Later we returned back to our holes. We sat very silent and cold.
The rain and cries I will never forget.
Along with this night to strange to be told.
As I was going to sleep my childhood returns reading GI comics
and the Ghost Soldier who save men at war.
Could it be that this was what happened to me?
I told no one of what had occurred this strange night. I was the
corpsman and I couldn't show fright.
Why did this soldier save me tonight?
Thirty years later I still remember the fear and cries of the night.
Thanks to this soldier who gave me a chance to live past that fright.
   Blanca Estela Gonzalez

Snowflakes Of An Angel
A glorious voice, that like the star of opera,
With an inspiration of God,
Performed in the distance
amongst the stardust of the heavens
as the cold wind filled with fine snow.

The angel declared, magnificence,
Awe-inspiring the escapade
with her child-like charm and innocence,
the ceremony of feather light snow crystals
that wandered aimlessly.

As the snowflakes performed,
the wind composed
an archaic complexion of song
over the snow whitened hills, valleys, and mountains.

While the depth of her winsome sound,
Unfathomable, yet reaching beyond the zenith
of the ascending stairway of heaven.

Angelic, enchanted snowflakes,
Dance to a symphony in the wind.
   Bonnie J. Bowers

Unconditional Love
Love is the confidence in knowing that God is the same
yesterday, today and forever. Love has ties that won't sever.
Love is endless, love is free — true love is for eternity.

Love is the assurance that when you and your love ones
are apart, there is always that deep affection in the heart.

Love looks up to others — not down. Love greets with a smile —
   not a frown.

Love is setting each other free to be what God has called
us to be. Love is patient and love is kind; love enables us
to have peace of mind.

Mutual love is free so why not share in God's true liberty.
   Carol Belue

Ode To The Brown Farm
Ah the quietness sweetening the vast north lands
With air as pure as gold.

Ah the quietness of formidable glaciers gracing
The majestic mountain-side seen for millions
of years only by animal eyes of yore.

Quietness welcoming the sounds of river ripples
Flowing upstream to ocean waters.

Quietness broken by the summer rustling
of leaves on trumpeting bending trees
As the winds give chatter.

The quietness heralding the sounds of newly homed
chicks - welcoming the bays of newly corralled
horses - the bees buzzing as they carry pollen
to newly planted flowers in virgin soil - vegetables
silently growing to feast the nurturing hands.

Ah the quietness applauding the youthful sounds
of glee - the laughter - romping through the tall
grasses - the woods - greeting the voices of the
newly arrived little beings whose happiness joins in -
With all the wonders of nature's magnificent world.
   Grace Brown

Summer Lightning
Orphaned black
With a wave of his hand
Said goodbye to all
And died.
Jaw slapped shut
Closing my ear to the mind of truth
That laughs in the crowd milling about like ants
Through the sand.
Dark spots arc-
Form a line from outside our world.
Ask God-if you know him.
Walk and wonder if you don't.
Church bell drones and the line moves a bit
But you and I may crawl back to the sea
To float above the dirge of time's tune
Hearing soft water wash our bodies clean.
   Burnham Lewis

Five Little Fingers
Five little fingers reached up and wrapped themselves about mine.
With a look of trust, they tightened, as two little legs stood firm
Ready to go. Confident I'd fulfill his every need. He welcomed my
outstretched hand, I helped him to stand. Here, this little one so new
in his talent of walking, soon to be talking. Once his five little
fingers gripped mine, he was ready to go; I walked behind. His
steps were small, yet he knew what to do, putting one foot in
front of the other, in his new shoes.
I marveled at his confidence and trust, I reflected on my own faith in
Jesus. Was I as willing to go where I was led? Was I humble to be
spiritually fed? So God spoke to me through five little fingers, a
sermon helped me to recall that little ones bring him glory, unspoken,
manifesting God's presence. Thank you Lord! For this lesson so clear,
for using little ones so dear. May I be as willing to reach up, accept
your hand, you'll give me the best you can. May I be as trusting
that where you lead, I will follow, gladly accepting all. Yes five little
fingers revealed God's heart to me; I stand in awe, as he instructs
helps me to see, little wonders, are ever before us. We must be quiet,
sensitive, to connect them with Jesus. Thank you Lord for these five
little fingers entwined; with your help Lord, I'll grow in you and no
longer walk as one who is blind.
   Judy Miron

My Blue Overalls Grandpa

The tall, thin frame,
wire-rimmed glasses,
and wispy, gray hair.
Wearing blue overalls.

The old, red pick-up truck,
cigarettes in a blue and white package,
taking me to feed the dog at the farm,
getting a drink from the old tin cup by the water pump.
Wearing blue overalls.

Taking a fall—
breaking your hip,
going to the nursing home,
memory fading,
but never forgetting your family.
Wearing blue overalls.

My tenth birthday,
you left this world.
Watching from above for twelve years now.
I remember you—
my blue overalls Grandpa.

Jenny Plager

Remembering

October:
  Windows ablaze with flaming hues,
  Arresting me,
  And I,
  Reminded of another time.

  "No playing out-of-doors today."

  We made a game
  Of watching raindrops on the windowpane.

December:
  The world a-hush with falling snow.

  Cathedral-like,
    As through a nave,
    I see it falling on my little one's grave.

  We made a game
  Of watching snowflakes on the windowpane.

Ann Walko

Only The Chosen

Who will be worthy, to carry the ark?
Will there be a blameless, without a little fault?

Who will find the stones, the twelve did lay?
Only the Chosen, did my Lord say.

Only the true Believer.
Only the pure in heart magnified in his glory.
Can touch the Covenant of God.

Who will lead the way, to the promised land?
Will there be a circumcision, before we part our way?

Who will know the way, in the blind mind dark?
Only the chosen, did my Lord say.
Only the chosen, will know the way.

Only the true believer only the pure in heart magnified in his glory,
Can be God's scout.

Who will enter the Kingdom?
Who will carry the Ark?
Who will lead the way, in the blind mind dark?

Only the chosen, only the pure in heart.
Magnified in his glory, only the father's choice.
Amen.

Geraldine H. Wooley

Blessed Be He - Whom God Hath Made

With the sun beaming down so hot, as if it
will surely drain my mind; the sand in my
eyes, as to blind my sight,
so strong at times - I fall to my knees,
and ask the Lord for my daily bread.

I ask for sight, he gave me his hand; I asked
for bread, he gave me a kiss; I asked for drink,
he cleansed me with love; I asked for strength;
he put his arms around me; I asked for courage;
he lead me; I asked for my gun, he wept.

I asked him why he wept, (the Lord replied)
"I gave you daily bread where there was none,
and you ask for guns!

But Lord, I am but a small ant upon these sands,
compared to you, I am not as strong as you;
I am but a blade of grass beneath my feet.

Lord you have the strength of ten thousand armies.
I have but only strength of a fallen leaf of a tree.
I ask for guns, not to take a life; but to save
ten thousand.

Ermaka Campbell

Isn't It Funny

When you are born, will someone care,
Will someone dress you and comb your hair,
You don't know, but whose face do you see,
Smiling down on you proud as can be,
This is the person who will always love me,
You know in your heart, right from the start,
Isn't it funny
You grow up leave home to make a life of your own,
But do you ever look back, or pick up the phone,
You watch her grow old, her hair has turned white,
Complains of aches and pains, never seems to feel right,
This is the time she needs you now,
To listen and be there for her somehow,
Isn't it funny
She wants to help - still needs to be useful,
You tell her to sit down, she can't do what she used to,
Don't criticize her so much and tell her what she can't do,
Because she knows that much better than you,
Be happy to see her and take her along,
Because before you know it, she will be gone.

Frances C. Mazzeo

Mom's Treasures

dedicated to Travis Proveaux

Personal collections that mean so much to me
will some day be part of my legacy.
What joy or pleasure in the future could there be
if my treasures were not passed on through the family?

Would they not mean so much
if they were not for my child to touch?
To pass on to his children and grandchildren,
if not appreciated, what an affront to my chagrin.

For to me, part of the joy of living
is my collections to my child I'm giving.
To know that I am not really gone,
part of me, my treasures, will be passed on and on.

If not to have a child to leave my treasures to,
they and I would be gone without much ado.

My treasures are a part of me,
they are my legacy.

Deidra Proveaux-Cox

What's On My Mind? (Class Of 96)

Twelve steps, now I've reached the top
Will I keep walking or will I drop
My future is distant and still untold
My father has been found, but some secrets shall unfold
My sister has been found, will we meet again
Does she have time for her brother or am I just a friend
Me and my friends act like brothers
But now I've been moved and have to find others
Do I walk alone or is my mom on my side
My feelings sometimes are hurt, will she help me hide
Maybe she's my sister, she'll love me eternally
But I need someone to walk beside me
hand and hand, I need her to stay
Mutual respect, I'll meet her one day
until then I have a family I adore
My uncles, aunts, mamas, and cousins to live for
They'll help me pack when I go on my way
to find my destination they'll hope and they'll pray
When my learning gets higher I'll look at my past
My future will unfold as the wind blows my mast.

Demetrius N. Blevins

Just Wondering

Just wondering little Christmas Tree
Will I be here next year
To dress you up
And let you wear
The pretty tinsel in your hair,
And colored balls hung here and there
To make you look so gay and fair?

Or, will I be in another world
No need of moon to shine by night
Or sun to shine by day,
Just light and loneliness abound
No need for Christmas lights to glow
Christ, light of the world is there and everywhere
Eternally, if we but know!

Edris L. Guenther

"A World Of All Colors"

In a world of all colors it's hard to see
why people can't treat each other equally

I saw a child crying; I asked him why...
he said, "Cause I'm not like the other guy"

We may look different, we may not talk the same...
but we all must live together in a world with the same name.

We need a revolution, at total change of mind...
our exteriors aren't important cause our souls are the same kind

We're all God's children, he loves us though we sin...
but the world will stay unequal until we see past the skin

Debra Simon Williams

Where Are You Going

Where are you going, my child, with your smiles and laughs?
Will you return? Will you remember?
I hope.

Where are you going, my friend, with your hopes and dreams?
Will you chase them? Will you catch them?
I hope.

Where are you going, my loved one, with that special part of me?
Will you keep it? Will you cherish it?
I hope.

Jonathan M. Yuschock

Meeting Someone New

For who are you, I do ask;
Why I wonder, it's such a task
Oh, how rude of me to lecture?

Have our paths crossed before;
if they have, through which door;
And simply, are we friends?

Know you I must, not I forget,
Is it pleasure or of great debt
To which I owe the knowledge of this encounter?

I know you not; for friends, let's be
I for you and you for me,
just to leave this state of standing.

Daniel Hines

I've Gone Home

Sometimes it's hard for us to realize
Why God's work is full of surprise.
We go thru life without a care
And never send God a simple prayer.
He looks down on us each and everyday
Just for a kind word to say.
Our loved ones have taken their place
And left behind an empty space.
They knew their time was not long.
Bodies full of pain, and laughed off the wrong.
They are at home to get their reward.
Their journey was long hard but they look forward
As they gave to you and others,
continue on my sisters and brothers.

Geralyn Allen

Brothers

There are a couple of brothers
  whom I love very much
And the same goes for their mother
  with her tender loving touch.
The amazing thing about these kids
  Is their love for one another
Which does much to enhance the intimacy
  Between two different aged brothers.
The youngest is six and the oldest is eight
  But age is merely a statistic
They both are very studious in school
  And show signs of being artistic.
They are both the same height and do dress alike
  Which cause people to think they are twins.
Both enjoy sports in their respective age groups
  And show sportsmanship no matter who wins.
Their sense of humor is astonishing
  For a couple of kids so young
And I must admit that I'm partial
  After all, they are my grandsons.

Arlie T. Lewis

To Sister In Law On Her Seventieth Birthday

Dear Mary Liz:

Seventy birthdays! What a blast!
Whoever thought that you wouldn't last?
You still have your looks, a remarkable chassis,
Truly the envy of many a lassie,
Seventy birthdays! Oh what fun!
Before you know it, you're seventy-one,
When friends ask, "How old?" why just let them guess,
Many happy returns from F. J. S.

Your Favorite Brother-In-Law

Frank J. Sweeney

Love(Hate)

The wrench is tightening in my chest,
Who was to guess the pain it would produce?
This was not even something to choose.
Unsolvable thoughts fill me with vengeance
that calls the name of Wordsworth.
Sell out, hypocrite, some ignorant thoughts.
"Together forever," was many a times spoken,
Little was it known to foretell the token
of the lies and unworthy love.
The devil's bed, a halo on your golden head.
Misnomers and missed feelings.
You ate of my flesh to feed your want,
Leaving me fleshless and uncurable.
Distraught it seemed, the curser of life.
I will build your cross and hammer the nail.
Quickly the evil will not die, death it may cause.
All truths in the domestic creature.
She, the monster, lives to kill,
kills so that she may nourish and move on.
"Death becomes her," said the louse.
Bryan Moore

The Sparrow

There once was a bird who thought she was a sparrow
Who tried to follow a crooked arrow
Aye! Said she, "Looks straight to me!"
Everyone told her she couldn't see
But the bird denied her fate, not knowing it was too late
So she kept on dreaming her dreams and thought things were as they
  seemed
But one day came a hunter who's arrow did shoot the tiny sparrow
Too much to bare for so small a sparrow
Much too large was the Hunter's arrow
If only the bird could have been a swallow, it may have seen the
  future of tomorrow
Christine E. Haupt

Untitled

Perhaps we are parallel, two rivers
Who shall never cross. I wish to be free,
But the geometry of life loathes me.
How I denounce structure and ask favor,
Wash and flood away all the partitions,
That towers square and taut fall in our wake,
Bricks and mortar old crumble for love's sake
So the land will be engulfed in passion.

Yet the square taut towers will rise again.
The walls that separate to persevere.
Topple the walls! Let us go someplace bright,
Where we can be one away from the pain.
Where I, not the lion, hold your veil near.
And a kiss, the mulberry fruit is white
Hao-Kai Chen

Fair Warning

You never know what's around the corner,
Whether you live or die, you can never be sure.
When you see your life flash before your eyes,
What to expect is to your surprise.
What you've done you may not know,
But in the end the damage will show.
You never know what's going to happen next,
So you should always do what you think is best.
No matter who you are,
Remember that death isn't very far,
And to be careful out there,
Because sometimes life isn't always fair.
Annette Koch

"H.I.V."

I met a man a few years ago.
Who said he was H.I.V., when I met this man a few
years ago it really did frighten me
The man I know has a heart of gold
A wonderful human being
I asked myself why this was I couldn't quite comprehend
All I know is I was proud he picked me for his friend
I don't care what they say
I'm going to love him anyway
I wish I could make people comprehend
This disease that will one time come to an end
The man that I know has a way to go
But isn't it giving up the fight
God bless his soul he's trying so hard to have people see the light
My man with H.I.V. is just asking of all of you
To understand of what he's going through
H.I.V. isn't pleasant, H.I.V. is always present
He's hoping that the next few years
We can eliminate everyone's fears
Let's show my man that we love and understand and we also care
Patricia Keller

Stirred Memory

Who-oo who-oo on this lemon-colored night
Who-oo who-oo so soft, to sweet, so mellow.
Are you calling for someone far from your sight
You wise, superb, soft-feathered fellow?
Who-oo who-oo sang the sentry of the night
Who-oo who-oo from the winter-dead tree.
My whole body quivered with delight
And there stirred within my mind a memory.
Who-oo who-oo called our nocturnal friend.
Who-oo who-oo answered Rolen from the sill.
This sudden who-song with the night sounds blend
Taunts my memory and makes my heart stand still.
Your soft haunting call of who-oo who-oo
My husband can no longer answer you.
Elsie E. Bastian

Gratitude

I stand here at the sink
Who knows how many times?
Scrubbing dishes, pots and pans
Mixed with prayers for peace
Over the years

> World War II, SALT, Iron Curtain,
> Walls tumbling down,
> Conflicts resolved, small and large,
> Release of captives, men and women.

One final wash—
This huge crock-bowl of deepest brown
With simple edging of light beige around the top,
My mother's and her mother's before her,
Yields an overflow of yeast-filled thoughts
Wafting fragrances of warm, homemade bread.
Fern Fugman Clarke

Untitled

I want to go back to the land that meets Penobscot Bay
where tides ebb way far out,
With tide pools in the scooped-out rocks.
Where tides rise high to meet the fertile soil,
to places where there is no sand or dune,
no gradual transition from edge to edge
and green apple trees drop their ripened globes
to float in tidal pools,
where land meets sea abruptly.
Gloria Olson

As I Count My Blessings

As I count my blessings, given from God above,
Who gave me a Mother, anyone would love
She was my Teacher, my pal and best friend
Giving her love and love to no end
Next a kind hubby, after I had grown
Displaying great kindness and a love all his own
Then the joy of my wonderful children and their children too,
Without all those blessing, what would I do?
Now last but not the least, my old friends and the new,
Accept thanks dear God, all of this, made by you.
   Gloria B. Brown

After Albuquerque

Flat on my motel bed and hyperventilating
who can I call ten minutes after midnight?
So much yellow silence has exhausted me;
and the horizontal line of mesas, plugged
into the blue and yellow eye of afternoon.

Outside my window the scorpion moon
crawls to the west and from the ceiling bulb
light falls in one long vertical to pluck
eyes from their sockets, marrow from my bones.

Oh zip code man, I gasp into the telephone.
Give me the zip code for Brule, Wisconsin,
where rainclouds like a band of desperadoes
hold up the sun, and windy, needle-pointed pines
avert catastrophe.

Yes ma'am, 54820. Mighty good fishing, those parts
in Wisconsin. Night now, and have a good evening.

And all the blue and yellow weight of silence
changes to the rippling confusion
of a rise of speckled trout
leaping at mayflies.
   Cicely d'A. Angleton

The One Called

   He walks upright in the Spirit of love, to represent the one
who came from above. To share the gift with all who grieves,
Benevolence, Charity and Prosperity. For giving to those who need
he reaps the rewards soon to achieve.
   Come one, come all to hear, the fruits of The Spirit you will
bear. "Love," "Joy," forever clear, following the path of the one
who cared. In giving the gift of life, he made the ultimate
sacrifice.
So in your life bear the cross, given freely by the BOSS.
Be an example for all to see...you be you, and I'll be me..
"THE ONE CALLED."
   Arthur E. Gibson Sr.

I Need You, My Comforter

   I sit here as the hour approaches 12 o'clock, all but your big
white ZXE T-shirt on. I felt like letting all feelings that are
miserably locked inside this prison of a heart out. No, my heart
doesn't always feel like a prison for the angst-ridden pain that
tears at my inside. It just slowly goes through a metamorphosis,
from a big, warm, knowing, loving heart to a small, desolate, cold,
ignorant heart that needs desperate attention and delicate help.
This is what happens when we have a little "disagreement."
   This is why I try so desperately hard to hang on to you when you
want to let me go. I know that it is only of your best intentions,
and I know that it is your way of healing your hurting heart...
but can't you hear the needing cries of the silence when you say
good-bye? Doesn't that which frustrated you, let you know that
I need you? I do not wish to make situations worse... I just
need my soul mate, my other half, to cling on to.
I need you to be my comforter..
   Elaine Garduque

November

I am living in the abundance tree
White flowers are blooming in my garden
My hopes are plucked, shadowed and let go, free
How long to complete, and wholeness harden?

I do not resist whiteness of flowers
Or tell stars how and when to shine on me
They are steady in infinite powers
I am swinging on the abundance tree.

Eternity, to be, eternity
Is immediate and ends with no time
Brothers and sisters, my fraternity
Awards are not to win but to refine.

Reflected abundance on the same tree
Ready or not, The Thank Tree shakes us free..
   Bettye Hammer Givens

Alaska, Uncle Sam's Attic

   The sea can rock you, like a baby in a cradle.
While the silence of the night plays you a lullaby.
   The moon shimmers on the water, icebergs
gleam like diamonds, while the stars flicker above.
   The mountain tops are glistening white,
while water trickles down the side.
   So far you can see, only mother nature.
Yes, it's her and me, surrounded by water.
   Then there are times, you see nothing at all.
Those times, the fog is so thick, you've got to slice through it.
   The stormy sea lashes out, the breakers
thrust against, anything that gets in the way.
   The provoked water beats against your flesh,
with an infuriated sting, and you can taste the salt in the air.
   The tide will stop you, unless you want to try
and defy her.
   The sea is a passion, all of its own.
   Cynthia L. Allen

Sheep Mountain

Infinite mountain meadows reaching for the sky
While the bleating of the herds echo on high;
The queen of the range in majestic splendor
Uses many faces to reign in awe and wonder.

Spring's freshness crowned by her snowy heights
Gives her water power for summer rights;
To mellow her meadows lush with grass
To feed the sheep when they ascend en masse.

Storm clouds billow and hover round her
Bringing sweet rain to blossom her clover.
Beneath the rainbow her throne is tremendous
With fog rolling at her feet she seems suspended.

Sunset tranquilly paints her a golden glow,
Followed by purple of twilight seeming to grow
As it descends into the valley below,
While the moon in rising silhouettes her crown.

Sunrise brings the sweet warmth of awakening
While it stretches its arms to the mountain beckoning
All its creatures with the strength of a new day
To grow and explore life in every way.
   Carrie M. Free

Forevermore

Dedicated to Brendan Skelly

Once upon a ten o'clock dreary,
   while I laid in bed all weak and weary.
Over many a quaint and
   curious songs I've heard of before.
While I nodded, halfway napping,
   suddenly a tragedy was happening,
As if someone was unfortunately
   dying, crying out once more.
I didn't know this until late,
   that this person was crying out once more.
This and only this, forevermore.

Ah, I distinctly remember it was
   in the darkest March.
I had wished it to not to be
   true as it was before.
And each dying thought would soon come to an end.
For my thoughts of sorrow —
   sorrow for the one lost more.
For the rare and radiant friend who I'd known before,
This and only this, forevermore.

Debbie Conner

Ethnic Cleansing

The sun shines hot upon the squalor beneath,
While Apollo holds it fast to pour forth its heat,
And mix with the cries of pain and bursts of bombs.
In their shabby camp, a mother sits beneath a leafless oak,
Whose scorched trunk and limbs fail to tame the sun's rays.
She strokes her babe's head as it suckles a dried teat.
A naked lad crawls toward the river for a cooling drink,
But scoots back to his father when a bomb falls close.
A bony cat returns to her dying master, only to search anew
When pains of hunger burn her empty belly.
A half-eaten chicken smokes on the open fire,
Its savory odors blend with cordite in the air,
But like other days for her there's naught,
Yet she hopelessly awaits a bit of scrap.
Abandoned by their breed, abused by the Gods,
They will soon die, defeated and alone,
In this their perilous and defenseless home.

Bart Tuffly

Untitled

To Achieve perfection is a terrible climb. One which only ensues pain and frustration without promise of ultimate redemption.

To desire perfection is a foolish dream. One which should remain out of a mans reach, unless to forebode the damnation of man's soul (as to eat from the tree of knowledge).

To change ones perfection is to change ones mind and soul. What was once will never be again. What is unseen will never be understood until its too late and knowledge seals your fate.

I only wish I was still a foolish man with foolish dreams that remain beyond my reach.

James A. Carroll

Dreams

The world of dreams has miraculous powers
Which I never came to appreciate until one particular night
When I decided to check on my little brother
Who had become remarkably quiet.

I found him asleep on his bed in his room
Which had an essence of the baby powder
That had apparently been sprinkled all over the carpet
Which would not be easy to clean up.

My eyes traveled with scorn to my brother
Who was lying there so peacefully
With a lopsided smile on his face
Which suddenly seemed so innocent.

He seemed not a nuisance anymore
And all his mischief was forgiven.
It was then that I realized
How powerful the World of Dreams really is.

Faye Chang

Oklahoma City

When disaster strikes with its silent force
Whether its by nature of some man made source
It leaves in its aftermath of destruction a path of debris
Shattered lives and broken dreams

Nature will heal what it produces but it takes man a long
Time to find a solution as to how he can pick up the
Pieces when his life is torn apart and there's so much missing

No one can search and find enough words to put together
All the reasons some of us treat each other
When something happens like Oklahoma City
Where one split second can change the lives of so many
We try our best to understand while reaching out a helping hand
When the dust has cleared and the search is through
We find the world doesn't change - people do

Bob Johnston

The Circle Will Not Be Broken

I wandered down a country road,
Where we once walked,
He loved me and it showed,
By the way he smiled at me when he talked.

My dad was big and I was small
He just knew everything,
Why always in the cool fall,
Leaves turned red and yellow, but pines stayed green.

The years passed by and I was grown,
Then I went away,
To walk streets made of stone,
But I knew I'd go back to that road one day.

Today I walked that old dirt road,
A child was by my side,
I watched as his face glowed,
When I told him why in autumn all leaves died.

   And though by him not a word was spoken,
   I knew that the circle would not be broken.

Joan Gurganus

The Vision Of A Perfect World

The world we live in is a grand and wonderful place,
Where we all have come together regardless of race.
We exhibit love and understanding of our fellow man,
And we reach out to others to lend a helping hand.
There is no room for prejudice in our world - it's in the past,
We build relationships with others that endure and last.
Who we are, what we do, and how we act it the measure,
We look for differences in others as traits to treasure.
We know that different thinking is what makes us strong,
And that sometimes our opinion can be wrong.
We reach out to the north, the south the east and west,
We're all equal, working together to be the best.
We teach our children that loving all people is right,
And there is no need to argue, kill and fight.
Respect of others is our guiding value every day,
We listen carefully to what others have to say.
we let our conscious be our guide to what is right,
And know that everyone is precious in our maker's sight.

Judith W. Stevanovich

Poets Paradise

There's a place in the world where poets roam,
Where they write their songs about life and its storms.
They write about loved ones and the trials they face,
And they always write with beauty and grace.
Its a place where poets can speak what they choose,
And not be criticized about their views.
It's a place where beauty is spoken in rhyme.
It sounds so perfect it nearly stops time.
The place for all poets is not on a map,
But a picture in our mind that we keep under rap.
Some poets are different, but most are the same.
Life is too short to play this game.
We all have a place where we go in hard time.
The poets paradise can be yours and mine!

Donald Barker

For The Children

On this evening many the earth be at peace.
Where there is hatred may it come to cease.

As the children watched for a bearded man from above,
  Others heard the voices of love.

The crackling sound of the fire was there.
  Around us indeed were hearts that did care.

But it was not the presents or the lights on the tree,
  Or how far along this world has come to be.

As the children learned to know right from wrong.
There was magic around them, it was very strong.

  A child asked why do people fight?
As I looked into his eyes I saw a light.

I knew what the wars of the world created.
  The children said that is what they hated.

For each and every single creation,
They will bring forth peace of a new nation.
  As they grow standing side by side.
For the children, they will bring love as their guide.

Darlene C. Crifo

A Mother's Sorrow

I gaze at the bed
where my child once lay
Empty - not forgotten
With what else must I pay?

The unshed tears begin to fall
I cherish her pictures on the wall
I can no longer bear to see the neatness of her room
Her unused dolls, in silence sit, like statues in a tomb.

Her empty table setting accuses me each night
What was it that I did not do that could have made it right?
Where is the little gold-haired girl I bounced upon my knee
and snuggled safely in my arms and now there's only me?

Does she still remember me
and search the passing faces?
Will our memories hold strong
or something time erases?

Deborah J. Bostock-Kelley

Sunset Sleep

Awakened by a midnight's dream...disturbed. Oh love of mine, where might thou be? I took a moment to say a prayer for my love. How I long for my love's well being, for his joy and happiness to be fulfilled.

My lover's soul calls out to me at night...I lay asleep to listen to what he would say. Be silent oh mind of mine as I hunger for my lover words. I whisper, "Here am I, fill my heart with elation." Images now come to me at intervals. I see my thoughts but I hear the chatter...oh damn these scatter thoughts! Be quiet as I wait to hear from my love...chatter...chatter talks cloud my mind. I am restless, I toss and turn...moments by moments go by.

My eyelids now half open see the bright orange light beaming through my window, the venetian blinds chime with one another. I feel a breeze. Chatter talks continues...I hear a rattle at my door!...Thumping noise follows, they seem to be drawing nearer. I brace myself and look up, there, in front of me stands my lover. The radiant orange rays behind him makes him a splendor. What a sight, my heart gleams with joy as we embrace; our happiness
is fulfilled.

Carmen Lydia

Without A Prayer

A woman and son play in a field
Where freedom and laughter grow wild
Another will fight for a box in the streets
To sleep with her nine year old child

A weathered old man walks down to the banks
Of the river, to watch the rain flow
As another in rags, stumbles and falls
In a mound of filth, he calls home

The star of the team throws the pitch of the year
Under lights that shine through the dark
While angry young men, throw stones and tease
A wino who's drunk in the park

On a bright sunny day, men swing away
With a club in their hands, on the course
And a boy's seeking drugs, from a man in a club
It's his one and only source

Many hope for relief, in a world full of grief
Trying to make life better
While others, go, to sleep at night
Praying for things that don't matter.

Dori Dennis-Vasquez

"Old Loves Die"

Old loves die, and new loves spring into being.
   Where are the dreams of yesterday?
Old loves die in a kaleidoscopic swirl of memory.
   And tarnished are the dreams of yesteryear!

Old loves die, buried in the ashes
   of yesterday.
Enmeshed in the memory of the touch
   of a hand;
Forever haunting the heart with the
   visions of yesteryear.
And the dusty dreams of those
   taunting green eyes!
Hazel J. Bruchalski

Ode To A Northern Lights Territory

There is a northern region
   Where air and water remain constantly pure
And icy-azure heavenly color complements
   Massive opaque mountains poised
With territorial glacier lakes of
   Crystal clear turquoise.

An unspoiled Canadian habitat,
   Where colossal trout frolic and endure,
Keeps secret arctic places concealed
   From strangers with fishing lures
And fancies nature's symphony of
   Rippling, splashing, dancing creature noise.

The illuminated sky, crystal glacier lakes,
   And streams flowing clear
Display the natural treasures of a
   Pristine Yukon paradise,
Where travelers experience a sense of loss
   When leaving its awesome wilderness.
Carolyn K. King

Alone

Do you know what it's like to be alone?
When you think you have friends,
but then again you don't.
When everyone else prefers someone else over you.
When you're incapable of speaking to anyone new.
When you think you have love,
but then again you don't.
When you think what might be left
to live for is nothing.
Only waiting,
the waiting to die,
the waiting for joy,
the waiting for love.
the love you have, but cannot touch.
The love that is so far away, as if
in another world.
Colleen Rising

America

About my country I feel so strong
Where freedom, where love, and I belong.
In war we fought
With all our might
The flag still stands from that victorious night.

To this day I'm proud to say
I love my country more each day.
A land so beautiful
People are free
This is the way it will always be.
Angie Kabo

Tears

Tears are shed over many reasons
When you think of them.
   Death comes to mind.
You see tears from a mother
   who is crying over her daughter's graveside.
You see a child crying
   realizing she will never play with her sister again
A couple in the distance, crying,
   their granddaughter past on.
The girl's father never comes,
   he's too heartbroken to be there.
Her boyfriend is heartbroken,
   he just lost his one and only true love.
Her brother's upset too,
   he has no one to pick on.
While her friend thinks of the last words said to her
   "You're my best friend;"
Her boyfriend thinks of the last words
   she ever said
"I love you..."
Amanda Jose

My Mother The Truck Driver

You said you'd stay with me until the very end.
When you hurt my heart, you said it would mend.
Last night, you call me and told me that you love me.
You told me that our love would fly like a bee.
Once, you told me that you cared.
Then you hung up and I was scared.
You told me that I should be calm.
Then I knew you were my Mom.

Every weekend you call and we talk.
When it's time to hang up I balk.
Even though I can't be with you.
My love for you will always be true.
We count to three, which is our game.
But this doesn't make the end the same.
I know there is a semi for you to drive.
That's what keeps your heart alive.
As we say goodbye my heart has a load.
You get back in the semi and hit the road.
Amber Gager

Just A Thought

It often hurts so very dear,
When we loose someone very near,
The days, the times, won't make it go away,
Sometimes it seems worse than a previous day.
The one's passed on would want us to be glad,
But we are selfish and want to feel sad.
They show us a rainbow and a bright, bright star,
Just to let us know they aren't really far.
We think of their jokes, their thoughts
and their rhymes, which make us remember;
ONE DAY AT A TIME.
They could be our Guardian Angels,
Or pop in just a minute, to check up on us
and see if their JUNK really was a menus.
So here's a thoughts I think they would share,
IF YOU DON'T NEED IT TRASH IT, OR GIVE IT TO
SOMEONE WHO CARES!
Christina Lee Braswell Hucks

Peacemaker

There's a time when deception can take heed to our hearts!
When we look to our thoughts it's evil pulling us apart!

We're writing our own doom because were so lost!
Think back remember who died on the cross!

We're all humans we shouldn't deceive one another!
Because in "God's" way we stand as all brothers!

I say this message not for one certain race!
Because its in each country and happening every place!

We think that we're better by the color of our skin!
Well if that's the concept wouldn't it be posted as a sin!

Technology is the fault of mankind to a degree!
We strive for it so much its taking over mortality!

Clarence L. Grover

An Ode To Charles Cutler (1908-1994)

That time of year I could in you behold
When the sun loses strength, and the air turns cold,
Or lifelong sinners rush to make their plea:
Atonement for life spent not on bended knee.
As the gnarled oak defiantly stands
In the face of nature's endless torments;
With similar scorn you faced time's waves of sand,
Shunning Death's touch, to enjoy life's essence.
A coin has two sides but only one in sight,
The smallest of efforts brings the other to light.
But effort met with pride, and pain was never shown.
If something was wrong, friends would surely have known.
  Your lifeless state reveals your change of thought,
  Why choose this end for a life so well fought?

Eric M. Carlton

Spring

You know it is Spring,
  When the flowers begin to bloom,
  And the birds begin to sing.
  The leaves on the trees are turning green,
  Everywhere splashes of color can be seen.

When you hear the laughter of children,
  Playing and doing their thing,
  Glad to be outside again.
  When baseball fever is in the air,
  Who will win the series this year?

Time when old things are made new,
  After the winter snows, sleet, and rain.
  Being able to open our windows again,
  Letting the fresh air and sunshine in,
  Giving everything renewed strength within.

Time to set new goals and directions,
  Knowing not what tomorrow may bring.
  Worrying not about tomorrow,
  Thinking only of today, because its Spring

Annette Branch

The Journal

An empty page must beckon every eye
  to wonder what therein must soon be writ:
the promise of a life as yet untried
  but authored well by courage, faith and wit.
Had I the years before me as this book,
  with firm resolve of mind and pen in fist,
'Twould be my aim to live so none might look
  upon a heart unmoved, or life unfit.

Gina Stepp

"The Ways Of Fall"

Fall is a beautiful season,
when leaves fall for some reason.
The leaves turn brown, gold, and beige,
and at dusk there's a reddish pink haze
  The squirrels and chipmunk are very active,
scurrying through the leaves which are attractive
The birds are also changing color,
but their bright shades are getting duller.
  The breeze is becoming colder,
the leaves colors are getting much bolder,
The wind is blowing very strong,
and it's lasting all day long.

Christopher Evans

Fall Day

Ah, yes the time of the year
When leaves change and disappear
Red, yellow, green or brown.
The wind comes to blow them down.
Seasons come seasons go,
But no other season is known to blow
Quite as much as that fall day,
When it was warm enough to be May.
I was walking when a gust of wind lifted me up,
I floated up to a cloud and it cuddled me like a cup.
While I slept I floated down,
Down, down, down to the ground.
When I woke up, I was in my bed
With the pillow under my head.

Annie T. Smith

Chronic Illness, My Constant Companion

There was a time not so long ago,
when it was my decision whether to come or to go.

Then suddenly joined by my new companion,
my choices were taken.
My dreams were forsaken.

But life must go on whether it's good or it's bad,
my companion remained not giving a tad.

Well the day would come when a choice I must make,
would I let it take over, my spirit to break?

My decision was long and ever so hard,
I'd join it, not fight it, that was the card.

Now we coexist in an uneasy way,
when overdoing I know I must pay.

My life is much different, that I must accept.
But for the small beauties in life I've gained new respect.

So for all of you out there who are still fighting the fight,
I hope that this poem will give you insight.

Elaine Sanderson

Adversary

Though religion and through war
we seek to find the answer to the questions aching in our minds.
  On we go lamenting,
our cries toward heaven aimed,
it's God's adversary that we came to blame.
  Direct the weeping to life's hell.
If what is above is down below as well.
  To keep our faith, we erect an invisible moat.
And how easy, to grasp a likely scapegoat.

Annette Go

The End Is Near

Loneliness is what I see
When is happiness to be a part of me?
I just sit here staring blankly and look around
Seeing people with worried faces
Only seeing traces of an ending world.
Walking through the misty clouds,
Pushing through an empty crowd.
Where did everyone go?
How simple it would be to tell a child,
"Don't worry, it's just a dream."
Tomorrow the sun's rays will gleam."
But who are we trying to fool?
This world is just as cruel
As a nightmare coming true.
What shall I do?
Teach him of the things to come.
Don't help him turn away and run.
And pray he'll never suffer
Cause tomorrow's just another day
And the end is yet to come.

Esther Maria Garcia

No Boyish Dream

When I was a boy... Oh! How I would dream
When I would see the world and its wonders
From the low crawling things to the high flying birds
From the small blade of grass.... To the tall towering trees

What wonders there are for a small boy to see!
What does it all mean?
What's in it for me?
Where do I fit in this grand plan I see?

I hope it will last.... These wonders for me
But now I've grown.... And much time has elapsed
The things that I see are not like the past
For the birds are few.... Like the tall towering trees
I become faint at the things that I see

But no more do I tremble or faint out of fear
For now I've found hope in the future that's near
For soon they'll be plenty.... You wait and see
For his boyish hope is no pipe dream you see
This grand hope I know is for you and for me!

Gerald L. Campbell

Marie At A Distance

Then there was Marie
Who was not who she should have been
Far and away and late at night
Voice trailing, tentative, tenuous
Sucked through under-sea cable
Whizzed and singed by orbiting telesat
Alone and quiet on her bed
Me in full cry
Buzzed, Angeleno style, nothing getting away.

By now I am half aware.
The pull of the line
On the hulk of this transmogrified persona
Thickened and stained with the seep of Los Angeles and hazy.
Conversation, like a Dylan song
In the key of transatlantic hiss and spit

And maybe we wait for a message in a bottle
Carried along on a tide that runs high
But I sat for a while when our whispering ended
And thought I saw pink in the gray L.A. sky.

Jeremy Mathews

Living Love

There was a time in my childhood
When I wondered
  What was prepared for me?

For I was lonely and ready to shout
  "What is life all about?"

Suddenly my eyes were opened and I knew.
  God had a place for me.
  What a glorious feeling!

"Love is the fulfilling of the law."

As obedient children, we go forward.
Feeling God's love, we journey on
  To live Love.
  To feel the joy of Soul.

There is no other way to go, for God IS Love.

Like the hymn: "I love Thy way of freedom, Lord,
  To serve Thee is my choice."

Now I know the way to go:
I will be a ray of sunshine, leading my friends
  All the way to our heavenly Home.

  Amen!

Blanche Maxwell

My Teddy Bear

I remember having a stuffed teddy bear
When I was very little.
He was brown and had the softest fur,
So every night with him, I would like to cuddle.

I took my teddy bear to bed with me at night,
So when I held him I wouldn't feel scared or alone.
He was my friend and confidant.
He didn't mind if I cried, and always listened to my woes.

My teddy bear never complained or told on me,
If I happen to do something wrong.
I'd tell him stories of what happened during the day.
He always listened, never caring if my tales were too long.

My teddy bear got a little dirty and ragged looking
From giving him so much love and cuddling,
So when I out grew him one day
My mom gave him away.

Today, when I sometimes feel afraid or alone at night,
I wish I still had my teddy bear
To cuddle with and be able to talk to him.
Then I know, I wouldn't feel alone and have nothing to fear.

Dolly Braida

A Mother

A Mother is someone who's there night and day,
When I wake in the morning, and night when I pray.

She's someone who gives of herself all the time,
So caring and loving, I'm glad she'll all mine.

Since I was a child, she was mother and friend,
A strong and proud woman, who'd fight to the end.

She's no longer here, I miss her so much,
Her smile, her voice, her sweet gentle touch.

I know she's with God, looking down upon me,
But I wish things were back, like they once used to be,

As I sit reflect on those wonderful days,
I loved you dear mother and God bless you, always.

Julio E. Velazco

To My Fiancee

When I look at you, I see my knight in shining armor
When I think of you, the raging seas grow ever calmer
You are the only one that my heart does ever want
You're in my soul and life; your kisses and breath do taunt
I want you forever in my life, and I want you now
I want us to be together; let's walk and make our vow
I have a hunger deep down that only your touch can feed
I have been searching for so long, and you're the one I need
Our love is forever blissful; it's always been known
Even when I didn't think it, in my heart it was thrown
We've known our friendship was special, for the longest of time
I want to be yours for eternity, and you to be mine

Jessica S. Turner

Untitled

I don't understand these feelings I have.
When I see you the anger fills me inside,
When your gone the tears fill my eyes,
You preoccupy my mind, this I can't hide.

I run the other way, to avoid your eyes,
They're knowing and cruel looking, searching
All I want is the pain to go away
But it's like a bird watching and perching.

I opened my heart which you broke like glass
The wound won't heal no matter how hard I try.
Pushing you away won't help me at all,
I've tried and I've tried but inside I cry.

My life, I felt, was over. Without you how?
I cannot bear to see you, but I can't stay away.
You played me for a fool, why couldn't I see?
You used me for love and sex, and you didn't stay.

Now I'm on my own. With my tarnished reputation
Burned forever, never to be fixed, the past always follows.
I'm moving on slowly, your out of my life,
The pain my heart feels, forever it wallows.

Alicia Vien

Imagine

I can imagine the day I first opened my eyes;
When I looked into yours with great surprise,
Marveling at their brightness and size.

I can imagine the day I first smiled at you;
When I didn't know who your smile was to,
Thinking it was for someone new.
I can imagine the day I first experienced pain;
When I saw your tears shaped like the rain,
Wondering if they would ever stain.

I can imagine these things and much more,
I can imagine but you may ask what for.

Well, mother, imagine what you can do for us on this day,
A very important fourteenth day in May,
To make us love you in the most special way.

Imagine what you can do.
Imagine what we want from you.

Don't imagine too long,
Because all we want from you on this special day, and on every day to come along,
Is for you to be healthy, happy, successful and strong.

Allen Rabinovich

Loss Of Innocence

I prayed continually for days in vain.
When I finally broke, I cried out in all my pain,
Why have you deserted me?
Why did you not save me from what has come to be!
My eyes swollen and heavy,
I felt the ending and was ready.
I knew no longer what was right,
only that I had no strength for the fight.
A deeper sorrow for the girl heaven sent,
for I could no longer protect her from their murderous intent.
One last prayer for her safety,
brought a small amount of serenity.
He appeared before me in a long white gown.
Ashamed of my weakness, I could only look down.
He called to his child with compassion and love.
The beautiful child emerged and joined him above.
Her innocence made me feel the immediate loss,
I had a choice but I did not cross.
I went back to those who meant to protect me.
They said they loved me, then why their need to change me?

Jean Johnston

A Memory

I refuse to remember from two Junes to two Decembers
when he was there waiting for release and rest.
A severed leg propped upon a pillow, pride put aside.
Old and ill now, life all but done, he spoke of eternity
and of a hereafter.

A dynamic man a few years back standing straight and
true, virile and tall and strong.

I remember as a little child barely up to his knee the
adoration and love I felt. I knew he would always love,
and look after me.

I went one wintery day to see where he might be.
The family name fashioned out of stone,
and now this is his home.

A memory only of laughter and love
brief now is the sorrow.
And knowledge that time here is only ours to borrow.

Catherine Saly

A Sonnet To Mom And Dad With Love

I'm overcome with pain sometimes at night
When blackness of despair becomes my guest.
I writhe and pray for coming of Dawn's light
To free my soul and leave my mind to rest.

So long as daylight's friendly smile is near,
My mind remains impervious to dreams
Of childhood hate, the agony and tears
Wrought by the blind, never-ending screams.

Just let the sunshine frolic o'er my face
With fingers warm; and playful patterns jest
The bitterness will slowly leave it's place
Within my heart; withstand the grueling test.

'Tis strange the sadness mars a young child's view
Of security, happiness, and you.

Deborah McKnight Lawson

Untitled

Clumsy air, swallowed words, eyes to the ground
When a minority appears, black, yellow, brown...
an excellent screening device
to get a sense of what's expected
I long for such a defense mechanism
from those who are affected.
Standing vulnerable,
merely labeled "pretty," "warm," "bright"
initially, all that is seen is skin of light
They like who I am, they like simply me
they can't see my color
and the words become free.
"You're Jewish?"..."Oh, please don't get me wrong
you're different,"
and they sing their patronizing song.
Color me Jewish, God...color me green
for it hurts to get close
and then have your color seen.
Color me Jewish, God color me too
orange will be fine, I'll even take blue.

Darlena Goetz

The Mask

When I'm "out there", I wear a mask
Whatever is needed - I do
It's a kind of role, a survival task
A way to make others comfortable too.

The mask, it hides what I really feel
It gives me a sort of - tough look
A pillar of strength, someone made of steel
Even though my hearts an open book.

Those who've "been there", know about the mask
And understand why it is worn
They too have softened the truth when asked
Rather than reveal a heart so torn.

Without the mask, I'd feel naked and bare
Exposed for all to see
So, instead I put on it's constant stare
And hide what's really me.

Someday the mask, I hope to shed
When some of this pain is gone
But until that day, my head and heart
The "deception mask" - will don.

Jill M. Wagner

Abstract

Life is abstract
What you think isn't really what it is
A relationship isn't a relationship
With out love from both sides.
A president has no power, the people do
Death, there is even in we who are
Still living and breathing
Love is not love unless the other loves back.
Money is not money unless there
is something to spent it on
A child is not a child unless treated like one.
You are not being used unless
you let the other use you.
A life isn't a life unless you make it a life.
You're own personnel hell is only
a hell if you allow it to be.
You let life control you instead
of you controlling it, you really
don't have a life
  Abstract, see it and survive

Daniel Post

"The Writer Of My Dreams"

I dream of the day I become a writer.
What would I write about?
Would it be poetry or stories, biographies or guides?
In my dreams I am all those things
And in my dreams I write endless themes...
Does the writer of my dreams end
For the writer of my life to begin?
Or is it the consolation of one's destiny
To know that somewhere in the depths of my "self"
lies another "me?"...
I wonder about the writer of my dreams...

Gloria E. Vargas-Willis

Bird Of Omen

I won't be the one to hold you down.
What will we do when we are free?
Aren't we not hopeful? I think so just restless.
So what's holding us back?
Maybe we focus on the pain?! Maybe...maybe not.
Do you know? Inside deep down it's there.
Find it, challenge it, conquer it.
And when you think you've looked everywhere, have you?
  No.
The answer is...
  Your choice.

Hana Rhodes

Poetry In Seclusion

   Words clear the path of confusion,
what is this ongoing force that won't ease?
It keeps me yearning and learning beyond the
obvious for what is buried deep.
I have to express it...this desire rules my
soul...guides my thoughts...to a place I've
only dreamed of...

I do not prophetize like Gibran, I do not know
what purpose rhyme or reason has.
I hoard the lyric and suppress destiny,
for it is mine to wallow in alone.
So I cry in isolation, while I strive to satisfy
your soul...shedding tears cleanse the pain,
only bare truths remain.

Poetry in seclusion, waiting for your love
to set it free.

Elizabeth Briggs Wilson

A Reflection

The lonely Coyote, the lone Oak tree,
  What is the difference in thee?
    You're one of a kind, a special breed,
      And only you are responsible for your need.

Yet, are you really all alone,
  Or a creation on your own?
    Does one not hear the answer to your howl,
      Or at night do you not feel the owl?

Yes in the quiet of the night,
  Do you not feel the shiver of delight?
    As the coolness surrounds you,
      And the wonder of something there too!

A presence distant, and far,
  And yet there you are,
    The lonely Coyote,
      And the lone Oak tree.

Elaine Koch

Prison

Prison.
What is it?
One can define it as an encasement,
Where there is limited space.
A jail.
A confinement.
Then, is the world not the prison of the human race?
Is there an escape?
Maybe in our minds,
Maybe in our souls,
Maybe only in death,
But in the end, there is only a larger prison.

Angie Moy

"My Friend The Full Moon"

My friend the full moon
What am I going to do
I was hoping that you might help
My broken heart to find someone else
The tears I cry don't show
These brown eyes won't let them go
I need your advice so I can move on
My life's a mess and the dream is gone

My friend the full moon
I hate to bother you
But I thought you'd know what to say
I need the wisdom to send this problem away
The pain I feel is inside
These deep wounds open up each night
I've come back again to hear your voice
To get an answer before I make the wrong choice

Wait just a moment am I hearing you right
The man that I know wouldn't give up without a fight
Brush yourself off get back on that horse
Find another shooting star wish upon it once more

Cory Iiams

Life Begins At Ninety

Life begins at ninety!
What a ridiculous thing to say!
Bear with me as I relate today
A few attainments on my way
To reach this goal at ninety!

As a youngster at school reciting a poem
I was fortunate to win second place.
Later in a jelly making race
I was happy to win third place.

My score in tennis was only average.
I played second violin in my college orchestra
I was accepted but never the best,
At a recent art show I won second best.

The greatest honor came to me
When my poem, "Rare Little Toad"
Won in the top three percent best
In the National Poetry Contest!
Life began at ninety for me!
This little poem bringing the greatest honor of my life!
As I look in gratitude and joy I say all: Keep trying!

Etta R. Sharp

Dear Son

Each year as you break your promise that you made to me when you were three, "I never grow up mommy, I stay your baby,"
I'm so thankful that little boy's promise is broken to me.

I praise God for you! He gave you to us to raise in Him. We give you back to Him. For you are our son for only a short time of an earthly journey. You are God's son for Eternity.

You are growing up to be a fine young man and we are so proud of you! Proud in you and the things you do, not proud of ourself but praise God for the wisdom to raise you.

We dedicated you back to the Lord six months after you were born. You are His but you are coming of age to choose the path of life, God's or the world's. We pray each day that it is God's path of life you wish to walk upon.

The World will throw things in your path and sometimes God too, to test you but don't forget who is there, no matter what, to help you! It's not mom or dad. Call on Him always and He will be there always.

LOVE FOREVER, MOM AND DAD.

Darlene M. C. Hill

Willie Wee

Once I had a little snake and I named him Willie Wee.
We were constant companions, he went everywhere with me.

When I'd walk to the market, he'd slide along by my side
And he kept every secret that in him I would confide.

We had a fine arrangement and of him I was quite proud.
Our only problem ever was when we were in a crowd.

Strangers got so excited when they spied him slithering.
I fear it hurt his feelings when they ran away, poor thing.

We played lots of different games; his favorite - hide and seek.
He loved to keep me guessing, sometimes I'd search for him a week.

One rainy day while reading, I sensed Willie's restlessness.
He wanted my attention focused just on him, I guess.

That silly snake did something he had never dared before,
Sidled into the kitchen sink just as Mom walked through the door.

I never really blamed her, at least I tried to pretend,
It wasn't hers but his fault, Mom dispasaled my best friend.

Anne A. Carpenter

The Love Of A Parent!

In the early sixties, when we both were beginning,
We traveled this wet road - Together.
A bond of friendship - devotion - and love,
We became "like" birds of a feather.

Kids with a purpose, goals that they set,
With parents to back them up.
Coaches with patience — knowledge and care
Made Dolphins from little seal pups...

We became so involved, those early years,
Swimmer's creed became a way of life...
The wins and loses — sweat and tears...
All the joys and yes, — all the strife.

Our golden years are blessed indeed,
 For you still have time to share.
  Your hopes, your goals,
   your meets, your fun
    with us older folks who care.

Dorothy Graham

The Way Of Nature

We scan the spot for glimpse of life or green.
We sense the molding earth beneath the leaves.
We search for signs of beauty there last seen,
Lest recall of the spot our mind deceives.

But nature is not hurried on her way,
Her secrets to reveal or beauty flaunt.
One waits with patience for the hour or day
The birth of life within the hidden haunt.

Soon circled sun, its warmth and light bequeath,
And gift of rain from dark clouds overhead
Bring yellow, purple, white from underneath,
And crocus speaks to us, "Not all is dead."

What faith can come from nature's lessons taught!
From beauty viewed in that which God hath wrought!
Emma Warnock

1

Deep within the darkness of Being,
We reach for the word:
   The word that sustains and engenders
   The being of all nothingness,
   That nothingness within.
   For in nothingness all beingness emerges:
By the word that is spoken,
By the word that is felt,
By the word that is received.

2

By the word that is spoken—
By the word that is felt—
By the word that is received,
   The being that is crushed,
   The soul that is bruised and made fragile
   May return to the nothingness of all beingness
   Within the darkness of Being, and
Hear the wholeness that is spoken,
Feel the wholeness that is felt, and
Receive the wholeness that is.
George Campbell Hage

Gratitude

When we are grateful and thankful in all things
We open the fountain of joy in our soul
As the fountain of living waters bursts forth
We will fulfill every worthy goal

When we are grateful and thankful in all things
We shall indeed become forever glorious
In all accomplishments and every tragedy
We will be unfailingly victorious

Because out of the fountain of living water
Flows the joyous ecstasy of the spirit divine
Filling our hunger for love and peace
Quenching the thirst of all mankind

Gratitude brings unfailing abundance
Depending on how we will behave
We have free will to make the choice
To be the master or the slave

When we can love with every fiber of our whole being
We are assured of every treasure life can give
Glowing with joy, our light shines forth
In everlasting splendour as we live!
Henry Kotschorek

You And I

If I were you and you were I
We look at each other eye to eye,
Things about us are carefully decided
In order to be all the time united.

When I plan for our tomorrow
You'll be involved devoid of sorrow,
Because you are truly very truthful
That your image is certainly beautiful.

I don't know if we were designed
To have mingled each others mind,
Just in case you will be mine
Oh! I know that it's really fine.

When you and I happen to forget each other
Try to recall those days when we were together,
Those memories were sort of treasure
For they were sources of our pleasure.

If some days both of us are lucky
I'm inclined to believe it's divinity,
Now and then we will always pray
That our CREATOR will bless us each day.
Elpidia A. Garcia

"Vacation"

You were here,
We laughed and talked, ate, slept, and played.
It was fun now it's done.

You left now it's quiet and still.
No chatter and laughing no hustle and bustle.
And no children to play in the creek.
It's lonely.

But now there are ghosts who lurk in your places.
At the table for coffee-outside for the sun
Four smiling faces who say
"We're still here."
Feryne C. McCammon

Influence

Are there ding bats in the wind?
We jump into a fight with a friend.
We look and look, but do not see!
What shall we do with you and me?

The weather and crops are safe for talk;
with our dogs only, we go for a walk.
The sounds we hear, and are they new?
What shall we do with me and you?

News of the day brings food for thought,
Politics, economics with problems fraught.
Loud noise called music, hear that cry?
No mystery why many young ones die.

When the stars grow old as fossils are,
Perhaps more people will sing in the choir,
And all babies have parents that love and care.
"When hell freezes over, is the negative dare."

Beauty in the eyes...of the beholder is.
Eye...or mind? Think on that quiz.
Where does the mind receive its spark,
And can think of such a quaint remark?
Gladys Michaels

Fragile Hearts

There are fragile hearts in all of our souls.
We hide these hearts behind faces hard and cold,
Believing that we are strong when we are weak,
Never letting anyone in to take a peek.
Some of these hearts grow cold from neglect,
Some grow weary with time and regret.
There are those that are broken and in need of repair,
But one thing is true for hearts everywhere.
They each need the love of some one close by,
For without this love every heart dies.
   Donald C. Graham

Vietnam

Only nineteen, still almost a boy
We gave him a number, just like a toy
What he'd seen through his eyes
Could not compare, as his best friend dies

In the bush you know what it means
Hoping when you wake, it's only a dream
Things that were done, they couldn't believe
It took over their minds like a disease

The lives that were taken
Left most of us shaken
If the truth were to been known
That American boy would have come home

As our boys came home from this place
Soon they became a terrible disgrace
Some were spit on at the airport
Very few would give him support

To all you troops who did you part
And all you Americans who still have heart
Whisper a prayer for that soldier boy
It's not his fault, he was played liked a toy
   Donald D. Zimmerman Jr.

The Fear

A touch, a hug, a kiss,
we feel each other the way we wish.
The passion grows stronger, but it's time to stop
but he won't, he begins to tear off my top.
I push him away, but he comes right again
I fear that my body will be torn limb from limb.
I yell "NO!" but my scream goes unheard.
He just keeps on going without a word.
I grit my teeth and scream in pain.
"Damn you man, you are insane!"
And close my eyes knowing it won't do good
I'll wait till he leaves and then do as I should.
He finally pulls away, and grabs his shirt
And all I can hear is a silent bird chirp.
I pull on my blanket, my body I curl.
"Why do you cry you dumb little girl!"
I look at him and want to reply
but all I can do is simply just cry.
He walks out and slams the door.
How will I be the same anymore?
   Christal Brooksbank

Daddy's Girl

I was Daddy's girl right from the start;
We each held a piece of the other's heart.
When I as troubled or had a bad scare,
When I needed help he was always there.
He taught me to love, to give and to share;
He taught me of life, of hope and of prayer.
He showed me how Indians snagged trout with bare hands
And scrubbed out their pots with coarse river sands.
A mattress of pine boughs he made for my bed
With a pillow of fern leaves to cushion my head.
I learned of the clouds, the stars and the moon;
I learned to read tracks of the deer and the 'coon.
Woods creatures and birds and plants of the earth,
His love for them all he taught me from birth.
He's gone and I'm grown, and now I'm a wife,
But I'm still Daddy's girl for the rest of my life.
   Barbara S. Weppener

Christmas Time

Christmas is a special occasion,
  We celebrate our dear Savior's birth.
When we sing from the hymns, what joy that they bring,
  Makes us feel there is peace still on earth.

We're privileged to live in this country,
  The land that we call, "the free."
Compared to so many nations,
  We strive for tranquillity...

Some parts of the world will be laughter.
  Some parts there'll be tears in ones eyes.
Some will have food on their table,
  While some will go hungry and die.

Let's strive for a better tomorrow.
  Lets give to the folks who's in need.
Lets help the lonely and homeless.
  Give your time, sacrificial let's be.
   Dorothy Horrell

Friendship

Just as a flower needs sunshine from above
We can give our rays of pure true love

Just as a flower needs rain to grow
Our mental inspirations can be showered I know

Just as a flower needs air to live
Our cheerful spirit we can also give

Just as a flower needs rich soil to flourish
Our emotional sharing we can give to nourish

And if friendship has all of this it will be
Just as a flower — a cherished beauty
   David Kaaialii

Drab Days

Sitting on my comfy couch.
Watching autumn leaves dancing about.
Winter's chill can now be felt, and a drizzling rain
Onto the browning grass now pelts.

All look drear compared to summer,
but thoughts of spring I dream asunder.

With fireplace warm and glowing brightly,
I know I'll endure this winter spritely.
   Barry Baggett

Special Guest

"Come into my parlor" said the spider to the fly
"We can be good friends, you and I
You are so handsome, big, and strong
If you come into my parlor, you can sing me a song."

"I will wrap web around you to keep you warm.
I would never, never do you any harm.
Your wings are so pretty, I do like your style.
Please come into my parlor, and sit for a while"

"I'll dress up my table with the best
You will be my special guest."
The fly said to the spider "Oh me-Oh My"
"You have such charming ways, I don't deny."

"I'll come in for a minute, just promise me
As soon as lunch is over, I may go free.
I know I'm handsome, and hard to resist.
I'll come in just to please you, if you insist."

He flew into the web, and to his dismay
He knew he could not leave, he was there to stay.
Let this be a lesson to all who are vain
If you fly into that web, you'll never come out again.
Emma Lucille Clough

A Shadow

We don't laugh, sing or love
we are separate from the living
but not from life
Complete in our silence, filled with darkness
No one can ever get close enough to touch you
but you are always there
Never part of the radiance that creates you but
cast off from reflections of many
In death there are no shadows or reflections
only the light that makes you
and so we are finally free.
Juli-Anne Lakritz

Deep Water

The last glow of a sunset.
Waves meeting and rushing away from the sides of the ship,
White water, cool wind.
Sea spray, ever so light, ever so faint.
Darkness encloses the end of the day.
The sea is mysterious, with knowledge of a past you might
not know, though it is sensed all around you, enclosing you
In, taking you back to another place, and time.
A rhythm of its own, peaceful.
No notion of time, endless, eternal.
Jennifer L. Milosavljevic

The Day Passed

This day is gone;
What did we do?
Did we contact someone along the way?
Cheer up a friend who shared our day?
Did we speak kindly to a stranger?
Rescue something from any danger?
Did we discover ability in other folk?
Exercise caution before we spoke?
And now we see the die is cast,
Was this day spent as tho' it were our last?
What did we do?
Jesse R. Bull

My Father's World

I stood by the oceanside looking over its great span,
Watched the waves roll in and knew it was at God's command.
I saw the morning sun come rising in the sky,
It was a gift from God, a new day for you and I.

I felt the gentle breeze blowing gently on my face,
Watched the graceful birds flying high above his place.
I saw the busy creatures making holes into the beach,
Running here and there to hide from harmful reach.

I sat upon the sand and watched the rolling tide and
Pondered on the things that only God could provide.
He made it all in six days, the big things and the small.
He put them all together so man could enjoy it all.

As the day was fading and the night began to fall,
I stood upon the sand and marveled at it all.
As the breakers hit the shore, the moon shone on the water.
My thoughts could only be, "HOW GREAT MY HEAVENLY FATHER."
Gloria Fraser

Moonbeam

Alone, I walked the street,
Watched the leaves fall.
The sun had set below the city.
The clouds shaped inanimate forms.

I passed a man with sullen eyes longing —
Longing for pity.
He looked up, his eyes drilled into my soul.
I wanted to stop and wipe away
The tears.

This man needed love and a kind heart,
To see the world as he saw it.
I waved off my grief, began to leave, but something drew me back.
I needed to understand.

With those eyes he asked, "Please stay to listen, hear my story."
So I sat. And heard.

When he finished, I looked to the sky.
And there I found the answer among the stars.
Reaching into the heavens,
I grasped a gift that would compare with no other.
To him, I gave a moonbeam.
Jennifer M. Fenton

Remembering Our Vets

I guess what this generation remembers best,
Was the war that caused a great protest.
It was a war that didn't make much sense,
And the injuries incurred were very intense.
The President and staff weren't very wise,
When the war started in '66 and ended in '75.
The war in which I speak on,
Is the one with the Vietcong.
Their methods were sadistic, and their punishments mean.
One could not imagine what the prisoners had seen!
To remember those boys, who, God made answer their call,
We guilt ridden citizens erected a wall.
Engraved upon it were the names of thousands of men,
Who were sent to fight this worldly sin.
The few who came back all in one piece,
Faced a life of failure and deceit.
Some of you, though, came back less than whole,
And are faced with a life in a Veterans home.
Our hearts are open to you all,
Those whose bravery that did not fall.
Gale Dazzo

Gone

I never thought the day would come when we would say good-bye
was our whole relationship started and ended because of some secrets and lies?
I kept your secrets and I believed your lies for over a year and a half
you've almost killed me with pain but I didn't try to hurt you back
this wasn't intentional though I know you won't believe
and I'm sorry though the apology you won't receive
I never meant to hurt you though you've hurt me way too much
will I ever see your smile again? will I still have your hand to clutch?
everyone make mistakes; I'm sorry I make more than most
is our relationship like this subject? will it remain forever closed?
I hope you can forgive me - one day, near or far
but do believe that from now on my heart will have a scar
as far as you're concerned our friendship is forever lost
every time I make a mistake will this be to final cost?
you were my best friend till the day you ended it all
and now you have seen the last tear that from my eye will fall
this was your choice, good or bad
and if it upsets you, good, this time I want to see you sad
don't see me as selfish; you know it's just not true
the only thing I regret is simply losing you!

Amber Huffmann

True Friend

Upon the never ending river of time
was it chance that caused us to meet?
I discovered with you a friendship
With which others sorely fail to compete.
Helping me to face the painful memories
That lie buried from years before.
Looking past my protective facade
And shaking up my very core,
Revelations of sub-conscious motives
I have refused to even consider.
Showing me decisions based upon a heart
That for many years has remained bitter.
Reaching down past dread emotion's wispy veil,
Finding there my greatest fear
Is one that I may fail.
Making someone face their thoughts,
A mark of a true friend, sets you apart.
Opting to decline dispensing advice, only,
You say, reconcile your mind with your heart.

Darrell W. Sutton Jr.

The Grove

The grove I knew when as a child
Was filled with stately trees and wild
With birds that chirped with many a song.
And squirrels quickly scampering along.

The grove was fun for boys at play
Who dug a cave for their hide-a-way.
Many secrets hidden within those walls
As boys retreated till mother's calls.

The grove contained special treasure too
Chokecherries galore in brightest hue.
Boys and girls filled buckets, a few
Hauling from grove for Mom to view.

Mom put the kettle upon the stove,
Pealed and cored apples grown apart from the grove.
Cooked up the most delicious chokecherry-apple jam
Placed in large jars; so tasty with pheasant or ham.

Thank you, Lord, for memories today
Of happy boys and girls allowed to play.
And Mom who toiled from day to day
That what was good would not waste away.

Effie Ruth Larson

An Elusive Emotion

The elusive emotion called love
Was a gift to us from God above
For our hearts to forever remain elated
Never to feel slighted nor degraded

Many times the gift of love has been misused
Wrecking lives and leaving souls abused
Seeking solace we suppress the hurt
Hiding the fact that we feel like dirt

Entering our lives special at first
Leaving us empty with a heart that has burst
Embracing our souls with childish joy
Abandoning us like a broken toy

Pessimists say put self before another
Focus on your needs not your lovers
Optimists say give before you take
By being sincere not a fake

Many people believe love must be expressed
Straight from the heart or it will not be blessed
The reason why love is so elusive
Must be discovered and made conclusive.

Anthony S. Williams

The Whispering

The whispering invaded my days without
  warning, without substance or shape.

The whispering touched my sleeping nights,
  waking me, then fleeing into the
  shadows behind the moon's glowing cape.

The years went by and seasons would reflect,
  the whispering I tried to grasp, and failed,
  much to my regret.

Until the moment came as I stood in the quiet,
  between night dark and morning light,
The whispering became clear and did not take flight.

It was I, all this time, and always the same,
  softly, with love, whispering your name.

As I felt strong arms surround me, holding me tight,
  holding me safe,
I knew it was you, your heart, your face.

My heart's love, my soul, had at last broken free
  from life's chains that had not let me see,
My life, my love had always been you...
  together with me.

Cynthia Marie Chantry Carlson

Crossroads

We live from day to day
With the hopes of a healthier way
Vitality sometime seems very troublesome
And each day, we hope, we can observe a better day

When you reach the crossroads in your life
And you don't know which way to turn
You wish, you knew what the future contains
But you know, that is privilege information

Remember your beliefs in time of sorrow
Because there is always tomorrow
If dreams don't come true, never be blue
Because GOD will never desert you!

Daniel Cole Jr.

"Fullmoon Is Dancing On My Breath"

I want to breathe in open air
Warmonger breaths are hanging around
Blasted bombs clouds the breath of civilization
In Adam's breath was smell of apple.

Beside mass graveyard
Widows are inhaling breath of protest
Breath crosses virgin land
To reach dawn of human era.

Couple engaged in love need open air
Breath of nature is confronting damn massacre
For the spring time
On the point of my pen is scrawl of breath
On this blank paper breathless sculpture.

Breath of youth is irrepressible pace
Breath of child has innocent joy
A dying man is seeking some more breath
Fullmoon is dancing on my breath
I am reaping the harvest of breath
For the peace of future generation.

Abu Bakar

All Saints Day

Mother: remembering, Novembering.

A dull maroon world burnished rich by
Warm topaz and garnets' dignified mourning that
Melds with autumns' last, deadest, frail grey-brown leaves.

Your birthday.

Deep-set, window-wide-open eyes regard me quietly.
Pain-honed, they glow darkly love-filled and allow
Buried, unquenchable humor to flicker and sing earthy songs.

Your presence.

The essence is prenatally, pre-consciously familiar, tinged acidly
With the awareness of disappointing human limitations.
Ever-pervading — the constant reassurance of peacemaking.

Quality to depths unplumbed, unfathomed.

Ginny Garrett

The Loneliness Disease

I have lived amongst the ruins of a heart that's been neglected;
Waded through the muck and mire to find only misery.

Sang love songs to a woman, who walks the street at midnight;
Shared my body and a bottle, on a bed of sympathy.

Whiskey soothes the bitter loneliness of a man locked inside a heartache
It opens up his voice, in conversation with the rest.

But the words that need to be set free, remain captured by a heartache;
While he foolishly becomes someone, who says all things in jest.

But a tear-stained pillow mocks the laughter, as the jester cries in slumber;
Muffled sobs heard only through the keyhole in the door.

Awakened by the voices in the hallway of deception;
Where passers-by, lie and deny, pretending life is not to be abhorred.

Living life without someone is a morbid aspiration;
But never having known, will force you to walk on your knees.

Clinging to a gesture, a comment made in passing;
Perchance it be, the one to cure, the loneliness disease.

Glyn S. Johnson

The Centaur

Girlish wishes, still hopeful housewife dreams
Visions herself silhouetted by moonlight
Riding fast on Pegasus, in designer jeans
Still yearning, for that Knight in shining white

Oh Men! Why can't you be more like the Horse?

A Friend she's proud to be seen with
Strong, to carry her over the rocky roads
A friend she can be quiet and alone with
Reliable, there to help with heavy loads

Oh Horse! Proud, intelligent, noble force!

The trick is to train, but not the spirit break
The secret is trust, the answer, gentle hands
Lead with loving lessons, watch him come awake
Adventuresome teammate, one that understands

Oh Centaur! Why this Image do you Enforce?

Man/ Horse a combination not so bizarre
Cowboys and horses, they're really much the same
Begin to realize, It's just the way They are
Neither likes fences, nor thoughts of being tame

Oh Woman! What recourse, what must You Endorse?

August Knittel

End Times?

What has happened to the human race?
Violent crimes are always taking place.
Disasters and murders are everyday news.
Children are carrying guns to school, but
Prayer in the classroom is against the rules.
The rich use their money to do as the please;
A poor man spends more time on his knees.
   Everyday I pray to God above,
    please protect me from madness with
   your Great Love.

Deanna L. Vento

Nothing Ventured

Ten years passed and this Sunday last,
Venturing home from a picnic feast,
I unexpectedly saw you from the corner of my eye
As I drove by.

Sitting solo on your porch,
You waved to the faint recognition
Of a familiar, but long-ago forgotten face.
I knew you,
But I only smiled
At the child I remembered as a friend
When dreams were free tickets to the dance,
Or whispers beneath the willow tree
That hid us in our secrecy.
When each beginning had no end
And every love was just pretend.

I never travel down your street
More than twice a year,
Where your memory lies along the road
Like empty cans of beer.

Cynthia L. Snyder

Society

What is Society
Us feeling comfortable
In a land of strangers
Society is a reassurance
That everything is okay
When it's not
Without it we are afraid

Lonely

Society gives us a sense of identity
We are no longer afraid
No longer
Lonely
However Society can also be a harsh winter night
It blows us from belief to belief
Leader to leader
It can blind the truth
And destroy young saplings
Aspiring to be great trees
Society is both
And neither

James Reich

Her Fantasy

If I should draw,
Upon a quiet stretch of sea,
An island of mauve loam and beige sands,
I would have a place
For you and me.

Sand: Stippled green with ocean finery.
Sand: Gold evoked by silver shine.
Mountain: Jutting red and blue-gray spine.
Mountain: Steep enough for just one to climb.

A darkwood schooner, sheets taut,
Lines stretched as myriad tendons,
Exposed keel and polished hull.

Secured from passing ships,
Ringed by a sky of marshmallow down,
Only the darkwood schooner,
Sure and yaw, can heed the need
In the island's call.

Barry Baker

Cousin Or Sister

One day she's content and fine
Until you realize she's crossed the line.

Suddenly you hear of what she might do
and spend the morning realizing what she means to you.

Remembering when you were small
taking crayons and coloring on her walls.

Now you're older things have changed so much
death shall not bring its deadly touch.

Her innocence robbed memories remain
no one could ease her misery and pain.

But your caring words made her understand
that if she left, you wouldn't have her to hold your hand.

She's someone to help you with all your thoughts
Someone to untie the mangled knots.

So you see that I need you more than ever could be.
Without you there is no me.

Amber Reed

The Divine Wine

Bring ye the cup of Red Wine to thy Lips
until thy Heart of on'rous Poison weeps.
Heed not the cries of thy despondent Soul
Give in to That which at your Spirit chips.

Keep watch as the bright Light of your Soul dims;
take no heed and satisfy all thy whims.
The Brilliance above, thine eyes should not meet
for all its light comes down in blinding beams.

Take light, gay steps as you descend into
the Pits that are a murky, dusky hue
and Hades comes and takes you by the hand
Alas, there is no one to pity you!

For since you complied with the World's Design
and raised to thy Lips the sweetened Red Wine,
you suffer, for you the World did deceive;
'tis the ivory, White Wine that is Divine.

Ella Nkhoma

Exodus

Twenty years of sand and twenty more to come
Until there's none of us left to spoil the nation.
Nobody ever came so close to the promised land
And no one ever was so destined not to reach it.

We live feeding on hope and manna from the skies.
Our ignorance and our faith - two pillars that support us.
We know we are God's chosen, and his prophet's leading us,
But this is half the truth, and that's why we're still going.

We were born in slavery, we will die in the sands.
It all is long decided without our knowledge.
We're just a heavy burden of subjugated minds.
We can't be put to blame, but to save us is impossible.

To reach the Common Good, we have to be destroyed
It could be our blessing, and it could be our curse
How can I be the judge? What do I understand?
For we are slaves at hearts and this is why we must
Be a generation sacrificed to save the people.

Elena Nabieva

Los Angeles Blues

I never knew what sadness was
Until the day that we did part.
But now I know and can't forget
The pain that's in my heart.
I feel my soul has been stripped away,
No feeling left inside, until the day we meet again
From this pain I cannot hide.
Memories are what I have left of you.
But memories are not enough to ease this unforgiving pain,
The happiness I shared with you was more than any other gain.
I'd give up my soul for you my love,
For you are my only guiding light, cause without you I'm a broken man,
A stranger in the night.
So while I'm here and you are there,
My mourning will repeat,
I count the days, with a broken heart
Until these two souls shall once again meet.

Christian D. Monroe

Dreamtime Canticle

Come to my Dreamtime land:
Undivined universe of silent sounds.
Soft stones. Concrete clouds.
Fragrant timbers of sculptured castles,
Breathless hurricanes of luminous shrouds.

Come to my Dreamtime tower:
Infinite needle of dazzling night.
Warm snow. Frozen fire.
Gem and eye wresting in futile submission,
Darkness forbidding my fear to climb higher.

Come to my dreamtime cave:
Exquisite galaxy of crystal tears.
Liquid pebbles. Tremorous tides.
Indelible visions of smoothness and warmth,
Jewel-eyed anthem of longing, forever inside.

Cradle my pain of wisdom
In endless joy of ignorance:
Distil my cry of knowing
Into tears of carefree laughter.

Be still my Dreamtime world.
Clive B. Pascoe

Untitled

A unicorn on the lonely mountain
underneath the setting sun
So beautiful, so rare
this creature atop the jagged cliff
looks down upon the humbled Earth below it
and nature gazes back in envy.
Its mane, long and fair
pure white as snow
flowing in the breeze
blazing like the tail of a comet among the stars.
Her eyes, black as coal
look to the orange horizon
contrasting the deep, blue waves
rolling over the deserted beach.
On her head, rests an ivory tower pointing to Heaven.
It sparkles in the fading sunlight
as she raises up on her hind legs
in a gesture of farewell before galloping into tomorrow.
Another miracle of life to welcome into your dreams.
Gerald Phillips

Just One Moment More

Just wishing there was one moment more
Uncertain of the challenges that lie ahead of us
Searching for strength and comfort for just one moment more
The sands of time drift slowly through our days

Overcoming the loss is the hardest step we must take
Nights seem to be never-ending in darkness
Ever longing for just one little glimmer of hope

Memories have taken the place of happenings
Over and over we play those special times
Minute by minute we try to forge ahead
Ever mindful that those we loved so deeply
Never really want us to be so sorrowful
Time, we are told will lessen the pain, just one moment at a time

Memories will soon bring smiles through our tears
Overpowering those feelings that sometimes capture our minds
Reach deep into your heart for peace and contentment
Everlasting will be that bond of love we shared together
Joni Francano

Unborn Hope

I once was conceived by two little seeds;
Two hearts, entwined, that met in time as me.

My mom and pop are all aglow.
This nine months of waiting sure will be slow.

Conceived in love and from God above,
The love they share brought me to bare.

Now soon I'll be born and in their care.
I hope, to them, I will be a soul unique and rare.

Together they will lead me down life's many trails,
But, no matter what they will all end in smiles.

They are strong and full of hope.
I know we shall always be able to cope.

Because of this, and our love,
We shall become the stuff families are made of.
Jeannie Hubbard

Pride In Georgia

Be proud you were born in Georgia, Son!

Her name from nobility came.
Two centuries past were plans begun
For greatness and fame to proclaim.

Her wood made "Old Ironsides" strong.
Like her, make your constitution one
Of strength that endures e'er long.

With heart in her hand she has reigned
Through blood and the tears of wars not won,
And wears yet attire that is stained.

Plateaus greet her coastal plain rise,
And - Listen! - her mountains strum n'er done,
Depicting her love - longing sighs.

And climb like her Cherokee rose
To heights of success by deeds you've done,
A pattern for friends and for foes.

And strive to be wise, to be just,
Be moderate, too, in all things done,
Remember in God always trust.
Jeanne Palmer Moss

Cry For Relief

The pain, the pain!

Here I stand at doorway's view
Trying to get a glimpse of You.
I show You my suffering through drenched tears
And distorted face and words from fear.
Awake and see the suffering!
These years of pain explode through me.
Always I ask, then yell. You didn't respond.
Hear me, see me, love me, Oh, God!

Abused when young, prayed not to hate.
When all alone, I prayed for a mate.
My mate turned hostile, my marriage then ruined.
I prayed for a baby, my heart though so wounded.
While my love for my baby was most intense,
I've held anger so dearly ever since.
Help me forget, forgive, look ahead and mature.
Give me hope and happiness that will long endure.

The pain, the pain!
Christine Cecchini

Think

So here I sit with pen in hand
Trying real hard to understand
What it was from the teacher I heard,
So quickly I jot down the spoken word.

But still the words didn't let me know.
Where is the knowledge? Where did it go?
So I ponder, I stare, at last my eyes blink.
A light comes on, the answer I think!

For the reading, the writing and listening is grand,
But the thinking is essential to understand.
So add to the lesson one more goal.
Put that brain in gear, then you'll know.

For knowledge is more than a paper and pen.
It's a wonderful thing that comes from within.
We all are different in the knowledge we store,
But we all have the capacity to hold so much more.

The wisest people may not read a novel a week
Or get up in public and eloquently speak,
But ask them a question, find the missing link.
They'll give you an answer - they know how to think!

Dema Puckett

On Days The Sun Is Hot And Dry

On days the sun is hot and dry,
Try eating some apple or cherry pie.
I guarantee you'll feel better fast,
Believe me it's worked in the past.

If you don't want a piece of pie,
Try a glass of water when the temperature is high.
If that doesn't cool you down,
Don't worry, you'll smile not frown.

If you still feel dry and very hot,
Try ice cream if that's all you've got.
Melt it, drink it, slurp it too,
Just eat it up whatever you do.

I know these methods aren't the best,
Here's the best one, take a rest.
Then maybe it will seem,
When you were hot was all a dream.

Allison Shoger

"The Kiss Of Death"

For a kiss from one as gentle as a whisper is to be praised,
treasured,
cherished it would be,
locked deep within my heart,
In a distant chamber of my being,
Yet never forgotten.
As I await near slumber,
I dream of her image.
Feeling an inner warmth surpassing all emotions,
I see beauty greater than beauty itself.
By the sensual touch of her lips, I awaken.
Anticipating pure bliss,
My spirit bursts as my mind and body are paralyzed.
Locked away it cannot be.
Gasping for breath,
Reaching for life as I know it,
My eyes seal slowly,
My heart flutters as a sensation of pure evil entwines my soul.
I feel no more.

Jeremy Seibold

N.Y. City Sky Line

Awe inspiring demi-gods of steel and cement
Towering spires reaching for the blue firmament,
Dwarfing man's stature, pushing him clear to the ground.
In this winding maze of buildings
you might never be found.
Loudly blaring auto horns, cars
rushing everywhere,
People always in a rush, no time to even share.
Yellow haze hanging like a blanket in the sky.
The sun, a red ball nearly hidden, from every human eye.
This mighty city standing on
the Hudson's rocky shores
A door way to the U.S.A., this
land that we call ours.

Helena O'Keefe

Of Lines And Echoes

Morning fog rolls memories
toward the edge of the sky at sunrise.
In the cool breath of autumn
yesterday hums behind me.

Those mornings when mist tangled my bangs,
licked my cheeks,
dry leaves crackling against my plaid knee socks
as I skipped toward the schoolhouse.
That door, scarred with time
opened to the world of paste,
new books, sweat and vegetable soup.

We drew houses with wide rooms
and rock gardens on the playground
and lived out our dreams
until the rain beat down on the rocks
and washed the lines away.

But the sun of September had warmed
a child's simple scrawl in the dust
passed by, and believed, and never forgot.

Doris Toppen

Starlight

Sleep escaped me throughout the night
Tortured by love that didn't seem right
So I looked above to the omniscient stars
Longing to find just who we are
Are we lovers forever or sympathetic ships
Sharing the ocean on fleeting trips
As I searched for answers on moonlit skies
Sorting the truth from clouded lies
I pictured the stars that reminded me of you
Bright and beautiful; I could tell they knew
They formed a flower - a rose in bloom
A perfect portrait except, there was too much room
For next to your flower I imagined a kite
With a fanciful tale ready for flight
It shone with your passion and echoed your song
It pierced the night "I must be moving on"
And reinforcing what the stars seemed to reveal
A fallen star silenced the blue cried field
Our love is like that shooting star
What now seems so close is soon to be so far.

Jay Vardin

Coffeehouse Perk

Damn you beatniks with your gorgeous black tights!
Tonight you serenade me with your hollow, heart felt prose.
I'll have a large coconut cappuccino please.
   She sits next to me on the table, steaming like an ember-red
   fire about her life. I ignore her in her little espresso cup world.
   Latted in a sublime vision, My cappuccino lover.
Her love scorched my tongue. Blisters malaced
forward. Bitterness is the residue of coffee
grinds left over. They fill the deep crevasses of
my teeth, like a diseased cavity. She dehydrates
me. Diuretic! Taking, stripping me of all resources;
leaving me tense and shaking. My cappuccino gigolo.
   I love her with her coconut spunk, flavored
   generously with whipped cream and cinnamon
   curled hair. Her strength, as if it were black magic,
   stimulates me in the insomniac nights and in the early
   morning rituals. My cappuccino woman.
So you beatniks stand up there, in the spotlight, and read
to me your paused cries of your turmoil; I'll sit right here
in calm misery and sip my lover goodbye.

Brant J. Wardner

Today

Today's steps are all I need to take.
Today's decisions are all I need to make.
I'll leave tomorrow alone, I don't know what it holds.
There is joy in not knowing what tomorrow might unfold.

Today, I'll live the fullest that I possibly can.
I'll savor the sights, the sounds, and even the smell of the land.
I'll learn from the past that has taught me so well,
To grow in love and understanding, and try not to fail.

When today is finished, I'll lay it gratefully aside,
And know that tomorrow will be another, with nothing to hide.
I can be thankful as I finally find the time to rest,
And go to sleep, knowing, that I have lived my best.

Joyce Campbell-Reese

Walking Tall

   In times of famine and great distress, someone should put him
to the test. Test his power and you will see! He is great and mighty
able to set you free.

   Free from what? you may ask, I'm not in bondage at all!
Oh but yes! you are my friend, otherwise you would walk tall.
   But I am walking tall, can't you see I'm standing up straight!
No my friend you are crippled, you see your mind in filled with hate.

   Is this not bondage, that you refuse to give him place. Beware,
beware be very careful for we all must see his face.
   All must tell him why my friend, they did not choose to hear his
voice. He was there from the beginning, giving you that very choice.

   He is calling you from the roof top and from all the city streets.
You that are sick and hungry come and join him at the feast.

Arnold Hayes

Son

As I sit here in my old chair and rock, my mind wanders back
to the years long past.
The tears roll down my cheeks and my heart saddens at the thought
of you; the times we shared together at work and play.
I keep hearing your voice, saying "Mom everyone should have
a mother like you".
My mind wonders why, my heart tells me that God had a reason,
but still I wonder why you were taken from me before I could
give you all the love you deserved.

Barbara B. Keetch

Life Is Choice

Fly by night on wings of gold
to the place future holds.
Grow and learn and be set free
as you fly through time,
passing up many years of your would-be-life.
Fly by night while others sleep by day.
Your journey may be dark,
but you will be set free.
Life is not to die for
but yet you do as you fly by night
while life is choice.
You have of life
to live life or let it go.
Take a hold a life
and use it as you may,
let it go to fly free
for you have a choice.
Fly by night with life
the forgiven choice.

Dianna Troxell

Thanksgiving

Thanksgiving is a day to look to God.
To thank Him for a bounteous harvest, is not odd.
We gather around the table with glee,
And praise Him because He keeps us free.

We forget about heartaches and sorrows this day,
And we think of the gladness and joy as we pray.
Burdens are lifted as we accept His grace,
As we gather at dad's and mother's place.

We welcome our families with our smiles
Also defeat the evil one all the while.
As long as we tenderly hold them close
No one will murmur about the way we choose.

We linger some and talk of old times,
And doing this the clock sometimes chimes.
The more we visit and share our joys,
Our way grows so much brighter for each girl, each boy.

The day comes to a close and its getting dark,
We head for our homes with a friendly spark.
As we drive down the lane and wave our goodbyes
We can all thank the Lord who with us abides.

Helen Addleman

Paid Stranger

She talked to someone who was paid to listen...
To someone who only knew her first and last name from a filing folder
in a gray cabinet; she talked about her deepest, darkest secrets,
about the things she swore she'd never tell another soul, but now, she
easily spilled them out in small notes of smooth agony to this one
listener. One listener, who she had only met an hour ago. And why
she did not come to me, is a mystery I hold prisoner in a dark room in
my mind. I had come from her; I was part of her, but she chose a
stranger over me because possibly she felt I didn't have time to
listen, or maybe I didn't want to hear her pains and catch her tears.
She was very wrong. Maybe today, as she enters the office, her hired
"friend" for an hour recognizes her face. Maybe this time, her
listener can distinguish between the other patients; maybe her image
is as fresh as yesterday's wind; maybe today, for just a moment, she
will become more than just a name on a file folder...but who knows?
I watch her pay the routine fee, enter the quiet room, and release
her tragedies of the day to a stranger
She paid to care.

Ginger Smith

How To Say Goodbye

To someone so much a part of me
To someone somehow the heart of me.
To rampant emotions, confusing ideals
Whose counterfeit loyalties anyone steals.

Whose immature wisdom and instincts are led
But the greatest of pitfalls, whose heart rules her head
With corners of mind so decisively cut
No breadth for expansion or knowledge of it.

To smugness of ignorance, smugness of youth
To trim little parcels with labels of truth
To sureness and certainly (both good and bad)
To unfailing optimism (equally mad.)

To both judge and jury of all that was viewed
With justice and tolerance. (According to mood)
So truthful, so honest, emotions laid bare.
Turned fleetingly faithless and placed blame elsewhere.

So long to have waited, so sure to have been
This ending so final can last comprehend
The day that her parents have waited for nears.
Their daughter has grown up in more than her years.

Elizabeth Angelone

Silence New Participant

Silence to some is an experience,
To some it is a way of living;
For me it is a genuine feeling,
Never ceasing - always giving.

To be silent is indeed a blessing,
Often silence is like a dressing;
Sometimes sour - sometimes sweet,
But to God - it is a quiet peace and stillness.

Of being tuned to the world, and yet,
Being the master of the lease;
A free country! At last peace!
With the world at least.

Peace with thy soul and above all, a silence
heard throughout the world which, was indeed our goal.
And now that we have attained our goal -
Let's be careful that we do not disturb it.

So years from now we all can say
Silence is golden in the USA and that
Silence is here to stay - we pray
We will never be at war - no not for a day.

Doris E. Heefner

Tomorrow's Love

When I woke up I found myself already living tomorrow.
To shut off trauma and go ahead seemed the plan for sorrow.
The pain and hurt from yesterday I left back in today.
Piece by piece I go back in time, it's like a game I play...

Each day I do what I deem right; that lesson I have learned.
I'll not give in without a fight, for what becomes concern.
Each one I've trusted failed, I expected them to win.
The stamina of others wears, their focus becomes dim.

Go ahead, laugh at me; you think I do not see.
Look in the mirror, my denying dear, and your reflection's me.
We are the same, but different yet, and I can tell you why,
The bitterness set into you and gladly passed me by.

I will not live in the past and hug old memories.
I will not let the hurt and pain my disposition be.
I close those thoughts to clear the way, and push into tomorrow,
So another chance for love will come and soothe my aching sorrow.

Barbara Haynes

Going-Going-Gone

I'm 18 and I'm ready to soar
to see where life leads me
to open new doors.

I'm a freshman in College and I'm ready to fly
to reach out to people
to touch the sky.

The minutes pass slowly,
the hours they stall
I want a new world
to experience it all.

I'm afraid and elated and very excited,
there's a party called life
and I've been invited.

I can't wait for what's out there
I can't wait for what's new
so wish me good fortune and bid me adieu.

Cassandra Creighton

A Christmas Prayer

Dear Lord....

May you give me sight,
to see and appreciate those things which are good about my life,
may I remember to give thanks.

May you give me knowledge,
to know that my life has been blessed with a wonderful family, and
friends, to know and act upon what's right for those I love and
care about.

May you give me balance,
that I may give the best of what and who I am to my spouse and
family first, then others.

May you give me strength,
to channel my energy towards those relationships that give me
unconditional love, happiness, and peace of mind.

May you give me courage,
to humble myself and acknowledge when I've been less than I
could be, or should be, and to say I'm sorry.

May you give me a new beginning,
one that puts balance and harmony between self, family, and friends.
And just as important, one that makes you a part of my life.

All this I pray for you.

Esther Brown

Gone

It's the hardest thing to do,
To say its okay for them to go
But when they leave their presence
Lingers and reminds you they were here
And that you willingly let them go
You thought when you told them to leave
They wouldn't really go, but they did.
Left you abandoned in a world of memories.
No real sense of life. An empty shell of
What used to be. Later when you grow up
Alone in a world of illusions, nothing seems
Tangible. Nothing within your reach. And all
You could remember was that you told them
they could go.

Heather Friedman

ARMOR
Dedicated to my very dear friend Evan...
He wears an invisible shield of armor,
    to protect against the unknown.
A barrier to obstruct intimacy,
    a barricade to hinder attachment.

He keeps her at an emotional distance,
    not allowing feelings to surge.
He battles evolvement,
    and struggles with involvement.

She questions his reluctance,
    and is perplexed by his ambivalence.
Yet she compelled to strip him of his armor,
    and expose his soul.

Surrender your heart she requests,
    and bestow your love.
What you'll discover,
    is that the war will be over.
       April Tamuty

In Memoriam To
In each generation from the hand of God, a great life is given,
To proclaim God's piety,
    charity and intelligence to every person livin'
Robert was a man whose life was given by God,
    to this impossible task, day by day.
Whose magnanimity could never be comprehended in a lifetime,
By us or you, in any way.
His brother John, too, was touched by the hand of God, and swept away,
Because, our country, their Judas, must be heard, must destroy,
    must have their say.
Are these Judases so powerful, they will decide the destiny of these
    United States?
Can they fell such great men, and play God,
    and decide this country's fates?
No! So God took them, to hurt, but you should not be hurt:
You must understand and see,
Because of Robert and John, Peace in the world,
    in these United States,
will come to be!!
    Joanne F. Wisener White

"Friendship"
When a new friendship begins it's like a diamond in the rough,
To polish it, "two must agree to disagree" or foresee a sharp rebuff.
The above phrase would be an asset if chosen as a seed to sow,
Bringing harmony to a friendship that will blossom and grow.
A kindred spirit has the qualities of a friend and on whom one
can depend,
Respect is visible in words chosen, deeds done and actions taken
by a friend.
If a situation or a problem arises one may seek advice from
another source,
A friend will try to guide and you will decide the best course.
One needs a confidante to listen and encourage when the other
has to unwind,
A confidence betrayed is a friendship misplaced and a violation
of one's peace of mind.
When one deceived is by another poor judgement of people
becomes a real concern,
The distraught individual will be more judicious in giving another
acquaintance a turn.
Some friendships prevail and others fail when one chooses not to
fully invest.
Learning the difference between an acquaintance and a friend is
a judgement test.
Those whom acquire a true friend have accomplished this quest.
    Anne Devine

Parody On 'Over The River And Through The Woods'
Over the highways and through the skies
To our children's home we go.
The cars in our lane and the lines for the plane
Make travelling seem so slow.
We don't cross the river and we're not near the woods;
The condo is five stories high.
The thing that we smell as we ring the doorbell
Is Mrs. Smith's Pumpkin Pie.
The turkey looks odd — it doesn't have legs;
In fact, it is only a breast.
The vegetables come from freezer and can,
The microwave helps with the rest.
Modern days and modern ways,
We still have lots of fun.
In one accord we thank The Lord
For all that He has done.
    Jean Zimmerman

O Father, My Father
"How great thou art" 'tis the praises I sing
    To my father with me, and my heavenly King.
Made in their image, and nurtured by love
    Guided by instincts and help from above.
Conceived to this world as only God can
    Be taught as a child, to teach as a man.
Blessed to be a father and a father I will be
    As my father before me, and his father before he.
I use their great wisdom for decisions I make
    And given my freedom for directions I take.
Encouraged and strengthened for each passing day
    They give my faith and light up my way.
I grow in their wisdom to live fatherhood
    To raise up my children and lead them to good.
So thanks to my father for all of life's things
    And thanks to the Father for blessings you bring.
So should the day come and I'm called to go
    and my soul to rise must be,
Never you fear, I'll always be near, with my fathers
    along side of me.
    Frank P. Nauss Jr.

Untitled
    Sometimes you care to much,
to much to know or realize what lies
stand behind those big brown eyes.
Her mind knowing to much.
She gains what she needs through persuasion and touch.
Her fears and mistakes would leave minds a musk.
She can drive you insane with the sound of her voice.
She draws you in trapping you, leaving you no choice.
You pay the price as you see her sting.
Bells of confusion and self hatred begin to ring.
The end is near, you can hear it's call.
Her treacherous ways end it all.
    Guy Cornell

Season's End
The dried leaves fall in autumn;
their miraculous green goes...
In the trees, no musical tones;
the flowers are dead, their dresses torn...
Upon the fury of winds, sometimes and some day,
in autumn, the splendor ends... with the leaves,
it ran away...
    Germaine J. Sorel

Unsung Hero

The common man working hard
  to meet the common man's needs,
Exhausted, ragged looking, going home,
  dragging his aching feet behind him;
Never too tired for a kind word to his woman
  or a listening ear for his children.
The fate of life stings us with turmoil
  and conflict,
The agony of its endurance leaving us
  feeling defeated.
Some men: Escape through drunkenness.
Some men: Curse and lash out at their spouses.
Some men: Put up barriers to distant themselves
  from their children.
Some men: Drift in and out of other people lives
  like a runaway train.
Unsung Hero - Just a common man
  Still standing there with a
  Kind word and an understanding ear.

Jamie L. Arbuckle

Tameless Mold

In the mold one has settled, deciphering the chaos abound
to many this is secure, others cannot be so sure

When does the mold release all ambition and let fruits ripen full

It is difficult to sail your thoughts when secure often means one wind
from our lives a breeze comes by - a challenge, a risk,s not a certain win

How can you attain that pinnacle destination, without losing ground
repetition of the step must be mastered for you to have absolutely found

Once free or without the mold, how will one fare
limitless winds to sail, ideas that refuse to bail -
certain satisfaction, security one may not bare

Ah yes, that underlying blanket, what can it truly hold
appeasement to those around, yet continuance within the mold

But what for the mind, essential in this plan, yearning to escape
follow your heart, sail this day, pull back that long dreary drape

In no one but you shall it derive, with your self-initiative it shall survive

Gain that extra breath and wipe your brow
for your goal can be reached, maybe later, maybe now

Salute your beliefs while your emotions release
it is you, as great as you see - the mighty storm, the quiet peace

Whichever you choose, whomever you are
remember your dreams, for they will surely guide you far

Jonathan Cutler

Crumpled Foil

Here's a crumpled piece of foil that resembles Christian life,
When we're crumpled, like it's crumpled, we all reflect much more light.
God crumples us through childhood, and through our teenage years,
Through happiness and joy times, through grieving times and tears.

After all the crumpling our faces show the signs,
Of all that we have been through with laugh and worry lines.
And all those lines upon our heads are light reflecting faces,
So that we can help others, in different times and places.

Help them with the Savior's love, and all that He has taught us,
Tell of those who hated us and also those who sought us.
Then after all of life is over, and we've fought the final fight,
We'll be bright crumpled foil, reflecting all His light.

Ica Lyndsay Root

Your Party

You chose for your life to be like this,
To know that death, you will glimpse.
You made the bed you lie in.
You know it's wrong, but you get up and do it again.

You wanted to get messed up.
Now you are sick and that's tough.
You have a problem and need help,
Open your eyes; the world is telling you that you need help.

You don't even know why,
But there is something about getting high.
You fools actually think you are going to fly.
All you are going to do is die.

You land yourself in the hospital.
You will eventually end up in the coffin.
And all you can say, when you start to turn blue,
Is "It's my party and I'll die if I want to."

It's terribly sad,
Because you thought you were rad.
How unfortunate for you, and those who heard,
Because those were really your last words.

Donna Church

"A Prayer For Dad"

Here's a prayer for you, our beloved Dad.
To have to let go has made us all sad.
We pray that you will have no more pain.
That your passing away will not be in vain.

We pray that each and everyone of us will be
A better person for having known thee.
Your friendliness, your smile, and the love, you did show
To all of us, wherever you would go.

We pray that you will be happy not blue.
For you will be with Mom and Grandma, too.
You will see Grandpa, and friends so true.
We pray God will bless and look after you.

We pray God will help us, each and every one
To live our lives well, and to get the job done.
We pray you will be our guiding light
To watch over us, both day and night.

So we will not say goodbye to you,
Just so long for now, until we are through.
With this old world, and all that is bad,
We love you, we will miss you, God bless you Dad.

Eve Parsons

Translate Only If You Must

Don't hurry to transcribe the poet's thought,
  To risk losing in a loose translation
The essence of a spirit, as if naught,
  And fail to capture pure distillation.
Vibrant words, thoughts like vapours condensating
  On glass funnel of alchemist's retort,
New fluids forming and compensating
  With a crystal dross, diamonds turned bort.
So with a poem, the words must surely flow
  Or truth stagnates, to sicken and to die,
Each verse with lively words must always glow,
  A poem must be fluid, else a lie.
A journalist with words and phrases sports,
A bard must rhyme and scan or art aborts.

John Gerson Davies

A Tribute To Courage

To describe the strength and courage it takes,
To go through life never knowing what awaits;
It takes a certain person, to say the least;
To go through the pain and fight the "Beast".

You are that person!
You're special you see
You're fighting the battle,
Trying to find the right key.

Your courage and spirit is ever present
Within our hearts and minds,
And that, to me, is the most
Precious gift anyone could find.

Your life sounds like a rainbow
With bold and lively colors;
Like a bright blue sky with a great big smile,
Always showing concern for others.

You're an inspiration to all of us,
A special message you seem to send
Whatever you do, wherever you go,
Don't ever say can't and always stand tall!!!

Carolyn McFarland

Thanksgiving

Thanksgiving is a Special Day,
to get together with God and Pray.
It's a time to say grace, and time to rejoice,
a time to stand tall and project your voice.

Thanksgiving is a special time of year,
a time for Joy and a time for cheer.
a time to rejoice, and a time to Pray,
it's a time to give thanks on this special day.

Let's all give thanks to the Lord above
for He gave us all a reason to love.
Let's all join hands, for a special prayer,
and give him thanks for being there.

Thanksgiving means a lot to me,
for I know that I am finally free.
When He died on the Cross at Calvary,
He took the blame and set me free.

Jerry Anne Bickell

The Bridge

A quiet place where I could go to sit and think.
To get away from my parents and their world.
The responsibilities given to me.
This is my place.

A short walk from home along a gravel road.
Down the slope of a steep ditch and under the bridge.
They never knew where I went. They never even asked.
They wouldn't understand why I went there.
I did it for me.

I hear the cars pass over me,
As we pass by the little things around us every day.
The drivers never knew I was there.

Down there I could relax, I could dream, I could cry.

Last year they tore my bridge out and replaced it with
Concrete and steel.
With it, they tore out a part of me.

Craig Lytle

The Journey's Man

No choice, without decision
To find the way, to cautiously envision
Travel straight and narrow with blurred vision.
A thousand dead stones a thousand souls have risen.

Walk down predestined darkened corridors
Unsure laughter and wicked whores
Where to go or where to be led
Chapters of our life something unseen said.

I've seen this place, replaced by much haste
Not the free wild times, surely the smoke was laced?
Frivolous memories can't hold the same, sigh for the waste
So soon, so real, what is it here?
With what am I faced?

I know you don't see through the eyes which I look
Slip silently now, ancient lay, my salvation it took
Come unaware secret thief
Breathe so freely now, a tree a leaf.

Chris Korth

My Peaceful Valley

For years I've searched the world over
To find a place like the picture in my mind.
I've named this place "My peaceful valley."
And that is where I want to spend the rest of my time.

Do you know the way to my peaceful valley
A place where all troubles will stay away
Oh, how I've searched for that valley
Surely I'll find it someday.

The years have passed by so quickly
All pleasures of life have ended in tears
My last hope is of finding my peaceful valley
And there spending my final years.

Age has over taken my old body.
The picture of my valley is so cloudy in my mind
There is no more hope that I'll every find my peaceful valley
Because for me I've ran out of searching time.

If by chance someone should find my valley
This is my last request
"Please tell others of the peaceful valley"
So that they may enjoy that peaceful rest.

James R. Pinckard

To Be Or Not To Be

I was working very hard to be more careful
To eliminate "to be" verbs, just for you.
'Till my fingers took a cramp
Willie Mouse yelled, "Let me nap!"
And Thesaurus was a'groanin': With the flu?

I found another note, then, you had written—
I start with "I" too much, please leave "I" out.
Was I ever going to be
Astute enough to see
How to be a better writer??? I had doubt.

But now that I've completed all the rewrites,
Of the rewrites that I wrote for this great class
There is much that I have learned—
And your salary you sure earned!
If I don't deserve an A, just let me pass.

Julaine B. Kern

Wish He Was Mine

Wish he was mine, to love and caress.
   To dance with and touch, to nightly undress.
Wish he was mine, to have and to hold.
   To laugh and to cry, to slowly grow old.
Wish he was mine, in good times and bad.
   His ex doesn't know, what a good man she had.
Wish he was mine, to be held in those arms.
   To see his smile daily, z'only part of his charm.
Wish he was mine, would loved to be kissed.
   If I couldn't see him, would sorely be missed.
Wish he was mine, but he doesn't know it.
   I have a hard time, and no way to show it.

Becky Lou Hanson

Time

Tick-tock goes the clock, never ceasing
To clutch each second into its firm grip.
Tick-tock goes the time, once caught never releasing
Its hold on things past, never returning a snip.

Whether it be tick-tock—boing, blip or cuckoo
Clocks are greedy, heartless, uncaring inventions.
Time doesn't care what it swallows up or who;
To release any part it has no intention.

If we destroyed all man-made time
And cast all calendars into the fire,
And had no sense of rhythm or rhyme;
Do you think some past we could hire?

Once ticked, it's gone, once tocked, it's dead.
One little second at a time does fly.
If in this world there were no time to dread,
No days, weeks, months, or years — how would we get by?

If time disappeared, would we grow old?
If no one heard, would it do away with sound?
If ages and noise left, would the earth fold,
Or would everything just go round and round?

Giula S. Wiggs

"Waiting For You"

Tonight I sit waiting for you
To build one heart made for two
This precious gift we call love
Is so often taken advantage of
But someday time will stand still
And we no longer will trudge uphill
Peace and harmony walk hand in hand
And love and meaning meet demand
We are so blind to not see change
When we both see nothing staying the same
We find ourselves being so involved
In a misrepresentation that some call love
Time is so valuable in this life we live
Yet we give no direction to our efforts still
If elation and content is for what we strive
Then the sooner it will come as we look inside
We know from past that we have only ahead
But contrast our feelings and change instead
Tonight I sit waiting for you
To build one life composed of two

Chris Jacobs

An Ode To A Wet Christmas In July

The world is much bigger so I need a head start
to beat out Toys R Us and K-Mart.

My nose is all red from a late summer cold
(But a new box of Kleenex will help, I am told).

I'm wet and I'm soggy and my suit won't stay dry.
The reindeer are mad and say they won't fly.

I rushed to the airport and there I was told
that because of the weather the planes were on hold.

To find other transport, I phoned around town
But after one phone call, the lines were all down.

I'll need an Arc for a sled in this awful rain.
I knew dealing with Noah would be a real pain.

Renting the arc came with one major hitch.
A one-of-a-kind rental with one little glitch...

I could take the Arc, but with all of it's freight.
I couldn't say no, it was really too late.

Noah and the Mrs. were dancing with glee.
They now had a sitter and I'm afraid it was me.

Merry Christmas in July and to all a dry day.
But I hope you have shovels and plenty of hay.

Gloria Barltrop

My Son

I look at my son and what do I see? He is supposed
to be an image of me...and yet he is not like me,
he's different, he's special you see.

My son is retarded, anyone can see, and yet he has
something I can never have. If only I could get
inside his head to see what he sees, to hear what
he hears, to feel what he feels, then maybe, just
maybe, I could accept and love so unconditionally
the way he does. My son, Tom, is so special to me.

Donald L. Balsley Sr.

"Awakening"

Awaken to the dawn of morning,
To another day of dismal forlorning;
Try to put on a cheerful face,
For this is truly a wondrous place.

This is a land of freedom and splendor,
Which not even war or hatred can render;
A place where courage for believing can save,
A home for the restless hearts and the brave.

Open your eyes and see the truth,
Live out your life and your fulfilling youth;
For there is a yearning to be good in you,
A blessing so great that you shouldn't be blue.

Go, be daring and live out your destiny,
And life will reward you with bounty and plenty;
Listen to the bells in your mind that ring,
For you never know what another day might bring.

Catherine Cone

"The Glory Is God's"

God created the heavens and the earth,
To all creatures he did give birth,
He made man with a mind to choose,
Whether heaven to gain or loose.
The beautiful snowcapped mountains high,
The ocean wide and the bright blue sky.
To mankind he has truly blessed,
Peace, happiness and all the rest.
His yoke is easy, his burden light,
But to be pleasing, you must live right.
God made man with different colored skin,
To praise one more than others, would be sin.
Whatever your color, it don't mean a thing,
It's what in your heart, joy will bring.
Don't blame God for your aches and pains,
Ask God for strength, and you will sustain.
Ability, not disability is what counts in life,
We all have our struggle and strife.
Give God the glory for the good you have done
Remember Christ died on the cross for everyone.

Crystal L. Jackson

"My Neighbor"

My neighbor's name is Sonny, and he bought an arctic cat
Tis a sassy little bugger, and it travels just like a scat.
He travels on the icy lake at sixty miles per hour
there's very few that pass him, until the plugs go sour.

He is a little heavy in the rear, as he's riding on this thing
but all goes very wonderful until he breaks a spring.
He goes roaring down the old back roads and up the snowy trail
the most that one can see of him is his kitty's old black tail.

It seems he liked this cat so well, that he bought wife Bert one too
where you used to see one kitty, you will probably see two.
Now Bert has her problems too, as you can plainly see
while riding on her pussycat she ran into a tree.
The bumpers sprung, the cowl is broken, the skis are badly bent
she sees when riding snowmobiles cost dollars and some sense.

While all these things have happened to my good friends next door
the arctic cat's still running and they will for evermore.
These cats will carry Bert and Sonny all through the winter snow
up and down the trails and where they want to go.

Tis nice to have their friendship, as one can plainly see
for anyone with eyes at all, know they ride with Doug and Me.

Don Sharp

October Tears

October tears fall early this year.
Time has eased our pain.
When the Lord called her away,
Our loss was Heaven's gain.

She was small in statue but mighty in wisdom.
There when needed, silent when not.
Her greatest love was her family.
Of this we're all aware.

Her mind was not on death that day
as they wheeled her away.
I leaned to kiss her and whispered, "I love you."
With a loving smile and a shake of her finger,
She didn't say good-bye.

Take care of your daddy was her last commanding wish.
I knew, that mom was soon to die.
October tears fall early this year.
Time has eased our pain.
When the Lord called her away,
Our loss was Heaven's gain.

Jo Ann Vennebush

"Looking Back"

Laughing and twirling all around,
till my dress came far from the ground.
Running through the fields of wheat,
remembering the cool breeze beneath my feet.
My little pink dress so full of lace,
perfectly matched my angel-like face.
All those picnics were so much fun,
flying my kite under the hot, bright sun.
Swinging high under the big oak tree,
trying to reach my toes to the leaves.
I followed the colors of beautiful rainbows,
hoping to find that huge pot of gold.
My eyes were like diamonds, glittering off my face,
The sparkle of heaven, had once more taken its place.
Those joyous memories, run through my mind,
only to realize its been a long time.
Oh, How I wish to go back there,
so free and happy without a care.
Being a child you have a lot of dreams,
and most of all of them you truly believe.

Anna Oberst

Ten Second Setback

While cleaning the bathroom, there,
tightly fastened to the drain,
was a solitary black hair.
Yours.

Like a Phoenix,
ephemeral visage, there you were...
standing beneath the shower's cascades,
facing me, arching back,
fingers and shampoo filtering through midnight waves,
Ireland's eyes and supple mouth in silent prayer,
rivulets traversing down your neck,
wrapping around your breasts and over your belly,
stealing down between slender thighs and calves,
across the arch and disappearing into chrome and tile.

Somehow, a solitary black hair has managed
to fasten itself and has hidden, until this morning.

Wresting it from security,
I washed it away with disinfecting suds.

I wish my memory of you was so easily dismissed.

Alexander W. Steel

The Heart Asks More

The heart asks more than life or love can give.
Thus pain is born to fill the space between
What is and what is yearned for. I should live
Somewhere outside the heart upon a mean
Unflowered field where music makes no sound,
Where no bird sweetly sings to cut my heart,
And no breeze gently brings its arms around
My lonely self. I play the foolish part
Of lover, struggling in a web as prey
Yet freer than the one who will not dare
Urge life and love above their common way,
And thus evolve the "more" the heart holds rare.
The seeking heart will fill with pain
While meeker lovers wanting will remain.

Anne Firth Murray

Lord

I think of my life as a rose and you are my stem.
Throughout my life I have lost many
petals from wilting or just plain falling.
But somehow you, my stem, always stands strong
and provides the nurturing needed for survival.
It seems in my most desperate time for strength
either you sprout a new bud or you revive what is
left of my wilting petals to form a more
beautiful, stronger, blooming rose. And in the
happiest moments of my life you are there. For
you have delivered the nutrients of love to me
so I can open my life to others and let them
know that they too, have a stem.

Heather Champlin

Silence

Through the silence no one heard her cries,
Through the silence no one knows she died.

But the pain still flows deep inside,
and yes the tears fill up her eyes.

Then he comes back for more.
The evilness is ignored.

Someday she will not fear the voice of someone so near,
As he whispers something in her ear.

And tells her not to fear because daddy is here,
As she tried to push him away he ties her to a crate.

As she looks up at his face, he shows a face of hate.

Jeff L. Goodwin Jr.

Hope

After the storm the sky cries out
Through shapeless forms and formless shapes.
With tones of gloom berimmed with light.
It cries of life - of love - of hope.
Its colors show my way.
They're not the red, red, red of love and war
But the rosy tint of peace and solitude.
"No more on earth," it seems to say,
"Can man find life and love.
Oh, look to me for I am hope,
The only hope for life."
I look upward now and feel within
The peace that settles down,
For all around and outward from my view
Is only ravaged man.
And over there midst clouds of black
A circle hueless - vast,
A bottomless abyss that rises to the sky
To reach the rosy cleaner air of life —
Of love - of hope.

Barbara Reichel

Untitled

MOIRA......................Everymind,
Through introspection and knowledge of the world,
Sorts out that which protects itself from discomfort,
Placing these jewels of thought in the innermost
Recesses of its private lair...much as a lioness
Settling down her cubs in a cozy nest.

As sometimes happens, we may meet kindred souls
Along the way who laugh at danger after our fashion,
Or paint the colors of our own rainbows,
So we add them to the treasures of our restful minds
In wonder, love and gratitude.

George T. McWhorter

Untitled

Thoughts of you run thru my mind,
thoughts of more joyous and happier times.
Over the years your devotion has dwindled,
your passion has died.
Love that was once genuine and true
is now tainted with heartless and hateful words
Cold winds have long ago extinguished the flames.
This loneliness I feel breaks my heart.
And I long for the days when you and I were one.
When hostility was not part of our world,
only fiery kisses, tender caresses and kind words.
I realize now that our relationship
will never see that beautiful love again.
So I ease the pain of reality
with thoughts of more joyous and happier times.

Heather Casdorph

Friendship

Friendship is a state of mind
   Thoughtful, merciful and very kind
It is not measured by the hour
   Rather by its staying power

Friendship to us is never free
   Most often bought down on your knee
Tho you have money, you cannot buy
   There is no need for you to try

Friendship, my kind is tried and true
   Give me a chance I'll share it with you
Hard work will always make it pay
   Giving of yourself day after day

Friendship is good and always right
   It doesn't matter if you're black or white
It's not an order that you can heed
   It's not a word or offered deed

Friendship, you say, it cannot be
   We are different colors, don't you see
God our creator, I'm sure he knows
   We are created equal in different clothes

George C. Parker

City Pain

This pain is killing me making me cry;
though the drugs keep selling, there's still drive-bys
Helicopters circling; should I go inside?
False alarm; it wasn't close by.
Why is the pain still stuck in my head?
The pain hurts so bad I'd rather be dead.
I wish those bad memories would just disappear,
the memories that cause all of my fears.
I moved away but the memories came back;
I wish I could put them all in a sack.
I don't feel sorry for those who are dead,
I just think it could have been me instead.

Candice Chavez

Golden Windows

My little girl craves windows of gold,
   To her that would be ideal.
Each morning she looks at our neighbor's house
   And thinks that the gold is real.

We came home last night as the sun went down
   From this neighbor's on the West,
And what was her surprise to find
   Her own windows as gold as the rest.

Dorothy Kelley

She's Ours

God gave us this child to raise as our own.
Though problems we know there would be;
To raise this child is like a raising our own.
To watch her grow and learn,
And to show that life's no picnic where children are concerned.
She hurts, she cries, there are tears of joy,
Her laughter, her smiles, the look of concern,
To watch, to listen, to praise "Well Done!" and go on.
To teach what life's all about,
The years go by so fast,
But we know this child we raised is really our own.
You see we raised her - from baby 'til now.
She came to us long time ago;
Her father and I could ask for no more.
You see God gave us this child to raise as our own.
   Helen D. Hoehn

Untitled

The angels came to see me today
Though it's not time for me to go away.
The beauty of their appearance stays with me
And what they tried to tell me, I just can't see.
I told them how weary I had become
But my life's journey is just not done.
Could they understand all my pain, I asked?
Yes, they could and at times it was like
   a hard driven rain.
Don't give up they said, and the sun will soon shine.
An internal, eternal peace would soon be mine.
I saw my loved ones who had already departed;
They all sang, danced, and had praises from their hearts.
Be patient, for some day all things will be revealed to me.
Just don't lose my faith, they said, and all things will come to be.
Make sure everything in my life is right
For the end is not for from sight.
   Cathy Anne Bales Wilder

Weeds

Moving, sitting staring at a synonym for what I think is an hour,
though it may be different, waiting to see if what I get
in return is anything like want, what I got.

Hoping, craving some remorse from this torment
that I have adopted to my own self
to be part of my history in writing my future.

Friend, wanting what I can never have,
that it may come someday and I will not be
anywhere to receive what I wish,
only out to be looking for some other.

Father, one that I never knew.
I am of your flesh and share yourself,
bound in pain and fear of discovery,
you are me, I am you, why?

" 'Tis a difficult road we tread,"
we rest when we can and hunger for more,
never remembering that it was never enough to
sustain for even a short time.
In the field we let grow weeds.
   James Wantz

Best Friends

BEST FRIENDS are those that are together day by day.
Those that always listen to what the other has to say.

BEST FRIENDS are those that will always be there.
Those that will always love you and always care.

BEST FRIENDS are those that share the good times and bad,
Those that everyone really wish they had.

BEST FRIENDS are those that are loving,
Those that are caring and forgiving.

There will be times when there will be a doubt,
But they always tend no work things out.

BEST FRIENDS are those that are true from the heart.
They always feel close to matter how far apart.

BEST FRIENDS will never forget the day they met.
Those special memories they will never forget.

BEST FRIENDS are those that always understand you,
Those that stand by your side in whatever you do.

BEST FRIENDS are forever and they always will be.
BEST FRIENDS are those like you and me.
   Francis G. Lopez

Feelings

Passion, Love, Romance
Those of which can wash away the pain
Pain that inflicts the deepest scar
The scarring of the heart
Depression, Loneliness, Frustration, Heartache
The grief, the sorrow it brings
I sit there thinking
Thinking of better times
Times when I was happy
Times when I was grateful
As I sit here all alone
I will sit alone every time
It's like I'm shut out
I am being shut out by the cold world
Burned and rejected by the world
No, it's not Happening
Not to me, I can't hear what you say
Not when I don't want to hear it
I will block it out, Then it will go away
It's not leaving, why isn't gone?
   Cassondra Jane Blackburn

Today I Am A Bride

Today I am a bride.
Those around me, fixed in envious stare
see not beyond the trembling lips, the veil,
nor beyond the flowers in my hair.
I was promised as a child and now must wed
this stranger in the shadows there,
and share, obediently, unwillingly, the marriage bed.
If I could but dance and sing and smile
and dare to dream,
if only for a little while.
I'll not release this flood of tears filling me inside.
Let others celebrate,
while I pretend;
for today I am a bride.
   Connie Hess

"Pain"

My silent sorrow looks in this place,
This motionless picture that used to have a face
Now nothing more than a place to roam
This desolate land I once called "home"

This shallow grave I stand before
That no one looks at anymore

I've tried to say that it's alright
But still I know I'm lying
Without a bark it tends to bite and leaves me slowly dying

I walked through millions of centuries searching for my lost youth
It's poisoned with salt within rivers of blood, the downside to power and truth

And I look through a present picture now, so silent and discrete
the darkened winds that blow through life
help me stand alive with acceptance and be with thou'
Until my journey is complete

Stand with me here till the ends of time
Through light and through darkness always be mine
And keep this bond within thine heart
then the winds and us shall forever be apart...
Clay Herdman

Untitled

You're so indifferent to the regard I bestow on you.
This materialized in the course of our exchange.
I do not comprehend you and your impassive manner.
I'm led to be of the opinion that you fancied me,
But under present conditions, I am not so convinced.
Who are you?
Why make yourself known to me and then become aloof?
My emotions are not a pastime — they are genuine.
You have time for your avocation, but none for me.
We are nothing, as of yet, but nonetheless, you are in my reflections.
As I contemplate your character, a smile cannot help but emerge on my mouth.
Your gentle ways combined with your rugged demeanor,
Make you all the more alluring in my perception.
However, I yearn for you to manifest your feelings.
Reciprocate the sentiments I dispense to you.
All would not be lost on me.
In fact, I would be obliged in knowing.
I will continue to await your echo as long as needed...
You are worth every instant.
Cali Day

Rebirth

"Let the little children come to me"
This is the way the Good Book reads
"Man shall work by the sweat of his brow"
This is the way it was, do we change it now?

For this cycle of life to be complete
First man and woman need to meet
In sharing their love, a life they can return
This is what makes our Great World turn

I would like to live to see
The year of 1996 A.D.
And still thrill to the eternal joy
Of the tender love of girl and boy

Let's Hope by then men will have agreed
To let Faith and Love become their creed
That women will rejoice in giving birth
Leaving Charity to reign all over our earth
Anona Bourassa Walker

Life

Happiness is in the eye of the beholder,
This is for my dreams growing ever colder.

Trying to scorn my beauty folded,
Fitting me into a life molded,

Life and love not understood,
Hiding under my fragile hood,

My life is much worse than thee,
Floating with your heart so free,

Getting to love who you want,
Not wondering on the location of your next haunt,

Melodies and tunes fill my head,
Dragging my feet made of lead,

Like a bird in a cage,
Killing itself on bars with rage,

And as my life's blood seeps,
Through the cracks, ebbs and neaps,

It is then like the flowing tide,
Free to crash upon the sand's side,

Do not mean to catch you suddenly,
And keep your life for mine so sullenly.
Carla Sitterlet

The Grant Gift

We all are given a grand gift.
This gift may last a long time or it may last a short time.
In the end this gift wears out or does it?
This grand gift is called life and this gift seems to wear out the quickest to those who we love most.
This gift can last if you only remember the good times as well as bad.
These times that you have had with those who have died should be shared with those who have not known who you have lost.
So say you will never forget those simple moments.
Even if those moments were only one you should still keep and share them so that those who you have lost will live!
Promise those who you have lost to share those moments and lessons that you have learned with others so that they may live forever!
Carey Houtz

Unwanted Puppy

I sit in my cage filthy and wet
thinking of the people I've met,
  Few pats on the head mostly kicks
but every hand I tried to lick.

I'm so hungry and very cold
man's companion I've been told,
  All I wanted was someone to love
all I received were prods, kicks, and shoves.

I shiver and quake in total fear
my matted coat feels a tear,
  I look to heaven and a radiant face,
etched in sadness at the human race.

Some are loving but some so mean
abuse and cruelty is all I've seen,
  A loving hand erases the past

Thank God, I'm loved, loved at last.
Helen M. Ahern

The Cat Ladies Of Centre Street

I know two ladies you'll never want to meet,
They're the "cat ladies" of Centre Street!
They have cats here, and cats there,
They have cats almost everywhere!
Cleanliness is a virtue, but not to these two,
The baths they have taken are entirely too few!
They dress in clothing that's been sprayed by each pet,
An odor more foul has never been met!
Each day that I see these ladies, I pray to God above,
Please help their cats find homes where they will find love!
For most cats are creatures that are excessively clean,
And these ladies to their cats are being excessively mean!
Please Lord also help us to find,
A place to put these ladies that will give peace of mind!
Help them to know there is help from us all,
Preferably before the end of this fall!
We care for their welfare, and that of each pet,
They're an example of a situation we've never before met!
Please Lord hear our prayer, and give us some release,
In a way that will give us all some inner peace!

Allen P. Rothlisberg

Goodbye

A crowd had gathered where he stood, and sensing his deep pain
They sympathized that he was brokenhearted once again.
Their relationship seemed perfect with the love they two had shared,
But lately there was trouble, and at times her temper flared.
She had promised they could work it out; she just needed time and space,
And so she walked out through the door, determination on her face.
As he waved goodbye he wondered, while she drove into the night
When she'd be coming back to him to end this silly fight.
Now with grieving heart he promises his love will never end,
And just then he caught a sparkle from the diamond on her hand.
She had wanted him to have it back..."had no use for it now,"
But he refused...believing it would be all right somehow.
The circle draws in closer; all his friends have misty eyes,
For they knew how much he loved her, it was never in disguise.
So he bent his head and kissed her, the tears no longer hid...
He softly said his last goodbye, and gently closed the lid.

Alison R. French

Hear The Children Cry

Why can't you hear the children cry
They cry loud with their silent hurts.
No one ever really knows what it's like to not be heard
Until you have been a child who has been hurt silently, but cries loud, and yet no one hears.
The most devastating of all the wounds is the wounded heart,
Broken in some places, torn in others, ripped to shreds here and there and pierced in other areas.
Why can't you hear the children cry, their cry is so loud, that it doesn't make a loud noise.
Scars tell a story that a normal boo boo don't, burns have a stench that playing with fire did not cause, outburst of anger that a fight did not provoke, shyness that isn't given by nature, tears that weren't caused by a fall, slothfulness, not due to the lack of ability, and fear, not because of a horror movie. Why can't you hear the children cry. They cry loud with their silent hurts.

Etta M. Davis

If I Could/I Would

If I could turn back the hands of time
These are the things I would keep in mind

I would warn the people all over the earth
That the next generation may not have a birth

I would remind them how the dinosaurs died
And we could be the next if we don't try

To save our trees that we badly need
Because they give us the air we breathe

To keep the oceans and seas always clean
So all the waters can be visibly seen

And not overfish so they can multiple
Because they'll feed us numerous times

To look up in the sky and see the sun
And all the damage that we have done

The ozone layer that protects us all
Is being destroyed because of silly laws

So while we are here on this beautiful earth
Let's take these words for what it's worth

Brenda Spellman-Rock

Ode To Tax Season

Once more it is that time of year,
There's no more Joy and no more Cheer,
'Cause Uncle Sam dropped us a line,
With a form he's asking us to sign.

To Uncle Sam we don't wish to be cheap.
But most of our cash we'd like to keep,
It's so hard earned through blood and sweat,
And it's tough to stretch what little we get.

So find yourself a good C.P.A.
And listen to what he-she has to say,
If there's a way around it they will find,
But always of the legal kind.

Now, make your appointment A.S.A.P.
Nowhere to go? then come and see me,
We'll do our best to show you they way,
And make April 15th a happier day.

Cynthia Dumbleton

Untitled

When I dream, I'm scared at what I see.
There's no beauty, there's no peace, only death chasing after me.

I see guns, and crack dragons,
its wicked and nasty pain.

I cry for help, my eyes darken,
its blood that has begun to stain.

I leave my dream, entering this nightmare of fear.
I find no hope, I find no security, the meaning of life is unclear.

Where is the smile, the laughter,
the happiness of old?

Has anguish taken over,
the pain of life gotten so bold?

I want out of this terrifying pain, is the answer in death?
I have no answer, I have no gun, yet I feel the dark angel's breath.

David Cheloha

Birth Of A Snowflake

As the gray clouds of a winter storm gather in the sky,
There's expectation in the air of a snowstorm by-and-by.

A snowstorm brings the promise of loads of winter fun,
Building snowmen, snowball fights, and sledding will be done.

A snowstorm brings the chance to learn more about God's creation;
How snowflakes form inside the clouds by the process of "sublimation."

No two snowflakes look alike as they fall through the clouds.
They grow 'till gravity makes them fall, and moisture 'round them enshrouds.

Where single crystals join as they descend in such a storm,
They twirl and swirl, and blend and merge, until the snowflake's born.

Seven types of crystals can be seen as they float in the sky,
As they blend together they produce the snowflakes as they fly.

Early on a winter morn when a layer of mist hangs high,
These tiny crystals can be seen dancing and twinkling in the sky.

The storm is over, the snow is deep; a blanket of white shrouds the earth,
We enjoy the landscape's beauty and forget the snowflake's birth.

Colene White

A Little Boy

When the weather is beginning to turn windy and colder,
There's a flake of snow that lands softly on my shoulder.
I feel like singing and dancing for what reason I don't know,
But it is the feeling in the air and the spirit that people show.
When there are mistletoes and people start buying things to give,
And all the sadness and angers within you no longer live.
You'll feel like jumping and shouting for joy,
For it is a happy day, a jolly day, a birthday of A LITTLE BOY.
When the streets are covered with snow and full of glittering lights,
And no matter where you go love and peace linger in the night.
With the carolers are singing high and spreading the good news,
And the holiday performers are spinning across the stage with their dancing shoes.
People are passing, smiling and listening as the angels pray
That on a cold winter night - wisemen bring gifts to A LITTLE BOY born on Christmas day.

Ivan Dinh

A Friend Made Of Clay

If I had a friend that was made of clay
There'd be so many ways that we could play
He'd be what ever I wanted him to be
As small as a mouse or as tall as a tree

When I want to play sports, he'd be the ball
He'd be soft as putty or hard as a wall
He'd be any animal under the sun
Or change into a shield, a sword, or a gun

He could be anyone in a movie or book
When I get hungry he'd be the cook
I'd have a partner for video games
He'd guard me from bullies (I'm not naming names)

If I had a friend that was made of clay
There'd be so many ways that we could play
But if I had friend that was made of snow
The sun would come out and away he would go

E. M. Cox

In The Eyes Of A Child

When you look into the eyes of a child
There is so much there to see.
He is seeking the answer to the age old question,
"Do you think you could love me."

"Could you care if I'm cold and hungry,
With only rags to wear,
If I'm alone and frightened when dark time comes,
Are you the one who could care?"

"I won't always be little,
I'll be all grown up some day.
But if no-one can love me, now when I'm little
I will have forgotten the way."

These are questions you will have to answer,
For deep in your heart they are filed.
These are questions you cannot help but see,
In the seeking eyes of that child.

Alice M. Starrett

Always There

Through my times of rage and torment
There is only one who will stay by my side
One who will care whether I stay or go
And will love me no matter how bad things may get
There is only one who will remind me
Of the true roads to travel upon
To steer me away from the lies of Lucifer
No one could have as much compassion as He
He is with me every step of the way
To protect me and guide me
To the light of another day
There is no need to feel alone
Because if you look in your heart
And search in your mind
There will always be Jesus
Standing right behind.

Amber L. Giovinazzo

Puppy Love

I once had a puppy, I loved him I did.
There is nothing more special, than a puppy and a kid.
  We played all over, through the house we would race.
Having all kinds of fun, as we tore up the place.
  I've got in more trouble, than I have fingers and toes.
But staying in there with him, because that's the way love goes.
  And then one day, my happiness came to an end.
I looked out in the highway, and there laid my friend.
  It hurt me so bad, seeing him lying in the street.
Because an untimely death, my best friend did meet.
  I couldn't stop the water, that ran from my eye.
As I said to my mother, I'm O.K., I'm not going to cry.
  I'd rather this happen, than again ever age.
Because I just couldn't see, my puppy locked in a cage.
  This was my first time, with the experience of love.
But I know my little puppy, looks down from above.

Douglas Pettiford

Winter

  As the icy winds rustle through
the trees. Birds flee. Winter is coming
now or never. Bears hibernate. There is a
chill in the air. Snow starts to fall.
Days get shorter. Night get longer. Winter
is coming; there's no stopping it.

Jennipher Fullerton

Untitled

To my dearest Family
There is no document that can make a man a servant of God,
Nor can whatever enter man's mouth damn his soul in sin.
But to worship the son of God, our brother Jesus Christ,
Shall determine the worth of our soul, thru the spirit that dwells within.
We must walk the narrow path, never stumble nor be led astray,
We must put our faith in Jesus as we journey thru this life, as tho
Jesus came, and looked us over yesterday.
I may not be able to get down on my knees, as some people think I
should, nor speak in tongues to save my soul,
But as long as I worship Jesus every moment and be good, I know my
name will be spelled right, when it's added to the SACRED SCROLL.
James E. Daniels

What Does It Take?

What does it take to be a poet?
There is no answer, yet I might know it.
Frown when you're happy, smile when you're sad.
Laugh when you're angry, cry when you're glad.
You must see the world from all sides.
Look at and peer into other people's lives.
Feel sorrow in you soul, love in you heart.
Hear music in your head, and act the right part.
To a poet life can be boring and lame
Or be a fun and challenging game.
But I am not sure, this may not be right.
Poets are people whose imagination takes flight.
So stop asking questions, go grab a pen!
Sit on the sofa or lie in the den!
The words will come, as easy as pie.
To be a poet, you only have to try.
Julia M. Schwab

"The Friend"

It is just amazing that amidst the strife and woe,
There is comfort never ending from the one who loves us so.

Why we spend our time in anguish, when he is waiting for our call,
Why we go through life so stricken, makes no sense to me at all.

There is peace without ending, there is joy to replace pain,
There is happiness and comfort, there is sunshine to dry the rain.

Yet we wander through our lifetime thinking we can make it all alone,
Thinking we are ever powerful, we can manage on our own.

When all we have to do is ask, and he will happily reply,
He will comfort and protect us, and dry the tears from our eyes.

How can we disregard this special friend who knows each step we've
trod?
You know his name, for he's always around, his friends all call him...
God.
Judy Turner Beard

Paris

As we are sitting in our tour bus
There's a young man sitting in front of us
His companions and all else he regales
With remembrances of his first trip, (Parisian tales)
We listened as if to a travel guide,
Thrilled, enthused continued our ride...
To the Eiffel Tower, over the Seine and to the place we stayed
Back and forth each day a trip to the Louvre we made,
We would cross over the Seine from the left bank
Proving us to be art lovers of the first rank!
When I think of Paris; it's pictures painted, pictures to besigned,
And the bus tour comes to mind.
Alice L. Lawrence

Untitled

Life a precious gift, presented with certain reservations
there are no guarantees, of any great expectations

The game is afoot, the play is continuous
with elements of chance. The only force indigenous

You play the cards, that fate has dealt
and win a few. And exultation is felt

Then at another time, you surely will lose
the game goes on, and you must choose

To stay the course, and come what may
to win or lose. You still must play

When the game closes, you did your best
with fortitude and courage, you met every test

And playing the game, and you never faltered
the score is tallied. It cannot be altered

The next game begins, you know not where
all things being equal, you will be there

Every ending a beginning, of a new game
the field is different, the play the same

And so it is, nothing is ever discarded
a variety of existence, each soul is awarded
Ira Gay Sealy

If Only You Could See

If only you could see through my eyes
Then you would see all of the beauty that I see in you,
If only you could see how much you've touched my heart
Then you would know that you've reached down to my very soul;

If only you could see what I see so clearly
I wish I could put into words why I love you so dearly,
If only you could see my thoughts that are always about you
You are the dream come true and allow me to believe in forever,

If only you could see the love we already possess
I no longer feel the pain of my past, or the emptiness,
If only you could see that it is you that I desire
You allowed me to love again and I will always remember;

If only you could see that I come to you with a naked heart
I bare my soul to you now as I have from the very start,
If only you could see you mean the world to me
I would gladly share with you all that I am and have for eternity;

If only you could see through my eyes
You are all that is good and all that is right with my life,
If only you could see me as I see you
If only you could see;
David Alan Robinson

Ashley Love Of My Life

She was so precious, asleep in her crib,
Then later so cute, with food on her bib,
So independent when she learned to walk,
Spurting words clearly, when she learned to talk.

In school she blossomed, came into her own,
Learning and sharing things unknown,
I feel blessed to have had her these years,
Loving and caring for her through laughter and tears.

Through all these changes, I have watched her grow,
Now comes the hardest part, I must let her go.
Ann Hurley

Fat Is Out And Thin Is In

I eat and eat and eat some more.
Then I'll throw it up like I did before.

I'll flush it away. It'll all disappear,
but I see a crying face in the mirror.

I'll make sure I hide it really good
and start eating right like I know I should.

Or maybe I'll just not eat again;
You know fat is out and thin is in.

I lost some fat, so close to a goal,
but soon all my work will take its toll.

I get really grumpy, a real b*t*h,
and all my friends I want to ditch.

I'll hide in my room and hear my heart beat,
or just lie in bed and have dreams sweet.

But then I can't cause people will suspect
that it's my body that I neglect.

I don't know when it started or how it did begin;
All I know is fat is out and thin is in.

Debra Burdick

One Solitary Night

I awoke with the sun as it shone on my face,
then I looked at the sand and thought, 'What a place.'
Gently did the waves come and lap at the sand,
and as gently did I reach out and take your hand.
I looked down at you, fast asleep by my side,
and listened to music played for us by the tide.
Now a flock of sea gulls have joined in our song,
I only wish it could last all the day long.
But the sun rises higher with each beat of the heart,
and though I don't want to, I know we'll soon part.
For one solitary night you belonged to me,
you lifted me up and set me free.
Now one small memory may I keep,
and when I think of you, I'll try not to weep.
I just want to say thank you, for my dream came true,
for one solitary night, you let me love you.

Deborah Davern

Reflections

I woke in the early morning and heard the sweet song of birds.
Their tune was clear and pleasant, no thought or need for words.
The message came so clearly I paused to smile and pray,
"Thanks, God, for the gift of hearing.
Let me hear good things today."

I labored all day without ceasing, so much for hands to do.
The whole house needed scrubbing, and I must get a meal or two.
I was tired as I went to my bedroom to settle in for the night,
But I thought of the day and its blessings,
"Thanks, God, for the gift of sight."

So much of the time I keep busy without thinking a how or a why.
I take all too much for granted; the use of an ear or an eye.
When I hear the cry of a baby, or look up at a bird in the sky
It is best that I pause to consider,
"Some folks aren't as lucky as I."

Hazel F. Hickson

My Little Jewish Elf

There is a place where there the Irish play
their music with the Scots
And...sings, and...dances a young Indian child girls voice,
As I make my vows to a Jewish elf;
And so because he loves all things, especially me..
That's why he gave me his heart,
Something more precious than gold or even a leaf;
Of course the fairies were jealous...
but not of me...but of their own souls
And never do they worry...but always
do they laugh. Why? For the way the sun hits their nose;
What did you say? The sounds. They the
sounds, lift me from my toes
As I carry my elf with me in the sky in the snows;
And the clouds around...They may never
carry me nor my beloved elf
And though I've been told they don't
I think I hear a sound...
"My love, where does the wind come from?"
"I don't know."

Janice Berry

Friends

Growing up together, you're invisible to the world.
Their lives can be stolen, as can a precious pearl.
Although we cannot predict what the future holds
Things may happen that seem cold.
We love them, yet we cannot say goodbye.
Taken away before their lives were lived, in silence we cry.
Unknowing of where they have gone,
Remembering them as beautiful as a love song.
Even though they're not here in body, they're here in mind.
Friends like them are hard to find.
Jackie, Jamie, Ed and Greg, we'll miss you so.
In your absence, our love for you grows.
Heaven is beautiful and peaceful, you'll see.
When it's my turn, I hope you'll be there to guide me.

Colleen Martin

Upside Down 60'S

The 90's are the upside down 60's
The world has gone crazy - violent - and there is little love......
Random acts of senseless shooting are on every street
A woman is battered every 15 seconds in our land
A MILLION MAN MARCH happens in Washington, D.C.
HATRED, FEAR, AND PERSONAL SECURITY ARE FLEEING
Remember the time when LOVE AND PEACE WERE EVERYWHERE
Young people gathered on street corners with flowers in their hair
Brotherly love for all mankind abound
MARTIN LUTHER KING, JR. lead the civil rights movement to
our nation's capitol
FREE LOVE, HAPPINESS, AND HARMONY WITH MOTHER
EARTH LIVED
WHERE HAVE ALL THE FLOWERS GONE?
WHERE ARE PEACE-LOVING HIPPIES OF YESTERDAY?
Let's turn the 90's back around to a gentler time
We need compassion, understanding, and
cultural awareness of each other today
Pray for PEACE—Pray for LOVING CONCERN—pray for HOPE

Cindy Lowry

The Woman In The Mirror

I looked into the mirror, and I was shocked to see,
The woman was my mother, looking back at me.

It took me back in time to days when I was young and free,
And the Woman in the Mirror was taking care of me.

With a patient hand she'd try to guide to keep me out of strife,
For I was much to eager then to get a taste of life.

"Oh, Mother," I would say to her, "You cannot understand!"
"All the other girls are, please, let me go as planned!"

It seemed unfair and cold that God had given me,
A mother that was stupid and unable to perceive.

But now that I am older, I can see that she was right,
And she has grown much wiser; I never thought she might!

Today I think I'll call and say that she has grown much dearer,
And ask her if she knows about the Woman in the Mirror.

Aleta L. Richardson

Tin Men Dancing

Listen.
The wind chimes sprinkle sound
so softly in the distance,
in the slow stagger of a breeze.
A calm, slothful air drifts on benign barges of humidity.
And carried within that slight and heavy movement,
the song of a thin metal ever so briefly
embracing its partner.
They bend and sway and touch:
A waltz not a battle—just
Tin men dancing on a gentle wind.

Look.
A bird, a dark blur that fades into a crescent
of a swallow wheeling and dipping
past my head, my eyes, making me duck and smile
at the early morning foolishness of thinking, just for that instant,
a creature of such agility and grace
would actually, clumsily, bestow on me a feathered brush,
a touch, a silky connection
of a swallow and a man in the just-light morning.

Dan Yarbrough

Darkness

The darkness is angelic.
The way it holds me to it,
lies to me to keep me near.

Yes, I know the darkness cares.
Protects me from the searing light of the sun,
whispers stories of eternity in my ear.

The darkness is soft.
It's cloak is dream woven,
Keeps the demons at bay.

Yes, I know the truth behind the darkness.
Only the truth never seems to matter,
as it enshrouds me where I lay.

I know the darkness is me.
My own personal everlasting night,
to hold me close,
after I've finished pretending everyone thinks I'm alright.

Allison Pope

"A Moment"

As I stare out the window I watch the sky
The trees move yet I sit still
I think of my life and what has happened
You came into my life and I started to change
It is such a good feeling to have something to live for
I have no reason to cry anymore
Just a reason to smile
Thanks to you I can live again
Now the sun is shining and so am I
All because of you.

Julie Wright Weintraub

My Shattered Mirror

I walk blindly in the darkness as rain drips from my eyebrows.
The trees branches crackle around me in the night air.
Lightning serves as my only hand of guidance.

My blood boils rapidly I begin to run
Its fury chases me
I feel its presence growing behind me
I run faster, afraid to look over my shoulder
I'm almost out breath as my feet pound the gravel below
Frightened as its terror fills my body, I turn and face it
My frown is its snarling grin and my misery is held by its never
   ending grip
Fear stares me in the eye

From the clouds above, bravery strikes my will
Strength arises inside me
Through piercing eyes, courage looks back and confronts it
I stand tall, shoulders broad
My first step toward uncertainty shatters the will of fear in front of me

The rain stops and the clouds blow away
My sun peeks over the mountains as flowers smile on the hillside
Lightning of will struck the fears inside me

Bruce L. Sanders Jr.

Twisted Oklahoma Epitaphs

"My home, my home," I raged and thickened my grip, tears treading
   the tar.
                              ME

To their last chair, scheming and bare, with pointed stares,
   their eyes bulged, soaking their hair.
                              BOMBERS

Communist-stricken blood-letting slipped across stale screens and
   magazines.
                              MEDIA

Nuclear scalpings and glass arrows sliced the sixth, sick
   civilized tribe.
                              AMERICA

The Plains techno-skirmish sided decidedly with the tied-hand
   white-man.
                              HUMANITY

The sly-eyed serpent stamped into their scooped eyes, and so
   sickened, sent them cloudless and down south.
                              PLANET EARTH

Elizabeth Barb

Chat With An Angel

For a great many days
the soft grays ghosts of my soul
have been roaming your body
searching for a weaker seam
to let me in and see from your eyes.
My body always asking "Will you maybe love me?"

You have been touching my nakedness
with gloved fingers
withholding the answers I've been looking for
while I hoped with every ounce that one day
you would lay aside your fears and let me crawl inside you.

I stand before you boldly focusing all the strength within me
on showing you who I am telling you what I am looking for
hoping that you want to see and praying for a guardian angel
to stretch protective wings over our heads
and allow us to open to each other
like the small fists of sleeping children.
    Diana Juhasz

Untitled

The touch of a tiny hand
The smile on a little face.
A little heart pounding fierce
Hair as soft as silken lace
A giggle that brings you joy
A little bump that needs a kiss
A first to be remembered
A moment not to miss;

To have a child is the greatest gift that you
  could ever receive
Someone who loves you unconditionally more
  than you can believe
They bring you joy, happiness, and as they
  get older some pain
But to hurt a child is the deepest wound
  that always will remain;
Return the love twice over and always try to understand
A child may not always be perfect, but they are gift
  so blessed and grand.
    Anita Johnson

The Snow

The moon has gone down and the sun does not show its face.
The sky has turned blue and hazy gray.
The white flakes scatter randomly, seeking refuse from the wind.
Each flake falls silently to the earth as it gives one last sparkle.
The tree branches reach out in a gentle motherly way to save a few flakes.

On the ground and on the trees the flakes die,
never again to fly about carefree.
They are heard giving their last breath of life as the crowd walks
by them and on top of them.
Didn't you ever wonder why snow made a noise when you
walked upon it?

When warmer weather comes,
all the flakes are melted,
and just like the caterpillar,
it lives again only transformed.
    Cheryl Lynn Cleland Haralson

"Myself"

In my room of old books and old places
The shelves of pictures family of all faces
My trunk packed with memories to share
With those who one day will care
In my room is a part of me in all traces
Going through my life in all spaces
This is my worldly shelter to mediate
Where my mind of past and future concentrate.

In my room whatever I leave behind
I am sure a clue to my life they will find
For I hold no secrets of heart
From those who had a very large part.

Another year
A laugh - a tear
It can only get better
As I write this letter.
    Dorothy I. Brown

"Evening Skies"

I love to sit by the lake at night,
The setting sun is such a delight.

I've done this many times before,
The brilliant colors, I just adore.

The heat of day has passed me by,
Soon the moon will rise in the darkened sky.

The gold reflecting path on the waters calm,
Shows me the way of the westward bound sun.

I sometimes want to follow that path,
In hopes this day will never pass.

When the background, tree shadows begin to darken,
The whip-poor-will call, soon will harken.

As the last glimpse of day slips slowly away,
I have my thoughts, but what can I say.

Night is upon me, for now it's a fact,
The sunset is gone, I can't bring it back.

One last pause, to cherish the day,
I have no control, I know it's God's way.
    Derk J. Vander Yacht

Friend?

Even though the tempest rage, blowing like the winds of hell
The sands of time abrase my flesh
Though the clouds of dread pass fervently overhead.
Resolute my faith stands in the LORD.
I offer myself up into His open and loving hands.
All life's perils pass meekly away.
Alas the clouds part revealing the light from above.
I cast my eyes about,
Behold GOD'S beauty manifested in nature's treasure trove.
The air crisp and clear fills my lungs.
Vibrantly life's blessings fill my soul.
This life a precious gift from GOD above.
How precious and fleeting the time here on earth.
We've naught to do, but learn to love.
Why is it then, we can truly call, so few FRIEND?
    Gordon L. Bush

This Wonderful USA

When I stop to wonder - how great this country, the United States and
throughout I want to stand up and yell, scream and truly shout!

This wonderful country of 200 plus years old
Started with men and women who were truly brave and bold

We have the Constitution of this United States
That has allowed us to be a free spirit, with no enemy crossing our gates

3,000 miles from one border to the next
And the rest of the world knows our strength and shows its respect

Our president, congress, state, country, city, town government is the
best there could be
It's just one of the wonderful things within us that has allowed us to be free!

You could not find a government country that has opportunity knocking
at every door - and isn't big enough, you are free to go beyond these shores!

Why has God allowed this wonderful, magnificent country to survive 200 years?
I would imagine it's because taken a lot of blood, sweat and tears

People often ask why is it folks from all over the world want to live
in the USA its because of one human dignity that we allow,
 it's called freedom, I would say

Will we, the USA, last another 200 years as free as we are?
My guess is it's up to God, working through us,
to see if we will make it that far

This note of excitement about us the USA and the freedom
we hold so precious to our heart
Let us hope and pray that anyone who asks us if they can be like us,
we will have the ability and love to give them a start!

Gary Vochatzer

Bridges

There they stood, on opposite sides of the river,
Wondering what the other was thinking.
Curious if they would ever meet.

Slowly, brick by brick, and layer by layer a foundation is laid.

Each layer after, made with thought and care.
Till finally, the top layer is made from trust, hope, understanding, and love.

Now the two meet in the middle and admire what they have made.
Ever so slowly watching the not so understanding river, swiftly gnaw
and weaken a foundation that was thought to indestructible.

They struggled to patch the holes, but were unable to keep up with
odds that were against them.

They stopped fighting and returned to the river bank from whence they came.
And there they stood, on opposite sides of the river knowing what
the other was thinking,
And ready to try and build this bridge a little farther downstream.
Where the river doesn't run like lies off a snake's tongue.

Cynthia J. Stone

Sister

Life has brought us together
Time and space have sometimes separated us
Different experiences have brought us different perceptions
Similar experiences have brought us understanding.

Love connects us, and
The Spirit holds us together as ONE.

Let us honor the SPIRIT that binds us,
cherish the love that connects us,
and celebrate the relationship that
is uniquely our own!

Emily Austgen-Greeley

Let Go

If you really love someone
   you've got to learn to let go,
You've got to see they have a life
   of their own.

You can't hide them from the rain
   behind your raincoat,
You can't shield them from the pain.
Even though pain hurts you've got to
   let them go.

They have to challenge life
   they just have to see
How much they've got to learn,
   from you, from me.

You can shield them so much, and even so
One day you'll just have to let them go.

Jennifer Lagerstrom

Untitled

Loving you is so easy to do
you're the one that makes it so easy
when I'm with you
I want nothing else
you fill my life with laughter
and brighten up each day with joy
without you my life would be so empty
the days would seem so long
the months would go by so slow
loving you was so easy because
it was a two way thing
you loved me and I loved you
the times that we had
are forever with me
when your lips were on mine
it felt so good
I would want it to be that way forever
If I had another chance
I would never want it to end

Ana Zissu

Untitled

Whenever I need someone to talk to
You're right there to help me through
Sometimes I feel like giving up
And giving into my fears

When I think of someone special
You're the one who comes to mind
Knowing you understand me
More than anyone of our kind

The love I have for you
Grows and grows stronger every single day
There's not a day that goes by
When you're not on my mind

We try to be together
But our situation keeps us apart
Every time I see you
I long for your kind and tender touch

Together forever I do pray
Longing for our wedding day
Happy ever after that's the way it should be
For our love will last all eternity

Dorothea Helma Haupt

Sheet Of Music

Your body is a sheet of music,
your tempo is PP very soft,
your pulse moves like a d. (scato),
your kiss is like a soft note,
your hands are soft,
softer than words on a measure,
your body moves like a soft note
off the piano, I love every
line, every word, every measure,
every note, and every beat,
so let me play you, with love.

Angela Schutte

My Sweet Muneco

I remember your first touch,
Your lips being pressed onto mine.
I never knew I could feel so much,
During such a short time.

Looking into your eyes of brown,
I know what your thinking, without
You saying a sound.

I want you to know exactly what I feel.
How much I care, and that my love is real.

I want our love to continue to
grow stronger.
I want to hold you forever,
and much longer.

Jennifer Drain

"Baby"

You come into this world so innocently.
Your first cry, your first smile touch
my heart so deeply.
You rely on me for your every need.
You bring such joy to my life, so much
fulfillment to me.
I look into your eyes and see how
much love you have for me.
The love I return to you makes me whole.
There is no greater love than a Baby.

Gwendolyn Broussard

Again

If you cut corners in life,
you will end up where you started,
again, and again, again, and again.

If you cut corners in life,
life will bring you back from
where you once started,
again, and again, again, and again.

As life has it
you will lose everything
but everything that you think that
you don't have
again, and again, again, and again.

As life would have it
you will have more than you
would have bargained for,
again, and again, again, and again.
Again, is just one letter short of A gain.

George Miles

To Someone Who Is Still Pure...

For you is poem is written,
You, who unknow the sin,
You, who believe in love
As pure as you have been.

You, who still in your bosom
Keep the virginity pure,
And that is a great treasure
In this fragile and dangerous tour.

If someone tells you it is wrong
About the pureness that you keep,
Ignore those stupid things
And sing a beautiful song!

Keep the smile on your lips,
Keep your pureness in your heart,
Until the moment comes in...
And you can give all to him,
Everything you have kept in.

Javier Girarte

If I Were A Tree

Sitting by the window,
you think a lot of times,
of how it would be,
if I were a tree.

A bird sitting here,
some new leaves growing there,
oh how grand it would be,
If I were a tree.

Little children climbing up me,
squirrel's scurrying around me,
but this is just a dream,
for so it's not true,
cause if it were true,
you would be under me.

Carrie Vaughn

Golf Ball's Nightmare

You take me outta your pocket.
You set me on a tee,
you hit with your driver,
you knock the hell outta me.
I soar thru the air
as far as you can see.
I fall in the grass,
you start looking for me;
you hit me, you bruise me, you cut me deep,
you throw me in the junk pile
and there I'll forever sleep.

Derwood Sweaza

Truly A Teacher

You can be good and sweet and kind,
You can encourage the girl who is behind.
You can be the mother who isn't there.
You can teach the children how to share.
You can be wrong today and right tomorrow
Sometimes the world seems full of sorrow.
You can tell them God is always around;
For joys and sorrows always abound.
The years may come and the years may go,
But rewarding years come very slow.

Blanche Langdon

The Wind

There's something strange about the wind
  you never see its face.
Yet you feel it everywhere you turn
  you see it every place.
It whistles thru the trees at night
  its song so soft and low
And if you listen carefully
  a message will unfold.
It tells of places far away
  of people old and new.
It tells of people deep in love
  and yet, brings sadness too.
So when you feel the wind one day
  give an ear or two.
Listen for its message cause,
  it could be meant for you.

David A. Wright

Black Man

Black man
You looked so good at the
Million Man March

Black man
Black man
Take pride in who you are
For you must be all that
God created you to be.

Black man
Black man
Heal all old woes, move forward
Forgive all wrongs, move onward

Black man
Black man
Love your women
Raise strong black children
Love that strong black man
You see in the mirror
For guess what Black man God created that man!

Bessie Thomas Mahone

Ragdoll

Ragdoll,
You listened to my cries
Stayed by when I was ill,
You heard my temper fits
You heard my secrets and
Never told them,
You listened to my fantasies
And never laughed.

Ragdoll,
You have been my truest friend
Never complaining,
Never crying
We have shared the good times
With the bad times.

Ragdoll, I love you!

Bonita Whitmire

"You Left One"

You were a part of my life,
You have a place in my heart.
You made me laugh,
You never made me cry,
 till the day you left without
 a goodbye.
You meant so much to me,
You were so special to me.
And you will always hold
 a special place in my heart.

Becky Fry

My Friend Jean

Friendship is like a sunbeam,
You feel its warmth when you're cold,
And admire its beauty as it filters
Down through the tree tops overhead.

Friendship is like the babbling of a brook
That soothes the jangled nerves,
Calming the troubled soul and
Putting a smile back on your face.

It's like a gentle ocean breeze
as you walk the beach at night,
Listening to the pounding of the surf
and feel the warm sand on your feet.

Friendship is like the song of a bird
as you listen in the stillness of the dawn,
Enjoying the serenity of the moment,
Preparing you to face a new day.

Jean you're all of the above
Wrapped up in a personality
That sends a smile from your heart
Bringing comfort and joy to my life.

Earl Gosvener

Past Present Future Tense

It was spring
You didn't see life's
Beginnings as you had begun

It was summer
You didn't see the showers
Or hear the songs sung

It was fall
You didn't see the harvests
The sunsets at its best

It was winter
You didn't see life's
Scheduled rest

You were a child, then 20, then 30,
 then middle age, then more
And you didn't see what you wanted
 before your life was o'er

God gave you life, God has given you time
But the wisdom you longed for, only comes
When you ask for, in kind.

Austin G. Morrow

Nightly Dreams

Like a dream
 you came suddenly one night
From the moment I saw you
 I thought that you were right
But like every other dream
 I awoke and you weren't there
And nightly I searched for you
 but you were no where
People say "Don't live in memory
 it's wrong and it's bad"
They say "it causes confusion
 and makes people sad"
But memory is all I've got
 or at least that's what it seems
Cause I only see you
 in my nightly dreams

Judy McKinnon

A Mother's Cry

You are my angel
 you are my love
 you are my precious child
 that was sent from the one above.

You are my everyday
 you are my pride
 you are that sweet baby
 I carried inside.

You are my friend
 you are my pal
 you are the only one
 that knows your mothers cry.

You are my life
 you are my touch
 you are that special someone
 that I love so much!

Greaves Denise

Against The Wind

Before the raven
 You and I stood
Knowing our faults
 And our merits.
We saw the trees and mountains
 above us collapse.
Separated we stood
The ground quivered
Its core wrecked
 Suspended in air, we stood.
The stars above us fell
A whole galaxy disappeared
 Still we stood.
And when the air ceased to exist
We flourished and became everything
 Together we stood...
 and became a seed
 which grew.

Jacquelyn Lopez

Plague

Awake in the night,
Yet still asleep.
His face floats in my head.
I'm losing my grip on him.
He floats away,
Always.
He can never come back
Except in my head.
He seems so real,
I think he is.
But then he leaves again.
He never stays.
Every night this happens,
And everyday he is gone.

Heather Rook

Missing You

We're so far apart
Yet so near
Each and every minute
The loss of you I fear.

For the short times
We are together
I love being with you
Wishing that it would last forever.

I know you cheat
And probably lie
With love I am giving you
I cannot see why.

I cannot help wondering
What you feel
The distance between us
May never heal.

A few small words
Will never say
How much I miss you
When you are so far away.....

Jody Buice

My Door

My door is but a little door
Yet it swings open wide
To let five children in at four
An eager, jostling tide.
My door has one small curtained window
Through which I can see
My neighbor coming up the walk
To chat an hour with me.
But best of all. When shades of night
Are crowding out the day,
A gray car stops within the drive,
My dear one comes this way.
With tired tread yet gleaming eye
He comes. Yes, I can see.
Oh! Sweet embrace in tired arms
That work so hard for me.
The shade is drawn, the key is turned
The world without may roar.
A host from yonder heaven reigns
Sweet peace within my door.

Eleanor Jewett

Untitled

It gets you high for the moment
yet it leaves a bitter taste
and smashes your hopes
like a kite
beating in the wind
held together by a thread
never knowing when it'll snap free
and some clever child will rip it
from the clutches of a tree
somewhere far away.

John S. Hastings

I Am The Wind

I am the wind so big and strong, and
yet I'm tender like a beautiful blond.

But when I am mad I tear down trees and
pretty much do what I please.

I have taken part in many disasters
for example the one in Lancaster.

I can be peaceful like a newborn baby,
but today I think I'll just be lazy.

Fernando Gonzalez

Untitled

Happiness and friends
yes, they are one
the happiness is there
when we're all having fun.

As long as we have friends
friends so dear to thee
we shall be happy
and smile cause we are free.

And if those friends
on occasions let you down
try to pick it up
and they will come around.

Because friends who are yours
and friends who are dear
will never leave you
year after year.

Jennifer Day

God

Is he there
Yes he's there
I was looking for him
But he wasn't lost
through the crack in the pipe
through the sniff of the snow
through the dead of the night
He brought me through
was he there
Yes, he's always there
The smoke is all gone
The snow has blown away
The night came to light
Now, I know
Yes, he's there (as I smile)

Elenora Maxine Graham

Words

Words can hurt or harm
Words can please or charm
A king uses words the same as I
To speak the truth
Or to speak a lie
If it were not for words I fear
None of us would be here

Ernest G. Fox

Confusion

The confusion in my head
Won't leave my head alone.
The confusion is kept alive
By the drugs that make
My life liveable.

The confusion in my head is
Fed by not knowing what
The future holds. Not knowing
If I will succeed or fail. Will
I be alone or will someone be there?

My mind has been withdrawn
From reality. Everyone knows
But no one cares. All I need
Is something to share. Someone
To talk to someone to be there.

My head filled with confusion
My heart filled with loneliness
My body filled with shame
What has happened to my life
It just isn't the same.

Andrew Swagler

A Light Turned Out

The child so perfect in every way,
won't come home from the hospital today.
The great things this child could have done
will never be known.
Or was the world saved from his wickedness?
No one will ever know.
His light extinguished before any of his
good or evil could be seen.
But we see the cruelty and wickedness
that turned out his light forever.
Nothing great can come of this.

Deborah G. Church

"Sun Rose On Fire"

Lubbock, one morn,
woke from retire,
in the eastern sky
sun rose on fire.
From the horizon
it took flight,
warming earth
with its light.
Streaking westward,
high up it flew,
blinding bright
on crystal blue.
Sun takes off
once each day,
yet comes back
the same way.

Jack Overfield

What If?

What if we lived in world
  without war?
What if we lived in world
  without hate?
And what if we lived in a world
  where everyone was equal no
  matter their color or creed?
If we could live in such a world,
  that would be a wonderful
  world indeed.

Janet Simmons

Child Abuse

I was sent to my room
Without being fed
All because I wet my bed
You tell me that
I'm stupid and dumb
The emotional hurt
Has left me numb
You must stop making
Me your excuse
For your actions
Of child abuse
The bruises you can
No longer hide
In someone I must confide

Christine D. Braxton

Nowhere

Above the world, a sky lies clear,
Without a cloud, no need to fear.
Across the way, a man stands tall,
Wondering what happened to it all:

A house that could only be called a home,
A yard in which the dogs could roam,
A playground where the kids could play,
A city where that man could stay.

But then there came a mighty wind
That wiped away each one of them.
So now the man just stands and stares:
His home, his heart, he stands...nowhere.

Angela M. Brown

My Darkest Moments

Life had lost its purpose
with the loss of my spouse
and yet I had so much:
My children and grandchildren,
the paradox made me sad and glad.
I began searching my soul
for meaning to make me whole.
It took me by surprise,
maybe it was the sunrise,
But I found God!

Joan DeLeon

Circle Of Life

She came in
With the first fallen
Leaves of autumn,
Petite and fragile,
A true creation
Of God.

Like a bird,
She never stopped singing,
Or a flower
She never ceased to bloom.

Her time on earth
Was like the wind
Whisking the last warm
Moments of summer away,

For while she was here
She was sunlight,
Shimmering, full of life,
And when she left
The leaves were preparing
To fall once more.

Amber Jenkins

Untitled

Mary could have been alone,
With the child she called her own.

Forsaken by those whom she loved,
Walking only with God above.

Her father so ashamed to see,
His daughter "O how could this be".

Even Joseph feels betrayed,
By the one his love he gave.

Yes Mary could have been alone,
All through life's long, dreary road.

God himself intervened,
And sent an angel in a dream.

This child is God's, he did say,
Hold Him, love Him, and guide the way.

Compassion and mercy should be given,
For Mary and this child from heaven.

Yes Mary could have been alone,
But God chose his love to be shown.

Alice Gail Dowis

Untitled

Now the summer passed us by
With memories that make us cry
We made new friends
But now they're gone
Soon our words
will renew the bond
So many great times we shared
with the people who really cared
I miss them so
But we shall see
more great times that will soon be

Ann-Marie May

Inappropriate

I walk by
with tears in my eyes
my heart
in my hand
my childhood
on my sleeve.
You see me
and you want to
wipe my tears..... away,
but you can't
and you shouldn't.
Between ethics
and therapist-client relationships
there is a fine line,
a boundary not to be crossed.
You cannot
wipe my tears
because although
you see me
you are not supposed to.

Donna M. Hir

Battlewound

Is it not strange? Thirty years ago,
With scarce a thought beyond my mind.
I did my job and earned my pay;
Was averagely happy, I'll be bound home soon.
Lo in my little groove I was content,
Seeing my life run smoothly to the end.

When presto! Like a bubble goes my dream:
I leap upon the stage of Splendid Deeds.
I yell with rage; I wallow deep in gore,
I, that was a clerk in a grocery store.

Stranger then any movie I've seen,
Here on the reeking battlefield I lie.
Hit on the spine, legs cannot move;
And though I yell:
I cannot hear a sound.

Under the grey sky, propped up by a comrade,
But calm and feeling never pain at all:
And full of wonder at the turn of it all:
For of al the dead that fell before me,
If I die, I have no right to whine.

Joseph O. Rodrigues Jr.

Untitled

From the days
with rainbows
over an ocean
filled with jumping dolphins,
to a dark day
with no one
to be with,
with no one
you care for at all,
with an empty heart
and a sad sway,
you long to see those
dolphins play,
Under the blue sky
and rainbow

Jessica Loffredo

She Walked Passed Me

She walked passed me...
With perfect hair and gentle smile..
She walked with liquid grace...
I could see her for a short while.

But at that brief moment...
My thoughts were relaxed...
Oh, if I could touch her...
Or hear her playful laugh...

And with that touch, her warmth would fill me...
And her voice could calm and soothe my mind..
She walked passed me without a glance....
But, beauty in her I will always find.

Harry Phillips IV

Feed Your Dreams

Feed your dreams
With passion and fire,
For it's our dreams
We soon retire
And trade for the
Shoelaces of life instead
To make easier the paths
We must tread.
But lifeless are we
without passion and fire,
For it's our dreams
We have retired.

Carrie Thompson

Living Our Life

By our touch we feel
    with our feelings we touch

Through our eyes we feel
    through our feelings we have vision

When we listen we feel
    when we feel we hear

Through our taste we can
    feel the bitter and sweet

Through the smell of nature
    we can feel the decay and blossom

Through our senses our lives
    are lived to the fullest

Open our life to feelings
    for feeling is living

John D. Hammer

Untitled

I sailed my ship out to sea
with my love and memories.

Love letters would keep us close you see.
My first true love
would come back for me.

Out of the blue, a dark cloud came.
And with it took my love in vain.

I stumbled down life's lonely road,
just to see, what my life would unfold.

Years have passed. I shall never see,
the ship, I once sailed out to sea.

Eleanor Everly Thomas

Acceptance

Three weeks ago I took a ride
With my companions by my side.
We saw a movie where we cried.
Two weeks ago my darling died.

It was not unexpectedly.
We faced it with reality
And fought it knowing utterly
'Twould take its toll eventually.

We knew the journey would be tough,
A blind man's hoax that had no bluff,
A ballot box we could not stuff,
A slow decline into the rough.

I watched my sweetheart slip away
A little more from day to day.
My love was such I could not stray
And did not wish to look away.

We shared the agony in tow.
In different ways we suffered so
And knowing what there was to know
We said good-bye a year ago.

Gary Welch

To Amy

Eyes that twinkle,
with mischief and joy.
A smile that turns me
into a little boy..

When I hear you laugh
my troubles are few.
Your plotting, and skullduggery
are a part of you.

I dwell on your good
and accept your bad.
Both with out
would make me sad.

To watch you work
feels me with glee
To loose the chance
to costly a fee.

I have these words
that are so few.
To say my feelings.
I Love You

Harrold H. Black Jr.

Shadow

Shadow, dark in the night
with just a whisper of light.
Follows you round all day.
Sometimes it seems he wants to play.
Shadow will stay with you,
Never leaving your side.
Shadow is a friend you see,
Just a puppy dog for you and me.
We pet him and feed him.
He will be loyal even as his eyes dim.
He plays all day within your sight.
Shadow, dark in the night
with just a whisper of light.
Shadow guards our home wherever it may be
He keeps his eyes and ears tuned in.
When there's no danger, he crawls in his den.
Shadow, dark in the night
with just a whisper of light.

Dalphne Kile

My Papa's Funeral

As I say good-bye to you, Papa,
With all the love in my heart,

I know that you will still be there,
Listening to me as I say this prayer.

I speak for everyone here today,
We'll all miss your kind and thoughtful way.

You gave us joy and happiness,
And you deserve the very best.

So in heaven I hope you'll find,
Peace and comfort all the time.

And while you're up there looking down,
Just remember you'll always be around,
In our hearts and everywhere,
We love you Papa,
And we still care.

Jennifer Broberg

Books

I went to the library on a hot sunny day.
With all of those books, I think I might stay.
I like reading books.
I'm hooked on books!
You should be hooked on books too!
Books are cool, as cool as can be!
I'll go again next year.
You go and you will see.
I'll go to the library on a hot sunny day,
With all of those books, I think I might stay.

Jennifer Crowl

The Thornless Rose

She deathly marches down the lonely lane
With a solemn pace silently
And in her white hand she holds
The fairest of all roses

Its thorns the eye cannot behold
Yet it holds some mystery
The prickles upon the stem
Have gone somewhere else to be

For behold, if you step nearer
You can find that roses nails
Follow the blood that trickles
Down the lady's arm that pales

Chelle Lynne Miller

The Critical Eye

Now this is to all
With a critical eye.
Don't pass harsh judgment
On my verses gone by.
Just read once again
Giving serious thought
That not creed nor solution
Are the goals that I sought.
Just an inspired moment
Not foreign to all
A spontaneous gesture
Encouraged with gall.
No claims of artistic potential
Or hint of professional stock.
Just compatible words flung together
Intended to stimulate thought.

George N. Dufresne

"For Someone"

You're an angel
with a perfect smile
hiding all your pain
and I remember the night you cried
I know I'll never be the same

I wanted to hold you in my arms
and tell you everything would be alright
I wanted to tell you that I could be
your guiding light

But I felt if I got too close
you would push me away
there was nothing I could do
and there was nothing I could say

You're an angel
with a perfect smile
hiding all your pain
and I remember the night you cried
I know I'll never be the same

David Hodnett

"You My Love"

Your smile lights up my eyes,
with a glow whenever you're near;
My heart skips a beat too fast to sleep;
Could love be growing when we meet
with these signs portrayed so neat.
To share a touch would surely explode,
the glow of you, and bring forth tears
like the morning dew.
The dampness of my tears on your flesh
would only create emotional stress.
Thus, when the birds stop singing;
The flowers stop blooming;
The angels in heaven stop caring,
It is then that you and I cease to hold
onto the love that we are sharing.

Gloria Elaine Deering

Untitled

You'll die all alone
with a bottle by your side
to this fate you have resigned
and from it you cannot hide

You've refused to accept
the love and the light
if you would open your heart
it would be in plain sight

Yet in your loneliness
you'll continue to grieve
hiding from that
which you need to receive

Take what I give you
the offer is good
yet I often wonder
if you even could

Christine E. Rideout

Memories

Awake. Now.
Now becoming then.
But this is now,
I live in the past
Of memories
Because everything is a memory
And so am I.

Lyanne Abreu

Twinkles

Soft brown hair that is soft as silk,
with a body the size of a pumpkin.
Shining blue eyes like crystals
watch over me.
A soft paw touches my face.
Slowly the brown furry animal
lays down beside me, purring
with happiness.
Then drifting off to sleep in
a quiet way.

Janet M. Bell

"Sunrise On The Lake"

As I awake and go to the
window to survey what lies before man
in the coming day, I open the curtains
And the beauty that greets me is
indescribable, every color of the spectrum
has been interwoven and painted
upon the early morning sky.
The subtle colors do homage to an
artist of excellence that no pen
is empowered to define. The wind
gives movement to the trees with
rhythmic motion and sound that
no conductor has yet put to
score. I seize the opportunity to
steal this moment to pen and
canvas, but try as I will, I fail,
for no mortal has created this
And I realize that God has
Awakened before me and has
Painted and composed another Master Piece.

Edwin F. Blalock Jr.

Fishery Epitaph

Coffee colored roses,
Wilted in their poses.
A tainted symphony.
A silenced timpani.
Seasons full of closure,
With no time to measure.
Era from ancient days,
Now gone in foggy haze.
Melody left behind.
Harmony came to mind.
A porpoise in a wake,
Glides silently to Kake.
Chinook feeds the eagle,
That soars high and regal.
Who will free the troller,
Wooden double ender?
Lifestyle of distinction.
Livelihood extinction.

Joan M. Greene

Why?

Why is the sky so blue?
Why are the clouds so white?
Why is the water nice and clear?
Why is black the color of night?

Why is life so long?
Why is my sister in a bad mood?
Why are the Red Sox so good?
Why is there so much food?

Alex Dombroff

Journey Of Love

Reach down, dear Lord
Willingly, I take Thy loving hand
And drift with Thee
Over Thy threashold.

If Thou will, O Lord
Look down upon my loved ones
Precious gifts from you
That filled my life with joy.

Brush their brows
With Thy gentle hand
To let them know
Of my love unending

Let them know
Of Thy love
Greater and stronger
Than any other.

Doreen (Oehlers) Pekarek

Someone

Will no one come and help me?
Will no one dry my tears?
Will no one hear my cries,
And help me through these years?

No, no one is there to help me,
I'm just a child crying alone.
There's no one I can confide in,
There's no one to carry me home.

I need someone to help me,
To hold me through the night.
I need someone to tell me
It's going to be all right.

As I'm crying all alone,
Someone comes and dries my tears,
Someone comes and lifts me high,
Someone comes and soothes my fears.

Jesus is that someone,
Who came when I was alone.
Jesus is that someone,
Who has come to carry me home.

Elizabeth Wallmark

The Grim Reaper

The grim reaper cautious and sly
Will never let a chance pass him by
Young or old, weak or strong
A visit from the reaper is never wrong

He is lurking around, open your eyes!
Dusk to dawn, anytime he may arise
Treacherous, thoughtless, frigid and cold
What right has the reaper to be so bold?

He may snatch your loved one
Any moment, any second of the hour
For with the Reaper, this is easily done
Who carelessly gave the reaper this
   horrendous power?

The reaper exists in all reality
The past and present and thru all eternity

Deborah L. Hann

Twenty-Three Years

"Come share my life," said he.
"Why yes," he answered.

"Abandon all else," said he.
"Follow me. Follow me."

"Come dance with my soul," said she.
"Not I," he answered.

"Come fly with me"
"Not I," said he.

"What seek you here?" She asked.
"Diamonds and gold," he replied.

"I offer my life and my love," said she.
"Is that all?" He asked.

"I offer the fruit of my womb," said she.
"Oh bother," said he.

"What seek you here?" She asked.
"Diamonds and gold," He replied,
"And sex without end," said he.

"Come dance with my soul," said she.
"Not I," said he.

Goodbye.

Joanne L. Bachmann

God's True Master Plan

There is no way to understand
why waves retreat from off the sand.

Or why God keeps giving morning light
and glorious sunsets before the night.

We're only told to have faith and obey
and He will show to us the way,

To live in peace and harmony with man.
  GOD'S TRUE MASTER PLAN

To teach our children how to love,
our greatest gift from God above.

Then they in turn will do their best
to teach their children peace and rest,

Finding favor with God and man,
  GOD'S TRUE MASTER PLAN

With our children grown and raised
by our grandchildren we are praised.

Their lives we have helped shape
and when we enter heavens gate,

We will know we did the best by man,
  GOD'S TRUE MASTER PLAN

Janet Mack

Untitled

Desperate, desperate, desperation
Why is it —
Some people can extract your very
lifeblood,
Leaving you to panic
to struggle
Only to become more ensnared
and ultimately—
More desperate

Carol Harding

Confidence

In the sunshine or in the rain
Why doesn't it shine all the time?
I'm quiet and insecure
Because I'm young I guess...
But who wants to get older?
Children make the world a brighter place.
How can I teach them to trust in
Themselves and aspire to new heights...
Regardless of their setbacks?
God made us all different and that
Was a blessing so we can all share
Our expertise with the people who feel
Inferior and give them CONFIDENCE
In their skills
Making even the sad, brighter,
And the poor, richer.
   Julie Lantis

"Run Away"

Why did you have to hurry?
Why did you run away?
Couldn't you hear me calling
Come back, come home - please stay
Didn't you know I loved you;
Didn't you stop to think.
Couldn't you hear the terror in
a heart about to break?
Where are you going?
What will you find?
Is there a love that's greater than mine?
You aren't really ready.
When you are - I'll let you go,
I'll kiss you softly, and bless you, and
help you right along.
Stop and look behind you before you
close the door.
Maybe what you're leaving is what your
looking for.
   Frances M. Shetterly

Rested Soul

Where did you go
Why did you leave
You knew the pain
That I couldn't see

In the hospital you walked
Never to leave
'Til this day
It's hard to believe

And through your eyes
You tried to explain
Something went wrong
I feel very strange

The tubes held you back
Sleep soon came
Rest your soul
In the Lord's name

The burden is gone
There is no more pain
Memories of this day
Will always remain
   Genevieve Semones Adams

"Echoes Of The Heart"

Why can't I see the stars above?
Why can't I feel the rain?

Why can't I find the chartered
   path, to rise above the pain?

Why does my inner self proclaim
   a fear that halts all joy?
Seems all that happiness can render,
Is like a broken toy!
Listen to your voices shadow,
an echo that is near.
Memories are futures past
and present is our peer.
Happy high and sadly low
Counting dreams that will not grow.
The hopes and fears we have within,
The war of peace, the good can't win.
To every life, the tranquil flurry
Slowly ending in a hurry.
   Ellie Espina

"I Am My Father's Masterpiece"

Little girl sitting there speaking German,
Why are you sad?
Has someone made you mad?
You're a precious little thing,
Why do you not sing?
I see many potentials in your eyes,
Please don't cry.
Your Daddy's little masterpiece,
All that is good and pure is what you are.
From the time of your birth,
We knew you would grow into a shining star.
That is why you share our name,
It's your passport to a life of fame.
Sit up straight,
Daddy's soon to walk through that gate.
The war has taken your daddy away,
But don't fret he'll return some sunny day.
So daddy I won't cry, I'll dry my eyes.
Dad I want to make you proud, sing out loud.
I'll forever be your masterpiece.
   Dorleen Chism-Kabia

Why? Because!

Why? Are we too quick to judge?
Why? Are we too uninvolved?

Why? Are we to cautious?
Why? Can we not love?

Why? The sun is shining brightly.
Why? The flowers smell so sweet.

Because. The sun is shining brightly,
the flowers smell so sweet.

Because. We choose to love, we will
not quickly judge.

Because. Were not too cautious, we
end to get involved.

Because. We all are human.
   Cathy A. Rainey

"The Elements"

The roaring thunder throughout the night.
Who's to fear the lighting, wind and rain?
   Thunder so loud and clouds so
low and so far away.
   Even now, flakes of snow falling
gracefully, like feathers in the wind.
   Elements of old and new.
Here for now and maybe here after.
   Oh help me understand that
this is reality.
   It's sometimes frightening.
Yes! It frightens even me.
   Billie Brooks

The Sorrows

They have arrived, powerless I whispered;
Whom? Helen questioned me,
with affliction I answered: "The Sorrows,"
everyday they keep coming back,
like waves that recede from the shore
miles perhaps, yes, many miles..........
we wish they will never come back,
and always our hopes are vanquished;
because when one wave goes away,
there is another one, that takes its place.
   Eduardo Noriega DelValle N.

Moments More To Go....

It's November of 95, and I have a daughter
who soon will be forty
Kathy was born November of 55
that was the year when our love came alive
to grow through the years
with humor and tears
And being 39 isn't so bad
wait till Kathy gets to the years
her 61 year - old mother had
that she'll find out that
being 39 was glad.
   Dorothy Raybe

Control

The days of our lives are like insects,
   Who labor intensely at their choirs.
Only to end up stepped on,
   forgotten, unknown, and no more.
Time ravages our lifelines,
   but continuously unseen.
Fate shows who's superior,
   in ways our minds can barely glean.
For who is to say,
   and who is to blame.
For the paths we have taken,
   our success and our shame.
And only when the reaper takes,
   our very last string of breath.
Will we know the very truth,
   the cost of knowledge...death.
   David G. Embrick

"My Angel"

I know I have an Angel,
Who keeps me company.
His love is never changing,
It's constant as can be.

I feel my angel touch me,
When life has got me down.
He takes my spirit to a place
Where glory can be found.

I look to him for guidance,
I soar upon his wings.
He guides me through my daily chores,
At night, he fills my dreams.

At times my Angel talks to me,
As silly as it sounds.
You see, he is my best friend,
The best that can be found.

Because I know he's with me,
I walk a different road
My Angel holds my hand with love,
He's always here, I know.

Brenda Koch

No Rain's The Same

Red lights flashing on the wings,
White lights splashing in the sky;
Unserenely I float along.

Only thoughts can roam and ask,
"Why am I here?"

Blurred stars give no light;
know not the pain of his dark night.
Mine is no race with time;
Only a silent sign of Love.

Jessie Dawson Wilson

'Tis Morning

The morning breaks, light intensified,
White clouds float across the sky,
Bright sunlight rays flow through,
'Tis morning.

Birds sing their shrill songs,
Awake for a new day dawns,
The squirrels scurry down the trees,
'Tis morning.

A robin lights on a branch nearby,
Cocking his head to hear the cry,
Of baby robins in their nest,
'Tis morning.

The hummingbird darts to and fro,
His unseen wings all aglow,
To sip the nectar from the flowers,
'Tis morning.

The budding flowers burst open
To great the sunlight ray
On this bright and beautiful day,
'Tis morning.

James H. Mero

A Winter Scene

The snowflake storm tossed its
White blanket over the highest hills,
To melt and slide streamer-like
Downward to ice crusted valley rills.

Pine cones wear soft white bonnets
Upon their brown wizened heads;
Nearby the fashionable shawls of other
Trees are wind frayed into shreds.

The sun reflects off cotton balls of snow
On bushes delicately bared branches,
Placed by Mother Nature, believing sparkling
Jewels on every finger greatly enhances.

A scene of little color, painted with
Icy strokes of blue white cast,
Later to be reworked in green when
Winter is the season just past.

Claire Ellen Martin

Spin Fall

Time stops,
While the world turns.

The rain cools,
The passion burns.

My mind is set,
My hopes are high.

Time has been so good,
To you and I.

Time stops,
While the world turns.

The rain cools,
The passion burns.

My body is wet,
My mouth is dry.

I'm in a spin fall.
Then I hear your sweet sigh!

Brenda Hammond

The Downpour

Silently, the morning dew moistens the grass
While the birds chirp loudly above.
Drops of rain melt like butter
Into the already dampened ground.
Soon, showers pelt at the earth
Like a million darts from the sky.
Sycamore leaves begin to droop
While hundreds of bugs huddle
Under the protection of a natural umbrella.
As the sun turns red, the rain stops.
Evening fire flies brighten the gray sky
While the gutter continues the
   drip-drop
   drip-drop
That lulls even babies to sleep.
Then,
The day ends as quietly as it began
With evening mist moistening the grass.

David Martin Nickerson

Crickets

I love the sounds of crickets
while I'm laying in my bed,
The summer nights while I'm at camp
I just don't want the song to end.
The chirping sounds are music
that help me sleep and dream
of great outdoor adventures
and places I wish I could have been.

Emil Crystal

"In Search Of"

I must have missed the warning sign
which pointed to the narrow line,
that would give my life direction.
For my quest of all perfection,
resulted in these scrambled thoughts of mine.

If it's true there is a book
perhaps someone forgot to look,
plotting each soul's destiny.
I stumble on blind, but steadily,
in search of my personal nook.

Someone should be here to guide me,
don't they hear my heartfelt plea.
This is the only ride of my life
peppered with happiness, not only strife,
as my choices dictate what will be.

Elena Schoen

Serenity

I have learned the secret of life
Which is always to be content,
Not dependent on circumstances
Nor the amount that can be spent.

When I cried to my God for help,
He was only a breath away
The One who will not forget me,
HIS grace is sufficient each day.

There's contentment in a person
Christ will supply our every need
A believer can live in peace
When God's word alone one does heed.

As the stars shine in their beauty
Piercing the darkness of the night,
Serenity at that moment
Removes every barrier of fright.

What a joy there'll be in heaven
When the king of kings we shall see,
We shall be content forever
For the Savior has set us free!

Carolyn F. Marquis

Halves Of A Whole

There is a good little fairy,
Who lives within my heart,
Warming the blood flowing through my body.
She will not show her face however,
Because she is afraid of the demons,
Holed up inside of my brain,
Chilling my thoughts going through my mind.
I have the power and the choice,
To let one of these loose,
To reek havoc around my world,
Good or bad.

Abigail Bertumen

Morning Comes

Whisper to me softly
Wherever you may be.
   Think of me
When thoughts are blind
If you wish to see.

I offer what I can
   as a boy
     as a man
Forever I'm adrift
   without direction
    or a plan.

Have your dreams
Grab your dreams
For some they
Do come true

Take it from a dreamer
Who once dreamed
He really knew.

Gregory House

Follow The Rhythm Of Your Heart

At the end of the tunnel,
Where the pleasing essence of roses
Mesmerizes every soul,
There's a light, for you, that glows.
   At the end of the tunnel,
   Where the sun kisses her hair,
   And the body that's now yours,
   Take the time, my friend, to stare;
Contemplate the gem you claim.
Your heart, did it skip a beat?
Does the world still look the same?
Do you see it more in pink?
   Before the sunset occurs,
   Posses her in your firm embrace;
   Take the flowers she offers,
   Run your hand on her delicate face;
    Brush your lips against her eyes,
    And don't glance behind in the dark.
    There are more noble surprise
    When you follow the rhythm of your heart.

Claire Judine Saintil

Created For Glory

Father, help me to understand,
Where I fit in your great plan.
Help me to pray, Thy will be done,
And to accept the things that come.
I, the created, seek your face,
Asking for your perfect grace.
Death is certain, that I know;
It is life's uncertainty that puzzles me so.
Beyond my existence, may I see,
That men's souls won to Jesus
Is Thy greatest priority.
Grant me with more tears to pray,
For your servants near and far-away,
Who may be called to lay down life,
So that sons of man can see Thy light.

Brenda Cochran

Oh! Jenny!

Oh! Jenny!, Oh! Jenny!
Where have you been?
I haven't seen you since,
"I don't know when".

You're the joy to your mother
Who loved you from a child
To the girl you are now
So tender and mild.

You're a friend to all those
Who know you so well.
They know you keep friendships
And their secrets you don't tell.

They trust and believe you
Because you don't lie.
You're a very true person
On whom they rely.

You deserve lots of credit
For being just you;
A young lady who is loving
And a friend who's so true.

Jack A. Feldman

Oh God Oh God I Cry!

Where do I dwell
where do I die
oh blackened bones
my soul is lost
in times unknown
oh scream of hell
oh agony
what are there wills
surrounding me
what are these chains
upon my feet
the smell of rats
lost roses sweet
all dreams of life are
gone to stay
do all dead prisoners
die this way?

Eva Long

A Guardian Angel To Watch Over Me

Whenever I was lonely
whenever I was sad
you were there to cheer me up
to take away the bad

Then when there was happiness
fun times to be shared
there you were once again
to show how much you cared

You were like a shadow
always one step behind
you were my guardian angel
of a very special kind

Although you've gone away now
and we have to be apart
you'll always be in my memories
forever in my heart

Holly Ashford

Time

It seems like time will never end
When you're without that special friend
So slowly the days go by
So quickly the nights fly
For your heart's sake
You don't want to wake
But as you open your eyes
And look up to the skies
You try to draw hope from the new sun
Thinking he won't be the last one
There will be plenty more
Each better than before
Next time his love will be true
He will belong only to you
And as you lay by his side
To his heart you will confide
Time is no longer feared
The loneliness has disappeared.

Angeline Diptee

Untitled

The intense feeling of no fear
when you take control of the wheel,
is an immense RUSH of energy
as you hurdle the jumps
and soar through the air
like a bird in flight.
With the saying, "Everything that goes up,
must come down,"
you land with such a jolt,
that a surge of electricity
travels throughout your body,
as your fingers squeeze the throttle
to greet the sky again.

Danielle N. Dionisio

Manna From Heaven

God snows manna from Heaven
When we're tired and in despair,
Giving us little blessings
To send away troubles that are there.

We hunger in this desert
In life's wandering here on earth.
Our struggles are distressing
When we wonder what it's worth.

But now and then
It's nice to receive
A special moment to treasure
That helps to bring a smile of relief.

Life, though, can be awfully tough
When fighting with the devil,
But when we get our strength back,
It keeps us on the level.

Lord, snow us with this wonderful bread
That feeds us when we're starving,
And we will sing a continual praise
While in your joy we'll be thriving.

Carol Joy Nunley

How Will It End

How will it end, we contemplate
When we sit at this machine.
We know someday we'll be of late.
We'll be an old has-been.

You'll wonder why, when you look around,
Searching for the bones of me
That there's nothing left but a plastic mess
Of our ideology.

Now do not fret; we brought it on
It was meant to set us free
But it took our minds and will to think
So now just let it be.

Gerald E. Hoffman

Fifty Years

It only seemed like yesterday
When we had come together,
The trials and tribulations
We naturally had to weather.

We had four beautiful children
Three lovely girls and a boy,
But God needed another angel
And came to get our joy.

Those probably were the worst days
When we thought that He had left us,
But on every day and in every way
The Master chose to trust us.

With blessings came our day-to-day living
And it soon became apparent,
That our love and devotion for each other
In both of us was inherent.

We held on to our happiness
In doing what God told us to,
And that love has lasted fifty years
Which makes each day brand new.

Arnetta F. Davis-Carpenter

Crescent Eyes

I peer into your eyes of golden twilight
When the starlit heavens
And the waning light of the moon
Sear through your world of eternal morrows
And burning into mine
Of crescent fates
Dancing to implore the blackness
Of macabre sorrows

The tearing of my cold heart
Unto the splintered pieces of wilted blood
From your fading passions of beauty
   Of your crescent eyes

So cordial and heartfelt
Pleading for your heart's desire
So desperately beseeching the broken love
My shattered soul confides
   Of your crescent eyes
Finessing and caressing my hatred
   With your crescent eyes
The golden twilight covets

Aaron A. Cotton

When The Parting Time Has Come

Who speaks for the little children
   when the parting time has come,
When Mom and Dad go separate ways
   each to a different home?

Who hears the breaking of their hearts
   who sees their tear-stained eyes,
Who shares the loneliness they feel
   amid their silent cries?

Who knows the anger that they hide...
   the hurt of one so young,
Who speaks for the little children
   when the parting time has come?

Josie Harris Goodwin

Untitled

There comes a time in life
When the battle finally ends
The arguments cease
And peace falls upon you
Like the morning dew
Refreshed and back to life
You venture forth
And the treasures of your heart
These things we treasure
and search for
Have always been there
Like so many things we search for
They are found in the last place you look.

Julie Ann Sheppard

Untitled

"I knew you once so long ago,
   When I was young
   And still among
The immature and gentle flow of life.

And as I grew in love of you,
   I came to know,
   And yet so slow,
The richness of this love I knew t'was mine.

And now I'm growing old, and yet
   My life is new
   Each day with you,
And love for me is as we met - so young."

Elizabeth Houchens

The Fall

I fell off a chair once
When I was three or four.
I fell down the stairs once
And tumbled to the floor.
I fell off my bicycle
And skinned my knee real bad,
My grade point average fell a bit
Which made my parents good-n-mad.
I even fell off my bed
When I dreamt it was a cliff.
Fell for the empty wrapper trick
When offered gum with nothing left.
I thought the chances of me falling
Would discontinue as I grew,
But now I see that falling's fun
Because I fell for you.

Brian A. Myers

To Teddy

As I toddled up to you, back then
When I was only two,
I fell in love with you, back then
With your button eyes of blue.

Perched upon the highchair seat
At Malleys Department Store,
I reached for you and called you "mine,"
And meant forevermore.

I held you in my arms, so tight,
And turned you into "real."
I loved the fur right off of you
There's so little now to feel.

I've had to mend your well-worn scars
And fix your eyes for you
Just like my Mom did, years ago,
When you weren't quite so new.

And now, dear one, the years have passed
And you are forty-four.
I loved you then, dear Teddy,
But now I love you more.

Gail Baldwin Whipple

Are You Ready

So many times I've heard them say,
when I told about the Lord.
I'm just not quite ready yet,
to listen to God's word.

You've got a choice to make my friend,
and you don't know how much time.
Before the Lord will call us home
to spend the rest of time.

You have the chance by the grace of God,
for the gift of eternal life.
The spirit will surely guide you,
and help you through your strife.

The choice is this for you to make.
God loves us with all his heart.
And he died upon the cross one day,
to give us another start.

That makes me wonder every time,
how would this world be set?
If Jesus Christ himself had said,
I'm just not ready yet.

Elmer F. Dunn

Feeling Love

You can feel it in your feet,
when I run to you aid.

You can feel it in your arms,
When I hold you from all your fears.

You can feel it in your muscles,
when I relieve you with a massage.

You can feel it in your eyes,
when its the truth I tell you.

You can feel it on your lips,
when mine are touching yours.

I love you. Can you feel that in your heart?

Bruce Boman

Wrong Love

Everything I had I gave it to you,
When I gave you my heart
You tore it all a part.
When I gave you friendship
You gave me end ship.
When I gave you light.
You couldn't stand the sight.
When I gave you a song
You said we don't belong
When I gave you my years
You gave me tears.
I have given you all I have
I have nothing left to give
Have you ever had
this feeling as I did?
My feelings are hurt
You treated me like dirt.
How can you be so cruel
How could I have loved
  a fool like you.

Andrea Blum Dichoso

"I Need To Know"

I need to know when I'll feel his touch,
When he'll feel for me and just how much.

I need to know when I'll find a man,
When all my feelings he'll understand.

I need to know when I'll feel his heart,
When we'll become one never to part.

I need to know when he'll be with me,
When his love is one thing I can see.

I need to know when my hurt will leave,
When happiness is what I'll believe.

I need to know when he'll feel the same,
When my heart and soul will stop this shame.

I need to know when this will be real,
When his love one thing I can feel.

I need to know when this will be true,
When I'll be able to be with you....

Jessica Lynn Shoup

Untitled

She remembers
When driving was such a big deal
Learning how took forever
Two months, almost
She used to get so nervous
Now
It's like every time
She slides behind the wheel
There is an automatic response
She no longer has to think about it
It's all instinct.
Love is like that, too.
Her love for him is deep
But there is no thought or logic behind it
Not anymore.
She obeys the rules
Only to avoid accidents
And she's not nearly as meticulous
As once she was.

Amanda Wojciek

Olivia

I met you in your youth -
When all the world was at your feet.
A timeless image my heart made -
An eternity to keep.
As the years go by -
And your hair turns grey -
And lines appear where there were none.

Although the world may see
That time has fled -
In my heart you'll be -
Forever young.

Albert Marrero Salas

It's Time For A Poem

It's time for a poem
When all else seem bleak
I want to shout, live and seek.

I want to be happy and maybe I am
but the winter's cold air is biting
and life seems on hold.

So I think of good living
and laughter and cheers
Remember the pen is mightier
than all my fears.

I write a few words
a smile slowly descends.

Yes, the days are like glaciers
slipping onto my soul
But the thoughts of tomorrow
keep me happy and whole!

Anne M. Ehmann

Horizons

Let men who dream
Whatever manner of greatness,
build their home by the sea.

And there not be bound
by fences nor worry
over limits, for their
horizons shall be forever
beyond their grasp.

James W. Fee Jr.

Silence

My speechless child,
What stifled sobs or soundless laughter
Die behind your silent lips?
Childhood dreams
Created by your eager mind
Remain imprisoned there
Shaking the locked door
And crying for audible release
And understanding.

Catherine W. Phillips

Love

What is love.
What is love to you.
What is love to me.
What could love be.
Is love sin.
Is love hate.
Is love a key to a sacred pleasure gate.
Is love true.
Is love war.
Is love the knocking on a demon door.
Is love nice.
Is love great.
Is love a passion for a human's mate.
If I have love let it be.
That love is me.

Dwayne Lee

Take A Look

Our society...
What has it become?
Where are our values?
What have we done?
There's murder and violence,
Greed and pollution,
Drugs and gangs,
What's the solution?
There are kids having kids,
Kids killing kids, too.
Runaways, homeless,
Do we ignore what is true?
Racism, gay bashers,
Bombings and rape,
AIDS and abuse,
How do we escape?
Our children are suffering
And I feel the shame,
For a society gone crazy,
For we all are to blame.

Angela Michele Johnson

Love Insane

Do you know,
what flows,
through the veins,
of Love INSANE?

Sweet caressing.
Pure and Black.
Never held back.

Love INSANE,
my second name.
When I'm with you...
this is true!

Wild Heartbeats.
Soft and Unique.
Comfortable Touch.
Can't get enough.

Love INSANE,
never a pain.

You control my thoughts.
You have relaxed my heart.
I'm in captivity to you...blaming LOVE INSANE.

Andre' T. Briscoe

What Do I See

When I look at the sky
What do I see
The color blue
Like the deep blue sea

When I look at the sun
What do I see
A gleaming face
Looking back at me

When I look at the stars
What do I see
A field of diamonds
Glistening for me

When I look at a child
What do I see
Innocence, beauty, created with love
A gift from the creator up above

When I look all around
What do I see
Nature's wonders
Boy, am I lucky

Barbara Schwarz

All Hallow's Eve

Demons lurk the streets tonight
Werewolves howl with all their might
To summon the spirits from beyond the grave.

Ghosts will haunt you house tonight
Vampires will try to get a bite
And Jack-O-Lanterns will come alive.

You can stay inside,
And try to hide,
But the goblins and ghouls will find you.

Witches will cast a spell or two,
And it might be put on you.
So beware.

The day is dawning, they disappear.
But they will come again next year.
So be prepared for another night of fright.

Jeannie Tudor

The Mission

Like passing ships in dead of night,
We're souls from far off ports,
But in the essence of ourselves
United in our thoughts.
Though we go our separate ways,
You live a life of lust.
I live mine the way I do
Simply because I must.
I cannot rest until I do
What I was put here for:
To soothe your wounded, battered souls
And put an end to war.
My vessel has no armament,
Yet while I sail the seas,
You fear my unarmed vessel not;
You fear your own disease.

Gary S. Fried

The Rain And The Shoes

Bump, bump, bump
Went the rain.
Clump, clump, clump
Went the shoes.
The rain went
Tip, tip, tip, tap
And the shoes went
Tip, tap, tip, tap.
Clickety-clap, clickety-clap
Went the shoes.
And the rain
Went splat!

John D. Jackson

Untitled

You may say I'm "Old Fashioned,"
Well I'll tell you daughter dear;
I may have done things "The Hard Way"
But I've lived for many a year.

To an electric dishwasher
I never would succumb,
And as for a garbage disposal,
They drive me both deaf and dumb.

The drivel on TV bores me
I don't like modern art,
The "Comics" simply leave me cold
and rock-n-roll breaks my heart.

I never take a cocktail,
Cigarette smoke makes me ill,
I would never rely on "Geritol"
Nor a "One-A-Day" vitamin pill.

You say I'm too Old Fashioned,
Well I'll tell you what I'll do,
I will hie me away for a Bridge Game
and leave all the rest to you!!!

Aura Inez Rader

Awakening

As the clouds parted,
we sat in the sun
with the oak between us.

The touch of your skin,
how soft, but yet how hard,
so near, but yet so far.

How safe I was surrounded by wood.
Softly the music played.
My hands holding in the warmth
that I wanted your heart to feel.
The smoke was curling up.
The eagle soared above.

Carolyn L. Carvalho

For Fear We Lose

For fear of looking bad
We hold ourselves restraint
For fear of looking silly
Most times we ain't
For fear of saying wrong
Although we may be right
For fear of being hurt
We sometimes lose the fight
For fear we don't enjoy
The things we would
For fear we lose
When winning we could

Edmond P. Rutigliano

Love All

Love all far and near, we see,
We feel, we hear

Love all far and near, do your best,
Do not fear

Love all far and near, we have heart,
We are dear

Love all far and near, Be thankful
And share

Love all far and near, reach out,
Don't let help be rare

Love all far and near, all children who
Are our future, we love, we care

Love all far and near, pray a prayer,
Jesus will hear

Hilda Bellamy

In Time

There are things in life
we don't understand
We read and write
in hope that we can
How the wind blows
The cold when it snows
Why a bell rings
how a bird sings
We try so hard
to make up our mind
But we tend to forget
It all comes in time.
In life we feel
things are not fair
But that doesn't mean
that people don't care
In everyone's life
The sun will shine
But you have to be patient
Cause it all takes time

Derrick Dampher

Brothers In The Sand

We were called to fight a war
We did not choose, but we are there.
To fight together to right a wrong.
We are brothers in the sand.

When the war is over and we are gone.
We'll remember our brothers in the sand
They are left to rebuild their land.
So once more proudly they can stand.

This new world has come about.
Shoulder to shoulder we now stand
Of freedom won in this great land.
With our proud brothers in the sand.

Now we leave this far off place.
Our job is done as we leave this land.
But some of us still must stay,
To stabilize the current fray.

When out heroes, they come home.
Let's not forget the burdens born.
We welcome them home with open arms.
We leave our brothers in the sand.

Chester R. Yell

The Walk To The Sky

As we walk to the sky,
we cannot be afraid to die.

As we go through the
heavenly gate, we will know
that we're not too late.

As the time comes for us
to meet our maker,
we will then truly know
that he is our taker.

Charmaine Santresa Fuller

Grandma's Song

We both have laughed.
We both have cried.
There's so much love.
Between you and I.
And, yes it's true,
time after time.
That me and you,
could not see eye to eye.
But with every day,
and beautiful night.
You have meant
much more to my life.

Eleanor Rainey

Flame

As I sit here patiently,
Watching this flame before me,
I see it burn so gold, so bright,
It leaves me chilled with fearful fright.
And yet there seems so pure and bold,
This flame that burns so bright and gold,
A warmth so rare and comforting,
Yet it could be a danger to me.
I hear it kills with burning screams,
And homelessness beyond our dreams,
It has two meanings, of good and bad,
A flame so happy, a flame so sad.
It dances before me so fast and tall,
The music is silent, the dancing and all,
There need not be a fright for me,
For it warms me with uncertainty.
Starting out small as it came,
I knew the warmth of this gold flame.

Carole Strehle

The Mist

Standing on the mountaintop
Watching the mist slowly rise
Wondering if it will ever stop
This violence before his eyes

He glances over the vast expanse of land
Watching the mist steadily rise
Dreaming that it will stop
This destruction before his eyes

Knowing he died a wrongful death
His mother cries at his graveside
His brother vowed to avenge him
The mist swirled before his eyes

Francine Shephard

"Finding Comfort"

The day we said goodbye to you
Was the hardest thing I've had to do

I stood beside your grave to grieve.
Wondering why you had to leave

My swollen eyes were filled with tears
Wishing we could have more years

Then as the tears ran down my face
I realized, you were in a better place

A place where there was no more pain
A place where we would will meet again

Because though our time on earth is through
There will come a time I'll be with you

But until that day we meet above
You'll be sadly missed and always loved

James Dayon

Untitled

Long ago when I was young, time
was slow and days were fun.
I remember running thru the
fields, so green, playing cowboys
and Indians till no light could be seen.
Now I am old and time is dear,
just to remember my childhood, keeps
my mind clear.
For the days are short and the
time is fast as I sit here
remembering my far away past.
Nothing to do, nowhere to go,
but into the past, where memories grow.
Just once more, to run and
play, cowboy and Indians again, one day.

George Thomas Angel II

Children Did You Know

Children did you know it
was only fifty years ago;
That so many of our country's
men went off to fight a war?

I wonder if you understand
how different your world would be,
If they hadn't left their home
land to fight across the seas?

Has anyone told you of the
sacrifice they made?
Their chance to raise a family
and die in their old age.

You say the world has changed
in every way since then;
But that was made possible
because of these special men.

You may not remember history
just the way you should;
But I know this world would
be a better place if only you would!

Carleen Bagley

"Merging Souls"

Two tortured souls.
Warily observe the other.

Recognize a kindred spirit.
Know the bond without mere words.

Calling forth a steadfast vigil.
Stealthily circle, with judicious tone.

Drawing closer upon each prowl.
One makes the heedful move.

Provoke the other, acknowledge this tie.
With brazen prowess, the other responds.

There could be no choice, but to commune.
Misery suffuses into ecstasy.

Andrea Maddack

Fairy Grandmother

One day I was walking,
Walking by the sea,
When suddenly a fairy,
Appeared in front of me.
She told me that I knew her,
Someone from my past,
I thought and thought about it,
And it occurred to me at last.
She was my great-grandmother,
Looking after me.

Aubrey L. Smith

The Doctor

If you would find me
Walk where the lightning splits the skies
And thunder claps the hands of God
In reprimand of errant earth
Drench in the spray of an angry lake
That beats upon the breakwall
And comes as gentle waves
To wash away my footprints
In the sand
Step softly past the silent sickrooms
Where anguished minds in restless slumber
Weep the long night through
Then search the purple mountain mists
And hear the west wind's vesper song
On harps of alder and aspen
In anxious quest to know all truth
I found calm in the tempest
Strength in the storm
Purpose in work
And faith on the winds

Dr. Edward R. Krivda

Lovers' Lament

I am afraid, but still I'll peer
When hearing the laughter of lovers near.
I envy your closeness; is it real?
You seem content, but your eyes reveal
A bewilderment you can't conceal.
What's in your heart that you can't reveal
Has been triggered by a past full of fear,
By stormy times that confuse and steer
You into a world of tears.

Elizabeth A. Kirk

Wooden Heart

Painted wooden rocking horse
Waits patient in the yard
Treasure of a lifetime
A child would not discard
Her colors cracked and faded
Stubble tail and shaggy mane
Saddle twisted sideways
And a single leather rein
Can't be compared to other ponies
She's green and blue and red
Where others feel the spark of life
Beats a wooden heart instead
Tell her child she's make-believe
The words fall on deaf ears
Her pony might not be the same
But still cries wooden tears
A believing child will fold her hands
When day comes to an end
To say a prayer for family dear
And her little wooden friend

Douglas Lenhart

A Silent Lullaby

Hear a child's silent cry,
Waiting for a mother's lullaby.
As the years go by fast,
all the memories seem to pass.
Thinking of what might have been,
But you keep soul searching within.
That special day comes along,
And all of the pain is gone.
No one would have ever guessed,
That we were truly blessed.
You can no longer hear that silent cry,
But only the voice of a mother's lullaby.

Christina L. Moak

Nature And Flowers

Roses are red
violets are blue
nature does her work
you should do yours too

Help keep the earth clean
you'll make her happy
if you do your work
she'll bring the light
and everyone will be full of delight!

Jennifer Crabtree

When

When is everything going to be alright,
When is everything going to work out,
When will the struggles pass,
When does everything go by,
When will everything turnout,
When will life get better,
Will life ever get to that stage?

Jennifer Elkins

Uneasiness

Heavy clouds,
Violet, blue, grey spot of light
Foretelling tempest,
Colours gathering up best
Uneasiness and fright.

Crazy sky of Van Gogh,
Hamlet's weird monologue.

Violet, blue, grey spot,
Thunderstorm
Thrilling harmonies a lot;
Liszt-Preludes,
Timpani din
Echoing the sin.

Heaven is pouring bright rain
From its bowl
Over my violet, blue, grey uneasiness.
This way
It is changing the stress
Of my soul
Into a rainbow ray.

Constantin Stoicescu

Remember The Angel

Something tiny,
Utterly defenseless,
   lying in what appears to be a cage.
An angel looks over,
Wings sparkling,
   making everything perfect again.
Someone worries,
Guilt inside.
   What will tomorrow bring?
Thinking of death
Only brings it closer.
Remember the angel,
Her sparkling wings,
   the glimmer of hope in her eyes.

Allyson Larke

Betterment

What's best for
Us all
Can cause us to stall
What we have seen
Can cause us to
Be very keen
With this in mind
We could become
Very divine
A new approach
Is sometimes
What is needed
To promote that
which has been seeded
It's best to look
High and low
To soften the blow
This we need
To grow
In order to soften the blow.

Edward T. Philpitt

An Open Hand

My hand now rests here openly,
   Upon this sea of sand.
My love sleeps on so peacefully,
   Here upon my land.

As he dreams of quiet streams,
   My secrets I shall speak
I am within those waters, Love...
   So soft, so pure, so deep.

He came to me yea long ago,
   When life was, yet so young.
How could we know that here today,
   Our song could still be sung.

What joy in knowing loving trust,
   Which keeps him in my sight.
I stroke his brow...I touch his lips,
   While night time turns to light.

Who is this beauty...at my side,
   Dark eyes in quiet sleep?
A love this simple maid doth know,
   An open hand shall keep.

Bonstance

God's Handiwork

Majestic mountains lay row,
upon row, as they fainter,
dimmer grow, with ethereal
grandeur against the sky,
up where the eagle and
ravens fly.

The lofty ridges rear their
heads, and rich green valleys
make their beds, down
where lichen and mosses grow,
and streams ripple to rivers below.

I see God's hand in
everything, I feel his
Presence near, and as I
Wait and meditate, His
still small voice I hear
in song of bird and gentle
breeze, wafting thru the
rustling trees!

Alice Chaussée

I Wish...

I wish I could fly.
Up where the wind runs wild,
and never die.
I wish I could laugh at pain,
and never cry.
I wish the sun never set,
the sky was always blue,
and the things that make me sad,
I wish I never knew.
I wish I was invincible,
I'd run and never stop.
And there would be no bottom,
And there would be no top.
And I would just go up, and up, and up,
and never fall,
And the world compared to me,
would be so very small.

Erin O'Neill

Future's Eternal Fight

Alone in a world
Unforgiving to most
No end in sight
All exits are closed

Nothing to view
While looking around
Can we not see
Nature's natural beauty

Air too bitter
Even to breathe

Must we strive
Through all eternity

Continue to struggle
Till the end of time
To save our planet
For future's eyes

Jason M. Boyer

Summer Song

Softly singing summer's song,
Twittering, trilling thrilling tunes;
Birds, brashly, brandishing, babbling,
Choruses crisply colored, choralled.
Earnest entreaty elegantly entered,
Holiness highly held, happily.
Flaunting freely, feathered flight;
Wildly wallowing with westwind.
Permanently perceived precious paintings.

Israel Baron

A Walk On Swan Street

floating up the sky way
twisting, through
the unchained melodies
misting my heart

when, the silver queen rises
two figures sway
on swam street we play
enclosed by Luna's luster

blinded, hands attached
with crickets, we dance
hearts clasp, wind
stirred wheat

Helios drives
the queen west
my Sandy, heart and eyes
behind are left

hopes lift, to drift
dreaming again

strolling, my queen and I
down swan street

Bryan Ludwig

Cold Breeze

The sunset fell on my face.
While the breeze stung my eyes,
I listened for the footsteps of my mother,
coming up the wide dusty road.
It started to rain. I heard my Mother
coming. There she was. I ran to her;
she was wet.

Elizabeth Lake

Self Deception

If self deception,
Turned into perception,
The misconception
Of life would remake.

If truth were derived
From old reason, revived
And not just contrived
For convenience sake,

Then civilization,
No longer, sedation,
Would with elation
Attend its own wake!

Bunny-Anne Lindsay

Barrel Of Gunpowder (Tornados)

Locomotive gales lacerated the night,
Trees bowed down, acknowledging their might.

Windows tattooed by needles of rain,
Houses once flourished, now splinters remain.

Masses of black swallowed the land,
Demonic funnels allowed nothing to stand.

In expectations swept the earth,
Scales of misery just gave birth.

Dawne C. Bielefeld

The Town God Loved

Gentle breezes of wind against my face
Trees blowing in the wind
One hiding the moon
Nature's opposing lights burning
false lights

Over all of man's sins watch the mountains
Gazing at us from above
Wondering why we all are here
Why some love nature
And others kill it

The stars becoming fainter and fainter
They used to be clear
When nature's opposing lights weren't here
They tell us our fortune
But we never listen

Most of all the moon
The moon that is so bright here
This must be a special place
And we all should praise it
It's from God's grace.

Bettina Antionette Judd

Untitled

In the night water is still
Trees blow silently across yards
Waves of the ocean are still.

Owls hoot, bats screech, dogs bark,
Cats meow. The moon shines bright across
The fields til morning begins again.

James Henry Bichler

By The Grace Of God

Sometimes the flowers and
trees bend to the winds.
As the winds die out and
the storms pass, the flowers
and trees rise up again.
SO BE IT
May we bend with our
private winds and storms.
But by the Grace of God,
May we stand straight and tall
before the night becomes total
darkness.
SO BE IT

Jeannette L. Strother

Hands

Hands, the tools of feelings,
touching, holding and shaking,
patting, squeezing and grasping.
Touch of a hand says so much.

The wee hand of tiny babe
chubby and sweet reaches out,
your face to meet.

Before we know it this hand finds another
new paths are taken, souls to awaken.

Hands work at many things
strong and skilled, soft and gentle
holding firm, with love caressing.

Hands too are for rings and pretty things
Some hands are injured or just grow old
thin and bony, swollen and sore
not pretty or strong anymore.

These hands will always be caring
feeling and loving and sharing.
Saying so much by the way they touch.

Barbara H. Miller

Loss In My Life

Nights living awake,
Tossing,
  Turning,
    Yearning.
Why did this happen to me?
Did I deserve it?
Am I destined to be...
Crying,
  Hoping,
    Praying,
      Worrying,
        Wanting,
          Wishing,
That someday soon
I will
Be whole again when...
My voice returns!

Amy M. Hamill

Van Gogh At Arles

The mistral tortures the landscape
Trees twist and bend in agony -
And the leaves -
They scream in terror
At a landscape aflame
with color.

George W. Coderre

Vacation's End

So glad you liked your camping trip
   Too soon to end, 'twas quite a gyp.
Although you like the outdoor life
   For me it's really too much strife.

To me the song of woodland thrush
   Is just a lot of stupid mush,
And, too, it would disturb my poise
   To hear the birds all making noise.

I could go on forevermore
   Relating nature's faults galore.
But I am different from the rest
   I think the city is the best

You sit beneath the shade of trees
   While bugs and ants crawl on your knees.
The rare perfume of skunks that roam
   Should make you wish you were back home.

And so I say to you my friend
   'Though your vacation's at an end,
In fifty weeks or more or less
   You will again find happiness.

Arthur A. Meola

I Remember

Whenever I feel life's troubles are just
Too much to bear,
When I feel I'm alone and no one
Seems to care,
I remember someone who was
More alone than I.
When I remember His great works
My troubles seem so small,
And all my nagging worries seem
Nothing at all.
When I think of Him I try to see
His eyes,
Those loving eyes that see past skin
To where true beauty lies.
And I am comforted when I recall
This, the greatest man on earth,
This man who died upon the cross
To give me second birth.

Jenny Wise

Untitled

WOMEN Strong and self-assured
Together we create a team
Full of love and self-esteem
Tearing down the walls that formed
No longer willing to conform
We've had the knowledge through the ages
Trust the wisdom, Learn from sages
Once I learned to stand up straight
A power came to stop the hate
This is my strength, my will, my might
A trusting love, a guiding light.
Know yourself, get on your feet
To love yourself is not conceit
Feel the power, trust your guide
I understood this once I tried.
Show yourself, hear your voice
And happiness becomes a choice
To live your life, create the dream
This, I've found is self-esteem.

Christina Sawelenko

Nurses Are A Special Breed

On call to adhere
To your every need
They follow their creed
To be sure they will weed
Your every vein
To give an I.V.
For you to be fed
So be kind when you meet
A nurse so neat
The strife in their life is tough enough
So be patient—patient
Whenever you call.

Alfred V. Santillo

Untitled

When you go
to whom it may concern...
This is to my
love
To whom it may concern...
I am dying
I feel as though my
spirit has drifted
To whom it may concern...
I am dead
but to my love
I went trying

Amy Toole

Your Tears Are Pearls

YOUR TEARS ARE PEARLS
THAT ANGELS GATHER,
To whisk away those jewels to me,
A precious symbol of your caring,
And that your love will ever be.

Those happy times we shared together,
The things that we enjoyed so much,
Let these dear memories be your solace,
That nothing sad can ever touch.

Just make your life so rich in living,
That there is no time for past regrets,
Take time you need for love and giving,
And save time for God; lest you forget!

Speak not of me with grief and sadness,
For I have your tears all tucked away,
A sweet remembrance of our friendship,
Knowing we shall meet again one day.

It's time to go on with your life now,
Look forward to a Brighter Day,
For sure as there are stars in Heaven,
God surely will show you the way.

Chris Dowdall Schult

Firewood

   There was a tree I loved
to play on, but then it was
cut down for firewood.
   There was a tree I loved
to sing on, but then it was
cut down for firewood.
   But that old tree I loved
to play and sing on, kept me
warm for winter.

Jacqueline Jones

The Cross

It was probably just some limb of a tree
To which He was nailed for you and me.
We don't know what color it was at first.
But it was dyed red as He cried, "I Thirst!"

That ugly old piece of wood
Held Him—the only one who could
Purchase for me salvation
By His humiliation.

His so-great pain
Bought such great gain
For you and me
On that ugly old tree.

Janice Hocutt

All In A Day

One giant step
to then fall behind
lose my balance
lose my mind

To clearly define
all in a day
lose my sight
lose my way

To befriend
no friend at all
lose my touch
lose my all

Dennis P. Fish

Listen

I love to listen to the brook and the bees,
To the whispering of the trees,
To the murmur of life each day,
I hear God this way!

He calms my soul and leads me on,
As I listen to these sounds,
For the world is His and all therein,
To enjoy when we slow down.

Thank you Lord for lending to me,
These moments we can share,
For my world is certainly better,
When I pause to find you here.

Ada V. Eppler

Oasis Of Chance

Loneliness on a tumbleweed,
Traversing a boundless wind,

Rolling across hate,
Erase the fault of men,

Reputed conspirator,
Entranced a third world spiral,

Blind not, the child mind,
Trouble not, their spirit

Fruitful growing persona,
This land dubbed natural expectation,

Wave my flag harmony,
Before a serious civilization

Planting seed, at the peace moment of cause,
Mirror an unknown, rainbow into waterfall,

Arthur R. Collazo

The End

From the moment you live
To the moment you die
How far you reach and
How long you strive

Is all you will see
From now till the end
I'll help you with all I can
I'll help you my friend

Later on in this lifetime
You'll see and touch
Remember why
You can't learn too much

And the end of the world
Will come to all
When the sun and the moon
Both shine through our hall

And if all you want
And you need
I will help you
If you let me be

Denny Matisin

"Autumn Leaves"

There Is No Wonder Like a Book
To Take Us Far Away —
Except The Fall of Autumn Leaves
And All Their Mystery —
They Filter Down and Fall Around
And Blow To and Fro!
They Warm Our Hearts
And Cast Their Glow
Of Yellows, Reds, and Browns, and Gold.

Joe Hix

Encouragement For A Friend

I know you're scared
To take care of your Dad
But think of your Mom
How she'd be proud
She's watching down
From up above
And showers you
With all her love
She trusts in you
To watch her man
You think you can't
She knows you can
She likes the son
That you've become
And now can rest
Her job is done

Judy Dresbaugh

"One Painful Teardrop"

One of many tears
To make up for all fears
Your memory kept in heart
With pain as piercing as a dart
It all went so fast
I wish it wasn't in the past
This memory I'll keep forever
Along with a single tear shed for you.

Jennifer A. Germanton

Having All These

Having all these things to read,
To study, to enjoy,
To roll in like a cat
In catnip,
Makes my life
The great gold pleasure that it is.
It piles up high around me —
Stacks of magazines, old newspapers
Too often on the floor
Though carefully (with the latter)
On a piece of plastic bag.
No dirt of newsprint then
To soil
My lovely yellow carpet.
And the books - on shelves
And shelves and every table top,
Not ever on the floor.
Neat, orderly, a sort of sorting,
Some dusty, some most aged and
All dearly loved.

Barbara C. Jensen

"Sojourney"

A far mile trek did undertake,
to see the sea's the reason,
from far atop my mountain's home,
in Terra's sweltry season.

Did fall beneath the briny wave,
to speak with Davy Jones,
within the Mother Ocean,
where she does keep his bones.

We passed around the bottle, boys,
and raised up a most raucous noise,
and spoke of all our earthly joys,
of sailing ships, and other toys.

When conversation turns to round,
and leave at dear man's beck,
and next to night did undertake,
to go return the trek.

George A. Crawford

Seeing Rainbows

Sometimes it is so very hard
To see the light of a distant star,
For the night itself is so very dark,
As it wraps so closely around us.

When troubles seem to stack themselves
One upon the other,
It's often hard to see what blessings
May rest within life's shadows.

We can, at times, spend so much time
Midst all our pain and sorrow,
That we forget to search among the tears,
For smiles that are hidden there.

What we need to always remember,
When our day begins to darken,
God never sends the clouds to us....
Without sending a rainbow, too.

Barbara I. Brown

"I'd Like To Write A Poem For You"

I'd like to write a poem for you
To put into your book.
One with a catchy title
To make readers say "Oh, look!"
But when I think of those I love
Or sentiments so dear
It seems my heart goes speechless and
My eyes begin to tear.
My husband and my Mom and Dad
My precious boys so sweet
Mean more to me than words can say
When heart and mind do meet.
So when I try to capture love
With paper and a pen
It seems my soul just must explode
And words fail me again.
And so I must apologize
For taking up your time
Unless you're saying as you read
"These thoughts, they could be mine."

Jennifer Stone

The Unsung Symphony

God gave to me my Symphony
to pull me from my pain;
Symph taught me I had naught to lose
and everything to gain.

Step by step, ever careful he kept
me secure upon his back;
Hour after hour, day after day
we plodded 'round the track.

Many times a day my balance strayed
but never did I fall;
Symph felt my shift, swerved under me
to keep me sitting tall.

Still, in my dreams at night it seems
my accident ne'er occurred;
The music swells, I'm jumping well
and the lion in me purred.
Symph gave me back ME and set me free,
A gift which ultimately;
Can ne'er be taught and at no cost be bought —
He restored my dignity.

Bobbi Groover

Fall Is Here

I came outdoors this evening
To our patio in the rear
The wind is rather chilly
But the sky is nice and clear

There is noise out on the free way
There is a plane flying up above
Although fall is in the air tonight
It is the season that I love,

I should be in my apartment now
Listening to the evening news
But all the news today somehow
Bring on a severe case of the blues

I have many friends and loved, ones
I could call them on the phone
But every one is busy
And sometimes its good to be alone

It is nice and peaceful now
It's been a pleasant day
Soon it will be to cold out here
So I'll enjoy it while I may.

Bertha J. Buffington

The Meaning Of Marriage

When two people make a vow
To love until the end,
It does not matter why or how
Or what life does intend.

A sacrifice indeed occurs,
For each gives all there is;
His goods, his name, his self are hers,
And she is completely his.

The risks and dangers life deals out,
They'll face them now together;
As a team there won't be any doubt
There's no storm they cannot weather.

Just as a plant starts from the seed,
Their love will change and grow;
And each for the other will find a need
That before each did not know.

The two, once separate, now are one,
The union of groom and bride;
No more alone the race to run,
A partner is now alongside.

Henry M. Ditman

Prayer Answered

I prayed to God this morning
to lead and guide my way
to help me use the gift
that abides with me each day

He heard my prayer and helped me
to do my very best
to listen and think humbly
and then he did the rest

To use the gift he gave me
was not as I thought
I thought it would be a fight
but instead I found delight

I believed God when I awakened
and a special day it was
as always he upheld me
in his care and with his love

Crystal Spencer

"The Men Of Peace"

They came in peace
To heal our lives
To turn hate into tolerance
And tolerance into love.

One man lived long ago - in Nazareth.
His name was Jesus.
Another man lived in India.
His name was Gandhi.
Just recently, this time Tel Aviv,
Lived another man of peace named Rabin.

All these enlightened men of peace
Were extinguished by forces of darkness.
But their light did not die
No, their example will shine forth forever.

Will men ever learn to turn away from hate?
Will the world ever know true peace?
The answer is within the hearts of all
Who can recall the men of peace - and
Follow their example.

Jack R. Mertz

Fun In The Past

Why do we work so hard it seems
To go home and watch TV.
Or to go to the local pub and drink
When things aren't going so easy?

Where did we falter
Are we still in a dream-
Do you ever think we will find
That land of peaches and cream?

When we were younger, years ago
Things didn't seem so hard
There were places to go and money to spend
Now everything is put on a credit card.

Well, Christmas is nearly upon us again
God, the years have gone fast-
The bills are all backed up again
We had a lot more fun in the past.

Cerelda Spalding

Susan B. Anthony

Susan fought with all her might,
to get what she believed was right,
to have all people be treated alike,
woman or man, black or white.

She would stand up and fight,
fight for people's rights,
listening to her heart day and night.

Susan worked to get her dream,
no matter how impossible things would seem,
working with her friends as a team.

Susan fought with all her might,
to get what she believed was right,
to have all people be treated alike,
woman or man, black or white.

Jessica Marts

To You — My Love You'll See

To see us as another dream,
To gain knowledge of life's stream.

To care enough to be concerned,
To be aware of what I've learned.

To come to terms and to accept,
To forget the many nights I wept,

To realize when it's time to change,
To make the time to rearrange.

To seek myself and strength in me,
To turn my back — to let you be.

To believe in God — to let you go,
To hide the pain you'll never know.

To have a heart that can forgive,
To find the peace one needs to live.

To smile each time I recollect,
To feel your touch and its effect.

To show my feelings in such a way,
To respect you enough to walk away.

To sacrifice my love — you'll see,
To you — this is a gift from me.

Desirae J. Riley Corso

"Yesterday's Pain"

A new day dawned and I was on my way
To finish the chores of a usual day
I looked at the clock, only to see
The pain from a year ago, haunted me

I relived each moment all over again
The grief was renewed with stronger pain
Oh, how will I make it without you here
Momma, this has been a struggling year

Tomorrow is your birthday, too
I promise to sing, just for you
A special tune, a familiar song
As you listen, please sing along

I try to keep my eyes on the Lord
To find comfort in His Holy word
His grace is sufficient to get me through
Yet, I will forever be missing you

Sometimes I find laughter in a day
But underneath it all, there is dismay
I want to be happy, as in the days past
To live each day fully, as if it's my last

Bonita H. Dunlow

Some Poems Sleep

The poet's mind wanders
to clear blue skies
imaginary gardens with butterflies,
roaring waves amidst the sea
the essence of flowers
and the rustling tree.

Some poems lost
because of high sounding interpretation
and never reach the poets designation.

The poet's mind pushes
before the poem is washed away...
and becomes invalid.

Some poems lost
through hesitation
in the poet's bewildered imagination.

Some half finished,
incomplete,
hands cannot grasp the poems
that sleep.

Joyce Unsworth

Nature/Life

Mother Nature has the gift
to bring life from ashes
From the fallen leaves to
the coverlet of life renewing snow
The promise of Spring.

And, so it is with us humans
who are an inborn part of nature.
If only we would listen
with our soul—to her gentle
whispers.

So shall we be reborn to the
promised Spring
to blossom in the sun.

Jannis Candill

The Old Home Place

I had to say goodbye
To an old friend today
I took plenty of pictures
Before I went away

I thought of all the good times
Of all the memories we shared
Of all the family and loved ones
This good friend has loved and cared

The nights my children slept in peace
The days they played away
The many family get-togethers
The storms that passed our way

All the rooms, all the doors
The big yard, the hardwood floors
The bay-window, the ceiling fans
All my neighbors and even the old mail man

If only these old walls could talk
Think of the stories that could be told
I had to say goodbye today
The old home place is being sold

Dianne Fenner

Precious

Hold your breath a character
timid with sharp image
hold your breath a character
timid with sharp image
ambitious precious
Precious precious
outspoken open on
her toes no villain or
foes precious precious
precious tender shiny
shiny hair responsive daring
pretty in the clothes she's wearing
precious precious precious
understanding a glide stride a sparkle
in her eye precious precious
precious witty soft to
caress your my interest
precious precious precious

Eric Granda

Moon Candy

At times the moon is shaped like a bowl...
tilted
I used to think that peppermint butterscotch
chocolate covered
chimes
would pour from it
My mother would hold out her shirt to
gather the candy
In the kitchen I saw her pull peppermints
from the beaming bowl
I'm still thinking about it...
How could she climb so many stairs?
Did an angel lure it down by rope,
Or did she call God and ask to borrow it?
Now I can place my hand on the
moon's heart
grasp peppermint chocolate
happiness
Now I know my mother's shirt is
free from the spewing candy

Albert J. Kelly

Untitled

Thumb your life
Thumb when you need a ride,
Thumb down to your side,
Thumb in your eyes,
Thumb when you cry,
Why thumb?
Don't be dumb,
Take a bus, train, or why not fly?
Seek a job, don't be a slob.
"Thumbs Up"

Deborah L. Rypple

To The One I Love

To the one I love I give my heart,
    thru good and bad, till death do us part.
The one I love is someone sweet,
    someone who is special from head to feet.
The one I love is so very caring,
    someone whose life I'm glad I'm sharing.
This someone is very beautiful too,
    that someone my love, is you.
I love you so much,
    that I tremble with your touch.
The only place I want you to be,
    is safe in my arms with me.
Always remember, I love you
    wherever you go and whatever you do,
Forget the bad times, remember the good
    then we'll go on as true lovers should

Bambi Lynn De George

To The One I Love On Any Day

There are special days
    Throughout the year
For traditional gifts
    To wish good cheer

But, this is to say
    I love you much
Your sparkling eyes
    Your gentle touch

Sure, we have
    Our ups and downs
Sometimes we laugh
    Sometimes we frown

When we get mad
    It's not for long
Because we know
    Our love is strong

This is how
    I wish it to stay
'Cause honey, you're special
    To me every day!

Bobby Purcell Sr.

Waves Crashing

As I was walking
upon a shore,
I found seashells on
the shore,
Washed up by the
crashing waves,
I also found someone
special waiting just
for me.

Jenny Nguyen

Snow Dance

Night comes and one can see
    through the window
the mesmerizing beauty of the
    swaying snow,
dancing its way down
    from heaven.
Mounds of flakes cradle
    delicately in the branches,
as a dressing upon the trees.
Warm reflections glisten from
    its blanket of light,
as though millions of stars
    have fallen.

Carole Lee Garrison

Wind

The wind is calm and blustering
through the trees so silently
and very gently, now the wind
is mad and tearing through the
trees knocking over limbs and ripping
through the leaves.

Alex Tice

Ole Beautiful Spring - Begone!

From my window I used to see,
Through the boughs of a leafless tree,
The one I love - but she not me
Perched to muse on her balcony.
But now that pleasure is no more
To gaze on her whom I adore,
For leafy spring is here, damn her,
Cloaking the boughs of that leafless tree
Hiding till autumn that dear one from me.

Dante Vezzoli

A Mother's Love

A mother's love is an amazing thing,
through summer winter fall and spring.

A mother's love is always there,
through smiles, laughter, hurt and Despair.

A mother's love is happy and bright,
all through day and by night.

A mother's love is like a dove,
a definite gift of the heaven's above.

A mother's love is an eternal flame,
Never going out,
Never the same.

Alicia Alvarez

Untitled

My head is racing...
Thoughts of you bombard my mind
Like the raindrops
That sound against my windowpane.

Like the flower
Seeking its nourishment from the rain
So I would be
Nurtured by the strength of your love.

Jennifer Lucera

Life's Embrace

It is yes I said to life
Though part we must aghast in strife
We did our part both you and I
And now my time draws near to die
Though tears be hidden in masks of smiles
Warrior you not I to face these miles
One last time we embrace ourselves
Stealing time from blessed bells
As your hand cedes mine for the last
Let go the body and thank the past
For your love has born my soul
And given strength where worries toll
I leave here now with only love
And only you to thank for all above
So walk from here and shed the old
With chin up high to stars behold
Focus anew the shimmering night
And promise me Yes, you say to life.

Brian P. Gaucher

Throw-Away Cards

Not often used
   Those cards we get
That come by mail
   They usually set
Upon some shelf
   Where they just lay
Until one day
   They're thrown away

But I have found
   Good use you bet
For one such card
   It is to let
You know I'm glad
   You thought to say
"John Gadd we need
   Your poem today!"

John A. Gadd

Advice For Bad Love

Beautiful, but young as buds on the Crocus,
This was the one he took as his love.
Each in the time of their seasons,
she in the springtime,
he in the winter.
Yet, she was younger than the years
marked off on her calendar.
Fragile, lacking direction, like a
baby bird who fell from its nest.
Growing like a woman, yet nestled in
her thoughts like a child.
And this was the woman that he chose.
And he heard the sound of the Siren
chanting her call.

Irving Weinberg

Memories

Dreaming, just dreaming of times gone by
Thirty years in the space of a sigh
Moments experienced taken for granted
Becoming a fantasy ever enchanted

Weaving a web of euphoric illusion
Memories comfort in tortured confusion
Recorded forever on passage of time
As magically sorrow becomes joy sublime

Betty Stulgin

Lost Youth

She wept - she knew not what to do.
This surely had destroyed her life.
Her dreams were never viewed this way.
She always thought she'd be his wife.

She was so young, but no one knew.
She dressed much older, like her peers.
She thought it gave her self-esteem
And somehow helped to calm her fears.

She drank a little, smoked a little;
Who remembered what was next?
All she knew was she was ready
For a night of love and sex.

But now she cries out all alone;
Where is the man who vowed his love?
She lay there on a street of filth,
With no one but the Lord above.

And as she struggled through the pain,
She thought how she had been beguiled.
She stood up slowly, wiped a tear,
And walked away and left her child.

Boots Mertens

The Poets' Walk

Step outside with us.
This perpetual morning
we are here waiting.

Walk slowly ahead.
We find realms of subjective
as concrete grass waves.

No words are spoken.
In this clear sense classroom
we breathe metaphors.

Like Sisyphus we
labor ceaselessly. Our words,
struggling upwards, run.

Adam Kaufman

Me, Myself, And I

I'm all alone in this world,
this little world of mine.
this caring world,
this loving world,
but not thru my eyes.
I have just three people in my life.
I'm not alone with them.
They listen to me,
talk to me,
and are always my friends.
I'm not afraid with them,
I'm never bored with them.
I laugh with them,
cry with them,
sit with them,
and shine with them.
I thank these three people.
They mean a lot to me.
For with out them who would
I be?

Elizabeth Gentry

"The Best Gift Of All"

Christmas comes but once a year!
This day for me, is very dear.
   The woman I love most of all,
came by to see me, and help deck the halls!
   We sat and talked, we laughed,
and smiled! She stayed with me,
for quite awhile!
   I felt so good, and warm inside.
While she was sitting, by my side!
   I think the best gift, you can
get in life! Is to have someone special,
like a lover, or wife! To share those
times, when your happy or sad! To
help pick you up, when you feel,
really bad!
   For without this gift, that I speak of!
There's no point in sharing, his
gift from above!

James M. Kostkiewicz

What Is Time?

The young of man called children
   Think that time moves much too slow,
Wishing only it would go faster,
   Then they ask "Where did it go?"

For some it is a burden,
   Saying it's never just or fair,
All just wanting to be younger,
   Most of which "touch-up" their hair.

Others think of time as money,
   Measuring it only by their dough,
Spending most of their waking hours
   Gathering items made for show.

Then there are those who think of time
   As something without end.
But the end of time for man, I fear
   Is just around the bend.

For time is that which passes
   At a pace that's much too fast.
It rolls along not knowing man,
   Most of which live in the past.

John LeGros

Eagles

They fly high
They fly low
They even sometimes
Dive in to the snow
And get all white you know
Take a bath in a pond
Then fly again far and beyond
The more we see are extent
See their very few at
The pue, but if we see
one we will know cause
in the moonlight it will
Glow in his eye as
for you and I an eagle's
Great in God's fate.
Eagles.

Barbara Mayo

"Before You Go"

Before you go
There's something I must ask you.
Before you go.
I'd like to know.
Will you return when 'ere you lonely;
Or will you wander farther on.

Because when you leave,
You carry all my thoughts of you;
And I'm no good until you return.

So, before you go,
I'm still wondering;
Will you miss me, when lights are low.
Or will the past be cast behind you.
Won't you please tell me.
Before you go.

Frederico B. DeRichardes

There's No Time

I really need to talk to you,
There's never any time,
I need to tell you so much,
There's really a lot on my mind.

My mother sometimes understands,
My father doesn't have a clue,
You know it's a lot different,
For me to talk to you.

There's so much going on right now,
So many things are new,
There's never any time for me,
To spend time with you.

There's so much work so little time,
The day flies by so fast,
When I think there's time for talking,
The time to talk is past.

All that I can say right now,
It's I'd like to talk to you,
Maybe the day will come,
When there's more time for me and you.

Cassandra Crawford

Tiny Angel

Pale as a spring moon,
there you stood. Why
did you have to leave so soon?

Death's habitual grip
wedges his scythe between us,
you, pale as a spring moon...

His ways still haunt me.
I try to grow and forget, forgive.
Did you have to leave so soon?

Like a dream, you are
just out of reach; I cannot touch
you, pale as a spring moon.

Unasked, death descends and
in time we all must dance his tune.
But why did you have to leave so soon?

When foresight frays, often
silent judgment streams behind.
So pale you were, like the spring moon.
Why did you have to leave so soon?

Debra L. Woodruff

The Pain

Child, the day you were born
   there was pain,
Your first steps and falls
   there was pain.
Your first day at school
   there was pain,
Through your teens
   there was pain.
When you married and left home
   there was pain,
For you, your first baby
   there was pain.
Your separation and divorce
   there was pain,
But drugs and prison
   what we called pain!
Was not the crying, lonely, never-ending pain.
That all of us suffer now
   this is pain, terrible PAIN!

Alice C. Limpach

Words Down Under

When you go down under
There are words that you should know,
For Australians speak pure Aussie,
But don't you get the joes.

A bagman is a drifter,
The cobber is your friend,
A shiela is the lady
Waiting round the bend.

A ranch is called a station,
A jumpbuck is a sheep.
The brumly is a wild horse,
Dare you one to keep?

Dingos, drangos, galahs
Are people without class;
The doggers chase their dingos,
Now don't go all aghast.

Learn the Aussie saying,
While in this foreign land,
Then you can knock them bandy
With all you understand!

Ellen Bourgeau

The Puzzlement

Like the King of Siam
"There are times
I am not sure of what
I absolutely know..."
With the king, I identify
In regal status not
But in confusion's lot.
A puzzle to me am I,
A jig-saw all apart,
A crossword left undone,
A tick-tack-toe unwon,
A riddle with no key.
I fight to recall the face
Reflecting back the chap
Behind the mask,
The self he never found.
I am a puzzlement
Maybe not to God
Nor even to my wife
But certainly to me.

Gus Wilhelmy

"To Love"

O Lord help the helpless that I see
There are so many children across the sea.
Children we've seen in need of love,
Clothes and shelter
and a mother's helping hand,

The world is in need
of a touch from the master.
We are in turmoil,
distrust and disaster.

May the children of the future
be wise, and armed with truth,
so the Lord can get back
in touch with us.

The Lord's promise is clear,
as long as we follow his footsteps near.
Hold on to each other
and have the love
the Lord said we should
for the whole human race.

Betty Legeness

You And Me

I gave birth to you
Then you were gone
To make someone else happy
Then came sorrow and pain
Years went by not knowing
I knocked on door after door
Still no answer of where
If only could find
It's true as can be
You found me
What a "Miracle"
No matter who or what
If only you can forgive me
Now we are a "Family"
Let's make new beginnings
That means you and me

Diane Bartlett

Grandpa

An angel came and touched your hand
then took your soul away
If I could only join you now;
But it's not my place to say.

Your soul gone but your pain stays here,
dormant in my heart;
Right next to the love I have for you,
that's been there from the start.

"Let not your heart be troubled,"
I know I should believe;
Your happy now, I should be too,
But all I do is grieve.

I wish just once I could hug you again;
and bring back your faithful smile
to have my heart laugh and feel content;
at least for a little while.

Just one last time to comfort me;
as I lay my head on your chest,
But I know that you are happy now
in your peaceful time of rest.

Christina M. Patterson

Prairie Storm

Prairie winds sigh deeply,
Then rise and run in rage
Stirring dust and tumble weed,
Ripping at the sage.

Wind tossed seas of waving grass
Go rolling oer' the hills,
While tempest tossed, the creatures,
Seek shelter by the rills.

The drum deep roll of thunder,
Comes tumbling down the way,
And jagged fingers, all on fire,
Pierce the clouds of gray.

Then rain falls down in torrents,
The sweet wet kiss of time,
While puddles grow to rushing tides,
And dash to get in line.

Then quickly, as it passes,
Its wake is filled with mirth,
For this heaven-sent thunderstorm
Has just refreshed the Earth.

Alfred H. Schoen

The Silence...Too Loud!

If our hearts select no burden
Then our hands pay no debt
When we sing the Truth in secret
We stutter a false duet
But the silence is still loud!
Like the quiet before the hail
Or the smile of a deaf child
Or ex-lovers unanswered mail
So hands and hearts redeem yourselves
And change the way you feel
Mr. and Mrs. Jane and John Doe
It's time we pay the bill
Though everyone is wearing black
To grow we all must wean
Fear not the storm
The dark won't last
The rain will wash us clean.

David B. Allen

"Nobody's Fool"

First I met this girl
Then I made her my wife.
We're celebrating twenty nine years,
With her, I'll spend the rest of my life.

I look to the future,
I remember things from the past.
I'll always remember her,
Our love will always last.

I've seen the summers and winters,
The falls and the spring.
I will be looking forward.
For happy days our love will bring.

Sometimes we are together.
Sometimes we are apart.
Which way makes no difference.
We carry each other in our heart.

You can keep all your money.
You can treasure your family jewel.
Me, I'll keep my family,
Because I'm nobody's fool.

Donald W. Morse

When Petals Bloom On Roses In The Spring

When petals bloom on roses in the spring,
Their fragrance lures the others to its place,
Where beauty meets the eye before the sting,
And captures many hearts just by its face.
But life goes on and as it passes by,
The beauty it possessed begins to wane;
Its smooth red skins all shrivel up and die;
So momentary, it cannot remain.
Begin and end - the way that life must go;
When grown in age the handsome turn to vile;
If not in mind and physical be so,
Is fading life and failure in the trial.
But one's true being lasts if one can give
To memory, in heart forever live.

Christine Choi

Pussy Willows

As I was walking through
the woods one day,
I found some pussies
that wanted to play.
Their soft fuzziness
tickled my arm
as I walked by
And I almost thought
I heard them cry (meow).
Now these were not kittens
or even cats
but pussy willows along the path.

Anne Jessen

Days Come Days Gone

Seating in my room looking out.
The window of my life silently slip by.
Dreary days wind breaking limbs of trees
Lost loved ones.
Sunny clear days bringing
Love-children home.
Snow flakes fall. Hair white.
Soon re-birth green leaf trees.
Grandchildren come home.
I wonder when my tree will fall
Then no more will I see days go by.

Angelike Platis

The Other Spirit

Her entrance is soft,
The whisper of the closing of a
  refrigerator door.
Her laughter the tinkling of ice on glass.
Then the strong pungency of her scent
As she the color of warmth
Walks hand in hand with my husband
A twosome in my presence.
She is sly, and with slurred words
Urges him to rant at my short comings
And how only she can comfort
The stress that life inflicts.
A demanding mistress she has proved.
Her love is at a price,
Besotted, he is powerless in her embrace.
They lie together
And I in anger sit and
watch the lost expression on his face

Daphne Sparrow

The Old Sea

I walked alone by the troubled sea,
The waves swept up over the sand to me.
How old is the ocean?
How old is the sea?
It is as old as eternity.

God made Adam first.
Then He made the universe.
He made the skies so fair,
The cattle, and fishes and fowls of the air.

The moon divided the day from night.
In the daytime the sun was bright.
As I sat and listened to the roaring sea,
I felt so happy and fortunate to be

On this earth with flowers and trees,
The birds soaring above
The gentle breeze.
Oh! How beautiful life is to me.

Eloise N. Collin

The Valley Of Tears

While I walked thru the valley,
The valley of tears,
I saw thru the teardrops how love
disappears.
Each teardrop shows a bitter scene,
With emotions felt sharp and keen.
Now alone I often wonder,
As my spirits lift from asunder;
How I made it thru,
The Valley Of Fears.

Elizabeth A. Troudt

A Message To My Son

In the final seconds of the game,
The two teams have scored the same.
Loud and noisy yells the crowd,
But in the end I'll still be proud.
Of my son who played so hard,
Playing the game with all his heart.
Down and down the seconds fall,
Soon the kids must shoot the ball.
One second left the ball is shot,
Right there in that exact spot.
The shot from my son's hands,
In the basket I hope it lands.
I hear the buzzer sound,
The ball goes through the net
and hits the ground.
The game is over and we won,
Especially my son.

Bryan Parker

The Popsicle Man

Whatever happened to the popsicle man
The truck to which I so often ran.
With my dime held in my fist
My eyes would gaze up and down his list.
So many things from which to choose
My favorite popsicles were the sky blues.
The fudgesicles too were truly a delight
My tummy laughed with each yummy bite.
Oh popsicle man I miss you so
Where...Oh where did you go?

Gayle Seymour

Heaven On Earth

Ah, the beauty of the hills,
The trees — such glorious splendour!
The rushing brook, the babbling rills,
Only God can render!

Ah, the beauty of the lakes,
Reflecting those glorious trees,
The rippling wakes the lonely loon makes
Helped along by the breeze.

Ah, the beauty of the leaves!
Such a riot of colour they bring
Swirling down to their bed on the ground
Warming the mayflowers till spring.

Ah, the beauty of the fields
Their golden harvest rip for reaping.
Tall stalks of corn at early morn,
Their yearly vigil keeping.

Yes, the beautiful trees,
The crystal pure lakes
The riotous leaves —
God's heaven on earth makes!
Evelyn Stata

Winter Consumes

Her news hits me
The thunderous crash
I try to ignore her
The snow plummets closer

I am Buried
I can no longer listen
My body's cold and numb
If she keeps on talking
I will never be discovered
John W. Mayle III

Gratitude

Dear Father help me understand
The tasks set forth for me.
Upon my shoulder place a hand
To guide me nearer thee.

Confused, discouraged, and dismayed
I turn my thought above
Thou art the way, your light displayed
Resplendent, filled with love.

'On this straight path your feet must tread'
My thought rejoicing hears
'Onward, upward, without dread,
Nor pain, nor fear, nor tears'.

Dear Father thank you for this gift
Of truth which sets us free
To know and cherish and to lift
Our spirits up to thee.
Helen-Lane Jessop

Shenowa

Years past, hearts Linger
their lone for sure.
Their eyes grow gray,
as their minds stay pure.
Their touch for wisdom,
stands, their touch for gold
they sit,
Their mind Linger,
Deborah Harris

"Home"

The beautiful sky,
the sun shining through
the clouds,
the green grass beneath
my feet.

All this beauty is so sweet,
this beautiful place we
call our home is no
more than a resting place,
we are just passing
through on our way,
on our way to heaven.
Eryn Sandifer

First Feelings Of Love

The first time that I looked in your eyes
   The sun cleared away the rain
The first time I held your hand
   I no longer felt the pain
My troubles seemed so far away
   As long as you were near
I'm glad that I found someone
   Someone who'd really care
With you in my life
   There is no more looking back
This feeling of love
   I'm sure it's going to last
Never before has there been another
   Who's felt the same as me
Every day with you
   Feels like eternity
But when the sun goes down
   And the stars fill the sky
There is nothing brighter
   Than the sparkle in your eye.
Cliff Colella

Sweet Mystery

This morning as I woke
The sun brought her long fingers
Into my room,
Caressing my cheeks, tantalizing
My eyes
To open and awake
To embrace the day
On wings of a dove —
Soaring high into the blue sky
To experience the warmth, colors,
Wonders
Of the enchantment below

In every voyage
And the Sun's gentle touch,
Lie thoughts of you, dear Michael
Dana Eichert

Spring

The flowers are blooming.
The snow has melted.
The sun is shining.
The people have jogged for the day.
The bees are buzzing.
The dogs have been walked.
This spring day is ending.
Wait for a little, and
You will see another
Spring day will appear to thee.
Giulia Capriola

"Sounds Of Surf"

A man is blest when he can see
   The splendor in the restless sea —
To feel her touch and hear the tone
   That speak to us when we're alone.
She tells of strength - unwavering will
   Of tenderness, of power to kill
Consumes the vain, denies the bold
   And keeps her story much untold.
She counts no years, reveres no name
   Forever changing, yet the same.
She reaches out her beckon hand
   To touch the shores of every land.
In common tongue she speaks to all
   Who hear the sound and heed the call.
What does she say to you and me
   Of life and love and destiny?
She gives to each a secret key
   And no one else can hear but thee.
Floyd A. Balman

Torn Between Two Lovers

   Torn between two lovers as
the song goes.
   Where it will bring us
we won't know.
   We can't move too fast,
we can't move too slow, for
when the right time comes
we both will know.
   Our love a secret we must
hide, for no one must know
or I'll surely die.
   When we both get married
and go our separate ways, when
we say our vows we will both
leave our love
   In vain.
Denise Reid

As Time Goes On

Magnolias and moonlight
The smell of grass and sea
Moss, and warmth and gentle breeze
They mean so much to me

A slower pace gives me a chance
to reflect on childhood dreams
The early years of wedded bliss
and what such happiness means

Thoughts of babies all grown up
with babies of their own
Whose smiles and ways did so much
to make our house a home

Friends who have gone before
and those we still hold dear
Even when they're far away
they seem so very near

Time goes by so very fast
You don't know where it went
Lingering thoughts of things long gone
Memories are permanent.
Elizabeth S. Bush

So I Dance With Joy

The silver mountain moves me.
The silver mountain lifts my spirit,
It takes me to the gates of heaven
Like a prayer at the Pieta.

The trade wind moves me.
The trade wind buoys me,
It sways me up and down
Like the branches of a willow-tree.

The golden sun moves me.
The soft light enters my soul,
It carries me with it
So I dance with joy....

Cleo Laszlo

Friends

As we travel through life searching for
   the security and happiness life
   promised us throughout our childhood,
We seek evanescent rainbows to fill
   our hearts with the rewards
   from false ideas and dreams.

Seldom do we stop our searching to learn
   that many times our pots-of-gold
   wait in the hearts of our friends;
And treasures stored in true friends'
   generous hearts are always available
   —just for the asking!

Becky J. Richardson
Marietta, Georgia

"Apprehension"

Silently he moves across the frozen lake
The rest of the pack waits at the shore
He sniffs the air and freezes
Then slowly backs away
Following his own footsteps
To return to the safety of the shadows
The woods around him are silent
No call to echo through the trees
A strange stillness falls
On the darkening forest
As the wolves scan the hills
And peer into the trees
Searching for the source of their tension
A telling scent or trail
But no sign is forthcoming
No tell-tale puff of breath
Just the pervasive apprehension
That man has entered the woods

Jeffrey S. Williams

The Truth

People smile not knowing,
they think that you are always happy.
If they knew what you feel inside,
would they still smile the same?
The hurt will never go away,
the pain will always stay.
You can cover up the truth,
by putting smiles on your face,
the laughter that you fake,
and the words that you say.
No one will see through,
There's a shield of metal around you.
They will never know the truth.

Jennifer Engel

"Rain"

Like a leaf on a tree...
the raindrop falls from the clouds.
Never, ever so hard to see,
the clear water is set free.
The sound of rain falling on the
ground is like a heartbeat
sound. Pound, pound, the rain
falling to the ground and the
world still spinning around.
When it's always the feeling
of pain, it is now to be
healed by rain, and the
day I run in the field
in rain, is an April day, in
forever I'll pray.

Gina Trombetta

Bitter Winter

The glittering snow shows no mercy to me
The piercing, frigid cold has a hold of me
Lost and alone on frozen land
The wind reaches out and grabs my hand
The end this time I cannot see
My mind slipping away fantastically
From this terror there is no shelter
Death will come in helter skelter
The mouth will open to release its roar
Sounding out forevermore
Ice driving deep into my soul
A few more steps, my final goal
Blackness crosses into my path
Standing absolute to face the wrath
I'm off to see the secret show
Lost eternally in the snow

Jeremy L. Elliott

Until That Day

The first love that never lasted is
the one I shall miss the most
For a long time he was all that I lived for
Almost what I died for
He was so much to me
I'd like to have him back
I think it would kill me though
I miss him so much
I can't go on with my life
My tears fall like the water from a faucet
I try to go on with my life
He'll always be in my mind
I'll stay to try for him
My life will eventually go on
I'm just waiting for that day
The day my mind becomes free.

Diane Michelle Dees

Untitled

"When I was six, I had a best friend
Then I moved away.
When I was nine, I had a best friend
Then he moved away.
When I was nineteen, I had a best friend
Then God took him away.
When I was forty-eight, I had a best friend
And she led me back to God.
Nothing can ever take this friend away!"

Gordon W. Schoen

Late Autumn

I love to watch and see
   the oak's remaining leaves
     spin
       and dance
In morning's breeze.

not brown and sere
   are they,
But shades of tawny deer
   below the gray
Autumnal skies.

My heart lilts too
   as do the leaves
As bits of blue
   when gray sky cleaves
Shine through.

Gwendolyn Y. Walker

The Day Dawns

The day dawns
the night appear
please awake
Jesus draws near

No time for sleeping
no time for play
we must keep marching
till the end of day.

Keep your head high
it'll soon be over
cross the finish line
we will make it on time.

Fannie Jones

Untitled

The holidays are over,
The new year is here,
The skies are cold and gray,
I have little reason to cheer.

I wait for spring,
I want the temperature to rise,
I want to hear the water running,
To look up and see blue skies.

I can not wait for the April showers,
When trees, shrubs, and flowers bloom,
I walk outside into the wind now,
All I feel is frigid and gloom.

Do not take me wrong,
Winter can be beautiful, peaceful, quiet,
But, I herald the coming of spring,
For this is the time God lets nature riot.

Amber L. Lackey

September Day

As I sit underneath the maple tree
The wind kisses my face
And the sun smiles at me.

A tiny bird
Flutters away
All the world is cheerful
On this September day.

Amanda Bernier

My Mind's Eye

In my mind I can do
The most wonderful things;
I can conquer the Alps
Or play polo with kings,
Dive deep under oceans,
Jump out of high planes,
Trap lions in jungles,
Lead bull fights in Spain.
My bravery, daring,
Bravado, and more,
Are spread far and wide,
I am worshipped, adored.
The mind is a gateway
To magic and fame.
We all can be heroes
In life's many games.
Carolyn R. Perry

Wild Berries In His Hand

The slight wind rises from the north
The morning shadow of the sun blinds the
  Tall grass

The dew still clinging to the meadow
Stretches in a fog along the road
The sounds of an outsider invade
  This peace

Along the crisp new grass and weeds
Stalks a man with wild berries
  In his hand

Breakfast is consumed along the way
As the man paces off down the road
  Following the empty highway.
Jake Michael Schindler

These Things I Love

I love the flowers and the trees,
The moonlit nights - the gentle breeze
I love a hoot owl's mournful cry.
A tender smile - a lullaby.
I love a firelight's warming glow
A baby fawn - a buffalo
I love to watch the children play.
I love to hear a donkey bray.
I love the silence of the night,
A flock of geese that's in full flight.
I love to hear a dear one's call
A loving smile - a waterfall.
I love the mist upon my face,
A baby quail - a quiet place.
I love the mountains and the hills,
A field of yellow daffodils.
The man who has these things for free
There's none so blest by God as He,
And if he would be doubly blest,
He'd love his fellowman the best.
Bobbye Brooks

The Ice Rink

I love the ice rink,
The cool, crisp air,
The music, the hockey games,
The powder white ice shavings,
Everything that's there,
But most of all
I love the atmosphere!
Elizabeth Johnson

Island For Two

Walking along
the moon tattered sand
the gleam of the ocean
we walk hand in hand.

The sound of the water
pounding the beach
the breeze in the air
a smell that is sweet.

The trees are all flowering
a time to bear fruit
the sun is now rising
to see such a view.

Asleep on the beach
feel the sun's warmth
rush to the water
wash it all off.

The foods are quite plenty
the people, so few
we're all alone
on our island for two.
Julie A. Burns

Dream Keeper

The knight is dark and mysterious.
The moon shines radiantly on cold steel,
And stars flicker like dark blue eyes.
The wolves howl pierces the knight,
And the screech of an ancient knight Owl.
Shatters the silent darkness.
Lightning crashes like steel on steel,
Thunder roars like frantic hoof beats,
From a dark rampant stallion.
Rain falls randomly, like the lives of
Opposing armies from the past...
The clouds vanish like distant memories.
Day breaks and the knight dissipates,
And leaves behind a light,
Simple teenage boy.
Brandon Vaughn Braithwaite

Seasons

Fall comes and I welcome it.
The maples are shedding,
for some, only skeletons remain.
My father is in his Fall.
His hair now faded to a brilliant gray.
Chicken prints lie by his eyes.
Up steps, where he once ran,
he now walks.
His wait is over
preparing for the Winter ahead.
I remember my grandfather's Winter.
Waiting inside his den,
he grew envious of Spring and Summer.
Thin skin exposed his skull,
and his hands,
hands that were as brittle
as the icicles mirrored in his eyes.
Feeling that cold,
I cover under my Summer blankets.
John Louis Perry

Promises

Promises that are never kept
The lonely times that I have wept

My heart is full of doubts and fears
I cry the many lonely tears

All of my dreams apart keep breaking
Oh how much my heart is aching

I feel like nothing goes my way
Certainly not yesterday nor today

People do you wrong and do you dirt
Oh how I get so tired of the hurt

The abundance of pain that's in my heart
one day it stops and the next it starts

God please take me up above
Where there is no pain only love

God please show me there is a better way
In another world, in another day

Maybe soon I will be blessed
The Lord my soul will put to rest
Ellen L. Love

Native Americans

Indians lost in life
The life we all live

The promise we said
The promise we broke

The life we give
Do life like hell

All they ask is freedom
Freedom we stole

Native Americans
Last in life
Forever.
Cristina Quintero

Seasons

I awake in the morning
The leaves fill my yard
I awake in the morning
The leaves are gone
I awake in the morning
The snow fills my yard
I awake in the morning
The snow is gone
I awake in the morning
The rain fills the streets

I awake in the morning
The sun is bright time to rejoice
until it is night
Bruce Doering

The Catnip Mezzanine

Angus is up
The Jimmy tree,
Vigilant
Through Martian moons,
And sniffing the flutophone jazz
That hangs askew
On Nocturnal mist.
Cheryl A. Fazenbaker

With Giving

With giving comes new life
The joy and expression of pain,
The grasping of hands
And imprinting of tiny feet.

With giving comes new strength
Blessed be the Lord.
A blessing that chimes wisdom
Hope, fear and love.

With giving we create new horizons
For the new life escaping our dreams,
As we capture the innocent in our arms
May God trust the babe in our lives
forever.

Ernestine Pina-Sandoval

Nostalgia

Tread lightly along the path,
The hidden violets hold
Secrets of your yesterdays
as memories unfold.

Speak softly as you climb
the hilltop where is carved,
the initials of your first love.
Also disappointment; marred.

Touch gently the wooden seat...
So many joy filled hours,
Look! The vast horizon,
once your ivory tower.

Now the turning seasons;
live again the moments gone.
Then trudge down to reality,
Sunlight of another dawn.

Dorothy Hom

A Widower's Lament

Foggy eyes peer unseeing through
  the haze of memories
    of her-

Dried up pools of sadness
  forever trapped
    in tearless eyes-

Silent grey hours, days slide into years,
  endless empty moments;
    he must perform

The daily rituals of life
  without her steady
    guiding hand-

Thirty-five years melt soundlessly
  into the hollow carcass of
    his defeated heart-

Love gone, love lost
  abandoned helplessly to wait
    patiently-

    for his turn.

Claire P. O'Sullivan

Challenges

The past is a reality,
The future a dream;
The present is life's awakening.

To strive for perfection,
Daily struggles and strife.
Look to a higher being
Beyond the sky.
For guidance in our life.

The mind like a maze.
Which path to follow;
Confusing at times.
Full of dreams and ideas
And at times empty and hollow.

Concentration and focus is the key.
To strive and succeed in life.
TO BE ALL THAT YOU CAN BE!

Blanche L. English

One More Dawn

The ugly thing has reared its head
The dreaded word we hate to hear
Cancer they say it is cancer
The ugly mass that we all fear

The doctor says it is terminal
This puts a heavy load upon the heart
They can't be right. It can't be so
It is more than just a bittersweet tart

It is so good to have you home again
The day of hospital long are gone
Prayers we hope nightly will be answered
To have at least one more dawn

Janet Farnsworth

The Seasons Of Jesus

Through the gray storm clouds
The downpour of warm spring rain
Pray, you will feel Jesus there.

Over the grassy hills
Through the forest green
Look, you will see Jesus there.

Sun turns harvest gold
Leaves began to fall
Watch, you know Jesus is there.

The blustering winds of winter
Peaceful flurries of white snow
Listen, you can hear Jesus there.

Connie Lowe

Bombus Americanus

One day I saw a Bumble Bee.
The biggest one that the there could be!
He was all fuzzy-black and yellow
Really quite a handsome fellow.
His legs were packed with pollen dust
That from a daisy he had brushed.
Then buzzing loud and buzzing clear
He had to rush and fly from here.
Maybe to a hole in ground
Where his honey comb is found.
Bee bread from his legs he'll make
To feed his children. Good like cake!

Grace Frenkel

Autumn Song

Pumpkins dot the countryside
The cornstalks stand like tepees tall
Goblins and ghosts move about unseen
While the golden moon keeps a watch over all.

Tis' time to gather the harvest
The wind is cold and strong
The frost covers all like a mantle
As Autumn sings her song.

Dame Nature is dressed in her glory
Red, orange, gold - yellow and brown
Mr. Winter is waiting to wed her
And tomorrow she'll wear a white gown.

So welcome the changing seasons
In nature there's no right or wrong
There's only the hope of tomorrow
When Autumn sings her song.

Jenny Travers Bouza

Nature's Best

I love the sound of the ocean
The color of autumn leaves
I marvel at the endless stars
The awesome depth of the seas
I enjoy the brightness of the sun
The softness of new fallen snow
I'm in awe of nature's splendor
Everywhere I go
To see a beautiful rainbow
After a summer rain
Or glimpse a figure made of clouds
A mystery the skies contain
To hear the chant of sea gulls
While drawing in the sand
Is music to my aching heart
Hope in a desperate land
So, I ponder in my romantic mind
How precious life will be
When man and nature both allow
The other to be free

Deborah White

Summer Palette

Today the wind is very high —
The china blue of the sky
  Is pure.
No mark of wisp or cloud.

Two red-tailed hawks
  Above the ridge
Pursue and dive and chase and wheel.
Their wings are close enough to touch —
  Well, almost touch.

Their short but penetrating call
  Not sweet—but surely tender
    To one of the pair...
Their tails clear coral
  In the crystal air.

The leaves of the red maples quiver
And near at hand the singing river.

How lucky to be midst it all!

Frances E. Mendenhall

Alcohol

A medicine that became
  the biggest lie on earth.

L eaving even the strongest
  homes and families broken.

C asting its shadows at
  every village and town.

O f all sickness
  yet its the legal one.

H ow could I show my people
  to leave it alone.

O h God! Help us to
  overcome this misery.

L iving to one's potential
  has to be alcohol free.

Aqpik-Robert Mulluk Jr.

Take Heed

I once knew a girl,
the best in the world;
And she meant a lot to me:

She is now gone,
and I'm on my own;
It's the way things were meant to be:

I don't know why,
but I sometimes still cry;
At least when I think of her:

I wish I'd forget,
or still, better yet;
I wish things could be as they were:

But that's not to be,
for she left me you see;
And it was my fault, this I know:

The pain felt inside,
is due to my foolish pride;
And the fact I couldn't say, ... Please don't go.

David R. Jenney

Dreams

The ending of tonight,
  The beginning of tomorrow.
The ending of the goblins,
  The beginning of the angels.

The ending of the dark,
  The finding of the light.
The resting of the body,
  The awakening of the soul.

Charles Haugland

The Sparkle In Your Eyes

I wonder if you realize,
The beautiful sparkle in your eyes.
Makes the day seem bright and clear,
I enjoy it so when you are near.
I only see you now and then,
But I will look for you again.
Down the hall and past your door,
A glimpse of you, I smile once more.
The day will end it always seems,
Sound asleep, and you a dream.

David Schumaker

The Final Farewell

Alas dear one,
That you will leave.
There goes my sun,
And I am left to grieve.

And I am left,
To a fate worse than death,
All was in jest;
Echoes of Beth.

I thought it would be always.
Something that wasn't bought.
Now, it's empty hallways.
And you love me not.

Why my fair one,
Did we have to part?
We had just begun,
to make a start.

And I am left,
To a fate worse than death,
All was in jest;
Echoes of Beth.

Bill Fleming

Tribute to Trubby

He sauntered with high nonchalance,
That witching night in June,
Along the rocky garden path,
Out to the sandy dune.
His tail a black-ringed question mark
Against the rising moon.

Lordly Lord of all the feline tribe -
He paused a moment brief.
With eyes that seemed to focus on
A distant wind-swept reef.
Yet watched a most momentous
Swaying shadow on a leaf.

And if, when late he sauntered back,
His dreamy eyes alight.
Inscrutable phosphorescence in
the blackness of the night,
the dunes held one mouse less -
the king had claimed it as his right.

Gladys H. Robinson

My Lord

The sun just a little more brighter,
The sky a little more blue,
The wonders he's created,
And the things he does through you.

The peace that he has given,
And the light to you he's shown,
The things you never understood,
Are now to you made known.

The doubt that once lied within,
Is erased and taken away,
And a new you is risen,
Like the sun on a brand new day.

The freedom he has granted,
Insecurity left far behind,
His spirit wanting to dwell in you,
In your heart your soul and your mind.

The picture you have painted of yourself,
Is now to you made clear,
He has found a home in your heart,
And to you will always be near.

Chris Jones

Nature's Windows

Are our lives in such a hurry
That we can't spare a little time
To look out through a window
See what's on the other side?

If I feel lonely or distressed
A simple cure I have found
I check through windows of my home
Tension leaves, seeing beauty all around.

Each four seasons of a year
Puts fourth beauty of it's own.
Ole Sol can shine on all of it
Seeing the best of each day's form.

I see the weather as it changes
From dark clouds and elements of gloom.
Then once again the sun bursts forth
Like a beautiful earth in bloom.

We've heard "Stop and smell the roses".
No harm does that impose.
You will appreciate what really matters,
Values passed up may have been your rose.

Elva P. Rowe

Twilight

I will not tell you, dear,
That to my eyes you look,
As first I saw you.
Time and the years with me,
Have etched their marks upon you,
And I love you the more for it.
Year by year.
We can sit together,
The two of us,
In silence for long, long moments,
No words spoken,
None necessary.
And yet, we commune,
In comfort, ease and love,
Aware one of the other,
And that is true communication,
True love.

Ib Melchior

"Gods Light"

God is the light
that makes things right.
If you follow him
you'll be alright.
God gives us the might
to put up a fight
against all odds.
God gives us the light
to win the fight
to get rid of evil
with all our might.
If you follow God
he'll give you the sight
to see in the night
so you can fight
with all your might.
Put God in your heart
to see the light
to get things right.
Love God with all your might.

Diane R. Broughton

You

Can it be you
That made me stronger
Able to face the sadness of life
Feeling calmness
That did not exist

Can it be you
That made me understand
A feeling of love
Never before felt

Can it be you
Who helped me
To enjoy moments of closeness
Never experienced before

I have never known
This special world
Until I found
You

Donald C. Porchia

Moma's Tears

Moma's tears won't stain the pillows
That lie upon the bed of roses
Moma's tears won't stain the sheets
That lie upon the bed of clouds

God's angels from above
Will look over moma daily
Moma's tears won't stain the streets of gold
Nor will they cry out loud

Moma is here with us now
And not a tear within her eyes
She loves each and every one of us
And to us she replies......................

I love you my dear children
Each and every one
Forever we will be together
Until the victory has been won.

Jamie Fitzsimmons

The Fifth Season

I am freer now, now
that I've retired
my old spirits, my old guardians...
I can pass the dark corner
in my own silence, certain
of the shadows' insubstantiality,
or walk the churchyard
full of ancient, tilted stones,
and bear witness to the dead dead,
now that my soul
has let in the brisky winds
of a more reasoned rationality.

Emptied of the fearsome burden,
I feel full with life, and can laugh
and nod in tolerant fashion at old tales
told by old wives and their old men
in the evening after sunset.

George T. Jones

Don't Promise Me

Don't promise me forever
That isn't yours to give
Just tell me that you'll stay
For without you I cannot live

Don't promise me the sky
You'll never reach that high
Just tell me that you love me
And never say good bye.

Don't promise me the moon
Or the stars that brightly shine
Just hold me close to you
And tell me that you're mine.

I need you here with me
We'll find a way somehow
To always be together
The way we are right now.

Jamie Griggs

Ode To A Word

Ode to a word
That I might with it
Capture what I see.
Or like Van Gogh's paintings
That I might write what I feel.
To bring to life a moment
To capture humor
To write of passion that
Love awakes.
Or things of a crying heart
When love brings heartbreaks.
With a word
To capture the things etched
In my heart, soul and being.
Ode to a word, that written
It might be seeing.

Dawn Ungersma

"Memories"

"Memories" like phantom ships,
   that haunt my every dream;
Drifting past in shadow forms,
   with now and then a gleam.

"Memories", like April tears,
   the soothe my feverish, thoughts;
Cooling fresh - as if to quench
   My hearts, dull aching drought;

"Memories", like sun upon,
   a crimson rose, full - blown,
As if, to bring again to me
   old love, that I had known.

Apikia Shaw

Details

I like to pretend that my tail is small
that my nose is long
that my eyes see all

I like to pretend that my feet are round
that my skin is wrinkled
that my mouth won't frown

I like to pretend that my voice is shrill
that my tusks are sharp
that my life's a thrill

Jonathon D. Tuttle

Flowers

Flowers, they are nature's treasures
That God has given to us all.
They hold tender meaning with their
Colors and sizes, large or small.

On special occasions or any time
There is in them magic power.
The gift of flowers to those we love
Brings joy for each to snare.

Flowers give strength to people who,
Are sick and those who are well.
Flowers speak soft, warm and sincerely,
So no tongue could fully tell.

I thank God for giving us this
Gift to help brighten our ever hours.
What would this world be like
Without the gift of flowers?

Adeen Cantrell

Work Of Art

Life is like a work of art
That glows with promise at the start,
The canvas seems so cold and bare
But capable of colors rare.

The work requires an artist's touch,
The stroke of genius can add much,
The kiss of an inspired brush
Converts the bare to an awed hush.

Life is like a block of marble
Quarried from the lions of earth,
Solid, gleaming, pearl of stones
Yet nothing 'til the sculptor hones.

We make of life a work of art
If we progress from careful start,
But only if the bare and tragic
Are transformed by touch of magic.

Harold Putnam

At Dawning

At dawning when I wake and see
The rays of morn streak o'er the sky,
Who can create such mystery?
Just why is it that night rolls by?

Why does the darkness fade away?
Who makes such glory come to view?
Our majestic world is born each day
Sent lovingly from God, for life anew.

At dawning I arise and go
In morning prayer to him I love.
Humbly unfolding all my woe
I pray for help from God above.

Dear Lord, at this sweet hour of day,
Help me to live a worthwhile life,
Guide me daily in your way
Be with me always in my strife.

And when my tide of life drifts on
And the battles of life are hopefully won,
Many I be lain to rest at dawn?
But oh! dear Lord, thy will be done.

Jean Nabhan

A Life Too Short

It was a dreary, dismal day
The sun refused to shine
There was sadness in the air
The day that Johnny died

His friends and family gathered
When Johnny was laid to rest
At only fourteen years of age
He had already failed the test

The struggle for the good life
Most times it's very rough
He tried escaping through drugs
He just wasn't strong enough

Becoming a member of a gang
He believed he was so cool
The day the fatal bullet hit
He realized he'd been a fool!
  Carol Ann Riddle

Untitled

My little girl isn't curly or bouncy.
The clothes that she wears, aren't
 ruffled or flouncy.
For tripping over her feet, she has
 quite a knack.
You don't know whether to hug her,
 or give her a whack.
A zit on her chin can give her
 a fit.
She's sometimes an angel, and
 sometimes a twit.
For all of these changes, we
 haven't any clues.
We just chalk them up
 to the "Puberty Blues"
  Beverly Layne

Changes Of Season

Winter is here
The birds have gone away
And the sky is full of clouds.
The trees are naked
And the roots of thee are frozen.
Inside the house
The fireplace is still burning
Just like my love for you.

Will the change of season
Bring effect upon us?
Will our love be renewed
When the birds come back?
Or will it fade away....
Like the frozen water
Melting down the stream?
  Angella A. Focas

The Harvest

The farmers harvest has begun.
The frost has nipped the pumpkin.
The leaves are turning crimson red.
Winter quilts are on the bed.
The air is crisp the nights are clear,
Thanksgiving day will soon be here.
  Charlotte Whitmore

Tell Me, Tender Me

In Loving Memory of Virginia Roan
Tell me about the flowers in Summerland,
the roses grown by a loving hand.
One that used to place beauty on my table
Would I take a deep breath of surprise
as their beauty sparkled before my eyes?
Tell me about the flowers in Summerland,
their fragrance must be soft and sweet as
the loving hand that tendered them still tenders me.
The hand that says I love you still reaches from beyond,
bringing me comfort...
A mother's love
I did not lose
I just had to learn again how to talk with you
Tell me about the flowers in Summerland
I'm sure there's a bouquet for me.
My heart has missed you much.
Now once again I thank my light you're here
I feel your loving touch...
Tell me about the flowers in Summerland.
  Angela Williams

He, I And The Moon

The moon was full
The room was noisily quiet
Through all of the darkness of the room
He could be seen in the lights of my eyes
Does he see me as I see him?
When he looked my way, his eyes met mine
So much was said without a word
Those once hidden thoughts are now well known
When our smiles touched, who was to blame?
With stars in our voices
We asked one another who was to blame
He says I, I say him
Blame it on the fullness of the moon.
  Donna S. Petrone

Hope

I am the light in the room of darkness
The rainbow in the midst of a storm
The flower blossoming among weeds
The smile in between the tears
I am strong in greetings
But weak in farewells, yet
Even death cannot fully crush me
I am what pushes the young to dream
To strive toward their goals
I am found in the strong, the happy, and the ambitious
While desired by the weak, the sad, and the lonely
I am part of the present as well as the future
Dreams die when I die
  Catherine Dulay

Peace In The Valley

The sun sets on the mountain
The shimmering moon takes its place in the sky
A firefly dances across the field
Light breezes are felt across your sleepy head
The quiet sound of a whippoorwill heard in the distance
Shadows of the trees swaying in the moonlight
The rocking of your chair on a creaky porch
Maybe a laugh or two
A bright smile from a special friend
Barn cats meowing
The sound of silence
Peace in the valley
  Frances Betlyon

A Mind Affair

The question was asked, "Where did the black man come from"?
The question was asked, "Where did the white man come from"?
Who knows, I know
We are from the same land.
Its a mind affair.

The first earth was destroy by a flood.
One man and his family brings forth this population.
They are the parents of every nation
Regardless of your complexion
Is not this a mind affair.

The black nation have a right
The white nation have a right
Cling to your creed and complexion
Think of another nation as your brother in need
Its a mind affair.

There is no white blood in a white nation.
There is no black blood in a black nation.
All nation blood run red.
Re-think, re-bound. We must be one.
This is a mind affair.

Janeta Williams

These Days In April And May

In our land so filled with stress,
The people thrash with restlessness!
What progressed our country to come to this?
These days in April and May.

And who so ever shall be found,
Not guilty in the eyes of those plastic clowns.
The people are ready to tear us down!
These days in April and May.

Who shall pay or has paid the most?
Was it Rodney King or some unannounced ghost?
Time's running short. We're cutting it close!
These days in April and May.

Havoc and horror have filled the air!
Pillaging and killing with no despair!
How one can hurt another and not even care?
The hatred is everywhere!

I can't understand this, my God, I swear!
And the pain won't go away.

Charles Misner

Jetsam

We stand upon the shore and mourn
   the passing of a friendship,
its timbers strewn by a mighty storm.
   How lovingly we built that ark
which carried us through years of
   sharing life's woes and pleasures.
Only to watch it dashed to pieces
   by harsh words and deeds.
Bittersweet memories lap the sand,
   revealing treasures, like precious shells,
some well-formed, others only fragments
   of what had been
Can such timbers be reclaimed
   by words of understanding and acceptance.
or has the force of anger destroyed
   the very form and substance of what was?
The wind blows, the waves crash,
   the timbers shift. We mourn.
We have not strength to reconstruct alone.

Carol R. Steele

War is Hell

"On the battle field of war after all is clear
The only sound that you will hear
Is the spirits as they go into the light above.
To say that Heaven is all Love!
As these spirits arise with a mighty yell
to all mankind that War (with its memories) is he only Hell!"

Donna Crowder-Yates

A Letter Of My Death

My memories have drained to a few.
The ones I have, are hard to recall.
I wish I had more to be proud of,
But I'm left with the truth, and that's all.

I'm laying under a mound of soil,
I can feel the coldness on my skin.
Bitterness in eating at my soul,
But it won't erase what I've been.

With each breath I take, I grew weaker,
The air I breath is hollow and cold.
Old feelings escape with each short pant,
And I cry for the life I had sold.

Never again will I see real light,
For my sins will bury me deep.
So I'll leave you with thoughts of my past,
But years of pain, I am forced to keep.

Jill Arroyo

Untitled

   Alone and pregnant such a feeling of doom,
The once sun filled skies now look so gloom.
   No one to turn in times of despair,
Is there any one out there who even cares?
   What did I do to loose the love from my groom,
That once was so plentiful and started life in my womb?
   A new innocent life grows within me every day,
How can I be strong enough for this little babe?
   Who will be my strength when labor nears?
Who will soothe my heart and calm my fears?
   Who will help me push when I grow weak?
Who will wipe the tears from my cheek?
   A painful trying time yet filled with such cheer,
The childbirth now over a new baby appears.
   So pure and innocent laid on mother's chest,
With peaceful contentment now eyes close to rest.
   No more will mother feel unwanted or alone,
For this little babe fills the void in her home!

Doris J. Hetzler

Untitled

You stumble through
the night on filmy, nearly
invisible wings. Searching, unendingly,
For a light that singes
those same wings in a flash of fire, leaving
you flightless. And you must wonder as you
lay here at my feet, why
those arms of yours led you
to the promise of a light
that killed you in the end. The same thing
you searched for all your short, uneasy
life
betrayed you
leaving you now
unable to fly.

Gretchen Colman

Love Poem

As the stars and gems of the earth mimic your eyes,
The music of the God's own harpists will not warm me as much as
  your smile,
Even your presence makes me feel refreshed and new.

Your voice is the sound of golden church bells ringing on a
  Christmas morning.
Your inner beauty is unequaled in the world of men,
It is the same beauty as crystal water glistening in the moonlight.

My thoughts and feelings have only been skimmed on the surface.
My trust for you is deep in my soul,
My love for you is deeper, spanning ages, centuries, going back
  to before time.
You are as perfect as the flowers on the tree of life.

My feelings for you will never cease,
The sun will rise and set for the last time,
But my love for you will endure.
This may sound foolish,
But true all the way through.
I love you.
  Christopher W. Beltz

Seeing Through the Rain

Life is strange, I know you know,
  The more you think, the more you don't...
    Understand what has to be,
      When yesterdays are all we see.

We think we've grown, we know there's more
  Still we move through half open doors,
    Wondering why we're on the same old track,
      Like ocean waves that pull you back.

Yesterdays weigh on your soul,
  Tomorrow sometimes feel so cold.
    The day will come; the sun will rise
      And life will, again, be in your eyes.

Still today seems to be all wrong,
  We all try to sing the future's song.
    But our paths are set, we can only wait,
      Crying won't determine fate.

Day to day is all we can live,
  I wish what you needed, I could give.
    Yet the darkness in your eyes remains,
      You must learn to see the sun, even when it rains.
  Colleen A. Jeffrey-Ruth

Seasons Change

Seasons change as time goes by,
The love we shared will never die,
Feelings felt have passed us by,
Your tender touch was just a lie.
Moments together now are memories,
Your loving caress was just a tease.
How could you hurt me and make me blue?
Why couldn't you see, "I was in love with you?"
Your warm smile, your gentle clutch,
Loving you just wasn't enough.
Away from me you tore my heart,
Left my world in pieces.
And my life in the dark.
Seasons changed and so did I,
When you left my world and said, "goodbye."
  Ann Marie Johnson

Soul Mates

Words cannot express
The love I feel for you
but on this day, your birthday
words will have to do.

Quiet often after becoming a man
I prayed each day for a wife
A woman who could and would stand beside me
A companion to be cherished for life

After years of hoping and praying
the Good Lord sent someone my way
an angel, though I couldn't see it then
who meant more to me each day

We struggled, and we hurt each other
suffering a clash of differently worlds
But through all this we blended our lives
and the molds of our lives together were poured

Each day we became closer
closer and closer, as one
finally we settled our souls together
alas the Lord's will had finally been done.
  James M. Huling

A Chain is Broken

The chain is broken, another one is gone.
The Lord has called another one home.
First a dad-then a brother.
Please dear Lord, let me keep the others.
It's breaking my heart to see Mama's bowed head
As she hides the tears I know she must shed.
It's so hard to lose a dear older brother.
I know the pain is much worse for
My dear, sweet mother.
We love her dearly and we let it show.
Please Dear Lord, give her strength
As she has to let go.
  Beverley F. Riley

To Ciarra

Tonight I held your precious hand and could not believe my eyes
The little hand that once held mine is now a grownup size.
The years have flown and you have grown while I worked as I should
But I'd go back to yesterday. Oh, only if I could!

To hold you in my arms once more and wonder at the skill
It took for God to create you, I marvel at it still.
You have always been my shadow, or so the others cried,
No matter where I walk or work, you're always at my side.

You fought the lure of growing up when all your friends gave in
Childhood is a treasured time that you knew must surely end
Yet you and I have still stayed close, we've traveled and we've played
We've camped beneath the star filled sky, I wish we could have stayed.

You've been right there beside me through the good times and the bad
You are but a child, but still, you're the best friend that I've had
You've walked so close beside me, that you were a part of me
I would not trade my time with you, for all eternity.
  Barbara Keel

No Interest

I carelessly dropped a coin down a deep well, only to hear silence.
Still silent.
I am the coin. You are that well.
I plead, "Spend me that I might drink to quench this thirst."
The deafness is bearable. It's these eyes that I wish were blind.
  John S. Rulka

A Day With Grandpa

Grandpa, why are we walking so slow?
The little girl asked with a gleam in her eye.
"Because I love you, my dear, that's why".

I want to show you the daisies so yellow and bright,
And look at the tall trees - look up real high.
Be very quiet, and you might hear -
The chirp of a bird; shhh. - it sounds so near.

Oh Grandpa, look down on the ground,
Here is a little fuzzy worm -
See what I found!

The time passed too quickly as we walked hand-in-hand
Looking at God's creation - the would around us,
His perfect plan.

At the end of our adventure as we shared discoveries
Of the day gone by, the little girl asked with a
Gleam in her eye, "Grandpa, you're so neat, can you
come out tomorrow and play with me?"
Dorothy LaPlante

Rain

When the shards of saliva descend from the virgin heaven
the land shall be filled with a thick wetness
of descent through holy earth to evil hell and back, not with
vengeance, but with humor, knowing that he will never venture
down below the living again.
"I have seen pain," he said,
"and it hurt."
Oblivious to the world revolving
he spun in his own misery.
The light that shown down on her that once kept her warm now turned
white not and as their hearts beat to the same rhythm,
the mauve light touched, smelled, heard, filled their senses,
and it too was oblivious to the white hot pain.
Fortunately night fell,
cooling them,
bathing their bodies in cool sunlight
without the suns harsh gleams.
It was the cool sunlight reflected off the moon and onto their faces,
their solemn faces which were attacked
by shards of saliva, onslaughts of rain.
David Feldman

Untitled

There is no way that you can own anything you see -
The land, a car, a house, a boat - not anything, not me
It's all just an illusion to cause suffering and pain -
Disappointment is achieved - when fulfillment is not gained

Even when you have achieved the object of your desire -
You soon become so obsessed - your heart's consumed with fire
Once it was an object just for you to own -
Now you must call it master - and serve it in it's home -

Another of the illusions in life's bag of tricks -
is something we all crave - so much that we get sick
Security like a mirage, we all keep trying to attain -
Through money, possessions - your job, your name

You do the right thing, in order to make it so -
Then everything collapses - and you don't even know
How you could be so stupid to think you had control -
The mirage has once again - withdrawn so you will know

When minutely dissected, and held under the light -
Life becomes an occurrence - without significance or bite
We can then just sit and be - not frantically pursue
The things we think will make us happy, but rarely ever do -
Catherine Armstrong

Forbearance To Testamentary

The vikings have swerved censure;
The knights have fluted;
The warriors have immigrated challenge;
The dragon has acrimony;
Combined it has the third generation and its diversity.
Vikings cajole the mission and their heritage;
Knights are the radiance in shining armour;
Warriors are the vengeance of their foes;
Dragons are covenant to Nang and Wang;
A diphthong is of the British Charter;
The colonies have an emergence in its grueling times.
Long live the King takes the enforcement of the knights;
The vikings apart from the warriors are divided.
The dragons purports to Nang and Wang;
Treaties are forbearance to combined diversity;
The States are the sanctioned ruled;
the Covenant is the new assembled;
The righteous will be of their beliefs;
The Lords will be of their testimony;
And the king will reign.
Jenette Matanane

A Mother's Life

I get up every morning and get ready for work,
The kids are yelling and I'm going berserk!
I grab my purse and my keys, backpacks and shoes,
We head out to the car, but first we choose.
Is it Kyle's turn or Cody's to sit up front?
This is driving me crazy, so I let out a grunt!
Just get in the car, I don't care about this,
If you don't settle down, I'll give you a kiss!
To them it's a threat, so it works every time,
I don't know how I do it, but it's my moment to shine!

I get home every evening and have dinner to cook,
I'd really much rather be reading a book.
But there's clothes to be washed and kids to be fed,
Ooooooh, I can't wait till they go to bed.
When homework is done and their things put away,
I shout, "Okay everybody, it's time to play!"

Sometimes I get tired of this everyday life,
I try to be a good mother and wife.
I may rant and rave till my face turns green,
But I love those kids and hope they always have sweet dreams.
Jana Joswiak

Los Angeles

Carefully arranging the plastic wrapping on the bus bench
the homeless man ignores the awakenings of the City.
A lawyer, businessman and a housewife pass by with rigid
gazes determined not to recognized reality.
Just as well. He lies on the plastic and curls
inside its womb. It is time to rest
and the hopeless have no nocturnal clock.
A City suffers through fire, flood, riot and earthquake
but is always reborn with evangelical fervor.
A person suffers through disease, unemployment, racism and despair
and some cannot survive the quest for a life of quality.
The homeless are sacrificed for the greater societal good
and must not be acknowledged for fear of mass guilt.
Los Angeles rises to live again and the homeless man
closes his eyes. Sleep comes quickly and with no pain.
Whether he rises again is out of the control of man.
Go with God.
Joseph Gunn

More Than You'll Ever Know

Words cannot illustrate what my heart knows —
the heart made of flesh but born of soul.
It is not my hand but my soul
that guides my pen as it swiftly flows.

My soul wants to sing and dance —
it has never experienced love until now.
What a joyous song it wants to sing —
it knows that this will be its only chance.

The words you want to hear I don't say enough.
They remain in my heart, locked up.
Sometimes I feel embarrassed or ashamed —
but know my lips are weak but my spirit — tough.

Communications of love through flesh is easy to do —
but our flesh is only a temporary home.
What really matter is how our soul feels —
because the soul is forever and mine wants you.

Jason Thomas

All Hallows Eve

Sibilant cries emulating the lyrical nocturne.
The ghastly air dwelled with dire scenes
Enacted upon the dance on all Hallows Eve.
Where the ghouls and dryads praised the cosmos,
Viciously feasting upon flesh with delight and
Concupiscence.
The exhumation of cadavers, where the enviable
Goddess intoned her earthly creatures for the ritual
Of invigorating the dead.
Where the spirits roamed and lurked in the deadly night.

Alina Callender

The Foundation

Limerocks from an old chimney lay crumbling,
The forsaken homeplace is covered in brush.
From the boughs of a stalwart oak tree nearby,
The wind scatters notes of a warbling thrush.

Here once had stood a farmhouse filled with love
Although there were many chores to be done.
When the work was finished, the crops laid by,
There was time for rest, and also for fun.

Here girls became women, boys became men,
Learning the rewards of an honest day's work,
That promises made should be promises kept,
And that some duties you must never shirk.

The foundation of the old house is shaky,
But it matters not now we can surely say,
For principles instilled in minds nurtured there,
Still remain unshakable unto this day.

Jean Ikner

Storm

Rain assaults my window a thousand times over.
The fiendish lighting comes madly dancing.
The wrecking-ball-smashes of thunder so bold.
Hear them all come one after another.
The lighting is jiving outside my window,
And the thunder laughs at my fright.
The rain watches me shake and shiver,
All through the night.

Donna Merry

Strangers Of The Night

One morning I awoke with a shadow hanging over my head.
The feeling gave me such great chills.
For I lost all my womanly skills.
As I approached my point, I was stricken with fright.
For all I could see was the darkness of the night.
No lights, just the softness of the raindrops.
As I places the key, In a shadow I saw he.
What I was to do but be me.
I was spoken to like dirt.
Afraid of being hurt.
Do as you are told.
Don't act bold.
For I looked in the night, A gun they did hold.
Give me the money.
All I could think about was my Honey,
Die by the hand, this I couldn't stand.
For an instant I was blind, but all I had to do
was use my mind.
Lucky me, the shadow past, for my love was here to last.

Billie Leininger

Mother

When I look in the mirror I can see
The eyes of my Mother smiling at me
She has been gone for a very long time
But I can visualize her face right in mine
I never thought I looked much like Mom
But as I grow older, I'm looking more
like her all the time
I love and miss her very much
I miss her voice and her touch
Mother was a great inspiration to me
She taught me no one was better than me
She said anything they can do you can do too
But do it in a way that you can follow the rules
My Mother was the best in my world
She loved us all very much
She had 2 boys and 2 girls
They say you never miss your water until
the well runs dry
Please children show love to your Mother
while she is still alive...

Earnestine Jackson

In The Tender Act Of Care

We can connect to share
The energy pure and strong

Fearlessly it proceeds
No thought of self corrupts the charge
The spark of light ignites the flame
The cosmic flare of care
Suddenly we rise above the early toil and snare.

A light with life's insights we rise to meet our higher self.
Our pure purpose unknown yet unbroken,
aware at last the way made clear.

The only true reality
"It must be lived,"
and never can be owned, you see
the purpose, dear,
is reality.

Alive we are, a light for evermore,
ablaze because we simply care
we learn to step aside and let the selfless power guide
throughout eternity.

Brenda K. Oswalt

Untitled

Slag runs thick down the mountain side.
The demon cannot be found for the demon doesn't hide.
The garbage of immortality smells of the stench of time
For the foulness of justice is buried under grime.
Monuments of man are torn down in a blink
But no man wonders just how to think.
Happiness takes flight but is always shot down.
The jester killed the king and now wears his crown.
Sadness feeds on the belly of the worm,
Under the sun it starts to wither and squirm.
Over all hovers the outreaching limb of a tree.
Looking for the never but there's nothing there to see.
Stars stop shining but their light is still seen,
The eyes of the night are beautiful, yet teasing and mean.
The universe spins inside of a fragile crystal ball,
Balanced precariously on the brink of a fall.
Bryan Fender

Love The Essence Of Life

Just as the moon and sea need each other to change
the delicate rhythm of the tide, so do lovers need each other.

Just as the flowers and trees thirst to be kissed by the
succulent raindrops, so do lovers need each other.

Just as the morning earth covered in dew awaits the
rising of the sun and warmth and comfort of her
embrace, so do lovers need each other.

For without one, the other could not exist.
Love the essence of life.
Janifer O. Rizzuto

In Deepest Sympathy

In deepest sympathy, were sorry about your life,
The deeper the symphony the steeper the knife.
We regret our lies and our mind games,
We push upon you all our dirty crimes and shames.

All this we do is in sympathy,
When you become one, only then will you see.
We do understand your troubles and all your pain,
We feel without another we'll all go insane.

We all do regret what you'll soon be,
All of this we give you in deepest sympathy.
Deborah Patrick

Split Second

There is nothing more important than
　the life you live,
　but we don't always realize it,
　we take it for granted.
Sometimes when we're mad,
　we hang up on the phone,
　but in a split second, that person
　could be gone.
People kill people, like it's nothing new
　but in a split second, that person
　could be you.
People are raped, bruised and battered
　and in a split second your world
　could be shattered
No one lives life day by day, we're too wrapped up
　in the future and not thinking about today.
Lives are short, some lives are sweet, but if
　you live in a race, your score will be beat.
So slow down on the track, be happy you're on the team.
Don't worry about the finish line, it's closer than it seems.
Heather T. Silva

The Battle

How did we lose the battle that day? We had won so many times before
The death cry of a nation was heard today for we would win no more

Could it be that God was on their side
When we marched toward their hill,
Or, was it Death who turned the tide, and laid our boys still

Bullets are flying now, cannons spout death
Closer and closer, there's no turning back
Running and falling, no time to catch breath,
Voices ring out "attack, attack"

We fire our guns, and stab at the Blue
Pushing them back from their court
But now we are alone, we can't get through
Where in the hell is our support

Slowly the Blue wave forces us back
They pursue us like the hound, no more do we think to attack
As we run over the blood soaked ground

How did we lose the battle that day?
Where now are the men that Pickett once led?
The death cry of a nation was heard today
For the battlefield was Gray with dead.
Fred N. Reynders

Spring

Spring has come with all of its many delights
The days are getting longer and shorter the nights

Flowers in bloom, trees with their buds, my what a sight
Filled with anticipation of life and birds in their flight

To light on their limbs and branches and sing a happy song
And proclaim to the world, its spring, and it's here we belong

Hearts swell in the chest of young people of all ages
For spring brings love and happiness etched on its pages

Love abounds in the air, in the land, seas and stars.
With cupid poised ready with his arrows and darts

To awaken the sleeping giant of winter's long sleep
And quicken the heart of young lovers, and put a dance in their feet

Winter is over, we can all give an applause and load cheer
We may even want to raise a toast, if only with a beer

So open your eyes and heart and enjoy this great show
It is now playing before us, right here, don't you know

Lift up your hearts to God for spring to us He has given
For today it is yours to enjoy, tomorrow just a vision

Life is like nature with the seasons predictable, but still
always changing
For only what we know for sure, who's doing the arranging
David Carlucci

Tropic Madness

The silver shadows of the night haunt my sleep;
The whispering voices of the palms disturb my slumber.
Sometimes I toss and turn in fretful hotness;
Sometimes I lie and gaze into jungle blackness.

What holds me here when my heart cries for release?
What strange magic compels me to stay?
Can that scourge of all the whitemen be ingrained within me?
Has the gnawing at my mind o'er come the hunger of my heart for home?

Perhaps I am the victim of some strange malady;
Or perhaps my quinine is too weak.
Whate'er the cause, I hope and pray sincerely
That the madness of this climb has not befallen me.
Harold N. Faucher

"Lasting Love"

The time has come to watch and pray I'd live to see that wondrous day;
The day my love comes back to me from what seemed an eternity
Of waiting, watching, keeping time; hoping always she'd still be mine.

She's inspired me to achieve more than ever I would believe
I could grasp, think, or understand; when I offered to take her hand
In mine, she smiled; and we both knew that our love was pure,
   through and through.

When we were out alone one night, we argued and began to fight.
This fight soon caused us to divide and break each other's hearts
   inside.
We knew we'd have to reconcile - but be apart a little while.

She packed up and went on her way, promising to come back someday.
Love is patient I must admit; it brings me pain down in the pit
Of my heart, soul, and empty head to know she left for what I said.

She will return someday, I know. If she didn't, I could not go
On living in this agony. I know she is my destiny:
That is why I watch and pray, longing to see that wondrous day.

Craig Kopas

Look At The Cross

Look at the cross, what do you see
The cross is empty tho he died for me
My Jesus died to save the lost
He's waiting in heaven he's not on the cross

Jesus shed his life's blood for me
Because he died my soul is now free
Oh won't you come and meet him today
The holy bible will show you the way

Please call my name each time you pray
I'll meet you in heaven some wonderful day
Jesus came to this earth he came as a man
To live and die to fulfill God's plan

He died on the cross and arose the third day
He was the first to go that way
On God's word I'll take a stand
Because Jesus is the son of man

Betty J. Nolen

Green's Peak

The wind is whistling through the pines singing me a song.
The creek is bubbling joyfully it has no worry at all.
Nodding bluebells wave to and fro as the breeze blows across the
   meadow.
Red Indian paint brush standing in a long line, like soldiers guarding
   its hidden fortress.
Tall mountains stand proud and strong looking out over its beautiful
   Eden.
Golden eagles soaring high above the lush green hills its wings glide
   through the air of freedom.
The proud bull elk prances with his herd of cows and calves through a
   maze of pines and quaking asps.
Buckskin antelope stand proud as they look across the meadow.
Small purple flowers blossom in a bed of moss like amethyst lying
   in a bed of emeralds.
Spiderwebs strung between branches like silver threads strung with
   diamonds as if angels had done their weaving there.
A paradise of wildlife, enjoying the freedom of this sight.
As the sun sets and turns the hills red with its fiery glow, the moon
   rises over this peaceful land.
Until the silence is broken by the howl of a coyote singing to the
   moon of this glorious place.

Grace Ann King

Habitual Halloween

Young mummies in gauze and ghosts in white sheets,
The children prepare for Halloween night.
And soon they'll be searching for tricks or treats,
As they beg door to door without respite.

Yet strange it seems, for these creatures of youth,
To mask their true selves and hide what is real.
Time has not shown them the harshness of truth,
And children should have the least to conceal.

But wait 'til the present becomes the past,
And fear makes a home inside of their hearts.
Then this evenings strangeness will cease to last,
As they learn the lessons that life imparts.

Then donning disguises won't seem so queer,
And they'll wear a mask each day of the year.

Allison Marie Elliott

Hidden Beginnings

My life has left me,
The children are gone,
I cannot find them,
I've searched through the years.

They were born: beautiful, healthy,
Eager to live, as I wanted.
I gave them love, nourished them lovingly,
They grew, and learned, and responded with a natural verse.

School: an advantage they could add to their status.
Sometimes they left,
Even though they were there,
Will I ever see them again?

Marriage for them,
Love canceled, another love holding true.
Time has passed,
We meet, we speak, we are glad.

Barbara L. Hackett

If Ever You Never Saw...

If ever you never saw
The brilliant spring morning dew drop
Perched still on a poppy red rose petal.

Felt the warmth of a flame orange sunrise,
A palette of colors splashed across the horizon.

Heard the late-morning breeze, gently,
Ever so softly rustling through the treetops,
Like the inadvertent bump of young lovers in crowd.
So innocently, their eyes meet
He smiles,
Her cheeks slightly reddened.

And it all stops,
just for a breath.
The world doesn't spin
and two hearts become one.
Together they are splinters of arctic starlight,
Exploding over and over into the darkness
Despite the ease of disappearing to the day.

Jeffrey L. Bernstein

Childhood Memories

Tree-lined street, quiet, peaceful street.
The bright sun making strange patterns on the grass
through the treetops.
Small, but comfortable, split-level houses.
No fences to keep anybody out.

Summertime, ninety degrees and scorching.
My friends and I, opening the fire hydrant and splashing in the
cool, refreshing water.
Running through the soft grass,
barefoot and playful, the birds accompanying
our laughter with their music.

Wintertime, thirty degrees and chilling.
Tall, bare trees resembling forlorn, scary skeletons.
My friends and I, building snow forts and having
snowball wars, sledding behind the City Hall,
our scarves flying behind us
like brightly colored flags of surrender.

Angelique Ensrude

A Sonnet

I saw the man fall onto the cold ground,
the blood ran from his mouth onto the floor.
To his ears he heard not one single sound,
asleep and dead his red heart beats no more.
His love and memories don't matter now,
his friends and family are unknowing.
To come back and live, he doesn't know how,
in life his grief and pain were not showing.
He strained very hard to keep them hidden,
no time now to pray for his many sins.
Fear, love, hate, and courage, were forbidden,
the burdens of life no longer are bold.
Just thoughts of a society gone cold

Jay Lovett

Cathy

I look up in the sky and see
The beauty which Cathy can never know
Which she can never show
To a friend like me.
Why, oh why, did she have to be this way?
I say,
"Cathy, see the pretty bluebird."
And a feeling comes over me,
A choking kind of feeling
Because I know.
But Cathy never shows how sad she is.
She plays and talks as though she were in a world of bliss.
But she can't hide from me
That feeling of hers.
And since sometimes it's not good enough for words
She just slips her hand in mine
And I know she doesn't like being blind.

Anna Barton Jensen

Griefwork

This is the part of the dance where we leave
the ballroom floor to pirouette among
minefields of sudden loss. Step gently here:
though you follow successful-seeming tracks,
avoiding footprints that stop mid-stride,
there are no sure paths. More than once,
confident the worst was past, but missing
the silent choreographer, I have waltzed
onto solid-appearing ground only
to land in a pitfall of guilt, pierced
by possibilities, impaled on old pain.

Jennifer Marvin

A Winter's Solstice

A winter's solstice envelops
The aura of our being.
The feeling of tranquility is here.
The sounds stimulate the body, the smells stimulate the soul
and then we lose control.
The feeling of being in the tranquil land of serenity.
The love of the grasp taking you by the hand.
Leading you astray to the unending vortex of tranquility.
No engravings. Nothing.
Just the grasp leading you,
to a place you won't ever be.
Not in this life.
Over the high plains of jaded souls
that let go of the grasp.
They plummeted to their demise.
The umbrage of you is just a trifle,
for you won't let go.
Until the winter has ended.
Then we will fade into ourselves,
and become our former selves once again.

Chris Golden

The Gate

A weathered barnlot gate barely hangs on hinge
the ancient poplar holds no paint
its been three decades since it did
seasons cured the rough sawn planks
through summer's heat and snow
carefully sized by older hands, in times we'll never know
The boards won't crack when children climb
only a splinter now and then
they help their dad at feeding time, like only children can
The hinges squeak when opening, as if to cry in pain
on colder days it barely swings
as if to show its age
At night we sit out on the porch
and talk of life and things
sometimes for reasons we can't know
the gate begins to swing
we figure it's the farmer's ghost
who built the gate back then
full moon he checks the gate and post
to see if it still hangs

John Emile Perrault

"What's Within"

People judge people by the way they dress,
That's one of the reasons this world's a mess.

Also they look at what color of the skin,
Instead they need to look at what's deep within,

No matter how short or tall, even if they're thin or fat.
God made us all, why can't people except that?

If everyone's heart was like a window,
then they could see the pain.
Then maybe it would soften their heart
and they would try again

If you read this, don't judge someone
by their color or if they're poor, say Lord
let me look at what's within, let me
open a new door.

Billie Jean Mayberry

Friendship

What more is friendship than trust and love?
That's all that exists there.
Telling each other anything and everything,
Knowing the other always cares.

But then something arises,
And shatters that sacred trust and love.
Ruins that relationship, and threatens others.
In this time many surprises surface,
Many of which cut like knives.

Now your love is gone.
All caring for you has vanished.
All because of what we've done.
Like a naked and shivering child,
I am forced to face this cruel land alone.

Heath Sweatman

Natasha

An infectious giggle on a summer's day,
That smile that never goes away
Those gorgeous eyes, pure Wedgwood blue
That tentative voice, determinedly sounding "moo"

The puddle-duck waddle, when you've tired
Those cute retro-boosters, occasionally fired
Your pink lizard tongue, protruding in fun
That precious shriek as you start to run

You, my dear Natasha, so full of joy,
Have become this grown-up's favorite toy.
As we share time together every day,
The world can never appear to be gray.

Celeste J. Glaser

Our Love

The distance is never so far that the spirit of our love is not present
That our thoughts are not mirrored in the minds of each other
That the loneliness does not echo within our hearts

We are kindred
More closely bound that the blood of families or contracts of marriage
Time and space cannot be measured by our love

Wherever this life may lead us
We are one as our hearts beat in unison
In the eyes of our soul we are infinite
We are everlasting
We are forever

Georgeann Brown

Poem To Justice

Stab me once more with your words
that make me bleed pain.
Let me feel the stares of your criticism
that make me cry blood.
Yes my dear old friend stab me once
more with your angry words and eyes of hate.
Let me hear the sounds of the demons
inside screaming to get out...to get out.
Let me see the strong arms of your
mind scream out the weak words of your soul.
Let me fall once more into the sorrow
that comes from your brain.
No, my friend feel no shame, for I beg you to give me pain,
without your companionship I would most certainly go insane.
Once more stab me again,
my dear old friend.

Jennifer Marcum

Not Giving Up Yet

I've quit wishing on the first star I see at night
that I'll be alright.
I've quit blowing at loose eyelashes
hoping that someday I'll be free from these hostile flashes.

Haunting me, taunting me, stealing my thoughts
Giving me ideas that are not mine, couldn't be!
What is this thing called "Mental Illness"
And how does God decide who suffers?

I've hurt my friends and the ones I love,
lost a few along my way
When I lost myself, I didn't know what to do.

I am lost, so often alone
sometimes can't face these thoughts of my own.
I want to die more often than live.

But!!! from time to time
I have a great day!
Where I can happily and clearly see my way

If I give up on myself, all is lost.

Judy T. Hurt

Naughtia

Naughtia has given so very much,
That I of one eye saw everything then,
Within the bowels of dog days that did clutch
And daze all again, when as she did lend

And borrow, as my sight swims and is torn.
It is hard to return for I am soft.
So she swears and whispers that all is mourned.
Beginnings, ends, and middles are lofted

And thrown aside for no reason, but she
Demands daintily a return of it,
That which was her worth and promise to be,
So fulfilling for us, reward of wit.

I wait for Naughtia; she'll surely come.
Then give me what she achieves, and then some.

Ashton John Fischer Jr.

In My Dream...

So many lilacs stand before me
That I do not believe what I see
A blanket of purple, a light shade
By God this work of art was made

I lay under a willow tree, asleep
It is so peaceful, my thoughts are deep
I feel safe in my humble home
A house of nature, a beauty dome

An ocean so blue
So vast and so true
I stare out on it, and glee
Takes over me

The world is quite beautiful, yet we do not see
It's so great it couldn't be bought for any fee

Jessica McGonigle

Friendship

I thought I'd drop you a note to let you know
that I care; that you are in my thoughts every
time things seem so bare.
When I think of you - I see friendship that's so true;
Then I wonder - what would I do without you.
I would probably be sad and disappointed if I didn't
know you, because without you there wouldn't be
anyone to smile and have things to do.
I treasure your friendship with all of my heart,
for without your love - I would probably fall apart.
I thank God everyday for bringing me to
you - you to me, for without this wonderful
God - "we" wouldn't be.
I look forward to seeing you soon. For I
have lots to say to make you bloom.
Well, good-bye for now and have a good day.
The next time I see you we can share our faith.

Jill Krause

The Roc

The Roc,
that hideous bird,
haven't you heard of that foul bird,
the Roc?
It all started long ago,
In the land where nobody goes,
there was a bird quite big,
who was searching for certain fig tree.
It was called the darkest tree,
the bird knew what was in the land of man.
He searched the orchard to the darkest of man,
the humans fussed when the tree was taken away.
Why the humans and the Roc are still fighting today!

Clark Sturdevant

Welcome Home, Friend

While you were gone, I wrote this song
That has little tune or rhyme.
Just a note, to say a quote,
"You've been gone a long, long time!"

The weather there I hope was fairly nice.
But, sometimes I wondered,
Do those ships really have mice?

Days went by and end of the month was here.
I heard from a young girl, one day,
"They're here! They're here!"

Overjoyed was I when I heard her cry
That on that morning you said, "Hi!"
So, welcome back to the grind.
Cause all of us here are slowly losing our minds.

Sit right down in your usual chair
And wait a while to roam.
I'm so happy you're here.
We can now say, "Welcome home!"

Gracie L. Willett

The Golden Time

September brings us Autumn
That golden time of year.
When frost is on the pumpkin
And harvest time is here.

Breath taking are the cotton fields
Resplendent in their glow
Beyond the far horizon
The fields are white as snow.

Leaves are brightly gowned
in a multicolored hue, skies are crystal clear
And grass is bathed in dew.

September is nostalgic, a golden bittersweet time.
When man and earth enjoy
A partnership sublime

There's beauty in each season
Enriching one and all.
But matter mature shares
Her glory in the fall.

Johnnie Mae Ponton

Diary Of A Reluctant Expectant

It was rocky road ice cream
that first gave the clue
that aliens had landed there, here
in my most nether cushy parts

Within a septet of moons
you might have fought your rosy way
forward through the primordial maze of tissue
and blood
screaming the sound of light and life

Doubt and rage intermingled to form a blockade
to the tiny tunnel's aperture
collective unreadiness.
lingering
unwillingness to be the sacrificial lamb
unlived self-fulfillment,
a scar on the inside

Heidi Sauer

Midnight Madness

You are the gentle summer breeze
That comes over me in the middle of the night
In the darkness of my lonely room,
Driving me to the brink of madness
With your soft sigh,
Your teasing caress,
And the lingering scent of your sweet perfume.
All the while whispering to me
Promises of things yet to come.
Promises of great loves and noble passions
That stir my body
And send my heated blood racing through my veins.
I have touched you.
I have tasted you.
I have possessed you for one magical moment,
And I now know
I shall surely go insane
If, in the middle of the night
And in the darkness of my lonely room,
You come to me not again.

Becki Dodson

Untitled

Thanks for the memories
Thanks for the memories...thou some were bluer than
blue, I'd do it over again with you

It's been wild, a trip, a blast
but we know nothing even last

The warmth, joy, happiness was such
I hope I've given you as much

We laughed shared some tears
Where did they go, the years

The love you so graciously gave
I will cherish and carry to my grave

And how supportive you've been
stuck by me, thru thick and thin

Forever we will be
In our thoughts, you'll see

Gone, but never forgotten
but still, good bye, how rotten

Thanks for the memories..thou some were bluer
the blue, I'd do it all over again with you.
   Frances Carter

Thanks For

Thanks for all the love we've shared.
Thanks for showing me you've always cared.
Thanks for your time, to laugh and to cry,
Thanks for answering my questions, of why,
Thanks for my upbringing and continuous support,
Thanks for keeping everything in rapport,
Thanks for picking me up, when I was down,
Thanks for making me smile, instead of frown,
Thanks for doing every little thing you do,
Thanks for being a very special two,
Thanks for wiping away my tear,
Thanks for motivating me, from there to here,
I guess what I'm trying to say is,
Thanks... Mom and Dad... for being there.
   Janis S. Luce

Violence In The World

When I wake up each morning, I think
Thank you Lord for blessing me.

With all the violence in the world today
We shouldn't make the children pay.

What have the children done to make it like this?
Nothing!
The children have done nothing!

Joining gangs and doing drugs,
Ending lives and pulling plugs.

Pulling plugs from someone's life
Would not lessen the children's strife.

Who is it that dies when drugs are sent?
A future doctor, a teacher, or maybe even a president.

If parents had loved enough to guide,
The innocent youth may not have died.
   Dalita Brown

"Fame, Fortune, And Popularity"

Who seeks more fame and fortune
Than the "Popularity" seeking regimes?
But they never can tell the masses
The cost that this entails it seems.

The rich and the famous sometimes rise
To the level of receiving a Nobel prize,
And for a time they seem to be popular you see
But this too is temporal as with every degree.

This world system of ours is perverted
And society is contaminated at its best
The capitols of this world are crumbling
For a lack of true leadership is stressed.

So if you're one who seeks fame and fortune
And popularity among men is your goal,
I fear for your uncertain future
And the uncertain destiny of your soul.
   Cecil C. Lawrence

"Thanks To My Mother"

She was courageous and stronger
than most of us will ever be called upon to be.
In her heart she knew what was best and allowed my "Mom and Dad"
to adopt me. To thank my mother, I know not how...

She gave me the gift of life...
Then let me go, so as a child I would suffer no strife.
To thank my mother, I know not how.

Wherever she is, I want her to know that her decision was the best
for me... I've had the greatest parents who never concealed the truth,
and told me from the start that I was an adoptee.

They told me I was special and now at 43...
I can truly see that I have been blessed to have not two loving
parents, but three. To thank my mother I know not how...

She needn't worry nor feel any shame...for in my heart there's no one
to blame. I pray that by now she has found happiness with a loving
family who brings her no pain.

To thank my mother, I know not how...
Except to say thank you for the life she gave to me,
and the courage that she displayed.
For without my mother's love, I wonder where I'd be.
   Colleen A. Hubert

Champ Or Chump

When you are in a duel
Testing your skill against your foe
Show your courage when you are felled
By rising up - ready to continue
The bloody bloody bout!
For this is the stuff champions are made of

To challenge the many problems of life
For winners in life facing certain defeat
Turn seeming odds into glorious feat
The rule in life is thus summed
To rise above the ashes of the ruin
Basking under the luminous light
Holding his the torch of victory

That all may see that you deserve
To have your name etched on the cup of victory
Thus the world will applaud your heroic deeds
And place you on a pedestal deserving such success.
   Arnold H. Chow

Forgive And Forget

Forgive and forget should be a required course,
Taught and learned with no regret or remorse.
Always try to handle others with the greatest of care,
Kindness is without a doubt one of the greatest things shared.

Be honest to yourself and to others be true.
Then there is nothing more that can be asked of you.
Come clean when you're steppin' up to the plate,
No hidden insecure feelings insure a good fate.

Always goin' to be those times when ya gotta bite that tongue,
But holdin' it back often elevates ya to the next wrung.
So when ya get wronged and it will occur
Forgive and forget - it's the ultimate cure.

Julie Kay Phelps

"Vacation"

Ocean waves, a crystalline topaz blue rarely seen,
Tall palm trees with their tufts of green,
Flowers-red, yellow, orange-everywhere,
Exotically perfumed air,
Five days and nights without a care.

Moonlight reflected on the night-darkened surf,
A gentle evening breeze,
The contented sighs of the trees,
My mind is mellow and completely at ease,
The fragrant night air,
Five days and nights without a care.

Cynthia L. Cooke

Letter To A Warlord

Take this
Take that
My white glove cracks across your face
Granite crashes to the floor
With a hollow echo
I have been deceived I shout
Warlord strategies
Strangle me with soft pillows of indifference
Form bars across my windows
Stop it I gasp
Let me go.

P.S. it's funny how the weather changes
First it's sunny, bright, warm
Then a storm comes
Ice cold breezes stab my chest
And I have to stay home for the weekend
They name hurricanes after women, you know.

Janine Scammell

Old Billy

Old Billy was a Morgan horse—a noble hack
Trained for buggy or saddle on his back.
He pulled the buggy when the folks were courtin'
In warmth he moved with ease and in the cold was snortin'.
His gait was stylish—none better could be had
And forged a sentimental tie with Mom and Dad.
They often said that Billy knew
The homeward course though daylight flew.
They trusted him without a hand upon the rein
After going where directed to bring them home again.
In his day he pulled the buggy rain or shine
And good old Billy served 'til he was twenty-nine.
Now Dad and Mom are on that distant shore
And I wonder if old Billy led them home once more.

Gail E. Balman

Remember When We Laughed

Thoughts disappear in the wind
Sweet memories of days gone by.
Our hearts were filled with joy
Makes me pause and wonder why

When we slept in forests
I kissed the mornings mist upon your face
When we swam at midnight
   and warmed our naked bodies in embrace

When we walked to rivers
   and hungrily made love upon the ground
We ate from candles lights
   to gaze in special words we couldn't sound

We would sing and do silly things
   our hearts were filled with joy
We had our play times to fill the hours
   words were our only toy

When we danced barefoot on the beach
We made a fire, built castles in the sand
The magic I could reach, you would hold my hand
Life was simple, remember when we laughed

Judy Jagerman

Jackson

A Mexican prairie dog without a home,
Survived nature's worst and had done it alone.
This new found love god meant it to be,
I did not find him rather he found me.
I gave him a name and gave him my heart.
Jackson was loyal, was brave, and was smart.

I knew my vacation would come to an end
And it would be time to say goodbye to my friend.
Soon enough it was time for me to go home,
I had to leave Jackson how I found him,
Alone.

Every night that I went to sleep,
I would think of the dog that I could not keep.
All that remain are memories of mine,
Of that Mexican prairie dog that I left behind.

Anthony Shaun Carini

Plastic Superhero

So you think you're tough, well so do I
Superman did and we watched him die.
The "Man of Steel", hope he didn't rust
Made of aluminum, he'd bend or bust
So what would a superhero be made of today?
The new government plastic everything's made of, it may.
We'll recycle, recycle, recycle again
Until everything's made of plastic my friend.

Jeffrey Sykes

"The Darkness Is My Friend"

The darkness is my friend.
This is the day of birth, the first day of my life.
No one knows who I am, no one knows my name.
I am hungry.
I cry to suckle my mother's breast.
She does not hear me.
Motionless.
I cannot hear her breathing.
Mother!!!
The darkness is my friend.

Dale A. Weed

Evening Sunset

At the end of the day I saw a beautiful sight
Sun setting over the lake giving spectacular light.
Looking out the window sixteen floors above the street,
This view gave my eyes a very special treat.
The sun's rays sent alizarin crimson, lemon
Yellow and cadmium orange across the lake,
The lake was calm, glistening as the
Reflections danced a little shake.
A lighthouse was a pleasant sight
In shadows and the sun's brilliant light.
Then I saw sail boats on an evening trip.
White sunlit sails in the water's mist.
God has given us a relaxing sight,
All this happening just before night.
   Ethel M. Shannon

The United States Of America

America is a miracle come true,
Such a dream come true
Is the United States of America,
for me and for you.
The United States really rates,
In all of the Fifty States.
Let us all reach for the stars together
Our country is rich in every way,
It has class like no other.
To live here with thee,
Is heaven to me.
The greatness of our Country is brought
out in the beauty of our people,
and their principles, ideals, and philosophies.
From the Atlantic to the Pacific
Our country is truly, breathtaking.
I can't begin to tell you America, how much
I love you.
My family and friends and all people
everywhere, who have made my life so worthwhile
   Edmond Korrinhizer

Waves

Before my eyes I spy the ocean waves
Stumbling and falling over themselves
Struggling and yearning to reach the protection of the shore
Swallowing the weaker, more unfortunate curls and
Conquering the brutality of the massive combers
The weary traveler dissolves into a breaker;
Its lifetime goal is finally reached
Only to be lost once again
Because the wave knows that it cannot linger
Where it longs to be - drawn back into the unmerciful
   pelagic waters
The cycle begins again and will live forever
   Jessie D. Turner

Just This One Time

   I had to go to the doctor the other day - I knew the
the price I would have to pay, a big tall gent came strollin'
in, said, "He saw my double chin and Ma'am - you've got weight
to loose, means life or death - you'll have to choose" and off
he went, left me stunned, but returned with a diet you'd
through he won. "But Doc" I said, "is there anything sweet? I
have this urge I have to meet," he laughed, shook my hand
and wished me well - handed me an awful bill. I turned to go
and said to myself, "I still have goodies on my shelf, I'll go
on this diet but first - just this one time - I've gotta quench
this thirst and have my way - just this one time and that's today."
   Jean M. Smith

Stuff 'Neath The Sink

There's stuff for the windows and stuff for the doors
Stuff for the cupboards and stuff for the floors
Stuff for the silver
Stuff for the pans
Stuff for the dishes
Stuff for the hands
Stuff for the furniture
Stuff for the plants
Stuff for the roaches and stuff for the ants
Stuff for painting
Stuff for the brass
Stuff for bushes
Stuff for the grass
A can of old grease
A nut can of screws
A sample of dish soap
A bottle of booze
With all of this stuff it got me to think
How lucky I am for the room 'neath my sink
   Arlene K. Schroeder

Prairie Rose

I kept telling myself to be fair.
   Stroke not, that pretty hair.
Gaze not, into those lovely eyes.
   Speak softly, and tell no lies.
Taste not, of those sweet lips.
   Notice not, the body nor the rounded hips
shall I tell her?
   Or was it too soon?
But I looked up
   and there was the moon.
I realized daylight had faded away,
   and there was something I wanted to say,
But when we stopped where the roses grew,
   there was love and each one knew.
Far a touch of love like a fire glows.
   And I kissed a "Prairies Rose."
   Ann Campbell

Untitled

   The plastic mold on our once brand new door
stretched earthward. Every window in our house
teared stains of defeat. Blackness hollowed its
way in and out of every crevice. Soot clung to
the damp air all around. The sofa I loved so
much sat upside down, shamefully helpless among
the debris. Everything that was here during the
time of the attack became distorted in size and
color. Despair enveloped our walls of hope,
exhausted and eaten through. The blood of life
smoldered in the flames, camouflaged by the
charcoal remains on all, except the windows.
   Jennifer M. Jorgensen

Amber

She's the light of my life,
The apple of my eye,
She's growing so fast as time passes by.
The touch of her hand,
The smile in her eyes,
The love she inspires is no big surprise.
I want you Amber to know how I feel
It's a grandmother's dream so true and so real.
I want to thank our God up above,
Cause he's sent me my kids and my baby to love.
All my love grandma D.
   Debra Dowling

Autumn

Footsteps are echoed by leaves in their falling;
Streams retreat lazily as to rivers they run.
The woodlands caught up in adornment of color;
Set afire by shimmering spears of the sun.

Hillsides are touched by bleeding of sumac;
Midst browning of bushes already at rest.
Brilliance of colors culminating in beauty;
Rendering a sadness hard to suppress.

Sadness that blends with peace and contentment;
Bringing joy to the soul in measures untold.
Sighting of geese is communion with nature;
and life takes new meaning as autumn unfolds.
Darlene Cree Johnson

Out Of Darkness

She sauntered through the darkness
stepping softy into the light
The ardent glow embarrassed her
and gave to her new sight
she noticed all the flowers
then knelt and picked a bloom
The ambiance it captured, her
soul and senses too.
The garden that she walks in
if you understand her mind
was not made of seedlings but memories in time.
The darkness fell upon her from
pain of a reticent past
The light comes from the touch
of an honest man's hand
so when she says she loves you
know that it is true
for you are the sun
that gave aura to the bloom.
Darlene Brandafino

Beacon Of Light

It doesn't matter, let the past
Stay where it belongs
Today I traded my past of sin
For the light that will lead me home.

I'll take my cross with him I'll walk
It's shame I'll gladly bear
For beneath the shame, came forth great light
God's love for all to share.

I had walked away, from the cross that day
But my Saviour chose to stay
He knew some day the cross would give light
When I turned to show me the way.

The shame is mine, it was my sin
The Saviour had to bear
And out of darkness shone his great light
My Saviour's love and care.

Yes it was my sin, that made the cross
That Jesus bore that day
As a beacon of light, it shines for all
That you and I might find the way.
Dorothy Thornburg

Untitled

A printer for a check-up, to the doctor did go
Stating that his actions, and pace were slow

The physician, after lengthy examination
"Rx'd" a pill, that was thought a sensation

Printer neglecting to have, this "Rx" filled
Placed it in his wallet, not needing the pills

The illegible "Rx", hard to interpret
The printer as a "bus pass" showed it, "you bet!"

He entered illegally, to large "Broadway Shows"
Confusing many, even those on their toes

Plus the time he entered, a symphony concert
Featuring a renowned, gastronomical flirt

One day the "Rx", was somehow mislaid
His daughter found it, and delightfully played

She won a scholarship, to a music conservatory
This however, is not the end of the story

A note to the druggist, was the doctor's intent
Scribbling deciphered, all angled and bent

Was as follows, you certainly can be sure
"I got mine!", "Now you get yours!
Clyde Wilson

I Sometimes See

In the morning I sometimes see her face
Staring lucidly into some forgotten memory,
The smile ever so light,
As if to tell a secret which would spring hope into my awaking heart
Her breath ever so calm
Lying next to me wanting nothing but the moment
Slowly I awake to the brute emptiness of the bed

In the mirror I sometimes see her face
Watching with a playful look
Her eyes dancing like children, urging me to come out and play
I can almost hear her laughter
Beckoning from the reflection
I turn to find an empty room

At night I sometimes see her face
Staring lovingly into my eyes
Calling to me to hurry on my way
I can almost hear to voice as my name rolls off her tongue
Butterflies rise from my stomach
I reach for the night embracing only darkness
Sometime I can see her face
Dave Swenson

"Nature's Serenity"

Night quietly comes to a close.
The last star leisurely flickers out of sight.
Crickets slowly cease their monotonous chatter.
Morning innocently commences.
The sun struggles to pass over the horizon.
Soft breezes rustle the beautiful leaves of autumn.
Clouds dance across the pale blue sky.
Water trickles gracefully to the weather-beaten shore.
No one in sight,
No noise to be heard,
Only the complete serenity of Nature.
Julia K. Holem

Two Cents For Your Thoughts

What causes oneself to sit immutable as a stone Buddha
staring into space?
An inept conscience stuck as wet pages of an undisclosed coda?
Being lulled to sleep by the opiate lackadaisical
therein my spirit wanders thru the universe of the deep.

Finishing up my breakfast with strong coffee
a stimulant to induce the 'snapping out of it,' is this the key
that might work? Throughout wearing my bathrobe my usual clothes
in experiments futile as trying to wear out a pig's nose.

When out of the blue a question thrown
(a discobolus couldn't have done better).
"Two cents for your thoughts"!
Being at ebb tide this jolted me out of my reverie.
With this delving over evaluation of my
innermost thoughts, the thief of time Lethargy
an unwanted companion dredged up
from I know not where, now resides within me.

Haven't forgotten, I do remember
the center piece, a glass vase with several droopy stems
where rose petals lay scattered in pitiful disarray,
amidst the floral debris a mauve card phrased in endearing terms.
Benjamin Katcoff

Roller Coaster

In the line you wait as the speeding cars go by,
standing there impatiently, your heart begins to fly.

The people then come rolling in from their previous thrill,
you step into the warm, dry seat, as you go in for the kill.

The jerky car starts up the ramp your partner at your side,
you near the top and as you do the tracks are your only guide.

Suddenly, you are pulled down a hill as whiteness fills your face,
the cars are pulled left and right at a fast and even pace.

Quickly you are thrown into a loop, upside down and out,
all the people in cars behind give a screeching shout.

You're sucked into a deep dark hole, just waiting for the end,
when finally out of the tunnel you're thrown into a bend.

Gliding slowly into the station house that's where you did begin,
you race to get back into line you want to ride again.
Emily Alger

My Missing Angel

Angels don't float from the sky,
They grow from within your heart.
You can feel them spreading thru your heart
Into your mind and filling your soul
With peace and joyfulness.

Angels, halo of the sign
I used to be an angel
My halo was brighter than any other
But, no longer.

My angel has fallen
Where is my angel?
Where has my halo gone?

Why have my eyes deceived me again?
My angel is missing and I can no longer see
For my halo used to lite my unguided ways.
Cynthia D. Kemp

How Or Where Or When

What is this disease that's going around,
spreading dissension, disaster bound?

Ridicule, rioting, racial unrest,
a few of the symptoms, this disease at it's best.

Striking equally our young and our old,
cutting with criticism our brave and our bold.

Alienating the child from his peers,
instilling hostility, disquiet and fears.

Most pathetic of all is its blinding power,
closing our eyes to the grief and the sorrow.

Dividing our people and causing them strife,
obliterating all of the other man's rights.

Who can tell me where it began?,
this perverse epidemic that sweeps our land.

Caring not what is left in its inclement wake,
death, destruction, and of course heartbreak.

Who can tell me if it will end?,
or how....or where.... or when...
Charlene A. Perry

Beatitudo (Bliss)

I am spinning,
　Spinning with the wind while making my own,
　　Thematic moments and less real ones,
　Each carrying its own weight,
And carrying my weight with them,
　The lines of age, wisdom, and joy drop their boarders,
　　I can only see one line,
　It encircles me,
It is the world,
　Or at least all that concerns me.
　　I cast my gaze outward,
　　I avoid looking at myself,
There is nothing to be learned there.

Details demand my attention,
　And my attention they shall receive,
　　But not until I have slowed down,
　Or seen all I wish to,
Or stopped outright,
　Or stopped spinning.
Colin Marshall

Walk With Nature

An autumn walk with nature sets my inner spirit free.
Soothes my mind and lifts my heart that I may clearly see
Nature's grand finale, a magnificent display,
Touching on my heartstrings this Indian summer day.
Leaves and grasses whisper a compelling invitation.
Music of the natural world, a powerful invocation.

Walk in the morning hours with dawning and first light.
Since autumn days are cooler, frost steals in at night.
There is no lovelier brilliance, for all the world to see.
Than the diamonds in the crystal frost on every plant and tree!
It's sad to see frost fade away as the sun bursts on the scene,
Bringing life and warmth to us in its vibrant, golden sheen.

There are those who walk at midday in lovely sunlit places,
Enjoying the radiant sunshine kissing freckles on their faces.
Others wait till later to walk and talk and play.
Evening shadows stretch and grow, all along the way.
Lift your eyes toward heaven, it may take your breath away.
God made a lovely sunset to bless the close of day!

Take a walk with Nature. God's world is truly grand!
For every person needs to feel the joy in Nature's plan.
Caroline Hopkins

Love Is

Love is, to me, simple and sweet,
Sometimes painful yet keeps you weak

Love is communication greetings and salutations
And much needed interpretations.

Love is a love letter used to make
Good times and good things better.

Love is a new birth, husband and wife
Bringing new life to earth.

Love is remembering that special day
Anniversaries, birthdays the kids school play.

Love is, fast, love is slow, love is
Happiness needing to grow.

Love is trust in God, for he knows how.
And love is what the world needs
NOW...
Harold R. Miller

For My Friend

Our children are like roses, each beautiful and unique.
Sometimes like roses, our children die.
Our thorns are usually the pain of watching
our children struggle through life.
The piercing thorn of the death of a child is the most
severe pain of all.
Unlike the death of a rose, our memories and love will never die.
The love we share with our children transcends through all
space and time. It is eternal.
I believe that my daughter is one of many angels,
who watch over me and my family.
Each person must choose their own belief
Whatever helps them to endure
the incredible pain of the death of their child.
It has been seven years since my daughter died.
I cherish and value life more now than ever before.
God has been my rock and my salvation.
Many loving friends and family have helped along the way.
You can still live life after your child has died.
There is life after death.
Georgia Dunfee-Hamilton

It Only Takes A Moment

How rare it is to find
Someone who wants to unlock
The spiritual doors of your heart.

To listen and understand who you are.
Bonding enough to let yourself be true
letting God's light shine in you and through you.

Each one of us has a gift to give to one anther
A talent a kind word, a jester,
and yes even a smile.

It only takes a moment.
With that one moment
your world becomes alive,
the door has opened,
light is shining through
and the beginning of a new friendship
has just begun.

"It only took one moment"
Deborah Schroeder

He Says But I Feel

Feelings so deep inside but they are confused,
Someone so special to me I only hope not to lose.
Afraid of rejection and getting hurt like before,
Unable to recover being left, my heart being stolen and torn.
He says it won't happen that he'll always be true,
He ways he'll love me eternally but I feel like a fool.
His caring, his life and love-all these I want to conceive,
I feel so negative but his words and thoughts I try to believe.
Promises made but all promises were broken,
Feelings were kept and words went unspoken.
Jealousy and guilt which riddled the mind
I sit and think of all the tears that I have continually cried.
He says he'll be there to share my life together,
His feelings won't change, he'll leave me never
He says there's no other there's no reason to regress.
Rich words of happiness nothing he says ever less.
For the knot in which there's no untying,
Without him near I feel a sense of dying.
A love for two we shall always endeavor,
Then bind the love to last forever.
Brandey Palmer-Fogarty

Surroundings

Green trees and honey bees I have seen them all today,
Some clumps of grasses and moustaches along the way.
A butterfly, a dragonfly gliding through the air,
A duck preening here upon the sands, another there,
And pretty birds flying almost everywhere.
Life is good; no, in fact it's great!
What have I done to earn this fate?
Is it perhaps because I've walked and though not far
Instead of driving my old car?
You too may never know what you might have missed,
Perhaps a toad or frog you could have kissed!!!
Bill King

My Room

My room is the best place to be.
Solitude is for me.

In my room, society cannot judge
My thoughts and words.
In my room, society cannot influence
My behavior.

In my room, I am free to think and act as I please
Because there is no conformity.
In my room, I am one, single mind.
Fitting into the crowd is impossible.

In my room, there is no judgement.
In my room, there is no molding of actions.
In my room, there is no regulation of thoughts.
In my room, there is no intrusion by society.

In my room, I can always smell the roses.
In my room, I am truly myself.
James A. Gargiulo

Five Sense Worth

The majestic vision of a mountain, or a meadow,
The fragrant perfume of a dainty flower's petal
The cherished sensation of a loved-one's embrace,
The Thanksgiving dinner you can't wait to taste
The sound of children at play in the park,
These are the senses held dear in our hearts.
Dyanna L. Arnold-Willis

Destiny

Love goes door to door
Soliciting happiness and sorrow,
Constantly pushing our Hearts to soar
One way or the other - into tomorrow.

Allowing yet another
Day to uncover the Heart's love -
Waiting; waiting to sequester
That eternal eternity from above.

Giving Hope that one day there will be a light
That forever shines for two -
So Fear can be put to flight
And the Heart's pain can be withdrew.

Jennifer O'Brien

Knowing You

She hit me by storm,
  so sure of herself, so aware, so warm.
Where was she decades ago?
Did we cross paths and not even know?

But then, years later by chance,
  some common interest, an event, a dance.
I couldn't hide my emotion
  and as we danced close, it excited me, her knowing.

Mixing our worlds is too often tough.
But when they merge, time is shut out with an embrace; a laugh.

Is this like a soap opera I see on TV?
Now it's confusing as it happens to me.
How to react; a script there is none.
We live out each scene with calls, cards or dates made opportune.

Talk, otherwise stifled and short,
  now flows from our lips with no ridicule or guilt.
We rue the clock; it cuts short our meeting.
Aah, next time short kisses goodbye, we'll embrace at our greeting.

The frustration is great, with rewards far and few.
Yet each has been enriched; and I by just knowing you.

Jerome M. Fudurich

Rainbow Dreams

As evening comes I hunger for your face, your hand, your touch.
So much you have to give and lavish on me with such style.
I think of your smile.
My heart dances, and prances, you seem so supreme.
I do my face, my hair and wait for you with a heart full
Of rainbow dreams.

Janice C. Johnson

A Passing Cloud

So many years carried away on a passing cloud,
So much time tossed about by the forceful wind.
All of the memories clear as the blue sky above,
All of our love spilled out like a wave on the sand.

As an eagle soars freely the heavens so high
So we, too, must soar our separate sky.
But forget you not the Father above,
Who strengthens us daily with His unending love.
He is the stronghold, should a storm pass through
To give a haven of rest gladly to you.
And now with memories and courage weighing your heart,
With trust and dependence in Him we must part.
Now with fear and hope, tied together with love
Soar those heavens that are so high above!!

Cassaundra Hope Paul

Nothing Without You

My Father says I'm one of a kind,
So how come a steady boyfriend is so hard to find.
When you were here, I had something to do,
Now that you're not here,
I am nothing without you.
People talk and people stare,
People whisper and people glare.
But I don't care about what people say or do,
Cause like I said before,
I am nothing without you.
You may think that this is a lie,
Or you may think that this is true.
Follow your heart like a true man does,
And the rest will come to you.

Star Patterson

A Plea For Mercy

As I lie awake and think about the past, my first love I remember;
So full of love, so full of life, and hope for future splendor.

Naive and trusting as I was then, I became a mother;
But he turned his back and walked away, and walked down the aisle with another.

Then he came back to rekindle the flame, just as my tears had dried;
I realized then, though years had gone by, that my love had never died.

I raised our little girl the best that I could, but riches they were few;
Except for the love that I gave everyday, I tried to give love for two.

I wonder what he thinks of in his mansion on this earth, does he care one way or the other;
Or does he somehow think that he's right in a way, because he honored his mother?

On Judgment Day when the book is open and the choice is life or slaughter;
Will he look in His eyes and whisper these words,
"But Lord, I have no daughter"?

Betsy Koch

"Petal In The Wind"

You are like a rose petal in the wind
So beautiful and delicate
You move with such ease and gracefulness
Waiting for somebody to find you
When you are found you are just another
Petal waiting in the wind
You fall gently to the ground
Waiting for the next breeze
The breeze picks you up so delicately and carries
You off to the next destiny
What lies ahead you do not know but soon
You will find the one that will not say
"You are just another petal in the wind"
He shall pick you up and never let you go
Because you are part of the special rose
He has been looking for

Anthony Underwood

Heaven

How I would like to go to HEAVEN, dance among the clouds,
Say hello to those who have gone before me.
Leave the life on earth behind me as my soul leaves my earthly body and my family weep in a soft and gentle tone.
I would say, "Don't cry for you will soon join me in this glorious place entitled HEAVEN".

Johron Jones

Blue Sky

Blue sky my sky so blue so high,
so always there when in despair, lit up till
night to keep all in sight and to make sure were all there.
Blue sky so beautiful and all so big,
with clouds flouting all around in the wind.
Blue sky with different features
and different thoughts, I sometimes feel like
giving you a big hug, but then I cannot.
Blue sky all so round and all so
nice, it sometimes reminds me of sugar and spice.
Blue sky I wish I could keep you
but you're down and I'm a frown.

Heather A. Bauer

A Look From The Inside

As I sit in my room of glass,
Snow is covering the once green grass.

Flocks of geese can be heard and seen,
Heading south so graceful and lean.

Rabbit tracks are present in the snow,
Hiding from the wind that starts to blow.

Squirrels and chipmunks nibble at the feeder,
As I sit cozy and warm by the heater.

God's gifts are abundant and beautiful to see,
Be thankful of what he has given to you and me.

Bethel D. Ebert

Untitled

CLICK, CLICK, CLICK,
snap, snap, snap,
CLICK, SNAP, CLICK,
transpire down one after another
CRASHES ON THE SIDEWALK
sticks to me like a little brother
MULTIPLIES AS IF COHORTING ON CONTACT
congregates on everything
RUNS ON THE SIDE OF THE ROAD LIKE A DOG CHASING A CAR
stay together as if they are confidants
THAT ARE THERE FOR EACH OTHER
crawls along the gutter
AND BLAZES DOWN THE SHUTTER
RAIN
IS
AN
ASTONISHING
EPISODE

Amos Corralez

Love And The Tugboat

The Tugboat was moved by the Ship it just met and with every
small tug the ship was impressed.
A tug at the fore and a tug at the rear and with every small
nudge they knew love was so near.
In fact each was elated.
And although the catastrophe had caused a big wreck and many
rich people got terribly wet.
The Tugboat mused, "life is certainly quaint, the sad things in
life just ain't what they ain't and more often by far they're
not what they are.
I've finally found what I longed for years and although I
admit I never shed tears, life for me was lonely ordeal, like
when you're not even content after a glorious meal.
But now I'm so happy this ship's my "Big Lug".
And for the rest of my life I have someone to hug.
Thank you "Love", to you I cling.
"And each day to "My Lug", your virtues I sing".

Joseph Giorgio

My Fantasy

I've been away for fourteen years,
Slept through the cries and the tears.
I've been in a dream far away,
So I could be happy and live each day.
I've spent nights away from harm,
Opened my doors and still felt warm
I've been in love one million times,
But never heard the ring of wedding chimes.
I've spent many days on a cloud,
Dreaming of what would make me proud.
I've ridden on bright moonbeams,
And sat among other's wishes and dreams.
I've gone to journey for new worlds,
and walked through pools of diamonds and pearls.
Then only a day ago or so it seems,
You woke me from these dreams
With one look at you,
All my fantasies came true.

Ashley Wade

Confidence And Fear

My dreams are filled with wondrous springs of rain
Sleeping so softly, seldom do I try
My mind passes through stages without pain
Subconsciously my hand reaches the sky.
My entire body so light and free from despair
Oh, tell me why can I feel such relief?
When I open my eyes and no one seems to care,
Reality does instill my belief.
I've broken through the locks of depression that bind
So I can wonder to a place I know,
And finally see that the world is kind
Where all the flowers and trees do grow.
With the air of freedom I spread my wings
And fly to a place where my sad heart sings.

Diana Steinman

Underneath Shades Of Time

To fear death is to burn in the ball of rotting dirt with the serpents skin,
bleeding in an uninformed fortune.
When night denies you tomorrow's life
you hide calling the dark evil.
Crouching in a cache because you cannot, or do not understand
what is shrouded by the black smog.
Yet the radiating light reveals the melancholic sin that lives in you
and all around you.
So the fear of death only proves your lack of faith.
Afraid to see what someday we
all must face.
Faith in what? You ask
A prince of love, of more than life
deleting fear from ones thoughts.
To live in fear is ruining life
Trials come like flying fire flies
let them pass, retire with the sun and start over
A new day is for forgetting nightmares.
To train your mind on new cares

Ethan Andrew Holub

From Above

Jesus sent you from above because he knew I needed
someone to love.
He picked you out from all the rest, because he
knew I'd love you best.

Anna M. Hildebrand

Back From A Party

In a neat little social circle we spent the evening.
Six or eight couples in apparent close contentment.
Yet, how many with surface stripped away
Would show desperate longing
For life or love or talents unfulfilled?

Dear God, how do we break our molds
And still be true to self and Thee?
A desperate yearning to grow and change
Without harm to those past or present
Loves and loyalties
That are distant from us,
So far distant, but within our reach
If we choose.

We are separated by so many barriers.
Some we cannot cross, some we choose not to
For fear of harming others,
Or by reflected hurt,
Ourselves.

Dick Butler

Tangasseri

Ninety-nine acres embraced by the tranquil waters of the Arabian sea
Situated off the coast of Kerala, south of India,
Is a heaven for the Indians and visitors.

A colorful arch is the rainbow of its gateway,
Feathery coconut palms ruffle in the air of sunny skies
With the season change, monsoons quench parched wells,
At sundown fishing boats glide over waves of hope
As the beacon of peace is cast from the towering lighthouse.

Surfs of joy rush to the shore, as gleeful children wet their feet
While the gentle wind caress the cheeks of elders cushioned on the
  sandy beach;
Bonavista hill, kissed by the aura of the setting sun harmonizes
  teens and lovers,
Weary travelers find solace in the summerhouse.

Remnants of a fort keep history alive,
Graves of Portuguese and Dutch soldiers are traces of a bygone war.

Mount Carmel, Fountain of education, flows through generations
Whilst the Infant Jesus enriches the people's Catholic faith,
Chimes of the Holy Cross tick the clock of time;
As you walk the streets that depict,
The stations of the cross, you behold
The golden peninsula, Tangasseri

Erma Whittle

Ode To A Friend So Close

Pray for me my friend that in my life I might live it to the fullest.
Sing to me a new song so that I may dance gleefully along the way.
And grant to me well wishes that I might go forth secure in the
thought that someone cares.

When you have time, walk with me to keep me company. Tell me a story
of life and love that I may cherish in my days of loneliness. Throw
your arms around me and give me the warmth I may otherwise lack
on cold days.

Write to me in a time when from each other we are absent.
Recount the good times and the bad times we've shared
to keep us close.
And end it with a thought that is good so that I may never forget
you if we never meet again.

Call me sometimes and share in camaraderie with me. My love for you
will not founder as we move along the continuum of life. But, if
nothing else, remember me with the deepest love you have; for,
that is how I'll remember you.

Jeffery R. Shelton

Worms

As I pressed the shovel in to the ground screams of pain
shrieked through my ears, but yet I did not know where
they came from.

So I continued, I hurried to finish the hole where I would plant a
seedling. Many months later as I sat on a warm spring night
watering and nurturing my sapling, I noticed several little
bodies below my lawn chair.

MY GOD what had I done? How could I justify one life for another?
But it was too late; I could see the shovel marks through their
tiny bodies severing them in half.

Why didn't I stop when I heard their screams?
Oh GOD I am sorry I never knew I could or would hear worms SCREAM.

Armand Powell

Hurricane Hugo

The winds came so furiously in the middle of the night.
Should we hide in a corner, or stay up and fight?
A tree came down at the windows on the side;
Do we peek out and look, or do we run and hide?

The trees were swaying all around,
Many of them uprooted from the ground.
What a sight to see - these majestic trees
Fallen and lying like October leaves!

The freezer was melted, the refrigerator was hot;
There was no ice to be bought.
You panicked around all over town,
Only to return with a great big frown.

The rains came, the winds slowed down,
There was devastation all over town.
It got hot, and you sweated;
But darkness was the thing that you most dreaded.

Where is my nightgown? Where is my bed?
I need a place for my weary ol' head!
You stumble, you falter, you swear, and you pray:
Dear Lord, may tomorrow be a brighter day!

Carolyn M. Furr

The Ashes Of Eden

Streaks of electricity
shooting from the sky,
striking upturned claws,
dead branches reaching for the sky,
blood red sky.
Earth, cracked into a thousand hardened pieces
like scales on some beast
greater than the mind can comprehend.
Scattered clouds, storm clouds,
static in the sky.
Balls of dust and ash roll across the broken ground,
bouncing, spinning in the solar wind.
Sun and moon, ringed by halos, peek
through the bleary sky,
watching the dead planet.
On a raised plateau in a valley,
A statue still stands, corroded, headless,
but still she lifts her torch to the heavens.
It glows, sometimes, with an unhealthy light,
welcoming visitors to a world that once was.

Holland Mihai

Descent

And I stand over the lake,
Shivering above the placid surface.
Fatigue creeps over me as I am spent,
Sent tumbling into the waters.

And I am falling,
Cold and pure and forever.
In this new, frame-frozen world
The pain escapes, and I can feel him no longer.

But somehow I knew he had gone.

The burning tightness in my lungs
Forces me up. Crashing
Into the air, I leave
My sanctuary where hurt fades,
Forgotten.

And I stand alone on the dock,
Dry above the rippling surface.
Wind washes over me as I wonder,
Have you ever fallen?
    Eileen Kelly

My Love

Your hair, as blonde as the sunlight
Shining down upon the ocean.

Your eyes, as blue as Bermuda waters
Crashing against the sand.

Your smile, as bright and warm as the sun
Beating down on a beach-comber.

Your heart, warm and caring
And as big as the universe itself.

Your hair flows gently,
As the cold winter breeze whispers through it.

Your eyes stare into mine,
Revealing your love.

Your simple smile,
Brightens up my life.

Your heart beats strongly, each beat for me,
You are my love, and will always be.
    Danielle Avery

A Dying Sun

Through clouds of mist, the sun peers over
Shedding light upon sunflowers, poppies, and clovers.
It nourishes crops in a farmer's garden;
The molds of life are beginning to harden.

It will rise and reach its highest height
Like an eagle caught in the air, mid-flight.
The sun will shine its last earth-warming ray;
Not a single soul shall see the light of day.

Lost in a world of blackness and confusion,
We will realize our life was simply an illusion.
For we were controlled by the sun's currents of power;
Now that it's gone, we all shudder and cower.

What did life ever have to give
When it's up to fate whether we shall live?
There's nothing more to do but wait
Until darkness shatters - along with hate.
    Jennifer Clemens

She's Gone Away

My gram went away today;
She was in so much pain.
The place she rests is far away
and that is where she will remain.

Her face, her smile, her quietness
and her big bright blue eyes,
She will be remembered for her tenderness;
we all thought her quite shy.

Gran's strength we took as weakness;
we found out how wrong we were.
She loved us all, now there is a bleakness;
her strength was not deterred.

There is an emptiness today
because she's gone away.
We'll love all our memories and all that they'll bring:
the love, the joy, and just about everything.
    Joyce E. Gray

Love In Bloom

A beekeeper loved a milkmaid,
She was a farmers daughter.
They wished to wed, but the farmer said,
"Can you support her like you oughter?"

The beekeeper replied to the farmer,
"It's true, I have no money.
But my bees will swarm, love will keep us warm
And we will live on milk and honey."
    Alice M. Gadberry

Solitude

Solitude stands by the window
She turns her head as I walk in the room
I can see her eyes, she's been waiting
Standing in the slant of the late afternoon
And she turns to me with her hand extended
Her palm is split with a flower with a flame

Solitude retreats to the doorway
I am struck once again by her black silhouette
By her long cool stare and her silence
I suddenly remember each time we've met
And she turns to me with her hand extended
Her palm is split with a flower with a flame

As she takes my wrist I feel her imprint of fear
And I say I knew that I would find you here

I turn to the crowd as they're watching
They're sitting altogether in the dark in the warm
I wanted to be in among them
I see how their eyes are gathered into one
Then solitude turns to me with her hand extended
And all my instincts, they return
    Hollie Pack

Goodnight Sun

Innocent old world colors of yellow and gold
Streamed from the sun
Touched the walls of the pure blue sky
Said goodnight to the clouds
Who tucked him in to the mountainside
Guilty new age colors of gray and black
Dripping from the sky
Touching the walls of the dark brown earth
As if the sun has forgotten our world
Clouds smother him, not faithful as in his youth
    Angela M. Marino

Mother

My sweet little mother is one of a kind
She never hesitates to speak her mind.
She's loved by all who know her might
That her bark is louder than her bite
On politics, Medicare, neighbors-you name it
Alcoholics, nudity - disrespect she'll, blame it
Women's lib, hippies, motorcycles are outrageous
And to argue with her-you must be courageous
Mothers who work and let her kids run wild
Her retorts are quite a bit stronger than mild
Stray Dogs, fleas, Mary Tyler Moore
Are things disliked with a very high score
Lawrence Welk, Blue Knight and Hawaii Five-O
Are enjoyed a lot as she stitches and sews
She's compassionate, generous - Helpful towards others
She's my sweet little Mama
The best of all mothers.
   Dorothy Goldman

With A Nod Of Her Head

Day by day as her life unfurled
She learned to control her own little world,
With a smiling nod or a sharp shake of her head
She finds that no words need be said,
It's a yea or a nay, but mostly a nay,
With a nod of her head, she gets her way.

It wasn't long before she "loint"
That all she had to do was point.
So now Miss Princess on her throne is sitting
While those about her do her bidding.
Any hour of the night, any minute of the day,
With a nod of her head, she gets her way.

She's not spoiled
She's adorable
She's my granddaughter.
   Jo Colan

Loneliness

Loneliness is being alone within yourself,
She is the one that cries out for the company of others.
She lives a life of silence in her own little world.
It started when she was three and she could
Fall asleep in her dad's arms as her mother sang.
Though at age six her life was cut in half,
The one that held her was gone.
Her life could never be the same.
She didn't want to believe it,
So her life began to fill with lies,
From then on she lived life in a false way
Because she didn't want others to know who she was.
Now that she is older she still looks back,
But now all she sees is a big wondering hole.
   Codi Kissick

A Poem For My Mother

My birthday is your "birth" date
   The night in which you stayed up late
You gave me birth on the bed which you lay
   Fourteen years ago on this very day
With tears in your eyes that glistened and glowed
   In which all your joy and happiness showed
I was in your sight and there was a grin on your face
   You took me in your arms and I felt your embrace
Oh how warm, mother, was your chest
   And how great were our feelings, oh the best
      Emily Marxkors

COMPANION ON THE ONE GREAT JOURNEY

SHE hallows, even as we drink in the chronicles of past and now,
She hallows even as we curse her,
   languid in her youth, and we wonder of tomorrow,
   swift in age, and we fear the morrow's certain fortune.
She hallows with her memories and ego fancies of wisdom,
   the early ones of pleasure, the later reaped by heed
      to countless follies.
For what does this companion demand and reward,
   a spirit for the slave, and yet sometimes master,
      a span of splendor, so often stayed by sureness of ordeal,
         and anguish.
So, embrace the dear companion, she is faithful, of engaging subtlety,
   who will leave you but once.
Till then her joys we relish and we hold,
For her departure is squired by the close of all,
   splendor, anguish, and light.
Oh companion. Oh, great journey.
   John Stuart Maitland

A Broken Something

   A twist in reality a fall of
shadows. You can see it coming
you know that it's there. So look deep.
   There is a truth in darkness
that takes a grip on a broken
something. A heart that wants to
be full which is only full of
emptiness. That twist of fate,
that downfall of lies.
   Now lays there a broken
something. A something full of rain.
   What do you say of the
present emptiness, sad and true?
   The call of the raven lies before you.
Eternal peace being your only thoughts of escape.
   Once full of love and the light of a flower,
now so empty with holes left where a heart once stood.
   I can never forget the look in
your eyes in the hopes that love
may prevail, my dear emptiness.
   Erica L. Miller

A Sanctuary for Shannon

A brick was laid in a desolate land,
Set in place by an infatuous hand;
and there while the wind impaled the blue,
The next brick was laid which made the base true.

Composed of more than Earthly matter
Bricks as these will never break or scatter.
Yet to know their substance, lives as a must;
The substance of these is mainly our trust.

And yet, trust is only a pawn of Love,
Which crosses the skies like a feathered dove.
And as a dove soars the heavens so true
I will flutter my wings of love for you.

Like the Egyptians did so long ago,
A pyramid of trust in us will grow;
Block over block of affections so bold
Layered in purity shining like gold.

Our beginning now, must come from our ends,
And all that we have to each other lend.
To explore new beginnings we commence;
The future can only be as intense.
   Edward Santa Cruz

Thanks-Giving

It's just a special time
Set aside by mortal man
When two of earth's enemies
Learned how to become friends.

It certainly wasn't an easy task
For each could have hurt the other
But God placed love within their hearts
That made them give so as a true brother.

Are we such a different people today
Wrapping Thanksgiving up with only special food
Stuffing ourselves with all the victuals
Being thankful for what or who we see as good?

Or could we learn to relive that old tradition
Of forgiving when it could possibly hurt
Only our pride that is merely temporary
To make our thanks-giving really work?

Elaine Willinhart

Will

Will the newborn children of this year see how beautiful the tall
Sequoia trees are?
Will they survive the pollution we have left for them to breathe?
Will the rainforest still be there for them to see and touch?
Will they ever see a Panther or Zebra without going to the zoo?
Will the rivers still sound peaceful and filled with harmony like
They are now?
Will they be able to go home and not worry about being hurt by a criminal?
Could they save themselves from what politics we have left for them?
Will the national deficit be paid off?
Will we leave them a strong education and enough
Knowledge so that they can fight for what is theirs?
Could they prevent or cure viruses with good medicine?
Will our technology from today give them hope for their tomorrow?
It is too extreme for us to understand but, will they?

Becky Contreras

Soldiers

Rustic leaves flocking in spiritual breeze.
Sent as soldier souls, earth dormant trees.
Across your path they fly, sudden glimpse eye.

Trees breeze sends us these soldiers flight.
Grim reapers plight always in sight.
Earthly air needing to share souls delight.

Earthly desires endless, so graceful and tasteful.
Seeing everyday life's waste will lay.
Soldiers war begins, leaves float to earth's light dim.

Rain drives them to the ground, soldier tries not make a sound.
Soldiers life may end suddenly, autumn drives leaves soon.
They'll take their place, world's sudden gloom.

Bruce E. Dittrich

Autumn

How beautiful is Autumn...with colors aglow.
Seems The Master Painter has touched His brush below.
The leaves are colored with green, yellow, orange, and brown,
Soon to be wind-tossed, tumbling to the ground.
Summer's toil has ended, the harvest almost done,
The shocks of corn and pumpkins are drying in the sun.

Soon frost will come...the colors will fade from radiant to faded brown,
With crackling leaves beneath the feet, an icy air renown.
God in all His glory must be pleased to see,
His mighty works, His changing moods...created for humanity.

Betty M. Waugh

"...Depths Of Lonely Wells"

Ever look into a lonely well at night and
See the starry sky reflected there?
Ever drop a pebble, see them dance upon
The rippling surface deep below?
Ever think how far it is that nature
Reaches out to paint such jeweled loveliness?

If you have, you've found, dear one,
A bit of deep infinity to share;
You've found a bit of godliness
'Cause stars have danced for you.
You've found God's secret cache of joy,
Within a lonely, sparkling well.

Donald S. Mayo

Kinship With A Tree

Have you ever embraced a tree, and felt her breath?
See, she reaches her branches to heaven, as a mother in prayer
In breathing, we give her only some of what she needs.
Unselfishly she gives back much more in return.
She cleans our air, she gives us shade to cool us,
And gives us a place to rest.
She gives our children a place to play,
And she gives us wood to keep us warm.
Have you ever embraced a tree?
We all need to, to feel her breath.

Janet Marie Burton

Fantasy

Look out my window, out through my mind.
See my world, see survival of my time.

Rambling through whispering sands.
The kingdom now is sadly only mans.

Pretend you're me, I'd be you, let me be free.
Would it change if I took away all the keys.

All doors would be open, the walls and corners gone.
Loving all living things, no reasons left to con.

The deep unsolved waters care not for this life.
He and she, black and white, with husband and wife.

It's just one more careless intruder on her beach.
Almost getting there, the dream so far from reach.

She shares no secrets, but still inviting.
Read the Bible it's all there in writing.

Always removing past foot traces.
Never uniting with all our races.

Aimless the blowing sand with one embraceless sweep.
All the sadness of nature evolving is why I weep.

Laughing and crying deep beneath the crystal water.
Her revenge is soft and controlled in the Name of the Father.

Deborah Klugman

Thoughts To Suicide

Mixed emotions are coming from you to me.
Sorrow and despair is what I feel.
Love and compassion is what I need.
Protection and a champion is what I want.
A light to follow is what I must see.
A road to nowhere is were I must go.
Today or tomorrow, but I must leave soon.
For one day it will be too late and no one will know
All the torment I have to put up with
Or the feelings that made me feel this way.

Amy Michelle Ward

Windows To The Soul

Look into my eyes; these eyes of mine and tell me what it is that you see
Is it that you can't hear my voice of heartache and loneliness?
A voice of grief?
Is it that you can't hear me talking? Is it that you can't hear my plea?

Can you see my hunger? Is it that you can't see my pain? A tear
trickles in my eyes; it runs down my cheek; a tear drops in the rain

Please don't pass me by and show me the way towards the door;
my tears still trickle from my eyes; these tears do fall
they fall into a puddle; they fall out on to the floor

Look into these eyes; these eyes of mine and remember all that you see
The most important in my life, is what lies within
It's everything that lies within me

C. Huston Wamsley

Echoes Never Heard

You made a mess in the life of that little girl's room
Secretly, you walked away, her innocence consumed
You took her daydreams, and gave her nightmares
A life time memory, of your cold hard stare

Each step slower than the first one, her down in shame
It was time again to take a nap, to play that grown up game
Her pleading cries of innocence were echoes never heard
A brand new pair of shoes for never saying a word

Feeling so empty inside, her pillow wet, from tears
She tries to seek protection but sent away to face her fears
Her loneliness, her only worth, failure, her only guide
Pain is all she's ever felt, from an open wound inside

A slave to the silence, a secret with no name
Her precious soul was dying from eternal shame
She knew she was losing before the game would start
She knew she had lost by the numbness of her heart

She had no choice when push came to shove
She didn't know she was worthy of any other love
An empty life, a murdered soul, and games she'd always lose
Her innocent love, and trust betrayed...all for a pair of shoes.

Dona Jean Freed

"Wild Flower"

I walk through the forest of flowers...
Searching in my heart, but not in my mind
Hoping one day to find... a wild flower,
Step by step I see, I grab one, and I bleed.
Tired of the endless journey, I stop and breath
I close my eyes and pause
My pause is timeless, no boundaries there for me
I listen to the sounds that fill the air
They encompass my body like a sweet symphony....
I take a deep breath, breathing in the air so fresh
Such a potpourri of aromas it sets my mind free.
As I hear the water trickle across the sand in this barren land.
My eyes open slowly, very slowly, and my breath-stolen for a moment
As quickly returns, my heart pauses - there before me in this
Forest of weeds, sits swaying in the gentle breeze
My wild flower, graciously at ease...with petals I can't describe
For the immaculate colors I see, aren't what others perceive
A beauty of the sweetest cologne not known... I kneel in
Awe, of God's power with the creation of this wild flower.

Chris Levy

Handwriting

Signatures make significant displays.
Scribbles exhibit what the writer didn't say.
Inking on paper gives shape to the vapor of words.
Tension in the pen strengthens and disturbs.
Clues are pursued, patterns detected
In drooping loops and letters unconnected.
Pressure heavy, forward bound
Or carefree, loosely circling around,
Scrupulous dotting of every "I",
Useless garlands and varied size,
Crowding, cut-offs and omissions
Speak loud of lost and found ambitions.
Ink spots along the trail.
Dug up to tell a tale.
Pen-pointing evidence, casually planted,
Says to the writer, "You had a hand in it."

Genevieve Griffin

Ribbon Of Steel

Drilling deep - cold steel kept probing Alaska's tundra land,
Rugged men in Arctic gear withstanding nature's hand.
Black liquid God discovered - news of "OIL" boomed the states.
Man...they all came running, as they did in "98".

Blueprints by the thousands, maps for every turn.
Before Congress gave the "go-ahead" and wheels began to churn,
"To protect Alaska's beauty" must be written in the plans,
The wildlife, their roaming grounds, the natives and their land.

Alaska's pipeline-so majestic, testing - so precise.
Rugged mountains-swirling rivers - earthquake shifting-moving ice.
800 miles to cover from Valdez to Prudoe Bay,
Big rigs of all description, scattered along the way.

It takes a "special" breed of people resisting nature's hand,
"Deceiving" is her beauty - "Unforgiving" is her land.
Still men and rigs kept rolling, puffs of diesel upwards reel,
Building bridges-blasting mountains-moving earth-welding steel.

Snaking low beneath cold tundra, the "Ribbon of Steel" unwinds.
Crossing rivers, winding forests, crawling jagged mountain sides.
An "800 mile" pipeline weaving Alaska's vast domain,
Now pumping hot crude oil, 2 million barrels a day.

Jean E. Petersen

Grandma's Rocking Chair

I can't remember a time when grandma didn't have white hair.
She always sat in the corner in her old wooden rocking chair.
Her rocking seemed as though she was keeping time to some
unknown tune and never skipped a beat.

Everyone in the household knew, that old chair was Grandma's
reserved seat.

It wasn't uncommon to see her worn Bible in her hand, an afghan
over her knees, and her glasses sitting on her nose.

Once I opened her Bible and pressed between the pages, was a
picture of Grandpa and a dried up rose.

Sometimes when my house is quiet, I can hear the rhythm of that old
rocking chair.

I wish Grandma was here today, we'd have a lot to share.

Diana L. Smith

God Asks Of Us "Why?"

The wings of dawn sweep in through the darkened sky,
Rosy streaks paint murals upon the pale golden hue.
As morning comes with its new fresh beginning,
God asks of us "WHY?"
"Do you not know that I Love You?"
"I AM, that you stop sinning."

We careen down the road of Life in such a rush,
Passing all who would reach out to touch us.
All God asks is for us to hear Him call,
"Come home My children, great and small."

Take a moment now, to contemplate what God could mean.
His call is sweet, the time left is short.
Hear in your heart God's cry and glean
Understanding of His Rapport.

Listen now and hear of the Love God gave.
Cruel Calvary's tree sacrificed His SON'S blood.
But His ultimate price was meant to save
You and me in that Wondrous Flood.
God asks of us "WHY, DON'T WE HEAR HIS CRY?"

Jo Anne E. Hall

Ovid's Star

Publius Naso saw the bright 'star'
Rise in the dense ebony morning that began
His sentence: Exile from Rome forever.

Two thousand years later uneasy sleep
After my sweet complex love had died
Would bring me to the window
Where, drooping in the southwest
Over the night shaped cityscape, Venus shone,
Paradox because the wide bed reflected in the pane
Was disordered only on the left side.

Grief looks for odd comforts and so,
Flattering myself, I wanted my planet
To be the poet's star.

A book, not a papyrus roll, gave rich names
For the brilliance whose light stung Ovid
Near the Capitaline hill;
Lucifer, and Phosphorus
('Bringer of light')
Radiance our cities' morning shared.

Eloise B. Segal

Falling

There I was
riding along
on Belle.
I started to slip,
  Slip,
    slip away.
Slip down that new leathery saddle.
There it was
my life
right in front of my face.
I whispered quietly to myself,
"Goodbye, Mom. I love you."
"Halt!" my instructor Mark shouted loudly.
My body was weak; I couldn't think straight.
I couldn't stop.
"Help, help!" my body was saying to me!
Then Mark came over and helped me stop Belle.
He helped me up and gave me a big long lecture about how I am not
supposed to hold on to the saddle.

Julia Puckett

The Train

This mighty behemoth roars along
rending the air with its strident song,
you hear its whistle, see its light
feel the ground shake as if in fright.
First come the engines with power to pull
then the freight cars, how many empty or full?
Heading for somewhere away down the track
to pick up, deliver, then maybe come back.
They criss-cross the country
from sea to shining sea,
from Canada to Mexico serving places in between.
Day and night they're rolling
through rain and wind and snow
so you might see one anytime anywhere you go.
Hear it, see it, rushing on
all a clattering noise
then——gone.

Alfred R. Pears

Winter Detritus

Cleaning up the detritus of winter—
Remnants of autumn leaves
Drifted behind the potted plants and beneath the patio bench;
Seed pods fallen from the locust tree;
The twigs pruned by storm-sent wind and rain.

No more lazing now in complacent hibernation,
Cocooning near a crackling fire.
It is time to clear the cobwebs from my head,
Expiate the lethargy and excoriate the ennui
To prevent a horrendous clash of seasons.

For already the tulips are poking through the soil,
The wisteria on its trellis is beginning to bud,
And the sweet smell of new life permeates my environment.
Spring is not somewhere around the corner;
It is ready to burst forth.

Winter's detritus must be raked and swept away.
The patio and pathways must be cleared;
My flowerbeds freed from their imprisoning layer of leaves.
I must strip the shaggy cloak of winter from my garden and my mind—
The season of renewal is at hand.

Janice A. Fauber

A Journey

Sitting alone, yet nor forlorn
Reminiscing of a journey of foot,
omnipotent in my mind — travels afar,
peaceful recollection of a Eastern European journey,
where moments are experienced,
where the future tedium of the work day is not discussed,
consciousness unhindered by responsibilities of future moments,
observing the smiling faces of embraced mothers and daughters,
of trams filled with adolescents holding hands,
of medicinal baths filled with the community of all ages,
carefree swim of senses, rest and relaxation,
their eyes do not inform of the desperate times,
of the inflationary spiral,
concern, frustration — yes,
and yet, their eyes always turn to their children,
touching their cheeks,
a smile always surfaces.

David J. Tyrrell

War And Peace

Wars have raged, battles have engaged.
Religion against religion, race against race,
countries against countries, face against face.

Why is it that we must fight,
in order to prove who is right,
or to preserve our respect,
by putting battle plans into effect.

Why are the governments so cold-hearted,
can they not see that the world has parted,
into sectors of religion and race.

Death is laughing at our face,
and is looking down at us with disgust and disgrace,
for he has seen what we have done,
and what we have become.

If we do not stop the carnage,
and heal the bruise which our hatred has started,
hell will find its way to roam,
and it will find the salvation
for which we call home.

Edgar Poureshagh

"Go Lightly, Receive Gracefully, Release Easily"

Solid Nike running shoes
quiet on the dark ground of
oak leaves and dirt;
I do not run,
pounding the earth
with my heavier lifting weight;
rather, I walk slowly, feeling
this soft land under my feet.

I pick up small acorns,
their centers intact even
as the shells crack from the fall.
These tiny trees
grace my palm with their
rough, embryonic brownness.

I walk through most of the afternoon
in the dusty dry park, collecting
light patterns and bird songs.

Then, as shadows
stretch from tree to tree,
I give the acorns back.

Darlene Lasher

Fixing Things

With a puzzled face, a small boy asked the
question, "What'cha doin' Grandpa?
To which Grandpa replied, "Sonny,
There are five kinds of broken things
in this world.
There's the kind, when they are broken
can never be fixed.
Then there's the kind that will fix themselves,
if you leave them alone.
And there's the kind, that's none
of my business.
Somebody else has got to fix them.
Then, there's the kind when they are
broken, you should never worry about them,
Them, only God can fix.
Now, there's the kind I got to fix,
Which is what I'm doin'
Fixing this gate."

Dorothy J. Mitchell

School Days

Our school day begins
Promptly at 8.

The lockers clang,
The kids congregate.

Off to class, anxious to learn,
Algebra, Geography, and does this world really turn?

Problems to solve,
Some easy - some hard.

How we fare is displayed,
In our quarterly report card.

A break in the action, a time for lunch,
Friends each gather in their own separate bunch.

Then back to class, to finish the day,
Oh please no - not homework, not tonight please, I pray.

Finally it rings, the bell says you're done,
Time to relax, see your friends have some fun!

When all's said and done - let me just tell you all,
I really do love school, homework and all!!

Amanda King

The African Mask

We are all descended from one of two common
Procreators of our race.
Our DNA proclaims this in a very real space
Along the spiralled staircase of the double helix chain
Our common great great Grandmother reaches out in pain
"Although your skin is snow white,
And your hair like golden corn".
"Forget me not; my skin shown dark".
"My hair was jet; my dress not smart"
"But I alone did bore you"
"I cared and didn't ignore you"
"Do the same for me now; acknowledge me!"
"We're family"
"The human race"
"Comes from one space"
"A common womb, we know that"
"Our great great grandmother issues this plea"
"Take your place beside one another"
"You're sister and brother!"

Francine Dolan

My Father's Voice

My father spoke so many times and prayed that I would hear,
Proclaiming things he felt were true, thru laughter, and thru tears

Sometimes, he felt the need to shout, to circumvent life's din
But words, to reach the mind and soul, the ears most enter in

This I surmised when just a youth, and so it seemed to be
My ears now hear myself quite well but loved ones don't hear me

Do ears alone sort out the words they think that we should hear?
and words that hurt our foolish pride, will ears allow them near

Thoughts linger now on bygone days; was that my father's call?
Remembering times I heard him well and others, not at all

Deep in my heart, he knew someday would ring echoes of his calling
When words deaf ears had turned away upon my heart are falling

Earl E. Wright

Reflections

Reflect, hey World upon vacancy and darkness,
preceding the phenomenon of light.

Reflect, hey World upon a watery expanse,
no partition midst above and below.

And then he created; Lord of Thy universe,
light and dark, heaven, waters and dry land.

Adorned with a carpet of grass and fruitful trees,
stood the "world" in its grandeur and splendor.

Yet could we consider her complete,
without those luminaries on which so much depends?

Upon God's command his waters produced fish and amphibians,
to sustain their species.

And on earth God placed animals,
which unlike humans function according to instincts.

Tell of what purpose would be a world of such great workmanship,
other than to serve Mankind?

Thus in His infinite wisdom,
the Author of our being created us to serve him.
Kayla Montal

A Groom's Prayer

Heavenly Father listen to me where I stand, I pray that you will bless me to be a little bit of everything to the woman who is about to take my hand. I pray that a picture of her is in my mind each morning before I wake, and that her name is the first word I call out before every breath I take.

Bless Me O'Lord, touch me with your precious grace, help me to love this woman you created for me to fill this empty space. Make me a cloud O'Lord, fill me with cleansing rain, and when the time comes release me to wash away her pain.

Build me up, make my body strong, let her use me as a refuge when she is weak, to rest her head upon all the night long

...And at times when I am weak, and at moments when things are rough, dear father fill me with your love and rejuvenating spirit when my love isn't enough.
Darryl Williams

Old Age

Now, my eyes are dim
Poor sight. I am sad.
Life is sweet. So real.
My ears - dull tones. Why can I not,
hear my cat meow, the bird sing, or
the bull frog croak, yet life goes on.
A joy, my mind is still sharp,
not a ball of wax, a clear view,
I can still think of my time and space.
My weak limbs, so slow a gait, yet I walk near and far,
on the open road. Now the path is steep, I tire,
the end is near. No! Not yet, I have things
to do. I guess it is best not to fret,
as the close of day nears.
Carl Arguello

Untitled

I'm lost
Please help me!
  So long we were bonded as one
  Half of me now is gone

    No more sunsets, no joys nor sorrows to share
    Your death - so sudden - so much to bear

    Friends came - now are gone
    Children are busy
  I'm all alone

    No one to cuddle, or hold my hand
    No one to guide me and shore any plans

    Void: Darkness: Where is the light?

    Please help me
    I'm lost
     I'm lonely tonight
Jacquelyn F. Owens

Untitled

Guardian Angels given power from God's own hand,
Please come to my child and by his side always stand.

Angels flap your wings to rustle my child's hair.
Hold him in your arms and shower him with care.
Wrap him in your wings with warmth, comfort, and love.
Please, always watch over him from your home high above.
Never let him stray in the wrong direction, far from your sight.
And always keep him safely, tucked in your wings, during the night.

Guardian Angels, God's special helpers, second in command.
Stand by my child and always hold tightly to his hand.
Christina M. Ward

Sea Dream

During the waking day, she calls to me on the songs of gulls and terns.

She entices my eyes to follow her fairy dance of sunbursts that playfully caress her cool green skin.

She moves back and forth over me, gently teasing me with her finger tips, beckoning me to join her.

I close my eyes and walk into her waiting arms. She envelops me with her form, I feel her touch all around me, I am awed with the strength of her presence, time stands still.

I open my eyes to the sleeping night, I hear her voice whisper on the wings of night flyers. Her breath is soft upon my face as she gently strokes my hair. Her skin is smooth and darkened from the night, she sparkles from moon beams dancing upon her. Her dark eyes twinkle with the radiance of starlight.

I feel the breath of morning return, I hear my mate move to the call of waking. I gently touch her warm soft body. I feel her heart beat in rhythm to my own as we embrace. We are filled with each other's essence. We are one and the world stands still, as wave after wave of love flows over and through us.

We part and we awaken again to the world. The cool salt sea breeze blows gently through the open window, the sun warms our faces, the sound of morning birds drift on the wind. We kiss, touch, and breathe deeply into our souls our mixed fragrances of love.

We rise and begin our day.
Gerald Bichler

Mirror Images

I used to look in the mirror and hate what I saw
Picking out all the flaws and the wrongs
Never understanding there was so much more to see
You opened my eyes to all the beautiful things
That I had never seen in myself before
Now I can face the mirror and smile
Because now I can see me as you do
I am a good person - I like what I see
Thank you.

Allison Kelly

The Wise Owl

There once was a wise owl
perched high in the trees.
Watching the array unfold below.
Waiting until the time is right
to bring forth its wisdom of life.
Bringing to light of day,
things of the past and present.
Of things longing to be buried forever,
but will never be.
Only until life's misfortunes are faced with the owl,
will its wisdom help guide the way.
So take heed, whoever you may be, the wisdom of the owl.
Life will go without the wisdom,
but it will never be as free.

Charles Cook

Passages

Birds on their southerly trek
pepper the sky
as grain flung into the wind.
We run, laughing,
through a patch of young birch trees
and tumble onto a golden bed.
You hang your honey-brown face over mine,
while beneath my sweeter curious fingers
pluck ripe raspberries.
A languid orange haze from the west disappears.
And as we watch for the aurora borealis
our breaths catch.

Delores Norman

A Spiritual Love

A spiritual love is a love that comes from two
people, who are a match for one another.
A Spiritual love is a love that is sent from above.
A spiritual love is a bond that has magnet
force that becomes as one love.
A spiritual love is a love that comes in many
ways on expressing one spiritual love.

Deborah R. Booked

The Beast

In the shadows there lies a beast.
People say when he is gone we will have a feast.
But I know behind that beast there lies a man.
Who only needs a helping hand.
To rise his spirits soaring high.
Just like a bird when he learns to fly.
So if you ever see a beast.
Look past his face,
and see a man that is a friend,
that you can lend a helping hand,
to look past his face and to a far better place.

Autumn Dawn Self

Giving

'Tis the time of twinkling bright lights, indoors and out,
People laughing, singing and skating all about.

When many tiny snowflakes cover the ground,
Drifting, floating, never making a sound.

Then we pause.

For we must NOT forget the homeless, the sick or poor,
Some may even come knocking at your door.

Most importantly it's a time for giving,
To appreciate things that make life worth living.

A time for loving, for hugging and for caring,
NOT for fighting and shouting, but for sharing.

Then we pause.

We think about long, long ago-on a very special night,
When shepherds came from miles and miles, guided by a light,
To see a baby in a manger, OH what a beautiful SIGHT!

And then we remember Mary and Joseph, who were blessed,
And amongst them were the dear animals at rest.

Then we pause.

So in your heart dig deep and don't forget,
To give a little of yourself, for this you won't REGRET.

Helen Hunter

Peace To All

Peace to all men.
Peace to my friend.
Peace to my father and mother.
Peace my sister and brother.
Peace in the west, peace in the east.
Peace in the world not to say the least!
Peace to the children without any home
Peace to the ones living in a war zone.
Peace to the ones living on the street.
Peace to the ones needing food, love, and heat.
Now I've said it once, and I'll say it again;
Peace to the world and love to all men!

Elissa Rainer

The Circle

It all begins with the twinkle of an eye.
Passionate love, sigh.
That slap on the butt, they listen for your cry.
Mommy can I stay up late? No dear, time for beddy bye.
I'm not tired, I don't understand, Why?
Santa doesn't exist? It was all a simple lie.
Is it OK to cheat, to lie?
Eventually you grow up, mom and dad, good-bye.
They taught you well. Spread your wings, now fly.
I met a girl, I'm in love? I don't know why.
Look, there's that twinkle in your eye.
9 months, Slap, Cry.
Deja vu, no dear it's time for beddy bye.
Before you know it, in the blink of an eye.
Your kids are grown up. Look at them fly.
Life was tough but we always got by.
You look back on it all. You can't help but cry.
I lived a good life, didn't cheat, steal or lie.
I'm getting old. Soon it will be time for me to die.

Charles Martin Jr.

Thank You God

Thank you God for the life you have given me
particularly for the genes
One can't be too choosey or particular it seems
in receiving those sort of things

It's rather a toss-up we often say
(who gave you yours by the way?)

If you already know my secrets
and you stay just as you are
What have you got for my future?
Will you fool me, maybe, by far?

Elizabeth Parker Kase

Friday Nights

Friday nights were velvet, pure velvet -
pale melting candles - flaming, flickering
sweet lilacs and violets, scenting and swaying
gentle velvet curtains, rippling around the Torah
Old Testament Psalms, whispering in Hebrew
black velvet yarmulkes, embroidered with pearls
murmuring voices chanting, wailing, crying Kaddish
purple plum filling, nestling in rich pastries
crimson wines pouring, splashing into glasses
my red velvet dress, shimmering, quivering -
and later your hands, velvet, pure velvet

Florence Wallach Freed

The Forgotten Kid

In the dark house where I used to live
Pain and sorrow are all they give.
My thoughts relinquished, overwhelmed by darkness.
My room is empty, overruled by sadness.
So many unknowns I need to know
Help me out, I need to go.
I walked the streets in search of nothing,
My mind is restless, my heart is beating.
My hands are cold, my pocket's empty
Please, someone stop this whole mystery.
Like a thread through the eye of the needle,
Let me breath the air of hope, and break this riddle.
Could I close my eyes and make it go away?
Could I wave my hand and make it fly today?
Touch me please, I can't feel anymore,
Hug me please, like you did before.
Tears in my eyes, I cannot show,
This is my life, I feel so low.
I cover my face, I'm full of shame
You know who I am; is there someone to blame?

Ann Becerra-Globus

Easter Morning

Soft light of the morning
Spreads its waking arms,
Bathes the earth in myriad hues,
Lighting up its charms.

Dogwood trees ablossom out along the rill
And a rude cross towers on a lonely hill.
The woods at daybreak echoed song of thrush's trill
And warblers filled the air with music soft.

The dogwood petals spread their nail print palms
And redbuds stretched their burdened arms aloft.
'Tis Easter morn and glory fills the soul
For Christ arose to make a sad world whole.

Bertha West

The Rape Of The Pencil Willows

We were planted here as tiny sprigs,
overlooking the pool and the cool green
grass and hills,
Nurtured by soft winds and frosts,
and westerly gales, and gentle rain.

Then, one day they came. Oh, precious heaven,
they came.
They wanted us, young and untried,
To make more of us. Their great claws
tore at our limbs,
So lean and fine, and filled with youthful blood.

They cut off each new bud and branch
around our feet.
They took their fill, and left us, naked
to the ground.
Our very soul was stripped from us that terrible day.

They went away. Singing and happy they were, never glancing behind.
Slowly, and in anguish, we breathed in the beautiful air.
It was no good. The strength in us was gone.
We died.

Judy Forell

The Spider

The effluvium of deceit spews forth in noxious odors,
Overcoming the unwary victim she entraps.
With leg advantage she does a dance maneuver,
Rolls her eyes, entices him into submission,
Swings him in her hammock of passion.
He is a perfect hunk
To mold, arrange and rearrange.
Her every wish is his command.
She cajoles and wheedles him
While she saps all his love,
All his strength,
All his vigor.
When no longer complete and perfect in every way,
No longer the object of her affection,
With invective, she bounces him off her trampoline,
Sits and waits, rolls her eyes,
And waits, and waits,
For another conquest to come her way.

Flora Adams

Backroom Passions

Wintry skies bring drifting snow
over and over the moon shines its light
morning after morning the creeping dawn
  breaks up the dark of night

Easiness follows the flow of understanding
because the top performance
  is always spontaneous

Plans get entangled — the heart corrupts them

Floating around my head are harbingers of fear
—wails of dark night's despair

Yet hallowed beings strengthen these footsteps

The difficulties of trauma are calmed by truth

For in the backroom, and under our passions
lie the sleeping haloes of angels

Dwight Cosper

The Urge to Write

Sometimes the urge to write comes straight
out of the blue, and puts ideas on the page
never before thought through.

You realize that the written page, never
before seen, is just exactly your feelings,
just what you mean.

As you write your words, often with a
necessary correction, you find you may have
written new insight, new direction.

The method here is just like telling a friend,
having a sounding board, another ear to bend.

You have now added such a degree of pleasure.
Seeing the words you write, using them as a measure.

So pick up a pencil, write your
impression. You'll find a new freedom, a new
way for expression.

Jerry Matthews

Blessed

The sky was dark and wet, the clouds a gloomy gray.
Out I went with toast and cup, as many other days.
Tho as a lighthouse beacon, a ray slid through the clouds
It settled on the poplar tree to chase the darkness out.

Raindrops turned to diamonds, bark to burnished gold.
I sat and held my breath, and watched the scene unfold.
More rays come down gleaming bright,
  bringing colors with the light.
Emerald grass, violets blue, stars of gold,
  the iris bed of purple hues.

God blessed my life this morning!
As He does most every day.
He let me look through His window, to see the angels play.
Painting flowers with colored brushes
  forming clouds in skies of blue,
And turning drops of water, into diamonds for me and you.

Ina M. Adkins

The Ice Age

In Eskimo lore of days gone by, they left the aged in the cold to die.
Out beyond help in the freezing snow,
Till their life expired on a cold ice floe.
That's where I am in this life of mine,
Alone on that ice floe-deserted and dying.
My family is gone (not literally so),
And loneliness, loneliness is all that I know.
There is no comforting hand, oh God
To help me along in your footsteps to trod.
No one to keep me on the road so narrow,
To appreciate love that comes from my marrow.
I wait and I wait (pray me patient to be!)
I wait for the one who will rescue me.
Who'll take me away from this freezing death,
Who'll breathe within me a living breath.
One who'll strengthen my shaking knees,
Who'll put out a hand to comfort me.
Please send him soon, I beg you Jah, before this death has gone too far
My breath is feeble, my life bloods lost,
Help must come soon or I'll die of frost.

Elizabeth A. Rickert

"Our Tree"

There was a tree beside our family home, and it was tall and strong
Our tree held back the winds and rain, and gave us shade all summer
  long
I felt safe among its leaves and branches, and grew strong climbing
  in it's limbs
But though our tree has been cut down, it's memory never dims
You were that tree who sheltered us, and kept us safe for years
You had a way of bringing smiles, to little eyes with tears
With a voice that could calm an angry child, you watched our family
  grow
You gave your love and time to us, till God called you to go
But yet today, when the weights of trouble try to make it hard to
  stand
I will not fall for I am steadied, with the spirit of my grandfather's
  hand.

Gary Tom Smith

Friend

A friend is a friend who only knows
  our special kind of love and how it should grow
To be confident in thought when I am confused
To bring a special kind of meaning to things I can't understand
A friend is a friend who can only tell
  when my heart is distraught and how they can help
When my mind is filled with discouragement
  a friend fills my senses with encouragement
When life has come to a glorious state
  a friend will be there to share in its grace
Tough love is something difficult to convey
  yet a friend will be there and able to be brave
Friendship is a bond held together by love
  that can only be sent by a power from above.

Daryn Gibson

The Crossroads

We met at the beginning and we began our walk through life.
Our roads intertwined, but you had a road block - an obstacle that
couldn't be moved.
So we parted and as I walked, I felt the stones that you threw to
get my attention; I ignored them.
After awhile I stopped feeling the thud of your stones.
I looked back to see if you were still there and I saw you.
You were crying for the bruises on my back, but I reminded you
that they were on my back; I could always leave them behind.
So we walked on, not speaking to each other.
Then, you passed me!
You sped ahead, never looking to see the sign that read,
  "Danger Ahead! Veer Right!"

You continued wrong until you came to that cliff where you stand
now trying to save yourself.
Now, I pass you. I know that I cannot save you.
I cry for you instead.

Gerria E. Johnson

To My Husband, Ed

Each time I spend an hour with you
Our love grows stronger through and through.
Each time I see you smile
My love rekindles for a hundred miles.
Each time they play our song
It reminds we with you is where I belong.
Each time I feel like crying
You happen by and send my spirits flying.
With each day of love that surrounds us,
Happiness, joy and all that compounds us,
Let's not change but grow in the love that binds us.

Elizabeth A. McDonagh

Our Log Cabin

Come, come with me so you can see,
Our little, log cabin built among the trees!
It's closely enveloped by a porch so wide,
A garden of roses covers every side.

A cistern of rainwater to fetch a cool drink,
A wooden swing nearby; sit, rest and think.

Come, follow the pathway, so you can see,
A pond with catfish big enough to eat.

Encircled with shady spot, sit, rest your tired feet.
Azaleas so beautiful, they can take your breath away!
Come follow me, but please don't stray;
There's butterflies, bumblebees, and squirrels along the way.
Clusters of velvet, green moss covering much of the ground,
A baby chipmunk scampering by, not making a sound.
Come, once more so you can see
Our little log cabin built among the trees!

Eulene Tanner

The Unknown

Our Universe
Originates from the Unknown
Terminates with the unknown

We too human beings
Come from the Unknown and end up with the Unknown
But between two Unknowns, we fight for being known

We talk about races and live with biases
Cheating and lying are our basic mantras

We eat everything, vegetables and animals
If a tough time follows, we eat even humans

When we are unhappy, we visit religious places
Try to convince our God, please forgive our vices

Eventually we forget what we promised to Him
By the end of the week we are ready to face Him

Indeed! No one knows about the Unknown
But He is the owner of all the known

Dhirendra Kumar Pandey

Ten Seconds

It only takes ten seconds to snuff out a precious life
Or to kill tender feelings from deep in the heart with words that can cut like a knife.

It only takes ten seconds to make me feel like a queen
To give me a gift, not a mansion or jewels—but the thoughtfulness my eyes have seen.

When your chariot takes us exploring and you open your door to get in,
As I wait by the side, how it does hurt my pride when a button you push lets me in.

But it only takes ten seconds to be just the hero I know,
To open for me, with your own magic key, my door to the chariot and go

And when we're out seeking adventure, hand-in-hand and side-by-side,
I feel like much less than a cheap mistress when you walk ahead and leave me behind.

But it only takes ten seconds to show me and the world you care,
Just to wait for me and accompany my heart, mind, and body so fair.

Yes, it only takes ten seconds to make me feel like a queen,
To give me a gift, not a mansion or jewels—but the thoughtfulness my eyes have seen.

Amber Taylor

"Perfect Together"

Shall I begin this poem about your style and grace
or should I write flattering words about your beautiful face

Should I ask you the question I've been dying to know,
will you hold onto my body and never let go

I could tell you I love you but that wouldn't be true,
Lots of pain, lots of heartache is all that would do

I could ask what I've been wondering with so many questions in mind

Would you let me be your one and only
Would you let yourself be mine

I could tell you how my fantasy of making love to you is like
or how the mere presence of yourself fills me with delight

I could write about the times that I wonder what love has in store for me

How I think of a love that's stronger than thunder with feelings as deep as the sea

Now with an affluent sense of companionship and a legitimate reason to say

I'll think you and I are perfect together and perfect together we'll stay

Derek Cain

Life

Dost thou know life, tis just a dream or thought
Or maybe a fantasy of yourself
Or a superior being that brought
A vision of truth in one's boastful self
Or reproduction took a turn throughout
A reflection of blush mist in ourselves
This image of defiance could be sought
In the darkness of the woods in himself
In the light of day, is the heart that ought
To have been a frank man to God and self
This meaning of life has no end for thought
But has meanings of occurrences in himself
Men do not know real meanings of life brought
By the great Almighty who made ourselves.

David Leon Speyer

Trinity

Touching my feet in the future
Only to re-unite with my childhood.

The bridge that took years to build
Had to be crossed alone.

We cannot run away from us
We are always there.

People come and go and we love them
But who really knows us?

Who can see our spirit rise and fall?

Only ourselves can make us joyful.
We pray to God for support and we always receive it,
Only sometimes it's foggy.

We cry in the rain because we feel its pain.

We laugh in the sunshine because it's warm and friendly.

We long for our missing self,
Not understanding that we are whole with God.

Why must it be this way?

Whenever two or more of you are gathered in my name,
There will I be, also.

Franco Pepe

Racism

Why do we make a division in society
  only to divide people by the color of their skin?
Why do we allow ourselves to form an opinion of someone
  based solely on the pigment of one's skin?
Why do we feel the need to place ourselves superior
  to others of the same species simply because of their skin?
Why does society continue the ignorance toward
  those who are different for the reason of their skin?
Why do parts of society isolate itself from others
  just because of the differences in pigment of their skin?
Why does society create separate sets of rules
  for dissimilar persons built on the basis of one's skin?
Why do people teach hatred for various groups of humans
  only because of the diversity in the color of their skin?
Why do people construct such harsh barriers between races
  since the only conflict is the pigment of their skin?
Why do people of the same country with the same dreams
  divide themselves with the only incentives being their skin?

Why do you accept these prejudices in your country?
Why do I have to live my life accepting these prejudices?
    Jamie Cox

Madness

Madness is the color of a blank page.
Only the person who feels the madness can hear the
  noise it makes, like the crying of a newborn baby,
  destruction, and life caving in on him\her.
It tastes like a bitter rage.
It smells like smoke from a raging fire of a burning
  building.
It looks like a demolished city from destruction of war.
Finally, madness is in everyone, people feel differently
  about it; overall it makes people feel unwanted and
  like life is slipping away day by day.
    Deanna Smith

Mother

Mothers are God's helpers, placed here on Earth.
Only Mothers can take away the pain that hurts.
They're always there, you've been there since my birth.
Having patience, always, with our impulsive spurts.
Every so often, I get the chance to prove she is special to me.
Really Mom, you are very special especially when myself you let me be.

Many women can give birth to a child these days
  but don't you know it takes someone special to be a Mom.
May all you future days be filled with joy always,
  nine months you carried me, from your womb is where I am from.

You scolded me when we both knew I was wrong
  you gave me tenderness when I came home crying.
You'd argue with me when'ere I was on the phone too long,
  you gave me love and care when sick, I thought I was dying.

I wish I could be there to present this gift from me to you,
  but, I hope you know with special care it was made.
My best wishes for a good year, all year through.
I'm sending this wish, may the joy of your life never fade.
    CoLetta M. O'Neill

An Unforeseen Journey

A dreamer is like a shooting star
Only God knows where she will land
Each night voyaging the world of imagination
Always trusting God to lead her
Through the darkness of the night
    Elizabeth Graham

Lost And Found

One lost heart searches to find true love the only
one of its kind.

It searches and searches leaving nothing unexplored or
left behind.

Until it stumbled upon a lost soul. Heart: (To the soul)
"I want to love and share is there anyone who really cares."

Soul: (To the heart) "You must learn to understand and
value these feelings, is this why you search for such things."

"You have been broken much like me I understand why you seek
such things." The heart understood and the soul held the
broken heart.

Their search was over, for the heart found an understanding in
the soul and the soul healed the broken heart.
    Elizabeth A. De Condo

The Little Child

Watch him play in the yard so big,
one minute the explorer discovering new uncharted lands.
Next the engineer,
making bridges and tunnels with great vision and skill.

Look at the actor,
A cowboy hero or the indian hunter so brave,
...John Wayne would be put to shame.

The child does not seek material wealth.
Never worried about being somewhere at two o'clock sharp.
He is happy to imagine and play,
content and even fascinated with his surroundings.

A spirit so free is in every child.
Something every grownup should recapture,
and hold close to the heart.

Remember always...the little child inside.
    Dalton Jerry Ruddlesden

Without Tears

As leaves fly away from their limbs;
one day my Aunt fell asleep and never woke-up again.
I tried so hard not to cry.
But it never seems to pass me by.
Three years have passed and
I think to myself and say
that I was the one to see her last.

I think of her as I think of her then.
When I picture her in my mind I see myself within.
And I'll never stop loving her till the end.
    Jessica M. Traugh

The Family Bath

Mother boiled pots of water on the flame
one after another to prepare a family bath.
She filled a large tin tub and we each came
in turn to wash ourselves. It makes us laugh
now that a daily shower comes with ease
and need not be shared with anyone.
Yet the comfort and convenience can't decrease
our pleasure of that old time, warm and wet
and settled naked in that big round tub;
the front room fire stoked high to heat the air
around our humble sauna. We should scrub
ourselves with homemade bars of soap; our hair
the same. We were like remnant pioneers,
momentos of a life that disappears.
    Ila Marie Goodey

The Mountain

It will lure you with its majestic formations
Once you are captive to the beauty it will not release you
Shadows play among the trees shrubs and rocks
Inviting you too seek all that is - it is all there
The musical winds flowing through and around
Carrying the soft clouds across the vivid blue skies
Birds glide along as the wind spirals
Their songs fill the air the purest of pleasures heard by all
The secrets of the mountain lie quietly as the small and large
Scurry from in and around unnoticed with barely a sound
From the smallest of hummingbirds to the grandest of eagles
Butterflies to elk to the bears
Some will not let you know they are even there
Streams of icy waters trickling down from snow capped peaks
Descending over and around the many rocks collecting in a pool
Only to flow quietly in its own stillness
Inviting all who pass by to share in its abundance
Of cooling waters
Share in the secrets
Of the mountain
Judie Edwards

To Mend Well The Clouds For Fall

I carried the scattered cloud
Once I gathered it all.
With this view I've been vowed,
And my thriving doubts,
I am mending well the clouds for Fall.

The sky has remained diverse
By the many clouds I saw.
And like a sonata of misty winds, in verse,
The sky has adhered to me,
A bright, pillowy Fall.

This omnipotent space that harbors the clouds,
The space we may name our upwardly call.
Though, by dawn, the sky is still broad at morning's sound,
Granting me another cloud
That I may mend it well for Fall.
Jack Eugene Larson

Young Visitors To Life, Please Watch And Wait

Young visitors to life, please watch and wait.
Once dormant tongues take to life when hair greys;
The road less traveled may lead you to fate.

Like Elder who wasted life with debates,
And now, in old age, yearns to seize each day;
Young visitors to life, please watch and wait.

Like Father who, blinded by love, dictates
Your life because his own led him astray;
The road less traveled may lead you to fate.

Like friends who criticize each word you state,
Now at feet, since your uprising, do lay;
Young visitors to life, please watch and wait.

Like you, opaque and confused, with new slate
Which to carve in, crying "Come What May!"
The road less traveled may lead you to fate.

And I darkness behind and since headed straight
State, please consider all that others say!
Young visitors to life, please watch and wait;
For the road less traveled may lead you to fate.
Joe C. Millar

The Hand

This is the hand that held so tightly to my mother's
on that first remarkable, incredible day of school.
This is also the hand that let go to creep tentatively
into the deep, grand sea of life beyond the backyard.

This is the hand that will lead me along the intense,
obscure, emotional paths and curves of my life.
It will not remain uncalloused or unbruised,
but the calluses will smooth, and the bruises will heal.
The wrist may grow limp at times;
the nails may chip now and then, but the fingers will still curl
to make a fist when threatened.

This is the hand that will build the foundation needed to make my
life strong, solid, and successful.
This is the hand that will explore all possibilities,
and hold tight to all opportunities.

This is the hand that will protect my heart, my dreams, my desires.
It will build an impregnable wall around all that I hold sacred,
and it will DARE anyone to intrude.
Angela Alongi

Pray God Rule The Day

Cities were bustling as morning broke day
On farmlands the livestock was rustling the hay
Children were sent off to school for to learn
And babies to day care for love and concern

Bursting the midst of a fine morn begun
A blast and the news a grievous crime had been done
Screaming for help was heard near and far
As the guilty would run fleeing justice from the bar

The Commander-in-Chief promised swiftness for sure
For hatred and fear made their minds so impure
The federal building's demolished, it's true fact
Hundreds of lives were quenched just like that

Amidst pain and anguish men search through debris
Hoping some sign of life soon they will see
Doctors are called on to help the bereaved
As Oklahoma City buries its deceased

Now I pray that our God will soon intervene
To handle the persons who've killed sight unseen
He says "Vengeance is mine, I will repay."
Grieving our losses, let's pray God rule the day.
Eulalia M. Greene

The Quest

I long to slumber, I cannot
Oh, mind, bound by muddled thoughts
I yearn to write, I've not a pen
Thoughts turn to slumber once again
I thrash about, yet find no peace
One lonely pen, for my release
In desperate need, I rise from bed
To find this tool, to ease mine head
I scrounge and scour, yet not a find
I breathe a prayer within my mind
Still, I've not which I desire
I resign my quest, again I retire
I draw back the sheets and there, on the floor
My object of prayer, "Oh, thank you Lord!"
I take up my pen in sheer delight
Alas, I am saddened, my pen will not write
"Oh Lord, why does my pen not work?"
Said the Lord, "Tis cause of a mortal quirk.
In your desperate plea you did not think,
You asked for a pen, you did not request ink."
Cheryl A. Seals Manuel

Thanks Lord For Keeping Me

When I wake up in the morning I look around and see
Oh how beautiful and graciously thou has supplied for me
Realizing in my situation I no way was able to understand
But believing God's word "No more than we can bare be put on man"
Knowing my mind so wavered, heart so broken and body so weak
Look to my Jesus; "Please put a special touch on me to be humble
   and meek
My heart so full of love, ("Buckets of tears from my face) to the
   floor I kneel
Praying, "Lord if I have the strength to lift my hand a little-please
   let me feel
Your precious hand pulling me to help to be strong and push on
For Lord: They're several little life's here with me depending upon
My love: My strength and my support to see them be happy in growing up
My thanks Lord for keeping me close to you as whining a little pup

Faye Twigg

Violence

My writing of violence to whom are concerned,
Of violence in video games and things that churn.
Red flowing blood is all they see,
True to "Primal Rage," "Killer Instinct," and "Mortal Kombat 3."
All critics are trying to bring it to an end.
Like all critics, they're not friends.

Can we teach children wrong from right?
Or is "finish him" to be the end of a real fight?
Moms, come on, let them have fun,
But kids are smart not dumb.
All we know, it's not going to end.
Take my advice, game violence is the new trend.

Josh Lomax

Untitled

No I will not pluck off the petals
of this beautiful red rose
I do not have to destroy the beauty of it
For the answer of a question I already know

I will not destroy the beauty of it
As you will not destroy me
I will not let you pluck my heart from my body
I gave you a chance at love and you let it be

So I'm leaving the flower as it is
which is the promise I want from you
I want to live again
It's over - forever - we're through

I'm keeping this flower forever
For it's shown me the way
When you want me back again
I'll look at my living flower and remember the
price I'll have to pay

Janice Brown

My Grandfather

My grandfather is like the gum tree, both
  of them tall and proud.

The rustling of leaves is like my grandfather's
  soft whisper.

And the tree trunk is the slightest bit coarse
  like my grandfather's face.

I can imagine my grandfather when I look at
  the Gum tree, because the tree's branches

Remind me of my grandfather's outstretched
  arms ready to give me a jug.

Ashley V. Bender

The New Generation

Overflowing with beauty, they amble towards you from out
Of the pages of past generations—young innovative women
With long silky hair—swaggering in tight classic jeans and
Cropped boxed spandex tops—their designer spicy perfumes
Wafting through the air painting a blossom trail of haunting
Feminine mystic as they saunter confidently past you in
Shades of vanilla and chocolate pigskin granny shoes...

Graceful spirited creatures from the past—emerging now in
This new generation—adorned in metallic gold slip dresses
And curly cascading tresses—asymmetrical straps and
Black scalloped high heels—reviving Retro Hollywood glamour
Again in swing skirts and T-backs—savvy awareness too in
Pinstriped suspended pants and herringbone leggings...whisper
Light drawstring pants in satins and velours only make us stare
At these damsels of yesterday that much more...

Sophisticated and beyond our wildest visions in their fluid
Softness and broomstick and crinkled skirts, they have come
Temporary as it may be—a form of art to see—and we await
Breathlessly the turning of another new look, in another season,
From the chapters of their fashion history book...

Judith Durnbaugh

Presence Of The Wall

I stand beside the wall wondering and unaware
Of the life that stands beside me afraid and alone
I feel his presence beside me
His strength and grandeur
But will he ever leave the wall from which he hides?
Does he know that I stand here,
Alone?
Behind this wall
Behind the life from which I hide
Or from the loneliness I call home

Does he see me standing here?
Does he feel my presence?
Will he come around the wall and hide no more from me?
I hide behind this wall of life
Strangely unafraid
For his presence is beside me
From wherever he may be
I stand beside this wall wondering and unaware
Of the life that stands beside me afraid and alone.

Catherine Thompson

Forest Idyll

What causes me to dream such dreams
Of flowing streams in forest green, moist and deep
And chilled nights of hibernating sleep -
Where only the woods as my cover,
Fallen needles and leaves my carpet, the sun my beacon by day
The stars and the moon gently illuminate my night.
For the air is always so richly endowed,
With the scents of the purest that can be offered -
  The dew that wets the morning grass -
  The cleansing smell of the pines.
A trout breaks the water in the distance.
Slapping the water hard, the sound reverberating briefly.
It's Freedom! The freedom of nature and all that is beautiful -
  that lives in our world.
Come with me, and drink from the cold and pure
  springs that flow from the mountains.
Escape your nightmares of boredom and drudgery that hold us down.
For even if it's only a transient daydream
We keep it alive in our minds while the deep green forest
Silently awaits our true return.

Anthony Gallo

Untitled

Here at the start I stand, to tell the tale,
Of evil and good, of rain and hail.

Born to the dark, my nature is grim
My heart painted black, my mind full of sin.

I escape my curse, many moons ago,
I found the light, and hid in its glow.

I tried to live in the light, all of my years,
Fighting the dark, and facing my fears.

But my soul has grown old, and my lights grow weak.
My fears have made friends, and my Demons now speak.

The dark has come back, to claim my soul,
And I wish not to fight, but I wish not to go.

I cry, and I weep, and I call to my friend,
As I'm dragged from the light, and called by my end.

I am the heir to the throne, the son of the dark
Dragged back into terror, ending up where I start.
   Bobby Benjamin

Always Be Aware

The earth is round, so they say,
oceans, land, rivers if you may.
   Full of people all colors and size,
teaching their children to be honest and wise.
   Oh so many people and places to go.
   Oh! wait and be aware of the unknown.
When I was young life was caring and free,
   Oh! wait and be aware of the unknown.
Carjackings, rape, murder and crime.
Oh what have we done, life's so unkind.
   Oh! wait and be aware of the unknown.
Lock your doors, lock your windows, hold
tight to your purse, don't shop alone,
you hear bumps alone in the night.
   Oh! wait and be aware of the unknown.
The earth is round, it's always been,
people all colors and size.
   Please keep your children honest and wise
So we can sleep and be peaceful at night.
   Always be aware of the unknown.
   Janice Sheppard Jaffer

My Haven

I stare out the window to a magnificent view,
of dirt roads, rolling hills and the ocean blue.

Strolling along wind swept, sandy beaches,
I admire all its unique, exquisite features.

Mist encased mountains, pounding waves,
finding precious shells and mysterious caves.

Wading through the crystal clear waters of the ocean,
watching its calm, peaceful motion.

As the sea breeze gushes through my hair,
I feel relaxed, free, without a care.

I go to bed listening to the sound of the waves
crashing against the shore,
Fairhaven, my favorite place, will be part of me
forevermore.
   Emily Incledon

Whom The Lord Calls, He Qualifies

Joshua was chosen by God as he lived so long ago.
Obedience was God's prerequisite for his mighty power to show.
Faith is so broadened by each step taken on our own.
Maps are not given, each step will be guided by Him alone.

Whom the Lord calls He qualifies and draws closer to His breast.
Whom the Lord calls He qualifies and fills with His best.

The world may have laughed at Joshua, they may have thought him odd.
But the mighty walls of Jericho fell as Joshua followed his God.
Chariots could race upon those walls, yet they fell as if they were
   paper thin.
Joshua followed his God and God provided the victory that was theirs
   to win.

Whom the Lord calls He qualifies and fills past the brim.
Whom the Lord calls He qualifies and draws closer to him.
   Bonnie R. Parvino

Searching...

As I am resting under the shade
of a single old tree
I cannot remember anymore
in what town, in what street
in what road, in what ally
I've been looking for you

It's been so long
I don't remember...
what desert, what marsh land...
What mountain, what river
I have crossed to seek you

At time I don't remember your face, your voice, your touch
at times I can't get rid of your face, your eyes, your smile
you are in my dreams in my thoughts in my soul

In the middle of nowhere
as I pack all my hopes
I don't know if I am still searching for you...
It is the flame of your memory, my existence,
and the frozen time in between...
   Bruce Rezvani

I Shall Remember You, My Love, In This Way

As a flower,
   nurtured and now unfurled to its utmost
beauty. And when it has faded and lost it's bloom
I watch the petals fall, softly, one by one. Never
to forget it's beauty.

As a good book,
   wishing it would never end. For as I turn
each page they become a companion to me. When I
finally close the cover on the last chapter I am
saddened. But I shall remember the contents well,

As a symphony,
   or more a sonata. As I listen to the melody
thrilling to it's vibrato. Only to hear the final
passage which brings it to a formal close. Its
tempo pulses with-in me.

As a sunset,
   radiant in the west. I gaze at God's canvas
in the heavens, in silence and wonderment, until
it sinks. Its decline manifests a feeling of
reverence in which I revel. And my faith is renewed.
   Doris Renniger

"Wishing You Were Here!"

Seems it's been so long, since I've seen your face.
Now you're gone and are in Gods' Grace.
So many things I wanted to say.
To tell you just how very special you are.
I know there will come a day,
When our paths will cross again,
On my way to my distant star.
I miss your smiling eyes,
They were so pretty and the color of God's blue skies.
I miss the hugs you gave when I was down.
I really miss you just being around.
So many things I miss, now that you're not here.
Even all the little things are now so dear.
There were to many things we could have done.
No matter what they were, I know they would have been fun.
I thought I had more time—time to tell you all the things my heart needed to say.
Like I love you Mom!
Why did you have to go away?
  Brenda L. Hendricks

A Very Special Woman

Let me tell you about a very special woman my friend
Now let me see, where do I begin
She can comfort you on a rough day
And no exactly what to say to make your worries go away
She can cradle you in her arms where you feel safe
And presence there will make you believe and have faith
To touch her skin is like touching the wings of a dove
Her hypnotic gaze will make you surrender to her love
And to taste her moist lips, to kiss
This is something not to be missed
It is like crossing a desert for days thinking that you are whipped
And to finally taste that drop water, a sip
This is everything you could ask for
And there is nothing in the world I want more.
  Jim Bell

Fade To The Past

When she loved me for the first time I had someone to be with.
Now as I look back, I see things I would have done differently.
The only thing that I know is that I still love
her and she's not there anymore.
He gives her attention I forgot to;
Now my mistakes have cost me her love.
She is all that I think of from when I wake until when I dream.
The part of her that love me has died,
So now I must think of her as a ghost.
It's hard to be alone after you have shared so much,
But for now I must fade to the past of her love.
  Joe Easley

Those Few Things

I'm plagued by a penchant for prattle
not very unlike Tourette's
and yet, few of the things that I've said
I can honestly say I regret.
But, I would be remiss if I did not say this,
there were those few times, I've found along the way,
there were those few things, that I didn't say.
And so, unsaid, they remain with me still,
a burden to this day,
and there I fear they'll abide, Forevermore,
each a debt I never paid.
  Douglas Wilson

Forever A Friend

A friend is something that lasts forever,
not something you lose because of change or distance,
and not something easily forgotten.
A friendship is a gift from God,
and a friend will always be...
someone you can laugh with,
someone you can cry with,
and yes, even someone to say goodbye with.
A friendship is more than making memories but remembering them too.
And this friendship through pain, joy, and even tears
has shone through like the sun on a cloudy day,
and will always remain this way.
So over the miles we have laughter, tears, and lots of love.
But most of all we have a friendship to adore,
a friendship that with such wonderful
memories will never die.
A friendship that can grow and will.
A friendship that has many more years and many more
memories to share.
  Corinna M. Wilhelm

I Am

I am a picture hung on an empty wall. Unimportant, overlooked and not meaning much at all.
I am framed with loneliness, depression and guild.
I am on a wall in a house that hasn't been built.
I have tried to build it, but it keeps falling down. Maybe I am building it in the wrong town.
I am an exit ramp leading to an interstate. Run over constantly at a steady rate.
The only time people stop is when there is trouble or when they break down, then they're gone on the double.
I am a girl, confused and sad. I am so young, how can I be this mad?
I can't believe that I tried to grow up so fast, I wish my youth could just last and last.
I have made so many mistakes, why can't I take them all back
Why did I try to please everyone? Did I want to be friends with everyone under the sun?
I've tried to be good, I've tried to be nice, I guess from now on I'd better think twice.
  Angela R. Etterle

I Confess

Thinking of you and living in the past, holding on to a love that did not last.
Dreaming of you and the times we shared, back when you were here to show me you cared.
Have you forgotten about me? I thought I was your destiny.
I wonder if you ever think of me, what we had and what we could be.
Will I ever see your face? I miss your kiss and warm embrace.
My dreams are of you and me, my hopes and fears are kept secretly.
Did you really love me when you were here? Were the words you spoke truly sincere?
How come you don't call? Not a word from you, nothing at all.
I feel mislead by you, Is that what you intended to do?
Why can't I just forget you? Is that the best thing for me to do?
You left me feeling so good inside, now I feel like I want to hide.
I want to run away from the pain, It hurts to think you don't feel the same.
I'm hopeless thinking of you, it's time to go on, I will leave the door open, but for how long?
Maybe one day you'll come back to me and it will be the way it used to be.
I long for your love in my heart, it hurts so much to be apart.
All I have left is time, so I'll wait for you until your mine.
It could be tomorrow, it could be never, but I would wait for you forever.
  Betsy Mahsoul

A Christmas Car Ride

The rain let up; we ventured out to sights upon the highway.
   Not knowing what God had in mind as we went along our way.
We were very surprised as we happened upon the many scenes
   Of various activities that were so seemingly very routine.

Purgatory! Skiers flying down the mountains and the hills.
   With my camera, I climbed the snow and stood so very still.
The skiers saw me and they turned making the snow spray.
   While I took pictures, they parted around me on their way.

Upon the highway we saw families as down the hill they slid,
   On the sleds, inner tubes, cardboard strips, trash can lids.
Over-tipping, laughing as they made their downward slide.
   Then the walk back to the top, to again repeat the glide.

Next morning so very bright with the beautiful, glorious sun.
   Spirits lifted, and happily we went out to have some fun.
Again we went on the highway, to an appointment we must keep.
   After a while, we parked the car. The snow became too deep.

Here, we took a long, long ride in a one horse open sleigh.
   Our eyes opened wide with awe at the many sights on our way.
The strips of bells upon the horse were so merrily a-jingling.
   We sat on the seat and in the crisp cold we were a-tingling.
     Ada Stein

Capture The Excellence

When you wake up each morning, which is
not guaranteed, and say — "Thank you Lord"
I can fill a special need

When you say, "Dear Father," what a wonderful
day, and know He wouldn't have it any other way

When you look in the mirror at that pleasant
face, and realize the excellence to capture is
already in place

When you know, your best partner is the Father
above, and to see Him spread everywhere "His
God-given love"

When love is balanced, from day-to-day, being
who you are — it had to be that way

When you unfold and bloom, like a favorite
colored rose — to Capture the I am, and
know you were chosen
   Donald F. Swift

No Parking At Anytime

We've become a society of "No Parking" sign readers
No time to pause

Afraid to driving in the slow lane
Wouldn't think of stopping along the way

Pass one more
Gotta be first

Anxiety, fear, unknown
Rush life

Park yourself, put your feet up
Listen to a hoot'n owl sing his song

Watch the stars sparkle in the night
The ocean rushing in

Hush! You might hear those worries being chased
By a gentle breeze

Slow the speed
Continue on
   Jacqueline Joyce

Life Of A Clown

There stood a clown so jolly and round,
No time for his head to hang down.
His schedule is filled with things to do.
He goes to hospitals to visit the kids,
And to birthday parties too.
He's at the circus to entertain you.
His big red nose flapping up and down;
As he does his flip flop and lands to the ground.
He's at the rodeo to guard the men
The bull comes a running and he jumps in the barrel.
His big feet sticking in the air, he stands with a grin;
then jumps out and does it all over again.
   Ella Stuver

"Night Time"

Night time is here again, another sleepless night
No sleep, bad dreams, and so much uptight

Wishing you were here holding me tight
Making me feel alright

I think about you all the time
Wishing everything was fine

Night time is so lonely and blue
Just not the same without you

In my life there is just no other
Can't have any other lover

I love you more than you'll ever know
Please, say you'll never, ever go

In my heart there is only room for one
Who gives me pleasure and so much fun

What you do for me, no one will ever know
The happiness that makes my heart glow

You take the sadness right out of my life
I never feel that I could ever be your wife

But in my heart for you I have so much love
Has God sent you down from Heaven above
   Carlta J. Setlock

The Little Black Girl

I was born by a river shortly before midnight,
No one witnessed my mother's plight.
Living her life amid suffering and pain,
She bore me and knew no shame.

I've heard that this is "...the land of the free,"
But with no one to watch over me,
Am I destined to become one like the rest?
Or will I rise up and be put to the test?

My father, whom I will never understand
Longed for the life of a better man.
Before attempting to change his lot in life,
He abandoned his children and his wife.

I remember, now that the deed has been done,
We were once ten, we were once one.
I don't dwell on this now that the die has been cast,
His presence in our lives is a thing of the past.

With different standards for blacks and whites,
I strive to the top with all of my might.
And I'll make it, you shall see,
In this "...sweet land of liberty"!
   Gwendolyn A. Dixon

"True Love"

True love is so hard to find,
No matter how you search for it,
In this day and time.
But by and by, it finally comes your way,
And you pray to God that it's here to stay.

A kind word,
A gentle lovin' touch,
You never thought could mean so much.
Each day in, each day out,
It feels so good to talk about,
What it means to find true love.

Now that you have finally found your one true love,
Drop to your knees, and give thanks to the "Lord above."
Hang in there and you will see,
That this "true love" was meant to be.
Carrie B. Neal

Untitled

No words to utter, that you could understand.
No hope your heart will ever hear my heart's cry.
Alone I walk dark, lonely streets on rainy nights
And the tears I shed, mingle with the rain.

How wrong I was, how wrong, oh God, how wrong!
I took the glass heart for the crystal one.
But even after so many sharp swords were thrust into my heart,
I still saw some light in the dark.

All of a sudden then your cruel hand
Just plucked the last star from my dream-land.
And no matter how hard I tried to see the sky,
By total darkness only was surrounded I.
Grazina Nemunis

Treasures

Through life's dark maze I tread
No fear invades my bed,
For my soul's thirst for life's best on earth,
And I continually dwell
On things not for sale,
Like the smell of a rose,
An eagle as it flies,
And the stars in the sky,
The soft brush of a breeze,
And the rustle of autumn leaves,
The warming rays of the sun, and a life that's just begun.
A lesson learned, and a friendship returned.
These are the treasures I seek, for they provide both
Both comfort and relief.
Cheri Olson

Nature And The Seasons

SPRING is a time of new beginnings; the resting shall unfold to new birth and new fruit.
SUMMER is a time of utter amazement. We see the beauty of new life reaching its fullest ... looking forward to a grand harvest.
FALL Before coming to a restful sleep, everything must show its grandest colors ... and, as we watch everything go from brilliant to brim and bleet, we await another new season,
WINTER with all its peace and splendor. Its beginning is pure and clean, and, in many areas of the world, the resting are comforted by a blanket of heavenly wonder. As it ends, its beauty lessens, but, it leaves all in a state of hopeful rebirth.
Joanne Elizabeth Sly

Room With A View

There is a room with a view that I've heard somewhere
never seen, never been, never thought I'd dare
cross the boundaries of myself to reach this so called view
even though the room is what I thought I knew.

I do not fear not knowing, not being what I am.
The question isn't whether, or how, or why, or when.
There is no answer for this view, not this view that I am.
The reason lies within me, and you, and us, and them.
Behrad Fardi

Duplicity

And they walk around eyes closed, bumping into obscenity
Never really realizing immorality
I cock my head from side to side watching as they go
fabricating lifestyle, from their view you know
They speak with true emergency
They chatter and they spout
demanding that you live your life
in the framework that they tout
Their souls are very dark
but this you do not know
because they are so gifted
in the sagacity that they hold
Perhaps these little blind-things like knocking all about
confident the way their world is, confused and full of doubt
The sad part about these dark-things, they're scattered all about
so be wise and very careful when sorting this all out.
Chari Spears-Coffey

The Irish Pride Of Johnnie Keane

Irish silence so untamed, proud of those who kept their names. My name was McKinney, for my grandfather I feel, they changed our name but my anger lies still. We've gone so far with our backs to the wall, so dash away soldiers, dash away all!

For Irish I am and Irish I'll be, praising my father who gave it to me "Honor thy father, comfort your mother, protect your sisters and fight for your brothers." We tell our mother when it's safe outside while our father's prayers keep us alive. What a strong man to carry these burdens, he knows freedom will come and shall come without sinning.

When you're Irish, true Irish, you put yourself last, denying your future in search of your past. I look at my sons and my daughters agree, my dedication takes time so they will be free.
It's all for them I've fought all my life, my persistence respected through support from my wife. I can't take back the stress that she feels, her innocence rewarded as our freedom prevails.

From the North I was raised and hold many regrets, unwelcome memories I can't put to rest. But it's great to be living and the sun will rise, I live to wipe tears from my mother's eyes. The wind will blow in a special way, in the year 2000 on St. Patrick's Day. Those who ran seeking leprechauns, will return to Ireland and forever belong!
Edward J. White

Old Man On A Porch

Yes sir, we've had a lot of whipper snappers,
'Round here lookin' for their forgotten pap'ers.
The life they got won't 'nuff for these.
What they han't got yet them still got ta sees.
Most of them's Fathers I knows,
Now there helpin' the grasses grows.
Lookin' for some more they can take
Or s'more mistake to make.
They should a stay in them sky scrapes
In them cities full of dem rapes.
And leave us old folk to ourselves.
Our lives is our only wealth.
David Hayes

Life Light

I stand atop the sun drenched peak
naked, yet warm
My whole life passes before me in a streak
into the oncoming storm

Brilliant stars tumble from the sky
as I grab hold of the moon in fear
it lifts me high.
Suddenly, I feel numbness as the heavens appear

Looking down upon the earth glistening
my life becomes all too clear
I can hear nothing, but I am listening
the luminous light is oh so near

With my weightless arms outspread
I soak greedily in the vastness
In learning to love, not dread
my life before me - is greatness

Angela C. Cappel

In Fear Of The Flip Side

Holding the blue ink pen I created letters of my meaning,
My words form to the rhythm fingers as they dance across my page,
Line by line the picture becomes more clear - more vivid,
Rat ah tat tat, I can hear that sound - that beautiful music.

Words eluding the meter of the measure, but I like it,
R...at, oh the crescendo loud and on beat, hitting the paper on cue
I twirl the drumstick to the flip side, wanting of a new note,
Yeah.... that's smooth; composition halfway there.

Woops, no more flute sounds I say to the red tip rubbing the page,
My baton is slowing down,
Hands moving to the beat of a different drum,
And then only left with movement void of meaning.

Take it from the top,
Take it from the top,
Fingers still dancing to the caged rhythm drummer,
Cursed cursive causing confusion on my pages.

Too many empty phrases, lines,
Come on, a one and a two and a three...
I hear the triangle ring,
That's not what I wanted.

Julian Martin Lloyd

Beauty Of Trees

I sit in my house, a fourth mile from the creek.
  My view, through my picture window, is clear and slick.
After a hard freeze, there is a change in the color of the leaves.
  And I gaze, at the leaves, as they float away in the gentle breeze.

Some, their leaves have fallen to become dust;
  Others are green, red, golden, and rust.
It won't be long, this beauty will leave.
  The winter is coming, I can perceive.

The different trees, I know by name.
  Some look similar; but they are not the same.
There are walnut, hackberry, ash, maple, willow and cottonwood, too
  Intermingled together, they make a beautiful view.

With the breeze today, the trees changed a lot;
  Because, many leaves from the trees did drop.
After the leaves all drop, I'll enjoy seeing a neighbor's place too
  Across the creek with a winter view.

Many Norway Spruce around my farmstead grow;
  They keep their green leaves the entire year, you know.
I'm sure glad, that windbreak is there;
  As I sit and rock, in my old rocking chair.

Clifton E. Wiseman

Most Precious Treasure

Many years ago when I was very young,
My thoughts would wander incessantly
About conceiving my first child.

She would look somewhat like me,
possessing beauty in and out - a spirit of compassion
And all people she would beguile.

Her smile, her eyes, bright like radiant sunshine
And her voice so small so sweet,
Would always attract all people she would meet.

Her nature 'blessed-given'
In the form of angel-sent,
By God's purpose - special meant.

I would spend many waking hours
To her, singing songs of love,
And making-up the words and tunes
As I rocked my soft baby dove.

Her eyes would peer up at my face
While songs and kisses I'd embrace,
Her every look, her every gesture,
Would tell me that she's my precious treasure!

Dolores F. Church

"Daddy Gordon"

  On a rainy December morning we laid to rest
my stepfather, Gordon. As I was leaving the grave site,
I reached over and touched your casket.
I felt a sense of relief when I did.
  I always thought you would be here when I needed you.
My life has changed since your passing.
I have learned to appreciate things more.
  Your pain and suffering is over now.
I will always love you and look forward to seeing you
in the after life.
  I will always remember that rainy December morning
in 1991.

Annette Heironimus

Dancing With The Woman Of The Wind

On the wings of the wind
my soul is lifted to unmeasurable heights

With the slightest most undetectable shift in pressure

I am slammed to the rocks below.

With the same impish grin
that allows me to soar with the eagle,
my flesh is slashed to the bone

And she leaves me
aching and alone.
I am dancing with the woman of the wind.

As if a gentle breeze,
she caresses my mind
and grants me rest in the sun.

She convinces me of the good in the word,
only to prove the opposite exists.

I feel the kiss on my neck
And the force at my back

The music plays on.
Once again I will take to the sky.

I am dancing with the woman of the wind.

Christel Henderson

Osmosis — Me And The Sea

Look ahead — friend, see upon the clear
My ship it sails, e'er so gently, the wind to bring it near
Can you feel the strength within its bows — 'tis minute,
   a speck of light
Look ahead — slowly she nears, the sea is her home,
   her best is in flight
The light is white against the sails, the clouds in contrast dark blue
   If only to be lost between the two of them
   my dream of life come true
Look — afar — ahead — can you see?
The ship and I we share, the most common bond for us, my friend,
   Our love — the ocean and its warm salt air
But, alas, the sailing ship is gone, outlining shadows remain
Into the sunset — that speck of light — will gently return again
   Jeannine Simonian

JUDGMENTS

Bend your ear to hear my plea
My people bleed for not being free
We lick the feet of drugs and alcohol
   because you have not answered your call
So we try to survive ourselves
   but it's hard since we've been taught slavery
   to the ones who put us on their shelves
   and told us to conform is an act of bravery
It's time we transcend our means
It's time to give more than our screams
   for our words are easily confused
   connotations of meanings abused
I don't want to gun between my lips
   nor to bear the brunt of the master's whips
The machine marches on my bended knee
   it hurts so much I cannot see
I remember my rage is nothing but a dose
   of what will descend from God's host
And you that have not bent your patronizing ear
   will then understand the true meaning of fear.
   Bill Meadows Jr.

Enlisted Men

When I was five years old
My mother put me to a kindergarten school
First she told me that she does not want me
To come home with a black eye.

Son she said, when you grow up to be a man
I do not want you to be a husband man
You must fight back so your life be protected
Be a brave boy and you will be respected.

When I turned seventeen years old
I remember what my mother had told
That she does not want a coward boy
Fight back, fight back, she buoy.

And when I was eighteen
I volunteered to go join the Navy
Because my country needed me to protect her
For I am loyal to her not a coward man either.
   Guillermo Pescador

My Mom, My Forever Friend

So many daughters cannot say
"My Mom is my friend in every way"
I'm one of the lucky ones who'll always know
My Mom is my friend and this poem will show

Through my growing up years
There was one person to wipe away the tears
From falling off bikes to boys breaking my heart
Helpful words of advice from someone so smart

Independence was given with a watchful eye
Instilling trust and told not to lie
Mistakes were forgiven, punishments light
Smiles and praise for all the things done right

This allowed me to grow into the person I am
From your stern morals yet loving hand
You've always had a good insight into the feelings I felt
Making me deal with the hand I was dealt

Then the day came when I married a man
Letting me go with a loving goodbye
My Mom, My Forever Friend
Wishing us well for my new journey in life
   Dawn Michaelle Plummer

Twisting And Turning

My life keeps on twisting and turning
My mind, my soul and heart are always burning.
I know something great is going to happen
Only if I pull my life together.
I tell myself wisdom is knowing the difference between right and wrong.
So live your life from day to day,
But from drugs please stay away if you don't, your life will end
And you won't be able to know the difference.
So I looked up and saw the sunset.
It was different from any sunset that I had ever seen.
It was truly magnificent with some of the most vibrant and
beautiful colors.
Looking at the sunset made me forget all my troubles.
It gave me hope as I stood there and gazed into space.
I wish it would never fade, but as time went by so did the sunset.
Now these images are locked in my mind as if it was a dream.
Now I know what it is to see God's beautiful nature
And to know that our unhappiness can become hope,
While my life keeps on twisting and turning,
I've got to keep the faith, love God and live, hate God and die
Even while my life still keeps on twisting and turning.
   Eugene A. Parkes

A Birthday Gift

On this birthday, you gave me a great gift
Something to look at and my spirit to lift

I know that it took love and time
That means more than a thousand dimes

By that picture I know how much you care
It is family love that we give and share

Sometimes its not money that can bring love to our hearts
Its prayer, wanting to help, and family that loves sparks

It meant a lot to me to see what you had done
I hope it meant as much to you and that you had fun

To all three, I want to say thank you
And from my heart, I want to say I love you
   Adell Rejcek

Two Clasped Hands

It is in my quiet time that the rest I seek overwhelms
   my mind and soul;
The absence of sound encompasses even my racing heart; for
   quietness and peace reign in my moment of wondrous imagination.
This tranquility I seek and seem to find speaks no words, for
   This time is mine.

To bow my head, to slumber in thought or reverence to the creator,
   Breaks to my inner sanctum the purpose of my existence.
For the groanings deep within my person shake the foundations
   That speak of the creation and all that it has to offer me;
Wondering in utter amazement that the inner cool refreshing
   I emulate is the presence of a higher being?

My hands sweat, my grip tightens as my body becomes in deep thought.
When my life has meaning and quietness is no longer just a
Friend but life sustaining to all that is of me.

For as I rest again, I hear laughter, a break of silence as
The earth rejoices in its bosom.

That for a fleeting moment I was else where, for I am here now with
myself, my creator, my imagination and my two clasped hands, for
he is in me and my quietness.
   James M. Thompson

Untitled

Last night while I was quietly asleep,
my inner self reached into the night so deep,
across one hundred-fifty miles of space
To place a kiss on your dear, sweet face.

You must have known it, sweetheart;
For your lips moved slightly apart
And you smiled with movement slight
As if you knew and would have returned it, if you might.

You smiled and stirred on your pillow;
your breast swelled as you quietly sighed,
happier than you'll ever know.
I stole away. My heart was satisfied.
   Emmett A. Snyder Sr.

My Imagination

Often I imagine there is a wonderful and fascinating place where all my hopes and dreams can never really die. It's a very special place where flowers can bloom forever, inside my secret world of imagination where my most intimate wishes are just waiting to come alive.

I have opened the doors to a magical world when I ride past on the tail of a shooting star, only to discover all the hidden secrets of life and love I never new existed in my life before. I've climbed the steps to a magnificent rainbow, to a mystical place which time seems to have forgotten.

When I close my eyes I know deep inside my mind I will find my most vivid imagination. I imagine the pure softness of a beautiful young woman who gives me a soft tantalizing kiss. If only I could savor the mysterious sensation of her love, which she has placed upon my unsuspecting lips.

All my senses are alive when I inhale the refreshing fragrance from the silky red rose petals which seem to cling to her soft delicate skin. I try to reach out to caress the petals inside my hands. To my amazement they seem to be fading inside the strange enchanting winds.

Suddenly the doors to my imaginary world have started to close. One of the hardest things in my life is knowing when to say goodbye. Now all I have left is a strange feelings emptiness along with my imaginary teardrops. Why do I feel as if I have to cry?
   Dana K. Ryder Sr.

Because Of You

Because of you my life has changed in a positive way.
My heart sings with joy and my lips echo laughter.
My eyes feast upon your beauty every day.
My face will bask in your love until the hereafter.

My ears strain in anticipation of you calling out to me.
My hands tingle with delight at the touch of your skin.
My arms reach out and hold your body with glee.
My fingers want to rub your face and lips again and again.

My legs and feet are swift to run after you.
My body aches and longs for your touch.
My heart for you beats strong and true.
My darling, when we are apart, I miss you so much.

My source of joy, excitement, and pleasure comes from thee.
My days are filled with hope and anticipation of the next day.
My nights are filled with peace and tranquility.
My being in your presence lights my way.

My love for you will never end.
My affection for you will grow and grow.
My care for you I will forever tend.
My devotion to our love will forever flow.
   Chris Rider

My Heart, Behind

Wherever I go, whenever I go -
My heart does not come -
It stays behind an indefinite amount of time -
Until, one day, it comes back to me -
When it does, it is not whole, parts have been stripped away.

My heart stays behind an indefinite amount of time -
And as it tries to follow me it is being held down -
Almost pulled back, if it were not for its loyalty to me -
It struggles to move forward and stumbles across the ground -
Leaving pieces, fragments behind on the place I left -
Days-months-years pass -
Those pieces will always be there, with that place -
The place will change, people will forget -
But the things that touched me about that place will always hold -
those pieces of my heart, forever -

My heart stays behind an indefinite amount of time -
And when my heart finally reaches me, it is not all there,
It will never be the same -
It's tired from the journey and from being torn between its two loves -
This is when I fell that maybe I should have stayed and not left -
My heart behind!
   Heather Shively

Daddy's Flowers

I stood in front of the grave
My head bent low
My lips moving in silent prayer
Daddy, I called softly,
But no reply.
Just the sound of trees moving
Daddy, I brought you flowers
The roses are your favorite flowers
I took the fresh cut flowers and laid them down
Next to a small marker,
A tear trickled down my check

For tomorrow
The flowers will be dead
Because nothing lives forever
No daddy, nothing lives forever.
   Danielle Smith

Window Seat

Here sitting on my window seat, I see the blocks of light on my floor that my window lets through into my room. I see the shadows of the trees as their leaves billow in the breeze. I watch the children frolic and play. They ask me to come but I have nothing to say. Cause I can no longer frolic and play ever since that fateful day. It seems like only yesterday when the car swerved in Mama's way. She tried to stop she really did but it was to hard for our car. The cars screeched them slam, next I saw the hospital wall and braces on my legs. The doctor said, "I'm sorry dear you'll never walk again." Mama cried and Daddy did too, everyone was sad and I didn't know what to do. Karen brought me letters from all my real good friends and Tyler brought me flowers and still does, every weekend. He says will say together because he loves me so very much, but ever since the accident he hasn't keep in close touch. I wish I could stand up and run into his arms, ride my bike one more time, and swim under the night time skies enchanting charms. But all I can do is sit here and watch the blocks of light, all I can do is sit here as day turns to night.

Amanda S. Murray

That Night

Even as the scent fills my rose
my eyes mist, and take me back, back
to that wonderful night and him
Children lost in a world of adults pretending, pretending
I close my eyes and remember everything
Him in his tux, me in my dress so yellow, yellow
We talked, made promises, and twirled
it was like a dream, but dreams end, end
I found myself cold, lonely, looking
but the man in the moon was looking back, back.

Christa Abbott

The High Spirit

When I am ensconced in my celestial domain
my beloved, remember, the spirit never dies.
When you feel the winter sun on your shoulders,
that's me, giving you a big warm hug.
When the summer breeze moves the tender branches,
that's me giving you a friendly wave "hello."
When the leaves are falling in the autumn winds,
that's me reminding you not fall by the wayside,
but walk straight and tall with your eyes
on the white tipped mountains. And
when the "green up" times come in the spring,
that's me reminding you to nourish the seeds of
wisdom sprouting within.
When the red waning sun sets on the horizon,
that's me remembering the three "red letter days"
when each of you were born and
when you see the first bright star
twinkling in the blue of night,
that's me giving you a sly old wink.

Cecelia Fortener

Console With The Deep Blue

Grasp the breezes of the fresh ocean smell,
Observing the breaking of the waves, the format, and how they fell.
Feel the adhesive wind, as it blows through the fine morsels of your hair,
The grainy sand that slithers between the clefts of your feet so bare.
Note the sensation of the open heavens, the widely spread space,
How water and land come together, creating this wondrous place.
Feel the gathering on your moist skin, from the dampened chilled air,
Taste the salty atmosphere, as it breathes through your skin so fair.
Staring across the forever blue, as images contain your mind,
A sight not to pass, whereas a moment of no other you will find.

Amanda Schrey

Acting And Playing A Part

You came into my life like a ship out on the ocean parting waves,
Moving everything close to me and far away.

You were sitting in a high place shining down on me,
like the stars above,
And your light was so bright that you blotted out many satellites.

You played the part of a "knight in shining armor."
The waves of your command moved me out of my true being or creation,
And I believed in you and knew this was the way.
For many years I walked in the moonlight with you and enjoyed
the sun freely by day.

In times of trouble we worked hard, prayed and stayed together;
success was never far from us.
So one day you decided to step up to higher ground, it turned out
to be a step down.

That's when we ran into many dark clouds...and they burst!!!
And oh! how it rained....only on me.
For years I walked the earth wet, sorry and despaired.

Oh! How it rained. Oh! How wet I was. Oh! How sorry I was.
Oh! How despaired I was.
That's when I realized you were only acting and playing a part.

Cleo C. Kohlman

Life's Simple Pleasures

Enveloped in warm, soothing liquid,
Mother's heartbeat sings her lullaby.
Silky softness of her pale blanket;
Arms that cradle 'neath the winter sky.

Hot, crunchy sand nibbling at the toes,
Flowing through small and dimpled fingers.
Ocean lapping and circling the feet;
Crabs and crawly things without stingers.

Arm in arm, skipping with schoolyard friends;
Socking the ball higher than before.
Wind burnt cheeks, legs racing up the hill;
The smell of hot cocoa through the door.

Chills, sighs, feeling love's eyes pierce the heart;
Whispers, "He loves me, he loves me not."
Two straws, one malt, the touch of his hand;
Dancing, twirling, whirling, time forgot.

Sticky fingers and chocolate kisses;
Children asleep, angels in repose.
Crackling fire and mugs of hot wassail;
Arms that cradle 'neath the winter snows.

Carole Woodland

Daymares

Tears fade away in the subtle moonlight.
Memories of hate-filled nights flash
Through my mind in an instant of pure rage and peace.
Loveless drops of dew bead up and roll
Down my wretched, yet colorful, face.
Silhouettes metamorphosize gracefully.
Shadows materialize with a whisk of fresh air.
Life is scarce in this corner of hell.
Serene undulations drape across my body
To set me to sleep in a sea of darkness
Where I find my only sanctuary, my only escape.
"Give me freedom, Lord. Give me an outlet,"
I scream at the heavens.
Thunderous silence is my answer.
Hopeful discouragement fills my bleeding soul.

Gary L. Barton Jr.

Pond

Day is awaking, sunrise peeks through tree.
Morning fog rising, willows swaying in breeze.
Gazing upon water, morning winds gently blow.
Sitting on dock, legs dangling below.

Senses dulled by daily work.
Come alive to birds delicate chirp.
Reflections on water of clouds in sky.
School of fish swimming gently by.

Turtles sunning, on nearby rocks.
Mother nature their guide, no need for clocks.
This pond is more than water and weeds.
It's home to creatures with similar needs.

Dragon flies darting here to there.
Loons surfacing for breaths of air.
Water sustains life is a well known fact.
Ripples appear from fogs jumping at snacks.

Water bugs playing tag, in seemingly random fashion.
While twilight approaches, caused by earthly rotation.
Night time sound are filling eve.
Day is resting, sunset peeks through tree.

Bill Sherwood

Momular Science And Momular Songs

   We are locked into words like popular science
     Momular science opens the pregnancy deliverance
       Which then opens the psychic memory
     While we shared with mother and deuteronomy
Momular opens architecture poetry and medicine
Evolving his story to her story to our story win
Our story is hour story the time to make a baby
He brew evolves to she brew finally to the our brew
   The new clear solution opens linguistic evolution
     Language gives off pheromones and toxulation
       As Momular songs delineate feminine pursuits
     Planets will be as genes for loyal suits
Momular science and songs will open reproduction
Ovulations and menstruation fulfilling production
Opening group will fulfill the promise of woe-man
Whose time behind bars causes the rage of women
   Momular science and songs is the new clear truth
     We are all connected thru new clear techno proof
       Those who dream color have opened a black white
     Barrier next you feel you're in a dream a momular height

Alexander Galahad

Moments

Moments in my life that have come to pass,
moments I wish I could change, moments that last.
When moments with you go through my mind,
some make me laugh, some make me cry.
If in my life only one thing I do,
I hope I show the undying love I have for you.
Though I've failed you in the past,
your love for me, you say will last.
Love like that is hard to find,
how could I have been so blind?
Now I see and now I show,
over the years our love is sure to grow.
I will never stop loving you,
my last moment will be loving you.

Anthony M. Hill

Autumn Changes

As we watch in awe, the painter of fall
mix his colors of brown, orange, and green;
Oh yes, red and yellow, that makes the soul mellow,
as he finishes fall's colorful scheme.

While the leaves frisk and frolic
in the North winds that blow,
It makes us a bit saddened to know;
That soon they'll stop playing,
for they'll be quietly laying,
beneath the Winter's cold freezing snow.

Beverly Rensink

Happy Birthday - Old Friend

Lazy layers of searching smokey vapors
Mingle with and rise to hover over - BIRTHDAY LAUGHTER —
Louder each year!
Between, among, and from friends who need this moment
To reflect on passing years.

We need you once again with your one year older lungs
To blow out more candles than ever before!!
Birthdays, marking space between time . . . and time,
Are as elusive as the smoke
Soaring above cold nights and warm people.

With steady hand, the cake is cut and served.
The guest of honor's smile freezes on lips that
Could say, but won't say the question.
"Have I used my time well?"
And the Heart responds, "There is yet much to do!"

"May I yet have another year with friends
And share the laughter and the joy that they deserve?"

To each you give great peace as they take from you a piece
Of the glowing and burnt out symbol of passing time -
One candle from your flaming birthday cake.

James D. Young

The Theory Of R .. Evolution

We look in awe at God's vast sky across the miles so far,
Measure mankind on this earth to find out who they are?

Three billion years it maybe was when life on earth began,
Terrestrial forms of this and that all part of God's great plan.

A curious mind did one day ask what brought me here to be,
Not one could answer for the lot blind souls who could not see.

And so began a crusade forth for that which saw the light,
Men of knowledge stood the test they searched both day and night.

Anthropologist dug the earth so deep for want of facts to tell,
Found holy men to argue with who threatened them with hell.

The first brave man disputing all he called it evolution,
A step by step progressive way that near caused revolution.

Emergence from the sea he said when life on earth began,
When living creatures climbed ashore and transformed into man.

And when it comes to measures worth mixed emotions come our way,
The Bible's quote of Adam n' Eve or the scientists with their say.

Then someone boggled all our minds they monkey-wrenched this plea,
A complex question one did ask what's the missing link to thee?

John R. Page

Dream Coma

I've fallen into a coma. No one is with
me. Just me and my thoughts. I'm alone
in a dream. A dream of my memories. I'm
free from my pain now. My continuous
pain and sorrow. My mind is wandering
farther away. I'm drifting into a deep
sleep. My body has gone numb. I can't
feel anything anymore. I can no longer
hear the people of my past. I think
I've finally escaped. Escaped from my
life of hell. To this wonderful world of a dream.
   Darlene Wood

That Special Guy

As I think about what we could have,
Me and you all glad,
Makes my heart fill with glee,
So I drop right down to my knees
Hoping you would rescue me.

I don't know if you know I existed
So I try to act like Miss Priss.

Every day and every night I think about you holding me tight,
Waiting for your lips to press on to mine,
Oh I wish I could hold that moment in my mind.

But I know I got to let go because,
You don't know how I love you so.

I'm trying to keep my hopes up high but I just can't seem to fly

I know you've seen me around but I guess,
I'm just another person in the crowd.

I wish you would make a move and ask me out,
Because you can't hear the love I got for you,
Unless I let it out loud
   Heather L. Bohara

The Unspeakable Gift

It came wrapped in swaddling clothes, in a manger the gift for you and me;
A Savior and a Redeemer for all the world to receive.

"Oh such a pretty baby," I trust said a few;
little did they know for what he'd come to do.

A Wonderful Counselor, Healer, Comforter and the Living Water that
   never ends;
Our Righteousness, our Mercy and an everlasting Friend.

We were full of sin and shame, living a life full of pain;
living a lie and doomed to die, but God stepped in!

This Gift was given to all the world, so we could be set free;
Freedom to live a life full of victory.

A life of joy, a life of peace and love;
A life full of truth and purpose given from God above.

This Gift was carefully thought out and prepared for me and you;
Something to help us in everything we do.

Understanding and wisdom in our hearts to help us along the way;
to be holy, just and blameless each and everyday.

God the Father gave to us his only begotten Son;
Oh such an Unspeakable gift, because now the victory is won!

Have you accepted God's unspeakable gift of Jesus Christ today?
It's free of charge, waiting to be received all you must do is believe.
   Alexis D. Smith

First Love

Some days I wonder, "Was it meant to be?"
Maybe someday people could see us
as a couple standing there together, just you and me.
When I'm at your house and I know it's time to leave,
I push back that last tear with the corner of my sleeve.
The feeling I feel inside, I cannot explain,
Because you are the one causing all my pain.
I wish for one day you'll be my first kiss.
But I know it won't because my mind already tried, but only
missed.
   Jenni Crippin

The Last Rose Of Summer

From May to September, as part of her weekly plan,
Mary came to my office with roses in her hand.
Friendly and unassuming she arranged them with grace,
Positioning them on my desk with a radiance on her face.

The aroma so sweet perfumed the very air I breathed,
Completing her task, she then quietly takes her leave.
Was the fragrance that of the rose ... or was it Mary?
Thoughtfully my eyes upon the roses would tarry.

Mary will never know all the love she has bestowed,
While giving so generously of herself through the rose.
The last rose of summer, more precious than the first,
So like a reflection of Mary, and the purity of her mirth.

Though summer is gone now, and with it the rose,
Indelibly etched in my memory in treasured repose.
Like the miniature visits with Mary, so lovely, so dear,
Forever to remind me of her when a rose a near.
   Janet Humphries

Little Box Of Mine

Little box of mine so strong and secure,
marred and scared down through
the years, but you still endured.

It seems you were shipped in from Havana filled
with cigars three for twenty cents.
Now you sit on my curio shelf all beautifully bent.

You once stayed in Daddy's highboy on the bottom shelf,
holding eight, ten cents, life policies to be
used in case of some child's death.

You've held receipts for things bought down at the
hardware store:
Figures and measurements for someone's new floor.

I sometimes miss the strong hands that held you and
put everything in its place,
And I will forever cherish the fond memories you embrace.
Little box of mine.
   Clara Bowe

For Your Love

When I was young I could not see.
My soul was tender and had yet to live and let be.
You were a mystery, a puzzle to solve.
Little did I know you were the answer, my resolve.
Now, the years have weathered the person I once shown.
What was once certain has revolved to the unknown.
But I take heart when I remember we are one,
For your love is as constant as the sun.
   Belia Felix

Untitled

It all depends on the tip of a pen
Marital beginnings in holy vow
Confirmed by blood and ink
Then with shameless finality of broken promises
Ended by dual signatures
It all depends on the tip of a pen.
A child's new name, a final grade
Someone's financial gain, another's loss
Commitment to a new home
Where life's happiness and despair resides
It all depends on the tip of a pen
Letters from friends and lovers
Exhale wonders of the spirit
The swelled heart of a little boy
Seeing his name appear on a team roster list
Nations crumble and war rages
Documents of peace follow
Like wools wrapped around the chill of the soul,
Dreams can come true.
It all depends on the tip of a pen.

Cheryl Blanchard

Forever, We Will Last!

Forever they will last together.
Marching on in married vows.
Pledging to stay loyal forever.
As a knight does when he bows.
Their future brings some fear, some pain.
As they await their time of joy.
Nothing's to lose, everything's to gain.
Knowing pain is a mere decoy.
Will their love help ease them past,
Those tremendous times of mess?
Is it good enough to last?
Oh God, for Our sake, Yes.
Together we are destined, for doing just fine.
Aging to perfection, like an admirable French wine.

Jason Mayeu

Shadow Of A Tree

One night I could have walked for miles, because I was burdened with many trials.
I walked with my head hung down as I watched my shadow on the ground.
Walking into the shadow of a petrified tree I looked up
and noticed a full moon in the midst of dead limbs with no leaves.
The tree had been beat and battered by my storms.
Yet, it stood even though it suffered great harm. Then the Lord spoke to me, "Be like this tree-Stand and go through your trials."
The burden lifted, and I was relieved. The next morning
I saw the moon through an opening of many trees covered with leaves.
The Lord spoke again, continuing from the night before,
"And I will bless you abundantly."
I was happy and content the rest of the day. While on my way home
I glanced up a certain way only to see a white moon in a clear blue sky.
The Lord spoke for the third time, "and in the world to come Eternal Life". Since then the storms of life have done much harm,
but I will continue to stand and be like this tree, because of the words the Lord has spoken to me —

"Be like this tree — Stand and go through your trial,
and I will bless you abundantly, and in the world to come Eternal Life."

Gerald E. Davis

Behind His Eyes...Beyond His Soul

In his eyes many times I've seen anger,
Many times, worry and fear,
But today his eyes were different,
I could not turn away.
Impossible for me to halt my mind from that memory...
It would not erase.
His mood seemed to humble,
His mind seemed to race,
He looked at me but did not see,
As I gently touched his face...
I know now what pierced his eyes,
It was beyond his sadness, worry, or fears,
It was death's door,
And it seemed closer than tears.

Christina Blasi Miles

What Price Freedom

They fought a war and they fought it well-
Many felt they were trapped in an earthly hell.

Now they are at peace in the sleep of the dead.
As a field of poppies blossoms overhead.

The cost of freedom runs very high
And to pay the price many must die.

But there must be something that can be done
To save someone's daughter - someone's son.

We cannot continue to take and never give
And expect our freedoms to continue to live.

For freedom is not free you see.
We all must pay - all - even you and me.

So when you see the poppies of blood red
Don't just remember those who are dead.

Remember the country for which they died,
The flag - the freedom - America's pride.

You heard it said many years before,
But I'd like to say it just once more.

Ask not what America can do for you.
Ask for America what you can do!

Earleta N. Selm

A Nurses Aide Day

We hear the stories time and time again.
Many days we don't even know where to begin.
As we listen to their aches and pains.
While seeing the frustration and anguish as well.
Along with other things that seem never to fell.
We try to smooth away their fears
As we gently wipe away their tears.
We share their joys and sorrows
While hoping things will be better tomorrow.
We try are best to meet their physical and mental needs.
As we try to do are good deeds.
Many become cherished friends.
As we sit with them to the end.
We do for them what they can know longer do.
And once in a while we get a hug or two.
But still it would be nice if we could hear.
We really appreciate you for all that you do.

Cheryl R. Oxford

Monarch Butterfly

Hello beautiful butterfly.
Many are our euphonious names.
In Italian, Farfalla
In German, Der Schmetterling
In Japanese, the polite O Cho Cho
In French, Papillon
In Spanish, the most beautiful of all, Mariposa!
Are any creatures as fortunate as you and I?
Who are Monarchs here on earth.
With blue sky overhead and green grass below and the sun to warm us.
With colorful flowers to delight us
And their sweet nectar to give us nourishment.
Warm summer breezes offer us currents to ride and glide on.
Higher and higher, then lower again.
Men measure their lives in years
But how many of them are wasted?
Our time is short, but we live each day joyously.
And thankfully and beautifully.
Who of God's creatures could ask for more?

Eileen Barton Lisman

The Quiet Man

For years the quiet man tagged along, as the wife said "Lord save my man!" In quiet trust the man Thanked The Lord, as the wife said "Lord save my man!"

As the word was preached could the quiet man be reached? As the wife said "Lord save my man!"

The quiet man looked bored, as he Thanked The Lord for what was in store. The quiet man looked tired, and sad, as he quietly told the Lord why he was mad.

"Look into my heart, and into my face, for it is Your Grace that I am saved" said the quiet man. As the wife said "Lord save my man!"

Then came the Judgement Day, The Lord opened His Arms to the quiet man.
"But What About Me?" Asked the wife who always said "Lord save my man!"

Up Went The Lord With The Quiet Man!

(Inspired By The Holy Spirit)
Amanda J. Caputo

Together (for: Jason)

All those yesterdays came and went
Making memories of the time that's been spent...
Together.

The laughter, the tears, all the smiles and pain
The sunshine, the snow, the endless nights, the rain
We have shared...
Together.

I can look into the past and see memory upon memory
Our love so sweet and true
I'll always be able to see me and you...
Together.

No matter what anyone says or what anyone tries to do
I promise from the bottom of my heart
That I'll always love you and only you
Yes, I know we can make it...
Together.

I'm still hearing the sweet words and feeling the gentle touches
That make our love burn so bright
And just the two of us are perfectly alright...
Together.

Angie L. Shepard

Dripping Picante Sweat As He Lunged

Dripping picante sweat as he lunged...
Lunged for the blinking piquant buzzer, the color
of the illuminated lipstick red Mexican tomatoes
He'd used in the Squid Punch with Liverwurst Salsa: yesterday's menu

Plump ripe baby cherry
Baby he was, all right
She licked her deli-meat lips and watched
As he blurted sizzling steamy the sultry ingredient
In polyester piped pineapple-shaded pants.

"Calves' Feet Popovers with Pig Belly!"
Pizza smile. Eyeing her culinary lover, contesting tasty on sound stage, she sighed, breathing strawberry breath
The pungent scent of competition inhaled

Watching her ravishing radish love redden,
He quickly augmented his response, (the game guy with his jello jiggler stomach slumped,
Expectant in corduroy green, munching on a pink jambon appetizer) "Calves' Feet Popovers with Pig Belly...

A la mode! "Yes! Yes! Yes!" green sigh
Flashing lights redgreenyellowblue
An inordinate cash prize...famefortune...and le gateau du chocolat!

Dina Cheney

Teach Only Love

We teach our children judgment by judging them.
Love does not judge.
We teach our children fear through anger, attack and hatred.
Love is the opposite of fear.
We teach our children inequality through discrimination.
Love does not discriminate.
We teach our children scarcity by not giving fully of ourselves.
Love has no bounds.
We, the parental generation can change our ways.

We can teach a child to listen by taking the time to listen to him.
We can teach a child his value by paying attention to him.
We can teach a child respect by offering our respect to him.
We can teach a child peace by being peaceful.
We can teach a child honesty by speaking the truth from our hearts.
We can teach a child equality by treating others equally.
We can teach a child abundance by giving abundantly of ourselves.
We can teach a child Love, for that is what we are.

Gina Montalbano-Fenske

Abandoned

Happiness from within? Memories no longer suffice.
My need is to share but you are not here.
My only companion, despair.
Grief is the penalty I pay for love.
I am consumed with fear destroying hope, reality, to love, to be...
Mournful cries from my anguished heart fall on deaf ears.
Nobody cares; least of all, me.
Empty days and tumultuous nights stranded on this island of life,
the oppressive darkness turns almost brilliant, is it my light?

Dolores M. Hess

Untitled

So tattered and torn, so barely worn, so comfortable but thin.
Now, as I hold you by two fingers with an unsightly grin,
I remember only the long roads and exciting places we've been.
But, as sad as I must say, it's time for a new pair of tennis shoes today.

Gordon B. Herold

95 Years Is Not So Long

I was recently looking at photos that were taken just three months ago
of our family united for Thanksgiving which we do every year as you know.

But this year a thought really struck me, though it's something I've
always known. If it weren't for Grandmamma Sallie I'd be staring at
background alone.

The impact you'd have on the world was not known when you first became
a mother, and I know I speak for us all when I say we thank you for
each other.

Even those who married into our group are grateful for your life.
Without you they'd not have the children they do, not to mention their
husband or wife.

You've given the world several teachers and some who like cattle and
farms. Did you realize just what you had started when you held your
first child in your arms?

When reflecting back on your accomplishments you must look forward,
too. For every achievement each one of us makes, to you also some
credit is due.

However, the greatest thing you have done which will bring you
eternal reward is the life you have led as a Christian and the souls
you have led to the Lord.

Because your blood runs through all of us your life will never end.
In our family each time a new baby is born you get to start over again.

So 95 years is not so long when you look at it as I do.
You've been blessed with immortality by the lives God created through you.

Carrie R. Franco

Zodiac

*(A poem dedicated to the stranger in Haight Ashbury Cala Parking lot
who told me of the Chinese Way)*
His Stranger in the Cala Parking Lot, who helped park the groceries in my car.
You told me of the Chinese way. You told me how this Buddha left one day.
You told me how he called the animals to stay.
You told the stories to my child. But I was taping every word you spoke,
In the silence of the Parking Lot.

So let me count the ways you told me of the Chinese way.
First, there was the **Rat** that always took the opportunity.
Then there was the **Ox** that ventured out too far.
And then there was the **Tiger** that pounced to kill the Ox.
And finally, there was the **Sheep** sharing pastures green.
Next there was a **Dragon**, fierce and bold in 1988, who shed his wings to be a **Snake**.
Then there was the **Rooster** in the silence of the Parking Lot.
And the car alarm that made the tape go blank.
Mr. or Mrs. without an "s" in the barnyard of my dream.
Mouse and **Rabbit**, my daughter guessed that right.
And then the story of the **Dog** that had to learn the way of life.
That had to wear a smell chicken necklace, to love the way of life.
And finally the **Pig**, the **Boar** of life, that bites the piece.

Thank you stranger in the Parking Lot.
You gave me Love, Life and Peace in the Chinese Way.

Françoise Herrmann

I am a withering rose,
reluctant to let go of my last living petal,
my link to the comfort of home, family, high school;
Yet eager to move on
to create stories yet untold,
to unveil the shadowed, uncertain future
that impels me by creeping closer minute by minute,
forcing me to be overtaken by reality.

Ginger Raines

"Our Heavenly Father"

Our Heavenly Father
  Thank you for our church,
    our Sabbath schools,
     our Bibles, and
      our missions throughout the world.
  We thank thee for our country;
    to guide our government, and be with,
     and protect our servicemen.
  We ask you to help us work well with our
    friends at church, and at school, and
    to be happy with our friends.
  We give thanks
    for gifts of love,
    for strength, and
    courage.
  Forgive us when we fail our families and
    our friends,
  God, help us to know your will,
    to understand your will, and to "Do" your will!
In "His" Precious name we pray. Amen!

Diane M. Spencer

Man in the Moon

The man in the moon,
tells me a secret each night.
I promise not to tell,
but to you I just might.
He tells me about the stars,
and how they twinkle so bright;
then he whispers your name,
and my soul is in flight.
Just like a bird,
it soars through the sky;
my thoughts filled with you
and a spark of love in my eyes.
Then the man in the moon,
he whispers again,
this time so softly,
so my dream will never end.

Birgitta Peterson

"Lonely"

Walk with me, someone
Talk with me each day
I'm so very lonely
Life seems oh so grey.

Lets enjoy a rainbow, someone
Lets find a pot of gold
I'm so very lonely
Sometimes I feel so old.

Let's share the seasons, someone
We'll celebrate each one
I'm so very lonely
My life needs some fun.

Let's wine, dine and dance, someone
Enjoy music, plays and shows
I'm so very lonely
For me boredom grows and grows.

I know you're out there, someone
Can't you hear me call
I'm so very lonely
You could change it all.

Bonnie McDowell

"Successful African Woman"

I have been taken by the hand,
taken by the hand of a man
called "power."
Power has given me a place in life.
In life, indeed, I have become
his dove, his wife.
I feel him and he feels me.
Thank God my brothers and
sisters help set me free,
free to obtain all the
comforts that power can bring me.
Bring me love; bring me joy.
Don't forget my expensive toys.
Power you are my man,
and I am your woman.
You are definitely someone
I will never stop lovin'.

Cheri L. Humphrey

Death Wish

O Lord, take me now,
Take me please, I care not how.
Life is useless it gives me nothing,
Take me away from what I am loathing.

I have nothing to live for,
Life is bitter, it needs me no more.
Take me to where I will have no worries,
Money is not, no one hurries.

A place where I will have peace,
No one to bother me, no one to please.
How I long to go away,
Take me now Lord, take me today.

Judy Woods

"The Simple Things"

Country roads and birds that soar
Take me back to days of yore,
A one room school house on the hill,
Jumping rope, oh, what a thrill.

Walking three miles in the snow.
Trying to learn what we needed to know,
Recess was fun, happy were we,
Happy as larks in that big oak tree.

Simple things, like the old country lane,
We even loved being caught in the rain.
Life was precious in the days of yore.
Oh, let us return, just once more!

Life has changed so much today.
Where is the joy of ole yesterday?
The old country roads, flowers on a hill,
Simple things, oh, they gave such a thrill!

Folks look so worried that we see today,
Where is the serenity of ole yesterday?
Pack up your bags and see what it brings,
Go back to the joy of the simple things.

Jane Stutler

Untitled

The roses you gave me
so long ago,
still rest at my bedside
in an innocent white vase.
Once they were blood red and proud,
but now, blackened with age,
they bow their heads.

Callie B. Leaper-Nettles

Life's Just Begun

To my children yet to be
take from the bellows
What's left of me
my remains my children dear
Spread amongst the timbers near
without a tear remember me
think often of my memory
As I will live inside your heart
Til from this world you may part
Together again we'll be one day
Souls free to dance and play
In God's eye we will be one
Fear not death,
Life's just begun..

Cindy Anne Watkins

Sea Shells

Sea Shells
swimming in the sea.
Sea shells
sticking all over me.
Sea shells
buried in the sand.
Sea shells
as I lift my hand.
Sea shells
as I turn and leave
Sea shells
that I left on the beach

Cindy Morgan

Sleeping Over In Granddaughter's Room

Lying awake in Emmy's bed,
Surrounded by the Grateful Dead,
Posters, posters, everywhere.
There's a new one over there.
Where did Van Gogh go?
Doesn't anybody know?
The last I heard,
From a little bird,
Was that Van Gogh had said
About the Grateful Dead,
Some very nasty words,
That hurt the noisy nerds.
Guess he hates to share wall spaces,
With those ghoulish faces.
Wonder what will greet me here
When I come back another year.

Donald C. Stiles

Dust Devil Lake

Under an empty sky
surrounded by fault block mountains
rising, like islands, out of a sandy sea,
lies dust devil lake.

There on it's powdery dry bottom
they weave and dance.
Two, three, sometimes more,
they spin their veils of whirling dust.

Raised from the dust by the sun
and drifting with the wind,
they bend and sway and finally,
settle to earth - exhausted.

Edward J. Tschupp

My Mary

They say young love
Surely is the best
The flame of passion
Burns brightly in their breast

But what about
An older love
That's grown throughout the years
Yet now you wake alone
To a misty vale of tears

Her pillow now is empty
Her fragrance no longer there
You can't take her in your arms
And say how much you care.

And like me one day you'll awake
And your heart will turn to stone
For you will finally realize
You are all alone

John J. Hayes

Great Day

Great day
sun hidden in a drowsy slumber
shadows hover over
smothering the weak of heart
constant battle
sun breaks through
the clench of day
only to stumble in darkness
tears of rage
bloom then decay
wither in embrace
struggle to escape her deadly touch
when it becomes too much

Angie Derr

Fallen Child

A fallen child once more.
Summoned, to God's open arms.
God's great golden gates
open to all, fallen children.
All angels soon to be
with wings of pure white.
A bright white light has.
Has guided my fallen child.
Through the halls, to the Lord's throne.
To all I must convey.
I have wept and will weep again.
Always retained alive within.
A heart of memories kept.
My fallen child is not dead,
in my heart.

Dale R. Patchen

Hate

Those beady eyes
Stare with a stone cold face.
You misinterpret everything I say.
I do not trust you
Or like you at all.
You are so selfish
You can not see,
This bottled hate for you
Which is within me.

Cheryl Briggs

The Coming Of Summer

When flowers are in bloom
Summer is coming soon.
We know from the smells in the air
The days will be sunny, bright, and fair.

The birds are chirping to their mates
Getting ready for their lovely dates.
The leaves are all pretty and green
The colors are the purest ever seen.

Insects are buzzing all around
Some of the meanest ever found.
When summer is in full bloom
Everyone sings a different tune.

Surfing, swimming, and flying kites
Fishing and playing with all our mights.
Taking turns in batting a ball
Which always last through the fall.

I like summer best of all
That's the time when we have a ball.
The sun is hot all over town
I promise that I'll never frown.

Delois J. Sykes

Together Again

The beat of our hearts, the
suffering and the smart. Sweet
children's charm and your warm
affectionate arm. How can it be
we all have sight and still cannot see?
The cold hearts, the warm
hearts how can it be? Our time
is so limited and yet so strong.
Is forever real or just an idea
of our human minds? We all
need kindness and in time we all
find this. I hope we'll all be
together again. Someday in a
type of peace and serenity we
cannot even fathom.
Are friends, friends, or
just a person to condemn?
In the end I think it will be
splendid in one way, yet so sad in another.
I hope in the end we can all be friends and
have time in

Amanda K. Hobbs

Order

What is this world that it reveals
   such awe-inspiring sights
As rainbow-painted afternoons
   and star-strewn velvet nights;

What is this world that nature's order
   rules moon, sun, and tide,
And holds the planets in their orbits
   where they won't collide;

What is this world with all its beauty,
   indescribable,
That gives a poet inspiration,
   indefinable;

This is the world that God created
   with His mighty hand
To be protected and explored
   by his creation, Man.

Gladys Harmon Birmingham

Birthday Blossoms

I'm grateful to have known you,
Such a dear and loving friend;
Sharing adventures old and new,
With magic moments for pretend.
In song and dance our voices would blend,
Youth's spirit so easily we could spend.
Mysterious engaging prophesies,
For promises to pursue.
The love of one forsaken,
As in beauty once begun.
The silence of a springtime heart,
Before garden's felt of sun.
The battles we have wagered;
The wars we never won.
Illuminating with the madness;
Soul's survival on the run.
When time shall race beyond us,
We may know a steady slowing age;
Pondering many of youth's passions;
As history turns yet, another page.

Farr North West

Scarecrow

I'm a little scarecrow
   stuffed and puffed,
Wearing borrowed clothes,
Full of hay and itchy stuff,
When the crows begin to leave
and the snow begins to fall
Say good-bye to me,
   For I'll see you next fall.

Chanel Thomas

Our Changing Love

Our love has changed and grown
Steadily from the start.
I keep you in my mind
And always in my heart.

I've wondered many times
At the love between you and I.
There is so much in my heart;
It could reach farther than the sky.

I've changed so much since the first.
Some things I'll never miss.
I've come to know one thing for sure,
And that one thing is this:

When we come together,
You and I as man and wife,
I will be forever complete
With you apart of my life.

Christina Lamont

Halloween

Halloween comes but once a year,
Smiles, candy, and lots of cheer,
Bats, witches, goblins, and ghosts,
You don't know what will scare you the most!

Julie Lois

The Sculpture

I gaze upon a sculpture
standing there alone.
A fantastic man of marble
with a heart of stone.

A darkened solitary vigil,
against memory's shadow he doth guard,
as he stands there lonely watching
with eyes so cold and hard.

From morning tide to evening mist,
through time's eternal sea,
his expression never changes
and I find he stares at me.

His glare is unforgiving
with no pity and no grace.
There's not a shard of sympathy
upon his chiseled face.

And I vaguely hear the question
at the corners of my mind,
"Is this image that I look upon
a statue's face...or mine?"

David E. Nettles

Our Moon!

When the moon rises up into our sky
spreading her soft light from way up high,
making trees, homes, fields and waters glow
with magical pastels from blue to yellow!
This wonderful shine of our full moon shows
us for a while, the silvery high and lows
of mountains and valleys of the earth
changing everything like into a new birth.
Lifting up our wounded souls as to forget
our worries or things we really do regret.
For that evening we feel truly bathed
into a forgiving light, that is not laced
with animosity or ways for the next play
planned maybe for the coming day!
Standing outside looking at our moon
somehow, it gave me rest, in the middle of June
I can sit there, watch it and look
It even inspires me, wanting to write a book!
About this old world, its people, its past
alas, for little old me, it's too complicated and too fast!

Johanna A. Garretson

Nature Path

There is a love of nature,
that goes beyond compare;
A walk along a nature path -
one finds contentment there.

The fallen leaves - a russet rug,
to walk upon and savor;
The changing Season in the air
to look upon with favor.

A flower that was blooming
gives way to a hearty plant;
the cool crisp air invigorates;
bare leaved trees stand so gallant.

Friends and lovers like a walk -
no matter what the Season -
you feel so close to Love itself,
There is no better reason.

Dorothy Moshier

...Tock

Seconds pass and minutes go...

Each one new and never again
spent and lost, never to regain
  or enjoy anymore.

Seconds pass and hours are gone...

Sleeping or not, the ticking
marks its past with a silent sweep
  of its hand once.

Seconds pass and days go by...

Filled with waiting and watching
the time as it circles
  joining its ends

Seconds pass with years of time...

All for naught.
  All wasted.
    All spent.

Gone.

Dennis K. Winger

Love Wonderful Love

  Love is the most beautiful
sound I have ever heard.
It's more than a feeling,
It's more than a word,
It helps us make it's
the next day.
It's what we live for,
It's what we say.
What is it like to be in love?
It's something you can't get enough of.
The green grass,
The wind through the trees,
A warm summer day with a
cool frequent breeze.
Almost anything I can think
of is somehow linked to the
beauty of love.

Jessica Corwin

Mother Dear, So Near

See in my window
Song of my heart
Dream of dreams
Hummingbirds sing
Why did you die, die, die
Spring is your smell
Your mane to your waist
Slender and style
Touch me once more
Oh! Your grace

Barbara Williams

Untitled

We understand one another no more
Than the fallacious dictum
We will fully incarnate
Not for love or virtue
But for the blind accord
Of smooth sail...
As amos to the jews - beware
The cataracts are coming

James Leckie

Son Of Mine

Son of mine,
Son of mine,
Please don't grieve after me
I'll always be in your heart
  Son of mine.
  Son of mine.
Please don't cry for me
I won't be here, but I'll be there
Son of mine,
Son of mine,
I'll always love you
Always and forever!

Courtney Leanne Shorthouse

Thoughts

It's so soft when it rains
Sometimes we hide all the pain
Why-oh-why does it hurt so
It seems to makes us grow old
As time goes by we become cold
Just as it hides a fallen snow
Heaven help us each passing day
So one day we can roll in the hay
As life goes so slowly on and on
Some day soon we can sing a song
Soon the sun starts to shine through
Now we can finally shed the blues
It helps to know we are loved
It was sent from a heaven above
Before long we feel we have self-worth
Today we chose to not end up in a hearse
Rejoicing death is near at hand
We know we will end up in the land
All our hurt will be forever gone
It's time to sing our own special song

Bonnie Page

Clean Once Again

When I take a bath at night,
Sometimes it's a horrible sight.
The water is all stagnant and grey,
And all the bubbles have gone away.
It starts off hot and ends up cold,
When you get out you look real old.
Your all wrinkled and white,
Your looks are a terrible sight.
It's hard to get out you get such a chill,
Sometimes you wish you were on a strong pill
Then when you get out and towel off,
You stayed in so long that you
start to cough.
But in the end, you'll find it's
worth it, cough and all you look perfect.

Brenda Lee Fuentes

Death

Oh Death, sweet realm of
solitude, come, I welcome
thee.
Whisper softly in the night
as a prince taking a bride.
Oh Death be thou kind
release my soul from
my troubled mind.

Derinda Kero

Pathway Of Fun

Often I wonder
Sometimes I pray
Must the condition of life
Continue this way?

Conflict - Resolution
Conflict - Resolution
Am I always required
To find a solution?

Am I two people?
And I left or am I right?
This dichotomy of mine
Is such a great fright.

I feel enlightened; then guilty.
I feel strong; then weak.
My God give me grace
Your pathway to seek.

For in this your pathway
The two become one,
And life's constant struggle
Is turned into fun.

Frank E. Bianco

Life

Life is so funny
Sometimes ever so short
Life's filled with all types of people
All colors, all sorts
First love so sweet, so precious, so pure
And not many things we can say
are really for sure
We cry at new births
We mourn our love ones gone
but these tears should both
be of joy - for they allow life to go on.
So keep your chin up
in life's mud don't wade
When in life handed a lemon
Go ahead make lemonade.

Brenda C. Williams

Feelings Of Hallow

A feel of hallow dwells within.
Something knocks, wants to come in.
Its presence fills the arid air,
With echoes of renewed despair.

A feel of hallow dwells within,
Stretching, reaching seeks to get in.
It's looming with its frigid hand,
And chills one's soul it can.

A feel of hallow dwells within.
Scorching thoughts it brings.
Thoughts of hurtfulness and sorrow.
Shallow feeling, thoughts of hallow.

A feel of hallow dwells within.
Tormented souls, it brings.
Within one's self, it will not part.
Its nest within, one's swollen heart.

Carlos C. Torres

A Girl From Spain

In high school classrooms, there's no doubt,
Some knowledge is absorbed by all,
As for me, just one thing stands out,
Something said in assembly hall:

About a girl from Spain, age eight,
Who, while seeing London by train,
Burst out crying for its children:
No grand view appeared for children!

Art Juntunen

A Flower Fades

Crying
  Sobbing
    Wailing
      A tiny flower fades.
Winter's come;
  Life is gone;
    Dawn's turned into night.
Dreams have been taken;
  Hopes are gone;
    A little child dies.

Donna Morris

Wildflowers Of Easter

The wildflowers bloom
so vivid and bright

It's God's way of showing
He started new life

Where homelessness hunger
and disease abound

He's given us something
to soften our frown

Then maybe one day
we will all understand

That Jesus thru flowers
is holding our hands.

Deanna Ward

I Think I Care?!?

Whispers blowing in the wind
So shrill it cries between the trees
Entwines itself in tiny webs
Its wrapped its arms around my knees.
It stopped me from the tracks I've made
It focused me upon one thing
It opened doors which once were closed
It grows like flowers that bloom in spring

Like tiny pebbles along the shore
Swept with every passing wave;
A piece of my heart consumed again
Leaving me with little to save.
In many days.. that will arrive
How much of my heart, will be left to spare?
Before it's taken away from me.....
No!!! Given... to whom... I think I care?!?

Evelyn Alexis Solano

Who Is This Man?

So bright was his radiance,
So kind was his face,
How humble was this man,
Who gave such sacrifice
To atone for us,
So we could live with him again.

Through him we'll live,
Through service we give,
And to pattern our lives after his
Who is this man?
The son of God,
Who atoned for all our sins,
Who is this man?
He died for us
Who is this man?
He loved all and healed the sick and the blind.

Who is this man?
He is Jesus the Christ.

Delores Olmstead

Ode On A Mountain

It sits there
So incredibly powerful in its majesty
Yet so innocently quiet and serene;
It sits there.

At constant war with the heavens
Its vicious body tearing apart the sky
Without mercy
Without purpose;
It sits there.

So bold in its divinity
As if it were of God's doing
So humble
So graceful;
It sits there.

Kingdom of monstrosity
Peril among giants;
It sits there.

But why?
Its purpose, its being, its beauty, its secrets
In the eye of the wonderer; it sits there.

David Tawfik

I Wish

I wish I was a butterfly,
so I could spread my wings and fly.
I wish I was a mocking bird,
so I could cheep a song.
I wish I was a letter,
then I could really travel.
I wish I was a grain of sand,
and lie among the pebbles.
I wish I was a tortoise,
who races with a hare.
I wish I was so many things,
that I know I'll never be.
For I am but a woman,
who hasn't got a dime.
For I am but a human,
a racing with the times.

Carol Martinez Gaona

This Day

This day may I begin it with a smile
So I can laugh a little while
And then present its goodness too
To everyone within my view.

I dare not start this day without
A call to God for strength to fight
Away the evils day and night
So that my life will yield the light.

May I this day be firm and strong
To show that love can conquer wrong.
That faith and beauty still prevail
For those who follow the Master's trail.

This day I shall leave within my wake
A path that others may desire to take.
A path that brightens up the life
of those who have not seen the "Light."

This light is Jesus. He's the one
That teaches what is right or wrong.
O friend, this day I pray that you
May see His light within me too.

Dewey R. Winchester

The Roses Will Bloom Tomorrow

It's hard to believe it's all over,
So hard to go it alone.
All the years we spent with each other
I can't believe they're all gone.

The roses will bloom tomorrow
Some will have faded and gone.
The soul is much like the roses.
The good ones will bloom on and on.

There is always thorns on the roses.
From the stems they all grow.
The bees stay on top of the rose
For they know there's no honey below.

This life a short time it's over
Let me live it the best way I can.
Let me stay on top of the roses.
And reach out with a helping hand.

Grady W. McCurry

Galumphing

Galumphing through life
Smelling the roses
Eating watermelon
Best I ever tasted

Mama was so weary
Midwife was so tired
Daddy was just a farm boy
Who went to the springhouse
Brought a watermelon for the BABY

It still comforts me
Building castles anew
More towers and turrets

Three wonderful boys
The greatest gift of life
Glory be
and
They all like watermelon

Eunice Lanning

Adoptee's Plea

Birthmother, birthmother, take a look at me,
Sitting on a branch of your family tree!

I'm balancing, teetering, hanging on,
Although you wish I'd soon be gone.

Adoption hid my blossom many years,
But I emerged, through all the tears.

Tears of grief for what was lost
Gave courage to search, whatever the cost.

I am the fruit from off your vine,
Seeking acceptance from those who are mine.

Blood from you runs through my veins
In the same amount that each sibling claims.

A birth certificate proves it true,
That long ago I was born to you!

Adopted children you love, you say;
But certainly, you don't treat me that way.

I am your child, and that's a fact,
And God in heaven knows how you act.

Birthmother, please reconsider what you do,
And grant me the acceptance I seek from you.
Betty Allman Kampa

Alone

Tonight, I sit here alone
Sitting by the telephone
You are gone from home
Why must I be alone?

I cry and cry, alone
Sitting by the telephone
It doesn't help you come home
Why must I be alone?

I don't like living alone
Will you call me, on the phone?
I pray you will come home
Why must I be alone?

I dream each night alone
I dream you call me on the phone
You tell me, "I'm coming home."
Than I awake, I'm still alone.
Dorothy V. Farkosh

The Puffin And The Walrus

The puffin and the walrus were,
sitting by the sea.
The walrus to the puffin
"Come on down, for tea,"
The puffin to the walrus
"That I'll never do, you'll drink
the tea, eat the cake, and then
you'll eat me too!"
The puffin and the walrus were,
sitting by the sea,
The walrus very hungry and
the puffin very free!
David W. Cobb

Anyway The Wind Blows

Sing a song of life.
Sing a song of soul.
Sing and song of the whole world.
Anyway the wind blows.

Hold your head up high.
Hold your head up proud.
Hold your head up any which way.
Any which way the wind blows.

Keep on running.
Never stop.
Keep on sharing, everlasting thoughts.
Keep on loving and caring for life.
Anyway the wind blows.

Anyway the wind blows holds
A secret for today.
Anyway the wind blows
holds a promise for tomorrow.
Candice Neidy

Helena

Over fifteen years have passed,
Since I have seen my sister last.
I think about her every day.
She's in my thoughts each time I pray.
'Twas forty years since I left home,
To start a family of my own.
She was young, her skin so fair.
I close my eyes and she is there.
Her smile so warm, her eyes so bright,
I often see her in the night.
In my dreams, to home I go.
My family's love I'll always know.
In the winter of our lives,
To see you again my heart still thrives.
Oh, dear, sweet sister of mine,
Have our lives been robbed of time?
I know that we will meet again,
By God's side, in His Heaven.
Julie Beaulieu

Untitled

Swimming in a Black hole,
Silence, so deafening, I hear—
Had confinement by a white wolf
I feel down like a dear—

Holding down a weak soul
Without knowledge—breath plain to steal—
Struggling like a ghost,
Evidence, now and then, so real—

Now, left with no pity,
I stumble, but stand—in—I moan—
Dreaming is but a dream—cropper
One more—take Hand, You're not alone.
Constance Jackson

Untitled

The Garden
often, I come to my garden
for awhile
To where the trees, grass, and
sky are close to me.
Lonely, yet happy to be alone
I walk, quiet with my thoughts
Away - from the noise of the world.
Jesse J. Kuehn

Last Rose Of Summer

A single rose peeks through the snow,
Shrugs off the morning frost
Its summer season long since gone,
with blush and fragrance lost.
No more its perfumed petals spread,
its sweet aroma each day at dawn.
The bees that kiss its silken face,
sip the nectar and are gone.
Its many friends have spread such joy,
to loved ones far and near.
A bouquet for a blushing bride,
a corsage for mother dear.
The last rose of summer always makes me sad,
when at last it's gone from view.
No more to carry my silent pledge of love,
that I can send to you.
John Endrigian

A Puppy's Promise

Home I came; I gave a sigh.
Should I laugh? Should I cry?
My comforter with flowers abloom
Was torn and strewn from room to room,
Fluff and feathers made a path
From bedroom, hallway, to the bath.

Aloud I yelled, "What have you done?"
Inside I said, "It must be fun."

The older dog ran up the stairs.
The younger barked, "She really cares."
He looked at me and cocked his head,
And with his eyes, he quickly said,
"I promise never, never more to chew."
He ran away - with my favorite shoe!
Bev Robertson

Power Over the Night

Though the days grow long,
short grows the journey
And the law of the light
grows stronger.
For golden is the light
  Growing through the night.

Night lifts its veil
bowing to the light
and the light holds on
to its own.
Great is the light
having gained its power
  Over the night.

Glorious is the day
when light yields its colors
And silver tears
break the pattern of the sky.
The life giver yields only to its own
  And gathers those who obey.

  While the night must stand alone.
Ellsworth A. Berget

Flashback

The back door slams
she sobs quietly
life desolate again...
Cassandra Ward

Candles On The Altar

Candles on the altar
Shine out on Christmas Day
Bidding precious welcome
To little hearts that stray.

Lighting paths of memory
Back through the many years
To Christ the babe of Bethlehem
Who banished sin and fears

Like sweet angelic voices
To guide us on our way
Candles on the altar
Shine out on Christmas Day.

Celia Hampson

Clouds

Billowing, all dark and light,
Shimmering in the sun,
Hidden by the night.
Faces forming, a limb, a bear
Floating so far, drifting so near.
Fluffy glaziers, mounds of snow.
Changing positions, to and fro,
Some so high, some touching the earth.
Pushed by the winds, enhanced by the tide.
They know no exception, they're seen nation-wide.
Clouds, large and small watch them and ponder,
God's work so amazing, a gift full of wonder.

Dorothy R. O'Brien

A Soul's Whisper

Slow down
Shh...still the racing mind
Listen to the rustle of leaves

My soul cries for
Simplicity
Silence
Solitude
Stillness

Ease up
Do nothing
Simply be

My ego does not understand
How can I be?
I must do!

And some days my soul wins the struggle
And I understand
My being is enough
And peace embraces me

Elizabeth D. Rembisz

Patriotic Pride

Why am I so proud, and want to say it loud
"I am an American"
I look up and see a Blue sky.
White clouds and Red sunsets
and I think of our Beautiful
Flag and our Beloved Vets
they made it a reality for you
and I to be Free.

Helen M. Williams

"The Mask"

If he could see behind the mask,
  she's worn for all these years
He'd find her eyes are not so bright;
  they've drowned in lonely tears
The person that she hides in there
  is tired, used, and worn
She made the mask some time ago
  to hide her heart that's torn
And only she can tell him
  of who she really is
She's not the one he thinks she is;
  he'd find she isn't his
And trying to convince him
  that her love is strong and pure
Is only one of her great lies;
  and one of many more
So, whenever she is with him
  she'll always wear the mask
He never needs to know;
  he'll never have to ask

Dina B. Doughty

Farewell To Us

A week before Mother went to her new home
She told me of the beauty at the throne
The flowers so colorful and bright
She said, "You cannot imagine what a sight."

It wasn't time for her to stay
So she came back with us to pray
She said she didn't want us to grieve
Daddy was waiting—she was ready to leave

He was waiting for her, a new life to begin
She had seen him at the tunnel's end
Gone from this earth but not my heart
I'll see them again when this world I depart

Everyone that came to her room
She told about the flowers in bloom
Her last wish was granted from above
To see her great-grandchildren with love

The doctor had told me two days before
Her weakened heart could not stand anymore
I held her hand and saw the last breath
She smiled so sweetly, not afraid of death

Bonnie R. Hart

Ghosts

Vodka russhin' down my throat
Scream reversed
The car backed into the street
over the homeless person asleep
at the wheel, back on the road
Nowhere to go when always at home
Delivery man brings it to de stable
Nowhere to go
set a better table
Take out a girl on a date
sitting there she looks great
She's in my car
Where is the matchbox
Look in the glove department
A lost Government Bureau
Dresser drawers
of Mr. Ex-president
Who could never express
smiling
The plight of the "dispossessed"

Clay Schonberger

"Little One"

They called her Amy, I call her little one;
She is as warm and bright as the morning sun.

She has taught me much of life;
Of love even during times of strife.

Yesterday she was but a child;
Sweet at times and sometimes wild.

Looking towards her tomorrow's;
Still willing to deal with today's sorrows.

Now a woman of her own right;
Courage and ability took her to flight.

"Little One," how proud of you I am;
A sensitive, caring and loving gem.

I thank both you and God;
For I've become richer than sod.

To God be the glory;
For you are His story!

Cheryl Anne Seese

My Mother-in-Law

My mother-in-law is as sweet as can be
She always takes good care of me
She makes me laugh, she makes me cry
But most of all, she's by my side
She always helps me when I'm alone
She treats me just like one of her own
She loves me, and that I know
And for that, I thank her so
She always shows me that she cares
She's always willing to share
Whether it's something big or small
She always takes the time to call
Even though we're not yet kin
I do consider her my true friend

Janice Carol Spencer

The Starling

A crimson mist towards
shadows flow
Twilight pierces the night
like arrows and bow
A fluttering passion echoes
by night
Whispers the song of a starling's
flight
Elusive dreams soar through
dusk to dawn.
Before his wings no boundaries
spawn.
The tender enchantments of
night belong
Amidst the heart of a starling's
song.

Holly Schultz

Jesus

Oh how wonderful to know
Peace and joy
Comes from above,
Love and laughter
Blessings now and ever after,

Ida Carpenter

Valley Of The Setting Sun

See the Valley of the Setting Sun
shadows dance as the day is done.
I am there and cannot run.

Cold and snow, they are everywhere
covering lies that were spoken there.
No one seems to ever care.

All alone with the Earth and sky
silence broken by an eagles cry.
Why did they all have to lie?

Now a path stretches before me
filled with things that just shouldn't be.
Many trails, they wait for me.

Fear is not even in my mind
for I know what it is I'll find.
I can see, I am not blind.

See the day as the dawn has come
peace of mind as my journey's done.
I'm alive and know I've won.

James McCarthy

Tyrant Shoes

Gazing out across the land
Shadows cast below his hands
Strange sights come before
Piercing his mind to the core
Idle drops of carbonation
Barely wave on his frustration
Comically a jest betroths him
Only to see his face grow dim

Tears bubble behind his eyes
Aches made of bounding lies
Searching for the final part
Which would complete his lonesome heart
Scars set into the bone
By a father not his own
The price for living as a clone
Is to be left all alone

Brian Hagmann

In My World

In my world of empty places,
shadowed minds, with twisted faces.

Yearning hearts that long for love,
blurry visions from above.

The flames of earth are burning fire,
Rising from hell higher and higher.

For I am here, I don't know why.
There is no difference from ground nor sky.

In my world where everyone's dead,
The people aren't real, they're made of lead.

Brenda Bousquet

"Winter Joy"

Snow gently falling to the ground,
snowflakes blowing all around.
Children sleeping unaware,
of elves working with tender care.
Carolers merrily singing a song.
Santa delivering the whole night long.
Presents waiting under the tree,
those presents are waiting for you and me.
The joy of Christmas is here,
everyone's merry when Christmas is near.

Alicia Curtis

Untitled

Wind from the shadows
Settles the night
Like the affectionate whisper
Of a pretty girl,
As the fragrant moments
Gain momentum
As touches lengthen
And motionless eyes
Deepen with study
While two new worlds
Gently collide
Causing unseen ripples
In time.
Saved for the moment
By dusty brown eyes.

John M. Gootee

Semester Exams

Heads are whirling, books are strewn;
Semester exams are coming soon.
I fret, I worry, I dread the day
When tell-tale grades will have their way.
From math and physics I want to flee;
The books and I just don't agree.
How can "X" be two and "Y" be three?
Oh, please explain these things to me.
History too is almost as bad.
Why didn't I read those notes I had?
Did Ferello sail the ocean blue?
And what on earth did Magellan do?
I can't get Latin, no sir, not a bit.
But studying would help, I must admit.
And in English I'm shut in a daze;
What is a sentence, a clause, a phrase?
If I get an "F" I won't ever pass.
Shall I cut that fourth period class?
There's only one question I want to be asked
And that is "Aren't you glad that you passed?"

Joyfully Jane (Jane Martin Johnson)

Freedom School

Children will do creative learning
Self-express inside yearning
Art to create a feeling
This is inside revealing
Show what one feels inside
Picture form of self-pride
Emotion in a drawing to see
Expression of freedom to be
Not afraid to show an ideal
Picture expressions that are real
Minds working for a common cause
Active minds have no pause
Creativity in many a form
Breathtaking like a storm
Just want to be free and live
Not to take but to give
Creative minds saying a whole lot
Look at the talent children got!

Andrea V. Garcia

Star Light...

Venus shine your light this way.
Plant the seeds of love this day.
Love is wanted, love is desired;
aid me in granting me this
love favor.

Amanda Strong

Window To Your Heart

I feel the hurt you feel,
see through your eyes and see such pain
But you say you are happy,
and only put yourself to blame
Everyone depends on you
to help them through their though times.
Now I think it is your turn
to get support in your binds
Someone to guide you,
someone to care,
someone to always be there,
I want to be that someone,
so open your eyes and open you heart
cause' I will always be here,
and never ever part,
I want nothing in return,
all I need is your love,
so please give in and let me help,...
and I'll never let you down!

Alicia Seidl

I Close My Eyes

What I did to make you feel that way -
Saying it was over, you couldn't stay -
Racing my mind to find an answer -
I close my eyes.

Wanting the time to spend on your own -
Is that the truth, it isn't known -
Searching my heart to find an answer -
I close my eyes.

My heart is filled with what if and pain -
There are no answers, myself I blame -
Sleepless nights of wondering why -
I close my eyes,...and begin to cry.

Jonathan Bryce

Leave Weave

Oh this tangle
Said to be a web
With a tear
We call weep
And the worry
  of repeat

I walk the strands
Searching the net
For the catching of
My own doings
I feed like a pet
As on and on
  I weave
That's life until
  I leave...

Jeffery Roy McVey

For Mark - Eyes Of Love

I know you child,
so fresh and sweet of face,
though in my mortal vision you
dwelleth in another place.

Only your eyes speak, not lips
nor wave of hand, nor quirk of brow.
your mind knows what I know not,

How I love you
yet shan't receive requited love
but God's leave.

Cynthia Blounts

Mustang

Behold! A pale horse
Running through a canyon
Free of man.

Mane and tail flying,
Galloping with the wind.
No restraints.

Plunging down canyon walls,
Fording streams of water.
One with nature.

Blue sky, sweet air flowing,
Green grass for gazing.
God's creature.

Western sky blood red,
Shadows on the canyon floor.
Herd sleeping.

Jane A. Pierce

Coming Home

Curly locks a bobbin,
Running in the wind.
Watch out my little man.
or, you'll skin your shins.

I know you see your daddy
coming down the street.
Mommie wants to meet him first
But, come along my sweet.

Jane E. Jensen

Forever Lost

Deep in the forest I run away
Run away from what has gone astray
Catch me, catch me if you can
Closer it came the longer I ran

As I gaze into the black sky
Angels of mercy are standing by
For they know that this will be my last
Stone on the pile of life that I cast

Thunder and lightning strike the ground
I can feel the presence all around
I struggle with myself to escape the hold
From something that wasn't foretold

Deeper and deeper within myself I lie
Feeling the internal tears I cry
Now I take my last scream
For it has got me or it may seem

Now my body lies dark and cold
Upon a forest bed I can't withhold
As I close my eyes to feel one last tear
I see what killed me was my own fear

Carli Horner

Eternal Embrace

They gaze into each others eyes,
Smitten by the smiles,
Each face glows with excitement,
Each heart skips a beat,
Each heart beating as one,
Feeling the closeness...touching the moment,
Each touch feels the warmth,
the passion, the love
In a final embrace...the love comes forth
To be one forever...in an Eternal Embrace.....

Barbara A. Sherin

Washed Away

My insanity is on a wheel, spinning
round and round. Confusion from others
I steal, as they peel my emotions off
the ground. Though I sit and watch
and wait as my thoughts get polished
and primmed. 20 ccs 40 ccs I inject my
infected broken mind.
My addiction is of great multitude
I have no need of waist. I'm
prisoned by my attitude and watch
my life turn to paste. I remember
a young boy, gathering in a
school yard of fears. My enemy
stares, my areas condemned. I
hide a bleed tears of stone. Now
I sit oceanside, draining my life on
a beach. I've rolled the dice, I've
made up my mind. For some kids
I hope this will teach, for with life not to
play. The tide rolls in, then I'm simply
washed away.

Dillman Sean Thomason II

The Bright Summer Sun

The bright summer sun,
rising in the eastern skies,
bringing the bright day.

The bright summer sun,
soaring across the blue sky,
lighting the dark earth.

The bright summer sun,
falling in the western skies,
bringing the black night.

Daniel Coes

Sun Flower In The Aqua Blue

Silently the smoke clears the screen
Revealed is a young spirit
With a clear makeshift view of pleasure
Unlike that of the beast who hears only time
The tick of the lovesick chest
Then went the imagination
Dried up love and a magician
Pick a flower from the lapel
What's it say about the divine?
Listen close while it whispers
With patience in your stomach heart
You knew all along so you placed it home
With a twist of the wrist
The tick of the lovesick chest stopped
The flower was the key
the passage to the other side
Now smile as the sun kisses
The pale face of the once dead
Walking out of the foreign movie
Fallen in some love

John Allin

My Life

My life and his life are as one life.
Our feelings and doings are shared as
on life. Together forever we will
always be one life. We will always be
together, for the rest of my life, for
the rest of his life. Together we will be
always and forever for the rest of ours lives.

Frankie Mae Deloney

If I Should Hear The Call Again

The falling leaves surrounding me
remind me of a distant past,
so filled with pain and misery,
with dying friends...and broken hearts...

This endless search for my lost youth,
this never-ending, silent pain,
could I once more heal someone's wounds
if I should hear the call again?

I hear them calling me, I see
their faces filled with pain and fear,
and in their hands I see the blood,
still warm, in spite of all these years.

A walking wounded I've become,
a prisoner of my own pain,
and my release will only come,
if I should hear the call again...

Ines Rivera Acevedo

A Phantom In The Night

I gazed across the brightest midnight sky
Remembering the darkness of the moon
The feelings of immense, impending doom
That now did seem to fade in yonder nigh.

I know not why the night can make me cry
For there I see in peacefulness the moon
Can tell a thousand tales, it sings a tune
So beautiful, we hear but when we die.

The truth, I know, is that I hide from light
I know that I'm afraid to see my face
I do not want to know what it would tell.
But when I look into the raven night

My still-spent spirit then can find its place
And then it is, I truly see my self.

Arthur Sobczyk

Reflections

Your attitude in life
    reflects what others see,
Much the way a mirror
    can image you and me.
For someone else to see a smile,
    there must be a light that shines.
The good things done from time to time
    leave reflections in the mind.

Barbara Nickelson

Guest Commentator

I look at the glass and see me
reflected as I sit on the couch
a passive vision implanted

amidst the action and movement
laughter, screams, fear and fantasy
playing out on the small tv screen.

I watch with rapt attention
interactive in all the events
ghost guest commentator
spontaneous critique no replay.

How reflective of life it feels
until the projective lights go out.

Clara M. Frieder

My Baby Blanket

Baby born on an April morn
Received a blanket all nice and warm,
She was lucky it was not torn
The baby fit the blanket in perfect form

Lovingly made by her great-aunt Claudine
She was an aunt not so mean
Creative, kind, and just plain keen
She wanted the baby pretty when seen

The blanket had many special flowers
It helped the baby sleep her night hours
She was not afraid during daytime showers
Cuddly, soft, and security were its powers

Now the baby girl is quite grown
The blanket is still neatly sewn
Her own dolls are kept in a cradle down
Wrapped securely in this cover of renown

Allison Nawoj

June

Spinning figures confused
reality is near
not at all amused
a lost love I fear

The day will come too soon
our dream I have awoken
a month away in June
my heart will be broken

As memories fade away
I know I'll be his past
Because he'll never stay
This kiss may be the last

Amy J. Barton

Gloom

The gloom approaches
    reaching out its deathly hands
How should I avoid it
    or should I take a stand
It stares at me from afar
    waiting to make its move
I see it grow impatient
    debating on what I'll do
Every second I collect my mind
    gathering my defense
It wants to be hasty, come at me now
    but it has more sense
As I prepare
    a death battle awaits
Finally I flinch
    open up the gates
My power flowing fully
    I engage upon the air
Bewildered, for a second,
    by something never there.

Jesse Brown

Life of Love

The love of life
Or life of love
Which of the two is greater?

The love of life is surely fine
and altogether good
but without love, life is not good

So, life of love is better.

Jason G. Crabbe

Nature's Wonders

Clouds darken the sky
Rain begins to fall
Lightning flashes and thunder crashes
But we're able to face it all

Mist in my eyes
Sun upon my face
My shadow follows me around
To my hiding place

The sky turns blue again
Flowers begin to grow
Birds, we can hear them singing
Rivers begin to flow

Fish jump out of the pond
Frogs leap from shore to shore
Bees buzz and they are not the only ones
A neighbor knocks on my door

Clouds darken the sky
Rain begins to fall
Lightning flashes and thunder crashes
But we're able to face it all

Alicia Colson

"America"

America, america a melting
pot, many beautiful colorful people
all in one pot, different kinds
of clothes customs and many
attire. Just make you realize
that America is a great Empire.
America, America land of the free,
There's know other country that I would
rather be America, America
a melting pot the country my brother
father uncle serve, and never forgot
America, America what a melting
pot, freedom to walk talk and
that means a lot
America America land of the free,
there's know other place I would rather be.

Dorene Cooks Abdelkhalk

Tears

Crystals of sadness
Pool at my feet;
The petals of roses crumble
To lie in pain
Throughout the lonely night.

Sands of love
Sift through my fingertips;
Waves crash against the shores of my heart
But do not touch.

Diamonds of the night,
Deathly still in gloom,
Carry stolen light
And die in torment,
Never to laugh.

The moon in the sky
Cries on moonbeams,
To illuminate the sadness,
As tears flow down my cheek.

Christina Mize-Jette

We Need New Poets

We need new poets:
Poets who can see
With the eyes of Science,
Beyond the obvious.

Sophocles long ago looked at the Aegean
And Matthew Arnold from Dover Beach;
But I saw a composite picture taken
From the Galileo spacecraft
As it left our solar system.

Looking back from there,
Our earth was a blue dot.
A tiny blue dot! Nothing more!

Then, like North Sea Tide,
The spacecraft retreated, its batteries dead,
Down the vast drear edges,
Not of a sandy beach, but of unimagined
Melancholy light years of dark silence.

"Ah, love, let us be true to one another";
For beneath the world of old poetry
Lie the quanta, and Heisenberg's uncertainty.

Edward R. McGrath

I Was So Proud to Be a Pumpkin

I was so proud to be a pumpkin
Plumped with pillows in an orange shell
My mother created the costume
And I was glad she did it well

That night I went door to door
Showing off my special frock
I knew they would smile
So I didn't fear to knock

All night I ran in the dark
And I never was afraid
I got bags and bags of candy
To sort and share and trade

I enjoyed myself immensely
Everything seemed to go right
The night I was a pumpkin
Was for me a special night

JoAnne Baese

Earth's Diamonds

To walk, to run, to feel, to ski[
Pleasures unthought of
Before my movements clipped.
Some consolation found in
Seeing the dewdrops cluster.
Like the rarest diamonds found
Frozen by natures fancy
Into the rarest gems.
The sky at night
Bedecked in navy blue
Holds yet more diamonds
In her beauteous locks.
Yet the diamonds
That hold the greatest worth
Are those reflected in the eye
Of one that's loved
And lovingly returns
The sparkle of these diamonds
In her lover's eye.

Edith T. Hillman

Release

Show me how to release thyself "I cried"
Please please; I've tried God, I can't
Do it all by myself
I must repent! I confess, "I'll do my
part", and please you do the rest.
Every time I push please pull; "I cried"
I must release!
God says:
Quiet my child, through Faith
Your soul I will restore
As long as you promise not to close
Thy door.

Connie M. Papion

"We Are All Alone"

Don't make me go to sleep.
Please I won't go and complete.
I can't care to obtain fortune and fame.
Is their someone to blame?
Can this be one persons shame?
I am afraid to live.
Others are afraid to die.
Someone please take my hand.
Someone please show me where to stand.

Jason P. Stoughton

A Mother's Prayer

Dear God, up in your heaven so blue,
Please hear my prayer tonight.
I have a son on the battlefield;
Keep him safe till morning light.
He is just eighteen, Dear God,
Just my little blue eyed man.
It seems only yesterday,
That I led him by the hand.
You'll surely know him, Dear God,
He's blond and very tall,
He has a kind, unselfish heart
And winning ways with all.
he doesn't want to kill, Dear God
For, by your book, I taught him so;
He is just a happy, carefree lad,
Who will soon older grow.
When you visit his foxhole tonight,
I pray he will be sleeping in peaceful bliss;
Touch a finger lightly to his brow
And let him dream it's mother's kiss.

Emma E. Parish

Life's Harvest

Our movie screen the idle mind,
past images we'll see.
Evoking scenes thru memories,
unfettered thoughts your key.

Use caution whilst you wonder why,
as danger courts this task.
Frustration's surely close at hand,
obscuring answers asked.

Futures cast within this mirror,
show fruits in life you'd reap.
Reflected then proceeded seeds,
whose destiny you'll keep.

Resolving echo's yes! or no!
these options yours to make.
This time elapsed whilst you reply,
foretells each route you'll take.

Bruce Allen Siems

Prayer Of A Simple Man

My dearest Lord, Jesus
Please hear me if you can
And answer if you will
This prayer, of a simple man

My life has been so lonely
I have traveled a long, hard road
During my life my sins were many
I now carry a heavy load

My drinking has driven me crazy
The drugs have driven me insane
It seems these years of living
So far, has been in vain

Today, I come to you Lord
Upon my bended knees
Giving my heart, and soul, to you
Forgive me, my Lord, please

I believe in you, with all my heart
And beg you to understand
Please answer this old simple prayer
This prayer of a simple man!

Charles S. McGary

Untitled

Dreams are like sandcastles
plan them in your mind
mold them with your hands
into your own private design.
But if a storm comes through
they're gone, never built the same
blown away through the air
your hands once felt.
So you get up the next day.
Mentally blueprint one more...
Hoping this castle will be strong enough
To withstand the next storm to come.

Brenda Wilson

The Ascension

I ascend to our "secret place" on
petals of the sweetest abandon.
With you beside me, above me,
beneath me, I am enveloped in the
purest form of our ecstasy.

I soar ever higher and higher, and
when I plummet back to reality,
it is you who caresses me, enfolds
me——and as I see the depth of our
passion reflected in your dark eyes,
the ascension begins again....

Christine M. Harmon

Chewing Tobacco

I took a chew of tobacco,
Reckon what I done?
I got sick, turned green,
And died,
All rolled into one.
They say it takes a man
To chew that stuff,
So a boy I'll always be.
For if I took another chew,
They would have to bury me.

Dickie E. Troxell

Untitled

This night brings quiet
  Passing
Filled with gentle wind and light
  Moon and stars,
But here shadows miss my thoughts
  My way.

I wonder at this age
  at my time
So glad that there are things that men
  will never know
So glad that reasoned mind
  will never fully comprehend
  A shadow or a star.
That even now
  Magic my be found
  In a trodden moon.

So glad each trembling day
  still may bring unmeasured wonder
In a cricket,
  A remembered smile.

James T. Hubbell

Apollo

A bright green hue,
paints the sky,
the shade beams familiar, blue?
Yet none could see,
or,
retrieve the key,
there are mountains,
at an impossible slant,
magical fountains,
scraping the coast,
of a purple ghost,
Their stars are made,
to never fade,
but all would die,
and that's the great lie

Jeff Borgardt

Desert Daybreak

Waking, bronzed, red-glow
painting pinkly, in passing,
wild, white, windblown
fluffies.
OLD SOL climbs,
reaching ever higher,
glaring at his backtrail
the deafening silence
of demonic vengeance;
screaming bitter laughter
at a beaten-down creature;
seemingly saying
in sardonic superiority
"you cursed me...
accursed man!"
resuming toward
the pinnacle of heaven
as sure of each foot hold
as if he climbed there
every day.

Bryan Seelye

Halloween

Happy Halloween,
paint our faces green.
You can have fun,
but keep it clean.
On All Saints Day.
when the sun goes away.
All ghosts and goblins,
come out to play.
When the moon is out,
they moan and shout,
as bats and witches
fly about!

Erica Baruffi

Fatal Decisions

A vacancy of heart
Pain reaches deep
The anguish of reality
So slow to seep

Something was wrong
You fought not to see
Because the effects
Change eternity

Slaps in the face
You tried to ignore
Until he revealed
Love was no more

It touched all near
Magnifying the loss
A separation of love
Regardless of cost

The house still stands
No blood is spilled
Yet hearts cry out
A family is killed

Donna Leverant

Mt. Elbert

Many steps up
   over the dust-slickened rocks

An inviting slumber
   amongst the highest of evergreens

Across a bright
   snowfield of white
     tinged with mountain blood

Many steps up
   higher into the thinnest of air

Elbert welcomes
   with gusty winds of mountain spirits

Many steps together
   together and apart

An acquaintance
   may blossom into a friendship.

"The Traveler" (James G. Maki)

"Daybreak"

Coldness swept its sheet of warning,
Over the countryside to show morning.
Homes and hollows opened their eyes,
To meet the sun's awakening in the skies.
Power and mighty has the wind unfold,
To shake loose the sleeping leaves so cold.
Crashing clouds in the sky,
Only form pillows to be low and lie.
Beneath the sun's magna heat,
Over the field of golden wheat,
And the wind still cries daybreak,
For man and a life to make.

David F. Drzewiecki

Wishes

How "I wish you had the wings of an angel,"
Over land, over sea you could fly,
You would fly to be with me, my darling;
These tears I would no longer cry.

How I wish I could hold you and kiss you,
And sing my sweet praise to your name;
For I know from the first time I kiss you,
Our two lives will not be the same.

How I wish you had wings of an eagle
And would seek me and find my sweet nest;
For I know there'll be two happy people,
On that day when the East meets the West.

I've waited so long for you, darling,
And I've wondered, "Will love ever be?"
Then God found an Angel, so charming,
And I know he will bring her to me.

I wish there were more people like you
In this wearisome world where we dwell;
Then true peace would at last be our virtue;
For through God's blessed grace, all is well.

Clayton G. Moseley

"Why Am I Me?"

There is a big world
Outside of this room.
I know — I've seen it.
And here I am.

There are many people
Out there in that world.
I know — I've seen them.
But, I am HERE.

There's mountains 'n valleys
And oceans and rivers.
I know — I've seen them.
Yet, HERE I am.

But where IS our world,
And why so many people?
How so? Do you know
Why we are HERE?

Oh, we are all somewhere,
And we are all someone.
But how — how did I
Come to be ME?

Fay Brookins

As Winds Blow Cold O'er The Water

I sit by the lake, and think of you,
   our precious son and sweet daughter,
How lonely I am, without them here,
   as winds blow cold o'er the water.
I think of your dear, each time I see,
   fish swimming to flee the otter,
For our love has died, it's destiny,
   as winds blow cold o'er the water.
I think of our love, and see a vase,
   gingerly held by the potter,
He finds it broken, hurls it away,
   as winds blow cold o'er the water.
My memories of you, remind me dear,
   of lambs being led to the slaughter,
I've blocked you out of, my entire life,
   as winds blow cold o'er the water.
When you cross my mind, once in a while,
   I see the days of the squatter,
Take all the man's got, he down and out,
   as winds blow cold o'er the water.

David R. Clukie

Life Of Abyss

Formless void;
   orbiting our subconscious
Lost souls
   searching for life

I am among
   the innumerable Godless
Stabbed cold;
   loneliness knife

Pain within;
My unbearable sadness
   grips me
   stealing my smile

Lonely death
of my life's directness
Pain free;
   poisonous vial

Brandon Gregory

Time

Speak not to me of growing old
   Or time so swiftly passing by
Of fearing naught and being bold
   You cannot know the thief that lies.

For yesteryear a river bright
   So promise filled with endless time
Has tumbled madly always right
   And stolen what I thought was mine.

Had I but known that torrent would
   Take all I loved and held so dear
Time swindled me because it could
   Make all my days a mindless fear.

And when I reach this river's end
   To find a shore and join the sea
Time will laugh and mock me then
   It knows despair that should not be.

So speak not now of growing old
   'Till you have run this river's race
For sure the thief has left your soul
   Since time had fixed your heart in place.

Edith M. Stanger

Missing Person

Lost
Or is it found
How do I look?
How do I sound?
For when I look, there's only white
And when I cry, I cry at night.
Lost
Is what consumes me
Aches my bones, races through me
Come run my maze of rage and madness
Of hate and doubt, of puzzled sadness.
So, pick up here and drop off there
Do I look good, do you care?
Please look some more, have some hope
Search the closets, sweep the floor
I know it's here, it has to be
What did I lose?
That's right, just me.
Carolyn Kavanagh

Untitled

I sort out my feelings
Or hate I thrive
Neglect my emotions
A liar am I

Buy your clothes
Put them on
Call it pure
But its not

Just an image I portray
Just an image it will stay
Just an image quick as gone
Just an image that lives on.

I hate to love
I love to hate
I have no regrets
I've made no mistakes.

Chanted my thoughts
Danced in my moon
Wallowed in pain
Salt in my would
Holly Bussey

Rain

Can be warm as friendship
Or cold as anger
Can be soft and gentle
Or hard as hail

Drawn naturally to the earth
Lays on top of the ground
Penetrates deep inside
Trying to germinate life

The earth wants the rain
The rain gives itself to no other
They are attracted to each by strong forces
Together they are as natural as love
Albert Arruda

It's Hard To Let Go

Oh how she will be missed
Only the ones that loved her will know
Oh how we miss our mothers
And yes it's hard to let go

From the minute life began for us
Our closeness began
With the beating of her heart
She gave us this new start

As the new start of life
Starts to grow to be strong
It seems that the strength
From her she gives is gone

It's a sad thing you know
And this is why it's hard to let go
But for our mothers
Our love will grow and grow
Bonnie Hanks

Florida

Wind, blowing cold off the lake, no more
Only the heat of the sun
Beating down upon my head
Sweat trickling down my brow
Running down my back
'Til my clothes are wet
And clinging to my skin
The sun, turning my skin more brown
more wrinkled by the day
My hair whiter
But....
'tis truly paradise.
Anne Lee Assante

Time Warp

Without traveling away, leaving
Only growing away
Our search for youth, evasive!
Our sedative for today

Can you go back
To the place of youth
And feel it as it was,
Or the lack?

On a lake shore or street is where
Feet came and went
Winter or summer, so different
Where is a trace we left there?

This was all ours, then.
In my mind it is now!
No recognition from the locals
Of us, or was there a when?
Jim Mample

Untitled

   Set your sights sailing
on a sea of glass
   so calm, so placid, your
soul is whirling fast
   to the purple crystal castle
with a starlight turquoise door
   Then back again you drift
to the warm and sandy shore
Bill Marino

Twelve Roses

One rose to blush your tender cheek,
One rose to quell your sighs,
One rose to catch the radiant light
That's shining in your eyes.

One rose to greet the morning dawn,
One rose for soft sunset,
One rose to thank the Lord above
For the day that we first met.

One rose to share your laughter,
One rose to dry your tears,
One rose for precious moments
I'll cherish through the years.

One rose for being who you are,
One rose for all you do,
And one last rose, my angel,
To tell you, "I love you."
Brian Murray

I Lost A Dear Friend The Other Day

I lost a dear friend the other day
One of this life I once knew and
Now I find it difficult to say, "Yes
I'll come see you some way,"
But, as time rolled on and days grew long
Another year slipped from sight.

I lost a dear friend the other day
Thirty three years of fifty two
Was the length of time we once knew
That one day we would reunite, but,
Instead we continued to write as
The many years did go by.

I lost a dear friend the other day and
Now I hear my heartbeat say — "I let
This friend get away" and failed to take the
Time to say "I love you and missed you today."

I lost a dear friend the other day —.
David C. Hester

A Dream

I wish you had a dream to dream,
One I know could come true,

A light to shine within your soul,
And hope to pull you through,

A dream that would give you strength
To hold your head up high

One that would fill your heart with joy
And be reflected in your eyes

Something you would share with everyone
Something too wonderful to hold

A light so bright within your heart
You couldn't help but let is show
Frank D. Mowell

A Fantasy Declared

In the dark of night
My own heart's delight
Came to me a'creeping
He kissed my hand
And he kissed my mouth
But alas,
I was only sleeping
Bonnie J. Gustafson

"When I See That Woman"

As both of our eyes focus upon
one another it is if I am making love
to her mind and soul. I purge through
her soft willing eyes and penetrate her
craving, yearning soul. It feels like
passionate foreplay to the both of us.
I see her beautiful smile so far content
with desire. I can almost feel the smooth
curves of her body with both of my hands.
She and I definitely longing for more.
I cannot help but to stare, and admire
her shiny, flowing hair that reminds me
of a clear sparkling stream. Her lips I
can almost taste. Her body is of art and
is like the sunrise over the mountains.
The sun illuminates all the smooth
curves and turns of the hills that are
suppose to be there. Two, things I regret
are one, I don't even know her name
and two, her beauty makes her almost
unapproachable.

Gordy Guillen

Goodbye

Come wrap me in your coat
  once more
And spin me with the old
  delicious mischief
Into that Cotton Candy
  world
Where we did naked
  cartwheels
On a moon reserved
  for two.

Lift up the silver
  chalice
That we once shared
  with Gods
And toast our life!

Then tell me how it
  goes with you
Before you fly.

Esi Tremblay

The Pedestal

What do thou dream?-
On thy pedestal so high.
What may I gleam
In the sound of one's sigh?
What perfection knows of
So far from hand's reach
The ordeals of love
That many can not teach.

What deeds place thee there?
So high by one's own cares.
People, one once held dear,
Held firmly still by their fears.
What sorrows lasted,
Untouched upon thy shrine?
An erratic die casted
To rend a woe so fine.

Jennifer Wong

Last Summer

The leaves
  on the trees have changed color.
It's fall
  I am melancholy summer is over.
Last summer
  was especially
  warm for you and I.
We spent time
  in your boat
  sharing, laughing, swimming
  on Canandaigua Lake.
How I laughed
  as I saw you
  pick corn in the rain.
I was happy last summer
  I had a friend as well as a lover.
Memories of you
  and last summer will always be with me.
Fall brings cold weather—no more boat.
  Will you still keep me warm in winter?!

Jessica F. Santora

Cliche

There is nothing except the blue cup
on the table, with white specks.
Dishes splashed on the floor
splinter my feet with ivory daggers.
Through the filmy panes
his shadow follows him to his
truck, dulled red.

Water slips from the faucet,
sliding over my fingers in quiet
wails. My heart pumps beneath the
withered cotton of my dress.

Toward the handle reaches his hand.
Calloused fingers, thick
slide over the steel.
Blood snakes down my legs,
splattering the ivory chips
and my lips sigh
at the smell of burning tires.

Jennifer Sheldon

The Ballet Dancer

I see her twirling, twirling,
On the stage of her dream,
High above on the tips of her fingers,
Down to the tips of her toes,
Twirling her slim body,
Craning her beauty, a swan-like beauty.
In front of millions of beaming eyes,
And thousands of floodlights,
Innumerable applauses, in appreciation of her
  graceful, precise movements,
On the tips of her toes.

Jean G. Guerrero

Rain

Blackness fills the sky
Loud thunder comes and dies.
As the rain pours down from up above
Clouds circle the Earth like a dove.
The rainbow appears, and the sky's so blue
Everyone seems to know what to do.

Diane Pierce

Renewal

The morning dew glitters
on the pink petal of a rose

The morning light shines
the cool, crisp wind blows.

As I step out of my cabin
sipping my tea...
The snow owl hoots
from up above the tall trees.

The birds now sing a new tune...
For spring is coming
The cold nights are
leaving us, Jack Frost
is running, running away.

Brittany Daniels

Saint Luca Day

Quietly, quietly do I creep,
on the darkest hour of the year.
I put on my white gown,
adorned with red sash,
and crown of ivy and candles.
Slowly on a tray I lay coffee
and rolls. I awake my family
from their slumber to eat and
drink this warm treat.

Jessica Reeves

God's Precious Gift

The beauty that laid in my arms
On that Sunday winter morn
Was more than I could ever dream;
'twas the day that you were born.

I watched the doctor with his skill
Deliver you with care.
And I realized the precious gift
That I had come to bare.

For God intrusted you to me
And I feel that I've been blessed,
For tho He gave me only one
He gave the very best.

And now my dear, you're leaving me
And going to start your life.
Today's the day you say, "I do"
To become a young man's wife.

I hope that he will come to know
The joy you've given me
And cherish you as I have done
For all eternity.

Joan Colpaert

Sorrow (A Lover's Prayer)

Now I lay me down to sleep,
Oh Lord, please don't make me weep.
Take away all this sorrow
Make it be gone tomorrow.
So the memory of us I'll keep.

Please don't let him forget me,
For I love him, can't you see?
Please take away this sorrow
And let me be free tomorrow
For without him, I am not me.

Julie Ann Davis

Fantasy Love

She comes alive
  on paper,
radiant,
   deer-like eyes
    and downy hair,
naked,
  wanton,
   and sensuous,
virgin
  on a white sheet,
colored by desire
  and reality,
touched only by
  imagination,
drawn up
  from the deep hollows
   of my mind
    and heart,
     and,...
      now yours.
       Bo Wring

Electrical Outage

I lie next to you
on our bed
in the dark

Waiting for the electricity
to surge once again
lighting our lives

Banishing
the darkness
between us

Tired of waiting
I try to feel the way
back on line

I touch your skin
no charge, no spark, no tingle
we remain disconnected

For a long time
our lines have been down
maybe forever
    Christopher Halvorsen

Rocking Chair

Come little one lay your head
On mommy's bosom.
Lets drift to dreamland in our
Rocking chair.

So soft your hair all
Tousled and fine,
So sweet your face
Lifted towards mine.

Asleep so soon my lovely one?
How good to hold you near.
I know too soon like a resounding slap,
You'll not want or need your mommy's lap.

You won't mind if I linger awhile.
As I hold you close and stroke your hair,
I will always remember the love we shared,
In our rocking chair!
    Allene Hobbs

Living-Now

Life shines/sparkles
  on me
   eyes-tears-trees
Dew on leaves

The sea
  waves-water-wind
Where ever-when

Colors
  bright-reds-greens
Life schemes

Seasons
  winter-spring-summer-fall
Life welcomes all

Dreams
  love-wisdom-faith
THESE LIFE MAKE
    Callie L. Stewart

Impressions

It's magic, magic how it rises
On its silvery wings;
Its big propellers whirring.
You can see the earth receding.
Green, brown and yellow patches
Soon are far below.
And the houses look like doll ones
For they're small and very low.
The roads wind round like ribbons
On which toy cars move to and fro.
It's a magic carpet!
My! How fast we go!
    Ione Peeke

Excelsior

Charging into the fray of life
on galloping steed of determination,
pulsating waves
of vulnerability and excitement
pummeled his armorless being,
now causing him to cry out in anguish,
now to exclaim in exultation.

He sought the center of the thickest action,
entering exposed
into the heart of the maelstrom —
And then returned,
blessed with bruises of growth
and wounds of openness,
sitting tall and triumphant
in the saddle.
    Ben-Joshua Jaffee

Untitled

Shattered dreams and pictures burn,
No matter what the world will still turn.
It's sad to know what is, is not
And nothing is what we had thought.

Our thoughts are lost in endless sound,
In our world, we can't touch the ground.
Hanging lifelessly on someone's words,
A concrete future you think is assured.
Pleading ignorant for what we know,
For what we know we're afraid to show.
    April Strickland

An Ordinary Day

Reflect, if you will
On an ordinary day

From that instant called dawn
'Til the sun comes out to play

Earth's creatures arise
Their day to pursue

Not knowing what life
Will present for their view

How many dreams will be fulfilled
How many plans will fail

Is really not important
From an earthly scale

For as earth turns on its axis
Showing to the sun

The wonders of a universe
When our day is done

As we close our eyes in sleep
We cannot help but pray

That we will live to see
Another - Ordinary Day!
    Grace B. Campbell

Woman With Scarves

A portrait painted in polyester
On a windy corner
She stands scarves draped
across the cylinder of her arm
Who will
buy her
wares?

Season
After
Season
ALONE
The 14th
Street hub
passes her by
Who will approach
this lone soul?
Ask to see a pattern unravelled.
Folded and
Unfolded
Bagged and carried.
    Bonnie Worthman Goodman

Dream Goddess

Night dare not touch her,
Nor take the sunlight from her eyes,
Or tresses of stardust which adorn her
Like a million fire flies.

With worried heart I cry,
"Wish she would walk across my sky,
As nature plays her lullaby
And give her love before I die".

Night do not tread here,
Nor veil in darkness this angelic vision,
Leave the kiss of each glistening tear,
For this dream goddess is my heaven.
    Eugene Chelland

Somebody's Mother

Somebody's mother
Old and Gray.
But remember, she wasn't
Just born that way.

She earned her gray hair
And wrinkles too.
With loving concern
And anxiety for you.

She shared your joys
And many heartaches,
But she was only human
and so — made mistakes.

She was very mindful
of these and so
Would trade some of her tomorrows
To just have you know.

How oft she prayed
Your life would be blessed.
And hope you truly understand
She tried her best

Florence Hackl

Best Friends

My friend Vel
Oh! what a gal
In my lifetime of friends
I found a real pal
you could do the same
If you'd play the game, of life
and take everyone as they come.
You'd gain friendship and love, then some
Blessing from God's love,
From heaven above.

Bernice N. Powley

Concerns Of The New Cook!

Up in the morning and out to work.
Oh! Oh! My legs do hurt.

How am I doing, how do it look.
Well I'll be, you sure can cook.
What was it that you wanted to bake.
Was it sugar cookies or was it cake.
Third period lunch is about to start.
Getting this meal prepared was truly an art.
Look at our students, look at your lines
Will they get lunch, will they have time.
Well my new cook, here they come again
I am sure you cooked enough
Lunch, for period ten.

Eloise C. Jackson

Soul!?

Oh, my tortured soul,
Oh, my tortured soul;
Oh, where can it go?
Humanity once had a goal,
  Oh, where did it go,
  Oh, where did it go,
I asked high, I asked low?
  But nobody knows,
  But nobody knows!?

Bill McReynolds

The Sunset

When the sun sets
off the bay

Signaling the end of
another day

Though the light of day
has passed us by

Shades of pink and
orange are in the sky

Soon millions of stars
will shine

Bringing visions to
your mind

Even though the day
is through

Remember this
I Love You

Josh Boltz

Footprints

footprints in my mind
of when you were a child
learning to walk, wobbly steps
and innocent toddler smile

that first day of school
you were all dressed up
I shed a mother's silent tears
letting go's first lonely step

learning to expand your mind
the value of right and truth
cornerstones, life's building blocks
footprints of your youth

what's gone before, what lies ahead
your years of growing up
memories made, horizons sought
God's blessing, and gentle touch

footprints in my mind
first steps you've walked and run
I'm holding on to letting go
to you, and the you that's yet to come

Jean A. Grensten

The Fairy And The Ladybugs

A fairy lived, in a tiny mushroom.

She had brilliant wings
  of diamonds and pearls.

The mushroom glowed day and night.

The ladybugs that landed on this
  magnificent plant were filled
  with gentleness and joy.

As they flew away their little,
  red bodies turned into
  sparkling silver.

God's smallest creatures lived,
as beautiful as the
heavenly, majestic angels,
because, of one lovely, fairy.

Elizabeth Hall

Anniversary V-J Day 1995

Memories mesh with TV scenes
Of tears and fears and brutal war.
Then smiles and hugs and shouts of joy.
The horror's gone, the strife no more.

When you left for foreign shore
We agreed our lives would cease.
We'd wed when this world once more
Lived in harmony, love and peace.

The years were long, the war was grim,
The past was gone, the future dim.
You wed a new love and smiled again,
For she was now and I was then.

Then war was won and you were free
And asked to spend you life with me.
I loved you still, but trust was gone,
So needed to build marriage on.

When we both bid this life adieu
And joyous, pass through heaven's door,
Perhaps our lives will start anew
And we'll share love forevermore.

Dorothy Goetzheimer

Castles

There are castles in our minds
Of clouds, and gold, and water.
And there are castles that we find
In children, son and daughter.

Castles come in different kinds,
Some place worth in fortune, fame,
While other castles, over time
Bind themselves with wish and hope,
Forever in our brains.

Eric Hogle

Lady Child

With all the curves and features
of a woman, she is truly a child
and though you may see a lady as
she smiles, can't you also see a
frightened little girl? With dignity
and grace laced with elegance she
walks across a crowded room, in
the same room a small child weeps
alone. So many masks with painted
lips trying to cover their real faces,
not the ones you may see, but
the one that feel and hurt. At
times there is joy but also sorrow,
in the child there is sorrow, but the
lady never lets it show. The frightened
little girl stays locked inside as the
lady glides across the floor.

Jennifer Howe

"Dreams"

Sometimes I visit another man's dream
Not taking part, watching the scene
In my own I can fly and do marvelous things
Or suffer and fall, chased by hideous beings

Frightened to death or laughing aloud
A minuscule nothing, or feeling so proud
Kaleidoscope, vortex, a fantasy world
Bits and pieces remembered
While in bed I lay curled.

Barbara Ross

The Poor Man

Sitting on a corner
Of a busy street,
You see an old poor man,
Counting pennies by his feet.
You kneel down beside him
And try to say hello,
But all he does is sit there,
Very calm and very mellow.
Suddenly he stands up,
And looks up to the skies.
You look at his old wrinkled face,
And notice tears in his eyes.
He reaches into his pocket,
And looks into the sun.
He closes his eyes tightly,
And pulls out a gun.
He checks if it is loaded,
He points it at his head,
You yell at him to stop,
But he is already dead.

Justin F. Armstrong

My Mother

The person who gave me life, my mother.
Nurturer, counselor, and my best friend.
Only she is mother, like no other.
We are always together till the end.

Adventures we have each and every day.
Memories that only we two can share.
Many times we work, many times we play.
Together or apart we know we both care.

Feeling that my mother is my teacher,
Showing me things as I proceed to grow.
There for guidance, but never as a preacher.
My support, no matter how high or low.

She is someone I can always talk to,
Whether I'm feeling happy or sad.
She will never laugh at me when I'm through.
And she will never make me feel bad.

When I leave she will be unencumbered,
And our love will continue to grow stronger.
She is someone who should always be remembered,
She is my mother, and I will love her forever.

Amanda Herrick

The Turning Of The Page

Crisp, slash, colors by far,
Numbers quickly flash, how bazaar.
Pictures of people,
Works of art,
A church and a steeple,
The colors dart.
Poems, stories,
Love and hate,
Fights and glories,
Topics to debate.
Gold, blue and red,
Lines and dots,
Nothing being said,
Measuring in watts.
Neon and dark,
Black and beige,
A question mark,
It all comes to
The turning of the page!

Aundra Martin

Rock And Roller

Used to love to travel:
Now my nerves unravel.
So I rarely go outside,
To my hearth I'm tied.
Would rather take a trip
In my rocker
Back and forth from south to north
Is my endless goal
As I rock and roll
Can go places fast
and make it last
Or stay in one spot
which I like a lot
I'm a chair recliner
find nothing more diviner!

Bella Wein

Sherri

I met a women of hair golden fair
Nothing withstanding I had to stare
Her red dress vibrant in sexy song
Could this be the women I long

A face of beauty matched by none
A smile as brilliant as heavenly sun
A master of wit and lady like charm
A sculptured body give goddess alarm

The masses surround this isle of beauty
It's fragrance enticing is thy booty
Many have tried to swim the land
All I wish is to hold her hand

On this thy sweetest day
The only thing I must say
Sweetness aimed and did not miss
I would do anything for one long passionate kiss

Jim Maguire III

Erase The Color Line

When harsh words are said
Nothing can take them back.
But what is those words were said
Just because the color of your skin is black?

But what if your skin is white
And harsh words were said upon you?
Who would you blame it on?
What would you do?

Would you go and blame it on a certain race
or would you blame it on the soul
Who said it in the first place?

We're all the same in many ways
and we all have special gifts that
   we can give away.

So now all we have to do
Is find a way so that when people see you
They see your mind, they see your soul
And not your race as a whole.

So try real hard and free your mind.
Remember we're all the same, erase the color line

Jason Kelsey

Love And Care

A friendship starts as a small seed
  not planted in a row
For it needs space and lots of time
  to go where it must go

In rocky ground or tender soil
  the root seeks as it must
For if that friendship is to grow
  it must find love and trust

With time, a flower is blossomed out
  it's fragrant smell a blend
Which bonds the hearts of those it's touched
  a seal that does not end

No darkened skies ran then conceal
  the worthy thing you share
This cherished bond is not achieved
  without great love and care

John Sauvageau

The Road To Nowhere

The silence is all around me;
Not one dog howls or bird sings.
I've been walking for miles
But no sound have I heard,
Not a dog or a bird.
The one continuous sound to be heard
Is the tap of my own feet
Against gravel.

What have I done to deserve
This fate? I say to myself.
Why am I forced to walk
This road of loneliness?
I have to walk alone.

Holly Scheuhing

My Problems

My problems make me feel dirty.
Not on the outside, but on the inside.
My problems make me feel ashamed.
I am learning not to be ashamed,
because a fire has been lit
and has destroyed everything.
Why do I have to feel the
way I do? You wouldn't
like it if it happened to you.
All of my friends say they
want it to happen, then
they become excited and go off laughing.
Please God, tell me, why doesn't
anybody understand; is it
because my feelings have built a dam?

Jessica Houser

Home Sweet Hell

As I can feel the heat
Of the flame burning my face
I can smell the sweet aroma
Of human flesh burning
With human bones melting
In the internal flame
With their epidermis
Raped from there naked carcasses
Then I saw my father sitting on his thrown
This is more than home sweet home

Derek Ray North

day or night

I lay here in such wonderment
Not knowing day or night
All I know is what's in my heart
And the future brings me light.

Just holding you and feeling you
And knowing the warmth of your touch
My darling what I'm saying is
I love you oh so much

The hours go by slowly
Until we touch again
I want you here beside me
Where our bodies know no end

I lay here in such wonderment
Not knowing day or night
I'll drift to dreams to hold you
And love you with all my might.

Catherine Ertl

A Sister

A sister is a person.
Not always related by blood.
Who will love you for who you are.
She is your one and only bud.

You can tell her all your secrets.
Hidden deep inside.
She knows everything about you.
Even what you try to hide.

Sometimes you will fight.
Sometimes you won't think you care.
Sometimes you'll want it over.
Sometimes you won't want her there.

But then you will make up,
Like every time before.
You know it will happen again.
But sisterhood is never a bore.

Claire Bolander

Untitled

I am here neither to defend
nor debate, nor postulate.
We hold self-evident that each
human being must decide their own
destiny.
To do so with integrity and
fortitude will bring joy.
To do so and be loved will
bring meaning.

Daniel Deakins

Opening Letters

Not to take these literally
(no, no, Gargantuan feat
when drawn from artist's pen)
as thought rings ABCs with gems
mined by Midas point...
for seen inside the alphabet
a way to cross each word
appears signalling hope's message
shining out of season's wreathes
grace has spring-like intertwined
while figuring them out of gold leaf.

Jane R. Harwood

DELIGHT I FIND IN MANY THINGS...

Walking in the Summer rain,
Noisy wee-folk in their play,
The hush that stills a boisterous day,
In waterbeads on windowpane.

In bell-clear tones when Robin sings,
Dew-kissed web a spider weaves,
Red and gold of Autumn leaves,
And fairy-flakes that Winter brings.

A gentle pat upon my cheek,
In glancing moonbeams on a lake,
In happy laughter children make
While wading in a rushing creek.

In wind that plays in willow trees,
And angel voices in a choir,
The crackle of an open fire,
And tulips nodding in the breeze.

In silky strands of milkweed pod,
In sparkling grains of sea-washed sand,
The courteous clasp of Friendship's hand,
And in a dialogue with God.

Anne Shannon Demarest

Butterfly

You're so beautiful when you fly
No place to go just anywhere
Fly so high for you have no cares.
Some would like to catch you
That you know.
But you'll fly away - untouched
Fly so high soar like an eagle
So beautiful you butterfly
No place to go
Just fly on by
I wish I was a beautiful,
beautiful butterfly.

Betty Andrews

Taken By Surprise

It was Sunday morning
  No one to be seen,
To church we were going
  All was quiet and serene,
Upstairs older children
  Their dressing were doing,
Downstairs with the youngest
  The father was helping,
And I at the sink
  My teeth were a washing,
When round the corner
  Bathroom duties the mission,
I was caught by the youngest
  His eyes nothing missing,
When out he came
  His hand on the knob,
With quizzical brown eyes
  A watching the job,
In wonder and shocked expression, he sings
  "Does daddy know you've got those things?"

Belva Shaull

Feeling Homeless

How's it feel too be homeless
  No one really knows
To feel down and out, and all alone
  With no place too really go

For the only thing you can call home
Is a card board box or a park bench
Or worry if you make it through the night

Too sit in a doorway or on a side walk
Just too watch people pass on by
for the only thing they wonder
Is how you got that way

For all your personal possessions
Could fit in a plastic bag
So you carry it around with pride
No matter where you decide too stay

If people would only realize
  or if they only knew
That one day or another
This could wind up being you

John C. Frazee Jr.

"The world gone wrong"

The world gone wrong,
no one is strong
to put up with all

The hate people are creating

The world is supposed to be beautiful
at one time it was a safe place
not too many people being shot: Where it
used to be you could leave doors unlocked

Now you bolt them with many locks

The world is not always safe
elderly people getting beat up
kids shooting kids; for what?
their jackets and shoes

For what is the purpose?
the world gone wrong with many people.

Angela C. Cran

The Invisible Helper

I am the one that no one sees.
No one acknowledges my pain,
yet I am always present.
I am there to lift you up
When you are in your depths of sadness.
I am always patient.
Always there to pick up
What you have carelessly discarded.
There to guide you
when you are lost,
to protect you when you are hurt.
Your pain
becomes my burden,
your health
an investment of my time.

Francine M. Morris

Darkness

Darkness,
No illumination,
No colors,
No sight,
Just black.

If we all live in darkness,
We would all be the same,
All of our features,
Only to be seen by,
Our hands,
And hands are not prejudice.

In this world
Everyone is equal,
Nothing to compare,
But only the sounds of,
The voices,
Even then,
How bright could one voice be heard.

Greg MacDonald

My Grandpa

My grandpa is a genius
No doubt about it.
If he wanted to
He could invent a rocket.
He's tall, he's thin,
he lives in a house.
He's quiet, oh, so quiet,
but he's not a mouse.
He's got a wife
Who takes care of him right
Ad she is, oh, so bright.
He is a math wiz and
Boy is he wise!
I love Grandpa,
No doubt about it.
When I think of him
I just want to shout it.
He is an inventor and a wonderful mentor.
He is wonderful man.

Jennifer Kruse

Ghost Town

They may not be so obvious;
No complaining specters with
Greater-eyes looking for handouts
Of revenge or pity will you
Find floating over the witch-finger
Nails of the floorboards.
Can't ward off these ghosts
They are the remnants;
Disemboweled buckets housing no
More rain water, gears missing teeth
(Upper-cut by age),
Bones, embedded in dirt instead
Flesh, like railroad ties.
Can't number this population:
It expands as the uselessness does
The walls cry, the floors buckle in
Loneliness, the frantic curtains
Flutter in a wind whose language
They can no longer decipher.

Andrew Robbins

The Dead Night

The day is short
night grows cold and long.
The hour is death, everyone joins,
in the meeting of dead souls.
Moaning together in harmony
no one knows why.
The night so dark tonight
we walk hunched over in hurt.
Pale skin, the smell of death
flesh decomposing, bodies rotting.
All together the ring of hate
We all join hands; sit alone.
Dark as night, stench of gone
the smog so dense; something crawls out.
The candle lit blowing in the wind.
The wreath of greed sweeps over the
haunted ground.

Heather Harney

The One

Before things were spoken of
Never understood
Love brushed a cheek
Hope stilled the pain
That nothing ever could

Tears in blue
Bloody and sore
Embraced as God looked down
For all have dreamt and wished
Desiring what has been found

Lay yourself
Into the arms
Bringing comfort through the night
A peaceful calm, an angel
Shines its brilliant light

Surely things are spoken of
Now clearly understood
Love is a gift
From God's own heart!
These two, blessed by the one

Charlene Skylar Paight

The Paths Of Life

Twisting, turning
Never ending.
These are the paths we take.
These are the paths of life.

Some are dark,
Some are light,
Most are shades of gray.

Fraught with danger and delight,
Full of choices,
Filled with obstacles,
Our choices determine the outcome.

And when we reach the end of our path
And leave the mortal realms,
We hope our friends and loved ones
Carry on with their lives
And carry loving memories of us down
their own path.

Joel Hacker

Heaven

A white wood frame house
nestled back in some trees.
Front porch swing sways gently
from the cool afternoon breeze.
Daisies grow in flower boxes,
bright green grass on the ground.
The faint laughter of children
makes a magical sound.
These things are precious,
there is no counting their worth.
Heaven is not up above,
it's right here on earth.

Henry S. Pflanz III

Thank You

Are the words "Thank You"
needed
when eyes meet in gratitude?

Are those words "Thank You"
necessary
when lips smile in acceptance?

Are these words "Thank You"
noticed
when hands touch in warmth?

Nay, nay said the closed world.
Yes, yes said the laid-open heart.

Frances Zepponi

Change For The Better

A transformation is taking place in me
Namely from good to better ... then best
My wagon is hitched to the star of
  perfection

I ascend on the wings
Of wisdom and zest

My human self begs me be careful
Lest I would stumble
Or fall on hard times
But my spirit soars on
Past all of the hurdles
It knows neither limits
Nor space, nor time.

My journey goes on everyday of my life
I think and I pause
And I see inwardly
Evermore of the heavenly beauty
My Father God reveals to me.

Jesseca B. Roberts

Dreams

Walls of blue surround
my vision,
Threatened by this childish
way I've been given.
Settled on the ocean floor,
drifting slowly all the more.

Grief and sorrow above
me at last,
While I sleep and dream
letting go of the past.

Danna A. Blanco

On The Steps Of St. Mary's

If I close my eyes I can almost see
My too oppressive destiny
That speeds to overpower me
   in night, in light, ruby-bright.

The trees around me turn to stone;
In a crowded church, I'm all alone;
If I cannot whisper, I only moan
   through ice, paradise, seen twice.

I confess my sins and try to pray,
But I never mean what I actually say;
I just want some time to sleep and play
   so cold, almost old, never told.

I tried to cry but couldn't force a tear;
I know I feel the end coming near
I just want to get away from here
   thin traces, no aces, quiet places.

My will died so long ago,
I have no other place to go
   deep ice, paradise, lost twice.

Ariana Almajan

The Dark Stares Back At Me

I lie awake in the darkness,
My thoughts are running free.
My heart fills with emotion,
And the dark stares back at me.

When suddenly I'm aware of
A feeling from within
That this part of my life is over
And a new life must begin.

More than fifty years together,
That's a very long time.
I know that you have found your peace,
Now I need to find mine.

Thoughts of the past come forward
As tears to my tired eyes creep.
There are memories that are precious
And memories I don't want to keep.

As I struggle through the feelings
Of this burden I must bear,
I know that God will show the way,
And to him I turn in prayer.

Ethel Dehnart

Hear The Silence

Empty house, ain't it loud,
So much noisier than any crowd.
Look around, how can it be,
An empty house is so noisy.
Hear the ticking of the clock,
Loudly reminding that time doesn't stop.
And that creak, was that the floor,
Or was that today, closing the door.
And that noise coming from the hall,
Was that already tomorrow's call.
And that loud whisper, was that the wind,
Or was that tomorrow trying to get in.
Did the whole house just heave a sigh,
Or was that today saying good-bye.
And that bang, was that a shutter,
Or was that today's final utter.
Strange how all these thoughts commence,
Just by hearing the silence.

Colleen Thesing

Wind Song

A gentle wind blew

I knelt by the pool
my tears had formed
my dreams
my hope
gone

A gentle wind blew

As I gazed longingly
lovingly
into the pool
a voice sang
softly

It touched my heart
lightened my soul

My memories stirred as it led me
away
A gentle wind sang
"It was time...
to let go"

David Pelloso

Night Flight

Come to me my Raven
   My shining, silver bird.

Come embrace me in the night,
   My vivid red and gray,
Splashed against the light.

Come to me my Raven,
   My lethal, silver bird,

Release me to eternal flight!

Jeanette B. Raymond

Some Day

"Mommy read this book to me."
My precious baby said.
My heart stopped, my breath caught
And I was filled with dread.
How could I tell this innocent
"Baby, mommy cannot read."
When all these years I've made up stories
Of knights and fiery steeds.
She can read herself now,
She knows what the words say,
But she wants to spend some time
With me, I can't turn her away.
Maybe it is time for me to toss
My pride away,
And call someone who will
Help me learn to read, someday.

Brenda K. Ivie

Twist, Wiggle And Squirm

I have no legs or bones
My two ends look like ice cream cones
Fisherman use me for bait
But sometimes I escape
My skin is soft and wet
I do not make a very good pet
I like to twist and squirm
Because, of course, I am a worm.

John David Bryan Jr.

Remembrance

When twilight illuminates the western skies
My mem'ry turns to my home and you
In the land far away across the seas
Missing the love and care I knew

The golden marigolds that quiver at my touch
With diamond dewdrops in their petals afresh
And dancing willows on the breeze a-flutter
Nodding and swaying in the nearest cluster

Snake-like boats glide softly by
Splashing their oars ever so nigh
And myriad arrays of twinkling lights
Add sparkle to the fading sights

The butterflies flitting from flower to flower
Bring back the days that we did roam
And the shimmering backwaters lent a glow
To the golden rays that touched our home

Remembrance takes me back to land
And eases the tumult of my inner soul
The Almighty stretches his soothing hand
And calmness engulfs me as a whole

Bridget Thommi

To You

You are my man among men
My king without a crown
The captain of our ship
My unpainted clown

Although we aren't gadabouts
We do like to dine and dance
There's you across the table
Giving me a special glance

Dear, there aren't words enough
To declare my deepest feelings
The only thing left to say is,
To me, you're always appealing

Evelyn R. Lewis

Missing You

Each night I dream about you.
My heart is full of joy and Love for you.
   Each morning and days my heart is sad;
Because you're not here with me.
I am waiting for the day;
We are going to see each other again.
Then I will smile and be happy again.
For now I'll close my eyes and I see;
your beautiful face, your great smile,
and us holding hands, hugging and kissing.
My wonderful gentle love.
   And then I ain't sad no more.
But I wish that you would be here;
With me to hold me close and nor let me go,
With your strong arms around me.
I miss you, my love.
Yours forever. Your love.
Until the day I will see you again.
I love you, I love you, my dearest heart.

Amalia Carbonetta

Tortoise shell cat's tail
Performs plies and arabesques
Feline aerial ballet

Barbara Brandes

Whispers In The Dark

In the still of the night
My heart is filled with tears,
Here in my bed out of sight
Lamenting the torment of years

Pain fills my every crevice
Muscles, bones, and brain,
Oh why must I endure this?
Surely there is solace to gain!

Then somewhere in sorrow's depths
There glows a little light,
A voice is speaking to me
Hold on, hold on real tight.

You are not alone dear
Your spirit only sleeps,
Hold my hand forever
And your soul I'll always keep.

This time is just for testing
Your body is crumbling clay,
Look to me and smile dear
Soon comes a brighter day.

Delores Fore Wertz

The Love I Lost

Crying without you,
My heart fills with pain,
Reliving the memories,
For me to stay sane,
Hoping and praying for our day to come,
When the skies will open and let in the sun,
Gleaming and sparkling,
White as the snow,
Praying on my knees,
Prayers to many to know.
My head full of anger,
My heart filled with pain,
Why did you leave me,
And leave my heart slain,
Now I look back at the pain you
    caused,
But I still miss you,
The love I lost.

Jessica Ferguson

Dry Tears And Silent Cries

I'm a soldier of my souls army
My head is held up high
Although a prisoner of war
No liquid sheds my eye

My neighborhood a battlefield
And I'm on battlegrounds
Surrounding me are obstacles
Mental shackles hold me down

The pain, the stress, the agony
1000 enemies
A war I'm in against my sins
Until I no longer breathe

I can't break down I must stand strong
This war I fight to win
The struggle will help me appreciate
The victory at end

Jonathon Stone Jarrell

"Generation Ex"

Piercing my soul with indignity,
my hands clench into iron fists —
vice-like on the throat of humanity.

Stripping the fleshy skin of courage
I fight for control, for the pride the
    years in my heart —
cutting like a razor
spilling the sap of humanity toward
    the ground.

I stop and wait for the ringing to at
    least yield enough for my sanity
    to sleep and tumble back into my head —

from closed eyelids clenched tight,
a tear streaks my face and I turn away
    in bitter disgust knowing the
    wrong that has been done.

Fading, we are unable to finish
    what we have not begun.

Chris Schultz

Craters On The Moon

I will die as sure as I have lived.
My existence renders my very being.
I often wonder if the life I have
lived will remain, even after I am gone.

Will I leave a trail of broken dreams,
or a path for others to follow?
Will my children's eyes set upon the same
star, or will they focus on the moon?

Never knowing or comprehending all of
God's creations - I will wander forever,
aimless. I shall wonder with a
questioning heart, and an open mind.

I have felt the touch of triumph.
I have seen the heavens burst with
Angels descending. I know of
Miracles so true. I have seen
the craters on the moon.

Heather Gariepy

Saskia

I see in you
my daughter,
grasping her baby crib.

I see in you
a flower,
with a thousand petals.

I see in you
a river,
strong and demanding.

I see in you
a cornfield,
embracing an abundant bounty.

I see in you
a woman,
in life's full glory.

I see in you
the world,
and all that it holds...

Johanna A. Spee

My Child

My child is love
My child is life
He makes me smile
He makes me cry
I hold him oh so very tight
I watch him change
I watch him get into things
I watch him crawl
I watch him walk
I watch him run so very fast
Is he growing up at last
I wonder what he thinks of me
Am I liked
Am I loved
Am I doing all things right
Am I holding on to tight
I wonder what he thinks of me
Am I all that I can be
His Mom...that's me

Joane L. Pappaterra

Brothers We

I'm nothing like my brother
My brother's not like me
Even though you might see other
We won't admit to be
If even once you looked my way
It's very plain to see
That his image you could say
Quite nearly mirrors me.
The measure of our voices
Resounds with perfect blend
If you'd ask about our choices
We'd argue to the end.
I claim to meet life as it is
While he plays hard to get
His gripe is that life's lost its fizz
But I'm not quitting, yet,
Our spirits stand uniquely tall
As really it should be
For underneath this crust and all
My brother's part of me.

Barbara Kinney

Thinking

I am...
music, lyrics and words
harmony
out of tune
Bugs Bunny
in the Bahamas
melodic laughter in Looney
Tunes
the impelling hand
of conduct in symphony
exhaling taskmaster
counseled by my sighs
the forth and fifth hand
on the clock
and the "-"
in tick-tock
guessing
as I wish to believe

thinking of something to say...

a Butterfly's opinion

Lightning

Words have to come from a place
much deeper than words
They have to come from a place
where words never go
  Like subatomic particles
    that appear
     and disappear
      in the void
       too fast for mortal vision
words have to flicker
in and out
  like lightning
   in April
And I have to stand in the dark
  with a kite
  and a string
  and a key.
Janet Rees

Mothers Day

Mothers day is a day for a
  mother happiness.
For the kids it's let's try
  not to make mom mad day.
Dad is the one who asks what
  day is mothers day?
But deep down in his heart
  he really loves my mom.
Mom gets extra special gifts,
  hugs, and all.
Mothers Day is a day to love
  and help your mom with anything.
So for this mothers day lets
  try not to make mom mad.
Amanda Miller

Her Children Rise Up To Bless Her

I have been blessed beyond measure by the
  mother God gave to me.
She is everything, and more, that a
  daughter hopes her mom to be.

She taught me to cook, stand straight,
  be strong, kind and such.
She imprinted my life with her
  permanent, loving-touch.

I can see she went without, so her kids
  could have their wishes.
She put up with our messy rooms, and she
  usually did the dishes.

Although we were close, we did not always
  see eye-to-eye.
But she was forgiving when I hurt her,
  or made her cry.

Now "Her children rise up and bless her."
  Thus, I pronounce this decree:
I have been blessed beyond measure by the
  mother God gave to me.
Ann C. Glenn

Mother Made Cookies

Mother mixed the sugar and flour with love
Mother cut the dough into shape, with care
Mother baked the dough with patience
Mother passionately decorated it
Mother proudly presented cookies
to the world on her 16th birthday
Connie Sandoval

"The Jungle Chateau"

Filled with dread, I went to where
Most men would fear to tread
Land of the cursed jade idol
And the shrunken head
Where barbaric tribes beat angry drums
Of human skin and skulls
Boiling pots of flesh
Make no mistake, they're cannibals

At the jungle chateau

Last night I watched the fog
Surround the outskirts of our camp
Near bubbling pools - malaria
Thriving in the damp
Unseen beneath the mists
But we all knew what was there
Beyond the trees
The leering face of death
Hissed "YOU BEWARE!"

At the jungle chateau
David Vollmar

Dreams' Turn At Bat

Dreams, more than synaptic meanderings
More than wonderful waves
Far above gossamer mind images
Every day a free prospectus.

A path of aims toward stubborn steel
Slow, steady persistence brings reality
Compromise perhaps a later approach
Flexible leniency of the game.

The other side of the picture bolts in
Burrs, doubts, and hubs snared
Feelings of release and easement
The whole of satisfying wonder.

A long reach for so-called impossibles
A long walk where angels enter not
Where winds are briskest, dreams riskiest
Long-term advantages to dreamy goals.

A thing called eventuality
End of challenging airs
Golden daybreak in the morning
Heart's balm in full reality.
Beth Sudduth Wills

Untitled

Overhead a full moon
moon, moon, my two year-old grandson says
—the dark side there but not seen

In Sarajevo
the moon's light brushes
charred walls, spills into streets
a woman and son look out
Bosnia
dark in their eyes
and behind their eyes

And farther behind
that
which has no name
Grace Herman

Childless

Childless mother mourns sadly;
Month after month after...
year after year after...
the loss of her unconceived child.
Guiltily, sadly, jealous;
she seeks a different destiny.
Child abuse? Birth control abortions?
Childless mother mourns sadly;
sometimes crying inside when she sees a child,
mostly she just looks away,
a mother's love dormant in her soul.
Gayle Whittle Jackson

Too Late For Emotion

They lie side by side
Mismatched and angry
Over some misunderstanding!

But her love for him
Is pure, deep and total...
And he's too sick and hurt to care
So he just takes her for granted!

Mismatched?
Indeed!
But soul mates nevertheless!

The one who makes you cry!
Sometimes holds you in his arms
While you cry...
Jack Ferreira

Shadows

Ceremonies of tranquility
Mind at peace
Continuous versatility
Windows watch
Soul at rest and no release
Truth and lies at dread
Dawns decade
Mummified emotions
Open thy heart, free thy mind
Speak of silenced opinion
Confide in new faith
Attempt to expose inner shy expressions
Absence of flesh
The past is put to rest
Day of contentment
Defy unlawful judgement
Rescue freedom
Reason to know, curiosity to follow
Embrace the forgotten
Weave a web of light, light shed in the shadows
Debra Anne Seeley

Mike

Mike is the boy I look up to
Mike is the boy that I like
He is my knight in armour
Whenever I dream at night
He is the one I'd love to hold
Hold in my arms so tight
And never, never let him go
Until the night is bright
Yet I cannot have him
Because he is not mine
To have and hold to love or cherish
Until the end of time
Ann S. Capizzi

All The Same

Dogs and cats
Mice and rats
Are all the same to me
Pesky gnats
Are the same as bats
No difference I can see

A truck and a car
Can both go far
So they're the same to me
Buses and trains
Both do the same
What difference could there be?

The only difference in the world
Is found in every boy and girl
The difference is not hard to "see"
For it's simply personality
One may do this and another that
And it's inside you where the difference is at!
Jason Jones

Immortality

If from the heart, we could obtain,
Mere mortal words, our best refrain,
Meet on paper, with pen and ink,
Once in this life, make people think,
Rhyme with meter, that sings a song,
That beings keep, however long,
And they shall pass, their days grow short,
Like winter wheat, at last report,
Immortal means, eternal fame,
That burns so bright, a mindful flame,
Your memory, will give these lines,
Journey through time, for other minds,
Endless are words, properly set,
Remember this, lest we forget,
It's from the heart, it's better yet.
Jeri Heidrick

Come Out

Come out of the dark,
 meet me in the sun.
 Don't you know 2 hearts
 can beat as one.

Come out your shell,
 why do you hide.
 Come light my fire,
 we can take a ride.
 I wish I could tell you
 how much my love grows,
 I try to tell you, but
 it never shows, so here
I am,
 awaiting your call.
 I'll catch you forever,
 every time you fall.
Come out of the dark
 meet me in the sun and
 our 2 hearts may beat
 as one.
Angie Pacheco

Your Point Of View

Your view, a step or two from mine,
May differ more in thought
Than words can ever show,
But let me spend some time with you
And soon I'll know.

I may see the spaces
Fit between the lines that draw
Those silhouettes of loneliness
That stress a world of awe!

But you might say,
In quickened thought,
That space is nothing there.
But I would say at once returned
That space is brightened air.

It's more the way you look at life
Than how it passes by.
It's more the space between the lines
That spells a truth a lie!
John A. Fosse

Truth Cuts

Through the jester
Marked and violent
Dark, choking on his tears
It shines revealed, obvious
Why did I never see it?
Natural, flowing trance
Gliding, spinning
Into the lowest lie
Fire searing
Rapist breaking out
Dead-end grooves
Guilt cuts
Jimmy Lutz

There's Another World In The Sky

There's another world in the sky,
Made up of cotton and fleece,
Cats and dogs, horses and frogs,
Ducks and swans and geese.

Roses and carnations and tulips,
Raccoons and zebras and kangaroos,
Ferns and trees and eucalyptus leaves,
It's a garden, not just a zoo.

Floating above the world;
Racing through the sky.
Just look up,
You'll see something by and by.

An imaginary place,
That isn't imaginary at all,
Just look up,
Winter, spring, summer, and fall.

It's so much more,
Than I can say,
So when life is just too much,
It's splendid to get away.
Catie Almirall

Flag Of The Free

I'm glad and honor this flag of mine.
Made of cotton with stars and stripes.

Rich of a history
Of these great United States.

This is the flag of hope
For those fortunate souls

Around the globe.
Flag of tears and joy

And the symbol of freedom above all.
As it sways with pride in the breeze

Over countless buildings
Over numerous ships on the high seas,

And standing firm and tall
On the moon where we first landed,

As the final frontier in space.
Portraying images of peace, liberty and democracy,

And reminding all its people
That they are free

To pursue their dreams
As that of all immigrants in the U.S.A.
Eugene Conrad Chorosinski

I Want To Splash In The Puddles

I want to splash in the puddles
made by the rain
I want to laugh when I jump
and laugh when I fall
I want to reach for a whale
and run from a moth
I want to hear every sound
I ignore through the day

I want to say yes and no,
yet know not what they mean
I want to sing songs of Pooh
caring not how I sound
Every day will have sun
and every night will have peace
Every moment that I live
I want to be with my daughter
Brad Davis

Fallen Leaves

I wish to be like fallen leaves
Lying on the water
  Their colors at rest
   Nestling one another
   Forming a pool of tranquil beauty

Above them
Gray skies linger
November's chill remembered
  As a sudden gust of wind
   Disturbs the quiet waters
   and sends autumn leaves dancing
once more
  before their death and decay

I wonder if they are rejoicing?
  And can I do the same?
Gary Scarbeary

"Love Is Eternal"

A baby's smile, a child at play,
Lovers strolling on a sunny day.

A flower in bloom, a bright full moon,
Thunder and lightning, a cozy room.

Mountains and Rivers, Valleys below,
Snow flakes falling and solitude.

Peace from all wars and harmony,
Love for each other eternally.

Growing old together, a reminisce,
A soft little sigh, When we kiss.

A shelter to keep us safe and warm,
and never doing each other harm.

If there's a need let us be there,
to show each other that we care.

Thanking God together for loving hearts,
for creating Angels, the earth and stars.

For giving us life and liberty
and a love for each other for Eternity.
Glennis Colbert

Untitled

There is a breeze, and the
lovely sea, and in this
world is lots of anger and
hostility.
I dream, I pray for the
day - we join in peace in
a heavenly way - and not
let our skin color get in
our way
Betty J. Brager

Total Love

Jesus brought me here.
Love will keep me here.
And I made up my mind to stay here.

The mind can't do nothing if we're not here,
Love is the reason we, are here.
Love is the healing of our soul.

I totally love you,
I really do.
Constance Davis

Love Is

Love is not blind
Love see's the soul that
  is really US!

  Love see's beyond,
the facade we paint. The
part we hide for no one
to see. It brings out the
best in us.
  Love is forgiving,
it is strong enough to
let us grow.
  Love is not prejudice
or bigoted....it knows
no color, race or creed
  Love is freedom, acceptance
and the right just to be me!
Carol A. Wold

Love

Love is special,
Love is sweet.
Love is what makes life complete.

Love is giving.
Love is kind.
Love is joy and peaceful mind.

Love is laughter seldom tears
Sharing and caring throughout the years.

Love is more than words can express,
  but mostly LOVE is Happiness.
Johnny Strong

Sonnet 27

What is love?
Love is a crow
Or a bright, white dove.
Love is something that grows.
Love lasts forever.
That is what some believe.
Love can be very clever.
Sometimes it can deceive.
I think love is an emotion.
The possessor holds the key.
They must put it into motion
Or else it wasn't meant to be.
Love is a gate.
Some get through first and others must wait.
Allison Utrup

Untitled

Thou shall be an abundance of
Love in thy air
and Peace throughout thy ground
which we stand upon.

Kindness and Forgiveness shall rise
and give Life, Love and Happiness
forever and ever.

If He that is Love
shall attain unto our needs;
the Faith and Love shall overcome
Discomfort and Anger...

And the bond of our loved ones
shall forget not the heart of the world.
Jay Nelson Parks

"Tomorrow Lord"

If there be a tomorrow,
Lord lend it to me.
I will take my tomorrows,
And share it unto thee.
All of my tomorrows,
I will try to see,
All of the sorrows,
of others in need.
Because tomorrow belongs to you Lord,
I will give it back to you.
Betty R. Faile

Tick, Tock

Listen to your ticking clock, please dear
  Lord don't make it stop,
Just to hear the tick and tock of that
  beautiful sounding clock,
Thru morning light and evening shade
  it seems to say why it was made,
To tell the time of each long day the
  ticking of our lives away,
And when that tick and tock does stop
  then you hear your coffin lock
Dead and buried you will stay your
  ticking clock has passed away.
Arthur Picone

Upside-Down Smile

Oh, this little clown
Looks happy enough
With the smile on his face
And his knapsack full of stuff!

But, oh he can't see
What's happening under foot,
Nor feel the load
On his shoulder he's put.

With holes a-comin'
In the bottom of his sole,
And the load he's a-building,
Oh where is his goal?

Oh, he's loose alright
With shoeless sore feet.
His load is too great,
And problems he can't meet.

So, think a-fore you
Throw in the towel;
And just face the music
Before you go on the prowl!
Barbara J. Allen

Star Gazin'

  Star gazin'
Lookin' into infinite
  for something
that I know nothing of

  Just lookin'
at the stars
  relaxed, peaceful like
Enjoying life, takin' it all in

  Only sitting
and waiting
  for the next impact
of this life to come

  While the stars
fly high
  and I sit below
the mighty ORION'S grasp

  Just waiting to appear
back in the sunshine
  of this life again,
at some near time.
Brian Gilbert

Little Fellows Sharing

They marched up the path and stopped,
Looked at the big tree there with ladder.
Climbed up into their tree house
Inside was so much better!

They could look at fields of wheat,
Which would become seas of blue.
A tall slender tree became a spaceship,
Watch out clouds, we're coming through!

This clubhouse held their treasures,
It became a fort when they needed battle.
It was a station when they were policemen.
A wagon when they herded the cattle.

A great retreat, home away from home.
No parents, no rules, no hassle.
But every once in a while Sister would come,
Bringing dolls and junk for a castle!

Joyce Hubbell

Untitled

Gone are the roses
   Long, long, gone
Gone is the laughter
   Long, long, gone
Gone is the sudden enchantment
   of spring
Gone is the ecstasy
   Long, long, gone
Grey is the daytime
of what once was warmth
   only the memory
     and that almost gone!

Hortenze Kopple Heisel

"Addiction"

Locked in a hell with no answers
Locked in a hell slowly die
Falling slowly to no where
They all sit back and ask why

The rage and anger inside me
Eating away at my soul
Losing touch with reality
The days go by I get old

Tired of going in circles
The battles have taken their toll
The war is almost over
The story still untold

So I gather up all the pieces
My final quest has begone
Using all that's inside of me
for a war that can't be won
for the war of one on one.

Guy P. Mone

Memories

We all have memories of things in the past,
Memories that will always last.
Memories that just make you cry,
Of short "hellos" and long "good-byes."
Memories of times with family and friends,
Times you wish will never come to an end.
Memories of things we always said we'd do,
But most of all, memories of YOU.

Elme Vivier

Homesteads

Old forgotten homesteads,
little piles of rubble,
all that's left are shadows
hiding in an old man's mind.

The apple tree is gone.
The barn has fallen in.
All that's left are shadows
hiding in a little child's mind.

Memories don't know time
like shadows and old men.
They stay alive in wonderland
like Alice and Peter Pan.

So maybe old homesteads
and memories never die
as long as there's a little child
still hiding in an old man's mind.

Johnie Sue Hall

Lovely Things

I asked, "What is a lovely thing?"
Little David, newly two,
said, "My hand,"
And held it up to be kissed.
Jonathan, about to be four
said, "I know, raindrops -
raindrops on my head."
For David's second turn he said,
"My other hand."
Jonathan made more choices
"A butterfly, a bluebird,
a pretty flower, and finally -
broccoli."
And now, reflecting back my choices are easy.
Lovely things....
Jonathan and David.

Erma Carstens

Accept Me:

I walk with my head held high.
Listening for your voice, I wonder why?
With the blue sky above, and the ground below
I do not know where I am going to go, or
do I really care.
All I want is for you to be there.
I want to be near you.
I want you to accept me for who I am.
I want to feel your arms around me.
With you I always want to be.

Is it so wrong to love you?
Is it so wrong to tell you my love is true?
Questions, questions is always on my mind.
Answers do not come to me at anytime.
Think about me each day I live.
Because my love to you I am willing to give.

Janice Haugabook

Haiku

Shepherds of heaven
May have been sharing their sheep.
Floppy clouds float by.

Elizabeth Hulbert

The Spirit Of The Song

If you wake to find me gone,
Listen to the music of the song.
Feel the chords, the sound, and the blend,
Watch the conductors baton upon the stand.
Notice crescendos and notes on every line,
Look at the metronome to keep the time,
My heart may not beat along,
But I am there, within the song.
I cannot play again with you my friend,
But just remember I am in heaven,
And I play in the greatest symphony of all,
The one created for
The spirit of the song.

Allison Hicks

Each Of Us

You and Me
links on a chain, beads on a string
drops in a bucket, knots in a rope
   You and Me
part of something larger,
    grander,
    better,
    sadder,
    gladder

Each link is unique,
each bead is its own color,
each drop is so critical,
each knot is required,
each of us will contribute.
Each of us (us) ((us))
   each of us
Blocks in a tower, bricks in a building
   petals in a rose,
   people of the world

Anna Mracek

Soldiers

My emotions
like weary soldiers
come marching back to me

   Exhausted
   Exhilarated

   I count their numbers...
   no fatalities

Honorable soldiers
they come back to rest
   learn from mistakes
   prepare new strategies

Happy to be of use,
   now wiser...

My emotions
like exuberant soldiers
go marching out from me

Dana Ralston

Highway Dancers

They stand there
Like dancing girls
All in a row,
Wearing multicolored
Autumn clothes,
Ready to shed them
At the slightest hint
Of a late autumn breeze.
Shapes vary from
Thick to thin.
Their height from
Short to tall.
But no matter
Which shape or height,
All stand with arms outstretched,
Reaching for their place in the sun.

A. Perry Adams

The Gift

The sky gazed down upon the meadow
Like a mother watching her children
Nod off to sleep.
The sun was like a great orange eye,
Blinking out its vision as it disappeared
Over the horizon.
The animals were quiet, realizing the
Serenity of the moment at hand
And honoring it with their silence
And reverence.
The stars blinked into view, one
By one, casting their brilliance
Upon the sight in the center of the
Glade as the child stood and
Proclaimed his gift with a laugh,
Like the clearest crystal bells.
His hand rose up, reaching out for
The moon, offering his gift of
The lemon yellow flowers to
The world.

Christie Satterfield

Walking Through The Paths Of Life

Crash, in the distance
Lightning flashes, skies roar,
Ears of many hurt with this disturbance.
Rain drives wildly forcing me from my path.
Wind howls and whispers
Deadly secrets to my ears
Calling me in taunts and leers.
And I come not knowing
What lies in the future.
Remembering the pains of the past
The wind of the storm tells true.
Lightning lights my way.
Like a fawn
Seeking its mother
I seek a new dawn...

Amanda Leigh Miller

Untitled

Love is a great feeling
It's a feeling of securement
It's a feeling of support
You know that someone
Will always be there
When you need them most

Heather Nelson

The Lovers

Hello Darling,
Life had given me a hard heart
And it was hard for love to start
I thought my life would never be complete
But God has given me someone to meet
Who has softened my heart
And allowed love to start
Darling, you have made my life complete
And with all my heart I promise to treat
You with all the love and kindness
That will keep our lives out of a mess
And we can begin to live out our lives
To the fullest and without any strife
I will love you forever
And Darling - hurt you never...

Love Always

Dale Roach

Father To Daughter

Well, my daughter, I will tell you,
Life for me has not been so easy.
It's had nicks in it, and needles,
and places with no carpet on the floor,
wood.
But all alone, I have been climbing on,
and reaching into the sky, and turning
corners and sometimes walking in the dark,
where there was no light.
So, my daughter, don't you look back;
Don't fall down on the steps
Because you will fall harder.
Don't fall now,
For I see you climbing, darling,
and life for me has not been easy.

Anthony Ford

The Words I Never Heard

You always tried to make
Life easier for me
I recognized that from the help and toil
You sacrificed for me

In years gone by, I tried to show you
All my love and voiced it often, too
I longed little words of love to hear
But alas, to commit to voice
Was not at all your choice.

Now those years are late
And lost words of love
Are very out of date,
So please don't tell me now
As it is quite too late
To hear those you left unsaid
For you know I cannot hear you now,
Now that I am dead.

Irene N. Wehde

Love

Love is a wonderful thing,
It's when cupid takes you
Under his wing. You
Could be left with a
Broken heart or even a
Smile, but in the end you
Will realize that it was
All worthwhile!

Dana Blackman

"Cherish The Woman"

Within her heart her beauty
lies, let us not forget those eyes.

As blue as the sky can be
bigger than you and me.

In her soul she often cries
no one likes teary goodbyes.

Of her heart mind and soul
the latter two she can control.

Time and time again she will
Turn her head from sin.

As her patience is often tried
she will never run and hide.

If you know of whom I write
please don't let her from your sight.

Jay DuBois

The River Ends

The river runs silently and deep,
Let the quiet monster stay asleep,
Till the dam breaks its slumber,
Then its cascade roars like thunder.

Amid the noise of churning water,
The setting sun creates such splendor,
A rainbow arched above the mist,
Seem to muffle the roar to a hist.

Further down stream it changes course,
Meandering with much greater force,
Everything in its path raked by erosion,
Unnoticed amidst such monstrous
commotion.

The giant serpent moves through plains,
Ever swelling with the summer rains,
Like tiny eels the streams join ranks,
Penetrating points along its banks.

Tamed by nature it ceases to be,
Like a wonder engulfed by the sea,
A new cycle has silently begun,
Miraculously drawn up by the sun.

Cliff Robinson

Effluence

Let the rain come down!
Let the dust of living
stream from me in rivulets
in torrents
down to the sea

Let the rain come down!
And wash my cares free
that I may find peace
in the soft damp
of morning sun.

Elizabeth Hall

Acme

Now I will leave thee
Lest this wondrous fulfillment
Be the death of me.

Alice Faye Singleton

My Shadow, My Shadow

In an ageless age, so young you
left this earthly place. Near death
you reached me. You came in love;
strong in smiling spirit, yet weak in
a body that was soon to be shed.

Oh, my lovely shadow! My memory
fades and yet propels me. Presently my
tears fall upon moistened cheeks, a warm
salty taste enters my senses as I yearn
for memories of your presence.

Again chaos enters my heart. I drift
backwards in deep sorrow. I hear a deep
inner urge, crying inside as my soul
acknowledges your trusting presence.

Now, I can remember looking
into your trusting calm-fired
eyes—like a deep lighted mirror.
I sense a bridge, a communion
with the luminous world beyond.

Ina C. Adams

Gone...Too Soon

Gone...too soon
Left...so suddenly
Suffering...no more
Physically...you left me

Gone...too soon
Young...too young to die
Heaven...called for you
Leaving...questions as to why

Gone...too soon
Love...you left behind
Forward...we'll meet soon
Constantly...you're on my mind

Gone...to soon
Rest...in peace
Always...in my heart
Memories...will never cease

Gone...too soon
Far...away from me
Now...my guardian angel
Yet...always my beloved mommy

Annette Ho

Desert Days

The blazing sun wilted the dry land
   leaving all things thirsty
   for a drop of rain

   dead brown grass crunches
   breaks
    under each footstep
   like burnt black bread
   stuck to a pan

   each leaf curled
   like hair burned by a cigarette

   trees tilted downward
   toward dehydrated streams

   And the land wept
    hot dry
    tears of dust

Belinda Jo Hays

"The Boxes"

The boxes...far back, and behind
   lay closed within my mind.
They must eternal lay they be,
   closed...only summoned out if by me.

Thy lids are sealed with lock tight,
   viewed only seldom...if I might.
The contents painfully hidden away,
   refused entry until today.

Inside each box...a story told,
   remembrance chills thy body cold.
Not one...or any, could ever understand
   all the boxes secrets...as only I can.

A million boxes...pushed far back.
   desire to keep hidden...forever I lack.
Never easy to view...never easy to see,
   the contents of those boxes...those boxes,
   hidden within the "mind" of me.

Gladys A. Walker

Heart-Felt For The Heartland

People going about their business, not
Knowing what was yet to come.
Little children playing with toys, whose
Lives had barely begun.

It's sad to see so much crime,
In our streets these days.
We have to stop and wonder,
Will this pain ever go away?

It will be hard and it will take time,
but as a nation we will heal.
We know evil did this to us.
This was not God's will.

Just remember, God is with us always.
He knows our grief and feels our pain.
He was crying right along with us.
We were so blind, we thought it was rain.

Now, President Clinton, you are our leader.
Can't you change the rules?
Please give this nation what we need the most.
Let us have prayer back in our schools.

Denise Shindler

Alone

Awake, I listen,
Knowing-
Beside me you sleep,
Your innocence
Showing.

Asleep, I dream,
Fearing-
I cannot escape,
The shadow is
nearing.

Awake, I watch,
Caring-
Wanting you with me,
This ghost to be
Sharing.

Asleep, I die,
Screaming-
I cannot wake up,
Though I'm only
Dreaming.

Diane J. Storie

Faces

You look at her and
know her thoughts
in times of deep despair.
Born together, looking alike,
and sharing so much more.
Childhood memories
of terror never leaving you.
We wear many faces but
there's no face to call our own.
Keep looking to paint a future,
knowing deep inside
there just isn't one
to replace the faces
you learned to wear.

Dale Davis

"In My Heart"

Your words and advice I've always
kept in my heart
that's something I'll never part

You taught me the gift of giving
you taught me the meaning of living

But in my heart I know, that one day
we all must go

There's not a mountain that can't move
the ground you walked on,
you were even there the day I was born,

But now you're gone and it's hard to believe
It's hard to accept that your illness
caused you to leave

But in my heart I know you're in good hands
We'll meet again in the Promised Land

Juanita Wimberly

The Blossom Within

Trapped in a shell
Just waiting to blossom.

Bursting forth! An array of colors
Yet to be seen.

The trials, tribulations
Undaunted, unrelenting.

Yet these necessities must thrive
And endure I must.

For when properly honed and cultivated
I will burst forth!

An unsurmountable beauty!
Perseverance and strength my adornment.

The blossom within.

Barbara A. Dannemiller

Thoughts

Live your life by helping others,
listen or ease a pain.
Help someone in their sorrow,
in this you will always gain.

Beauty in life is always around us,
don't search for it diligently,
But 'do unto others' and always be kind,
and you will always, beauty, find.

Ann M. Kenney

Life And Death

A day has passed again
Just like the days of
Fifteen years that I've lived.

And I am still alive.

This is so amazing,
Truly incredible.

While so many people are dying
In the outside
Or in my home,
I'm alive

Living without
Thinking of people
Who exchanged their life with death

To make me live.

Jung Lee

"Here I Lie"

Here I lie with soul and heart.
I've served my time and done my part.
The Lord took me into his hand.
If only they could understand,
That life is not a continual show -
You live your life, and then you go.
I said my prayers to the man above
Just to show Him my Christian love.
Because of these things, here I lie.
The Lord picked me, of all, to die!

Charlie Ridgeway

Anticipation

I'm filled up with anticipation.
I've lost all my concentration.
I feel so eager, it must show.
All who look at me must know.

I feel like a kid on Christmas morning.
I start to giggle without warning.
I wonder just what waits for me.
What could the biggest "package" be?

I go through life in rapt suspense;
I wonder if I seem real dense
To those who say I do not hear,
But only smile from ear to ear.

I fear they think I must be daft,
That I don't know what's fore or aft.
It's just that I enjoy life so
I can hardly let a moment go.

Life is so grand, I know it is;
I wake each morn and say, "Gee whiz,
I think that I will celebrate,"
And thank God for what I anticipate.

Gloria Apfel

Essence Of Time

Yesterday was never here
It only dwells in the past
Tomorrow never comes
For when it does, it is today

And today always is . . .
A never-ending here and now
But now is your last chance
To make the best of today

Diana Len Henderson

"Of Water"

The ocean laps against the shore
Its tongue is licking every pore
Of sand and shell and rocks and green
The hungriest water ever to be seen.

A friend to fish and fowl and earth
It's been around since everyone's birth
It covers much of our land
Making the presence of water so grand.

From where did the water come
A mystery to all or to some
A cloud burst at earths creation
Water deposited in every nation

So many reasons we'd love to know
Did all of our original water come from snow
And while our creator took a nap
Was there a melting of the arctic ice cap?

Janice E. Butz

Life Is Life A Glass Of Wine

Whether it's fruity, sweet or dry
It's lovely to behold.

With many flavors and colors
It's better when it's old.

So smell and taste and savor
You can't just look, be bold.

Take up your cup and drink it dry
Or it will stale and mold.

Jackie Larson

To Jesse

I dream of you so much
  It's like you're still alive.....
  Space inside —
  Partly died —
  Left on the road with you.....
My buddy —
My music man —
So much left to
  Teach you
  And share
  And learn from you.....
What a man
  You would have been
I miss you. My angel.

Henry C. Beukema

The Leader

The banner unfurls to the eyes of all
Its brilliant colors ablaze,
Raised above so to stand tall
Above the murky haze.
And so the light that shines upon it
Beside it now turns pale,
The flagpole just a narrow picket
A flimsy piece of rail.
Yet below its reign of red and white
Of crimson and of bleach,
None raise a hand in hate or spite
And none of him beseech.
For he is King and Lord of all:
The man who passed the test,
Yet they cannot, for wont or call
See he's just like the rest.

Daniel Richards

Real Love

Real love is unspeakable
It's a feeling that you'll know
A whisper in your heart
That clings unto your soul
Real love is a silent thing
Shared with only two
Inside your heart begins to sing
And never are you blue
Real love is a binding force
One that makes you blind
Never will you feel remorse
It is always kind
Real love is a spirit
In perfect harmony
And if you ever hear it
Your soul will be at ease

Diane Drishell Waddell

Wilderness

Wild, unkind, furry animals
Itching, scratching, sleeping people
Listening, frightened, little animals
Digging, hungry, grateful rabbits
Eager, tiny, just born deer
Racing, dancing, wonderful sheep
Nested, tired, fearless birds
Endless friendship, endless time
Sightless dread of fire
Sunset's night light in the sky

Ariane Benito   1994

The Game

I blinked my eyes and shook my head,
It wouldn't leave my sight,
And there it sat
Atop my ball
A smirk from left to right.

I quit the game long ago
I thought I'd seen the light.
For me the game became a chore,
My coach became the blight.

Yet there it was
My favorite ball,
And there the little guy sat
To remind me of a friend I lost....
Ignored and lost respect.

With twinkling eyes and a pointed cap
The leprechaun seemed to say:
Remember baseball, it's just a game,
A game that made your day.
Cherished memories that made you a man...
And they'll never go away.

Barrett Burke

Sparrow

Petite, supple, and seemingly frail,
Lasting in rain, snow, sleet and hail.
Sparrow how do you sing,
The alluring tunes you continually bring.
Out in the cold and hot,
How do you live in such a small spot.
I wish I were you thinking your thoughts,
Maybe have eggs with little black dots.
I wish I could do the things that you do,
And live my life exactly like you.

Joshua D. Fowler

One Wish

If I had one wish to wish
It would be for freedom's sweet bliss

To tiptoe to your room in darkest hours
And pave your path with fragrant flowers

To place a kiss upon thy brow
To hold you close here and now

If I could wish for love so true
My wish would be for only you

If I were free of duties ties
I'd fly with you through starry skies

If I could wish away the chains
I'd dance with you in springtime rain

If I could wish a wish today
I'd wish for you to always stay

If I could wish one wish for you
I'd wish your dreams would all come true

Carrie Mastronade

"My Last Home This Side Of Heaven"

When I first moved into a "Highrise"
It was a questionable day indeed.
I never thought in my wildest dreams,
My home I'd ever leave.

Somehow when I was young.
And busy as a bee,
In my home I'd stay forever,
No matter how bad things might be.

Little did I realize,
As the busy days flew by,
That God would call my loved one home,
To be with Him in the sky.

But life is full of changes,
Nothing ever stays the same.
Thank God for the Grace He gives,
When we call on His Holy Name.

Every comfort of life is mine,
Even the view from the window I see.
I'm thankful to God for "Highrises"
And paradise my next home will be.

Ann Cooper

Solid Foundation

A Foundation is something seldom seen
It support the super structure with
   Its huge iron beams.

The storm may come and toss about
But this building will hold, it's
   strong and stout.

Almighty God is just the same
If you believe in Him and trust His name

Then you to the storm of life can stand
While you walk with Him and hold His hand.

Hildred E. Paxton

The Red Rose

A rose is red
It smells so good
Sweet just like sugar
It makes me feel to
Drink some wine
I feel good when
I am fine. I love
Roses and they love me.
Red red wine you make me
Feel so fine.
Do you love roses?
You can give them to
Anyone you love with
Chocolate. Now, isn't
That nice? Roses are
Cool it makes you feel
Good are you in the
Mood to take a rose in
Your hands and think about
Something good?

Bidjawatie Ragoobeer

The Wind

The wind is like a kid,
It runs all day,
And likes to play
The wind is like a kid.

The wind is like a slug.
It doesn't like to play.
It's as slow as a bug.
On a cool spring day.

The wind is like a cat,
It moves with lots of grace,
It flies like a bat,
You can't carry it in a case.

Brent Gauspohl

Lightning

Lightning is dangerous
it is not fun.
It is really scary
Oh, please bring out the sun.

Lightning is hot
it can burn down a tree.
I wouldn't want to go near one
because it can burn down me.

Lightning is yellow
the sky is blue.
I wouldn't want to be burnt
if I were you.

Lightning is zigzag
thunder is boom!
I wouldn't want to go up in an airplane
because it would crash and go boom!
Boom! Boom!

Danielle DeLuca

Feeling

Nothing left inside
My feelings came out that I tried to hide
Staring into nowhere without a decent care
Just sitting alone in a place unknown
The room bright, the hopes risen high
I find out the rejection, as I let out a sad sigh.

Ginger Herron

"Love"

Love is something greater than life
it is more than just a feeling.
It's something that's inside your heart,
that can never be taken away.
No matter what you love is for,
it is sure to be true.
For if it is the real thing,
the empty hole with no love,
will be filled with you.

Amanda Curtis

I Saw It In The Sun

Light so bright
it hurt my eyes

Light so bright
all of God's heavens
opened up wide

Light so bright
peace flowed
through with
all its might

Light so bright
serenity was
impossible not to feel

Light so bright
"The Great Amen"
could be heard
world wide

Light so bright
with heart overflowing.
came the image of you,
saying, "go on be happy.
to thine own self be true"

Janet Minnick

Choose Life

Life is like a roller coaster
It goes up and down and all around
Living is hard, death is easy
Choose life and take a breather
Please don't throw your life away
Therefore drugs will lead you a stray
Once you die, you can't come back
Take my advice and be on track
Let's start serving the almighty Lord
It will be a blessing on one accord
Life is serious, so don't be curious
When you choose to live or die
Don't make the choice when you are high
Choose life right now today
Cause tomorrow you might not be here to stay
Choose life! Choose life

Gail L. Shelton

O Ye...

O ye faithful
O ye bound
O ye store
O ye shop
O ye money
O ye buy
O ye clothes
Buy and buy
O ye bankrupt
O ye no more.

Emily Howe

What Shadow Is This?

What shadow is this of mine, which hides the sun itself?
Looming high and dark, towering over me.
What illusion of light darkens my world?
I turn to the north, the east, the west and the south.
I have the compass, I have the directions, I have the map.
And yet what blindness overcomes me
that I cannot face the sun?
I have heard of the power of the sun.
The brightness that dispels, the heat that warms.
What senses do I need to feel the sun?
I know it is but my shadow;
I know it is but a cold and senseless thing
that feeds on me and grows...
What strength does it weaken?
What weakness does it make more strong?
What shadow is this of mine, which hides the world itself?
What shadow is this of mine, which shrivels Me up and becomes me?
   Anitha Murthy

Take My Hand

I walk in darkness 'neath the shining sun:
Looking, searching for the right one.
As I travel far across the land,
Will you be there and take my hand?
To a crowded city with cold granite stone,
That somehow still makes you feel alone.
To a distant desert, with its drifting sand,
Like a fiery furnace, will you take my hand?
To the frigid Northland and its never ending snow.
To towering mountains where only eagles dare go;
Even they, flying so high, have a mate
Somewhere in that sky.
And maybe sailing on the high sea,
Will you take my hand and be with me?
To a steamy swamp, with ever watching eyes,
The sounds of animals and their strange cries.
Even a sparrow is not alone, in a tree
Will you take my hand and walk with me?
   Charles H. Small

Where Were You When I Was Your Friend?

Where were you when I was your friend?
Looking over the ocean for what might have been?
My love stood by you through thick and through thin.
And I heard all of your words begin and then end.

Where were you when I was your friend?
I gave you hope to start over again.
I made you see that your world didn't have to be
So dark, so cold, so lost and lonely.

Where were you when I was your friend?
Your heart was still warm but your love was held in.
I needed you more and more every day
But your love kept slowly slipping away.

Where were you when I was your friend?
You never knew I had my own wounds to mend.
I had no one to listen to me.
I had no one when I set you free.

Where were you when I was your friend?
Where were you when my world did end?
I needed you as you once needed me.
But you were still looking over the sea.
   Cynthia D. Hyatt

Look Out World

We're all caught up, we have our bills all paid,
Look out world, I think we've got it made.

Have a car in the driveway, and the kids are being fed,
We can finally start to save for our own little spread.

Work so hard for our money, just to pay the rent,
Seems before we get them, our paychecks have been spent.

At last, I think we're even, and it's time to get ahead,
Has to be the first time, since the day that we were wed.

Then suddenly I hear it, the telephone starts to ring,
Familiar voices begin talking, I refuse to comprehend a thing.

"Honey, call a wrecker, because I didn't get too far,
Don't worry about the deer I hit, you should see the car!"

"Mom, I need some money and this really cannot wait,
The prom is next week Saturday, guess what, I have a date!"

"Your daughter's teeth need braces, as I've suspected for awhile,
The procedure is expensive, but it will improve her smile."

"Your dog is in my yard again, and he dug my flowers up,
I do expect you'll pay for them, since you intend to keep that pup."

It seems we'll never get ahead, although we try our best,
Whatever made us think that we could be different from the rest.
   Debbie Piette

Mind, Body And Soul

MIND - from the day of birth I am taught the fury, torture and long suffering of my black ancestors. Made aware of my heritage, and the long legacy of accomplished dignitarians. By their example, I know what I can do, and what I can be. In my mind I know that I am black.

BODY - It's not the color of skin that perceives blackness. But walk, talk, attitude and feelings towards those that tried to keep you suppressed. In my body I know that I am black.

SOUL - From the core of my heart, I can feel the hurt, anguish and pain that was exempted upon every black man and woman. It touches the center of my eternal being to know that there are some people who can accept what has happened to us over the past hundreds of years. In my soul I know that I am black. To be black is to be proud, and not be ashamed of our tempest past. There are some of us who do not wish to remember their past, and try to shy away from who they are. And their are others that try to duplicate and copy us. Black is not a race of color it's mind body and soul.
   Curtis L. Wright

Summer Night

I came by tonight, from the place where I live, to the place where you live.
Because the rain had seemed to wash the earth,
And the scent of the earth filled by nostrils, and all my senses came alive.
And the moon would peek out from behind a cloud now and then,
And it was as though it would burn on a portion of my brain,
And I would think of how it feels when you hold me,
And how I feel in my heart when you say you love me,
And my need for that,
Like my need for the moon, and the sun and the rain.

I came by because the evening came after the rain, on a cool summer breeze,
As if to block out the day, which was tumultuous, and painful.
And with the peace of the evening came the yearning to be with you,
As we've been a thousand times before.
To share that peace with you who understand.
   Dorothy Burns-Putman

Just One Precious Baby

She was lying there wrapped in a blanket, her
little face was all aglow.
　She was born with aids, her little body was limp,
would she live, they didn't know.
　Oh Father in heaven, this can't be your will for
this baby to suffer this way.
　If no other prayer ever gets answered, please
answer this one today.
　She's not even mine, but the pain that I feel, is
tearing my soul apart.
　What was her mother thinking, where was her pride,
her feelings, her love, her heart?
　Surely she knew what would happen, when she starting
tempting fate,
　This innocent baby is carrying her sin, she can
overcome, it's not too late.
　Send this baby an angel Lord, wrap his wings around
her little bed.
　And if you must take someone away, Lord, would
you please take me instead.
　　Glenda Meeks

Summer Breezes

Whisps of summer breezes on the air.
Little children playing everywhere.
Sunshine and laughter in everything
The time when birds sing and bluebells ring
And people relax and share memories.
As birds go soaring high, we sit here, just you and I;
Sharing stories of summers past and glances cast at one
　Another. Letting memories control our actions.
Now we've moved so close together there's no room left
　Between us.
Now our hand are linked and we move even closer.
Just as our lips are about to brush, my baby cousin starts
　Making a fuss.
As I pick her up, calm her down, we both realize the truth.
You lean against a tree, look at me, and smile.
I guess some things were never meant to be.

　　Amanda Gerken

Flowers Of Spring

For spring they make their first appearance
Little but growing are they throughout spring.
Our eyes can't keep up with how fast they grow.
When do they get so big and where was I?
Each one grows at their own pace meeting up in the end.
Rows of them with more every day.
So beautiful are they.

　　Julianne Guercia

Listen

Listen to their voices, hear the words they say,
Listen to the stories they're telling us today.
Can you hear the meaning disguised amid their tone?
Can you hear them saying that they feel all alone?

Listen to their laughter ringing through the air.
Can you see the suffering showing in their stare?
Listen to them crying when they think no one's near,
Listen to the message displayed in every tear.

Listen to them screaming, pretending they are mad.
Can you hear that through their tone they're saying they are sad?
Now that you have listened, tell me what to do.
I want to help but they've a wall that I cannot break through.

　　Anna Christine

Send Me The Soulless Graduation Subject List, On The Manichean Ungodly Sacred Brain?

Send me the soulless graduation subject
List, On the manichean ungodly sacred brains.
Don't you know sweetheart "that" it's the god EA who makes it rain.
So, will you send me the soulless graduation subject
List on the manichean ungodly sacred brain?
"So," Darling, I can love on proudly with the souls of the
galaxies originally of the plain.
From the Milky Way Galaxies of god Masai created the divine couple
Under the beautiful Eurydice birth by producing the bright heavenly
Peoples with the eternal of life the first.
Then god Masai sent some children on through the god Rig-Veda created
Biachholes for the spaceship's trips to the Lumerians Earth.
So, will you send me the soulless graduation subject list, on the
Manichean ungodly sacred evil brain.
So, Darling, we can love on proudly with the souls of the galaxies
originally of the plain.
So, Darling, we can love on proudly with the souls of the galaxies
originally of the plain.

　　Harold Gabriel McNairy

Waiting

Memories drip through my mind
like the rain drips through the air outside,
beating a syncopated rhythm upon my brain.
They slide down,
into the sewer of my conscious.
They wait in the dank, dreary silence.
They wait.
They whisper softly to each other of things forgotten,
waiting for the day when I will have
the courage to open the sewer,
find them, bloated and vaporous,
and bring them back out into the light.
To shake them out and dust them off.
To rediscover what I already knew.

　　Grace Doty

Echoes Of My Mind

Memories drifting through my mind,
like shadows seen in a twilight rain.
Some have a joyous and lasting warmth,
others lurk and pounce with a sudden pain.
Your children's births, and so swiftly grown,
your mother's love, and your father's pride
The nightmare war of freedom for another race,
the journey to hell, the friend's death, and you cry inside.
The long slow healing, the readjusting of my mind,
to relearn my humanity, and in the end find faith.
I have a gentle loving wife, who walks by my side,
She helped me find God, and walk with a smile on my face.
As I prepare to enter the middle years of my life.
My wife and I seek our happiness and serenity.
We take great pleasure from life, and joy from family.
Steadfastly believing in God, in preparation for eternity.
As I sit gazing out over the green and gold ocean,
Sometimes it seems to me a faint and distant dream.
But it is only memories and echoes of memories,
that only God and I can perceive, or so it would seem.

　　Edward L. Hilliard

To My Mother

You are calm,
   Like a lake that is placid and still.
You are strong,
   Like the eagle that builds its nest in the hills.
And when I think of you,
   I think of lovely music
Softly played upon a master's violin,
   Of blooming flowers,
A symbol of terrestrial beauty.
And dearer,
   Than all the wealth the world could hold.
More precious,
   Than all its stores of silver or gold,
You are loyal and true.
   Home is my great mansion
When you are there;
   And life, a melody,
Beautiful and rare.

Doris W. Dixon

Yours And Mine

Life is a moment in time
Life is yours, Life is mine.
You can hold it in your hand
You can walk with it across this land.
Sharing it with someone is nice
Still others choose to be like ice.
There are so many ways to look at life
Sometimes it's taken away from another with a gun or a knife.
It doesn't seem worth it, who are these rebels without a cause
It doesn't seem worth it, blood splattered on our walls.
A mother is crying for someone she loved
A father is enraged and damns them all.
Within a moment of time
Brothers and sisters want an eye for an eye.
Others that look on are wondering why
Is it really worth it at this moment in time
or is the truth in a few lines.
Yours is Yours
Mine is mine.

Donna L. Vasilis

Try The Commercials

If you're feeling tired and sort a blue
Let the commercials make a whole new you
Alka Seltzer Plus helps you fight bad weather
Lady Speed Stick fights wetness and odor together

An Ivory bath will make you feel fresh and new
Have a cool drink, "you'll like the Sprite in you"
Eat raviolis for a good tasty hot meal
Take Maalox plus if bloating you feel

Take daily exercises; don't wear a frown
Tylenol for the pain, will never let you down
If your house smells stuffy when you come in late
Freshen the air right away with Room Mate

If breathing is bad, can't sleep, turn and twist
Get up and use some Primatine Mist
Use Fleischmans margarine, fight heart disease
Take Metamucil, get regular, feel at ease.

Ellen Collins

Second Chance

Hi there young man! That was officer's morning greeting
Let me see your driver's license, because you were speeding
Officer! Please! I just got this job of mine
I am trying to get to work, on time

You see, our child was sick all night
He kept me awake, when he cried
Please! Give me a second chance, your honor
Young man said.
I am not a judge, as you know
I am the officer, enforcing the law

Ouch! It hurts officer said
When in his squad car he sat
That someone else kidney, sometimes feels bad
It's not a bad day, I happened to be your honor
To his surprise on the driver's license he sees "organ donor"

Give me second chance, the words came to the officer's mind
When he saw the eyes of the young man, that almost cried
Hospital bed, came in front of his eyes, when he remembered his own
cries, give me a second chance, he prayed
Young man, drive carefully, slow down, this is your lucky day

Chester Kaminski

Untitled

Hear my cry, hear my plea, oh Lord,
   Let it be. Let it be. Let it be.

Lord step aside and let me by, I am coming inside.
   And I will be satisfied.
To lay my head down to rest,
There will be no more sadness nor pain,
   No more sorrow, and no more tears will I shed.

Oh Lord, hear my cry, hear my plea,
   Let it be. Let it be. Let it be.

Oh Lord I have laid my head down to rest.
I have made my home with you oh Lord.
Lord I know you will take care of me,
Oh Lord, you have heard my cry,
You have heard my plea.
So let it be, let it be, let it be.

Geneva Brown

First Love

Conception to three is vital to me;
less than fourteen hundred days to imitate
what I hear, feel, see.
Surrender your loyal, sturdy, trusting support passionately.
Because of you better than best I'll prove to be.

A matchless present above any given me
is certainly the tireless love, firm guidance and deserved
discipline applied consistently.
Confirm my ability to face challenges no matter the complexity.
Contribute your best example as the key.

Vested wisdom others will see in me.
Around my waist welded snugly they'll find
a belt of security.
Respect from them will grow gradually as will sure success
nurtured by my first love — my family.

Jessie Smith Morgan

My Own

Once again, under tree of sorrow,
leaves of pity, just drops of blood, fall on my face.
It turns colder now, in the forest of 'morow,
as the bitter wind, comes and goes, with no haste.

No lesions to show, the pain I suffer.
Just the ground and tree at my back to comfort.
Still the breeze here, while I still love her.
And dangling branch stays, when I say..."I loved her."

Sweet branch hangs lonely on my neck,
   giving little forgiveness,
but lending enough to let me through.
I feel the light shine without fearfulness,
Who will lead me to love so true.
   Conner Rythems

Costume Creation

Question: What do you get when you combine at
least a dozen tattoos with a leather jacket, a torn
Sweatshirt, and an old pair of jeans?
Answer: The perfect halloween costume. It's a
great way to look like a totally wild member of a
heavy-duty motorcycle gang!
Solution: The trick is to apply the tattoos so they
can be seen if you're wearing warm clothing. Put
most of the tattoos on your neck, face, and lower arms.
Then find an old sweatshirt and cut off the
sleeves just above the elbows. If you want to wear
this costume for halloween, put a few layers of
T-shirts underneath the sweatshirt. Add a leather
jacket if you have one. Just push up the sleeves so the
tattoos show. If you don't have a leather jacket,
that's okay, too. Covered in tattoos, you'll look
cool enough without it!
The best part of this costume is that it lasts for days.
That means you'll probably get to wear
it to school!
   George H. Marcum

Seekers Of Moonshadow

The wisdom of mankind and the beliefs of our world
Lay spread out before us, beliefs of reason and chaos.
I, seeker of knowledge, of passion, of love and of unity
I, creator of words and words am scarred in mind and soul.
The boy, the dreamer, the angel of creation, demon of lust
Hunted by you, bitterness, and the pain of mistrust.
Intuition tells me what you do not, that my soul is good but torn
Inside, pure and light... outside the sounds shroud and poison.
I became the healer of the torn and the armor of the pure
After countless lessons, mistakes, trials and rewards.
Resulting in an avatar of freedom, hope, and dreams
A one with a spirit and art, one with sight of good in mankind.
Unable to thrive in the life of everyday man
Given ability to live inner desires so the rest can...
All of us, friends bound in spirit and in kind
Nothing hidden from view or unsolvable with understanding.
Created by mind, desired by soul, needed for dreams
Believe in the magic, strive towards unity, seekers of
Moonshadow...
   Justin D. Steele

A Glorious Day

I am soaring with eagles,
Laughing in the rain,
Swimming in rainbows.
I am high with an energy force
That keeps beating through my veins,
That comes from the very depths of my soul.
Savoring every moment that this feeling is upon me.
Enjoying the presence of my guides.
Giving gracious appreciation to God and all His wonders.
Basking in joy, peace and love.
Life is full within my being.
This day is for me, this day is real,
This day is glory in all its colours,
For this day is what I made it to be.
From the warm glow of the sun and the gentle breeze.
To the bright moon shining against a backdrop of twinkling stars.
It's good to live in the present.
No past to think of.
No future till it arrives.
Living for the moment in one glorious day.
   Eva McMullin

A Beauty Forevermore

Where beauty lies beneath blue skies
Lands mountains meadows valleys and blue lakes
Those wondrous things that God gave us
Not from man's mistakes

The beauty of a woman that the eyes can mistake
For the beauty of a heart in disguise
For there in lies a simple fact

A women's beauty we may adore but that beauty
Will not last evermore
A heart that is pure with love has real beauty
A beauty that is for evermore
   Edward David

Thomas N. Melton

   Today, we are sending You one of our best, better I have not known yet, and I doubt I will.

   He leaves us knowing his love lives within us. He leaves us now, having known the joys of his parents, having known the joys of a beautiful woman for 46 years. He leaves us now, having known the love of three children, he leaves us now having known the joys of brothers, sisters, grandchildren and many, many friends.

   Yes, Lord, we are sending You one of our best, better, I have not known yet, and I doubt I will.

   Yes, we can cry, yes we can hurt, yes we can heal. But thru these windows we can look for an answer, and there is only but one answer, God's love is strong and great and He chose this man for His work.

   Thomas N. Melton was a man who lived with kindness, generosity, laughter, gentleness, and was loved. He is what God is needing now.

Today, we all live in a smaller world and now we have sent to You
One of our best.
Better, I have not known yet, and I doubt I ever, ever will.
We all love you, Dad, and we always will.
   Craig N. Melton

In Memory Of A Loved One

Here I sit in my husband's favorite chair
Knowing that in my heart he is not here
His illness gave us pain and now he's free
And as the time goes by his Spirit will remain with me
Oh how true those ups and downs, happiness, joys, and tears
God brought us 6 beautiful children, 8 grandkids and 45 1/2 years
It has been five months that I said my last adieu
So farewell my dear, and may God Bless You

Cathy Apuzzo

River Below Me

I sleep, high and serene above you,
Knowing full well, the power of your
possible seduction of me.
When I first knew you, when we were both younger.

Now...whirling, bubbling, swirling,
rushing, circling, but always flowing
against the horizon, level with my sleeping eyes,
you move.
River, do you care if I still dream about you?
In dreams of higher thoughts,
in my yet unrequited love for you?

Or, am I just a sleeping spectator,
a lonely, loving, admirer of your beauty?
Someday...In my dream,
when I awaken to myself,
as well as to you,
I will tell you, river, of my love for you,
and how I feel about you.

Henry Glynn

Infinite Angel

Think, of what's going on
Know, something's going wrong
Don't be too blind to see
What it is,
You might hang for yours
like he did his.
What's behind those eyes
Is it evil cries, or
an infinite angel that lies
deep in the soul when the body dies.

Watch, of changes that come
Notice, where you started but already began.
You are born with no one else,
Study you to become yourself.
Close your eyes and beware what you see,
Imagine you are your best friend and you will be,
An infinite angel that no longer lies,
Its wings rise, it now flies,
What is behind those eyes?

Christopher D. Moody

A Prayer To The Sun

Heavenly sunlight shine down on me.
Let your rays embrace me with their tender touch.
Guide me through each glowing day and through
  the rest of my life.
Let not your absence be my misfortune, let it be
  my inspiration.
Oh how blessed are your golden rays of delight.
Shine on me always and be my eternal friend.

Faith E. R. Merideth

My Courage, My Children

You have both always thought that I have courage, little do you know, it wasn't courage but, sheer determination to never let anything or anyone drag me down, to the depths that I've been and never knowing if I would be able to climb back up again. I protected myself by building a room in my heart, where I can hide all the hurtful words ever said, all my sorrow and pain. I faced them and sealed the room. Only sometimes does a crack show through, I'm an expert on sealing up this room, a crack appears and I hide more hurt and pain, and then I seal it back up again.
You both have rooms that are sealed, do you know what you hide? I know at least a large part of it. First face these things, accept your responsibility for them, and then you hide them. And you wait For another day that the hurt is too great, and the problems unsolvable, then you start all over again.
This is the key to "courage" you never surrender, you find another way to deal with it, you accept your mistakes, learn from them, then put them in your room, so you can never be hurt by the same things again. You may children, my pride, my joy, and this room was and is the only things that keeps me going, if that is courage, then I guess I have it. Your both have this same ability use it.

Carolyn Sue Allen

The Still Small Voice

The still small voice from the back of my mind
Keeps repeating my name, but I remain blind.
Before I search for the meaning, I must silence the roar
And quiet the banter from the front of the floor.

This serene sweet messenger whispers its story,
Persistent and patient, a herald of glory.
It comes and it goes, yet a continuous expression,
Completely independent of my ability to listen.

Unperturbed by the challenge to top the crowd's babble,
It continues the tranquil, the peaceful sweet fable.
A tale without time and a phrase without form,
Its peaceful cool chat surrounded by storm.

The storm of advice and opinions of others
Swells up to include the voices of brothers.
The forceful report from the mind's other voices,
Thunderous in volume, complicating my choices.

This calming informer delivers its speech,
Revealing its secrets and intuition to teach.
From way in the back, the quiet informant
Foretells of a time when I say "I knew that."

John C. Johnston

The Heart's Desire

Two hearts collide then pass by
keeping a rhythm neither can control.
Their souls beating: wandering, wondering
will they ever meet again
Soar, circle, spiral, swoop
how will they keep the imperfect time destiny dictates?

The hearts search to wed with
the unutterable visions in their minds
Knowing without speaking, feeling without touching
searing like a dying star.
When one heart is split between two
will the embers of desire fade with the fire?

Dana Tanksley

The Hourglass

Take a good look at me in the eyes
Just what exactly do you see?
Only the darkness and emptiness my eyes reveal
Somethings are just better, left sealed

Dying is all I seem to think about
I'm so angry I could scream and shout
There's only so much I can take
And for me it's already too late

Take me and show me there's a better place
Seems there's nothing left to do in my case
I went from a winner to a loser
With nothing much left to live for

I'd like to love and be loved, but there's no way
I'm slowly dying, and only want to live for today
Take it one day at a time they say
Only I'm running out of time and no change

Time to put myself to rest
Maybe tomorrow there will be a new test
Bring me sunshine bring me rain
Most of all bring me something for this pain.

America Ray Garcia

The Knuckleball

The batter steps in and stares at the pitcher,
just waiting for the pitch.
The pitcher stares back and then to the catcher,
for the signal.
The batter takes some warm up swings,
then positions himself for the pitch.
The pitcher grips the ball,
then pulls back his arm and throws the pitch.
The batter awaits for the ball as it dances through the air,
up and down and side to side.
The pitcher follows through with his pitch,
and hopes the ball will pass by the batter, untouched.
The batter, now not knowing where the ball will pass him,
swings and misses.
The pitcher once again regains control of the ball,
and walks back to the mound, successful.

Jayme Laughton

God's Will

Just to be tender, just to be true
Just to be glad the whole day through

Just to be merciful, just to be mild
Just to be innocent as a child

Just to be gentle, kind and sweet
Just to be helpful with willing feet

Just to be cheerful when things to wrong
Just to drive sadness away with a song

Whether the hour is dark or bright,
Just to be loyal to God, who is right

Show me your God, a doubter might cry: That's easy

Just point to the flowers that smell so sweet, and the birds in song,
Their call to meet. Just show him two lovers walking hand in hand

Just show him the deaf, who seem to hear his call;
Just show him the blind who seem to see it all.

Just show him that love and understanding is God's plan;
To stop the hurry and take time for our fellow man.

Just tell him to think from deep in his heart and he will see,
That IS God's will for you and for me.

Circe Bileschi

Please Pass the Peassandra

Robert Andrew Brian McSneeze
just simply would not eat his peas.
His mother begged so very hard
but Robert said boldly, "I'd rather starve.
I'd run buck naked through brush and trees
before I'd eat those dreadful peas.
I'd sit upon a hive of bees
before I'd eat those ugly peas.
I'd kiss a girl upon the cheek
and eat raw onions for a week.
I'd go to school for five years straight
and never be a minute late.
I'd do every single one of these
before I'd eat those disgusting peas."
Suddenly his mother said, "Start undressing, Robert.
First are the brush and trees"
Then Robert replied with an embarrassed look,
"Please pass the peas."

Drew Amoroso

I Am The Warrior

I've heard your words on the wind for weeks now calling, Joseph. I too, am tired. My heart is weary. There is nothing left of my strength. Yet, I am not allowed to quietly just cease participation. Oh, no. From battle, to battle, I must continue on. Like the ragmen in wars gone by, moments of exhausted numbness, my only hope of comfort. Or the seemingly, out of the question, the slumber of the saints. But, some of us are hard to kill, apparently quite necessary cogs in a greater plan, and sentenced to live a long, long, time. Joseph, is your rest sweet now? If you had to do it all over again, would you even try? Would your heart break any less? Would your earthly success, please you more? Would the other spirits on the wind, delight in a moment greater than the sum of your life-force effort? Oh, how I long to join you in your teepee. But, my trail looms ever before me, and I know not how or when I'll rest. Say a prayer for me, Joseph. In moments of rejoicing, I am with you trekking north. The children, like children always do still find things to laugh about, mothers still hum, and you Joseph, full of hope in your heart, know that one day this will all end. There is still some warmth from the sun, and light in the sky. And that is enough to dream by.

Jamie L. Rabideau

The Barn

The old man stared at the barn, long and hard...He could see tiny Johnny
Barely standing...trying to walk...smiling
He stroked his white beard that had withered many seasons ago
Small Johnny was there...skipping around, swinging under the old tree
He shook and small Johnny was gone...

His ears began to rattle...Deep thunder filled his mind
His eyes glazed and turned gray
He looked at the barn again and saw nothing
He glanced once more...Little Johnny was playing games
Running from his friend Bang! Bang! The other boy shouted
Johnny put his hand to his chest and went down

The old man closed his eyes tight, closing them hard and keeping them shut
Shaking...he let his tension go...A time long past
Teenage Johnny was doing his chores
So diligently and hard working
Feeding the hogs and the chickens, milking the cows
He flinched...The squirt from the cow and Johnny laughing
Held fast in his mind...
He wiped the milk off his face

ALL he had wiped were tears.....

Ellis Michael Ott

Best Friend

Since I was just the lady of 10,
I've had the very bestest friend.
She vowed our friendship would never end,
I guess she lied.
Cause it began to bend.
The memories we shared together,
will stay with me forever.
In the hallways at school,
I sometimes feel the tears in my eyes.
But I know we must say
our good-byes.
Have I ever thanked you for being my friend?
Maybe not, but now I see what you truly mean to me.
I know you care and love me too,
In all endeavors I go through,
so, I give all my youthful thanks to you.
Amanda, this, is your "Q".
Jennifer Simon

Untitled

I sit alone and wonder how my life has been shattered
I've finally realized my life has no meaning and I don't matter
Why must my life go on when it has no meaning
My mind is racing and my heart is always screaming

I've been walked on all my life and treated like dirt
I guess they don't realize how much it can hurt
This hurting inside eats at me every day
I've tried oh so many times to make it go away

What did I go to get this life that I've leaded
It was just love and affection that I needed
Not this pain that is with me wherever I go
The scars that it left are starting to show

Neither bandage nor Band Aid could cover these wounds
I just wish the good Lord would take my life soon
Christina Anuszewski

Love, She Cried

Love is cruel, she said and it has cut me deeply;
I've been hurt and I've been disappointed by it.
It is abuse and mistreatment that hurts, I told her.
Love doesn't injure; it is tender and caring.

Love is hard and cold; I've spend many nights alone
And it's coldness has turned my warm tears to ice.
It is callousness and indifference that's cold.
Love is togetherness; it is soft and warm, I replied.

Love, she said has caused me grief and heartache
And my heart had been broken many times, you see.
It is malice and spite that causes you misery, I said.
Love is compassionate; it is kind and considerate.

Love has passed me by like a stranger on the street
Without a nod or even a smile, she tearfully told me.
To receive love one must be willing to give it, I said.
Love is a harvest; what you sow is the crop you grow.

Love and realization brought misty tears to her eyes.
I have eyes but could not see; now, it's crystal clear.
Love is an extension of the soul that comes from within;
It shines from the eyes and reflects from a smile, she cried.
Charles E. Stone

Selling Out

It's hard to watch it crumble,
it's sad to watch it go,
to witness this place dwindle
from the great years of long ago.

This farm was once a beauty,
a shrine set off the road,
with a great house, a dairy,
and a large family to uphold.

The years have taken its toll on the
people and property alike,
it is the end of an era,
the end of our families farm life.

This house and the land will belong to another,
but our spirits will always remain,
for that's the one and only thing
that the buyer can not claim.
Anita Brendelson

The Real Meaning Of Christmas

It's Christmas once again and I want you to know,
It's not about Santa, trees, lights and snow.
To keep the real meaning of Christmas in your heart,
Let us go back almost 2000 years, to the very start.

It happened in a stable far far away.
A child was born whose bed was made of hay.
He was placed in a manger in the shadow of the Cross.
It's the gift of His love that we celebrate most.

He was born to save the world and to make all men free.
Giving us a gift that will last through eternity.
So as you put up the tree and decorate with lights,
Remember that child born on the most holy of nights.

After you've opened your gifts and return to your bed,
Say a Happy Birthday Prayer to Jesus then rest your head.
Dream of the gift that was given to you so long ago,
AND REMEMBER IT'S NOT ABOUT SANTA, TREES, LIGHTS AND SNOW!
Judith C. Sample

Depression

A sad state of affairs depression can be
It's feeling down, out and full of gloom
Not willing to communicate with anyone
Just waiting for an impending doom

It's sitting in the dark with a bottle of brew
Watching television for no particular reason
A soft chair in the corner becomes your friend
But your slowly enlarging belly betray's you with treason

Dreams, hopes, wishes come and go through your head
But day after day you find little has changed
Lack of money in the pockets is one excuse
No one is fooled however and former friends become estranged

Moodiness and a serious state of mind become you
One minute your upbeat, the next your mad
You want to change your life, leave home, see new things
But that will only change the place that you are sad

Suicide, running away, these ideas play in your mind
A rut you are in frustrates any happy thoughts
Finding yourself alone with no one who understands
You wish to be happy but even that can't be bought
Fred Harris

A Guard's Prayer

'Tis a stormy night on Mindanao
It's dark; it's raining, and the wind does howl
As I walk my post I feel so all alone
So my buddies may sleep and dream of home.

I pray to God we'll not shed our blood
In the muck and mire of this island's mud
And if it be so we'll survive to pray
With His good graces we will go home to stay.

So we face this battle with shot and shell
We will know that this is close to hell
But we must win this fight as well the war
Though some may die at victory's door.

As I walk I know that there is nothing I can do
So that all my comrades will see through
I must pray to God to do what he might
And I will watch over them for tonight.

John D. Gogerty Jr.

The Sound Of Running Feet

It's changed-the world, I mean, since yesterday.
It's changed-and yet, somehow, I still remain the same.
The same old me with sandy hair,
The same bright eyes and laugh still there.
I feel just as I did last year-and year before the last.
Will I ever, never, see the boy-with-youth-now-gone-on-past?
I can almost hear him leaving me
To play, perhaps, another game with someone I shall never see.
"Oh, please come back! I'm all alone-Don't leave me now..."
The words are formed upon my lips; it's such a simple plea.
But ah, my cry is wasted word. The youth has slipped away...
Just the sound of running feet-the echo of some yesterday.

John Edmond Thomas

Trail's End

Life's trail of dreams is winding to an end,
It's best offerings lie behind,
No great fulfillment awaits beyond the bend.

In retrospect life's joys and sorrows blend
With routine daily toil and grind,
Life's trail of dreams is winding to an end.

To look ahead and dream is but to pretend,
For at this point we truly will find
No great fulfillment awaits beyond the bend.

In awareness I can but recommend
Discarding dreams that held a heart entwined,
Life's trail of dreams is winding to an end.

Long range goals no longer have hopes to lend,
And as the skeins of life unwind,
No great fulfillment awaits beyond the bend.

One's youthful dreams I ever would defend,
Such dreams serve now but to remind,
Life's trail of dreams is winding to an end,
No great fulfillment awaits beyond the bend.

Gwyndolyn Smith

Untitled

I feel too deeply when mortar and bricks are removed.
My garden and bed behind my sanctuary feel naked, strangely naked.
My head in my hands are the only comfort.
How long has this been going on?
Not as long as it took to hide behind these walls.

Gilbert G. Gordon

Anything Poem

Any ANYTHING POEM...is just that.
It's a poem about anything...even a hat.
And if not a hat...maybe a ball.
You see it is anything...anything at all.
How about a bear cuddly and cute?
Or a kitten playing in a boot?
An ANYTHING POEM can be great fun
It can be anything you wish under the sun.
Why don't you try one when you feel sad.
You know what it does? It makes you feel glad.
It brings out the sunshine and chases the rain,
Makes a gloomy day bright, makes you happy again.
I wrote one myself on a cold snowy day,
I found myself laughing the blues away.
I felt so good I walked through the snow
Watched snowflakes make a picture of winter's glow.
Now it's time for my poem to come to an end,
Do hope that it cheered you a little my friend.
Next time you are lonely and feeling blue,
Try an ANYTHING POEM and you'll smile too.

Eleanor F. Basinger

Preach Love

If it were my decision to decide what was to be taught,
It wouldn't take me long nor would I have to think a lot.
I would stand up and shout it for I feel it deep within.
Preach the word of love for "love covers a multitude of sins."
Love can tear down "strongholds" that's been there for years.
Love has torn down bitter enemies, to melt their hearts in forgiving tears.
As a mother loveth her children, this is the path we are to trod.
After all, are we not "joint-heirs and children of God
To feed the hungry, clothe the poor, and help the blind to see?"
Jesus said, "If you've done it to the least of them, you've done it unto me."
Even to give a cup of water and to give that in love
Will help build your mansion in your heavenly home above.
The greatest commandment is to love one another,
To reach out across the miles to help a fallen brother.
For God so loved the world, that He gave his only begotten son.
Then before Jesus was crucified, he cried, "That they might be as one"
"One" in unity together, for now and forevermore.
I believe "love" is the key that unlocks heaven's door.
Your life might be the only Bible that a lot of people read;
So if you want to lead people to Christ... let "love" be your seed.

James C. Bash

Thoughts Of Love For A Wedding Day

A special love has come into my life.
It welcomes me with open arms which wrap around and pull me into a world of happiness and security.

The protective arms hold me gently and I begin to feel a warmth as I close my eyes and experience a sense of love that I have never known before.

A reassuring voice comes from above telling me that I am no longer alone and that we will be together through eternity.

A soft hand gently touches my shoulder
and helps to guide me toward my goals and dreams.

A heart beats next to mine with the anticipation of sharing our lives, and in unison, exploring every corner of our world together.

Thoughtful eyes look upon me, eyes that are filled with sincerity, devotion, honesty, and humor.
I feel them gazing deep into my heart where they intertwine with my soul.

My senses are heightened as I realize how fortunate I am
to be sharing this feeling with another person.

A special love has come into my life and I smile as I lean back in the secure arms that hold me close, and I bask in thoughts of happiness.

Yes, a special love has come into my life and that love is shared with you.

Heidi Rouleau Whitehair

The Book

There's a book that was written ages ago
   It was written for you and I
It's the oldest book that I know you can read
   with the author standing close by

God has preserved his Holy Word in this book
with his Righteousness, power, wisdom and grace
When you read this magnificent Holy Book
You'll meet God face to face

There's many wonderful things written in this book
   Just for you and I
It's the oldest book that I know You can read
   with the author standing close by

Don't take just anyone's word
for God's most Holy word on high
The prophecy of Jesus was told in this book
for this world's salvation, he was sent to die

So stand mightily in God's word from day to day
accept only God's truth and not satan's lie
It's the oldest book you'll ever read
while the author watches close by.
   Edward C. Burks Sr.

The Precious Gift

I will never forget the way you smiled at me for the very first time.
   It was worth more to me, oh so much more, than the worth of a dime.
For that simple smile, turned my whole life around.
   You gave me self-esteem that I thought would never be found.
You helped me realize I was worth more than I thought.
You helped me fight the battle I thought would never be fought!
You see, I have cancer and I am not sure if you knew,
   the years, months, and days I have left are very few.
I grow weaker and weaker every day.
   But I will never forget the smile you gave me last May.
It was in the hallway in the west wing
   when you gave me that smile, then walked on and started to sing.
When our other classmates learned of my cancer they would not look at me.
   Then you smiled at me, you opened the door, and you gave me the key.
You gave me the hope, the strength that I needed.
   You were never rude and never conceited.
Now through that simple smile you gave me last May,
   I have been able to live one more year, one more month, one more day.
Now it is time that I must go, I have come to my end.
   But I just wanted to thank you for the smile that you were able to lend.
   Heather J. Stillman

Life

We've known each other for some time now.
It was the past spent together which has brought us closer, even now
Regardless of the distance that separates us.
There is such a deep familiarity in what we share-in our connection.
We've weaved a web of our own so special and intricate
Only we can comprehend its very depths.
Like a puzzle we fit together, we feel comfortable with each other.
Even though we get lost along the way our paths always seem
To bring us back together allowing the pieces once again to
Fit the puzzle we've created.
As our friendship expands we deepen our understanding of the
Important roles we play in each other's lives.
A piece of us will always be a precious part of the other
In this intricate, unending puzzle called life.
   Holly Carnine

Life's Mirror

I once had a hand held glass mirror
It was old, hand carved and even beaded.
Every little niche and every little bead was so intricately placed
That the mirror was just one of a kind.
So many would hold and admire the mirror and the beauty that it possessed.
Until one day the mirror fell off of a stand and broke.
Oh, how I cried, because the mirror was so special to me.
Because it was a gift; a gift from someone who loved me so dearly.
As I picked up the broken pieces of the mirror,
I was picking up the pieces of my life.
Every hurt, every tear, every joy, every pain;
Even every failure and success arose to my mind from the broken pieces.
As I placed it back together to make one whole piece,
I knew that my life was like that mirror; it had to be broken into pieces
Before it could be put back together again into a whole piece.
   Joyce Servey

Our Love, Our Angel

MOTHER, we love you so much, you are an ANGEL.
It was, I guess, GOD's will
To take you from us and make you happier still.
You taught us everything we know,
Guided us when we were on the go,
And when you sensed what a mother senses, you said "no."
We can see your frown and we can see your smile,
When we were wrong, or when we walked down the aisle.
Now we need you, we miss you and we look toward HEAVEN.
If you have a smile, it contains your blessing,
If you have a frown, we better do some correcting.
You walk with us, you smile with us and you sing with us.
You talk to us, you cry with us, you relax with us and laugh
   at out silliness.
Every day we thank you for bringing us up the right way,
All you did and what you put up with every day.
We shall follow your path and always say,
"Thanks to our ANGEL...who's in HEAVEN today."
   Hope Argumedo

Fonda's Rock

Fonda's rock is a special place where I can feel so serene
It sits on top of the mountain in the waving grass so green.

At Fonda's rock majestic mountain peaks meet the soft blue sky
From there I can see the eagle as he spreads his wings to fly.

From Fonda's rock I can see a golden sunset at the end of day
When I am perched on top, I just cannot help but be inspired to pray.

From Fonda's rock I can see thousands of tall stately trees,
Their colored leaves in the fall or summer nest for the bees.

From Fonda's rock I can see the starry heavens on a moonless night,
Or catch a glimpse of a young spotted fawn as she leaps away in fright

From Fonda's rock I can hear a turkey gobbling in the spring
Or watch the pretty bluebirds flutter and listen as they sing.

From Fonda's rock I can watch a groundhog sneak into his den
Or watch the dainty wildflowers gently swaying in the wind.

From Fonda's rock I can see a rabbit dashing to and fro
Or watch the softly floating flakes of a chilly wintry snow.

From Fonda's rock I can hear the echo of the proud hunter's gun
Or watch the men tap the maples and see the sugar water run.

Fonda's rock is such a beautiful place to which I love to trod
Where I can meditate and be thankful for this great gift from God.
   Fonda Anderson

"Childhood"

A moment in time,
It seems to last forever, then it's gone.
You wake up and everything is smaller than it was.
Every day seems shorter than it was.
Every day goes quicker than it did.
A moment in time,
You dream about tomorrow, and wish for it to come.
The things you took for granted,
Swinging on a swing, jumping on the bed, playing with your friends,
Are long gone.
A moment in time,
Something will always remind you.
The aroma of a breeze strikes a memory,
You feel like a child again, and in a moment,
It's gone.
Cindy Dela Rosa

Golden Eagles In The Orchard

I saw Golden Eagles in the Orchard.
It really wasn't very absurd.
They went along with everything I
always heard.
They were the most beautiful sight I ever
saw in my life.
I was sure that they would suffice.
The golden eagles were spread out all
over the place.
They were beautiful like pink and scarlet lace.
The flowers in the orchard were red and white.
They were a very beautiful sight.
I saw them in the sun's light.
Some of the eagles began to fly.
I don't believe I'll ever see them again if I tell a lie.
And I know I'll never see them again
until I die.
John A. Britt

Night Voices

The night is mine,
It is time again, and she calls to me.
I begin to walk—-
Dark shadows hold secrets
And winding paths are full of things that might be,
Moon light tangles in the shadowed branches,
Spirits drift by like smoke.
The spirit that I am was never born of man.

The spirit that I am
Has lived in the guise of man years now,
But at night when other men sleep
I must walk — long and far and wondering
I walk in shadow and the moon hastens to follow,
Fearful of losing one of her children,
The winds blow through me
And tug at that shadowy and ghostly wraith of my soul.

I have been a man much time now
But I know, one night I will walk
  and not return.
Juliana Boyd

Return My Soul

Don't look into my soul, not today,
It is deep, dark, and empty.
Where did it go to anyway?

My soul was ME, full and rich.
It held excitement, laughter, and love
All washed down some drainage ditch!

Oh how, I MISS what used to be!
My insides ache with loss and pain.
If you find it, send it back to me.

RETURN what is MINE, it isn't fair!
Give "ME" back to me, please!
You took it away, why can't WE SHARE?

WE shared it once, YOU and ME,
I let YOU IN and bared it all.
YOU LEFT and took it AWAY! Why can't you see?

If WE can't have EACH OTHER, give it back!
YOU don't need it, your's is complete!
To be WITHOUT MINE MAKES ME BLACK...
Della J. Mitchell

The Future

A door swings out of the shade and opens to you
It has been waiting
Revealing a new sun, a new sky and numberless
Stars that glisten
Out of the cloud on a wider world than before.

Welcome it, explore,
Test the new creatures and partners ready
to saunter along for this hour

The hour is a long one and curves out of sight
but always it curves back
Suggesting this night
Jessie Kachmar

To Be Alone

When you're out there and you're all alone,
It feels as if you can't go home.
As you wipe away that single tear,
Do you have anyone that will always be there?
When you have a pain it's not to be fixed,
You just roll with the blows and take your hits.
You want someone to hold you tight,
And to be your friend all through the night.
Why try to fix the problems you have,
Because nothing can be done about the past.
I try to live in today and do my best,
But these pains keep coming up like a bad pest.
No matter what you do to put them out of you head,
These pains that trouble you can't just be shoved under the bed.
When I try to get close to someone I love,
Warning signals go off and they come from above.
When I get close I get pushed away,
The pain starts all over and it's new from today.
It's all a cycle that starts with pain,
Pain that keeps coming over and over again.
Amanda Glenn

"Multiple Sclerosis"

Multiple Sclerosis
It could be quite atrocious.
But we get up every day and do our thing,
never really knowing that the day will bring.

With research, studies and money galore,
why are we still knocking at the back door?
There still is no cause, which means no cure.
So the future for me is still unsure.

But I know what I want and I'll try to achieve,
And that you can count on and truly believe.
MS Is what I have and maybe you can't see,
I have MS but it doesn't have me.

Elizabeth A. Krause

True Friendship

A friendship is like a season,
It changes from day to day.
Its hard to depend on the weather
And with friendship you can never say.
Yes I've had my share of friendships,
Some turned more bitter than any winters cold.
But like the changing tree's in autumn,
Some turned more precious than gold.
Yes there is more than one season.
But true friendships, are fewer than those.
Some end as quick as a summer storm,
some blossom like an early spring rose.
Its all through trial and error,
I guess that's how I've learned
There's no other way around it
True friend, has to be earned.
There's a certain bond in friendships,
That's shared between so few.
That's why I'm really grateful,
That I have a friend like you.

Harry Lee Van Buren

God's Special Rose

God planted a "Rose" no one thought was any Good
It came up so beautiful like he knew that it would
The essence of that "Rose" was tender and rare
That's why God kept it in his very own care.
He nurtured it with love and kept it from harm
He carried it every where he went safely in his arms
When it had grown to the size he wanted it to be
He placed it out in front for the whole world to see
The strength of this "Rose" was like no other
This "Rose" I speak of was my Dearly Beloved Mother
Even though that "Special Rose" has withered away
The petals from that "Rose" still remain here today.

Charlethea Johnson

Special Wings

Parts of my heart had been sadly burned,
lessons of life I had lived and learned.
I took a chance and reached out into the dark,
Hoping my hand would touch a gentle lark.
Unseen through darkness the Lark was there,
with feelings of warmth, with feelings of care.
The presence of him was difficult to explain,
Except that his hand made it possible to
bring sunshine through my rain.
The Lark made my darkness into light
and took away my pain.

Cheryl Reid

Life Blood

It rushes, it rumbles, it roars
It bubbles, it trickles, it seeps, it springs
It's water...the lifeblood.
It runs, it sinks, it floods
It freezes, it boils, it flows
It's water...the lifeblood.
It's seeks out, it fills, it covers
It waves, it ripples, it stands still
It's water...the lifeblood.
It's gives life, it drowns
It makes food, it can wash away
It's water....the life blood.
It's blue, it's green, it's black
It's kind, it's gentle, it's mean
It's water...the lifeblood.
It quenches, it heals, it soothes
It sustains, it nourishes, it makes the world
For it is the lifeblood...it's water.

John Wallace Yardley

Music

Music is one of the single-most greatest creations on this earth
It brings happiness in times of sorrow
It heals, soothes and enlightens
Music is a very powerful tool that can be used for
Positive or negative confrontations

For the ones who God gave a voice to sing, treasure it,
For all it may bring
Sing high or sing low
Just let the funky sounds flow
Keep making the world happy with your treasure
For music is a creation you just can't measure
So sing to the world you funky divas
Keep singing and don't ever leave us

Gwendolyn A. Bush

Love In Bloom

You have taken this withering rose, replanted and tenderly nourished it,
And now it has begun to grow, into a delicate thing of beauty lovingly aglow.
The petals of softness that once belonged, fell dried to the earth, their softness gone.
Upon them you came, and breathe the warmness of your love, and once again they bloomed softly, like the cooing of the dove. The greenery of the leaves had begun to fade, until the drops of your dewy kiss upon them played. The crooked stem that seemed not to grow straight, reached with the strength of your caring, as if to welcome the petal, its mate. Taken have you, the roots falling apart, replenishing them with loving kindness, giving the growth of a new start,
and now this rose is in full bloom, complete, basking in the sunshine of your love, ever so sweetly, so sweet.

Benie Edwards

Belonging

To confront the world and all of its beauty
is to focus on nature in its fullness, clothed
with life colored and boldness.
To undress the world naked from birth is to
give it beauty with creativity and love.
To size the world is to become one.
To love the world is to love self and the creator.
To change what's in the world is to come face with the truth.
To shut out the world is to die.
To be hidden from the world is deny self freedom to
explore, to be part of and belong.
To understand death we must understand life.
The world is a beautiful place. We are placed in it, not it in us

Deborah Baker-Railey

A Dream In My Heart

I open my eyes to see the sunshine, wondering;
Is there really life at the end of my run.
Compassion, love is the things that we seek,
Coming together the strong and the meek.

Soaring to the highest, the highest of peaks,
Above the pits of despair and the depths of defeat.
In my heart I find, where my dream is glowing,
Shining full of love, straight as a beam.

Desires oh! Give me what I want, I crave,
Reality is not my dream, for I'm dreaming.
I keep it deep, so deep in my heart, my mind,
Is it the right moment, the right time.

The heart, oh! My aching, hurting heart,
Dreaming of floating and walking on air, dear heart.
Can it be, should it be, will it be, humm,
Looking from my heart to my mind to see.

A dream in my heart, this is where it starts,
Let it go and wish it well, fly, fly, fly, fly.

John W. Washington

Tom

In my heart were love lies
Is the love for you that never dies
You are the one that I hold in my heart
But the thing is, your tearing it all apart
You have no idea in your mind
Why I'm being so kind
When you say mean things about my friends,
But I still love you til the end
Why do you say the things you do
Why do you make my world so blue
Why do you judge people like you would a book
You look at the cover, its only important the way they look
Open the pages and you will see
They are human, just like you and me
I wish you could see the way I feel about you
But I don't think you want to
Cause you are too blind to see
That I wish you and me were to be.

Julie Ringgold

Millbay Shore

Are bluebells still in bloom on lone Knockcree?
  Is the heather still as purple as of yore?
When roaming on the Braes, as we did in other days
  Can you taste the sea breeze salt, from Millbay shore?

I see the rustic bridge in Laurel Glen,
  The primroses and violets by the Mill,
And as the sallies sway, I see the brown trout play
  In shallow pools, the waters clear and still.

Are fairy thorns still growing on the hill?
  Can you hear Whitewater sighing ere the rain?
Does the corncrake in Park Bawn call as shrilly at the dawn?
  Or the cuckoo pierce the air with his refrain?

I hear the sheep still bleating on the Mournes,
  As peacefully across Slieve Mor they roam;
And though far away I dwell, today I still can smell
  The yellow gorse around the fields of home.

Are bluebells still in bloom on lone Knockcree?
  Is the heather still as purple as of yore?
When roaming on the Braes, one wee prayer for me please raise,
Then I'll taste the sea breeze salt from Millbay shore.

Christina Cunningham

Direction

What course to confront the racists, what is to be the path?
Is the direction compromise, or a vengeance journey of wrath?

Should one erase the memories past of treachery and deceit,
Abound with inhumanity and liberty's defeat?

Forgetfulness is not the route, surrender is not the rule.
An eye for eye, tooth for tooth is anger's path for the fool.

Prejudice spreads wider every day by those of every hue;
Ridding the earth of this terrible blight, must begin with you.

You must be the leader and you must take a stand.
Be the inspiration that bolsters a righteous plan.

Making the world a peaceful place would be our greatest endeavor.
Should everyone to this quest be true we'll live better together.

Justice for all must be the goal, vigilance the mode,
Integrity the compass point and a March for Truth the road.

Frank W. Terry

You Are Not Alone

The power we possess to mold our earthly life
Is sometimes overshadowed by our pain and by our strife.

We possess the power to turn a frown into a smile
Although we feel that life is long, we're here just a short while.
We have to grab the moment, seize the times that mean the most,
And hold each moment of happiness to help us when we coast.

Not every day is sunny, but the rain's important, too
For without the clouds and a little rain, there'd be no life anew;
Without the wind, there'd be no breeze to scatter seeds around
And without the wrong, there'd be no right and chaos would abound.

The answer to our happiness is carved within out hearts,
And God is there to carry us through life's most difficult parts.
If you believe His perfect love will guide you through your plight
Then there will be no fears and tears to wake you through the night.
So trust in Him and hand your life to Him to make it right
Just ask Him and I promise you....He will shine the light!

Dorraine G. Asparro

A Special Bond

The bond between father and daughter
is one that can never be broken.

From the time she is born
her father is there to protect her from every thorn.

He cradles her tightly in his arms
and protects her from harm.

As she grows up and goes her separate way
she always holds her father dear in every way.

Though the miles may separate them now
she never forgets how....

Her father's love got her through
whenever she was blue.

She cannot always tell him how she feels,
but deep down he knows her feelings are real.

Debbie Alpaugh

Truth Satisfies

To leave one's family
Is not very easy,
It seems to be destiny;
So there should be satisfaction
In the lands of reconciliation
Where everyone is so busy.

To leave the churches
Was my displeasure
For so many souls the sermon touches,
Why! There is always time to do a good deed
Not worrying about colour, race or creed,
For all Churches are what everyone treasure.

To leave one's country
Is just another case,
Cause the mineral, sea, water wakes everyone sultry;
And all people live in unity, peace and love
As God sends his rich blessings from above
And that's why much sunshine is on everyone's face.

Ionie Smith-Donalds

Something To Leave Our Children

It's not sweet perfume we smell coming from above,
is mostly our gasoline vapors flying into our sky.
Car makers say "do you see black smoke from a car.
Now where does the vapors go, we can't see fly by?

Sightless vapors not be seen but smell in our air,
millions of cars on our roads in everyday driving.
We know that the oil we used falls to the ground,
be careful in the rain, makes most car go sliding.

Yellow stuff, we call smog, goes floating our sky,
excuse they say it will go away, we dumb to agree?
On a clear night in future. No star will be seen,
when down with no air, where do our children flee?

How long do we wait to protect lives and children?
Someday they may get it right and not to be alarm.
Thinking however this world, no flowers will grow,
we leave children on earth, only the biggest bomb.

Ben Silber

Star Search

How will I find the way to my star?
Is it gentle or bright, beside me or far?

Will it outshine all the rest, like the eyes of a bride?
The choices seem endless, an ocean so wide.

At times it seems that I've found it at last,
Only to leave me, a tide that has past.

From where will it come in a cosmos so vast?
I can't bear to miss it, a lure I shall cast.

Like a fisherman waiting for the water to ripple,
My spirit grows limp at the lack of a nibble.

Perhaps, it has always been waiting for me,
I need not search, at my side it shall be.

An angel enveloping me, it's always been there,
The comfort beside me that doesn't compare.

As a rainbow falling from heaven to earth,
It is timeless and ageless, immeasurable its worth.

My soul mate awaits me, together we'll endure,
The journey before us, the love that is pure.

Constantina Theophilos

Love And To Live

Love
  is all but a hollow shell trying to reach
  richness and fulfillment.

  For time is of no essence it enters the heart
  of every unsuspecting fool.
And
  to love is to see into the bleak darkness of
  another world.

  It has no shape, no color, no boundaries, it is
  all but meaningless to the naked eye of man.
To
  breathe, to hope, to see, without love is a
  lifetime no man could endure.

  For he would swiftly die in life's hardened
  calloused hands.
Live
  in love breathe the wet sweet fragrance of
life.

  For love is a river flowing towards the sunset
  of eternity.

Angela Shaw

Living One Day At A Time

Living one day at a time I truly say
Is a philosophy that gently guides me on my way
Through these declining years with no qualms or fears
Of that which lies in store for me near or far away.

  And yet that philosophy should have a guiding star
  To provide a long range goal that one would dare
  To achieve notwithstanding sorrow of today and tomorrow
  Which constantly attempts that goal to mar.

Many birthdays have I taken in steady stride
Some nostalgic while others with pride
Giving thanks to heaven to have reached seventy seven
In the crucible of life sorely tried.

  There is no denial of the fact of life
  That the flesh is weakening and aches are rife.
  Yet, if one's thoughts are simple and the mind nimble,
  Then the spirit will surely soar above the strife.

That is precisely what is happening to me
As I journey on my way merrily
Living one day at a time in a state of freedom sublime
From anxieties of what the future may hold for me.

Ernest Dudley

A Mother's Prayer To Mary

Mary, be the mother of my home. Bring your warm love
into my home, and embrace my children.

Mary, be the mother of my children.
Protect them when I cannot.

Mary, be the mother of my husband.
Give him guidance, wisdom, and patience.

Mary, be my mother. Teach me to love my children
the way you love us and the way you love your son, Jesus.

Mary, teach me to love my husband the way you love
the church and the Lord, God Almighty.

But most of all, Mary, be my mother and teach me to love,
worship, and glorify our Lord and Savior, Jesus Christ.
Amen.

Inspired By The Blessed Mother

Diane Gandero

Relationships

A relationship is a wonderful possession,
Involving true passion and the deepest obsession.

It needs two lovers to make it spark,
Like a Wintergreen Lifesaver does in the dark.

They share all their feelings and secrets with each other,
She's like his sister, he's like her brother.

And the personal things that both of them share,
They keep to themselves and don't spread anywhere.

When the awkwardness leaves, and they both feel in place,
They bring themselves closer, and begin to embrace.

There may be an argument once in awhile,
But they look past the quarrel and dig deep for a smile.

They laugh and they joke and have a good time,
If this quality is lacked, they're committing a crime.

They never get bored of each other's company,
And their happiness together is a true guarantee.

When their love for each other hits the final stage,
Their eternal unity they decide to engage.

And that is when the love is real,
Because it's the greatest thing they'll ever feel.
Erik John Langley

Thinkingness

In the vast and deep soil of your being
(into whom deeply I've been)
I've met the mad hordes in dreams created.
Boisterous disclosures of some and others
Lead me into chaotic desperations of myself.
With you I am and I am not;
I pretend to be; and I want to be.
But the great universal unknown
Gets much more on me than the
Little cockroaches that inside the street drain
Reflect the moon's halo.
I agree with you and your eighty-three
Juxtaposed roles.
I've stopped, but just to continue.
Now.

Ivan Costa-Pinto

Untitled

Sitting on a hill alone, in despair, waiting for life to be put back into it.
Continually night, for the trees that drop over the house, shed it no light.
A woman's touch is needed to brighten up this dreary place.
A masculine house it was with bold antlers hanging over the porch and a
bear skin rug slapped onto the front door which creaked in the wind.
Inside on the window were torn pieces of cloth which tried to preclude the outside world.
Plastic kitchen utensils and paper plates were still sitting on the counter top from the last time he had eaten.
He was an unhealthy man said the pile of cigarettes and empty beer bottles.
And now he is gone.
Jens R. Trull

In Favor Of The Truth

Perversion of the truth is running rampant
Instead of being absolute, the truth is perceived as relative
Instead of being final, the truth is perceived as debatable
Instead of being objective, the truth is perceived as subjective
In sum, disrespecting the truth is conducive to disrespecting
Laws which are meant to protect us
But if the truth is disdained
Then advocates of the truth
Will feel powerless
In the face of a runaway locomotive predicated on falsity
Careening on a path of destruction
So now is the time to stop that same locomotive right in its tracks
From inflicting more damage.
Henry T. Sarnataro

Untouched

Sometimes...
Inside me there is a feeling of great pain;
A pain that breaks my heart and numbs my mind.
But where there is pain, there is life.

I can feel in me the pain of
A lover separated from his beloved...
A mother unable to console her precious child...
A little girl unable to understand death and illness...
A man hurt by a world unable to see greatness.

But to my amazement and delight,
In searching my very depths..
I find a part of me unscathed and untouched.
Not a scar, not a mark, not a sign of the pain
Oh my surface.
Oh! What glory. Oh! What bliss.

I hear my inner voice impart to me the wisdom of the experience.
Live life to the fullest,
Fearing not failure, pain and sorrow
And you will return to the origin...
The spirit, the untouched.

Amita Kohli

"Foolish Heart"

No one understood, they all had that look on their face,
Inside I felt the emptiness and the disgrace.
Not wanting to ever look back at the past,
Knowing deep down inside, it was not meant to last.
Trying hard to forget the love I once knew,
I held my head high, as my confidence grew.

My heart kept speaking, but I concentrated on and in my mind,
For I knew that love could be nice as well as unkind.
The pain got worse with each passing day,
My mind got stronger and wiser for what the heart would say.
Tears had become my best friend....memories my past time pals,
And love my worst enemy...yet I longed for it,
There were some sweet times, I had to admit.

Now I look back and I sit for a while,
Then my lips slowly come apart for a smile.
"Life is like a challenge, a mountain and an ever-changing time,
Where sometimes you have to up the mind for the heart or the heart
 for the mind,
For without either one of them the other would be surely blind."
It now became easier with the passing of time,
Where it once had hurt so much, oh yes, that foolish heart of mine.
Claudette Ramos

Don't Neglect Your Wings

With spiritual bliss witness nature's applause.
Indrawn children pull pulsating heartbeats from the depths
of voiceless shadows,
Exit from their mouths chartreuse powdered butterflies,
which gracefully flutter, chase one another, drop, gyrate,
rise, perform a centrifugal spin, elaborate
The rate their pattern of flight ends.

Aviators reach unmeasurable new heights,
With opalescent glazed peacock wings
These angelic beings reinforce a lost, fading sunbeam,
With a hypnotic yet humble voice to the children they speak.

Do not neglect your soul,
It should blend well with sunset,
Conquering the angry moon when covering your eyes,
Prepare your own wings, sketch blueprints of the seasons
Wake with the sunrise, deliver hope, trust, love,
your only reasons to reflect.

Perpetual breeze, feathers stroke a brilliant harp,
With gentle rhythmic care aviators drift towards peaceful
atmosphere.

Gregory A. Farrell

Untitled

The deep red light permeated every
   inch of the town.
It shone dark against the leaves, the
   homes, the streets.
Animals scurried for cover
   amongst the branches of the trees.
Insects hid within the flowers
   and shrubbery.
People headed into their homes.

The red light crept across the
   sky.
It grew
   darker and greater by the second.
All of a sudden, there was
   a quick flash and the red light disappeared.
The town was hushed.
Night had fallen.

James M. Larmon

"We're All Soul Brothers"

We're all soul brothers
In this great world of ours.
Earth is our home,
They're our sun, moon and stars.
One small planet in the great universe;
We must stick together or the whole thing'll burst.

Our great Creator made a wondrous plan:
The beautiful world;
Then He made itty-bitty man.
Itty-bitty man, but with mind, heart and soul
To tend His great wide world was His goal.

We're all God's children in this great wondrous plan.
Each of us brothers given heart and hand
To fight for the right; that love conquers all,
Even the least one so small.

Even the least is my "brother" said He.
Only with love can there be victory.
When we all fight just to conquer sin
Then, with God's help, we will win.

Catherine R. Thompson

How He Made Us

Carefully He made everything unique;
In their own way each thing can speak.
Though maybe not to human ears or in
Human ways, each sound brightens every day.
Without one the chain would be incomplete,
Leaving nothing but a hole to fill the chirp or peep.
Eventually the hole would grow,
Leaving everything on Earth to woe,
For together we are all entwined,
Leaving nothing to divide.
We all depend on each other,
And in God's eyes we are sister and brother.
So together we shall stand,
Everyone hand in hand.
The strong shall care for the meek,
For that is how He made us.

Jessica Willey

Creation

Roses now bloom,
In the sparkling sunlight of gold.

The clouds sing out for glory,
In the great sapphire sky.

The angels eat colorful fruits,
In the Heavens above.

The Fairy Tern flies of pure white,
Through the sky singing a song of color.

The wind blows lightly,
Through a lush green jungle.

A path takes the deer and baby fawn,
To a clear, sparkling stream that bubbles for the Lord.

For it was He who makes the Ivy White Wind,
It was He whom made this Creation.

Anne Baatstad

Questions Of War

How many fights must be fought,
In the hardest lesson to be taught?

How many battles must we brave?
How many lives can't be saved?

Why must a soldiers fall,
Who had once stool tall?

Why must lives apart be torn,
With messages of regrets to inform?

Who must respond to the duty calls,
Only to add their name to the wall?

Who of those who survive must live with their fears,
Every moment for the rest of their years?

When will enough shots be fired,
Before all arms can be retired?

When will hate and greed be put aside,
So that peace can be something worldwide?

Elizabeth Leigh Deck

Thank You

Sometimes,
in the aloneness of my thoughts,
I recall
my moments of great despair,
and how you,
in those same moments,
lifted me, held me in your arm's,
helped me to realize that without you
I would be truly alone
and how without your love
and my loving you
I would have no meaning, reason, or purpose.
So, I thank you, warmly, from the depths of my soul,
for loving me, for being there,
for allowing me to love you, and for making
despair a stranger to me. Thank you.
Donald L. Rath Jr.

Off The Boardwalk

A clement breeze caresses the boardwalk
in the advancing dusk.
Off to the West, high in the dimming light
the Sun, retiring,
sprays pink and purple pastels,
Crimson rays, sand tones and greys,
as Laser displays, through the vastness
of the evening sky.
But now, off to the East, far to sea,
a full silver moon ascends majestically
out of the darkeningness of the Atlantean sky.
Power puff clouds, dark earthward,
silver heavenward, accommodate escort.
Ethereal alchemy slowly morphs the silver orb
to gold as it soars to the beyond.
Ah!
Thus, the resplendent panorama plays it's role,
fades, and unerringly transforms
to nightness.
John R. Clarke

Affaire D'amour

In my dreams I awaken to you
In another world where dreams come true
There is no worry about where I belong
And being with you is never wrong
I can tell you I love you without feeling guilty —
And our desires are fulfilled so easily
I don't have to lie for the sake of another
And our time together never has to be over
I can give myself to you wholly and without hesitation
And our passion can grow with endless intensification
We are soul mates on a pilgrimage to re-connect our souls
And in my dreams our journey is complete and we are whole
But when I awaken there is someone else beside me
For a moment I was able to escape from reality
I am not distressed that my dream had not come true
Only hopeful that one day I can be with you
Gayle Schism

My Spirit

My spirit soars high as no bird can fly
It reaches the heavens and sings and dances among the stars.

It is so close to Heaven it can hear the angels whispering
A beauty only my spirit can see.

As my spirit swoops down, let me bring a little bit
of Heaven with me.
Anita A. Andrus

Arthur Lee

It was many and many years ago,
In a house down by the sea.
There was a boy who you know,
By the name of Arthur Lee,
and this boy with no other thought,
to be love and loved by me.
He was a boy and I was a girl,
In this house down by the sea.
But we loved with love that was more than love,
By my darling Arthur Lee,
For wedding bells were ringing for him and for me.
And this was a long time ago,
In this house down by the sea.
A wind blew out the clouds at night,
Killing my Arthur Lee,
But our love was stronger for from those older than we.
Neither my father nor even my
mother, who live down by the sea,
Can ever know how much I
love my darling Arthur Lee.
Elois Littleton

Untitled

In a cold dark room I am drifting away into my own world,
In a cold dark room I hear my music playing on in my head,
In my cold dark room no one enters no one exits,
I hope you don't hate me and my cold dark room,
In my cold dark room there are no windows to the outside
    world there is just a door,
In my cold dark room I hear a knock it disturbs my music,
I go to the door and open it, the person is discouraged and
    turns the other way,
In my cold dark room once again I am alone,
In my cold dark room the music starts up again,
In my cold dark room I am slowly fading, but no one
    person is there to care,
I am shivering in my cold dark room, but I still just sit there
    staring into the shadows,
In my cold dark room I am fading quicker and quicker as
    days go by,
Someday I will never be seen again, but no one from the
    outside world will know that the day has come that the person in
    the cold dark room is not around anymore for the music to play on.
Amanda Kotkin

Kimberly Poupee Juneau

Kindly, gentle and tender, you're blessed with a life serene,
Immortal youth and ebullience of yours enliven every scene;
Melody, ineffable, are you with a haunting, bewitching rhyme,
Beauty everlasting, never fading whatever the passage of time;
Enduring love that springs evergreen, destined are you to find,
Rivers of gold and silver too, and an ethereal peace of mind;
Lovingly you impart to every setting happiness and tranquility,
Yearningly desired by the wisest from of yore to eternity.

Pearl most priceless of the orient, of the purest clearest ray,
Orange blossom flowering ever fragrantly all through the day,
Understanding, sympathetic, you shine as the stars in the sky,
Prosperity, and quiet contentment are your gifts from on High;
Elegance, nobility and grace escort a will to seek what's right,
Enchanting you'll forever be, a comely vision of sheer delight.

Jewel precious and lucent as you there is not one under the sun,
Unconquerable spirit and will of yours ensure all battles won;
Nestled in a garden in this happy land there is a stately bower,
Endowed in due course to you to have as heaven's special dower.
Arise, intently pursue the fulfillment of your wishes and dreams,
Unlatch you'll the gates of learning against all hurdling streams.
Elijah E. Jhirad

After All Child, I'm Only Human

I wear many caps in your life.
I'm your mother, your dad's wife, I'm a nurse.
I take care of your daily needs.
You get mad at me, many times, you think I am unfair.
When you are in pain, you know I'll be there.
I'm the one who is supposed to know what is always right.
Even when I'm wrong.
I can't run interference in life's plan for you.
But your tears are mine, as well as your pain.
Experience is the best teacher. So I let you stumble and fall.
Sometimes I won't pick you up, sometimes I lend you a hand.
I want you to grow up to be an independent woman, man.
When you want my knowledge, I give it to you.
If you absorb it as a sponge, and go from there, you will learn.
If you choose to play with fire, child, you will get your fingers
burned. I'm your rock of Gibraltar, but I'm human, not made of stone.
My apron strings I've untied, so go.
A part of me leaves with you, my child. It will never die.
But I'm human child, and when I close that door,
you'll not see me cry. But because I'm human, I will.

Bonnie Seefeldt Kaminski

The Beach

We're walking on the beach, hand in hand.
I'm your girl and you're my man.

The tide rolls in, and the waves rush out.
Undressing the grains of sand,
revealing their whereabouts.

A fat pregnant moon is shining very bright.
Breaking its way through the cloudy dark night.

The air is solid, and very warm.
I'm safe when I'm with you, away from all harm.

A breeze blows very smooth; it smells of a sweet rose.
Its scent fills my nose and lingers on my clothes.

Hand in hand on the beach; what could be better than this?
To have you close to me and to feel your kiss.

The spirit of the beach blows through my hair.
When I look into your eyes, I know you care.

The beach holds my wishes for love, and dreams I want to come true.
The dreams of someone special, someone like you.

Danricka Lute

Season

Seasons, what are seasons anyway?
I'll tell you what they are.
It is the weather changing from one day to the next.
There are four seasons a year in all.
Lets start with fall: it's when the green leaves turn to brilliant
golds and browns, then fall down to the ground.
Then there's winter next,
and when it comes it covers the ground with fields of white gold
called snow.
After that spring comes.
You'll know it's here because the grass, and the trees will be green,
and flowers will start to bloom once again.
Then the last one to come is summer.
It starts to get real hot and birds come back,
well until August.
It means it's time me to go have fun in sun.
At last it's all over and the seasons start all OVER...

Jessica Mead

Alzheimer's

You may not remember me but I'll always remember you.
I'll remember your eyes and all the things they tried to say.
I'll remember the lessons you taught me without speaking a word:
Lessons of pain, of hope, and of how hard it is to live life just to forget;
To dream dreams just to forget them all;
To speak beautiful words only for you to hear;
To see a beautiful young child but not to remember his name;
To become a truly beautiful woman inside and out,
but your life turned silent, empty, lonely.
When I think of you,
I'll always remember everything you gave to me
without even knowing it.
You're in peace now, and I'll always admire you.

Elizabeth Lutz

Wild Woman

Relishes a grimace, primal scream, or a belly laugh
Ignores dust kittens in the corners
Encourages the weeds and flowers to flourish side by side
Serves the same meal three days in a row
Even though she's told that it tastes like eating old socks

Wallows in dressing outrageously
Sees beauty at any age as she stands naked before her mirror
Strong, ready for action

Immerses herself in the essence of the sea
Going over, under, tumbling in the surf
Observes the ever changing surface
Listens to the breakers booming and the wind howling

Enjoys her own company
Is true to herself and trusts her intuition
Can recognize and side step gilded cages
Remains open and present

Created at the beginning of time
She joyously sings
As she dances surefooted, head thrown back
And merges with the sand, the waves, and the wind.

Chris Martin

Quarterback

He is a quarterback in the pros and one you can't miss
If you were to put the top five on a list,
Although young and inexperienced, he will indeed be around
Luckily for New England Patriots they were the ones who found,
With his potential and aggression he has been seen everywhere
But perhaps the fans of New England are the only who care,
In the near future there will be awards for him to hold
Only the ones he achieves in the hot and humid or cold,
He's one for the future and most people know
With his records and talents, he is Drew Bledsoe.

Elisha Kabanuk

Shoes

Shoes a walk but not a lot.
If not worn they don't a scorn.
If not a sprayed they smell like spades.
If they're light they fly like a kite.
If they eat they don't have seats.
If they don't sleep they don't keep.
If they laugh they'll (most likely) have a calf.
If they write they'll probably bite.
If they're rubber they'll probably slumber.
If they're dressy they're probably fussy.
Shoes are shoes don't laugh nor write nor talk nor cry.
You get the point, they don't even try!

Jenni Maylene Cavazos

Lamentations

I've heard it cried, throughout this life,
if I had only known. To what avail?
Can a wish change a time that's been cast in stone?
Let not your ego think what God has done, can be undone.

Let it not be said after friend or foe has
gone to his reward. If I had only known.
I missed my chance to help him along salvation's road.

Let it not be said in my defense before
the Judgment Throne. If I had only known.
Let me only have to say, in Christ have I trusted.
And to Jesus my life, given.
For He alone gave his life for this unworthy soul.

So let me never have to say, if I had only known.
Let me live this life as if I have always known.
For who knows?
In the next moment I may be home.

Bill Lemmons

Flying

I often wondered what flying would be like?
If flying is as free as a bird on the end of
The wind, or is flying being as free as a kite
Caught in mid air, I often wondered what it
Would be like to fly, to be free and sail
On the wind of the air.
  Or is flying just a dream of mine,
I wonder if so?
  Or will my dream come true, will I fly
Some day soon!
  Will that day ever come,
That's a question to ask?
The wild blue wonder is for me.

Harlan R. Pernu Jr.

Christmas Dream

A Christmas dream twinkling glow all in a row
Ideas flow children's dream and gleam for go

A Christmas dream snow flows trees with branches hanging low
Decorated cookies all in a row

A Christmas dream chorus of carolers singing in a stroll
Benevolent people in churches bow their heads low

A Christmas dream deck the halls with fragrant holly tied with a bow
Silver bells ream

A Christmas dream astonished guest in appropriate attire glow
Candles illuminate low owe

A Christmas dream red and green decorations all in a row
Deemed a valuable acquisition reanimate with each passing year grow

A Christmas dream popcorn balls one another love to throw
Christmas cheer with one swallow too tow

A Christmas dream romance of Christmas love greatest gift of wow
Man's Christmas love of rings and woe

A Christmas dream pretty packages all tied up in a row with a bow
Silver bells ream

A Christmas dream families gather together to give thanks for heavenly
Love of Christmas long ago

Connie DeLawter

Call Me From Heaven (David's Song)

Call me from Heaven - today after two,
I'd really like - to talk with you.
To know that you're happy - that it's so real,
Please won't you call me - and say how you feel?

Are sweet angels singing - a beautiful tune,
As clouds chase the sunset - then follow the moon?
Does God bless the children - and hear as I pray,
Please call me from Heaven - I can't find my way.

I got your message - last night after two,
As I danced on the edge - waiting for you.
You called me from Heaven - and filled me with love,
The light in my heart - now blessed from above.

I'll see you in Heaven - when my time has come,
And when my eyes open - I'll know what it's from.
Beautiful memories - remain in my heart,
But God blessed the children - and they'll never part.

Donna J. Smedley

Abandoned Child, Abandoned Child

From when I was a little child, Oh! How
  I'd cry for you.
My tender little heart would stay say, "How
  could they leave and walk away?"
The years went by and how I'd cry
  for each and every new abandoned
  child, that was left behind.
My aching heart would long to find you,
  run and take you in my arms, and say,
  "Don't worry child, I'll care for,
  love and cherish you, and I will never walk away."
One day I had a child, and I
  gave him all the love you yearned for.
But now abandoned child out
  there, can you hear my broken
  heart, crying out from here?
I've now become like one of
  you, you see.
For now my child's abandoned me.

Gloria Grandstaff

The Tree House

IF I HAD A TREE HOUSE
I would build it in my back yard.
I would build it out of wood, high up in a tree.
My Tree House would have a ladder,
  so I could climb up and down.

A Tree House, a Free House,
A Secret You and Me House,
High up in the leafy branches
Cozy as Can Be House.

A Street House,
A Neat House,
Be Sure and Wipe Your Feet House
Is not my kind of House at all -

LET'S GO LIVE IN A TREE HOUSE.

Dale M. Gipe

One Last Look

As I sit here by the fire, all snug and settled in,
I wonder how I happened here, and when it all began.
Through travels, miles and miles I roamed.
What was I looking for?
The perfect place, a friendly face, a nice and even score.
A place of comfort, joy and peace, to make my life complete.
As I look back, it's over now, as with my Lord I meet.
He takes me by the hand,
And says; "I truly understand.
Your search is at the end, my friend,
Though it was quite the task.
I could have helped you out my child,
If you had only asked."

Donna Fryer

The Strong Black Woman

I AM A STRONG BLACK WOMAN
I will get through this
I've been through more, worse
I SURVIVED.
I AM A STRONG BLACK WOMAN
I've had my heart taken and crushed
My spirit stolen and killed
But my soul still lives on.
I AM A STRONG BLACK WOMAN
I've been used, abused, talked about, and beaten down
Taken for granted and taken advantage of.
But through all of this,
One thing is always left for me to hold on to,
   HOPE
HOPE that one day everything will be okay,
HOPE that I will get through this,
HOPE that I'll never go through worse,
HOPE that I'll stay
    THE STRONG BLACK WOMAN.

Angelique Michele Smith

A Place

I went over the hill and into the wood,
I went to the place where an elm tree stood.
The scent of flowers filled the breeze,
The grass was so green as were the trees.

The sun how it shone from blue patches of sky,
The bubbling brook as it flowed nearby.
The twittering birds as they flew from their perch,
From an oak, walnut, chestnut or birch.

The breeze as it went sang a sweet melody,
Though flowers and leaves from every tree.
All the four footed creatures came out in the sun,
To frolic and play and have some fun.

I loved to see and hear the animals play,
And listen to the wind on its merry way.
It's so cheerful and peaceful, and cool, and serene,
Just to be sitting there is just like a dream.

All Spring and summer to this place I come,
When not feeling well, or feeling so glum.
Away from the daily toil and strife,
God put this place here to enjoy for life.

Charles Semenick

Forgiveness

I remember the moment clearly still, when,
I was one of the first to yell, Crucify Him!
As I watched the soldiers pierce His side,
Out flowed blood and water! My eyes grew wide!

No! What have I done? I cried!
I've caused Him to be mocked, beaten, tried!
Hanging on the tree; Olive skin, nails forced under!
Hanging on the cross, all dignity torn asunder!

I feel to my knees, my hands cover my face...Shame!
I know now we wronged, yet He took the blame!
In my hands I weep, What He said was true!
I've helped crucify Jehovah! What am I to do?

He came because of our sin, and died from our hate.
In my heart now I have this unliftable weight!
And now I wonder, Can I be saved after what I've done?
Here a Man stood before me saying, Salvation lies in the Son!

I realize now, even though I had arranged the kill,
And I had crucified Jesus, He loves me still!
I ask to preach for Him. He answers, let it be!
I've murdered the King, and yet He died for me!

Chance Springfield

Looking At A Child Today

I was looking at a child today, and he was looking at me.
I wanted to be like him; I could tell he wanted to be like me.
Innocent blue eyes,
Soft, curly hair.
His little body burning with energy, with years ahead to spare.
My eyes are bloodshot and cold.
My head is hanging down.
My body is weak and torn within.
Yeah, I've been around.

So innocent, so fragile,
Son, stay young while you can,
Because soon you'll be out on your own,
And they'll force you to be a man.
And there's one thing I can guarantee:
When you're grown up and playing this game,
You'll stop and look at a child one day
And wish you were the same.

Jeffrey Woodley

Moving Beyond Death

I've read so many tragic stories these days,
I used to be angry for losing you.
At times, I still am, but I know now that heart-pain is universal.
Each person has a story to tell and a tear to shed,
and they should.
I haven't forgotten you,
but the joys and sorrows before me now demand my attention, my
direction, and so I must move on.
I must not ever forget,
but it does no good to hold on to pain or anger.
I will keep your memory strong
and you shall be known to my little one - she reminds me of you.
There is a certain look that is only yours,
so through her your memory lives on.
I hope that you can someday meet her,
I know you would be charmed.

It's like a human chain - we are linked by blood and love.
We pass a little on to those who remain after us,
and keep our core - our essence - to linger
long after our shells have been shed.

Diane S. Hunter

To My Rosemary

I closed my eyes,
I turned my back.
I did not want to see that you had gone away from me.

I wrung my hands.
I shook my head.
I cried and cried.
My heart was dead - shattered within me.

Yes, you were gone.
Away from me all of us who love you.
But then I felt a peace come over me.
And, all at once, I knew God had made a big decision.

As he looked down at you.
And saw your suffering and pain
He said, "Enough, there's nothing more to gain"
And reached down and gathered you in his arms.
And, in His marvelous wisdom, he took you home.

He cradled you in his loving arms.
Where there is no pain or stress.
Just everlasting happiness.
Florence V. D'Incau

Jesse's Song

In loving memory of Jesse L. Dunlap, 9/14/31 - 10/21/93
As I kneel in the crisp leaves to pray
I try to think of the words that I'll say

I need not think, the words come with ease
carried by him in the fresh Autumn breeze

I hear the song of the geese flying south
I taste the salt as the tears reach my mouth

It must be my father's sweet gentle kiss
For as I pray, it's him that I miss

The geese grow weary, their flight shall be long
But fly they must, to sing Jesse's song.
Greg Dunlap

Thanksgiving

I thank you Lord, for the years you've given me
  I thank you for my mother, who gave birth to me
I thank you for my father, who taught me to see
  I could be whatever I really chose to be.

I thank you for a husband who worked so hard to see
  I had all the nice things that meant so much to me.
I thank you for his tenderness, and all the love he gave
  His body now lies sleeping in a lonely grave.

I thank you for our fifty years of happiness and love
  I thank you for Eternal Life, and for our God above
I thank you for my lovely daughter, who means so much to me
  You gave me a diamond, when you gave her to me.

I thank you for our church, Dear Lord; in its entirety
  And for all the Christians, who worship there with me.
I thank you for our Pastor, who is our guiding light
  And for the guidance he gives to us, every day and night.

  Yes Lord, I truly thank thee!
Helen W. Haines

A Choice For Rejoicing

What is death?
I tell you it's not a myth!
When you die,
Let's hope you go to the sky.
As you take the walk through the valley of death,
We hope and pray that you have made a choice.
We hope it's a choice that we'll all rejoice.
We pray that you walk God's way.
If you're faithful you shall never go astray.
This place I speak of is Heaven.
It's a place for God's faithful servants, men and women.
The other place is not all that swell.
It's hell!
It's as if you've been thrown into a burning well.
You can make you're choice of life eternally.
So why not start to get ready?
It's your choice,
So please give us something to rejoice!
Jeremy Jarrett

Past Is Present

I stand in the elevator, suspended by a cable
I stay still, for it not to break, I am not able
This metal enclosure falls at an alarming rate
It takes me through time to a forgotten date
The floors are that of cobble stone
The walls are that of brick
Felt with disease, the smell of decay makes me sick
Glancing around, I view figures
Men they are in cloaks
Standing on a pedestal a jester spills jokes
By the light of the candle
Given off by the flame
I see the fingers that point at me
As in to blame
They grab at me
Violently determined to cease my heart
Though this is not their extent
It is only their start
As I fade I realize this is not of the past
It is what present day society, has given me at last
Anthony P. Strong

"What I Will Miss"

A gift of life is what I've received,
I should not treat it as if it will leave.
But their is no telling what can be conceived,
When someone has vengeance for me.
My life would be gone,
And no more to see.
The time has come for the angel to read,
My name was on the list,
And now I must go,
Without ever seeing a young child grow
I missed out on things I wanted to do,
But I guess my time just came way to soon.
Jessica McCloskey

Laugh!

Laugh, Tiny Child!
Laugh with the joy that is your right.
Laugh with the innocence of your child's heart,
For it is still yours to claim.
Shriek and squeal with abandon—with the glee found fresh in your
  child's soul.
For there is goodness yet in this world
And where there is goodness—there is hope.
Dorothy H. Evans

Thoughts Of A High School Graduate On Graduation Day

Gee, I can hardly believe this day has finally come
I should be so happy, but yet I feel so glum
And as I gaze around me
At all these gals and guys
I noticed that they too, have tears within their eyes
With memories of the basketball, football games and such
And all the school activities
That we loved so much
Remember the high school play
We had a lot of fun
I'll never forget our senior prom
With that special certain someone
It seems like only yesterday
That I walked through these halls
Feeling like a big shot, feel ten feet tall
If I only knew how quickly the years would pass
I'd cherish every school day and try to make them last
Well this is it, here I go
They just called my name
Good bye high school years, life will never be the same
   Dorothy J. Kolb

Twenty Third Psalm

The Lord is by boss
I shall not be lost

He makes me learn
He leads me into new ways of worshiping

He restores my mind
He leads me into paths of scripture

Yes, though I walk though darkness
I will fear no evil for He is with me

He prepares my accounts in the presence of co-workers
He anoints my heart with love

Surely debits and credits shall balance the days
Of my life in the Lord.
   Barbara Martin

Memories Of You

My days are filled with thought of you,
I see your face so clear.
There's days I cannot make it,
Its your voice I need to hear.
I have my thought and memories,
The life and love we share,
These memories will always be.
I take them everywhere.
I think of things, the child we had that acts so much like me.
You gave her all your beauty, it's you through her I see.
I think back in time, when we first met, my angle from above
Special moments come to me in thought,
Time just spent making love.
These memories I keep with me, no one can take them away.
They help me when I'm feeling down, they brighten up my day.
So when I wake and feel alone, and cannot make it through,
I close my eyes, remember times I just spent loving you
   Dareen W. Gray

Untitled

In this New England eggshell sky
I see summer's broken flame
when ferocious August hammered on the porch deck
brazen blues
lemon-soaked hair
and heat so deep your own heart beat made waves in it,
going
BA-BOOMBA-BOOMBA-Boom
and I go back to shoveling snow.
Oh, the present blankets the past
like winter washes away sunburn.
   Elise Bochinski

Reflections

When I stare in to a pond,
I see my own reflection,
Dark, against a blue sky.
Nothing mars my place with the clouds,
The pond surface is without disturbance,
Like a plate of glass washed across the surface.
So clear and motionless it scares me,
For my reflection tells me truths.
And I stare in to a pond,
As still as the water, while I reflect.
   Hannah Russin

I Really Can't Say "I Love You"

I looked into your eyes one day
I saw that our love was not far away
the Chemistry back and forth as it flew,
but in my heart I really knew that I
could not say, "I love you." We went out
and did things together, I felt inside
deep down that we would be forever.
Holding hands while walking down the street,
feeling safe and secure so complete. Listening
to you as you play the baby grand piano,
watching you as you sing nice and slow.
Knowing that my heart should belong to you,
but I really can't say that "I love you."
   Cynthia C. Cox

The New Baby

My baby brother came home from the hospital today.
I saw him in the blanket—but he seemed too tired to play.
Mommy is going to feed him in her bedroom
   because she doesn't want to hear him cry.
I bet he'll never tell her that he needs to be made dry.
He doesn't look at all like me.
The teeth he has—I cannot see.
When will I be able to share my toys?
How long will it be before he'll be a big boy?
How can they treat us both the same?
If, when you call him he doesn't know his name.
   Hetty F. Noble

Reflections

As I sit here all alone, looking across the water,
I reflect back on my life and the choices I have made,
I have taken many paths and learned many a lesson,
And if you asked, I could not count, how many were of transgressions.

As I grew, I came to realize I needed a source of hope,
But what and where to find it I really didn't know.
Until one day I heard His name mentioned among a group,
And decided to look Him up in a book they called "The Word of Truth."

As I read, I found there to be many stories from the past,
Of people who were just like me, alone and lost and sad.
And like them too, I saw His light through the Holy Spirit's love,
And followed Him unto the cross and watched him shed his blood.

From that day on my heart was full, with Him guarding the door,
And though I stray every now and then, I know He's still my Saviour.
And like the pearl within its keep, I know I am protected,
From the daily evils I may face until I get to heaven.

Courtney Kirschenmann

Memory

I see you there, you sit alone, while I sit here my heart forlorn.
I reach out, then you reach back.
When you love me you have a knack, to pull a passion from deep inside,
and a love I tend to hide.
When I love you I come alive, but if one day I wait, and you do not arrive.
I will not mourn the loss of you.
If anything what I will do, is cherish all our happy times,
not waste your time with silly rhymes.
I will find someone new to love to love, so you may brood with your new dove.

Someone new to hold me tight, someone to love all through the night.
Another's kisses I will need, another's words that I will heed.
But always in my memory, will be the love you gave to me.

Michael Wilson

Wishing True

When we're apart,
I quietly close my eyes and imagine you here with me.
I spend so many quiet moments of my own,
Thinking how much I miss you,
And how hard it is to be away from you.
I miss your embrace,
I miss everything you did.
But sometimes I feel you don't have the same feelings as I do.
I just wish I could do something to bring us back together,
So I won't have this awful feeling inside me.
You told me you didn't forget about me,
But now I feel you have.
You said you love me, and nothing will change that,
I wish I could believe you,
But nothing yet has changed my mind.
You know I will always love you no matter what.
But I just don't want my heart to fall apart.
If you could only show me and make me realize you're for me
And that it's true you love me too,
Cause you know that I'll always love you!

CariLee Yachiyo Nakamura

Silent Prayer

Now I lay me down to sleep,
I pray to God my soul to keep.
Let my spirit rise above, and be free to fly,
Even though my mortal body lays down to die.
Give the goddess of love my heart,
So maybe one day, cupid will hit it with his dart.
Sprinkle my dreams over the glistening sun,
So they can dance come true, and have fun.
Man on the moon you better pay attention too,
Cause mother nature will shoot my hopes straight to you.
As for my passionate running emotions,
Please turn them into a spiritual potion.
When all is done please send my body adrift,
On the river to heaven, that beautiful gift.
Now I lay me down to sleep,
I pray to God my soul to keep.

Allison Sayner

Missing You

You've been gone so long, but I need you here.
I need your help and your cheer
What can I do, you're gone for good.
I miss you now a lot more than I thought I could.
The time we spent together was great,
But I'm loosing my trust in fate.
I hate the disease that took you away.
It made us both have to pay.
Where are you now, and why aren't you here?
I just need one more chance to be near.
I want the chance to tell you goodbye,
So night after night I don't have to cry.
I'm sure the pain will never go away.
And always and forever there you will lay.
I'll never forget the times we have shared,
And I'll forever remember how much you cared.
I love you.

Eryn Senter

Leaving To Find

Leaving to find something that I need...
I need to feel the comfort from someone.
I need to feel the love
Or even feel the pain
From these tears falling.
Leaving to find the love that has been lost between us...
For at one time, our love was so strong
That nothing could ruin it.
I need to find the love
My heart felt for you once again.
Leaving to find maybe another love...
Someone who could give
And show me what I want.
Someone who would understand my love
Which I know you never could,
So just let me go
And save what is left of my heart.

Amanda S. Smith

Seasons

In autumn the trees of rustic brown, deep red and light, golden leaves
have started falling in the gentle, cool breeze
In the winter the frosty rain turns into ice and freezes.
In the spring the crocuses, tulips and forsythias weaves
its colors of pink, white and red in a colorful maze.
In summer it turns to hot humid days.
Enjoy the seasons in their special ways.

Helen Guckenheimer

The Past

The past entraps my mind, holding me back from moving on.
I must make my peace with it, so I may see tomorrow's dawn.
Learn from the past, and live for the future.
Allow the old to crumble, and build a new sculpture.

Life is cruel and full of despair,
But I must go on, for there are no repairs.
I remain in the shadows of mistakes in the past.
People remember and judgement is cast.

Never regret the past, nor mourn,
there is no changing it, allow it to be torn.
Tomorrow will be brighter.
Problems and worries will become lighter.

Some say our lives are written by fate.
This I must escape, and open my own gate.
I must pull away from the pain of the past.
Live my life to the fullest, up to the last.

Yesterday must be forgotten and laid to rest,
or be held in the pain of righteousness.
Life is beautiful if allowed to be,
change is here for all to see.
    Jamie Stamps

I Miss The Girl Who Used To Love Me

I miss the girl who used to love me,
I miss the look she once had for me,
This girl is special, she's like no other,
Her rays are sunny, her eyes are thunder!
I miss her subtle surprises,
Iced teas with love, and a smile from heaven!
I miss her voice, I miss her smell,
I miss the girl who knew me so well!
She taught me patience,
She taught me love,
She gave me her heart,
And touched me with her soul!
I love the girl I miss so much,
Her tender smile, her gentle touch,
I'll pray for her again tonight,
Ask God to bless her, and restore her sight!
I let her go, and now I know,
I miss the girl who used to love me!
I thought her love was real?
And I miss that love it made <u>me feel</u>, again!!!
    Daniel John Dobner

Prisoner Of Untold Secrets

I look outside and see freedom,
I listen and hear the laughter,
I open the window and see the innocent smiles.
I breathe in the air and close my eyes,
I remember back when I was carefree, but now it's just a memory.
As the visions return I feel the pain return.
No matter how many times I block it out, it always returns.
So I shut the window and lay down to cry.
The feeling of betrayal, hate, and shame returns from its empty hole.
But now the worst feeling inside is the regret,
  the regret of keeping it a secret deep inside every time.
    Devonia Renee Summersill

The Path

As I look down the dark path I see no light
I listen and do not hear a sound in sight
But then I hear a sound in the leaves
Could it be death coming for me
I look around in anger
To see if there is a man pointing his finger
Then the man said it's your time son
For your spirit to break away and become as one
But I don't know which road I will be taking
Because in church I was never one of decision making
I ask will it be heaven or hell
I wonder if I will here the glorious bell
Because believing in God is must
My soul is nothing but a pile of ashes and dust
    Jason Rice

The Bus

I'm standing on the corner, waiting for the bus
I left work 'bout an hour early to beat the evening rush

I board the bus at 4:15 and grab a window seat
The air conditioning's really cool, it sure does beat the heat

I close my eyes and stretch my legs while starting to relax
Then suddenly I feel the bumps that come from railroad tracks

I sit straight up and turn my head just in time to see
A big and shiny Metro-liner staring right at me

I try to scream but nothing comes, I only feel the pain
Of being hit square in the chest by a speeding southbound train

Then all at once I'm wide awake and sitting back at work
I must have fallen off to sleep, I feel like such a jerk

I think about my little dream, it's great to be alive
And as for taking off at 4......I think I'll work til 5
    Fred A. Nauton

Questions

Dedicated to Stephanie Lyyn Palmer
I know I'm here, But where are you?
I know your with someone, If I only knew who.
Are you with God or Satan, are you in Heaven or Hell?
Did you complete your life, or did you fail?
Can I see you again, or was your death day my last?
I thought you hated me, or was that in the past?
Are you happy there, were you happier here?
Or when you left this place, did you cry your last tear?

Answers
You are on earth, only across the vail.
And I am in Heaven, Not with Satan in Hell.
Yes I completed my life, But God needed me here.
We will see each other again, and I will hold you near.
I did not hate you, I only had trouble expressing my love.
I was happy there, but I am happier here above.
When you get here, you will see,
that there's no need for tears, cause together as a family we'll be!
    Christiana Palmer

Spirit Of The Soul

A soulful medicine man sitting on the cliff, the eagle soaring
in the sky his eyes searching earth, are the eyes for the
medicine man. Majestically gliding down and round the canyon
of life in search of the "White-eye" who will right the call
of the wings of an eagle spread full it's seven feet calling
to it's mate bringing life as they flow through time and
space with grace and beauty to land in the hearts searching
and pressing the loosed winds.
    Elizabeth Lowry

I'm Sorry

Honey I'm sorry for doing you wrong
I know you have been uncomfortable long
I wish I could turn back the time
In order to clear the wrong from your mind

I hate to see that you are upset
Because it makes me start to regret
The thing I did to you yesterday
That is making you very silent today

I don't like to say the word sorry
But for you I'll get it out of me
Now I feel good having you in one arm
Because I am able to kiss you and keep you warm

But honey I will do anything for you
If you ask me or want me to
I don't mind spending a little money
On the girl that I call my honey

I love to see you smile whenever
Because you're mine forever
But I will continue to take care
Of you honey because you're my teddy bear

Chinedu Dean Ogbuike

Pain

Pain all around me
I know when it all started
but when does it end?
In this deep hole, there are many faces
faces of confusion, faces of hate, faces of helplessness and anger.
Scars, gashes, tears -
that's all I'm made of.
I want to be loved, but I can't.
I want a free life, but I can't.
I want death to be come part of me
but nothing lets it happen.
I want to run, but it will run after me
the pain is so strong, it isn't fair
So the tears shunt fall from my face
I won't let them
I will fight "pain" and I will win
Win happiness, not the pain
Pain all around me

Donika Moon

My Love For You

Just as the eagles fly in the sky,
I know my love for you will never die.
We have conquered the past,
And the dye for our future has already been cast.
No one will ever stop our love
Since it is sent from only above.

Did the Father place this love inside of you and me,
So that we may be joined in Heaven for all of Eternity?
I need you like the grass needs the morning dew,
Like the ocean needs the sun's radiant hues.

You were sent from God and you are a priceless treasure,
But I can't count the cost because love has no measure.
No one will ever know the depth of our faith in each other,
The only thing they will see is how we love one another.

So just as the eagles fly in the sky
Our love for each other will never die.
We have conquered the past,
And the dye for our future has been cast.
Allow me to love you forever
Just as the Father's love between us will never sever.

Amy E. Moore

Say You Love Me

When my time has come and they lay me down to rest
I hope that they can fill my last request
To bring in your pretty face so I can see
To hear those three words from you to me
Just say you love me that's all I want to hear
Just say you love me, whisper in my ear
There's one thing I want to know
Is that you love me, so I can smile when I go
There's only one thing I truly want
It's not a fancy home or big ol' yacht
It's just to look in your beautiful eyes
And know you love me when we say goodbye

David J. Wilson

A Mother

My babies so tiny and dependent
  I held them close when they cried.
They squirmed to get away.
  "Colic," the doctor said.
Rocking two hours a day I'd spend
  hoping to take their hurt away.

I reach for my child's hand.
  He withdraws and runs ahead.
I dart to catch him if I can
  before he finds the danger that lies beyond.

Teens, I want to share with you
  The joys and sorrows of my youth
but you have your own life to live.
  I seem to have nothing left to give.

Where are the arms to cling to me,
  The hand reaching to say protect me?
I'm still here with my rocking chair.
  My arms are empty, hand still
reaching, my heart still cares.

Jane Meeker

Gotta Go

She called to me from her dying bed,
I heard her voice so weak and slow,
"Help me, help me " was what she said
But my reply was "Gotta go."

All he wanted was a friend to see,
A friend whose hand warmed with a glow,
"Help me, help me" said he, said he,
But his friend's reply was "Gotta go."

The child looked at him with tears in her eyes,
The ragged clothes that spoke of woe.
"Help me, help me" were her cries.
But all he could say was "Gotta go."

She couldn't remember her name this day,
Or where she'd been, or where she'd go
"Help me, help me" was what she'd say.
But all she could hear was "Gotta go."

The Twenty-first century looms ahead,
With promises bright with glow,
Computers helping us bring home the bread,
May God help us, we've all gotta go!

Evelyn Bland Lipscomb

Sounds

    Through the slamming sounds of waves on rocks,
I hear the screeching of a sea gull.
    Through the screeching of a sea gull,
I hear the barking of a seal.
    Through the barking of a seal,
I hear the chirping of a sandpiper.
    Through the chirping of a sandpiper,
I hear the clicks of a crab.
    Through the clicks of a crab,
I hear the whoosh of waves on the beach.
    Through the whooshing of the waves,
I hear my mother calling me.
    Through the noise of her voice,
I hear her love for me.
    Carrie Margeson

The City

As I awake in the morning I see the bright sun through the window and I hear the birds singing. In the distance I hear the cars, horns and sirens ringing. Life in the city is loud and crowded yet in my backyard I feel the breeze and see the beautiful leaves as they change colors and drift to the ground.

Hear the planes overhead as the city wakes up, see the squirrels in the trees up above. Turning my head I see the streets so full of people hurrying to work, impatient, and I frown. I look back at the trees and listen to the birds sing, can't let it get me down.

It's a race to the end of the day business must go on, in the evening the sky is so nice can't always be so clear with factories and such so near. Goodnight big city another day goes by, in the distance I hear an owl as he cries. So much more quiet at night, so goes the city life.

    Debra A. Garcia

Who's Who

I sit curled up in a corner scared half to death.
I hear someone near me and feel her warm breath.

Is this real or my imagination.
Is she here or is this a hallucination.

I'm scared to move I may get hurt if I do.
But I must get out I must break through.
To tell everyone who's who.
    Jessica A. Micewicz

My Journey

I have lost sight of a new sunrise.
I have walked on sheets of blood,
crossing rivers,
Exploding on mountain's tops.

Yearning an incredible desire
to shoot across a northern milky way,
experience death.
Talk to the mormons and enchant the snakes
in this darkened hall of confusion and fears.

As I walk on sheets of blood,
and thru the walls around me,
I can't smile nor cry
my soul is numb with anguish and despair...
the strangest feeling...I have ever known.
    Christian Ferry

It's Time For Me

I finally know just what I want
I have to live for me;
I've thought and thought of the other guy's needs,
Till they were all that I could see.

I've spent what seems like all my life,
Living for someone else:
Well, DAMN IT ALL, it's time that I stop,
And do something JUST for myself!

And now seems like a pretty good time —
Just as good as any;
I'm tired of problems clouding my mind:
There really have been so many.

From here on out, it's "Bonnie first";
The others will have to wait:
If I don't make this decision NOW,
Tomorrow may be FAR TOO LATE!!
    BJ Reese

Little Boy, Little Boy, Where Did You Go!!!

My little boy where did you go?
I have searched for you day and night.
You left me so many years ago.
Oh, how I have missed you so.
How I have longed to hold you and to love you.
You where my world and a part of my life.
You were my first born.
You were meant to be my blessing.
But, how the tides turned,
my world turned upside down when you were gone.
How I longed to hold you and to love you,
you were my precious son.
I can still recall your smile and your eyes
for your shined like diamonds in the sky.
If you only knew how many buckets of tears I have cried for you.
For you were my little boy.
    Diana Macal

Looking Back

As my work takes me on many roads,
I have opportunity to explore;
I like to look at the countryside,
And picture it as it was before.

There were fields of grain, corn and hay,
As far as the eye could see;
As they waved in the breeze along with the trees,
They were a beautiful sight to me.

I remember the many fine horses,
And their harnesses all decked with brass;
A man could plow from dawn to dark,
Without the stench of gas.

Our transportation was simple,
A horse and buggy fine;
They always seemed to get us,
To town and church on time.

Yes, as I look back o'er the years gone by,
And view our nations great range;
My eyes are filled with burning tears,
When I see the way things have changed.
    Carol A. Atwood

Birth Of A Dream

In my heart and soul there has always been a dream waiting to be born,
I have held and nourished and grown with this dream since I was born.
Everyone has a secret little dream hidden in their heart and just won't let it start
To unfold and grow, become a reality, to be born and hear the first beat of its heart.
I'm letting you out my special little dream, lets grow together and share with everyone
Our sincere thoughts, our loving, laughing, caring and sharing and crazy things we've done.
It's time we strutted our stuff, put it in print, send it in and show the world that together we can,
Take the test, shine with the rest, "guess what Dream", we have just taken our Stand.
    DREAM JUST BORN

   Judy Thomason

My Pride And Joy

The Suwannee River is my pride and joy.
I have fished from its bank since I was a boy.
It flows right through my home town,
I learned to swim so I would not drown.

I have fished the creeks and I have fished the sloughs,
And when I can't go fishing I get the blues.
I fish with a pole and a rod and reel,
I usually catch enough for a good meal.

When I get enough I call it quits,
Go home and cook them with a pot of grits.
Bread and pickles round out the dish,
And I thank the Lord for Suwannee River fish.

   Edgar L. Tompkins

The Answer

My vision blurred, yet ever sharpening,
I have come to see more clearly.
Days upon days, marking the time of learning
And integration, to fumble until I see.

I searched, unknowing, the ultimate truth,
Shrinking yet growing under heavy load.
Soul in torment, I did not know, one aim only.
Pain brought by me, confused my soul.

Nearly blind, by my own blinding. Yet gaining,
My soul seemed to expand and nearly grasp,
My body waning, yet beautiful in maturity
Seemed perfect for undeniable mystery.

One thought came clearly, mocking the complex
With the simplicity of freedom.
The truth, the aim, the panacea, the solution
All contained in one word and action. Love

   Helen Atwood Stark

Untitled

The other day when you came my way
It was a thrill to see you, still
It was no surprise when I saw your eyes.
Our bodies were feeling and our minds were reeling.
It's been a year, but I had no fear
I'd see you again, we'd always be friends.
So as you drove away, I knew that some day
I'd look up and see someone else smiling at me!
So until next time, would you be so kind
To come my way another day.

   Debra Lyn Witherspoon

Hurt Me No More

My pride hangs loose on my bones;
I have barely escaped from your cast stones.
Have pity on me, for you are my friends.
Why must you torment me with your mocking amends?
Why must you strike me down, for I have done you no wrong.
You say it will end, but with that you only prolong.
All the things you've called me should
Be written in a book or chiseled in stone,
So that all may look and remember your harsh tone.
I know there is someone in heaven that will come at last to my defense,
But only when my body is dying of lost sense.
Yet while still in this body, I shall see God
With my own eyes.
He will tell me no lies,
For he will not be a stranger.

   Cathryn Karashin

I Loved School (Back In The Days)

Back in the days I used to love school,
I hated to miss; I thought it was cool.
All my classes - I thought they were fun,
I did all my assignments, every last one!

I tried very hard and got the best grade
I did reading, reports - projects were made!
I was a good student, got A's on the test
Going to school was what I loved best.

Things changed fast; my love for school didn't last.
I lost interest and lost my will; school had simply lost its thrill.

If I had a choice, I wouldn't go at all
I'd skip it altogether and hang at the mall.
I don't need school with its figures and facts,
In my opinion, excitement it lacks.

The teachers are boring; the books out-of-date,
For every class I'm showing up late.
If it weren't for sports, I'd barely show up at all
I need a 2.0 to continue to play ball.

Back in the days I used to love school,
I hated to miss; I was such a fool!

   Dan Feldman

Addiction

Addiction is all that I want.
I go to any length to get what I need.
I don't care if I live or die, but I want that addiction.
I got a bad attitude and I can't think straight.
But I want that addiction.
I wanna look so nice, but I wouldn't think twice,
About that addiction.
Floating on high, that addiction,
Makes me think that everything is so great.
Can't face life on any terms, so I need that addiction.
When I do my drug or my alcohol.
I can look at the world no conscience at all.
My addiction!
Everyone says I need an attitude adjustment,
But I just need that addiction.
Floating high above the clouds;
I'm looking back and thinking out loud, about my addiction.
I do have to face my past
With a much higher power than myself.
I wonder how he feels about my addiction.

   Irene M. De Cata

My Father

Wisdom and knowledge
I gain.
Soothing comforts of his smiles,
my heart fills with love.

Watching miracles at work,
the possibilities of this man!
What seems impossible quickly changes.
Testing the boundaries of a storm filled life,
the courageous heart.

Who could this man be?

Holding himself with confidence,
using his charms.
The word hate has no meaning to the
human race no longer.

As I hear the mind's questioning,
I proudly answer,
"He is my father."

Josefina Hellsten

Never Too Late

I was born before my time, you see, I was never wanted.
I found out for sure as I grew older.
I had love in my heart yet the emptiness kept getting bolder.
As a child I lived the lonely life, as a teen I was always told
to get gone.
I didn't think anything about it until I started wishing I'd
never been born.
As a young girl I married quickly so I wouldn't be alone, but I never
felt real joy 'til I heard the Dr. say "my dear you have a boy".
I had 5 children and tired to shield them all. Give them all the love
I never had, I looked around all too soon they were grown and gone,
I had to realize again I was all alone.
My mother passed and I could not feel real sad,
for I felt in my heart how can I miss what I never had?
At the age of 57, I divorced and am trying to live
for it seemed I was dead, I had no one to love me and nothing left to give.
There is no hurt like an empty heart, so I fell down on my face,
I prayed to GOD before I die please send me love that I could return
He took away the built up hate and sent me Thomas in it's place.
I do believe with prayer you can change fate
and I THANK GOD IT'S NEVER TOO LATE

Frances A. Wallace

Archetype

Across these steaming seas of silt
I flap my leathern wings: I fly
Aslant my weary shattered kingdom.

Soaring through ashen-coated skies
I watch the groaning carcass of Pangaea
Rip open on the plasma of the globe.

On the icy mirror of my reptilian eye
The kindred shapes of prey grow dim.
Africa slides away — a cargo of carrion.

My ages-old dominion smells decline.
Godwanaland is gone - its glory fades —
My endless fern plantations shrivel in a blazing sun.

Asia beckons to India astride her brittle shell
Of a blazing tortoise paddling molten rock.
This world my great wings enfolded

Explodes toward rodent principalities
Who will inherit my probing fossil beak.
I sleep — and wait my dawn in the garden.

John Atherton

"Insignificance"

As I look at the world around me,
I find myself so insignificant.
Compared to the starvation and war,
I don't matter at all.
What can I do to help?
How can I show that I care?
Can one man make a difference,
If nobody else believes in the cause?
I have tried before and have failed;
Should I try again?
Yes, I shall try again. I will be insignificant no longer.

Jason Bolicki

The Christmas Gift

Last night I sat with down bowed head
I felt so depressed and blue,
Christmas Day was approaching fast
And I had no presents for you.
The beautiful lights and the caroling sweet
Found no echo in my heart;
In the happy throng of shoppers gay
It seemed that I had no part.

Then I thought as I sat in the shadows gray
Why ask wealth, when you'll leave it behind?
Did our Savior purchase with silver or gold?
The great Gift He gave to mankind?
Then lifting my eyes, as my soul filled with love
For the Spirit of Christmas, at last
Had found place in my heart, and our Dear Savior's Love
I had found it, what more could I ask?

Christina Herbert

Sleep

Sleep!
I dreamed of you last night
and in that darkness that lets me dream
I saw you sunshine-smile on me again.

In my mind, I think, the light
and deceived myself with what I would have seen.
Your face was younger, happier, than
I ever knew you while you were alive.

And now questions, long-neglected, like my friend,
undemanding of conversation or understanding.
Awakenings, as a product from my sleeping, thrive.
These are, they say, only what is inside coming out.

Great mysteries are answered within a magic ring
Portents, wise men, crystals; myths are come alive
Psychologists, theologists; questions and answers now
There explain my dream, and death, and love.

The answer to my only doubt:
Last night I dreamed of you;
Were you dreaming, too?

Dan Griffith

Rain!!

I SEE: Dark, gloomy clouds when it rains outside.
I HEAR: The loud, pounding rain as it dribbles down my window.
I TOUCH: My wet, knotted, messy hair when it rains.
I SMELL: The hot chocolate my mom makes and the smoke from the
  neighbors fireplaces.
I TASTE: The nice, sweet, warm hot chocolate and fresh baked cookies.
I FEEL: Nice, and cozy in my warm house when it is raining.

Casey Shumate

Dreams

I dream of our never ending embrace.
I dream of your touch to my face.
I dream of you being near me.
Could this possibly be?

I dream of us hand-in-hand.
I dream of us sharing a plan.
I dream of you holding me.
Could this possibly be?

I dream of us walking outside.
I dream of us side by side.
I dream of you hugging me.
Could this possibly be?

I dream of us looking into each other's eyes.
I beam and you smile to my surprise.
I dream of us sitting by the sea.
Could this possibly be?

I dream of us not letting go.
I say I love you, which you know.
You dance and only with me.
Could this possibly be?

Glenda Bedneau

Love's Prayer

I think of you by day.
I dream of you by night.
I wish I may,
Hold you in my arms tonight.

If I could, everything would be right.
With the stars shining bright above.
Dancing under the moonlight,
With my love.

You would bend down and kiss my cheek.
I would stretch up and kiss your lips.
We would then notice that we were unique.
Then you'd gently put your hands around my hips.

We would start walking down the beach.
The waves rolling over our feet.
Then to me you would reach.
I'd start to feel your body heat.

We'd make out in the sand.
Only if my wish would come true.
Then everything would be grand.
If only I could be with you.

Jennifer Behnke

Imagery

I sleep a dark succumbing sleep,
I dream a dream I wish to keep,
Of heroes and damsels in distress,
Ruffle shirts and a flouncy ballroom dress,
Of swordplay and moonlight romances,
Tall Sir Lancelot fighting men with lances,
Of a remote castle, a green dragon, and of evil witches,
Then I saw bright colored switches,
Red nobs, blue buttons, gray hammers, and green nails,
Worked by and old man with hands pale and frail,
Suddenly I was awake sitting in my bed,
Oh my poor aching head!

Jean-Marie Venturini

Ode To The Disadvantaged

They must think I'm a pigeon, good for nothing at all
I don't sing in the choir, I'm not big and tall
I can't play like the others, run and push and be shoved,
But I have feelings like others, I know the need to be loved.

They must think I'm a pigeon, good for nothing at all.
My body is broken and twisted, sometimes I can't move at all.
But life still flows in my body, I see what for others it holds.
For me there is little to hope for, as each new day unfolds.

They must think I'm a pigeon, good for nothing at all.
They look for beauty and stature, I'm both ugly and small.
No wonder they joke and reject me, I don't fit in their crowd.
But I have a right to survival, and I can succeed if allowed.

They must think I'm a pigeon, good for nothing at all.
They make sport of my trying, its like running into a wall.
All I ask is my freedom, promised by God up above,
I may be less than they hoped for, but give me a chance if not love

They must think I'm a pigeon, good for nothing at all.
They'd be amazed at my talents, bet I could pack the hall.
But they'll never know my secret, they'll never let me try.
'Cause they just think I'm a pigeon, they'll shoot me before I can fly.

George E. Saurman

The Dream

I see your face but it's in my dreams
   I don't know you yet somehow I do.
I search through discards of these broken loves
   still I find no clue.
There is something out there
   something hidden from view.
How long must I search; will I know it's you?
How many times will my heart break
   with these passing loves?
When do you call quits and accept your fate
   that it is nothing but a dream
   something never meant to happen to you.
The hope that the One you see in your dreams
   will find you. Somewhere. Someday.
And as these years pass on by
   there is still the hope; the want
   stronger, yet much more distant.
Oh, why can't I see or touch you
   but only in my dreams.

Anne M.

Thanks God, For The Thorns

Lord, I've stood very close to death today—
   I didn't ask for the opportunity to serve you that way,
   But I guess you knew where I belonged.
It's hard to give thanks for having walked through the
   valley of shadows myself,
But I thank you for having led me even there so I could
   later share that walk with others.
Thank you for the long night of pain shared with a sister.
You knew the pain would not disappear, but yet could be eased
   by talking about it openly.
Even as you gave your disciples words as needed, I thank you
   for making my timid soul bold enough to care and share.
Today I understand more fully with the Psalmist who says,
   "The Lord is my shepherd, I shall not want."
I have emptied myself into the life of another's pain, and yet
   somehow now I have more room to receive of your love!
Lord, I won't even try to explain it—but I accept it, and I
   give thanks!

Howard N. Palmatier

Untitled

My heart you held in the palm of your hands,
I dedicated my love to only one man,
A man that has totally changed my life around,
The meaning of love was something I had found,
I had it once, and lost it again,
The meaning of love has come to an end,
You left me here to suffer alone,
With a heart that has turned from grass to stone,
You broke my heart and showed no shame,
You played with my feelings as if the were a game,
An everlasting game that shall never end,
Love became my enemy and hate was my best friend,
My feelings for you refuse to part,
You closed my hand and crushed my heart,
A man I loved and always adored,
Your shadow will follow me forevermore,
You took the love that cannot be replaced
The ever lasting smile has been striped from my face,
A man I loved and thought that I could trust,
Who neglected a relationship, and settled for just lust...
Heather Renee Stahl

The Answer

Deep down within the abyss of my mind,
I constantly search for something all men have failed to find.
A perfect life filled with contentment and love,
In a world of calm, guided by the Supreme Being from above.

Why must there by quarrels, wars, and relationships full of strife?
While all men pretend to lead the godly and benevolent life.
Why must each have more possessions than other men,
While logic derives it matters naught in the end?

To live out his life span each day ready to die,
Is a goal whose attainment each man should try.

When all men are brothers in a world peaceful and free,
My search will have concluded;
The answer found for me.
Edward Harrell Hinson

Paranoid Woes

I tighten the black yarn around my wrist.
I concentrate on the force of my blood beating against it.
I release it when my fingers turn purple and the life giving liquid flows.
I do this to verify my mortality.
I do this to prove to myself I can still feel.

I tighten the rubber hand around my arm.
I can once again feel my blood beating against it.
I prick my skin with the poison needle.
I can feel it touch my vein and flow up my arm.
As soon as it hits my brain I can breathe again.

My emaciated spirit traps me in this room.
The little red devils called society wait outside to stab me with
  their pitchforks.
I can see the way they leer at me; I know what they want.
I'd give it to them if I knew they wouldn't just take it and throw
  me to the side.
I'd give it to them if I could release it and I knew wouldn't abuse it.
But I know better.

Whatever it is they want, it stays with me in hibernation.
The poison I inject helps to keep it in my brain and helps me
  deal with their leering eyes.
The poison I inject helps me go one step closer to the immovable state.
Jenn Bull

I Know How Your Feeling

I see through your smile, the hurt you try to hide.
I can't think of what to say to make it alright.
  But I know how your feeling!

You see I've been through loves hold before,
and loves grasp sometimes lets go and you fall,
  so you see, I know how your feeling!

I don't know how to make you feel better.
I wish I had enough smarts to write it in a letter.
  But, I do know how your feeling!

It takes awhile to get over the hurt, and
the pain lingers on for a long time.
  You see, I know how your feeling!

Someday tho, you'll find the right person
to fill the void you now have in your heart.
  You see, I know how your feeling!
  can you see how I feel for you?
Deborah Rocks

Not Goodbye

The golden dawn that brightens my door
I cannot share with him anymore.

The first snowflake with its thrill
And delight of winter's new chill

Are mine alone to view
While I suffer the loss anew.

Standing here by his final resting place
His death I have come to face.

And on this cold December day
I realize with shock and dismay

That grief has forced me to forget
The wonders he strove to share since first we met.

His love lost in death? Never!
It shall remain forever

With me each step I wander
While nature's beauty I remember to ponder.
Janet Koerner

Goodbye to Heartache

Through the smile and the dimples,
I can see that the heart is crippled.
Recent pain and heartache has taken its toll,
Laughter and happiness has fallen into a lull.

Looking for reasons and explanations,
Wondering why you feel these sensations.
A tear rolls down my cheek for you,
I've been there, I know what you're going through.

I want to take you in my arms and hold you tight,
Whisper in your ear, "It's going to be all right."
Only time can heal the wounds and ease the pain,
In the end, you will be amazed at the strength you've gained.

Hold on to the good memories and cherish them forever,
Learn to let go of the bad and let their ties sever.
Figure out from this experience what it is you were to learn,
Say goodbye to the heartache and let the pain adjourn.
Holly K. Sharer

"Rainy Days"

As I sit looking out of the window,
I can see little drops fall on the ground.
They fall on the leaves and trees so quietly,
They can't be heard at all.

As I sit looking out of the window,
I can see little boys and girls jumping in the puddles.
Watching them, thinking of my own childhood.
Remembering how I used to be.

As I sit looking out of the window,
I can see the crystal-clear dew on the grass
   after the rain has stopped.
Thinking to myself, "Today will be a wonderful day."
But I'll miss those rainy days.
   Aleia Nichole Banks

Terror In The Heartland

   I know I cannot even imagine your pain,
I can only hope your heart, life and spirit survive the strain.
   For all the precious and innocent lives that were lost,
Throughout our lives we will all carry the cost.
   Wondering, are we really safe anywhere?
And how many others can take lives and not even care?
   As I put my children to bed at night,
I am so tempted to never let them out of my sight.
   And I think about the parents, who's cribs are now empty,
Forever wondering what their kids were meant to be.
   I don't think any of our lives can ever be the same,
Because of the lives that were lost, and maybe a bit of shame.
   Shame that human life has so little value to some,
And that some say the worst is yet to come.
   I can't seem to explain to my five year old son,
Why there are bad guys, and why they want to hurt someone.
   "But you won't let them hurt me, will you dad?"
For all the Daddy's like me, who made that promise, I feel sad.
   There were a lot of people and promises that died that day,
And many more "I Love You's" left to say.
   Greg Miller

My Morning Walk

I really enjoy every step of my morning walk
I can hear my Creator talk
As the cool breeze ruffles through my hair
He whispers softly: "How much I care!
I'm with you in your daily affair!"

I really enjoy every step of my morning walk
I can hear my Creator talk
As the birds hap'ly flutter their wing
And through a sweet melody they sing
He tells me: "My child, keep on praising!"

I really enjoy every step of my morning walk
I can hear my Creator talk
As the fresh air I deeply inhale
New hope surges through my soul, though frail.
He vowed: "With me my child, you'll ne'er fail."
   Anneke G. Simorangkir

John Brandy Jason — Our Fight

Another day has gone by with a song left undone.
Holding your hands tight — trying not to show my fright.
Hugging you for as long as I can, while the tears gently
fall on your head, hoping it won't be for long.
Just one more "love you" before I have to say — please
remember "I didn't want it this way."
Smiles passed only to be gone, now your on your way —
believing the tears will stop, but the love will not!
   Carrie Schmidt

Mom

From my childhood memories,
I bring to my adulthood the positive affects
   a good parent has on my everyday life.
You have quietly watched me
   through many changes, starting from birth.
The complexity of all this made easier,
   only be someone who cares.
You have been and are a big part of my life,
   of me.
Thanks for helping me grow to the woman
   I am today,
For being able to express myself
   through the gift of poetry.
   Cathy L. Daniels

Where To Go, L And O

What's this?
I asked confused.
Standing on the fine line separating light and dark,
Not knowing when to rest.
Not knowing awake,
But subconsciously turning to dark.
The dark,
Lying down in darkness,
Lying down with my shaken friends.
Still being miles away.
The light?
Resting in the light?
Not feeling at home,
Feeling insecure.
The light too bright to see into.
Still being in two places at once,
Looking for the soft comforting pillow to rest upon.
Finding the place most like home,
I turn to darkness,
And sleep...
   Jonathan Ortiz

Through The Field

   I see your eyes peer from behind the trunk.
I am timid, weak, fatigued, but you seem not to care.
   I turn to see the presence of someone else,
but no one is there.
   Surely it is not me at whom you stand and stare?

   I see you step forward
and the soft grass whispers beneath.
A sound as slight as the turning of a leaf.
   What is it in me that you see?

   Your arms are extended.
An undefinable force beckons me.

   We embrace with the comfort of the sea.
Your heart must be singing in a different key.

   For the world, so cold and lonely,
However, this is all I had.

   Until you found me-I am so glad!
With you near, there is not a thing to fear.

   Your hand in mine,
Mine in yours,
We walk through the field, towards...
   Jenni Crowley

The Thinking Man's Game

I love to play chess.
I am the King,
the pawns are my personal guards,
my queen, the most powerful,
the bishops, merely decoys,
tricky are the knights, my loyal queen-stealers,
the rooks are strong like castles, tending to my needs,
until finally the ruler of another kingdom stands trapped.
Because I am clever,
all but one kingdom can I consistently raid—
the Kingdom of Chandler.
His knights are strong but bishops are weak,
similar to mine,
I order the pieces to win,
sometimes they do not.
The Kingdom of Chandler I will defeat.

Aaron Swiggum

"Till Then"

I hate to leave this world that is full of life
I am sad to leave my family and friends at this time
But death is always around for everyone
It only gets to you when it's your time

Don't feel bad nor sad for me when I'm gone
For I will feel the same for you
Just come to say goodbye and see me go
I will be happy to see you all around

Let's just remember all the happy times
For we can't do a thing for this sad time
Make this day a happy one for me
When you all get together and keep me company

As I go on to my long journey beyond
Let me take with me the love and peace from all of you
So when I get to face our Heavenly Father above
I may say that my life on earth was not in vain

May we have peace and love in our hearts
So when the time comes you can hold your head up high
And say, I am at peace to face the Lord
For I have loved all of you in this world

Erlinda G. Delos Santos

Birth Date To Remember

This thought, and mine alone, to celebrate:
I am not quite as empty as before.
My bid for motherhood that lonely date
Let me see you as through a louvered door...
That sunbeam, not persuaded by my glance,
Would seek companions of its kind...Along
the angels' path, eager to join their dance,
Would learn the words and music of their song.

You'd see the world as yours at sweet sixteen
And claim, I hope, your father's hazel eyes.
You'd choose a dress-some shade of summer green?
(Were golden wings that day your first surprise?)

Tonight the sky is wearing royal blue
While heaven lights a special star for you.

Hascal Vaughan Stewart

Untitled

When I hear the roar of thunder, or see the falling rain,
  I am left in wonder, is God crying out in pain.
And when I see the lightning flash across the sky,
  Could it be the heat of wrath aroused by you and I?

Or could it be the lightning is but flickering candlelight,
  To guide the step of Angels who tend him through the night?
I wonder if my mother is one of those who share
  That flickering candlelight, as she gives Him tender care.

And could that falling rain be teardrops from his eye,
  Because we show so little love, that he is want to cry?
Father I am sorry for all sin you see,
  And I ask you to forgive the wrong you find in me.

I pray all your children, rich and poor, from every land,
  Will follow in your footsteps and obey your command.
And when I see the blue sky, with sunlight peeping through,
  I will believe my prayer was heard, and all is well with you.

Grace Kephart

Untitled

As I sit and watch the spectacular sunrise,
I am in complete awe.
To see the first rays gleaming off the water.
Lost in thought as if nothing really mattered.
Only able to think of you, to my surprise.

Just as the darkness gives away to the sun rays,
My troubles give away to your smiling face.
And my heart beats to the pace,
Of an Indy 500 race.

Just as the sun is true;
Especially so, is my love for you.

Justin Antonellini

Jesus In My Heart And Soul

With Jesus in my heart and soul
I am filled with a great deal of joyfulness and gladness
In my heart and soul wherever I have been and wherever I go.
No matter what the circumstances are
Jesus is always right with me as close as my fingertips.

The love of my life dear Jesus has been
And I do always trust in him.
He takes care of all my needs and his great
desire is always to please those who belong to him like me.

While I have been handicap all my life it's
been Jesus the sweet savior who has favored
me and released the pain and hardships (thorns).
Jesus has taken care of all my needs, all my life
And always does what is right that releases the pain out of my life.

The matters of my heart he knows and he is truly
with me and a blessing wherever I have been and wherever I go.

Jesus truly has been my Love and Justice and best friend to me.
Jesus is the one I truly depend and we are
made as bookends for each other.

Catherine D. Feathers

A Servant Of Humanity

I am a nurse, a servant of Humanity.
I am a mother, a servant of a household.

As a nurse, I serve the patients their meal trays.
As a mother, I cook and serve the meals to my household.

As a nurse, I dispense medications as prescribed.
As a mother, I prescribe and medicate the members of my household.

As a nurse, I provide an clean environment for the patients.
As a mother, I clean the environment of my household.

As a nurse, I assist patients with their clothing.
As a mother, I wash and prepare the clothes of my household.

As a nurse, I was educated at a school of Nursing.
As a mother, I was educated by the self-taught method.

As a nurse, There is a co-dependency from the patients.
As a mother, My household depends on me.

As a nurse, I have received awards and honors.
As a mother, I am honored by my household.

As a nurse, The shift's hours are long.
As a mother, The shift never ends.

As a nurse, I am love by my patients.
As a mother, I offer unconditional love.

Betty Hill-Johnson

Dedication

O God, great master smith,
I am a dull, bent plowshare in your hands.
Melt in your scorching flame my stubborn will;
Lay me upon the hard, unyielding anvil
And rain your ringing hammer blows upon me;
Temper me, try me, fit me for your use.

Fit me to plow a furrow straight and true,
Burying deep Earth's sodden, dead debris,
Bringing to light its mellow, fertile soil
That it may bloom anew.

Everett L. Refior

A Husband's Prayer

I am the onion that makes you cry
I am a bear that you tear
I am a fox that sneaks at night
I am the I lamp that doesn't work
I am the chandelier shining in the room
I am the crow that calls your name
I am the ash tray you made in school
I am the comet that brakes the night
I am the twinkle in your eyes
I am the rain that falls
I am the window you just cleaned
I am the fog in the morning hours
I am the cup of coffee you hold tight
I am the infant inside you, I am the roses that you grow

You see, I am who I am
  I stand for your love
  I stand for your hate
  I stand for your confusion
  I stand with you always
You see, I am who I am

Michael D. Smith

Waterfowl Pilgrimage

From eggs, thoust do emerge
hurry quickly, oh young ones
forever your fate is sealed in the grass

The wetland edge, a burden lifted
swim behind mother, alongside your brother
secure your sustenance, in waters shimmering of glass

As winds blow, and day length withers
feathers grow, preparing for the sojourn ahead
Mother declaring you, as travelers en masse

You are harbingers of fall
silver linings winging to new lands
cutting the tow, in harmony like a band

The air, the smell, the clouds and the leaves
patterns evolving once again
dancing around Her winter grip, all in hopes of furthering your end

To the north, lured by Mother's friendly retreat
a niche waiting in the sea of grass, oh elegant daughters
to witness your young, from eggs thoust will emerge

John Brian Davis

Prescription For Peace

It's in the making...
Humankind's prescription for peace:
  a Multicultural Quilt.
Reach out and join the chain of hands
  across the lands, the seas, the oceans...
Find your place in the Multicultural Quilt
  and let it grow as generations come and go.
So be it...hold on and don't let go.
Together as one multicolored fabric of humankind,
  share a vision of one world, a better world —
With one voice in all languages,
  one shade in all colors,
  one tune in all songs,
  one big step in a million steps
  towards PEACE.

Aida A. Joshi

To My Darling Daughter

To my darling daughter, I just wanted you to know
How wonderful it's been, to sit back and watch you grow.

I remember those days, when I first brought you home
I knew in my heart I'd never be alone.

You are my life and my love, the biggest thing in my heart
And I wanted you to know we'll never be apart.

It's hard for me to believe, you've grown up so fast
Your childhood years just didn't seem to last.

But now you're a teenager, the years just slipped away
I didn't see it coming with each passing day.

You're no longer a child, not an adult quite yet
Mixed emotions and feelings, unsure of how to act.

I'll always be here for you, through the good times and the bad
Teenage years are rough, sometimes can be quite sad.

But one thing you can be sure of, no question in my mind
I'll be here for you, any day, any time.

Thirteen years of growing, you're thirteen years old today
Your teenage years are here, adulthood's on the way!

Judith Ticer Donaldson

How Often

How often do you long for someone for care for just you?
How often do you not care just for someone?

How often do you sit in loneliness wishing for a friend?
How often do you not offer yourself as a friend?

How often do you want to feel trusted and needed?
How often do you not offer trust or need?

How often does your heart cry out for the feeling of belonging?
How often do you close your heart to those who wish to belong?

How often do you wish to share your good fortune and happiness with others?
How often do you find fault in others good fortune and happiness?

How often do you wish to be accepted for what you do and what you are?
How often do you not accept the same in others?

How often do you wish forgiveness for something you have done?
How often do you not show forgiveness?

How often do you wish to reach out for someone's hand in the Spirit of love?
How love do you hold your own hand back?

Let us all search our hearts for the answer to how often?

Joanne C. Jansen

My Angel My Daughter

My daughter, I love you so,
How much, you could never know.
You've been a joy from the day of your birth,
Bringing me only happiness, never any hurt.

Your beauty is like a rose in bloom,
You shine like the sun, stars and the moon.
All life's sparkle I find in you,
Making me only proud, as I always knew.

Some people don't know what a real gem you are,
They've hurt you with words, I wish I could bar.
Don't let it bother you cause God only knows,
You've been an angel since the day I counted your ten little toes.

It really doesn't matter what they say,
Their actions are not God's loving way.
Time only for themselves is all they see,
I hope and pray so greedy they learn not to be.

May they someday soon realize,
The loss of an angel in their lives.
Of someone so caring, lovely and true,
God knows, my daughter that angel is you.

Christine Swetland

Soul Of My Soul

Soul of my soul, where do I know you from?
How many lifetimes ago were we one?
In silence, I know you intimately...deeply.
But as you speak the knowledge vanishes,
the gates come crashing down,
and I'm returned to the present facing a stranger.

Looking deeply into your eyes,
I search once again for the union that we shared,
but only a stranger stares back.
You don't remember me,
but I'm haunted by the absence of you.

Soul of my soul,
remember me, return to me.
My love,
My life
My Breath.

Chayris Burd

Glass

When glass tells a story
How is this true?
When the sun beams down
Through the deep reds and blues
These windows of pictures revealed by the light
These picture windows in churches
Are teachers of Christ
Without motion or sound or script or paint
Illumination through glass projects
The stories of saints

Garrett Pearson

"Flutters Of Growth"

How strange the paradox through which learning is born,
How harsh the lesson do first appear.
How lovely when insight comes crashing through,
How long we await the removal of fear.

The blocks and the turmoil, twin devils of fate,
They twist and they torture, we writhe in our pain.
Then somehow, somewhere, from a source undefined,
Comes a message of comfort, we sought not in vain.

What form this can take is not up to us,
Though fantasy brings a rigid release.
Again and again, we picture our needs,
Confused with desires, they grant small surcease.

We stumble and shudder, afloat with ourselves,
Convinced of answers spun from the mind.
Bent on a course, we decide what is right,
Barring the truth, our souls in a bind.

Then, barriers topple, welcome light does appear,
As again we transcend our misguided desires.
This shimmering quest, one of natural joy
Ignites tumbled ego with spiritual fires.

Jeanne Meyer

Unknown

I stay on the surface not wanting to know
How far or deep I could really go
I don't want to face my fears
I am at a perfect state of being
I sit listening to the rain
I can feel it flow throughout my mind
Finally I plunge to the bottom of the dark hole
Only to find that there is no bottom
How can this be?
All the lingering on top for nothing?
So I make my way back up to the surface
I am relieved and confused

I realize that some things are left better unknown.

Amanda Beth Kafaf

A Sterling Home

Quarter moons and Stars of Sterling,
How did they come within your grasp,
Rocking Horses, wooden lions, warm thoughts always last.
Cozy corners, fire light, fragrant flowering roses,
Soft beds, furry kittens, cold puppy dog noses.
Blue skies, green grass,
The symphony for two,
Everything nice brought together,
My memory of you.

Jack DeYoung

"Another Unfinished Song"

When I close my eyes you invade these thoughts.
How can I survive knowing what I lost?
You're no longer mine to have and to hold.
All our dreams are gone; our love's been sold.

I am empty inside without a memory.
What I believed in with all my energy
Is now awashed into the ocean's blue.
Did I ever think I would be without you?

Yes I played our love till it wore too thin.
Now it's turned to dust; I am all alone again.
I was just a fool to hurt you that way.
Can I get it right; can I make you stay?

Only time will tell just where we stand.
All that I can do is reach out my hand.
Will you take hold of it once more
Or turn away and forever close the door.

Feliza L. Maggay-Hill

Sisters Of Life

Flaming, majestic, spectacular, serene.
How can anything earthly come close to your splendor?
You take my breath away,
Breathless, awestruck.
Molded by the hand of God, your true form you show to but a few.
Thank you for choosing me.
Many would imitate you, but never fool you.
From above it all you conquer all, envelop all.
Dominate all.
You start as a mere shining in my eye, but you grow quickly.
Quickly you become me; my soul; my hope.
You are life. You give life and you take it away.
Please don't take it from me now.
You, sunrise, and your twin sister love, are one and the same.
You rise above everything and make the world turn.
The sisters of life.

Jill Rodgers

Of The Tomb, And Of The Cemetery

How beautiful the flowers, that graced your lonely tomb!
How beautiful their fragrance, like exquisite perfume!
Immense the sea of green grass, immaculately, kept!
'Neath clouds and skies, and sunlight, I knelt in prayer, and wept!
With arms outstretched to'ards heaven, like ghostly silhouettes, they stand:
The trees! The sentinels, the guardians of man's sacred land!
Glist'ning headstones o'er the land, of gentle rolling hills under the sun:
God's vigil lamps that brightly, guard, the soul's eternal sleep that's just begun!
Oh, sacred soil, where fragrant flowers and souls of men, in death's embrace entwine,
The boy you cradle in your bosom, is the son that once was mine!
Alone, and badly broken, my soul must bear life's grueling test:
My life shall pass so swiftly, upon your bones, my bones shall came to rest!
Illusive peace and solace, not meant for me upon this earth:
With you, my son, I'll find them, beneath the soil that gave us birth!

Alejandro B. Murillo

A Stillness In Our World

Our world stopped for there was a stillness that had not been expected.
We couldn't move and all we had was this aching in our hearts,
And the silence was broken with our voices saying, we loved him.

Bill Albright

Alabama

From tall pine forest to white sand beach
Hospitality is the hallmark of Alabama's reach.
Fed by rushing water, calmed by peaceful lake
The land gives much more back than it could ever take.
We fish the gurgling streams, crab the tranquil bays,
We hunt the deep, pine forests on frosty winter days.
In summer the fields are covered in cotton sparkling white;
Our farmers are the bedrock strength of Alabama's might.
Pecan trees shelter grazing cows from blazing summer sun;
They wander back to the sheltering barn when the long, hot day is done.
Azaleas and camellias, and moss-hung sturdy oaks
Draw the snowbirds from ice and sleet to just be "down home" folks.
Yes, Alabama is the state to visit and to stay.
You'all come to see us, hear? Don't waste another day.

Janet S. Mayer

Oh God...

Oh God can you hear me tonight praying for what is right,
Hoping that the world will not, end up in eternal night...
Hoping you can end the pain, the bitterness of acid rain.
The needless evolution we partake, in a path like junkies to cocaine...
As humans we struggle for a faith waiting for a sign that You are here.
Some of us cling to the falsest God, is it fear that the end is near?
Truly You can understand the suffering of a woman and a man,
Living in an America with propaganda that we're selling out to Japan...
What do we need, who do we believe,
When to trust is simply another way for us to deceive?

Oh God I read the Bible, the holy book of riddle and rhymes
Questions within more questions, an endless ladder to Heaven I climb...
And to not believe is sin, even the winner can never win
I'm another fool in a world of fools in this crazy world I'm in...
Jimmy Jones called himself Jesus, Charles Manson tried to kill the world,
But in the end faith kills us all and all that's left is being fooled!
What do we need,
Who do we believe,
When to trust is simply another way of us to deceive?

Joshua D. Dressel

Crumbled, decrepit old hands
hold hers - equally old and stale.
The life they had flashes through her mind
the marriage, the children - who never call anymore -
a fine "thank you for raising and guiding me through life."
They fought to give it all - the world to them.
That first home they owned
the one that burned in '54 during a union strike
the one he stubbornly worked through -
thanks for many years of hard labor.

The bled knuckles that built the new house
the one they now live in.
The walls don't even whisper any more
they only weep at the loss of life.
they decay from neglect - unconscious.
She gasp a hard breath - air is hard to find
He leans to her, kisses her cracked lips.
He feels the last warm breath they'll share
at 10:45 the next day the coroner pronounces them dead.

Chris Griffith

Ancient Warrior

I saw him shuffling down the street, an elderly gent on leaden feet
His pace was not a steady gait, confusion had become his mate
The once straight frame was bowed with age, his speech was awkward, slowed and frayed
Oh time had taken its mighty toll, and now he's cast as that poor soul
Yet beneath that aged and wrinkled skin, a once proud warrior still lives within
And though his earthly shell is worn, the soul beneath is strong not torn
The big store window reflected the street, including the man on leaden feet
He gazed at what the world did see, and wondered aloud, "Is that me?"
Then shrugging his shoulders and shaking his head, he turned and pondered what he'd said
Yes, time had ravaged his earthly shell, yet still he had so much to tell
Oh those that have no time for him, may one day pay for that small sin
Earth's aging process is the fate of all, and their time may come to walk that hall

David G. Turner

A Daughter's Love

There is a man I love so much
His guiding words, his gentle touch.
He is always the one I can turn to with my joys and my fears.
He is always the person I share my laughter and my tears.
He is always there for me day or night.
To take the days wrong and make it right.
Our time together goes by so fast.
With each passing moment we make memories that will last.
I feel so safe when I'm by his side.
My feelings of love for him I could never hide.
To the world he is just one man.
To me he is very special, you see he's my dad.

Donna M. Anton

The Old Dog

He is old and wise.
His face is filled with scars.
His body is slender and white.
He stands proud with his head held high.
For he knows something we don't.
But he will never tell us his story.
You look into his eyes and see love and hatred.
Physically he never got farther than the end of a chain.
But mentally he traveled the world.
His toys would become deer and birds, chasing in his mind through deserts, mountains, and fields.
He reached the top of this world, then looked down at us and frowned.
For he knows the truth within us that we will never know.

Danielle Mehlenbacher

Fishing

Ice cold water rushing before my feet.
I step in, carefully placing my steps
My boots tighten but no water will seep.
Cast after cast but I've caught nothing yet
The fish takes the bait and the fight starts now.
The hook embedded in the fish's mouth
The fish is strong I hope I'll win somehow
Suddenly the fish began to head south.
I finally reel it in and I find,
Could be small but I hope it's big one,
A twenty-inch Brook trout, one of a kind.
I let it go because my day is done.
I'm standing sadly at the car wishin'
That once again I can return fishin'.

Jason Drew

Airplane Ride

Up through the stench and toiling haze I rise,
Higher, and still higher, till trembling,
I burst through the cracks of forever.
Wild and pure; a clean, blue, ever-shining,

Where my heart throbs so very small
In all this immense, shimmering eternity,
Which fills my eyes and wrings my soul,
Leaving behind only a joyous, uncomplicated me.

Would that I could spring from this bird's womb!
And dance across a puff-cotton, white peace dream-
Yes, go out there! And perhaps see my Lord
Walking among the sunbeams and silver lining;

And hold His hand, and ride these gossamer clouds
Together into a timeless blue; I am this day
Born in flight, conceived in grace, forever to be
Closer to heaven, closer to God, closer to thee.

Isabelle Barbour

White Horses

I'm really not a foolish old man who thinks
He's going to ride into the sunset
Beside a youthful maiden
With such beauty, she's a living minuet

I've learned though, as I've grown a little older,
Feelings are much deeper and just a little bolder
Not only are emotions so much stronger
The yearning seems to last a little longer

So is it any wonder, when an Angel's on my mind
I'm filled with such desire
I forget my logic courses
And start wishing I could find
A couple of white horses

Donald R. Hall

She's A Gem

I know a girl who is a treasure,
Her works are fine and without measure.
The love she gives is so apparent.
It must be God, in her inherent.
She will receive and without censure
What she gives, despite the pressure.
And so, dear God above
Let her know this is my love
To her expressed in some small way, to repay.
I'm writing this because you shine like a star
and I want you to know just who you are!

Helen R. Moreno

"This Child Of Mine"

This child of mine not yet quite three
Her stay on earth so brief
Was she really here or was it just a dream
Like a soft breeze on a cool summer eve
This child of mine not yet quite three
I look to the skies and there in the clouds I see
This child of mine not yet quiet three
Oh yes! I miss her as of yet
But the memories in my heart and in my mind entwined
Never to forget
In my eyes she will always be not yet quite three
This child of mine, Michelle Marie.

Donna M. Robinson

The Dryad's Tea

The sun shone down upon her cherry-colored cheeks,
Her smile long and light I'd dearly love to meet.

The sand was soft and heavy to her fairy feet,
And upon the soft, soft sand she calmly took a seat.

'Twas there she laid a pretty set for tea,
Each tiny cup was filled with dew; sparkling, silvery.

The cakes she sets upon the tray were iced with green,
Four lovely, lacy napkins set about none err had seen.

Quite gracefully she let down her golden hair,
And set on it a wreath of rosebuds from her lair.

Her dress was green with flowery bouquets,
Sprinkled on in sweet array.

Her mouth was sweetly shaped with dimples at the corners,
And pleasantly it softly curled into delicate forms.
AND THEN THEY CAME!

Stepping, skipping, leaping, running, skirts of petals gently rustling;
Coming, coming, swiftly coming; never stopping always running.

Then they saw her near the water, waving slowly, singing softly
Come wee fairies, come; please come to tea; and sit with me.

Elizabeth Ann Baker

DORI

Do we love her? Of course we do.

How can we do without this tiny, curly baby.
   Her name is Dori, she's very black and such a little lady.

She loves to be snuggled and is free with a kiss.
   She plays in the yard, and this she wouldn't miss.

Dori picks each piece of food up before she takes a chomp.
   And takes it to her mat to eat, then does a little romp.

She goes back, then, for another piece and really makes it last.
   For her, the joy of eating is not to eat too fast.

She loves to play with all of her toys.
   But her favorites are ones that make the most noise.

Dori rules our home and already it's better.
   We enjoy her so much that that's why we let her.

She misses us greatly when we're not home.
   And doesn't seem to want to roam.

She's quite content behind the gate.
   But really doesn't like to wait.

Yes, we love Dori, she's our special friend.
   And upon that, you can sure depend.

Becky Combs

Fishing

Ice cold water rushing before my feet.
I step in, carefully placing my steps
My boots tighten but no water will seep.
Cast after cast but I've caught nothing yet
The fish takes the bait and the fight starts now.
The hook embedded in the fish's mouth
The fish is strong I hope I'll win somehow
Suddenly the fish began to head south.
I finally reel it in and I find,
Could be small but I hope it's big one,
A twenty-inch Brook trout, one of a kind.
I let it go because my day is done.
I'm standing sadly at the car wishin'
That once again I can return fishin'.

Jason Drew

Fading Into Dusk

She struck upon morning with midnight's stare,
Her hopes of freedom all but lost in the moonlight glare.
They who have found themselves imprisoned in Felisha's heart,
Carry regret with them through the blindness of the dark.
She came into strength ensued by nightly whispers,
All her childhood dreams broken, burnt to cinders.
The recklessness of finding one's self true romance,
Has left the mind to wander, the soul to dance.
Midnight has shapened her with all of its nightly glory,
So tells us the beginning of the end of the story.
She weeps not now, nor never will,
With that which she has given to you, let it be now mine to steal.
Far better prisons are held for thee,
Do not let her fool you, never let her see.
When she cries for tomorrow's passing, fading into dusk,
May you there find your strength, let your heart be the one you trust.
Take back your shining rays of nightly glory,
'Tis not yet, the end of the story.
Let your love be the strength of your way,
You control the fate of your heart, always on this day.

Denise Sanborn

Lost Love

As the misty eyed girl cries, I cry too.
Her glassy gaze rips apart my thoughts.
My heart is shattered as the beats pummel to a stop.
No more nights are shared upon the grassy knoll.
Vicious thunder crashes my desires amongst her tears.
Fear of loneliness stings the veins, soaking the pores
   with ever most coolness.
Her Southern Belle smile touches my soul no more.
I reach out in hope of finding a falling star
   but none can be found.
My wish will not come to rekindle this day.
Havoc has been released on my unbounded soul,
   as I cannot control all actions in which it acts upon.
Blue Jays chirp in the distance but their
   cheerful melodies are of no meaning here.
Clamping my fist I tire my lungs with screams for forgiveness,
   but no reply can be cast down upon me.
My life is not over but in a blink of an eye
   my love is gone.

Joshua Williams

She Walks

She walks as light as air, as if laying on a cloud
Her entrance is not red carpeted but well noted
She smiles at a passing wonderer
Her teeth as white as snow, sparkling in no one's direction
Her dress sways from side to side, side to side

Seeing her brings hope and dreams
Although you know none will be attained
When she looks into your eyes you know she is the one
But only if life were that easy

Life is too short to be trivial
Too short to play the game that most of us spend months and years
hoping that we will win
But when you glance into her bottomless eyes you convince yourself
that the game is worth it and can be won, even though it is usually for not

We know better, but love is just an excuse to act foolish
To hide feelings that need to be shared

She walks away, once again as light as air but she will always be
heavy in my heart

Derek Worlow

Seeing Through It All

Wallace Stevens' poetic feel
Hemingway's classic zeal
van Gogh's impressionistic appeal
How it is all benevolently surreal

Einstein's determined will
Perseus' famous kill
Diogenes' cynical skill
How they influence us still

A volcano's beautiful might
A rainbow's colorful bright
The hurricane's destructive plight
How they are all a majestic sight

Witnessing an amazing feat
Experiencing love by a heart's missed beat
Hanging on by the edge of your seat
How life can be an unexpected treat

Given the seed put to sow
A flower breaks through and struggles to grow
For what beauty it holds, time can only show
Because like life, the flower is mundane until see its radiant glow

Jason Bolyard

Give Your Soul To God, Sam

Give your soul to God, Sam, give your soul to God
He'll help you make decisions, son, as thru life you trod.
It would make your mother happy, son, it would brighten up her day
She would know that you would be safe whether near or far away.
I want you to see angels, Sam, when you pass from the earth.
Then, you will know, Son, the true meaning of his birth.
Jesus gave his life, Son, so we could all be free.
It really doesn't hurt, Son, take a tip from me.
He'll be a friend forever, Son, and he'll never turn on you.
What are you waiting for? The decision is up to you.
I hear the phone a ringin', need to put this old pen down
My son Sam is on the Phone, what an uplifting sound!
"Just wanted you to know," Mom, "since I'm so far away"
"The holy spirit talked to my heart, and I gave it to Jesus today"
"Seemed awfully strange tho - this voice that kept coming thru"
"It sounded awfully familiar, Mom; sure sounded a lot like you!!"

Ellen Kaye Webb

Pondering Life

I've sat all alone pondering about life, thinking about all the wars, heartaches and strife. Where did it all began, when will it end, I don't really know, but then it all depends. On whether or not the nations will cease, all activities that causes war instead of peace. But it's not just nations, it's also people, who act cold toward each other not, peaceable. The natural love has cooled off from being hot; Loving someone today demands a price like a coin in a slot. And then there's the threat of nuclear war, that some people seem to think will happen for sure. This whole planet gone, blown out of the sky; No one will be left alive to ask themselves why. The environment itself is in threat of extinction; luxury or life, for many it's hard to make a distinction. But we fail to realize we won't survive for long; If there's no ozone layer, we would all be gone. Will men wait until that time comes to start doing something; by then all efforts to reverse damages will be nothing. I hope for mankind's sake the nations will wisen up, and start making a decision to drink from one cup.

James David Joseph

To My Beloved

Thou, beloved, art the essence of things my
  heart, soul, and mind hast longed for.
Only a mortal man, yet, thou hast ascended
  to angelic heights and more.

If only thou could see me for what
  I am, Thee do I implore!
And not just a perception of someone
  thou hast known before.

I seek only to bring to thy eyes the
  sparkle of joy restored,
To lighten thy heart and smooth thy
  path through this life, no more.

Come down from thy lofty heights upon
  Mt. Olympus; accept this human sacrifice.
Offered to thee out of endless love and
  with no thought given of price.

Barbara Batchelor

Things Adored

The special moments in life that I adore.
Hearing locusts singing in the fall.
Looking at a memorable picture on the wall.
Reading a letter from a dear friend,
or watching a leaf blow away in the wind.
Staring up at the stars in the night sky,
or watching fireworks explode on the fourth of July.
Looking out of a window on a snowing day.
Watching a tree glow on Christmas day.
Getting a hug from someone you love,
or simply being thought of.
Sipping cocoa in front of a warm fire,
or watching a balloon float higher and higher.
Smelling an aroma of fresh baked goods,
or taking a walk in the woods.
Watching a young girl become a wife,
or simply adoring life.
There are so many special moments in life to adore,
for without them life would be a chore.

Jennifer Hawkins

"The Spirit Of The Wolf"

Once you talk he will stalk moving back in your track
he will find you like a cat, you can try and fight but

You are never right, he is the one that can move at the
speed of light all through the night

You can run but you cannot hide, he will find you
because he is The Spirit of The Wolf

You can be the cowboy because he is the Indian
You can be the hunter because he is the warrior

You can have the guns because he has the tomahawk
Just remember he is The Spirit of The Wolf

If you sin you will never win he is full blooded Indian
He comes from the tribe of Mohawk

So do not try and walk or try to talk him out of getting
you because he will attack and you won't know how to react

He is one of the great fighters among those such as
Crazy Horse, Sitting Bull, Yellow Hawk, and Thunder Heart

Running through the forest you have no part and no clue
And that is why The Spirit of The Wolf will get you

Aaron J. Sandstrom

Sound Effects

To My Friend Bob Solomon — Saxophone Player

Accompanied by the wind, while birds are asleep
He takes over, sings into a night. And clouds are sobbing.

He plays saxophone into a starry night
On dream theaters of the souls.
Plays jazz to the stars. And dreams are shattered.

Stops at the moon light. Moon full, floating, disappearing
Gives him directions. And the sun is away on a trip.

His music lifts him up to unreachable spheres.
He dances with the stars on the gliding skies.
And does not know how to come down.

His band: The moon-drums, the wind-castanets
Skies, stars, played and played, accompanied by his saxophone
On dream theaters of the souls
Transforming caterpillar into a butterfly.
   And seed became a sprout.

Waiting for another wind, another starry night
Another trip of a sun
In meanwhile taking lessons from a butterfly
Composing dreams.
   And he does not know who he is.

Dragica Radic

Fears

Am I losing the love I hold so dear?
He seems so far away, even though he's near.
We were always together, never apart,
Now is something changing in his heart?
Does he run from me for a little freedom?
I fear the days coming that he might be leaving
I'm still the same woman that he once lived,
I pray for guidance from above.
I know there's a little of my heart that's changed
But its all for the better and I should not be blamed.
Hold me now and don't be concerned
For there are things I must learn.
Don't shut me out because of your fears,
For now my love I need you near.
I myself don't know what's happening to me
For I need you now, its meant for us to be.
Hold me and love me like you use to.
For I need to hold and love you true.
Don't run from the love I hold so deep in my heart,
I love you more now then I did from the start

Jo Gurewicz

My Dreams

I had a funny dream, about a man who needed a room
He said he was over 2000 years old
Though he looked not a day over thirty
How would I know Him if he came for bed
At the Inn where I'm working today?
Would he be wearing a robe (and needing a shave)
Or a fine flannel suit of grey.
Will he be walking or driving a car
What would his license be,
Shall I ask him a all these questions
If he's the Man from Galilee?
Some day he will be among us
And maybe he will ask
What became of our beautiful world
Did he give us too great a task
I'm glad it was only a dream I had
I couldn't answer him
It took millions of people, and many years
To make our world so bad.

Evelyn Mooers

"Father"

A man who is a father is a special man indeed,
he provides for his family keeping them warm and fed
and gives them comfort of security when they all lay down to bed.
A father is not always recognized for the sacrifices he makes
but he does them anyway because he'll do whatever it takes.
A fathers love is sometimes silent when we need to hear it most
but through the good times and the bad times there's one thing that I can boast,
and that is you're the greatest dad that a son could ever have.
And the day the ALMIGHTY decides to take you up above,
you won't go empty handed, because you'll have my undying love.

Brian L. Rickord

Freedom Lover II

The freedom lover knows no fear; he gives his heart away.
He offers all the love he has, to pave life's rocky way.
He asks for nothing for himself; he wants no guarantees.
He offers only freedom...to do just as you please.
The freedom lover has a heart he wears upon his sleeve.
His arms are always open...you're always free to leave.
He is a free and gentle soul; he'll never let you down.
His love requires no boundaries...total freedom does abound.
The freedom lover offers peace; he offers love and trust.
He knows true love will bring you back...your freedom is a must.
The freedom lover knows the truth...true love will be his own.
If it is given freedom, his true love will come home.

Janna L. Botello

Untitled

So in love with Mr. Right,
he makes me long for him every night.
The way he brings my desires to life,
cutting out and stealing my heart, he's a knife.
He's the delicate breath of my every waking day.
He's laughter of children at innocent play.
Sweet and gentle, he's my May flower,
after every solitary April shower.
He brings my heaven down to earth.
He's the perfect miracle in every birth.
He's the wind that makes me soar,
the strength in every lion's roar.
The yearning for him that exists in my heart,
my Romeo, he plays that part.
My cloud 9, my guiding light,
Yes that's him, my Mr. Right.

Amanda Solomon

"Angels"

What is an angel? I asked the little boy.
He looked at me so innocently. With eyes that danced with joy
Oh! That's easy she looks like my mother.
Only wings added to make look like another.
I smiled and said, "You're right, my child"
But what I have to tell you will really seem quite wild

It could be the old man, who walks the street
With his back badly bent
Or an elderly lady, whose back is humped
She could be heaven sent.

You see Angels take on different faces
And you can see them in familiar places.
The people that we meet each day.
Maybe the angels God sends our way.
Just a smile, hug or pat or perhaps a friendly chat.
A drink of water, or a piece of bread.
A place to rest on a warm bed
A kindly deed to pass the test
When we enter into our rest

Helen Witham

"Tests of Endurance"

The epic hero Odysseus, departs from Calypso's isle.
He is the son of Laertes, whom he hasn't seen for a while.

He lived in the town of Ithaca, before the Trojan War.
He fought for Greece his homeland, sailing shore to shore.

Trying to find his way back home, he sailed across the sea.
Many dangers lied ahead, for the crew, the ship, and he.

He landed upon Circe's cave, where he started to build a life.
But nothing she gave, made him happy, because he missed his wife.

Setting sail a second time, they drifted 'til day ten.
Where suddenly they came upon, groups of lotus-eating men.

Next they came to Cyclops' cave, where they became trapped inside.
Driving a pole in Cyclops' eye, he was blinded but had not died.

Arriving in the Land of the Dead, he received a lot of advice.
After talking to Tiresias, he made a sacrifice.

Singing Sirens were next on the trip, and Odysseus was tied to the mast.
His crew put bees wax in their ears, avoiding spells that she might cast.

The journey isn't over, for Odysseus and his crew.
But if he's made it this far, he can surely make it through.

Janice Pierson

The Oak Tree

Eyes on the eagle high on his wing,
He is an oak tree, he is a king.
Tall and proud, he guards the brook,
Offering shade to all who look.
He chose the duty of the hard and brave,
An image not silenced, even to the grave.
His wooden mantle is steely and strong,
But inside a heart, which can do no wrong.
Fighting the storms, he stands in the wind,
Knowing full well the elements will win.
But his acorn is here to shadow his way,
Waiting to grow on his own someday.
For when he is gone, it will survive,
And the memory of his life will surely revive.
So dread not that day on which he will die,
Honor and love him while his branches still sky.
And take his hand and cherish his smile,
For he is my father and I am his child.

Al Danny Brown

An Example

One of my best friends is the ocean,
he is always there for me.
No matter what the weather looks like,
he greets me with a refreshing breeze.

My friend is a very generous fellow,
he has connections all over the world,
let's all the ships sail from harbor to harbor,
communicating everywhere.

Why don't we take the majestic ocean
as an inviting example to be
more generous and open to people,
what a great place the earth then would be.

Ilse Roffler

Untitled

You close your eyes and see Him there, smiling at you,
   He holds out His hand and you take it.
The world is shining, at peace with itself.
   He shows you the world, as He sees it—
With fatherly love, and you see its beauty too.
   You smile in delight. He shares your joy
and you begin to understand the peace of the world,
   then you open your eyes and see utter chaos.
You close your eyes to the dark
   And open them into pure, white light
And see Him smiling down at you.
   You never want to open your eyes again, but He gives you strength
with His presence, and so you know what you must do.
   You open your eyes
And start to see the worlds as He does,
   And you begin to understand His love, and His pain,
and finally, you understand, when a child reaches up to hold your
   hand, and you smile down at him in wonder, the child in innocent,
trusting, and again in your mind, you see His smile, and it gives you
   strength.

Jennifer Prior

Of The Great Tactician Is Divine Fight And Fate

The Poet,
He, Himself, He
sees the world through different eyes.

The Poet,
He, Himself, He
speaks the truth of the soul's reprise.

The new birth of his fallen spirit,
the revelation fuels his impassioned blaze
and ignites it further into a wild flame.
The treasured ink in his pen, the blood of his soul
the two become one in the same.

He presents a challenge to the bewildered masses,
to look past the fleeting golden lusts
and gaze upon the majesties of world to come
To this fight he'll raise a toast,
and it is the liquors of the spirit to which the poet succumbs.

The Poet,
He, himself, He
will live through the fabled future's demise.

Banks Pappas

Cowboy's Life

Every night he nods his head to signify the start.
He has no apparent fear in his heart.
This time is the same.
He came out to win this game!
He has his eye on a gold buckle.
The thought of losing makes him chuckle.
He isn't afraid of being hurt.
Or thrown off the bull into the dirt.
The chance he awaited finally came
For him it ended in shame.
The mighty cowboy who thought he couldn't be hurt.
Wound up lying dead in the dirt.

Brad Gordon

Blind Trust

He looked at me; I looked at him too
He had a smile so bright, eyes so blue
What a flirt he was

He said, "Hi" to me; I said, "Hi" too
We went out to lunch
What a nice guy he was

He wanted to have dinner; I wanted dinner to
Wine by candle light, with an ocean view
What a romantic he was.

He kissed me real soft and held my hand
What a gentleman he was.

He wanted to lay down; I did not want to
He unbuttoned my blouse, pushed me to the ground
What a violent guy he was

He wanted more; I wanted no more
He forced me, he made me
What a criminal he was

I wanted him in jail; he did not want to go
I called the police, they arrested him
What a victim I was

Elizabeth Ceballos

A Call To Our Savior

Our heavenly Father is as great as can be
He can flood the earth to rid it of sinners
And part, the sea to help the good flee.

He gave us his only Son to bring peace on earth
But emperor Pontius Pilate, to his despair had Him crucified
And while he was dying people mocked him to their mirth.

He preached to the good and all the Mankind
He healed the sick, the crippled, and the blind.

Jesus was loved by children, ladies and men
And if there was no food he would bring about water,
Fish, and bread to stop the famine.

Dear God we need you here now to bring peace and love to our land
We need you to guide us, please take us by the hand.

We have fallen to temptation, we have fallen to sin
Let us all find you dear Lord please rise again -

James H. Black Jr.

Memories Of Childhood

Kites soaring while flowers push fancy
Hats through moist soil, brother waking
Mother's rocker creaking, brown owl

Hooting his evening lullaby, leaves falling
So colorful they fly while gray squirrel
Saves before cold skies drop flakes of white

Now wood crackling to firelights dancing
With smells of baking flowing merrily through
My mind, skaters smooth sailing over icy

Ponds combing into my memories of a time
Long ago, the big house where we were young
Where cotton clouds made pictures in the sky

Agnes B. Moyer

The Colonel's Widow

Before her eyes open to light or she
Has left the warm cocoon where she forgot
The cruel vagaries of ailing flesh,
Her brain signals: This place is not my home!
And she remembers she was stripped of her
Belongings (as becomes advancing age
And life beyond one's usefulness) and brought
To this strange town to live in little rooms.
Dying in odd new ways, she is asea
In idleness and can recall no real
Reason to quit her bed. There is no one
In these dark shadows; only silence here,
And emptiness. But schooled through many years
Of waking to desires of others, not
All loved, she rises. Daunted by the fact
That she has come somehow to be her sole
Reason to live, she marvels that nothing
She ever learned before trained her for this
And wonders how to care enough about
Herself to want to learn to live alone.

Grace Roberson Hicks

Where Has Our Love Gone

Where is the love we felt just a short time ago...
   has it dwindled and faded and lost all it's glow

Can it be found in a touch or a hug...
   that love we once felt not so long ago

Can we recapture that feeling of bliss we felt
   towards one another each time that we'd kiss

It doesn't seem such a long time ago when we were
   together and couldn't let go

Where did it go...When did it leave...
   that love we once felt between you and me.

Carolyn Breen

Wisdom's Choice

The Constitution of the United States; a well written plan,
Has for two-hundred years, shown others where we stand.
Phrased in simple language, strong, truthful and fine,
It is easily understood by open heart and seeking mind.
Distant angry voices are heard to shout, "Wrong, wrong!",
Yet, no plan nor schedule is sent forth from the throng.
No written achieving effort, sent to fulfill America's need,
Nor author yet discovered to plant anew, and nurture the seed.
Thus, the centuries old message still stands strong and clear.
"All are created equal," is a truth that many still hold dear.
"Equal" in life, the Constitution states; this applies to all.
And kindred souls throughout the world have heeded the call.
"Life, liberty and the pursuit of happiness," equality foretold,
It is to those who seek freedom, more precious than gold,
As it begins, "We, the people," and many who have heard,
Believe it unlikely that one alone could formulate the word.
Surely only God, aware of the world's great soul felt need,
Through divine grace has helped Constitutional wisdom to succeed.
It may not indeed, be perfect; but at least, we have a voice;
And the United States Constitution still remains wisdom's choice.

©Beulah Marian Marshall

Love

An emotion to which I am unfamiliar,
Has enshrouded my soul.
Your face, your voice, your stride, your smile.
To these visions are all I can take a hold.
A blanket of joy warms my forsaken heart,
Behold my trust and love,
Please, don't tear it apart.
Everyone knows by the look on my face,
That your being has taken sanity's place
My forlorn soul sings of gaiety unsaid,
The song is not hard to hear, to learn,
Straight to the inner most of my heart - you'll be led.
Please don't damage this soul of mine,
Treasure it and it will endure 'til the end of time.
Gillian Swaim

This Silence

This silence which whispers in my skull
Has a tone, grey and dull
It is such that exists in the dim morning light
It is that which is present during the bleakness of night

This silence which speaks in my head
Has a home in the coffins of the dead
It's voice is present in times of sorrow
It is there from eve until the morrow

This silence which yells through my ear
Has a voice none other can hear
But it exists I am sure of this
It is the fog and the dark sullen mist

This silence which screams through my soul
Has upon us taken its toll
It lurks behind all charitable and kind
Sits there letting its evil unwind

This silence speaks to us all
So quiet we cannot hear its call
But in truth it rages through our hearts
Slowly, subtly wrenches us apart
Anika Clark

Green

Poisonous is the virtue of the keen predators,
harping on a complex society...
being unpredictable by the means of justice,
which surrounds various groups of achievers.
Climbing over every boundary,
each obstacle of unsuitable words
dispersed from plagiaristic mouths - they swoon...
creeping into the broaden minds of the honest survivors.
Working to prick the single bone of life
incorporated by pure jealousy, the venom secrets.
Flowing out and around from their seductive lips,
into the shadowy haze of the successors deep eyes...
Challenged to speak of truth,
green is the envious color, shading the depth of their skin
when acknowledging in their hateful and deceptive manner -
Preying upon the weak,
to destroy the innocent...
and to reign over the righteous man.
Benjamin P. Bower

"Sonnet To A Friend"

We know each other well.
Happy hours were shared and cherished.
Staid feelings were developed.
There was no need for words.
Our hearts knew every thought.
Laughter shook us to our very souls.
Innermost secrets were revealed.
All masks were dropped; ourselves brought forth.
Time has been transcended.
Fleeting years have not altered out love.
The ties remain intact.
We speak of other times, memories refreshed.
Our humor yet is visible.
We know each other well.
Betty L. Wansor

Farewell, Dear Heart of Mine

Happy Anniversary Dear Heart of Mine, This June
Happy Anniversary dear heart of mine, this June
But years are spinning past too soon
Will you always be with me in times of stress?
We have been together all these years, our very best
But roll on they do; will you be with me if time doesn't anew
And treat us kindly as our due?
But it will be golden years we'll share
But at best we will together bear
But it didn't work our that way, forever to stay
Alone I relive our lives
But tears dim my eyes as I think of you
And I pray we will be together in the hereafter
Never to part, dear heart
Dot Luria Nadler

A Time To Die

Oh, how I dread Father Time to lay his
   hand on me.
Age has a way of coming too soon.
Then it comes, sick and helpless like a baby,
Lying, waiting, waiting for what?
Tubes and needles, all running through my body,
Staring into space motionless, unable to speak,
White sterile women coming too soon to
   turn me this way and that.
Oh, the pain, but I can't speak to
   them, leave me alone.
Leave me alone to die in peace.
Why must I go on?
If I could only tell them,
Tell them "Let me die."
The smell of death saturates the walls
   of my room,
Life is but time in a bottle,
Slowly, slowly, evaporating.
Emily J. Nulph

Mothers

Mothers are special to everyone,
Her sons and daughter who are very
young. She loves them with all
her might and prays for them to
do things right. The moon that's
bright, the stars twinkle white;
She Prays to her Lord who's her shield and sword.
Mothers are special to everyone.
She cares for her children who are ages of all.
Cemone Glinton

Of Meredith

Eyes like emeralds, teeth like pearls
Hair of gold that sometimes curls.
Skin as soft as a worn in quilt
Such youthful vigor, it will never wilt.

Delicate hands whose touch drives me mad.
When your arms are around me I cannot be sad.
Your lips are heavenly, perfect and divine
I crave them incessantly as a drunkard craves wine.

Eyes and lips and hair of gold
Skin so soft and hands to hold.
These things are nice, they set you apart
But what is important is what is in the heart.

Share, O share, share with me your heart.
It's destiny for you and me, I've known it from the start.
The world is cruel and full of lies
But I see heaven when I look into your eyes.

Your eyes are beautiful, pure, and revealing.
When I gaze into them I'm consumed with a feeling
Of boundless love. What a wonderful gift.
From you, my love, I will never drift.
Jason Michael Price

By Way Of My Grandmother

My grandmother fought the war one bead at a time,
Hail Marys and Our Fathers rattling like tank fire
into the mine fields of hell to free her son and save
the world. She would not give credence to telegrams.

She could not join the war department in presumption
of his death; she chose instead to know that he would
walk safely through the valley of death's shadow, flee
the confines of POW camp and battlefield and return to her.

Her prayers carried the heavy packs of the liberating forces
and turned the locks on barbed wire gates and powered
planes and ships to carry her oldest son back to New Hampshire,
home to meet my mother; to fall in love; to become my father.
Carol Willette Bachofner

"The Golden Years"

I've been around for quite a few years
Had lots of laughs and shed lots of tears
Raised up my children some grandchildren too
And have no regrets as some folks do

And now come like golden years ailments and all
But they will not stop me from having a ball
No rocking chair for me. I'll deal with the strife
And when its all over I will have had a great life
Christine Blake

The Chosen Flower

Fair flower, rare flower
growing more each hour
the Sun feeds your fragile life
each day bathing you in loving light
spew forth your holy seeds into the wayward wind
can the prophets know each seed's chosen end?
You, flower of wonder, will give birth to many mirrors of yourself
to spread the Sun's song upon the troubled earth
so all of nature will proclaim
"Glory to God in the highest"
Allan H. Lambert

The Gift

The blue waves tipped with the white pearls of the sun
   greeted her toes and bestowed a gift.

And like a Good Samaritan, the waves left without
   hearing the words of appreciation.

Not adorned with rare jewels or tarnished with pure gold,
   Unaccompanied by a symphony of harps, the gift
   Could easily be mistaken as invaluable.

With its weathered jagged lines, the gift could trace a miracle;
   It could reflect the collage of a life, and reveal the
   Sparkles of the spirit of the truth.

And at the precious moment, she slipped her fingers
   Underneath, the gift and brought it...
   A mirror to her face.

Without hesitation she saw a miracle.
Ann Emelson

Time Of Fall

Crisp apples and crisp air and leaves of yellow, rust, and red
Green of trees and misty morns and skies that show no dread;

Halloween is past and Thanksgiving draws near;
With family and friends and all we hold dear;

But, just in between and barely out of sight;
Are memories of other years and other times and oh, so much delight;

When we were young and full of life and dreams were made of gold;
And, never, never, ever could we think of growing old;

But, years come and years go and really after all;
The best of times come back again with each new, lovely fall.
Judith L. Cox

Homework

Homework homework, what will they think of next?
Grab a pencil grab a text.
What now?
How can this be!
That evil teacher is staring at me!
What should I do?
What should I say?
May I go to the bathroom Miss Adilae?
When I got to the bathroom, guess what I found?
Liesel's homework on the ground.
I erased her name and put mine instead,
then went upstairs and handed it in.
When the paper returned I received an "F".
Boy, that's the last time I ever cheat on a test.
Ashley Segelke

Felicia

November one nineteen ninety four
God came unexpected and knocked on her door
She entered our lives for a short time
Left lasting memories and us still asking why
So much to live for
So young you see
So much left unfinished
At least as we see
A young daughter she left behind
Her baby brother she carried inside
Her deeds on this earth are over and done
She now lives with God she and son.
Esther M. Langford

Reflections From The Heart

But is this love, that in my hollow breast
Gnaws like a silent poison, till I faint?
Is this the vision that the haggard saint
Fed with his vigils, till he found his rest?
Is this the hope that piloted thy quest,
Knight of the Grail, and kept thy heart from taint?
Is this the heaven, poets, that ye paint?
Oh, then, how like damnation to be blest!
This is not love: it is that worse thing-
Hunger for love, while love is yet to learn.
Thy peace is gone, my soul; thou long must yearn.
Long is thy winter's pilgrimage, till spring
And late home-coming; long'ere thou return
To where the seraphs covet not, and burn.
And never let thy colours think to cast
A brighter splendour on her beauties past,
Or venture to disguise a fancied flaw;
Let not thy painting falsify my rhyme,
But perfect keep the mould for after time
And let the whole world see her as I saw.

George John Guerin

Sailing Along The Sea

As a sail along the sea
gliding through the waves
I sing a pretty tune of faraway places.
The sea so never-ending
is a paradise in itself
which helps me bear the long, tedious journey.

My gaze turns to the horizon,
so far off and mysterious;
I dream of what lies ahead
and long to reach my destination
when the love of my life
will be waiting for me with open arms.
Then we shall embrace each other
and go prancing on our way
in the streets of the faraway places of my dreams.

Jeffry Weisenthal

"Recurrences"

The wheat in the fields sways in the sunlight; it seems frail at first glance, yet it thrives amidst wind, rain and sun until nature signals it to surrender its life-giving grain.

Standing there amongst the golden wheat gives one a sense of belonging and of becoming a participant in a ritual of the seasons.
We seek its constancy.
We crave the nurturing that is here on the plain.

The harvesting brings families, strangers and machines together for one single event.
Toil, laughter and friends descend on the wind-swept prairie lands.

All is done. Machines have ceased. The strangers have sought wages elsewhere.
Friends and families settle back into their daily routines not unlike any others across this land.
There is one exception, the aroma of freshly baked bread that delights the senses.

The pumpkins dot the landscapes surrounding the white-washed houses, and the newly painted barns remind us of a holiday painting on a picture postcard from a long time ago. Orange jack-o'-lanterns, red barns, green vistas are the flavorful colors that remain.

The crows fly over the fields in anticipation of what is left behind.
The storm clouds finally come and the cycle once more, repeats in the rain.

Donna B. Barham

"First One At The Altar"

We're standing here together side by side
Giving our hearts away with nothing to hide.

The joy that abounds in the presence of this holy place
Is sacred and pure on the look of his face.

We exchange our vows meaning every word we say
Promising to put him first in our lives each new day.

The time has come and two is formed into one trust,
Yet the first one at the altar makes three with us.

You see God was the first one there waiting patiently.
Giving us hope and love to grow more spiritually.

He gave us time to understand what we both shared
And he smiled when we found out how much we cared.

Now here we all are, there standing strong
You, me, and our Savior right where we belong.

Cynthia Atkinson Rivenbark

The Beauty Of It All

The magnetic beauty of a Sun Rise,
gives promise of the day to be.
Viewed from a point of vantage
stretching outward over the sea;
reveals the majestic beauty,
nature has prepared for you and me.

Drops of moisture, kissing the tender breath of a leaf;
pearls of water linger, and bring innocent relief.
The dewy eyes of an awakened child,
views it's mother's face and timidly, conveys a smile.

Long stemmed roses - red,
received in tasteful grace,
are scented, caressed and softly embraced.
A lover's kiss, sweet, gentle and kind,
is rendered over and over in a sleepless mind;
as one inebriated in a tie that binds.

Nature closes the fruitful day,
chores are reviewed and put away.
The sun will set slowly in the West;
and all life's beauty, will temporarily, be stilled in rest.

Elva B. D'Antoni

The Mountains

I sat upon the Mesa way up High.
   Gazing at the mountains as they seem to piece the sky.
My windows seem to dim
   When the clouds began to roll In.
I cranked up the motor to move my van
   Through my windows appeared this weird looking man.
What's your name? He gave no reply,
   Rolled up my window and said Good-bye.
I took one more look for the mountains in the sky
   The clouds had moved in to wave them by.
I love the mountains with their snug heads of gray,
   Then look to the valley below all dressed in green so gray.
What an artist our Creator has been,
   He also gave us the snow, rain and wind,
Which reminds me, we could not live without them.

Clark Miller

One Million Men Or More

Today, I saw on television, 1 million men or more
gathered for an atonement speech, gathered for remorse.

They vowed to take responsibility for their children in this world,
they vowed never again to wreak havoc and sorrow upon the world.

Some promised to help their brotherhood. Some promised to clean up
their neighborhood; 1 million men or more praying, crying, and
embracing for love, hope, and swearing off of dope.

They pledged to be good husbands to their wives and to do away with
guns and knives. Never have I seen so many brothers gathered
together that weren't trying to kill each other.

I was astonished and surprised, it made me want to cry
to see a million or more black men retreat with so much hope and pride.

On the news today, I heard the pundits say,
"The Million Man March was all a squander,
these men will never ponder the idea of being self reliant and stronger."

"We'll give them time and see if crime will ever cease, it's all in
their genes..." They say, "Those guys will never act,"
that most of them are on crack.

That's what society expects of them, "They'll never be responsible,
respectable, intelligent black men." Oh?!! I wonder?

Mia Warren

The City

It stalks me silently,
   gaining strength with each step of concrete.

It laughs from the shadows,
   surrounded by greed on 'crack corner'.

It stares out in numbness,
   as the homeless search for warmth.

It charms with its beauty,
   coaxing with views and sunsets...
     like a lover who says, "Please, stay a little longer."

It wraps its arms around me,
   and smiles at me with grace....

Begging for forgiveness,
   as the blood runs down its face.

Aimee Jo Craft

The Quest Of Time

Backside coming up,
Frontside going back.
We rock like babies in a crib.
Darkness surrounding, not seeing what's out there,
Not caring.
Formed from a mold that has since been broken.
Flowing through time carefree.
The void grows larger and less is known.
The more you learn the more you forget.
Time and life natural enemies,
Spend time till you run out of life,
Run out of life and you have no time.
To feel the sensation that you know you're dreaming,
And have absolute power to control.
The child runs free with parent,
Lift him.
"Oh Child, What do you see?"
"I see what can be!
I see a tree!
I see myself laughing and loving so free!"

Joel E. Richardson

Slipping A Disc At The Disco

When you Disco with Farrell your whole body's in peril,
   From your toes to the top of your head.
He twists you and jerks you and pulls you around
   Until sometimes you wish you were dead.

His "Basics" are great — it's the "Turns" that I hate.
   My poor spine is a bundle of nerves,
For as hard as he's tried, he can never decide —
   Is it "INSIDE or OUT" on turns?

So he sends you BOTH ways to make sure that he's right—
   And slipped disc and all - THAT'S YOUR LAST DANCE TONIGHT!
The HUSTLE is fun — but somehow I'm offended
   If I'm all out of joint when the music has ended.

So Farrell, get your act in gear - and do the dance right Honey,
   No double clutching on the TURNS - It really isn't funny!
Turn "INSIDE" — "OUT"— "SWEETHEART" without the reverse action -
   Or you'll soon run out of partners - THEY'LL ALL END UP IN
   TRACTION!!!

Do your "Taps" and Bumps" and Turns"
   While the band plays "BURN BABY BURN"
And hope when it ends and you head for your table
   That you're all in one piece and still perfectly able......

Joanne E. Johnsen

Mother

To my mother who I have loved so much,
from your scoldings to each gentle touch,
Mother, there is one thing you must
understand. This son of your is now a man.
We've both grow older and I've left you den.
My love now is stronger than it's ever been.
I know it's hard to watch part of you
walk away. Both of us know we're still
together each and every day.
Even though the distance has set us apart,
I still feel that grasp of yours around my heart.
Mother, in flesh I may not have here;
Mother in soul, I feel with each tear.
So, thank you great lady for always being
there, and for your unselfish love
you're so willing to share.
To finish this poem, I have one thing
left to do — Mother, that is to say
I love you.

Jeff Chrisco

Unfulfilled Desire

Love's longing stilted
from transcending ambrosia fields
of the exalted Olympic heights.

An enkindled passion erupts
inwardly upon itself without escape
toward freedom of ethereal expression.

Ardor chokes as a festering wound
succumbing to clot and rot and filth
eroding the suppleness of beauty's creation.

Angels fall lamenting such grievous loss
and the heavens crack at the arrested ascent
of once inspired desire collapsing into dust.

Eugenia A. Nero

God's Love And Grace For O.J. Simpson

O.J., O.J. Why did they say you were guilty
from the very first day?
Didn't they know that "What they sowed so
shall they reap"?
That's why their case went down in a hoop!
I believe, I believe in God you see
that's why there was F. Lee
Lies and deception we could all plainly see
coming from prosecutors and detectives couldn't we?
That's why we needed F. Lee
Dream team, dream team can't you see?
You were sent from heaven with all "God's Glory"
to break down their "Lying Story"
To shower O.J. with God's love and grace
Now he'll go down in history without disgrace
I love you Christ
    Betty J. Miller

The Story Of Noah

This story is about God's love and a man named Noah,
From the Bible, one of many I know of.

Noah lived among corrupt men, but in God's eyes found favor,
His fellow men ridiculed him but Noah's faith did not waiver.

With God's instruction he assembled the ark,
Forty times God said, "I'll send the light and the dark."

And, when you've finished building - gather all your kin,
Two of a kind; animals, birds and creatures will come in.

Just as He promised Noah, they began to come two by two,
God sent them, just like He sent His Son for me and you.

After Noah and all with him were safe, the rain began to fall,
Listen to the cries as on God's name others began to call.

But, it was too late, only the faithful were saved,
As God did for Noah, Jesus the way for us paved.

The ark was their home, till Noah released the dove,
What a wonderful story of OBEDIENCE, FAITH and LOVE.
    Gail Nichols

Ten Mile River

Route 17 goes to White Lake, high in the mountains green From here
it's not far to T.M.R. the place of which all Scouts dream You're away
from the heat of a city street and the air that you breathe is clean
The time has come for a barrel of fun, how long is this been going on?
Your by the shores of a mountain lake as it reflects the heavens
blue in a camp that's fair near the Delaware like me you'll love it
too this is the home of the otter, the deer, the raccoon and the bear.
As you roam around new sights abound if you keep your eye on the
ground. Did you ever fire a rifle, or try your hand with a bow?
Have you ever done much fishin or paddled your own canoe, can
you swim a mile in real Scout style, there's nothing beats trying to. Now
I've seen a lot of what Canada's got and been south to the Suwannee river
and the land between can't beat the scene of life at Ten Mile River.
I've seen the best of the mighty West and without a doubt its grand
but here's a spot that's got an awful lot and it's pretty darn close
to home, so pack your gear and have no fear this place was meant
for you if fun's your game, remember the name Ten Mile River.
    George Rabus

Widow

Who will stay the terrors of the night?
Friends will install a new burner in my oven,
new license plates on my car; friends will
mend my kitchen floor, unstop a stopped-up
drain, bring me supper when I'm ill...

But who will stay the terrors of the night?
Who will comfort me in storms, shield me from
the buffeting winds, hide me from the jagged
lightning, whisper love things through the
thunder? Who will be my umbrella?

Who will guide me when I have lost the way,
seek me out when I need to feel needed, or
hold my hand and mourn with me the empty nest?

Who will sing of dream when dreams have died
and songs have ended?

Who will bring me coffee in the morning?
Who will bring me coffee in my mourning?
    Dorothy P. Hickman

Heart of the Matter

Living in outer space. Untouched by reality. Untouched by people, friends and family. Untouched by self. Not thought for tomorrow but by time. Seconds, Minutes, Hours, Days, Nights, Weeks, by Months by Years. Running against time, people, places, things. Running as a Motor Robotic. All thought turned to nothingness. Feelings as motionless pictures. All things processed within. In through the ears, eyes, and nose. All is processed by recording, motion pictures, and memory of scent. This Motor Robotic is strong with outer appearance, but touch of a button, electrical surge, Memory bank overload, leads to destruction and surges of mixed up, confused data input. Causing unexpected uncontrollability and behaviour. Fuses blowing and electrical wiring melting finally shutting Motor Robotic down. We fix-and plug in to recharge, replace old blown chips with better chips - and ship him out for trial again. Til he blows again and again. The brain is smoking with power oversurge, major melt down, and bloop-blop-bleep-crackle-pop= Silence... Motor Robotic beyond repair...
  It's not the outer body we need to keep in working order or
repair, but the heart of the matter within.
    Diane Dellar

God's Eternal Light

God's eternal light shines so bright
For you and me this night
He sent His son for his love to show
So very long ago

To believers or not he's always near
With strength and love so clear
So I compose this poem today
With tears and memories, Gods love won't fade

To reach out to everyone
He even brought forth his only son
So all his eternal light they'll be
Full of love and harmony

To all mankind, I hear him say
Worries and problems will be cured for those who pray
And this story is near its end
Look for God's eternal light from within
    Bob Wilson

That Was When

The day was when, in my youth, the stars twinkled in my eyes
for the one who was a real man in every aspect of the word;
truly a man among men, like a lion among cats or an oak among trees;
strong, powerful, competent, firm, bold, brilliant, knowledgeable,
gentle, caring, classy, charming, great lover, exciting, good friend.

The time was when, as the moons passed by, the twinkle was
still there for this certain real man, but he found his love
in worldly things, the wrong things and he was no longer there,
he disappeared from my life, "whereabouts unknown,"
my man, my lover, my friend, gone!

The year was when we, he slipped into the recesses of my mind
but nobody ever stood in his stead.
The winds of life continued to blow, 'til hearts and minds traveled
the road to face each other again,
Life bestowed upon the newness afresh; new man, new career,
hand-in-hand, heart-to-heart, twenty two years later
united in wedlock "til death do us part."

Bette Nevarez

A Dedication Prayer

Dear God, you sent this precious child from heaven above,
So that we may protect him, raise him, and show him our love.

As parents we ask for you guidance to teach him the way,
To overcome the challenges he will face day to day.

Please give us the patience as we help him to grow,
For the pathway he'll take is one you only know.

Lord, hear our dedication prayer and take this young hand,
We ask that you guide him, be with him, and make him a special man!

Jamie Nicholson

Power Of Love

She healed the sick and those in pain,
Her heart and soul are pure.
They kept coming to her, the sick and the dying,
Despite society's glitter and lure,
She kept on healing, and living her life to cure.
Her mother was dying, but she did her best to keep her alive.
Her boyfriend was stricken and in terrible pain,
Like a Saint, she worked endless hours, to keep him alive.
She nursed him back to health, so he could survive.
His pain was unbearable, but she kept on loving him.
And the power of her love helped him to get well,
No one will ever know who this person is,
Because she told me not to tell.

Bruce Horaz

We Call Him Papa

When I was born he called me little wonder.
He was there when I got stitches.
He taught and took me canoeing.
He also taught and took me all kinds of ways to ski.
He took me on the ferris wheel at the state fair
and we got stuck at the top.
He was the best softball coach I ever had.
Papa is my dad.

Heidi Crook

Stormy Eyes

Oh, how the soul mourns the loss of your presence when once again you leave me. You know not my sorrow, for like a drama, my lips speak only those words of a comical clown, and I bare not any emotions.

You have become my passion and my pain entwined for all eternity, and the forbidden fruit that I crave. When you go away, my heart returns to sleep knowing another stormy season is upon it. Let the rain flow with my tears, let the wind dry all my fears, and let the soft white flakes of the winter snow blanket my grieving eyes. Only then can all my concealed emotions be liberated.

Oh, but did you know that through the veil of all those tears, it is your vision I clearly see? The reflections of your incandescence eyes and compassionate smile permeate all the destitute inside of me and suddenly like a miracle, I feel whole again. You must know I asked not for you and fought your presence. But for some reason known only to him, my wings flew too close to the ground and like a butterfly I'm caught up in your web.

Release me oh my soul, so I may fly again. This love I have I cannot share. Though fervent love bleeds profusely for you, our lives must undeniably depart. Remember this though, within thy heart, that somewhere in time our spirits will once unite and be free to bond into one everlasting.

Anastasia Frendreiss

Liquid Life

Sunburst heaven and dionysus tonight, we drink and be merry
for tomorrow we die, with the crazy starlids posthumous undertakings
we lift our eyes, and howl, with grinning curiosity, and our muse speaks
the song and dance wed our ancient revival, filled with lead
heavy and content on our wanderings, through ultra violet webs spun
in confusion and the desperate silence of the placid night
it's all escape, fantastic profound minds, linking.

Out of the social domain I peel my rind, layer after and juice flows
to no revelation, I finger the solitude, from my blurry vision outwards
and extend my gratuity to the love and passion in the ominous void
and everyday I hitchhike up to the plateau, in strange trance
the lonesome traveler of short distances, brooding over my quiet veracity.

Below halogen bulbs burning, I find companionship and need to hide
with Ti-Jean taking me for a ride on the highway pulchritude
leaning left on the road, and Stevie Ray sets the tone of glory
and I poised, in my window to the world, my own private Big Sur
bent mad with raging rippling waters around, locked and bound.

Jonathan Michael Bitz

TO MY MOTHER

(Dedicated to my adorable mother, Francisca Casas-Rivera, may she rest in peace)

Dear Mother, when I hear the holy call for me to enter the tunnel of light that will guide me to the other side of the mountain where my final rest awaits, I only ask God to give me the happiness to cuddle again in your arms forever, like when I was a child, and in the warmth of your bosom, feel myself once more loved, secure and protected...

We are what we are and you, like the Lord, love, bless and forgive your children, for only the love and heart of a mother are eternal, sincere, noble and truthful, and that is why when we lose you, there is no consolation and we suffer for an eternity...

Jenny Sarria-Casas

Circular Breathing

Circular breathing, waiting to exhale,
It gets built up, must hold the note
The sound cannot waiver, cannot change,

Cannot let the mystified know my secret
It gets built up, need move air
  more!
  more!
  more!
Wait to much, I have to much air,
Could it be possible to change?
Rotate my circle of breathing backwards?
Haven't held it long enough yet
Not good enough, they won't be impressed
It gets built up,
must exhale,
Try backwards
it worked
I need more air,
Not too much.

Jim Jenson

Death

You never know when it will strike you;
It can happen to anyone.
You enjoyed the memories and joy.
Your heart is broken.
My eyes are filled with tears.
When someone dies,
It's hard to say goodbye.
You keep on loving.
It's hard to love without you.
You shared the good times.
We ran and played.
We went to the movies
I wish you were here,
To hear your voice,
The laughter and happiness.
As we say our goodbyes
to the burial our loved one,
As we put the dirt
on the urn, we see you
again and it will be in heaven.

Elizabeth Berrsch

The Faucet Leaks

(A leak from the faucet)
It builds a puddle
The puddle becomes a stream
The stream a river
The river rough rapids
The rapids a lake
The lake keeps filling from the leak
The leak becomes an ocean
I drowned when the first drop fell.

Audrey M. Austin

Searching

Does life begin where life ends?
Is this what the delicate balance lends?

Does it take great loss to make great gain?
Is this the reason for all the pain?

Do others die so we can cry?
Is this where in the wisdom lie?

Do others suffer so we can see
how precious life should be?

Dawn Snow

The Dark of the Night

The dark of the night,
  is like a bird in flight.

It's dark shadowy wings,
  filled with frightful things.

Like a big dark beast,
  on your flesh it will feast.

It will invite you in,
  and let you think you can win.

In your dreams it's alive,
  Through your screams it will survive.

You will have pain beyond knowing,
  All the while it is growing.

In a pit of despair,
  It likes living there.

At the end you will die,
  and no one will hear you cry.

Dallas Clifton

Serenity

A Jewel in the Crown of Southwest Florida
Is Lehigh Acres for sure
It's serenity and loveliness
Give us much happiness

People more friendly you'll never find
Mostly due to their peace of mind
The beauty of the flowers and trees
Adds fragrance to the gentle breeze

Walking along at crack of dawn
Enjoying the view of the rising sun
The new mown lawns on every street
Give promise anew to tiring feet

We thank you God for each new day
To make our way to work or play
The birds sing out in joyous song
To keep you company all day long

Eileen A. Millett

Life

What is life all about
Is it fishing, or catching trout?
Or is it to learn
Or maybe to discern.
The answer I do not know
Nor which way I will go.
I have no knowledge
If I will go to college.
Even if the world will end
With no reason or bend of fate.
Everyone is trying to get money
But for what reason?
It does not matter what season.
People will even commit treason!
I do not know what life is all about
Is it to try to beat you out?
To produce more goods?
Production makes more than we can handle,
Pollution in our streams is a terrible scandal.
So please tell me, what is the point to life?

Curt Canine

Love

What is the meaning of true love?
Is it as pure as a white morning dove?
Is it something that is to be known?
Or just something to be shown
For each sharing of such affection?
With a heart binding connection
Just to be joined internally for eternity
Maybe that is the meaning of true love.

James E. Johnson

The Child Within

The child within,
is hurting so deep.
Inside the wounded,
never does she sleep.

The child within,
is always aware.
Something that happened,
To hear it is a scare.

The scars are visible,
but only to those who share.
Those who know what happened.
That life was truly unfair.

The child within,
was tainted and then blamed.
Touched in a way,
that made her cower with shame.

The child within,
will always fear,
until the day comes,
when she sheds her final tear.

Annalise Blanchard Jensen

Communication Via Expression

A face in repose lacking expression
Is changed in an instant if there's a digression.
A slur or a criticism elicits a frown,
But a smile will greet a tumbling clown.

A face reflects what is in the mind,
Whether anger or sorrow or joy unrefined.
A tear in the eye expresses grief,
A laugh means happiness however brief.

We communicate in many a way—
Talking, writing, to what our bodies say.
A clenched fist, arms open to hug, a thumb to a nose,
A grin, a tongue sticking out, a peaceful pose.

Jo-Ann Segall

A Lonely World

A world without music
is a sky without stars
A colorless, meaningless blank
A world without song is a dull quiet space,
like a silent movie—
A world without love is a world without joy,
a flat existence - a girl without boy!

Carol Gehrhardt

Beauty Of The Rainbow

The beauty of the rainbow
is a gift from rain and sun,
The color is a specter of
what is yet to come.
The mythical pot of gold is
for all who finds its path.
I for one prefer the beauty
that lies within its grasp.
Not having to travel to seek
what may be, but to lie
here and see the beauty God
granted to me. Blue, pink
and yellow it's all here to
be seen. So tell me who'd
give all this up for alleged
gold, when all these colors
are here to behold.
And you'd find nothing more
than considered fool's gold.

Diane Kerrigan

Cold Fire Bird

Walking cock-sure, the
   iridescent energy form
struts his shimmering
   ultramarine blue fire
for a blue-struck
   observer...

   Am I as cock-sure as he?
Does his deep fire shimmer also
   in me?

George E. Cauthen

Separation Individuation

Now I step quietly, gently, curiously
into this new world
of the dying
uncertain of the way
as a child beginning to walk
faltering at times and falling
yet filled
with newborn possibility and challenge
the call of the unknown...

For in your death and dying
you taught me not to fear
and boldly now I leave your side
and let go of your hand
step out alone on new terrain
listening to your soft refrain
treading gently and courageously
living in your legacy
your death teaching me
no fear.

Bonnie Parsons

Untitled

When I look
Into the future
And all that I
Hope to be...
A wish is that
My children
Have a
Father...
Like the one
You are
To me

Audra Sigan

Nemesis

If it were you
   we'd run through dew-kissed fields
     into the warm sun

You'd hold my hand and
   put daises in my hair

Sometimes you'd sing but
   mostly
     you'd laugh
     chasing me and grabbing
at my legs to make me fall
   but you'd catch me

A whirlwind of lilting laughter
   and twinkling tiptoes
     is where we'd live and
   you'd never let me go

So I don't really think
   it's you

Jill Beauchesne

Gone

The sinking sun has gone
Into the ocean.
I did but look away
One short moment,
To Life ..to the passing of Life
To Love and memories of other days,
lands, joys.
So quickly it was gone
   Completely!!
Into the ocean.
Like life on this plain
Goes quickly
Causing No sound.
Unnoticed, it slips
Over the edge, into the ocean.
And we are left to weep,
And to rejoice, for the Freedom
Of those we loved so passionately!!

Izetta Karp

EVOLUTION

Regret is my eyes,
   infinitely focused on my
   mistakes.
Unappreciation is my ears,
   patiently listening to the surrounding
   conspiracy.
Self-pity is my mouth
   painfully ingesting
   bureaucracy.
Sorrow is my abdomen,
   fat and overflowing with
   sweet nothings.
Selfishness is my hands,
   carrying all of my unwanted
   baggage.
Despair is my legs,
   taking me forward into
   oblivion.
Indifference is my shadow,
   looming over all of my
   accomplishments.
I have become an
   American.

David C. Battaglia

"Pristine"

I've been here all my life
   inexperienced, a virgin
Not yet mature, not accepted with the "in
crowd"
it's almost time to become a man
I go through doors for the first time
walls on each side, I'm one now, a man
it doesn't get any better
the finish rushes to me
day is over
   I must return tomorrow
a real man,
   the ninth grade.

Anthony E. Holland

Reflection

The sparrow,
in Winter,
dines,
not by candlelight
with Asti in fine crystal
and St. Honore.

Frances B. Ricci

The Stars Came Out

The stars came out as I walked home,
In the silent campus, all alone - and yet...
Across the fields with stone and street
The flashing lights and autos steep,
And near the sounds of rushing feet,
I searched in vain for peace and love.

The stars came out as I walked home.
The shadows on the corner street,
Beside the post of light beneath,
Encircled with a ring the rays,
Blue or purple, red to white - ghosts...
All flesh, all visions, in the stars tonight.

I seemed to see them stare
From hallowed deepest trenches up there,
Upon my brow and on my hand,
Upon that sand beneath my feet,
Those rushing steps, that noisy street:
The battered flesh, the twisted bones,
The wailing people wrought in the stars,
About us now...came out tonight.

Bojana Russell

Seeing Red
(A Child's Reaction To Bosnia)

A shot rings out
In the middle of the night.
A war is on our hands
We have got to fight.
A bang and a blast
And we're all dead.
Why do people
Want so much bloodshed?

I do not understand
The fire in the night.
Does the outside world
Understand our plight?
A scream and a cry
And we all die!

Jordan Marx

R. T. Alias Superman

I showed up on your doorstep
In the middle of the night
You picked me up with caring arms
And mended my broken wing

If only for one night

I remember fondly
The kind man, the gentle soul
A space in time
The steel facade was cracking
Superman was weakened by my kryptonite

If only for one night

Gray Wolf

An Ode To The Sparrow

Oh I would go where the sparrow flies,
  In the far blue skies
    Where the mountains rise.
    See his sights with sighs
    Where the sparrow flies.

Oh I would go where the sparrows sing.
  Go on feathered wing,
    Where there treetops swing
    Where the sparrows king
    Where the sparrows sing.

Oh I would go where they fly the sky.
  Hear the sparrow's cry
    When they soar so high
    Where the heavens lie
    Where they fly the sky.

Oh I would go where the sparrow flies.
  sever all my ties.
    Become sparrow wise.
    See with sparrows eyes.
    Where the sparrows flies.

D'Mar E. De LaTor

Vernal Gift

Stone silent I sit
  in pine-sifted sunlight.
Winter weary, my spirit sighs.

Then songbird sweet choir
  in spring-gilded sky flight
Chirps away my thick arctic guise.

Bold butterfly lands
  on work-whitened Levis —
Uninspiring, with folded wing.

Not daring to breathe
  in gathering surprise
Watch I this sacrosanct thing,

As wings slowly open
  of sun-sparkled new gold,
Then flash upward in crystal skies.

Still breathless, my soul's
  own frost wings now unfold.
Vernal gifted, I smile and rise.

Gary A. Schuler

Windows

She opened windows of glass
In our home,
Worshipping the
Breezes of the seasons.

She opened windows of beauty
In our souls,
Painting her canvasses
For all to enjoy.

She opened windows of mirth
In our lives,
Laughing, joking, poking fun
As a way to love us.

She opened windows of understanding
In our travels,
As we packed and unpacked
In strange environs.

She opened windows of love
Within our hearts, and
By leaving so soon,
Left us these gifts.

Jack L. Boland

Untitled

If a star was to fall
In midst of the rains,
It would follow path
Of its true conduction.

Through the wire; but
Which is water, it would...
Fly — as; if
To race to
Its final.

Destiny, aftermath, then
May he be seen; or
Discovered, as
If he'd been...
Hiding...
And only those who luck;
That fate allows a look
Will have seen to testify
Yet, another marque of God.

Arabella Brandes

A Sight To See

A world of mist,
in it I exist,
Looking for light on a cloudy day.

A sight to see,
a forsaken tree,
Finding the sun, a lonely ray.

The end has come,
'tis good for some,
The tree's golden glow saturates the haze.

The tree has grown,
yet it's not alone,
It shall be remembered for the rest of its days.

Edward Weiss

On Justice Street

I passed a woman
In her usual sprawl,
She held a scale,
For weighing,
Anything.

"Is it correct?" I asked,
"Is it balanced?"
"Are there any adjustments
Necessary.—?"

My questions remained
Unanswered;—
Her lips formed words,
But she was mute,
Her unseeing eyes, blankly
Desperate;

I dropped a coin into her
Outstretched grimy hand,
She gave me a quick nod,
Waiting for the footfall
Of the next passerby.

Joan J. Grant

Forever Yours

There comes a time
in every couple's life
when they decide
to become husband and wife

It's a beautiful moment
to cherish so dear
close to your heart
eyes overflowing with tears

Then finally your life begins
without any rules to follow
getting through the twists and turns
and trying not to wallow

When you start to feel this way
just remember and always say...

  I Love You

Bernadette Russo

Marionette

Celebrating each day
In damnation, family feud,
Whirlpooling, spiders webbing,
Crying mad-laughing smiles.
Secrets
Melancholy, my best friend,
Rewards the unloved,
Sinful, and chosen
Sugar coated sleeping pills,
To ease the pain.
Bete noire,
Go deep enough, you may not come back,
Point of no return for the intrapersonal,
Hemorrhaging, humanoid-dummy
Entombed in silence.
Skeletons
Temptations,
Stumbling through existence
To hope for a death
That is more than certain.

Derenz M. Perez

Pursuit Of Soul

Into the night I ride my steed,
In blind pursuit of my one.
need.

I do not know what Devils wait,
to drive me to some other fate.

They haunt me, taunt me, pierce
my mind,
To hide away what I must
find;

For if I find it, they will be,
Compelled to let my soul
go free.

Billie M. Macy

Irish Tea

A sunset on the beach is magnificent.
In a split of a second
   to be seen only by a telescope
In that instant there is a
   beautiful shade of emerald the
   naked eye cannot capture.
Have you seen it?
Not in your imagination
Nor in your dreams
But on a distant shore.
Allow only you,
Perhaps the luxury of your favorite
   warm tea,
The writings of a poet.
Then dream yourself
Believe yourself
And you'll be there
In Ireland or wherever
You and only you
Wish to be.

Debi Maynor

Arlington Army
(Farewell To My Father)

He was laid alone
in a sea of stone
company of comrades
consoled the cold sleep
where old roots run deep.

End of war, he fell ill
weary to the bone
pain became prison
Freedom led him home.

So proudly he hailed
a Clarion call
beyond all rank and file

Flags wave our soldiers brave
marching one last majestic mile.

Josie Deaton Hoalcraft

Angry Water

Raging white water, burning and boiling
into the canyons so far below
Raging white water, burning, yearning,
she knows she has so far to go.
Boulders, rocks, clay and sand, all are
carried in her hands, always to the sea.

Craig S. Carlsted

Weird Widow

A darling old lady waits for her courage,
In a room with only a tea kettle.
Asking when valor will be back?
But he is not coming back no more,
Upon this earth among the living.
Looking through the window everyday,
Hoping smiles will come.
Every time door makes a sound,
her heart leaps to the call,
A little bird flew upon the window sill,
whispering "oh mystery is gone forever.
The secret one is resting in nether,
in the land of the unknown forever."
Teardrops fell from her eyes,
"Asking oh where, oh where is strength."
Every letter that she receives,
hoping her voice will write.
But the little bird is saying,
"Oh joy is gone,
and comfort will never he back."

Jerry Pinckney

Pretty Penny

It's importance magnified
In a material society's eyes
Lies the penny and paper bill
Controlling like a false God
Void of happiness or love.
Worshipped for its pleasures
A car, a business, a home
But never is it seen
Mending a broken heart
Or strengthening one's soul.
Misguided ones taken in
By this evil tyrant called cash
The ones who sleep alone
With no loved-one by his side
Making his millions worth nothing.

Jennifer Watts

Hilltop

I stand on a hilltop
In a faraway place
Among pine trees and poppies,
And I see your face.

I see shadows shift
Into evening's repose,
And I see your eyes
In the soft afterglows.

Afar from my hilltop,
You may see the sky
Enraptured forever, and
Know it is I!

Jenna V. Ownbey

My Addiction

How do I describe my feelings for you?
I want to be with you,
Every moment, waking or not.
I will do anything and everything for you,
To keep you.
I love you.
I'm hooked.
Love is an addiction,
And I'm addicted.

Jocelyn Hill

Soul Remembrance

I remember how you loved me
In a different time and place
With arms wrapped tight around me
In a passionate embrace

A lifetime that was long ago
Yet, here we are again
This time things are different
But a part of "us" remains

You tap into those feelings
Once dead but now alive
Can't you feel the passion
This memory has revived

And yet I am so grateful
That at least we are close friends
And the love that we once shared
Is forever, without end.

Jo Lee

Untitled

I'm writing a poem, to write it.
I'm writing it down just for fun.
My rhymer's not trying to fight it,
and my good time has just begun.

I do not know where it is going;
where I'll end up, I haven't a clue.
I don't know the title or content
nor whom I am writing it to.

It will flow wherever it's going.
It could soar like a bird through the air.
It can sail to port or to starboard
without reason and nary a care.

It makes me feel happy creating,
without rules with which to abide.
When I'm finished, I know it will leave me
contented and happy inside.

If there's something that makes you happy,
something that you like to do,
don't be put off by critics and doubters;
just do it and follow it through.

Ellen Silverman

"The Best"

The going thought now is
I'm the best!
At simply me.
The only way I can get beat
Is if someone else becomes me,
And gets better.
Same thought applied by all.
In the city of stages.
Drives of life towards,
Best you and not,
Beat other.
With no competition
But yesterday's self.
Everyone's the best.
Sharing ourselves for ourselves,
No one could do it better.
Living for the us within our chests,
Famous the masses at the least.

Jason D. Wall

Untitled

You came from nowhere into my life
I'm so glad to have you and I know you
Are glad to have me
Your sweet sensitive ways
Our feelings grow strong
How could these feelings of love
Be leading us wrong
There is a narrow divide
That we may not cross
Cause all that we know
Could quickly be lost
So, we must continue
To love in our own way
And hope that sometime
Somehow or someway
We have to keep silent
Until that day
Billie Fairchild

Please Take My Hand

Please take my hand...
I'm not that strong...
I can't handle much...
At least for not long...
I'm slipping into a large dark hole...
Please take my hand...
I can't find my soul.
They say things get better...
Just be strong and endure...
But please take my hand...
I'm not really sure.
Janice A. Horsley

Destroyed By Love

I haven't stopped thinking about you...
I'm definitely drawn to you somehow.
Everything reminds me of you,
and the great times we have shared.

I'm not ready to fall in love, but
these feelings for you won't fade.
I know we share the same hurt,
we've both been destroyed by love.

I never felt such a want before,
I want to hold you really tight,
I want to help ease your pain,
And then maybe, I can ease my pain!
Julie Ann Johnson

"The Setting Sun"

Like a fireball, the sun
Illuminates the sea,
Leaving it stranded over
The endless grains of sand.

As the eternal tides shift
Toward the desolate lands,
They recede back to the
Everlasting depths of the water.

Mirror reflections of the
Sun's rays leave
A playful mixture
Of radiant colors.

Above, the abstract assortment
Of clouds can be seen,
Imitating a countless
Number of characters.
Ivy Whitlock

Wondrous Love

My heart is soft, forever sweet
I'll wait for you to sweep me off my feet
I'll stand here waiting for you to come
Because my love for you is never undone
You look at me, then turn away
Then I think of what to say
I dream of you day and night
And wonder if this is right
I write your name one thousand times
Then strain to hear the church bell chimes
I always take quick glances at you
And hope you do the same thing, too
I try so hard to make you see
She's not the one who loves you, it's me
I wonder if you'll ever know
How much I truly love you so
As he goes, I see him wince
And wonder if he'll ever be my prince.
Erika Rio

Why?

Why did it do it?
I'll never know.
Why did I leave him?
He loved me so.
He's all I could ask for,
And even some more
the respect, the looks,
not looking to score.
Maybe patience and time,
Should have been the key,
Not only just thinking of me.
When I hear the rain,
fall from the sky,
I think to myself,
Why?, Why?, Why?
Brandi Carlton

Untitled

Come into my life
I'll let you see my soul
We'll become one
Under the shadow of the moon
But when the morning comes
When the light shines
Don't run away
Share the light; share the warmth of the sun
Who knows what will happen
Who knows what the future will bring.
Each moment must be lived to it's fullest.
But when all is said and done
We must remember why we are here
together
To share our lives
To share our love
To share our souls
Christine Cahill

Thoughts

Roses are red violets are blue,
I see a thing; how about you?
You're the thing so what I am.
I am a bird just like you.
If I am a bird then how do I fly?
I guess I fly like an eagle so high.
Now I am done with this verse so
I can get on with the rest of my life.
Jennifer Shay

I'll Be Waiting

Don't cry for me when I'm gone.
I'll be with Jesus, I'll be home.
No more heartaches, no more tears,
No more struggles, no more fears.
This old body is tired and old,
It's time to walk the streets of gold.
I'll be waiting for you there
each one you see,
In that beautiful Kingdom
God promised for you and me.
Teach the children in their
faith to be strong,
then when you're finished
come tarry along.
When all your work is done
and He says no more,
I'll be waiting for you
on that heavenly shore.
Helen L. Serio

Reinvigorate

If you are lonely
If you need a friend
If times are tough
If you think it is the end
If you are upset
If you are mad
If you are feeling pain
If you are sad
If you are angry
If you are in a fight
If it is morning
If it is night
If you are in trouble
If you just want to talk
Give me a call
We'll go for a walk
We can forget the world for a while
So we can remember our love
And how it truly was sent
From the heavens up above
John Rigg

Untitled

Crossing the street is the right thing to do.
If you don't want anything to happen to you.
Before you cross, you have to look each way.
And you'll get home safe each and every day.
So always remember, do it right
And you'll be crossing at the green light.
Crossing the street is what you have to do
And that is what I am telling you.
When crossing the street, look both ways.
This way you'll get home safe always.
Crossing the street is what you should do
So that nothing happens to you.
Look both ways before you cross every day.
You know you should do it the right way.
Before crossing, you have to look both ways
And then you'll get there safe always.
You know you should do it the right way.
Looking before crossing is what you
   should do everyday.
So always remember what you should do
Because that's what I have told you.
Allen Christopher Trembone

Life

If life is a flower, let me bloom,
If life is space, give me some room,
If life is a book, let me read,
If life is a warning, let me heed,
If life is words, let me say,
If life is Bible, let me pray,
If life is music, let me sing,
If life is flying, give me wings,
If life is a wind, let me blow,
If life is a seed, let me grow,
If life is a spirit, let it be mine,
Because life is for such a short time.

Alexandria Wise

The Mysteries Of Life

Why am I who I am
If I had not been myself
who would I have been
why did I enter this world
at the time and place I did
there were so many periods in time
that I could have appeared

Why were my parents selected
to start my creation, I could
have entered this life in so many
centuries, so many countries, so
many families, so many races, so
many religions, and so many cultures

When you consider all the human
beings of all time and all the
possibilities, you must conclude that
this is all orchestrated by a higher
power which is almighty God
and to him - all this is no mystery at all
...that is why I am, who I am

David W. Brown

Forgive Me Baby

Forgive me baby
if I ever made you cry
Forgive me baby
if I ever told you a lie

Forgive me baby
if I ever broke your heart
Forgive me baby
for tearing you apart

Forgive me baby
I never meant to hurt you
Forgive me baby
for not knowing what to do

Forgive me baby
for everything I've done
I'll try to make it up to you
in the years to come.

Forgive me baby
cause I love you so
Don't ever leave me
cause I won't let you go

Elidia Garcia

I Can't Help It!

Is it wrong to laugh out loud?
If I did, I would draw a crowd!
People can't laugh without being accused.
I can't help it, if I'm suddenly amused!

Is it wrong to let tears flow?
If I did, everyone would go!
People can't cry without being left alone.
I can't help it, if I wanna give a moan!

Is it wrong for me to be nice?
If I did, they'd all think twice!
People can't help without being strange.
I can't help it, if I want that to change!

Is it wrong to say what I think?
If I did, they'd all call me a fink!
People can't speak without being tormented.
I can't help it if I'm alive, not dead!

Joanne Leah Canganelli

How Will I Watch Over You

When you see a flower, I'm the drop of dew.
If by chance you spot a flying gull or two
Or as you gaze above at a sky of azure blue
That is me every moment watching over you.
As you catch a fish far out at sea,
Remember that fish is beckoning to me.
When you have a moment of joy,
I'll be there
Kissing your cheek, stroking your hair.
We all have happy days and days
That are very sad.
I'll be there to share your
Pain, every need that you have.
Don't think because I've (vanished)
From your sight
That I will not be there.
Look up!
I'll be on the face of the moon
and in the bright sunlight.

Irma Hircsh

Grandmother

I always felt it mattered not
If a grandmother I became
But after my first grandchild was born
I didn't feel the same
The joy of holding a newborn
The love and pride you feel
Sweeps over you like a tidal wave
As your heart they gently steal
So innocent and pure are they
It's been so long since I've felt this way
Memories of years that have passed
Wondering how they flew by so fast

Now your children all are grown
And although a grandchild is not your own
They're a bit of heaven here on earth
And the best part is
You didn't have to give birth

Joan Lenhart

The Play Of Life

After forty years of rehearsal
I wrestled my thoughts to a reversal.
There was no script,
The actors unknown.
A live broadcast,
To walk-ons we're prone.
Forget what your taught.
Shut down your thought.
To best play your part,
Act always from the heart.

John W. Allen

If I Could Give The World A Gift

If I could give the world a gift
  I would give it peace and love
I would teach everyone to care and
  to share...
If I could give the world a gift
  I would give it peace and love,
    peace
      and
        love
          from
            above.

Ashley Maney

"If I Could Give The World A Gift"

If I could give the world a gift
I would give it a flower
It would bring a rain shower
That shows the earth's great power
It would bring eternal love
From the good God above.
It would have the power of healing
It would give us each a good feeling
It would help us in troubled needs
If we planted its seeds
It would lead us the way that's right
And bloom day and night
This flower cannot be bought or sold
For its value is far greater than a
Mountain made of gold.

Delila Clements

The War

As I look up to you and pray
I wish the best in every way.
Innocent people getting hurt,
Countries bombed, building's burnt.
As I sit beside my bed,
Thinking of innocent people being dead,
I sometimes wonder what could it be.
Why can't all countries just become free?
Why can't we stop this mistake?
Can you answer God, for heavens sake?
If everybody in this world became friends
It could stay that way until the end.
I pray for soldiers to be all right
Even though they're not in sight.
Will this war ever end?
Will we all just become friends?
I can't depend on anyone more,
So God please try to stop this war.

Brenda Nygren

I'll Remember

My lonely heart cries again.
I will miss you so —
Your smile, your touch,
Your tender kiss —
Are gone. I'll never know
How this story might have ended
If we had had the chance
To spend more time together,
To get to know each other,
Perhaps again to dance.

So I will just remember
The good times that we shared —
The laughter, the warmth
Of your tender loving —
I'll remember that you cared.
And though my tears are falling
I know that they will dry.
I will one day be whole again,
Though cold and dead inside,
Til, lonly and alone, I die.

Betty Anne Jeffery

Requiem To A Pup

You were here yesterday
I watched you at play
Laughing and teasing
Chasing troubles away.

I threw you a ball
You caught it so quick
Then deeming it too small
You brought me a stick.

You couldn't catch the stick
But denying defeat
You gave my hand a lick
And dropped your bone at my feet.

You were here yesterday
But you couldn't stay
Now off chasing rainbows
In heaven you play.

Barbra Kathleen Meina

Soul's Flight

In the deep and silent night
I watched the moon climb and
Swell in gay delight.

As I watched and soft music played
I felt my soul gently slip away.
It left its earthly home to fly
Toward the moon in a starlight sky.

I watched it sway weave and wind
As it left me further and further behind.

It stepped upon the moon and began a
Dance to a heavenly tune
My soul was free dancing thru the universe
Released from all its earthly curse.

It jumped and leaped with graceful line
Among the stars in rhythmic time.

Then to face its eventual plight
It stopped, sighed, and began its earthly flight
It returned to me and I was aware of this
My soul looked back, smiled, and threw a kiss.

Betty Tinsley Darby

The Windows Of Her Soul

Last week my Mother died
I was with her through it all
As needed, we prepared for visitation
For her friends and family to come to call.

The family gathered first to view
Our little Mother dressed in pink
She looked strange — unreal to us
We surely did not know what to think.

Suddenly, it dawned on me.
Her eyes were closed in her rest.
No sparkle, no twinkle, no loving shine
We were missing a trait that was her best.

Mom loved people and was a great host.
Her warmth and welcome was very true.
You could not stop to visit or to call
Without a warm hello.. "How are You?"

So those eyes, the Windows of her Soul
Are not ours to share as they were
But, now, we know that her living love
Needs to glow through us, for her.

Dolores A. Spieles

Remembering

I was thinking of my mother today,
I was thinking of all the things
I didn't say.
I wish I could see her one more time
To tell her what is on my mind
Gentle mother, gentle dove,
You taught me wisdom,
You taught me love.
Oh for the touch of a vanished hand,
The sound of a voice long gone,
Why is it I wait until you depart
before saying the words I hold
in my heart.

Ali O'Grady Kalitan

Love At First Sight

Enchanted by the first sight
I was blinded by her light
Lost in her beauty
I heard nothing
And nothing else mattered
My heart over flowed
With a love do never known
Hot chills of emotions
Pure energy flow
A natural high for the soul
Although we are not lovers
Although we are not friends
I think of her often
I'm just in love
In love at first sight

Daniel Solorio

Untitled

With open arms,
 I wait in pensive mood.
Our reunion,
 the bliss of my solitude.

David Cahoon

Thanks To You

Sometimes I wondered if I'd make it
through.
I wanted to quit
until I saw you.
You gave me the strength I instantly knew.
The race was won
thanks to you.
You stood by my side
when I wanted to give up.
You gave me support and self pride.
You made me do my very best.
Thanks to you
I beat the rest.

Chris Susee

Untitled

I remember the night
I wanted to fly away
To the upper edges of the stars
So that my heart could soar
Like the dancers
Who move through
The easy atmosphere of space
But I was led away
By a force
Which shackled my hands and feet
And took me off to war!

David Nillo

Tell Me That You Love Me

'Neath an ethereal bit of a moon
I traveled the boardwalk to the sea;
And sat alone with thoughts of you -
Thoughts of you and me.

That night we touched so long ago -
The night we held and kissed;
Your arms around me so lovingly
Couldn't be more missed!

I wanted more; you wanted less -
You conveyed that in your note.
I wonder if the things you felt
Are the same as those you wrote...

Cindy Sharpe Coffin

Feelings Mixed

What dream is this, where peace is lost,
I thought this was that land
of knownst, I could fly,
But my wings are clipped,
I dream of a land, not over the rainbow,
But inside the rainbow,
Can you feel the colors,
Can you taste the music,
Our senses are twined,
Why would they mock this,
Do they not conceive that they
place that color of night upon thy soul,
Through a dark cloud of mist,
Into a dream of mystic blue,
Let's take a trip towards the clouds,
Let's soar to the sky,
Together we can enter the rainbow,
And together we will fly...

 Be blessed
 And peaceful

Henning Larsen

As Days Go By

As days go by.
I think of you.
I can see the worries
The confusion
The thoughts that are
troubling you.
But you should hold your
head up high because
I'll be there to catch
you if you fall.

Even though we both seem
to be running into
brick walls hopefully
one day those brick walls
will be able to merge
together and build a
castle built for two!!

Carla M. Koch

Before I Sleep

Before I go to sleep,
I think about the
good times we've had.
Maybe it was meant to be
  Like this...

Broken hearts,
Crying nights,
Thinking if you loved me or not???
Well it doesn't matter anymore...
It's over, and done with.

Like they say:
  Forget the past
  Look into the future...

Carolina Camus

Woman's Flight

You, the spider.
I, the insect.
Your words, your web,
The one I fell into.
My body, your nourishment;
And, just before you devoured my soul
The wind came with the rain and it was fierce,
But it got me away,
Away from you.

Now, the storm is gone.
I am free to fly again,
Weary of ones like you,
Who want to suck my life away.
You can't.
I got away from you.

Jamie Johnson

I Found A Little Pup

As I drank from a cup
I looked over and saw a pup
His coat was red,
As the blanket on my bed
He was as fury and small
Like a round little ball.
He didn't look more than two months old
But the color of his fur was very bold

Erin A. Moore

Apart

Out of love and adoration,
I talk to you each day.
Even though you cannot hear my voice,
I say it anyway.
I tell you that I love you.
I tell you I'll be true.
I tell you that you're in my heart.
These days we're going through.
For you see this separation,
Is only for a while.
And then we'll be together
To make each other smile.
If only dreams sustain us,
Then let those dreams be bold.
For in the end it's you and me.
We'll have each other to hold.

Joseph Allen Ward

Revelation

As the evening shadows fall,
I stand watching in my hall.
A spider spins on an outside pane.
I think, "How silly to work in vain!"

For I will sweep his work away
In the light of dawning day;
But, lo, I discern his scheme;
And this I simply will not demean.

He aims to catch insects in flight
Trying to escape dark of night.
By moving toward the lamp's glow,
They will meet a fate they can't know.

When morning once more has its way
And there is light of a new day,
I go to check the spider's fare
And find only shambles are there.

I leave with a deep, mournful sigh
With a truth I cannot deny.
Brilliant as we think we can be
Nature has the final decree.

Betty Nichols

Without Heart

I walk around in daydreams
I sit in a fog of memories
I sleep in a nightmare
I awake with despair
I get through the present by forgetting
that it exist.
No plans for a future because there
is no tomorrow.
Without you there is no Love,
Without Love there is no heart,
Without heart there is nothing.

Grace L. Wilson

Summer's End

I went on vacation
I looked in the woods.
The tall trees, leaves green,
falling from the trees.
It started to rain.
The birds flying, flowers growing.
Summer is almost over.

Christopher Del Gaudio Jr.

Our Freedom

Independence Day
I sit all alone
Thinking of soldiers
Who left their homes

Left their babies
and left their wives
Walking toward
the end of their lives

They battled and fought
and could only silently cry
as they lay bloody and wounded
Knowing they'd die.

They fought for a cause
they fought with their might
Never lost their dignity
They're in Heaven tonight.

Remember your freedom
as fireworks explode
Remember those brave men
who fought long ago.

Jessica Scott

My Mind's Eye

My eyes grow dim
I see the grayness now
Rising in the distance
Things are not so bright as once they were

I shudder and grow cold
Knowing that the dimness
Will increase the gray
And I cannot control the image

Still I struggle to see the beauty
Of the world and of you
Before time casts its shadow one last time
Upon my fading view

My mind's eye will remember you
Trying to soothe the despair within my soul
Forever the visage of your beauty
Lingers in my mind

Your beauty swells and my heart with love
Then the dimness is all around
And I am alone in the world
Of my mind's eye.

Al Hallberg

Losing A Friend

In the midst of all this confusion
I see the face of depression
Could this possibly not be true?
How come the rest of us look so blue?
A smiling face turned upside down.
Why so blue and such a frown?
They have said a friend has died
It's ok we have already cried
You think the tables have been turned,
You think you have been burned.
We both can cry
And say good bye
She's now in a better place
With all the time and all the space.
No longer with the crowd
Rather buried 6-feet under ground.

Hope Green

When I Look Out My Window

When I look out my window
I see beautiful trees. Majestic mountain
and clear blue streams.

When I look out another
window I see thing I can't
believe I see drug, I see hatred
and I see guns all scattered on
the street

I wonder where those beautiful
trees majestic mountain and clear
blue stream go?

I realize this is real
not every thing is beautiful
trees majestic mountains and
clear blue streams

Julian Jackson

Emptiness

In the midst of my chaos
   I search for spiritual release.
And freedom from desire
   Leads to inner peace.
Who me?
   Oh yes, I am a child of the
      human kind.
   I am as curious as anyone around,
   Yes, I am a child who wants to
      reach up to you.
   I am giving you unconditional love.
Oh yes, I keep reaching up and my hands,
   as well as my heart keep touching
      Nothing but
         Emptiness.

Isabel Salam

A Bethlehem Star

On a clear and crystal night
I saw it in the sky
The brightest of the heavenly stars
Wondrous to the eye
Glowing like a coal afire
Spreading love and joy abound
Just as it did so long ago
In the town where Christ was found
I in awe took in its splendor
Praising God who caused to be
This sign of everlasting life
And light for all the world to see

James T. Huckleberry

Untitled

As time goes on
I realize that all is done
I think that everyone, everywhere
Everybody is going to realize
that time goes on.

Time holds secrets in the future
and sometimes it holds onto the past.
I realize that when joy comes
You need to hold onto the joy
You never know when it could return.

Jessica Baker

A Planet Erased

The scientists tell us our planet is young
I picture it colorful and spry,
But everywhere I look around
The things so young soon die.

Our waters all run black with oil
Pollutants fill our air,
Hazardous waste upon the land
Acid rain so hard to bear.

Species gone we will never meet
And others that we know,
Will soon have faded from out mist
Without a chance to grow.

Rain forests gone with insects and plants
Later generations will pay,
The medicines and cures we had
Are now just gone away.

War for some, hunger for others
Disease and lack of nature,
I fear for our planet still so young
For we soon face erasure.

Gloria A. Van Wagner

"Mother and Child"

Mother! Why did you leave me?
I need you"

Mother! Please holds me in
Your arms.
"I need you"

My child! My child!
The Lord called me.
"He needed me."

My child! My child!
You are not only in my
Arms but also in my
Heart.
I will always be with
You in spirit.

Francie Bryant

Soul

Within me now the feeling grows
I must reclothe my soul;
The ever and eternal stirs...
I would again be whole.
For She once more awakens
And from me drops the spell,
She uses for a respite
And in which She dwells
in other states of consciousness,
experience sublime
Preceding the combustion of
the incandescent time.

Gloria Scott Cole

Forever In The Wind

I'm as powerful as I want to be.
I can spread my wings as far as
the eye can see.
As I wander through the clouds
night and day I continue my
adventure as I seek for a prey.
Back and forth time and time again.
I will ride forever in the wind.

Christy Berry

Home Sweet Home

I miss it so,
I miss it so,
one day I'll return
But tell I do I'll
Always be sad an
long for you.

When I'm back,
I'll be back for good,
No more tears,
Soon I'll be where
I belong.

I hate it here,
So miserable and dumb,
I wanna be happy
But I don't know
How?

Angela Sullivan

Who Am I

Who am I without his love.
I loved him with all my heart and soul.
He was my lover,
He was my best friend,
He was my soul mate
but, he is my past.
We can't go back.
She is now what I once was,
She is now envied,
She has a lover,
She has a best friend,
She has a FUTURE.
All is forward.
Will I ever get to tell him,
"I love him".
And hear an echo or ditto.
Who am I without his love.

Cynthia Mastin

"I Just Don't Know"

Hi, Bye,
I love you, I hate you
Let's kiss, let's fight.
I don't know it's just not right.
When I think about it,
All I want to do is shout it.
But I don't know what I want to shout.
Someone, please, don't tease
Just tell me what it's all about.
I have the words in the top of my head,
If only I could get them out.
Sometimes I want to stay
Sometimes I want to go.
Someone, please help, me I just don't know.
Well, I guess I've figured it out.
So, let's not cry and let's not shout,
Just keep it inside and never let it out.
It happened so fast,
I wish I could have made it last,
Longer than all the rest.
But to leave and forget must be the best.

Janice Reed   12 ½ years old

A Lasting Love

I love you for who you are,
I love you for being you.
You're so very special,
No one else will ever do.

I love you for always listening,
To my troubles, problems, and cares.
I love you for being so understanding,
And for always being there.

I love to listen to your laugh,
And see your friendly smile.
You're someone I can count on
To go the extra mile.

I love you for being concerned,
And for talking to me each day.
For being so loving, kind, and thoughtful,
Each step of life's way.

I'm so very thankful,
To have someone like you.
So trusting, sweet, and kind,
Someone who will always be true.

Brenda Parker

A Beautiful Tree

Receiving my sincere admiration
I love a tree, this magnificent creation.
The cottonwood, the oak, the elm
And others that are in God's realm.
But, most of all, I think the first
Is the lovely weeping birch.
Its stately branches and narrow leaf
Allow me to forget my grief.
It has its own personality
And brings out the creativity
In me...and makes me yearn
To study more and to learn
About lovely, mossy shady nooks
Cool and rocky babbling brooks
There I could dream away my days
Thinking of God's wondrous ways
And my mind would rise to higher things
Where eternal nature springs.
And underneath this lovely birch
I feel like I am in God's church.

Edith Wagner

"Hope Eternal"

Today the earth is cold and white
I look on it with awe.
I wonder about the living things,
Only yesterday, I saw.

Will they survive
and again arise
as the earth begins to warm?
Seeking the joys of life
After weathering another storm

Eternal life is for us all
sometimes it seems so bleak
We have to weather some turbulent storms
to find the peace we seek

Although the Earth seems cold and still
life is still within
Once more it will emerge
A new cycle to begin.

Beulah C. Gazay

Two Directions

As I move on to yet another calling,
I look back at what became.
Became so expressionless,
That few an eye could see.
Yet nothing explainable,
Could ever reach the heights, we soar.

Without a whisper,
We came to be.
The clouds descended,
Finally we could see.
Love lives on.
Tranquility flows through,
For us to hold.
We transcend through waves,
The darkness has lifted.
Without grasping for destination,
Here we'll be.
Ever without you, we climb.

Amanda C. Roberts

Joseph To Mary

I am here to care for you
 I like your pretty name
Though I am old Mary dear
 I love you just the same.

We must hurry now to bethlehem
 To pay our census sums
I hope and pray we make it
 Before the baby comes.

Oh they mocked us and they told us
 Nothing good has ever come
Out of these hills of nazareth
 How could they be so dumb?

Little donkey's ears are flopping
 In rhythmic joy today
He will carry you safely
 And the rugged way.

Better days will come for us
 just you wait and see
I love you and I dare to hope
 That you in turn love me.

John Altman Sr.

Eyes Of The Beholder

I like the land, I like the trees
I like the wind, I like the breeze
I like the flowers and the farms
I like the earth with all its charms

But one thing I don't like to see
Is all the buildings and the streets
I like the dirt and the rocks
But not the cement and concrete blocks

I like the open, not the enclosed
I like the smell of roses, not the decomposed
I like the quiet, not the noise
I like the sound of birds, not motored toys

I like the sun yellow and bright
I like the moon that shines in the night
I like the sea, I like the sand
I like the animals, I like the land

Christal G. Hardenburg

To The Woman I Love

When I look into your eyes,
 I leave the realm of reality.
And drift away, into the universe,
 Letting each star represent a dream of you.
And each cloud a tender caress,
 Tied with a ribbon of moonlight.
While the first rays of the golden sun,
 Penetrates the sands of time,
While the tides of the sea beat a tattoo
 Against a tomorrow that will never end.
And words of parting are never spoken,
 And vows are never broken.
 And vows are never broken.

Cooper C. Cowan

"Reflections Of Innocence"

As time draws near, my darling dear,
I know that you have a lot to fear;

It's almost time to spread your wings,
No one is certain what our future brings;

As you leave, hold your head high,
No need for us to say goodbye;

No need for tears sweet daughter of mine,
There are lots of hills for you to climb;

Give your new life a fair chance,
Your future, you surely will enhance;

Yet it's true, I will miss you,
And I know, you will miss me too;

I know you will do yourself proud,
At graduation you can stand and yell out loud

"Look Mom", "I made it"! "Look at me"!
Yes, my beautiful "Baby Girl", I can see!
I see a reflection of me

Gloria Baker

Two Stolen Hearts

My heart was stolen from me
 I know now when and where.
You stole it when you kissed me
 standing in the garden there.

You stole it without knowing it
 for I was very shy.
And I didn't want to tell you
 "Cross my heart and hope to die."

I didn't want to tell you
 but I guess somehow you knew,
For you looked at me and whispered
 that your heart was stolen, too.

Evelyn Gardner

Dad And Mom

When I was young, and growing up.
I lived in a world where there wasn't much.
Except a father love, and a mother's care.
Some how we knew they would always be there.
A year ago they went home,
Leaving us kids all alone.
But as day's pass, and life goes on.
I know someday they will welcomed me Home.

Edna L. Darden

Personal Springtime

As Persephone made her descent,
I knew this year would be different
My connections going deeper than
Where she reigns as queen.

I sat beside her in the dark unfamiliar
Cave where there are no words only
Symbols. Then after autumn mournings,
After we slept through winterdeath
And prayed for light, I felt her stirring.

Longing to rise from those depths, I
Spoke to her. Awake Persephone and ascend!
Your arrival is announced
In the budding Maple.

Diane Segal

The Homeless

Why are people homeless?
I just don't understand.
Millions of them everywhere,
All across the land.

At this very moment,
We have things others do not,
And that is because they were fired,
Or they just went bankrupt.

Just because you have a home,
Doesn't mean you'll stay that way,
Anyone can become homeless
It could happen to you any day.

Even if you have the least amount
Of possessions, please take
every advantage of them that you can,
And think of the least fortunate,
The homeless, who have nothing
to take advantage of.

Celena Guerrero

Visiting Hours

Within these walls
 I hide
People come and go
They stare
 and look away
I hide my face
 my feelings
My body is not mine
I watch the door
To see who comes
you are not there
and darkness
fills my soul.

Barbara McRea

Your Angel

Your angel
I always think of you
In every prayer,
That the angel,
Will always be there.

Angels bring rainbows
And dreams it seems,
No matter where you go
The angel will always be there.

Cheryl S. Walver

Hopeful Illusions

As I sat by a silver river
I held on tight and began to shiver
As the cold winter rain began to fall
I rolled myself up into a ball
As the acid rain fell from the sky
All the flowers began to cry
I lifted my hands to cover my ears
As the rain mixed together with my tears
The wasteful rivers that I could see
Had filled all the fish with mercury
With my animal friends gone I hated to think
That they had all died and now were extinct
And there seemed to be a hole in the sky
That kept on making people die
When I looked for some kind of answer
I discovered I too was infected with cancer
For what rolled in was some kind of fog
That burnt my lungs with a luminescent smog
And as I awake at my dreams conclusions
My heart was filled with hopeful illusions

Andrew Balasa

Our Children

Yesterday I cried
I heard a baby girl had died
The family car, they say
Had turned the wrong way
Why would they want to shoot
A little girl so young and cute

Yesterday I cried
I heard two teenage brothers died
Just boys riding in a car
Not going very far
The shots rang out that night
They cause us all such fright

It's today I cry
I heard more children died
Our little children gone
What in the world is wrong
Our world's not safe, I fear
Not with these guns so near
How can our children play
With our world this way

Carla Aday

Resting Place

I look across the face of the ocean deep
I hear it whisper to me soft and sweet.
Come, come and I almost go
But something inside me whispers no!

Come, come, I hear it beckon me.
From tears and broken dreams you'll be free
You can ride the wind and waved with me.
We'll go down to the ocean floor
Come, come, my lady, weep no more.

Not today my dearest friend
Tomorrow I say, I'll come again
I turn and as I walk away
Come, come, I hear it softly say.

Wait I whisper soft and low
Tomorrow to you I'll surely go.
You can caress my body and kiss my face
And carry me off to your resting place.
I'll dance on your waves and ride the wind.
And never, never, weep again.

Dorothy Crosby

Flame

My icy blue flame of deception
I have used countless times
to burn away the deadwood of
lostlove and nevercaredfor friends but
I have never burned myself on my
tongue as I have this night
with you As a pale wind
you pushed this fire back
at me melting my
artificial face What is
left I do not understand I cannot
believe that I am this trivial
Nothing special Just crispy skin
and blackened bone and sharphotpain
I am the chinese dancing dragon
and you have seen the feet that move me
We step forward to play our roles
of something in nothing
Now I pray I am the understudy left to watch
I pray you finally blew out my flame

Annie Krause

An Artist's Sunset

The blue across my canvass
I have swept
But now the sun is sinking low
I add a touch of yellow gold
Then suddenly earth's sky is bold.
Stay, let me capture nature's bliss
Of azure blue and gold
And pinks and lavender so pale,
Before your sinking rays
Tint these to reds and purple deep.
My brush can't hold your magic sun
So sink, and go to sleep
While I will copy lifeless color
On my screen
And wish a hundred times
I could have painted
What I've seen.

Edna Pack

Unforgotten Friend

I've loved you since the day we met,
I have not stopped thinking of you yet.
Not yesterday, today or tomorrow,
I'll be there to wash away your sorrow.
All I know it what I say,
I will not have your love today.
I want to feel your love inside,
But when you get close my love I hide.
I wish you could feel this love of mine,
I'll remember you till the end of time.
At this you may laugh or start to cry,
But I'll be there to dry your eyes.
Love is an object pure and hard,
to survive you must keep up your guard.
When I close my eyes you're all I see,
As long as it's you it makes no difference to me.
Some say my heart is cold as ice,
But those who know me say it's nice.
The love I give is warm and true,
And if you say yes it can be for you.

Joshua C. Leonardy

I'm A Strong Black Woman

I'm a strong black woman
I have no doubt that I came
from Kings and Queens and sometimes
I have to shout! I'm a courageous
woman and my grandmother
and mother before me were
strong. I'm in every sense of the
word to tackle harder things
in my life than I deserve.
Being the best I can is what
I must do. I'm teaching my kids
to have respect too. I'm
a mixture of mystery and desire;
strong are these two things
to set your heart on fire.
I must never give up on the hope
within to show love whenever I can.

Jo Helen Pettigrew

Rejection

I have known rejection for an eternity.
I have been kept weak yet strong.
Paralyzed into uncertainty,
Aggressive when it's all wrong.

So easily wounded by unconscious words.
Should be desensitized by now,
But it becomes more painful
Than I had ever thought somehow.

Bad choices, I've made a million.
Got a million more to go; you see
Sickening visions of poor decisions
Have brought me to my knees.

I want, no, I need to be wanted
When libations are no where in sight.
When music assuages the atmosphere
And conversations linger into the night.

I don't wish to be that last resort
Only because I am there; No never!
Because someone thinks I'm better than nothing,
And nothing lasts forever.

Andrea Glauberman

Illness

I didn't know.
I had no idea.
It was just there.

They cut it out,
performed chemo,
radiation.
What was left was
weakness, pain.

I reflected.
What was important
is not now,
I need to set
new priorities.

Life is different,
I am selective now.
I am surrounded by
loving family,
sweet caring friends.

It's a new life!
I have a second chance!

Fran R. Fordis

Sleeping

I can't sleep
I guess I should count sheep
Sleeping is cool
There isn't one rule
When I sleep
I've never seen a sheep
Dreaming is cool
You are never the fool
When you dream
You can be king or queen
When you have a nightmare
Things aren't fair or square
Nightmares are usually scary
But rarely about a fairy
I guess I should try to get to sleep
Without counting sheep

Jason Donahe

The Time Of Sunset

As the sun set on the mountains,
I felt the warmth of its glow.
The streaks of red among the clouds
Slowly began to flow.

I thought of time that is passing by,
As age does come to all;
And I know that there's a setting sun for me
At the Master's call.

Still, we can feel its gentle glow,
If only we walk with this Master,
And His love we come to know.

Jacqueline D. Roberts

A Personal Prayer

Father, there are two things
 I don't like about myself; no, three;

Guide my thoughts and
 throw out the chaff
Every thought that is not
 pleasing to you, Lord.
Whatever is true and honest,
 let it be in me.

Humility is lacking
 thinking wrongly that
I can have knowledge and
 goodness without Your help.
Thinking that I am important
 not walking humbly with You.

Prayer is needed to give
 myself completely to You
To have You in my mind
 at a moment's notice without
Thinking of myself first.
 Oh, to have prayer without ceasing.

Eunice Kauffman

Fly

I can fly like a bird.
I can soar in the sky.
I can open my wings,
And fly up real high.
Until the wind stops,
Than I'm in trouble!
So, I flap my wings,
And fly on the double!

Jennifer Armenta

Roads Of Life

I'm lost.
I don't know where I am.
I don't know where I've been.
I don't know where I'm going.

Won't somebody help me?
Show me the way home?
Teach me how to do it myself?
Help me understand?

Give me a map,
Maybe even a map with a key.
A key to unlock my problems.
And a map to show them the roads out.

Find me, show me, teach me, help me
and then maybe I can face the world alone.

Aurora-Jillann Hall

Busyness

You sure keep busy, he wrote
I didn't answer it's because of him
When I practice my choral music
I don't think of his inviting mouth
His promising eyes, his empty arms.
When I'm typing the membership list
I can't think when will he come
Will he come
Will he invite me there
When I make change for a bake sale
customer
I can keep from wondering
Does he like me
Does he love me
Does he think about me
But work doesn't always work
Arranging flowers for the awards dinner
I'm free to think
How his smile gleams
How his eyes held mine
How I love him.

Barbara R. DuBois

My Love For You

As I watched TV last night ...
 I did it all by vanilla candlelight,
I found myself coming un-glued ...
 all because of the woman in you.

Your voice, so soft and smooth ...
 makes my heart do a triple beat.

Your skin, so soft and smooth ...
 gives me warm feelings, thru and thru.

Your touch, so tender and kind ...
 gives me a tingle, all down my spine.

And as the days go by so fast,
 I often look into my looking glass.
There I see the woman in you,
 standing tall, so warm and true.
And again I find myself un-glued,
 all because of wondering of you.

Come each night, I wish upon a star,
 I hope and pray you won't stray too far.
If I had a wish that could ever come true.
 I'd wish each day to spend with you.

James C. Crawford

My Dream

To be with you again it seemed,
I could only dare to dream.
To be loved by you once more,
was all that I wished for.

The day my wish came true,
at the altar we said I do.
My love for you I cherish,
and as one we will never perish.

This poem for Valentine's Day,
hopefully tells you in my way,
how special you are to me,
so I pray thanking God our love came to be.

Jonita Hogan

The Moment You Laid Your Eyes On Me

I cared for you
I cared for you
The moment that I saw you

I yearned for you
The moment that you
Laid your eyes on me
And tried to get to know me

But there was one thing you said
It sounded like you and I were made
Made to be together

How did you know my lover
That your sweetness
Had turned my heart to its deepest
From the moment you laid your eyes on me

Carmel Victor

Healing Hearts

I'm so confused between hate and love
I can't even talk to God above

I have so much pain inside
All I want to do is run and hide

So many feelings that won't come out
It seems that all I do is scream and shout

So I have to go out and find the key
to open the door and set me free

I'll take it slow from the start
And let my blood flow to my heart

As time goes by I'll care about others
And think of mankind as my brothers

I see it now so plain and clear
all I have to do is listen and hear

Look closely, and you too will see
that it's not just about you and me

The whole picture comes into play
If you take it step by step, day by day

Go forward to face the fear
Hold on tight your dreams are near

Beverly Cook

Untitled

Don't tell me what
I cannot do,
I'll never know until I try.
Don't tell me what
I have to do,
The only one who knows is I.
You do not rule me,
I am myself.
Do not judge me,
Judge yourself.
My soul is what I make of it,
Not for what you choose it to be.
I cannot live up to the
Standards you set,
So why not just let me be me.

Amanda Riddle

November

The leaves have begun to fall
I can smell you in the air
If I only knew then
What I know now
I would have changed my ways
Did you really know how much I loved you
If only I could express how I feel to you
The lump in throat when I remember you
The guilt used to over flow my body
I believe in God
I know you are still here with me
I know you have forgiven me
I love you Granny

Brandi Bosetti

Love

When I look into your eyes
I can see a love restrained.
But darlin' when I hold you
Don't you know I feel the same.

It's hard to keep and open ear?
There's a time and place for
Everything
For everyone like me and you.
But love is hard and it worth it,
But I love you with all my heart,
If you could heal a broken heart.

Sometimes I need sometimes on my own.
Sometimes you need sometimes all alone.
Everybody needs sometimes on their own.

David Matthew Vanover

I Am!

I live
I breathe, I see, and I hear.
I think...therefore, I must be.
I am a promise yet to be fulfilled,
I am a fury...waiting to be unleashed!
I am always seen, though seldom
Heard,
Rarely happy, I am always smiling.
I am we whose souls are soaring,
Our matters anchored,
By "The Dream"!
I am the creation of Divinity,
I am the result of Morality,
I am what I see, I am what I hear.
I am as I think, I am what I am.
No more, no less!

Jasper Anthony Jordan

My Son

As I sit and look upon your face,
I bow my head in disgrace,
For failing you in your time of need,
When all you wanted was to be freed.

To lose the demons in your heart,
To not feel so far apart,
You filled your life with games and drugs,
When all you wanted were the hugs,
Love did not come easy for you and me,
All we wanted was to be free.

I remember the day you came,
I new right away it was not a game,
The life I gave, God took away,
I wish you could have stayed.

I made mistakes along the way,
I'm sorry you had to pay,
Now I go to see your grave,
I wish to God you could have stayed,
Please forgive me for all I've done,
You were my first born, you were my son.

Anita Diane Henson

A Pray To All The Runaways In The World

Dear Lord,
　I am writing you this letter on
behalf of all the runaways in the world!
Pray you keep them safe, from all harm,
For when its, may you keep them safe from
warm, cause you are so strong,
When they are hungry, may you provide
for them, and as you look upon their
fears and sorrows
For only you know if there is or will
be a tomorrow,
May they not despair because of the
fears, may you bless them in your
own way, may you soon send them
back towards our way,
Dear Lord,
　I am writing you this letter on behalf
of all the runaways in the world!

Beverly Armstead

A Senior's Lament

Who am I? My inner thoughts do say.
I am woman in most every way -
Caring, loving, curious am I
Needing, wanting, I look at the sky.
I ask my God to watch over me
Now that I feel so alone without he.
We are in the same house, we both built.
Quietly we sit thinking how we had felt
When we were young and things were exciting.
Now it's silence or with lots of fighting.
What's for supper, and where are you going.
Do this, do that, the lawn needs mowing.
He orders and I ask that this be done.
His way, his time and he has won.
So I go my way with all my friends
All the time wondering how this ends.
We are two seniors, who are supreme
Supposed to be silent and never seen?
But I love, I live and have much to do.
Is it a journey alone or will I be with you?

Flora Calef Hammond

Stay

Today I can honestly say
I am thankful in so many ways
God is in my life looking over me
Every minute of every day
Working miracles along the way
As I continue to grow I am here to stay
Because God knows the only way
So there's not much else I can say
Except that I only have this day
Knowing that I am here not only for this day
Wondering not only what it would pay
So I can only say that I am here to stay.

Gary P. Kooken

Delayed Reaction

No! I am not all right with that.
I am not with you on that.

I don't want to condemn you.
I don't want to confront you.
All I want to do is tell you
I am not with you on that.

You come to a party with your
hatred and toxic shame and
I am not with you on that.

Out of your mouth, in a room
full of strangers, comes a
genocidal n*g*er joke and
although everybody laughs
except me
I am not with you on that.

I took on your shame and by
My silence I took on my own shame.
I am not with me on that.

John F. O'Donohue

Eternal Day

I am time and dominion.
I am dust and great winds.
I see the seasons prodding forever onward
circling eternity again and again.

Time... in its old age
folds up and is changed.
While every little simple thing
speaks of subtlety and of great pains.

Life, draped softly over
like some frozen waterfall,
has captured in its crystals
a fleeting image of us all.

On her banks desperate hopes sway,
screaming in the breeze.
The pollen of some silent answer
settle softly and we breathe.

Spirits stare across fertile plains,
spawned from the depths of night.
It dawns on me, I am celestial being
borne into eternal light.

Ivory Dean Jones

The Algonquin Round Table

Wit can devastate,
   Hurt gives way to hate;
      Was I ever like that?
So hard to forgive,
   Forget and let live;
      Can I ever do that?
Alone in the din,
   Mortal and human;
      I was ever like that!

James Foresti

Presence

Her pride was pure presence touching
human souls in wonder watching
petals glowing roots clutching
earth goddess ever reaching
future past present teaching

I am your rhyme I am your reason
I am your time I am your season
stop look listen see
fragile power reality
'sans' me on earth you cannot be
'ami' your worth depends on me
as I live to grow I have no voice
as I grow to die I have no choice
in this you and I are similar glories
attend me now 'fore cold destroys me

Once again remember my roots
strengthen my sleeping tender shoots
conspiring to leap into flower fruitful
divinations giving rise
to future past present lives

Audrey Wilkins Byrd

Looking Back

How foolish we were;
how young.
Following blind faith
with an impetuous moxie
known only to warriors.
Are we smarter now,
or simply smarting from
past abrasions?
Life goes on but the
memories burn,
like warnings to the soul.
You ask me if I regret our past.
How could I? It made us
who we are.
You ask when the memories will
finally fade.
Never, I hope.

Dawn Josephson

Still

I'm lost somewhere between high and low.
   How far gone, I just don't know.
Roaming aimlessly describes my mind.
   Searching for something I cannot find.
What that is, I couldn't say.
   The answer hasn't come today.
Someday soon, I hope it will.
   Until then, I wait here - still.

Amy O'Shay Guibert

Untitled

I want to tell you
how you make me feel.
How when I look at you,
I see with my heart.
And when you talk to me,
I hear with my soul.
I want to tell you
how when you kiss me,
I feel fire;
and when you hold me
I know love.
I want to tell you
that, for the first time in my life,
I know how it feels
to need someone so much
it makes my heart ache.
I have many things to tell you,
but I just don't know the words.

Buffy Broncato

Uncle Kelley

Trailing laughter in your wake;
How would I know you'd leave heartache.
You brought joy to all around;
I can still hear your voice's sound.

Me and my siblings you did rear;
And you us you had no peer.
When my parents were gone, you were there;
And it never seemed you had a care.

You had a presence like no other;
Loving and helping your big brother.
You taught me how to laugh and sing;
And now you're with our Heavenly King.

You had so many things you wanted to do;
And now you're a cold and lifeless hue.
Two weeks and four months have past;
And yet in you thoughts you still last.

The pain of you death is ever near;
Along with many a miserable tear.
I loved you much and miss you so;
More than you can ever know.

Crystal Nicole Bale

Reverie At The End Of A Year

What a gray November day!
How to keep the gloom away?
   A fire's glow, a cup of tea,
   A friend to keep me company.
   Work to do and letters to write,
Keep me busy til the night
   Drops its curtain much too soon
And wraps us in its dark cocoon.

This is the fall and so it'll be
Til cold December's days I see.
   From gloom to gleam the days will flow,
Gliding in on glistening snow.

The final seasons of the year
   Bring with them both some gloom and cheer.
Find each day some deep content
   And you will find the year well-spent.

Carolyn Lea Scott

Nature's Miracles

Did you ever think about nature
   How the seasons come and go...
How they seem to be timed perfectly
   Within a week or so?

First comes the welcome springtime
   When the tulips poke through the ground...
Then the birds come north to nest
   And budding trees are all around.

Summertime brings many more flowers
   And the roses smell especially sweet...
Laughing children are out of school
   And they think vacation time is neat.

Autumn is cool and invigorating
   After those hot and humid days...
The mountains display beautiful foliage
   Resemble an artist's palette in many ways.

As the starkness of winter approaches
   Jack Frost etches the windowpanes...
The snowflakes glisten like diamonds
   And the miracles begin all over again.

Blodwyn L. Newcomer

My Little Julie Rose

You don't know my little girl
How special she is to me
So let me tell you from my heart,
For she's young and so carefree.
My darling little wonder of life
A miracle of our love.
A great event to him and me
She finally came to be.
Her name is Julie Rose,
And a perfect rose to us.
We give thanks our God above
To have blessed us with so much.

Jodi Robertson

Let Thunder Be Our Song

Dreams of golden hair,
How sad I know not the touch.
Dreams hold little respite
For the treasure I covet so much.

My dearest dream of all,
How I cling to you so tight
In the darkness of my solitude,
On cold deceptive night.

Every star will fall,
Not every wish comes true,
Desire burns endlessly
Such is my longing for you.

If I looked into your eyes
And told you of things to come,
Would great love ease the pain,
Could our love then be as one?

Love hear my tender plea.
Dearest touch me soon.
Let thunder be our song,
Our limits to golden moon.

Alan Paine

Ode To A Loved One

Your hair so soft and fluffy
How like the feel of a cuddly puppy
Your nose so straight and fine
How like the sculpt of Venus divine
How like the stars, your eyes
That twinkle in yon azure skies
Your lips how like the Rose
So luscious red in meadow grows
To you so lovely and so fair
I do my ardent love declare.

Herman G. Minter

Unattainable Love

How I see him in my dreams
How I feel him in my dreams
How I love him in my dreams
How I made love to him in my dreams

In my dreams
My heart aches, my mind wanders,
My desires, my passion, my pain,
My tears, my emotions...rise.

In my dreams
We walk along the beach, my heart beats,
My mind wanders, my body tremble,
As his come close to mine.

In my dreams
I wrapped him in my arms with warm tender love,
I cared, I listened.

In my dreams
We had a chance to be lovers, he chose another.

In my dreams
My love for him will eternally be.

In my dreams

Birelee Bryant

Too Young

I was too young to ever see
How good you would have been for me.
To see you grow from day to day
I wish they didn't take you away.
I try to forget, but I never will
There is always that void to fill.
Everyone said it was better this way
I never could have made him stay.
Of us, he didn't want no part
And this really broke my heart.
I hope you'll forgive me for what I've done
Without you baby, I never really won.

Camille DeLuca

What Time Is It?

It's time, it's time, for me to see,
How good my God has been to me.
When I was in darkness I cried to thee,
Oh Lord, oh Lord, please deliver me.
Suddenly, I felt the presence of love,
That came from my God up above.
What great joy I felt you see,
Because my God heard my plea.
He's an awesome God of hope,
He's an awesome God of peace,
I know His love will never never cease.
What time is it?
It's time for me to see,
How good my God will always be to me.

Cynthia Elaine Sanders

"Seasons"

We've reached the autumn of our life
   How could this be - so soon?
Just yesterday we were young and vibrant
   Seeking maturity; keeping in tune.

Our steadfast love for each other
   Has stood the test of strife.
Each child was accepted with open arms.
   As a new chapter in our life.

The daily challenges that test us
   Are accepted, as always, with faith
That the good Lord above
Will allow His love
   To help us to travel on.

Joyce D. Droege

A Boy Named Randy

   The easter bunny came to my
House and gave me lots of candy
   I wonder why he didn't give the
Boy down the street named Randy?

   I know that his Mommy sick
Maybe she couldn't come to the door
   Neither could his Daddy cause
He's not around know more.

   Maybe its cause Randy was a
very naughty boy
   Naa, Randy always sits and plays
with his one and only toy

   I don't want this candy, I might
get a belly ache.
   I am going down to see Randy and
my candy I will take.

   "Hey Randy, wanna hear something
very awful funny?"
   I got your candy by mistake
that dumb ole Easter Bunny."

Joan Cleland

Summer and Fall

Summer
Hot lake
Swimming jumping biking
Birds flowers leaves colors
Raking falling fishing
Colorful crispy
Fall

Jesse Jack Gober

My Little Rocking Horse

Rock my little rocking
horse,
Up and down we go.
Rock my little rocking
horse,
In the fields and snow
we go.
Rock my little rocking
horse,
To the mountains oh so
high.
Rock my little rocking
horse,
Rock me beddy-by.

Dorothy Palladino

Lingering

I stopped by for a simple kiss
Hoping to fade into utter bliss

But you weren't there
I said, "I don't care"

And left with simmering madness
Which turned to glimmering sadness

For a kiss I came about
Leaving I acquired doubt...
Jille Jennifer Neiman

Summer Shade

Shadows in the cry
Hoping sunshine falling from the sky
Choking rainfall in the mist of
melting pain
Green fields breed yesterday's shame
Multi race
Half in half
side by side
As we hold hands
Let the colorful rainbow reflect
Peace in who we are
Christopher T. Burns

Buried In A Reflection

Look at my reflection so tall and thin
Hoping so much that it would be true on in
Wishing for a body like that
Knowing that it is all just fat

Somebody put a mirror in front to me
And made me realize that I could never be
I'm buried in a reflection wanting to move
Where's my genie to give me that groove

Always wanted to be like that
My reflection...
Jenny-Rebecca Prohaska

"Loving Someone Special"

Do you know the way I feel about you
Hopefully the way you feel about me too
I love you more than words can say
More and more everyday
Every time I see you face
I think of a special loving place
I think you're sweet I think you're divine
And forever I hope you'll be mine o mine
April LaTishe Parker

Soul Of Wondering

I watch the time and wait for what,
I watch for the day and wait for who,
When I watch I wonder, why I wonder I
do not know. When I watch I know not
for who, when I wonder I know not for
what, I will continue to watch so that
I may ease my mind, and I will keep
wondering so that I may find the
purpose of my pondering ways, the things
that always keep me in a daze.
Darryl McIntyre

Fading Dreams

A poet lost his dreams
  his thoughts flowing into the streams
Drowned in the whirlpools
  are images of love and whims;
An angel lost her wings
  broken by the blowing reckless winds
Falling down from the heavens
  she's never known such grave fear;
A fairy stood alone
  in a desolate place away from home
The enchanted forest now is gone
  her heart has turned to stone;
A philosopher prayed to God
  begging for a little peace of mind
He always believed in the truth
  but its the truth he could not find;
The rainbow have faded
  gone are the colors of the day
Not a raindrop would fall
  but tears roll down from a soul...
Joselito C. Enriquez

Just A Breath Away

I saw him stroll along the sea shore -
his tanned body ever so pronounced
against the gleaming white sand.
His hair streaked with gold glistened
in the sunlight. He was magnificent.
  But he never noticed me

I watched him from across a crowded
theatre, yet I could distinctly hear his
laugh - a wonderful laugh that was as
captivating as his smile.
  But he never knew I was there

Once he even brushed against my arm
as he passed me by - so close that I
could see his eyes were the color of a
clear winter sky. And for a moment
the world stood still.
  But he never acknowledged me

How sad it is to love from afar and yet
be just a breath away
Dori Schindel

Hidden Love

He lights up my day when I see
his smiling face,
and it warms my heart in
a special place.
  I brush his shoulders as I
am passing by,
hoping I will catch his eye.
  I speak to him in my mind,
thinking someday he will be mine.
  Is he as great as he seems?
Or only like that in my dreams?
  If I was with him, I'd make
him my world,
And I'd pray I'd always be
his special girl.
  I must tell him how I feel inside,
maybe,
he too,
his love he did hide.
Amy Bracheen

Highway Cowboy

He stood beside the interstate.
His life lay by his feet.
Those eyes, they had a tired look.
His stature said, "I'm beat."

His saddle, rope, and bedroll,
Told a common tale:
A cowboy on the move again,
Who'd spent a night in jail.

Lost his job to some machine.
He didn't know his boss.
The spread was sold to movie stars.
They always showed a loss.

He's pretty sure he hit someone,
Maybe in that bar.
The last three days seem lost for good.
He knew he'd rolled his car.

He's sure he'll find another ranch,
Where cows and hay need men.
And values that he's always held
Will come to life for him.
Ed Shuey

Translucent Swami

No stutter could suffice;
His language simple, and precise;
Not hidden by the veils of mystic speech.

Dare not his spoken words obscure
perceptions altered from before,
revealing points of view well within reach.

Elevate intelligence;
separate states of consciousness;
refuse to settle for the same or less.

Always progress shall depend upon
desire to extend potential capabilities;
Success.
Jason Andrew Smith

Sharing

  He smoked his pipe and rocked in
his chair, with a wrinkled face and
graying hair.
  The stars were shining and the sky
was clear, when up to the doorway
a small figure appeared.
  "Come talk to me","his eyes seemed
to say, while sitting alone, most of
the day.
  "I'm Sam," the youngster said,
with a tear in his eye. "My folks
are in heaven, way up in the sky."
  The old man reached out
and held him tight. "You're
welcome to stay with me tonight."
  Their friendship grew and each
played a part, of sharing the love,
each held in their heart.
Jeanette Piel

Addiction

He's a big strong man but a side of
him that's gentle as a kitten. He stares
at you with hurtful brown eyes that you
think any minute he's gonna burst. He's
hurt you, his family so much guilt he
doesn't know what to do with himself. The
monkey that's on his back he's trying to
detach it but he's grown to love it as
if it were a pet. He says to himself
do I kill you? No, he thinks to himself
that would be killing a part of me. So
He says to this monkey I cannot
love you anymore I must set you free
and when I see you on the streets
I'll see you there and acknowledge you
but I will never accept you again.

Fonya Gately

The Trial

Turn on the light that
hides shadows of hate,
And let its conjuncture
deflect the ravaged minds!
For its ruins are sightless
and priceless to contrive...

Why torture the innocent
yet a suspect while the real
killers watch with fainting smiles?
To plunder the candor of respect,
denied to a human by the unjust
the feeble and the vile.

Precious is the chant to freedom
and freedom will never destitute
a smile, with a grin of hate and grue;
So is the rage that lingers in our minds
in search for the dimmest beam of truth!

Carlos Hower

A Writer Bares Her Soul

A writer bares her soul to the world,
Her life, her being, her heart.
I want you to know me, to hear me speak.
I'm competent, worthy, and smart.

My life is filled with happiness, grief,
With sadness, with peace sublime.
I want to share my feelings with someone,
But someone cannot find the time.

My mother said "Go outside and play!"
My father was rarely there.
My brother didn't want to get involved.
My sister said "I just don't care!"

So I am frequently too alone.
I spend too much time at home.
I am jealousy selfish with my life,
For creative thoughts like this poem.

Now, I am quiet, an introvert,
Trying hard not to impose.
But I will confidently bare my soul
Through poetry, music, and prose.

Bonnie Cantrell West

A Mother's Day Gift

Softly without a whisper
her gentleness I'm showered with:

Though my wild spirit roams
freely in the night she looks
upon me only with love:

Sadness grips my heart
as the gift I have
for her are words, instead
of pearls of gold I can
only send my love

Bryon Harrelson

"Corisma's Great Adventure"

She trots the ground the earth,
Her eyes lit all a glow.
Her hooves hit the frozen ground,
Of newly fallen snow.
Her chestnut coat plows through the white,
She comes upon a yellow light.
A sense of home drifts through the air,
A cold breeze tears and whips at her hair.
As she comes towards the fence,
She hears a noise that makes her tense.
"What could it be?" Thought the mare,
The snow is so thick, it just wasn't fair.
The sound approached her in the snow,
"Come on Corisma, time to go."
The sound she heard was a friend,
She thought the night would never end.
The snow was like a heavy shield,
As they walked back across the field.

Brandi Nylen

Childhood

I hear a child laughing,
Her eyes bright with glee.
I hear her say nothing more,
Than, "Mommy look at me."

I see a playful child,
Swinging on a swing,
Running to the slide she goes,
Up and down the bars she flows.

I feel a little hand,
Pull upon my skirt.
Climbing up to my lap,
A tender hug she gives.

I remember a childhood,
So long ago it seems,
When I was running to and fro',
And scampering to a knee.

So long ago it was,
When that little girl was me.
Now I sit here holding,
My little girl of three.

In my antique rocker,
The one I grew upon,
When I was perched upon the knee,
Of my dear loving mom.

Bridget Forge

My Bill

My Bill has gone to his
  Heavenly home
No more to roam
  This earth
He said goodbye to all
  The aches and pains
Thus closed his eyes
  In peace he lies

Though he is gone and
  I remain
I am really not alone
  For all the years he had
Together, will keep him
  With me for ever and ever
Until that day when I
  Close my eyes and join
Him in our heavenly home

Cloamae Suiters

Fellowship

The fellowship of kindred souls
  Heartwarming at the least
An inspiration for living
  A joy of life for most!

To see the little children as
  They grow so straight and tall
True love exhibited by them,
  And we just love 'em all!

As Christ loved the little children
  They learned of His Great Love,
Awakening their parents, too,
  Like angels from above!

And in "Everyday confusion"
  With "Tempests in teapots"
We overlook the child-like faith
  That surely means a lot!

Remembering as once we were
  The children of our faith
United, we can do all things,
  Through Jesus, as he saith!

Anne M. Jensen

My Friend, Dick

Dick he thought he was well liked,
He sure did live an illusion.
He forced his way into my life,
My gosh, he was an intrusion.

Dick, I'm getting tired of you,
Your everywhere I go.
You interrupt each thing I do,
Now Dick, you'll have to blow.

He seems to know just when I eat,
Taking morsels from my plate.
Ignoring everything I say,
No, Dick is not my mate.

It is late and sleep won't come
Cause Dick won't take his leave.
I think I'll bury him nice and deep
And Dick I will not grieve.

Not many turned up on that day,
Just me to wave bye, bye.
There's nothing more for me to say, except...
"Here lies Dick the dead fly!"

Jenny Dever

Untitled

He tossed and turned,
He opened his eyes, dropped his bag.
She broke and burned,
The bedraggled old hag.

She says she'll do what she can,
Laughing at his cost.
He closed his eyes again,
His mind is what he had lost.

A flash on the mirror,
A bright light in his eye.
They told him not to fear her,
Frightened by the blackness of the sky.

When through with the release,
And the morning after.
He'll always find peace,
In the coldness of her laughter.

Cheryl Montrone

"What If"?

If a person lives with tolerance,
He learns to be patient.
If a person lives with encouragement,
He learns to be confident.
If a person lives with praise,
He learns to be appreciative.
If a person lives with acceptance,
He learns to love.
If a person lives with honesty,
He learns what truth is.
If a person lives with security,
He learns to have faith.
If a person lives with approval,
He learns to like himself.

Arturo Obregon

Sorrow

See the lonely one.
He kneels before the grave in a puddle
    of mud and crushed leaves.
The moon watches
    through the canopy of the trees
As his heart is wrenched out and
    dashed against the stone.
He writhes and shakes as he clutches
    the last remnant of his love:
A cold stony grave.

Gregg Nelson

You Can

You can climb the highest mountain;
He keeps your footing sure.
You can run the fastest race;
He will help you to endure.

You can sail the mighty ocean;
He's the wind that fills the sails.
You can face the fiercest storm;
His anchor will prevail.

You can swim the deepest river;
He gives strength to meet the tide.
You can walk the longest road;
He will be there by your side.

You can come into His presence;
He waits for you to come.
You can love for all eternity;
God's blessed holy Son.

Janet Lee

Gentle Acceptance

I've given my life to God
He has a plan for me.
So I'll accept each day as it comes,
Knowing it was meant to be.

Trials are part of His plan,
To help me learn and grow.
So I'll accept each burden in trust,
Knowing He loves me so.

Good times are meant to be cherished,
A blessing from my Father above.
Make each moment a memory,
Granted by God with love.

Each day of my life is a gift,
Made possible by God's only Son.
So I'll accept what God has to give
And waste not a moment - not one!

Dixie Battles

The Origin Of Love

When God made the stars
He gave to us wonder
When he parted the sea
He built in us faith
When God gave us music
Our hearts learned to sing
When he gave us the Word
The Word gave us strength
When God gave us night
God gave us rest
When he gave us the dawn
With it came peace
When God gave his son
His son was our hope
But when God gave us friends
It was then we gained love!

Eva Marie Lounsbury

Jesus Is Reverent In Our Lives

Jesus is reverent in our lives
He brings us joy!
He brings us peace!

He showed us His love with all His heart.
He died on the cross to save us all.
He took a path in this world-
A path that lead Him down a road of blood.

He loved mankind with all of His heart.
He died on the cross the save our souls-
I love Him so, I love Him so!
He means so much I cannot let Him go.

I love His Father for creating a Saint-
A Saint so holy and so full of grace.
A King who is The King of kings-
A King omnipotent in all things.

He is so wonderful, He is so great!
Jesus is the only one who can bring
Amazing grace.
Yes, Jesus is reverent in our lives!

Jewelean Jackson

Goodbye To Dreams

And I, being poor,
Have none, nothing to offer,
But this precious sand castle.
Please walk softly, gently,
For you might step,
Upon this fragile sand castle,
And wake, the anger sleeping before.

Then, you stepped upon my treasured,
Sand castle.
The anger leapt with deadening downpour.
A world was ripped because of anger.
My sand castle vanished like a phantom,
My sand castle drifted and left me,
In silent humiliation.

I waded to oblivion.
Self-pity was my companion.
Self-knowledge a vindication.

Carmelita Ledesma Agnas

A Lucky Man

A big inspiration of my life
Has been inspired by my wife.

My affections are possessed
By a love that is the best.

Great admiration is the key
Filled with truthful loyalty.

Loving her is a joyful duty
I am delighted by her beauty.

I know she has a magic power
Like the beauty of a flower.

There's romance in her heart
I have enjoyed from the start.

I appreciate her tender care
With happiness that I share.

I am so proud to be her guy
My love is hers until I die.

I'm the luckiest man on earth
Since God gave my angel birth.

Howard Golley Jr.

Change Of Seasons

The clouds are blue-trimmed fair,
Hanging like pillows in the air.
The sun sinks low, in its daily flight,
To open the door, for the coming of night.
The wind whispers softly to the trees,
As it playfully ruffles their leaves.
The crickets are waiting, as if on cue,
To supply the sounds, as it's their due.
All must know as summer clouds scurry by
A cycle is born, a cycle must die.
It's echoed in the whippoorwill's cry.
as night comes after the day,
Autumn comes winding its way.
The winds hurry the clouds, with a call
To welcome the golden beginning of fall.

Bonnie Dallas

Sorrow In My Heart

When the day you and I
Had to part,
I felt sorrow in my heart,

For it was like a heavy load,
Had came to my heart and gotten
A hold,

And even after all these years,
I still weep and shed tears,

But I know you don't feel any pain,
And soon happiness I will gain,

Because now I know in every way,
That you and I will again meet
Someday,

Janita K. Jackson

Episode At Dawn

The beacon kept on flashing
Guiding the helicopter
to the hospital
As the full hunter moon
sat momentarily
on the horizon
like a golden dome
on the cathedral of the world.

Bede Eckart

The World Of Make Believe

Tasting pure savor from sweetest dreams
Guiding each movement by hand
Creator of joy and childish schemes
Mounting those castles of sand.

Timing all seasons to days and years
True judge of right shapes and size
Sunshine of smiles and rain cloud of tears
Able to change and revise.

Founder of breezes that stir the night
Protector of weak and fair
Idol of worship, throne of delight
Endower of help and care.

Fantastic hopes so easily gained
All pleasures and joys to reap
High walls surmounted, prestige attained
Great master of fortune's heap.

Existence passes in single file
With honors that dreams conceive
On one among many, fame does smile
In this world of make believe.

Frank Hundshamer

The Weeping Willow

The willow's bows bend with grace to the ground
The weep in the wind without making a sound
The trunk is burdened with lots of strife
And the roots grasp deep, hanging on to life
Yet as the weeping willow stretches tall
Its trunk stands firm, it shall not fall
I embrace its strength and graceful woe
My roots give me courage, not to let go

Allysan F. Drew

A Gray Sky

The skiff's keel grates on rock,
Grinding slip, quickly free.
The oars dip together.
A cold rain. A gray sea.

The painter is made fast
at the stern. A sail flaps
sullenly, wet and rough.
Overcast sky. Dark shore.

The gaff rises up the mast.
An anchor weighs slowly
Spilling chain on the deck.
Heavily, the boat heels.

Set a course. Steer toward
the thick, dim horizon.
Leave something, everything
on the land. Gray leaving.

At sea now, and alone,
the sloop rises to the swell.
But dripping, from cold rain
Tears, under a gray sky.

John B. Shaul

When Comes The Storm

The grandeur of a summer storm -
God's mighty power displays.
The lightning, wind and thunder, all
Speak of his wondrous ways.

Then comes the rain to wash the earth -
God's blessing from above
Like all good things He gives to us,
It tells us of His love.

So when the dark clouds fill the sky
and winds begin to blow -
God's in control and all is well -
This, you can always know.

Tho' storms of life may come your way
and cause your heart to fear-
Be calm, my child, and look to God
For He is always near.

Evelyn A. Anglin

"Walk And Talk With Jesus"

There was a man called Jesus.
God sent his only son.
He let him die on the cross at Calvary
And His life had just begun.

I have talked to this Man called Jesus,
And He told me of His coming again.
He walked with me through my sorrows,
He showed me His nail-scarred hand.

He told me of His dying on the cross,
And the blood He shed for you and me.
I knelt down on my knees in prayer
And he touched my soul so tenderly.

Jesus said let me walk with you
And I will be your friend.
I will stay by your side forever,
Never to leave you again.

Anita H. Walton

I

I am the sun
   God of the day
I stream my magic upon
   daisy-dabbled fields
   snow-cloaked mountains
and transform
   elf-greened leaves
into
   hue-dyed flags
My power is a flame everlasting.

I am the moon
   mistress of the night
I shed my eerie glow upon
   the star-studded sky
   sheathed in black velvet
and transform
   tear-hushed waters
into
   storm-raged seas
My power is a depth eternal.

Colleen Seely

A Tribute To Elvis Presley

To the ecclesiastical choir in heaven
God called the Mama's boy
To be with brother Jesse
and be heaven's joy...

The world will long mourn him
Dixie's famous son
His music art and charisma
He had something for everyone...

This one voice I heard in my lifetime
America's uncrowned king
His style was like no other
He made the heavens ring...

You weren't meant to grow old, Elvis
Your life on earth is done
May you find peace in heaven
With God's chosen son....

Gloria W. Sicina

Soul

I will not down to the waters go,
go gaze at reflections, azure blue,
with oaken bucket, held just so.

Nymphs dance on water, they dance to show,
show soul's reflections, mirrored too.
I will not down to the waters go.

Some dare angels, unaware, they go,
go gather to the waters view,
with oaken bucket, held just so.

The secrets that those waters know,
know now the angels secrets too.
I will not down to the waters go.

Down to azure waters, some still go,
go gaze alone, cold, naked, blue,
with oaken bucket, held just so,

To learn the secrets held below,
below blue water, safe from view.
I will not down to the waters go,
with oaken bucket, held just so.

Carole J. Maxim

TV

Held in place by one small view.
Glued in place by the intense action.
Swallowed up within the story.
Losing all my identify.

Sitting spellbound hour after hour.
Compelled to watch night after night.
Homework mounting higher and higher.
Not caring or desiring to work,
Only to sit in front of the TV!

Joann Chevrier

Eternity

A Gull caught the Wind and
   glided over the Sea.
He picked up a grain of Sand
   on the bottom of the floor
   and dropped it on the Shore.
A Gull caught the Wind and
   glided over the Sea.
He picked up a grain of Sand and
   dove for one more.
One by One he dropped each
   precious grain on the Shore.
This Gull who caught the Wind
   and glided over the Sea was
   destined by God to scatter each
   grain into Eternity.
There is no end to the Sands of Time.
So spread your Wings, catch the Wind.
   learn to glide and you'll sail
   into ETERNITY.

Elaine M. Adams

tiny feet

tiny feet
glide through timelessness
tiny hands
hold everything together

tiny beings
create separate spaces
for tiny echoes
to escape into

love is creation
taking tiny selfless steps
which has no echo
and does not wish to escape

Edward J. Malone

Words

Will the words I speak today
help lift a load of care?
From some poor weary heart
imprisoned by despair.

Idle words are freely cast
about us every day.
Should not I speak a gentle few
when hope has gone astray?

All our words are tools indeed
though brief their message be.
It's always wise to choose the best
and speak them carefully.

Gladys L. Stokley

Keep Washington State - Ever Green

Oh stop! - Man in your great onslaught.
Give thought to what your greed has wrought,
Retract your vain mythology
And live by sane ecology.
Give honor to our mighty trees
That withstand tempest, storm and breeze,
Their stateliness is unsurpassed,
From seaside crag to forest mass.
Cedars, tall spruce and towering pine
Reach up to heights that dwarf mankind.
We stand beneath the awesome fir
Proud hemlock, yew and juniper,
Oblivious in our years of youth
At what past age these trees took birth.
As 'neath a canopy serene
We pause within the forest green,
Let each in grateful, humble tone
Thank God - for trees of Washington

Hazel M. Palmer

Jesus Teach Me

Jesus teach me how to pray
Give me love and grace each day.
Forgive my sins and make me learn
How to reach the heaven I yearn.

Teach me to be humble too
That I may be, much more like you
Teach me to forget my pride
Forever keep me at your side.

Teach me to forgive the sinner
Help him to become a "winner"
And when my time on earth is thru
I give my heart and soul to you.

Justine Bowen Shawk

"Freedom"

Let my soul be free,
From these sorrow chains
That cause me so much pain.

Let me be free,
So I can reach the stars
Within a deep sigh.
Let me be free,
And open my wings;
Flying for my goals and dreams.

Let me be free,
So you can be proud,
Raise your head to the clouds
And see on how high I can fly.

Let me be free,
And follow my road
Reach the freedom that to my heart
belongs,
And remove those chains,
That fasten my days,
And look for the happiness that I long.

Please let me be free..

Erika Karla Ochoa Rascon

Mother

From the various depths of anguish;
from the silent torture of rage;
Rise forth, rise again and relinquish
Ready for the coming of age.

For your seeds have become roses,
filled with pricks and thorns and yet alive.
Ranting, to destroy the roses
Remember your womb brought these alive.

For when the gardener plants the seeds,
fulfilling the heart's desire,
rejoicing in the fragrance it leads;
(Rapture!) the prick is the fire.

Resurrect from amidst the ashes.
Recall the color and fragrance.
For though there is fire is roses,
from these, the fragrance is sublime.

Isabel Caldera

The Battle

You see through rose colored glasses,
From the outside appear in no pain,

Although within you lies a burden,
One searching to find its claim.

It's evil with strength and force,
Stabbing you when times seem worst.

It seems as if an enemy,
Conniving with actions of curse.

The battle can be very lengthy,
A time that's hard to cope,

But I know that you can do it,
Climb that long and twisted rope.

Remember all those who love you,
Who will talk and share your pain.

For they will help you to see the outside,
With those rose colored glasses again.

Abbie Smith

Untitled

I was riding around the other day
from one place to another
thinking of the special things
that makes someone a mother
my head soon filled with a thousand things
that all came from my heart
like how she is encouraging
She's loving and she's smart
a Mother is two separate people
as fragile as she's strong
a saviour and a guardian
who rights me when I'm wrong
her smile shines like sunlight
Her warmth can melt the snow
her voice is filled with buoyancy
it lifts me when I'm low
and though I fail to say it sometimes
believe me mom it's true
of all the living things on earth
I love none more than you

Dan Voelker

Heaven And Earth

As I walk through my garden
from nine - until noon, I think
about what God holds for my future
or what will be coming to me soon,
   I wonder about my life and my
family too. When they die, when
I die what should I do? We think
of heaven as home away from home
what its like its not really known,
   But what we do know it to hope, pray
and have faith that more will come
to the heavenly gates.
Brandy Chambers

My Daughter

I love her dearly
From her head to her toes,
From her crooked smile,
To her Grandpa's nose.

She's the only girl I have,
She has two brothers tho.
I know they truly love her,
But they won't tell her so.

She's a good girl
And a joy in every way.
Someday a young man will come
And take her far away.

They say you don't lose her,
You gain a son.
I really don't relish
That day to come.

I wish I could keep her,
Just the way she is.
I know it's impossible
Cause someday, she'll be his.
Fanny Lee Baker Shaw

From Agony To Infinity

Unattended, agony rushes out
From behind the cover
Of the curtain of calm
Like conglomerating mercury

Molecule
By molecule, her forces
Join as fear and loathing
Make a shocking
Connection

For the sake of recovery, this circuit
Must be interrupted:
There is no balance
When pain is no longer
Being recycled, and no
Regeneration when the relationship
Between the actual
And the possible is severed
Caitlin Sullivan

Souls Forever Paired

From a seed - A tree
From a page - A book
From a sound - A symphony
From your eyes - A look

With a step - A journey
With a note - A song
With a thought - A fantasy
Dreams - that made us strong

From a drop - A river
From a ray - The sun
From a breeze - A mighty wind
Carries us - Along

In a touch - A feeling
In a poem - A rhyme
In a love - A healing
To the end - of time

All our past - Our history
All our present - Shared
All our future - Mystery
Souls forever - Paired
Dale Neel

Retired

Now in retirement, I should be
Free as a bird perched in a tree.
Able to travel to places new,
Never planted to where I "Grew."
Not confined to that "Same Old Grind,"
Dreaming of all I hope to find.
Eager to seek some new pleasures,
Perhaps to find a few treasures.
I went about but always found
More of the same, on some new ground.
Life is only as good as prize,
As are the thoughts we do surmise.
Bernice DiBernardinis

Precious One

Precious flower from the East
fragile and wilted after the long summer
hot and dry from the lack of nourishment
attempted to tap all the sources
an indigent blossom looking for your
    own trunk in the West-

Precious flower in the West
searched out one to walk with
supplier of water for the roots
tunneling under all the walls
willing to find a way to your
    smiles in the altitude of the sun-

Precious flower of the garden
breath in the energy of the chant
frost of the neck chills the body
signs of life wanting to reach out
turning to the strength of your
    tree for the limbs to be squeezed—
Duane R. Neff

Your Choice

Jesus did I hear you say,
"Forsake your sins, repent today"?
Take up your cross and follow me
And I will change your destiny
But Satan's voice within me cried
That cross is heavy on which he died
Come take the easy way with me
No cross to bear, you'll feel quite free
"Oh no, he said my way is life
Where place and gladness dwell
The other path which is of sin
Will only led to hell.
Now choose the one
Whom you will serve
And let that choice be me
Because I bring you peace and joy
Through out eternity."
Doris Ferguson Meek

Bewilderment Of Humanity

In burgeoning centers of civilization
forbidding effigies eternally somber
tall graceful spires
allegorize the human virtue
of integrity
which makes us all
quintessentially human.

Beyond the gamut of cityscapes
plans envisioned the archetype
planned obsolescence
on impact of new modes
and manners
expulse eternal vigilance
of sovereign state.

Progenitor of noble echelon craftsmen
consider these idioms archaic
bound by incessant scrutiny
of statesmen alluding
to the truth
deftly practice their skill.
Frank Davis

Untitled

Think only of today,
   for yesterday is past,
And tomorrow is only
   a vision of what
   today might have been.
Think only of today,
   for there will only be
   one like it.
Just as there is a
   new moment to follow the old.
Think only of today,
   for tomorrow will leave
   memories of a day well-lived.
So live each day
   to its fullest extent,
And make each moment the happiest.
Dee Ann Malesich

October

Again we reach the time of year...
For witches on a broom
And smiling jack-o-lanterns...
To brush away the gloom.

The spooky black cats...
With backs arched high
Remind us of Trick or Treats
Of times gone by.

Remember bobbing for apples...
Skeletons hung,
Hot cider in mugs
So smooth to the tongue.

Our memories are precious...
Each one we recall,
So enjoy this special season
Before Santa comes to call!

Fran McCarty

My Everything

You are everything to me, my Love,
For which my soul doth pine;
The freshness of April showers,
The excitement of creative design.

You're like all the lovely flowers,
That gently bow their heads;
You're like the trees in autumn,
As their fluttering leaves are shed.

You give to me a language,
As spoken by the silent sea,
You brighten up the moonbeams,
That gently float on me.

Your strong arms remind me
Of eagles as they soar,
Of love and adoration,
And time, to be no more.

Time vanishes at your special touch,
I know it's just because
I love you so much!
You are my everything!

Georgia Justina Harper Curry

Patiently Waiting

Patiently I'm waiting
for the Lord to carry me home
Where I will never suffer
and never walk alone

Jesus knows I'm suffering
while walking here below
But he promises me salvation
and will free me of my pain

When its done and over
I will feel so serene
For I will be resting peacefully
in my eternal home.

Iva L. Foor

Heaven Bound...

I am so proud my loved one,
for the call you made today.

By asking JESUS in your heart,
His love's with you to stay.

Keep Him with you always,
you know you're safe and sound.

You made the call that's always answered,
1-800-Heaven Bound...

George W. Coquillard III

My Little Angel

You were in my arms
for some minutes

And you are right now
my little angel in heaven

I will always send
you my love

One day we will meet
and be together in heaven

Love you my little
Angel

Dawn Felella

A Prayer To Those Special To Me

I often say a heartfelt prayer
For my friends who mean so much
I ask our Heavenly Father
To Bless everything they touch.

I ask Him for the graces
That they will need each day
To solve their doubts and problems
And to take their cares away.

I ask that He will fill their lives
With sunshine after rain
With success to crown their efforts
And with comfort for their pain.

I ask that He will give them friends
To brighten daily living
And hearts that know the lasting joy
Of loving and for giving.

And every time I say this prayer
One thing I always do
Is to ask these blessings — especially
For a favorite person...you!

Alice J. Mills

New Eyes

At first I thought I had no room
For love...no extra place
Then you came into my life
And made enormous space

Once I thought I had no time
No precious days to spare
Now I look into your eyes
And find my moments there

I used to think I had no wealth
My clothes are never new
But since you came into my heart
I know I'm rich with you

Bev Steward

The Starling (This Bird's Life)

He came to me this bird one day,
for it was his passage; death decreed
a brief imprinting stay.
He cried in silence, this bird of mine,
and waited out moments of time.
It was from him I learned a pain
that changes the soul. I am not the same
and beyond all this comes the light,
flickering, piercing deep in the night.
Fly little spirit bird; fly high to your Lord,
for in tender arms you will forever soar.

Corinne Hernandez

Crossroads

Standing in my solitude
for I have pushed it all away
And now that the dust has settled
a dirt road has led to this day
At the eye of my life's divergence
some choice awaits being made
Though be it with tepid patience
knowingly, its path soon to be laid

I see around me four directions
one deeply etched in mind
Clearly leaving three to ponder
although there are only two to ever find
Turning one way while recalling the other
as Time shall wait no more
Summonsed upon a simple decision
and all that stands beyond my door

Andrew S. Reiss

How Long Since You Wrote To Mother

How long since you wrote to mother,
 for her the hours must fly.
The hours become years to your Mother,
 when the postman passes her by.

How long since you wrote to Mother,
 and told her little cheerful white lies,
To read to her friends and neighbors,
 with tears in the grand old eyes.

How long since you wrote to Mother,
 better get that letter done,
For Mothers like flowers soon fade,
 when there's no word from her
  wandering son.

Doyle E. Wallace

Love, A Priceless Treasure

Whenever an act of love is shown
God is making His presence known.
He commands we love one another
Not judge or hate our brother.

Love is a many splendored thing
Happiness to others it will bring.
Express your love to someone today
God will bless you in every way.

When you give love in good measure
Within your heart lies your treasure.
Pure love seeks nothing in return
The love of God we can discern.

Catharine E. Kusior

The Race Of Life

I strive to beat my opponents
  For goals or money to make;
My heart is set on competing,
  To win for winnings sake.

But is the race worth winning?
  Can I ill afford the gain?
Will the promised ecstasy of victory
  Outweigh my growing pain?

I long for a simple assurance
  That every hurricane has an eye;
And divine power will control this age
  Unchanged as the world rushes by.

So herein lies my own true peace,
  Cradled all up inside.
For victory is not in reaching a goal
  But accompanies an eventful ride.

Alvin G. Haworth Jr.

Untitled

I boiled the salt out of your tears
for finger nail scratches by another
a weeping penance cleansing our flesh
with searing red hands
that have traced anothers' sin

The church of guilt chants
Its hymn for the beggar son
hedonism my heaven and hell
and the pit bull of denial
eats me for its last supper

Join me in my self-denigration
a ration of rotten water
that aggravates my thirst
the satiated savior
spits at my life as pornography

I linger in the sieve of forgiveness
too substantial to pass
between its generous perforations
lying with the other filth
in the gutter of your malaise

Brett P. Michael

Freight Elevator, Stuck

Dear freight,
for fear of your
weight
They discovered my emotional
state
Not new to me
But plain to see
Sitting so still
So as not to be spilled
or crushed like an apple crate.
Yelling, "Elevator Stuck."
He replied, "You outta luck!"
Not understood by me
his words said with glee
I asked, "How long it will take?"
"You'll just have to wait."
So I shut my trap
while my sister's lips flapped
philosophy so free.

Akwelle Vallis

Reflections

I climb the ladder a step at a time
For every step, a joy is mine
I can't look down for I may fall
And miss the meaning of life's great call.

I don't look up to see how high
I fear the heights, I fear to try
So just one step, I'll do my best
To take the day and pass the test.

I will not fret if once I fail
For life is mine, I set the sail
You too can climb above the ground
Discover worlds yet to be found.

Feel the joy of each success
Instead of all that harmful stress
So take each thought that comes to mind
And some good thing, out of it find.

You too will see a better way
Because you climbed that step today.

David L. Whittaker

Never Mind

Never mind, I have nothing to say.
For each thought I don't convey
  an idea breaks; I cry,
  I bleed, and I do die.
However, I've no life be as it may.

I am lost in the whole world a play,
I sleep, I wake, I work in a drudgery way.
  To think and not speak, a fateful lie
is my never mind.

I leave the thought as it lay.
Tip of the tongue but not to say
  to you: I've a world to defy,
  but it passes a whisper, a sigh.
I do not rest, I've nothing to say.
Never mind.

Carissa M. Thornock

Destructions Eve

The world will have to change
For all of us to survive,
We cannot win at war
We cannot go on living a lie.

We have to do it now
As we stand straight and tall,
Speaking well of others
And giving peace for all.

Why can't they understand
When will they ever learn,
For all of us to live in peace
For all of us are concerned.

No more death and destruction
No more shedded tears,
No more loss of loved ones
Now and throughout the coming years.

Danny Payne

My Gift To You

If I had just one gift to leave,
for all eternity
it would not be of gold or jewels,
but just a part of me.

I'd leave you all the memories
of all the fun we had,
the way you used to hold my hand
the way you called me "Dad."

The times we laughed, the times we cried,
the sad times and the good;
No matter what life had to give,
it seems we understood.

The gifts of love and happiness
are gifts you gave to me;
I could not have been more blessed
nor ever richer be.

So carry this deep in your heart
and know it to be true;
my gift to you is part of me,
to be a part of you.

Clark Beardslee

A Toast

Pop!
Foam
Fizz, Ah!
What frosted bliss
is this!?
Decadent
Effervescent
Thousand Bubbles
Oh so pleasant
Cold, Golden
Fascination
Tinkle...

Clink!
Anticipation...
Sip, Ahh...
(Nose Tickle)
Slurp
Gulp
"Burp"
(Giggle)

Debra Livingston

Transitions

You touched me I became a bird
flying high above the Earth
then through the clouds I flew
down to become a silhouette
then I was sitting man
without an estimate
then I was about to die I stared
down deep into the ground
the ever moving one.

Then I found myself in tears
and sinking inside out with fears
I looked up high and screamed,
but then the forest echoed it
in its quiet stream.
Then the storm deprived me
from my sight by doing so I realized
I had a vision and then at last
I stood strong high above it all
as mighty Pegasus
was now in my control.

Daniel Dentchev

Love

Love is like a river,
   flowing from the heart.
Love will be there,
   from the very start.
Love is like a breeze,
   blowing through the willow trees.
When feeling down,
   love is always around.

Cynthia A. Geisler

At Easter Time

Easter time is here
   flowers ever where
Little birds are singing
   and flying in the air
Christ the Lord in risen
   this lovely Easter morn
God gave His Son to die for us
   on he old rugged cross
So that all of us would have a right
   to Everlasting and Eternal Life.

Catherine Bradley Ezzard

"Tapestry"

Summer's closing scene, and lazy days.
Flowers all have blown away.
Scattering seed over hill and dale,
Next year once more to hail.

The tapestry of autumn,
Spins a cloth of gold,
As crispy days unfold.

Sunsets brush of colours,
Spread across the land,
As we stand in awe of nature's gifted
hand.

Floating leaves scurry by,
As gusts of wind,
Chase and whirl them to the sky.
To settle restlessly,
In carpets deep, beneath the mother tree.

Glorious autumn paves the way,
To celebrate Thanksgiving day.

Eileen E. Szabo

I Think Of You

Dedicated to My Husband Dan Myers
Sitting in a beautiful meadow of
flowers,
the peaceful sound of the breeze
flowing by me,
I think of you.

Sitting here believing in the beauty
that I see,
and having faith that this is how it
will always be,
I think of you.

Sitting in a cloud surrounding me
with love,
knowing that the love is also inside
of me,
I think of you.

DeeLola Myers

Weeds

You and I are dandelions
flowering weeds of this land
drink-up all the sunlight
give back what we can

Pass away if you must
knowing I will follow
fleeting, fiery, flashes
among an unmarred field

So burn with stolen sun
blaze out your message
of dawn and warmth
and priceless dewdrop diamonds

Scream of chill night stars
of moonshown showers
and making love in cool air
under cobalt skies.

You and I are dandelions,
flowering weeds of this land
stubborn, worthless, hated
perfect.

Jason Lees

"Walk Slow"

You feel the wind
Floating thru you hair
Recognize it...
It there!
Don't run or hide
But try to face another
Day of fury at your own pace
You don't put it together
It's like lace
Soft cord that makes a form
If you're fortunate
You'll never see the storm,
just feel loved and warm

Jacquelyn I. Dowd

An Autumn Song

An Abundant harvest,
Fix'd in numberless diaries,
Erupted in colors,
And painted the morning.

A solemn gray,
With sails and oars,
Captured the sun,
And lengthened the night.

The single-minded wind,
Indifferent in extreme,
Eroded our resolve,
And hardened the earth.
The silent snow,
Stainless in beauty,
Forgave us our sins,
And ended the cycle.

David Neff

Of Life And Death

In her lifetime, she consumed:
Five vacuum cleaners
Indeed, against dirt, she always stood
Nine lovers
Nine is her lucky number
Seven cars
Eleven toasters
Ten dishwashers
Three husbands
All of Caucasian type
Fifteen neighbors
Running short of favors
AND ONLY ONE MATTRESS!
And when she died
From a very bad case of consumption
She left behind
One hundred thousand fifty pounds
OF STEEL AND BONE TRASH
She had NO WILL.

Jacqueline Hahn

Closure

Sparks!
Fire!
Blaze!
Surely, at one time, it was there.
Both of us will attest to this.
The heat was strong.
I never thought the intensity would die.
I did not know it had.
But now I know!
I am so glad you came to visit.

Justin G. Kravetz

Cemetery Rocks

A simple poet
finds shelter in his dreams
where everything is innocent
and the spark of life still gleams.
He thinks about his friendships
his lovers
a deep depression takes his eyes.
He wonders what to trust
and what to disregard as lies.
In the heat he begins to sweat
he keeps his hands in his pockets
eyes to the ground a few steps ahead.
A lonely poet walks.
He walks to find his laughter
somewhere in the next few blocks.
He swears he's getting closer
and trails along the cemetery rocks.

Frank Grimm

"A Poet's Mind"

A poet's mind. It's a wonderful place!
Filled with visions, like outer space.
It's there nostalgia and present meet.
Like dreams and reality, bittersweet.

Words and rhythm flow and dance
And the weary mind has equal chance,
To live again in another sphere.
In a poet's mind all things are clear.

A poet's job is to point the way,
From past into each coming day.
To show the futures constant flow
Toward each truth we all should know!

Juanita Hall Weiche

"Visions"

This is a day in the life of me...
filled with anxiety.
Like a wheel my head is spinning.
As visions dance.
Filled with anxiety.
My heart beats fast...
Like a wheel my head is spinning...
As thoughts of the past come rushing back.
Why do I feel so much pain?
As I cry...
I can see just what's bothering me....
what's wrong with me?
As visions dance...
This is a day in the life of me.

Cindy Parent

School Bus Drivers

Driving is nice, except when you
fill your seats twice. You'll hear
screams and schemes, but sometimes
you're never seen. Through all the fear,
comes a care for each smile or tear.
We will drive them safely here or there.

I drive a school bus and boy what
fun we have, some fights or no
one wants to sit nice. We have
good days and bad days, that's true.
But the kids on our buses help
us through. We love what we do.

Dawn Clevenger

Shadows On The Wall

Extended bodies without life,
figurines of black
not deep enough for a knife,
but lusting after what they lack.

They feast on the brightness of my soul,
but I fight not to succumb.... to be being
a dark shadow on the wall.

My memory continually shows me the past,
of which I do not wish to view,
but my heart is as numb to the pain...
as a shadow on the wall.

Cold and hardened by hard fought battles
lost, my life pump can no longer spread
vitality...through this shadow on the wall.

Dancing ballerinas of darkness circle around
me...laughing... As I struggle to free my
spirit from the confinement.... of this
shadow on the wall.

Autumn Foushée

Mr. Bird

See the bird in the tree over there?
He sings as if he doesn't have a care...
as if life's overwhelming problems
vanish in the air.
Can I too find this peaceful "don't care"?
My friend, Mr. Bird, has the answer for me
sitting there singing from his lofty tree
If only I would open my heart and see
the healing love of the man from Galilee.

Juanita Wallace

Freedom's Fight

In a cavern there dwells a lonesome tree,
Fighting for freedom, like you and me.
Reaching its boughs up to the light,
Living almost, in eternal night.

No pleasant wind, with whispering sounds,
That in the outside world abounds.
No loveliness, of bird or bee,
Comes to enhance, this forlorn tree.

Its thirst is quenched by limy drip,
Encircling its roots, from tip to tip.
His neighbor close by in this forest of night,
Stands mighty and tall, a cold stalagmite.

A wintry gust, did one day blow,
And carried its seed, onto the snow.
Along came the thaw, and melted down,
The little seed, now touched the ground.

Our freedom fight has now been won,
Our forlorn tree, has had a son.
Out of the caverns, dark of night,
This off-spring traveled, into the light.

Jean Eastin

When We Make Love

When we make love, you look in my eyes.
Feelings so strong, it comes as a surprise.
I've searched so long for what we share.
In my dreams, could never compare.
My heart used to feel empty and cold.
Your precious love has touched my soul.
Our love is strong and true.
Forever, it'll be me and you.
Till very death do us part.
A new life together, we'll start.
Our love may lead us to shaky ground.
Feeling so strong, it won't bring us down.
Come the tribulations we must endure.
Of anything, I've never been so sure.

Gina J. James

Confused

I am so confused,
feeling used
trying to figure out what's in her head.
The tears I shed upon my bed
not knowing what's in her head.
Living life from day to day
not wanting to keep away;
losing each day,
the love I gave away.
To her everything seems okay.
She has my heart,
and seems to be tearing it apart,
each day goes by not knowing why
or what she is thinking about.
To her there may be no doubt.
I want to know, is there hope for us?
Or am I making a big fuss,
over something that is not going to be?
I wanted to say "marry me,"
but it looks like she would rather be free.

Jason Williams

My Friend

There are times in my life when I'm
  feeling quite low.
Misery surrounds me, I've nowhere to go.
The walls of disappointment are closing in.
The light of happiness is beginning to dim.
The sun up above refuses to shine.
The moon at night seems so unkind.
When I feel I've hit bottom and
  there's no way out,
You are my friend, I haven't a doubt.
You lift the clouds on a rainy day.
You take hold of my hand and show
  me the way.
You're at my side when I'm feeling alone.
You brighten the path that leads me home.
You are my friend, a special love.
You were sent to me from God above.
I could never have asked for a friend so true,
Than the one I am blessed with,
  my best friend, YOU.

Debra Cosby

"Fantasies Could Be Real"

Up close we see a rainbow
Far away we see the stars,
If we keep on going,
Will we finally get to Mars?

Is that where we want to be
out among the stars?
Will we have to walk to work
or can we bring our cars?

If the planets do intrigue us
should we leave this world behind?
Must we search for other worlds
Just to find the other kind.

We have bombs with mighty muscle,
We have men with vision strength,
If we all decide to ride the rocket
to find our friends in skies immense.

But when they came to search and find us,
We had left to search for them.

Herman L. Larsen

Untitled

The snow,
Falling.
Soft,
White.
Landing,
Melting,
Running.
The silence,
Broken by a siren.
Someone is
Dead.

Andrew Thomas

Earthly Ties

When sadness overcomes me when tears
fall from my eyes.
It's then I look toward heaven
and throw off my earthly ties.
It's only when I do this that light
seeps to my soul.
How precious is the love I feel
How near my final goal.

Grace Munoz

"Asleep"

Lying down you take your rest
Eyes closed so shallow in breath.
Your eyes move and twitch back in fro.
What's in your dream I'll never know.
Sometimes you twist toil in grief
Then a peaceful wave you're beneath.
How many places and faces you see
I wonder if some were of me.
The reason for the escape unknown.
We all go there you're not alone.
Maybe some night we'll cross paths
I'll wave to you and tip my hat.

Calvin B. Welch

Wilderness

Wilderness
Exciting and beautiful,
Quiet and graceful,
Jagged mountains
Climbing to the sky,
And valleys, far and wide.

The fallen snow,
White as can be,
In patterns
On trees,
Or mountains,
Is beautiful to me.

Mountain streams,
Glaciers,
And lakes
All a beautiful blue.

A quiet place,
An exciting place,
A cruel place,
A wilderness.

Cara L. Crouter

Carried Along

Carried along by the happiness of dreams,
everything is not like what it seems.
Riding along on a day without end,
feeling as if I'm summer's best friend.
Swept away by a gust of air,
sorting out feelings, life's not fair.
Staring out the window, watching the world,
everything's perfect, just like it should be.
Hope keeps me going when nothing is right,
crying away in the darkness of night.
But when everything's going my way,
there's never enough time in the day.
Yet I am still feeling strong,
Being carried away by life's great song

Beth Sharkey

Tennis

It's in, it's out, it's into the net,
Game after game, set after set;
A racket, a ball, some common sense,
A positive attitude and confidence;
Lobs, slices, drop shots too,
There are so many shots for one to do;
A shot down the line, one would hope to catch,
It's just point, game, set, match!

Cristen Leaper

My Buffy

My dog Buffy gets older
  everyday.
Sometimes she plays and
  sometimes she lays.
I wish she was getting
  younger, not older
I wish she could live
  forever!
But, her time comes just
  like you and me
Because no one lives for
  an eternity.
She will leave my house
  one day
But, in my heart she will
  always stay.

Jennifer Rinkel

You Are...

You are the circle of my life.
Every step I make
on every road I take
always leads back to you.

You are the seed of my life.
Whatever I do
and how I make it through
grows from the center of your love.

You are the peace of my life.
Every word I say
when every night I pray
is thanks to God for you.

You are my love, my life.
When all is said and done
together, we are one.
And from my heart I say
I Love You.

Andrea Fournier

How The Candle Flickers

How the candle flickers,
Every jump of the flame
Another pause in pulse
of our love blood pumping.
Forever changing shadows moving
across my ceiling.
Constant changing moods threatening
to blow out my flame.
A steady flame, a constantly growing flame
Melts away non-revealing wax leaving
Only yellow-orange reflections on the glass.
Wax takes space and hides the true
beauty of our clear container.
So the candle burns on and on
  to melt our wax;
Slowly I begin to see through your glass
  and you through mine,
'Til all that separates us is
  the carcass of a once glowing, hot,
  Wick.

Derek J. Reckard

A Child

A beautiful child
Every child is the
most beautiful child
in the world.

A child's love
The love of a child
is beyond compare.

A child's laugh
Hearing a child's
laugh can bring a
smile to the most
hardened face.

A child
A child is everything
good in the world.

Amy Peelman

The Jesus Christ Poem

Just and perfect man.
Everlasting life He gave when He rose again.
Sins were forgiven through Him.
Understanding He was to people's problems.
Storms even obeyed Him.

Crucified He was for our sins.
Healed many people He did.
Risen He was on the third day.
It was done through the power of God.
Son of God was He.
Temptation He overpowered with the Word.

John H. Tuttle

"No More Pain"

A tiny Soul,
ever full of pain,
A Mother's cry,
For it all to end.

A prayer of hope,
Some shred of release,
ending the pain,
a soul at ease.
An innocent child,
no longer fights,
Now living in heaven,
in God's perfect life.

Gin M. Poeske

"The Pillow"

If I lay my head here,
Even if by chance
Will I remember the shoulder
Will I remember the dance
Will I hug this pillow
And think of the nights
Holding you close
Eyes blind to the lights
Will I cry at the way
My memory will pay
For the happiness
It does not have.

Alan J. Pentaleri

Where's The Moon

It's dark and gloomy
evening song long silent
God's creatures are sleeping
Where's the moon?

The stars are high and sparkling
The wind is silently moving
sweeping the dust from the streets
Where's the moon?

Midnight is over taking
yesterday's forgotten memories
in anticipation of a new day.
Where's the moon?

Daybreak is arriving slowly
God's creatures are waking
A new day beginning
Where's the moon?

My two little daughters
tumble sleepily from their beds
and crawl into my lap
And now I see the stars, sun and moon.

Judith Barnes

Memories

Memories are so soothing,
even with the tears they bring.
Memories are heart warming,
even with the sighs they bring.
Memories are so picturesque,
even with their faded images.

Memories come and go,
they never leave.
They partly fill the space,
of past living souls.
We get desperate to touch them,
bring them closer to us;
In order to dismiss their non-being.

But, how long can we go on dreaming?
Reality calls us back, to return
to the land of the living.

Hanna Stark

Betrayal

Consumed by deceit,
Entranced by betrayal,
Mind taken over,
Love of no other;

Hated by hell,
Loved by no God,
Dreams of the end,
Sins I can't mend.

Clever to be,
Dull is to end,
Life to begin,
Wounds never mend;

Traitor to you,
Betrayal by all,
Heaven and hell,
None ever call;

Given no mercy,
Committed all sin,
Forgiveness none of,
Never to win.

Brian S. Daneski

Rain

Some folks think rain is depressing
energy suppressing
When in actuality
it is somewhat refreshing
It is earth cleansing
and
soul replenishing

Rainy days give us a chance
to reflect
on the nature of things
and things of Nature
and
soak in her beauty

For without the feast of
gentle rains
where would nature be
let alone we

Dianne A. Diersen

Mother's Love

The ocean...
Endless...as far as the eyes can see.
A mother's love...
Endless...as deep as the heart can feel.

The waves...
Follow...one after the other...
Relentless...unfailing.
A mother's love...
Always there...
Never ending.

The waves...
Reach out...lapping at the sand...
Only to release it and begin again.
A mother's love...
Reaches out to pick you up after a fall
To let you go...when you, again, stand tall.

The ocean...
Made by God.
A mother's love...
Given by God.

Dawn Currie

Heath Cliff

For her own reasons
Emily dragged me from the shades,
Forced me to live
Numberless seasons
In the house of Earnshaw.

What memory fades?
None. Tortured by Hindley
Made mad by Cathy,
I lived like a beast
Naught could I give.

To living person naught
To Linton, my own son, least,
Only unremitting hate
Save for Cathy, love beyond law,
And with her I often fought

Till Emily placed her in the grave
Leaving me alone to keep
Unwanted life, my soul it ate.
Thru sheer will I sought my death,
At last embraced the final sleep.

Edmund Brunner Jr.

Christian Life?

Pieces...put together.....His glue
Edges rough, scar tissue, of wounds
so deep....!
Pain in every movement...
Stretch those limbs...
Smooth the edges (says He)
Work the new tissue...let it
grow!
Time will pass...blended
is the new and the old.
Show yourself to Him (says He)
Now,...you are
just like
Me!

Chris B. Weber

The Quiet One

The quiet one sits by herself
eager to talk and eager to listen,
but only if someone will do the same.
She looks around for a friend,
one she knows and can talk to.
But no one is around.
To hear her cry.
To hear her tell her story
of how alone she feels.
Of how she would like a friend.
One that would stay by her side.
But she has no one.
She never has.
Except for once,
and she smiles upon the memory.
But she was torn away.
From the only one who listened,
The only one who cared.
And now she has no one.
So she is just alone.

Jennifer Burrill

Ripples

Life is like a ripple in a wave,
Each ripple is different, like life
Each experience is different.

As each ripple ends, a new one begins.
With each ripple the flat plane of
Life changes.

The beginning of a ripple is
Strong and vibrant, and as
The ripple ends so does the vibrancy.

Life's ripples are not always
Perfectly shaped as ripples in the water.
But unlike water, you can choose.
What kind of ripples life has to offer!

Beth Lewis

Midnight Snow

A purple shroud of silken coldness
entombing the night;
While flakes cautiously balance
themselves on their perches,
occasionally being brushed away by a
cold hand of wind.
The darkness giving away life with a
welcoming embrace of whitened silence.

Daniel L. Young

Life

Life is like a deck of cards
Each hand dealt, is the player's chance
But beware, the fiddler must be paid
If you expect to dance

On life's highway, we play the odds
And hope to come out even
Hoping the other cars
Are by sober players driven.

We gamble on tomorrow's sunrise
And worry little about today
When today is all we really have
And that could suddenly be snatched away.

So let us live one day at a time
And do the very best we can
Thank God for every blessing he gives
And ask no more of any man.

So when the dealer, in the game of life
Who sent the king, his son
Deals the final trump, then we will know
By the nail prints in his hand, we've won.

Frances Cooper

Every Day Can Be Christmas

I wish it were Christmas
  each day of the year
With joyful bells ringing
  so sweet and so clear.
You see people smiling
  that don't often smile.
Makes the todays and tomorrows
  all seem worthwhile.
There's much loving and giving
  this time of the year
And friendly card greetings
  from loved ones so dear.
People helping the poor,
  the sick and the blind
And it seems that we all
  are just extra kind.
But each day can be Christmas
  a time of good cheer.
Keep Christ in your life
  every day of the year!

Doris Hastings

"Friend"

So filled with emptiness,
Dying of your loneliness,
Sinking in the ship you made,
Didn't know till this very day.

But I'll always be there for you,
To me you're a friend that's true,
I'm sorry I couldn't help you more,
But you didn't tell me what I was
needed for.

Moments passing away,
Couldn't find the courage to find a way,
There was so much more you wanted to do
  with your life,
But you didn't have the time.

But I'm still here for you,
You were a friend that was true,
And I wish you didn't have to
leave so soon,
But I'll always remember you.

Jamie Wilson

This Earth I Love

Before I do exist
During my short stay and there after
this EARTH is here
For us all
Its ground of solid rocks
Among forests and fields
Oceans with its nature
millions of creatures
On it
Oh! Beautiful all over from beginning
While some enjoy and cherish
others destroy or tarnish
Soon it will no longer furnish
its bountiful source of life
As Mother Nature provides
We, the best creature of then all
"PEOPLE," such a title
With feeling, knowledge surpassing all
Please do something
To save it.

Cathy T. Nguyen

For Joanna

Bare arms in a small pink cotton
dress and she waved I love you
to the Spring colts in the field.

A soft white I love you in the
shape of a polar bear from Carmel
Clint I call him, after the mayor.

I gave the bear to my daughter who
needing the reassurance of soft love
at night on her pillow carrying dreams

Of expectations, adolescent exchanges.
A gift of thank you's that stopped a
moment when you understood but didn't
ask, why I was late.

Felicity Johnson

Deja Vu

When the snowbanks loose their riv'lets
Down the gravel of my lane,
And the shadows turn to azure
O'er the frozen, white terrain;

When the tops of trees are yellow
Up against a blue, blue sky,
And a winter-hungry robin
Gives my suet cakes the eye;

When the willow buds are swelling
From an inner urge to grow,
And an old, black, sleepy beetle
Lumbers stiffly on the snow;

When the squirrels use my maple
For their private jungle gym,
and a grackle lifts his feathers
At the rival on his limb;

And I hear a titmouse "Kew"-ing
Then my spirits soar and sing,
For I know the land remembers
And is resurrecting spring.

Beatrice E. Andrews

Untitled

Tears are streaming
Down my cheeks,
Each single one is a friend
I cannot replace,
You support my decisions
Though you don't always agree,
I know I've messed up
Time and time again,
You were constantly there
Right by my side,
You pull me through
Still now like then,
I hope we remain.
Friends
Always,
Forever,
Until the end.

Cameo Danielle Stahl

Minds Apart

Around the world, across the street,
Down avenues of thought I race
Seeking some small sequestered place
Where our once-attuned minds can meet.

Alas! I stop daring not to face
The chasm all at once too wide.
Behind walls of small talk I hide
From the terrible truth I find:
The once far-reaching robust mind,
A pallid prisoner of time and place
Impaled upon the stagnant status quo
Not knowing, nor caring elsewhere to go.

When the awful answer finally came,
Giving her evil illness a name,
Her beautiful brilliant mind pulling apart;
Every shining shattered piece piercing my heart.

There is nowhere on earth to hide
From my mother's slow steady slide
Into the jagged jaws of Alzheimer's
Mocking senile smile.

Emma Mai Ewing

The Door

Look through the crack
Don't touch the knob
Memories flood in with the light
Laughter tiptoes quietly in
Sshh!
Embarrassments bang on the door
Regrets and mistakes join in
The door gives way
Laughter sits quietly in a corner
Surrounded
Sadness dances around
Trapped
In the recesses of your mind

Jean Misola

A Dream

Dreaming is a step towards tomorrow
Don't let your heart be filled with sorrow
In dreams you lose your heartaches
For a dream is a wish your heart makes

Jack Stuver

Hope Human And Wild

Don't bitter my love life
Don't put your noisy lucid eave
Your guess is extraterrestrial
Hope human and wild

Don't gladiate my deepest space
Alienor eliminate
Don't be an independent guess a mate
Hope human and wild

With a zillion
A billion on line
Sophisticate a signal meet
Hope human and wild

Decimate my definite
Lure to success a cede
Joke to separate
Hope human and wild

Isabelle Hunter

Positive Healing

Don't let yourself be taken in
Don't let the hurt dig deep,
It's only in a shallow mind
That fools will make you weep.

I throw away the negative
And shout up to the sky,
The positive will only win
They'll never ask you why?

The healing fills your mind and soul
You know you've done no wrong,
Life is full and reaching out
And the road you trod is long.

But at the end you'll find the spark
Of forgetting simple minds,
Forget, let go, and don't look back
For life is too sublime.

Bettye Lopp

The Ambitions

Come to me tonight my love,
don't let me be alone,
And I shall give to you a love
this world has never known,
I've been waiting for a lifetime,
for this moment to arrive.
In you I've found my paradise,
And I thank God I am alive;
you shall never have to worry,
nor shall you ever be alone;
For the love I hold for you in me,
is solid as a stone;
It cannot be trampled on
nor can it ever be torn apart;
For it is locked away in safety.
In the very bottom of my heart;
And as life is still unfolding,
we have much yet to force;
But right now the only thing I need,
is you, the night, and me!

Eric Foley Saucier

If You Can't

If you can't be good to me while I'm here
don't cry for me when I'm gone.

If you can't love me now
don't ask me what went wrong.

If you can't be my friend
don't be surprised when it comes to an end.

If you can't love me now
don't bring me flowers when I'm dead.

If you can't accept me like this
don't tell your friends what you miss.

Diana Hodgin Grein

Nature's Love

See the flag;
Dogs tails do wag!
The sun fell into fall,
But shadows are against the wall.

Winter is on its way.
Snow! On a nice sunny day!
Ice fishing is a decent thing.
Listen to the snowbird sing!

Here comes spring!
Ice melts away:
Fish jump the day away.
Shear the coat of wool off the sheep.
Seeds sown; soil tilled.

Now, it's summertime - so
Salute the flag;
Everything is happy.

David Wood

To DSS - With Love

Cold, bitter and hurt
Doesn't anyone care anymore
Can you not see all the dirt
I am so tired and sore

You used a baby to satisfy yourself
With not a care in your world
I cried loudly for help
But like a thief in the night, you stole

You have had your glory for now
But you have not yet won
For I have not thrown in the towel
Just wait for the next dawn

Christina M. Levens

The Courage As Love

Stand by me. Hold my hand.
Don't let me go. I am afraid. I am lonely.
I am lost.
Listen with a open heart. Accept
me with all my faults. Be my friend.
My heart aches. My insight not
so clear. My trust is diminished.
Show me how to smile, how to
clear my mind, how to hold my head
up because of who I am.
My heart cry's for warmth, my
body craves a touch. My mind
yearns for laughter.
Help me down this rugged road,
so that I may know the courage of love.

Daphne K. Bunn

Dead Beat Dad

Do you love your Dad,
Do you think he's bad,
He thinks money buys love,
Money is not better than a hug,
He calls once in a while,
He can't see you smile,
Do you sometimes cry,
Then wonder why,
He don't come to see you,
And you don't have a clue,
Why don't he visit,
Or come by and sit,
Is there another girl,
Who is in his world,
Does he love another,
And not your mother,
He says he loves you,
He doesn't even know you,
Does this make you sad, don't worry
He's just a DEAD BEAT DAD!

Deatrice A. Smith

What Is This World Coming To?

What is this world coming to?
Does anybody know?
Does anybody care?
I know these answers...
This world is coming to a living Hell!
Nobody really cares.
Our future depends on this world but
nobody wants to fix it!
Our children's future depends on it.
It isn't safe anymore.
You can't walk out the door without
getting robbed, shot at or beat on!
The world is becoming a scary place to live.
What is this world coming to?
Can or will anybody help fix it?

April Hamling

The Garden

Have you walked through the
garden of love?
If you have then you
know
Just how far love can
go
Have you walked through the
garden of life?
If you have then you
know
Which way in life you
will go
Have you walked through the
garden of hope?
If you have then you know
Just how far hope can go
Have you walked through the
garden with Jesus?
If you have then you know
Just how far that walk will go.

Donna Langley

Creation

Electricity flows from your fingertips,
Connecting with my bare skin
   sending surges of pleasure
     through me.
Your kisses open the window
   to my innermost feelings.
The love and desires found there
   are overwhelming,
     yet compelling.
The moment you enter me I
   become lost in waves of passion,
     barely hanging on to reality.
Then you look deeply into my
   eyes and I become one
     with you.
Bonded in soul and spirit,
   never to be whole again outside
     the entity we've created.

Linda Garcia

Sophie Was Dancing

Sophie was dancing
Dancing in the hall
Dancing the two-step
The Cinderella of the ball.

On a Saturday morning in the wind
Sophie burned the trash
Beneath the willow.
Brown dry leaves, twigs and branches
Papers and dried flowers
From the graves.

The flames licked the perfume
From her hem,
Caught her sash and then her hair,
Sophie, screaming, ran into the wind.
Now Sophie is an angel Perhaps
Sophie is dancing on the head of a pin.

Eunice B. Lanzl

Call Girls Lament

I would like to lay with you
Get all tangled and askew
Caught in love's little web
Trying for ecstasy in bed
No one knowing
But we two
Carrying on
So old so new
Touching, kissing, loving, mad
Afterward feeling, so good, so bad
So good, it was, at least for me
So bad its over, you have to leave
Take with you
A memory
My love I give you
Oh so free

Anita Del Castillo (Anita Stanke)

"Grim Reaper"

Cat, bat, rim of hat,
Halloween, hide, head of hair,
Skeletons, ghosts, of a pair,
hiding away in a lair.
Bony fingers, and its nails,
Children screaming out their wails.
Frogs, teeth, curses, and smoke,
maggots, scars, murders of blokes.
Potions, brews, stews, and warps,
bodies, blood, grave of corpse.
Someone dies of being sick,
as the grim reaper dampens the
candle wick.

Joanna Lynne Berny

I Did It For A Purpose

It happened on a Sunday
I did what I had to do
I murdered my best friend
I did it all for you
I did it for a purpose
I thought of doing it all the time
First, I thought of our relationship
And other things too
I made sure she was dead
I did it all for you
It was for a lot of things that she said
That she loved you
I could never live with knowing that SHE could
Love thee
So, then I have decided that I have to kill me

Tiffany Ann Smith

Night Time

When the night comes and I put out the lights,
I lay lightly on a soft bed, made up of white
crisp sheets, dried slowly by the light of the sun,
cooled from the morning breeze with the smell of honeysuckle
I nestle next to you, feeling the beat of your heart as
if it was my own. I look at you, as I slowly but
ever so gently move my hands over your body, feeling
every curve of your strong, beautifully sculpted frame.
I can feel your manhood come alive. I raise my body up
on yours, kissing you passionately; feeling your skin moving
gently against mine, I become overwhelmed by the heat
caused by the friction of our bodies. After completing
our dance of love, you take me in your arms and hold
me next to you. I, without any struggle, fall asleep
only to awake the next morning, realizing, it was all a dream.

Marsha Pennie

In The Dark

In the dark I lie awake and I can see
   them dance for me.
A voice is calling and I shall go,
There is no reason to dawdle more.
Now the children have stopped singing,
and there are no birds.
The sun has stopped shining,
and there are no words.
To speak would be murder.
To move tempts suicide.
And the children are gathered and
   sacrificed to him...

Erin Hearn

"Do You Remember Me"

Do you remember me?
I was the boy laughing, reflecting happiness.

Do you remember me?
I was the boy who kissed
with the fear of being kissed.

A languid motion
A deteriorating victory

A virgin,
how did I hold on so long?

You must have shaven off the follicles
that disturb my ability to love.

Now I must cast you away,
compassion is gone.

I'll be a corpse in the morning.
Robert Masters Jr.

Jester

I have seen the sick cow
  inside the one I love.
   Such eatingbreathinglyingdown, mechanical
repetition to disgust...
my sense of ego: so affronted-
by you-animal!

Sick Cow who I would be Bull for
likening my thoughts (cow's tongue)
to maggots in heat
cloven feet I see
such dark interpretation,
But I can not bear vacation
from your face and our embrace
I race to meet you
in a fabled city
as fast as I can
You must believe.
Odonnell

Untitled

I'll put a gun in my hand
Last resort of unhappy man.
Into the shadows of darkness I creep
Following no one to my solemn sleep.
A poet's rendition of my life
Too many a**holes that aren't my type.
A clueless lie I leave behind
Your darkened future still blind.
Dreaming not for your life
Face the truth, yield the knife.
Painful place in my perception
A lie if thought, to be the exception.
This is the last resort of unhappy man
As I've put a gun in my hand
B. J. Cappozzi

"The Beginning And The End"

Beneath me were thee, my loins surround you.
Oh! masterful fearless steed. My long white dress
your mantle. Golden hair wrapped my neck,
down to my bosom I could feel it.

Run Steed, run, loose it. Whistle softly at
the gate as we pass by. I have the reigns.
Oh! let us fly you and I. Beneath me I
feel the growing surge of pleasure.

Past the cove I hear the ocean's mighty roar.
Hearts pounding now, we've reached the waves,
"Ebb Tide," endless, flowing never ending. Gentle
ripples along the shore, reveal the life
beneath the sand. Out of breath now my
cheeks incandescent as I feel the mighty rush.
"Omnipresence" here abounds.
"Alpha and Omega."
Helen DiMente

Dark Christmas

Christmas beckons amidst frivolous cheer.
  Remorse amasses from a wasted year.
Remorse amasses, instead of snow.
  Bringing on Christmas, a Christmas of woe.

Insults flew, feelings were hurt.
  She made it clear, I was nothing but dirt.
My son knew no better...it was over his head.
  She was his leader, and he was misled.

My wife had betrayed me, one week left to the year.
  Seeking revenge, I have nothing to fear.
Although I was right as I firmly believe.
  The score must be settled...this Christmas Eve.

The score will be settled, but no one will know...
  what action I've taken or where I did go.
I could be a coward, it'd be easy to run.
  Instead, rest my head, at the end of a gun.
Bradley Joseph Wallach

In My Skin

Judging from where I've been, I don't think you want to be in my skin.

I am the one who shuffles down the street. Carrying a weary soul on blistered feet. I argue with the voices I hear in my mind, as people pass and pretend they are blind. They think that I'm oblivious to my pain, yet I know that I'm completely insane.

I am the one who is abused. I pride myself that only my body is bruised. I try to tell you to stop, but all my hope is lost. But tonight was different from any other night. You finally broke my spirit and won your fight.

I am the one that was born the wrong sex. Trying to learn the right behavior makes my life complex. Living life this way seems to be my fate. I am a prime example that sometimes nature makes a mistake.

I am the cold and the heartless that no one wants to see. I don't give a sh** about anyone but me. I whisper no prayers before I go to bed, because I know inside I'm already dead.

Judging from where I've been, I don't think you want to be in my skin.
Taryn Simpson

The Fall Of 95

It was flower power then
Summer of 69
One, two, three, four,
We don't want your f***ing war

Today Keith emptied his clip into Joey
Today they were both 8th graders
Keith's face was empty as he shot thirteen times
Don't have to take Joey's sh** no more

Today young soldiers fight their own wars
On hallway battlefields between classes
Hit the lunchroom floor when gunfire flashes

"Teach Your Children Well"
This ain't no Woodstock Nation
"Teach Your Children Well"
This ain't the peace and love generation

A mother holds her son close
She wipes his eyes
She sings him a lullaby
Christy Newcomb

"Me Against The World"

I'm sick of people pretending to care.
The pain they cause me I wish wasn't there.
The ache in my chest won't seem to go away,
I miss my mom who could not stay.
   It's me against the world
My family doesn't want anything to do with me.
I break the law and they think I'm crazy.
They give up on me, just like everybody else.
I don't care, I can depend on myself.
   It's me against the world.
Runnin' from the cops one day;
Did a crime and had to pay.
I was a fool with the big girls, breakin' all the rules;
I guess I'm learnin' things the hard way.
   It's me against the world.
Just f*** the world cause I'm all alone;
I can make it on my own!
Cheyenne

"In The Eyes Of The Beholder"

Burn my fire burn, kill, kill.
The smell of flesh burning,
And the children screaming,
Oh, the glorious colors and sounds.

The pits of hell scream for you darling,
Spread your hatred over this land of nothing.
Eat its people for me, my love.

The wicked don't desire to live with us.
So, burn them in your coat of color,
Let them suffer the way I suffered.

Make their flesh bubble and melt.
Make the smell suffocate their nostrils,
My fire, my friend, burn for me, burn,

..... and I took one more
look into the fireplace and turned away.
Heidi Theule

Public Bathroom Blues

Sitting with a crowd around me
Toxic gases, they surround me,
Wondering why I came in here
To this public castle of fear.

Perched upon my porcelain throne
Being chilled right to the bone,
Fearing attack from a social disease
Crabs, or lice, or even fleas.

Listening to the choral refrain
Of tortured men in mortal pain,
Seeking to be free at last
From Sunday's lunch or Monday's gas.

Now that my plight is nearly through
And my body is turning blue,
I cast about for the sacred tissue
And empty roll, what an issue.

Sound the alarm, hoist the flag
Has anyone got a paper bag?
Matchbook, Band-Aid, I'll not refuse.
Cause you can see, I'm trapped here by the Bathroom Blues!
Bradford A. Deel

"Rape Me"

Take me, rape me, make me, hate me
Poison my mind with dirty ventures
Send me a chill with the scariest calenture
Teach me to abuse my body and learn from these cruel experiences
Push my heart to bleed while, my soul it dances
With a thrust I shall repeat these words as song,
Take me, rape me, make me, hate me,
Explore my body in a forceful way, when all the while
  you'll hear the words I say
I know you love what's on my mind,
All the wrong in the world your passion will blind,
In hate you are my teacher, my master. In fear our are my mind
In love you are my heart, you will hear me say as we part
Chanting, screaming, loud as hell
Take me, rape me, make me, hate me,
Will you ever know or believe the power and strength invested
  in me,
Today you are destined to see...
Stacey Goodwin

The Meaning Of A B*t*h

Some don't understand as to why I feel this way,
Not so much a bitterness, but an indifference towards men of today
Most try their suave, sweet talk tricks
And only play childish mind games
Plucking music to a woman's heart
To lure them into their "bed game"
Others try a different trick
To get exactly what they want
Disregarding another human's feelings
Materialistic things is what some hunt
But on account of these very few
It's the good ones who get judged too
Because the NASTY DOGS are the ones
Who make good men seem too good to be true
But not all negativity comes from a woman running into a dog
She becomes more and more strong minded
Learning to beat the game before the dog
So if, my reader, you are a dog, trying to play those mind games
Remember that in the process you'll CREATE
A woman who will beat you to your own game... A B*T*H.
Miriam L. Smith

Society

I don't know how to feel,
I don't know what to do
I don't know what to say
I wanna die.
I wish I could just walk away
Far away from everything
I wish I could be the only one here
Nobody else; well, maybe just one
Someone to talk to, once in awhile.
I wish I could hurt people
Really, just hurt people
For no good reason, just for being a**holes
People suck!
You do something wrong
I always get blamed
I can't control this anger inside me!
One of these days, I'm gonna blow!
People get so offended
When you tell them to "F*** off"
I don't.

Carin A. Sutherland

"Craving The Day"

   Craving the day for a man to stimulate
my mind, to give me love, truth, understanding
of God's kind. To make me feel strong and not so weak,
to make me feel whole and not incomplete.
Craving the day for a man to touch my heart
so nothing in my world will ever fall apart.
Thoughts of passion that runs so deep to be with a man
who's in love with just me. Waiting for the touch of your
tender loving hands across my breast and up to my
chest to caress me like no other man can.
Craving the intimacy of real love, searching
for the right one to give me that love.

Lisa Miller

A Woman's Eye View

Woman,
of Smooth flesh,
sinuous arms,
and shining eyes.

Lapping up
life's essence
which you
oh, so sweetly
   provide

Would that I
could stand
behind
not touching
simply breathing
in your
tantalizing scent.

Until, Woman
you shudder
deliciously
in my arms
and take
   away
   my soul.

Love you,
would I
and see
passion
in your
heated movements

Diana Lee White

Soule

In the thinkthicket strewn of eye echoes and milk-born polliwogs walk my mother's shoes-slower than ice-amidst the furious fire of unheard sighs and sights and fallen porridge roots of the slanted daze, list with the open yawns of gaping brain typhoons in the season when eve wildest bone trees sleep-

Shaken snows peppered come the bought to crown the laughing proph of the marrow with many a viral seastone: they always got fat from the wear-Puffer o puffer swim up the sockeyed seasee and pop nard on my middle bud: mother whispered them on the raven frost of my back neck. Tickle twiddle cat rubs and puppy cologne salted with 'coon hands around twiddle cat rubs and puppy cologne salted with 'coon hands around a grape, and out with the pouring of days and years. The pitcher's cork unearthed and now mows the chained ghost wine over my rust-sunken ember fields of withering eight

Gandhi spun laces stroke the marionette that is my beagle hound belly: my soul hears only the sole sweet violin played across the sifting floors

Who taught us all to summon up the Muse at dirge of day, and cockles at babe after stars have purchased in their will the minefire again? Yes, the acorned pair grow the passion fruit that bricks my house, and evermore shall I haunt in sea garden tombs.

Lawrence Wayne Brooks

Buzzard Breath

They buzzed me overhead
To make sure I was dead.
As I was enmeshed in barbed wire.
Then the time came.
They tore at my frame
With their vampirical - wanton desire.
I watched overhead as "Mr. Dread" —
The Head Buzzard tore at the part that held my heart!
Insipid reasoning thrown from afar
Like finding a treasure hidden in a jar—
Washed upon the shore of mankind's reef.
The thief—
Pulled my heart apart — as I stood above it all.
Oh! too much for my baby!?
Too much and too soon?
How far is the earth from the moon?
I must try to sound dumb; and be nothing but numb,
As they censor the very rest of my beast.
And, I sayeth, "I do smell buzzard breath,
right after my living — death."

Ronald Joel Ragan

Enchanted Love

Naked hosts engulfed in love,
Pure as snow white turtle dove.
Raging lust entombed, released,
Never ending, never cease.
Power great enriches souls,
Heaving breasts now taking toll.
Blissful screams as soul now spills,
Into another in equal thrill.
Parallel bodies resting still,
Greater lost controls the will.
Hatred lost and serenity gained,
Passion now replaces pain.
World is one in their eyes,
Only by love hypnotized.

Loren Stroebel

Gross Body Thoughts

Slumbering souls sickled into marrow of joints and
cavities. Phantom pain cramped intermittently,
boring, yet, malingering.

Fractured promises plastered to wasting and degeneration.
Weeping egos punctured, creeping into venular pit to burrow.

Blastic crises lyzed, vasospastic, shearing forces lipping
the occludens. Gangrenous sorrows amputated, odoriferous
as swarm of maggots feasted the debris.

Stalky pedicle of truths twisted, clockwise,
180 degrees, counter-clockwise depriving nervi ergentes
to sustain.

Newgrowths of hope, puncuate, cerebriform to cancerous
slowly shifting malignant pressures
palpable catatonia unstoppable
as drooping lids, drooling liquids
suffocate the life, the body
into apoptosis.

Joseph Herrera Balatbat

Hidden Evil

He smiled showing white teeth
He smiled hiding the evil beneath.
He laughed with such hidden anger and hate.
Before I realized, it was too late.
Oh my God if only I'd known I would
of handled it all on my own.
But someone I love more than life
became involved.
He thought by just talking things
could be solved.
But this evil being, that I once
thought was human, struck out with
intent to kill.
All that saved my loved one was
prayers and God's will.
The judicial system let us down,
they set this monster free, to
maim and may be kill.
But his day to pay will come and it will
be God's will.

Dolores M. Regalbuto

Mary, Mary

Mary, Mary quite evil how
does your evil garden grow
With hanging toes and heads
Blood splatted on the wall
Cuffs chained to the bed
Your grandma laying on the
floor with a stone through her head
Hands of people on the wall
still moving
The dog eating your mother
Mary, Mary quite evil how
does your evil garden grow

Megan Stiltner

The Beginning

I triumph over the dunes of time,
For reasons of naught remorse.
A place to repent for guilty crimes,
I've found through route and course.
My duty is to find the key,
To life for which we're born.
In the after-life do we finally see,
The true torture and scorn.
To complete the journey I go alone,
Transcending through love and glory.
I must be cleansed, stripped past the bone,
And here begins my story.
To establish my perseverance, I exert a loud cry.
Another journey is ahead of me, I take a deep breath and sigh.

Joshua D. Watts

For One Night Of Pleasure

For one night of pleasure as you're out in the night
For one night of pleasure for someone to hold tight
For one night of pleasure as you see him
For one night of pleasure he will give you a grin
For one night of pleasure he will ask you to dance
For one night of pleasure you will take a chance
For one night of pleasure he gave you chills
For one night of pleasure he gave you thrills
For one night of pleasure his memory fades
For one night of pleasure he gave you AIDS
For one night of pleasure he was the best
For one night of pleasure as they lay you to rest

Anita J. Watkins

A Night On Black Mountain

Everyone scurried to get to their shack
For it was getting dark on the mountain called Black
This happens the same time, every night, every year.
It is a mountain no one would live near
The mountain rose out of the ground too high in the sky
Its top was impossible to see with just the naked eye
Now was the time, the time of the damned
The people of the city's shacks were now jammed
As the prince of darkness emerged from the depth of hell
He brought with him an acidic like smell
No one ever falls asleep,
You're always wide awake and breathing deep.
While the souls of the dead come out to dance
The demons arrive in a zombie like trance.
This goes on all night and early unto dawn
As they dance and they dance they might never be gone
Until the sun comes and scares them away
The Devil is screaming to bring the new day.
Now the living come out again and work there way to dusk
The dead will rise once more in their disgust.

Andy McClelland

Life Of A Comb

With cigarette butts n' snot-caked rags
I'm carried along in a dirty pocket.
I welcome daylight cause then I get t' eat.
I rush through the butts n' rags.
My meal of flakes n' greasy tangles
is kinda like the 15th Street Mission spaghetti.
I'll get t' eat again today
if I'm lucky.
If not,
guess I'll stay in the dirty pocket.

Amy L. Boardman

The Irish Gift

A gift to the Irish is almost unseemly
For he carries within him the gift of himself
He needs not the excess to make him affluent
His unbounding depth is the source of his wealth.

When he booms at you, listen!
For his temper's a terror,
Though his love can be sweet
As an even tide prayer.

He understands shadings of life as the happen
He questions not that which is his to endure
To be known and be loved by those he holds dearest
Are all of the gifts he feels need to procure.

Be he rough talked, or gentle,
Whatever his way
Know that deep in his soul
Lies the best of each day.

Berniece C. Smith

"My Son"

The brightest star in the heavens is the sun............
For a mother with a boy - he's the only one............
We teach him to talk, to walk and to grow...............
And reap the blessings that we bestow...................

When he's little - and always under your feet..........
It's hard not to give in - to total defeat.............
It's feeding and bathing and tucking into bed..........
And always there are the prayers to be said............

As they grow up some - and start to school.............
There's always an empty nest - as a rule................
Where did the time go? Where's my baby boy?...........
He's now beginning to mature - oh, what a joy..........

Before you know it - in high school he'll be...........
And now it's happening - the less of him you'll see.....
The other women in his life - they too now are about....
It gets frustrating at times and you want to shout......

As the boy turns into - that fine young man............
He's ready for the world - to make his stand............
From my baby to a man - came way too soon...............
For now my house - has an empty room....................

Angela Redman

A Thoughtful Transition

It is very difficult to provide a definition
for a common household word,
counterclockwise,
when wearing a digital watch.
It is also difficult to explain how to
dial a telephone in an
environment of touch tone phones.
That these have passed from our use
is due to the ever-evolving technologies
changing the way we communicate information.
So subtle are the changes,
we do not notice the difference
until we are at loss for words
or lack the skills
to complete a task.

Beverly Enns

The Fool

Patience,
  I wait so disparately
    for a change that may never come.

Uncertainty,
  like thin ice under my feet.

My glaciers of tears,
   layered by your cold tendencies,
    will melt away one day.
One day when you open your soul to me.

Do not fear love,
   for you will not become a fly captured in my web,
    but a caterpillar,
     cocooned by fears, wishes and desires,
    Waiting to become much more.

Patience,
I wait for both of us.

Dawn M. Taylor

An Airman's Vision

I will hear the bugle blow,
Flags will dip to my body below.

In my honor a salute they will fire,
My child shall lift his head even higher.

Soldiers will pass, a tear will form,
Memories from the past, they are torn.

Ladies too, will pass and ladies will cry,
All for a soldier who was willing to die?

My soul is dead, but my spirit shall soar,
Unlike the eagle, ever more.

When the salute is fired,
The thunder will rumbled in the grave below.

This is when one to one a Nation will say
"...on this fine Memorial Day, here a soldier lay

One who loved his country, his freedom, and this land.
One who loved his family ever so great, ever so grand."

Giacinto A. Lucci

Purpose And Memory

I relax and with outstretched pen
find in me little speeches
so I shift things to my inspiration
and search for purpose; reach
draw into myself, smother myself
in the seams, the scenes of things
and reach to a shelf which holds
something inside it that sings

Memory of space, in time   it's cold
Months younger in me, on concrete Indian style
There were red metal lockers on the school campus, It was old
It was old - the subtleties - my smile
the new blotches of yellow, the yellow sun
easy shades, and change. It was old
the dreamy thing continued to run
sneezing breeze kindly; folds
Event folds, times, its lumpy continuity
streams of feet and people, strolling, restful
blue cool, grass, brown roofs, seas
Things, things, appearing, I lunched on an apple...

Aaron Zaritzky

Season Of Love

Heavy pouring raindrops,
filling the ocean's water floors.
Raging winds,
causing waves of turbulence.
Exhausted thunderstorm,
filling the land with crackling scare.
Winds that blow,
hundreds and thousands of miles away.
Black haunted skies,
Waiting for the morning sunshine.
But as the world goes around,
the storm quiets itself down.
be stilling the oceans overflown water floors.
Morning has arrived,
sunshine fights the battle to move every cloud in sight.
A victory succumbs,
for the storm is gone.
  Evelyn Justiniano

"A Place For Pain"

I open the door pain walks in
filling my home with darkness and discontent

I open the door love walks in
replenishing the bedroom

I open the door faith walks in
illuminating my living room

I open the door hope walks in
filling the kitchen with wonderful smells

I open the door joy walks in
I explain that she has the wrong address
she should be next door
she comes in anyway
joy like pain knows not of manners or proper protocol

I open the door humor walks in
It fills the empty spaces

Pain is still here but it has little room.
  David M. Jacobson

Lanie's Lament

"I can never love another," she cries.
For the heart of my heart has been ripped from me
And lies scattered from the warmth of the sands beneath the
bougainvillea to the glow of the northern pines.
My soul is a wasteland.
Filled with grief I stand alone to face an eternity of despair.
He was to me as vital as the very air I breathe;
The love that happens once and forever.
And I will not promise another that which I am unable to give."

"My love," he murmurs softly on the wind. "Do not mourn so;
For the enormity of your pain diminishes my spirit.
I will soften your hardened heart with each gentle fall of twilight.
And with the velvety caress of every drop of rain,
I will replenish the endless wells within your soul.
Someday you will find within another what you found in me.
Listen not for the sound of my voice, but for the music of my soul.
For our souls were intertwined before time began and shall be ever so."
  Joyce E. Carver

Love Dreams

I don't know exactly what it was that made me care and caused me to
  feel what it was that made me care and feel for you so true.
  And I'm not sure of the exact moment or the day in time,
  That exactly day I fell in love with you.

I don't know why I did fall so hard and fall so fast,
  Why I fell so fast for you at this point in time.
  I don't know why I didn't pay more attention to the warnings,
  Why I simply chose to ignore all the signs.

I don't know if it was your laugh, your soft voice or simply the look
  in your eyes, these things I would long for so deeply and so much
  Maybe it was your friendship and your thoughts and your dreams of
  true love, I'll never forget your passion... and feeling the need
  of your touch.

I don't know why I opened up and let you so deep inside,
  Why I let you inside me so deep and so near.
  I don't know why my heart wasn't more careful of the pain,
  Why my heart got confused and over came all the fear.

I don't know why you made me feel you were so different and so special
  You stood out from the rest or so it did seem.
  But now I do know I'll feel a fool when I stop and I realize,
  If I wake up to realize...you were only just a dream.
  Brent J. Kechler

One Day To Live

If I had but one day to live, I wonder what I'd long for? Perhaps to feel the warm winds gently touch my face or the cool running water of a mountain stream at my feet. Or perhaps I'd sit atop a mountain ledge and gaze down upon the splendor of God's creations. Maybe I would sit quietly in the grassy fields and smell the sweet perfume of the flowers or lie next to a friend as we playfully perceive the clouds as something only we can imagine. Perhaps I'd just rest and think of all the good times - the most enjoyable times - when life was free and laughter came easy - and I'd smile. But of all these things, by far, I'd long to see your face, to touch your hands, and to feel your warmth one last time. For it is all these things - the beauty of nature, the creations of God, and the touch of a friend that gives life meaning. And I hope never a day passes that I shall forget this, for life is to be lived one day at a time.
  John W. Blaskowski

Somewhere

Somewhere, a corporate paper shuffler slices his finger on a fax, the blood congealing on his nail in a small pool. His sandy eyes look warily about as he presses his finger to his lips, the acrid taste satisfying a deep perverse desire in all of us . . .

Somewhere, a junkie bathed in chilled sweat stands on a ledge as the wind knifes through him. A marionette to the crowd below him, he hears the murmur and call of the critics. The curtain rises and he begins to soar . . .

Somewhere, a dark lonely road is invaded by two beams of light. The car speeds around the bends between painted lines. It hits some small unidentifiable animal in the dark dead of night, but the whine of the engine does not change . . .

Somewhere, a woman sobs in a cold linoleum corner. Her face is swollen and blood dries on her slackened lips and chin. She hugs her knees as she hears her husband's stupor fade into sleep . . .

And somewhere, a child screams, protesting his untimely rip from the womb, into a world so alien . . . and cold.
  Daniel R. Haller

Love's Cycle

He came unexpectedly...
Fate brought confusion, excitement, anticipation,
Heart wrenching decisions
Love and pain.
My life was changed,
Nothing was the same.

He left unexpectedly...
Death brought confusion, emptiness, anxiety,
Heart wrenching decisions
Loneliness and pain.
My life has changed,
Nothing will ever be the same.

Donnaclaire Taylor

I Wonder

I enjoy watching people. They may
fascinate me in different ways, but they
all make me curious.

I wonder why some people must always have
companions near them, while others insist on
solitude.

I wonder why it is a difficult task for some
people to figure out who they are, while others
pretend to be someone they are not.

I wonder why some people weep for forgiveness to
clench their regret, while others feel no sorrow
for wronging themselves or others.

I wonder why some people value lives that
bring them pain, while others end lives that
bring them pleasure.

At last I wonder why everyone can not accept
other people for who they are, since it is
impossible for everyone to be the same.

Beth Welsh

Just Like You, Dad

I always wondered what was wrong with me. You were always
    distant—so far away.
You said, "I love you," and you thought taking care of me with money
    proved it.
You showed little emotion and, at times, you seemed cold and almost
    unfeeling.
I always wondered what I was doing wrong—why you wouldn't let me in.
You had that business tone every time we talked. When I tried to get
    closer, you'd be farther away.
I asked how you could build walls around you and not let anyone in.
    You said, "That's just how I am, but I do love you."
Pushed to the point of unresolved hurt and of failure at trying to
    become that perfect person you'd open up to,
I said the one thing I wish I had never said—"I hate you."
Now, I see I've inherited your talent of construction, of building
    walls.
I can distance myself from others and also experience the "numb" state
    of unfeeling.
I now hear myself talk in that business tone and think, "That sounds
    familiar."
And, although I try to control it, I can't. It's part of me now.
"That's just how I am"—just like you, Dad—and I do love you, too.

Darla McCool-McMurtry

For All Luv's Worth

When I wake up in the morning, with a smile upon my
face and I feel you lying next to me, as I hold you in loves
embrace. That's when I realize that I love you, I'd follow
you to the ends of the earth. Oh God, I'll love you, yes, I
love you. For all love's worth.
  Now it's time for me to get up, to get dressed and go to work.
I've got eighteen long hours, to put in before my return.
You know I love you and I need you. I'd follow you
to the ends of the earth. Oh God, I'll love you, yes, I love you.
For all love's worth.
  Well, the hours move so slowly, when you're away from me.
I feel I just want to squeeze you and kiss you tenderly.
You know I love you and I need you. I'm so glad you're my wife.
Oh God, I'll love you, yes, I love you for all my life.
You know I'll love you, yes, I love you. For all my life.

James F. Baker Sr.

The Face Of A Nation

This is a face that reeks of hypocrisy
eyes rotten with irony
black with love and lust
teeth broken, bleeding with trust
imploded ears ringing with a cheap word
a paranoid nose refusing to smell
a tongue pierced with the badge of the Republic

The rotten eyes on Dow Jones
a chipped tooth in the Vice Presidency
a nose broken and set in the post office
cheap ears exported
dead tongues imported
an exchange to keep the body polarized
to keep the body happy

In spite of the face

Carol J. Stratman

As We...

As we drift through the sky, never opening our
eyes, and we feel the warm sun beating down,
we begin to understand the whole master plan,
of who we are and why we came to be.

We are the distant cousins of the stars, the planets
and moons are our friends, the universe is our
creator, and we all live together as one.

As we float through the sea, never stopping to
breath, and we taste the salt water that surrounds,
we know the fish and seals are our brothers, the
dolphins and sharks protects, the sea is our father,
and we all form together to be one.

As we dance all around, never touching the ground, and
we see the wind whipping through the air, we realize the
trees and flowers are our sisters, the deer and lions our
aunts, the earth is our mother, and we all love each other
as one, yes we all love each other as one.

Jessica Oisen

Life

Life is a STORY BOOK filled with
fantasy, and dreams, hopes, wishes, memories, disappointments.
Choices that we face are PAGES to turn.
All of the pain and sufferings are PICTURES of lessons we have
or have yet to learn.
PAGES fill and turn as we make and reach goals.
The question is: DO I READ THE END BEFORE STARTING THE
BEGINNING?

Jessica C. Dombrowski

Success

What is this word Success?
Exactly what does it mean?
It holds many definitions
Through various stages of our lives we may see.

How can one measure success day by day
When money sometimes will get in the way?

Our wealth can be found deep down within.
What can one do today to make this joy come around and stay?

We should live each day to the max.
Who knows how long they will last?
The quality of life we lead
is something to be scrutinized, especially.

Hold your own with your head up high.
Never let those standards slide by.
Are we good to others and hold ourselves with pride?
Do we really like what we always see inside?

Success is yours when you are true.
What counts in the end is a special you.
Dru Kolb

How Can It Be?

Life gives love a beginning to be,
Everyone has abilities, even you and me.
To love someone more dearly every day,
It takes time to build love in many ways.
God is in this plan, to make it a success,
It all can be there, even if you think it has regressed.
His wings of tender love and care are a miracle we share.
I only know that God is always there.
Thanks to Him for my life, a gift from parent's love.
It can always be far greater, when we know the gift of Grace came from above.
Heaven is an open door within the soul divine
Peace from deep inside surrounds the hurts and to
forgive and then forget makes the pain go away.
The ticking of an old or new clock each day,
Makes one happiness in his or her own way.
Faith unlocks the door and is the key to find our destiny,
He makes the moves and sets the scenes in our lives
Just as the hangs the stars out to shine in the sky
A miracle is, how can it be?
Betty Marie Garth

Are We There Yet?

Are we there yet, the children chime?
Every time you take them for a ride.
They can't wait to get where they are bound.
They miss the joy of the trip every round.
We think, what a shame, why don't they relax?
And enjoy the scenes along the way.
But don't be so hard on the children, my dear.
Did you stop and smell the flowers today?

When we were little, we wanted to be grown.
We didn't enjoy our youth, cause we griped and we moaned!
We were in such a hurry to reach adulthood
Cause we thought everything would be so good.
Well, I wish my friend, that I were young again!
I wouldn't be in such a hurry then,
To be so grown and all alone.
But the old saying is, "You can't go back home."
Are we there yet? Still rings out in our ears,
How many times have we wondered all these years
Are we there yet?...and do we know where we are?
Carol Rich Meshelle

Awakening

Like a god of bronze I placed her before me
Every curve of her body covered my shame
Her soft lips hid my faults
The touch of her embrace enveloped my fears

I longed to have her close to me, to keep myself away
A symbol of my guilt that stool before my eyes
Someone to attack and ease my pain
A dressing for my wounded soul

How very dark is that place I hold inside
It fears the light that will save it
Searching the world for captives of relief
Holding others and myself in chains

"Open your heart," cries the voice inside
"Stand naked, fearless before your brother"
The darkness has power when hidden
It disappears in the spirits light

Never again will I need a bronze god
The God of truth dwells within me
Standing tall with courage, accepting my self
His love will light the way
David Wendling

Echoes In The Night

Somewhere in the night, a tiny voice calls
Ever so faint, it echoes from my walls
Whispers of love long since lost
Memories of the past, reminders of the cost

Evading my touch, answers unclear
In the darkness, none see my tears
Alone in the night, untouched by love
Begging for mercy from heaven above

No one feels my beating heart, aching to be held
The burning in my soul, longing to be felt
Passionate thoughts, roaming in my mind
Nor the tender emotions I hold deep inside

Still the voice calls, a tortured soul
Weeping for the past, longing for more
Cries go unheard in the absence of light
A whisper from my heart echoes in the night
Brad Stefanko

Keep On Keeping On

In life, many battles I've defended,
Even when life seems to have ended.
I claim the victory, with God's love in my soul.
He filled my heart and made me whole.

This is the trend I pray will blend,
Within the hearts, of all my family and friends.
Keep on keeping on, and never give up,
"No matter how rough it gets, keep holding on...
...to God's unchanging hands." Our lives belong to God.

"Give, when you've given all you can gave,
reach back and give some more."
Give your best, withstand the test,
Put it in God's hand and he'll do the rest.
My spirit will be close to you,
Wherever you may go.

When the armor is worn, the body torn,
My heart says, keep on keeping on.
Johnny A. Tyson II

My Father

There comes a time when a heart must be broken.
Even though you passed away,
I still have to I... I... I love you!
I love the way you cared...
When I was down.
I loved the way you held me when no one else was around.
Those moments were so dear to me.
But...But now they are just a precious memory.
We had special times every minute we were together.
You'll be in my dreams always.
I love you so much Dad.
Daddy, I'll miss you every hour of every day.
Forever and always you'll be in my heart.
Daddy I love you.

April Dawn Zambrano

Alcoholism

It destroys people, families, communities and yes,
even nations.
It is a disease that has no cure,
leaving its victims recovering,
always recovering and never completely cured.
It is a demon that ruthlessly controls
both the young and the old,
who get hooked on its innocent looking lure.
It promises relief from your problems,
but it only brings despair and destruction.
It promises friends and popularity—
neither of which is kept.
It leaves many a child crying alone in the dark,
because a role model has fallen victim
to this highly preventable disease.
Prevention is the key to eliminating this terrible disease.
Never, oh please, never pick up the first drink and
please don't be fearful of taking your last one.

Dawna Snethen

Blackberries Are My Pick

There's something I love about picking blackberries
Even if I get chiggers and pricks and the hot sun makes me weary
I feel so much seclusion out there by myself
And when my buckets are all full, I feel so much wealth
The berry season only comes once a year
Soon the berries are all gone - quickly they disappear
In the winter I gaze at the bare vines
And the dream of their fullness comes to my mind
When once again it's that favorite time of mine
To pick blackberries for my family, from the blackberry vine.

Joy Hoyle

"Sharing My Thoughts"

I'm wondering will we share
feelings for one another...
And will these feelings grow deep...
Will I ever hold you in my arms...
And passionately yet slowly fall asleep...
Will we ever spend the night in a very romantic place...
Just to wake up the next day looking deeply
into each others face...
Holding hands and listening to our favorite song...
Knowing with all our hearts that this
is where we belong...
We could spend most of our time looking at the stars above...
And whisper softly into one another's ear as we slowly make love...
How I wish that all of this would come true...
So until that day comes I'll always share my thoughts with you...

Diane Tarkington

The Language

Having a language, waters speak. quiet flows...
encircling
coaxing
suggesting

Swift currents... pulling
persuading
moving

Rough shoots... enveloping
tumbling
telling

This language known only to waters,
humans will never understand it
yet, in an attempt, many make the waters a way of life.

I will never be able to speak it s native tongue.
But God allows me to hear it.
And it is with the language of the waters
that I find peace.

Jennifer E. Nelson

DESOLATION

There seems to be such desolation all around
Emptiness   Loneliness   Aloneness
It's a though a dry, unyielding desert surrounds me
Hot   Windy   Blowing
My face is scorched by the ruthless sun
Laughing   Mocking   Sneering
My body cries out in its unquenchable thirst
Begging   Pleading   Dying
I see with hollow eyes
Vacant   Empty   Silent
Other hollow eyes look back at me
Dull   Sunken   Depressed
People everywhere
Cold   Listless   Uncaring
Silence abounds
Hush   Soundless   Stillness
Save only the dreadful wind
Eerie   Ghostly   Mournful

Cynthia E. Rhodes

Love Is More

Love is more than mere heart expressions
emotions, desires and sweet caresses

More than just a passing phase
writing a passage or quoting a phrase

More than eyes filled with adoration
fleeting desire - unspoken passion

It is that which is not spoken
of covenants that will be broken

Of steadfastness in troubled times
friendship, partnership, ties that bind

Of oneness, a choice made by two
not led astray by what another might say or do

A cord of three not easily broken
promise made in a vow - softly spoken

Love is not rather to be taken lightly
but in it's freedom, binding us together
in God Almighty.

Chris Hollenbeck

"My Daddy's Last Night"

My daddy's last night on earth with me,
emotional pain caused him to plead.
He held my hand, asked me not to leave,
I stayed with him 'til he fell asleep.
To my daddy I tried to never say "No!"
On his last night I did, and so I did go.
I reflect now because of my leaving,
because of my pain and so much grieving.
I told him, "Don't worry, you're finally eating,
A couple of days and home you'll be greeting."
He said "you stay" and grabbed my hand tight
he worried me because of his fright.
He finally decided to give up the fight.
and so he was gone by early next night.
I didn't know my daddy was dying,
I long for his hug to keep me from crying.
Now he rests in God's hands to keep,
Waiting for him to waken from sleep.
His eyes will be opened to no more fears,
And God will wipe away all his tears.

Gloria Jean

Rural Nights

How peaceful the nights on the farmhouse porch
Embraced by the black blanket of night
dotted with a myriad of stars
Vaguely aware our hearts were beating
to the rhythm of the squeaking swing
All our senses drinking in the serenity
of country sounds and smells
Hound dogs baying in pursuit of a fox
Voices of crickets and tree frogs chirping
in harmony, relax, relax
Our nostrils treated to the perfume
of honeysuckle and clover
How pleasant to submit to Nature's
anesthetic, easing tensions of the day
A wondrous rural night providing
biofeedback for a weary soul

Jean Ann Sanchez

A Lover's Stare

With a heavy heart and mind that is light, the thought of his lover's
embrace overtakes him this night. Amongst strangers and friends all
gathered to dine, he sets himself down lost in a void without space
or time. With slight look up and eyes a blur, he gazes across the
table longing to find her. Just as if destiny had no time to spare,
his intense green eyes clasp on to her chair.

She knows he is there, but she does not look,
for she remembers last night and how she shook.

With eyes for hands he caresses her hair,
yearning for her to see him seated there.

Like the beauty of the morning sun,
she glances up to see her loved one.
Memories flood her soul and mind,
of how his touch was so powerful yet kind.

He grabs her soul and steals her air,
as he magically holds her face so fair.

With innocent eyes she touches him with care,
both caught in the embrace of a lover's stare.

Holly Hislop

"The Bat For The Young"

In a little red rocker at the stage of two,
Eating raisins I can't even tie my shoe.
Father, as I know it, is sitting on the couch.
 the more of a grouch.
I spilled some raisins on the hardwood floor,
Father snatches me up and hangs me on the jamb of our door.
Dangling and hanging, screaming and meaning
To be heard and taken down but I only got a beating.
Taken down after two hours of hanging by my shirt,
I was beaten with a plastic bat and, oh!, did it hurt.
Boom! Boom! Boom! Pleading for the chaos to end.
Agony! The bat for the young is there again.
I say to all, "Off with his head, or let him melt!"
And, to those who don't make it, our efforts were heartfelt.

Christopher Donnan

Goodbye

She said goodbye to me. It was so plain and
easy for her, as if she left everyday.
Maybe she was used to this. She didn't mind
leaving at all. I did. I didn't want her to go, I'll miss her.
She didn't even turn her head when she was walking away...
maybe that's good, -an' maybe that won't give me a picture in
my head to cry about. At least she didn't see me cry.
She wasn't willing. She wasn't frowning, either. She
was blank. I couldn't read her face like I usually could.
She was thinking about something - I hope it was me.
I hope she'll miss me like I already do her.
Her head just floats so innocently on her shoulders.
Gracefully bobbing with each step. Her ponytail followed behind.
Each step squeezed another tear. I shouldn't have let her go.
She'll forget me. I hate knowing I'm going to be forgotten
Why didn't she say more? Just one word to sew up the relationship.
If she could've said anything more what would it have been?
Would she have told me that she loved me? Did she ever? She
said she did. I know I loved her. I always will. Goodbye

Charlie Burnett

The Dogwood

I never look so deep in the woods, as when the dogwood blooms.
Each tiny blossom lights a path, casting out darkness and gloom.

The warmth of each blossom, hugging each infinite space,
Brings joy to my soul and a smile to my face.

Tiny rocks in trickling brooks, a cabin my eyes consume.
Never before seen the naked eye, until the dogwood blooms.

Scattered through the trees and over the terrain.
Blossoms dancing all around, bring attention to minute things.

In summer, fall and winter, visions of woods are trees.
When dogwood petals spray their depths, it sets the hidden
things free.

The dogwood serves a purpose, bring forth how we tend to miss,
The hidden secrets of the woods, that glow with beauty bliss.

Elaine M. Brewer

Rumors And Truth

Rumors and truth go hand in hand,
each are told by a different man.
The man who tells rumors, his heart is cold,
and the man who tells the truth happens to be bold.
Rumors go out quickly and do so much damage,
wherefore, the truth can help to heal and be like a bandage.
If truth went out like rumors so quickly received,
men would say come now Lord Jesus, I'm ready, I believe.

Debra Mighty

A Stranger

I took a step, then another,
each one bringing me into the future and the danger that there was to come.
Suddenly, I was there.
My face turned pale, my breath froze and my body shut down.
I was left awkwardly standing there trying to scream.

Scream at that stranger in my mother's car.
I wanted to hit him or worse, but I couldn't!

I abruptly realized that he was unconscious, probably from too much beer.
That knowledge let me realize that Mom was telling me to move away from the car.
"Should I call the police?" I wondered
but I couldn't call the police, not even if I tried!
I stared at the stranger in my mom's car, stared,
stared blankly at that man that had broken in and fainted in the back seat.
I didn't quite know what was happening but I knew I was scared;
that I could be in a lot of danger.
Danger, that word didn't make sense, I couldn't be in danger, that only happened in stories.
Finally the police arrived, they weren't even scared! I was!
As they drove away, it was as if the event was still going on,
It will always go on inside of me!

Brenna K. Bray

Just Can't Wait To See You

I'm bored for you; are you bored for me. Thinking about you each day, cress crossing my railroad tracks located in my brain. Ohhh! I'm so damn bored, wishing you were here to relieve my sorrow. Is it physically or mentally. I have no idea because, the way you make me feel is like a pill, when you take it to relieve your headache, or refreshing you might say when you drink a cool, calm drink, in a way you never drank before because, you are so thirsty. Being around you I must not let down my guard or something like that, but showing you a side of me you never seen. I feel funny because, you're my love and when you express the way you feel to someone you love, it's excellent. Keeping my stamina I clinch on to your every word, whisper by whisper. Length by length, sometimes we argue and then break up the ice all over again, in shattering the disagreement. But like I said I'm so bored. How bored can I get. Eager to talk, eager to walk, eager to show my love and respectfulness to you.

Alfred C. White II

God's Love Vs Fear Of AIDS (etc.)

F orgetting God cares for you -
E ntertaining doubts -
A llowing fear to rule and control you -
R elying on yourself - to get by -

O pened arms that now are closed -
F amily and friends - keeping their distance -

A ccepting the inevitable -
I ncreasing your independence -
D enying that you are solely responsible -
S taying away - from those who care.
   Fear takes over when Satan realizes - that **you've** given up-
   Not God - but you. He'll sneak in and rob you of **any** hopes you may have left.
   FEAR is a four (4) letter word that loses its power whenever you think and remember that **God Loves You** and you are **important** to Him.
   Forget your fear (s) - and cling to the One who died for you. God bless you.

Emily M. Brown   Nov. 6, 1995

Behind The Picture's Glass

I open a window into the past,
dust off the picture and gaze through the glass.
The photograph captured all of my pain,
My eyes swollen red looked down in shame.
I can still hear the little girl cry,
the whole time just wondering why.
Why all the cruelty,
Why the abuse...
Why the brutality and the misuse.
On raging madness I begin to soar.
The picture is hurled onto the floor.
Broken glass shatters;
the wooden frame scatters.
Emotions and tears start to pour,
My body collapses in a fit of horror...
As blood runs free a glimpse is cast.
If the pain is behind me
it's all in my past...
Then how...how do I get out of pain's tight grasp?

Cammie Van Rooy

"Hunger"

   As he sits and watches the sweat forms as big as rain drops on his forehead,
   As he sees the golden brown prairie dog, he starts to walk slowly... slower... stops.
   The cold dew makes his toes cold and his heart jump. As he starts to run his heart throbs with anticipation and roars with incredible hunger, his legs shake and his knees hit together. As he runs his tongue drowns in saliva, as he runs the iciest winds blow across his face.
He pounces and can already taste the blood in his mouth.
When he hits the ground he clamps down and can taste the blood, 5 minutes of gnawing and he opens his eyes and sees know food but only his paw in his mouth and his stomach roars with 'Hunger'!
   As he awakes he relies that it was only the bad dream in his mind.

Jessica R. Patton

Spirit Of Christmas

Christmas trees sparkling tinsel and lights.
Drinking hot toddies on cold winter nights.
Laughter and singing, friends to be found.
Snow slowly falling on wet trodden ground.
Bright wrapping paper, ribbons and bows.
Is there a santa, nobody knows.
Silently, silently, someone comes calling,
   for presents are found on a cold Christmas morning.
The meaning of Christmas - a mother giving birth.
A child who was born, to save us humans on earth.
A time for goodwill and peace to all men,
Until next year, when it's time to start over again.

Helen Capacchione

Hello

As you sit in the cafe.
Drinking coffee and staring
In space the waitress refills
Your cup and you give her a blank look and say
Thank you. She smiles and goes about her way,
With nothing to say.
You sit there with that look
In your eyes,
But you know when someone sits beside you
Puts their arm around you,
Gives you a gentle hug and
Says hello.

Debbie Noe

The Beauty Contest

Black-eyed Susan with her golden hair,
  Dressed up with a certain flair.
Shy violet rose from the forest floor
  And assured herself she could do no more.
Cool Daisy smiled and head held high,
  Thought haughtily, "It has to be I."
Wild rose, with scent so rare, was clad
  in pink, her nose in the air.
The Master looked down on the colorful array
  And observed his work, all done in a day.
He said, "I cannot choose who should win,
  As all are beautiful without or within."
They turned to each other, surprise in their eyes,
  For on this day, they had become wise.

Joyce Hill Holden

Dream's Not, Ash Clay

Wyvern breaths rise from dust life had cometh.
Dream's not, ash clay sundering from one kind.
How's One love without love of that which lives,
Of ye, the mid of heart, but yet had mime
With white paint tempests of perils of drone.
Without thee eternal beckoning brine
That was wellspring and once unwielding throne.
Yes without! Ye in saddest of pine,
O'er busts where melodious chimes had ring.
But earthstar eyes, ears, heaven will wake
To gift of lofty leaf where breasts unseen
And to well the love of life astray.
  But ones of hybris halls will not be seen,
  For they glean not, nor love, a virgin clay.

Jay Robb Jr.

Horizon Over The Hill

There it is, a bright new horizon.
Don't you see it?
It's right there, over the hill, beyond the stars,
Farther than the sun, in the deepest, darkest corners
Of your mind.

It's amazing, it's exciting, it's challenging, and rewarding!
CAN YOU SEE IT? SURE YOU DO! REACH OUT AND GRASP IT!
Now don't let go, don't give it up.
Keep it alive and you'll stay alive.
Make it big, make it huge, make it Awesome!
Then, go for it and stick with it.
Watch the illogical become logical and the unreal become real.
It's mine, it's yours, it's ours for the hoping, the believing,
The taking.
DO YOU SEE IT, NOW?
It's right here in the palm of our hands.
IT'S BEAUTIFUL, ISN'T IT?
GO ON, TAKE IT, I DARE YOU!
I dare you to dream and find your next horizon and MAKE IT REAL!
Go on, I dare you, I DARE YOU!

Jenna Shook

Boredom

The time of feelings lost,
Drifting out in space thinking of something to do,
Wishing there was a person there to talk to.
Sitting by a corner in the dark,
Watching people walk by,
Laughing,
Smiling,
Just having a good time,
And me sitting by a corner, in the dark.

Dawnel Pettingill

Brotherly Love

Sometimes I'm too hard on you and treat you harsher than someone I don't know. At times I'm critical of you and think, how can this be my brother? Sometimes I look at you and see everything I want to be. Sometimes I realize the things in you that I criticize are what I want most for myself. And, at times, just when I think I know you and how you'll react, you change. You grow when I'm not looking and become exactly who I need. I look to you for a love I can't get anywhere else. I go to you because, it seems, you can love and support me no matter what I do or say. Somehow I always make it through, but never alone. Together you and I have taken great steps toward improving and shaping my future. Without you, I would not be me. You are my fiercest competition and my biggest supporter. You're my worst enemy and my best friend. Without you I wouldn't have a reason to try harder or go longer, or reach for the things I need or want most.

Bettianne Flanders

The Circle - Mother And Son

Let me introduce you to the world my son, mine to hold till each day is done.
I am your mother, oh tiny one, a title guarded with love bar none.

Together we'll set the world ablaze as we discover this new and magic maze.
Oh look, a first step I see, it seems but just a few days to me.

I work to nourish the growing man, a job taken with tired hand.
You are my life, my heart, my spirit, my son.
Hello mom! Thank you for caring dusk to dawn.

Wings spread to meet the challenge, I will not flee, you raised me undaunted by life, and full of glee.
Let me take your hand, together we go, weathering smiles and trials, through life we row.
I must rest my son, the time has come.

These arms reach out to carry you on, my guide, my spirit, my heart my mom. I am your son oh precious one, a title guarded with a soul, never done. Carry on my son, my spirit your guide.

Lift her up on angels wings, carry her away with worry of not a thing.
Let her rest, and dream, a heavenly endeavor, until we meet across that bridge to forever. I am your son, I love you mom.

David W. Reid

"My Nanny"

She sits on her rocker, her hands crippled and worn,
Doing her needle point, her face full of forlorn.
She tries to stay busy, to brush off the pain,
Dreading the thought of another operation again.

Each line on her face, has a story to tell,
Her life on this earth, has been a drawn out, living hell.
I can see her dear, sweet face, and her graying white hair,
as she quietly does her needle point, in her favorite rocking chair.

A strong woman once, she's now so weak and brittle.
Wasn't she once bigger? Dear God, she looks so little.
Is this the woman who once bounced me on her knee?
Who mended my clothes, who was always there to take care of me?

She takes to her rocker and sits down with care,
My heart aches to see her having more pain than she can bare.
As long as I can remember, she has had it tough,
Her road traveled in life, always up hill and rough.

She struggles to make it to her bed to sleep,
Thinking of her youth, she lies quietly and weeps.
She prays to the Lord, her soul to keep,
With a sigh of relief, she falls fast asleep.

Debbie Geiger

"Ma Belle"

Tell me about your soul.
Does it tingle when gently caressed by a warm soft heart,
or faintly outlined with the tip of an eyelash?
Would a firm embrace satisfy a "Wyld" desire throughout years of growing,
or would you turn and run when the rivers edge found its way to dampen your sorrows?
Does it scream with passion when I swallow you whole,
or would you push me away when you realized I was getting through your walls of pent frustration and tainted emotions?
Dream the wish of love,
only if your soul aches beyond ultimate repression and true self denial.
Does love make you sad,
knowing you cannot have that which is mystically correct?
Could coincidence be the beam of light
as it passes through the stained-glass wall of destiny?
Would you acknowledge my spiritual existence,
or would you weight me down with judgments from false fears of a previous life?
Should I already know you dreams and have the means to obtain them?
Am I looking directly into your blinding sun, or am I dreaming myself?

Bruce Michael Anthony Hanley

If?

If you are there
do something about your defective invention.
They've given you praise and credit,
this cracked world you've supposedly ignited.

If you are there
open your sleeping eyes; be aware of the chaos.
They've gone mad,
your prized possessions,
They've gone mad.

If you are there
wake up from you, dream world and face the horror.
It's not working,
this huge pinwheel you've started a 'spinning with your white breath,
It's not working.

If you are there
arise your mighty self; let your omnipotent power be known.
If you are there —
If?

Carly Berger

Enlightenment

Possessions, possess me not!
Do not bind me...
Let me go empty handed
When in my turn to go
Up to the Almighty.

Just let me take along
The scent and colors of the flowers
The songs of birds, the smile of children,
The melancholic memories of dusk,
The lights of a sunrise.

The beauty of a clear stream cascading
From a mountain, the colours of October leaves,
The falling of the rain on tin roof.
The shining of the stars on a dark night...
The joy of old friendships...
My love for life, for all mankind.
And please, give me no promises
But those of plowed fields and ripe vineyards!

Emilia Cordova de Sicard

Lightning Ballerina

On a warm midsummer's night, in the far
  distant sky with only silence in the air
A beautiful ballerina of light was dancing,
  in the darkness lighting up the sky
Flashes of lightning streaking across the
  midnight sky with all of such beauty
As the ballerina dances across the night sky,
  revealing the hidden shapes of dark clouds
  moving so slowly with silence and ease
The ballerina continued on with her dancing,
  showing strength yet softness, beauty and
  grace with each of the flashing movements
  of lightning speed among the hidden clouds
Silently and patiently the moon awaits in the
  wings for the beautiful lightning ballerina to
  gracefully come to a end of her performance
  in the sky...

George J. E. Borovicka Jr.

Vernissage

Cold ceramic faces and wet clammy hands, dissecting.

Butterflies fluttering slick wings, fresh from chrysalids, newly hatched in your stomach.

Issuances of sweat from your over-heating body, cooled by refrigerated classification cabinet eyes.

The distinct smell of moth balls and formaldehyde surround a silk clothed desiccated smile presented on a stone dias.

Bubbles are carried to the surface of the champagne on conveyor belts, while thin fragile hands clutch the crystal.

The bottles hiss and the butterflies quiver, thoraxes gently rubbing against the inner walls.

James S. Bouchie

Can I Learn To See Life Your Way?

Do I see what you see, or do my eyes project a whole different picture.
Do you see what I see, or does our vision differ.
Is this dead world full of life to you.
Can you not taste the bitterness of death.
Do you not gasped for every dying breath.
Can I live in your world of dreams, for my reality is a nightmare.
Do hopes die in your world, do people care.
Do you ever reach the top, here you just die trying.
Can I be whole again without society picking me apart.
We must not see he same, my world has no heart.
Can I learn to see life your way?

Alexander Garcia

The Epic Of The Butterfly

Butterfly winging freely on high
Floating, dancing against the sky.
Butterfly jewelry enhancing a dress,
Creating an image of more from less.
Butterfly decorating a wall where it lies,
Butterfly captured, immortalized
By one who failed to warn us, to tell
Her hands were nevermore to cast their spell.
These same hands too suddenly in stillness lay,
As the warm flesh cooled, so did the light of day.
Therein lies the answer, the reasoning, the why
Of the depth of my love for the fragile butterfly.

Beverly A. Miles

Wide Eyes

Peeping through those big wide eyes
Did you know you hold the key to life inside
Our ancestors had their time and space
Now it's your turn to take their place

Crystal ball of our future is in your hands
God gave us a gift to share with every man
Bold yourself with challenges that have not been met
Let the world know they ain't seen nothing yet

Good and bad lie in wait
Choose one and it shall be your fate
Love God with all your heart
You will have no problem doing your part

Let wisdom and knowledge guide you through life
You'll embrace life's opportunities with all your might
So, wide eyes, help us understand what you see in this land
That brotherhood and love can be shared by every man

April Robinson Yokley

Who Is God?

Who is God is a question often asked?
Did He make this universe and make it to last?
Who is this God who made the stars, moon and earth?
He who gave man and woman their birth?

Who is this God who gave mankind all,
Then stood and watched as they took their fall?
Who is this God who set His people free?
Is He the God that loves you and me?

Yes! He is! He is my God, my Creator, my Father!
He is to me my lifelong partner!
He is my hope, my life, my all!
He listens to me and answers when I call.

His praises forever we must always sing,
For up to heaven His faithful He will bring.
So all of you of little belief or faith,
Please get to know God, before it's too late.

Joyce Hebert

Field-Stone Wall

Picture a man behind the plow,
Determined face, sweat drenched brow,
Followed by sons big and small,
Carrying rocks to the field-stone wall.

Structural squares on checkered fields,
Gray shale products of ancient harvest yields,
Obstacles, hindrances to settlers new,
From rock strewn forest, fertile farmland grew.

Feel the stones with your out-stretched hand,
Locked in place by a colonial man,
Symbols, monuments of determined toil,
Man's continual battle with stubborn soil.

The men are gone and trees did grow,
But the field-stone walls in silent rows,
Continue to stand and fight to remain,
Withstanding the passing of time, snow and rain.

Frank G. Vurture

Untitled

Her words fell like angels breath
Familiar, comforting, like soft voices that call you home soon after
death all calming, soothing, steadies me when I'm weak
such is the beauty of her nature, the euphoric rush when angels speak.

George Orange

DISCOVER YOUR GIFT

Let not past conditioning nor programming
    deter your own sense of what your Creator
    has freely given you
Do not abandon your dreams because of
    opinions of others, or an overly logical
    mind
The gift is there, whether expressed fully now,
    or still lies dormant
Listen to the quietness of your soul, for
    there in lies a quest, and great hopes for
    everyone to seek, experience, and
    eventually find

Ann Blakely Rice

Virtues

VIRTUE, savored like a fine tasting wine,
demanding chastity, delightfully divine.

HONESTY, and PRUDENCE, rather a boring sort,
though needed for nature's sport.

CHARITY, a true test to mankind,
revealing ones soul and spiritual mind.

JUSTICE, reality playing with fear,
retribution sought by those far and near.

HOPE, a true seeker for peace and love,
an offering from above.

FAITH, a glorious solution, a reprieve,
if one has the courage to believe.

TEMPERANCE, self restraint learned as a child,
enhanced, but not always so mild.

These are some VIRTUES needed by one and all,
to make us strong, proud, and tall.

Anita G. Scott

Lost Days

Somewhere in my head memories linger of days once lived
days of happiness and comfort lost
oh what I would give
just to see the light of one moment glisten in my eye
instead a mist of darkness erases my thoughts
and only a damp street corner listens to my cry
a cry for the way things were so long in the past
Thanksgiving dinners and a Christmas tree on Christmas Eve
But all those things drift behind me in a cold windy draft
can my old friends imagine me here today
I don't know
do they even remember me
oh so long ago
now I am alone living on a street
with only lingering memories of the way things used to be

Jessica Latterman

The Gift Of Friendship

The package may be large, or the package may be small
But the contents within, will bring happiness to all.
It need not be gaily wrapped, or with ribbon in bright array
To hold the gift of friendship, we all need each day.
Such a simple gift to give,
With value of the greatest wealth.
Remember when you make a friend—
It's a gift you give yourself.

Jean Linenberger

Ballet Of Leaves

Hues of reds, yellows, browns and gold,
dancing in the breeze on the deep green lawn.
In unison they twist and flutter, flashing their colors proudly.
Pivoting on stems, seemingly anchored to the ground.
The sun reflects from the gilded tips,
like fingers reaching r-e-a-c-h-i-n-g for the wind,
to carry them off center stage.
While others lie silently still,
waiting for their cue, to add their contribution to the performance.
The wind sings and whistles musically,
through, and around the Mother Tree.
Bending with the wind,
she directs her prodigies with her baton-like branches.
Another year nears it's end,
as Mother Nature in all her brilliance, renders her;
Ballet of leaves.

Janet A. Margetta

A Silenced Pain

Mommy, Mommy, what have I done, I just wanted to show you
  love and fun.
Daddy, Daddy, why are you so mean, I just want to grow like you,
  strong, smart and lean.
I did not mean to make you mad, I did not mean to be so bad.
Mommy, Daddy, look into my eyes, my soul is pure and for both I
  idolize.
Mommy, Daddy I gave you my trust, I have no figure, no bottom or bust.
I take the hellish blows, the pain, the sorrow,
Because I hope to win both your love...hopefully tomorrow.
I did not mean to learn so slow, out of love.
  I take your punishable blow.
Mommy, daddy, why did you lie; you gave me life, then you let me die
And now you're sorry, confused, and now you sigh; well it's too late
  to even cry.
There is no way to change the past, just live your lives,
  feeling suffocation as though your body is in a full body cast.
As my spirit floats away, finally feeling no pain, I see my body lay,
As I rise to a heavenly place I shall stay.
May my story be heard, let the other children hear my words,
Don't be afraid...be bold, have faith in your God to give you a
  protective hold.
Don't let my life or story go in vain,
  don't be like me or grow up insane.
Please don't live a silenced pain.....

George Michael Villega

Denial

What I've just been told, isn't true.
For, "see you later", I just heard from you.

So much to live on for, you're still young.
Why would you be gone? Your life has just begun.

My head is spinning, so dizzy I feel.
Why would they tell me this, if it's not real?

You are my love and my life, my best friend.
We promised to be there for each other, until the very end.

Laughs and loves, and secrets we've shared,
Each other's troubles we've always beared.

Tomorrow I'll see you I know I will,
You can't be gone, I need you still.

How lost I'd be, if this lie was true,
A cold and lonely world it would be without you.

Everyone's crying, can't they see?
There's been a mistake, it just can't be.

"I'll see you later" is what you said.
Therefore, my heart says you can't be dead.

Emily Gentry

Snail

Crawl slowly heroic little snail a life of one;
Created by the image of God flowing from his trail.
Knowing one and knowing best, who dare's to challenge me?

Yet battered and beaten by the rain,
Floods of tears from those that lost.
Where does the Sun go hiding behind the big tree?

Sun, you are strong, you are bigger,
But gone!
But why all this, the torture from you, leave us be.

Hunters of the shadow are rising,
SMASH!
Another one gone, Another one missing.

Where did he go I ask?
Answer! Answer!
The hunter was bred to kill, not to care.

Slowly but surely he makes his mark,
On the cold and dying concrete.

Hoping someone will follow his trail,
Weird, winding,
Wiped away by a giant flood.

Brian Edward Maulhardt

Quiescence

I have been wanting silence lately
Cool breathy sounds almost somber so smooth
Drawing me out of myself floating through every window
Natural sounds if there are such things
Simple sounds Wind Water
Orchestrated rumblings and crashes only
Mingled with the silence in light
A shaded sun a down turned light
Or candles old and dusty with their shadowy warmth
And silence in people
Talktv tvtalk talkshows toughtalk talkradio sales talks
It's not that interesting but it's the only way we talk to each other
Of course I just want it all turned down
Grab the big central volume knob
Just jump right up and give that knob a good spin to counterclockwise
Because it's silence all around and within I want
Just to walk down the night time street
With all the tones joining one another mixing like all the colours making black
So that I can hear only the nothing without
And I can discover that I too am silence

David Kennedy

To David

I have waited and prayed for so very long
for the day a true love would appear
And when all in my life was so desperately wrong
I awakened to find you here.

I knew you were coming but didn't know when
in my faith there is no doubt
My spirits been willing, my hearts been open
surely love's what it's all about.

Love is life, life is love, it's a journey to share
with another who knows your soul
It's a bonding of spirits of people who care
two as one to become a whole.

Are we blessed, you and I, with this oneness?
Is our love truly heaven sent?
God made you, He made me, was He done yet
or is "us" what he really meant?

Cindy Hulstine

Tiny Rose Buds

Heaven's a resplendent garden mere mortals can't conceive,
containing sights that we'd have to see first to believe.

Some down here were daisies, filled with cheerful joy.
Others were patient orchids, hard works they did employ.

Some were bright as sunflowers, standing straight and tall.
Their brave seeds of faithfulness were planted in us all.

But the purest hearts who came here, could not stay to grow.
The hidden mysteries of why this is, we may never know.

Until the light of knowledge imparts the reason to our soul,
we endure this awful pain and loss, never feeling whole.

These precious little ones, who left us grieving all to soon,
are now cradled in an angel's arms, kept in perfect bloom.

Tiny Rose buds left unfolded with thorns that never formed,
tender eyes unopened, witness no sin, no shame, no scorn.

These chosen few have not one inkling of the earthly trials we meet.
For they were gathered back to sit 'round our beloved savior's feet.

They face no toil or strife, have no heavy cross to bear.
Basking in God's presence, awaiting us to join them there.

We have to trust our dear Lord loved those tiny rose buds so,
he's keeping them in his own garden to these and grow.

Jinx Kinneer

Theme From The 605

Once again I'm here sitting, the same sounds are pounding.
Consumed in my nothingness, admittedly drowning.
As colors change constantly, used forms are everywhere,
yet none seem to interrupt my unseeing stare.

The door squeaks now open, and in strolls blind Marty
singing "I'm Looking Over" completing our party.
It's Bake in his bill cap shouting loud and with force
and tone deaf old "Red" on piano of course.
On the floor dreaming tangos are Mac and Sal at their best,
she in her rummaged shoes, he in his vest.
There hugging his corner is catatonic Cal,
in his glass is his only and very best pal.
His body unmoving, his forearms tattooed,
he hums in soft consonance his own interlude.

It's a night in the life of the 605
and things are as they should be
the once-men are hung in their places with style
thus spicing our strange fricassee.

James R. Cravens

Memories

My most cherished possessions are memories
For memories are the keepers and images of the soul.
They arouse and awaken the feeling world —
    unfolding the patterns that shape our lives.

Memories persuade me to realize...
    that there really are no goodbyes.
For it is through memories,
    that we come to understand the paths simply cross and
    sometimes shift into separate directions,
Leaving us with memories that provide us comfort when we
    stand alone.

Memories soothe our weariness and fill the void of loneliness.
They pay homage to our past, nourish the essence of our being
    and reshape of bring healing to our sorrows.

Dara Willett

Hold Back The Darkness

Hold back the darkness, deny not the light
Conceal all your cares away out of sight.

Listen to the melody the rustling leaves bring
Watch the sun glisten on bells as they ring.

See flowers blossom and brown turf turn green
Laugh at wee creatures jumping sun-beams.

Examine each leaf, each pebble, each flower's shape,
Observe the miracle of their colors and scape.

Make kindness your aim without reservation,
Forgive those that wronged you without limitation.

When the rain falls, and light's hidden from view,
Let your heart cleanse, let good thoughts accrue.

Spread your arms wide, raise your head high,
Let peace surround you, bid sadness good-bye.

Hold back the darkness, deny not the light
Rejoice as the sun and you reunite.

Dixie R. Krueger

Husband And Wife

Close your eyes and hold me tight
Comfort me throughout the night,
Relax your body quench our heat
Let's take our hearts and make one beat.
Touch my lips caress my face
Hold my soul with your warm embrace,
Whisper softly in my ear
Shelter me from all my fear.
Take my hand you lead our way
We'll take it slow day by day,
And with our love we'll build a life
We'll be committed husband and wife.
We'll work together as our children grow
We'll in store the values that we both do know,
And when our hair turns the color gray
The words I love you we still shall say,
And than at last our resting place
Side by side until God we shall face.
And he'll look proudly on us two
For keeping our love so honest and true.

Elizabeth Hatfield

Tingles And Warms And Wooly-Bear Charms

Tingles sneak in from over and under
Cling to arms and legs when they are at slumber
Appear from thin air, from sinks, and from drains
With ants beneath rocks they emerge when it rains

Warms arise to be spiteful to frost
In bowls of apple crisp and blankets so soft
After-bath robes, a loved one's deep kiss
Around our icy heads their steamy hands wisp

Thawing cheeks are tingle nests
Laughter and mysteries and under-door drafts
Symphonies, scary tales, and climax of song
Ghosts and scripture and memories thought gone

Warm is a nectar, bless thine cup be full
Through water and skin, through heartbeat and wool
In bitter black coffee spiked with sweet Irish Creme
To be wrapped in the things and people we dream

They tickle the spine, give aid to the soul
Tend flames of the heart and shelter from cold
We receive them in life, each in our turns
Through tingles and warms and wooly-bear charms

Carl Knickerbocker

The Crow

Beautiful black shiny creature, you are a survivor
City dweller, you know the world's ways, but
you make up your own rules and lead a simple,
peaceful life.
Highly intelligent as you are, you could outsmart
even the most brilliant of animals.
The king of the beasts has nothing on you.
Far from the most ignorant of animals you
will never become an endangered species.
And it wouldn't surprise me that
at the world's end,
You, the crow, will be left standing,
like an omen of the impending
doom of mankind
Watching the end and laughing at
our ignorance from some perched elevation,
like some dark angel or sentinel,
knowing that you with your wisdom
could have taught us how to live.

Debbie Steen

What I See

What do I see? I'll tell you what I see
Children, so many children around me
Depressed, unhappy always glassy eyed
Seeking constantly whatever makes them high
Many intelligent lives wasting away on dope
So readily available there doesn't seem much hope
They could be happy but they're always stoned
They can't leave this awful demon alone
Why can't they see what I see?
Come back children and face reality
The parents who love you have given you life
Are willing to help, willing to fight
Because they too see what I see
And they want you back so desperately
Stop what you're doing, take a look around
Then help your friend up off the ground
Life is very precious, don't waste it away
Look and see what I see, give up drugs today!

Dorothy Beagin

Movement Of Air
(The Bombing Of Oklahoma City 4-19-95)

Lives torn apart, hearts shattered.
Children left without parents.
Parents left without precious children.
Pain and suffering discharged without remorse.
Firefighters searching in the ruins leaving a scrap
of themselves with each step.
A nation raped and validation cannot be found.
A nation in agony grieving, together.
A moment where time stopped then chaos supervened.
Now we try to make sense out of nonsense.
Our hands too fragile to hold, our hearts too fragile to mend.
Our minds without understanding.
We grieve.
We hope for a future where terrorism
isn't found in the name of God.
When the rubble is cleared and each
daughter and son is found,
silence will hit our state - our nation.
Nothing can replace what was lost and our
healing will never be complete.

Donna Parks Tomlinson

Nostalgia

I always remember the moments that we had together when we
were children.

When we use to run through the woods playing and singing
together with lots of smiles.

You were always there for me, to defend me, to help me, from
everybody and everything.

But while we grew up and the responsibilities came for each
one of us.

We started to draw away slowly.

Until the day came that you drew away from me completely.

I will never forget the day when you boarded the ship to go.

My heart broke in pieces when we said goodbye at the entrance door.

When I got home I turned off the lights and just cried and cried
the days turned into weeks.

While time past, I waited for your letters that came regularly.

But was not the same like when I had you beside me.

Gloriela E. Devorak

"Feelings You Deny"

Let me look into your eyes.
'Cause they won't tell me no lies,
It's the feelings you deny,
That they won't let you hide.
Now I'm not trying to bring pain in your life.
'Cause I know he's been good to you and made you his wife.
But was that loneliness kissing me last night?
Or what you really feel deep down inside.
So I met you yesterday.
And I held you tonight.
Be my friend always.
Be my love for life.
And with our passion that burns so brightly,
Will it only get stronger with time!
And if you ever were to leave him.
Forever my lady be mine.
And I met you yesterday
Will I hold you tonight?
Will you be my friend always?
Will you be my love for life?

Brian K. Wedding

The Fairies Of Spring

The fairies of Spring have been at work,
For now a month and a day,
And it is wonderful what they have done.
Making the wide country gay!
They've roused the daisies and buttercups,
The lilies, bluebells, and phlox,
They've redressed the drooping fern,
That grows in the dampish rocks,
They've called the butterflies and bees,
The spiders, worms and ants,
Every creatures that hastens the growth,
Of the lowliest or loftiest plants,
They've sent messengers for the birds,
Who make their nests round here,
Oh, pretty is the sight of our feathered friends
But sweeter their song to the ear.
Yes the fairies of Spring have been at work
And grateful we are to them,
They've renewed our hopes, refreshed our faith,
And gladdened our hearts again.

Ann R. Mills-Price

Loneliness

Loneliness feels like you are all alone, without someone to love and
  care for you.
Loneliness is the feeling of emptiness, when you are use to feeling
  full with love.
Loneliness is the sorrow of a loved one's death, knowing they are gone
  forever and you will never feel the warmth from within them again.
Loneliness hurts when it's all locked up inside, with no one to
  release your pains or joys and hopes or dreams with.
Loneliness belongs to the child whom doesn't know his family. He's
  all alone in the world, all by himself, with no one to discuss how
  his day went. No brothers or sisters to teach him the ways of life.
Loneliness looks like a fearful, dark, cold, bitter place, where no
  life exists. The lonely side is so fearful that a lot of people
  would rather die than be in that lonely state of mind. They would
  much rather be just across the mirror on the happy side where
  it is full of life, cheerfulness, and many wonderful colors.
  I know I would rather be there.
Loneliness makes no noise, everything is very still. There are no
  traces of life. No human voices, no animal talk, nothing, not even
  a whisper of a gentle breeze. Occasionally you will hear a voice,
  your voice, screaming out "HELLO" as it echoes on forever.
The sad
  part is there is never a reply. That is when you finally realize
  you are all alone.
Alone is a very feared word. It is the feeling that no one loves you,
  cares for you, or accepts you. Loneliness can sometimes fall into
  depression. I know I would rather be dead than alone, here.
See, death would mean that I could finally be with all my friends
  and family that have left me behind to be alone.
I would finally be loved and wanted again.

Amye Lauth

Tye Dyed

There is a heaviness to the very air
Cannot get a grip on reality, not clear
The very air is so foggy - so dense
A great weight sets upon the eyes - the being
Feel like a tye dyed shirt, crunched and banded.

Heat sears the soul - paints the eyes. The body bloats, get so heavy -
bulky try to lift, to sit up - so difficult why try? What is the
purpose to rise? Feel like a tye dyed scarf, bunched and banded.

Try to grip a table aide to rise arms hurt, hand screams, finger
snaps. Cannot grip, finger, oh the pain, to the roots. Pain flows
like water, finger to spine. Feel like a tye dyed belt, lunched and banded.

Ride the current of the pain; try to think. Is it physical?
Maybe that and emotional? Does one pain go more than one way?
Can it be like a web from the center - out?
Feel like a tye dyed soul, lynched and branded.

It is all a game, a play on words and feelings. See how pretty the
pattern of the pain; the light. See the colors as they weave their
magic in and out. Light equals color which equals shades of pain.
Feel like a tye dyed spirit, pinched and expanded.

Donna J. Miele

Someday

I live in a place of beauty, where everything tastes sweet
Children laugh and play, carelessly in the streets.
You listen to your parents, say prayers at supper time
Politicians aren't corrupt, ten cents is worth a dime.
Everybody gets along, regardless of their race
No one talks behind your back, or slaps you in the face.
Drugs are not a problem, gangs do not exist
Guns are used for hunting, violence is off the list.
No one's over worked, or even underpaid
Unemployment lines are gone, equality is made.
If you like this place, come with me tonight
You to can have a piece of the dreams I have in sight.

Elijah M. Poulos

Knowledge

In the dark caverns of her mind, the clock creeps as the
candle flickers with foreboding doom.
Although she mules thru page after page with painstaking
care, the application of reality weighs like a sunken
treasure chest hidden between her ribs. At intervals
she inhales sharply with confusion.
Her dreams protrude catch her daylight, and they
are always the same. Just one strand short of the woven
vest she retreats as it is pulled, unravelling to everyone's disdain.
She tries frantically to go grasp a corner of the threadbare
fragment but it slips thru her fingers to the wooden
floor which groans as she genuflects.
Alone tear escapes and she dashes it with a
wave of curl as she turns toward the table.
The shadows recede as the clock creeps and the
candle flickers with her uncertainty. She turns
back to the book.

Donna Sullivan

Fate

Fate, fate; art thou really true?
Can I believe all they say of you?
Do you really sit and watch and wait,
knowing what will happen, the hour and date?
Or can I, a mere creature be,
control you, instead of you me?
If you really exist, then why should I groan
and work my fingers down to the bone?
For I could but sit and let you decide
a problem or two, the way of the tide
For if something's to be, then let it be,
cause it wouldn't help to have efforts from me.

But he question of your truth
is still one to be proved.
And only when proved can my problems you soothe.
So until you've been checked, your values to me told,
you'll sit side by side with my own self control.

Henry William Young

Infestation

In the mirror, it is apparent, no amount of make-up
Can hide the hate on the face of my twin — ugly as the grill of a
  cockroach.
All he ever saw when he looked at me was a frail body,
Useful only for his primitive satisfaction.
Yet, the whetted steel needs little weight behind it.
Given life by the heart's joyful black parasite
It rips, rends, and rives the redness out,
Feeding on the writhing, the squirming, and the surprise.
I can no longer look forward to a warm bed,
But hide under the cold black covers of my mind...

Erek L. Barron

I Wade

I wade upon a lake of passion.
Calm at times, often stormy.
So powerful is the undercurrent;
That which no one sees but can feel when they are close.
One may realize, yet never put their finger upon.

Appearing like a warm spring day;
While ice and fire fight for control.
I am misunderstood many times.
Struggling through the woods I have found a forest.

Wade on?
I Will.

Edward F. Fissinger

Hang Up And Die

"Not a hospital emergency madam; you will have to leave,
Call your primary care physician at your local H.I.P."
Former Mayor Koch now shills for H.I.P.
Seems he sold his soul for a fat piece of cheese.
Consulting firms and insurance companies write all the rules;
And not being doctors, they are simply money making ghouls.

Most H.M.Os. respond by phone on robotic sounding tapes,
Give your butts to God folks, for it could be too late.
A live response asks for I.D. numbers "before" you get any help,
And if you are dying you may surely go to hell.
Thanks to our Congress, the new merchants of death,
They will solve our economic woes and to hell with all the rest.

Anthony Torres

My Love

　Come soar with me to the sky, so we can see more
butterflies.
　Look through the clouds and see the trees, feel the
wind whisper through the leaves.
　Sit with me on a mountain high, take my hand so we can fly.
　Along with the eagles in the sky, isn't it grand to be
alive.
　Sit with me beside a brook, we will ponder the mysteries
just you and I.
　I will tell you all the things I have locked inside, if you
promise me you'll learn to fly.
　Unlock your heart, let love in, for you may never get a
chance again.
　Take my hand, let's walk through a stream, tomorrow this may
all be a dream.
　The angels are singing, they're playing their harps, for
only one man who holds my heart.
　Treat is gentle, don't let it drop, remember your standing
on the mountain top.

Ethel Bartlett

I Wish

　I wish I can hear your voice
but you're too distant for me to hear
　I wish I can share your laughter
but your laughter is too far for me to share
　I wish you were here to hear my stories
but my stories will only trail away in the wispy air
　I wish I can see you smile even for only a moment
but I can only see you in my memory
　I wish you were near enough to comfort my fears
but it's only my heartbeats that I hear in the dark
　I wish I can hold you to calm myself in a storm
but rather the storm is what I touch
　I wish I can be near and snuggle close to you
so your warmth will tale out my weariness
but you're gone too far for me to feel
　Yet I will continue hoping that someday
all my wishes come true even if I wait for a lifetime
　For you made me realize who I am
and gave me understanding of the little thing called love.

Annie Dela Cruz

Reach For Dreams

Our hopes and desires lie far away, far up high.
Every star in the sky is a dream from you and I.
Those who reach will touch their stars.
If you have many dreams you have many stars to reach.
Once you touch your star and your dream is reached
the feeling of succeeding is complete.

Hilary Nat

O.J.

Is washing blood from your hands as hard as they say
But you're innocent aren't you O.J.
They screamed and they cried before they died
But that was O.K. O.J.

Black gloves and knife would end a life
The end you knew would come soon
You didn't wait long to end their song
On the night of the 12th of June

The trial flowed like syrup too old
The judgment was bought for cash
The Doctors and experts had their stories told
And nothing came out of the trash

The lawyers harangue even glove salesman sang
The media had such a time
People grew warts and stopped watching sports
And then even I made this rhyme

The versus could flow as older I grow
But who wants to hear all this stuff
The lawyers were paid and justice was stayed
And we've all heard just 'bout enough

Bradley A. Arnold

Our Mom And Dad

I was asked to write poem just for you,
But words were hard to find to describe a mom and dad like you.
In what order do you put the words to say how we feel,
Because they don't always come out like we want them to.
Is it to much, or is it to little?
These are the questions I've asked myself,
And what I came up with seemed so inadequate.
For you have always been there for us,
Loving, caring, kind and so strong.
You've always given us a helping hand along the way,
Whether it was advice or just a shoulder to lean on.
Your arms have always been a warm place to be,
Your hearts and home open as a haven from the world.
Thanks for never giving up on us,
For all your prayers, love and laughter,
For you are the best,
But most of all we love you and are very proud to call you our
mom and dad.

Carol Fox

"The Eye Of The Storm"

From the very first, things were simple,
but very hard. Everything and everyone
worked hand in hand as a team.

Although times were tough, it was through
these times everyone pulled together.
Unfortunately, through time there was a storm
brewing. It came so slowly that hardly anyone
became aware.

Now, from the cause of the commotion slowly developing
through the years, has come into being... the eye of the storm.
No more is the pulling together through tough times
hardly ever seen; the unity of people working hand
in hand as a team.

What you see now is technology so high, simplicity
almost lost. People evolved around themselves and
making judgement upon others.
The cause, the reason...
The eye of the storm.

Joyce Herrin Boutwell

Families

What's happened to families? I really don't know;
But they are so different from long time ago.

Fathers, mothers, and children too;
Seemed to have had a lot of together things to do.

Churches, picnics, and rides through the park;
Now all of these things are left in the dark.

Movies, carnivals, even the zoo;
These are the things that they used to do.

Family dinners with everyone around;
Not one would be late and let the others down.

But families now are all out of place;
It seems to be such a disgrace.

Everybody's going here and there;
Without each other and don't even care.

What's happened to families? I don't understand;
How did they let it get out of hand?

What I believe and is in my heart;
These families will have to make a new start.

They've got to get like peas in a pod;
And give themselves back to GOD.
Cecelia E. Washington

Mother

They say the ones you admire the most will let you down,
But there is one that will always be around.

The one that will love you more than any other,
This is the one, the one who is called your mother.

My mother is there when I am depressed,
No matter how hard I try, she will always be impressed.

The hardest times of my life, she stood there by my side,
With tears, she always had her arms held, opened wide.

You are very special and dear to me,
As my mother, you will always be.

As mother and daughter we have a bond that will always last,
We will keep it strong just like it was in the past.

If I was to start my life again,
I would want you from the beginning to the end.

And as my mother, I love you so much,
I'll love and cherish, your tender touch.
Connie O'Neil

Autumn's Song

The orange, flaming sun beams down, piercing through the trees
Causing the bountiful leaves to shine and gleam
An array of colors...brown, orange, yellow, but seldom green
Flowing down towards the earth like a rainbow colored stream

The leaves blow gently in the wind, landing sweetly at my feet
Recognizing when nature stops to lend a hand
Taking in the fresh air, allowing the season to be complete
Only now, fully understanding what our Creator had planned

Thinking of the time when the harvest is truly plentiful
Friends come to carve pumpkins, and thankfulness is strong
When earths scenery blooms, becoming more than just beautiful
That's when all of creation gathers to sing autumn's song
Jeni Berdecia

The Looking Glass

It's nice to have friends who you care for and talk to.
But take your own time and see what you find.

Search your soul and do it completely,
and your heart will set apart those feelings down deeply.

So here is a LOOKING GLASS for you to peer in.
Take a deep look, a deep look within.

Will it be FRIENDSHIP or PASSION or LOVE that you'll see.
If you're honest with yourself it may be all three.

FRIENDSHIP is joking laughing and talking,
telling a secret as you hold hands walking.

PASSION is like a raging wave, it comes in, hits you, and takes you away
it's hard to distinguish between Passion and Love,
'cause as the wave of Passion takes you away,
it will be Friendship and Love that will make you stay.

LOVE is not a fireworks display,
but it can explode with the joy you give one another each passing day.
The look in your eyes or the smile on your face,
can say so much more than words can replace.

So gaze into that LOOKING GLASS and see what you feel
they're your FEELINGS inside and they're totally real.
Christine E. Balletto

A Woman and a Man

I fell in love with you to stay
But some how we got lost along the way.
Let us find each other darling if we can.
Here's the story of a woman and a man.

Through the years some others came along
And taught our hearts to sing a different song
But it was really you the lyrics always ran
That's the story of a woman and a man.

Time and time again I remember when
The world was meant for only you and me
Songs were sweeter then, days completer then
Darling come back to me.

Let's pick up the pieces where they fell
Cause oh my darling, this I know so well,
We have loved each other since our lives began
That's our story. I'm your woman you're my man.
Dorothy Rae

You Just Wait

When I grow old, I'll drive 2 mph on the freeway,
but people won't care, since I'm old they'll give me leeway.
I'll wear bathing suits in the wintertime,
but because I'm old that'll be just fine.

I'll pull my socks up over my pants,
and will get much pleasure from farming ants.
I'll wear floppy hats with big silk flowers
and go out roaming the streets til unthinkable hours.
In my house, I'll keep 35 cats,
and chase relatives around with baseball bats.
People may think I'm not perfectly sane,
and they're probably right.
Emmye Mosley

Time

Sometimes we need a break,
   but not for long.
Time to stop.
Time to take notice.
Time to listen and understand.
Time to put it all together.
Just time to make it right.
And then in the end there is nothing but time to share.
Time together
  Smiling
   Laughing
   Playing
    and Enjoying each other.
Just Time -
Well spent before the end.
Two hearts as one
    Sharing and Caring, Honest and True
     need the time
Just time..... time..... time.

Barbarette Williams

Helen

Reality hits harder than any fist I've known
But my tears stay hidden...to no one else they're shown
A part of me has died inside but I don't know what to feel
Oh, God please reassure me that this isn't real
Wake me from this nightmare...it hurts too much to care
give me back my apathy because life is so unfair
I close my eyes to loose the pain but it won't go away
It sits in the dark corners of my mind calling me...
but I don't want to play.
It teases me intently and seems to know my weakness
and knowing me the best of all...it works on my uniqueness.
I cannot make much more sense of this
my mind is slipping fast
Oh well at least now I know that she is free from pain at last.

Jessica Lynn Day

Heavens Gates

Twenty years ago is crystal clear,
but my last thoughts fade like a shooting star,
my friends no longer worry about their problems,
I wish that I could sleep along side of them.

My legs are crippled and my back's hunched,
I walk with wheels today,
I struggle for every breath,
my life flows from a tank I carry with me.

All the nutrients I need flow into me through a needle,
my hair is gone, and the teeth I have are not my own,
I tell you that I'm not young anymore,
I wish to follow my friends.

Yesterday I saw my wife,
she has been gone ten years now,
we were together for over 50,
she told me to hold on as long as I can,
but I am ready to knock on heavens gates.

Chris Rouleau

The Mystery Behind Our Existence

We didn't ask for it,
But it's why we are all here.
We wonder what it holds,
Yet even if we had the chance, most of us would decline.
We complain about it,
And we still pray that God will let us keep it.
We try to rush it,
Just to find ourselves trying to slow it down later.
We risk it,
While all the rest of the time we try to keep it safe.
We try to rule it for others.
But at the same time we fight for self-rule of ours.
We want to make it worth while,
Knowing this is the only chance we will get.
We wonder what it would be like if it was over,
Only to find out then how precious it really is.
We take it for granted,
Forgetting how easy it can be snatched away by others.
It is LIFE...
Our chance to make the world great.

Joshua Herndon

Interior Truth

I see a reflection,
  but it is not me.

I see a girl with a smile on her face,
  a girl who is not herself.

I see in her eyes pain that won't go.
I see a girl who wants to change.

I see how she feels as she walks down the street.
I see how she is by the music she plays.

I see what she is thinking when she confesses to herself.
I see a girl who has wisdom in her years.

I see a reflection,
  but for the first time it is me.

Janet Hrehowesik

"Your Son Is Grown"

You have your new family, so far away,
But I think of you most every day.
For most of my life you've been gone,
Do you realize dad, your son is grown?
There's a void in my life made by you
Memories of a father are so few.
With no second chance to relive my childhood
I wish you'd been there like you should
To throw me a ball, to shake my hand
And give me advice on becoming a man.
You choose to put the miles between us
I guess you figured I would adjust.
But dad you've missed out on a lot too
The day to day things not shared by you
Yes I've become a man, but not overnight
It's been an uphill battle, a long hard fight.
I'll always love you within my heart
Tho most of my life we've been apart
Dad please remember the next time you phone
I have become a man, your little boy is grown!

Faye Thomas

"Scattered Dreams"

I paint a picture of what I'd like to be
but I know simply that, that could never be me
woman of few words spoken out loud
I look through a fantasy overlooking a cloud
my dreams are fading in my head
some would say they might as well be dead
Through dreams untold and hardships unnumbered
My scattered dreams have broken to crumbles
Some days I feel like I can make it
Other days I feel why even fake it
Evil is surrounding my weaken mind
What is this dream I'm hoping to find?
Each day I sit and wait to see
What simply is to become of me?

Caronda Parker

Wonderful Friend

This life for me will soon come to an end.
But I don't mind, I have a wonderful friend.
He guides me along each step of the way,
He is my strength from day to day.
Before I knew Him, he watched over me,
To guide me along, O'er land and sea.
But how my life changed when I met him that day.
His name is Jesus; He is the way.

Ida Gordon

Beyond

To the memory of Shirley White 4/13/44 - 10/24/94
There is always sadness at the end of time
  but happiness will come as her spirit flies,
Up and up, away she will go
  to heavens light as peaceful as snow.
He'll comfort her and treat her
  like the child she is inside,
No longer will she need to fear
  or pain will she have to hide.
Her wings carry her gracefully through
  the endless beauty of heaven so true,
Happy again to be free and loved
  with all her family below,
  and the Lord and her above.

Angela Kelly

Answers

The things in my life many times I sat and pondered.
But from these paths, I often found I wandered.
The many hours wasted making wishes into dreams,
And when morning came, nothing was as it seemed.
I tried and tried with all my might,
Unto the end when I gave up the fight.
Alas, I lack the strength in me,
The answers to my quest to be what I want to be.
Until the time came and the answer I was to find.
Was right there before me, how could I be so blind?
With a gentle grasp, I took up the key,
Unlocking the door for everyone to see.
For with God's help, the day will soon come,
When my dreams become real and my work is done.

Colleen Kaye Lockrem

I Love You Not

I love you not for what you are,
But for what you are to me.
For loving, trust and faithfulness,
You've helped my heart to see.
For all the joys and happiness,
The precious hours we've shared.
I love you not for being proud of worthwhile things I do.
But more because it means so much to hear it come from you.
I love you.

Ida Gregory

Shoo Fly

I have a memory of a rainy day
But every time I think of you it seems to go away
Thunder would cease and be replaced with the sun
Shining its warmth down on each and everyone
The rain would cease its beat upon the ground
And with such quickness I would be to astound
The bluster would slow to a mere summer's breeze
Bringing the Thunder, Rain, and Wind gods down to their knees
Every time I think of you it seems to go away
The memory I have of a rainy day

Edmund A. Byfield

My Poem

I tried to write a poem one day,
But could not think of a thing to say.

Write of the new puppy who has come to stay
Who with the children is eager to play.

Write of the Spring, which here at last
Ends cruel Winter's snowy blasts.

Write of school days soon to end,
Joyous students with happy teachers blend.

Write of the summer—of swimming, picnics, gardening, play
Sun-filled, joy-filled, many a happy, happy day.

Ideas tumble—thoughts rumble—and yet
Nothing makes sense or rhymes you can bet.

Poems are written by others 'tis true.
but my efforts always leave me feeling blue.

Eloise C. Brown

Spark

As it lay there in its stony grave
Burning like the hell, trapped like a slave
Nowhere to run, nowhere to hide
The glory of death lay hidden inside

Orange and yellow, now it's blue
No chance to save it, nothing to do
Call the hospital, even the cops
Cradled kindling, dwindles and pops

In the mourning, there was no more
Except some ashes upon the floor
So alas you can see
There's no justice for a creature such as thee.

Eric T. Cronin

Sorrow

The rain on the roof, the constant patter, the huge raindrops;
Buckets;
Is like someone crying.

Who makes the rain?

Far away, a girl is crying for her poor dead bird, murdered by an outlandish house cat.

The rain succeeds from that distant place, moving far, far away.
All the while, a constant rumble, steady stream of all the elements;
Wind, rain
A rush of light, a deep boom.

The rain dies down; the girl's hot stream of tears, too.
The heart-wrenching sobs become more and more like muffled words.

Just as the storms fury has left behind devastation, the girl's soul is permanently scarred.
But time will heal it.
And all that will be left is a wet pillow, and a damp ground.

Erica Puopolo

A Woman's Love

Once a creature, half woman, half lover, half angel
brushed against me, and of a sudden I knew,
that when a woman gives herself to you,
You possess all women.

Women of all age, race, kind and creed -
The moon and stars, all legends and miracles.
The dark skinned women who inflame your senses,
The cool yellow headed ones, who entice and
Escape you, the gentle ones who serve you, the
Slender ones who torment you and the Mothers
Who love and suckle you - all the women whom
God created out of the teeming fullness of
This earth, all these are yours and more in
The love of one women -

Arthur A. Vallee

Christmas Meaning

Christmas season arrives each year.
Bringing us all hope and good cheer.

People hustle about forgetting the reason.
What is the true meaning of the season?

They shop in the malls with all the crowds.
Thinking in silent, but speaking out loud.

Everyone works so hard to set up a tree.
Working so hard with joy and glee.

The commercial meaning has really spread.
The true meaning of Christmas is all but dead.

It is time we gather to worship and pray.
Jesus Christ was born on Christmas Day.

His birth gave sights of a new tomorrow.
This allows our soul to make it through sorrow.

The carols are sung with a joyful sound.
So there are smiles on faces all around.

Keep the true meaning of Christmas in your heart.
Way down deep and never let it depart.

Don't let your thoughts ever sway.
Remembering Christ on Christmas Day.

Donald A. Woodson

Snowflakes Of Autumn

Autumn colors, red, yellow and gold,
Bright leaves falling to signal the cold.
They let go of branches and float through the air,
Tossed by the wind until the trees are all bare.

Snowflakes of autumn, red, yellow, and gold,
Lay heaped on the ground, like a story untold.
They blanket the earth, like a quilt against frost,
But gradually the hues of autumn are lost.

Bright autumn colors, red, yellow and gold,
Fade and wrinkle as they become old.
They then turn brown and are covered with snow,
But add mulch to the dirt through which flowers will grow.

Diana Lee McGinity

The Snake Catcher

The snake catcher no doubt, is the
bravest of them all; his stories are chilling
and his tales are tall. But at the end
of this day, when he's home with his prey,
He can't ever hold her or teach her to play.
Straight to her cage, and that's where she'll
stay. She's sure with her plan, for a strike to
the hand, you see in the eyes of a snake;
she's going to catch her a man. That's just
life in the wild, to each they are game;
nowhere to point the finger, no where to
place the blame. If the hunter wants
something he can hold so dear, kiss it on its
feet or right next to its ear, to wipe up a
tear, free from all fear;
If he desires a heart he can fill full
of love, hunt what I've hunted,
go after the White Dove.

John Harb

Just Open Your Eyes And See Nature's Beauty

A flower's life is short but sweet,
Born in the earth in wet, rich soil.
Its fresh spring scent, and petals neat,
Green leaves and vines twist to a coil.
The sunlight and beauty in most of them,
Moonlight and love in the rest.
I wish all flowers could be my gems,
I guess I just must pick the best

The soft, gentle wind sings to the flower,
As it secretly steals pollen and petals.
Seeds will land and bloom after a shower,
They will stay until the wind calls.
The flowers will bloom again in the spring,
But will die when Winter fairies start to sing.

Jenelle Analisa Burd

Silver Moon

Silver moon way up high shining on the sea
Casting off a brilliant light that covers you and me

Mesmerize our minds and thoughts with a
single beam
Shattering the midnight skies as if a
piercing scream

Carry our hearts and our souls to a different place
And let us dance among the stars in the
never ending space

Christine Chico

The Assessor

Dusk has come and gone, the sky is dark
blue, earth red brown,
And something is sitting on my bed!
Clicking on the floor, a hot breeze came by me,
Wafted from the bat like wings flickers
from the horns on it's head, bright green eyes.
And a big grin on it's face, "Oh" a
shiver ran down my spine,
Who are you I said? You know me it said,
I'm here to help you, it explained and
What am I?
Well sometimes I'm your friend,
I'm the IRS, CIA, FBI.
The Building Inspector, Priest your Local Government
Health Department, Park department,
"HOLY COW" that can't be, I said, and then
with a very big grin oh yes it said
you see, I "LIVE" OFF the "EFFORTS" of others,
I'm your friend.
Now move over I'm "TIRED".

Guy F. Ruff Sr.

Stardust

A tiny speck of stardust floated out of heaven's
  blue,
Drifted down onto a white rose, its petals kissed
  with dew.
It shimmered and it sparkled, it glowed with joyous
  light,
All the colors of the rainbow, against the petals
  white.
The rose then shyly whispered to the stardust
  lovingly,
What brings you to my world from yours of pristine
  purity?
I'm light divine, I'm in all things
In all life you'll see me glow,
For what's above you will someday see, is the same as
  that below.

Daisy M. Collins

Father/Daughter Dialogue

Basking in the searing sun
Blinded by the shining sea
Deafened by the ocean's roar
Reeling in a whopping tuna, I am at peace.

I can see, Father, it matters little
We've wrenched you from your moorings.

What are those burnished shadows rumbling by?
I hear the ocean droning

It's freeway, Father.

Don't confuse me
I have a century's worth of sand in my shoes.

Without your steady rudder, Father
I'm adrift on an uncharted sea.

Take hold the tiller, focus on Polaris
You'll sail through those treacherous shoals
You are my daughter.

Father, don't leave me
I need your measured good sense
Your gentle balance
Your long clear view.

Elaine C. McGee

Remembering...

Amid the fragrance of fresh, damp earth, and new
blades of grass having just found their freedom
from the seeds that held them dormant until the
early days of Spring, we silently clasped our arms,
each around the other.

With soft, billowing clouds drifting lazily by, their
whiteness touched with gray contrasted by the blue of
the heavens, we tingled in the joyous, ecstatic moment
of our perfect union.

Now and then a blue jay, halting in its quest for food,
twittered its approval.

Leaving our little paradise, we left behind our shared
experience which had left its impression on the soft,
young blades of Spring.

Fiora Stone

Take No More

You took the yellow iron from our rivers and mountains, we call the
  Black Hills.
You carved the faces of your great chiefs on the cliffs of our
  sacred mountain.
You cut our green forests down and sent the trees away to build
  your teepees.
You brought the iron horse across our prairie, where our buffalo
  trails were many and now are none.
You sent the mountain man and trappers up our rivers and
streams,
  and took the beaver from our people.
You sent the settlers to our land of the buffalo and plowed under our
  prairie grass until it became dust.
You opened up the heart of Mother Earth and took her copper,
  turquoise, gold and silver.
You strip mined her great basin and took the black rock you call coal.
All these things you have plundered with greed and put nothing back
  in return.
Now I say to you, your great chiefs never honored the treaties, for
  now you have finally taken all our land and left our people to live
  on the land you call a reservation.

Dale L. Sharp

Children Of The World

Indian and Caucasian
Black and Asian
We are the children of the world one and all
Each standing so proud and tall
Hand in hand
Together all walking across the land
In harmony singing a new song
Of PEACE forever long
Come sing along, sing along
In harmony singing a new song of PEACE forever long
We will dare
To dream of PEACE and freedom everywhere
Blessed PEACE is our constant prayer
Indian and Caucasian, Black and Asian
We are the children of the world one and all
Each standing so proud and tall
In harmony singing a new song of PEACE forever long
We will dare
To dream of PEACE and freedom everywhere
Blessed PEACE is our constant prayer

Billie Jeanne James

Scars

The scars of love
Bite deep into one's heart.
I myself have felt them many times.
I know how love is constructed.
It is a fragile infra-structure
Which is easily shattered.
Not from within
But from without.
Sometimes it can actually consume itself, though.
But in doing so, it strengthens itself
When it is next built up.

The scars of life
May also be looked upon in this same way.
Like stepping stones to some greater purpose.
Sacrifices are made so the whole is more complete.
But they are there, these scars,
As memories and experiences
In which to grow on, learn from,
And live with.

James S. Cleary

Untitled

Blue eyes beckoning me onward.
Billowing clouds, like ballerinas dancing across pristine skies.
Open fields, holding captive dreams of serenity.
The embodiment of Nirvana.
A perfect state of grace.
Struck down on the road to Damascus,
I lay captive to her being.
Roll away the stone, dear Lazarus.
Set me free from my slumber
So I may rise and live.
Breath in the cool air for the first time,
And be immortal in her touch.
Carry me across the sands of eternity
And set me gently into her arms.
For it is there that I shall find satisfaction.
And it is there that I shall find peace.
Captured by the jailer.
Sentenced for life in a dreamland,
Where I will gladly live forever.

Jason Dana

The Trip

Dad at the wheel, Mom beside snapping her Juicy Fruit gum
Big brother and I, short legs sticking to the vinyl
Eye one another across an imaginary border.
At lunch brother and I empty
Our water glasses just to see the waitress
Refill them. We excuse ourselves
To go to the bathroom.
With my tight fist I rap five times on the wall.
Brother answers with two raps from the other side.
Back in the '54 Mercury wagon we play the alphabet game.
I carefully scan the billboards on my side of the car
For a word that begins with "A,"
Then with "B" and so on.
I whine if brother gets too far ahead.
Mom sticks her arm out over the dash
She chirps cheerfully that she has
Crossed the state line first.
I nod off to sleep dreaming of
Drip castles, skee ball and miniature golf.

Anna S. Lacher

My Impossible Dream

You are my impossible dream
Beyond an arm's length away yet close enough to smell your perfumed breath
It tantalizes and invites me at the same time mocking my foolishness
Seeing in your eyes an undying invitation
And on your pillow lips a constant goodbye.
The refreshing breezes on a scorching day
are like the safety in our distance from one another
If we get too hot the trees will dance in the air and we are relieved.
We have the insatiable burning of a candle's wick
Killed with a single exhalation.
You are the mountains and the ocean, I am the sun
Each day you make me rise, you give me unsurmountable energy
Yet without fail you swallow me up every night and extinguish my light.
My dream, my impossible dream
Is to forever shine in the midst of the sky
You along with me, the earth my escort.
We revolve around each other
Independent, but survival impossible without one another.

Josie Stroud

A Vietnamese American Visiting His Birthplace In Vietnam

A black skeleton of columns and beams
Beside puddles of water and heaps of trash;
A section of wall ruined by many a rain wash,
A wild garden where a yellow flower gleams;

A hammock where Mother sang many a song
Now half buried under layers of dust.
Where the altar of ancestors was a must
Now only clouds of flies throng.

As the setting sun begins to glow
A raven comes and sits on the wall
And utters a harsh cry as of sorrow

In empathy with the returnee and all,
For so much destruction and sufferings
In a country covered with a gray pall.

The black raven again flaps its wings
And, in the dark, crows somber forebodings.

Hach C. Nguyen

The Five Stages Of Life

<u>The First is to Live</u>
Being born, this is the dawn of life.
From babyhood to childhood, then adolescence,
   and growing into adulthood
<u>The Second is to Work</u>
In adulthood, one makes the choice of their life's work.
It's essential to become self-sufficient and self-supporting.
<u>The Third is to Love</u>
To love someone enough to make them your life partner.
To marry and share the joy of parenthood with a family.
A true fulfillment in life is a stable and lasting love.
<u>The Fourth is to Learn</u>
Always to keep on learning throughout one's life.
Thus enabling growth both emotionally and mentally.
<u>The Fifth is to Make a Difference</u>
It's the importance of making a difference to
   others during one's life.
That our many years of living have been productive
   and worthwhile, not in vain.
It is the legacy we leave "Having Made A Difference."

Irene Kanter

Mistress Of The Waves

Riding quicksilver waves of gold
before the sun sinking in crimson
just a glimpse, perhaps his imagination
a vision of buoyant floating breasts
and the salty charms of wave tossed hair
of a stone cold beautiful Goddess
empress of whitecaps breaking into spray
casting a timeless ancient smile his way
lured by the fluid watery harps
the sailor dreams appropriately enchanted
longing for one ephemeral embrace
and the lust of forbidden pleasures
listening to whispers of imagined conversations
her deepest secrets revealed in brine
and the cool scent of her misty breath
evaporating with her silken tresses
best to forget the perfect
wake of her sultry bathing
not a muse but a siren
vanishing in the waves
Dodd C. Schweinfurth

The One Who Got Away

He settles fights with his fists. She takes the blows
because she's his.

What makes a man react this way? To inflict pain on his wife
watching the tears stream from her face.

The kids watch on thinking that it's okay for daddy to hit
mommy that way.

We continue watching wondering when he'll ever stop - the
violence that separates us. Is it our place to interrupt?
We voice that it's no way to settle fights. He tells us that
it's none of our business - continues the fight.

He drives away with his wife and kids in the car. My sixth
sense can't help to wonder if she'll be alive or dead the next day.

Where to we draw the line? When do we intervene? We know
it's wrong? We can't seem to convince her of what we foresee.

Despair is all we feel - not being able to save her from the
man she married or thought she could trust. For only she can
help herself.
Jennifer S. Sholler

God Made Us Twins

God made us twins, by name Lee and Dee.
Because I need you, and you need me.
Both of us are here, for each other.
We've shared a womb, we share the same mother.
I know sometimes, we don't get along.
But together, we can make each other strong.
When we were little, we were the best of buds.
Do you remember, how we used to play in the mud?
You with the sugar, me with the cream.
All of those good times, you and I've seen.
We can understand each other, without saying a word.
Our voices, don't even have to be heard.
I know it's tough, growing older each day.
But we're doing it together, every step of the way.
We'll always be twins, no matter the cost.
Our special bond, will never be lost.
Maybe one of us, was just supposed to be.
But God created both of us, the ones that make, WE!
Jennifer Dee Grissom

A Rose Bud

Standing erect in the Sunlight a rosebud awaits to blossom
Beautiful, trusting, Naive, Pure, Innocent
Stares of lurking spectators holds an uncertain future
Eventually disturb, not allowed to blossom in its own time
Forced to take on a burden brought on by those parasites
Who raped, handled, ravished, and stole its innocence
Their main goal, filling their hungered bellies until
Satisfied with the sweetness of this naive bud
Now there is a silence, but listen, you can hear the pain
And the spills of its tears as it drops to the soil
Through fearful eyes, confuse by what's reflected back
An unknown reality now floods its peaceful mind
Invading its taught, its emotion, and while polluting its being
There's a silent cry for those lost friends
The ones familiar to the bud who now whispers their names
Beauty, Laughter, Trust, Peace, but there's no answer
Replaced by unknown creatures rapidly becoming familiar
Confusion, Fear, Loneliness, night, now is its reality
Drooping in shame, faltering to the soil you sprang out of
Perhaps to find those friends, and sleep in peace again
Hannah Belcher

The Mockingbird

Such a peaceful innocence.
Beautiful singing, joyous laughter.
The children of today.
Not only on the outside, but the heart within.
The innocent heart beating wildly to stay alive
in today's unjust society.
   Injustice?

Do children understand?
The meaning of life is to keep
that childhood innocence.
We are giving up that innocence by prejudice.
Where do we learn it?
The adults of yesterday.
Not only by hearing,
but by the actions we see.
Will it stop?

The mockingbird slowly dies.
   Peacefully.
Becky Gall

Pied Sports

Glory be to God for Athletic things......
For eternal fields of grass and clay lined with white chalk;
For clubs to smash and pulverize a ball into the deep blue sky;
For nets big and small to catch spheres kicked and thrown and hurled at them;
For the tackle, the pass, the catch, and the kick of that most sacred pigskin;
For the flight of the ball as it's shot off the tee, chipping and
putting until it comes to rest in the cup - only to be hit again.

Yes, thank Him for the delicate white flakes that fall upon a hill;
Only to be thrown and kicked and cut by a pair of freshly waxed skis;
The speed, the power, the flight as they fly down the mountain turning
and cutting, lifting, spinning, thrashing, again and again by each
move of the body.
The sharp cut of the snowboard, the turn of the mono-ski,
 the speed of the skis all in perfect harmony with the flakes.

The running, the jumping, the kicking, the throwing. All the stamina,
agility, energy, endurance, power, nerves, courage, sweat, strength,
speed, intensity, the thrill of victory, the agony of defeat. All the
beautiful and perfect things an athlete holds sacred will live on
through the spirit of the creator.

Praise him.
Brandon Edward Dusick

Jealousy

If someone wants something that I own
Be my guest...everything really on loan

The one thing that's mine and no one can take away
Is my mind and spirit developed over many a day

Jealousy should never be used as a weapon or tool
It exists only in the heart and mind of a fool

Tolerance is kind and compassion a need
But jealousy a feeling designed in the mind thru greed

Wanting something my neighbor has is lust
And desire to take or steal becomes a must

Sarcasm and pettiness move in on our side
The way becomes slimy and actions hard to hide

The bitches move out to cut down their own kind
And bastards come forth to hand out their line

The innocent victims of all this trash
Are the children who stare in alarm at the bash

Must I go that way to fulfill my desires
And burn in the hell created by my own fires

Rave on jealousy and beat on your chest
Look around and go after someone else's best
Jean Sublett

How Long?

Till when must I dress, and assist this tie? Till heaven and earth
   be mine, I sigh.
It was never this way before, goodbye was always at my discretion.
It was I, bored with the conversation, eyeing the door, suddenly
   leaving.
But now the words seem to be getting an edge of feeling.
How long without cutting my hands? Only just now you left me,
With those very words and no choice in the if or when.
Sweet Queen, bring me your healing. Hello with no chance for dealing.
How long? Till you're mine, the Lord revealing,
Till time stands still, and there's no more feeling,
And that's how long I will love you.

How long is it going to be before I stop counting the cars on the
   street,
Looking for yours and almost seeing it?
How long before I stop opening the door,
Expecting to see you, and finding someone else?
How long before I stop answering the telephone and waiting for your
   voice?
The days are passing like clouds and my life goes with them.
How long? Till you're mine,
The Lord revealing.
Till time stands still and there's no more feeling
And that's how long I will love you!
Ian Alexander

The Angel Who Doesn't Leave

I have an angel, that never leaves, he's my grandson and will forever
be. He came into my life, a baby was he, precious and cuddly for all
to see, through those brown eyes, he captured me. He gave me strength
when I had none, always keeping me on the run. That's my angel that
never leaves. As anyone can see, he gets my praise constantly, his
hugs and kisses right from the start, will forever be in my heart.
Some day he's sure to be a good man, and I hope to be there to do
what I can. That's my angel who never leaves.
Juanita Z. De Frese

Einstein's Interface

the often minuscule delta of the empirical and the transcendent
ballooned in Einstein's being
more like an enormous sound
flooding the boundaries between the disparate fields

such freedom he must have felt

navigating between the poles
delighting in the dissolving borders
bringing us glimpses
of the gymnastics of physics
and the dance of the divine
Jenifer Kolkhorst

Sweet Winter Night

Down through a nighttime slough, down winter's slippery edge
Back up through a spare strand of trees on a midnight hike
Cold weather parties behind me, fewer concerns with every step
This is my time alone
Until coyotes laugh, much closer to home than I am
Trees cover the moon with bony hands
Under a silvery glaze, brown survivors of summer crunch
beneath my feet

This is so safe, where I belong, the finest time of day
For my kind. Dark and unique, not noticed by many, accessible
to only a few

I am not modest, don't need to be
I am not embarrassed, there is no reason
The moon shares its glow and every thing glistens
but is still dark

And the dark is as protective as a tigress, and
a tigress has never seen these winter pastures
Except on nights like these
Christine Wakefield

Always Friends

Over the hills and far away my friend Christine has moved
away. With tears in my eyes and sand on my feet I wander
off to where we might meet. As I walk along the sand with
fear I wonder if I'm drawing near. I walk up a hill with
wind in my face to see if I've reached my far off place. As
I reach the top of the hill I hear someone say, "Are you my
friend from far away?" As I stumble down the rest of the
hill I wondered if that was my friend. Standing quite still
when I reached her, she looked me in the eyes and gave me a
big hug, for she had known from my eyes that it was me.
Now time has passed on by and by and our friendship will
never die.
Christine Marinello and Sarah Ellis

Losing Uncle Bart

When someone you love so much is slowly fading
away and all you can do is pray
for a miracle,
That is pain.
When the tears flow endlessly and you are unable
to catch a breath between the sobs,
That is pain.
When the only word that you can utter is
why, yet there is no answer to be found,
That is pain.
Intolerable, excruciating pain.
When only one emotion can consume
a person's heart as much as the pain,
That is love.
Brenda Dolan

To My Love

I try to profess, as one would a faith, the woman I love:
   Auburn hair like spun copper,
     framing with delicate caresses
       a face of unsurpassed loveliness.
Eyes which shine forth
   the joy of life and its gifts.
Supple lips which warm the heart
   with gentle smiles and offer hope
     through words wise or winsome.
Delicate nose, and ears which
   not only hear but truly listen
     to the hurts and hopes of others.
Feet which walk the way of peace,
   carrying one strong woman
     in her desire for justice
     and firm in her commitment to heal.
With helping hands,
   gentle and full of power,
     she molds new worlds
       for those she loves... and there is Eden.

David W. Hook

Prove Yourself

How far would you go, to what length, what degree, to capture my attention to really please me?
You claim I am the focus of all that you desire, you say that you need me, I set your soul on fire.
To complete your life, I'm the only one, you say, if only I'd acquiesce, stop holding you at bay
There is a simple answer for everything you ask, but something is required of you that seems to be a task
If I'm so important, if I mean that much you, what I'm asking in return you could easily do.
Why do days, sometimes weeks pass, no word from you at all, again I ask, if you want me, at least, just make a call
Don't let time pass, days and weeks, refuting all your claims that I'm your dream, your everything, please stop playing games!
What comes from your heart, will touch my heart, a proverb tried and true reach out to me with sincere love and I'll reach out to you
Stop wasting time with flowery speech before it is too late
Just be yourself don't talk, just act, I may reciprocate

Ann Murrell

The Race

You are getting so much older and I'm getting younger every day!
At one time I was ten times your years and while I began to gray,
You began growing up and suddenly, I was only five times your age.
But time ticks on and with the turning of another page.
I woke up one morning at twenty, while you were turning ten,
So, see I'm only twice your age and the pattern begins again.
Today I'm sitting here smiling, breathing a gentle sigh,
Waiting for that day - one day when you will pass me by.

Jeffrey Howard Morrison

Color Of Heart

Taken from the red man, his land.
Black man chained at hand.
Does white tear hope and faith away?
Will tomorrow dig under yesterday?
Was pale greed born in his blood?
Is the heart sacred in today's flood?
Yellow man taken down in a political manner.
Yet the brown man still pledges our banner.
America...home of the free?
What color am I supposed to be?
So many answers I search to find.
Yet these questions rain from my caucasian mind.

Chet Tucker

From The Heart

October one nineteen ninety five
At one p.m. he took a bride
with all the happiness and the joy
Today I lost my little boy
With vivid memories both good and sad
I remember his childhood
As I said a prayer
God let them be happy, live a long life as one
The little boy I lost
Today was my son
He became a man to cleave to his wife
His child like ways he has put aside
A good husband I'm sure he will be
Hopefully a father, of one, two or three
God bless and keep them all in the palm of your hand
The little boy God gave me is now a grown man.

Esther M. Langford

Hubert's Lament

On Grandpa's farm one summer day,
At nap time I, on my pallet lay.
When everyone was settled down,
I went outside to look around.
There on a tree limb, I found,
A Red Wasp nest, high off the ground,
I went inside, for the old highchair,
Still too short so; I put a box up there.
When I climbed up, the box began to rock,
With a long stick, I gave that nest a sock.
Now you can guess the rest.
Wasp don't like it, when you disturbed their nest.
A wasp flew down and stung me, right between the eyes,
I fell off that highchair, with cursing, and cries.
Remember this was nap time, folks came out every door.
Grandpa's Farm, never saw, such a commotion before.
Quick as lightning, my eyes were swelled shut.
If I wanted to see things, I had to lift my eyelids up.
I promised the Good Lord, if He'd just let me see,
The next time I saw a Red Wasp nest, I would let it be.

Florine Nolen Hollan

The Unthinkable

It is unthinkable but true, I am a happy person.
At last the years of frustration and pain have met their Waterloo.
The promised joy of life has come, poignant, unnatural to my expectation of when it should occur.
My youth has past and likewise middle age.
My hair is white, my right hand trembles,
but my soul is free as a bird soaring in the sky.
I am ascending to a higher level of life.
Time is rich as thick cream, tasty as the raspberries of fall.
The wind carries fragrant smoke of smoldering fires
from lost dreams, but also sparks of new hope.
More than ever before, I can appreciate the sun rise and set.
I know what rings true and what does not,
so I'll not envy anyone, rather boldly say
the unthinkable thought from my wrinkled brow,
"Thank God, I am a happy person."

Joyce Morey

Fear

What is it that I fear inside, that keeps me awake at night?
It does not take on a physical shape nor fade with the morning light.

This fear harms me indirectly, leaving me so insecure.
I feel as though it takes from me all that I adore.

I sometimes take it out on others, I hope this, they can condone.
For my greatest fear if you have not guessed is the fear to be alone.

Heather Hayden

May-December

But for the difference in the times in eternity
Assigned to us for our births, who knows?
Only rarely in one's lifetime are we graced
With a chance meeting with a kindred soul,
And we know only too well within ourselves
That the presence of this very special and dear entity
Shall reside within our hearts and our very beings
Our whole lifetime...
This rarest of gifts, given to me by the Power above,
I accept without question, and shall treasure and
Embrace it within my heart of hearts;
Knowing, without asking...
That it is a link which will be there,
In silence, always...even until the end of time.

Gena Hawkins

Distant Love

Constantly I cry at night
Because you are so far away
You tell me to think of you near not far
But, no one is there to wipe my tears away

It's hard to think of you near
When you're really gone
But I guess there is still more I need to learn
Instead of crying all the time,
I need to be more concerned

Carmelitta J. Redmond

A Toast To Forty

Right now is a time of happiness and joy
Between two people, a girl and a boy,
Of forty years together that shall never part,
Of two loving soul and two loving hearts.

And now we raise a toast to two that care,
Two that love and two that share,
Two that shall stay happily ever after,
A whole lot of fun and a whole lot of laughter.

Carolyn Marie Beasley

Guardian Angels

He flies off into the light of dawn,
Back in the dark of night.
Everywhere he goes he's well escorted,
He's always in their sight.
Saudi Arabia was quite a trip,
This worried mother nearly lost her grip.
She cried, prayed to the "head man",
Please, Dear Lord, keep him safe, as only you can.
It was not an easy thing to cope,
Then God stepped in and gave me hope.
Lying in bed with tears welling up,
Everything seemed to become very still,
I realized that God was exercising his will.
A feeling of warmth went from my head to my feet,
I was experiencing God's Special Treat.
A Guardian Angel had laid hands on me.
My mind was flooded with relief.
Worrying about my son would bring no more grief.
The Guardian Angel had taken care of my fear,
Leaving me knowing, for my son, they would always be there.

Belk N. Robinson

Life Is A Game

Life is a game in which we play, we are the actors and live day by day. Days may be sad and days may be glad, we all have our ups and downs. The body may say no when we want a yes, or situations may arise which take away our zest, things look bad and clouds descend upon us, HOW DO WE GET OUT OF THIS MESS! Well in this game of life we see, to enjoy it we must actually be.
We are born with special talents to take use and watch grow, but some of us may never realize what we have to show.
We have a choice to let it live or die.
Liveflowing through us or die before our eyes. And so perhaps we think we've failed because everybody else wears a grin. Could it be that in this game, I FORGOT I WANTED TO WIN! What can I do so I may win and sing with the birds and run with the wind? Perhaps I ought to stop and learn the rules which guide me on, so I may join the winning team and sour way beyond. How powerful is the human body, how powerful is the mind? Think for a moment and REALIZE YOUR POWERFUL GOLDMINE! FOR IN YOUR BODY AND THROUGH YOUR MIND YOUR TALENT MAY POUR THROUGH, THE ONLY ONE WHO CAN STOP IT IS THE POWERFUL YOU. AND SO YOU CAN SAY YES AND LET THE GAME OF LIFE PLAY ON, OR WITH THE FLICKER OF A THOUGHT TURN IT ALL OFF AND WONDER WHERE LIFE HAS GONE.

Elizabeth Langlois

Untitled

There you stand barefoot on your pedestal
At the dawn of the twenty-first century
And you shall pursue, Beloved Liberty
The dream you have borne as your ideal.
Blessing the hungry, the poor and his pal
You enlighten the spirit that you embody.
You have opened the gates of a kingdom
For you have given them hope and freedom,
Your task is as noble as it is colossal!
In promising to shelter and nurture
You have accomplished their endeavor
And in glory your name shall perdure.
Protecting your children from what they abhor.
You have in the past and shall in the future
Remain Liberty, stronger than any dictator.

Isabelle Cabaza

October The Eightieth

Our Father which art in Heaven, this congregation of Worshippers and I come before you this morning with questions, with thanksgiving and with humble hearts.
Questions because of the multitude of winds that blew since we were last in this place. The winds of the actions of the forces of nature, the winds of the actions of men seeking retribution and justice and the winds for one who travels to unite with a message of hope through social equality.
Thanksgiving that we are here to worship and to today to seek your answers, and in,
Humbleness of heart for the promise kept that you sent your Son, our true hope and deliver.

DeVere W. McGuffin II

Untitled

Dear Grande,
　Happy Fathers Day!! I have prepared a poem for you:
My Dad has a Dad,
Who cheers me up when I'm sad,
Smart, he likes to be,
Strong, he tends to be,
But he likes me!

Eric Siegel

Time

The time you took my hand and asked
me that one important question a
teenage girl urges to answer, your deep
dark eyes took me to a far away place.
Time could only tear us apart. Our
lives changed and our relationship
did too. The time you took my hand
and slid the ring on my finger, we
vowed to stay together forever. The time
I stood by your side the day you died.
As the time went by the days
grew darker. The life, the love, and
the time that made us grow, just died.

Leslie Corrine Smith

Silent Scream

What exactly is a silent scream?
Maybe it's a scream that can't come out
Or maybe one that can't be heard.
It could be from the spiritual world
Only heard by the chosen one.
Trying to mess with your mind,
Driving you insane,
Following you all the time,
Until all that you can hear...
Is the Silent Scream.

Lisa Champ

Zodiacs Fable

The twin of two
marks three
by the sign of the universe
as Castor and Pollux
did birth to be
another learned heir
and bright
is their newest constellation
who is asking
ever asking
seeking learning
sometimes masking
but always
always
always asking
how?
why?
where?

Kimberly Anne Ensign

Maggie

Some dogs are nice, but
Maggie beats them all.
She scampers all around the rooms
And up and down the halls.

She looks into my eyes,
Then she moves a little bit
To see how close she can get.
Now she runs to get me

She made me fall down.
Oh, no now she's here
A nibble, a bite
On the ear she might.

Kirsten Moore

My Love For You

I remember when I fell in
love with you
  I saw things differently, the
world seemed new.

  Then you left. I don't know
where you went.
  It made me feel like my
heart bent.

  You only visit me when you can;
you're supposed to be my true man.
  I write you every week. I think of
you every day.
  My feelings for you will never
fade away.

  But I feel like you don't care.
Since you left, there's only empty air.

  I look at your pictures, and
I try to see
  The thoughts and feelings
you have for me.

Kimberly Burgess

Loneliness

I am within, yet outside
  looking in
They move about me
I hear their chatter and laughter
I see their bodies
  Moving; interacting with
  one another
Someone call out my name;
  I turn and smile
But how can that be, for
  I am all alone

Mary E. Josey

Untitled

You
Looking at me
Like that...
I got lost in your eyes a couple of days,
And stumbled across your face.
I finally returned to
That slap-in the face-burn
To find only,
You
Looking at me
Like that.

Megan Michael

Angels

Angels we hear
Most high
Unveiling their wings
Against the sky
Prayerful watch
Bestow upon us
Looking through the
The stainless glass

Nannette Dulcie

A Teenager's Ultimatum

Decades have passed,
Long before I am borne.
I await her decision,
It is a hard one to make.
Life or death,
That is hers to decide.
She is the judged,
She is the jury,
She may even be the executioner

My life,
My death,
That is the issue here.
Some say I am not alive;
Some say I am alive;
What do you say?

To be terminated,
or to be borne;
To be a mother,
or to be a teenager;
That is her ultimatum

Kenneth L. Holley

"The Way I See Me"

Sometimes I wish I could
  live my life over,
To be able to be loved as
  I have wished on a clover.
All I have wanted in my life,
  was a man to love me as
  his equal and wife.
I have a man now, but his
  love is not for me.
I will keep loving him, as
  long as God can see.
My life is what I made it,
  so I should not complain,
But one day I will have to
  explain to the man upstairs
  who watches over me.
For now I know just what
  God sees,
It's all in the way "I look at me."

Louise Vestal

"When Friends Aren't Friends"

"Look at her, what's she wearing?
Look at her hair."
  I hear it everyday, but try to pay
no mind. It hurts, it makes me feel
worthless. I try and try to be liked,
respected, known, but the more I try
the more I'm hurt.
  These feelings come from people
who are supposedly my friends.
  Why are they doing this?
  All I'm left with is the feeling
that one day, when I'm rich and famous,
I'll be the one pointing at them saying,
"Look at her. What's she wearing?
Look at her hair."
  Then I'll add, "See that girl?
she's one of those people who works
in the mailroom of my office building."

Michelle Butler

Direction

I need to catch the wind
Like an untimely petal
I'm falling
Where will it end?

Can't keep reaching out
Like a child of its mother.
Can't keep running in lines
Lines of infinity in my book of life.

Will I find
Find what my wondering
Eyes are looking for?
Confusion in hazy minds
Direction
Where to find it?

I'm running like water
Will a small river catch me,
Or will I run into the sea?

My heart is open to the wind
Take my heart and give me.
Direction...

Nicola Crofts

The Technology Wind

Faster, Faster, We spin
like a mighty tornado
technology the driving force
creating and recreating

Faster, Faster, We spin
like the moving wind
across the desert
devoid of humanity

Faster, Faster, We spin
like the sirocco
hotly, quickly, swiftly
lacking, the feeling of humanity

Faster, Faster, We Spin
like a fire storm
wind creating wind
devour all before
leaving only ash and
memories of the pass

M. J. Knepper

Mood Swing

Depression, elation
  like a light switch
  on then off in a flash
Tears of sorrow
  for loss, for self-pity,
  for decisions poorly made.
Tears of joy
  for God, for luck,
  for happy surprises
All within one
  rotation of the planet
As the earth turns,
  so can your life.
Never lose hope.
Never lose faith.
Never take for granted.
Never forget.

Kenneth E. Hahurst

Love And Respect

Parents hug your children,
Let them know how proud you are.
Do not ridicule them ever
For that will often leave a scar.
Be sure to listen to them
And when they ask you for advice,
Do your best to give them counsel,
Which quite often will suffice.
Let your children know you trust them.
You expect them to be true.
Then you'll have a happy family,
For they'll have respect for you.

Lois Kahl Davis

Without A Doubt

Have you troubles along your way?
Let prayer and praise guide your day
By His love and blessings plenty
Stated so within Psalm twenty

Gods promises in The Good Book
Are often misplaced or mistook
Receive His SON, His WORD impart
To seek the KNOWER of your heart

He teaches love that all would prize
Without measure, without size
A simple love and faith that cries
When will MY children realize?

That Love has sent Him for awhile
To teach us how to reconcile
So when life's ripe for death or pain
It's really only for our gain

Now in HIS LIVING WORD alone
New life begins and faith is honed
Where all the troubled souls embrace
The victory of His Saving Grace!

Amber Rose Lighthouse

A Pilot's Dream

Come, let me be your wings,
Let me set you free.
Free beyond the threshold
Of necessary activity,
Far from frustration's grasp.
Free to chase the sun
And play amongst the clouds.

Though you were born on earth
To live on earth,
Your home is — here in the sky.
The comfort and ease
You have not known,
You will know
For I will make it so.
It shall be your most natural instinct
To fly — with me.

Marshall Kline

An Astronomer's Lament

On my judgment day,
If God should say.
Are your affairs in order?
I will say nay, nay, nay.
I studied your galaxies far, far away.
And, I forgot.

Melvin James Cotterill

Peace And Prayer

There are mystical places where I go alone.
Leaving all the bad news on TV at home.
Atop a mountain or by the seashore.
I know I will find peace of mind once more.
On this mountain I stand so high.
I feel suspended between earth and sky,
And I see for miles out into space,
Feel the soft moist clouds caress my face.
God's creation is all around to see.
All is relative as its meant to be.
I feel as one with all creation
Peace come to me a healing sensation.
Love and compassion fills my heart and mind.
For this earth and all life combined.
I hope that humanity will know and see.
God's love for all creation, it's given free.
For those in pain and hunger I prayed.
People in power, the thousands enslaved.
This wonderful planet, home of life and birth.
Lord heal humanity, and this living earth.

Katie E. Edwards

Perspective

Dishes in the sink
Leave me on the brink

Laundry to the sky
Makes me want to cry

Homeless on the street
Not enough to eat

Shivering in the cold
No clothes for them to fold

So I'll reduce each pile
Giving thanks all the while

Michelle Johns

Untitled

Take heart, my sweet
Lean over my shoulder and whisper
"I love you, my handsome dove"
And I will smile, coy and still
Whisper, whisper, my sweet
"Tender is the snow
That cold dry water of our tears
Frozen in a wasteland of men's fear"
I will follow you
My love and fateful one
To curve and curve
To thigh and breast and sigh
No one else is here, my sweet
So whisper in my ear.

Kellie D. Gore

Our Flag

  Our flag is just of plain design.
It was made of compass, square and line.
  Colors of red, white, and blue,
Stand for the brave, proud and the true.

  Our flag that men have died for.
A flag that stands for peace and war.
  Our flag is just a plain design.
I am proud to call her mine

Leisa Marie Jarvis

Oklahoma Children

Rooms filled with
LAUGHTER!
Faces full of
SMILES!

Tiny lives with a
FUTURE AHEAD OF THEM!
Tiny hearts full of
LOVE!

Tiny ones given to us
By God above,
Precious blessings
Here on earth.

Everything stolen,
Everything lost-
Innocence, purity,
LIFE!

19 dead,
ALL wounded-
May God forever
Be their healer.

Krisinda Taylor

Who Has Time

We've heard that time is of essence.
Just keeps on tickin'
But who controls this thing called time?
Could it be a child, world leader,
an animal perhaps.
But how do these mere mortals
and creatures stay up infinity?

There's only one person on this
earth with the patience and
perseverance.
So logically speaking it has
to be my Lord and Saviour
Jesus Christ.

With a clap of his hands, a tap
of Jesus' mighty toe, or a spoken word.
Time could be over with just
a blink of an eye.

Thank goodness Jesus has time instead of
a
wretch like me.
For no one is as perfect as he.

Ophelia Denise Groomes

"Call To Heaven"

There was a call,
Just before seven.

A call for mother,
To go to heaven,

Yes, mother was,
Called to heaven.

My prayers answered,
Her times of pain over.

She was taken gently,
While she slept.

She was,
Taken to heaven.

The call came.
Just before seven.

Mattie M. Stewart

Nothing

I am a useless machine
Just another character in God's dream
A worthless being
Devoid of meaning

I am just a grain of sand
In God's master plan
A senseless existence
I'll just fade into the distance

I am at my dyer's eve
My last breath I'm about to breathe
God's joke finally gets the last laugh
As my time has passed

I am just a fleeting memory
Of a person that used to be
In death I am still the same
I am nothing

Mark Andrew Shiltz

Soundless Sound

Can you hear it snowing?
It's such a soft sound -
Hearing stillness and silence
As flakes touch the ground.

The heavy air deadens the silence
Until, you feel it is growing
And it's hard to stand still,
As you listen intently - it's snowing.

Did you hear the flakes
As they touched - down on down,
Like the petals of roses
On a velvety gown?

Ah, wait! Of a moment
I did hear the beat
Of their soundless gyrations,
As the flakes touched my feet.

Marion Bussino

Untitled

A cactus is a metaphor for love
it's dry brittle hard
seemingly
unapproachable with its thorns
the barren environment within which
it needs to survive
belies the life and joy
waiting inside
to be discovered yet
if one works diligently
to get
beyond the thorns
taking and giving freedom
to the life entombed
the cactus gives of its very essence
with joy
the life-restoring juices within and
isn't that love

Nancy Susan Armstrong

Untitled

My guest at tea
lemon wheels of eternity
in our tea.

Kathryn Nancy Weldy

Love Is Lost Forever

Sitting here looking out my window
It's dark outside and the stars are aglow
Wondering where I went wrong
Where is my love that is gone

Life is like a looking glass
My love is lost and I cannot pass
People stare and see right through
The silence in my heart which is true

To share, to laugh, to cry
My love is lost but will never die
Just to hold and embrace
It's like a food you love to taste

Love maybe lost forever
But in my heart we will always be together
A smile, a hug, a kiss
This is the love you will miss

Mary Ellen Bines

Life

Life is like history,
It won't be repeated
When it's over it's over
There's nothing you can do.

Life seems so long,
But is so short.
You only live once
So why not have fun.

Be yourself all the days of your life
Because before you know it,
Your life will be gone.

Life goes so quick,
But seems to last forever.
Life comes and goes,
Without hellos or good-byes

So do all you can
And say what you feel.
For the end is the same
In one final domain.

Kevin Commeford

Tearsome Lost

It was cold.
It was dark.
The wind was howling
But where was she?
She was lost, I guess.
Would she find her way back?
How would she get there?
She had no one.
She had no way.
Why was she there?
How did she get there?
It didn't matter,
No one was looking for her.
Even if they were,
Nobody could get to this place.
Why would they want to?
It was dreadful.
It was dismal.
It was tearsome.
But she's still lost.

Meghan Anne MacKay

Christmas Joy

Christmas is coming...
It soon will be here
Bringing with it
Good news and cheer.

Christmas is coming...
Santa is on the way
Following him is reindeer and sleigh
Bringing good children
Toys to play with everyday.

Christmas is coming...
Each day brings
The joy of our Lord
Whose praises we sing.

Christmas is coming...
The star on each tree
Gives off a glow
To decorate a tree
For you and for me.

Kerrie Edwards

Untitled

I'm tired of trouble, sorrow and pain.
  It seems it will never stop.
I try to be brave and sing a refrain,
  But every time it turns out a flop.

What do I do then; do I just give up
  In trying to overcome?
Do I just roll over and say it's too much?
  Do I just give in and succumb?

It doesn't sound like me the lady of courage,
  The one who never says die.
So pick yourself up and lift your head high,
  Don't you dare give in and cry!

There are others in sorrow, trouble and pain,
  Others that need my help in their need.
I must go on and see to their sorrow,
  In so doing my problems are eased.

As long as we live we should always look up,
  Even though in deepest despair.
For whatever happens good can come,
  With blessings for others to share.

Mildred Schmitt

Untitled

The tenderness of your embrace,
it never fails to surprise and warm me;
How one so large,
hands so big, arms so powerful,
can be so gentle,
The sweetness of your smiles,
brighten my life,
the sun can do no better;
Blue eyes so clear,
announce the feelings harbored there,
all this for me, this love this depth,
my heart is full.
A man so strong, so full of ideals,
who lives his life standing tall,
an oak in the wind.
A man complete within himself,
a balance within,
surely his love,
a mere mortal woman,
would live and die for!

Katherine L. Parke

Madness

Can you see the madness?
It is raging in our eyes
And tearing away
At the heart of the world.

Can you feel its power?
As it seeps into our lives,
It takes away our common sense
And our knowledge of right and wrong.

The madness is taking over
And there is no place to hide.
We are deep within its maze
And have lost our way out.

Lisa M. Blakeslee

Generation X

This thing they call our youth by name
Is generation X.
Morality is gone and shame
Comes only when we hex

Could it be that AIDS is God's way
Of giving us a task?
Adultery is fun and play
Without even a mask.

Generations come and go but
What lifestyle do we lead?
Parents work to give their all but
What they give is their breed.

Where are we going I ask you
This generation X:
Will the next be more lose and to
Be classified as X?

Natalie Boswell

A Moment Of Glory

The featherless turkey
is a lonely drink,
to the memory
of a lost eagle;
Devoured,
by the flames of life.

The Featherless Turkey
is a drink of acid;
To excite memory,
and live the dead.

Add wildeberry
that eats turkey feather.
Berry and turkey marry,
love to tether.

A toast to the warrior,
fallen;
on the battlefield of life.

Norman E. Murphy

Gracefully

Time is running out for me
I watch my life go on
Faster now
As water flows down hill
My thoughts go with it
The last trickle before the pond
Pats on a smooth round stone
Like the ticking of an old gold watch

Lynda Dodge

Your Pain

Coming from your heart
Into your soul
Scaring your thoughts
Confusing your mind
Drumming in your voice
Into my ear
Entering my soul
Weighting my heart
Releasing the pain
Place it on me
I'll do away with it
I'll set you free

Kara Duffy

Missing You

Night slips
into waterspun
silken threads
dreams splashed
with lovecrazy
color
I wander dodging
pangs
like bullets
which graze flesh
and pierce nonvital parts
enough only to bleed

Lisa Winfield

A Hawk's Flight

Extreme heights explored
into
dark crevasses
he emerges
touched
by man
and all
his enemies
To be branded
virgin
no more

Michael T. Putney

Ode To New York

I love the city called New York
In which is found the club named Stork.
  I see here many streets and cabs
  And waiters handing out the tabs
Numberless theatres, all alike,
To which hats and gowns so hurriedly hike.
  You arrive by plane, you leave by boat,
  Or vice versa - but take your coat.
The food is grand, if you know the place.
But more than all, you must save face.
  Don't let the captain or waiter sneer
  Behind your back or in your ear
Because you leave a five dollar bill
When twenty is needed to assure good will.
  There's more to tell - it never stops
  The auto horns - the whistling cops
The artist's dream - the actor's hope
The Yankees with whom the Mets can't cope.
  But I must leave tomorrow night
  So put me aboard the airplane tight.

Laurence M. Weinberg

Panes Of Mist

People come, people pass,
In this world we think we know.
But, their hearts are made of glass,
Misty glass with panes so cold.

In a foggy haze we walk
Never stopping on our way
To show we care or sit and talk.
In this gloom is where we stay.

Though somewhere far off shine a light
This could about me's much too thick.
Although this light is flaming bright,
We ignore it, dim its wick.

I can not see a sweet azure;
My life's consumed by gray.
I don't know if I'm quite sure
Why I live this way.
    Marie Kauffman

Always, Your Friend

Tall green grass and sweet bright flowers
  in the meadow of my mind.
Sing a psalm of friendship, we fashioned
  with our time.

A shared idea, a laugh, a cry cinched
  our spirits in.
To form a band of caring, and strong
  love between two friends.

Though miles may be between us, our
  spirits still will blend.
I'll be with you forever, my most
  treasured prize, my friend.
    Linda S. Pittman

Special Person

There are so many things
  in our lives
Sometimes we seem to forget
  about the people in our lives
But you always remember
  one special person
A person who knows you
  better than yourself
A person who has been there
  for you when you need a good laugh
Or when you need to talk
  and have a good cry
A person who will forgive
  your faults
And sometimes we will
  have our bad times
But we will always remember
  our good times
To me, that special person
  is you my friend
    Lorena Yvette Villegas

Untitled

I'm sorry I make you late all the time
I hope in your heart you really don't mind
It is just that I enjoy your company
And time flies by so rapidly you see
So please don't be angry I ask once again
Because I consider you to be a friend
    Kory Conrod

A Black Voice

I am a weed
in my life's garden,
or so you would regard me.
But all your poisons
and attempts to mow me down
are doomed to fail.
I can take root in the
barestone walls in the meanest jail.
Push up through sidewalk cracks,
crumbling city blocks
claiming my rightful space.
Until you see I have an
Equal place. I will be free!
    Mel Alegria

Into A Dream

Behind the window
In front of my door
Beside my bed
Upon the floor

Beyond reality
Inside of a dream
Over a river
Past a stream

Inside of my body
Within a lie
Except for the fear
Of when I die

From this world
Of pain and hunger
This is a life
Of dreams and slumber
    Kim Crystal

This World

I have so many different friends,
In different shapes and colors.
Some I see more often
Than I get to see some others.

What I cannot understand,
What I cannot comprehend,
Is all the fighting in this world.
Will it ever end?

I think about my daughter
And all the hatred that I'm seeing.
When will people look around
And realize everyone's a human being?

I think about my daughter
Growing in this world we live in.
Will she too be judged
By her beliefs or color of her skin?

I teach her to respect herself
And each and every person.
There seems to be a lack of this,
Although it's an extremely important lesson.
    Miriam Pacheco

Oak

The Oak it stands so big and strong,
I wish that I could come along.
But only those who are born of earth,
Can hope to gain a second birth
    Michael G. Madison

John's Song

Could you behold such as I perceive
in a sheltered driftwood fire
in a plaintive sea gull cry
in a sunset of gold embrace?

I am a voice drifting along the sand.

Strange that love arises from death...

Could you comprehend such as I realize
in a silent granite spire
in a tide of infinite sigh
in a wild and lonesome place?

I am a touch gentling a forlorn hand.

strange that death ends not a love...

Could you cherish such as I discern
in a kiss of purling desire
in a moonrise sailing nigh
in a smiling windblown face?

I am a kite wheeling aloft the strand.

enduring love and undying death...

no less wondrous to you and I.
    Kathy Rose Joseph

I Wish...

I wish I could fly over the moon,
In a rocket ship.
I wish, I wish,
I wish I could dance,
On a stage at midnight.
I wish, I wish,
I wish I could be the president,
Of the United States.
I wish, I wish,
I wish I had a room full of flowers.
I wish, I wish,
I wish I had a garden,
A secret garden.
I wish, I wish, I wish.
    McKenzie Miller

"Autumn"

I remember this time
In a mood of melancholy
Yellows and reds
Rain and wind
They remind me of you.

We hunted, we walked
Explored the surrounding fields.
The dogs always in front of us
Their noses sniffing at
The crisp but pungent air.

Our races were quick
You always let me win.
Now I run alone.
My path not always my own.

Then I remember
What you told me
Life is like autumn
A time to change.
    Lisa A. Barker

Friends Forever

Friends forever we stand together.
In a moment of truth, the
brightness of hope.
We have shared the joys
and the blues.
We understand each other's
pain and sorrow.
We understand each other's
wishes and dreams.
Now we know why we stuck
Together because we'll always
be friends forever.

Kourtney Schuler

River Refuge

The life I lead is caged
Imprisoned I am alone
My dreams are someone else's
My destiny not my own

My only refuge lies with nature
Out under God's blue sky
With the soil beneath my time worn feet
And the river rushing by

Yes the river brings consolation
As it gurgles at my side
It has seen sorrow glee and agony
Hatred love and pride

Beside this river I now cry
Have cried-will cry
For the pitiful souls such as mine
Who were born and lived and now must die

River you have been good to me
Listening and giving your love
So I leave you now and commit my soul
Into the heavens above

Lauren Maggio

I Am A Woman!

I'm not supposed to be hit upon.
I'm supposed to be loved and not hated.
How could you hit me blow by blow and
Not realize you're hurting me?
You're hurting me physically and mentally.
You do not take time out to apologize
because you "think" you're too much of a man.
Well you are not too much of man
If you spend your time beating on a woman!

Karin Cleveland

Mum's The Word

This poem was made by me.
I'm only nine, just a boy, you see?
If my friends were to know,
They'd call me a nerd.
They'd laugh so hard,
If they ever heard.
That I like the sound of
Of words that rhyme.
Of lingo with rhythm
That keeps good time.
Well, I'm only nine, just a boy, you see?
So don't tell the guys
This was written by me!

Mathew E. DeVore

A Moonlight Miler

The moon, a motorcycle headlight,
 illustrates your svelte silhouette,
  against a flashbulb popping sea.
You sprint along the shore,
 with your fired hair,
  flaring in the breeze.

The waves, a scouring pad,
 erases your flux footprints,
  obliterating your pulpy path.
You pass in perfect stride,
 with your sinewy gait,
  sweeping along the sand.

I, a platonic figure,
 planted on the barren beach,
  scan the swarthy sea line.
I track your passage,
 with laser-guided accuracy,
  staring at you posterior.

Michael Gentzler

Untitled

My love, don't feel depress
 I'll be back before you
  know it
My love, don't feel sad
 My love is here for you
My love, don't feel lonesome
 My soul will be here
  with you.
My love, don't feel deserted
 I'll be back before you
  know it.
My love, feel the happiness
 When I come back to you
My love, feel the joy
 When I come running
  into your arms
My love, feel the love
 the love will bring
  us together soon.

Nancy Boothe

Internet

You'll always be what you think and say...
I'll always be what I know and what is...
Don't follow your dreams in
 "a world of virtue"...
  ... reality...
  ...thought...dream't...
  .. knew....
Wasn't there..
 mind..., dream't...
with surrounding feeling...touches..
and real.,never there...
I am...I cry...I felt.

Moon Star

Fallen

Falling leaves
in a copper moon
like the years hesitate
then tumble.
Turning spinning to the ground
falling,
they fall on one another down.
Do I want them back?
Not with this burning in me now.

Marilyn Lenzen

Nowhere

There's nowhere to run, nowhere to hide.
If you want to see reality open your
eyes wide. It might be good, it might
be bad, you might be happy, you might
be sad. There's nowhere to run, nowhere
to hide, must stand tall, must stand
with pride, must keep yourself going
never frown, always look up never down.
There's nowhere to run, nowhere to play,
must take it each day by day. Don't let
anyone say you're wrong, just stand
there and look strong. There's nowhere
to run, nowhere to play if you
see the horror on the streets of
today. Kids with gangs, and guns, and
drugs, why won't the world just give
out hugs. There's nowhere.

Melissa Traversa

Untitled

Dear Santa...you remember me?
I wrote to you last year
I wasn't very nice at all and
I'm not much better, I fear.

My sister, she's a wise one
Always blaming stuff on me!
Though it was I who tripped her
She knocked over the tree!

But Santa, I tried very hard
To be a real good boy
So come this Christmas morning
I'd find a brand new toy!

My Mother says I'm naughty
And she really has her doubts
My sister says that she'll get lots
And I'll have to do without!

But Santa, I was thinking
It could work just like they say,
It's the giving and the thought that counts
So I can have gifts anyway!

Linda Mead

Trust

Trust me,
I won't hurt you.
I won't bash you in
I'll be as kind as I can,
If I can have your trust

I will love you, like you,
and learn to respect you.
You will honor me for my trust.
I wont blab or steal
My trust, my friend, is real.

I'll be that shoulder
no going through a bolder
I'll be that smile
I will talk for a while,
with all the trust I have.

Trust me, if you will,
and I will trust you.
You can trust me.

Mary Jo Dennis

I Am

I am smart and a fast runner
I wonder what I'll grow up to be
I hear the kids in my old neighborhood
I see the beach
I want a '67 Mustang
I am smart and a fast runner

I pretend to have my dream car
I feel the ocean gently kissing my ankles
I touch the wet sand
I worry about my future
I cry when I think of my old friends
I am smart and a fast runner

I understand why I moved
I say the glass is half full
I dream I never moved
I try to do my best
I hope I'll make lots of new friends at Acadia
I am smart and a fast runner
Lisa Srok

Heart Of Light

Beaming thru the darkest night
I woke to see a light
So brightly shining

It was Angels
Calling for me

Heaven can't wait
you see

Let me share one soft touch
A kiss to at last seal our vow

Unbroken even in the darkest hour
Lynn King

Fragile Strength

Spoke the flower in November,
"I will not lay down and die.
If there is sunlight in the days ahead,
Through the nights I will get by.

For I have not finished living yet.
There is much I need to do.
I have more buds that wait to bloom,
More seeds to leave for you.

The time will come for me to rest,
Under Winter's blanket white,
When I have done my best, left my mark,
And lived with all my might.

You must disregard my crumpled leaves,
Withered brown by frosts of past.
Look instead to the beauty I have left.
The best, I saved for last."
Karen Vinson

A Thought

As I think of love,
I wonder what a wolf with ice encrusted paws
Must feel like after spending a harsh winter
Searching for warmth and nourishment
The day the first rays of spring shine.
Mike Urash

Cover Of Tears

I gave you a cover of tears,
I watched you go down the isle,
I followed you out to the garden,
I longed to see your sweet smile.

The memories come back to me now,
The love and the heartache we shared,
The growing we all did together,
The thoughts and the feelings you cared.

I gave you a cover of tears,
I touched you as you went on by,
You were my Maria Theresa,
In you I reached to the sky.

You gave me all that was yours,
In life and now that you're gone,
I'll try hard to go on without you,
My heart will carry your song.
marion murphy

I Believe

Whisper you love me,
I want to believe.
Tell me you need me,
Then you up and leave.
How can I go on,
Pretending it's real?
Cause, I believe in fairy tales.
Do you believe:
In story book times?
Hanging on clouds?
And flying on high?
Soar like the wind?
And float like the leaves?
I'm hanging on chances!
Oh! Do you believe?
I believe in Cinderella!
I believe in miracles!
Tell me now,
While there's still time.
Mr. Prince, will you ever be mine!
Luellen Short

One Being

He glares,
I turn.

He screams,
I turn.

He attacks,
I turn.

He bruises,
I turn.

He is mournful,
I turn.

He weeps,
I turn.

He kneels,
I walk away.
Michelle Paton

Lost Love

You left so quietly, little bird,
I thought you were content.
I believed your quiet little song,
I thought you would consent.
You had me fooled, little bird.
I put my trust in you,
So, I left your little cage door open,
And, in the night, away you quietly flew.
You went without warning, little bird,
I never thought you felt confined.
I would have given you your space,
Maybe then you would have felt I was kind.
Could I have done anything, little bird,
That would have made you stay?
Did you feel you needed to travel the world,
To see the mountains and the bay?
You broke my heart, little bird.
I know it may sound absurd.
I'm starting to understand, my love,
Just lying here, thinking of my lost little bird.
Kelly Thomson

Untitled

In a different state
I tell you
That of truth
You and I and all
We've found together as friends
A person I see
Can bring a smile to all
Of us who cries a tear
To those who care enough
And a beautiful sight to see
You are to me
A person I will love
Till time stops
And all the joy you bring
To the life I possess
And troubles I see
Through your eyes
I mourn for us
For you are me
And I love you
Kevin Kretser

Untitled

What makes someone special?
I suppose it all depends
It's what unique in each of us
That we will share as friends

The difference is the differences
Maybe great or small
Variety adds spice to life
So we should celebrate,
Your you and I'm me

If there was only one note
How boring life would be
I'm glad there are so many notes
In many different keys

I hear each voice singing
With a special quality
And when we sing together
We bring music to the earth.
Keilen Holben

"Wake Me When I Die"

I'm human.
I suffer.

I want to die
and feel no pain.

When I arrive
to immortality from reality
I will be happy.
Wake me when I die.

Karen Lynn Franke

The Dream Of Dreams

The new kingdom, the new kingdom
I see the new kingdom. Though my
life is filled with Kayoas, though
it is filled with fear. Though my tears
flow like a river, I see the new
kingdom. It's a place where my dreams
will be fulfilled. In this kingdom,
I live near the roaring sea. I play hoops
on the sand. I fly like a bird.
I dunk as "Air Michael-Jordan."
The people, the people in this kingdom are
of a simple mind and of a simple place.
Off in this kingdom we humble ourselves
even though the streets are filled with
Gold! I see, I see, the dream of all
dreams, it's a childhood playground!

Michael Meloro

Now You're Gone

As the sun arose this morning,
I saw your smiling face.
The soft pink clouds made a silhouette
of beauty, charm and grace.

The silhouette wears a smile,
just as you always do.
A smile of warmth and friendliness,
I know, my love, is you.

And as the clouds did fade away.
I wept, for you were gone.
And yet I smiled, for as we know,
Tomorrow is another dawn.

Linda Zimmerman

Down On Lorain

I saw you a minute too late but
I saw you as I lit my cigarette
in the window with my fair body
exposed. I could not tell your exact
expression. Were you amused?
Were you shocked?
 Shortly thereafter I came back
to see if you were still there and
found you door closed.
Were you embarrassed?

Old woman don't worry.
I am nothing more than on image
of what you once were,
And you are nothing more than
a picture of what I will be.

Kathy Robinson

Spring

I saw you drive away the snow.
I saw God cause the plants to grow.
And all around I saw your face
In every flower in the place.

Oh! Spring so lovely and so fair,
In all the gorgeous gowns you wear.
I saw you deck the trees in green.
I saw you crown the May Day Queen.
And all around sweet odors swept,
From blossoms fair as pedals wept.
Oh! Spring so happy and so gay,
You change our darkness into day.

Marian A. Swieringa

Deadly Silence

As I sat wishing and waiting,
I saw a world of people died;
now I wish I acted on beliefs,
as all that's left is me, so I cried.

From the beginning to the end,
a darkness so profound;
always willing to lend a hand,
yet hardly making a sound.

Ever a war, or man, to serve its needs,
waiting for a time to strike again;
plenty of lost souls, to do the deeds,
for do we not have a world insane?

The madness spreads its wonders wide,
we see how quickly, man helps man die;
and so we see the silence and pride,
as dwindling man gives a gasp or sigh.

For now you see, I...the silent majority,
as the good man waited to long alone;
now all that's left from the hate,
is our flesh being eaten, raw to the bone.

Rhyet

The Fellow Traveler

Yesterday,
I saw a dust Devil
Dancing in the empty field,
Along the traveled way.

Today,
I saw another Devil
Dustily-whirlwinding—
Following me.
Fading out to a ghostly whisper
Then in a moment
It became
A full-blown whirlwind that
Materialized;
Dipping,
Swirling,
And just as quickly disappeared
And I was alone
Once more.

Not even a dustmote was left
Floating there!

Norma V. Yandell

Midmorning's Ride

At morning's light that day in March
I rose to mount the hairy arch.
With head dropped low and ears laid back
With might and mane both fierce and black
He eyed me with a curious eye
As tho to say, "Mount me and die."
And so I did, Oh, foolish man.
It's thus my odyssey began.
He backed, he turned, he fought the rein
And I aboard his back remained.
And then he reared, and then I fell.
The fall to earth; the sound of hell.
And then my eyes looked toward the sky
As down he fell where I did lie
To crush my bones, to break my flesh,
My very soul he did immense.
The sound from out my wounded lips
Moaned, as the great apocalypse.
And yet I rose to greet the day,
Broken and bloodied, but okay!

Myles B. Knape

A Friendship Mirage

As I cross a desert in my mind,
I realize all I left behind.
I lost my friends,
I'm at the end.
What can you be?
You didn't help me.
In my mind, you are air
Although I thought we were the perfect pair.
What will I do
Without a friend like you?
But you're an illusion,
Not a friend.
I should have known I was at the end.
Although, maybe without you,
I can just forget about you.
Because I do know right from wrong.
What doesn't kill me, makes me strong!

Melissa Leitman

Untitled

Just the other day,
I looked into your eyes.
Somehow things had changed,
it hurt to realize.
You seemed so annoyed,
at every thing I did.
So back in my little corner,
is where I painfully hid.
You know you really scared me,
I thought you were gone for good.
Somehow this day was turning out,
nothing like it should.
There was rain inside my head,
it kept coming harder.
As the day went on,
you slowly went farther.
Somehow you came through,
the light shined again.
It's not only that I love you,
I'm also your friend.

Lydia Nelmes

Quaking Aspen

Tall, slim, milky white,
I look at you in an inspirational light
standing erect among the pines,
a Mother to trees of all times.

The slightest breeze makes you quake,
a legacy among the trees to make
you bring them up with gentle care
and gladly help them their troubles bear.

When your adopted children have grown high
reaching majestically for the sky
their massive shade blocks the light
causing you to lose the right for life.

Laura Williams

My Dreams

I am not a bird that flies above
I live on earth which I love.

I dream of seeing the earth revived
Without wars, without crimes.

The cruel actions would not exist
And all the peoples live in peace.

He who spent his life on earth
Would leave a good name after his death.

Mira Brokhin

Fear

On the pillow of darkness
I lay my head.
When the moon comes out
I wish I were dead.

You're scared, you're frightened,
You don't know what to do.
Maybe after tonight
Your life will be through.

Inside, your body's filled
With anger and hate,
It's not my fault
You're in trouble -
You stayed up too late.

You think tomorrow
Birds will sing and
Flowers will bloom.
Try not to worry about the night filled with gloom.

You're scared, you're frightened,
You're about to burst in two.
What are you to do before the night is through?

Nathen Phillips

Time...

However the Appearance
it remains the SAME.
Always here and there
but Never the same.
Change is what it Is.
Motionless when Acknowledge.
flashing if unnoticed
Different so it is Called.
A place, moment, or sequence
Mysterious to all.

Kristine D. Boudreau

After The Chorale

To all the angels in my life...
I hear the flutter of your wings.

I wish you peace said the magician
and right be fore my eyes
I heard the angel's wings.

I was on a mountaintop looking into the
snowfall from the sky and
I heard the angel's wings.

I was listening to the beautiful voices
singing songs of Christmas and
I heard the angel's wings.

I was envisioning the magic of faith
in the spiritual and
I heard the angel's wings.

I was experiencing the fulfillment
of friendship and
I heard the angel's wings.

Liz Allman

Me

I was born a bad birth in June.
I have learned not to sin.
I have heard my parents fight.
I remember catching bees.
I was the first child.
I bought a penny for a dollar.
I have collected the whole He-Man set.
I've been bit by ferocious dog.
I got shot by a paintball gun.
I was the kid everyone laughed at.
I once left my house when I had enough.
I flew across the United States.
My dream is to live on my own island
I was thrilled to receive my first bike.
I used to always bite when I was young.
I have gone from soccer to football,
and skating to surfing.
I was always scared of myself on Halloween.
I have lost my pet parakeet.
My cats have disappeared.

Kory Wilde

The Message

As I started to work very early one morn
 I had no idea of the message borne
By the heavens there before me

My thoughts were of much
 About orders and such
Things to do when I got to the store

Tho the time was still night
 The moon big and bright
Made country side shapes you could see

Then the east caught my eye
 And the glow in the sky
Told me sunrise was almost in view

And I knew that the moonlight
 That first had seemed so bright
Was no match for light of the day

This is like life at the end of our days
 A glimpse of the light as we finish earth's maze
To show what's ahead will be glorious

Lila M. Spear

A Lesson From Childhood

As I walked upon a field today,
I had a funny feeling.
While picking through the clover,
The deja vu was reeling.

Back to another place in life
When time went just a little slower,
And yards were full of interest
'Cause we just had a hand mower!

There were necklaces to make from clover,
And dandelion puffs to blow.
Imagination could run wild there
On spots where no grass would grow.

Today we've created a monster.
The perfect yard is a must.
It seems there is a new motto,
"No weed grow here or bust!"

It all set me to thinking
That maybe we drive ourselves crazy.
Frankly, I think I'll change my ways,
Watch the clover grow and get lazy!

Marguerite Pons Williamson

"Four Walls"

In all my dreams I praise these walls,
I glance with love at every turn.
No one will ever steal away,
The memories seen at every nook.
Generations will come and go,
The stories they tell will never end.
Those photos on the walls can tell,
That life will always live within.
Don't fret, don't cry we're here not gone.
Preserve the stories of life foretold.
If these walls could speak,
You could always hear;
Our love for you and me will never end.
These treasured walls will forever live.

Louisa DeLeon

Broken Heart

I loved him so much,
I gave him my heart,
But he took it for granted,
And broke it apart.

He left a scar in my life,
I crumbled to pieces,
The pain never stops,
It haunts and increases.

If I had a fresh start,
I would make no mistake,
I'd find the right man,
Then my heart would not brake.

Kim Epperson

Dreams

At night when I go to bed,
I dream of wonderful things in my head,
Castles with dragons prowling around,
Gardens where magical fruits are found,
Fair ladies imprisoned in a tower,
Or lost in an enchanted bower,
While knights and horsemen ride by streams,
That border all this land of dreams,
I find so clearly in my head,
At night when I go to bed.

Nathaniel High

Sometimes...A Lull-A-Bye

Sometimes life's confusing,
I don't know which way to turn,
Love has taken so much from me,
My heart no longer burns.

My friends all live so far away,
There's nothing I can do,
There was a man I cared for here,
But he has left me, too.

Sometimes life's so crazy,
I lose my mind to liquor every night;
People make me so angry,
I want nothing more than a fight.

Sometimes life's so depressing,
I just want to die;
But death is way too final,
So all I do is cry.

Sometimes, life's so tiring,
I just want to weep,
But I have no energy for tears,
So I fall asleep.

Lisa R. Burris

Individual In One

I am black
I am white
I am red
I am yellow

I am a man
I am a woman

I am disabled
I am foreign

I am young
I am old

I am homosexual
I am lesbian

We have all been created in the image
of God and we have all been created equal.

Mickey J. Carson

Do Not Label Me

Do not label me...
  I am not a sign.
Do not call me names...
  I am not an enemy.
Do not mock me...
  I am not a comedian.
Do not identify me...
  I am not a thing.
Do not stick it to me...
  I am not a wall.
Do not hit me...
  I am not numb.
Do not pass me...
  I am not gas
Do not neglect me...
  I am a person.
Do not label me...
  I am not a sign.

Kristen Denecker

Me

Who am I?
I am my mother,
I am my father,
And I am my peers,
But I am not me.
I try to be me and no one accepts who I am.
I try to be them and I hate myself.
I have no feelings,
I feel what they want me to feel.
I have no opinions or thoughts,
I think what they want me to.
When I tell them the truth,
I am lying to myself.
I try to find who I am,
But don't know which parts of me are mine.
Who can help me find myself?
Only I can.

Lindsey Wentland

Asking God's Help

Now, my good life has ended
I am exhausted and weary
Discouraged, downcast and low
I am not happy living alone
But, there is no foreseeable answer
I have no place else to go

I kneel down in desperation
And slowly start to pray
Then, God did not answer me
Which I expected right away
Since he did not hear my plea
Why should I bother to pray

I am very nervous and anxious
I am too impatient to wait
I must believe and have faith
He doesn't answer too soon or too late
Since he did not answer promptly
In my heart, I know in my heart he's delayed

Mary Grace Nicholson

Disintegration

How the hours have rushed in panic,
How the time has swiftly sped.
My mind keeps turning backward
and I cannot look ahead.
There's a devil in the foreground,
there's another on my back
and the imp that is my conscience
has me ever on the rack.
I cringe from wailing voices
that aren't really heard.
I flee from monstrous shadows
that leave my vision blurred.
There's another me inside me
that turns and twists my brain.
That plays upon my nerve-ends
until I'm all of me insane.

Morris Ginsburg

A

A crocodile is not a gator
A wasp is not a bee
A frog is not a toad
A bush is not a tree
Oh, I just don't see the difference
But I know: A you is not a me.

Kevin Kammeraad

Times Of The Great Depression

I'm thinking about my mother
how she had to sell her wedding ring.
I was little, and now I'm old
but I'll never forget how calm she was,
just a reddening of the eyes.
Our home ('til the bank foreclosed)
was in a nice suburban neighborhood,
a mecca for transients, indigent and weary.
I remember clearly, still, a lovely woman,
very young and lone; so neat, so clean,
so pale, frail and wraithlike that
the edges of her seemed sheer
like wings of moths.
Mama fixed her toast and two fried eggs —
it smelled so good.
The lady could not eat.
She apologized to Mama that
her stomach was
too shrunk for food.
There are many kinds of wars.

Nancy L'enz Hogan

Holding On

I never took the time to notice
how she had changed.
I was always busy,
Appointments rearranged.

I would sometimes drop by
Just to say hello,
And when I'd leave
She'd always smile,
But wished I wouldn't go.

Now sitting here beside her,
Hand in hand since dawn,
My mother died this morning,
But I'm still holding on.

Lawrence Klepinger

Lady Bug

Lady bug, lady bug
how red you are.
With all of your spots
you shine like a star.
Eating and protecting
the flowers that smell so bright.
You bring good luck
wherever you go.
You might as well come on down.
My crops are dying and turning brown.
So please come on down and give me luck.
I'll give you all the leaves you can eat.
Don't worry about paying it's my treat.
Lady bug, lady bug
how beautiful you are.
Bring me some luck.
I think you see why I need it.
Very much!!!

Lucas Redmond

A New Star

There's a new star in Heaven tonight.
A way up there shining so bright.
Sending to Earth a lovely light.
I wish, I wish with all my might.
That I could hold that star tonight,
Oh, wouldn't that be a glorious sight.
Holding that beautiful star tonight.

Ovella Easter

Birthday Wish

Today is your day.
Hope your birthday is
bright and sunny.

It's the right time
for fishing and golfing.

Cake and ice cream
are being served.

Because you're an
Uncle who is deserving.

This is wishing you
Love and lots more
in the year to come.

Mary M. Valeu

Untitled

Masking the pain inside.
Holding the fears of life.
No one ever knowing
how hurt you're feeling inside.
Putting on a smile
when really you want to cry.
Feeling so much hurt
and nothing no one can do.
Angry and frustration.
Where is all the love
sent from Heaven above?
Yet we are nothing
without His love.
God will love, all
you have to do is ask.
So pray to Him, when
you're feeling sad and
you may just get
a laugh.

Kimberly Fowler

"A Memorial To Jim Morrison"

The words of somber poet
He's gone
But not forgotten
Out of sight
Not out of mind
A treasure like gold
To have and to hold
Oh gentle spirit
I wish you this
Your eternal peace
Peace be with you
As you rest
Though it's hard to
To say goodbye
Peace be with you
Where you lie
Peace to the poet
Whose words made the Doors
Those are the words
Forever yours

Lori Kunz

Sister Sun

The sun is large and bright
it illuminates eternal night.
It contains pure light
and darkness runs in fright.
The sun stands alone
and on the earth is shone
her life-giving light.

Michelle Marie Prendes

Pleaful Cry

Dear God up in heaven,
hear my pleaful cry.
Forgive me of my sins,
and teach me not to sigh.
Teach me Lord not to be jealous
of what my neighbor has.
Teach me not to covet
for things I do not have.
Teach me Lord instead,
to be very very thankful.
And to know that you and you alone,
provide what I have.
Help me Lord not to be weary in well doing
but do it all day long.
Teach me Lord to forgive and understand.
All of what others have was provided
by your hand.

Maudie Litton

His Hands

With his hands
he touched the blind to see
With his hands
he hung and died for me
Oh when I see those hands
I can't understand
Why he did it all for me

He picked me up
when he heard my cry
gently drew me to his precious side
then set me down upon the solid ground
and that's where I stand
since he touched me with his hands

Sinner take your hands
and pray with me
Let his blood
come and set you free
Oh won't you take his hand
he'll help you understand
Why he died for all eternity

Neisha Cochran

Growing Gracefully

Retired, but with determined grip,
He sets his jaw and bites his lip,
As he surveys his joys and trials;
His folks and friends his pills in vials

He wonders, will it balance out;
Can good off set the bad about?
Does he some good influence bring,
To cause some hurting souls to sing?

He looks to check some things he's done;
Accomplishments, or battles won,
That might off set his loss of vim;
And some "get up and go" in him.

If daily gains exceed the losses,
And joy for others lifts his crosses,
He has a pleasant living style,
Though growing older all the while.

Melissa Moczulski

Son, Brother, Father, Friend

When I walked on a wall
He held me up when I would fall
He would hug me tight to calm my fear
Wherever he was
   He was always near.

He was a teacher
   In his own way
He was a scholar
   In what he'd say
He was a giver
   To the lives he touched
He was a comfort
   And was loved so much.

His family was important
   Of this there's no doubt
They are a reminder
   Of what his life was about
He shielded the pain and sorrow
   Showed us hope and love
Now he protects us from his home above.

Karen Ward

My Red-Haired Boy

He looks at me with eyes of grey;
He does not ask for very much.
Calm, trustful in baby way,
He thinks I hold a magic touch.

Late sunbeams through the window
Fall upon hair of burnished gold.
I pray, "God, let his hair remain this way;
Don't let it fade as he grows old.

And now my sleepy little boy
Toddles toward me with a yawn;
I tuck him safely into bed
He knows I'll be there at dawn

The house is quiet, I gaze at him
And picture him on life's hard road.
I think he'll bear his burdens well
And smile, no matter what the load.

When grown to manhood years from now,
His locks may match those eyes of grey;
In memory then I still will see
The red-haired boy I love today.

Norma Ruth Sanders

The Ocean Blues

If you look at the ocean,
has a beautiful blue
and has a magic potion.
Nothing can destroy it, not even you.
Its fish swim free,
and feed on the seaweed,
all happy with glee.
With great speed,
the sun's light shines down.
The sea life is peaceful.
The ocean bottom is a deep dark brown,
The waters are cool.
The wind blows to make waves,
as sharks look for fish.
Sometimes I feel it is all just a wish!
I call it the ocean blues,
as blue as perhaps my shoes.
The ocean is so blue,
and so wonderfully true.

Kosha Patel

Sisters

Two people
Growing together
But living
As strangers
Till one day
Their minds meet
Surprised at the thoughts
Of each other
only to find
They are the same
　Nancy Allen

Mommy

Mommy don't let me
grow up so fast
Let me walk and talk and play
Let me kiss and hug and say "I LOVE YOU"
In my trusting and childish way

Soon enough I'll be all grown up
With the worries that grown-ups face
So, please, try now to tolerate me
And my all too rapid pace

Enjoy my childish mannerisms, Mom
While still they linger on
I need for you to understand
That I won't be a child for long
　Nicole L. Hodson

Rainfall

An angry sky
Greets us today,
As rain falls like tears
Along our way.

The frantic winds
Sway each moist leaf,
Which gleams as it falls
To ground beneath.

Then comes the morn -
All earth is still,
And the sun breaks forth
Upon the hill.
　Lorette Murphy

Rest The Heart

Hear the music of bird-songs
Greet the morning sun;
Excited chirping from joyful hearts
And flowing notes of pure melody;
These little throats were fashioned
For the sound of beauty
Such exalting trills could never be writ;
These little hearts know only
The message of cheer;
Like life itself they present
Moments of wonder and delight
To be savored now and held
As long as memory lasts.
　Olive E. Bergquist

Untitled

It is with sadness that I say
Good-bye to your dear friend.
I know although we must now part
Our friendship will not end.

For many years we did together
so many pleasant things
We share the sorrow and the joys
That destiny us brings.

Of one another precious dreams
And hope we always knew
And wished for one another that
All of them would come true.

If we at times did not agree
As do that best of friends
We never did not hesitate
To quickly make amends.

Because you have in my life played
Such an important part
Our friendship I am sure will stay
Forever in my heart.
　Marshall L. Berman

No-One But Me

It's in the river,
Going to the sea.
No-one will notice,
No-one but me.

Flowing, flowing,
Continuously,
Stopping for no-one,
No-one but me.

Bringing the treasure,
That no-one can see
No-one will know,
No-one but me.

It's in my heart,
It is the key.
No-one can feel it,
No-one but me.
　Michelle Bruhnke

Paula

Rock fountains, soft support
Godly touch to assist along
A passable trail, encouragement said
His creates temporal strong.

White satin birds, majestic oaks,
Transparent river streams
A walk through His paradise fulfilled,
His promise, mortals dreams.

Nature, birds, support I pray
Thankful to God above
He gave me you, my walking stick
And angelic dove.

Right filled eyes in blessed join
pair life on sea and sand,
An answered prayer, a sacred act,
To me, thine loving hand.
　Mike Bensen

Destiny

Seasons colors have
given way to inevitable
changes life must bring.
A mother's heart cries,
as painted skies tell
stories, lessons learned
hard with more to follow.
The sun sets on
another page and a child's
heart cries - darkness
falls on the miles that
bind - bound by love
torn hearts cry together.
　Nicole Peltier

Dream

To live with joy
gathering all those things
that our inner wavers...
and all the effort won't bring.

But there are them.
For us, in eternal fantasy,
chase them in vain,
relishing the wants
and making up for joy.

In early autumn
they come up looking.
All the wants gone.
No much of joy, present.

Under the skin we feel
the resilience of not having
attained our will.
Soul gazing over
the abyss that reigned.
And what is left of joy,
surrendered!
　Marco Mercado

Little Girl Lost

Daddy please come back
From wherever you've gone.
Mommy can't stop crying
And feels all alone.

Brother and I are sad
Cuz you're not here to play.
Instead of riding my bike
I cried on my pillow today.

Tell God to send you back.
Brother is turning two,
And I will be six soon,
Birthdays can't be without you!

Through tears and sadness,
Mommy explains about you,
But God doesn't need you...
Not like I do!
　Katrina R. Grant

The Nut

They cracked my shell
And looked inside.
They saw but raw meat
They ate me.
　Merrill Neave

Voice of Heaven

O Angel fair, please bring us word
   From this God we have not heard;
Tell his news to those who grieve,
   And enlighten those who disbelieve.
Be not elusive, show your face,
   Be sublime and full of grace.
Tell us how we came to be,
   Show us things we cannot see;
Explain to us this Master Plan
   What God intends to do with man;
If you can, please clue us in
   On how to turn away from sin;
Tell us, in a minstrel's song
   All the ways that we've gone wrong,
Then show us how to make it right,
   And guide us into heaven's light.
O Voice of Heaven, Angel fair
   Take us to the heavens there.
     Laura McConnell

No Longer

No longer do we gather eggs
   from henhouse or hidden under sheds.
We stop for them at the supermarket
   and pay a whopping price instead.
No longer do we can our meat
   or smoke or fry it down.
We purchase a super-freezer
   and buy all our meat in town.
No longer do we take to mill
   the rye and wheat we've grown
To get the flour for making bread,
   we don't know how to bake our own.
No longer do we save the seed
   to plant garden the coming year.
The trucker hauls our produce in
   we're too involved it would appear.
No longer is there relaxation
   in doing jobs that should be done,
We must keep up with Mr. Jones
   though we miss a lot of fun.
     Nora Newman

Intimate Passage

Soft words spoken
from deep within.
Yearning to feel the warmth
of your skin.
Kiss me, kiss me, my
imagination races.
Trying to capture the lust of
your embrace.
Dreams beyond the furthest star.
Ecstasy surpasses
all by far.
     Martha Alice Fields

It's Christmas Time Again

Good wishes, glad tidings and
   holiday cheer;
Fruitcake, bright lights and
   a Red-nosed Reindeer?
Prayerfully healthy and wiser
   this year,
Merry Christmas to you and
   Happy New Year!
     Mary E. Dacey

Untitled

Bright
   freshly-painted
     Carousel

Twirls

Up high
I can see
   lush, green meadows
     clear azure hues

Down low
   I view
     grime
       greasy
Axles turning wheels

Tears
   fall on
noisy motors

I ride
   the
     silent thoroughbred.
     Luci L. Olsen

Untitled

When the billow of your smile
found no quietness in smiling
I took your head and
put it to my chest
And the beating of it all
laughed you in meeting kiss
the sweet intricate little-ness
of all my heart
And in you
     Nathan Whittemore

Best Friend

My Lord is right beside me.
Forever my best friend,
through thick and thin together
with love until the end.

We are always side by side
together we won't sway.
Right beside me my Lord stands
Forever he will stay.
     Katie Leigh Emerald

Self

Ask the mirror of your reflections
   for your true self
to find out:
   It is not you.

Ask time, mother of predictions
   for your future
to find out:
   It is not your future.

Ask your mother - reason for existing
   for her thoughts on life
to find out:
   It is not your life.

Nagging questions, restless and confused
You try to live, searching for your true Self
To find out:
   It is not lost.
     Nicole Henzler

Our Footsteps Of Love

I had searched the whole world over.
For such a dream as you.
One who could love me for myself.
And thrill me the way you do.

We have each other My darling
To love, honor and trust.
To hold our love so sacred
Till we both shall turn to dust.

For God gave us each other, Sweetheart.
To travel the rugged road as one.
And I shall never forsake thee Darling.
Till my last breath is gone.

We'll live each day to the fullest
We'll build a home of happiness sublime
We'll leave behind for our children.
Our footsteps of love, in the sands of time.
     Marney L. Norwood

Untitled

Live every day to the fullest
   for it might be your last
Give to the poor
   for it might someday be you
Open your heart
   for the Lord will speak
Take chances
   for they may never come again
Fear nothing
   for God is with you
Talk to your angels
   for they will listen
Always smile
   for others will do the same
Respect your parents
   for they gave you life
Give of yourself
   for others may be in need
Love the Lord
   for he will always love you
     Miranda Walding

My Strange Elephant

My elephant is really weird,
for he's yellow with a purple beard!
He's got some stripes and polka-dots,
and likes to eat in parking lots!

He's pretty tall and round and fat,
and always wears a bright red hat!
He's got big ears and a big nose,
that looks just like a great big hose!

His name is Marvin Malard Moe,
and he has a huge humongous toe!
He's got brown eyes and great big thighs,
and has a lot of different ties!

Some ties are big, some ties are round,
and one is green that Marvin found!
Marvin has the chicken pox,
that matches with his red knee socks.

Marvin gets a lot a mail,
that's always from his friend the whale.
Him and Marvin are great friends,
with them, the fun never ends!
     Katie Clark

Heaven Is My Home

Do not grieve when I am gone
For God is standing by...
He knows our thoughts, our hopes
Our soul, he does not let us die
Do not grieve nor feel the strife
As we pass on to eternal life
If we believe in what God said
There is no thought that we are dead
Our life goes on, we live again
In God's planned world, all void of sin.

Mona Morris

"For Use To See"

I think I have the soul of an artist
For each morning as I drive along
I see so many beautiful sights
That fill my heart with song.

A stately tree, stands unchallenged,
Against a meadow green.
The drifting low hung clouds of fog
Seem like pictures on a screen.

Over the wooded hills, the sun
Rises like a huge ball of fire,
Revealing the beauties of nature
Garbed in her grandest attire.

The beauty of earth, in his painting,
Man often portrays so well,
But God, in one fleeting moment,
Creates the scenes, which excel!

Leona S. Detwiler

"A Prayer From The Heart"

Thank you oh so much Dear Lord
For all the sweet wonderful blessings,
You have given me in this life!
The divine joys that only you,
Could truly bestow upon a person.
I'm sincerely grateful
In all the precious treasures
Only from your loving hands they come.
Keep me safe in your tender care;
My mind is constantly filled
With glorious praise towards you.
Master of my life,
Protect of my spirit,
Captain of my heart!
Help me win this race called "Life on Earth."
That I must take part in.
Give me courage please I pray!
In order to make it on over
To make it on over
Into your Eternal Kingdom called "Paradise".

Karen Kenyatta Moody

Night

Night is hypnotic
Fluid as a water lake
Delicately it hums.
Night is a beautiful monster,
so delicately devised
mysterious as lovers.
Night is a selfish child that
suffocates day...languidly.
Night is deception washed clean as
the fiery sun crests over the ancient hills.
Night

Michelle S. Cilia

Liquid Attitude

Open spaces and the wet eyes
Flowing tears like rain from skies.

I try to die, I dine on pain,
But all that reaches is the frozen rain.

The empty space in which I dined
Cared more for me than you, I'll find.

I've trapped the rain, cloud and thunder
Maybe I'll break this spell I'm under.

I'm trying to die with smooth grin and pride
Like rain that falls and ends up as tide.

Loraina Floyd

Flowers

Flowers are beautiful,
Flowers are colorful,
Flowers are wonderful,
   Looking that is.

Flowers are reds,
Flowers are pinks,
Flowers are purples,
   That's what I think.

Flowers are roses,
Flowers are tulips,
Flowers are pansies,
   That shine in the sun.

Flowers are dull,
Flowers are bright,
Flowers are shiny,
   In the night.

Flowers are short,
Flowers are tall,
Flowers are low,
   In the ground.

Nicole Nauyalis

Our Love

Moonbeams across the lake
Flame of love's embrace
Sitting hand in hand
A love we can't withstand
The sky's shining light
Falls with quite a sight
Never knowing a destination
You stare with inspiration
Relax through your mind
A tingle down your spine
Destination clear and true
My love I share with you

Kenneth A. Key

Untitled

Dreamers own the world
for they have what it takes
Everyone's a dreamer
but some are jarred awake
Be it sports, models, or writers
some in other extremes
To be a dreamer, a fighter
you must know what it means
To be that famous person
who must live out their dreams

Melissa L. Varga

A Childhood Memory

Snow fell
Fire crackled
Wood smelled
Burn-y
Mama made
Snow cream
Tasted
Vanillary.

Snow fell
Fire danced
Logs smelled
Woodsy
Daddy sang
"My Blue Heaven"
Sounded
Warm and merry.

LaVohn W. Waddell

The Glory Of Christmas

I would like to tell you a Christmas story
Filled with happiness and glory.
It all began one Christmas Eve
That's what people say and believe.
In Bethlehem where a baby was born,
He lay in a manger where sheep are shorn.
A baby who would be a king
Throughout all nations His name will ring.
This child called Jesus is God's own son
He lived and died for everyone.
He died on a cross far away
To pay for our sins that occur ever day.
Thank you Lord Jesus for your tender care.
I know when I need you - you will be there.

Mary White

Autumn's Shadows

Branches of color all around,
Falling leaves upon the ground.

Harvest moons shining many nights,
Jack-o-lanterns glowing by candle lights.

Costume strangers at one's door,
Apples, pumpkins, festivals - yet more.

Flocks leaving above the sky,
Preparations for holidays seeing nearby.

Frost coming with a chill,
Winter is approaching - Autumn's still.

Karen M. Wilson

Cinderella

Tears glitter in bright blue eyes,
Faded bruise mars her shoulder,
Dark green velvet over midnight lace.
Bright smiles paint her mask,
Murmurs flow freely on air.
Reaching into the void within,
She stretches for a feeling,
Just one she can call her own.
Surrounded by people, though
She's alone in mind's abyss.
Will you reach in and save her?
No! The fairy tale is dead.

Katie Chaney

Rebirth

Plant a seed in the
early spring
And watch it sprout
while the raindrops sing.
Watch it bloom when
the sun comes out
Then wither and die
in the autumn drought
To return again to
Mother Earth
and its cycle of rebirth.

Martha Murphey

Falling Apart

Vivid memories from a solemn past
Eagerly racing through thoughts of the mind.
Aggressively screaming out in unison
When cast behind.

Inner turmoil, internal pain
Coursing through mind, body and soul.
Bravely fighting it off
until insanity gains control.

Consumed by panic and fear.
All reason and meaning utterly lost.
The mind's perceptions made unclear
Not much is left of myself.

The turmoil and the pain
Now it all seems the same.
No more fighting to be done.
The struggle was lost.

Body racked by distress
Falling apart from the inside out
One last thing do I ponder:
What was this life all about?

Matt Barnes

That's Magic Wouldn't You Say?

Magic occurs each second of the day,
During the birth of an innocent life.
That's magic wouldn't you say?

An individual is born with a special way.
Personality, love, independence and pride.
That's magic wouldn't you say?

A new opinion comes into the world.
We hear their cry, Why? Why! Why.
That's magic wouldn't you say?

When answers unfold
as we grow old.
That's magic wouldn't you say?

A microscopic spark ignites
an explosion of ripples we call life.
That's magic wouldn't you say?

It's magic wouldn't you say,
If we all looked at life this way
Starting each glorious day
Knowing its our new birthday
That's magic wouldn't you say?

Mark Dwane Mullins

Parting

Life on the rocks
down by the sea
We take our walk
Just you and me

One hot summer's day
Out on the beach
with nothing to say
both out of reach

We set on the sand,
as the clouds go by
you wave your hand
I try not to cry

I know it's the end
as we say good by
I know you're my friend
I don't ask you why

Kenneth Gary Sargent

Dawn

Don't ask me why.
Don't ask me how many times I tried.
To reach you with my soul,
my heart, my mind...

It always happens at dawn,
When the stars are almost gone,
and the moon is not so bright,
but it still has so much light.

And I hear myself calling,
wishing, sobbing:
Are you there?
Can you see me?
Do you care?

Don't ask me why,
but I'll continue to try,
To reach you with my tears,
my eyes, my life...

Maria Penha

What Is Love?

What is love?
Does anyone know
Just how much,
Can some people show?

And what do you do,
When you love someone
With feelings so true
It shines like the sun

Then that person hurts you
More than you can bear,
And what you thought was true,
Was never really there?

Melissa Marie Duffy

Kathleen's Perfect Day
(Diamante Poem)

Day,
Clear, blue,
Cheering, shining, wakening,
Birds, sun, bats, moon,
Darkening, frightening, sleeping,
Dark, scaring,
Night.

Kathleen Snyer

Everything That's Me

I don't feel very special
  Deep inside,
But I have feelings,
  And I have pride.

People never look beneath
  The surface of my skin;
At my mind, my heart, my soul,
  The love that lies within.

When my hand touches yours,
  There's something I can't explain.
Time subdues all memories,
  And eases all the pain.

So here I am, wondering
  Thinking about you.
Tell me, my special friend,
  Is this a dream come true?

So I am sharing a secret,
  Others can not see.
Finally, I am opening up,
  And sharing everything that's me.

Michelle Johnson

Childhood Observations

  Life is birth and then life is death.
  Life is sweet and then life is sour.
  Life is laughter and then life is crying.
  Life is happiness and then life is sorrow.
  Life is vacations and then life is work.
  Life if family and friends and then life is loneliness.
  Life is love and then life is betrayal.
  Life is long and then life is shorts.
  Life is growth and then life is decaying.
  Life is only for a moment.

Marah Reece

Days Of Toil

Lonely the walk that travels the feet
Daring the back that moved from its seat
Treacherous the path to soaring heights
Where eagles fly
At the height of craved success

Bitter the pain you have to endure
When all you want is a pampering break
Tearful the eye that reveals the dreams
Of what you wish to be

Oh, world of turning currents
Mighty sea of shocking torrents
Give me chance to stare at the moon
Reflecting the fruit of my days of toil

Kadija Diallo

Untitled

Angels play
Dancing, under deep velvet skies
Gleaming, brilliant stars glow
  as scattered candles
The gentle breeze carries the voices
  of sweet innocent laughter
As angels play games, as though
  children breaking for recess
Twilight slowly creeps in
  as shadows draw nearer
The sun begins to rise
  As I watch...
Happy angels disappear

Mark Rindahl

Daddy

Daddy goes to work
Daddy goes to sleep.
Daddy goes to heaven
When he rests in peace.

Daddy has a truck
Daddy has a day
It is for him that's what
I say

Daddy gets a gift
Daddy gets a hug
Daddy gets a kiss and
Best of all is love.

Laura Grose

You

When I'm with you, I can laugh,
cry, sing, dance, shout, etc.

When I'm with you, I can let my
hair down and let all my emotions show.

When I'm with you,
I can let it all hang out.

When I'm with you I can let all my
feelings show and not have to say,
"Oh, what will he think."

With my family and friends, I can't
always be myself, but when I'm with
you, I am myself and I am what I am.

When I'm with you, I love with all I
have and all I have to give is all of me.

Margarett Howze

A Mother's Farewell Prayer

Oh God you've laid me down to sleep.
For troubles and burden, I no longer weep.
For joys you gave me, I rest in peace.
And now my graces I do reap.

My children are now grown and gone
And for their happiness, I do long.
God keep them safe and help them be strong
Now that I'm here where I belong.

I've taught them to be loving and to care
And now it's theirs to give and share.
Dear God please help them through despair,
For I no longer can be there.

Margot M. Neary

I Feel You Sitting There

With sorrow, I feel you sitting there,
  Crouched, hands tangled in your hair,
    Not knowing Savior's grace.
      Stains He can erase!
My heart embraces you tenderly,
  Yet I stand here helplessly.
    Can't see your preciousness?
      God has made you blessed!
Though quiet, you rage from lack of peace.
  Happiness swiftly decreased.
    Worthy are you of love,
      Granted from God above.
Unable to feel that you are adored
  By your Father, by your Lord?
    You are glorious in His eyes.
      Always calling, He cries.
Your life is filled with only despair?
  Aching, I feel you sitting there.
    His desire for you will reign!
      Let Him ease your pain.

Myriah C. Roberts

On Becoming An Artist

You moved across the stage
creating poetry
in every line
a lovely legacy of motion

I watched bewitched
as lights leaped in duet
with your lyric limbs
coming to rest fleetingly
on your glowing and beautiful face

You were web-caught in time
an airborne
an exquisite
an essence
expressing pure joy
at being alive
at being a dancer

Because I love you daughter,
I said a silent goodbye from the wings
and forever joined
the audience of your life.

Nora Ortiz

Our First Year Of Marriage!

  Our first year of marriage has
come to an end. A year full of good
times and also some bad.
  Whatever the feelings or moods have
been, they've brought us closer together
and deeper in love.
  A love that's grown so intensely
since we said "I do". It's doubled
and tripled each day passing through.
  You're my husband, my friend, my
life and my love. I cherish you honey,
because you're a gift from the man
up above.
  Yes...our first year of marriage
has come to an end, but, our
life time of happiness has just began.

Michelle Ann Potts

The Pickup Kiss

You leaned against the pickup glass
come hither was your style
and I enchanted by the pass
moved closer with a smile

Your neck was sweet with silken tress
that fell upon my hand
and jeans of blue held fond caress
reposed against her man

I leaned against your womanhood
urged on by eyes of guess
and found that love was understood
in lips that teased me...yes

I felt more heat than I could know
as springtime breathed me on
and wonder sparked impassioned glow
my senses all but gone

Breathless now I close my eyes
enthralled by all the bliss
and plant my heart between your sighs...
abandon in my kiss

Lanny Wade

Understanding Color

Hello, goodbye.
Colorlessness tastes
Of gunpowder
In a cold room,
Cold floor violating
Thrift store armor,
Cold barrel teased with
The tongue of many
Before, when
Love tastes black
And hate smells loud,
But stifled,
And the only thing missing
Is blue,
And the warmth of a cold
Hand.

Karen DiBenedetto

Winter Now Is King

White is snow upon the land.
Cold is starlight upon stone.
Wild is sea upon the shore:
Winter now is King.

Daystar is far now,
Brief does its light shine
To brighten the dark:
Winter now is king.

Castles bright on hillside,
Cottages of thatch,
Each glow with firelight,
Peatsmoke heralds night.

Forgotten is springtime
As the flowers whither deep.
Hearthlogs brighten dark hearts:
For winter now is king.

Harpers tell in stories
of how springbirds gaily sing.
But long shall be the snowqueen's reign,
For winter now is king.

Maryclaire Norton

Poland 1942

Death is marching in Poland now.
Claiming young and old.
Big and small.
Death is marching on.
It doesn't matter if you're rich or poor.
It doesn't matter who
As long as you are a Jew.
It is dressed in the uniform of the SS
Doing what it does best.
It is merciless and cruel.
How many are dead now?
More than the stars above.
They say 6 million, can you understand?
6 million mothers, fathers, sisters, brothers.
6 million who we loved and cherished.
Are all gone now and perished.
And I am scarred, scarred for life.
You can't see the scars
They are deep inside.
Leah Fier

The Ascension

On wings of love and wisdom,
Christ met us in the air.
He gave the love that understands.
He took away our cares.

He touched our eyes that we might see
With a light that never fails.
He caused our spirit to be free
And our body to be healed.

On wings of love and wisdom
We lifted through the veil.
The fear of sin and death are gone
In God awareness here.

Separation is no more.
We saw it all unfold.
A land of radiant beauty
Where no one need grow old.

Life and death merged into now
And time just ceased to be.
The angels bow before us
As we step into eternity.
Maggie Gallimore

Buried In The Sandbox

The park can be a beautiful place.
Children rising like soft songs;
the slides, swings, carousels
up and down
round, round.
Today it stinks;
I ripped my stocking on the slide
fell off the swing
a little boy spit on me
my dress tore... breast exposed,
knees bleeding, I cried
and no one came to me.
As night stepped in the sandbox,
I buried all but my face
I am not afraid of the dark.
The park begins to swirl;
above me
laughing children,
swings, smells of bubblegum,
and pretty dresses...
Nicole Mouton

The Sun

Timid, the sun peeks over the horizon
Cautiously studies its surroundings
Casually it spies its neighbors
Gaining confidence, the sun shines brighter

Reaching, natural companions lean toward it
Warming, the sun rises higher
Brighter, more commanding
Warming hearts
Sparkling boldly, the sun smiles on

Slowly, gracefully the sun dims
Frustrating slow it wanes
Staggering on, friends yearning
Grasping at the final rays

In a blaze of glory
Bright hues, final farewell
The sun dives below the skyline
And prepares to rise again
Lindsay Salmon

The Granite Stone

Speckled hues of amber gray,
carved letters remind us of the past.
Surrounded by sorrow,
generations cry.

Sharing the same blanket of grass,
its warmth covers me with peace,
forgiveness lies nearby.
Patriotic homage - a symbol of courage,
to the war hero beneath.

The battle of fatherhood,
is where I remember him best.
Seasons turn full circle,
the stone is not forgotten.

A promised return is whispered,
a teardrop falls,
and kisses..,
the granite stone

Goodbye
Marla Ault

Are You Listening?

Dear Lord, are you listening?
Can you hear me calling you?
My heart is deeply saddened,
By the sins we humans do.

Teens are murdering each other
With weapons in the street.
Poor families are dying needlessly,
From lack of food to eat.

Innocent babies have been thrown
In trash bins, gagged and bound.
Some deliberately tossed over bridges,
Or seatbelted in a car to drown.

Women are raped by the minute,
Often left to die in shame.
There is no way to deny it,
We've only ourselves to blame.

Dear Lord, are you listening?
I have even more sad news.
I too, am dying slowly,
From an ailment called...the blues.
Karen Shahidi

"On Modern Conveniences"

The television repairman
Came to fix my V.C.R.
Now the Oldsmobile repairman
Says he needs to fix my car.

Last week I had the plumber,
And Ray, bless his heart,
Spent two whole days with me
Fixing my golf cart!

I've got to get my doorbell fixed
And the oven's on the blink;
Since the dishwasher isn't working
I have to use the sink!

The stereo won't record,
The ice-maker won't drop ice,
My inspection sticker has expired
And I think I have some mice!

I forgot to go to a bridge game;
Oh, I was home, baking bread!
Now all I want to know is
Who can fix my head?
Nancy Hunt Creason

Inspiration For A Dream

A soul's strings are plucked
By the heart's constant yearning.
No problems are ducked
For love's blessed earning.
Real love is a melody,
Played with two 'in tune' hearts,
So creating true harmony
From incomplete parts.
Resonating as one,
Moving forward as two.
The love lingers on,
Through all that we do.
With life's trials and tides
Washing through each soul's life,
Love is the rock,
Countering strife.
Mark Boothby

Bible Writings

The Bible has been written
  By learned men - we're told
Their stories are all true
  worth their weight in gold
In the beginning we do learn
  How earth came to be
God - Powerful mighty
  Created all for man to see.
How could one e'er question
  when the Son shines so bright
When stars and moon come out
  So brilliantly at night?
Who - but God had this power.
  To make the waters part
To give us trees and flowers
  From whence - did they start?
Life holds much beauty
  And some sadness too
But God is omniscient
  He'll guide you through and thru!
Louise J. Davis

Just At Dawn

The giant sun: Cut in half
By a cloud bank

Rises above a mist covered ship
Standing in to shore

The sea: A desolate grey
But bright gold: The half sun

A lonely gull wings away
One lonely shark glides along

But a far, far lonelier human
Walks the hard packed sand

Black and white stands the light house
With it's still gleaming lamp

In the distance
A fog horn blares

Early, early morning
On the Atlantic shore!

Onalee Ann Butler Weaver

I May Not Live To Be A Hundred

I may not live to be a hundred
   But there's a lot of living yet;
Things to do and things to see—
   Maybe even fly a jet!

I may not live to be a hundred
   But there're dreams instead of cares;
I may want to write a poem
   That will live a hundred years!

I may not live to be a hundred
   But there're many smiles to share;
Smiles for loved ones, friends and strangers
   As my journeys end draws near.

Yes!
I may not live to be a hundred
   But you better bet I'll try;
The last thing that I plan to do
IS TELL THIS WORLD GOOD-BYE!

Lily Higdon

Love All Races

We are born to love,
but taught to hate.
Nonetheless evil penetrates
and teaches us to hate.
The message of killing is
very clear to kill all those
people of other races. We must
spit in the face of evil and take
the course of good. For when we pass
to live with the lord above.
We shall surely be judged by the look
of love upon our faces.
Please love all races.

Michael Montemarano

Love's Voice

Through day and night, the fire rages bright,
Brilliance magnified ten fold.
Second to second, blinding all sight,
Feel its talons take hold.
Taste the heat, a passionate thing,
Both pleasure or pain its choice.
Never to know what it will bring,
Love and its strange voice.

Melanie G. Selby

When I Pay My Last Respects

I thought I would have more time
But now you've passed away
I never got to tell you
All the things I had to say

I never got to tell you
In all my eighteen years
And as I pay my last respects
It all comes out in tears

I wish I could have told you then
What I'm gonna tell you now
Maybe I couldn't find the words
Or I just didn't know how

So listen to me father
Listen to what is next
I am going to tell you now
While I pay my last respects.
I love you daddy.

Keith Sowder

Fleeing

In my room I do watch the phone
But no one now is calling
I feel a future all alone
My socialness is falling
In my room I do read a book
But none a plot is making
Out the window I sneak a look
With legs and arms all shaking
I watch the people strolling by
Of me they are not seeing
What wonders see those on that side
Society I'm fleeing

I see a crippled man grope past
I think about my days
His life must have been very vast
I think about my ways
I see a face inside my head
The image is agreeing
My conscience self will soon be dead
My future I am fleeing

Nicholas Rezanof Rinard

Blinders

Truth's cries I hear,
but never see,
for blind we are
in insulation.

Propaganda's
comfort, I squirm
within silent
threats, misled.

Misconceptions,
free press, how "free,"
subjective slant,
hypocrisy.

What for wonder?
Miasma is
thick, polluting
free thought within.

Michael Brower

Youth

Youth is a thing we all strive for,
But it only lasts for a time.
Growing older is a fact of life;
Growing old is a state of mind.

Everyone loves the young at heart
They are a pleasure to be around.
A zest for life is a wonderful thing,
And laughter is a beautiful sound.

Looking young is very important.
At least that is what we are told.
But looks are not the important thing;
It's our minds that shouldn't get old.

Life will have its ups and downs,
But we'll find we'll be able to cope.
God will always supply the strength,
Our friends and family the hope.

To sum it all up in passing,
Forever stay young in heart.
Then life will always be a joy,
And from youth you will never depart.

Kathy Dunn

Country Children

Hear the children's voices ring
Busy as they play.
Echoing over the peaceful plain
Anytime of day.

Gayest chatter, whirring wheels,
Bicycles and toys.
Little girls in pinafores,
Freckled little boys.

Toothy grins, sometimes tears,
That's the way they play.
Up and down the road they go,
Any time of day.

Mary Corish Gawlik

Where Joy Is

Hunger for living
Burns deep inside
A struggle against pain outside

Faith like a light
Carries into the night
The awakening to
Overwhelming confidence

In the continuation
Of living
A never ending paradise
Filled with promise

Reinforce a knowing
That lifts beyond
And flutters with
Angels wings

Awaken in me
Knowledge and understanding
Of everlasting joy
Let my soul rise to meet eternity

Margaret Wilkinson

Goodbye

My life is enclosed in a box,
Boy I wish I could run like a fox.
   I can hear the sounds,
I want to play on the grounds
   I try to fight out of this place,
That's all I can do to save face.
   My place is dark,
Some light shines in just for a lark,
   I sit here by myself and cry,
Left alone I will surely die.
   As I slowly lose my breath,
There is only one way but death.
   As I say hello to the dove above,
I say goodbye to my only love.
GOODBYE!!
   Ken Winnen

How Many More Miles, Lord?

Molly watches the wind
Blowing the thin curtains
Through the open window.
Graying light passes to dusk,
And still there is more work.

Yet she is very day-weary
And her heavy eyes close.
She lays her head down,
But the desk is cold
And hard beneath her.

She feels so tired that
Every muscle, every bone
In her whole body aches.
Still she must keep pacing,
So Molly raises her head.

She has to keep running,
For she is not home yet.
The distance looms far,
But she must get there
Before darkness falls.
   Mary Sullivan

Song And Sky

Raucous bird songs
beneath icy blue sky
the sun warms
my disconnected limbs
not touching
the chill that
fills my chest
and spills out over
the back of my neck
inner shivers
echo in knotted voids

I try to rest
a tangle of noise
a thin shell
between emptiness
and song and sky
   Michael K. Jones

"Faith No More"

Behind the dark there lies a light
Beyond the light there is no end
Without belief your faith is dead
Why go on with nothing ahead
   Michael Cossette

Sweetheart

I sit here and my focus is on you
Being the unselfish person that I am
You know that I won't abandon you
Even though we will be apart
Trust me on this "my love"
In my heart "we are one"
So there is no separation
Only of the body
Our mind and spirit are joined together
You love fills my heart
And I can only "smile"
Because "one day" we will be joined
In body, mind and spirit
That is the day "tears of joy"
Will come from these eyes
"When I first lay my eyes on you!"
   Linda Dianna Price

The Love I Feel

The love I feel keeps growing
because of you,
Sunbeams suspended in my heart,
Beams of peaceful joy.
Your love purifies my soul,
Your tenderness shelters me
From the cold...
The love I feel.
   Mark Steven Torcasso

The Christmas Gift

'Tis the time to be Jolly
Because Christmas day is here.
A time for Christmas trees and holly,
And to spread our love and cheer.

But we should celebrate Christmas,
Not for gifts that Santa might bring,
But for one who is far greater,
Because He is the mighty King.

His gifts are far more precious,
'Cause he gave His life for men,
That they might be delivered,
From the awfulness of sin.

His love is His gift to you,
That's just beyond compare,
And all the wealth of heaven,
He wants with you to share.

So on this glad Christmas day
Make God's love the major part,
And as you are celebrating,
Make your gift to Him - your heart.
   Nora E. Hurley

Lord, Be My Partner

Dear God above
Be my partner
Be my friend
Take my hand
Hold it tight
Be my guide
Stay close beside
Me day and night
Keep my life shining bright
That I may lead others,
To Jesus and into eternal life —
   Mary Eva Taylor

Night And The Poet

A dream and a poet
at the edge of the world
helplessly awaiting a line
or chasing a word.

Yearning for a time...
when the darkness around the mind,
would melt
and the simple human thought
will be released.

Time goes by
and every day, the sun leaves while I cry
for every day,
is another way
for the dream to die.

Oh, Lord...
if love only becomes reality,
if hate was shot down forever dead,
then peace will exist
and the poet might rest.
   Kamal B. Bashir

"I Will Be Waiting For You"

As I dropped off my child
   at the child care place,
I spoke the perfunctory words,
   "I'll be back for you, dear,"
To which she replied,
   "I will wait for you here."

We're said these same words,
   my daughter and I,
Many times as we've said good-bye,
   Then—came news of the bomb!
And, I called out your name!
   But, this time, there was no reply.

Now, I've always thought
   that I'd be the one
to be waiting in heaven for you,
   But, you'll be the one
who will once again say,
   "I will be awaiting for you!"
   Kay H. Ingebrigtsen

Hate

Hate is like a sharp threaded needle.
At first, it will puncture you.
After awhile it will string its thread
down into your soul.

Tearing at your heart,
every little chance it gets.
Sewing up your feeling like
a newly knit sweater.

And in the end, you will be
as cold as an ice chest.
You will have hate
flowing thick in your blood.
   Kelly Fick

To My Grandchild

I look into your eyes
And there I see
Love, hope, joy and the future
But, more, much more
The validation of my very existence.
   Linda Lankford

A Touch Of Essence

Nature and natural
Assimilate as one
Centering on the
Meridian sun

Creature and creator
Sorb the light
Basking in radiance
Acquiescing to night

Mary Olympia Eichenlaub

Little One

Little Babe,
as yet unborn;
here is this letter, handled and worn.

I want you to have this,
as I have it now,
lovingly wrapped in a cream satin bow.

The contents are
precious and very dear.
Written, I'm sure, with a joyous tear.

Many mothers
have passed this down.
Now, little Babe, it is your own.

You'll pass it on
to a child so dear,
on it will go for many a year.

For in this letter-
'tis a welcome, you see.
'Twas given to Grandmother, Mother and me.

Marilyn B. Andrews

Untitled

May we fly the wings of love
   As we past through life again.
May the love I have, we share
   As weightless as a feather.
May we always see the care
   As to whatever the weather.
May the sun also bring rain
   As we learn by it together.
May this love never complain
   As the love lives on forever.
May God's Will teach us our grace
   As darkness turns into lace.
May we find the Eternal Place
   As we seek, to what was told.
May our hearts discover the space
   As our souls once more be whole.

Lynne Cutsogeorge

A Poem

Insomniac Dreams
Are walking the borders
Of my mind
Silent nomads wandering
The badlands

Everyone has gone home
Before the last show
I know they're not there
Because I CAN hear them

Larry Frantzen

Untitled

The pain is much too deep
As inwardly I weep
How can I lose this love
I ask of God above
As a child when first we wed
I followed, as he led
Through years of work and play
Together we would stay
And watch our children grow
With pride and joy to know
Our union was so blessed
And now, this final test
To carry on my life.
Stabbed as if by knife
That twists inside my heart
Knowing we are now apart
Upon his grave I kneel
And pray that I may heal
To carry on with life
This man's shattered wife.

Nancy Bartling

Illusion

Darkness fills the world around me,
As I watch everything go.
I can't have you now,
And this I know.

Look around you,
Can't you see,
We must be together
Just you and me.

Dark clouds continue forming,
And the rain is falling.
In the distance,
I hear somebody calling,
Is it an illusion,
or is it you.
The trees are trying to tell me,
what I must do.

It's not you,
It's just the wind.
Is this true,
Is this how we must end.

Melissa Martinez

A Moment Lost

My eyes frozen in sorrow
As I looked in awe upon
The dying thought of love.

For an ephemeral moment
The communion of our souls
Touched a hope, a question.

Love is now a shadow memory,
Too effervescent to survive.
The question remains alone.

Desire is embers once again.
All is safe and sound
And hope has flown to fate.

A lingering taste is all that's left
To remind me of that moment.
Is the answer in the taste?

Kimberly Dietert

"I'm Hurrying"

I'm hurrying to school now,
As I do almost every day;
Monday, Tuesday, Friday,
I don't have time for the play!

When I play my piano,
I must be the quick,
Because I don't have time
And I am to sleep.

Narcisa Uzunalich

The Summer Of Her Life

There once was a beautiful butterfly
as free as she could be,
Who brightened up her social life
with fun and gaiety.
She flitted here and flitted there
from one beau to another,
And treated all of them alike
as though they were her brothers.
The summer of her life flew by
she gave it little notice,
Until one day she realized
her friends had flown,
   and so 'tis
A story sad we have to tell
of days of fun and laughter,
Without a thought of summer's end
and the time that soon comes after.

Leona Schweikert

Losing My Mother

I'm losing my Mother day by day
As Alzheimer's steals her mind.
My advisor in life is disappearing
Her brain is going blind.

Her mornings are full of awareness
Of most everything around.
While evenings change to confusion
And yearnings for home abound.

This once vibrant lady so full of knowledge
Wrote many fine stories and plays
Now she struggles to complete a thought
Her words resemble a maze.

My Dad has become a stranger
She calls by many names.
He knows she's in her own little world
And plays along with her games.

I know the day is coming
When she will cease to be.
But until then I'll cherish each moment
With my best friend and me.

Mary F. Brady

Reprieve

The fog strolled in on little cat feet
and then it sat, the big fat cat
hovering over our mouse of a house

Swished away the sun with its great tail
just laid in wait, for a great plate,
of rain, then, arose and sashayed away

Mousey me and my little mouse son
saw it was gone, ate honey buns
laughed, and joined in a big snuggely hug.

Mary McLean

As

A whole cut in half
As a cry turns to laugh
A fire fueled by ice
As free you pay a price
   A tree without leaves
   As wind without breeze
   A bike without wheels
   As wound that never heals
A watch without time
As song without rhyme
A book without a cover
As me without you, my lover
   A stream without water
   As mother without daughter
   A memory without a pace
   As person without a face
A house with no door
As earth with no floor
A sky with no blue
As me without you.
Krista Miller

America The Beautiful

   You welcomed strangers with open arms from many different lands and cultures, when you were but a child.

   Then you grew and become arrogant, your hunger for power and wealth turned to greed, selfishness.

   You lost yourself respect your beauty is fading, you have a racist mind and a hardened heart for those that are different.

   Turn back, please turn back before it's to late, turn away from greed and corruption

   Please don't grow old with a bitter soul, perverse and evil, pray for healing, lest you die at a young age.

   Lord have mercy on you, you who were to set an example for the rest of the world.
Letha Rose Webb

Wind

The day I become the wind...
I will play with the leaves
of tall trees and help them
settle to the ground as they fall
I will dance with wheat fields
and together we will make
wave-like patterns
I will carry a butterfly from
flower to flower until the
end of it's journey
I will play with a child's
hair and enjoy every
minute of it
I will embrace you with a
draft and whisper your
name a thousand times
The day I become the wind
will be the most joyous day
of all, for it is then
that I will be free.
Maria Fuentes

The Sounds Of The Wind

The sounds of the wind
Are the cries of the souls
That never could leave us,
That never grow old.

They need to tell us
Warn us somehow,
Of why they are with us
Protecting our shadow.

The sounds of the wind
Are voices of fear.
They are telling us something,
We just do not hear.

Until we are one of them;
Screaming out your name.
All along knowing,
It is all in vain.

There is nothing we can do
To spare you our sins.
That is why they call us
The sounds of the wind.
Mary J. Swiderski

Key To My Heart

I had closed the door upon my heart
And would let no one come in.
I had trusted and I'd been hurt
But it would never happen again.

I had locked the door, and thrown the key
As hard and as far as I could.
Love would never enter there again;
My heart was closed for good.

Then you came into my life
And you made me change my mind
Just when I thought that tiny key
Was impossible to find.

That's when you held out your hand
And showed me I was wrong.
Inside it was the key to my heart,
You've had it all along.
Linda Yang

Amber's Moment

I saw her coming down the aisle
And when she appeared,
I was startled - transfixed:
All I could say was "MY - WORD!"
I'd seen her a few weeks before
All elbows, gawky, but lovable.
Today her step was a bit more firm;
Her face glowed a kind of assuredness
Not seen before, though her
Wide glasses gave still an owlish
Impishness that had clung to her.
Now she was like a butterfly
Just out of the egg with wings
Stretched out to dry in the sun
Before taking flight - a split second
Time of becoming!
Certainly she was no more than
Three days after awkward, but angels
Were letting fall golden dust of promises
And she would change again!
Louis D. V. Palmer

Alone

I stand here alone
And watch the dark water swell
In angry terror

I'm lonely, hurting
The waves cry out
As they crash at my feet

I think of what there is
What there was
The white foam washes back to sea

Far off in the distance
The waves last forever
Just as my dreams

They keep coming back
Only to wash away again and again

The sun sets
On the edge of my happiness
All hope is gone

I stand here alone
And weep over the vast emptiness
And my tears become part of the sea
Lorie Beaumont

Blind

Of memories faded much from time
   And visions smudged in greys
Your presence rests among my thoughts
   Within my heart it stays

The years have passed by like the wind
   First here and then - just gone
And as the rainfalls do return
   Again we meet as life goes on

Upon two different roads we've walked
   Though at intervals they cross
We each have felt both happiness
   And the empty pain of loss

Now once more we're face to face
   Between us there's no change
The comfort felt when we're together
   Leaves feelings which still remain

Tell me why each one of us
   Still searches desperately
For the right one to complete our lives
   And fulfill the love we need
Linda M. Lett

You're My Dad

I only have one life to live,
And this, to you, I would give.
I'd give you all nine or ten,
But I only have one to send.

I had a heart, and it was true,
But now it's gone from me to you.
God picked you from all the rest,
I guess He knew I'd love you best.

That special day of yours and mine,
Comes every April, on the nine.
The day that you became my dad,
And made me feel no longer sad.

If I could say one thing for sure,
Through all the days that I mature.
I'm really, really, really, glad,
Mom chose you, to be my dad.
Kelsey Hamilton

Flow

As the wind does blow
And the years do flow
She now recalls
Her triumphs and falls

The ups and downs
Memories and sounds
Of yesterday
And though she lost her way,

Down the wrong trail
She has yet to fail
She does not look back
For this is where most people lack

But sometimes she may ignore
Who she is doing this for.
Is she content,
With a soul to rent?
Lindsey Smith

Death In Autumn

When the leaves start to turn
And the tree boughs its head.
The leaves tumble down
And soon they're all dead
I looked at their colors
"Oh what a sight to see!"
And then I soon discovered
The trees were a lot
Like you, and me,
I heard the tree whisper
It was sad you are gone,
And the wind blew out
A sad lonely song
Saying, "Awaken my friend,
Your life's like the trees,
As you lost your loved one
The tree lost its leaves."
Mary A. Newhouse

Miss Me — But Let Me Go

When I come to the end of my road
And the sun has set for me
I want no sorrow in a gloom filled room
Why cry for a soul set free
Miss me a little but not to long
And not with you head bowed low
Remember the love that once was shared
Miss me — But let me go

For this is a journey we must all take
And each must go alone
This is part of the master's plan
A step on the road way home
Mark Abrams

Helping Hands

Take these helping hands away
And save them until I've decayed
So many hours I've been delayed
By your filthy helping hands.
I showed you once there was no need
But after proof you still proceed
Take them away forever I plead
Your pitiful helping hands.
How we could have spent those hours
gazing at the trees and flowers
Hours wasted by the powers
of your helping hands.
Kevin Belanger

Choice Of Life...

When you feel down,
and nothing is right.
Lift up your spirit,
and look to the light.
Cause what you decide,
is based on your choice.
Perk up your smile,
and highlight your voice.
For you know He is with you,
always He will be.
When you journey down the road,
or cross over the sea.
We show Him our love,
with the goodness we do.
Don't ever turn back,
for the bad will tempt you.
You have to be strong,
and survive with good will.
For that glorious day will come,
when the good forever lives.
Katina Whiteside

Yggdrasil

Plant a tree upon my chest,
and nestle there its roots to rest.
With spring sap I rise assure,
and brush the sky, my green verdure.
Divine the part that pierced the blue,
to think a while life's lesson through.
And if I come again for kin,
I shall don a coat of skin
and plow the earth with better tool
one honed sharp in other school.
And plant the seed eternal hope,
Life beyond our present scope.
Miles B. Wells

Sebastian; My Cat

When my brother is very annoying,
And my mother gets on my case,
And when my dad reads the paper,
I turn to Sebastian's kind grace.

I tell him all my problems,
He doesn't interrupt.
He sits upon my bedspread,
He doesn't even but.

He looks at me with big yellow eyes,
His low purrs are meant for me,
Deep inside Sebastian, I know,
He knows exactly what I mean!
Katherine Bosch

Love Is A Drug

Love is a drug
I don't won't it

Of cause I miss the highs
But I don't miss
the worry
the pain
insecurity

Don't you want me anymore?
Of cause I miss the rapture
No more earth shattering sex
Love is a drug.
I don't want it
Nina L. Woods

Integrity

Seek in life to be your best,
and live not as have the rest.
Seek integrity where it's found,
and that your method be sound.

A vision for your future,
full of character and sure.
Full of dreams that move they soul,
set to accomplish your goal.

Trust the great power that be,
shine thy light for all to see.
Live with integrity and grace,
and shining forth in thy place.
Lloyd F. McGill

A New Dimension To My Sight

In spite of life's experiences
And its toll upon my soul,
I've gained a new dimension
To my sight.
It is to view all things
Within this earthly life
Not only with the eyes of day
But with the eyes of night.

I've learned to love the shadows
Lurking behind trees
And to respect God's creation
In creeping, crawling things.

On the road that takes us
To place where all may win,
Where aspirations for
All higher things begin,
It's important to acknowledge
And to even love our pain
To remember we are but travelers
Traversing earth's domain.
Marcia M. Walsh

School Days

When the summer days are over
And it's time for school to start
I meet it with mixed emotions
And joy down in my heart

The radio will be silent
The T.V. will be dark
The stereo will not rumble
In my rocker I will park

I'll just sit there all day
With a book upon my lap
And maybe I'll read awhile
And then I'll take a nap

But as I see them off to school
Their faces all aglow
In my mind I'm saying
Thank goodness, there they go

And faintly in the distance
Like the rolling of a drum
I can hear their teachers saying
My goodness here they come
Nell W. Cooley

The Rose And I

I put a rose up to my nose
And it did smell so sweet.
How do you manage lovely flower
In this excruciating heat?

You look so fresh, still drops of dew.
It takes so long until I'm through
With my lengthy beauty task,
And then this question I must ask,

Did I achieve your lovely blush
On my visage with so much fuss?
To you it comes so naturally
But I'm not you and you're not me.

Malou Wylie

Untitled

When I was young
   and in my prime
I thought I knew it all
   but I found out in time.

Growing up is hard to do
   but if you have love
you can make it through

Watching my kids grow
   strong and tall
I know now it was
   worth it all.

Parents today don't realize
   what they have

Tell them how much you love them
   and you will be glad

Then they will grow up
   strong and tall
Then you can say
   it was worth it all.

Mona Mahan

One Constant

Some mornings are cheerful and bright
and I know that all will go right.
It's always joy on such days,
Having one constant there always.

There are days when all is so dark
I know I'll never reach my mark
But whatever may cloud are my ways,
My one constant is there always.

When grief comes that overwhelms me,
When there is no path that I see
And I roam many dark byways,
There's still my one constant always.

And so no matter what I seek,
I realize each day is sweet
for no matter how my life plays
I have my one constant always.

That one constant that my life tenders and cheers
Is my husband, my love of many years.

Marvel K. Sundin

The Empty Chair

I have often wondered why,
And how true love could ever die.
Have I been there before?

A family had so much to share,
Then there was an empty chair;
I still remember the closing door.

She never thought he would cheat or lie,
When he did she could only cry;
All her dreams were gone.

She raised her sons all on her own,
Her will to live made her strong;
She is strong, so very strong.

She now lives with her younger son,
Rarely hears from the older one;
Who was so much like his dad.

When I am gone she will start anew,
Carry on with cares so few;
Closing the door will make her sad.

But then, she has been there before.

Micah David Allen

Grandma's Boy

Grandma's boy is full of love
And has got a lot of charm.
He looks at you with loving eyes
You take him in your arms.

Grandma's Boy is full of grace
He sits upon your knee.
He cuddles up, kisses your face
Oh, so tenderly

Grandma's Boy is full of life
And that is plain to see
He's not quiet like a mouse
He's full of energy.

Grandma's Boy is fair of face
That's as it should be
For after all he's Grandma's Boy
And he is kin to me.

Marion Monger

Christmas

At Christmas we celebrate Jesus' birth
And give praise to Him here on earth.
Christmas is a time for giving and for joy
Spreading our love to every girl and boy,
Spending time with the homeless and the old
And giving them shelter from the cold.

If with the less fortunate we would share,
Open up our hearts and show that we care,
It would make their Christmas brighter
And their heavy burdens a little lighter.
At Christmas we should go all out;
That's what Christmas is really all about.

Gifts and food we all could bring
And Christmas carols we could sing
To their broken spirits give a lift,
Which would be a wonderful gift.
Now wouldn't that be the best way
To say Merry Christmas on this special day?

Leona Moore

A Grieving Nation

When someone takes another's life
and gets away scot-free
his riches surely made the difference
this fact is plain to see.

The flaunting and the taunting
are too much for me to bear
as a member of the human race
he ought to pay his share.

He ought to tell the world the truth
so he can make his peace with God
for if he keeps this to himself
in hell he'll get a nod.

We lost our innocence this somber day
a country is in mourning
two lives were taken viciously
the world should heed this warning.

The grieving shall continue
until justice can be served
I would not hold my breath dear friend
the scales of justice, they are curved.

Kristine Weiner

Close Your Eyes

I want you to close your eyes
And dream of colorful flowers
Growing underneath the blue skies
Near the rushing river

I want you to feel free
To travel the highest mountain peak
Or swim the greenest sea
Seeking love by the trickling creek

I want you to discover
The hottest passionate fire
Or the sweetest golden nectar
Of love and spiritual desire

All my life and here after
Will dedicate my life for you
Through storms and sunny weather
Think of me, my love is true

Mark Allen Fee

"The Perfect Rose"

The Lord must be a gardener
And daily as he sows,
He must be on the watch
For a most perfect rose.

And He must have called you
Before you were fully grown,
because you were the Perfect Rose,
He wanted for His own.

To know you are his angel
As I look at the sky above,
Life is somewhat easier,
Knowing you were mine to love.

The bitterness was hard to shed
because He took you from me.
Then I realized He needed you more
So He could plant the most perfect seed.

Then at that moment the sadness went away,
And at last, I was at peace with what had
happened on that day.

Lisa M. Carlock

Lost

Many times when we're lost
and can't find our way,
the safe well-lit path
can lead us astray.

For when we enter some waters
untraveled, unknown,
no maps are we given
no paths are we shown.

But follow not only your mind,
but your heart as well
and you'll become unlike others
who tumbled and fell.

Fell because they did not
look with their heart,
but relied only in their mind
to see in the dark.

The dark of tomorrow
matters unknown
the journey we travel on,
our paths always unshown.

Melissa Mena

Rights

What right do we,
An incorrigible creature,
Have to destruction
Of something not wholly ours?

Are our rights right;
When we cannot be bothered
To help another
Who is an unfortunate.

Because we live
Is it our price to pay up?
Should we try to love,
Or to not ever love?

Should we even try
To ponder a question
That could never bother
Ours, but our child's life?

Karla A. Kopf

"Jagged Edges"

Wayward winds prevail
Amongst the cliffs high,
Sandy sounds around,
Jagged edges lie.

Peaks slapping the sun,
Clouds rupture the view,
A shy background light,
The color of blue.

Steamy weather swells
Just past the midday.
Dust sketches the swirl,
No reason to stay.

Finding the fruit sweet,
It was worth the while,
To blister and singe
In complete exile.

To this baron land,
On the outside seems,
In ruins, too dry,
Fine honey it bleeds.

Matthew Laurence Morgan

Waves

The waves are rolling,
along the beach.
I love to watch,
them grasp and reach.

They move the rocks,
they move the sand.
Waves can make changes,
in the land.

Some of the waves,
can be high and fast.
They can stop rolling,
or they can last and last.

Echo sounds,
the waves do make.
It's so peaceful,
along the lake.

Mary Paver

Tropical Notions

Tropical palms
Almond trees
Soothing breeze
stir banana leaves
Sun is setting
ships going by
Birds are flying
way up high
Grass so green
Mountains serene
Glorious sunsets
can be seen
A tropical evening
is truly a dream!

Mariana C. Webb

A Teenager's Day

The feelings inside me are calm.
All of the sudden they scream;
Let Me Free!
I want to scream and shout and run all about.
Then all of a sudden, I felt so confused.
How do I feel and what should I do?
I think, but I do not know.
After a while, I am happy.
I put all those feelings behind me.
Everything is O.K.;
nothing really happened today.

Michele Lambert

Blind Love

Is that you?
   Could it possibly be?
True love that has gone,
   are you coming back to me?
I see your face and the truth
   in your eyes.
Is this just another
   disguise?
You fooled me once and made
   me believe
Am I setting myself up to
   be deceived?

Nichole Orman

Untitled

O'er head the winged wild ones fly
Against a dark and pitched grey sky
From miles around, one can hear
their enchanted, piercing cry——

The white-washed pattern, hovers,
   oh so high
And the sound that fills the air
Stops my breath and makes me sigh —

Are they anguished?
Why scream so much?
Excitement at the homeward rush —

As the wind twists and turns
So do they —
Some eerie accompaniment

As though keeping
Perfect rhythm with the wind

Lang Windsor

Greetings

I stare at a useless sheet of paper,
after not talking to him.
It's filled with words and letters,
but they say nothing.
Everything goes blurry,
and then he's there,
looking at me, stumbling in my eyes,
Still not saying a thing.

Kimberly Dowda

Recalling Memories

Beyond the blue horizons
   Across the misty seas
I hear your voice calling back to me
   As I glance across the waters
Your image reappears
   The softness of your whisper
Echoes gently in my ears
   Many words were spoken
To many left unsaid
   But memories keep us gathered
In this life that lies ahead
   Smiles bursting everywhere
Where once the black clouds hung
   Life is everlasting
Tis a new life that's begun

Marion H. Wright

Soldiers Song

Oh soldier, oh soldier
across the blue sea
is fighting and fighting
for you and for me.
Out the whole night
no sleep in sight
A vigil he keeps while
everyone sleeps.
Oh soldiers, deep soldier
you are so brave
Helping them all
who could have been saved
A new day has begun
here comes the sun
I'm hoping to see
my dear soldier
home with me.

Martha Lester

"Living" The Moments

"Its gallery of radiance
  a wonder to see
How precious these moments
  they're special to me!"

"Life's moments can mean
  much more than all
Of this world's possessions
  Both the great and the small!"

"The touch of your hand to mind
  made my heart skip a beat
Much rushed than before
  from way way down deep!"

"Clinging together as if this
  was the last
Time to be spent
  With no more to past!"

"Living out each moment
  sharing as we go
Our time on this earth
  is precious you know!"
Nellie M. Wilson

Shalom, Friend

He was in his youth
A warrior with gun
Although he searched for truth
Israel's enemies on the run
Shalom, friend
He saw war's terrible bloodshed
He laid down destructive arms
He saw lives in shreds
War has no redeeming charms
Shalom, friend
Olive branch in his hand
His escort was a dove
His family strength to stand
For peace was their love
Shalom, friend
Freedom's beacon via human race
Bullets from a terrorist gun
Ended his freedom run
Shalom, friend
Leona F. Lee Lein

The Voice Of Courage

From the deepest depths it comes,
a voice.

At times it bubbles up slowly, meekly;
calling to be heard, begging attention.

At times it rushes out forcefully;
a screaming outcry, compelling action.

A powerful voice in meekness or mightiness.
Could it be the voice of the soul...
offering direction.
Purpose,
possibilities,
self...
offering freedom?
Listen to the voice.
Laurie Shiparski

Mussel Grove

Moon-lit ripples
A twilight sea,
Shore rushed waves,
A lonely heartbeat;
Morning bird sleep.

Sea gulls scudding
In scattering light,
Dark silhouettes
Above the shoreline.

Long-tide rolls back,
New life exposed-
Found lying helpless
In a mussel grove.

Thieved from hunger
Taken to the sky
Let go with forgiveness

Waves of circular motion
Sinking to dark water -

Falling with such grace.
Matthew Beery

The Wave

The cry of a gull rang out like a bell.
A swift breeze smothered the shore
With microscopic beads of sand.
Just then a sea gull swooped down and
Lay silently afloat on the salty blue ocean.
The smallest, calmest, coolest wave
Barely tipped the gull's left wing.
After the wave quietly tip-toed
Back to the clear sea,
A little black shell was left
behind.
Nathan Alan Roberts

This Autumn Eve

In the beauty of the night
A soft rain falling
The moon lite shining
on the silvery wet
leaves on the trees
on this autumn eve
a beautiful sight to see
so quite and peaceful
on this autumn eve.
Lillian Brown

Untitled

It's really not that I don't need
A woman to be close to
It's really not that I don't want
A person not to lie to
The things that count, I really want
Some definite compassion
A taste of humor subtly
A touch of the old fashioned
A breath of air to fill the day
To hold but not to cling to
A sight to see, and yet not grasp
My soul I'm sure to sing to
Mark F. Coulon

A Friend

A friend is like a flower
A rose to be exact

Or, maybe like a brand new gate
That never comes unlatched

A friend is like an owl
Both beautiful and wise

Or perhaps a friend is like a ghost
Whose spirit never dies.

A friend is like those blades of grass,
You can never seem to mow,

Standing straight and tall and proud
In a perfect little row

A friend is like a heart
That goes strong until the end

Where would we be in this world
If we did not have friends.
Melody Music Sanders

Memories Of Old Astoria

Once again I see the hills of home,
A river wide, and ocean's foam.
Softly city lights in twilight show;
The river shines back the sunset glow.

No place compares with such rosy skies
As seen by childhood's unworldly eyes.
'Tis sad to think how memory fades
All this brilliance into lighter shades.

The pilings once held the streets up high;
Their planks rumbling as the cars went by.
We saw on bright rails the street cars go
While the waves caressed the shores below.

Art's perspective lines to me were taught
By shine of nail heads in wooden walks.
As nail heads seemed to approach the sun
Closer together the lines would run.

Still ships sail out with the evening tide
To cross the bar; meet the ocean wide.
May all the farewells be a happy song
Long after we and the ships are gone.
Mae Sallila

"I Stand In Line"

I stand in line-I stand in line
A right I did not hither.
Other women I am among,
My true soul sees and withers.

Yet I sought
To tie the knot
And be his special kind.
But, here I stand
Behind this band
Of his women of earlier time.

"Be gone," I say, "of pride I beg!"
So to be his beauty charmed
So fresh I stay for the day
My soul would be disarmed.

I stand in line-I stand in line
With purpose of no other,
Than to forget
This man I met
For shame I'm not
His mother.
Mary Ellen Sieck

"Plight Of A Horseman"

Torn from that perch,
a refuge of protection,
and hearing hoofs a dancing,
inflicting pain unasking.

The horse's lance of which,
with pain staking aim,
still keeping rhythm the same,
until a horseman lay lame.

And looking back,
a horseman not the same,
and on that day,
God graced my way.

And knowing its full meaning,
living and experiencing life,
I shall always keep in memory,
the "Plight of a Horseman."

Leonard Dee McGee

The Black Hotel

I know the sadness that you hide from them
A recluse inside for no one to see
I feel that desolation too, my friend
Paralyzed like a hollow redwood tree

I'm the only friend you have left now
Refuge in an ocean swell
I'm the only one who knows where you live
Across the hall from me in the black hotel

The windows are a purple gray
Stale whisky is the only smell
Faint whispers with no one to talk to
That's life in the black hotel

You laugh and try to hide from yourself
You wear a convincing disguise
But I've got your eyes....memorized
Pools of winter under the fire...lightening in
the summer sky

I listen to your anecdotes with curious fascination
So many smiles to sell
I'll pick you up and carry you home
And it's back to the black hotel

Monica Goodman

That Lost Feeling

Thinking Human Beings are born;
A question in our minds arise.
When people start to scorn,
Our answer continually dies.
What are we? Where do we go,
When no one cares?
Our future dies and happens slow,
Decaying our civil mind that stares.
Too many have died from within
Because of that lost feeling.
Sticking in like a sharp pin
And unable to be seen.
That lost feeling - What is it?
You must prove your answers true.
Finally it will fit,
That lost feeling is YOU!

Marcy R. Mumford

The Hunt

I know a place
A point in space
That only I embrace.

A bird may fly
At six feet high
Or a mole in its contour lie.

It is absurd
Me, below the bird
Yet this was the given word.

The bird sizes his goal
While I join the mole
And burrow for coal.

The bird finds a worm
I seed in turn
More than a mole can learn.

Life watches the river
Strife changes the giver
Arrows are time in my quiver.

Louise G. Kioski

Past, Present, And Future

Look into the past
a long time back
and see what you can see,

There was love and friendship
with all your kinship
yes a world just filled with dreams.

Now this is the present
where we all resent
planting buildings and not enough trees,

There's hatred and death
and the smog fills our breath
and the rest pollutes our seas.

Now what's in the future
what does it feature
what's in store for me?

There's probably destruction
of today's construction
which afterwards will no longer be.

Leonard R. Palmer

Love

Love is something you cannot see,
A feeling so special between you and me,
It's something you can't explain,
It can make you happy, but can also
cause pain.

Love has a mind of its own
It can make you scream, cry, and also moan,
It has no limit to what it can do.
But you know when you have it because
the feeling's so true.

Love is a very strong word
some know how to use it, some abuse it;
love is what I feel each and
everyday I'm with you, and without
any doubts you should feel it too.

Karen Lind

"Woman Of My Dreams"

Woman of my dreams,
speak to me in verse
Come within my heart
Satisfy my thirst

Paint with living water
on the canvas of my soul
in the richness of your colors,
ocean blue and aspen gold

Brush with gentle strokes
the oils that breathe with life
conceived within the union
of matter and of light

Lead me in the dance,
woman of my birth,
Surge within my footsteps
vibrant rhythms of the earth

Fill my body opened
with the music of the spheres
Whisper of your joy
to my waiting, listening ear

Martha Helm

The Lighthouse

From faraway, a friendly light
A soft warm glow
In a dismal night
A mighty fortress
On solid ground
Stately and tall
Without a sound
A silent message
Sent over the sea
Come to the shore
And rest with me
The lighthouse stands
So strong and brave
It weathers the storm
The sailors to save
Come to the light
Where all is well
Rest your weary body
Then, set your sail

Melinda W. Chance

Now

People live,
And people love.
Go as you will,
Free as a dove.

"Carpe diem."
Seize the day.
For come again,
It never may.

Live your life,
But give more than take.
And only leave smiles
In your wake.

For happiness
Is where it's found,
In the air
And all around.

Owen Jones

Mortality

Did you ever feel your heart flutter?
Did you ever hear a voice mutter?
far away, far away,
"None of us is here to stay."
I did.
I felt no fear,
only
utter dismay.

Mary Ann Griebling

Sunflower Fields

As the winds blow lightly,
The sunflowers sway softly,
And the sun shines ever so brightly.
The birds are chirping,
As the sunflowers are growing,
And the bees are busy with their buzzing.
The clouds with gleaming faces,
Looking down with streams of blue laces,
This is my favorite of all places!

Megan Caroline Trehern

Battered

Helplessness bolts in,
Escaping from its cause.
Smashing her breast bound soul,
Against the camouflage.

No standing - too infirm,
Falling - there she lies.
Where the faucet drips,
To drown her cries.

Sounds of empty walls,
Take the echoes from her head.
Robbing her reason,
Ripping out her sense.

Wounded and prey,
Beautiful and frail.
Under the crack of the door,
Beholds the baneful spell.

Here behind the barricade,
The locks, and screams, she's free.
'Cause in the dark room,
She's lost her sanity.

Michael Navarre

Happy Birthday Mom!

All ripples
Concentric circles
Magnetic vortex swirling
Energy whirlpool universal black hole

The passing of the ages
According to the sages:
From Piscean
To Aquarian!

The eye of the hurricane
MIND OF GOD
Closes...opens again

For new millennia
Of creation...
Hail to the Messiah!

Kristine Lorance

Would You Mind?

My blood pressure's gone sky-high,
And the doctors don't know why,
But I do.
I've no more little dog to hug
To wrestle with upon the rug.
I miss you!
You knew my every ache and pain,
You'd walk with me out in the rain.
I'm so blue!
You traveled with me where I dared,
And licked my face to show you cared.
You always knew.
Although you're gone, my little friend,
Your memory I will always tend.

So, would you mind if I went out,
And looked around and all about
And got a new, wee Pierre true
Just like you?

Loris Edsall Kerekes

My Husband's Sons

You are not my children,
although you seem to be.
Not of my blood, but in my heart...
Sons, chosen for me.

Who knows why things happen,
of what God's final plans.
Yet, He took you as little boys,
and placed you in my hands.

Now I watch you becoming men
and it truly baffles my mind!
My two little boys have grown so tall,
each of you, 'one of a kind.'

I know there are tough days ahead,
and many days, also of joy.
But, all too soon, it will happen...
You'll never again be a boy.

So don't grow up too fast, my sons.
Enjoy your youth while you can.
I'll love you and help you through it,
just as I know is God's plan.

Linda J. Agee

Untitled

I feel a rush, a surge of energy that
magnetically pulls me toward you.
Your eyes, draw me closer,
inviting me to end my curiosity of you,
encouraging me, evermore, to follow,
like a child chasing
a fluttering butterfly.
The child does not chase to capture,
but...to light upon the awe
of its magical wings.
The child wonders over
natures breath-taking beauty;
this beauty I've found in you.
I do not follow to possess you,
but to be fulfilled by
the faith in human beings
that you have restored in me;
I found good in man,
because you found good in me,
and the butterfly.

Linda Drumright

Mary Jane

She lays there, knowing he can't resist.
She waits for him to touch her, even though I'm there.
(his girlfriend).
He doesn't fight the urge, and brings her to his lips.
As I watch, tears burning my eyes.
He's always with her, when we're together.
She never leaves him alone.
She has been there longer, through all his pain.
She gives him the feeling, no one can.
I could, if only he'd let me try.
I watch him everyday, knowing I can't change him.
Hating her, because she is what he lives for. Not me.
They ask me why I don't like her. I just shrug.
They would laugh at my jealousy.
She is the person everyone loves. She's everyone's girl.
It might be silly, to envy something like her.
But I can't get over his want of her.
So as he blows the smoke out, from the blunt he loves.
I have to hold my breath and look away.
How I hate knowing he loves weed, more than me.

Kristi South

Pass On By?

May wonderment never fade, amazement never cease;
  May curiosity never wane, and discovery decrease.

How would we find the answer, who would we ask?
  Future scientists and astronomers, may have the task.

The one question that prevails, since humans lived on Earth;
  With most generations, and birth after birth.

When in awe of God's celestial orbs we ponder;
  "Is anyone else out there", we ask and wonder?

If God can set in motion: Suns, Earths, Mars;
  He could create other people, beyond our stars.

Do we think so little, of His power and ability?
  Some suffer from delusion, of His great enormity.

I pray to be alive, still asking not "if" but "when";
  And "where" will they come from, waiting 'til then.

I hope they stop to meet us, our "neighbor-in-the-sky";
  But, seeing the pollution and cruelty,
    They'd surely Pass On By.

S. Brownlee-Cobb

I Love A Girl

I love a girl ... her name is Kim ...
She sticks by me through thick and thin!
My love for her will never die...
For she is the apple of my eye!

I think of her, when we're apart...
As she is forever in my heart.
I long for the day we're together again
To live and love as woman and man.

Her beauty is such that I just can't describe
It's more then her looks...
It goes deep down inside.

She's my love and my life, my joy and my friend.
I'd die for her safety again and again.

Yes she is one I'll love, till the end, that girl
is my lady her name is Kim!

Mark E. Butler

Fractions Of Love

So tender is a mother's loving touch,
She seeks to give without assured return,
And like the sea, a boundless, buoyant crutch;
But Susan Smith knew well young lungs would burn.

The brotherhood of friends is love's other
face, vast and varied as the contoured land,
Its hand extends beyond age and color;
But even earth can quake and run as sand.

Fragment lovers unite in hot embrace,
Consumed by passion, flesh and thought afire,
The bonfire snaps a beat to their timed race;
But post-explosion, cools to dying pyre.

God's love is whole-some, alone agape,
Sum of fractions, binding primeval clay.

Linda Mei Douglas

Last Goodbye

As his eyes closed and she watched him slip away
she realized then this would be his last day.
She watched him and cried wishing he would stay,
but in her heart she knew this was the best way.
He was going to a better place now
where he could escape the horrible pain.
She stood in grief and took a farewell bow
and kissed his hand trying to keep sane.
Everyone said their last goodbye to Jon
until they meet again some where, some day.
It's still so hard to believe he is gone
he touched our lives each in a different way;
Make educated choices in all you do
and remember AIDS can break your heart too.

Nicole Myers

A Special Lady

My mother was a special lady, that always put her family first
She could do anything, it seemed, even when she felt her worst

From cooking in the kitchen to opening a clogged up sink
She'd even help my daddy push his car, when it went on the blink

She took care of everyone she knew, who wasn't feeling well
No doctor could have done any better, to get you feeling swell

She'd cook up a storm in the kitchen, for us every day
There always would be good food ready, if we asked company to stay

She'd take a piece of cloth and sew without a pattern to use
The davenport would have a new cover, before there was time to lose

And even when she got older and would tell grandchildren nursery
  rhymes
With them she'd dance and jig as if she was still in her prime

I can still see here in the yard, sawing the tree's branches off
Then she'd mow her lawn and paper walls, instead of being out just
  playing golf

There never seemed to be anything I saw, she just couldn't do
A mother, like her, it seems to me, there are only too few

I guess she drew her strength, to do these things, from God above
I know for us, she did so many things, out of her love

Marilyn Bublitz Berning

Who Will Share My Joy

Who will share my joy?
Shall that someone be you?
No I see, for sorrow takes your time.
My ears were ope'd to your crying,
And my heart shed drops for you.
And I cared so much it cut a gorge deep inside my soul.
But who will share my joy?
There are no eager bidders.
I set aside my sorrow,
The grief and pain of life.
I pruned away the briars
To let in precious light.
But who will share my joy?
Not a soul alive.
So I'll wrap it up with wisdom,
And tuck it back inside
I shall not put upon thee, the burden of myself
But continue on my journey
And hold dear, my inner wealth.
    Margaret Kist

Untitled

I, barefoot on a windy beach.
servant to the powerful waves that
push and pull at me as I walk.
My thoughts pastel with simplicity,
colorful with their wonder, race
across my brain like a soft blanket of rain.
I lay down and let the warm waters
caress my body, luxuriating in their wildness.
The soft white sand sifted through my
fingers like fine sugar.
I knew then, I was the water, the
sand the sky
A moment in time, a dim recollection
that might be remembered, again...
    Kathleen Borbet

Seasons Change

A crimson bloom in winter's glow,
Seen out of time, when the chill winds blow,
Spawned in a season when roses grow.

T'was caught in a sheltered spot,
Bright sterling jewels, and blemished not,
Red as a drop o'blood from a broken heart.
A fiery torch viewed no more,
The flames have fallen through years of war,
But t'will arise from consistent lore.

Fear not, sweet flame, smothered on the moor,
The winter rose doth promise in the fading ruins of yore,
That the ardor once found will again be restored.
    Kristiann Louise Powell

Mother And Sons

The birth of a son is a mother's greatest joy.
She tells all her friends about her wonderful boy.

When that boy becomes a man, she tells all her
friends about her wonderful man.

And whether her son takes a wife, depends on
how his mother affected his life.

So, mothers take heed, in love keep a balance,
or your son may turn out to be like Jack Palance.
    Marlene C. Locke

True Love

Sometimes the world seems so unkind
seems you're in total danger,
You don't know where you'll find a friend
when everyone's a stranger.

But if you get lucky
just once in your life,
You'll find that special someone
and make her your wife.

Though strange it may seem
It can make you wanna shout,
You'll get to know the way she works inside as well as out.

But in the search for that part of you
There's something you must beware,
Don't settle for the first who says 'I love you,'
There's a lot of phonies out there.

But when you find her I think you'll know,
Just don't give up if she wants to go.

You'll have to take a chance on love
That's the way it has to be, if she's the one
She'll come back just you wait and see!
    Mary J. Carey

Native American Dream

A tribe of lonely wanderers
searching the mountains
for a long-ago home.

The piney fragrance of the air.
The men go out of hunt.
I skin the rough, slimy meat
of a newly killed deer.

Black hearted vultures of a light skin
come greedy for our land, and a golden treasure.
They come in herds, larger than the buffalo.
They circle,
closer, closer, closer.

The swoop down one by one,
taking all that I have left.

The black, starry night is gone,
an icy frost covers the land.

The bitter taste of hatred,
replaces the feeling of peace, joy, and happiness
From this bloody war the people of a great nation,
were lost forever.
    Kelly Sink

Untitled

I am at it again,
    Searching for a way to make you understand how I feel.
      Lost for the proper string of syllables to express my love.
I have been here before,
    You are so imprinted on my senses,
      That I can smell, touch and taste you from afar.
I am struggling,
    The absolute power and quantity of emotions
      Makes it almost impossible to concentrate or compose.
I will continue the quest,
    To assemble the lines that have evaded me again,
      All the while knowing, it is only three words that are needed.
    I love you.
    Larry A. Stanton

A Special Angel

My world was full of deep despair when he came to me.
Searching and reaching where no one else dared.
Willingly accepting the hurt inflicted upon him
from a friend who felt nobody cared.

Entering the darkness he slowly took his time,
cautious not to hit the wall he tried to get behind.
His countless attempts to conquer this wall opened my eyes to see,
he did all this because he cared for me.

God picked the perfect angel to enter in my life,
for he fought the wall with all his might.
The angel came to realize the hurt that built the wall,
and the pain that I'd experience should I take another fall.

Gently he took me in his arms and wrapped me in his warmth.
Giving me comfort until once again I ventured forth.
Gradually he let me see how special life can be,
if everyone had someone to always be with thee.

I love this special angel, a friend he'll always be.
Unfortunately........he doesn't belong to me!

Karen J. Janulewicz

"I Miss You"

The waves crash against the shore and splash caps of white onto the sand.
The deep blue sky is full of white billowy clouds.
The sun sets and turns an iridescent pink as the water reflects the color.
In the distance the water is so smooth it looks like a mirror.
Pelicans fly overhead and circle.
White long necked cranes with yellow eyes scream out
as my heart longs for you. "I miss you."

Time feels suspended. Like sand that drips in an hour glass—each moment
feels eternal. My soul longs for your touch.
My eyes search for your stare, but you're not here.
The stars glimmer in the heavens above, with each one appearing brighter.
I call out to you in my mind—each cry becomes louder until
I can speak no more.

The warm tropical breeze turns cold as lightening flashes across the sky.
The thunder roars.
I extend my arms for shelter in your embrace — tears fall like raindrops
down my cheeks.
It feels like forever since you have held me in your arms.
"I Miss You."

Lori L. Spencer

"Cast My Past"

It seemed so long that this went on, the time
released abuse; that was to lure, without a cure,
Disease was self induced.
The coverage plenty, in short some twenty, to
actually take its toll; day to night, unknowing my
fight, would be harder to reach my goal.
While something felt, my knees had knelt, my
conscience had been caught; and so off guard, I'd
played so hard, for gambling was self taught.
But even then a prayer began, and was heard
to help my way; though not to know, my faith would
grow, much stronger by the day.
And now I look outside my nook, from countless
tears from fears; being lifted out, without a doubt,
that which had cost me years.
Compulsions gone that were so strong, my second
chance at last; to live for me, that is to be,
he's cast aside my past.

Katt E. McCray

Surface Tension

A bug crawls softly atop a wall of water,
Rippling as he goes along the glassy stage.
Unsteady fingerprints. Ice skating—
His blades unequipped to mar or sculpt.
Will a crack result and he be plummeted to unnavigable depths?
A fatal fall to match a fetal flaw?
But only a babe,
He tappity tiptoes like a child's fearful hushhhhh...
Learning guided by caution.
With each step a stitch of artistry newly interwoven.
No, he fears no fall, no slide off the ice into a shadowy valley.
He sees only the mirrored dawn beneath his feet
And instinctively knows only that
Spring is here.

Melissa Caldwell

Madigan Chronicles

Ashen beauty eddies atonal consciousness, astigmatic nonsense rhyme and narrative wax lyrical, to size and breed in captivity enhanced and gasping for truth. Venus variation, familiar complex shapes make intellectual demands, coaxing chameleons and lady bugs to negotiate lofty ransom. The record was made to be broken, secrets told to be sold, dizzy atop San Francisco we shared Jaffa oranges and globes of wisdom, cones of brick not yet immortalized. Mark the wizened watchword, excel in Windsor inks forever bordered by favorable impression. Madonna lilies black-on-white powdered chalk and mimicry echo chronicles substantially ciphered. Harpies and harridans haunt the atelier overturning baskets of whelk and polished jasper to leave sketchy portraits in oxblood. Hidden in the depths of chlorophyll Wellingtons is the password scratching briars against chromatic wheels. Abandon the chiffonier, escape the warren for welkin blue restraint, awkward axioms stacked like layers of verdigris in the palette box. Leave the changeling in the bower, arrangement severs emotion. Be not vaulted and deceived by Tuscan collaborative lament. Taffeta whispers snare and repeat fractious secrets tied in envious chartreuse bundles, hollow accolades bronzed for eternity.

Karen A. Gitzen

Untitled

Dear Dad,
Remember when I was your little girl and you loved me very much?
I remember your promises and your sweet and tender touch.

Remember that special day you saved me from Mom's harsh hand?
I remember when you would listen and you would always understand.

Remember other special days when it was just you and me together?
I remember those special days, but they didn't last forever.

Just like you, they've come and gone - never to be seen again..
If I can't have you as a father, can't you be my friend?

It's hard for me to face the truth and look at reality
I'd be better off if I could live my life like my fantasy.

Even in my dreams, well, nightmares really, it seems like you don't care,
And in reality, it's the same way - you don't even know I'm there.

I wish you understood the feelings that torture my mind,
For it's a father and a friend that I am trying to find.

I keep the pain locked in my soul—locked so very tight
And it stays there and won't come out until the very night.

I just wish that you would tell me what I want to hear
Because thinking that you hate me is what I very much do fear.

Just say that you love me, and please don't lie again
Because I don't want a father unless I have a friend!

Melissa J. Pena

Alexander Joseph

He is dawn dancing on a twilight sky
   Rays of morning dappled with starlight
    Flashes of shadow enveloped in color
Red-blue-yellow
Primary, primal
Possibility

He is truth, dancing in a ballroom of truths
   A mind in motion
    Gliding and whirling, twirling to rhythms
Bass-Conga-Flute
Structure, form
Improvisation

He is family, dancing on a sea of souls
   A living history of raging, passionate hope
    Calmed by glimmering, twinkling memory
Yesterday-Today-Tomorrow
Mother earth, sister moon
Opportunity

Nicola Wickl

Gifts To My Children

I whispered in your tiny ear
Quietly so none would hear.
All the dreams I'd hoped to dream
I gave so willfully to you.
But what could I give to those I loved
My heart, my soul wasn't enough,
Courage, I whispered, to be the person inside.
Bravery to stand the path of misfortune
Grace and dignity for humanity,
And love the sweetest of the gifts,
Love embraced with tenderness
And as I drew you near
One last wish fell upon your ear
Quietly so none would hear,
That someday you would pass these wishes too,
With all the dreams you'd hoped to dream
And life would flow on as a stream,
Quietly so none would hear
Whispering in a tiny ear.

Mari-Lynn Cooley

I Wonder Why

   Every night I wonder why, why do I get put last on his list? Why can't I please him? Do I ever do anything right? Does he love me? What did I do to him? Will I ever be good enough? Everyone says he does it because he cares; but is love supposed to hurt? I don't remember a time that he talked to me as a friend or someone he at least cares about. Maybe I'm feeling sorry for myself but if I don't then no one will care at all.

   The other night I remember we got into a fight. I went to bed shortly after and I had a dream. I got up from bed, walked out the door and I heard a slight friendly voice say "I'm sorry," "I love you," and gave me a hug and kiss, then I wake up and it was all a dream. I got up from bed walked out the door, everything looked the same, I waited for a minute or so and was destroyed by the silence of my father.

Mario Eloy Garcia

My Destiny

I was walking with others on Life's highway
Pushed along with the crowd, with humanity's sway
But I knew not the goal of this busy throng
So occupied with life, so merry with their song
I was but a drop in a down-pouring rain
Not knowing the spot, where my resting place lain
Just blown along with the elements, that be
Blown along as a leaf from an Autumn tree
That I wearied of the way, drew apart from the noise
Useful I wished to be, not one of elements toys
Desire giving birth, I found a lone by-way
In solitude I knelt, burden-pressed to pray
And deep in prayer, my heart with wings was shod
Its burden lightened, it found its way to God
I knew at last the path my feet should follow
No more they need, in indecision wallow
A tool I would make of my unworthy soul
A tool in God's hand, for me shall be my goal!
A useful tool, that none can easily sway
For these feet of mine are on, my "Kings Highway!"

Lillian Freiermuth

Twins

Sweet child, smiling face
Pulling, yanking green, white threads of yarn
Voice gasping in dismay.
Bigger, bigger grows the space.
No longer semblance of a sweater.
Tossed aside. Philip, Joshua, to whom belongs the face?
New grounds to chase.
Sweet child, smiling face
Refrigerator door ajar. crash, carton to the floor,
Milk, milk, splashing on the kitchen floor, hand to mouth.
Joshua, Philip to whom belong the face?
New grounds to chase.
Sweet child, smiling face. Water, water, everywhere.
Soaping ships, shampoo suds, shower, shower made.
New grounds to chase.
Sweet child, smiling face, Onto sleep.
Dreams of merriment, mischievous smile on your face.
Was it Philip? Was it Joshua?
Who can say, who can say.

Mary Stachowski

Valleys Of Green And Pots Of Gold

'Tis the land of my ancestors long ago, valleys of green and pots of gold.

Where you do a jig and drink some brew, the pubs almost beckon to you.

The Emerald Isle as it's also know, kiss the rock of Blarney stone.

Shamrocks are the national emblem there, and March 17th is celebrated everywhere.

Lakes, mountains and valleys to see, some ancient castles older than trees.

'Tis the Irish in my blood that calls to me, come see Dublin and Lake Killarney.

Top of the morning to ya las, some day I'll be there to answer back.

I haven't been there yet I know, it's one of the prettiest places to go.

Ireland the home of ancestors long of ago, valleys of green and pots of gold.

Nova Mangan

A Mother's Plea

Oh Lord, who created her through me,
  Please help my child
She was been so hurt, body, mind and soul.
A frightened child, in a woman's body.
I want her back Lord, she didn't do
anything wrong! She is a good, thoughtful
caring person.

Let her know, in her heart, that the
medicine she is taking (For her mind) and
the over eating... is just another way
of "Hiding ... Self Denial. Let her know
she's loved, and that she's a valuable human being

Take the pain away, that's tormenting her mind,
Let her live ... if just for awhile...
  Happy!
I would give my life... instead of hers
She deserves a happy life, with people
who love and respect her

If not Lord, save a peaceful and happy spot
with you in heaven, who loves her most.
   Karen Ziegler

Prayer For The Unborn Child

Oh, my unborn child resting within the womb
Please be still for now - your time for birth's not soon
You're only five months grown and it's early yet
Your seed in love was sown while the sun was set

We're waiting your arrival and looking for the day
But we'll try to be patient for God to have His way
While you're growing in Mom's womb you're growing in our hearts
We'd love to see you soon but for now we'll be apart

You've been 'specially created formed by God's own hand
His mercy and His goodness will keep you safely in His plan
No, your time is not completed although your body parts are formed
We'll trust that God will finish the work His miracle to perform

And when the danger comes and you cause Mom's heart to sway
We'll place our trust in God for there's really no other way
Our faith is in the Heavenly Father knowing all things work for the best
We're praying for you, grandchild, claiming health, joy and rest.
   Marsha McFarland

Voices

Sweet voices enter the realm of my heavy soul, calling to me,
pleading with me.
Foreign to my mind, I refuse to acknowledge this plea.
Too far lost upon my own self-conscious, I lie in wait,
for a time that I may break these walls of bitter conformity,
leaving all that once mattered,
in the shadows of my giant wings. For one day
I shall fly...high, above a world of reality and shame.
Above a world that I once loved.
Boredom flashes through my mind, a queer device of selfishness,
a bitter escape from time.
For time is the only boundary of human antiquity.
The key to life, that I once held, has fallen,
far below, deep into my tainted soul,
stopping momentarily, upon the steps of self-worth.
Not long enough for me to view this life through borrowed eyes,
yet long enough for me to realize that I
have lingered here within this destiny
one breath too long.
   Kimberly Halcomb

Tiny Angel

(Words from a mother to her terminally ill child.)
Holding you in my arms, you look at me and smile,
  Placed here in my life for just a little while.
When I'm holding you the only thing that I can see,
  Is a precious, tiny angel smiling up at me.
Oh, little one, I cannot take your mountains away,
  Or create for you another path that is easier to take.
But in every challenge that you face a lesson waits for me,
  As you have become my teacher - a debt I cannot repay.
I watch you fight life's battle and struggle to be free,
  Confined within a form that you did not choose to be.
Unable to express yourself to all those around you,
  You remind me that it doesn't matter what you can or cannot do.
You see, tiny angel, God made you just as you are,
  Here, safe in His world for a little while in my arms.
He let you teach me, tiny angel, that all that matters in this life,
  Is the spirit within you and the love you leave behind.
   Laura L. Gill

"Pulling Memories From The Fabric Of Time"

Pulling memories from the fabric of time,
Pictures of happenings from a time long gone by;
Sweetened by the passage of many long years,
And made precious by the spilling of laughter and tears.

Pulling memories from the fabric of time,
Memories of family and friends of mine;
Memories worth more than any money could buy,
Of pictures that were painted on memory's fabric of life.

Then when I have looked at some of yesterday's best,
I put them away again into life's memory chest,
Until some night when sleep eludes or some day's loneliness,
I pull them out to warm my heart once again.
   Opal Sallee

There Is No Fool Like An Old Fool

An old fool feels stupid and confused.
People take advantage of these poor souls who are good and honest.
They don't realize that people are not honest and truthful.
They find out to late that their friends have changed.
Their friends lie and pay not attention, they have no
  reason to be so deceitful but they are.
When the old fool finds out, he's left with great pain and anger.
Life is much too short for people to do these terrible things.
What should the Old Fool do? End this beautiful
  friendship, forget all the precious memories they shared?
Should he forget, forgive and start all over again? Definitely not.
In the long run the Old fool is the better person.
The old fool has learned a good lesson, poor dear old fool.
   Nancy Attraente

Matthew

Matthew, let's build a castle along the beach
  please
A chocolate brown sand castle
Laced with emerald-green seaweed
And trimmed with seashells
The colors of the rainbow
We'll make your beach towel into a robe
You can be the king - and rule your land
A grown-up king - wise and good
And I - I shall become your age
And stand in awe of our magnificent creation
It feels good to be a child again!
   Maxine Joy Hansen

Quiet

I like the quiet; it gives me peace,
peace that's so hard to find
in this day and time.

I like the quiet; it does not disturb
anything beautiful,
anything superb.

I like the quiet for it surrounds me with peace,
peace that is so lacking,
peace I want and need.

It lets me think and be and pray;
it lets me know that I'm okay.
It gives my power back to me
that went away somehow from me.

I'm glad I have it whenever I want.
Peace is good, it comes with time.
I'm so glad that quiet is mine.
   Kathryn R. Bezemes

"Wonderment"

Perched on rocks above the thundering surf,
Peace pervades the senses and body.
Wind blowing through hair,
Smelling the salty sea air.

Calmness returns to a disquieted mind.
Problems are now seen through unjaundiced eyes.
And clarity returns to find answers
So far unrealized.

Power filters through the entire body,
For the healing of the magnificent ocean
Has once again reclaimed sanity.

We listen, we feel, thankful for the healing,
Thru the immensity of this vast ocean.

Sea gulls wheeling and crying
As if to answer the roar.
From the depths of this tidal wonder
Created and birthed by an inexplicable power.

As renewal takes place,
And we are once again whole,
The world becomes a much better place.
   Mary Elizabeth Long

Time

Land, trees, grass,
passing at a speed where
only a vague remembrance of it is left.

They no longer sit, count and observe,
my sprouts;
no time, no time,
everything rushing, leaving, fading...

I could have spotted the red flower,
the bud,
giving birth to the purity left,
but-
this life was a pond of jungle darkness.

My flowers, my beauties,
my existence; oh! bring me back my innocence,
wash me clean;
endow me thy orchid: the shelter of my feathers.
   Lavinia Bensley-Bromilow

Visioning A Soiled Mist

Breathing life into question,
paranoia, searches for the answers.
Elaborate murals written in stone,
erased; dilate.
Lunar equations descend,
claiming zodiac signs walking in the desert,
illuminating our perception detailed on every page.
Possibly, another portrait for the season,
crashing off shore ceasing the tide,
breeding naivete in.
Grace, deemed to failure,
becomes a lost utopian festival.
   Larry Boggs

The Fish Bowl

Peering out from the inside,
Our land lives while others have died.
Goals here of peace and prosperity;
Results there of turmoil and poverty.
Some leaders and rulers conceited;
Their heinous deeds and wars repeated.
Kings and queens beheaded;
Bullets in bodies embedded.
A wall surrounds us — transparent—
Freedom — yearning to reach out and share it.
Masses of people living in fear,
Oh, Wishing to unlock their doors and bring them here.
Compelled to do something dutiful —
To emulate every country after America the Beautiful.
   Michele Irene Wilson

Dreams

Have you ever looked at the sky on a bright blue day?
Or the clouds that sprinkle white pillows along the way?

Have you ever seen the mist on a cold winter's morn?
So quiet, so still, just peace forever more.

Have you ever looked up in the sky at night to see?
The twinkling of the stars that glitter so bright for you
and for me?

You then see a star falling so gently and swift
You know that soon you will get your wish.

Have you ever looked up to a building so high?
At the top you see a vision of a red heart with
love on its side.

That's when you know.
It all seems so clear.
The magic has always been amazingly near.

Wake up to your dreams.
   Kerry F. Verrinder

You

Except for you I'd never known what love is
or how it feels to have a dream come true.
But now I find my world no longer lonely,
the way that it would be except for you.
One by one you mended all the pieces
of a heart that someone broke in two;
you fill my days with happiness and sunshine
that I never would have known except for you.
You brought all the rainbow colors to a world of solid blue.
There's nothing prettier than rainbows except for you.
My love I wanted just to tell you this heart
won't beat again except for you.
   Lucille Trent

Nature's Own

Did "yew" ever hear a "dogwood" bark
Or have a "catnip" "yew"?
And did you know that if a "boxwood" spar,
It "wood" knock the sap out of you?

Have you ever dreamed of the "golden chain"
Or heard the "weeping willow"
As you lay in your cozy bed at night
With your head on a "downy" pillow?

Would you like a coat of the lovely "fir"
Or one of a "cottonwood?"
It's "plane" to me that even a tree
Would make "locust" coats so good.

Then there was the whine of the lofty "pine"
Hey!! "Eucalyptus" way too short
And the crop of seeds that the forest needs
This year we will abort.

Now is the time to send this rhyme
To judges, not a few,
And hope they say to "Missy May"
I like this subject too.

Lily May Lynch

The Choice Is Ours

The choice is ours, to heal or to hurt.

A life is precious no matter what.

When one gets hurt, do we stand still and watch,
  or do we do whatever we can to help.

There are no reasons for war, but if we were
  to all just try to help each other,

Instead of blaming, the mass confusion would quiet.

Enemies or not, we are all people,
  and we should all do whatever we can
  for one another.

Am I dumb for putting my life on the line for another,

No I only care, and that is not wrong.

Judge if thou want, but judge me fairly,
  for I am I and not what thou want me to be.

Maria A. Tchinchinian

"Me"

On this journey of life, I seem to climb one mountain
Only to find another, I run into one brick wall
Only to find one higher, I travel down roads
Of frustration and anger, roads of anxiety,
Fear and confusion, all in search of me.

I find myself going down avenues for information,
Seeking truth and quoting affirmations.
I am on a quest of who is this and what is that,
Just to find out where am I really at.
All search of me.

Then one day a realization. I know there is a
"Great Spirit," a love so powerful and strong,
A feeling that could never be wrong,
A strength so bold and full of courage.
The truth finally surrounds me,
That God and I are one!

Marilyn L. Radiff

Undefinable

Labels, names, abstract definitions, titles and designations all mean one thing - limitation. Our society finds its security in making things small and controllable by labeling limitations. Yet, this I declare unto you, label me not for I am not what or who you think I am or was or will be. Limit me not for I shall be all that I can and want to be.

How dare you say because I am black or white, male or female, young or old, Christian or Jew or whatever else I am or am not that I "belong" here or there or that I can only be this or that? How dare you try do define me - the undefinable, ever-changing being that I am? I am everything and anything I want to be and grow to be. I belong wherever I want to be and come to be.

You cannot define me for your own security to limit me to your mental underclass society! I was born like any other and each day renewed with new knowledge, understanding and growth. Everyday a different person from the day before or/and the day after.

I am ever-changing and growing - I am undefinable and therefore, unlimited in what I can do and be. Defined in life I will never be - only in death will the world be able to attempt to label my memory -

for I am undefinable and unhindered by the limits of your labels.

Lynn Welch Hargrove

The Greatest Gift

There was a Wonderful Gift, sent from above,
  One that was gladly given to me.
This Gift was wrapped in swaddling clothes,
  And not in bright paper you see...
No strings were attached to this Precious Gift,
  Which was given out of a Heart of pure Love.
Born around a stable, but yet he was able
  To prepare us for those Mansions above...
No box was needed for this priceless Gift,
  And you can't buy it with silver nor gold.
Oh, this Special Gift, God offers to all,
  From a Great Story that never grows old...
We thank the Father for this Glorious Gift...
  So if you are lost and will only believe,
The Perfect One was given, that we might have life
  And is the Greatest Gift we will ever receive...

Leona Tiller

Someone Else To Blame

If it's not your fault,...and it isn't mine,
one of us must prove this claim.
Who made the mistakes that caused many heartaches,
...maybe we need someone else to blame.

Love came too fast,...so fast it didn't last...,
each other we didn't get to know.
And soon it would change, it wasn't the same,
...maybe we need someone else to blame.

A marriage commitment we didn't expect,
...our wedding vows we'd both soon neglect,
a stranger now slept in my bed.
She made the call,...or it wasn't at all...,
If I didn't comply, many threats of 'good bye'
...maybe we need someone else to blame.

Disillusion and disappointment soon bred hate ...now
there's a separation of late..., but it was never my aim
to cause pain. Will she ever see it was not only me?
...maybe we need someone else to blame.

A destructive game, but our lives we'll reclaim;
...maybe we'll get past the need to blame.

Lois L. Irving

Unity By Love

One song we sing, your song, my song,
One love we bring, your love, my love.

A flame burning deep within us yet miraculously bright,
A flame so tender that we hasten and stutter to ignite.

The hatred, one to many an overlapping, but there
lies a frail small light, so small do we dare to
kindle, to acknowledge, to recognize its presence.

To absorb its warmth and relish it in unending delight,
to join hands and take flight! To become one body!
One unity! One faith! One fight.

But not against each other, do not engulf the flames
of hate, distinguish it but still one will remain and prosper.

The flame of hope, and of right judgement, of care and peace,
and let it burn hard and bright.

For though some love may be fragile and thin, true love
comes only from those who believe it's deep within.

Madu Onwuka

Seasons

In the busy 'down-below' world of daily work-a-day fretting,
One is accosted by the dull sameness of days spent sweating.
One day succeeding another never weather report needing,
But up here on the slopes the turn of clock bears repeating.

The frigidness of winter with her brittle breezy kisses,
Stays the crackling dryness broken by steamy kettle hisses.
The wind-driven bare fingers of once leaf-shaded trees,
Play their incessant tapping of staccato yuletide reprise.
With the pellet sting of snow clusters that on once's face alight,
One tends to grow weary of day light-strings dimming in our sight.
One longs for Summer's temperance, her warming soft embrace,
Whose bright seed-pocket promises Winter hues erase.

When the cool Summer breezes bring the scent of deep pine forest,
One then knows the fulfillment of the Seasons is before us.
The gossamer web of Earth's temperament reminds one to see,
Just how perfect in their timing God's Seasons were meant to be.

Mara Schramm

In The City Of Orchids

And the night spills its darkness over the sky;
on the streets, a conspiracy of colors, neon lights and spot lights;
in the air, fireflies and butterflies and flying mice with paper wings.
Everywhere, fresh like flowers, black and white orchids,
young girls, wild with desire, flying to reach the moon,
reaching the edge of darkness, sweet flesh against the sky,
shy angels, wanting to bath in fire, their wing tips mercilessly clipped;
black and white doves dragged by their wings
on the streets of the city of orchids,
where roses die early with petals half open
and stars crumble on deluded skies, like brittle yellow flowers in
   the evening wind.
And the night trembles toward morning,
the longing in her heart becomes a cry
as she lies fragrant on the bed of a stranger;
nothing around her but the predictable truth;
and she cries in shame a river of tears that reaches the sky.
Shy angel gone wild with desire,
having bathed in fire, wing tips mercilessly clipped,
run away from the city of orchids,
away from fireflies and butterflies and flying mice with paper wings.

Maria Minakis

Untitled

A sampan drifted along the riverside.
On it stood an old man holding a baby.
I stopped my work to watch them glide by.
He asked, "Would I like to join them, maybe?"
But I had so much work to do
That I would never get through.
I had things to build and things to sell.
I wanted to, but I had to tell, I couldn't go.
I asked who would take care of them on their journey.
The old man said with a toothless grin...
"The sun is our father, the river our mother,
And I won't die
And the baby won't cry
As long as we have each other."
Soon their little boat was no longer near.
He waved back, and in my eye a tear, as
I realized with deep sorrow, that I had nothing
And they had tomorrow.

Larrie Ervin

Santa Claus Is Running Out Of Presents!

Now Dasher, now Dancer, now Prancer, and Vixen.
On Comet, on Cupid, on Donner, and Blitzen. Dash away, dash away
dash away all. Down the highway and to the mall. Don't worry
children stay calm and rest. I'm trying to get presents I'm
doing my best. Calm down, there's no need to cry. I'll
get you some gifts, believe me I'll try. I buy all the presents and
go to each house, I slide down the chimney quiet as a mouse. Then
I put down the presents from one Chaumburg Place. I'm so proud a
smile comes to my face. A toy train for Jerry, a doll for Mary,
clothes for Carrie, G.I. Joe's for Larry. A book for Jenny, a poster
for Kenny, a ball for Lenny, a mitt for Penny. A book for Johnny,
markers for Ronnie. A hat for Ryan, a puppy for Brian, a teddy bear
for Holly, and a clock for Molly. Now all the children feel much
better. I gave them what they wanted, I know from their letter.
As I walk to my sleigh I almost have a stroke. Now I realize that I am
broke, I already gave the cashier the check, oh what a wreck. I'll go
to the bank on my way north. I'll do that, then I set forth. I get
my money and am gone in a flash. Flying through the air with handfuls
of cash. Now I'm through Rome, on my way home, I hold myself
tight and yell: "Merry Christmas to all and to all a good night."

Lauren Weber

Lost Dreams

Outside, the sky is dark,
   Ominous, and foreboding
      Indeed, it is a reflection of my moods.

It seems a day of mourning,
   for death of love is much like death in life.

Loss of hopes and dreams,
   words that will never be spoken,
      and what could have been, but now never will be.

Alone I wait, willing the phone to ring,
   But of course, it will not.
      It is a game between us now.

Without you, there is a silence to my life.
   My heart breaks, but you will not hear it.
      My mind speaks out, yet there are no longer any words.

Tears, long thought forgotten,
   now flow freely, as if to erase the memory of you.
      But, they cannot.

For you, will always be
   in the deep, dark wound
      called my heart.

Laura Renee Jennings

If I Were Made Of Stone

If this heart be made of stone, it shall not perceive the anguish of tormented memories and that of disregarded love. For it shall have not one memory, for this cobble has only coldness and pummeled gravel as its valor.

If these eyes be made of stone, they shall not gaze at that of such a vicious and battered humanity as this. They would not sting at the sight of dissolution. For bittersweet tears from them shall not fall, for they are as wintery as the ocean air.

Thus, if my whole union of members accordingly be as pebbles and that of tombstones, the agony of endurance it shall not comprehend.

Yet, comfort is brought to me. This heart, if stone it has become, then it has not felt the touch of its beloved. It has not triumphed in the exultation of its perseverance.

These eyes as if boulders they were, have not seen the endless sea overlaid by its sable blanket of diamonds.

Therefore, pain shall be felt; yes, this we can not elude. But misery shall make this very essence stronger. Yes, tears of sorrow shall fall from these eyes, yet tears of joy descend more unwavering!

Upon this I reflect, of what could not be seen, felt, or touched if I, with everything that I am, were made of stone!

Kelli Michelle Graves

Why God Made Boys

God made the world out of his dreams,
Of majestic mountains, oceans, and streams,
Prairies, plains, and wooded land,
Then paused and thought, "I need someone to stand,
On top of the mountains,
To conquer the seas;
Explore the plains and climb the trees—
Someone to start out small and grow,
Sturdy and strong like a tree," and so—
He created boys, full of spirit and fun,
To explore and conquer,
To romp and run,
With dirty faces and bandaged shins,
With courageous hearts and boyish grins,
And when he'd completed the job he'd begun,
He loudly said, "That's a job well done!"

Matthew King

Strength's Eclipse

In photographs I spy sweet memories of ole,
Of happy times, of moments shared, and of things that made me whole.
Phrases spoken days in number, of the things we longed to do.
Dreams spun golden on campfired nights, 'neath brilliant stars and skies dark blue,
Now mirrored images show tell-tale signs of strength's eclipse.
The changes revealed in shapes of ghosts, 'ere once we ceased to be,
Mine shape I see it toys with me, as parts of me receding,
Betray the memories portrayed in times preceding.
To appreciate what once you had, needed is some to perish,
As we look back we will recall the warmth of all those cherished.
When in mirrors you see betrayal and the body's harsh eclipse,
The shaking hand and subtle tremble in voice and smiling lips.
The Lord's bestowed times of past in our hearts to help brighten strength's eclipse.
So child of young, do all ye can to taste what life will give,
Look not for back enough in years to pain thee.
Squander nary grains, for precious few are the crystal sands of time, and stroll by my side to the end of my path as friend, companion and kind.

Maria Mitchell

Autumn Song

Skies are painted with patches
of fluffy white on blue.
Maples and oaks are glowing
with a red and golden hue.

Mountain streams are gurgling
as they meander from their source.
Hillsides are speckled with cattle a grazing;
Yonder echoes a neighing horse.

The air is crisp; the wind foretells
an approaching change of weather.
The sunset darkens the evening sky
as a chickadee rustles its feather.

Summer days of sun and pleasure
have escaped us once again;
But the glorious song of autumn
is ready to begin!

Mary Wisham Fenstermacher

Prayer For The Selection Of A President

As we come again to the crossroads of the selection
Of a president, God, please give us direction,
And forgive me when I seek for ME and MINE.
Rather, help America choose who's best: Let us YOUR choice find.
Please guide us as a nation and as a people, too.
Help us as we work, think, plan and do.
Lead us so that SELF is not the measure that we use,
But grant us wisdom, Dear God, to rightly choose
So that our choice fits completely in YOUR plan.
We thank you, God, knowing that only YOU can
Motivate and move us for the good of ALL.
Please guide and forgive us. Let not America fall,
But direct and lead us in the "paths of righteousness for thy namesake."
We thank you, God, and beg that YOU our choice make
So that America may continue to reach for peace,
Prayerfully led, a "nation under God". Let our faith increase,

Marie Eubank Turner

All The Difference

The simplicity of the presence, from Day to day,
of a kindred spirit, similar in soul and mind;
Understanding fully what Adam spoke
when confronted with Eve;
Having found, "Bone of my bone, and flesh of my flesh."

Expectation to experience, hope and faith to reality.
Better than what was hoped for, beyond the feeble
capabilities of a mind to expect.
"Exceedingly, abundantly beyond all one could ask
or think."

A believer, in one accord, made also to be one flesh.
No comparison to the past, no need to.
Faith and hope in Christ, for us,
has made all the difference.

True love found! But still the challenge of intimacy.
Thankful for a lifetime to understand those
intricacies.

Foundational love, knowing its true source.
The blessings of security that, for us,
have made all the difference.

Mark Mathew Ahrens

Our Love In Later Years

The ultimate of completeness
Of a beautiful beginning——

All of the candles and matches around the world
Ignited at once in my heart when you first said, "I love you"

Every musical instrument on earth was playing
At peak crescendo at our first kiss.

What joy, what bliss starting our own home.
And being a part of God's miracles as we gave birth to children.

The golden glow of sunsets——
The pitter-patter of refreshing spring rains

The quiet unfolding of a beautiful rosebud——
Into the most gorgeous fragrant complete flower——

Are all reminders of our love
As it has grown and deepened through the years.

As now we walk hand in hand, heart in heart
No words need to be said.

The fire is still there — glowing softly——
The "Oom-pa-pa" still in your kiss for me.

Thank you, and thank God, for
The quietness and completeness of OUR LOVE.

Norma Jean Tarnow

My Stepping Stones

I felt humbled...as I stumbled
O'er a stone in the rough road,
As I trudged with a pack on my back.
  But I picked myself right up
  And I headed down the road
  With my very heavy pack still intact.
And I tried to dodge the rocks
That lay before me in the road,
As I struggled to keep intact my heavy load.
  And then there were places in the road
  That were filled with muck and mire,
  And my feet had trouble
  To maintain a steady pace.
I was tired...yes, sore and hurt...
And I was chilled from skin to bones...
'Til I used the stumbling blocks...in the dirt...
  As my stepping stones!

Michael S. Mapa

Love 101

The teacher presents his lecture.
My mind says to listen,
But my heart is busy thinking of you.
Why are you in my thoughts so much.
I'm usually in such control.
I would fight it, if I could.
I'm helpless but to submit to my emotions.

I want to make you laugh to play with your hair
  to kiss your soft, sweet lips
  to tell you that I care.
Agony is wanting and not receiving.
I miss you, though I just met you.
It is confusing to me.
Tell me how you have done it,
No other has been able to.
Is it a spell, a charm, or just you.
It doesn't really matter.

My heart is beating fast
And my thoughts are a blur.
Somewhere unheard, the teacher lectures on...

Louis Krivanek

Night Symphony

What limpid beauty, this golden night
Numerous night birds persist in flight.
Their crescendo calls, the still disquiet
Oratoriously announcing their winsome plight.

An enchanting symphony seems to begin.
It's repertoire wantonly in aria contend.
In full discord, each to rend
Their soulful sounds to heaven ascend.

The Whippoorwill voluptuously fill
The wayward breeze with a reverberating trill.
Calling its mate from the distant hill,
Its intrepid tonality, tranquility instill.

Virtuosos flaunted, chaotically float
As crickets chirp their humdrum note,
Dramatically magical, their billowy dote
Chanting the arrangement its celestial composer wrote.

Their ecstasy wanes and inadvertently decline
As a rapturous concert mellows to a harmonious chime.
Blissfully undaunted by thematic rhyme
Its phrasing repeated thru eons of time.

Lois L. Wathen

No Words

What words are there, other than, "I'm sorry?"
No words can take away the pain
No words make things the way they were again
Now comes the question "WHY?"
Why my son?
Why my brother?
Why my friend?
No words will ever answer that one
No words can make us understand why anything happens
They just do and some how we are left to just accept it
It may make us sad
It may make us angry
It may make us cry
But the one thing death always does is to make us stronger
Stronger to live life better
Stronger to love a little better
Stronger to step back and take a look at what we have
And to appreciate it
No words can heal the hurt inside only time will make
It fade NO WORDS

Laura A. Thoman

White House Counsel

O Mr. President,
  Mr. President!
Please! Please! Please!
I beg on my knees,
  ONE BIG FAVOR.

Keep IT clean, clean, clean,
Positive, positive, too.
Let candidates ALL, work wonders
  On this score.
Gently, gently, but firm as Gibraltar,
Genuinely presidential in intellect, word, substance.

Verbiage diminished, non-redundant,
Without bias or prevarication.
  Tell it LIKE IT IS.
Action increased and super-abundant,
Based on ethics pure and simple;
Not personalities - good or bad;
But pressing issues, complex, knotty.

Serve the present, not the past.
The IT above? Your next campaign, of course.

Mary Joyce Schladweiler

To My Grandma

To grandma with all of her loving ways,
　No wonder I'll love you all of your days,

Thank you grandma for being just you,
　Thank you for helping me with the pain I've been through

Tho you've toiled many a years, don't worry grandma,
　God saw every one of your tears

Grandma with all of life's ups and downs
　Grandma I could always depend on you to be around

And so we celebrate another birthday today,
　Your love for us is here to stay

So thanks for all the good advice,
　Grandma you never had to tell me twice

I thank God for giving me the words to this card,
　Believe me grandma it wasn't hard

I love you now, I love you then,
　Your life is an example for all to live free from sin

I love you grandma, there'll never be another,
　I'll stop right here, don't need to go any further.
　　Mary A. S. Lemon

She's Gone Home

So young, and yet so free.
No other place I'd rather she be
Than with our Creator, watching over me.

She had beautiful brown eyes and hair,
Tinted with gray from years of worry and despair.
Changed over a few hours, with no longer a care.

Our first thought - had she just been drinking,
But when we saw her we knew our ship was sinking
And all we could ponder was what she was thinking.

At some point, none of that no longer mattered,
For we realized that all of her worries were shattered
And all of the good seeds had been scattered.

Although we miss her dearly,
No one is more deserving, sincerely.
She had a heart of gold and I will always hold that near me.

She was our Mother, like none other,
To me, two sisters and a brother.
　　Misty D. Stitely

A Lonely Child

When I was born no one was there
No one to love me no one to care
I lay in my crib at the end of my rope
They said I wouldn't live, the Dr. gave up hope

Then a man and a woman came to my aid
They gave me their love so I wouldn't die
The day I left the hospital they took me into their home
With 7 brothers and sisters I wouldn't be alone

When I turned ten they took me to court
The judged asked me if I was happy I said of course
Now every thing is legal I carry their name.
I am finally some body that no one can change.

I will always be thankful I'll pray to the Lord
For he helped my pain he took out my sword.
Yes they have given me everything I wanted and thought I'd never have
For that man and woman are my mom and dad
　　Linda C. Faulkner

I'm So Glad There Is Jesus

If it wasn't for Jesus, there'd be no alter call,
No one to cling to, when I stumble and fall.
If it wasn't for Jesus, there'd be no mansions above,
Built by his nailed-scarred hands and filled with his love.

I'm so glad there is Jesus, who loves me every day,
He leads me by the hand, so I won't go astray.
He shares my burdens and carries my heavy load,
He gently leads me down victory's road.

If it wasn't for Jesus, the Bible would not be,
No plan of salvation, nor a heaven to see.
If it wasn't for Jesus, oh, how weary life would be,
There'd be no cross on dark Calvary.

If it wasn't for Jesus, there'd be no eternity,
That's where I want to live, when he reaches down for me.
If it wasn't for Jesus, there'd be no streets of gold,
Nor a land where we'll never grow old.
　　Mary Ellen Mays

"Our Father's Pride"

Many of stories have been written of true love.
No one knows or wants to understand, but the one above.
For most of us on this land.
It takes an honorable person to take this kind of stand.
To set a good example for all man kind.
You must have humor, love, discipline, and a very strong mind.
Some men are weak, and some are very strong.
Some take command and others do wrong.
The love is for America and what a Nation.
With all the pride for this land our ancestors brought
　forth such organization.
Many soldiers fought upon foreign soil.
To save mothers, fathers and children from chaos and turmoil.
Blood from bodies have been shed.
Many brave young men have a permanent bed.
So sad they couldn't have shared the fame and glory.
Without these great men how could he have written such a story.
They gave their life to save ours.
Upon their grave stands a shining stars.
On a plaque bear the names of these men.
They only did what was expected of them.
　　Nancy Carol Chatlas

The Bogeyman

Night descended slowly, blanketing her in empty quietude.
No dulling routine remained to blunt the ever-present fears
lurking just below her conscious reflection.
She sits alone shrouded in her misery, silently whistling
in the face of anticipated catastrophe,
and offering up promises to perfidious Gods.
A frightful game of "Bogeyman", executed with an adult's
rejection of the inevitable, and a small inner-child's surrender
to the monster in the closet.
Unchecked, her tears fail to deliver the release she covets,
and hope flickers too feebly to revive her wearied spirit.
Exhausted, she waits for the first pale rays of morning,
it's warmth to soothe her restive soul,
and chase the night's long shadows into the sun.
　　Melsyne Montgomery

Night Wing

I stand at the edge of the world and open my arms to embrace the dark night.
The stars on high watch like millions of unblinking eyes lit by an unholy light.
The full moon sends its beams down to brighten my dark twisted path.
A misty rain falls gently to clean my weary soul in its warm wet bath.
A breeze caresses my body knowingly like an old familiar lover's hand.
I close my eyes and listen to the sounds of the dismal land.
I can feel the cool wet earth beneath my bare feet as I turn to face my eternal fate.
Cursed forever to hunt my next blood date.

I cry out in rage to the black Gods of the night.
Why must I hide from the sight of light?
Forgive my sins and bless my lost soul.
A creature of the night denied the warmth of day.
Denied the sun's bright golden rays.
Doomed to wander the earth at night longing for the touch of man.

A mist silently forms in response to my pleas and holds me tight.
A ghostly lover's embrace that somehow feels right.
I know in my heart that I will always be a creature of the night.
Destined to flee eternity the sight of daylight.
Cursed until the end of time.
I open my arms and welcome the dark demons of night.
   Linda Myszka

Waiting

And when I see you, no matter from how far
My whole being responds in love.

Must I absorb all your pain to make it go away?
I have walked with you through the doubt
Lived the sadness that tears at your heart
Experienced your anger, misplaced, still loose
Cried for the wholeness of one torn apart
And waited for that time when forgiveness
will finally set you free.

Oh, would that I could grant you that forgiveness.
Allowing you to move peacefully into tomorrow,
Unfettered by the pangs of guilt
Open to one who cares so very much
Free to trust a waiting heart
And ready to open your being to the
fullness of life—and love.
   Maureen Price

Lost And Found

All alone in this strange place, just another unknown face
My spirit sighs to meet, my master on this street,
My heart leaps with joy, for the touch of a boy,
Long have I roamed, and this wilderness combed
Searching for familiar lands, and the stroke of loving hands.

Many days my feet have trod, upon this dusty sod;
Long nights I've cried, and watched the sky
All alone with my fears, until the dawn reappears
Once again to face my woes, and bypass all my foes
Hoping that I may view, kind faces I once knew.

Then from the wind an echo blows, his childish voice I know
Out of the purple night, and gradually into the light
A smile I see, Ah! my master...it is he,
Though I'm just a wayward dog, fate wrote upon my log
That to me she would be kind, so my master I could find.
   Lydia Pauline Dunlap

Took A Chance And Moved Far Away From Home

Far away from everything I've ever loved or known.
My heart was broken, my body bruised, thought suicide was the
Consequence for letting myself be used.

Pulling myself together, the best that I knew how, I came to this big
City wondering, what do I do now?

Painful memories started dissipating into the lock-box inside my head,
Thanking God each night for the new chance; resurrecting my
self-esteem from the thoughts of being dead.

I've still had the up's and down's here, but at least I am now free;
free to be a woman, and free to just be me!
   Nina Marie David

Call Of The Wind

To my deepest sorrow and dismay
my greatest love lives among the wild hunting for prey
This great grey wolf holds claim to me

He calls to me in the dead of night
a piercing howl that cause many fright
Yellow eyes shining so bright
captured my heart at first sight

This magnificent creature has beauty and grace
leading the pack on a glorious chase
A boundless energy carries them far
as they travel under sun and stars

Curiosity has taken them away many times before
leaving me with an emptiness until their safe return once more
Silence surrounds me on this cold winter day
high above snow clouds roll in not far away

The strong winds carry to me the most heart-warming sound
my beloved pack is homeward bound
Moving at a steady pace
racing for my warm embrace
   Lisa West

A Prairie Saga

That Sunday the sky was dark and mean, but out to the field I crept.
My Father stood with his head hung low; I could see that he had wept.
The stand of wheat lay flat on the ground, as far as the eye could see
The darkened sky held the black top-soil and it flew on the wind to me

The wind had begun the night before, and it howled the whole night long
My dad had listened while mamma prayed, 'till they fell asleep at dawn
Now black dirt lay on the window sills, and black dirt on the floor.
It settled into the cups and bowls through cracks in the cupboard door

Our drinking water and dipper too, so muddy we would not use.
I heard Dad say "I've had enough! To Calgary we'll have to move"
Seven crops my Dad had planted and only three of these were saved.
The "Dust Bowl Days" had just begun, in spite of the way they slaved.

While tumbleweed and thistle might over-run the plain,
I still see the broken and shattered stalks and the ruined crop of grain.
Whatever happened to the puppy I loved, and the horse Kate
  drove to school?
Did some other kid get the wagon we pulled, full of buffalo chips for fuel?

I wonder if Dolly still lies in the field, where I left her one summer day?
Her arm broken off and her hair not curled, still waiting for me to play?
The prairie land where I grew up once again grew crops that paid.
And we got used to the city streets, but my heart on the prairie stayed......
   Margaret L. Bartholomew

Living LaRoux

I am an ocean, and you are the sun.
My body is sometimes warm and welcoming,
Sometimes cold and forbidding.
I have storms and rages;
Some days the pressures of my own self cracks down my sanity.
I am full of mysterious depths, waiting
  to be explored and discovered.
Angry winds mess with my emotions, and I
  may lash out my deadly waving arms at loved ones.
I hold many unseen treasures,
And I can bring you happiness and make you cry.
I am full of myself and my greatness sometimes,
But other times I follow the moon in hopes
  that she will give me the love I need.
I have many levels, many feelings and hopes
  and dreams and nightmares,
And you, the jealous sun, barely shine your
  life-giving light beyond my thin protective exterior surface.
You try to compete for my affections.
Look deeper, and you will see in me what only the bravest have found.
Lisa Overbeck

Plummeting Dreams

More than just someone to hold me,
More than just a friend,
Just someone I can love.

Pure white flakes plummet to the ground,
They elude the ears, but not the nose;
The silent beauty of the snow.

Watching, dreaming, longing;
He sits by the window staring blankly,
The snowflakes pass the window, like the dreams in his mind;
Slowly a warm arm slides across his chest,
Without looking he clasps her hand in his,
Silently, she opens her heart and pulls him in.

Watching, dreaming;
He gives thanks for dreams come true,
  and bids farewell to the longing.
Mathew Thomas Jett

Locked Together In Love

Upon an altar I see myself with the man I love,
Minister before us, friends behind,
Flowers surround us, sweet scents fill my nose,
Beautiful music fills my ears,
Love fills my heart,
Here I stand entranced by my life long love,
  I am oblivious to any words spoken,
I see only him.
The altar fades only he and I remain, our eyes meet,
  as if for the first time again neither of us are able to look away.
All I see is his love for me,
Love that is strong,
Love that has brought us together again when we were blinded by the advice of others,
Now our love for each other is known to all and nothing will separate us again,
We are eternally joined by our love.
Devon Alexandria Rose

For The Love Of A Man

For the love of a man...I would cheat myself out of what is best for me.
For the love of a man...I would throw away my peace of mind and harmony.
For the love of a man...I would ignore the pain down inside, in order
  to be what he wants me to be, it's my real self that I hide.
For the love of a man, I thought I would do anything; until I saw the hurt to myself that it did bring.
For the love of a man....I would no longer lose myself, in order to put him up on a shelf.
Myself I will not steal, kill or destroy, or over him lose my joy.
I will not be a puppet or statue, allowing me to be me is what he will have to do.
I will not stand like an ostrich with my head buried in the sand, or agonize inside, for the love of a man.
Nadine Vazquez

O' Grandfather

O' Grandfather,
May your spirit soar though the skies,
Let your eyes - follow our lives,
To look upon us - a family of Reardons,
To watch the nest - you helped create,
To see us grow - through time and through fate,
To be there to greet us when we too pass through the gate,

I'd like to thank you now - for I may not have in the past,
For building a swift, strong, ship with two powerful masts,
I know grandfather - that if I miss a step or run aground on hard times,
That I'll just look back - and smile with awe, - remembering the man I call grandpa.
Mike Reardon

All Hallows Eve

Two teen werewolves dare the path to my door,
masked and hungry
for full size candy bars.

Hiding supper in the hall
I eat quickly
waiting for a knock.

Am I a witch sometimes,
angry and yelling, scaring my children?
Are my children sometimes
angels and vampires; showing wings or fangs?

No one knocks.
Eating, I stuff in candy kisses
waiting for a knock.

A knock, and my son is home with candy
Not an angel, or a vampire, nor a witch
But a Ninja and his mom.
Linda A. Sjoberg

Untitled

  My friend, you are a jewel that sparkles in the night when there is no other light. Not because you are a diamond or a crystal. What I see is your heart and your sparkle mind forever seeking knowledge, almost like mine. Seek peace, my friend, contentment seek deep within your heart and you will find the center for forgiveness. Set yourself free, let love and mercy be.
Margaret R. Guarogno

Through And Through

The heart is like my home, broken yet together.
Many challenges and hard times spent there but sooner or later
overtaken by the laughter and love shared throughout.
Day by day spent at this place, night by night slept through and
yet it builds stronger with every laugh and every tear shed
throughout it.
You have to tend to its needs or it could fall apart.
Cherishing every moment that is yours makes it seem like nothing
will ever harm it.
Yet in one second something could happen.
The boards and the nails and the plaster holding the walls together
could all be torn apart just like when it is your time to go.
Your feelings no longer felt, your thoughts no longer thought,
your voice no longer spoken.
The times may cease but the memories are forever flowing in this
wonderful place I call home.

Lindsey A. George

Thirteen

God sent you to me in His love and grace
Making room in this world for your special place.
I felt your life from deep within; a bright new future waiting to begin
I cherished you then, right from the start.
My love for you was from the heart.
And then the day you entered my life —
Free and innocent, no fear or strife.
You were my joy and strength to go on.
Once a baby — Look again, she is gone.
We had our time, though it never lasts.
We have to look forward and ponder the past.
You are my being — My hope untold.
You are the life I long to unfold.
I know my love will guide your way
As you become a teen on this, your day.
You make me proud, the daughter you are.
In a sky of brightness you are my star.
My best friend you are to me,
For mother and daughter we were destined to be.
My little girl has grown so much today.
She is a young lady now. Do not stand in her way.

Louise M. Bistrick

"Take God With You"

Take God with you my children as you start this long journey today
Make sure you have God with you to lead the way
Just trust in him with all your heart
And he will help you with whatever you start

As you start in a new home
Please know that you are never alone
Just be sure God is number one in your lives and in your hearts too
For he will love and take care of you

Put your thrust in him with whatever you do
And you can be sure he will always take you through

Notie L. Welles

"She"

God saw she was getting tired and a cure could
not be found. So he put his arms around her
and whispered, "Come to me."

With tearful eyes we watched her slowly fade
away. Although we loved her dearly we knew
she could not stay.

A golden heart stopped beating, hard working
hands put to rest. God broke our hearts to prove
to us he only take the best....

Karen A. Piazza

Catcher's Prayer

Lord give me the arm to throw the ball,
Make it good, so there's no need for a call.

Help me to set my feet and throw
Then let the short stop make a tag that is low

But if the throw is not too great,
hopefully the back up will get it before it's to late.
Around third base the runner will go
but, I'll catch the ball and take the blow.

But first, dear Lord, on a bad pitch I ask
please, don't let, the ball go past...

Mary Jo Raughley

A Tribute To A Tree

She was so stately and so tall, she from a seedling grew.
Majestic in her height and girth for all the world to view.
She reached her arms up Heavenward, fought wind and rain and sleet.
The winter snows hung heavily, she withstood the Summer's heat.
She swayed and bowed in Autumn's breeze and sheltered us from sun.
Provided nests for countless birds; made a place for squirrels to run.
Bare of leaf as seasons changed each and every year.
But budded forth with boughs of green when Springtime did appear.
Through all she stood so grandly for such a long, long while.
She was graceful in her splendor, she had much class and style.
Then came a dreaded illness that made her branches die.
It ate away like cancer; she almost seemed to cry.
Those men that came so swiftly, in no time chopped her down.
They sawed and hacked and chewed her up 'til naught was left but
  ground!
This was the purpose of their task; they did not beauty see.
In so short a span she was all gone, as it was meant to be.
And although I dearly loved her, she is now a memory.

Katherine Lottman

Emotional Strain

Bodies lying in halls.
Lying on beds, lips moves, lungs gasp for breath.
You wish for a cure, but only get pain.
Life's non-existent, emotional strain.
Tubes and needles, needles and pins
Wonder where, just where your mind is.
Friends and relatives here to see you.
What in the world will the doctors do.
Feel no pleasure against the grain.
I'll forget your face, forget your name.
Silver white hair, flimsy robe on.
No one will remember you when you're gone.
I can't forget the misery, the pain you live through, the agony.
Only now do you begin to refrain,
Your life's null and void, emotional strain.
Lying down in your hospital bed.
You wish for a dream,
Dream you were dead.....

Michael Maccarrone

A Father's Love

  I long for his touch, the feel of his small hand inside
of mine. I miss the noise of activity, his wide eyed wonder,
his cheerful smile and full belly laugh.
  As I sit alone in this small darkened room, the sound of
silence echoes in my ears. Time seems to stand still, but
I know that I will be with him again soon. Closing my eyes,
remembering brings him home again. A smile comes to my lips.

Michael J. Rice

Girlish Dreams

Ever since I was a little girl I have dreamed of being
   loved and loving someone like you.
Someone I hated to say good-bye to and
   longed to see again.
I never in my darkest dreams thought my
   girlish dreams would come true,
   till I met you.
I have come to realize just how much you
   really do mean to me.
I don't know what I would do without you.
I never want to lose you.
I love you always
   Leasa Garrett

A View

I, with many, share a view all on subjects that aren't new
Love, religion, and politics we all need without tricks
Many are confused by the lies brought on by people who
disguise
Their view with an illusion of self-sacrifice.
An illusion all want to believe, trusting in the words said by
These stealthy sirs but many know and have seen too well
The illusions to fall victim again and again.
Many are too naive to listen to the words being said
Implicated meanings are given to fit the needs of the listeners
No matter who they may be.
These listeners, too, will fall victim to the stealthy sirs
Manipulating by words and implications are their tricks
No self-sacrifice is seen when the words are the screen.
To you I say with all my heart, listen to and trust
The spirit and the soul
For they do not lie as we all know.
   Mary Ann Lee

Love Is Emotion

Love is emotion, so painful, and so deep,
Love is a storm, pours rain, and strikes thunder,

you can't seem to sleep,
When you fall for it, you can't even bare,
To be alone, or to be awake,
already its too big of a mistake,
Love will take you high, and take you low,
is there ever anything left to show,
But still more despair, forgetful of those affairs,
The more I think, and the more I fight,
I wish to God, I had been left alone,
in all those cold, and lonely nights,
It stirs quick, cuts you sharp,
stabs you painfully through your heart,
Loudly quiet, and lying still,
lurking on the moment of thrill,
I can't believe, mostly I can't bare,
that I had to fall in LOVE,
with that EMOTION out there!
   Meghan Kerins

The Emigrant's Song

When I was a young boy from across the sea,
My mother said to me "Be good, kind as wise as you can be
that all may come to thee."
I grew to man's estate, had done as she had said.
Now all of America is here for me!
   Marjorie A. Stone

Untitled

You only live once, that's what they say
Live it to the fullest, live it day by day.
Yet the pain I bare just can't go away.
I feel so lost and so upset,
Feelings like this, I'll never forget.
Sometimes I wonder if they really care,
It's so depressing having nobody there.
It's like being born, yet rejected,
I'm not praised or respected.
I stand on my own when times are rough,
I believe in myself because nobody will
They leave me upset and catch their thrills.
They think I'm in control, because I pretend I'm fine
But the pain I bear will just blow your mind.
I hide the pain, and I hide it well
So little do you know, my life is a living hell
I look like I'm so happy but it's all an act
Oh I hate my life so much
And that's a fact.
   Natasha Canionero

Life

L -
Live for today, hope for tomorrow, plan for the future, be thankful
for the past.
Longevity is a desire for all.

I -
In the wake of the dawn, lift up thy hands in praise to the Lord for
all that he has done for mankind.
Spirituality brings forth peace. Internal peace brings forth joy.

F -
Forever is not promised, but we can all dream.
For those who dream envision a tomorrow.
Some will follow their dream, while others will lose their dream.
Both will have memories.
Fortitude and vision will influence what becomes of their dream.

E -
Every moment of life should be treasured.
We must attain fulfillment, peace and love.
Eternity is the life of our soul. God is the light of our life.
Mankind influences our life-style. Energy is a necessity of life.
God has provided us with energy through his spirit and love.

Longevity, Internal Peace, Fortitude and Energy are characteristics of life.
Life is a treasure. Life is a dream. Life is what you make it.
   Lorette F. Nixon

My Brother

My friend, my protector, my brother was he;
little lady, little sister, no one bothered me.
Following him around, being a tomboy too,
meant trying to follow everything he could do.
But he left for war, then college and more;
his stained glass windows became his main chore.
England called him to do "window of the crusades"
and so many other windows followed after this brigade.
A champion fencer and black belt holder was he,
singing with local bands just filled him with glee.
Teaching, dancing, training and even more;
on he went getting accolades galore.
Alas, on that sad and fateful August day
"goodbye everyone" was all that he could say.
My friend, my protector, my brother was gone,
leaving memories forever like a sad lonely song.
   Losita Stewart

The Process of Healing

The beat of the drum growing musical.
Listen to it; it's comfortable and silky soft.

The beautiful gleam of the stars.
People stare from the unroofed cars.
The flowing rapid river.
The air sends a comfortable quiver, releasing the pain and joy
To play with a simple toy.
The toy called painless joyless life.
Flying on a stringless kite with all of your inward spite.
My heart, what are you stealing?
Nothing of your peeling.
How come you have no feeling?
It's the process of healing.

The music renews your feelings of everything within the world.
So my world crumbles to an ash.
Sun shines deep and vividly bright.
The blindness of all painful joyful feelings is once again.
We've left to proceed the creed.
Melt the lava that eagerly burns your midnight away.
To harden the stoned cracked heads with the spreading fume of healing.
Lance Briley

The Happiness The Leaves Bring

The leaves were falling to the ground
like the rain.
A smiling little boy runs in the
leaves and kicks them up.
His smiling face shows how the
colorful and plentiful leaves
makes him happy.
He jumps and rolls around in them.
He runs and runs forever in the
leaves until the darkness come.
Even then his desire is to keep
running and listening to the crunching noise
as he runs over them. The leaves make a
blanket over the dead, brown grass.
The mother looks out the window at her
little boy and smiles with great awe
over the beauty of the blanket on the
ground and the trees that are still
full of God's great colorful leaves.
Kelly S. Smith

Just Open Your Eyes And See...

JUST OPEN YOUR EYES AND SEE the twinkling silver stars
like diamonds resting on an enormous, black velvet pillow.

JUST OPEN YOUR EYES AND SEE the vividly-colored rainbows
stretching across the sky as the raindrops fade away.

JUST OPEN YOUR EYES AND SEE the brilliant shades of jeweled
sunsets so blinding.

JUST OPEN YOUR EYES AND SEE the flowers
awakening, opening their bright petals towards the blazing sun,
their pungent fragrance like sweet perfume.

JUST OPEN YOUR EYES AND SEE the calm, sparkling lakes
flowing along.

JUST OPEN YOUR EYES AND SEE the long powerful fingers of
the ocean
crashing onto the shore, roaring like thunder.

JUST OPEN YOUR EYES AND SEE the majestic eagle
soaring above the white-blanketed mountain peaks.

JUST OPEN YOUR EYES AND SEE the joyful smiles of little children
scampering across the green silky grass of never-ending meadows.

JUST OPEN YOUR EYES AND SEE the power of love.
Megan Stokesberry

"The Manifestation"

Sculptures carved by life are standing tall
Like columns in front of the house
Towering over the entrance

Images of life whispering in the dusty air
A manifestation of a time lived long ago
The keeper of memories

The success is noted in the book of life
Judged by a scale of standard
Performance is honored with eternity

The music of NOW is filtered through the display
Tones of existence caressing the monuments
Smoothing away the edges to perfection

Our award will come
A pedestal for the future
The base for progress
Marianna Linder-Madsen

"My Mother"

The night emerges into a quick darkness.
Light is scarce in our vivid minds.
He sends a dim light of hope;
With a quick flash it is embraced by a cloud.
The thought of light enriched out minds.
The memories of her glow on,
Like moonlight on a winter night
His sight is forever captures in eternity,
Amidst the radiance of her smile,
Illuminating the loneliest moment.
    Shining through our souls we cope,
    Relying on dreams, relying on hope.
Michael P. Irwin

DNA - Learning The Code

Simply complex, organized chaos... a system where part is the whole.
Life energy surges taking direction from this implicate code
Self-similarity, from micro to marco... emerging covert to overt
    manifest form.
A spirit beyond time, or dimensional boundaries.
Symmetry, synergy... this newborn energy
Spirit wearing a face, not a mask
Eyes that tell, no deflection needed
Touching to know, not take
Sharing joy, knowledge, fulfilling needs... knowing pleasure, knowing
    itself.
Sensing self, sensing whole, sensing one
Spiritual truths still visible each day.
Lynne Riedy

A Day To Grow

Goodbye Dad, don't go away, I wasn't done with our lesson today.
Now who is there to hold my hand and tell me it's OK when times go bad?
I know my partner will always nurture when times are uncertain,
but it seemed a job that had to be certain,
and done by a man who carried me through my childhood,
Not judging my life and how I lived it but always looking on with
    loving wishes.
Today I grow up and give up some childhood dreams, but I know
    in my heart that Dad will still be with me.
In some spiritual way he has taught me his way, to guide me through
    the rest of my days.
Karla Simon

Happy Birthday America July 4, 1976

In this our "Bicentennial" year,
Let's all stand up, and proudly cheer.
As we are nearing the "Fourth of July,"
Raise your head, with a tear in your eye,
Proud as we watch our "Flag," in the breeze,
High above the towering trees,
Our lovely colors of "Red, White, and Blue,"
Will go on forever because of "You",
Happy Birthday, "America," this "76,"
We will defend you always there will be no tricks,
Our flag's stars will shine, bright and true,
For this "Country" we love, through and through,
Remember our "Men," who have given their lives,
Their "Loved One's" they left, "Mothers, children and Wives,"
God grant they did not die in vain,
We know they suffered, anguish and pain,
So to all our "Men" who are resting below,
If we keep on praying, I feel they will know
This great "Country" of ours, "Will Never Let Go."
Mary E. Schubert

Sobriety

As we achieve a day of sobriety
Let us remember a new life of variety.
Daily we lived by that old Serenity Prayer
So, take the wisdom or drink if we dare.
This is a challenge of our lives to be
We ourselves only hold the key.
Let's open the door and be on our way
A new beginning, a new meaning, not tomorrow but today.
Endeavor the twelve steps bit by bit
If it works don't fix it.
Staying sober means striving within, reaching out
Don't throw in the towel for you can win the bout.
There are groups of people out there who share
Attend a meeting and pull up a chair.
There's more to life than a bottle of booze
The decision is yours to live or to lose.
So if in doubt go pick up the phone
Give a friend a call you're not in this alone.
For if you slip there's no crime
Just remember 'ONE DAY AT A TIME!!'
Mark Dean

A Change Is Going To Come

Come my rebellious children of the world
Let us not seek a single love affair
We'll strive to a universal understanding
Spreading our newfound knowledge everywhere.

Our ideals, the dreams of men once reluctant to speak
Hear us now, for we are the vibrant new breed
We possess hearts bursting with sincerity
And that is why we are destined to succeed.

We are a generation full of love, laughter, and song
Loving, laughing, and singing each and everyday
It's a very passive way of life we live by choice
And our hope is to make it the overall accepted way.

Knowing that the old makes way for the new
We've a lifetime for obtaining those goals within our reach
We'll be the ones to practice the meaning of equal rights
Racial equality is only the beginning of what we'll preach.

Influencing everyone with our unwavering persistence
As we solve world hunger and strive for worldwide peace
We'll make legal revisions to maintain a modern justice
Making love for our fellow humans our ultimate masterpiece.
Len Johnson

Colors

As time goes on and changes us - as it often does,
Let me remember the dream the way it was.
To always put our best foot forward,
To keep in our hearts, the peace of the Lord;
To have the strength in our minds,
That someday our soul would find;
To see things not just as they are,
But, each as its own blinding star.
Though we go through time endlessly,
As people on a forgotten sea,
There is a dream that I foggily see,
But, also one in which I strongly believe:
To see the people of the world hand in hand,
To see them all-together stand,
A people of a thousand faces...
Of all colors; of all races.
This is the dream that fills my heart,
One in which the people of the world-play apart.
For together in life - we are but one,
But, separate and apart - we are, none.
Lori A. Zboran

"Did You Hear Me?"

Did you hear me? When I whispered your name
late last night — but you never came.

Did you feel me? As I moved from our bed to the window
and the warm wind that lit my heart all aglow...

Of thoughts of you and I in times gone past
and of days to come — can we make it last?

Did you smell my scent? As it drifted with the breeze
across the miles to the place that holds the keys...

Of the present and to the future
but only if we hold fast together can we be sure.

Did you see my face? In the light of the moon
hoping for the day that I'll see you soon.

Did you taste my lips? Touching yours so lightly,
my arms wanting to hold you so tightly...

But you're not here and so I must wait
for the day that will come when they unlock the gate...

And to your arms I will run and hold you so tightly, while I gently kiss your lips and breathe in your sweet scent that drifts with the breeze, as I behold your handsome face under the summer moon.

But for now I stand at the window each night
waiting for you to come and I whisper your name...Did you hear me?
Karen M. Toranzo

Oh Child, Oh Child

Oh Child, Oh Child where can thee be.
Oh Child, Oh Child come play with me.
I wish you would not hide from me,
For I would like to see who you might be.

Oh Child, Oh Child lets go to the park,
Oh Child, Oh Child not in the dark.
I cannot think where you are,
Let me guess if you are near or far.

Oh Child, Oh Child who can you be?
Oh Child, Oh Child please look at me!
I finally can see while your petting the cat,
That it was only a mirror that I was looking at.
Matt Cimino

Empty Boots

Once a member of this mighty band; Now he's left us in this foreign land.
A symbol of a fallen warrior - empty boots upon a stand;
Once filled with life so strong, now empty of it all.
They journeyed far to protect; yet now they only stand.

Boots that became a part of him, like boots of soldiers past,
Do not follow on with the soul, only stand as testament he was here.
Might think he deserves more - NO; simple - direct - blunt.
The symbol of a soldier's life, testimony to trials and faced.

Though the life is simple, survive; the man is complex.
Though the boots are basic, the meanings are multiple.
Reasons unknown to each other, each man here became a soldier.
Pride, patriotism, adventure, tradition, a job - whatever the cause.

The heat, the tears, the loneliness, the cold, the rain, the bullets,
the adrenaline — each man shares with the other.

And the boots march on in time, as a symbol to forever recall.
   Michael J. Francomb

Long Lost

Here I sit in the dark corner of my mind
   knowing that you will not return,
and when I ask myself how I feel
   I can only say to her...empty.
I understand now:
   you showed me what it was to be alive
      so you could leave me to die.
   Will it ever end?
I can feel my heart beating slowly now
   synchronized with the dripping dew of midnight.
      Such a soft blanket of dust.
Everything around me is aging before my eyes
   as I drift in and out of consciousness.
I am quite comfortable in this corner
   as if it were the one place in the world
      where I was meant to be.
I think I'll stay here a while
   for I have become exhausted through thought
      ...and I have time.
   Kwei-Yuen Chu

For My Sweetheart

Happy in a crowded room of strangers,
   Knowing that her smile breed smiles
      in those she touches with her eyes.
Touching me, I feel her eyes
Soft caresses from across the room.

Pulsing through her, energy untapped
   Accentuates the brightness of her smile
   Makes her stride not steps but happy hops.
Skipping into my life, I watch her come
Close, but not such that I cannot move.

Honest in her manner and her speech,
   Understanding the power and potential of truth
      to open wide the doors to trust and hope.
Talking to my heart, I hear her speak
Words assuring me of future love.

An accent to my life in countless ways,
   I feel that her strength has made me strong
      Or rather has accepted half the load.
Filling all my gaps, I am complete
Completely happy and completely in love.
   Ken Milano

Untitled

Though you may move to another place,
   know that your friendships cannot be erased.
One of Gods greatest gifts is a friend for all times.
One you can laugh with, share with, and cry.
So as you move on to that far away land,
   always know you have friends who will give you a hand.
Friends who will think of you often in thought,
   and those who will wish you were there, more often then not.
No matter how far the distance becomes,
   just pick up the phone and all will be well.
For your friends will be there to find out what's new,
   and you'll find they'll be time for a visit or two.
New friends you will find. It's just a matter of time,
   and friendships will finally bloom.
Just remember who made those friendships for you,
   and thank God, for he knew you were worthy of two.
Where ever you go you will touch people lives in one small way or another.
Fora person like you, will be looked up to, as one whom one can lean on.
That too is one of Gods special gifts, so take pride in who you've become.
And know that some day, up in heaven we'll pray, that we'll all be together again.
   Melissa Waddell

Angels Amidst

Such is the spirit of an Angel;

One that seems to lift us up so high that God
Kisses our foreheads ever so softly.

Such is the spirit of an Angel;

A whisper of comfort, a sudden breath of kindness,
A tearful wish from an unexpected friend.

Such is the spirit of an Angel;

The silence that brings peace to our souls, the joy
That breeds inside our hearts, forcing us to smile.

Such is the spirit of an Angel;

That which makes us fall on our backsides in the snow,
Stretch out our arms and legs,
Vigorously waving away our cares.
   Mary Ellen Wellbaum

L.A. Mode

My L.A. Mode; no more eastern dress code.
Keep your starched white shirts and airs of authority.
Rigid rules and phoney ways, of ridicule.
I need not adhere to your politics; no more ground rules.
I'll play in the sand; run in the surf build
castles, and lie in the sun - adrift in
thought - careless and free living a fantasy
fulfilled by a child's dream, of endless skies
Salt - filled waves pounding out the pain of
yesterday's unrelenting refrain.
Crashing waves over falsehoods; illusions
blanketed by the mist...Coolness; clean and
Fresh waiting to begin anew.
Come, take my hand. Teach me to
trust, to hope, and dream. Bring me
into your world of reality. Truth.
   Katherine R. Perna

Death Of A Tear

slipping down the glass
joining the others below
tired little raindrops
on a car window

creeping for a second
existing for a breath
then the wipers destroy them
a droplet's insignificant death

those same, short-lived raindrops
are tears from a pessimistic sky
crying for a misplaced world
for what; we are all going to die

they are also tiny prisms
reflecting colors that are so beautifully real
colors that run so bright and alive
changing the world into what we feel

to change this world seems imaginatively transcendent
but constant change never changed a thing
through happiness, sadness, anger, and madness
all these tears still sting

Miranda Hawkins

Do You Know Jesus?

In a far off land across the sea
Jesus was born, lived and died for me
Angels heralded His lowly birth
With songs I cannot sing on earth;
But because God sent His only Son
To earth as a sacrifice for everyone,
When I have accepted the truths in His word
In the hereafter those songs will be heard.
I thank God for Jesus every day
That I have been able to find His way
I would that everyone else could know
This Jesus who suffered here below;
To hear Him, believe Him, confess Him as Christ.
To obey Him through baptism, then live a life
Of obedience and love, teaching each other
And striving to live like Jesus, our brother.
So though He was born in a far away land
Because He's my Saviour He'll hold my hand.
From His birth 'til His death we know the story.
Let's sing hallelujah and give Him the glory.

Margaret Good

Love Will Prevail

Take courage now, there's much power in prayer!
  Jesus is very near to help in all our despair,
Joy and comfort will be if we trust in Him!
  Then all our fears, will grow strangely dim.

We all grow weak time and time again,
  Thanks be to God, we're in Jesus' hands!
He's just as near as we want Him to be,
  So let us take care, His blessings to see!

Look beyond others faults, and see their needs.
  We as Christians, need to plant the seeds!
Help uphold our faith in all we do!
  To find the Glory of Jesus come shining through!

Mary Frances Hamlin

"Star-Gazer"

All my life I've longed to find, that special man with whom to bind.
I've looked real high and searched so low,
  men would come and men would go.
Staring outside at the stars so bright,
  I'd wish for you on shooting light.
Until alas you came along, I've never felt a love so strong.
You make me feel so scared inside, but I'll face my fear,
  not run and hide.
Although at times we disagree through each other's eyes we fail to see.
We have to enhance our listening skills,
  and follow through with what we will.
To not only hear what's said but what we mean to say,
  worlds can't always express our feelings the right way.
I love you so, how can I say, daily it grows in every way.
The love and kindness you give out, is what my love is all about.
To hold you close and feel your chest,
  to hear your breath sets me at rest.
I've looked so deep into your eyes, with no words I see no lies.
I want to spent my whole life through, with no one else but only you.
My one-in-a-million, just perfect for me,
  the best thing in life we've got for free.
I've won your heart and you've won mine, together we sit,
  high on cloud nine.
A dream come true is what you are, I have caught my shooting star!

Mandy Ellis

Maria Scuderi

Here I am, just like a little toy, perched high up on the shelf.
It's time to play, so here you are, you take me down and wind me up.
I smile then laugh, talk and sing, dance and run, embrace and love,
sigh and cry.
I'm off the shelf for quite a while, sometimes an hour sometimes a night.
It's time for you to leave, so back I go
Days have passed and here you are, once again you wind me up,
this time I'm wound a bit too hard, I'm crying more than laughing,
loving a little less.
Please don't put me back high up on the shelf, you don't listen so
up I go, you don't like the tears so we don't play.
Finally you come again, oops this time you drop me, I fall too hard,
a tiny piece is missing, looks like a tiny heart,
now you can no longer fix me,
you no longer even try
and now your little toy is broken
But you're happy because now you're free
You leave behind this little toy, a toy who once was me...

Maria Scuderi

The Coldest Of Lovers

There is nothing warm or hot about our love
It's one of a kind sent from heaven above
The year doesn't care about our 3 months with each other
It was especially designed from the nature of our mother
Sowing seeds could remind us how our love could grow
But the temperature forbids and freezes it with snow.
If only we had heat to warm our icy relationship
I couldn't get one kiss due to the frost bite on the lip
There must be something we can do as I said to Mr. Frost
Let's have a party, invite spring and summer, no matter the cost
Christmas brought her lights and decorated a tree
All the presents gave us a blissful smile that the world could see
We love spending all our time under the warm covers
The coats, hats and gloves all prove that we are the coldest of lovers.

Marie A. Erby

The Way - A Magazine Of Energy

A group of chelas all lending a hand
It's like a garden of many flowers
But each has a name, as Roses, Violets, etc.
So in this garden of names
Each is offering a piece of his own thoughts
Adding their names, filling a page
The more names, like a garden, it grows
All of life has a name.

And each one wants to sow his seed
A group of hearts beating as one
Can you feel the beat, beat?
More energy, more energy, until it is love
And anther name for love is caring, caring,
The way to go, ever upward
Chelas, God's Garden of Names.

Lynne Albert

Betrayed Angel

Saying one thing and doing another,
It's just not right, why is it always a fight?
When will we learn to just take flight?
Spread your wings and learn to sing.
Betrayed angel, I feel betrayed.
Promises broken, lies spoken, they leave me so open.
Dream with me and you will see, what's meant to be!
Give your best, take time to rest.
Show me your soul and please let go!
Betrayed angel, I feel betrayed.
The winds of change are blowing, so let's start
showing and keep love growing.
Create no hate, don't deviate and always communicate.
Look inside, for we must avoid this genocide!
Betrayed angel, I feel betrayed.

Michael Hall

Beautiful Hawaii

Oh, how I loved beautiful Hawaii
its friendly and easy going people.
The many islands and sandy beaches,
soft music and happy songs and dances.

When young people welcome you as a guest
and just flower lie around your neck;
it gives you a feeling of peace and happiness
when your vacation starts with friendliness.

Interesting are the big palm trees
with coconuts, figs and bananas.
Pineapple and sugar grows in the fields;
Macadamia nuts and coffee beans in the hills.

Unforgettable was the big "Hawaiian fest"
at the new "King Kahamaha" beach Hotel,
where Hawaii's history was told in songs,
when we enjoyed delicious food and wines.

When the sun goes down in the blue sea,
and the velvet black darkness then comes;
peacefulness falls over beaches and homes,
a soft brisk rattle the leaves on the palm trees.

Karen Marie Fjelle

Reflections

"I sit in contemplation, reflecting on the past.
It's experiences, once future thoughts now shape eternity.
"Decisions made and carried out, influence now, my life throughout.
How will I license them... their effect on me?
"I have a choice, of this I'm sure. Will I dwell on past mistakes,
decisions errant, only to face a dismal and defeated end?
Or, shall I learn my lessons well, be accountable:
accept responsibility?
"Questions upon questions run amuck in mind; 'Will I have to answer?
Will of ought I be ashamed?'"
"These and many questions same will yes the answer be?
Yea, afraid to say, will the answer be!
"What's done is past and only lasts in thought or word, or deed.
My choice decides posterity.
"What matters most is not what's been but, what will be."
"When things seem hopeless, without cause;
draw strength from where you've been."
"Then as said by someone past, 'Rest if you must, but please,
don't quit.'"

Kevin Spargur

The River

The river runs wild, as does my soul
It's always crossing vendors but doesn't pay a toll
It's always looking for trouble and trying to get free
Nobody seems to understand, that river is me

It's the heart of a woman and the strength of a man
It's a child's glory when he finally learns how to stand
It's the truth of a good man and the lies of a thief
Nobody understands, that river is me

The river will flow, 'till it runs dry
It'll just stop meeting the ocean but nobody will ask why
Everyone will know, it's something you cannot mend
Everyone know I have reached my end

Lisa Cash

Loving You

Hurry, hurry, wait, stand in line
It won't wait, it can't wait, there's really no time
It won't last forever as songs say it might
For always and forever, I'm under your light.

It's giving and taking, a smile and a grin
Like saltwater taffy, it tastes good, like a sin
It's there from the start and it grows so very tall
Like being next to a tree, it's big and you're small.

It's not what you have and it's not what you get
It's that feeling I felt when you and I met
Like chocolate in cookies, like ice cream and cake
It's a feeling of forever, like no other can make.

It's security and compassion and sharing that lasts
It's not where you go, it's not in the past
Like a flower in spring, each day a new bloom
It's as long as the distance from here to the moon.

It's the way I feel when you whisper in my ear
Or the sound of your voice, whether it's far or so near
It's knowing the peace that I feel in my heart
Like the romance and the loving there's been since the start.

Michael Lipe II

In Loving Memory

You were taken from me when I was very young,
It wasn't time, there were still things to be done.
It was so simple, so easy to see,
We made quite the team just you and me.
The day you left me a part of me died,
All that I felt was anger towards God when I cried.
I wrote this for you to let you know I'll never forgot,
The things you said, the lessons you taught.
People keep telling me you are in a much better place,
But sometimes I just want to be with you and see your face.
I want you to know just how much I love you,
And someday I'll be with you again I know it's true.
But until that day I will remember you in my heart,
That way I know we never have to part.

Lorraine Crumbliss

The Emerald Sea

I remember my first garden
It was parsley and I was only three
And it was way higher than my knee
And as green an emerald as you ever did see

It was my first glory, it was first joy
It would have been nice to have know you then
To see what grew in your garden
When you were only three

I can tell from the way you look at me now
Love was the only thing it could be
Now we're both way past thirty-three
And each year it still amazes me

To see the love in your eyes
As once again we plant parsley
And wait to look at each other
Across that tall emerald sea.

Myria Newman

Fire

There lie in the woods, a little house burned in the cold fire.
It was once a house full of laughter and gayness.
But now it stands alone.
What once was such a place full of memories, is now gray and sad.
How could this be, you say? It is easily done, for the things that built the memories have grown up and forgotten the place of their childhood.
But the memories live on in the house burned in the bold fire in hopes that one day the memory makers will return.
So until then the house burned in the cold fire stands alone in the woods with the beloved memories of laughter and gayness, just waiting.

Kathleen McCullough

The Garden

Long, long ago a garden was made,
It was filled with a single flower that was only one shade.
Gradually different flowers came there to bloom,
At first this was okay but then it brought a lot of gloom.
The flowers came from many different seeds,
This caused them to have a lot of different needs.
Some bad weeds came into sight,
This brought confusion and very little light.
Many of the flowers tried to bloom with perfection,
By hurting all the others that suffered with rejection.
The flowers' conflicts soon showed up.
This caused many of the flowers to give up.
No one can understand why they just can't get along,
Because long, long ago one flower stood so strong.
The flowers in the garden will always be there,
As long as we take the time out to care.

Nicole Garda

The Big Old Tree

Across the street stands a grand old tree.
It stands like a monument for all to see.
It doesn't fear the wind and the rain.
You would never know if it feels pain.
Some limbs are gone, and its trunk is scared.
Yet its proud I know to grace the yard.
It shades the house from the summer heat.
The birds nest there and sing so sweet.
I sit by my window and look each day.
At the big old tree across the way.
For he's waiting like me for time to come.
When our purpose on earth will all be done.

Mabel Jean McCuan

Russell's Sunflower

I noticed it yesterday while mowing the lawn
it shouldn't even be blooming
    this late in the fall

but there is was
audaciously lifting its golden summer glory to face a wan and chilly autumn sun,
oblivious of its own impending demise
    radiantly saffron
        brazenly saucy
            wantonly cheerful

what a joy to see it there
    nestled
        next to the house
    sheltered
        from the turmoil of the season and the tempest of the winds

shining out into the chill grey clouds
lighting up its corner of the yard
beaming with lustrous gold

mocking the approach of
    winter

Lydia H. Wirkus

Untitled

My life is out of order. Everything is falling in around me.
It seems to go faster and faster. I'm loosing ground.
Falling behind, running out of steam. I need time to recuperate.
Time to focus. Time, time, time. To find my way. A new way.
The old has been lost, destroyed.
I need to find the new me. The me that must go on.
The me that must go on even though he doesn't want to.
The me I must find. Find to go on.
Go on without looking back.
Leaving old baggage behind. Looking for new, new, new baggage.
Baggage to make me happy.
To keep me happy.
That is what I need.
I need help.
I need friends, good friends,
Friends to help.

Matthew Troso

Demons Knocking

Demons knocking at my door, should I let them in like I've done before?
Demons knocking at my door; leave me alone I'll tell them once more.
Demons knocking at my door; Come in! Come in!
I let them engulf me as I lie upon the floor.

Lucionna D. Mellow

Untitled

Life is so full of beauty.
It seems so synchronized and yet so complex.
Every day the sun will rise and will set again.
The summers are warm and the winters are cold.
Our body works in harmony taking on the challenges
of whatever confronts us each day, until one day,
for some unknown reason our spirit will flee.
Like a bird leaving its nest in the cool autumn
months to find a place of warmth and comfort.
Setting out on a journey to where no one knows.
It's scary, and yet reassuring to think that
someday, somewhere we will meet our creator
and shall understand this life we have lived.

Mary Ann Estep

Love

Love is a feeling that two people share.
It is something you express to show you care.
If you give someone love it should be from the heart.
Once you fall in it you can't stay apart.

Love is something that is hard to find.
It should be gentle, precious and kind.
Love is priceless, it has not cost.
Without my one love my world would be lost.

I love to share all my happiness with you.
There is nothing in the world I'd rather do.
Your smile is what I look forward to everyday.
You are the perfect one in every way.

Your gentle kiss that warms my cheek.
The touch of your hand makes me weak.
The sound of your voice is music to my ears.
You make me feel safe and take away my fears.

When I look in your eyes my heart skips a beat.
I think to myself this love is pretty neat.
I remember and cherish every little thing you do.
What else can I say except that I love you.

Larae Tuller

The Loneliness Of The Abused

There is a pain that cuts to the depths of my soul
it is a pain in which others can not see.
There is a child within me that is hurting;
that has experienced such pains beyond herself.
No one to hold me, no one to hug me,
No one to love me not even myself.
Afraid of the shadows and no one to hear my cries.
Too afraid to cry aloud - I keep it within and
bury the pain in the depths of my soul.
Now as time passes by this pain eats away at my soul.
I become a lost child, visions of life disappear,
fading in the incense of drugs and alcohol.
A child young and innocent was destroyed by
those who said they loved her.
Who now can I trust, who will I turn too?
Isolation and depression become my companions now.
The loneliness of the abuse, no one cares, no one knows.
I carry this pain alone, never trusting yet,
yearning to share it - to be rid of these flashbacks.
I cry silently, alone in the dark where it all began.

Maryann Ramshaw

Cloud Watching

Did you ever make shapes out of clouds in the sky?
It is a game mother taught me to make time fly.
A better game that counting cars while on a car ride.
Look up at the clouds the next time you go outside.

Pretend you can float on a cloud like a magic carpet ride.
Let your mind wander to a far away place;
You can be a rocket floating in space.
See a cloud that resembles the human face.

A cloud can be anything you want it to be,
Image depends on what you see.
If you are bored on a nice day make shapes out of clouds, and
boredom will go away.

Used imagination when watching clouds in the sky.
Watch the clouds...
You can see wonders with the human eye.

Mary Lou Adams

It Is...

It has pierced my heart, yet I do not bleed.
It has taken control of my mind, yet I am sane.
It is a dream I had longed for, for many years.
One, I never expected to come - but it is here.
I lie awake, alone - yet I am not.
As it lingers in my blood, my veins,
Filling my entire body with its presence.
In my dreams I see it.
In my thoughts it is always there.
I can smell it, when I smell a rose.
I can hear it, when a bird sings or a child laughs.
It has the purity of snow,
And the strength of a storm.
It brings me peace and warmth.
I will cherish it forever.
It is - your love.

Maura L. Hechim

Getting Ready To Go Home

I went down the other day to see Mom and Dad,
It has been with them the very best of times I've had.

They have had a long and wonderful life,
Dad would never have wanted a better wife.

Dad's doing great but he will soon be eighty-three,
They wanted to have a long talk with me.

They began to talk about things I just didn't want to hear,
Things that to them were precious and dear.

For over fifty years from state to state Dad has gone,
Preaching and teaching of what some have only heard in song.

Many lives through his work have been reached,
His life has been an example of what he preached.

His whole life has been at peace because he knows,
Of a place and time where there won't be any woes.

And there Heaven awaits to swing open its door,
Others will be there too who have gone before.

And there, I'm very sure one day, at Heaven's pearly gates,
Will be my Father's open arms as for my arrival He also waits.

Life can be both happy and sad during our roam,
For you see, Mom and Dad were getting ready, getting ready to go home.

Olin Fulmer Hutchinson Jr.

THE INEVITABLE EVIL

It begins innocently - a trivial thing in an indifferent world.
It grows, as does a seed, sprouting in soil filled tissue
    amongst the rocks bordering a road.
    First the roots stream forth   small
    creeping   entangling   sapping all
nourishment from this substance which unknowingly
    blindly nurses it through infancy;
    and it grows steadily as time is created.
A stalk   twisted   covered with food-seeking talons
    as it crawls toward the sky
Clinging to this terrible mutation is a bloom   a bloom
  of such hideous appearance and horrid stench that none
  except the ignorant and willfully innocent
could pass without tearing it from the ground and dashing it
  to pieces for fear of its spreading.
    People come.
    People go.
  Time removes the plant   untouched by man
    A seed remains.

Michael Krizak

Ancestral Impact

Ancestral Love is with me everyday
It gives me strength to make it along the way
Prayers for protection, wisdom, salvation and guidance
Were consistently rendered before the masters throne
Our ancestors knew, without them we would never see our
heavenly home
I feel my ancestors presence
I think their thoughts
Yes, my ancestors are in every move I make
Certainly, in every step I take
Early morning and late night wailing at the saviour's feet
Impact generations upon generations
As I cry out to my heavenly father for direction, wisdom and
salvation
For my life, my children, their children and all in my loins
I realize ancestral love and care transcends space and time
I cry and thank God for ancestors who were so wise.

Lore A. Boyd-Williams

The Past

The past is lost in someone's pocket then found again,
It flows out their mouth and into the ears of listeners like a
  waterfall falling into a river,
The past is Christopher Columbus, Martin Luther King Jr. and
  George Bush,
The past is having more time to do the things you can't do now,
The past is good times and bad,
The past is lost high in a tree out of everyone's reach,
The past is gone, lost in the future.

Michael Scott

The Power Of Feelings In The Heart

The power of feelings within the heart
It can take you to places you've never been
It posses the warmth, tenderness and love one holds
It also posses the hurt, pain and struggle to survive
Each person posses these powers
You must choose which way to use it
Only you can determine which way to use it
Only you can determine the outcome
Reach out
Touch someone
It is well worth it

Laurie L. Smith

Night Walks

I love to walk at night;
it calms me, and gives me serenity.
It is a quiet time to pray, meditate and dream.
The night wraps around me like a comfortable old blanket...
familiar, like a loved and cherished friend.
Sounds carry for miles at night.
As I walk, I am surrounded by an orchestra...
crickets, passing cars, katydids, rustling leaves...
I am lulled by the rhythmic click, click of a passing train.
The moon seems to seek my soul;
the stars hang brightly suspended in time.
The houses are bathed in the soft romantic glow of porch lights.
Every time I walk, I am renewed and revived spiritually.
When I walk I am myself...
not a mother, not a friend, not a co-worker or a care giver.
Just myself.
Walking lets me look inside and touch my own reality.
I love to walk at night.

Lisa Marie Stoers

The Labyrinth

Entering once again the sanctuary of the mind, I was
interrupted by a thundering splash
Confusion resting its timely feet gave rise to an unforeseen lash

Realizing that there was no time for fortification, I headed for asylum
Disillusion formed its familiar wall while entwining and
twisting my body numb

Casting his erroneous notions like shadows, he enforced the
waves to break against the splintering night
Illusion smashing, bashing the lingering thought that he
might stumble while diving and not perceive the light

Swimming among those other carnivorous creatures the ripples
began to unfold
Solution, poised like a mannered man, bowed its head for the
ruthless bold

Sinking was never anticipated nor could it be swallowed like this
Intrusion was not a slight offense and nor was the obvious
encroaching hiss

Drowning though unforeseen blossomed like a fruitless tree
Confusion brought with it death but was it me or was it he?

Karen Terese Young

The President Of The Philippines

Freedom fighter for democracy, world-renowned political figure
Intellectual person, a vigorous leader, first Filipino Protestant,
  elected President, inspiration of the younger generations
Devoted man to your family and country
Energetic President, Commander-in-Chief Armed Forces of the
  Philippines, Westpointer, former Secretary of National Defense,
  Chief of Staff AFP, Vice Chief of Staff and Chief Philippine
  Constabulary
Leadership and outstanding achievement is the key to your success
  and your children's success in life
Vietnam, Korean and World War II veteran
Religious, warm hearted, soft spoken, a very supportive human being
  with a Christian heart
A man of integrity and courage, leader of the famous EDSA 1986
  revolution
Man of the masses, pride of the Filipino people
O fall the good things you have done for the nation, you'll always
  be remembered
Son of former Secretary of Foreign Affairs, Narciso Ramos, noble
  professional family and very humble person.

Leonides S. Sales

Like A Sparrow

Through hot summer days, and long winter nights, I searched,
   Indeed, I searched for one good friend, companion or mate,
   Who would, indeed, make life's burden a little lighter-this
    my fate
But, to no avail, I found not one that "always" by my side would be,
   Who'd bring humor to the plot, or some stability to my lot.
Learn had I, through much turmoil, and strife,
   That none can give what they do not contain!

Then, one day, a sparrow in my garden came to stay,
   So patiently, and without a care, for food he looked, here and
    there, and everywhere!
In that brief moment, I saw "The Light" as the sparrow flew away.
"Seek not perfection in man's love, I heard a voice say,
   But, as the sparrow, place your faith and trust in the "One Above!"

What peace since then, I've found that like the sparrow, I, too-
   Look not to man, kin or kind, but, to "Our Heavenly Father"
   Who knows my every care, pain and need.
So, to Him, each day I go, for "He," alone-
   Hears my every call, prayer, and plea!

Now, to "Him" each day I talk,
   Now, with "Him" each day I walk,
   And, in "Him," each day I rest!

Marguerite Rocco Orsomarso

"Listen To The Children's Cry"

Listen to the children's cry everywhere,
In their hearts they want to share.
Their love with us near and far,
It doesn't matter who they are.

Listen to the children's cry in their life,
They may have a lot of struggle and strife.
They are beautiful children wherever they may be,
The children should be loved and be free.

Listen to the children's cry when they meet,
Drug dealers walking on the street.
Trying to give children drugs of all kinds,
Anything that will affect their minds.

Listen to the children's cry when they turn to go,
We don't accept drugs, we just say no.
No matter if the children are young or older,
They need someone to lean on their shoulder.

Listen to the children's cry, dear Jesus from above,
Take their hands and show them love.
From your heart to all of theirs,
Each night please keep them in your prayers.

Margaret L. Rodkey

Silence

Silence,
in the darkness of the night
creeping in, enveloping, overwhelming

Silence,
the closing of a door
imprisoning the mind

Silence,
locking the voice into a cell of muteness and isolation
time goes by, life goes by
you, in silence, go by
never expressing a thought, never expressing a word
passing by as a wraith, a specter
haunted and terrorized, possessed by some crazed demon

Your spirit has taken cover
buried deep in the silence of a grave

Nataly A. Bortolutti

Where Do I See God?

In the laugh of a baby, full of glee
In the care that He's taking of you and me
In the beautiful sunshine, the rippling brook
In the words that are written in His precious book
In the face of a friend, in the birds that fly
In the beautiful moon way up in the sky
In the flowers that bloom, and the stars so high
In the bees that are buzzing, and the butterfly
In the rocks and the rivers and mountains, too
He's given so much to me and to you
But most of all, the love of His Son,
Who died on the cross for every one.

Nell Watkins

Magic Scent Colors, God Sent

Fresh is the fragrance sent
in the aromatic air of pine lumber smoke
or the eucalyptus and the earth's dirt,
Where tulips, daffodils, lilacs and roses
are sewn and how the cedar chests,
shampoos, soaps, baby powders, leather
jackets new cars and new crayons have magic
scent in reality of colors, God sent!
in the aromatic air of pine lumber smoke
or eucalyptus and the earth's dirt, where
tulips, daffodils, lilacs and roses are sewn
and how the cedar chests, shampoo, soaps, baby
powders, leather jackets, new cars and new
crayons have magic scent, in reality of
colors, God sent!

Lonita Mullins Krantz

To An Airplane Pilot

To you who ride the skies in sun and rain
In stalwart flight and then come back again,
Who play with clouds, outrace the birds in flight,
Whose wings gleam silver in the moonlit night,
To you - who are so high above us all
Stay close enough to always heed our call
Lest, when you look upon us from afar
You'll sense how infinitesimal we are
And pledge your whole allegiance to a star.

Mildred M. Carlson

Oklahoma Children's Story - The Tragedy

As we lay beneath these concrete beds
In GOD'S hands, we lay our heads.

We did not know of your ghastly intent
Or give a prayer, before we went.

Mom, Dad, please don't cry
We think of you, of where we lie.

Our bodies are cold, but not our souls
Our spirits are there to console.

We see you from our heavenly nest
We've gone there to get our rest.

For to those that made us part
We still love Mom, Dad - with all our hearts.

From this heavenly place, in which we dwell
We'll seek out the ones, and your secret, we'll tell.

Mom, Dad - dry your eyes, but later meet us there
We'll be waiting - just beyond the stairs.

Louis F. Green

Eternal Moon

I have seen your eyes gleaming blue
   in a pale light under the moon.
Reflecting signs of love to be
   reflecting future love for you and me.

I have tried to love once and have failed
   searching for a love I have ailed.
If you should go; what would I do,
   I have never met any one like you.

I know this feeling inside is right
   so therefore I am praying for an endless night.
Look into my eyes and see that I am sincere
   hear my heart beating and pull me near.

Our love together is so strong,
   if we listen to each other we cannot go wrong.
Your skin so soft, oh so very soft to feel
   this feeling is true and this love is real.

I cannot hide it anymore
   you are the only one that I adore.
So forget me not, I am so true
   just remember that I will always love you.

    Michelle Baxter

Pathways Of Life That Enrich Or Ruin

Education's Pathway opens careers for each and all,
Importuning parents and schools to help every child learn.
An invitation to do something special, great, worthwhile,
While others seek lawlessness, a pursuit for which they yearn.

Family's Pathway provides responsibility, deep love,
Requiring more achievement the world truly endorses.
Abortion, AIDS imperil the fragile family make-up,
While destruction boasts an ascendant tide of divorces.

Money's Pathway is strewn with amenities, benefits,
With chance to show that a caring charity is not rare.
Charlatanic wizardry brings loss to the unwary,
While ill-gotten fortunes crumble in desolate despair.

Forest's Pathway provides satisfying pristine beauty.
Waterfall watches as wind and flower dance with finesse.
Robin's early morning greeting echoes in dewy pines,
While sun chases ghostly phantoms into waning darkness.

Spirit's Pathway has a profound well of eternal life.
Its pure, "life-giving" water, quenches thirst forever more.
Unbelievers lose Christ's grace, God's love, spirit's fellowship,
While holiness, made in God's image, enters heaven's door.

    Max Culbertson Bee

My Soul's Asylum

Ignorance is my soul's asylum,
I'm unknowing of the worldly pain.
I don't care who's near or right behind me,
Not knowing or needing has made me insane.

A mere victim of this world's hateful desire,
I sit alone and lonely in this dreadful room.
Wondering what happened and where you've gone.
I know I'll die here in solitude in this dark black tomb.

I stare at you in the mirror on my wall and
I gulp another of the doctor's healing pills.
I stare at my icy, shaking hands
Wondering how I'll make my next kill.

    Michelle A. Womble

Let Go Let God

Get out of my way, I'm busy
   I'm important, I'm going places.
Can't you see me?
Look at me.
   Wait, look and really listen
Who do you see. Nothing??
   Let go, Let God.
Now the peace comes
Now love is here
   Seeping through my body like a melting snow
     when the sun rises.
   Don't leave me -wrap your love around and
     around so I'll never figure a way out
I need to go nowhere but here.
And now your love is my love.
And my love slowly transcends me
Until my love is your love
And we all connect..
   But first let go, let God.

    Marsha Marie Barnes

I'm Free

Don't grieve me now, for now I am free.
I'm following the path that was laid down for me.
I could not stay another day, to laugh,
To love,
To work,
Or to play.
I found that place at the close of the day.
If my parting has left a void,
Then fill it with memorable joys.
A friendship shared, a laugh, a kiss,
Oh yes, these things I too will miss.
Don't be burdened with sorrow,
I wish you the best for tomorrow.
My life's been full, maybe a little too much.
Good times, good friends,
To have your touch.
Perhaps my time a little too brief.
Lift up your heart and share with me,
God wanted me now,
So He set me free.

    Kim Morales

To My Wife On Valentine's Day 1994

Sweetheart I love you and
I'll be home before you know it.
This separation has brought out the poet.

Waiting and dreaming 'bout our nights together,
Picnics on the beach, like birds of a feather.
Spending two weeks making love every night,
Lounging on the weekends without any fights.

So many times I've missed your smiling face,
Lost in thoughts while looking out in space.
Together again is where we'll be,
In love's sweet embrace for all to see.

I miss you more each passing day,
True to your love in every way.
This trip has been special, there's no doubt,
But my place is with you, in our own little house.

On March 10th, you'll be by my side,
Safe, together, my heart filled with pride.
So while we're apart, be careful, be smart,
For it's your love that's sustained me and
Been my guiding light in the dark.

    Michael Lee Cowart Sr

A Mother's Prayer

If ever you need me and I'm not there just bow your head and pray
I'll always hear you no matter what and help you through your day
If not in sight or touch or voice, I'll always hear your prayer
'Cause I'm your Mother, dear heart of mine, and forever I'll be there

Sweet baby girl, your name reflects a child as good as gold
I'm here for you sweet baby girl although you see me old
Don't shut me out sweet child of mine please keep me in your heart
For we together, sweet baby girl, will never be apart!

Your heart, your soul, your mind and self can only cause you joy
So remember Kandi all the time that life is not a toy
Sometimes it seems that life's not fair and so sometimes its not
But always follow in your heart the goodness that you've got

Its up to you and only you to make your dreams come true
So just go forward, catch all you want and get your dreams for you
Its not your family, friends or foes that you will do this for
Its all for you and only you to open up this door

Karen Laumann

The Midnight Sky

Have you ever took time to look up at the midnight sky,
if you have I know you've said those simple words "Oh my".

The stars in all their splendor are there so shiny and bright,
the moon in all its glory makes the most beautiful light.

So, you don't know the constellations and you think "Oh who cares,"
just take time to do it, you will find something to share.

It's up there, so let's enjoy it, let's take the time to sit,
look up, stop and listen, like me you will be bit.

The night and all it's glory is a wonderfully grand sight,
how can you help but feel it, doesn't it bring you some delight.

So take time to do it, grab your coffee and your chair,
go outside and sit there, look up, and just stare.

Linda Jean Bowman

Curiosity

It's interesting that some always want and need to know why
If one learns what they wanted to know they sometimes may cry

If people were not so distant we would not have to yearn
Our hearts and souls could avoid things that hurt or burn

Why is it there are some who play those silly games in life
As if anybody truly needs any additional and added strife

While there are so many complexities that make up our being
Our eyes may occasionally play tricks and alter our seeing

There is so much involved to make us who we finally become
As we grow we need to remember where we have come from

We must not ever forget to look forward to the future
Permitting ourselves ample time to absorb and nurture

Is there really more to someone than meets the naked eye
I believe so but once again I want and need to know why

Margaret E. Male

Terror In The Heartland (The Oklahoma City Tragedy)

When men make themselves sovereign,
   in attempt to dethrone God,
Making their reasoning a standard,
   absolute of right and wrong.
Then children in their innocence
   are broken, lifeless, still.
And terror hits the heartland,
   leaving a void which can't be filled.

Marla Sue Cross

If I Was A Bill

If I was a bill would you spend me now?
If I was your friend I would wonder, "How?"

Although similar there are differences.
Both are earned but one is kept forever.
One is green but two will be together.

Two friends will then depart on their own ways.
Each searching for the money they will spend,
Forgetting what is important in the end.

Remember to think, remember to save.
Remember the joy the other one gave.

Take time, you can never be too careful.
Watch out, before you know, it is gone.
A friend is forever, but now too late
You are in pain, you feel the hate.

Now you know what ought to be known,
If I was a bill would you spend me now?

Michael V. Nguyen

With Our Hearts

If not for the love of you
I would have no other reason to stay.
My greatest desire is to always be close to you,
Loving you, day after day after day.
When I looked into your eyes the first time
I knew you were the one for me.
And the way you smiled and touched my hand,
There were tingles, that still tingle me.
Time brought us so much closer to each other.
We learned to give and share without hesitation.
We learned to take each moment
With great anticipation.
You were the only love I had
And your love was the healing power.
So when the ups became the downs
We were able to stand for each other.
I celebrate this love with you tonight.
Destined to be here from the start.
Some may say it's just simply black and white.
We never loved with our skin, only our hearts.

Neil Ray

Scared And Alone

I am scared and alone.
I wonder why the darkness only covers my heart.
I hear voices from my past, coming back to haunt me.
I see faces of the ones I loved, but when I reach out, they are gone.
I want my life to be complete again.
I am scared and alone.

I pretend that I never hurt the people who cared for me.
I feel a sharp knife cutting my heart into pieces.
I touch the face of the man I once loved.
I worry that he will never forgive me.
I cry when I see the sadness hidden deep in his eyes.
I am scared and alone.

I understand that my horrid past cannot be changed.
I say that it wouldn't have mattered anyway.
I dream about being free again - in mind, body, and soul.
I try to forgive myself for the secrets I keep, but I cannot.
I hope my mind will be put to rest soon, for I am slowly dying inside.
I am scared and alone.

Katherine Slick

LIFE

Wandering thoughts, I sit and stare
I wonder if, why, where
where do they travel to, do they get there
or drift on into eternity

A pensive mind and a puzzled frown
where do I go from here
all my sorrows I could drown
and wash away my fear

Agitation, botheration, the mind races on
leaving no time to sit and think and realize life's a con
for if you sit and think too hard about where life is at
there is only one way for you to go, and there is no coming back

So free your mind and think anew
and bless every day that comes to you
for life is short, so live and gain
and reap the benefits, not the pain.
   Maureen S. Abney

"I Am"

I am a lively girl who loves the earth.
I wonder if they will ever stop cutting down the trees.
I hear the people crying for help in small countries.
I see the tragedy going on in Oklahoma.
I want there to be peace in the world.
I am a lively girl who loves the earth.

I pretend to be a magic genie.
I feel sad when someone dies.
I touch the gold at the end of a rainbow.
I worry about the earth blowing up.
I cry when innocent little children die.
I am a lively girl who loves the earth.

I understand that I can't live forever.
I say don't pretend to be someone else, just be yourself.
I dream of travelling all around the world.
I try to always find the good in people.
I hope that I will be a teacher when I grow up.
I am a lively girl who loves the earth.
   Kara Eaton

I Am

I am compassionate and an individual
I wonder about future technology
I hear the wind though the trees
I want to clean up our world
I am compassionate and an individual

I pretend I am much older than I am
I feel and when kids are abused
I touch the soft grainy sand
I worry about how life will be for my kids
I cry when I see people killing others
I am compassionate and an individual

I understand about how what we can do affects others
I say people should not be judgmental
I dream one day I will each all my goals
I try to help others younger and older than myself
I hope someday to make a difference in the world
I am compassionate and an individual
   Meghan Stallmer

I Want To Say Thanks

Who ever you are, that left me your eye
I wish you knew, how much it means to me
To see blades of grass and planes in the sky
I'd like to say thanks, for all I can see.

When people walk down the street or store isle
There's something I wish everyone would do
Give everyone you pass bye, a big smile
And you will see, they will smile back at you.

Thank You, God, for the sight you gave me
And bless that person, who gave me their eye
Let me help someone who might need to be
I will be grateful till the day I die.
   Minnie Louise Martin

Reach

Reach for my hand
I will show you the way.

Reach for my hand
I understand.

I have traveled this road before
I know the corners along the way.

I can carry your burdens when the load seems heavy
Trust me my friend
Let me hold your hand.

I know life seems endless with so many decisions to make
Reach for my hand
I know the way.

I will take you through this passage
You need not be alone
Take my hand my friend
I will lead you safe to home.
   Mary Bline

A Dance For The Lord

Let me dance for you my Lord
I will dress in white
With a wreath of flowers in my hair
It will be my delight
To dance a spiritual dance for you
To music of intense beauty
  and sound

And it will bring out the spiritual part of me which I feel
  to be so profound

The movements will show my love and awe for you
As I dance with humility and purity of soul

The dance will make feel humble to you and yet I will
  feel completely whole!
   Mary Perifimos

Jewel

On a lighted shelf in a dark room, there is a
Jewel
encased in glass it stands alone.
On its stand it shines with the light.
When you look at it your eyes can see nothing else.
Its greatness overwhelms you, you see the
Orange bounce off the mirrors that surround it.
You may need to sit down, or look away for a moment.
It will always shine, nothing can stop it.
   Lauren Harvey

My Perfect Sister

To me a perfect child was sent
I will do everything for her to be content
Years have passed and...
Lots of people have put her last.

She doesn't act her age
Which may send others into a rage
Her advancement may be slow
Improvement might not show.

She may do things in an unusual way
She may need extra attention many would say
Raising your voice at her doesn't work
You must have patience... or she'll hurt.

Treating her as if she's normal
Will make her feel loved and so much warmer
Many will laugh at her and call her retarded
But I call her... "my perfect sister."

Kellie Ruleman

Grandpa Kiha

"Kupunakanes" (Grandfather)
  I went to the Island that you
came from, to get a sense of you
  To somehow feel how you must have
felt leaving, so small a boy so innocent and true.
  Across an ocean to a strange land
and people, whose customs were not yours,
where you longed for your Makuahine. (Mother)
  To never again hear her voice
or feel her touch, how hard it must
have been, never to see your Makuahine (Mother)

Maravene Kurtz

Christmas and My Childhood Memories

As I sat staring out my window on a snowy Christmas Eve,
I watched the snowflakes gently falling and clinging to the trees.
I thought of all the Christmases, long in the past
Of how we were so excited and our hearts beat hard and fast.
We looked forward to old Santa's visit that we knew would come that night
We longed so much to see Santa and his reindeer in their flight.
Of course that never happened, as to bed we had to go - before he would show
But oh what joy we shared with all, when on that Christmas morn,
We would find our Christmas stockings filled with goodies and maybe a horn.
For you see, we did not get the finest things, nor even the very best.
But you could not convince us of that, when we put it to the test.
My heart goes back to long ago and all the memories
And I would gladly give my all for just one more of these.
Christmas morning shared with all my family - it's Christ's birthday you know.
Love, joy and happiness - shared by all the way it was meant to be.
God blessed us gave us life and every thing we own,
But few of us remember to give "thanks" for all that He has done,
So please thank Him everyday for all the blessings we receive,
And help us all to always pray. "God bless us and teach us to believe."

Lucile Smith

I Love My Wife

I love my wife, because she's kind and loving.
She brings me love and warmth when I need it.
I love my wife when she comes to me in need.
Because she's my wife I love my wife more than me.

Michael John Nowotarski

Beauty In Wisdom

I watched as the silent hills were covered in white,
I watched as birds headed for thickets at night;
The world was silent and tranquil.
Nothing could ruin my view,
But in vein did I find the joy of winter
That as a youth I once knew.

It wasn't the cold of winter, but something inside of me.
It's what I was told by my doctor
That won't let my spirit be free,
"Your days on earth have been numbered;
Find joy in the time that you have had."
So I look out my window and remembered
To revel in God's beauty and be glad.

I thanked the Lord for snow and wind gusts,
And I thanked Him for birds to see,
I settled back in my warm bed
And let His beauty be a lesson to me.

Myrtle Lambert

Shattered Dreams Of Realism

   What could have been isn't!
I was walking along the shores of life
desperately struggling to be mother and wife
when you came along like a Robin's song
how could anything so right be so wrong
I met you and you met me
Our hearts soared together in joyous glee
But I'm afraid for us, we haven't the answer
Its bound to consume us like a deadly cancer
So go ahead and have a good life
Go back to being a husband, go back to your wife.

Marjorie Douville

God's Beautiful World

At six this morning the alarm did ring
I was so sleepy and lazy I ignored the thing.
A moment later I sprang to the floor
I stretched and dressed and went to the door.

I looked to the east and what did I see.
God's great big sun as beautiful as could be.
I called to my sister that was still in bed
Come here for a moment you sleepy head.

In a very short time she stood by my side
When she looked out the door, her eyes opened wide
As she stood there with delight
I heard her whisper, "What a beautiful sight."

Mother and Daddy came in to see
What was so interesting to sister and me.
The birds were singing and playing around
First in the trees, and then on the ground.

It seemed to us, they were trying to say,
Thank you God for this beautiful day.

Leonard L. Hays

Christmas

This is the time we celebrate Christmas
It brings out the cheerful spirit in us
It's a time we put up the holly and hang up the wreath
It's a time when Santa Claus is generous to the children beneath
Tuck up the little ones, tuck them up tight
For they await the presents brought over night
It's time for jingle-bells to ring through the air
They ring, yes they ring but no one knows where
It's a time for love, a time for mistletoe
When it's time for Christmas, you'll be sure to know.

Kathryn Wells

I Cried

You left me today, and I cried.
I wanted to hold you,
I wanted to tell you how much I would miss you,
How much I love you.
But, I knew I would cry.
I don't want you to be sad,
I want you to be happy.
This is a new part of your life,
A new beginning.
Starting on your own, it's your time now.
I missed my Mom today,
And I cried.
She left me a year ago.
I wanted to talk to her,
To tell her how much I would miss you,
She would know how I feel.
I bet she cried for me.
You left me today,
And I cried.

Norma Engstrume Baker

Standing Still

Standing still, the rain begins to fall on my face.
I want to run, but my feet slip out from beneath me,
I am paralyzed.
I close my eyes only, to hear the crashing thunder that
is exploding all around me.
I see only for a second the flashing lightning that blinds me.
Crying out loud only to be humbled by the power engulfing me.
I feel helpless.
I have no where to hide.
Only when I have the courage to lift myself above the storm,
will I see that the storm is only the fears I hold above myself.

Katherine Brown

The Gift

When God created mothers
  I think somehow He knew
He couldn't make all mothers
  As special and dear as you.

So, He searched for the one
  He thought the most worthwhile
And to that particular mother
  He gave your gentle smile.

Then, He formed new stars in heaven
  To place into your eyes
And filled your heart with a love so sweet
  That makes all mothers wise.

I waited impatiently 'til He whispered, "Go now.
  Her kind are so few
So as my greatest blessing
  I'm giving her to you"

Louise Lutz

"Wish Upon A Star"

I gaze into the sky at night
looking at all of the stars shining so brightly
Wondering if you are doing the same.
There's a certain star
I look at each night and that star I call you.
You are just like it,
you're always shinning full of light
sometimes I wonder if in the same
because I get to lay beside you
and stare at your beautiful blue eyes every night,
dreaming of you holding me tight.

Karen L. Spain

The Last Tango

My room is dark and lonely and cold
I talk to myself, "How soon I grew old!
Is this really me, so frail and so gray?"
Family and friends are all gone away.
They bring me food, I seldom go out.
My wants are few, what's left to care about?
Only my memories, still bright and clear.
The beautiful young girls, the boys so dear.
The lovers I've had I remember the most
Sweet lips and strong arms, holding me close.
Life was a song, so sweet and so wild.
How could we know, it lasts only a while?
Oh! Let me exchange the bitter dregs of the wine
For one night of music and dancing and passion sublime.
Oh! Let me dance the tango, one more time.

Mozelle Woodard

My Dragon And Me

I rub my hands on its dark green scales
I take the time to clip its dirty toe nails
I run my hands over its round round tail
Now its time to fly and sail
Up I go my dragon and me over the beautiful beautiful sea
Up above the clouds
Up above the sounds
Up above everything
It's just my dragon and me up above the beautiful beautiful sea.

Kafui Attoh

A Cowgirls Prize

Once upon a time, not so long ago
I spent a lot of time at the Rodeo.
Oh, I loved the Rodeo with all its noise and thrills.
I used to whistle loud an yell when cowboys took their spills.
My hair was always combed just right
My clothes were spic and span
My nails were filed and polished
You see, I was trying to catch a man.

Now I still love the Rodeo with all its thrills and noise
But it scares me half to death when bulls chase after boys.
"Watch Number 5," the clown announced; my heart would give a leap,
Then the bronco would dump his man into a crumpled heap.

My nails no longer be; I've chewed them to the quick,
The chances all the cowboys take, it nearly makes me sick.
See, I caught one handsome cowboy amongst the other guys.
He brings home the winnings; but I brought home the prize.

Kathy Park

The Flight

Soaring as the eagle soars,
  not all creatures can fly so majestically.
For those that try there is a constant challenge.
There are mighty winds that blow,
  but the creatures have to glide through the tumultuous streams or air.
There are storms that cloud the sky,
  but the creatures have to see through to the brilliance of the sun.
It is the durable strength of those broad reaching wings
  that carries that mighty bird.
The challenge is never easy,
  to soar as the eagle soars.

Laura Jasper

In The Dark

In the dark,
I see no one.
Not me, not I, not myself.
In the light,
Still fuzzy.
The being all have known,
yet do not know.
Not the boisterous, or loud, or funny one.
Only emptiness, lacking afraid, hateful,
Somehow.
The light that blinds always leaves the aggravating dots.
Screaming.
Trying to block the naive Eustachian.
Crying.
Turmoil.
Knowing the light is there to aide,
Continually I walk,
over the cliff,
into freedom.
Lisa Deaderick

A Small Cafe

As I passed the small cafe last night
I saw you dancing and holding her tight
All I could remember was the things we'd done
Little things that were so much fun...

Your face was so happy and hers so new
Leave, I told myself, before he sees you
But I could not see through my tears
We had been married so many happy years...

Then I remembered your bad temper when you're mad
And your beautiful tears when you were sad
Your sweet words telling me how you loved me
Your understanding mood when I forgot my key...

Your happy look when you saw our little girls
Your wonder when you saw our little boys curls
Your crazy look when we have to go
Your tender lips kissing me so...

All these things I can so well remember
We were a family and all its members
I've got to find a way back into your heart
There is no reason we should stay apart..
Mary Anne

A Celebration
Dedicated to Becca, 1990-1995
I've never witnessed a more beautiful funeral than hers.
I saw a church full of loving hearts and many tears.
I saw the innocence of a young daughter gently place her head upon
her mother's shoulder.
I saw a young boy try to comfort his mother, grandmother and sister.
I saw a man and a woman hold one another.
I saw a group of friends embracing.
I saw flowers and balloons symbolizing life.
I saw students break down in their teachers arms.
I heard meaningful songs that touched everyone's heart.
As my eyes filled with tears, I saw an aunt dance gracefully for her niece.
But most of all, I experienced a celebration for a little angel and
her new life.
We all miss you!
Lynda M. Battaglia

My Brother, My Friend, My Dentist

My brother, my brother, an interesting fella'
I remember the night he was born -
Daddy had a gleam I never had seen
I thought, wow! A brother, how keen.
By the time he was five I had serious doubts
Hanging 'round Leonard led to wrestling bouts
All kinds of attention he seemed to capture
Sometimes I wondered - such praise and rapture?
I couldn't compete with his brown eyes and curls
Exchange him right now, bring home a girl!

As Leonard grew up we were all proud
He always seemed to stand out in a crowd
I remember our parents often would say
He'll be your best friend come whatever may
Mothers and Fathers are really profound
That's why it's important to have them around
Lo and behold somehow they knew
At his 60th Birthday I'd need him ACUTE
Because wouldn't you know it?
I chipped my front tooth!
Lorraine Donohue

"Our Place To Hide"

As I lie on my bed on a rainy cool night,
I regret every word that I said in our fight.
With the sounds of the rain so closely outside,
I wish there was a place for just the two of us to hide.
As I slowly close my eyes and dream of you so near,
These fantasies of you and me seem to be so clear.

When you wrapped your arms around me together with our cries,
Time and time before we had said our last good-byes.
As you gently lift my head and wipe away my tears,
A sudden feeling of love eliminates my fears.
You whispered three words I swore I'd never say,
And if I hadn't I'd regret it to this day.

Now as I still lie on my bed
And thoughts of you run through my head,
And as the rain still falls outside,
I listen to the gentle wind sing
In hopes to find our place to hide
And wait to see what future may bring.
Lauren Durkin

Perfectly Fine

Now that your back I want you to know
I really missed you,
But I was perfectly fine without you.

The sun didn't shine once while you were gone,
At least I didn't see it.
But I was perfectly fine without you.

The birds didn't sing their morning song.
At least I didn't hear them.
But I was perfectly fine without you.

When my co-workers asked how I was
They jumped at my "I'm Great!"
But I was perfectly fine without you.

Each night when my eyes closed you appeared in my dreams.
Loneliness filled my heart when I would awake.
But I was perfectly fine without you.

But I am so much better when you're around
The sun shines, birds warble their songs.
And I'm perfectly, wonderfully fine with you.
Lynda L. Woolf

The Attic

The attic is dark,
I pull the light switch,
But the light won't come on.
Dusty puzzle pieces are scattered all over the attic floor.
I look at the puzzle box one more time
and try to see how the pieces would fit together.
Suddenly they do.
The light comes on.
The math equation is solved.

Kim Bruha

My Prayer

For the heart that knows only emptiness; I pray for thee!
I pray that the essence of a meaningful life will be found.
Amid the darkness is the hope that all will be forgiven.
And out of the depths will arise an awakened soul,
A soul that sees only beauty and knows only happiness.
For the heart that knows only emptiness; I pray for thee!
I pray that through this emptiness the dream will be kept alive,
For what a dream it is!
A dream to love when there is only hate.
For the heart that knows only emptiness; I pray for thee!
I pray that from this emptiness comes strength
And from strength comes courage that will nurture the soul.
Courage to keep the soul endeavoring even when there seems to be no hope.
For the heart that knows only emptiness; I pray for thee!
Because that heart is me!

Michael Polcari

Skipped Through Time...

Skipped through time,
  I move.
Like a rock across water.
Touching only once,
  perhaps twice.
Causing ripples across the mirror,
  which quickly fade.
Returning the surface to peace.
Seeming as though I had never passed.

Slowly across the sand,
  I walked.
Quiet footsteps follow close behind,
  hurriedly cleansed by the tide.
Every sign of me is gone.
Only the waves whisper my near forgotten presence.

I have skipped these stones,
And walked these shores,
  a million times passed.
But every time results the same,
  marks that never last.

Meleah Trice

I Like...

I like the wind blowing in my hair.
I like the stars glistening in the air.
I like the birds chirping in the trees.
I like the grass rustling in the breeze.
I like the sand going through my toes.
I like the smell of a red, red rose.
I like nature where there are so many sights to see.
I like the sound of a busy bumble bee.
I like a world where peace is far and near.
I like a world where there is nothing left to fear.

Neda Bolourian

I Followed The Light

A beam of light which shined from afar,
I mistakenly conceived to be a burning star.

This beam of light steadily drew me near,
As I tried to determine from whence it appeared.

I reluctantly followed, gazing through tears,
As my steps became shorter and my destination near.

I finally reached the point where the light was overbearing;
I decided to end my journey - so I tarried.

After some time, as I watched and waited,
A heavenly voice said, you've been faithful and dedicated.

So for following the light through the sun and the rain,
And for tarrying despite heartache and pain;

I'll always lead and guide thee in the things that must be done;
I'll always watch and protect thee when evil falls upon;

Finally will I forever bless thee and make thee a light unto me,
So that others can follow thee as you have followed me.

I trust by now you know me — as I have come to know thee;
I am the light of the world, the Lord God, omnipotent
That's me.

Michelle D. Sloan

This Chance To Live

The sun shines thru the window making him a silhouette.
I look up from the pillow and his words I can't forget.
There are no tears, I've built a wall. See, I fore told my fate.
The symptoms forced the issue and I've no more time to wait.

My life must chance, but change is life. I can no longer be
As I am now, my mind projects the more imperfect me.
Soon I embrace these huge machines, they're welcome to assist.
My frantic multiplying cells cannot their power resist.

I lay alone, oh so alone, inviting all the rays
To penetrate my tender skin and please extend my days.
A nurse whose hands betray her heart, injects into my vein
A clear mysterious liquid that keeps rebel cells in rein.

We sit at each side of his desk, the surgeon (young) and I.
My eyes search out this pair of hands, there may my future lie.
I take the prep, I take the drugs, depending now on care.
Thru drowsy haze I fix my eyes on surgeon bowed in prayer.

A brilliant mind guides skillful hands and soon a year has past.
I love myself, I love my earth, and I've been greatly blessed.
I've learned to trust, I've had to take, 'til I again can give.
Forever I'll be grateful they gave me this chance to live.

Lavone Johnson

Sounds

Sometimes, when I'm out to play,
I listen to sounds, whether night or day.
I listen to the sounds of the rustling leaves,
And wonder what's behind the trees.

I hope I'll live just one more day,
And I hope I'll see June and May.
And when it's nighttime, and the moon shines bright,
Well what can I do, but listen to the sounds of the night?

What is that I hear from my room?
I think it's a wolf howling at the moon.
And there's a cricket, I hear that too!
It's amazing what sounds I can hear from my room.

Katie Ellen Wallace

Winter's Start

As the cold and dreary weeks drag on
I know the last warm days have now all gone
The sun it seldom ever shines
It only plays havoc with our minds
The north wind blows strong and harsh
Over the now hardening crystallized marsh
And the once green trees are now all bare
And all that's left are the skeleton-like branches that flail the air
Kathleen A. King

Wonder.....

I sit here wondering where you are,
  I know not if you stand beside me,
    or if you are further then I would ever imagine.

Not having you beside me,
  is like having a piece of my heart torn away from me.

I had always wondered what it was like to be happy,
  and with you I know.
You always knew how to make me laugh and smile,
  especially when I was down.

When I was with you I felt so safe,
  as if nothing could hurt me.
Now that you are gone,
  I feel so scared,
  not knowing what could be around the next corner.

All I do is wonder why you left me,
  just sitting here crying,
  feeling all alone.

And I have no one to turn to.....
Monica Morales

Cher

If heaven were to do again,
I know it would thank you and when
The skies burnt blue, they couldn't pretend,
That you were not to thank again.

And when the sea, its breeze blown in,
And how the gulls fly high and then.
They gaze upon you with intent,
To thank you properly once again.

And when the mountains weep with tears,
They cry with happiness when you're near.
Without you they are well aware,
They're height and beauty would despair.

And oh the meadow would not fair,
With all its splendor it could not prepare.
If you were not to watch and glare,
And keep the meadow from drying bare.

And if you were to fall elsewhere,
To somehow grieve or despair.
The heavens, seas, and mountains, all here,
Would certainly perish without you there.
Michael Kicenski

Colors

Beautiful, beautiful colors, waving in the sky.
I see them all before me, the magic touches my eye.
Nature is an artist, life becomes her palette.
Have you ever seen a sunset that didn't dance upon your eye?
We gaze upon natures artistry, with wonder and surprise.
Megan Brotzman

Untitled

The well worn pages of an old journal are among the treasures
I keep in the many boxes that store my life's memories.
I read with detached interest thoughts that were once
important but I have long forgotten why.
I study photographs that hold precious images of old friends
that no longer exist in my world.
This saddens me for a while but I brighten with the knowledge
that I am better because they were in my life for a time
and gave me more than they'll ever know.
I repack my memories for another day and give thanks
for all those who made them my reality
and not theirs...
Lynn Purvines

Grandma

I love you so,
I just don't know,
what I would do without you in my life,
without your love, without your care.,
I often wonder how life could ever treat you unfair,
You glow so bright, that every night,
I wonder what I would do, without a Grandma like you!
Kristin L. Goss

Awakened To Spring

As I awoke this morning when life was oh so still
I heard a robin singing outside my windowsill.
I got out of bed real softly I didn't want to scare,
The little bird that sang so sweet and filled the morning air.
As I looked out across the land the wonders I did see,
For there were trees filled with leaves as green as green could be.
The yards were full of rolling grass birds were everywhere,
Flowers bloomed across the land to fill the sweet warm air.
I ran outside and looked around, it made me want to sing,
When I woke up this morning God showed me a touch of spring.
We went to church on Sunday, my family and I,
On each side of the pulpit lilacs caught my eye.
The inscription on the altar read "In remembrance of me"
I remembered all the beauty of spring I'd just seen.
O God if things are pretty here, our love we give and share.
Tell me what it's going to be when we get over there.
Spring will be everyday, flowers everywhere, and birds
Will sing all the time to sweetly fill the air.
God touched me today.
Mary Lou Goff

My Best Friend

I have looked far and I have looked wide;
I have yet to find a friend closer than the one at my side.
He is the sunshine and brightness of my day;
By constantly uplifting my spirits each and every way.
He is my guiding light who leads me through the dark;
By illuminating the path to insure I never miss the mark.
He is the strength that carries me through hard times;
By helping me to cope, usually by my own designs.
He is compassionate and caring and knows me better than no other;
By listening to my deepest secrets which I could never tell another.
He is loving and tender and constantly fills me with desire;
By being passionate and romantic and kindling my inner fire.
He is honest and sincere and treats me with respect;
By listening when I speak and not criticizing my intellect.
He is witty and funny and always makes me laugh;
By complementing my sense of humor and being my better half.
He is generous and giving and touches my very heart;
By enjoying our time together and missing me when we are apart.
He is my husband, my partner, but most of all my best friend;
Who will always be there for me, right up to the very end.
Kristine M. Whitty

The American Way

When I was just a little girl, my father said to me,
"I have to go to war, my dear, to keep our country free.
Someday, when you grow up, I hope you understand,
There are worse things than dying for your country or your land.
To live without the freedom to express your thoughts, would be
An awful state of being and a much worse destiny.
So child, I'm in the Army; I'm a Chaplain for our men.
I've been in two World Wars and I'd do it once again.
My duty to America, I do for you with love
And hope to keep your freedom with the help from God above."
The Colonel has been buried, but his Spirit marches on.
It lives within the hearts of every generation born.

If daddy were alive today, I'd thank him - tho then I cried.
I'd kiss his face with tender love. I'd hold his hand with pride.
I've lived the life of freedom, for which men gave their own.
I know I'm ever thankful that America's my home.
So when I hear opinions, to which I disagree,
I remember, that's the freedom, men fought for - for you and me.
And even though, I may not like, the things you have to say,
I'll stand up for your freedom to live The American Way!

Mary MacCombie Fietsam

Momma, Oh Momma

Through the course of my years,
I have had my share of female encounters,
and I have taught and been so taught by them.

Most have come and gone,
passing through my body and soul,
but one always remains within and its prime.

How lucky I am to share such a being,
as that in my mom.

As I skip along this pavement and smile so,
a piece of my brain recites the refrain.

Momma, oh momma when I have been hurt,
you soothed the pain and offered the gain.
Momma, oh momma when I have been strong,
we laughed and we played on the prices I paid.
Momma, oh momma how do I deserve,
such good love from you?

My youth was full of mixed feelings,
and emotions ran rampant with the tides.
But throughout it all I suppose I stood tall,
since my love for you will never subside.

Matthew Fogel

Don't Cry For Me

Don't cry for me, for don't you see?
I've already live longer than what ought to be
Don't cry for me you'll need your tears;
Save them for your true future fears.
Don't cry for me, cheer instead
For the lives I've touched and souls I've lead.
Don't cry for me
Life's too short to be blue;
But discover who you are
And try to lead others too!!!

Linder D. Anderson

"My Rose"

As the wind blows across the skies,
Its rustling within the trees,
One cannot help but notice the eyes
Of a grandmother so loved as thee.

As a child, I remember it well,
Staying overnight with my Granny, such a treat,
The laughing, the playing, the stories you would tell,
A true adventure indeed.

You have always been there, my loyal friend,
Never once did I need look far.
You gave me advice and that beautiful grin,
Do you know how loved you are?

Have I ever told you what you mean to me?
The memories? What your love has meant?
You are the wind that moves through the trees
Of my live, giving me strength.

As an adult, nothing has changed,
My love for you still grows.
Your beauty and love are still the same
I love my Granny Rose.

Michael S. Edwards

Past The Darkness

Reaching with outstretched arms
I gathered the warmth of the sun.
My feet sank beneath crystal white sand
To feel the strength of where a thousand
Barefoot feet have trod.
Memories of emotions encased my being
And the wind off a nearby cloud
Hit my face with the reality of life.
An angry mass covered the sun
And changed soft rolling waves into tempered peaks.
A vicious current reached for its victim
And tossed it helplessly into darkness.
Sitting in disbelief, I looked past the anger.
In the mist of the confusion of what I was dealt,
I saw hope
A small glimmer of golden sunshine.

Lynne M. Handsel

Autumn's Window

Sunrise greets me with a hue of yellow gray,
In assurance autumn is underway.

Trees lose their leaves,
Through the sometimes gentle breezes.
The remains of summer are gathered,
To welcome the coming season.

Reds, orange, greens and tans,
Elude capture, with a whirling sophisticated dance.
Fields of gold once fortressing to the sky,
Bow low beneath the combine, rendezvous with heaven denied.

All of nature anticipates the yearly retreat,
Collecting, storing, harvesting, preparing for the coming feat.
Ghastly visions that flash through my head,
Give way to thankfulness, for the good life I've led.

As nightfall engulfs the earth below,
I beheld it all, through autumn's window.

Lubertha McClairen

Echoes

As I walked along the shoreline echoes cried out from the deep and the
sadness on the lonely wind made me stop and weep.
Empty sounds resounded as waves softly kissed the shore, and as I
listened closely creatures sang from the ocean's floor.

A murmur starts the singing as the moon rose to its peak, softly,
sweet and gentle, lowly, mild and meek. A soloist was humming a
haunting lullaby, and far off in the distance another duplicates the
cry. I stood in silent wonder as the minute began, and far off in the
heaven's timid thunder was their band.

Together now in harmony they begin their serenade, I'm feeling
blessed and honored to hear what God has made. The moon gives the
hour of midnight, all is quiet on the land, The only sounds around are
lapping waves upon the sand.

From asunder comes a rolling roar of which I've never heard before
it rumbled o'er the landscape, seemed to shake the ocean's floor.
With echoes of the roaring still hanging in the air
a silhouette danced over a high-moon's polished, golden glare.

Was a love song they were singing, they sang a song of love, peaceful
Solomon beauty as a star fell from above. No empty sounds resounding
no sadness on the wind, but dancing, prancing flips and spins,
Happy splashing playful fins.
Karen Kuerbitz

The Tree That Sits In My Backyard

The tree that is in my backyard,
Must have been there for a million years.
Every night I sit and I talk, and it listens to me.
It has feelings that only I can understand,
Me, and only me, can see it, and hear its glee.
The tree that has become my best friend,
Is the only one who understands me.

None of my friends know about this tree,
For if they did they would not believe me.
I love this tree with all my heart.
I'll love it forever, like I did from the start.
Megan Laskoski

The Poet's Pen

Ah - what beauty lies within the words a poet pens, they make a soul
rise then bring it back again to home and hearth and love
unfeigned, to verdant forest floor and sun-drenched rolling plain,
to city streets and country lanes, to oceans wide and wild, to fields
of golden grain - the beauty of a child.

For eyes that cannot see, the poet paints a sunset red, a blue bird
in leafy tree - a glorious flower bed.

For ears that cannot hear, the poet's pen becomes the sound of gentle
rain on silver pane or splashing on the ground or mighty thunder roll
from mountain top to valley floor, a poet's pen can sound all these - and more.

For feet that cannot walk a poet guides their path 'cross shining
desert sands, to jungles, there and back, to meadow grass and pebbled
path, to mountains lofty climb, past blossom scented trees - in summertime.

A pen becomes a magic wand in every poet's hand to share the beauty
held within with those who cannot see or hear or stand with those
who long for distant shores or places found in dreams, a poet's pen
can take you there - or so it seems.
Melba Buttars

Troubles

Sometimes I'm asked what
do I think of the world
And sadness fills my heart.
I look around at all the grief,
And I think to myself where do I start?

Do I begin with the homeless,
or the starving children,
or all the racial fights;
maybe the young and old people,
who can't walk the streets
because they're afraid of the nights.

The gangbangers, child abuse,
I can go on; there's no change.
To live in a peaceful quiet world,
would that be so strange?
Donna Kuknyo

Bitter Is The Taste

Bitter is the taste
distant is the warmth
that flees from my
wandering eyes

I feel as if
I am torn apart
two noble directions
with no quarter given

I sit here
an echo of what
will come, and maybe
what has been
Jeffrey T. Wallin

The Meaning Of...

The thought is mortal,
dismiss it with the mind,
never the soul, undying and pure.
The sunset, a dream in this world.
Darkness with the absent moon a reality.
Cold and lonely we wander this earth.
always hoping
hoping for that fulfilled dream of desire.
Each with our own Pandora's box.
To quench our thirst in fantasies is one way,
to explore life another.
But where does this quest end?
There is no end.
Only time as an ultimate barrier.
Jim Larens

"Why?"

Just as a single star twinkles in the sky,
a lonely tear drop forms in her eye.
She promises herself she won't cry.
Why did he have to die?
Why? Why?

The day came that I was on my own,
but I'll always know I'm not alone.
Why did he have to die?
Why? Why?
Kyle Witt

Who

Did you ever think
Did you ever wonder

Is this really real
Is this just a dream

You could just be
A figment of my imagination
Put here for my amusement
Or me yours

Imagine this is true
We never know with who
Wonder what would happen
If we both wake up

Who would be
Me or you
Donnie J. Decker

Untitled

Verbal tidal waves
destroy and conquer the mud walls
enclosing my core
allowing floods, thought after thought,
flow; molten mercury solidifying into prose
and emotion. My literary voice screams
dividing this winter might into two beings,
one hideous creature named thought
he hurts me, always did.
His counterpart, known as literation
burns cobwebs and
clears the murk my thoughts provide.
My pen, my Jesus
saving my soul
from the damnating pit
I always
think myself into.
Gary Eckman

All People Smile
In The Same Language

All people smile in the same language.
Despite differences in family heritage
From which personalities stem,
People smile in ways most suitable to them.

No matter who does the smiling,
A smile is beguiling
And glows from within
Whether masculine or feminine.

No matter the human condition
Or their nutrition,
People smile natural and true
Sharing themselves when they do.

No matter cultures are not the same,
A smile is a message to proclaim
Goodwill, personally sent,
Freely given - excessively spent.

A smile is never wasted or passé.
It is meant to be thrown away.
A smile is a language all people share:
A language spoken everywhere.
Howard C. Rolfe

Love Comes Late

So Many Wasted Years
Desires unfulfilled—heart battered.
Wrong choices—dreams shattered.
Feelings concealed—surfacing never.
Continuing on—trying forever
   to change things
   which cannot be changed.

Energy drained from this body so frail.
Soul may depart—time will tell.
True love never known 'til much too late.
Obstacles hinder—this love must wait.
   Cannot be recognized...
   Must remain obscure.

But, through it all, contentment abides.
True love, at last, in heart resides.
No one can take that love away.
Whatever fate—it is there to stay.
   Never to die...
   love immortal.
Ida Lea Johnson

The Invitation

Chained by fears, the girl waits.
Depression has come, her existence bleak.
A dark foreboding secret

Beyond the window lies the forest.
Howling winds.
Like banshees, they call her name.

Carlaine

Death is everywhere
Stench permeates the surrounding walls
Sweet pungent odors have come to entice.

Clearly the invitation calls
Seething within shall cease.
Fears will depart.

Polyandrium awaits.
Carol Crawford Lewis

Fly Away

Today you left,
dear love of mine;
to cross the river wide.
Spirit fly, fly away.

With God, you now abide,
and angels walk,
at your side.
Spirit fly, fly away.

Beneath the cold,
dark Earth, you lie;
where neither sun nor moon,
upon your face may shine.
Spirit fly, fly away.

Now in God's warm,
and loving embrace,
you rest.
Spirit fly, fly away.
Janis Wheeler

Dead

"Dead" I heard them say.
Dead? Or just away?
A body here, a voice there:
Can the soul transcend?

"Dead" I heard them say.
Words reverberate off
Gleaming sterile walls
Echoing in silent dark hallways.

"Dead" I heard them say.
It cannot be. It must not be
The scarlet lips scream
The litany unheard in the night.

"Dead" I heard them say again.
Dead? Or just away?
A spirit here, a voice there.
Dead? No, just away.
Barbara H. Carson

The Rich Man

On and on,
day after day, he talks,
continuously,
never stopping,
no one heeding.
Nothing said by him taken seriously-
by anyone.
On and on
he continues anyway,
not realizing, no one cares;
he doesn't even consider, that maybe,
   someone - anyone - isn't listening.
Alissa Greenwood

Creating A Frigid Love

Crimson, ebony
dark and cold
Tears fall painlessly
   on petals of fresh flower.
So pure and true,
So warm and soft
   but lonely just the same.
Swirling in torment,
engulfed by sweet and tender kisses.
Cinnamon incense permeates my thoughts.
Still smoke,
like the waves in the midnight hour,
Lost in a swirling sea of emotions,
I light the last Camel Light.

Losing love, is death to a heart.
Danielle Banfield

Autumn Leaves

Autumn leaves under a sky of blue
Dancing to the hum of the wind
Bright hues of rust, red and gold
A beautiful sight to behold.
The happy faces of children
The sound of merry laughter
As they gaily tumble among the leaves
Under a sky of blue.
A story told as of old.
Helen Hellman

The Portrait

Faded lines that
Curve to form
An old forgotten face.

Red outlines in wavy curls
The paleness of a rosy cheek.,
Pink lips are formed
Into a sweet, gentle smile.
Eyes shine blue and innocent;
And creamy, frilly, lacy dress
Blends with the milky flesh.

It makes one wonder,
Is anyone alive who remembers
That sweet face?
Did she marry?
Was she mourned by all
When she breather her last?
Is she remembered still?

Everyone sooner or later,
Becomes a nameless, faceless
Faded portrait.

Dawn Anne Manske

Star

Little black cat
curls up on my lap,
purring contentedly,
while I stroke her
shiny, smooth fur,
that has the feel
of fine silk.

She used to be
frightened and
hide - would barely
allow the tentative
touch of my patiently
outstretched hand,
but now has learned
to trust and relax.

I always loved her,
but she did not know...

Edda H. Hackl

Secret Sculptor

Little Hautvan child of pain,
crippled by the hooves of horses;
made his bed among the clover,
protected by the unseen forces.

Not like other boys around him,
strong and fearless braves were they;
Little Hautvan made a pony
from the river's bed of clay.

Stole the dyes from bark and berry;
Painted bright his horse of clay,
as silently he labored o'er him;
Made the mane of sun-bleached hay.

What he finished was a steed,
perfect quite in all detail;
agate eyes of river stone,
hooves sculpt from the mountain shale.

Made by his hands with love and talent,
though crippled little boy was he;
Now stands this stallion proud and mighty,
for all the tribes of earth to see.

Doris F. Peach

Untitled

Black as night it comes,
Creeping up on you
Scaring you what it seems like to death,
Though, it is Death
It wraps around you,
Like a hungry snake,
Strangling, choking
For a minute, it gives up
Only to come back with
Such a force that
Your body wrenches at the sudden attack,
Then it lay stiff, unmoving
For the rest of Eternity

Carran Cain

Shadows

Shadows during the day,
covering my way.

Shadows at night,
postponing my flight.

Shadows all the time, yet,
it's my time to shine.

Why won't they go away, I'm
not living my life, a big delay.

Mother, Father, Brother, Sister,
their looks all so sinister.

The shadows are bigger, engulfing
me, leave me alone, go away.

Shadows during the day,
covering my way.

Shadows at night,
postponing my flight.

Shadows all the time, yet,
it's my time to shine.

It's my time, to shine.

Carrie Stockwell

Someone's Crying

Someone's crying
Could it be you?

Someone's crying
I hear it too!

Soft and low barely heard
Now and then I hear a word.

In early dawn of another day
Please oh please make the crying go away.

Beth Napoleon

Simulation

Today, I discovered
  a "new" color
    in my rainbow,
And that color is "YOU".
  Brighter is this arch
    of magnificent hues,
      warmest sensation,
        courageous
          and true.

Kathy M. Pennigar

Dune Sand

Woman is sand
Cool or warm
Depending on the closeness of the sun.

Blown about
Constantly reshaping
Enduring and grounded in the real.

She supports
The creatures and the life forms
Who live within her dune space.

Sand cleanses
Reconstructs and renews
From a spirit that is always there.

Sand is woman
Firm and nurturing
Shifting, supportive yet free.

Erline D. Goodell

Essence Cubed

Brown squares - boxes
Contents sorted, wrapped and packed
Carefully, so as not to break.

Taped cocoons for portable memories
Like children's blocks, stacked
Top on top, side by side, end to end.

Forlornly standing sentries
Watching o'er empty chambers
Casting shadows on the wall.

Storehouses for accumulated treasures
Sorrows and fears now tucked away
Spirit contained, but not controlled.

Enduring symbols - boxes
Segments of life, hopes and dreams
Readied now for new frontiers.

Judith Townsend Seime

Life Is What You Make It!

What goes around,
Comes around!
Think about it.
There's so much truth to it.
I've learned that
When you do a friendly deed,
It comes back to you!
A smile given,
Is returned when most needed.
A hand offered,
To help out a friend,
Comes back again and again!
Put into life
What you expect to receive.
You may be surprised,
With what you achieve!

Connie Mezak

Night

As I walk in the night
Before the dawn's early light
At the dark sky, I do stare
To see a falling star, with such bright glare
I ponder, then wonder to myself
How lucky to behold such a sight
As I walk in the night
Before the dawn's early light

April Delbrugge

Devotion

Every time you need a drink,
Come to me, I'll quench your thirst,
When your pain becomes unbearable
I'll take away your ache,
Whatever the problem, no matter
how large or small, I'll help
you solve it.
You're here on earth for a
purpose, you'll remain in my
heart for eternity.
Once in a lifetime, a love like
ours comes along. Life is our
playground, happiness, our destiny.
Betty J. Behrendt

Since I Met You

I'm sitting on a cloud up high
come join me in the sky
it's a scene that must always be
   for you and for me

Through the air we will swing
with a rainbow for your ring
it's a dream that must always be
   for you and for me

There will always be a star
to guide us near and far
it's reality that must always be
   for you and for me

From east to west we'll go
with never a sunset below
it's a life that must always be
   for you and for me

Over oceans and mountains we'll sail
our love will always prevail
it's a forever that must always be
   for you and for me
Harry F. Jenkins

Toy Angel

Little toy angel, alabaster face,
Come alive and give me grace.
Touch me, kiss me, lips so kind.
Give me strength that I may find
all my dreams come true.
Bless me with your out stretched hand.
Let me rise, let me stand,
Let me run and let me fly
towards your distant friendly sky.
Little toy angel with dress so white,
Pull me up with all your might.
With your sparkling, magic wand,
Bind us with your heavenly bond.
Upward, upward into flight,
Lift me up into His sight.
Little angel, sign of joy,
Are you just a little toy?
Charles D. Sears

Innocence Lost

All around me
closing in
painless death
to my soul within
shadowy fringes
drawing nearer
a moonless midnight's
image of mirror
a rasping voice
whispers my fate
the voice of humanity
seething with hate
all around me
no escape
a painful future
naivete's rape
Cree Ross

Magic Potion

Perpetual Motion is the ocean
   churning up a magic potion.

First it's calm, then wild it seems
   yet deep beneath it is serene.

All looks dirty, then all is clear
   the waves go out and then come near.

Through dirty grays the sunlight streams
   the colors change to blues and greens.

Life is like that moving ocean
   searching for the magic potion.

Sometimes a smile, sometimes a frown
   emotions go round and round.

The moods of black and gray recede
   and rainbow colors take the lead.

Serenity deeper than emotion
   supersedes the elusive magic potion.
Donna J. Smith

Life

Fear not, darkness, Unknown
Cherish every moment, Memories
creating a life well sewn.

Life closes slowly with time
Many feel to quickly
Unlike Birth, Death is blind

Warmth not cold
Should fill your soul
Your loved one's in GODS hold

Heartfelt thoughts
Good and Bad
Come together in your head

Living, loving, feeling
Baggage for your journey
Grief and sorrow, parts of mourning

Be at peace within yourself
Simplify Destiny...
Cheri Fecker

Miss Katie Love

She makes me feel glad
Cheers my heart
and makes me laugh.
While I dust and clean
She plays hide and seek
Popping out here, and
Peeking under there.
Morning noon and night,
She greets me with loud purrs
With her funny face,
and sweet ways
She's so dear, soft and furry.
She's part of all the hope,
Love and beauty
God has created.
She's my kitten,
Miss Katie Love!
Dorothy M. Hammer

Cat's Game

With my cat, life's a game;
Chase a string, capture a prey,
Teasing or torture, she's not to blame,
But I was glad it got away!

A nocturnal huntress, we'd find
A dead thing at our door;
A token of her prowess, like a sign;
Of the wild beast's roar!

Birds a favorite catch,
As they perched in the tree.
Slinking, crouched before the snatch;
Pouncing adroitly, almost with glee.

I do not blame her hunting ways,
Mercy not natural or innate;
We made not earth nor direct sun rays,
Nor take blame for a creatures fate.

And yet, cuddle she would in my lap,
Sweet and loving as can be;
Innocent, faultless, takes her nap,
And leaves such thoughts up to me!
Clarence A. Skinner

It

I never knew something could be like this,
Changing, making life feel like total bliss.
Life and Love change in a flash,
Just like winning Lottery cash.
It brings to your life great joy and delight,
And makes everything feel completely right.
Your mind starts to see in a brand new way,
Making things look more beautiful and gay.
The many days and nights go by so quick,
As if they're done in a magician's trick.
Some cannot prepare for this lover's curse,
but receive it without any reimburse.
I should probably thank the sky above,
For this wonderful thing that I call love.
Amber Dobbins

My Silent Siren

She brings a
Certain beauty
To
A
Perfect rain day
Turning up the hue
Stunning the view
...the view
She's
  out
    of
      reach
From you
Her too
Reaching, searching
So blue
The sky above
Cocked, from the whiplash smile
Bewildered and betrayed
She steals away...with love

Ben Nichols

Untitled

Today I think I need a walk,
'Cause when I walk I sing and talk,
I sing to birch and maple trees,
And hail the cooling, soothing breeze;
I love the sky, I sing out loud,
Enjoying each and every cloud;
The outdoors is the best place
To calm the nerves and slow the pace;
I love it all, come rain or shine,
For when I walk the whole world's mine;
And it's important in my life
To get away from daily strife;
It turns my "daily strife" around,
Head in the clouds, feet on the ground;
It wipes away "too much to do,"
And happy thoughts come smiling through;
My life is good! There's little wrong
That can't be cured with walk - and song!

Janet C. Williams

Puddled Reflections

Cast a stone into the water
catch a ripple, hold it now
slowly turn and reach inside
the future's waiting for you there.

Peer inside the rippling haze
through the broken face
gather all your wits to ponder
of this place so far away

As you feel the warmth engulf you
the dreams will pull you in
the sounds that echo deeper
are just droplets out of place.

Debbie Smedley

Our Flag

Red white and blue
Burning our flag you must never do
Each new star shows how we grew
Keep it safe from birth to the new

Carolyn Bunting

My Place

Dream poet:
Cast off those furtive looks
From the shadows.
Drink of this, the air
Here is where I live
Let earth trickle from grinding hands
Hands weathered and eroded
By the wind which carries my words
and is my teacher.
No more unblemished flesh
And ignorant bliss.
Yours is to be muddied
Your soul is the planting ground
Sparse among the weeds
Will the flowers grow
Let the rain pound upon you
It is my drink.

Costas Hanjis

Après Earthquake

Butterfly, bless this house.
Carry our cares away on your wings.
Guide us through the faulty maze
Where we are cursed to spend our days.

You fly above it all
Except the day when in you flew
And landed in our living room.
Monarch against lily walls.

I see you as an omen of better days to come.
When all is finished, patched and fixed,
Mirrors hung, bugs undone.
All shiny and anew.

Curse begone! Oh, Evil One!
How dare you darken my front door!
Be at peace, evermore.
Thank you, butterfly, my friend.
You came through, in the end.

Carole Knaul Williams

Hillbilly Knight: Country Wildflower

Aaron,
Carolinian hillbilly,
Charging like knight,
Singing with lively animation.
Fantastic!

Fantastic!
Bulldozer style,
Giving Tippin all,
Loving every stage moment.
Fans.

Fans,
Many devotees,
Growing in number,
Appreciating wild exhilarating performances.
Wildflower.

Wildflower,
Country serenades,
Blooming on stages,
Sowing everlasting musical love.
Aaron.

Betty Luddington

Farewell

Snowflakes on hair,
Caressing
Nose and cheeks.

Bundled forms forlorn,
Conceal longings
Of endless smiles.

A distant shrill
Pierces the night;
Foreboding Winter.

Summer memories
Fleetingly linger,
As glassy eyes meet.

Beating hearts merge
With steel and steam;
A train beckons.

In cold embrace,
Fall leaves swirl
Around hesitant feet.

A last farewell
To a passing season.

Adrian C. Vroegindewey

Lost People

As autumnal winds
caress my face,
simultaneously harass trees
to strip them of summer.
The winter interlude
of depression soon comes,
and covers destitute souls
like a blanket of fog.
Those who survive
to see summer children,
bronzing in the day
under azure skies.
The sun is pushed away
by night's cooling moon,
as the day scavengers
slip out of sight,
out of mind.

Bruce P. Boysen

What's The Difference?

WHY do you act as if they're different?
CAN'T you see they're the same?
LOOK beyond their color
AND call them by their name.

WHY do you act as if they don't belong?
CAN'T you see they do?
GOD put us all together
SO see. He loves them too.

CAN'T you put it all behind you
AND learn to get along?
CAN'T you see being prejudiced
IS really very wrong?

WHO cares about their color?
IT'S only their skin.
WE should be more interested
IN what they have within.

SINCE we're all on earth together
CAN'T we just be friends?
ISN'T that the message
WE should want to send?

Jennifer Young

Day After Day

My heart for you is yearning,
Can't you see, my soul is burning.
No one makes me feel this way,
Thinking of you, day after day.

I know you've been with me from the start,
As I live without you, my lonely heart.
The day we move to that perfect farm,
My dream's coming true, I'll be in your arms.

What we have has always been true,
That's how I know I'll always have you.
Please don't ever let me miss,
The way you hold me, the touch of your kiss.

I now have someone to love,
We shall remain, now and above.
I know that you love me in every way,
Now we have each other, day after day.
Connie Beard

Blind Date

Nervous
Can't sleep
Can't seem to rest my feet

   I've seen your shadows in pictures
    Beautiful contours
    Beautifully formed

I feel your movements within me
Your soul takes over mine
God's creation confined

   Tomorrow we meet face to face
   My spirit lifts me
    Loving unconditionally

Big bright eyes
Like Big Sister's
Smiles like Daddy's
Sentiments for Mommy.

   I Love You
   Just wanted you to know
   That
   We longed for your coming.
Jeanne Mawak-Breen

Empty

   I'm empty, something's wrong
can't figure out what it is
   keep making the same mistakes
over and over again
   I have what is takes
   I say to myself
   and others say to me
But I never do it or get it done
   I need to fulfill what's to be
   I can be more
   but I never am
   Can't motivate the soul
   The body and mind are stuck some place
   That should have been left far behind
   but it holds me back
   Drags me down
   Pulling me backwards in line
Jackqueline Gass

You Are

You are the starlight of the evening
   Candle like moonbeams in the night
Warm sunshine on a cold grey morning
   You are my heart's memories delight.

You are the lark song in the meadow
   A peaceful river flowing calmly by
Wild flowers painting a grassy hillside
   You are the gentle raindrops in the sky.

You are my first kiss and my last kiss
   And I knew someday you'd die
But how I sorely miss you
   You are the teardrop in my eye.

You are finished with your journey
   But mine has yet to come.
Dearest I'll hold you again in heaven
   When my last long day is done.
You are my one true love,
   You are my setting sun.
Drew Von Watson

Gold Strike

In the early days, along the canyon floor,
came the men to claim the golden ore.
Shacks sprung up; then families came,
living only to play the hunting game.

From one to another, the words were told,
that in Galena Canyon there was gold.
More and more came, as word went around;
crowding in by the score, to dig the ground.

Laughter of the children, at their play,
sounds of the picks all through the day.
Early and late the men worked their claim;
Silently praying to strike the richest vein.

Some where so very lucky, hitting it big;
hopelessly, others continued to dig.
Many stayed on, but with hidden fears
others left with heartache and tears.

Now they are all gone, but those who sleep,
leaving the canyon, her treasures to keep.
Today there is a hush on the canyon floor...
....no one is there claiming the golden ore.
Billye Freeman

Remembering

   At the time we parted darkness
came...now I strike a match and hold a flame...
   Your picture in hand and a crack
in my heart. Searching for answers
in a glowing spark...
   Longing a glimmer to see in your
eyes. A movement if any would be a great
surprise...
   Looking back at the moments we shared
in time. With that sparkle in your eyes
and also in mine...
   Looking back at the times you were
here by me. Never would have thought,
now apart we'd end up to be...
   Glancing above at the stars and the sky.
I'm so lost and confused, expecting some
reply...
   The match now shrivelled, and it's
light in doom...Reality is I'm alone
in my room... Remembering
Darcey Starnater

Rubber Duckie

I'm sitting in a little pool
called a rubber kayak.

Swing dip.
Swing dip.

I paddle out to battle.

Ludwig, yes, Ludwig
my big fierce enemy.

Swing dip.
Swing dip.

A rush of water
a rush of nerve.

Push.
Push.
Push.

Faster.
Faster.
Faster.

The wall of water goes
SMACK!
In my face.
Etta Taylor Meyer

The Drunkard's Warning

Again the ale doth have me
by the scruff and by the tail.
And soon a man will grab me,
Then through the door I'll sail.
The sidewalk's there to greet me.
It's cold upon my face.
These things to men aren't strangers
who drink at such a pace.
So, if the spirits call you
with merriment in mind,
The key is moderation,
or concrete's kiss you'll find.
With you I leave this warning,
but if you fail to heed,
at least, go to a country inn
where in the grass you'll bleed.
David A. Haack

Untitled

I'd rather spend the night
by the fire in your heart
in it
I feel the warmth
that frees me
like a breezy summer night

I'd rather spend my time
at least a good part of it
watching the sun sleep
feeling your heart beat
knowing our love grows
like the meadow grass

I'd rather spend these golden moments
here by the ocean
digging my feet in the sand
next to yours
feeling your touch
your kiss
knowing you and finding myself
in your love for me
Deborah Elizabeth Foss

A Helping Hand

It follows you all your life
But you don't know it's there
It follows you all your life
But you don't even care
You never see it coming
And then one day you do
It's been coming for a long time
Then it jumps out at you
First you don't accept it
Then you know it's true
Someone who you love has died
Was it because of you?
You ask this question in your mind
Many times over again
When the answer you don't find
What will you do then?
It's hard to believe
And it's hard to understand
And you just won't find relief
Without a helping hand

Erica S. Harbatkin

Where Have You Traveled?

Waves, you slide up the sands,
But where have you been? To foreign lands?

To China? Or England? Spain? Or Rome?
Tell me where you make your home.

Possibly Norway? Maybe Sweden?
Do you stop? Where does it end?

Are you greeted kindly in every place?
Or does mankind simply turn his face?

Have you seen the peace and maybe war?
Been met by rich folk? Maybe poor?

Tell me great waves, with bubbling breath,
Have you dined with rats? Or met Elizabeth?

Tell me of adventures, then tell me this...
May I come, too? I won't be missed!

Please take me waves to your fantasy lands
And guide me there with your drifting hands.

As you glide off again, away from dry sands.
Send greetings for me to your wondrous lands.

Amanda Ingram

Corrupted World

At a distance
bullets fly through the air.
With the cops assistance
the fight still isn't fair.

The scream of pain.
The silence of death.
Are those people really sane?
Do we have the faith?

This world will never change.
People die because
they don't want to change.
Drugs are the cause.

Now an innocent child is dead.
When all his parents wanted
was for him to be safe in bed.

He was in the wrong place
at the wrong time.
All because people are greedy
just to make a dime.

April Young

Living In My Greatest Fear

The room is full of people,
But there's no one here.
My heart is filled
With my leftover tears.

This mask is working —
People think I see the light.
They don't look any deeper —
They don't think it's right.

The sky is crying,
For it understands;
It knows if help doesn't come,
Bloodshed will be my land.

My sleep is peaceful,
It's the only time to escape.
My everyday reality
To suffer is my fate.

The flowers bloom,
To spread fake cheer.
To live in pain and suffering,
Is my greatest fear.

Angela S. Barrow

The World Keeps Spinning

People laugh, people cry
But the world keeps spinning around.
People love, people hate
But the world keeps spinning around.
People live, people die
But the world keeps spinning around.
Despite of all that happens
The world keeps spinning around.
I wish I could deny
The world keeps spinning around.
No matter how hard I try
The world keeps spinning around.

John T. Barbouletos

The Fight

Life seems so great
   but the pressure is getting tougher
All my beliefs aren't straight
   and the road is getting rougher

My lips keep saying no
   While my heart and mind say yes
Is there any real way to know
   Without taking a guess

Some say it's wrong
   while the others say it's right
Will it take long
   to finally end this fight

If I choose the wrong way
   let it be right
Cause there will be a day
   when I will end this fight

Jennifer Lohse

Untitled

As I walk down the seashore,
and I see the sun fall.
It looks so big,
but it's really so small.
It's orange and yellow but,
it's so far away.
I wish I could catch it, very soon or today.

Annette Doyle

Dear Family

It isn't the NUMBER of gifts by the tree,
But the depth of love in the heart,
   that we see

Sometimes the heart and the gifts,
   SEEM like one
But our purses... and yours are all flat
   when its done

The wrappings are torn and the bare floor
   and tree... cry out,
"No No No! Just LOVE....
   You and Me!"

So, think of our Savior
   Who gave us this love
and mended our hearts by his love
   from above

Forget all the trappings of gifts
   by the tree
And keep the deep love in the heart that we see.

The family, the dinner... a gift here and there
Is all we could wish for... an answer to prayer

Eleanor M. Barnhart

Life

I try to touch the rainbow
But it's out of my reach.
So many lessons need to be taught
But no one wants to teach.

I've tried to see the sunlight
But the clouds won't part.
I've tried to find the answers
But my head contradicts my heart.

I've tried to ask the questions
But no one wants to hear.
Maybe they don't know how to reply,
Or maybe they just don't care.

I've tried to keep a bird in my hand
But it wanted to be free.
I guess my love wasn't good enough.
I guess it didn't need me.

I try to touch the rainbow
But it's just too far away.
That dark cloud's hanging over me...
Hope it's not planning to stay.

Crystal Singh

Untitled

The lost tear must fall
But its not for you at all
It there within, and cant be called
Till I know for whom it shall fall.

The well of tear's is empty now
Except for one more
who far?
When shall it come?
It may never fall
And stay with in the well

To know it there
Releases the despair
For I know
I have one more tear to fall

John W. Pallone

Untitled

There is a longing in me
But I know not how deep it has become.

It carries me upon a raging wind
  to cool waters of its well within.

And I feel as blossom yet unbloomed
  but beautiful and graceful
    as a yearning bud can be
  when she knows
    deep inside
    a blossoming soon will be.
Deitra McMahon

The Valley

I walk in the valley of fear
But I do not care
I want not to live
I want not to love
I will try anything once
I'll stay on it for good
For I walk not in the valley of fear
For I fear nothing
Not the death that I welcome
And wait for the day I cannot walk by
Anne M. Arndt

Do I Know You?

I know we've met somewhere before
But I can't remember when.
We've played in fountains pure and clear
We've walked a grassy glen.

We've seen the birds soar in the sky
As they sing their songs of praise.
Oh, tell me please, oh tell me do
When were those precious days?

I know those eyes, I've seen that smile,
And dimples that come and go.
Were we together in the some far land
And did our friendship grow?

I close my eyes and see us run
Up a steep and flower decked hill.
The haunting memory just won't stop
My heart will not keep still.

Do you also feel the chord
That binds us in some way?
I wish the cobwebs in my mind
Would let the memory stay.
Berniece MacGregor

Can I?

The light is on,
but I can not see.
I can't hear,
but the voice is there.
The woods are talking, saying, come on.
Can I turn on the light in my head.
I can hear the voice that says,
I am taking you to a world
with no,
Name,
No end.
I must die,
With a bullet through my
Head.
Jessica Stengel

Child's Fantasy

The grown people call me a child,
but I am God too
because all the palaces
and roads in the sand
under Grandfather's cottonwood trees
are mine, and the people are mine too,
and they are happy
because I am good to them,
and when I tear up their kingdoms,
I build them back every time.
David L. Hyde

Memories Of Our Hours

It was a night knowing no shame
But having moments of fear
It was not just a game
For the memories I hold dear.
But are these memories of our hours
Yellow roses and baby's breath
Or are they artificial flowers
Without life
But then without death
So then, he may go
The man I didn't know.
Judith H. Vierra

For Romance A Crumb

For romance a crumb,
but for the miracles of saints
the immoderate eye had done
where poet and verse pain
to win of its couple one;
astir line to bring
the mind and rose to heart;
for a lust uncomprehending
when the souls depart
and the sore unrelenting.

For each a finer course
the gilded soul will side by want
and saddle encumbered horse,
but from his stead will flaunt
the prize of loves recourse;
thorn and rose conspire
to court and scratch the gallantry;
mend and wound the old desire;
kiss and burn chivalry;
then stir the ash and fire.
John C. Welch

Bliss

Her arthritic fingers
brushed the white hair
from her wrinkled brow.
She sat on the porch
in her old rocking chair
and watched as the children
frolicked in the big yard.
Her life's struggles and
heartaches seemed so trivial now.
Her only regret was that her
lover and partner of some fifty
years was not there to share in
the laughter and the joy.
But then again, perhaps he was.
She smiled as a warm gentle
breeze softly caressed her skin.
Deborah S. Reed

Brave Hawks

There's evil on the ground
But Brave Hawks survey the land from above
They scout the world
They seek a home for their eggs
Eggs they sit long hours upon
Even the wind will not harm them
Brave Hawks know eggs become birds

Light pierces the night of the shell
And the days exist for the young
They do not fly
They do not hunt
But their mothers persist
Though many a fall
Though many a fall

Brave Hawks know students become teachers
For they see greatness
When there is but a shell
They see talons before there are feet
And they see flight before there are wings
John Hassler

I Got Gravy On The Brain

Granny made the bread
But Auntie made the gravy
They stood by the stove
They watched the oven quick

Salt and pepper exchanged hands
A little sugar with flower flowed
They rattled those pots and pans
the gravy drove you crazy
The batter simply glowed

All golden and brown
were these treats of creation
As warm and lovely
Were those expressions on their faces

To sit down to the table
and say Grandma pass the butter
While Auntie holds the ladle
cause I Got Gravy on the Brain.
Gary B. Nichols

Preconscious

It comes like an ocean breeze
But across the ocean floor,
Shimmering in the shifting sands
Of a time long ago.
Still it quickens the heart
And ripples the soul.

"The albatross, far from shore,
Follow him...
For he has some answers now."

But its Sunday and I can rest.
Tell me I don't have to fly.
Slow my heart and bind my soul
The view is fine from where I lie.

Is this my father speaking;
The poet who never wrote them down?
What good immortal words
When we each are just as gone as he?

"Grab that shaft of light
Before the crash of thunder rolls
And time stands still...."
Al Gietzen

To Wonder

It was not a command performance
But a voluntary volution of
A play of pigeons in ballet of flight.
Twelve there were before me facing west
In silhouette 'gainst the rain-promising sky
Fluid motion sustained as a single phrase
Borne aloft on Pacific currents.
Swirl of the corps in upwind spiral
To reveal soft blue of belly side.
Whorl of diving descent to display
Darker shadings of top grey wings.
In unison they banked, glided,
Came to rest on Spanish tiles, and
Drew in their wings for closing cadence.

With empathy and wonder
I stood in suspension to reflect -
What is your secret?
What do you know?
What mystery lets you
Fly so unfettered and free?

Julia S. Bailey

Anything But A Man

If I could be any thing
  but a man
I would be something as
  free as the wind
and white down on my
  fin
I would have a voice
that start's the day
and chases the rain
  away
the sky would be my limit
and on a mountain top I
  would sit
living in a cherry tree
loving the world I see

So if I could be anything
but a man, I would be
a bird in the palm of
GODS HAND!

Charly R. Davis

Fire

Fire is a force
burning in my soul
Fire is a red inferno
when put out a coal
Fire is the planet
in a million years
Fire is my enemy
or my worst fears
Fire is the look
in your sorry eyes
Fire is very dangerous
and somewhat a surprise
There's a fire in my soul
and it's burning bright
help me wash away the sun
and stop that endless fight.

Andrea Laggart

Curing Criminality

Today our world is overrun with crime
Brutality and killings are the norm
More police are offered as a cure
But changing the result does not end crime

The eschatology of crime has roots
Stages of community gone wrong
These episodes of life should be our boon
But when they fail, development is crushed

The story of our lives begins with home
A place children grow aright with care
Education is the second phase
Where mind and job development are prime

Next is joining the economic sphere
Where work begets a share of GDP
Then the citizens social life appears
Meeting people helpful in distress

Community of governance is last
With binding contract promoting common good
Community should be the order of today
And peace will reign in our society

Eugene E. Rennekamp

Untitled

Fantasy visits at midnight,
Breaking darkness in half.
Descending a sheer, treacherous wall
Made of vile things.
Forever, it seemed.

Suffocating on acridity of atmosphere
That choked sobs from satan himself.
Foul vapors of death and sickness,
Raw terror and agony,
Burnt and decaying flesh.

Balancing on a strip of ledge,
Dodging arrows of charging flame
Between endless abyss and bottomless pits
Of damnation.

A sea of tormented souls
Wailing, moaning, begging me.
I outstretch my hand. They theirs.
We cannot touch.
Our worlds separated by an inch
Of eternity.

Don Mathis

What Is Love?

Hands that raise the down and out,
Comfort who sorrow are in doubt,
Feet to walk among the poor,
Give them crumb they ask no more,
Ear to hear aborted children cry,
Unwanted, homeless old man sigh,
Eye to see where misery is,
Share hearth good will do this,
Voice that speaks gently to,
Abandoned, their smile comes through,
Heart that feels love has no end,
For one and all as a friend
   This is Love.

Amelia Nyers

Brandon Montana

Born on this day; my son,
Brandon Montana — Bradley Joseph;
A legacy has begun.

As he continues to grow older
I will love my son
And he will love me, his father.

He will be a gentleman
Brave, kind and wise
Beyond my expectation.

Behold, from my own blood; my son
I will see him crawl,
Then walk, then run.

He will run to win his place
Among the struggles and triumphs
Of life's rewarding race.

From the flicker of helpless infancy
To the blaze of gallant manhood,
He will enrich our noble legacy.

James Wesley Young

Fire

Like a flame
Bound under superior
Running undercover
Claustrophobia,
Chained by seclusion
Recognized excursion.

Like a flame
To a fire,
Genus to a race,
Nominating dermatology
Excluding democracy.

Like a flame
To a fire,
I'm trapped in hysteria,
Searching for a way out,
You see my desire...

Aron Chambers

The Sun And The Moon

Two heavenly bodies of wonder
Both high in the world up above
Each shows itself at a moment
Apart or together... that's love
The sun warms the waters of moonlight
The moon takes the heat from the day
One is so bold and bright shining
The other of mysterious ways
With moonlight comes calmness and peace
An ease to the fast racing day
The sunshine streams warm and almighty
Each soothes in their own special way
Two objects created for reasons
They both have a soul purpose why
You may see them apart while gazing
But they're always together in the sky.

Dawn Sharp

I Am

I am a daughter,
  Born to my parents,
    in a tiny town,
      BASSETT, ARKANSAS.

I am a Sister,
  I have Brothers and Sisters,
    from my family,
      Of which I am a part.

I am a Mother,
  I have a Daughter,
    Born to me, and her Dad,
      In St. Louis, Missouri.

I am a Grandmother,
  I have two Granddaughters,
    and one Grandson,
      All born in the State of Maryland.

I am a Great Grandmother,
  even though the twins died.
    All my blessings came from GOD.
      I am Forever "THANKFUL"!

Connie James

Together As One

Marriage is a loving
bond in which two people
become as one.

They will begin their
journey of married life
together as one.

Marriage is a road of
loving, knowing and respecting
one another and putting behind
the past and looking to the
future of sharing life
together as one.

Life of marriage can be very
enjoyable and, at times, unhappy.
But, as long as you have each
other and God's love in your hearts
You can take the good as well as
the bad, honoring and
respecting each other always.

Barbara Stefany

Whisper

Cold November air
blowing the dead leaves
across the frozen ground
They whisper to one another
Seasons change
My cold empty arms
held you but once
Now my heart whispers
to my soul
I want to hold him again
Seasons change
Let me hold you
Allow my soul to
Whisper to your soul
Allow my heart
to heal your heart
Let this become
A season of love
Let me whisper
Sweetly to you.

Jennifer Baughman

Love

Love is like a burning candle
blowing in the wind.
Taking all my hurt and loneliness
within.
The wind is whispering
like a shadow inside
your mind.
It feels sorrow
and crushed
and can't confide
love is a feeling
that everybody
has.
And all the hurting
is in the past.

Amanda Harris

Bless The Lord

Bless the Lord my brothers
Bless His holy name,
Thank Him that He saved you
From sin and death and shame.

Bless the Lord my sisters
For He has saved you too,
Love one another and work for Him
Be always kind and true

Bless the LORD together
Souls are there to save,
So get out there and witness
Be strong and bold and brave.

Bless the LORD ye children
Now your time is near,
To do your service for the LORD
Because HE is so dear

Gladys Olden

Kiss

the desert sigh
blazing stars
blind my eyes
heightened
awareness
no fear for the
blessed————warm air
      cool breeze
        comfortably
          forsaken thee
Across the endless night
the moon shines bright
everlasting love and life
begin tonight————
such an odd sensation
the flight of imagination
    rapture
      our destination
        you and I

Anne Ilgenfritz

Past, Present, Future

The past is energy;
burned. Stored in memory
are the past's by products.
The present is energy;
burning; using the fuel
stored in the future!

Joyce Kersell

A January Day

I awake to a rose-tinted dawn,
Black tree limbs with ice crystals on
Diamonds sparkling on pure white snow
Frost-white vines in the garden row,

January should bring a weary day
With endless time to while away
To dream of spring and flowers fair
And golden sunshine in the air.

But tell me, is not such a sight,
When everything is wrapped in white
A thing of beauty to behold
With bright jewels shining in the cold?

For twilight's pink I shall be glad...
Not waste my time with feeling sad
I would not wish my life away
I'll revel in this lovely day!

Doris E. Stebbins

Alaska

Alaska!
Black spruce
Struggling trees, stunted,
Scattered on rocky fields and mountains
Scarcely soil enough in which to cling.

Alaska!
Areas of wild summer flowers,
Lavender firewood, orange-yellow poppies
On quiet lakes, golden pond lilies.
Families of dark ducks swimming peacefully.

Alaska!
Majestic mountain peaks towering
In the distance, snow capped.
Huge rocks and boulders appeared
To be moving down the mountain sides.

Alaska!
White spruce
Tall, wide, beautiful, reaching skyward.
White barked birch, aspens, too.
Scattered patches of tundra, some in
bloom.

Berniece E. Warner

I Was Born

I was born bonded nor free,
Black nor white, good nor bad,
Right nor wrong. For I am of God's
earth, and who is to say whether it
be bound to any man or free to the winds
or whether it be bright as the flower gardens
or solemn as the graves of earth or whether
it is good soil for the harvest or soil
where only death may reap. Whether it
should prosper or stand motionless.
No, I know not why that I am or
what I must do. Yet, by God's wisdom
I will succeed for I "WAS" born.

Janet L. Bell

Candy Coated Rain Drops

  Falling on your head,
around the tears, that you left
beside my flowered bed.

Melissa Bragadin

Free

Yesterday
Bitter words, a slammed door
Today
A passionate embrace
But what of tomorrow?
Together - so far apart,
Alone we excel
Together we flounder.
The field
Our hearts once laughed and played in
Has turned to swamp.
It is with relief
I bid you good-bye
Good-bye
I am free!
I am free.

Chandra Elayne Downs

Difference Of The Sexes

There are many differences
between men and women.
 Most women are feeling, using
their emotions to touch the world.
While men uses his mind to solve
the world.
 If he can't see it or touch it,
it doesn't exist.
The total existence of most women
is that it doesn't have it exist to
exist. If she feels it than it is so.
If she can imagine it then it will be so.
 Too often I wonder why man can't
use his emotions for such knowledge.

Alicia LaVonghn Caesar

Adrift

He's gone.
Bereft, alone, empty.
Aching to speak with him, afraid to call.
"Let him take wing," they say.
He's free.
But where is my anchor?
No longer grounded.
Drifting, purposeless, drowning.

My son has left for college.

Diane Speare Triant

Untitled

I have fought the dragon
and slayed the beast
I've conquered the oceans and
have made the highest mountains
my sand castles
I have watched throughout time
As man has gone from strong
and daring
To weak and thoughtless
Watched cities of beauty crumble
Under greed and hate, people
forgotten, dreams shattered,
hopes set ablaze
I've seen true and blinding
Beauty twice on my long journey
upon your lips
And in your eyes

Dominic Faletti

In The Know - I'm Educated

How can I be so haughty, so proud,
Being in the know I'm educated.

If others would only know that
You don't know
How much you have to know
In order to know
How little you do know!

But then, I'm educated
You know, in the know!

If up-front I'm so haughty,
Unseemingly so very proud,
Then I don't know nothing
About being in the know.

But then, I'm educated,
You know-in the know!
Now that we're all educated
Let's remember to be knowledgeable.

Alfred Sheldon Hanly

Special Time

There is a special time when men
begin to think what they will do
with long eventless days ahead
and there is an end to strife

That time when men
measure their accomplishments
and check their headlong pursuit
of the golden fleece of life

That special time means
something else to you my love
with scarce a pause to speculate
Now catch a breath to evaluate

Facing new problems and challenge
Discouraged even in lonely fights
Still gallant in your wall
to redirect, turn wrong to right

Yes, there is a special time
When men like you so rare
Grasp the chance to live and love
Consider timed to dare

Eugenia Hummel

Emotional Turmoil

My anger - I suppress
Because of love - I transgress
My dreams - reality shatters
My hopes - some joy, some laughter
My nights - lonely and cold
My tears - multiply tenfold
My happiness - always taken away
To keep my sanity - each night I pray
My fears - bombarded by constantly
My future - I dread to see
My hate - each day gets greater
Bad experiences - made me braver
My life - filled with so much pain
Pessimism - I try to reframe
My heart - broken beyond repair
My brain - distracted by so much despair
My weakness - I'd rather not say,
My strength - hope for a better day
For now that's all
The bottom line - emotional turmoil

Cheri Miller

All Alone

The anger builds up inside me,
Because nothing can I think of,
Will punish him for what he did,
To the friend I love.

He hurt her so horribly,
She is now damaged for life,
Having to deal with the pain,
Hoping she won't result to her knife.

It kills me to see her like this,
It makes me want to kill him,
I want her to stop crying,
But the chances are (so) slim.

I want to hug and hold her,
Tell her it's alright,
But the chances once again,
Are ever so slight.

The only way I know,
Is she called me on the phone,
But because we live so far away,
Now she's all alone.

Emily Leonard

Worship

Worship is sacred to me,
Because it cleanse me and sets me free.
It makes ne offer everything to God,
And in doing his will, we will
never be apart.
I love God, more than I can say,
And I offer myself to him
each and everyday.
Let me always glorify thy name,
And never ever, worship you in vain.
Let my worship be true in every way.
for I hive to serve thee every day.

Gregory Kelly

"A Daily Prayer"

Raindrops on my window
beam of light shining through...
blades of grass are glistening
with early morning dew.

I'd reach out to touch it
if it didn't fade away...
even if it dries up
tomorrow's another day.

I hear the birds are chirping
chanting their sing - song tune...
here in my secret garden
where all my flowers bloom.

To touch a single petal
I'm feeling a new life...
enchanting as a fragrance
a man would give his wife.

The sun it sets suddenly
giving a dark warm glow...
A sigh escapes my lips
as I wait on the morrow.

Jeanette K. Elkins

Thoughts In A Graveyard

Then stranger let no ill timed tear
Be shed for those that slumber here,
But rather envy them the sleep,
From which they ne'er can wake to weep

Yet if thou hast learnt to seen
With feeling eyes the fate of man,
Go weep for those still doomed to sorrow,
Who mourn the past nor hope the morrow

For those whose tears must ceaseless flow,
Whose minds of pain each morn renew,
Who if they dream but dream of woe,
And wake to find their visions true.

Burton L. Strid

My Special Friend, You

I'll be kind, I'll be happy;
Be it at home, at school, or at play.
I'll reach out my hand in brotherhood,
For I want to be your friend always.

I want to be there in your time of great joy,
When you win the trophy or game.
I want to be there when you're hurting too,
And you go on crying in the rain.

I also want to share in your laughter and fun,
With a beautiful rainbow in view.
I want to walk the long dusty trail,
With my special friend, you.

Florence E. Weaver

To A Bride And Groom

May the beauty of this moment
Be forever in your dreams.
May the world and all its ferment
Ne'er intrude upon your schemes.

May you always hold to tenets
Which this holy day fills your heart.
And may all those distant planets
Ev'ryone be gone before you'd part.

May the words of one much older,
Who has traveled down the road,
As he speaks across his shoulder...
Would you listen... may he be heard?

Each, please, give to one another,
Your tomorrows you may not see...
That is lovers secret. No other...
Love you give. Else love cannot be.

Chris W. Carr

Thoughts Of Sand

Lay me on the shore
Bake me in the sun
Sweep me into the waters
Let the waves crash upon me
Squish me between your toes
Play with me and take me home

Mix me with water, and change my shape
Build me into a beautiful castle
I am the makings of an hourglass
Change me into glass
I endure the changes of time
I always was and always will be

Brandy Dzerigian

Untitled

Asleep in my hollow body
Awake in thy mind
So refine and so solid
Is my soul. It allows
Me to feel nothing evil
But at the same time it
Is always in control.

Fear has no place in my heart
Cause I have no time to be
Fearful. My destiny is built
Around my fate as my fate relies
On my actions. If at any point
In time. I shall grow weak, my
Body will become the dirt you walk
On and my soul shall become the
Air you breathe. Take my thoughts
And devour them like nutrients
For everything I think of will
Later become food for life.

Ebony Joy James

Seasons Changing

Summer's gone, been put to bed.
Autumn's here with shades of red.
Winter's waking with it's frigid wind.
Spring's far away, like a long lost friend.

James K. Bright

Petals

If I could gather all the flowers
At the first hard frost.
To put in old books I've never read.
Drying on yellow paper and grey letters,
With crushed perfume in musty words.
Could I capture the golden autumn light?
With the faded glory of petal and scent.
Or would someday they flutter out?
Tissue thin and brittle.
To break on the floor
Without a memory.

Carri Gunderson

Untitled

I visited the sea one day,
At the brink of dawn.
And as I sat there at its side,
Its hand reached out to mine.
And it whispered in my ear,
"I love you."
And to this I answered,
"How can you love that which you know not?"
And laughing like a gentle breeze,
It whispered back to me,
"How can you not?"

David J. Ciesla

Quiet Time

Come rest a while in the quiet meadow,
As the twilight dusk grows deep.
The silent edge of the night grows still,
As the world is lulled to sleep.
The song of the wind in the rustling leaves,
Is a lullaby born of love.
And the mist rolls out, in a blanket as soft
As the down on the wings of a dove.

Grace Behabetz

Precious Daughter

In memory of Bonnie

We feel you beside us each day,
As the sunlight dances in the wind,
And delicate stars twinkle at night.
The dew of early morning
The rain that touches our face.
The glorious shades of the rainbow
That promises God's love.
We know you're waiting for us
Beyond tomorrow's sunrise.

Brenda G. De Boer

Ode To A Gallant Lady

Soft winds sigh their requiem,
as the sun sinks gently in the west
Saying thoughts of a gentle lady,
at peace in her eternal rest.

May the love of God,
in his own immortal way
Take her into his presence,
at the close of her mortal day.

Herman A. Wedemeyer

Four Seasons

Sunflowers are as golden
As the summer sun.
White carnations are as white
As winter snow.
Fall is like children playing in the leaves.
Spring is a young child's
Voice in the wind.

Adrienne Elizabeth Kinsey

In God's Time

A touch of sadness in the air,
As summer comes to end.
The lazy, hazy days are gone.
Cold winter's around the bend.

Singing birds have disappeared,
From their nesting trees.
Summer gardens are now bare.
Except for falling leaves.

Things change, but God does not.
To everything there's a season.
We can not know what his purpose is.
But in God's time there's a reason.

Faye Teague

Little Storms

When two satanic clouds collide
And turn the twilight sky to dust
The whipping wind cannot abide
That these two forces join in lust
Their only purpose to destroy
The marriage of the sky and sea
The thrusting thunder clouds employ
Disrupts the perfect harmony

Till climax rides on silvered light
That bursts the darkening sky to flame
And every creature quickens flight
Refusing parts in nature's game

Then morning sun peeks out and warms
The dying chill of little storms.

Barbara Vecchione Yablansky

Untitled

I witnessed something special today.
As seconds became minutes,
on how darkness avoids light.
Vice versa...
The making and ending of
friendships and friendships to be,
struck my attention.
And a new relationship was discovered.
Bringing light to the dark.

Later, I rediscovered that
my minutes became hours, and so on.
Vice versa...
The creation of smiles and laughter
and laughter from smiles, caught my eye.
As a door was shut and a wave goodbye.
And for a brief moment bliss was bred.
Bringing light to the dark.
   Jason Tickle

The Question Of Life

I'm alone in heart and soul
As my mind keeps telling me so
Feelings always in my way
The tolls of life I have to pay

I try to look at the good
But in my life who could
I dream of love and of marriage
Wake to a nightmare my empty carriage

Should I give the reaper his token
After these words I have spoken
Should I torment everyone
My peace of mind has been undone
   Jim Darling

Of Dreams To Run Again

Asleep last night a dream swept by
   as mountain air was still;
Out there I ran cross-country high
   once more along the hill!
This time I wore a business suit
   each foot a reg'lar shoe;
Yet seemed to glide in fast pursuit
   all steps again were true!

As I awoke from slumber low
   with body still as sore;
No fleetness of the years ago
   nor speed of hours before!
Now cane to balance struck-down gait
   as slow each step has been;
But I must tell you as I wait
   of Dreams to run again!
   Joe Wehrly

Spinning

As a child I played with time
   as it went spinning by,
Turn, turn, turn, more silent
   than a sigh.
Green to gold, gold to black,
Time will never bring green back.
Faster and faster time raced on,
I tried to catch it but it was gone.
My youthful years have gone
   away I'll be a child nevermore,
For time has silently shut her door.
   Julia Miller

Mysterious Orb

What mysterious orb meets my eye
As it slowly passes by —
Sailing through the starry night
Like a graceful bird in flight;

Bathed in gentle luminous glow —
White as silk and soft as snow;
Hidden by a veil of clouds
That Mother Night alone enshrouds;

Noble as a ship of state
That's gone to meet some watery fate,
This orb that sails on through the sky
Shall never falter, never die;

It's there for all the world to see,
To know the common destiny
That binds all mankind with creation —
Flowers, creatures, every nation;

God, from His great Wisdom Store,
Has given us an open door
Through which, if we but try to see,
Lies Heaven and Eternity.
   Judy Koopman

Today...

My mind burns with a flame-like intensity
as it experiences the confusions
of today's people
Love is diminishing
hate is demonishing
my eyes your eyes
his eyes her eyes
scarred with the visions
of all of our actions
and reactions
We're killing our own nation
on this so-called God's creation
as the excavations
of our expectations
in ourselves
begin
leading our future
into the vacant world of
extinction
   Jeffrey Tovar

Life

   Life moves pretty fast,
   As I sit here I think about
all the days that have whittled
away,
   All the people that have
died,
   When is it going to be my
time?
   Will my clock stop an hour
late or early?
   I wish I could wind the clock
back up,
   But that's only a dream,
   You can't get another
lease on life,
   Once it's expired that's it,
   Don't let your life go to
waist.
   Cindy Blinn

Thoughts Of You

Thoughts of you dance in my head,
As I lay awake in bed.
Through the nights come my fears,
As thoughts of you bring me tears.
As I walk alone at night,
Thoughts of you hold me tight.
When we're so very far apart,
Thoughts of you flood my heart.
When I hurt and cannot cope,
Thoughts of you give me hope.
When there's nothing else to do,
I remember thoughts of you.
   Heather Ann Hipps

Prayer Of A Planter Fir Tree

Dear God above,
   As fir tree small I lend my worth
   To help Keep Christmas on the Earth
   Once hopefully I yearned to share
   A ballroom grand, an urban square,
   Bright life aboard a ship afloat,
   Homes fires of those of wealth or note,
   And to know the thrill of gay array

Now, God,
   From thoughts mundane I turn away
   Hence prayerfully I live to cheer
   Someone in circumstance austere,
   A lonely child in Hospice kind,
   The halt, the needy, yes, the blind.
So, God,
   If I may scatter joy some way
   Then well I'll keep your Christmas Day!
   Hope Hathaway Kent

A Simple Countryside

I'm not pretending to be busy
   As by my fire I sit,
With thoughts so dark and gloomy
   As a room e're lamps are lit.

But then I chanced to look outside
   And lo! The gloom is gone!
A miracle has taken place
   Since breaking of the dawn

Did you ever hear the quiet
   Of a thousand snow flakes falling?
Did you ever feel the beauty?
   It's really quite appalling.

Each flake works its awesome magic
   As it falls and settles down,
Covering with lacy petticoats
   The ugliest of the town.

There's no ending to the joys
   Of a simple country side,
If only one will take the time
   To let the quiet abide.
   Inez Barlow

California

   On the outside I am dry
and hot but on the inside
I am moist and damp.
I am very big with trees and bees
and I am getting crowded with people
and things.
   Clayton Keeling

The Passing Of Autumn

Could it be that winter's close at hand,
As autumn creeps o'er all the land?
She sweeps the green of summertime
In mounds of color with dots of pine.
And with her brush, so wide and bold,
Paints the world in shades of gold.
Yellow, brown and crimson too,
Are splashed against an azure blue.
Fall spreads her cover over all,
'Til man can only gaze in awe.
Now she's touched the very sky
And in her haste she hurries by.
And though we long that she might stay,
Season's need she rush away.
Then comes the soft and rustling breeze,
With sunny days and falling leaves,
"Til trees stand dark and bare.
And with that special chill to air,
Frost coated fields she leaves behind.
Even autumn yields to God's own time.

Ida Mae Hill

Black

Black black
As a witches cat
As a starless summer nights sky

Black black
As an endless ditch
As a tree at night whooshing by

Black black
As a frozen dream
As the blink of a wizards eye

Black black
As the stillness of night
As the deep dark waters lullaby

Jennifer Venn

Reclaiming My Spirit

The darkness enclosed over my spirit,
as a void had clouded my mind.
The thoughts I'd lost and good I fought,
was very hard to find.

And as my skin turned hard and cold,
I saw in the darkness, a light.
I light to guide me through
the evils that I was to fight.

And in the most inner parts of my heart,
I felt a warmth return.
And soon it felt as if my veins were
about to boil and burn.

In horror frozen eyes I saw the
stillness of the quiet.
For all the time of never listening, I soon
became ready to buy it.

With wallowing might and piercing scream,
I shattered the disturbing peace around.
And in a rush of love and hate my
thoughts I'd finally found.

Anna Smith

Ode To Debbie And Gail

Your loving, caring hands,
 are busy every day;
Molding things more precious
 than little bits of clay.
You're shaping little children,
 Our Lord's favorite things.
Building up their bodies,
 to grab life's highest rings.

The times we've shared together
 in the past and still to be;
Are cherished inspiration,
 To parents such as me.
We often take for granted,
 that very special one;
Who does the very hardest task,
 and makes it look like fun.

My prayer each day to God above,
 is one of thanks for you;
For sending you into our Lives,
To help make our dreams come true.

Judy Cooper

Words Can't Explain Your Feelings

anger accumulates inside you.
You're in a great state of confusion.
Your mind goes blank and
you don't know how to reply.
People begin to keep their distance;
Nobody can feel your pain.
There are many things you wonder about,
questions that can't be answered.
Your knowledge can only go so far...
In love

Anna Lee Sanchez

The Lord's Test

As each little tragedy strikes
 and your world seems to fall apart,
Grab, hold and stand to fight
 don't let depression start.

Feeling you've tried your very best
 and your mind wants to close and rest,
Remember the happiness of yesterday
 yes remember -
 but most of all pray.

As this is all in the testing of God
 His goal is to make you so strong,
So He lets life seem so hard
 yes - He lets it all seem so wrong.

And though He knows you can make it alone
 He wants you to see the rewards
Of having yourself to help you always
 of having passed our
 "Test of the Lord."

Arlene Colorusso

Silver Cinders

Silver cinders cling to tips of cedar hands
After a summer's rain, late afternoon,
Lush residue immobile in a silent sleep —
Until man's lights, unseeking, sweep a swathe
Across the lair of shyly lingering drops,
And thousand liquid eyes smile love's reprise.

John Lenox

The Beauty Of Love

Look into the true beauty of love,
And you will feel a movement in your soul.

Experience the glory of love,
And your heart will dance.

Follow the path of love,
And you will always be guided.

Plant seeds in the garden of love,
And they will always bloom.

Stop along the way to smell the flowers,
And you will bask in their perfume.

Be intoxicated with the emotions of love,
And feel an eternal natural euphoria.

Never stop believing in the strength of love,
And your soul will never feel alone.

Elizabeth Scruth

Fall Fantasy

I went for a walk in the woods today
And you were there with me.
Of course we didn't really go.
It was a fantasy.

I never saw the sky more blue,
The aspens more aglow.
The mountains shone majestically
Covered with new snow.

The air was crisp, the sun was warm,
Our heartbeats were in rhyme.
Each moment etched a memory
To brighten some dark time.

The leaves would rustle as we walked.
Their fragrance filled the air.
With every breeze more tumbled down.
One landed in your hair.

The sun is sinking in the west.
Our fantasy must end.
Come soon and walk again with me
My gentle loyal friend.

Clara J. Keske

Night

If I were a star
And you were the night
Off in the far
I'd shine for you bright

Seen in the eyes
Piercing so bright
Reflecting the skies
The beauty of night

Taking your breath
Howl the wind blows
Dark as near death
Yet casting shadows

Bright as the moon
My love I will shine
Never to soon
Will I make you mine

Take off your cast
So let it be
Let our love last
Eternally.

Johnny Crouse

Passage Of Time

The sun will rise, the sun will set
And yet another day is met.

Awakened from a world of dreams.
Yesterday's gone so far it seems.

And now a new day we must face
Prepare ourselves to keep the pace

Try to make the hours last
For soon another day will pass

Tomorrow's fast approach is near
The passage closes year by year

Take each day as it comes
And learn to live another one.

Sane in mind and sane in soul
Is good for me as I grow old

Stars that shine is time reflected
On your passage that's unprotected

Like an hour glass that spills its sand
Your futures fate is in times hand.

Allen Becker

I'll Not Think Of Her

When all the tears are shed and dried,
And waves have fled the ebbing tide;
When there's no warmth in summer time,
And verse has lost both rhythm and rhyme;

When I forget that there's a sky,
And bumble bees and bluebirds fly;
When I forget in dark of night
That with the morning comes the light;

When sound is mute from beaten drums,
And it's not cold when winter comes;
When there's no heat from raging fire,
Then, I'll forget my heart's desire.

When I lose thought of yesteryear,
And everything that I hold dear;
When other thoughts are left behind,
There'll still be someone on my mind.

When sleeping lovers cease to dream,
And love is not the poet's theme;
When the final shooting star's a blur,
Perhaps, then, I'll not think of her.

Charles E. Mieir

No Boundaries

The voices I hear in my head
are only whispers from the past.
Reflections at the side of my bed
are only images that won't last.
Midday nightmares floating in my mind
crumble to dust and ash.
   Live, for the power.
   Love, for love's sake.
   Die, say never.
The cards that father fate deals to me
are only rhythms for my purchase.
Limitations on abilities
are only locks that I have cast.
Late night crossroads calling to my soul
rumble a lustful wish.
   Live, for the power.
   Love, for love's sake.
   Die, say never.

Carole J. Eberly

"The Awakening '93"

Today arrived
   and ushered in
My prior visions
   and my dreams.

My anxious search
   and constant cries
Have led to paths of
   tangible replies.

I'll cross my rivers
   and my streams
On shallow waters
   I may swim.

Hurdle my mountains
   and my sloping hills
Challenge my heart
   my intellectual trails.

My faith can anchor,
   doubts and fears be gone
Rain me Ethereal Power
   I am not alone.

Elma Diel Photikarmbumrung

To Remember

Gettysburg, Pennsylvania
The ground is covered with stones of gray,
And under each a soldier lay,
Never again to see the rain,
No more to feel joy or pain.

For they have nothing more to dread,
No sounds of war or ground blood red,
No more to face the rivals gun,
For them the final battle's done.

All were brave no cowards here,
They died for what they held so dear,
Preserve the Union at all cost,
In doing so each life was lost.

The names of some beneath the sod,
They're known only to their God,
While others here beneath the stone,
Their date of birth and name are known.

But names mean nothing to these dead,
Each has a stone above his head,
Among the trees and grassy hill,
In our prayers you're remembered still.

Jim Crosiar

Weathering The Storm

If we have stormy weather
and trials to bear,
Just remember God has
lovingly put them there,
For like roses need rain to grow,
Before they can let their beauty show.
So these heartaches we must bear,
That we may know, God's loving care
Into his beauty then we can grow,
And to those around us it will show
Then in their hearts, they surely must
Know how it pays in God to trust.
So let's bow our heads and without pain
Praise our Lord for the rain

Donald Berry

A New Beginning

I watched the morning sun come up
And touch the trees with gold.
The birds awoke to greet the day
With voices sweet and bold.
Breezes wafted gently in
With honeysuckle bred.
The room was filled with brightness
And all the shadows fled.

A rooster crowed to let the world
Know a dawning had arrived.
That through a dark and lonely night
A spirit had survived.
My mind was filled with gladness
Despair was there no more.
I turned and said goodbye to grief
And softly closed the door.

Betty Jeanne Tatum

Kamaaina

The Salts have seen the China Station
   And too, the Red Lead Row,
But when they want to settle down
   Then here's the place they'll go.
The jewel of the Pacific, where the
   Rich man takes his bride
To watch a cloud-swept sunset
   Fade out at eventide.
There's a garden at Moana where
   They serve the finest rums
'Neath the overhanging branches
   Of a Banyan's spreading runs.
In the gentle shades of evening
   When the moonlight comes to rest
And the silken surf rolls inward
   Then recedes back to the West.
Where the rhythm of the palm trees
   Is melted into song
And leis of floral splendor
   Spell Aloha, warm and long.

Burton Flower

Untitled

I could sit here for hours
and think to myself over and over
"What am I feeling inside?"

But I don't think I would
find an answer. Maybe because I am
trying too hard to figure it all out.

All I know is that I have this
feeling inside — this uncontrollable,
undeniable feeling. It's a feeling that
misses you as soon as we walk away
from one another. It's a feeling that
leaves me thinking of you late at night
when I am trying to sleep and it's a
feeling that puts you on my mind before
my eyes are wide open in the morning.

It's just this feeling, this uncontrollable,
undeniable feeling, that won't go away...

I guess if that's what love feels like
then I love you.
It's that simple.

Jennifer A. Therian

Reflections

I stand here looking,
and there you are
Gazing back at me -
Admiration shining in
your eyes!

As I twist and turn
Your movements are
in tune with mine,
Graceful, alluring,
fascinating.
What a precious gift
is mine.

Satisfaction shivers
through me
And I see you,
self-confident,
Gazing at me,
knowing you are
Reflecting the best
in me there is.

Eleta Creutz

The Sea

Rolling high are its salty waves,
And then in gentle motion,
They cease to roll, they settle down,
Thus the way of an ocean.

A sailor boy loves for the wind to blow,
But the fisherman prays for calm,
The fisherman and the sailor boy,
Get aught from the sea as alm.

When man he braves the ocean waves,
And takes to the wild rough sea,
He should go with a fearless heart,
And without a family.

Because the demon that he braves,
When he takes his life in his hands,
Would gladly take that life at stake,
And wash it dead on the sands.

Annie Coggin

I Have Set Flight

My frustrations were high,
and their expectations were low.
I wanted to soar,
they wouldn't let go.

To me, God is a Man
and my Dad hung the moon.
Men are presidents
and no woman would be soon.

I fell into place
and quit trying to fly.
My place in their world
was just to BE, and then to die.

Now I've broken the rules,
and I'm out on my own.
I've entered a world
that I've never known.

I am a woman and a person,
and my future is bright!
I am strong, I am smart,
and I have set flight!

Elaine Jarrard

Someone

The future's always far ahead,
and the past isn't far behind.
Always trying to be something more,
more than who we are.
Searching for an identity,
one we can call our own.

Looking for someone to remember us,
to comfort us,
to be like us.
We drift among the stars,
trying to find someone, something,
so we won't be alone.

Jamie Whitmire

Always

When the sun has burned out completely,
  And the earth has turned red as rust.
My soul will love you as sweetly,
  Though my body hath turned into dust.

And always will have a new meaning,
  As each star in turn fades away.
Until only one light is left gleaming,
  And the end of time is that day.

Then nothing shall stand between us,
  When our essence is not clothed in flesh.
As the end of life brings a stillness,
  And the strands of our souls enmesh.

Carol Grubbs

Stay By My Side

When the spinning gyrations stop
  And the center doesn't hold
  Stay by my side

When things falls apart
  And troubles flood our lives
  Stay by my side

When the moonlit nights have lost their glow
  And darkness fills our time
  Stay by my side

When love doesn't attract you any more
  And faith has lost its hold
  Stay by my side

When communication has lost its thread
  And silence stills our thoughts
  Stay by my side

When the journey of life is done
  And death cloaks our souls
  Stay by my side

Harshi Syal

The Marker

I touch the marker, trace the name.
Can it be real? Are these the same?
The granite is cold, though touched by sun.
I can't believe, I feel so numb.
So short a time and you were here,
To talk, smile, touch your face so dear.
Oh, God I ache. Tears wet the grave.
I miss you so - I must be brave.
I stand and turn to leave alone.
But part of my heart lies neath that stone.

Alphretta Meginnis

Untitled

As the sun sets over the water
And the beautiful day comes to an end
Many thoughts of you pass through our minds
Happiness for the peace that you'll now find

Memories of you, we have to treasure
Times of joy and times of pleasure
We know our lives will never be the same
But in our hearts you'll always remain

The tears we shed are tears of love
For now you walk with the Lord above

As we go on from day to day
We cherish the thoughts that we'll be
together again some way.

Barbara Melo

Stand Still

There is only one answer.
And the answer is to face
whatever comes your way.

Turn those obstacles into opportunities.
In time, you will find the way.

Don't let your past drag you down.
Don't let your future worry you so.
Don't let today be an ordinary day.

Let yourself be free and spontaneous.
Let today be a juicy and a sour moment.

Amy S. Ng

Oscar The Oyster

Always at a clambake
And swimming with the crowd,
He would shimmy and shake,
But not very loud
Because
Oscar the Oyster
Didn't have a pearl
To rattle his shell.

When courting he went,
The ladies were so fickle,
To sea he was sent,
Since he could not tickle.
Oh
Oscar, poor Oscar
Didn't have a pearl
To get him a girl.

An outcast he became,
He wondered what to do;
So Oscar gave up the game
And now rests in a stew!

Hank Forte

A New Day

I awoke this morning to the light of the sun.
And then I knew a day had just begun.
I heard the chirping sounds of the birds.
And they were so beautiful, like foreign words.
Awaking with the sun so bright.
I know now the real delight,
of seeing heaven come alive with the sun.
And knowing of this day's new fun!

Darlene L. Graham

My Potpourri

I opened a ginger jar,
And sweet fragrance filled the air
Of an old-fashioned garden,
From the contents that were there.

I envisioned sunny days
And bees among the flowers,
Butterflies and trilling birds,
A sundial counting hours!

A garden of long ago,
Sealed in petals in a jar,
Still living in the spirit,
As all my memories are.

All kinds of flower petals
Make sweet-smelling potpourri,
Just as sad and happy days
Make up my memories.

As time goes by, the mixture
Of my recollections, grows,
The loss and tears are spices,
Joys, the petals of the rose.

Anna Belle Jeffries

How The Spirit Is Born

When windy waters blow,
and stars shine so bright they blind you,
There are spirits roaming the moon,
Waiting in line for a new life,
to enter into the world.

When a child awaits a spirit,
it is waiting for a mind,
power and a personality.

Then in one cry to the universe,
a child is born.
The spirit is welcomed into a new life.
That is how the world has been changed;
Spirits have changed it.

One day my body will die,
and then I will be free from this life
To be welcomed to start a new one.

Angel Nava

Reflections

Of all the guys I ever knew
And soon put down with no regrets
No one could love the way you do
And every kiss went to my head

If Valentino played the game
You really do put him to shame
All avenues of love explored
And every single one adored

Though I can't tell you face to face
I write these missives in their place
I want you so to know I care
And should you need me
I'll be there

And sometimes when I'm alone
And had a busy day
Reflections of the past we knew
Stay with me every day

Evelyn Carter

Frustrated Fisherman

The other day I got my pole
And some of my fishing gear
Put on old clothes, and donned my hat
And drove down to the old pier

I baited up and tossed in the line
Out where the pilings lay
And waited oh, so patiently
Like an ancient bird of prey

The hours pass, and still no move
From weary bobber floating
My patience gone, my nerves are taut
My face in anger, bloating

Oh wily fish, I'll snare you yet
From fortress dark and deep
I'll find some bait that you desire
To make resistance weak

And when you take that first big bite
Don't wait for a second try
Then I will be the conqueror
And you'll be my fish fry.

Francis D. Getman

Something To Think About

If we could look into the future
And see just a few years ahead,
If we could have all we ask for
And be pleased with all that is said
If we never had to worry
And need never to plan ahead,
Do you think we would all be happy?
With nothing at all to dread?
What would we have to live for?
Why even get out of bed??
That's why GOD gave us rivers to cross
And tall steep mountains to climb.
HE knew it would keep us busy
And that's why he gave us a mind.
That's why HIS book tell us,
Just take one day at a time.
HE will comfort, rest and soothe us
And help us to stop and unwind.
And we will get an extra BONUS
HE WILL GIVE US PEACE OF MIND

Gladys Cox

One Of A Million

In me there is a thunderous calm.
And I know Malcolm...Medgar...
And Martin...are at peace
smiling down on this sea
of Black Masculinity.
Gathered in full view of the world
standing tall shoulder to shoulder
brother to brother bonded in unity.
All hands reaching back lifting up.
One small step on a road too long
untraveled.
One million plus gathered before
symbols of former slave owners
and he...who coincidently
broke the link of bondage
still we struggle to unravel
the chains.

James Mel Brooks

Love On Silver Wings

Though I might get angry
And say things I don't mean,
There's a battle going through me,
Though unheard and unseen.

There's a side made of anger,
Of hate and unconcern;
The other side is love and hope
And beautiful things in turn.

Though I say things falsely
And say some awful things,
I want you to know, I
Have a love on silver wings.

It flies above every mountain,
It soars through every sea;
It dances on every loving, lis'ning heart,
And it returns to me.

So if I do ever hurt you
Or "cut you down" to tears,
My winged love will fly back to you
And bring you hopeful years.

Elizabeth Eckert

The Human Condition

I glanced upon a rock,
and saw its simple form.
It had no special beauty,
but a certain warmth.

I picked it up I hand,
to get a closer look.
And then I noticed,
its surface... like a book.

The scars deeply embedded,
yet the exterior shows no signs.
Like a boulder that is weathered,
but smoothed out over time.

This complex object so rugged,
not noticed far away.
I get a new opinion,
in a sympathetic way.

I begin to see its beauty,
and consider it some more.
And then I simply throw it,
as dirt upon the floor.

Dianna L. Bargerstock

"Recipe For Happiness"

Take a little sunshine
And put it in a smile
Show a little kindness
and it will all be worth your while
If you lend a helping hand
To someone who needs it too
This is the recipe for happiness
But it all depends on you.

If you show some kindness
Some one's heart may gladden too
Even tho you get discouraged
And you may stumble that is true
Just take time out to pray
And God will see you through
This is the recipe for happiness
But it all depends on you.

Hazel H. Smith

The Fisherman

I'm out of bed
and on my way
Looking forward
to a peaceful day

My first cast
a perfect arc
A fish does rise
and lights a spark

The sun is high
so are my hopes
To catch a few
and treat my folks

As evening falls
the breeze grows cool
And sunbeams dance
across the pool

The day is done
I've had my fun
A few to fry, a few to bake
thank you Lord for a peaceful day.

George M. Blakney

Scream Of Angels

You hear their cries of anger
and of fear.
Their screams are all but
whispers that flutter in your ear.
You see the faceless people
That in your mind are so bold
You're scared to sleep at night
Afraid of what the night
dreams behold.
When you have nightmares,
You wake up to a tear-stained
pillow
And your mind; your thoughts
are drained.
For you cannot forget the
scream of angels
When they cry you feel the
pain.

Elekta Damron

Bunches Of Violets

When I was young
And my children were small
In May they picked violets,
One and all
Purple bunches,
Bright and bold
I put in cups and bowls,
To behold
All of that beauty
For the world to see
Those bunches of violets
They picked for me
They grew on a hillside
Where the sun came through
To shine on bunches of violets,
Purple, violet, and blue.

Carole L. Herrle

Creative Fire

Peace brings me,
and many others,
blazing creativity.
Stress smothers
the sacred desire
which ignites creative fire.

Drew Ian Wild

I Know

She will draw a crowd,
and make me so proud
she's like a lone cloud;
so quiet, yet so loud.

Having her near
makes me want to cheer.
She's like a small deer,
with nothing to fear.

I am a knight, fighting for right.
I will fight with all my night,
I will scratch and I will fight,
I will walk into her light.

She will shine over me,
and I will feel such glee
I will beg and I will plea,
but sadly, she will only flee.

Jonathan Cerny

Rain On My Window

I wake at night on rainy days
And listen to the sound
That Heaven's teardrops make
Upon my windowpane.

Have you ever really listened
To the music that rain makes?
If you listen closely, you will hear
A sound that has echoed throughout the years.

An eternity of rain has passed
Older than the human race.
It has beat upon a dino's hide
And hit against your face.

Have you ever *really* listened to the rain?

Jennifer A. Kestner

My Love

I'm so glad to have found my dream.

I've searched and sought in great despair
and just before I gave up you were there.

You're always near day or night whenever
I feel I might need you by my side to
hold me, listen, and to be my guide.

I can finally open up my soul and mind
And together we will find new discoveries,
good or bad; whatever it may be we'll
be together endlessly.

Thank you so much; words just can't
say how I feel about you from day to day.

Just remember you're always in my heart
and mind, and I'll be there for you
until the end of time.

Angela Antetomoso

Inner Peace

I feel pleasure in a simple task
and joy in fleeting ways,
the warble of a meadow lark,
an early morning haze;
the way the sun shines through the trees
in patterns on the ground;
A tiny little pine cone -
a feather I have found.
The fragrance of the cedar chest,
the blankets stored within;
a pair of antique pillowslips
so delicate and thin.
The flaming glorious sunsets that
follow cloudy days;
small happy feelings come in many
unexpected ways.

Barbara Barton

My Lost Love

I listen to the wind,
and in the wind,
  I hear my lost love.
He is always there.
  When I walk the trails
that we once walked.
  I can hear my lost love.
He is always telling me he loves me.
  But still, even though I know
He is there,
  I still feel lonely and lost without him.
If I could have one more glimpse of him,
  I would feel whole again.
But life has taken him away,
  Never to return.
Oh, how am I to go on?
  listen, do you hear?
My lost love is telling me he
  loves me.

Becky Libby Rumery

Provincetown, 1960

You play the wave
And I the salt-sea foam
We'll learn what game time plays
When left alone,
And like a lonely light
Cold as the moon
Time will swirl away
The lyric from the tune.
You play the rain
And I the wind-tipped cloud
And time will hear us splash
And laugh aloud.

George N. Braman

Fairy Ballerina

I once saw a fairy ballerina
  and was she a pretty sight

I once saw a fairy ballerina
  and she was very polite

I once saw a fairy ballerina
  she let off a sparkling light

Oh, how I wish I were a
  fairy ballerina.

Jennifer Nelson

Tomorrow

I have known joy
  And I have known sorrow.
    But, always I've known
      There will be Tomorrow.
        Now many Tomorrows
          Have come and gone,
            And so many I've loved
              Have gone beyond.
                My days are lonely,
                  The nights are long.
                    Maybe soon I'll know
                      How it will be
                        When there's no
                          Tomorrow.
      Frances R. Martin

For My Love, Maria

I met someone some time ago
And I feel that I have more in my life.
When I go to sleep, I know somebody is
Thinking about me.
And when I finish the day, I know
somebody is waiting for me.
Now I can't explain in a few words
What's really happening, but it's nice
To think and feel, that you belong
To somebody and I feel good to know,
That this person is you.

I'll be with you always
and you will be always in my mind,
in myself, in my heart, in my dreams,
in my feelings, in my life.
I love you like the earth loves the sun.

I love you, my beautiful chiplionic.
      Erick McDonald

"The Band Played On"

The unsinkable ship sank
  and hundreds met their fate,
But the band played on.
Our own kind was killed
  by the hand of our brothers,
But the people looked away.
A child cried out in pain
  for the hunger that they had,
But the soldiers marched on by.
Our prosperity was lost
  by the fears of our life,
But the sun still shone.
Friendship perished
  to a world filled with blame,
But that same world continued to turn.
Our past became forgotten;
  Love existed no more.
And the band played on.
      David Dinwoodie

Halloween

Halloween is coming,
Coming, coming for you,
Trick or treating, eating,
Pumpkins, costumes
BOO!
      Emily Torre

This Is My Moment

This is my moment
And how I choose to
Use it is all mine
No one knows what this
Moments is to me
It could be a moment
Of hurt and sorrow
A moment of disappointment or despair
How I decide to deal
With it is my choice
This moment could be my moment
Of great happiness and joy
A moment of peace and serenity
If the moment permits
I could share it
However, my decision on how to handle
this moment
Rests with me alone
For I alone am the only one
That truly lives this moment
      Edward Williams II

Creation

Dear God,

When first you took some clay and sand
And held it gently in your hand,
Did you intend to make a world,
Or just by chance your finger curled
And thus was our beginning?

Perhaps you thought our land was plain
And so you took great mounds of grain,
To sprout and grow and multiply,
And cast their brilliance to the sky?

Thus was our beginning.
Perhaps you thought the land was bare
And so you had a certain plan.
The first beginning of a man —
Or was he modeled with such grace,
To take the image of your face,
A benediction on the land?
      Claire R. Fiddyment

The Auto-Car

I'm glad I'm not an auto-car,
And have to run both near and far
At speeds that are hard to tolerate
To save my boss from being late.

I'd hate to live on gasoline
With sips of oil, like Valvoline.
A spike in tire, like nail in shoe,
Is something that will never do.

A spike in tire, like nail in shoe,
Is pain, and hurts, I'm telling you!
The car will run for miles with nail,
While I, a man, will "Ouch!" and fail.

The time when I'd have greatest fear
Is when the boss drinks too much beer.
He'd drive me fast and very wild;
A threat to cars, to man, to child.

I'd have to wait in snow and sleet
And parked out on a dirty street
While Boss enjoys his drinking bar.
I'm glad I'm not an auto-car!
      Haydn A. Fox Sr.

Come Fly With Me

Come fly with me the birdies say
And have a very special day
High in the sky one sees
The mountains, plains and seas

Watch the squirrels stash their nuts
And the bears prepare to hibernate
Fish swim here the water is warmer
Crops are harvested by the farmer

Then winter comes along
With snow so white, the winds so strong
Moisture penetrates the ground
And things will grow again, we've found

So let's all say a "Thank You" prayer
To God above for everything
And appreciate nature everywhere
Isn't His universe something?
      Alice Marshall

Cry Of Angels

You laid me down
And gave this breath of life to my soul
When I crawled into your
Arms from the cold
You laid me down

You raised me up
You led me through my fears by my hand
And followed me from innocence to man
You raised me up

But now
I lay you down
And if you listen
You can hear the cry of angels
As it echoes
Through this empty broken heart
And though it's the hardest thing
Your son will ever have to do
I lay you down
I lay you down

In Memory of Patricia Peluso, Loving Mother
      Jerry Peluso

To A Brook

It winds its way around each hill,
  And enters every valley
It glides so smoothly on, until
  Fate challengers its folly.
It ripples over pebbles white,
  in its descending journey,
And travels on through starry nights,
  Bending, twisting, turning
It nears a distant cataract,
  To bound...to bounce..to quiver,
The white waves seem to hold it back,
  To save it from the river.
But no! it will not stay its pace,
  Held in captivity,
It enters, once again, the race,
  That ends in some far sea.
      Herbert Victor Corney

Rainbow Hue Or This Is My Wish For You

I would ease your toil
And end your pain
Give you sunshine
And gentle rain.

I would place in your heart
Peaceful thoughts
A smile on your lips
And dreams you've sought.

I would perfume the air each day
With fragrant flowers
To line your way.

Around your shoulders
Always would be
A lovely rainbow hue
Of health, love, and laughter
Constantly following you.
This and even more
I would do.
This is my wish for you.
    Benita C. Patrick

Kids

When the kids get out of hand
And don't listen to your command
When they get out of line
And really start to whine
Remember they're just your kids
When they're quiet as a mouse
you better check your house
When they argue, fuss, and fight
you can send them to bed for the night
But remember they're just your kids
When you think you're going crazy
and things start looking lazy
When you start to feel depressed
All you need is a little rest
And remember they're just your kids
When they really are a problem
Just thank God you have them
no matter how bad they get
Please mom don't forget
they're just (my) kids
    Antoinette Famuyiwa

Man's Kind

Fish and fowl
and dogs that howl
and trees that grow so tall
Live in peace
without beauty cease
in thanks to the Mighty All
Then here is man
Who by His hand
Would have it all be changed
only to find
He had lost His mind
Then wish it rearranged
    Frederick Shayne Moore

The Playful Sun

The sun came out to play
  and brighten the day;
It lifted my spirits
  and made me smile.

The trees reached up
  to catch its rays,
And flowers were kissed
  by butterflies.

The old cat stretched out
  to soak in its warmth,
And puppy-dog tails all
  started to wag.

Oh! What a beautiful
  sight it was,
The day the sun came
  out to play.
    Judy L. Wilkinson

Thoughts

I stepped outside this morning
And as I looked around
The air was cool and brisk
The dew still on the ground;

Looking back behind me
I saw the mountains high
Standing there so boldly
Beneath a clear blue sky;

I saw two rabbits playing
Beside my flower bed
Doves were feeding next to them
Wild geese flew overhead;

So many things of beauty
I could hear and see
I thought how blessed I truly am
How thankful I should be;
That I was born a citizen
Of a country that is free
And I have been so fortunate
To live in Tennessee!
    Barbara Sides

Conceding

Children spill from next door
And across the street.
Six voices clamor.
My heart disengages from my mind.
I surrender.
Clinging to a centimeter of choice,
I listen for sanction.
The "firefly story" shrills
Above the "long-dog story."
Heart surges cautiously.
A small victory.
I race to find the blue binder.
Twelve eyes focus.
I begin to read:
"Lester Lightning Bug...."
    Julie H. Crooks

Hide Away

A gawky smile
And a skittish giggle
Alters your individuality
With reasons I can't explain
Lights turn out
And you?
The same
To face another day in the rain
To trip and fall
Just once again
Then to hide away humiliated
You put on a clumsy smile
To try to show that you have no shame
But way down deep inside you have a fear
Of everyone else's impression
You hate to think they will abandon you one day
So you try to live up to their standards
But you know you'll never really change
    Danielle Scatena

The Supreme Gift

There's a brightness to this season
and a freshness in the air;
a Gift of Love beneath a star
lays in a stable bare.
The Christ child brought this holiday
both kings and shepherds found
that giving is the gift of love
for which the child was crowned.
See the stable and the cross
the stones been rolled away.
May the Christmas Spirit stay alive
in every heart - I pray.
    Florence N. Troll

Untitled

A journey into life
An original poem
Dedicated to Christian, Christopher,
Damien, Darien and Jennifer

All began blessedly a miracle
from heaven, an adventure
beyond distance far in earth
Life, space, world, planted
rooted, soiled, life in a prairie tree
    Charmaine Glover

Walking

Downcast heading
an introverted King
"land, land without Gods!"
was saying.

But his notion turned
while downcast he learned
a flower in tombed inklings:
then guessing the scent
"I wasn't, love, I am!"
the flower screamed.

To the scent or God
the King stalled
and his joy was extreme
'til the inspirited flower
indeed it did cease.
    Eduardo Rodríguez

Angelic Voices

I hear a whisper,
An angelic voice,
This is something,
To rejoice!

Voices of angels,
So sweet to hear,
Not to be seen,
But oh, so near!

Angelic voices,
Call to me,
Whispering words,
In times of need!

There's no one around,
When I look to see,
My guardian angel,
Must it be!

Debbie Camberg

I'll Be Going

This green
Among the reds and whites
I've seen
Sunny days
Turn to starry nights
Purples and blues
Are the colors I'd love to use

Describe the sky
Then the earth
Death comes
Long after
The awaited birth

Sitting at a window
I see myself and you
You walk around the tiring tree
I sit and understand
Why all is all
Soft underfoot
Make that silent call
Then I'm gone

Daniel Larson

Lyric For A Loved One

Love is heart's acorn,
Among polished leaves.
Silent as soot it lies
In secret it weaves.
Green hope for tomorrow
Sunshine and rain.
Hold it and hug it
Again and again.
It is a mystery from heaven
Elusive as smoke.
Cherish it, trust in
Star high as oak.
Give it to your dreams
Your tears and your laughter.
Forever is its goal
And the day after.

Bobbie S. Carr

Alone No More

Atop this hill a tree does stand
Alone except for wind and land
It reaches forth to gasp for air
The limbs expanding stripped and bare.
And then a seed from heaven falls
To plant itself by woody walls
The roots dig deep and firmly grasp
At soil and water and time does pass
As all God's love runs still and deep
The birth of a tree from this seed does seep
As spring and summer runs to fall
Time brings growth and soon its tall
Now a lonely tree no more stands
For love was found through God's hands.

Betty J. Crossno

Easter Lily

She was like an Easter lily
All white...and gold inside,
Long limbed like a filly
Filled with dignity and pride

He was mature and worldly
Well-travelled and well-read,
Somewhat less than godly,
But suave and quite well-bred.

He approached her gently
With gifts to turn her head,
Trusting that eventually
She would follow where he led.

He thought that he would surely
Take her in his stride.
Alas, his Easter lily
Will become a pure June bride.

Edwin G. Murphy

Our Scottie

Loving - protector - friend,
All these he was to the end.
Soulful dark eyes and curly hair,
Ready to play and willing to share.
Part of our family, so faithful was he,
Tho' only a dog - we loved him you see.
We miss his glad bark and soft padding feet,
If dogs go to heaven I'm sure we shall meet.
"Hi, Duffy," I'll say as I hold him tight,
A wet nose on my cheek and all is made right.

Anna M. Hoffman

The Skycatcher

She stood on the windy hilltop,
Arms lifted to the brilliant azure sky.
Ankle deep in the browning grass,
She lifted her head and let the
Autumn wind catch her ebony hair.
She whirled in circles, her head
Thrown back and her arms outstretched,
Her eyes drinking in the sapphire beauty.
Around and around and around she turned.
Her heart beat faster as she twirled.
At last she dropped exhausted to the ground
And let the liquid sky envelop her.

Catherine A. Lutz

To My Children

It's hard for me to put into words
All the things I'd like to say
My heart fills with love and pride
As I think of you everyday
You are children to be proud of
And I love you all so much
I wish for you only good things
A kiss, a smile, a gentle touch
As you've grown we've had our joys
Our fights, our laughter, our tears
We shared the good times and the bad
We shared our hopes and our fears
But if I could give you one last gift
Before my time on earth is through
I'd give you the hope and courage
to start each day anew
I'd give you peace and laughter
I'd take away the strife and woe
I'd do this oh so gladly
Because my children I love you so

Darleen Hurst

The Observe

The world turns dark
   all seems silent
All there is,
   is a gentle wisp
And the soft sounds
   quiet and indefinite
wholesome and protecting
   as though someone's watching
   you can't see him
But you know he's there.

Angie Andrews

"This Would Be Heaven"

If I could hear the newsman say,
all nations are at peace today;
all black-outs, blood-shed, better - tears,
will not be heard by listening ears.
If I could hear the doorbell ring,
and see my sweethearts face again;
I know my aching heart would sing,
because the fear of war is ending.
If children, people, cities, nations,
would, kneel to God in meditation
and ask for all to love thy neighbor
   "This would be Heaven."

Evelyn E. Trask

Soul Quest

Sweet, gentle soul I sought thee out
Across all space and time.
Sweet, gentle soul who's heart beats soft
A rhythm sweet like mine.

Dear peaceful soul, your music swells
Like a bird my heart takes wing.
And lifts my spirit gently up
To hears the angels sing.

Oh wondrous soul your light shines forth
Its brilliance sets me free
To look within and find at last
My God, myself and thee.

Jim Gaffrey

When The Children Cry

Children crying everywhere
All around them people stare
Cardboard boxes are their homes
Scraps of garbage coat their bones

Here we sit in our ivory towers
What do we care, their not ours
Faces smudged with dirt and grime
What did they do, what was their crime

To be born in the good old U.S.A.
Home of the free, land of the brave
No one cares about fellow man
Why can't you reach out to hold one hand

If each of us just took the time
To look around, scrape off the grime
They're only children after all
Please open your heart, don't let them fall

With our help they can survive
They have the will, they have the drive
So next time just hold out your hand
Save a place in your hear for your fellow man.

Deborah Blanchard

Untitled

I saw a falling star tonight
again, I think of you
A flash across the horizon
then vanished from my view

Could only I defy the law
that governs nature's might
That star would all upon my lap
and I would hold the light

To wish upon a falling star
would old cliches be true
Fate would turn her smile toward me
and I would soon hold you

As long as I may take a breath
as long as I have sight
I'll save my luck and all my charms
to bring me that one night

Jim Allison

The Death Of My Heart

We walk together,
after the bell has rung;
i was like the moon,
in place of the sun;
only because i knew

She is my stream,
She has run dry
She is my love,
and the light in her tower
shines no more

Her eyes are
my future seen;
and she
is not
within them

Her tears flow,
like my stream;

   and down
    the river
     i go.

Destry Griffith

Life's Line

Afraid that good times can't last forever.
Afraid of deaths edge, power to sever
the earthly ties between family and friends
without whose love happiness would end.

But if the rope is made of more than twine
and the bond is stronger
then earths strongest line,
deaths edge against a line like this
is weak, dull, and powerless.

David A. Zerafa

Arrest

Within every mountain
Above its jagged peak,
Bullet hole in the hand
Running on bloody feet.

Nailed to a Swastika
Battered, swollen, and bruised,
Twisted and conformed to its shape
Controlled, raped, and used.

Driving the spikes.
Pounding the nails.
Killing young minds.
My heart grows pale.

The blind leading the blind
With trust put forth as a lie,
If they can murder King
They all deserve to die.

Arrest me, beat me
Bruise me, kill me.
But remember this
You can never break me.

Bates J. Pugh

In The End

I have been thinking all day,
About everything you had to say.
And I won't make this a fight,
About what is wrong or right.
And I won't hold it against you,
No matter what you decide to do.
You do what you think is best,
And forget about the rest.
For no matter what that is,
Just remember this,
When it all comes to an end,
You can still call me your friend.

Jessica M. Williams

My Grandfather

It was a time of grief,
A time of no tomorrow.
When my grandfather died,
He left me full of sorrow.
My grandfather and I had a special bond.
He used his wisdom like a magic wand.
He kept me dazzled,
He kept me in suspense.
I will always miss,
The time we spent.

Camiel Renieta Vidal

The Answer To Life

When I sit here I think
A young man dreaming

Wondering where my life will lead
I want to live

The more I think
I want to die

To leave this world
Never to cry

I look to the old
For simple answers of the past

Sitting in the corner
Gun pointed at my head

Answers, answers, answers
Before I am dead

Pull the trigger
They scream in my head

Answers, answers, answers
Darkness

No answers, no answers, no answers
Why a cowards death

Jonathan D. Korb

"God's Green Earth"

On distant hills the forests stand
A work of art by God's own hand
He, the maker of us all
Made those trees so straight and tall,
Made the soil that gave them birth,
Thus we call it God's green earth,
In the valleys and by the streams
Nature in her beauty gleams.
Roses red and violets blue,
Many others of every hue
They bring us joy, gladness, mirth
Thus we call it God's green earth.

Inez Jack

"Ways"

I love you in all the ways
  A woman can love a man;
I love you because you
  reach out your hand,
A hand that is strong yet gentle
  and true,
A hand that says you
  love me too!
Love, Fidelity, Commitment,
  Loyalty and Trust —
These five virtues
  Are a must.
The activities and interests
  We share,
Show each other
  just how deeply we care.
I love you, my unforgettable man.
  I am your woman,
Your ways, I understand.

Connie Rigsby Jones

Music

Music
a tone
held lightly above
a gently playing
melody.
The harmony
senseless
to the emotions
it has expressed,
unleashing hearts,
and explaining lost loves.
Thinking not
of what it does.
Floating softly down
into the mind
of the disturbed.
Healing their pain,
and yielding all thoughts.
Until they are one,
one with the music.

Crystal Kegebein

Crop Circles

It was only a fuel stop, then
A tiny gap in the electromagna-doorway
Steam cleaning the chaff was a pastime
Shaping it was the art

Over the years it was left to wild pickers
And up for grabs now, the beneficiaries
Cultivate memories of the imminent
Warlords in the name of heaven

And the caretakers dare to prohibit
Ancestral trespassers, in a mutant attempt
To capture some time-travelers
Paying their respects

In a frightening language too ancient
For crop dusters to copy, copy, copy?

Two more Popes to Paradise...
And there won't even be a bruise.

Cheril C. Carrington

I Can Hear The Oriole Singing

If only for just a moment,
a sweet voice dances
on the breeze

Longing eyes of blue and green,
so full of spirit
and wonder,

Sweep the yard, hoping for a flash
of the minstrel's black
and orange

No luck today as the song fades
away into the
sunlit sky.

Time may come tomorrow when she
will listen and say
"I can hear the oriole singing."

Casey Haley

In Your Eyes

The morning, sitting watching
A sunrise come up
The wind warmly caresses
The chimes they ring
Clouds bringing showers
To be loved under
That fills the canyons,
Lakes and rivers...
With their water
Birds sing, plants in bloom,
And flowers, fills my senses
A rainbow, love me under
To watch a sunset fall
Experience the color it brings
The Lord, and all that
His creative nature brings
It's all at peace
The way things make
Me see this
In your eyes

Arthur James R

A Southern Daisy

From everywhere the softness bloomed.
A Southern Daisy breached the loam
And met the freshness of the spring.
Affectionate desire sings.

As summer rains did wash her bare,
Her fertile blossom rose to share
An air of love embracing her.
The warm breath of the sky was stirred.

The fall was dressed in honey-gold.
Above the autumn moonlight glowed.
She reached up to its tender kiss
Which beamed amidst her flowing tress.

Then winter slowed her growing stride.
Last season's seed still held inside.
She dreamed beneath the open sky.
Sweet memories could never die.

Carol Thomas Horton

One Night

A woman screams,
A siren blares,
A man is yelling orders.
Woe to those who love the night.

The woman faints,
The siren flashes,
The man begins to worry.
Woe to those who love the night.

The woman bleeds,
The ambulance races,
The man assists the woman.
Woe to those who love the night.

A baby screams,
An ambulance stops,
A man is checking a pulse.
Woe to those who love the night.

The woman passes,
The baby cries,
The man is saddened by death.
Woe to those who love the night.

C. H. S.

A Tear

The wind blows gently on the rose,
A sign of love, and sweet repose
The strength of man did fail to save
This hapless soul a somber grave.

The mourners clad in shades of night
Sang dirges in the fading light
The vestige left of one so dear
Was but a mem'ry and a tear.

Donna Van Hofwegen

The Shape Of Silence

I sit beside the shape of silence
   A shape not oval, round or square
Yet all of these and more.
   A silken thread, down soft
Beguiles me with its tender quiet.
   Enter here, my friend, and find
The sound of silence too.

But I sit, afraid to enter there
   For fear I'll lose myself
And forever wander, lost within
   The strange mysterious shape of silence.
I would withdraw from noise
   From bellow, blast and beat
And sometimes from the sound
   of voice and feet.

Quiet, quiet, quiet, I whisper in despair.
   But still, I sit beside the
   Shape of silence
Immobilized by fear.

Isabelle C. Melville

I Can't Leave Her Behind

There upon a bench,
a sad little girl sits.
Tears stream down
her pretty little face.
"What's the matter?" I ask.
She looks up mournfully,
saying nothing.
Little girl, little girl,
please come with me,
let me wash your face,
and free your eyes from tears.
I know of a happy place,
full of laughter and joy.
Where tears and sorrow,
they are things of the past.
Please little girl,
please come with me.

Dawn Miller

Love and Devotion

A day of sun
A day of rain
A day of fun
A day of pain
We'll live this life
We'll live it through
For this whole life
I'll live for you
We'll see the best
We'll see the worst
and through it all
I'll put you first.

John R. Dryer

My Two Ones

I don't believe, nor have I seen
a reason to believe.
When I count 'one' — then add just one
the sum is two — not more.

And yet I'm told by those who've "seen"
that "more" exists somewhere,
and two is never quite enough,
nor the process even fair.

"It discounts my feelings!" Is the cry.
"The logic is cold, detached."
"Facts cannot be truly known,
and I'm certainly sure of that!"

But my world is just The World, it seems
and "more" I'll never need.
And my two ones together
will never more than two exceed.

Joseph Kane

That's My Dad

A strong hand with a gentle touch,
A powerful force that I need so much,
A nonchalant way that I understand,
A friend, indeed, like no other man.

Someone to lead me in the right direction,
In life, while I strive to learn perfection,
Always there to give me a little nudge,
Full of optimism with words to encourage.

Punishment, when necessary, to give heed,
But lots of love to balance the deed,
Handling each situation with great finesse,
Softening each problem with a sweet caress.

What would I do without his calm attitude,
I'd probably be somewhere singing the blues,
His soft assurance, yet firm grip on things,
Is the reason for my pride and why I beam.
   That's My Dad!!!

Eddie B. Cloman

Father

You see your father standing strong,
a picture you have always seen.
My father is a great man,
we shared many days together.
His words, you heard, you listened,
I admired this man, my father.
If I inherit just some of this man,
could I be as grand a man as he.
My father has come into the quite
time of his life,
a time of reflecting of years passed.
I a reflection of him, standing in
front of my father.
And now my son growing into a man,
a reflection of my father and me.
My he will be a grand man,
just as his grandfather and father.

Deborah M. Vanderwood

The Death Of A Child

Painfully stricken
A mother awakes
Only to learn
Of her child's mistake

It was bitterly cold
On that dark winter's night
When her child instilled
The most horrific fright

Trying to save
An innocent girl's fate
He was forced to kill
While interrupting a rape

Innocent he was
But wrongful indeed
Searching for help
For someone in need

With only the hope
Of his weeping mom's prayer
He stands alone
In a world with no care

Amy Lurentzatos

"Whatever Happens To A Child"

Whatever happens to a child when
A mother and father gets a divorce?

What ever happens to a child?
I would like to know where
Does a one, two, or three year old
Child go?
What do they do, and how do
They feel?
What ever happens to a child?
I ask you my mother and father
Please. Please don't depart and
Break a small child's heart.

Whatever happens to a child?
Whatever happens to a child like
Me at one, two or three?
When you lose your love from me.
Whatever happens to a child?
Whatever happens to me?

Daniel D. Duliba

Old Friend

I hear a song
A melody of days long gone,
And I miss you.
It's just knowing
You are no longer
A part of my world
I long so to tell you
How much you meant to me.
Not as a lover,
But as a friend.
So many times
You helped me through
difficult times.
And now you are beyond my reach.
Perhaps - perhaps
In God's own time
We shall meet again.
Until that time
I will cherish the memories.
I miss you old friend.

Elsie S. Dillon

Untitled

And the toaster dies.
A mechanic milks the car,
and I frown a smile.

Andy Wietecha

The Love A Mother Is

Is a treasure of gold
A love that never gets sold.
It's a high that can only get higher.
The kind of love that never dies.
I can feel her love around me.
The kind of bond that's never taken away
Even though there comes that day,
The love of a mother will always stay.

Debra McFadden

Ecstasy

Ecstasy is a moment in time.
A love and joy shared by two people.
A caress or holding of hands.
A moonlight walk on the beach.
A glance across a crowded room.
It is also love and a primal need,
the giving of a kiss, the sharing of dreams.
But most of all it is the joy of being a part
of someone else's life.

Carmen L. Daignault

A Lover's Curse

One warm and windy day brought this,
A look from you, like a lover's kiss.
My captured soul you charmed that day.
I love you too you seemed to say.
Hearts danced so close and then away,
To play the games that lovers play.
Though I love you and you know,
My prison lies within my soul.
The prayer I made for you came true.
Now what in the world am I gonna do?
You're everything to me and more,
How could I close this open door.
Would you understand or rage and weep,
At these hidden feelings dark and deep.
This love for you turned to a curse,
To love myself I must do first.

Joan Groover

Sweet Re-Union

A voice - somehow, familiar
  A look, a smile, a gesture
The flash of memories treasured
  the fleeting, pain-tinged pleasure
Reminders - so unexpected re-open the
Wounds, by time protected.
The hurt, the loss, the feelings re-awaken.
The heart recalls those loved ones taken.
Yet mixed with grief and lonely yearning;
A message of hope is there for learning.
The lessons they taught as they touched
Our lives; we now share with those
Whose lives we touch.
Until, sweet re-union with loved ones
We've missed so much.

Gayle T. George

Loneliness

A desperate heart
a longing tear
a soft gentle cry
and made worse with
a careless sigh

A desperate heart
a longing tear
a soft gentle cry
has now turned to
a gaping try

A desperate heart
a longing tear
a soft gentle cry
has lessened to
a care beside.

Angela Brock

Garden

In San Francisco
A lone green Jolly Roger
Flies in the cool breeze

As the flag flutters
Under the air's magic spell
Wind chimes improvise

Melodies playing
Wisps of incense climb slowly
Butterflies descend

Nearby, carved in stone
A sun God and Buddha
Share this time and place

Arthur Bourque

The Little White Lie

I spy with my little white eye
A little white lie
Fairly harmless
Seems so doubtless
It is humanity's worst enemy
And satan's favorite tool
He likes it himself
When you lie to your self
Then you twist your own mind
And that's less work for him and his kind

Doug Mott

Stone Life

The stone is chiseled
a life takes shape
harsh features appear
sharp jaw
stern brow
bold structure
compelling eyes
soft nose
delicate lips
connects present to the past
forever to remind
of a love
that never should have been lost
but the artist has
a surprise message
the statue is called "me"

Julianne Blommer

Untitled

A bird in flight, is truly a sight.
A language of freedom is in their flight.
Singing away on a bright sunny day,
Not a care in the world, for in God's
hands do they lay.

Our dreams are God's seed to reality

Barbara L. Jenkins

Edward, Prince Of Wales

Thirteen-thirty, a prince is born
A lad his land will too soon mourn
Aged sixteen he knew first glory
In Crécy's battle, victory!
Knight of the garter, this king's son
In warfare could not be outdone
From Bordeaux to Narbonne he strafed
The land for his father vouchsafed
Then on to Poitiers he flew
A general who only knew
His fathers kisses he desired
And dazzling combat that transpired
Against the foe and their array
The gallant prince was heard to say
To his men that none could deprive
Their triumph while he was alive
The challenge of disease was met
With lasting pain in Navarette
Near forty-six his life was gone
His wasted dreams, alas, anon

Cathy Davidson

"The Laughing Eyes"

Out of the mist come
A joyful sound and laughing eyes.
Oh Lord, 'tis what I need!
Why then, the cast away glance
And down ward head?
When the laughing eyes
Are yours to give - and
The world needs so much

Fred Royal

Darkness

The dark of night blocks out the sun,
A human soul whose life is done,
The caw of a crow as it rides the wind,
Carrying a soul to hell again,

As shadows dance by the light of the moon,
An evil has risen far to soon,
A thick gray fog of solemn, despair,
Envelops me from shoes to hair,

And if this dark should ever end,
I'd have a sense of hope again,
But since I've been here for so long,
My sense of hope is so far gone,

The dark around blocks out the light,
Filling me with icy fright,
So if a crow should next fly by,
I would not be afraid to die,

The dark of night blocks out the sun,
I wish my suffering was done.

Bill Garrity

Restoration Heaven

Destination heaven
A Hope deeply hidden
Profoundly entrenched
Yet Truth soundly quenched
The Sanctum of Him
Set in the heart of men
Infused by His grace
Delivered in Him being raised
The ancient promise fulfilled
In the Son Emmanuel
My Spirit lifted up
Unto overflow He fills my cup
Restoration heaven
A gift freely given
Through His salvation mission
By my humble belief and lowly confession

Edmundo Oranday

"My Sorrow"

The tears stream down my face, sorrow,
a flower so deep and rich,
its beauty rarely appreciated,
disguised by loss.
My soul is emptied,
emotions so intense,
feelings so strong.
Lighting a candle
I draw you into me,
filling the emptiness I feel.
You have left this earth
but you will never leave my heart,
even after the tears have ceased,
over the years,
not until we are joined again,
sometime,
some life again,
soon I hope.
Goodbye dear, dear friend.

Anthony Guthmiller

Garden Of Love

A garden of love as you can see
A flower blooms for you and me

Where ever a certain seed is planted
A burst of love is definitely granted

So find the soil and let go
Your heart will help the love to grow

Through your heart something will shine
To grow this little garden of mine

So follow your heart and make it grow
When you grow love you will definitely know!

Holly Marie Vermette

"Silent Whisper"

The silent whisper echoed through the night,
As I hid in fear of what I had done.
I fled from myself not knowing who I was,
But feeling proud that I had won.
He faded off to sleep as a tear left my eye,
Knowing that soon it was my turn to die.
Who killed this child? I'll never tell,
For it cost me life to spend in hell.

James A. Varela

A Fine Line

Human nature is
a fine line
between genius and insanity
between mediocrity and shine

Every day we walk
a fine line
between good and bad
between the profane and the divine

Everything we desire is
a fine line
between need and want
between to have and to pine

Every situation that occurs is
a fine line
between perception and reality
between a six and a nine

The world we share is
a fine line
between love and hate
between yours and mine

Hean Tat Keh

Grandfather

A mother gives you birth.
A father is your guide.
A grandmother gives you so much love,
and from a grandfather you gain your pride.

A pride in who you are.
And from where you've come.
A pride in all your family,
that can never come undone.

Even though you have left us.
My grandfather, to join God's son.
I'd still like to just say thank you,
for all that you have done.

Our roads have gone on different paths.
We've all moved far and wide.
But our hearts know we'd be nothing,
if it wasn't for our pride.

Debra A. Towle

Ranch Life

Ranch life is
  A dream come true
From dark night
  To sunset's hue.
Each day brings
  Some happy times
A bird sings
  But puppy whines.

Who am I
  To write this poem?
I who spend
  My days at home
I who feed
  The cats and dogs
Chickens, ducks,
  Even two hogs.

Life goes on
  I'm glad to say.
I'm grateful
  For every day.

Alice T. Peachey

Green Sea

A crown on a mountain of velvet
a clown in the face of mimes
A wish in a moment of silence
a sea in the rhythm of rhymes

Sounds of symphonies
and hands that speak
slither by sadly
it doesn't keep

How quickly things wear
how slowly they tear
when silk white skins fair
things seem to go nicely

The love of her lips
are stuck to his hips
and they fall through the seas together
in every kind of joke of green
what a terribly wonderful complex dream

Camille Davila

The Childless Woman

You are the child within my mind
A child that was never conceived
But you live in my heart
In my soul
In my dreams
In all that I have ever believed

I will never know what it's like
To hold you close to my chest
But I feel your heart beating
Your tender skin
Your soft hair
The warmth I feel from your breath

Some may say that I do not understand
The special love it takes to be a mother
But I will just smile and I will know
In my heart
In my soul
In my dreams I will always be
  A mother

Angela Johnson

Without Someone To Teach

Without someone to teach
  A child can never learn to hurt,
  A child can never learn to lie,
  A child can never learn to hate,
  A child can never learn to cry.
Without someone to teach
  A child can never learn to love,
  A child can never learn to play,
  A child can never learn to hope,
  A child can never learn to pray.

We are the teachers.
  We choose the curriculum.

Brook Lamb

Untitled

A tree huddles, bent by the wind
A bird hides, sheltered by the tree
I am the tree
I wish I were the bird

Dale R. Myers

The Dolphin

Adrift in a human sea,
a castaway
in the blue eternity,
longing the play of yesterday.

Gone are my kin,
netted in treasures
from poverty within,
drowned by humanity.

Whose waves smother the breeze,
pressing down
the struggle to be freed
to the land beyond the tides.

Of two worlds I come,
needing the deep
to a touch of the sun,
as each cannot meld in one.

I sway from sea to sky,
for below the skin
chokes a futile cry,
forever I swim alone.

Brian Zielinski

River

There's a river running under
a bridge streaming through my back
yard, where it waits for me to touch
it's current and feel it's sense of peace
and usefulness.

Alongside the flowers bloom
making an elbowed torn where it
faces my house. On the river the wind
blows and night calls the river
that is alone crying for someone
to touch it, to make it feel alive...

Ida Gonzales

That Night

One night,
a boy and a girl went for a walk.
They walked the beach that night,
with hand in hand.
Love was blowing like the wind that night.
Her eyes were sparkling,
as they walked together,
like the moon sparkling on the ocean water.
As he looked into her eyes,
he knew she was the girl of his dreams.
As they stood in each others sight,
they both kissed that night.
This is a dream that I hope comes true,
but I know someday it all will come true,
because love always finds a way.

Daniel Reidl

My Wish For You

I wish you days of sunshine
  And nights of shining stars
A friend to lend a helping bond
  No matter where you are
And as a little afterthought
  To carry day by day
Remember Lord is always near
  To guide you on your way.

Evelyn Vinal

The Bond

Parents and children have a special bond,
   A bond that could never be broken.
A bond of unconditional love,
   A bond that could never be spoken.
When I was young and immature,
   I never knew the love you had for me,
But now that I am a parent myself,
   I could not understand more completely.
You don't know how much you are appreciated
   Each and every day.
You're the best parents anyone could have,
   In each and every way.
You both are so valuable to me,
   More than you will ever know.
You've helped me in so many ways,
   Your love can't help but glow.
So this is Thank You and I love you,
   For all that you do and show.
For that bond of unconditional love,
   That will always continue to grow.

Gwendolyn Johnson

"When Gods Die"

What happens when the Gods begin to die?
A blanket of black covers the sky,
the clouds cry...
Confusion; hysteria, chaos; the clouds
cry, and the Gods die.
Innocence last, children burdened by
responsibility and necessity, death of
Gods; this is the cast....
Afraid to pray, what would we say?
Why should we try?
We know the Gods will die.
Childhood; a luxury, bought and
traded on holidays and special times.
This lie of immortality fresh in our minds.
Born of reality, no desire to try,
because we know, the Gods die.
Nurture with truth, full aware
life is a moments dare,
because the Gods are dying
everywhere....

Debra Williams

"The Finest Of Gold"

I went to Him in the rawest of form,
A battered ship destroyed by the storm.
Broken dreams, determined to make the
Finest of beams.

I gave up, often said I Quit.
He formed my life with the best
Of the steel bit.

Love His materials, My life His
Concern, My Faith in Him He knew
I needed to earn.

A product now complete, A fine piece
Of work the Devil could never defeat.

In the End I was nothing but the
Finest of Gold.
God's Finest of work Raw Steel
To the Best of GOLD.

Diane Gardner

Infinity

Infinity
Destiny, Balance
Purpose, Strength, Spirit
Earth And Water, Wind And Fire
Mass, Distance, Time
Man, Woman
Change
Growth, Survival
Process, Intent, Practice
Vision, Focus, Love, Commitment
Chaos, Complexity, Creativity
Destiny, Balance
Infinity

Bart Barthelemy

Love Is Born

Whisper where the coolest summers are
and to the yellow moons that
hearts are round like balloons

Imagine the color of peace
or the song of rain on a tree,
Or time jumping inside
clouds

And the slow music in the
stars,

And the cries of cats like
babies talking
And who puts snow in my garden at night?

Follow her dreams as they flew far
flowering upon
a red sky

Love is born, fly child fly

Yes, joy has magic to live for, glowing
sunny
light and big butterfly wings
All together you have...

Spring!!

Haley Van Dyck

Christmas Tree Heaven

'Tis so sad to see
A Christmas tree
With it's head buried
In a trash can.
I'm sure that's not the way
God meant it to be
Not even a part of his plan.
I believe that he has a place
For each little tree
In "The greatest forest of all"
With their feet firmly planted
And their heads held up high
So they can keep on forever
Growing tall!

Evelyn Mitchell

Our Children's Future

The curse of the land,
comes from our own hands,
because we refuse to see!
That if we don't make a stand,
to give morality a helping hand,
malice will take over our society.

It's been proven in history,
when a nation revels in debauchery,
it is certainly soon to fall.
For it's from this immorality,
there comes a spiritual liberality,
from which our selfish desires call.

So while presidents come and go,
one thing the past will certainly show,
their decisions do affect our course.
In the way our children will grow,
into the future that they will know,
within a world that shows no remorse.

Danny Matheny

Lost Love Found

An essence here that words can't show,
Nor ever quite define
Our tender inner beings know,
And share 'cross space and time.

I know I'd shared a life with you.
You're young and I am older,
But when I saw you standing there,
A rainbow 'round your shoulder,
A thousand sweet remembrances
I gleaned from years gone by
And now I know that they are true.

I know that you and I
Will once again repeat the plan
We started long ago.
We'll touch our lips and fingertips,
And let the mem'ries go.

But should this life forbid our tryst
Two hundred years or more
I'll gladly wait at least that long,
For you're worth waiting for.

Betty Santa

Untitled

Closed faces stare at you daily
fragments of pleasure
glimmers of hope
leave a stone pulsing inside you.

Days become months moving slowly
through clouded years
curtains drawn tight
contain the driving storm within.

If I could I would release you,
wish for you more than you could imagine,
smile as I watch you soar upward,
dissolve the stone
calm the storm
set you free
walk with you on the other side,
reaching out to your open hand
knowing the instant of that touch
will make you smile
for the first time.

Jane Jensen

Her

As my mind wonders subtly,
I fix on the shadow upon the wall.
There she stands, in the essence of purity.
Curious of the thoughts in her head
I venture slowly and cautiously toward her soul.
A vibrant young life full of dance and laughter.
I must pause.

Pause, so that this moment of our passing
will last a second longer.
Pause, so that a flicker of passion
may be exchanged.

The wetness in her lips spread
the sweet grin I have yearned for .
The smile that my heart has imprisoned.

I use imprisoned literally.
For as time effortlessly passes
her body may age and mind grow with confusion;
the innocence of those lips will warm
my heart that of the deepest winter
flame of eternal life...
Matt Dunlap

Fame

Chasing myself in my dream again,
I feel your presence in a distant flame.
The tribal doll I find by my ocean,
Is the bearer of true and pure emotion.
And as I trip and fall over your thoughts of distress,
You sit alone with nobody else to impress
And I've wondered why you've felt such pain
As you crouch down in the cold winter rain,
You shed your tears in the iridescent sky
Searching for the time that just went by.
So we now find ourselves with nothing to claim,
Chasing one another in my once forgotten fame.
Moses Munoz

Untitled

You told me you loved me with all your heart
I feel better now that we are apart.
You've hurt me so much these last few years
All fighting, pain, and many of tears.
I tried my best to change for you
just to end the things you do.
The pain never stopped and the tears still fell.
Why must you put me through this hell?
I was afraid to leave yet putrefied to stay.
You never got the hint to just go away.
You will never understand the way I feel
And the scars you gave me will never heal.
Michelle Homick

The Sun

I saw you race across the far reaching firmament and plunge it's
depths, into a sea of yellow, into the sea of death.
Fear, Loneliness, Despair
I saw you rise awakening eye, our glorious sight fills the sky.
Passionate colors dancing high, warms the spirit, all from your light.
Exhilaration, Joyous, Peaceful
I saw you race across the far reaching firmament and plunge beneath
its depth, into a sea of yellow into a sea of death.
Fear, Loneliness, Despair
Mark Stephens

Feelings

When I heard what went wrong,
I cried all day long.
I don't understand the reason to die.
I didn't even get to say goodbye.

I am in so much pain,
The tears fall off my face like rain.
I want you to know we will never part
Because you will always have a place in my heart.

You never showed to much sorrow,
Not knowing what would happen tomorrow.
My love for you will never end,
You weren't just a grandma you were a friend.

We had some great times,
Too many to be told in these rhymes.
For you to die, I was scared,
This day I had feared.

We had a blast but these times went by so fast.
My memories of you are far from few,
Grandma, I want you to know "I love you"
Mike Leblanc

The World Today

The world today has become angry, why?
I cannot say

The world today has become unimportant, why?
Again, I cannot say

The world today doesn't care about our environment, why?
I wish I could say

The world today ignores our children's cry, why?
I have no answer

The world today ignores God's commands, why?
Because we didn't listen

The world today is frightful and scared, why?
I cannot say

The world today has so many questions
that can't be answered. Why?
Meoshameka L. Taylor

Inside My Mind

I got in kinda late, and you were on my mind...
I called you... 'cause you were on my mind...

I woke you... 'cause you were on my mind...
I tried to explain...that you were on my mind

You didn't care...if you were on my mind
I'm sorry! For having you on my mind...

But you were!

You chuckled at the thought...of you on my mind
Because, in your dreams...I was on your mind...

So go back to sleep...with me on your mind...
Because you are still on my mind....

And tomorrow...we'll wake up smiling...

Together!
Michelle R. Langford

"Penetrate Vitality"

I partake on a long journey with a direction unknown.
I begin traipsing through a foggy wood, and my ankles silently moan.
All the while, a murky swamp crawls up my legs,
And levels at just below my knee. The smog violently sucks the air
out of my lungs, and my teary eyes strain to see
Any obstacles in my path, but the attempts remain fruitless and vain.
For the turbid air prevents any kind of foresight, and illusions pluck
  at my brain.
Reaching a mountain base, I begin to climb—higher, faster, grappling
  with slithering vines that continuously clutch my limbs.
I swiftly grab for any protruding rock. Working my way upwards,
I am mysteriously propelled by some divine force.
At long last, I reach for the summit of this unyielding elevation
And peer around, finding no feelings of remorse?
Deliverance! This be the motive behind my strenuous migration.
the sole reward - simply reaching the ultimate destination!
Atop this marvelous peak, I behold an entire world of wonder down
  below.
Surrounded by velvety clouds, I relax to observe a living earth
  prosper and grow.

Kelley Sue Maria

A Departure

As I sat waiting for your ship to depart
I became aware of a knowing pain in my heart
I sat nervously poised on the jutting rocks
Watching the lines freed, one by one, from the docks
Soon your ships engine began the roar
And the ship edged out the channel more
Finally, I saw you up your hand to say goodbye
I could feel hot, burning tears form in my eyes
I put up my hand and waved until I couldn't see any more
Then ran, brushing away my tears, to the edge of the shore
As your ship drifted farther toward the sea
Tears rolled down my cheeks, suddenly a sob burst out of me
I strained watching your ship turn into a dot
Then stared unbelieving at an empty spot
I turned and ran, stumbling, blinded by tears
My heart loud pounding filled my ears
I made my way through the sand, then over jagged rocks
Jumped in car and sped by the now empty docks
Each night I stand on the same shore, searching the horizon
Waiting for the sea to bring back to me again

Lucille Fritts

Well Of Life

Water is a life source.
I am a spring.
Drink from me purely.
Drink deep, drink deep.
Nourishing creation,
Life upon life.
Let my waters,
Flower fields of plenty
With new life, young life
May adults of all ages
Drink for sustenance,
May all of creation drink as one;
Drinking the potion of peace and tranquility,
Drinking the waters of pure love.
So come to my well and drink deeply.
Pour my waters over your drought-dried flesh,
Quenching your thirst and setting your soul free.

Nicholas Osgood O'Reilly

Ain't It Fine Today

Sure this world is full of trouble,
I ain't said it ain't
Lord I've had enough and double,
Reason for complaint.
Rains and storms have come to fret me,
Water with the wine
I've had my trials and tribulations.
But Lord ain't it fine.
Cause it's today that I'm a livin,
Not a month ago-
Havin, losin, taken, givin, as time wills it so.
Yesterday a cloud of sorrow fell across the way.
It may rain again tomorrow,
But say, "Ain't it fine today!"

Marguerite Twigg Fitzgerald

Wasted Innocence

Children made from ignorance running a nation of disease
Hypocrites at birth, they close the world down with their
insubordination and unwillingness to be
What has happened to the lives that once brought promise and hope
The congregations have turned bitter and the skies have begun to choke
Once all stood on common ground now we began to separate
Vengeance reins its weary eye towards empty minds of indecision
They lock themselves in circular rooms where visions just repeat
Without the corners of a square, the game would not breakdown
See the songs of white lies and watch them grow into
creatures of your destruction
They have been brought up in a twisted metamorphosis of
anger and despise
Who can fix the thrown off balance caused by blind minds

Laura N. Webster

Nature's Creation

I lifted this intricate and mysterious creation of nature, and was
hypnotized by it's grace and deceiving simplicity. As I glared upon
the chalky, desolate, almost moon-like surface, I was engulfed by the
rough, course terrain of this creation, and it reminded me of a very
proud, kind, elderly man who had worked hard all his life to
accomplish nothing more but coarse arid, callused hands, and the signs
of aging deeply engraved into the palms. When I slowly and very
observantly wondered to the underside of this magnificent creation of
nature, my eyes extract what first appears to be a shiny egg yolk
film. As I venture further into the immeasurable yet frivolous
canyon, I find stripes, like a tiger fish or a cub. Down deep in the
consecrated cavern, I see nothing but the soft glow of pink, like a
newborn baby. This magnificent creation of nature that I hold,
resembles the existence of all things living and not.

Kristina Wolski

Oh Little Dog

Run, run, little dog
How you run to me as I approach you
When you retrieve a stick, or try to drag a log
and when you chase your tennis ball all around the house.

When everyone is gone and the house is dark
I always wonder what you do
Do you bark?
Do you sleep?

I love it when you're waiting for me
After a long day at school
you're a special friend that I always love to see
Oh little dog, you are so cool.

Matt Wehrle

Confusion, Anger And Peace

The smile you gave so freely,
How could I deny the pain you had buried so deeply?

You always told me to "keep your chin up and move on"
So please help me to understand why you gave up and now you're gone.

We had so many good times and bad times to cross together.
Now I am without you and I feel lost forever.

Getting through one more day is hard enough.
Not being able to tell you how special you were to me is far more tough.

I will never know everything on your mind, rather
I will think of the happy times and how you were so kind.

The day you took your own life and mine fell apart,
Was the day I lost the biggest piece of my heart.

My dear Aunt Yo-Yo you meant everything to me,
You were always there with your wisdom and helped me to see.

And now as I look into the deep blue sky
And slowly wipe away the falling tears from eyes,
I am able to smile and cherish memories and more
because I know that one day we will meet again at heaven's door.

Mary H. Rodriguez

Rebecca's Song

Masked behind uniformity, I know not what each day brings
Hour upon hour of monotony where my heart does not sing

I look into the clear blue sky in a world of mum
Yearning for my soul to roar and cease it's stagnant hum

All things seem in solitude though I am not alone
A melancholic serenity, a feeling quite unknown

With many a friend my love is shared each day through and through
But all who know me know too well I long to be with you

The memory of the love we shared hovers in still air
My every path haunted by green eyes and auburn hair

The rumble in the streets, all seems to pass me by
I have no need for earthly things....I need what is in the sky

The sun's warm rays, God's good grace, and a star to steer me through
That every path and road I take may lead me back to you

I know not what I want from you....or maybe then I do
I long to stop thinking it...and share my life with you

What good is life if it is passed merely just content
Days and dreams not fulfilled - are lives not well spent.

Kwame Ofori

Listen, Love: A Sonnet To Bob

A melody — pink soft, subdued — had long
Held timid, hidden hope — a doubtful dream
Of sparkling smiles, of rhyme-and-dance-beat strong.
Persistent tune, but pastel-pale with obscure theme.

Oh, I'd known love, but so oft tinged with dread,
Concern would overstrain the tenderness,
Would inundate and drown the love it fed
And yearning lyrics die, still unexpressed.

But your love is passion-peace. Kindling flesh,
It smothers care; it ignites the hungry brain
And soothes the soul. Alighting hope afresh,
It turns moon to sun, grey flood to summer rain.

So listen, love, to words freed when you came —
To music from my heart enshrine your name.

MaryAnn Blakely Wagner

You

I know I'm not all you dreamed of, perhaps your expectations are too high
You see my imperfections, but refuse to see my other side

I don't think you realize your control over me because I'm not considered part of your life
But your touch or a kind word would fulfill my dreams at night

I am scared and sometimes I don't know what to do
So I end up over reacting, making life more difficult for you

Though it may seem I want to ruin your life, this has never been my intention
But through the hours, days, and months, I've only wanted an explanation

And this I know I deserve more than anything from you
Maybe if you would give me an answer I'd be willing to part with you

Sometimes I wish to see what you see, then I would know what it's like to be you
But that would require me entering your mind and giving another piece of me to you

Only I have been in your mind before and I brought with me a box of crayons
I wanted to make everything beautiful, so you would have wonderful things to look on

You didn't turn me out then so why do you choose to now
I've always been there for you and you no longer care for me, how?

I hope I find my way out...and I hope you do too
For this maze we're traveling through, would be easier to conquer with two.

Katie Cox

Those Amazing Plural Nouns

The farmer's wife found three blind *mice*
Hiding in the *houses*, not the *hice*.

The men's lunch, while they're plowing with *oxen*,
Contains bagels with *lox*, not with *loxen*.

Good old Tarzan and all of his *children*
Roam around the *wilds*, not the *wildren*.
Amid ducks and wild *geese* and big *moose*, not big *meese*,
Where the peaceful grazing *sheep* aren't disturbed by noisy *jeep(s)*.

Through the forest they run on bare *feet*,
For they wear neither *boots* nor *beet*.
They chew plenty of *roots*, not *reet*.
From the lake, which provides for their *wishes*,
They eat mostly fresh *fish*, not fresh *fishes*.

The fishermen's laughter and *shouts*
Disperse all the *trout*, not the *trouts*,
And the hunters' *jeers* over their *beers*
Scare away the fine *deer*, not the *deers*.

Coming home late, the police *chiefs*,
Quite perturbed in their righteous *beliefs*,
Found a break-in by *thieves* (not by *thiefs*)!

Kerry Weinberg, PH.D.

Views

One eye is blue, the other is blue,
I am a person and so are you, they say I'm crazy,
But I disagree,
The world is dying,
And so are we...
But life's not fair;
So live with it!

Natalie Varrone

Endings

Yes, I see the man, the one sitting back there;
He's so drunk he can't see me, please don't ask me to care.
You want someone to help him, he's a sick man you say;
All alone and so lonesome, drinking his life away.

Well, I'll tell you a story of this man I know;
Just bring me a short one then I have to go.
Once he had all the good things the Good Lord bestows;
Then, he got him a guitar and the wine quickly flowed.

His home and his children were forgotten for days;
As he played his guitar and sang thru the haze.
Many women adored him, wanted him for their own;
He just loved them and left them, his heart was of stone.

His wife finally divorced him, she'd had all she could take;
And I've often wondered, did that stone ever break?
Don't tell him I saw him; what's my name? Mona Lee;
I just hope I haunt him, his ex-wife? Yes, me.

We found ways to go on, tho he darkened our days;
We just cared for each other and got thru the maze.
Those games of 'power' and 'victim', I won't play again;
He needs help? You do it, I've had enough pain.

Millie Kastet

Six Up.....Six Down

Sunrise.....

The mist dances on her body slowly
Her mind gently warms his imagination with soft blows

Temperatures rise as the sun continues to flow
Flow with them and around them
Covers them with Heat and Passion
   Racing hearts
    Racing minds
     Racing bodies

We're almost there
We see the rays of the sun setting
   Temperatures drop
   Emotions high
    We are there
     The mist is gone
      Sunset....

Kelley Dumas-Wright

Precious

As walking along the beach was I,
Hearing the darkness - Heav'ns cry,
The sparkling gems so wond'rous,
Like the eyes of a maid'n - so languorous,
The thrumming silence, silv'rn light,
Shone upon the moonlit night,
The blanket of darkness swallowed the cove,
Glittering diamonds in a king's treasure trove,
The grains, so tiny in my with'red hand,
Slipping through my fingers - grains of sand,
I stood watching, fascinated,
The dreams of my life emancipated,
As slowly the grains were slipping through,
I knew there was utterly nothing I could do,
I watched in horror, the last grains fell,
Burned by the fires of the deepest Hell,
The blanket of blackness grew deeper still,
A void in my soul no soothing could fill,
Time froze - damned was I,
He who let the last grains fly.

Matthew Kruer

John, better than God, John

There's a light in his eyes
He writes to disguise
He sees, but doesn't feel
But he feels love is real for you and me
He has no faith, but in self
His wife, a lonely girl
He tries not to please her but always does
His hair is no longer a legend
We call him hero now,
For causes, he speaks out
No history book rebel here
Only our hearts and minds will record him for times to come
So, as the karmic wheel goes around
We sees him in us all
All of us in him
We've come together, John, over you
May you feel peace, fly free as a bird
Amen, Brother
John Lennon 1940-1980

Mary Jane Cilreb

Spring

They were so young, and son in love
He knew she was sent from Heaven above
He wanted to marry, gave her a ring
The answer she gave "Not until spring,"

The winter was long, time moved so slow
He loved her so much, and needed her so
She was sixteen, he barely seventeen
She still insisted "Not until spring."

He built her a house way up on a hill
Her childhood memories form there lingered still
She gave him good new, a child she would bring
Only to be born, of course, in the spring.

Time for the baby, the pains would not ease
He gave her a kiss, her hand a gentle squeeze
The labor was cruel and death made it's sting
When the baby came, he named her spring.

Sometime life has no real rhyme or reason
Live life to the fullest no matter the season
If you find that one, and love he can bring
Enjoy that love in summer, winters, and especially spring.

Mary T. Fulcher

Untitled

Look at the lonely man crying
He found out today the girl was lying
At the doctors he found out he was dying
He finds it hard to believe
The lonely man has HIV
He knows it won't be long till the can know longer see
The lonely man knows there is no cure
What happened to the days he was immortal, it's all a blur
Only one thing is absolutely sure
In a short time he will die
At least he won't be around to see his family cry.
The only comment he can make is why
How could this happen to him
He remembers the lights going dim

Nycol Lyn Shepherd

Thank You, Shannon!

Once there was a little elf, who stood in silence on a shelf.
He couldn't dance, he couldn't sing, he couldn't do a single thing.
And yet, somehow, he always knew
The things that he would like to do.
He'd like to jump, he'd like to run,
He'd like to be out in the sun.
He'd like to dance, he'd like to sing,
He'd like to do most anything,
But all he could do was watch the girls and boys
Who came in his room to play with the toys.
One day Shannon said, "Watch!", and she started to throw
Her belts and hair ribbons, wherever they'd go,
And one landed on elf, as he sat on his shelf,
And from that moment on he never felt like himself.
First he moved his fingers, and then moved his toes.
He felt of his hair, and he wrinkled his nose.
His eyes grew quite big, and he turned like a top.
He said, "I'm so happy, I don't want to stop!"
So you just keep thinking what you'd like to do,
And if you wish hard enough, it could happen to you!

Mary S. Lee

What Have You Done For Me Lately?

What have you done for me lately?
Have you lent me money, bought me a car,
made me feel like a rising star?
Have you boosted my ego, given me praise,
told me you'll love me all of your days?
Have you treated me to dinner, mowed my lawn
rented me a movie, walked my dog?
Have you sent me love letters, bought me
something gold, defended my honor in front of my foes?
Have you paid for my vacation, bought me new
clothes, listened to my problems, sent me a rose?
Have you thrown me a party, gone the extra
mile to lift my spirits and make me smile?
Have you made me soup when I was ill,
brought me water to take my pills?
Have you fluffed my pillows, sat by my bed,
kept me company, rubbed my head?
Have you soothed my heartbreak,
helped me forget my past? Do more for
me, please. What you have done won't last.

Kathleen Kolar

Word Search

Every thought that has come to mind
  Has been embedded somewhere, in some soul
Since beginning of time

A poet yearns for his words to be new
  And this is what I yearn for, as I write for you
Dare I speak of love and try to find
  A secret wisdom to it all, somewhere in my mind

I long to leave you a precious gift
  A gentle muse through which you might sift
To find in the thoughts embedded there
  The universal secret God placed with care

But there are no new words to be spun
  For God says nothing's new under the sun
So there's no great magic in these words of mine
  That hasn't been said by some master mind
But oh, I searched from the depths of my soul anew
  For something so special, my dear for you.

Maxine Price

"The Stars Above Mapletown"

The stars shone about over a moonlit night,
Happy wanderers of Mapletown sauntered under the pale light,
The twinkling stars in their eyes, golden white,
And the little children recited,
  "I wish I may, I wish might."

Little humble Mapletown rested beneath their vigil care,
With no sound but that of footsteps about the air,
The hazy look around the bright watchers,
Gave a safe feeling to all the late night walkers.

The glimmering images off Mapletown's shadowed river,
Reflected the marvelous show that the stars delivered,
The stars winked to the passers-by,
From where they laid deep in the midnight blue of the sky.

The stars and their ethereal shine were disclosed,
The stars, with pureness, perpetually glowed,
The stars of the sky shimmered like a resplendent gown,
They are,
The stars above Mapletown.

Mary Alyson Eylers

Journey for Peace

Like a beacon shining bright
Guiding my way as if deep in the night
I felt comfort and peace of mind

Death came, comfort and peace are left behind

The sands of time have passed
Pain and sorrow still hath last

The want of heart and mind
Struggle with doubt yet undefined

The journey for comfort and peace
Is not an easy goal

I pray to God to show me how to once again
Fill my heart and soul..........

Laura Tafoya

Untitled

When I was little,
Gramma would come over.

She would sit in her chair
at the dinner table, look around
to see if anyone was watching,
and secretly slip some food underneath the table
to our dog that she named Daisy,
who would wait there expectantly.

She would let me paint her nails in a bright, bright red,
and color her face with makeup,
and do her hair however I wanted
before going back to the Nursing Home.

Later ...
She would look at my face, but not see who I was,
She wouldn't recognize us, when we came for visits,
She would forget almost everything,
She would die.

But ...
She never forgot to feed Daisy when I was little
and Gramma would come over

Marianne Leah Suelzer

Once A Baby, Now A Soul

There's life before death and sometimes after
going through at different paces, some get there faster.
There are places to be chosen and seen
you and only you can decide where to lean.
I like where I am which is where I've been placed
but I went through something that I hope others won't face.
I always wonder what I would have been like
and if my name could've been Betty, Susan, Kreig or Mike.
Where would I have lived? How would I have looked?
Who would have raised me? Could I have read a book?
Would I have had friends and gone to school,
played with dolls or used a tool?
The answers to these questions will never be known
for my human body, one day was unsewn.
Being torn apart, limb by limb
I owe it to my mother who made it all come to an end.

Kim Dominique

Grandma's Little Angel

Grandma's little angel, you will always be,
God sent you down from Heaven, for Daddy,
Mommy and Me.
My Grandma Alma loved me special, but
God took her back you see.
My little Makayla, I have all this love
that my Grandma gave to me, and now I
have a little angel to share it here with me.
Your Grandpa and Uncle Wade love you so,
you can't imagine the joy that you sow.
Grandma loves it when you come, to spend
the day with me.
Your tiny little hand in mine, feels so
good to me.
Your little hugs and sweet little kisses
brighten up my days, even when they're gray.
I just wanted to let you know that
I love you so,
Grandma's little angel, you will always be.

Linda Chaffin

In Case We Part Again My Friend

A friendship that has grown strong,
gives you and I a special bond.
Although someday distance may pull us apart.
You'll always live within my heart.
If the day should come, and you should go.
I'll miss you very much I know.
To your desire I set you free,
Even if it takes you from me.
I don't know how to break my dream
we must go on like the stream,
That stream of life that twists and turns.
as we go on and continuously learn.
I'm a part of you, you're a part of me.
connected we will always be.
We bonded the night we met.
A bond as unique as a sunset
Even if we part again.
I know I'll see you soon my friend.
Wherever you go, whatever you do.
Just remember I love you

Leah J. Nadeau

Hurricane Marilyn

Marilyn was a Hurricane that if wasn't hard to tell. With great
fury and destruction came to our Island straight from hell.
So furious a Hurricane was she that Marilyn flung the fish
and salt out the sea
The transformation is reminiscent of a magician's trickery. Burned
trees to brown and all around flung boats blocks from the shore,
killed mariners who braved the storm, now never as before, my
beautiful St. Thomas is beautiful no more. Almost every living plant
has been ravished until dead. It seems that this has happened just
as the bible said. I am passing through a forest of a ravished burnt
out scene, dead trees dried by wind and salt are where
beauty once had been. Severe destruction all around, jeeps on
jeeps and boats on ground. Galvanize is everywhere and wires
and poles and such. Marilyn's destruction, all is simply much
too much. All creatures were affected by this unholy mess.
And each and every one of us has our lives touched by stress.
Hurricane's cause destruction and unmitigated pain; please enter
hell and stay there, do not came back again.

Olga Rasmussen Lopez

M. S. Who?

One of many,
Full of life within
She taught art
She shares her heart.

Creative minds that can not talk,
"Hand lift the brush, add a shadow or cast the light."
There is no blame but lack of understanding,
This tragedy with a name.

Courage she has, more than I.
She laughs and beams with love
Inner strength she exudes,
But she can not talk or hold your hand.

Yet, she is still teaching
Those of us more fortunate.
Live each day, Love, Brother and Sisterhood.
Less important, life's meaningless concerns.

Her name is Jill and it's name is M.S.
She is my wife, I love her very much.
Multiple Sclerosis, what is this thing?
We're still learning, each of us!

Michael L. LeBlanc

Linda Blaine

Down by the sea near the eroding docks,
A lone old salt, puffing his briar,
Sat and stared at the rising sun,
Wizened face and long white locks.

It was a morning just like this,
Fleecy clouds went drifting by,
The red-gold sun bright-flamed the brine,
A spirited wind passed in bliss.

Suddenly there appeared a hazy mist,
That engulfed the seaworthy Linda Blaine,
She whirled and spun and tossed about,
And then began to shift and list.

Then men were thrown about like straw,
As the captain gripped the mast with fear,
Speeding on in wild abandon,
It seemed they entered a gaping maw.

His arms felt bound, he was in pain,
Being lifted to his feet, he was made to stand,
Two men in white escorted him in
The private office of Dr. Linda Blaine.

Harold Sampson

Words - Like The Wind

Words are like - the wind that blows
   From where they come - no one knows

Some words blow hot - and some blow cold
   Some words praise - while others scold

Some words are written - with pen and ink
   Telling others - just what we think

Describing things - we buy or sell
   Or roses that - we see and smell

Libraries are filled - with books and words
   About all subjects - including bees and birds

Some words are found - only in the dictionary
   Some are true - and some only fictionary

Whether we attend - grade school or college
   Words are used - to expand our knowledge

Words written in Braille - can also be felt
   But what they say - depends on how they're spelt

Some words fill poems - much like these
   Full of fiddle-faddle - and lots of fiddle-de-dees

But the wind and the words - finally cease for the day
   And it's a time of peace - and a time to pray
     Lloyd G. Nicholas

Sour Grapes

In this old world there are lovely things,
   Fringed lemony leaves and emerald rings.
There are shafts of sunlight and drops of dew,
   Crisp ruffled curtains and grapes of blue,

   AND GALL STONES!

There's the smell of bread all crusty and warm,
   The feel of velvet and the sound of a storm,
The aroma of coffee and Mulligan stew,
   And the sight of roses with buds anew,

   AND GALL STONES!

There's the smell of Christmas and spices rare,
   Goblets molded of silver and short fluffy hair,
The sight of wild roses and a meadow green,
   And things that our eyes have never seen,

   AND GALL STONES!

There's a baby's soft neck and his fat little hands,
   A bowl of steamed pudding and Old German bands.
There are bold colored flowers of fuchsia and pink,
   There's more to this world than you might even think,

   AND GALL STONES!
     Lynn Spencer

Was It You?

A woman stopped along the road.
Clearly anyone could see she was
speaking with someone.
Her voice remained low, extremely so.
There appeared to be no one near.
One could not get close beside her to hear.
She cupped her hands as if to someone's ear.
She slowly resumed her walk along the road.
Pointing here, picking a flower with loving care.
Then speaking again as if in prayer.
Was it You, I'd like to know.
Did you quietly accompany this
woman along road?
Offering an ear, warmth and cheer,
keeping pace in a friendly mode.
     Katherine L. Bond

Darkness

When the night is dark
Forbidden creatures take it to heart
They come out to play and have their fun
Then they go back in and laugh at the damage they've done

They only come up to try and destroy
The peace that is born in every girl and boy
At first they play with the feelings within
And the next thing you know your life is covered with sin

So let me tell you beware of the dark
Whatever you do, don't let it grow in you heart
Once it's inside you it's hard to get out
You'll hurt the ones you love the most, without any doubt.

I was one of them that let it in, by trying to be cool
Now, I can't see how I became such a fool.
I guess I just wanted to be the one friends wanted around.
And all they did for me was get me hell bound.

I believe satan would have taken me all those times, I liked to have died
But the good Lord wouldn't let him, because Christ still lives inside.

Now if your life is filled with darkness the devil will have his way.
But if you'll just let the Lord in, there ain't no way he can stay.
     Mitchell Lee Nichols

A Special Kind Of Mother

The love of a mother cannot be too highly emphasized
For she represents God's creature
So visible in our lives

Our lives, our hopes and dreams
Are cultivated by our mother
One who shares, cares, loves, understands,
   encourages, and disciplines
She is one who prays like no other

Your faith and love lifted our house into a home
Filled with laughter
So many times conquering the storms
Your love even reached out to comfort a friend
With whispers of hope and prayers
That lingered to the very end

Thank God for you dear mother
My faith and love still grow
I cannot put into words
How much I love you so.
     Maggie Sanders-Strickland

To Be With You

You are more than a dream come true,
For I was meant to be with you.
When I am with you,
in my heart I know,
This love that we were meant to share,
began so long ago.

From the beginning to the end of time,
I was meant to be yours and you were meant to be mine.

Since the day the world began,
I know that God has had a master plan,
he made the sky to hold the sun,
he made the sands to hold the sea,
and he made you for me.

Through all the days and the darkest light,
our love will be the guiding light.
With every breath I take,
and every day I awake,
the love I have for you will never fade,
in fact, it just grows stronger with each passing day.
     Maria Albrecht

"Dear Mother"

God bless you "Dear Mother" in heaven above,
For giving me life and a family to love.
We did dishes, sang songs and shared all the chores,
You gave sunshine new meaning, we never were bored.
Oh dear, it's my birthday, 44 years today;
What happened to time - it all flew away.
Red roses, hugs, and kisses I honored you with,
For my birthday each year, you deserved it, you did.
I love you and miss you so much on this day.
In exactly 2 weeks, 3 years ago today,
God sent down his angels and took you away.
Even though there are no roses, hugs, or kisses to give,
I have memories, sweet memories, to honor you with.
If I had one wish and it could come true,
I'd wish on my birthday to spend it with you.
When my time comes along and angels appear,
We'll celebrate together all my birthdays each year.
But today with honor, "I thank you with love,"
All my respect, hugs, and kisses on the wing of a dove.
Till we meet in heaven love forever and ever
Nancy Morgan Wuesthoff

Robin's Arrow

Before I was a man, I was an arrow
Flying through air straight and true
My shaft perfectly crafted and balanced
My feathers trimmed and neatly glued
My arrowhead honed and polished
The target squarely before me
   As propelled by the twang of a tightly strung bow
   My archer sent me spiraling through air.

Then it happened
My fine wooden shaft splintered and scattered
My feathers torn, floated off on drifting currents
My arrowhead, tumbling round and round, fell.

Naked when I awoke
I rose from hands and knees
Blood seeping from cuts and tears
And walked as a man through air
In which once I flew.
Kirk Ridgeway

My Painted Glass Window

Looking out at the world through a painted glass window.
First thing in seeing, flecks of dirt on the glass;
unfixable things on worlds this is one
not degrading the earth nor stripping its beauty.
See it not through the eyes of the beholder,
but as one on the out looking in.
Incompleteness still stands so my eyes search for more.
Beyond breaths a world of technology, metal embracing cement;
cold, hard, unfeeling soul wishing to shine, but out of luck.
For some things in nature remain unchangeable,
as old as the earth, but new as babe
blazing yellows, oranges, reds, and blues
lord of the sky, the sunrise.
Its endless gaze looks down on me,
past my painted glass window to the depths of my heart.
Finding whatever truth it is seeking, leaving,
to come again when whim commands
as I sit here thinking in my steel walled room.
Kristina Jutzi

If You Wanna Be A Dreamer

If you wanna be a dreamer,
Fill your pockets with silver and gold
Sail into the moonlight
On a ship - that's a sight to behold.
Follow that illusive rainbow
You may never see again.
Oh I was such a dreamer
Please don't ask me when.
I followed that rainbow- searching for its end.
But it was always just around the other bend.

If you wanna be a dreamer,
There's so many wonders you can find.
Make sure they're all of a lasting kind.
Build your dream house with treads of silver and gold.
Make it shine like a beacon, as both of you grow old.
And as the years go by, your dream and you
Will never ever die.
Oh the world needs such a dreamer.
You may have guessed - that it was I.

Yes the world needs such a dreamer.
Michael Joseph Kobak

A Time And Place

Are you emotionally stuck in a time and place
Feeling family and love ones don't care
It was something said or done in the past
That won't allow you to share.
Put pride and ego aside, learn to listen
You can let go of fear, and find love there.
Try love unconditionally

One day when you're all together you will see
Pain and fear on their face
And understand they are also emotionally
Stuck in a time and place.

Hopefully time will allow you to release
The pain and fear
You all will share the love that's there
All will have smiles on their face
And no longer be emotionally stuck in a
Time and place...
Leroy Price

Happy Fathers Day

On this special day,
Fathers all around the world,
Are highly being appreciated
For their kindness and hours of hard work.
So, let me be the first to say, "I thank you,"
Not only for the shelter, and protection,
But for helping me with my job, as a Mother
When I needed you the most.
Thank you for holding me close
When the pressures ran deep.
And for the many tears you dried
As they fell down my cheeks.

You may not wash the dishes,
Or even pick up your clothes.
But that's O.K., it keeps me busy,
As I'm anxiously waiting for you to come home.
Thank you, thank you, thank you,
I don't know what else to say.
Except, I love you very dearly,
And I wish you many a happy Fathers Day.
Michelle Hughes

A Friendly Face

Silence of the screaming rage
falls further away than remembrance can reach
seeking madly, he runs through the darkness
tripping, falling in the cold damp woods

The end is not far now
a drop from the trees sharp needles
falls upon the forehead of the victim
who has lost all that was his to the fear of what never was

When death is imminent a hand falls to his head
lifting it to the sight of a friendly face
who lightens his back from the wet soil

Slowly, he walks away
unaware that no longer has he the burden
of the terrified body lying in silence.
 Lucas Burbano

Walk With Me

She asked her, to take a long journey with her,
explaining to her that they could take nothing
with them. They would come across all that
they needed. Shelter would be found if the
wind was to blow to hard or the skies began
to cry releasing their pain. If their stomach
became restless their mother had already
prepared food for them along the way, and if
their bodies hungered thirst there would be
liquid awaiting their presence.
And then she reached out to her, her eyes
softly awaiting the final glance. And she
asked...will you allow me to bathe you
in the many ways God has given me the
ability to? Will you walk with me now,
bare in naked form, allowing me to provide
you shelter, food, and water beginning from
within? Will you take my hand? Will you
walk with me?
 Krista M. Ryan

Beach Walk

Ocean Breeze, salty and pungent
exhilarating to the senses
The sun is warm and soothing,
a golden ball suspended
over a turquoise sea.
Our steps are synchronized
to the rhythm of the pounding surf
calming our scattered thoughts
as they tumble aimlessly..
in and out,
like the tangled seaweed
in the shallow breakers.
The stretch of beach ahead runs on forever
and the sand is wet and gritty under foot.
I think of you
Your comforting presence, your carefree spirit
Side by side
Touching..
yet not touching at all.
 Lauralynn Healani DeNisi

"To Know"

Sometimes in life
Everything we don't know
No matter if we study
To realize
That with experience
Much more we know
Listen to the one who speaks
When he knows something
Write in your book, what others know
And when time passes, you'll realize
How much you have learned of what others know
A lot of people in life
Haven't had schooling
And if you hear them you'll realize
How much they really know
And it's because of their experience
Of what one listens and learns in the streets
If you take what's good
You'll have a school by helping others
Of what you've learned
 Olga Frontela

The Greatest Gift

Christmas time is a special time,
everyone will agree.
We put our special gifts under the pretty tree,
but the greatest gift that comes to my mind,
is the precious gift God gave for all of mankind,
and he didn't put our gift under the tree,
but upon it for you and me.
The Gift wasn't wrapped in pretty paper,
but wrapped in the color of red.
Pretty ribbons surround our gifts,
but a crown of thorns surrounded his head
I know that during Christmas time,
the babe in the manger comes to our minds,
but I also remember the man on the tree.
He is our gift from God above,
and no greater gift could we give or receive,
than the gift of life Jesus gave for you and me.
 Nancy Lafferty

Dreamscapes

Life within life, is this a dream?
Don't wake me up; I like what I see.
Dreams upon dreams, overpower me,
A circle of water, nothing it seems.
Filled with things that never before touched me,
Whispers of feelings dance, doesn't it seem?
Life within life, this feels like a dream,
Please, wake me up I don't want to remember these things.
Nightmares with masks, trees hidden by leaves,
Where is the face that I need to see?
Close your eyes forever if you don't want to be,
Remember if the mask is taken off, you awake from the dream.
Life within life, is this really me?
Dreams upon dreams, I don't understand a thing,
The fall is soon to come I need help, stand with me,
Holding your hand just another life of dreams.
 Leah Metzger

The Answer

You asked me today
"Do you think you ever sin?"
Anytime I fail what His Word commands.
Even in my ignorance there is no excuse.

Did He not say
"For the lack of knowledge My people perish"
It is up to me.
Do not the lines and shadows on my face
Tell of the disappointments from leaning on me?
He has said, "Cast all your care on Me"
"Trust Me, lean not to your own understanding."
Yet even now - I long my conscience He prick
And my face reflect His grace
No guile, no deceit be found in the recesses of my soul
That His glory be seen
This my heart's desire, my goal.

Mary E. Squyres

Just Look At Yourself, God

Just look at yourself, God.
Do you see what I see?
The reflection of sun on orange autumn trees,
The tiny slit of moon among fast moving clouds,
The deadness of rain as it nourishes the earth,
The brightness of newborns as they squeal and squirm.
God, just look at yourself.

Just listen to yourself, God.
Do you hear what I hear?
The whizzing hums of bumblebees defending their nests,
The creak of a rocking chair full of lonely night tales,
The shrill clink of a cash register ringing up bread,
The early morning bird demanding I wake,
God, just listen to yourself.

Just think about yourself, God.
Do you think what I think?
Those shocking colors of autumn that caress the lawns,
And rain and newborns and birds spiking at worms.
This is the world that I see, that I hear, that I know.
God, just think about it.

Mary E. Benecke

Night Sky Oratory

I went and sat at the feet of my beloved.
Distractions. Mind wandering. Me talking.
Stop and listen! Window! Clear receptive window!
The sky burnt umber. Light pops on the canvas. White flash.
The cross stands tall. Flowers dance with candle.

I sit at the feet of my beloved.
The energy lights up the room where the two of us meet.
Lightening wavers across the night sky.
Wow! From one end of the canvas to the other. What a picture!
Distraction...if only I had my camera...I'd do this angle...
Tripod...stop..focus where you are.
Look! listen, feel!
God! Speaking God! Lightening! Noise!
Canvas painted with God's hands. Power! Majesty! Awe!
Beauty!

I sit at the feet of my beloved!
Creation fills the inner and outer walls.
Light pops highlighting the trees.
Wind blowing. Trees dancing to rhythm.
Water falls! Unto me...God watching.

I sit at the feet of my beloved and my thirst is quenched.

Karen L. Savant

Healing Journey

there is only the glass surrounding me; it is thick and cloudy and
dirty with the evil of ages.
the Child is trapped inside the glass, and the essence of the Child
is truth and freedom and life.

there are cracks beginning in the glass;
I reach in - the glass shatters and cuts, bringing blood and pain;
a sliver of glass imbeds itself in my chest, my heart, opening the wound.
it will not stop slicing until it reaches my center,
ripping me open;
what is inside is black and thick and heavy like chains binding me
to the walls of my terror.
it will not stop spilling out until the blackness is gone, and it
runs red and free, cleansing, healing.

I must keep my hand, my arm, my self inside the glass
and not pull away, until I touch and hold the Child within
and stand with her looking out, at the cracking of the glass that
surrounds us; I reach out
shattering the prison of lies, fear, shame, until we stand together
surrounded by the clarity, the colors of healing, freedom, wholeness

Lydia Dorn

If It Isn't Clean, It Must Be Dirty?

Clean is clean.
Dirty is dirty.
If there is dirt; try hard not to say, 'It is dirty'
Consider instead, that it might not be clean.
If the dirt is gone, (which is not to say it had been cleaned)
Then the dirt must have deserted - or de-dirted, as dirt does at times.
... And, if the dirt is gone, it should be clean.
... But, ,if the dirt comes back to this same place,
it has to be pretty stupid dirt to go thru this all over again!
Let's just say the dirt comes back. Then, it is dirty again.
But what about this "IT" that supports all this dirt anyway?
"It" can't be dirt cheap, that's for sure!
And if the dirt keeps coming back to this "It", what is "IT"?
I know! I know! "ITS" DIRTY!!!
STILL, why would this dirt come back to the same place in the first
   place?
Was it because the second place might have been dirtier
than in the first place?
Or could it just be the dirt knew it was not necessarily
Dirty even when
Clean is Clean.

Margaret Bennett

West Side Girls

Born on the East Side, raised on the West Side,
Dayton, Ohio, West Side Girls.
Small apartment, apartment life, share with many
in need of a home.
One bed for three girls, tiny feet on cold floors.
Jack Frost on our windows, our fantasy world.
Mom's in the kitchen, Mom's cleaning now, Mom's at
the sewing machine, No time for fun.
Quiet! Be quiet! Dad is asleep. 11-7 shift, No time for fun.
Side walks our playground, movies our friend, school
and Church our refuge from War and war at home.
Grow up West Side Girls with kids of your own.
Give love, hugs and time, REMEMBER REMEMBER.

Lou Rinda Sexton-Hill

Almost There

I'm almost there; the end is near. Perhaps it'll
creep at night to greet me or come at dawn to engulf me.
Will it be quick or take its time?

The glimmering blue of virgin snow capping the mountains
will be no more; the happy chirping of spring birds
nesting silenced forever; the jubilant splashing of little
feet in summer waters never to be. Will it be quick or take its time?

Long summer walks, memories gone; horse back rides
through country settings smelling of wet grass, lost forever;
obliterated. Will it be quick or take its time?

Prepared I am for what must come. If nothing else
memories I hold, deep in my mind, deep in my soul. If life is
granted elsewhere, I will conform cause I've prepared for
what's to come. Will it be quick or take its time?

Reeking with the aroma of honeysuckle, my body anointed
with precious oils and cleansed of evils prepares
to meet whatever awaits. I'm almost there; the end is near,
Perhaps it'll creep at night to greet me or come with dawn.

Maria A. Ortiz

Maturing Love

How dare them, come into my life and make it dim.
Courting, pursuing, stalking, then capturing me on some conqueror's
 whim.
How dare them!

Why did he bring his sunshine smile to honor me?
Curtseying, prancing, twirling, then bowing deep into my glee.
Why did he?

When did our lives entwine, unite, bloom then slowly sour?
Ripening, sweetening, fading, shriveling with each succeeding hour.
When did ours?

Time will come when we two shall surely equal one.
Straining, convening; replacing strife with thoughts we both have won.
Time will come.

Then we will look into love's mirror; clear, serene and real.
Searching, probing, seeking to divide our image, yet preserve our seal.
And then, we will.

Maxine Brown Gloyd

Sterling Silence

Oft are times when gazéd words we worship,
Courting feelings found in tacit friendship.
Silver-treasured strangers smoothly swaying,
Golden-garbéd orbs, so suavely preying.

Primal powers peering render passion!
Whence evolved seduction . . . tender fashion?
Eye to eye enrapt enticing entrance,
From the womb of Wonder born is Romance!

Beauty being served, communion beckons;
Ret'cence profound, grandest parlance reckons!
Heartfelt secrets shared so sweetly certain,
Stage the setting for the final curtain:

Dreams inspired create fantastic presence . . .
Drama ended — Fate vows sterling silence!

Michael S. Centala

Cops

Mowin' my yard
Cop drive by - look at me hard

Go inside
In my drive he do slide

Gonna kill dat cop
Gonna kill dat cop

Cop broke my gate
Dat cop I do hate

Hit my dog with his stick
Grab my gun - his head I hope I don't just nik

Gonna kill dat cop
Gonna kill dat cop

Bust down my door
Shot him - now he lay on the floor

That sucker not gonna put me in the can
Ah, heck, dat was just the mail man.

Lee Hartley

If Tomorrow Never Comes

If tomorrow never comes, I can only hope that I had
completed yesterday;
That the things I set out to accomplish were done
with satisfaction.
Perhaps I have spread a faint touch of joy.
If tomorrow never comes, I hope that I will have
set right any harm I may have caused;
That the uneasiness has dissipated and peace reigns anew.
If tomorrow never comes, I pray that I could have
looked back and no tears of regret would have filled my eyes
no sorrow would have clouded my heart.
If tomorrow never comes, I would know that I have
Served my friends well, and perhaps the memories will be precious.
If tomorrow never comes, may God and the ones
I truly love have forgiven any debts of pain I have left owing,
and find a place for me in heaven and heart.

Michele O'Donnell-Imran

Who?

See nodding flowers or gently waving grass;
Clouds building castles, waiting for storms to pass.

Hear crashing pine cones or wildly pounding rain;
Vintage oak trees moaning, creaking out in pain.

Feel splashing ripples or cool refreshing draughts;
Chills sending shivers, spinning down spinal paths.

Taste tangy, salty ocean or bitter burning smoke;
Jasmine offering sweetness from beneath its silken cloak.

Smell pungent blossoms or spicy desert sage;
Dust devils hover, whirling in constant rage.

Senses madly working;
Who evoked this strange barrage?
Oh, it's only the wind —
That fantastic mirage!

Karen Kerman

A Perfect Place

Black and white, women and men,
Christian and Catholic, and no one with sin.

Heavy and light, wealthy and poor,
Older and younger, and so many more.

People and places, love and no fights,
Feelings and faces, and so many sights.

Everyone loves everyone, that they come to see,
Caring and sharing, as free as can be.

All these things, belong to one place,
Which is difficult to find, just through your face.

You must look inside, to find this place,
Inside the eyes, that lie on your face.

Peace and love, is all that lie,
Beyond the light, that's in your eye.

This place is deep, and hard to find,
Not in one, nor two, but every mind.

This place seems perfect, and is to me,
But how can we live, being troublesome free?

And now that you know, what this place means to me,
I hope that when you find it, you will agree.

Kristin Witte

Untitled

There are children born in sorrow beneath the golden sun.
Children wanting families, not being only one
They grow in fear with no one to love,
They grow alone like a lonesome dove.
They're poor little children who don't know where to go,
poor little children who might not see tomorrow.
If a child could speak you would hear them say:
   I want to live; I want to grow
   I want to share what I know
   I want to give, I want to try
   I want to reach a star in the sky.
The world will be here after we're gone
it's up to the children to lead me the world on.

Kim Bartolatta

Untitled

The end of the world is here
Can you envision it all around us?
Our technology has surpassed our intellect
Our society refuses to accept the abnormalities
That Mother Nature endows
Rather than explore the vastness of our disregarded minds and souls
We are left feeling isolated from the world
In the desolate dark we seem to cower
It collapses apart on the inside, through our cultures and customs
It crumbles apart on the outside, from the war and the hatred
We choose to make weapons that kill ourselves
We ask the never answered question: Why?
Is it instinct?
Is it the way it's supposed to be?
Or is it we just cannot cope
With the feeling of being outcasted from others?
Our correlation with humanity is fading
It is the end of the world
Are you ready for it?

Nathan Charlan

The Maze

Isn't it amazing that one little door,
can seemingly lead to a cluster of many, many more
Webbed in confusion, the middle man am I,
standing in the plush greenery of this complexity in time

Duplicated so precisely are the flowers cupping each
   monumental thicket
Adding to this mind-boggling mid-day walk are the fine
   layered brickets

Leaves fall from the tall oak trees high above,
enough to pave a trail into the adventure
The noonlight dances in the sky
Heated is the sweetness of the summer that prevails
Noon bells ring sweet music through the sultry mid-day air
High above are the towers clocking time

My betrothed and I are nestled between the shaded shrubbery
   Finding love in the existence of a Rubik's cube

Maria Conzo

My Love Forsaken

Love given endlessly, never replied
By your dark heart, but see fit to pulp mine.
You mock me, but even Cupid breaks stride,
Bow prematurely nocked, gives her the sign.

I found my love for you unquenchable,
My desire to kiss your lips unsatiable.
To hold your ethereal body tight,
Hard, but to my dismay, my fright,

My love, it is unrecompensed, in a lull;
Slated clean as the River Styx
Washes me with blow after blow
And spins me lifelessly against the bricks.

From the Heavens high, to the underworld
Far below, all creatures name us the match.
From the naiads to the nymphs to twirled,
Tiny color wing-worms we were to watch.

Still, you distaste me through it all;
Cut to the chase, dark one, why do you stall?

Morgan A. Wallace

School Daze

The school-house doesn't sit
By the side of the road today.
Sadly the blackberry vines are scarce
And the sumac in disarray.

Those who sought and got
Their education there,
Are thinning like the blackberry vines, and,
If still living, white, like snow invades their hair.

DON'T sell that education short,
It was tough to stay the course.
Hot days, cold days, all good days.
Molded mankind into force.

My wife and I do have the right,
to expound that history.
We got our education there —
we're survivors, DON'T YOU see!

Kenneth Findley

Untitled

Explain these changes of exterior behavior
by the changing of interior beliefs.
Hypocrisy, it becomes my stumbling block.
I sit alone in this wooden pew,
I feel like the only one,
I feel your eyes cast on me,
I cannot go.
Don't you see that the sanctity of these elements,
the symbolic measure of their sacrifice,
it weighs heavy...
it holds value,
I cannot tread upon it lightly anymore.
I am renewed by this man's conviction.
It sustains re-entry for my faith to submerge into.
This is my body which is broken for you,
take it in remembrance of me.

Melissa Short

All Alone

All alone sitting, waiting for your call.
But yet the phone does not ring.
All alone sitting wishing you were here,
Right here beside me holding me and telling me
You love me and no one else.
All alone sitting remembering the way you made me feel,
Remembering the way you touched me,
The way your soft lips would touch mine.
Our bodies so close, you could feel the warmth of our hearts.
Our hearts racing with each breath we take.
The soft music we would listen to, as the candles and their
Dim glow shined as bright as they could.
Remembering the sweet words you whispered in my ear.
All alone still waiting for your call,
But still the phone does not ring.

Lisa Marie Rocha

I Loved You Once

I loved you once
But will I love you again?
Or has my chance past?

I hurt over you still
Will the pain ever stop?
Or will I hold the pain forever in my heart?

I cry tears, tears of you
Will my eyes ever dry?
Or will my tears flow into rivers of blue?

I think of you constantly
Will you ever fade from my mind?
Or will you become my thoughts all of the time?

I think of the day when you'll be mine
Will my thoughts become true?
Or will I always be dreaming of you?

Lisa Kuthe

I Thought

I thought I was the one to cheer you each day,
but instead you cheered me.
I thought I was the one to pray for you each day,
but instead I found out that you prayed for me daily.
I thought I was the one to make your unpleasant
experience an enjoyable one, but I found out that I
looked forward to seeing you, as you gave me a good
feeling that I truly was helping someone.

Lucile Maxian

Symbol Of Love

Our love is strong
But we know it's oh so wrong
For we know we can't be together
Even though we want it to be forever.

My father told me it would be a sin
To date a person of a different skin
But I want to be with him in every way
All my life, everyday.

We had one passionate night of love
The angels must have been watching from above
After that night we agreed to part
As I walked away I felt a growing ache in my heart.

I see him pass me everyday
And not a word does he say
Nine months has passed and gone on by
I feel his son grow in me, and I want to cry.

The time has come and I waited so long
But God help me I think something's wrong
Looking down from the heavens with the stars above
I'm able to watch him, holding the SYMBOL of our love.

Kimberly Denise Archie

"A Misty Fog"

   Alas, the love of a man is hard to find.
But the admiration of a woman is easily given,
and it is the hope of hope that the eternal love
would be found. For no one can control completely
their emotions. But it can be said well
of one that is able to hide them.
Like a misty fog on a flowery field.

Kristine Campbell

I Have Never....

I have never pressed a flower between the pages of a book,
But, still, I have poignant memories that can be recalled
   by just one look.
As I walked down the street and passed a clutch
   of dandelions lying on the road,
I wondered....
What mother missed a small happiness that could have been
Had her child not dropped them while he strode.

Karen Bernardy

Lost Love

You are hurt and the pains are unbearable
But don't look back at your lost love.
Look up and fly like an Eagle.
Take a walk and let the air relax your mind.
If he hurts you, he will hurt you again.
He will be like the wind in a pile of leaves,
Scattering your mind whenever he leaves.
Look to the sky and fly like an Eagle.
Be free of the lost love who leaves you empty hearted.
The pain may not seem to go away, but focus on something else.
Time heals and gives you a new sense of direction.
He is not the only one out there.
Why are you letting it seem that way?
Fly like an Eagle and let it go.
Take my word for it because I know.
You are still in a dream world you know.
Let go because I told you so. When you strive for a goal - it's
destiny. So make a choice or lose your mind.
Reach for your goal. Think hard and forget that lost love
which wasn't meant to be.

Naomi A. Rose

Old Girl

"I'm tired, 'Old Girl,' I'll see you tomorrow,"
But in his voice was a tremor of sorrow.
He stroked her side with a gnarled old hand,
Limped down the dock and across the sand.
Tomorrow, somehow, never came.
That beloved voice never called her name.
But she held her bow high, in an expectant way,
Waiting for her captain, who would come one day
To varnish her decks and shine her brass.
He didn't come, - and the long years pass.

She's waterlogged now with a bit of a list,
And her bow spirit has developed an odd kind of twist.
Her wood is rotting, she's got no paint;
The name, "Old Girl" on her stern grows faint.
With a heart full of hope, her bow sinks low,
And her dreams drift back to the long-ago;
To the sun in her rigging, and the wind in her sails,
To salt caked decks, and the lust of the gales.
Still she searches the deserted shore
For the face of her captain, - who will come no more.

Marjorie Millison

The Nature Of The Boy

Blue eyed child in the springtime of his life,
Bursting with energy for the ecstasy of his existence,
Dwells in a home whose hearth is rustic,
Nestled in the sunshiny mountains and shaded valleys of the Blue Ridge.
He tempers himself to follow nature's path and harmonizes with it,
In ideology becoming the self-same leaf his wakeful eyes behold
Gently drifting to earth.
His child-eyes witness the sweetness of the land,
Recognizing each creature for their wild and weary nature
And innately comprehending the macrocosm of the world.

From the rise of the sun,
When shadowy creatures emerge from their night's cloak
And stand revealed in dawn's lucency,
To the twilight of the day,
When the boy,
Immature in body put mellow in understanding,
Stands fall and waves goodbye
With small fingers and glistening eyes to the ageless scene,
Man and beast honor their species,
If just on this small hill.

Maryah Rose

Motives

What matters the population's ruminations?
Burden of proof is on the prosecution.
Speculating on the jury's motivations?
Examine your own!

Court system "best for the children" determinations
doesn't know theirs or my devotion.
Blame assignment, guilty until innocence authentication?
I know my motivations.
Examine your own!

Are civil wars the world's jurisdiction
if we don't agree with the confrontation?
Judging a person's, culture's, nationality's motivations?
Examine your own!

Who among you lived my situation?
Why do you question my motivations?
Examine your own!

Mark F. Huber

A New Day

Night gives way to dawn of a new day,
Bringing new ideas, and dreams to try.
Unknown are the wonders and joy in store.
Unknown the heartbreaks it may bring.

But, with quickening anticipation,
I face this dawn of a new day.
The wonders and joy embraced and accepted,
Savoring and basking in their warmth.

The heartbreaks and sadness I ignore
With the hope — go away they will,
All the time knowing, they will not,
And in the end face them I must.

For, facing the heartbreaks and sadness in life,
How I overcame and rebuilt
Is what makes me what I am,
What builds my strength for yet another day.

At the beginning of this day
I was armed with knowledge
"That at this day's end,
A different person I would be."

Kenneth A. Tucker

Peace Reigns

Peace reigns in the still of the night,
Bringing joyful sounds from the people in the town,
Making light of all pain within her bounds,
Each giving until their hearts make sounds,
with joy of Praise for this small town.

The streets are bright with the full moon light,
Giving the picture of a very peaceful night.
Church bells ringing, giving meaning to our life;
Merchant's doors opened wide, to each passerby,
To purchase the goods they offer inside.

LOOK!!! What's this I hear, coming down the street?
A terrorist has brought the whole town to its feet!!
Watching with anger stirring inside,
As bullets were flying all through the air,
Taking with it a man in despair!!!

Sirens all blowing, screams of panic fill the air,
As the policemen shot down the terrorist with a gun.
HEY!!! The lights are back on, and peace is restored!
People are hurrying about once more, because
PEACE, I SAY, PEACE IS RESTORED IN THIS SMALL TOWN!!!

Nancy Williams

Snow Star

A warm breeze caressed the stars,
  Brightly glittering flakes of snow.
Her fur, soft against my cheek,
  The warmth of sunlight on a summer's day.
The clouds came,
  The rain stung my face, the sharp point of a needle.
She left... all too soon,
  The promise of the future... gone.
Like the mist of dew from an afternoon rose,
  Left, only the dreams of what could have been.

Marcy Desmond

Know Thyself

Close your eyes.
Breathe deeply and go inside.
Further than you have ventured in a long while.
Be not afraid.
The path is known to you, though somewhat cluttered by the
Undergrowth of disuse.
Look into your soul.
Blow away the dust of neglect and look closer.
Be not sad. The soul is forgiving.
It knows that, that which is often neglected is that
Which is most cherished.
Be not angry. The soul is patient.
It will wait for you forever and beyond.
Your essence is ever quietly present.
Listen closely.
The wisdom is innocence and experience reside there.
Embrace the root of your being.
For therein lies your truth.
Rejoice in yourself.
For therein lies beauty and love.

Katie Brais

Something By Beethoven

I feel the piano keys flow under my fingers as I seek to please both Beethoven and my teacher.
My fingers trip on a black key and a harsh chord escapes the piano.
I caress the keys again and command my hands to play beautifully, like my grandmother.
Grandmother's piano is all I have left of her.
Play something from Beethoven, Grandmother commanded me.
But, afraid of mistakes, I always told her I was not good enough, not like her.
When Grandmother died, I couldn't play at her funeral.
It was her wish—play something by Beethoven.
My teacher taps out the tempo on the polished mahogany.
Someday I'll play for Grandmother, something by Beethoven.

Marianne Sloan

Winter's Storm

Crystal ice and snow, blow into snow banks.
Blustery winds blow cold and sharp, snow drifts
Against the house; rise higher as the wind changes
sky of winter white crystal flakes; falling, blowing
Icy against the trees; limbs covered with winter ice
And snow. It stops and all is quiet;
Standing in winter beauty.

Maureen L. Smith

Definition Of My Life

Life is like a piece of trash
Blowing down the never ending streets
Never knowing what it will encounter
Experiencing new things everyday
And dodging new obstacles

Life is like a piece of trash
Being run over in rush hour traffic
Being swept off the ground and put in the garbage
Only to be knocked over
Only to be stepped on again

Life is like a piece of trash
It blows in the wind all its life
And when it reaches its final destination
It rests in peace
And is never disturbed again

Kristin Strathearn

Pedestal

The seeds get placed into the ground, just like in the beginning when you found a place in my heart. As the flowers grow, we grow together. In the rain we still laugh, in the sun we still cry, in the storms we shake but hang on; throughout it all, we grow and become strong, together.
As days passed and evil came, nothing was done wrong, but it came to you, you fought long, you fought hard, yet with all your goodness, with all your beauty, evil conquered and took you away.
Now with each flower petal that flutters to the ground, a tear gets shed for you, and that pedestal that I once put you on is now higher and eternally yours.

Nancy Burns

March Of Time

Striding through the centuries, time tramps all things
Before him; evil and good alike mere grist
For his continuously grinding relentless mill.
Civilizations rise and fall as he advances
With but pyramid and potsherd in his wake.
Few things survive Time's unremitting scythe.

Man's inquiring mind, his yearn for knowledge
Defy Time's indiscriminate forward journey;
His love of brother man resists assaults of Time,
As does deep need for something larger than he,
As told in myth and ancient lore.
Candlelight of wonder and understanding
In eyes of little children never dies.

Perhaps, just perhaps, Time destroys the unimportant,
Enabling man to build a better world
Could he but recognize, then undertake the task.

Marie F. Ryno

Dying Day

Once in a lifetime we shall dance on our grave.
Before eternal sleep comes the end of this winding maze.
Give me the chance to reminisce until a dying day.
I saw the remains of what used to be,
this vision so beautiful, someday you'll see.
We frolic in our youth as our minds grow old,
cherish this sweet memory, your life I shall behold.
Once there was a dream that together we would share,
How could time erase the chance to breathe this new found air?
A frown was placed upon your lips,
and silence filled the room,
how dare I speak to you my friend,
this shrine was all to soon.
Once in a while I look back on when we lived on a dying day.

Lindsay Niemann

Shared And Lost

When we met, it was a dream come true.
Everything in life we wanted to share.
Now the dream is gone and all is lost.

We shared a part of our lives, I lost a companion.
We shared our time together, I lost a year.
We shared some secrets, I lost a friend.
We shared our families, I lost a new home.
We shared many a dreams, I lost a few.
We shared a few tears, I lost a shoulder.
We shared joy, I lost a happy heart.
We shared a relationship, I lost a lover.

Your life has touched a deep part of me.
Always and forever I will remember you.
I'm glad we shared each other.
I'm sorry I lost you.

Kelly D. Burnaby

A Thank-You Poem From A Bi-Polar Manic Depressive

For such a long time I was frantic
Because you see I am manic
It was a bad ride
But you stayed by my side
When all seemed a loss
I would become very cross
When all was fair
All I could feel was despair
When things were somewhat right
My mind would be in flight
Now with some legal drugs
I'm working out the bugs
For you see
Now my mind is free
Life is now newer
So bad days should be fewer
Thanks for standing by me.
Mark Saincome

Magic Touch

You feel lonely inside your heart,
because the hope you had is gone.
You don't have to worry about anything,
nor be at all alone.

The savior awaits in the heavens,
for you to cry out his name.
So that he can give you a magic touch,
to wipe away the shame.

The touch is full of happiness,
joys, laughs and love.
Pushing out all the pains, as evil
flies away from you and flutters like a dove.

Evil fears the magic touch,
and the strength and power that it brings.
That makes you want to thank the Lord,
with a special magical blessing.

So don't give up believe in yourself,
take also my advise.
The cries and tears will give up hope,
when God's magical touch gives you a magical, brand new life.
Michelle Tompkins

Thoughts

A rose is but a gift of God —
Beautiful, delicate, yet strong in nature.
Your friendship is God's gift to me —
Warm, tender and always treasured.
Speak to me from the depths of your soul
  and I will listen quietly.
I will take each thought and contemplate —
  then give back to my love.
For it is of you I speak with love and admiration.
Pure thoughts and words do I give nothing imitation.
Listen to my words and you will hear my silence,
Listen to my silence and you will understand.
Lynn Walsh

Magic

The crystal ball said,
"I am more than a ball.
I can show you it all,
I'll show you the sea or the shore
Nothing to you that is a bore!
I can make the golden bells chime.
I'll make you a memory that'll last a lifetime."
Kathleen Marie Tschampel

Taken A Hookin'

Walks to the gate, comes the hush of the crowd. Names announced, beast and rider both proud. Riders heart skips a beat, a lump in his throat. He swings his leg over and tightens the rope.

The gate masters ready, prayers are said, visions of winning run through his head. A slap on the hand, a nod of his head, should be take a hookin', his dreams may be dead.

Now the gate opens, the clock has begun, a good ride, eight seconds, a buckle he's won. Out of the gate, the bull turns a back, the rider he wonders, what did I lack.

Hitting the dirt, hears a stomp then a roar, rider jumps to his feet, fleeing in horror. He runs to the gate, his foot is a miss. Taken a hookin' means years he'll be missed. Hail to the rider, his soul it does fly. Up to the bull riders heavenly sky.
Laurie Champion-Daigle

On Age

When I recall past chapters of my life,
Beam present light on images long spent,
Rash words fall mute, bold colors fade. Where strife
Cried out and combat flashed its wild intent
Hushed voices now half reach the inner ear
As, from afar in some cathedral, prayers
Administered forte arrive unclear;
And age-borne shadows tame the crimson flares
Kindled by a contending youth. My year
Is nearly written out; these final scenes
Complete the canvas of a spent career.
I rest, now certain what this record means:
Whoever reads or looks can never know
The painful pathway traveled long ago.
Kirk Browning

City Life

Little bird, happy bird,
Bathing in a mud puddle.
Do you know? Can't you see?
You will never be clean
in a mud puddle.

This city
This dirty, busy city:
Lonely faces, Run-down places,
Nasty children, Desolate races.
A veritable freak show,
Ladies and gentlemen!

It is hard to believe the STATE
that this CITY is in...

Why are you so happy, birdie?
How can you be so carefree, chirping and flitting about?
Can't you feel the pain that is in the air?
Of course, you realize that you can fly away from your puddle;
You are not condemned to live this way.

If you had the strength to take these people with you
on your flight, WOULD YOU?
Karen C. Burnstad

Shawn

He was more than a friend in away.
He always set aside time to play.
The one thing that his sister said to me that really
got to me was...
"He never had the guts to tell me but he always
had a crush on me."
He may look gone, but I know the real Shawn
will never be gone."
Leslie Evanoff

The Remains

Your remains lie in state today
At Beanblossom's Funeral Home,
Decked out as for a party,
Red suit, red earrings, against your brown skin.

Beautiful in death, more beautiful in life,
Today I visited the remains of you,
Your hair, your sparkling eyes, your smile,
Gone from us soon. Gone from us forever.
It is commonly thought that the body is one's remains.
Not so, Bernice.

When you are dust,
When the red suit fades,
When time has filled your niche with lesser things,
We keep the things you gave
Your love. Your touch.
These are your true remains.
    Nell Moses

Day Dreams

What are you thinking my lovely child?
As you lie so quietly with a pensive smile.
Do you dream of castles and shining Knights?
In countries away on some foreign sites.
Or do you dream of missions beyond the stars?
And a life of adventure in a place like Mars.
Do you dream of heroes and their shining deeds?
As they gallop through life on their great white steeds.
Are those silent words on those soft red lips,
All about strange people on bright space ships?
Dream on sweet child with innocent bliss.
You'll awaken some day with one sweet kiss.
And return again to your place of birth,
And a simple life on this planet Earth.
    Madge Reynolds

Untitled

I am the rose under the tree
As you can see I am small as can be
Under the tree — small as can be.
I feel the pain is bigger than me — just like the tree.
As the loving wind goes by kissing away the tears that I cry.
I am the rose under the tree
Thinking to myself how beautiful a rose I must be,
Under a tree as people walk by admiring me.
A rose as small as me.
Under a tree that's bigger than me.
Not knowing my pain is as big as the tree
Big as the tree that's bigger than me.
    Kathryn A. Beam

Friends With Depression

My pain and I find quality time
  for each other.
It's not fun. But it's comfortable.
We've bonded.
Tell no lies; keep no secrets.
What friends we've become!
It keeps us alive,
  wondering why...
But we need each other
  and meet regularly.
God is in attendance (we know)
  listening...guiding...never judging.
In the quiet,
answering questions not asked.
Gently, mysteriously easing the ever-present pain.
    Leslie A. Starr-Schmick

"Going Home Now"

It's as though you've been round-the-block,
As though you've been around a lot.
You should know what you want.
Maybe you will tomorrow.
Thinking about going home now.

Hope some old things and feelings are waiting,
Hope things have not changed like you have.
You appreciate them all now.
Like tomorrow you might appreciate today.

Can imagine yourself being at home.
So much to do, so much you can do
But you might not do anything.
Success, failure, fear, choices, chances, hope.
Will experience them all when you get home.

Are you leaving anything of value here?
You will come back. Sure you will? Why?
Here was a purpose, meaning, something real.
There still are but they are for someone else,
Taking my memories and going home now.
    Mark H. Leblanc-Lewis

Ode To Inked Skin

The spirit and dreams of one's soul become visible
as the virgin skin becomes inked. The skin starts to
become a permanent tapestry for all to observe in awe
and wonder. The ink is like a suit of armour and can
be the eyes into one's heart and soul. For one who has been
inked has been transformed from a caterpillar into a butterfly
and is perceived in a new light by a unenlightened brother.
For some fear the enlightened because they don't understand the
reason behind the ink. Some are fascinated by the ink because
of the illusion that it creates. For we all are equal in the
dark, but allow the sun to dawn and the difference is there
for all to see. For once ink is applied to the skin you are
who you have been, but you will never be the same. So remember this,
for those that haven't been inked yet, beauty is only skin deep, but
inked skin may be the most glorious sight there is.
    Lee Stockman

Untitled

In the dawning of each and every day,
  as the sun sheds the surly bonds of the horizon,
    I see the brilliance of your smile
      streak brightly across the sky.

Through the heart of the day,
  in the rush of the wind through the trees,
    in the sounds of wild flowers growing,
      I hear your name spoken softly.

In the blaze of each sunset,
  and all its attendant majesty,
    I feel the warmth of your voice calling to me.

And when the night cloaks us in its velvet,
  I see the sparkle of your eyes,
    so intense in the glitter of myriads of stars,
      scattered over the heavens.

Your touch is the caress of the butterfly's wing,
  and I see you in all the wondrous magic of nature.
    I see you...and my heart smiles.
    Norman C. Kohlstrand

"Rain"

The wet, moist droplets fall from the heavens
as the sky guides the way,
walking through the mildew filled grass
hoping for a new bright and sunny day.
Rain will come and go as it pleases
bringing excitement or a steady calm,
relaxing in its melody
or sounding a thunderous noise to a child's alarm.
A storm has a sense of thrill
and excitement as it passes through,
running for shelter
while the rain comes pouring down on me and you.
Water fills the nearly empty streets
as if a river has taken its place,
the roaring sounds of rainfall
come trickling down our face;
thinking back to remember
the child's fear, as she prays on her knees
to God and his grace.

Kevin Popovits

As We Grow

I want to be the one you love, want and desire
As the moon glows upon the open sky
As you are the one I lust and admire

Our lives change every day just like the autumn leaves
Sometimes I freeze just like the winter trees
And I am honestly so sorry

I am warm, gentle and true
Just like the spring air and dew

The summers come with love and joy
Just like our little girl and boy

I can change just like the weather
As long as we are always together

Melissa M. Brown

Eternity

All but to thee are as the wandering shadows fall,
As the homing pigeon returns answering his mate in call.
The sun sets on another day where sky and mountain meet,
As two lovers' hearts share a unitary beat.
Darkness spreads its mystical veil once more,
As the cessation of day ends its daily chore.
Eventide brings with it moments that entrance,
Created for men and women thrown together by fate and chance.
All beings catapult into a world of sighs and laughter,
So thankful for the instant and blissful hereafter.
And how and why has this all come to be?
Our God and Maker is the One with the golden key!

Marilyn Kriney Tonnesen

"A Poem For You"

It seems like only yesterday when you and I first met
And as the years went by so fast I've only one regret
That I didn't know you all the years before
You are such a special man I couldn't love you more
You touched so many peoples lives with kindness, joy and care
Your bright blue eyes revealed your heart your love was everywhere
My thoughts keep going back in time to all the special ways
You showed your family all your love each and every day
The other night I listened close as I heard the chime bells ring
I thought of you, you're an angel now…I knew you got your wings
So I say goodbye to you for now I'm so sorry we must part
But know that you are always here living deep within my heart

Melanie Marasco

Song Of The Prairie

The smoke rises slowly toward heaven
As the campfire lights up the night
We'll sing sad songs about life out here
While we wait for the coffee to boil
We tell one another our troubles and about
the miles we have yet to run
With a star-studded sky for our blanket we shiver
As a coyote's howl pierces the night
Sometimes we sure do get lonesome,
and the comforts out here may be few,
but I'm just a cowboy who chose this life,
and there's nothing I'd rather do
Yep, tomorrow I'll climb back in the saddle
And the warm sun will soothe these old bones
Giddy-up Dan, though you're weary
We've been through a lot you and me
I guess someday we'll die on the prairie
when all our work here is done
We'll ride one last time toward the sunset
And our last Song Of The Prairie is sung.

Lauretta Brockman

NEL COUR DELL'UOMO

Disappearing in the shadows is a broken heart,
As suspended fires of the evening unite with fury.
The trembling waters came alive under the silent moon,
I am drowning in beauty as I look into your eyes.

The radiance of the flame of a candle lives in my heart,
How red your lips are, bella mia, they give me great joy.
I wait for you to secure my love in precious stone,
My sighs are so violent for you bewitch the sunshine.

Tonight there will be no peace for me in the world,
Love holds me in a prison and I do not protest its presence.
As the winds reach the heavens over the sweet stars,
I release the beauty of love in the crimson flowers.

Remember how you stood on the white marble balcony?
I suffered then when my heart was carried to paradise
Hidden in its glowing flames I was overcome by its power,
Bella mia, I have given you my heart. How much do you love?

Marcia Schwartz

Dance

"Georgie Girl" played on the radio in a different day and time
As Mom swayed to the music, we sat on the sofa
Watching, giggling, slurping our chicken noodle soup.
She wasn't supposed to act silly being a mother and all
At maybe thirty years old.

We wouldn't let Mom step back into the confines of childhood
And she would only let us grow-up so high.
We needed her to be a grown-up, she needed us to be her children.
And yet, we all needed a little of what the other had.

As though wishing for myself to be that small again
Though not in size or stature, but, so free
In thinking, in feeling, in being a child
I can transform myself, and now at nearly thirty-five
I can look back from the edge of the sofa
And watch the spirit of the child in Mom,
Dance.

Kim J. Ozment

"Eternal Youth"

Don Quixote's search goes on and on...
As Man awaits the distant dawn.
Of answers to his burning quest,
Knowledge to add longevity to life.
And yet, we seem to overlook,
The fact that these answers are in THE BOOK.
It is human nature to dwell on strife,
Completely overlooking the Joy of Life!
A pessimist dwells on sorrow and fear,
While an optimist holds Life so dear.
Therefore, let us strife to find the Joy,
Not only in living but also in dying...
For that is the process that frees the soul.
As the butterfly ascends from below,
Leaving the cocoon that it has outgrown.
Man too must leave his mortal body and all he's known.
In order to fulfill the mythical search,
And live forever but not on this earth.

Norma Jean McMacken

Prospector

I was lost and all alone,
As I wondered for days,
Cold-weak and weary,
I knew my time was near.
As I lay in the snow,
My body felt warm and within,
There drifted love and peace,
And when I saw the halo
and heard his voice.
I knew the Lord was with me

He said, What's wrong son?
I said, Your looking at a lonely, lonely man.
I'd give all the gold that's buried in this land,
for one little walk with Jesus to the sweet promise land.
Where the holy water is as sweet
as the mountain dew, the mountains
are high and the rivers are wide.

The Lord spoke and said,
Son take my hand and I'll take you home
to a place more precious than gold.

Leonard Orr

Spiritual Lifting

Once upon my darkest hour
As I gazed from my third eyes tower
I looked around for a sign of hope
As I struggled to grasp my life's rope.
I had spotted one small light
Amongst this gloomy self-shrouded night.
The gleam was neither dim nor bright,
Yet steadily shining to give me sight.
I raced towards it, when I caught it's glimpse;
Wild and happy like Bacchus and the Nymphs.
Closer now, it's warm and healing
I embrace it sealing it there.
What is this which raises me up form deprivation?
Why all it is, is self-belief and salvation!

Mark T. Snyder

Red

I am blood, stained, on a used battle ground
condemned fires beneath, which demons surround
I am the anger that burns deep in men
a rose, showing off, at the top of its stem
the wine of an old man remembering when.

Michael Mehaffey

Ode To Bid Whist

Bid whist originated in the South during the slavery age,
As a release from the chains and the master's cage.
For families who were separated; mostly on the auction block,
It was important to have an "universal" game - one solid as a rock.

So Bid Whist was developed and the rules were made.
The bid would open with 3; end with 7 is how the game would be played.
A low bid would take out a high bid and then a no,
To get the bid, the next number you had to go.

Now logic says a high bid should take out a low, in those days, it wasn't so.
'Cause if master knew the game, he'd take it away,
Since he couldn't understand the logic; it was okay to play.

Now, there were "field Coloreds" and "house" ones, too. And we all know what the "house Coloreds" do.
They tried to incorporate bridge from the master and his miss, into the game and added a twist.

The "field Coloreds" said, "No, hold up — this ain't so,
Take your master's game and back to the big house you go."
So the "house Coloreds" left and started their own game,
And made the high bid take precedent for the "house Coloreds" who came.

So, when folks talk about bid whist from here or there, tell them to come on by and pull up a chair.
Share with them how the game really began, and how the "house Coloreds" messed up the Bid Whist plan.

Minnie Reynolds

Reunion

Like a favorite photo album in the pages of my mind
are warm days in Carolina, Carolina in the pines

Grandpa, he was a carpenter, as his dad was in the past
when time came to build his house, he built it to last

Grandma was a gracious lady, she'd find good in everyone
she'd wear hats on bargain days, and to church when the week was done.

Generations of pine trees, with roots planted firm and deep
add a smell that I treasure to the memories I keep

But those trees aren't the only ones, with roots deep and strong
wind and rain won't shake us, as our family tree grows on

Bonnets, quilts and butter churns, add a country flavor
packing up to go back home, with mementos sent to savor

Fond memories of cousins and relations, light the corners of my mind family gatherings are even better with the passage of time

Kathleen Brady

"The House Below The Hill"

There's a house below the hill where the road runs by,
Alone and empty, the grass grown high.
I've traveled the road many times,
I climb the steps and open the door as I have many times before.
I stand inside and look around, then turn my eyes to see
All the things the house is to me.
A cold winter night by the wood burning stove.
A warm spring day with purple crocus blooming on the hill.
Swimming in the summer by the old windmill.
In the fall a day filled with sunshine and ripe yellow grain.
The old house still stands by the road.
A windmill turns when the wind blows cold.

Lillian R. Jenkins

All That Is Me

The wonders of my soul
Are always changing
Yet the beat remains the same
Dark and scary, only momentary, on and on I go
Rays of nature's pure light
Filters through cracks in the wall
Yet shadows refuse to fade
Bright and merry, only momentary, on and on I go
The wonders of my soul
Hold love that's unconditional
Yet the scars remain the same
Deep and buried, only momentary, on and on I go
The healing salve of life
Slowly penetrates the pain
Yet aches refuse to fade
Cool and airy, only momentary, on and on I go
The wonders of my soul
Is what I see, feel, touch, love, breathe
Is all that is me

Nikki Kage

Listen

Listen to your beating heart
And you will hear the voices within
Telling you God has been there from the start
If you'll only listen and let him in

Listen to your dreams
For they can be a stepping stone
Into a life with many streams
To follow, but never alone

Listen to the voices
For they are telling you
To go ahead and make your choices
And have faith in whatever you do

Listen and you will find
The peace you are longing for
And you will hear God's answer in time
And the turmoil within will be no more

Marilyn Sisson

Chairs

Ma'ma, can I sit there? Oh, it's so high!
And what's that tray for? Oh, I see.
I'll be very careful and try not to get it dirty. Oops!
Thanks, Ma'ma.

Mommy, can I sit there? Is this really mine?
It's just like Daddy's big one. It rocks and turns,
And I can lean back and put my feet up.
Thanks, Mommy.

Mom, I don't want to sit in this thing. People here
make fun of me - the way my face looks; my crooked legs.
Why couldn't God have taken me instead of Dad?
Someday that man will pay for your loneliness.
I love you, Mom.

Mother, forgive me for not contacting you in so long,
But they don't let people write or use the phone here.
I'm so sorry, I never meant for it to happen. Anyway,
They have a new chair for me, so I must go now.
Please remember...I love you very much, Mother.

Linda J. Weigand

My Book

I stare at the blank pages
and they stare back...so lifeless and empty
hoping, waiting for me to share my deepest thoughts.
My life unfolds page by page
confined to these little blue lines
How can thoughts be put into words
How can your soul be expressed on paper
I ponder this as I stare at the empty blue lines
But without warning...the pen tears across
the vacant page.
Each letter is a part of me
They make words, which makes thoughts
which fills a book that is me
My letters, my words, my thoughts, my book,....,me.
Each page feels my pain, shares my tears,
dreams my dreams, and reminds me of the good times.

Nicole Smith

Sometimes

Sometimes you think of their smile or their cry;
And then you just sit and wonder why?
Darcy and Glen, Amen.

Sometimes you question is there a God,
Or how could there be?
As he took your children away from thee,
Darcy and Glen, Amen.

Sometimes, you cry or just sit and stare,
But time is short, so look to your heart,
As they are in there.
Darcy and Glen, Amen.

Sometimes, think of the good times you had,
And how they always made you proud,
Hopefully, this will ease the pain
And you can try to start over again.
Darcy and Glen, Amen.

Maureen Metzinger

Faded Honor

The knights have long since lain away their armor
And the mighty kings have lain aside their swords
And Chivalry and Loyalty only live in fantasy
Beside Truth and Honesty and Lords.

Gallantry rides slow upon his charger
And Romance has been scattered to the winds.
Honor lives in fairy tales, and dreams inside of wishing wells.
Innocence is full of rips and rends.

Where now can a tender heart go wandering?
Where now can a gentle dove light down?
Among the torrid races? Their empty echoed graces?
Silhouettes; dark shadows on the ground!

Our heroes have ridden past the sunset.
The fires inside their noble breasts burn low.
Their passions lie in memory, written down in eulogies,
Their courage faded into weakened glows.

Alas, the age of Honor has departed
To be replaced by something less within
Taking all its Glory, to live inside of History
Never coming back this way again.

Karen Hoofard

California Landscape

There are native lilacs blooming,
And the grass is green
Along the valley floor,
For the valley is beloved by Spring
And sweetly does she flaunt her treasure.

But the muffin hills are jealous
For they, too, have courted Spring —
Receiving merely glances in return.
Now, baring nubile bodies to the sun instead,
They seek release of pent-up passion.

The sun, whose heated rays
And brazen glances they implore,
Caresses them so warmly
As to burn them, blush them brown;
His searing kiss consumes them.

While still the valley flirts with Spring,
The sun has consummated union
With the naked, prostrate hills —
And prematurely from their bodies
Wizened Summer issues forth.

Kay E. Kuter

Tranquillity

To My Beloved Bethaney Cobun
As frail candlelight intrudes the undying evening,
And soft waves of moonlight caress its shadowed shores,
And gently in my ears your heart is singing,
And on the rose is dancing the Faery of Azure,
Slowly I wander into slumber wondering if I'm dreaming,
For if I am I wish never to wake; my Love it is you I adore.
My celestial angel blooming in the Sea of Tranquillity,
My winter rose, my Bethaney.

Nicholas Toscano

Primal

For those who learn to know truth,
And seek to give, without the plans to take,
Prepare to meet thy God,
In all his hope and glory.
Within the moments after dusk,
Before dawn takes first place,
Let all sorrow filled salty water seep from thyne eyes
To cleanse thyself from within
To touch, to taste, to feel
The first stirrings from the new day.

Let this be the dawning of awareness
For all the world to know:
To sip from the glass of once pure self
And know no more suffering from within.
The original child has spoken
Let it be so.

Kathryn Benson

Spoken

As I feel, I have a long way to go;
A multitude of memories speed through my head;
Of people, places, and faces that I have known.

Souls drift and spirits shift;
My reality hangs by a thread.
Who is to say;
That when children play,
A few kind words could not be said?

Michael Gathings

A Letter

To you I write:
and my fingers fly
over the keys of this old machine
as my tongue would fly, if you were here.
If I put in what I should put out,
and put out what I should put in,
you will know what I mean, you are such a dear.

I don't erase. So the errors remain—
some typographical. You must know
that I'm careless because I am fond of you.
Because of true confidence, not disdain,
but great admiration, my letters are so.
I even imagine you're fond of me too
when I write to you.

Nell Esslinger

A Family Is One

A family is one who knows how to care
  and love that will not wear
A family is one who knows each others feelings
  so as one we can start the healing
A family is one who knows how to smile
  even in an unending mile
A family is one who knows how to stick together
  through hell or high water
A family is one who knows how to be
  just one big happy family

Kathleen Price

My Life Walks With Me

As a child of five, I watched kites in the air
and longed to be flying with them...
Now, with planes soaring high overhead
My thoughts are carried to His diadem.
I liken that unto my daughter and son
Once they were babes — now parents too.
As I could not fly with the kite or plane,
I cannot travel in their shoes.
Recalling days of my childhood...
And those of my glorious 'teen' years...
Slipping forward into thoughts of romance
And of the long hours of becoming a mother
...Now, facing the status of today...
It finally dawns on me
My life walks within me.
I am not a mere observer of life passing by...
The actor has always been present...
I ponder - forewarned
What kind of actor am I
Is God pleased with the character formed?

Mildred Lucas Reddoch

"AIDS"

There is a disease going around our nation
and it's killing all of God's creation.

It may not sound fair,
but it is very hard to bear;
with the situation that lies ahead to those of us who care.

Many families must say goodbye
to the ones they love that soon will die.

Although we have to go on with our lives,
we must take the days in very long strides.

Through this we all will become
a better nation that will fight as one.

Laura I. Liposky

Timeless Love

They meet by chance as their eyes took a glance
And it took but a moment for their souls to touch.
With just one kiss their fates were sealed,
For none are to old for love to take hold.
Down the aisle they walk hand in hand,
Eyes full of love as they say their vows.
And they start their new life as husband and wife
To share happiness and joy forever and ever.

Nancy Lou Foye

The Parts Of A Child's Mind

Though I'm not perfect I thought of this rhyme
and it took a bit of my time.
The parts of a child's mind are mixed,
once they are scarred they cannot be fixed.
A child is a person just like you.

Children are small, they run in the hall,
they don't answer when you call.
But all in all children are small
and sweet and pretty neat.

Children are our fate
they will save our planet before it's too late.
So take care of the young
even if they do stick out their tongue.

The parts of a mind are fine and delicate.
So take care of them, they decide all our fates.

Michael Douglas Younke

It's All About Injustice

We need to silence the violence
And increase the peace
It's all about injustice
That people can't see.
Too much killing, too many drugs,
Lots of mass murders, and many a thug.
Some people are living out on the street,
Scavenging their way, for something to eat.
There are too many robbers, stealing people's dreams,
Just so they can go along with some stupid scheme.
Many young children cry themselves to sleep at night,
Cause Mommy and Daddy are fighting with spite.
Why do we let this happen?
It sounds terrible, I know.
So lets silence the violence,
And bring peace to everyone.

Lysa Ackley

To A Friend

I saw a tear in the eye of a friend
And I wished there was a message I could send
To relay my thoughts that lie within
And tell my friend her faith will win.

Somehow it's always so hard to say
What our hearts long to convey
But I hope my friend will somehow know
Without an outward display or show.

That the reflection of grief upon my face
Is heartache that is taking place
And I hope her burden of grief is less
Just knowing a friend has shared her stress.

Mary Vion Hoover

"When You Are Near"

When You Are Near,
And I may see,
The softness of your eyes,
There are no shadows on the ground,
Or any lonely skies.

For I am happy in my heart,
Each moment of the day,
And I am blessed and comforted,
by every word you say.

I am encouraged to succeed in everything I do,
And I am grateful to my God,
That I may be with you.

But every time you leave me,
And we have to be apart,
There is an empty feeling,
In the center of my heart.

And all I do is wonder then,
How long the time will be,
Until the shadows disappear,
And you come back to me.

Kim Grinolds

True Love

True love is a feeling, no words can describe
and I know I can't, but for you I will try

It's a feeling of closeness, that never fades
instead it grows, with each passing day

It's a feeling of warmth, when I see your face
or just feel your presence, or find a small trace

It's a feeling of tenderness, which gives us both grace
so we can tread lightly, in each others space

It's a deep bonding trust, that both of us share
with no room for doubt, because of how much we care

It's a gleam or a sparkle, in each others eyes
it's that twinkle you get, you just can't hide

It's a bonding of hearts, that no one can break
we both give, as much as we take

It may happen suddenly, or it might happen slow
but it will fill your heart, until it's ready to explode

Linda M. Christensen

Look

Written for and dedicated to Miss Jara D. Belcher

Take a long, deep look into my eyes,
and have a quick look into the farthest
regions of my heart.
　If the picture that you see is moldy
and gray, close your eyes and come back
tomorrow.
　If by chance you sneak a peak of the
other side, that's untouched and pure as the
driven-snow.
　Sit down, take your shoes off, and put
your feet up, and prepare yourself for an
　experience of astronomical proportions and
and dimensions; for the eyes are a portal
to the heart and the soul.
　Instituted in my heart is chivalry, etched
in my soul is loyalty.
　As strange as it may seem, even in these
troubled times, and it still might be hard to
believe. That all things are in reach only
if you look.

Leslie G. Rembert I

Untitled

I love you,
And great wings beat in my heart,
Carrying me out over vast shadowy depths
Where your voice sounds amid the towering crags,
Luring me ever onward.

Louise Glynn Barr

"The Landlubber's Lament"

The ship rose and sank on an uneven keel;
And from the top of the yardarm to the hold, you could feel
The waves lash and break with unlimited fury
Upon the decks, then hastily scurry
Down the scuppers to renew the charge
Of Father Neptune's resentful barrage.

As I lay listening to the unrelenting splatter,
Remorsefully I asked myself what was the matter
(As my stomach tried dogmatically to complete
Unscrupulously with the movements of the fleet
Rising and falling, 'round and about,
And seemingly, every moment turning inside out)?
Then along came a wave with an usual swell
And all of a sudden my stomach got well!
Now you'll find me on the bounding main
With never a twinge of seasickness again.

Marvin H. Cheshire

Our Land

Quietly I lay beneath the trees
And felt the wind in every little breeze.
I looked across the field and plain
And saw the wind sweeping over the grain
"This is my land", I thought, "My homely land"
It's soil, its trees, its prairie sand.
Its mountain towering high
Far beyond the cloud and the sky.
Flowers and trees together sown
Into a form of beauty it has grow.
Our land, free to walk, and free to roam
A land which we call home.

Kay Odom

Dad

It doesn't seem that long ago that I was only three
And every time you turned around there with a smile was me.
Remember when I'd put on your shoes and pretend that I was you?
You were the best man I had ever seen and I hoped to one day be as
  good as you.
Remember all the times you came home after a hard day's work
And stumbled over some old toy I had left lying in the dirt
And every time my heart got broke you were there with loving smile
To help me through the ups and downs we go through as a child.
And now that I'm all grown I don't tell you often enough
How very much I miss those days when I was growing up.
Any one can be a father but it takes a special man to be a "Dad"
And every time I say that word, inside I feel so glad
So glad to have a Dad like you who has taught me the things I know
That has helped me each and every day to live, and learn, and grow.

Lisa A. Cooper

Yggdrasil

The World Tree shivers in the empty silences
and echoes twist around the ancient limbs.
The aging roots that clasp the living worlds
move gently with the light born cosmic hymns.

The Myth Tree dances in the hopeful living
with just a chance that it may be released
to live—or to be killed by its creations
in an agony of violent disbelief.

This tree that bore first man and beast then tears
the start of wisdom, war and wondering—
it bears the Earth like Atlas through the years,
a mocking world with no more time to sing.

  Until the ancient green dome withers, turns
  to brown-gray dust in winter beaten by sun,
  destroyed by weather—It will not rise again.

Yggdrasil will not rise again at all.
The magic mighty tree gone back to dust
was set throughout forever for this fall.
Our world, once cradled gently in its arms,
is dropped.

Letitia Rizzuto

In The Seats

I scratched the bumpy sticky wall;
And dunked myself in my hard plastic seat;
The big radiant green and orange field;
Shined in my face;
The sizzle of my Coke;
Going down my throat;
I sigh, peacefully, Ah!
  Then the sight of one of the best players,
Gary Sheffield made me jump out of;
My seat with delight;
  The smack of the ball sounded;
Like mighty thunder;
  My knees were trembling;
As the game was tied;
The "boo" of the crowd sounded;
Like the horn of a truck;
  In that moment I knew the game;
was lost.

Neil A. Lyn

Wake To Reality

Steady upon the stone where my thoughts are voiced,
And deemed pathetic in this golden existence.
Let me crumble! I say to the rhythmic drum.
So it takes me upon the deep rapids
Waking me to the day's end.
Clear is the sun that drowns in the ocean,
Like the moon's illusive radiance holding me safe.
I break from this cage of a sleep-filled night
To welcome the nothingness that is arriving.
Where I stand is no longer relevant,
For my foundation rests upon a dying stone.
But not once did I expect to remain sheltered
From the blaze of dusk that burns into the stars
Of nothingness

Lisa Ball

The Indian

Once there was a nomad,
An Indian, an explorer.
His homestead he would leave, to explore the plateau.
He did not have an atlas to lead him around.
One day when he awoke, his mighty father, who had enriched his life,
Revealed that the mighty powers did legislate that they
   would move to a reservation.
The Indian boy then made a declaration,
"Some democratic nation!"
Kelly L. Walding

Spirit Quest

No family ... few friends ... purposeless drifting
An alien of sorts in this world, afraid it will never end
...my state that is.
I try to envision a different time, of graceful community
...where I belong,
A new life paradigm...history rewritten by me.

A right place...a right time...truth, or yet another illusion to chase?
Fellow sojourners, worn on the path of becoming,
...won't perchance to a state of grace;
Where judgement are left outside the soul, where spirit and will may co-exist,
In unified communion of purpose, bringing healing essence to the earth.

The color is pink, of the softest hue, the texture too...
The rules all righteous, governing lovingly me and you.

Now, denial banished, the death covenant broken,
Light displacing darkness, the sting now removed
Fear no longer stealing the show, with acts of powering, towering over...

Love...the great equalizer, prevails at last...we heal the past, and now live
Present in the future.
Mimi Ellison

Light

There are so few bright, shining stars
amongst us whether near or far.
I feel grateful for every personal
contact that I make.
I want to share. I want to reach out and help;
give them a break!
I do not need any material
in return.
A candle within me now eternally burns.
I'm still not perfect; not even near.
But that won't stop me. We are ALL God's
children, precious and dear.
The spiritual friends I carry very close
to my heart
have begun to fill a void I never thought
would ever start.
Thank you, God, for carrying me once more
to a more than appropriate spiritual door.
Lisa Lindstrom

A Promise Kept

A thunderstorm passes through the night;
A child cries out with his fright.

"Hold me, Mommy!" said with tears,
As his mother draws him near.

"I'll hold you near all through the night.
There's nothing to fear - Mommy holds you tight."

So - a promise is made, only then the child sleeps;
Held fast in Mommy's hands, her word all night she keeps!
Melissa L. Siciliano

"Parents Are Forever"

Parents are forever, they say everything right;
always being there everyday and every night.
They hold out their hands to guide you along the way;
holding you up through rough water, when your life goes astray.
Parents have an intuition in knowing how you feel;
they can show you the answers, that you, yourself could not reveal.
They listen to your dreams and watch you follow them through;
and if you should fail, they will still be there for you.
Parents are always there to help through the good times and the bad;
and no matter what you're going through they're still your mom and dad.
Because of their loving and caring, they have produced a great result;
for now they have watched you grow up and become a fine adult.
And as time passes by, and they start to grow old;
a parent's love, the heart will always hold.
So as you go out and start a family of your own;
the love for your children is the same your parents have shown.
A parents love is bonding with which no one can ever sever;
and passing their love on, proves;
Parents are forever.
L. Matthew Mattison

Fantasy

I gaze above from out terrace
Alone on this night in June
It's the kind of a night for dreaming
There's a softness and round full moon
A plane just flew over with blinking lights
And I thought could it possibly be
That it wasn't a plane in the midnight blue
Or did you wink down at me,
The night was all stillness then a breeze brushed my cheek
And traveled across my lips
I know that I wasn't dreaming
For I felt your finger tips
I'll never cease to fantasize
Tho the years have spun by in a whirl
There once was another night like this
Then we were just by and girl
So patiently wait up there for me
And together sometime well fly
On gossamer wings among the stars
In another June night sky
Mildred Rey-Snyder

To My Lost Love

My feelings have faded to memories of the past.
Alone in confusion, I don't know how long I'll last.
Now I'm lost in the grips of loves insanity,
why did she do this; do this to me.
She came looking for love,
I gave her all she would need.
Then she ran away, leaving me to bleed.
Now that she is gone and I try to find my way,
I'm lost in the thought of a better day.
One where I can hold her so close in my arms.
One where I can kiss her and feel that old charm.
One where we can walk together through the day and night,
sharing our love through the morning light.
For now I'll sit alone and hope to feel her love again.
I know she hides her feelings and one day she will learn.
As for the love she pushed away, she'll wish for it's return.
Norman H. Luck Jr.

The Rose And Her Butterfly

Within a garden grew one red rose, her petals soft and velvet,
Alone, brave, prickly thrusting thorns on her slender stem,
Her heart locked frozen with memories, trampled and crushed.

There on a blue summer day swaying gently in the breeze,
came passing by a butterfly that lit upon her perfumed petals,
like a soft kiss in the summer rain.

He came to her, those summer days, brushing her with beautiful wings, til she slowly bloomed and kissed him back, the thorns melted and transformed was she to ruby red.

As she sang the song of love, came the day he kissed goodbye,
and away he flew with another butterfly,
into the whispering winds of the east and west.

She bent her velvet bloom and tears fell gently to the ground,
as tiny slivers pierced her heart, again she grew her prickly
thorns and wrapped her petals so very tight.

She stood alone within the garden, sunshine hidden in shadows,
as dewdrops danced upon her heart, while singing the silent song
of the memory of her butterfly.

Nancy Quinn

To My Son

I'm sorry I can't give to you
All the things you want
Lately all I can give to you
Are things that can't be bought.

Things like love and security,
Time and your own space.
Many years after I'm gone
These things won't leave a trace.

But I hope you know how much you're loved
And my life I'd give for you
You're the best thing that has happened to me
I know you love me too.

I just hope after you're grown
You can look back and say
My mom did the best she could
And I don't regret one day...

Kathy D. McIntosh

Thanksgiving Day (Oklahoma Style)

From the Hills of California to the Gulf of Mexico,
All our folks are getting ready for the time is set to go:
To the land of Oklahoma, to the tepees of our tribe,
To our Pow-Wow of the Autumn — cares of time we cast aside.
Greet the oldest, meet the youngest — raise your voice above the din,
Hear that chatter on the back porch-open the door and help them in.
Oh, their hands are full of more food — where in the world will we put it all?
Someone with an eye for tomorrow hides pumpkin pies out in the hall.
Kids play in the crisp cool weather—jackets, caps of brightest hue,
Raking leaves to build a fortress—tears it down and builds anew.
Count each one and set the tables, get in line to fill your plate,
Turkey, dressing, and all the trimming—worry tomorrow about your weight.
The young folk in by the fireplace, dignified dads rate the dining room,
Gabbing Gals around the kitchen table—while kids in the den let the T.V. boom.
Pass thru these rooms and join each small group, deeply breathe this Atmosphere.
For Thanksgiving is so lovely and it comes but once each year.

Lucile G. Harvey

Effects

I'm sure you have felt it, at least once before.
All of us want it, some just much more.
A meaning although words cannot describe.
Tremendous effects of which we can't hide.

Comes on without warning, as too it can end.
Can be very tragic, believe me my friend.

Some call it a gift, a blessing I hear.
Trusting each other with something so dear.

For some only sadness this brings to mind.
If ever you've been there, surely you'll find.
A wall even stronger, no one will get near.
A soul very lonely, a heart full of fear.

So, what is the answer?
I'll let you decide.
For you are so different than I am inside.
This mysterious thing, the one I speak of,
Just one little word.
That thing we call...
LOVE

Lori Phillips

Life Goes On

As I stand here looking out the window,
All my precious memories of your love
Flash back into my mind.

We had a love that I thought would last forever.

Now you have gone from my life
And my heart is breaking in two.
I never thought I would see the day
When we would say our last goodbyes.
But I guess no one ever knows.

You were my everything, my reason for living.
But now I know the time has come for me
to try to forget the love that we once shared.
I still love you and I always will.
And my heart is overlapping with pain.
But life goes on though I wish it didn't.

Lisa Davis

"Feelings Of An Unborn Child"

Hello, Mommy, I'm the child you have to send away
All because you Daddy, said, "I'm not to stay"
I heard Mommy ask you, I heard you tell her no
I felt Mommy crying where her tears will never show
I almost thought to tell you, "Daddy wipe away her tears"
Then remembered I could never tell you, not in a million years
Because after its all over and they remove me from inside
I won't even get the chance to tell you both goodbye
Mommy, I'll always love you for when you wanted me
Love you more for the pain you suffered knowing I would never be
Daddy, I'm not mad at you, you see I love you too
Even though it was your choice you too are somewhat blue
Because as much as you would like to have Mommy give me birth
Right not it's just impossible with all this friction here on earth
Mommy, Daddy I think I understand
Although I'll never get to see you, love you, or hold your hand
Mommy and Daddy I love you both
And I do understand! Goodbye Mommy and goodbye to you Daddy, too!

Linda Pacheco

"Always Loving You"

Why must I feel so lonely inside?
After the pain was gone,
I still cried.
The morning you died:
A part of my heart was lost;

I couldn't go see you in the hospital that day
not knowing how much our love for each other cost.

You left and I didn't have a chance to say good-bye.
The morning I heard the news,
all I could do was scream and cry.

I thought you'd never leave me,
but I should have known that wasn't true.
But I want you to always remember that
I Will always Be Loving You.
Orlantha Moore

My Love - Defined

Passion, seduction, devotion that fills;
   Adoration, infatuation, intoxication that thrills.
Goosebumps, butterflies, hot flashes and lust;
   All of these things I feel when we touch!

Erotic, sensuous, delicious and rare;
   Ecstatic, zealous, salacious without a care.
Exhilarating, satisfying, provocative bliss;
   All of these things I feel when we kiss.

Perfection, obsession, adulation, quintessence;
   desire, exaltation, captivation, concupiscence.
Beguiled, enticed, allured and beloved;
   All of these things I feel when we love.

Contentment, fulfillment, realization of all dreams;
   Felicity, euphoria, and unabridged self-esteem.
Elation, gratification, and actualization of perfect life;
   All of these things I would feel if you were my wife.
Michael J. Berg

Untitled

Pictures of people, all covered with paint
achieving perfection, flawless restraint -
Striving to be the most beautiful girl;
how did they do it? Perfect like pearls.
Wanting so badly, needing much more,
mimicking dreams, an unending shore...
Where do they come from, these frivolous creatures
tricking us all with their flawless features?
One by one the girls wither away,
food is the enemy of each passing day.
Sickly and pale, yet still pushing on...
obsession is cruel - I think we've been conned.
Who says that you're perfect when you equal a feather?
Oh where did they get these standards of measure?
Kasey Lee Edwards

Choices

Choices are voices from deep down inside,
A haven for experiences that refuses to hide.
We struggle each day with life's constant array,
Of decisions to be made come as they may.
We stand on the brink of an embattled wall,
Where an unsteady move may result in a fall.
Eager and ready to make that daring leap,
There are goals to reach and promises to keep.
So remember as you travel along each day,
That a voice from inside will guide your way.
Minnie G. Muldrew

The Early Risers

Night thus spent, the morning's cool
Absorbing golden rays
Rising like that early sun,
Pleasing with her ways
Puddled beams spilling through
Place wet shadows ever new
Around the gardens, in the trees
Liquid sunshine paints a frieze
An orchestration planned in time
Beauty with no bounds, the morning coolness unaloof
Comforts awakening sounds
Bringing warmth to opening eyes
Ascending with a steady rise
To feel her touch and listen in
Perhaps to join her songs
Nature's music scored so well
Each tiny note belongs
The early risers with the sun
Lift up God's window shade
To sneak a peek and share the joy, the hand of Him has made.
Nason E. Allen

Work—I Quit

The man who said — and I quote —
   "A woman's place is in the home"
Was very wise — and if more loudly spoke
   These fast graying hairs — he could atone!

The placid contentment of children's screams
   Should never have been exchanged
For screaming phones and men who shout
   Always of something they know nothing about.

When Johnie, Mary, Joan or Lee
   Track mud on the floor in their joyful glee —
There is no eviction notice — no one to say GET OUT —
   We just mop again — and sometimes maybe pout.

Yet in the office — we do a job to perfection
   Only to have it returned for correction
Now, we cannot anticipate a child's action
   But trying to please my boss man
Is driving me to distraction.
Margaret H. Hardcastle

Images

The images fade - a new one appears.
A trees shade - or the drop of one's tears.
The seasons change - in different places in a sphere.
The rhythms change - in different patterns to steer.

To steer the unfortunate one's - to start the good luck.
To place the humble one's - to start to afflict.
To drop the one's tears - who had been struck.
To see the new image appear - to part the conflict.

The celestial horizon - a line to form the boundary.
The lonely one - a time for wondering.
Hopes are gone - the dreams are broken.
Faith is gone - nothin' else but a token.

Faith's bad schemes - but not lost forever.
One's broken dreams - trying to put them back together.
A lonely one - Wondering why.
A boundary line - between Earth and sky.

Thoughts are held - trapped inside.
Dreams of wealth - lost pride.
You might find yourself on the stage.
But always remember - Images fade.
Michael P. McGovern

Troubled Times

You place me here
a tragic scene
to relive painful memories
of places, faces, troubled times
and upon this man you lay the crimes

and though no bounty man shall come
to lash the rope at setting sun
nor shall we hear, the silent scream
of one last breath perhaps, one last dream

but rather a quiet man
with secrets kept well inside a tainted bottle
he'll choose to hide
and tears, like blood
shall soon drain his lifeless soul
while death becomes the friendly foe
welcomed by a broken heart
of dreams, of passions, torn apart.
Matthias Morris

Unaware

I knew not love, then you were there.
A tender heart, you took such care.

I dare not speak less they see,
Oh please, don't think less of me!
You read the book, took some time,
had a look. Whispering softly in my ear,
don't despair you've much to share.

Of self-worth I had none,
you helped me see I'd just begun.
You reached out, took my hand,
pulled me up so I could stand.

The reflections in the pond were always she,
never me. You touched my shoulder,
turned me around, somehow I knew I'd been found.

Finally free, a brand new me!
"Oh no" you say, "can't you see,
you were always there—unaware."
Mavis R. Richardson

Victoria

Crashing, tumbling, so many feet
A rumbling roar that sounds so sweet.
Mist that upon wings to fly
Rainbows arching o'er the sky.

And no mankind to spoil the scene
Of sparkling water pure and clean.
Bushes grow right to the edge
And drop their dew below the ledge.

She's been falling for eons of time,
Not yet has she reached the peak of her prime.
She'll go on falling long after we've gone
Untouched by the problems that around her go on.

And joy to the man David Livingstone
Who first looked upon what the Creator'd done.
And David said, "I christen thee,
Victoria Falls, forever to be".
Kathleen McBride

The Eternal Refuge

In this day and age, I know everyone needs
    a refuge to which they can turn.
There is one Man who is this refuge, you see,
    and there's a book from which you can learn.

This Man's name is Jesus, and He was born to die
    so our sins would be washed away.
The Bible tells of this Man and His Father,
    so pick it up and start reading today.

In this Great Book, you'll learn that God and His Son
    walk beside us everyday.
If you'll ask Him into your heart, He will never forsake you
    and stand with you all the way.

The only everlasting refuge, my friend,
    is our Father in Heaven above.
Depend on Him and ask forgiveness of your sins,
    and He will bathe you in eternal love.

We can stand on His promise that one day He will take us
    to live with Him forever.
When this earth ends, and New Jerusalem begins,
    a refuge we will search for never.
Kim Stacey

I Have Found A Place

A place where my love is music
A place where I am in Divine Spirit
A place where nothing exist - only us
A place where the Sky above and the Earth below
    smile in harmony
A place where there is you
A place where time is still
A place where the air is calm and the water is in
    passionate, ragging, spirit
A place where love is God
A place where love is beauty
A place where there is peace, laughter and joy and
    the true essence of being-being in Love with You
A place where you and I are ONE.
Kirti Kohli

Alone

I walk alone on winter-cold cobblestone,
A naked spirit wafting in the gray and scarlet of dawn
Down silent urban avenues, boulevards, and lanes—
While on my bed of death, my life in balance hangs.

Serpent-eyed demons, black-robed and hooded, fly
From bedsides of sleeping mortals whose cry
Foretells the horrors that rule in deep Sheol
For lost souls for whom death-bells somberly peal their toll.

As spirit only, I pass through bed-chambers of maidens
Who seductively lie, watched by spirit ravens—
Demons in disguise—whose kind 'round my bed
Also wait—since by death and darkness are they led.

Alone I exist 'twixt life and death in shameful, seamy decay—
A hovel cold and dim—of fallen ruins and stark dismay.
Stalked by tragedy—stalked by malady to my door,
I lie in coma—unknown, unmourned, friendless, and poor!

My candle-flame of life now snuffed by death, I spirit-roam
The worlds of both the living and the dead—alone.
Alive in death, I strike my swords against life's altar stone!
I curse curses that impel me into battle immortal—alone!
Mitchel Walters

"The Season Of Fall And Halloween"

"The fallen leaves lay on the ground,
A myriad of colors peeking through the trees —
The season of fall is with us now,
The fall foliage is lovely, and aims to please."

"Now's the time to take a trip,
The scenery is great. —
The trees in their changing finery,
Bring joy to all, so don't be late."

"Pumpkins, Goblins, witches and Ghosts,
Give Halloween that eerie feeling —
And seeing those dancing Skeletons,
I nearly hit the ceiling."

"What would fall be without Halloween?
And the time to go trick or treat —
Don't forget to check all your goodies,
Be careful of what you eat."

"Why do people do such things,
Putting needles and pins in their candy? —
That day will come, when they'll get caught,
To the hoosegow they'll go, won't that be dandy?"

Marty Rollin

Many Religions, Races, And Places

How would you like to be,
   A Muslim across the sea?
Worshipping five times a day,
   But all you do is pray.

Another religion developed in the Middle East,
   Included Arabs and Muslim priests.
The Christians were among these two,
   And also there were the Jews.

Buddhists believe in reincarnation,
   But that's the way of their civilization.
They think if they live righteous lives,
   They will achieve higher and higher stage of life.

No matter what the race may be,
   Mexicans, Blacks, or Chinese.
We're all a part of this big world,
   So let's give each other a bit of peace.

Kimberly Hardee

A Man

A man so tall, so gruff, so gentle, so loving.
A man who knew how to laugh but one who wasn't ashamed to cry.
Who always put us first. Whose legacy was his children.
We look at each other and see a part of him.
Some have his height, some his features, some the color of his hair,
But the one thing he gave us all was his heart.
He's the bond that ties us together. The center of our world.
We always wondered how we would live without him. Now we know.
He gave us his strength, so we would be strong enough
   to face the fight, life has for us.
When we get tired and weary, he'll always be there telling us to go on
We thank God for that special man
Who was so tall, so gruff, so gentle, so loving.
A man, we knew as Daddy.

Kathy Teague

A Little Bit Of Yesterday

I took a little walk and saw
A little bit of yesterday
Along a country road
I saw a yard now full of weeds
Where little children once played
And an old house standing there
Lonely without the sound of voices empty and bare
Broken window panes, sagging doors
A little bit of yesterday gone
The house so vacant, so forlorn
Once spoke of happy days
It held laughter and sorrow
And faith and hope for a better tomorrow
Thank God for a mother and father
Thank God for precious memories along life's way
Thank God for an old house
And a bit of yesterday

Mildred Oldham

Just To Live

A life filled with hopes and joys
A life full of sorrow and pain
A life I thought by now would surely have reached an attainable plain
Up the hill I went
Down the hill I strode
Stuck right now in a very destined mode
Tears from my eyes, slowly they crawled
Nobody noticed or gave a dam at all
So many people to busy to care
Only worried about how they can steal their fair share
In a lonely life such as mine
The only thing left
Is the reward of death
To outshine even your lifeline
My simple life lost in a sea of misery
Tell tale signs we glorify daily in living color scenery
The story of life in a world so cruel
Once made me feel glad
"Just to live and obey the rules"

Kendall W. Scott

Good-Bye

We stood together hand in hand
A friendship to cherish for a lifetime
Together we formed an unbreakable bond
When times got rough we tightened our grip
To ensure our presents and strengthen our security
But along the way your grip loosened
And I, somehow, began slipping away
I don't know where I went wrong
But the struggle to hold on is to heartbreaking
So today I'm letting go of your weak hand
So we can go our separate ways
Hopefully, each of us stronger than before
But I will grieve for my lost friendship
But cherish the happiness I gained from it
And maybe in time will join hands again
And continue life's journey together
But until then I'm saying good-bye

Kelly Spivey

To Do Or Die

On a beautiful December morning, they came, but the doors were closed.
A family broken up in the blink of an eye, without a warning.
Where do all the boys go now? Will they still be bound as family?

Now the news comes many times, like a thief in the night.
It tells of one who could not bear life's burden.
To take his life was the great escape, not all were strong to carry on.
There was no greater loss for those who worked beside him.
It happened to him, it happened to them.
So many gone before their time, too soon they're taken from us,
Leaving behind the memories and a world of broken dreams.

No longer would they be together
Spreading down new avenues in different places.
They were family, apart from their own
Tied by common bonds, sharing trials and joys,
United by greater bonds than blood.
And each time that the sad news comes,
They know what they are feeling.
In heart and spirit, they are still united.
The tears flow from their broken hearts
They are and will always be . . . the boys of Pan Am.
Marian Caruso

Prelude To Spring

A note whispered by a Robin
A blossom blows a kiss to the sky,
The gentle steal of brooks and streams -
Yesterday's snowflakes - from a mountain high.

The wonderful promise of heaven
Brought by a dove on the wing,
These are the prelude -
The prelude to spring.

The hum of a honeybee
A love-song from the lark,
And ripples flowing across the pond
Where lovers skated arm-in-arm in the park...

So gently virgin breezes
Caress everything,
Bringing joyful tidings of
The prelude to spring
Mel Scott

Untitled

I needed a healthy heart,
A black man's family gave me his,
I'm well again.
I needed a working liver,
A black lady's family gave me hers,
I'm healthy again.
I needed a new lung,
A black neighbor gave me one of his,
I'm breathing easy again.
I needed prayer, consolation, and help when I lost my only son,
A black friend saved my sanity.
God gave me a soul and intelligence,
He gave my black friends the same things.
My skin is white, my hair is blonde,
My neighbor's skin is dark, his hair is black,
But we cry alike, we love alike, we hate injustices alike,
We are brothers.
Margaret R. Youngren

Our Utopia

I sure could use a smile
even if just for a little while
time is of essence
and we have not much to spare
taking and giving what we can
is all we have to share
the look, the touch, the force, the feel
is so gentle, yet strong, but soft, and always, always, sure
tell and show which one, if not all are real
if not asked, how much can be touched, felt, and received
before total submission is achieved
when you're near, strong is the desire
absent and the reverie takes over
enchantment transcends me, as I proceed higher and higher
curiosity eludes me
and I stop.
For I know it should never be
but...
for that short while
it was my.......our brief UTOPIA
Monica Anderson

The Camp

Tired
Tired
Tired from crying.
Wanting
Wanting
Wanting to go.
Wanting to stop weeping and go;
To leave this horrid camp of torture.
My eyes sting from tears.
Dad says no.
No!
No, I can't go and leave this horrid rotten place.
Anger and pain pour out of my mouth and through my tears.
My fists pound on the blue and ashen carpet.
Katie Machowski   Age 11

Thrush Gone

Brisk, the winds November brings;
Nature's essence, the chilled fragrance
Of sterility.
Autumn's multicolored primer coats hill and dale,
Void now of thy ethereal melody.

Acquiescent to its fate, the vale lies,
Unaware, or unconcerned of the trespasser within.
Torn between the now lost music of its recent past,
And the coming of December, and its ensuing din.

Who shall keep thy song alive?
Who shall sing us lullabies and chase our fear
Of dark away?
Who will speed the metamorphosis of winter's night
Into the dawn of spring, and finally summer's day?

Spread thy wings, thou songbird!
Catch the express currents en route to yonder
Meadow green.
Taint not thy freedom with sullen afterthoughts
Of songs unsung, or things that might have been.
L. C. Fahrendorff

Santa's Dilemma

When Santa makes his rounds this year, he's not happy as before
He thinks he lost his credit and card, in a "toy" department store

His little elves quit early, with much more work to do
It seems the workshop personnel were stricken with the flu

The reindeer have decided to take a holiday
they feel they won't be needed, there's no snow anyway

"Just as well" said Santa, as he packed the toys away
I noticed that the rudder, is broken on my sleigh

His boots don't fit, his suit's too tight, and his hair is getting thin
Still, I know he'll be here Christmas with his old familiar grin

There will always be a Santa, of course you must agree
as children's eyes are glowing, around the Christmas tree
Meredith A. Anderson

My Idea Of Heaven

My idea of heaven is some say, a bit far fetched.
A big, huge land of ice and snow and beauty never sketched.
Up here in Alaska where friends you make are true
If you are in some trouble some one will see you through.
The air is pure and healthful, we live off of the land
We've berries, fish and venison and furs to trap and tan.
In summer fish, in winter trap, as seasons come and go
The north winds blow and parka wrapped a visiting we go.
A hearty welcome you will get at any place you stop.
The latch strings out and smiles are big while fires crack and pop.
You can keep your city life full of hurrying, strife and smoke
I'll stay here in Alaska where folks are really folks.
Marylee Walton

Mysticism

I found eternity caught in the web of my dreams:
A beautiful woman of one thousand faces
who loved me, wiggled and struggled, cursed
and threatened, and begged for release.
But I wanted to keep her and so I refused.
Then suddenly for a brief moment the heaven opened
and GOD appeared, smiling, and with a stern voice
commanded: "Release her right now or else:
Your world will collapse to a tiny black hole."
I obeyed, set her free with deepest regret.
She danced away, laughing, and never looked back.
my world then collapsed. I felt guilted by her
and deceived by my GOD. But after much thought
I know now that God only saved me from her web,
I have been caught in, all the time, without knowing.
Kurt Lehovec

Flower Poem

Each Day I look at The Rose of Your Affection.
A perfect bud, whorled in, tightly coiled, waiting to...
Now, you're slightly open. A Cave, revealing just a few chosen secrets.
The full aroma. You can be smelled to the far reaching corners of the room.
Today, you are slightly tired. Drooping a few petals over the Coke glass, resting.
Tomorrow, possibly shedding a few parts of your life, scattering gracefully around the phone machine. Dropping softly onto the floor.
Leaving a stem and yet another bud, with a crown of delicate feelers, reaching towards the sky.
And this bud grows and glows a ripe orange-crimson. Awaiting a curious, clumsy soul to crush you, revealing the Jewels of your insides to the harsh winds of life.
Nina Kaufman

These Are The Things I Love

I love the flavor of coffee and brandy in the morning
even better than ice cream and hot boysenberry pie.

I love sitting up with the wind blowing through the ends of my hair
on the back of a red motorcycle racing the sky.

I love blowing on dandelions and seeing their seeds spread
through the air and picking delicate wild flowers
in sunny fields by sparkling clear streams.

I love loose messed up bed covers and long morning loving.
All that hugging and kissing and kissing and hugging
makes me long to follow my dreams.

I love laughing, dancing, singing and camping and fishing.
And jumping in water and splashing and wishing.

I love soft morning sunrise out somewhere in nature,
and sudden storms and rainy days.
Those evening sunsets of my past,
that's what I'm really missing.
Lynn Marie Cecchini

Untitled

In my mind's eye I see a blanket of darkness,
Empty,
A black canvas,
Imagination, life, mine.
Do I have the courage to cover my life's canvas in an array of colors,
  even to give it a splash?
Do I want to take the chance, that the color I choose cannot be erased
  that I will be forever haunted by one mistake,
  to have my life end and still be asking the question what if?
What if I had chosen a different color, a different path?
What if I chosen a different decision?
Do I have that courage?
I cannot tell.
I may not tell till I have made the decision and I paint my canvas.
Will I then here myself utter the words
What if?
Lori Knight

Reflections Of My Happy Thoughts

It makes me happy when I think of watching the sun rise with grandma as she stirs her coffee, in her teacup, with her finger. Ooh!

Listening to granddaddy crank up his old Ford truck and hearing the motor sputter - putt - putt and after a few times it decides to catch on and run smoothly. Ah!

Skipping in the rain with my cousins through puddles and watching the little pools swirl round and round our water-logged oxfords. Uh, uh!

Running to an fro after butterflies as they flutter amidst the lilies in the fields. Gee!

Tasting the sample cake that Mama bakes before the real thing. Yummy!
Walking to town with the sun upon my brow anticipating a bag of popcorn from Sears and Roebuck. Yes!

Going to the picture show once a month to see a great western. Hotdog!
Daddy kissing my knee when the scrape from a fall is too much to bear. My oh my!

Everyone sharing their stories at the same time about the events of the day. Wow!

Laughing uncontrollably over a joke that's funny because my sister is laughing. Hey!

What is the meaning of family? TIME TOGETHER. Love ya!!!
Karen Hardin

The Lady On The Train

The soldier with the winning smile
Asked to share my seat
I nodded, and so Our journey began.

We enjoyed each others company and in parting vowed
To keep in touch, and I cherish the letter
He wrote to the "Lady" he met on the train.

Married after the war, we were blessed with family and friends.
Our love grew stronger and life was fulfilled
For the couple who met on the train.

The years slipped by, life has taken its toll,
His more pronounced than mine.
He walks with a shuffle, just can't remember
And sometimes he shouts in a rage
But he's always the soldier I met on the train.

I tend him with loving care
I'm pained as he gazes with eyes not so clear.
It's then that I embrace him and pray,
Lord please let him always know,
I'm the "Lady" he met on the train.
Alpha M. Keaton

A Wish For Your Happiness

I wish you both the best in life
As you walk together as man and wife.

If you think that marriage is give and take,
A fifty-fifty proposition, that's surely a mistake.

If you give 100 percent, love will abound,
And you'll have triple when it all comes around.

Don't be petty and a miserable nag,
Or you will truly turn into an ugly hag.

Put beauty in the world you make,
And your husband, never forsake.

It is said that the woman creates the mood,
So give positive feelings to your man, not just food.

And, when you come in from working and feeling tired,
Hug her and tell her how much she's admired.

An encouraging word is cherished in your heart;
A bitter remark will never depart.

If you keep her best interest high on your list,
She'll hold you dear, and you'll always be kissed.

A word from the wise, this is what I've been told:
"Always take time to be sweethearts, and you'll never grow old."
Janet Mumau

People

I walk along the hurried street,
A concrete slab beneath my feet.

I watch the people as they pass by,
The women speak, and the children cry.

As daylight ends, and night falls near,
The faces of homeless people appear.

With greasy smiles and tear-stained eyes,
While crouched in corners weep starving cries.

They scramble through the twisted trash,
They beg and plead for coins and cash.

In tiny boxes that they call home,
Their dirty children play alone.

When the light of day draws near,
The people of the street disappear.
Michele Gasaway

My Love For You

This love I have, will bind us as one,
As we explore life together.

Our life together will lead to respect and trust,
Both the foundation of a final commitment.

Along the way I promise; to protect, be supportive,
trust, hold, touch, kiss, adore, not criticize,
But understand, while being sensual without reservation.

For my life would lose meaning without you and this,
My special need, would grow into selfish loneliness.

If I could demonstrate all of the above
In an instant, I would, for time is fleeting.

I beg of you, let us seek that love,
As if there is only the moment.

This love will reach out in all directions,
Attracting all, as is the moth to the flame.
And, those attracted will bath in splendor,

For as the flame does; our love will purify,
Bring light to darkness, show direction and,
Surround all with warmth, ESPECIALLY US.
John Nevshemal

"The Carousel"

Children laughing, jumping with joy
As they view this great big toy

Young and old are riding it today
Hearts uplifted, in round and round play
Horses all shining bright, colors bold
Never tiring of numerous mounts we're told

Melodies fill our ears with happy circus songs
Suddenly all is quieted...something is wrong

Repairmen are summoned, they promise to mend it
Day's turn into years, it goes unattended

Faces haunt me, sad all chipped weathered worn
Blank eyes stare, raindrop tears from a storm

Dusk at day's end silhouettes the carpenter man
Sweating from working with a toolbox in hand

Children are laughing, by the light of the moon
Then my ears distinguish a familiar sweet tune

No more waist high weeds to hide the treasure
Sparkling like a diamond, I see with pleasure

  The Carousel...begins again
Dorothy A. Wise

A Priceless Love

God has given you thy peaceful pleasures of life,
As thy own love anchor a mystery of joyful healing,
That is tender to the richness of many unspoken hearts,
While mankind struggle for its own lost moral sight.

I lift my eyes to gaze at such a priceless moral gem,
Which silently gives me unselfish beautiful dreams,
And filters the essence of reality in my rising faith,
Where by the inner soul finds a sensational loyalty.

It is the hope of an everlasting precious moment,
Found truly with the warm loving passion you bring,
That provides honor to unbelievable revelations,
To the hidden thoughts of Cheryl's quiet serenity.
Herman Renoir Hill

Responsibility

..And so I'm left alone again, this warm summer evening
As the light softens and disappears into night -
I can hear the traffic passing taking people there or there
But I sit here alone again, not going anywhere.

It's left for me to ponder the problems of the year
   And how to find solutions so others won't have to fear -
But how I'd really love to hear some very good advice
   And feel someone's arms around me -
To tell me it will be alright.

But the truth is, no one's coming -
   And it's really up to me
To find the strength inside me to deal with what I must.
So let me try remembering the good that's in my life -
   To find the courage somewhere to go on with my life.
But I don't want to waste it, in sad soliloquy -
   For as long as there's tomorrow, there's hope that I'll be free.

Claudia De Laas

As The Children Play

As the children run and play; I hear the sounds of laughter
As the children run and play; it makes me want to follow after
As the children run and play; it makes me feel young again
As the children run and play; it makes me think of old friends

As the children run and play; my day becomes better
As the children run and play; it's good that they play together
As the children run and play; it makes the day seem so good
As the children run and play; they get along the way everyone should

As the children run and play; I can feel my youth coming back
As the children run and play; of time, I tend to lose track
As the children run and play; the world seems at peace
As the children run and play; all my troubles seem to cease

As the children run and play; it brings back good times
As the children run and play; it gives me peace of mind
As the children run and play; things seem as they should be
As the children run and play; I think, "Why couldn't that be me?"

Billy Smith

A Love Once Counted

Where is my beloved gone, the one whose love I once counted
As sure as fire from a thousand suns rising fierce, undaunted?
  Come in from the cold and bolt the door
  Oh man of love, oh love no more.

Where, now, the one whose sigh I once dreamed
Was carried on mystic lake-shore waves,
Lapping among the willow reeds?
  Shake the fairy dust from your boots so worn
  Oh man of love, oh love no more. (And yet again he asks)

O where is my beloved gone, the one whose lips I once pressed
Upon my own under the temple stars, dreaming simple truth professed?
  Eat the bread, drink the wine by the fire warm
  Oh man of dreams, oh dream no more.

She has grown tired and drunk of Lethe,
And sleeps at mem'ry's gypsy feet —in the darkness—
Behind a thousand falling suns, beneath the waves where stillness runs;
Between the stars of temple night,
Where altared truth and grace do cry.
  "What footfalls down the corridor?"
  Oh man of dreams, oh dream no more.

Bryan Adams Hampton

Drawing The Short Straw

I have to take grandma home.
As she says her goodbyes, I rush her things out into the trunk.
Helping her down the steps, cane and all, she complains about all her
aches and pains on the trip from porch to passenger seat.
Fully strapped in, I shut her door
Then ready my mind for the trip South.

She immediately chimes in with the radio, a one-sided conversation.

She complains about the weather and how it plays havoc with her
  arthritis.
She comments on all the grandchildren and
  how they are all growing like weeds.
She reminds me of Grandpa and how next Tuesday it will be 10 years.

The rows of corn run along with us.
Countless small towns slow us down.
Livestock in every pasture greet us, the only car on the road.
My eyes search for the water tower.
Not a moment too soon, our station just went fuzzy.
We make our final left and head into town. Cullom, Population 350.

Backing into the driveway, only five more minutes or so.
A slow crawl up the sidewalk. Suitcase under one arm,
Her clenched fist strapped around the other.
A quick trip to the bathroom and I'm outta there.

I peck her cheek lightly. She squeezes me with her best effort.

The ride home will be longer.

Domonic J. Delrose

Remembering

The lilt of her voice rang familiar
As she greeted me atop the stairs
The baby blue eyes were ever present—
But the wrinkles were long and deep

And the auburn hair, now as white as the fleece
of a sheep
The tight embrace was strongly remembered
Through tears of skinned knees and bicycle falls

The smile was warm and automatic
But somehow dimmed
In the golden, yet fading
Twilight of her years

Helen Noorigian

Now And Then

There's more than one she thought with a smile
  As she felt the little one move.
But onward now, no time to waste;
  A place to hide, make haste, make haste!
Into the dark, get out of the light;
  They're coming now; make sure your flight.
First came her son so healthy and tall;
  Then followed Hannah, lively but small.
She nursed them and kissed them and watched as they grew;
  Pride watered her heart like her thirst from the dew.
Food was not easy to get in those days
  But Sarah, wise Sarah had her own special ways.
She nursed them and kissed them but now what is this?
  What is that noise? What could be amiss!
The light! It's so bright!
  And her heart stopped dead-still.
Oh, what will they do; they've discovered her house?
  Yes, what will they do for I'm but a grey mouse?

Gaylene Lelko

Bride

She came — and a love caught flame;
As she entered with delicate step in the dim
She intended her loveliest moments for him.

She sighed — and an Angel cried;
Would the Author of exquisite graces approve
Of the one she determined her veil to remove?

She stopped — and a pulse-beat dropped;
In a lull of the breeze — in the hush of the night
Could she conquer with courage this instant of fright?

She stared — and a soul was bared;
She was placing her life and her love in his hands
With no question of even the least of his plans.

She smiled — and a heart grew wild;
She declared to the world by this tender appeal
Her dependence on One whom no mind can reveal.

She knelt — and a prayer was felt;
As she gave him her hand, all her radiance confessed
That the Lord of all Nature her union had blessed.
George Barbary

Birthright

Our belly swells and bulges with life
as lying naked, cold, awake
we touch the stretch marks of time.

These scars carved without a knife
furrow our flesh with yesterday's ache
and are hidden with clothes except at bedtime.

The wind in the fences begins to fife;
a tune that we heard at the planted seed's wake.
We pillow our face to extinguish its rhyme.

Through the skylight of a stillborn life,
which we once had bloodied opaque,
the moon and the clouds dance a requiem mime.

We sob the tears of future strife,
bathing our wounds in a salt mattress lake;
diluting the stains of first fetal slime.

On blue flowered sheets, huddled; husband and wife,
wrapped in the guilt of our flesh, we forsake
the hope of removing the stretch marks of time
with the cry of our first born's namesake.
Cliff Clark

"One Evenings Tribute To Life"

An eagle soars high near the snow capped peaks
As the sun goes to sleep in the hills.
The shadows stretch long into deep shaded streaks,
And the cool wind the heated air chills.

The high mountain green turns a deep shade of blue,
And the sunset hits sheer granite walls.
The eye beholds colors of every hue
As the light hits the spray from the falls.

The eagle looks down from his effortless flight
At the work of his Master on high.
And, beholding the earth as the day fades to night,
He gives praise with an ear-piercing cry.

His cry splits the air like the edge of a knife,
And the earth far below understands.
She too loves her Lord, the Creator of life,
And she lives to obey His commands.
Aaron Bronson

Circles Of Loneliness

Night falls and the world sleeps.
As I walk in lonely circles,
only the half glow of moonlight suggests,
that others are waking to the dawn.

I am alone tonight.
There are a few sounds that strike
at the unsuspecting ear,
heard against asphalt, cement or rocks.
In time these sounds are gone.

Surrounded by black, the darkness hides the tears,
the disfiguring of a once gentle face,
to memories of abuse and misuse.

I am followed by trails of light.
They disappear around corners of buildings, and trees.
The falling snow, the warm breeze, rain on my face,
the chill wind, and the peaceful calm.
Sometimes there are a dozen seasons in the night.

I roam in circles to forget, to pray, to think.
Just as there is darkness, as I walk in lonely circles,
so is there gloom in the heart.
David M. Blackner

"Between Dimensions"

A reposeful sensation surrounds my soul
as I slip past supraliminal stimuli.
A vindictive world is left behind;
substituted by an artificial reality.
Here, only imagination exists.
The disgruntled person is transformed
into someone only a supernatural vision could create.
Possibilities that were once finite become limitless;
visions that were once fantasies become tantalizingly tangible.
The mortal limit of the imagination is the only boundary
which separates this experience from God.
Then suddenly, with a blink of an eye,
my own private panacea begins to quickly fade;
to be forever lost in the black abyss between dimensions.
Jeffrey P. Cupo

A Rainy Day At A Cafe On The Lower East Side

The rain sets in during the morning hours.
As I sip my coffee, I watch the monotonous shower.

Faces pass the window; a man tucks up his collar
to shelter himself from the penetrating rain.
He buys the paper vendor's umbrella for a dollar.

I finish my coffee and ask for more, then I feel
Someone looking at me through the sticky door.
She comes in soaked to the bone.
She has coffee also; she finishes it and is gone.

As the noises pass outside, winding through the heart
Of the city, my mind wanders off, trying to find
Its way, twisting and turning through all the memories.

As the waitress startles me out of my day dream,
I suddenly remember that I have to run
through the rain to catch a train.
Angella Trulove

Whispers In The Night

Whispers in the night, are calling out my name,
As I reached for the light, the voices fade away.
To darkness I return, once again I try to sleep,
Tossing and turning I soon begin to weep.

The shadows in the room, shape into someone I know,
A silhouette of you, my mind begins to go.
Memories beyond control, draw me back to you again,
I miss you my darling, my heart will never mend.

As I drift into a dreamless sleep, I can not stay awake,
I pray for morning, oh! How long can it take,
Awakened by the light, the sun begins to shine,
Night finally fades away, the day starts to unwind.

Gaye Horta

Whispering Wind

The sound of the wind whispers through my mind
as I listen to the rustling leaves crush behind.
The moment to escape the worries of the day
takes a hold of my spirit as I leave behind the workday.

I embrace the feeling of warmth as I nestle
releasing the problems that I have wrestled.
Here I am free to think, ponder and roam
easing into the space only known as home.

Here I seek to discover what occupies my innermost nature,
in order to find the dreams that will create my genuine signature.
Deeply I hope that my words will touch another's soul,
with depth and vigor to set their mind aglow.

Christina Glassman

That Moment

His only gift was sorrow, wrapped in a black bow
As he sat, bathed in darkness during the season of birth,
A solitary tear rolled down his cheek
That had known years of bitter cold and happy warmth.
The salty prism captured blinking colors from the blurry glow:
Red, blue, green, yellow ...
I watched him silently from around a corner;
His thoughts were my thoughts
And for a moment, his memories were mine.
To this day, an instant doesn't pass
That I don't think of her - her laughter, her smile, her touch
And I wonder exactly what went on
During that moment in his mind.

Denise R. Frank

Happily Ever After

Intense feeling of warmth covered me,
As he looked in my eyes,
Undressing my mind,
Relating to me like no other had before.
I am the adventure that he explores.

Loneliness is just a memory.
Time is now something to look forward to.
Emptiness is replaced with joy, comfort, and warmth.

Oh what a grand feeling.
Better yet, what a incredible reality to have
him touch me, as the sun the sky.

Bridgett J. C. Kimble

Morning Awakes

Today I beheld a beautiful sight,
as God drew back the curtains of night,
and he golden face of the morning sun,
Was exposed to show me the day had begun.
Shadows of darkness slunk slowly away,
Reluctant to face the light of the day.
As if to give thanks, a flower looked up,
Forming its petals, and making a cup.
It drank the dew and opened up wide,
Stood sturdy and tall, showing its pride.
And in answer to show he was
pleased with his specter,
He placed a honeybee inside to taste of the nectar.
Dear Lord I know its not anything new.
To see a flower tasting the dew.
Or giving its nectar to a honeybee.
But I'm so glad you let me see.
For if such care is taken for a
flower and a bee.
You must have gone to a lot of trouble for me.

Charlotte L. Keck

Time For Truth, And Truth In Time

Truth lies buried deep in shackled silence, because of the cunning
    artifice of treachery,
Bound, but patient, Truth awaits her turn, to be exhumed and freed
    from unfair wretchery.

Hours, days, years, perhaps eons pass along, but Truth awaits with
    Time to speak,
But Truth exists, and ever will, despite the delusion that liars
    always seem to seek.

Like a spring beneath the desert floor, Truth at last will surface
    from its place.
To stand erect, yet intertwined with Time, it's friend, woven as a
    lovely lace.

Contrarily the Lie will crumble, and Time will cause it rot and gore,
But Truth will come to surface with the Time to triumph ever more.

Liars deny that Truth exists or is, fail the Truth to know at all,
But someday the Depth of Truth will cause the liars feet to trip and fall.

Perhaps Time must protect our mortal bodies, and allow us strength to gain,
For what might be too much at once, Time spreads out, to lessen shock
    and pain.

Bonnie Zinnante

Envious

Strong, black physique well sculptured
arms of steel and gentle hands
bristle or curly dark haired man
upon a handsome face with mesmerizing eyes

A turned up smile as bright as the sun
rugged chin smooth to the touch of my lips

Strong, black physique upon powerful legs
capable of withstanding the toughest of gains
baby soft feet smooth to the bottom of mine
a physique like that viewed from the front as well as behind

Also includes a brilliant black mind
useful, willing and able to learn
from the simplest of things to the complexities of life

Hard working body and mind
A perfect combination of the envious
Envious of the scent of strength from the mold
out of God's own hand upon this earth
Creator of this beautiful black man

Juliet Grimble-Morris

Windows

If we were but a window what many things we'd see
Are there cob-webs in the corners
Lets think just you and me
Are we filled with little webs of sorrow or of grief
things we haven't left behind but carried as a thief!
Are we filled with unforgiveness stopping God's great flow,
Are we carrying little things around even through we know
Let's look into our lives as windows through we see
For Jesus wants the best for us
To bless both you and me.
Arise and take another look and see what you will find
Are we swept clean by the Blood
Or do we really mind the webs that clutter up and in our lives they bind
Take another look and you will see
The blessing that our God wants for you and me.

Joyce A. Moore

Resolution

The belligerent waters of bitter words
Are now, like an infant, being lulled into serenity
By the gentle, melancholy humming of the conscience.
The waves flow softly toward
The dawn's golden rays,
Which at first sting tear-trodden eyes,
For while light appears beyond the horizon,
One's heart still sees darkness.
Forgiveness and Hope walk along the shores,
Collecting what's left of shattered emotions,
And then, hand in hand, they sail off to a new place,
A strange and desolate land called Resolution.

James D. Montague

Never Give Up

Never is a word that you should not have to say.
Anything you want to do you can if you try and pray.
So always think positive, never doubt what you can do.
God can help so much, but the choice is up to you.

Give is something that you should always try to do.
Help the one's that are less fortunate than you.
When you give always try to give all that you can.
Don't just give to one, give to every man.

Up is used because you should always aim for the top.
Don't let anyone tell you that your dream should be stopped.
God, Our Lord and Savior is up above.
If you NEVER GIVE UP then you can be with the one we love.

Delmesa Long

The Tree

Have you ever gazed upon a tree
   And wondered what he's seen,
Or how many other creatures
   Have also gazed and stood amazed
At his splendor?
   What has stood here next to him?
How many loyal companions have fallen?
   I'm curious...
Have two young lovers crept from their cozy houses
   To meet under this tree
So that their midnight kisses
   May be hidden by his limbs and leaves?
What mysteries does this tree know?
   Is he keeping secrets?
The tree stands strong
   In wisdom!
~~Behold~~
His silence!

Heather Hosford

Just For Her And My Death (Stanzas When I Lived)

I figured the Stygian shore needed me so I decided to create another elegy.
Death has called and answered my rain, from my eyes of drear
love has caused my tears and slain my life and death is me.
No more Romanticism eloquently.
Once again obit has torn another lovely girl and a family
has been divorced by the pearl of my sanguinous suicide...,
and even in death I still clamor for the love of my bride
and she cries on my tomb and Magnolia's wanting to be by my
side, but my love was just for her and my death tyrannically rides.

No not a sonnet or ever a stanza can explain my suicidal,
deathly bonanza.
Even in real love not ever was I sustained and no one cares
insanity is who to blame.
The ebb of life has done her apart from me
but even with my body in earth I still love my Erica Lee.

Lee is me and me and Lee will never be separated
because mortality has its clefts.
My love is just one; just for her and my death...

Eliezer Ferrer

"Summer Rain"

The drops beating against my rooftop
Announcing the arrival of a summer rain
A brief respite from the season's heat
A gentle reminder life can be sweet again.

The smell of the air is fresh and clean
Nature's own special perfume
All around the earth's senses come alive
As its given fresh water to consume

I remember a very special day
When you and I looked out a windowpane
The sound was like a romantic lover's song
As we experienced a lovely summer rain

The shower it seems has ended now
And today I look out the window alone
But the summer rain has brought me a memory
Of a time when our love really shone

The fresh air brings to mind that all is new
Hearts get replenished just like the earth
So there is hope that I'll know love again
The summer rain reminds me to continue the search

Felix Valdez

My Baby

   From the day you were conceived I felt so happy and so free waiting
and wondering what you would be. Hoping and praying for the day when
you I would see. The sound of your heartbeat the movement of your feet makes me long to touch you; that day will be so sweet. The sickness in the morning, the sleeplessness at night makes me wonder if
I'll make it through all right. The time is now approaching when we meet at last. Waiting to hold you in my arms and kiss your tiny head. The day is here I'm ready to go; the pain is strong and very low. Your head is starting to appear, the excitement of it all makes the pain disappear. One last push and there you were, my baby boy, with strong lungs. When I saw you for the first time, my tears of joy could not be stopped. I love you more than I ever thought. When they put you in my arms, I knew that God had planned it all. My baby boy you are so sweet; God loved me so he gave you to me.

Crista Murdock

Untitled

I have seen the springtime coming, many years I've watched it come,
and with bold anticipation looked for battles to be won.
I have felt each ray of sunlight spell an end of damp and cold,
and would set my youthful spirit after glory...after gold.
A cause was what I wanted, trumpets sounding, watch bells ring.
For a fair and tender maiden, for a just and noble king.
As the years continued flowing, into manhood I was thrust,
still the promises of springtime left my reason in the dust.
I have seen my dreams of glory fade and tarnish year by year.
I've watched the gold so seldom won trickle off and disappear.
The winter chill has weakened me, last summer's dreams are gone.
It's clear the path to follow is a steady cautious one...
Yet I know that spring is very close, quiet now I'll watch it come,
and with renewed anticipation look for battles to be won.

John Stuart Graham

When There's No One Beside You

When you are alone,
and when you know there is no one beside you...

An angel is looking down at you from the high sky.

Then you will feel something inside you
that will make you happy.

And then you will think you have
a friend beside you.

Emily Pegoda

Deer Sir

They live not very far away
And we're taking away their homes every day.
With the offices and factories and buildings we make,
Very selfishly we these things take.
We take these without a thought
While they for new homes have constantly sought.
They are running out of hope.
They haven't a clue how to cope.
Their delicate ears they use with skill
For if they don't they might get killed.
We are the predators and they are the prey.
And they can't to us even one word say.
To tell us to stop, "Can't you humans hear?
We mean no harm. We're just gentle, peaceful deer."
Even though they cannot speak we should be able to see
With our own eyes that we have the key
To stop all of these thoughtless things.
Because of these we to them harm bring.
But they still for their lives must race.
The cause of this: THE HUMAN RACE!!!

Dawn Henley

Michigan Summer Sunsets

I sit on jagged rocks
And watch the sun go down.
The sunlight begins to fade
The reflection of the bright water is in my face.
My heart is full of excitement,
Waiting for the sun to fall behind the awaiting water.
Finally it's about to fall.
The sun is right above the rippling water
Where my feet lie dead upon the edge of the rocks,
I turn my head
I see the blazing color, bright, red as fire
And an orange light rippling through the air.
Finally it sets, still, you see it's
Wonderful dimming colors and then
You see no more.
I sit there in the dark, just thinking.

Aaron Hoeber

Shadow Dream

I paused to mingle with the crowd
and wandered from the light of my soul.
Thrust into the darkness of my uncertainties,
cowering like a mouse in the gaze of the cat
I fail at the ebony curtain
severed by the tide of civil-ization.

Free as the wind yet shackled by the world
I struggle to float with the autumn leaves.
A damselfly stilled by the shadow of the frog
I fear to sing and flutter free
lest I be swallowed into the emptiness
lost in my fear of the abyss.

I climb the mountain searching for my soul
and embrace my vision-peace.
But it fades to mist, a whisper on the wind
I grasp the cloud but the air is thin
and darkness begins to settle.
And still I dream.

Joseph D. Engler

A Day On The Trail

The winding trail is weary, long and dry
and vacant is the vast blue vault of sky.
The wind swept eagle swoops with shrieking cry
while searing sands through canyons soar and sigh.

The overheated branding iron glows
and anvil mesas sound with ringing blows.
Old stream beds sleep and dream that water flows
where creosote in prolonged anguish grows.

The sagebrush sifts the sandstorms grain by grain
and tumbleweeds toss seeds across the plain.
The cactus flowers thirst but bear their pain
and devils tears are not as rare as rain.

From buried boulders deep bass groans are sent
to lofty rim rocks roaring in lament.
The burdened arch with breaking back is bent
and moans for endless eons not yet spent.

The tired day is done as is the chore.
Cool shadows quench the iron lands once more.
While moonrise chills the cattle that now snore
the bunkhouse beckons warmly from its door.

Delbert Park

Intervals Of Sunshine

When clouds hang heavy over your head
And troubles pile one on one,
No matter how dark it may seem to you,
Just wait! You will see the sun.

If things continuously went just right
With never a worry or care
We wouldn't appreciate all that we have.
There'd be no way to compare.

So when things seem dark, and you've lost your way
Don't give up — be hopeful instead.
Remember, no matter how bad the storm
The sunshine is just ahead!

And when it breaks through those clouds above
Spreading its golden rays
You'll forget the hurts and tears of the past
And remember the happy days!

Eleanor Trevithick

Untitled

Baby's born so sweet and small, it seems you blink
   and they've learned to crawl
Changing diapers, making bottles and potty trained already!
First steps so exciting "steady now, steady."

Before you know it they're everywhere
   underfoot, on each leg, and in you hair.

Now the sun is shining, the kids are whining, what a way to
   start the day.
"I skinned my knee" "she's pinching me!" So innocently they play.
"It's time to go we have to leave, and stop wiping your nose on
   your sleeve!"
It seems that's all I say
"I was here first", "I'm dying of thirst," "Are we almost there?"
"How come his piece is bigger than mine - that's no fair!"

All morning through and afternoon too, they laugh, cry and pretend
But not one peep while they sleep, for the day has to end.

Despite all this it's one small kiss that makes it all worthwhile
And this beautiful gift that makes my heart lift,
   is wrapped up in a child's smile.
     Jeanette M. McCue

Time's Requiem

The sun keeps rising; the moon keeps setting;
and the world keeps turning round;
The clock keeps ticking; the hands keep moving;
and the sand keeps trickling down.

The wheels keep rolling; the miles keep clicking;
and the cars keep whizzing by;
People keep milling; but no one's smiling,
and I'm not questioning why.

I must slow-it-down, make time stand around;
It flies while I crawl; I don't have time for it all.

The work keeps piling; the bills keep growing;
and I keep getting behind;
The house needs painting; the lawn needs mowing;
and neighbors aren't being kind.

The years keep coming; people keep dying
and I'm forgetting to cry;
I can't be dreaming; I can't be hoping;
for I'm barely getting by.

I must slow-it-down, make time stand around;
It flies while I crawl, I don't have time for it all.
     Dana F. Eddy

Dreaming

"With most men, unbelief in one thing
springs from blind belief in another."

Falling into dusk
here am I
by my open window
dreaming that one man might dream of me,
that I might whisper softly in his ear
a secret he would not reveal:
Dreaming that in my middle years
I would bring forth joy and light
and he would claim,
"This light is mine
let no man stand within it."
     Barbara Grippe

Sugar Plantation Memories

I dream of fields of sugar cane dancing to the rhythm of the breeze,
and the mango and sweet papaya fruit growing among guava trees.

I think of the little plantation houses with their noisy screen doors,
topped with tin roofs, shady porches, and painted wooden floors.

I remember the work men who would sweat on the land,
burning cane, carrying machetes, and poisoning weeds by hand.

I can still smell the molasses weaving its scent throughout the town,
that sweet, sugary syrup so tasty, golden and brown.

I recall the village stores where we'd stop to check our mail,
and mothers gossiped ruthlessly while their babies would cry and wail.

I stare at silent roadways so empty and so clean.
The falling stalks from cane trucks no long litter the scene.

I hear now of the industry that is silent, still and done.
The once-thriving commerce is quiet and the laborers gone.

I grieve for ones still struggling there and wonder how they will cope.
Are there jobs? What will they do? Is there any hope?

I share my plantation memories with my children of today,
tell stories and show them pictures of how we used to dream and play.

I say good-bye to an era that has faded and in the past,
yes, Aloha to the sugar fields of Hawaii, may the memories forever last.
     Angela Lapinid Ponce

Lullaby

Night has fallen
and the darkness has come,
the moon and its expanse to the midnight sun,
above I watch,
the crystal stairs aglisen,
longing to hear the love song that I have been missing.

I have no come
to this spot over the horizon
to clear my soul and let go of the oppression
I long to hold
the hand of my love
he left me above the darkness like the wind under the dove.

I have never
laid my eyes on one so lovely
and yet each time we meet it becomes more heavenly
oh, the marriage
is near, forever it will be
the time he can have my heart and unlock it with the key
     Dawn Marie Vowell

Summer's Gems

The darkness flees; the glowing sun appears
And sheds o'er earth its golden TOPAZ rays,
Which slither gently through the misty haze
Absorbing silently each CRYSTAL tear.
A meadow dressed in TURQUOISE green is near;
A stream bedecked with DIAMONDS slowly strays,
The EMERALD stones which it so proud displays
Remain to beautify each passing year.
The PEARLY clouds, in yonder SAPPHIRE sky,
Are wafted gently o'er the RUBY ball,
Whose rays are slowly drowned in sea of JADE —
Their watery bed, where they're content to lie,
While darkness then descends and covers all;
A blanket, ONYX-hued, star-decked, is laid.
     Jean F. Vistica

Mirror Image

Upon the boundaries of reality, I stand on the edge

Contorted views of the world confront my soul,
and shatter my daily thoughts, my morals catch the eye of a needle
and weave into a straight jacket of conformity.

Uncontrollably I stagger, peering into the darkness of my spirit

Past, Present, and Future collide into a corrosion of existence
Where have I been?

Into the depths of hell I'm eager to journey,
forbade by my synthetic days as a charitable girl

Who shall hold my hand or shall I just fall into the curtain of the
odyssey I yet not know

Bridget Pilchak

Life On The Internet

While surfing the Net, I'll find a place,
and set up shop in cyberspace.
When I do I'll let you know,
so you too will know where to go.

We can watch the traffic as it goes by,
traveling by land, water and sky,
and enjoy seeing the economies grow,
in areas of the World we begin to know.

We shall see the development, with NAFTA and GATT,
and how the lean of the World will begin to get fat.
Will this make us rich? We will wait and see.
Just being here is reward enough for me.

Joseph D. Rudloff

Aunt Mary

The old porch swing sways in the wind
   And reminds me of times long past
When I used to wander down the road
   To a wonderful house on the hill.
An old porch swing and a white picket fence
   Stand out so clear in my mind.
Morning glories twined 'round each little board
   And pansies grew 'neath the tree in the yard.
Old Butch is napping by the front door —
   There's my Aunt Mary in that old swing.
I sit by her side and she holds my hand
   And together we talk and sing.

Now the porch swing is gone
   And the house is run down,
Old Butch — he just wandered away.
The pansies don't grow in the yard anymore
   And Aunt Mary can't hear me sing;
But surely she knew right from the start,
   She was making memories for a child's heart.

Jo Bess Burris

Another Day, Another Time

Fingers of fire brought forth from my mind,
   are frozen in memory, recaptured from times distant past.
My want to revisit this fullness of life,
   spawns even more vivid thoughts.
So, I'll harvest the best from these rapturous sights,
   brought so clearly to the fore.
And savor the journey of again discovering my dreams
   another day, another time.

David G. Sheriff

Shop Before You Marry

Forget the high school sweetheart, the girl next door,
And pure who pulled you through Psych eleven four.
In mall or city hall, giant or tiny cash-and-carry,
Waits the girl you will want to marry,
To reveal lasting love's light,
Giving a hard time is all right.
Perhaps a painting for the entry hall?
So to Wentworth's Gallery in the mall,
What caught the eye and shot a dart,
Sophisticate in ecru, not the art.
Composed: "Way up there: Renoir picture of the West."
In 'Ecru', discreetly: "No, Darvas, one of his best."
"May I see it lower? Now, in better light.
"Must think about it over night.
"Still better, set it aside.
"I'll know when on house colors I decide."
Sophisticate, no way ready to bawl:
"No trouble at all."
Not the moment to heed psychologist's plea,
Right then: "Will you marry me."

Joseph Rutkowski

Lest We Forget

Many young and old are confused today
   And progress is ahead in this relay,
Forgotten in this technical tidal wave,
   Are things in life including feelings of joy,
When seeing first hand a bird in flight,
   Or the thrill of a firefly in the night.

Punching a key and watching the screen
   Is surely not the same as the real thing.
Let them not take over as human emotions
   And nature do really need more space
While living our lives at such a fast pace.

Helen L. Nelson

Content

In a land forgotten there is a walled garden where time is forgotten and overgrown with the passions of life and the wilds of lost words... tomorrow forgotten, yesterday may have passed... Love remembered in the grass and wilted pedals of flowers blooming on their own accord as a dare to a gardener who has forgotten them... within the walls safe from time and time's demise and the lost words...unneeded. A wordless moment with the sheer joy of death and decay as fragrant as the wild roses caught in the branches overhead. A hermetic well stands as old as the walls that surround and the shade. A well whose waters still hold mystery within, and four points around...What secrets have been traded between these walls? As unimportant now as the future is to yesterday. Will you smile again? Will your eyes look at mine with blinding truth...Truth that could will me to scream until I have only a frogs voice to ramble with? Let us just sit in the quiet shade in these walls.

Erik Rogneby

Untitled

The mysteries of the world are an amazing sight to see
And there's one mystery that just plain magic to me.

A riddle I propose to solve this magic pun
Is one mother nature established before she was done.

If a hawk can go a hawking while flying in the sky
And a cat can go a stalking while moving on the sly

Why is it that a horse can go while walking by?

Harlan L. Gordon

The Liberal

While running his cunning campaign, he visibly smiles at bag ladies,
and offers spent aluminum cans to itinerant rummagers.
He does care for the ill-willed sick, and eschews jelly beans;
all the while trying to oppress the latter day viscounts.

"Is he a liberal?" We query. No worry!
He's generous on occasion, but singly he's stingy.
Yet he's all for rockets via jingling pockets, and
doesn't favor and flavor of high fiber ice cream.
Come to think: after ponderous declarations, he winks.
He shrinks from arguments on tin tinkle tubes and foot stools,
especially if they're collectibles. He adores checks and balances,
especially if they're collectibles.
And by all means, let the owners of Mercedes also owe the taxes.
He makes no rules for us to make for him.
Now that we know him; who are we?
   Charles Jacob Miller

Relieving Tears

Sometimes I feel like crying...
And not for my own trivial woes - but for all the world's!
For the children without parents; the adults who've lost
their children. Everyone need to cry sometimes.
But will crying truly remove the hurt?
Many times, crying merely removes the tears from our eyes
leaving the hurt still deep inside.
Yes, I've felt sadness, as we all have at sundry times.
But I've not brushed against a fraction of the atrocities
seen by millions everyday.
As a child, a good cry would make all seem better.
How I wish we could all revert back to that age of innocence
and simply cry the sadness, fear and despair out of our hearts.
   Jared Clavin

A Pleasant Dream

I was so tired when I sat down
and my brow was furrowed with deep frowns
My day had been so song and hot
what a pleasure just to sit and rock.

The rocking soothed my jangled nerves
and soon my head began to droop
and like a peaceful flowing stream
my nerves relayed I began to dream.

Of a garden of flowers nodding and sparkling
all wet from the showers
There were beautiful daisies and pansies so bright
With their heads held high in the bright sunlight.
And in a far corner with the sun shining on it
Was a spray of baby's breath
With raindrops like tears shining on it

My dream was so pleasant I hardly could hear
I tiny voice speak close to my ear
Saying "Grandma" I got you a present.
A fat little puppy "Ain't" he a dear.
   Genevieve A. Krafft

Life As I See It

A tale too pretty for mere words, but I try.
A world too far inept to make any sense of anything.
A universe so large as to encompass us all - Too small for such
thoughts as diversity.
Yet one world in many have extraordinary events, pass by like the wind.
So large yet so small;
understanding nothing;
the Tales, just great memories of our past.
   Cheryl K. Schmeidler

Untitled

The mind has greater windows than the eyes
And more opened are the doors of the soul, where all things
   can be seen at a glance.
A greater vision the eyes of the spirit has.

It amazes me how much more we can see with our hearts than with
   our eyes.
Go inwardly and you will have the whole world opened for you.
Go outwardly and the world will close on you.
The world will become a blank wall for you to stare.
Nothing is greater than the opening of the inside.
Nothing shows more clearly than the clear blue skies of our
   inner self.
Nothing more clearly than a clear inside, an idea in the mind.
The soul is an open window where you can free the today forever.
The soul is an wide open window where you free all the desires
Of your mind, and they fly like white doves in the middle of
A widening sky. Then I feel that the spirit is an open world
   of love.
   Joseph Moctezuma

Spirit

It's hard to be happy when castles all fall,
And life seems more hardship than fun,
It's easy to say "what's the use of it all,"
And then leave the battle half-won

It's hard to take failure when all of your dreams
Have centered on glory and fame.
It's easy to let all your plans and your schemes
Fall apart and leave you in shame.

But the one who can weather all storms with a smile
Who has spirit that never will bend
Is the one who at heart is really worthwhile
And will come out on top in the end.
   Evelyn L. Splitt

Images Of Red

Candlelight burns across our embrace,
And leaving me unsatisfied
Is your shadow molding against mine.
Pushing through every hour,
While telling myself that I need you.
Despising your vulgar tongue that slashes against me,
I accept you against my will
   (in a lie).
Longing for an excuse to shut you out,
Yet dying for your stay out of loneliness.

As incense burns jasmine musk.
We hold ours together the best that we can.
As I lie with you once more
I close my eyes and see another.
   Jason Gantt

A Child's Love

From me to you, I give thanks.
And I praise and praise all the wonderful saints.
As days go by, I can't in any way,
Think of a time my mind whisked you away.
When I think of you, I think of flowers,
Standing in the breeze for hours and hours.
When I'm with you I feel safe and good,
Like a baby deer, hidden in the wood.
I've got a message I want to say,
But when I try to say it, the words are so far away.
I love you, I love you with all my heart,
I love my mother with love in my heart.
   Aaron Tiller

Untitled

Time heals a broken heart
And it takes a little time
Its really kind a hard
To let an old love die

If you don't try to love again
You find yourself alone
And its really kind a lonely
Cause you find yourself never leaving home

There's other love out there
If you just give them a chance
Don't make this old one your last dance

A broken heart takes time to heal
But it doesn't last that long
And if the love leaves and breaks your heart
It was never meant to be from the very start
   Chrissy Tennison

Watch Your Step

I walk upon a solitary pathway
And it seems that this has always been my place.
And though friends come to call upon occasion
They are careful to depart without a trace.
For it seems the trial is difficult to follow.
Designed with much irregularity.
I understand, its surface can be awkward
And yet it is appropriate for me.
I'm familiar with the feel and the appearance
And the narrowness of this kind of terrain.
I've been walking here for ever and for ever
And when I've rested, this is where I've lain.
In the middle of the silence of a pathway
Where the corridor accommodates but one
Who is traveling the ages on a mission,
Where a solo flyers work is never done.
   Anne W. Brunelli

This Decade

This decade drops a curtain on my heart
and in its folds are thoughts
no power can part from memory,
from you and me,
and I stand dazzled.

Our love has traversed all the stony shores,
like timbers wrenched from off a bolted door
to let the sunlight in,
and I stand dazzled.

Reality embraced a dream
where nothing was quite as it seemed
upon the tangled paths we trod,
known but by you and I, and God,
and I stand dazzled.
   Carol Denham Baines

Thank You Lord

Thank you Lord for making me
and for loving me, for being with me.

And I thank you Lord for giving me life,
For all you done, for believing in me,
For saving me and walking with me.

Thank you Lord for being with me.
For day to day and night to night,
We thank you Lord for being with us all the time,
And forever until we come home to you Lord.
   Billy Huey

A Call To God

If you're tired and weary with the pain you bear each day,
And if you feel you're so alone and no one really cares
And if your heart is breaking and the tears are hard to hide,
Just turn your eyes to Heaven and His arms will open wide.

He will tenderly enfold you and hold you oh so tight,
And with His strong but gentle hands,
He'll brush your tears aside.

For He knows the cross you carry and,
He knows the pain you bear.
For He's your Heavenly Father and,
He's heard your every prayer.

So when your heart's too heavy with the burdens of the day,
And your footsteps falter with the passing of each day
Just call to God for comfort and He'll give you strength anew,
And the courage to accept all things that lie ahead for you.

For He loves you oh so dearly,
For you are a child of His.
And He's here to help you bear your cross,
Just like His Father did for Him.
   Charlotte Wolf

The Woman I Admire And Why

The woman I admire surprises me everyday
And I would like for her to know that she makes my day.
She believes in me and she has faith in me;
This is one reason why she is very, very close to me.
She knows me, she loves me, she wants the best for me,
And when we're apart, so is a piece of my heart.
I don't think she understands how I need her in my life,
So hopefully this poem will share a little light.
I love you, I love you, if she only knew how much.
When she reads this poem, I know her heart will be touched.
The woman I admire is a very special friend,
Whom I'll always love to the bitter end.
To you, Christina, my beautiful child,
You're the best I've seen in a long, long while.
So continue to believe and have faith in me,
And I promise you, I'll be all that I can be.

Love Mom
   Carolyn Browder

The Anecdote

Your love was so seraphic
And I misjudged it for endearing,
Let's not get enthusiastic
'Cause I went the wrong way caring.

Sorry I never told you
All I wanted to say,
I never showed you how I felt
Assumed you'll always be there anyway.

So I'm writing this tryst to confess
To all the things that were susceptible,
And I'm so glad that I had met you
'Cause you were so very incredible.

So forgive me, for the decision I made
I'm so very thankful for all the love you gave.
And I knew in my heart your love was always true,
That's why I'll always remember you.
   Carmen Trishell

A New Year's Wish

Let's all gather our thoughts this eve,
And hold hands around the world.

From family to friends, our love
Will help keep all flags unfurled.

Gazing at the stars this New Year's Eve
Will strength our love and friendship,
What more could we achieve.

Freedom and peace is on the agenda
That love and togetherness will be with us, forever.

"Happy New Year Everyone"
Beatrice A. Delorier

The Alchemist

She takes me in her hands as the base metal that I am
And gently exposes me to her elements.
Earth, fire, water and air
All hiss, smoke, and spin before me.
Through her tender esoteric care
The transmutation begins.
As the steam clears, I settle to the bottom of her alembic
And though I contain all qualities necessary
To become pure,
It is only through her exoteric permutation
That I may become gold.
Did Arnaldus and Albertus fail to look at the obvious?
Or, have I, through some random quirk of fate
Simply stumbled on that one rarity in a million,
The "philosopher's stone?"
Soon my sublimation will be complete,
My molten body will be poured into the mold,
And all I am to do
Is hold her in my arms
Giving my heart as my body cools.
Everett E. Le Grande

The Corner Of Time

Have you ever stood at the bend in the road
and gazed for a moment or two,
wondering what was around that bend,
wondering what it would hold for you?

Have you felt the tug of the safe know way,
the comfortable space you knew,
and wondered if, after all's said and done,
the old ways were the best for you?

Then having decided and ready to turn,
going back the way you came,
did the bend in the road seem to call to you
and draw you into its game?

When you finally followed the urgings within
not knowing the reason or rhyme,
weren't you glad you stepped out in faith
and turned the corner of time?
Hilda Kellis

Angels

Angels
Appear unexpectedly, often unbidden,
A flash of light
A soft touch
A whispered sound
Pale outlines that emerge from the shadows, then quietly disappear
Leaving a peace, kissed by their presence
A calmness anchored in their love.
Joanne F. Jones

A Season Of Meaning

There's shopping and baking and fires burning bright
And folks softly humming strains of Silent Night
Bright lights twinkle gaily from windows and trees
And suddenly all kids remember to say "Thank you" and "Please"
There's good cheer and laughter and spirits are high
And with last minute details, the days seem to fly
Then snow begins falling, and everything's just right
Giving us the pleasure of a Christmas of white
But have we forgotten the cheer has a meaning behind it
Is it buried so deep that we'll never find it?
Let's look beyond the gift wrap and ribbon
And remember the reason for the gifts we are giving
That this was the day the Christ Child was born
And there was no santa on that first Christmas morn
So after the kids have all squealed with delight
And dinner is eaten down to the very last bite
Let's reflect for a moment, just how blessed we are
To have had this day of happiness to share
Then let's look ahead to a year bright and new
And please, let me extend Christmas Greetings to you!
Barbara Seesholtz

For Your Special Birthday

There are friends who may share the year,
and family who may share the month, but
only you can hold this one date dear.

This is your 18th birthday and it is golden,
since on an October eve on the 18th day
you were my first born child I was beholden'.

There are memories of you that I hold dear,
a smile, a step, odd moments both good and bad,
such as diapers that could make my eyes tear.

Like the summer you fell off the boat,
or teaching you jacks stretched upon the floor,
and your lesson in flight - thanks to Miss Goat.

There were several things I wasn't there to see,
big achievements, small victories, so many firsts,
but our future ones together are enough for me.

Happy Birthday to my daughter who is now grown,
off to see the World both near and far, take with you
all of your Mother's love - which I hope I have shown.
Bonnie Younger-Scott

My Farm

It nestles in the valley of Ohio's rolling plain
And every night at sunset I stroll down the shady lane,
My soul is filled with deep content, my heart is filled with love,
for my dear old rambling farm house, with deep blue sky above.

Fearlessly it stretches forth, with fields of ripened grain
Rippling gently in the breeze, as though it can't refrain
From sending forth a song of peace for the world to see
Knowing not only that we are at peace, but also that we are free!

Free to rise at the crack of dawn and hike about o're the hills
Free the stroll through wooded glens and listen to the bird's
   warbling trills;
Free to live, to laugh and to love, as is everybody's right;
And for this freedom, we're ready indeed, to take up our arms
   and fight.

These are the small things I've worked for, treasures to me, everyone!
I would not trade for a mansion—fearing I'd lose the sun,
Yes, fearing I'd lose the pleasure of digging down into the soil'
Of working and reaping the harvest,—Ah yes, T's worth all the toil.

For, here on my farm in Ohio, with it's fields of goldenrod,
One cannot lose sight of nature—One cannot forget about God!
Florence Pyle

Storm Cloud

    Gray puffs drifting southward;
and early looms an ebony sky.
    Whither onset cast the smile of morning sun.
unveils her now a blissless pout.

    Dialog elapsed into obfuscated discord,
reason diffuses to umbrageous wigs.
    Immutable hearts wrangle, grapple...
augmented with reproach and refute.

    Restlessness reigns wherest heaven
cradled formerly her promising kiss.
    Zephyrs squabbling chase leaves about
as claps of fury shatter amity.

    Tempestuous yawps pierce the air.
Souls unalterable spate acrimoniously.
    Resounding maelstroms-austerely cast barbs
bring on the deluge of despair.

Byron Halvorsen

Untitled

I pranced across the fields of green
and danced before eyes unseen
an innocent heart, so pure and light
my soul so free and full of delight.

Sometimes I return to that place in time
and find somehow the perfect rhyme
my mind free of the all too familiar worry
and my body free of the all too familiar hurry.

All too often I lose my place
when cramped within my daily space
sentiment of life is lost to priority
and peace becomes a minority

Still I continue to search for that child
who still runs along free and wild
well all the world continues the same
and sometimes I hardly remember her name.

Beverly J. Gale

Dear Whale So Gentle

Dear whale, so gentle, and so great.
A more gentle creature than you
our Creator did not create.

As you swim there,
both deep and shallow within the sea.
Malice is a trait, that is not within thee.

You do not wish harm upon any man.
And why man wishes to harm you,
this poet does not understand.

In some countries,
your meat is considered a delicacy.
A while these puny men
satisfy their palates, they are destroying thee.

It seems to me, dear whale, that they don't care
if they completely destroy all of you.
For they have already diminished your number, down to just a few.

These are a terrible people in this poet's point of view.
Terrible people, once you have destroyed all of the whales,
then to please your palates, what will you do?

Michael D. Jones

Christmas Eve

She was pressing her face against the glass watching the people laugh and dance around the tree that was so bright with color. Frost melted with the warmth of her breath as music froze the tiny girl that stood without moving, without noise. I wanted to touch her and ask her where she was from, on a night as cold as this. There was a calm inside her that I sensed, a feeling that had no words. I remember that this was Christmas Eve and that is when I'd seen her.

The smell of wood burning and the paper bags with small lights in silent rows, on walls and steps and walkways. Thousands of lights burning and glowing; no sound, just soft warmth, like knowing eyes and memories waving. I thought of all that we have and all that we do not really feel that makes us glow inside. It's a warmth inside so strong that Anything is possible and Everything is real. I watched her staring, torn and tattered, little hands on glass. The cold did not touch her, she had no feeling, just eyes like candles glowing. I knew inside her heart was warmth and that she knew far more than any of the people in the fancy clothes; their empty shells, with painted faces and icy hands held out. I watched her walk away, down the walk ways and along the walls, the candles still burned on. I could not feel the cold now either and hoped I'd caught the spell. Maybe I was dreaming; and then I caught her coat. It ripped away - a small footprint lay melted in the snow. I felt my hand grasping a torn bag of sand. My breath was warm on glass and music swayed inside me. I thought of all the things I had and knew I had the greatest gift. A memory of a candle, in a bag full of sand.

Ann Eager

"Questions"

What if green was blue
and blue was green
would be witnessing a different scene
or would it be the same
only going by a different name.

What if white was black
and black was white
and no one had the gift of sight
would we judge people by the cold of their face
would there be a minority race

What if you were me
and I were you
would you still judge everything I do
or would it be the other way
and I'd judge you every day

What if I were right
and you were wrong
would there be a reason to write this poem
I think the answers clear as day
everyone sees things a different way

Anthony Gewinner

The Black Boy On The Beach

Seashells, waves, the nice warm sand were all in easy reach
and as I watched, a little boy appeared upon the beach.

He stretched his arms up to the sky and welcomed in the sun
the happiness upon his face made known to everyone.

For all the world a frisky colt he frolicked in the sand
His color mattered not at all, nor did he understand.

He'd stumbled on a white man's beach and would be turned away
and told to find another place where colored children play.

So as his fine sand palaces the waves would soon destroy
a tide came up and washed away the childhood from that boy.

I wonder if I'll ever see - a contrast - day or night
that's sharper than a boy's face in learning black from white!

Jean Brown   1948

Autumn Memories

'Twas October on the calendar, as the seasons roll around,
And as I searched my memory, this is what I found —
That pile of leaves in which we rolled and so happily played,
The tang of the cool cider that grandfather had made,
The tolling of the school bell that called us from our play,
Oh, life was calm and simpler in that remembered day.
Today the rush of business keeps me running all around
As I try to do those simple things in which that joy was found.
Time will not turn back, no matter what I do,
But the memory of those happy days still warms the heart of you.
And so, amid the dancing leaves, a certain peace I find
As the memory of those happy days keeps coming to my mind.
When we see the leaves a falling, we know that winter will soon abide
With its ice and snow and wintry wind to drive us all inside.
But then there'll be the fireplace, with all its warmth and cheer,
To bring back those fond memories that we all hold so dear.

Howard J. Lockward

Night Sky

Just as the last crimson highlight of a forgotten sunset fades,
and a sparkle from the first star can be seen,
the night sky comes.
Darkness falls like a blanket, slowly inducing deep slumber
Tic-tock on the clock, chimes sound as the hours pass.
The ghostly silver moon rises like a giant beacon in the night,
shining a path over the waters.
The stars in their constellations, as eternal children play
timeless games in a field of sweet dreams.
A myriad of shimmering gems against the black velvet night,
so real,...yet so far away.
Cool breezes caress my face. Black clouds silently glide by,
now joined by others. They grumble in thunderous tones.
The scent of newborn rain on the night's breath,
forewarns me, of the coming storm.
Lightning shatters the darkness and the clouds reply with a
deafening
boom of thunder! The sky weeps mournfully.
The quarrel eventually ends sending the clouds apart.
Orion and the Big Dipper disappear into the morning.
The night sky, but a memory.

Bethany Joy Healani DeNisi

The Ride

He was an ornery old man
And a practical joke was always the plan
He came home dragging a trailer behind
With a smile on his face, Circle D was on his mind

A gold palomino was saddled and bridled
He was backed in the trailer and ready to straddle
They pulled and pushed and cattle prodded, too
That ornery horse just didn't move

Then grandpaw came up with the clue
He came saddled and bridled, so ride that jewel!
He will give you a good ride, there's no doubt
So sit straight in the saddle, son, he's coming out

Well, he came out of that trailer like the chute at the rodeo
But only the ornery old man enjoyed that show.

Calvin Roney

Into The Arms Of Destiny

A feeling, that comes only once.
An understanding you'll know, without
a doubt is there.
A smile, more radiant than any other.
For your eyes only, to see.
A tear, that has its own soul; a
single drop that means more to
your heart than any others have.
A breath, held in your throat.
When release comes, gradually so does knowledge.
A heart, passing a beat. Only to
reassure you, on return, you are
still full of life.
A poem, in your eyes, that is consumed
by reality. Perhaps to others, just
words to be read; perhaps not.
A single person who cares, who
enfolds you, into the arms of your destiny.

Danyelle Umsteadt

Suppressed Rage

Years of suppressed rage
An anger that will, and shall, never cease
All of one's tears fall like raindrops
Tears of rage and sadness
All of the rage
Like an angry madman stalking his next victim
All of the suppressed rage
All of the deaths and fears
All of the anxiety of the year passed
The rage suppressed for so long, waiting to be released
To blow up like a bomb
Just waiting for the fuse to be lit
The "bomb" will eventually blow up
Waiting for the right time
Again and again the tears fall
As if running from a spigot, never to be shut off
All of your emotions strewn about,
　like a tornado just struck
All of the sadness, rage, and anxiety will not leave you
It will always be with you

Jessica J. Wahl

The Song Of The Heart

The song of the heart can be as sweet as
an angel's singing voice.
The song of the heart can be as gentle as the
light rain that kisses a rose at dusk.
The song of the heart burns true, like a
burning candle lights the pathway on a
dreary winters night.
The song of the heart beats strong like the
promise of pure love will never fail.
The song of the heart is as innocent as a
newborn baby's first breath.
The rhyme of the heart's song remembers, and
knows only love, and the beauty of joy.
The song of the heart last forever, even when
the body passes from life into death.
The song of the heart always stays the same,
yet it will always be a mystery.

Andera Gunter

Fathers

Father you are faithful, a foreseer and a friend,
An advisor, admirer, anxious and able to guide to the end.

You are thoughtful, thankful, thorough and strong,
Helpful, humble, hopeful, showing happiness as you hold
to God's teachings all day long.

Father you are easy to talk with, eager to help, even forgiving
when mistakes are done,
Real as you instruct, ready as an example, reverence to God
teaching he's the only true one.

Father your relationship means so very much to me, but
maybe you don't know,
If I'm a daughter you are my first love; and if I'm a
son you are my hero.

Gertrude V. Brewer

Untitled

Am I just a teardrop, in another pond?
Am I only a day in another year that has gone?
I'm a fraction of a second of a day that is done,
In a crowd of millions I am just one.
A tree in the forest, set away from the rest,
Never can be good enough, always second best.
Just another star in the darkness of the night,
Just another wrong in an endless sea of rights,
I'm just another shell, lying on the beach,
A dream, a hope, just barely out of reach.
Just another person, never to be known,
Just another person, to live her life alone.

Debika Paul

Season's End

Another day in the crow's nest, with summer drawing nigh.
Although we dread to think of it, the snowflakes soon will fly.
But all the glorious colors, that fall is sure to bring,
The reds, the golds, the oranges, the crickets when they sing
A lot of the birds will leave us, to find a warmer place,
But there's always new arrivals, and each day a small new face.
The tiny little winter wren, she always makes you smile,
To watch her very busily, search the wood that's in a pile.
The groundhog's ceased his wandering, in the fields of grass so deep,
He's curled up in his burrow, for a long and peaceful sleep.
Though summer seems elusive, each season has it's time,
A time for birth, a time for rest, as the years go quickly by.
The birds nest all stand empty now, the little ones gone and grown,
They'll fill the nests once more next year, with babies of their own.

Helen Sheets Moore

Untitled

To some, to exercise is a way of life,
Although the ways of exercising are rife.
A brisk walk is the best way to go for some,
To others, any kind of walking is dumb!
The true joggers think running is to jeer at,
While true runners think jogging is to sneer at!
The "running up steps" precept also has fans,
Whether the action be of woman or man's!
Some people claim jumping rope is for the birds,
And using a trampoline too dumb for words!
Yes, swimming is good too, but as you should know,
It is not very good to do in the snow!
All things considered, it comes down to this,
Do that exercise in which you can find bliss!

Dan Nelson

Gold Colored Rose

A rose colored a hue of gold
Allows your mystery to unfold.
It started a long time ago,
When we were not lovers but foes.
Hating, but lovingly we touched each others souls,
When we walked by each other to and fro.
So strange it seems that now we are together
And from the way things look it could be forever.
So when you gave me that gold colored rose,
You proved to me that wherever I go your love goes.

Christy Langston

Tears

Tears are a watery collection of
All your pent-up feelings that become
so large that have to roll down a cheek,
form a creek.

A rivulet of dashed hopes,
Long suffering, joy turned to pain,
Sadness over something lost — perhaps never had.

Splash.

But they stop, you know,
After a while, they stop.

And life goes on.

On until
Your heat overflows into your eyes and
you feel.

Cloudy weather.

The only difference between one tear and another
Is that the last
Has been here before.

Jim Lee Morgan

Words Of Truth

People are wondering why, and who's to blame
All they have to do is believe and praise His name.

Just take the time; read His words; you will find
That God's words are the truth, and
He gave it to all mankind.

The words of truth, God gave to me and you
The words of truth, they are written down as proof.

He gave us the laws of the Ten Commandments
And he meant for us all to know and understand them.

He said who that believe shall also understand
For after all, He has the whole world in His hands.

The words of truth God gave to me and you
The words of truth, they are written down as proof
The Words of truth, you got to believe, people
You know they are true. the Words of truth.

Clifford Duane Roseboro

I Love The Boardwalk Of Miami Beach

I love the boardwalk of Miami Beach
All the way to south point as far as it will reach
You can feel the ocean breeze and hear the ocean talk
I love Miami Beach boardwalk from south point to fountain blue
You view ocean parks hotels and Susie Q
A walk where lovers hold each others hand
And sometimes vow to wedding plans
The beautiful baby from the official stalk
The beautiful Miami Beach boardwalk

Dominick Murillo

Peace

The waterfalls I hear are very distant,
all the meanwhile they flow persistent.
I listen to the leaves, I listen to the trees.
It is peace I hear, I know I have nothing to fear,
for it's peace I hear.
    And for a moment, it seems to almost touch me,
then I feel a little glee.
As the happiness comes over me,
I think of the way it used to be.
I clear my heart, as the sadness does part.
It is peace I hear, I know I have nothing to fear,
for it's peace I hear.
Peace speaks to me in a sweet and gentle way,
as I lay in the sun on a hot summer's day.
    For when silence comes creeping this way,
the peace will be here to drive it away.
Peace destroys troubles and pains
because peace is life.
    Candace Johnson

Hands

The joys of love formed from life's sands
All shaped and molded with just two hands
Hands gently caressing to help love grow
Hands to comfort when spirits are low
Hands to guide through the darkened places
Hands to fill in the empty spaces
Hands to guide to that future we'll reach
Hands strong to endure lessons life will teach
Hands to hold steady and never stop trying
Hands to comfort a small baby's crying
Hands clutching in embrace just to help show
Of a whole life devoted to loving you so
Two hands, there's nothing that they can't do
When one belongs to me, and the other to you
    Bill G. Willis

To My Grandma With Love

I remember when I was young,
All of the songs that we had sung.
The dreams that we shared,
The disappointments that we bared.
As I lie in bed awake at night,
I think of you and know that everything will be alright.
I love you Grandma with all my heart,
And I know that we will never be apart.
I'll never forget the fun that we had,
As I stood there alone and feeling sad.
I waited and waited to see you that day,
To say goodbye in my special way.
I know that heaven is a wonderful place,
And you will be welcomed with a warm embrace.
I'm scared and lonely without you here,
But in my heart you will always be near.
The memories of you will never fade,
For these are what we have made.
I'll always love you Grandma and this is true,
For I lost a part of me when I lost you.
    Heidi Nikole Gwinnup

All I Have Is This Poem

I can't give you a present.
All I can give you is this poem.
For I have no way to get you anything.
So I'll have to write exactly how I feel about this very special day.
It's a time to celebrate with the ones you love.
A day filled with presents and memories.
All I can give you is this poem.

You opened every gift and liked them all quite well.
Somehow mine was the very last gift to be opened.
You carefully unfolded the paper and read the words I'd written.
A tear came to your eye and you said this is the best gift of all.
You didn't spend a lot of money,
but I know you spent a lot of time.
Because I can feel the love overflowing with every single word.
And all you gave me was this poem.
    Deb Harnden

My Special Grandma

I was once happy and outgoing, but now I'm not sure where I belong.
All because a train came and took everything beautiful away, I may
    be young, but I hurt just like you.
The parents that were once together are apart and with someone new.
My only question is Why?
Now that my Grandma is in her new Home I wonder why God took
    someone so dear.
I feel alone, confused, and misunderstood.
I know She's watching over me and I know She's wondering what
    happened to her little girl, the one She knew was the strongest
    in the world.
But I know that my Grandma also knows that it's not me, but the
    people around me has hurt me too.
My Grandma is with me in more ways than one, She's with me in mind,
    and spirit and She'll always be my best friend and the Best
Grandma
    in the world only to me.
So, when I'm sad, mad, and happy I know that She'll be here with me
    to experience the pain, sorrow, and the joy that I will endure in
    my lifetime.
And as God has always said; I'll never leave your side... Never Alone.
    Bernadette Fink

A Small Chance For...A Child

Peter won't see, because of Mommy dearest.
Alison didn't even take a breath, because of Mommy's secrets.
Sally won't sleep she is only going to cry, Mommy
gave her NO chance to be a child.
Sally is only five days old and already she has a drug addiction.
    There is no chance... she will be normal.
Peter and Sally will maybe live, what type of life
No one can ever know.
Alison had no chance at life, Mom's final fix is what has
placed Alison below a cement slate, which only states;
    Alison Doe (baby)
    Born 5/ '95 - Died 5, '95
No one will cry at this grave site, nor a flower placed.
A child without even a chance to cry... to the world in
which shall never crawl upon.
These are only a few, very few of a small amount of the young,
whom will never have that.....
    Small chance for life as
    A CHILD.
    Cheri Tracy Larssen

November

Gray skeleton trees appear, almost a surprise
After October's brilliant show.
Rake scrapes sidewalk and gravel
Creating mounds of mulch.

Soft rain and overnight frost.
Leaves uncaptured, form hard mats
Unyielding,
A handy excuse, to let them be.

Good news for the weary gardener,
Cold ears, blistered hands,
Longing to be inside
To dream of spring and bulbs in bloom.
Judie Hansen

Of Emily

Amber sunbeams warm an upturned cherub face,
Adding blush to apple cheeks.
Cherry blossom breezes gently ruffle golden curls
As a button nose perks at a familiar scent,
Syrupy sweet, floating like music in the spring air.
Tiny toes tickled by soft green grass
As they creep towards the wafting scent.
Azure eyes, shadowed by feathery lashes, widen
As they spy tangled vines
Heavy with fragrant ivory and butter trumpets.
It's honeysuckle!
The smell of her favorite blanket and Mommy's hugs.
She smiles.
Errin Cain

The Prayer That I Pray

The smell of flowers in blossom on an early spring day.
Accompanied by joyous laughter drifting my way.
Just over the fence, several children at play.
Our comes Mom with milk and cookies on a tray.
Consumed by the youngsters without delay.
Back to their playing in the dirt and red clay.
Thank you God, for sharing this with me today.
Let Mommy nor Daddy neither one go away,
Keep them safe and warm, is the prayer that I pray.
Nothing else in mind. That's all I want to say.
Jeanette Trauth

The Carousel Of Life

The carousel of life goes round and round,
and it goes on into eternity
all the brightly painted animals
have their paint chipped off,
for them life has lost all its color.
all the people are dying and sick,
for they are constantly rained on by the
problems of this carousel.
Many of them are crying to get off,
because even though the music hasn't stopped
the ignorance of the people has made them deaf to it.
After all life is dead,
the carousel will still be turning
for one morbid lady in rags
who is a princess in disguise
once known as mother nature still lives,
but she, too, is dying.
Though as long as she lives,
the carousel of life goes round and round,
and it goes on into eternity.
Hadas Marcus

Convergence Of The Minds

Gather round the table and talk, talk, talk
about the affairs of the world.

Peace treaty, The Armament's Pact, and all of that
endless, fruitless stream of dialogue...

Going nowhere, despite the convergence of the minds —
great and small. A waste of time...A waste of
money...A waste of energy...

For talk is cheap and no sooner said, one
would say he's been gypped.

Where have we gone wrong? For all these years of
trying and achieving nothing but
temporary respite from guns and bombs...

Maybe we need a change, not of the mind, but of the
heart...the giving up of selfishness, the I, I, I.

We need not try to convince others of how we grieved,
rather ask ourselves how we can help erase their
bitterness and dread.

Together we could do it, when we start to recognize,
we are truly one, for we live in the same land,
breathe the same air and are warmed by the same sun!
Audrey B. Abrera

What You Mean To Me

"To love, and be loved, is the greatest thing on earth."
A year ago, these were just empty words to me.
However, now, because of you, they are a reality.

Since I've met you, you've taught me so many wonderful things
I never thought I could know:

Understanding; believing that we don't need to be exactly alike
and knowing that we can accept our differences as blessings.

Honesty; knowing that you know everything I say and do is sincere.

Faith; that with persistence, and God's help, we can conquer
anything together.

Trust; allowing my heart to be completely vulnerable to you,
believing that you'll never break it.

Commitment, promising to myself and you I'll be ever faithful
to this relationship, during the good times, as well as the bad.

And finally...
Love; giving you all my love, with no strings attached, seeing your
weaknesses, and loving you regardless, just as I know you love me.

Understanding, honesty, faith, trust, commitment and love.

This is what you mean to me.
Jessica Schwingel

Untitled

A word, a name, a person, true love.
A word has a meaning, a name symbolizes a meaning,
and true love is a bond between two people
that care a lot about each other.
If you have a true love and their heart is in your hands,
then you should be obligated to take care of it,
meet its needs, and fill it with love and joy.
So if you think or know that you can't obligate yourself
to a person at the time being,
then be honest with them even if it hurts their feelings.
Because if you mislead them, their feelings can get hurt
much more than you could imagine.
Bridget Wise

The Leaves Of Autumn

It seems like only yesterday dear, when you became my bride. Oh! what a wonderful day. I was so filled with pride. The leaves of Autumn were so brilliantly arrayed. I think the Lord must have arranged this spectacular display.

25 years of marriage-how swiftly it has passed. Sometimes it seems like the flicker of a match. Yet some particular days an eternity could have passed.

But like the leaves of Autumn, our marriage is a testimony to God and nature's plan. The leaves must endure to be so grand. And so with our marriage, the road is not always smooth, but the beautiful days of Autumn remind me of my eternal love for you.

John F. Shubert

Wondering

New worlds unfold, Sunlight streams onto a child's face.
A woman dies to save another.
The sun rises, drying the dew on sweet clean grass.
Two girls enter the room, their voices breaking the beauty of my
Silence. "I love your sweater!"
"Thanks, I got it at the Gap. So, are you going with him or not?"
"I don't know, he can be really annoying, but he is cute."
A pause, silence, for a moment they are...
Lovely. Will they see that they say nothing
not one important word,
and think
even less than they say?
The silence ends,
the girls go on as they always have,
forgetting the moment as it ends.
A beautiful flower,
New worlds created, The clouds of a storm...
For me, and for them, I shed a
Tear.
And I Wonder...

Christina Heath

Molding The Mind

Some people change, even you. After not seeing them for a while, you grow not to notice them by their look in the mirror, but by their look in your mind. You're not pals like you used to be, and soon, even laughter begins to fade away into the dark shadows that lurk behind you. Even though they're still the same person, you begin to loose respect for them, and after a while, they are just another face in the crowd. It's funny how people forget. I forget, and I have forgot, and I dearly regret it. Remember that with each and every look, you should mold their character in your mind so that you will never forget, and they will seem the exact same as they did many years ago.

Ann E. Ritz

Untitled

For the last time, I see your smile, you just sit there and stare for a while. I want to say, "Look inside, and you'll find me," but the drugs are making my eyelids heavy.

Very quietly I hear the doctor say, "Sorry sir, she won't see another day." As you start to cry, I pray, "Please God, don't let me die!"

The life machine beeps in my ear, one more time before I sense the fear, The fear that tells me, I'll soon be dead, the pressure is building up in my head.

One more time I smile for you, to tell you my life is through. As you touch my shoulder, the beep is constant and all is over.

As I pass away with a smile on my lips, the last things I hear is you say, "Honey, I love you, and I'll see you... someday..."

Jessica Nodes

Fatherhood

On the day you were born, from the moment I saw you,
A warmth swelled inside, as I reached out to hold you.
and you nestled and cooed, in my arms all the while.
I studied your face, there was a trace of a smile.

Oh the feeling of pride, that inflated me that day.
Just opened my heart, in a strange sort of way
And now I'm a dad, it's a feeling quite rare.
For the rest of my life, I'll be walking on air.

So this is what it's like, to be a parent at last.
I'll savor each moment, cause they grow up so fast.
and the powerful feeling, that's over and above.
Is the strong sense to give, is the meaning of Love.

I thank you Lord, for allowing me to give,
So much of myself, so our child can live.
As hard as things seems, I'll wish more than our share.
To prove to you always, all our love that we'll share.

For isn't it true, that after hardships have passed.
Our eyes show a sparkle, a flame that will last.
And our smiles always broaden, after storms go their way.
I'll long to see rainbows, on your face everyday.

Dale Coppin

The Awakening

First there was a darkness engulfing, possessively,
a vast and useless universe
Then came a rosy dawn, hopefully encompassing
the murky depths of black
Reaching and enlightening as it went
groping for the truth
That which chose it was uplifted
But knowledge became at once a blessing and a curse
A blessing in that it enabled mankind to see the folly of the past
A curse in that it became the rule
with which to measure and deceive
Those less fortunate than ourselves

Hector Ramirez

"Silently Screaming"

He was her firstborn,
  a tiny gift from God,
    rocked in her arms a thousand times.

Then a small boy, happy and carefree,
  smelling of rain and sunlight,
    running to her for hugs and kisses.

That boy, grown to manhood, tall and handsome,
  became a man, cold and hateful,
    lost in a world of delusions, hallucinations and fear.

They, who knew about those things,
  told her it was schizophrenia,
    an illness with no cure or closure.

She, stunned and heartbroken, shed countless tears in anguish, for his pain and terror;
  prayers unanswered, she often wished she had never been born.

But, because of her love for him, she would always be there to help,
  day after day, year after year!
    Silently screaming: Why?

Cloie J. Teitler

Reflections Open Your Eyes And See

I open my eyes and see
A teddy bear worn with love, symbolizing my childhood
A frightened child in her mother's warm embrace, showing
my early fears
Curious eyes eager to learn and experience; my will to learn
I see the past.

I open my eyes and see
Challenges at every turn
New found friends and fun everywhere
Hopes and dreams for my future
I see the present.

I open my eyes and see
Numerous choices and chances
A happy family of my own
A successful, fulfilled life
I see the future.

The past holds memories of joy forever
The present holds my key to the future
The future holds my life and new endeavors.
   Julie Lee

A Stand For Freedom

A blood-stained battlefield upon a devastated land —
A tear-stained handkerchief in a mother's trembling hand —
A young country's beauty now ravaged and marred.
A young soldier's body lay trampled and scarred.
For righteous ideals and with bravery he fought,
Clinging only to God's love and the freedom that he sought;
A mother's prayers were answered as her son became a man,
He had yearned for what was right as he lay dying in the sand;
And though the costs were greatest for those who took a stand,
Still a mother and her precious son lay nestled in God's hand;
The Comforter had dwelt with them when the world appeared benign,
Their unwavering faith had carried them, unfolding God's design,
For a land where freedom reigned supreme and peace was symbolized
By an eagerness to fight for truth and a willingness to die.
   Cathy Robinson

"Wayne"

  As I lined your fingers with mine, I felt
a surge through my body that gave me a sign,
that somehow I knew you in a past time.

  Maybe we loved as far back as the beginning
of time and that maybe our souls have been
intertwined. Meant to meet specifically - past
to present joyfully.

  Maybe we met in Egypt - I was Cleopatra
and you my devoted lover Marc Antony. And then
again we met on Mt Olympus in Greece, you Zeus
and I your enchanted wife Hera.
  We became one another, and our souls
seek out and search for one another until joined
again your inside my heart and mind, and we
carry each other always.

  I lost myself until we were reunited.
I love you again and again - we shall love
forever among the stars and your name hangs
heavy on my lips - Wayne
   Heidi G. Evans

My True Friends Of My Old Hometown

Growing up as a child, I had dreams of who I wanted to be
A superstar of something, and well-known, well that could surely be me
I'm now no longer a child,
I'm no star worthy of world renown
But I have the honor and blessing of my true friends
Of my old hometown

Looking back at those days as a child, I see how much I have grown
How many places I've been, what I've done, how many people
I've known
Although I haven't seen times when
I was part of something going down
I have been a witness of legends, they're my true friends
Of my old hometown

No politician, no actor, no musician, no big name that you know
Will ever even come close to make a difference in my life as a whole
I am left with some memories
That will never let me carry a frown
'Cause to me they're a living tribute to my true friends
Of my old hometown.
   Joe Hetzel

"Burning Love"

My love for you is like a river,
A summer breeze that makes my soul shiver.
One look from you is more precious than gold.
I've tried to tell you, but I'm not that bold.
There's a hole in my heart that I need to fill,
And only your love fits the bill.
Living without you is like living without air.
I'm the one who will always be there.
So, let me be the one to love you and the one to care.
I vow to be faithful.
I won't make a promise that I can't keep,
And if you tell me to "Shut up," I won't make a peep!
Take a chance with me,
And make all my wishes come true.
Every moment that we spend goes by too fast.
Let me be the one for you.
I hope that you feel the same way too!
   Janna SuEllen Atzenhofer

Along Life's Paths

There is a yearning in each of us.
A striving need to be loved and give love in return.
We each follow innumerable paths reaching to fulfill this need.
We frequently follow wrong or incomplete paths,
Which end in despair and trepidation.

Our true paths also have branches which we invariably follow,
Hoping we will find a short cut to reach our yearned for goal.
However, each branch eventually rejoins our original path,
And we see how our delusions made our trip longer and more arduous.
We realize, not for the first time, that we create our own roadblocks
through self-deception and delusion.

Though our trip through life along our chosen paths is long and arduous,
Though we sometimes blunder along blindly, seeking more in
desperation than full heartedness,
Though we sometimes relinquish our long sought goal because
we don't recognize it there,
In the end we will drop our blinders, shake off our self-deceptions
and finally see that which we failed to recognize before.
That which we yearned and strived for so long is right where we
left it, in front of us, waiting to be recognized.
   Duane R. Bowers

Only Now In Books

Only now in books can I catch a gleam,
A snatch of old California of America,
Like Stephen Vincent Benet's phantom deer.

There'll be a sigh, a stir, a faint, clear
Shadow on the edge of my inward eye,
And my heart will break for a moment.
But raucous, rough, unruly, glaring shards
Of disorderly society drive them off.

El Camino Real, The Santa Fe Trail, Route 66
Lead nowhere now — no one uses them anymore
Or wants to go where they went.

And so I read and read, and try to bury myself
In the folded hills of Stewart Edward White
Or in the western chivalry of Louis L' Amour —
Gone, all gone now, if it ever was.
The walk along land's end has ended.

But we do have a new shopping mall
With a magnificent view of the Pacific.

The coastal access route is just a mile
Down the road.

Hope A. Jeter

Untitled

Before a charred cooking pot on open flames
  a shadowed duck bows low and
    pecks the ground thrice, then rises up
      on outstretched wings.
A curious ritual there beneath the glowing,
  singed palm fronds
    and closing darkness.
What causes her to rise up so in the
  quiet, dripping aftermath of pounding rain
    and penetrating cold?
Earlier—
  The rain, running muddy rivers round her feet
    offered drink and play and gaily, she accepted.
  An element of joy when those around sought
    shelter, warmth from that intruder.
  Perhaps, compatible with such a force gives
    rise to an instinctive pride and calls for
    just a moment of such curious celebration.

Cindy Schmickle

The River

There was a river
  A river so very high
  A river in the mountains
How it started no one knows when or why

Our love is like that river
  Flowing through out time
And heaven only knows I will never change my mind

For you my dear are my love
  To share my love and time
And heavens only knows I will never change my mind

As time goes by
  The river does not die
    It just keeps growing
      As the winds keep blowing

Our love is like the river
  Growing bigger and stronger throughout time

For you see my dear this must be clear
  I will say it again so that you can hear
    I Love You

Angela B. Hoth

The Wonders Of The Clouds

Between each equator there are large masses of clouds. Each cloud is a reminder of the beauty of the omnipotent God. The openness of our eyes, our hearts and our minds. The feeling of God's presence as if I am being lifted into the clouds. The clouds are represented by a love that never changes, a greater understanding, a deliverance, calmness, prosperity and peace. The wonders of the clouds bring reassurance, tranquility and rejuvenation. There is such a connection that I must reiterate the beauty again. Most importantly, I thank God for His beautiful creation and allowing me the opportunity to write this. I give God all the glory and the honor. I extol him to the highest. How beautiful and exotic they were made. I have had several visions of being in danger but was sustained by the clouds. Sometimes they are moving in two or more directions with different colors depending on sunrise or sunset. When raining they look like mountains. Whatever the circumstances might be, the clouds always give me a reason to rise and sing the praises. As I walk away I see many miracles, a greater understanding, unbiased, unbroken and unconditional love.

Dorice Douglas

Winter Rapture

Greeting the frost-covered hill on an early morning walk:
A morning for thinking, no need for talk...
Yonder there I see from a night-born heavy mist and
I became amazed; a dazzling new world did exist!

Tiny brave sunbeams had pierced the morning haze
Reflecting ice crystals from a forest of evergreen maze.
A wonder to behold; no artist would try to capture.
This day was made for me, my own Winter Rapture.

I walked on through this God-given paradise
As the wildlife scampered busily in the sunrise.
Soft, sincere thanks were uttered to the Creator we know;
So, in strolling back to the house, I'm now wishing for snow.

Donna L. Swope

The Angel

Stars glowing high a sigh comes from the wind. Why say good-bye
a mere question found amidst
confusion. Her love was scarce when found in hate.
The sight of death, SOON whispers the winds of time.
Why say good-bye asks the angel
I see her face so much like an angel or so it seems...A smile, so
generously dedicated to love to a
family.
She like the angel until that night, so cold, so desolate, air
scarcely found.
Her breathe taken away in a second.
Stars glowing high, a sigh comes from the wind
Tears fall from the angel,
Why say good-bye..
Life says
the winds of time.

Jessica Paula McClure

Waterfall

W hite and majestic like a ghost gently creeping over the rocks,
A soft calming flow into the
T eal blue waters at the base of a bride's fabulous dress.
E ager to dive into the crystal clear pool under the dazzling
R ainbow, magnificent and glorious. Drops
F alling slowly like a fairy's breath.
A we and wonder fill your mind.
L et the crisp blue sky fill the air.
L ovely and dramatic are the falls.

Dina Warnock

"Remember"

Remember, oh, my brothers, that God sent you one day,
A man who rose before us to cast our fears away.
Remember, oh, my sisters the one who spoke for you,
and bravely fought the battles for peace though some unsure.

Remember all God's people the roads that we once trod.
The goal still in our future, our hopes still very strong.
Inform all generations the cross that they must bear,
To win the type of freedom that one day all will share.

Remember he who died to make our dreams come true.
The vision that God gave him, that gift for me and you.
Therefore, we will remember from whence we have come,
And carry on this journey till nations live as one.

Fight on all of God's children!
There's love and peace to win, the King we will remember
Till we unite again.
The prize still stands before us, God leading, as before,
Our faith our courage stronger, than ever before.

Faith Evans

I Cry At Night

I go through the day with a smile on my face.
A look of sadness, why there's not a trace.
But when the world's not looking and I turn out the lights,
I lay in the dark and I cry at night.

My day is filled with noise and laughter.
I've got things to do, and tasks to look after.
But when the day winds down and all is quite,
Reality sets in and I cry at night.

When no one is looking, when I'm all alone,
It's then that I face my pain head on.
I accept the truth that I fight to hide.
I lay in my bed and I cry at night.

Clarissa J. Payne

Untitled

The first time I saw you, you lit up my life
A long time ago that seems like yesterday
All these years later, you are still my wife
I am the happiest, wealthiest man ever to say...

I LOVE YOU!!!

We're shard so many experiences with each other
That have brought smiles and warmth deep inside
I hope and wish that you are always my lover
For there is one thing that I can never hide...

I LOVE YOU!!

I always think of the wonderful things you do
Bringing out the best in everything you touch
I am the most thankful man for being with you
And I have to say and mean this so very much...

I LOVE YOU!!

This sincere wish for you from deep in my heart
Hopes you have happiness that will always last
You and I are a team that will never, never part
I honestly feel these words I've said in the past...

I LOVE YOU!!

David Edward Brown

The Mighty Oak

Down in the woodland pastures brown
A little thing occurred.
A little seed was dropped to the ground,
And the earth by some hoof was stirred.

Through the days that followed, then,
Some were very cold.
Touched by the beating sleet and rain,
And wrapped by the winter's snow.

Then the days of springtime came,
The sun grew bright and hot.
The trees awoke, the grass became green,
Its sleep of nature forgot.

Twas only an a corn small and brown
That had lain through the winter's snow,
But its little roots soon pierced the ground,
And leaves began to grow.

Those branches reached our for the summer sun,
And with beautiful foliage were clothed.
That acorn, though small, thru time,
Became a mighty oak.

Elmer G. Carr

There Is A Light

There is a light that is very bright and full of life,
A light that is always there when your life feels wrong,
That light is of our Lord Jesus Christ.

There is a light that brightens everybody's life,
A light that is always within our grasp,
That light is of our Lord Jesus Christ.

There is a light that is always there to help us,
A light that will always be there for us,
That light is our Lord Jesus Christ.

There is a light that will give us eternal life,
A light that is full of life and love,
That light is our Lord Jesus Christ.

There is a light, that when we see, we are on our way,
A light that shows us the way to our new home,
That Light is our Lord Jesus Christ.

John Tensley

My Favorite Place

A platform in the trees
A late summer's night
After everyone is asleep
Water lapping on the shore below
Platform creaking in the wind
The luminous moon emerges from behind a cloud
It reflects onto the rippling water
The trees sway back and forth with the breeze
I pull my knees close as a light wind touches my bare legs
And sing a soft song
I wish to go back to those heavenly limbs
So I may be awed by its splendor once again.

Brianna Rebecca McGibbon

In Memory Of Grandpa

They worked hard all their lives building their dreams.
A house, two kids, and love was all they'd need.
Their years together seemed to just roll by
Then it was time for her to say goodbye.
Time and sickness took its toll
The one he loved now left him alone.
The day she left a part of him left to.
His last words to her was I'll be with you soon.
The rest of his days he spent alone.
Wondering where all the good times had gone
You could see the pain, the tears in his eyes.
There was nothing to fill the loneliness he felt inside.
And then one cold and rainy night his final wish came true
He left us in a peaceful sleep to be with the only love he ever knew.

Annette Lynn

Little Hands Tree

Once upon a Christmas tree, when my girls were very little
A holiday mystery developed, with a single branch in the middle.

Colorful balls and tinsel adorned our lustrous tree.
But very active little hands removed them, for you see,

While the splendor of a festive tree gives us time to celebrate.
Sometimes, from a child's height, it's just too tall to appreciate.

My twins, and their older sister, enthralled with it all,
Worked silently together, rearranging every sparkling ball.

One limb, barely two feet high, they decorated with care.
Other nearby branches they left empty and completely bare.

Now, Mom and Dad restored each limb to its former luster.
But the girls returned that singled branch back to its pretty cluster.

Many years have passed, adults they have grown to be.
Yet, every Christmas season, I envision the "Little Hands Tree".

James C. O'Donnell

Falling Stars

The patience of pointillism pervades on the sky;
A great artistry grown by millions of years,
sought on the canvas of astronomy's eye,
and brought to light by the moon's dusty tears.

An evening unfolds to exhibit its show,
as the artist looks out toward his master;
And the depths seem too cold with iridescent glow,
so much the stars twinkle so faster.

And tonight, the painter with his deep desire
can be seen on some drawn constellation,
streaking 'cross stars in such a great fire
with his acrobatic coalition.

And we, bearing wonder, watch them all prance
about this one wisp of magical delight,
still holding hands as they boastfully dance
to colour the plane oceans of night.

And tiring from the evenings work at hand,
beauty washes it's brushes in the sea,
and dazedly drifts closer to land
For, it's art is always and only for we.

Dana Smith

Solitary Sail

When the waves turn under and the roof of the sea lies sleek,
A glaze of azure hooding hazards deep,
Then I turn on rock and sand and scorn the meek
Whisper of wavelets, soft as maiden's weep.

And leave the green of tide and its meager surge
To graceless clattering craft and gaseous gusts
Of infernal engines smoking a siren's dirge,
A pelagic pillager's savage noisy lust.

But let Neptune's shoulders heave and roll the main
And Zephyrus sound his Westwind horn of gale,
I must fling my tiny craft to sea again,
To chain the glory of the wind to serve my sail.

Poseidon's power, briny breath compelled
To briefly yield God's sway to mortal will.

Hoyt Foucault

Astrea

I look deep into the night sky
   a gently rolling sea of blue-black waves
     softly undulating sheets of nebulous algae
and I fall with the waves in violet harmony

A dark sea afloat with silver anemone
quietly blooming and bursting with mystery
   the sky above me
   the sky beneath me

I am adrift
   lying on the starboard bow
   of a shining blue vessel
When I gaze into the sea
I am one with the ship
   sleepily spinning and rocking

The sea breathes
   and I sigh in echo
   dreaming in the fathomless deep

Donna Marie Smith

The Snake Charmer...

the piper's pipe is calling my name
a game of chance to glimpse the dance...of the hooded snake
I awake...to your intuitive calm
and your fluted charm...has alarmed the cobra inside my woven basket...
the casket of thought that I undoubtedly wrought upon myself
Yet you charmed me with song
The melody had been pounding...resounding in my head
as my heart played dead all along
Now you soothe me with song!
Could I be wrong?...Is it only a game?
...a shame they couldn't see the scared little child
bent down on her knees, crying up at the sky
Alive...in so many ways, but always alone...unknown
...and made to atone for her silence
Now this wide-eyed girl is in love...with the world!
She's romping in the rain again...running barefoot in the mud again
And no one knew
she had a heart of straw
packed deep in the grandest mud pie of them all
...baked in the sun.

Joy Buckhout

Why

As I stop and think awhile
A frown takes the place of a once before smile
My life is changing and so is my mind
My once normal life is left far behind
The pressures, the decisions are what I face today
I wish I could change but is there a way?
Late at night I spare a moment to cry
Some times I wish that I could die
These are the times I wonder why
I never knew life could be such a maze
I suppose I could just be facing a phase
I find myself starting out into space
I feel as if I am in a never ending race
One I cannot win because I have no pace
Only God can help me at this stage
Why is thirteen such a difficult age?
Where does my future lie?
Why must the question for me always be why?

Colleen Harvey

A Real Friend

A Friend is one who smiles when your joke isn't funny.
A Friend is one whose bright when the sky isn't sunny.
A Friend you can trust with a secret you have told.
A Friend is a person with whom you can be bold.
A Friend can respond when you hurt from the heart.
A Friend gives you a lift when that old car of yours won't start.
A Friend will stick with you through thick or through thin.
A Friend will even join in a little bit of sin.
A Friend isn't perfect in everything they do.
A Friend is only human and that makes you human too.
A Friend can be a little crazy, even be a little lazy.
A Friend could have the name of Daisy, but I think it's JOAN STOCKHOFF.

Betty Mae Eaton

Ode to Sleep

Sleep drug of my heart-
a free addiction resting reality from the reality of pain -
feeding loneliness
play'r mind trick s oul...in illusionary games of being more than real
escape solutions from ambitions - you drug of death born to restfully
deceive me to be more than you actually are:
you drug on and drug off
'r serious time
I hate to love
you disturb my search for life
numb my involuntary limbs
(n)ever sleep everyday wave up appearances
illude me into being more than...sleep why can't you be real with me
like awakening from joyful pain
you ware me off
grant me time to live without you..restless beast of shame laughing
with guilt of sheetless hopes - idol without guilt demanding your war
shipping time drugged up healing
I hate you whatever you do come
take me away again to time less souls of needful help
but will always remain sheepishly- ode to sleep

Isabel Mueller

Lost Yet Found In The Wood

The forest sweet and pungent,
A fragrance that embraces the senses as in a dream
Still and somber, sometimes foreboding
Yet fragile and inviting, uncommonly serene.
A haven, a place of comfort, introspection, discovery,
And eventual transformation
A shedding of the skin, new life emerges, of hope and confirmation.
How every much like love, the feelings it creates
Excitement taunted by fear, the secret there within awaits.
A risky thing to enter and hike along this trail,
Safer to stay in the familiar, but never to avail.
You navigate, I follow, and dusk fades into dark
The path now obscure, forward on a journey of trust we did embark.
Up and down we scurried;
Through trees, over branches, thicket and briar
Another new experience, anticipation as fierce, as love is to desire.
Visions of the wolf and fairy tales racing through my head
I chose to trust your senses, and as always, to safety I was led.
The bond grows ever stronger as well in time it should
A unique and cherished memory of being lost
Yet found...in the wood!

Elise H. Bennett

Untitled

What could be better than having
A family, an extended family, and a God family?
My God mother, Karen, my God father, Chuck...
Their children,
Kristen and Angela, my God sisters,
Chuckie, my God brother...
Karen's mother, my God grandmother
And father, my God grandfather...
Chuckie's wife to be,
My God sister-in-law to be
And Angela's husband
My God brother-in-law...
Their son, Tanner, my Godnephew
And daughter, Jessica, my God niece and my Godsister,
My real mother being her God mother.
My mother's best friend, my God mother,
Her husband, my God father...
Once a close New Jersey family...
Now a separated Arizona family
with families, extended families, and God families of their own.

Julie Rogers

College...

There comes a time in one's life where not everything's clear,
a decision must be made and that's what you fear;
Not knowing exactly which one to choose,
what you gain at one is at the other you lose;
Lonely and lost is how you feel,
not ready for your life to become this real;
Looking for an answer waiting for a sign,
there's no one there to help you and you're running out of time;
The pressure is amazing, the anxiety too,
for this will decide your future and all you plan to do;
So as you look for support and parting time draws near,
gather courage from your past and let faith conquer fear.

Dina Fisher

Yearning For Yesterday

Remember long ago, when hearts were filled with joy
  a <u>decade</u> or two recalled...by every girl and boy

Remember long ago, when love passed through all hands
  a <u>year</u> or two recalled...by a bond that firmly stands

Remember long ago, when smiles turned into laughter
  a <u>month</u> or two recalled...by dusk, dawn, and after

Remember long ago, when children sang one song
  a <u>day</u> or two recalled...by churches miles long

Remember long ago, when rosebuds bloomed in full
  an <u>hour</u> or two recalled....by sheep with coats of wool

Remember long ago, when crime seemed obsolete
  a <u>minute</u> or two recalled...by a human whose life is complete

Remember long ago, when the world spun slowly 'round
  a <u>second</u> or two recalled....by all of creation heaven bound.

Beverly Withee

My Sister, My Friend

A small innocent child looking up into the eyes of her sister,
A child just the same, curious as to why she's here.
One sparkle from her sister's eye tells her why she came.
I am here for you as you are for me.
You, my sister, are the best birthday present I could ever receive.

You, my sister, my teacher, taught me how wonderful,
how difficult life could be.
You, my sister, my leader, showed me the path in which I should
follow, those that I could not see.
You, my sister, my doctor, have cured my heartache, healed my
wounds, and eased a lot of pain.
You, my sister, my therapist, have wiped away my tears, and have
kept me sane.
You, my sister, my friend, have brought joy to life and
laughter to my ears.
You, my sister, my angel have kept me safe and helped
me face my fears.

A young woman looks into the eyes of her sister,
A young woman just the same, no longer curious as to why she's here-
Only glad she came.

Deah McClain

My Little Pal

Abbie was a sweet old gal; My friend, my bird, my little pal.
Our relationship was special to the core; As life with Abbie was never
a bore. She loved to cuddle on my chest and thought it was her private
nest. She was a bird, but humanized she thought; Other birds were a
nuisance, to me this she taught. She'd watch me make dinner with glee
in her eyes; Waiting her turn for her own surprise. She loved all
people and would let them know; By demanding their friendship,
she wouldn't let go.

Abbie was a sweet old gal; My friend, my bird, my little pal.

Her eagerness to show her love for me; Became her downfall, she
couldn't let be. She laid eggs for me, without being mated; Perfectly
oval, they were A1 rated. She even laid eggs while sitting on my lap;
I thought she was just taking a little night cap. On Friday morning
she laid an egg; On Sunday morning she was dead. Another egg
she tried to lay; But with her life she had to pay.

Abbie was a sweet old gal; My friend, my bird, my little pal.

On August 13 I laid you to rest; My cockatoo for 19 years, you were
the best. That's why it's so hard, I'm still so blue; If only you
had given me some kind of clue. Abbie I love you and always will;
I think of you often, I can't get my fill.

Darlene T. Carver

The Battle Of Our Lives

Battered, bruised, torn and broken.
A battle fought?

Not a battle of justice or peace.
Not a battle of right or wrong.

This battle is seldom won,
and rarely are all sides pleased.
The battle is more vicious than the most violent war.
The battle is life...

Fought for love and acceptance,
Fought for hope and forgiveness.

This battle does not end easily, and no one wishes to lose.
Everyone is fighting, and you must also continue to fight.

For after the battle is won,
happiness will be found.

Amy Johnson

Wild Bleeding Hearts

Wild bleeding hearts grew along the creek beside the barn,
a barn smelling of mice and hay and tractor parts in grease;
oil seeped into the earth along the back but the bleeding hearts
bloomed in clumps with fern-lace leaves despite the oil,
despite the little girl who regularly picked them clean.

From branches in my cherry tree I spied on bantams
you gave me to name: Mr. and Mrs. Sad Eyes.
Cows held by barbed wire chewed at wet grass;
Bosco once broke free to eat your lilac by the door.

Even though we tramped the woods in spring searching trillium and
fiddle-head ferns, even though we crunched madrona leaves
ankle deep each smoky-smelling fall, even though you helped to dig
the well and haul the hay and birth the sow, that farm was never yours.
Fingers trained for Schubert and Chopin
were plucking chickens on the porch, were snapping beans.
Bleeding hearts and sad eyes followed
your escape down the gravel drive
in high heels, bearing one bag and a violin.

Erin Walsh Moncada

Sleigh Ride

Give me the jingle of sleigh bells on a cold and starlit night
When I'm warmly tucked in a buffalo robe for sledding through fields of white
The kluff, kluff, kluff of the horse's hooves is a rhythm I like to hear,
For a sleigh is a wonderful place to be when the night is cold and clear.

Give me the biting wind that blows the glittering snow about
That bears on its breath a lone dog's bark and a neighbors friendly shout
Let the gaunt limbs creak with a frozen sound, for the night is all too still
As I merrily glide on the slippery snow through the valley and over the hill.

Give me a full moon in the sky, let it follow wherever I go
And twinkle on icy branches and sparkle on drifted snow,
My breath like a puff from a friendly pipe to float on the freezing air
There's a smile on my face, a song in my heart, for heaven is surely there!

Irvin C. Kreemer

The Point Of No Return?

Are you at the point of no return? That never is the fact! As long as there is breath to breathe, and life to live, anything else is all part of the act. To return is to be able to go back to the works and joys in life that have meaning, inspire hope, and instill a song in your heart from which the melody, you never wish to part. And as long as this anomaly is true, the whole world is still open to you.

Your day in the Sun was ever so bright and no one can dim your brilliance. But sometimes, the Lord has other plans for the brilliance of our light. He knows the proper place that suits his needs and for us that is right. Our brilliance is a gift from him with an intended purpose in mind. Not to be depleted by man, prematurely, and man will if man can. But thankfully, the light of our soul is not in man's hand. This area is strictly God's plan.

And God does not allow his children to stumble, unless to show a point for all to see, while through it all we remain ever humble. God gives us the power to do his will wherever we are to go. At the time, we may not understand and grieve with all our might for things not really in God's plans for now; but in all things, lean toward him and you will surely be alright.

Cecelia Marie Polford

Inside Me

Inside my heart there are many feelings to share.
Inside my heart there is betrayal, love, understanding, hate, and care.
Inside my heart there are many words that I don't say because of pride,
words that have never been shared, have been hidden deep inside.
My feelings are like sand on an ocean floor, quickly washed away.
Not away like gone for good; away like walking far astray.
Inside my heart are infatuations, wishes and desires
as well as knowledge, hopes, dreams, yearnings and inquiries.
Among those feelings inside my heart that are increasing more and more
is the need to find out all that's hidden, to unlock the bolted door.
I will sit and dream everyday and feel what is inside of me
and soon, one day, I will find the key that will set my secrets free.

Ashley Waters

Springtime

Springtime! Oh my Springtime! Where have you gone?
Hmm, seems as if yesterday, I looked toward summertime and being grown!
So many plans, dreams, hopes! I just couldn't wait!
But then, so swiftly here's autumn, its getting colder—too late!

I look back on life, and feel a dull pain—what a waste!
I've sped through youth, adulthood, middle age with hardly a taste!
And all those things I planned and anticipated so eagerly,
Through sad luck or fate, have enjoyed so few, and those, but meagerly.

Sad, the "Muses of an 'Old Man'," aching in spirit and body from pursuing a mission, during a lifetime of misuse and abuse by self, the world, and profession.
No longer can I rise to challenge, take on the world and it's sorrow,
But only envision, a different path, to have taken, towards tomorrow.

Yet despair not my plight, I've loved children, grandchildren, family, even life.
And in these final years, found peace and happiness, with a wonderful wife!
God meant me to run life's course, and battle just as He'd laid out,
But in my frailty and faults, there was always His love, of this, I've no doubt.

So, as I approach winter, its colder, dismal—there's little to anticipate, I've had my chances, missed opportunities, endured times that I hate, and tho I really can't complain, nor disparage others, the decisions were mine, I can't help but reminisce, of days long ago, when I was in my SPRINGTIME.

Calvin T. Gibson Jr.

Life

Life is flying by like a bird
flapping in the wind
the ice clinging to its wings
but nothing stops the flight of life.

Life is crying at us while
we waste our lives like garbage
people think they'll live for ever like the needles of a pine
but before you know it's gone like a lilac in the fall.

Life is smiling at the joys of the people
while the birds are singing in the trees
as the flowers bloom in the warm spring day
we treasure these moments as the shadow of death lies on us

I am
wanting life
cherishing it
coloring it
protecting it
loving it
living it.

Alon Payenson

"Mr. Sun"

At approximately 6 am, the bright California sun makes his rise into another day; nothing unusual, just another day the same as the one before.
Few awaken to indulge in his beauty, except for maybe an occasional surfer walking along the beach in the early hours of the morning; but then again, he's probably too worried about the oncoming sets to concern himself with the sunrise.
Mommy awakens at the sound of her alarm, her daily signal to start the children off to their day of school.
Daddy, the executive, has already gone, and is busily working in the privacy of his office preparing his briefs for a meeting to be held later in the day.
The sun sees it all. He is always there, waiting and pleading for recognition, hoping to one day share his beauty with all humanity.
He rises every morning, satisfied if he is able to reach even one solitary soul.
He tries and tries throughout the day, and at the point of exhaustion, he takes a rest, always in hope of tomorrow.

Allison June Olsen

Longing

It's Sunset,

Another day has slipped by,
The surroundings offer me peace,
Birds chirping, moon shining, flowers smelling, buildings shining

But where are you?

Are you walking on a beach? Swinging at a golfball? Slamming at a puck, painting a new world; filled with visions of hope, joy and beauty, massaging moms shoulders,
spreading smiles with your witty, corny humor...

It aches me to think and wonder that you're with another,
for you were come once mine-so tender, sincere completely demure-
so trusting and supportive...
I let go of that, so tossed of needing to be true to myself,
for the first time in my life.
I get lonely you know,
lonely for you.....

Christina L. Pino

"Inner"

I can't understand how the "inner child"
Has the wherewithal to give me guidance
If when I was young I was oft beguiled,
What help would I gain from adolescence?

When the Good Book says, "A child shall lead them"
"Them" is referring to the animals
Children leading adults contrives mayhem
...Instead, they belong within our controls

What inner child profit is there to heed?
All it can offer are it's pains again
As an adult now, trying to succeed,
The last thing I need is "inner" burden
Everyone's life has it's measure of pain
But life moves forward, it doesn't reverse
Trying to resolve the past is in vain...
In fact, if you try...it only gets worse

Quit wasting your time in what you can't change
Today is to love...tomorrow, to plan
If it's strength you seek, you'll have to exchange
You inner child for the Lord's "inner man"

Bob G. Martinez

Clashing Forces

Love is like the clouds in the sky
  always observing with a tender eye

Hate is like an angry bee
  stinging anyone it can see

Love and friendship work hand in hand...
  their strength like waves upon the sand

Hate despises working relations
  he alone wants to ruin the nations

Love is passion, understanding, and trust
  Hate is murder and blood is a must

Honesty describes Love unconditionally
  while deception and Hate work diligently

Both forces of Love and Hate are strong
  only one can remain...the other is wrong

Who will win the battle? As of now, no one knows
  we can only await until the future shows

Whatever the outcome, we must stand tall
  and hope and pray that Love conquers all

Jill Kietzmann

"Army Of Faith"

A small band of warriors defend themselves
against the deadly throes of the enemy.
Cut off from reinforcements by an inflamed arrow
storm, they valiantly stand their ground,
unto their very last breaths.
Not to be gripped by fear, they call upon the King,
Most High for spirits, and strength.
Though in number they are few, in their faith, they
are a formidable army.
With a demon bashing battle cry, they charge from
their rampart safe haven, to take up the offense.
They attack!
As gladiators of truth, they battle the darkness
with heart strong courage, and honour.
Though in flesh they may be slain, in faith, and
spirit they have already won.

Gabriel Unbehaun

The Butterfly (A Two Person Poem)

The butterfly
        The butterfly
        So graceful

So lovely
        As she flies on delicate wings

I am a Caterpillar
        I creep along

Eating leaves
        Getting fat

I'll build a nest with my thread
        And when I come out

I am a butterfly
        I am a butterfly
        Narrow escapes

From net
        From bird

My tender wings
        With flashing color

Attract bird and human
I am a butterfly
        I am a butterfly
With loving eyes
        And graceful flutter

Ashley Teal Hulen

'No Place To Cry'

There's a place for pleasure; there's a place for all our toil,
A place for the happy and there's a place for pure joy.
There's a place for success, and a place for those who win,
But there's never a place for the heart that's caving in.

No place to cry Lord, no place to cry.
No place to cry Lord, no place to cry.

There's a place for success and a place for those who win,
But there's never a place for the heart that's caving in.
Then I hear a whisper, and my spirit tries again.
I hear my Lord calling, "You use my arms to cry in."

"You need a hiding place to renew your soul within."
"There'll always be a place for the heart that's caving in."

Someplace to cry Lord, someplace to cry.
Someplace to cry Lord, someplace to cry.

I need a hiding place to renew my soul within,
And there'll always be your love when my heart is caving in.

Esther M. Thomas

Sleep—What Is It?

An irrepressible need
An escape
An illusion
A silence of our perceptive existence allowing us a brief glimpse into another world
Sleep is like a novel comprised of dreams that can be full of peace or mashed with horror where we are not always its author
Sleep is a liberation of all our mental imprisonments
A nourishment for our conscious-starving dreams
An exploration of our own desires and fears, as well as a revelation of our masked truths

Jennifer R. Jackson

Great, Great Uncle

When I was a young lad and times were bad,
I would pledge allegiance to the flag.

My spirit would soar high like the Eagle flies;
Riding my soul on the words to another shore,
Where woes were foes against, this region of peaceful bliss.

The words of my magic carpet were '... one nation
Under God indivisible, with liberty and justice for all.'

I am poor white with a proud white heritage;
My Grandmother before she died talked about her
Mother's brother who had fought for the Confederacy.

My great, great uncle fought for the Confederacy.
He was blinded in some battle, I don't recall which one.

I have often wondered about this man; my great, great uncle
Who paid the price of his sight for the Confederacy.
He and I are somewhat alike, and Brother Farrakhan was not right
By saying there are two Americans Black and White.

My great, great uncle gave up his sight for the Confederacy;
I gained Brother Farrakhan's right by being innocently crippled in a
Racial riot. Yes, I am proud to be a Disable American with a
Great, great uncle who lost his sight for the Confederacy.

Jerry Thomas Hopkins

A Mother's Prayer

A mother's prayer is truly this
A baby's smile, a child's kiss
A life that's yours, but yet its own
You love and care for till it's grown
Which at that time they spread their wings
You feel so proud, your soul sings
You wish them good life, luck and love
Then say a prayer to the Lord above
Please bless them Lord their whole life through
Happiness in all they do
A dependable partner to have in their life
To cherish and help them with everyday strife
Children to love, enjoy and share
This is truly a Mother's Prayer

Caroline C. Smith

The Sea

As I walk upon the sand dunes that line the misty seashore, my aesthetic love for the sea encompasses my being. This beautiful wonder I see before me is truly one of God's best creations; the sea. It is the center of my material wealth, a wealth so great the humblest of men can feel rich with emotion. It's vibrancy makes my spirit come alive and renews my faith.

As I look outward upon this bounty of feminine gentleness, the sunlight is reflected on the soft undulations of the swelling white-caps. This omnipresent light is so pure in spirit, I feel in my heart it is the true bread of life.

With a staunch gust of northeastern wind, the sea air is perceived through my senses. Such memories I hold with this salty smell; my childhood and present life.

Beyond the western horizon, gray clouds cover the brightly lit edifice of a vast city. The clouds soon pass, and this city of light casts shadows on the murky sea water. I feel a single tear roll down my cheek and disappear into the sandy floor; what beauty before me. God has truly blessed this sea of utopia, and I will keep it in my heart forever.

I soon realize I am only a detail, in a world so beautiful I can only admire it from afar.

Amy Leigh Foreman

November

The trees and shrubs have lost their leaves,
A COLD BREEZE, MIGHTY WINDS FROM THE NORTH
Buxom bears asleep, ice forming on oceans deep
Some birds have gone south,

Materials in nature, eminent domain,
perhaps pervasive
facts of all reality will remain.
TIME for warm caps, scarfs, ear muffs.
REMEMBER, the poor do not have a home, food or warm clothing.
Prepare your family feast,
COUNT your blessings, you will rewarded.
With thanks for giving

Florence G. Axton

Not As Cold As Your Love

My baby and I were standing on the river bank. The wind was blowing 35 m.p.h. The temperature was 4 below zero. I looked at him and said:
The wind is cold baby, but not as cold as your love. I sleep with you at night, do your cooking and wash your clothes everyday. You never tell me that you love me. You never even hold me tight. You don't even kiss me good night, so this wind is cold baby but not as cold as your love. If you don't do any better baby, I'm going to find me another man and when I find him, I'll be leaving you because your love is so cold. The temperature done drop below zero between me and you. And I just can't stand it any longer because your love is so cold.

Ella M. Bailey

On The Death Of My Father

Time had ebbed the boil of my blood
And eased the indifference of my sanity
The hair was thinned, the body gaunt
Nothing remained in his visage to daunt
No longer had I the anger to engage his remorse
The pain I had wished - on his face - ran its course
I held him for a time insignificant to me
But measured and meaningful - in the time left to he
In that instant the past resurrected - and was done
And all that remained - a father and his son

Alan Paul Gillan

TVH-2

Stars and stripes light up my nights
as I look at the pictures you gave me,
Oh God - I wish your love was mine
you are the only one that can save me.

I've fallen fast into your arms,
will you fall so softly into mine?
So in tenderness I can hold you,
and love you for all time.

Oh, how my heart so yearns,
to kiss you tenderly,
my soul bleeds without your love,
please hear me, can't you see?

I would give my entire world-my everything for you
to love, hold, and cherish
(That's if want me to)
so if I perish tomorrow,
do not feel any sorrow -
place your picture on my tomb,
for in my heart there will always be room,
(only for you...)

Eric Christy

I Love You Mama

I love you mama, for giving me birth.
Wiping my tears, every time I got hurt.
When I was sick, you were always close by.
You'd sing me to sleep, with a sweet lullaby.
I'd hear you pray for me, when I was ill,
You'd bow your head, by the bed you would kneel.
Lord up in heaven, I'd hear you say.
Make my child well, Lord while I pray.
When you were through, you'd raise your head,
Thank God, for hearing the prayer that was said.
You'd tell me everything's gonna be alright,
Take me in bed, and kiss me goodnight.
Tell me to sleep tight, and don't let the bed bugs bite.
Then you would get up and turn out the light.
I LOVE YOU MAMA.
Mary Ann Gehrmann

Do Your Hear Him?

The night is still and very dark.
The floor boards creak neath the rug.
Not because anyone is there.
Mother Nature has blown her cool breath over the land.
She is announcing that Autumn is here.

Soon there will be a chill in the air.
We'll have to close the windows at night.
I lay in my bed and listen.
Listen to the stillness in the absence of light.
I feel the cool breeze cross my brow.

I am content for the moment.
Content to be here in this small moment of time.
Content to hear the rustle of the leaves on the trees
As the breeze gently sways the branches and whispers hello.
I am in tune with nature and with the one who gave her.

What a mighty God we have.
Why don't more see that?—Oh oblivious.
Why don't more hear that?——Oh oblivious.
It is He that allows it all.
I am humble in His presence.
Trudy Finch

"You're The One"

You're the one,
The one I adore.
You're the one,
The one I want to soar,
Soar through the clouds with forever.
The one I would kiss the open
Wounds to make better.

You're the one,
The one I would go forever to find.
You're the one,
The one I want to be mine.
Jeremy Gilliland

Honeymoon Suite

Rising like a Red Sea moon
her Universe parts,
Black Hole fissure missile launch.

Rising like a Challenger
his passion explodes,
White puffs across burning skies.

Rising like a leaven'd seed
Earth colonizes,
sleeping with them in her womb.
Jeff Logan

Relevancy

Slick back your hair
damn man

Polish your teeth
pearlie white

Whale out a laugh
While the years are young
Run, run, run the race

Shine your shoes
On the corner
Down at the shoe shine stand

Kick up your heels
Damn man and dance, dance, dance,
Run, run, while the years
are young

Grab you a pretty black girl
Black boy
Ask her hand
On bended knees

Smile as she says, "I do"
"Black boy Marry your kin"
Dorothy Breedlove

"Freedom"

I woke up this morning to the chirping of little birds
  on my windowsill.
I laid there wondering what they were thinking.
They sat there looking at me as if to say,
  "I'm Free, what's your problem?"
It's strange, I haven't a clue.
Even at night, a good fairy doesn't sprinkle sweet dream dust
  on my head.
Only nightmares invade my supposed to be peaceful nights.
I hate to rise and face the day.
Of course, no one said it would be easy.
I have this amazing ability to go through the same routine
  over and over and over again.
Yeah, I wish I could fly away with those little birds.
To fly into the breeze would be the ultimate high.
Better yet, I'd love to jump on a Harley and ride into the wind.
Forgetting my past, not thinking about the future.
I'd ride and live for the now in all its glory.
I suppose I'd be like the little birds on my windowsill;
  I'd be free!!!
Kathy Seibert

Many Religions, Races, And Places

How would you like to be,
  A Muslim across the sea?
Worshipping five times a day,
  But all you do is pray.

Another religion developed in the Middle East,
  Included Arabs and Muslim priests.
The Christians were among these two,
  And also there were the Jews.

Buddhists believe in reincarnation,
  But that's the way of their civilization.
They think if they live righteous lives,
  They will achieve higher and higher stage of life.

No matter what the race may be,
  Mexicans, Blacks, or Chinese.
We're all a part of this big world,
  So let's give each other a bit of peace.
Kimberly Hardee

Super Mom

18 Times she became a Mother
So for us, there could be no other!
The noise, the fights, and all the fuss,
Was often enough to make her cuss!
Though lots of work - with little rest,
She always tried and did her best,
With 8 more still, to love and raise,
She really deserves our Love and Praise!
So as you can see, there could be no other
Then the Super Mom, who is Our Mother.
Stephanie Banik

Verve

Enter the realm of the forever dead.
A silver river of severed limbs onward into the void.
Skeleton fingers lurk beneath a thick mist.
The stench of something foreign looms within the wetness.
A thin film of sticky green covers everything.
Her hair is a light, her eyes a deep purple.
I follow her heavenly dress as it slithers along.
One candle is lit in desperation.
"What may be this hell I am trapped?"
Cries fall upon deaf ears.
My mouth opens wide but my teeth fall out with clumps of blood.
My lungs hurt as my ribs feel to crush inward.
My angel is swallowed whole by all my false hopes.
No one sees, no one cares.
My love is no longer my life.
My life is no longer my love.
I will never fall in love again.
My body left as a rag doll thrown by an infant over
   the rail and forgotten forever.
A misconception-black is not a color, it's an emotion.
Nathaniel Darwin Kennedy Kline

Let's Go Out Into The World

Let you and I go out into the world
To reveal our one dream to everyone;
That we are recognize as individuals with dignity and value.
Using the world motto as our guide; "UNITED WE STAND, DIVIDED
WE FALL"; we will feel the pride of the liberation of oneself.

Let you and I go out into the world
To conquer it and everything in our reach;
To avoid negative things which are self-destructive
And overcome obstacles in the path of our success.

Let you and I go out into the world
To build a kingdom; glorified with love.
This will be our gift to mankind.
In our kingdom, we shall rejoice in the world at peace.

Let each of us go out into the world
To enrich the earth with the children of generations to come.
Let us conquer the world before death arrives, you and I.
E. Faye Stallworth

Mother, Oh Mother

Mother, Oh Mother are you here?
Where is your sweet voice I so long to hear?
Mother, sweet mother where can you be?
Are you in this room, here with me?
The way you do things are slowly being forgotten.
Like the way you cooked, cleaned, sewed, and spun cotton.
As I look upon your grave in great despair.
I remembered how you used to play with my hair.
Mother, oh mother, please kiss me goodnight.
So you can protect me from fear, horror, terror, and fright.
Michelle Correll

Untitled

Your memory's still here
And that will never change
Deep down inside my heart
You will hold a sacred place
But the pain is slowly fading
And the tears no longer fall
They say time heals all wounds
I guess they were right after all
I used to cry myself to sleep
Wishing you were here with me
But now I've finally realized
That dream is never going to be
I know it's time to let you go
And give up on this dream of you
But I'll always remember what we shared
And I will never stop loving you
Kim James

Whispers

Above the tree filled mountains
And within the sky above,
There's an image of your beauty
A piece of you I love.

It's like the freshness in the air
After the ground is full of snow,
That best describes the emotions
Through you I've come to know.

Like the blue jay in the morning
That flies and sings his song,
We both have this in common
We know where we belong.

I'm thankful that your with me
I'm grateful that you care,
You awake the sound within me
Like the spring fresh morning air.

So if you hear a voice
As winds whisper through a tree,
It's a song of joy God sings
A dedication to you from me.
Frank Alanis

Caught Between Two Fires

She sits in a dark corner feeling confusion
In the distance she sees a dim light
Though she cannot feel its warmth
The light gives her the half knowledge
She needs to reach her final destination
As she slowly falters along the faintly lit path
She finds herself descending from the warmth
That has saved her from his cold touch
This same burning feeling has thawed her
From the inside out and sometimes from the outside in.
She is puzzled from not knowing which way to go
She understands that if she follows each one to the end
It will result in being severely burned
Either by the light from the outside in
Or by the warmth from the inside out
So she sits alone
Caught between two fires!
Shannan Ingraham

Interlude

It was a special day my friend
It will not come again
That special day.

Another one perhaps
Another time, hour day or year
And then you will appear.

Your smile so quick and warm,
We'll meet with outstretched arms.
There will be another day
A special day, in some far time.

LeeOra Jacobe

I Love You Mom

Mom, life has not been easy
but yet you carry so much
bondage of love to share beyond
the souls of those you love.
You give without asking for nothing
in return and all you receive is hurt
and not love.

Life has not been easy but yet you
showed me to love and to care to forgive
and forget to hope and to pray and with
all the suffering destiny has caused you, you
still took the time to put me in your arms
and tell me "I love you, you are my shining star of life."

You gave me so much hope and so much
love, that my life without you would have
no meaning to me. You are my destiny
and all that I love, the mom who never
surrendered, you never gave up, never let
go because the true meaning of life
was always by your side.
   I Love You Mom.

Raquel R. Perez

Acceptance

This is a poem to the one I adore most.
Does he realize the loyal love that is felt for him?
His strong arms, and youthful body, please realize
That you are not invincible.
Bright blue eyes that have such hidden pain.
Why can't he let it go?
I promise that the pain won't linger.
Has the sickness been passed on?
Can't he see that it will cause excessive pain?
Lack of hope, apathetic numbness,
It can be easier! I wish he could visualize.
Don't act like it doesn't matter.
His consistency is becoming more relevant,
And sweetness is apparent,
Lightheartedness and humor follow him.
Please know that to be serious is just as intriguing,
Or more so.
I don't want to see him burdened.
I will be his comfort just as he is mine.

Katharyn Grace Rykert

One Cloudy Winter Day

As I walked through the woods one cloudy winter day,
I came to a tree that was old and decayed.
It had fallen across the path that I choose to travel on,
But its roots were still deep and its trunk was still strong.

As I walked through the woods another cloudy winter day,
I happened upon a lake that was dry and sprinkled with hay.
But its hollow was still deep and its banks were still strong
So I knew that the lake would not stay that way for long.

As I walked through the woods one cloudy winter day,
I reached the little old shack where my dear sister stayed.
But as I stepped on the porch and entered through the door
I knew that my dear sister was not alive anymore.

So as I walked through the woods the next sunny winter day
Tears slid from my eyes as I journeyed on my way.
I left behind the shack and the lake and the tree
And pushed my sister's baby in a stroller by my knees.

Natasha Thomas

St. John's Chapel, The Tower Of London

Aloof and pale,
Your oranged pillars' thickened stone
And deepset window eyes,
Distort our suns to a soft glow.
Those ancient panes, below a vaulted head,
Reflect the steps of those who paced:
Remaining birthdates marked on stone-crossed floor.

You are a reverent place,
Where even far beginning Norman Kings
Paused death in monument.
Those great stones matched upon your walls
Show not a twinkle of the tears:
They are the softness of a faith...the dignity of years.

Little one,
You are God's greatest house.
The privacy of faith has sealed you here,
And kept your walls a cloak
Against the ages man has prayed:
A mighty hour's audience...a minute's breath alone.

Sydney Tyler-Parker

What Am I

I come from a garden that was planted with a kiss
A garden of many which grows within a soul
I come to you with tenderness from deep inside of a heart
I live to be yours briefly only to die like so many before me
There are millions like me but I am special I am yours today
My purpose is as clear as your tears I am a token of affection
I am a messenger from the one who last held me before you
I'm telling you someone cares I'm saying someone is thinking about you
My color is of everlasting friendship my fragrance is of everlasting hope
My petals hold moments of happiness never before known
Happiness that came suddenly and will never come again
Soon I'll wither away and die another flower is waiting to take my place
With your acceptance I will live once again
For as long as you want me I'll always come back
You could save me and remember or discard me and forget
What am I, I am a rose a yellow rose.

Daniel F. Gomez

Fire And Ice

This fire that burns inside me is true
It feels like it's red but I'm sure it's true blue
It rages in me only for you as does my
mind in all of your truth.
Though it does not miss and it
does not hug, it only remembers
your true love, sometimes in '
states of bliss it can feel your
mouth warming kiss, but before all
this is done, I swear I had none.
It was as my fire was lit by your unknowing
peck on my cheek.
Sometimes it freezes and hurts
like desire, but I think to myself
I must rise higher. Not to push
it down but to let it all out
even if it means to cry out loud.
And when I miss you (which is a lot), my emotions
get scarred but never my heart.

Randall Scoll Perry IV

To A Broken Friendship

While meandering through the wooded brush.
I came upon a fallen willow tree.
Its massiveness took me by surprise
As it lay there helpless, guise by night.
Its solid foundation, is ere diminutive stump,
Rotting away from the dampness and the cold.
Its branches bowed in reverence to the earth,
Some kissing the ground Gaea trod upon.
Rivulets of rain flowed through the wrinkled bark
And sprinkled upon a few remaining leaves,
Most a faded, homely looking green.
But standing out amongst all the others,
A healthy, lush green leaf swaying steadfastly
On a weary twig. The cord is snapped,
Letting the beautiful leaf be on its own,
Away from the weeping willow tree.

Craig Cazeau

My Little Nephew

I have a nephew,
Who is so kind and sweet.
He watches every move I wake;
Just remember he's only three.

As each day goes by,
I look down, he is beside me;
When I walk to town, he walks with me.

As time goes by,
I pick up Garron, when I drive he always looks.
He starts to speak, and what he says is,
Uncle there's my church.

I want to count
My many blessings,
And thank God for Garron,
Just remember he's only three.

Joseph Smith

Upon the Return of My Beloved

In soft meditation, I sit;
I shudder, and I sigh.
For when to draw nigh
The carriage of my beloved,
In anticipation, crouched,
Perched at the gates, I wait.
Still I stay, and unmoving,
Until with leaps of joy
I move at the coming of
my beloved. My heart leaps,
And races within. I am a
cup that is full; a portion
That is filled.

Randy Blohm

Untitled

Please learn your lessons
Please count your blessings
Making the world cruel
Deceived and made a fool

Please learn to think
Please delve in deep
All is not what it seems
Reality actually a dream

Please learn to listen
Please feel compassion
Capacities are lost
Love is a ghost

Please learn to live
Please try to give
Everyone is sleeping
They leave me weeping

Candace Elaine Proctor

Untitled

Blood stains my hands
Stains my blade
And stains my memory
The senseless slaughter
Of souls never met before
And never to be seen again
I've condemned myself
To a life of burning memories
And eternal damnation
For the sins that my forefathers
And I have committed
We shall burn eternally
In a pool of brimstone and fire
We are the warriors of this world
And our legacy will never
DIE

Timothy Coulombe

On Desert Rain

The rain is falling softly:
The desert drinks it in.
Hidden seeds, so long in slumber,
New life will now begin.
A stirring is felt beneath the
Once dry, baked-hard earth,
Becoming a clamor of color, and
A riot joyous mirth!

Fran Stott

Chieftain And Child

When the shadows take their place,
with the ageless lady of night,
and the symphony of nature begins to slow,
the heavenly bodies, focus and form,
below the classic moon, atop the hills overlooking their world,
standing hand in hand, like timeless works of art,
child and chieftain, stare and wonder, like any other.
And when the west wind blows the fields in a wave,
the woman child dances for her naked Indian.
And they make love hidden by the deep grasses,
but the warrior soon gets his call;
he hears the war cries of his tribal brothers,
and he runs to the sound of the pounding drums,
the drums of his ancestors.
Even nature herself screams,
when the chieftain falls.
He died in a warrior's dance, never any fear in his eyes.
The child and chieftain, their love is eternal,
she now dances with the wind, and stares into the night,
and wonders, of her warrior, like any other.

Mitch McKnight

A Birth In June

Movements of life
in time beating
like sudden bursts
of breath pressing
forth in light
and nigrescence
comes to pass
in the present
sun interstices moon
of the sky I know
only clouds of you
floating further forward
your aura upon me
so close
mysterious
your flesh descending
beyond my womb
arriving through
God's keyhole
of life.

Sharon Redding

To All That Care For Me

I sit in my room in my wheelchair
Waiting to see if someone will care

I look out the window or glance at T.V.
As my time goes so slow, I have no one to see.

I once had a family, and reason's to live
I was so happy, I had so much to give.

But now as I sit here, I wonder and worry
Will I bother you, you seem so much in a hurry.

My legs and arms are not the same
I guess that old age is the one to blame.

So as my turn comes to care for me,
I pray to God, to give strength to thee.

I now know someday, you to will grow old
and I hope someone will care for you
   with a heart of gold.

So now as this night draws near, I thank you
from my heart, if you really do care.

Susan Barnhart

"Melt, The Lonely Heart"

Ah! The great sword of the Excalibur,
Slowly melts the frozen shell
Of the ice queen,
And deeply thrusts
To find her hidden dove.

But alas, a lack,
Even the heat of his great steel
Cannot unleash
The mysteries of her love.

But again, and again
He thrusts, and softly, gradually,
Her love begins to rise
Until she eagerly greets
His penetrating heat.
Their fingers touch,
And their souls rise to meet.
But alas, a lack,
Her heart begins to ache within,
For her frozen shell
Will never mend again.

Jean Rose

Untitled

In the dark forest of the soul
   all shadows menace and mimic demons
Sounds return and echo back our fears
Beliefs coronated to Kings of our realms
The sleeping dragon arises to meet our
   shuttering footsteps approach
Spewing fire that lights up reflections of our face
   upon it's hardened scales
Our trembling hands strike out-fighting gallantly
   upon this battlefield -in this rank battle for the soul
With laboring heavy heavens we strike
Weariness seeps deep as time stretches out like
   strands of web
Death brushes a handshake across our fingers
   and splits open numb
We will strike one more blow
With calculated heave we wield this sword
And take down this dragon of our night
And crown a new King to a new land
Our soul throws flowers across our conquering path

Bonnie L. Cannon

Happy Fathers Day

On this special day,
Fathers all around the world,
Are highly being appreciated
For their kindness and hours of hard work.
So, let me be the first to say, "I thank you,"
Not only for the shelter, and protection,
But for helping me with my job, as a Mother
When I needed you the most.
Thank you for holding me close
When the pressures ran deep.
And for the many tears you dried
As they fell down my cheeks.

You may not wash the dishes,
Or even pick up your clothes.
But that's O.K., it keeps me busy,
As I'm anxiously waiting for you to come home.
Thank you, thank you, thank you,
I don't know what else to say.
Except, I love you very dearly,
And I wish you many a happy Fathers Day.

Michelle Hughes

Waterfalls

Thunderous earth shattering feelings
He awakens in me
Arousing every fiber of my entire being
Soaring me into heights that I dare not to have dreamed
Pleasuring my mind until my body quivers
With unheard screams

Kisses raining like a waterfall...
Cascading all down my back
Reducing me to a smoky blaze of fire
Left smoldering in a track

His breath brushes my ear
and while lying in his arms, I know not fear
Sweet kisses stir so gentle a breeze
caresses calmly stirring the seas
His touch sends shivers up and down my spine...
Until a thought of my own...at that moment...I cannot find!

His body sends lightening crashing throughout my chest
But I know—after the storm, in his strong, loving arms—I rest

sending him away seems a fate worse than jail
I'm reeling through withdrawal...Not a lot unlike hell!!
Sharon Kay Johnson

Wind

There is a whisper in the night
   that only I can hear.
There is a song in the night
   that sings softly in the ear.
There is a voice in the night
   that calls only to me.
There is a ghost in the night
   that only I can see.
There is a hand in the night
   that gently touches my cheek.
There is a feeling in the night
   that makes my heart beat.
There is the wind in the night.
Valerie J. Duckett

A Baseball Poem

Baseball is fun to play
On a hot summer day
before summer ends
go get your friends
break out the ball, and bats
and throw on your hats.

Make sure the teams are fair
don't worry about errors
for fun is the reason you're there.
Brian Michael Roe

You

You not them I say
All your life is like a book
You the book is rated
For all your life is rated
You are told what to do
I say go by your heart
You may or may not know
but life will find a way to tell
Candy Hill

Assassination

There is war, tonight, in the Holy Lands.
Where Jesus once walked
His brothers are killing each other.

As two halves of the same nation
Shed blood over God given land,
Our Saviour weeps.

One man raised his voice
In a song for peace.
Now, silence answers the rain of bullets.

Will his life's work be meaningless?
Or will his death
Cease the children's tears?
LaRaine K. Etheridge

Behind The Wheel

I am a pair of bright red dots.
Just one in a line of angry luminous eyes
that snakes a way up and to the left
of your view as you swoop
low overhead: A liberated
investigating bird.

I am part of this rippling serpent.
You might see me as a mere segment
hive me off and the whole would heal
seamlessly as the accelerator behind
responds to the lazy depressing foot
of the yawning silhouette thinking of home.

My two crimson drizzle-fuzzy eyes
may be all, in your perspective
but I am more: Skull, thoughts, capillary networks
Though I struggle for my significance, my meaning.
But watch me die, you high-flying contemptuous bird
and know that someone will miss me.
Tex Dunstan

It's Never Going To Happen (For Us)

No matter how I try to live positive I can't change
this world I live in.
I will always be considered different and you will
always be distant.
So it's never going to happen for us

To unite and not fight would be a wonderful sight
we've got to know to show love.
But it's never going to happen for us.

Our immorality doesn't let us see and if we continuing
Being afraid then ignorance will always be.
Starlet Reid

Looking Glass

How can you stand there and throw your guilt at me as if I were a mirror?
A mirror that knows all too well how to cry,
Hang me on a wall.
Seen never heard through the mind by few with true vision.
The hole in my heart can't compete with the horrible things,
you believe in me.
How can you stand there with my heart in your open hands?
I don't think you took the time to find out who I really am.
You reflect me in your looking glass.
Carrie Moonier

Summer Memories

Bumbleberry pie, apple juice
Family of mine, family of goose
Swim in the lake, fly a big kite
Watch - the mosquitos really bite!

Apple juice, bumbleberry pie
Baked in oven - rises so high.
Serve with a big fork. Steaming hot!
Homemade pie is better. Not bought!

Family of goose, family of mine
Time of memories for us - nine.
Mother makes pie, father cuts wood,
Kids chase geese as fast as they could!

"Fly a big kite, swim in the lake
Stop chasing geese for goodness sakes!
Find a friend or play together,
Run through the meadows in the heather."

Watch! The mosquitos really bite!
Run real fast while you fly your kite.
Stand still and you will take a chance,
It might be good to wear some pants!
Cheryl Anderson

"What Will I Say"

When the Lord chooses to take me,
What will I say I have done?

Have I given my food
To those who go hungry?

Have I given my shelter
To those who have none?

Have I given my heart
To those in need?

When the Lord chooses to take me,
What will I say I have learned?

When I've felt anger,
Have I walked away?

When I've felt hatred,
Have I chose to love?

When I've felt temptation,
Have I used restraint?

When the Lord chooses to take me,
What can I say?
Barbara Frasca

Untitled

Have you ever studied a cup on a tray
Look closely, it comes alive, so they say

The handle begins to look like an ear
A copper stain seems to represent a tear

Keep on staring and a voice cries out
I'm not happy here it hollers and shouts

As if it were some being, inside locked up
Trying to escape from that horrible cup
Trying so hard and getting no where
And all you can do is sit and stare

Then the voice is gone and you will find
You made it up in your imaginative mind

You realize then, there was no man locked up
You look again, to find only a cup
Anne Konnerth

Silence

Lord, silence this inner commotion,
that I alone cannot control,
Father, please bring silence
to a weary soul.

I need a touch from you Lord
to quiet the turmoil inside,
A small blessings Father,
to still the raging tide.

Heavenly Father, I beg for Peace,
Peace inside my heart,
Calm my weary thoughts,
Let the storm within me depart.

Take away the fear within
and give me a moment's rest,
just a little stillness
inside my weary breast.

Oh Lord, grant me this I pray,
a little silence to my restless mind,
without you God,
This on my own, I'll never find.
Mary M. Long

The Kiss Of Two

Two people lips so close at the shudder of a breath. And the moment is gone, to be replaced by another. Yet here in the heart it's frozen forever. The memory of such a sweet embrace. Like a picture, captured in the pages of my mind. The kiss of two people who know at the same time that love has taken over. Their destinies not their own, joined together as a single path. In this way they carry on bounds stronger than before. Not even bands of iron have this strength. The ability to stand fast before anything thrown their way. No tempest could destroy the foundation they have built. And until the end of their time it should always be the two of them. Now, and on down this single lone path.
James D. Williams

"Mother Dear"

I'm probably the first thing on your mind
When you awake to a new day
And the last thing on your mind at night
When you bow your head to pray
I know how you must miss me
And oh how hard you've grieved
And I just want to comfort you
And put your mind at ease
Leaving you know, was not my choice
But it was my time you see
The Lord above had greater plans
So he sent angels after me
He brought me home to his promise land
And it's so wonderful being here
So please don't worry about me
And please don't shed a tear
When you think of me just give a smile
For we'll be together in awhile
For some sweet day he'll bring you here
'Til then just remember "I love you" Mother dear
Lisa Efird

MEMORIES WILL NEVER DIE...
In memory of Scott Michael McClure
"Do You..."

Do you realize the love and pain I hide,
the anger and depression built inside.

Do you realize the need I have for you,
You'd be here if my dream came true.

Do you realize over the years I've tried to go on,
with you I could communicate, we got along.

Do you realize that I am lost, who do I have?

"Nobody..."

Nobody understands me, the way you did,
you cared what happened to me as a kid.

Nobody will ever be as good of a brother,
there's no way I would replace you with any other.

Nobody could ever duplicate your choice of word,
the good ones that gave me confidence I heard.

Nobody would be able to copy your influence on me,
I just wish you were here to see.

Someday we will meet again,
But I have to move on until then!!
 Jaimi Lyn Tromp

My Snowmobile

Riding my snowmobile is fun;
I like to ride it under the sun.
Riding my snowmobile is loud.
I like to ride it under a rainy cloud.

Riding my snowmobile is cold;
It's as shiny as precious gold.
Riding my snowmobile is bumpy.
When it's too rough I get grumpy.

Riding my snowmobile is past.
This line will be my very last!
 —*Joshua Lisowski*

Life

I looked out this morning and thought, "It's going to be a great day."
Everything around me seemed to prove this in every way.

There were flowers blooming in the yard.
The birds were singing without a care.

I knew there were things that could mar this day.
But I thought to myself, "they wouldn't dare."

But even as I stood watching; it was proven just how wrong I was.
All of the sudden things began to change; even the bees seemed to
 loose their buzz.

The clouds started rolling in; the winds began to blow.
A terrible storm was brewing; I knew there would be trouble for
 everything below.

When the storm finally ended, it did leave destruction in its wake.
But the most surprising thing of all, my life it didn't take.

The storm had raged on and on, but I made it through.
My life was given back to me; and I know who I owe that to.

Because you believed in me; I recognize you for what you are.
Even in the midst of a terrible storm, you are a bright and shining star.
 Tamla Copes

Brother Against Brother

From 1861 to 1865.
Over 600,000 men had lost their lives
They fought in over 10,000 places
Both men of black and white races
It was the end of slavery
The end of Southern Plantation aristocracy
It began April 12, 1861 4:30 a.m.
Boys as young as 12 soon became men
Grant and Lee both men of honor
In this horrible war of brother against brother
From McClellan to Grant the North won in the end
Robert E. Lee was the South's one true man
Their colors were blue and gray
some people still honor them to this day
Didn't we believe in 1775 that, "All men are created equal"?
At that time in all 13 colonies slavery was legal
Although slavery was the meaning of this war
Racism cannot be ignored
Racism still exists, will it ever end?
Will brother against brother ever happen again?
 Kathleen Mae Fisher

Oh Gentle Thy Hand, Fate

He was born to a queen
 The son of a king
  And they reared him
   And watched him grow.
Just a seedling was he
 When he played near his tree,
  A friend of so long ago.

How he cleaved and he cleaved
 To his old friend, the tree,
  But fate took his hand,
   It was stronger than he.
And it lead him up there
 To a pure golden chair
  Where it crowned him,
   It crowned him a king.

Yes, fate took his hand
 And lead him up there
  Where he was anointed, a king.
 —*Katherine Lisowski*

Nature

From mountaintops to ocean shores
From grassy meadows to swampy moors,
There's nature everywhere from far to near;
Nature you can see, nature you can hear.

The bees that buzz from here to there,
The birds that fly everywhere,
You can see the trees grow so tall.
You can hear the robins waking call.

And when you see those beautiful deer,
The song of nature you will hear.
There's nature everywhere from far to near;
Nature you can see, nature you can hear.
 Christina Haddox

"Love"

Love
Is it worth the pain you get sometimes?
Or do you do it
so you can say you did?

Love
is a word used often but
defined wrong so many times.
Even if you fall in love with someone
that is when you normally treat that person the worst.

Love
is a word you should say to the person
that makes you feel so good
whenever you talk to them
or even just when you look at them

Now tell the truth...
Is just one little word worth all that pain and suffering?
Or am I lying to you?
I guess you will never know
unless you said
"I Love You" to someone
Sunshine Acosta

Reflection

Was it yesterday you reached for the stars or was it just today?
I saw your hunger for a new beginning.
Was it yesterday or just today that filled my eyes with tears?
To see you struggle, to see your pain and watch you meet your fears.
Was it yesterday or just today confusion filled your mind?
A world of twisted troubles and answers you can't find.
If not today then surely tomorrow all of this will end.
It may have been true yesterday but things have changed since then.
Your strength and your conviction have led you on your way.
And it's tomorrow you will soar
And then tomorrows evermore.
Theresa Ormsbee

Rand-McNally Daydream

With friend in hand I shrug the worldly rush
And finger-brush a corner-curling face,
And wonder not aloud how is it now,
And map-empowered in my mind I smiling
Run the wrinkled length of painted ribbon
Mountain ward, where lurking grandfathers
Stand in patient purple: Welcome home,
Welcome to the sky. Then caught in a flush
Of mindless wanderlust I wake to trace
A different path to peace. The sun-capped brow
I quit as I race through countless red-lined miles
Of infant corn rocked in a rolling crib,.
Drawn to the sea, where faction cannot bother me,
And thought dissolves in roar and foam.
Gary Mills

He

He smile the smile of geniality;
Showcase the state of respectability;
Nod to those of affluency;
Shades his hatred towards those in abject poverty.

He mimics compassion and sincerity;
Exhibits impartiality contingently; and
Wounds the mind and soul towards people like me.
Cassandra Covington Coker

Untitled

My hidden pain
   Hurts like a blazing fire
While I am left to blame.
   I am left with much said, a liar.
They circle me like vultures with no food
   But their food is me and my own.
My pain is the flesh being ripped from every bone
   and my tears are the blood to quench their thirst.
Trying makes no sense from me to them.
   All I have are shadows as once a friend.
With whatever I do...I think is right
   but to them is only left,
and their minds are so cramped, small and straight,
   never accepting me as one and their lives to be my fate.
Charles M. Edwards

"In The Light Of Hope"

Fear is dark and it can hide deep in our souls.
So deep, that light will fail to enter into our hearts
if we choose to allow the darkness
to shut out the light.

We are afraid to show our vulnerable side
in fear we may be hurt.
Instead, we side-step our neighbors, passing up
those golden opportunities to truly love and care for one another.

Fear will be our future,
if we continue to journey down this dark and aimless path.
Say "no" to fear and the light will break through
the darkest of clouds, defining the way to truth.

The window of truth will open to let the stale air of fear out,
and the refreshing fragrance of hope in.
The heart will begin to heal and the soul will see joy
amid the sometimes harsh, natural realities of the earth.

For even in the presence of the natural pain we may feel today,
tomorrow will always offer a new start,
to search and to fly toward the light
in the hope of finding eternal love.
Joseph J. Nicholosi

I Used To Wish I Was A Boy

I used to wish I was a boy
With blond hair and blue eyes

You used to say that was what you wanted
Before I came on the scene

I grew up thinking that was what you really meant
Even tho you denied it all the time

I know now it was an unconscious thing
And you never meant to hurt me

I tried so hard to do boy things
I wanted to do sports

That was not the things girls do
So I was told "You Will Not"

It created great confusion
Not being able to please

And now I know
It was never meant to be

I used to wish I was a boy
With blond hair and blue eyes
Shirley Helman

Circumstances Of My Birth

I should have been
born in Italli.
I love lasagna,
pack in parmigiana,
ravish ravioli,
masticate mostaccioli,
dig rigatoni,
smack macaroni.

I insist, in Italli
I should have been born.
I yearn for vermicelli,
moats of mozzarelli;
I mangle manicotti
and spindle my spaghetti;
I fete to fetuccine,
and I'm zany for succhini.

But Mama Mia
Who disliked pizzeria
Was exiled to Flint, Michigan.
    Dawn Escoto

"Parents"

Parents are large people
Who frequently declare
That "Other Children"
Eat their meals and
Sit straight on a chair.

"Other Children"
  wash their hands
According to My Parents
They never yell, or lose their caps
  or fight, or be a bother
"Other Children: They say
  speak when spoken to;
    they answer "please" and "thank you"
  the way I'm s'posed to do.

I'm sorry for my parents,
  Just as sorry as can be;
  They know such lovely children,
  Then get stuck with one
  like me!!!
    Sandi Pfeil

For Michelle

We know you will wait
Just past the moon
For those of us that love you
And those that you have loved

You're in our hearts forever
No one can take away
The remembrances and memories
We carry with us each day

We know you're looking down
When we're looking up and see
The brightest star in the black of night
You're saying "keep on with life peacefully"

You've touched our lives so much
Whether a day, year, or more
You'll continue touching our lives
Now as much as before

No one can surpass
The love for life you had
You lived life to the fullest
In the short time you had
    Shirley Vandine

Biographies of Poets

ABBOTT, EDWARD E.
[b.] December 18, 1907, Franklin, MA; [p.] Dr. C. Edson Abbott and Lillian F. Abbott; [m.] Beverly Abbott, February 2, 1983; [ch.] Dr. Carol Montgomery, Margaret Herrick; [ed.] Dartmouth College - AB Degree, George Washington Univ. Law - D. J., Georgetown Univ. Law - LLM degree; [occ.] Retired; [memb.] Elks - Masonic Lodge, AARP (Shrine Temple), Almalaikah of Los Angeles, Society of Former Special Agents of the FBI; [hon.] Former Honorary Mayor of Big Beer City, CA, served on Local Boards of: Hospital District, School District, Community Services District, Local Agency Formation Commission; [oth. writ.] Book "On Mountain Tops"; [pers.] Service to my country and community and preservation of environmental values.; [a.] Big Bear City, CA

ABDELKHALIK, DORENE COOKS
[b.] July 16, 1967, Brooklyn; [p.] Frances Cheatham, Frank Cooks; [m.] Nadiem Abdelkhalik, October 16, 1994; [ch.] Shavvona, Ieesha, Jessica, Natasha, Ebony; [occ.] Housewife, I have five children whom I adopt.; [memb.] Trinity Baptist Church, Jamacia Queens; [oth. writ.] I have been writing poems since age 9 yrs. old, something I really love to do and I hope that the many poems I wrote it touch someone in some kind of way.; [pers.] My poem is for all men that die in this country serving in the military. And also my beautiful foster kids whom I had for 7 yrs. And my husband, I love you all.; [a.] Jamacia Queens, NY

ABRAMS, MARK
[pen.] Shira Stone; [b.] September 3, 1982, Cincinnati, OH; [p.] Arthur Abrams - Ruth Abrams; [ed.] Peebles Junior High; [occ.] Student; [pers.] I would like to say that poem writing is a gift not a talent, and everybody has the talent it's just some people do not show it.; [a.] Peebles, OH

ACKLEY, LYSA CHRISTINE
[pen.] Lee; [b.] April 1, 1981, Meriden, CT; [p.] Carl and Christine Ackley; [ed.] K - 9th and Still Continuing, K - 8th St. Joseph School 9th Platt High School; [occ.] Student; [hon.] Academic And Special Achievement Awards; [pers.] First, I would like to thank my mom and my dad for their love and inspiration - I love you guys! Second, I would like to thank my sister Amy for being a great critic. A special thanks to ALL of my relatives in CT, VT, and SC. And most of all, to the National Library of Poetry for letting my poem be in this beautiful Anthology.; [a.] Meriden, CT

ADAMS, FLORA BOLLING
[b.] Wise County, VA; [p.] Henderson Bolling and Laura Boggs; [m.] Kelsey Adams, October 22, 1945; [ch.] 2 boys, 2 girls; [ed.] Flat Gap High, Radford State Teachers' College, (now Radford University) University of Maryland - Master of Education - 1970; [occ.] Retired Educator; [memb.] Church: Alpha Delta Kappa Honorary Teachers Sorority, International, Local Community Organizations, Political Party, Education Organizations, National Trust for Historic Preservation; [hon.] Nominated for Outstanding Member Leadership of ADK; [oth. writ.] A few unpublished stories for young people, a number of poems, plays for children, church, and organizations, a play "The U.S. Constitutions on pull out section of newspaper Norton Press, Curriculum writer of Language Arts, Social Studies, Health; [pers.] It is important to me to weave a thread of moral integrity in at least one character of my stories whether they are set in times past or present. The goodness of a human being makes it possible to accept and tolerate the aspects of his life which are not perfect.; [a.] Williamsburg, VA

ADDISON, WILLIAM
[pen.] Bill Addison; [b.] April 26, 1956, Riverton, WY; [ed.] Graduated from High School; [occ.] Raising Horses; [hon.] Outstanding Student Award in High School; [oth. writ.] Writing down thoughts brain storming.

AGEE, LINDA J.
[b.] June 2, 1952, Wellsville, MO; [p.] Floyd and Bernice Banks; [m.] Mark E. Agee; [ch.] Dana and Anna Poindexter and Ben and Joel Agee; [pers.] My poems express my feelings for the people I love. I thank God for all of them.; [a.] Mannford, OK

AGNAS, CARMELITA LEDESMA
[pen.] C. L. Agnas; [b.] December 28, 1939, Roxas City, Philippines; [p.] Ricardo Agnas Sr., Cristita Ledesma; [ed.] Bachelor of Science in Education, University of San Agustin, Iloilo City, Master of Arts in Teaching, Marikina Institute of Science and Technology, Metro Manila, Philippines, Bachelor of Laws, Roxas City, Philippines; [occ.] Teacher (Mathematics); [memb.] Filipino American Movement in Education; [hon.] Certificate of Merit for Mathematics Instruction, Certificate of Recognition on Teachers' Assestment, U.S.A., Certificate of Merit, Scholarship, Department of Education, Philippines, Editor's Choice Award in Poetry, 1994, 1995-Nat. Library of Poet; [oth. writ.] "This Heart! This Heart" and Other Poems, "Search for an Identity and People's Power", "Dance of the Ricestalk" "Affection is Forever"; [pers.] "Let my teaching drop as the rain, my speech distill as the dew, as the droplets on on the fresh grass and as the shower on the herb." Deut, 32:2; [a.] San Jose, CA

AHRENS, MARK M.
[b.] January 22, 1969, Prairie du Chien, WI; [p.] Lowell and Nancy Ahrens; [ed.] B.S. in Psychology - V.W. Platteville, Platteville, WI, A.A. Biblical Studies, Marilyn Hickey Bible College Denver Co.; [occ.] Student; [hon.] PSI CHI National Psychology Honor Society, Two Year Scholarship - Marilyn Hickey Bible College; [oth. writ.] "A Tender Hope" - collection of poetry inspired by the Holy Spirit; [pers.] The words I write are a feeble attempt to express words, thoughts, feelings and ideas that can only truly be lived and experienced, not described.; [a.] Prairie du Chien, WI

AL-SHALCHI, OLLA NAJAH
[b.] February 20, 1982, Pittsburg, PA; [p.] Huda and Najah Al-Shalchi; [ed.] 8th grade student at Katherine Stinson Middle School; [occ.] Student; [hon.] National Junior Honor Society; [pers.] Islamic Dua- Waqur-rabbi-zidni-alama. English translation "O my Lord! Advance me in knowledge."; [a.] Helotes, TX

ALADA, ROBERTO V.
[pen.] Bob Ken; [b.] August 16, 1954, Manila, Philippines; [p.] Mr. Romeo P. Alada and Mrs. Amparo V. Alada; [ed.] Lyceum of the Philippines, Northern Marianas College (NMC) BOE Certification and Continuing Education; [occ.] Language Arts teacher, self-contained teacher Tanapag Elementary School, Saipan, MP 96950; [memb.] Marianas Association of Filipino Educators (MAFE), Association of Commonwealth Teacher (ACT); [hon.] Tanapag Elementary School Teacher of the Year 1993, Government Scholarship Grant Regional Language Centre, Republic of Singapore, 1989 (Course 602 B), One of the Ten Outstanding Teacher Jaycee International Manila, Philippines, 1984; [oth. writ.] Manual For Creative Drama for Secondary School, A Proposed Syllabus for the Teaching of Drama Using the Communicative Approach for 4th year Student in the Philippines.; [pers.] Man's purpose in this changing World: Living or simply existing? It is painful to be hated, it is dreadful not to be loved, but it is most devastating to be a victim of indifference. For man has a soul and a heart. Let us then love one another. I am advocate of realistic and romantic poems.; [a.] Saipan, MP

ALBERT, LYNNE
[b.] May 10, 1912, Brooklyn; [p.] Frank Albert, Antoinett - Mother; [ed.] Art Schools I Point; [occ.] Retired; [memb.] Summit; [hon.] For fashion; [oth. writ.] Throne Room

ALBRECHT, MARIA ELIZABETH
[b.] August 14, 1971, Piedra Niegra, Mexico; [p.] Duff and Jo Mills; [m.] Warren C. Albrecht, April 7, 1995; [ch.] Caelum McKenna Albrecht; [ed.] Angelo State University Sul Ross State University; [occ.] Housewife; [pers.] Life is short, so I'd like to express that happiness, along with true love is magical. If you have that then you have solved the great mystery of life.; [a.] Lewisville, TX

ALBRIGHT, WILLIAM E.
[b.] February 11, 1931, Falls City, NE; [p.] Helen L. and William J. Albright; [m.] Joan V. Albright, August 2, 1976; [ch.] Barbara, William S., Craig D. Kristin; [ed.] Bain Ed, Peru State College, Peru, NE, Med., Oregon State University, Corvallis; [occ.] Retired Public Educators formerly - Counselor/Teacher, Santa Rosa, CA City School; [memb.] Sharpsteen Museum, Napa Co., Calistoga Friends of the Library, VFW; [hon.] 1989 Secondary Teacher of the Year Santa Rosa, CA, Kappa Delta Pi, Who Award California Teachers Association; [oth. writ.] Monthly local publication The Grapevine; [pers.] Questions should be one result of any writing. Questions which may only have answers to be sought not immediately answered.; [a.] Calistoga, CA

ALEGRIA, MEL
[b.] September 7, 1980, San Jose; [p.] Mel and Gloria Alegria; [ed.] Attending High School; [occ.] Student; [memb.] Member of many High School Clubs; [hon.] I have been in the Honor Roll several times. Athletic Participation Awards in Cross Country Track and Wrestling; [oth. writ.] Several writings published in high school literary magazine.; [pers.] I have been greatly influenced by my family, teachers and friends. I strongly believe that anything is possible if you believe with your heart.; [a.] San Jose, CA

ALGOSINO, PHIL
[b.] January 6, 1954, Bornxville, NY; [p.] Josephine and Phil; [ed.] Half Hollow Hills H.S Stony brook Univ. N.Y.; [occ.] Writer; [oth. writ.] A place in time, monkey's thumb, fox's box; [pers.] I always like to be original. My poems to think and feel, so they are important to me; [a.] Ridge, NY

ALLEN, MICAH DAVID
[b.] October 28, 1969, Garland, TX; [p.] Clayton Allen, Melva Thorpe; [memb.] Environmental Preservationists Friends of the Forest Wolf Sponsor; [oth. writ.] Have written many other poems and songs since I was a child. Have also written for local publications.; [pers.] The poem in this book was actually from a song I wrote when I was fourteen regarding my parents divorce when I was five. You never know when love begins but you always know when it ends.; [a.] Garland, TX

ALLEN, NASON E.
[pen.] Nason, Nasonallen; [b.] February 26, 1925, Erie, PA; [p.] Heber E. Allen, Marion Nason; [m.] Margaret (Shaw) Deceased, September 2, 1950; [ch.] Kathleen, Barbara, Judith, Craig; [ed.] Lakewood High School Cleveland College Ohio Wesley University Lakeland Community College; [occ.] The sole Proprietor, Owner Shade's Gray, Studio. Owner Bramble Bush Farm. Editor Madison Historical Society Times Chairman of Board - United Methodist (Park U. M. Church) Madison OH.; [memb.] Member Madison and Ashtabuga. Fine Arts Center Madison Historical Society Lake Coun-

ty Historical Society Bay Crafters Bay Village, Ohio. Delta Tau Delta, Mu (Past Pres.) Phi Mu Alpha, Nat. Music Honorary. American Marketing Assoc., (Instructor) United States Navy Veteran (43-46) Pacific Theater - 7 Major Campaigns, Destroyer Escort L. C. Taylor (De 415).; [oth. writ.] Short stories, poems editorials. Many published in Local Papers, Madison Historical Society Times, Ohio Wesleyan Transcripts now in process relating unique, art perspective; [pers.] Retired sales and marketing executive commencing (new) career to sketch, paint, and write of the good life in words that are black and white shades O'Gray (in between) and with full color in those words. (And Rhymes); [a.] Madison, OH

ALLEN, PENNY
[b.] March 7, 1962, Urbana, IL; [p.] Linda King; [m.] Steve Allen, November 22, 1983; [ch.] Chasity, Chad, Chelsee; [occ.] Publix Bakery Manager Florida; [oth. writ.] Personal kept folder; [pers.] In every person there are many. Roads to travel. Each leads to a new city, and then come the dimensions.; [a.] Port Saint Lucie, FL

ALLEN, THERESA C.
[b.] February 23, 1955, Princeton; [p.] Frank and Roberta Carl; [m.] Michael C. Allen, August 1, 1975; [ch.] Stephanie, Pamela, Heather, Christopher; [ed.] Early Childhood Degree, Amboy High, Sauk Valley College; [occ.] Day Care Directress; [memb.] NAEYC, Illinois Day Care Association, DeKalb 4-Cs, Association for Child Development; [hon.] Dean's List, DeKalb 4-C's, Lee County Family Child Care Provider of the year; [oth. writ.] Several poems published in local newspaper, contributing writer for Golden Notes.; [a.] Dixon, IL

ALLISON, ROBERT
[b.] June 23, 1968, Danville, IL; [p.] Gary and Nancy Allison; [ed.] Hope Christian High School, Danville Area Community College; [occ.] Computer Operator, Temporary Employee of R. R. Donnelley in Danville, IL; [hon.] Honor Paper Carrier Award, Dean's Scholastic Achievement Award; [oth. writ.] Previous writings have never been published before.; [pers.] I write poems which reflect the happenings in my life, along with those of the world.; [a.] Tilton, IL

ALLMON, CECELIA ADRIENNE SWANSON
[pen.] Tede Adrienne Allmon; [b.] April 20, 1915, South Bend, IN; [p.] Anton Swanson and Florence Boudinot Swanson; [m.] Francis Elwood Allmon, June 6, 1936; [ch.] Robert Elwood Allmon, son Diane Elaine Covert, Daughter; [ed.] BS Lincoln College, Wisconsin Taught elementary schools in Wisconsin and South Bend, In, (Madison) School, first through eight grades, IU Graduate Parliamentarian, PR, Journalism School, drama and public speaking, ballroom dancing under BEA Teeter Studios, political science: Taught and served on election board Lifetime volunteer (50 year) community:; [occ.] Freelance Writer, Publishing FEA BIOG./ 96; [memb.] (Hon. State) Delta Kappa Gamma, Nat. Soc. DAR PP Schuyler Colfax Chp) 2 NS PR Ch, Memorial Hospital Aux. PP, news Ed., PR and Prog Ch., Vol. Coordin., Speechcraft YWCA Orgz, PP, PR, ED, City Chair USA Constitution Bic., PP Ladies of the Elks #235, 1st Presbyterian Church Women PVP: Hearing and Speech Aux. St. Joe Co. PP: S.B. Kiwaniannes PP (2); [hon.] NSDAR Outstanding newsletters/programs/historic plays. 50 year service South Bend Community (mayoral): Chief Justice Warren E. Burger nat'l 5th for SB USC bic. achievements (1987), S.B Trib. two feature stories front page (68 and 87): DKG for comm. service, Alexis Coquillard, CH. Sons of Am. Rev. good citizen award, SB Kiwanis Club-comm. Service: Memorial Hospital Men's Board citation for volunteer recruitment and fund raising $200,000; [oth. writ.] "South Bend Then and Now" history for opening brochure/program of Century Center 8 million dollar complex as city historian, "First Ladies of Indiana" Program, also cast, prod. a and narrated, S.B. Tribune - "Historic St. Joe County Bridges": "Mrs. Robert Morris Requests" - play of wives' day of USC signing with final tableau of Signers, cast, produced, costumed, directed, Daily countdown two weeks before signing broadcast on NBC-WNDU TV station. Series of historic editorials of founding father's lives, families and letters/ speeches in SB Tribune.; [pers.] I try to influence young American all ages to study American's patriots as role models in today's world. Inspiring them in excellence of goals with good citizenship will, through love of country and others before self, return the nation to its leadership in the world and its citizens of the future to great happiness of its children in love, security, success and regained world respect.; [a.] South Bend, IN

ALONGO, UNO I.
[pen.] Uno I. Alongo; [b.] June 23, 1907, Amasa, MI; [p.] Isaac Alongo; [m.] Helena Alongo; [ch.] Five Boys and One Girl; [ed.] 10th Grade; [occ.] Retired; [a.] Saint George, UT

ALSTON, RONALD
[b.] October 25, 1958, Long Island, NY; [p.] Walter, Muriel Alston; [m.] Divorced; [ch.] Lemar Alston, Tiandra Alston; [ed.] Berklee College of Music (composition) Sawyer School (Broadcasting, Rhod Island North Carolina, T State Univ.; [occ.] Consultant (Teaming Empowerment, Diversity) Student; [memb.] Toastmaster Int.; [hon.] Merit Award (Building Organization Teams); [oth. writ.] Currently seeking a publisher for my first book. "The Resurrected, A Motivational Guide" for self help and empowerment.; [pers.] I want to contribute my experiences to help educate others. I have been motivated by the million man March.

ALTMAN SR., JOHN
[b.] January 29, 1911, Harmony, IN; [p.] John and Mahala Altman; [ed.] 8th grade; [occ.] Retired - from growing and caring of trees.; [oth. writ.] Eight or ten song poems - not published. Short stories - namely "The Tree that Talked - Book one", "The Tree That Talked - book two".; [pers.] I have spent a long life of seeking the spiritual approach to the harmony joy, and love. The success that I have attained has been a journey not a destination.; [a.] Sandusky, OH

ALU, KURSTIN
[b.] August 30, 1934, Laramie, WY; [p.] Esther Clanu and C. R. Burrell; [m.] Tony Paul Alu, April 14, 1992; [ch.] Toni Mari Alu and Joseph Alu; [occ.] Housewife; [oth. writ.] I've written several other poems I am hoping they'll be published in the future.; [pers.] My poems that I've written express my feelings. I also want to thank my family for believing in me I love you all.; [a.] Ely, NV

AMADOR, RHONDA
[b.] March 12, 1959, Albuquerque, NM; [ch.] Four; [ed.] 12th grade graduate; [occ.] Homemaker and waitress; [oth. writ.] Tears; [pers.] I have a variety of poems, they came straight from my heart. From personal life experiences.; [a.] Albuquerque, NM

AMOROSO, DREW
[b.] February 8, 1984, Sayre, PA; [p.] Ginny and Vince Amoroso; [ed.] 6th Grade-New Albany Elementary, New Albany, PA; [occ.] Student; [memb.] Wyalusing 6th grade Basketball Traveling Team, New Albany Football and Baseball teams; [hon.] Bradford County Library Book Writing Award for Poetry - 1993, 6th Grade Honor Roll, 1996 Towanda Elks Lodge, Hoop Shoot Contest 1st-place, made 22 out of 25 baskets; [oth. writ.] A personal collection Of Christmas Poetry, Poem published in local newspaper (Wyalusing Rocket Courier)-December 1995; [pers.] I enjoy laughing and making others laugh through my poetry. I owe a debt of gratitude to all my teachers and family who encouraged me and to Shel Silverstein who sparked my interest and desire to write.; [a.] New Albany, PA

ANDERSON, J. WALTER
[pen.] Walt Anderson; [b.] September 24, 1919, Aurora, IL; [p.] Henry and Anna Anderson (Deceased); [m.] Hazel Pontious, August 31, 1941; [ch.] Jill, Glenn, Jonis; [ed.] High School: West Aurora High, BA, North Central College, Teacher's Credential from Stanford, IL, M.A., Azusa-Pacific; [occ.] Retired college professor, freelance writer; [memb.] American Golf Writers Assoc., Commissioner on the City of Redlands, CA, Recreation Commission, B.P.D.E., Merit Ridge Counselor, BSA; [hon.] "Who's Who among College Students", Soc., U.S. Olympic Games Committee, Water Polo, Coach/Mgr. USA Swim Team for World Championships of 19973 in Belgrade, Yugoslavia, President National Interscholastic Swim Coaches Assoc., elected and inducted into Fort Lauderdale's International Swimming Hall of Fame, 1992, awarded "Outstanding Contribution to Swimming" by Nat. Assoc. of Interschool Swim Coaches", South Calif. "Athlon" award for "Outstanding Contribution to Swimming"; [oth. writ.] Feature writer and Assoc. Editor of a regional golf magazine, columnist, Swimming World Magazine, columnist (Golf Feature Stories) Redlands Daily Facts, several poems published in a local and a national publications. I have written a series of potential children's story books in rhyme not yet submitted, also a rather long "History of Golf" that I have researched and been working on 3 years. (Not finished yet); [pers.] I try to use humor and nostalgia in my work. Preferring unpredicted rhymes to free verse.; [a.] Redlands, CA

ANDERSON, LINDER DIANNE
[pen.] Detroit, MI; [p.] Mr. and Mrs. Isaiah and Bernadette Woolfolk; [m.] Larry James Anderson, Capt. USAF/Ret; [ch.] Tamika, LaShun, Mariam Katrea, Teesha Meredith; [ed.] Kettering High, Wayne State University BBA; [occ.] Business Owner; [pers.] When you feel insecure, abandoned and betrayed, or when life seams hopeless, don't panic, but remain calm in the face of unexpected changes. Listen to the inner voice that assures you that everything is going to be all right and remember that although you may not always have a choice regarding situations that are presented to you during your lifetime, you do have a choice in the way you wish to react to them.; [a.] College Park, GE

ANDERSON, MARYANN
[b.] January 9, 1951, Passaic, NJ; [p.] Nina and Vince Costa; [m.] Dale Anderson, June 17, 1973; [ch.] Daniel, Dana, Keith, Kyle and Karly; [ed.] MA English, Montclair State University, BA English, Montclair State University; [occ.] Teacher of English; [hon.] Salutatorian High School Class '69, Third Place in Poetry Contest in Ingenue Magazine at the age of 18; [oth. writ.] Two novels in progress.; [pers.] Writing makes possible the sharing of human experiences and feelings without the barrier of time.; [a.] Wayne, NJ

ANDERSON, MATT
[b.] April 8, 1982, Dodgeville, WI; [p.] Steve and Janet Anderson; [ed.] Currently in the 8th grade at Pecatonica High School; [occ.] Helps on the farm doing chores etc.; [memb.] FFA; [hon.] An originally award for a story in 1989 from the school.

ANDERSON, SANDRA
[b.] August 22, 1947, Richwood, WV; [p.] Charles

and Glendine Sears; [m.] Dr. Charles N. Anderson, August 21, 1981; [ch.] Thomas; [ed.] Brentwood High, MCC (Community College); [occ.] Bookkeeper; [memb.] WACO Women's Bowling Assoc., Auxiliary of TVMA; [pers.] I write about my feelings for my family. I thank the Lord for all that I am and all that I can be.; [a.] Lorena, TX

ANDERSON, WILLIAM O.
[b.] December 11, 1942, Brownwood, TX; [p.] William O. Anderson, Sr - Sybol Hedrick; [m.] Verna McClain Anderson, July 8, 1983; [ch.] Scott Anderson, Sean Anderson, Bruce Wayne Rose II; [ed.] Tarrant Country Junior College A.A.S. Degree 1995; [occ.] Free Lance Legal Assistant; [memb.] Associate Member of the International Society of Poets; [hon.] Editor's Choice Award 1995; [oth. writ.] The yellow rose a sea of treasures ISBN 1-56167-274-2; [pers.] The Universe is Based on Balance and Harmony, every thing in its own place at its own time.; [a.] Granbury, TX

ANDREWS, MARILYN B.
[pen.] "Ma"; [b.] March 2, 1934, Pittsfield, MA; [p.] Henry and Louise Flebotte; [m.] Robert Hansen and Jerome Andrews, February 2, 1954, July 26, 1974; [ch.] Mark Hansen and Rebecca Hansen; [ed.] Classical High Springfield, MA, Asnuntuck Community College at home (ret.) Supervision printed Circuit Co. (memb) CT. Soc. Genealogists, Parsons Assoc., Kelsey Kindred Shepherd's Chapel.; [memb.] Several Animal Orgs. Republican, formerly very Active, worked for Thomas Meskill (gov.) Robt. Steele (cong.) invited to Washington DC; [hon.] For 5 days for 1 pt. inauguration president Richard Nixon, Meskill prayer breakfasts, Governor's Ball - etc.; [oth. writ.] Many animal stories, poems written showing GOD's love for all HIS creatures. Written for my 3 grandchildren, but about 5000 people have read them. All other poems are narrations of a bible story. I guess I was influenced by Coleridge.; [pers.] I try to teach the Bible with my stories for young children. Hobbies Genealogy, Rug hooking arts and crafts, History-ancient and American.; [a.] Stafford, CT

ANGEL II, GEORGE THOMAS
[pen.] Tom Angel; [b.] July 29, 1941, Washington, DC; [m.] Katherine M. Angel, August 20, 1983; [ch.] Four; [ed.] 12th

ANGELONE, ELIZABETH C.
[b.] June 27, 1939, Brooklyn, NY; [p.] Margaret and Eric O. Wilson; [m.] Leroy Angelone, August 20, 1955; [ch.] Karen, Rick, Allen, Christopher; [ed.] 2 yrs. College, Quinnipiac College, New Haven, CT, Business Administration; [occ.] Travel Agent and Professional Astrological Counselor and Teacher; [oth. writ.] Many poems, newspaper letters and memoriams printed.; [pers.] Poetically most influenced by Emily Dickinsen and Ella Wheeler Wilcox; my astrological spiritual mentor - Isabel Hickey. My philosophy is simply to express with sensitivity the truth, beauty, and aspirations within us all!; [a.] Wallingford, CT

ANGLETON, CICELY
[b.] April 8, 1922, Duluth, MN; [p.] Aubert and Helen Autremont; [m.] Jawes Angleton, July 17, 1943; [ch.] Three; [ed.] BA Vassar College - Phd. Catholic Univ - Medieval Studies; [occ.] Retired; [hon.] 2nd Place Passager Poetry Contest 1995; [oth. writ.] Poet Lore. Delos. Asha, Hungry as we are (Wash. wretern publishing Cens'n).; [pers.] In writing poetry, dead material comes alive and so do I.; [A.] Arlington, VA

ANTIS, KATHLENE LILLY
[b.] January 25, 1951, Easton, PA; [p.] Homer Lilly - Betty Findley; [m.] Steve J. Antis, August 24, 1992; [ch.] Reed R. and Joseph R. Mangino; [oth. writ.] I have written many poems in as many years this is the first one I have ever sent to anyone.; [pers.] My husband was the inspiration for this poem. I cherish his love. My dad had a God given talent for writing poetry and songs. I believe God has seen fit to bestow the same gift upon me. I thank them both.; [a.] Easton, PA

ANTONELLINI, JUSTIN LUV
[b.] February 5, 1977, Heartford, CT; [p.] Mike L. Antonellini, Jolene Antonellini; [ed.] Manchester High, DeVry Technical Institute; [pers.] I would like to dedicate my poem to my Grandma, Peggy L. Campbell. I would like to thank Eric, Alice, Cordy, and Ted Jones for their help in teaching me how to express myself freely in my writing. And a very special thanks to my parents.; [a.] Richmond, VA

ANUSZEWSKI, CHRISTINA
[b.] November 24, 1974, Wilmington, DE; [p.] Gerald and Melinda Anuszewski; [m.] Single; [ed.] Newark High School - GED; [occ.] Custodian - University of DE., Deli Clerk - Country Maid Deli; [oth. writ.] I only have pomes that I've written and kept to myself.; [pers.] I like to write poems that reflect on my life whether they are the trying moments or the greatest moments that have occurred in my life it also reliques a lot stress when I write.; [a.] Newark, DE

ARBUCKLE, JAMIE L.
[b.] September 1, 1958, West Palm Beach, FL; [p.] Elwood and Nancy Taylor; [m.] Robert Arbuckle, October 31, 1977; [ch.] Son - Taylor James Arbuckle; [ed.] GED 2 years - Lenawee Votech; [occ.] Folder Operator Braun-Brumfield Inc. Book Manufacture; [pers.] I've always loved the writings of Kahlil Gibraw. His writings and poems have help me through life on a personal and spiritual level.; [a.] Dexter, MI

ARGUELLO, CARL J.
[pen.] CJA; [b.] April 22, 1920, Trinidad, CO; [p.] John and Isabel Arguello; [m.] Mary E. Arguello, April 30, 1939; [ch.] Betty, Kathrine, Isabel; [ed.] BA Social Science; [occ.] Retire Postal: Worker; [memb.] Distinguished Member of International Society of Poets; [hon.] Achievement Award from International Society of Poet; [oth. writ.] Various essays and poems; [pers.] I love poetry, it is so symmetrical, it comes from the heart, it is certainly the power of the word.; [a.] San Francisco, CA

ARMSTRONG, STEPHANIE
[b.] January, 8, 1963, Soul Ste. Marie, MI; [p.] James H. Hindmarsh and Sheila Schell; [m.] Carl Armstrong, October 18, 1986; [ch.] Jacob David Armstrong; [ed.] East Hampton High School, New York Crockett High School, Austin, TX.; [occ.] Technical Contractor CDI Corp for IBM; [memb.] Faith Evangelical Free Church, Cub Scouts; [pers.] "Never say never", the older I get, the more I realize how much I'm still learning, and have yet to learn. It's interesting how my opinions on some things have gone full circle over the years.; [a.] Round Rock, TX

ASPARRO, DORRAINE
[b.] January 22, 1950, Long Island, NY; [p.] Edward and Christine Manser; [m.] William Asparro, May 17, 1970; [ch.] Tracy, Adam and Lyndsey; [ed.] Half Hollow Hills High School and Secretarial School; [occ.] Bookkeeper and Office Manager; [memb.] American Legion Auxiliary Local Organizations; [oth. writ.] Poem entitled "Letting Go" published in book "Reflections of life" by EPS publishing Co. "Holiday Inspirations" a collection of holiday poems copyrighted and awaiting publication offer.; [pers.] My poems reflect my life experiences and the life experience of my family. I am fortunate to be a part of a very spiritual and loving family who inspire me every day.; [a.] Babylon, NY

ATHERTON, JOHN
[b.] October 17, 1916, Minneapolis, MN; [ed.] Amherst College BA '36, Univ. Chicago MA '40, PhD. '52; [occ.] Writer; [memb.] Phi Beta Keppa, Delta Upsilon, National Maritime Historical Society; [oth. writ.] Work in Progress: Steel Empire: A History of the Isthmian SteamShip Company.; [a.] Claremont, CA

ATKINS, RUTH
[b.] November 4, 1943, Burnsville, NC; [p.] Ernest Wilson, Evelyn Wyatt Wilson; [m.] Charles Atkins, January 7, 1962; [ch.] Charles Richard, SherryLynn, Kimberly; [ed.] Grad. of East Yancey High School; [occ.] Pastor, wife; [memb.] North Lenoir Church of God; [pers.] I desire that someone's life maybe renewed as they read "Hope".; [a.] Lenoir, NC

AULT, MARLA
[b.] July 14, 1958, Walla Walla, WA; [p.] Jay Glatt, Nancy Glatt (Step); [m.] Dayton Ault, February 27, 1982; [ch.] Allison, Donovan; [ed.] Woodburn High School, Eastern Oiegan State College, Patricia Waalkes Development Workshops; [occ.] Land Developer and partner Tukwila Golf Course Community, Woodburn, OR; [memb.] March of Dimes Birth Defects Foundation Supporter, Lake Oswego Public School System Advocate, Woodburn Tulip Festival Association member, and Boy Scout Troop #129 Co-leader; [pers.] My first published poem symbolizes my belief that one never knows their own true strength until they're forced to pick themself up and start all over again. This philosophy has seen me through my struggle with dyslexia and has led to my accomplishments as a writer.; [a.] Lake Oswego, OR

AUSMUS, STEVE
[b.] April 16, 1971, Pasadena, TX; [p.] Don Ausmus, Jean Sherbenou; [m.] Kim Carver Ausmus, September 15, 1992; [ch.] Levi Kurtus Ausmus; [ed.] Raceland High School, Raceland, Kentucky; [occ.] Inland Mariner; [hon.] National English Merit Award; [a.] Flatwoods, KY

AUSTIN, KENNETH K.
[pen.] Keith Austin; [b.] June 13, 1947, Springfield, MO; [p.] L. L. and June Austin; [m.] Barbara S. Austin, January 18, 1969; [ch.] Angela, Jason, and Amanda; [ed.] B.S. Degree in Civil Engineering; [occ.] Contractor, Heavy Construction; [oth. writ.] A Rose, A Woman, A Wife, (Not published - a poem I wrote for my wife on one of our Anniversaries); [a.] Fayetteville, AR

AVERY, DAN
[pen.] Daniel Dane; [b.] December 10, 1955, Bellflower, CA; [p.] Paul and Alma Avery; [m.] DeLinda Dane, January 26, 1985; [ch.] Sophie (yellow lab); [ed.] American High, College of the Redwoods, Cabrilla College, Ohlone College, Chabot College, Laney College, College of Alameda, California State University Hayward, Life; [occ.] Executive Officer, S.S.S. Sea Fox, Student, Teacher, Arborist, Horticulturist; [memb.] Sea Scouts (BSA), Island Yacth Club; [oth. writ.] Illusive Dreams, True Friends, Viewer Discression Advised, Sailing in Paradise.; [pers.] Children are the most important natural resource on earth, racism is a blight on our planet. Writing is an amazing tool of life, it can sort out feelings, emotions, and priorities. If we all wrote and read more this world would be a better place.; [a.] Alameda, CA

AVERY, DANIELLE
[b.] June 19, 1977, Haverhill, MA; [p.] Brenda and Gary Avery; [ed.] Pentucket High School; [occ.] Retail Sales Associate; [oth. writ.] Many un-pub-

lished, unknown poems.; [pers.] I started writing poetry when a good friend, Beth Brodie, was murdered in 1992. Sadness was my inspiration. The poem' 'My Love' was inspired by happiness and the love of Mark Delle Chiaie.; [a.] Groveland, MA

AXTON, MRS. FLORENCE M. G.
[pen.] Florence G. Axton; [b.] March 6, 1915, Saguache, CO; [p.] Agnes, Gordon Galtheef Deceased; [m.] Y. Tracy Axton Jr. Deceased, January 7, 1939; [ch.] Tracy Axton Jr.; [ed.] Saguache, CA, Elementary School High School Finche College, N.Y.C. Degree Dramatic Arts PhD Kr 2 Evergreen Christian College Evergreen CO; [occ.] Poet - Historian Dance Library Denver CO - Denver University; [memb.] Mother Cabrini Shrine Aux. National Biographical Assn. Flower Denver at Museum Denver Lyric opera Aux. - Central City CO. opera - Nt'l. Kidney Foundation Cystic Fibiosis Assn Woman's Club of Denver; [hon.] 5 Awards American Cancer Soc. English 5 playing honor denver Symphony Guild Award Membership - Randall Moore School Emeritus Education Golden Poets Awards - over seven; [oth. writ.] Denver Press Club poem - Article Clean Water, Cleaniu - Colo Club, Women - Public Relationship Denver Symphony Guild, Gourmet Relapses; [pers.] Those to live a beautiful devoted Christian Life; [a.] Denver, CO

BACHMANN, JOANNE L.
[b.] May 21, 1947, Madison, WI; [p.] Joseph H. and Lois M. Klein; [m.] Divorced, August 24, 1968; [ch.] Two sons, one daughter; [ed.] B.S. Elementary Ed from Univ. of Wisconsin - Madison, MBA from Tulane Univ.; [occ.] Doctoral Program in Anthropology - Tulane Univ.; [a.] New Orleans, LA

BADIANG, REMEDIOS H.
[pen.] Mer Barn; [b.] August 13, 1949, Bayombong NV, Philippines; [p.] Eusebio Badiang, Salvacion Hermosura; [ed.] Saint Mary's College (to Elementary College) Bayombong NV, Philippines, Degree: Bachelor of Arts and Bachelor of Science in Education (English), M.A. Units; [occ.] New Immigrant on Job Hunt, Former English, Literature and Journalism Instructor of M. Marcos State Univ., Philippines; [memb.] 1) M. Marcos State Univ. "Theater on Wheels," 2) Phil. Historical Association, 3) Inter-School Association of Advisers of Campus Writers, 4) Gumil (Association of Ilocano Writers); [hon.] 1) University Demonstrator in English, Resource Speaker for Secondary Schools Journalism; [oth. writ.] 1) Essay writing entries in local Inter-School contests (Phil.), 2) Award-Winning Oratorical Pieces for Inter-School, 3) Short story as entry to international contest, 4) Poems for local Phil. magazine, some 5) Pageants for School programs (Phil).; [pers.] My life experiences and trials, coupled with strong faith, patience, humility, and great love keep me steadfast. To wellmore, I dearly love, life is worth-living. To him this work of art is lovingly dedicated.; [a.] Glendale, AZ

BAGGETT, BARRY
[b.] April 17, 1955, Clarksville, TN; [p.] Steven and Catherine Baggett; [m.] Debbie Baggett, March 20, 1984; [ch.] Jason, Jamie and Jeremy; [ed.] Henry Ford Community College, Dearborn Michigan; [occ.] Operating Engineer, Detroit Newspaper; [memb.] Phi Theta Kappa, Honor Society; [hon.] The National, Dean's List; [a.] Livonia, MI

BAILEY, WALRON V.
[b.] November 16, 1915, Monterey, CA; [p.] Oscar H. and Lois Viola Bailey; [m.] Edna (Balliet) Bailey, October 26, 1948; [ch.] Christine, Geraldine, Mary Ann; [ed.] 8 years otherwise, self-educated; [occ.] Retired; [memb.] Member Veterans QE, Foreign Wars; [oth. writ.] Numerous poems of greater length than accepted by National Library for Publication. None of which have I attempted to have published but have been encouraged to do so; [pers.] Because of the many adversities that I have endured, I find it a great pleasure to make those who surround me smile a little, for I know that a smile can erase even the worst of thoughts even if for just a few memories; [a.] Sacramento, CA

BAINES, CAROL DENHAM
[b.] February 25, 1943, Portland, OR; [p.] Mike and Sylvia Denham; [m.] Paul Baines, November 24, 1967; [ch.] Caroline Baines and Paula de Sanabria; [ed.] Brookings-Harbor High School, University of Oregon; [oth. writ.] have never published my writings, 'til now. Perhaps, like so many others, living and dead, who have enriched my own life, I too should share.; [pers.] With thoughts, understanding is everything. Thoughts are complicated and tangled, like lives. When written down they flow straight and the improbable, yea the impossible, make sense and again expression. Expression gained is the first step to understanding.; [a.] Okanogan, WA

BAIRD, THOMAS
[b.] September 17, 1953, Asheville, NC; [p.] Melvin T. Baird, N Charlene Putnam; [m.] Virginia M. Moore, January 9, 1982; [ch.] Elizabeth A. Baird, Joseph D. Baird; [ed.] North Buncombe High School, Asheville Buncombe Technical Inst., University of Tennessee, Knoxville; [occ.] Structural Drafting, designer; [memb.] International Society of Poets; [hon.] National Library of Poetry semi finalist, 1995 Editors choice award; [oth. writ.] Publications of poetry in book "A Sea of Treasures", a poetry anthology, CR 1995; [pers.] "You only live twice: Once when you are born, and once when your look death in the face. After bassho: Japanese poet, 1643094.; [a.] West Columbia, SC

BAITY, KRISTIE F.
[b.] May 14, 1971, Klinston-Salem, NC; [p.] Hoke and Linda Flynt; [m.] Travis E. Baity, September 18, 1993; [ch.] One on the way!; [ed.] B.S. Degree in Criminal Justice from East Carolina University, Greenville, NC; [occ.] Police Officer - Gaston County Police Department; [memb.] Pleasant View Baptist Church; [hon.] Received the Lt. Aaron Tise Colleague Award - Winston - Salem Police Department (12/93); [oth. writ.] I have written several poems for family and friends to enjoy. None of my poems have ever been published.; [pers.] Always put your faith in God and know if one door closes another will open.; [a.] Gastonia, NC

BAKAR, ABU
[pen.] Abu; [b.] August 14, 1959, Dhaka, Bangladesh; [p.] Khaled Bauksh and Sona Miah, Shaila Begum-Hanufa Begum; [m.] Sahida Akhter-Ruma, July 20, 1989; [ed.] Gandaria High School, Hill's Little Flower School, S.S. College, Central Law College, Dhaka, A Grimsby College and Dhaka and Hull University Graduation Master, Doctoral Research; [occ.] Nutritionist; [memb.] Member of various social organization, in Bangladesh, member of school committee, member of college organizing bodies; [oth. writ.] Poetry books published in Bangladesh. Several poems and other articles published in Bangladesh, Calcutta and London newspapers and magazines; [pers.] Materialistic and romantic poets and writers of late 19th, Beginning and mid of 20th century nurtured my thoughts. Their works inspired me favorably to paint the sufferings of peoples. Statement and struggle joy and judgment love and life live and let live is the philosophical notation in my life. Always I try to reflect the dialectical aspects and ethics of life, struggle and love in my writings.; [a.] Buena Park, CA

BAKER, ELIZABETH ANN
[b.] February 3, 1981, Grand Junction, CO; [p.] Kenneth and Theresa Baker; [ed.] I have been homeschooled since 1st grade. I am now in mu freshman year of highschool, during an extended homeschool program called Deep River High School; [occ.] I am employed at the Grand Junction Gymnastics Academy as an Assistant Secretary; [memb.] Mesa County Public Library; [hon.] I have received swimming, Gymnastics, Golf, Taekwondo, Ballet, and School Awards, Certificates, Medals, Ribbons, and Trophies; [oth. writ.] A Sunday afternoon (a poem), Israel's Descendants (a poem), Happy Anniversary (a poem).; [pers.] If my writing makes someone think, I will be content. If I makes them smile, I will be happy. If I makes them laugh, I will be thrilled.; [a.] Grand Junction, CO

BAKER, GLORIA
[b.] May 26, 1957, Torrence, CA; [ch.] Caren and Melisa; [occ.] Homemaker; [oth. writ.] I do other poems about people in my life. Parents, children, friends, grandparents/which they all get copies.; [pers.] I have found that through my writing I am able to express myself in a very personal way.; [a.] Shingle Springs, CA

BAKER, RENZA MOSCATELLI
[b.] July 19, 1929, Ancona, Italy; [p.] Decio Moscatelli, Vittoria Moscatelli; [m.] Harvey B. Baker, March 11, 1967; [ed.] Teacher Collegio D. Agostino Roscelli Genova, Italy, University of Texas, Austin Austin, Texas; [occ.] Lecturer on Early Childhood, Education, Artist (Painter); [memb.] American Montessori Society (Teachers) Windcrest Art League (Member and past president); [oth. writ.] More poems, Two unpublished books; [pers.] Helping children in the awareness of nature and mankind and teaching respect and concern for both.; [a.] San Antonio, TX

BAKER, SANDRA
[b.] October 18, 1938, Abington, PA; [p.] Maiden Metz; [m.] William H. Baker, July 7, 1956; [ch.] Sheryl, Steven, Scott, Suzanne; [ed.] Graduate of North Penn High School, Lansdale, PA; [occ.] Homemaker/Retired Switchboard Receptionist; [oth. writ.] A few poems of personal reflections; [pers.] During the time my husband was considering retirement, I was inspired to write this poem.; [a.] Telford, PA

BAKER SR., JAMES F.
[pen.] James F. Baker Sr.; [b.] February 11, 1951, Hempstead, NY; [p.] Bernard and Winafred Baker; [m.] Shirley M. Baker, May 9, 1971; [ch.] James F. Baker Jr., Jill Anne Marie Baker; [ed.] Commack High School, Commack L.I., N.Y., Suffolk Community College, Selden, LI, NY; [occ.] Field Agent for the Knights of Columbus; [memb.] Knights of Columbus; [hon.] Past Grand Knight, former District Deputy of Calf., Field Agent; [oth. writ.] Alone; [pers.] This poem was written for the sole purpose of expressing my love to my wife Shirley. She means everything to me. I love her, for all Luv's worth!; [a.] West Covina, CA

BALAREZO, OSCAR FUXA
[b.] February 23, 1932, Peru; [p.] Antero Balarezo, L. Grocida Fuxa; [m.] Kolene Uhre Balarezo, April 24, 1977; [ch.] Ronald Robert Donald, Dennis and Katherine; [ed.] Graduated from L.A. Valley College plus 12 units, Nebraska University 24 units, Northridge University 3 units; [occ.] Waiter at Musso Frank Grill Hollywood; [memb.] Republican Party Santa Anita Enter, Stock Holder; [oth. writ.] Wrote 25-30 Poems.; [pers.] I write and recite poetry English, Spanish since I was 12 years old.; [a.] North Hollywood, CA

BALATBAT, JOSEPH HERRERA
[pen.] Centrum 63.16.1.; [b.] January 16, 1963,

Manila, Philippines; [p.] Enriqueta Balatbat, Zacarias Balatbat; [ed.] Doctor of Medicine, University of Santo Thomas, Manila, Philippines; [occ.] Physician; [hon.] Gamma Beta Epsilon, Dean's List 'Cum Laude'; [oth. writ.] Former Associate Science and Literary Editor for the Purple GAzette College Journal; [pers.] In my writing, I am inspired from individuals who have strangely embraced life's wrenching pain, who molded the course affirmatively and who have risen to enjoy the richness of life regardless what society propagated as acceptable behavior; [a.] New York City, NY

BALDWIN, LEANN LORRAINE
[pen.] Leann L. Baldwin; [b.] February 28, 1971, Lynn, MA; [p.] Mr. & Mrs. Robert W. Baldwin; [ch.] Joel R. Baldwin; [ed.] Beverly High School, Plymouth State College; [occ.] Lamson Library, Penodicals Office; [memb.] The Association of Non-Traditional Students (94-95); [hon.] President's List (94-95) National Dean's List (1994) Academic Scholarship (1994); [oth. writ.] The Continuum (The Magazine of PSC), Voices from the Center (PSC Woman's Center Anthology), The Different Drummer (ANTS Newsletter); [pers.] My writing has been greatly influenced by my son and his curiosity of the world around him. I awe my current success to the hopes and dreams I hold for his future.; [a.] Laconia, NH

BALDWIN, PENNY KAY
[pen.] PK Baldwin; [b.] April 2, 1965, Towanda, PA; [p.] Jack I., and Ethel C. Rifenberg; [m.] Ronald B. Baldwin, April 27, 1984; [ch.] Amanda Sue and Katie Marie; [ed.] Northeast Bradford High, and Keystone College; [occ.] Teacher Aide, BOCES-Alternative Learning Center; [memb.] Paraprofessional Union, PTA, Foster Parents of PA.; [hon.] Honor Society and Dean's List.; [oth. writ.] Poems: Rag Doll 1985, Sleeping in Gods Hands 1989, in books of collection of poetry.; [pers.] It is my belief that ideas, words, and writing are the most important elements of life. They can make peace as well as war, and they will out live in all.; [a.] Warren Center, PA

BALE, CRYSTAL NICOLE
[b.] January 19, 1979, Caldwell, ID; [p.] C. Duane Bale, M. Elaine Bale; [ed.] Junior in Homedale High School; [memb.] Business Professionals of America; [hon.] All-American Scholar, Who's Who Among American High School Student; [pers.] The lives of friends and family are two of the most important things in my life and I try to express that through my writing.; [a.] Wilder, ID

BALLARD, RUBY N. HARRISON
[b.] November 20, 1935, Franklinton, LA; [p.] Alex and Lenora Harrison; [m.] James M. Ballard Sr., February 22, 1959; [ch.] James Jr., Portia, Kevin, and Deidra; [ed.] Washington Parish High, Southern University, and Southeastern Louisiana University; [occ.] Retired Elementary School Teacher; [memb.] Sweet Home Church of Chris (Hol.), Alpha Kappa Sorority, N.E.A., Washington Parish Retired Teachers, Louisiana Retired Teachers, Riverside Pink Ladies Auxiliary, Southeast Spouse Abuse Program, Churches Help Center etc.; [hon.] Church's District and Diocese Youth Group Leader for 1995; [oth. writ.] None published; [pers.] I have always harbored a deep love for writing poetry, but have written very little. I have written jingles that I set to music to help my students learn various math skills. Tried to help my students "see" the poetry in things around them.; [a.] Franklinton, LA

BALLETTO, CHRISTINE E.
[b.] July 15, 1964, Haverhill, MA; [p.] Edward and Eleanor Balletto; [ed.] Georgetown Jr. Sr. High and New England Hair Academy; [occ.] Eastpak - Customer Service Rep.; [pers.] Thanks for good friends and family who had faith in my work. Thank God for the talent brought forth to me. To rich my inspiration for this poem.; [a.] Haverhill, MA

BALMAN, GAIL E.
[b.] July 8, 1923, Rozel, KS; [p.] Fred Balman Christina Riedl Balman; [m.] Nan Poston Balman, January 14, 1951; [ch.] Steven Kent Balman; [ed.] B.A. Wichita State University, M.A. Wichita State University, Emeritus Central State University; [occ.] Retired Pol. Sc. and History; [oth. writ.] Articles and book revues in Professional Journals; [a.] Edmond, OK

BALOCATING, SAMUEL G.
[b.] August 5, 1965, Manila, Philippines; [p.] Alfred C. Balocating, Alicia G. Balocating; [ed.] A.S. Degree (Skyline College), Western Career College (Pharmacy Tech.); [occ.] Pharmacy Technician; [memb.] California Pharmacists Association; [hon.] Army Achievement Medal, Air Force Good Conduct Medal; [pers.] I am greatly influenced by God and parents. Everything I do, say, write, think, feel is based on their kindness and gifts. To the Almighty Jesus, and mom and dad — thanks and love.; [a.] San Francisco, CA

BANKS, ALEIA NICHOLE
[b.] November 2, 1980, Bronx, NY; [p.] Margaret Banks and Timothy Banks; [ed.] The King's Academy (private school); [occ.] Student; [pers.] I have been greatly influenced by my mother's love of reading and poetry.; [a.] Mount Vernon, NY

BARBARY, GEORGE
[b.] December 4, 1922, Havre de Grace, MD; [m.] Euma Wilbert Barbary, June 8, 1946; [ed.] Susquehanna Township High, Harrisburg, PA Dickinson College, Carlisle, PA - B.A. Columbia University, New York City, M.A. University of Denver College of Law, Denver, CO J.D. cum laude, University of Denver M.A., Stanford University, Ph.D. Graduate Special Philosophy Work, Thru Residence, Orals and Thesis Rewrite; [occ.] Attorny at Law - Admitted to U.S. Supreme Court, Supreme Courts of Texas, Tennessee, Colorado, U.S. Court of Appeals for Third, Fifth and Sixth Circuits; [memb.] Texas Bar Assn, College of State Bar of Texas, American Bar Assn, Federal Bar Assn, National Assn of Scholars, Southern Society for Philosophy and Psychology, American Society for 18th Century Studies, U.S. Marine Corps League, First Marine Division Assn.; [hon.] Omicron Delta Kappa, J.D. cum laude, University of Denver College of Law; [oth. writ.] Professional Treatises: "Constitutional 'Freedom To...' Or Sociological 'Freedom From..?" Wash. Legal Found. (1993) "Constitutional Principals and the Bork Hearing," Prepared for U.s. Senate Use (1987), "Immigration Law Concern for Business and Corporation Lawyers", Texas Bar Journal (1983), "The Structure of Pure Law," Private Publication (1979), "Resolution: Definition of Death", American Bar Association House of Delegates (1975), "Psychoanalysis and the Law—Universal Triadism", Memphis State Law Review (1973), "Journal Issue: Tennessee and Federal Rules of Produre", Memphis State Law Review (1973), "Social Ideals in Anti-Trust Law," Dicta, University of Denver Law Review (1953), "Colorado Prefers Vesting — Future Interest," Dicta, University of Denver Law Review (1951); [pers.] The poem, "Bride," here published by the National Library of Poetry, was one of a dozen poems written while Euma and George Barbary were spending a summer in the Colorado Rockies.; [a.] Dallas, TX

BARBOULETOS, JOHN T.
[b.] August 19, 1982, Salt Lake City, UT; [p.] Paul and Marjorie Barbouletos; [ed.] 7th grader at Finn Hill Jr. High; [occ.] Student; [memb.] Speech and Debate club, Washington Teen Institute; [hon.] Hope of America award, Honorable mention for Reflections 1988; [oth. writ.] None published; [pers.] I have an older brother named James and a younger brother named Stephen. I am a Christian and I believe God has given me a great talent and love for poetry. I have always enjoyed reading and writing poems. I sincerely hope others enjoy reading and learning from my poetry.; [a.] Kirkland Seattle, WA

BARBOUR, ISABELLE
[pen.] Susan Bates; [b.] May 20, 1954, Marion, IN; [p.] Roy and Patty Sidebottom; [m.] Duane Barbour, February 9, 1991; [ch.] John Bates, Shannon Graen; [ed.] Pima College, Tucson, AZ, Social Work, Boise St. V. Boise, ID, Social Work, Ark State U. Beebe, AR, Grad, Eng. Studies; [occ.] Substitute Teacher, Little Rock School District, Freelance Writer; [memb.] Volunteer In Public Schools (VIPS) Arkansas Screen Writer's Association; [hon.] Nominated - Jane Mendel Award for Volunteer In Public Schools, Little rock, for outstanding Volunteer Service to the Little Rock Central High School Band 1990-93.; [oth. writ.] Columns, News, Features, Essays, Various Local Newspapers, Tucson Lifestyle Magazine, Tucson, AZ, 1994, also Local Photography.; [a.] Little Rock, AR

BARDIN, JODY
[pen.] Jay Vardin; [b.] November 2, 1960, Houston, TX; [p.] Helen C. Bardin, J. N. Bardin; [m.] Alison Bardin, December 27, 1987; [a.] Dallas, TX

BARHAM, DONNA BRUCKSE
[b.] March 24, 1938, Portsmouth, VA; [ch.] Donna Bruckse Barham; [memb.] A Poetic Offering; [pers.] Made her poetry debut with the poet's domain, vol. 12, 10195. She lives in Glen Allen, VA, where she is currently working on a collection of Children's Stories/Poetry and a second work titled Intimate and Heartfelt, a poetic offering.; [a.] Glen Allen, VA

BARKER, TONY
[b.] February 14, 1962, Biloxi, MS; [p.] John and Gail Barker; [m.] Lisa Barker, February 1, 1982; [ed.] High School, Extensive Travel, Hard Knock University (honor grad.); [occ.] Radio Station KYYD, Operations Manager; [oth. writ.] Many, many songs, which I perform live.; [pers.] In the entertainment business, there must be a balance between "Entertainment" and "Business". I seek that balance while striving for excellence in both. (Also available for parties and weddings...); [a.] Abilene, TX

BARNES, MARSHA M.
[b.] March 8, 1953, Alton, IL; [p.] Frank and Rosalie Brice; [m.] Gary L. Barnes, February 14, 1982; [ch.] Erika Lynn and Lara Renee; [ed.] Palomar College, Free Enterprise Institute; [occ.] Homemaker; [memb.] Vista Junior Women's Club; [oth. writ.] Unpublished short story; [pers.] Our mission here is to create peace and love within ourselves and then we can't help but spread it to others.; [a.] Vista, CA

BARNETT II, JOHN WAYNE
[b.] November 30, 1972, Ruston, LA; [p.] John Barnett and Gail Barnett; [m.] Kristie Michelle, May 25, 1996; [ed.] Caldwell Parish High School, Northwest Louisiana University, Mississippi State University; [occ.] Research Associate LSU Agricultural Center; [memb.] McGuire United Methodist Church, LA Farm Bureau; [pers.] The only true darkness is our own closed eyes; [a.] Saint Joseph, LA

BARR, KATHY VERNA
[pen.] "Moon-Maker"; [b.] June 5, 1957, Frederick, MD; [p.] Atlee and Pauline Sanbower; [ch.] Jason 19, Emmilyn 16, Jonathan 8 year; [ed.] High School Diploma Loudoun Valley, Purcellville Virginia; [occ.] Kathy's Keepsakes Sole Proprietor and

Manager; [memb.] New Jerusalem Lutheran Church - Lovettsville VA, Eagles Aux- Brunswick, MA, Lovettsville Elementary PTO; [hon.] 1990 Volunteer of the Year, Army Community. Robinson Barracks, Germany 1992-Army Dedication and Support Award; [oth. writ.] Personal journal, love sonnets for friend's weddings, dedications to inspire love ones. Shorts story, and other numerous poetry; [pers.] I write to reveal warmth in people's spirit and goodness in their hearts, So that they may find love and peace from within their soul. Just to live and find happiness in life!; [a.] Lovettsville, VA

BARRETT, SHAWN
[b.] March 28, 1979, Dallas, TX; [p.] Bill Boor, Kaye Boor; [ed.] Currently Attending Sterling High School; [hon.] All League Defensive back - 1994, All League Honorable Mention, Running Back - 1995; [a.] Sterling, KS

BARRON, EREK LAWRENCE
[b.] February 20, 1974, Washington, DC; [p.] Melody B. Barron-Carson and Bradford L. Carson; [ed.] Episcopal High School, Alexandria, VA, University of Maryland, College Park, MD; [occ.] Full-time student majoring in English Language and Literature; [memb.] Thurgood Marshall Pre-Law Society, The CARing Program (Children At Risk); [oth. writ.] Part-time writer/editor for school newspaper - "The Eclipse"; [pers.] Interested in reading and writing works which best interrogate the human mind and shed light upon the human experience.; [a.] Silver Spring, MD

BARTHLEIN, SANDRA M.
[b.] October 25, 1946, Norfolk, VA; [p.] George William (Deceased) and Mary Frances Murden; [m.] Jimmy Dan Barthlein, October 14, 1978; [ed.] Princess Anne; [occ.] Retired Executive Secretary for Federal Gov't.; [memb.] National Piano Guild - American Diabetes Assn. - Norfolk Savoyards, Ltd. - Hospital Volunteer Committee - Norfolk Theater Productions - National Modeling Academy, Sweet Adalines.; [hon.] Beta Sigma Phi, VA., Volunteer's Award Committee, over 2,000 hours, Plank Owner, U.SS. Mississippi; [oth. writ.] Poetry and short stories featured in various newspapers, magazines and periodicals. Reporter for local Gov't., and Civilian, newspapers, including fashion columns, ect.; [pers.] My love and appreciation for the fine arts has been inspired by praise from my family and friends which has greatly influenced my writings.; [a.] Norfolk, VA

BARTHOLOMEW, JESSICA LYNN
[b.] April 16, 1983, Grand View Hospital, Perkasie, PA; [p.] Dawn and Steven Bartholomew; [ed.] Emma Havens Young School, Pleasant Valley Middle School, Homeschool; [occ.] Homeschooler; [memb.] New Covenant World Outreach Church, Youth Group, Previous member of girl scouts of America; [hon.] Successful completion of fifth grade, Baptism, Promoted to 3rd grade class at church, Completion of Here's looking at you, 2000, Outstanding homework, completion D.A.R.E. Program, honor roll, membership of New Covenant World Outreach Church; [pers.] Let the wise listen and add to their understanding (learning), and let the discerning get guidance. The fear of the Lord is the beginning of knowledge, but fools despise wisdom don't discipline.; [a.] Saylorsburg, PA

BARTHOLOMEW, KENDRA
[b.] November 16, 1980, Perkasie, PA; [p.] Dawn and Steven Bartholomew; [ed.] Pennsylvania homeschooler, Pleasant Valley School District.; [occ.] Student of Pennsylvania; [memb.] New Covenant World Outreach, Youth Group, Former Flutist and Girl Scout, Siberian Tiger Sponsor; [hon.] PATIT reading and Development Program, Principal Honor Roll, outstanding performance in Physical Education, successful completion of 5th grade, 8th grade Honor Roll.; [oth. writ.] Why get involved (not published) nothing ever published before.; [pers.] Walk in the way of understanding. A generous man will prosper, he who refreshes others will himself be refreshed.; [a.] Saylorsburg, PA

BASCKO, SHIRLEY ANN
[b.] August 24, 1946, Augusta, AR; [p.] Monteen McCurdy, Roy Elvin Murray; [m.] Richard Bascko (Deceased), September 28, 1973; [ch.] Regina I. Bascko, Kenneth Ray Bascko; [ed.] Searcy High School, Lasalle University, Chicago, Illinois, Artex University, Beverly Enterprises; [occ.] Central Supply and Ancillary Clerk Beverly Health and Rehabilitation Services, Inc. Seacry, Arkansas; [memb.] Jesus Name Church Paterson, Arkansas; [hon.] Arkansas Children's Hospital, Leisure Lodge Nursing Center of Searcy; [oth. writ.] Magical Moments Do Right 93 and Share the Spirit in '94, was written for Beverly Enterprises 24 Karat Customer Service Program; [pers.] I strive to reflect true enter feelings of love and understanding of life and God's people. I have been totally influenced by my life experiences, family, and friends who surround me. I enjoy reading poems of all kinds; [a.] Searcy, AR

BASH, JAMES C.
[pen.] Jim; [b.] September 18, 1947, Indiana, PA; [p.] Clarence and Evelyn Bash; [m.] Margaret Peggy Bash, June 3, 1967; [ch.] Melissa, Rebekah, Timothy, Suzanne; [ed.] Ligonier Valley Senior High School Full Gospel Assemblies Int. Ministerial College, Don Steward Evangelistic Association; [occ.] Truck Driver/Pastor; [hon.] Safe Driver Awards for 7 years; [pers.] I desire above all else to do God's will for my life. To reach out to those who have been hurt and cast aside.; [a.] Ligonier, PA

BASHIR, KAMAL
[b.] July, 1960, Omdurman-Sudan; [p.] Lila Hamed and Bashir El Ajab Bashir; [m.] Lisa Bashir; [ch.] Mahadi and Mohammed Bashir and Step-son Marcus Stapelton; [occ.] Owner of Small Business "Artistic Innerscapes"; [a.] Omaha, NE

BASS, MONA LISA
[b.] November 23, Birmingham, AL; [p.] Richard and Annie Graham; [m.] James A. Bass, May 4, 1976; [ch.] Tracey Melissa Bass and Casey Diana Bass; [ed.] Brighton High School, Alabama State University major - Art, minor - English; [memb.] Montgomery Art Guild; [hon.] Editor's Choice Award, presented by: The National Library of Poetry; [pers.] Now is the time to create good memories that in time will bring smiles to the faces of those we leave behind.; [a.] Montgomery, AL

BAUMANN, JUANITA
[b.] July 6, 1957, Batesville, AR; [p.] Tommie and Wando Smith (Deceased); [m.] Larry Baumann, September 12, 1981; [ed.] 12th Poughkeepsie High School and Central Votech in Wichita; [occ.] Home Maker; [oth. writ.] One published in church paper, To God Be The Glory. Those Not Published The Persian Gulf War, God Has A Plan, Home Is Where The Heart Is, She Sleeps Now, A Mother's Love, Hears Of Gold Without You Lord, That's My Dad and more.; [pers.] My poems reflect how I feel about, God, family and friends. I sent copies of "The Persian Gulf War" and "Hearts of Gold" to our troops in Saudi.; [a.] Wichita, KS

BAUMLE, LAURIE JO
[b.] February 10, 1957, Evanston, IL.; [p.] Joe Mallman and JoAnn Motch; [m.] Douglas Baumle, October 24, 1987; [ch.] Katie, Alexandra, Natalie; [ed.] High School Grad. Glenbrook North; [occ.] Homemaker; [memb.] New Apostolic Church; [pers.] When your spirit is low, listen to the cry from within. It will bring you up...to the heights preserved there in.; [a.] Broomfield, CO

BAXTER, MICHELLE
[b.] December 13, 1973, Michigan City, IN; [p.] Robin and Timothy Covert; [m.] Michael Baxter, June 25, 1994; [ch.] Victoria and Twins on way; [ed.] River Valley High School; [occ.] Housewife; [hon.] Presidential Award, American Legion Award; [oth. writ.] I have a collection of poems that are as yet unpublished.; [pers.] My poems were written to inspire teenagers. They were all written during a very trying time in my life. I hope to one day publish them so that others may benefit them.; [a.] Shoreline, WA

BEABEY, JIM
[pen.] J. B.; [pers.] Born years ago, lived and died many times, still hope, still dream, looking forward to the end. There are some few days left, but I will a summer make of them and spend them wisely on hopes, dreams and deep skies of billowing clouds.

BEAL, ANTHONY
[b.] September 6, 1974, Bronx, NY; [p.] John H. Beal Jr., Bettie Cofield Beal; [ed.] Cardinal Spellman High School, Mandl School of Allied Health; [occ.] Medical Secretary Montefiore Medical Center, NY; [hon.] National Library of Poetry Editor's Choice Award 1995; [pers.] Although the love and gratitude that fill me transcend human abilities of expression, it is my hope that through my poetry, they are at least partially communicated to both the woman I love, and to God for allowing me to sign my name to the gift He's given me.; [a.] Bronx, NY

BEARD, CONNIE
[pen.] Inga; [b.] March 23, 1979, Cottage Grove, OR; [p.] Russ and Judy Beard; [m.] Cliff Price (Boyfriend); [ed.] Home schooled through "American School"; [memb.] Several horse associations: AQHYA, ABRA, PSBHC, WSH, KSC.; [hon.] Grand Champion Horse rider. Honor student.; [pers.] I wrote this poem for my wonderful boyfriend, Cliff. I enjoy reading, and riding and showing my buckskin more.; [a.] Olalla, WA

BEASLEY, MARCINA PLEASHETTE
[pen.] Pleashette; [b.] June 13, 1977, East Orange, NJ; [p.] Wanda K. Beasley, Michael, Beasley; [ed.] Arts High School. 1 majored in drama for three years attending arts.; [occ.] I am working at "Food Of Our On Design" Decorate and Box Cakes; [memb.] Emmanuel Church of Christ (P.A.W), Pentacostal Apostolic Assemble of the World Pastor Suff. Bishop James D. Churchwell Sr.; [hon.] Awards along with mental are birth from track. Love to run! I ran track in elementary school on to high school. Other wards came from my performance in drama and being honored as a good student; [oth. writ.] (Spiritual poetry - "Example", "Watch Out") (Encouraging - "Can You See the Beauty", "Genuine Men") (Childhood - "Laura Victoria Mcay", "Gossip") (African -"Garden of African", "Heroes") and my more.; [pers.] Who is willing to carry in their womb success? Me, I am willing! I am determine! and with this mentality I am in delivery everyday; [a.] Newark, NJ

BEAUCHESNE, JILL MARIE
[b.] November 11, 1978, Virginia; [p.] John and Jeannie Beauchesne; [ed.] Broad Run High School, Ashburn Virginia will graduate in June 1996 will attend University of Virginia in fall 1996; [hon.] H.S. Literacy magazine editor-in-chief, National Merit Commended student; [oth. writ.] Several poems published in school literacy magazine; [pers.] If I did not have an outlet through which to create I think I would shrivel. "Rage, rage, against the

lying of the light." - Dylan Thomas; [a.] Sterling, VA

BEDDOE, DOROTHY CAROL
[pen.] Dorothy Beddoe; [b.] February 19, 1926, Sunnyvale, CA; [p.] Maude Allison - Raymond Andrade; [m.] Div.; [ch.] (5) Gary, Robert, Kathy, Allyson, Richard; [ed.] High School, (Brevard Comm. Col,) Nursing Asst. Certificate (Grad. with 40 Aver); [occ.] Retired; [hon.] Several letters published in today newspaper artist (als) received best of show award 1990 (Harris Semi Conductors Art Festival) Palm Bay FL.; [oth. writ.] I manuscripts unpublished (novels) for youth readers; [pers.] I love writing, and just day to day living has so many moments that inspire me I am ashamed to say, that I do not take the time to put what I feel on paper but I am changing my lifestyle and will in the future be more productive.; [a.] Palm Bay, FL

BEDOLLA, PHIL
[b.] April 26, 1942, Willcox, AZ; [p.] Marcos Bedolla, Librada Bedolla; [m.] Tova Bedolla, August 17; [ch.] Lance, Aaron; [ed.] BA Spanish - English Ariz. State University, MA Counseling ASU; [occ.] Writer; [memb.] United Methodist Church, AEA, NEA; [oth. writ.] Several poems published in magazines and in treasured poems of America; [pers.] I like to have readers speculate about their feelings in different situations and current issues. I enjoy Emily Dickinson and Robert Frost; [a.] Sierra Vista, AZ

BEHRENDT, BETTY J.
[b.] November 26, 1961, Carlisle, PA; [p.] John H. - Emmie M. Foose; [m.] Charles W. Behrendt; [ch.] April L. Foose - Leann Behrendt; [occ.] ADW-Warehouse; [pers.] Attitudes are essential for our physical and mental well being. Learning to cope with our emotions will enable us to take the appropriate action, need to solve our problems. Focus on the positive attributes in your life. Success will be your reward.; [a.] New Bloomfield, PA

BELCHER, HANNAH
[pen.] Ann Elect Chance; [b.] July 9, 1960, Guyana, South America; [p.] Rudolph and Lettie Chance; [m.] Eric A. Belcher, November 28, 1982; [ch.] Four boys and one girl; [ed.] Forest Park High, Baltimore International Culinary Arts Institute, Advanced Career Training; [occ.] Secretary for Back to Basic, Medical Transcription Program; [memb.] Elect Ladies of God, Trailblazers, The Smith; [hon.] The Highest GPA for A.C.T., Graduated with Honor from Baltimore Culinary Arts Inst. Honor Award Parents Assisting Teachers Program - James McHenry Elem. School.; [oth. writ.] Songs, Poems, Taughts children (Stories) books not published as yet.; [pers.] "She openeth her mouth with wisdom: And in her tongue is the law of kindness." Proverbs 31:26 I am greatly influenced by my sister Esther Chance.; [a.] Baltimore, MD

BELL, RANDY
[b.] July 30, 1956, Cherokee County; [p.] Matril Bell, Joe Dean Bell; [m.] Divorced; [ch.] Katie Marie Bell; [ed.] Blacksburg High School; [occ.] Operator at Timken, Roller Bearings, SC; [hon.] "I Dare You Award" for qualities of leadership (Senior Year); [oth. writ.] Safety and Quality Slogans at (Timken) work and poems in local newspaper and co-wrote a gospel song at age 15.; [pers.] As a divorced father, I have been blessed with an adorable daughter to raise. My poem is dedicated to her with love.; [a.] Blacksburg, SC

BELLAVIA, ROXANA
[pen.] Rocky Bee; [b.] May 7, 1967, Irving, NY; [p.] Samuel C. Bellavia II, Patricia Bellavia; [ed.] Graduate of Lake Shore Central High School and Willis Carrier Center of "Horsecare".; [occ.] Bush Industries (Boring Operator); [memb.] Alabama Fan Club; [hon.] I have hundreds of song/poems but none that I have ever shown to anyone but close friends and family.; [pers.] Life is a challenge and when I have reached a certain challenge I always move one and look for another. (The game of billiards is a great challenge for me cause there's always another cool shot to make.)

BELLEMARE, KENNETH R.
[b.] August 11, 1933, Hartford, CT; [p.] Mary McCarthy, Arthur O. Bellemare; [m.] Barbara J. Perron Bellemare, May 16, 1965; [ch.] Patrick Sean, Shannon Dean, Cherise Marie; [ed.] Graduate Glewdale College, Cal State Northridge; [occ.] Retired; [oth. writ.] Numerous poems and short stories. I am currently collecting them in a personal Anthology for possible future publication.; [pers.] A man's life is not measured by the fortune he has amassed, but by the smiles on the faces of those he left behind.; [a.] Palmdale, CA

BELTON, SHARAE
[pen.] Sharae; [b.] October 24, 1980, Yonkers, NY; [p.] Arnold and Quinetta Belton; [ed.] Saunders H.S. in Yonkers NY studies Architecture; [memb.] Secretary of Mt. Carmel Youth Church, Corresponding Secretary of Mt. Carmel Jr. Usher Board, Member of the African-American Club in Saunders H.S.; [hon.] Won the Mt. Carmel, Mt. Luther King award for writing; [oth. writ.] That Night, Brokenhearted, Disappearance, My Forever Friend, Respect, The Crush, A Lost Love, Afraid of Falling in Love, A Shattered Reality, and the Summer that Changed Our Lives; [pers.] Put and keep God or whomever your superior being is first. Remember your family and your true friends will always be there. Everyone has a purpose in life and I hope mine is to keep everyone happy when they read my works.; [a.] Yonkers, NY

BELUE, CAROL
[p.] Mr. and Mrs. Belue - Fred and Ezelle Belue; [occ.] Clerical/Data Entry January In my writing my aim or desire is to glorify the Lord and to describe his unconditional love.; [a.] Muscle Shoals, AL

BENECKE, MARY ELIZABETH
[pen.] Mary Elizabeth Benecke; [b.] October 16, 1934, Omaha, NE; [p.] Walter and Frances Merriam Benecke; [ed.] MS in Pathology Sciences; [occ.] Retired Medical Technologist; [memb.] Toastmasters Club Omaha; [hon.] Honorable Mention Atlantic Monthly Poetry Contest for High Schoolers; [oth. writ.] Two novels, several short stories and poems not yet published; [pers.] All my writings have the pavement of God in them, are serious with humor, are uplifting, as in poems are happy endings as in stories my last half of life spent writing; [a.] Omaha, NE

BENGARD, RYAN PATRICK
[b.] November 18, 1978, Los Angeles, CA; [p.] Tom and Kim; [ed.] Self taught (school of hard knocks); [occ.] Student (High School); [memb.] Many Psychiatrist's Institutions, Gyms, Piano Concert Making Cists, Boxing, Clubs, Pharmisists, no Gangs... (Dead -End Lifestyle), Football, Guitar; [hon.] Football Sportsmanship Award. Future's High School 1995 Poetry Award. Defensive Player of the Season Football Award 1994. Most Aggressive, 1st Place 40 Yard Sprint, 1st 50 Yard Sprint 1st 100 Yard Sprint. Squat Record for my Weight 450 lbs, Squat 300 lbs Bench; [oth. writ.] numerous poems: "The Call," "Before the Demos Start," "Shattered Soul"... shorter fiction stories song lyrics, and research on schizophrenia, and other mysterious mental illnesses.; [pers.] "End Racism," "Don't Mess With What You Don't Understand," "Use Your Anger for a Just Cause," "Never Surrender or Submit," "Stand by Your Morals." "Never Take on the Role of a Victim"; Man is not a victim of circumstances, environment; make your own decisions.; [a.] Laguna Hills, CA

BENNETT, CHELA
[pen.] Chela A. Bennett; [b.] April 4, 1970, Beverly Glen; [p.] Sharon and Craig Bennett; [m.] Joseph Lucero, March 1, 1995; [ed.] College creative writing, Creative writing from mind to manuscript journalism.; [occ.] Labler, Crafts with style; [hon.] Work bonuses at Christmas at Earth Island; [oth. writ.] Letters, bills other poems, short stories; [pers.] Poetry helps me free my anger, without poetry I would not be so happy.; [a.] Woodland Hills, CA

BENNETT, RENEE GORHAM
[b.] May 3, 1947, Rocky Mount, NC; [p.] Bill and Mittie Gorham; [m.] Bert Bennett, December 25, 1988; [ch.] Tiffany Huddleston and Brook Wadsworth; [ed.] North Edgecombe High School, East Carolina University; [occ.] First Grade Teacher at East Carolina University; [memb.] St. James United Methodist Church, North Carolina Assoc. of Educators, National Education Association; [hon.] Pi Omega Pi Honorary Society, Nominated for Teacher of the Year, attended North Carolina Center for the Advancement of Teaching; [pers.] I try to write what I feel in my heart.; [a.] Tarboro, NC

BENNETT, VELMA JEAN
[pen.] Abena Keeping Hollers; [b.] September 29, 1942, FL; [p.] Deceased; [m.] Divorced, May 2, 1957; [ch.] 4 Daughters, 2 Sons; [ed.] G.E.D. - State College Undergraduate Degree - Harvard Extension School Course 1995 Fall; [occ.] Teacher, Grandmother 14; [memb.] Black Educator's Alliance; [hon.] Editors Award for Poetry Merit Award of Poetry; [oth. writ.] 'Be Strong' 1994, 'Volcanic Beginning' 1995, 'Become the Very Best You Can', 1995 'Eye See' 1994, 'Beans and Peas' 1995, 'Color-Then' 1995; [pers.] Through the stroke of a pen I have been able to relive many memories and get clear about some experiences - my poems reflect a part of my life then and now and hopefully your's too!; [a.] Jamaica Plain, MA

BERG, MICHAEL J.
[b.] November 21, 1967, Duluth, MN; [p.] Charles Berg, Katherine Berg; [ch.] Dakota December 94 to April 95; [ed.] Cloquet High School, Thief River Falls College; [occ.] Airline Instructor; [oth. writ.] My Woman, Tsunami of Desire, How Much Do I, My Sweet Baby, She is Gone, Pain on Jour, The Traveller, Was There Possibly A Way, When I Think Of You; [pers.] I have been called a poetic Barbarian as an analogue of my passion and rage. May true love find us all.; [a.] El Segundo, CA

BERG, ROBERT
[b.] October 9, 1979, Phoenix, AZ; [p.] H. Robert Berg Jr., Cynthia L. Berg; [ed.] Brophy College Preparatory; [occ.] Student; [oth. writ.] Several unpublished poems in own personal collection: Wrob's writings and wramblings, a play produced by his school: Escape from Eden; [pers.] Unfortunately, the human race does not evolve as a collected. It takes limitless strength and endurance to take the strugglers in two. Nonetheless, we are all on the eventual road to greatness.; [a.] Scottsdale, AZ

BERGER, LARRY
[pen.] Larry Arnold; [b.] October 18, 1937, New York, NY; [p.] Emanuel and Rose Berger; [m.] Callie Y. Berger, October 18, 1969; [ch.] Kurt and Larelle; [ed.] Miami Beach High, U. Cal., Long Beach; [occ.] Physical Therapist; [memb.] Kiwannis, Elks, American Legion, Juvenile Justice Commission, El Dorado Co.; [pers.] I enjoy writing poetry, lyrics and short stories: My writing expresses, the length and the

breath of me, and I'm sure to continue, right up to the.... end.; [a.] Placerville, CA

BERGERON, KARL T.
[b.] September 30, 1946, Hanover, NH; [ed.] BGS and UNH Psych/Sociology; [occ.] Special Education Teacher; [oth. writ.] Vietnam Chaos - unpublished; [pers.] I've been a social activist since returning from the Nam in '67; [a.] Concord, NH

BERGET, ELLSWORTH A.
[b.] January 15, 1936, Silverton, OR; [p.] Mr. and Mrs. Arthur J. Berget; [m.] Mary R. Berget, December; [ch.] Scott, Michelle and Christopher; [ed.] Ph.D. Syracuse University, Secondary Reading, Master Ed. (M.Ed.) U of Illinois, AB Brigham Young University; [occ.] Professor of Education Cal State University, Hayward; [a.] Pleasanton, CA

BERGH, NICOLE
[b.] January 9, 1980, Twin Falls, ID; [p.] John and Gay Bergh; [pers.] If I win all I want is the cash, and for my name to be at the bottom of my poetry.; [a.] Hagerman, ID

BERGMANN, TOM
[b.] December 6, 1953, Hanau, Germany; [p.] Karl Bergmann, Ilse Bergmann; [ch.] Philipp, Sven; [ed.] MSC. Human Nutrition at Justus Liebig University, Glessen; [occ.] UNICEF's Emergency Country Program Coordinator UNICEF Kigali, RWANDA; [memb.] National Audubon Society; [hon.] Scholarship, Ruebel Foundation Dominican Republic 1978; [oth. writ.] Technical papers on Nutrition, Food AId and Disaster Preparedness. Various poems (unpublished).; [pers.] The future belongs to those who believe in the beauty of their dreams (Eleanor Roosevelt).; [a.] Kigali, Rwanda

BERNAL, ANGELA R.
[b.] October 8, 1969, Walton, NY; [p.] Shirley Chase and Tom Mills; [m.] Jorge F. Bernal, April 30, 1991; [ch.] Julia - 3, Chelsea - 7; [ed.] AAS Degree from S.U.N.Y Delhi (Delhi, NY); [occ.] Housewife/Mother (and proud to be); [memb.] Member of Phi Theta Kappa, A National Honor Society for 2 yrs. Colleges; [hon.] On Dean's List my Last 2 Semesters of College; [pers.] I am my family love God. We study and believe his word and we're very thankful for his goodness and kindness to us and to all of his people.; [a.] Kyle, TX

BERNIER, AMANDA
[b.] July 14, 1982, Brunswick, ME; [p.] Ivy and Joseph Bernier; [occ.] student; [pers.] Even though I am young I have a love of poetry and would like to thank my special friend Matt for standing by me along the way.; [a.] Brunswick, ME

BERNING, MARILYN HELEN
[pen.] Marilyn (Bublitz) Berning; [b.] July 27, 1938, Winona, MN; [p.] Donald and Helen Bublitz; [m.] William E. Berning, September 13, 1958; [ch.] Son - Jeffrey and Jason Berning Daughter - Peggy Lynn Berning (Deceased); [ed.] Spring Valley, MN. High School; [occ.] Small Business Owner and Homemaker; [memb.] National Society of Poets; [oth. writ.] Various; [pers.] Poems are an expression of one's inner soul. They are an expression usually not expressed if not written. You can reveal much of oneself through writing poetry that could otherwise remain hidden; [a.] Stewartville, MN

BERNTSEN, THOMAS
[b.] August 6, 1965, New York; [p.] Joanne and Ragnuald Berntsen; [ed.] B.A. Utica College of Syracuse University (1988) M.S. Indiana University (1991) Ed.D. University of Massachusetts (expected 1998); [occ.] High School Math/Science Teacher Wilmington, Vermont; [oth. writ.] Article, "Let it Snow, Let it Snow" in The Physics Teacher" Article, "What if" in The Science Teacher (February 96); [pers.] As the title of my poem states, Look Up! There is a better day ahead for you and me.; [a.] Brattleboro, VT

BERO, ROBERT
[b.] October 6, 1950, Seattle, WA; [p.] Nick and Lillian Bero; [ed.] BA in Latin and Greek, Classical Languages awarded by Gonzaga University, Spokane, WA, 1973; [occ.] Senior Systems Engineer at Hughes Aircraft Co. Los Angeles, CA; [oth. writ.] Most of my poetry has been written as personal gifts rather than for publication.; [a.] Playa del Rey, CA

BERRY, WILLIAM L.
[b.] August 9, 1927, Corydon, KY; [p.] Douglas and Rose Berry; [m.] Angeline, September 18, 1954; [ch.] Nancy William, Judy and Kathleen; [ed.] High School through correspondence courses; [occ.] Retired; [memb.] Barbershop Quartettes, Northwest Chapter, Chicago, IL; [hon.] Sold a poem to company I worked for about the service. I'm also an inventor and sold a novel idea to a Novelty co.; [oth. writ.] I've written many poems, I have put two of my poems to music.; [pers.] It's only human to forget but, you can't forget what you didn't learn.; [a.] Franklin Park, IL

BERTSCH, ELIZABETH
[b.] September 19, 1962, Albany, OR; [p.] Robert - Deolores Bertsch; [occ.] Unemployment; [oth. writ.] 1 poem; [a.] Portland, OR

BEZEMES, KATHRYN R.
[a.] Nahant, MA

BICHLER, GERALD
[b.] August 28, 1955, Cut Bank, MT; [p.] Janet Bichler, Elmer Bichler; [m.] Nancy Bright, August 29, 1992; [ch.] Marlene Bichler, Kristian Bichler and Micah Bright; [ed.] Sheldon High School, Lane Community College; [occ.] Manufacturing at Rosboro Lumber Company; [memb.] National Geographic Society; [hon.] The honor of living life from the heart; [oth. writ.] A few unpublished poems shared with close friends.; [pers.] Yield to the living light of creation, cast open the window of awareness. Become one with the light, oh the ecstasy of none.; [a.] Springfield, OR

BICHLER, JAMES HENRY
[pers.] Jamie's poetic words caught the attention of family members when he was very young. His talents are many: athletically gifted, mathematically talented. He aspires to be a hockey player or an artist. We love you, Jamie. Your sensitivity and talents will take you far.

BIDJAWATIE, RAGOOBEER
[pen.] B.J.; [b.] February 26, 1981, Suriname; [p.] Bishnoe and Gomtie Ragoobeer; [ed.] P.S.7, I.S.171, now a freshman in Franklin K. Lane High School; [occ.] Attending school, baby sitting and writing; [hon.] Reading award, bronze award; [oth. writ.] A story published in a magazine named skipping stones.; [pers.] I love getting my writing published. It makes me feel better. I never thought that I had talent in writing poems but I was wrong.; [a.] Brooklyn, NY

BIFANO, MELISSA A.
[b.] March 26, 1977, Toms River, NJ; [p.] Mary Ann LaVista, Denis Bifano; [ed.] Toms River High School Northk, presently at Ocean County College; [occ.] Unit Management at St. Barnibas Medical Center, Livingston, NJ; [hon.] Certificate of Achievement in a Creative Writing Class; [oth. writ.] I had poems published in the school literary magazine; [pers.] I like to write about what I feel, and about situations that are happening in my life.; [a.] Manasquan, NJ

BISHOP, VICKY
[b.] July 15, 1950, Banner Elk, NC; [p.] Frank L. Hicks, Earlene Crump Hicks; [m.] John Bishop, June 28, 1968; [ch.] No natural children but many of the heart; [pers.] Lived most of my life in Johnson City, Tenn. My writing began as one way of talking to my Lord or a way to tell my husband that I love him. Some of my work are funny, cute, or silly, but many deeply felt. Whatever the outcome of a piece may be, I give credit for any talent to Jesus Christ.; [a.] Gray, TN

BITOUSHANA, LORI E.
[b.] November 24, 1964, Susquehanna, PA; [m.] Paldin Bitoushana, November 6, 1993; [ed.] Deposit Central School, Deposit NY, Broome Comm. College, Binghamton NY, Central CT State University; [occ.] Account Executive, Automatic Data Processing; [memb.] Faith Baptist Church, Enfield, CT; [hon.] Editors Choice Award, National Library of Poetry; [oth. writ.] Several poems in local newspapers, other publishing in previous Nat'l Lib. of Poetry releases.; [pers.] God has given me the ability to write. I pray that my work will glorify and touch others for Him.; [a.] Vernon, CT

BJORNSON, ERIKA
[b.] July 5, 1983, Saint Joseph Hospital; [p.] Jan Bjornson and Jeff; [ed.] Berg Elementary, Hagen Jr.High; [memb.] United Methodist Youth group; [oth. writ.] Poems for school; [pers.] My poem is about how I felt and delt with my fathers death at the age of five.; [a.] Dickinson, ND

BLACK, GASREL L. M.
[oth. writ.] "The First Snowfall of Winter", published book of poems "On Moonstones, Pearls and Crystal Wings".; [a.] Anacortes, WA

BLACK JR., HARROLD H.
[b.] July 21, 1956, North Kingston, RI; [p.] Harrold H. Black Sr. and Betty Jane Black; [ch.] Harrold III, Joeann E., Jenny M., Polly C.; [ed.] Bayside High School; [occ.] Tank Shop Forman, Uptegraff Mfg.; [hon.] Honorably Retired from U.S. Navy; [oth. writ.] Article for Carolina Country, several articles for ship newspaper while in the navy

BLACK, LORRAINE MARGUERITTE GARRELL
[pen.] L.n. Garrel Black; [b.] July 12, 1952, New York City; [p.] Eugene and Padette Garrel; [m.] Tracy Eugene Black, February 14, 1978; [ch.] David (17 years) and Adam (15 years); [ed.] Graduated from East Hampton High in 1970 Attended Jonestown C.C. 70-71 then transferred to Suffolk C.C. 72; [occ.] Homemaker. I am learning fortune telling with cards; [hon.] Golden Poet Award 1988 Award of Merit Certificate 1988, 1991 from World of Poetry; [oth. writ.] A book of poetry titled on moonstones pearl and crystal wings. I am researching for a novel (s); [pers.] My poems have been published in newspapers, Literacy magazines and Anthologies. I plan to write a novel in the future. My interest in the spiritual realm has been life long and I plan to study in depth. Every minute of life is important. Live well, laugh often, love much; [a.] Anacortes, WA

BLACK, MICHAEL
[pen.] Michael Black; [b.] May 6, 1978, Albany, GA; [pers.] I go to wherever my muse takes me. I do not, concern myself with the styles of others. I enjoy the psychedelic and esoteric forms of literature.; [a.] Albany, GA

BLACK, MOLLY
[pen.] A. White; [b.] June 11, 1976, Wichita, KS; [p.] Monty and Marilyn Black; [ed.] Dodge City

High School, Dodge City Community College; [occ.] Gunfighter at Boothill Museum and Front Street, Waitress; [oth. writ.] Stories and poems published in Jr. High, High school, and college papers and anthologies. Novel excerpt in Kansas Voices five year anthology 1990-1994; [pers.] I greatly thank my favorite authors, Mercedes Lackey, Tanith Lee, and Stephen King. I also thank my brother for giving me needed competition.; [a.] Dodge City, KS

BLACKBURN, BRENDA S.
[pen.] Brenda Bousquet; [b.] February 21, 1961, Norwich, CT; [p.] Prescott and Catherine Bousquet; [m.] Donald Blackburn, September 12, 1987; [ed.] Putnam Catholic Academy, Killingly High School, Huntington Institute; [occ.] Transportation Assist. and Kaman Aerospace Corp. Moosup, CT; [oth. writ.] Private Collection of unpublished works.; [pers.] My writing is based on raw emotion in all facets.; [a.] Sterling, CT

BLACKNER, DAVID MICHAEL
[b.] September 24, 1963, Murray, UT; [p.] David Blackner, Marian Johnson; [ch.] Erin E. Blackner; [ed.] Weber High School, Weber State University; [occ.] U.S. Treasury Department; [memb.] Sigma Alpha Epsilon, National Honor Society; [hon.] Eagle Scout BSA, On my honor award LDS/BSA, duty to God award LDS Church; [oth. writ.] A collection of 54 unpublished poems/sayings about my life as an abused child.; [pers.] I write to help survivors heal, and to help they non-abused to understand us.; [a.] Ogden, UT

BLACKOWSKI, JOHN W.
[pen.] Jason Ripp; [b.] March 28, 1958, Ladysmith, WI; [p.] Jacob and Clara Blackowski; [m.] Patricia Blackowski, September 29, 1979; [ch.] Jacob, Michael, Jay; [ed.] WWTC, LaCrosse, WI Electronics WITC, Rice Lake, WI Telephony Science Ladysmith-Hawkins High School, Ladysmith, WI; [occ.] Communications Consultant PTI Communications, Cumberland, WI; [hon.] National Outstanding Musicians Award, French Horn; [oth. writ.] I've written a multitude of poetry on my past experiences and use them for reflecting on when I need a lift.; [pers.] Writing is the best way to look inside your heart and expose it to those around you.; [a.] Cumberland, WI

BLAINE, TRACY
[b.] September 13, 1977, Scranton, PA; [p.] Jennie Longcoy, Julio Garcia; [ed.] High School; [occ.] Student at Wallen Paupock Area High School; [hon.] Golden poet Award from the World of Poetry in 1989; [oth. writ.] I wrote a poem called "Outside" when I was 10 years old. It was I published by the world of poetry 1989 in world treasury of great poems.; [pers.] I'm 18 years. old and I've worked to be a writer all my life. I feel as though I was blessed with a gift. I have the key to open people's minds and touch their souls if they only hear my words.; [a.] Hawley, PA

BLAIR, PATRICIA V.
[pen.] Tricia Vee; [b.] October 19, 1937, Dayton, OH; [p.] James and Gertrude Jackson; [m.] Frederick L. Blair, February 25, 1956; [ch.] Martin Shane - Ned Anthony Trudae Elayne; [ed.] Miamisburg High School, Pensacola Jr. College George Stone Vocational G.E.D; [occ.] Student - Institute of Children's Literature; [memb.] Several letters of appreciation for volunteer charity work (March of Dimes American Lung Assoc. Kidney Foundation, Etc); [a.] Orlando, FL

BLAYLOCK, RONALD F.
[pen.] Ron; [b.] March 8, 1956, San Marcos, TX; [p.] W. J. and Sarah Blaylock; [ch.] Amber Blaylock; [ed.] Southern High MS, TX Christian University, University of Arkansas; [occ.] Auto Service Director; [memb.] Optimist Club, Lions Club Automobile Clubs; [hon.] Optimist International Citizenships Award, Class President; [oth. writ.] Poems published, articles published in Readers Digest's, San Antonio Newspapers Sports Writer-Herald; [pers.] This poem is dedicated to Tricia Wright. Tricia I love you!; [a.] San Antonio, TX

BLEILER, RALPH W.
[pen.] Arby; [b.] December 24, 1938, Philadelphia, PA; [m.] Barbara Bleiler, June 13, 1875; [ed.] Degree in Liberal Arts, Humanities (Dean's List) from the Bucks Country Community College.; [occ.] Retired from a Career in Electronics; [memb.] American Chess Federation First V.P. and 2nd Pres. of P.P.A. Volunteer Counselor for those born with birth defects and their families.; [oth. writ.] Many inspiration writings. Since retiring, I have devoted myself to fiction and non-fiction short stories, essays, and my greatest love, poetry.; [pers.] From being involved in the civil-rights movement in the 50's, I have come to love the hindu proverb which tells us "There is no nobility in being superior to another: True nobility is being superior to your former self." I have devoted myself to understanding human attitudes, logic and emotions.; [a.] Doylestown, PA

BLINN, BRIAN RENE
[pen.] Brian Rene Blinn; [b.] October 28, 1971, Haverhill, MA; [p.] William and Jane Blinn; [ed.] U.S.A.F. Tech School; [occ.] U.S. Air Force; [memb.] V.F.W.; [hon.] A.F. Achievement Medal, A.F, Humanitarian Service Medal, national Defence Service Medal.; [oth. writ.] Personal collection of thoughts on life, the universe and everything. Love Ya! Doug!; [pers.] If we call ourselves the human race why do we not act humane. "I'm not weird, I'm misunderstood!"; [a.] Vacaville, CA

BLUNDON, JACKIE
[b.] February 20, 1980, Milwaukee, WI; [p.] Lynn Blundon; [ed.] Currently a Sophomore in High School; [hon.] Who's Who Among American High School Students Award, USNAA (United States National Art Award); [pers.] My first has been my one true inspiration. For that I thank him.; [a.] Montello, WI

BOHARA, HEATHER L.
[b.] August 2, 1984, London, England; [p.] Stephen and Judith Bohara; [ed.] 6th grade; [occ.] 6th grade student; [memb.] The club that I've been in is, the baby-sitters club; [hon.] Soft-ball awards, all-star soft-ball, and also many school awards; [oth. writ.] I've written other poems and 1 book but never been published.; [a.] San Antonio, TX

BOLAND, JACK L.
[b.] February 8, 1943, Youngstown, OH; [p.] Henry and Eva Boland; [m.] Kathryn (Deceased), November 26, 1976; [ed.] B.S. ED., Youngstown State Univ., '67, M.S. ED., The University of Akron '76; [occ.] Middle school Language Arts teacher, Head of English Dept. Kent Middle School, Akron, Ohio; [memb.] Akron Eduction Association; [hon.] Who's who in American Education, 1989-90; [pers.] Writing should be clear, succinct, and to the point. If the right words are chosen, they should reflect an economy. If writing comes from the soul, I doubt that it can be a renewable resource.; [a.] Uniontown, OH

BOMAN, BRUCE
[pen.] Bruce Boman or Billy Goat; [b.] June 11, 1976, Pontlac, MI; [p.] Mary and Carl Boman; [ed.] East Kentwood, High School; [occ.] Stocker; [hon.] Football Conference Champs; [oth. writ.] Normal; [pers.] I am an abstract poet. One in my own. I use no set format. (Relation to my life); [a.] Kentwood, MI

BONTON, SHANNON
[b.] September 3, 1968, Vicksburg, MS; [p.] Eddye Bee, Nora Bee; [m.] Mark A. Bonton, August 15, 1989; [ch.] Brittany Lynette, Jared Morgan and Anthony Michael; [ed.] Vicksburg High, Jackson State University, Southern University; [oth. writ.] "Timeless" published November 1995 in *Poetry Ink*, An electronic Magazine; [pers.] I believe that everyone we encounter in life leaves an imprint on our souls. It is these imprints that make us who we are. My imprints have caused me to be a hopeless romantic with a twisted sense of humor.; [a.] Baton Rouge, LA

BOOTH, LINN R.
[b.] June 13, 1948, Yonkers, NY; [p.] Deceased; [ed.] 3 yrs College; [occ.] Dept Veterans affairs appraiser, Musician, jeweler; [pers.] To raise awareness of big governments opportunistic practices, oppression and racial apathy.; [a.] Seattle, WA

BOOTHBY, MARK
[pen.] Mark E. Boothby; [b.] October 7, 1951, London, England; [p.] deceased; [occ.] Writer (Yet to be sold!); [memb.] Screen Actors Guild; [oth. writ.] Books awaiting agent and publication: *Feelings On Paper* and *Mutterings From An Absent Mind*; This is my first published work; [pers.] For 'Jacee' There is no pain or struggle in love; There is only pain and struggle on the journey toward it. [a.] Valley Vlg., Los Angeles, CA

BORBET, KATHLEEN
[b.] May 25, 1955, Lousiville, KY; [m.] Stephen Borbet, June 30, 1979; [ch.] Jason, Daniel, Timothy; [occ.] Nursing Student, Suffolk Community College; [a.] Nesconset, NY

BORING, PATTY
[pen.] Patricia or Patty; [b.] June 23, 1960, Minnesota; [p.] Ralph and Joan Niznik; [m.] David A. Boring, May 1, 1992; [ch.] Marisa and Markie; [ed.] Fullerton Union High School also Chaffey College four years; [occ.] Self; [hon.] Food handlers certificate; [oth. writ.] A Christmas Story, A Touch Of Love and A Children's Story; [pers.] I really enjoy writing poems and stories, my favorite one is children's poems and stories.; [a.] Ontario, CA

BORKE, SHARON GRIFFIN
[b.] December 22, 1965, Jacksonville, NC; [m.] John Thomas Borke, August 29, 1987; [ch.] Daniel (13), John (5); [ed.] 12 Grade Grad.; [a.] Richlands, NC

BOSAH, AUGUSTINE ODI
[b.] January 1, 1960; [p.] John Nnaemeka and Theresa Obiannju Bosah; [ed.] College of Medicine Graduate; [occ.] Medical Doctor; [pers.] Always fascinated by literary sculpturing ever ready to add to it if only to increase my fascination.; [a.] Staten Island, NY

BOSWELL, NATALIE
[pen.] Natalie Boswell; [b.] February 10, 1971, Provo, UT; [p.] Gary Boswell, Janice Boswell; [ed.] Tintic High School Weber State University; [occ.] Customer Service Representative, Ballard Medical Products, Draper, Utah; [memb.] International Association of Business Communicators; [hon.] Tintic High School Valedictorian; [oth. writ.] Several news articles published in the Signpost, Weber State University.; [pers.] There is a great deal to be learned from other people. I wish for everyone to be as fortunate as I am in being influenced by the greatest.; [a.] West Jordan, UT

BOVEE, TAMMY
[b.] February 12, 1966, Salem, OR; [p.] William and Karen McCutcheon; [m.] Jove Bovee, August 10, 1986; [ed.] Bachelor of Science, Human Develop-

ment and Performance, University of Oregon 1990.; [occ.] Health Claims Analyst; [memb.] Confederated Tribes of Grand Ronde, in Grand Ronde, OR; [oth. writ.] None, except more personal poetry, not of it published.; [pers.] I want people to feel hope for the future. I feel my poetry can do that by teaching them about Jesus, and the wonderful gift He offers.; [a.] Springfield, OR

BOWE, CLARA
[b.] August, 1936, Danville, VA; [p.] William and Mary Brown; [m.] W. Curtis Bowe, August 30, 1958; [ch.] Timothy; [ed.] Southside High, Blair VA, Philadelphia College of Bible, Langhorne PA; [occ.] Retired; [memb.] Living Word Bible Fellowship, Blackwood NJ; [oth. writ.] Other unpublished poems; [pers.] Currently working in poetry of childhood events; [a.] Berlin, NJ

BOWER, BENJAMIN P.
[b.] November 15, 1970, Santa Maria, CA; [p.] Raymond C. and Helen S. Bower; [ed.] Current Arizona State University Student, Junior; [occ.] Research and Development for Motorola; [hon.] Theta Chi Fraternity; [oth. writ.] Many other poems, and short stories and screenplays and soon to be published.; [pers.] "Today I strive to achieve every bit of creativity which lurks behind the meaning of this life I live from day to day. Tomorrow... I will accomplish more.; [a.] Chandler, AZ

BOWMAN, LINDA JEAN
[b.] November 3, 1959, Richland, WA; [p.] Hank and Joyce Prest; [m.] Patrick Bowman, May 14, 1988; [ch.] Travis, Ramsey, Lee Riley; [a.] Arnold, CA

BOWSER, KELLY
[b.] August 20, 1962, Minot, ND; [p.] Herbert Braun, Darlene Braun; [m.] Curtis Ratcliff, March 30, 1996; [ch.] Marie Danielle, Isaac Alan, Kevin Alexa; [ed.] Bishop Ryan H.S., North Dakota State University; [pers.] Significant events influence me most: The births of my two children, being a surrogate mother for two couples, falling in love, losing my grandmother. Maybe one day I will succeed at expressing just how deeply grateful I am for all I have and all that I love.; [a.] Collinville, IL

BOYD, PAT
[pen.] Trisha; [b.] December 17, Saint Johns; [p.] Mr, Miss Marion Boyd; [m.] Carla; [ch.] Al, Mike, Julia Michelle; [ed.] Reed spring high School; [occ.] Clean-Care of elderly; [oth. writ.] High School newspaper; [pers.] Feeling based on experiences.

BOYER, JASON MILES
[pen.] Jason M Boyer; [b.] June 26, 1973, Witchita Falls, TX; [p.] Franklin Miles and Judith Ellen Boyer; [ed.] Senior year at University of Denver, plan to go to graduate school of education at the University of Colorado of Denver; [occ.] student; [memb.] Beta Theta Pi fraternity; American Diabetes Association; United States Ski Instructors Association; [hon.] Who's Who Among American High School Students, People to people Student Ambassadors Program; [oth. writ.] None published, although many other poems have been written. [pers.] The influences in my writings are vast. I have studied many poets from many eras and styles; therefore, my writings encompass all styles. Currently, my favorite poet is Robert Frost. --"For the sake of our future, we must understand the mistakes of the past."-- [a.] Denver, CO

BRADLEY, ARNOLD
[b.] May 13, 1936, Brooklyn, NY; [ed.] Junior High School and Law School; [oth. writ.] After, Itzak, and other poems.; [pers.] Horatio Alger lives! This author at age 38 entered Law School. Without the benefit of college or even one semester of High School. Mr. Arnold is now practicing Law in Van Nuys, CA.; [a.] Van Nuys, CA

BRADLEY, TAMMY LEE
[pen.] Tammy Lee Bradley; [b.] December 28, 1970, Mt. View, CA; [p.] Joseph Asciutto, Sharon Asciutto; [m.] Divorced; [ch.] Jillian Lee Bradley; [ed.] Escalon High School (Escalon, CA), Modesto Junior College (Modesto); [occ.] Law Student; [memb.] American Red Cross, Delta Blood Bank Donor, Kiwanis Club; [hon.] Poetry award from Treasured Poems of America and Writer's Digest; [oth. writ.] "God Took The Dead," "Alone," "Heart Alone," "Saved..."; [pers.] Never leave your feelings alone, always question and soon you will understand. [a.] Oakdale, CA

BRADSHAW, LINDA
[b.] March 24, 1942, Marshall, MO; [p.] Arthur Kirk, Elizabeth Kirk; [m.] John Bradshaw; [ch.] Randy, Jeff, John; [ed.] Marshall High, Northwestern State, LA; [occ.] Office Manager, Springfield Striping and Sealing, Springfield, MO; [oth. writ.] Few poems published, many written for special people at special times.; [pers.] I love to write and have always loved music. I would like to combine the two someday.; [a.] Springfield, MO

BRADY, SARAH ELIZABETH
[pen.] Sarah E. Brady; [b.] February 12, 1986, Tucson, AZ; [p.] Diane Brady and Thomas Grubaugh; [ed.] Presently in the 4th grade; [occ.] Student; [memb.] Catalina United Methodist Church Sunday School Class, Jefferson Park School Orchestra; [hon.] January 96' Student of the Month at School; [oth. writ.] I have other poems and stories that I have write.; [pers.] I write poems to express my ideas about animals. I love all animals and I have 6 cats, 2 dogs, 1 bird and I mini hamster. I also love to dance. I take ballet, tap and jazz classes.; [a.] Tucson, AZ

BRADY, VIRGINIA J.
[pen.] Virginia J. Brady; [b.] April 8, 1924, New Canaan, CT; [p.] Margaret and Anthony Savatsky; [m.] Peter R. Brady, April 22, 1946; [ch.] Virginia Joanne, Patricia Margaret, Peter R. Brady II, Margaret Elizabeth, Katheryn Mary; [ed.] New Canaan High School, Kings County School of Nursing; [occ.] Retired; [memb.] U.S. Army Nurse Cadet Corp.; [hon.] Editor's Choice Award by The National Library of Poetry; [oth. writ.] One poem published two to be published.; [pers.] In my writing I try to bring out mankinds emotions in life. The humor the love, the storms and the sunshine that is granted to us as we walk the path of our life.; [a.] New Monmouth, NJ

BRAGADIN, MISSY
[pen.] Melissa Marie Bragadin; [b.] September 6, 1985, Westland, MI; [p.] Diane and Nick Bragadin; [ed.] Elementary 5th Grade; [occ.] I'm in 5th grade, 101/2 years old; [memb.] 4-H in 4/96 New Member; [pers.] After my grandfather passed away, June 95, I wanted to write this lovely poem for him. And share my poem to Mankind; [a.] Monroe, MI

BRAGG, SHIRLEY
[b.] September 22, 1940, Dallas, TX; [p.] Paul and Juanita Hall; [ch.] Teri Duncan and Scott Crump; [ed.] Woodrow Wilson High, Draughons Business College, Brook haven Jr. College; [occ.] Surgical Services Co. Ordinator - Mary Shiels Hosp.; [oth. writ.] Many - but only one published in a Church newspaper about AIDS a subject very near to my heart.; [pers.] From the heart - thats where my poems come from.; [a.] Dallas, TX

BRAIDA, DOLLY
[pen.] Dolly; [b.] April 17, 1937, San Francisco; [p.] Joe and Louise Dougherty; [m.] Arthur Braida, August 25, 1962; [ch.] 2 Sons; [ed.] High School and 6 weeks Business School; [occ.] Homemaker and poet; [memb.] WUJ President of Epiphany Mother's Guild. Served on the Parish Council for one year. Lifetime member of ISP; [hon.] 8 editor awards; [oth. writ.] Written a collection of poems - published last year (1995) came out in November called From Sad Beginnings to Happy Endings - A Child's Book - it's a lullaby with music called "Sleep My Sweet Baby" - not published; [pers.] I'm a wise, Mother and grandmother. I love writing poetry. I hope to help change some of the hate and prejudice to love in the world today. If God gave me this talent this late in my life. I want to do some good with it.; [a.] Windsor, CA

BRANDES, ARABELLA
[pen.] Jenny Jia Yim; [b.] April 16, 1971, Seoul, Korea; [p.] Samuel and Jennifer Yim; [m.] Robert F. Gordon, (1997); [ed.] St. Mary's Ryken Preparatory Leonard Town, MD; [occ.] Model, Actress, Freelance Writer, Musician; [pers.] Knowledge is power, money gives time but God and love are everything to me. Grace Be With You; [a.] Scottsdale, AZ

BRENNEMAN, PAULA MARIE
[b.] March 10, 1963; [p.] Joseph R. Batsa, Sarah K. Batsa; [m.] Brian James Brenneman, June 22, 1991; [ch.] Ryan James Brenneman; [pers.] This poem is dedicated to my son Ryan James Brenneman; [a.] Pasadena, MD

BREWER, ZACHARY B.
[b.] October 20, 1987, Bay City, MI; [p.] Bryant and Tracy Brewer; [ed.] Currently enrolled in the third grade at Pinconning Central Elementary School; [memb.] Barney Club, Sunday school, little league and summer school local library club.; [hon.] Trophy for most valuable player for T-Ball- 1995.; [oth. writ.] I write poems and stories on a weekly basis.; [pers.] I read books all the time and it gives me ideas for writing.; [a.] Pinconning, MI

BRIGHT, JAMES K.
[pen.] J. Kevin Bright; [b.] April 23, 1963, Robinson, IL; [p.] James W. Bright and Edith V. Bright; [m.] Pamela S. Bright, July 11, 1992; [ch.] William, Clayton, Amanda; [ed.] Neoga High, Lake Land College; [occ.] Cutter Operator Petty Co.; [oth. writ.] Several poems and short stories for family enjoyment; [pers.] In a fast paced world, I hope my poems and stories help people slow down and enjoy what is around them.; [a.] Effingham, IL

BRINAR, PAMELA
[b.] January 8, 1961, Phoenix, AZ; [p.] Royce and Gloria Lambert; [ch.] Shana Janelle and Jacob Dylan; [ed.] San Luis Obispo High School; [occ.] Executive Assistant, Towers Perrin; [memb.] Professional Secretaries International, Women's International Bowling Congress; [pers.] My goal is to write from the heart, to make people feel something - maybe even catch their breath.; [a.] Arvada, CO

BRISCOE, MARGARET M.
[pen.] Peg Briscoe; [b.] March 16, 1922, Westminster, MD; [p.] Eurath B. Ed, Donald M. Myers; [m.] James F. Briscoe, July 12, 1942; [ch.] Susan Briscoe Huse, J. Douglas Briscoe; [ed.] Samuel Ready School for Girls in Baltimore, Md Western Md, College Westminster Md; [occ.] Retired; [oth. writ.] Only poems nothing published; [pers.] At my age I write for fun about life as I see it and things that touch my fancy.; [a.] Fort Myers, FL

BROCKMAN, LAURETTA HELEN
[pen.] Lauretta Brockman; [b.] September 27, 1936, Bristow, IN; [p.] Onan and Marie Aders; [m.] Arthur P. Brockman Sr., June 9, 1980; [ch.] Karin, Greg, Becky, Mike and Lorie; [ed.] Bristow High School

Graduate, Hank Hanna School of Cosmetology, Western Wisconsin Technical College; [occ.] Receptionist at Odd Fellows home in Saratoga California; [memb.] VFW Auxiliary, Post 1994 At water CA, Sutter School PTA-Santa Clara, CA, Institute of Children'S Literature, West Redding, CT; [hon.] Published in sparkles in the sand 1995. Received the Editors Choice Award. Was inducted into the International Society of Poets at the Convention held in August 1995. In Washington D.C.; [pers.] Poetry is like walking through a meadow strew with flowers. Or through a forest of tall Stately trees. Sights and sounds of poetry puts us in touch with the splendors of all seasons of life.; [a.] Saratoga, CA

BRODSKY, IDA
[b.] May 15, 1920, Brooklyn, NY; [p.] Sarah and Joseph Emerman; [m.] Jack Brodsky, May 19, 1946; [ch.] Dr. Joel Brodsky and Michael Brodsky; [ed.] B.A. Degree from San Jose State College, Art Major 1972; [occ.] Retired; [oth. writ.] Two poems published in sacto-bee-my time is spent mostly in painting.; [pers.] I am a people watcher - I have concerns of the world around me - I love my country and I'm so proud to be an American.; [a.] Discovery Bay, CA

BRONCATO, BUFFY LEIGH
[pen.] Buffy; [b.] February 4, 1969, Buffalo, NY; [p.] Pamela Probst, Ronald Broncato (Deceased) Stepfather - Roger Probst; [ch.] Ronald Shaine; [ed.] Mt. St. Mary Academy, Cornell University; [occ.] United States Air Force; [memb.] Alpha Omicron Pi Sorority; [oth. writ.] This is my first published work.; [pers.] All of my work (and my love) is for my family, especially my beautiful son, and for the special people who touch my soul and fill my heart.; [a.] Laurel, MD

BROOKINS, FAY TEMPLETON
[pen.] Fay T. Brookins; [b.] August 26, 1929, Dayton, OH; [p.] Chas and Hazel Templeton; [m.] Edward V. Brookins, October 8, 1949; [ch.] Ann Lorraine and Carol Jane; [ed.] Tucson Sr High School and Woodbury College in Los Angeles, CA a BA degree from L.A. Valley College in L.A.; [occ.] Housewife; [memb.] Formerly a member of the Puppeteers of America 86-93 until 1993 and Lakewood Arts council '89 to '95 Lakewood, Co; [hon.] "Journalism Assoc. of Community Colleges", Second place in 1987 State competition (calif.), "Bigger isn't better, magazine news feature for a book review Humanscale by Kirkpatrick Sale was published in the LA Valley College quarterly magazine "Crown" (spring 1987 issue); [oth. writ.] Many skits for puppets from 1987 to 1994 a series of short plays written for children to perform. I wrote them for a summer drama workshop I taught at the La Canada Youth House in La Canada, CA sponsored by the Creative Arts Dept. of the Assistance League of Flintridge; [pers.] I feel that the earth is finite (not infinite) and the Human Population is out of control. The earth has limits and cannot effectively sustain so many people. (K.SALE's book deals with this!) "HUMAN SCALE" published in 1980.; [a.] Aurora, CO

BROOKS, ANGELA D.
[b.] Charlottsville; [p.] Sandra Ryder; [ed.] Louisa Middle School; [memb.] S.C.A., Wrestling; [hon.] Science Fair 2nd Place, Young Authers, Art Festivals (3); [oth. writ.] On Flash Cards Inside; [pers.] I like sports such as baseball, basketball, tennis. Have a little brother named Jimmy Brooks III; [a.] Louisa, VA

BROOKS, LAWRENCE WAYNE
[pen.] Gerrn Brrfdrm; [b.] December 27, 1960, Charlotte, NC; [p.] Clyde W. and Mildred T. Brooks; [ed.] Charlotte Catholic High School, UNCC (one semester at UNC-CH) BA degree in English (yet I started out in my best subject - math, and switched majors later on); [occ.] Apostle of Jesus Christ (Christian Minister); [memb.] International House in Charlotte; [hon.] Elected "Most Intellectual" of the school at Junior High School graduation, Termed their best student of all time by my French teacher and Russian professor, Qualified for Mensa, Studying five languages (French, Russian, Mandarin, Modern Hebrew, Tamil, and will add two others (African language and another East Asian); [oth. writ.] Two other poems: Crestlicker, and Hellhole Filled Two other poems in the works: The Cinnamon Forest, and Colossul; [pers.] Some have likened my writing to Gerard Manley Hopkins and James Joyce when it all comes down to the end most important thing in one's life will be how he answers this question: "Are you born-again?" Remember: comedy is no laughing matter! Ha I say!; [a.] Charlotte, NC

BROOKSHER, LARRY V.
[b.] October 14, 1942, Galveston, TX; [p.] Clovis Vaugh and Ruth Brooksher; [m.] Judy J. Brooksher, January 17, 1990; [ch.] Kelly, Sherry, Todd, Joy'l, Lynn; [ed.] Vienna High School, Vienna, Ohio Marion College - Marion, IN; [occ.] A&A Home improvements Sale Manager and president in Peru, Indiana.; [memb.] In the daily human race to encourage every human you see are meet that "They are OK and I'm OK" - Have hope and be happy.; [hon.] "A challenge to a president" written for the debate between ducacas and bush in the winston salem news paper before their debate. The selection of my poem "Abandoned, wife's on jury duty: for printing in, The Rainbows End in Summer of '96.; [oth. writ.] Numerous poems friends at weddings, graduations, anniversaries, and birthdays as a free gift to them for their thoughts and happiness.; [pers.] I admire my step father because he has done so much with his hands as a carpenter in building things and when I credit him, he says in tribute to me, "You can teach someone to build but you can't teach someone to think and writer to think and write deeply, they must develop their own gift."; [a.] Logansport, IN

BROSH, RON
[b.] November 14, 1980, Tell Aviv, Israel; [p.] Dr. Hezi Brosh, Sarit Brosh; [ed.] Lawrence Woodmere Academy, High School; [occ.] 9th Grade student; [hon.] First prize in a video contest (November 1995) made to this song. This poem was first published in The Jewish Post and in two Israeli newspapers.; [oth. writ.] A song named: I Am The King.; [pers.] Special thanks and love from the bottom of my heart to wonderful sister, Shani, a medical student, who inspired me to write this song. After the assassination of Yitzhak Rabin, The prime Minister of Israel (November 1995) I dedicate this song to his family and to all the people who care for peace.; [a.] East Rockaway, NY

BROUGHTON, DIANE ROBERTA
[b.] January 2, 1956, Brooklyn, NY; [p.] Abraham and Sylvia Blustein; [m.] Gary Lewis Broughton, April 7, 1990; [ch.] Stepchild-Todd A. Broughton; [ed.] College of States Island - Susan Wagner High School; [occ.] R.N. - Disabled; [memb.] N.Y. Audubon Society; [hon.] Awards at work for (fast thinking and saving pts. life, and helping out in a dangerous situations.; [oth. writ.] Poems for family; [pers.] Believe in God and you will have everything you can ever want in life.

BROWN, AL DANNY
[b.] July 17, 1947, Baton Rouge, LA; [p.] John C. Brown Sr. and Anna M. Brown; [ed.] Istrouma High School, Baton Rouge, LA, Louisiana State University - B.A. Journalism; [occ.] Communication Director-Louisiana Dept Of. Revenue and Taxation; [memb.] LA. Association of State Communicators Public Relations of Government Communicators Editorial Advisory Board - LA. State Voice Newspaper; [hon.] 2nd Place Feature Writing-Associated Press Services, 1st Place LA. Sports Writers Association, 1st Place United Press International - Sports 1994 State Fax Communications Award; [oth. writ.] Novel "Tomorrow's Treasure" numerous feature stories, news articles, and photos in local newspapers, State Wide Magazines, and National Publications.; [a.] Baton Rouge, LA

BROWN, BARBARA I.
[b.] February 9, 1951, Plainview, TX; [p.] Homer and Dorothy Inscore; [m.] James Roy Brown, November 28, 1970; [ch.] Ryan - 20, John Adam - 13,; [ed.] High School, Texarkana College; [occ.] Chief Deputy Tax Assessor, Nevada Co.; [memb.] Central Baptist Church, VFW Auxiliary; [oth. writ.] Poems and articles in school publications. Mostly I share copies with a growing circle of friends who ask for them.; [pers.] I think God gives each of us a way to deal with everything in our lives. My poems are a sort of journal, that help me see the way God is there in all things, good or bad.; [a.] Prescott, AR

BROWN, DALITA LINEA
[b.] February 15, 1983, Plainview, TX; [p.] Wilma Brown; [ed.] 7th Grade Attending Hutchinson Jr. High. I am a Honor Student; [hon.] I am a honor student. I was also nominated for the spirit of a west Texan Award in May of 95. I hold a title for Little Miss Black Metroplex 95-96 Little Miss talent for the year 94-95, 95-96, Little Miss Modeling 94-95 Little Miss East Lubbock 94-95, 1st runner up Hospitality Queen 95-96 1st runner up modeling Queen 95-96 and 2nd runner up Miss Petite Lubbock; [oth. writ.] My poem was published in a book. Also publish in local newspapers.; [pers.] Due to my many accomplishments, I must first thank the Lord and my mother for being there by my side. I have been influenced by many things and in the future I plan to strive for bigger and better things and hope that the Lord will answer all my prayers.; [a.] Lubbock, TX

BROWN, GRACE V.
[pen.] Agnes Nessie Darling; [b.] May 1, 1922, Canada; [p.] Deceased; [m.] George James Brown, November 11, 1943; [ch.] Marilyn J. and Boy Murray; [ed.] Matriculation High School - Two years St Mary's Academy College - Winnipeg Manitoba - Canada College Real Estate Business College; [occ.] Semi-retired realtor; [memb.] Universal City - North Hollywood Chamber-Commerce, California - Canada - Canada Chamber - Commerce past president - Los Angeles Woman's Canadian Club; [hon.] 1959-Canadian Press Women's Club, Real Estate Awards, Covering Opening St Laurence Seaway, Covering Queen, Elizabeths B.C. Tour-Covering Pre-inaugural Propject flight across Canada - 1954-CPA; [oth. writ.] Unpublished fiction novel "Forever The Child" by Lines as women's editor of prince Rupert daily news prince Rupert B.C. Canada; [pers.] The words of my small grandchildren when moving to the farm my son bought in the Bulkley Valley surrounded by woods and mountains in Northern B.C Lent contrast to our San Fernando home of palm, crypress, rubber fruit trees-each providing peace and beauty valley village; [a.] North Hollywood, CA

BROWN, NANCY L.
[b.] November 4, 1957, Springhill, LA; [m.] Terry Michael Brown, May 20, 1976; [ed.] Taylor High, Eastfield College; [hon.] (H) Phi Theta Kappa, (H) Secretary to Student Commissioner staff, (A) Distinguished Service to Phi Theta Kappa, (A) Outstanding Service to Student Commissioner Staff, (A) Outstanding Service to Eastfield College; [pers.] My

grand parents, John Walker Toms and Idell Burns Toms, gave me a unique understanding of love and people. I miss them very much.; [a.] Dallas, TX

BROWN, STEVEN D.
[b.] September 11, 1967, Spokane, WA; [p.] Jimmie and Bettye Brown; [m.] Kyong - Hui Brown, July 26, 1989; [ch.] Andrew Daniel and Rebekah Keren; [ed.] 1 year DTC; [occ.] Asst. Manager (Total Petro.); [memb.] First Love Christian Church; [oth. Writ.] Eternity (At Waters Edge); [pers.] I originally wrote this poem for my wife in 1988, just a few months after we met. I gave my heart to her and I never want her to let it go.; [a.] Aurora, CO

BROWN, TAMIKA
[b.] August 29, 1981, Kinston, NC; [p.] Sandra Bryant and Edward Brown; [ed.] Currently in High School; [occ.] Student; [memb.] Member of beauty spot M. B. Church and other church organizations. I am also a member of FHA/HERO at Douglas Byrd High School.; [hon.] I am on the "A-B" Honor Roll list throughout the year. I won the school spelling bee.; [oth. writ.] I have written a host of poems and I am now currently working on a play that has not yet been titled. I have written several stories also.; [pers.] Most of my work consists of my inner personal feelings at that time which I write.; [a.] Fayetteville, NC

BROWN JR., WAYNE H.
[b.] July 27, 1978, Indianapolis, IN; [p.] Chong Fletcher, LeRoy Fletcher; [ed.] Full time student at Atlantic Community, H.S., will be attending University of Indianapolis in the Fall of '96; [occ.] K-mart modeling associate and model for Elle modeling agency.; [memb.] Success without drugs (affiliated with the Indianapolis Colts); [hon.] Honor Roll Award, Eagle for excellence award, numerous athletic awards; [oth. writ.] Several poems were printed in the school newspaper.; [pers.] My philosophy is simple. You take something ordinary and plain, and make it unique and extravagant.; [a.] Boynton Beach, FL

BROWNING, KIRK
[b.] March 28, 1921, NYC, NY; [m.] Barbara Browning, 1947; [ch.] David and Sean; [ed.] Avon Old Farms, Conn. Cornell Univ.; [occ.] TV Director "Live from Lincoln Center"; [hon.] 5 TV Emmy Awards, Harris Foundation Award, International Opera Award. Award, Monitor Award, City of NY Crystal Apple Award, Silver Circle Award (Nat'l. Acad. of TV Arts and Sciences)

BROWNING, PAMELA J.
[b.] November 28, 1960, Hamilton, OH; [p.] Doyle and Shirley Browning; [m.] Single; [ed.] Supervisor for TCI Cablevision, Middletown, Ohio; [oth. writ.] Several other writings - unpublished; [pers.] This poem was written in memory of my special friend Toni M. Pfeffer who was called home August 31st 1987.; [a.] Trenton, OH

BRYANT, LYNDA JEAN
[pen.] Lynda Jean; [b.] October 13, 1941, Washington, DC; [p.] Virginia Mae Lamm Darden Zierdt and Jesse Robert Darden, Sr.; [ed.] Suitland Sr. High School, MD, Eckerd College, FL (BA 1984), and Capitol College, VA (MS 1996); [occ.] Program Manager - Computers, Communications, Controls and Audio/Visual; [memb.] Washington Farm United Methodist Church, Information System Audit and Control (International) Association, and small writing groups; [hon.] Federal System Integration and Management Center performance awards, Scholarships, Speaker at the Federal Data Center Directors Interagency Conference ('90) and other business, educational, and church groups; [oth. writ.] Several technical articles published in Federal Computer Week and various personal poems for friends, families, and fellow travelers.; [pers.] I strive to reflect faith, hope, and understanding in all my writings both for fun and business. Communication with each other (worldwide) and GOD is critical. Thanks to my friends and family for the encouragement to learn, write, and persevere towards my dream; [a.] Alexandra, VA

BUCK, TAMMY L.
[pen.] Tammy L. Buck; [b.] May 23, 1961, Easton; [p.] Beverly and John Mostow; [ed.] Wilson Area High School; [occ.] Ship Control, Journal of Commerce, Philippsburg, NJ; [oth. writ.] My own personal keepsakes.; [pers.] I believe that life's greatest gift, is the friendship of another.; [a.] Easton, PA

BUICE, JODY L.
[b.] June 14, 1969, Lilburn, GA; [p.] Joseph L. Buice, Marcial Buice (Deceased); [m.] Wade A. Franklin, June 1, 1987; [ch.] Joshua Wade Franklin; [ed.] North Gwinnett High School Devry Institute of Technology; [occ.] Home maker, mother; [oth. writ.] I've written at least 50 poems. This is the first time that I have attempted to have any of my work published.; [pers.] I am a romantic in every sense. I try to bring this out in all of my poetry. I feel that my words are moving to any one who reads them.

BUNCH, MEL
[hon.] OHCA Resident of the Year

BURDICK, TERRI JO
[b.] May 11, 1973, Massillon, OH; [p.] Dave and Laura Price; [m.] Mark C. Burdick, April 24, 1994; [ch.] Luke William Burdick; [ed.] Strasbury-Franklin High School, Bradford School - specializing in Hospitality and Travel.; [occ.] Homemaker; [memb.] Supporter of March of Dimes; [hon.] Honor Student at Bradford School also Tips Certified; [oth. writ.] Many personal writings, no other publications.; [pers.] Do not put things off, do them and have them taken care and do a job you'll be proud of. Always put love first in your life.; [a.] New Philadelphia, OH

BURKE, BARRETT DALE
[pen.] Barrett Burke; [b.] April 28, 1966, Parsons, KS; [p.] Kenneth and Patricia Burke; [ed.] West Jefferson High School, Harvey, LA, Louisiana State University A&M, Baton Rouge, LA, BA Psychology; [occ.] Mental Health Therapist, St. Francis Hospital, Federal Way, WA; [memb.] Registered Counselor - State of Washington Professional Licensing Services; [hon.] All Metro Catcher - Baseball, All-District Catcher-Baseball, New Orleans, LA, Dean's List, Scholastic Award for Sports, MVP - Baseball; [oth. writ.] Honey comb hereafter (Adventure Novel - currently unpublished), Working on and novel currently; [pers.] I strive to bring to life the ordinary and mundane things of the world in which we live. I have been tremendously influenced by Charles Dickens.; [a.] Kent, WA

BURKE, FRED G.
[pen.] Fred G. Burke; [b.] January 1, 1926, Collins, NY; [p.] Fred and Sophie Burke; [m.] Carol Sterling, December 22, 1986; [ch.] Rebecca, Fritz, Dan and Adam; [ed.] BA Williams, MA Princeton, Oxford, Ph D Princeton; [occ.] Retired Senior Fellow Phillips - Stokes Fund; [hon.] "Festchrift" 1990 CT. Academy Arts and Science or 1985 Doctor Law Rides colleges 1979 Awards for excellence, Ed Press Asso 1973 Or Law Bryant College 1971 Kimborough-Owen Award American 1958, Political Science Association 1930; [oth. writ.] Public Education - Who is in charge 1990, sub-Sahara Africa 1966, Africa's Quest for order 1964, Local Politics and Government in Legarda; [a.] Milford, PA

BURKE, KERRY ANDREW
[b.] December 17, 1956, Gary, IN; [p.] Joseph and Geraldine; [m.] Brenda Kay Medrano Burke, September 5, 1990; [ch.] Renee, Michael, Angelia, Kerry, Nicholas; [ed.] Crown Point, High School; [occ.] Warehouse Supervisor, Midwest Siding Supply, Lowell, IN; [memb.] Cedar Lake Civil Defense; [hon.] Employee of the Month of June 1995; [oth. writ.] "The love within me", "My Three O'Clock Girl", "Remembering", "Like Oak", "My Dearest Darling"; [pers.] In all my life, I've never known anyone who has brought out the feelings and emotions that my wife, Brenda Kay has.; [a.] Cedar Lake, IN

BURNS, NANCY
[b.] November 14, 1977, Glendale, WI; [p.] Late Patricia Burns; [ed.] Nicolet High School; [occ.] Student; [hon.] 1994 and Editors Choice Awards; [oth. writ.] The National Library of Poetry *Seasons to Come* and *Beyond the Stars*; [a.] Glendale, WI

BURNSTAD, KAREN C.
[b.] March 8, 1972, Norfolk, VA; [p.] Donald Carmack And Linda Hedrick; [m.] David C. Burnstad, July, 16, 1994; [ch.] Kali M. Burnstad (Step daughter); [ed.] Salem High School in Va. Beach, VA. (major in English Education); [occ.] Bank teller at Adams Country National Bank in Hanover, PA; [memb.] People for the Ethical Treatment of Animals, The National Council for Teachers of English.; [hon.] Dean's List at ODU; [oth. writ.] None published as of yet.; [pers.] The inspiration for my writing is directly linked to my personal feelings, relationships, and experiences. If I can simply evoke emotion from my reader, then I feel like I have accomplished something wonderful.; [a.] Gettysburg, PA

BURRIS, LISA R.
[b.] January 17, 1978, Muncie, IN; [p.] Teresa D. Burris; [ed.] 10th G.; [oth. writ.] I have a lot of poems, I have written for family and friends, but I don't have anything published.; [pers.] I write what I feel, in my heart I can write what my friends ask me to write about

BURTON, JANET MARIE
[pen.] Jan Phillips; [b.] April 12, 1948, Allentown, PA; [m.] Howard Burton, October 9, 1982; [ch.] Michael, Steven, Don Allen and Maria; [ed.] Oley Valley Area High Sch.; [occ.] Homemaker, aspiring writer; [pers.] There is so much more to life than materialism, if only we would stop for a moment to recognize and appreciate it.; [a.] Del Norte, CO

BUS, GLORIA JEAN
[pen.] Gloria Jean; [b.] February 28, 1943, Hamburg, NY; [p.] Earl and Katherine Bogardus; [m.] Joel Thomas Bus, September 23, 1961; [ch.] Joel Leon and Jeremy Earl; [ed.] Orchard Park, Central School, International Institute of Reflexology; [occ.] Reflexologist; [pers.] Poetry has been a source of comfort, reviewing the joys of my youth and eagerly seeking my happy future. Everyone should try writing poetry at least once in their life.; [a.] Blasdell, NY

BUSH, GWENDOLYN A.
[pen.] Gwen; [b.] November 10, 1957, Wintergarden, FL; [p.] John and Mary Tucker; [ch.] Tamara; [ed.] A/GS in General Studies pending B.A. in Business Admin. from Wayland Baptist University Graduated H.S. in Atlanta, GA, B.T. Washington.; [occ.] Secretary for 408th Signal Company at Fort Wainwright, AK; [oth. writ.] Several unpublished writings.; [pers.] I pay attention to everything around me and learn from the different experiences, then I put it in the form of a poem.; [a.] Fairbanks, AK

BUSTAMANTE, RUSSELL D.
[b.] July 13, 1977, Albuquerque, NM; [p.] Dale

Chavez-Griego and Randy Bustamante; [ed.] Albuquerque High School graduate, Now attending TVI Vocational School; [occ.] Swift Leader at Arroyo Del Oso Restaurant; [hon.] 95 Student of the Week at Albuquerque High School, TVI honor role; [oth. writ.] I like to write poems in my spare time. I have written many other poems, but none have been entered in contests or articles.; [pers.] I would like to thank everyone for helping me, become what I am today. I love you Mom and Dad, and best wishes to everyone who I love and care about. Bebes, I love you so much. God give me strength to make difference.; [a.] Albuquerque, NM

BUTCHER, MYRTLE
[pen.] Myrtle Butcher; [b.] August 17, 1916, Ricetown, KY; [p.] Ed and Callie Hill; [m.] McKinley Butcher, April 1937; [ch.] Dr. Maxine Nichols; [ed.] 12th grade, Booneville, KY; [occ.] Retired from construction business with husband (now deceased); [memb.] A.R.C. of N. Ky., Trinity Church Episcopal, Republican Women Club, I do T.V. commercials now in 7 states; [hon.] Lifetime Member of Internation Society of Poets, First filmed acting part in T.V. commercial going national; [oth. writ.] one poem published and two others to be published, two Friendship poems for *Poet's Corner*; [pers.] My writings reflect my feelings of past and current times. [a.] Ft. Wright, KY

BUTTARS, MELBA
[pen.] Melba; [b.] June 10, 1923, Newton, UT; [p.] James Sands and Mable Benson Hancey; [m.] Clair DeVerl Buttars, June 22, 1940; [ch.] Clint, Cris, Brent, Lance, Lisa, Gail, Aaron, Robert, Lorna and Holly; [ed.] High school - many Art Classes, Home Study Course, Chicago School of Interior Design; [occ.] Retired; [memb.] Utah Artist Assoc., Utah Water Color Society, Past Member of Idaho Writers League; [oth. writ.] Title (Traveling), 2 page poem published in Ideals. (Vacation issue 1968). 2 other poems accepted but not yet published (Ideals). Lyrics accepted by not yet produced by Mormon Tabernacle Choir stories and poems in trade magazines poems, lyrics, play for many civic and church org.; [pers.] From an early age I have been able to appreciate the beauty of the world around me and to visualize other times and places, I feel the need to share these feelings with others through the written word.; [a.] North Salt Lake, UT

BYFIELD, EDMUND A.
[b.] August 8, 1975, Brooklyn, NY; [p.] Herbert Byfield, Doreen Byfield; [ed.] Art and Design High School, Hunter College; [oth. writ.] Published in a collection of poems by college and university students entitled "The Poets: Anthology"; [pers.] Every conceivable form of fiction from the prose to the poem to the short story and novel is autobiographical. If is to believe otherwise that one finds himself in the mist of true fiction.; [a.] Brooklyn, NY

CABAZA, ISABELLE A.
[b.] February 23, 1968, Nantes, France; [p.] Jean-Francois Pelle, Clementine Pelle; [m.] Victor Cabaza III, December 23, 1994; [ed.] France; [occ.] Awards Coordinator, International Advertising Awards Agency, NY; [hon.] Bronze Medal Winner at a French Speaking Poetry Contest (1991) "Halaf" (Haute Academie Litteraire et Artistique de France).; [oth. writ.] French Poetry, English Poetry.; [a.] New York, NY

CAIN, CARRAN
[pen.] Carran Cain; [b.] February 11, 1983, Salem, OR; [p.] M. David and Virginia Cain; [ed.] I go to Cascade Junior High School.; [occ.] Student; [memb.] Cadet band - I play the flute; [hon.] All American Scholar; [a.] Aumsville, OR

CAIN, DEREK
[b.] March 29, 1974, Andalusia, PA; [p.] William Cain, Elizabeth Pellicciotti; [m.] Single; [ed.] St. Charles Borromeo Bishop Egan High School; [occ.] Warehouse Laborer; [memb.] Andalusia Community Theatre Rated #1 in the best of Bucks County; [pers.] When writing my poems it makes my heart want to dance with a feeling of joy and a whip of romance; [a.] Andalusia, PA

CAIN, ERRIN
[b.] February 13, 1970, Glen Dale, WV; [p.] James P. Clark Jr., Linda J. Clark; [m.] Mark D. Cain, September 22, 1991; [ch.] Emily Renee, Dalton Alexander; [ed.] John Marshall High School, West Liberty State College; [occ.] Homemaker and Mother; [hon.] Dean's List and National Dean's List, 3.48 Graduation GPA; [pers.] My writing has become lighter and more inspired since my marriage and my children. I receive tremendous support from my family which keeps me writing.; [a.] Moundsville, WV

CAIN, RICHARD EDWARD
[b.] December 14, 1939, Plattsmouth, NE; [p.] Richard Charles Cain and Velda Bernice Cain; [m.] Sharron Lorraine, June 13, 1964; [ch.] Lorina Lee, Richard Zachary; [ed.] Woodland H.S., Woodland, WA. B.A. English, M.Ed., Dev. Reading, PhD. Ed. Psych. - Univ. of WA, Seattle, WA; [occ.] Writer; [oth. writ.] Article, Jour. of Correctional Ed., Poetry Sou'Wester, Portland Review, Kansas Quarterly, fiction Imagination Friends, "The Wimp", Lighthouse Publications, "The Cake".; [pers.] Kill the computer, bring back the horse and buggy, and recognize overpopulation for the threat it is.; [a.] Edmonds, WA

CAINE, TALANA LYNN
[b.] April 5, 1984, Modesto, CA; [p.] Agnes Gaylor, John Caine; [ed.] Hughes Elem., Modesto, CA, Teel Middle School, Empire, CA; [occ.] Student; [hon.] Traffic Patrol 5th Gr.; [oth. writ.] Poem published in local newspaper; [a.] Modesto, CA

CALLENDER, ALINA
[pen.] Joselyn, Zibi, Mr. Williams; [b.] June 7, 1979, South Shore Hosp.; [p.] Amina Callender and Vincent Callender; [ed.] Lawrence High School, Conflicts: Ms. Greenlee, Psychology; [occ.] Lens Direct, General Operator, Reader's Market; [oth. writ.] Special thanks to family (Veena and Stephen, Mary, Chris, Adrees, Dede, Alli) and Mr. Williams for encouraging me. Every way to smile and forget if only we could, and make believe we never needed anymore than this.; [pers.] "Moment's become memories. Memories that linger are the secrets of the heart." (Anonymous). Akasha a.k.a. the 5th element, the omnipresent spiritual power that permeates the universe. Projective energy, visualization.; [a.] Inwood, NY

CALMES, SHIRLEY THOMPSON
[pen.] Shirley Calmes; [b.] July 27, 1947, Vero Beach, IL; [p.] Paul and Lessie Thompson; [m.] John W. Calmes, September 6, 1991; [ch.] Two; [ed.] Graduated from Vero Beach High 1966; [occ.] Owner of a florist shop; [memb.] Member of Vero Beach County Club; [hon.] As a young child, I won art contest in school. Today it's a hobby one that I enjoy; [oth. writ.] Yes, I've written several more poems, some I have, framed and on display in my floral shop, along with the one to be published.; [pers.] I feel very good and thankful for the talents I was given - people say I should sell my work. I give it away, it's something I can give freely; [a.] Vero Beach, IL

CAMBERG, DEBBIE
[b.] August 18, 1957, Saint Helens, OR; [p.] Donald and Roxie Timmons; [m.] Adam Cambery, September 2, 1992; [ch.] Nicholas and Nissa Villeneuva; [ed.] St. Helens High; [occ.] Self employed Videographer for a business I own named: Video Memories since 1990; [oth. writ.] Several unpublished poems and short stories about angels, miracles, NDE (Near Death Experiences); [pers.] I was inspired to write a poem for each chapter in the book I'm writing, thanks to the encouragement from family and friends and those who've shared to experiences.; [a.] Saint Helens, OR

CAMPBELL, GERALD L.
[b.] May 5, 1938, Toronto, Canada; [p.] James L. and Evelyn P. Campbell; [occ.] Landscaping Contractor; [pers.] The future I see for mankind is almost beyond words. The hope of everlasting life in a paradise earth - soon to come through owe loving creator Jehovah God. Psalms 37:10-11 - Isaiah 11:6-9; [a.] Orange, CA

CAMPBELL, T. ANN
[b.] October 7, 1948, Ogden, UT; [p.] Ana Maria Garcia; [m.] Don L. Campbell (Deceased), April 28, 1988; [ch.] Tracy, Cristy, Cindy, Robbie, Lee, David, Shawn; [ed.] Weber State College of Nursing U. of Utah; [occ.] R.N.; [memb.] American Cancer Society - etc.; [hon.] Too many - do not like to brag.; [oth. writ.] I have several poems I have written, but non published at this time.; [a.] Corpus Christi, TX

CAMUS, CAROLINA
[b.] January 28, 1980, Chile; [p.] Ricardo Camus, Marvin Morales; [ed.] Going to high school; [occ.] Student; [oth. writ.] I have a lot more others, but not published; [pers.] I like to write poetry because I like to express feelings on paper, since its too hard in person. So I often write how I feel or how I see things in life.; [a.] Miami, FL

CANGANELLI, JOANNE LEAH
[pen.] Joan Canganelli; [b.] January 30, 1955, Indianapolis, IN; [p.] Dr. Vincent G. and Beverly Canganelli; [m.] Vince Robert Parman, August 19, 1978; [ch.] Julia Candace Parman; [ed.] West Side High (West Laf., IN) Purdue University BA-HU-77, majoring in European History; [occ.] Photo Lab Manager, Kerr Drug; [memb.] Shaklee representative, The Rose Preservation Foundation, Cousteau Society, Association for Research and Enlightenment, NOW; [oth. writ.] I have written over 60 other poems none of which have been published.; [pers.] I believe we were all put here on Earth for a reason and that we spend our whole lives trying to solve one simple question - why? And the only answer is that we must learn to love.; [a.] Apex, NC

CANIDNERD, NATASHA
[pen.] Tasha; [b.] September 25, 1973, Honolulu, HI; [ed.] Leilehua High School, Travel University; [occ.] Cashier for Chevron (Bionic). Hey, it pays my bills!!; [pers.] I know there are people out there having a very difficult time in their life, and that pain is only temporary, but that does not mean what I'm going through is not hurting me. Yet it is what we experience, which makes us who we are!!; [a.] Wahiawa, HI

CANINE, CURT
[b.] April 27, 1981, Kansas City; [p.] Debbie and Mark Canine; [ed.] Currently in 9th grade; [memb.] Hickman High School Wrestling; [hon.] Honor roll; [pers.] I write about whatever comes to mind. I like to write imaginative and fictional stories.; [a.] Columbia, MO

CANTWELL, RHONDA J.
[pen.] Rhonda J. (Parton) Cantwell; [b.] August 7, 1952, Chickasha, OK; [p.] L. Paul Parton and June G. (Loughridge) Parton; [m.] David G. Cantwell,

June 12, 1970; [ch.] Jonathan David, Matthew Aaron, Paul Andrew; [ed.] Duncan High School; [occ.] Halliburton Energy Services as an International Support Coordinator; [memb.] Bethel Assembly of God Church; [oth. writ.] Numerous poems about family members; [a.] Duncan, OK

CAO, PAUL
[pen.] Ma Ngo, Cao Phuoc; [b.] January 7, 1959, Saigon, Vietnam; [p.] Mai-Diem Thi Nguyen, Lam Quoc Cao; [m.] Mai Cao, June 19, 1991; [ed.] L'e'toile de Mer High, Marie Curie High, Pedagogical University of Saigon, Vietnam, Movie Acting School, Saigon, Virginia Community College (U.S.); [occ.] Business, student; [memb.] Movie Acting Research Club (V.N.), Phi Theta Kappa Fraternity (US); [hon.] Honor student (1992-1995), Summa Cum Laude for International Business (AAS) 8, 95. Summa Cum Laude for Business Management (A.A.S.) 01/96. B.A. in V.N.; [oth. writ.] Poems published in Vietnamese Society of Amateur Poets, several poems published in Vietnamese newspapers, short stories published in Vietnamese magazines, some short stories and poems unpublished; [pers.] I often deserve nature, people, and life that reflect my feelings and thoughts in writing. Writing in impulse of heart, feeling of soul, and imagination of mind that God loves and gives us, especially for someone who enjoys literature.; [a.] Sterling, VA

CAPPOZZI, KEVIN A.
[b.] July 3, 1976, Manchester, CT; [p.] Peter A. and Belinda Cappozzi; [ed.] Completed 4 years highschool in 9 mos. at Lee Adult Education Center Lessburg, FL; [memb.] Boy Scouts of America; [hon.] Many high achievement awards for drawings and writings during his school days.; [oth. writ.] Some minor publications through local newspaper.; [pers.] Nobody ever truly understands another. Secrets are always hidden.; [a.] Clermont, FL

CAPUTO, AMANDA JEAN
[pen.] Jeanie Caputo; [b.] November 22, 1941, Walsenburg, CO; [m.] Frank Caputo; [ch.] 3 Son - Joe, Tim, Steve, 7 grandchildren, Krystle, David, Joey, Yvonne, Timothy Tyler, and Robert.; [occ.] Retired Grocery Clerk and real Estate Agent; [memb.] Catholic Rainbow Outreach Prison Ministry; [hon.] For voluntary service at prison (Life in The Spirit Seminars) Youth, and Anti-Gang reallies, Mexico Outreach.; [oth. writ.] Share Love-Trust Me Count Your I's - Because He Lives God! Where Are You? - You And Me Lord Because He Lives; [pers.] Put Jesus Christ first in your life! Love unconditional just love and forgive.; [a.] Santa Ana, CA

CARBONETTA, AMALIA
[pen.] Amalia Carbonetta; [b.] December 6, 1956, Italy; [p.] Ottorino Pasquini Rosa Pasquini; [m.] Anthony Carbonetta - Deceased July 10, 1977; [ch.] Laura Carbonetta; [ed.] High School in Upper Darby; [occ.] Home maker before I was a child carework; [pers.] I love kids, animals, people all ages. I'm very sensitive person, and with my poem if I can make people feel good, or any difference, in they're day. I will be very happy and proud. Thank you.; [a.] Drexel Hill, PA

CARDONE, NANCY ANN
[b.] October 6, 1955, Astoria, Queens, NY; [p.] Daniel and Edna Demato; [m.] Christopher Mark Cardone, October 1, 1995; [ch.] Robert, Alex and Rebecca; [ed.] St. Gabriel's Elementary School, Brooklyn, New York, Sachem Senior High School, Ronkonkoma, New York, Multiple Medical Courses, presently taking a Counselor Training Program for Alcoholism and Addictions. Accepted for 3/4/96 start of Nursing School. Advanced Emergency Medical; [occ.] Technician - Critical Care; [memb.] Past Member, Rocky Point Volunteer Fire Department (1988-1994); [hon.] R.P.F.D. Co. 2 Captains Award - 1990, Mather Memorial Hospital E.M.T. of the Year - 1990, Town of Brook Haven Certificate of Appreciation - 1990, St. Charles Hospital E.M.T. of the Year/Scholarship 1993, Suffolk County Ems. Leader of the Year 1994, Proclamation Suffolk County Legislator - 1995, Proclamation Suffolk County Executive - 1995, New York State Assembly Citation - 1995.; [oth. writ.] Still working on them!; [pers.] To remember that equally important as learning something new everyday, is to unlearn something old everyday as well.; [a.] Ronkonkoma, NY

CAREY, SOFIA SCHODOLSKI
[b.] November 11, 1982, Mexico City; [p.] T. Elaine Carey and Vincent Schodolski; [2ed.] 7th grade Countryside Preparatory, Northridge, CA; [occ.] Student and Artist; [a.] Northridge, CA

CARLSEN, PATRICIA J.
[b.] 1950, Utica, NY; [ed.] New Hartford School MVCC College; [oth. writ.] Two poems published recently - other poems and notes of feelings not yet published; [pers.] My poems reflect heart felt experiences. I hope others will identify with these feelings.; [a.] New Hartford, NY

CARLUCCI, DAVID
[pen.] Dave, Roe Manse; [b.] June 25, 1942, New York City, NY; [p.] William Carlucci Sr., Fanny Carlucci; [m.] Regina Carlucci, September 12, 1962; [ch.] David W. Brian A.; [ed.] Hillside High School, County College of Morris, Monmouth College; [occ.] Senior Buyer; [memb.] National Association of Purchasing Managers, Calvary Assembly of God; [hon.] Lambada Sigma Tau, Honor Society, Bell Altantic Climber's Club; [oth. writ.] Journal of Purchasing and Material Management, Annual International Purchasing Conference, BA - Purchasing Gazette; [pers.] To convey the seemingly uninteresting Adventures of everyday mundane living, through a romanticized vogue.; [a.] Randolph, NJ

CARNINE, HOLLY A.
[b.] September 19, 1971, Austin, TX; [p.] Dr. Al and Nancy Carnine; [ed.] Bachelor of Arts Degree in Communications and an Associate of Arts Degree in General Studies (December, 1993); [memb.] Phi Eta Sigma Honor Society, Omicron Delta Kappa Honor Society, Alpha Chi Honor Society, Dean's List; [hon.] Graduated Magna Cum Laude, Dean's List.; [oth. writ.] Published poem, "I'll see you soon"; [pers.] My philosophy of life is summed up in the following quote, "The way to happiness: Keep your heart free from hate, your mind from worry. Live simply, expect little, give much. Fill your life with love. Scatter sunshine. Forget yourself, think of others. Do as you would be done by."; [a.] Joplin, MO

CARPENTER, IDA
[b.] July 2, 1938, Baltimore, MD; [p.] Pauline Carpenter, James Carpenter; [m.] October 11, 1974; [ch.] Four Children; [ed.] 9th grade; Mother and Father, with 11 children unable to further education; [occ.] Housewife, Retired and Raising 2 Grandchildren; [hon.] Just things I feel in my heart. I sit and just write in my spare time in school I had wrote a poem which was years ago. My school put this in the paper this all what I feel; [oth. writ.] I just write Snow and Wind - Whetel as Crimson, Wind Blowing Better, Families Closer Together, People Helping Each Other, Plowing Forward, God's Grace and Goodness for His Children; [pers.] In my spare time, I like to write what is in my heart mainly about how the Lord has brought me through so many heartaches in life.; [a.] Baltimore, MD

CARRELL, RHONDA
[b.] October 17, 1956, Excelsior Springs, MO; [p.] Johnny C. Jones and Doris J. Jones; [m.] A. Stephen Carrell, March 19, 1994; [ch.] Christy Lynn, Nell Marie and Jed Allen; [ed.] Palestine High School, Maple Woods Community College; [occ.] Homemaker; [memb.] American Heart Association, American Cancer Society, Humane Society of the United States; [pers.] I write what I see and feel. I write compassion, what everyone has but few acknowledge.; [a.] Needville, TX

CARRIER, DONALD L.
[b.] October 7, 1952, Rochester, NH; [p.] Wilfred Carrier Jr., Laurette Carrier; [m.] T. French, October 15, 1983; [ed.] Master of Arts in Counselling Psychology (Holistic); [occ.] Crisis Clinician; [memb.] Mass Assoc of Mental Health Counselors; [hon.] National Library of Poetry Editor's Award; [oth. writ.] Poem published in National Library of Poetry, A Sea Of Treasures; [pers.] A heart open to life's possibilities, with faith in a higher power, is a soul open to countless adventures, celebrate the journey.; [a.] Malden, MA

CARROZZA, ROSE
[b.] November 7, 1938, Brooklyn; [p.] Maria Carrozza; [oth. writ.] Angel Of The Night

CARTER, ROSELYN
[pen.] Rosie; [b.] April 1, 1920, Spring Field, OH; [p.] Dan and Mary Walsh; [m.] Dr. Leland M. Carter, July 25, 1942; [ch.] Three; [ed.] High School; [occ.] Housewife; [oth. writ.] Just a lot of poems; [pers.] I like humour and the way to express my admiration and liking of other people; [a.] Gresham, OR

CARTWRIGHT, ROSALIE
[b.] March 23, 1922, Barrington, RI; [p.] Rose Jacobs LePage and Louis LePage; [m.] Norman Cartwright, December 30, 1944; [ch.] Rosalie Cartwright Hainey; [ed.] High School Institute of Childrens Literature - Long Ridge Writers Group; [occ.] Writer - Poet; [memb.] Matthews Seniors Volunteer; [oth. writ.] The thirteenth floor for I am - light and shadow day break - my tree - old tree - lost love cruel, cruel world ghost ship - imagination; [pers.] If I had a penny for every thought, I would be a millionaire.; [a.] Pawtucket, RI

CASBY, DEBRA
[b.] July 21, 1963, Monroe, MI; [p.] Howard and Elizabeth Yentz; [m.] Mark Casby, July 16, 1983; [ch.] Mark David, Miranda Rana and Matthew Howard; [ed.] Jefferson High School; [occ.] Child Care Provider; [memb.] Secretary of Parent - Teacher Organization; [oth. writ.] Several poems and Children's book (none published); [pers.] My family and friends are the greatest source of inspiration and joy in my life.; [a.] Bronson, MI

CASTILLO, NICOLE
[b.] January 10, 1979, Port Huron, MI; [ed.] Port Isabel High School; [occ.] Full time high school student

CAUDILL, JANNIS MAE
[pen.] J/C; [b.] September 8, 1929, Dayton, OH; [p.] John L. and Evelyn (Slaven), Davidson (Deceased); [m.] Richard K. Caudill, August 7, 1952; [ch.] Mark, Kathleen and Amy; [ed.] Patterson High School Dayton, Ohio Stated College at 53 yrs attended Ohio State U, Newark Ohio for help attended IL. Rank; [occ.] Re-tired - volunteer for boy scouts of America - Ass it District Commissioner for Licking Co Ohio; [memb.] Kiwanis, order of Eastern stars, past worth matron - 73 - grand page Dist - 12 78, Sec-tres Dist 12 - 78 - 81 Democratic party; [hon.] Friends of scouting fund raising for Licking Co - Commissioner

Crest of Service Award; [oth. writ.] Kept daily personnel diary since 6, 1st poem published in national library of poetry - 1995; [pers.] My poetry writes it's self. Very seldom edit - once written, I put them away and pleasedly surprised when I read. My interest: The universe nature and the events that surround our daily lives thus - the poetry springs forth and becomes the word.; [a.] Heath, OH

CEA, VINCENT
[pen.] Vincent James, James Vincent; [b.] October 14, 1947, New York; [p.] Vincent Cea, Rose Cea; [m.] Carol Ann; [ch.] Diane Chiopalo, Vincent James, Joseph Paul, Nicholas Anthony, Samantha Lynn; [memb.] International Society of Poets; [hon.] Editor Choice 1995; [oth. writ.] Several poems published in books, also published in local newspapers.; [pers.] I believe the care and the love you give in your life, shall always be returned to a heart filled with true feelings.

CEBALLOS, ELIZABETH
[b.] November 13, 1967, San Bernardino, CA; [p.] Leo Ceballos and Emilia Ceballos; [ch.] Pet - Lil' bit; [ed.] San Bernardino High School San Bernardino Valley College California State University - San Bernardino Western State Univ. - College of Law; [occ.] Law School Student; [hon.] First place winner for short story/essay contests at the University.; [oth. writ.] Various articles in school newspapers, poems, and short stories submitted into local school magazine.; [pers.] Writing in communication, a way to put life in paper. Jotted down feelings and paper. Jotted down feelings and thoughts is the most touching and thoughts is the most touching from of expression, whether it be in a newspaper articles, stories and poems, or in greeting cards, letters, and small notes.; [a.] San Bernardino, CA

CECCHINI, LYNN MARIE
[pen.] Pink Cloud; [b.] June 5, 1954, Bakerfield, CA; [p.] Robert and Kathryn Ramey; [m.] Gregory Cecchini, May 25, 1983; [ch.] Michael Gregory and Kathleen Nicole; [ed.] East Bakerfield High School, Bakerfield College, Cal State Univ. Northridge; [occ.] State Farm Insurance agent since Jan. 1982; [oth. writ.] I started writing poetry to make sense out of some of my experiences in life and to relive through certain poems some of the best experiences in my life.; [pers.] "Sometimes it helps to write a poem, to organize the words - thought by thought. In a certain order of motion and beauty. Sometimes stuck for a rhyme, like a knot. Pink clouds drifting in a pretty blue sky, that's what I often see at sunset or dawn. I watch the sky changing colors, clouds turning pink them gray, then moving on".; [a.] Burbank, CA

CENTALA, MICHAEL
[b.] February 5, 1952, Rogers City, MI; [p.] Robert and Dolores Centala; [m.] Dine Marie Sample, November 18, 1983; [ch.] Jessica, Angela, Leandra and Michael; [ed.] St. Paul Seminary, Rogers City High, Alpena Community College and Ferris State University; [occ.] Teacher, Social Workers; [memb.] Boy Scouts, Fraternal Order Police, Eagles, Civic Theatre, ZBA, Licensed, General Contractor, Licensed Social Worker Registered MHSAA Sports Official; [hon.] Cum Laude Graduate; [oth. writ.] Numerous poems and short stories; [pers.] Live by the Golden Rule; [a.] Alpena, MI

CHAMPLIN, HEATHER MARIE
[b.] January 14, 1974, Aberdeen, SD; [p.] Dave and Jan Champlin; [ed.] High School - LD. Bell High - Bedford, TX - Diploma College - ITT Technical Inst., Houston, TX - Associate of Applied Science Degree in CAD; [occ.] Substitute Teacher for Elementary - High School; [memb.] ITT Alumni Association, Who's Who Among American High School Students; [pers.] Though I have never shared my writings before I have always hoped they would be used as a tool of inspiration.; [a.] Spring, TX

CHANCE, MELINDA W.
[b.] November 21, 1950, Columbia, MS; [p.] Stephen Williamson and Vannie Williamson; [m.] Burney D. Chance, July 3, 1970; [ch.] Alice Adelle - Jared Burney; [ed.] Bunker Hill High School, Pearl River Community College; [occ.] Personnel Office, Columbia Cable Manufacturer; [pers.] I am sentimental person. I value love and happiness more than material possessions. I have been influenced by Helen Stiener Rice; [a.] Columbia, MS

CHAPMAN, CAROL
[b.] August 1, 1955, Newport News, VA; [p.] Oliver Chapman, Annie Chapman; [ed.] Colonial High, Mercer University, Valencia Community College; [occ.] Substance Abuse Counselor (Intern) Orlando, FL; [oth. writ.] Currently working on collection of poems and short stories; [pers.] I have a deep appreciation for the classics, as well as contemporary poetry. My writing attempts to merge an intensity of emotion with the integrity of expression; [a.] Orlando, FL

CHARLAN, NATHAN ARTHUR
[b.] November 11, 1981, Libertyville, IL; [p.] Leonard Charlan, JoAnn Charlan; [ed.] Johnsburg High School; [memb.] National Rifle Association; [hon.] District 12 Young Authors; [oth. writ.] Antarctica's Dead Man Trail, The Cry of the Wolf, An Ocean Ordeal, Avalanche; [pers.] The secret of life is to live every day to the fullest; [a.] Johnsburg, IL

CHATLAS, NANCY
[pen.] Nancy Chatlas; [b.] July 27, 1947, Uniontown, PA; [p.] Jane and Carl Gaskill; [m.] Stephen A. Chatlas, April 16, 1966; [ch.] Robin, Rebecca, Susane; [ed.] 12th Grade, High School Graduate; [occ.] Store Owner; [oth. writ.] Non published children's stories.

CHATMAN, ANITA L.
[b.] July 28, 1972, Washington, DC; [p.] William C. Chatman and Bertha L. Chatman; [ed.] Northern Virginia Community College, AS: Business Management, Marketing, General Studies; [occ.] Secretary for the Assistant Director of Security at INS; [hon.] Honored by many friends and relatives who had recognized my talents and believed in me before I believed in myself.; [oth. writ.] Many writings trying to get published and recognized for.; [pers.] Always find your strength within and don't be afraid to let it grow. We all have something within us that needs to grow.; [a.] Washington, DC

CHEN, SISTER SHERYL FRANCES
[b.] April 16, 1957, Princeton, NJ; [p.] Prof. Francis F. Chen, Edna Lau Chen; [ed.] B.A. Religious Studies, Cum Laude Yale 1979, Work toward M. Div., Notre Dame '79-'80; [occ.] Cloistered Cistercian Nun; [oth. writ.] Catechumenate Magazine, Spirit and Life, U.S. Catholic, Vision '92, Vision '95, Onward, Inter-Varsity Student Leadership Journal; [pers.] May my words give glory to the World who became flesh and lived among us, full of grace and truth.; [a.] Sonoita, AZ

CHERRY, SHARON REISCH
[b.] October 27, 1963, Washington, DC; [p.] Benjamin and Betty (Simpson) Reisch; [m.] Edwin Monroe Cherry, April 6, 1984; [ch.] Jessica Marie, Jennifer Nicole; [ed.] Grace King High-Metairie, LA. George L. Wallace Community College; [occ.] Secretary/Bookkeeper; [memb.] Southeast Writers Assoc. and Associate member of the International Society of Poets.; [hon.] Graduated with honors in English.; [oth. writ.] Poetry published in local newspaper, poetry published in Where Dreams Begin, Best Poems of 1995, Recipient Editor's Choice Award - poem "About Forgiving" published in New South Poetry Chapbook.; [pers.] My writing is a way to share my love for our Lord Jesus Christ who gave us eternal life. I dedicate this particular poem "The Sacrifice" to my late dad whom I miss very much. This is for you Benjamin W. Reisch.; [a.] Pansey, AL

CHEVRIER, JOANN
[b.] May 13, 1955, New Brunswick, NJ; [p.] Eugene Chevrier, Eva Dorothy Chevrier; [ed.] Madison High, The King's College, Briarcliff Manor, NY; [occ.] Missionary, BCM International; [pers.] In my poetry, I write about things that I've observed or experienced. I have an ability to be empathetic with others and their needs, and this shows up in my writing. Jesus Christ is my personal Savior and the center of my life. He gives peace, stability and fulfillment beyond our impossible needs. You can have that fulfillment too.; [a.] Lititz, PA

CHOPANE, YUSHERIA
[pen.] Nikki Chopane; [b.] April 6, 1981, Beaumont, TX; [p.] Stephanie Chopane; [ed.] Banning High, and looking forward to going to Howard University.; [occ.] Student; [hon.] Magnet Program; [oth. writ.] Entered poetry in contests and some in our local newspaper, the Beaumont Enterprise.; [pers.] I enjoy writing, poetry of any kind and hope to be a famous poet someday.; [a.] Carson, CA

CHOW, ARNOLD H.
[b.] November 15, 1908, Huelo, Maui (U.S.A.); [p.] Mr. and Mrs. Chow Lai; [m.] Annie L. F. Chow (Deceased), July 24, 1937; [ch.] Mrs. Anita K. Y. Terry, Mrs. Audrey K. M. Lum; [ed.] St. Anthony School, Wailuku, Maui; [occ.] Retired (Commercial Artist); [a.] Honolulu, HI

CHU, KWEI-YUEN
[b.] August 8, 1974; [p.] Tyrone Chu, Shu-Ching Chu; [pers.] Beauty exists in the most-unlikely places.; [a.] Modesto, CA

CHUNG, MUOI
[pen.] Purple Martin; [b.] April 3, 1968, Bienhoa, Vietnam; [p.] Lac Phan, Xieu Chung; [ed.] 2 years college at Evergreen Valley College San Jose California; [occ.] Embroider; [pers.] I try to create the connection between human and nature in my writing. I also express my emotion of being young. My writing is influenced by the joy of life.; [a.] San Jose, CA

CLARK, ANIKA
[b.] August 1, 1981, Pasadena, CA; [p.] Richard and JoAnn Clark; [ed.] Currently attending Westridge School (Freshman); [hon.] Member of the California Junior Scholastic Federation, received Excellence in Performing Arts Award (middle school); [a.] Pasadena, CA

CLARK IV, GEORGE WILLIAM
[b.] May 17, 1971, Nashville, TN; [p.] George and Barbara Clark; [ed.] Franklin High School, B.S. Middle Tennessee State University; [occ.] ACZ Laboratories, Steamboat Springs, Co; [memb.] Sigma Chi Fraternity; [pers.] There is no grater joy in life that happiness, have fun!; [a.] Steamboat Springs, CO

CLARK, RUTH M.
[b.] October 7, 1919, Devon, Montana; [p.] Harvey and Athena Lyseth; [m.] Joseph Daughaday Clark, June 21, 1947; [ch.] Douglas Edward, Anne Louise, Mary Ellen, and Karen Elizabeth; [ed.] Hinckley High School, Minnesota School of Business; [occ.] Homemaker; [oth. writ.] Several articles and poems published in local newspapers and church bulletins.; [pers.] I am approaching the age when my thoughts,

and therefore my writings, tend to reflect memories of my childhood of or "how things used to be", also a deeper appreciation of my heritage and God's continual provision for my life.; [a.] Brooklyn, MN

CLARK, SALLY
[pen.] Salome Adkins; [b.] May 17, 1931, Tucson, AZ; [p.] Charles Adkins and Mattie Adkins; [ch.] Robert C. Graham, Bruce Cabot and Judy Cabot; [ed.] Empire Elementary School, at Sonoita, Ariz, Sunny side High School, Tucson, Ariz; [occ.] Retired Homemaker; [oth. writ.] Several poems, some published in Manatee Glens Senior Center Newsletter, at Bradenton, Florida; [pers.] I try to write helpful, encouraging poems to give others a chance to learn from my experiences and observations.; [a.] Holmes Beach, FL

CLARK, SHARIE D.
[pen.] Sharie D. Clark; [b.] April 4, 1941, Ontario, Canada; [p.] Margaret May Deline; [m.] Divorced; [ch.] David, Shennon, Stephen; [ed.] High School, English and Drama Arts coarse at Brock University. Also three years training and travel with Covenant Players (Christian Touring Theater) some courses in Water Color.; [occ.] Writing short stories, poetry, some water color paintings.; [memb.] Church of the Resurrection, World Vision Canada, Smithsonian, Wild Life Assoc, Covenant Players of California; [hon.] Recognition in some water colors, and service in a prison ministry, Award in performance and person, from Covenant Players, greatest award as a mother and friend.; [oth. writ.] Taking a coarse for some children's stories I want to publish (Institute of Children's Literature) Have written some plays for church, dialogue for fashion shows, for recovery groups along with picture therapy. Poems for the Christian Artist.; [pers.] Let us run with patience the particular race that God has set before us. Hebrews 12:16; [a.] Niagara Falls, NY

CLARK, SUSAN E.
[pen.] S. E. Clark; [b.] May 8, 1966, Medota, IL; [p.] James and Margejorie Clark; [ed.] Completed High School and 6 years of Community College; [occ.] Ink Roller Assembler, Poetry Columnist, Editor, Beginning Poetry Instructor; [memb.] 2 Memberships with the International Society of Poets; [hon.] 2 Golden Poet Awards, 3 Merit Awards, 2 Earned Awards with the Famous Poetry Society, an Editor's Choice Award from the National Library of Poetry. I have been published extensively in different anthologies and publications from the years 1991-1996. I am also a published song writer with Tin Pan Alley.; [pers.] Believe in God, pray to Him, and let Him work in your life. You won't be sorry!; [a.] Tucson, AZ

CLARKE, JOHN R.
[b.] April 15, 1913, Saint Paul, MN; [p.] Johna Anne; [m.] Opal, December 16, 1939; [ch.] John, Carol, Dale, Richard, Susan; [ed.] M.S. Purder; [occ.] Retired; [memb.] Florida Freelance writer's Ass'n.; [hon.] 3rd place Florida Writer's Competition - 1989 "Who's Who - Writers Editors and Poets." 1988; [oth. writ.] Book "Executive Power How To Use It Effectively" - Practice Hall Mise Articles; [pers.] Life is good; [a.] Boca Raton, FL

CLEMENS, JENNIFER
[b.] January 29, 1981, California; [p.] Barbara and Joseph Clemens; [hon.] Westminster Teachers Association Award 1992 and 1995, Girl Scout Silver Award, Rotary Club, National Junior Honor Society

CLEMENTS, DELILA A.
[b.] February 16, 1983, Redford, VA; [p.] Mark S. Clements, Lila Goff; [ed.] 7th grade; [occ.] Student at Great Bridge Middle-North; [memb.] Virginia Marine Science Museum, and Somerset Place Foundation NC, Pleasant Grove Baptist Church; [hon.] Young Author '93, '94, Chesapeake's 30 Birthday poster 2nd place '93; [oth. writ.] I We What We Ate, Bill My Snowman, The Moon and Stars; [pers.] I like to write and sing because they bring out my most inner feelings. I have been greatly influenced by many people and objects but what influence me the most was the outdoors.; [a.] Chesapeake, VA

CLEMONS, RICKY T.
[b.] March 15, 1958, Suffolk, VA; [p.] Mr. and Mrs. Robert Lillie Bonnier; [m.] Mrs. Nancy A. Clemons, April 7, 1993; [ed.] High School Diploma some college education; [occ.] Security officer; [memb.] I'm a delicate member of Capernaum Seventh-Day Adventist Church and a Gold Star member of the price club.; [hon.] Soldier of the month for October 1977 in company C, 65th Engineer Battalion, in 25th Infantry Division at Scofield Barracks, Hawaii. Special honor for serving as Deacon and Sabbath school chorister at Capernaum Seventh-Day Adventist Church; [oth. writ.] "Our Transparent Wall" copy wright not publish yet; [pers.] I strongly believe that when you put God first in whatever that you do, he will give you showers of blessings.; [a.] Suffolk, VA

CLIVER, CAROLYN E.
[pen.] Carolyn E. Cliver; [b.] October 27, 1935, Indianapolis, IN; [p.] Frederick and Frieda Packer; [m.] Dean O. Cliver, August 13, 1960; [ch.] Blanche, Frederick, Carl, Margrerite; [ed.] BA and MA - Indiana University; [occ.] Retired Social Worker; [memb.] Attruks High School Alumni Assn. No. 14, AAUW, AARP, volunteer at International House at University of California in Duris; [hon.] Unsung hero from NAACP in Madison, Wisc.; [oth. writ.] Presently writing a book.; [a.] Davis, CA

CLOMAN, EDDIE B.
[pen.] Eddie B. Cloman; [b.] April 13, 1941, Houston, TX; [p.] Eddie J. Cumbo Jr. and Hazel McGlee; [m.] George W. Cloman, January 4, 1965; [ch.] Erik V. Cloman and Scott J. Cloman; [ed.] 1958 Graduate of Phyllis Wheatley High School and 1963, Graduate of Texas Southern University's School of Pharmacy; [occ.] Retired Registered Pharmacist; [memb.] American Pharmaceutical Assoc., California Employee Pharmacy Assoc., Central Los Angeles Pharmacist Assoc., and National Pharmaceutical Assoc.; [hon.] Several poems appeared in publications Mt. Triumph Bpt. Church Trustee Board, Mt. Triumph Bpt Church Hero of Fund Raising, Mt. Triumph V.P. Mass Choir, Commissioned to put Citizens of Zion Bpt. Church (Compton, Calie) 50 yeara history to poetry and traveled to Calif. 12-3-95 to deliver and received Honorarium, Guest speaker on 4 occasions for Church Annual Affairs, wrote and performed a Concert of Poetry and Song at 2 Churches in California, Guest Soloist many times for Churches, Weddings, and other Private Affairs; [oth. writ.] Book "Feelings of Yesterday Today and Tomorrow", "Bits and Pieces", "Raw Material", "Clearly Delivered"; [pers.] My poetry is a gift from God which served to save my sanity and my life. It's purpose is to deliver it's reader from some burden or problem and point the way to hope or inspire someone.; [pers.] My poetry is a gift from God which served to same my sanity and my life. It's purpose is to deliver it's reader from some burden or problem and point the way to hope or inspire someone.; [a.] Boyce, LA

COE, TRILBIA D.
[pen.] Trip; [b.] July 22, 1942, LA; [p.] Drusiella and Harry Duncan; [m.] David Coe Jr. (Deceased); [ch.] Diane Thorpe (Deceased), Leah Thomas, Yolanda Duncan, Renita Anderson, Benny Anderson; [ed.] 3 yrs College; [occ.] 30 yrs Nurse, aspring writer semi-ret'd; [memb.] Past member NNA - past member Ladies Auxiliary VFW - Member of International Poets Society; [hon.] Editors Choice Award from Nat'l Library of Poetry Seal of Nev. under Gov. Mike O'Callaham Adm.; [oth. writ.] French Bertha (poem) "Abuse" The Naked Truth to be released in May of 1996; [pers.] I express my feeling about others in my writing. Dedicated to Diane from all the family; [a.] Las Vegas, NV

COFFMAN, KERRY
[pen.] Kerry Coffman; [b.] September 1952, Eureka, CA; [p.] Joseph and Peggy Browitt; [m.] Leroy Coffman, March 4, 1989; [ch.] Joey Jon, Jade Joy; [ed.] Issaquah High Renton Vo-Tech; [occ.] Housewife; [hon.] I am honored to be a mother of a 1992 Naval Academy graduate (my son), and my daughter just awarded me with my first grandchild Trista Lane; [oth. writ.] None that that have been published; [pers.] I love to read so much, that its hard for me to believe, there are people who hate to read! I have learned a lot in my life through the pages of many books; [a.] Renton, WA

COHEN, JIMMIE RUTH
[pen.] Jimmie Ruth Cohen; [b.] East, TX; [p.] James and Cora Harrington; [m.] Herman Cohen (Deceased), June 24, 1943; [ch.] 2 sons and 1 daughter and 5 grandchildren; [ed.] High School and Business College; [memb.] First Baptist Church 7401 Katy Freeway Houston, Texas 77024-2199; [pers.] Kindly include my middle name, RUTH, spelled out as I never go by only my first name or even my middle initial. In the future I shall appreciate your using my entire three word name which is Jimmie Ruth Cohen.; [a.] Houston, TX

COLAN, JO
[b.] Factoryville, PA; [m.] John Colan, February 5, 1949; [ch.] Laura and Cheri; [ed.] Tunbhannock, PA High School, Scronton State Nursing School Columbia University; [occ.] Financial Consultant, Registered; [memb.] Principal with N.A.S.D. member of very large family about 90 positive. We (my husband and I) waited 12 years for our one and only grand child one of my many poems about her is "With a hod of her head" (Cody was about 1 year old); [oth. writ.] Numerous personal poems for special events.; [pers.] I write poems from the conclusions I make from what I observe what I observe all around me, family. New York City, anything; [a.] New York City, NY

COLE, GLORIA SCOTT
[ed.] B.S. Criminal Justice, Grad study - Law; [hon.] Alpha Sigma NU - Natl. Jesuit Honorary Society

COLE JR., DANIEL
[b.] October 31, 1953, Hempstead, TX; [p.] Mr. Daniel and Reatha Cole; [ed.] B.S. Degree in Computer Science Prairie View A and M University Prairie View, TX; [occ.] Senior Programmer analyst H.E.B., San Antonio, TX; [pers.] Express what you feel in your writing.

COLELLA, CLIFF
[b.] April 9, 1971, Lynn, MA; [p.] John and Catherine Colella; [ed.] Hood Elementary, Lynn, MA Eastern Junior High, Lynn, MA English High School, Lynn, MA; [occ.] Star Market "State St. Lynn" Grocery Clerk; [oth. writ.] "Crystal Rose" (not published yet); [pers.] It's better to lose at Love, than to have never loved at all.; [a.] Lynn, MA

COLEMAN, SHARON L.
[b.] August 5, 1936, Princeton, IN; [p.] Charles Mauck, Lena Mauck; [m.] Harold L. Coleman; [ch.] Tonja and Tamara; [ed.] Owensville High School, Lockyears Business College and University of Evansville; [occ.] Bookkeeper and Treasurer of South Gibson Sch. Corp.; [memb.] First Christian Church,

Disciples of Christ, Various Club Organizations; [oth. writ.] Various poems, not yet made available for publication.; [pers.] My many blessings in life have been my inspiration for writing, and I plan to continue writing in hopes that my words might help someone in their lifetime.; [a.] Haubstadt, IN

COLLINS, TRAMELL L.
[pen.] Tramell; [b.] November 17, 1971, Chicago, IL; [p.] Sheila Wilson, Larry Wilson; [ed.] Grant H.S., and Life; [occ.] Maintenance Administrators Pacific Bell, N. Hollywood, Ca.; [memb.] Weskose Residents, Ghetto Natives; [oth. writ.] Scores of poems, songs and essays for personal enjoyment.; [pers.] Everything I am and shall be, I owe to GOD and my hero, my mother. For without them I'd be nothing.; [a.] Lancaster, CA

COLOM, KIAMESHA-SYLVIA GABRIELLE
[pen.] Kabrielle; [b.] December 18, 1980, Bronx, NY; [p.] Arlene Rivera and Wiliam Colom; [ed.] Academy of St. Joseph Brentwood, NY; [occ.] Student; [memb.] Glee Club, Girl Scouts, Basketball team, track team, adopt a-family committee; [hon.] Ambassadorship to Australia; [pers.] My poetry symbolizes the strength of a child the methods she uses to deceive her parent, who does not look behind the surface image that she portrays.; [a.] Coram, NY

COLSON, ALICIA
[b.] January 18, 1978, Kettering, OH; [ed.] Centerville High School; [hon.] Editor-in-chief of high school newspaper/magazine; [oth. writ.] Articles published in school newspaper/magazine; [pers.] The biggest reward for me is when people read and enjoy what I write; [a.] Centerville, OH

COMBS, BECKY
[pen.] Becky Combs; [ch.] Emily Combs Biasini; [ed.] Bachelor of Arts Science, Master's Degree - Supervision and Administration Principal's Certificate; [occ.] Retired Principal (currently Guided Tours - Kennedy Center volunteer); [memb.] Friends of the Kennedy Center, Md. State Teacher's Retirement System Mgmt. Co., Maryland Principal's Retirement Assoc., Women's Committee for the Nat. Symphony Orchestra, Sorority - Md. Beta Chapter A.D.K.A. National; [oth. writ.] Interpretations for School Guide Book - Stories and poetry, Choral Speaking Tapes for schools in Montgomery Co. Md.; [pers.] I write written poetry for my own enjoyment. I have been encouraged to write poetry for publication. This is my initial try.; [a.] Silver Spring, MD

COMPTON, PHYLLIS
[pen.] Reva Barr

CONE, CATHERINE
[b.] March 4, 1981, Miami, FL; [p.] William Cone and Estella Cone; [ed.] Our Lady of Lourdes Academy (high school) (freshmen); [hon.] The American Legion Award, Valedictorian of eight grade class, President's award for Educational Excellence; [oth. writ.] Several other poems and some short stories but none have been published; [pers.] I write to demonstrate that there is hope in the youth, if only people had the courage to believe in us.; [a.] Miami, FL

CONLEY, RENE LYNN
[b.] October 8, 1961, Bartlesville, OK; [p.] Theron Kroeger F., Betty Skye M.; [m.] Gregory Alan Conley, March 9, 1991; [ch.] Dustin, David, Hilary, Kasi, William; [ed.] Labette Co. High, Altamont Kansas Dewey High Dewey, Oklahoma; [occ.] Housekeeper Hotel Phillips, Bartlesville OK; [memb.] New Hope United Methodist Church Dewey, OK; [hon.] Veterinary Science Award; [oth. writ.] Several poems unpublished; [pers.] I wanted to share with everyone the reality that when we get older we are not reaching the end, only the beginning.; [a.] Dewey, OK

CONNORS, RICHARD D.
[b.] November 12, Aurora, IL; [p.] Jack and Helen; [ed.] Marmion Mil. Acad. Univ. of Arizona; [occ.] Teacher and Baseball Coach.; [hon.] The first foreigner to be a sunctioned H.S. Baseball Coach in Japan. September 1, 1994, Suijo His. Mito, Ibaraki.; [pers.] Enjoy each day, and be happy being yourself, also "do your best" each day of your life, don't worry about failure!; [a.] Tucson, AZ

CONROD, KORY E.
[b.] June 15, 1968, Southington, CT; [p.] Richard and Anne Newell; [ed.] Our Lady of Mercy, Plainville High School, Connecticut Center for Massage Therapy; [occ.] Massage Therapist; [memb.] American Massage Therapy Association; [oth. writ.] I have a few unpublished poems that I've written.; [pers.] I enjoy writing poems. The environment is my inspiration.; [a.] Plainville, CT

CONWAY, MARGOT
[b.] August 6, 1954, Brighton, England; [p.] G. R. Conway and G. E.; [ed.] Coral Gables High School, Charron-Williams Para-Medical College. Miami Dade Community College.; [occ.] Medical/Legal Assis. Miami, FL.; [memb.] American Medial Technologists, World Wildlife Fund, No Shore Animal League.; [oth. writ.] I've never tried to have anything published before, but have written for years for my own enjoyment.; [pers.] I write about what is true to me, whether on not others agree with my views. I can find beauty in the little things sometimes over looked by others.; [a.] Miami, FL

COOK, CHARLES
[pen.] Chuck; [b.] July 9, 1958, Baraboo, WI; [p.] Norman Cook and Vera Cook; [ch.] Marcus Ryan, Brandon Tyler, Ashley Zara; [ed.] Adams Friendship High School; [occ.] Chief, Information Management, United States Air Force; [oth. writ.] An article for the base weekly paper; [pers.] This was the only poem I have ever written. I woke up one morning and wrote down these words. The poem will mean something to everyone.; [a.] Eglin AFB, FL

COOK, LESLIE MAXWELL
[pen.] Blue Guns; [b.] May 9, 1950, Detroit, MI; [p.] Carrie and Melvin Maxwell; [m.] Tim Cook, April 30, 1994; [ed.] 1) Mumford High School, 2) Univ. of Michigan, 3) Laney Cosmetology School, 4) Computer Learning Center, 5) Diablo Valty College/Environmental Engineering Dept.; [occ.] Environmental Field Technician, Poet; [memb.] Glide Methodist Ediscopal Church, S.F., CA, 2) National Cosmetology Association, Look Good Feel Better Program/Cancer Makeover; [hon.] Burgandy and Blue Honors Club at Mumford High, Computer Learning Center (Graduated with Honors) Editors Award for True Blue Love; [oth. writ.] Published: 1) True Blue Love, 2) Stillness Waits, 3) Understanding Us, 4) Cat Woman Do it, 5) Passage. Extensive collection of poems focusing on joy, peace, and life and suffering of womankind and mankind and humanity.; [pers.] I pray for continued grace and mercy from God. I live a life filled with passions that create a "boil that cannot be stirred down".; [a.] Walnut Creek, CA

COOLEY, MARI-LYNN
[b.] July 14, 1956, Utica, NY; [p.] Anthony Mastrino, Dolores Mastrino; [m.] Rory Cooley, May 21, 1975; [ch.] Anthony, Erin, Christa, Daniel; [ed.] Walt Whitman High School, Huntington, New York; [occ.] Adult Instructor, Self employed teaching computer software; [oth. writ.] Several poems, short stories and articles written privately - not published; [pers.] Through teaching and my writings I try to touch the lives around me - to wipe a tear, give a smile, embrace a soul. I have been inspired by the writing of Nesbit and Elizabeth Barrett Browning's love sonnets.; [a.] East Northport, NY

COPPA, MRS. TERRI K.
[b.] April 5, 1947, Oakland, CA; [p.] James C. Travis, Danielle Elliott; [m.] Stephen J. Coppa, July 10, 1993; [ed.] Ojai Valley School, University of the Pacific, Humphreys Business College; [occ.] Housewife, volunteer worker, in N. Providence and Woonsocket, RI, respectively; [hon.] B.S. Degree with honors at University of the Pacific; [oth. writ.] A book of Poetry yet to be published and a Diary, "My Impressions of Poland", also awaiting the opportunity to be published.; [pers.] I have a deep love for nature and animals. I also entertain a wonderful hope that someday the earth will be restored to its original beauty when people who really care achieve supremacy. One of my favorite poets is Rod McKuen.; [a.] North Providence, RI

COQUILLARD III, GEORGE W.
[b.] August 13, 1961, Goshen, IN; [p.] George and Laura Coquillard; [ch.] George, Dustin, Ryan; [occ.] Mobile Home worker; [memb.] Wawasee Heights Baptist Church; [oth. writ.] My letter to Jesus published in Famous Poems of today by the Famous Poets Society.; [pers.] I have been greatly inspired by my love for Jesus Christ.; [a.] Syracuse, IN

COREN, SUSAN HODGES
[b.] September 17, 1959, Norfolk, VA; [p.] Jerry and Jayne Hodges; [m.] Lance S. Coren; [ch.] Amy Elizabeth Coren; [ed.] Fresno City College/Fresno State Univ.; [occ.] Registered Nurse (RN); [hon.] Outstanding Young Women in America, 1987-1988; [pers.] I wrote the poem "My House" in 1976, during my senior year of High School. It was based on a home I had once lived in and loved as a young child.; [a.] Prather, CA

CORLETT, KEVIN
[b.] May 22, 1961, New York, NY; [p.] Joan and Ernest Galfus and Walter Corlett; [m.] Eileen, June 11, 1988; [ch.] Eric James; [ed.] Connetquot H.S., University of Richmond, VA; [occ.] Principal, Trinergy Marketing Group; [a.] Kenersville, NC

CORNELIUS, RUSSELL B.
[b.] September 9, 1921, Virgin, UT; [p.] Henry and Emma Cornelius; [m.] Ruth Call Cornelius, January 7, 1943; [ch.] Russell K, Shauna, Harold, Steven; [ed.] Masters Degree Educational Administration, BA - History; [occ.] Retired; [memb.] Phi Kappa Phi; [hon.] Governors Award for Volunteerism President Antioch Education Chairman Washington Co. Solid Waste District.; [oth. writ.] Poetry and now completing a history of Dry Farming on the Mesas; [pers.] I was inspired to write this poem from recollections of reading and being influenced as a youth "The Great Stone Face" by National Hawthorn; [a.] Hurricane, UT

CORRALES, PATRICIA M.
[pen.] "Patico"; [b.] March 10, 1964, Cocha Bamba, Bolivia; [p.] Filo Corrales and Martha Veisaja; [m.] Joaquin Talleda; [ed.] Edgewood High School, Mt. St. Mary's College, Univ. of Colorado School of Law; [occ.] Attorney; [oth. writ.] Several poems; [pers.] My spirit is moved by my life experiences that God places in my path.; [a.] West Covina, CA

CORRALEZ, AMOS
[b.] February 4, 1972, Chickasha, OK; [p.] Frank and Esther Corralez; [m.] Jacque Corralez, July 21, 1993; [occ.] Carpenter; [pers.] Writing is a release of my imagination I start the pen, and it flows like

butter off a hot pan. I was influenced poetically by my 6th grade teacher, Mrs. Helen Lawson, of Deer Creek Middle School.; [a.] Springhill, TN

CORRELL, MICHELLE LYNN
[b.] January 19, 1983, Springfield, OH; [p.] Sheri Correll and Scott Correll; [ed.] 7th grade, St. Clare Catholic School; [occ.] student; [pers.] All of my poems are dedicated and influenced by my deceased uncle, Kent A. Correll. Kent was my best friend and his love and faith shone even in his worst of health. [a.] O'Fallon, IL

CORSO, DESIRAE J. RILEY
[b.] April 15, 1955, California; [p.] Daughter of Dolores Cruz, Riley and the late Daniel; [m.] Burton Riley Sr., Divorced; [ch.] Daughter: Brandon Debra Corso; [ed.] Graduated in 1973 from Manteca High School (Manteca, CA located in San Joaquin County; [occ.] Administrative Secretary I- San Joaquin Co. Office of Education; [oth. writ.] Specializes in writing personal orders to be given as gifts.; [a.] Manteca, CA

COSPER, DWIGHT H.
[b.] January 19, 1953, Jackson, MS; [p.] William H. and Alice R. Cosper; [ed.] Western Washington University, B.A. 1974, Jack Keroval School of Disembodied Poetics, attended '75-'76; [memb.] P.M. and L. Theatre, Antioch Il.; [hon.] Senior Study Grant, Dean's List; [oth. writ.] Contributing Editor for "Exhausted Ramblings" literary journal, poems in "Mirror Northwest" and in "Bumper Crop"; [pers.] Poetry can be a path of discovery, taking our best understanding into the heart of confusion and chaos and arriving with excitement at new insight.; [a.] Island Lake, IL

COWAN, COOPER C.
[b.] July 31, 1930, Sylvan, NC; [p.] Thad and Nora Lee Cowan; [m.] Marjorie (Nee) Campbell; [ch.] Caroline, Shane, Michael; [ed.] High Schools - Webster N.C. - Sylva, N.C.; [occ.] Retired; [oth. writ.] An original hunting story published in the Sylva, N.C., Hearld; [pers.] Always listen to the meadowlark sing Marvel at the beauty of a murmuring stream always seek the far-away places and forever search for the hidden dream; [a.] Sedro Woolley, WA

COWART, MICHAEL LEE
[b.] May 11, 1958, Bay City, TX; [p.] Clyde Coward and Mary Cowart; [m.] Catherine Cowart, May 26, 1990; [ch.] Michael Jr., Rebecca, Collin; [ed.] Bay city, High School, City Universities, Seattle, Washington; [occ.] Active duty military US Navy Damage Controlman Chief; [oth. writ.] Other poems have been written to my wife during the same time from me.; [a.] Chesapeake, VA

COX, JUDITH L.
[pen.] Judith L. Cox, Rusty Cox; [b.] April 9, 1935, Los Angeles; [p.] B. G. and Mabel Goodwin; [ch.] Cathy, Connie, Susian and 10 grandchildren; [ed.] Graduated Cal-Poly Pomona 1976, with 40 G.P.A. in special studies, graduated Catherine College, 1993, with 40 G.P.A. Admin. Asst. Course; [occ.] Sr. Admin. Secretary; [hon.] Awarded plaque as Outstanding Admin. Assistant Student from Catherine College 1992-93.; [pers.] I have been writing all my life and I am truly honored that my first published work is to appear in "A Tapestry of Thoughts" for the National Library of Poetry.; [a.] Sunland, CA

COX, PATRICIA
[pen.] Patricia Cox; [b.] June 7, 1928, Detroit, MI; [p.] Fred Pardon, Esther Pardon; [m.] Phillip E. Cox, November 7, 1945; [ch.] 7 - 16 grandchildren; [ed.] St. Gabriels Detroit MI, Sacred Heart High - Dearborn, MI

CRAFT, AIMEE JO
[pen.] A. J. Craft; [b.] October 14, 1960, Newton, IA; [p.] Ivan John Craft, Mary Kay Stevens Saxe; [ed.] Newton Sr. High School - 1979, Des Moines Area Community College, A.A.S. - 1983, University of San Francisco, 1991-1992, Berkeley Psychic Institute 1993.; [occ.] Minister, Church of Divine Man, Berkeley, CA; [memb.] Dejavu Publishing Company's Board of Directors Committee - 1995, Church of Divine Man; [hon.] Vice-Chancellor, Church of Divine Man (1995), Who's Who of American Women, 16th Edition (1988), Dean's Lists, Associated Collegiate Press and American Scholastic Press Assoc. (1983) Both 1st Place Awards.; [oth. writ.] Articles published in the Psychic Reader Newspaper.; [pers.] It is an amazing time to be one this planet. Spirit is manifest in the Universe, and we are all part of it. We need to forgive ourselves and our society and focus on consciously creating life as we want to live it.; [a.] Oakland, CA

CRAWFORD, ALISTON
[b.] December 14, 1950, Belize, Central America; [p.] Elphin and Boadica Crawford; [m.] Jillanna Bell Crawford, December 14, 1991; [ch.] Ezequeil, Jemuel and David (1st son); [ed.] St John's H.S. Belize Downey - CA West Angeles Bible College Los Angeles; [occ.] Reservation Sales - Amtack; [hon.] Baton of honor - 1971 Police Academy Belize Central Representative at Barbados, WI - Comforta - 1981; [oth. writ.] Published in amanda press Belize, (Central America and other periodicals - (Pen Name David Alston); [pers.] Psalm 127:11-15

CRAWFORD, CASSANDRA
[pen.] Cassandra Crawford; [b.] April 2, 1982, Georgetown, OH; [p.] Charles and Twila Crawford; [ed.] Presently attending school; [occ.] Student; [memb.] Was Captain of school Safety Patrol, Nursing Home Volunteer, Junior Aux. Member of American Legion. Volunteer at Seamar Community Building; [hon.] First place in fifth grade Science Fair, First place in 8th grade Science Fair; [oth. writ.] Numerous unpublished.; [pers.] I would like to dedicate my poem to my grandmother, Ruth Miller. She wrote many beautiful poems and always wanted to write a book about her life raising 10 children, unfortunately she died before she accomplished her goal. My paternal grandmother, Geneva Crawford, is also a great influence on my writings.

CRAY, MS. VERDELL
[b.] October 7, 1943, Detroit, MI; [ch.] Twin boys one girl; [ed.] Willard Jr High, Berkeley Calif., Berkeley High School, Berkeley California Contra Costa College, San Pablo Calif.; [occ.] Preschool Teacher in Oakland California; [hon.] A.S - A.A. Degree in Early Childhood Education and numerous certificates and awards in the Fields of Early Childhood; [pers.] I give all praise - honor - recognition - love - and acknowledgment to the good Lord who has given me the ability to put words on paper.

CREIGHTON, CASSANDRA
[b.] June 6, 1977, Pittsburgh; [p.] Michael and Gail Creighton; [ed.] St. Mary of the Mount Elementary School, Our Lady of the Scared Heart High School; [occ.] Freshman at Duquesne University; [memb.] Youth Group, Basketball, Softball, Drama Club, Volunteer at St. Mary's Church, Newspaper Committee; [hon.] Most Improved Player Sophomore Yr. on the basketball team. Student of the Month 1995, lettered in girls b-ball junior year in high school; [pers.] I try to live life for what it's worth and have no regrets. I have been influenced by the Chinese poets whose messages are not to ignore the simple things in life.; [a.] Pittsburgh, PA

CRENTZ, ELETA C.
[b.] November 25, 1931, Hancock, IA; [p.] Dr. Homer D. and Eva H.; [m.] E. H. Crentz Jr., June 3, 1968; [ch.] Homer Ernest and Julia Mayroe; [ed.] B.A. and Brigham Young U.; [occ.] Retired; [memb.] Church of Jesus Christ of Latter-Day Saints, Sheridan School district Special Ed Advisory Committee; [hon.] Church, Scouting, Teaching Certificates; [oth. writ.] "I Speak For Democracy" Contest. Mainly for my own pleasure. Mother's Day poem in Toilette paper, Poem in High School booklet, etc.; [pers.] "I" (I) Praise the Lord: Obey His command, give to others with a helping band. (I) Learn each taste as it combs along. Take each step and sing a song. (I) Let rainbows shine through the tears. Struggled much across the years. (I) Made my mistakes repented too. Wish as much for all of you!; [a.] Englewood, CO

CRIFO, DARLENE C.
[b.] November 17, 1963, Worcester, MA; [p.] Louis Crifo, Phyllis Crifo; [ed.] Johnson Elementary, Nahant Jr. High Lynn Vocational Technical Institute course Interior Exterior Painting and Decorating 1982 graduate; [occ.] Sales Clerk BLDG 19 Lynn MA; [oth. writ.] For The Hostages written on January 22, 1981, published in the Daily Evening Item Lynn MA January 29, 1981, Local Paper; [pers.] I work very hard in writing my poetry in hopes that people who read my work will realize how wonderful people and things in life are. My writing reflects on how I feel about life and should be treated with respect and appreciation. Maybe if all of mankind did this our world would be a little more peaceful.; [a.] Lynn, MA

CROFTS, NICOLA
[b.] March 19, 1972, Scotland; [p.] James and Elizabeth Crofts; [pers.] I believe in sunshine, rainbows and real emotion, my inspiration being! "Our Father"; [a.] Grand Blanc, MI

CROSIAR, JIM
[b.] February 2, 1939, South Bend, IN; [p.] Mary Dzierla; [ch.] Heather, Sean, Mary; [ed.] Washington H.S., So. Bend, in graduated 1955; [occ.] Programmer; [memb.] Volunteer - Columbus and Franklin County, Metropolitan Park District; [oth. writ.] Several poems published in the local newspaper and work place papers; [pers.] I believe I write best when I'm taken up emotionally with what I'm writing about; [a.] Worthington, OH

CROTSENBURG, MARLENA A.
[pen.] Donielle Drakkaar; [b.] October 22, 1966, Dallas, TX; [p.] Charles and Bonnie Crotsenburg; [ed.] Graduated Schroonlake Central High 1987 at 20. I am really proud of my diploma!! WNCC and YVCC; [occ.] Sales; [memb.] Union Local 1439 Mystery Guild; [hon.] Certificate of Appreciation- Peer Leadership first place speech class; [oth. writ.] Cold Lonely Nights (not finished) Color Me An Addict: Chameleon Living Autobiography (unfinished).; [pers.] I keep promising friends and family, "Some day you can go into a store and buy a copy of me".; [a.] Yakima, WA

CROWLEY, JENNI
[b.] November 10, 1980, Alexandria, KY; [p.] John and Carol Crowley; [ed.] Saint May Grade School, Bishop Brossart High School; [occ.] Student; [memb.] American Tae Kwondo Ass.; [pers.] Keep a smile on your face, especially through the hard times. It can brighten up anything.; [a.] Alexandria, KY

CULLOUGH, MARILOU
[pen.] M. Vernon; [b.] December 7, 1942, Downey, CA; [p.] Robert and Ruth Walker; [ch.] Clint; [ed.] Bellflower High School Rio Hondo College; [occ.] Order entry/customer service BFS, Santa Fe Springs, CA; [memb.] BHS Reunion Committee; [pers.] Writing is very meaningful to my life. I find that

poetry can express my feelings like a song of words, and always from my heart, Norm Lewis, my writing teacher, helped me understand the value of writing.; [a.] Whittier, CA

CULVER, DARA
[b.] August 21, 1967, Tyler, TX; [p.] Toinette Collier, Ed Collier; [m.] Donald Culver, November 24, 1995; [ch.] Holly Morgan Culver; [ed.] Collin County Community College, Texas Women's University, University of South Alabama; [occ.] Practice Manager, West Side Family Medicine Center; [pers.] Poetry mirrors the soul. It is a true reflection of who we are, what we want to become and where we've been.; [a.] Gulf Breeze, FL

CUMBO, PAUL
[pen.] Paul Cumbo, P. Andrew Cumbo; [b.] July 14, 1965, Bridgeport, CT; [p.] Joseph Cumbo, Catherine Connors-Cumbo; [ed.] Samuel Gompers Secondary School, Miramar College, San Diego State University; [occ.] Student; [memb.] Project Read San Diego; [hon.] Science Fair-Botany, Dean's List, Won 2 Poetry Contests; [oth. writ.] Short stories, satires, poems, and many articles published in school newspapers and employee newsletters.

CUMINALE, RAYMOND J.
[b.] August 24, 1948, New York City; [p.] Joseph and Carmela; [ed.] Fashion Inst. of Technology, and N.Y. University; [occ.] Interior Designer, and Visual Merchandising Consultant; [memb.] National Arts Club V.P., Board of Directors, Alumni LA Guardia High School Board of Dir. Member, Alumni Fashion Inst. of Technology; [hon.] Diamond Homer, Famous Poets Society P.O.P.A.I, for display design accent magazine grand prize for display and packaging (twice), She is also a poet and semi-finalist in the 1995 open the poetry contest.; [oth. writ.] Copy writer, seminars and visual merchandising programs.; [pers.] As an artist and designer I write poetry visually, I see the words and paint the images with my pen. I dedicated my poem Tomy sister-Maryann C. Jaczko.; [a.] New York City, NY

CUMMINGS, WILMA FAYE
[b.] July 2, 1945, North Little Rock, AR; [p.] Ida Mae and Herman Fulmer; [ch.] Terrell - Michael - Angela - Tanya; [ed.] Sylvan Hills High; [memb.] Liberty Fellowship Church; [hon.] Typing Award; [oth. writ.] Poems - songs; [pers.] I find great comfort in writing my poems, and songs along with playing several instruments - It gives me peace within myself and comfort to others.; [a.] North Little Rock, AR

CUNNINGHAM, CHRISTINA
[b.] December 24, 1941, Co. Down, Ireland; [p.] William and Ellen Cunningham; [occ.] Retired. (Part-time Hotel Receptionist.); [hon.] Phi Theta Kappa National Junior College Honorary, Scholastic Society) Boise. Idaho '59. (Nursing Major); [a.] Seattle, WA

CUNNINGHAM, PETER J.
[pen.] Pete; [b.] January 1, 1953, Alexandria, LA; [p.] Howard S. and Doris B. Cunningham; [m.] Janice S. Cunningham, August 21, 1976; [ch.] Jeremy Dewayne; [ed.] Vinton High School, Vinton Louisiana North Western University, Louisiana South Plains College, Levelland Texas; [occ.] Electronic Service Tech; [memb.] First Assembly of God Levelland, Texas; [hon.] Honorable Discharge-Army; [pers.] When ever you feel that you are alone and hurting, remember that there is always someone listening and ready to talk to you.; [a.] Levelland, TX

CUNNINGHAM, REBECCA
[b.] January 21, 1965, Virginia; [m.] Michael Cunningham, 1993; [ch.] Two; [ed.] High School writing class; [hon.] Second place in a short story writing contest.; [oth. writ.] Short story published in local paper as second place winner in contest, two novels I am trying at present to get published.; [pers.] For me, writing is a way for my spirit to soar through fantastic adventures while my feet must remain flat on the ground.; [a.] Baton Rouge, LA

CUNNINGHAM, SHARON
[pen.] K. C. Mallory; [b.] January 25, 1973, Lufkin, TX; [m.] Paul Cunningham, May 20, 1994; [ed.] BBA from Stephen F. Austin State University; [occ.] Records Management for a bank (Scanning documents and maintaining database); [oth. writ.] None as of yet, still trying to finish at least one short story or novel; [a.] Nacogdoches, TX

CURTIS, TINA L.
[b.] November 7, 1966, Wattsburg, PA; [p.] Raymond Tanner, Jani Tanner; [m.] Crispin L. Curtis, November 1, 1991; [ed.] Seneca High Southeastern College of the Assemblies of God; [occ.] Wattsburg Youth Center, Director 1988 to present; [memb.] Wattsburg Area Scholarship Fund Committee, 1st Assembly of God of Union City; [hon.] Erie County Community Star Award - 1995; [pers.] Through the beauty God has created I have found a solemn place. It is in this natural setting that God has given me the works to use in my writing.; [a.] Wattsburg, PA

CUTLER, JONATHAN S.
[b.] June 27, 1972, New York City; [p.] Penny Cutler, Steve Cutler (divorced); [ed.] New Rochelle High School, New Rochelle, NY 1990, The American University, Washington, D.C. 1994; [occ.] Public Relations; [oth. writ.] Numerous poems, short stories and other writing works.; [pers.] Dreaming provides an escape, believing will ultimately create we must all believe in our dreams.; [a.] New York City, NY

DACEY, MARY E.
[b.] January 22, 1952, Santa Monica, CA; [p.] William F. and Donna Sahlen Dacey; [ed.] BA in Graphic Communications - San Diego State University; [occ.] Police Service Representative for the LAPD - also free-lance illustrator; [hon.] Awarded 1st prize in employee writing contest. Illustrations Published in Medical and Travel Journals.; [pers.] As a Born-Again Christian inspired by God, I hope to honor Him through my poems, illustrations and crafts.; [a.] West Lost Angeles, CA

DAGUE, MANUELA MONIKA
[b.] May 27, 1976, Germany; [p.] Gisela Dague, Matt Arnold; [m.] Single; [occ.] Student, Hostess; [oth. writ.] My burning soul hate and fear, autumn life yours and mine friend, opening and others that are all unpublished; [pers.] My writings are a way of expressing my self and I am happy to have the privilege to share it with others may you all enjoy them too. Thank you.; [a.] Colorado Springs, CO

DAIGLE, LAURIE I.
[b.] April 16, 1962, Michigan; [p.] Ronald Bunce, Lyn Kuhl; [m.] Stace Daigle, September 1, 1994; [ch.] Ashleigh Besk, Shanay Stone; [ed.] Chief Sealth High School, South Seattle Community College; [occ.] Sr. Workers Comensation Claims Examiner; [memb.] President Missoula Insurance Women, National Association of Insurance Women, Missoula Adjusters Association, Seattle Adjusters, Association, child and family resource council; [hon.] Editors choice 1994, 1995; [oth. writ.] Cye, enlightened love, day by day; [pers.] A note for my daughter Ashleigh: Keep your dreams alive, I love you.; [a.] Lolo, MT

DAIGNEAULT, LOUIS M.
[pen.] Luigi; [b.] July 20, 1964, Leominster, MA; [p.] John P. Daigneault; [ed.] Leominster High School, Wilbraham and Monson Academy, Merrimac College, Assumption College; [occ.] Chef and Owner of the IL Camino Restaurant, Singer; [memb.] Worcester AIDS Action Committee; [hon.] Various awards for singing, various publications about my family's restaurant and our food; [oth. writ.] Mostly songs; [pers.] I wrote this poem for my mother, who died in a car accident back in 1982. It's time I share it with others.; [a.] Leominster, MA

DAILEY, VERLINDA SHARRON
[b.] January 3, 1956; [ch.] Carlo and Jeremy; [ed.] Snohomish High: Everett C.C., Lifetime Career School; [occ.] Landscape Architect; [memb.] World Wildlife Fund, Nature Conservancy; [hon.] SHS Top Ten Scholar, Friends of Animals; [oth. writ.] Haiku Nature Poems (unpublished); [pers.] It is time for humankind to become the caretakers of nature and all of its living inhabitants.; [a.] Arlington, WA

DANIEL, JAMES
[pen.] James Daniel; [b.] June 12, 1977, San Diego, CA; [p.] Teri Popp "Curtis Daniel"; [ed.] Billing's West High School; [occ.] Songwriter, Poet; [oth. writ.] A little Boy's Prayer, The Dream Dreamt Goodbye...; [pers.] I've worked so hard to get when in at now. I dream of one day having a book of my own using my Poetry to bring the condition of our mother earth to the worlds attention. (Life isn't now it is it's what it can be.); [a.] Billings, MT

DANNEMILLER, TINA
[b.] November 13, 1964, Athens, Al; [p.] Jimmy and Sadie Clay; [m.] David Dannemiller, August 14, 1993; [ch.] Jeremy, Lisa, Nick, and Sara; [ed.] West Limestone High, John C. Calhoun College; [occ.] Mommy, Family Manager; [memb.] American Heart Association, American Cancer Society; [pers.] Since my visit to Paris, I have been very inspired to write romantic poetry to my wonderful husband, Dave. I am blessed with 4 beautiful children and I also enjoy photography.; [a.] San Francisco, CA

DAUPHIN, SALLY
[b.] September 5, 1936, New Orleans, LA; [p.] Alex and Pearl DeCoux; [m.] Francis T. Dauphin, November 19, 1955; [ch.] Four; [ed.] High School, Adult Ed. some College Courses.; [occ.] Retired, was Manager of Apartment Housing for Elderly 1981-1995; [memb.] Empoyled for 13 yrs. member and Director of St. Landry Parish Suicide Prevention Program 1984-1995; [hon.] Humanitarian Award OPelousas St. Landry Chamber of Commerce, 1989, Outstanding Community Service, Frontiers International Club, 1988; [a.] Opelousas, LA

DAVID, C. BORDEN
[b.] May 14, 1930, Attleboro, MA; [occ.] Owner - multi Insurance Associates, Insurance Marketing; [oth. writ.] Appeared in various magazines of Companies and local newspapers.; [pers.] There are three types of people. Those that learn from their mistakes, they are lucky. Ones who learn from the mistakes of others, they are fortunate. Those that learn from neither one, they are foolish.; [a.] Agoura Hills, CA

DAVIES, JOHN GERSON
[pen.] John Gerson; [b.] February 17, 1936, Wales; [occ.] Realtor; [memb.] International Society of Poets California Federation of Chapparal Poets, Palm Springs Writers Guild; [oth. writ.] "An Orchid Nosegay For My Love" Janus publishing Co. London. ISBN No. 1 85756 174 O. "Democracy, rush Limbaugh Et Al", "Where Eagles Soared". 1 a 2 (poetry) 3 (novel) 2 a 3 not yet published.; [pers.] I tend to write about my resound experience. People I've known, places I've been. My first language in Welsh but since I'm now married to an American

lady I've had to adapt myself to the English.; [a.] La Quinta, CA

DAVIS, CHARLES R.
[pen.] Charly R. Davis; [b.] August 30, 1977, Conway, AK; [p.] Paula Davis; [pers.] A special thanks to Martha S., Linda M., Sharon S., and the Lord for all the encouragement and Belief in my work.; [a.] Corrigan, TX

DAVIS, CONSTANCE L.
[b.] September 10, 1951, Atlanta; [p.] Queen Grier; [ch.] Phillip, Larita, Gary, Corey, Drayton and Maru; [ed.] Sih Archer High, Atlanta Aear Tech.; [occ.] Salad-Cook; [hon.] Editor Choice Award 3 times; [oth. writ.] Seven poems published by the National Library of Poetry and several other unpublished poems; [pers.] "He who offer nothing, has offer his soul to Satan"; [a.] Atlanta, GA

DAVIS, ETTA MARIA
[b.] January 17, 1971, Lynchburg, VA; [p.] Lacy C. Nowlin, Lorraine D. Nowlin; [ed.] E.G. Class High; [occ.] Residential Provider for Central Virginia Community Services; [pers.] I want to reflect hope, survival and triumph over the battles and wars that occur on the inside, which are often not seen because some people can't see deep enough but in the same taken, it takes a special heart with a vision to see beyond what presented to them; [a.] Lynchburg, VA

DAVIS, GERALD E.
[pen.] Gerald; [b.] September 13, 1950, Dallas, TX; [p.] LA Salle Davis and Beatrice Davis; [m.] Carolyn Davis, December 20, 1980; [ch.] Gerald II, Alysia and Arnesia; [ed.] F.D. Roosevelt High, East Field College; [occ.] CAD Drafter/Designer MCI, Richardson, TX; [memb.] Minister and Founder of Church in your Heart (Outreach Ministry); [hon.] Art and Calligraphy; [oth. writ.] Beyond shattered dreams, sin's no friend, etc.; [pers.] In my writing, it is my desire to throw out the lifeline of encouragement and hope, and rescue as many as possible from the troubled waters of life.; [a.] Dallas, TX

DAVIS, JOHN BRIAN
[pen.] J. Brian Davis; [b.] March 24, 1964, St. Louis, MO; [p.] John and Barb Davis; [m.] Single; [ed.] B.S. Univ. Mo. Columbia M.S. Candidate - Miss St. Univ.; [occ.] Graduate student, biologist Wildlife Ecology; [memb.] The Wildlife Society, Ornithological Societies, Ducks Unlimited; [hon.] Welden Wildlife Foundation Scholarship; [oth. writ.] Several popular articles about waterfowl published in California Waterfowl and several newspapers, brochures, etc.; [pers.] My goal is to promote resource stewardship, and, to educate the public, primarily youth, about ecology, hunting, and outdoor ethics, through speaking and writing. The writings of Aldo Leopold are a tremendous influence.; [a.] Mississippi State, MS

DAVIS, JULIE ANN
[b.] July 25, 1948, Platea, PA; [p.] James and Elizabeth Cook; [m.] Kenneth P. Davis, March 17, 1992; [ch.] Two; [ed.] B.A. Our Lady of the Lake Univ.; [occ.] Writer (free lance) Artist; [pers.] My poems reflect my feelings at certain points of my life; [a.] Sugar Land, TX

DAVIS, LOIS KAHL
[pen.] Lois Kahl Davis; [b.] November 21, 1909, Burr, NE; [p.] Gustave and Lois Basses Kahl; [m.] Jack L. J. Davis, June 19, 1941; [ch.] Jacquelyn, Edward and Daniel; [ed.] R.N. - from Bryan Memorial Hospital, Lincoln, Nebr. in 1933 Wesleyan and Lincoln Nebr University Courses, Taught country school 2 yrs in Rockford School, School Nurse 9 years in Lincoln Nebr.; [occ.] Retired; [memb.] Austin Poetry Society 1963- 2 vice pres 9166-67, pres 1968-69 Poetry Soc. of Texas - Life Member, First Cumberland Presh Church, Channel Choir, Care Givers, Love in Action; [hon.] Took many 1st, 2nd, and 3rd awards in Austin Poetry Society's, monthly and annual awards contests; [oth. writ.] White Dove Divine 1983. Contributed to, Poetry classical and contemporary (anthology), Nat'l Library of Poetry Best Poems of 1995, American States - man, Missionary Messenger, Cumberland Presbyterian, Austin Visitor, First Cumb. Press Journal; [a.] Austin, TX

DAVIS, MARA
[b.] August 5, 1943, New York, NY; [p.] Florence and Harvey Schwartz; [m.] Divorced; [ch.] Ashira Beth, Joshua Ari; [ed.] Calhoun High School, New York University College of Arts and Science, 1966. New York University graduate school of social work, M.S.W. 1972 Postgraduate Center for Mental Health.; [occ.] Training in International Ballroom Dance; [memb.] National Association of Social Workers, Academy of Certified Social Workers, State Certified in New York and Florida; [hon.] Graduated High School with a distinction in Latin. Graduated College with a Founders Day Award, Dean's List and Phi Beta Kappa, accepted to Columbia, Berkeley and N.Y.U. for graduate school English, went to graduate social work.; [oth. writ.] I have been waiting poetry since I was 17 years old, and seriously writing for the past 13 years. This is the first poem I have ever submitted for publication.; [pers.] I write a great deal about nature and man's oneness with nature. Most of the time, I try to instill my readers with the hope and faith that I feel daily.; [a.] Tucson, AZ

DAVIS, PATRICK LANE
[b.] November 28, 1969, Alton, IL; [p.] Barbara Jim-George and Vernon Davis Sr.; [ed.] Castlemont High, Oakland, CA; [pers.] I write from the delicate balances of the joy and the pain within my heart. My writings are a reflection of my environment and personal experiences.; [a.] Oakland, CA

DAVIS, PEGGY ANN
[b.] September 17, 1926, Woodbury, NJ; [p.] Arthur and Marian; [m.] Raymond Butcher, January 10, 1975; [ed.] High School Wdby.; [occ.] Retired Mobil Oil; [memb.] Housewife; [a.] Thorofare, NJ

DAVIS, PETE
[b.] January 22, 1934, Sheridan, WY; [p.] John B. and Dorothy Mae Davis; [m.] Cynthia (Cindy) J. Davis, October 15, 1977; [ch.] Diane, Dan, Krista; [ed.] Barnyard and Range, Kellogg ID. High School, Sheridan College, University of Wyoming; [occ.] Retired Vo Ed Teacher; [memb.] St. Margarets Catholic Church, Knights of Columbus, Credit Unions (Past Officer); [hon.] Who's Who in Am. Jr. Colleges, Wyoming Honors BS, Dean's List, President's Honor Roll, Phi Kappa Phi, Kappa Delta Pi, Pride of Wyoming Cowboy poet '92, Man of the Year St. MCC '91; [oth. writ.] I've had cowboy poems in various state, National and International magazines, I write custom cowboy poems for families. I submit very little for publication; [pers.] I write to preserve old cowboy sayings, ways and thinking, then I present it in performance. I follow many successful western writers in not using any profanity in my writings as "It ain't ole cowboy ta swear in front of any woman or in public".; [a.] Riverton, WY

DAVIS, PHILIP E.
[b.] January 29, 1916, Newarks, OH; [p.] Irwin and Helen Davis; [m.] Jean V. Davis, June 10, 1944; [ch.] Edward, Vicki, Mary and Paul; [ed.] B.A. Denison U Granville, Ohio 1939, Ohio State M.A. 1935 C.A.G.S. Boston U. 1951; [occ.] Retired Teacher Coach; [memb.] Wellesley Baptist Church Massachusetts Teachers (Retired) N.E.A. Teachers (retired); [hon.] Coach of year (Soccer) Treasure (Wellesley Teacher Association); [oth. writ.] The Little Golden Wasp, Novel - UP From the Dumpster unpublished 26, poems by Philip Davis published in book form (limited edition for friends and family; [pers.] I learned to love poetry as a child and feel it is the expression of the inner self.; [a.] Sherborn, MA

DAVIS, REBECCA LYN
[b.] December 30, 1973, Lubbock, TX; [p.] Randy and Carla Davis; [ed.] Slaton High School, South Plains College; [occ.] Receptionist at Lubbock Digestive Disease Associates; [oth. writ.] Other poems for my own personal collection; [pers.] My goal in life is to work with handicapped children. If I can make a difference in one childs' life my goal will be accomplished. I have a brother with a disability who inspired this poem.; [a.] Lubbock, TX

DAVIS, SHANNON DENISE
[pen.] Piercy; [b.] September 25, 1970, Las Vegas, NV; [p.] Eloise Holmes, Thonroe Davis; [m.] Fiance Ontorio Thontgomery; [ch.] Cameca Willis (4), Kadejah Thontgomery (2); [ed.] Clark High School, Class of 88; [occ.] Asst. Manager Taco Bell; [memb.] Economic Opportunity Board of Education; [oth. writ.] Thy first in National Library of Poetry, I've write for 8 years at home; [pers.] I hope my poetry touch alot of peoples heart. My work is influence by a lot of early romantic poets of love.; [a.] Las Vegas, NV

DAVIS, SUE
[b.] November 23, 1940, Kentucky; [occ.] Secretary; [pers.] I am not a writer. This poem, which has 60 lines in its original form, is for and about my two grandsons who are 9 and 11 years old. I have taken care of them much of the time since they were toddlers, and three years ago I was given legal custody of them. My hope is that through this poem they will know how important they are to me and how much I love them.; [a.] Huntington, WV

DAY, JESSICA LYNN
[pen.] Daze; [b.] December 10, 1977, Virginia Mason Hosp. Seattle, WA; [p.] Mr. and Mrs. John P. Day and Janis; [ed.] St. Catherine of Science grade school and Blanchet High School; [occ.] Part-time babysitter; [hon.] 2nd Honor Roll Student as 10th grader in Blanchet High School and Student of the Month in Geometry as a Junior (this year) (11th grade) at Blanchet High School; [oth. writ.] Near Death, a poem published in the Blanchet Art's '93 journal, Voices, Mute in Blanchet's '94 Voices.; [pers.] Uncovered dreams and pain kept behind closed doors stirs much poetry inspiration, but only love can release the pain and open your dreams to the world. And though reality can kill, friends can bring a will to live when nothing else will serve as a salvation. Such is an influence for my poetry and life.; [a.] Seattle, WA

DAZZO, G. GALE
[pen.] Gale Dazzo; [b.] September 19, 1951, Alexandria, VA; [p.] Emma Edith and Samuel Edward Bechtel; [m.] Dan L. Dazzo, August 26, 1972; [ch.] 2; [ed.] High School - Radiographic School for X-ray; [occ.] Med Tech/Radiographer Orthopaedics; [memb.] ARRT, ASRT, MSRT, Internat'l Soc. of Poets; [hon.] Twice champion of MWSCCA in Autocross multiple champion in Porsche Autocross Series Potomac Chapter; [oth. writ.] My Life as a Porsche Owner's Wife, The Runaway Teen, Remembering Our Vets, The Last Event; [pers.] My poetry is written as a story written in verse. I try to deliver feeling as well a kind of reading that flows; [a.] Owings, MD

DE BOER, BRENDA G.
[b.] July 4, 1939, Franklin, MA; [p.] Fredwin and

Mildred Clark; [m.] John De Boer Jr., October 19, 1957; [ch.] Sandra, Debbie, Bonnie, Barbara; [ed.] Franklin Mass High Grad., Wrentham State Sch. Nursing; [occ.] Housewife; [memb.] American Heart Assoc., Liberty Baptist Church Cystic Fibrosis Foundation; [hon.] Top 5 Distributors in Nation (4 yrs. in a row); [oth. writ.] This is my first.; [pers.] Writing brings me comfort and peace. This poem is in loving memory of my daughter Bonnie.; [a.] Orlando, FL

DE LUCA, CAMILLE
[b.] January 12, 1952, Brooklyn, NY; [p.] Thomas De Luca, Angelina De Luca; [ed.] Abraham Lincoln H.S., Kingsborough Community College; [oth. writ.] Several unpublished poems written throughout my lifetime.; [pers.] My poetry has helped me cope with life's ups and downs. Each one reflects my innermost feelings and thoughts.; [a.] Brooklyn, NY

DEADERICK, LISA
[b.] January 24, 1979, Camp Springs, MD; [p.] Barton Deaderick, Karen Deaderick; [ed.] Chula Vista High School; [memb.] African American Student Union, Associated Student Body; [pers.] I try to portray my deepest, innermost thoughts through my poetry. Whether they be about me or those around me.; [a.] Chula Vista, CA

DEAN, MARK
[b.] May 20, 1964, Pittsfield; [occ.] Tax Coordinator, Kay-Beg Toys, Inc., Pittsfield, MA; [memb.] Alcoholic Anonymous/N.A.; [pers.] I strive to enrich others and to fill their lives with peace and love. To remember patience and one day at a time.; [a.] Pittsfield, MA

DEANNAE, CYNTHIA
[pen.] Amanda Howard; [b.] March 31, 1972, Hollywood, FL; [p.] Sandy Cooper - Dean Schaeffer; [ch.] Andrew Dustin, Courtney Dangle; [ed.] General Subjects High School Graduated; [occ.] Artist - traveling from city to city; [hon.] Won Amateur Contest at Madona's Club on South Beach of (for Dance Ability); [oth. writ.] Snowflakes - 7th Grade First Place. In process of writing a novel..."The Angel and The Leprechaun"; [pers.] There is an angel inside the heart of every person. Weather to choose to listen to your angel or not is your choice - good luck to all the angels.

DEAR, NINA K.
[b.] March 29, 1967, Dallas, TX; [p.] Amelia J. Mercey, Paul B. Hill; [chi.] Bryan A. Dear, Natalie N. Dear, Joshua L. Dear, Kristina M. Dear, Bianca R. Hernandez; [pers.] I love all of my family dearly and I thank them very much for all their love and support that they have all given me. I hereby dedicate this poem to Sergio Vallin for whom inspired me. May we be together again someday. Love Always Nina; [a.] Tyler, TX

DEBLANC, SANDRA LEE
[pen.] Sandy; [b.] January 4, 1943, Sea, WA; [p.] Sam H. and Leora E. Jones; [m.] Daun J. DeBlanc, October 26, 1969; [ch.] Samuel, Robby Anne, Teva; [ed.] Quit school at 16, got my G.E.D. at 38 yrs. of age in Anch., Alaska; [occ.] Home maker and also raise pygmy goats; [memb.] Amer. Legion Aux. Palmer, Ak. National Pygmy Goat Asso., Tennessee Dairy Goat Asso., Memphis Commodore Users Club; [oth. writ.] Some newspapers, read-on radio shows. I have bee writing poems and stories and songs since I was a little girl. Mostly for an emotional outlet or just my own pleasure or my children and friends.; [pers.] My grandmother, Gladys Jones and Aunt, Lucille Robinson-Bonomi, have both been poet Laureate for the state of Washington. Also many of my cousins write or paint - The arts seem to be a big part of my family. My daughter Robby Anne seems to have picked it up also.; [a.] Byhalia, MS

DECATA, IRENE M.
[b.] July 22, 1938, Somerville; [p.] Joseph and Elvira Lo Souto; [m.] John P. DeCata Sr., September 14, 1958; [ch.] John P. Jr., Irene E. Valentine, and Jane Groder; [ed.] College (Fitchburg State), Teaching; [occ.] Cosmetologist; [memb.] Cosmetologist Assn; [oth. writ.] None published just wrote for myself. I love to write but ever thought what I had written was good. I just thought this time I would try. I want to write a book.; [pers.] If I could send a message to the earth, I would like the world to realize what drugs do to people. We have choices in our lives, to live or die. Drugs is death. Without drugs we do have a chance at life.; [a.] Woburn, MA

DECONDO, ELIZABETH A.
[b.] December 19, 1968, Westward, NJ; [p.] Robert Speer, Alice Speer; [m.] Anthony Decondo, March 10, 1991; [ch.] Amanda Marie; [ed.] Bergen County Academy for the Advancement Science and Technology; [occ.] Cake Decorator Baker; [memb.] Y.K. Park Tae Kwon Doe; [oth. writ.] A High School Publication of Tek Neeks; [pers.] There are many coincidences or reoccurrences that seem familiar but you can't place it. These are the things that make the majority of us tick. The minute we settle is the minute we stop ticking.; [a.] Paterson, NJ

DEERING, GLORIA E.
[b.] North Fork, WV; [p.] Carrie Deering, Isaiah Edwards; [ch.] Judith Scott; [ed.] Douglass High, Huntington, W.V., University District of Columbia, Howard University; [occ.] Retired (Technical Writer) U.S. Govt.; [memb.] Director, District, Government Employees Federal, Credit Union (Wash., D.C.); [hon.] Gamma Phi Delta Sorority, Inc., various certificates from organizations; [oth. writ.] Various magazine articles, Articles for newsletter for a Rehabilitation and Nursing Home.; [pers.] My greatest goal in life is to provide love, and assistance to my fellow man and the ability to experience joy and share it with those around me.; [a.] Silver Spring, MD

DEL GAUDIO JR., CHRISTOPHER
[b.] December 16, 1987, Jersey City, NJ; [p.] Chris and Kelly Del Gaudio; [ed.] Third Grade; [hon.] Awards in track and baseball; [pers.] Likes to read and hopes to write more poems.

DEL PRADO, LINA GARCIA
[pen.] Lina Del Prado; [b.] February 2, 1950, La Habana, Cuba; [p.] Ernesto M., Esperanza M.; [ch.] Maria-Lina Noy; [ed.] Dr. in Mathematics, Cuban Academy of Sciences; [hon.] National Award "Pablo Miquel" from the Cuban Mathematical Society; [oth. writ.] Several papers in the field of Mathematical Programming, published in Optimization, Rev. Inv. Operational, etc.; [pers.] The poem included in this anthology is dedicated to my father, Ernesto M. Garcia Alzola, distinguished Cuban writer, author of several books including four collections of poems, and winner of various national literary awards (Cuba 1945, 1952, 1953).; [a.] Santa Barbara, CA

DELAS CASAS, WALTER
[b.] February 3, 1947, Havana, Cuba; [p.] Mario and Aracelia DeLas Casas; [ed.] Power Memorial Academy, Iona College (P.A.), Hunter College (M.A.); [occ.] High School Teacher; [memb.] American Association of Teachers of Spanish and Portuguese; [hon.] Americanism Medal For Essay on same granted on June 1965 by American Legion (San. Post 1110 A.L.), B.A. Cum Laude; [oth. writ.] (Spanish Verse) La Ninez Que Dilata (1986) and Libido (1989), (English Verse) Tributes (1993) Articles: "Curriculum Guide for Spanish Native Language Arts" (Hispania, May 1987), "El Genio Del Lugar: Un Estudio Comparado De El Greco Y Toledo De Gregorio Maranon Y El Greco O El Secreto De Toledo De Maurice Barres," unpublished poetry manuscripts: (Spanish) Hojas Dispersas, (English) Discourse.; [a.] Brooklyn, NY

DELEON, LOUISA
[pen.] Louisa DeLeon; [b.] March 8, 1913, Bent, NM; [p.] Esquipula and Leonor Gallegos; [m.] Santiago DeLeon (Deceased), September 15, 1929; [ch.] 4 - 10 Grand - 10 Great Children; [ed.] High School, Postal Operations thru, Okla. State Un. several courses pertaining to employment.; [occ.] Retired from 25 yrs. as Postmaster and Management; [memb.] NAPUS: National Ass'n of Postmaster - VFW Auxiliary, AARP, Spanish Club, RSVP: Retired Senior Volunteer Program St. Therese Catholic Church; [hon.] South Dakota Centennial Governor's Award for Involvement in Celebration of State's Centennial 1876-1976, 100 yrs, Blue Ribbons: Senior Olympics 1985-86-87; [oth. writ.] History on family tree. In the 60's News on Community for Newspr's have written articles never published - I keep in my files.; [pers.] Winning on a senior citizens writing contest I had been in Mexico attending a bull fight from my experience I wrote "Strictly Bull Amigos"; [a.] Rapid City, SD

DELLENBACH, CORY
[b.] March 18, 1981, Rhinelander, WI; [p.] Lora Rustad and Terry Dellenbach; [ed.] Pine Lake Elementary, James Williams Jr. High School Washington School, Ocento Falls High School; [occ.] Student - 9th grade; [memb.] FBLA - Future Business Leaders of America; [hon.] Honor roll student; [a.] Oconto Falls, WI

DELMENICO, GENE
[pen.] De-Geno; [b.] February 17, 1923, Switzerland; [p.] Deceased; [m.] Lila Jean, December 31, 1979; [ch.] Two; [ed.] 8 years - 2 years of College in Switzerland, Speak Fluent - Italian, understand several others; [occ.] Realtor; [memb.] The Sirs #95 Sunset Whitney C.C. SP. Inc.; [oth. writ.] I do have many other poems short stories, I am working on a book "The Immigrants" the story of countless people that came to this country very interesting!; [pers.] You made me very happy to choose me as a finalist. I have not try to hard to expose my work for the simple reason publishers want money up front I am not rich yet.; [a.] Cameron Park, CA

DENECKER, KRISTEN
[b.] September 1, 1976, Manhasset, NY; [p.] Thomas and Susan Denecker; [pers.] To my parents Tom and Susan for always believing in me and to my brothers Shawn, Ryan, Keith who always support me in everything I do. I love you guys.; [a.] Middlebury, VT

DENISE, ROBYN
[b.] September 22, 1963, Canandaguia, NY; [p.] Dorothy and Arnold Wager; [ch.] Ted, Nicki, Jeramiah; [ed.] High School graduate June 1982 will graduate in May 1996 with an associates degree in human services alone, with a gevontology certificate; [occ.] Mom-full time student believer in dreams.; [memb.] Parents helping parents lifestream personal growth seminars.; [hon.] Deans list 3 times; [pers.] I take the time to believe in dreams no matter how big or small, realistic or ridiculers I believe. The rewards of this belief have been a true gift for me.; [a.] Lima, NY

DESMOND, MARCY
[pen.] Marcy Desmond; [b.] November 8, 1937, Minneapolis, MN; [p.] Axel and Helen Wahlquist; [m.] Joseph, April 17, 1970; [ch.] One daughter, two stepchildren, four grandchildren by my daughter; [ed.] Assoc. of Science - De Anza Junior College and Nursing Degree (licensed registered) San Jose Hos-

pital, School of Nursing, San Jose (Calif.) State College (now Univ.) and De Anza Jr. College, Cupertino, Calif. 1970 School of Nursing; [occ.] Retired; [memb.] German Shorthaired Pointer Club of America, North American Versatile Hunting Dog Assoc., (I have raised show and field dogs for over 25 yrs. many champions and dogs in other countries); [oth. writ.] Articles and poems related to dogs published in nationally distributed breed magazines as well as two books related to dogs.; [pers.] The unconditional love of a dog has often times become the line line between loneliness and total acceptance, depression and a joyous, warm reason to live. The untimely loss of this furry friend can change your life forever. I know 'cause I've been there.; [a.] Hayden Lake, ID

DEVER, JENNY
[b.] August 20, 1953, Griffith, New South Wales, Australia; [p.] Margaret Allen; [m.] Paul; [ch.] Melanie, Marcus, Anthony; [ed.] New South Wales and Queensland, Australia; [occ.] Owner - memories in print; [oth. writ.] Numerous short stories and poems; [pers.] To find joy in all of life's trials is something I treasure. I believe it is a gift from God.; [a.] Cape Coral, FL

DEWEY, KATHLEEN PEREZ
[pen.] Kathleen Perez; [b.] July 27, 1957, Sturbridge, MA; [p.] Joseph Perez, Geraldine Boudreau; [m.] Daniel Dewey, October 7, 1990; [ch.] Daniel Christopher, Jeffrey Alexander; [ed.] A.B., Smith College, Religion, M. Div., Weston School of Theology, M.S., Wheelock College (in process); [occ.] Student of Early Childhood ED, Homemaker; [memb.] SGI-USA, Women's Division District Leader; [hon.] M. Div. "With Distinction"; [pers.] I write to save lives, including my own. I hope to communicate faith, the greatest of all gifts. I chant Nam-Myoho-Renge-Kyo and "That has made all the difference."; [a.] Cambridge, MA

DIALHE, KADIJOI
[pen.] Charlotte Bronte; [oth. writ.] Maiden of Silent, Dreams Kiss of An Angel, An Egyptian Lotus; [pers.] "A poet is a romantic"; [a.] Washington, DC

DIAMANTE, SAUNDRA
[b.] January 12, 1959, Baltimore, MD; [p.] Lt. Cdr. Stanley A. Taylor and Rose Marie Taylor; [m.] Gil P. Diamante, October 25, 1985; [ch.] Gil Jr., Robert, Timothy, Ariel, Athena Diamante; [ed.] I graduated from Serverna Park High in 1977.; [occ.] Homemaker; [memb.] I'm a member of the International Society of Poets. In 1980, I obtained my FCC license and work at the Maryland Public Broadcasting Station in Summers of 1980-1981; [hon.] I have two awards from the International Society of Poets.; [oth. writ.] "The Balance" published in the *Sea of Treasures* "September" will be published in *Spirit of the Age*.; [pers.] Pursue your dreams and there will always be hope.; [a.] Daly City, CA

DIAZ, GLENMORE FITZGERALD
[b.] December 27, 1976, Los Angeles, CA; [p.] Marine R. Diaz; [ed.] As of now, a Freshman at California State University Northridge; [occ.] Student, Sales Associate; [a.] Northridge, CA

DIERSEN, DIANNE A.
[pen.] Dad, Anne Deer; [b.] July 8, 1949, Howell, MI; [p.] Leo and Wanda Saunders; [ch.] Melissa Katherine; [ed.] J. W. Sexton High, the Institute of Children's Literature; [pers.] Poetry is the best conveyance of the heart through the mind's eye. I have a deep love and respect for nature and all animals, and hope to portray this through stories and books for children.; [a.] Petoskey, MI

DILLON, ELSIE
[b.] August 24, 1919, Elizabeth City, NC; [p.] Lena and Clyde Seymour; [ch.] Billie Valley and Paula Gregory; [ed.] High school and several college courses at College of the Albemarle.; [occ.] Second Female Parole Officer in the State of North Carolina; [memb.] First Methodist Church; [oth. writ.] Many poems, a few short stories.; [pers.] Being able to put my thoughts in poetry form has always helped me to sort out my deepest feelings.; [a.] Swansboro, NC

DILLON, GABRIELA NOREEN
[b.] November 26, 1960, New York; [occ.] Communications Consultant, First Bank St. Paul, MN; [pers.] My poetry paints pictures of human emotions that transcend beyond what our eyes see in the world around us. Just as art elicits different feelings in each one of us, my poetry strives to uncover the beauty that makes us all so unique.; [a.] Lake Elmo, MN

DILLON, LISA
[b.] December 29, 1978, Carmel, NY; [p.] Thomas Dillon, Louise Dillon; [ed.] Sophomore - Pawling High School; [occ.] Student; [memb.] Religious Education Teacher at St. John the Evangelist Church, Peer Leadership; [hon.] High Honor Roll, Who's Who Among American High School Students, All American Scholar, National Science Merit Award

DIMEO, FRANCESCO A.
[pen.] Prince Machiavelli; [b.] November 6, 1964, San Bernardino, CA; [p.] Ronald and Helen Cremo, Giovanni and Angela DiMeo; [m.] F. A. Dimeo; [ch.] Cory and Kenneth Cremo; [ed.] BA Liberal Arts Suffolk University Boston, MA 1962 High School; [occ.] Financial Consultant/Investor/writer/Housewife/writer of poetry; [memb.] LUAnn's statement to promote better understanding amongst peoples of the world.; [oth. writ.] "In Triumph" Published in England/Arthur Stockwell, Ltd. 1994; [pers.] Man must develop the International perspective in order to promote harmony and reasoned judgment amongst men and women of all persuasions, which ultimately leads to world trade and less conflict amongst people of the world.; [a.] Lawndale, CA

DINSMORE, L. BLANCHE
[pen.] L. Blanche Dinsmore; [b.] August 18, 1937, Hopewell, MD; [p.] Maston and Ruth (Haga) Hall; [m.] Robert Fulton Dinsmore, Jr., August 17, 1956; [ch.] Robert Scott Dinsmore and Pamela Ruth (Dinsmore) McQuary; [ed.] Graduated 1956 Bel Air Senior High School, Bel Air, Md. various private courses; [occ.] Self-employed in sales; [memb.] Dexter Community Betterment, Dexter Chamber of Commerce, Calvary Baptist Church; [hon.] Received highest honor as Associational Clerk in Maryland for Susquehanna Baptist Assn. for nine years was one of 75 out of 3,400 to receive this award; [oth. writ.] None published except news articles for local paper. Poems written for personal occasions; [pers.] The writing I do hopefully, is entertaining and/or helpful to these who read it.; [a.] Dexter, MO

DINUNZIO, SYLVIA
[pen.] Syl D.; [b.] October 7, 1966, Boston, MA; [p.] Anna DiNunzio and the late Louis DiNunzio; [ed.] East Boston High; [occ.] CNA (Nursing); [memb.] NFA, Pro Bass, Animal Shelter Cash Inplan; [oth. writ.] Several others that have never been read by anyone; [pers.] On days that the world seem empty sit down and write to bring joy to others. Not only to yourself.; [a.] East Boston, MA

DISCHINGER, THERESA
[b.] December 9, 1948, Atlanta, GA; [p.] Duane and Bernice York; [m.] James Dischinger Jr., May 19, 1970; [ch.] Jennifer Christine; [ed.] H.S. Douglas S. Freeman, Pan American Business College; [occ.] Homemaker; [memb.] MADD, ISP, The Saints, Houston Diamonds, WIBC; [hon.] Greater Council of Garden Clubs - Slidell "Blue Ribbon" winner; [pers.] Poetry for me is a way to express my inner thoughts, to release my imagination, and to capture memories of places visited so that I can revisit them again when I read my poems.; [a.] Houston, TX

DITMAN, HENRY M.
[b.] July 24, 1945, Baltimore, MD; [p.] Luther S. Ditman, Rosina M. Ditman; [ed.] Balt. Polytechnic Institute, B.E.S. Elec. Eng. Johns Hopkins Univ. 1966, M.S.E., Elec. Eng. Univ. of Pennsylvania 1968, Ph.D, Elec. Eng. Univ. of Pennsylvania, 1979; [occ.] Retired as of July 28, 1995 from Naval Surface Warfare Center in Silver Spring, MD.; [memb.] I.E.E.E. (Institute of Electrical and Electronics Engineers); [hon.] ETA Kappa Nu (Elec. Eng. Honor Society); [oth. writ.] One poem ("Blue Bird It Is") and several articles published in NABS (North American Blue Bird Society Journal); [pers.] To write meaningful poetry, one often must resort to vicarious experiences.; [a.] Westminster, MD

DITTRICH, BRUCE E.
[b.] August 18, 1961, Brattleboro, UT; [p.] David Leward and Joan Dittrich; [ed.] Keene High School; [occ.] Chef, Poet; [oth. writ.] My Angel, Let Your Spirit Flow, Learn to Live, You Make Me Want to Live, Song Sweet Song, Miracles, New Days Delight, ECT.; [pers.] I have a message for the entire world through my writing and songs, I will inspire millions of people, my fate is sealed, my destiny is very clear.; [a.] Brattleboro, UT

DIXON, DORIS WIRTZ
[pen.] Doris Vivian Wirtz; [b.] June 4, 1922, Baltimore; [p.] Myrlie May McCleary and Lawrence Vernon Wirtz; [m.] Widowed; [ch.] Carolyn May Anderson; [ed.] Western High School (June 1940); [occ.] Retired (wanting to retread life's scenes); [memb.] AARP, Wednesday's Choice Sr, Club, Parkville VFW, Hampden United Moth. Church; [hon.] Recd. $10.00 for poem on village of Hampden used in publication here in 50th anniv. annexation to city of Baltimore, 75th and 100th annv. 1988. In 1938 won gold watch essay on history of Hampden. Read poem "Mental Steeds" on radio program "Bards of Baltimore." "Keep on Tryin" published in HS yearbook June, 1940; [oth. writ.] Many poems for church programs and publications. Throughout school life poems, essays, new words for songs. Community celebrations. Personal poems of consolation, friendship, love, nature, church and family celebrations.; [pers.] Poetry to me is music in words—and been since age twelve. I dearly love God and write to Him, about Him, and for Him to help and comfort, encourage and bring my joy in Him to others. I never studied by inspiration. Poetry — I write as my heart is moved; [a.] Baltimore, MD

DOBRICK, RUBY B.
[b.] March 15, 1954, Alamogordo, NM; [p.] Richard E. and E. Pauline Smith; [m.] David M. Dobrick, June 21, 1990; [ch.] Henry-Don Sartin; [ed.] Alamogordo High School, Eastern NM University; [occ.] Secretarial; [pers.] Romantic at heart, Procrastinator in the mind, and love of the physical outdoors.; [a.] Louisville, KY

DOLAN, BRENDA
[b.] October 24, 1972, Ridge Crest, CA; [p.] John Dolan, Mary (Walsh) Dolan; [pers.] This poems is dedicated to the memory of Bartholomew T. Walsh, my loving Uncle, father-figure, and friend.; [a.] Dedham, MA

DOMBROWSKI, JESSICA L.
[pen.] Jesi; [b.] January 31, 1979, Syracuse, NY; [p.] Stanley R. and Kim M. Dombrowski; [ed.] High

School Senior; [occ.] Student; [memb.] Theocratic ministry school (bible class); [hon.] Merit role honors 4 yrs. in a row.; [oth. writ.] Poems published in the "Pen and Palet" school magazine; [pers.] Push yourself or you are standing; [a.] Tully, NY

DONOHUE, LORRAINE
[b.] October 28, 1928, Los Angeles; [m.] Robert Donohue; [ed.] L. A. High Class '46 U.S.C. Class '50; [occ.] Grandmother, housewife; [pers.] This poem was written in fun as requested for a surprise 60th birthday in his honor (Dr. Leonard Silauglate) How shacked we were when he died suddenly and unexpectedly a few months later. He was 3 years younger than me and and is surely missed by me and his family and many relatives, patient and friends.

DOUGLAS, LINDA LEE
[pen.] Linda Brandt, Linda Mullican; [b.] May 26, 1945, Louisville, KY; [p.] John W. Douglas, Wilanna Sandifer Douglas; [ch.] Steven William, Gregory Douglas, Michael E.; [ed.] Anne Arundel High, Rota, Spain School of Art, Montgomery Co. Adult Education, Creative Writing, American Sign Language; [occ.] Starving Artist and Author; [memb.] Louisville Baptist Church, Laytonsville Baptist Church; [oth. writ.] Various articles and letters. *The Washington Post* Newspapers, *The Damascus-Courier Gazette*, *Woman's Day* Magazine.; [pers.] There will always be a good, always be a beauty, even in that which is dying, a beginning, to each and every end.; [a.] Westminster, MD

DOUVILLE, MARJORIE L.
[b.] February 17, 1935, Minneapolis, MN; [p.] Geo and Margaret Thompson; [m.] Philip L. Douville, August 10, 1958; [ch.] Jon, Michele and Renee; [ed.] High School, Airline School, Cosmetology Training Center, EMT School - CPR Instructor Police Training; [occ.] Beautician - Estate Sales Part time Police Officer.; [hon.] Volunteer of the Year Award Golden Valley Police Dept.; [pers.] It gives me a warm feeling to extend myself in helping less fortunate people and watch their progress develop from nothing to something.; [a.] Minneapolis, MN

DOWDA, KIMBERLY GAYLE
[b.] June 14, 1980, San Antonio, TX; [p.] Ron and Liz Dowda; [ed.] Two years of High School so far; [occ.] Student; [memb.] High School varsity choir, Who's Who Among American High School students.; [hon.] One time Region Choir, one first place Vocal Solo, three first place Vocal Ensembles, four first place VIL Vocal Ensembles.; [oth. writ.] One poem in lasts years National Library of Poetry book.; [pers.] I use my personal emotions in my poems.; [a.] San Antonio, TX

DOWNER, KRISTIN E.
[b.] April 22, 1959, Petaluma, CA; [p.] Fredrick W. Klindt (Deceased), Donna S. Klindt, (step-father) Irvin E. Dellinger; [m.] Ronald J. Downer, January 26, 1979; [ch.] Ten Children; [ed.] I attended: West Yellowstone High School, W.V. Mt., and graduated Heritage Christian School, in Bozeman, MT College; [occ.] Housewife, joyful M.O.M (Mother Of Many); [memb.] Pastor's wife and member of Gateway Fellowship Home Church; [hon.] My only "Honors and Awards" are my 10 children: J.D. Daniel, Philip, Stuart, Tonia, Stephen, Constance, Erica, Charity and Grace!; [oth. writ.] Over 80 other songs and poems, yet unpublished.; [pers.] I write what I live: Faith in Christ, love, joy, home, family, marriage. Life is an unending adventure - a process of change... Each poem or song I write is an expression of that life that dwells in me.; [a.] Big Sky, MT

DRESSEL, JOSHUA D.
[b.] May 6, 1974, Lacey, WA; [p.] Carol and Dennis Akehurst; [m.] Sheila Dressel, October 17, 1994; [ch.] Mai Kayla Diane Dressel; [ed.] Hillsborough High School, Tampa, FL, San Diego City College, San Diego, CA; [occ.] Professional Driver; [hon.] Honorable Discharge U.S. Navy; [oth. writ.] Just completed my first novel, "The Hall of Windows" and am in the process of trying to get it published. I have written over seventy different works of poetry. Working on my second novel, "Peppermint Tribe"; [pers.] I look at the darkness and anger of our society and I try to alleviate it through words. I think of life as being very much like the poems "Richard Cory" by Edwin Arlington Robinson - sometimes having everything we can still feel we have nothing.; [a.] Spring Valley, CA

DREW, WILLIAM LINCOLN
[pen.] W. L. Drew; [b.] September 30, 1931, Boston, MA; [p.] Mildred Alice and Wm. H. M.; [m.] Martha A., April 2, 1966; [ed.] Roxbury Memorial H. S., Boston, Mass., American Academy N.Y.C., C.B.A. (Eqiv), Lee Strasberg NYC (Advanced) (1958-1962); [occ.] Retired broker 4/95 (Stock Market); [hon.] Various and Sundry (other vocations); [oth. writ.] Poems - Historical, etc., TV play and Lyricist (song) (unpublished); [pers.] Think Nobly, Remember Honor, Give Anonymously, Meditate Humbly, Love Always, Protect Health; [a.] North Hollywood, CA

DRYER, JOHN R.
[b.] December 15, 1969, Moline, IL; [p.] Ervin Dryer and Linda Avila; [m.] Michelle M. Dryer, December 12, 1992; [ch.] Alexander James Dryer; [pers.] If you try to focus a lot of attention toward your spouses romantic needs with genuine intentions your marriage will be a most fulfilling lifelong experience.; [a.] Cleveland, OH

DU-LONG, PATRICK
[pen.] Du, Phuoc Long; [b.] May 31, 1921, S. Vietnam; [p.] Du Phuoc Thuan; [m.] Van Anh Du-Long, November 2, 1943; [ch.] Five; [ed.] Ph.D. in Human Resources Management, B.S. in Foreign Services, International Relations; [occ.] Youth and Family Counselor and Consultant, Asian Organized Crime Consultant, Public Speaker, Author.; [memb.] Vietnamese PEN Club; California Law Enforcement Association; International Asian Organized Crime Association, President; Vietnamese American Social-Cultural Council; [oth. writ.] Subjects: Political, Social, Economics, Cultural issues and problems; [pers.] Love - Peace - Freedom - Harmony - Fairness; [a.] San Jose, CA

DUBOIS, JACQUELINE J.
[pen.] Jacqueline Joyce; [b.] April 4, 1944, Kingman, AZ; [p.] Daughter of Jacqueline Gariepy; [m.] Warren, December 9, 1988; [ch.] 3 sons and one grandchildren; [ed.] Canoga Park High - California Mesa Comm. College - Ariz; [occ.] New Home Real Estate Sales - 12 years; [memb.] Tucson Assoc. of Realtors Antigue Airplane Association; [hon.] Private Pilot Licence Top Salesperson 1994, 95 for the Doucette Co; [oth. writ.] Articles in Aviation Publications. Children's stories "Me and Bear" and the gold smell in Burro"; [pers.] There never seems to be enough time to spend with our loved ones "Put laughter and tenderness into the minutes shared".; [a.] Tucson, AZ

DUDDING, LAURA VEOLA
[b.] December 7, 1930, Grantsville, UT; [p.] John C. and Eva J. Brown; [m.] Earl B. Dudding, August 4, 1953; [ch.] Laura Marie, David L., Dorothy and/ Grantsville High, Grantsville, UT; [occ.] Choral Arts Society of Utah; [a.] Woods Cross, UT

DUFRESNE, GEORGE N.
[b.] June 4, 1933, Lewiston, ME; [p.] Napoleon Dufresne, Gratia Plante; [m.] Nancy Rinaldi Dufresne, October 24, 1953; [ch.] 4 Girls, 1 boy; [ed.] 11th Years; [occ.] Retired truck driver; [memb.] Democratic party, Roman Catholic Church, A.A.R.P.; [hon.] Korean War Vet, Combat Infantry Badge Purple Heart, Honorable Discharge.; [oth. writ.] Miscl, Poems Black Fire, Emerald Pond, Poems to Pictures, Philosophical Daydream, Yonder shore The Love Embrace, Roots of Heaven, My Lords Prayer, Meditations on Heart, Mind and Spirit and more; [pers.] While education is very important. The wellspring of creativity is truly spiritual based on your gift from God, and the genes of your ancestors.; [a.] La Habra, CA

DUMBLETON, CYNTHIA
[b.] June 12, 1945, Summerset, England; [p.] Alex and Rebecca MacGregor; [m.] Robert (Bob) Dumbleton, November 13, 1964; [ch.] Paul Dumbleton (28) Amanda Mazer (25); [ed.] Educated in Scotland and England; [occ.] Assistant to owner/CPA of a small accounting practice. Our clients are mostly from the entertainment industry; [oth. writ.] Some poems scheduled to be published in the "Children of the Night" newsletters '96. Write mostly poems expressing my feeling for family and friends as well as experiences.; [pers.] I started writing as my children married and left home. Also, I find it a way of dealing with my emotions. Since turning 50, I find that I want to leave a little part of me with my family after I've departed from this "crazy" world.; [a.] Sherman Oaks, CA

DUNCAN, WILMA M.
[pen.] Willie; [b.] June 12, 1950, Beelic Knob, WV; [p.] Harold Shuck; [m.] Betty Shuck, May 20, 1967; [ch.] Elmer E. Duncan III, David H. Duncan; [ed.] Marvin L. Duncan; [occ.] Freelance writer; [memb.] Greenbrier Valley Interagency Council, Dean's List; [hon.] Dean's List; [oth. writ.] Several poems published in local newspapers, articles for Woman's World, Inspirer.; [pers.] I strive to be a brave soul and attempt communication with my fellow human beings with my writing.; [a.] Dawson, WV

DUNLAP, MATTHEW L.
[b.] November 10, 1977, Boise, ID; [p.] Jim and Sarah Voss; [ed.] Graduate Ocosta High School June 96; [occ.] Student

DUNLOW, BONITA HELEN
[pen.] Bonita Helen; [b.] May 5, 1956, Eldorado, IL; [p.] Gene and Marilyn Smith; [m.] Donald E. Dunlow, July 7, 1973; [ch.] Donita Jean, Donald Scott, Timothy Wayne; [ed.] Norris City Elementary, Garner Senior High, Wake Technical College; [occ.] Food Service; [memb.] Stage Road Free Will Baptist Church, Jr. Church teacher, Assistant Sunday School Teacher, Choir Member, Bulletin Publisher; [oth. writ.] I have written many poems, submitted only a few publications. Garner News, Garner Times newspaper. "On This Your Wedding Day" printed in my daughter's wedding program as a gift of consent.; [pers.] I want to share my poetry with others and dedicate it in loving memory to my Mother, who influenced me and took great pride in my love for poetry. I write from personal events of those near and dear to me. I have always enjoyed Helen Steiner Rice's writings.; [a.] Garner, NC

DUNN, DANA
[b.] April 30, 1964, Noblesville, IN; [p.] Ron and Marilyn Byrd; [m.] Todd Dunn, August 31, 1991; [ch.] Tara, Alyssa, Dylan; [ed.] South Putnam High School; [occ.] Self Employed - Secretarial Service; [memb.] Glad Tidings Assembly of God; [oth. writ.] "Don't be afraid" published by the National Library of Poetry in window of the soul - 1996.; [pers.] I have been greatly influenced by my daughter Tara Nicole Dunn.; [a.] Lizton, IN

DUNN, ELMER F.
[b.] February 7, 1956, Coatesville, PA; [p.] Walter A. Sr. and Helen M. Dunn; [m.] Ruth E. Dunn, May 28, 1995; [ch.] Four children, two step children; [ed.] Downingtown High School; [occ.] Roller Operator; [oth. writ.] Had a poem, "A Price For Peace", published in local newspaper, Daily Local News of West Chester, in March 1991.; [a.] Sadsburyville, PA

DURHAM, MYRTLE BARBOUR
[b.] September 2, 1932, Pine Level, NC; [p.] Thurman-Irene, Woodard Barbour; [m.] March 1953, Divorced 1966; [ch.] Kathy Durham, David Durham, Lorna D. Christie; [ed.] Smithfield High, Wayne Tech, Johnston Tech; [occ.] Retired; [hon.] 1990 Silver Poet Award World of Poetry; [oth. writ.] 11 poems pub.; [pers.] My poem is dedicated to the people I came from (Barbour, Woodard, Ellis, Flemming, Blackmon, Wood, Somerlin, Overman, Massengale, Phillips, Thompson, Bennet Walker) and to the ones who come after me. Remember the past that the future may be better. Protect and love the child, for God does not forget.; [a.] Clayton, NC

DUWE, ROBERT R.
[pen.] Robert R. Duwe; [b.] October 21, 1937, Cleveland, OH; [p.] Otto and Anna Duwe; [m.] Sandra A. Duwe (Walkley), April 28, 1962; [ch.] Robert Jr. and E'Lise; [ed.] An AS Degree from Cuyahoga Community College; [occ.] President of Sales with High Performance Asphalt, Inc; [memb.] I am a Jehovah's Witness since 1973; [hon.] I've received two Editors Choice Awards from The National Library of Poetry 1994 and 1995; [oth. writ.] I've written many long poems and some short stories that haven't been printed as of yet.; [pers.] Every man, woman and child, no matter what race or station in life. Has many things to contribute to this world. From their writings to their different forms of art and inventions. But most of all is their faith love and obedience to their God Jehovah; [a.] Brook Park, OH

EAGAN, MIMI
[b.] August 28, 1926, Syracuse, NY; [p.] Leo T. and Eleanor Eagan; [ch.] Margot Papworth, Muffine Wilson, Chris Cheney; [ed.] B.A. from Georgian Court College, Lakewood, N. Jersey; [occ.] Retired; [memb.] Several local clubs; [hon.] Editors Choice (5), Distinguished Poet of Merit Award; [oth. writ.] "Bittersweet", Book - published by Watermark Publisher; [pers.] I write about everything and everyone I love. I'm very anti-war, and write about the wasteland of war.; [a.] Fayetteville, NY

EARLEY, OTIS LEE
[pen.] Otis Lee Earley; [b.] July 31, 1928, San Benito, TX; [p.] Lester W. Earley, Crystal B. Earley; [m.] Joyce Raybourn Earley, February 14, 1951; [ch.] Gene Earley, Vonnie E. Eidson, Darcy E. Talbert; [ed.] Graduate, san Benito, High School - 1945, College courses, Speak Spanish as second language; [occ.] Retired - Longshore man, Master Electrician, Supervisor of Bldg. Maintenance, Texas State Tech. College Harlingen, TX; [memb.] Baptist Temple Church, Antique Tractor Club; [hon.] One of my poems was recited at a Veterans Day Memorial Service at a local College. I was interviewed by a local T.V. station due to this Veterans Days Service. Excepts of the same poems were used in a local newspaper in a Memorial Day edition. Copies of this poems have been framed and hung in lobbies of various Veterans facilities.; [oth. writ.] I have written sixteen poems on various subjects, several humours. Among the sixteen poems is an epic poem about a childhood friend who was killed in Word War II. "Jesse and the crew of the trembling Gremlin," is a documentary short story I wrote as a follow up for the poem. I am about half way finished with my autobiography; [pers.] I believe in Jesus Christ and incumbent basic Christian values, honesty, the sanctity of marriage, devotion to my children, respect for my contemporaries, love for my country and dedication to solid work ethics.; [a.] Harlingen, TX

EASLEY JR., JOE B.
[pen.] Joe B. Easley Jr.; [b.] October 3, 1966, Tyler, TX; [p.] Joe and Peggy Easley; [m.] Donna Easley, July 27, 1994; [ed.] Central Texas College, Trinity Valley Community College; [occ.] Grievance Investigator T.D.C.J.I.D.; [oth. writ.] Published in High School Newspaper/Editor of Newsletter.; [pers.] These were early writings in which I was still capable of love.; [a.] New Boston, TX

EASTBURN, SHIRLEY
[pen.] Shirley, Eastburn; [b.] November 11, 1927, Galesburg, IL; [p.] Mr. and Mrs. Hilmar Nelson; [m.] Robert S. Eastburn, April 10, 1951; [ch.] Michael Lee, Gary Robert, Christine Ruth; [ed.] Grade School in Galesburg Ill. Jr. High Hilchock Jr. High Galesburg Ill. H.S. Santa Monica High S. Monica Calif. and Moreno Valley High Moreno Valley Cal.; [occ.] Housewife; [memb.] Plymouth Congregational, Church Women's Society, Senior Citizens; [hon.] Several ribbons for crocheting in State Fair in Ida.; [oth. writ.] Poem - called fourth written for Advocate (Newspaper) in Cascade, Ida, for July 4, 19-article to reader digest, rejected have numerous poems cause I love doing it; [pers.] I write poem because I enjoy it and its a way of expression what I feel.; [a.] Oshkosh, WI

EATON, BETTY MAE
[pen.] Betty Mae Eaton; [b.] July 8, 1935, Indianapolis, IN; [p.] John W, Fishback and Dorothy L.; [m.] Charles H. Eaton Jr., November 19, 1977; [ch.] Penny Jo Shumaker, Cynthia Ann Smith and Mark Allen Smith; [ed.] Tech. High School Jr.; [occ.] Cashier at Roselyn Bakery #43 Of Indpls; [memb.] O.E.S. #465 Beech grove Ind. Chapter for 33 years was chaplin in O.E.S.; [hon.] A poem put into a capsul to be opened in 100 yrs. October 1, 2091 Pegasus Time Capsul. World of Poetry's Who's Who in poetry 1992 Edition Golden Poet 1980-91, Editor's Choice Award 1993-94 Honorary Charter Membership 1993, International Society of Poets; [oth. writ.] The time is now. Family tree, Moma's Hands, Colors, Chase away the Blues, I am a Poet, my son, A woman's place is in the home, and several others in the Library of Congress.; [pers.] I write from real life, to make a point and to make others feel they count and are important to me. Life itself is poem. You only have to look at it through my eyes.; [a.] Indianapolis, IN

ECKART, BEDE
[b.] December 27, 1916, Subiaco, AR; [ed.] BA Hist. Mt. St. Scholastica Atchison, KS. MA Hist. St. Louis U. St. Louis MO, CPE Clerical Pastoral Ed. Bethany Med. Center K.C. KS-Ark. Children's Hospital Little Rock, AR.; [occ.] Retired teacher and school administrator — Ret. Hospital Chaplain; [memb.] Benedictine Sisters, Ft. Smith, AR. NOW Natl. Organization for Women Feminist Majority WE Women's Empowerment; [oth. writ.] Poem published in Lydia Sigourney—An Anthology in Memoriam (1791-1865) Bristol Banner Books, 1995 Poems published in community and school papers.; [pers.] Jesus taught about the acted on a domination-free system, a system of relationship. I believe that the evil stemming from the male domination system in the world and in the church is the chief cause and purveyor of the injustices in the world.; [a.] Forth Smith, AR

EDDY, DANA F.
[b.] September 24, 1959, Sistersville, WV; [p.] Arthur and Corena Eddy; [m.] Marla J. W. Eddy, August 8, 1987; [ch.] Jason and Daniel; [ed.] B.A., Salem College, Salem, W. Va, J.D., Harvard Law School, Cambridge, MA; [occ.] General Counsel Office of Governor, West Virginia; [oth. writ.] Poem, Walk Through Paradise, various legal writings; [pers.] My wife's beauty is an inspiration I cannot repress, her love is a motivation I cannot resist.; [a.] Charleston, WV

EDDY, S. N.
[pen.] Sariah Dawn; [b.] January 25, 1952, Topeka, KS; [p.] Celia A. Eddy and Ronald N. Eddy; [m.] 1M-F. R. Winston, 2M-Terry Lynn Adams 1M-July 10, 1972, 2M-December 19, 1988; [ch.] 1M-Steven Scott, Ronald Lawrence, Nicholas Foster, 2M-Stephanie Nichole.; [ed.] Seaman High, Washburn Univ., S.U.N.Y. at Cobleskill and Black Hills State Univ.; [occ.] Admin. Bookkeeper, USD Barracks, Fort Leavenworth, Kansas; [memb.] My Church (The Church of Jesus Christ of Latterday Saints), My Country (U.S.A. citizen), and My Family (proud parent and spouse).; [hon.] Officially: A 20-plus year career in the U.S. Air Force, and the Bowling Congress "7-10" award. Unofficially: I share in the honors and awards of my children as they are a reflection of myself at a younger age.; [oth. writ.] Personal life and narrative poems all unpublished.; [pers.] "...All things are possible to ye that believeth", no wish too small, nor dream too big. Dreams DO come true, and miracles abound in all of our lives daily, if one will only pause, long enough, to recognize them.; [a.] Fort Leavenworth, KS

EDGERTON, ROY
[pen.] Roy G. Edgerton, R. Garland Edgerton; [b.] January 29, 1950, Laurens, SC; [p.] N. Bruce Edgerton, Emma Edgerton; [m.] Mary Edgerton, August 9, 1982; [ch.] John Michael, Mark Ryan; [ed.] University of South Florida 1972, BA Advanced Liberal Studies; [occ.] CEO, Nations Leading Durable Medical Equipment Co.; [oth. writ.] "Mama" an inspirational work based on my love for my mother; [pers.] "Today I shall judge nothing that occurs."; [a.] Tampa, FL

EDMUND, RUBY
[b.] June 29, 1938, Exeter, NH; [p.] Wilfred Lamott and Stella Lamott; [ch.] Three; [ed.] Hampton High School - College Course, McIntosh Business School, Institute of Children's Literature Art Classes; [occ.] Newspaper Carrier Portsmouth Herald Artist and Writer; [memb.] Firemens Auxiliary Junior Women's Guild - United Church of Christ; [hon.] Cheerleader - Miss Foot ball - Class of 1956, Sports Credits Music - Special Chorus Glee Club, Director - Rhythmic Choir; [oth. writ.] Several poems; [pers.] I create my writings in variety form.; [a.] Hampton, NH

EDWARDS, JUDIE
[b.] Staten Island, NY; [ch.] Todd, Mathew, Melissa; [ed.] San Fernando Jr. Col.; [occ.] Disabled stroke in 1991 November Left with cognitive difficulties with impaired speech-damaged nerve in left leg-muscle disease fibromyalgia; [oth. writ.] Currently finished a manuscript depicting struggle with coping disabilities from stroke - fight for social security set out along leaving family in California. For a new life in Colorado includes poetry and letters from White House - finding peace within and love. A few poems published in local newspapers; [a.] Green Mountain Falls, CO

EDWARDS, MARGUERITE K.
[b.] October 5, 1913, Floydada, TX; [p.] Mr. and Mrs. Ben Keltz; [m.] J. E. Edwards, July 2, 1938; [ch.] Patricia Lane, Tom Edwards; [ed.] College: BA, MA, Postgraduate. Teaching specialties: Eng., Hist., Span. and Math; [occ.] Retired School Teacher; [memb.] El Progreso Study Club, Mary McCoy

Baines, D.A.R. Baptist Church S.S. Teacher; [pers.] "Trees" by Joyce Kilmer has always been a very special favorite of mine. My daughter who has a lovely voice, learned the song when the words were set to music and encouraged me to write the poem.; [a.] Matador, TX

EDWARDS, STEVE R.
[b.] May 13, 1976, Jamaica; [p.] Lorna Tulloch; [ed.] I graduated High School in "95", plan to attend college in Fall of "96".; [occ.] United States Marine (Reserved); [hon.] I once received a writing award for a report I wrote during school. Over all I did not perceive very much.; [oth. writ.] "Me", a Broken Heart, and Last Night.; [pers.] I try to write about life itself and how people often forget the importance and faith of life.; [a.] Germantown, MD

EDWARDS JR., WOODROW W.
[b.] September 29, 1939, Clinton, SC; [p.] Woodrow and Mae Edwards (Deceased); [m.] Inge, September 19, 1995; [ch.] Joyce, Phyllis, Linda and Chad; [ed.] Armstrong High, Washington, DC; [occ.] Department of The Army Civilian, employed in Germany.; [oth. writ.] Numerous poems and songs. None ever published; [pers.] I believe in being me, more than anyone I've ever seen, I'm so busy being myself, there's no time to be anyone else.; [a.] Germersheim, Germany

EDWARDSON, RUTH M.
[b.] November 8, 1925, Carve, MN; [p.] Carl and Mae Johnson; [m.] Deceased, April 24, 1946; [ch.] Cindi, Gary, James, Patricia Charles, Darrell, Theodore, Shirley; [ed.] Dist 22 Elementary Caver MN. Belle Plaine High Belle Plaine Mn. 3 3/4 yrs. Nursing, Little Falls Mn.; [occ.] School Bus Driver for special needs kids - 35 yrs.; [memb.] American Legion Aux 566, UFW Aux 6583, American Cancer Society Columbus Lioness, UOSH International. Incarnation Lutheran Church Chaplain 10 yrs. Vet's Council Anoke Co.; [oth. writ.] Other patriotic poems, many miscellaneous poems; [pers.] Poetry writings are spur of the moment thing.; [a.] Lino-Lakes, MN

EHMANN, ANNE M.
[b.] New York City; [m.] Robert B. Ehmann; [ed.] St. Barnabas High School, Herbert H. Lehman College (B.A. Degree).; [occ.] Administrative assistant to the President and Chief operating officer at Chyron corporation, a Computer Graphics Company based on Long Island, New York.; [memb.] Member of "The Filmaker's Network" c/o the Long Island Film and T.V. Foundation.; [hon.] Graduated College - Cum Laude, Dean's List; [oth. writ.] Several poems published in "The American Poetry Anthology" by Robert Nelson, and in the anthology "Our Western World's Greatest Poems" by John Campbell.; [pers.] Strive to live life to your highest level, see and experience everything around you with the awe and innocence of an inquisitive child.; [a.] Babylon, NY

EICH, PATRICIA
[pen.] Pattay; [b.] June 5, 1945, Jersey City, NJ; [m.] Richard; [ch.] Rick, Christine; [pers.] Anyone can write a poem or story. The problem lies in trying to get people to read your work and hopefully they will be touched by it, which is where all the rewards are.; [a.] Aurora, CO

EILEEN, COPELAND J.
[b.] November 13, 1927, Bakersfield, Kern Co., CA; [p.] Charles Andrew Shultz, M. Martha Viola Boring; [m.] V. Alvin Copeland, August 29, 1947; [ch.] Charles Randolph, Rebecca Alana and Robert Alvin; [ed.] Kern Co. H.S. - Univ. CA at Sacramento, CA; [occ.] Retired Sch. Teacher from Placerville Elem. in CA.; [memb.] Regent daughters AM. Rev. Hon. and Life Mem. PTA and NEA, V Pres. Colonial Dames-Priscilla Alden Shop, Music Co-ord. Hillcrest Wd. Lds Church Orem UT and various Gen/Hist Groups; [hon.] Teachers of the Year - Rotary Club Outstanding Achievement Award -El Dorado Board Education Cub and Blazer Awards of Achievement Outstanding Teacher - PTA; [oth. writ.] Co/Author of "Speech Way to sounds" for teachers. "Color Me Gold" for children for Marshall Gold Discovery Site, Coloma, CA "Tallac Historical Guide Book" for U.S. Forest Service in CA. Lake Tahoe; [pers.] I write according to my moods with honesty. This poem was written as my oldest son, Charles, was dying in Mar. 1995.; [a.] Orem, UT

ELLIOTT, ALLISON
[b.] April 10, Rochester, NY; [p.] Tom Elliott, Judi Elliott; [ed.] J. L. McCullough High School; [occ.] High School Senior; [memb.] National Honor Society Explorers; [a.] The Woodlands, TX

ELLIOTT, JEREMY L.
[b.] September 18, 1970, Salem, IN; [p.] Frank S. Elliott, Lawanna L. Benham; [ch.] Justin Michael and Amanda Nicole; [ed.] Salem Highs School, Community College of the Air Force, University of Alaska; [occ.] U.S. Air Force; [oth. writ.] Angel Dust, The Color Of My Nightmare and Until The End; [pers.] I hope each day for peace in life.; [a.] North Pole, AK

ELMER, MARY ELLEN
[pen.] Mary Ellen Elmer; [b.] November 12, 1933, Battle Creek, MI; [p.] Carl W. Grim and Hannh L. Moffiett Grim; [m.] Ralph S. Elmer, May 2, 1953; [ch.] 5 - 4 boys, 1 girl; [ed.] High School, 2 years college at KCC in Battle Creek.; [occ.] Factory worker retired made "Girl Scout Cookies"; [memb.] Women's Bowling League Local 815 Union Baker's Retail Aflcio. PTA Y-Center, First Hot-Air Balloon Flight, Saint Phillips Church; [pers.] I was greatly influenced by my dad who use to take time out with us children and read poem's and stories and play games with us.; [a.] Battle Creek, MI

EMELSON, ANN ELIZABETH
[b.] August 17, 1972, Daly City, CA; [p.] Gloria and Earl Emelson; [ed.] Graduate in Psychology with a minor in Business from Sonoma State University (1995); [occ.] Licensing and Contracting Assistant at Legacy Marketing Group; [memb.] Member of the Humane Society of Sonoma Country; [hon.] Honor Student - member of Psi Chi Honor Society at Sonoma State University.; [pers.] There was a time when all I would do was run, even from my own shadow. I have been fortunate to be the recipient of love and devotion from my parents, brothers, and Dan. With their support I began to embrace life and allow myself to see a miracle.; [a.] Rohnert Park, CA

ENCISO, MICHELLE
[pen.] T. Kipper; [b.] February 21, 1979, Caloocan City, Philippines; [p.] Marlon Enciso and Claireen Enciso; [ed.] Student at James Madison High School; [hon.] Received awards with the James Madison Color Guard; [oth. writ.] A few poems published in Heritage, a Literary Magazine at School; [pers.] Poetry's is one that touches the soul through poetry, I collect my feelings and thoughts, happy or sad.; [a.] Vienna, VA

ENCK, LAURA
[b.] May 6, 1945, Texarkana, TX; [p.] Fred K. Newberry, Meredyth McCracken; [m.] Douglas Lee Enck, August 20, 1966; [ch.] Troy and Scott; [ed.] Highland Park H.S. Dallas Gulf Park Jr. College - Gulfport, Miss Richland College - Dallas, TX Special Education - Major; [occ.] Housewife; [hon.] Being Doug's wife and a mother and grandmother; [oth. writ.] I have written many poems over twenty years that I tuck away. This is my first time to enter a contest - I'm so thrilled with the results.; [pers.] Well known in my family making up songs that make sense. I am totally deaf since 13 yrs of age - My goal is to have one of my poems sung by a country western singer. I write from my heart to yours.; [a.] Toledo, OH

ENGLESTAD, MATILDA
[pen.] "Malene"; [b.] Istanbul, Turkey; [p.] Joseph Haigezen; [m.] George Dewey Englestad, 1934; [ch.] Carole Joyce, Barry and Steve; [ed.] American Girls High School, Istenbul, Turkey - Valedictorian UCLA graduate with teaching credential; [occ.] Retired, lost my husband after 25 years of a very happy life, live alone.; [pers.] Traveled extensively on tours. 1) 'Europe in 90 days' by bus. Covered every country. 2) 'Orient Odyssey' included Russia, India and from Bali to Kathmandi and Himelayas. The travelogue was written in a small magazine in 4 sections. My outlook - 'Positive and Spiritual'; [a.] Thousand Oaks, CA

ENSIGN, KIMBERLY ANNE
[b.] April 25, 1953, Toledo, OH; [p.] William James and Joan Marie Kennedy Ensign; [ch.] Ryan Williams Ensign; [ed.] Bachelor of Arts, Ohio Dominican College 1980, Post graduate study in Quality Improvement Processes, Adult Learning and Training; [occ.] Criminal Justice Policy Specialist, National Crime Prevention Consultant and Trainer; [memb.] Advisory Board Member - Village to child, Ohio Dominican College, Member - Ohio Victim Witness Assoc.; [hon.] National Award Winner Outstanding Young Women of America (1986), National Library of Poetry Contest 1996 "Tapestry of Thoughts"; [oth. writ.] Poetry, children's stories/plays; [pers.] ...Pursue the truth what is to be without neglect to whom is He, whose gifts bestowed upon the land reveals the tale when times at hand...; [a.] Dublin, OH

ERBY, MARIE A.
[pen.] April Winters; [b.] April 7, 1961, Birmingham, AL; [p.] Ilena Erby, Woodrow Foster; [ed.] Wenonah High, Lawson State Comm. College, UAB; [occ.] Mail Processor, U.S. Postal Service, B'ham, AL; [pers.] I hope that my writings will some day surface to the top.; [a.] Birmingham, AL

ERNI, REBECCA COLE
[b.] December 22, 1917, Neosha Rapids, KS; [p.] Ed and Gertie Rages; [m.] Clarence Erni, June 29, 1975; [ed.] Bazine, KS High School, BS in Educ., Univ of KS, 1940 MBA 1964 Univ. of Denver; [occ.] Retired Teacher of 36 yrs.; [memb.] Delta Pi Epsilon, past member of Alpha Delta Kappa, Meth Church. VFW and Am Legion Aux; [a.] Topeka, KS

ESQUIVEL, MICHAEL A.
[b.] October 31, 1971, Long Beach, CA; [p.] Delfina Esquivel; [ed.] Dima Community College; [occ.] Student; [memb.] U.S. Marine Corps Reserves 1991-1997; [pers.] There is no such thing as a failure, rather, it is a chapter in a book of success.; [a.] Tucson, AZ

ESSLINGER, NELL DANIEL
[pen.] Nell Esslinger; [b.] Huntsville, AL; [p.] Blanche Russell and William Francis Esslinger.; [m.] Divorce April 5, 1995, August 18, 1979; [ed.] Vocal Certificate Agnes Scott Coll. BA Univ. of Alabama, Voice Major, Journalism minor. MM Univ. of Illinois., (with vocal recital).; [occ.] Retired, but publishing music and music books. Owner of "The Notation Press."; [memb.] Honorary Life member, The Huntsville Music Study Club. Member of the first poetry club formed at Agnes Scott College. Member of The First Church of Christ Scientist, in Boston, MA., and of its branch in Decatur, AL.; [hon.] Award from GA. Science and Technology

Commission for creative Ability, 1968. Later listed in the National Music Museum, London, England. See also: International Who's Who in Music, Melrose Press, Cambridge, England, Marquis Who's Who of American Women, '93-94, and Marquis World Who's Who, 1996.; [oth. writ.] Textbooks: "Revised Notation" (New and Shortcut to the old) "The Variety of Voice" (with poems). Choral Works: "Magnolia" 3 female voices, in 13 pages. "Ode to Summertime," 4 voices, 22 pages. Suite of "Three Christmas Carols" mixed voices. Solos: "Immortal," "All for Alabama," Over the Railroad," etc.; [pers.] Although grateful for the rich background of music, I find the inspired word of the Bible sufficient.; [a.] Decatur, AL

EVANOFF, LESLIE GAYLE
[pen.] Les Evanoff; [b.] March 24, 1983, Overland Park, KS; [p.] Pam and Gary Evanoff; [ed.] Stanley Elementary, Stilwell Elem., Blue Valley Middle School; [occ.] Student; [memb.] 4-H Club, Soccer, and Soft ball; [hon.] Honor roll student; [oth. writ.] I've written a lot of work, none of them have been published. You have to realize I'm a 12 year old kid and and I may look young but I'm a mind full of words.; [pers.] I want to thank some of my friends who gave me courage to share my poems and make me feel good about them. (Azita Linsey Bridge - Kristin, Ryan, Ablay, Anne, Kris, Tara Ms. Hartzler, Ms. Jones, Ms. Lowland, Ms. Holmes, Ms. Muelback.; [a.] Overland Park, KS

EVANS, DOROTHY H.
[b.] May 13, 1945, Raleigh, NC; [m.] Albert L. Evans III, August 28, 1965; [ch.] Bert, Laura; [ed.] Main Clinical Psychology, MS in Social Agency Counseling BSN (nursing); [occ.] Psychotherapist; [memb.] Several Child Abuse Organizations, several Environmental Protection Agencies, several Professional Organizations; [hon.] Civilian Meritorious Service Award (for work in child advocacy), Citizen Reviewer of the Year (Court organization to protect children in Poster care); [oth. writ.] Numerous other poems, some prose, none published; [pers.] I am a survivor of severe childhood abuse. My writings came out of my attempts to get past those old memories and feelings. I now write to help me connect with my clients and as political statements about society's ways of dealing with child abuse.; [a.] Centerville, OH

EVANS, HEIDELINDE G.
[pen.] Heide Evans; [b.] December 1, 1972, Dover, NJ; [p.] William and Audrey Thompson; [ed.] 2 years of college, Country College of Morris, 4 yrs of high school at Morris Knows H.S. -Denville; [occ.] Data entry typist Fulco Denville, NJ; [memb.] 1st presbyterian church of Rockaway; [hon.] Published in H.S. literary magazine, College newspaper youngstown edition ent. staff writer, K. Kulik Vocal music scholarship.; [oth. writ.] Many poems, but none published as of yet.; [pers.] I believe I have a unique style and hope to achieve greatness, not only in my writing but as well as music. I strive to be the best at everything I do not I hope others will enjoy my work as much as I do; [a.] Rockaway, NJ

EVANS, MARY EMILY
[pen.] Mary E. Evans; [b.] May 3, 1919, Osceola, NY; [p.] Albert and Jennie Steadman; [m.] William D. Evans, August 18, 1940; [ch.] William H, Dean L, John J.; [ed.] High School, several college courses; [occ.] Housewife; [memb.] Camden Presbyterian Church, Camden Public Library; [oth. writ.] Many pieces of verse. "The Crying Stone", a book published in 1968. Several children's stories. One being "Herman the Little Green Worm" which has become very popular but not published; [pers.] Look at the bright side of life. No matter how hard your life is, it could always be worse. Forever be humorous, never carry a grandpa, never look down at another forever have faith.; [a.] Camden, NY

EVANS, RODERICK F.
[b.] January 21, 1977, Bessmer, AL; [p.] Carter and Katie Evans; [ed.] Washington Park High and Dayton Jobs Corps, WI; [occ.] Taco Bell, WI; [oth. writ.] "The Garden of Love," "Simplicity to Complexity back to Simplicity Again", "What You Son, That Shall You Reap," and Reality; [pers.] I am a man of God and I strive to spread the Gospel throughout the world. I also strive to help the world understand God from God's perspective, through the Church; [a.] Racine, WI

EVERTON, MISS SARAH
[b.] May 23, 1944, Montgomery, AL; [p.] Robert and Lillian Everton; [m.] Single; [ed.] St. Jude High School also went to Trenholm State for Childcare Worker; [occ.] Sitter-Take care of sick Elderly People; [hon.] Received four of Five Honorable Mention Certificates from World Wide Poetry; [oth. writ.] Had one or two poems published by world wide poetry; [pers.] I wish for peoples are all over the world to have peace and harmony with one another. My poems reflects personal problems some people have.; [a.] Montgomery, AL

EZZARD, CATHERINE B.
[b.] August 2, 1943, Orangeburg, SC; [ed.] Wilkinson High School, Atlanta Area Tech; [occ.] Nursing -27 years; [memb.] Missionary Society King's Chapel A.M.E. Church; [pers.] Let the Lord be your guide in every thing you strive to do.; [a.] College Park, GA

FAILE, BETTY RAMSEY
[b.] September 29, 1932, Rock Hill, SC; [p.] Rev. and Mrs. Walter Ramsey; [m.] Rev. Perry Joe Faile Sr., June 27, 1953; [ch.] Wanda, Perry Jr., Belinda and Carla (four), seven grandchildren - Heather, Jarod, Matthew, Joshua, Justin, Logan, Jordan; [ed.] 11th; [occ.] Retired Ministers Wife; [oth. writ.] Two songs I am fixing to have copy write. Started a book, about my Dad. Working on another poem.; [pers.] My writings pertain to my walk with Jesus - influenced by my father.; [a.] Rock Hill, SC

FALLAHAEE, J. D.
[b.] January 10, 1968, Arlington Heights, IL; [p.] Richard and Mary Fallahee; [ed.] A.A. William Rainey Harper College, A.S. William Rainey Harper College, B.A. Blackburn College, M.B.A. University of Phoenix (4/97); [occ.] Industrial Sales; [oth. writ.] Articulations from Apathy 2 Zeal.; [pers.] "Let the fury of words be the winds of change!"; [a.] Schaumburg, IL

FALOR, LAURA E.
[pen.] Bun; [b.] November 6, 1970, Tecumseh; [p.] Bennett Palmer and Darlene Palmer; [m.] Robert Falor, April 9, 1994; [ed.] Associates degree in applied Arts and Science. I graduated from Addison High School and from Jackson Community College; [occ.] Registered Radiologist Technologist Specializing in Cat scan, W.A. Foote Memorial Hospital in Jackson Mich.; [memb.] This is not the kind of Membership you may have wanted but I am a member of a Fantastically Supporting Family.; [pers.] I have been writing for twelve years, and feel as though you can always be successful if you put your heart in it. My best friend has been my biggest inspiration for my poetry.; [a.] Jackson, MI

FARKAS, JENNIFER M.
[b.] Ontario, Canada; [p.] Wayne and Beth Fenton; [m.] Stephen; [ch.] Jonathan; [ed.] Ingersoll District Collegiate Institute, Victory Memorial P.S.; [occ.] Secretary; [memb.] Trinity Lutheran Church; [hon.] Gold Medal County Architectural Drafting Contest 1991; [oth. writ.] Published poems high school yearbook. Currently working on a children' story.; [pers.] All my poems come from dee personal emotions. As a writer, I have to feel th situation before I can express it.; [a.] Kissimmee, F

FARRAR, R. SARAH
[b.] October 10, 1941, Pittston, PA; [p.] Edward and Susan; [m.] Edward B. Farrar, August 20, 1957 [ch.] Michael E., Steven C., and Douglas C.; [ed. Associates of Arts Degree; [occ.] New Homes Rea Estate; [memb.] Disabled American Veterans; [hon. Graduated with High Distinction, Dean's List, an member of Phi Theta Kappa, National Scholasti Honor Society; [oth. writ.] Wings of a Magi Carpet, Crown of Light, Nature's Connection, Moment Away, The Mask; [pers.] I have a passio for thoughts that are expressed with select words an phrases that depict vigor and imagination, bot symbolically and realistically.

FARRELL, GREGORY
[b.] February 23, 1971, Whibdey Island, WA; [p. Wanda Delores, Roger Lee Davis; [m.] Tracy Farrell August 1, 1996; [ed.] Woodrow Wilson High School currently taking vocational classes for Build and Trades, future prospects for Ecology (Environmental Sciences); [occ.] Student; [oth. writ.] I have a few journals of poetry and a couple of short stories, but I have never tired publication or entered a contes until now.; [pers.] We are surrounded by art, (Macrocosm). The Universe within each individual soul creates an inner art, (microcosm). Let's preserve the natural arts.; [a.] Beckley, WV

FARRELL, MELVIN V.
[pen.] Bud Farrell; [b.] November 5, 1935, Millville; [p.] Virgie S. Henrietta Farrell; [m.] Marcille, October 29, 1967; [ch.] Lerri Sandee and Kenny; [ed.] High School graduate, Graduate of Western College of Auctioneering in Billing, MO; [occ.] Rancher Al Lechican Auctioneer; [pers.] I love to see people laugh it make for a brighter day, also I like to write about children that needs homes.

FARRIS, ROBERT S.
[b.] November 18, 1956, Dayton, OH; [p.] Fayetta Farris, Spencer Farris; [m.] Lorraine K. Farris, March 11, 1978; [ch.] Stephanie Mae, Tara Elizabeth, Michael Lloyd Robert; [ed.] A.S. Monroe County Community College Miamisburg Sr. High School; [occ.] Partner - (Two o'l Dogs, D.J. Service and writer's garret); [oth. writ.] Poetry and thoughts Vol. I and II not published as of yet. (Vol. II still in works), this was the first poem I've ever submitted anywhere.; [pers.] Open your "real" minds eye, take it all in, sort it out, look deep to find the hidden meanings, and delve into that which interests you. Thanks to Lord Byron and T.S. Eliot who had the guts to put their thoughts into words despite all the adversity. And to Jack Staas, my psychology professor for opening up new worlds of my mind realm.; [a.] Petersburg, MI

FAUBER, JANICE A.
[pen.] Jan Fauber, Janice A. Woodruff; [b.] October 10, 1942, Duluth, MN; [p.] Robert J. Woodruff, Muriel E. Woodruff; [ed.] Berkeley High School, Berkeley, CA, University of California, Davis, CA. - B.A., Art and History (2 majors), California State University, Sacramento-completed all course work (27 semester units) towards an M.A. in History; [occ.] Writer and Editor (self-employed); [hon.] Award of Merit from the American Association for State and Local History for the book, City of the Plain, Sacramento in the Nineteenth Century (editor); [oth. writ.] Author of several booklets and feature articles on local history of the Sacramento area, editor, *City of the Plain*, Sacramento in the Nineteenth Century (hardcover book), managing editor, *Western Museums Quarterly*, 1971-1973,

published by Western Regional Conference of the American Assn. of Museums, managing editor, *The California Historian* (quarterly magazine), 1974, published by the Conference of California Historical Societies, editor of several newsletters and numerous technical reports, advertising copywriting for several local advertising and public relations firms in the Sacramento area.; [pers.] I especially enjoy writing about Man's interaction with nature and the environment, and about the history of the local area in Sacramento and northern California.; [a.] Carmichael, CA

FAUCHER, HAROLD N.
[pen.] Frenchy Faucher; [b.] July 17, 1924, Minneapolis; [p.] Narcisse C. Faucher; [m.] Hilma Faucher, 1948; [ch.] Dorothy, Gene, Richard, Tom, Jerry, Kenneth, David; [ed.] Hopkins High School, Univ. of Minnesota, graduated 1951; [occ.] Commercial Real Eastate Broker and Appraiser; [memb.] VFW, Amer. Legion, Disabled Vets, Lions Club, Board of Realtors (Local, State and National), Knights of Columbus, China Marine Assoc.; [hon.] Graduated Beta Gamma Sigma (Dean's List) from U. of M. School of Business Admin. Bachelor of Business Admin.; [oth. writ.] "Crickets of Fagassa Pass" prose and poetry of a U.S. Marine in World War II; [pers.] Life must be lived and enjoyed to its fullest extent. Sorrows are things of the past and should remain as nostalgic memories.; [a.] Hopkins, MN

FAULKNER, LENA WEBSTER
[b.] May 13, 1939, Boligee, AL; [p.] Reuben and Frances Webster; [m.] Grady Faulkner, January 22, 1967; [ch.] Grady Jr., Keith Jeffrey Earl and Dennis; [ed.] Greene County Trg School and Baruch College; [occ.] Computer Operator for NYC Parking Violation Bureau

FAULKNER, PAMELA D.
[pen.] P. D. Faulkner and/or a.k.a. P.D. Angel; [b.] August 16, 1958, Detroit, MI; [p.] Philip and Lenora Angelevski; [m.] Graham William Faulkner, August 16, 1986; [ch.] Kevin Philip-William, Kyle Graham-William; [ed.] Crestwood High, Oakland Community College; [occ.] Administrative Assistant; [oth. writ.] Runner up in local newspaper and local college writing contest, many short stories, poems, memoirs and tributes to family members and friends, and several songs. (Unpublished); [pers.] Writing has always been a very special hobby in my life. Most of my writings have been influenced by personal experiences - both happy and sad and some imaginary.; [a.] Garden City, MI

FAZZONE, MARSHALL J.
[b.] April 6, 1956, New Haven, CT; [p.] Lorraine and Marshall; [ch.] Joey and Kenneth; [ed.] Wilbur Cross High, Northern Maine State Tech., Institute of Children's Literature; [occ.] Self Employed Contractor and Math Tutor; [memb.] I.C.E. International Car Exchange, Antique Auto of America, Piedmont Model Railroaders; [hon.] Award given for Service to the New Haven Fire Dept. Award in Tutoring for Aware; [oth. writ.] Various poems and children's stories not yet published.; [pers.] "Life is what happens when your busy making other plans." (John Lennon) I live life to the fullest.; [a.] Lyman, SC

FEATHERS, CATHERINE DORENE
[pen.] Sunshine; [b.] November 22, 1952, Darby, PA; [p.] Sarah H. Byrne; [ed.] Collingdale High School, Adelphia Business School; [pers.] My poetry is based on the love and inspiration I receive by Jesus and the Holy Spirit.

FELICIANO, MENDIOLA
[pen.] Ella Joy; [b.] August 14, 1977, Philippines; [p.] Juan Feliciano Jr., Erlinda Feliciano; [ed.] Camiling School for Home Industries, Philippines, Kailua High School, Windward School for Adults; [occ.] Part-time Student; [hon.] Honor Roll at Kailua High School; [oth. writ.] Three poems sent to cader publishing was approved for publication and qualified for the final round; [pers.] Things that hard to explain and to express to others are the major contents of my poems.; [a.] Waimanalo, HI

FELIX, BELIA
[b.] March 11, 1956, Fresno, CA; [p.] Joseph M. Gonzales, Mary E. Gonzales; [m.] Gilbert Felix, February 4, 1973; [ch.] Jeffrey, Jessica, Edward; [ed.] Bakersfield High School, Bakersfield College, Fresno City College; [occ.] Homemaker; [pers.] I admire people who have a gentle way but affect millions such as Mother Theresa of Calcutta and Maya Angelou.; [a.] Bakersfield, CA

FENDER, BRYAN KEITH
[pen.] Doc; [b.] August 12, 1973, Pittsburgh, PA; [p.] Leona and Richard Fender; [ed.] Currently attending California University of Pennsylvania (Psychology Major); [occ.] McDonald's Crew Person; [pers.] Time kills.; [a.] McDonald, PA

FENSTERMACHER, MARY WISHAM
[b.] April 11, 1952, Bridgeton, NJ; [p.] Charles D and Mildred M. Wisham; [m.] Todd E. Fenstermacher, September 2, 1972; [ch.] April Dawn, Angela Marie, Abigail May, Aaron Matthew, Arik David; [ed.] Bridgeton High School '70 (N.J.) Catawba College '70-'72 (N.C.) Kutztown State University '75 B.S.; [occ.] Elementary Education, Teaching piano lessons; [memb.] Home start Home schooling Portfolio Review Committee; [hon.] Babe Ruth Sportsmanship Award (H.S.), Ellsworth J.C. Flexer Memorial Scholarship Magna Cum Laude (KSU); [oth. writ.] Several articles and stories in conjunction with the Institute of children's Literature Writing Course Assignments, West Redding, CT. Numerous poems used in teaching and personal writing.; [pers.] Language is a special gift from the Lord. In my writing I seek to proclaim God's love and power and the majesty and beauty of his creation.; [a.] West Peru, ME

FERGUSON, REBECCA
[b.] March 13, 1958, Piggott, AR; [p.] C. Laws Cargill and Inis O. Cargill; [m.] Larry Ferguson, May 15, 1981; [ed.] Piggott High, Arkansas State University, Jonesboro AR, Northeastern State University, Tahlequah OK; [occ.] Floral Shop Owner; [pers.] I believe creative writing, as with any artistic endeavor, awakes the inner beauty, resilience of spirit, and hidden strengths that lie within us all.; [a.] Tahlequah, OK

FERRY, CHRISTIAN
[b.] June 4, 1971, Santiago, Chile; [p.] Jeremy Ferry, Paulina Ferry; [ed.] High School, Coral Park Sr. High in Miami; [oth. writ.] I have so many more, since 1986 and I'm writing and painting.; [pers.] In this generation we need some one who understandings these minds and touch them with wisdom and inspiration. So I will try my best to do that.; [a.] Eastridge, TN

FIETSAM, MARY
[b.] January 22, 1938, Lynn, MA; [p.] Dr. Herbert E. Mac Combie and Amy Campbell MacCombie,; [m.] Robert Fietsam Sr., P. E., June 8, 1956; [ch.] Dr. Robert Fietsam, Jr. Terry Young, Wendy Gould, Darcy Luadzers, Cindy Matz, Randall Fietsam, Chadley Fietsam, Skotti Gray, and Karolyn Tomayko; [ed.] Mrs. From Chio State University; [occ.] Elected Official Treasurer of the Charter Township of Shelby; [memb.] Michigan Class Pool Trustee (Elected) Shelby Township Building Authority Treasure; [a.] Shelbytownship, MI

FILKOHAZI, PATRICIA R.
[b.] January 15, 1941, New Brunswick, NJ; [p.] Rose and Wm. Kunsevich; [m.] Andrew R. Filkohazi, III, July 9, 1960; [ch.] 5-2 Boys 3 Girls; [ed.] Roosevelt Jr. High and North Brunswick High School New Brunswick, New Jersey; [occ.] Housewife; [oth. writ.] God's hands Choc. eyes and curley hair grand daughter "Alex" someone touch my shoulder; [pers.] I write my poems, when I lose a loved one, or I feel I have to write down may feelings.; [a.] Forked River, NJ

FINK, BERNADETTE
[b.] January 24, 1970, Sugar Land, TX; [p.] Elizabeth Duke and Donald Hyde; [m.] Charles Fink, April 24, 1987; [ch.] Charles Jr. and Dustin; [ed.] Lamar Consolidated High School, Alvin Comm. College; [occ.] Homemaker, Mother; [memb.] PTA; [pers.] Feeling plays a great role in what I write whether it be pain, sorrow, or happiness. I have to feel what I write otherwise what I write means nothing and I want what I write to mean something to someone.; [a.] Needville, TX

FITZGERALD, MARGUERITE TWIGG
[pen.] Marguerite Twigg Fitzgerald; [b.] April 4, 1897, Paris, IL; [p.] Hanson R. and Nellie Twigg; [m.] Jerry B. Fitzgerald, June 12, 1929; [ch.] John, Patrick Paul, Jerry, Joan, Rose Mary; [ed.] Graduate of University of Illinois 1919; [occ.] Teacher for rural schools teacher of mentally, physically handicapped,; [memb.] St. Mary's Catholic Church, Catholic Daughters of America, Alter Society, Koinonia of Springfields and Eastern Illinois, Edgar County, Retired Teacher's Assoc. Right to life Edgar County,; [oth. writ.] Several poems, not published; [pers.] "God said it, I believe it and that settles it."; [a.] Paris, IL

FJELLE, KAREN MARIE
[pen.] K.M.F.; [b.] November 30, 1918, Norway; [p.] Elizabeth and Harald Most; [m.] Kaare Andreas Fjelle, June 14, 1947; [ch.] Carl Ingvar Fjelle; [ed.] Making Lady's Dresses Men's Clothing; [occ.] Retired Writing a Book: Elizabeth's Fam.; [memb.] Sons of Norway - 30 years Lief Erikson Lodge Nr. 1, Westkystens Nordmorslag member since 1951; [hon.] For a story published in "Allers" OSLO - Norway, Stories Recorded - At 1050 AM Radio Station K.B.L.E. - Seattle some in the late 1970, I was recorded and aired for Christmas in Scandinavia - 1995; [oth. writ.] Thru the years I have written stories who has been published in newspapers in my home town Kristiansund N. Norway and in Wester Viking in Seattle-Wash. Pen-name K.M.F.; [pers.] I wish I could have used the scholarship. Principal E. Kvenbo offered me. But my parents turned it down. Because I was the oldest in my big family and was needed to help at home.; [a.] Seattle, WA

FLANDERS, LOUIS H.
[pen.] D'Mar Emral DeLator; [b.] March 22, 1917, Knoxville, IA; [occ.] Retired; [oth. writ.] None published; [pers.] Would that the world could be blessed with more people with the intelligence of William Shakespeare!; [a.] Hamburg, NY

FLENNIKEN, CEILS BANKS
[b.] April 26, 1909, Mount Nebo, TX; [p.] William Banks, Donna Banks; [m.] Arthur Flenniken, January 28, 1939; [ch.] Michael Banks, Laurel Ceils; [ed.] Naples High School, University of Texas, Nixon Clay Business College; [occ.] Retired - Austin School District; [memb.] Grace United Methodist Church; [hon.] Gold Medal in Declamation, Naples High School First place in debating, Naples High School Essay Awards in College; [oth. writ.] A number of short stories, many poems through the years (1926+), a novel that has never been typed, The Other Man in Mark Twain, Articles in South

Austin Newspaper, The banks of Sulphur River (1977) my two sisters and I published this book in 1977 about our growing up years in East Texas.; [pers.] Writing has been one of my great pleasures as far back as I can remember.; [a.] Austin, TX

FOGARTY, BRANDEY L. PALMER
[b.] October 24, 1973, Torrington; [p.] Leslie and Darlene Palmer Jr.; [m.] Kevin Terrence Fogarty, June 17, 1994; [ch.] Kevin Terrence Fogarty, Jr.; [ed.] Oliver Wolcott Technical School, Northwestern or Comm Tech. College.; [occ.] Homemaker, home typist; [memb.] Volunteer for Visiting Nurses, Inc., St. Francis of Assisi Church, Women's Volleyball of Torrington and Women's Volleyball League of NW YMCA.; [hon.] Who's Who Among High School Students and Dean's List, High Honor Roll, Student Council, Community Youth Award, Student Council Representative, Chrmnowts Auto show, Elks Award, PTO Shop Award Graduated Top 10 Students 1992, Varsity Valleyball; [oth. writ.] Numerous juvenile novels - unpublished, several poems - one published in the local paper as well as my yearbook.; [pers.] I enjoy writing novels which reflect humor for young adults. I also write poems to portray the true feelings not only "spirituality but also romance; [a.] Torrington, CT

FONTAINE, JOHN G.
[p.] Gordon, Virginia, Fontaine; [memb.] A.A.; [oth. writ.] Wonder, Today; [pers.] Learning to fly on my own wings. Still searching. Written for Sandra Barnes; [a.] Green Bay, WI

FORTENER, CECELIA
[b.] December 30, 1914, Indiana; [p.] Mary E. Clark - Edw. Vianco; [m.] George Fortener, [ch.] Three; [ed.] 2 yrs. college; [occ.] Retired; [oth. writ.] Attended Parochial School studies piano music as a child. Husband and I built a complete house (Cottage type) single handed. At the age of 52 attended college; [pers.] Become a critical care registered nurse (was on dean's list) now retired but active.

FOWLER, JOSHUA D.
[pen.] J. D. Fowler; [b.] November 10, 1983, Austin, TX; [p.] Larry and Sherri Fowler; [occ.] Full Time Student in the 6th Grade

FOWLER, LARRY GERARD
[pen.] Lgfowler, Lgerand Fowler, Lgenard; [b.] May 21, 1956, Saint Louis, MO; [occ.] Electronic Computers and Switching Systems Craftman; [pers.] No is no force greater than the "Peace" within me.; [a.] Glendale, AZ

FRANCANO, JONI
[b.] January 14, 1945, Philadelphia; [p.] Mary and Dan Boyd; [m.] Angelo (Late), November 27, 1982; [ch.] 4 step (Angela, Tom, Maria and Stephen); [ed.] St. Maria Goretti High, Stenotype Inst; [occ.] Executive Legal Secty; [memb.] St. Maron's Church; [oth. writ.] Poem published in Local Hospital Quarterly Book; [pers.] I write with a sense of personal feelings from my heart - to try to give a little joy to family and friends.; [a.] Philadelphia, PA

FRANCISKOVICH, ROBERT J.
[b.] December 25, 1921, Chicago; [p.] Marion and Marie Franciskovich; [m.] Corinne Franciskovich; [ch.] 2 Boy; [ed.] High School; [occ.] Self-employed; [oth. writ.] Approx. 50 verses; [a.] Palatine, IL

FRANDSEN, BENJAMIN W.
[pen.] Benjamin Wiley; [b.] February 25, 1974, Westwood, CA; [p.] Robyn K. Frandsen and Thomas W. Frandsen; [occ.] Currently triple majoring in Biology, Theatre Performance and English (Technical Writing) at boise State University. (No Bachelors Degree yet); [occ.] Full-time student, apprentice to master craftsman (stained leaded glass); [memb.] Kim's taekwondo, BSU Theatre group; [hon.] Torrance area reading council ('88) - first in poetry, National Council on Alcoholism '89 Editorial on Children of Alcohol, 2nd place; [oth. writ.] "Chameleon," "Ailiteration Analysis," "Sense", "Whisper," and "The Pain of Knowing" (Published writings relate respectively to awards: "Orcinus Orca" and "Donna's Dad"; [pers.] "Poetry words to express that which words cannot express" by me; [a.] Boise, ID

FRANK, DENISE R.
[b.] July 3, 1974, Dearborn, MI; [ed.] Deer Valley High, University of Arizona; [oth. writ.] Editorial columns for the Arizona Daily Wildcat and the Arizona Summer Wildcat; [pers.] Throughout our lives, there must be a constant flow of truth and knowledge.; [a.] Tucson, AZ

FRANKLIN, BRIAN
[b.] October 25, 1971, Connecticut; [p.] Edward Franklin, Marilin Martin; [ed.] Coventry High School; [occ.] Writer; [memb.] Powerhouse Gym.; [oth. writ.] Searching for myself Licacs in the field the flower time is near time is near the meaning of Christmas; [pers.] My goal is to reach as many inquiring individuals as I can. I feel as if my poetry focuses on heartfelt feelings that many of you will enjoy; [a.] Esmond, RI

FREDERICK, SHIRLEY
[pen.] Mikes Mother; [b.] September 27, 1937, Dixon, IL; [p.] Cyril and Dorothy Ryan; [m.] Roger Frederick, September 3, 1960; [ch.] Bryan, Tom, Ted, Mary, Mike; [ed.] R.N.; [occ.] Retired; [memb.] Church open Bible; [oth. writ.] Wall, My Wondering Heart, Mushroom Family, My Baby; [pers.] The son I lost had my talent.; [a.] Morrison, IL

FREED, FLORENCE WALLACH
[b.] May 31, 1933, New York City; [p.] Frances and Irving Wallach; [m.] Charles Freed, April 16, 1956; [ch.] Lisa and Josie Freed; [ed.] Barnard College - Bachelors Degree, Harvard University - Masters Degree, and advanced Study Certificate; [occ.] Professor of Psychology Middlesex Community College, for many years; [memb.] Psychological Organization, Concord Musical Club, Lincoln Poetry Group; [hon.] High School Valedictorian Barnard College - Phi Beta Kappa, Cum Laude Grand Harvard School - Pi Lamba Theta and Tinkham Feloowship; [oth. writ.] Poems and short stories published in the Lincoln review and many other literary journals. Psychological research published in psychology journals.; [pers.] I try to present personal experiences realistically, and beautifully.; [a.] Lincoln, MA

FRONTELA, OLGA
[b.] February 27, 1927, Cuba; [p.] Juan Gil, Dolores Montes De Oca; [m.] Arsenio Frontela, January 21, 1962; [ch.] Olga, Arsenio, George Frontella; [ed.] Elementary School; [occ.] Cosmetology; [pers.] Like a human being I love God and I love my family. I wish that all humanity is full of faith and love as also our fellow being. I wish the very best always to everyone in the whole world. Never, will I do wrong to others, not even if their my enemies. Although I do not think I have any, only God alone knows. I like to write compositions and read.; [a.] South Gate, CA

FRYER, DONNA
[b.] November 11, 1949, South Milwaukee, WI; [p.] Fred Raether, Lorraine Raether; [m.] Robert Fryer, December 9, 1967; [ch.] James Robert, Lori Beth; [ed.] South Milwaukee High Mid-State Technical Institute Milwaukee Area Technical College University of Wyoming; [occ.] Fryer Realty; [memb.] Wyoming Scribes, Christian Women's Club, Wyoming Board of Realtors, Certified Residential Specialists, Women's Council of Realtors, Wyoming Writers; [oth. writ.] Poems and short stories; [pers.] Born in Wisconsin, transplanted in Wyoming. Living in the splendor of the Big Horn Mountains writing reflect searching changes and growth especially the Christian Walk.; [a.] Sheridan, WY

FUENTES, BRENDA LEE
[b.] November 21, 1961, Greenfield, MA; [p.] Kenneth C. Barton and Evelyn M. Barton; [m.] Reymundo Fuentes, May 23, 1981; [ed.] Cleburn High School, Fort Worth Skill Center; [occ.] Construction Laborer at Seven Oaks Dam, Highland CA.; [memb.] HOD Carriers and Laborers local #783.; [a.] Adelanto, CA

FUENTES, MARIA
[b.] July 7, 1970, Jalisco, Mexico; [p.] Alipe and Margarita Fuentes; [ed.] University High, West L.A. College -A.A. Degree in Liberal Arts Humanities; [oth. writ.] Several poems in Spanish and English not yet published, as well as children stories; [pers.] I write hoping that the reader will be touched in more ways than one. My brother Martin's memory has been my biggest inspiration.; [a.] Los Angeles, CA

FULCHER, MARY T.
[pen.] Mary T.; [b.] June 27, 1947, Henry, CO; [p.] Cletus and Dovie Turner; [m.] Richard D. Fulcher, April 14, 1995; [ch.] Donna, Lynn, Brian; [ed.] High School - Fieldale VA, Management Training thru Bassett - Walker Ktg. Co., Inc.; [occ.] Supervisor, Bassett - Walker Knitting Co.; [memb.] Hillcrest Baptist Church Spencer, VA; [oth. writ.] I remember well - I also have a collection that has not been published.; [pers.] My writings have been inspired by my grandchildren, and a brand new husband.; [a.] Critz, VA

GAGER, AMBER
[b.] September 9, 1982, Dearborn, MI; [p.] Patricia and Gary Gager; [ed.] Federal Hocking Local School; [occ.] Student; [memb.] Fox Kids Club, Olympia; [hon.] 2nd Grade (2, 4th place Field Day Ribbons, a Certificate of Achievement) 3rd grade (3rd place field day ribbon) 4th grade (Certificate of Appreciation) 5th grade (Student council) 6th (Play, yearbook staff.); [pers.] My Maternal Grandparents adoptive me since my mother is a truck driver. They gave me the inspiration to write my poems.; [a.] Guysville, OH

GALINDO, JOEL
[b.] August 8, 1959, San Antonio, TX; [p.] Mr. and Mrs. Emilio G. Galindo; [m.] Divorced; [ch.] Vanessa Galindo; [ed.] Antonian H.S., graduated from St. Phillips H.S. 1977 (Battle Creek Mich.), attended San Antonio College (45 hours); [occ.] Board Certified Orthotist (BOC), Board Certified Pedorthist (BCP), Orthopedic Shoe Tech, 3rd Generation Cobbler; [memb.] American Diabetes Association, B.O.C. (Board for Orthotist Cert.), B.C.P. (Board for Certified Pedorthist), P.A.D.I. (Professional Association of Diving Instructors), U.S.A.K.F. (United States of America Karate Federation), I.S.P. (Associate Member of International Society of Poets).; [hon.] Editor's Choice Award (*Beyond The Stars*); [oth. writ.] Published poem (*Beyond the Stars*), Advetorials in S.A. Business Journal and Bulverde Standard; [pers.] Someone once said "Life is a poem, and each one of us are the verses to the poem" I want to be the verse always remembered.; [a.] San Antonio, TX

GALLIMORE, MARGARET MARTIN
[pen.] Maggie Gallimore; [b.] March 20, 1947, Winston-Salem; [p.] Mr. and Mrs. Hollard Martin; [m.] Timothy M. Gallimore, May 9, 1986; [ch.] Andrew, Amy, Alan; [ed.] Attended High Point

College; [occ.] Communication Associate with AT&T in Winston-Salem; [oth. writ.] Numerous poems and songs Solitude, Faithful Friends put on sound of poetry and published 1995 National Library of Poetry, other poems published in local newsletters; [pers.] To inspire and uplift through poetry.

GALLO, DR. ANTHONY A.
[pen.] Dilan Jones; [b.] December 19, 1956, Providence, RI; [p.] Barbara and Antonio Gallo; [ed.] Country High School, University of RI, B.S. Psychology, Zoology and Pre-Med Dean's list 4 years University of Mexico School of Medicine, D.D.S. at the University of George town; [occ.] National Champion in Martin Arts; [memb.] National Dental Ass., CT Dental Ass., Waterbury Dental Ass.; [hon.] Dean's list college and medical school. All shate football, wrestling and track in high school 4-years. 10 years Nationally Rated Martial Artist. National and International Champion 1991-1992. Junior Olympic Champion Wrestling (Silver Metal); [oth. writ.] Torment Of A Dying Soul, Ghostly Shadow Of Death, Change Of Sensons - Change of Heart, Slumber, Ego So Humble, To A Friend, Revival to Life; [pers.] So many beautiful things go unnoticed in our world or they are misunderstood. I hope my poetry awakens people and helps to learn a little more about our world, our dreams and ourself.; [a.] Bristol, CT

GAMBLE, WESLEY
[b.] May 4, 1970, Buffalo, NY; [p.] Ella Cawein and Wayne Gamble; [ed.] City Honors High School, Cornell University B.S.E.E. '92; [occ.] Computer Consultant; [hon.] National Merit Scholar, 1980; [pers.] Lifelong learning is where it's all!; [a.] Houston, TX

GAONA, CAROL MARTINEZ
[b.] August 16, 1949, Hamlin, TX; [m.] Jose G. Gaona, March 29, 1992; [ed.] GED (76) 1 yr. Wharton County Jr. College; [occ.] Housewife; [hon.] Golden Poet Award 1989 and Award of Merit Certificate for An Aim.; [oth. writ.] "An Aim" published 1990 in a book called Great Poems of the Western World by John Campbell Editor and publisher. Eddie Lou Cole, poetry editor; [pers.] My work reflects my thoughts and dreams for life. And I thank my college English professor who encourage me to write after he read some of my poems.; [a.] Snyder, TX

GARBARINI, GERALD C.
[b.] October 22, 1929, San Andreas, CA; [ch.] Mitch, Matt, Teryn; [ed.] B.A. Degree, San Jose State Secondary Teaching San Jose State; [occ.] Retired; [pers.] Pizza is good, but a poem can be better.; [a.] Jackson, CA

GARCIA, MARIO E.
[b.] February 4, 1979, Pueblo, CO; [p.] Eloy and Tina Garcia; [ch.] Have three older sisters; [ed.] Junior at Centennial High School.; [occ.] Student; [memb.] Bootball, Wrestler; [hon.] Third place winner in an outer space invention sponsored by University of Southern Colorado when I was in fourth grade; [oth. writ.] Only I could fly name of book: Castalia by: Mile High Poetry Society age:13; [pers.] Work hard to accomplish your coals in life.; [a.] Pueblo, CO

GARCIA, MICHAEL
[b.] August 23, 1960, Houston, TX; [p.] Macario and Eva Garcia; [m.] Margarita (Divorced), October 10, 1994; [ed.] Mary Brantley Smiley H.S.; [occ.] Salesman; [pers.] Education is always the key for a bright future it opens doors wherever you wish to go in this world; [a.] Houston, TX

GARCIA, STEPHANIE ALAYNE
[pen.] Khyttin; [b.] May 6, 1971, San Antonio, TX; [p.] Stephen and Barbara Doumit; [m.] Rogelio G. Garcia, April 16, 1992; [ch.] Roger D. Garcia (Stepson); [ed.] Thomas Edison High; [occ.] Layaway Manager, Wal-Mart #765; [pers.] My heart is always open to these who are in need and for whom I know I can depend on when I am in need. Within my heart, is all children striving to be free.; [a.] San Antonio, TX

GARDUQUE, ELAINE
[b.] December 16, 1977, Guantanamo Bay, Cuba; [p.] Eduardo Garduque, Rosalinda Garduque; [ed.] Lemoore High School, West Hills Community College, Accepted to San Jose State University; [occ.] Student; [memb.] California - Scholastic and Federation, Future Business Leaders of America, Filipino - American Association of Kings County, Asian American Citizens Club of California; [hon.] Honor Roll, 1st Place Talent Show for Vocal Performance, MVP-Tennis, MVP-Cheerleading; [oth. writ.] Several articles for the Tiger Tribune, several poems published in "Valhalla", High School Literary Magazine.; [pers.] I personally love the arts and all types of literature, because it is through your words and through your pictures that you have the power to stir up emotions. Through your own creations you can inspire people to really think beyond the facts. The best literature comes from the heart.; [a.] Lemoore, CA

GARFIELD, MICHAEL
[b.] February 7, 1917, New York, City; [p.] Maurice Garfield; [m.] Sadie Garfield, Second Marriage, September 11, 1993; [ch.] Barry Garfield; [ed.] Brooklyn College Graduate - 1939 Training in Air Corps. Mechanic Crew Chief in World War II Studied Art After War (Kann Institute); [occ.] Retired Computer Salesman - Top Sales Man; [hon.] Top Sales Man in Company - Best Short Story In College Magazine - Poems published in local newspapers; [oth. writ.] Completing adaptation of play called "Unhusk The Heart Of Fear" for motion picture company; [pers.] Poems reflect love of nature and relationships of people towards each other; [a.] Los Angeles, CA

GARIBAY, STANLEY B.
[b.] May 9, 1905, Philippines Island; [p.] Simon D. Garibay; [m.] Julia C. Bauzon; [ch.] Five children; [ed.] M.A.; [occ.] Retired - Instructor; [memb.] Filipino - American National Historical Society; [oth. writ.] Please see page of "A Question of Balance" of 1992.; [pers.] There might be thousand of them, that we might meet in life stream, but few of them will give brighter beam, that might make by a sweeter dream.; [a.] Fairfield, CA

GARIEPY, HEATHER
[b.] December 18, 1978, Dalton, GA; [p.] Don and Jennifer Gariepy; [ed.] Claxton High School - junior; [occ.] Student; [memb.] Drama Club; [oth. writ.] I have a collection of poems including: "Hit Me", "Colours", "Guilt", "The Sweetest Song I Never Heard", "Untitled", "Bourbon By My Bedside", "That's Not Love"; [pers.] I have my bout with demonds, as does everyone, but I always try to remember that these demonds help drive me towards my accomplishments - no matter how major, no matter how minor... I would also like to add that I have two of the most wonderful sisters anyone could ever ask for. And I have a very special friend, John, who's "There" with me.; [a.] Reidsville, GA

GARRETSON, JOHANNA A.
[b.] January 14, 1917, Passuruan East Java, Indonesia; [p.] Jan Karel Van Haastert (was an engineer), Rudolphine H. F. Van Olden both were born in Indonesia, the was 3rd generation born in the East Indies or Dutch Colonies.; [m.] Johnnie D. Garretson, May 4, 1954; [ch.] 2 sons (adopted); [ed.] Elementary School/Dutch/in Indonesia, High School and Junior College/Diploma 5 yr. H.B.S. in East Java, Indonesia. Was trained for Assistant Librarian in Surabaia/East Java, worked there, till World War II; [memb.] The Senior Citizen's in Glendora, Ca. next door to San Dimas from 1977-1992, 15 yrs I was a volunteer in Palomar Hospital in Escondido, Ca.; [hon.] Only a 7,500 hour pin for my work in Palomar Hosp. Escondido, where I used to live from 1969-1992; [oth. writ.] Just for myself, some essays, or compositions and longer poems, never publised anything. I loved to write as a teenager everything was lost WW II (all in Dutch language); [pers.] My husband worked for Mobil Oil Comp first in Columbia S - Am. Oil was found in the deep virgin jungle, were the Motolonie Indians were living and used born and arrows to shoot. We lived there from 1949 - 1965, my husband that is, I joined him in 1954 after we were married. We went thru 2 revolutions here. There in 1965 we were transferred to the Sahara desert in Libya, N. Africa We went thru, the middle East War in 1967. We had to flee. I become a U.S. Citizen in Aug. 1965. I believe in the Creative God, the Holy Spirit and Jesus Christ. I'm a protestant, but I'm not affiliated with a church.; [a.] San Dimas, CA

GARRETT, VIRGINIA
[b.] August 3, 1939, Saint Paul, MN; [p.] William J. Walker and Margaret Strope Walker; [m.] Thomas C. Garrett, August 3, 1990; [ch.] Martin Schleuse, Stuart Schleuse, Paul Schleuse; [ed.] B.M. Ed. Univ. of Houston, M.M. Univ. of Houston; [occ.] Director of Education, Houston Symphony; [memb.] Houston Symphony Society, Houston Symphony League Board Young Audiences of Houston, Board University of Houston Moores School of Music Friends Board Houston Yacht Club La Porte Heritage Society St. John's Episcopal Church, La Porte; [hon.] Fredell Lack Award (for outstanding contribution to arts and education) Yachtsman of the year Houston Yacht Club; [oth. writ.] "The Musical Kid", puppet show, "Paul And Papa Haydon", "Carnival Of The Animals" narration, "Gideon And The Space Ship" all concept scripts with symphony orchestra; [a.] La Porte, TX

GARTH, BETTY MARIE
[pen.] Betty Garth; [b.] June 4, 1923, Portland, OR; [p.] Lawrence and Myrtle Whitman; [m.] Wilfred Lovell Garth (Deceased), August 8, 1989 First marriage August 2, 1941 to John Henry Nelson December 19, 1987, (second marriage); [ch.] Jack Nelson and William Nelson; [ed.] High School (Van Nuys, CA) La Salle Accounting Business Accountant Course H and R Block Tax Course; [occ.] Retired - writing is my most intense interest; [memb.] Baptist Church (newhall, CA) Senior Center - Newhall I attened the Village Church at present. I plan to become a member.; [hon.] Received Certificate of honorable mention for poem my father, a great pad. The contest was held in New York. This poem was published in our Local Newspaper" The Signal". As poem of the week for father's day; [oth. writ.] Short Story for Children, a family book "Street/or Skeletons in the Closet" I am working on my book and hope to complete have written so poems. Some of spiritual nature.; [pers.] I have a strong faith in Jesus Christ. My children and family are very and ear to me. I have two sons, four stepchildren, two sons and six step grand children two daughters. Four grandchildren and one great granddaughter due February 6, I have five great grand sons.; [a.] Valencia, CA

GATELY, TONYA
[b.] January 13, 1977, Stoughton; [p.] John Green and Charlene Green; [ed.] I am a Senior at Bridgewater Raynham Regional High School and plan an attending College out in California; [occ.] I'm a part time

worker at Dunkin Donuts; [hon.] This is my first Award concerning writing I have received other award concerning sports.; [pers.] For the people who read my poem, I hope you all enjoy it, but most of all to look deep inside of who you really are, don't turn to other substances it doesn't solve anything but cause more confusion.; [a.] Bridgewater, MA

GAUDET, VIOLET F.
[pen.] V. F. Gaudet; [m.] Married now for thirty-four years.; [ch.] One adult daughter and one adult son, five grandchildren; [ed.] A degree in Mental Health; [occ.] Home - Writing; [oth. writ.] I am presently working on a mainstream novel titled "Women, Children and Their Conversion Vans." I also have other poems that I have written but have not submitted for publication.; [pers.] I have been shy all of my life, sometimes painfully shy. I become very uncomfortable in any social situation. I get very anxious and feel insecure much of the time.; [a.] North Andover, MA

GAUSPOHL, BRENT ANTHONY
[b.] April 15, 1985, Indianapolis, IN; [p.] Jill Rosengarten Gauspohl, William M. Gauspohl; [ed.] 5th Grade Student Spring Hill Elementary; [memb.] Webelo Scout, Den 3 pack 91; [hon.] Arrow of light award; [a.] Columbia, TN

GAWLIK, MARY B.
[b.] December 15, 1920, New York; [p.] Edward and Elizabeth Corish; [m.] William Gawlik, December 27, 1942; [ch.] William, Jane, McGloine, Sue Perzchanowski, Gerard; [ed.] Our Lady of Wisdom Academy, Dominican Commercial High School, Mc Lane Art Institute, Suffolk Community College; [occ.] Retired Housewife; [memb.] Hibernian Society (Historian), Citrus County Genealogical Society, Former Member Withlocoochie Poets Society; [oth. writ.] Many other poems unpublished.; [pers.] I am an avid genealogical researcher and specialize in Irish history, culture and celtic literature. I have a large collection of authentic Irish history books and am constantly searching for more.; [a.] Inverness, FL

GAY, KIMBERLY
[pen.] Kim; [b.] November 21, 1976, Baytown, TX; [p.] Brenda Saunders, David Saunders; [m.] Larry E. Gay Jr., August 1, 1995; [ch.] Hayley Mechelle Gay; [ed.] Robert E. Lee High School; [occ.] Housewife and mother; [memb.] Abundant Life Church; [hon.] Drawing Awards in School Contest.; [pers.] My wish is for my poems to help someone through the hard times and also to make them laugh.; [a.] Baytown, TX

GENECZKO, STACEY LYN
[b.] October 9, 1978, Northampton, MA; [p.] Thomas Geneczko, Nancy Geneczko; [ed.] South Hadley High - will graduate in spring, 1996; [memb.] South Hadley HS band, Young People's Symphony, Field hockey team (at school), Softball team, Youth wind ensemble; [hon.] Made original french hornist in the western mass district concert band my senior year (1996), National Honors society at school - Junior and Senior yrs. Member of all-state concert band in Mass (playing french horn); [oth. writ.] A quote published in 21st Century newspaper, two poems published in local newspaper in seventh grade (1991); [pers.] As rare as the truth may be, we must try to ascertain it. Our lies become so believable that they deceive us—killing our love and innocence. Lies are the walls built to divide us from reality. Mysteries are the doors that when unlocked, our fate can be recognized and the truth revealed.; [a.] South Hadley, MA

GERKEN, AMANDA
[b.] October 1, 1980, Amarillo; [p.] Cindy and Garry Gerken; [ed.] Oskaloosa High School, I'm currently a freshman; [occ.] (Freshman) Student and family owned bowling center; [memb.] I'm the president of a youth bowling league.; [hon.] TIP Talent Search State Recognition Award, Presidential Academic, Fitness Award, A Honor Roll; [pers.] My writings are based on how life is seen through different peoples eyes. I tell it like it is and I don't paint disguises or try to hide the truth.; [a.] Oskaloosa, KS

GETSINGER, STACY
[b.] July 30, 1982, Erie, PA; [p.] Bruce and Christine Getsinger; [ed.] Franklin Middle/High School, 8th Grade; [occ.] Student; [hon.] Honor Roll, Principals List; [oth. writ.] Franklin Middle School poetry reading for parents, teachers, and classmates. Christmas poem published in local newspaper.; [pers.] Special thanks to Mrs. Hornbeck and Mr. Kuzneski.; [a.] Franklin, PA

GEWINNER, ANTHONY J.
[b.] April 4, 1975, Omaha, NE; [p.] Robert Gewinner, Elaine Garrett; [ed.] David City Public High School; [occ.] Factory Worker; [pers.] I believe people need their eyes opened to what they see every day. I just try to give a different perspective, I was, and am, greatly influenced by James Douglas Morrison.; [a.] David City, NE

GIBSON JR., CALVIN T.
[b.] December 16, 1934, Choctaw, OK; [p.] Calvin and Opal Gibson; [m.] Rita C., December 16, 1992; [ch.] Shaun, Michelle; [ed.] Choctaw High/Roosevelt Univ., Chicago/many AVN. Schools; [occ.] Ret. Mil. Pilot/Ret. Automotive Retailer/Wholesaler; [memb.] Ret. Officers Assn./US Army Assn./US Army, Air Force Assn./AARP/SPCPSSA/Mil.Ret. Coalition; [hon.] Mil: DFC, BSM(2), AM(8), plus 16 others/Diamond Homer Trophy/Inducted 1995 Int'l. Homer Soc. of Poets; [oth. writ.] Weekly newspaper publications/several publications by 3 poetry societies/OKC Bombing Memorial Display (permanent)/Vietnam Vets Memorial Wall "writing" used for ceremonies/over 100 poems in locally reproduced portfolio; [pers.] I write as the mood or a particular subject deserves attention and addressing (age brings up many topics).; [a.] Lawton, OK

GIBSON, OPAL
[b.] March 16, 1929, Cyril, OK; [p.] Claude and Winona Long; [m.] Oren Gibson, July 17, 1984; [ch.] Judy, Connie, Tienna, Glenda, Brenda, Mike, James, Jeff; [ed.] High School; [occ.] Retired; [memb.] Lifetime member Int'l. Society of Poets; [hon.] Editor's choice awards for poems published in "Sparkles In The Sand" and "A Delicate Balance" - Nat. Lib. of Poetry; [oth. writ.] Several Poems, only 3 published so far but I love poetry and scribbling on anything that comes to hand.; [pers.] I feel my poems come through me, more than from me, as I will be thinking about something and all of a sudden the poem will just flow through my mind. So I feel I have help from the spiritual world on them.; [a.] Cement, OK

GIEBLER, RUTH KINZIE
[b.] October 26, 1946, Staunton, VA; [p.] John Kinzie, Anne Kinzie; [m.] Gary Giebler, April 12, 1969; [ch.] Dennis Quinten; [ed.] William Fleming High, Monroe Business College, Winchester, VA; [occ.] Home-maker/Secretary; [memb.] Redeemer Lutheran Church, Richmond, Virginia, L.W.M.L.; [hon.] Letter in Concert Choir, William Fleming High School, Roanoke, VA; [pers.] Poetry is a particular mood in a particular space in time. It is my desire to share this mood and space with all who read my poems.; [a.] Midlothian, VA

GIGO, SAIHOU OMAR
[b.] November 7, 1969, Banjul; [ed.] Student at Shaw University, Majoring in Mass Communication; [hon.] Presidential Scholar, Several Academic Achievement Certificates and Medals, All-American Scholar (1996); [oth. writ.] Currently working on two inchoate books, My professors always commend my writings — prose and verse. I hope to actualize the faith they confide in me through a racy pen.; [pers.] A proper historian must be successful for he is not a loaded chip, but a formula - translator My poem is a reflection on history. Incidentally Timbuktu did not impress me as much as it has intrigued me.; [a.] Raleigh, NC

GIORGIO, JOSEPH
[b.] March 5, 1923, Boston, MA; [p.] Deceased [ed.] Seminole Community College Sandford, Florida (Music Major), Queen College, NY, (Music Major), Berkley School of Music Boston; [occ.] Music Teacher; [hon.] Music and Theatrical Director Montessori School Forest Hills, NY., US Navy Musician on USS California, Dove into Pacific Ocean to Save a Clarinet, Have 40 poems to my credit...All ready to be appreciated, Night Club Comedian for years...Still very funny.; [oth. writ.] Currently promoting a story entitled "Have a Gluey Christmas". It is about children in an orphanage who spread glue around the Christmas tree to capture S.C...wrote story and "8" original songs.; [pers.] Some attain success when very young... I shall attain it in the autumn of my years. I will make a great deal of money and I am dedicated to "Covenant House" (Here in NY) for homeless children.; [a.] Glen Oaks, NY

GLASER, CELESTE JANELLE
[b.] August 6, 1974, Temple, TX; [p.] Stanley J. and LaVelle Glaser; [ed.] Buckholts High School, Texas A&M University, A.A. in Biology from Temple Junior College 1994, University of Mary Hardin-Baylor; [occ.] Senior at UMHB pursuing B.S. double major in Biology and English and University of Mary Hardin-Baylor Academic Support Counselor; [memb.] Hope Lutheran Church ELCA Women, Phi Theta Kappa, Sigma Tau Delta, Association of Texas Professional Educators, National Beta Club, International Society of Poets Lifetime Member, International Society of Authors and Artists, the National Authors Regis- try, Poets' Guild, Poetry Society of Texas; [hon.] UMHB Vice President's Honor Roll, TJC Honor Graduate, Dean's Honor List, and Dean's List, The National Dean's List 1992-95, Who's Who Among Students in American Junior Colleges 1994-95, Who's Who Among American High School Students 1988-92, United States Achievement Academy All American Scholar 1992, The National Library of Poetry Editor's Choice Awards '94 and two in '95, Famous Poets Society Diamond Homer Trophy '95, Who's Who in New Poets '96, Nat'l. College Poetry Contest Honorable Mention Fall Concours '93, '94, and '95; [oth. writ.] Poems - "One Perfect Dream", "Heaven Sent", "My Mother", "Searching", and "A Meditation." The poem-"Natasha" was inspired by and written about my precious, two year old niece, Natasha Lauren Ramthun. She's the daughter of my sister, Jocelyn Lanice and her husband, Ricky.; [pers.] Writing poetry has become a wonderful adventure! I feel that it is a God-given gift that "keeps on giving." Along with playing the piano, oil painting, and reading historical novels—writing poetry is very relaxing and a great creative outlet.; [a.] Buckholts, TX

GLOVER, TENA
[b.] September 6, 1971, Fayetteville, NC; [p.] Herman and Etta Mae Edwards; [m.] Randy Glover, May 25, 1994; [ed.] Triton High School Graduate; [occ.] Inspector with Morganite (Dunn, NC); [memb.] Grace Chapel Church; [hon.] Beta Club Honor Graduate; [oth. writ.] To date, I've written 51 poems. I just recently started writing. My first poem was written Sept. 1995, I hope to write a book

of poetry.; [pers.] I feel my poems are a gift from God. I never had the ability to write poetry until recently. Most of my poems are about the Lord, and I use them as a form of witness. My poems touch the hearts of people.; [a.] Erwin, NC

GOBER, JESSE JACK
[b.] November 23, 1984, Marquette, MI; [p.] David and Marie Gober; [ed.] 5th grade student at Scenic Park Elementary in Anchorage, Alaska; [occ.] Student; [memb.] Boy Scouts of America, Fox 4 Kids Club, Burger King Kids Club; [pers.] Treat everyone like you want to be treated.; [a.] Anchorage, AK

GOETZ, DARLENA
[b.] April 9, 1956, Hollywood, CA; [p.] Leon and Thea Schafer; [m.] Tommy Goetz, May 14, 1987; [ed.] BA Sociology, California University at Long Beach; [occ.] Writer; [oth. writ.] Teleplays: Movie of Week (optioned), Sitcom Pilot (optional) spec - mini-series and feature. Many sitcoms specs, a children novel (unpublished); [pers.] My writing seems to be drawn toward unearthing denial in it's many forms to regain hope.; [a.] Hollywood, CA

GOGERTY JR., JOHN D.
[b.] August 4, 1922, Cumberland, MD; [p.] John, Twila; [m.] Loretta Nee Yomnick, June 8, 1949; [ch.] Kathleen, John III, Bridget, Brian, Veronica; [ed.] Fort Hill High Cumberland, Md. Trade School Cleveland, Ohio; [occ.] Retired Postal Service; [memb.] American Legion V.F.M.; [hon.] Military Medals earned by making five landing in the South Pacific in WW II.; [oth. writ.] Two other poems being published by your Library and one more accepted as well as this one.; [pers.] As I started writing poetry when in the army I sure didn't know why, it must be in Irish genes as we all know there many great poets from the Emerald Isle and I hope that I inherited a little of there wit and charm.; [a.] Cleveland, OH

GOLDMAN, RUTH PHARES
[pen.] Ruth Phares Goldman; [b.] May 25, 1913, Indianapolis, IN; [m.] Deceased; [ch.] Richard, Marilynn and Jon; [ed.] The usual - plus business college, and the most supreme educator of all: Life. I have been a most attentive and appreciative student thereof.; [occ.] Keeping in close touch with family and good friends of long standing who are scattered from eastern Canada to Hawaii.; [oth. writ.] Reader's Digest: A small offering long ago. Occasional tidbits to Honolulu Magazine during my eight years there. Sporadic exchanges with various columnists and the occasional contribution to newsprint personalities when invited. World of Poetry Anthology, Great Poems of the Western World, Vol. 2.; [pers.] I have been blessed with a rather imperturbable attitude toward life. This enables me to absorb whatever comes my way without drastic reaction, sparing me harmful emotional upheavals. I am grateful for this for I have led a full life, lived in many interesting places and loved every minute.; [a.] Vacaville, CA

GOMES, NOELLE JULIET
[pen.] Noelle Juliet; [b.] January 19, 1966, Newport, RI; [p.] George Thomas and Marie Louise Corey; [m.] Robert Joseph Gomes, March 23, 1985; [ch.] Katelyn, Nathaniel Krista; [ed.] High school selected college courses; [occ.] Homemaker, pre-school teacher; [oth. writ.] Journals for my children, poems to friends and songs to sing in workship on sundays. Short stories and handmade books for my children.; [pers.] All my writing is directed to my children, and grandchildren to come I have been influenced by my love of scripture and the passing of "Truth", to inspire, and encourage future generations.; [a.] Portsmouth, RI

GOMEZ, TED CRUZ
[b.] September 16, 1983, San Jose, CA; [p.] Maximo Custodio Gomez and Rufina Cruz Gomez; [ed.] Robert F. Kennedy Elem. School, J.W. Fair Middle School (Present); [occ.] 7th Grade Student (J.W. Fair); [memb.] Honor Society; [hon.] Outstanding Academic Achievement (1995), Principal's Honor Roll (1994-95), State Mathematics Award (June 1994); [a.] San Jose, CA

GONZALEZ, BLANCA ESTELA
[b.] October 14, 1957, McAllen, TX; [p.] Argentina Alvarado Gonzalez and Marcelo Gonzalez Jr.; [ed.] PSJA High School 1976, Pan American University 1980 BA Psychology and Elementary Education Texas A and I University 1985, MA Reading Texas Teaching Certificates Elementary Education, Psychology, Reading Specialist, Supervision and Mid-Management; [occ.] Reading Specialist, Teacher at PSJA North High School 15 years teaching experience in elementary, secondary, and college; [memb.] Texas Computer Education Association, The International Society of Poets (New Member), Poetry Society of America, Texas Class room Teachers Association; [hon.] Poem published in After the Storm, First division for two years in ensemble band, Second Division for one year in ensemble band, Psychology scholarship for tuition, President honor roll; [oth. writ.] Article published in local paper, Poem published in the following books, After the Storm, Best Poems of 1996, A Delicate Balance; [pers.] I believe that through education anything will be achieved. A goal is accomplished through hard work and determination. The stars can be reached.; [a.] San Juan, TX

GONZALEZ, FERNANDO
[pen.] Nano; [b.] August 12, 1984, Dallas, TX; [p.] Ramiro R. Gonzalez and Margarita C. Gonzalez; [ed.] 8th Grade, Gospel Lighthouse Christian Academy, Elementary School: M.B. Henderson Dallas, TX., 75224; [occ.] Student; [memb.] Western Heights, Church of Christ; [a.] Dallas, TX

GOOD, MARGARET
[b.] February 4, 1933, Estancia, NM; [p.] Claude and Bertha (Crider) Brown; [m.] Paul W. Good, March 16, 1963; [ch.] Dena Sue Roberts, Edward F. Good, Steven W. Good; [ed.] Ewing School, Torrance Co., NM Estancia High School, Estancia, NM Harding University, Searcy, ARK.; [occ.] Retired Secretary; [memb.] Church of Christ International Society of Poets; [hon.] N.M. Girls State, 1950 High School Salutatorian Scholarship to Harding College; [oth. writ.] Anthologies of High School - 2 years Sermons I Poetry - 2 years College - 1 year Famous Poets Society today's great poems famous poems of today National Library of Poetry Best Poems 1995 and 1996 Plus 12 other Anthologies Vessels Several poems 1993-1995; [pers.] I credit my 6,7,8 grade teacher, Mrs Eulah Watson, deceased, for getting me started writing poetry. My writings consist of things with which I am familiar, specific events, people, religion.; [a.] Stephenville, TX

GOODWIN, STACEY
[pen.] Anastasia; [b.] October 24, 1977, MA; [p.] Bea Goodwin; [ed.] High School (Our Lady of Nazareth Academy) entering freshman year of college.; [occ.] Day Care Assistant Teacher in Massachusetts; [oth. writ.] I've been writing for myself since I was a child. I have hundreds of poems which I've never had published before.; [pers.] I endure great pleasure in expressing myself in poetry. And I encourage anyone with the desire to do so.; [a.] Medford, MA

GOOTEE, JOHN M.
[pen.] Jonathan; [b.] June 11, 1948, Indianapolis, [p.] Glenn and Ardella Gootee; [m.] Mary H. Gootee, March 3, 1990; [ed.] Graduate: Indiana University; [occ.] District Manager of National By Products, Inc.; [memb.] I belong to the Log Cabin's Senous Fireplace on a Raspy Leaf Autumn Saturday night; [hon.] Accolades from strangers; [oth. writ.] Anonymous Chapters left on book shelves in college library.; [pers.] Life is a song looking for a tune.; [a.] Brownsburg, IN

GORDON, HARLAN L.
[pen.] H. L. Gordon; [b.] September 30, 1924, Morgan, TX; [p.] Deceased; [m.] Doris E., August 24, 1951; [ch.] Michael Lee; [ed.] Ball High, Corpus Christi State Univ.; [occ.] Retired USAF, retired Tex. Prison Employee; [memb.] VFW, Amer. Legion, Elks Lodge; [oth. writ.] Outdoor columns for Huntsville item newspaper, Novels.; [pers.] My poems are based on the humor side of life. I write for the fun of it. I believe that to create is to recreate.; [a.] Weslaco, TX

GORDON, SCOTT BRADLEY
[b.] January 30, 1982, Santa Barbara, CA; [p.] Gary Gordon, Janet (Eckert) Gordon; [ed.] Washington Elem. La Cumbre Middle School, Santa Barbara, California; [occ.] Student; [memb.] La Cumbre Middle School Jazz Band and Yearbook Staff; [pers.] I like my inner thoughts to be reflected in all my writings. My writings also reflect my hopes and dreams for the future.; [a.] Santa Barbara, CA

GORODETSKAYA, YELENA
[b.] December 10, 1975, Beraichev, Ukraine; [p.] Yuriy and Yergeniya Gorodetsky; [ed.] Student of Pace University, New York; [hon.] Pace University Dean's List and Pace University Trustee Scholarship; [oth. writ.] Other writings are also about a beautiful feelings of love.; [pers.] My poems are not written. They just happen one after another, merging into the song of my soul.; [a.] Brooklyn, NY

GRAHAM, DARLENE L.
[b.] October 22, 1964, Novi, MI; [p.] William E. Parker, Katherine A. Parker; [m.] Thomas W. Graham Jr., January 23, 1981; [ch.] Tommy, Kathy and Charlie; [occ.] Artist and Self-employed; [memb.] Very Special Arts Association, Mobile Art Association; [pers.] Sometimes life is a rough road to follow, but I think that even bad times can make us better people. If you can see good things through the bad, you can learn to cope and carry on...be happy and healthy!; [a.] Citronelle, AL

GRAHAM, DONALD C.
[b.] July 10, 1966, East Liverpool, OH; [p.] Donald and Betty Graham; [m.] Annette R. Graham, January 26, 1985; [ed.] East Liverpool High School Graduate; [occ.] Warehouse Worker; [memb.] White Dragon Warriors Society; [pers.] I try to look into the heart of an individual rather than look at just what they appear to be; [a.] Kissimmee, FL

GRAHAM, ELIZABETH J.
[pen.] Libby; [b.] January 20, 1983, Wichita, KS; [p.] Mattie Cargill and Don Graham; [ed.] 7th Grade; [occ.] Student of Holy Cross Lutheran School; [hon.] Honor Role; [pers.] "There are two things that connect life fate and destiny. You can't control your fate, but your destiny is in your own hands." Elizabeth G.; [a.] Wichita, KS

GRANT, KATRINA R.
[pen.] Kat Grant; [b.] July 18, 1967, Missoula, MT; [p.] Don Erickson, Penny Erickson; [m.] Mark A. Grant, November 8, 1992; [ch.] Bethany Dawn, Nathaniel James; [ed.] Loyola Sacred Heart High School, Univ. of Montana; [occ.] Public Relations; [memb.] Lutheran Church of the Good Shepherd; [pers.] In all situations act lovingly and you will not look back with regret.; [a.] Salem, OR

GRAVES, KELLI MICHELLE
[b.] May 12, 1979, Carmichael, CA; [p.] William Graves, Tedi Graves; [ed.] Currently in Walnutwood High; [pers.] I would like to dedicate this poem to my beautiful mother and my four exceptional sisters for not only telling me to reach for the sky, but for giving me the stars to take me there! I love you all.; [a.] Carmichael, CA

GRAY, JOYCE E.
[b.] July 7, 1956, Saint Louis; [p.] Arthur Lehmann, Gladys V. Chamineak; [ch.] Lisa L. Gray, Kasie L. Wiegand - Gray; [ed.] Fox High School; [pers.] I feel deeply that this is a profound Phil. State our destiny is pre-ordained not one of us to live the same. God's given us a gift, he wants to see what we do with it.; [a.] Arnold, MO

GREELEY, EMILY AUSTGEN
[b.] March 26, 1941, Chicago, IL; [p.] Margarita and Anthony Lofrano; [m.] Donald F. Greeley, December 21, 1980; [ch.] Jeffrey, John, Joseph, (grandchildren) Jason, Arynn, Jeffrey, Joseph, Jacob; [ed.] B.S. Art, Cum Laude, Univ. Wisc. 1980 M.S. EDC/Guidance and Counselling Univ. Wisc. 1989 Cert. Spiritual Direction - Center in the City 1994; [occ.] Social Work; [memb.] NASW, MSSA - Twin Cities Marriage Encounter; [hon.] Outstanding Service Awards - various agencies - 1975, 1977, 1981, 1982, 1992, 1996; [oth. writ.] Journal writing, essays, short stories, unpub. poetry school publications.; [pers.] My writing releases my inner most thoughts and feelings. It is inspired by the divine spirit, those I love, and the life and energy of the Universe.; [a.] Stillwater, MN

GREEN, LOUIS FREEDLAND
[b.] April 31, 1931, Canandaiqua, NY; [ch.] James, Jon Green, Joan Mason, Janice Bailey; [ed.] B.S. - Vocational Education, Souther Ill. at Carbondale MPA - Public Adm. - Troy Vn. - AL; [occ.] Ret.-Air Force; [memb.] VFW, NCOA, AFSA, AARP, Ill. Alumni, Troy Alumni; [oth. writ.] Process of copyrighting several poems.; [pers.] I would like to be a good black poet - A personal goal; [a.] Mary Ester, FL

GREEN, PAULA
[b.] July 22, 1970, Falon, NV; [p.] Leigh Keller; [m.] Michael Green, July 17, 1993; [ch.] Morgan Taylor; [pers.] I'd like to thank my sister, Rhonda, and my mom for the thoughts of them on paper. I love you both. I love you Michael and Morgan, and my mom for the thoughts of them on paper. I love you both. I love you Michael and Morgan too.; [a.] Chino Valley, AZ

GREGORY, BRANDON
[b.] July 11, 1976, Mount Vernon, IL; [p.] Steve and Jettie Gregory; [ed.] None past high school, too lazy and apathetic to attend college; [occ.] Delivering for Pizza Hut; [hon.] My inclusion in *Tapestry of Thoughts* is the first real honor I have received I hope it might make a good springboard to get more work published.; [oth. writ.] I have several note books filled with hundreds of poems of varying moods and/or themes. They are basically diaries of however I feel at the moment.; [pers.] My writings have almost always been used as a release valve for the emptiness that fills me from time to time. Sometimes I think that if I didn't release all that negative energy on paper, it might come pouring out in other, violent forms. So obviously, writing is a rather important aspect of my life. I just hope that others like me will read my words and realize that they are not alone in how they feel, and that violence toward themselves and others is not the answer, no matter much fun it might be at the time.; [a.] Mount Vernon, IL

GRIFFITH, DANIEL W.
[pen.] Dan Griffith; [b.] July 28, 1938, Kingston, PA; [p.] Willard Griffith, Gertrude Wright Griffith; [m.] Shirley Merrill Griffith, June 23, 1975; [ch.] Kate, David, Stepchildren: Robert, Bill, Valerie, Susan and John; [ed.] Valley High School, Syracuse University: BA in Business, Masters in Education; [occ.] Educator; [memb.] Camillus Sportmen's Club, Cornerstone Church, Mad River Club, Syracuse Marching Band in College; [hon.] Full Scholarship to Syracuse University, Regents Scholarship Recipient; [oth. writ.] Poems yet unpublished.; [pers.] Nothing happens by coincidence. Each of us has a special place in the universe only we can fill. Mine, I believe, is teaching young people to be all they can be.; [a.] Baldwinsville, NY

GRIFFITH, DESTRY
[b.] December 8, 1979, Casper, WY; [p.] Julie Griffith; [ed.] Central High; [occ.] Student/Part time Handyman; [memb.] International Studies Club, Asian Studies Club, SCUBA Sciences, Boy Scouts of America, Alternative Fuel Vehicle Club, (E.V.T.C.); [hon.] 1994-95 A.S.U. Science Fair 2nd Place Winner; [pers.] Poetry is one way that I make my feelings immortal and available to all, to have someone inside of me, living me, breathing me, and truly knowing me, that is my dream.; [a.] Phoenix, AZ

GRIMSLEY, WILLIAM E.
[pen.] Will E.; [b.] November 22, 1937, Pensacola; [p.] W. E. and Elaine Grimsley; [ch.] Jean Elaine, Wanda Elizabeth, William III; [ed.] B. S. South Mississippi; [occ.] Public Health Officer; [memb.] FLA Public Health, FLA Environmental Health National Health Assoc.; [hon.] Coach of Year Little Flower Football Scholarship Univ. Of South Mississippi.; [oth. writ.] Kathy Kristmas, Blue Angel Who Couldn't Fly, Where Have The Bell South Giali Gone; [pers.] At this late day in life I wrote my first poem with hope that someone's life would be better if only we would think before we lose what's not our's to start with.; [a.] Pensacola, FL

GRIZZLE, K. RENEE
[b.] February 17, 1962, Wakefield, MI; [p.] Bernard and Karen Pedrin; [m.] Frank Grizzle, March 17, 1990; [ch.] Anthony, Kaitlyn; [ed.] High School Grad, working to get kids to College my dream is to have my children have more than I ever had.; [occ.] Extruder Operator; [oth. writ.] An writing songs now, also a book.; [pers.] When things look their worst, don't give up for God helps those who help themselves as well as others in despair.; [a.] Sheboygan, WI

GROSSO, JUDY OWEN
[b.] Montgomery, NC; [p.] Wm. and Cora Owen; [m.] James J. Grosso, April 29, 1961; [ed.] 2 year college; [occ.] Retired; [memb.] E. Green Dr. Church of God; [hon.] Honor Student High School and College; [oth. writ.] This is my first poem.; [pers.] I love poetry and good reading. My personal aim is to live a life that might be of benefit to those with whom I come in contact.; [a.] High Point, NC

GROVEN, MR. DENISE L. B.
[pen.] D. L. B. Groven; [b.] September 18, 1950, San Diego; [p.] Martha Peters, Raleigh Peters, Alphina Bond; [ch.] Three sons and a daughter and grandbabies; [ed.] San Diego High, E.C.C. College; [oth. writ.] Poems from the Heart. I sent my poems to Carlton Press Corp. They said my poems have meaning on life's joy and pleasures, etc., etc. I'm waiting for them to get back with me.; [pers.] I strive to reflect on every day life. The way it truly happen, am the blessing that we receive. My inspiration come from Tah Tah and his family and my beautiful babies He bless me with. I give thanks to Tah Tah.; [a.] Palmer, AK

GUARAGNA, MARGARET RUTH
[pen.] Hutchi (Hut-Chi); [b.] November 17, 1942, Porto Alegre, Brazil; [m.] Gino Guaragna; [ch.] Ana, Maria, Joseph, Renata (four twins); [ed.] H.S. Leagues Chines Art/Portuges, German, Italian, Eng.; [occ.] Self Employed Artist, Counselor; [memb.] Eckankar, Yoga Connection, Desert M.; [oth. writ.] (Spirit is my Ireland) (yesterday's garden).; [pers.] We all are like a mirror reflecting in each other. Life is nothing more than on experience. I have gratitude in every day I'm in.; [a.] Tucson, AZ

GUENTHER, EDRIS L.
[b.] September 12, 1907, Leedey, OK; [p.] Kenneth F. and Laura A. Wilson; [m.] Paul A. Guenther, December 23, 1929; [ch.] Kenneth Arno and Carole Lina; [ed.] High School, Leedey OK, Lamar H.S., Enid, OK, Grad. 1926, 1 yr. OK College for Women, Chickasha, OK; [occ.] Retired; [memb.] World of Poetry, International Soc. of Poets; [hon.] First Prize, Leedey Times, Essay Contest, 1918 on "Drinking and Driving", World of Poetry Silver Poet Award 1989, Golden Poet Award - 1990, 1991, 1992, International Soc. of Poets, International Poet of Merit Award 1995; [oth. writ.] Miscellaneous poems - some published in World of Poetry and ISP books.; [pers.] Love thy neighbor as thyself, which is the "Golden Rule", be honest and true to yourself and others. Be just and kind to others old or young alike. Do your best in whatever you do, the reward will surely come. I've had a wonderful life. I'm 88+ years old. I was blessed with three talents: Painting, voice and poetry and/or writing. Thanks be to God who has kept me free from harm this long life through, and provided me with all I need. "Thank you God for these."; [a.] Port Hueneme, CA

GUERRERO, JEAN G.
[pen.] Gene G. Guerrero; [b.] February 1, 1929, San Mateo, Philippines; [p.] Vidal Ponce Guerrero, Simeona G. Guerrero; [ed.] Bachelor of Arts, Bachelor of Science in Education and CNA; [occ.] Pre-Board Screener (Security); [memb.] International Society of Poets, World of Poetry (Past Member) Member of the Filipino Community, Member of Volunteers in Teaching English as a Second Language, and the Sacred Heart Charismatic Prayer Group; [hon.] Silver Poet 1986, 1989, 1990, Golden Poet - 1987, 1988, and 1991, Topaz Pin for my 10 Years Service and Swedish Hospital Medical Center - 1991, A Medal of Merit Award - 1991, as one of the Best Outstanding Poetry Writer in the World of Poetry; [oth. writ.] 1) My Mother Dear, 2) You are as Beautiful as a Yellow Rose, 3) Uncertain Love, 4) Unrequited Love, 5) Tessie, 6) DiDi, 7) I am a Mustang, 8) Bridges, 9) Paluan Strand, 10) Cherry Blossoms.; [pers.] Writing is a way of conveying my feelings and emotions, of past and present experiences in my life. And also in appreciating the beauty of my environment that surrounds me.; [a.] Federal Way, WA

GUILFOYLE, SISTER THEOPHANE
[b.] February 1, 1904, New York City; [p.] John and Mary Guilfoyle; [ed.] English major, Training in school art, B.S. in Secondary Education; [occ.] Retired; [memb.] Poverty Program in Hartford, CT for 2 years, 4 years - Handicapped Program in the Diocese of Brooklyn; [oth. writ.] Community paper, a published account of my work in the Handicapped Camp in Brooklyn, Poem: Liberty or Heritage, published in community newspaper Contact; [pers.] The gifts God has given me, I hope to see for the benefit of others. Literature has always been my first love, and art a second. During sickness my Mother always read Longfellow, Stevenson, and Field to me. Later I studied the Romantic poets.; [a.] Columbus, OH

GUILLEN JR., GUILLERMO
[b.] August 4, 1975, Bakersfield, CA; [p.] Guillermo Guillen; [m.] Rosalva Guillen, November 24, 1993; [ch.] William Rene Guillen III; [ed.] Virginia Avenue, South High, Bakersfield College; [memb.] Budoshin Ju-Jitsu; [pers.] My loving wife and son are my inspiration for my writings.; [a.] Bakersfield, CA

GUILMETTE, MARY F.
[b.] December 5, 1965, Canon City, CO; [ed.] Canon City High School University of Southern Colorado; [occ.] Barton School of Medical/Dental Office Assisting; [hon.] Outstanding Spanish IV Student 2000 Hour Pin as a Volunteer in a Nursing home; [oth. writ.] Four poems from a creative writing class in a booklet made by the school newspaper. Some articles when I was on the staff.; [pers.] I like my poems to reflect how much the world needs peace and love.; [a.] Canon City, CO

GURGANUS, JOAN
[b.] August 12, 1937, Walker Co, AL; [p.] Garland and Lois Pounds; [m.] L. T. Gurganus Jr., December 18, 1955; [ch.] Quena Mears, Michael Gurganus, Robin Gurganus; [ed.] B.S. and Master's Degrees from Univ. of AL in Birmingham, AL, but did most of my studies at Sophia Univ., Tokyo, Japan; [occ.] Housewife, but my husband and I were teachers at International Univ. in Kieu, Ukraine (former Soviet Union) last year and we plan to teach a summer session there in May-June 1996. I was an assistant English Professor. I also taught English at Japan Ladies Academy in Hokkaido, Japan, my husband and I spent 10 years in Japan as Missionaries, I also worked 10 1/2 years as a Social Worker for Walker Co. Dept. of Human Resources.; [oth. writ.] I am planning to publish a book of short stories. I also write country songs and children's stories. I won 1st place in a Ghost Story Contest this Halloween published in a local newspaper.; [pers.] Writing should be entertaining as well as informative.; [a.] Cordova, AL

GUTOWSKI, RAYMOND WALTER
[b.] May 21, 1978, Long Island, NY; [p.] Lorraine Wolz and Joseph Onufrak; [ed.] Mattituck High School, Accepted to Gettysburg College, will be attending after graduation; [occ.] Work Part Time in Print Shop; [pers.] I am not a Philosopher, the world is cruel.; [a.] Mattituck, NY

GUTTZEIT, SUSAN
[b.] October 1, 1947, New York; [p.] Margery and James W. Anderson; [ch.] Karl Guttzeit; [memb.] NOTIS (Northwest Translators and Interpreters Society); [pers.] On August 6, 1993, Lisa Mulholland, a 19-year-old daughter of my dearest friend and partner, was horribly murdered in Seattle, WA. Her parents, relatives, friends, fellow students at Cornish Performing Arts College, and myself were touched by her deep compassion, love, generosity, vivacious spirit, and artistic talent — we lost a precious human being. I was inspired to write a poem in her memory.; [a.] Kalaheo, HI

GWINNUP, HEIDI NIKOLE
[b.] May 9, 1972, Elmhurst, IL; [p.] Bonnie and Dennis Gwinnup; [ed.] St. Charles High School, Elgin Community College; [occ.] CNA at McAuley Manor in Aurora, IL; [pers.] I use my experiences in life in my poetry, to help people understand what is going on in their lives.

HAAPANEN, PAIVI
[pen.] Rainchilo; [b.] July 12, 1981, Finland; [p.] Raija and Ali Haapanen; [ed.] Still in school at Chattahochef High.; [occ.] Student; [memb.] "Spiritual order of young minds".; [pers.] "Love is a flower, you've got to let it grow". To think is to dream, yet to dream is to live.; [a.] Alpharena, GA

HADDOX, MAXINE
[m.] Donald Haddox; [ch.] Jesse and Shan Genetin; [occ.] Painter AKA Jesshan Oils and Acrylics, Former Art teacher; [hon.] Editor's Choice Award 1995 (The Garden of Life) and (A Delicate Balance); [oth. writ.] What are you searching for Marie? (The Garden of Life), "Dear Little One" (A Delicate Balance) Short story (Trailer Mag) Other poetry not published; [pers.] Poetry is the "Silent" song within the heart. "Love From Two" is written in memory of Grandmother Verena.

HADEN, BLANCHE L. ENGLISH
[pen.] Lari English; [b.] April 11, 1954, Bluefield, WV; [p.] Wendell L. English Sr. (Deceased) and Christine English; [m.] Divorced; [ch.] Stanford R. Haden II and Christopher M. Haden; [ed.] Bluefield High School attended - Bluefield State College Blfd and Prince Georges Community College, Mercer County School of Nursing - Largo Rd Princeton WN; [occ.] Nurse at Southern Hills Rehabilitation Center President Ebone; [memb.] Gold a Special Club - Corprised of Professional Women - with a Genuine Interest in Making Society Better Member of Ana, American Nursing Association; [hon.] Member National Honor Society, in High School; [oth. writ.] Poem accepted for publishing 1992 - national library of poetry - several poems written in a collection for a legacy for children - article published in local newspaper "letter to the editor" several years ago.; [pers.] Society is a direct reflection of the times. We all must have a genuine interest in the improvement and education of the people, thru whatever means necessary poems, writings books.; [a.] Bluefield, WV

HAFLIN, ROBIN ELIZABETH
[b.] June 13, 1960, Glens Falls, NY; [p.] Duanet Betty Green/Bill and Sue Hagel; [m.] Brian Richard Haflin, November 6, 1993; [ch.] Christopher, Jennifer, Kelly Ann; [ed.] Schuylerville High School, Schuylerville, NY; [occ.] Homemaker; [oth. writ.] A poem published in the book Tomorrow's Dream.; [pers.] My poems are inspired by special people, places and memories, that have filled my life with love.; [a.] Bayonne, NJ

HAGE, GEORGE CAMPBELL
[b.] November 12, 1944, Huntington, WV; [p.] Campbell Joseph Hage, Martha George Hage; [m.] Ellen Elaine Hage, July 1, 1972; [ch.] Shauna Kristin Hage; [ed.] Ed.D. - Curriculum and Teaching The University of NC at Greensboro (12-19-90). M.Ed. in Social Studies Edmonton. The University of NC at Greensboro (5-15-84). B.A. in Music Education - Marshall University, Huntington, W.V. (12-18-71). BA in Religious Education, Washington Bible College, Lanham, MD (5-15-71).; [occ.] Youth and Family Counselor, Ordained Minister, Teacher of Philosophy, Social Studies and Music; [memb.] American Counselling Association, Winston-Salem Professional Piano Teacher's Association, The National Council of The Social Studies Advisory Committee on Religion in the Schools, Appointment from 11/86 - 11/90.; [hon.] Who's Who in the World (1995-1996), Who's Who in the South and South West (1993-1994), Who's Who in American Education (1987-1989), Chi Alpha Omega Honor Society (1969-1970), National Dean's List (1980-1981), Finalist - The International George Herbert Memorial Poetry Competition, The Perish Life Institute, Notre Dame, IN (7-23-82); [oth. writ.] Poetry: "The Peace of Light" in "The Poetic Churchman (1982), "Striving To Know", in Fleet Street Poet (1983). "Luke 2:14" in Lawrence of Notthingham (1985). Published Disser to her: A symbolic Analysis of The Dimensions of Holiness in American Culture and Curriculum: Toward a Symbolic Synthesis of Holiness (UMI 1990).; [pers.] The wholeness through the awakening of the creative self. This creative self that in intrinsic to the life of the artist is potentiality in every person. For me, counseling, teaching and ministry are the means through which I create others to realize this creative energy. This energy is the heart of life and, therefore, the heart of knowledge.; [a.] Winston-Salem, NC

HAH, WON J.
[b.] November 30, 1971; [p.] Ok Jah Hah, Sang Ho Hah; [ed.] Wellesley College; [occ.] Student; [memb.] DAR Scholar, National Honor Society; [hon.] Summa Cum Laude, Phi Beta Kappa; [a.] Worcester, MA

HAHN, JACQUELINE
[b.] February 1, 1941, Marrakech, Morroco; [m.] Dr Lewis C. Hahn, December 22, 1970; [ch.] Four Children; [ed.] M.A. in English (E.S.L.) Main French/Spanish English is my second language - I speak five languages I can write poetry only in English; [occ.] Teacher/Professor; [hon.] Best instructors award in 1992 at U.C.I. (University of Irvine, where I am a professor; [oth. writ.] "Moroccan Cuisine" "Entre Vouset Moe" a french text book; [pers.] I would like to point out some short comings of our society of consumption, all my poems are extracted from my book called, "Poet Reverie on our times; [a.] Laguna Beach, CA

HAHN, THOMAS TOMMY
[pen.] Tommy Hahn, "Peace"; [b.] October 25, 1963, Milwaukee, WI; [p.] Thomas M. Hahn, Lolita Galecki; [m.] Divorced; [ch.] Jason Christopher, Serena; [ed.] Milwaukee Tech. College, Navy Aviation Training Ctr., The Streets of America; [occ.] Musician; [memb.] Dads Against Discrimination; [hon.] Cherished and valued consultant to family and friends.; [oth. writ.] Numerous songs from rock to country, poetry, short philosophies stories. This is my first published poem.; [pers.] I find writing to be the best way to share a feeling or moment. I hope to publish an autobiography using poems and philosophies I've written over the years, in hopes of teaching the "Brighter Side" of life's hardships.; [a.] Las Vegas, NV

HAIUNGS SR., MARCH C.
[b.] April 5, 1967, San Francisco, CA; [p.] Otto and Henrietta Haiungs; [m.] Stephanie, April 14, 1990; [ch.] Marc Conrad Jr. and Michael Vincent; [ed.] Oakmont High School, Sacramento City College; [occ.] Acting Senior Deputy, Kern County Sheriff's Department; [pers.] This poem was written for and is dedicated to all the Law Enforcement Officers everywhere, who have fallen in the line of duty. Hopefully, someday we will all get the respect we deserve!!; [a.] Tehachapi, CA

HALES, KELLIE J.
[b.] October 12, 1964, Vancouver, WA; [p.] Ernest R. and Ida Mae Horne; [m.] Garland V. Hales, April 5, 1986; [ed.] I am in the process of earning a degree in the field of Journalism.; [oth. writ.] Signal, Winter 1994; [pers.] My writing is inspired by my faith in Jesus Christ and the endless supply of encouragement I receive from my loving family and friends.; [a.] Cottage Grove, OR

HALES, PATSY
[b.] May 29, 1936, West Allis, WI; [p.] Harry and Ramona Potton; [m.] Hal James Hales, September 5, 1954; [ch.] Linda, Vicky, Hal Jr., Ramona, Nancy, Larry and Robyn; [ed.] Tri County High - Plainfield, Wis.; [occ.] Childcare (Infants) Kinder-Care, Vancouver, Wa.; [memb.] New Heights Baptist Church, Vancouver, Wa., I was a member of a sweet Adelines for many years. I really enjoy singing!; [oth. writ.] My poems have been used in singles groups, retreats, and in a relationship work shop.; [pers.] I've always been a lover of poetry

Helen Steiner Rice is one of my favorites, and God; [a.] Vancouver, WA

HALL, JO ANNE E.
[b.] October 21, 1940, Warrensburg, MO; [p.] Howell Wendell and Katherine May Everts; [m.] Fayette Lyon Hall Jr., January 15, 1961; [ch.] Fayette L. III-34, Melanie Lynne-29, Justin Wendell Hall-26; [ed.] Olathe, Kan. Senior High, Hayes Hairstyling Institute, Zoe College (Christian Counseling) 3 yrs; [occ.] Semi - Retired Hairdresser; [memb.] Zellwood Historical Society, Orlando Christian Center, College Park Baptist Church; [hon.] Ft. Pierce Cosmetology Asso., 1st place competition in hairstyling 1960, Miss Ft. Pierce 1960; [oth. writ.] This is my first; [pers.] God loves his creation and through people like me, He wants to encourage and lift the spirits to know how much He does.; [a.] Zellwood, FL

HAMILTON, WANDA ARGATHA
[pen.] Merchant "Gat"; [b.] December 17, 1919, Thomastown, MS; [p.] James H. and Annie Mae Hamilton; [m.] Divorced, 1960; [ed.] Degrees AA, East Central JC, BS University of Sov - MS, M.S. University of Sov - MS; [occ.] Retired taught 40 years in Miss Schools; [memb.] PTA, MEA, CTA I was the Dean of Women at Three Jr Colleges where I have worked; [hon.] I was honored by USM for outstanding service to the university I taught undergraduate courses while a student and worked my way through $60.00 is the only compensation I paid USM I had night classes so I could work during the day; [oth. writ.] I have written articles for Miss. Educational advance I am a Health Physical Education and Recreation Major? I also have 30 hrs in miscellaneous subjects I enjoyed very much; [pers.] I am a water safety instructor I have been all over the USA because I was a WSI. In demand at Campo Calif, Colorado Texas Tenn and got to see from the other half level beside.

HAMLIN, MARY FRANCES P.
[pen.] Granny; [b.] December 6, 1918, Tuscaloosa, AL; [p.] Rev. W. T. Moore and Ophelia W. Moore; [m.] W. O. Parker, Robert G. Hamlin, July 37 (deceased), February 14, 1975; [ch.] George, James, Linda Kay; [ed.] 17 yrs. of Home and Public Schools. An A.U.G. degree approved under God, a small amount of wisdom!; [occ.] Volunteer 2 days per week at local V.A. Hospital; [memb.] A small child of God's! A large human family and church. Retired Mental Health State Workers, Past Worthy Matron in O.E.S. and many others!; [hon.] Love of God! A blessed assurance of my own salvation, plus an abundant joyful life! In our Lord Jesus!; [oth. writ.] Poems and others never published, but with God's help in the near future work, is used in teaching and church. An unknown writer, free lance; [pers.] Always keep an attitude of gratitude! Never under estimate what God can do through a human! Try hard to love the unlovely! Have a profound love for the soul of man.; [a.] Tuscaloosa, AL

HAMMER, DOROTHY M.
[b.] September 4, 1915, Plevna, KS; [p.] Deceased; [m.] Edmond M. Hammer, August 29, 1965; [ch.] 2 girls - Husband girl and 1 boy; [ed.] Graduated from Blackwell Okla. High School - 1935; [occ.] House wife; [memb.] Riverside Baptist Church in Wichita, KS. Taught Sunday School for 10 years; [pers.] I enjoy playing my dulcimer for my church and church groups. My hobbies have been sewing (I make most of my clothes) crocheted afghans, sweater (knitted) for grandchildren.; [a.] Wichita, KS

HAMMER, JOHN
[b.] October 20, 1950, Brooklyn, NY; [p.] Richard, Bertha; [m.] Divorced; [ch.] Christopher, Jessica, Evan, Andy, Stephen; [ed.] John Glenn H.S., Huntington New York Institute of Technology Old Westbury, N.Y.; [occ.] Architect, Business Owner, Writer; [memb.] American Institute of Architects, National Trust for Historic Preservation, Long Island Housing Partnership, Long Island Country Music Association; [pers.] Writing from the heart is a courageous act of self expression. To know oneself is to know our creator to write, is to be creative.; [a.] Northport, NY

HAMMIL, SHIRLEY J.
[b.] May 9, 1936, Freeman, SD; [p.] Leo M. and Elda Roth; [m.] John M. Hammil, June 17, 1956; [ch.] Jeffrey Donn and James Allen; [ed.] B.S. Education; [occ.] Retired - Teacher part time - Puppeteer and Ventriloquist; [memb.] YWCA, Presby, Church, RV Clubs; [hon.] Who's Who in Education 1992-1993; [oth. writ.] It's Child's Play Curriculum Vol. 1 and 2, It's Child's Play Patterns Vol. 1 and 2; [pers.] My love of animals is second to my love of children - A child's smile is precious.; [a.] Oklahoma City, OK

HAMMOND, BRENDA KAY
[b.] November 16, 1952, Columbus, OH; [p.] Patricia Overturf, Don Howard; [m.] Timothy Charles Hammond, August 22, 1970; [ch.] Jeremy, Amy, Angela, Jason; [ed.] Graduated from Pleasant View High School and Paul C. Hayes Tech. School in 1970; [occ.] Homemaker; [oth. writ.] Observation and other poems.; [pers.] Every day is a gift, don't wait until tomorrow to be thankful. Writing is my way of expressing thanks.; [a.] Columbus, OH

HAMPTON, COLLEEN
[b.] June 8, 1964, Ohio; [p.] Maureen and Gary Hampton; [pers.] This poem was written for my best friend who I love more than anything in the world. Love and friendship are the greatest inspiration for me. As I go through life I will continue to love as God intended and hope one day the races will come together.; [a.] Oak Park, IL

HAMPTON, STEPHANIE
[b.] October 2, 1980, Denver, CO; [p.] Phyllis and Stephen Hampton; [ed.] 9th grade, Westminster High School; [occ.] Student at Westminster High School; [memb.] National Guild Assn. for Piano, Westy Singers, Westminster High School Girl's Basketball.; [hon.] Several academic and music award; [oth. writ.] None published; [pers.] There is an essence to life that I try to reflect in my Poetry, that essence is kindness and understanding.; [a.] Westminster, CO

HAMRICK, WILLA
[pen.] Billie Hamrick; [b.] Deceased; [p.] Gordon Hamrick; [ch.] Two; [ed.] High School; [occ.] Writer, Musician, Play Guitar, Sing, Writer Songs; [hon.] Had children's story published in the Children's Hour in *Atlanta Journal* when I was nine years old. Won some singer's contests, some writer's contests. Won 1st Place in a writer's contest on "Stars You Love To Hate". Published in *The National Inquirer*. Short pieces in other magazines. Wrote and recorded my original songs.; [pers.] Love to write and sing songs that are spiritual and uplifting. Have had my own radio show, a 10 years T.V. show of music and singing with my husband in a duo, husband plays mandalin.; [a.] Jacksonville, FL

HANLY, ALFRED SHELDON
[pen.] Bo Hanly; [hon.] Use one currently on computer which was published in "The Garden of Life" and amended by my Ltr. to include mixed doubles win 135+ combined age in the Huntsman's World Senior games both in 94 and 95.

HANSEN, KRISTIN
[b.] October 11, 1977, Glendale; [p.] James and Mariann Hansen; [ed.] Currently attending School at Simi Valley High School; [occ.] Working at a Fast Food Restaurant called Del Taco; [hon.] Had a poem published in Simi Valleys Local Paper entitled "Homeless" also had a poem published in the National Library of Poetry's Book called Walk through Paradise, the Poem is entitled "The Bagpipes"; [oth. writ.] None that were published besides those under honors and awards.; [pers.] Knowledge is the key that will open any door to life's mysteries.; [a.] Simi Valley, CA

HANSON, RONALD J.
[pen.] R.J.H.; [b.] May 29, 1970, Anoka, MN; [p.] Raymond and Arline Hanson; [m.] Jane M. Hanson, March 27, 1992; [ch.] Crosby - Ironton High School; [ed.] CNC Machinist; [oth. writ.] I have written several poems and I have recently started a western novel. I may seek publication of these in the future; [pers.] The poem "The Pioneers" was inspired by the 50th wedding Anniversary of my grandparents Raymond and Delores Hanson. If my writing can touch the heart of one person. Then I'm honored to have written it.; [a.] Upsala, MN

HARDIN, ROSHAWN
[b.] November 17, 1968, Germany; [m.] Andre Hardin I, September 9, 1990; [ch.] Andre Hardin II; [pers.] To know one's heart is to know one's soul.

HARDING, CAROL
[b.] April 12, 1945, Yonkers, NY; [p.] Lillian and Frank Skrobola; [ch.] Edward, Matthew; [occ.] Administrator, Gov't. Agency

HARJO, SENA KOLEEPKV ANN
[b.] February 5, 1981, Rose Medical Center in Denver, CO; [p.] Mody B. and Lisa D. Harjo; [ed.] College View Elementary School, Henry Middle School, Abraham Lincoln High School and a 6 week Summer Math camp at Mt. Holyoke College in Mass.; [occ.] Freshman in high school; [hon.] Optimist Award, National Junior Honor Society; [a.] Denver, CO

HARMON, CHRISTINE RAY
[pen.] Christi Ray; [b.] May 29, 1960, Kankakee, IL; [p.] George Ray and Rita William Hastings; [m.] Divorced; [ed.] 1978 graduate of Henry - Senachwine H.S., Henry, Illinois; [occ.] Aspiring writer; [memb.] FCC - Licensed Radio Announcer, Kidney Foundation; [hon.] Various Awards in Elementary School for Literary Arts; [oth. writ.] Several poems published in local newspaper; [pers.] Through my writing, I have learned to look much deeper than just on the surface in all my relationships.; [a.] LaSalle, IL

HARRIS, BUTTERFLY
[b.] August 24, 1963, Chicago, IL; [p.] Jeannie Stringer; [ch.] Patrice and Joshua Harris; [memb.] Art Institute, Writer's Voice, Duncan YMCA, Women of The Word; [pers.] I close my eyes... and I see, I close my mouth.... and I speak, I open my mind and close the reasons that say I can't a butterfly's opinion.; [a.] Chicago, IL

HARRIS, FREDERICK
[pen.] Fred Harris; [b.] February 7, 1963, Auburn, NY; [p.] Arthur and Katherine Horr; [ed.] Port Byron H.S. BS Davis and Elkins College, Hospital Corp School U.S. Navy; [occ.] Surgical Technician; [memb.] Association of Surgical Technologists, Association of Central Supply Sterile Technologists, U.S. Navy Reserves, various running clubs; [hon.] Who's Who of U.S. College Students 1993, numerous running awards, Beta Alpha Beta; [oth. writ.] Two poems published "Run Hard" and "Cats" by N.L.P., two articles in college newspapers "The Senator"; [pers.] I enjoy reading and running writing poetry is an enjoyable hobby I do not often enough do; [a.] Auburn, NY

HARRIS, GWENDOLYN RAY
[b.] San Antonio, TX; [p.] Wayne Neal, Joyce Beaudin; [m.] Stephen Harris, October 11, 1988; [ch.] Six boys; [ed.] Simi Valley, High, Sierra College; [occ.] Student/Homemaker; [memb.] The Interplanetary Society; [oth. writ.] The child is not safe: Child poverty in America. Eng. 1A; [pers.] "I just want to know God's thoughts, the rest is just details" - Albert Einstein.; [a.] Grass Valley, CA

HARRISON, LEWIS S.
[pen.] Theophilus; [b.] November 8, 1916, Moulton, IA; [p.] Mr. and Mrs. Ray Harrison; [m.] Opal Maple Calef Harrison, August 30, 1940; [ch.] Donald, Linda and Charlotte; [ed.] BA, Wm Penn College Oskaloosa, IA; [occ.] Retired, Tech, Ed, Engr Writer; [memb.] ISP, IEEE; [a.] Cedar Rapids, IA

HARRISON, MICHAEL J.
[b.] June 26, 1957, England; [p.] Roy W. and Lilian I. Harrison; [m.] Mary Therese Waitkus, February 9, 1995; [occ.] Radio and T.V. Personality, working in major U.S. Market - (Detroit); [hon.] An award winning radio personality and the only english national to have a successful and growing penetration of a major U.S. radio market.; [oth. writ.] On going lifetime compilation of poems. Also advertising copy personality campaign concepts, comedy writing and other occasional literary endeavors; [pers.] I'm a believer in the beauty and grace of oral and written communication and the infinite possibilities they offer with the tremendous joy of striving to achieve a small measure of success in self-expression; [a.] Saint Clair Shores, MI

HART, TIMOTHY P.
[pen.] Tim Hart; [b.] July 27, 1964, Detroit; [p.] John and Ann Hart; [m.] Divorced; [ch.] Matthew J. Hart; [ed.] L'Anse Creuse High School; [occ.] Engineer; [oth. writ.] Currently writing Murder - Mystery; [a.] Mount Clemens, MI

HART, WAYMAN CLYDE
[pen.] Wayman C. Hart; [b.] December 27, 1956, Hardin County, KY; [p.] Jane and Lyman Hart; [m.] Eva A. Hart, August 21, 1976; [ch.] Wayman Chad Hart, Mirand Dee Hart; [ed.] G.E.D; [occ.] Heavy Equip. Oper.; [oth. writ.] Several unpublished poems.; [pers.] All was given, all is given for the under standing of faith.; [a.] Elizabethtown, KY

HARTFORD, TIFFANY ANN MARIE
[b.] September 8, 1976, Morgan City, LA; [p.] David and Dale Hartford; [ed.] Graduated from Patterson High School. Attended Louisiana State University and Nicholls State Univ.; [occ.] Customer relations; [memb.] Member of Speech and Debate Team, Member of Quiz Bowl, Member of SADD, Member of French Club; [hon.] Honor roll, Member of Parish Honor Band for 7 years, attended State Honor Band for 3 years; [oth. writ.] Had stories published in a book at a young age. I have written about 10 other poems. I wrote the poem for my junior class ring ceremony.; [pers.] The poems just pop into my head. I usually write about problems my friends are having. Very few poems reflect my own feelings.; [a.] Patterson, LA

HARTLEY, LEE
[pen.] Pilot micro fine superball; [b.] February 16, 1960, CA; [p.] Two; [ch.] 10-12; [ed.] Bachelor of Science: Thermal Duct Deployment - M.I.T./ Magna-Cum Laude. Degree in Floral Arrangement and Hotel/Motel Management From Sally Struthers School.; [occ.] Poet and Floral Duct Deployer in Motel 6.; [memb.] Alien spoor growth society, Minnesota Militia, President: Timothy McVey Fan Club.; [hon.] Special Forces Operation and Survivability award of excellence, AK-47, AR-15/M16 Expert award, Special Forces: Art of Death Award, Disruptive Terrorism award, Explosives for sabotage award, advanced combat tactics and techniques, spelling award-4th grade.; [oth. writ.] A couple of letters to my Mom, Three threat letters and a variety of stalking notes, unemployment application; [pers.] Damn, I'm a poet an didn't know it!; [a.] Anadarko, OK

HARTMAN, SCOTT
[b.] July 2, 1976, Milwaukee, WI; [p.] Robert and Barbara Hartman; [m.] Courtney Cox, March 14, 1995; [ed.] Lynbrook High School, presently attending University of Wyoming (UW) in Loramie; [occ.] Student/Scientific illustrator; [memb.] Society of Vertebrate Paleontology; [hon.] Winner of Dinosaur Essay Contest of University of California at Berkeley; [oth. writ.] Predation in Tyrannosaurus Rex (scientific paper); [pers.] "Life is too important to take seriously." Emily Dickenson and Edgar Allan Poe have been strong influences on me.; [a.] Grand Junction, CO

HASHBARGER, KENNETH J.
[b.] October 4, 1932, Bristol, VA; [p.] James N. Hashbarger, Roxie Hashbarger Wright; [m.] Lucreta Anne Hashbarger, January 24, 1953; [ch.] Andrea K. Wright and Daina L. Parker; [ed.] Thomas Jefferson (Elementary) Virginia High School Bristol College; [occ.] U.S Air Force (retired); [oth. writ.] Since February 91 have written more than fifteen hundred poems and songs. About every subject that come to mind.; [pers.] My poems and thoughts like many other's may never be fully known. Maybe God only intended that I utter them for his glory, as I stand beneath his heavenly throne.; [a.] Bristol, TN

HASTINGS, JOHN SILAS
[b.] March 29, 1976, Mesa, AZ; [p.] Eldon Hastings, Carolyn Hastings; [ed.] Gilbert High, Eastern Arizona College Chandler-Gilbert Community College; [occ.] Customer Service Representative, Factor's Clearinghouse, Gilbert, AZ; [memb.] Secretary of Sigma Gamma Chi EAX chapter, Member of Eastern Arizona College's A Capella Choir; [hon.] Eagle Scout, World Conservation Award, nominated Freshman Homecoming Prince; [oth. writ.] For my closest friends, I wrote many poems and short stories and I put them together in a soft-bound cover book that I entitled: Literary Freedom.; [pers.] I finally got published! Warmest thanks to my love of a lifetime and inspiration, Camille Flake. I would be nothing without you.; [a.] Gilbert, AZ

HATCHER, VERONICA M.
[pen.] Luv Lee; [b.] April 25, 1969, Cheverly, MD; [p.] Theodore and Antoinette Hatcher; [ch.] Teonna, Crystal, Michael Hatcher; [ed.] Suitland Senior High School Graduated in 1987; [occ.] Asst. Teacher at Alexander Graham Middle School and Lance CO; [memb.] Future Business Leadership's of America (F.B.L.A.), Big Sister United, President of Sounds of Praise; [hon.] (F.B.L.A.) Awards Church Committee Award for (Excellent Teacher) for Sunday School; [oth. writ.] They would be listed under luvlee anthology also true thoughts. Several poem and lyrics of creative works would be found here.; [pers.] My writings reflect on life styles of many modern people of today. Wanting my writings to reach out to people under the same perdicament and allowing them to know they are not alone.; [a.] Charlotte, NC

HATLEY, RENEE PREWITT
[pen.] Renee; [b.] October 8, 1959, Dallas, TX; [p.] Jack Prewitt; [m.] Bill Hatley, December 31, 1988; [ch.] Somer Holly, Clint Holly, Tessa Hatley, Kelia Hatley; [ed.] Jr. College; [occ.] Research; [memb.] National Wildlife Federation Greater Forth Worth Sierra Club Save Eagle Mountain Lake, Inc.; [hon.] Black and White Photography Honorable Mention in the State Fair of Texas, 95; [oth. writ.] Is someone there change? The words are just words, me; [pers.] Respect; [a.] Forth Worth, TX

HAUGLAND, CHARLES WILLIAM
[b.] November 6, 1984, Cape Girardeau, MO; [p.] Jerry and Susan Haugland; [ed.] Birth-age 5 Center for Child Studies, K-5 Alma Schrader School; [occ.] Student; [memb.] Primary Enrichment Program (Gifted Education) Explore Program (Gifted Education); [hon.] Missouri Council of Teachers on Mathematics Award, Math Olympiad; [oth. writ.] Stories published in locally distributed books.; [pers.] I dedicate this poem to my brother, Michael William Haugland.; [a.] Cape Girardeau, MO

HAUPT, DOROTHEA H.
[pen.] Dottie; [b.] February 6, 1973, Baltimore, MD; [p.] Mrs. Doris R. and Mr. Donald W. Haupt Sr.; [ed.] Garrett Heights Elementary, Hamilton Middle School, Chesapeake High School, Baltimore, CO; [occ.] U.S. Navy Active; [oth. writ.] I have written are: 2 songs called Calling From Afar and Look Inside. Also other poems Life Is It Worth, Calling From Beyond, Dream World, and Wedding Day. These have not been published. Only family and friends have seen and read them.; [pers.] When I write I want people to put themselves in the poetry and let them feel and think. Always try your best and no matter what don't let others put you down.; [a.] Edgewood, MD

HAVENS, WILL H.
[b.] November 21, 1910, Douglas County, MO; [p.] B. Ray and Mary E. (Tooley) Havens; [m.] Clara (Keeler) Havens, December 2, 1933; [ch.] Ivan, Ruth, Ann, Bill R.; [ed.] Self-educated beyond high school by home study courses, Correspondence and Seminars; [occ.] Retired Minister; [memb.] Ava Gen. Bapt. Church, Am. Bible Society, AARP, Int. Society of Poets, White River Association Presbytery; [hon.] Editor's Choice Awards for poems published in "The Desert Sun", "Edge of Twilight", "The Garden of Life". Award for 50 years pasturing plus one for 8 plus years of Ministry; [oth. writ.] Two books of essays, one book of Meditations, three books of poems, many poems and articles published in the local and regional papers; [pers.] I want to be an encourager for those who meed a spiritual lift. It is my hope and prayer that my writing will bless many souls even low, after I am gone.; [a.] Ava, MO

HAWKINS, GENA FALLEN
[pen.] Gena Fallen Hawkins; [b.] September 28, 1942, Ennis, TX; [p.] Gordon Leon Fallen Sr. and Doris Burke Fallen; [m.] Jerry Hawkins, November 12, 1976; [ch.] Brent, Bryan, & Lance; [ed.] Ray High School - Corpus Christi, TX; Trinity Valley Community College Athens, TX; Navarro College - Corsicana, TX; degrees - Legal Assistant & Computer Science; [occ.] Computer Lab Supervisor at Navarro College - Corsicana, TX; [memb.] First Christian Church National Honor Society, Phi Theta Kappa, Psi Beta, President's List, Dean's List; [pers.] I endeavor to instill in my reader an acute awareness of the existence of the relationship between time, space, and the evolution of the soul.; [a.] Ennis, TX

HAWKINS, NEWELL A.
[b.] February 11, 1928, Alabama; [m.] Idel Garmen Hawkins, May 26, 1951; [ed.] BA in Psychology with graduate studies in Education and Theology; [occ.] Retired teacher; [memb.] American Legion; [hon.] 4 Golden Poet Awards; [oth. writ.] Abiding Grace, Modern Beauty, Guiding Light, The Pearl You Keep, The Book of Life, and many more; [pers.] "All honest daughters become believers"; [a.] Signal Mountain, TN

HAWLEY, C. PATRICK
[b.] June 28, 1967, Seoul, Korea; [p.] James and Pamela Hawley; [pers.] "I'd like to thank my parents for helping me to realize my dreams."

HAYES, ARNOLD
[pen.] Peru Adu; [b.] August 1, 1964, Los Angeles, CA; [p.] Odella Hayes, Reginald Hayes; [ed.] Mt. Sierra College, Computer Learning Center, Nathaniel Nar Bonne High; [occ.] Artist, Poet, Consultant (Computer); [hon.] 4.0 Graduated with honors; [oth. writ.] Only A Kiss (Peru Adu) Love Shines, Lost In The Dessert Wind, Still A Man, Walking Tall; [pers.] In love we find our existence, and in truth we find our purpose. I try to bring love into clear focus through my poetry and I hope to touch the world with my thoughts.; [a.] Los Angeles, CA

HAYES, DAVID
[pen.] Jay David; [b.] December 28, 1979, New Haven, CT; [p.] Rocky and Cherie Cioffi; [ed.] New Covenant High School; [occ.] Poet; [oth. writ.] Poems and a play (unpublished); [pers.] The eye is the window of the soul. The tongue is a window of the heart. Poetry is the window of both.; [a.] Seymour, CT

HAYES, EVA
[pen.] Maria Hayes; [b.] November 15, 1980, San Diego, CA; [p.] Celia J. Hayes; [ed.] I am in the 9th grade. At Newark High School; [hon.] Basketball Awards, Merit Roll at School, Awards for Keeping a 3.5 grade average; [oth. writ.] I wrote poems for school.; [pers.] A person once told me that I would never be anybody, I proved them wrong.; [a.] Newark, OH

HAYS, STEPHEN
[b.] October 15, 1958, Laramie, WY; [m.] Married; [ed.] MS: Counseling, BS: Health Science, Minors: Computer Science, Zoology, Sociology; [occ.] Property Management Entrepreneur, Storyteller; [hon.] U.S. Army Honorable Discharge, Academic All American; [oth. writ.] Articles in local newspapers and Western Tourism Magazines; [pers.] Lifeskills: Athlete, outdoorsman literature, Human Resources and Management. Prolific writer of fiction and poetry, seeking further publication.; [a.] Denver, CO

HAZZARD, JOSEPH L.
[pen.] Leo-Jo; [b.] May 6, 1920, Ottoman, VA; [p.] Chester and Eliza Va. Hazzard; [ch.] Jo Ann Watts; [occ.] Retired; [memb.] Carrottoman Baptist Church; [hon.] Ordained Baptist Deacon; [oth. writ.] In church bulletins, various epitaphs to friends passing and read at their funerals; [pers.] In a personal relationship and belief and faith in God, the inspiration for my works were born; [a.] Lancaster, VA

HECHIM, MAURA L.
[pen.] Maura L. Woodruff; [b.] October 7, 1970, Flanders, NJ; [p.] Norton and Evelyn Woodruff; [m.] Matthew Hechim, October 21, 1995; [ed.] B.S. Biology, William Paterson College, Wayne, NJ; [occ.] Fermentation Operator - Chiron, Emeryville, CA; [memb.] Tourette Syndrome Association, Environmental Experiences Inc.; [hon.] Dean's List, Beta Beta Beta - Chi Ro Chapter, Biopsychology Honors Program, Most Outstanding Senior in Biology, Dean's Award; [oth. writ.] Author in "Don't Think About Monkeys", several poems published in the above mentioned book as well as in school magazines and newspapers.; [pers.] Dare to dream - and experience worlds once unknown, through the words of life.; [a.] Brisbane, CA

HECK, RACHEL
[b.] January 15, 1979, Peoria, IL; [p.] Daniel Heck, Carol Heck; [ed.] Cypress Creek High; [memb.] National Honor Society Mu Alpha Theta; [hon.] Principal's Honor Roll, Superior Rating on Flute Solos, Highest Grade in Geometry and Algebra II, All-American Scholar 1993, National History and Government Award 1993, Who's Who Among American High School Students 1994/1995; [pers.] Both poetry and music should be made more of emotions than of words and notes. They should both aim to touch the heart.; [a.] Orlando, FL

HECKENBERG, RON
[b.] June 22, 1952, Burlington, IA; [p.] Loren and June Heckenberg; [m.] Susan Heckenberg, July 8, 1969; [ch.] Amy and Doug Heckenberg; [ed.] West High School Phx Az., Glendale Community College, Glendale, Az; [occ.] Operations and Maint Superintendent; [memb.] Toastmaters; [pers.] Have an interest in using poetry to keep safety and work practices and methods fresh for those I work with.; [a.] Phoenix, AZ

HEISHMAN, NANCY
[pen.] Nancy Quinn; [b.] May 30, 1945, San Mateo, CA; [p.] Quinn and Joan Campbell; [ch.] Erica Ann, Tony James, David Michael, John Jacob, Michael James; [ed.] Mexico City College; [occ.] Medical Administrator/Marketing, owner of Alpha-West Environment System Business; [memb.] American Marketing Assoc. Business, Leaders Chapter of Business Network International, Local Poetry Group and Writers Guild.; [oth. writ.] Short stories of the orient, children stories, book of poetry; [pers.] For those who have found true love, may they treasure the joys and sorrows of magical moments that forever light up the heart.; [a.] Las Vegas, NV

HELLSTON, JOSEFINA
[b.] June 20, 1980, Santa Monica, CA; [p.] Margareta and Bongt Hellston; [ed.] Cardem, OLM, Webster to Crossroads; [occ.] Student; [hon.] Malibu Optimist Award; [oth. writ.] Journal writing; [pers.] The purpose of my poetry is simply to express my emotions and lingering thoughts.; [a.] Malibu, CA

HELM, MARTHA
[pen.] Martha; [b.] January 24, 1953, Cincinnati, OH; [p.] Jim and Jean Geyer; [m.] Don Helm, June 1, 1974; [ch.] Christopher James, Jonathan, Russell, James Michael; [ed.] Purdue University; [occ.] Homemaker; [memb.] Administrative Board Christ Methodist Church; [hon.] Phi Beta Kappa; [oth. writ.] Letters written to Sean in South Africa exploring the path to true freedom and the fulfillment of dreams.; [pers.] My poetry expresses emotional pain and the path to healing through the love of Jesus. I have been inspired by the truth and poetry of the Bible.; [a.] Memphis, TN

HENAUGHAN, MARY E.
[b.] March 8, 1933, Akron, OH; [p.] James and Bridget Henaughan; [ed.] BSE St. John College Cleveland, OH. ME Ohio University National Beauty College; [occ.] Nurse Aide and Cosmetologist; [memb.] NCEA, INSP, HM Community National Parks Association; [hon.] Teacher of the Year East Ohio GAS 1988, Poet of Merit ISP, Editor's Award NLP; [oth. writ.] Article written in Chatanqua's Writer's Convention Newspaper, Poetry Booklet published by New Life Center, Poem In *Sea of Treasures* published by NLP.; [pers.] I believe the vitamin pills of my life are centering, being real, living in the now moment to the fullest give me energy, peace, joy and control in my life.; [a.] Canton, OH

HENDERSON, DAWN E.
[b.] March 7, 1977, Baldwin Park, CA; [p.] Teralei Henderson; [ed.] Burney Jr. Sr. High School 95 Graduate; [occ.] Hopeful Writer; [oth. writ.] Several poems, I completed children's story (not yet published) and 2 short story's in progress.; [pers.] Don't try to figure out the past for it's already done. Nor look to your future, for what you do now pertains to it.; [a.] Auburn, WA

HENDERSON, DIANA LEN DICK
[pen.] Diana Len Henderson; [b.] May 25, 1963, Dallas, TX; [p.] Hartman R. and Taeko M. Dick; [m.] Raymond Neal "Randy" Henderson, June 25, 1988; [ed.] A.A.S. with Honors 05/86, North Lake College of the DCCCD, B.S. with Highest Honors 08/89 and B.A. with Highest and Special Department Honors 12/89 The University of Texas at Austin; [occ.] Intercultural Consultant, Japanese Teacher. Airshow Announcer Aerobatic Club of America, Aircraft; [memb.] Owners and Pilots Association, Experimental Aircraft Association, International Aerobatic Club, International Council of Airshows, Central Region Council of Airshows (Secretary/Treasurer), MTTOF Club (Director), Professional Airshow Performers and Producers Association, Gold Seal Award 1992; [hon.] Certificate of Appreciation I.A.C., 1986, 1987, 1990, 1992, College Scholar, U.T. College of Communication, 1988, 1989, First Runner-Up, Mrs. E.A.A. 1989, Golden Key National Honor Society, Honor Society of Phi Kappa Phi, The National Dean's List, Award of Merit: 1986-1987, Certificate of Merit, 1988-1989, Outstanding College Students of America 1989-1990, Outstanding Student Award, U.T. Dept. of Speech 1987, 1989, Outstanding Young Women of America 1991, The Phi Beta Kappa Society, Phi Theta Kappa National Honor Fraternity 1985, Who's Who Among Students in American Junior Colleges, 1985-1986, Who's Who in American Universities and Colleges, 1990.; [oth. writ.] Articles for association newsletters: International Council of Airshows and Professional Airshow Performers and Producers Association; [pers.] I began writing poetry for creative writing assignments in grade school. As a teenager, my poems allowed me to explore and share my feelings with others. Although I have not written much new poetry of late, I still hope to someday publish my works in book form—perhaps just as a gift for friends.; [a.] Frisco, TX

HENDRICKS, BRENDA L.
[b.] January 16, 1958, Brigham City, UT; [p.] Linda and Robert Benavidez; [m.] Paul D. Hendricks, September 1, 1979; [ch.] Phillip and Charles; [ed.] Graduated Elko High School, Elko, NV, 1976 - College; [occ.] Production-Ad Department, the Leader Newspaper; [memb.] First Baptist Church, Tremonton, UT, MAD; [hon.] This is the only honor I have received besides ribbons for photography and art work.; [pers.] I wrote this poem for my mother - Linda Benavidez - (March 28, 1940 - August 25, 1995) she was killed in an alcohol related accident. She was my greatest inspiration. I dedicate this publication to her.; [a.] Tremonton, UT

HENDRICKS, SHAWN
[b.] October 25, 1976, Danville, IL; [p.] Roger Hendricks, Cindy Hendricks; [ed.] Hagerstown Jr.-Sr. High School; [occ.] Head Chef at a successful local restaurant; [hon.] Being published by "The National Library of Poetry"; [oth. writ.] This poem is an excerpt from a more extensive piece entitled "Know" which is previously unpublished as a whole.; [pers.] Thanks to: God, my parents, and my brother Jason. Special thanks to: Jodi Marsee for getting me started and the Chad Cortner for putting it all together. My love to Lisa always.; [a.] Hagerstown, IN

HENSON, ANITA L.
[pers.] Dedicated in loving memory to my son Donnie. As long as he lives in the hearts and thoughts of others he will never die. You will always be in our heart and in our thoughts forever. We will

always love you.; [a.] Hemet, CA

HERNANDEZ, EDGAR
[b.] November 25, 1976, Bronx, NY; [p.] Benancio and Julia Hernandez; [ed.] Fordham Preparatory High School Fordham University; [occ.] Student; [memb.] National Honor Society National Geographic Society; [hon.] National Honor Society 2nd Place in Academic Olympics (Religion); [oth. writ.] Several other non-published poems; [pers.] My poems reflect the inner struggle of a teenager in matters of love, direction, and faith; [a.] Bronx, NY

HERNANDEZ, MARIO
[b.] September 27, 1969, El Salvador; [p.] Candelaria Quintanilla; [ed.] United College of Business; [occ.] Computer System - Operator; [hon.] Honored with the right for creating and painting a "Logo" that represents my Junior H. School in El Salvador; [oth. writ.] "Fantasy Girl" (poem), "Vanessa" (poem), several other poems never published.; [pers.] "We can not become what we want to be by remaining what we are"; [a.] Van Nuys, CA

HERNANDEZ, SERGIO EVERARDO
[b.] September 13, 1979; [p.] Agustin Hernandez, Estelita Robles; [ed.] Corona Ave School, Nimitz Middle School and Bell High School; [hon.] Not at all. Yet the utmost honors to me is the honors, I've received by my family, cousins, ye, and my fiance; [oth. writ.] I've acquire a few more poems, nought yet published, yet millions await in my future. I also procure a drama, which I merely outset, but hope to be a success when all polished.; [pers.] In my poesies I intent to aid the injured, ope eyes to the blind and cede sunshine to the eclipsed, I have been persuade by the wisdom derived through my own perception.; [a.] Bell, CA

HERNDON, JOSHUA MICHAEL
[b.] July 3, 1978, Indianapolis, IN; [p.] Mike and Marilyn Herndon; [ed.] Morristown High School; [occ.] Student; [memb.] Spanish Club, National Honor Society Member; [hon.] Chosen as Teen of the Year by the church I attend, the Hugh O'Brien Leadership Seminar in 10th grade.; [oth. writ.] I write just for enjoyment. I hope to get my other works copyrighted and published some day.; [pers.] I would like to thank my family for being supportive of my poetry works. Most of all, though, I would like to thank God for giving me this talent. I hope I can use it for Him.; [a.] Shelbyville, IN

HERRICK, ROBERT L.
[b.] September 13, 1930, Brookfiled, MO; [p.] Lowell Herrick, Dorothy Herrick; [m.] Darlene Herrick, August 15, 1954; [ch.] Mark, Scott, Kristina; [ed.] Independence High, Independence Jr. College, York College, United Theological Seminary, University of Chicago, University of Illinois; [occ.] Retired College Professor (Sociology); [hon.] Sear-Roebuck Teaching Excellence and Campus Leadership Award - Westmar College; [oth. writ.] A few sociological articles and book reviews, a few poems in college publications.; [pers.] I am grateful to those friends, relatives, and colleagues who have encouraged me to keep writing.; [a.] Green Valley, AZ

HERRLE, CAROLE
[pen.] Carole Herrle; [b.] October 8, 1931, Pittsburgh, PA; [p.] Harold and Rose Billingsley; [m.] William Herrle, October 16, 1951; [ch.] James, Joe, Theresa, Bonnie, Bill, Sue, Stef, Gina, Mary, Cathy; [ed.] 12 years - Langley High Graduate, also Connelley Skills for Nurse - Aide Work; [occ.] Mom, Grandma, Nurse Aide - Sunday School Teacher and Rainbow Helper; [memb.] Smithsonian, Allison Park, Assembly of God Church; [hon.] Sidewalk Sunday School Helper; [oth. writ.] Many poems, small play - started 1st chapter book, poems as gifts; [pers.] I love God and all of God's creation, I love to pray. Prayer is a poem. I like Robert Frost, Thoreau, Emily Dickinson, Millay, Lowell, Kilmer, Emerson, Hughes.; [a.] Pittsburgh, PA

HERRON, PEGGY LOU
[b.] January 30, 1929, Ft. Smith, AR; [p.] Mr. Otho and Mable Swink; [m.] Widow; [ch.] 1 daughter, 1 granddaughter, 2 great grand children; [ed.] Finished High School; [occ.] Nursing in home care; [oth. writ.] Song, life story, many poems. This is my first time for evaluation of my work; [pers.] Poetry comes from the very depth of our soul. Creative talent from my Lord to bless me, and to bless others is my desire!; [a.] Burleson, TX

HESTER, MARK BRYON
[b.] May 9, 1963, Visallia, CA; [p.] William F. Hester and Elizabeth E. Hester; [ed.] South View Sr. High; [memb.] Oak Society; [oth. writ.] Various poems, essays, etc... all of which are yet to be published.; [pers.] I will not blindly follow any institution or person. I search for the truth in all things and act accordingly.; [a.] Hope Mills, NC

HETTERICK, ROBERTA ANN
[pen.] Roberta Holland; [b.] December 3, 1962, San Antonio, TX; [p.] James and Carlene Holland; [m.] Ralph Thomas Hetterick, July 25, 1981; [ch.] Monica Nicole, Heather Elizabeth; [ed.] 1-12, 2 years drafting joint vocational school; [occ.] Housewife, make crafts, sell Avon, Farm, Raise Tobacco; [hon.] Craft awards, chosen "81" Miss Teen pageant; [oth. writ.] Poem, aired on local radio station working on current book. A collection of poems written since High School; [pers.] I use my writings as an spiritual and moral way of enduring events in life, reflecting an important scenarios and events, giving these events poetic. Remembrance.; [a.] Moscow, OH

HETZEL, JOSEPH R.
[pen.] Joe Hetzel; [b.] March 16, 1957, Cleveland, OH; [p.] Robert and Dorothy Hetzel; [m.] Mary Ann Sparenga Hetzel, September 25, 1982; [ch.] Daniel, Rebecca, Andrew, Leah and Rachel; [ed.] Bachelor of Civil Engineering, Cleveland St U., 1979; [occ.] Professional Engineer, Patio Enclosures, Inc.; [memb.] Order of the Engineer; [hon.] Dean's List, Employee of the year, 1992; [oth. writ.] Has written lyrics and music to over 100 songs. Released copyrighted CD, "Love And Beloved" in 1995.; [pers.] Through my writings, I want to inspire and encourage others, and that they may have a positive impact in other's lives.; [a.] Macedonia, OH

HETZLER, DORIS J.
[b.] June 15, 1961, Greenville, OH; [p.] Monte M. Baird and Delores J. Houston; [m.] Gary T. Hetzler, June 3, 1995; [ch.] Tracy Danielle Harris, Samuel Allen Hetzler, Angela Marie Harris, one on the way; [ed.] Greenville High School; [occ.] Emergency Medical Technician/Security Officer; [memb.] Gettysburg Fire and Rescue, Tri-Village Rescue; [pers.] No matter how bad life may seem at times, I believe one must keep their chin up and always look forward to a brighter tomorrow.; [a.] Gettysburg, OH

HEVERLY, PATRICIA A.
[b.] September 19, 1947, Bellefonte, PA; [p.] George N. Emerick, G. Louise Emerick; [m.] Thomas L. Heverly (Deceased 1983), January 31, 1969; [ch.] Sean Derrick, grandchildren Brittany Linn, Sean Thomas.; [ed.] Bellefonte Area High South Hills Business School; [occ.] Assistant Counselor, The Hub Inc. Bellefonte PA.; [memb.] St. John Lutheran Church WELCA, ELCA Mission Action Committee St. Mark Lutheran Church.; [oth. writ.] None published; [pers.] Writing is a stress-relief for me. I have kept a daily journal since 1983. I have just recently added a poem journal, gratitude journal and a sketch journal.; [a.] Bellefonte, PA

HEWES, SHELLEY LYNN
[b.] February 6, 1974, Yakama, WA; [p.] Linda and Lee Mason; [m.] Frank N. Hewes II, July 3, 1994; [ed.] LaSalle High School Three Rivers Community Tech College; [occ.] CT Army National Guard, Groton, CT; [memb.] National Beta Club, Who's Who Among American High School Students; [hon.] Presidential Academic Fitness Award; [oth. writ.] Nothing published; [pers.] I write what I feel in my heart. I just want to express myself.; [a.] Norwich, CT

HEYWOOD SR., RAYMOND ALEXANDER
[pen.] Raymond A. Heywood Sr.; [b.] February 21, 1955, Saint Croix, VI USA; [p.] Mr. and Mrs. Abraham and Beatrice Bland; [m.] Kerri Lynette Heywood, June 21, 1986; [ch.] Quianna Raynell Young, Darian Heywood, Raymond Alexander Heywood Jr.; [ed.] George Wingate H.S. (grad.) Brooklyn, NY, 2 yrs Associate Degree U.S. Navy, Retired (U.S. Navy); [occ.] "Senior Court Clerk" at Fulton County Superior Court Atlanta, GA; [memb.] Peace Lutheran Church, Decatur, GA; [oth. writ.] Several poems published in the U.S. Navy Mediterranean Cruise Book 1981, Uss Coontz (DDG-40) Norfolk, VA; [pers.] Poetry to me is the ears, eyes and the heart of a world of emotions brought to life for all humanity fulfillments.; [a.] Rex, GA

HICKEY, MRS. MARY PATRICIA
[pen.] Mary Pat or Mary Patricia Hickey; [b.] May 4, 1920, Philadelphia, PA; [p.] Theresa and Frederick Wickman; [m.] Deceased, May 8, 1989 (Austin F.), May 8, 1945; [ed.] Holy Spirit H. S. High School Atlantic City - New Jersey; [occ.] Retired; [memb.] A.A.R.P.; [hon.] 1st prize 1974 Pencil Drawing of A Mt. Vernon Art Assoc.; [pers.] I'm grateful for the few accomplishments in my life, being a self taught artist, having won 1st prize in 1974 for a "Portrait of a Man", I've written poetry, but this is my first time in submitting one. I love Life and all "It's ups and downs".; [a.] Mount Vernon, NY

HICKMAN, DOROTHY P.
[b.] July 6, 1919, Duquesne, PA; [p.] Bessie and Joseph R. Kennedy (Deceased); [m.] Everett I. Hickman (Deceased), March 12, 1949; [ch.] Susan, Eric and Terry; [ed.] Got as far as College Sophomore - Through Correspondence Courses - Ohio University at Athens, Ohio; [occ.] Retired; [oth. writ.] A book, unpublished, about growing up during the great depression, "The day before," A lengthy poem about the atom bomb. "I'll call every day and write once a week," he said. A humorous poem about unrequited love., "Curtain going down," About the after math of nuclear destruction., "Conflict," An essay.; [a.] Cedarville, OH

HICKS, LARRY
[b.] November 1, 1927, Chicago; [p.] Donal and Lorna Hicks (Father Deceased); [m.] Beverly Hicks, December 2, 1961; [ed.] Elkhart Lake High School - Wisconsin Commercial Art School America Academy of Art - Chicago I was commercial artist 14 years followed by cartooning and water color painting - employed by State of Illinois 19 years before retiring at 62; [occ.] Retired; [memb.] U.S. Navy 1945-1948 Honorable Discharge, American Legion Post Gurnee, Ill Doris Day Animal League Peta - people for the ethical treatment of animals; [hon.] My wife beverly and I were presented VIP awards from pet rescue, Bloomingdale, Illinois for outstanding loyalty and dedication efforts of behalf of animals. We were volunteers for Disabled Veterans - little brothers of the poor delivering hot meals - mostly to elderly volunteers for pet rescue to aid

homeless animals - 3 years; [oth. writ.] I wrote numerous letters to Editors of Newspapers and one poem. Wrote hundred of other poems, but never submitted them for publication I have other hobbies such as writing humor, jokes and quotations.; [pers.] My quotation: "When my Irish Malarky brings happiness and laughter to the elderly, I have then been blessed with rewards far exceeding all the riches in the world."; [a.] Gages Lake, IL

HIGH, NATHANIEL
[b.] January 25, 1983, Chattanooga, TN; [p.] Ben and Beverly High; [ed.] 7th grade student at Columbia Academy; [memb.] Volunteer Junior Civitan Club, First United Methodist Church, Williamson County US Swim Team, American Youth Soccer Association; [hon.] Spelling Bee Attendant, third place Math Olympics Winner, Summer Reading Award, Dare Graduate, Achievement Administrator's List and Presidents List, Perfect Attendance Award, Math Award, Language Award, Swimming High Point Award, First Place in Track Meet; [oth. writ.] Good Night, The Willow, The Fair; [a.] Columbia, TN

HILL, FELIZA LYNN MAGGAY
[b.] October 6, 1965, Charleston, SC; [p.] Guillermo and Marie Maggay; [m.] Glyn Phillip Hill, February 24, 1990; [ch.] Geoffrey Eric Maggay, Reed Alexander Hill; [ed.] Berkeley High, Trident Technical College; [occ.] Customer Service Mgr. Fool Lion, Inc. N. Charleston, SC; [hon.] Who's Who Among Amer. High School Students, Dean's List, Graduated A.S. Horticulture Cum Laude, 1987, 1988 World of Poetry Golden Poet; [oth. writ.] Several poems published through high school paper and in other poetry anthologies.; [pers.] I hope to achieve within those who read my work a deeper sense of human emotion reflected in the triumphs and tragedies of every face of life.; [a.] North Charleston, SC

HILL, IDA MAE
[b.] May 17, 1922; [m.] Miner N. Hill, June 22, 1940; [ch.] Three Daughters; [occ.] Retired, still speaking at Local Ladies Groups; [memb.] Member Grace Bible Church Teacher Ladies Class; [oth. writ.] Author of Jr. Church Curriculum, Contributor to many different Church Newspapers, Many poems and article, some published.; [pers.] I am a born again christian. I like people and have always been interested in wild life and the world of nature. I desire that my writings reflect God's grace and His love for all his creations.; [a.] Hagerstown, MD

HILL, T. GREG
[pen.] T. Greg Hill or T.G. Hill; [b.] September 12, 1970, Houston, TX; [p.] Terance Copeland Hill and Elizabeth Ann Hill; [m.] Single; [ed.] Clear Creek High School, League City, TX, (B.A.) Political Science from Texas A and M University (12/93); [occ.] Substitute Teacher - Currently Looking Elsewhere; [pers.] Find what is good and right, and apply it in your life from day to day.; [a.] Houston, TX

HILLGER, LINNIE RENEE
[pen.] Nae - Nae (Candy); [b.] June 29, 1969, Midland, TX; [p.] Robert Wayne Phillips, Alma (Tina) Lee Walker; [m.] Tracy Del Hillger, June 28, 1986; [ch.] 3 + 1 = still born son (6 yrs. old) October 31, 1989, + 1 St. Daughter 9 yrs. old August 16, 1986, Robert July 21, 1990, C. Hillger, 1 Daughter 3 yrs. old August 10, 1992; [ed.] 10th Grade Mabank High and Malakoff High Loved Reading and Spelling, Typing a little Journalism, Music and Art Class; [occ.] Reseptionist at Gulf Shore Tel - Com; [memb.] V.F.W. Ladies Aux., Sam's Club; [hon.] Kite 1st flying Contes 1976, 1st place poetry contest for Henderson County Library; [oth. writ.] Tears (1st), Love Is, Growing Up; [pers.] I get my ideas through lifes experiences. By the things that happen to me. I am very much inspired by those kinds of poems. I enjoy writing songs and sing. I've always tried hard at any thing I set my goals to.; [a.] Kemp, TX

HIPONIA, MARIA CONCEPTION GARCIA
[b.] December 8, 1974, Manila, Philippines; [p.] Cesar and Florecita Hiponia; [ed.] Baltimore Polytechin Institute, 3rd-year student at Univ. of MD, College Park, double major in Journalism and Chinese; [occ.] Student at Univ. of MD, College Park; [memb.] Filipino Cultural Association, East Coast Asian Student Union, Public Relations Student Society of America; [hon.] Phi Eta Sigma, Office of Multi-Ethnic Student Education Certificate for Outstanding Achievement; [oth. writ.] Articles in various Univ. of MD publications; [pers.] The most important thing I can do as a writer and a human being is to always look for beauty in the ordinary; [a.] Baltimore, MD

HIPPS, HEATHER
[pen.] Ann; [b.] October 10, Eureka, KS; [p.] Steve Hipps, Nikki Hipps; [ed.] I'm a Freshman at Valley Center High School; [occ.] Babysitting; [oth. writ.] I have written many other poems, but they have not been shown to many people.; [pers.] I love to write. Most of all that I have written has come from the heart. Poem dedication: My two best friends - Eva Guhr and Katrina Rubenich.; [a.] Valley Center, KS

HISLOP, HOLLY
[b.] December 30, 1967, Oceanside, CA; [p.] Judy Ahrend, Errol Lewis; [m.] Marshal Hislop, September 24, 1988; [ch.] Hayden Hislop; [ed.] Mt. Cormel High Mira Costa College; [pers.] Live through your senses. Taste, touch, see, smell, and hear all that life has to offer. Feel life instead of controlling it, and the pages of time will turn and your adventure will unfold.

HIX, JOE
[b.] Texas; [occ.] Owner - Book Store; [memb.] Historical Society's Book Associations; [oth. writ.] Several poems.; [pers.] Operate bluff park, rare books in Long Beach, California. Also sell autobiographs and collectibles and do book searches on the internet.

HO, ANNETTE A.
[b.] October 11, 1948, Okinawa; [p.] Shizue Yoshimoto (Mom); [m.] Joseph K. Ho, July 5, 1983; [ch.] Nahoko Ahlo, Michael Miyashiro, Keoni Ho, Kaila Ho; [ed.] 1967 Kalani High 2 yrs University of Hawaii, AA Degree Leeward Community College; [occ.] Homemaker/Part Time Secretary; [memb.] Hawaiian Club, PTA, Line Dancing Club, Family Child Services; [hon.] My children.

HOBBS, ALLEN SALYER
[pen.] Allene Hobbs; [b.] April 9, 1936, Fort Worth, TX; [p.] Frances and Austin Salyer; [m.] Lindsey Ferris Hobbs, July 1, 1966; [ch.] Kirk Hobbs, Sandra Radosavljevic; [ed.] Stephen F. Austin, Computer courses, Austin Community College, Management courses, State of Texas; [occ.] Real Estate Assistant - Tejas Spicewood Real Estate; [oth. writ.] Have written many other poems, two novels,, and a short story.; [pers.] Writing, muck like your eyes, is a reflection of the soul. Do no harm to others so that what goes from you, returns to you, pure, harmless, and joyful.; [a.] Spicewood, TX

HOEHN, HELEN D.
[b.] February 7, 1938, Lehighton, PA; [p.] Verna Moyer; [m.] John D. Hoehn, February 25, 1983; [ch.] 12 Stepchildren and 1 adopted; [occ.] Housewife and mother; [oth. writ.] Several others; [pers.] All my poems are inspired by my adopted child and husband; [a.] South Roxana, IL

HOGG, MARTHA MOLINE
[b.] October 27, 1931, Dickson, TN; [p.] Hattie and Seamon Trother; [m.] Cecil Hogg (Deceased), July 1, 1950; [ch.] James, Gary and Perry Hogg; [ed.] High school graduate, Shawnee High School Louisville, KY.; [occ.] Home Maker; [hon.] Faster poem won Second Place in High School Easter Poetry contest; [oth. writ.] Poems and short articles; [pers.] Many of my poems reflect the hand of God in nature; [a.] Louisville, KY

HOLEM, JULIA
[b.] Junes 29, 1974, Lake Forest, IL; [p.] Judy Smith, Terry Holem; [ed.] Riverview High, Manatee Community College, Sarasota School of Natural Healing Arts; [occ.] Administrative Assistant; [hon.] National Honor Society, Who's Who of American High School Students (1991 and 1992); [oth. writ.] This is my first publication.; [pers.] Poetry is my way of expressing myself, I don't write for others (to bring them pleasure), but rather for myself (to bring me pleasure) although it's always nice when both happen at the same time.; [a.] Lake Bluff, FL

HOLLAN, FLORINE NOLEN
[pen.] Florine Nolen Hollan; [b.] February 19, 1924, Louise, TX; [p.] Loudell Davison, Warren L. Nolen; [m.] Hubert Samule Hollan, December 8, 1945; [ch.] David, Darrell, Leroy, Carolyn; [ed.] Louise, High, S.W. Business Univ., U.S. Air Force Instrument School, Art, Music and Computer courses; [occ.] Accounting for Husband's business for 50 years, Piano teacher; [memb.] First Baptist Church, Organist, Janis Hindes Art Class; [hon.] Accomplished Artist, Many Awards In Oils, Cooking Award, "Bluebell Ice Cream" contest; [oth. writ.] Several poems and short stories.; [pers.] I have mastered the computer, can sew, sing and paint a picture. I can play the organ, even cook, write a poem, or a book, I would prefer, above all other, to be remembered, for my roll, as mother.; [a.] Fowlerton, TX

HOLLER, DIANNA LYNNE
[pen.] Dianna Christy Holler; [b.] March 10, 1951, Grove City, PA; [p.] John and Mary Christy; [m.] Joseph A. Holler, December 28, 1968; [ch.] Samantha, Shelie, Josef, John; [ed.] High School graduate, Grove City Sr. High, one year business, ITT of Youngstown, OH; [occ.] Homemaker and business owner; [hon.] My children have all honored me by graduating high school. I am awarded three grandchildren so far. Bobby Alexander-Ashley.; [oth. writ.] I have over 200 poems written. This was truly my first attempt to publish.; [pers.] I want very much for people to think about the gifts they all have been given so they can really appreciate them. To find the silver lining. In all life is a blessing by itself.; [a.] Wade, NC

HOLMER, VIVIAN
[b.] April 24, 1946, Detroit Lakes, MN; [p.] George and Virginia Riggle; [m.] Jerry Holmer, November 23, 1974; [ch.] Dave Wayne Riggle, Rita JoFeldt, grandchildren - Xavier David, Laken Jo; [ed.] High School - Frazee MN, Cascade Locks Oregon, Grade School - District #65; [occ.] Logistics Engineer, Retired School Bus Driver; [memb.] United Blood Services; [oth. writ.] Heather (poem); [pers.] Spending time alone or with a friend, I live one day at a time and enjoy each moment.; [a.] Frazee, MN

HOLSEY, STACEY LYNN
[b.] April 18, 1978, Wichita, KS; [p.] Shirley J. Holsey; [hon.] Will attended College this fall; [oth. writ.] Has wrote several other poems for mother's day, birthday life etc. started when she was about 11 yrs. old; [pers.] Stacey wrote this poem at age 16 after being told of her Grandmother's illness, whom she always had called Nana, and that she was terminal with ALS and had been given 3 to 6 months to live.

Stacey - her brother Brian were the only grandchildren and very close to her.; [a.] Wichita, KS

HOLUB, ETHAN ANDREW
[pen.] Rastaman, Ski Bum; [b.] April 5, 1978, Eugene, OR; [p.] Andrew and Terri Holub; [ed.] Pleasant Hill High School; [occ.] Student (Senior) High School, manage farms including Ken Kesey's (the author), construction; [memb.] I run several drug awareness groups in my high school. Run a Bible Study with over 50 members. Direct Youth for Christ for Jr. High Kids. Sing in Jazz Choir and play in a Jazz Band, etc.; [hon.] Lane Country, Register Award, Newspaper Student of the Month, KMTR Student of the Month, Vice Pres. of National Honor Society, Captain of 3A State Football Team; [oth. writ.] I love to write and have many poems, short stories and have started a book. I plan to publish a book of poems in the near future, community newsletters to parents of students. I love to write music.; [pers.] I live for Jesus Christ. He is my main goal in life, sharing his word. My poetry is about life, death, relationships, God, and the world in a teenagers mind. I thank my friends, family and God most of all for my talents.; [a.] Pleasant Hill, OR

HOLZMAN, S. LOUISE
[b.] March 18, 1915, Spartinburg, SC; [p.] Williamm and Sarah Lance; [m.] William Holzman, June 2, 1994; [ch.] Six; [ed.] I went only to 7th Grade; [occ.] Retired seamstress; [memb.] Redeemer Lutheran Church, Tucson, AZ; [hon.] I was awarded 1 dollar in 3rd grade for being best reader in that class; [pers.] I left my first husband, before he died, after he almost killed me. I was alone when I met, William, my present husband.; [a.] Tucson, AZ

HONDA, TOSHIKO
[b.] April 3, 1939, Japan; [p.] Haru and Moto Honda; [ed.] MA California State University, Northridge Social Psychology; [occ.] Real Estates; [oth. writ.] It's Me! Collection of my poems in English and Japanese. Self-published; [pers.] Life is to pursue real self.; [a.] Santa Monica, CA

HOOKS, VIVIAN
[b.] January 8, 1908; [p.] Mr. and Mrs. C. F. Springer; [m.] Roger W. Hooks; [ch.] A son Charles; [ed.] University Carbondale-Ill. University of Michigan-MA Degree and most of my doctorate - AM Hist. and Government; [occ.] Retired from Memphis City Schools; [memb.] Delta Theta Tau. Sorority Graceland Baptist-Church Retired - Teachers Assoc.

HOOVER, MARY ELIZABETH
[pen.] Mary Vion Hoover; [b.] January 10, 1939, Enid, OK; [p.] George Edwin Vion and Jacqueline Potter Vion; [m.] Roger Lewis Hoover, February 24, 1957; [ch.] Diana Dee, Karen Kay and Jeffery Jay; [ed.] Leuzinger High School, Lawndale, CA, Winner Business School, Los Angelas, CA.; [occ.] Housewife; [oth. writ.] Poems and I am working on a historical novel of the 1600's. Based on my 13th removed great grandmothers life coming to "The New Land" in 1632.; [pers.] I would wish for my writing to always be a pleasure to read with a message of hope to all who should read it.; [a.] Riverside, CA

HOPKINS, CAROLINE
[b.] October 3, 1940, Sidney, IA; [p.] Roy and Doris Driever; [m.] Robert Hopkins, July 17, 1960; [ch.] Bradley and Brent, and two grandchildren; [ed.] Graduated High School - Sidney Community School, Teacher Degree - Peru State Teacher's College, Masters in Education - Northwest Missouri State University; [occ.] Elementary School Teacher at Farragut Community School, Farragut, Iowa; [memb.] National Education Association, Iowa State Education Association, Farragut Education Association, United Methodist Women, Iowa Conservation Commission, Southwest Iowa Birdwatchers, Cornelia Rebekah Lodge; [hon.] Fremont County Southwest Conservation District Photography Contest 1995 Winner, Interests - Poetry, Photography, Nature, Antiques, Pets and most of all my Wonderful Family; [oth. writ.] Poetry for special events at school.; [pers.] I strive to help others to see, understand, appreciate, promote and preserve nature through my poetry.; [a.] Riverton, IA

HOUGH, DAWN M.
[pen.] Dawn Marie C.; [b.] December 26, 1969, Buffalo, NY; [p.] Edward and Jane P. Seifert; [m.] Gregory D. Hough, June 30, 1990; [ch.] Haley-Jane Helen; [ed.] Maryvale Sr. High - Regents diploma; [occ.] Mother, survivalist, cellist; [memb.] Holy Name of Mary Church; [hon.] D.E.C.A. Awards and music awards from high school, MHS class of '88; [oth. writ.] Personal journal of my life to give to my daughter one day of 'How it was in the late 1900's in America: Generation X'; [pers.] Have seen too much sadness on T.V. Why can't people just be? Leave me alone, don't you throw that stone. Words can cut like a knife. I choose peace and love for my life.; [a.] Corfu, NY

HOUTZ, TOBY L.
[b.] June 25, 1968, Lock Haven, PA; [p.] Raymond Houtz, Lois St. Clair; [m.] Amy Marie Houtz, August 13, 1988; [ch.] Brittni Adriana, Logan Dakota; [ed.] Lock Haven High, Lock Haven University; [occ.] Student at Lock Haven University; [hon.] Dean's List for Spring 1995 Semester; [pers.] I write most of my poems strictly out of my head to gain the most heartfelt response possible.; [a.] Lock Haven, PA

HOWARD, SARAH
[b.] December 11, 1979, Fresno, CA; [p.] Jane Hussey, Steve Howard; [ed.] Right now I'm a sophomore in Yosemite High School, Oakhurst, Ca; [hon.] White head Memorial Art Award; [oth. writ.] Have written many other poems but this is my first time sending one in to be published; [pers.] I find that when I put the feelings inside me into my writing it reflects and shows and great many things to different types of people and can be interpreted in differingly ways; [a.] Oakhurst, CA

HOWARD, SYLVIA D.
[pen.] Syl; [b.] March 2, 1938, Portsmouth, VA; [p.] Julia G. Howard; [m.] Deceased, 1958; [ch.] Two sons; [ed.] McClymonds High, Alameda College, Western College; [occ.] Self employed, Special Education; [memb.] First Presbyterian Church; [hon.] Deans List in College, USNR- Outstanding Sailor Numerous Awards and Certificates, Editors Choice Award for Poetry; [oth. writ.] Several poems published by The National Library of Poetry, Owings MD, have written over 100 poems, not published yet.; [pers.] We know that life is really about a spiritual unfolding that is personal and enchanting and through my poetry, I like to see the beauty of life.; [a.] Oakland, CA

HOWE, JENNIFER R.
[b.] August 1, 1966; [p.] Paul B. Howe, Donna B. Howe; [ch.] Jessica Catherine Howe; [ed.] Ocean View High School; [occ.] Self emp. child care provider; [hon.] My most precious award is my daughter Jessica.; [pers.] There is therapy in writing, also a chance to look back and see growth, then look forward and see promise.; [a.] Garden Grove, CA

HOWELL JR., PAUL MARVIN
[b.] February 14, 1984, Providence Hosp., Mobile, AL; [p.] Fhom and Renee Fowler; [hon.] Fitness in Sit-ups Sports; [oth. writ.] This is my first.; [a.] Mobile, AL

HRANJ, REBECCA E.
[b.] April 23, 1982, Bremerhaven, Germany; [p.] Albert Hranj, Daniel and Inge Van Reenen; [ed.] 8th grade at Aberdeen Middle School; [occ.] Student; [memb.] Student government; [hon.] Presidential Academic Fitness Award, 12 Honor Roll Award (School); [oth. writ.] Poem published in Local Newspaper - 1992; [pers.] I have been greatly encouraged by family and friends, especially my real Dad and I would like to thank them.; [a.] Aberdeen, MD

HUBBELL, JAMES T.
[m.] Mary Ann Hubbell; [ch.] Four; [ed.] Cranbrook Art Academy, Bloomfield Hills, MI Whitney Art School, New Haven, Conn.; [occ.] Sculptor, Architectural Designer; [memb.] Hon. Prof. of Valdivostok Technical Univ., Valdivostok-Tijuana Sister City Association, San Diego-Tijuana Sister City Association, Co-Founder Valdivaotok-San Diego Sister City., Founder of Ilan-Lael Foundation; [hon.] C-3 Revelle Award 1989 Honary Professor of Vladivostok Technical State University, Vlad. Russia Interfaith Forum on Religion, Art and Architecture 1987 and 1993; [oth. writ.] Emerald Gate, 1993 - Love Letters To The Earth 1975-77-82- Poetry Book - Is There Life After 50 Form Old Hate 1988 Poetry Book; [pers.] I believe, in beauty, as the edge between the pathos and joy of being human. That matter and spirit are intermeshed. That wisdom is a balance of what often seems as opposite and ambiguity. That art is the making real of what is first an inner world. That art is the refashioning of our myths to bring us into balance with a world everchanging. That for the artist, after discipline there is only trust.; [a.] Santa Ysabel, LA

HUCKLEBERRY, JAMES T.
[b.] September 17, 1943, Olympia, WA; [m.] Linda L. Huckleberry, June 30, 1974; [ch.] Eric, Michael, Sheri, Sheila; [ed.] M.A. in Communication University of Northern Colorado; [occ.] Computer Systems Analyst; [hon.] Meritorious Service Medal, Army Commentation Medal, Defense Meritorious Service Medal; [oth. writ.] Published poems (World Book of Poetry) "A Child's Equation of Love," "Mistletoe," "Twilight," "Twilight Peace," "Wailing In The Wilderness" - one recorded song, hilltop records "That's What It's All About."; [pers.] Hidden feelings die unspoken; [a.] Middletown, MD

HUCKS, CHRISTINA BRASWELL
[pen.] Chrissie Hucks; [b.] January 3, 1970, San Diego, CA; [p.] Frank and Linda Braswell; [m.] Randy Leverne Hucks, February 14, 1988; [ch.] 2 daughters Jessica and Kayla; [ed.] Conway High Graduate 7 years of Music; [occ.] Palmetto Animal Hospital Medical Secretary; [pers.] I would like to dedicate this poem in loving memory of my Father: James Francum Braswell July 27, 1939 to November 9, 1994. I will always keep you close to my heart. Pooh; [a.] Conway, SC

HUDSON, SETH
[pen.] Seth; [b.] April 27, 1980, Memphis, TN; [p.] Lynda Hudson; [ed.] Pittsburg Independent School District; [oth. writ.] I have a book of nearly 100 poems in which I plan to publish in the near future; [pers.] Every one gets lonely, I still, every one needs to be alone sometimes.; [a.] Pittsburg, TX

HUEY, BILLY JOE TROY
[pen.] Billy Joe Huey; [b.] June 9, 1972, Clouderport, PA; [p.] Martha Robinson; [occ.] Good times Skate I am a D.J. and a skate teacher; [memb.] Lake Athens Church; [hon.] Student of the year of Athens TX, 75751 Athens High School; [oth. writ.] None, my teacher Mrs. Cruseturner Taught English and taught me how to write and express myself.; [pers.] I enjoy writing how I feel and express myself to write how you feel to touch other people's hearts. It just feels

good to write how you feel all of the time.; [a.] Athens, TX

HUFNAGEL, MARIAN A.
[b.] June 19, 1932, Newburgh, IN; [p.] Rosalia and Russell Windels; [m.] Raymond E. Hufnagel, October 17, 1952; [ch.] Three adult, three grandchildren; [ed.] Reg. Nurse - Extensive Background in Psychiatry; [occ.] Retired Nurse - now using skills to serve as a volunteer in many areas of Church Work eg, DEACON, Health Minister, Coord. of Acolytes; [pers.] Though my dreams occasionally black my writing, reality is my inspiration.; [a.] San Diego, CA

HUGGINS, STEPHEN C.
[pen.] SCH; [b.] October 30, 1962, Tallahassee, FL; [p.] Louis Huggins, Dorothy Huggins; [m.] Barbara Huggins, September 28, 1991; [ch.] Cameron Blair, Jeremy Daniel; [ed.] FSU; [occ.] First V.P., Investments, Dean Witter Reynolds; [memb.] Parkway Baptist Church; [hon.] Dean Witter President's Club; [pers.] I thank God for my new family, and my parents for creating such wonderful childhood memories.; [a.] Tallahassee, FL

HUMMEL, EUGENIA
[b.] August 30, 1923, Watsonville, CA; [p.] Mr. and Mrs. Mitchell; [m.] Don Hummel (Deceased), December 27, 1947; [ch.] Donna, Diane, Clifford, Charlene; [ed.] Stanford AB and Secondary Degrees; [occ.] Homemaker, [memb.] Arizona Watchcolor Guild and Museum of Art - Ass. member, [a.] Tucson, AZ

HUMPHREY, OWEN E.
[b.] October 25, 1920, Wautoma, WI; [p.] Marion Humphrey, Flora Humphrey; [m.] Billye Cox (Deceased), April 6, 1946; [ch.] Reba Humphrey, Rick, Ivye Humphrey; [ed.] Wautoma H.S. B.S. Univ. of Wisconsin, Whitewater M.S. Univ. of Arkansas, Fayetteville Ed. Sp. University of Illinois; [occ.] Retired school teacher/admin.; [memb.] Asoc. for Supervision and Curriculum Development (Hon.) National Education Assoc. (Life), Phi Delta Kappa, Kappa Delta Pi, Collinsville Area Theatrical Society.; [hon.] Phi Delta Kappa Service Key, 1984, Creativity Recognition Award, 1972, George H. Reavis Associate Award (PDK), 1991, Granite City Area Council PTA Award, 1979, Military Service Awards (Bronze Star, 4 ETO battle stars), 1942-45, Biog. Sketches: Dict. of Intern. Biog, Who's Who in Amer. Educ., Who's Who in Midwest, Who's Who in the World, Two Thousand Men of Achievement, Creative and Successful Personalities of the World.; [oth. writ.] Poems pub. in A Delicate Balance, Famous Poems of Today. Articles in various IASCD Newsletters, contributor to Illinois School Research, author of The Greening of Gateway East, A History of Chapter 1097, PDK.; [pers.] At age 75, my retirement years are stirring up renewed interest in the poetry-writing I first started at age 16. My time is largely filled with writing and acting in a local theater group.; [a.] Granite City, IL

HUNDSHAMER, FRANK
[pen.] Frank Hundshamer; [b.] Syracuse, NY; [m.] Judy, 1948; [ch.] 4 children, 12 grandchildren; [occ.] Chairman of Board Orange Credit Service, Lake Elsinore, California 30 years; [oth. writ.] Numerous poems, songs (words and music), short stories, novels. No attempt to enter commercial fields.; [pers.] Many of my poems composed while in Marine Corps, WW 2 and Korea. These writings were a stabilizing mental "escape hatch" to the reality of war.; [a.] Arcadia, CA

HUNTER, HEIDI HENRIKSON
[pen.] H. H. Hunter; [b.] September 1, 1951; [occ.] With husband, William, own and operate, Bacchi's Inn, the oldest, singly family owned Italian restaurant at Lake Tahoe.; [pers.] Have lived at Lake Tahoe, Calif., all of my life. I have traveled extensively world wife, but have never found a place in which I would rather live. Through my poetry I try to express my feelings and personal philosophy. My views of the future, can be optimistic, true to life and death, or pessimistic. My poetry vacillates between three.; [a.] Tahoe City, CA

HUNTER, ISABELLE
[pen.] Isabelle; [b.] February 16, 1927, Fayeville, PA; [p.] Alex and Lucy Jackson; [ed.] High School, North Eastern University, Fisher Jr. College; [occ.] Volunteering; [memb.] Museum of Science Boston Public Library Mustic Valley RR, Life Study Fellowship; [hon.] Life Study Fellowship, St. Anthony's; [oth. writ.] I flicked a dream.; [pers.] I live from day to day.; [a.] Boston, MS

HUTCHINS, SHARLEEN
[b.] January 28, 1961, Monroe, WA; [p.] John Hutchins Sr, Patsy Esserdonhof; [ch.] Sonja Shambaugh and Chris Peterson; [ed.] Snohomish High School; [occ.] Caregiver and Owner of TWS Ltd an errand running service; [memb.] The International Society of Poets and National Society of Female Executives; [hon.] Commanding Officers Accommodation award, two Editors Choice award from the NLP; [oth. writ.] "A Muse to Follow" the NLP, "Best of '95" the NLP, "Dance on the Horizon" the NLP, "Dusting off Dreams" Quill Books, Listen with Your Heart" Quill Books; [pers.] Peace and harmony must be reached in the world, if we all work together it can be.; [a.] Snohomish, WA

HYDE, NELMA
[b.] January 2, 1937, Port Arthur, TX; [p.] Lean, Horace White; [m.] Peter Dawson Hyde, June 5, 1959; [ch.] Rebecca Fike, Ruth Nethery; [ed.] College Graduate; [oth. writ.] "When Will We Cry?", (Journal of my mother's suffering, and death with Alzheimer's Disease.), "Grandmother, Grandmother!!" (Vignettes about the grandchildren), "From Pilgrim's Pen - The Incredible Journey.; [pers.] What I have "touched" when journeying "inside" is REAL: The stuff of ordinary life lived in the extraordinary awareness of Divine Presence.; [a.] Paris, AR

HYSLOP, MARLENA MARIE
[b.] January 28, 1965, Indianapolis, IN; [p.] John and Bonnie Phillips; [m.] Gregary A. Hyslop, April 4, 1991; [ch.] Zackary Posey, Teren Posey, Sarah Posey, Amber Hyslop, Thomas Hyslop; [ed.] Completed 8th grade; [occ.] Homemaker; [pers.] I write from my heart of personal experiences. I know others have experienced some of the same things that I have. This is my attempt to let them know that they are not alone, and may God bless you all. Although not as educated school wise as some, I have learned through numerous heartaches and joys this thing called life. Working on my third marriage, I have finally begun to realize some of my dreams. To be able to write of my feeling, and God willing, to touch others. I finally have a husband who supports my dreams, and pushes me to attempt what I don't think I can. I have learned, through him, that nothing is out of reach. All you need to do is keep trying, and never let your heartaches stop you from trying to realize your dreams. This is one of my dreams, and I have finally had it come true.; [a.] Apache Junction, AZ

IMMELE, JENNIFER MARIE TOLES
[pen.] Lady Turtle, Jennifer Toles; [b.] November 22, 1976, Huntsville, AL; [p.] Rhonda Jo Palmer, Roger Dale Toles; [m.] Richard Kirk Immele, November 23, 1995; [ed.] Sierra High School, Simla High School, Pikes Peak Community College; [occ.] Salesperson, Mervyn's California, Colo. Spgs. Co; [hon.] Editors Choice Award for "Friends Always" published in Dance on the Horizon by The National Library of Poetry; [oth. writ.] "In the Summer" Of Diamonds and Rust, "Our Love" Quest of a Dream, "Friends Always" Dance on the Horizon [a.] Colorado Springs, CO

INGEBRIGTSEN, KAY
[b.] March 18, 1924, Minneapolis, MN; [p.] Leonard and Esther; [m.] Jeanne, July 29, 1950; [ch.] David, Mark, Kathy, Kari, Jeni; [ed.] Marshall H.S., Minneapolis, MN, Beach. of Mechanical Engineering, Bach. of Science, Doctor of Dental Surgery, University of Minnesota; [occ.] Retired—I am currently writing poems and songs.; [hon.] Several poems published in various publications.; [pers.] I write poetry to bring to life and to illustrate realistic situations, some of which are from personal experiences.; [a.] Fridley, MN

IRWIN JR., MICHAEL P.
[b.] March 11, 1976, Buffalo, NY; [p.] Michael and Sharon Irwin; [ed.] Sophomore - University of North Carolina at Chapel Hill (English Major); [occ.] Student; [oth. writ.] Personal poems and essays; [pers.] I have been strongly reference by God, Emerson, and the Romantic poets. My writings embody peace and strove to present the light on our universal world.; [a.] Chapel Hill, NC

JACK, INEZ I.
[b.] January 11, 1914, Kansas; [p.] Calvin and Carrie Twibell; [m.] John Jack (Deceased) April 12, 1936; [ch.] Two Foster Children; [ed.] High School grad.; [occ.] Widowed since 1993; [oth. writ.] I wrote many poems during WW II. Spouse was prisoner of war in Germany; [pers.] My poems express humor, family values and my love for nature; [a.] Tacoma, WA

JACKSON, EARNESTINE
[pen.] E. Jackson; [b.] April 5, Chicago, IL; [p.] Robert and Lucille Jackson; [occ.] Administrative Assistant; [hon.] Golden Poet Award 1990

JACKSON, GAYLE LYNN
[pen.] Gayle Whittle Jackson; [b.] November 19, 1956, Tampa, FL; [p.] Winston C. Whittle and Dorothy Henry Hazlett; [m.] Karl Willi Jackson, October 21, 1994; [ed.] Leto High School in Tampa, Secretarial Vocational NFJC, Madison, FL, Electronic Technology - FCCJ, Jacksonville, FL; [occ.] Disabled; [oth. writ.] None published; [a.] Melbourne, FL

JACKSON, JEWELEAN
[b.] February 21, 1949, Vallejo, CA; [p.] Beulah Jackson, Lete James Jackson; [m.] Divorced; [ed.] Vallejo High, Soleno Community College completed Certified Nurses Aide, Human Health Aide Trainers Vallejo Convalescent Hospital; [occ.] Home Health Aide, Private Duty Vallejo Calif; [memb.] Church of Christ, Vallejo Calif; [hon.] Deans list, Certificate CNA, NHA; [oth. writ.] Wrote other poems and songs as a hobby; [pers.] Poetry and songs writing is a way for me to express my deepest feelings. I choose to write a religious made for my love for God. I hope to have longevity as a poet and song writer; [a.] Vallejo, CA

JACKSON, ST. CLAIR CONSTANCE
[pen.] Constance St. Clair; [b.] February 5, 1974, Arcata, CA; [p.] Mr. and Mrs. Warren Jackson; [ed.] Bishop Manogue High, Senior at University of Nevada, Reno; [occ.] Full-time student; [memb.] Gamma Phi Beta Sorority - Alpha Gamma Chapter; [oth. writ.] Have written several poems, however none have been published until now.; [pers.] Expressing yourself is but an art. I choose to do it with the combination of the words we speak and my imagination.; [a.] Reno, NV

JACKSON, STEPHANIE
[pen.] Stephanie J. VIII; [b.] December 28, 1956, Miami, FL; [p.] Felix Smith, Roberta Jackson-Smith; [m.] Single (for now); [ch.] Gabriel Lamont, Clearon Jermaine; [ed.] GED, Miami-Dade Community College, Victory Bible Institute; [occ.] Dietary, Hillcrest Medical Center, Tulsa, OK; [memb.] House of Prayer, Choir, Grace Tucker, Pastor; [hon.] Dean's List, Management in Food and Nutrition; [oth. writ.] This is my first poem ever submitted and published.; [pers.] This publication has been such an encouragement to me. My poems are inspired by God's love, share your gift.; [a.] Tulsa, OK

JACKSON, TRACEY A.
[b.] May 29, 1961, Baltimore, MD; [p.] Ann E. Fletcher and the late Robert L. Fletcher; [m.] Gary Jackson, February 17, 1989; [ch.] Gary Jr., Justin; [ed.] Francis Scott Key high A.A. Degree - Catonsville Comm. College, B.A. Degree - Western Maryland College; [occ.] Rehabilitation Counselor, Granite house Inc., Westminster, MD; [memb.] Church of the open door, MADD, concerned Women for America, Alliance for the mentally Ill.; [hon.] Dean's List; [oth. writ.] Several poems written for special occasions and special people.; [pers.] My poetry is a colorful display of the many wonderful people. Who's paths I have been fortunate to cross. All credit is due to my creator, who has richly blessed me with all my abilities.; [a.] Westminster, MD

JACOBSON, DAVID M.
[b.] December 21, 1957, Rochester, NY; [p.] Israel Jacobson, Rose Jacobson; [m.] Laurie Anne Jacobson, June 30, 1985; [ch.] Shira Sheva, Samuel Richard, Yosef Paul,; [ed.] Arisona State Univeristy, Suny at Brockport NY; [occ.] Manger: Dept of Volunteer services, University Medical Center, Tucson, AZ; [memb.] National Association of Social Workers; [hon.] Jim Elliot Award: El Tour de Tucson, Silver Medalist. Governor's Office for Children appointment to: Children's Justice Task Force, Cum Laude graduate.; [oth. writ.] Currently working on first book on subject of health and humor "My left Elbow". Several articles in a news papers and magazines regarding authors use of humor to cope with athritis.; [pers.] I wish to inspire others to use the power of positive emotions in facing life's adversities.; [a.] Tucson, AZ

JAMES, BETTY
[b.] September 9, 1941, South Carolina; [p.] Deceased; [m.] Robert, April 28, 1958; [ch.] 5 Kids, 8 Grands, 1 Godchild; [ed.] Mayo High School; [occ.] Home Health Aid; [memb.] Christ United Church Choir Member; [hon.] Mother's Day Award, 3 Awards Nurse's Aid Course; [a.] Brooklyn, NY

JAMES, GINA
[pen.] Gina James; [b.] March 26, 1971, Sandusky, OH; [p.] Shirley, Richard James; [ch.] Galadriel, Adeline Corrine; [ed.] LaPorte High, Butler High Beville State Community College; [occ.] Student of Pre-Veterinarian Medician; [oth. writ.] Songs, poetry dealing with my present state of mind.; [pers.] I may not achieve all I care to, but at least I've tried. "Can't never could do anything," as was told to me.; [a.] Hamilton, AL

JAMES, JOANNA
[pen.] Jani James; [b.] February 21, 1959, Steuben County; [p.] Shelda J. Ford and Alta R. Ford; [m.] Jimmy L. James Sr., May 23, 1983; [ch.] Eric James, Jennifer James, Jimmy L. James Jr.; [ed.] High School Graduate; [occ.] House wife; [memb.] The Hamilton Fish and Game Club; [hon.]; [oth. writ.] Have written several things since High school but had never pursued it seriously.; [pers.] Never let anyone stop you from being everything you can be.; [a.] Hamilton, IN

JAMES, TAMMY S.
[b.] May 7, 1965, Fort Smith, AR; [p.] Bill James, Marsha Lensing; [ed.] Southside High School, Univ. of the Ozarks, currently a student at Univ. of AR at Fayetteville; [occ.] Student, part time receptionist at Mercy Crest, a residential care facility; [hon.] Who's Who Among American High School Students, National Honor Society, Mu Alpha Theta, Thespian Club, editor of college newspaper, Dean's List; [oth. writ.] Several poems published in literary publications in High School and college; [pers.] Each day I try to make the world a better place, even if it is just in my own little corner. I use humor and laughter to reach out to others. I, also, use my writing to express my feelings and hopefully touch someone else's heart.; [a.] Fort Smith, AR

JARRARD, ELAINE
[b.] February 25, 1966, Savannah, GA; [p.] William C. Petty, Anita Louise Wilkens Perty; [m.] Jerry Dean Jarrard (Divorced), March 2, 1984; [ch.] Jessica Delaine, Melanie Beth, Shelby Lee; [ed.] Rockwall High, North Texas State University, Northeast Louisiana University; [occ.] Realtor, Century 21 Real Estate Professionals; [memb.] First Baptist Church, Bossier Chamber of Commerce Diplomat, National Association of Realtors, Shreveport Bossier Board of Realtors; [oth. writ.] Several non-published poems.; [pers.] My goals include touching peoples lives in order to help them believe more in themselves.; [a.] Bossier City, CA

JAUS, JENNIFER P.
[pen.] Jenny P. Jaus; [b.] June 13, 1973, Bloomington, IN; [p.] Hal and Vicki Jaus; [ed.] McClintock Jr. High School, East Mecklenburg High School, Wesleyan College, Macon, GA, and UNCC, Charlotte, NC; [occ.] I work for the Charlotte - Douglas Airport; [memb.] Bally's Health and Fitness, Surfer Mag., Surfing Mag., U.S.A., Junior Volleyball Assoc., Sardis Presb. Church, Charlotte Choral Society!!!; [hon.] I've won many talent (voice) comp. and Volleyball Awards!!! Life is my own reward and honor!!!; [oth. writ.] None!!! I like!!! My first poem, but I like to write short stories and mysteries!!!!; [pers.] Life is a one big obstacle course. If you want the ultimate thrill, you have to pay the ultimate price!!! Enjoy life, don't take it for granted!!!; [a.] Charlotte, NC

JEFFRIES, ANNA BELLE
[b.] Washington, PA; [p.] H. Floyd Jeffries and Irene K. Jeffries; [ed.] Graduate of Washington High School and Penn Commercial College of Washington Pa.; [occ.] Church Sec'y of the Church of the Covenant, Presbyterian Church (USA) in Washington, Pa.; [oth. writ.] Poems published in an Anthology of High School Poems by National High School Poetry Assoc., and "Love Poems" Book by American Poetry Assoc., Honorable Mention in a Poetry Contest By Xi Beta Alpha (these several years ago), recently - poems published in "Harmony of Hearts benefiting the local Humane Society, Honorable Mention in the EDCO Poetry Contest of Rockford Business College Rockford, Ill.; [a.] Washington, PA

JEFFRIES, LOREN TERRELL
[pen.] L. T. J.; [b.] July 14, 1962, Denver, CO; [p.] Vernon and Rose Jeffries; [m.] Nancy J. Jeffries; [ch.] Terrell, Cody, Ashley; [ed.] Wetminter Colorado Schools; [occ.] Musicians, Writer, Working Class; [memb.] N.R.A.; [oth. writ.] Many, many more writings and music; [pers.] Follow your dream were ever it might lead youu.; [a.] Denver, CO

JENKINS, AMBER MICHELLE
[b.] December 11, 1983, Norfolk, VA; [p.] Billy R. Jenkins and Barbara A. W. Jenkins; [ed.] 6th Grader at the Norfolk Academy Norfolk, Virginia; [memb.] First Baptist Church of Norfolk, Norfolk, Virginia; [hon.] The Simcoe and Celia Glasser Poetry Award, 1st place in 5th grade Essay Contest of Great Bridge Chapter of the National Society Daughters of the American Revolution, High Honor Roll Student; [oth. writ.] Poems published in the Norfolk Academy publications "Luminary" and "Rings and Strings and Other Things", the Thomas Jefferson Memorial Foundation, Inc. publication "Monticello", and "Virginia Writing". Articles and essays published in The Norfolk Academy "Cornerstone" and "Literary Bullpup".; [pers.] I like to write poetry that stirs people's emotions. "Circle of life" is in memorium of my friend Allison McCall.; [a.] Virginia Beach, VA

JENKINS, STEPHANIE C.
[b.] May 15, 1957, Norfolk, VA; [p.] Frank and Sarah Chancey Sr.; [ch.] Rury T. Jenkins II; [ed.] Junior - Norfolk State University; [occ.] Student; [memb.] Second Calvary Baptist Church, Norfolk VA; [hon.] Civil Service Award 1986. Post Office; [oth. writ.] "Trojan Man," "Its A New Day," "He Gives Me Joy"; [pers.] I am the mother of one son. This is my first endeavor to write, although I've always wanted to. I through the "cannot" word out of my vocabulary after my son was born. I say to my readers. Always follow your dreams with hope in your heart until they become a reality.; [a.] Portsmouth, VA

JENSEN, JANE
[b.] January 20, 1957, Maryville, MO; [p.] Darrell and Melissa Jensen; [ed.] B.S. English University of S.D., M.A. Library Science USD; [occ.] Librarian; [hon.] Phi Delta Kappa, Margaret Sanger English Scholarship; [a.] Yankton, SD

JENSON, JAMES SCOTT
[b.] October 6, 1978, Vallejo, CA; [ed.] Currently High School Senior; [occ.] Trombone Player; [memb.] School Bands, Honor Bands, Local Y.E.S (Youth Empowerment); [hon.] 1994 Most Improved Low Brass, 1995 Most Valuable Low Brass; [pers.] Beyond words, you find voice, beyond voice, you find emotion, beyond emotion you find meaning. Beyond poetry you find yourself.; [a.] Napa, CA

JHIRAD, MR. ELIJAH E.
[b.] April 6, 1913, Quetta, Pakistan (Then British India); [p.] Khan Sahib Ephraim Jhirad and Mary Jhirad; [ch.] David, Sarah, Ephraim, Rahel, Yigal; [ed.] B.A. (Hons.) 1933, Barrister-at-Law of Lincoln's Inn, London, England 1937; [occ.] Semi-retired, writing history of the Jews of India etc.; [memb.] Freedom, Lincoln Lodge B'Nai B'rith (President 1976-95), Jewish War Veterans, President, Congregation Bina; [hon.] Member of the Most Excellent Order of the British Empire. Conferred by King George VI, on January 1, 1946, for distinguished war service World War II in the Navy, other war medals and decorations. Also granted war service rank of Commander for life; [oth. writ.] Significant law books and publication in U.S.A. and India; [pers.] "Look into thy heart and write." You will discover there fond memories of a leaf, of a bud, of a flower.; [a.] Briarwood, NY

JIMENEZ, MARIA
[pen.] Maria Jimenez; [b.] January 29, 1974, Cuba; [p.] Daisi Jimenez, Jose L. Jimenez; [ed.] High School Coral Gables Senior High School; [occ.] Recording Artist (D.J.); [memb.] American Red Cross, The March of Dimes; [oth. writ.] Hundreds of poems written in Spanish and English but never been published; [pers.] My poetry is extrictly base on passages of my life. Hopefully people will see through my poems what is like to be me.; [a.] West Palm Beach, FL

JOEDICKE, LINDA
[b.] October 20, 1960, De Soto, MO; [p.] Oscar,

Reva O'Harver; [m.] Steve Joedicke, October 21, 1978; [ch.] Steve Jr., Travis, Shelly May; [ed.] De Soto High School; [occ.] Housewife and mother; [pers.] Writing poetry is like stopping to smell the roses, if you don't take the time you, will never know the sweet smell of a rose of the beautiful sound of a poem.; [a.] De Soto, MO

JOHNSON, ANGELA
[b.] August 23, 1971, Dayton, OH; [p.] William Lehman, Judy Lehman; [m.] Larry Johnson, May 21, 1995; [ed.] Miamisburg High School; [occ.] Teacher; [oth. writ.] A poem of mine was published in the 1989 class year book, Miamisburg High School. Another poem was published in the local newspaper.; [pers.] My poetry is my release. It is a way to express my emotions and feelings in a positive manner. I only wish more people knew how to express themselves in this way, maybe the world would be more at peace.; [a.] Dayton, OH

JOHNSON, BETTY HILL
[b.] January 19, 1955, Black; [p.] Mr. and Mrs. Paul D. Hill; [m.] Mr. Otis Johnson Jr., August 15, 1992; [ch.] Tierra Nicole Johnson; [ed.] Southside High School, Greenville Technical College; [occ.] Registered Nurse; [memb.] Allied Health Educational Committee, American National Nephrology Association, Health Task Force; [hon.] Chi Eta Phi Sorority Inc., Talent Show Awards; [oth. writ.] I have written several poems but I never have had any of them published.; [pers.] I strive to utilize all of the talents that God has bless me with to uplift some one else spirits and to touch the human heart in us all.; [a.] Greenville, SC

JOHNSON, CAROL MANGGET
[pen.] Carol Johnson; [b.] December 15, 1954, Georgetown, Guyana; [p.] Samuel R. Manget and Lilian; [m.] Neville M. Johnson, March 18, 1988; [ch.] Shaina Ashleigh, Lauren Brittany; [ed.] Lilian Dewar College of Education, University of Maryland, College Park, MD.; [occ.] Home Maker/ Writer; [memb.] North Highland Assembly of God, G.C.H.E. (Gwinnett Christian Home Educators); [oth. writ.] Several short-stories and poems (not yet published). Children's story manuscript in progress.; [pers.] I hope my writing encourage readers to not only ask but find answers to those questions we find so intrinsic to life and living; [a.] Atlanta, GA

JOHNSON, DARLENE
[pen.] Darlene Cree Johnson; [b.] September 16, 1935, Amery, WI; [p.] Wayne Cree and Fay Cree; [m.] Charles A. Johnson, June 8, 1957; [ch.] Marshel - Angella - Michael; [ed.] Amery High School; [occ.] Home Maker; [oth. writ.] Poems - unpublished; [pers.] First Poem I have ever shared; [a.] Amery, WI

JOHNSON, GERRIA ELAINE
[b.] September, 4, 1977, East Chicago, IN; [p.] Maxine and Jerry Johnson; [ed.] Stewart Elementary, Lincoln Middle School, Wooddale Jr. High, Wooddale High School; [occ.] Student; [memb.] Explores, Mu Alpha Theta, National Honor Society, DECA; [hon.] National Leadership, National Honor Roll, Who's who Among American High School Students, French and Marketing Student of the year, all-West Tennessee Band Alternate; [pers.] To create a Utopian Society, we must all return to the innocence of a newborn baby with the wisdom of our grand parents; [a.] Memphis, TN

JOHNSON, MS. JACQUELINE
[b.] January 10, 1960, Ohio; [p.] Ms. Mary Johnson and Jack Foster; [m.] Single; [ch.] Three; [ed.] Dramatic writing; [occ.] Musician; [memb.] The New World, Griots, The Optimists, Writers; [hon.] Top Songwriters, Short story, colorlines and hopefully one from you (TNLP); [oth. writ.] "Special Moment", "A Race of Color", and "The Force"; [pers.] I am currently dissecting scripts. Reared as a child, the support of my family and friends, renew my strength.; [a.] Palmdale, CA

JOHNSON, JAMES E.
[b.] September 7, 1963, Cosby, TN; [p.] Carl E. and Annie Lousie; [ch.] Brian James, Victoria Kay; [pers.] I feel that through poetry you can touch someone's heart and soul.; [a.] Sevierville, TN

JOHNSON, JAMIE
[b.] August 14, 1975, French Camp, CA; [ed.] Currently working toward a degree in English; [occ.] Student; [oth. writ.] Short Stories, Essays, and Poems; [pers.] I feel fortunate to be writing in a time when women are being recognized for their literary talents and I am grateful ot women like Ann e Bradstreet, Zora Neate Hurston, Kate Chopin, and many others who cleared the path for writers such as myself; [a.] San Jose, CA

JOHNSON, JANE MARTIN
[pen.] Joyfully Jane; [b.] March 22, 1936, Yakima, WA; [p.] George and Betty Martin; [m.] Ed L. Johnson, July 28, 1979; [ed.] Yakima Senior High School Whitworth College; [occ.] Housewife; [pers.] I thank God for giving to me the gift of writing in poetry!; [a.] Yakima, WA

JOHNSON, JANICE C.
[b.] July 20, 1951, Richmond, VA; [ch.] Michael, Christian, Levern Johnson Jr., Jannita Johnson; [ed.] Facilitator, steril concepts Inc. Richmond, VA.; [oth. writ.] The poem each of us published in Tomorrow's Dream.; [a.] Richmond, VA

JOHNSON, LAVONE E.
[b.] January 28, 1940, Fremont Co., IA; [p.] Joseph E. and Grace E. Lorimor; [m.] J. Arlen Johnson, December 26, 1959; [ch.] Jana Blair, Jenise Carl, J. Alan Johnson; [ed.] Farragut High School; [occ.] Owns and operates 900 acre farm with spouse, is potter and dollmaker, several dolls featured on Hallmark cards.; [memb.] First United Methodist Church; [pers.] The land provides the substance for life and the arts provide my zest for living. Lindsy, Alyssa and Nathaniel, Grammy loves you.; [a.] Clarinda, IA

JOHNSON, MARGARET
[pen.] Peggy Johnson; [b.] August 13, 1956, New York; [p.] Thomas and Mary Archer; [m.] James, May 13, 1979; [ch.] Ashley and Megan; [occ.] Nursing Assistant; [pers.] I miss my mother very much. Her death has been the hardest experience of my life. A part of my heart will always be sad. If she can hear me "I love you Momma".

JOHNSON, MILDRED A.
[b.] October 31, 1925, Baltimore, MD; [p.] Eugene Gough and Sadie Gough (Deceased); [m.] George R. Johnson, June 5, 1948; [ch.] Seven; [ed.] St. Peter Claver's Ridge, MD, Cardinal Gibbons High Ridge, MD; [occ.] Housewife; [memb.] NAACP, St. Vincent de Paul, Catholic Charities; [a.] Baltimore, MD

JOHNSON, PORTIA CRAWFORD L.
[b.] May 28, Washington, DC; [p.] Carl and Jessie Crawford; [m.] Robert E. Johnson, June 29, 1996; [ch.] Tyvon Jerome and David Allan Crawford; [ed.] Suitland High School, Creative Nails Institute - (Nail Tech.), Southern Md Nurses Assos. - (Assistant Nurse's Aid); [occ.] U.S. Postal Worker for 23 years; [memb.] Lane CME Memorial Daughters of American Revolution; [oth. writ.] Various poems, short stories, non-published; [pers.] One should always express feelings of the heart, being a class A romantic, I try to reach all romantics in the world.; [a.] Clinton, MD

JOHNSON, RACHEL A.
[pen.] Rena Fehren; [ed.] High School in St. Paul and studied the Arts in College University of Utah. [hon.] Awarded a Bachelor of Science Degree in Music Education (Ogden, Utah); [oth. writ.] Unpublished "Wintertime" and "Reflections" and "Harvest". One other presently in preparation for print, is "Songs of the Desert".; [pers.] In the Springtime of 1995, I began writing my first poems. Writing poetry is an experience of writing I cherish very highly.; [a.] Tucson, AZ

JOHNSON, SHEILA R. NOEL
[pen.] Sheila R. Johnson; [b.] December 10, 1960, England, AR; [p.] Billy and Ocie Noel; [m.] Theodore R. Johnson, June 7, 1995; [ch.] LaQuittah 15, Tre'Nina 5; [ed.] England High School 12th Grade Completed; [occ.] Producers Rice Mill Stuttgart, Ark. Rice Parker; [hon.] Several poems published in "The England Spotlight" and "Producers People", local paper X-mas poems, holiday poems personal poems for special People Terminally Ill, Lovelore, Desert Storm Military personel, Birthdays Tribute for Accomplishments.; [oth. writ.] When the poem hits me I just start writing. The house is usually quiet or the people ask for a special writing. Especially when our military personal went to war.; [pers.] These writings come from my heart. If a person wants a poem written, I must get personal data, and in about 15 min., with a quiet house in my favorite chair, I write.; [a.] England, AR

JOHNSTON, ROBERT L.
[pen.] Bob Johnston; [b.] March 25, 1923, La Grange, GA; [p.] J. D. and Lovie Johnston; [m.] Joy (Shipman) Johnston, March 7, 1968; [ch.] Two boys and three girls; [ed.] High School - Chipley, GA (Now Pine Mountain) some special training - radio-TV business; [occ.] Retired; [memb.] Life member VFW - Member American Legion Hebron Lodge - Scottish Rites - Akdar Shrine Temple - First Baptist Church; [hon.] High School Letter - some WLV 2 medals; [oth. writ.] Ten songs (never published) only copyrighted.; [pers.] Live each day with the thought of being your best and help someone along the way if possible.; [a.] Cleveland, OK

JONES, CHRIS
[pen.] Slate Wooderson; [b.] June 9, 1974, Asheboro, NC; [p.] Tiffany and Susan Jones; [ed.] Eastern Randolph High, Guilford Tech. Comm. College Associates Degree; [oth. writ.] "The Eyes", "You've Seen It"; [pers.] I strive to show what some may consider to be small or insignificant ideas in life and show their importance in my writing.; [a.] Greensboro, NC

JONES, CLAUDINE
[b.] January 18, 1975, Jamaica, West Indies; [p.] Rosalind and Virgo Jones; [ed.] Rancocos Valley Regional High, 3rd year student at Jersey City State, College Jersey City, NJ; [occ.] Student majors, Secondary Education Math; [hon.] Volunteer Mentor for Urban League of Jersey City, Jersey City State College Opportunity, Scholarship Award Certificate for G.P.A. above 3.0.; [pers.] Each day live life to the fullest.; [a.] Mount Holly, NJ

JONES, CONNIE RIGSBY
[pen.] Connie Rigsby Jones; [b.] May 31, 1947, Huntsville, AL; [p.] Charles E. Rigsby and A. Sue Cagle Rigsby; [m.] Thomas Ward Jones, D.D.S., December 7, 1973; [ch.] E. Todd Pierce; [ed.] Lee High and Sparkman High, University of Alabama at Birmingham, Univ. of North Carolina School of Dental Assisting, Lakeshore Business Education Program, Birmingham, Al.; [occ.] Medically Retired Secretary, Univ. of Al. at B'ham School of Business/Retired Certified Dental Asst.; [memb.] 1) Valley Christian Church (Disciples of Christ), 2)

Voices of Valley - Literary Published poems and Musings.; [hon.] National Certified Dental Assisting Professional Honors: 1974 Winner: Alabama State Dental Assistant's Paper Trophy - "Your Hands Active Dental Assistant", 1973 Clinician: American Dental Assistant's Association National Meeting, Houston, Tx., 1972: Winner: Tennessee State Dental Asst's Table Clinic, "The Isental Assistants Role in Cardiopulmonary Resuscitation"; [oth. writ.] Poems published in the following: 1) On The Threshold of a Dream 1988, p. 73. "A Very Special Visit," The National Library of Poetry. 2) The National Poetry Anthology, 1988, p. 63. "Morning Dew." 3) Poetic Voices of America, 1988, p. 109, "If You Must Go". 4) Many Voices/Many Lands, Anthology of Poetry, Spring '88, p. 122, "A Very Special Treasure". 5) New American Poets, '89 p. 61 "Why Do You Have To Leave Us?"; [pers.] I was put on earth to serve my fellow man and my gifts to mankind are the poems which I pen.; [a.] Pelham, AL

JONES, GEORGE T.
[pen.] George Jones; [b.] November 7, 1922, Greenwich, Ct; [m.] Deceased; [ch.] Vinson, John; [ed.] New Rochelle HS (New Rochelle, NY), Howard U. (Wash. D.C.), BA, MA in Philosophy; [occ.] Retired; [oth. writ.] Book of poems: "Pure Black Nights", 1989 Carlton Press, NY; [pers.] We are born to ignorance: The Gods decree it. But not to arrogance: For this we are condemned by Gods and men alike.; [a.] White Plains, NY

JONES, JACQUELINE SUANN
[pen.] Jack or Jackie; [b.] January 9, 1982, Oktibbeha County Hospital; [p.] Jed and Charlene Jones; [ed.] I attend Maben High School and I am 14 year old in the 8th grade.; [memb.] I'm in the Oktibbeha County 4-H and St. Paul M.B. Church.; [hon.] A and B Honor Roll in all my classes at school. Trophies for highest average in Earth Science, Math, and English. Received Distinguished Citizen Award 4-H.; [pers.] I wrote this poem when I was 11 years old.; [a.] Starkville, MS

JONES, JEANETTE JACKSON
[b.] September 17, 1946, Opelika, AL; [p.] Palmer D. Jackson Sr. and Lucy Jackson; [m.] Freddie Leon Jones Sr., April 3, 1965; [ch.] 3 Sons; [occ.] Poet/Writer; [memb.] International Society of Poets; [hon.] Distinguished member international society of poets, golden poet 1990, golden poet award best poem 1989, from world of poetry editor's choice award. 1995; [oth. writ.] Best poems of western world Vol II, at water's edge poems free and sunday morning by the river, best poems of 1995.; [pers.] I would like to dedicate this poem to my dear husband of 30 years.; [a.] Fredericksburg, VA

JONES, MICHAEL D.
[b.] February 17, 1942, Crowell, TX; [p.] George and Bertha Jones; [m.] Frances A. Jones, November 12, 1983; [ed.] 7th grade; [occ.] Own my own company; [oth. writ.] Over 3,000 poems and 300 songs. This is the third publication of one of my poems with the International Society of Poets. No other publications; [pers.] I love the Lord Jesus Christ with all of my might. And my hearts desire is to be precious in His sight.; [a.] Houston, TX

JONES, MICHAEL KEITH
[b.] March 4, 1956, Atlanta, GA; [p.] Leonard Jones, Sue Jones; [ed.] Eastridge High, Kankakee, IL, University of Illinois; [occ.] System Engineer, Jet Propulsion Laboratory, Pasadena, CA; [a.] Pasadena, CA

JONES, NATASHIA M.
[b.] February 10, 1972, New Orleans, LA; [p.] Diana St. Julien and Bryan Thomas; [m.] Byron M. Jones, July 29, 1994; [ch.] Atia Renai Jones; [ed.] Benjamin Franklin Sr. High, Xavier University of Louisiana, and The University of Northern Iowa; [occ.] Currently I am still in school; [hon.] Dean's List, Graduate Scholarship to Univ. of Northern Iowa; [a.] Cedar Falls, IA

JONES, RAPHAEL B.
[b.] March 24, 1922, Valdosta, CA; [p.] Charles and Anna (Robinson) Jones; [m.] Betty Rae (Deceased), June 27, 1947; [ed.] High School - 2 yrs. college level; [occ.] Retired (Government); [memb.] Church the Refuge church of Christ (Apostolic) Phila - PA; [oth. writ.] Over 150 other poems of mostly religious and philosophical care nature; [pers.] My poetry reflect my personal philosophy along with the inspiration of the Holy Spirit of God with whom I become acquainted at the age of Heaven. And has become the center of my life.; [a.] Philadelphia, PA

JONES, WANDA
[b.] Harlan, KY; [p.] Andy and Eunice Pack; [m.] Jackson Jones; [ch.] Tim and Jason Jones; [occ.] Housewife and I spend a lot of time writing; [memb.] I S. of poets and Various others; [hon.] Various awards for my work accomplishments like employee of the year customer service awards etc.; [oth. writ.] Poems published, The Butterfly, Imagination, Where Dreams Have Been; [pers.] I absolutely love to write poetry I have always been able to sit down and write poems and songs it comes easy for me I would love to write and whole book of poetry.; [a.] Norwood, OH

JONES, WILLIAM H.
[pen.] William Henry Jones, W. H. Jones, Bill Jones; [b.] April 1, 1924, Black Diamond, WA; [p.] Helenor Jones; [m.] Barbara A. Jones, May 17, 1960; [ch.] Denise, Lynn, Williams, Robert, and Jeffrey Jones; [ed.] B.A. San Diego State Naval School of Hospital Administration of poetry; [occ.] Captain, U.S. Navy (Ret); [memb.] (1) Federal Health Care Executives Institute Alumni Assn., (2) Fleet Reserve Assn. (3) Distinguished Member - International Society of Poets; [hon.] Legion of Merit (Navy) Numerous Service Medals and awards, Graduated with honors 5 military schools, Advanced from Apprentice Seaman to Captain during Naval Career; [oth. writ.] (1) The National Library of Poetry, "Beyond the Stars", "Best Poems of 1996", "Spirit of the Age", "A Muse to Follow", (2) Sparrowgrass Poetry Forum, Inc., "Treasured Poems of 1995", "Poetic Voices of America", "Treasured Poems of America", (3) Oriville Register, Oroville, CA., "The Infamous Still in Oroville"; [pers.] I believe in personal achievement, inspiring others to fulfill their dreams, at peace with self and others, all with a sense of humor, dedication and perspective.; [a.] Lake San Marcos, CA

JORDAN, JASPER ANTHONY
[b.] April 3, 1974, Pasadena, CA; [p.] Justina Thompson and Margaret and Herman Jordan; [ed.] John Muir High, Health Careers Acad., U.S. Navy, Knoxville College, and life!; [occ.] Student; [memb.] The Human Family!; [hon.] Knoxville College honor roll.; [pers.] Tell it like it is! (Tell the children the truth.); [a.] Knoxville, TN

JORDAN, JOIE
[pen.] Joie Jordan; [b.] January 22, 1980, Atlanta; [p.] Mary and Fletcher Jordan; [ed.] Sophomore, B.E. Mays High School; [occ.] Student, Veterinarian Assistant; [memb.] Color Gaurd, ROTC program. Former member of Kawanis Club Builders.; [hon.] High Honor Roll, (7-9 grade), Veterans day Commemoration, Certificate of Commendation (ROTC); [oth. writ.] Several poems written and one notarized, poems for school activities also.; [pers.] Poetry is a state of mind that lets you open doors to thoughts trapped inside and encourage you to let your own strengths be your guide.; [a.] Atlanta, CA

KAAIALII JR., DAVID
[b.] March 24, 1950, Honolulu, HI; [p.] David Kaaialii, Puna Kaaialii; [ed.] Copperas Cove, High School, Central Texas College Texas State Technical College; [occ.] Carpenter; [oth. writ.] First letter to editor published in column in local newspaper; [pers.] Life is ultimate mortal experience for an immortal being, governed by the laws of nature-proven (physics), not yet proven (metaphysics) and Divine Providence.; [a.] Copperas Cove, TX

KABANUK, ELISHA
[pen.] Boogie; [b.] February 5, 1976, Fargo, ND; [p.] Elliott Kabanuk, Denise Kabanuk; [m.] Single; [ed.] High School Diploma in '94 and currently a sophomore at the University of North Dakota; [occ.] Student Athlete; [memb.] Student Athletic Advisory Committee, Member of St. John Lutheran Church; [hon.] Student of the Quarter in High School Senior year, most valuable player junior year in soccer and basketball, player of the game junior year championship game in basketball.; [oth. writ.] Several poems for english classes in high school and college; [pers.] Humans are the only creatures, who, when lose their way, run faster!; [a.] Fargo, ND

KAFAF, AMANDA BETH
[pen.] Amanda Beth Kafaf; [b.] June 16, 1980, Morristown, NJ; [p.] Richard and Elizabeth Kafaf; [ed.] 2nd year High School; [memb.] High School Literary Magazine Spanish Club, Chefs Club, S.A.D.D.; [hon.] Music Educators of America Piano Award, Karate Award; [oth. writ.] Prose and Poetry.; [pers.] Writing poetry is a way of releasing my emotions and feelings. Most of my poetry is an expression of what's happening in my life at that time.; [a.] Randolph, NJ

KALOSS, VICTORIA
[b.] September 28, 1961, Red Bank, NJ; [p.] Dr. William A. Kaloss, Hilda A. Kaloss; [ed.] Monmouth University, Rutgers University-Graduate School of Social Work; [occ.] Social Worker; [memb.] American Federation of Teachers; [hon.] Who's Who Among Students in American Universities and Colleges; [oth. writ.] Poetry/Children's Stories/Short Stories; [pers.] I write from the heart as my spirit guides me through the ebb and flow of life.; [a.] Red Bank, NJ

KAMINSKI, BONNIE J.
[pen.] Bonnie Seefeldt Kaminski; [b.] February 24, 1950, WI; [p.] Lawrence and Adeline Seefeldt; [m.] Donald L. Kaminski, October 3, 1970; [ch.] Corre and Tirsa; [ed.] Lena High School (68), NWTC (84); [occ.] Licensed practical nurse; [hon.] Poem "Time" in a muse to follow. The National Library of Poetry, Mis for moments bought by Blue Mountains Arts is in its and printing. They own poem, but my name Bonnie Seefeldt Kaminski, son card as the Author; [oth. writ.] Freedom Prayer, Colors of Beauty to hide the sorrow for rainbow house collection of poems in essentials of mental health care. Planning and Interventions 1986, WB Saunders CO; [pers.] When God gives you a gift. With his help you use it for good. Sometimes you give it away as I do with my give away poem to help others deal with the loss of a loved one; [a.] Coleman, WI

KAMINSKI, CHESTER
[b.] September 11, 1951, Poland; [p.] Wladyslaw and Stanislawa Kaminski; [m.] Mary, July 6, 1974; [ch.] Bernadette, Matthew and Joey; [ed.] High School Rezin Orr Chicago IL; [occ.] Machinist at Commercial Machine Services; [memb.] Polish National Alliance Lodge 3246 St. Margaret Mary Cath. Church; [hon.] U.S. Army Honorable Discharge IL, National Guard Honorable Discharge

Certificate of Achievement 1st Infantry Division, The Big Red One; [oth. writ.] "Prolife Prochoice" in *Between the Raindrops*, "Trial of the century" *Best Poems of 1996* Oh! No! Community poems for the lost seven in Fox River Grove; [pers.] Tell the way it is; [a.] Algonquin, IL

KAMINSKY, DANIEL
[b.] November 19, 1971, Anaheim, CA; [p.] Isabelle and Eric B. Kaminsky; [ed.] Trabuco Hills High School, California State Polytechnic University at Pomona, University of San Diego Law School (currently); [occ.] Law Student; [oth. writ.] None others published.; [pers.] It is not the words that are truly moving, but rather the human events that caused the inspiration.; [a.] San Diego, CA

KAMMER, NANCY C.
[b.] July 12, 1962, Evergreen Park, IL; [p.] Robert J. Savage and Margaret J. Savage; [m.] James M. Kammer, Jr., May 20, 1983; [ch.] Ryan Patrick, Colin James, Daniel Robert, Sean Francis; [ed.] Elizabeth Seton High School, Illinois Benedictine College, Southwest School of Business; [occ.] Homemaker; [memb.] St. Dennis Church; [oth. writ.] Published Poetry: The Road to Life, The Wow; [pers.] Believe in yourself, believe in life and believe in love. A little respect, honesty, patience, understanding, generosity and love goes a long way.; [a.] Lockport, IL

KAUFFMAN, ETHEL C.
[b.] April 6, 1921, Berns, KS; [p.] Orville and Leota Hoover (Deceased); [m.] Ivan O. Kauffman, January 5, 1946; [ch.] Three girls and one boy; [ed.] High School; [occ.] Retired; [oth. writ.] I have written mostly religious poems since, 1974. Some titles are The Cross, Walking on the Water, A Talk with Jesus, He covers us with his hands, many, many more.; [pers.] I read my poems at Nursing homes and in Church and use them to help people to know Jesus love.; [a.] Zephyrhills, FL

KAVANAGH, CAROLYN MARGARET
[b.] September 16, 1964, Worcester, MA; [p.] Joseph W. Kavanagh, Eleanor Harris; [ed.] California State University, Nothridge, CA; [occ.] Account Executive, Howroyd Wright, Inc.; [memb.] Accounting Association; [hon.] California Scholarship Federation, United Way Bronze Award, Dean's List; [oth. writ.] "The Window", a short story.; [pers.] The greatest influences on my writing style have been Dorothy Parker and James Joyce. I try to convey the high and low triumphs of the human spirit in my work.; [a.] Glendale, CA

KEARSE, TATINA ELIZABETH
[pen.] Tee-Tee; [b.] July 19, 1974, Long Branch, NJ; [p.] Johnnie Mae Kearse; [ed.] Graduated from Sweetwater Union High School; [pers.] I would just like to give thanks to my mom and my very best friend for 5 years Chad Clebert Hays. Thank you for all of your help and support.; [a.] Chula Vista, CA

KEEL, BARBARA HAGANS
[b.] July 28, Opelika, AL; [p.] Albert C. Hagans and Helen Hughes Hagans; [m.] Kenneth S. Lunsford, December 31, 1992; [ch.] Jason L. Keel, Victoria K. Keel, Brody Hagan Keel, Ciarra Jade Keel and 3 stepson - Guy, Tom, and Pat Lunsford; [ed.] Opelka High School, Auburn University, Auburn, AL; [occ.] Professional Wildlife Artist, Author of Children's Books; [hon.] 1st Woman in history to paint a 1st of State Duck Stamp, Al, 1979 - 1st place winner at 1st International Wildlife Art Exhibit; [oth. writ.] "George, Sam and Harry", "Furby the Monster Eater", "Arnold is a Werewolf, Run! Run!", "Grandma May's Ghost", Co-Authored with daughter Ciarra, "Doorway to Forever", "Tori's Decision"; [pers.] My children and my relationships with them have always been an inspiration to me both in my writing and to my very existence.; [a.] Auburn, AL

KEELE, CHRISTY M.
[b.] February 8, 1979, Riverton, WY; [p.] Raymond and Sheryl Keele; [ed.] Junior (11th grade) at kelly Walsh High School Casper WY; [occ.] Student; [memb.] Upward Bound; [hon.] Second Honor Roll; [a.] Evansville, WY

KEGEBEIN, CRYSTAL
[b.] April 30, 1982, Tift County Hospital; [p.] Linda Kegebein and Donald Kegebein; [ed.] G. O. Bailey Elementary School, J.T. Reddick, Middle School, and Tift County Junior High School; [occ.] Y-Club, Beta Club, Science Club, Student Council and Tift County Junior High School Band; [hon.] Writing Fair Contest winner, bandsmen of the year 1995, Honor Court, "superior" award at "Solo and Ensemble" competition, and all district participant (for band); [pers.] I strive to reflect the wonderful enjoyment of the arts in my poetry.; [a.] Tifton, GA

KELLIS, HILDA
[b.] February 28, 1924, Weiser, ID; [p.] William Oliver and Ruby G. Turnidge; [m.] Marvin L. Kellis (Deceased), March 9, 1947; [ch.] Four adopted children, 13 grands and 15 great-grands; [ed.] Grade School and High School at Weiser, ID, Graduated from Northwestern Business College, Spokane, WA, writing classes at Whitworth College and Spokane Falls Com. Col., Spokane; [occ.] Unity Minister; [hon.] Appreciation and praise from many, many people whose lives seem to be touched by the words that appear at the end of my pen.; [oth. writ.] Poems published in Unity Daily Word, Unity Magazine and the former Weekly Unity. Over 40 years poems and articles in our local church pub. Poems published in the Spokane Daily Chronicle, the Spokesman-Review, Spokane, also newspapers in surrounding areas.; [pers.] I am most grateful for the gift of writing and the ability to share with people "where they live." I believe that the all-loving goodness of God transcends all matter and matters. If conveying this personal truth to others thru my poetry, fans a flame of awareness in them, then I am doubly grateful. What blesses one blesses all!; [a.] Spokane, WA

KELLY, ALBERT JAMES
[pen.] B. C. Sunset; [b.] March 12, 1974, Kingston, PA; [p.] Patricia Ann Kelly; [ch.] Chris and Jeff Kelly; [ed.] Middletown Area High School, Kutztown University; [occ.] Senior Student at KU, Majoring in Secondary Ed (English); [oth. writ.] Published in several Pennsylvania Magazines (The Pennsylvania Review), also recognized in a few Midwest Publications recently published a Fantasy Novella: The Spool of Thread Wept.; [pers.] Something happened after I built my own universe: I had to prove that my world co-exists with the world we inhabit. I accepted this responsibility with pleasure.; [a.] Middletown, PA

KELLY, GREGORY
[pen.] Gregg Kelly; [b.] June 17, 1951, Memphis, TN; [p.] Lon and Mary Kelly; [m.] Leona Kelly, October 21, 1994; [ch.] Latoria, Gregory Juan, Gee Martel and Sherrell; [ed.] 12th grade; [occ.] Warehouse manager for (Fleming, Furn Co.); [memb.] Norris Rd, Church of Christ; [hon.] Employee of the year, for 1985 and 1986 I'm a member of the President's Club of Fleming Furn, for being a 10 year employee.; [oth. writ.] I write spiritual poems, for people that are trying to find God. And I also write love poems to my wife.; [pers.] I live only to serve and do the will of God in everything I do. And to bring the lost to Christ and His Church.; [a.] Memphis, TN

KELLY, WILLIAM R.
[b.] May 18, 1956, Tacoma, WA; [p.] Mrs Phillip Wendt and Ted L. Kelley; [m.] Divorced; [ch.] Wesley Lynn Goodall, Trever Dylan Kelly, Candice Elaine West and Sammantha Ann Kelly; [ed.] Stadium High School Tacoma Wash. "74"; [occ.] Rec Supervision Boys and Girls Club Kenai, AK; [memb.] Si-Fi Book Club; [oth. writ.] Song Writer; [pers.] Don't give up love the children peace.

KELONE, DIANE
[pen.] Samantha Rose; [b.] March 12, 1958, Corpus Christi, TX; [p.] Al Rankin and Flo Rankin; [m.] Artie Kelone, April 9, 1982; [ed.] Woodsboro High, Southwest Texas State University; [occ.] Accountant; [memb.] Save the Manatee Club, Woodmen of the World Society; [pers.] One can choose to see beauty in almost anything.; [a.] Port Neches, TX

KELSEY, JASON M.
[b.] January 4, 1978, Pennsylvania; [p.] Ken and Marie Kelsey; [ed.] Deland High School; [occ.] Church's Chicken; [pers.] When you look at someone, look past the color of their skin and see who they really are. And help others to do the same. Stop racism, erase the color line!; [a.] Deland, FL

KENT, HOPE
[b.] December 26, 1908, Sandusky County, OH; [p.] James B. Hathaway and Hazel Hathaway; [m.] Virgil F. Kent, June 10, 1934; [ch.] Karen Elizabeth, Alan Hathaway Kent, Shirer; [ed.] 3 yr. M.S. N.C. Yr Silanti, Michigan after High School Monroe Michigan 1926; [occ.] Retired; [pers.] Taught grade school Monroe, Michigan; [a.] Defiance, OH

KEPHART, GRACE A.
[b.] June 23, 1925, Lyons, KS; [p.] Arval and Alice Baldwin; [m.] Thomas W. Kephart, April 14, 1945; [ch.] Gary Kephart and Lyn Maish; [ed.] High School; [occ.] Retired; [oth. writ.] Many poems working on a book; [pers.] Many of my works are based on memories from childhood.

KERSELL, JOYCE
[pen.] Joyce Pairett; [b.] January 14, 1954, San Antonio, TX; [p.] Charles M. Pairett and Bernice Pairett; [m.] Lee F. Kersell Jr., January 27, 1971; [ch.] Kirsten J. Kersell, Lee F. Kersell III; [ed.] Roosevelt High; [occ.] Artist, Painter; [oth. writ.] I've written some other poems. They aren't published yet.; [pers.] Try to do the things you love.; [a.] San Antonio, TX

KETHLEY, DIXIE LEE LENE
[b.] November 22, 1942, Port Arthur, TX; [p.] Wilfred and Orie Lene; [m.] Jack L. Kethley, July 17, 1964; [ch.] Jef and Jeremy; [ed.] B.S. in Education (Elem.), Masters in Edu. Supervision; [occ.] Classroom teacher 4th grade; [memb.] ATPE, TSTA, PTA, (life member), Faith UMC, Amer. Bible Society, (Edu. Chairman - Faith UMC) BSA Committee member; [hon.] Teacher of year - 1986, Who's Who in America's Teachers, Silver Beaver in BSA.; [oth. writ.] Short stories; [pers.] My desire is to write poems and stories that reflect God's love.; [a.] Beaumont, TX

KETTERER, WENDY LEE
[pen.] Wendy Lee Ketterer; [b.] October 14, 1968, Chicago, IL; [p.] LeRoy and Lois Ketterer; [m.] Paul Vincent, June 14, 1992; [ch.] Cheyenne Lee Vincent; [ed.] Barron G. Collier High School; [pers.] Find beauty in all that you see, find something to respect in all whom you meet, be kind to all living things, it will come back to you ten-fold. Life is too short, don't observe...participate!; [a.] Tampa, FL

KIA, RACHEL
[b.] October 14, 1975, Boulder, CO; [p.] Janie

Sprayberry and Larry Roach; [m.] Norman Kia, March 21, 1992; [ch.] Kyle; [ed.] Homemaker; [pers.] Writing is my outlet. It is the best form of communication to express my feelings.; [a.] Portales, NM

KICENSKI, MICHAEL
[b.] September 20, 1969, Lancaster, CA; [pers.] This poem was inspired by and is dedicated to Cheryl Lynn Albrecht. The only woman I ever really loved. Cher, your a star in the face of the night sky and these will always be a piece of me that will love you.; [a.] Santa Monica, CA

KILDOW, NANCY L.
[b.] January 11, 1940, PA; [p.] Geo. Mulhorn, Jennie Mulhorn; [m.] Raymond N. Kildow Jr., June 19, 1960; [ch.] Richard, Michael, Kimberly; [ed.] Catalina High School, Tucson, AZ; [occ.] Homemaker; [pers.] This poem was written in 1957 by me and about wonderful Sunday evenings spent with a youth fellowship and the man I have been married to for 35 yrs.; [a.] Bullhead City, AZ

KILE, DALPHNE MAE
[pen.] Dolly; [b.] May 25, 1952, Burley, ID; [p.] Mildred Bennett and Luther Bennett; [m.] Widowed (November 18, 1993), May 26, 1975; [ch.] Three; [ed.] Some College - Gen Ed.; [oth. writ.] None published.; [pers.] I have written several short stories and poems. I hope to write an autobiography.; [a.] Salem, OR

KIMBLE, BRIDGETT A. C.
[m.] William Kimble; [ch.] Monticue-15, Brittany-10, Malik-5; [ed.] Holds a C.D.A. (Child Development Associatship) and is a continuing student attending local writers' workshops and seminars; [occ.] Home school teacher; [memb.] Black Book Writers Network (Denver, CO) Third World Poets' Coolition, "I Can Do It" publishing Group; [oth. writ.] Currently working on a collection of poetry entitled, "Black, In Little Pieces"

KING, KATHLEEN A.
[b.] April 23, 1945, Granite Falls, MN; [p.] Joseph A. Riley, Viola E. Riley; [m.] Jerome R. King, February 19, 1977; [ch.] MaRyia Lynn; [oth. writ.] Several poems and thoughts have been written for family members and own personal enjoyment.; [pers.] To put on paper what's deep in my heart, has been a soothing medicine to me and an enjoyment to others.; [a.] Eden Praire, MN

KING, MATTHEW
[b.] July 24, 1981, Fairfield, IL; [p.] Randy and Vickie King; [ed.] Freshman at Fairfield Community High School; [occ.] Student; [memb.] Math Club, Spanish Club, Scholastic Bowl Team, Fairfield Country Club; [hon.] American Legion Award; [a.] Fairfield, IL

KIOSKI, LOUISE DEVINE
[pen.] Weasy; [b.] July 20, 1918, New Brighton, MN; [p.] William Henry Devine, Otillia Schmalzbuer; [m.] Bernard Thomas Kioski (Deceased June 21, 1995, June 23, 1945; [ch.] James (6-22-1946), Teresa Elaine, Kioski Kennedy (1-26-1949), Louise Anne Kioski (3-30-1954); [ed.] District 18 School, Rural Ramsey County 8 years, Murray Jr. High School, St. Paul, MN 1 year, John Marshall High School Mpls. MN. 3 years, BS Univ. of WI Stevens Point, WI Jan. 1964, MS Stout State Univ.; [occ.] Menomonie, WI, 1969, 1995-Golfer, Author, Investment Doubler.; [memb.] AZ Women's Golf Assn.; [hon.] 3rd place, A Point in Space, Catholic Daughter's of America, 1964. Journalism Fellowship Award, 1966.; [oth. writ.] The Sleeper, Sept. 1962; Who Paws There, June 1962; The Hunt, Sept. 1962; Columns: Louise Adds, 1950, "Book Tracks to the Library, 1962; [pers.] Be true to yourself.

KIRBY, VIRGINIA
[b.] July 1, 1941, New Bedford, MA; [p.] William and Beatrice Kirby; [m.] Divorced; [ch.] Michael J. Gambell; [ed.] New Bedford High, Kinyon School; [occ.] Unemployed on disability; [oth. writ.] "The Song in My Heart", unpublished collection of 25 religious poems, misc. unpublished poems.; [pers.] I just love the Lord - and life - and I am able to express myself poetically thanks to His gifts to me.; [a.] Anaheim, CA

KIRSCHENMANN, COURTNEY
[b.] September 14, 1976, Bakersfield, CA; [p.] Tim and Christine Kirschenmann; [ed.] Community Christian H.S., Bakersfield College, California State University; [occ.] Secretary; [memb.] Children International, International Society of Poets; [pers.] We all have something we believe in strongly. For me, it is my faith. My savior has gotten me through many difficult times. Without him I would have no hope or inner peace.; [a.] Bakersfield, CA

KLEIN, SHAWN
[pen.] Doc; [b.] September 12, 1980, CT; [p.] Denise Panzera Klein and Larry P. Klein; [ed.] Fishburne Military School; [occ.] Student; [memb.] JROTC, Wrestling team; [hon.] Many JROTC Ribbons, and Medals; [oth. writ.] Many untitled poems; [pers.] I would like to say "Thank you" to the beautiful Shannon Lee Woodford for inspiring all my poems.; [a.] Killingworth, CT

KLINE, SUSAN L.
[b.] May 20, 1961, Fort Laud, FL; [p.] Art and Nadean Royal; [m.] Paul Kline; [ch.] Steven Tucker; [ed.] Retired Medical Assistant Hospice Care giver; [occ.] Homemaker; [memb.] National Multiple Sclerosis Society, National Multiple Sclerosis Association Of America, International Society Of Poets. (New Member); [hon.] Editors Choice Award; [oth. writ.] "Paid In Full" "The Land Of The Free" and Why Don't We Care? 4 anthologies, 3 sound of poetry tapes; [a.] Tamarac, FL

KLUGMAN, DEBORAH
[b.] June 17, 1950, Indianapolis, IN; [p.] Ward and Opal Wolfe; [m.] Douglas Klugman, July 9, 1993; [ch.] Son - William Goldman III, stepson - Bryan Klugman; [occ.] Dental Asst. Washougal, WA; [pers.] I'm greatly influenced by the heartache in mankind. I hope reading my words will help others to know they are not alone in life's experiences; [a.] Vancouver, WA

KNITTEL, AUGUST
[pen.] Toby King; [b.] August 24, 1937, Oxnard, CA; [p.] Anton and Rosa; [m.] Bonnie Joyce, November 27, 1993; [ch.] Angela, Anton, Alyssa and Adena; [ed.] Moorpark Memorial Union H.S. Ventura junior College University of California and Davis B.S. in Animal Husbandry; [occ.] Farmer - Cattle Rancher; [memb.] Calif. Cattlemens Assoc. National Cattlemens Assoc.; [hon.] Being married to Bonnie and having four fantastic children; [oth. writ.] Scientific and technical research papers, reports and studies for major Agric. Companies also some poems and articles published in local newspapers; [pers.] I enjoy writing about real life farm and ranch experiences as well as animal and nature studies. I would like to explain the many positive aspects and products of ranch life to our city neighbors; [a.] Auberry, CA

KNOLL, DORIS JEAN
[b.] May 14, 1934, Salida, CO; [p.] Russell Peck, Leone Peck (Deceased); [m.] Robert Eugene Knoll (Deceased), February 12, 1954; [ch.] Deborah Denise, Robin Irene, Robert Scott, Dawn Renee, Bobbi Jean; [ed.] Salida High School, 3 semester in Oil Painting, Garden City Community College Outreach Program, Kansas; [occ.] Retired, ranching; [memb.] Prairie Winds Art Association Charter member, Kansas, WMU Mt. Zion Church, Reach to Recovery Volunteer, Member of two cancer support groups; [hon.] Ranked third in H. S. Graduation class, National Honor Society; [oth. writ.] Wrote first poetry April 1995; [pers.] I give all the glory to the honor of my Lord Jesus Christ Who gave me this gift.; [a.] Washburn, MO

KOCH, BRENDA S.
[b.] September 2, 1951, Charleston, WV; [p.] Joseph and Atha Walker; [m.] Divorced; [ch.] Kevin Kenneth, Shane David; [ed.] South Charleston High, W. Va. State University; [oth. writ.] Songs, short stories, holiday and love poems published in Local Newspaper.; [pers.] Poetry is an idea that flows gently from the deepest reaches of the soul. My dream is to use the gift that God gave me.; [a.] Saint Albans, WV

KOCH, CARLA MARIA HEINRICH
[pen.] Sunshine; [b.] February 10, 1963, Beloit, WI; [p.] Naomi and Paul Heinrich; [m.] Larry Koch, November 25, 1995; [ch.] 4 Daughters, 3 Stepdaughters; [ed.] I went to Beloit Wisc schools my whole life; [occ.] Roofer; [memb.] Our Saviors Lutheran Church; [hon.] At church and my children schools and in high school; [oth. writ.] Dreams, The Branches of the Weeping Willow Tree, Friends, and lots more poems; [pers.] This poem is dedicated to my husband for being the greatest person in the world and being my best friend when I need one!; [a.] Beloit, WI

KOCH, MRS. ELAINE
[pen.] Elaine Koch; [b.] June 5, 1947, St. Louis, MO; [p.] Robert Simpson Nye and Dorothy Foley; [m.] David T. Koch, September 29, 1972; [ch.] Kurt Koch; [ed.] Ass. in Comm. Art., Mo. Board Nursing, L.P.N.; [occ.] Retired Hospital Treatment - Med/Surg L.P.N.) - Housewife and Mother; [memb.] Com. Ch. Boy Scout Troop 450, Church goes of St. Davids Church in Arnold, Mo.; [hon.] Once got printed in Scouting "Duffle Bag" month paper; [oth. writ.] Scouting printed. I have other poems, but none of them became published.; [pers.] I try to listen to world around me, and put it in poetry. Poetry is the spice of living.; [a.] Arnold, MO

KOERNER, JANET DIANNE
[pen.] Jannette Dianne Murphy; [b.] May 30, 1943, Los Angeles, CA; [p.] James Murphy, Ernestine Read; [m.] Robert Howard Koerner, December 26, 1964; [ch.] Robert N. Carl, James and Terry; [ed.] Birmingham High School Kingsborough Community College; [occ.] Assistant Director, Small Fry Cottage, Brooklyn, NY; [memb.] Boy Scouts of America, National Association for the Education of Young Children, KCC Early Childhood Club, KCC Returning Adults Club; [hon.] Dean's List, B.S.A. District Award of Merit, B.S.A. Training Awards, N.Y. City Council Citation, B.S.A. Woodbadge Beads (Boy Scout and Cub Scout Program); [oth. writ.] Several articles published in college newspaper; [pers.] I would like to know that I made a difference in the lives of young people that I introduced them to the "Special Person" within themselves.; [a.] Brooklyn, NY

KOHLMAN, CLEO C.
[pen.] Cleo C. Kohlman; [b.] New Orleans; [p.] Theodore Carter and Lillian Carter (both deceased); [m.] Louis F. Kohlman (Deceased), October 4, 1954; [ed.] B.A. Degree; [occ.] Field of Arts; [memb.] Adler Planetarium Member, Meta Center, Chicago Alumni Association, International Society of Poets; [hon.] Phi Theta Kappa; [oth. writ.] A collection of poems written by myself gathered in book form (book has not been published); [pers.] I have

to thank, my mother, for my inspiration as a poet. She was an unpublished writer of poetry. 1st Place Award achieved from a Sculpture University. This sculpture is recorded in the Library of Congress and his name is Alpha.; [a.] Chicago, IL

KOHLSTRAND, NORMAN C.
[pen.] Encie Kaye; [b.] April 15, 1946, Detroit, MI; [m.] Kathleen, May 4, 1968; [ch.] John, Kelly and Michael; [ed.] Schoolcraft College, A.A.S., Madonna University, B.S. (Honors), Detroit College of Law, J.D. cum laude; [occ.] Attorney at Law; [a.] New Boston

KOONTZ, DANIEL
[pen.] Danny K.; [b.] January 26, 1961, Bellflower, CA; [p.] Leonard Koontz and Carol Koontz; [ed.] Cleveland Elementary Haskell Jr. High Cerritos High School, Long Beach City College; [occ.] Song writer, composer, certified massage Therapist; [memb.] Friends of the Ocean (Dolphin), World Wildlife Fund (Tigers); [oth. writ.] Poem titled "Come" in the release of *A Muse To Follow* hard copy book by National Library of Poetry; [pers.] "To be alive on Earth and to be creative is an 'Expression of Human Rights'".; [a.] Cerritos, CA

KORRINHIZER, EDMOND
[pen.] Edmond Korrinhizer; [b.] October 5, 1933, Saint Louis, MO; [p.] Lillian and Joseph Korrinhizer; [ed.] Arlington School Samuel Cupples School; [occ.] Retired Formerly Aeronautical Chart and Info. Center-Vending Maching Business, Book and Record Business, Printing Business, Owned outright my own Business; [pers.] I love american like nobody ever. I am a third generation american and I want to bless our wonderful country. Have a wonderful everything, always, america God Bless; [a.] Chesterfield, MO

KOSS, WILLIAM S.
[pen.] "Shortfellow"; [b.] May 19, 1927, Glendale, CA; [p.] Otto Koss, Ida Koss; [m.] Mildred G. Koss, November 23, 1985; [ed.] Jordan High Long Beach City College; [occ.] Retired 43 1/2 yrs. at Rockwell International; [memb.] American Bowling Congress; [hon.] Outstanding performance-Rockwell International; [oth. writ.] Joy of the Season, The Greatest Mother, Daylight Confusion Time; [pers.] The English had "Long Fellow" thought America should have "Shortfellow".; [a.] Victorville, CA

KOSTOULAKOS, STEPHEN J.
[b.] August 29, 1921, Dracut, MA; [p.] Demetrius and Mary Kostoulakos; [m.] Irene, December 22, 1946; [ch.] Marcia and Stephanie; [ed.] Dracut High School Bentley College; [occ.] Retired; [memb.] AARP Rotary; [oth. writ.] I write many poems for birthdays, Anniversaries and other special occasions I have a louse leaf folder full of them and many happy people who received them.; [pers.] The poem I sent in "Without A Radio And No Television" is just a part of some 200 verses of a poem I wrote about my family titled "Someone Up There Loves Us" showing one family's struggle to survive through poverty without public assistance; [a.] Nashua, NH

KOVACH, KATHLEEN MCNEIL
[pen.] Kathleen McNeil; [b.] August 14, 1952, Pittsfield, MA; [p.] William McNeil, Jean McNeil; [m.] David William Kovach, June 10, 1995; [ch.] Joseph and Tara; [ed.] Adams Memorial, H.S., Berkshire Community College Westfield State College California State University, Northridge; [occ.] Homemaker, sales; [memb.] Autism Society of America Friends of the Civic Arts Plaza Democratic Association PTA; [hon.] Dean's List 1989 CSUN; [oth. writ.] Poetry and entertainment reviews unpublished; [pers.] I try to capture experience through heart-felt emotion. I believe that good writing is meant to inspire and illuminate, because it comes from the soul. Emily Dickinson, Wordsworth, Shelley; [a.] Camarillo, CA

KOVACH, KATHY L.
[b.] May 24, 1956, Toledo, OH; [p.] Howard and Esther Shue; [m.] Ernest S. Kovach Jr., January 3, 1989; [ch.] Kari A. Everett; [ed.] Rossford High School graduate, Penta County Vocational School; [occ.] Managing Beautician for 21 years.; [oth. writ.] Poem published in local newspaper (The Toledo Blade).; [pers.] Everything in life around me, inspires me to write.; [a.] Rossford, OH

KRACHT, SANDY K.
[b.] January 24, 1967, Omaha, NE; [p.] Donald Burns, Sylvia Burns; [m.] James D. Kracht, August 5, 1995; [ch.] James, Sierra, Justin, Candi, Jayden; [ed.] Storm Lake Senior High School in Storm Lake, IA and Iowa Central Community College; [occ.] Housewife, Tupperware Sales Consultant; [oth. writ.] I have writing poems for other members of my family, though this is my first time to be published.; [pers.] I find that my thoughts are best expressed when I put pen to paper.; [a.] Peterson, IA

KRAFFT, GENEVIEVE A.
[b.] December 2, 1910, West Braitore, CO; [p.] Mr and Mrs Lucius Mallehan (Deceased); [m.] James B. Krafft (Deceased) April 26, 1931; [ch.] 10 - 1 Living; [ed.] Grade School 9th; [occ.] Am a widow, am a quilter, pianist at church; [memb.] Member MP. Church Womens home makers; [hon.] Nothing only a life of work; [oth. writ.] A few short stories at times our club wrote a few sacred song's etc. I was to busy to with much I was a self made musician piano, organ, guitar, etc.; [pers.] I worked help raise my family help my husband I did the work help of my little boys husband worked away he was a timber man. At that time our address was a local caress.; [a.] Sutton, WV

KRAFT, MARLON
[b.] July 7, 1926, Bellerose, WY; [p.] Margaret and Michael Bungert; [m.] Edward Kraft (Deceased), September 1, 1946; [ch.] Robert, James, John Kraft, Janet Contento; [ed.] Sewanhaka High School L.I. Class of 1944; [memb.] Ladies Aux VFW Albany, N.Y. 6776 Aux - American Legion Post 104 Pinellas Park, FL. Aux - Amvets - Post 7467 Pinellas Pk, FL.; [hon.] Aux. President VFW 1979-1980; [oth. writ.] WWII and Desert Storm poems - never submitted. Letters to editors - Pub. "To Presidents, Congressmen, Mayor Koch (N.Y.), Atty. Generals, etc.; [pers.] Mostly write situation poems, articles and letters. I have strong feelings about a lot of things going on in the world today.; [a.] Pinellas Park, FL

KRAVETZ, JUSTIN G.
[pen.] J. J. LeBlanc; [b.] August 4, 1967, New York City, NY; [p.] David Kravetz, Selma Kravetz; [ed.] Clarkstown H.S. North, B.A. - Alfred University - May 1989, M.S.Ed. - Iowa College - May 1992, M.S.-S.A.S. - City College (current); [occ.] Social Studies Teacher, The Mirabal Sisters Intermediate School, New York City, NY; [memb.] UFT, ASCD, The Concord Coalition, Rockland Center for Holocaust Studies, Friends of Lincoln Center; [hon.] Induction into Phi Delta Kappa - a professional education fraternity; [oth. writ.] Reviews/critiques of various N.Y.C. area nightclubs published in a variety of N.Y.C. area nightlife publications.; [pers.] I hope the time I have spent here has helped, in some way, to make the world a better place.; [a.] New York, NY

KRIVANEK III, LOUIS W.
[pen.] L. W. Krivanek; [b.] November 7, 1970, Mustang, OK; [m.] Lacey Krivanek, May 19, 1995; [ed.] B.S. in Mathematics University of Oklahoma; [occ.] Math Teacher and Football Coach; [memb.] Kappa Sigma Fraternity, Mustang Assembly of God Oklahoma Coaches Assoc.; [hon.] OU Football Letterman, OU Dean's List and President's List, and National Honor Society.; [a.] Oklahoma City, OK

KRUER, MATTHEW
[b.] April 2, 1981, Bethpage, NY; [p.] Rick Kruer Eileen Kruer; [ed.] High School Student - Mountain View High School; [occ.] Student; [hon.] Honor Roll; [pers.] "If you bring forth what is inside you, what you bring forth will save you. If you do not bring forth what is inside you, what you do not bring forth will destroy you." Jesus Christ; [a.] Mesa, AZ

KRUSE, JENNIFER
[b.] July 5, 1982, San Diego; [p.] Charles and Elise Kruse; [ed.] I'm in eighth grade at Pensacola Christian Academy.; [occ.] Secretary for my Dad's church; [memb.] I'm in the 4-4 Club.; [pers.] "With God all things are possible." Matthew 19:26; [a.] Westminster, CA

KUBASZAK, PAUL
[b.] April 10, 1950, Chicago; [p.] Harry and Josephine Kubaszak; [m.] Julie, April 24, 1970; [ch.] Son Christopher; [ed.] High Sch. at T.F. North, in Calumet City - 4 yrs Pipefitter Apprenticeship; [occ.] Maint. Foreman at Bethlehem Steel, Burnsharbor; [memb.] St. Peter's Lutheran Church, Member of International Society of Poets; [oth. writ.] God's Best in "Best New Poems" (Poet's Guild) - 3 others in National Library of Poetry, Anthologies, including "Best of 1996" Backyard Window"; [pers.] Be careful what you pray for, you may get it.; [a.] Portage, IN

KUEHN, CHRIS EDWARD
[b.] October 4, 1955, Houston, TX; [p.] Edward Charles Kuehn, Alice Joy Kuehn; [ed.] Glendale High School, Glendale, Ca., U.S. Coast Guard Training Center, Cape May, New Jersey, Grays Harbor Comm. College, Aberdeen, Wa., South Seattle Comm. College, Seattle, Wa., Green River Comm. College, Auburn, Wa.; [occ.] Flight Test Expedite Support for the Boeing Co.; [memb.] YMCA, National Geographic Society, Renton Athletic Club, NAUI (National Assoc. of Underwater Instructors); [hon.] Marksmanship Medal for Expert Rating with M16 Rifle at Coast Guard Training Facility in Cape May, New Jersey.; [pers.] Do at least one good deed each day for another person, including strangers, to make their day much better. It makes the world a better place, you feel good about yourself and, practiced enough, it can be contagious.; [a.] Everett, WA

KUNZ, HEIDI
[b.] July 15, 1977, Mc Henry, IL; [p.] Albert Kunz, Anita Kunz; [ed.] Wauconda High Sam Houston State University; [occ.] Student at SHSU (Freshman); [memb.] 4-H; [pers.] If a picture is worth a thousand words, does that make talk cheap.; [a.] McHenry, IL

KUUMBA, UMOJA
[pen.] Umoja; [b.] September 5, 1953, Trinidad; [p.] Joan Jerome, Joseph Jerome; [occ.] Leather Craftsman, Self-employed; [oth. writ.] A-Question, Feelings, Mother, Beauty, Unity is Strength, etc.

LACEFIELD, GEORGIA
[pen.] Ann Fields; [b.] March 10, 1958, Davenport, IA; [p.] Hardin Lacefield (deceased); [ch.] Tracey, Timothy, Felishia, Victor, Jeffrey; [ed.] Sangamon State, Illinois Central College; [occ.] Credit Manager; [hon.] Cover Girl for my High Schools Vocational Training Program 1974-1975 Booklet, Modeling; [oth. writ.] Many poems and short biographical

tories yet to be published.; [pers.] "Life on earth is a journey...Only those who have direction from within can actually "obtain" rest at the end of life's journey."; [a.] Charlotte, NC

LACHER, ANNA S.
[b.] August 1, 1947, Montreal PQ, Canada; [p.] Walter Herton Schaellkopf and Eleanor Flood Schaellkopf; [m.] W. Scott Lacher, December 16, 1972; [ch.] David Flood and Peter Graham; [ed.] National Cathedral School, Helten-Arms School, Western High School, Hiram College, University of South Carolina - B.A. History; [memb.] Served for years on board of Historic Aiken Foundation; [hon.] My photographs have been exhibited in local gallery; [a.] Aiken, SC

LAIB, BARIZA
[b.] April 10, 1947, Constantine, Algeria; [p.] Salah Laib, Rabia Ounas; [ch.] Lamia, Aida; [ed.] University, Constantine, Algeria, Cartography, Geomorphology, remote-sensing Environment; [oth. writ.] The branch in selected shorts all write! Investigation on inhabitat, North Algeria, study on the desertification around Chott Ech Chergui, Algeria.; [pers.] No one deserved to be killed because of his appearance or believes. We have to struggle to maintain our differences which are intelligence and beauty in this world. Any culture has to survive. If uniformity were imposed it would be the end of humankind and we would face the worst form of slavery. For the sake of the darkness, and for the peace.; [a.] New York, NY

LALA, EULA E.
[b.] July 16; [ed.] High School Graduate; [occ.] Retired Elderly Homemaker; [memb.] Church Bywater, A Neighborhood Assn and Sr. Center for over 18 years; [oth. writ.] My Mudbug in *Edge of Twilight*, Editor's Choice Award No. 3 1994, Sent In My Private in 95, Sent in B.C. said to be wonderful verse in 95; [pers.] Do unto others as ye'd have do onto others" The Golden Rule I always true to help others and pray for all. Including you all.; [a.] New Orleans, LA

LAMB, BROOK
[b.] August 6, 1980, Nampa, ID; [p.] Jim Lamb and Tina Szurgot; [ed.] Passed GED; [occ.] Student; [pers.] As a student, teachers are very important to me. I believe that we all contribute to the curriculum of life, but we each give something different.; [a.] Queen Creek, AZ

LAMBERT, STEPHANIE NICOLE
[pen.] Nicole Whytower; [b.] June 18, 1979, Iowa City, IA; [p.] Mike and Debbie Lambert; [ed.] High School and hopefully to college; [hon.] Creativity Award; [oth. writ.] None of my poems have ever been publicly noted.; [pers.] My love for poetry is more than any physical loves. Poetry is apart of how I express myself.; [a.] Las Vegas, NV

LAMOTHE, DAVID A.
[b.] August 8, 1971, Woodsocket, RI; [p.] Arthur and Kathy Lamothe; [ed.] 12 Years of Schooling (K-12) Burrillville High School - Graduated 1989; [occ.] US Navy - Enlisted in 1989; [hon.] Veteran of the Persian Gulf War. Was stationed on the USS Seattle which is a ammunition, explosives and oil carrier.; [oth. writ.] Limited poetry and short stories.; [pers.] Judge a man not on "where" he has been, but "how far" he had to go to get there.; [a.] Harrisville, RI

LANGLEY, ERIK JOHN
[b.] March 9, 1979, Cambridge, MA; [p.] Marlene Langley, John Langley; [ed.] Burlington High School; [occ.] Full time student; [memb.] National Honors Society, S.A.D.D. (Students Against Drunk Driving) and Collab (I am an Editor of this Literary book which published students' writing); [hon.] Honor Roll Status (Sophomore and Junior Years), Academic Excellence Team Ward; [oth. writ.] Poems published in my high school literary book "Collab"; [pers.] Poetry allows me to escape the frustrations of everyday life and is my way of expressing my feelings, be they happy or sad. I've enjoyed writing poetry since the age of 9 and have grown to truly value it.; [a.] Burlington, MA

LANTIS, JULIE ERIKA
[b.] August 11, 1974, Fargo, ND; [p.] Mr. and Mrs. B. T. and Sara Lantis; [ed.] Graduate Notre Dame High School, Salinas, Calif., presently 2nd year College, attending Clark College Vancouver WA; [occ.] Student in "Early childhood Ed. degree"; [memb.] Volunteer at Ingham School Monterey, Ca. for physically and emotionally challenged children.; [hon.] Grand price Monterey County, Calif. Science Fair 1988; [pers.] My writing is inspired by people with physical and mental challenges who show immense determination to succeed in life.; [a.] Vancouver, WV

LARIVEE, TARA ANNE
[b.] January 31, 1983, Sacramento, CA; [p.] Dan and Sharon Larivee; [ed.] Currently a 7th grade Student at Scott Valley Junior High, Fort Jones, CA.; [occ.] Student; [memb.] Gate, Ski Club; [pers.] I enjoy writing and illustrating my own stories.; [a.] Etna, CA

LARKIN, ROBERT C.
[b.] March 18, 1959, Philadelphia, PA; [p.] Donald and Anne Larkin; [ch.] Dylan, arrive in June; [ed.] "Lot's of Colleges across this Great Country"; [occ.] Health Care worker for the Elderly; [oth. writ.] Several poems published regionally ⸺ several poems submitted nationally; [pers.] "Still Dreaming of Mercy, Little One."; [a.] Bloomsburg, PA

LARMAY, KRYSTAL LYNN
[b.] November 2, 1969, Oconto, WI; [ed.] Lena High school, University of Wisconsin-Green Bay (BA German), University of Wisconsin-Milwaukee (MA), German Literature; [occ.] German Teacher, Lena Public Schools; [oth. writ.] Several poems completed, but did not attempt to publish as of yet.; [pers.] Always take time to appreciate the beauty and wonder in all things, for even in the simplest stone, a crystal slumbers.; [a.] Lena, WI

LARSEN, LINDA
[pen.] Linda Larsen or Linda Potts; [b.] June 19, 1947, San Francisco, CA; [p.] Niels and Margaret Larsen Jr.; [m.] David J. Potts, August 16, 1969; [ch.] Michael, Stephen, Stephanie; [ed.] Middlesex Community College, A.S. (1968), Piedmont Bible College, Bre (1972), Attended: Univ. of Hartford, Moody Bible Institute, Central Conn. Univ, Morse School of Business; [occ.] Administrative Assistant; [memb.] Tenth Muse Poetry Guild N.C. (1972), Connecticut Poetry Society (1988-present); [hon.] Evangelical Press Assoc. Scholarship, Deans List (MCC), Phi Beta Labda Honor Society (Morse) Editor and Chief of Yearbook and Newspaper (MxCC), The World's Whose Who of Women (1978), Outstanding Young Women of America (1980), Whose Who in the South (1975); [oth. writ.] Pegasus - 1964-68 (National Poetry Press, 1968), Poem published: "The Wilted Rose", The Clover Collection of Verse, Vol. XIII (Clover International Poetry Competition, 1976) Poem published: "Judas Love", New Voices in American Poetry - 1977 (Vantage Press, 1977), Poems published: "Sweet is the Death" and "Consuming Death", World Treasury of Great Poetry, Vol II (World of Poetry Press, 1989) Poem Published: "Upon Entering New York", God's Potpourri, Vol. II, (Rainbow's Edge Publishing House, 1995) Poems Published: "In The Midst of a Thunderstorm" and "How Far Does Your Vision Go?", Sparkles in the Sand, (The National Library of Poetry, 1995) Poem Published: "Can't Say No to the Blithering Joe"; [pers.] "Let your light so shine before man, that they may see your good works and glorify your father which is in heaven." (Bible); [a.] Wethersfield, CT

LARSON, JACK EUGENE
[pen.] Maison Odin Douchist; [b.] December 1, 1973, Woodstock, IL; [p.] Kathy, Bill, Jack, Susie; [ed.] McHenry High School (And a private tutor in my head, teaching me the inspirations I now have!); [occ.] Cellular phone manufacturer for home, troubadour for survival and life; [hon.] In my early schooling years, I outspelled every one, I won little awards, but great to my hopes and for my encouragements by peers, or from my self; [oth. writ.] I have purchased blank-paged, leather-bound books that are now filled with short stories, poems, and eulogies for past artists.; [pers.] If the world was a desert, perfection would be just a cactus. I strive for perfection that emulates eloquent poetry, short stories, or philosophical writings that I have with me now. I will be changing my name to: Maison Odin Douchet, (Legally, also); [a.] McHenry, IL

LARZELIER, RADIE M.
[b.] December 27, 1956, Houston, TX; [p.] David L. and Nancy M. Schrader; [m.] Henry Paul Larzelier, July 26, 1975; [ch.] Wade P. and Nancy Joyce; [ed.] Scarborough High School Houston, TX; [occ.] Self employed in the Automotive Transportation Industry; [pers.] My writing tends to reflect experiences in my life and feelings that all people can relate to.; [a.] Houston, TX

LASHOONES, RICHARD H.
[pen.] Richard Xavier; [b.] March 14, 1950, Pittsfield, MA; [m.] Dianne C. Lashoones; [ed.] Siena College; [occ.] Disabled; [oth. writ.] Currently working on a short collection of poetry entitled "Through The Looking Glass - Darkly".; [pers.] My poetry a stream of consciousness validation of feelings that I believe are experienced by those similarly disabled.; [a.] Marshfield, VT

LAUMANN, KAREN MCLENDON
[b.] November 23, 1953, Baltimore; [p.] Shirley and Kenneth McLendon; [m.] Vernon Laumann Jr., May 27, 1972; [ch.] Kandice and Vernon III; [ed.] Graduate - Western High, Some College: Un. of MD.; [occ.] Word Processing Operator Scientific, UM.; [pers.] This poem was written by me in 1991 to give to my daughter, to help her through some hard times. It comes from my heart!; [a.] Baltimore, MD

LAUTH, AMYE
[b.] July 14, 1977, Wayne, MI; [p.] Rebecca Lauth and Al Lauth; [ed.] John Glenn High School, senior class; [occ.] Rave, Sales Assoc.; [memb.] Westland Police Explorers; [pers.] The death of my father inspired me while writing this poem.; [a.] Westland, MI

LAVIN, SHAYNA CELIA RUTH
[b.] May 26, 1955, Lost Angeles; [p.] Norman Lavin, Carol Lavin; [m.] Gary Michael Adler, August 15, 1993, Divorced August 28, 1993; [ed.] Dr Joseph Pomeroy Widney High School, Medical Careers Program, CCOC, LACC, LATT, SMC, Culver City High ROP EMT, Program, EMT Recert. Midway Hospital; [occ.] Certified Emergency Medical Technician (Currently Unemployed); [memb.] American Heart Association, Sierra Club, Nobles, Athenians Humane Society, LA GOAL, Chaverim; [oth. writ.] Several other poems published in school news papers from age 12 on this was my very first poem.; [pers.] I try to show the many beautiful things in this world in my writings. I also try to show everything in the most positive light possible; [a.] Lost Angeles, CA

LAWRENCE, CECIL C.
[b.] August 2, 1914, Kentucky; [p.] (Foster-Parents) James and Pauline; [m.] Helen Louise (Harrison) Lawrence L., February 8, 1948.; [ch.] Patricia, Doris, Lee, Joy, Faith, Grace and Hope.; [ed.] High School (Ged), Tennessee Temple College (A.A. and Thg. Degrees); [occ.] Baptist Missionary to Hispanic people in Georgia.; [memb.] Rome Baptist Temple, Rome, GA., Missionary with (Word for the World Baptist Ministries, Ft. Oglethorpe, Georgia. Have been members of various mission boards over the 44 years in which we have been missionaries to Hispanic People.; [oth. writ.] Several poems, including the poem on page 22 of the anthology, "Beyond the Stars" entitled "Senior Citizens".; [pers.] You'll notice that I didn't put anything under "Honors or Awards" because as a missionary I have tried to honor my Lord by giving out His word to others and it is reward enough when others receive Him as their Lord too.; [a.] Rome, GA

LAWRENCE, PAMELA
[pen.] Pam Lawrence; [b.] March 31, 1959, Washington, DC; [p.] Dorothy Lawrence; [ch.] Richard Jr., Edward, Daniel Jr.; [ed.] Armstrong Adult Education Center; [occ.] Resident Service (Laundry); [memb.] So Others Might Eat Food Club; [hon.] National Education Center Certificate (Business Operations); [pers.] My son's are my heart, that keeps pumping courage and determination through me.; [a.] Washington, DC

LAWSON, SINGINN ANDREW
[b.] July 26, 1982, Phila, PA; [p.] Sheelah and Charles Lawson; [ed.] 7th Grade at Wendler Jr High; [occ.] Student; [hon.] Principle Achievement Award A&B honor roll since 2nd grade, Principle Reading Award Certificate of Reading Award; [oth. writ.] My Grandmother, a poem I wrote about my Grandmother, wasn't nominated for any awards.; [pers.] I write my poems about the people I love, and good times and bad times. My poems are spiritual, emotional, and about good people.; [a.] Anchorage, AK

LAYMON, WHEELER
[pen.] Wheeler Laymon; [b.] December 14, 1932, Dale, IN; [p.] Isaac Laymon, Bernice Laymon; [m.] 1st Norma Logan, 2nd Barbara Brown; [ch.] 1st 1952, 2nd 1966; [ed.] 2 yrs. High School at Reynolds IL.; [occ.] Retired Iron Worker, Carpenter, Millwright; [hon.] Honorable Mention - 1990, and Golden Poet of 1991 for poem "Lover's Moon" from World of Poetry. Editors Choice Award from The National Library of Poetry in 1995 for poem "Daddy's Boots"; [oth. writ.] I have written over 80 poems. Most over the 20 lines allowed for contest, on almost every subject.; [pers.] I am very much like my father, what life deals me, just roll with the punches, and there is no use to complain.; [a.] Lincoln, IL

LAZENBY, GWENETH BRATTON
[pen.] Wendy Lazenby; [b.] February 27, 1978, York County; [p.] Dr. and Mrs. William Jordan Lazenby; [ed.] Senior at Westminster Catawba Christian School Rock Hill, SC; [hon.] National Honor Society, Who's Who in America's High School Students - All American Scholar, Sewanee Award of Excellence; [pers.] In order to express yourself, you need find your peace with God.; [a.] Fort Lawn, SC

LE GRANDE, EVERETT ERIC
[b.] March 25, 1960, Fresno; [p.] Dale and Patrisha Le Grande; [m.] Robin Le Grande, July 18, 1992; [ch.] Keith, Katarina; [ed.] BA in English - California State University Fresno, Minor in Literature; [occ.] Teacher Middle Girls School - S. Korea; [oth. writ.] Numerous poems, currently working on my first novel.; [pers.] It is the pen that validates the world we live in.; [a.] Santa Monica, CA

LEE, MS. JO
[pen.] Jo Lee; [b.] May 11, 1949, England; [occ.] Corporate and Government Billing and Collections Specialist for Cellular Co.; [oth. writ.] Several poems I am in the process of getting published; [pers.] All of my poems have been inspired by life's experiences be they happy or sad. Wanting what I have, not what I and practising unconditional love in all areas of my life; [a.] Laguna Niguel, CA

LEE, KENT-FUH
[pen.] Kent Lee; [b.] May 24, 1985, West Covina, CA; [p.] Lorraine and Johnson; [ed.] Mesa School; [occ.] Student; [memb.] Student Council; [hon.] Principal Awards, 1st Place in Continental Math League; [oth. writ.] Pollution; [pers.] Music interest - piano, saxophone, recorders and guitar.; [a.] West Covina, CA

LEE, VIVIAN
[pen.] Washington, DC; [p.] Lola Robinson; [ed.] Attended public schools and University of D.C.; [occ.] Retired government employee; [hon.] Employee Awards for Meritorious Service; [oth. writ.] Book of Poetry, "Come Share My Love" presently writing a book about corruption in the system and how it impacts innocent people. Also, simultaneously a book tentatively titled "God Is My Judge" is being written.; [pers.] If God is for you, who can be against. Help a child, insure the future. Love for fellowman, end racism.; [a.] Washington, DC

LEFKO, RANDY
[b.] September 13, 1960, Elizabeth, NJ; [p.] Margaret and Thomas Lefko; [m.] Cathy, December 23, 1991; [ch.] Amy, Jennifer; [ed.] Ocean County College (NJ), Cabrini College (PA), Univ of Alabama, USAF; [occ.] Photographer; [hon.] Parade Magazine Annual Photo Contest "Champions" theme Florida Press Association - 1990 - Best Sports Photographer, 1990 - Best Sports Writer, 1989 - 2nd - Sports Photographer, Cabring - Maga Cum Laude, Dean's List; [pers.] My wife is my passion, my writing reflects that.; [a.] Lake City, FL

LEGENESS, BETTY
[b.] August 5, 1946, Los Angeles, CA; [p.] Edward James Howells and Sadie Howells; [m.] Francis Legeness, February 7, 1970; [ch.] David, Elizabeth, Bridgit, Jamie and Jeremy; [ed.] Fremont High School, International Correspondence School of Pennslyvania; [occ.] Mother, Housewife; [memb.] Christian Coalition Paralyzed Veterans Assc.; [oth. writ.] Just started but had one published by National Library of poetry; [pers.] It is important for others to learn what real life is.; [a.] Los Angeles, CA

LEGROS, JOHN EDWARD
[b.] February 7, 1956, Fresno; [p.] Alexander J. and Gladys May Legros; [m.] Janice Colleen Legros, November 5, 1977; [ch.] John Edward Legros II; [ed.] Tulare Union High School; [occ.] Data Entry; [pers.] Its all on the wheel - what goes around comes around; [a.] Modesto, CA

LEININGER, BILLIE JEAN
[b.] November 21, 1962, Gladewater, TX; [p.] Bill and Nancy McConathy; [m.] Raymond Dale Leininger, February 15, 1995; [ch.] Shane Bryant, Casey Lee, Angelo Vincent; [ed.] Hallsville High, Mansfield Business School.; [occ.] Breakfast Mgr for Braums Dairy.; [hon.] 4.0 Grade Average, Accounting diploma; [pers.] My writing comes from personal experiences I have went through. Comes from within the heart.; [a.] Balch Springs, TX

LEMMONS, W. F.
[pen.] Bill Lemmons; [b.] March 22, 1947, Los Angeles, CA; [p.] Frank and Juanita Lemmons; [m.] Joyoe Kay Lemmons, December 7, 1973; [ch.] Eri Lee, Jennifer Kay, Judith Karyn Lemmons; [ed.] Mesquite High School, Eastfield Jr. College University of Texas; [occ.] Food Broker, Licensed Minister; [memb.] Chaplain - Lake point Hospital, Rowle TX; [hon.] Central Marketing Broker of the Yea 1976, Life Saving Award-Dallas Police Dept. 1978 National Broker Rep of the year-Ori Foods 1993 [oth. writ.] River To My Soul, Southern Shepard' Dream, The Lonesome One, Wind Within M Heart, Gone Tapping, Brothers Twelve Upon Th Sea, A Rose That Wept, Victory's Ground, Messi ah's Face, Prayer Warrior, Farewell Old House o Clay, Elijah's Walk, Cosmic Junk, Last Fligh Hummingbirds and Apple Pie, Youngest Child [pers.] I am committed to preset Christ, the christia walk and the need of each person to live his life a if each day is his last. That the next breath he take will be before his creator. I h ave been greatl influenced by life's experiences. Both joyful, an painful, the warmth of love, and coldness of fear. [a.] Rockwall, TX

LEMON, MARY SATTERTHWAITE
[b.] March 21, 1949, Bath, NC; [p.] Fenner and Hellen Satterthwaite; [m.] Matthew Lemon Jr, June 19, 1993; [ch.] Derrick, Rozonia, Krystal; [ed.] Beaufort County High School, Greenville Community College; [occ.] Medical Clerk (Typing), Womack Army Hospital, Ft. Bragg, NC; [memb.] Queens Chapel Disciple of Christ Church; [hon.] Musical Certificates, Letters of Recommendations; [oth. writ.] Several poems written but not published yet.; [pers.] Through the inspirational of God, I was able to write my poem to my grandmother. She lived to be one hundred years old. I pray that the poem (To My Grandma) will touch the lives of others.; [a.] Fayetteville, NC

LENHART, DOUGLAS C.
[pen.] Duke Lenhart; [b.] March 9, 1956, Fort Riley, KS; [p.] Charles H. Lenhart, Hollis J. Mason; [ch.] Rabecha and Jennifer Lenhart; [ed.] Wenatchee High School; [occ.] SPLSM Clerk, USPS; [oth. writ.] Several poems published in local newspapers, numerous poems and short stories published in 'Portals' magazine.; [pers.] Friends are more dear than a perfect formula for impossible dreams.; [a.] Wenatchee, WA

LENHART, JOAN
[b.] December 9, 1935, Pearl River, NY; [m.] Charles Lenhart, October 5, 1955; [ch.] Linda, Charles, Edward; [ed.] Nyack High School; [occ.] Homemaker; [memb.] National Humane Education Society, ASPLA; [pers.] I have no formal training in writing poetry. I enjoy creating personalized poetry for my family and friends. "Grandmother" was written for a friend who became a first-time grandmother.; [a.] Haverstraw, NY

LENZEN, MARILYN SEVERSON
[pen.] Marilyn Lenzen; [b.] June 4, 1935, Madison, WI; [p.] S. Howard and Clarice Severson; [m.] Louis C. Lenzen, May 17, 1970; [ed.] Northwestern University, BA Literature 1957, Art Institute of Chicago - Fine Arts Painting San Francisco Ballet; [occ.] Commercial Model, Film Extra, Amateur Choreographer (Ballet); [memb.] Museum of Modern Art, New York Museum of Modern Art, San Francisco World Affairs Council, San Francisco, San Francisco Ballet Association; [oth. writ.] Various poems over the years, lots of letters, travel articles and some prose. I have never sought out a publisher and am delighted now at the response to my poem, "Fallen".; [pers.] I seek to capture and to treasure the moments that are given me, both in my writing and in my everyday living. Writing is a descent into myself. I write because it makes me see clearly. It

...akes one exquisitely aware.; [a.] Belvedere, CA

EON, RAYZA
[b.] January 6, 1974, Miami, FL; [p.] Alfredo [Ra]mirez, Vidalina Ramirez; [m.] Hector Anthony [Le]on, April 25, 1993; [ed.] Miami High School; [occ.] Graphic Designer, Raleon Graphics and Advertising, Miami, FL; [oth. writ.] Personal compilation of unpublished original poems and music compositions; [pers.] I admire poets who incite their readers to reflect and reason upon matters which would ordinarily be overlooked. I try to accomplish this in my work. I primarily enjoy writing about topics which have affected our society and the human condition in the past and present.; [a.] Miami, FL

EPPERT, SUSAN
[b.] October 15, 1957, Frankfurt Germany; [p.] Jack and Beth Hammond; [ch.] Jesse Ryan; [ed.] Daleville High School, Enterprise State Jr., College C. Wallace Community College; [occ.] LPN, Behavioral Med. Unit, Southeast Alabama Medical Center, Dothan, AL.; [pers.] This poem was written in memory of their Jeffcoat, RN, BSN - co-worker and friend, who tragically ended her own life May 21, 1995. We all loved her and miss her. May peace be with you now, Teir.; [a.] Dothan, AL

LESTER, MARTHA
[pen.] Martha Lester; [b.] October 19, 1942, Great Barnington, MA; [p.] Laura and John Moro; [m.] Norman Lester, August 14, 1975; [ch.] Scott, Vicky, Faith, Sarah; [ed.] High School; [occ.] CNA Certified Nursing Assistant; [memb.] Red Mountain Christian Center, Mesa AZ; [pers.] Just love to write; [a.] Mesa, AZ

LETT, LINDA M.
[b.] October 28, 1951, Rockville Centre, NY; [m.] William R. Lett, January 28, 1983; [ch.] Travis William, Chelsea Lin and Greydon Bernard; [ed.] Baldwin High, North Country Comm. College, Certified Riding Instructor, BHSI, Student of Art and Drama, Horsemanship and Horsemastership; [occ.] Horse Trainer, Instructor, Breeder of Shires and Shirecross Sporthorses; [memb.] Amer. Shire Horse Assoc., Amer. Horse Shows Assoc.; [oth. writ.] Non-published compilation of poetry and prose in a book entitled "An Inner Collection". Several short stories; [pers.] My treasures in life are my husband and children. My luxuries are my horses. My writing has been my therapy. It has balanced both despair and exhileration. I have been a release for the emotions of the heart and needs of the soul; [a.] Franktown, CO

LETTRE, MELISSA
[b.] November 22, 1974, Berlin, NH; [p.] Robert and Catherine Lettre; [ed.] Berlin High School Class of 93, The University of Vermont, Plymouth State College (Psychology major); [hon.] Dean's List; [oth. writ.] "Do Not Let Me Go" - a poem published in a tapestry of thoughts, as well as many other unpublished poems.; [pers.] I want to dedicate this poem to the inspiration for this poem - Kimberly - this one's for you. The love of my life and perfect companion. 1-4-3!; [a.] Plymouth, NH

LEVENS, CHRISTINA MARIE
[b.] January 4, 1968, Cook County Harvey, IL; [p.] Ken and Nellie Levens; [ch.] Jacob Lee Molinari; [ed.] Alexandria Elementary - Alabama Wheeling High - Illinois, Cypress College - California Colorado Mountain College - Colorado; [occ.] Nurse Assistant (CNA); [hon.] Certificate for completing a computer class; [pers.] I write because it helps me when I write about how I am feeling. People always say that I will make nothing and do no good in my life, I go to school and work because I want to prove others wrong.; [a.] Glenwood Springs, CO

LEVY, CHRIS
[pen.] Lev; [b.] October 26, 1972, Melbourne, FL; [p.] Richard and Mary Anne Levy; [ed.] Melbourne High School, Brevard Community College; [occ.] Cook; [oth. writ.] None published; [pers.] To have all, is to desire nothing; [a.] Satellite Beach, FL

LEWIS, ARLIE THOMAS
[pen.] Arlie Thomas Lewis; [b.] December 21, 1921, Plymouth, PA; [m.] Kathryn Lewis, February 2, 1946; [ch.] Doctor Kathy Lewis Iversen; [ed.] Plymouth High School, 1940; [occ.] Retired (FEd. Gov't.); [memb.] American Legion, Veterans of Foreign Wars, Tall Cedars of Lebanon, Masonic Lodge #302, Grace Lutheran Church; [hon.] Numerous WW II medals; [pers.] I am not a trained poet, but merely an ordinary man who enjoys developing poems. I have written 50 plus poems that are intended to entertain and perhaps have the reader to reflect on his or her own life.; [a.] Camp Hill, PA

LEWIS, BETH
[b.] May 19, 1970, Commerce, GA; [p.] Robert Lewis, Doris King; [ed.] Banks County High, Gainesville College; [occ.] Statement Rendering Clerk; [pers.] My inspiration comes from my family and especially my mother. I write from the heart to encourage people to see a brighter world.; [a.] Baldwin, GA

LEWIS, RONALD J.
[pen.] R. J. Lewis; [b.] July 16, 1958, Monrovia, CA; [p.] Donald and Beverly E. Lewis; [m.] Kathleen Ann Lewis, August 8, 1986; [ch.] David, Mandy and Lawrun; [ed.] High School and two year college, (A&A degree and A&P Lic); [occ.] Aircraft Tech. (Mechanic); [hon.] Employee of the month and numerous achievement awards related to my job. (Aircraft mech.); [oth. writ.] I also dedicated a poem, writing to my late sister Carol Lynn Lewis, who also died of cancer.; [pers.] My poem was dedicated to my wife in memory of her father who passed away last year of cancer. (Samuel Mendola), I believe that everybody has a hidden gift inside themselves.; [a.] Saugus, CA

LEWIS, TRAVIS
[b.] April 26, 1974, Houston, TX; [p.] Karla Lewis; [pers.] I like writing poems, but I really love to draw. I have written and illustrated two comic books. And I'm working on the third.; [a.] San Marcos, TX

LIBBY, MICHAEL J.
[b.] April 25, 1984, Santa Monica, CA; [p.] Gerold Libby, Carol Libby; [ed.] The Mirman School; [occ.] Student; [memb.] School Sports Teams, Stephen S. Wise Religious School, American Entertainment Club, Camp-U-Server-Online, Forums, including the comics and Animation forum; [hon.] Recipient of Johns Hopkins University Cty State award - 1995 (both Math and verbal), third highest school score in the C.A.M.L. Math competition, and highest school score in C.M.L. competition.; [oth. writ.] Young Author's Fair books: World Quest, Knocked Right Out, and My Worst Nightmare. Poem's published in Anthology of Poetry by Young Americans, and in At Day's End, The Silver Rain in progress.; [pers.] I would like to thank Mrs. Candice Corliss for her guidance in poetry, and Mrs. Natasha Lubin for helping to continue my development as a writer. I am also influenced by my comic books.; [a.] West Hills, CA

LIBUTAQUE, LORI G.
[pen.] Laurie Libutaque; [b.] January 26, 1973, Cagayan De Oro, Philippines; [p.] Panfilo S. Libutaque, Rosario G. Libutaque; [ed.] Cabatuan National Comprehensive High, West Visayas State University; [occ.] Registered Nurse; [pers.] The fewest of words sometimes convey the deepest meaning. A smile, a nod... Lira, you and I we understood.; [a.] Chicago, IL

LIGGETT, WALTER STEWART
[b.] April 15, 1909, West Chester, PA; [m.] Sarah Dewing Liggett, 1993; [ch.] Dr. Walter S. Liggett Jr. (1940), Dr. George S. Liggett (1943); [ed.] B.S. West Chester M. ed, Temple U., Teacher - Philadelphia (1929-1945), McBurney School, Manhattan (1945-1971); [occ.] Retired, I have always responded to the moods of elemental forces. At sea I generally am on an upper deck for an hour at dawning and another at sunset. I usually spend on hour before going to bed on moonlit nights studying the sky.; [a.] Gaithersburg, MD

LILIENTHAL, LINDA K.
[b.] June 14, 1951, McCook, NE; [p.] Alfred Matthew and Maude Olive Plourd; [m.] John Arthur Lilienthal, August 29, 1971; [ch.] Lisa Aleta, John Ace, Jacob Luke; [ed.] BA in Ed, 1971, Kearney State College, Kearney, NE, MA in Elem. Ed/ Reading 1991, Univ. of NE. at Kearney; [occ.] Farm wife, and Kindergarten Teacher at Hayes Center Elementary, Hayes Center, NE.; [memb.] President of Hayes Center, Education Asso., Vice President of Hitchcock County, Farm Bureau, Member of NE. State Farm Bureau Political Action Committee, Member of Hitchcock County Farm Bureau Administrative Committee and Country Farm Bureau State Affairs Chairman, Member of Student Assistance Team at Hayes Center School, Member of Southwest Nebraska Interagency Team for Children with Disabilities, Member of International Society of Poets, Member of Phi Alpha Theta, Kappa Delta Pi; [hon.] 1995 Editor's Choice Award from National Library of Poetry, Girl Scout Helping Hands Award; [oth. writ.] Several poems published in National Library of Poetry Anthologies.; [pers.] Poetry is dedicated to the memory of Heidi Jo Lilienthal.; [a.] Culbertson, NE

LINDSTROM, LISA MICHELE
[b.] August 8, 1961, Minneapolis, MI; [m.] Jeffrey Rollin Lindstrom, July 25, 1992; [ed.] Hopkins Charles A. Lindbergh High School, 1 year U. of Minnesota; [occ.] My full time occupation at this time is Housewife and Poetry Writer-Publisher.; [memb.] Distinguished Member - International Society of Poetry; [hon.] Editor's Choice Award for Poem "Unfantasy" in "At Water's Edge".; [oth. writ.] I've just been accepted into a fifth anthology and I have just published my own book of 30 poems entitled "Adequate Justice", Beginning Healing Through Poetry January 1996. I plan on many more.; [a.] Yorba Linda, CA

LIPE II, MICHAEL
[b.] November 11, 1961, Russellville, AR; [p.] Michael and Sherry Lipe; [m.] Linda Sue Boggs Lipe, August 1, 1987; [ch.] Kathy, Kristy, Kelly; [ed.] High School graduate, one year vocational school of nursing; [occ.] Truck Driver; [oth. writ.] Numerous personal poems that have not been published.; [pers.] I strive to reflect the simple aspects of life that go un-noticed or over looked as we rush thru our life.; [a.] Riverdale, GA

LIPOSKY, LAURA I.
[b.] January 24, 1972, Toms River, NJ; [p.] Joseph Liposky, Carene Schmidt; [ed.] Lacey Twp. High School, Miami-Dade Comm. Coll., Ocean County Coll., Capri Inst. of Design, and Barbizon Modeling School; [occ.] Sales/clerical for Coopers Florist; [pers.] At the time I wrote the poem, AIDS had become a worldwide issue. I felt sincere about the

situation and felt I needed to express myself with this poem.; [a.] Jackson, NJ

LITTLETON, ELOIS
[b.] June 3, 1935, Madison Co, AL; [p.] Mr. and Mrs. Leatha Ingram; [ed.] 10th grade; [occ.] Housekeeping

LITVIAK, ROBERT C.
[pen.] Morris; [b.] December 31, 1955, Chg.; [p.] Edward, LaVerne Litviak; [m.] Carolyn, November 17, 1976; [ch.] 6; [ed.] Bogan High SWCC, UICC; [occ.] Shop foreman mng; [oth. writ.] Collection of other short poems; [pers.] To be the best parent I can be to our children, To be the best husband to my wife

LIVINGSTON, LAYRON
[b.] May 14, 1985, Mesquite, TX; [p.] Ethel Livingston; [ed.] 5th grade, gifted and talented, A.I.M. Program, Barbizon School of Modeling Graduate, An Honor Student (all A's); [occ.] Currently enrolled in Barbizon's Acting School; [memb.] Boy Scouts, Bridge Club, Science Club, Paw Print (School Paper), Active Youth Church Member, Turn Around Terrell Drug Fighters, Volunteer and UIL Participant, (Art Smart and Ready Writing); [hon.] Outstanding Male Model Award Sept. 1995, Young Author's Extravaganza during 2nd grade for writing and illustrating a book; [oth. writ.] "A Friend Is Someone Who" by Layron Livingston, a book he wrote in second grade that won Young Author's Recognition; [pers.] "I treat people the way I want to be treated."; [a.] Terrell, TX

LOGAN, GEOFFREY JOSEPH
[pen.] Jeff Logan; [b.] February 2, 1947, Philadelphia, PA; [p.] Dorothy Logan and James Logan; [m.] Divorced; [ch.] Michael Joseph, Anne Michelle, Thomas Daniel and Brian James.; [ed.] Monsignor Bonner High School, Univ. of Scranton (1.5 years); [occ.] Writer; [memb.] 700 club (no joke here), Vietnam Veterans of America, VFW (Vets of Foreign wars); [hon.] (none literary), Bronze Star, Army Commendation Medal, Purple Heart, Parachute Badge, (only ones military, sorry).; [oth. writ.] "Key Rings" (vol. of poetry as yet unpublished), "Street corner 101" (vol. of poetry in progress); [pers.] Mission to readers: "I don't much care who this guy, Logan, is... But I think I might like to know his God".; [a.] Granada Hills, CA

LOHR, ROBBY
[b.] January 24, 1978, Uniontown; [p.] Bob and Patty Lohr; [m.] Girlfriend Sarah Dennis; [ed.] Senior at High School, but plan to attend Penn State; [memb.] Member of a cities in school program to help small children with school work; [pers.] I wish that everyone who has seen or felt love be happy and not let that special someone slip away. Always remember how much you love someone, for love comes from inside for no apparent reason, it is just there; [a.] Mount Braddock, PA

LOREMAN, SARAH
[b.] June 12, 1982, Norristown, PA; [p.] Mary Loreman, Barry Loreman; [ed.] Eagle View Middle School Student - Cumberland Valley School District; [occ.] Student; [oth. writ.] Collection of short stories and poems; [pers.] I try to write from my heart and soul. My friends and family are always a part of my poetry.; [a.] Mechanicsburg, PA

LOWRY, CYNTHIA L.
[b.] November 2, 1953, Cleveland, OH; [p.] Mr. and Mrs. John Tymoc; [m.] Mr. Robert R. Lowry, November 19, 1977; [ed.] 1972 - Cerritos Jr. College 'AA' Medical Secretary - have continued education at FJC and Rio Hondo; [occ.] Self-employed Quorum person - company name - Cynthrian International; [memb.] Woman's Leadership Network, Sacred Dance Guild, and Baby Boomer's Grp at Presbyterian Church; [hon.] Outstanding Service - Humanitarian Action Forum - Rio Hondo Jr. College - May 1992 Outstanding Service - CROP Walk - February 1991; [oth. writ.] October 1995 - published in Whittier Daily News - Letter to the Editor - also, three other times in the L.A. Times, Orange County (same section) - Letter to the Editor; [pers.] My poetry is an integration of personal experiences, thoughtful reflection, and a holistic approach to humankind and the world beyond.; [a.] Buena Park, CA

LOWRY, ELIZABETH
[pen.] Beth and Hatti O'Dell; [b.] June 17, 1948, San Diego; [p.] Robert and Virginia Bizzell; [m.] Widow, July 11, 1983; [ch.] Michael Richard, Casey Wayne, Alexis Michelle; [ed.] Cupertino High School, Kings River Community College, working on Associates of Art Degree; [occ.] Cosmetologist; [memb.] Mountain Christian Center, Christian Women's Club Shiloh Ranch Idaho, Fresno Pavaralo House; [oth. writ.] None published, one book, six poem; [pers.] My intent is to stir the heart of man's soul to the awaking of man's truth.; [a.] Coarsegold, CA

LUCARD, ALEXANDER J. C.
[b.] September 17, 1971, Brownsville, TX; [p.] Deceased; [ed.] M. I. Vernon High School Alexander VA., U.S.A.F. Medical Service Trains School Sheppar AFB TX, Surgical Technologies; [occ.] Surgical Tech, Volunteer Fire Fighter; [pers.] The only words of wisdom I can give are inscribe on the family seal "Loyalty Above All Else Except Honor"; [a.] Centerville, OH

LUCAS, MARY CHRISTINE
[b.] January 18, 1958, Kirkwood, MO; [p.] Frank and Patsy Lucas, Donna Lucas and Gary Bustraan; [ed.] Hillsboro High School quit freshman year; [occ.] Disabled; [memb.] Belong to the rose of Sharon Pentecostal Church DeSoto MO; [hon.] Editors Choice Award; [oth. writ.] Many other writings all from my heart one published by you in sparkles in the sand one newspaper article; [pers.] I thank God for the heart I was given. I suppose I was inspired by the death of my baby sister, by that I mean don't ever wait to long to tell someone how you feel for you see time might be taken away from you.; [a.] DeSoto, MO

LUCCI, GIACINTO A.
[pen.] Gino; [b.] April 24, 1971, Aliquippa, PA; [p.] Michael and Caroline Lucci; [ed.] United States Airforce (Mechanic); [occ.] Kitchen Designer; [memb.] National Kitchen and Bath Assoc., Pennsylvania Air National Guard; [hon.] Desert Storm Veteran, Airforce Achievement Medal Outstanding Unit with Valor, Southeast Asia Service Medal, General Billy Mitchell Award, Private Pilot Rating; [pers.] Life is not a story to be told yet an adventure to be lived and a romance to be loved.; [a.] Monaca, PA

LUDDINGTON, BETTY WALLES
[pen.] Betty Luddington; [b.] May 11, 1936, Tampa, FL; [p.] Edward and Ruby Luddington; [ch.] Irene Losat, Daniel Schmidt; [ed.] Plant High School, USF, Tampa, FL: 1980 BA American Studies/History, 1982 MA Library, Media and Information Studies, 1986 Ed.S Gifted Education; [occ.] Media Specialist, Dowdell Jr. High School. Tampa, FL 33619; [memb.] HASLMS (Hillsborough Association of School Library Media Specialist), Country Music Fan Clubs, ISP (International Society of Poets.); [hon.] Phi Alpha Theta Outstanding Student Award, Golden Signet Award, Who's Who Among Students in American Colleges and Universities, Honors: Phi Kappa Phi, Kappa Delta Pi, Omnicron Delta Kappa, Phi Alpha Theta, Pi Gamma Mu, Honors Council, Honors Convocations, and several graduate scholarships.; [oth. writ.] Publication: "WITAN: A simulation activity for gifted students." The Gifted Child Today, September October 1986 and poems in several Country Music Child Fan Club Newsletters. Newspaper article "Librarian uses poetry, country music to reach students at Dowdell." The Tampa Tribute, December, 1992.; [pers.] Inventing a poetic style that flows forward and backwards with accents along the way..... Making life a poem, a bouquet of words, that turns each day into something special. My Daughter had twin boys Feb. 5th (first grandchildren). My son is in the Army.; [a.] Tampa, FL

LURENTZATOS, AMY
[b.] September 4, 1972, Brooklyn, NY; [p.] Elia and Evelyn Lurentzatos; [ed.] Graduated 1990 from Valhalla High School, Bachelor's Degree, 5/95 from Long Island University, C.W. Post; [memb.] Alpha Xi Delta; [hon.] Alpha Phi Sigma, Dean's List; [pers.] Live for the day, for tomorrow may be gone; [a.] West Harrison, NY

LUTZ, CATHERINE
[b.] November 20, 1940, Mercedes, TX; [p.] Lil and William W. Richards; [m.] Ronald Stephen Lutz, February 3, 1964; [ch.] Lisa, Karri, Michael; [ed.] MS - Education/Supervision MA-English Texas A&M University at Kingsville (TAMUK); [occ.] Instructor - Texas A&M Kingsville, writing; [memb.] NCTE, N&A-TSTA, AAUW, First Christian Church - Education Chairman; [hon.] 1994 Third place State-wide By-liners writing contest, Children's story National finalist in KODAK-NEA-Photography in the classroom 1985; [oth. writ.] Poems, short stories, children's stories.; [pers.] I enjoy writing, especially children's stories. I feel that it is very important to encourage children to express themselves through writing and artistic activities.; [a.] Kingsville, TX

LYN, NEIL ANTHONY
[pen.] Neil A. Lyn; [b.] September 2, 1983, Fort Lauderdale, FL; [p.] Cobden Lyn and Sharon Lyn; [ed.] Boca Raton Christian School; [occ.] Student grade 6th; [memb.] Boys scout of America, West Boca and Lumber Jack Youth Basketball, St. Gregory's Episcopal Church Youth Group, Boca Raton Christian School Boys Basketball and BRCC Heirborne Middle School Ministry.; [hon.] Grand prize winner - GCC Pocahontas Essay Contest (1995), First place Scout Poster contest (1994), Cub Scout Arror-of-light, (1994), honor roll every year of school life, Presidential Award for Excellence in Education (1995); [oth. writ.] Essay writing contest winner, My favorite event in American History, The Declaration of Independence. BRCS- Grade 5 - fiction and non fiction stories-classroom publication; [pers.] I like writing and I think it is enjoyable. As a kid I like to write poetry and essays.; [a.] Boca Raton, FL

LYNCH, LILY MAY
[b.] March 15, 1915, Oklahoma; [p.] Ollie May, William L. Kizziar; [m.] Stephen H. Lynch (Deceased), February 25, 1943; [ch.] Kathryn Louise and Carolyn Ann; [ed.] High School, College, Nursing, Reg. Nurse; [occ.] Retired; [oth. writ.] One short story while in college. Poetry through the years. None offered for publication before this.; [pers.] A good Christian life, a good husband, lovely children - that is what makes our world go 'round.; [a.] Monticello, GA

LYNN, ANNETTE
[pen.] Annette Lynn; [b.] July 31, 1964, Statesville, NC; [p.] Kenneth and Sherron Taylor; [m.] Jeff Lynn, January 21, 1988; [ch.] Justin Ryan, Jeffery Caine; [ed.] West Iredell High, Trismith College; [occ.] Army wife; [pers.] I write mostly about my life experiences and things I see around me. I want

y writings to affect people in a positive way or to ..uch hearts.; [a.] Salisbury, NC

YON, MARJORIE W.
..] August 17, 1930, Washington, DC; [p.] Channing .. Walker and Helen C. Walker; [m.] Harvey E. ..yon, November 4, 1955; [ch.] Harvey C. Lyon and ..nger S. Lyon; [ed.] BA, Smith College, 1952 ..dwell Friends School 1948; [occ.] Retired; [memb.] .. Matthews UMC, Smith College Alumnae Assoc.; ..on.] Amer Legion Nat'l Merit Scholar '48 Ph: ..eta Kappa '52; [oth. writ.] Devotional booklets, ..oetry in several anthologies sermons; [pers.] I ..elieve a gift is to be shared - my devotional works ..ave been used by many organizations without ..harge.; [a.] Fairfax, VA

MACAL, DIANA
..] March 6, 1954, Rio Grande City, TX; [p.] Elias ..nd Concepcion Macal; [ch.] Jacob Lee Villarreal ..nd Chris R. T. Fincher; [ed.] McAllen High/Mcallen ..chool of Business/Full Gospel School of Ministry; ..oth. writ.] A prisoner in my own body; [pers.] This ..s dedicated to my oldest son Jacob because I lost my ..on at the age of 3 years due to my being very ill and the ..aw being bought by my ex-husband; [a.] Houston, TX

MACCAN, CLAUDETTE
..pen.] Claudia De Laas; [b.] San Francisco, CA; [oth. ..writ.] Various poems - as yet unpublished.; [pers.] ..My goal is to touch the human heart and mind.; [a.] ..an Carlos, CA

MACDONALD, GREGORY
..pen.] Greg MacDonald; [b.] January 6, 1978, San ..imas; [p.] Linda and Steve MacDonald; [ed.] ..onrovia High; [occ.] Manager, Foothill Grand ..lam; [memb.] National Honor Society, Scholar-..hip Society, Interact, A.S.B., Peer Counselor; [hon.] ..cademic Excellence Award for U.S. History, Math ..tudent of the Year in Algebra II and Geometry ..onors, Baseball Iron man Team Leader Award; ..oth. writ.] Several poems and essays published in ..y school newspaper.; [pers.] As sand through the ..lass, our time has passed, leaving all to move on, ..he times now gone, and for what's to come and ..what's behind, is for me to know and you to find.; ..a.] Monrovia, CA

MACKAY, MEGHAN ANNE
[pen.] Adelaide; [b.] February 6, 1981, North Kingston; [p.] Beverly J. and Richard W.; [m.] Michael D. MacKay; [occ.] Student at North Kingstown High School; [memb.] Symphonic Band, Marching Band, Orchestra, Latin I, Class of 99, Drama Club; [hon.] All State Honors Band, Clarinet, Solo and Ensemble, Poetry, Education, Academic Honors; [oth. writ.] Other expressive poems called "Gone Forever," "Never," "They're Always There," "Just Building Up," "To Be There," "Reality Dreaming," and more to come.; [pers.] I think that depression is a state of mind, not an illness. I think that life is a learning process, not hell. I think that poetry is an expression of thought and who you are, so embrace it.; [a.] North Kingstown, RI

MAITLAND, JOHN STUART
[pers.] The words of man - spoken, sung, written, bards of old, bards of now, the infinite pinnacle - man, mind and communication. [a.] Newhall, CA

MALE, MARGARET E.
[b.] January 10, 1957, Redbank, NJ; [p.] Henry A. Male Jr., Ellen Wright Male; [ed.] Abington Heights High School, Attended East Stroudsburg State College; [occ.] Fiscal Clerk, Keystone City Residence Inc., Scranton, PA; [memb.] The Church of the Epiphany Choir; [oth. writ.] Articles in the local newspaper.; [a.] Clarks Summit, PA

MANCINI, RAY
[b.] June 14, 1957, Phoenixville, PA; [p.] Lou and Adelle Mancini; [occ.] Driver, Oil Painter, Writer; [oth. writ.] I have written other poems reflecting God's creations. I am currently working on short story's telling how good will overcome evil. I hope, by God's grace, to someday have my stories published.; [pers.] I enjoy writing because it enables me to share my God-given abilities with others; [a.] Phoenixville, PA

MANEY, REBECCA ASHLEY
[b.] July 22, 1985, Roswell, GA; [p.] Ronnie D. and Rebecca L. Maney; [ed.] Attends Ball Ground Elementary School - 5th grade; [memb.] Cool Springs Baptist Church; [hon.] Honor student, 1st place winner for poetry in the "Reflections" program at Ball Ground Elementary.; [oth. writ.] I write all the time, mostly for myself.; [pers.] I love writing and hope to be a great poet someday.; [a.] Ball Ground, GA

MANUEL, CHERYL A.
[b.] September 8, 1961, Bessemer, AL; [p.] John and Patricia Seals; [m.] Kalani Manuel, March 23, 1992; [ed.] Carson High School; [occ.] Retail - Manager; [oth. writ.] Poem published in world Poetry Anthology (Cheryl Chunn).; [pers.] Growing old is mandatory, growing up is optional. Greatest inspiration - my husband, Kalani; [a.] Lomita, CA

MANWEILER, SUSAN A.
[p.] Susun A. Manweiler; [b.] July 15, 1959, Norwalk, CO; [p.] James and Francene Manweiler; [ed.] High School Graduate; [occ.] Bookkeeper for A Condominium Association; [pers.] I solely dedicate my poem to my parents, James and Francene Manweiler for their affection and devotion has awarded me with the gift of courage of face all of gifts challenge... past.. present... and future.; [a.] Hallandale, FL

MAPA, MIKE
[b.] August 26, 1916, Hilo, HI; [p.] Ruperto and Isabela Mapa; [m.] Dolores Windsor Mapa; [ch.] Mike, Gene, Gary, David and Jon; [ed.] Graduate of Salinas Junior College (Hartnell College) Salinas, CA. Attended Monterey, Hollister and Santa Barbara High Schools. Graduated from Santa Barbara in 1938.; [occ.] Retired from Federal Civil Service in 1981.; [memb.] Gideons International 23 years in Auburn, Ca. Faith Lutheran Church, in Meadow Vista, CA. And in the Sixties I served as a Scoutmaster for the Scout troop sponsored by Faith.; [hon.] At Hartnell College I was captain of the boxing team and won the conference welterweight title. I also had the male lead in the school's operetta in 1940. I also had the male lead at Santa Barbara High School's Operetta in 1938.; [oth. writ.] I have written more than 2,000 poems of all sizes and thoughts. They are still waiting to be published. Also, my true short stories...based on what I have done or felt in my 79 years...have been assembled as 77 chapters in my roots novel that soon I will submit to a publisher.; [pers.] I can't forget that I am the oldest of 10 who grew up as migrant field workers and experienced that life where food and a place to sleep came by searching for work in the farms of California. I learned to read and gained my love for writing in Bay View Grammar School (New Monterey, CA, just above Canney Row).; [a.] Monterey, CA

MARGULIES, ROBERT A.
[pen.] Robert Alan; [b.] April 28, 1932, Manchester, England; [p.] John and Betty Margulies; [m.] Holly Brooke Margulies, January 10, 1987; [ch.] Keith, Kevin, Kraig - 1st marriage, Stepchildren: Tom, Joanne - 2nd marriage; [ed.] Woodron Wilson High Washington, DC, BS University of Maryland - College Park, MD, MBA California State University - Long Beach; [occ.] Senior Principal Specialist McDonnell Douglas; [memb.] Society of Competitive Intelligence Professionals, Global Business Development Forum, McDonnell Douglas Long Beach Management Club, 1st Presbyterian Church of West Minster; [hon.] Phi Kappa Phi National Honor Fraternity, Fellows Award - Society of Competitive Intelligence Professionals, Man of the Year - Douglas Aircraft Co Management Club; [pers.] Poetry allows me to express my experiences, observations, and perceptions about the past, present, and future.; [a.] Westminster, CA

MARINO, BILL
[b.] June 28, 1970, Manatee Memorial Hosp.; [p.] Michael and Virginia; [ed.] Tabernacle Christian School although I have studied Guitar, Piano Multitrack Music recording, comedy I also have an interest in Acting, anything Artistic; [occ.] Country Mail Clerk/courier (for now); [memb.] Humane Society of Manatee County, I'm not a joiner; [hon.] My name is on one of the plaque at the Humane Society of manatee country for volunteer service which I have been doing for 2 1/2 years.; [oth. writ.] (None published) Several other poems/songs written: Optimistic, pessimistic, happy, sad, angry, philosophical, stupid, funny, imagery, bleak, meaningless, meaningful, doom laden, lifegiving irrevarant, reverent, chaotic, focused etc....etc...etc...; [pers.] Truth will be found by those who seek it, I don't believe, in politics or overcompetetiveness not a crowd follower, my religious views are uniquely my own. I have a strong belief in God I'm quite skeptical at times yet quite sure at others. (A person's destiny is based upon their actions and attitudes.) (with or without God).; [a.] Bradenton, FL

MARSHALL, BEULAH MARIAN
[pen.] Beulah Marian Beulah; [b.] February 19, 1929, Calhoun County, TX; [p.] Harrison Corroll Hartzog, Virginia Faye (Brecheen) Hartzog; [m.] Willie Clay Marshall (Deceased), June 29, 1947; [ch.] William Harrison Marshall (Deceased), Marian Lei (Marshall) Harrison; [ed.] Began reciting poetry and scripture and age 3. Usual education through college. Further educated by very well educated, talented, and caring family; [occ.] Writing and dramatizing poetry.; [memb.] First United Methodist Church, Poetry Society of Texas, Woman's Study Club of Port Lavaca, Texas. Mary former memberships.; [hon.] Art, Parade, Personal Honors Awards etc.; [oth. writ.] 1976 - Letters/Worthy Mothers of Texas, published by DAR, Book - "Kids of Calhoun County", Book - Snooka and Big Yellow Ball", Book - The "Indianola Doll", Book - "The Gift A Heritage of Love"; [pers.] There are so many things time absorb it all. Every day offers so many choices of enrichment. There is one thing I've learned and want to share. We to share. We upon this Earth, are "Spare people". My best to my fellow Earthlings.; [a.] Port Lavaca, TX

MARSHALL, COLIN R.
[b.] December 9, 1980, Los Alamos, NM; [p.] Bob and Mary Marshall; [ed.] Currently a freshman at Pojoaque High School; [occ.] Student; [memb.] Chess Club, Unitarian Universalist Church of Santa Fe Teen Group; [oth. writ.] Unpublished volume of poetry; [pers.] The mind works in rhythm, and poetry is the essence of rhythm, thus I write from the patterns of spontaneous thoughts of my mind.; [a.] Santa Fe, NM

MARSHALL, MINDY LOU
[b.] July 13, 1958, Somewhere in NJ; [p.] Lou Weisberg, Lorraine Weisberg; [m.] Joe Marshall, April; [ch.] Tori Marshall; [ed.] Still in infancy stage; [pers.] Success in a Journey, not a destination the child is the Father of Man.

MARSHALL, SERENE T.
[b.] Grenada; [p.] B. Marshall; [ed.] Colgate University, BA English/Uncchalotte, M.A. English; [occ.] English Instructor; [memb.] Southeast Writers Association; [oth. writ.] Several poems. Local Newspaper Article.; [pers.] I hope that those who read my works would in some way be touched and positively influenced. Honesty, clarity and simplicity are my primary ingredients.; [a.] Charlotte, NC

MARTIN, MICHAEL A.
[b.] February 29, 1940, Akron, OH; [p.] Beatrice M. Gorcoff, Albert L. Martin; [ed.] Diplomas in Hotel/Motel Mgmt. Claim Adjusting/Accident Investigation. H.S. Grad-Passed College Entrance Boards/Test, Received/GED. Received Strategic Air Command and U.S. Air Force Europe; [occ.] Conspicuous Educational Awards Professional Security Officer Casino Surveillance Technician.; [memb.] Master mason-32nd Degree Mason Scottish Rite-Shriner-Member Post #8 American Legion. Distinguished Member of The International Society of Poets. Song Writer for Hilltop Records.; [hon.] Received two (2) major Educational Awards in U.S. Air Force. Presidential Security in Military. Received several Editor's Choice Awards for Outstanding Poetry and nominated as a "Best Poet" for 1995 by The National Library Of Poetry.; [oth. writ.] Published in Las Vegas, Nevada by Gorman Inc. Published Author-"Atlantis Secrets Revealed" and "Noet You Poet" published by Watermark Press. Lyric Writer for Hilltop Records - published Poet by The National Library Of Poetry in several Anthologies. Dance on the Horizon-Echoes Of Yesterday-Best Poems of 1995 - Beyond The Stars - Walk Through Paradise -The Voice Within-A Muse To Follow-A Tapestry Of Thoughts - Where Dawn Lingers Hilltop Records Featured "To Eva My Love in their "Album" "America"; [pers.] To strive for perfection in all I do. To write the very best books -Poetry-and Lyrics for Songs. To make my Book: "Atlantis Secrets Revealed" successful.; [a.] Las Vegas, NV

MARTIN, MINNIE L.
[b.] March 3, 1928, Henrietta, OK; [p.] Ernest Ward, Suzanne Ward; [m.] Edward Martin, March 2, 1991; [ch.] Charles, Suzanne Howard, Hal, Ernest McDanie,; [ed.] High School - Michigan School for the blind; [occ.] Housewife; [memb.] Elba Lions Club Auxiliary; [pers.] A cornea transplant operation that restored my sight inspired me to write this poem; [a.] Lapeer, MI

MARTIN, SUNNY
[b.] March 10, 1913, Ft. Bragg, CA; [p.] John Wm. and Lena Giesler Meyers; [m.] Alphonso Martin (Deceased), June 28, 1958; [ed.] East Ely Grade School, White Pine High School, Ely NV, Heald Business College, Oakland CA; [occ.] Retired - Former Accountant; [memb.] United Methodist Church, Rainbow Girls (Life), Ely Riding Club (Founder), American Bashkir Curly (Horse) Registry (Founder), Western Music Association, Western Folklife Conservancy, White Pine Women's Bowling Assoc. (Founder), W. P. Museum, W. P. Historical Soc.; [hon.] J. C. Penney Co. Golden Rule Award (Conservation), White Pine High School Athletic Hall of Fame Award, Nevada Governor's Senior Samaritan Award and Sen. Richard Bryan's Senatorial Recognition Award for Volunteerism, etc.; [oth. writ.] Poems include "Dreams" - "Pa and His Danged Old Cows" - "Never Learn to Milk a Cow" - "Bang for the Buck" - "Ode to the McGill Smokestack" - "Our School" - etc. Have also written skits, many articles for norse magazines and our local newspaper The Ely Daily Times, plus Artwork for many organizations; [pers.] An primarily a cowboy poet, and am invited to many Cowboy Poetry Gatherings to recite my poems and those of others, including the National Cowboy Hall of Fame at Oklahoma City OK, Gene Autry Western Heritage Museum at Los Angeles CA, plus many others.; [a.] Ely, NV

MARTINDALE, SARAH
[b.] March 19, 1982, Carlsbad, NM; [p.] William Martindale and Sharon Martindale; [ed.] Currently 8th grade student at Chipman Junior High; [a.] Bakersfield, CA

MARTINEZ, BOB G.
[pen.] Bob G. Martinez; [b.] June 7, 1949, Las Vegas, NM; [p.] Mary Jane Martinez; [m.] Annette E. Martinez, February 10, 1973; [ch.] Lita - 18; [ed.] High School: Denver North in 1968; [occ.] Security Guard at Denver Merchandise Mart; [memb.] Distinguished Member of NLP-ISP... C.E.O. of the prestigious "Martinez Family"; [hon.] Currently up for publication of poetry in ten anthologies, four of which have received "Editor's Choice Awards".; [oth. writ.] Compilation of poems titled, (Sidetracks)... also, a personal journey of my life and times from birth to grandfather... one unbroken poem of 302 pages.; [pers.] Ideas, reflections, and images can well represent this author's mascots... Through them, all poets in their languages weave a poetic tapestry of thoughts.; [a.] Denver, CO

MARTINEZ, STACY
[b.] July 17, 1970, Winchester, MA; [p.] Richard Corduck, Edith Hodge; [m.] Jose Martinez, September 12, 1994; [ch.] Amanda, Savannha, Angelina; [ed.] Hilmar High School; [occ.] Housewife; [pers.] Most of my poems come from reality but all touch may hearts and lives all over.; [a.] Salida, CA

MASETTA, SERENA
[b.] March 7, 1980, Cleveland, OH; [p.] Antonia and Russell Masetta; [ed.] I am a sophomore at Solon High School; [occ.] Student; [memb.] Member of SADD Students Against Drunk Drivers; [hon.] Merit Roll; [oth. writ.] I write poetry all the time but this is the first poem I've ever had published; [a.] Solon, OH

MASON, MARY
[b.] August 15, 1955, Chicago, IL; [p.] George W. Mason, Dorothy Rousselle Mason; [ed.] St. Mary-of-the-Woods College (B.A.—Applied Music, B.A.—Speech and Drama), Northern Illinois University (M.F.A.—Theatre Arts); [occ.] Writer/producer/designer for masonart (amalgamated production service), also freelance project specialist (corporate environment); [memb.] Shakespeare Assoc. of America, American Federation of Television and Radio Artists and the Catholic Actors Guild of America, Downers Grove Choral Society, St. Isaac Jogues Choir, Chicagoland Radio Information Service Volunteer; [hon.] Mu Phi Epsilon International Music Competition (Vocal Finalist); [oth. writ.] Corporate training scripts; [pers.] "The soul is touched...the soul speaks...my heart listens."; [a.] Clarendon Hills, IL

MASSEY, KIMBERLY
[b.] March 16, 1975, Monterey Park, CA; [p.] Patricia Massey, Frederick Massey; [ed.] Currently attending Saddleback College with a major in Nursing, Trabuco Hills High School; [occ.] Nurse Assistant; [pers.] Much of my writing originates from my life experiences, which God has so greatly blessed me with and without him I would have no poems to publish.; [a.] Lake Forest, CA

MATANANE, JENETTE MARIE
[pen.] Jenette Matanane; [b.] May 9, 1930, Oakland, CA; [ed.] Graduate Oakland Technical High, January, 1948, attended Merrit Business School, Feb.-June, 1948, graduate Laney College, May, 1992, Oakland, CA; [occ.] Clerk (semi-retired), City of Oakland, Oakland, CA; [memb.] Young Christian Women's Assn., Oakland, CA; [hon.] yrs. certificate, Civil Service Employee, 196; [oth. writ.] I have written 22 poems but have n gotten around to having them printed. They are compilation of different topics. The reason I hav ot had them printed thus far is because some poen could have photos, or drawings to compliment the writings.; [pers.] The poem that I have sent in poetry anthology is a factual writing of the times a the events that are heretofore of one's testame tary and beliefs. A person who reads differe poetry, may come across in this poem a philosop ical passage of their own character or beliefs, ar would relate to other subjects and references.; [a Oakland, CA

MATHENY, DANNY LEE
[b.] August 6, 1952, San Antonio, TX; [p.] Milto M. Matheny and Ellen Joyce Matheny; [ch.] Ta Lee Matheny; [ed.] Graduated from High School Mobridge South Dakota in 1971; [occ.] Truc Driver/Miner in Silver City, N. Mx; [hon.] I won State poetry contest in South Dakota when I was years old.; [oth. writ.] A family affair (Modern Da Poems By A Family of Modern Day Poets - chapter 1 and 2/A family affair) (A Literary First by a Famil of South Dakota Poets (pending release) in m family.); [pers.] There are 10 poets over 3 gene ations (so far) from my mother Ellen Joyce to m Daughter Tai-Lee we're currently in the proces establishing that claim.; [a.] Silver City, NM

MATHIS, SHANNON
[b.] February 9, 1978, Phoenix, AZ; [p.] Denni Mathis, Kathy Mathis; [ed.] Cactus High School [occ.] Student; [memb.] Varsity Club, Medstar Club, Varsity Cheer - Captain, Clinical Medica Science; [hon.] Academic Award, Honor Roll, Var sity Award, United States Cheer Leader Achieve ment Award, State Cheer Award, National Chee Award, Blue Ribbon Circuit Awards; [oth. writ.] Have written short stories, songs and other poetry for pleasure; [pers.] I often write to express my feelings. In the future I would like to continue my education to further my writing abilities and hope to obtain a career in medicine.; [a.] Peoria, AZ

MATOSICH, PHILIP
[pen.] Philip Riley; [b.] December 30, 1963, San Francisco; [p.] Rick and Rose Matosich; [ed.] Four years of high school, 1 1/2 years at Diablo Valley Jr. College, Studied acting privately for five years; [occ.] Bookkeeper/Bartender and waiter; [oth. writ.] The Friends Not Chosen, A Friend Put Something In My Ear, Better To Be Blind, Only That Of..., Touch Gently This Life, The Message, As If I Were A Page; [pers.] "Once you've tended to the weeds in your yard, you'll be more apt to notice the roses in bloom in your neighbors' yard!

MATRISCH SR., RONALD A.
[b.] February 25, 1953, Springfield, IL; [p.] Deceased were William and Edith; [m.] Linda Matrisch, October 1, 1994; [ch.] Ron Jr., Kriste, and Cheryl Matrisch; [ed.] Lanphier High, Corresponding with Lael College and Graduate school for becoming a Minister.; [occ.] But driver for Springfield Mass Transit District, and studying for the Ministry; [memb.] Amalgamated Transit Union; [oth. writ.] The Choice, The Word Christmas, Special Star, Judas, His Angel Watches Over Me. Warnings, Wasn't Good Enough; [pers.] My goal if it is God's will, is to try to bring other people closer to God, and to show them that God is the only way in these present times we need God more than ever.; [a.] Virden, IL

MATSUMOTO, MICHAEL WARREN
[b.] October 16, 1981, Los Angeles, CA; [p.] Kathy Finley, Chris Matsumoto; [ed.] Grammer School at

enter for Early Education and Junior High but I'm all in 8th grade at Campbell Hall. I will continue gh school at campbell hall. I have taken classes UCLA; [memb.] I play golf at Riviera Country lub; [pers.] I'm often Influenced by being out in ature. Its one of my favorite things to do. I'm 14 ears old and love to freely write. I also play the iano and trumpet. I'm very good at digital imag-ing and drawing.; [a.] Beverly Hills, CA

MATTHYS, LILA RUTH STOKES
[pen.] Lila Matthys; [b.] November 3, 1918, Cheapside, TX; [p.] Verner E. Stoke, Opal Carlin Stokes; [m.] Fred H. Matthys (Deceased, January 7, 1984), July 31, 1940; [ch.] (1) Fred Matthys Jr., (2) Ann M. Smalley, (3) Gail M. Beauford, (4) Eric Todd Matthys, (6) Matt A. Matthys, 10 grandchildren, 12 great grandchildren; [ed.] Baylor V. Waco, TX. (3 years) (Bachelor of Science With Honors) (2) University of Texas, Austin, TX. (Master of Education), (3) Southwest Texas State University (Correspondence course New York) (4) Newspaper Institute of America (Journalism); [occ.] Retired Elementary Teacher, Kindergarten (Have taught 2nd grade); [memb.] First United Methodist Church, Path Finder's Club-Federated-Study Club, Crenshaw Athletic Club - Aqua Fitness, Susanna Wesley Bible Class - Teacher, Fred H. Matthys Men's Bible Class: Teacher, Wednesday Afternoon Bible Class (Home); [hon.] Phi Kappa Phi - (U.T.), Kappa Delta Pi - (U.T.), Full literary Scholarship - Baylor G., Pres. Baylor Twin Club (1939) (fun!), My most rewarding honor (last 12 years) was to be elected to teach on the fifth Sundays the men's class, which my husband taught over 35 yrs. and named for him after his death, and to teach on the 4th Sundays - the Ladies.; [oth. writ.] My First poem published in Liberty Vindicator, Liberty, TX. at age 13. These three things: Published in the 1970's in the Austin American Statesman, Keep Daily Journal, Write/ Research Lessons - I teach for two Adult Classes, Writing my biography for my children.; [pers.] I was born a fraternal twin. My parents and 2 grandparents taught school, My father was a minister. My husband was a school administrator. I taught 32 years: 12 in public school - Austin Independent Schools. Owner Matthys Pre-School (Private Kindergarten). All my children are married and have children. Nine in family taught/teach in the public schools. I love children and people, art (amateur), music and outdoors. [a.] Austin, TX

MATTISON, LEONARD M.
[pen.] L. Matthew Mattison; [b.] January 31, 1971, Corning, NY; [p.] Gary Mattison, Valerie Mattison; [m.] Susan L. Mattison, September 9, 1995; [ch.] Joshua Mattison, Ryan Mattison; [ed.] Corning-Painted Post West High School; [occ.] Manager, Pizzaria Unos, Henrietta, New York; [oth. writ.] Have many poems, most not published in the Addison Post.; [pers.] My parents and family are what makes my desire for poetry so strong. They have influenced the "Parents Are Forever" poem.; [a.] Rochester, NY

MATYOK, MARGARET S.
[b.] May 9, 1937, Toledo, OH; [p.] Julius and Margaret Fodor; [m.] Lewis P. Matyok, June 20, 1959; [ch.] Pamela Sue and Lewis P. Jr.; [ed.] Graduated from Waite High School, Food Service Course in Sanitation, and Nutrition and Management; [occ.] Server at Parkvue Retirement Community Center; [memb.] St. Stephen United Church of Christ, Chefs Ass.; [hon.] Nellie Arthur, family, husband, friends, poets, poetess, the Bible, God who gave me talent and Jesus my friend.; [oth. writ.] To name a few God Made Our Tears, The window of Life, and my first to be printed in your book Beyond the Stars, God Painted First and I thank you so much.; [pers.] My grandchildren are the light of my life. As God gave me the gift to write, I share them with others, as others have share theirs with me. My writing have given me the strength to go on no matter what events came in to my life.; [a.] Sandusky, OH

MAXWELL, BLANCHE STARRATT
[b.] October 9, 1900, Queens City, Nova Scotia; [m.] Linwood Maxwell, 1932; [ch.] Douglas Maxwell; [ed.] Normal College, Nurses training. Taught school 6 yrs. RN for many years, Christian Science nurse for many years.; [occ.] Retired; [pers.] I have been a nurse for many years. I gave loving care to patients which I enjoyed doing and for which I was rewarded. Having the talent to give harmony in my piano playing which many enjoyed, I was led in this era to write poetry. For all this good, I give God the glory.; [a.] Southlake, TX

MAYLE III, JOHN W.
[b.] November 21, 1971, Detroit, MI; [p.] John, Fran Mayle; [ed.] De La Salle High, Ferris State University; [occ.] Safety Professional; [memb.] Michigan Association of Young Authors, American Society of Safety Engineers.; [oth. writ.] Several poems published in small and collage press.; [pers.] My writing reflects the reality of man through my own personal experiences.; [a.] New Baltimore, MI

MAYORGA, PATRICIA ANN
[b.] March 16, 1952, Sacramento, CA; [m.] Stephen Mayorga, June 20, 1973; [ch.] David, Teresa, Stephanie, Sarah, Melanie and Linda; [ed.] University of the Pacific, BA, MA; [occ.] Teacher (Multiple Subject, 6th Grade) Taylor Elementary Stockton, Calif.; [memb.] Association of Mexican American Educators, Affirmative Action Advisory Board Member; [hon.] Honors Delta San Joaquin Delta College; [oth. writ.] Publications in the National Library of Poetry, Local Newspaper publications, Book of Poetry entitled Days of Thirst; [pers.] Life's journey is not an isolated experience, rather the journey is the gathering of a bouquet arranged in a vase called friendship.; [a.] Stockton, CA

MAZZEO, FRANCES C.
[b.] October 20, 1937, Boston, MA; [p.] Mary A. Mazzeo and Anthony Mazzeo; [ed.] Roxbury Memorial High, Brockton Business College; [occ.] Bookkeeper, Space Building Corp., E. Taunton, MA.; [memb.] Smithsonian Institute; [pers.] I always wanted to express myself by writing a poem or a song.; [a.] Avon, MA

MCBRIDE, KATHLEEN SHANK
[pen.] Kathleen McBride; [b.] January 27, 1956, Wenatchee, WA; [p.] Robert and Wanita Shank; [m.] Larry L. McBride, June 1, 1992; [ch.] Pamela, Jeremy and Laura; [ed.] B.S. Degree in Accounting from Central Washington University, Ellensburg, Washington; [occ.] Financial Manager for USDA Forest Service; [hon.] Graduated Salutatorian from Entiat High School, Entiat, WA 1974, Graduated Cum Laude in Accounting Program, Central Washington University, 1979; [oth. writ.] Poems and short stories, none published.; [pers.] I began writing at an early age, mostly poems and short stories which I would take to school and share with my classmates. Victoria was written when I was in Jr. High School.; [a.] Roseburg, OR

MCCAIN, G. STUART
[pen.] G. Stuart McCain; [b.] April 6, 1963, San Antonio, TX; [p.] Arthur G. and Vera Gayle; [ed.] Graduated from Kilgore High School and completed 2 years at Kilgore College, I aspire to go into the mission field.; [occ.] Oilfield Security, and Minister of the Gospel; [memb.] The Church, The Body of Christ and the House Hold of God; [oth. writ.] "A Lot Like Lot", "Some People", "The Samaritan Woman at the Well", "one and All", "Resurrection".; [pers.] I am a Born Again Christian whose heart's desire is for all men and and women, young and old of every race and nations to receive the Lord Christ Jesus as Savior who alone can heal their hearts and save their souls.; [a.] Kerrville, TX

MCCARTHY, KERI-ANN
[b.] December 28, 1971, Yonkers; [p.] Kevin and Joyce McCarthy; [ed.] High School graduate. Presently going to Connecticut Center for Massage Therapy, to become a licensed massage therapist.; [occ.] Working full time as a secy/recep at San mar Labs.; [memb.] Club fit at Jefferson Valley.; [hon.] I had, in the past, sent a fun poems into Teen Magazine, was offered an award in Washington DC. for my talent but could not make the trip to Washington to be honored.; [oth. writ.] I have a book that I keep which has quite a few of my favorites. A few are tired as follows: Inspired, My Guardian Angel, Sorry If I was Too Much, Silence; [pers.] One of the strongest statements, I've ever heard - that which inspired me to send my poem to you, I get from a movie his: "There's Nothing worse than wasted talent".; [a.] Manopac, NY

MCCARTY, SARA E.
[b.] June 5, 1977, Greenville, OH; [p.] Vicki and Tom McCarty; [ed.] Springfield North High, University of Toledo; [oth. writ.] One poem published in another anthology. A few published in my high school journals.; [pers.] My poems reflect my emotions that go one in my life. I have been influenced by other great poets and encouraged by many people in my life.; [a.] Springfield, OH

MCCLAIN SR., MICHAEL T.
[b.] June 12, 1952, Cincinnati, OH; [p.] Donald and Shirley McClain; [m.] Alice Charlene, September 2, 1972; [ch.] Amy Ruth, Michael Jr., Jenny Mae, Anna Louise; [ed.] Schwab Jr. High, Aiken and N.C.H. Sr. High, Cincinnati State Tech for. Aviation Engineering; [occ.] Jet engine production mechanic for G.E. (General Electric); [memb.] Calvary Pentecostal Church Board of Trustees, Advisory Board of Deacons and Recording Secretary Officer, also: Children's Church Coordinator and Sunday School Teacher; [hon.] Also: Member of The Calvary Pentecostal Church Orchestra (Violinist); [oth. writ.] Has written numerous unpublished poetry over the years...; [pers.] In dedication to my children and appreciation to my parents who have influenced my writings tremendously.; [a.] Cincinnati, OH

MCCLURE, JESSICA
[b.] January 12, 1977, Oregon; [p.] Cheryl and Norm McClure; [m.] Donald Owen, May 11, 1997; [ed.] Heritage Christian S., Madison H.S., Mt Hood C.C.; [occ.] Employee at the Disney Store, Lloyd Center; [oth. writ.] This will be my first work published.; [pers.] I feel that writing is a self-expression of life, love, tears, and memories. Metaphorically these details are expressed. This is my writing style.; [a.] Gresham, OR

MCCORKLE, PAIGE
[b.] January 17, 1981, Columbus, OH; [p.] Roger and Kathy McCorkle; [ed.] Homeschooled; [occ.] High School Student; [pers.] I want to include a special thanks to God almighty for giving me such special that I hope and pray that all my future pieces will be written for his glory.; [a.] Gahanna, OH

MCCORMICK, KATHERYN
[b.] February 24, 1934, Belle Glade, FL; [p.] Mr and Mrs George F. Webster; [m.] Fred L. McCormick (Divorced), November 2, 1952; [ch.] Michael, Patrick, Joseph and Mavy Kay; [occ.] Disabled; [oth. writ.] I'll Remember, Dredgeman Blue's House of Loneliness, Life is No Joke, Marie Marie Old Man

Hungry, Slam Bam (These have not been published); [pers.] I write about events that happened in my life, good or bad. And it seem's to come out in Poetry. Four angels in the sky is about my children.; [a.] Dade City, FL

MCCRACKEN, KEVIN
[b.] November 15, 1973, Detroit, MI; [p.] Jack and Patty; [ed.] Grosse Pointe South High School, Miami University, Oxford, Ohio B.A. in Business-Economics, August 1995; [hon.] Tau Kappa Epsilon; [a.] Grosse Pointe Farms, MI

MCCULLOUGH, KATHLEEN
[pen.] Kathleen McCullough; [b.] February 7, 1982, Guam; [p.] John and Colleen; [ed.] K-8; [occ.] 8th grade student; [memb.] Benson Middle School Choir, S.A.F.E.I. president student awareness for environment issues; [hon.] Honor Roll grades, 2-8; [oth. writ.] Currently writing "The Environment in Poems"; [pers.] Influence is the biggest deal in these days. Ignore it and be yourself; [a.] Benson, AZ

MCCULLOUGH, SHAWN
[b.] May 22, 1988, Kansas City, MO; [p.] Don W. and Shelly McCullough; [ed.] Attending 2nd grade at Orchard Elementary, 711 E. Gish Rd San Jose, CA 95112; [occ.] Take Music Lessons - Key Board; [memb.] American Bicycle Assoc. Won National on April 8, 1995. California Motorcycle Assoc. - Pee Wee Class.; [hon.] Student of the Week December 4, 1995, - placed 2nd in 2 separate "Race for Life" Contests sponsored by ABA for Leukemia - 1st place at Lemoore, CA Action Park BMX National Bicycle Race.; [oth. writ.] My "response" letter about a "Prehistoric Wipeout" was published in the October 6, 1995 issue of "Time Magazine for Kids" - I write songs.; [pers.] Every accomplishment, great or small, starts with the same decision - I'll try! And if at first you don't succeed, try and then try again, and again.; [a.] San Jose, CA

MCDEVITT, DEBORA LEE
[pen.] Debbie McDevitt; [b.] May 3, 1958, Steubenville, OH; [p.] Leroy McDevitt and Lena McDevitt; [ed.] Sylmar High School; [occ.] Unemployed was an Inventory Control Coordinator, Printer; [memb.] North American Fisherman Club; [hon.] An award for business logistics systems; [oth. writ.] I've wrote poems and songs since I was a teenager, I've never tried to publish any till now.; [pers.] Love is a main source of how I do everything in life, the Lord and my family, my mother Lena, brother Bud, his wife Sandy and their daughter Candice and my sister Kathy have always been my inspiration, we will always be there for each other and we help others see the love inside of them.; [a.] Chatsworth, CA

MCDOWELL, MARY B.
[pen.] Bonnie McDowell; [b.] September 25, 1923, Reynoldsville, PA; [p.] Julia Farr and Maine Senecal; [m.] Howard A. McDowell, December 31, 1945; [ch.] Bonnie Christine; [occ.] Retired; [memb.] Gold Star Wives; [oth. writ.] Several poems for my own enjoyment; [pers.] I am greatly influenced by "Happenings" in my life.; [a.] Federal Way, WA

MCFARLAND, CAROLYN
[pen.] Carolyn McFarland; [b.] December 7, 1946, San Antonio, TX; [p.] Dorothy Brown, Gilbert Brown; [m.] Glenn E. McFarland, March 2, 1974; [ch.] Kerry, Kurtis, Kevin, Duane, Christopher; [ed.] Jefferson High School, Sam Houston State University - B.S. Art Education; [occ.] Completion Fluids Specialist with Baroid Completion Fluid Services - Baroid Drilling Fluids, Inc. (17 years); [memb.] National Childrens Cancer Foundation (5 years); [hon.] Cecil B. Sampson Award for Outstanding Service in Little League (2) years, Little League Volunteer of the Year Award (1) year. Involved in Little League for 18 years, including Tournaments and Play offs.; [oth. writ.] Several poems - none published; [pers.] My poems are my special way of communicating when words are hard to come by.; [a.] Humble, TX

MCFARLAND, MARCALINE
[pen.] Marsha McFarland; [b.] August 6, 1952, Marysville, CA; [p.] Billy and Peggy Vaughn; [m.] David McFarland, May 13, 1972; [ch.] Amy and Matthew; [ed.] AA Music and Humanities Skyline College, San Bruno, CA., Berean School School of the Bible in Springfield, MD; [occ.] Music Minister, Freelance Writer, Song Writer, Singer; [hon.] College Graduate with honors 1982; [oth. writ.] Several articles published in Christian periodicals and newspaper. Editor of monthly church newsletter called "Life Lines" song published in 1982, "He's The One "Chestnut mound music"; [pers.] I love expressing my thoughts in writing-thoughts that inspire others to be encouraged, to keep on trying. My philosophy about life is that anyone can live it to the fullest if they try.; [a.] Sacramento, CA

MCGARY, CHARLES S.
[pen.] Charles S. McGary; [b.] June 29, 1963, Old Waverly, TX; [p.] Charles C. and Doris M. McGary; [m.] (Fiance) Patricia A. Kizzee, June 8, 1996; [ch.] Charles Selwyn, Jazman Lamar, Eumah Michelle and Enrique Michael; [ed.] 1981 Graduate of New Waverly High School New Waverly, Texas; [occ.] Construction Worker, currently preparing to enter college; [hon.] Having "People Born of Yester-Year" published in the compilation "A Muse to Follow", and this current honor.; [oth. writ.] I wrote a poem, "This Is My Country" which is read to every class since 1977 in the New Waverly, Texas Independent School District. I've written several other poems but never attempted to publish any before, until "People Born of Yesteryear" which is included in the compilation "A Must to Follow"; [pers.] I write my heart felt thoughts, in regards to social, religious and racial ills, as well as the need for the adult members of society to ponder the consequences of overlooking the continuously, needs of our younger people, who look to us for guidance, hope and change.; [a.] Huntsville, TX

MCGEE, LEONARD DEE
[b.] August 9, 1987, Frankfurt, Germany; [p.] Lucille and Howard McGee; [m.] Lucy T. McGee, December 5, 1992; [ed.] "AA" Music Education "AS" Electronics; [occ.] Mech/Electrical Tech.; [oth. writ.] Collection of 40-50 poems (nature and love themes); [a.] Indianapolis, IN

MCGIBBON, BRIANNA
[b.] March 20, 1983, Vancouver, BC, Canada; [p.] Brian and Brenda McGibbon; [ed.] Grade 7 - Crestview Middle School, Chesterfield Missouri; [occ.] Student; [a.] Chesterfield, MO

MCGRATH, ED
[b.] August 17, 1929, Brooklyn, NY; [m.] Alice M. McGrath, February 17, 1977; [ch.] Michael, David and Jewel; [ed.] Utica College N.Y. (English Maj.), BA and MA, Cal State Fullerton (Poli. Sci.) MA Cal State, LA (Psych), MA UCSB (Psych), incomplete PhDs, H.C. Irvine, UCSB; [occ.] Theoretical Scientist, Evolutionary Psychology; [pers.] My most profound poetic experience has been seeing the universe and human nature as a scientist. This vision is essential to any serious modern poet.; [a.] Altadena, CA

MCINTOSH, KATHY D.
[b.] September 1, 1957, Franklin, IN; [p.] William E. and Winnie Dillow; [ch.] Shawn; [sib.] Edinburgh High School; [memb.] Fair Haven Christian Church; [oth. writ.] Articles in the company newsletter. "Monthly Interest Report".; [pers.] I thank m Lord and savior for giving me this special gift ar for letting me express myself in this special way [a.] Franklin, IN

MCLEAN, BUNNY SWOBODA
[pen.] Buny Malean; [b.] April 25, 1933, L Angeles, CA; [p.] Raymond J. Swoboda, June Swobod [m.] George Edward McLean, October 19, 198 [ch.] Dane A. Schneider, Todd J. Schneider; [ed Torrance High, West Los Angeles, CA; [occ Student Ermitus College and Santa Monica Colleg CA; [memb.] Agape Church-Santa Monica Califo nia; [hon.] T.V. Emmy Award "Women to Wor en" Best Daytime Talk Show, Three special award for Public Speaking, Radio Broadcast Commercia for Six Weeks Hourly. KIIS-F.M. "Rick Dees Show [oth. writ.] *Poetry Science of Mind* Mag., *Palisade Post* Editorials Page, Agape Church Paper Poetr corner of several spiritual poems.; [pers.] "To writ is to harness one of man's greatest forms of com munications... Let us never lose sight of it's powe for when verbal talk is never quite heard, or perhap understood, the written page is always there."; [a. Pacific Palisades, CA

MCMULLIN, EVA
[b.] October 5, 1955, Ames, IA; [p.] Corwin Brown Edith Brown; [m.] Kevin McMullin, September 8 1979; [ch.] Anthony Corwin, Amanda Jean; [ed. Roland-Story High; [occ.] Homemaker; [memb. The Loft Literary Center; [oth. writ.] A poem published in a local newspaper.; [pers.] I like tc express myself and my experiences through my gif of writing. My contribution to others is to offer comfort, hope and understanding. Writing poetry is to encounter truth, uncut and reborn.; [a.] Cottage Grove, MN

MCNAIRY, HAROLD G.
[pen.] Hal; [b.] March 30, 1929, Alberdeen, MS; [p.] Frank and Valaria Maria McNairy; [m.] deceased; [ch.] Harold; [ed.] College Graduate, Motel Institute, Restaruant Institute, Law Degree and Accounting; [occ.] none; [memb.] Songwriters, Christmas Valley Club; [hon.] Purple Heart and others; [oth. writ.] Songwriter, amateur; [pers.] When you want something with honor, make up your own sensible mind, and go after it. [a.] St. Louis, MO

MCNAUGHTON, RUTH A.
[pen.] Samantha Rose; [b.] September 4, 1968, Hershey, PA; [p.] Harold George and Maxine Elizabeth; [ed.] Lower Dauphin H. S., Hammelstown, PA; [pers.] In respect and love for my life-long friend. For without the memories that we have shared, there would be no writing. You are my source of strength and inspiration. Thanks for all that you are. Stephanie Rose.

MCNEELY, RUTH
[b.] September 21, 1913, Forest City, SD; [p.] Frank and Clara Isabel McNeely; [m.] Matthew Schatz (Divorced, 1945), 1930; [ch.] Gloria, Ramona, Lelia June, David; [ed.] 8th grade mobridge South Dakota, 12 grade Lancaster, CA, 1 year college Los Angeles, CA, 6 months college Glendale, CA; [occ.] Retired; [memb.] Seventh Day Adventist Church, Friends of the Senior Center Lancaster, CA (Retired), National Right to Life; [hon.] Certificate of Appreciation for Outstanding Community Volunteer Service, Certificate of Service to Visually Handicapped; [oth. writ.] Songs "Sun Bonet Sue", "Love Me A Little Bit of Lots", story: "Adopted Daughter of the Sioux". Several articles published in local newspaper.; [pers.] Success depends on how you handle the small every day decisions we all have to make, they add up, as 100 pennies make a dollar.; [a.] Lancaster, CA

MCQUARY, PAMELA R.
[pen.] Pamela R. Fulton; [b.] May 28, 1963, Havre de Grace, MD; [p.] Robert Fulton Dinsmore and L. Blanche Dinsmore; [m.] Scott W. McQuary, October 6, 1984; [ed.] Dexter High Sch, Southeast MO St Univ - B.S. Bus Admin; [occ.] Printing Exec I, State of Missouri, Office of Administration; [hon.] 1979-80 Edition Who's Who Among Am High School Students; [a.] Jefferson City, MO

MEAD, JESSICA MARIE
[b.] January 5, 1981, Maryland; [p.] Bette Morrow, Patrick Mead; [ed.] Freshman in the Albuquerque Public School System, Albuquerque, New Mexico; [occ.] Full time student; [hon.] School honor roll from 5th to 7th grade. Also won a Drug Free poetry contest at Lincoln Middle School; [oth. writ.] Approx. 30 more poems written. Titles such as: The Way, Tears, The Part, Life, The Color, Reborn, The Killing And Wasting.; [pers.] Events in my life take place, some good some bad, and one of my escapes is my poetry.; [a.] Rio Rancho, NM

MELCHIOR, IB JORGEN
[pen.] Ib Melchior; [b.] September 17, 1917, Copenhagen, Denmark; [p.] Lauritz Melchoir, Inger Melchior; [m.] Merle C. Melchior aka Cleo Baldon, January 18, 1964; [ch.] Leif Melchior, Dirk Baldon; [ed.] Grad. Stenhus College, Denmark, Degree of Cand. Phil. University of Copenhagen, Special Agent, USA Military Intelligence Service; [occ.] Author; [memb.] Authors Guild, Writers Guild of America, Directors Guild of America, Manuscript Society, The Adventurers Club, American Scandinavian Foundation and others; [hon.] Hamlet Award - Best Playwriting ("Hour of Vengeance") by the Shakespeare Society of America 1992, Golden Scroll Award - Best Writing, by the Academy of Science Fiction, 1976, Man of the Year Award - the American Scandinavian Foundation, 1995, Knight Commander Cross of the Militant order of St. Brigette of Sweden, 1965, Several Military Decoration, USA and Denmark; [oth. writ.] 10 novels, 3 non-fiction books, 107 short stories and factional articles, 12 feature motion pictures, 7 TV scripts, and 41 documentaries. (No poetry!); [pers.] I believe in man's in dominatable spirit to conquer seemingly insurmountable obstacles, and often write about it.; [a.] Los Angeles, CA

MELI, ANTHONY I.
[b.] October 4, 1954, Brooklyn, NY; [p.] Tony and Ann Meli; [m.] Maria, July 21, 1974; [ch.] Jennifer, Elizabeth and Maria; [ed.] Longwood H.S., Suffolk County Community College; [occ.] Technician, for IPEC/Westech; [hon.] Dean's List; [pers.] One of the hardest things a man can do is place his faith in God, instead of himself.; [a.] Chandler, AZ

MELORO, MICHAEL
[b.] August 10, 1971, Atlanta, GA; [p.] Mary P. Meloro; [oth. writ.] A Street poet, Empires, Treasure Hunters, Love, A boy and his dog; [pers.] I enjoy writing about all aspects of life and the treasures that lie hidden in it.; [a.] Marietta, GA

MELTON, MISTY NICOLE
[pen.] Misty Nicole Melton; [b.] March 29, 1982, Dublin, TX; [p.] Janet Aleman, Niki Melton; [occ.] Student, Winters Jr. High; [hon.] Blue Bonnet Poetry Award, Writing Awards, Scholastic Awards; [oth. writ.] Several other poems and one other poem that has been published; [pers.] I love poetry. I have been writing it ever since 3rd grade. It is my favorite hobby. My grandmother is my inspiration. She has supported me all the way. Thanks Granny for all your help.; [a.] Winters, TX

MENDES, SANDRA REGINA
[pen.] Sandy Kira; [b.] September 27, 1964, Brazil; [p.] Manuel Roberto Mendes, Maria Ofelia Mendes; [ed.] Towson University - Languages; [occ.] Translator; [hon.] Silver medal 2nd place winner poetry contest; [oth. writ.] "Bailarina Cigana Do Tempo" (Book) "Impress oes I" (Book), "Impressoes II" (Book) "Cumplice" (single poem); [pers.] I strive in sharing with others my deep thoughts and feelings; [a.] Baltimore, MD

MENDEZ, ERIKA
[b.] February 27, 1979, Glendale, CA; [p.] Antonio and Lidia Mendez; [ed.] I am a junior (11th grade) attending Bell Gardens High School; [hon.] Selected to participate in the Humanities Pathway Honors Class; [pers.] I like to express the pain and frustrations many of us feel at some time or many times in our lives. [a.] Bell Gardens, CA

MENDOZA, SLYVIA DE LA FUENTE
[b.] November 28, 1941, California; [p.] Clementina and Luis de la Fuente; [m.] Xavier Mendoza, June 1965; [ch.] Marc, Damian, Eva; [ed.] Sacred Heart of Mary High School, East Los Angeles College, Mt. San Antonio College; [occ.] Administrative Assistant for Special Education; [oth. writ.] Other poems published in "Alchemy" a literary journals of Latino writers, published in "Dark Side of the Moon", The National Library of Poetry.; [pers.] Poetry is the reflection of man's inner thoughts and beauty of the human spirit, captured in the written word.; [a.] Hacienda Heights, CA

MERCADO, MARCO
[pen.] Don Marcus; [b.] June 6, 1938, Guanica, PR; [p.] Elvira Torres, Pablo Mercado; [m.] Gloria Gonzalez, August 23, 1980; [ch.] All adults (7); [ed.] Presbyterian Academy 1957, 4 yrs. college ed. R.U.M. University of P.R.; [occ.] Writing, crafts; [memb.] Adelphia Lodge #1 P.R.; [hon.] Ford Motor Co. Best Selling Award, Mason 32 grade.; [oth. writ.] Poem published. Short stories for local papers.; [pers.] To help other being over their minds with the help of goodness. Peace lay abundantly inside oneself. Humans need help on conquering their inners and transforming more bad into plentiful good.; [a.] Coral Gables, FL

MERIDETH, FAITH E. R.
[b.] September 21, 1956, Great Barrington, MA; [p.] Gladys M. Council; [m.] James E. Merideth Sr., February 21, 1979; [ch.] Jennifer E. Merideth, James E. Merideth Jr.; [ed.] Brockton High, Massasoit Community College, Associate in Science - Law Enforcement; [occ.] Homemaker; [memb.] Womens International Bowling Council, Spotsylvania County Parks and Recreation Youth Softball Coach Fredericksburg Area Youth Bowling Coach (YABA); [hon.] Honorably discharged from the U.S. Army November, 1979.; [pers.] I have always been an introvert who utilizes writing as my way of self expression and emotional release. Writing is an excellent way to have fun with words while letting the imagination soar and the physical boundaries in life dissipate.; [a.] Fredericksburg, VA

MESHELLE, MRS. CAROL RICH
[b.] August 20, 1943, Marshall, TX; [p.] Daisy Campbell, Garland Rich; [m.] David Meshelle, July 1974; [ch.] Connie, Bo, Chris, Doug, Rich, Robin and Ronnie; [ed.] High School, Waskom High School Waskom, Texas; [occ.] Chiropractic Office Manager; [oth. writ.] Have written several books that are in the process of being published. Rhyme time is the name of my books. They are light hearted poetry about life and its many ups and downs.; [pers.] I believe we ought to be happy and enjoy living and do our best to bring joy to others especially those who don't have as great a measure of faith and happiness as me. I'd like to think of myself as an ambassador of joy to lonely people. The world can always use another laugh, even if it's on me! Life can be a drag, if you don't use humor to get through it! I just want to help!; [a.] Richardson, TX

MEYER, JEANNE
[b.] August 18, 1944, Shreveport, LA; [p.] Herman, Gloria Meyer; [m.] Divorced; [ch.] Josh Lehmann, Jonie Lehmann; [ed.] Liberal Arts (English), LSU Baton Rouge; [occ.] Apartment manager; [memb.] Past - various Professional Associations; [oth. writ.] Previous newspaper and freelance experience; [pers.] "We shall not cease from exploration - and the end of all our exploring - will be to arrive where we started - and know the place for the first time" — T. S. Elliot.; [a.] Shreveport, LA

MIDDLEBROOKS, LEVICA
[pen.] Bobbye Brooks; [b.] May 21, 1916, Jack County, TX; [p.] John and Chattie Jamison; [m.] Archie Midole Brooks (deceased), September 30, 1957; [ch.] One girl by first husband; [ed.] Graduated Jacksboro High School - One term at Tarleton College - Stephenville, TX - and Southern Business College, Ft. Woryn; [hon.] Scholarship to College from Jacksboro Gazette; [oth. writ.] All kinds of poetry. ,Also some romantic Stories.; [a.] Jacksboro, TX

MIEIR, CHARLES E.
[b.] January 5, 1929, Perry, OK; [p.] Deceased; [m.] Helen B. Mieir, November 30, 1951; [ch.] Robert, Steven, Pamela (Jones), Sharon (Beck); [ed.] BS University West Florida, 1970, Southeastern Baptist Theological Seminary (1974-1976); [occ.] Retired Minister of Gospel; [oth. writ.] Poetry Volume, "1 Choose To Give Them Light", Weekly Newspaper Column "Sunday School Lesson" 1975 through 1990. 2 unpublished book length manuscripts.; [pers.] God is our creator, and Christ is our Redeemer. Real meaning in life is possible only in Him. To Him be glory forever.; [a.] Oxford, NC

MIELE, DONNA J.
[pen.] Wolfwind; [b.] September 17, 1945, West Virginia; [m.] James J. Miele, November 11, 1967; [ch.] Four; [ed.] BS in History with Minor in Anthropology from Towson State Univ.; [occ.] Disabled/Artist Native American, styled Bead Work And Artifacts; [hon.] Graduated 1991 Magma Cum Laude Dean's List - Dean's Scholarship Phi Alpha Theta (Historical Honor Society) Alpha Sigma Lambda (Adult Honor Society); [oth. writ.] None published; [pers.] I voice for the abused and a mystical Native American viewpoint.; [a.] Parkton, MD

MIGHTY, DEBRA
[b.] Queens, NY; [p.] Earline Dowdy and Sidney Dowdy, Sr. (D); [m.] Colin Anthony Mighty, April 29, 1990; [ch.] Candace Marie Mighty; [ed.] Working towards a BA in Corporate Training, minor - Business Education - I attend Lehman College; [occ.] Legal Secretary; [memb.] Bronx Seventh-Day Adventist Church; [hon.] Notary Public; [oth. writ.] Several poems, short stories and a play.; [pers.] Writing is a part of my soul.; [a.] Yonkers, NY

MIKKELSEN, MADELYN BOYCE
[pen.] Madelyn Boyce Mikkelsen; [b.] May 2, 1939, Hempstead, NY; [p.] James Boyce and Madeline Boyce; [m.] Donald Costello Mikkelsen (Deceased), November 30, 1963; [ch.] Kevin Christian and Kathleen Mary; [ed.] High School, College 3 years, Real Estate Broker, California; [occ.] Owner, Management Services a real-estate related loan servicing business.; [memb.] California Assn. of Realtors, National Assn. of Realtors, Lake Elsinore Valley. Canyon Lake Assn. of Realtors Charter Director Wildomar Chamber of Commerce.; [hon.] Past President, Lake Elsinore Valley Board of Realtors.; [oth. writ.] Various articles published in local publications.; [pers.] Life is living every day and seeing

joy in what we do and receiving happiness from just doing...; [a.] Lake Elsinore, CA

MILES, CHRISTINA BLASI
[b.] November 23, 1950, Alabama; [p.] Christopher and Nell; [m.] Warren "Bud", November 2, 1979; [ch.] 5; [ed.] High School and Computer School; [occ.] Housewife; [oth. writ.] Children's books and one personal tragedy biography; [pers.] Don't travel through life faster than your guardian angels can fly; [a.] West Melbourne, FL

MILLAR, JOSEPH C.
[b.] May 6, 1976, Lancaster, PA; [p.] Joseph Millar and Ana Turene Millar; [m.] Dawn C. Poirier; [occ.] Journalist for "Juice" and "Ink Nineteen, New Music Magazine" and teller for first Union National Bank; [oth. writ.] "Cherry Chapstick" in, Ink 19 "An Autumn Moment" and "The Yard We've Seen Before" in McKenzie's Last.; [pers.] For my family.; [a.] Greensboro, NC

MILLER, AMANDA
[b.] July 8, 1982, Abilene, TX; [p.] Todd Miller, Jeanene Box, Duaine Box; [ed.] Runnels Junior High 8th grade; [occ.] Student; [memb.] Vice President of Art Club at Runnels Jr. High; [hon.] 1st place in Howard County Fair, for a painting, A,B honor role; [oth. writ.] Write in spare time, none published; [pers.] My goal in life is to become a writer and an artist.; [a.] Big Spring, TX

MILLER, B. DAWN
[b.] February 23, 1979, Twentynine Palms, CA; [p.] Steven L. and Mellie G. Miller; [pers.] 'Whatever you have seen or heard, it's true. What ever you think you have seen or heard, that too is real. It's all true "This is my favorite quote from Celestial Navigations.; [a.] Cleveland, GA

MILLER, BARBARA H.
[pen.] Bobbie Miller; [b.] May 22, 1925, New Jersey; [p.] Roslyn and Arthur Halvorsen; [m.] John Miller; [ch.] Two Daughters, five grandchildren; [ed.] High School, Secretarial School some College courses and poetry-writing workshop; [occ.] Retired Hospital Admitting Director; [memb.] Goshen Writers; [hon.] Honorary member National Association of Hospital Admitting Directors; [oth. writ.] Poems and articles published in local newspapers and church papers.; [pers.] I believe my best writing is about relationships and unique life experiences.; [a.] Goshen, CT

MILLER, BETTY JEAN
[pen.] Betty Jean Miller; [b.] August 5, 1941, Meridian, MS; [m.] Harold (Deceased), Hazel Green; [ch.] Gary Boatner, Robert Boatner, Donald Vandersen, Ronald Vandersen (Deceased), Daniel Vandersen; [ed.] Kate Griffin Jr High 10th grade Meridian, MS; [occ.] Social Security Disability; [oth. writ.] Dirt Road to Hell (1959) not copyrighted (stolen); [pers.] I believe that God is the creator. If you have God in you heart you have love for all people. The Holy Spirit will guide you to make life better for everyone; [a.] Meridian, MS

MILLER, MELISSA ANN
[b.] October 20, 1978, New Orleans; [p.] Judith Clark and May Ann Clark; [m.] Roger D. Cox; [ch.] Abita Spung's Elementary and Jr. High School, Covington High School (Senior); [oth. writ.] I am in the process of writing my book of poetry called "A Stream of Consciousness". The words will set a mood of imagination.; [pers.] I would like to say I wrote this poem to Robert G. Cox, who pasted away on 1995. This is dedicated to you, Robert.; [a.] Covington, LA

MILLER, RICKEY PAUL
[pen.] R. Paul Miller; [b.] May 1, 1953, Oxford, MS; [p.] Herman P. Miller (shorty) and Rose Davis; [m.] Barbara Lynn (Watts) Miller, July 17, 1980; [ed.] Life in itself; [occ.] E 911 Department, Lafayette Co. Sheriff Dept; [oth. writ.] Several about police work. 1 Poem published in "A Sea of Treasure" the National Library of Poetry.; [pers.] Some good lawmen: Dennis Gossett, Paul Webb, Andy Waller, Bruce Jenkens, Andy Shacklford, ED Jones, James Perke, Scott Mills, Mike Wilson and the last of the good ones, F.D. (Buddy) East.; [a.] Abbeville, MS

MILLER, STEVEN P.
[b.] May 6, 1966, Holyoke, MA; [p.] Paul and Florence Miller; [m.] Tina Carter, May 18, 1996; [ed.] Holyoke High School, University of South Carolina; [occ.] Air Force Officer; [memb.] Make-A-Wish Foundation Toast-Masters Int'l; [pers.] All things are possible through faith. Faith in the Lord and in yourself.; [a.] Colorado Springs, CO

MILLER, TARA
[ed.] Clemson University; [oth. writ.] Poems included in school literary magazine; [pers.] My writing is like the wings of a bird, when it takes flight, I can take you anywhere and to any time. I love to write because I can release the reflections of my soul in various ways through the written word.; [a.] Smyrna, GA

MILONAS, H. MINOS
[pen.] Minos Milonas; [b.] April 28, 1936, Heraklion, Crete, Greece (US citizen since 1968); [p.] Maria Milona, Stavros Milonas; [m.] Elaine Mauceli, May 25, 1988; [ed.] Dorsey Adult High, CA, Los Angeles Pierce College, CA, California State Univ at Northridge, CA, Univ of Washington Seattle, WA Degrees: Assoc of Arts, BA, MFA; [occ.] Artist, Poet; [memb.] Poetry Society of America Greek-American Writers' Association; [hon.] Grant, U. of Washington, Poncho Sculpture Scholarship, U. of Washington, Burien Arts Festival/Redmonds Arts Festival, two monetary awards, Hellenic Cultural Center, Springfield MA, 3 first place monetary awards. MFA graduate award.; [oth. writ.] To Mikro Karavani, a collection of short stories published in Athens, Greece, An Ode to My Ancestors, poem, published in the Greek-American Review, Art Is - 500 Definitions on Art, video.; [pers.] Coming from the Greece culture, I am philosophical about life and nature. My poems are about people, art, nature, death and philosophy; because I am an artist, I use visual imagery in my poems.; [a.] New York, NY

MILONE III, LOUIS JOHN
[b.] April 28, 1981, Mercy Hospital; [p.] Mr. Louis J. Milone Jr.; [m.] Mrs. Jeanette C. Milone, January 16, 1971; [ch.] Louis J. Milone III and James M. Milone; [ed.] Now in 9th grade at Chaminade High School Mineola, NY

MISIANO II, ANTHONY ROCCO
[pen.] Tony Misiano II; [b.] July 16, 1985, San Diego, CA; [p.] Anthony and Kathleen Misiano; [ed.] 5th Grade Student Gifted and Talented Education Program; [occ.] Grade School Student National City, CA; [oth. writ.] Poems - Raccoons - Ice Dragon and Snowman Sniffles.

MITCHELL, DOROTHY J.
[b.] August 30, 1928, Robeson Co., NC; [p.] Josephine and Martin Jones; [m.] May 1, 1945 (spouse deceased); [ch.] 4-5 grandchildren, 2 great-grandchildren; [ed.] High School graduate, 2 years college, graduated LPN; [occ.] Retired; [memb.] First Baptist Church, NAACP, AARP, Black Caucus, Eastern Star, Rosenwald Alumni, several choirs, Pioneer Civic and Social Club, Robeson Christian Women's Club; [hon.] Award for 50 years of Singing; award for appearing in community activities, choirs, play and single performance; [oth. writ.] "My Mama published in West Va. in 1994 by Sparrowgra Poetry Inc.; [pers.] I enjoy reading, writing, singin and fishing. My children have been my greate inspiration. [a.] Fairmont, NC

MITCHELL, MRS. JOE
[pen.] Sunny Laird; [b.] October 4, 1915, Atlant GA; [p.] Alma and Roy Wright; [m.] Joseph an Mitchell, March 21, 1983; [ch.] Linda Culler, Dorothy Boyd, Tommy Lair, (Deceased) Gary Lair (Deceased); [ed.] High School Atlanta, GA; [occ House wife; [memb.] Columbus flower worksho organized 1950 - President, 1999. Life member o garden club of gat, Inc.. State member of Nationa Council of Garden Clubs. Middle GA. Judges Council Macon, GA.; [hon.] Won Award of Distinctio 1968-81-82-91 for design in flower show, won 3 to award in the American hemerocallis show for desig June 3, 1995. Hold master certificate as judge o flower shows of national council garden club; [oth writ.] Cutting the apron strings, talking to th flowers, togetherness I'm a millionaire! "I'm millionaire! (song) the wise old creator.; [pers. enjoy my family first but hope someday to mak time to have published book of poems titled "poem about people and ordinary "things."; [a.] Columbus, GA

MIZE-JETTE, CHRISTINA
[pen.] Christina Silverio; [b.] June 25, 1975, Mountain View, CA; [p.] Vickie Jette; [m.] Eric Silverio, July 13, 1996; [ed.] Westmont High, West Valley College; [memb.] International Wildlife Coalition Whale Adoption Project; [pers.] I thank God every day for my talent. If I find I have touched just one person's life because of it, I will be grateful rewarded. [a.] Campbell, CA

MOAK, CHRISTINA L.
[b.] June 5, 1967, Chico, CA; [p.] James Moak and Sue Malin; [ch.] One put up for Adoption; [ed.] West Valley H.S. Fairbanks, Alaska; [occ.] Clerk - Advertising Department; [oth. writ] Novice; [pers.] Dedicated to my birth mother, for whom I found in October 1993. For the wonderful memories to make in the years to come. Sometime in the future when my child searches for me. I'll be waiting with open arms.; [a.] Anchorage, AK

MOCZULSKI, MELINA
[b.] October 14, 1978, Woodbridge, VA; [p.] Barbara and Lawrence; [ed.] Catholic Preparatory High School; [occ.] Student; [memb.] Student against Drink Driving, Interact Club; [hon.] Award of Excellence for writing.; [a.] Oxnard, CA

MOETZINGER, JULIE
[b.] May 10, 1981, Thiells, NY; [p.] Carol Ann and Edward Moetzinger; [ed.] Presently attending Albertus Magnus H.S; [occ.] High school freshman; [memb.] St. Gregory Barbarigo Church Choir, North Rockland Soccer Asso.; [hon.] Christus Rex Award for Community Service.; [pers.] I attempt the very best that I'm capable of doing.; [a.] Thiells, NY

MOGHADASSI, CYRUS
[pen.] Elvis "King"; [b.] June 15, 1982, California; [p.] Mostafa and Fariman Moghadassi; [ed.] Woodland Hills Elem. School and I attend A.E. Wright Middle School, I am in 8th grade; [memb.] USA National Karate-Do Federation; [hon.] Trophies, Medals etc. from Karate tournaments; [pers.] I would like to dedicate this to my two favorite actors, Bruce Lee and Jean-Claude Van-Damme. I thank my family for giving me everything.; [a.] Woodland Hills, CA

MONROE, CHRISTIAN D.
[b.] March 10, 1972; [ed.] Graduated with a diploma from a high school in South Jersey. Then graduated from a two year school with an Associates Degree in Science.; [occ.] Actor; [hon.] Dean's List, Shelby Lee Griffith Acting Scholarship; [pers.] You can never turn back time. If you want something now grab it before it disappears, never to be seen again. You can also never change the past. Learn from your mistakes - change the present and the future Thank S.G.M.D. for your inspiration. You are truly my "Soul Mate" and I will love you always!; [a.] Northfield, NJ

MONROE, REID DOUGLAS
[b.] October 8, 1965, Hospital; [p.] Two; [ed.] Lots; [memb.] YMCA, Sexa Holicas Anonymous; [hon.] "You'r e One Sexy Man, Mr. Monroe"; [oth. writ.] Letters to DA President!, Spray Paint DA Walls; [pers.] Never say I can't, do anything!

MONTAGUE, JAMES D.
[b.] August 20, 1971, Raleigh, NC.; [p.] James T. Montague, Geraldine S. Haywood; [ed.] Needham B. Broughton High, Saint Augustine's Colleges; [occ.] Substitute Teacher; [memb.] Usher Board, Tupper Memorial Baptist Church, Sigma Tau Delta, English Honor Society; [hon.] Dean's List, The National Dean's List, American Scholars, Who's Who Among Students in American Universities and Colleges.; [oth. writ.] Poems published in various literary magazines and chapbooks, co-Wrote and co-researched major study and paper with Drs. Julia Dreyden and Rebecca Weatherford, writer and department editor for Saint Augustine's Colleges Student newspaper.; [pers.] I think of poetry as painting pictures of life with words.; [a.] Raleigh, NC

MONTEMARANO, MICHAEL
[pen.] Michael (Walkere); [b.] December 6, 1974, White Plains; [p.] Antonio Montemarano, Julia M.; [ed.] Graduate from White Plains High School Class of '93, currently student deciding to go to college.; [occ.] Friendly's Galleria; [hon.] Made the honor roll in ninety-three.; [oth. writ.] Currently working on the novel (The Abattoir), also have written other poems, which I will submit at a later date.; [pers.] My love of writing also reflects my view of life. The poem I have written and submitted is the truth and it is what I truly believe.; [a.] White Plains, NY

MONTES, TROY D.
[b.] April 9, 1970, Healdsbury, CA; [p.] Janice Montes; [ed.] Forest Grove High, U.S. Air Force Academy Preparatory School, University of Oregon; [hon.] Appointment to the U.S. Air Force Academy, Dean's Scholar, triple major - U of Oregon; [pers.] The most important things to me: Love, life family and friends.; [a.] Forest Grove, OR

MONTGOMERY, ARVIL RAY
[b.] March 1, 1938, Davin, WV; [p.] Dennie and Frances Montgomery; [m.] Christine Montgomery, December 5, 1959; [ch.] Steven, David and Teresa; [ed.] High School Man, West Virginia (1956); [occ.] Retired; [hon.] My biggest awards are our three grandsons. Bryan, Corey, and Austin.; [oth. writ.] Poems for friends and family albums. (Births, Birthday, Weddings, etc.); [pers.] I try to express what I feel in my heart.; [a.] Agoura Hills, CA

MONTOYA, ANGIE
[b.] December 18, 1952, Wilmington, CA; [p.] Manuel, Arsenia Montoya; [ch.] Kristy and Aaron; [ed.] "Early Childhood" Education, Music. Harbor College; [occ.] Child Care Worker; [pers.] Poetry, is a strong expression that can open-up your mind and soul, this is my way. Of reaching out touching one's life.; [a.] Long Beach, CA

MOODIE, MELINDA A.
[pen.] Mindy Moodie; [b.] January 24, 1973, Evergreen Park, IL; [p.] Edgar and Kathleen Moodie; [ed.] Chicago Christian High School, Moraine Valley Community College A.A. Judson College - B.A. Communication Arts, Media Studies. Watching People.; [occ.] Graphics and Communications Assistant at Fairview Ministries, Inc.; [memb.] Crossroads Community Church, National Honor Society; [hon.] Dean's List, Cum Laude graduate; [oth. writ.] Several news and feature articles in The Desplaines Valley Newspaper.; [pers.] As a mirror reflects the one who blew and shaped its glass, so I hope to reflect the image of my Creator through my life and writings. Jesus' choice to give me life - not once, but twice through salvation - thrills me and makes me long to capture His world through words. I have been influence by the music of Amy Grant.; [a.] Orland Park, IL

MOORE, AMY E.
[b.] September 3, 1971, Forth Worth, TX; [p.] Richard and Judy Moore; [ed.] Burleson High School, Harding University (B.A. in Child Development); [occ.] Computer Teacher for Compu Quest and Independent Sales Consultant for Pampered Chef; [memb.] (ACCH) Association for the Care of Children's Health: Child Life Council; [oth. writ.] The Essence of Passion published in a Pampered Chef Newsletter.; [pers.] Life is meant to be lived with passion. Passion is doing what you love and being the best at it. With passion, you go the extra mile in the marathon of life. Passion ignites a persons dreams and leads them to becoming reality.; [a.] Burleston, TX

MOORE, FREDERICK SHAYNE
[b.] June 6, 1964, Joplin, MO; [p.] Fred and Donna Moore; [m.] Stephanie Moore, July 18, 1986; [ch.] Leslie Reshay Moore and Savannah Rae Moore; [ed.] Elizabethtown High School Graduate; [oth. writ.] "A Collection of Poems by Frederick Shayne Moore", "Thoughts, Only Thoughts.", published, Kidd Lightning Publishing 1995, unpublished. Not completed; [pers.] Share your love with all. For only shared love will go on to engender such exhilaration that the mind, in it's finite state it is here, can not even imagine.; [a.] Elizabethtown, KY

MOORE, HELEN SHEETS
[pen.] Hassie; [b.] September 29, 1939, Huntingdon, PA; [p.] Lena and Harry Sheets; [ed.] High School - also a Certificate of Management in Animal Husbandry from Penn State University, State College, PA; [oth. writ.] Several true nature stories published in 554 magazine. Article published in PA state game news magazine.; [pers.] Enjoy writing short non-fiction stories, poems and reading. Avid lover of nature and animals.; [a.] Mill Creek, PA

MOORE, JUANITA E.
[b.] July 8, 1953, Philadelphia, PA; [p.] Warren Floyd and Ida Floyd; [m.] Leonard L. Moore, November 12, 1972; [ch.] On-Jonet Beychamel and Melaya Ijuan; [ed.] Overbrook H.S., Sawyer College of Business, currently attending Long Beach City College, and looking to transfer to C.S.U. Dominguez Hills soon; [occ.] Secretary, Banning High School, Wilmington, CA; [memb.] I am a member of the Gospel Memorial C.O.G. IC where I am very active; [oth. writ.] I have written several other poems just for the pleasure of writing. This is my first contest and publication; [pers.] My writings reflect the progress of my people, coupled with a spiritual insight, as a born-again believer.; [a.] Long Beach, CA

MOORE, KIRSTEN
[b.] August 8, 1986, Biddeford, ME; [p.] L. Ruth Varley, (nee Dulmage) P. Gary Moore; [occ.] Student, Morristown Central School; [hon.] High Honors; [a.] Ogdensburg, NY

MOORE, ORLANTHA
[b.] February 21, 1980, Monroe, LA; [p.] Glen Moore Sr., Monica Moore; [ed.] Sophomore Wossman, High School Monroe, LA; [pers.] As a teenager you have to be strong and always remember where you came from.; [a.] Monroe, LA

MOORE, ROBIN LINDLEY
[b.] April 9, 1962, La Mirada, CA; [p.] Les and Barbara Lindley; [ed.] Casey Moore and Katie Moore; [occ.] AA degree from Fullerton College, presently in National University obtaining my BS degree; [memb.] Bookkeeper; [oth. writ.] I am presently working on three children's stories.; [pers.] With today being so tough on children, there needs to be a little joy in their life. Children can always find hope, love and joy in a story. That is why reading is so important to children. Reading is a place children can go live dreams.; [a.] Buena Park, CA

MOORE, VIRGINIA E.
[b.] April 4, 1952, Los Angeles, CA; [ed.] Valencia High, Saddleback College; [occ.] Graphic Designer (Catalog and Support Material, Recreational Equipment, Inc. (REI)), Kent, Washington; [memb.] Parents and friends of Lesbians and Gays; [oth. writ.] Ongoing progress with nonfiction books of interviews and a novel.; [pers.] I write to encourage understanding, truth and acceptance of our human differences. I hope this poem will also encourage my fellow gays and lesbians to be true to themselves no matter the consequence.; [a.] Seattle, WA

MORAN, KENT
[b.] June 12, 1982, New York City; [p.] Joan and Fred Moran; [ed.] Greenwich Country Day School, Greenwhich, Ct. 8th grade; [occ.] Student; [hon.] 1991, 1993, 1995 Bill Hershinger Award - Outstanding Camper 1990, 1992, 1994 Most Outstanding Swimmer, 1990 thru 1995 All Star Star Swimmer, 1993 Academic and Effort Honor Roll; [oth. writ.] Other poems short stories and other such writings.; [pers.] Some of my poetry is written primarily for pleasure. However, most of my writings are done in order to send a message to the world on my different views on various subjects. I write to inform the world of different problems we are having, to make people aware of these present problems and in some cases try to provide a responsible solution.; [a.] Greenwhich, CT

MORANDA, ROBERT E. P.
[b.] June 1, 1913, CA; [m.] Verna Fay Moranda; [occ.] Retired; [hon.] Silver Star, Purple Heart, Bronze Star, Combat Infantry Man's Badge, Commendation Medal, Presidential Merit Citation, Korean War Service

MORENO, HELEN ROSE
[pen.] H. R. M.; [b.] April 10, 1924, Germaco, NM; [p.] John and Catherine Mukavetz; [m.] Divorced; [ch.] Michael, Renae, Edward, Lisa and Robert; [ed.] High School, C.N.A. Certified Nurse Assistant; [occ.] Retired; [memb.] Eckankar Church, Eck writers group, received honorable mention in poetry contest years ago.; [hon.] I have a natural gift of spiritual writing, friends who have problems confide in me, I pick up my pen and ask for information and receive immediate answers, I love to read, read in a spiritual.; [oth. writ.] Book the passage in which God said, when you write about me write only poetry, so now when something impresses me, I write about it and the poetry comes flowing.; [pers.] I come from a musical family, my uncle was a brilliant pianist, my mother who has a third grade education, had a natural talent as a pianist. I love to sing, one daughter sings, play guitar, one sings and plays the key board, I'm concerned about animals and work at feeding birds

and squirrels in the cold Michigan winters.; [a.] Berkley, MI

MORGAN, JESSIE SMITH
[b.] January 30, 1945, Port Royal, SC; [p.] Charlton A. Smith, Angerine Bennett Smith; [ed.] Robert Smalls High, Mather Jr. College Alderson - Broaddus College University of South Carolina; [oth. writ.] The Checkered Book Series' children book: Stories For A Pleasurable Night.; [pers.] I have an affinity for children and deeply respect their natural intellect, imaginative genius and insight for discerning true affection.; [a.] North Augusta, SC

MORGAN, MATTHEW L.
[pen.] Ian Scott; [b.] January 7, 1973, Holyoke, MA; [p.] Raymond L. Morgan, Katherine J. Morgan; [m.] Kelly E. Morgan, July 2, 1994; [ed.] Grissom High School (Hunstville, AL), University of Southwestern Louisiana (Lafayette, LA) B.S. in environmental and sustainable resources; [occ.] Staff scientist, Ambar technical laboratories, Laffayette, LA; [memb.] Soil and water Conservation Society; [hon.] Alpha Zeta Honor Fraternity, Dean's Lists; [oth. writ.] Other poems that have not been published.; [pers.] Poetry is something that I enjoy writing in a quiet and undisturbed place, in a calming atmosphere. "Smile" God loves you.; [a.] Lafayette, LA

MORGAN, SHIRLEY MAE
[pen.] T. C. Christie; [b.] June 29, 1933, MN; [p.] Gladys Zelmer; [m.] William D. Morgan, January 27, 1951; [ch.] Terry, Bob, Lisa, Grandchildren: Grandy and Heidi; [ed.] Snohomish High, Everett College; [occ.] Retired; [hon.] Ballroom Dancing Trophies; [oth. writ.] I've only begun; [pers.] I'd like this poem dedicated to Brandy Morgan and Heidi Davis my grandchildren which I owe the courage and faith to move ahead with my life. Thank you and lots of LOVE.; [a.] Marysville, WA

MORGAN SR., PHILLIP L.
[pen.] P. Luther Morgan, P. Luke; [b.] January 17, 1960, Knoxville, TN; [p.] J. L. and Z. (Floyd) Morgan; [m.] C. A. (Kimbrough) Morgan, December 13, 1985; [ch.] P. L. M. Jr.; [ed.] Fulton High, State Tech. at Knox (Real Estate Certification); [occ.] State of Tn. D.O.T.; [memb.] Cherry St. Church of God; [hon.] Knox Co. School System Chapter 1 (one), Distinguished Service Award for parent involvement, 1992-93; [oth. writ.] Poems in church publications, poems read orally at church programs, several personal writings never published or presented.; [pers.] Most of my writing is personal experience. The rest is from world events. Make the most from the talents God gives you.; [a.] Knoxville, TN

MORRIS, ELSIE D.
[b.] April 6, 1920, Beaumont, TX; [p.] Edward and Lula Durant; [ed.] Graduate of Huston-Tillotson College in Austin Awarded BS degree in 1943. A&S Masters degree from Denver University. Diploma from Institute of Children's Literature; [occ.] She was a retired school teacher with 30 years of employment; [memb.] Sigma Gamma Rho Sorority; [hon.] Port Arthur Classroom Teachers Association Port Arthur Independent School District, Port Arthur Public Schools Certificate of Merit, and The Texas Congress of Parents and Teachers - Honorary Life Membership; [oth. writ.] Poetic Gems, Stories and Poems, and Poems and More..; [pers.] The author has been an avid lover of poetry, simply for the relaxing soothing comfort and sheer joy that poetry brings into one's life.; [a.] Port Arthur, TX

MORRIS, JULIET M. GRIMBLE
[pen.] Julie Morris; [b.] August 5, 1960, Sacramento, CA; [p.] Otis Grimble - Alma Grimble; [m.] Jimmie A. Morris, December 24, 1979; [ch.] Jennea M., Jeniele L., Jillian N., Je'Anna L.; [ed.] John Cabrillo Elementary, John F. Kennedy Sr. High Consumer River Jr. College; [occ.] Administration Assistant; [memb.] ASCAP, NAACP; [hon.] Honorary mention for the poem "Blue Moons and Purple Stars" poem and published in Great American Poetry Anthology; [oth. writ.] "Reflections in a Water Pool", "Reflections in a Water Pool Dripping Rain" (collective poetry works) (not published yet "Blue Moons and Purple Stars" published in Great American poetry anthology; [pers.] I began writing poems in High School. I found that God not only blessed me with a fine singing voice, but also a gift of self expression from mind to paper with just a stroke of pencil.; [a.] Sacramento, CA

MORRISON, EUGENE L.
[b.] February 6, 1963; [p.] Louise and Clifford Morrison of Belize City; [ed.] BS in English from Northern Michigan University; [occ.] Technical Writer for Fortune 500 Companies; [memb.] Several writings Clubs, Toastmasters International Speaking Club; [hon.] Many writing awards; [oth. writ.] I have written two unpublished novels, and I'm working on my first Anthology of poems. Worked as Journalist for several years. Presently write for local and international papers (Freelance).; [a.] Westchester, CA

MORROW, AUSTIN
[b.] Hammon, OK; [p.] Sterling and Ruth Morrow; [m.] 1938; [ch.] Five; [ed.] Public Schools, Agriculture, Ranching, Trade Schools, Accounting, Drafting, Engineering, Welding, Carpentry, Construction.; [occ.] Farming, Inventing, and Manufacturing.; [memb.] Church of Christ; [hon.] Singing-several blue ribbons, Performed at Cowboy Poetry gatherings, Have U.S. patents, have articles in newspapers and magazines.; [oth. writ.] Have over 150 Copyrighted Composition classed Southwest Country Ballads with up beat in moral messages.; [pers.] My philosophy must be, the near sacred talents I see, drafting, inventing, writing and composing my Creator gave unto me. (I must use them or lose them); [a.] Portales, NM

MOSER, LINDA
[b.] March 4, 1961, MD; [p.] Edna and Roland Faulkner; [m.] Donald Moser, May 27, 1986; [ch.] 3 - David 10, Nick 5 - Ashley 2; [ed.] High School; [occ.] Housewife; [pers.] I wrote this one only from my heart. As I was born a sick child - Rejected by my natural mother and left in hospital was loved and adopted by my parents and after several operations I am whole again and have a wonderful life.

MOSES, NELL
[b.] November 19, 1931, Douglasville, GA; [p.] J. S. Thomas, Willie Thomas; [m.] Warren Moses, June 10, 1950; [ch.] Marion Anthony, Bruce Kevin; [ed.] GA. State College for women, GA. State College, Univ, of Indiana; [pers.] Poems are the way I find out what I know. I celebrate life and the human spirit, in it's joys and sorrows. I marvel at the awesome grandeur of God's Creation, from the mighty universe to the smallest atom.; [a.] Corydon, IN

MOSS, JEANNE PALMER
[b.] Albermarle, NC; [p.] William V. Palmer, Gertrude M. Palmer; [m.] James H. Moss Sr., February 25, 1961; [ch.] James H. Moss Jr. and Andrea Palmer Moss; [ed.] Albemarle High School, Duke University - English Major, College for Financial Planning; [memb.] Riverside Presbyterian Church - Stephen Minister Cummer Museum of Art and Gardens, Garden Club of Jacksonville, FL; [hon.] Valedictorian, Dean's List, Social Standards Committee, Honorary Education Fraternity, Honorary French Fraternity; [oth. writ.] First poem was published in North Carolina State Magazine while a high scho student; [pers.] It is gratifying to write with adm ration and gratitude, honoring outstanding indivi uals and geographic locations in God's world; [a Jacksonville, FL

MOSTELLER, TERESA M.
[b.] November 9, 1955, San Francisco, CA; [p Robert J. and Teresa E. McCabe; [m.] Gordon Mosteller; [ch.] Emily Nicole; [ed.] University Colorado Bachelors Degree in Business (Theat minor). Machebeuf High School, Denver, CC [occ.] Sales and Service, Mutual of Omaha; [memb National Traspian Society; [hon.] HIAA (wi Honors); [oth. writ.] Presentation of her origin play, "Mr. Lucky's," in Seattle, WA, Several publ poetry readings, freelance poetry - and lyric-wri ing, unpublished plays and short stories.; [pers Throughout life and as a writer, my biggest influenc has been my wonderful and fascinating family. enjoy the lighter side of life and specialize in humo and light satire. My greatest source of pride is Emily who inspired the selected poem!; [a.] Seattle, W

MOTL, MARY
[b.] September 29, 1935, San Angelo, TX; [p. George William Cates and Artie Wallace Cates; [m. Benjamin Ellis Motl, October 20, 1951; [ch.] Darlene Brenda, Daniel; [ed.] Lake View High, 9th Grade [occ.] Retired Motl Welding Shop, 33 yrs. co owner, book-keeper, receptionist; [hon.] No clain to fame; [oth. writ.] Music and poetry unpublished [pers.] To me writing poetry or music is a pleasure So, if I could share with you a moment of pleasure a smile, a tear, a bit of faith, or a glimmer of hope then my heart is glad.; [a.] San Angelo, TX

MOUDY, R. DEAN
[b.] August 1, 1948, Oklahoma; [p.] Jackson Arlo. Montrey Lou Moudy; [ch.] Heather Marie Moudy [ed.] University of Iowa, Central Missouri State University; [occ.] Human Resources/Personnel Management Consultant; [hon.] Golden Poet Award 1991 Quill and Scroll, Honor Society for Journalists Best New Poets of 1989, Who's Who is Poetry 1990, Silver Poet Award 1990; [oth. writ.] National Library of poetry - 1993; [pers.] There is nothing wrong with attempting perfection, have the courage to risk improving...it places you closer to the dreams of God!; [a.] Phoenix, AR

MRACEK, ANNA
[b.] December 21, 1981, Saint Louis; [p.] Ann Mracek and Richard Merritt; [ed.] Attending Mary Institute and St. Louis Country Day School, grade 8; [occ.] Student; [memb.] Smithsonian, Air and Space, Startrek Fan Club and Star Trek Nit Pickers Guild; [hon.] Highest Academic Award, Detur, for grades 5, 6, and 7, the MICPS Alumni Annual Writing Award, full academic scholarship to U.S. Space Academy; [oth. writ.] Various unpublished poems and short stories; [pers.] In all I do, I try to put God first and do the best job I can. The old statement, "Anything worth doing is worth doing right." Still holds truth.; [a.] Saint Louis, MO

MUELLER, LAURA E.
[pen.] Elizabeth Heart; [b.] September 2, 1957, La Grande, GA; [p.] Jean and Glenn Gray; [m.] Robert C. Mueller, February 22, 1980; [ed.] Linden High, Linden, Ca., San Joaquin Delta Community College, MTI Business College; [occ.] Homemaker, part time health care worker and artist; [memb.] The human race and the planet earth; [hon.] Honored that you recognized my talent and honored that God bestowed it upon me.; [oth. writ.] Numerous poems and short stories - unpublished as yet...; [pers.] I feel that connecting to our creative nature will bring peace to the human heart and new life to our souls. I greatly admire the work of Van Morrison, among

...thers.; [a.] Valley Springs, CA

MULDREW, MINNIE GILLESPIE
[b.] September 10, 1918, Sweet Home, AR; [p.] Rosh N. Gillespie, Hattie Gillespie; [m.] Fletcher T. Muldrew, August 19, 1967; [ch.] Sharon, Lita, David; [ed.] Dunbar High School, Little Rock, Arkansas, Hampton, Virginia, B.S. Degree, Louisiana State University, M. Ed. Degree, Baton Rouge, Louisiana; [occ.] Retired Educator; [memb.] Dunbar High School Alumni Ass'n. Alpha Kappa alpha Sorority - Founders Church of Religious Science - Association of Retired Teachers - California Teachers Association - National Education Ass'n.; [hon.] Valedictorian High School and Jr. College Classes - PTA Honorary Life Membership - Certificates of Appreciation for Services from the Los Angeles Unified School District, the Major and City Council. Certificate of Appreciation from the Parents of 99th St. School of Los Angeles, CA; [oth. writ.] Article published in the Arkansas Gazette, "Pets for Seniors", Edited School Newsletter for Parents and Staff, Organized Publications for Educational Programs in progress during periods of my employment.; [pers.] Understanding human behavior has always been an interest of mine. Educators must learn as much as possible about the influences prevailing in the lives of the children they teach.; [a.] Culver City, CA

MULLICK, PAMELA E.
[pen.] P. E. Mullick; [b.] March 13, 1967, California; [p.] Mr. and Mrs. W. M. Mullick; [pers.] My writings are from deep within me and full of true life meanings and actions. To know ones self is to rediscover yourself in different aspect of life.; [a.] Sacramento, CA

MUNOZ, TONY C.
[pen.] Tony C. Munoz; [b.] October 12, 1954, Mexico; [p.] Antonio Munoz, Olivia Munoz; [m.] Jane Bridget Tolan-Munoz, October 6, 1984; [ch.] Thomas Clayborn, Catherine Jane; [ed.] Watsonville High, Humboldt State University, BA Biology; [occ.] Food and Drug Investigator, State of California; [memb.] California Association of Food and Drug Investigators (CAFDI); [hon.] CAFDI Commendation for Public Health Protection; [oth. writ.] Private poems, never before published; [pers.] I enjoy outdoors and have been influenced by John Muir's writings on nature. I have high regard for the farm laborers in the local Pajaro and Salinas Valleys.; [a.] Watsonville, CA

MURILLO, ALEJANDRO BUENO
[b.] November 2, 1918, Ontario, CA; [p.] Benito R. Murillo and Aurora B. Murill; [m.] Julia O. Murillo, July 5, 1948; [ch.] Six; [ed.] Elem Jr. High Senior High Industrial College - Business College; [occ.] Retired; [memb.] Vets; [hon.] Purple heart - bronze star good conduct medal - pres. unit medal European African middle eastern medal - world war II victory medal combat inf. men badge; [oth. writ.] "America" - my little girl" "Where can you hide: That I won't find death you? "My silent prayer" Never dwell upon yesterdays loneliness" wrote artica on appenenes winter line 34th Div - April 16, 1945 Great religious depth observation etc.; [pers.] A life time spent in bringing love, brotherhood and God to all who come into my life, by sharing all that God has given unto me, food, shelter money, work and my inner most self!; [a.] Tujunga, CA

MURPHEY, MARTHA
[pen.] Martha Murphey; [b.] February 22, Lancaster, OH; [p.] Vernon Smith, Dona Smith; [m.] Randall Murphey (Deceased), June 5, 1937; [ch.] William, Nancy; [ed.] High School Cosmetology School; [occ.] Retired; [memb.] Bexley United, Methodist Church, United Methodist Women Central Ohio Kennel Club, West Highland White Terrier, Club of Northern Ohio; [oth. writ.] A few other poems that were written in my earlier years and some that were written more recently; [pers.] My poems to date have been based mostly or our Great Creator and reflect experiences that have entered my life.; [a.] Columbus, OH

MURPHY, CHRISTOPHER A.
[pen.] Chris Murphy; [b.] March 6, 1974, Santa Monica; [p.] Robert and Mary Fran Murphy; [ed.] Attended Corpus Christi (Grades K-8) Attended Crossroads for the Arts and Science (9-12) Sonoma State University (Freshman) Santa Monica City College; [occ.] I am a student at Santa Monica City College with a keen interest in music; [hon.] Pacific Palisades Optimist Club's Youth of the Month October 1987; [oth. writ.] Song Lyrics, screenplays, as assortment of poems ranging from the zanny to the serious, the open-minded to the closed; [pers.] In my writings I touch upon emotions felt and emotions lost. Until the inspiration finds me with pen in hand can the emotion become a voice. It is my voice which writes and sings my emotions. Thus there are words to live by.; [a.] Santa Monica, CA

MURPHY, KATHERINE
[b.] November 29, 1915, Vigo City, IN; [p.] Nellie and Charles Ferree; [m.] Albert T. Murphy (Deceased), June 30, 1934; [ch.] Marilyn June, Carol Anne, Robert James; [ed.] High School in Terre Haute, IN.; [occ.] Retired from many years of clerical figure work; [memb.] None previous: Penwomen's Club of Dupo, IL; [oth. writ.] Only for creative writing class; [a.] Belleville, IL

MURPHY, MARION
[pen.] Marion Giottocolucci; [b.] March 6, 1940, New York; [p.] Frank and Ida Colucci; [m.] Divorced; [ch.] Four; [hon.] Abraham and Strauss Professional Oil Painting. Interview and write up in Suffolk sun newspaper by Shirley Carlson society editor; [oth. writ.] Soul searching song lyrics, poems. Have begun writing on two books.; [a.] New York

MURPHY, NORMAN E.
[b.] May 12, 1967, Streator, IL; [p.] Sam E. Murphy, Janet Pottinger; [m.] Mary Ann Murphy, March 27, 1987; [ch.] Duane and Daniel Romero; [ed.] 2 yrs. Ad Lamar Univ.; [occ.] Registered Respiratory Therapist St. Mary Hospital.; [memb.] TSRA; [pers.] Poetry is the best vehicle for emotion and images. I wish to become the best poet that my abilities allow.; [a.] Bridle City, TX

MURR, STEWART J.
[b.] May 24, 1972, Winchester, VA; [m.] Stacy L. Murr, July 9, 1994; [ch.] Jess R. Murr; [ed.] John Handley High School, Lord Fairfax Community College, Univ of Southern Colorado; [occ.] USAF, McGuire AFB, NJ; [hon.] VA H.S. League State Championships 3rd place short story.; [oth. writ.] Stories, poems, lyrics, music. This is first publication of any.; [pers.] "Bouncing on beds, I remember from childhood, is a great depression reliever". Robert M. Pirsig, Zon and the Art of Motorcycle Maintenance.; [a.] Pemberton, NJ

MURRAY, AMANDA
[b.] January 17, 1981, OH; [p.] Mr and Mrs Thomas Murray Jr.; [ed.] West Jr. High in Columbia, Missouri and Lexington Catholic High School in Lexington, Kentucky; [hon.] Second place in the West Jr. High Speech Tourney - 1995 for Poetry reading, honor roll; [pers.] I believe strongly in the statement. "That which does not kill us makes us stronger".; [a.] Lexington, KY

MURRAY, TIFFANY
[b.] June 30, 1983, Danville, VA; [p.] Sarah and Jason Murray; [ed.] E. A. Gibson, Middle School Coates Elementary School; [occ.] Student, Edwin A. Gibson Middle; [memb.] The Bibleway Church: The Joy Choir Gibson School College Awareness Program; [hon.] Honor Roll, Perfect Attendance, Certificate of Merit from Nation's Bank, and awards for stories and poems.; [oth. writ.] "Just Open Your Eyes", "Boy Oh Boy What A Day", "My Mother" and "A Lonely Man's Sorrow".; [pers.] "For me life is like a non-ending street. I can only go forward, and never go back."; [a.] Danville, VA

MURTHY, ANITHA
[b.] September 21, 1966, Bangalore, India; [p.] P. L. N. Murthy, Lalitha Murthy; [m.] Pattabhi Sudindra, October 7, 1994; [ed.] Degree in Engineering; [occ.] Software Engineer; [oth. writ.] Articles and poems in local newspaper (in India) and in-house magazines.; [a.] Antioch, TN

MYERS, REGINA A.
[pen.] Gina A. Myers; [b.] December 25, 1981, Forsyth Co., NC; [p.] Richard E. Myers, Debbie M.; [ed.] Presently a student in the 8th grade at North Davie Middle School, Mocksville, NC; [occ.] Student; [a.] Advance, NC

NABIEVA, ELENA
[b.] June 3, 1979, Moscow, Russia; [p.] Rashit Nabiev, Tatzana Nabiev; [ed.] Junior at Los Altos High School; [occ.] High School student; [memb.] National Honor Society, California Scholarship Federation; [pers.] My writing reflects my search for truth - if one common truth exists at all. I have been influenced by 19th and 20th century poets, especially by Mikhail Lermontor; [a.] Mountain View, CA

NADLER, DOT LURIA
[b.] June 15, New Haven; [p.] Basia and Morton Conn; [m.] Harry Nadler De, June 15, 1925; [ch.] Morton and Gerry; [ed.] NYU and Art (Night studied Under two (H.S. English Men "Bridge Water" and Petit it 1920's; [occ.] AM. Vol. SEC. (15 years for Advisory Board in Government Center); [memb.] For of and RJOP Pres, (2 yrs) for the VU, won Div. of the Univ. (yrs schica) The Board of R Fun raising Chairwoman Captain for Amer. Heart and Amen Cancer and Red and (in my vill-connecting funs/the old-American; [hon.] Certificates 86-86-91 from Senior Artist of the yrs in "Whose Who" 1985 and '87 of poets and Author's" contributed in the a Mem. poetry anthology pub by John Frost Robert; [oth. writ.] Frost's Grand Son 1985 my 1st poem "a new day ha-dawned" pub in the school year book" I was 8 years old. Recited it in the auditorium; [pers.] "Reflections of Our Times" Published in '86. Wrote for the democrat (newspaper) 12 years and Sunday people to people) record.; [a.] New Haven, CT

NAGO, STEPHANIE
[b.] August 6, 1961, Kauai; [p.] Mervilyn and Take (stepfather) Yamashiro, Steven Iida (father); [m.] David, January 6, 1994; [ch.] Preston and LeeAnne; [ed.] Kapaa High School, Kauai Community College; [oth. writ.] "Piercing Winds of Hurricane Iniki," appeard in the "911" publication of Kauai Community College; [pers.] I believe that writing expresses a person's feelings in a precise manner, enabling the reader to actually visualize an imaginary scene in an extraordinary way.

NAVARRO II, THOMAS W.
[pen.] Gypsy; [b.] August 30, 1970, Dover, NJ; [p.] Thomas and Pauline Navarro; [ch.] Thomas W. Navarro III; [occ.] Professional horseman; [memb.] The American Legion; [pers.] "Love is for the lucky - and luck is with the LOVED."

NAWOJ, ALLISON J.
[b.] April, 8, 1983, Elkhorn, WI; [p.] James and Janet Nawoj; [ed.] Williams Bay Elementary School; [occ.] Student; [hon.] President's Outstanding Academic Achievement Award; [pers.] I like to write poetry because it expresses issues and feelings indirectly you can put a point across without saying exactly what it is about.; [a.] Williams Bay, WI

NEIDY, CANDICE ANN
[pen.] Bonkers; [b.] January 8, 1982, Wayne, MI; [p.] Aimee and Mark Hampton; [ed.] I go to Edmonson Middle School in the Willow Run district; [occ.] Student; [hon.] Certificate of appreciation from Ypsilanti Charter fire department for artwork, Public speaking award, Awards for science fair project and field days running track and soft ball; [oth. writ.] 'Clean Your Room', Messy Messy Mess Makers, Christmas and What It Means; [pers.] I'd have to thank my parents for pushing me towards this whole deal and telling me that my poems were really great and thanks my brother for listening to them.; [a.] Ypsilanti, MI

NELSON, GREGG
[pers.] My goal in poetry is simple, yet extremely difficult: to convey all the raw emotion that is present in one single moment of a person's life. I will not feel that I have fulfilled my debt to poetry until this becomes a reality.

NELSON, JENNIFER ELIZABETH
[b.] May 17, 1987, Englewood, NJ; [p.] Elizabeth A. Nelson, Bertil C. Nelson; [ed.] Preschool Grove Hill, Nursery School, K-3 Clifton School; [occ.] Student; [memb.] Clifton Stallions Soccer Team, TAG Program (Talented and gifted, troop to GSA Brownie Troop); [hon.] Soccer Trophies 1st place, honor roll TAG program, Bd of Ed reading certificate; [pers.] I love to write and the stories and words just pour out of my head.; [a.] Clifton, NJ

NELSON, MARILYN A.
[b.] October 14, 1963, Oklahoma City, OK; [p.] Betty L. Saunders, William R. (Sandy) Saunders; [ch.] Joshua Thomas, Daniel Aaron; [ed.] Roosevelt High School; [occ.] Billing Clerk, Clements Foods - OKC, OK; [oth. writ.] I write about anything that catches my attention or express an intense thought or feeling. I have great admiration for Bernie Taupin, lyricist for Elton John.; [pers.] Oklahoma City, OK

NELSON, PAUL
[b.] September 22, 1991, Chicago, IL; [p.] Paul Sr., Lesbia Pino; [m.] Janice Berk Nelson, December 31, 1985; [ch.] Rebecca Rose Nelson; [ed.] BA - Columbia College, Chicago, IL (Broadcast Communications) '83; [occ.] Radio Interview Host, Holistic Journalist; [memb.] President/Founder of: "It plays in Peoria Productions", A 501 (c)(3) dedicated to "injecting a little wisdom into the information age"; [hon.] Hon. Mention - "Excellence in Legal Journalism", WA State Bar Association 1992; [oth. writ.] Upcoming book of poetry: "We don't celebrate Halloween in Cuba (And other Stories from Auburn)".; [pers.] "Nothing is absolute, save the nation that Holism is the answer."; [a.] Auburn, WA

NELSON, STAFFORD
[pen.] Anthony Nelson; [b.] January 23, 1965, Jamaica, WI; [p.] Ina Simon; [m.] Wendy Nelson, August 13, 1995; [ch.] Andrew Nelson; [pers.] Living in a world of darkness, my wife Wendy is my light and my inspiration.; [a.] Silver Lake, CA

NELSON, WILLIAM R.
[b.] October 1, 1924, Racine, WI; [p.] Joseph B. and Tena M. Nelson; [m.] Kathleen Peyton Nelson, February 13, 1944; [ch.] Kathleen S., David J. and Peter B.; [ed.] Univ. Wisconsin 1950, BSCHE; [occ.] Retired; [oth. writ.] Short stories-family experiences; [a.] De Pere, WI

NETTLES, DAVID
[b.] June 18, 1965, Upland, CA; [p.] Darrell and Beverly Nettles; [m.] Rebecca Sue Nettles, May 28, 1995; [ed.] Community College of the USAF; [occ.] Business owner, writer; [memb.] Laubach Literacy Tutor, World Wildlife Federation; [hon.] Disabled Veterans Asso. "Americanism Award" 1990, Editor's Choice Award National Library of Poetry; [oth. writ.] The Carmichael Experiment, beyond this pointe, and storm maker along with several short stories, songs, and poetry; [pers.] Keep thy heart with all diligence, for out of it are the issues of life - Proverbs 4:23.; [a.] Upland, CA

NEVSHEMAL, JOHN A.
[pen.] John A. Nevshemal; [b.] October 14, 1935, Milwaukee, WI; [p.] Anthony Nevshemal and Beatrice McGann; [m.] Elizabeth, November 19, 1966, Divorced; [ch.] Kris, Tony, Marty, Mike, Joe; [ed.] B.S. Engineering (Mech), MS Engineering (Mech); [occ.] Chief Engineer; [memb.] American Nuclear Society Professional Engineers Society; [oth. writ.] Short story entitled 2027 Miscellaneous poems; [pers.] Love is the basic driving force in all aspects of life.; [a.] Parker, CO

NEWMAN, MYRIA
[b.] 1941; [occ.] Yoga Facilitator; [pers.] We have only to keep our hearts, minds and eyes open and life will inundate us with delights at every turn.; [a.] Auburn, NY

NG, AMY S.
[b.] November 17, 1972, Canton, China; [p.] Fong Chou Ng and Sai Chang Ng; [ed.] Group Health Foundation Fellowship Program, Washington DC, Western New England College, Springfield, MA, Chicopee High School, Chicopee, MA; [occ.] Health Maintenance Organization (HMO) Management Fellow, New York Life/HealthPlus, Greenbelt, MD; [memb.] Healthcare Financial Management Assoc., Managed Care Forum, American Health Planning Association; [hon.] Management Association Award, Alpha Lambda Delta Honor Society, James Z. Naurison Scholarship Fund, Dean's List, Cum Laude; [oth. writ.] Greeting Cards, Short-Story, Several poems published in local newspaper, The Springfield Journal; [pers.] I try to reflect the beauties, hardships, and wonders of our lives in my writing. I have been greatly influenced by the early contemporary inspirational poets.; [a.] College Park, MD

NGUYEN, HACH C.
[b.] August 8, 1918, Vietnam; [p.] Deceased; [m.] Nga Nguyen, July 19, 1945; [ch.] 3 boys, 1 girl; [ed.] Doctor of Law (Paris, France), Promoted through competitive exams, as university professor of Political Economy (Paris, France), Formerly Dean, the School of Law, Saigon University Vietnam; [occ.] Retired; [oth. writ.] L'Harmonisation Des Charges Dans Les Unions Economiques, Les The'ories De Croissance, Social Implications of Development, Development Planning In Less Developed Countries, International Transfer of Technology; [pers.] Different countries and nations have gone their separate ways through many varied phases of development. But it appears obvious that such individualized efforts will soon converge to form a communion pool to help raise human kind out its present predicament of endless conflicts and wars. I earnestly pray that love of other human beings and respect of the environment became everybody's motto; [a.] San Diego, CA

NGUYEN, MICHAEL VINH
[pen.] Mike Daddy Nagoogen; [b.] August 11, 1977, Alameda, CA; [p.] Lich Nguyen; [ed.] Rio American High, University of California, Davis; [occ.] Student, University of California, Davis (Pre-Med); [memb.] President of the Asian Student Union U.C.Davis, Deans list, American Cancer Society Founder and President of Economics Society; [hon.] Magna Cum Laude, Outstanding Service, Community Outreach, Phyz Master; [oth. writ.] Several articles poems published in the Rio American "Miranda". Founder and Editor in Chief of "The Macro/Micro Monthly; [pers.] I strive to meliorate the goodness of human kind through my writing. I believe that to dream of being a person you cannot be, is to waste the person that person that you are; [a.] Roseville, CA

NICHOLS, GARY BRANSON
[b.] September 15, 1952, Brooklyn; [p.] Elizabeth Williams, George Nichols; [ed.] Benjamin N. Cardozo High City College to New York; [occ.] Struggling Actor; [memb.] S.A.G., Screen Actor's Guild; [hon.] A.A.A. Citizenship Award; [pers.] Treat family like friends and friends like family.

NICHOLS, TRACY
[b.] August 30, 1984, Houston, TX; [p.] Don and Terri Nichols; [ed.] Student of Queens Intermediate School; [pers.] You are not a writer if your poem come from your head but only if they come from your heart.; [a.] Houston, TX

NIEMANN, LINDSAY
[b.] June 13, 1977, Austin, TX; [p.] Lynda Springer Gary Niemann; [ed.] High School Graduated; [pers.] I can express myself to the fullest in my writing. It becomes my escape, as well as my freedom.; [a.] Humble, TX

NIX, RUTH
[pen.] Ruth Nix; [b.] February 24, 1952, Oak Park, IL; [p.] Virgil, Virginia Nix; [ch.] Heather, Orion; [ed.] Loara High School, U.S.C. music preparatory division, life; [occ.] Music teacher; [oth. writ.] Beyond Survival, (self published book) Various songs, two books in progress; [pers.] My goal in writing is to evoke thought.; [a.] Westminster, CA

NIXON, LORETTE F.
[pen.] Tracy; [b.] August 30, 1963, Nassau, Bahamas; [p.] Regina M. Johnson, Francis Nugent; [ed.] MPA - Long Island University, Bklyn, NY, BA - Marymont Manhattan, NYC, High School - St. Augustine's College, Nassau, Bahamas; [occ.] (Former) Vice-Consul, Bahamas Consulate General, NY, Program Director - Center for African Development; [memb.] ASPA - American Society of Public Administrators, Society of Foreign Consuls, NY, Nassau Bahamas Association, NY, Castlehill Women's Softball League, NY, Other Athletic Associations.; [hon.] Honors Certificate, Masters Degree, Bahamas Consulate General Achievement Award - Outstanding Work in organizing Cultural events. Numerous Athletic and Academic Awards; [oth. writ.] Oh Sunny Isles, (Historical Poem, dramatized at Bahamas Cultural Extravaganza - 1992 - Fashion Institute of Technology, NY), 50 additional poems (To be published).; [pers.] My mind conceives and my brain receives the mystery of sound. The sounds are transcribed and my hands rewrite inspiring words that are profound.; [a.] Bronx, NY

NKHOMA, ELLA
[b.] September 8, 1981, Blantyre, Malawi, Africa; [p.] Christopher and Winnie Nkhoma; [ed.] I'm in my sophomore year of High School. I attend the High School of Medical Professions at North side; [occ.] Student; [hon.] Placed at district level of the University Interscholastic League in literary criti-

...sm, Tandy scholar; [pers.] In my writing, I often ...say to encourage others to not cache their anima... ...t to let it be manifested in them.; [a.] Forth Worth, TX

ODAL, JOSIE G.
..] May 27, 1933, Jerome, AZ; [p.] Deceased; [m.] ...seph Nodal, March 14, 1958; [ch.] Two sons, two ...aughters, four grandchildren, three greatgran; [ed.] ...2th, HS P.H.S.; [occ.] Retired from Broadway ...ertst now at Prescott High School; [memb.] Alli-...ce Bible Church, Awana Program I teach 3 yrs. to ...yrs. - cubbies sun school; [hon.] Awards and honors ...r teaching for 7 yrs. in the Awana Program I do ...cause I love children.; [oth. writ.] I was orphaned ...hen very young, I am writing a book, about my ...hildhood, being brought up by an older brother.; ...ers.] I love to write, when I do write it comes from ...e heart, and it becomes real to me.; [a.] Prescott, AZ

NOLEN, RUSSELL D.
[pen.] Russel O. Nolen; [b.] October 20, 1959, Little Rock, AR; [p.] Loy D. Nolen, Joy L. Richards; [ed.] Bryant High School, Henderson College; [occ.] Disab/Vet; [memb.] Sharon Baptist Church Former Member - Benton Poet Soc.; [hon.] 3 time Semi-finalist N.A. Open Poetry Contest; [oth. writ.] Waterspout, The Wind Has A Way, Stars, Tears of A Lamb, Places in the Heart...; [pers.] What the mind can see, and what the heart believes, can set the spirit free.; [a.] Benton, AR

NORMAN, DELORES KOSCIUSZKO
[p.] June Bush and Alphons Kosciuszko; [ch.] Forrest A. Norman II; [occ.] Singer and Songwriter; [memb.] Virginia Beach United Methodist Church, Son Rise Choir; [pers.] The Holy Bible is every person's biography. Bring a sincere heart to it's pages and the Holy Spirit will guide you into a joyous life of love and gratitude, embracing the promise of eternal paradise.; [a.] Virginia Beach, VA

NORTON, MARY-CLAIRE
[pen.] MaryClaire Norton; [b.] July 4, 1952, Los Angeles, CA; [p.] Edward and Eileen Sandborgh; [m.] David D. Norton, April 24, 1982; [ch.] Caryn Marie Norton; [ed.] Sunnyvalle High School, DeAnza and Glendale Colleges; [occ.] Legal Secretary; [memb.] Vice-President of Salt Lake City Chapter of Internal Folk Harpers and Craftsmen, member of the Cantabile Chorale; [hon.] Dean's List - DeAnza Col.; [pers.] Nature has many things to teach us. I always try to listen to her many voices, and sometimes to write them down as poetry or music.

NORWOOD, MARNEY LUELLA
[b.] October 5, 1927, Salem, MO; [p.] James McDowell, Ethel P. McDowell; [m.] Winford A. Norwood, April 10, 1966; [ch.] Michael R., Judith L., Linda J., Vicki C. and Theresa R.; [ed.] Ninth grade taking courses for "GED." Doing 12th grade work; [hon.] Numerous Golden and Silver Poet Awards. Poems published in World of Poetry and the National Library of Poetry. First poem published at age 10; [oth. writ.] "Love's Golden Pathway", "The Little Country Church", "Someone Cares" - "The Little Negro" numerous other. "For all the eternity plea."; [pers.] God gave me this gift and a wonderful husband inspired me.; [a.] Mansfield, MO

NOTARIANNI, SOFIA MARY ANN
[b.] April 3, 1932, Providence, RI; [p.] Louis and Sofia Magnani Notarianni (Deceased); [ed.] No degrees, started public schooling, one year early, then skipped two early grades, which totaled, being three years ahead, in early public schooling, private family tutor, all tutored in high morals, physics, chemistry and nuemours other subjects with hands on training, all were true environmentalists. Major modeling course at Conovers Career Girl School, New York 1955, Real Estate School 1972, Department Store Buyer-on the job training 1955, various and numerous courses, with private tutors, ballet, etc. 1948-1955-1960.; [occ.] Inventor, metallurgist, miner, self-employed 1982 up to the present.; [pers.] Poetry is spiritual, uplifting and peaceful, I tried to reflect that in my first poem. I hope I have succeeded. I enjoy poems in the Catholic bible and other bibles.; [a.] Rancho Mirage, CA

NOYES, PATRICIA
[pen.] Tryssa; [b.] August 27, 1975, Seoul, Korea; [p.] Patrick Scott Noyes, Chi Nam Noyes; [ed.] High school graduate, military occupational training; [occ.] Switching Systems Operator, U.S. Army, PFC; [oth. writ.] "The Beast", Echoes of Yesterday, "Dark Land of Magic", Best Poems of 1995, several unpublished poems and short stories.; [pers.] Life throws many difficult trials at us, but they can all be overcome. Even my pending court-martial will soon be a thing of the past.; [a.] Las Vegas, NV

NUCKOLS, PEGGY L.
[pen.] Lois Palms; [b.] February 16, 1946, Charleston, SC; [p.] David and Marie Nuckols; [ed.] BS in Psychology and Economics at MSCW in Columbus, MS; [pers.] The most amazing journey is along the road within yourself.; [a.] Helena, AL

NYERS, AMELIA
[pen.] Kathryn Raw - Molly Nyers; [b.] Benwood, WV; [p.] Stephen and Christina Nyers; [ed.] Business course 1944-45 University of Pittsburgh, Penna, Journalism; [occ.] Retired ballet instructor - still writing; [memb.] Amorc - San Jose, CA. Ladies Auxiliary VFW post 1167 South Bend IN; [hon.] Wabash College Crawfordsville IN, from Institute University San Francisco CA. 1983 New's Register Memo Marshall Co. West Virginia 1982, Library Network 1990, Mechen Public School W. Virginia 1941; [oth. writ.] Children's stories - family history from 1781, research from 10,000 B.C. Ural Altaic Region. Science for the betterment of humidity; [pers.] Advancement in literature for the advancement of our human family of man.; [a.] South Bend, IN

NYLEN, BRANDI
[b.] June, 24, 1981, Concord, NH; [p.] Carol Nylen; [ed.] I am in nineth grade at Merrimack Valley High. I have always gone to Merrimack Valley; [hon.] I won a gold medal for a poster of a horse and rider in show jumping and a certificate. I have won trophies for dancing for 9 years, and bowling for a 2 years.; [oth. writ.] I started riding when I was thirteen and I hope someday I will have a horse. My best friend Cathy Reid helped me start riding on her horse Shamrock, a more.; [a.] Penacook, NH

O'DONUHUE, JOHN F.
[b.] January 14, 1946, New York City; [m.] Agnes; [ch.] Jean, Kevin (Deceased); [occ.] Actor, retired New York City Police Lieutenant; [oth. writ.] "Your Eminence," (One act play); [pers.] Let's put dignity and respect, for everyone, to the fore front of our minds. This is dedicated to my son Kevin. May He rest in peace.

O'NEILL, ELIZABETH MEGAN
[pen.] Megan Elizabeth Fitzpatrick; [b.] September 9, 1983, Seoul, South Korea; [p.] Linda Fitzpatrick; [ed.] Sky View Elementary 6th grade, Peoria, Arizona; [occ.] Student; [memb.] Band; [hon.] High Honor Roll, ASU Award - for Martin Luther King Celebration, Perfect Attendance, Spelling Award,; [oth. writ.] Poem "Feline Secret's", unpublished; [pers.] I want to thank many famous poets and my teacher Mrs. Jones for inspiring the poet inside me.; [a.] Peoria, AR

ODOM, KAY
[b.] December 19, 1965, Kinston, NC; [p.] Roy and Hazel McNeill; [m.] Stanley Craig Odom, April 1, 1989; [ch.] Kailey Dia Odom; [ed.] North Duplin High School, Mount Olive College; [occ.] Office worker, Dean Pickles and Specialty Products Faison, NC; [memb.] Faison Presbyterian Church; [hon.] Leadership scholarship, Jan Brewer scholarship, Dean's List, Pickle Classic Queen; [pers.] I inherit my love for poetry from my late grandmother, Barbara Ray McNeill.; [a.] Faison, NC

OFORI-MANKATA, KWAME AGYEI
[pen.] Kwame Ofori; [b.] March 14, 1970, Ghana, West Africa; [p.] Michael and Doris Ofori-Mankata; [ed.] United Nations International School New York, N.Y., Cook College, Rutgers University; [oth. writ.] Several poems in university newspapers; [pers.] "They that wait upon the Lord, He shall renew their strength..." - "...O, none, unless this miracle have might, that in black ink my love may still shine bright." A.D.I.D.A.S....for, all day I dream...; [a.] New Brunswick, NJ

OHNSTAD, GLEN G.
[pen.] Shades Gordon; [b.] December 8, 1954, Minneapolis, MN; [p.] Kenneth and Joyce Ohnstad; [m.] Sandra, August 20, 1982; [ch.] I have 6 children and 2 step children, Sherry, Ken, Missi, Felicia, Michael, Joshua, Angel; [ed.] 12 years went to Thomas Jefferson Sr. High in Bloomington, MN.; [occ.] Machine Operator; [oth. writ.] Have many writings, most of which are about children. Once published in American Poetry Anthology "It'll be okay" once published in Quill books - live only for today; [pers.] I am a descendant of Henry Longfellow. I write mostly to help others if my writing can make even one person stop and think, I've accomplished my goal. I would like to someday win the pulitzer prize for my work.; [a.] Osseo, MN

OKPALEKE, OSITA
[pen.] Amazu, Osita; [b.] Nigeria; [p.] Ozobiahi Okpaleke and Ogbozo Okpaleke; [ch.] Ijeoma, Obioma, Osita Jr.; [ed.] Early Education in Nigeria. Bachelor of Pharmacy, St. Louis College of Pharmacy; [occ.] Entrepreneur; [hon.] Who is Who in American Colleges; [oth. writ.] Poems in local newspapers and magazines.; [pers.] I attempt to wear the other person's shoes and to understand and speak for the disadvantaged.; [a.] Saint Louis, MO

OLIVE, RENEE J.
[b.] June 30, 1965, Baltimore, MD; [p.] Bert A. Bailey, Patricia Kellogg; [m.] James R. Olive Sr., December 20, 1993; [ch.] Alexandria JoAnn, James Robert Jr., Nathaniel Lee; [ed.] Northeast High, Central Florida Community College, Lake-Sumter Community College, University of Central Florida; [occ.] Student - English Education; [hon.] Phi Theta Kappa, National Dean's List, Dean's List; [a.] Lady Lake, FL

OLSEN, ALLISON JUNE
[b.] July 27, 1965, California; [p.] Nancy June Olsen and David E. Olsen; [ed.] B. S. from the University of the Pacific (1986), Juris Doctor from Whittier Law School (1995); [occ.] Attorney; [pers.] Special love to my family and friends, and especially to Keith and Buddy.; [a.] Malibu, CA

OLSEN, ROY E.
[b.] February 16, 1951, Brooklyn; [p.] Doris and Andrew Olsen; [m.] Kathleen, May 26, 1973; [ch.] Eric, Christopher, Michael, Thomas; [ed.] High School; [occ.] Electrical Mechanic; [pers.] To realize change is to learn.; [a.] Brooklyn, NY

OMMONDSON, LORA L.
[pen.] "Mouse"; [b.] February 22, 1949, Bremerton,

WA; [p.] Anthony L. Gerovich and Helen E. Gerovich; [ch.] Phillips A. Lepper and Kenneth A. Herbert; [ed.] Mount Tahoma High, Institute of Financial Education; [occ.] Flight Attendant-United Express/Westair; [hon.] Certificate for Excellent performance, United Express/Westair, Certificate - Institute of Financial Education; [pers.] I dedicate this poem to Rick McDaniel, who influenced me this creation and other writings, and to my beloved brother BJarne.; [a.] McKinleyville, CA

ONWUKA, MADU
[b.] February 14, 1982, Boston, MA; [p.] Chuck and Ruth Onwuka; [ed.] Want to mostly Catholic Schools where I feel the education is better and also safer. (8th Grade); [occ.] Schooling; [hon.] A-B Honor Roll in School; [pers.] Everybody, no matter what physical or mental condition, has the potential to achieve their dreams. They just need to use it to its highest peak. And as they say, "The sky is the limit".; [a.] Gary, IN

OPAT, ROBERT A.
[b.] July 17, 1970, Wakeeney, KS; [p.] Barbara Opat; [ed.] Trego Community High School, Fort Hays State University; [occ.] Student/Resident Manager, FHSU McMindes Hall; [hon.] KSHSAA Citizenship Award; [oth. writ.] Several poems for family and friends.; [pers.] Inspiration for my writings comes from life experiences. Family, friends and relationships have been the biggest influences. Everything that I write comes straight from the heart.; [a.] Hays, KS

ORAM, CHARLAYNE
[pen.] Char Oram; [b.] April 19, 1954, Bridge Pork, CT; [p.] John and Shirley Sweebe; [m.] Richard Leroy Oram, December 17, 1988; [ch.] Three; [ed.] Lansing Community College Nurses Training; [occ.] Home Health Aide; [memb.] Flint Blind Bowler's Neighborhood Watch; [hon.] Neighborhood Watch from Mayor Stanley of Flint MI; [pers.] This is due to my son Matthew Alfred Singletary for support and understanding and to my other two children Mark and Lisa Singletary for encouragement and love that never gave up and to my mother and father husband; [a.] Flint, MI

ORR, LEONARD PAUL
[b.] August 3, 1944, Parksburg, WA; [p.] George Orr and Ethel Orr; [m.] Carol Sue Orr, December 13, 1968; [ch.] George Paul and Ginger Louise; [ed.] Parkersburg High, W.V.U. University, U.S. Army Aviation School; [occ.] Asbestos worker; [memb.] Church - word of God Ministries Veterans of Foreign War's; [hon.] Serving in the armed forces which guards our country and may of life. Numerous awards in many fields.; [oth. writ.] Several poems, song's and short stories for use in church; [pers.] Live to day as it's your last, live tomorrow as it will be forever; [a.] Walker, WA

ORSOMARSO, MARGUERITE R.
[pen.] Marguerite Angelica; [b.] New York, NY; [p.] Benjamin Rocco, Gilda Rocco; [m.] Dom. Orsomarso, July 2, 1955; [ch.] Donald F. and Gail M.; [ed.] Mother Cabrini High School, Hunter College (B.A.), Hunter College (M.A.), Graduate Studies - Cornel University, Teacher (Elem. Jr. High) Long Island NYC, Connecticut; [occ.] Retired, Volunteer (local hospitals nursing homes); [memb.] American Cancer Association and volunteer, Christian Assembly Educators Association; [hon.] Dean's List (4 yrs.) throughout college, Medals (high school - History, English), (College) Language (Romance) Medalist Iota Tau Alpha Honor Society, Alpha Phi Delta (College Societies) Education Honor Society; [oth. writ.] Numerous poems distributed to church papers, distributed to nursing home residents, and to individuals throughout the United States; [pers.] Through my poetry, and other writings, I endeavor to bring readers to the realization that their main focus in life should be to go the "Source" of their strength, their needs, their goals - The Supreme God - the "source" of all things!; [a.] East Islip, NY

ORTH, ANTON PAUL
[b.] June 21, 1967, Eitzen, MN; [m.] Jen Leslie Reed Orth; [ch.] Zoe Jade Angelina Orth; [occ.] Freelance Tatoo Artist; [pers.] Life is truly good if lived in love. From every adversity falls the seeds of greater and equal benefit. This poem is of the love that shines through every adversity and is devoted to my Loving Lady Jen, my wife, my friend.; [a.] Eugene, OR

ORTIZ, NORA
[b.] February 12, 1920, Los Angeles; [m.] Luis R. Ortiz, March 3, 1962; [ch.] Four; [ed.] High School, 2 years college, on going classes; [occ.] Writer; [memb.] Human race, LA Museum of Art, KCET; [hon.] Friends, my husband, my children, life itself; [oth. writ.] Twenty years of advertising, but that was "make a living" writing; [pers.] I have used poetry to try to erase the influenced cultural input and find the center of who I am and what I feel - from my authestic true reality as a woman.; [a.] Los Angeles, CA

ORTMAN, HERBERT M.
[pen.] "Herb"; [b.] September 14, 1909, Martin, ND; [p.] Martin and Eva Ortman; [m.] Ethel May Ortman, June 14, 1937; [ch.] Two (grown) Doris Almond, Art Ortman; [ed.] College, Anderson College, Anderson, Indiana, B.A., B.TH., Seminary, Oberlin Seminary, B.D. Degree, Oberlin, Ohio; [occ.] Minister - Pastor Now Retired Minister; [memb.] First Church of God, Grand Junction, Colorado, Ministerial Association, Grand Junction, Sunday School Teacher, Hospital Chaplin, Community, Started New Church, Rochester New Hampshire; [hon.] Ordination as a Minister, Held Various State Offices in Minnesota Church Work, on Trustee Board at Grand Junction Church; [oth. writ.] Article in local Christian magazine, poem in vital christianity, (National Coverage), story in national youth magazine, books - "Memoirs of a common man," "Spirit led journey through life," "dear friends, your moments with the master are here."; [pers.] The first third of my life I was a farmer, the second a minister, the third (into retirement) I try to write. I trust in God for his grace and his mercy, I enjoy my wife and family, I want to leave behind something of value to others.; [a.] Grand Junction, CO

OSHER, REGINA LYNN
[pen.] Gina Osher; [b.] February 11, 1951, Topeka, KS; [ed.] El Cerrito High School, El Cerrito, Ca., University of Oregon, Eugene, Oregon; [occ.] Employment Counselor Alameda County Social Services Agency, Oakland, CA.; [oth. writ.] I have authored approximately 70 poems to date. I have also written three children's stories: The Legend of Greenhorn, The Barefoot Boy and Sky and Clouds Together, as well, an article: "Journal of a Californian" about my experiences, observations, thoughts and responses in regard to the 1989 bay area earthquake.; [pers.] I believe people should be connected by the down-to-earth aspects of life and I revere Mother Earth. I try to reflect this in my poetry. I try to create poetry that will promote peace on earth and peace of mind and which is timeless and enjoyable to all.; [a.] Alameda, CA

OSTREM, LAURIE
[pen.] L. L. Ostrem; [b.] April 2, 1958, Yakima, WA; [p.] Norm Thomas and Elsie Thomas; [m.] Roger Ostrem, July 9, 1977; [ch.] Natalie Dalyn and Jeremy Ryan; [ed.] Lathrop High; [oth. writ.] Poems and songs, children's stories.; [pers.] Within the colorful threads of the tapestry of our lives, God has placed many gifts...courage, strength, hope, joy and above all undying love. I Cor. 13:13.; [a.] Fairbanks, A

OSWALT, BRENDA K.
[b.] November 30, 1945, Mansfield, OH; [p.] Evely George Geier; [m.] James, May 27, 1967; [ed.] Hig School - Madison, Mansfield, College, Anthropo ogy Grad Courses, Business Related; [occ.] Preside Dixie USA, Medical Supply Company; [memb A.R.E. (Association For Research and Enlighter ment); [oth. writ.] Cook Books, Short Stories, Cop Writing; [pers.] To Emanate Peace and Reflect Jo - "Mind Reflects Light to Projects Reality".; [a Houston, TX

OTT, ELLIS
[pen.] Ellis Ott; [b.] August 26, 1977, Eagle River [p.] Alvin and Janice Ott; [ed.] Senior - West Valle High School Graduate 1996; [occ.] Host - Jeffrey' Restaurant; [memb.] Fairbanks Shakespeare The atre, Swimming - 4 seasons high school, 1 yea Midnight Sun Swim Team, Wrestle - 1 season hig school, Student Council - Vice Pres. of Jr. Class [hon.] 3rd Place 100 Back Freshman and senior yea - 2nd Place 200 Free Relay Summer Long Cours Championship, West Valley Swim Captain Jr. an Sr. Year - Plaque - Most Inspirational Swimmer Jr Year - The Search Published (W. Virginia Poetr Forum) - 96 Wolf Pack Pride Published - 96 Wes Valley Yearbook; [oth. writ.] Romeo and Juliet Rap The Barn, The Search, Hippy Fish, Wolf Pack Pride; [pers.] Do everything as if you do nothing else; [a.] Fairbanks, AK

OTTOSEN, WENDY
[pen.] Ashley Aschenbach; [b.] November 5, 1960, Lakewood, CA; [p.] H.D. Ottosen and Joyce Ottosen Miller; [ch.] Kristina Renee; [ed.] Third years psychology major at CSU Dominguez, A.A. Degree from Cerritos Community College.; [memb.] PsiBeta Honor Society, PsiChi Honor Society, CSU Dominguez Psychology club, former President of Cerritos College Psychology club, honors program.; [hon.] Cerritos College Bronze Falcon Award, Metropolitan State Hospital outstanding volunteer award, Dean's Honor Roll; [oth. writ.] A collection of not yet submitted poems. (Do not include if tacky); [pers.] Vengeance and hate keep the cycle of turmoil - Love, intelligence and empathy slow it down. Quick-fixes are needed for now, but deep-rooted solutions helps prevent future adversity at every level.; [a.] Bellflower, CA

OVERHOLSER, SHAWN D.
[b.] October 27, 1966, Hastings, MN; [p.] Richard and Deloris Overholser; [ed.] Centenial SR. High Cambridge Community College; [occ.] Student; [pers.] You don't own anything unless your willing to lose it or leave it behind, otherwise it owns you.; [a.] Mora, MN

OWENS, ROGER J.
[b.] October 2, 1946, Hollywood, CA; [p.] John and Caroline Owens; [m.] Margaret Jean Ormond Owens, May 29, 1971; [ch.] Grant Cumberland; [ed.] Ph.D., Literature, Univ. of California, San Diego. M.B.A. Pepperdine Univ., B.A. English, Univ. of California, Berkeley; [occ.] Writer/Consultant; [memb.] Sterling Award Council of Orange County, Society of Technical Communication; [oth. writ.] "The Seven Deadly Sins in the Prologue to *Troilus and Cressida*," *Shakespeare Tahrbuch*, vol. 116 (1980). "Writing the On-line Procedures Guide," *Society for Technical Communication Journal*, Orange County, May 1995.; [a.] Laguna Beach, CA

OWENS, SHELIA
[b.] November 25, 1954, Grundy, VA; [p.] Simmie and Burgie Charles; [m.] Olen T. Owens Sr., September 9, 1972; [ch.] Teri Meadows Barbara Owens

Olen Owens Jr; [ed.] Graduate Grundy, Senior High Buchanan Co. Voc. School; [occ.] Nurse; [memb.] National Nurse Assoc. Primitive Baptist Church; [a.] Grundy, VA

PACE, JONATHAN PATRICK
[b.] July 17, 1981, Rocky Mount, NC; [p.] Ronald H. and Brenda B. Pace; [ed.] Springhope Primary School, Spaulding Elementary School, Southern Nash Junior High School; [occ.] High school student (9th grade); [memb.] Momeyer Baptist Church, Quiz Bowl (SNJH), SNSH Soccer Team, SNSH Indoor Track Team, SNJH Baseball Team, SNJH Yearbook Staff, SNJH Newspaper Staff; [hon.] Academic Achievement awards, Athletic awards; [oth. writ.] Articles and poems in school newspaper, unpublished poems; [pers.] I enjoy the literary works of Edgar A. Poe, J.R.R. Tolkien, Frank Herbert, Terry Brooks, Shel Silverstein, Robert Frost, and Lewis Carroll. I feel that imagination is one of the best possessions mankind owns. I feel that everyone should always drive to learn more.; [a.] Momeyer, NC

PAGE, JOHN R.
[b.] July 24, 1916, Brussels, Ontario, Canada; [p.] Rev. R. E. Page, Lillian I. Page; [m.] Gloria M. Page, January 22, 1953; [ch.] Karin Davis, Cheryl Holland, Michelle Gray; [ed.] Public Schools and Private Tuition; [occ.] Retired; [memb.] Life Member of the Art Students League, N.Y.C.; [hon.] World War II Unit Presidential Citations, U.S.A and Philippines; [oth. writ.] In the 1970's articles of the New Haven Register's "Nuttmegger" Re Humor in Rural Life during the great depression.; [pers.] Inspiration for much that I have done stems from my uncle, John W. Page of England, esquired by King George VI for his works in Anthropology and my grandfather, Reverend Henri E. Benoit of Canada whose preachings and Publications gave the world the amunition needed to find out why goodness outweighs evil.; [a.] Stuart, FL

PAGE, TALIA
[b.] April 15, 1981, Hyannis, MA; [p.] Debra and Douglas Page; [ed.] I am a a freshman in High School; [occ.] Student; [oth. writ.] This is my first published work.; [pers.] In my literary creations I strive for rhythm, and a deeper meaning than words put together only to look pretty. My poems usually say something about life in general and can be interpreted for individual purpose or meaning. I am greatly influenced by music, the world around me and various other poets.; [a.] Columbia, MO

PALM, WESLEY D.
[b.] March 1, 1955, Anoka, MN; [p.] Robert and Edith Palm; [ch.] Matthew Wesley, Melodie Kay, Mandi Ray; [oth. writ.] This poem is the first one I've tried to get published.; [pers.] I have been writing poems for years. I never thought they were good enough. Until my sister Mary pushed me to send one in. I'm influenced by life itself. About one third of my poems are true.; [a.] Brooklyn Center, MN

PALMER, CHRISTIANA NAOMIE
[b.] June 10, 1981, Idaho Falls, ID; [p.] David R. Palmer, Karen Palmer; [ed.] Freshmen in North Fremont High School; [memb.] Church of Jesus Christ of Latter Day Saints; [oth. writ.] I have written many other poems.; [pers.] I was inspired to write this poem when a traffic accident took my sisters life in January of 1995. I dedicate this poem to her.; [a.] Macks Inn, ID

PALMER, HAZEL M.
[b.] February 4, 1912, Canada on the Border of Washington State; [m.] Lawrence L. (Deceased); [ed.] High school graduate and 1 year college and 3 years Registered Nurse Training Graduation; [occ.] Retired; [memb.] Englewood Christian Church, Yakima, WA, Agricultural Museum Yakima Interdenominal Christian Service Circle; [pers.] I have always enjoyed poetry and memorizing many stanzas. I love all aspects of the "Great Out of Door", the sights and sounds, the beauty of the changing seasons, the flowers of summer and snows of winter. The serendipity of our great universe.; [a.] Yakima, WA

PALMER, LOUIS
[b.] December 12, 1914, Peckville, PA; [p.] Palmer, Louis D. and Sarah L.; [m.] Betty M. (Deceased, December 17, 1994), May 19, 1940; [ch.] Susan C., Priscilla S., Louis III; [ed.] College Prep. Wyoming Seminary, Kingston, PA '33 Syracuse University; [occ.] Retired; [memb.] United Methodist Church College, Sigma Chi Fraternity/International Relations Club; [hon.] Oratorical Contest Winner (prep school); [oth. writ.] "Summer Only Sleeps," 4th place "Jesse Stuart Contest," sponsored by "Seven" Oklahoma City 1971, Member, Ohio Verse Writer's Guild, Springfield, Ohio, "Writer's Club," 1965-1980. Book award honorable mentions (several).; [pers.] Managed little league baseball 6 years. Presently one of several tutors opschool children in Pascagoula. Inspired by Robert Browning's Ah, but a man's reach must exceed his grasp, or why what's a heaven for?; [a.] Pascagoula, MS

PANNELL, SHAREN PINKETT
[b.] June 9, 1954, Easton, MD; [p.] Paige Pinkett, late Hazel Pinkett; [m.] Harry Lee Pannell, June 16, 1979; [ch.] Kasha Elizabeth and Leah Evans; [ed.] St. Michaels High School, University of Maryland Baltimore County, Loyola College; [occ.] Special Education Teacher St. Michaels High School, St. Michaels, MD; [memb.] Council of Exceptional Children Easton Church of God; [hon.] Dean's List; [oth. writ.] Unpublished, but have written several poems as inspiration in teaching classes and for speaking engagements, write (co-author) monthly newsletter through a personal ministry; [pers.] It is my goal to share through testimony the person that Jesus Christ is to me, to share the faithfulness of God, and to reflect the lifestyle of Christ through the person of the Holy Spirit.; [a.] Easton, MD

PAPPATERRA, JOANE L.
[b.] April 23, 1954, Fort Bragg, NC; [p.] William and Geraldine Mayo; [m.] Martin, February 13, 1988; [ch.] Michael and Michele; [ed.] H.S. grad. and some College; [occ.] Assistant Teacher Day Care Center; [pers.] My two children are adopted. I wrote this poem while watching them develope and grow in the early stages of there lives. Michael is 4 1/2 and Michele is 20 months.; [a.] Hamilton Square, NJ

PAPRITZ, CAREN
[b.] July 2, 1962, Yosemite Nat'l Park, CA; [occ.] Cowboy/Rancher; [pers.] Live Deeply, Love Deeply, Never Have A Regret, And Drink Only Good Whiskey.; [a.] Patagonia, AZ

PARENT, CINDY L.
[pen.] Cindy Lena Parent; [b.] June 19, 1965, Burlington VT; [p.] Leonard and Ellen Parent; [ed.] Burlington H.S.; [hon.] Vt. State Champ-Discus-and Shot Put and 4th in New England - Discus.; [pers.] In loving memory of my mother. Thanks for everything.; [a.] Burlington, VT

PARKER, BRYAN MICHAEL
[b.] August 3, 1978, Yuma, AZ; [p.] Mike and Debra Parker; [ed.] Grade School Jr. Gradeschool - James B. Rolle Jr. High - Gilavista Jr. High School - Yuma High School; [memb.] Basketball (4 yrs.), Football (4 yrs.), Baseball (1 year), Little League Member, Dare Role Model; [hon.] Honor Roll (4 yrs.), A-Team (2 year), Renaissance Member (4 yrs.), Captain Football Team (1 yr.), Captain Basketball Team (3), National Honor Society (2 yrs.), Rotary Student of the Month, Math Student of the Month; [a.] Yuma, AZ

PARKER, ELAINE COURTIER
[pen.] Quanah Parker; [b.] September 1, 1945, Nottingham, England; [p.] Mr. and Mrs. H. M. Parker; [m.] Jerry A. Courtier, July 4, 1983; [ch.] Mark, Mike, Joel, Jackie; [ed.] BA English Lit - U of C Bentley Business College - MA, Harvard University; [occ.] Writer; [memb.] Los Escribientes, 4 writers workshops; [oth. writ.] Completed a manuscript for one novel and is at work on another and a collection of poetry at about of 60 poems.

PARKER, PAULINE
[b.] November 5, 1922, Collinsville, TX; [p.] James Paul Tinsley and Lignum Pilcher Tinsley; [m.] James Louis Parker, Sr., February 14, 1951; [ch.] Elizabeth, James L. Jr., Paul, Robertson; [ed.] Gainesville High, Gainesville Jr. College; [memb.] Former member Garland Poetry Soc., Texas State Poetry Soc.; [hon.] Local and State; [oth. writ.] Unpublished; [pers.] I believe that a continuing process of learning is essential to a personal sense of well-being.; [a.] Garland, TX

PARKER, SUZANNE I.
[pen.] Suzanne I. Parker; [b.] December 16, 1966, Topeka, KS; [p.] George H. Parker Sr. and Delores G. Parker; [ed.] Orem High School, Orem, UT, Utah Valley Community College, Orem UT Arizona Western College, Yuma, AZ; [occ.] Secretary, College Student; [oth. writ.] None published; [pers.] This poem was written to my niece, Carlee S. Parker on the death of her son, Christian.; [a.] Yuma, AZ

PARKS, JAY NELSON
[b.] October 19, 1982, Annapolis, MD; [p.] Joan and Gary Parks; [ed.] K - 8 (Present); [occ.] Student; [oth. writ.] Poems and short stories poem published in "Chesapeake Children"; [pers.] I enjoy writing poetry and am inspired to write what I am thinking about at the time. I strive to keep writing and influence other to write poetry.; [a.] Lothian, MD

PARKS, LA WANDA JEAN
[pen.] Ms. Parks; [b.] May 11, 1943, Spokane, WA; [p.] Brady Louis Curtis Sr. (Deceased '88, Rubye Keenard Kittrell (Deceased '90); [m.] Divorced, May 16, 1985; [ch.] Donna Jean and Debra Denise, (grandchildren) Megan, Matthew,Morgan and Cristi; [ed.] Cleburne High (TX. - Class '61) Richland Junior College ('75) various business and professional courses spanning twenty years!; [occ.] Community association manager owner - LPL Community Management, Inc.; [memb.] CAI (Community Association Institute) National AAGD (Apartment Association Of Greater Dallas), AMORC (Ancient and Mystical Order Rosae Crucis); [hon.] Cai-hall of fame, PCAM-Professional Community Association Manager, AMS-Association Management Specialist All National Designations relating to Profession; [oth. writ.] "To be or not to be" 1974 article published in Dallas times Herald "A Management Audit Thesis" 1988, 300 + page book-on file at Cai Nat'l. "A diary in prose" 1995, 80 + pages of narrative prose written in Epic form describing true events (not for publication); [pers.] This life affords such an abundance of freedom - to waste any would be a shame! I love God in the mornings, in the evenings, in my children and theirs, in this evenings, in my children and theirs, in this phase of my life and I love the Dallas cowboys! It will be my personal pleasure to leave something behind that will benefit another human being in some way...; [a.] Dallas, TX

PARO, SHARON
[b.] June 4, 1962, Logan, UT; [p.] Kay Murray and

Mardene Murray; [m.] Philip Paro, April 27, 1990; [ch.] Tawni Marie Stamm, Shannon Jacklyn Stamm; [ed.] Sky View High, Business College, University of Utah, Salt Lake Community College; [occ.] Executive Secretary, Utah State Office of Education, District Computer Service; [memb.] Utah and National Rehabilitation Association, various ministry programs through Salt Lake Christian Center; [hon.] Employee of the month award-Division of Rehabilitation Service, Secretary Service award-Utah Association of Rehabilitation Secretaries; [pers.] I strive to share with others the impact Jesus Christ has made in my life.; [a.] Salt Lake, UT

PATE, CAROLE S.
[b.] July 7, 1949, Glendale, CA; [p.] Clifford and Bette Stewart; [m.] Robert Burns Pate, August 4, 1984; [ch.] Casey, Corky and Shonee; [ed.] Lowell High School, Fullerton Junior College, University of Nevada, Reno; [occ.] Artists and Writer Retired Real Estate Broker; [oth. writ.] "Reflections" an Anthology of early poetry written between age 9 and age 40. "The Path of the Rainbows" A childrens book. Numerous other other poems, some published, some not.; [pers.] On June 7, 1995 I was diagnosed with end stage Cancer, although there had been no prior symptoms. I am still alive past the doctors expectations and I believe it is due in part to the fact that I have a great need to write a book about my battle with this disease and how it has changed me within my soul. Within great hope I will continue to live, love and enjoy this wonderful gift of life.; [a.] Truckee, CA

PATTERSON, JEWEL
[pen.] SAA; [b.] August 13, 1933, Lauden Dale County; [p.] Crlyle and Margie Patterson; [ch.] Donnie Holt, Deborah Gatlin; [occ.] Home maker; [hon.] 2 letters from President Clinton, Editors Choice Award, poems in local News Papers, 2 Books Sparkles in The Sand and Best Poems of '96, a member of International Society of poets '95 and '96; [oth. writ.] I have written three poems for National Library of Poetry, I have written some poems that have been published in local news papers.; [pers.] I have been seriously writing for about 5 years. My favorite subjects are personal feelings, my love for God and helping people. Who are in need. I would someday like to have a book published with all my poems.; [a.] Brighton, TN

PATTERSON, MS. LELIA
[b.] March 11, 1941, Los Angeles, CA; [p.] Chuck and Emma Barkley; [m.] Deceased; [ch.] Jim and Cristy; [ed.] High School - Downey, CA., Jr. College - Compton, CA.; [occ.] Disabled - Lumbar disc. disease; [oth. writ.] All personal for friends or self; [pers.] I've always loved poetry but never thought to seek publication - it's just personal satisfaction, a gift from God, to help me learn and gain wisdom. Now, I may decide to seek a publisher!; [a.] Downey, CA

PAVER, MARY
[pen.] Kandy Reed; [b.] January 15, 1956, Erie, PA; [p.] Walter and Alice Reed; [m.] Paul A. Paver Jr., August 20, 1993; [ch.] William, Stephen, Thomasina; [ed.] Harbor Creek Central School, Harbor Creek High School; [occ.] Housewife, Horticulturist; [oth. writ.] A poem published on a greeting cards.; [pers.] I've felt the need to express my feelings and opinions about love, religion, nature, and the world we live in, so I've been writing poetry since 1969.; [a.] Union City, PA

PAYNE, RAYMOND E.
[b.] July 8, 1929, Baltimore, MD; [p.] Raymond A. Payne and Frances O. Payne; [m.] Jeanette, October 27, 1951; [ch.] Brian; [ed.] High School; [occ.] Retired Quality Assurance Manager; [memb.] American Legion; [oth. writ.] Several poems and a novel. Nothing published. Also a short story of "Steam Boats on the Chesapeake Bay.".; [pers.] I have always been interested in writing. Since retiring in 1993, I have more time to write, but have not done so. When I do write, I omit the obscene phrases used so freely.; [a.] Glen Burnie, MD

PEARSON, JERRY DEAN
[pen.] Jobina/Andro Quan/C/SM Jambia; [b.] Paris, TX; [p.] Jerome and Tharmond Pearson; [m.] Jacqueline Dareeke Pearson, November 6, 1995; [occ.] Researcher/Writer; [memb.] C/SM (Founder); [hon.] Almost always remembered. Dareeke (my wife) Honor forever.; [oth. writ.] Valpine Wille, short Christmas Pain, stories Dareeke, Bio Exit poems, The Coming of Warm Baby (a novelle) in progress; [pers.] Seeker of the person's I have yet to meet and the places I have yet to be.; [a.] Pasadena, TX

PEARSON, RUTH
[b.] December 14, 1908, Balin, NH; [p.] Karen Andersen Sorensen, Herman Sorensen; [m.] Herbert M. Pearson, October 13, 1928; [ch.] Fred H. Pearson, Lawrence H. Pearson; [ed.] 4 yrs. of High School, random courses in Art, (oil painting) writing; [occ.] Retired in retirement home with husband; [oth. writ.] At present compelling memories of family tree. Have completed many short stories and poems, none published, just recently completed play, with 14 songs, wrote all lyrics, tunes and book.; [pers.] I look for the something "Special" in every one. Each one has his own niche in life, the extent of our education determines how much we can benefit from our talents.; [a.] Hagel Crest, IL

PEARSON, MRS. RUTH E.
[b.] July 11, 1914, USA; [p.] Alice and Louis Eckert; [m.] November 24, 1938; [ed.] Bethlehem Liberty High School Bethlehem Business College Secretary to J.P. Madden - Steel Co.; [occ.] House wife Cheer Lady here at Country Meadows; [memb.] Bethlehem Garden Club, Bethlehem Blind Board Y.W.C.A. of Bethlehem PA., Poetry Group Sessions United Methodist Church; [hon.] Garden Flower Arrangement - Blue Ribbon. Girl See A Bronze Medalian 3rd honor; [oth. writ.] I wright whenever someone wants me to write about country meadows and there staff or fun poetry about the people here; [pers.] Help people and all living things whenever or where ever it is needed Keep a happy outlook and a positive kind spirit and helping hand.; [a.] Bethlehem, PA

PEGODA, EMILY JOAN
[b.] June 19, 1989, Santa Cruz; [p.] Edward and Joan Pegoda; [ed.] 1st grade at Main Street School Soquel, Calif; [occ.] Student; [memb.] Coast Lands Christian Church, Awana Church Club.; [pers.] 1996 Goal is to be a kinder person.; [a.] Soquel, CA

PENNIGAR, KATHY MULLIS
[pen.] Kathy Mullis Pennigar; [b.] March 12, 1959, Union County; [p.] Roy and Madge Mullis; [m.] Josef M. Pennigar, January 14, 1978; [ch.] Jesica 16, Kristofer 12; [ed.] Sun Valley High School, Monne, NC, Anson College, Ansonville, NC; [occ.] Pediatric Nurse, Employment Place, Pediatric Services America, This is a 2nd career (My 1st an Office Manager for Insurance Co. for 9 years); [memb.] Poetry Society of America, International Society of Poets; [hon.] Editor's Choice Award; [oth. writ.] Journal of Nursing '96, (published short story), Three Foot Creature (Nat. Library of Poetry), Stimulation (Nat. Library of Poetry); [pers.] "One can do anything he wishes to do, if he tries". Influenced greatly by my wonderful husband.; [a.] Monroe, NC

PENWELL, SHAWNE MARIE
[pen.] Shawne Smith Dailey; [b.] September 5, 1951, Billings, MT; [p.] Edward and Betty Boyd; [m.] Rick A. Penwell, December 24, 1994; [ch.] Treyse and James Rios; [ed.] Lakes High School Tacoma, WA, Edmonds Community College Lynnwood, WA. A.T.A - Horticulture; [occ.] Propagator (Plant); [memb.] International Plant Propagator's Society; [oth. writ.] Moonchild and whiskey cheese.; [pers.] I write from my heart and life experiences.; [a.] Everett, WA

PEPPER, ROBERT L.
[pen.] Melmothhh; [b.] August 7, 1972, Brooklyn, NY; [p.] Robert E. and Patricia; [ed.] B.A. of Fine Arts in Brooklyn College; [occ.] Artist, and currently working as a florist.; [hon.] Graduated Brooklyn College with Cum Laude; [oth. writ.] none published; [pers.] I am very happy my work can shared with others. I am looking forward to continue my writing as well as my painting so others can enjoy my work.; [a.] Brooklyn, NY

PERCY, MILDRED R.
[pen.] Billie Runbeck Percy; [b.] April 11, 1918, Turtle Lake, ND; [p.] Deceased; [m.] Deceased, January 9, 1940; [ch.] James and Robert; [ed.] High School; [occ.] Retired; [pers.] I have written many poems, as a hobby. Now, I would like to make a bash or home them published in whatever way they should or could be. I do not know her to go about this so I would appreciate your telling me what to do.; [a.] Portland, OR

PEREZ, DERENZ MARTIN
[b.] November 9, 1978, Marikina, Philippines; [p.] Carina Perez Navar; [ed.] Bolsa Grande High, Granite High, Kearns High; [occ.] Student; [memb.] Granite Youth Symphony Orchestra, Utah Youth Symphony, Paleontology Club; [hon.] High Honor Roll, Academic, Citizenship, and Musical Awards; [oth. writ.] Several poems published in Harvest Staff Magazine; [pers.] Proverbs 3:5-7. Thanks Jesus, Mom (Carina Navar), and Ms. Huppi for everything! Pray and floss daily.; [a.] Kearns, UT

PERNU JR., HARLAN R.
[pen.] "Scouter", "Bulldog"; [b.] August 9, 1960, Virginia, MN; [p.] Harlan Sr. and Carmen L.; [ed.] High School Graduate; [memb.] M.A.H.C., Y.A.F., CAT Lover's of America; [hon.] Editor's Choice Award, NLP; [oth. writ.] My Life As It Was and is unpublished; [pers.] Live life as it is, and not what it's not.; [a.] Britt, MN

PERRY, CHARLENE ANN
[pen.] Charlene Ann Hill; [b.] October 26, 1940, Hamburg, IA; [p.] Cecil Spittler, Ferne Boldra Spittler; [m.] Jessie W. Perry; [ch.] Teri Lynn, Rock Delos, Katrina Sue, Tana Marie, Traci May, David Brian; [occ.] Self Employed, twenty-one yrs., Owner operator of a small business, Moreno Valley, California; [oth. writ.] Children's stories; [a.] Riverside, CA

PERRY, WILLIAM LEWIS
[b.] August 10, 1953, Philadelphia, PA; [p.] Raised by mother Janne Mae Perry and Godmother Leola Edwards; [m.] Sheila Elizabeth Perry, August 28, 1993; [ch.] Robert, Edrina, William, Sherrie, Edric, Charles; [ed.] South Phila. High, Community College of Philadelphia (Business major have not received degree yet); [occ.] Truck Driver, and Freelance Writer for the Philadelphia Tribune; [memb.] Consolation Baptist Church of Philadelphia; [hon.] Award winning student writer/reporter of Community College of Philadelphia (received award May 1994); [oth. writ.] Columnist for the North Philly Matters (Monthly Community Paper), Articles in the Philadelphia Tribune Magazine in the 'Up-N-Coming' department, where I write about up and coming talent. Article comes out every last Friday of the month.; [pers.] "I want to reach fame and

fortune, but I want to be best known in Heaven."; [a.] Philadelphia, PA

PERSAD, RAMSUNDAR
[b.] September 25, 1927, Trinidad, WI; [p.] Choon and Mynee Maharaj; [m.] Hemrajiya Persad, April 22, 1951; [ch.] Indra, Vidia and Saty; [ed.] 8 "O" Levels and 3 "A" Levels, University of London; [occ.] Hindu Marriage Officer, Justice of the Peace; [memb.] Executive Member of the Sanatan Dharma Maha Sabha and Member of the Pandits Parishad; [hon.] Two Award of Merit Certificates and a Golden Poet Award from the World of Poetry, Sacramento, California, U.S.A.; [oth. writ.] Booklets: Famous Women in Hindu Religious Literature. Glimpses into the Hindu Religious Heritage. Ram Bhakta Hanuman in Reverence to Lord Shiva. Hindu Marriage in Trinidad and Tobago.; [pers.] The world is one family.

PESCADOR, GUILLERMO
[b.] February 6, 1909, Philippines; [m.] Evelyn Pescador, 1949; [ed.] 5th Grade; [occ.] Retired

PETERSEN, JEAN
[pen.] Jean Petersen; [b.] May 28, 1923, Fort Dodge, IA; [p.] Clifford and Ruth Johnson; [m.] C. A. Petersen, June 30, 1962; [ed.] Riverside grade and High School, Fort Dodge, IA, School of Modern Photography, Writers Digest School; [occ.] Retired; [memb.] Alaska Press Club 1982 to 1988; [hon.] Kodak International Award - 1970, Special Commendation Award - Modern Photography, Writers Digest Award - 1978, Ocean World of Jacques Costeau - 1974; [oth. writ.] Anchorage Daily News - Poems McKinley Hotel Fire - Photos and Write-up Alaska Campfollower March 1977, Alaska Yukon Magazine Photo - Write-up; [pers.] People in work or play are a never ending phase of activity for writing with words expending their actions - words build strength and excitement.; [a.] Mount Vernon, WA

PETERSON, SARAH S.
[b.] February 7, 1963, Yuma, AZ; [p.] Howard and Bonita Warrington; [m.] Single; [ch.] Three; [ed.] Leavenworth High, Wenatchee College of Beauty; [occ.] Domestic Engineer; [oth. writ.] Many unsubmitted; [pers.] I believe it's all in the air. A consumption of time. My ribs as the keys of the accordion, my heart it's pleated bellows. The taker of breath. A compaction of thoughts. A compression of feelings, as the soul wells up. Creating a pressure until the note breaks. As it cries, life's reflections. Creating a arched rainbow over my world that radiates that last line of gold., Which is laid to rest upon paper. Creating a world of black and white, giving such character to my Lord Jesus Christ the author and finisher of my life.; [a.] Wenatchee, WA

PETRONE, DONNA S. NESTOR
[pen.] Donna S. Nestor; [b.] October 23, 1964, Moundsville, WV; [p.] Ronald and Bobby Nestor; [m.] Fiance John E. DiMarco; [ch.] Jennifer D. Petrone; [ed.] Grafton High School, Taylor County Vocational Center; [occ.] Computer Mrg, System Coordinator and Inventory Control; [memb.] Our Lady of Pertual Help Church Highlands NJ, FBLA Club in High School; [hon.] Concert and Marching band awards in high school; [oth. writ.] Several poems written in high school but never published.; [a.] Highlands, NJ

PETTIGREW, MRS. JO HELEN
[pen.] Jo Jo; [b.] March 10, 1948, Memphis, TN; [p.] Mr. and Mrs. Joseph Hardy; [m.] Mr. Edward L. Pettigrew Sr., October 21, 1970; [ch.] I have 4 children; [ed.] I graduated from booker T. Washington in 1966. I have a 12th grade education.; [occ.] I know work at Federal Express (Memphis Hub); [memb.] I'm a member of Temple of Deliverance (Church of God in Christ) I'm a child of God and love helping people. I'm a usher; [oth. writ.] I have many poems I have written but this is the first time I really felt like this particular one had meaning, I have written love poem, spiritual poems for my church also.; [pers.] I truly know this is the way for me to reach and express myself to my fellowman of all races. I really admire, Maya Angelou and the writings of Carl Sanburg the American poet.; [a.] Memphis, TN

PFAFF, VERDA E.
[pen.] Verda Fausett-Pfaff; [b.] December 19, 1914, Hazelton, KS; [p.] Almon and Ora Fausett; [m.] J. Newland Pfaff, February 8, 1931; [ch.] Richard, Bonnie, Darrell, Dawn; [ed.] Baptist Bible Seminary, Extension work (Greek) at U of Az.; [occ.] Preparing Bible Studies, Stories and Poems.; [hon.] 3rd 2nd 1st in Public Speaking, debates and Dramatic Reading, published in various magazines.; [oth. writ.] Translated New Testament Greek into Modern am English - Short stories, poems, etc.; [pers.] That man or woman is blesses whose children have a thirst for knowledge.; [a.] Green Valley, AZ

PFLANZ III, HENRY STANLEY
[pen.] Henry S. Pflanz III; [b.] December 8, 1958, Dayton, OH; [p.] Henry S. Pflanz, Karen A. Pflanz; [ed.] 1977 Graduate of Frederic Douglas High School, Upper Marlboro, MD; [occ.] Aircraft Overhaul Mechanic for American Airlines; [memb.] American Motorcyclist Association, Transport Workers Union of America; [a.] Broken Arrow, OK

PHELPS, JULIE KAY
[pen.] Julie Kay Phelps; [b.] February 3, 1962, Springfield, IL; [p.] Jim Wooldridge/Paula Ogden; [m.] Randy Phelps, January 19, 1990; [ch.] Collin; [ed.] Mason City High School, Lincoln Land Community College; [occ.] Farmer/Bookkeeper/Mom; [memb.] Ducks Unlimited United Presbyterian Church; [pers.] If you never build boundaries around the dreams you create-then there's nothing that you can't achieve; [a.] Easton, IL

PHILLIPS, ADAM N.
[b.] September 16, 1982, Iowa; [p.] Crystal L. Hartmann; [ed.] Currently attending West Intermediate Jr. High School 7th grade looking forward to graduating High School in year 2001.

PHILLIPS, TRACY
[pen.] TIP; [b.] February 2, 1965, Los Angeles, CA; [p.] Irvin Phillips, Rosemary Smith; [ch.] Christina and Charisna Deberry; [ed.] Military Education/High School Graduate; [occ.] Aspiring writer/Office Manager; [oth. writ.] I have written several sentimental writings for special events/newspapers.; [pers.] I would like to dedicate this poem to my deceased brother Keith Phillips and all my family and friends.

PHILPITT, EDWARD T.
[b.] November 15, 1926, Washington, DC; [p.] Isabel and Richard - both Quakers; [ed.] Graduate from Benjamin Franklin Univ. 1952, Washington, D.C.; [occ.] Part time poet and songwriter; [memb.] Int'l Society of Poets; [hon.] Int'l Society of Poets, Poet of Merit - 1995, selected six times for "Sound of Poetry" by National Library of Poetry in 1995.; [pers.] It's the contest, not the length that makes something important. Posterity is the written word - not the spoken word. Adaptation is the beginning of forward progress. It's through tireless efforts that we gain the momentum to move forward.; [a.] Washington, DC

PIAZZA, KAREN A.
[pen.] Kopas; [b.] January 9, 1957, New Brunswick; [p.] Frank Piazza, Claire Piazza; [ch.] Three; [ed.] High School Grad. two years Rutgers Univ.; [occ.] Social Security Disability Self-emp. Poet; [oth. writ.] Yes enclosed; [pers.] Please refer to "things I remember". I sent a copy because. There isn't enough space.; [a.] Highlans, NY

PICHÉ, NEAL QUINN
[b.] April 27, 1982, San Berdadino; [p.] Flower Fox and Perry T. Piché; [ed.] Still in school; [occ.] Student in eighth grade; [hon.] Honor Roll, Renaissance; [oth. writ.] Other poems, some put in school papers; also write stories; [a.] Joshua Tree, CA

PIERCE, PATRICK L.
[b.] October 19, 1958, Sault Sainte Marie, MI; [p.] Glen D. and Barbara Pierce; [ed.] Moberly High, Moberly, MO Linn Technical College - Linn, MO; [a.] Columbia, MO

PIERCE, TAMMY TOMBOLI
[b.] September 29, 1967, Little Rock, AR; [p.] Mr. and Mrs. Floyd Tomboli Jr.; [ch.] Twin sons Ronny and Chris, Ryan; [ed.] Honor Graduate, Accounting, Computers and General Business major, 8 yr. major in Accounting and Tax Prep. Honor Graduate of collection; [occ.] Professional model, owner of Pierces Collection Agency, Tax and Accounting Service Inc. and Photography; [memb.] N.A.T.P, N.A.F.E., Leader of Cub Scouts, BSA, NIPB, FTS, AIPB, N.A.F.T.P, N.S.T.P.; [hon.] Woman of the Year, International Woman of the Year, 2,000 notable American Women, Research board of Advisors, Honor Graduate, Key of Excellence, Super Mom Award, Excellent Mother Award, Biography in "2,000 notable American Women"; [oth. writ.] Published poem in "Treasured poems of America", Author of "Beebob of Rocksteady" and "Quardian Angel" - which are children books.; [pers.] I work to make a statement with any of my work. I was mainly influenced by Shakespeare and Frost.; [a.] Bastrop, LA

PIETTE, DEBBIE
[b.] July 3, 1956, WI; [p.] Robert Smith - Betty Smith; [m.] Michael Piette; [ch.] Casey Allen - Salina Allen; [hon.] Editor's Choice Award (by The National Library of Poetry); [oth. writ.]; [pers.] No matter how different each of our lives may appear, many of u share the same dreams, the same goals, and the same disappointments. Never giving up is the key to life's success stories.; [a.] Neenah, WI

PILCHAK, BRIDGE
[pen.] Kateri Goretti; [b.] June 2, 1975, Grosse Pointe, MI; [p.] Joe Pilchak, Clara Pilchak; [ed.] Capac High, currently enrolled in Long Ridge Writers Group.; [occ.] I work in the shoe selling business and as a cook at an Italian Restaurant.; [hon.] Editor Capac Yearbook; [pers.] Without the ability to wonder and imagine is ceasing the existence of life and all hopes to live.; [a.] Capac, MI

PINCKNEY, JERRY LEWIS
[pen.] Jerry Pinckney; [b.] September 22, 1952, Charleston County, Mt. Pleasant, SC; [p.] Abraham Rebecca Pinckney; [m.] Sherilyn Richardson Pinckney, Divorced; [ch.] Sheniqua and Alabor; [ed.] Claflin College, Bronx Community College; [occ.] Mechanical Tech. (Chocklyn o'nuts Coll.) L. U. President; [memb.] All my worker's comp. committee, safety and health committee, Zion Am Church, N.Y.S. Legislative committee union member, American Museum of Natural History mem.; [hon.] Editor's choice award (the Garden of life), Harlem's playwright award (1980's) acting and comentary awards (1970's), college scholarship to Claflin; [oth. writ.] Screen (Jips) ideas for screenwriters Indep movies screen ideas (stories) "Twilight of Winter" Current films Lord Of Illusions, "Water Spirit" magic in the water "Celestial

Child" powder "Rivers of Serpents" Twelve Monkeys, "In the Valley of Dry Bones" Eden Valley; [pers.] I strive to be the best I can be, and hold a great affection for great literary works.; [a.] New York, NY

PINSON, ROBERT T.
[b.] January 18, 1958, Birmingham, AL; [p.] William and Ruthelene Pinson; [m.] Nancy Ousley Pinson, March 13, 1982; [ch.] Adam Terrell and Oakleigh Chathrine; [ed.] Pinson Valley High Jefferson State College University of Alabama at B'ham; [occ.] Banker; [memb.] American Institute of Banking; [oth. writ.] Technical Manuals, contracts. Have a song in production in Nashville.; [pers.] I like to write about practical matters and the simple things in life.; [a.] Pinson, AL

PINTO, IVAN NERY COSTA
[pen.] Ivan Costa-Pinto; [b.] November 17, 1948, Rio de Janeiro, Brazil; [p.] Hugo de Aguiar Costa Pinto and Wanda Costa Pinto; [ed.] BA in English, FECL Notre Dame, Rio de Janeiro, Brazil; [occ.] Translator Free-Lance; [memb.] Smithsonian Institute, California Great Outdoors; [hon.] Mention of Honor, ATL, Teresopolis, Brazil; [oth. writ.] Poems published in Teresopolis, Brazil. Translation of Rimbaud published in Teresopolis, Brazil. Translation of Agatha Christie published in Rio de Janeiro, Brazil.; [pers.] Never give up.; [a.] Los Angeles, CA

PIRYAEI, ROHOLLAH
[pen.] R. P. Payvand; [b.] April 21, 1952, Iran; [m.] Nushin Asadi; [ch.] Shabnam and Tara; [ed.] B.A. Degree, Teacher Training University (Iran); [occ.] ESL Instructor; [oth. writ.] Many poems published in Persian Literary Magazines and Articles in farsi about African-American Native American and Latin American poetry. Published and edited a multi cultural magazine for young adults; [pers.] Through my poems I endeavor to reflect the reality of life and values of my culture; [a.] Antioch, CA

PITTMAN, ROSEMARY
[pen.] Rosemary Pittman; [b.] April 29, 1916, Auburn, IL; [p.] Amy and Ben Forsythe; [m.] Marvin Pittman II (deceased), August 4, 1949; [ch.] Nancy; [ed.] Univ. of Chicago, MS, 1947, Univ. of Iowa, RNBS 1940; [occ.] Retired Fac. U. of W. (Nurse), Artist; [memb.] Gray Panthers, ANA (Retired), Citizens for Imps. Nursery Homes, N. Wash. Retirement Assoc., New Lutheran Church; [hon.] Assoc. Prof. Emeritus, Univ. of Wa., Robin Wood Johnson - Fellowship, 1 year Univ. of Indiana, 25 - Award 1976. Vpl. Award State of Wa., Mohler Grant for Art 1992, Wash. State Cert. Commission has purchased my work, lost 3 years.; [oth. writ.] If you want my work its 15 pages or more.; [pers.] I have been interested on poetry since I was an only child on a farm in Illinois and used to write poetry setting in a favorite apple tree.; [a.] Seattle, WA

PIZZANO, GINA
[b.] March 23, 1960, Chelsea, MA; [p.] Eugene and Helen Pizzano; [ed.] Chelsea High School, Burdett College; [occ.] Secretary; [oth. writ.] Other poetry, letters, and narratives; [pers.] "Let me ride the wings of time so I can be what I want to be and do what I want to do."; [a.] Medford, MA

PLACE, MARJORIE E.
[b.] May 12, 1919, Clyde Park, MT; [p.] Clearance and Elizabeth Johnson; [m.] Merton Place, August 14, 1940; [ch.] Marian Place, Scott and Robert Napton (grandchildren); [ed.] Gallatin High, Montana State College; [occ.] Bank Merchant Teller (retired); [pers.] I write poetry for my own enjoyment and with the hope that it entertains others.; [a.] Santa Monica, CA

PLESSEN II, ROGER
[b.] September 4, 1971, Redlands, CA; [p.] Roger Plessen, Barbara Plessen; [ed.] Valley Professional High School Rio Hondo College; [occ.] Consultant/Movie Extra; [memb.] House of Joseph - Interfaith Trustee; [pers.] The most difficult task to accomplish is feeling and understanding the events around you.; [a.] Covina, CA

POGUE, GARY D.
[pen.] Pogo - Stick; [b.] September 5, 1951, Turlock, CA; [p.] Bill Joe and Loretta Ann Pogue; [ed.] Westport Grade School, Ceres High School; [occ.] Cashier - clerk; [hon.] Outstanding Artists and City Downtown Fall Festival; [oth. writ.] Several mini movies of the Mind, A Couple of Cartoons, A Couple of Games, Hundreds of Songs; [pers.] Earthadise; [a.] Ceres, CA

POMMIER, SYLVIA
[b.] May 7, 1945, Basel, Switzerland; [p.] Deceased; [m.] Luis W. Pommier, February 12, 1966; [ch.] Four; [ed.] Saint Nicolas School, (now Lakeside) in Seattle, WA, High school graduate 1962, University of Washington BA (spanish) 1966; [occ.] Sales; [oth. writ.] Other poems - 2 Children's Stories; [pers.] I believe each person is a unique and valuable part of the tapestry of life. In my poetry I try to capture moments in time so that impressions and feelings - however small - will be saved to be re-examined and wover into our own unique pattern of life; [a.] Rancho Santa Margarita, CA

PONCE, ANGELA
[b.] September 7, 1954, Laupahoehoe, HI; [p.] Basilio Lapinid, Benita Lapinid; [m.] Jonathan Ponce, January 6, 1974; [ch.] Melanie Ann, Laura Ashley; [ed.] Paauilo El. and Inter, Honokaa High, Hawaii Community College; [occ.] Hawaii School Advisory, Council Secretary; [oth. writ.] Poems published in local newspaper; [pers.] Practice finding good in people.; [a.] Hilo, HI

POPE, DANIEL TIMOTHY
[b.] January 30, Indiana; [p.] John and Mary Pope; [m.] Single - still searching for a good-natured/pretty/feminine female...; [ed.] 1991 Magna Cum Laude, University of Arkansas at Little Rock, B.S. in Education, 1989, Arkansas State University-Beebe (ASUB), A.a. in Liberal Arts; [occ.] Entrepreneur; [memb.] ASUB Ecology Club, The Gamma Beta Phi Society, The Honor Society of the Phi Kappa Phi, The Kappa Delta Pi...; [hon.] 1988-89 ASUB Citizenship Award, 1988-89 ASUB Ecology Club Award, Who's Who Among Students 1987-88 and 1988-89, Chancellor's List 1987-90, The National Dean's List 1990-91...; [oth. writ.] I have written several poems and songs that have never been submitted for publication consideration, I have written and illustrated a book for children (also unpublished).; [pers.] Try committing at least one random act of environmental kindness everyday — these acts will transcend, disseminate, and rejuvenate...; [a.] Penrose, CO

POPOVICH, SHARON L.
[pen.] She-she, Munchkin; [b.] October 31, 1948, Lackawanna; [p.] Glenn Curtis Cook, Lillian Prenatt; [m.] Robert Popovich, March 20, 1971; [ch.] Dawn M. Popovich; [ed.] Kenmore West High, Bryant and Stratton Business Institute; [occ.] Housewife; [hon.] Associates Degree in Commercial Art; [oth. writ.] Chosen words appears in a sea of treasures; [pers.] If just one person enjoys and gets something out of my poem, then I've done something good. Thats what really counts. The readers enjoyment.; [a.] Tonawanda, NY

PORCHIA, DONALD C.
[b.] September 18, 1932, Los Angeles, CA; [p.] Salvatore Porchia and Sadie Thomas; [occ.] Ar Director for Photo. Lab.; [oth. writ.] Nothing published but have written a series of poems abou Aitzhiemers Disease another series called "moments of love" and a series about "my love of Mexico"; [pers.] I try to paint a picture with words in every day language.; [a.] Los Angeles, CA

PORTER JR., JOHN DAVID
[b.] March 16, 1978, Atlanta, GA; [p.] John Porter and Suzanne Arnold; [ed.] Landmark Christian School; [memb.] First Baptist Church of Snellville; [pers.] We only live by grace and mercy. Take these away from your brother and they will be taken from you. Give these to your brother and receive them back abundantly.; [a.] Jonesboro, GA

POSSEY, JOAN
[b.] September 22, 1932, Ozark, AR; [p.] Vernon L. Andrews and Emma Gilbreth; [m.] James L. Possey (Deceased, October 11, 1992), August 4, 1949; [ch.] Joe, Debra, Phillip, Beverly, Lawrence, Joyce, Bradley, Emily, Jennifer, Leslie; [ed.] High School, 17 Credit hours West Arkansas College at Fort Smith, AR; [occ.] Retired from factory and grocery store produce manager; [memb.] Mt. View Freewill Baptist Church, Adult Sunday School Teacher, V7W Auxiliary - Hospital Chairman, Different Drummers Literary Club, American Legion Auxiliary, Mercy Choice Club, friends of Library, Charleston; [hon.] I am mother of 10 children all adults now. I have 24 grandchildren. I'm the over qualified babysitter for my family.; [oth. writ.] Have written a weekly column for my local hometown paper (Charleston Express) for these past 20 years. Special events Church plays.; [pers.] I try to write only the good things I see. Home-spun philosophy. Everyday down-to-earth knowledge. Also Christian love and fellowship.; [a.] Charleston, AR

POTTER, KATHRYN
[b.] April 27, 1914, Leyden, WI; [p.] Eugene and Nora Donahue Reilly; [m.] Robert J.; [ch.] Dennis, Mark, Marcia.; [ed.] Degrees in Elem. Education - 25 years teaching in Milwaukee, WI area (Elm Grove) schools; [occ.] Stewardess; [oth. writ.] Occasional compositions including poetry, to share with friends in an endeavor to keep alive the Art of letter writing and legible hand-writing.; [pers.] A way-of-life Stewardship in Tryon, NC giving fulfillment and dignity to tasks which help people and projects in need of assistance.; [a.] Tryon, NC

POTTON, SHARON
[b.] September 6, 1961, Midwest City, OK; [p.] David Leonard and Judith Ann Bachelor; [m.] Alan Potton, February 28, 1882; [ch.] Christopher Alan, Travis James, Alyssa; [ed.] Cy-Fair High School, Cypress, Tx., some college, PVAMU, Tx.; [occ.] Mom - Home-maker, Wife.; [memb.] Metropolitan Baptist Church 11 yrs.; [oth. writ.] Have written some poems for self enjoyment - none were sent in for publication.; [pers.] I am a mother of 3 and am constantly reminded daily, as I watch my children grow, that life is too short. We must stop, enjoy our children so they will have memories to pass onto their children, for we now are the memories they will have later.; [a.] Cypress, TX

POTTS, MICHELLE A.
[pen.] Michelle Keene; [b.] July 10, 1965, Ypsilanti, MI; [p.] Margie Rowe, Billy C. Keene Sr.; [m.] Randall R. Potts, December 31, 1993; [ch.] Brian J. Jason Allen; [ed.] Milan High., currently enrolled in NRI School of Writing; [occ.] Housewife and Mother (Domestic Engineer); [oth. writ.] Have written several poems, for personal. This is my first poem published.; [pers.] When I write, it's from the soul, in and out. My writings have true meaning.; [a.] Maybee, MI

POV, SOVONN
[pen.] Stacy; [b.] May 3, 1980, Thailand; [p.] Sarang Pov, Soun Ros; [ed.] Sophomore in Oakland High School, California; [memb.] Boys and Girls Club, Cambodian Club; [hon.] Outstanding Achievement in Math, Outstanding Achievement in History and English; [oth. writ.] Never been publish but I have write many poems and story that I've cherish until now.; [pers.] I have always wanted to be an artist and a poet. I think drawing and writing is what you see, feel and think in everyday life.; [a.] Oakland, CA

PRATT, NANCY J.
[b.] February 1, 1966, Sacramento, CA; [p.] Allan Pratt and Jane Alves; [m.] (Fiance) Alfred Saenz, October '97; [ed.] MA in Couns. Psych. from Santa Clara Univ. '94, BA in Psych. from UC Santa Cruz '88; [occ.] Substance Abuse Counselor for Economic and Social Opportunities; [memb.] Member of the California Association of Marriage, Family and Child Counselors (CAMFT), MFCC Intern; [oth. writ.] Poems published in Palo Alto High School collected works '84.; [pers.] When you are feeling powerless over a situation, hang on to your dreams with all your might and keep hope alive. Dreams do come true with hand work and persistence.; [a.] Mountain View, CA

PRATT, REUBEN
[pen.] David Keith; [b.] July 29, 1974, Monroe, NC; [p.] Gurney Pratt, Carolyn Pratt; [m.] Sakeena Pratt, May 20, 1995; [ed.] Monroe High School, ASI Insurance Ins.; [occ.] Outside Adjuster for Griffen Motors Co., Insurance Agent; [memb.] SADD, Monroe High Drama Society; [pers.] I try to convey to my reader a story in poetry. A thought that I may have. I also try to put myself in the character's shoes then try to get the reader to feel something. It's great to walk in someone else's shoes even if they are heavier than our own.; [a.] Monroe, NC

PRICE, JASON MICHAEL
[b.] January 7, 1976, Concord, NC; [p.] Van W. Price Jr. and Janet Price; [ed.] Student at Wingate University; [occ.] Theology Student; [memb.] CSU; [hon.] Dean's List, John Phillip Sousa Award, Semper Fidelis Award, Boy's State, NC Teaching Fellows Scholarship; [oth. writ.] Many unpublished poems and essays.; [pers.] The inspiration for this poem is Meredith Byrd, the love of my life.; [a.] Concord, NC

PRICE, MAUREEN
[b.] August 4, 1933, Pender, NE; [p.] William and Frieda Goede; [m.] H. G. (Bill) Price, July 30, 1954; [ch.] Denis James and Kent T.; [ed.] 2 yrs. college; [occ.] Real Estate Sales Associate - ReMax Assoc. of Topeka; [memb.] Nat'l Multiple Sclerosis Society Topeka Center for Peace and Justice, Our Savior's Lutheran Church, CASA of Shawnee Co, Inc., Local, State and Nat'l Bd. of Realtors.; [pers.] Writing poems and songs has been as natural for me all my life as breathing and in times of loss or pain has saved me. Only recently have I thought about sharing my feelings in this way with others. Than my family.; [a.] Topeka, KS

PRIOR, CARMEN D. SANTOS
[pen.] Karmen D. Santos-Prior; [b.] San Juan, PR; [p.] Jackie H. Santos de Thomas, Dorotea Rosa Fuentes; [m.] James G. Prior, August 29, 1994; [ed.] Bachelor of Science, Chemistry Major, University of Puerto Rico; [occ.] Project Manager for the U.S. Environmental Protection Agency; [pers.] Life itself is my best teacher. I recognize its limitless teachings and apply them to improve myself and succeed as a human being.; [a.] Dublin, CA

PRYOR, VICKY
[b.] March 8, 1954, Kewanee, IL; [p.] Mervin and Gwen Wallace; [m.] Emmett A. Pryor Jr., July 14, 1995; [ch.] Jeffrey, James, Bobbi Jean; [ed.] Toulon High School, Toulon, IL Black Hawk Jr. College, Kewanee, IL Houston Comm. College, Houston, TX; [occ.] Clerk, Secretary; [memb.] Jersey Village Baptist Church; [oth. writ.] Several unpublished poems.; [pers.] My poems are reflections of my life experiences.; [a.] Katy, TX

PUGH, BATES J.
[b.] September 3, 1980, Decatur, GA; [p.] Daniel and Jennifer Pugh; [ed.] Heritage High School Conyers, GA. - Class of '99; [occ.] Student; [pers.] As a friend once told me, never be afraid to do anything creative. The purpose in it should not be to please others. It should be done for one's self.; [a.] Conyers, GA

PURKEY, VERA L.
[pen.] Vera L. Purkey; [b.] January 2, 1915, Verdigris, OK; [p.] Noah and Effie Fisher; [m.] Rodger C. Purkey, September 28, 1934; [ch.] Morse, Julia, Peggy, Rodgelan; [ed.] Claremore High School; [occ.] Retired, J.C. Penny Co.; [memb.] Assembly of God Church, Senior Advantages Claremore, Senior Citizens Hospitality Club, American Diabetes Association, Arthritis Foundation; [hon.] Mother of the Year, 1976, Teacher of the Year, 1989 and 1991, Valedictorian 8th grade, 1929; [oth. writ.] I have been writing poems, Short stories and plays all of my life which has been used in my own community and church many times but I had never sent anything in for publication before.; [pers.] Imagine my surprise when on my 18st birthday I received your letter saying you wanted to publish one of my poems. Thank you one of the best gifts I could ever receive.; [a.] Claremore, OK

PUTNAM, HAROLD
[b.] February 15, 1916, Boston; [p.] Marlene Putnam, March 9, 1980; [ed.] Boston Latin School, '33 Dartmouth College '37, Boston Univ. Law School '53; [occ.] Lawyer/Poet; [memb.] Rotary Club; [oth. writ.] Editor, Dartmonth Book of Winter Sports Voice of Reason, 1995 Anthology; [pers.] I grew up on old English and early New England poetry. My favorites now are Walt Whitman and Robert Frost.; [a.] Vero Beach, FL

QUINTELA, PHILLIP
[b.] October 10, 1973, San Antonio, TX; [p.] Felipe Quintela, Rose Mary Quintela; [ch.] Phillip Quintela Jr.; [ed.] Fox Tech High School, Edison High School; [occ.] Floor Man, Retama Manor West, San Antonio, TX; [memb.] Krist the King Church, Boys Club; [hon.] Given an a Plus in English Class, and had my poems displayed on the wall.; [oth. writ.] Several poems written that were a project for English class.; [pers.] I feel what comes into my mind and heart should always be written for the world to see through my eyes and heart. I have been inspired by the nature of the Indians poems.; [a.] San Antonio, TX

QURESHI, HASAN A.
[pen.] HAQ; [b.] July 28, 1974, Lahore, Pakistan; [p.] A. R. Qureshi, A. W. Qureshi; [ed.] Hillcrest High, QCC; [occ.] A/P, J. Walter Thompson; [oth. writ.] I was a staff writer for a National Magazine, New York Casting. I wrote several articles for it, including a personal column, "Hasan's Head Shot Heaven."; [pers.] "Life in lake a piece of paper and humans are like pencils. If you make a mistake, remember there is an eraser on a pencil. "I have been greatly influenced by a man by the name of Gene Mann.; [a.] Queens, NY

RAASCH, TODD A.
[b.] December 12, 1961, Red Wing, MN; [p.] Arnie Raasch and Simone Raasch (Carr); [m.] Jara Raasch (Delong), October 20, 1984; [ch.] Zac; [ed.] Williston, H.S., Minot St. College; [occ.] Account Manager, Jesme-Lowe Food Brokers; [memb.] Board of Deacons, and School Board, Apostles Evan, Luth. Church; [hon.] Salesman of the Year, Eastern, Mt., William C. Brownfield Award, Outstanding 1st Year Jaycee Local District, and Regional level; [pers.] Living life loving the Lord while weighing my wife's whispers. Seeking nothing....except one more say in the arms of love and life.; [a.] Billings, MT

RABUS, GEORGE
[pen.] Subar; [b.] April 26, 1915, Brooklyn, NY; [p.] Charles and Florence Rabus; [m.] Virginia Rhatigan (Deceased), January 30, 1937; [ch.] Rita, George, Charles, Joseoh, Virginia and Michael; [ed.] Richmond Hill High School, New Lots Evening High School, Brooklyn Technical High School Poly-Tech Institute (Evening); [occ.] Car Inspector N.Y. Transit Authority (Retired); [memb.] St. Christopher R.C. Church Boy Scouts of America 1928-1993; [hon.] Silver Beaver Award B.S.A. Pelican Award Catholic Scouting St. George Award"; [oth. writ.] Autobiography Editor 127 News Tropp Newsletter Editor Eagles Tale Tropp Newsletter.

RADIC, DRAGICA
[pen.] D. Natasha; [b.] Yugoslavia; [p.] Radinka and Vasilije; [ed.] Nursing College; [occ.] Registered Nurse; [hon.] Golden Poet Award for Poem "The Magic" 1989, Washington DC, published in great poems of Western World; [oth. writ.] Short and long stories poems, working on screen plays: 1) Year of a Spider, 2) Undiscovered Genius - My Aunt Lilly Channel, etc.; [a.] Hungtington Park, CA

RADULESCU, SILVIA
[pen.] Silvia "Anini" Radulescu; [b.] August 19, 1910, Darmanesti, Suceava, Romania; [p.] Rachel and Gregory Chelariu; [m.] Widow of 28 years (Late husband: Vasile), July 3, 1938; [ch.] Ileana Hawkins, Maria Lichiardopol, Victoria M. Browne; [ed.] Graduate of the Biology and Geography - University King Carol II, Romania, 1932; [occ.] Retired High School Biology Teacher; [memb.] National Geographic Society; [hon.] Professor Emeritus; [oth. writ.] I wrote and published two high school textbooks for biology and geology. For decades, I wrote poems, essays and prose in Romanian. They brought me joy and relief. I call them: "My drawer literature" because I did not publish any of it before. This poem is my first in English and also my first presentation to public.; [pers.] I am fascinated by the mystery of Life on Terra, with all its interconnections and its impact on abiotic and biotic media. My life's logo was and is: "Never give up". Per aspera ad astra. And the most important: In God I trust.; [a.] Anchorage, AL

RAGAN, RONALD J.
[pen.] "Cotton-Head Joe" and "Bubba Ragan"; [b.] November 4, 1940, Spartanburg, SC; [p.] Mr. and Mrs. A. D. Ragan; [ed.] Spartanburg High School Graduate (1959), City College of San Francisco, Business Course at Night at S. F. State College" Cheney Bros. Truck Driving School"; [occ.] Retired Warehouse Worker and Professional Singer; [memb.] Spartanburg Chorus and Glee Club (Soloist). "Boy Scouts", "County Music Assn. of America", "US Army", Smithsonian Institute", Democratic Committee Head, V.P. of 11th Grade Church of Christ.; [hon.] Four Poetry Awards from publishers, two "Funniest Original Joke Awards" from magazines. Lead singer for "The Four Spades", "Joel Ragan and the V-8's", toured with Joe "Black Slacks" Bennett and "The Sparkle Tones."; [oth. writ.] Poems from "Rivers of Dreams", "I Lied", "Best Poems of 1995/Vol 3", "Nice Advice", "Tomorrow Never Knows", "Love Is Like A Winding River", "A Sea of Treasure", "Slip Silently", and "Sparrowgrass Poetry", "Treasured

Poems of American, 1996" - "Automatic Heart River" (A Prayer); [pers.] Life is experience. Life is also a grand-school. When we die (translate), we graduate. I want to show more understanding compassion and forgiveness. All people have hearts and souls!; [a.] Spartanburg, SC

RAINS, FERN E.
[pen.] Shrum; [b.] July 19, 1919, McAlester, OK; [p.] James F. and Mabel Shrum; [m.] Vinson T. Rains, October 10, 1938; [ch.] Patricia Eileen Sheffield, James W, Robt. T., Carl K., Boyce E.; [ed.] Graduated McAlester, Ok. High School, May 20, 1938 - Btan. little time. Fresno City College, Fresno CA.; [occ.] A tired old "lifelong ezcematic" who never quits!; [memb.] A Born Again Christian since 16. Want to say, "I've read Bible thru 60 times (60 yrs). But cannot! Got study guide 16 yrs: Read it thru 16 times. "The Lord is my life, joy, all!; [oth. writ.] At 7 yrs. decided "I must write a book and see my name on it!" That would be great! (I have tons of pages, no book yet except granddaughters' Baby Books - no title, no author); [pers.] I detest what I see happening in our great "Christian Nation"! Americans must restore righteousness on their knees since that is only path to greatness! Victory! "Thank you all!"; [a.] Fowler, CA

RALLI, SUSANNA
[b.] January 26, 1964, Washington, DC; [p.] Mary Jo Tecce, Joseph Tecce; [m.] James Ralli, October 17, 1993; [ed.] Wellesley High School, Boston College; [occ.] Freelance writer, Editor, and Proofreader; [memb.] Women's Business Network, Women in publishing (Boston), Freelance Editorial Association; [hon.] Member of the Alpha Sigma Nu Jesuit Honor Society. Recipient of Boston Colleges's O'Connor Award for Outstanding Achievement in English.; [oth. writ.] Several articles published local newspapers. Honorable mention as a semifinalist for short fiction in the writers of the future contest.; [a.] Natick, MA

RAMPANI, ROBERT
[pen.] Bob 'Eagle' Rampani; [b.] July 1, 1928, Saint Louis Co, MO; [p.] Mike Rampani and Etta Rampani; [m.] Divorced, October 23, 1950; [ch.] Steve, Gene, Ralph, Aaron-Rampani and Roberta Dame; [ed.] High school; [occ.] Retired McDonnel Aircraft Corp.; [memb.] Greater St. Louis Archaeology Society, 45 yr. - I.A.M Machinist Union Distinguished Mem. - I. S. P.; [hon.] Single male who raised (5) children parent, V.P. of G. St. Louis, Arch. Soc. many beat of show - Archaeology Society; [oth. writ.] Poem in "Mists of Enchantment" several poems in magazines and newsletters articles in Archeology journals; [pers.] I write from my heart mostly from personal experiences or thoughts. In my heart is a lifetime of stored away thoughts. I have so much to say, its like talking to someone. I am influenced by the old ways.; [a.] Bridgeton, MO

RAPOLD, JULIA PATRICIA S. URROZ
[pen.] Patricia Urroz Rapold; [b.] February 16, 1949, Key West, FL; [p.] Lila Urroz, Anastasio Somoza; [m.] Divorced; [ch.] Jean Sebastien and Nicolas Rapold; [ed.] Academy of the Holy Names Tampa, Fla., Mount St. Mary's Newburgh NY, Boston University, Boston, MA., Columbia University N.Y.; [occ.] Bachelor of Arts Political Science, Boston University 1975, Investor; [memb.] New York Society Library NY, New York Public Library NY, American Association of University Women, Washington DC, Metropolitan Museum NY, Central Park Conservancy NY, Museum of the City of NY, NY, Harvard University Parents Association Volunteer, Boston, MA; [hon.] International Center NY Volunteer, Certificate of Appreciation, 1988; [oth. writ.] Seasonal Living In The Northern Catskills. An Essay, Art and Poems, Birch Brook Press, Delhi NY 1994; [pers.] I am currently striving to compile memories of past life experiences into poetry. I investigate the relationship between poetry and memory, feelings and consciousness. How to create poetry. From recollection of past events is the process.; [a.] New York, NY

RAPOZA, NICOLE
[pen.] Nikki Kage; [b.] October 3, 1967, New Bedford, MA; [p.] Evelyn Rapoza; [m.] Martin Higgins; [ed.] New Bedford High School Bristol Community College; [occ.] Pharmacy Tech.; [oth. writ.] Several poems, short stories, songs; [pers.] Writing from the heart gives me the freedom to explore my inner most being and express all that I am.; [a.] New Bedford, MA

RASCON, ERIKA KARLA OCHOA
[pen.] Erika Rascon; [b.] July 1, 1971, Mexico City; [p.] Yolanda Rascon and Raul Ochoa; [ed.] Garside School Mexico City, Chula Vista High School, San Diego, Calif. Commercial Career and Teacher's Degree Helen's School Mexico; [occ.] Executive Bilingual Secretary; [hon.] Third place of my generation in commercial career; [oth. writ.] Several poems like: My Lord, Love, Have You Ever Wish, the wish, the wind, my dearest song, etc. and one short story named: A Tiny Secret. None of these have been published yet.; [pers.] "Let our minds and souls be open for understanding and love, for receiving the blessings from above, and be able to transmit them to the word."; [a.] Mexico, DF

RAUGHLEY, MARY JO
[pen.] M. J. and Meatball; [b.] January 10, 1980, Wilkes Barre, PA; [p.] Albert W. Raughley and Sandra Lee Raughley; [ed.] 10th Grade, Wyoming Valley West High School, graduate in 1998; [occ.] Work at Hogan's Deli; [memb.] Member of the W.V.W. Varsity Softball team and Lightning Strikes Softball Team. Member of the W.V.W. Varsity Field Hockey Team; [hon.] Letter winner in Softball and Field Hockey, 2nd team All-star in Softball and Field Hokey; [oth. writ.] Sitting, Caring, Best Friends, What Is This World Coming Too.; [pers.] "Think of the things you love, then write about them."; [a.] Plymouth, PA

RAYBE, MRS. DOROTHY WEAVER
[pen.] D. J. Weaver; [b.] June 4, 1934, Bridge Port, CT; [p.] Joseph, Elsie Weaver; [m.] George F. Raybe, February 7, 1953, Bpt. Conn.; [ch.] Kathryn Ann, George F. Raybe III.; [ed.] High School; [occ.] Still a happy housewife and "Grown-up" Mother of two; [memb.] Epilepsy Society, Cancer Society, AARP - Silver Threads Among The Gold, When Your Hair Has Turned to Silver; [oth. writ.] The joke from her childhood "so it had to be clean", says Dorothy. Here's the joke: There two people were locked in church together. They tried to get out, but all the windows and door were locked. How'd they get out?; [pers.] They played the organ with they got the right key. P.S. I won a Victor Borge Tape and my name was mentioned in my local newspaper that year in Visalia, California Key Radio Contest A.M. Radio 1400; [a.] Visalia, CA

REARDON, MICHAEL J.
[pen.] Mike Reardon; [b.] July 17, 1967, Long Beach, CA; [p.] Ken and Helen Reardon; [ch.] Tyra, Keri, Shelby; [ed.] GED - Cerritos Jr. College; [occ.] Full-time student; [hon.] Phi Theta Kappa, Dean's List; [pers.] The poem "O'Grandfather" was written and read at his memorial. A tribute to a great man!; [a.] Downey, CA

REASON, MARSHA G.
[b.] June 9, 1966, Chicago, IL; [p.] Tom and Christine Geerdes; [m.] Jeffrey M. Reason, June 23, 1984; [ch.] Joshua and Paul; [ed.] Murray High School, will be going to college in the fall of '96; [occ.] Housewife; [oth. writ.] I have written several poems and short stories for children and teenagers, but nothing published; [pers.] I write in the hopes that my poems will help someone find their way to Christ. Without the guidance of my parents, Tom and Christine, I wouldn't be where I am today!; [a.] Calvert City, KY

REAY, SANDRA L.
[pen.] S. L. Reay; [b.] April 18, 1949, Philadelphia, PA; [p.] Herbert and Harriet Leviton; [ed.] Arapahoe H. S., University of Colo, BA, University of Denver MC; [occ.] Computer Consultant, Photographer, Singer-Songwriter; [memb.] Historic Denver, Music Association of Swallow Hill, Colorado Bluegrass Music Society, Rocky Mountain Musicians Assoc.; [hon.] Dean's List, Finalist 1994 Walnut Valley Bluegrass Songwriters Contest; [oth. writ.] "Coyote's Song" poem published in American Poetry Anthology Summer 1995, several photos published in Bluegrass Publications photo - journalist for distinctive lifestyles magazine.; [pers.] This poem was influenced by Ghengis Khan, a friends divorce, a nighttime trip into a bad neighborhood, a photograph, and a 25-year-old memory.; [a.] Parker, CO

RECKARD, DEREK J.
[pen.] Gailen, Dak, Jareth Lerxst; [b.] July 14, 1971, Taunton, MA; [ed.] Taunton High School, Bristol College, Art Institute of Fort Lauderdale; [occ.] Sound and Video Systems Engineer, Freelance studio design; [memb.] The Nocturnal Sandcastle Building Club, and The Circle of Spheres; [hon.] AIFL Dean's List, Hometown National Video Award - "Best Professional Media Series" 1994; [oth. writ.] Several scripts and screenplays for local television and theatre, several songs and poems, and currently working on a first novel and a screenplay with hopes of possible film production.; [pers.] "Immortality is given to, not created by, us. Something earned by sacrifice, the blood of the courageous and creative spirit."; [a.] Taunton, MA

REDDOCH, MILDRED LUCAS
[b.] March 1, 1916, Texarkana, AR; [p.] Mr. and Mrs. R. A. Lucas; [m.] Elbert D. Reddoch (Deceased, since 1952), September 25, 1943; [ch.] Elbert David Reddoch and Ada Lynn Reddoch; [ed.] Master's Degree Drama Teacher of Children and Adults; [occ.] Retired; [memb.] (a) Second Christian Church, Houston TX, (b) Republican Presidential Task Force Washington, D.C.), (c) 1996 Presidential Trust, Crystal Cathedral Ministries Dr. Robert Schuller Ministry P.O. Box 100, Garden Grove, CA 92642-0100, Freedoms Foundation; [oth. writ.] So white the Lilies Short Stories; [pers.] Anyone can prosper by (1) Praising God and Jesus Christ (2) Close friends (3) Considering others (a) Especially children (b) elderly (c) people in need (d) pray for the lost (e) honesty and sincerity.; [a.] Houston, TX

REDMON, JANET
[b.] January 9, 1949, Erie, PA; [p.] Leo Garske and Kathryn Boam; [m.] Daniel Redmon, January 2, 1993; [occ.] Accounting Clerk; [oth. writ.] Short stories for children (unpublished), one poem published in the poem train (Rock Ridge publishing of Jarretsville, MD; [a.] Lompoc, CA

REECE, VIRGINIA MARIA
[pen.] Vickiey; [b.] November 2, 1959, Veracruz, Mexico; [p.] Fausto and Jovita Maldonado Perez; [ch.] Jesse and Joe Maldonado; [ed.] Teacher of Elementary school in Mexico; [pers.] I'm born with bend for make poems because of big influence, my romantic poets. The write for me given new life. I'm for love have naturals involve my original lock

or new spirit the inter persons persons forgotten this possibility what is real love.; [a.] Balch Springs, TX

REED, NAOMI R.
[pen.] Naomi Rondelle; [b.] August 12, 1979, Syracuse, NY; [p.] Ronald F. and Theresa A. Reed; [ed.] High School plus; [occ.] Student - Artist; [hon.] Artist Awards, (Drug-free) Elks Drug, Awareness Program. Many awards in art and writing; [oth. writ.] I have other transcripts of poems written since 1989 to present, still writing.; [pers.] I express feelings of how people feel, including my own. To whom reads my poems will realize what's going on around the world, maybe someday something will be done.; [a.] Syracuse, NY

REETHS, ARTHUR JAMES
[pen.] Arthur James R.; [b.] April 4, 1954, Yorktown VA; [p.] Art and Pat Reeths; [m.] Divorced; [ch.] Arthur Jamie IV, Shannon Marie; [ed.] St. Marys High and Glendale High, Glendale College and The Hair Stylist Barber College; [occ.] Phone Sales, for US West Cellular, and a licensed (Barber Stylist); [memb.] Salvation Army, Asst. to the Homeless during our Holiday Season, Thanksgiving and X-Mas. Member of Valley Cathedral and O.L.P.H. Churches; [hon.] Vietnam Vet. Honorable Discharge from the U.S. Navy - Degree in Tricology - Drawing Artist; [oth. writ.] Have had a couple of articles published in my home town paper of Glendale, AZ where I've lived 37 years. The papers name is "The Glendale Star" stories were about growing up and the changes of Glendale, name of article "Remembering When"; [pers.] Influenced by reading the Bible and my second chance in life, after a death threatening motorcycle accident. Never stop believing in your self, and our Lord Jesus Christ. Anything can and will happen through your faith. Just do it. I'm writing an autobiography.; [a.] Jerome, AR

REGALBUTO, DOLORES M.
[b.] August 4, 1932, Pedricktown, NJ; [p.] Carmen and Josephine Comardo; [m.] Anthony Regalbuto Sr., January 4, 1951; [ch.] Anthony, Nazareno, Rose, Vicky, John, Frank; [occ.] Thorough Trainee at Charles Town Race course; [memb.] H.B.P.A., A.A.R.P; [pers.] This poem was a truth that I had to write about. A release from my emotions; [a.] Charlestown, WV

REICHEL, JOANN HELEN
[pen.] Jody Reichel; [b.] June 2, 1940, Phillipsburg, KS; [m.] Robert T. Reichel, April 13, 1958; [ch.] Five children, nine grandchildren; [ed.] Graduated H.S. in Abilene, KS, 1958; [occ.] Semi-retired, career in social services. Currently a substitute school teacher.; [oth. writ.] Write children's stories that teach or inspire young people.; [pers.] "God needs me, Mommy" was written for my "Angel" niece. In all my writings I try to put feelings into words. My writings have all been inspired by my children and grandchildren.; [a.] Twin Falls, ID

REIDENBACH, RENE S.
[pen.] Rene S. Gillespie, Rene S. Reidenbach; [b.] June 8, 1967, Cleveland, OH; [p.] Eugene T. and Francis L. Gillespie; [m.] Divorced; [ch.] Lora C. Reidenbach, Thonek Reidenbach, Seth T. Reidenbach; [ed.] 1985 Graduate of Wooster High School, Akna University College; [occ.] College Student; [hon.] Cum Laude, Editor's Choice Award - The National Library of Poetry - Lonely, Award of Merit - World of Poetry 1987 - A Prison Cell, Accomplishment of Merit Creative Arts and Science, Honorable Mention - Iliad Press-Spring 1995, The Rope; [oth. writ.] The Rope, Lost, Silenced, Lonely, Prison Cell Conditions, Judged, Christmas, A Strange Man several unpublished; [pers.] I reflect life experiences. Love is not a lesson, it is a gift.; [a.] Wooster, OH

REISS, ANDREW S.
[pen.] A. S. Reiss; [b.] February 26, 1962, Inglewood, CA; [p.] Alvin Reiss and Sally Hinton; [ed.] Leapwood Ave Elementary, William H. Taft High School, California State Univ. Northridge; [occ.] Independent Representative; [memb.] Frontline Foundation; [oth. writ.] Previously published in "Poetry Revival," an anthology sponsored by the National Kidney Foundation in Los Angles. Selected poems are "Illusion?" and "I'm Death Comes Rebirth"; [pers.] My poems wish to elicit an emotional response from the apathy that surrounds our decaying society. Also, the turmoil from within in making decision that affect the direction chosen in my personal life.; [a.] Woodland Hills, CA

REITENAUER, SUZANNE
[pen.] Laura Rosemary; [b.] July 22, 1949, Mary'd, PA; [p.] George and Altreda Bligan; [m.] Ralph C. Reitenauer, February 29, 1988; [ch.] Timothy James; [ed.] Tamaqua Area High School; [occ.] Housewife, activities I play guitar and sing; [oth. writ.] Thank you letters in Pottsville Republican newspaper; [pers.] I like to express the feelings and events people go through in their life times. I have been influenced by Robert Frost and Helen Steiner Rice.; [a.] Pine Grove, PA

RENNIGER, DORIS
[pen.] Doris Poems; [b.] February 26, 1919, Bayonne, NJ; [p.] Gesiena and Albert Richter; [m.] Nelson L. Hadler, June 2, 1940; [ch.] Susan Dreyer, Nelson L. Hadler; [ed.] High School - Bayonne High School; [occ.] Retired; [memb.] First Federated Church, Bayonne New Jersey. Lutheran Church Bayonne, New Jersey, Momen's Club, Bayonne, New Jersey. Lutheran Church, Paramus, New Jersey; [oth. writ.] Poems published in the Horace Mann School Press. "Hello Daddy" published in a paper sent to our service men overseas during World War II. "The Fairlawn Flicker" - The dj read it on the Radio. "My Friend" recognized by a recent late night show host.; [pers.] Since I was a little girl I have enjoyed writing poetry. Mostly about my family. After reading my Doris Poems you would understand how blessed I am to have had them in my life.; [a.] Columbia, NJ

RHILINGER, VONDA ANGEL
[pen.] Vonda Angel; [b.] Boston, MA; [m.] Ringo Angel, Poet and Actor (Deceased), Edward Rhilinger; [ch.] James Angel and Alexander Angel, grandchildren: Alex Angel and Andrew Angel; [ed.] Leland Powers School (Television, Radio, Theatre) Girl's Latin School, Peter Faneuil Elementary School; [oth. writ.] Written poetry for inclusion in personal greeting cards and to commemorate and celebrate special occasions or events. Presently working on anthology of Ringo Angel's poems and routines from our early life in Greenwich Village. Also my own recollections and anecdotes about the excitement and colorful events of the late 50's and 60's in that artistic, Bohemian neighborhood. (I was a Beatnik!); [pers.] I was very much influenced by Shakespeare, especially his sonnets and speeches. Also such giants as Oscar Wilde, Dostoevsky, Camus, T.S. Eliot and many, many others. But perhaps the greatest influence in my life has come from The Bible, both the Old and New Testaments. I try to capture the deepest emotions of mankind in my writing. From love to despair - from beauty to ugliness - from Truth to error. Most of all, as an artiste, I seek to paint colorful pictures using words and language to create a piece of eternity ala Ginsburg, Ferlinghetti and Kerouak.; [a.] Boston, MA

RHODES, ROBERT V.
[b.] October 26, 1939, Pasadena; [p.] Virginia J. Voorhis, Robert E. Rhodes; [m.] Nancy A. Ravesloot, October 23, 1982; [ch.] Robert Jr.; [ed.] Art Center College Menlo and Menlo Business College UCLA; [occ.] President RUR Holdings, Ltd.; [oth. writ.] poetry, prose vignettes, short thoughts and sayings (Unpublished); "Bah Koo" - A children's story published St. Martin's Press N.Y. 1987; [pers.] I try in my writing to: Capture poignant circumstances, awaken memories, stimulate insight, thought and conscience, touch truly deep emotion and paint vivid lasting pictures of some of the things I see.; [a.] Pasadena, CA

RICE, ANN
[pen.] Ann Blakely Rice; [b.] May 28, 1954, Houston, TX; [p.] Mr. and Mrs. Browne B. Rice, Jr.; [ed.] BA Fine Arts - University of St. Thomas - Houston, Tx.- Cum Laude, Lamar High School - '72 - Cum Laude; [occ.] Writer, Artist, Musician, Teacher; [memb.] Women in the Arts and Two Health Clubs; [hon.] Cum Laude - High School and College. Yoga - 20 yrs. practice - now teaching 2 art shows, 5 songs published in L.A. Record Co. - Regional Performances of Original Music and Lyrics - 5 songs on Regional Radio; [oth. writ.] "Angel Wisp" 1993 Post Oak Publishing (Collection of Poems). "Forty - Transformation" - Collection of poems to be published at later date. Songwriting-original music lyrics - 10 songs.; [pers.] I believe that the Divine "spark" within each and every human being, is waiting to be ignited by Unconditional Love, Acceptance, Light, and Healing. I entertain great hope for the consciousness of all humanity to be expanded, raised, and touched by the Sunlight of a Benevolent Creator.; [a.] Center Point, TX

RICE, KEITH PATTESON
[b.] February 23, 1924, Washington, DC; [p.] Clyde Christian Rice and Esther Mae Pearson Rice; [m.] Virginia Mae Prange Rice, July 21, 1951; [ch.] Sue Ann and Thomas Keith Rice; [ed.] Attended Woodrow Wilson High School - graduated from Western Night School both of graduated 1949 The Pricipica Washington, DC B.A. Eron College Elsah, IL; [occ.] Retired; [memb.] Masonry, G.S. Navy, retired Christian Science Church; [hon.] Plaque from United Airlines Fellow Pilots on Retirement; [oth. writ.] Articles for United Airlines "The Mainliner" magazine (An Ln House Publication) "The Professional Pilot" and "Watch Dog" (about dispatchers) August 1967; [pers.] My aim is love for God and man.; [a.] Redmond, WA

RICE, MARTHA ALICE
[pen.] Martha Alice Fields; [b.] October 16, 1963, Kanawha County, WV; [p.] Floyd and Phyllis Rice; [m.] Up coming spring of '96; [ed.] Duval High School Graduate class of 1981; [occ.] An Accomplisher, otherwise kept woman; [pers.] I've always had a passion for writing. Most of my pieces have been inspired by my fiance. May the powers beyond this life protect cherish and love him as I do.; [a.] South Charleston, WV

RICHARDSON, BECKY JOHNSON
[b.] August 11, 1940, Newnan, GA; [p.] Elder Charles I. Johnson (Deceased) and Varon Broadwell Johnson; [m.] Divorced; [ch.] Ivy Louise Head, Daughter, born June 14, 1960; [ed.] Sardis High School, Boaz, Alabama, AA Degree from Snead State Junior College, Boaz, Alabama; [occ.] I retired from IBM (for medical reasons) after 23 years in the publication profession. I just started a small home-based greeting card business, which provides creative opportunities, both artistic and literary, to keep me challenged. I also use my computer to embellished artwork and to visit on the "net".; [memb.] Toastmasters, International (to learn publish speaking). Multiple Sclerosis organizations, because I have MS. The Association for Retarded Citizens because my

daughter is learning disabled. Sigma Tau Delta sorority (while in college). Drama Club (college); [hon.] National Honor Society (High School), Won High School National Spelling Bee (age 13) and placed second in county spelling contest, Dean's List several times (college), Several service awards from IBM, Won several speaking awards in Toastmasters.; [oth. writ.] "Mistakes Are Just Wisdom Happening!", to be published in *The Light Ahead* by The Association for Retarded Citizens, Georgia Division. Spring 1996. Poem "Rigidity" to be published in *The Rainbow's End* by The National Library of Poetry, Summer 1996. I use many of my original verses, philosophical thoughts, and hand-painted original art designs in my greeting card business.; [pers.] When I need closure to a personal tragedy or trauma, I write a poem that expresses the many emotions I experienced getting through the situation. My favorite one liner is: "Mistakes are just wisdom happening!" My daughter inspired it. She needed a positive viewpoint because she was trying but failing at a particular task.; [a.] Marietta, GA

RICHARDSON, JEANETTA
[pen.] Kat Landers; [b.] March 7, 1979, Minnesota; [p.] Georgetta and James Richardson; [ed.] Go to Park Center High School in the 11th grade; [memb.] ICA (International Clarinet Association), Sierra Club Wildlife), Member of GTCYS (Greater Twin Cities Youth Symphony); [hon.] B Honor Roll, Honor Band, Pirates of the First Class Award; [oth. writ.] I have written other poems that are currently being judged at poetry contests.; [pers.] Poems have brought me happiness and joy. I hope by someone who's sad or upset reads my poem and it brings a smile to their face like poems have done to me.; [a.] Brooklyn Park, MN

RICHARDSON, ROBBI
[pen.] Robbi Richardson; [b.] April 19, 1957, Lynchburg, VA; [p.] Bill and Donna Schreiber; [m.] Rod Richardson, July 4, 1985; [ch.] Alexandra Jaye, Nicole Lynn; [ed.] E. C. Glass High School; [occ.] Home School Teacher: Alenik Academy, Wilmington, NC; [memb.] North Carolinians for Home Education, "Gotta Dance" Booster Club.; [oth. writ.] Poems for family and friends.; [pers.] "Thanks be to God who gives us the victory through Jesus Christ, our Lord." Corinthians 15:57; [a.] Wilmington, NC

RICKERT, ELIZABETH A.
[b.] December 19, 1930, Bloomfield, NJ; [p.] Douglas and Marion Austin; [m.] Hugh S. Rickert, June 19, 1949, (Divorced April 1990); [ch.] Stephen Douglas, Scott Austin; [ed.] Donna Louise and Parent of Kerry Christopher and Darian Douglas. After raising my 3 children I had the privilege of "inheriting" my grandchildren in 1976 when their young mother died. Darian was killed in auto accident; [pers.] Regardless of tragic losses, Jehovah my God, has brought me joy, strength, friendships, and love.; [a.] Cedar Grove, NJ

RIDDLE, WESLEY ALLEN
[pen.] Keoni Aloha; [b.] April 19, 1961, Houston, TX; [p.] Walter A. Riddle, Gloria Riddle-Roe; [m.] Maria Aida Riddle, December 21, 1985; [ed.] Northbrook HS, BS United States Military Academy, M. Phil. Oxford University; [occ.] Assistant Professor, Department of History, USMA, West Point; [memb.] Phi Kappa Phi, Phi Alpha Theta, National Association of Scholars, National Alumni Forum, Intercollegiate Studies Institute, Library of Congress Associates, Heritage Foundation, American Legion, Veterans of Foreign Wars; [hon.] Richard A. Whitfield, Memorial Award for Forensic Excellence, Major John Alexander Hottell III, Memorial Award for Excellence of Modern History, General Omar N. Bradley Award for Excellence in Research in History, Sara Norton Prize for Excellence in American History Research, Bronze Star Medal for Gulf War Service; [oth. writ.] Misc., poems and book reviews, numerous essays on American history and public policy published in books and professional journals including Leviathan at War, Cambridge Historical Journal, and Mississippi Quarterly: The Journal of Southern Culture; [a.] West Point, NY

RIEDY, LINDA ROTH
[pen.] Linda Riedy; [b.] January 5, 1945, Oakland, CA; [p.] Gertrude and Elbert Riedy; [ch.] Julie McCafferty, Joe Koeplin Jr., Michelle Koeplin - Valverde; [ed.] Notre Dame High School, graduated 1962; [occ.] On leave of absence. Worked as Analyst for IBM for 26 yrs.; [oth. writ.] Poems dating back to 1960; [pers.] The story of my life is reflected in my poems. I started writing as a young teenager.; [a.] Fremont, CA

RIEDY, LYNNE ADELE
[pen.] Lar; [b.] March 24, 1957, Lansing, MI; [p.] Marianne and Victor A. Zucco; [m.] Mark R. Riedy, September 6, 1980; [ch.] Brad Raymond Riedy and Brian Victor Riedy; [ed.] Bachelor of Science in Nursing - College of Nursing, at Michigan State University in 1979; [occ.] "At - home - mom", Volunteer, "Free-lance-poet"; [memb.] Current Registered Nurse in Michigan. Badge certified Red Cross Nurse. Member of the Noetic Sciences, Member of the ISP (International Society of Poets); [hon.] Second year elected Chairperson for Antrim County's Child Abuse and Neglect Council - focusing on prevention and education. Representative on Antrim County's Coordinating Council, and Project: Share; [oth. writ.] Anthology - "Beyond the Stars". Anthology - "The best poems of 1996". Anthology - "A Tapestry of Thoughts"; [pers.] My poetry spans over twenty-five years, revealing a poet's spiritual journey. At times I feel the grace and oneness of divine flow through my pen, at times by "Nursing"; [a.] Bellaire, MI

RIHN, TONI A.
[b.] January 29, 1970, Racine, WI; [p.] Karen Kristopeit, Larry Rihn; [ed.] Union Grove High - Gateway Tech., Art Institute of Ft. Laud. - Milw. Conservatory of Music - Art Institute of Houston - Milw. Area Tech - John Robert Powers Madding; [occ.] Student - Music Degree, Master Controller at a TV Station-intern; [memb.] PETA (People Against Ethnical Treatment Against Animals); [hon.] First Place in Horse Showing; [oth. writ.] Poem published in local newspaper. Lyricist for local musicians.; [pers.] In my writings I excel to base my feelings on the problems in our world, racism, gov't faults, abuse, etc., to the most wonderful things in our world, love, peace, and unity.; [a.] Racine, WI

RILEY, BEVERLY F.
[b.] April 27, 1944, Palmer, TN; [p.] Buford L. Sissom, Gladys Overturf Sissom; [m.] Robert C. Riley, May 4, 1963; [ch.] Tami Jo (Riley) Lapp; [ed.] High School, Business Course; [occ.] Property Manager; [oth. writ.] Lots of poems/verses but nothing published; [pers.] My writing is a release for my inner feelings. Maybe someone will find comfort and love through my thoughts of love.; [a.] Elkhart, IN

RILEY, PATRICIA
[b.] February 16, 1939, Pittsburgh, PA; [p.] Eva (Roe) Riley and James E. Riley; [ch.] Sean, Brian, Brennan, Maureen, Kevin, Shannon (McCullough); [ed.] Saint Mary's High School, Colo. Springs, Colorado College and Colorado Univ., Colorado Springs (Communications); [occ.] Owner, O'Donnell and Riley, Promotions and Advertising, and Stand-Up Comic; [memb.] American Women in Radio and Television; [hon.] Regional and National Advertising Awards, (Broadcast), National Public Service Awards (Broadcast), Regional Service Recognition PTA, Red Cross, Boy Scouts and Girl Scouts.; [oth. writ.] "The Counter Clockwise Screw" (Novel, Science Fiction) "American Schoolkids and "The Streets of Gold", (Textbook), "Riley's World" (News/Entertainment Column); [pers.] I work to find new ways to communicate honestly ... to share my ideas with others, because I've always believed most struggles among people are the result of a failure to communicate properly.; [a.] Colorado Springs, CO

RINGGOLD, JULIA
[b.] October 11, 1982, Fulda, Germany; [p.] Gina and Tim Ringgold; [ed.] Attending Downingtown (PA) Junior High School; [occ.] Junior high school student; [oth. writ.] Author of several unpublished stories and numerous unpublished poems.; [pers.] I write what I feel nothing more; [a.] Downingtown, PA

RISINGER, KENNETH
[pen.] Ken Risinger; [b.] August 13, 1919, Rombauer, MO; [p.] Hartford, Bettie Risinger; [m.] Eleanore Hansen Messick, April 28, 1969; [ch.] James and Kathy Messick, step-children: Elizabeth E., Michael D., Michelle Risinger by deceased first wife, Ethel B. Cabral; [ed.] Univ. of Hawaii (Lit) Univ. Cal. (Acctg) and various military schools in Mgt. Light Aircraft Pilot, Civil Air Patrol; [occ.] Self-employed businessman, Retired USAF and businessman; [memb.] Vet. of Foreign Wars, Pearl Harbors Survivors Assoc. Disabled Amer. Vets.; [hon.] WWII Victory Medal, Pacific Theater of Operations Medal, Good Conduct Medal w/ 3 clusters, Pearl Harbor Survivors Medal, Amer. Theater of Operations Medal, Pacific Campaign Medal w/ 2 battle Stars, several letters of commendation for meritorious service; [oth. writ.] Many articles published in newspapers. Two magazine articles in magazines, one story. Completed two novels and one nearing completion. Have written several poems, some of which has been published.; [pers.] As a boy, to see daylight framed in the window always held a feeling of magic of what I would discover that day. At 76 yrs I still have that feeling.; [a.] Green Valley, AZ

RIVENBARK, MRS. CYNTHIA ATKINSON
[b.] July 11, 1974, Rose Hill, NC; [p.] Claude and Erma Atkinson; [m.] Mr. Jason Alexander Rivenbark, November 20, 1994; [ed.] Pender High School Burgaw, NC; [occ.] Factory worker at Chloride Systems, Burgaw, NC; [memb.] Sunday School teacher and Choir member at Shiloh Baptist Church in Watha, NC; [pers.] I thank God for my ability to write my poetry. I strive to make people look into their own hearts and souls to find some peace. Helen S. Rice has greatly influenced my writings of poetry.; [a.] Watha, NC

ROBERTS, LORRAINE
[b.] December 1, 1963, Springfield, MA; [p.] Roger Wapner, Doris Wapner; [m.] Glenn Roberts, April 25, 1982; [ed.] Classical High, St. John's School of Business.; [occ.] Database Technician; [memb.] Worldwide Church of God; [pers.] I want to be remembered with a smile. I hope to bring a little sunshine to my readers' hearts. To express love and peace.; [a.] Springfield, MA

ROBERTS, MYRIAH C.
[b.] September 20, 1975, Long Beach, CA; [p.] Cynthia Avila; [ed.] Currently studying at Franciscan University for Bachelors degree in Psychology; [occ.] Hope to be a Christian Psychologist for Adolescents; [memb.] Psi Beta; [pers.] Through my personal hardships with depression and my delights of knowing my Savior, I long to bring the lost sheep

ut of the darkness to the light of the world. This poem was inspired by a picture of a desperate, crouching Kurt Cobain, a prime example of those I desire to help.; [a.] Irvine, CA

ROBERTSON, WARREN A.
[b.] September 4, 1958, Gettysburg, PA; [p.] David, Carol, Robertson; [m.] Martha S. Robertson, June 21, 1986; [ch.] Grant W., Justine V.; [ed.] Littlestown High School, Delaware Valley College; [occ.] Cabinet maker, Painter, Restorations of Old Homes in Bucks County; [memb.] American Bass Association, Bass Anglers Sportman Society; [pers.] My first writing influenced by a picture of (Baby Baylee Almon) bleeding in the arms of a firefighter after the Oklahoma City bombing.; [a.] Doylestown, PA

ROBINSON, KATHY
[m.] Paul; [ch.] One son; [occ.] Co-owner of small business with Paul; [hon.] This is the first ever submitted experience; [oth. writ.] I've always written, I've always read. I admire Rod McRuen.; [pers.] I'm not a writer or poet. I just live. And sometimes those memories spill on paper. Living it is easy. The hard part comes in having those memories exposed.; [a.] Swanton, OH

ROCHA, LISA MARIE
[pen.] Lisa; [b.] June 13, 1978, Lowell; [p.] Carol Rocha, Robert Rocha; [m.] Wayne Beaudette (boyfriend) soon to be; [ch.] Samantha and Sarina Beaudette; [ed.] Culinary Arts student at greater Lowell Voke; [occ.] Mother; [oth. writ.] Several other poems written, but not published yet.; [a.] Lowell, MA

ROCK, ANTHONY
[pen.] Anton Tomas Rok; [b.] February 6, 1975, San Diego, CA; [p.] Orrin and Karn Anderson; [m.] My Girlfriend, Summer; [ed.] Boyceville Grammar and High School; [occ.] None, other than writing; [oth. writ.] The Book of the Baroque Cavalier. The Poem of Summer and the Purple Waterfall. The Book of Vowels. (All unpublished); [pers.] The works of J.R.R. Tokien are an immense value to understanding the majesty of poetry.; [a.] Wheeler, WI

ROCKS, DEBORAH
[b.] May 30, 1958, Milford, MA; [p.] Anthony Carl Rocks; [ed.] Mount Ida Jr. College Newton Mass, Oxford High School, Oxford Mass; [occ.] Assistant Manager Royal Guardian Gas; [hon.] 1st Publication in the National Library's "A Sea Of Treasures"; [pers.] Due to a troubled childhood I began writing to real sense stress and tension; [a.] Putnam, CT

ROCKWOOD, MARTHA MARGARET
[b.] May 6, 1947, Bremmerton, WA; [p.] George Emmett Rockwood and Martha Margaret Farrell,; [ch.] Troy Allen Cates, Kathryn Elizabeth Cates, Louanne Islene Cates, Kwametasha Craig-Rockwood.; [ed.] White Cliff Elementary and Ketchikan High School in Ketchikan, Alaska, The Southwest School of Medical Assistance for Laboratory Technicians in San Antonio, Texas, The Pioneer Ministry School for Jehovah's Witnesses.; [occ.] Minister, Care Taker for In Home Support Services in San Diego, California; [memb.] Jehovah's Witnesses, Coordinator for the Linda Vista Village Citizens Patrol in San Diego.; [pers.] I have learned that each day of life is an educational day in the field of wisdom. The result is I can live each day to the fullest of my life experience. As each day closes, I am happy and satisfied that I have done the best I was able in accomplishing a growth in wisdom.; [a.] San Diego, CA

RODGERS, JILL MAYRE
[b.] July 2, 1975, Peace AFB, NH; [p.] Paul Rodgers, Audrey Rodgers; [ed.] Stoughton High, 1993, third year student at Univ. of Wisconsin - Whitewater, English major, Journalism minor; [occ.] Student, Univ. of Wisconsin - Whitewater; [memb.] Editing intern for Auto/Biography Journal, UW-Whitewater Environmental Federation, Scripts (on campus writing group); [hon.] Dean's List; [oth. writ.] Poems published in on-campus publications, poems written during one semester in the Dominican Republic; [pers.] I express, in my writing, the oneness of all nature and mankind and the profound influence of one upon the other. I also attempt to illustrate the true glory and magnificence of the natural world.; [a.] Stoughton, WI

RODRIGUES JR., JOSEPH O.
[b.] July 27, 1943, Honolulu, HI; [p.] Joseph Rodrigues Sr., Sarah Rodrigues; [m.] Carol Berini Rodrigues, September 15, 1968; [ed.] Balboa High School, San Francisco, CA; College of Marin, Kentfield, CA; [occ.] U.S. Army Retired, Investor; [memb.] Paralyzed Veterans of America, Disabled American Veterans: Life Member; [pers.] I was inspired into writing this poem to honor Veterans Day, to reflect the goodness of mankind and the horros of war. [a.] San Rafael, CA

RODRIGUEZ, EDUARDO
[pen.] Eduardo Rodriguez; [b.] October 14, 1962, Mexico City; [p.] Ernesto Conde, Carmen Hernandez; [ed.] Architectural, Designer; [occ.] Freelance, Architectural Designer; [memb.] YMCA Sunnyvale, California, AIA San Francisco, Cal.; [hon.] Gold Ring - Architectural Design Mexico City; [oth. writ.] Several poems published in Stanford University Students' magazines, articles in local newspaper in Mexico City.; [pers.] Always strive for goodness either upward or downward like a fountain with thoughts.; [a.] Menlo Park, CA

RODRIGUEZ, RUBEN R.
[b.] February 6, 1976, San Antonio; [pers.] The world's fate is in our hands. "If we can learn that we're one we can overcome before this takes us all we'd better catch ourselves before we fall."; [a.] Houston, TX

RODRIGUEZ, TABATHA L.
[b.] January 31, 1970, Denton, TX; [p.] Teresa L. White, Lee Conklin; [m.] Noe N. Rodriguez, March 21, 1992; [ch.] Michael Scott, Justin Matthew; [ed.] Denton High School, University of North Texas; [occ.] Accounting Assistant; [oth. writ.] Many personal poems and short stories. This is the first one I've submitted for publication.; [pers.] I let my life and events I am involved in influence my writing. I draw from these experiences.; [a.] Denton, TX

ROFFLER, ILSE
[b.] February 28, 1940, Switzerland; [p.] Hans and Ida Schoedler; [m.] Hans Roffler, June 24, 1961; [ch.] Kathrin, Robert, Jean; [ed.] College and Trade School in Switzerland; [memb.] International Society of Poets, San Pedro Writer's Guild; [pers.] In my writings, I like to capture the values and meanings of life.; [a.] San Pedro, CA

ROGERS, MARTHA
[b.] August 12, 1942, Charleston, SC; [p.] Gertrude Maddox and Brice Maddox; [m.] Berton Rogers, Deceased, November 11, 1989; [ch.] Kinney Clerk, Jones Clark; [ed.] Rock Hill High School 1960, Medical University of SC, College of Nursing 1963, Indent Technical College, Assoc. Degree in Commercial Graphics 1993; [occ.] Registered Nurse at Charleston Memorial Hospital, Pediatric Emergency, Freelance Graphic Artist; [pers.] I try to use the gifts God has given me - poetry and art - to show his love for all people.; [a.] Charleston, SC

ROGERS, WAYNE J.
[pen.] Jerome McCoy; [b.] August 17, 1941, Rochester, NY; [m.] Nanci J. Rogers, March 27, 1971; [ch.] Two; [ed.] BA Biology, BS Microbiology Basic Medical Laboratories Procedures Course (US Army) [occ.] Principal Investigator Material Safety/ Stericity Assurance and Environmental Affairs; [memb.] American society of microbiology New York Academy of Science American Asso., of Medical Instrumental, Calif. Monuf. Assoc's Environmental a variety steering commille; [hon.] Eagle Scout Mith Palms Joycees, Idea Man, Winner's Circle (1993) Award Editorial Advisory Board for Medical Device Diagnostic Magazines Honorable Discharge from U.S. Army Peace Corps. Training; [oth. writ.] "How Environmental Movement is Greening the Medical Device Industry", "Industrial Isteralization: A Review of Current Principals and Practices "New ISO/FDA Biocompatibility Criteria"; [pers.] Everything must be what it's own equalities determine. Who is the who, who asks the question. When will all peoples good for each person's rule be like a shaft of light in our consciousness when we all have suffered.; [a.] Carlsbad, CA

ROHE, TARA POVERTY
[b.] May 8, 1980, Marlton, NJ; [p.] David Rohe, Patricia Rohe; [oth. writ.] I've written many poems but have never gotten any of them published; [pers.] In my opinion writing is the best way to express yourself.; [a.] Franklinville, NJ

ROLNY, PETER
[b.] April 3, 1966, Kosice, Czech; [p.] Andrej M. Rolny, Lenka L. Rolny; [ed.] Washington High, UC Santa Cruz, Western Seminary; [occ.] Computer Specialist, Student (part-time); [hon.] Academic Honors; [oth. writ.] Authored chapters for the book, clean coding in Turbo Pascal.; [pers.] My writing is dedicated to the personal God of history.; [a.] Santa Cruz, CA

RONDEAU, ROBERTA
[pen.] Bobbie, P.I.T.A.; [b.] July 26, 1963, Keene, NH; [p.] Terrance and Martha Quigley; [m.] 15 history going on Divorce, doesn't matter anymore!; [ch.] Chrystal and Eric; [ed.] High School (Dropout) but I went back and finally got my GED (6 years ago!); [occ.] Unfortunately homemaker (I'm permanently disabled); [memb.] R.S.D.A. (Reflex Sympathetic Dystrophy Association (the reason I'm disabled now (but always hoping for a miracle!); [hon.] This is an honor and a great reward for me to have this very special poem published!; [oth. writ.] Life is different everyday to be published in (a muse to follow) (this is great! I'm new to writing poems and they're both being published!; [pers.] I wrote this for my best friend - boyfriend and soulmate. Because if it wasn't for him I wouldn't be who I am today!; [a.] Troy, NH

ROSE, NAOMI
[pers.] Ms. Naomi Rose is now and Alexandria resident, and has completed two business colleges: Atlantic Business College and Programming System Institute. She has a home nursing certificate, NVCC Special Education degree, and attended Strayer College in Computer Information Systems. Ms. Rose has taught kindergarten and worked in the government. She has won second place in speaking contest in Jr. High School, and was awarded Salutatorian, the second highest rank in the school. Ms. Rose currently works at Patrick Henry Elementary School in Alexandria, VA. She works in the LAB as a computer technician, and teaches second through fifth graders. She gives students "hands-on" experience in the LAB. Ms. Rose has invented three products. One was awarded a patent. "Less Clean Up" is a unique, exciting new idea in adult hygiene. Another product is patent pending. Ms. Rose is a

poet. Her poem was published in *Walk through Paradise* by the National Library of poetry, and was chosen to be put on cassette. She has been asked to be interviewed on "Poetry Today" on Public Radio in New York City (WNYE 91.5 FM) - a listening audience of over 11 million people. Ms. Rose is a member of the International Society of Poetry (1995-1996) and is recognized for support of the Society's priniciples of Peace, Education, Accomplishment, Charity, and Equality. Ms. Naomi Rose was also presented and award from Patrick Henry Elementary School in Recognition of Distinguished Achievement in Technology - March 1, 1996. Her hobbies include ice skating, karate, singing, arts and crafts, designing and sewing new fashions, and decorating cakes. She enjoys helping others and encourages students always to do their best.

ROSS, ROBERT W.
[pen.] Dr. Bob; [b.] September 27, 1926, Akron, OH; [p.] Alba/Anna Ross; [m.] Nancy J. Ross, June 23, 1989; [ch.] Renee' (deceased), Randy; [ed.] B.A. Muskingum Col- 1950, 1953 M. Div. Pittxenia Seminary, D. Rel. 1974 - Geneva Thel. Col.; [occ.] Retired Presbyterian and UCC Minister; [memb.] Southeastern Ill. Presbytery-Eastern Ill. UCC Conference; [oth. writ.] 'A Surgical/Spiritual Journey in Faith Major' local newspaper articles when in active ministry.; [pers.] God, family and friends are most important in our lives and love is the basis for reach relationship with all three.

ROTH, DOROTHY HUBBARD
[b.] August 2, 1929, Phebe, MS; [p.] Thomas G. Hubbard and Ruth Doggett Hubbard; [m.] Robert F. Roth, MD, April 2, 1975; [ch.] Thomas, Laura, Joy Roth; [ed.] Millsaps College - B.A. Northwestern University (M.A. in Biblical Studies) Yonsei University - Seoul, Korea (Korean Language); [occ.] Retired teacher of Christian Education with the United Methodist Mission in Korea; [memb.] United Methodist Women, "Roanoke Sister-Cities International" (Links to Korea, Kenya, Russia, Brazil, Poland and China); [hon.] High School Valedictorian, National Methodist Scholarship, graduated with honors from Millsaps College and Northwestern University; [oth. writ.] Numerous poems and true stories or essays, reflecting missionary experiences in Korea.; [pers.] I pray my writings may become "Seeds of Peace", giving growth to God's plan for all His human children to live together in mutual caring and friendship.; [a.] Roanoke, VA

ROTHWEILER, NICHOLAS S.
[b.] March 3, 1985, Great Falls, MT; [p.] Merle and Annette Rothweiler; [ed.] Fifth Grader at Elmira Elementary School, Elmira, Oregon; [occ.] Student; [memb.] Student Council Member, Junior Member Wildlife Home Care Network; [hon.] Published In The Wildlife Home Care Network News; [pers.] My poem was inspired by all the injured and orphaned opossums that my family and I care for and love. I hope my poem will help people better understand the opossum.; [a.] Veneta, OR

ROUBAL, SUSAN
[b.] March 17, 1954, Los Angeles, CA; [p.] Joseph H. and Dorothy Roubal; [ed.] Glendale Community College; [occ.] Customer Service Rep; [oth. writ.] Poems for family and friends; [pers.] My philosophy is to write from the heart.; [a.] Glendale, CA

ROUSE, SHELLY L.
[b.] May 30, 1963, San Francisco, CA; [p.] M. A. Whitacre, M. Carroll; [occ.] Software Sales; [pers.] The animal kingdom looks up to us, please don't let them down!

ROUSSEL, GARY K.
[b.] August 12, 1955, VanKleek Hill; [p.] Shirley and Roland Roussel; [ed.] Perth and District Collegiate Institute plus the School of life; [occ.] Chef and poet and lover of human kind; [memb.] All America Karate Federation, Judo and Karate Academy, Aicondo Martial Arts Federation, Star Trek Fan Club of Canada International Society of Poets, Distinguished Member; [hon.] 3rd Degree Blackbelt Karate, First Canadian Poet published in Rock Mag called *Cream*. Name of Poem - Existence.; [oth. writ.] Book of Poetry called *Sweet and Simple Word Rhythms and Other Poems*. Plus song lyrics to country music, also poems of the heart mind and soul; [pers.] Wish to see the end of racism and bring a better understanding of worth to humankind through peace. My personal favorite logo is "Through A Whisper"; [a.] VanKleek Hill Ontario, Canada

ROWE, CHRISTINA F. Y.
[pen.] Tina Rowe; [b.] April 17, 1985, Detroit, MI; [p.] Wynona Rowe and Lonnie Hayden; [pers.] I am a ten year old Jamerican twin. My mother is an american. My father is a Jamacian. I began to write poems in the second grade. I believe God will bless me to grow up to be a block famous writer.; [a.] Lexington, KY

ROWE, ELVA P.
[b.] January 19, 1922, Indiana; [p.] Frank and Carrie Billhymer (Deceased); [m.] Virgil M. Rowe (Deceased), August 12, 1967; [ch.] Shirley, Judy, Ronnie, Marsha and Nancy; [ed.] 8 yrs. Elem. School 4 yrs. Emmerich Manual High School, Arsenal Tech Night School Business Machines; [occ.] Homemaker; [oth. writ.] Have written 19 poems concerning my life, individual poems for each of my children, family gatherings, pets, and nature.; [pers.] I wish to thank you for acknowledging my poems and to be a part of the next publication, a tapestry of thoughts; [a.] Martinsville, IN

RUBY, DONNA
[b.] August 19, 1958, Chicago, IL; [p.] Richard Ruby, Sue Southard; [m.] Deceased; [ed.] B.A. degree from University of Colorado, masters in progress; [occ.] Staff Development Specialist at a Alcohol/Drug Rehab Center; [memb.] IAODAPCA (Illinois Dept. of Alcohol/Other Drugs Assoc.) Nature Conservancy; [oth. writ.] Many poems - none published - I'm working on an autobiography; [pers.] Please Dedicated to Jon Williams. My writing has been a healing tool for expressing intense feelings, "Loss and Love". My inspiration is nature, my love who passed away 12/17/94, Kahil Gibran, Richard Bach, Hugh Prather and others.; [a.] Chicago, IL

RUCKMAN, PATRICIA A.
[b.] July 30, 1944, Barberton, OH; [p.] Andrew and Pascalene Ulichney; [m.] Isaac C. Ruckman Jr., June 12, 1965; [ch.] Bradley Scott; [ed.] Barberton High School Grad.; [occ.] Quality Assurance Technician, Babcock and Wilcox Co., Barberton, OH; [oth. writ.] Unpublished poems written for family members on their special occasion - personalized especially for them. (Dad's 76th B-day, Laura's Wedding, Angel Poem, 25th Wedd. Ann., Baby shower poems); [pers.] I had never written a poem before 1995 - where the idea came from leaves me and my family wondering. I enjoy writing personalized poems. "Nature's Way" was inspired by the bald cardinal that visits our bird feeder.

RUIZ, VERONICA P.
[pen.] Veroca; [b.] November 21, 1966, Lima, Peru; [p.] Victor Chalco E. and Lidia De Chalco; [ed.] Institute Pedago'gico Nacional-Monterrico, Monterrico Lima Peru: English Teacher San Jorge-Miraflores School (primary-secondary); [occ.] E.S.L. (English as a second language) Teacher at New York Bilingual Inst. (EHCCI-TAP#8), New York Language Center; [oth. writ.] Several unpublished poems and short stories; [pers.] I think that: 'It is better to look at the future ahead thinking of things that will one day be...of a much better taste'. Veroca; [a.] Jackson Heights, NY

RULKA, JOHN S.
[pen.] Long John; [b.] May 7, 1952, San Mateo, CA; [p.] Stan Rulka, Helen Carter-Deal; [m.] September 5, 1988; [ch.] Heather Helen, Miriah Charmaine Rebecca Marie; [ed.] Santa Rosa J. C. - Horticulture Landscape Design, Prunning, Grafting Cuttings Nursery Prac. - Pland, ID, English, Sociology, 1972-1974; [occ.] Gardener; [oth. writ.] Have them. [pers.] Life is only need be waited for, as a lady in waiting, no need to look but in the doing in proper she will appear. Doing the good and right, let's itself be known....life.; [a.] Santa Rosa, CA

RUSSELL, BOJANA
[b.] February 20, 1921, Hoboken, NJ; [p.] Dusan and Rose Trbovich; [m.] Frank D. Russell, March 29, 1946; [ch.] Karen Russell (Cox); [ed.] Degree in Arts and Crafts, National Academy of Art, Belgrade, Yugoslavia, Diploma, Secretarial School, New York City, studied Classical Piano for is years in NYC and Europe, studied Painting for 5 years under Moi Solotar Off.; [occ.] Worked for Columbia and Depauw Universities; [oth. writ.] Unedited and unpublished poetry, which she wrote most of her life, entry was written when she was 18. Studied poets from John Donne to contempory.; [pers.] In Christ's teachings lies the whole solution to man's inhumanity to man and animal.; [a.] Arvada, CO

RUSSELL, LALLY
[b.] February 14, 1961, Sri Lanka; [p.] Vel Mahadevan, Ranee Mahadevan; [ch.] Shermila, Shanthi; [ed.] 1) Medical School (3 years), School of Medical Sciences, Kumasi, Ghana, 2) B.S. Physiology, U.C. Davis, Davis, California, 3) M.S. Physiology, Penn State University, State College, Pennsylvania; [occ.] The Coordinator of Donated Body Program, U.C. Davis, Davis, California; [memb.] Hundreds of poems composed for birthdays and anniversaries for family and friends from the age of twelve to date.; [hon.] Our life on earth is so transient... that we should endeavor to make each individual day beautiful.; [oth. writ.] Davis, CA

RUSSELL, ROY
[b.] North Ogden, UT; [m.] Patricia (William) of Logan, Utah September 14, 1956; [ch.] Two sons: Kerwin and Darrin; [ed.] Assoc. of Sci. Weber State, Ogden, Utah, Bachelor of Arts and Master of Arts from Calif. State College Los Angeles, Life Secondary Credential; [occ.] Writing and "extra" work in television and movies; [memb.] President of Glendora Color Slide Group, 3rd Term-CTA and NEA; [hon.] Honors Graduate CSCLA, Meritorious Unit Citation Korea, Cert. of Honor Blue Ribbon Committee City of West Covina, Teacher of year 10 years Arroyo H.S.; [oth. writ.] Photo-travel articles in Desert, Wildlife News, Gems and Minerals, Friends Mags. I like the works of Ralph Waldo Emerson.; [pers.] I am a romantic and sentimentalist about life and liberty and care deeply about the state of "things" in America. I am influenced by Lloyd C. Douglas, Pearl Buck, Alistair MacLean, Edwin Arlington Robinson. My favorite poems are "Richard Cory" and "Mr. Flood's Party." Also "Thanatopsis" by Bryant and "Friendship" by Craik. I love the mountains and deserts and my writing and photo work is about them. I try to participate in the democratic process.; [a.] Covina, CA

RUTIGLIANO, EDMOND P.
[pen.] Edmond P. Rutigliano; [b.] May 7, 1955; [p.] Edmond J. Rutigliano (Deceased) and May Rutigliano; [m.] Deborah A. Rutigliano, September 29, 1979;

h.] Edmond J., (12) Dana C. (6) and Brandan M. (8 mths.); [ed.] Graduated Bishop Neumann High School in 1973. Completed one year at Community College of Phila.; [occ.] Produce Manager; [memb.] a member in good standing with The International Society of Poets 1994-1995; [hon.] From the National Library of Poetry I received the Editor's Choice Award for outstanding Achievement in Poetry. The poem for which I received this award titled "Time Heals All Wounds" was a semi-finalist in the 1995 North American Open Poetry Contest and published in the anthology *Sparkles In The Sand*. At present I have three other poems certified as semi finalist to be published in the near future.; [oth. writ.] "Why? Why? Why?" to be published in Summer of 96 by the National Library Of Poetry along with "After The Verdict". Also "Abuse" to be published Spring of 96 by The Modern Poetry Society.; [pers.] The death of my brother Frank, a car accident, depression, The National Library of Poetry Contest sparked the flow of words on paper from me. I have written over 75 poems in a six month period with different subject matters, different styles, different messages and feelings. I have never studied poetry. I write from my heart, soul, experiences as most do. I'm hoping to get published a book of my best poems. Describe the beauty, the ugly, the anger, the fear as you feel only you can. It hurts to read all the writer's pain although we look to relate. When I read poetry that's clearly a suicide note I wish somehow to help. I hope their writing helps overt their thoughts of suicide and their expression in words helps them realize how inappropriate that action is to any problem or problems. Get professional help to deal with such thoughts. Stay strong and keep writing.; [a.] Clementon, NJ

RUTLEDGE, TROYCE LOUISE
[pen.] Troyce Louise Turner; [b.] September 18, 1956, Monroe, WA; [p.] Henry E. Trenk, Louise A. Trenk; [m.] Richard C. Rutledge, November 24, 1995; [ch.] Amanda R. Morrill, Kimberly Louise Morrill; [ed.] Skykomish High, Friday Harbor High, Everett Community College (Business Administration); [occ.] Mother, Grandmother, Housewife; [oth. writ.] I have written since I can remember but mostly for self-exploration and self-examination.; [pers.] I try to reflect on the essence of the heart and soul. To remind people in one push and shove world that life was not meant to be difficult. That it is more essential now than ever, that we take time out to enjoy the simpler things in life.; [a.] Wilbur, WA

RYAN, SARAH
[pen.] Liv Anderson; [b.] September 23, 1983, Bartlesville, OK; [p.] Larry Ryan and Sherry Smid; [ed.] Preschool Norway/Iowa Kindergarten Iowa 1st and 2nd grade in Oklahoma 3rd in Texas/China Skipped 4th, 5th and 6th in China 7th in Texas; [occ.] 7th grader at Macario Garcia Middle School; [memb.] Garcia Pop Choir, 1995-96 Middle School Region Choir; [hon.] Duke TIPS Program, Garcia GT Program; [pers.] Bessie and Smokie were my mischievous cats. I had to leave them with a friend when I moved from China. I wrote this poem to help me remember their good traits.; [a.] Sugarland, TX

RYAN, SUSAN
[pen.] Susan Ryan; [b.] June 20, 1961, New Brunswick, NJ; [p.] Charles and Carol Ziegler; [m.] Robert Ryan, September 29, 1995; [ch.] Mitchell, Meagan and Monica; [ed.] Madison High School Graduate; [occ.] House wife and mother; [memb.] Lutheran Church of the Good Shepherd; [pers.] This poem was inspired by the love of my family husband, Robert Ryan, son Mitchell and daughters Meagan and Monica. I love you all always and forever.; [a.] South Amboy, NJ

SABESSAR, TINA
[pen.] T. T.; [b.] May 29, 1987, Boynton Beach, FL; [p.] Emma Sabessars and Joel Sabessar; [ed.] Third grade, P.S. 132, Ralph Bunch School Springfield, NY; [pers.] I love to write story and poem, you can do anything if you put your mind to it.; [a.] Springfield, NY

SACKOR, BROH
[b.] Monrovia, Liberia; [ed.] B.S. in Business Admn. from Bryant College 1991, Classical High '87; [memb.] Leadership Education and Development Program in Business (LEAD '86), National Association of Security Dealers; [hon.] Who's Who in American High School, Varsity Basketball Captain (College 2 yrs.); [pers.] "Man will be judge on their deeds and intentions in this life. Follow the path of Allah.; [a.] Providence, RI

SAILER, PAULA DIANE
[b.] January 27, 1960, Denver, Co; [p.] Robert C. Sailer, Madlyn Sailer; [ed.] Machebeuf High School, University of Northern Colorado; [occ.] Retail Clerk for Vitamin Cottage, Englewood, CO; [hon.] High School Valedictorian 1978, Dean's List 1979, Summa Cum Laude (UNC) 1984, High School Award for Excellence in the Study of the Spanish Language 1978, First Place Award for writing contest sponsored by the Mayor's Committee on Employment of the Handicapped (Denver, Co, 1977).; [pers.] My poetry is the result of the Holy Spirit's influence in my life as well as the influence of my Native American brothers and sisters.; [a.] Lakewood, CO

SAINTIL, CLAIR JUDINE
[b.] February 25, 1971, Port-An-Prince; [p.] Jean and Marie Andree Saintil; [ed.] AAS in Business Administration at Kingsborough Community College, BBA in Industrial Psychology at Bernard Baruch College; [occ.] Assistant Manages of the Intellectual Property Group at AKOO-TOREN; [memb.] Museum of Natural History Sponsor for children International; [hon.] Dean's List, Honors Option Program

SALAM, ISABEL ROSE
[b.] July 9, 1953, Central America; [p.] Father born Syria, Mother born Andalucia-Spain and raised Central America; [ed.] Completed High School and College I love medicine went to school for Register Nurse and Radiology Tech.; [occ.] Artist (Oil paintings acrylics Charcoals Some Sculptures; [hon.] Flying Samaritans; [oth. writ.] Several small poems non ever published; [pers.] Easy going I find myself as very observant, analytical, realistic, eclectic and fair I believe in "Leave and let leave". And see life from a different perspective. So I express my deepest thoughts by Painting and writing something, or poems that might change those imperfections that surround us.; [a.] Newport Beach, CA

SALAS, ALBERT MARRERO
[pen.] Albert Salas; [b.] April, 25, 1953, Habana, Cuba; [p.] Albert and Maria Marrero; [m.] Olivia Rodriguez, June 1, 1991; [ch.] Miriam, Albert, Annette, Alex, William, Noe, Genesis; [ed.] Marshall High School La Ca - Ramparts College Santa Ana - California; [occ.] Director of Estamos Unidos - Pro Immigrant Community Group; [memb.] ACLU - Amnesty International - Cuban American Foundation - Democratic Party - Church of Jesus Christ of Latter Day Saint (Mormon); [hon.] Director of Estamos Unidos - Elder L.D.S. Church - Father Son - Husband Friend; [oth. writ.] Articles in Los Angeles times - daily news - patria Newspapers - coming to Christ through the Book of Mormon. Articles in Protos Newspaper.; [pers.] As Stated by His Holiness - the Dalai Lama "My religion is kindness.".; [a.] Los Angeles, CA

SALERNO, PAUL
[b.] February 4, 1914, Passaic, NJ; [p.] Charles and Teresa Salerno; [m.] Lilian Scott, November 10, 1990; [ch.] 2 sons and 5 grandchild; [ed.] 8'th grade; [occ.] Retired; [memb.] A.S.C.A.P. and the International Society of Poetry all my songs are copyrighted words and music; [hon.] The Editor of the sea of treasure gave an award of achievement; [oth. writ.] Songwriter

SALGADO, LAURIE
[b.] May 20, 1979, Chicago; [p.] Mary and Michael; [ed.] Argo H.S.; [occ.] Student; [memb.] National Honors Society (N.H.S.), Jazz Band, A Cappella Choir, Theater Drama Club, Student Council, Track; [hon.] N.H.S., Augustana Jazz Festival Superior Musicianship Talent Citation.; [pers.] It's easy to be conquered by conformity but it's more rewarding to conquer your own ideas. - Laurie Salgado I own my own fantasies, my dreams, my hopes, my fears, - Carl Rogers.; [a.] Summit, IL

SALLEE, OPAL
[b.] May 9, 1920, Campbellsville, KY; [p.] Jesse Sullivan, Callie Sullivan; [m.] Lewis Sallee (Deceased-December 10, 1984), August 15, 1942; [ch.] Glen Allan Sallee; [ed.] American High School (A correspondence school); [occ.] Retired; [pers.] I write poems and gospel songs from my life's experiences and from the feelings in my heart; [a.] Hoover, AL

SALMON, LINDSAY MARIE
[b.] June 21, 1981, Eugene, OR; [p.] Tom and Rosie Nice, Martin Salmon; [ed.] Currently a Freshman at South Eugene High School; [hon.] Completed Middle School with Certificate in Academic Excellence; [pers.] Writing poetry provides a sense of fulfillment and release in my life. In my poems I try to reflect my thoughts and emotions as well as my perceptions of life.; [a.] Eugene, OR

SAMUELSON, ROSWELL L.
[b.] January 29, 1918, Boone, IA; [p.] Hugo and Emma Samuelson; [m.] Miriam A., August 22, 1943; [ch.] Lawrence Edward, Janet Elaine; [ed.] Boone High, Indiana Institute of Technology; [occ.] Retired, Quality Control Engineer/Product Evaluation; [memb.] Elks Lodge 251, DAV, AARP, Kenwood park United Methodist church Retired means club.; [oth. writ.] Limerick's; [pers.] I am a sentimentalist at heart and reflect this in my poems with beauty and thick substance. I am a realist art 1st and dabble in Photography.; [a.] Cedar Rapids, IA

SANDBERG, SUE PRESLEY
[b.] March 29, 1953, Richmond, VA; [p.] Eugene Dale Presley and Sharlene Keen Presley; [m.] Divorced, Ausust 6, 1971 to June 16, 1982; [ch.] Jon Charles, Kevin Michael; [ed.] Thomas Dale High School in Chester, VA; [occ.] Merchandise Assistant for JC Penney Furniture in Fairbanks, Ak.; [memb.] Faith Baptist Church; [oth. writ.] Personal letters to network of friends and family worldwide. Lots of checks to pay the bills.; [pers.] John 3:16; [a.] Fairbanks, AK

SANDERSON, ELAINE
[b.] July 16, 1941, San Francisco, CA; [p.] Herman and Kathryn Meyer; [m.] Gordon Sanderson, September 15, 1962; [ch.] Elaine, Julie, Robert and Kathryn; [ed.] Mercy High, McMaster Paine Business College, MTO Nursing School, University of California, Berkeley; [occ.] Disabled 1987, formerly Medical Officer Manager, X-ray Technician; [memb.] Co-leader of Chronic Fatigue Syndrome Support Group of Stanislaus County; [hon.] Certificate of achievement, awarded for the highest score in the history of my nursing school's licensing exam; [oth. writ.] Several poems published in the

(FIDS Chronicle); [pers.] In 1987 I became permanently disabled. Poetry became my creative outlet. This poem was written for my support group's newsletter, with the hope that it would help them cope, my goal is to write more poetry that shows the beauty in life that people never notice until they are physical challenged.; [a.] Modesto, CA

SANDOVAL, CONSUELO C.
[pen.] Sandoval, Connie; [b.] May 17, 1967, Los Angeles, CA; [p.] Jose Rodriguez, Genovava Rodriguez; [m.] Joe Sandoval, June 17, 1982; [ch.] Miguel A. Cervantes, Vanessa Sandoval, Consuelo Sandoval, Christina Sandoval; [pers.] Some poems are the reflects of our souls, yet some poems prove our love for one other, and some other release our memories, but some poems are a great delight just to read them, and that what a poem is to me.; [a.] Sylmar, CA

SANDOVAL, ERNESTINE PINA
[pen.] Ernie; [b.] October 10, 1961, Heights, Houston, TX; [p.] Mario Pina and Patsy Perez Pina; [m.] Lawrence Lee Sandoval; [ch.] Proud family of nine children; [ed.] Incarnate World Academy and Bachelors Degree-The University of Texas at Austin; [occ.] Director, Marketing,; [memb.] Child advocates-Board Member, Leadership Houston, BMA-Business Marketing Association, Lector-All Saints Catholic Church, University of Houston/HCC Board Member-Curriculum Study and Scholarship funding; [hon.] Houston-Outstanding Hispanic Woman in Business, LH-Leadership/State Academic Scholarships; [oth. writ.] Several articles published in local newspapers, monthly articles for Hispanidad Magazine and local business magazines; [pers.] This poem was inspired by my first nephew on my husband's side of the Sandoval family - Lee O. Barker. My writing reflects the people, the emotion, and the dreams I experience and or perceive others may experience. Great writers such as, Chaucer and Tolstoy allow me to feel thankful there is so much to be read, perhaps more to write and whether blithe or melancholy many dreams left to unfold.

SANTA, BETTY
[b.] February 7, 1928, Johnstown, PA; [p.] Ralph and Margaret Leidy; [m.] Found someone he like better so we liberated him.; [ch.] Jeff, Georgia, Terry, Charlie, Judy David, Mindy; [occ.] Retired L.P.N.; [memb.] I'm not much of a joiner but I love it when others join me! Ecumenical Church of Light in North Huntington, PA; [hon.] Still to be awarded! I've been told I'm an excellent nurse, a good mom, and there's nothing I can knit or crochet. I'm an adventurous cook, and I like to laugh at myself - a lot!; [oth. writ.] Still refining the plot of the "Great American Novel"; [pers.] Truth is what you believe in to be, and anything can happen when you're following a dream.; [a.] Johnstown, PA

SANTILLO, ALFRED V.
[pen.] Alfred Baker; [b.] September 2, 1922, Elizabeth, NJ; [p.] Passed away; [m.] Divorced, March 25, 1945; [ch.] Eight children; [ed.] P.S. #3 Eliz. N.J. 1927-1933 Grover Cleveland and Jr. High 1933-1936 Thomas Edison Voc. School 1936-1938 G.E.D. Plainfield, N.J. 1952; [occ.] Retired, Baker-Italian bread and pizza; [hon.] My daughter was 48 years old, when she got her diploma - I was - 52 years old when I received my GED.; [oth. writ.] You were content to complete and hold together, your family, your daily chores, mother, wife, secretary the stripe, that goes with every day life, with patients and fortitude your plan to achieve your goal, "A college graduate" hoping from my heart, some of my strength and knowledge was partly an emulation of you, so I'll shout out loud, I'm proud to be your father.; [a.] West Palm Beach, FL

SANTINI, TARA T.
[b.] March 1, 1970, Bethlehem, PA; [ed.] BFA Marywood College, MA - Marywood College, San Francisco Art Institute; [pers.] When the stars fall from the sky and the rains flood the earth, and your final breath escapes you - God's hand will reach down for you Soul, Relieving your pain while a single flower foreshadows a new beginning. Love all for life runs through all.; [a.] Phillipsburg, NJ

SANTOS, SONDRA
[pen.] Sandy; [b.] January 16, 1966, Harrisburg, PA; [p.] William Thompson, Elva Anderson; [m.] LeRoy Santos, September 21, 1990; [ch.] Robert Yellock Jr. Alexandria Thompson, Anastasia Santos; [ed.] G.E.D. 11th Grade, (HACC) Harrisburg Area Community College; [occ.] Nursing Assistant; [memb.] Non-member but attend Faith Deliverance Church; [pers.] I write about what's in my heart and what I see outside my spiritual rom. God appoints me to write the subjects, that it may minister to the world thru poetry; [a.] Harrisburg, PA

SARGENT, KENNETH GARY
[pen.] Gary Sargent Cisco; [b.] February 24, 1954, Louisville, KY; [p.] Susan; [m.] Debbie live in WI; [ch.] Hope K. live in WI; [ed.] Wilkerson Elementary Valley Station KY, Valley High School Valley Station KY.; [occ.] I restore Classic Chevies at my home (trucks) self-employed; [oth. writ.] Many poems and short stories some cartoons also. None of are published at this time. My cartoon is political. Some art also (abstract) and other paintings.; [pers.] Just when your ready to give up and drown, you get a brake, so never give up the struggle, the sun will be out tomorrow.; [a.] North San Juan, CA

SAVAGE, REX D.
[b.] November 9, 1936, Lambert, MS; [p.] Ollie Wolfe and Jack Brown Savage; [ch.] Kevin Dale S, Karina Savage-Stranjock; [ed.] BA MCL Univ of Ariz, Tucson, AZ; [occ.] Bus driver, Portland, OR; [hon.] Elected to Nat'l Honoraries 0BK and 0k0, Dean's List Grar with high distinction U of A College of Liberal Arts; [oth. writ.] Many poems not submitted for publication and one great play; [pers.] I am concerned with emotions and reactions to everyday occurrences, like ee cummings. I leave the philosophy to others.; [a.] Portland, OR

SCANNPIECO, LYNN MARIE
[pen.] L. Marie; [b.] September 4, 1973, Staten Island, NY; [p.] Richard and Debra Scannpieco; [oth. writ.] I hope to one day publish some of the many short stories I've written.; [pers.] Proverbs 16:1 "We can make our plans, but the final outcome is in God's hands". I have been influenced by J.D. Salingers "Catcher in the Rye" and the writing style of S.E. Hinton.; [a.] Staten Island, NY

SCHAD, PERRIE
[b.] October 5, 1983, Minneapolis; [p.] Paula Schad; [ed.] In 6th grade at Mounds Park Academy; [occ.] Student; [pers.] Plays soccer for St. Paul Blackhawks Dance, Swimming on Codessy of the mind.; [a.] Saint Paul, MN

SCHAFER, KAREN
[pen.] Carton, Martin; [b.] August 29, 1942, Terre Haute, IN; [p.] La Verne and Helen Martin; [ch.] Laura, Lorna, Jerry; [ed.] Adams City High, Northeastern Jr. College, Sterling, Co, Western State College, Gunnison, CO; [occ.] Social Services Director, Glen Valley Care Center, Glenwood Springs, CO; [hon.] Dean's List, graduated Magna Cum Laude; [oth. writ.] Several poems published in New Voices and Mountain Thought Review - College poetry magazines, non traditional student Columnist for College Newspapers.; [pers.] Be Bold, Be Free, Be Truthful.; [a.] Parachute, CO

SCHATZ, THOMAS R.
[pen.] Thomas R. Schatz; [b.] February 5, 1949, New York City, NY; [p.] Philip B. Schatz, Mildred E. Schatz; [ch.] Tamara A. Schatz, Anthony T Schatz; [ed.] Bishop Dubois High School NYC, NY American River College, Sacramento CA, California State University - Sacramento; [occ.] Public Safety Dispatcher - City of Sacramento - Sacramento CA; [oth. writ.] Miscellaneous Essay, poems and a one-act play; [a.] Roseville, CA

SCHILLER, MARJE
[b.] October 21, 1974, Janesville, WI; [ed.] Attending the University of Wisconsin - Green Bay where I am studying creative writing; [pers.] I write it cleanse myself, to figure out who I am and put it on the page for everyone to see. I strive to find the realistic essence of myself and hope that my words will help someone else find their own.; [a.] Green Bay, WI

SCHINDLER, JACK MICHAEL
[pen.] Jake, J.M.; [b.] August 2, 1961, Forest Hills, NY; [p.] Jeri Kaye and Lewis Benjamin Schindler; [ed.] Rhodes Preparatory 1977-79, Laguardia Community College - 1979, School of Visual Arts - 1980, Queensboro College - 1983, Queens College - 1985; [pers.] "Do good and kind things for others."; [a.] New York, NY

SCHISM, GAYLE
[b.] November 26, 1971, Denver, CO; [p.] Rosalie Hoffman and Stein Fredericksen; [ch.] Harrison Keith Schism; [ed.] North Gaston High King's College; [occ.] Executive Secretary, Part-time Modeling; [hon.] Dean's List; [pers.] No matter what happens in your life the only important that matters is finding the one person who is your soul mate.; [a.] Maiden, NC

SCHLADWEILER, MARY JOYCE
[b.] August 6, 1913, Farmer, SD; [p.] Joseph N., Anna Marie Schneider; [ed.] St. Mary's Academy, Cardinal Stritch College, University of Chicago - Reading Specialist, taught all grades from Grade K through undergrad level and graduate level the latter in Reading/Study Skills and Methods; [occ.] Retired/Card shop worker and attendant Catholic School Journal; [memb.] Formerly WSRA, IRA Lecturers for reading conferences, Social Science Diocesan Committee; [hon.] Teacher of the Month, May '79 Today's Catholic Teacher graduated "Cum Laude" from CSC Honors Award for time taught in Cardinal Stritch Reading Clinic; [oth. writ.] Articles on Education topics for: IRA magazines — elementary and secondary levels.; [pers.] Serving the "intellectually poor" is an excellent means of helping many "poor and destitute." Most articles for secondary level, Journal of Reading.; [a.] Milwaukee, WI

SCHMICK, LESLIE ANN
[pen.] Leslie Starr; [b.] November 24, 1944, Chicago; [p.] Mr and Mrs Robert Wilcox; [m.] Bruce H. Schmick, June 23, 1991; [ch.] Aaron, 22 and Corie, 28; [ed.] Attended Purdue Univ.; [occ.] Legal Secretary; [memb.] Member Board of Directors, MDDA; [hon.] Art, Spelling, Social Work; [oth. writ.] Personal journals, contributions to MDDA newsletters; [pers.] Make "friends" with your manic depression (or clinical depression) it tends to bring out a satisfying creative side you didn't know you had; [a.] Merriville, IN

SCHNITTER, SOPHIE E.
[pen.] Sophie E. Schnitter; [b.] February 2, 1907, Saskatoon, Saskatchewan, Canada; [p.] Max and Alice Schnitter; [ed.] B.A. University of Nebraska Lincoln, Nebraska, MA Stanford University Palo Alto, CA.; [occ.] Retired Assistant Development and Instructional Services Superintendent, Curricu-

...m, Santa Barbara County Schools, Santa Barbara CA.; [memb.] Pilambda Theta, Delta Kappa Gamma, Altrusa International of Santa Barbara, Santa Barbara beautiful, Tree Program. United Nations and Santa Barbara chapter.; [hon.] Resolution from State of Calif for 25 years of service to children of Santa Barbara County, Calif., resolution from fellow workers and staff members Santa Barbara County Schools Office Santa Barbara, CA.; [oth. writ.] Articles for Altrusa Club Newsletter, Teacher's Resource Units with committee help, personal family history for family use only, birthday and anniversary letters and poems.; [pers.] "Do unto others as you would have others do unto you!" And live each day to the fullest in the name of the Lord and for the betterment of fellow man.; [a.] Santa Barbara, CA

SCHOLES, MARSHA ELAINE
[b.] March 3, 1950, Denver, CO; [p.] Marshall and Regina Strawser; [m.] Divorced; [ch.] Jenny, Joe, Sarah, Zech, and John Scholes; [ed.] High School-Chofu High, Tokyo, Japan Graduated from B.C. Rain, Mobile, Ala U. of Washington, Seattle, Wash. Sierra College, Rocklin, CA.; [occ.] Medical Assistant/Transcriptionist Bruce D. Gorlick, D.P.M., FACFAS; [hon.] Several oratory awards, 1st place Dramatic Interpretation, selection to Experimental Dram Program in Seattle at U. of Washington; [oth. writ.] A wide variety of poems, published and lyrics to several songs, with 2 recorded.; [pers.] I am deeply influenced by the variety of feelings and experiences, both positive and frustrating, of existing as a person in our world of change. This shows deeply in my works.; [a.] Sacramento, CA

SCHRAMM, MARA M.
[b.] December 1, 1951, Pasadena, CA; [p.] Richard J. Murphy, Amiee Murphy; [m.] B. J. Schramm, September 28, 1979; [ch.] Benjamin Jacob, Rebecca Janine; [ed.] San Gabriel Academy, Art Center College of Design; [occ.] Graphic Artist; [hon.] Dean's List, Design honored by R. C. McFarlane, former National Security Advisor, Technical Drawings Award, C. F. Braun, Engineers, nominated for Who's Who (Women in the West); [oth. writ.] Lyrics for children's musicals; [pers.] I delight in making the ordinary special.; [a.] Frazier Park, CA

SCHREY, AMANDA
[b.] December 21, 1978, Mission Hills, CA; [p.] William and Diana Schrey; [ed.] Currently attending San Fernando Valley Professional High School, Senior year; [oth. writ.] This is my first time entering any contest, and my first publication.; [pers.] My main influence is natures own beauty. Life's confession creates it's own unique poetry.; [a.] Canyon Country, CA

SCHROEDER, ARLENE
[b.] January 7, 1923, Allegeny, NY; [p.] James Kanellis, Elda Kanellis; [m.] Milo Schroeder, 3 marriages; [ch.] One daughter; [ed.] High School, Palo Consolidated School, Palo, IA; [occ.] Retired from Southern Bell; [memb.] First Methodist Church, Telephone Pioneers of America; [hon.] Salutatorian of High School Graduating Class; [a.] Terry, FL

SCHULT, CHRISTINE M.
[pen.] Chris Dowdall Schult; [b.] April 27, 1916, Humphrey, NE; [p.] Louis and Catherine Hittner; [m.] Charles H. Schult, November 27, 1976; [ch.] Daniel, Michael, James and Richard Dowdall; [ed.] High School - St. Francis, Homphrey Ne., Bryant Stratton Bus. College, Chicago, Northwestern Univ. Chicago Ill., major English and Creative Writing".; [occ.] W.C. Artist, Sculptor, Poet; [memb.] Nat. Pen Women AWA - Az. Watercolor Assoc., NAWS - Northern Az., Watercolor Society; [hon.] Numerous Awards in W.C. Painting - AWA and NAWS; [oth. writ.] "Message From Haven", also copy- righted oder "Farewell My Loves for Now", in a 5 different poetry anthologies, latest of which is "Echoes of Yesterday", Nat. Lib. of Poetry, others published are "Evensong of a Grand Canyon on Sunset", "Thru the Eyes of a Child", "My Daily Prayer", "The Eternal Search" - Golden Poet Award Trophy in 1992.; [pers.] Working in the various art mediums enables me to carry out my never ending search for beauty and light, in the joy of giving to others, I find that life can be so rich in living.; [a.] Sedona, AZ

SCHULTZ, HOLLY
[pen.] H. P. Schultz; [b.] November 11, 1962, Abington, PA; [p.] Maurice Potter and Isabel Potter; [m.] Frederick W. Gonzales Schultz, March 1, 1987; [ch.] Sarah Schultz; [ed.] Wissahickon High School; [occ.] Housewife; [memb.] A. V. Society, Boehms Reformed Church; [hon.] Circle of Merit Award; [oth. writ.] Sweet Sorrow (poem), Autumn Mist (poem); [pers.] The Tapestry of our thoughts, are woven by the words of our Heart. I dedicate "the Starling" to the late Maurice J. Potter S.R.; [a.] Rehobeth, DE

SCHULTZ, LORRAINE O.
[b.] April 25, 1915, Martha's Vineyard Island, MA; [p.] Frank and Ada Schultz; [ed.] B.A. in Biblical Lit and Theology, B.S. in Nursing Education; [occ.] Retired Missionary (33 yrs.) Africa (Ch. of the Nazarene); [memb.] American Schools of Oriental Research (ASOR), Biblical Archaeology Society (Los Angeles Chapter), Christian Writer's Guild.; [oth. writ.] 40 + articles on Biblical Archaeology. Missionary Booklets (Children) Adventures in Africa, The Fish That Couldn't Swim, For adults: Moiambique Milestones Because Somebody Prayed and Misc. poetry.; [pers.] Writing has been a hobby much of my adult life. I served in Africa 33 years, mainly in teaching.; [a.] Nampa, ID

SCHULTZ, TIMOTHY ERIC
[b.] April 3, 1979, Green Bay, WI; [p.] John and Marea Schultz; [ed.] Algoma High School; [occ.] Student at Algoma High School; [oth. writ.] Numerous (43) other poems - unpublished.; [pers.] Sensitivity, and rage are heard; [a.] Algoma, WI

SCHUTTE, ANGELA
[b.] January 14, 1981, San Bernardino; [p.] James and Carlyon Schutte; [ed.] Azalea Middle School; [hon.] Student honor roll award. Pre-teen Mrs. American. Photogenic finalist; [oth. writ.] Love takes time, why I'm filled with your love.; [pers.] I'm surprised you like my poem, I never thought that it would be published I'm glad you like it and I hope other people do to.; [a.] Brookings, OR

SCHWAB, JULIA M.
[b.] October 18, 1980, Los Angeles, CA; [p.] Virgil and Carol Schwab; [ed.] Sophomore at South Pasadena, CA High School; [occ.] Student; [oth. writ.] This poem was written when I was 13 years old.; [pers.] I enjoy poetry and I, for one, am deeply inspired by Shel Silverstein who shows depth yet humor in his writing. I truly love the poem "Put something In", and will live by those words!; [a.] South Pasadena, CA

SCHWAPPACH, PAT
[pen.] Sometimes Referred to as Grandma Pat; [b.] June 2, Anoka, MN; [p.] Clarence Groth, Blanche Paul Groth; [m.] Robert C. Schwappach, December 2, 1977; [ch.] Steven and Michael Fichtel, Dau Julia Fichtel Tollgoard, Step-children Sharon Schwappach Nelson and Larry Schwappach, nine grandchildren; [ed.] Graduated Anoka High, Attended U of M, Anoka-Ramsey Comm. College. School of Hard Knocks! Ha!; [occ.] Retired Museum Director and Researcher. Current Story teller - writer; [oth. writ.] Have had several history related articles published, in History Magazines and in Local Newspapers and News Letters. Published my our Family History Book.; [pers.] Family is very important to me, family folk-lore should be preserved for future generations. History can be interesting. History can be interesting and fun to learn? Laughter is great medicine.; [a.] Elk River, MN

SCHWARZ, BARBARA
[b.] March 25, 1938, Boston, MA; [p.] Deceased; [m.] Frederick J. Schwarz; [ch.] Frederick, Laurie; [ed.] Flushing H.S., Flushing, NY; [occ.] Secretary; [memb.] St. Ann's Society, Catholic Daughters of America, EAC, EDO Corporation, CCD Program, St. Fidelis Church; [pers.] Poetry, to me, is the warmth and love within the inner soul.; [a.] College Point, NY

SCOTT, ANITA GWYN
[pen.] Anita Gwyn Scott; [b.] August 18, 1961, Greenwood, SC; [p.] Sandra Carole Scott; [ch.] Brandy Nichole Scott, Alice Nichole Scott, and Cassandra Alice Scott; [ed.] Albermarle Senior High, Spartanburg Tech.; [occ.] Production worker; [memb.] P.T.A., Girl Scouts Mom.; [hon.] Rotary Club of Albermarle; [oth. writ.] "Outward In" and "Can You?"; [pers.] Writing is magical especially during frustrating times. I've been writing since I was 8 yrs. old though I've just started letting people seen them. Besides my children, writing is the best part of me.; [a.] Spartanburg, SC

SCOTT, JESSICA
[b.] June 6, 1977, Franklin, KY; [p.] Rita Scott and Steve Scott; [ed.] Allen Co. - Scottsville High School; [occ.] Employed by Dollar General Corporation in Scottsville, KY.; [oth. writ.] Poems and short stories for school.; [pers.] Life is precious, make every second of it count.; [a.] Scottsville, KY

SCOTT, KENDALL W.
[pen.] Pieta (My God How I Love Thee); [b.] August 17, 1956, Manhattan, NYC; [p.] Mrs. Valerie C. Scott, Mr. Andrew R. Pearson; [m.] Mrs. Soraya Crowsley Scott; [ch.] Kenny William Scott 1st, Shavonne Dalika Scott; [ed.] Francis Lewis High School, Los Angeles Valley College, University of California, Los Angeles; [occ.] Film and television producer -- Assistant Director; [memb.] Black Filmmaker Foundation, The Entertainment Fellowship; [oth. writ.] Television script entitled "Music Video Expose"; [pers.] "Aspirations Are Dreams" "Achievements Are Noteworthy"; [a.] Queens, NY

SCOTT, MEL
[pen.] Mel Scott; [b.] Toronto; [occ.] Film writer; [memb.] Writers' Guild of America, International Society of Poets, Screen Actors' Guild of America; [hon.] Ontario Arts' Council: Film Grant award. 1995 National Library of Poetry "Editor's Choice Award," awardee; [oth. writ.] Journalism, Radio, Television and Stage; [pers.] Too often we are by our emotions, rather than guided by our senses.; [a.] West Hollywood, CA

SCOTT, SUSAN GAYLE
[pen.] Susan Scott; [b.] April 5, 1961, Dallas, TX; [p.] William and Gavina Lumpkin; [m.] Delroy Eugene Scott, July 9, 1988; [ed.] Mesquite High School, Fast field Jr. College; [occ.] Aspiring Writer; [oth. writ.] The poems, Sometimes In My Darkness Hour, Am I My Brother's Keeper, My Soul Yearns For you, and, No I'm Not God. Also a manuscript I'm trying to get published titled: Pursuit; [pers.] When I write my poetry, I feel I have special help. It may be an angel, or Jesus, or even the holy spirit. Whatever it is, I feel I always have someone helping me express what's inside my soul.; [a.] West Bend, WI

SCOUTEN, ELISABETH
[b.] March 17, 1982, Syracuse, NY; [p.] Wendy Scouten, Michael Kianka; [ed.] Lincoln Middle School; [hon.] Reading Excellence, Achievement Award, Gifted Classes, Literary (Advanced) Reading Club; [oth. writ.] Remember, Angel of Dark Apologies; [pers.] Everyone has a dream, don't let go of it.; [a.] Syracuse, NY

SCRUTH, ELIZABETH
[b.] October 25, 1962, Western Australia; [p.] Frank South (Deceased), Pat Scruth; [ed.] Kewdale High, Edith Cowan University; [occ.] Intensive Care Nurse; [memb.] American Association of Critical Care Nurses, Pediatric Society of Nurses; [pers.] "True love is perhaps the only glimpse we are allowed, of eternity"; [a.] San Francisco, CA

SEACAT, CASSANDRA DEE MANN
[pen.] Sandy Seacat; [b.] June 25, 1974, Richmond, VA; [p.] Betty Tosh Moore, Ronald Mann; [m.] Rex A. Seacat, June 27, 1992; [ch.] Stacy Seacat; [ed.] Reidsville Sr. High, Ben L. Smith High, currently student at Rockingham Community College; [occ.] Radio Announcer at 1220 WREV Reidsville, NC; [memb.] American Legion Auxiliary Unit 53; [oth. writ.] Editorial in local newspaper articles for College paper, The Rock; [pers.] My writing comes from my soul. It reflects my life, experiences, and beliefs.; [a.] Reidsville, NC

SEELEY, DEBRA ANNE
[b.] December 17, 1975, Wortsmith Air Force Base, MI; [p.] Debra M. Seeley, Glenn K, Seeley, stepfather - Charles B. Scheffler; [pers.] My pride and passion is writing. It is an expression of the mind and heart, and a reflection of the soul.; [a.] Las Vegas, NE

SEGALL, JO-ANNE B.
[b.] August 26, 1924, Des Moines, IA; [p.] S. Donald Butters, Aileen M. Butters; [m.] Edwin E. Segall, April 29, 1955; [ch.] Jeffrey, Lewis, Becky; [ed.] All but dissertation for Ph.D. in International Law and Relations, Univ. of Chicago. Masters in Library Science, Masters in Library Science, Catholic Univ.; [occ.] Head Librarian, Upper School, Sidwell Friends School; [memb.] Amer. Lib. Assoc., Foreign Service Women's Assoc., (previous) school boards of the International Schools in Belgrade and Djakarta, Beta Phi Mu; [hon.] Election to Beta Phi Mu, International Library Science Honor Society; [oth. writ.] A poem in Sidwell Friends School Literary Magazine; [pers.] Literature should inspire everyone to live an ethical life as God's image and likeness.; [a.] Washington, DC

SEIME, JUDITH TOWNSEND
[ed.] Bachelor of Science in Organizational Behavior, Northwestern University, Chicago, IL; [occ.] Writer, researcher and corporate communications specialist. Fields of expertise include message development, positioning, and targeting communications to reach the financial audience.; [memb.] International Association of Business Communicators (IABC); [oth. writ.] Press releases published in regional and national press, Articles on current events, weather and climate published as "Consultant's Comments" by Paine Webber, Inc, Short story about cultural adjustment used by YFU International Student Exchange in their training manual.; [pers.] I have read my poems at Poetry Slams in Chicago, IL, but his is the first time I have submitted any of them for publication. This poem was begun one evening as I was preparing to make my 16th move, this time from Chicago, IL to Danbury, CT. Living in 14 states and two foreign countries has made me an expert in packing boxes and moving.

SERRAO, LORRIE
[b.] December 1, 1956, Oneonta, NY; [p.] Manuel and Lydia Serrao; [ch.] Ben Serrao; [ed.] Franklin Central School, State University College at Oneonta; [occ.] Information Services Associate (Computer Analyst); [memb.] Dryden PTA, ITHACA Employees Association, Inc.; [hon.] NYS Regents Scholarship, National Honor Society; [oth. writ.] Short story in Catskill Review, poetry in B-D Review, enrolled in the Institute of Children's Literature; [pers.] I write what I feel in my heart based on personal events.; [a.] Harford, NY

SHA, JEANNE
[b.] July 18, 1947, Fergus Falls, MN; [p.] Roy and Marian (Grace) Sha; [ch.] Deidre Diane Fuller, Kyle Thomas Spooner; [ed.] Roosevelt Park Senior High, Solano Community College, Life; [memb.] Beautiful Savior Lutheran Church; [hon.] Dean's List; [oth. writ.] Newspaper Articles; [pers.] To my first born grandson, Akira Tadao Nishimura, I dedicate this first vital component of my legacy. More to follow!?! Novels? Poems? Short stories? Grandchildren? God willing—yes on all counts!; [a.] Vancouver, WA

SHAHIDI, KAREN
[b.] December 16, 1957, Cincinnati; [p.] Gerald Barrett and Sandra Robinson; [m.] Hans Shahidi, December 29, 1990; [ch.] Kari Yvonne, and Patrick Ali; [ed.] High school; [occ.] Homemaker; [memb.] International Society Of Poets.; [hon.] Received editor's choice award for "A Poem To My Mother"; [oth. writ.] A poem to my mother, published by the National Library of Poetry in the "Walk Through Paradise" anthology; [pers.] Once again, I am honored to have my poem published by the National Library of Poetry! Many thanks to my husband, and my dearest friend Paula for their support and encouragement.; [a.] Westlake Village, CA

SHAULIS, BONNIE RUTH
[b.] July 10, 1937, Sherman, TX; [p.] Charles Walcott Aylne Walcott; [m.] Jay A. Shaulis, November 7, 1953; [ch.] Daniel Jay, Bruce Allen; [ed.] High School; [occ.] Artist and Poet; [memb.] 2nd Place Ribbon for Animal Drawing McKinney Art Show Honorable for Sam Houston Portrait Drawing Plano Art Show; [oth. writ.] Poem published in local newspaper. Plano proud article for editor's choice award in local newspaper.; [pers.] That my writing will bring pleasure to everyone who reads it and will help them to feel positive about them selves as they read what I have wrote.; [a.] Plano, TX

SHAW, MISS APIKIA
[pen.] Apikia; [b.] August 2, 1923, White Plains, NY; [ed.] Classical Pianist Degree - BA - Doctorate - St. Louis Renaissance Conservatory, Artist - BA Degree from Virginia University; [occ.] Retained, partly; [memb.] National Library of Poetry (I'm proud and thanks); [hon.] Played with the NY Philomantic - St. Louis - KMOX Station Cleveland Chamber Music - Art Exhibits - Delfic Studio N.Y. City - Beuna Vista Musician in Cleveland - Ruth Coltor Hollary

SHELVEY, MADELINE
[b.] December 1, 1907, North Chittenden, VT; [p.] John T. and Margaret Harte Shelvey; [m.] Single; [ed.] Pittsford High School, Castleton Normal School, Extension Courses at University of V.T. Catechist in several UT. Areas.; [occ.] Retired Teacher, social worker; [memb.] Court Fanny Allen, Catholic Daughters of America, Living Rosary Association Our Lady of Fire, Colebrook, N.H. Burlington Writers Group.; [oth. writ.] Sent by burlington free press do feature articles on member of it. Legislature - poems published in local newspaper, also feature articles. Article in Hobby Magazine; [pers.] I am particularly a tuned to all nature especially to the manner in which God flamed he would in such perfection. Our whole world is in great need to return to the way of Fed.; [a.] Winooski, VT

SHEPARD, ANGIE L.
[b.] January 14, 1976, Shelbyville, IN; [p.] Jerry Shepard, Rebecca Shepard; [ed.] Connersville Senior High School, Connersville Indiana - Connersville Jr. High School, Grandview School (Connersville) Garrison School (Richmond) Baxter School (Richmond); [memb.] Kingdom Hall of Jehovah's Witnesses; [hon.] 1993 Editors Choice Award - The National Library of Poetry - Grade School Young Authors Of America Conference Awards - Physical Fitness Awards - Science Fair Awards - Perfect Attendance Awards - Citizenship Awards, Good Penmanship Awards, Spelling Bee Awards, Grade School, Junior High Honor Roll, Most Improved Student Award, Physical Fitness Field Day Ribbons (Baxter School, Richmond), Track and Field Day Awards, (Grandview School, Connersville); [oth. writ.] 2 unfinished novels, nearly 1,500 poems, collection of short stories, other short stories - songs, short stories in school paper, The Vagabond (10th grade) poem - "Autumn" published 1993, 2nd National Library of Poetry; [pers.] I would like to say thank you to my mom and dad for being such wonderful parents and for always guiding me in the right direction. Thank you! I would also like to say a special "I love you!" to Jason. Thank you for being here and believing in me. I love you! My out look on life - believe in yourself and you can make anything happen. My outlook on poetry - everything around me, every little creation of God, is inspirational to me. There isn't one thing I look at that isn't over flowing with poetry.; [a.] Richmond, IN

SHEPHERD, NYCOL
[pen.] Nyci; [b.] September 14, 1976, Riverside Hosp., Trenton; [p.] Joy Cole and Don Shepherd; [ed.] Graduated from Romulus Senior High School in 1994; [occ.] Sales Associate; [oth. writ.] I write a lot of poetry, but none (before this) have been published. My poetry consists of things I've experience or my friends have experienced.; [pers.] Anything can be achieved all you have to do is strive.; [a.] Dearborn Heights, MI

SHEPHERD, WILLIAM O.
[pen.] Bill; [b.] August 15, 1920, Sidell, IL; [p.] James Guy and Opal Allen Shepherd; [m.] Thelma Helen Shepherd, September 27, 1959; [ed.] 12-grade high school, college at Buffalo New York, University of Illinois, Southern California, and Chicago Illinois; [occ.] Retired - 45 years with the Veterans Administration as a Building Management Officer; [hon.] In 1986, Governor Robert Kerrey appointed me an admiral in the great Navy of the State of Nebraska, Outstanding Career Award from the Veterans Administration in 1988 the 29th of January, am an Interior Decorator and Designer; [oth. writ.] "The Last Human Race" first published work in 1990 and am writing my second book "Near the End of Time" which should be published sometime in later 1996.; [pers.] I have been greatly influenced by Jesus Christ and the goodness of men and women, who are and have greatly influenced me in my writings.; [a.] Hoopeston, IL

SHERIFF, DAVID G.
[pen.] Garth David; [b.] November 4, 1941, Iowa City, IA; [p.] Helen and Forrest Sheriff; [m.] Mary L. Sheriff, April 3, 1965; [ch.] David, Daniel and Scott; [ed.] Napa High, National University; [occ.] Retired; [memb.] AARP, NARFE, NRA, Past Deacon Carmel, Mtn. Baptist Church; [oth. writ.] Various poems, novice poet; [pers.] Enjoyment found in peening expression of thought and sharing the like from others.; [a.] Napa, CA

SHERMAN, ROBERT
[b.] February 25, 1925, Chicago, IL; [p.] Joseph S. and Ida Sherman; [m.] Divorced; [ch.] Daniel S. Sherman; [ed.] Dorsey High, Frank Wiggins A&D, Art Center School, Chouinard, Otis Art Institute; [occ.] Retired, Inventor, Poet, Calligrapher; [hon.] Merit award from Caltrans; [oth. writ.] Technical articles and instruction manuals for CALTRANS, Technical article for "Plan and print."; [pers.] My Quatrains are my commentaries on the many aspects of life as I have experienced them, as an artist - photographer - draftsman. I was originally led into poetry by the RUBAIYAT quatrains of Omar Khayyam.; [a.] Gardena, CA

SHERWIN, HELEN
[pen.] Ille Anna Lazar; [b.] March 10, 1924, Aurora, IL; [p.] Deceased; [m.] Deceased; [ch.] David F. Sherwin; [ed.] Self-educated; [occ.] Retired; [a.] Oshkosh, WI

SHILLING, FAYE O.
[pen.] Sookie; [b.] August 7, 1948, Conway, AR; [p.] Lenodis and Ethel Walker; [m.] Eresell Shilling, September 1, 1990; [ch.] Keith Lavell and Michael Paul Lattimore; [ed.] Three years of college; [occ.] Medical Technician; [memb.] West Angeles Church of God In Christ; [hon.] In the 11th grade I received an award for writing the article of the year, for my school paper.; [oth. writ.] Articles published in *Players Magazine*. "Miss Black America Pageant," "Todd Davis," and "Willie T. Ribbs".; [pers.] The seeds of Greatness are enclosed in every individual, but cultivation and blossom are left to the individual.

SHIVELY, HEATHER
[b.] February 21, 1973, Philadelphia, PA; [p.] Greg Shively, Ltc Keith and Linda; [m.] Fiance - Jay Nunenkamp Kuberek, December, 1996; [ed.] Virginia Polytechnic Institute and State University (BS-Biology) Graduated may 1995; [occ.] Army Officer-second Lieutenant, Ft Detrick, MD; [memb.] Virginia living museum, Langley Kennel Club, American Kennel Club, Association of the United States Army; [hon.] Early cycle 4 year army ROTC scholarship, Langley Kennel Club $500 Prevent Scholarship; [oth. writ.] "Ghost dogs," the barker May/June 1990, page 64; [pers.] Struggle and overcome, lie down be conquered.; [a.] Yorktown, VA

SHORT, FRANCES LUELLEN CALOWAY
[pen.] Luellen C. Short; [b.] October 15, 1963, Canton, MS; [p.] Shelby and Dan Boyd, James Caloway (Deceased); [m.] Robert Lee Short, February 4, 1982; [ch.] Jason Lee Short - 17, James Robert (Short - Rocky) - 12; [ed.] Canton Academy - in Mississippi, Graduated from Decatur High School in Decatur, AL; [occ.] Attending Calhoun Community College; [memb.] National Federation of music clubs, Supreme Emblem Club of the United States #127 Bethel Baptist Church; [hon.] All State Rating In Decatur Concert Chorus, 79-81, Superior rating 3 years in a row for playing piano, Public Service Award 95 from Few Chosen, INC; [oth. writ.] There are many more things, I've written, nothing ever published before I have also written 3 songs, I believe is one of my songs.; [pers.] Of all sad words of tongue or pen, the saddest are these: It Might Have Been.; [a.] Decatur, AL

SHOWALTER, ALMA LOU
[b.] February 11, 1937, Des Arc, AR; [p.] Dewey and Lula Holloway; [m.] Bobby J. Showalter, April 6, 1958; [ch.] Tammie Orlicek; [ed.] Des Arc High School, 2 years College Arkansas, State University Beebe; [occ.] Housewife; [memb.] The Country Chapel Sunday school teacher; [oth. writ.] Short story - just an old carp. [pers.] Just wanted to see if I could write a poem - first try and it was published in our local newspaper.; [a.] Cabot, AR

SHUMATE, CASEY
[b.] February 2, 1982, California; [p.] Barry and Michele Shumate; [pers.] Casey is a direct descendant of John Page of Virginia who was a Revolutionary War Patriot, Governor of Virginia and life long friend of Thomas Jefferson.; [a.] West Hills, CA

SICARD, EMILIA
[pen.] Emilia A. Cordova de Sicard; [b.] June 23, 1939, Arenoso, Dominican Republic; [p.] Antonio Cordova, Julia A. de Cordova; [m.] Guillermo R. Sicard, January 11, 1963; [ch.] Fausto Antonio, Julia Margarita; [ed.] Bachelor of Philosophy and Art, Immaculate Conception College, La Vega Dominican Rep., Elementary School Teacher (5 yrs.) School principal (2 yrs.); [occ.] Executive secretary and housewife; [memb.] Stark County Historical Society, American Medical Assoc. Alliance, Stark Country Med. Auxiliary, Timken Mercy Service League, Hall of Fame Tennis Center, St. Paul's Church N.; [hon.] High School Newspaper Editor and President. Dean list Immaculate Conception College.; [oth. writ.] Numerous unpublished poems in Spanish. Few short tales; [pers.] I truly love and respect all mankind. Have great fondness for literature and history. A romantic at heart. (Influenced by intellectual father) would like my epitaph to read! "She was good and wanted to be a poet"; [a.] Hartville, OH

SICILIANO, MELISSA L.
[b.] December 18, 1969, Charleston, SC; [m.] Raymond J. Siciliano, July 14, 1990; [ch.] Martin Glenn Siciliano; [ed.] Summerville High, Charleston Southern University; [occ.] Office Manager, The Junior League of Charleston, Inc., charleston, SC; [memb.] Distinguished Member, The International Society of Poets; [oth. writ.] "A Son's Prayer" published in Mists of Enchantment by The National Library of Poetry, several poems published in various local and military newspapers.; [pers.] Most of my poetry is a reflection of my life as a Navy spouse. For that, and for the inspiration he gives, I thank my husband Ray. I also must give my love to my son for the many times he has given me a reason to write a piece of poetry.; [a.] Summerville, SC

SIDES, BARBARA JEAN
[b.] June 13, 1941, Mentor, TN; [p.] James C. Anderson, Ruth Anderson-Cooper; [m.] Carl Webb Sides, August 20, 1991; [ch.] Joseph Carl-Shelby Renee-Tara Elizabeth-Robert Elee; [ed.] Everett High School, Maryville, Tennessee; [occ.] Housewife; [oth. writ.] Birthday-Wedding-Get Well Poems I write Gospel Songs and Sing them in church and on with radio in Lenoir City, TN weekly. I participated in Spirit Fest '95 in Henderville, TN, and recorded my own song on a video, May 1995.; [pers.] I always try to put into words what I feel from my heart. I never make up things just to make the poem sound good.; [a.] Maryville, TN

SIEGEL, ERIC NATHAN
[b.] April 9, 1985, Phoenix, AZ; [p.] Geri and Marty Siegel; [ed.] Heschel Day School - 5th Grade; [occ.] Student - 5th Grade; [memb.] International Society of Poets; [oth. writ.] Poetry published in S*kipping Stones* Magazine, *A Muse To Follow*, *The Garden of Life* and other local publications.; [pers.] I feel that I can express my true feelings thru writing poetry.; [a.] Encino, CA

SIKORA, PHIL
[pen.] "Paul Sikora"; [b.] December 5, 1959, Milwaukee; [p.] Barbara Rydberg, Donald Rydberg (Deceased); [ed.] 1978 High School Graduate of Milwaukee Tech. Milwaukee, Wisconsin; [occ.] Lumber-Building Materials Manger: Builders Square; [oth. writ.] Editorial published in the *Milwaukee Sentinel*. Several poems read on TV's bowling Game: The Epic of the Bowling Game, the Challenge of the Bowling game.; [pers.] I strive to someday use my writing talent to be able to work at a TV Station, if only given the opportunity.; [a.] Milwaukee, WI

SIMKINS, JULIA OTTICE
[b.] July 1, 1913, Kounes County, TX; [p.] Verna and Carl Blackwell; [m.] Ray John Simkins, June 8, 1940; [ch.] Two sons both deceased; [ed.] High School, I'm a member of an art guild due to an accident July 94 I'm in a wheel chair due to my determination I use a walker with half do my won cooking etc - but do have help 5 days a week

SIMMONS, ESI TREMBLAY
[pen.] Esi Tremblay; [b.] July 9, 1936, Oswego, NY; [p.] John and Hilda Turkington; [m.] Hon. Richard D. Simmons, May 21, 1994; [ch.] Cindy, Mark, Ross, Scott, Kathi, and Linda; [ed.] U. of Rochester, Columbia U.; [occ.] Retired R.N.; [memb.] Adirondack Mountain Club, Adirondack Forty-Sixers, Rome Twigs, Gore Organization of Frequent Skiers; [oth. writ.] Unpublished poetry and journals; [pers.] My love of poetry is genetic, through poetry my thoughts and feelings are made visible; [a.] Rome, NY

SIMON, JENIFER
[b.] August 8, 1983, San Antonio, TX; [p.] Pamela Simon, Harold Simon; [ed.] I am in the seventh grade; [memb.] Science Club, Young Astronauts, Energizers, (Singing Group) Girl Scouts, Story Spinners, Safety patrol; [oth. writ.] I have written other poems, and stories and stuff like that in school.; [pers.] I believe that if you want to do something you should be awe to do it. You should never think you can't do something because what people say. When you set your mind/heart to something you should just "go for it."; [a.] San Antonio, TX

SIMON, ROBERT
[pen.] Bob Simon; [b.] October 30, 1959 (died February 5, 1991), Saint Fords, NJ; [p.] Stephen and Josephine Simon; [m.] Michelle Klimek, November 27, 1983; [ch.] Natasha Lynne (5 weeks old at time of death); [ed.] High School 1 yr. at DeVry Inst. of Tech. - 2 semesters at Middlesex City. College - graduated air-conditioning/cooling/ice making machinery in north Jersey after his marriage.; [occ.] Bob died on Feb 5 '91. He improved on an ice-making machine for one of his employers. He loved the work and was proud of it. He was advancing quickly before his untimely death. Bob was an active Sommelier, having studied wine making in all its phases.; [oth. writ.] Bob was not a writer. When his cat Buckwheat died, he was devastated. During one his bleakest moments he poured out his heart. This poem, his only writing, is what resulted.; [a.] Fords, NJ

SIMONIAN, JEANNINE L.
[b.] October 23, 1947, Fresno, CA; [p.] Dorothy Moore and Robert Pinckney; [m.] Kenneth G. Simonian, March 12, 1980; [ch.] Monique Mays, Robert Paul Scrivner; [ed.] American Institute of Hypnotherapy Various Community College - Business Major; [occ.] American Medical and Dental Certified Hypnotherapist Reiki II Practitioner; [memb.] Reverend Universal Life Church Metaphysical Research Society of Spokane Washington; [oth. writ.] I have written other poems however, none have been published; [pers.] My life is filled with joy. What more could I ask for!

SINGH, CRYSTAL
[b.] September 10, 1981, Port of Spain, Trinidad;

[p.] Bharath Singh, Vashti Singh; [ed.] Murrow High School; [occ.] Student; [hon.] Valedictorian of the Class of '92, Camille Coccaro Barbieri Award, Science Award, Communication Arts Award, The Bertram Parks Memorial Award, The United States Achievement Academy Award.; [oth. writ.] Many poems, songs, and short stories - unpublished; [pers.] To make it in life, you should always see the good in a bad or depressing situation. Remember, after every storm, there is a rainbow.; [a.] Brooklyn, NY

SINGLETON, CARL R.
[pen.] Carl R. Singleton; [b.] November 10, 1968, Dallas, TX; [p.] Berthal Singleton; [ed.] L.G. Pinkston High - Dallas, TX, University of North Texas - Denton, TX, Bachelor's of Science in Industrial Engineering; [occ.] United Parcel Service; [pers.] Plan to teach on the college level some day and marry by honey (Elizabeth Washington).; [a.] Dallas, TX

SISSON, MARILYN
[b.] December 15, 1947, Paris, IL; [p.] Chester and Katherine Kirby; [m.] Robert F. Sisson, December 31, 1971; [ed.] High School Graduate; [hon.] I received an award in 1970 from the Famous Writers School for completing a home study course in fiction writing.; [pers.] My inspiration comes from my husband, Robert who served 2 tours along the DMZ in Korea and my brother, Mike Kirby, who served in Viet Nam. The pain of the mind, Veteran's suffer is often misunderstood and forgotten.; [a.] Paris, IL

SITTERLET, CARLA R. K.
[pen.] Laron C. Quest; [b.] July 14, 1980, Detroit, MI; [p.] Carl and Barbara Sitterlet; [occ.] Highschool Student; [oth. writ.] I have written over 20 other poems with such titles as: Dark Angel, and Hope. I am now in the time consuming process of writing a novel, and I am continuously finding a new things to write.; [pers.] If you read my poem, listen with your mind to what I see my life as, and let your heart hear my words and understand.; [a.] McAlester, OK

SLATER, MARY KATHERINE
[pen.] Kat Slater; [b.] September 29, 1980, Kingsport, TN; [p.] Jim Slater and Pam Slater; [ed.] High School; [occ.] Student; [memb.] Martial Arts Academy, Parent, Student, Teacher Association, East, North Youth Association; [hon.] Editor's Choice Award (1994 Power to the People); [oth. writ.] Power to the People (Echoes of Yesterday) several other poems as yet unpublished; [pers.] I want to give description and interpretation to the emotions of life as I experience it!; [a.] Greenville, SC

SLEDGE, LINDELL
[b.] September 7, 1959, Whitakers, NC; [p.] Mr. Sack Sledge - Mary Ethel Sledge; [ch.] Kaneesha, Gregory, Tanikka, Telly; [ed.] Nash Tech. College; [occ.] Vending Atta and Cashier; [memb.] Member of the Read Budd Holiness Church (Rev.) F.C. Barnes; [hon.] Never had any.; [pers.] I will let this be a lesson to me that I do have talent. Have lots of poem always been afraid to sent them off.; [a.] Rockymount, NC

SLY, JOANNE ELIZABETH
[b.] October 14, 1944, Traverse City, MI; [p.] Carl Joseph Miller and Dorothea Elizabeth (Warner) Miller; [m.] Herman Terry Sly, July 2, 1981; [ch.] Danny, Tonny, and Terry Sly; [ed.] Suttons Bay and Willow Hill Grade Schools, Traverse City Jr. and Senior High Schools, and Northwestern Michigan College; [occ.] Homemaker; [pers.] God inspired upon my heart the words to this piece to relay through nature His work of creation and message of salvation.; [a.] Traverse City, MI

SMEDLEY, DONNA JEANNE
[b.] February 22, 1958, Syracuse, NY; [p.] Don and Lucille Wood; [m.] Johnny Smedley Jr., September 10, 1988; [ch.] Amanda Lynn and Emily Anne; [ed.] High School Grad. in 1976 from R.J. Reynolds in Winston. Salem, NC; [occ.] Mother; [memb.] N.C. Victim Assistance Network. P.T.A.; [hon.] Poetry Award in the second grade. Was once offered an opportunity to write song's but declined after learning my name wouldn't credited for them.; [oth. writ.] Poems, music and lyrics, personal thoughts. A private collection covering 20 years of feelings, thoughts and happenings in my life.; [pers.] Feelings and thoughts area easier to express through your fingertips via a pen and paper. Since my brother's death. I've been able to express more spiritual feelings in my writing.; [a.] Raleigh, NC

SMITH, ANNA LEAH
[pen.] Anna Smith; [b.] December 4, 1980, Anchorage, AK; [p.] Bennett and Linda Fay Smith; [ed.] Community Christian School (K-7) Smokey Bay School (8) Currently at Homer High School, 9th Grade; [occ.] Student; [memb.] Homer Assembly of God Church Blazing Saddles 4-H Club; [pers.] I want to thank my friends, Brooke Rainwater and Liska Kendror for encouraging me to write poetry, I want for the hope of humanity. To give a special remembrance to Edward whose inspired me to write this poem.; [a.] Haines, AK

SMITH, CAROLINE C.
[b.] July 1, 1938, Illinois; [p.] Arthur and Agnes McAfee; [m.] Jack C. Smith, February 18, 1955; [ch.] Jackie, Shirley, Sandy, Grandchildren - Robert, Jason, Jillian, Ashley, Rachel and Adam; [occ.] Housewife; [oth. writ.] "My Lord's Touch" published in "Beyond The Stars" in 1995 thanks to my husband for encouraging me.; [pers.] I would like this poem dedicated to my 3 daughters, Jackie, Shirley and Sandy, my 6 grandchildren, Robert, Jason, Jillian, Ashley, Rachel and Adam, with love.

SMITH, GARY TOM
[b.] September 5, 1951, Hardinsburg, KY; [p.] Tommy and Dean Smith; [m.] Divorced; [ch.] Brandy Smith; [ed.] Breckinridge Co. High School, BFA Western KY University; [occ.] Art teacher - Irvington Elementary School, Irvington, KY; [memb.] KY Teachers Asso., Western Alumni, Beta Club Sponsor; [hon.] Honorable Mention at Gallary Show, Bowling Green, KY, 2nd Place Art Guild Show, Lexington, KY; [pers.] I was raised on a farm, with a very close family. With professional parents, I spent much of my summer time with my grandparents, therefore I feel my work reflects a small town country boy with close family ties.; [a.] Hardinsburg, KY

SMITH, IONIE DONALDS
[pen.] Iona, Elizabeth, Blossom; [b.] May 10, 1937, Jamaica, West Indies; [p.] Mr. and Mrs. J. A. Donalds; [m.] Mr. Hylton R. Smith, September 26, 1959; [ch.] Karen J. Smith, Collie R. Smith, Dwight Barrington Smith; [ed.] Graduate of Moneague Teacher's College, St. Ann Jamaica, West Indies, got a rounded education in early life in Preparatory Basic and all age schools in Jamaica West Indies; [occ.] Outreach Programme, Volunteering in Health, House to House, Research in Religions of America and Family Life Education. Attending conferences.; [memb.] Several Religious Organizations was a member of Community Organization leader of 4-H Club. (Jamaica West Indies) Past member of J.T.A. Citizen's Association Jamaica West Indies; [hon.] 4-H Club Silver Award Social Service in Community Award Mothers Trophy from (Son) Dwight Barrington Smith; [oth. writ.] Songs - poems not published, articles for the daily gleaner in Jamaica West Indies during the 70s; [pers.] I learn to have faith in God and I believe in Prayer I make my decisions through God's leading me. Not giving up Leadership of my family to anyone but myself and husband. The love of God and mankind will always be portrayed in writing as I continue to help people.; [a.] Jamaica, West Indies

SMITH, JASON ANDREW
[b.] January 7, 1978, Omaha; [p.] Steven and Diane; [ed.] Currently attending Millard North High School; [occ.] Local Musician; [pers.] Though I have no resume ti speak of, my passion for songwriting has driven me to explore poetry in a more insightful way. A poem should send a message as well as a shiver down the spine. I plan to continue improvement of my work.; [a.] Omaha, NE

SMITH, JOSEPH ARNOLD
[pen.] Arnold Smith; [b.] September 24, 1950, Elkins West King; [p.] Pauline Sirjord; [m.] Divorced; [ch.] "Girls" Haley and Misty Smith; [ed.] 12 years; [occ.] I work in House Keeping and done maintence also; [memb.] I belong first Baptist Church; [hon.] 1995 Editors choice award; [oth. writ.] I wrote a poem about on Desert Storm, and few more, that unpublished; [pers.] In my poem, Praise God, what He done for you, I like to tell people, that are lost, that God has a place for you, your rewards, will be in Heaven.; [a.] Hubbard, TX

SMITH, KAY
[b.] September 15, 1953, Marshall County, AL; [p.] Kathryn Naylor and David Naylor; [m.] Earl Smith, January 12, 1973; [ch.] Shaun, Amanda, Tonya and Tasha; [ed.] Kate Duncan Smith (D.A.R.) High in Grant, Al. I.C.S. School of Journalism; [memb.] World wide Church of God, Reader's Club and Pen Pals Club; [hon.] Creative Art Award; [oth. writ.] Several poems published in local paper. Wrote and illustrated a children's short story; [pers.] I like to write about the conflicts of people, the beauty and importance of nature, and the imperative need for world peace. I have been influenced by the humanity in the writings of Abraham Lincoln, and the mysterious writings Edgar Allen Poe.; [a.] Crossville, AL

SMITH, KELLY S.
[b.] June 20, 1977, Bangor, ME; [p.] Kenny Smith and Elaine Smith; [ed.] Central High School; [oth. writ.] A poem in take five, youth devotional; [pers.] I thank Sandy Hurd for encouraging me to send this poem to the National Library of Poetry. I thank God for being there for me and giving me this talent to write poems. I love my family and am glad they are there for me.; [a.] East Corinth, ME

SMITH, L. LAURIE
[pen.] LLS; [b.] May 4, 1960, Hobbs, NM; [p.] Howard and Rozetta Smith; [ed.] Clear Lake High School, Texas Tech. University; [occ.] Part of Corporate America; [oth. writ.] I have written other poems, the following have been published in the following books: *Sparkles in the Sand*, *Walk Through Paradise*, *A Delicate Balance*, *Windows of the Soul* and *Best Poems of 1996*; [pers.] All my writings come from my emotional feelings and experiences I have encountered due to my family, my extended family of unique friends and especially from past and present relationships. My writings are my way of dealing with life in general, as far as what is worth keeping and what is worth blowing away using a breath of kindness.; [a.] Lewisville, TX

SMITH, MANFORD PAUL
[b.] October 13, 1937, Missouri; [p.] John Smith and Ellen Smith; [ch.] Allan Smith; [ed.] BS Ed Major: Art Minors: English and History; [occ.] Artist and Writer, Teacher; [memb.] United Keetoowah Band of Cherokee Indians. New Mexico Art League; [hon.] Art Award, Best Of Show Awards; [oth. writ.] Poems, Essays, Native Writings and thoughts; [pers.]

ords, from the pen of the writer, reflect how the writer views the things which form his concepts, which pull to the surface his emotions and emerge form the thoughts which appear on his paper.; [a.] lbuquerque, NM

SMITH, MARCI MARIE
[b.] September 22, 1981, Atlantic City, NJ; [p.] Joe and Cindy Smith; [ed.] 8th grader at Emma C. ttales School, Absecon, N.J.; [memb.] School afety Patrol, Yearbook, Drama; [hon.] Honors udent, John Hopkins' University Talent Search articipant, Peace Poster Winner, Jr. Duck Stamp nd place; [pers.] My two life philosophies are: It ever hurts to try, and to live each day like it's your ast, and learn each day like you will live forever.; [a.] Absecon, NJ

SMITH, MIRIAM LORENA
[pen.] Lorena; [b.] November 23, 1973, Waukegan, IL; [p.] Liz Smith and Guillermo Smith; [ed.] Some College - College of Lake County, goal: to transfer to Clark Atlanta University in Atlanta GA; [occ.] Secretary; [oth. writ.] "Play or Be Played", "Turning the Tables" and several other poems used for lyrics for a Demo for Thomas K. Bustos; [pers.] I would like to first of all thank God for giving me the talent to write, second, I would like to thank all those men who motivated me to write this particular poem (you all know who you are), thanks for turning a negative situation into everything more than success for me!!!; [a.] Waukegan, IL

SMITH, MISTY D.
[b.] July 15, 1975, Lindsay, OK; [p.] June C. Smith and Lyle E. Smith; [ed.] 1994 Eastland High School graduate; [occ.] Kable news in Mt. Morris IL; [hon.] 1st place for FHA speech down state; [oth. writ.] Several poems for creative writing festival in white water Wisconsin; [pers.] I write about the way I feel or for other people I believe poetry comes from the heart and soul. Poetry is a life for believers.; [a.] Lanark, IL

SMITH, MRS. MOLINE
[b.] Tennessee; [p.] Marshell Davis; [m.] Loue; [ch.] One; [occ.] Housewife; [memb.] Song Writer Association in Nashville, Huntington Club I play the guitar, Chroma Harp Keyboard, I belong to Baptist Church.

SMITH, PAUL L.
[b.] January 22, 1918, Chicago, IL; [p.] Grover Smith, Goldie Smith; [m.] Lorna Smith, October 31, 1953; [ch.] Susan McKee, Barbara Strahlein, Charles Smith, Stephen Smith; [ed.] Pasadena Jr. College, BS - Calif Inst. of Technology, Post Grad - UCLA School of Bus.; [occ.] Retired/Engineering and Marketing; [memb.] Academy of Magical Arts; [oth. writ.] Unpublished poetry.; [pers.] I look for life's lessons with an extra effort, when appropriate, to find human.; [a.] Huntington Beach, CA

SMITH, RAYMOND
[pen.] Ray Smith; [b.] New York City; [p.] Edward and Dorothy Smith; [m.] Claire Virginia, January 30, 1979; [ch.] Raymond, Edward, Elizabeth and Kathryn; [ed.] Williamburg HS, New York Tech. Mondell Drafting Institute; [occ.] Retired technical writer and design draftsman; [memb.] Library of Congress Associate, Nassau County Board of Elections, Veterans of Foreign Wars, AARP, Smithsonian; [oth. writ.] Poetry is Beyond the Stars, "Doorway To Space" published in American Heritage (November, 1990), Technical Manuals and a variety of poetry in local publications; [pers.] I have written poetry about storms at see, Bowery bums, lost loves, a scandalous divorce suit filed by Santa Claus's wife, etc. Composing a line of verse gives me the same high that a dope head gets from sniffing a line of coke.; [a.] Oceanside, NY

SMITH, SHANNON
[b.] June 12, 1979, Redmond, OR; [ed.] Currently a Junior at Redmond High School; [oth. writ.] I have also published a poem in the "Children's Album", magazine in Feb. of 1989 when I was 10 years old.; [pers.] My friends and family are the inspiration for my poems, and I thank them for all they have meant to me.; [a.] Redmond, OR

SMITH, TRACY L.
[b.] January 7, 1971, Youngstown, OH; [p.] Rose Mary Mucci; [ed.] Fitch High School, the Ohio State University, Young Stown State University; [occ.] Nurse Assistant and Pre-Medical Student, St. Elizabeth Hospital, Youngstown, OH; [hon.] Dean's List; [oth. writ.] Published in School (YSU) newspaper; [pers.] This poems was written in the memory of my great-grandfather, Harry J. Sugar, whose life it reflects. My goal is to increase awareness of this disease and to make strides in order to find a cure, for who is a person really, who has not their mind.; [a.] Youngstown, OH

SMITH, ZELMAK
[pen.] Sissy Smith; [b.] July 10, 1925, Byrneville; [p.] Ben Byrn and Myrtie M. Byrn; [m.] Darrel K. Smith July 6, 1946; [ch.] Diana G., Darrel W., and Kevin B. Smith; [ed.] Graduated from High School 1944; [occ.] Housewife; [memb.] Reorganized Church of Jesus Christ of Latter Day Saints (RLDS); [hon.] I have a Silver Poet Award and a Golden Poet Award; [oth. writ.] I have poems written for friends, neighbors and spiritual. Anything of interest in our small town (less than a hundred people in our town); [pers.] When they tore down our bridge and replaced it with a new one. I wrote An Ode To The Byrneville Bridge and it was printed in our Local Newspaper.; [a.] Georgetown, IN

SNETHEN, DAWNA
[b.] March 1, 1979, Winner, SD; [p.] Lyle and Karen Snethen; [ed.] Junior in High School; [occ.] Student; [memb.] Yearbook and Spanish Club; [hon.] B Honor Roll, attended 1994 Prairie winds writer's, got Conference, got an award my 8th grade year from Young Author's Extravaganza; [oth. writ.] I've wrote some short stories and poems. I've also one poem published in the school newspaper and another one in the district newspaper.; [pers.] I usually try to address possible problems that people can or do encounter in life as well as possible solution in my writing. I have been greatly influenced by my friends and family.; [a.] Carter, SD

SNYDER, CYNTHIA L.
[b.] May 3, 1959, Lewisburg, PA; [p.] Jacob R. and Vivian M. Snyder; [ed.] Lewisburg Area High School, Harrisburg Area Community College, Susquehanna University; [occ.] Financial Technician for State-wide Foster care organization; [oth. writ.] Numerous published features and articles about forster care for newspapers throughout Pennsylvania, poem published in a Native American magazine: *Positive Notes* (12/95 issue); [pers.] "The Emotion conveyed in a poem is as important as the words used to write it".; [a.] Lewisburg, PA

SNYDER JR., EMMETT A.
[b.] December 15, 1915, Monrou City, IN; [p.] Alfred and Mande Snyder; [m.] Helen E. (Green) (Snyder), September 21, 1935; [ch.] Dolores, Emmett, Alan Mehen; [ed.] Attended Vincent Univ.; [memb.] Christian Church, Maronry, Scottish Rite

SNYDER, MARK T.
[pen.] Mark T. Snyder; [b.] March 18, 1971, Gloversville, NY; [p.] Frederic Snyder, Gloria Snyder; [ed.] Gloversville High School, Fulton - Montgomery Community College; [occ.] Meat/Seafood Clerk, Price Chopper, The Golub Corporation; [oth. writ.] None publicly published, but I do have a complication of other personal writings to be published.; [pers.] Where some artists captive life in paints and canvas, I use words and paper. If a picture is worth a thousand words, then let me paint an essay.; [a.] Gloversville, NY

SNYDER, MILDRED REX
[pen.] Mildred Rex-Snyder; [b.] March 28, 1912, Syracuse, TN; [p.] Walter and Jessie Warble Rex; [m.] Richard E. Snyder (Deceased), January 1, 1933; [ch.] Richard Rex and Mary Gail Ridenour; [ed.] Salutatorian of 8th Grade graduating classes of Noble Co. In., Salutatorian and class president of high school graduating class of Avilla IN. High School, graduate of International Business College; [occ.] Retired; [memb.] Poet of Merit for 1995, Rec'd. an Editor's Choice Award 1995; [hon.] Poem published in 1995 anthology "Beyond The Stars"; [oth. writ.] Mother was a pianist, organist and poetess, a cousin is an artist and I am a pianist and organist and entertain residents in a nursing home; [pers.] Fort Wayne, IN

SNYDER, SAM STUART
[b.] October 18, 1940, Los Angeles, CA; [p.] Lawrence Snyder, Goldina Snyder; [ed.] BA, MA, MPH, PE, Ph.D. LLB; [occ.] Psychologist/Consultant; [memb.] Fellow and diplomate Coordinate American Academy of Medical Administrators L.A. Co. Sheriff's Dept Reserves, American Psychological Society, National Society of Professional Engineers; [hon.] PSL, CHI Nat. Psych. Honor Society, Performance Award Veterans Administration, Honorarium-American Medical Association, Performance Award U.S. Selective Service, Sheriff's Relief Award; [oth. writ.] Malpractice An Overview, The Ring Of The Devil, Change, Spousal Abuse, Holiday Bluer, Suicide In Prison's And Jails, 12 Steps To A Successful Marriage; [pers.] A one eyed man is king in the land of the blind; [a.] Playa Del Rey, CA

SODERSTROM, STANCI JAN
[pen.] Stanci Cloud; [b.] October 6, 1972, Springfield, MO; [p.] Deidre and Larry Cloud; [m.] Eric Soderstrom, December 9, 1995; [ed.] BA in English from Central Missouri State Univ., BA in Theatre from CMSU; [occ.] Teacher; [hon.] Dean's List 4 years, Phi Kappa Phi Honor Society; [oth. writ.] None published; [pers.] Forgive; [a.] Springfield, MO

SOLLOWAY, M. ELISE
[b.] November 25, 1956, Dallas, TX; [p.] Ray O. Blakley and Wanda L. Blakley; [m.] Robert S. Solloway, May 28, 1977; [ch.] Jon Solloway; [ed.] B.S. Elementary Education from the University of Oklahoma - 1979 Master of Liberal Studies - Univ. of Oklahoma 1992; [occ.] Elementary teacher at Washington Elementary School 4th grade; [memb.] Professional Educators of Norman, National Education Association, Learning Disabilities Association, Council for Exceptional Children; [hon.] McKinley Elementary School's Teacher -of-the-Year: 1991 Who's Who in American Education: 1994; [oth. writ.] Poetry and story in an anthology by the Oklahoma Writing Project, a poem in Reflections, quarterly, a poem in *Between The Raindrops* and on cassette, a poem in *Best Poems of 1996*, poetry in an anthology from a graduate writing course with the University of Oklahoma.; [pers.] My success with poetry is due to Dr. Michael Angelotti from the University of Oklahoma, who helped me overcome my fear of poetry and my blank-page syndrome related to poetry.; [a.] Norman, OK

SOLOZABAL, EDUARDO M.
[pen.] Ed Solo; [b.] November 24, 1970, West Palm Beach, FL; [ed.] University of Florida, B.s. Engineering (aerospace); [occ.] Self-employed; [memb.] Florida National Alumni Association; [oth. writ.] Unused "Seinfeld" script.; [pers.] "We are the music makers and we are the dreamers of the dreams" - Willy Wonka. Opportunities are few, true friendships are even less, but most importantly, throughout this vast universe, there is only one of You. Find yourself and you will discover the meaning of life.; [a.] Jupiter, FL

SOREL, MRS. GERMAINE J.
[b.] November 2, 1927, Saint Marc, Haiti; [p.] Aline and Stephen Joubert; [m.] Fernand Sorel, July 17, 1954; [ch.] Donald, Marie-Michele, Patrick; [ed.] Graduated at Elie Dubois College, Port-au-Prince Haiti, as Teacher; [occ.] Writer and Community Service Worker - Poet (no publication in America yet); [oth. writ.] I recently publish a book: Paquito of Haiti Vantage Press in New York City. Another book on the way. "Long Live the Cardinal" not published yet; [pers.] I thank you for entering my poem into the competition.; [a.] Central Nyack, NY

SOTTILE, KATHLEEN C.
[b.] May 25, 1941, Charleston, SC; [p.] Mary C. and Henry C. Calder; [m.] Albert J. Sottile Jr. (Deceased); [ch.] Albert J. Sottile III; [ed.] Registered Nurse since September 1967; [occ.] Out reach Coordinator Pediatric Cardiology Musc.; [memb.] Pediatric Nurse Assoc.; [hon.] 20 Years Nurse in Division of Pediatric Cardiology Musc.; [pers.] This poem dedicated to honor Mr. William Doren cousin, friend, mentor.; [a.] Charleston, SC

SOULAGES, WALTER R.
[b.] October 12, 1940, Prescott, AZ; [p.] Hugh and Beulah Soulages; [m.] Cardith Soulages, March 10, 1984; [ch.] Kelley, Kimberly, Scott, Brett; [ed.] Prescott Public Schools, University of Arizona - BS Pharmacy, AZ State Board of Pharmacy - Dr. of Pharmacy; [occ.] Pharmacist; [memb.] AZ Pharmacy Assoc, American Pharmacy Assoc.; [hon.] Retail Pharmacist of Year for Owen Health Care - 1992; [oth. writ.] Monthly columns in newsletters and weekly column in newspaper; [a.] Bisbee, AZ

SOUSA, TONY
[pen.] Yankee; [b.] May 30, 1982, Providence RI; [p.] Maria Sousa, Antonio P. Sousa; [ed.] N.B. Borden Elementary School Kuss Middle School B.M.C Durfee High School of Fall River (freshmen); [occ.] Student at B.M.C. Durfee High School of fall river; [pers.] I enjoy playing and listen to the viola. I admire the poet Robert Frost for his attitudes in life.; [a.] Fall River, MA

SOWELL, DIANNA
[b.] January 23, 1963, Berkeley, CA; [p.] Ida Whitten; [ed.] Master of Arts in Organizational Management at the University of Phoenix; [occ.] Execute Assistant at major financial institution; [pers.] With much love, I dedicate "Sliver of Time" to the man that inspired the poem and inspired me to tap into my creative side.; [a.] Alameda, CA

SPAHR, JULIE CHRISTINE
[b.] December 10, 1977, Maryland; [p.] Michael and Deborah Spahr; [ed.] Present High School Student; [occ.] Fast Food; [hon.] The Imagination Machine; [pers.] This poem called "Will You Be There" was written in dedication to my beautiful and loving fiancee Johnny Ivan Chorak. I love you! Yes was the answer to the poem.; [a.] Fort Collins, CO

SPAWN, STACY LENA
[b.] March 18, 1979, Albany, New York; [p.] Thomas and Patricia Spawn; [ed.] Guilderland Central High School; [occ.] Junior at Guilderland Central High School; [memb.] National Honor Society, Secretary of Class, Key Club, AIDS Awareness Club, SADD, Choir, Mentor, backstage and costuming for the High School musical; [hon.] Academic Achievement Award (Freshman and sophomore year) for 2nd highest average in class, honor awards for all academic classes; [oth. writ.] Published a short story "All I need is Love" in a literary anthology titled Happiness: Little Joys of Life (a creative with words publication). Was a 3rd place 10th grade winner in the 1994 National Art of caring Essay contest for my short story "One of them." Published a poem titled "Thy Love" in the worldwide anthology Walk Through Paradise (The National Library Publication.); [pers.] My writing reflects the beauty of nature and the love God had given the world to enjoy and live happily. I write stories and poems that deliver a message about the goodness of life and improve the way the reader thinks about life.; [a.] Albany, NY

SPEAR, LILA M.
[b.] September 20, 1935, Wausau, WI; [p.] Herbert W. Pyan, Rosella Rogge Pyan; [m.] Joseph W. Spear, September 23, 1960; [ch.] Gary Schwarck, Lonnie Creed Christine Steptoe; [ed.] High School, Life Experiences; [occ.] Rural Housewife; [memb.] "Pet clean-up and feed society"; [hon.] None, (But the animals think I'm great); [oth. writ.] None published; [pers.] Sometimes the words just come flowing - can be anything from thoughtful, serious, to cute, witty or romantic. I prefer happy endings.; [a.] Maud, TX

SPELLS, PAULA RAE-KING
[b.] October 19, 1939, New York City, NY; [p.] Josephine B. King, James B. King; [m.] Henry Lee Spells, January 9, 1960; [ch.] Derek Joseph, Tracy Lysette, Le Rae Michelle, Jonathan Bramwell; [ed.] Morris High School - New York; [occ.] Disabled - unable to work; [oth. writ.] Article for anthology on Fibromyalgia; [pers.] Although being disabled has deprived me of my former lifestyle, I feel God has given me this time and opportunity to discover the enjoyment or writing and the sense of fulfillment it can offer.; [a.] Crowley, TX

SPENCER, JANICE CAROL
[b.] December 6, 1967, Marks, MS; [p.] James Spencer, Florence Spencer; [m.] Fiancee Ralph Jameson; [ed.] Sam Rayburn High; [occ.] Restaurant Manager; [pers.] I express myself through my poems. And to also have a part of me share with my children, and grandchildren. Someday when I'm no longer here on earth.; [a.] Pasadena, TX

SPENCER, LORI L.
[pen.] Lori L. Spencer; [b.] January 20, 1960, Blue Island, IN; [p.] Mary C. Spencer; [ed.] DePaul University - Chicago Liberal Arts Bachelor with an emphasis in creative expression and writing Rhetoric; [occ.] I am seeking employment in a creative arena where I can utilize my communication and strong interpersonal skills.; [hon.] Nominated for the Arthur Weinberg award and the award of excellence at DePaul University for a book I wrote on El Salvador titled "Received Wisdom."; [oth. writ.] Sierra Club Travel Piece; [pers.] I strive to produce work with a social consciousness. I believe to only takes one person to facilitate change. It is my goal, through my writings, to help and contribute to those less fortunate than myself.; [a.] Alsip, IL

SPETA, VIOLET
[pen.] Violet Speta; [b.] February 15, 1953, Grand Forks, British Columbia, Canada; [p.] Pete and Elizabeth Smith; [m.] Kurt, October 3, 1970; [ch.] Dustin (23), Katrina (14), Billy (13); [ed.] V.B.C. - Real Estate, Kooteney Regional - Nursing; [occ.] Housewife; [pers] I'm honored to share my thought with you.

SPINELLI, RONALD GERARD
[pen.] Ronald Gerard; [b.] December 30, 193.. Bronx, NY; [p.] Louis, Carmella Spinelli; [m.. Carmella, July 30, 1955; [ch.] 3 Boys, 3 Girls and Grandchildren; [ed.] Bayside High, Queens, N.Y [occ.] Retired; [memb.] A.A.R.P. in active Nassa Country Police Boys Club Past President-V-Pres dent Secretary Elmont. Unit.; [oth. writ.] Hav been writing songs, and poems, since I was 12 yea old. I have just completed a outline for a book, tha I have been working on for 12 years.; [pers.] I a a very romantic man, holding onto every goo thing, that has happened to me, as a boy, and as man. I also in my writings, try to reflect the lov between men and women and the importance of lov in families!; [a.] Bay Shore, NY

SPOONMORE, TOBRA
[b.] February 11, 1979, Pittsfield, IL; [p.] James an Shirley Spoonmore; [ed.] Current Student (junior) a Pittsfield High School; [occ.] Teen columnist fo local weekly newspaper; [memb.] Pittsfield Hig School Drama Club, Yearbook Journalism Staf KIDS F.A.C.E.; [hon.] High Honor Roll Studen (5.143 GPA), Who's who Among American Hig School Students, Washington Journalism confer ence nominee, 1995 Writing Talent Search, Joh Wood Youth Conference; [oth. writ.] "Tall Tale and Milk Pails" (narrative), "Tobra's Teen Rou tine" (weekly column for local newspaper, Pike Press), various articles for Pike Press.; [pers.] " hope that everyone can learn to live peacefully and appreciate nature. Use your imagination to creat a wonderful world, then express it in your words Become inspired by all the beauty of people and nature on this earth. Love one another, Peace."; [a.] Pittsfield, IL

SPRINGER, JO RHONDA
[b.] November 28, 1970, Cedar Falls, IA; [p.] Ronald Springer, Donna Springer; [ed.] Horizon High School, Scottsdale, AZ and Arizona State University (B.S. Economics); [occ.] Computers; [memb.] Ntl. Honor Society, Sociedad Honoraria Hispanica, ASU Alumni Assoc. Youth for Understanding Intnl. Exchange; [oth. writ.] Several poems in local literary magazines; [pers.] One bubble of happiness is worth a lifetime chewing gum.. Never stop pursuing your dreams; [a.] Scottsdale, AZ

SPRINGER, LUCY A.
[b.] October 12, 1947, McKenzie, Guyana; [ed.] Studies concentrated in Nursing, 1967-68 Columbia Union College Takoma Park, MD, Medical Technical Secretary, Diploma 1969, Washington Business School, Washington, DC, LPN, 1979 - Diploma 1980, M. M. Washington School of Nursing, Washington, DC.; [occ.] Certified American Red Cross First Aid Instructor, Presently working on RN Degree.; [hon.] Dean's List, M. M. Washington School of Nursing Selected on basis of scholastic achievement as delegate to the National Conference of LPN's Phoenix, AZ.; [a.] Richmond, VA

SROK, LISA
[b.] June 11, 1984, Chattanooga, TN; [p.] Ed and Dawn Srok; [ed.] Presently a 6th grade student, straight A's since beginning school; [occ.] Presently a 6th grade student; [memb.] Student Council, Chorus, Girl scouts, Yearbook Staff, Track, Ski Club, Art Club, Participant in John Hopkins University's Center for Talented Youths; [hon.] 1994-95 Presidential Award for Academic Excellence, D.A.R.E. Graduation Certificate, Won 100 Yard and 440 yard relay in track; [oth. writ.] None published; [pers.] Live by the Golden Rule — do unto others as you would have them do unto you.; [a.] Ballston Lake, NY

[S]TACEY, KIM
[b.] February 15, 1966, Eldorado, IL; [p.] Don and [Jea]n Richardson; [m.] Paul Stacey, September 7, [19]90; [ch.] Matthew David and Christopher Wayne; [ed.] Ridgway High and Norris City- Omaha High; [oers.] I've always loved poetry, and I've been [w]riting religious poems for a year and a half in the [ho]pes that one day they will be published so that [m]aybe some people somewhere will read them and [re]alize there is a God out there for them.; [a.] [Sh]awneetown, IL

STAMPS, JAMIE
[pen.] Cody Kane; [b.] September 6, 1978, Littlefield, [T]X; [p.] Jo Ann Stamps, Leonard Stamps; [ed.] [O]lton High School; [occ.] Playing Guitar; [memb.] [O]lton Country Club; [hon.] English Award; [oth. [w]rit.] Have written many other poems and short [st]ories; [pers.] I write about society and death. I [ex]press the life I have in my poems.; [a.] Olton, TX

STANGER, EDITH M.
[b.] June 4, 1925, Rigby, ID; [p.] George E. Marler [an]d Edith Elliott Marler; [m.] Richard F. Stanger [(Deceased), 1943; [ch.] Michael R., E. Bruce and [K]imberly; [ed.] Graduate - Wasatch Academy, At[te]nded University of Idaho, Graduate - Idaho State [U]niversity, BA Degree in Secondary Education; [occ.] Coordinator-Agriculture Curr of Eastern Ida[h]o Tech College - a contact position - I am supposed [t]o be retired. Secretary — Idaho Falls Presbyterian [C]hurch Executive Secretary United Way, Substitute [T]eacher Idaho Falls District #981, Teacher Shelley [J]unior High 1989/1990; [memb.] Currently Mem[b]er of: Idaho Horse Council (Past President), Idaho [H]orse Board (Past Chairperson), Utah Power and [L]ight Advisory Committee, Idaho Chairperson - [W]asatch Academy 2000 Capital Campaign, Idaho [C]ommissioner - AMERICORPS, Idaho Cattle Asso[c]iation, Salvation Army Advisory Board, Inter[m]ountain Appaloosa Horse Club; [hon.] Who's [W]ho of American Women, Zonta's Yellow Rose [f]or Women of Distinction, Bonneville County - [F]riend of 4H Annual Award, Eagle Rock Chapter - [B]ack country Horsemen Appreciation Award, Life[t]ime Membership Award: Intermountain Appal[o]osa Horse Club, National Appaloosa Horse Club, [D]istinguished Alumni Award 1995 - Wasatch Acad[e]my, Mt. Pleasant, UT for outstanding accomplish[m]ents in Business, Leadership in Community and [C]ivic Affairs; [oth. writ.] Have been involved in the cowboy poetry "Movement", wrote unpub. - in school - have not had time but, now starting book - sketches about life on our ranch - The Double Arrow and one on History of the Appaloosa Horse Club; [pers.] One does what one must! I guess that is why I have started writing again; [a.] Idaho Falls, ID

STANLEY, NIKKI
[pen.] Nicolette O. Stanley; [b.] September 24, 1962, Manhattan, NY; [p.] Mary and Frank Stanley; [ch.] Peter; [ed.] Catholic School in N.Y.C. Manhattan; [occ.] Designer/Tower Records Record Store, Clerical Supervisor/Buyer; [memb.] I am 10th out of 11 children; [hon.] Spelling B/3 Buddist Awards Certificates; [oth. writ.] Yes, Prince of Peace; [pers.] I am a Buddist, were unknown Artists. My son Peter is my inspiration.; [a.] New York City, NY

STARK, HANNA
[b.] September 5, 1937, Viena Austria; [p.] Friedrich and Yolana Mar Kstein; [m.] Morris Stark, February 16, 1964; [ch.] Debbie and Harvey Stark; [ed.] Institute Americano Bolivia Graduated High School 1955, one year College Santiago de Chile, Secretarial School; [occ.] Receptionist - Billing Drs. Aid Medical Center.; [memb.] Channel 13 Jewish Center of Jackson Heights. A.A.R.P.; [hon.] Many School Awards (H.S) in writing - General Studies.; [oth. writ.] Multiple short stories. Poetry German poems. Spanish Essays.; [pers.] My life has been very rich in different experiences of life and economic changes I was deeply touched by changes of countries I lived in and life and death which gave me the urge to write it down.; [a.] Queen, NY

STARKEY, MARGARET L.
[pen.] Margaret L. Starkey; [b.] May 6, 1912, Mogadore, OH; [p.] Ann and Sam White; [m.] Lorin D. Starkey, July 29, 1939; [ed.] Graduated in Education at Kent State U., Kent, Ohio; [occ.] Taught first grade for 31 years in Tallmadge and Robertsville, Oh. Retired School Teacher; [memb.] Social and Educational clubs in Tallmadge A.A.R.P., Member of First Congregational Club in Tallmadge.; [hon.] 25 years volunteering in Sunshine Club. Making articles for invalids, children and Senior Citizen's Homes; [oth. writ.] My first attempt except for writing little jingles to make it fun for the children to learn to read.; [pers.] I love children and the Lord. Hope to have a moral in my poems. Have written fifty poems this year since writing "My Destiny". This is how I spend my time; [a.] Tallmadge, OH

STATA, EVELYN
[pen.] Ev Stata; [b.] April 3, 1923, Haliburton, Ontario, Canada; [p.] Thomas and Clara Scott; [m.] Wesley Stata, April 5, 1941; [ch.] Richard and Sharon; [ed.] Grade 10 high school; [occ.] Housewife; [memb.] Sr. Citizens Club, Home Support Services, United Church; [oth. writ.] Numerous poems published in local newspaper. Some Humorous.; [pers.] Like to give people a chuckle.

STEELE, JUSTIN DENNIS
[b.] January 28, 1979, Royal Oak, MI; [oth. writ.] Several poems and pieces of prose published locally and self-published.; [pers.] I write about people and emotions. My own experiences in life influence my writing more than anything else. I have, I believe, an important message - trust in mankind...; [a.] Scottsdale, AZ

STEFFEY, TERRY L.
[b.] November 18, 1945, Omaha, NE; [p.] Merril and Ruby Steffey; [m.] Single; [ch.] Brent and Shawna; [occ.] Director of Support Operations; [pers.] Poetry observes the inter-reaction with humanity, nature, and one's belief. Through poetry one can discover understanding, truth, and deep hidden emotions that will not only enlighten, but allow growth for each individual.; [a.] Scottsdale, AZ

STEIGERWALT, DEBRA
[b.] February 7, 1955, Pomona, CA; [p.] Joe and Ruth Ruiz; [ch.] Andrea, Michelle, Steve, Jason; [occ.] Disabled; [pers.] My poems reflect mostly on the changing times, from my childhood to the world our children live in now.; [a.] Spanaway, WA

STEINMAN, DIANA LOUISE
[b.] May 3, 1972, Phoenix, AZ; [p.] Donald and Darlieh Steinman; [occ.] Certified Optician currently Patient Care Manager for a National Retail Chain; [memb.] AZ Chapter President of FBLA (Future Business Leaders of America) APICS Member; [hon.] Student Ambassador, 1990 Soviet Union, People to People Org., world of Poetry 4th place winner; [pers.] I have been greatly influenced by my family special thanks to Jason Waldenburg; [a.] Springfield, OR

STENHOUSE, MARY LIVINGSTON
[b.] January 9, 1935, Dryden, VA; [p.] Ruth Ward Livingston and Theodore R. Livingston; [m.] Divorced; [ch.] Mark David Stenhouse, Dana Leigh Stenhouse, Erin Dawn Stenhouse, Brett Loch Stenhouse; [ed.] B.S. in Business Education, Radford College (Now Radford University) Dryden High School; [occ.] Medical Secretary, Vienna, VA, Previously taught in both public and private schools for 18 years in Department of Business; [memb.] Vienna Seventh Day Adventist Church, AARP, Kappa Delta Pi (during college years - Previously belonged to Countryside Garden Club (now defunct) and many organizations during high school and college; [hon.] Kappa Delta Pi, Dean's List, Who's Who Among Colleges and Universities, Assistant Business Manager and Business Manager of college yearbook, The Beehive, Church Board and other offices in church, and School Board for Vienna Junior Academy, Treasurer of F.B.L.A.; [oth. writ.] Published in literary journal during college, presented readings of my poems for many social events and during worship services (including farewells, weddings, baby births, welcomes, etc., etc.) personal greeting cards - was featured in a special Christmas cards published by my local church; [pers.] People, plants, and poems are included among my passions. A natural curiosity propels me to try new endeavors. Life is good!; [a.] Fairfax, VA

STEPHENS, MARK
[b.] February 18, 1959, Austin, TX; [ch.] Shawn 12 and Amanda 10; [ed.] AA in Science; [occ.] Research Scientist, II Heart Valves and Vascular conduits; [hon.] Montgomery College honor roll; [pers.] Life is too short not to have fun.

STEVENS, ELIZABETH K.
[b.] February 11, 1931, Stamford, CT; [p.] Alfhild and James Torrey Kirkpatrick; [m.] Divorced; [ch.] Linda Friend Spencer, Peter Borden Friend, Susan Torrey Friend; [ed.] Cazenovia Jr. College '50, Southern Ct. State University '65; [occ.] Retired; [memb.] National League of American Pen Women as Artist, New Haven and Country Club, Milford Ct. Yacht Club, Wilderness (Naples FL) Country Club Port Royal Club Garden Club Woodbridge Ct, (DAR Free Love Baldwin); [hon.] Blue and Red, Ribbons for Flower Arrangements, entered juried shows and accepted some awards for watercolors; [oth. writ.] Many many journals of travels and poetry - won published never tried before; [pers.] To mommy 65th birthday. You will be wise when you realize that you are only a part of the debris by the sea; [a.] Naples, FL

STEVENS, MARK LAWRENCE
[pen.] Larry Stevens; [b.] New York City; [ed.] M.S. E.C.E. (Dean's Award - 4.- G.P.A), Baruch College, N.Y.C., B.A. Soc. Sci/Psych Hofstra Univ; [oth. writ.] Poems and Essays volumes I, II, II, IV, McFuudles Hotel (Children's Story), Leap of Faith (Original music, Lyrics, vocals and piano).; [pers.] The search for truth, both internal and external, is the driving force in my life. Finding harmony love, and fulfillment is the means. Poetry is one of the vehicles.; [a.] New York, NY

STEWART, RUTH
[ed.] Bachelor of Arts, Major in Foreign Languages, Univ. of Toronto and Feagin School of Drama, New York, Art Students League, New York.; [occ.] Actress (Gail Stewart) Portrait Artist.; [memb.] Beaux Arts Society, New York, Actors Equity Ass'n, Screen Actors Guild, Aftra.; [pers.] Speak several languages, sing in seven languages, have traveled extensively throughout Australia, Japan, Europe, United States and Canada.; [a.] New York, NY

STOCKMAN JR., LEE
[pen.] Joker, Renegade Prep.; [b.] August 28, 1965, Mobile, AL; [p.] Samuel L. and Norman P. Stockman; [ch.] Possible Son - (Has not been born yet); [ed.] W.P. Davidson High School Mobile College, A.R.E.I - (Real Estate); [occ.] Personal Security/ Body Guard Collection Officer/Security; [memb.] Mobile county Board of Realtors D.W.V.M.C. Gym

Committee, Basketball coach (Junior High); [hon.] Best Marching Band Mediallen (1993) (High School) Best sales person (Junior Achievement), V.I.P. (Sales) (Junior Achievement); [pers.] I believe in being on Individualist while still living or at least trying to live by society's rules. I believe you shouldn't judge other people at first sight and I strive to up hold that standard.; [a.] Mobile, AL

STOKESBERRY, MEGAN
[b.] December 4, 1984, Los Angeles, CA; [p.] Barbara and Ken Stokesberry; [ed.] 5th Grade de Portola Elementary School Mission Viego, CA; [occ.] Student; [memb.] Girl Scout; [hon.] PTA Reflections Contest - 1995 Principal's awards - academic wizard, outstanding achievement; [oth. writ.] It's alive - wow - (Story) "Rain" (Poem) "Ocean" (Poem) "Spring" (Poem); [pers.] I really love writing! It lets me express my thoughts and feelings. My mind can wander as freely and wildly as I want it to; [a.] Mission Viejo, CA

STONE, CHARLES E.
[pen.] C. Stone; [b.] September 20, 1934, Whitesville, WV; [p.] George and Myrtle Stone; [m.] Dorothy (Deceased), January 18, 1958; [ch.] 3; [ed.] Graduated - High School, Several Courses in Military and Union Carbide Corp.; [occ.] Retired but still writes; [memb.] West Virginia Writers, West Virginia Poetry Society; [hon.] Honorable mention for a poem entitled - "An Angel Who Couldn't Show Love." in West Virginia Writers Competition.; [oth. writ.] Working on third collection of poetry. 122 page Novelette entitled "The Flowers of Twilight."; [pers.] Besides salvation and eternal life, love is God's greatest gift to mankind.; [a.] Bloomingrose, WV

STONE, FIORA
[pen.] Fiora Stone; [b.] March 18, 1923, Detroit, MI; [p.] Edmund and Clementina Bastiani; [m.] Joseph (Deceased), October 7, 1966; [ed.] Valley State and UCLA; [occ.] Retired; [oth. writ.] Short book of poems for my own pleasure...This was one of those: "Remembering..."; [pers.] A quotation from Browning exemplified my philosophy of life: "Man's reach should exceed his grasp, else what's a Heaven for"...I was "Grown Up" when I read it for the first time and I realized then, that even as a child I was ever reaching for the brass ring; [a.] Los Angeles, CA

STOUGHTON, JASON P.
[pen.] Jack; [b.] October 18, 1921, Port Huron, MI; [p.] Sandra L. Stoughton, Jack Burningtrec; [ed.] Biloxi High, Jefferson Davis College; [occ.] College Student; [hon.] Honor Roll, Principal's List Elementary School, Drawing Contest Eight Grade Spanish Class, Nothing Important; [oth. writ.] My poetry is reflected through experiences I have had up to now through my life and will continue to write.; [a.] Biloxi, MS

STRATMAN, CAROL J.
[b.] March 1, 1971, Yankton, SD; [p.] Theresa Stratman; [ed.] Wynot High School, Mount Marty College; [occ.] Writer, Design Basics Inc., Omaha, NE; [hon.] Dean's List scholar, Who's Who among American College Students, College Volleyball Player, Captain Volleyball Team, Mass Communication Scholarship, Best sports reporting, Missouri Valley Observer, 1992 2nd Place; [oth. writ.] Published in *National Business Employment Weekly* - subsidiary of *Wall Street Journal*, wrote for several award-winning direct-mail publications.; [pers.] Each word of my existence is meant to draw me and you closer to the meaning of life. To me, poetry is the most beautiful expression of this daily adventure.; [a.] Omaha, NE

STRAUB, MACKENZIE MATTSON
[b.] December 20, 1976, Renton, WA; [p.] Daniel and Carleen Straub; [ed.] Graduate of South Whidbey High School, Currently attending college to be a Physical Therapist; [hon.] "Athlete of the year for Track 1995" State competition awards in track; [oth. writ.] I have written many poems, but not to be published or for contests, just for myself. This is my first contest and publication; [pers.] I write my poems to express my feelings on ideas. I hope that people will then be able to relate them to me.; [a.] Freeland, WA

STRID, BURTON
[b.] June 14, 1955, CT; [ed.] W.S.T.C., W.C.S.V., R.V., (undergraduate).; [occ.] Shipboard Marine Mechanic, Virginia.; [hon.] Quality Control Award (Trades) '73, High Honors List '72, '73; [pers.] There can be no substitute for life expresses when one expresses himself (herself) in writing.; [a.] VA

STRONG, ANTHONY P.
[b.] August 4, 1975, Thief River Falls, MN; [p.] Paul Strong, Marlo Strong; [ed.] Apple Valley High, Inver Hills College; [occ.] Credit Card Production; [oth. writ.] Wrote for School Newspaper; [pers.] I hope to take people to new places through word.; [a.] Eagan, MN

STRONG, DARRELL
[b.] October 22, 1970, Saint Louis, MO; [p.] Joyce Knox; [ch.] Devin Romello Strong; [ed.] High School graduate, Jennings High School; [occ.] U.S. Soldier; [pers.] In my art, I wish to let the human race know that life is worth living and we are the only thinking that'll make a difference... Be it bad or good!; [a.] Fort Bragg, NC

STRONG, JOHNNY
[pen.] Johnny; [b.] July 3, 1973, Denver, CO; [p.] Micheal and Janis Strong; [ch.] Sebastian - 6 yrs; [ed.] Graduated with honors McClain Community High School; [occ.] Warren Fluid Power; [memb.] Volkswagon Enthusiasts of Colorado Warrior Dojo Kickboxing Club; [hon.] Valedictorian, graduation class of 1993. Awarded personal development by the Optimist Club of Denver. Male of the Year 1993. Outstanding Psychology 1993.; [oth. writ.] Love Is For The Living, I Do Believe; [pers.] Love is...was inspired by the reality that surrounds us till we part from one another to live forever.; [a.] Golden, CO

STROTHER, JEANNETTE L.
[b.] July 23, 1950, Wheeling, WV; [p.] Wayne West, Vivian/Nettie West; [m.] John E. Strother, June 25, 1988; [ch.] Timothy, Felicia, Carmen, John Jr.; [ed.] Smithfield High School (Ohio), Bellaire Sch. Practical Nursing (Ohio) attending Wheeling Jesuit College, Student, Long Ridge Writers Group; [occ.] Retired L.P.N., Homemaker; [memb.] VFW (Aux) American Legion (Aux), DAV (Aux), St. Jude Catholic Church Lector, Mansfield Senior Citizens; [hon.] American Legion Certificate of Merit, American Cancer Society Certificate of Merit, Tarrant County Senior Citizens Poetry Contest (1st Place); [oth. writ.] Prize winning poem printed local newspaper, poetry published in Senior Citizens Monthly; [pers.] I enjoyed being raised by my Grandmother. She taught me not only the basics and the essentials but gave me a lasting love for the language arts.; [a.] Mansfield, TX

STUART, LAURA
[pen.] Laura Stuart; [b.] May 1, 1982, Richards, VA; [p.] Deborah Stuart; [ed.] 8th grade level, Junior High, Cardinal Newman School; [occ.] Student; [memb.] Girl scouts of America, Northeast Columbia Soccer Assoc.; [hon.] Principals Honor roll, National English, Merit Award; [oth. writ.] Poems and stories published in school newspapers.; [pers.] All I write is about what I feel, I love, and what inside of me, in my heart.; [a.] Columbia, SC

STURGES, SHERRY
[b.] September 3, 1959, Milwaukee, WS; [m.] Andrew Sturges, April 4, 1984; [ch.] Micah Andrew Caleb Samuel; [ed.] Concordia College Milwaukee; [occ.] Inner City Missionary, Jesus People USA Covenant Church; [memb.] Concerned Crafts Fa Trade Federation, Jesus People US ECC; [oth. writ.] Poetry chap books available concerned crafts; [pers.] I seek to know God more intimately, to see his love mercy and grace found within our daily human experience. And above all, to love him more.; [a.] Chicago, IL

SULLIVAN, DONNA
[b.] June 21, 1955, Wilkes-Barre, PA; [p.] Dolore and William Richards; [m.] Terry J. Sullivan, Jun 2, 1990; [ed.] South Suburban College; [occ.] Working towards Associates Degree in Science; [hon. 1993, 1994 Dean's List of Scholars SSC; [oth. writ.] Several poems written. This is my first publishe poem.; [pers.] I write based upon my emotional encounters with life, I enjoy nature and like to include it in some of my writings.; [a.] Lansing, I

SULLIVAN, TIMOTHY PATRICK
[pen.] T. Patrick Sullivan; [b.] May 31, 1972, White Plains, NY; [p.] Michael, Patricia; [ed.] White Plains High School, Boston College; [occ.] Show room Manager, Rugs by Robinson, Atlanta GA [hon.] Dean's List; [oth. writ.] A couple of poem published in local newspapers; [pers.] What a day i must have been for e.e. cummings when people ceased telling him he spelled his name incorrectly Good - Bad - who knows? Just a heck of a day.; [a. Atlanta, GA

SULLMAN, WANDA DEE
[b.] June 24, 1964, South County Hospital; [p. Beverly Mae Matteson; [m.] Michael Sullman, August 25, 1982; [occ.] Housewife; [oth. writ.] I have a lot of time on my hands, so if I am not writing poems I do oil paintings, portrait, landscapes. And I am a true animal lover. I would like to have this poem dedicated to my friend who past away, Leo La Port. He loved this poem I wrote; [pers.] I have been writing poems for years, in my personal diary. It is good way to express my feelings. I can express my feelings much more clearly in poetry than any other way.; [a.] North Kingstown, RI

SUNDIN, MARVEL K.
[b.] September 19, 1921, Decator, MI; [p.] Ransom D. and Florence R. Kinney; [m.] Robert H. Sundin DDS MA, June 20, 1943; [ch.] Robert K., James H., Jon R.; [ed.] Ph.D Counseling Psychologist; [occ.] Retired; [oth. writ.] Original Christmas Card in Verse for many years; [pers.] Love for God - caring for others, deep family attachment. Care of physical health in both diet and exercise; [a.] Saint George, UT

SUTER, SUZANNE T.
[b.] December 24, 1973, Covina, CA; [p.] John W. Suter, Sharon T. Suter; [ed.] BA in psychology (cum laude) from Pepperdine University; [hon.] Psi Chi National Honor Society in Psychology, Golden Key National Honor Society, Pepperdine's Dean's List, National Dean's List (16th, 17th, 18th editions); [a.] Claremont, CA

SVEOM, VIOLA B.
[pen.] Viola Sveom; [b.] October 17, 1913, Genesee, WI; [p.] Clair and Leora Rice; [m.] Henry Sveom (Deceased); [ch.] Loretta, Eugene, Mary; [ed.] Finished High School I was 75 I'm glad I took the GED and the HED; [occ.] Retired; [oth. writ.] The rose

...eaks of love silently in a language known only to ...e heart. How sweet it is.; [pers.] I am a happy ...rson, I love God, my family and all of my friends. ...woke up each morning with a smile. I do all of my ...use cleaning. "I Love Life"; [a.] Brodhead, WI

...WANSON SR., DR. FREDERICK C. B.
...en.] Cool Breeze - (The Incomparable Breezeman); ...] August 16, 1952, Salem County, NJ; [p.] John ...ddison and Ruby Ella Swanson; [m.] Edna Mary ...wanson, January 14, 1993; [ch.] Frederick ...lexander Swanson; [ed.] Penns Grove Regional ...igh School, Penns Grove, NJ, American Academy ...Broadcasting, Phila, PA, Nuernburg Drug and ...lcohol College Furth, West Germany, Dcc, ...anville, VA; [occ.] Professional Self-employed ...usinessman), Business Communications - Minis-...r; [hon.] Honorary Degree of Doctor of Divinity ...om: The American Fellowship Church Carmel, ...alifornia; [oth. writ.] Have written (3) three col-...ctions of songs and poems - The Breezeman ...ometh The Best of the Breezeman - The Breezeman ...as Come (And Ready for the World); [pers.] "We ...ll have a tendency to say that we'll be right straight ...ack, we have to keep in mind that the roads we ...avel on are crooked..."; [a.] Penns Grove, NJ

WIERINGA, MARIAN ALICE
...en.] Marian Alice Swieringa; [b.] October 18, ...915, Hungry Hill Prospertown, NJ; [p.] Racelah ...nd Mary Hill Ivins; [m.] Simon Swieringa, June 18, ...938; [ch.] Paul, Rose, Dale, and Charles; [ed.] A.B. ...n Education; [occ.] Retired Elementary School ...eacher Substitute Teacher; [memb.] Orthodox ...rysbyterian Church, Westfield, New Jersey AARP, ...dison Township Retired Teachers, NJEA Retired, ...EA Member, Treasurer of Timothy Christian ...chool; [hon.] Best essay on cigarettes while in high ...chool; [oth. writ.] Doctor, My Brother, Christmas ...tar, Cigarettes

...WOPE, DONNA
...en.] Gloria H. Watkins; [b.] May 2, 1941, Balti-...more, MD; [p.] Raymond and Maude Eyler; [m.] ...onald C. Swope, November 4, 1961; [ch.] Diane ...enise and Donald Lee; [ed.] Taneytown Jr., Sr. ...igh Sch.; [occ.] Bank Teller New Windsor State ...ank, New Windsor, MD; [memb.] (1) Keysville - ...etour Homemakers Group (2) Keysville United ...hurch of Christ Keymar, MD 21757; [hon.] Grad-...ated 2nd in High School Class of 1959; [oth. writ.] 'An Evening Prayer" "Our Part In Nature" 'Love sounds, Love Scenes" "Let's Take A Walk" 'To The Mountains" "Christmas At Home"; [pers.] I believe in living each day to the fullest of ...my capacity. Having a good attitude to look for the ...good in the persons around me is one of my goals. ...My own hobbies are wildlife, music, and crocheting.; ...a.] Taneytown, MD

SYAL, HARSHI
[b.] June 19, 1950, Nairobi, Kenya; [p.] Dharam Pall and Samitra Devi Syal; [ed.] B.A. Univ. of Nairobi, Kenya, M.A. Studies - Univ. of Nairobi Dip. in Education; [occ.] Medical Administrator; [oth. writ.] Poetry in "National Library of Poetry", antholo-gies "International Poetry" in India, and in several magazines in U.S. several short plays, one full-length play "God minus - the life of Buddha"; [pers.] Ultimately, I strive for humbleness, I try to be influenced by good wherever I find it.; [a.] Northridge, CA

SYKES, DIANNE
[b.] September 11, 1965, Boston; [p.] Dolores and Ed Sykes; [ed.] University of North Carolina Bach-elors - in Business/Communications; [occ.] Medical Sales Commercials; [memb.] American Medical Association; [hon.] 1995 Most Valuable Team Player Business Award, 1993 Best Performer Award;

[oth. writ.] Salvation Heaven Life; [pers.] I am greatly influenced by the love God has for each of his children my writing comes form his hand - I hope that this goodness and love is reflected; [a.] Manhattan, CA

TAFOYA, MICHAEL ALLAN
[b.] November 24, 1961, Pueblo, CO; [p.] Ismeal and Nancy Tafoya; [ch.] Zachany, Jonell and Joshua, Tafoya; [ed.] Pueblo, South High; [occ.] Cook, Dennys Restaurant; [oth. writ.] Several poems for private enjoyment; [pers.] To the people in my life that I have loved. This poem is for you, and my father that I lost this past year. Thank you for every thing you have given to me.; [a.] Pueblo, CO

TAGUE, TIFFANY MARIE
[b.] June 15, 1979, Cincinnati, OH; [p.] Donald and Beverly Tague; [ed.] High School Junior; [occ.] Student; [oth. writ.] Poem published in local news-papers also one in Henson press 'through the sycamores'.; [pers.] Dedicated to my grandma, Ernestine Knigga.; [a.] Rising Sun, IN

TALLMAN, EVELYN
[b.] November 13, 1922, South Westeylo, NY; [p.] Mrs. Hazel F. Mabie; [m.] Deceased, January 23, 1940; [ch.] One; [ed.] Attended Greenville Central High School, National Baking School, 835 Diversey Parkway, Chicago, Illinois; [occ.] Retired and write poetry; [memb.] Social Service by Albany Country, Social Security Benefits; [hon.] Golden Poetry Gram, 701 Dixie Anne Ave Sacramento, California 85815; [oth. writ.] Food Recipes was published in the Albany Times Union.

TARLE, NAOMI
[b.] October 26, 1980, Santa Monica, CA; [p.] Marci and Norman Tarle; [ed.] Currently a sophomore at Santa Monica High School, Graduating in 1998.; [occ.] Student; [memb.] Santa Monica Chapter of California Scholarship Federation, "Delians", US Rowing Association; [hon.] 1995 Principal's Hon-or Roll; [oth. writ.] Short story "Oatmeal Cookies" published in the magazine, Young Voices.; [a.] Santa Monica, CA

TAYLOR, DONNACLAIRE
[pen.] Donnaclaire Taylor; [b.] July 7, 1932, Port-land, OR; [p.] Donald C. and Madaline C. Ringle; [m.] Bill Lewis Taylor (Deceased), March 13, 1976; [ed.] Grant High School (Portland) University of Oregon (Eugene OR) BA Music and Masters Degree in Education (U. of O.); [occ.] Retired Elementary School Teacher; [memb.] Oregon Council on Eco-nomic Education, Alpha Delta Pi; [hon.] "The Apple Award", CBS, Koin-TV Channel 6 Portland, for Exemplary Service to Students 1989, Impact II Award 1993, Impact II Award 1994, Porltland, OR, creation ideas for classroom teacher; [oth. writ.] This poem was my first effort - I penned it shortly after my husband's death (July 26, 1995).; [pers.] I am a portrait artist and enjoy playing the piano and reading poetry.

TAYLOR, KATHLEEN L.
[b.] October 26, 1950, St. Louis, MO; [p.] Paul and Mildred Spahn; [m.] J. Curtis Taylor, September 28, 1974; [ch.] Jason (19) and Bryan (17); [ed.] Com-pleted 1st year of college; [occ.] Cashier-part time; [memb.] Sacristan at St. Stephen's Catholic Church, YMCA; [pers.] I have always loved poems, ever since mother goose. I especially appreciate Dr. Seuss and others who use words to their full maxi-mum. Like good wine, words should be savored, rolled about the tongue and appreciated.; [a.] Brandon, FL

TAYLOR, P. J.
[b.] December 2, 1946, Ottawa, IL; [p.] Leonardo and Lorraine Brockman; [m.] David Taylor, MMCS-Navy, February 18, 1982; [ch.] Anthony Wayne;

[ed.] Assoc. Degree Ill. Valley Community College Oglesby, IL; [occ.] Housewife; [pers.] I write for fun most of the time I dream a writing - wake up compose - average time 10 minutes goal in life to become published and someday write a novel; [a.] El Cajon, CA

TAYLOR, TANYA
[b.] December 27, 1978, San Diego, CA; [p.] Buena and David Taylor; [ed.] Now in High School Mad-ison High School; [memb.] Varsity Softball and Fox Kids Club; [oth. writ.] Many poems that were never published.; [pers.] I've always said that the easiest emotion to describe is pain. But strange enough I'm a very happy teen.; [a.] San Diego, CA

TAYLOR, TERRY LEE
[b.] July 14, 1956, Geneva, OH; [p.] Richard and Jume Taylor; [occ.] Entrepreneur, Crystal River, Florida; [pers.] I'd like to dedicate this poem to my best friend Jim and his new wife Wendy. May your union of love forever be filled with magic I love you both. April 27, 1966.

TAYLOR, WES
[b.] October 29, 1954, Washington, DC; [m.] Debbie Murphy, September 19, 1981; [ch.] Wesley IV, Kendall; [ed.] Surrattsville HS, TESST Electronics; [occ.] Technical Co-ordinator, Nat'l. Electronics Warranty Co.; [memb.] BPOE (Elks), Volunteer work with Salvation Army; [oth. writ.] This is my first published work; [pers.] Stepped in what? Keep smiling... it makes people wonder what you're up to.; [a.] Riverdale, MD

TCHINCHINIAN, MARIA A.
[b.] January 2, 1974, Montevideo, Uruguay; [p.] Roberto and Maria Tchinchinian; [ed.] Montclair State University: Psychology/Spanish Dover High School; [occ.] Supervisor at a CVS Pharmacy Chain Store.; [hon.] "Who's Who Among High School Students", "National Honors Society"; [oth. writ.] Have written other poems but I have never attempt-ed to publish them.; [pers.] I tend to write about our society today. Through my personal experiences I have learned lessons about life and through my poems I reflect my feelings on these lessons.; [a.] Dover, NJ

TEKAVEC, ROBERT E.
[pen.] R. E. Tekavec; [b.] December 4, 1969, Uniontown, PA; [p.] Donald and Sondra Tekavec; [ed.] Pennsylvania State University, Stephen Black Acting: Pittsburgh/Lost Angeles; [occ.] Actor/Poet/Singer, New York City, NY; [hon.] Received the Presidential Academic Fitness Award as a High School Senior in 1988; [pers.] This poem is from a short collection of unpublished poetry entitled, "Cocoons in the Hemlock." All are uplifting stories of life and love emerging from the darkest hours of death.; [a.] New York City, NY

TERRY, STEVEN
[b.] March 3, 1959, New York, NY; [p.] James and Elizabeth Terry; [m.] Engaged to Tracey L. Boyd; [ch.] Elysha and Brandon; [ed.] School of Perform-ing Arts, West Virginia College of Technology, advanced Technology Institute; [occ.] Student; [oth. writ.] "The Glass Hill" unpublished Science fiction novel (unable to finance it myself).; [pers.] If mankind were perfect, God could rest.; [a.] Virginia Beach, VA

THAI, KHIEM VINH
[b.] February 25, 1944, Vietnam; [p.] Thinh V. Thai, Trang Diev Thi Vu; [m.] Cam Van Tran; [ed.] Bowling Green State University Bowling Green, OH, California State University, Fresno, CA; [occ.] Writer; [hon.] Fred Gerlach Awards, Grant-in-aids; [oth. writ.] Others poems published one awarded "Honorable Mentions" in a poetry contest - fin-

ished a book on provers of Vietnam - writing one about Nguyen Trai - A 14th century Vietnamese Hero.; [pers.] I like to write to express my personal experience and feelings as an individual who faces the complexities and challenges in this modern time.; [a.] Fountain Valley, CA

THEOPHILOS, CONSTANTINA
[b.] May 29, 1963, Buffalo, NY; [ed.] BS Pharmacy, BS Life Science; [occ.] Pharmacist; [hon.] Editor's Choice Award; [oth. writ.] Lion Hearted; [a.] Rochester, NY

THIELE, KAREN ELY
[b.] August 20, 1922, Evanston, IL; [p.] Laurence Driggs Ely, Gladyce Ely; [m.] October 4, 1940; [ch.] Karen and Christopher; [ed.] Private schools - Hathaway Brown, Girls Latin, Elgin Academy, Ashley Hall School (For Girls - thru - The Chekhov Theatre Studio - Ridgefield, Conn.; [occ.] At my "Stage and Age" sorting out boxes and Foot Lockers of Notes; [memb.] Released Organized Affiliation long ago. Now focused on growing and expanding through deeper insights in being a "Member" of the human race; [hon.] Rising Like The Phoenix, Bird Out Of Life Threatens Diseases and Receiving the "Award" of life! From Learning and Overcoming I now have something to give - what greater "Honor"!; [oth. writ.] Many new songs, books etc. From years of notes, starting new script for musical written in 50's, Hot Time For Its, Recognized Beauty - Only Rock 'N Roll then original material for showcase I produced and years of lecturing; [pers.] I believe the written and spoken word to be the greatest power on earth - they should uplift, ignite and in spite their recipients there's a hunger and need in hearts today for these words. Any word, will travel with understanding, love and purpose!; [a.] Chewelah, WA

THOMAS, DAWN MICHAL
[b.] July 31, 1961, San Mateo, CA; [p.] Bud Brewer, Dianne Livengood; [m.] Richard Allen Thomas, March 25, 1990; [ch.] Michael, Richard and Sarah; [ed.] San Jose, Leroy Andersen Elementary, H.B. Rancho View Jr. High, Fountain Valley High: English Teacher - Mr. Fayk Golden West College; [occ.] Hair Designer and Domestic Engineer; [memb.] The Body of Christ!; [hon.] Treasures in Heaven and Eternal Life; [oth. writ.] "Short Story! (nonfiction) "Spine Tingling Lessons", and various other poetry. Personal poetry for others. "Life Dreams." "Daddy, Husband and my best friend."; [pers.] Poetry flows, as I am a vessel of my God, "Jesus Christ", come to show the Depth of the human heart, in which the glory of the Lord is revealed! "My Spirit" his temple"; [a.] Garden Grove, CA

THOMAS, ELEANOR
[pen.] Eleanor Everly; [b.] May 12, 1928, Star City, Morgantown, WV; [p.] Mr. and Mrs. Boone Everly; [m.] James Thomas, September 31, 1985 (second marriage); [ch.] Three; [ed.] 8th grade; [occ.] Housewife; [oth. writ.] Name of my other poems are Oh Sweet Love, My Life's Dream, I wrote for my son. Songs (How Could It Be), How Many Times and others. Non of them have ever been printed.; [a.] Fort Myers, FL

THOMAS, JASON LEE
[b.] June 8, 1973, Louisville, KY; [p.] Joseph and Jackie Thomas; [ed.] Bachelor of Science with a Degree in Telecommunications, Double Minor in History and Journalism, from Ball State University December '95; [memb.] Radio and Television News Directors Association; [oth. writ.] Articles for the Orient yearbook of ball state and the ball state daily news; [pers.] The soul - where it has been and what it will become - that is what interests me.; [a.] Floyds Knobs, IN

THOMAS, VAUDALINE
[pen.] Virginia Vaudaline Thomas; [b.] February 22, 1916, Sweetwater, TX; [p.] Deceased: Claude and Marguerite Rogers; [m.] T. T. Thomas, July 1, 1934 (Deceased); [ch.] Toby (Deceased), James and Modelene; [ed.] Master's Degree, Texas Tech University, B.S., Hardin-Simmons Sweetwater High School; [occ.] Retired Teacher, 32 years teaching; [memb.] Lubbock, Texas: Member, Story-Telling Club, Kiwanis, AARP, Retired Teachers Association, and Church of Christ. Sweetwater: Distinguished Member of the International Society of Poets, Lamar Street Church of Christ, Kiwanis, AARP Retired Teachers Association, and Member of the Scurry County Poets.; [hon.] Texas Health Volunteers, President, Sweetwater Classroom Teachers, Lubbock Retired Teachers Association; [oth. writ.] Plum Creek Memorabilia, Straightway to Heaven, Terms Related to the Exceptional - 3 books, Teaching Experiences, Legacies - 3 books, The Spirit of a West Texas Poet, Sharing My Dream (Book generated a winning a trip to New York, reading two poems at the International Society of Poets Convention in Washington, D.C., August, 1995; [pers.] I live for love, peace, understanding, and helping others.

THOMASON II, DILLMAN SEAN
[b.] September 24, 1971, Stocton, CA; [p.] Carol J. Wallcot, Dillman Sean Thomason; [m.] Amelia Thomason, September 9, 1994; [ch.] Courtney Ashley Thomason; [ed.] 12th Grade Graduate; [occ.] Student (English Major); [hon.] Letter of Appreciation, V.S. Navy; [oth. writ.] The hole I dug. The story of 2000 Redwood. I'm going to mar's. Place of Serenity. Paranoia Pulling on a nail. Window of life.; [pers.] You can't judge a vuiture, by what he's ate.; [a.] Reno, NV

THOMMI, DR. MRS. BRIDGET
[pen.] Baby; [b.] December 25, 1916, Kerala; [p.] George and Josephine; [m.] Kyprumbath Itteryah Thommi, June 15, 1942; [ch.] Five; [ed.] English School learning certificate - SSLC, College at Trivandrum, Kerala - Intermediate with Science, Bachelor of Science French with Physics and Chemistry; [occ.] MBBS - Madras - Bachelor of Medicine and Bachelor of Surgery - now retired; [memb.] FCGP fellow of the College of General Practitioners FAGE fellow of the Academy of general education published original articles in the medical bulletins also served as President Rotary Club and Rotary Anne published original poems in the Rotary Magazines.; [oth. writ.] Contributed articles and poems in the Rotary and other magazines while in Kerala and abroad. After passing and working in Madras selected to work in Malaysia, Sabah and Singapore worked as Area Medical Officer, came back to Kerala after the Chicalren finished their education, worked in various teaching institution for nurses and did free service for the needy and poor, twice a week attended free clinic nearby towns.

THOMPSON, DEWAYNE
[pen.] TEX; [b.] May 25, 1957, Fort Worth, TX; [p.] Ray and Sue Thompson; [m.] Debra Ann Thompson, May 25, 1996; [ch.] Twin son's Rusty and Dusty (15) Step children Garrett (18) Joey (16) Lisa (14); [ed.] Haltom High School 12 grade; [occ.] General Contractor; [memb.] American Legion Post #720 PRCA: Professional Rodeo Cowboys Assn.Redding Rodeo Assn.; [hon.] Student of the year 1975 Senior class PRCA title 1976; [oth. writ.] Book of APP 250 poems.; [pers.] God gave me the talent to write poetry and I try to use that talent each chance I can.; [a.] Sacramento, CA

THOMPSON, JAMES M.
[pen.] J. T.; [b.] June 9, 1959, Beaver Falls, PA; [p.] Ruth R. Thompson; [m.] Sylvia A. Thompso[n] September 10, 1994; [ch.] Step-son Joseph A. Vi[l]; [ed.] Beaver Area High School-PA, (College) F[ull] Gospel Bible Institute, (College) L.A. City Colle[ge] Pasadena City College, Mount San Antonio, Stud[y]ing or Seeking (A.S. Degree in Computer Infor[ma]tion Systems at this time); [occ.] Owner of T.J. Enterprises - (Part time self-employed); [memb.] Toastmasters International Chapter 1506; [hon.] Served as a Missionary-Teacher in Guatemala, Ce[n]tral America; [oth. writ.] My first published wo[rk] poem; [pers.] All that I am and all that I hope to [be] is an instrument of my creator to the heart, soul a[nd] mind of my fellow man.; [a.] La Verne, CA

THOMPSON, NEDRA
[b.] November 12, 1932, Johnson County, Garbo[?], AR; [p.] Ester and Mildred Casey; [m.] Billy T[h]ompson, June 1, 1952; [ch.] Gary, Paul, Casey; [ed.] Business College; [occ.] Retired public county se[r]vant; [oth. writ.] None published, personal pleasur[e] poems for friends, have saved material, hopi[ng] someday to compile it.; [a.] Lonoke, AK

THOMPSON, SEAN
[pen.] Sean Thompson; [b.] February 22, 197[?] Huntington Beach, CA; [p.] Terri Flanagan an[d] Ronald Thompson; [m.] Stacey L. Talbott-Th[ompson, July 22, 1995; [ed.] Lincoln High, studie[d] 2 years at Charleston Southern University in Sou[th] Carolina; [memb.] Crossroads Community Churc[h] Summerville SC; [oth. writ.] This is my 1st publica[tion, I'm correctly working on a book of poetr[y] which I plan to publish myself; [pers.] Poems are th[e] world around us. I write from life and my ow[n] dealings with it. Poetry is an emotion to me whic[h] I express with my pen. Jim Morrison in bigge[st] influence.; [a.] Stockton, CA

THOMSON, JOAN ALBERTA PLACE
[pen.] Joan Thomson; [b.] July 6, 1912, Chicago IL; [p.] Mark Hopkins Place, Ellen Crandall Plac[e] [m.] Godfrey E. Thomson, November 18, 1948 [ch.] Alice Ellen Jutras, George Edward Thomson [ed.] BA Cum Laude Milton College, Milton Wis[?] MA, English, Colorado College, Colorado Springs Colo.; [occ.] Retired; [memb.] American Associa[tion of University Women, Women's Internation[al League for Peace and Freedom Charter Membe[r] Unitarian Fellowship, Pueblo, Co. Nuclear Weap[ons Freeze Campaign United Nations Associatio[n] of the United State of America; [hon.] Regent[s] Scholar to Tn. University of Wisconsin, 1933 1934, Special Commendation for my teaching fro[m] the Senate of the University of the South Pacific Suva, Fiji, 1980, where I was in the Peace Corps 1976-1980. Who's Who of American Wome[n] 1993-1994, 1995-1996.; [oth. writ.] Winnowings An Autobiography in Verse 1993, Helicon Mile High Poetry Society, Denver, Colorado 1995, Beulah Valley Word, Chalice Lighter, Pueblo, Co. and various other local papers.; [pers.] Let peace prevai[l] on Earth.; [a.] Beulah, CO

THORNBURG, DOROTHY
[pen.] Dorothy Thornburg; [b.] August 14, 1930 Lake Village, AK; [p.] Claude and Minnie Reynolds [m.] Jack Thornburg; [ch.] Jack, Marie, Bobby and LaDonna; [occ.] Writing Poetry, songs, sewing painting; [pers.] I strive to be an encouragement to those around me to lift them up in time's of need through my poetry and being there with them to show them God cares.; [a.] Wagoner, OK

THORNHILL, NIKISHA
[pen.] Carnik Shell; [b.] April 28, 1978, Trinidad; [p.] Nelcia Fortune, Peter Thornhill; [ed.] Martin Luther King High School; [occ.] Student (Senior in

gh School); [memb.] Seamae Flyers Dance Group, Matthews Church Social Committee; [oth. writ.] write other poems for self satisfaction.; [pers.] The young mind has not been challenged enough in my writings, I try to let the readers minds wonder, instead of facts I prefer to write hints.; [a.] Brooklyn, NY

ICE, ALEX RENEE
[b.] June 10, 1982, Portland, OR; [p.] Robert and Kathy Tice; [ed.] 7th grade at Lakes Middle School, Coeur D'Alene Idaho; [hon.] Lakes Middle School Honor Roll for two years, Girl Scout for 5 years; [pers.] Congratulations Alex, we love you! Mom and Dad (1996).; [a.] Coeur D'Alene, ID

TIENNE
[pen.] Tienne; [b.] February 23, Philadelphia, PA; [p.] Edward T. and Dorothy C. Leonard. I was raised by my beloved grandmother Bertha M. Campbell and by my Aunt Florence and Uncle Jim Asher.; [ed.] Ankenau School, Central Bucks High School, and St. Joseph's College, where I have a 3.7 grade point average out of a possible 4.0.; [occ.] Supporter of the Elizabeth Taylor AIDS Foundation, Theater Guild sponsor for many years; [memb.] The International Society Of Poets, and have won several Editor's Choice Awards bestowed by The National Library Of Poetry; [hon.] Won several Blue Ribbons at various horse shows. Once, I have the great honor of having Ms. Helen Hayes, the first lady of the America theater, see me in a play at The Totem Pole Playhouse, in rural PA. Won several Editor's Choice Awards bestowed by The National Library of Poetry.; [oth. writ.] My poetry has been in an anthology published by Lincoln B. Young and also several of my poems have appeared in two collections of The Poet, published by Doris Nemeth. My poetry has been published by The National Library of Poetry, in several collections. I have collaborated with a friend writing songs, have been working on a novel for about 20 years, or so it seems, and am also trying to compile a cookbook. Over the years, I have written several short stories, and have recently had poetry recorded on cassettes, produced by The National Library of Poetry.; [pers.] My basic philosophy of life was best expressed by Tennessee Williams in his play, Night of the Iguana, "Nothing human is alien to me, save cruelty or violence." I love writing and the theater and currently reside in Lansdale, PA., with my partner and illustrator, Marie Stara and two cats, Minx, and Kimba. Tienne is my legal pseudonym and I use it for all my writing.

TILLER, AARON EDMUND
[pen.] Aaron Tiller; [b.] January 11, 1983, Dothan, AL; [p.] Noel M. and Laretha Ann Tiller; [ed.] Currently attending 7th Grade at Roulhac Middle School in Chipley, FL; [memb.] National Junior Honor Society Boy Scouts of America; [hon.] USAA National Leadership and Service Award, USAA All - American Scholar, USAA National Honor Student, Academic Awards, Honor Roll, Math Team -6th Grade, Spelling Bee Champion - 7th Grade, D.A.R.E. Essay Winner 5th Grade, Perfect Attendance - K thru 5 All-star Award - Football, Homecoming King - Football, Rodeo King; [pers.] I would like to dedicate this poem to My Mother who has helped me in life at every chance, and in every possible.; [a.] Chipley, FL

TILLER, MRS. LEONA
[pen.] Lee; [b.] December 28, 1929, Antlers, OK; [p.] John and Jewell Work; [m.] Aubrey B. Tiller (Deceased), September 30, 1946; [ch.] Five; [ed.] Only a 10th grade Education; [occ.] Core Giver; [oth. writ.] I am the author of 120 poems, written about family, friends, and God and the here after and home life; [pers.] 35 poems in the Shownee News Star Paper; [a.] Shawnee, OK

TODD, PENNY
[b.] July 21, 1954, Carrollton, IL; [p.] Keith and Rose Liesenfelt; [m.] Deceased; [ch.] Eric Thomas Todd; [ed.] North Greene High, White Hall, IL, Jacksonville School of Nursing, Jacksonville, IL; [occ.] Nurse-mother; [memb.] Hope Presbyterian Church, School #186 PTO; [oth. writ.] Over 20 years experience in writing poem. Several published in local newspapers.; [pers.] Writing is a personal experience for me and sincerely from the heart. The lessons of life have had a direct influence in my writing.; [a.] Springfield, IL

TOLAR, MR. PHILLIP
[b.] January 13, 1965, Cook County Hospital, Chicago, IL; [p.] Archie and Georgia; [m.] Mrs. Angela Renee Tolar, August 28, 1993; [ch.] Phillip Arias Tolar; [ed.] High School completed in 1983 (Thornwood H.S., South Holland, Illinois), Associates of Science in Avionics from (Southern IL, University in Carbondale), Bachelors of Science (S.I.U.C.) Advanced Technical Studies Masters of Science (Work Force Development and Education); [occ.] Automated Radar Tracking System Specialist of O'Hare Int'l, Chicago; [memb.] International Aviation Fraternity, Alpha Eta Rho (AHP), (NBCFE) National Black Coalition of Federal Employees; [hon.] Airway Facilities Honorary Award for Excellence in 1992, National Sector of the Year Award in 1989; [oth. writ.] The Mystic Light, The Beauty of Life, The One-Legged Man.

TOMPKINS, EDGAR L.
[b.] October 23, 1910, Branford, FL; [p.] Martin and RosaLee Tompkins; [m.] Mary Crocker Tompkins, November 24, 1940; [ch.] Mary Ann and Martin; [ed.] High School graduate and Barber College grad.; [occ.] Owner and operator of Eddie's Barber Shop - Retired; [memb.] Church of Jesus Christ of Latter-Day Saints, Archer Historical Society, Archer Friends and Neighbors.; [oth. writ.] Various poems and jingles for grandchildren and family members.; [pers.] I believe heavenly father made this beautiful world for our comfort and joy and we should take care of it. Be honest, faithful, kind to others and life will always be happy with many friends.; [a.] Archer, FL

TONGE, SYLVIA
[b.] April 7, 1950, Antigua, WI; [ch.] Floyd, Wayne and Nadine; [pers.] Time takes us beyond the horizon of new beginnings - as we proceed with the swells of circumstance into destiny. What is the meaning of life? The process of living, aging and dying? As we shuttle in the commotion of existence.; [a.] Bronx, NY

TORRE, EMILY
[b.] March 30, 1985, Clearwater, FL; [p.] Eugenia Robinson; [ed.] 5th Grade Lake Highland Prep. School; [occ.] Student; [memb.] Lake Highland Preparatory President's List - Outstanding Academic Achievement 4.0 GPA; [hon.] Robby Manly Award - Lake Highland Preparatory School: Most prestigious honor awarded to outstanding 4th grade student; [oth. writ.] Speech and poetry in honor of English romantic poet John Keats presented in June 1995 - John Keats Bicentenary - Keats House, Hampstead, London, England; [a.] Orlando, FL

TOSCANO, NICHOLAS
[pen.] Nicholas Toscano; [b.] June 27, 1978, NJ; [p.] Thomas Toscano, Jean Toscano; [ed.] High School 12th grade, College Bound; [oth. writ.] Poems published in Jitterview; [pers.] I am greatly influenced by romantic poets.; [a.] Morgantown, WV

TOSUN, SYLVIA
[b.] April 29, 1969, Connecticut; [ed.] Guilliard School of Music- Voice- BA/Post College - Literature and Communications - BA; [occ.] Singer, Songwriter, Interior Designer; [hon.] Outstanding Potential in Creative Writing Award 1988. National Talent Winner - Miss America Scholarship Pageant Program, Miss USO (2 time recipient 1990-1991), Miss Manhattan 1990/United Service Organization National Award of Merit (5 time recipient 1988-1993); [pers.] Thought reflected is discovering truth.; [a.] New York, NY

TOVAR, JEFFREY
[b.] October 17, 1976, Whittier, CA; [p.] Kaycie (died when I was 15) and Frank Tovar; [oth. writ.] Many other poems and writings never published or even seen by publishers; [pers.] I write what my emotions tell my hand to and I feel that the paper and pen are the best listeners. I also try to live by the words that my grandmother once told me: "To know is science, merely to think on knows is ignorance"; [a.] Cypress, CA

TRAUGH, JESSICA MARIE-LYN
[b.] October 3, 1980, Athens, OH; [p.] April M. (Young) Traugh and William J. Traugh I; [ed.] Attending Patterson Career Academy 9th Grade Dayton, OH; [occ.] Student; [memb.] JR. ROTC, Choir; [oth. writ.] This is my first poem; [pers.] Death of my aunt who had passed away 2 years before inspired me to write this poem. I dedicate this poem to Frances Hall.; [a.] Dayton, OH

TRAUTH, JEANETTE
[b.] December 22, 1957, Norton, VA; [p.] Helen and Kyle Jones; [m.] Dennis Trauth, February 14, 1987; [ch.] Walt Eric and Adam Wayne Massengill; [ed.] Appalachia High School, Chaffey Adult School; [occ.] Co-Owner, Electrical Contractor in specialized fields; [memb.] Disable American Veterans Commanders Club, Northshore Animal Shelter; [hon.] Honor Roll High School and Grade School; [oth. writ.] Voice of the Angel, Renaissance of Love, Motherly Love; [pers.] I only wish people could be as concerned about their children's happiness as they are about their own happiness. Unhappy children grow up to be unhappy adults.; [a.] Torrance, CA

TRENT, LUCILLE
[pen.] Lucy Trent; [b.] September 24, 1950, Tennessee; [p.] Alivs and Lola Atkins; [m.] Newman Trent Sr., March 30, 1988; [ch.] T. H., Michelle, Melissa; [ed.] Rutledge High School graduate; [occ.] Home maker; [memb.] Alpha Baptist Church Member of Alpha Choir, Member of Temple Sunday School Class (Teacher); [oth. writ.] Several poems.; [pers.] I have been greatly influenced by The Victorian Era - reading The Bible also early poets and history writers. And would like to think I could make the world a little better place to live.; [a.] Morristown, TN

TRIANT, DIANE SPEARE
[b.] April 15, 1946, Boston, MA; [p.] George Speare and Athena Speare; [m.] James W. Triant, September 24, 1972; [ch.] Virginia Athena, William Speare; [ed.] Dana Hall School Wellesley College, Harvard Graduate School of Education; [hon.] Phi Delta Kappa; [oth. writ.] Editor and writer for newsletters of Wellesley College and the Wellesley Public Schools; [a.] Wellesley Hills, MA

TRIM, DIANA HETTIS
[b.] June 15, 1954, Ithaca, NY; [p.] Paul and Lou Hettis; [m.] Alvin Trim Jr., April 14, 1977; [ch.] Alvin, Cory, Russ, Carla, Rob and Penny; [occ.] Florist - for 8 1/2 years - started my own business; [pers.] I asked??? "Why God, did you give poems to me?" He said, "Some for your growth", "Some as love songs from your heart to mine", "Some for others to enjoy."

TRIMMELL, STEVEN JOSEPH
[b.] December 8, 1984, La Mirada, CA; [p.] Dave and Elaine Trimmell; [ed.] Presently a student in the 5th grade of Eastwood Elementary School La Mirada, California; [occ.] Student (5th Grade); [memb.] Boy Scouts of American, Church of Jesus Christ of Latter Day Saints; [hon.] Principals Honor Roll (3 yrs in a row), Winner of the Norwalk/La Mirada School District Authors Contest 1995; [oth. writ.] Several short stories; [pers.] I enjoy writing poetry about nature and children's fantasies' short stories. My favorite reading is mystery novels.; [a.] La Mirada, CA

TRINGALI, SILVIO JOHN
[b.] Daly City, CA; [m.] Wilma Tringali; [ch.] Larry and Laraine; [ed.] Jefferson School San Mateo Co., Univ Southern Calif Public Admin Disaster Management, St. Marys Peace Officer School; [occ.] San Francisco Intl. Airport Operations Supt. (Retired); [oth. writ.] Shoot Stories - Poetry - Plays - Songwriter; [pers.] Just as an Artist uses color, I lime to use words that paint a vivid scene...a portrayal that evokes and emotion on the part of the reader.; [a.] Sunnyvale, CA

TRISHELL, CARMEN
[b.] May 1, Houston, TX; [p.] Groffie Trishell, Clarence Powell; [ch.] Brandy Lizarian, Vontre' Lizon; [ed.] Forest Brook High, Houston Community College D.S.U. Training Institution; [pers.] To touch the heart's of many and leave the feeling, that it always gets greater later.; [a.] Houston, TX

TROUT, THERESA A.
[b.] August 4, 1910, Glenwood Springs, CO; [p.] Tim and Kate Doyle; [m.] Alvin U. Trout (Deceased), June 25, 1927; [ch.] Alvin E. Evelyn Fay and Arden Lee; [ed.] Highschool, plus business and Junior College and continuing Coloraso Mountain College - Glenwood, Education to include some fine arts. Earlier years, small articals carried in Pittsburg Press...As well as Capper's Weekly.; [occ.] Retired: Except to host an Occasional Visit From 15 Grand Children and 32 Great - Grans and 1 Grand; [pers.] My early life was touched by the warmth and humor of James Whitcomb Riley, yet drawn to older writers like William Cullen Brant as they meditate on an our final one certain end. Reading still opens the world to me.; [a.] Glenwood Springs, CO

TRUELOVE, TRISHA
[b.] January 3, 1948, Fort Sill, OK; [p.] John and Grace Parker; [m.] Divorced; [ch.] Heath Ashley Truelove; [ed.] High School; [occ.] 29 years Service Rep. with Sprint Carolina Telephone; [memb.] Spring Lane Methodist Church; [pers.] I am very sensitive and high strung. When something happens in my life, I write a poem. Reading them again is like reading a diary to me.; [a.] Fayettville, NC

TRUJILLO, VIDABELL
[b.] December 25, 1953, Glendale, AZ; [p.] Virginia Leuenberger and Clarence Horn; [m.] Joseph Trujillo, December 11, 1989; [ch.] LaVida Lee Venard; [ed.] Dysart High, teacher grades 1-3 in accelerated Christian Education, Experience In Community Action Program; [occ.] Housewife and writer, grandmother of three; [memb.] Attend good news community church. Extra curriculum activities, charitable activities; [hon.] Written and oral thank you speeches, flowers etc....; [oth. writ.] Others poems published; [pers.] It is my desire to bring hope and encouragement through the inspiration poetry God has blessed me with. I was greatly influenced by Helen Steiner Rice; [a.] Broomfield, CO

TRUNCELLITO, SANDRA
[pen.] Sandy; [b.] April 3, 1943; [p.] Edward Kerr and Evelyn Kerr; [m.] Salvatore Truncellito, November 3, 1979; [ch.] Allen, Sally, Paul, Donna, Torre and Joe; [ed.] Union Hill High; [occ.] Waitress, Thunderbird Restaurant, Florence, SC; [oth. writ.] Several poems, none published yet. Just getting started, and more to come. This is my first poem published; [pers.] Since the passing of my sister June 18, 1995 I have been inspired by Aggie and God to let everyone know we are not alone with our feelings and thoughts.; [a.] Darlington, SC

TSCHUPP, EDWARD J.
[b.] August 5, 1925, Union City, NJ; [p.] Edward W. Tschupp, Hazel D. Tschupp; [m.] Jeanne Button, August 30, 1947; [ch.] Edward Walter, Jeanne Lynn, Lee Anne; [ed.] S.B., SM, Meteorology, MIT; [occ.] Meteorologist; [memb.] American Meteorological Society, American Association for the Advancement of Science; [hon.] Certified Consulting Meteorologist; [oth. writ.] Monthly Weather Outlook column for "Telltales" Magazine and numerous technical publications; [a.] Seabrook, TX

TUBOSNICK, MICHAEL
[pen.] Michael Tubosnick, T-Bird; [b.] July 21, 1978, Pottsville, PA; [ed.] Washington School; [occ.] Student of Life; [oth. writ.] Undiscovered poetry.; [pers.] Speak your mind, play by your own rules and be loyal to family and friends. Think before you act! Rock and roll forever!!; [a.] Mount Carbon, PA

TUCKER, SALLY DALY
[b.] June 5, 1956, Moberly, MO; [p.] Raymond W. (Bill) Daly, Dorothy Mariwether Daly; [m.] Michael D. Tucker; [ed.] Moberly Junior College, - Moberly, MO Graduate Realtor Institute (GRI); [occ.] Realtor-Sales Person; [memb.] National Association of Realtors, Phi Theta Kappa National Honor Society; [hon.] Who's who American High School Students 1973 and 1974; [a.] Columbia, MO

TUDOR, JEANNIE M.
[b.] November 24, 1982, New York; [p.] Louise and William; [ed.] Attending J.H.S., I.S. 25 in Queens NY; [hon.] Gold Scholastic Honor Roll, OUtstanding Performance in Art, Excellent in Social Studies, Excellence in Math, Excellence in Spanish; [oth. writ.] A collection of poems, Cats are the World, A Rose Blooms with Every Poem, Sammy and the Talent Contest, A Potpourri of Poems and Short Stories; [a.] Flushing, NY

TULLER, LARAE
[b.] September 17, 1975, Zanesville, OH; [p.] Mr. John Tuller, Mrs. Ruth Stichter; [ed.] Graduated New Albany High School in Ohio. Attending Ohio State University; [occ.] Daycare Teacher; [hon.] Honorable Mention and $25 Cash Award for a book of poems and short stories I wrote, in High School.; [oth. writ.] I wrote a book of 6 poems, and short stories for my senior project in High School.; [pers.] Writing is one thing I love best. I can express my thoughts and feelings through the words I write. My writings are great accomplishments to me, and I appreciate the recognition I have received.; [a.] Columbus, OH

TURNER, DAVID G.
[b.] June 6, 1939, Salt Lake City, UT; [p.] David S. Turner, Arlene V. Turner; [ch.] Seven; [ed.] Olympus High School, Brigham Young University, University of Utah, University of Maryland, Gardners School of Business; [occ.] Special Consultant on Training; [a.] Santa Rosa, CA

TURNER, JESSIE
[b.] August 16, 1981, Burlington, VT; [p.] Debra Geraw, Peter B. Turner; [ed.] Student at Hanover High, Hanover, NH; [memb.] National Honor Society; [pers.] True understanding brings forth true happiness.; [a.] Norwich, VT

TURNER, KIM
[b.] April 6, 1963, Utah; [m.] Mark Turner, Ap 16, 1983; [ch.] Two daughters; [ed.] Teachi degree Westminster College SLC Utah; [occ.] Stude

TURNER, PEGGY
[b.] June 29, 1951, Atlanta, GA; [p.] Paul and Do Johnson; [m.] Al Turner, October 14, 1986; [ch Rebekah; [ed.] Vernon High, Vernon Florida, Clayt State College, Morrow, GA; [occ.] Owner - Truckin Co.; [memb.] Christian Coalition Metro Worl Outreach Center; [oth. writ.] Jesus I Looked ar Found You; [pers.] The heart of my writing is lo and the greatest love I have found is in Jesus Chris [a.] Riverdale, GA

TUTTLE, MR. JOHN H.
[pen.] John Henry Tuttle; [b.] July 31, 197 Houston, MO; [p.] Glen and Mary Tuttle; [ed Coronado High School, 1988. I was an hon graduate there, Lubbock American Commerci College, 1990, Lubbock. I got a degree in Busines Computer Science; [occ.] I work at an office he in Lubbock. I am timekeeper there.; [memb.] I ar a member of The Star Trek Fan Club in Lubbock [hon.] The only real award that I have ever reall received has been for having nine years of Perfe Attendance in School.; [oth. writ.] My other wri ings besides this poem, has been mystery and Scienc Fiction stories or Novels, but none has been pu lished at this time.; [pers.] As my childhood frien of mine told me once, "Stand up for what yo believe in no matter what it may be." I try to ti this idea in all of my writing by having religious o moral impacts in everything that I write. So that does touch someone's life.; [a.] Lubbock, TX

TYLER-PARKER, SYDNEY
[b.] Los Angeles, CA; [p.] Dr. and Mrs. Harvey E Billig, Jr.; [m.] Mr. Minot H. Parker; [ch.] Mrs. Le Harris Tyler Argabrite; [ed.] BA English Lit. -- College of William and Mary, MSc -- Univ. o Southern California, Post Masters -- The Tavistock Institiute of Human Relations, London; [occ.] Author and Teacher, Associate Editor: *Think* Magazine, President, Thomas Geale Publications, Inc.; [memb.] Phi Delta Kappa, Association for Curriculum and Development (ASCD), Kappa Alpha Theta, California Association for the Gifted (CAG); [hon.] 2000 Women of Achievement, Great Britain, US Air Force "Greatest Contribution to Social Actions Offices World-wide" (1977), Kappa Delta Phi: Honors Classics Society; [oth. writ.] *Just Think, Stretch Think, Young Think, Think Quest* -- Curriculums to Teach Thinking, Articles on Thinking and Learning; [pers.] The ability to be creative can be encouraged and enhanced in every person, if we take the time to care enough about our youngest learners. [a.] Montara, CA

TYSON, WYCLIFFE E.
[pen.] Wycliffe E. Tyson; [b.] January 12, 1953, Nevis, WI; [p.] Samuel Tyson, Margery Tyson; [ed.] Trinity International University Miami Fl. B Sci Human Resources Mgmt, Biblical Studies, Miami Dade College, A Sci Dietetic Nutrition Car; [occ.] Student, Dr Naturopathy Clayton School of Natural Healing, Alabama; [memb.] First United Methodist Church Miami, International Society of Poets, American Naturopathic Medical Association; [hon.] Honorable Discharge U.S. Navy Vietnam Service; [oth. writ.] Author of book titled *Messages, Prayers and Poetry* currently writing second book titled *My Life in Poetry*; [pers.] Your dreams can come true; [a.] Miami Beach, FL

UDOH, UKO BASSEY
[pen.] Uko-Bendi Udo; [occ.] Newspaper Correspondent; [oth. writ.] A novel, and feature screenplay; [pers.] I pursue understanding in both my life

d writing, because it is a commodity that allows me to "travel light" through this life, without the heavy and debilitating burdens of ignorance and hate.; [a.] Long Beach, CA

DOSEN, OKOKON SAM
[pen.] Sammy Soothsayer; [b.] September 20, 1969, Akwa-Ibom State; [p.] Sylvester Udosen, Arit Udosen; [ed.] Akwa-Ibom State, University of Uyo; [occ.] Student, Dept. of Theatre Arts, University of Uyo, Uyo; [memb.] Student Member, Nigerian Institute of Public Relations (NIPR); [oth. writ.] Several poems and articles published and unpublished.; [pers.] As I write, I observe that my writings quite often seek to expose the bitter truth of reality in existence.; [a.] Uyo, Akwa Ibom

UNBEHAUN, GABRIEL
[b.] September 8, 1975, Saint Croix Falls, WI; [p.] William Unbehaun, Nancy Unbehaun; [hon.] 2 year 1993-1994) Poetry Winner in Mid-Western Talent Competition "Celebrate Life"; [oth. writ.] 1 other poem published in local publication.; [pers.] That which does not kill us, makes us stronger - Friedrich Nietzsche; [a.] Saint Croix Falls, WI

UNSWORTH, JOYCE
[pen.] Joyce Unsworth; [b.] July 22, 1948, England; [p.] Deceased; [ed.] Finished High School in Lancashire, England; [occ.] Disabled due to spinal injury inflicted from Spousal Abuse; [memb.] Member of the California Writers Club; [oth.writ.] Broken Dreams and It's Not An Illusion (Published in a book) "Finding Our Voices." This One's For The Children (Published in a Domestic Violence Newsletter) "Focus." The Season Of Brokenness, (Published in Church Newsletter) "The Epistle."; [per.] I am currently writing on my personal biography - title "The Sound Of The Sirens." Also an anthology on poems related to child abuse and domestic violence and I am interested in writing spiritual poetry. I am seeking publication.; [a.] Los Angeles, CA

UPHOFF JR., JOSEPH A.
[b.] April 15, 1950, Colorado Springs; [p.] Melva C. and Joseph A. Uphoff; [ed.] Shodan (Black Belt), Judo, Tae Kwon Do, Nidan, Jujitsu, Karate, Doctor of Divinity, Honorary Doctor of Letters, Honorary Professor of Mathematics; [occ.] Surrealist, Corps Diplomatic, Knights Templar, Examiner, U.S. Judo Association; [memb.] The National Judo Institute, The Institute of Martial Arts, Colorado Springs Fine Arts Center, Colorado Springs Art Guild, Poetry West, Fraternity Order of Eagles, First United Methodist Church, American Numismatic Association; [hon.] Dr. Baron of Camster-Burn, Caithness, Scotland, 1995, Knight of the Year, 1995, International Writers and Artists Association, Presidential Sports Award, 1992, 1995, Grand Council, Confederation of Chivalry, Sydney, Australia, 1993; [oth. writ.] Mathematical Theory for Absurdist Drama, 1983-1996..., 990 Pages Plus, Analytical Labanotation, Dance Parameters in Differential Algebra, 1991-1996..., 350 Pages Plus, Martial Arts Sets, 1985-1995..., 1100 Pages Plus, Chemical Geometry, 240 pages.; [pers.] Poetry includes the timing to the parallel, the hyperbolic parabola, between event, memory, documentation, and development, as such, all art forms contribute.; [a.] Colorado Springs, CO

URBINA, RALPH F. LOPEZ
[pen.] Rafas; [b.] September 30, 1934, Los Angeles, CA; [p.] Ralph Lopez and Helen Urbina; [m.] Isabel T. Fernandez, August 18, 1962; [ch.] Dana Marie, Raul and Ralph; [ed.] B.A., English, California State College, Los Angeles; [occ.] Youth Service Worker, Teacher, Ret. Freelance Writer; [memb.] Con Safos, Inc. A California, Nonprofit Public Benefit Corporation dedicated to promoting, developing, and supporting Fine Arts and Literary Arts in the Chicano Community.; [oth. writ.] Poems, and stories published in Con Safos magazine, The L.A. Times, The Eastside Sun; [pers.] My writing addresses a broad range of human predicaments or themes: Innocence, loss of innocence, comic and tragic absurdity, love, friendship, betrayal, alienation and estrangement, heroism and paradox. I've been deeply influenced by existentialist philosophers, writers, and poets, e.g., Heidegger, Nietzsche, Rilkgek.; [a.] Baldwin Park, CA

VACHON, GARY M.
[b.] August 29, 1961, Lewiston, ME; [p.] George Vachon (Deceased), Sandra Trafton; [ch.] Joshua David Vachon (12 yrs. old); [ed.] Graduated from Cony High School in Augusta, Maine 1980, Graduated from J&D Welding School in Tacoma, Wa. 1983; [occ.] Artist - original music/writer, performer, etc., also a "relief type" wood-carver.; [oth. writ.] Lyrics and music (original) on my recently published CD debut titled: "Here I Am" by me, Gary Vachon. Also been reviews on me and my Album in many music publications, etc.; [pers.] I'm dedicating my life, to my God-given talents to continue writing/creating/performing my original music, as well as my wood-carving, etc. etc. so that people can enjoy and relate.; [a.] Coastal Maine, ME

VAN DYCK, HALLEY
[pen.] Halley Van Dyck; [b.] May 1, 1986, San Francisco, CA; [p.] Janet and Tom Van Dyck; [ed.] 4th. grade at Neil Cummins Elementary School; [occ.] Student; [memb.] Tidalwaves Swim team, Corte Madera Soccer Team; [hon.] Swim Team, Gymnastics, Soccer; [oth. writ.] I've written some other poems, but this is by for my favorite.; [a.] Corte Madera, CA

VAN NOSTERN, SARA
[pen.] Christine; [b.] December 18, 1980; [p.] Rod and Kathy Van Nostern; [ed.] Lodi Middle School, Tokay; [occ.] Freshman in high school; [memb.] Stepps Volunteer project (San Joaquin Tobacco Prevention Youth) Church Choir CSC (Contemporary Singers for Christ) Sr. Elementary Band; [hon.] Participation in local Health Fairs Conferences.; [pers.] Thanks to all my friends for believing in me and encouraging me to continue writing.; [a.] Lodi, CA

VANDERWOOD, DEBORAH M.
[b.] November 20, 1950, Ilion, NY; [p.] Frances Benson; [m.] Barry S. Vanderwood, September 7, 1967, Alan R. Piotrowski, October 18, 1975; [ch.] Brandy A. Piotrowski, Dowen-Alan R. Piotrowski, Christopher M. J. Piotrowski, grandchild - Dekyse P. Dowen, son-in-law - Stephan D. Dowen.; [ed.] Utica Free Academy Pikes Peak Comm. College Peterson Air Force Base Dental Assistant School, College of I.C.S. for Journalism.; [occ.] Writer, Poet, Songwriter, Prior - Dental Assistant, Preschool Teacher; [memb.] American Red Cross, Y.M.C.A., P.T.A., International Society of Poets; [hon.] Nomination as Poet Of The Year 1995, Certificate of recognition for Preschool Teacher, Certificate of Recognition from U.S.A.F. Space Command for Dental Assistant Program, Two Editors Choice Awards, Certificate of Recognition from the American Red Cross for Dental Assistant Program, Certificate of Appreciation from Defence Commissary Agency Pikes Peak Community College for Dental Radiology and Math Science, Health division of Dental Assistant Program and Verification and Surgery. Certification of Degree for Journalism and short story writing from the college of I.C.S.; [oth. writ.] Several poems for - The National Library of Poetry, Mile High Poetry Society, Local Newspapers, 1. As Season's Change As We, In A Sea of Treasures, 2. To Every Thing There Is A Season, In A Sea Of Treasures, 3. To Every Thing There Is A Season, In A Delicate Balance, 4. Many Years Passed As I Waited For You, In The Rainbows End, 5. Mother's, In The Book Of Piera, 6. Grandparent's, In The Book Of Ariel, 7. A Poet's Dream, In The Book Of Ariel, 8. A Gift From Yesterday, Very Near To, In The Voice With In, 9. There Are A Million Reasons Why I... In A Muse To Follow, 10. You See Your Father Standing... In A Tapestry Of Thoughts; [pers.] As a new poet I hope that poet readers will feel the emotions in my poetry, and I hope to move their emotions with their souls, and their lives, as life is poetry. Though my poetry I leave a piece of myself when it is my time to move on. Than when someone reads me, they will think my what was she feeling or thinking or what message was she trying to give us? I want to thank my children for encouraging me and standing by me. My writings reflect my personal emotions and every stem of my life, based on my own mistakes and experience. And there in Thanks to every one in my family, My mother and father, brothers and sisters, and yes even to my ex's for if not for them I never would of experienced life. I have been greatly influenced by early romantic poets and Emily Dickinson.; [a.] Colorado Spring, CO

VANNOY, DENNIS
[b.] December 29, 1960, Seattle, WA; [p.] Charles Vannoy Jr. and Floreen Vannoy; [m.] Everlie Vannoy, July 5, 1980; [ch.] Dennis John III, Tiecha Marie, Floreen Terese; [ed.] Highline High 1979; [occ.] Cook; [oth. writ.] I've had a few poems published in local newspapers. Published in the World's Great Contemporary Poems 1981. Printed by World of Poetry Press; [pers.] My kinds and my wife are the loves of my life. Thanks to my brothers Dan, Darrell, Dave, and my beautiful sister Charleen.; [a.] Granite Falls, WA

VASQUEZ, DORINDA DENNIS
[pen.] Doris Dennis; [b.] December 23, 1956, Freeport, NY; [m.] Jim Dennis Vasquez, July 28; [ch.] Gina Marie, Carla Rae; [ed.] Camelback High, McLennan Comm. College; [occ.] Office Manager, Housewife; [hon.] U.S. Army Letter of Commendation and Honorable Discharge; [oth. writ.] Various unpublished poems and lyrics; [pers.] My writings are a cross between a hobby and a gift. I live my life by fate. I am content believing, everything is for a reason.; [a.] Goodlettsville, TN

VAUGHAN, ASHLEY ANN
[pen.] Ash; [b.] February 27, 1974, Florida; [p.] Christina Miles and Geoffrey Vaughan; [ed.] Senior in College; [occ.] Full time student; [hon.] MVP 4 yrs. Softball Dean's List all thru College; [oth. writ.] "A Personal Injury I Have Suffered"; [pers.] When you reach as high as you can - reach another inch higher.; [a.] West Melbourne, FL

VAUGHN, BENJAMIN
[b.] August 13, 1969, All Saints, Antigua Virgin Islands; [p.] Jenita and Ronald Benjamin Sr.; [occ.] Lead singer and principal song writer for Reggae Midnite Band; [hon.] United States Achievement Academy: Nat'l Leadership and Service Award - Nat'l Leadership and Merit Scholar Award - Who's Who among American H.S. Students, - Who's Who in Music (2 times); [pers.] The truth is heavy, will deny you rest - like a thousand pounds on a baby's chest.; [a.] Dayton, NJ

VEGA JR., VLADIMIR
[b.] December 23, 1935, Cabo RoJo, Puerto Rico; [p.] Wladimiro Vega, Rosalba Vega; [m.] Alba G. Vega, November 30, 1962; [ch.] Judith and Vladimir III; [ed.] Luis Munoz Marin High, San Mateo College, USAFI; [occ.] Quality Assurance Tech., PPG Industries, Torrance, CA; [memb.] Puerto Rico Jr. Red Cross, American Organization of Pilots Assoc.,

Assistant Post Advisor Boy Scouts of America; [hon.] Letter of Commendation by General Robert Cannon for VIII Olympic Winter Games at Squaw Valley, Ca. - Letter of Appreciation from Presidio H.Q. in S.F., CA. Cert. of Achievement from P.P.G. Ind.; [oth. writ.] I have written many articles and poems. None have been published.; [pers.] Thank you Reynaldo Silvestry for swaying me to find the door to inspiration.; [a.] Rialto, CA

VELAZQUEZ, REBECCA
[b.] January 29, 1980, Paterson, NJ; [p.] Phillip and Sylvia Velazquez; [ed.] Creative writing major at Rosa Parks High School of Fine and Performing Arts, in Paterson, NJ, (second year); [occ.] Full time student; [memb.] Member of Church of God and of the youth group for the same church.; [oth. writ.] Letter published in the Paterson Herald News about defending animal rights, an essay in publishing process about my grandmother in a literary magazine.; [pers.] My goal is to publish my own books of poems and novels, inspired by true life experiences including my own.; [a.] Paterson, NJ

VENNEBUSH, JO ANN
[b.] May 19, 1936, Kiamichi, OK; [p.] Roland and Alice Sutton; [m.] Joe Vennebush, July 2, 1955; [ch.] Barbette, Roland, Robert, David; [ed.] Delhaas High School, Lamar U. - Beaumont, Pt. Arthur, Tx., Mainland U, Texas City, Tx.; [occ.] Housewife; [oth. writ.] Newspaper Articles, other poems - Bended Knees, Morning Awakening, Sudden Soul, Teenagers, He wasn't Always There, Fishing and Wishing, Reality, Life is Like A Rose.; [pers.] I hope one day to publish a book of my poetry.

VIDAL, CAMIEL BENIETA
[pen.] Cornmeal; [b.] December 15, 1978, Jamaica, WI; [p.] Nerine Mowatt and Nedrick Vidal; [ed.] I am in the 11th grade. I love school, I love getting up early every morning to get there on time; [pers.] I was born and raised in Jamaica. I came to the U.S. when I was 9 years old, I was very close to my grandfather. When I was about 12 years old He died leaving me in grief. At this funeral I kissed his cold and fragile hand and told Him that I loved Him and He's always in my heart.

VIEN, ALICIA
[pen.] Nadine Hunter; [b.] November 26, 1977, Hartford, CT; [p.] Debbie L. Vien; [ed.] John Jay High School; [occ.] Burger King; [hon.] 2nd place in U.I.L. competition for comedy acting. Being recognized for the Who's Who Among American High School Students; [pers.] Most of my poems are a way of purging my soul of feelings trapped inside.; [a.] San Antonio, TX

VILLEGA, GEORGE MICHAEL
[pen.] Zen; [b.] February 2, 1963, Bronx, NY; [p.] Nicholas G. Villega, Ada I. Carmenate; [m.] Sherri Lynn Villega, October 28, 1984; [ch.] Nicholas Michael Villega; [ed.] High School; [occ.] Customer Service Rep. Health Plan Services, Tampa, FL.; [oth. writ.] Unpublished works - Mother child, My friend, The oppressed, Eternal pain, Clownies Christmas, etc. also silenced pain.; [pers.] The ones that influenced my life - my Lord, family, son and wife, all helped me with my strife, I thank my friends I have come across, who helped me when I felt loss, so I thank the Lord who's life I share, because I've met people who care.; [a.] Tampa, FL

VINAL, EVELYN D.
[pen.] Evey; [oth. writ.] In Parochial School at 14 yrs. old won essay contest out of 5 grades, 8th thru 12th. In Junior College took writing in Publication and Creative Writing. Become a beautician at an early age.; [pers.] I am married, have two grown daughter and two granddaughter. My desire is to write for me and for anyone who enjoys reading.; [a.] San Luis Obispo, CA

VINCENT, KATHERINE R.
[pen.] Katherine R. Perna; [b.] November 30, 1955, Revere, MA; [p.] Joseph H. and Eleonor S. Perna; [m.] Divorced; [ch.] Michael 20, Jennifer 19; [ed.] High School CNA class; [occ.] CNA; [oth. writ.] 'Once' in high school paper.; [pers.] Life is what you make it... Hang with loosers and loose yourself; [a.] Goffstown, NH

VINCENT, TIMOTHY
[b.] Baton Rouge, LA; [p.] Carl Vincent, Lenora Vincent; [ed.] B.A. Theatre Arts Southern University Baton Rouge LA.; [occ.] Actor; [memb.] SAG, AFTRA; [oth. writ.] Treatment for films and television.; [pers.] I have been greatly influenced the people I've met and those I will meet.; [a.] Valley Village, CA

VINNIK, POLINA M.
[b.] July 13, 1980, Minsk, Belarus; [p.] Alla and Michael Vinnik; [ed.] Currently - Stevenson High School in Lincolnshire IL; [occ.] Student; [hon.] Several Academic/Math honors.; [oth. writ.] Many unpublished poems and short stories, several of which have been published in school magazines.; [pers.] I strive to find truth. I have been influenced by the books I read and the Earth I live on as well as the people that live on it. All the answers are out there if one has the determination and courage to find them.; [a.] Vernon Hills, IL

VINSON, KAREN D.
[b.] April 12, 1961, Boulder, CO; [p.] James and Oralyn Hahn; [m.] Terry Vinson, September 6, 1991; [ch.] Stacie Renee, Hahn-Vinson; [ed.] Boulder High School graduated 1979. Boulder Colorado; [hon.] Accomplishment of merit award from creative arts and sciences Enterprises of New York - for poem titled "Patience". Fall 1995; [oth. writ.] Have poems published, and due to be released 1996, in poetry anthologies in Colorado and New York. (The Rocky Mtn Poetry Society) and (Creative Arts and Sciences Enterprises); [pers.] I have lived in the Boulder, Colorado area my entire life. I began writing poetry as a child, and through the years it has grown into my life-long passion. My dream has been-to become a writer to perhaps touch something inside of someone else, and to share the magic of words.; [a.] Nederland, CO

VIVIER, LINCKY ELME
[pen.] Elme; [b.] June 23, 1984, South Africa; [p.] Elizabeth and Lincoln Vivier; [occ.] 5th Grade Student; [hon.] Selected to be in the AIMS program for Orange County, Florida.; [a.] Maitland, FL

VOCHATZER, GARY J.
[b.] March 9, 1940, CA; [p.] Mary, Ed Kuhn; [m.] Shirley, March 23, 1990; [ch.] Herb, Liz, Susan; [ed.] High School; [occ.] Insurance Broker since 1962; [oth. writ.] Have many, many, many, many, many poems, stories I have written but have done with than except when I during on a personal basis I give it to whom written about.; [pers.] My goal is to reach folks throughout the world about how wonderful two things are in life 1) God and His love to mankind, 2) How wonderful God has blessed America and its citizens.; [a.] Stockton, CA

VURTURE, FRANK G.
[b.] January 20, 1928, Staten Island, NY; [p.] Edward Vurture, Sarah Vurture; [m.] Barbara Vurture, April 10, 1990; [ch.] David Alan, Steven Thomas, Gary Frederick, Richard William; [ed.] New Dorp H.S., New York University B.A., M.A; [occ.] Retired Supervisor of Special Education, N.Y.C. Board of Education; [memb.] American Legion, Association of Retired School Supervisors and Administrators, A.A.R.P., Ducks Unlimited, N.R.A.; [pers.] My poetry is strongly influenced by personal experiences as they relate to the great outdoors and the common bond of similarity, that flora and fauna have with mankind; [a.] Staten Island, NY

VYAS, SWATI
[b.] December 7, 1983, San Gabriel; [p.] Harshad and Sukirti Vyas; [ed.] 6th grade; [occ.] Student attending San Gabriel Christian School; [hon.] Henry Myers Awards for best Christian Character, Superior in Speech Meet; [pers.] I am trying to be a good Christian example. Through my writing I would like to bring people closer to Christ.; [a.] Alhambra, CA

WADDELL, DIANE DRISHELL
[b.] February 4, 1977, San Diego, CA; [p.] Diane Waddell, Washington Waddell; [ed.] James Madison High School, UCLA; [hon.] Military Order of the World Wars Award, Who's Who Among American High School Students, Senior Class Treasurer, Cheer Captain, Honor Roll, Debutante, Ladies of Distinction Treasurer, Mediator; [oth. writ.] Poems published in school Literary Magazine like Purple Rain Black Pride, and let us Love ('93-'94). Poem published in school yearbook ('94-'95). Speech and poem delivered at my graduation (June 15, 1995).; [pers.] My writings are straight from my heart. My words grow from within, creating amazing masterpieces that I never knew existed. My inspiration is in knowing that my conceive in this lifetime. I admire Maya Angelou for following her heart and her strong convictions. One's vision can hold magical direction in other's lives.; [a.] San Diego, CA

WADE, ASHLEY
[b.] September 21, 1981, New Orleans; [p.] Steve and Susan Wade; [ed.] Madison - Ridgeland Academy, Jr. High School; [occ.] Student; [memb.] Fellowship of Christian Athletes; [hon.] 5th, 6th and 7th grade most valuable cross-country (varsity), 7th grade class favorite, 7th grade (Jr. High) most athletic, and 7th grade (Jr. High) most valuable track and field; [oth. writ.] Other poems and songs.; [pers.] All I try to accomplish are the things that are hardest to reach.; [a.] Madison, MS

WADE, MARIA W.
[pen.] Brook Loren Stevens; [b.] July 7, 1970, Killeen, TX; [p.] Natividad C. Wade and David Wade Sr.; [ed.] Some College, Vocational, (Video Prod) Seminars, High School Graduate Local UAW for Laborers sent me to school for construction; [occ.] Video Productions and Promotions Singer/Dancer; [memb.] Chamber of Commerce, Trade Network Incorporated, various Video Production Organizations; [hon.] I have won various awards for my writing as a child as well as various awards, and certificates for some of my other talents but I really don't like to claim them because my true rewards is when I see the reaction I get from those individuals whom experience my work whether the reaction is good or bad. When I write I write to retrieve a reaction from the reader whether it is bad or good. I try to touch there emotions or relay an emotion, and sometimes even make them question their ethics and beliefs.

WADE, RUTH
[b.] July 13, 1932, WV; [p.] Mr. and Mrs. Daniel Wray; [ed.] High School Sewickley PA; [memb.] Mass Choir, Sunday School, Church, Corinthian Baptist; [oth. writ.] I love to write poems; [pers.] I think the goodness of mankind should be known.; [a.] Pittsburg, PA

WADKINS, PAMELA S.
[b.] April 1, 1959, Covina, CA; [p.] Robert and Donna Hall; [m.] Alton S. Wadkins, October 7,

'78; [ch.] Amber, Autumn, April and Amanda; [ed.] Graduated from Mt. Whitney High School, attended 1 year College of sequioas in Visalia, attended Washington Elementary all in Visalina a.; [occ.] Housewife; [a.] Visalia, CA

WAEYENBERGH, SARAH
[pen.] Sarha McBride; [b.] December 21, 1980, Hon., HI; [p.] Luke and Sarah-Arin Waeyenbergh; [ed.] Rhor Elementary, Thurman White Middle School, Abeka Home Schooling; [hon.] A and B honor roll from 1st-9th, 1st grade Poetry Award; [oth. writ.] Short stories and poems; [pers.] No one can do anything for you, you have to do it yourself.; [a.] Hunting Beach, CA

WAGNER, EDITH SCOTT
[pen.] Edith Wagner; [b.] April 7, 1911, Alliance, NE; [p.] James and Zilpha Scott; [m.] Reinold Wagner - Deceased, May 27, 1944; [ch.] David Scott, Lenora Belle; [ed.] Graduate Alliance High School, graduate Chadron State College, several graduate credits.; [occ.] Retired School Teacher - 15 years rural schools of Nebraska, 24 years Edgemont South Dakota; [memb.] American Heart Association, American Diabetes Association, Saint Agnes Catholic Church, Member Smithsonian Institute; [hon.] Unofficially named "Poet Laurette of the Village". Outstanding Teacher Award.; [oth. writ.] Many poems published in various newspapers and magazines. Also short stories published 1989 in "Poem of Great American Vol. II." National Arts Society, Pass Christian, MS; [pers.] My philosophy is to bring forth my love for God and His world and to portray this love through my writings. As a descendent of Sir Walter Scott, I have been greatly influenced by his writings.; [a.] Scottsbluff, NE

WAGNER, JILL MARILEE
[b.] June 28, 1946, Toronto, Ontario, Canada; [p.] William "Jack" and Dorothy Watkins; [m.] Harley Vaughn Wagner, July 18, 1980; [ch.] Darleen, Daniel (Deceased) and Dustin; [ed.] Associates Degree - Business Mgmt. and Marketing Associates Degree - Sales; [memb.] Phi Theta Kappa (Honor Society) Alpha Beta Gamma (Honor Society) Vietnam Veterans Of America LZ Chapter 89; [hon.] 1994 - Wall Street Journal Award, 1994 - Outstanding Marketing/Mgmt. Student Dean's List, 1994 - Management Certification (CM) through ICPM Through Lima Technical College/OSU; [oth. writ.] Over 3 dozen poems written in the last year.; [pers.] My poetry has been a personal to heal after the December 23, 1994 tragic death of one of my children. It's a personal journey through the grieving process.; [a.] Lima, OH

WAHIDI, ZHENUS
[b.] February 16, 1982, Afghanistan; [p.] Jahan Ebadi; [ed.] Antioch Junior High School; [memb.] Wildlife Reading Club Association; [hon.] Honor Student, Student of the Month, 4.0 GPA, Honor Roll mention for young authors, Honor Roll mention for the science project, ... etc.; [oth. writ.] When I first came to U.S., I couldn't speak English at all. I started school as a second grader, and I had trouble understanding my teacher and classmates. As the years went by, I made friends and I started getting acquainted to the American Culture. Right now I am in eight grade and I can speak English quite well.; [pers.] Before I came to U.S., I spent 2 years in Pakistan, until we heard that my father had a heart attack in Afghanistan. That heart attack took my father away from us. After my father's death, my Mother raised us and helped us with our school. She was a mother and father for us. I am really thankful for my mother for sacrificing her life for us. I have a diary of my life just to keep the memories from the past. I love to write and I like to create more stories and poems.; [a.] Antioch, CA

WALKER, CAMELA
[b.] April 30, 1959, McKinney, TX; [p.] Linda Purcell, Wayne Wafford; [m.] Arthur, June 4, 1977; [ch.] Charman Lin, Wesley Charles; [ed.] North Garland High School Garland TX Collin Country Community College Collin Country TX; [occ.] Secretary Tatum Elementary School - Farmersville TX; [oth. writ.] Several poems one published by the National Library of Poetry 1995; [pers.] I just want to bring glory and honor to my Savior Jesus Christ through my poems which are inspired by the Holy Spirit. To God be the glory!; [a.] Farmersville, TX

WALKER, JOSEPHINE A.
[pen.] Anona Bourassa Walker; [b.] February 28, 1925, Brownstown, MI; [p.] Lambert Bourassa, Ovie LeBlanc; [m.] James B. Walker Sr., March 2, 1946; [ch.] Nine sons and three daughters; [ed.] Ecorse High School Class "43", The Grace Hospital School of Nursing "43-46" Diploma RN; [oth. writ.] "The Bay", "Love And Let Live" and others unpublished.; [pers.] I truly believe as stated in my cherished reading "DESIDERATA" that "With all its sham, drudgery and broken dreams, it is still a beautiful world."; [a.] Livonia, MI

WALKER, LINDA G.
[pen.] Linda Burton Walker; [b.] December 30, 1950, McAllen, Texas; [p.] Mr. and Mrs. Bradford Burton Mr. Roy Vinzant and Mr. Ralph Phoenix - Step Father; [m.] Jimmie L. Walker, March 22, 1969; [ch.] Jimmie L. Walker Jr., son 26 yrs., Jimmie L. Walker III, grandson- yrs.; [ed.] Graduate of Greybull High School, Greybull, Wyoming; [occ.] Housewife Volunteer Work (Sound Room/Music Ministry); [memb.] Twin City Baptist Temple Lunenburg, Massachusetts, Former Member of Job's Daughters; [hon.] Past Honored Queen (1967-1968), Job's Daughters, Bethel II (eleven), Greybull, Wyoming, Plaque and Seiko Watch, Service Award for 12 years work keeping records at Twin City Baptist Temple Lunenburg, Mass. (1993); [oth. writ.] A few poems I have not tired to have any published before. Would like to write a non-fiction book about my parents/family.; [pers.] As a quiet person, I have found ways to express myself in writing and also singing. I try to include something in my poems about my faith and trust in the Lord and a spirit of Thankfulness to Him!; [a.] Fitchburg, MA

WALL, JASON D.
[pen.] Moonan; [b.] March 19, 1970, Wiesbaden, Germany; [p.] Dan and Martha Wall; [ed.] By Divine Intervention; [occ.] Singer-songwriter above all poet.; [memb.] Secret Society (The never die family); [oth. writ.] "Sir Moonan Dune" Chances yet to be published a book to help spending derive enough relations 180 of madness to overdrive the power of collective coincidence drama.; [pers.] The day will come for a chosen few. Which we will go from building a name to creating our identity. Know the two are as opposite as good and evil. One eternal, the other and end. We gain this level of consciousness, when through rigorous questioned of the scientifically hypnosized definition of life and death and what's in the middle. We are dawned by a message from beyond simply implying this by way of appreciation, don't use yourself to create your surroundings use your surroundings to create yourself.

WALLACE, FANNIE A.
[pen.] Frances Wallace; [b.] September 3, 1936, Cincinnati, OH; [p.] Ben and Fannie Cooper; [m.] Divorced at 56 after 43 years of marriage; [ch.] Gerald, Denise, Dennis, Darren; [ed.] Wood Ward High School Temple Bible College; [occ.] Retired; [memb.] Morning Star Baptist Church; [hon.] Mrs. Temple Bible College; [oth. writ.] A book of poem's for my personal use.; [pers.] My poems are the only way I can express my pain sorrows, Happiness etc.

I thank God for a way to relieve my stress, and hopefully help some one else.

WALLMARK, ELIZABETH
[p.] August 11, 1980, Bellflower, CA; [m.] John Wallmark, Zofia Wallmark; [ed.] Trinity Lutheran School; [occ.] Student; [a.] Rancho Palos Verdes, CA

WALLOW, TERRI
[b.] June 9, 1975, Colorado; [p.] Jeff and Shelly Mav; [ed.] In my first year of college; [occ.] Student; [oth. writ.] My poem Place of Fright has been publish by the Poetry Society in an Anthology called mirror to the Soul.; [pers.] I believe anyone can write well, as long as they write what they feel and what they know. It's a very healthy way to show your emotions, and define who you are.; [a.] Scottsdale, AZ

WALSH, LYNN
[pen.] Lynn Walsh; [b.] November 16, 1955, Queens, NY; [ed.] Point Park College - Pittsburgh, PA, Dance major - Ringling Brothers Bob Circus - 3 years; [occ.] Masseuse/Stuntwoman; [memb.] Prof. Stuntwoman's Asso., St. Francis De Salle Choir; [hon.] VA. State award for tap dancing; [oth. writ.] Several poems published in various anthologies; [pers.] You will be the best if you believe in yourself. Use the gifts he has given you to the best of your ability. Though obstacles will be thrown in the way there will always be an open door to overcome the frustrations of life; [a.] North Hollywood, CA

WALTON, MARY LEE
[b.] July 8, 1923, Waterloo, IA; [p.] Chester and Alta Dawley; [m.] Clive L. Walton, February 12, 1940; [ch.] Five; [ed.] 9th Grade; [occ.] House wife; [memb.] Assembly of God; [oth. writ.] Lots of Poems; [a.] Shelton, WA

WALVER, CHERYL S.
[b.] January 8, 1957, Watseka, IL; [p.] Mr, and Mrs. Cecil Houser; [m.] Richard Walver, January 16, 1980; [ch.] One; [ed.] GED; [occ.] Private Nursing; [oth. writ.] I have other poems that I have written. Also enjoy word processing; [pers.] I enjoy my work and the thought behind each poem I write.; [a.] Watseka, IL

WAMSLEY, CHAD
[pen.] C. Huston Wamsley; [b.] January 18, 1969, Bethesda, MD; [p.] Raymond and Barbara Wamsley; [m.] Carrie Calimer; [ed.] BA in Psychology from Salisbury State University; [occ.] Security Assistant Montgomery County Public Schools; [memb.] Tau Kappa Epsilon Fraternity, International Society of Poets, Montgomery County Police Intern, Contemporary Fighting Arts; [hon.] Editor's Choice Award (top 3%) by The National Library of Poetry for "Spare A Dime", "My Reflection" published by The National Library of Poetry; [oth. writ.] Spare A Dime, My Reflection, Whispering Words, My Solemn Prayer, Dreams And Tears, That Old Rose, I Will Show You The Way; [pers.] I write by using my thoughts, feeling my emotions and listening to my heart.; [a.] Germantown, MD

WARD, JOSEPH ALLEN
[b.] February 23, 1957, Burlington, NC; [p.] Dr. W.G. and Molly K. Ward; [m.] Julane Isley Ward, April 7, 1993; [ed.] Walter Williams High School Trenton Jewelry School; [occ.] Jeweler; [memb.] Brookwood Baptist Church; [pers.] I dedicate this poem to my wife Julane Isley ward for if not for the love I have for her it would never been written. With this love I have truly been blessed.; [a.] Burlington, NC

WARD, STEVEN JAMES
[pen.] Steve - O; [b.] June 19, 1963, Tusculoosa, AL; [p.] Daisy Ward and Willie White; [m.] Maurita Ward, June 18, 1995; [ed.] Hyde Park Career

Academy Kennedy-King College; [occ.] Chicago Police Dept. Detention Aide; [memb.] Chicago Municipal Employee Police Service Employee Local 46 First Church of Deliverance; [hon.] Creator of School Age Combination Age Combination Group Project Certificate in Social Services Youth Work. Editors Choice Award National Library of Poetry.; [oth. writ.] Many unpublished poems and plays.; [pers.] We are born with the ability to become what ever we want in life - Depending on the roads we choose will reflect our accomplishments and our success in life.; [a.] Chicago, IL

WARNECKE, TERRY ANTHONY
[pen.] Terry Anthony Warnecke; [b.] February 29, 1956, Saint Louis, MO; [p.] Harry Warnecke and Antoinette Warnecke; [ch.] Kathryn Marie, Daniel Anthony; [ed.] Lindbergh High, Carpenter Trade School; [occ.] Carpenter; [memb.] Missouri Botanical Garden Step-up-Saint Louis; [pers.] I write about my passions, to try to transfer my feelings to the reader and if it raises any emotions, my goal is achieved.; [a.] Saint Louis, MO

WARNER, CAROLYN M.
[pen.] Lynn Wynn; [b.] April 16, 1908, Brooklyn, NY; [p.] Elizabeth Farmer; [m.] Charles (Deceased), July 18, 1925; [ch.] Four; [ed.] Night School College; [occ.] Retired; [memb.] AARP. Local Writers Club at Joslyn Center for Seniors 750 Broodway Escondido; [hon.] Small Magazines Local Newspaper non/North Country Times Pennsylvania are Escondido CA 92025; [oth. writ.] Poetry submitted printed poets pouch writers digest 1994 National Library Editors 1995; [pers.] Tell the next generation how me moved on help them to "Press On"; [a.] Escondido, CA

WARNER, SHARON
[b.] January 21, 1951, La Porte, IN; [p.] John and Melba Schepel; [m.] Ronald Warner, October 23, 1971; [ch.] Christian and Aaron Warner; [ed.] Ivy Tech Ind. Licensed Practical Nurse - grad. 1970 now retired due to back injury; [occ.] Homemaker; [memb.] Member of Church of Christ; [oth. writ.] Many of my poems were published in my church newspaper and many were written and read at funerals. Many are religious and have a lesson or message to the reader.; [pers.] A wise man strives to continue to learn all his life, but a foolish man thinks he already knows everything.; [a.] La Porte, IN

WASCHEN, LEISA A.
[pen.] Leisa Ann; [b.] March 1, 1967, Phoenix, AZ; [p.] Harry R. Waschen and Geraldine Stockham; [ed.] Sunnyslope High Rainstar School of Massage; [occ.] Licensed Massage Therapist; [pers.] Life is full of many thing (lessons), some can make great poems, when you stop living..... there is no more to tell (lessons) or write about. The things we live, see and breath that are real: are the things that are the most interesting because of their content.; [a.] Phoenix, AZ

WATSON, TANDY LENORE
[b.] June 15, 1963, Anaheim, CA; [p.] Shirley Ann Shie; [pers.] I believe writing is one of the most in depth forms of expression from the heart, mind, and soul.; [a.] Reno, NV

WATTS, KATIE
[b.] March 5, 1962, Fountain Inn, SC; [p.] Millie Watts; [m.] Anthony Mitchell; [ch.] Brian Watts, Keith Watts, Tameka Watts; [occ.] Current working at Kemet Electronics. A Large Capacitor Manufacturer.; [memb.] PTA; [hon.] 1st Place Shorthand competition. 2nd Place Business Law.; [oth. writ.] I am currently working on several other pieces of inspirational material.; [pers.] Try to live a good and clean life.; [a.] Simpsonville, SC

WAUGH, MRS. BETTY M.
[b.] October 7, 1932, Forsyth County, NC; [p.] William Franklin Myers, Ethel Lineback Myers; [m.] Cecile Osban Waugh; [ed.] Registered Nurse (NCBH Neurosurgery) Most of studies for BSN at Gardner Webb College Forsyth Technical Community College Winston Salem State University for selected night classes; [occ.] North Carolina Baptist Hospital/Bowman Gay School of Medicine, Registered Nurse; [memb.] First Assembly of God Church, Knitters Guild of America, Cultures Purls Knitting Guild; [hon.] I cannot recall awards, but at work I am Preceptor, am Coordinator of U.S. Savings Bonds, and of United Way. Was Student Government Representative in College.; [oth. writ.] Few nursing topics for class; [pers.] To do my utmost in the time allotted to me in helping my fellowman to live in better health, and to be a better person by having passed my way. I strive for excellence and meaning seeking quality rather than quality as a rule for success.

WAYE, ROMAYNE
[b.] May 26, 1924, Melford, CB Nova Scotia, Canada; [p.] D. O'C Doyle and Catherine (Boyle) Doyle; [m.] Angus M. Waye, February 12, 1962; [ed.] Gr. XII, Port Hawkesbury High Business Course, Empire Bus. College Sydney, N.S., B.A. Credits, Thomas More Institute Mtl. Quebec, St. FX., Antagonist, NS Gr. V - Piano - Royal Toronto Conservatory, Great Books - Discussion Group - 3 years; [occ.] Patients Svcs. Chairperson- Canadian Cancer Society, Strait Area Unit since October 1989; [memb.] Social membership - P.H. Curling Club Evergreen Seniors Club, Port Hawkesbury Bowling Club; [hon.] Won Moyers Co., Halifax, Children's Poetry Contest (the prize was a cake); [oth. writ.] Poems "Forgotten Clay" and "To A Very Special Plant" published in local weekly newspapers. Poem "No Stone Unturned" published in the 1959 "Nova Scotia Book of Poetry", Limerick accepted by CBC for the G7 Summit in Halifax, N.S., June 1995

WEAR, MARY ANN
[b.] August 26, 1939, Covington, KY; [p.] Margaret and John Dunn; [ch.] John, Joseph, Lisa, Leanne, Danny Lee; [ed.] St. Mary High Alexandria, KY, 1957; [occ.] Nurse Companion; [memb.] St. Raphael's Church Englewood, FL; [hon.] Editor's choice outstanding achievement in poetry presented by National Library of poetry Member International Society of poetry; [oth. writ.] Secrets of my heart 1990 lost 1995 God's greatest gift of life. The man who forgot love 4190 Masterpiece 1989 My captain, 1990 My Precious Lord Hold My Hand Today The present 1990. A new song 1995 The Miracle of Danny 1974; [pers.] God's greatest gift in life is love. Written in memory of my dear friend Edward Joseph Duddy. Born March 22, 1926 in Brooklyn NY. Died August 18, 1995 May the road rise with you, and the wind be ever at your back, and may the Lord hold you in the hollow of his hand. An Irish blessing; [a.] Englewood, FL

WEAVER, ONALEE A. BUTLER
[b.] March 11, 1921, Clio, MI; [p.] Fred and Helen Crawford Butler; [m.] Glenn Burton Weaver, August 30, 1941; [ch.] Mikell, Melinda, Ryan; [ed.] High School; [occ.] Retired Mail Carrier Livonia, Michigan; [memb.] With Royalty Theatre Co., Clearwater Ladies of Royalty; [hon.] My poem "Have I" has already been set to music and is on tape, with a very good vocalist singing it.; [oth. writ.] Golden Poet Awards "Have I?", "Walking the shore", "Moods" "Divine power", "So Far to the River", "The Long Sleep"; [pers.] "Smile, it doesn't cost a cent"; [a.] Palm Harbor, FL

WEBBER, RINDA LORRAINE
[pen.] R. L. Webber or Rinda L. Webber; [b.] M 11, 1946, Modesto, CA; [p.] Robert and Lorrai Hutchinson; [m.] Thomas R. Webber, June 4, 198 [ch.] Jeff, Michael, and Nichole; [ed.] Ripon Uni High School and Modesto Jr. College; [occ.] Deput Sheriff II with the San Joaquin Country Sheriff Department.; [memb.] San Joaquin Co. Depu Sheriff's Assn., Peace Officers Research Assn. Calif. (PORAC) and Calif. Assn. of Police Traini Officers, and Calif. Peace Officers Memorial Fou dation; [oth. writ.] I have written articles for loc publications and I write poetry for my friends a family when the mood strikes.; [pers.] Poetry a writing in general gives me pleasure. I like "paint" with words. I think I inherited my poet skill from my Great Grandfather Frank Hutchinso My mother told me he liked to write poetry, but have never seen anything he wrote. The mor Share your writing good or bad.; [a.] Ripon, CA

WEBSTER, LAURA N.
[b.] December 2, 1975, Uniontown, PA; [p.] Russe P. Webster (Deceased), Diane M. Patrick; [pers It's time that we open our eyes and realize th children are the foundation of our future! We nee to start helping them instead of hurting them!; [a Uniontown, PA

WEDEMEYER, HERMAN A.
[b.] June 5, 1914, Columbus, OH; [p.] Arthur A. an Josephine H. Wedemeyer; [m.] Betty J. Wedemeye (Deceased), May 9, 1942; [ch.] Dianne E. Herma A., Jr.; [ed.] High School Graduate; [occ.] Retire from Ford Motor Company, Livonia, Michigan [memb.] Ward Evangelical Presbyterian Churc and all branches of Freemasonry; [pers.] "Ode to Gallant Lady" is inspired verse that spontaneousl came to me during sleep. I used it in a "Memorial to a deceased lady in a Souvenir Year Book of m Masonic Fraternity.; [a.] MI

WEED, DALE A.
[pen.] Dale A. Weed; [b.] March 24, 1949, Dowagiac MI; [p.] Robert and Mildred Weed; [m.] Nancy S Weed, May 4, 1974; [ch.] Erick and Brittany; [ed. Southwestern Michigan, Community College an Western Michigan University; [occ.] Disabled Reg istered Nurse; [hon.] Associate Science Degre Nursing, Associate Science Degree Chemistry, Luck ily I found out in time that formal education woul set up blocks to my creativity.; [oth. writ.] Approx imately 22 unpublished poems and a children's story "The Adventures of Gwillaby Goose" unpublished [pers.] I paint pictures with words in hopes o someday fulfilling a dream. My dream is to be able to help as many homeless and hungry people as Harry Chapin did. My other goal is to have a comfortable life for my family.; [a.] Kalamazoo, MI

WEHDE, IRENE N.
[b.] September 27, 1918, Cook, MN; [p.] Gust C. and Maria Nurmi (Owen Bergman - 1934, 1949 deceased); [m.] Albert Wehde Jr., August 27, 1960; [ch.] Joanne Bergman, Ph.d Treasure Island Fl; [ed.] High School Graduate; [occ.] Retired Telephone Operator, NW Bell Telephone Co.; [memb.] ITASCA Art Alliance, Grand Rapids, Minnesota 55744, Citrus Country Art League Lecanto, Florida 32661; [hon.] Awards and Ribbons in Local Art Shows, Membership Chairman, Citrus Country Art League (3 years) Historian, Citrus Country Art League, (1 yr); [pers.] Duty, Decision, Desideratum, Determines, Destiny; [a.] Homosassa, FL

WEHRLE, MATTHEW W.
[b.] June 17, 1980, Baton Rouge, LA; [p.] William R. and Antoinette T. Wehrle; [ed.] Currently a sophomore at Carolina Friends School Durham, N.C.; [occ.] Student; [memb.] P.E.T.A., SPCA

ociety, Holy Infant Senior High Youth Group, Carolina Friends School Clerks Committee; [hon.] Academic honors are not distributed as part of the Carolina Friends Curriculum practices.; [oth. writ.] Carolina Friends School Class Publications. First submission to an outside of source.; [pers.] I believe that each living creature, man or animal, is part of God's creation and therefore each is to be valued and appreciated. My writings generally try to reflect achievement, great or small.; [a.] Chapel Hill, NC

WEINBERG, KERRY
[b.] Trier, Germany; [ed.] European and Israeli undergrad. degrees (Engl., Latin, Judaica, Math), Master's Degree, English Lit., Temple University. Business Administration, Dept. of Ed., NYU and SUNY. Ph.D., Comparative Literature, NYU.; [occ.] Retired from high-school (Engl., Latin, German, French, Hebr.) and univers. Teaching (Anglo-Amer. and Compar. Lit., German, Research Writing, Creative Writing), SUNY, FDU, and Pace U. Now: Writg., Publshg., Profess., Lects.; [memb.] Various professional, alumni, and charitable organizations. Former program chair at Bnai Brith Lodge, etc.; [hon.] Scholarships at Temple U. NYU, fellowship at Princeton U. Honorary lunches, dinners in Rockld. County, NY and FDU. Innumerable guest lectures at colleges nationwide.; [oth. writ.] Engl. Textbk. for Gradtg. Studts, Tel-Aviv Book Eliot and Baudelaire, Mouton and Co., A Co-Authored Book Emunah/Horizons, Frkft./Germany, numerous essays on literary criticism in scholarly journals (MLS, Bulletin Baudelairien, The Classical Outlook, Die Neueren Sprachen/Diesterweg, etc. etc. Memoirs, Travelogues, Book Reviews, also several poems publ. in anthologies, profess., newsletters and local newspapers.; [pers.] It is important to look beneath the surface of situations and of human actions and to be mindful of the famous English poet's warning, "a little knowledge is a dangerous thing."; [a.] New City, NY

WEINBERG, LAURENCE M.
[pen.] Larry Weinberg; [b.] March 4, 1910, Long Beach, CA; [p.] Isaac and Nellie Weinberg; [m.] Marion T. Weinberg, December 29, 1939; [ch.] Nana and Ivan Weinberg; [ed.] Los Angeles High School 1926, (Los Angeles, CA), A.B. Stanford University 1930, J.D. Stanford Law School 1933; [occ.] Retired Lawyer; [memb.] President, Stanford Law Society of Southern California 1963-64, State Bar of California, admitted 1933, Los Angeles Copyright Society (Charter Member, President 1959); [hon.] Professor of Law, Pacific Coast University, 1939-42, Member Board of Visitor, Stanford Law School, 1964-67, Chairman, Rent Control Commission City of Rancho Mirage, CA 1980-86; [oth. writ.] "Financing of television productions," Continuing education of the Bar, California 1957, over 100 musical works, mostly popular music with lyrics, none published; [pers.] I believe in the brotherhood and sisterhood of all men and women. I believe every person has a right to adequate health care and the opportunity to live a life of economic security.; [a.] Long Beach, CA

WEINTRAUB, JULIE WRIGHT
[b.] July 22, 1960, Bottle Creek, MI; [p.] Hugh and Sally Wright; [m.] Dr. James R. Weintraub, June 7, 1987; [ch.] Jeffrey Rubin, Jenna Meredith; [ed.] University of Michigan; [occ.] At home Mom; [oth. writ.] Been writing poetry since 1978; [pers.] I feel we all need to do our part to make this world a better place to live in.; [a.] Ann Arbor, MI

WELCH, JOHN C.
[b.] March 28, 1951, San Pedro, CA; [p.] Benjamin and Beulah Welch; [m.] Elayne Welch, October 21, 1987; [ed.] V.C.L.A., Theatre Arts 0 1968 Cerritos Community College, Theatres Arts 1971 Royal Academy of Dancer - 1976 University of LaVerne, paralegal studies 1991; [occ.] Ballet Teacher, Real Estate Agent; [memb.] Royal Academy of Dance, Imperial Society of Teachers of Dance; [hon.] First American Male to pass the Imperial Society of Teachers of Dance exams (with honors); [pers.] We will never, with all our man made scientific and philosophical disciplines, understand the concept of inception. Inception is not a concept it is simply the pulse and anxiety of existence. We and everything else that exists are products of that indefinable process called infinity.; [a.] Huntington Beach, CA

WELCH, ROBERT BENLIEN
[pen.] Dana; [b.] February 21, 1960, Lawndale, CA; [p.] Sanda May Benlien; [ed.] Granada High School Livermore, CA 1974 to 1978 Barbazon Modeling School 1979 American Modeling School 1980 to 1981 Shirley Jones Acting School 1981 to 1982 Columbia School of Broadcasting; [pers.] My occupation in life, is living for today! The honor and award that I would wish to receive! Is the knowledge man has nothing to kill or die for but, living in life in peace! From 1967 to 1987 Commercial ADs Training Films Extra and Actor for motion pictures! My last debut for television was on March 17, 195 20/20 ABC.; [a.] Honolulu, HI

WELLS, KATHRYN R.
[b.] December 9, 1984, Raritan, NS; [p.] George and Sharon Wells; [ed.] J.F.K. Elem. School, Eischower Intermediate School; [occ.] Student

WELLS, MARTHA M.
[pen.] M. Sunshine; [b.] August 5, 1942, Price, UT; [p.] Matt Simmons (deceased); [ch.] Brent 35, Lori 34, Stephen 27, D.J. 23; [ed.] North Seattle Community College, Seattle, Wash. Columbia College Eastern; [occ.] Admin Aid, Toungo Point Coast Guard; [memb.] Station Astoria, OR; [hon.] Safety Red Cross, Sports Awards, PTA when children were in grade school; [oth. Writ.] Ocean Waves - '95, My Grandson Nicholas - '83, Quietness With In - '93, Christmas Season - '92; [pers.] Your ability is surpassed only by your modesty.; [a.] Seaside, OR

WELLS, MILES
[b.] October 22, 1944, Houston, TX; [a.] Houston, TX

WESSEL, PATRICIA A.
[pen.] Patricia Fanning Avery Bawcum Wessel, Patricia Fanning Wessel; [b.] May 11, 1942, Weehawken, NJ; [p.] James J. and Elizabeth C. Fanning, Sr.; [m.] James R. Wessel, March 18, 1989; [ch.] Deborah K. O'Mara and (Jayson Keith Bawcum); [ed.] St. Mary's High School Graduated 1960, Alabama NM, Attended The University of New Mexico and Technical Vocational Institute, Alabama, NM; [occ.] Retired Secretary, current occupation-Housewife; [memb.] The International Society of Authors and Artists 1996; [oth. writ.] Numerous poems in various poetry contests, some published no purchase of anthology required to insure publication. Other poems published required purchase of Anthology to insure publication of poems.; [pers.] Laughter is contagious! May we all catch it, as it is also the best medicine! Thanks to my loving husband, family and friends who encouraged my poetic endeavors.; [a.] Albuquerque, NM

WEST, SUSAN GERALDINE
[pen.] Farr North West; [b.] February 23, 1952, Elizabeth, NJ; [p.] William and Geraldine Kamin West; [ed.] Academic Diploma High School Alma White Prep School Zarephath, N.J. June 9, 1969, Elizabeth General Hospital Sch. of Nursing Elizabeth, New Jersey Diploma in Nursing June 2, 1972, College of Notre Dame/Belmont, Calif. B.S. in Behavioral Science 12/81, presently enrolled in MHA program at St. Mary's College of Calif. School of extended Education: Will graduate May, 1997; [occ.] Registered Nurse in Acute Hemodialysis at El Camino Hospital Mountain View California American Association of University Women Washington DC; [memb.] National Association for Female Executives, New York City, National Trust for Historic Preservation, Washington, D.C., American Nephrology Nurse's Association Pittman, New Jersey, BCLS Instructor for the American Heart Association, Volunteer Educator for the National Kidney Foundation of No. Calif, Smithsonian Institution Member, Washington, D.C., World Wildlife Foundation; [hon.] Volunteer awards for Patient Education for Ntl Kid/Fund/No. Calif., Certified Nephrology Nurse since May, 1990, American Nephrology Nurse's, Association National Kidney Foundation of No. Calif East Hooly Ave Box 56, Pittman, NJ; [a.] Foster City, CA

WEST, TONI
[b.] August 61, Whittier, CA; [m.] Chris West; [ch.] Jordan, Kristin; [oth. Writ.] The Game, Too Late Now, Searching, to name a few; [pers.] I hope to evoke emotions of some kind, from all types of people, with my writings.

WEST, TONY
[pen.] ISIL; [b.] August 14, 1968, Pinehurst, NC; [p.] Gerald and Pam West; [occ.] Compensation and Benefits Manager - St. Joseph of the Pines; [pers.] I write for those I love to show how much I love them.; [a.] Southern Pines, NC

WESTON, SHIRLEY
[pen.] Shirley Weston sometimes Eraddock; [b.] September 19, 1934, Pueblo, CO; [p.] Charles and Georgia Scolere; [m.] Herbert J. Weston, July 3, 1995 (2nd marriage); [ch.] John, Mark, Matthew and David Craddock; [ed.] B.A. Marycrest College, Davenport, Iowa (Social Science), M.A. Adams State College, Alamosa, Colorado, Degree in Secondary Education, additional Graduate Work at 3 universities other than above; [occ.] Retired High School Teacher (History, Government and English); [memb.] Phi Delta Kappa; [oth. writ.] Political articles in local news papers.; [a.] Cerritos, CA

WHEELER, G. EGAN
[b.] January 19, 1977, Salt Lake City, UT; [p.] Gerald Wheeler, Melanie Wheeler; [ed.] Leysin American School, Leysin, Switzerland, University of Utah; [occ.] Ski Instructor, Park City Ski Area, Park City, UT; [memb.] Professional Ski Instructors of America, National Honor Society; [hon.] Eagle Scout Award, Department Award for Senior English, A.P. Scholar Award, various Awards for Academic Excellence; [oth. writ.] An extensive, personal collection of poetry, analytical essays, and other writings.; [pers.] Strong emotions dictate the essence of my writing, providing a means by which my experiences, sorrows, and passions can be expressed.; [a.] Salt Lake City, UT

WHEELER, JANIS E.
[b.] February 9, 1935, Buffalo, NY; [p.] Lorna Yox, Stanley Scurlock; [m.] Alfred D. Wheeler, October 17, 1953; [ch.] Thomas A. Wheeler; [occ.] Part Time Substitute Teacher; [pers.] Strive to live each day in a way that will make someone smile for tomorrow is promised to no one.; [a.] Terreton, ID

WHITE, DEBORAH LYNN
[b.] January 9, 1955, Philadelphia, PA; [p.] Elsie; [m.] Leonard White, December 14, 1974; [ch.] Deneen Denette; [ed.] Deptford High, Gloucester County College; [occ.] Bus Driver; [memb.] Living Waters Church, Edith Ave Jolly Ranches; [oth. writ.] Nothing published.; [pers.] Do unto others as you would have them do unto you. We all should care

and lend a hand. If we all helped, there would be no strife in anyone's life.; [a.] Woodbury, NJ

WHITE, EDWARD J.
[pen.] Irish Eddie; [b.] June 18, 1958, Hartford, CT; [p.] Patricia and Edward F. White; [m.] Kimberly A. White, April 6, 1984; [ch.] Edward J. Jr., Kacey Lee, Saramarie; [ed.] Manchester High School, 1977, Matatuck Community College 1980; [memb.] Manchester Midget Football Assoc., Manchester Little League Assoc. coach; [hon.] Captain of High School football, baseball, indoor track, all league punter CCIL 1977, Captain of College football, baseball, Sports Editor of Matatuck Arrow School newspaper; [pers.] I feel my work can be appreciated by the average reader through the simplicity and readability of my lines. On the other hand, connoisseurs may enjoy the mood or tempo I try to create. To be a successful writer, I must alter my readers present state of mind plunging deep enough to create a picture without losing context.; [a.] Manchester, CT

WHITE, LILLIAN C.
[b.] November 24, 1921, New York City, NY; [p.] James E. Armour and Lillian; [ch.] Barbara Staeben; [ed.] High School Grad; [occ.] Retired, Bank of America 30 yrs of service; [memb.] "So. Bay Coasters", Retirement B of A. Club; [hon.] Several cash awards for cash saving ideas for B of A. operations "Suggestion Program"; [oth. writ.] More poems personal and artist - again personal pleasure; [pers.] Do unto others as you would have them do unto you. Share with others less fortunate what God has given you in abundance. Love without conditions; [a.] Los Angeles, CA

WHITE, MARIE R.
[b.] March 18, 1928, Tennessee; [p.] Amon and Gladys Randolph; [m.] Albert Mitchell White (Deceased), October 13, 1945; [ch.] Linda, David, Garry, Patricia and Jeff; [ed.] High School; [occ.] Seam tress; [memb.] Lakewood Baptist Church Donelson Pk at Emeny or Nashville TN 37214; [hon.] Daughter-wife-mother, Grandmother and great grand mother; [oth. writ.] Precious moments some of life's most precious moments are woven from threads of sorrow and hidden deep within our memory to lighten a load tomorrow; [pers.] Lord teach me to live one day at a time, that the future is yours and not mine; [a.] Hermitage, TN

WHITMIRE, BONITA
[pen.] Pulaski D. Ethridge; [b.] August 8, 1959, Baltimore, MD; [p.] John and Eva Lee Whitmire; [ed.] Southside High School 1976, Greenville Technical College 1979, University of South Carolina 1987; [occ.] Marketing Research; [memb.] Member Chancel Choir of Edwards Road Baptist Church, Pleasantburg Lions Club, Zone chairman - Zone Six 1995-96 (Lions); [hon.] Melvin Jones Fellowship 1992 - highest award that can be received by Lions; [oth. writ.] 2 poems Reedy River Review, 1 poem Palmetto Lion, 1 poem Glimpses of Grove, 1 poem SAM Newsletter, East of the Sunrise, Best Poems of 1996, A Muse to Follow; [pers.] My writing reflects the core of my being. Often, when I write, what I write pours out of me, as if I have no control over it.; [a.] Greenville, SC

WILBUR, LAUREL J.
[b.] April 8, 1962, San Jose, CA; [p.] Tonja Carlton and Cliff Millhise; [m.] June 7, 1981; [ch.] 3 Children; [ed.] 1st year college - Walla Walla College, Art Course, Personal Creative Writing Course; [occ.] Bus, owner; [memb.] Hockaday Center for the Arts; [oth. writ.] Reflections, Daddy, God's Prism, Musings, Marriage, Divorce and Co Dependency; [pers.] I want to make a difference in my world through poetry and oil painting. God's world can be a better place. Helen Sleiner Rice influenced my love for poetry.; [a.] Columbia Falls. MT

WILHELMY, GUS
[b.] February 17, 1935, Saint Paul, MN; [p.] George Wilhelmy and Emily Wegner; [m.] Mary Rose Valley, September 1, 1990; [ch.] Rochelle Marie, Todd Jerome, Rebecca Ann; [ed.] B.A. Passionist College, Louisville KY., M.A.'s University of Michigan, Ann Arbor, Michigan; [occ.] Fund Raising Executive; [memb.] American Marketing Association, American Management Association, Society of Fund Raising Executives; [hon.] Martin Luther King Community Service Award, Outstanding Young Man of America, Founder's Award, Safer Foundation, Editor's Choice Awards from National Library of Poetry; [oth. writ.] Numerous articles published in magazines and newspapers... Poetry in other magazines; [pers.] I seemingly write best about the pain, the struggle, the weakness of all of us... yet my view is hopefully romantic and touches the light within.; [a.] Chicago, IL

WILKIE, WILMA
[b.] June 24, 1899, Kansas; [ch.] Four; [oth. writ.] A tribute to Charlie, "A mothers Service Flag" "When My Boys Come Home" "Almonds in Bloom" "Virginias First Day" "Wayne and Wanita"; [pers.] After my boys left to go to the army during World War II, I got a job, working at a machine shop. It was very noisy and monotonous. I passed the time away by writing poems; [a.] Fremont, CA

WILKINSON, JUDY
[b.] October 18, 1955, La Grande, OR; [p.] Buddy and Reola Glenn; [m.] October 13, 1979; [ch.] David Wade; [ed.] Imbler High School, Western Business College; [occ.] Powerplant Operator, U.S. Army Corps of Engineers; [a.] Dayton, WA

WILKINSON, MARGARET M.
[pen.] Magj Wilkinson; [b.] April 7, 1926, Oregon City, OR; [p.] Melvin and Nell Cage; [m.] Michael S. Wilkinson, September 5, 1983; [ch.] I have 2 by 1st marriage; [ed.] Graduated High School 4 yrs Bible College; [occ.] Foster Home; [memb.] Lincoln City Art Society South County Artists; [hon.] I have many blue ribbons for art, but this is the first time I have enterer a contest for poetry.; [oth. writ.] I have written articles for newspaper; [pers.] Life is finally showing down enough to paint and write. My motivating force is love for my fellow human. My ability to love is a direct gift from a loving God.; [a.] Beaver, OR

WILLETT, GRACIE
[b.] May 22, 1948, Houston, TX; [p.] Fleet B. Self and Anna M. Self; [ch.] Ella Louise, Greta Rosanna and Karyn; [ed.] Deer Park High School, Durhamn Business School, San Jacinto Jr. College; [occ.] Data Entry Clerk Customer Service; [memb.] Memorial Baptist Church; [hon.] Best Supporting Actress, Superior Performer - 1968; [oth. writ.] Soldier's Story (written in High School paper); [pers.] Be kind - for everyone you meet is fighting a battle.; [a.] Houston, TX

WILLEY, SHIRLEY JEAN
[pen.] Shirley Jean (Cricket); [b.] November 12, 1946, Dover, DE; [p.] Louise Marie and Fred Willey Jr.; [m.] Divorced; [ch.] Five living now; [ed.] Going to Polytech in Woodside since last Sept. '95 trying for my diploma, C.E.A. 3, Ged., hoping to graduate this year '96.; [occ.] I'm a self house painting, I paint people homes, trailer, sleds, what inside and out.; [memb.] I'm a Seventh Day Adventist Christian. I became the 28th Memberships of our Churches. I have a certificate from New York, Forged and Dodds University for Nurse's Aid - 94.0 was my grade.; [hon.] I have received in my li many Bible Studies Awards and Award from Fing Hut Company for being a top number 1 payer buying things and paying for them as they asked too.; [oth. writ.] I love to write. When I wri something, I take my heart in it. When I wrote th poem - What is Life, Day After Day?... It was birthday it came to my heart. "Nov. 12, 1995. [pers.] I have always since I was little loved poem trying to make things rhyme and make people laug smile, and feel better in their life. I love people be happy and so me if sick get well. I make upcard and verses and I send them to people.; [a Harrington, DE

WILLIAMS, ANGELA CAROL
[b.] November 24, 1958, Fortuna, CA; [p.] John a Virginia Kotopoulous; [ed.] High School; [occ Electronics; [oth. writ.] National Summit, Newsle ter; [pers.] Feeling so grateful, I'm unable to spea my poetry is a prayer I love to read and remembe [a.] Mountain View, CA

WILLIAMS, ANTHONY S.
[b.] September 2, 1958, Pittsburgh; [p.] Genevie Maye-Hearn; [m.] Mary Martin-Williams, May 29 1993; [ch.] Tamiya, Donte, Anthony, Ashley an Dominique; [ed.] Alleghemy High School (1976 U.S. Navy (1978); [memb.] Buena Vista Methodis Church; [pers.] I maintain a belief that every livin being serves a specific purpose in life. Upo completion of that purpose comes death. Throug this death comes life with the experience gained b beings past.; [a.] Pittsburgh, PA

WILLIAMS, BARBARA
[pen.] Gypsy Gaines; [b.] June 15, 1940, Chicago IL; [p.] Artie and Linnie Gaines; [m.] Oliver Will iams Sr., May 8, 1960; [ch.] Three Sons; [ed. Englewood High, Chicago Teachers College, Lo Angeles Southwest College; [occ.] Retired - Fulltime Student, Psychology Major; [memb.] National Park Trust; [hon.] Gamma Beta Mentor; [pers.] I write to express the love for one who worked so hard, and left too soon, my mother.; [a.] Hawthorne, CA

WILLIAMS, DEBRA H.
[b.] February 11, 1953, Savannah, GA; [p.] Byron And Corrie Hatcher; [m.] Bruce E. Williams, September 4, 1983; [ed.] Groves High, Savannah State College; [occ.] Student; [memb.] St. Peter's Catholic Church; [hon.] Pathways Scholarship, Dean's List, Second Place History Essay Contest; [a.] Savannah, GA

WILLIAMS, GENEVA
[pen.] Geneva Williams; [b.] July 26, 1937, Leachville, AR; [p.] Walter M. and Bertha L. Hale; [m.] John K. Williams, September 11, 1965; [ed.] B.B. Elemen. School WT..C. - Jackson, TN Beech Bluff High; [occ.] Williams Piano Co (owners) (Husband and I) Devoted to Musical Industry; [memb.] Peoples Chapel Ch.; [oth. writ.] Gattingberg-Cristus Gdns./Local publication poem book/church publication.; [pers.] To be an inspiration to others through poetry. "A poem can speak to someone... when all else fails."; [a.] Jackson, TN

WILLIAMS, JANETA
[pen.] Jean; [b.] September 30, 1963, Jamaica; [ed.] Primary, Secondary Community College; [occ.] Companion Aide; [memb.] Brooklyn House of God Church; [hon.] National Saving Committee Jamaica in 1978; [oth. writ.] Several poems publish in Local Newspaper for children in Jamaica; [pers.] I wish to reach out to every nation in words of wisdom as a poetess.

WILLIAMS, JASON LEE
[b.] November 3, 1978, Englewood, CO; [ed.] High

:hool, Junior; [occ.] Restaurant Busser; [pers.] I rite what is in my heart.; [a.] Englewood, CO

WILLIAMS, LILLIAN HARRISON
en.] Lilian Harrison Williams; [b.] April 12, 1934, ouglas, GA; [p.] Lee Harrison, Rosa Hand Harrison; n.] Oliver F. Williams, September 19, 1953; [ch.] ary M. and F. Michael (William); (ed.] No formal ollege: continuing Ed. Courses in Insurance, Real state. seventeen years cover in newspaper publishng (most phases); [occ.] Semi-retired. Editor and oordinator of various county Ressuree Directoes; [memb.] Active in church work, enjoy children, randchildren and great-grands.; [oth. writ.] Feature riter and sales (Adv.) consultant for: Managing ditor - the Nicholls Observer 1980-84, Feature Vriter - the Douglas Enterprise 1985-91, Feature Vriter Reporter: The Coffes Country Progress 84-5; [pers.] With no college training I attribute any uccess I may have attained to faith and an enduring elationship with an Almighty God, who provides ne with inspiration for most of my writings.; [a.] Nicholls, GA

WILLIAMS, LORI
b.] April 27, 1973, Houston, TX; [p.] Larry and Ann Williams; [ed.] North Shore Senior High, urrently a Senior Student at Texas Southern degree with a Major in Biology and minor in Chemistry.; memb.] Beta Kappa Chi (Scientific Honor Society). Served as Recording Secretary 94-95.; [hon.] Texas Southern University Honor Roll Student 1992, 1994, and 1994. Listed in the National Dean's List 15th Ed. (91-92), 16th (82-93). 17th (93-94) and 8th (94-95).; [pers.] I have always used my poems as an outlet for the abundance of emotions that are inside my heart. I hope that by sharing my creations, I will remind others of the wonderful feeling of love that is inside each and everyone of us.; [a.] Houston, TX

WILLIAMS, LORIE A.
[pen.] Lorie Rice/Boyd; [b.] May 14, 1962, Saint Louis, MO; [ed.] McCluer North High School Central MO, State University/Univ. of MO St. Campus B.S. Business and Information Systems; [occ.] Computer Specialist Network Administrator; [hon.] Lambda Sigma Honor Society, Dean's List, National Honor Society Lions and Rotary Club Scholarships; [oth. writ.] Songwriter-singer Speechwriterspeaker, many more poems.; [pers.] The mind is a great battlefield waiting to be conquered. Have war with with your mind to force to the forefront your hidden skills, talents and abilities.; [a.] Saint Louis, MO

WILLIAMS, REANNE
[pen.] Reanne Williams; [b.] June 18, 1982, Sodus, NY; [p.] Richard and Lisa Williams; [ed.] Currently an 8th grade, student at North Rose - Wolcott Middle School; [oth. writ.] Journal writings and many other poems.; [pers.] I am an accomplished horseback rider and enjoy sailing on my free time. I am 13 years old.; [a.] Wolcott, NY

WILLIAMS, RENEE E.
[b.] September 3, 1931, Chicago, IL; [p.] Madeline and Mansfield Williams; [ed.] Wendell Phillips High, Chicago, Central YMCA College, Chicago, Asoc. Bus Adm, Los Angeles City College, and Currently attends UNLV pursuing BA in the film Studies; [occ.] Retired; [pers.] Relationship are difficult. I try to explore human experiences without being judgmental or sanctimonious. We learned and grow best when we understand why we do what we do, especially to each other. Human Drama is played out in relationships. My first preference is Russian Writers. I also try Haiku poetry. Haiku is fascinating because it sets a limit of 17 syllables in 3 lines of poetry. So the poet must expand, expand, expand — words, imagery, metaphor — within this limitation; [a.] Las Vegas, NV

WILLIAMS, SANDRA Y.
[pen.] Alexandria Williams; [b.] February 2, 1936, Camden, TN; [p.] Mr and Mrs G. M. Ferguson; [m.] Joseph V. Williams, October 21, 1951; [ch.] Joe, Gary, Lisa, Scott Williams; [ed.] 12 grade, Grove High, Paris, TN; [occ.] Gospel songwriting and children's books; [oth. writ.] Copyright 1995 Rice Fields music (BMI), copyright (copy of enclosed) "Wake Up America", Gospel Song in poetry, children's storybooks, poetry, gospel songs (submitted to Rice Studios and Blackwood Bro Publishing House), music and lyrics, Rice Fields Music; [pers.] The gift I have is a gift from God. My poem "Midnight" was written at age 14. Most of my writing has been done as an adult. I have been a Christian since age 21. The Lord has put this gift in my life. I just receive what he directs.; [a.] Memphis, TN

WILLIAMS, SHAREL RENEE
[pen.] Sharel White; [b.] March 7, 1968, Houston, TX; [p.] Micheal Raymond Warren, Linda Kay Corbin; [ch.] Talyna, Celia, Katrina; [occ.] House Mother; [hon.] Editor's Choice Awards for 3 of my poems published by National Library of Poetry; [oth. writ.] "Sweet Celia," "Cloud of Confusion," "Glimmer of Hope," "Brother" all published by National Library of Poetry in different books.; [pers.] May we as American's stop, cool off, and listen. And if we are still feeling like hitting someone, then hit the nearest wall instead. There are no excuses for abuse. Young or old we all have feelings. So stop the abused.; [a.] Ehrenberg, AZ

WILLIAMS, STANLEY
[b.] March 20, 1925, Near Sulphur Springs, TX; [p.] Byron, Lorena Williams; [m.] Dr. Dorothy Burns-Williams, November 22, 1958; [ch.] Lorena Ann, Thomas Byron, Stanley Jr.; [ed.] Naval Aviator Wings (3-3-47) Fighter Pilot Flying On and Off Carriers - Supersonic (1953) some formal school housing considerable time in college of Hard Knocks - colors black and blue; [occ.] Retired Naval Officer Aviator; [memb.] Piedmont Council Boy Scouts, Oakland Museum Association, San Francisco Art Museum, KQED, BPDE Elks 1250 Red Bluff, Ca.; [hon.] Piedmont Council BSA-Silver Beaver (1982), Scoutmaster Trooph (1974-1977), Vigil Honor in the order of the Ardon (1984), Member of 3 Man Team receiving the Silver Anvil from Public Relations Society (1963); [oth. writ.] Newspaper Articles and Feature Stories.; [pers.] Married Mary Rose McGlynn (9-2-50) in first military wedding Red Bluff, Ca. Dress whites swords in 113 degrees heat. Mary expired in Santa Monica, Ca (1957) I was at HCLA. I have liars, cheats, thieves. - Be yourself, tell the truth and try to make friends. - Your word is your bond. Living is fun.; [a.] Piedmont, CA

WILLIAMS, TIFFANY ANN
[pen.] Tiff; [b.] November 2, 1965, Chicago, IL; [p.] Alice Coward; [m.] Andre T. Williams, February 13, 1988; [ch.] Amber - 3 and Amanda Williams - 2; [ed.] College Northern Mich. Univ. Marquette, MI 2 yrs; [occ.] Home Maker - Wife and mother to the best family a person could ever have.; [oth. writ.] Poems: To Dream Another's Dream, The One Without A Home, Short Story - Anticipation; [pers.] I give all honor and glory to God. I thank God for this gift. Remember God is in control, and your life is in the hands of the one who loves you the most.; [a.] Woomera, Southern Australia

WILLIAMS, WILLIE C.
[pen.] Willie C. Williams; [b.] January 1, 1938, Hubbard, TX; [p.] Mr. and Mrs. Edward and Dollie Williams; [ed.] Waco High School TSTI (NOW TSTC at WACO, TX.); [occ.] Semi- Retired; [memb.] Fleet Reserve Association International Society of Poets; [hon.] Poet Awards from International Society of Poets Peans list at TSTI.; [oth. writ.] Other Poems Published, Honorable, Mention in State Conservation Contest in Jr. High School.; [pers.] Hope fully these writings will be viewed and read by others today and tomorrow.; [a.] Waco, TX

WILLIAMSON, H. L.
[pen.] Le Roy Herman; [b.] May 1, 1934, Oklahoma City, OK; [p.] Herman Alvin and Beatrice Williamson; [m.] Nancy Gall, August 23, 1975; [ch.] Kim, Jim, and Mark; [ed.] BSME and MSME Okla. State Univ.; [occ.] Retired Executive - Aerospace; [hon.] All American and Professional Baseball; [oth. writ.] Novel "The Engineer" pits an Engineering mind against Las Vegas.; [pers.] Writing is a form of freedom, you can be anyone you want to be, but don't expect to always like yourself.; [a.] Seal Beach, CA

WILSON, BRENDA J.
[pen.] B. J.; [b.] August 16, 1960, Boyd Co., KY; [p.] Anna J. Hamilton and Johnny R. Nolan; [m.] Willie Wilson, January 17, 1995; [ch.] Allison age 13, Michael age 10; [ed.] LPN; [occ.] Nurse; [memb.] 2nd Baptist Church, Ashland KY; [oth. writ.] Searching for a Rainbow, Thoughts of Tomorrow, I Need to be Me. Waiting for Happiness, Does Anyone Hear, Remember Me; [pers.] I enjoy writing, I thank God for giving me the talent.; [a.] Ashland, KY

WILSON, CLYDE
[pen.] Lex Argot; [b.] November 8, 1920, Alameda, CA; [p.] Clyde Sr., Melva; [m.] Barbara Darrimon Wilson, June 23, 1943; [ch.] Karna, Clyde III, Dean, Janinne; [ed.] Alameda High; [occ.] Retired Clyde Lewis Wilson Co, Pan Pacific Fisheries, Inc., V/P DePaolo Auto Smog Control Co, Director, Silver Pine Homes, Ass't Editor, Rail and Cable News; [memb.] Distinguished Member International Society of Poets; [hon.] U.S. Patent #3752766, MIT/CAl TECH "Clean Air Car Race", Editors Choice Awards, 1994, 1995; [oth. writ.] Reflections of Light, East of Sunrise, A Delicate Balance, Best Poems of 1996, Sparkles In The Sand, Shadows and Light, The Voice Within, Spirit of the Age, A Muse to Follow, A Tapestry of Thoughts; [pers.] "May your Mettle Surpass the Crucible of Challenge and Change".; [a.] Moraga, CA

WILSON, ELIZABETH ANN
[b.] April 23, 1962, Corpus Christie, TX; [p.] John Briggs, Terri Beecher; [m.] Larry Wilson, May 8, 1982; [ch.] Elena Margaret; [pers.] I write out of inspiration alone, not satisfied to be a "puppet or player, but only as a truth messenger.".; [a.] Port Saint Lucie, FL

WILSON, JANET ELAINE WRIGHT
[pen.] Elaine Willinhart; [b.] January 18, 1942, Louisville, KY; [p.] William Frederick and Minnie Mae Wright; [m.] Walter Wilbern Wilson, July 19, 1963; [ch.] Annessa Eileen Mitchell, Alicia Ellen Mitchell Andria Esther Cuffel, grandsons: John David, Matthew, Kyle, Austin; [ed.] DuPont Manual High School, Christ Gospel Bible Institute, Norton Memorial School of Nursing, Accredited Home Schooling Teacher, Missionary Representative in Waiter 16 yrs.; [occ.] Registered Nurse, Jewish Hospital Healthcare Services, Louisville, KY; [memb.] Kentucky Nursing Association, Christ Gospel Church Int'l Inc.; [oth. writ.] Several poems published in church bulletins and magazines, newsletters of Capitol Marketing Insurance, Hospital publications.; [pers.] I enjoy sharing moral principles interacting in our every day living.; [a.] Georgetown, IN

WILSON, NELLIE MAE
[b.] March 2, 1947, Pineville, LA; [p.] Mr. and Mrs. Louis V. Elie; [m.] Rev. Wilbert Wilson Jr., December 5, 1970; [ch.] Louis B. Wilson; [ed.] Graduate High School Business College, 6 months writing course at; [occ.] Housewife or Homemaker; [memb.] EI; [hon.] Basic Art Certificate, Art Instruction School, Minneapolis, Minn; [oth. writ.] None published short stories and poems; [pers.] "To express deeper wonders of life and it's unspeakable riches!" Spiritual writers as past time; [a.] Alexandria, LA

WILSON, RUBY ZUNDELL
[pen.] Ruby Z. Boedeker; [b.] August 11, 1911, Willard, UT; [p.] Charlotte Taylor, Daniel Zundell; [m.] Deceased; [ch.] Sherry S. Takes, Billy L. Boedeker, Bonnie Jean Thomas; [ed.] Box Elder High School - Brigham City, Utah, College Writing Classes; [occ.] Retired Illustrator and Draftsman; [memb.] Member of Blue Quill Brigham and Ogden Utah, L.D.S. Church; [hon.] Honorable mention from Earl Stanley Gardener at Blue Quill Club Convention for poetry, Salt Lake City, UT., poetry recited by Kenneth King KLO - Ogden, Utah Radio Host.; [oth. writ.] "Bus Stop" short story published - Alfred Hatchback Wong, 2 articles in the Alaska Sportsman Magazine and a book of unpublished poems; [pers.] I write from personal experience and deeply felt feelings and a great love of words.; [a.] Hooper, UT

WILSON, TERRI R.
[b.] December 10, 1944, Chicago, IL; [p.] Joseph P. Grove, Phyllis D. Grove; [m.] Jesse W. Wilson III; [ch.] Jeffrey Scott, Michael Eric; [ed.] Vallejo Sr. High School, Calif. State University, Chico; [occ.] First Grade Teacher; [memb.] International Reading Assoc., National Council of Teachers of Mathematics; [oth. writ.] Several unpublished poems written for and used with my first grade children.; [a.] Gold River, CA

WINCKLER, KAREN A.
[b.] February 18, 1964, Newark, NJ; [m.] Ms. Ena Sherman, June 25, 1994; [ed.] W. Orange Mountain High, Princeton University; [occ.] Bartender, Astrologer; [memb.] Unity Fellowship Church; [pers.] To be black, a woman, a lesbian and a loving human being in America: Chaos and drama. I strive to be the best human instrument I can be, and let God play me.; [a.] South Orange, NJ

WINFIELD, LISA
[b.] May 5, 1960, Los Angeles; [m.] Frank Liberatore, February 21, 1987; [ch.] Angela and Camille; [ed.] BA Political Science, UCLA 1982 JD - USC 1985; [occ.] Attorney; [memb.] Int'l Society of Poets; [oth. writ.] Poems published in previous National Library of Poetry Anthologies (sparkles in the sand and Best Poems of 1996), currently working on volume of poetry and a screenplay about my daughter's struggle to regain the power of speech; [pers.] Never lose faith in the healing power of love; [a.] Los Angeles, CA

WINGO, VICKIE K.
[pen.] Vickie K. Wingo; [b.] August 10, 1960, Greenville, SC; [p.] Trudy and Mike Mahaffey; [m.] David Mark Wingo, June 27, 1993; [ch.] Jessica Amber, Ashley Elizabeth; [ed.] Carolina High, Clemson University, Enoree Vocational School; [occ.] Disabled, Commissioned writer and poet; [hon.] 1994 and 1995 New Poet Award, State Wide Painting Competition, Published in 11 book this past year.; [oth. writ.] I write for the Cunningham Collection, we specialize in the stories of the wee-people with a twist of poetry. I have also bee featured in several anthology's. I've written for years and am currently working on a manuscript for a chapbook.; [pers.] My work comes from the heart.
I try to express a whole range of emotions, honesty in my work is important to me. If I touch one person then I've done what I set out to do.; [a.] Inman, SC

WIRKUS, LYDIA H.
[b.] April 15, 1950, Miami, FL; [p.] Leonard V. and Rosemary H. Wirkus; [ch.] Faustin (14), Russell (11); [ed.] BA Florida State Univ., MS Florida International Univ., Med - U.N.C. at Greensboro; [occ.] Special Education Teacher, Mat Su Alternative School, Wasilla, AK; [memb.] Our Redeemer Lutheran Church, Troop Committee, Boy Scout Troop 28; [pers.] I would like to dedicate the publication of my poem to the memory of Joel Kabatznik.; [a.] Chugiak, AL

WISE, BRIDGET D.
[b.] January 5, 1979, Montclair, CA; [p.] Ann Marshall and Lee Wise; [ed.] This is my sophomore year in high school. I attend Little Rock Central High; [memb.] Cheerleading, usherboard at church, and spanish club. I am also on the track team at my school and ran cross-country.; [hon.] Having my poem published in a book is an honor for me.; [oth. writ.] Paris, I put on a mask, and life.; [pers.] I hope to be a great poet like Maya Angdo one day.; [a.] Little Rock, AR

WISE, DOROTHY ANN
[b.] December 6, 1934, Weaubleau, MO; [p.] Dr. and Mrs. Harry Taylor, Lorraine (Deceased); [m.] William Wise (Deceased), October 8, 1955; [ch.] William D. Wise, Cereda Lorraine Adams; [ed.] Lewisville High School - Lewisville, TX, North Texas University - Denton, TX, 2 grand-daughters - Staci Lorraine Patterson, Brea Lee-Ann Adams; [occ.] Reservations-American Airlines; [memb.] Eastern Star, First United Methodist Church - Lewisville Texas; [oth. writ.] Lewisville High School - Alma Marta - School Song adopted - 1952; [pers.] Live each day for all it's worth - then move onto tomorrow.; [a.] Irving, TX

WISEMAN, CLIFTON E.
[b.] June 30, 1922, Sheffield, IA; [p.] Thomas H. and Myrtle Wiseman; [m.] Jane Hart Lowry Wiseman, February 29, 1992; [ch.] Suzanne Miller, Melvin, Wayne, John, Tom and step-son Mark Lowry; [ed.] Sheffield High School, Mason City Jr. College, Iowa State College at Ames, IA; [occ.] Lived on a farm all my life farmed for myself for 50 years.; [memb.] Farm Bureau, 4-H leader, 25 years on youth committee and Extension Council.; [oth. writ.] Published a 116 page hard cover book of poems, "Verses From An Old Farmer As He Recalls" and also a 55 verse poem in the local paper.; [pers.] I write very descriptive poetry of true happenings during my life as a child and as an adult and most are written so as to bring out a laugh or a smile to the reader. All are written in rhyming verse.; [a.] Sheffield, IA

WITHAM, HELEN
[b.] January 23, 1937, Albany, KT; [p.] Reuben Brown and Mary Pennycoff; [m.] Maxie Witham, July 2, 1955; [ch.] Timothy Alan, Jana, Dana, Deanna; [ed.] Clinton Co. High, Lindsay Wilson College, Tampa Cosmetology School Tampa Florida; [occ.] Cosmetologist, Beauty Advisor, Hair Dresser; [memb.] First Baptist Church of Albany Clinton Co. Historical Society; [hon.] Have had great success in writing articles and poems for the younger students in Sunday school and children's church; [oth. writ.] Short stories. And reports on historical events and places.; [pers.] I believe every person living on this earth. Should have the privilege of being the best they can be and pursue the happiness that they can attain to make their life on earth eternal joy.; [a.] Albany, KT

WITHEE, BEVERLY
[b.] December 26, 1967, Saint Thomas, VI; [p.] David Frederick Sr., and Pamela Brackett Withee; [ed.] Oliver Perry Walker Senior High School (May 1986), University of New Orleans, Delgado Community College, University of Phoenix (La. Campus); [occ.] Rehabilitation Technician; [memb.] International Society of Poets, Symphony Chorus Of New Orleans, Concert Choir of New Orleans, Aurora United Methodist Church.; [hon.] World of Poetry, Golden Poet (1992), National Library of Poetry, Editor's Choice Awards (1993, 1994, 1995), Published Poems in 5 Anthologies, "Whispers In The Wind" (1993), "Outstanding Poets of 1994" (1994); [oth. writ.] "Best Poems of 1995" (1995), "At Water's Edge" (1995), and "Walk Through Paradise" (1995).; [pers.] "To be loved by some one is the greatest feeling in the world." I wish that every person had someone to love them, because love never fails; [a.] Harvey, LA

WITT, KYLE LYNN
[b.] August 28, 1981, Colorado; [p.] Robyn Hitchin, Jerry S. Witt; [ed.] 9th Grade, Goshen High School; [occ.] Student; [memb.] Teen Inst. (Teens against drugs); [hon.] National Honor Society, 2 yrs. Honored by United States achievements academy, all star award (softball), God, flag, Country - Runner up in 8th grades Goshen Middle School Cheerleader; [oth. writ.] Frightful Nights (one-four), "Kendra", "What You Don't See", "Holidays", "By The Fire", and, "No More Will I Cry"; [pers.] Dedicated to the family of Charles A. Messmore; [a.] Goshen, OH

WIX, WYNDOM ALLEN
[pen.] W Wix; [b.] September 17, 1965, Lebanon, TN; [p.] Charlie and Sue Wix; [m.] Renee Wix, April 4, 1993; [ch.] Cassie-Mike-Allen Wix/Step: Jeremey-Brandon Ryle; [ed.] Macon County High School; [occ.] Truck Driver Sub-bus driver; [memb.] West Macon Rescue Squad Attend Haysville Missionary Baptist Church; [oth. writ.] Collections of poems for family and friends.; [pers.] The poems I write just come to out of the blue, but they are things that are on my mind and very close to my heart and with help from above, maybe they always will.; [a.] Westmoreland, TN

WOLFORD, SALLY SHEPPARD
[pen.] Sali Shappard-Wolford, grandma Sali; [b.] November 8, 1946, Santa Ana, CA; [p.] William B. and Virginia C. Sheppard; [m.] Robert E. Wolford, April 30, 1993; [ch.] Krista, Amber Stone, Autumn Star; [ed.] Anaheim High School; [occ.] Author and Illustrator, poet; [hon.] I appear as a regular on KLSR - Fox TV as "grandma Sali", where I read my storybooks to children on the Fox kids club.; [oth. writ.] "Color and keep" Storybooks (series of 13). Poetry for children. Novel: "Daughters of the Phoenix" Novel: "Dream Catcher" (Valley of the Skookum); [pers.] I believe the ills of our world could be cured if only our leaders would stop to listen to their own "child inside."; [a.] Elkton, OR

WOMBLE, LEOTHA
[pen.] Le Hicks; [b.] May 17, 1939, Jackson, TN; [p.] Rev. and Mrs. Bunyan and Margaret Hicks; [m.] Mr. Roger R. Womble, June 30, 1978; [ch.] Mr. Lonnie J. Sorrell Jr.; [ed.] Central High High - Grad., Grad. Durham Institute of Nursing, Grad. Watts Hospital School of Nursing; [occ.] Homemaker; [memb.] National Federation of the Blind, Quality Living Service, Zion Hill, Missionary Baptist Church Sunday School Teacher, Woman's Missionary Union; [hon.] Honorable award Woman's Missionary Union; [oth. writ.] Atlanta Bulletin.; [pers.] I've experienced and many things in my life face to face and I listen, so I write, to give a word for thought that will give a better light to the present for a good day,

or living each day.; [a.] Atlanta, GA

WOMBLE, MICHELLE A.
[pen.] Me'shel Anet; [b.] July 19, 1978, Davenport, IA; [p.] Michael and Lindy Womble; [ed.] I'm presently a senior in high school.; [hon.] 1994 - Who's Who Among America's High School students. 1994 - Nomination for student ambassador. 1995 - Who's Who Among America's High School Students.; [oth. writ.] (Short stories) - Till death do us part, The Ultimate Sacrifice. (Poetry) - Faith, Pain, Precious Angel, Dreams; [pers.] Envy is only ignorance because we envy those who are greater than us. Therefore, follow your dreams.; [a.] Grafton, OH

WOOD JR., KENNETH W.
[b.] October 1, 1975, Tampa, FL; [p.] Kenneth Wood and Judy Wood; [m.] Holly Loetscher; [ch.] Lance Phelan Wood; [ed.] Plant City High, Hillsborough Community College, Unversity of South Florida; [occ.] Pre-med student, Lab Assistant/South Bay Hospital; [memb.] AMSA (American Medical Student Association), HOSA (Health Occupation Students of America); [a.] Lithia, FL

WOODLAND, CAROLE
[b.] Los Angeles, CA; [p.] Florian Robak, Ruby Brown; [m.] Frank Michael Woodland, March 27, 1971; [ch.] Scot, Bonnie, Frank, John; [occ.] Piano Teacher; [pers.] Paul wrote, "Whatsoever things are true,... honest,... just, pure, whatsoever things are lovely...and of good report.." I seek after these things. (Philippians 4:8); [a.] Cerritos, CA

WOODS, JUDY S.
[b.] February 24, 1954, Cheyenne, WY; [p.] Lewis and Caroline Nation; [m.] Mark E. Woods, August 30, 1991; [ch.] Chris Michelle, Jeremy Douglas; [ed.] Earl Wooster High, University of Nevada, Reno; [occ.] Supervisor, Washoe Medical Center, Reno, NV; [pers.] I have always enjoy writing poetry and reading it as well. Ideas just come to me and I write them down.; [a.] Sparks, NV

WOOTON, W. T.
[b.] December 31; [p.] Alive, healthy, and enjoying a happy retirement; [m.] Single; [ed.] I had one!; [occ.] Health Care; [oth. writ.] Lots, song lyrics mostly. To see more write to me at P.O. Box 1246, Shepherdstown, WV 25443; [a.] Leesburg, VA

WORKMAN, KRISTY ELLIS
[pen.] Kristy Ellis Workman; [b.] October 14, 1958, Howell, MI; [p.] Bob and Joyce Ellis; [ch.] Sheena, Kendall and Jacob; [ed.] Whitmore Lake H.S., Central Michigan Univ., Glendale Community College; [occ.] Senior Benefit Specialist, Pfg.; [oth. writ.] The poem "Sunset" in "Mirrors of the Soul", Spring '96.; [pers.] My writings are greatly influenced by my emotional - inner feelings and what life has to offer.; [a.] Phoenix, AZ

WORTHINGTON, KARY J.
[b.] May 28, 1964, Portland, OR; [p.] Charles and Alyce Withee; [m.] Skipper R. Worthington, October 30, 1984; [ch.] Rachel, Amelia, Timothy and Alyce; [ed.] Grant High School Portland State University; [occ.] Sales and Inventory Manager Verifone, Inc.; [memb.] Sierra Club, Portland Audobon Society; [pers.] I use poetry and drawing painting as a creative release. Nature and family are my most common subjects.; [a.] Portland, OR

WRIGHT, BARBARA RENEE
[b.] August 7, 1965, Laporte, IN; [p.] Spencer Wright Jr. and Susie Wright of Michigan City, IN; [ed.] Elston High School, (Indiana Vocational Technical College) of South Bend, Indiana; [occ.] Creative Assistant, Graphic Designer, South Bend Tribune, South Bend, IN; [memb.] Colfax Cultural Complex Poetry Group.; [hon.] National Honor Society; [pers.] POETRY..... Planting words of expression on paper, that the seeds of One's experience, might take root, in the fertile soil of the heart of another, in order to produce blossoms of recognition, and a bouquet of familiarity. All Praises to God! Special thanks to Mom and Dad, Geraldine Woodard, Ms. T, Yolanda W. Kelly, and My Uppity Sisters of South Bend. God Bless and many thanks to all of the womyn and men who have taught me to fly and inspired me to soar; [a.] South Bend, IN

WRIGHT, CURTIS L.
[b.] September 21, 1972, Brooklyn, NY; [p.] Chris L. Wright, Irene Feaster Wright; [ed.] Satelite Academy, Brooklyn College; [occ.] Supervisor of Security; [pers.] In my writings I strive to enlighten others and help others to see the negatives and turn them into positives. Also to appreciate the beauty that this world has to offer in all its simplicity.; [a.] Brooklyn, NY

WRIGHT, DAVID
[b.] December 10, 1956, Roanoke Rapids, NC; [p.] Earl and Betty Wright; [ed.] Peterson High, San Jose University; [hon.] Editor's Choice Award; [oth. writ.] Poem published in the book, walk through paradise. Poems to be published in two upcoming books, and a newsletter.; [pers.] To express beauty in words.; [a.] Vancouver, WA

WRIGHT, EARL EDWARD
[b.] April 14, 1929, Saint Joseph, MO; [p.] Mr. and Mrs. V. F. Wright; [m.] Doris Ann Knight Wright, April 25, 1948; [ch.] Steven, Calvin, Roger, Doris Ann, Elizabeth, John, Eli, Barbara, Charlott; [ed.] 11th grade; [occ.] Cattle Buyer; [oth. writ.] Poems; [pers.] I confide, and contest, within my thoughts.; [a.] Brandon, SD

WRIGHT, ROBERT
[b.] February 12, 1956, Flint, MI; [p.] Earnest Wright, Marjorie Wright; [m.] Hazel Wright, December 18, 1992; [ch.] 3; [ed.] HS Diploma, Genesee Area Skill Center - Graphic Arts; [occ.] Waste Collector; [hon.] Mayor's Award; [oth. writ.] G-Man Blues (See Of Treasures) National Library of Poetry; [pers.] I write poetry for fun. I enjoy watching different situations come to life, on paper.; [a.] Flint, MI

WRIGHT JR., ROBERT L.
[b.] April 23, 1967, Tachecowa, Japan; [ed.] U.C. Davis; [occ.] Disabled (mentally); [pers.] I aspire to create an awareness of the beauty in diversity in a Western world, too often encompassed on anglo images as exclusive beauty; [a.] San Francisco, CA

WUESTHOFF, NANCY MORGAN
[pen.] Nancy Morgan Wuesthoff; [b.] March 30, 1951, Auburn, NY; [p.] Richard and Joanne Morgan; [m.] George H. Wuesthoff, July 2, 1981; [ch.] Gloria, David, Daniel, Cindy, Nathan, Matthew and Adam; [ed.] Kathleen High School - 12th grade Lakeland, FL; [occ.] Wife, mother, Domestic Engineer; [memb.] Amvets Auxiliary Post #32 2nd Vice, Lakeland, VFW Post 8002, Lakeland Fl, North Shore Animal - N.Y., Kathleen United Methodist Church League - Kathleen, Fl; [hon.] 2nd Vice President Honors - Amvets, Editor - Newsletter - Amvets (American Veterans) Helping organize Lakelands Awards First POW.-MIA Rally Outstanding Service - to Veterans - VFW Post 10477 2nd Place Teeball Team Coach 2-year President Chorus Class - High School (Delivering - my first Grandson 3/14/94 "Greatest Honor"); [oth. writ.] I've written poems as long as I can remember. Never one published. I write newsletter monthly for Amvets (American Veterans) I've written song words, stories I read to my grand children (5 of them) letters of love to my husband - George.; [pers.] There is nothing as great as a mother's love. When you too become a mother only then will you understand the true meaning of "bonding". You may become a wife, sister or what ever you want - no matter what you do - love your mother, cause when she's gone you'll always miss and love her - be good to mother.; [a.] Lakeland, FL

WYATT, HARRY W.
[pen.] H. Winfield Wyatt; [b.] December 3, 1942, Plymouth, MA; [m.] Sherri, April 14, 1984; [ch.] Michael, Simeon; [ed.] 1-12; [occ.] Sales Consultant Freelance writing and photography; [memb.] C.E.O. "Romantic Interludes" B and B Locators; [oth. writ.] "Horses Great and Small" (Canada), "Bed and Breakfast Adventures" (U.S.), Technical Articles for solid surface counters (S.D. Family Living Magazine); [pers.] "I came, I saw, I shopped!"; [a.] El Cajon, CA

WYATT, JOSEPH
[pen.] Joseph Wyatt; [b.] December 2, 1936, Phila., PA; [p.] Thomas and Rose Wyatt; [m.] Patricia Anne Wyatt, July 27, 1969; [ed.] 10th grade; [occ.] Unemployed.

WYATT, SHERRY L.
[pen.] Sher Why; [b.] February 11, 1961, Kansas City, MO; [p.] Bernell and Dorothy Wyatt; [ed.] Central High, University of Missouri, Columbia - B.A. psychology, California Western School of Law - J.D.; [occ.] Attorney-Estate Planning, Office Manager-RSD Financial; [memb.] Earl B. Gillian Bar Assoc., CA Bar Assoc., San Diego Volunteer Lawyers Assoc., San Diego Citizens Review Board on Police practices, co-founder of fulcrum Group.; [hon.] By The State Bar of California Board of Governors in recognition to the delivery of Pro bono legal services in California.; [oth. writ.] Booklet titled. "Class Actions: The ABs of Business Etiquette", Newsletter - "Family Briefs", "Creative Sentencing Writing, and "Electromagnetic Fields and Associated Health Hazards."; [pers.] Today is a perfect time to start "getting ahead" by balancing your life, finances and time - because "EACH DAY COUNTS".; [a.] San Diego, CA

YABLANSKY, BARBARA VECCHIONE
[b.] October 22, 1949, Brooklyn, NY; [p.] Victor Vecchione, Hilda Vecchione; [m.] Martin Yablansky, May 13, 1972; [ch.] Shanna Bridgette Yablansky; [ed.] Canarsie High School, CC, NY, Brooklyn College; [occ.] Mother, Homemaker, I design and craft and sell Costume Jewelry; [hon.] Goodman Short Story Award, City University Poetry Award; [oth. writ.] Short stories, pantoums, sonnets, haikus, ballads - some locally published.; [pers.] Writing traditional forms of poetry is the most joyous challenge for me because I lead a very undisciplined life. The structured boundaries of the traditional form really reign me in.; [a.] East Meadow Long Island, NY

YAGER, THEDA D.
[pen.] Lonnie Reed; [b.] December 19, 1936, Austin, TX; [p.] Rev. (Deceased) and Mrs. O. V. Stubbs; [m.] Donald E. Yager (A.F. Retired), June 21, 1957; [ch.] Alydia J. Wingard, Lisa L. Everett, Gail L. Waechter; [ed.] M. Ed. Southwest Texas State U., San Marcos, Texas BGS. Chaminade U. Honolulu, Hawaii (Cum Laude) 1995 Graduate of Institute of Children's Literature; [occ.] Licensed Clinical Professional Counselor; [memb.] Daughter of Confederacy, National Association of School Psychologist; [hon.] Cum Laude (BGS); [oth. writ.] Craft Articles for Home Life Mag. (1996), Article Montana in Baptist Mag., (1995), Newspaper articles. (No poems in print); [pers.] In my articles and

poems I strive to touch the heart and soul of the reader. As a result of the death of a baby daughter I am a counselor helping hurting families.; [a.] Thompson Falls, MT

YARBROUGH, DAN
[b.] March 29, 1952, Wenatchee, WA; [p.] Mrs. Vae Harnack, Hank Yarbrough; [m.] Cindy Johnson; [ch.] Amy and Dae (Yarbrough), Emma and J.J. (Lancaster); [ed.] Sommersett High (Calif.), Wenatchee Valley Jr. College, Eastern Wash. Univ. (current); [occ.] Student Eastern Wa. Un. Junior year; [memb.] Phi Theta Cappa; [hon.] Graduated with honors, Wen. Valley Jr. College, received Academic Merit Scholarship to attend Eastern Wash. Univ., Dean's/President's List - WVC, Dean's List - Eastern; [oth. writ.] Several essays, short stories and poems ready for submission; [pers.] I most appreciate poetry (and writing in general) written clearly.; [a.] Wenatchee, WA

YAROSLAWSKI, MARY F.
[pen.] Mary F. Yaroslawski; [b.] Febraury 14, 1938, Jacksonville; [p.] Francies and Hattie Willis; [ch.] Drusilla Davis; [ed.] High School

YATES, REV. LESTER E.
[pen.] Rev. Lester E. Yates; [b.] February 12, 1948, Waynesboro, MS; [p.] Alvin, Ollie Yates; [m.] Ophelia Yates, April 14, 1978; [ch.] Helen, Shelia, James Earl, Nicholar, Angerla; [ed.] Day Aduet High School, AA degree Indiana Christian University; [occ.] Mechanical Equipment Operator; [memb.] Boy Scout of American, Assoc. Minister Mt. Olive Church.; [hon.] Dean's list, Servant of the month; [oth. writ.] None published; [pers.] Look for the good in each day, build up the positive in life and shun the negative; [a.] Indianapolis, IN

YESAEIL, RAMINA S.
[b.] August 24, 1976, Oromieh, Iran; [p.] Albert Yesaeil, Panna Yesaeil; [ed.] Mather High School, Loyola University of Chicago; [memb.] American Assyrian Civic Club of Chicago; [hon.] Won a Gold Metal in All American Art Exhibit 1992, Certificate of Achievement 1994 in Soccer, Certificate of Merit Award 1993-94 for National Honors Society; [oth. writ.] Several poems published in school newspaper; [pers.] I contend to refine the merit of death, for this wicked world brings about the freedom after death. I'm a survivor of a war and so is everyone else who is breathing this very moment.; [a.] Chicago, IL

YINGER, MARTHA L.
[pen.] Martha L. Yinger; [b.] March 23, 1916; [p.] Mr. and Mrs. William Conaway; [m.] Lloyd Yinger, September 15, 1936; [ch.] Daughter and son; [ed.] Bachelor of Science in Education, Capital University, Columbus Ohio 30 years Teaching; [occ.] Retired; [memb.] Alumni Association Capital University State of Ohio, Retired Teachers, Choir, Member and Teacher Church; [hon.] Of the Nazarene 5 yrs. Supervisor Foster Grand Volunteer Work at Nursing Homes, Active Alumni at Capital University; [oth. writ.] Published "Circle of Love" for news letter for Foster grandparents.; [pers.] I endeavor to create a "new out look" to learn how to live in our fast changing world. The 3 RS important. My faith in God.; [a.] Washington, OH

YOKLEY, APRIL J.
[b.] March 13, 1954, Chicago, IL; [p.] Dolores and Emmett Dozier; [ch.] Dyron N. Yokley and Samuel K. Robinson; [ed.] Holy Angel's Grade School, Chicago, IL, St. Stanilaus High Chicago, IL, Daley College, Chicago, IL; [occ.] Frito Lay, now on disability; [memb.] Boys and Girls Club Boy Scouts of America; [hon.] Boy Scouts of America Awards; [oth. writ.] Have written other poems; [pers.] I believe in the power of God when you walk by faith and all things are possible through Him.; [a.] Pulaski, TN

YOUNG, DANIEL L.
[b.] November 18, 1937; [p.] Daniel Bradley Young; [m.] Rosella Elizabeth Bergman Young; [ed.] Mongalela H.S., Triangle Tech. Trade School, various Military schools, Occupational Training Schools, Corning Glass Corp.; [occ.] Retired, Corning Glass Factotum; [memb.] First Christia Church, Veterans of Foreign War, Elks Lodge; [hon.] Various Military Unit Citations, Scholastic Certificate of Attainment; [oth. writ.] 'Indian Past', published, 'Myself' not published, Steamboat, not published, Wide World of: Haiku, not published.; [pers.] I believe in a person's roots and fill strong of my own.; [a.] Charleroi, PA

YOUNG JR., HENRY WILLIAM
[b.] June 15, 1936, Memphis, TN; [p.] Henry Sr. and Evelyn; [m.] Pauline Johnson Young, August 6, 1994; [ed.] B.S. Tenn. State Univ. MA Central Michigan Univ.; [occ.] Retired from Federal Government - Audit Manager - DOD; [memb.] Association of Government, Accountants, Tenn. State Univ. Alumni Assoc.; [hon.] Who's Who in American University And Colleges - 1956, Outstanding Young Men of America - 1971; [pers.] I believe that the world needs more people who display love for one another and provide help for those in need.; [a.] Fairfax, VI

YOUNG, MARGARET B.
[b.] Januart, 10, 1924, Clark Co. KY; [p.] Anna B. and Thomas S. Beall Sr.; [ch.] Two grown - one deceased; [ed.] G.E.D. Medical Tech.; [occ.] Retired; [pers.] Poetry is such a lovely way of expressing such a variety of different subjects.; [a.] Frankfort, KY

YOUNGREN, MARGARET R.
[pen.] "Travelin' with Maggie"; [b.] September 10, 1915, Mount Cornel, IL; [p.] Russell and Lulu Stansfield; [m.] Geo C. Barnds (Deceased), August 16, 1934 and Harrison Youngren (Deceased) June 24, 1972; [ch.] One by first marriage; [ed.] Graduate of Mt Carmel High School Graduate of BS S.I.U. with 252 hrs. on 9/72 Master from Univ. of Texas (Marketing and Management.); [occ.] Retired but still traveling and publishing columns; [memb.] 50 years DAR - 75 Lutheran 50 years member of 100 year old Reviewer's Matinee, 50 years Member Hosp. Auxiliary, 60 years Delta Theta Tau Sorority Charter Women's Fed Club; [hon.] My life has been honored with many friends and my awards have been good health. A lively interest in everything, two wonderful husbands and a gifted artistic daughter.; [oth. writ.] Had daily chat program "Good Morning Maggie" on radio - 15 yrs. had interviewed program at S.I.U.-TV 3 yrs. written travel articles since 1992 about 73 visited countries and all 50 States all published.; [pers.] I've been a "Jill of Many Trades" running our 100 yrs. old family Dept. Store, Clerk of Selective Service 1940-1946 Taught both grade, High School and College, Radio and programs. Acted and sang in Theatre, given hundreds of programs.; [a.] Mount Carmel, IL

YUSCHOCK, JONATHAN MICHAEL
[b.] July 1924, 1960, Ashland, PA; [p.] John Yuschock and Mary Beddo; [m.] Susan Serovich, June 26, 1993; [ch.] Samantha Morgan; [ed.] Elementary St. Ignatius Centralia, PA., High School Lourdes Regional Shamokin, PA, Bloomsburg University Bloomsburg, PA; [occ.] Machinist/Machine Mechanic; [oth. writ.] Collections of poetry "Answers", "Dragon Song", "Rhyme And Reason" Collection of Short Stories, "The Notes of Prof. Izno" unpublished to date; [pers.] "Loneliness, that perpetual thing, never has a place to turn"; [a.] Mount Carmel, PA

ZACHERY, KEVIN M.
[b.] November 7, 1964, Paris, France; [p.] Michael G. and Patty Lou Zachery; [m.] Christine N. Bath Zachery, August 4, 1990; [ch.] Ashley Noelle Zachery; [ed.] Chugiak High, U.S. Naval Academy; [occ.] Naval Officer, Instructor, U.S. Naval Academy Annapolis, MD; [memb.] Surface Navy Association, NRA; [oth. writ.] Small poems for my wife in the newspaper valentine's section. And a humor item in Reader's Digest.; [pers.] I am inspired by my wife.; [a.] Annapolis, MD

ZAMBRANO, APRIL
[pen.] Sharon Zambrano; [b.] February 13, 1981 C.C., TX; [p.] Sharon Zambrano and Salvador; [ed.] Flour Bluff Jr. High and High School; [oth. writ.] Wrote a poem of Father and published in a news paper.; [pers.] I try to write from the bottom of my thoughts and try to do the best poetry can; [a.] C.C., TX

ZARITZKY, AARON
[pen.] L. Zaret; [b.] October 2, 1977, Winston Salem, NC; [p.] Melanie Vaughn, David Zaritsky; [occ.] Senior at Durham Academy upper school in Durham, NC; [memb.] Talent Identification Program, The International Thespian Society; [hon.] A number of high school awards; [oth. writ.] A couple poems published in the high school literary magazine; [pers.] I do not believe in restricting oneself to a certain type of poem. I believe experimentation and individual craftsmanship are at the heart of poetry. I also think that violence is the idiot's way to make conversation.; [a.] Chapel Hill, NC

ZELLER, RICHARD J.
[pen.] Richard J. Zeller; [b.] August 11, 1972, Santa Clara, CA; [p.] Robert and Shirley Zeller; [m.] Jennifer Stucky Zeller, July 15, 1995; [occ.] Software Support, IBM; [pers.] It is my hope, my prayer, that I may convey a feeling of hope, and peace though my works. I hope to share my understanding of this world, and increase my understanding of the next world.; [a.] Rochester, MN

ZIEGLER, KAREN
[pen.] Karen; [b.] July 12, 1943, IL; [p.] Ernest and Bea Kresen; [m.] John Ziegler, February 1, 1974; [ch.] Deborah Hernandez - 32 and Tamera Graff - 30; [ed.] Farruqut High; [occ.] Housewife; [memb.] Trinity Methodist Church (Mount Prospect - IL); [oth. writ.] Through out my years (52) I have written many (not published) because they were to private to share. Published by national Library of poetry. A mother's plea - siblings? Havent heard yet; [pers.] All of my work is reflected an my youth, siblings, husband, children, parents. I believe, you count write, what your heart does not feel.; [a.] Des Plaines, IL

ZIELINSKI, BRIAN
[b.] June 24, 1971, Salt Lake City; [p.] Margaret Zielinski, Ray Zielinski; [ed.] Kearns High School, University of Utah; [oth. writ.] Poems include: Womb, deafness, short stories: Gold Rush, Light Squared; [pers.] Poetry is a private art. Adorning diaries, letters, scraps...Expressing realms of ourselves to ourselves. The finest poetry can be at the bottom of a trash heap or the center of attention, but what matters most, it reflects from pen to paper, our private art.; [a.] Salt Lake City, UT

ZIELKE, PAULINE M. GOOD
[pen.] Pauline M. Good; [b.] November 1, 1922, Acron, PA; [p.] Norman Eshelman, Lizzie Hibshman Eshleman; [m.] Norman S. Good (Deceased), August 3, 1941, John W. Zielke, August 20, 1979; [ch.] Ronald E. Good, Robert, Harold, Richard Anna Mary and Randy; [ed.] 9 grades in Lancaster, Co, PA, GED in Hutchinson, KS (1990), courses in English,

Creative (1992) Writing a H.C.C. in Hutchinson, KS; [occ.] Retired, aspiring writer; [memb.] Buhler Mennonite Church; [hon.] This is the first time I ever entered a contest. I have been printed in Church Newsletter many times.; [oth. writ.] Rupert the Turtle, I have a books written out of 8 I have planned. Children's books, with a Christian vein.; [pers.] I write as I am inspired by occasion or as the Lord gives it to me. Sometime in the middle of the night and I have to get up and write it down, if I leave it till morning, I can't get it like it was given to me.; [a.] Buhler, KS

ZIMMERMAN JR., DONALD D.
[pen.] Zee; [b.] September 1, 1956, Great Bend, KS; [ch.] Melissa, Zachary; [ed.] Great Bend High School 1975; [occ.] President AAA-ZZZ Sports Medicine Promotion "LTD"; [memb.] Youth Outreach Supervisor and Coordinator of Special Events; [hon.] Evacuation of last pull out of North and South Vietnamese 1975, Participated in military response to Ida Amin Uganda Hostage Crisis 1976, Attached to COMPHIBRON SEVEN, a UDT/SEAL-Pearl Harbor, Honorable Discharge-United States Navy 1978; [oth. writ.] Autobiography "The Broken Promise"; [pers.] Sometimes the most controversial people are the most effective leaders.; [a.] Seattle, WA

ZIMMERMAN, GLENDA A. E.
[b.] October 6, 1950, Bloomsburg, PA; [p.] Rachel Ernestine Ernest; [m.] Russel B. Zimmerman, August 13, 1983; [ch.] Zachary Zebulon, Benjamin Russel; [ed.] Graduated Southern Columbia Area High School, Catawissa, PA; [occ.] Legal Secretary, Liever, Hyman and Potter, P.C., Reading, PA; [memb.] Good Shepherd United Methodist Church, Bloomsburg, PA, Central Berks Fire Co. No. 1, and Ladies Auxiliary, Centerport, PA; [oth. writ.] Beth Ann - poem celebrating birth of youngest sister in December 1964, poem for in-laws 50th anniversary in January 1991; [pers.] I attribute my love of poetry to my grandmother, Ivy Sophrona Getty Ernest, (one of 28 children) who would read to my sisters and me at bedtime or when we were snowed in. My inspiration for the above poem was several family deaths and terminal illnesses over the past year (1995).; [a.] Mohrsville, PA

ZIMMERMAN, REBECCA
[b.] September 28, 1972, Lewisburg, PA; [p.] Dorothy Jones, Lynn Zimmerman; [ed.] Shaker High, currently a student at Hartwich College; [occ.] Full time student; [memb.] Main St. Baptist Church, Campus Ambassador's La Christian Fellowship Group at my school, was on the Cross Country and Track Teams for my school; [hon.] Dean's List; [oth. writ.] Personal journal of other works including titles of the following: Stone Cold, Emerald Ocean, Puric Victory; [pers.] I strive to express my true thoughts and feelings, and my poetry is one way of doing this.; [a.] Troy, NY

Index of Poets

Butterfly's opinion 395
Abbott, Christa 370
Abbott, Edward E. 45
Abdelkhalk, Dorene Cooks 384
Abdul, Sadia 23
Abney, Maureen S. 562
Abrams, Mark 530
Abrera, Audrey B. 641
Abreu, Lyanne 306
Acevedo, Ines Rivera 383
Ackley, Lysa 617
Acosta, Sunshine 660
Adams, A. Perry 400
Adams, Elaine M. 469
Adams, Flora 357
Adams, Genevieve Semones 308
Adams, Ina C. 401
Adams, Mary Lou 557
Adams, Robert E. 77
Adams, Sandi 49
Adams, Sheri 103
Adamson, Richard Fritz 59
Aday, Carla 460
Addams, Mike 129
Addison, William 115
Addleman, Helen 285
Adkins, Ina M. 358
Adriatico, Angela 259
Agee, Linda J. 535
Agnas, Carmelita Ledesma 467
Ahern, Helen M. 294
Ahrens, Mark Mathew 544
Al-Shalchi, Olla Najah 230
Alada, Roberto V. 175
Alan, Robert 66
Alanis, Frank 653
Alberre, Kristen 226
Albert, Lynne 555
Albrecht, Maria 602
Albright, Bill 437
Alegria, Mel 513
Alexander, Ian 506
Alger, Emily 344
Algosino, Phil 198
Allan, Laura 248
Allen, Barbara J. 398
Allen, Carolyn Sue 408
Allen, Cynthia L. 268
Allen, David B. 323
Allen, Geralyn 266
Allen, John W. 455
Allen, Leoma Cardwell 144
Allen, Micah David 531
Allen, Myrtis 133
Allen, Nancy 520
Allen, Nason E. 621
Allen, Penny 37
Allen, Robert E. 70
Allen, Theresa C. 42
Allen, Warren A. 53
Allerheiligen, Shad 175
Allin, John 383
Allison, Jim 590
Allison, Robert 190
Allman, Liz 517
Allmon, Tede Adrienne 189
Almajan, Ariana 394
Almirall, Catie 397
Aloha, Keoni 216
Alongi, Angela 361
Alongo, Uno I. 178
Alpaugh, Debbie 415
Alpert, A. P. 194
Alston, Ronald 120
Altman Sr., John 459
Alu, Edna 258

Alu, Kurstin 61
Alvarez, Alicia 320
Amador, Rhonda 170
Amorella, Tiffany 21
Amoroso, Drew 409
Ander, Paula J. 76
Anderson 41
Anderson, Cheryl 658
Anderson, Fonda 412
Anderson, Kim 156
Anderson, Linder D. 568
Anderson, Marian L. 244
Anderson, Matt 146
Anderson, Meredith A. 625
Anderson, Monica 624
Anderson, Olive F. 254
Anderson, Robert R. 17
Anderson, Sandra 95
Anderson, Shelly 102
Anderson, Slade 111
Anderson, Terri 211
Anderson, Walt 71
Anderson, Walter E. 170
Anderson, William O. 108
Andrews, Angie 589
Andrews, Beatrice E. 477
Andrews, Betty 392
Andrews, Marilyn B. 528
Andrus, Anita A. 419
Angel, Vonda 37
Angel II, George Thomas 314
Angelone, Elizabeth 286
Angle, Kimberly Greene 245
Angleton, Cicely d'A. 268
Anglin, Dianna 261
Anglin, Evelyn A. 468
Anne, Mary 565
Antetomoso, Angela 586
Anton, Donna M. 438
Antonellini, Justin 434
Anuszewski, Christina 410
Apfel, Gloria 402
Apuzzo, Cathy 408
Arbuckle, Jamie L. 288
Archie, Kimberly Denise 608
Arey, Shawn M. 219
Argo, Michelle Lynn 147
Arguello, Carl 355
Argumedo, Hope 412
Armenta, Jennifer 461
Armstead, Beverly 462
Armstrong, Catherine 333
Armstrong, Justin F. 391
Armstrong, Nancy Susan 511
Armstrong, Samantha 91
Armstrong, Stephanie L. 40
Arndt, Anne M. 576
Arnold, Bradley A. 498
Arnold-Willis, Dyanna L. 345
Arroyo, Jill 331
Arruda, Albert 387
Arthur James R 591
Ashford, Holly 310
Ashleman, Rose 24
Asparro, Dorraine G. 415
Assante, Anne Lee 387
Atherton, John 430
Atkins, Ruth 192
Atkinson, Scott 88
Attoh, Kafui 564
Attraente, Nancy 540
Atwood, Carol A. 428
Atzenhofer, Janna SuEllen 643
Ault, Marla 525
Ausmus, Steve 71
Austgen-Greeley, Emily 301

Austin, Audrey M. 450
Austin-Thorn, Cynthia 260
Avery, Dan 22
Avery, Danielle 349
Axton, Florence G. 651
Axton, Shana 58
Baatstad, Anne 418
Babcoe, Leona 23
Bachmann, Joanne L. 307
Bachofner, Carol Willette 445
Badiang, Remedios H. 200
Baese, JoAnne 384
Bagby, Tonia 105
Baggett, Barry 278
Bagley, Carleen 314
Bailey, Ella M. 651
Bailey, Julia S. 577
Bailey, Rhoza W. 106
Bailey, Walton V. 39
Baines, Carol Denham 635
Baird, Thomas 66
Baity, Kristie F. 130
Bakar, Abu 281
Baker, Barry 282
Baker, Elizabeth Ann 439
Baker, Gloria 459
Baker, Jessica 458
Baker, Marolyn E. 132
Baker, Norma Engstrume 564
Baker, Raymond K. 223
Baker, Renza Moscatelli 42
Baker, Ruth E. 173
Baker, S. 58
Baker, Sandra 179
Baker Sr., James F. 486
Baker-Railey, Deborah 414
Balasa, Andrew 460
Balatbat, Joseph Herrera 483
Baldwin, Leann L. 133
Baldwin, Lovey 253
Baldwin, P. K. 88
Bale, Crystal Nicole 463
Balkam, Sarah 59
Ball, Lisa 618
Ballard, J. C. 204
Ballard, Wendy J. 217
Balletto, Christine E. 499
Balman, Floyd A. 324
Balman, Gail E. 341
Balocating, Samuel G. 96
Balsley Sr., Donald L. 290
Bamber, Tanya 102
Banfield, Danielle 570
Banik, Stephanie 653
Banks, Aleia Nichole 433
Banks, Latrice 234
Bannister, Mary 234
Barb, Elizabeth 299
Barbary, George 628
Barbouletos, John T. 575
Barbour, Isabelle 438
Barclay, Wilma J. 41
Bargerstock, Dianna L. 585
Barham, Donna B. 446
Bari, Mona 252
Barker, Donald 270
Barker, Lisa A. 513
Barker, Tony 86
Barlow, Inez 581
Barlow, Pamela R. 217
Barltrop, Gloria 290
Barnes, Judith 476
Barnes, Marsha Marie 560
Barnes, Matt 523
Barnett, Wayne 67
Barnhart, Eleanor M. 575

Barnhart, Susan 656
Baron, Israel 316
Barr, Kathy 153
Barr, Louise Glynn 618
Barr Sr., Raymond C. 193
Barrett, Rita R. 172
Barrett, Shawn R. 100
Barron, Erek L. 497
Barrow, Angela S. 575
Barthelemy, Bart 595
Barthlein, Sandra M. 87
Bartholomew, Jessica 256
Bartholomew, Kendra 132
Bartholomew, Margaret L. 547
Bartlett, Diane 322
Bartlett, Ethel 498
Bartlett, Sharron 10
Bartling, Nancy 528
Bartolatta, Kim 607
Barton, Amy J. 384
Barton, Barbara 586
Barton Jr., Gary L. 370
Barton, Rebecca 199
Baruffi, Erica 386
Barwick Jr., Robert 120
Bascko, Shirley A. 100
Bash, James C. 411
Bashir, Kamal B. 527
Basinger, Eleanor F. 411
Bass, Mona Lisa 70
Bass, Tim 49
Bastian, Elsie E. 267
Batchelor, Barbara 440
Battaglia, David C. 451
Battaglia, Lynda M. 565
Battles, Dixie 467
Bauer, Heather A. 347
Baughman, Jennifer 578
Baumle, Laurie Jo 232
Baxter, Michelle 560
Beagin, Dorothy 496
Beagle, Terry 108
Beakey, Jim 63
Beal, Anthony 208
Beal, Peggy 77
Beam, Kathryn A. 612
Beard, Connie 574
Beard, Judy Turner 297
Beard, Michele 244
Beardslee, Clark 472
Beasley, Carolyn Marie 508
Beasley, Eldora Andrea 260
Beasley, Marcina P. 247
Beasley, Raymond 72
Beauchesne, Jill 451
Beaulieu, Julie 380
Beaumont, Lorie 529
Becerra-Globus, Ann 357
Beck, Lois 158
Becker, Allen 583
Becker, Mary 149
Beddal, Dorothy 181
Bedneau, Glenda 431
Bedolla, by Phillip 118
Bee, Max Culbertson 560
Beery, Matthew 533
Behabetz, Grace 580
Behnke, Jennifer 431
Behrends, Scott E. 109
Behrendt, Betty J. 572
Belanger, Kevin 530
Belcher, Hannah 505
Bell, Janet L. 578
Bell, Janet M. 307
Bell, Jim 364
Bell, Mary Catherine 238

Bell, Randy 160
Bell, Wayne 38
Bellamy, Hilda 313
Bellavia, Roxana 24
Bellemare, Kenneth R. 243
Belmonte, Lisa 229
Belsky, Michelle 253
Beltz, Christopher W. 332
Belue, Carol 264
Belvin, Kay 253
Bembenek, Pauline M. 14
Bender, Ashley V. 362
Bendolph, Roger D. 26
Benecke, Mary E. 605
Bengard, Ryan 217
Benito, Ariane 402
Benjamin, Bobby 363
Benjamin, Vaughn 39
Bennett, Elise H. 647
Bennett, Margaret 605
Bennett, Nathan 249
Bennett, Renee Gorham 118
Bennett, Timothy J. 112
Bennett, Velma Jean 218
Bensen, Mike 520
Bensley-Bromilow, Lavinia 541
Benson, Kathryn 616
Beougher, Richard 28
Berdecia, Jeni 499
Berdichevsky, Konstantin 145
Berg, Michael J. 621
Berg, Robert 120
Berger, Carly 492
Berger, Larry A. 243
Bergeron, Karl T. 238
Berget, Ellsworth A. 380
Bergh, Nicole 111
Bergmann, Tom 57
Bergquist, Olive E. 520
Berlin, Martha 246
Berman, Marshall L. 520
Bernal, Angela 54
Bernardy, Karen 608
Bernier, Amanda 325
Berning, Marilyn Bublitz 536
Bernstein, Jeffrey L. 336
Berntsen, Thomas 113
Berny, Joanna Lynne 479
Bero, Robert 39
Berrsch, Elizabeth 450
Berry, Christy 458
Berry, Donald 583
Berry, Janice 298
Berry, Robin L. 65
Bertumen, Abigail 309
Besenhofer, William M. 44
Betlyon, Frances 330
Beukema, Henry C. 402
Beveridge, Macelle 241
Bezemes, Kathryn R. 541
Bianco, Frank E. 378
Bichler, Gerald 355
Bichler, James Henry 316
Bickell, Jerry Anne 289
Bielefeld, Dawne C. 316
Bieth, Roseann 120
Bifano, Melissa A. 143
Biggs, Meredyth 145
Bileschi, Circe 409
Bill O. 81
Billings, Timothy 107
Bines, Mary Ellen 511
Bingham, Lucille Gossett 243
Bird, Sandra 92
Birdsall, Rayna Michelle 112
Birks, Stephen L. 205

Birmingham, Gladys Harmon 377
Bishop, Vicky L. 37
Bistrick, Louise M. 549
Bitoushana, Lori 250
Bitz, Jonathan Michael 449
Black Jr., Harrold H. 306
Black Jr., James H. 443
Black, L. M. Gasrel 177
Black, Melody A. 132
Black, Michael 157
Black, Molly 124
Black, Roberta A. 54
Blackburn, Cassondra Jane 293
Blackman, Dana 400
Blackner, David M. 628
Blackwood, Sue 122
Blaine, Tracy A. 115
Blair, Melva Y. 249
Blair, Patricia V. 4
Blair, Yvette R. 12
Blaisse, Tom 160
Blake, Christine 445
Blakeslee, Lisa M. 512
Blakney, George M. 586
Blalock Jr., Edwin F. 307
Blanchard, Cheryl 373
Blanchard, Deborah 590
Blanco, Danna A. 393
Blank, Pearl 60
Blaskowski, John W. 485
Blaylock, Ron 218
Bleiler, Ralph W. 168
Blevins, Demetrius N. 266
Blevins, Marvin 230
Bline, Mary 562
Blinn, Cindy 581
Block, Lauren 246
Blohm, Randy 655
Blok, Sandra 197
Blommer, Julianne 593
Blounts, Cynthia 382
Blundon 109
Boadway, Tim 215
Boardman, Amy L. 483
Bochinski, Elise 424
Boggs, Larry 541
Bohara, Heather L. 372
Boland, Jack L. 452
Bolander, Claire 392
Bolicki, Jason 430
Bolourian, Neda 566
Boltz, Josh 390
Bolyard, Jason 440
Boman, Bruce 311
Bond, Katherine L. 602
Bonner, Ruby 41
Bonstance 315
Bonton, Shannon E. 103
Booked, Deborah R. 356
Booth, Linn 141
Boothby, Mark 525
Boothe, Nancy 514
Booy, Timothy J. 173
Borbet, Kathleen 537
Borgardt, Jeff 385
Borger, Sophia Simmons 219
Borner, Leeah 139
Borovicka Jr., George J. E. 492
Bortolutti, Nataly A. 559
Bosah, A. Odi 177
Bosch, Katherine 530
Bosch, Sharon L. 176
Bosetti, Brandi 462
Bostock-Kelley, Deborah J. 270
Boswell, Natalie 512
Botello, Janna L. 441

Botts, Michele Lee 141
Bouchie, James S. 492
Boudreau, Kristine D. 517
Boudreaux, Paula 64
Bourgeau, Ellen 322
Bourque, Arthur 593
Bousquet, Brenda 382
Boutwell, Joyce Herrin 498
Bouza, Jenny Travers 327
Bovee, Tammy 116
Bowe, Clara 372
Bower, Benjamin P. 444
Bowers, Bonnie J. 264
Bowers, Duane R. 643
Bowker, Patricia 25
Bowman, Linda Jean 561
Bowser, Kelly 157
Boxer, Pauline 46
Boyd 107
Boyd, Juliana 413
Boyd-Williams, Lore A. 558
Boyer, Jason M. 316
Boysen, Bruce P. 573
Bracheen, Amy 465
Brackett, Laura S. 243
Bradley, Tammy Lee 200
Bradley, Victor A. 124
Bradshaw, Linda G. 132
Brady, Kathleen 614
Brady, Mary F. 528
Brady, Sarah 84
Brady, Virginia J. 171
Bragadin, Melissa 578
Brager, Betty J. 398
Bragg, Shirley 56
Braida, Dolly 273
Brais, Katie 610
Braithwaite, Brandon Vaughn 326
Braman, George N. 586
Bramblett, Pauline 209
Branch, Annette 272
Brandafino, Darlene 343
Brandes, Arabella 452
Brandes, Barbara 394
Brasil, Melissa 227
Braun-Hille, Monica 153
Braxton, Christine D. 304
Bray, Brenna K. 490
Breedlove, Dorothy 652
Breen, Carolyn 443
Brendelson, Anita 410
Brenneman, Paula 116
Brenton, Margaret 236
Bressler, Lois Deal 247
Brewer, Elaine M. 489
Brewer, Gertrude V. 639
Brewer, Zachary 182
Brickle, Rose 44
Bridges, Diane 256
Briggs, Cheryl 376
Bright, James K. 580
Briley, Lance 551
Brinar, Pamela 213
Briscoe, Andre' T. 312
Briscoe, Peg 115
Bristol, Kendra 240
Britt, John A. 413
Britt, Wendy 23
Britton, Rochelle 162
Broberg, Jennifer 306
Brock, Angela 593
Brock, Lisa 237
Brock, Tacey Ann 34
Brockman, Lauretta 613
Broderick, Marie 154
Brodsky, Ida 51

Brokhin, Mira 517
Broncato, Buffy 463
Bronson, Aaron 628
Bronstein, William Robert 96
Brookins, Fay 386
Brooks, Angela D. 177
Brooks, Billie 308
Brooks, Bobbye 326
Brooks, James Mel 585
Brooks, Jean 226
Brooks, Lawrence Wayne 482
Brooksbank, Christal 278
Brooksher, Larry V. 238
Brosh, Ron 69
Brotzman, Megan 567
Broughton, Diane R. 328
Brouillette, Maurice J. 251
Broussard, Gwendolyn 302
Browder, Carolyn 635
Brower, Michael 526
Brown , Jean 637
Brown, Al Danny 442
Brown, Angela M. 304
Brown, Barbara I. 318
Brown, Dalita 340
Brown, David Edward 645
Brown, David W. 455
Brown, Dorothy I. 300
Brown, Eloise C. 501
Brown, Emily M. 490
Brown, Esther 286
Brown, Geneva 406
Brown, Georgeann 338
Brown, Gloria B. 268
Brown, Grace 264
Brown, J. Scott 77
Brown, Janice 362
Brown, Jesse 384
Brown, Karen 234
Brown, Katherine 564
Brown, Kenneth H. 127
Brown, Lillian 533
Brown, Marlena 243
Brown, Melissa M. 613
Brown, Nancy L. 246
Brown, Pamela Sue 85
Brown, Raymond A. 176
Brown, Robin A. 79
Brown, Sonya 121
Brown, Steven D. 203
Brown, Tamika 50
Brown, Tanya 179
Brown, Teresa 16
Brown, Theresa 10
Brown, Wayne 192
Browner, Sarah A. 6
Browning, Kirk 611
Browning, Melanie 150
Browning, Pam 217
Brownlee-Cobb, S. 12, 256, 536
Bruchalski, Hazel J. 271
Bruegger, Merrilee I. 245
Bruha, Kim 566
Bruhnke, Michelle 520
Brunelli, Anne W. 635
Brunner Jr., Edmund 476
Bryan Jr., John David 394
Bryant, Birelee 464
Bryant, Francie 458
Bryant, Kay 136
Bryant, Lynda Jean 233
Bryce, Jonathan 382
Bryttegard, Sabine D. 221
Buck, Tammy L. 42
Buckhout, Joy 646
Buckner, J. H. 113

Buffington, Bertha J. 318
Buice, Jody 303
Buitenkant, Jade 75
Bull, Jenn 432
Bull, Jesse R. 279
Bunce, Phillip G. 84
Bunch, Mel 131
Bunkley, Leisa 234
Bunn, Daphne K. 478
Bunting, Carolyn 573
Buoy, Rick 178
Burbano, Lucas 604
Burchett, Nikki 230
Burchfield, Virgie 199
Burd, Chayris 436
Burd, Jenelle Analisa 502
Burdick, Debra 298
Burdick, Terri J. 121
Burgason, Tara Lynn 160
Burgess, Kimberly 509
Burghart, Susan 167
Burke, Barrett 402
Burke, Fred G. 192
Burke, Kerry A. 229
Burke, Sharon Griffin 202
Burks Sr., Edward C. 412
Burnaby, Kelly D. 610
Burnett, Charlie 489
Burns, Christopher T. 465
Burns, Julie A. 326
Burns, Nancy 610
Burns, Nicholas 249
Burns-Putman, Dorothy 404
Burnstad, Karen C. 611
Burrill, Jennifer 476
Burris, Jo Bess 633
Burris, Lisa R. 518
Burton, Janet Marie 351
Burton, Lajuana D. 134
Burttschell, Simon J. 171
Busch, Tina M. 50
Buschow, Marissa 156
Bush, Elizabeth S. 324
Bush, Gordon L. 300
Bush, Gwendolyn A. 414
Bush, Shannon 227
Buss, Larry R. 228
Bussey, Holly 387
Bussino, Marion 511
Bustamante, Russell 100
Butler, Dick 348
Butler, Mark E. 536
Butler, Michelle 509
Buttars, Melba 569
Butz, Janice E. 402
Byfield, Edmund A. 501
Byrd, Audrey Wilkins 463
C. H. S. 591
Cabaza, Isabelle 508
Caesar, Alicia LaVoghn 579
Cahill, Christine 454
Cahoon, David 456
Cain, Carran 571
Cain, Derek 359
Cain, Errin 641
Cain, Richard Edward 85
Caine, Talana 93
Calabro, Maria 143
Caldera, Isabel 469
Caldwell, Melissa 538
Caldwell, Vera 53
Callender, Alina 334
Callister, Veronica 60
Calmes, Shirley M. 163
Camara, Nick 128
Camberg, Debbie 589
Cambridge, Ruth 119
Cameron, Ryan 172
Campana, Ray C. 111
Campbell, Ann 342
Campbell, Ermaka 265
Campbell, Gerald L. 273
Campbell, Grace B. 389
Campbell, Kristine 608
Campbell, LouEllen 250
Campbell, Sarah L. 112
Campbell-Reese, Joyce 285
Camus, Carolina 457
Canazzi, Salvatore A. 4
Candill, Jannis 319
Canganelli, Joanne Leah 455
Canine, Curt 450
Canionero, Natasha 550
Cannon, Bonnie L. 656
Cantrell, Adeen 329
Cao, Paul 106
Capacchione, Helen 490
Capen, Randy 224
Capers, C. Thomas 192
Capizzi, Ann S. 396
Caplan, Lydia 244
Cappel, Angela C. 367
Cappozzi, B. J. 480
Capriola, Giulia 324
Caputo, Amanda J. 374
Carbonetta, Amalia 394
Cardenas, Lynnette A. 252
Cardone, Nancy 157
Cardones, Sean H. 73
Carey, Mary J. 537
Carini, Anthony Shaun 341
Carleton, Kathy L. 232
Carlock, Lisa M. 531
Carlsen, Patricia J. 196
Carlson, Cynthia Marie Chantry 280
Carlson, Mildred M. 559
Carlson, Patrick 222
Carlson, Shandra 99
Carlsson, Vivian 63
Carlsted, Craig S. 453
Carlton, Brandi 454
Carlton, Eric M. 272
Carlucci, David 335
Carnine, Holly 412
Carpenter, Anne A. 276
Carpenter, Ida 381
Carr, Bobbie S. 589
Carr, Chris W. 580
Carr, Elmer G. 645
Carr, Sharon 45
Carrell, Rhonda 109
Carrier, Donald L. 111
Carrington, Cheril C. 591
Carroll, James A. 269
Carrozza, Rose 53
Carruth, MacKenzie 174
Carson, Barbara H. 570
Carson, Mickey J. 518
Carson, Viviane 83
Carstens, Erma 399
Carter, Evelyn 585
Carter, Frances 340
Carter, Roselyn 174
Cartwright, Rosalie 105
Caruso, Marian 624
Carvalho, Carolyn L. 313
Carver, Darlene T. 648
Carver, Joyce E. 485
Casdorph, Heather 292
Case, Willie Mae 115
Casey, Rebecca 120
Casey, Shannon Shay 44
Cash, Lisa 555
Castillo, Nicole 226
Catalani, Thelma 62
Cates, Susan 99
Catlin, Nicole Christine 229
Cauthen, George E. 451
Cavazos, Jenni Maylene 420
Caverly, Rachel 5
Cazeau, Craig 655
Cea, Vincent 5
Ceballos, Elizabeth 443
Cecchini, Christine 283
Centala, Michael S. 606
Cerny, Jonathan 586
Cervantes, Norma A. 127
Chaffin, Linda 601
Chambers, Aron 577
Chambers, Brandy 470
Chambers, Rose J. 34
Champ, Lisa 509
Champine, Sarah 205
Champion-Daigle, Laurie 611
Champlin, Heather 292
Chance, Melinda W. 534
Chaney, Katie 522
Chang, Faye 269
Chapman, Carol 16
Charlan, Nathan 607
Chartre, Kay 135
Chatlas, Nancy Carol 546
Chatman, Anita L. 33
Chatterton, Mick 234
Chatto, Peter 62
Chaussée, Alice 315
Chauvin, T. R. 85
Chavez, Candice 292
Chawla, Narinder Nath 228
Chelland, Eugene 389
Cheloha, David 295
Chemnick, William Neville 24
Chen, Hao-Kai 267
Chen O.C.S.O., Sheryl Frances 40
Chen, Susan Y. 124
Cheney, Dina 374
Cherrington, Mary M. 132
Cherry, Sharon Reisch 31
Cheshire, Marvin H. 618
Chevrier, Joann 469
Cheyenne 481
Chico, Christine 502
Chim, Wai-Ping 122
Chism-Kabia, Dorleen 308
Choi, Christine 323
Chopane, Yusheria 215
Chorosinski, Eugene Conrad 397
Chow, Arnold H. 340
Chrisco, Jeff 447
Christensen, Linda M. 617
Christenson, Laurie 240
Christian Lucard, A. J. 38
Christiano, Robert 177
Christine, Anna 405
Christman, Marie 234
Christy, Eric 651
Chu, Kwei-Yuen 553
Chung, Muoi 236
Church, Deborah G. 304
Church, Dolores F. 367
Church, Donna 288
Cibbarelli, William 105
Ciesla, David J. 580
Cilia, Michelle S. 522
Cilreb, Mary Jane 599
Cimino, Matt 552
Ciullo, Michael A. 248
Clark, Anika 444
Clark, Cliff 628
Clark, Katie 521
Clark, Richard D. 25
Clark, Ruth M. 211
Clark, Sally 44
Clark, Sharie D. 106
Clark, Susan 173
Clark, Vivian 180
Clarke, Fern Fugman 267
Clarke, John R. 419
Clavin, Jared 634
Cleary, James S. 504
Cleland, Joan 464
Clemens, Jennifer 349
Clemens, Vanessa L. 167
Clemente, Cynthia 260
Clements, Delila 455
Clements, E. Lynn K. 181
Clements, Robin D. 84
Clemmons, Tara 162
Clemons, Ricky 190
Cleveland, Karin 514
Clevenger, Dawn 474
Clevenstine, Toni 188
Clifton, Dallas 450
Climie, G. W. 32
Cliver, Carolyn Elaine 257
Cloman, Eddie B. 592
Close, Richard 52
Closson Jr., T. L. 163
Cloud, Stanci J. 104
Clough, Emma Lucille 279
Clugston, Carrie 262
Clukie, David R. 386
Cnoi, Sun-Ki 104
Coakley, Sara 23
Cobb, David W. 380
Cochran, Brenda 310
Cochran, Neisha 519
Cockriel, Terri S. 72
Coderre, George W. 316
Coe, Trilbia D. 97
Coes, Daniel 383
Coff, Rachel 224
Coffey III, Robert J. 105
Coffin, Cindy Sharpe 456
Coffman, Kerry 247
Coggin, Annie 584
Cohen, Jimmie Ruth 204
Cohn, Pamela 202
Coker, Cassandra Covington 660
Colan, Jo 350
Colbert, Glennis 398
Cole, Gloria Scott 458
Cole Jr., Daniel 280
Cole, Leslie A. 154
Cole, Linda 232
Cole, Paula 31
Cole, Ronda 13
Colella, Cliff 324
Coleman, Sharon L. 184
Collazo, Arthur R. 317
Collier, Margaret C. 153
Collin, Eloise N. 323
Collins, Daisy M. 503
Collins, Ellen 406
Collins, Paul E. 164
Collins, Tramell L. 201
Colman, Gretchen 331
Colom, K. C. 33
Colorusso, Arlene 582
Colpaert, Joan 388
Colson, Alicia 384
Colucci, Phyllis 164
Combs, Becky 439
Combs, Ray 50

Comfort, Mark 255
Commeford, Kevin 511
Compton, Phyllis 169
Conder, Tracy Noffsinger 124
Cone, Catherine 290
Conley, Kandy 238
Conley, Rene 51
Conner, Debbie 269
Conner, Zelda Marie 193
Connors, Richard 179
Conrad, Sara 166
Conrod, Kory 513
Contreras, Becky 351
Contreras, Teresa DeGreek 107
Conway, Lois 139
Conway, Margot 129
Conzo, Maria 607
Cook, Beverly 462
Cook, Charles 356
Cook, Leslie Maxwell 134
Cook, Mary S. 140
Cook, Randolph B. 92
Cook, Rebecca 195
Cooke, Cynthia L. 341
Cooke-Zimmermann, Ruth 4
Cooley, Mari-Lynn 539
Cooley, Nell W. 530
Cooney-Cummings, Pat 33
Cooper, Ann 403
Cooper, Frances 477
Cooper, Judy 582
Cooper, Lisa A. 618
Copeland, J. Eileen 177
Copes, Tamla 659
Coppa, Terri K. 119
Coppin, Dale 642
Coquillard III, George W. 471
Corcoran, Sandy 117
Cordero, Sharon 103
Cordova de Sicard, Emilia 200, 492
Cordoza, Virginia 42
Coren, Susan Hodges 86
Corlett, Kevin T. 233
Corley, Sharon 85
Cornelius, Russell B. 3
Cornell, Guy 287
Corney, Herbert Victor 587
Corning, Kristen 151
Corrales, Patricia M. 103
Corralez, Amos 347
Correll, Michelle 653
Corso, Desirae J. Riley 319
Cortes-DeJorge, Valerie 162
Corwin, Jessica 378
Cosby, Debra 474
Cosper, Dwight 357
Cossette, Michael 527
Costa-Pinto, Ivan 417
Costle, Robert M. 174
Cotterill, Melvin James 510
Cotton, Aaron A. 311
Coulombe, Timothy 655
Coulon, Mark F. 533
Courter Jr., W. A. 123
Cowan, Cooper C. 459
Cowan, Ruth 174
Cowart Sr, Michael Lee 560
Cox, Cynthia C. 424
Cox, E. M. 296
Cox, Gladys 585
Cox, Jamie 360
Cox, Judith L. 445
Cox, Katie 598
Cox, Patricia 42
Coy, Penny 220
Crabbe, Jason G. 384

Crabtree, Jennifer 315
Craft, Aimee Jo 447
Craig, Steven 188
Cran, Angela C. 392
Cravanas, Virginia 46
Cravens, James R. 495
Crawford, Aliston 60
Crawford, Cassandra 322
Crawford, George A. 318
Crawford, James C. 461
Crawford, M. Elaine 184
Crawford, Portia 173
Crawford, Samantha 168
Crawley, Patrice 67
Creason, Nancy Hunt 525
Cregar, William L. 28
Cregger, Lisa 142
Creighton, Cassandra 286
Cremo, LuAnn 12
Creutz, Eleta 584
Crews, Rhonda 60
Crifo, Darlen C. 270
Crippin, Jenni 372
Crofts, Nicola 510
Cronin, Eric T. 501
Crook, Heidi 449
Crooks, Julie H. 588
Crosby, Dorothy 460
Crosby, Roxan D. 160
Crosiar, Jim 583
Cross, Marla Sue 561
Cross, Roberta 170
Cross-Livingstone, Lisa A. 149
Crossno, Betty J. 589
Crotsenburg, Marlena A. 133
Crouse, Johnny 582
Crouter, Cara L. 475
Crow, Paul Jay 161
Crowder-Yates, Donna 331
Crowl, Jennifer 306
Crowley, Jenni 433
Crumbliss, Lorraine 556
Cruz, Edward Santa 350
Crystal, Emil 309
Crystal, Kim 513
Culver, Cathie Jean 259
Cumbo, P. Andrew 40
Cuminale, Raymond J. 64
Cummings, Wilma Faye 16
Cunningham, Christina 415
Cunningham, Pete 77
Cunningham, Rebecca 64
Cunningham, Sharon 210
Cupo, Jeffrey P. 628
Curley, Diane 258
Curo, Garold W. 226
Currie, Dawn 476
Curry, Georgia Justina Harper 471
Curtis, Alicia 382
Curtis, Amanda 403
Curtis, Tina L. 210
Cutler, Jonathan 288
Cutsogeorge, Lynne 528
D., Nina 233
Dacey, Mary E. 521
Dague, Manuela 229
Dahlstrom, Philip 166
Dahmen, Ute 117
Daignault, Carmen L. 592
Daigneault, Louis 48
Dallas, Bonnie 467
Dampher, Derrick 313
Damron, Elekta 586
Dana, Jason 504
Daneski, Brian S. 476
Daniels, Brittany 388

Daniels, Cathy L. 433
Daniels, James E. 297
Daniels, Marva J. 253
Daniels, Tiffany Leigh 123
Dannemiller, Barbara A. 401
Dannemiller, Tina 215
D'Antoni, Elva B. 446
Darby, Betty Tinsley 456
Darden, Edna L. 459
Darling, Jim 581
Daugherty, Kathleen 241
Dauphin, Sally 181
Davern, Deborah 298
David, Edward 407
David, Nina Marie 547
Davidson, Cathy 593
Davies, John Gerson 288
Davila, Camille 594
Davis, Brad 397
Davis, C. Borden 22
Davis, Charly R. 577
Davis, Constance 398
Davis, Dale 401
Davis, Etta M. 295
Davis, Frank 470
Davis, Gerald E. 373
Davis, John Brian 435
Davis, Julie Ann 388
Davis, Linda 150
Davis, Lisa 620
Davis, Lois Kahl 510
Davis, Louise J. 525
Davis, Mara 103
Davis, Michelle 255
Davis, Patrick Lane 219
Davis, Peggy Ann 67
Davis, Pete 223
Davis, Philip E. 162
Davis, Philip J. 28
Davis, Rebecca 3
Davis, Rick 112
Davis, Roswita B. 53
Davis, Shannon 113
Davis, Shirley 17
Davis, Shirley L. 73
Davis, Sue 219
Davis, Veronica 102
Davis, Wesley Chandler 76
Davis-Carpenter, Arnetta F. 311
Day, Cali 294
Day, Jennifer 304
Day, Jessica Lynn 500
Day, Kathi 250
Day, Pauline 175
Dayon, James 314
Dazzo, Gale 279
De Boer, Brenda G. 580
De Cata, Irene M. 429
De Condo, Elizabeth A. 360
De Frese, Juanita Z. 506
De George, Bambi Lynn 320
De Laas, Claudia 627
De Las Casas, Walter 55
De LaTor, D'Mar E. 452
Deaderick, Lisa 565
Deakins, Daniel 392
Dean, Mark 552
Dear, Nina K. 247
DeBlanc, Sandra 181
Deck, Elizabeth Leigh 418
Decker, Donnie J. 570
Deeds, Theresa Ann 192
Deel, Bradford A. 481
Deering, Gloria Elaine 306
Dees, Diane Michelle 325
Dehnart, Ethel 394

Del Castillo, Anita 479
Del Gaudio Jr., Christopher 457
Del Prado, Lina G. 46
Dela Cruz, Annie 498
Dela Rosa, Cindy 413
DeLawter, Connie 421
Delbrugge, April 571
DeLeon, Joan 304
DeLeon, Louisa 517
Delgadillo, Sandra Ivonne 91
Dellar, Diane 448
Dellenbach, Cory 162
Delmenico, Gene 13
Deloian, Victoria 20
Deloney, Frankie Mae 383
Delorier, Beatrice A. 636
Delos Santos, Erlinda G. 434
Delrose, Domonic J. 627
DeLuca, Camille 464
DeLuca, Danielle 403
Demarest, Anne Shannon 392
DeMille, Ronald 110
DeMoro, Madeline 232
Denecker, Kristen 518
Denise, Greaves 303
DeNise, Robyn Wager 76
DeNisi, Bethany Joy Healani 638
DeNisi, Lauralynn Healani 604
Dennis, Mary Jo 514
Dennis-Vasquez, Dori 270
Dentchev, Daniel 472
Denzel, Tom 60
DePalma, Kathleen Mae 148
DeRichardes, Frederico B. 322
DeRose, Robert 3
Derr, Angie 376
Desmond, Marcy 609
Detamore, Linda 127
Determan, Alison 263
Detwiler, Leona S. 522
Dever, Jenny 466
Devine, Anne 287
Devine, Rose C. 51
Devorak, Gloriela E. 496
DeVore, Mathew E. 514
Dewey, Kathleen Perez 191
DeWitt, I. Stewart 122
DeYoung, Jack 436
Diallo, Kadija 523
Diamante, Saundra 95
Diaz, Richard David 95
DiBenedetto, Karen 524
DiBernardinis, Bernice 470
Dichoso, Andrea Blum 312
Dieffenbacher, Yvonne 43
Diersen, Dianne A. 476
Dietert, Kimberly 528
Dietz, Sheila 30
DiGennaro, Robert J. 177
Dillon, Elsie S. 181, 592
Dillon, G. Noreen 172
Dillon, Lisa 151
DiMente, Helen 480
D'Incau, Florence V. 423
Dinh, Ivan 296
Dinsmore, L. Blanche 212
DiNunzio, Sylvia 7
Dinwoodie, David 587
Dionisio, Danielle N. 310
Diptee, Angeline 310
Dischinger, Theresa 64
Dishman, Traci R. 195
Ditman, Henry M. 319
Dittrich, Bruce E. 351
Dixon, Doris W. 406
Dixon, Gwendolyn A. 365

obbins, Amber 572
obner, Daniel John 426
obrick, Ruby B. 214
odge, Lynda 512
odson, Becki 339
oering, Bruce 326
olan, Brenda 506
olan, Francine 354
ombroff, Alex 307
ombrowski, Jessica C. 486
ominique, Kim 601
onahe, Jason 461
onahue, L. J. 52
onaldson, Judith Ticer 435
onnan, Christopher 489
onnell, Radka 103
onnelly, Susan 110
onohue, Lorraine 565
orn, Lydia 605
orr, Tom 112
ottore, Peter 191
oty, Grace 405
oughty, Dina B. 381
ouglas, Dorice 644
ouglas, Linda Lee 102
ouglas, Linda Mei 536
ouglas, Sarah B. 112
ouville, Marjorie 563
owd, Jacquelyn I. 473
owda, Kimberly 532
owell, Joe 258
owis, Alice Gail 305
owling, Debra 342
owner, Kristin 230
owning, Tessa E. 169
owns, Chandra Elayne 579
oyle, Annette 575
raghi, Raymond 108
rain, Jennifer 302
raine, Joan 262
resbaugh, Judy 318
ressel, Joshua D. 437
rew, Allysan F. 468
rew, Jason 438, 439
rew, W. L. 24
roege, Joyce D. 464
rowne, Ruth E. 204
rummond, Lynne 142
rumright, Linda 535
ryer, John R. 591
rzewiecki, David F. 386
Du Long, Patrick 80
DuBois, Barbara R. 461
DuBois, Jay 400
Duckett, Valerie J. 657
Dudding, Laura VeOla 134
Dudley, Ernest 416
Duerr, Robin 107
Duffy, Kara 512
Duffy, Melissa Marie 523
Duffy, Richard 165
Dufresne, George N. 306
Dulay, Catherine 330
Dulcie, Nannette 509
Duliba, Daniel D. 592
Dumas-Wright, Kelley 599
Dumbleton, Cynthia 295
Duncan, Shannon 161
Duncan, Wilma 28
Dunfee-Hamilton, Georgia 345
Dunlap, Greg 423
Dunlap, Lydia Pauline 547
Dunlap, Matt 596
Dunlow, Bonita H. 319
Dunn, Dana 162
Dunn, Elmer F. 311

Dunn, Kathy 526
Dunstan, Tex 657
Durkin, Lauren 565
Durnbaugh, Judith 362
Durrenberger, Larisa 155
Dusick, Brandon Edward 505
Duvall, Tawna 79
Duwe, Robert R. 214
Dwarka, Rajendra 82
Dyer, Sally 116
Dzerigian, Brandy 580
Eagan, Mimi 254
Eager, Ann 637
Eagle, Paul White 171
Earley, Otis Lee 142
Earner, Sara A. 113
Easley, Joe 364
Easter, Ovella 518
Eastin, Jean 474
Eaton, Betty Mae 647
Eaton, Kara 562
Eberly, Carole J. 583
Ebert, Bethel D. 347
Echols, Magill 237
Eckart, Bede 468
Eckerle, Philip A. 37
Eckert, Elizabeth 585
Eckman, Gary 570
Eddy, Dana F. 632
Eddy, S. N. 18
Edgar, Scott J. S. 198
Edgerton, Roy 55
Edmiston, Tamara 189
Edmund, Ruby 80
Edwards, Benie 414
Edwards, Charles M. 660
Edwards Jr., Woodrow W. 46
Edwards, Judie 361
Edwards, Kasey Lee 621
Edwards, Katie E. 510
Edwards, Kerrie 512
Edwards, L. P. 46
Edwards, Marguerite Keltz 230
Edwards, Michael S. 568
Edwards, Steve Robert 39
Edwardson, Ruth M. 202
Efird, Lisa 658
Ehmann, Anne M. 312
Eich, Patricia A. 98
Eichelberger, William 164
Eichenlaub, Mary Olympia 528
Eichert, Dana 324
Eiden, Paula 30
Eiter, Teresa 93
Elchoness, Monte 158
Elkins, Jeanette K. 579
Elkins, Jennifer 315
Elliott, Allison Marie 336
Elliott II, Robert Lee 26
Elliott, Jeremy L. 325
Ellis, Mandy 554
Ellis, Sarah 506
Ellison, Mimi 619
Elmer, Mary Ellen 135
Ely, Nathan A. 247
Embrick, David G. 308
Emelson, Ann 445
Emerald, Katie Leigh 521
Emmrich Jr., William A. 11
Endrigian, John 380
Engel, Jennifer 325
Engler, Joseph D. 631
Engler, Sandy 32
Englestad, M. 136
English, Blanche L. 327
Enns, Beverly 484

Enriquez, Joselito C. 465
Ensign, Kimberly Anne 509
Ensrude, Angelique 337
Epperson, Kim 517
Eppler, Ada V. 317
Eppley, Mary Jill 235
Epps, Sandra A. 98
Erby, Marie A. 554
Ercolano, Madeline C. 136
Erickson, Kathryn 147
Ericson, Lorrie 152
Erly, Sara A. 57
Erni, Rebecca Cole 102
Ernst, Kristin 228
Ertl, Catherine 392
Ervin, Larrie 543
Escalante, Karina 146
Escoto, Dawn 661
Eskew, Rachel 24
Espada, Veronica 68
Espina, Ellie 308
Espisito, Nancy L. 143
Esquivel, Michael 121
Essler, Susan 91
Esslinger, Nell 616
Estep, Mary Ann 557
Estes, Kimaree 150
Etheridge, LaRaine K. 657
Etterle, Angela R. 364
Evanoff, Leslie 611
Evans, Christopher 272
Evans, Dorothy H. 423
Evans, Faith 645
Evans, Heidi G. 643
Evans, Mary Emily 130
Evans, Roderick F. 217
Evans, Sharon B. 172
Evans, Shawna Collette Haney 198
Everton, Sarah 89
Ewing, Emma Mai 477
Ewing, Paula S. 108
Eylers, Mary Alyson 600
Eymann, Lyndsey M. 139
Ezzard, Catherine Bradley 473
Ezzat, Hilda Ann 173
Fabiano, Robert J. 50
Factor, Sarah 186
Fagin, Tamar 95
Fahrendorff, L. C. 624
Faile, Betty R. 398
Fairchild, Billie 454
Faitoute, Mary Lou 229
Faletti, Dominic 579
Fallahee, J. D. 114
Falor, Laura E. 238
Famuyiwa, Antoinette 588
Fani, Nabil Cyrus 137
farahay, m. l. 75
Fardi, Behrad 366
Farkosh, Dorothy V. 380
Farnsworth, Janet 327
Farr, Linda 154
Farr North West 377
Farrar, R. Sarah 18
Farrell, Bud 52
Farrell, Gregory A. 418
Farris, Robert S. 112
Fauber, Janice A. 353
Faucher, Harold N. 335
Faught, Tonya 69
Faulkner, Lena 140
Faulkner, Linda C. 546
Faulkner, Pamela D. 95
Faulkner, Tyrone 88
Faux, N. Y. 18
Faux-Fakis, Leanne 152

Favichia, Ray 111
Fazenbaker, Cheryl A. 326
Fazzone, Marshall 237
Feathers, Catherine D. 434
Fecker, Cheri 572
Federico, Raul M. 123
Fee Jr., James W. 312
Fee, Mark Allen 531
Feldman, Dan 429
Feldman, David 333
Feldman, Jack A. 310
Felella, Dawn 471
Feliciano, Mendiola 236
Felix, Belia 372
Fender, Bryan 335
Fenner, Dianne 320
Fenstermacher, Mary Wisham 544
Fenton, Jennifer M. 279
Ferber, Lee 238
Ferguson, Jessica 395
Ferguson, Mamie A. 236
Ferguson, Rebecca 103
Ferguson, Wilma W. 87
Fernandez, Wendy 182
Ferreira, Jack 396
Ferrer, Eliezer 630
Ferrier, Robert W. 115
Ferry, Christian 428
Fettis, Kate 137
Fick, Kelly 527
Fiddyment, Claire R. 587
Fields, Martha Alice 521
Fields, Robert V. 49
Fier, Leah 525
Fietsam, Mary MacCombie 568
Fifoot, Richard S. 94
Filkohazi, Patricia 45
Finch, Trudy 652
Findley, Kenneth 607
Fink, Bernadette 640
Fischer Jr., Ashton John 338
Fischer, Steven 203
Fish, Dennis P. 317
Fisher, Dina 647
Fisher, Kathleen Mae 659
Fissinger, Edward F. 497
Fitzgerald, Marguerite Twigg 597
Fitzpatrick, Lois 244
Fitzsimmons, Jamie 329
Fjelle, Karen Marie 555
Flanders, Bettianne 491
Fleming, Bill 328
Flenniken, Ceils B. 180
Fletcher, Vonda L. 62
Flores, Kathleen Williams 229
Flower, Burton 583
Floyd, Loraina 522
Focas, Angella A. 330
Fogel, Matthew 568
Fontaine, John G. 76
Foor, Iva L. 471
Force, Kanda LuAnn 240
Ford, A. 201
Ford, Anthony 400
Ford, Patricia 195
Ford, Sheila D. 60
Fordis, Fran R. 461
Forell, Judy 357
Foreman, Amy Leigh 651
Foresti, James 463
Forge, Bridget 466
Forte, Hank 584
Fortener, Cecelia 370
Fortin, Peter Benjamin 170
Foss, Deborah Elizabeth 574
Foss, Patricia 116

Fosse, John A. 397
Foucault, Hoyt 646
Fournier, Andrea 475
Foushée, Autumn 474
Fowler, Joshua D. 402
Fowler, Kimberly 519
fowler, lg 254
Fowler, Steven 205
Fox, Carol 498
Fox, Ernest G. 304
Fox, Richard A. 179
Fox Sr., Haydn A. 587
Fox, Stacy 175
Foye, Nancy Lou 617
Frame, Sandra 222
Francano, Joni 283
Franciskovich, Robert J. 104
Franco, Carrie R. 375
Franco-Cuevas, Rafael 224
Francomb, Michael J. 553
Frandsen, Benjamin 164
Frank, Denise R. 629
Franke, Karen Lynn 516
Franklin, Brian 71
Franklin, Sandra 7, 87
Franklin, Ted 43
Frantzen, Larry 528
Frasca, Barbara 658
Fraser, Gloria 279
Frasier, E. Lewis 11
Frauenberger, Wilma 21
Frazee Jr., John C. 392
Frazer, Tanya 106
Frederick, Shirley 60
Free, Carrie M. 268
Freed, Dona Jean 352
Freed, Florence Wallach 357
Freeman, Billye 574
Freeman, Rachel E. 216
Frehren, Rachel A. 45
Freiermuth, Lillian 539
French, Alison R. 295
Frendreiss, Anastasia 449
Frenkel, Grace 327
Fried, Gary S. 313
Frieder, Clara M. 383
Friedman, Heather 286
Friedman, Pamela 52
Friesz, Mary Franklin 233
Fritts, Lucille 597
Fritz, Kathleen Anita 147
Froilan, Vicente S. 45
Frontela, Olga 604
Fry, Becky 303
Fryer, Donna 422
Fudurich, Jerome M. 346
Fuentes, Brenda Lee 378
Fuentes, Maria 529
Fujimoto, Randi L. 41
Fulcher, Mary T. 599
Fuller, Charmaine Santresa 314
Fuller, Richard C. 161
Fullerton, Jennifer 296
Fuqua, Marni L. 240
Furr, Carolyn M. 348
Fusco, Robin 160
Gadberry, Alice M. 349
Gadd, John A. 321
Gaffney, Margaret 129
Gaffrey, Jim 589
Gager, Amber 271
Gaines, F. W. 208
Galahad, Alexander 371
Gale, Beverly J. 637
Galfano, Rosa Leonora 89
Galindo, Joel 104
Gall, Becky 505
Gallimore, Maggie 525
Gallo, Anthony 362
Gamble, Wesley 27
Gandero, Diane 416
Gantt, Jason 634
Gaona, Carol Martinez 379
Garbarini, Gerald 68
Garcia, Alexander 492
Garcia, America Ray 409
Garcia, Andrea V. 382
Garcia, Debra A. 428
Garcia, Elidia 455
Garcia, Elpidia A. 277
Garcia, Esther Maria 273
Garcia, Krystal 240
Garcia, Linda 479
Garcia, Mario Eloy 539
Garcia, Matt R. 232
Garcia, Michael 165
Garcia, Oralia Cortez 138
Garcia, Presilla 58
Garcia, Rubi M. 220
Garcia, Santos F. 16
Garcia, Stephanie Alayne 173
Garda, Nicole 556
Gardner, Diane 595
Gardner, Evelyn 459
Garduque, Elaine 268
Garfield, Michael 255
Gargiulo, James A. 345
Garibay, Stanley B. 79
Gariepy, Heather 395
Garner, Sue A. 172
Garner, Susan T. 65
Garretson, Johanna A. 377
Garretson, Yollanda L. 24
Garrett, Ginny 281
Garrett, Leasa 550
Garrison, Carole Lee 320
Garrity, Bill 593
Garrity, Sabra Lynn 172
Garth, Betty Marie 487
Gasaway, Michele 626
Gass, Jackqueline 574
Gately, Fonya 466
Gathings, Michael 616
Gaucher, Brian P. 321
Gaudet, Violet F. 66
Gaulrapp, Victoria N. 45
Gauspohl, Brent 403
Gawlik, Mary Corish 526
Gay, Kimberly 251
Gazay, Beulah C. 459
Gehrhardt, Carol 450
Gehris, Linette M. 151
Gehrmann, Mary Ann 652
Geiger, Debbie 491
Geisler, Cynthia A. 473
Geneczko, Stacey 204
Geneva, Rebekah S. 197
Gentry, Elizabeth 321
Gentry, Emily 494
Gentzler, Michael 514
George, Gayle T. 592
George, Lindsey A. 549
George-Demotte, Patricia 38
Gerken, Amanda 405
Germanton, Jennifer A. 318
Getman, Francis D. 585
Getsinger, Stacy 29
Gewinner, Anthony 637
Gibson, Daryn 358
Gibson Jr., Calvin T. 649
Gibson, Opal 151
Gibson Sr., Arthur E. 268
Gibson, Victoria 48
Giebler, Ruth Kinzie 89
Gietzen, Al 576
Gigo, Saihou Omar 165
Gilbert, Brian 398
Gill, Laura L. 540
Gill, Rosalee E. 86
Gillan, Alan Paul 651
Gilliland, Jeremy 652
Gingell, Paul Edward 113
Ginger, Lacee 128
Ginsburg, Morris 518
Giordano Jr., R. 22
Giorgio, Joseph 347
Giovinazzo, Amber L. 296
Gipe, Dale M. 421
Girarte, Javier 302
Gish, Velma Ruppel 7
Gitzen, Karen A. 538
Givens, Bettye Hammer 268
Glaser, Celeste J. 338
Glassman, Christina 629
Glauberman, Andrea 461
Gleeson, Vivian 67
Glenn, Amanda 413
Glenn, Ann C. 396
Glenn, Shamara 78
Glinton, Cemone 444
Gloria 6
Glover, C. LaReeve 111
Glover, Charmaine 588
Glover, Tena 110
Gloyd, Maxine Brown 606
Glynn, Henry 408
Go, Annette 272
Gober, Jesse Jack 464
Goetz, Darlena 275
Goetzheimer, Dorothy 390
Goetzinger, Whitney Jaye 61
Goff, Mary Lou 567
Gogerty Jr., John D. 411
Golden, Chris 337
Goldman, Dorothy 350
Goldman, Ruth Phares 46
Golley Jr., Howard 467
Gomez, Daniel F. 654
Gomez, Melissa Anne 87
Gomez, Ted 205
Gonzales, Ida 594
Gonzalez, Blanca Estela 264
Gonzalez, Fernando 304
Good, Margaret 554
Goodell, Erline D. 571
Goodey, Ila Marie 360
Goodman, Bonnie Worthman 389
Goodman, Monica 534
Goodwin, Josie Harris 311
Goodwin Jr., Jeff L. 292
Goodwin, Stacey 481
Gootee, John M. 382
Gordon, Brad 442
Gordon, Gilbert G. 411
Gordon, Harlan L. 633
Gordon, Ida 501
Gordon, Scott 164
Gore, Kellie D. 510
Gornati, Rudolph 41
Gorodetskaya, Yelena 48
Goss, Kristin L. 567
Gosvener, Earl 303
Goudie, Valene 121
Gowen, M. I. 123
Graber, Sarah 29
Graham, Darlene L. 584
Graham, Donald C. 278
Graham, Dorothy 276
Graham, Elenora Maxine 304
Graham, Elizabeth 360
Graham, John Stuart 631
Granda, Eric 320
Grandstaff, Gloria 421
Grant, F. R. 98
Grant, Joan J. 452
Grant, Katrina R. 520
Grant, Leigh 157
Gratz, Ruthie 45
Graves, Kelli Michelle 544
Gray, C. Edwin 200
Gray, Dareen W. 424
Gray, E. Russell 177
Gray, Joyce E. 349
Gray, Morning Star 234
Gray, Tom 35
Gray Wolf 452
Green, Hope 457
Green, Louis F. 559
Green, Paula 122
Greenan, Lori L. 140
Greene, Eulalia M. 361
Greene, Joan M. 307
Greene Jr., Thomas H. 59
Greene, Rita 183
Greene, William F. 113
Greenwood, Alissa 570
Gregory, Brandon 386
Gregory, Ida 501
Grein, Diana Hodgin 478
Grensten, Jean A. 390
Grewe, Rebecca J. 204
Griebling, Mary Ann 535
Griffin, Genevieve 352
Griffin, Marlene J. 231
Griffin, Samantha 68
Griffith, Chris 437
Griffith, Dan 430
Griffith, Destry 590
Griggs, Jamie 329
Grills, Shastyn 198
Grimble-Morris, Juliet 629
Grimm, Frank 473
Grimsley, W. E. 21
Grinolds, Kim 617
Grippe, Barbara 632
Grissett, S. D. 222
Grissom, Jennifer Dee 505
Grizzle, K. Renee 194
Grogan, Misty Dawn 233
Groomes, Ophelia Denise 511
Groover, Bobbi 318
Groover, Joan 592
Groover, Keith Allen 131
Grose, Laura 524
Grossman, Ruth 187
Grosso, Judy 263
Groth, Nancy 139
Grover, Clarence L. 272
Grubbs, Carol 584
Guarogno, Margaret R. 548
Guckenheimer, Helen 425
Guenther, Edris L. 266
Guercia, Julianne 405
Guerin, George John 446
Guerrero, Celena 460
Guerrero, Jean G. 388
Gugliotaa, Ralicia 83
Guibert, Amy O'Shay 463
Guilfoyle, Theophane 11
Guillen, Gordy 388
Guilmette, Mary F. 117
Gunderson, Carri 580
Gunn, Joseph 333
Gunter, Andera 638

770

urewicz, Jo 441
urganus, Joan 269
ursky, Sandra M. Ward 57
ustafson, Bonnie J. 387
uthmiller, Anthony 593
utowski, Ray 88
uttzeit, Susan 161
uynn, Patricia Stone 80
winnup, Heidi Nikole 640
aack, David A. 574
aag, Jamie A. 257
aag-Smith, V. Joy 118
aapanen, Paivi 49
acker, Joel 393
ackett, Barbara L. 336
ackl, Edda H. 571
ackl, Florence 390
ackney, Marie Matthews 144
addox, Christina 659
addox, Maxine 252
aflin, Robin 93
age, George Campbell 277
agen, Tamara Lee 165
agens, Lucie C. 240
agmann, Brian 382
ah, Won J. 9
Hahn, Jacqueline 473
Hahn, Margaret 232
Hahn, Tommy 78
Hahurst, Kenneth E. 510
Haines, Helen W. 423
Haiungs Sr., Marc 150
Halcomb, Kimberly 540
Hales, Kellie J. 154
Haley, Casey 591
Haley, Pamela J. 51
Hall, Aurora-Jillann 461
Hall, Donald R. 438
Hall, Elizabeth 390, 400
Hall, Jo Anne E. 353
Hall, Johnie Sue 399
Hall, Michael 555
Hallberg, Al 457
Haller, Daniel R. 485
Halvorsen, Byron 637
Halvorsen, Christopher 389
Hamid, Sam 181
Hamill, Amy M. 316
Hamilton, Kelsey 529
Hamilton, Shannon Marie 121
Hamlin, Mary Frances 554
Hamling, April 478
Hammer, Dorothy M. 572
Hammer, John D. 305
Hammil, Shirley J. 104
Hammond, Brenda 309
Hammond, Flora Calef 462
Hampson, Celia 381
Hampton, Bryan Adams 627
Hampton, Colleen 39
Hampton, Stephanie 96
Hamrick, Willa 15
Han Jr., Howard S. 260
Handsel, Lynne M. 568
Haney, Traces T. 88
Hanjis, Costas 573
Hanks, Bonnie 387
Hanley, Bruce Michael Anthony 492
Hanly, Alfred Sheldon 579
Hann, Deborah L. 307
Hansen, Judie 641
Hansen, Kristin 47
Hansen, Maxine Joy 540
Hanson, Becky Lou 290
Hanson, Ronald J. 14
Haralson, Cheryl Lynn Cleland 300

Harb, John 502
Harbatkin, Erica S. 575
Hardcastle, Margaret H. 621
Hardee, Kimberly 623, 652
Hardenburg, Christal G. 459
Hardin, Karen 625
Hardin, RoShawn 103
Harding, Carol 307
Harding, Shay T. 58
Hargrove, Lynn Welch 542
Harjo, Sena Koleepkv 215
Harmon, Christine M. 385
Harnden, Deb 640
Harney, Heather 393
Harpool, Robert L. 83
Harrelson, Bryon 466
Harrington, Mary Alice 127
Harris, Amanda 578
Harris, Deborah 324
Harris, E. R. 183
Harris, Fred 410
Harris, Gwen 192
Harris, Maureen Holland 127
Harris, Melanie 126
Harris, Patricia A. 10
Harris, Shelia 61
Harris, Stan 106
Harrison, Lewis 213
Harrison, M. 59
Harrison, Polly 74
Harrison-Ballard, Ruby Nelle 45
Hart, Bonnie R. 381
Hart, Tim 41
Hart, Wayman C. 113
Hartford, Tiffany 15
Hartley, Lee 606
Hartman, Renee 200
Hartman, Scott 161
Hartnett, Rachel 169
Hartnett Sr., Paul F. 212
Hartnett, Toni 118
Harvey, Colleen 647
Harvey, Lauren 562
Harvey, Lucile G. 620
Harwell, Tom 115
Harwood, Jane R. 392
Hasemeier, Matthew A. 132
Hashbarger, Kenneth J. 233
Hassler, John 576
Hastings, Doris 477
Hastings, John S. 304
Hatalla, Shannon 74
Hatcher, Veronica 199
Hatfield, Elizabeth 495
Hatfield, T. M. 211
Hathaway Jr., Richard N. 62
Haugabook, Janice 399
Haugland, Charles 328
Haupt, Christine E. 267
Haupt, Dorothea Helma 301
Havens, Will H. 216
Hawkins, Gena 508
Hawkins, Jennifer 440
Hawkins, Marilyn 249
Hawkins, Miranda 554
Hawkins, Newell A. 120
Hawley, C. Patrick 222
Haworth Jr., Alvin G. 472
Haworth, Ralph 178
Hay, W. D. 125
Hayden, Heather 507
Hayes, Arnold 285
Hayes, David 366
Hayes, John J. 376
Haynes, Barbara 286
Hays, Belinda Jo 401

Hays, Leonard L. 563
Hays, Stephen 178
Haywood, Shannon M. 87
Head, Ruth Gretchen 171
Hearn, Erin 479
Heath, Christina 642
Heath, Sarah L. 191
Heathman, Peggy 110
Hebert, Joyce 493
Hechim, Maura L. 557
Heck, Rachel 162
Heckenberg, Ron L. 24
Heefner, Doris E. 286
Heide, Paulanne 171
Heidmann, Susan 83
Heidrick, Jeri 397
Heironimus, Annette 367
Heisel, Hortenze Kopple 399
Hejtmanek, Rocquel Lynn 102
Hellman, Helen 570
Hellsten, Josefina 430
Helm, Martha 534
Helman, Shirley 660
Henaughan, Mary Elizabeth 246
Henderson, Christel 367
Henderson, Dawn 97
Henderson, Diana Len 402
Henderson, Lydia B. 234
Henderson, Shelia 94
Henderson, Wayne 182
Hendricks, Brenda L. 364
Hendricks, Shawn David 13
Henley, Dawn 631
Hennager, Sandra 116
Henningsen, Tiphanie M. 167
Henson, Anita Diane 462
Henzler, Nicole 521
Herbert, Christina 430
Herdman, Clay 294
Herman, Grace 396
Hernandez, Corinne 471
Hernandez, Edgar 51
Hernandez, Lisa 235
Hernandez, Mario 153
Hernandez, Ronald Jay 195
Hernandez, Sergio 34
Herndon, Joshua 500
Herndon, Regina 43
Herold, Gordon B. 374
Herr, Marcia 252
Herrick, Amanda 391
Herrick, Robert L. 175
Herrin, Michelle Lanier 229
Herrle, Carole L. 586
Herrmann, Françoise 375
Herron, Ginger 403
Hess, Connie 293
Hess, Dolores M. 374
Hester, David C. 387
Hester, Mark 237
Hetzel, Joe 643
Hetzler, Doris J. 331
Heverly, Patricia A. 27
Hewes, Shelley 25
Heywood Sr., Raymond A. 57
Hickey, Mary Patricia 142
Hickman, Dorothy P. 448
Hickok, Becky 256
Hicks, Allison 399
Hicks, Grace Roberson 443
Hicks, Larry 126
Hickson, Hazel F. 298
Higdon, Lily 526
Higgie, Vivian 34
Higginbotham, Tonya 43
Higgins, Tahnee 123

High, Nathaniel 517
Hildebrand, Anna M. 347
Hill, Anthony M. 371
Hill, Candy 657
Hill, Darlene M. C. 276
Hill, Herman Renoir 626
Hill, Ida Mae 582
Hill, Jocelyn 453
Hill, M. K. 9
Hill, T. Greg 125
Hill-Johnson, Betty 435
Hille, Robert Benton 164
Hiller, Sarrah Jane 112
Hillger, Linnie Renee 54
Hilliard, Edward L. 405
Hillman, Edith T. 384
Hines, Daniel 266
Hinson, Edward Harrell 432
Hinson, Neda 158
Hinton, Shelley 109
Hiponia, M. Concepcion G. 55
Hipps, Heather Ann 581
Hir, Donna M. 305
Hircsh, Irma 455
Hislop, Holly 489
Hix, Joe 318
Ho, Annette 401
Hoalcraft, Josie Deaton 453
Hobbs, Allene 389
Hobbs, Amanda K. 377
Hobbs, Roxanne L. 57
Hocutt, Janice 317
Hodnett, David 306
Hodson, Nicole L. 520
Hoeber, Aaron 631
Hoehn, Helen D. 293
Hoffman, Anna M. 589
Hoffman, Gerald E. 311
Hoffman, Robert Wayne 61
Hogan, Jonita 462
Hogan, Nancy L'enz 518
Hogg, Moline 235
Hogle, Eric 390
Hoglund, Patricia 188
Holaday, Marjorie 245
Holben, Keilen 515
Holden, Joyce Hill 491
Holem, Julia K. 343
Hollan, Florine Nolen 507
Holland, Anthony E. 451
Holland/Hetterick, Roberta 164
Hollenbeck, Chris 488
Holler, Dianna Christy 8
Holley, Kenneth L. 509
Holloway, Veronie 180
Holmer, Vivian 48
Holsey, Stacey Lynn 36
Holton-Muller, Regina 197
Holub, Ethan Andrew 347
Holzman, Louise 233
Hom, Dorothy 327
Homick, Michelle 596
Honda, Toshiko 8
Honquest, Tess 176
Hoofard, Karen 615
Hook, David W. 507
Hook, Penny 43
Hooks, Vivian 108
Hoover, Mary Vion 617
Hopkins, Caroline 344
Hopkins, Jerry Thomas 651
Hopper, Rhanda 42
Horaz, Bruce 449
Horner, Carli 383
Horrell, Dorothy 278
Horsley, Janice A. 454

Horta, Gaye 629
Horton, Carol Thomas 591
Horton, Rosia 218
Horton, Shirley Campbell 59
Hosford, Heather 630
Hoth, Angela B. 644
Hotop, Patricia 84
Houchens, Elizabeth 311
House, Gregory 310
Houser, Jessica 391
Houtz, Carey 294
Houtz, Toby L. 205
Howard, Sarah 194
Howard, Sylvia D. 93
Howe, Emily 403
Howe, Jennifer 390
Howell, Paul M. 119
Hower, Carlos 466
Howze, Margarett 524
Hoy, Susan 110
Hoyle, Joy 488
Hranj, Rebecca 10
Hrehowesik, Janet 500
Hrouda, Ursula 42
Hubbard, Jeannie 283
Hubbell, James T. 385
Hubbell, Joyce 399
Huber, Mark F. 609
Hubert, Colleen A. 340
Huckleberry, James T. 458
Hucks, Christina Lee Braswell 271
Huey, Billy 635
Huffmann, Amber 280
Hufnagel, Marian A. 230
Huggins, Stephen C. 228
Hughes Jr., Richard M. 65
Hughes, Michelle 603, 656
Hulbert, Elizabeth 399
Hulen, Ashley Teal 650
Huling, James M. 332
Hulstine, Cindy 494
Hummel, Eugenia 579
Humphrey, Cheri L. 376
Humphrey, Owen E. 146
Humphries, Janet 372
Hundshamer, Frank 468
Hunter, Diane S. 422
Hunter, H. H. 94
Hunter, Helen 356
Hunter, Isabelle 478
Hunter, Kathleen 238
Hunter, Tiffany Ann 110
Hurley, Ann 297
Hurley, Nora E. 527
Hurst, Darleen 589
Hurt, Judy T. 338
Husser, Sandra Marie 56
Hutchins, Sharleen C. 43
Hutchinson Jr., Olin Fulmer 557
Hyatt, Cynthia D. 404
Hyde, David L. 576
Hyde, Nelma 167
Hyslop, Marlena Marie 155
Iiams, Cory 276
Ikner, Jean 334
Ilgenfritz, Anne 578
Incledon, Emily 363
Ingebrigtsen, Kay H. 527
Ingraham, Shannan 653
Ingram, Amanda 575
Ingram, Susan 206
Irving, Lois L. 542
Irwin, Michael P. 551
Ishizaka, Sylvia 199
ISIL 17
Ivie, Brenda K. 394

Jack, Inez 590
Jackson, Constance 380
Jackson, Crystal L. 291
Jackson, Earnestine 334
Jackson, Eloise C. 390
Jackson, Gayle Whittle 396
Jackson, Janita K. 468
Jackson, Jennifer R. 650
Jackson, Jewelean 467
Jackson, John D. 313
Jackson, Julian 458
Jackson, Stephanie 174
Jackson, Tracey A. 3
Jackson, William Darryl 118
Jacobe, LeeOra 654
Jacobs, Chris 290
Jacobs, Lucky 249
Jacobson, David M. 485
Jaffee, Ben-Joshua 389
Jaffer, Janice Sheppard 363
Jager, Shirley 75
Jagerman, Judy 341
Jahich, Mustafa 170
James, Betty 34
James, Billie Jeanne 503
James, Connie 578
James, Ebony Joy 580
James, Gina J. 474
James, Jimi 131
James, Joanna M. 56
James, Kim 653
James, Shannon 112
James, Steven 19
James, Tammy 82
Jansen, Joanne C. 436
Janulewicz, Karen J. 538
Jarosz, Steven A. 64
Jarrard, Elaine 584
Jarrell, Jonathon Stone 395
Jarrett, Jeremy 423
Jarvis, Leisa Marie 510
Jasper, Laura 564
Jaus, Jenny P. 103
Jay, Michael 149
Jaynes, Vivian 29
Jean, Gloria 489
Jeffery, Betty Anne 456
Jeffrey-Ruth, Colleen A. 332
Jeffries, Anna Belle 585
Jeffries, Loren T. 138
Jenkins, Amber 305
Jenkins, Barbara L. 593
Jenkins, Harry F. 572
Jenkins, Lillian R. 614
Jenkins, Stephanie C. 90
Jenney, David R. 328
Jennings, Laura Renee 543
Jensen, Anna Barton 337
Jensen, Annalise Blanchard 450
Jensen, Anne M. 466
Jensen, Barbara C. 318
Jensen, Jane 595
Jensen, Jane E. 383
Jenson, Jim 450
Jessen, Anne 323
Jessop, Helen-Lane 324
Jeter, Hope A. 644
Jett, Mathew Thomas 548
Jewett, Eleanor 303
Jhirad, Elijah E. 419
Ji, Wong 86
Jimenez, Maria 156
Jimenez, Samantha 110
Joedicke, Linda 242
Johansen, Solveig 74
Johns, Michelle 510

Johnsen, Joanne E. 447
Johnson, Amy 648
Johnson, Angela 594
Johnson, Angela Michele 312
Johnson, Anita 300
Johnson, Ann Marie 332
Johnson, Candace 640
Johnson, Charlethea 414
Johnson, Darlene Cree 343
Johnson, Elizabeth 326
Johnson, Felicity 477
Johnson, Gerria E. 358
Johnson, Glyn S. 281
Johnson, Gwendolyn 595
Johnson, Ida Lea 570
Johnson, Jacqueline 52
Johnson, James E. 450
Johnson, Jamie 457
Johnson, Jane Martin 382
Johnson, Janice C. 346
Johnson, Julie Ann 454
Johnson, Lavone 566
Johnson, Len 552
Johnson, Lillian T. 231
Johnson, Michelle 523
Johnson, Peggy 177
Johnson, Rachael 162
Johnson, Shari 123
Johnson, Sharon Kay 657
Johnson, Shaunquetta 52
Johnson, Sheila Noel 63
Johnson, Ted 207
Johnson, Terry A. 213
Johnston, Bob 269
Johnston, Jean 274
Johnston, John C. 408
Johnston, Tyler Richard 16
Joiner, Martha Lynn 254
Jones, Chris 328
Jones, Claudine 37
Jones, Connie Rigsby 590
Jones, Fannie 325
Jones, George T. 329
Jones, Ivory Dean 463
Jones, Jacqueline 317
Jones, Jason 397
Jones, Jeanette Jackson 258
Jones, Joanne F. 636
Jones, Johron 346
Jones, Kathleen 237
Jones, Lisa A. 241
Jones, Michael D. 637
Jones, Michael K. 527
Jones, Natashia M. 252
Jones, Owen 534
Jones, Raphael B. 221
Jones, Thelma R. 213
Jones, Veneta 7
Jones, Wanda 196
Jones, William Henry 206
Jones, Wray Christine Stewart 26
Jordan, Jasper Anthony 462
Jordan, Jill E. 256
Jordan, Joie 182
Jordan, Leslie 236
Jordan, Willie M. 78
Jorgensen, Jennifer M. 342
Jose, Amanda 271
Joseph, James David 440
Joseph, Kathy Rose 513
Josephson, Dawn 463
Josey, Mary E. 509
Joshi, Aida A. 435
Joshi, Vishnu P. 218
Joswiak, Jana 333
Jotter, Virginia 105

Joy 112
Joyce, Jacqueline 365
Joyfully Jane 382
Jozwiak, Shelly 76
Judd, Bettina Antionette 316
Juhasz, Diana 300
Juliet, Noelle 179
Juntunen, Art 379
Jurischk, Tim 12
Justiniano, Evelyn 485
Jutzi, Kristina 603
Kaaialii, David 278
Kabanuk, Elisha 420
Kabo, Angie 271
Kachmar, Jessie 413
Kafaf, Amanda Beth 436
Kage, Nikki 615
Kalitan, Ali O'Grady 456
Kallonas, Phillip 63
Kaloss, Victoria 199
Kaminski, Bonnie Seefeldt 420
Kaminski, Chester 406
Kaminsky, Daniel 166
Kammer, Nancy 249
Kammeraad, Kevin 518
Kampa, Betty Allman 380
Kane, Joseph 592
Kanter, Irene 504
Karanfilian, Leigh Anne 240
Karashin, Cathryn 429
Karp, Izetta 451
Kase, Elizabeth Parker 357
Kastet, Millie 599
Katcoff, Benjamin 344
Kauffman, Ethel C. 169
Kauffman, Eunice 461
Kauffman, Marie 513
Kaufman, Adam 321
Kaufman, Nina 625
Kavanagh, Carolyn 387
Kearse, Tatina Elizabeth 83
Kearse, Yasmin N. 175
Keaton, Alpha M. 626
Kechler, Brent J. 485
Keck, Charlotte L. 629
Keel, Barbara 332
Keele, Christy 73
Keeling, Clayton 581
Keenan, Robert 203
Keetch, Barbara B. 285
Keffer, Ruth Ann 188
Kegebein, Crystal 591
Keh, Hean Tat 594
Keller, Patricia 267
Kelley, Dorothy 292
Kelley, Ruth Allion 201
Kelley, William R. 118
Kellis, Hilda 636
Kelly, Albert J. 320
Kelly, Allison 356
Kelly, Angela 501
Kelly, Eileen 349
Kelly, G. 188
Kelly, Gregory 579
Kelly, Teresa M. 189
Kelsey, Jason 391
Kemp, Cynthia D. 344
Kennedy, David 494
Kenney, Ann M. 401
Kent, Hope Hathaway 581
Keoviengxay, Vilath 35
Kephart, Grace 434
Keraghan, Robert Charles 25
Kerekes, Loris Edsall 535
Kerins, Meghan 550
Kerman, Karen 606

ern, Julaine B. 289
ero, Derinda 378
errigan, Diane 451
ersell, Joyce 578
eske, Clara J. 582
estner, Jennifer A. 586
ethley, Dixie Lee Lene 18
etterer, Wendy Lee 3
ey, Kenneth A. 522
gaphola, Godfrey M. 105
ia, Rachel 103
icenski, Michael 567
ietzmann, Jill 650
ilcran, J. J. 182
ildow, Nancy 138
ile, Dalphne 306
illinger, Pat 180
ilmurray, Tammy 13
imball, Susan G. 109
imble, Bridgett J. C. 629
King, Amanda 354
King, Bill 345
King, Carolyn K. 271
King, Grace Ann 336
King, Kathleen A. 567
King, Lynn 515
King, Matthew 544
King, Melodee 128
King, Rebecca 116
King, Theresa A. 176
Kinkead, Edwin Lyle 259
Kinneer, Jinx 495
Kinney, Barbara 395
Kinsella, Kristen 129
Kinsey, Adrienne Elizabeth 580
Kioski, Louise G. 534
Kipper, T. 109
Kirby, Mary Anita 251
Kirby, Susannah 117
Kirby, Virginia 47
Kirk, Elizabeth A. 314
Kirkland, Tammy 63
Kirschenmann, Courtney 425
Kissick, Codi 350
Kist, Margaret 537
Kittle, Stacey 79
Klein, Anne 262
Klein, Shaun 30
Klepinger, Lawrence 518
Kline, Marshall 510
Kline, Mary 232
Kline, Nathaniel Darwin Kennedy 653
Kline, Susan L. 96
Kline, Tiona J. 218
Klinger, J. Philip 103
Klugman, Deborah 351
Knape, Myles B. 516
Knepper, M. J. 510
Knickerbocker, Carl 495
Kniffin, Karen Ann 146
Knight, Lori 625
Knittel, August 281
Knoll, D. J. 65
Knoll, Suzanne Guinn 166
Knowles, Raymond W. 47
Kobak, Michael Joseph 603
Koceski, Paul A. 164
Koch, Annette 267
Koch, Betsy 346
Koch, Brenda 309
Koch, Carla M. 457
Koch, Elaine 275
Koelling, Shirley J. 168
Koerner, Janet 432
Kohli, Amita 417
Kohli, Kirti 622

Kohlman, Cleo C. 370
Kohlstrand, Norman C. 612
Kolar, Kathleen 600
Kolb, Dorothy J. 424
Kolb, Dru 487
Kolkhorst, Jenifer 506
Kontis, Kellie 249
Konnerth, Anne 658
Kooken, Gary P. 463
Koontz, Daniel 104
Koopman, Judy 581
Kopas, Craig 336
Kopf, Karla A. 532
Korb, Jonathan D. 590
Korrinhizer, Edmond 342
Korth, Chris 289
Koss, William "Shortfellow" 167
Kostkiewicz, James M. 321
Kostoulakos, Stephen J. 177
Kotkin, Amanda 419
Kotschorek, Henry 277
Kovach, Sandra R. 221
Kovach, Kathy L. 156
Kracht, Sandy K. 161
Krafft, Genevieve A. 634
Kraft, Marion 237
Krantz, Lonita Mullins 559
Krause, Annie 460
Krause, Elizabeth A. 414
Krause, Jill 339
Krause, Steve 120
Krauss, Melissa 231
Kravetz, Justin G. 473
Krawchuk, Alyson Nicole 257
Krebs, Tyler 59
Kreemer, Irvin C. 648
Kretser, Kevin 515
Kreycik, Sarah 167
Krivanek, Louis 545
Krivda, Dr. Edward R. 314
Krizak, Michael 558
Kroen, Stanley S. 89
Krueger, Dixie R. 495
Kruer, Matthew 599
Kruse, Jennifer 393
Kubaszak, Paul 80
Kuberka, Loni 232
Kubitza, Robin J. 190
Kubosh, Rhonda Ann 54
Kuehn, Chris E. 52
Kuehn, Jesse J. 380
Kuerbitz, Karen 569
Kuhn, Robert Christian 184
Kuknyo, Donna 569
Kumar, Tobi 163, 165
Kunz, Heidi 193
Kunz, Lori 519
Kurisu, Michelle 250
Kurtz, Maravene 563
Kusior, Catharine E. 471
Kuter, Kay E. 616
Kuthe, Lisa 608
Kuumba, Umoja I. 112
Lacefield, Georgia 212
Lacher, Anna S. 504
Lackey, Amber L. 325
LaCount, Sandra J. 88
Lafferty, Nancy 604
Lagerstrom, Jennifer 301
Laggart, Andrea 577
Laib, Bariza 104
Lake, Elizabeth 316
Lakritz, Juli-Anne 279
Lamb, Brook 594
Lambert, Allan H. 445
Lambert, Michele 532

Lambert, Myrtle 563
Lamont, Christina 377
Lamothe, David A. 49
Land, Shari 123
Landrum, Paula Ann 100
Landry, Sabine 169
Lang, Mary E. 143
Lang, Michael G. 249
Langdon, Blanche 302
Langford, Esther M. 445, 507
Langford, Michelle R. 596
Langley, Donna 478
Langley, Erik John 417
Langlois, Elizabeth 508
Langston, Christy 639
Lankford, Linda 527
Lanning, Eunice 379
Lantis, Julie 308
Lanzl, Eunice B. 479
LaPean, Larry L. 230
LaPlante, Dorothy 333
Larens, Jim 569
Larivee, Tara 105
Larke, Allyson 315
Larkin, Robert C. 108
Larmay, Krystal Lynn 250
Larmon, James M. 418
Larry, Shara 15
Larsen, Henning 456
Larsen, Herman L. 474
Larsen, Linda M. 174
Larson, Daniel 589
Larson, Effie Ruth 280
Larson, Jack Eugene 361
Larson, Jackie 402
Larson, Russell 21
Larssen, Cheri Tracy 640
Larzelier, Radie M. 224
Lasher, Darlene 354
Lashley, Sara Toni 86
Lashoones, Richard H. 32
Laskoski, Megan 569
Laszlo, Cleo 325
Latham, Mike 253
Lathrop, Royce L. 202
Latterman, Jessica 493
Latting, Lanette F. 251
Laughton, Jayme 409
Laumann, Karen 561
Lauth, Amye 497
Lauzon, Vickie J. 211
Lavin, Shayna 167
Lawbaugh, Tara 110
Lawrence, Alice L. 297
Lawrence, Cecil C. 340
Lawrence, Luella L. 144
Lawrence, Pamela 120
Lawson, Deborah McKnight 274
Lawson, Singinn 42
Laymon, Wheeler 163
Layne, Beverly 330
Lazenby, Wendy 101
Le Deoux, Tamika C. 208
Le Grand, Renee 172
Le Grande, Everett E. 636
Le-Sueur, Zora Shenete 183
Leaper, Cristen 475
Leaper-Nettles, Callie B. 376
Leavy, Thomas G. 122
Lebans, Ruth J. 4
LeBlanc, Michael L. 601
Leblanc, Mike 596
LeBlanc, Saffron 167
Leblanc-Lewis, Mark H. 612
Leckie, James 378
Lee, Dwayne 312

Lee, Janet 467
Lee, Jo 453
Lee, Julie 643
Lee, Jung 402
Lee, Kent 244
Lee, Mary Ann 550
Lee, Mary S. 600
Lee, Rebecca 97
Lee, Richard J. 38
Lee, Suzanne C. 212
Lees, Jason 473
Lefko, Sportshots Randy 38
Legeness, Betty 322
LeGros, John 321
Lehman, Ralph 72
Lehovec, Kurt 625
Lein, Leona F. Lee 533
Leininger, Billie 334
Leitman, Melissa 516
Leko, Patty 6
Lelko, Gaylene 627
Lemaster, Paula Ann 122
Lemmons, Bill 421
Lemon, Mary A. S. 546
Lenhart, Douglas 315
Lenhart, Joan 455
Lennox, Christine A. 257
Lenox, John 582
Lenzen, Marilyn 514
Leon, Rayza 47
Leonard, Emily 579
Leonardy, Joshua C. 460
Leone, Susan A. 40
Leppert, Susan 19
Lester, Martha 532
Lett, Linda M. 529
Lettre, Melissa 126
Levens, Christina M. 478
Leverant, Donna 386
Levy, Chris 352
Lewis, A. James 97
Lewis, Arlie T. 266
Lewis, Beth 476
Lewis, Burnham 264
Lewis, Carol Crawford 570
Lewis, Evelyn R. 394
Lewis, Mary R. 143
Lewis, P. J. 53
Lewis, Richart Drake 115
Lewis, Robert T. 73
Lewis, Ronald J. 113
Lewis, Ruth 182
Lewis, Travis 94
Liakos, Leslie 236
Libby, Michael 246
Libutaque, Lori G. 242
Licata, Sal 207
Liermann, ReAnna 125
Liggett, Walter S. 176
Lighthouse, Amber Rose 510
Ligon, Rachel 50
Lilia 245
Lilienthal, Linda K. 238
Lilly-Antis, Kathlene 152
Limpach, Alice C. 322
Lin, Quinn 55
Lind, Karen 534
Linder-Madsen, Marianna 551
Lindler, Ronnie 33
Lindsay, Anina 262
Lindsay, Bunny-Anne 316
Lindsay, Michelle M. 240
Lindstrom, Lisa 619
Linenberger, Jean 493
Linn, Paula K. 191
Lipe II, Michael 555

Liposky, Laura I. 616
Lipscomb, Evelyn Bland 427
Lisman, Eileen Barton 374
Lisowski, Joshua 659
Lisowski, Katherine 659
Little, Karen 253
"Little One" Gloria 12
Littleton, Elois 419
Littlewolf, Rajandra 57
Littman, Warren 120
Litton, Maudie 519
Litviak, Robert C. 102
Livingston, Debra 472
Livingston, Layron 149
Lloyd, Julian Martin 367
Lockard, Emily 263
Locke, Marlene C. 537
Lockrem, Colleen Kaye 501
Lockward, Howard J. 638
Lockwood, Marjorie H. 151
Loewen, Tonya 35
Loffredo, Jessica 305
Logan, G. Fred 191
Logan, Jeff 652
Lohr, Robby 42
Lohse, Jennifer 575
Lois, Julie 377
Lokey, Phillip Mike 178
Lomax, Josh 362
Long, Delmesa 630
Long, Eva 310
Long, Mary Elizabeth 541
Long, Mary M. 658
Longmire, Steven 161
Loomis, Paula 168
Lopez, Francis G. 293
Lopez, Jacquelyn 303
Lopez, Michele M. 130
Lopez, Olga Rasmussen 601
Lopez, Zazy Ivonne 29
Lopez-Urbina, Ralph F. 41
Lopp, Bettye 478
Lorance, Kristine 535
Loreman, Sarah 56
Lottman, Katherine 549
Louis, Maxine 131
Lounsbury, Eva Marie 467
Love, Ellen L. 326
Lovett, Jay 337
Lowe, Connie 327
Lowe, Rhonda H. 92
Lowry, Cindy 298
Lowry, Elizabeth 426
Lozier, Lacey 158
Lucas, Mary Christine 138
Lucci, Giacinto A. 484
Luce, Janis S. 340
Lucera, Jennifer 320
Luchene, Nancy 128
Luck Jr., Norman H. 619
Luddington, Betty 573
Ludwig, Bryan 316
Luppowitz, Theresa 16
Lurentzatos, Amy 592
Lute, Danricka 420
Lutton, Nicole 146
Lutz, Catherine A. 589
Lutz, Elizabeth 420
Lutz, Jimmy 397
Lutz, Louise 564
Lybbert, Thos M. 30
Lydia, Carmen 270
Lyell, Noreen L. 248
Lyn, Neil A. 618
Lynch, Kristy 141
Lynch, Lily May 542

Lynch, Tony A. 56
Lynn, Annette 646
Lynn, Lonnie 156
Lyon, Marjorie W. 101
Lytle, Craig 289
M., Anne 431
Macal, Diana 428
Maccarrone, Michael 549
MacDonald, Greg 393
MacGregor, Berniece 576
Machowski Age, Katie 11 624
Macias, Nika M. 239
Mack, Janet 307
MacKay, Meghan Anne 511
MacKenzie, Valerie 67
Mackey, Tara Ann 60
Macklin, Beverly 258
Macy, Billie M. 453
Maddack, Andrea 314
Maddux, MaryAnn 232
Madison, Michael G. 513
Maggay-Hill, Feliza L. 437
Maggio, Lauren 514
Maguire III, Jim 391
Mahaffey, William M. 17
Mahan, Mona 531
Mahler, Larry 251
Mahone, Bessie Thomas 302
Mahsoul, Betsy 364
Maitland, John Stuart 350
Major, Poppy 58
Maki, James G. 386
Male, Margaret E. 561
Malesich, Dee Ann 470
Mallory, Rene 75
Mallow, Peter 10
Mallow, Susan F. 19
Malone, Edward J. 469
Maloney, Wendy Caldwell 160
Mample, Jim 387
Mancini, Ray 49
Mandile, Jack 226
Maney, Ashley 455
Mangan, Kathleen D. 123
Mangan, Nova 539
Manginelli, Ralph 6
Mann, Sandy 194
Mansberry, Paul B. 53
Mansfield, Pamela S. 33
Manske, Dawn Anne 571
Manuel, Cheryl A. Seals 361
Manus, Thomas 110
Manweiler, Susan 163
Mapa, Michael S. 545
Marasco, Melanie 613
Marcincuk, Tara 175
Marcum, George H. 407
Marcum, Jennifer 338
Marcus, Hadas 641
Margeson, Carrie 428
Margetta, Janet A. 494
Maria, Kelley Sue 597
Marinello, Christine 506
Marino, Angela M. 349
Marino, Bill 387
Marino, Roberta 195
Maronyan, Lyudmila 246
Marquis, Carolyn F. 309
Marquis Sr., William 225
Marriott, Patricia 209
Marshall, Beulah Marian 443
Marshall, Alice 587
Marshall, Colin 344
Marshall, Melissa 249
Marshall, Mindy 145
Marshall, Serene T. 55

Martin, Aundra 391
Martin, Barbara 424
Martin, Chris 420
Martin, Claire Ellen 309
Martin, Colleen 298
Martin, Frances R. 587
Martin Jr., Charles 356
Martin, Michael A. 239
Martin, Minnie Louise 562
Martin, Robert D. 122
Martin, Robert P. 39
Martin, Rosamond C. 172
Martin, Sunny 20
Martin, Zilla 26
Martindale, Sarah 109
Martinez, Bob G. 650
Martinez, Melissa 528
Martinez, Stacey 222
Martinez, Yalit 81
Martini, Michael G. 147
Marts, Jessica 319
Maruoka, Kazu 142
Marvin, Jennifer 337
Marx, Jordan 451
Marxkors, Emily 350
Mary Ann 245
Masaitis, Paula J. 91
Masala 60
Masetta, Serena 168
Mason, M. G. 4
Mason, Mary 245
Mason, Ruth I. 78
Massey, Kimberly 255
Masters Jr., Robert 480
Masters, Rosemary 101
Mastin, Cynthia 458
Mastronade, Carrie 403
Matanane, Jenette 333
Matheny, Danny 595
Mathews, Jeremy 273
Mathis, Don 577
Mathis, Shannon 58
Matisin, Denny 318
Matli, Paula 121
Matosich, Philip 79
Matrisch Sr., Ronald A. 203
Matsinger, Michael 129
Matthews, Jerry 358
Matthys, Lila Ruth Stokes 230
Mattison, L. Matthew 619
Mattox, B. L. 113
Matyok, Margaret S. 251
Maulhardt, Brian Edward 494
Mawak-Breen, Jeanne 574
Maxian, Lucile 608
Maxim, Carole J. 468
Maxwell, Blanche 273
May, Ann-Marie 305
Mayberry, Billie Jean 337
Mayer, Janet S. 437
Mayes, Ronnie C. 206
Mayeu, Jason 373
Mayle III, John W. 324
Maynard, D. M. 186
Maynor, Debi 453
Mayo, Barbara 321
Mayo, Donald S. 351
Mayorga, Patricia Ann 90
Mays, Mary Ellen 546
Mazzeo, Frances C. 265
McAtee, Nathaniel Ray 128
McBride, Kathleen 622
McBride, Sarah 71
McCabe, Shari L. 180
McCain, G. Stuart 32
McCammon, Feryne C. 277

McCarthy, J. P. 220
McCarthy, James 382
McCarthy, Keri-Ann 234
McCarthy, T. L. 114
McCarty, Fran 471
McCarty, Sara E. 79
McClain, Deah 648
McClain Sr., Mike 244
McClairen, Lubertha 568
McClary, Lorrie Sue 81
McClatchy, Patty Rachel 107
McClelland, Andy 483
McClelland, Ryan Lee 32
McCloskey, Jessica 423
McClure, Jessica Paula 644
McComb, Terry J. 46
McConnell, Laura 521
McCool-McMurtry, Darla 486
McCorkle, Paige 189
McCormick, Katheryn 236
McCormick, Nicole 246
McCormick, Sandra 31
McCracken, Kevin 148
McCray, Katt E. 538
McCuan, Mabel Jean 556
McCue, Jeanette M. 632
McCullough, Kathleen 556
McCullough, Marilou Vernon 159
McCullough, Shawn 124
McCurry, Grady W. 379
McDevitt, Deborah 99
McDonagh, Elizabeth A. 358
McDonald, Erick 587
McDonald, Patricia Coffey 8
McDonald, Thomas Porky 210
McDonnell, Laura Beth 233
McDowell, Bonnie 375
McElduff, Kristen 137
McFadden, Debra 592
McFarland, Carolyn 289
McFarland, Marsha 540
McFarland, Sarah 109
McFeely, Sean 29
McGary, Charles S. 385
McGee, Elaine C. 503
McGee, Leonard Dee 534
McGehee, Markeeta 144
McGibbon, Brianna Rebecca 645
McGill, Lloyd F. 530
McGinity, Diana Lee 502
McGivern, Maureen K. 150
McGonigle, Jessica 338
McGonigle, Patti 87
McGovern, Michael P. 621
McGrath, Edward R. 384
McGraw II, Stephen B. 53
McGuffin II, DeVere W. 508
McIntosh, Kathy D. 620
McIntyre, Darryl 465
McKibben, Robert 82
McKinnon, Judy 303
McKnight, Mitch 656
Mckown, Kyle 245
McLaughlin, Lisa 152
McLaughlin, Michael 248
McLean, Bunny S. 199
McLean, Mary 528
McLean, Vanessa 213
McMacken, Norma Jean 614
McMahon, Deitra 576
McMullin, Eva 407
McNairy, Harold Gabriel 405
McNaughton, Ruth A. 84
McNeely, Ruth 221
McNeil, Kathleen 191
McPherson, Kristie 152

McQuary, Pamela R. 159
McRea, Barbara 460
McReynolds, Bill 390
McVey, Jeffery Roy 382
McWhorter, George T. 292
Mead, Jessica 420
Mead, Linda 514
Meadows, David 261
Meadows Jr., Bill 368
Means, Will 116
Meci, Rob 108
Meek, Doris Ferguson 470
Meeker, Jane 427
Meeks, Glenda 405
Megginson, Paula M. 62
Meginnis, Alphretta 584
Mehaffey, Michael 614
Mehlenbacher, Danielle 438
Meina, Barbra Kathleen 456
Meiners, Patty 209
Melchior, Ib 328
Meli, Tony 194
Mellow, Lucionna D. 556
Melo, Barbara 584
Meloro, Michael 516
Melton, Craig N. 407
Melton, Misty Nicole 241
Melville, Isabelle C. 591
Mena, Melissa 532
Mendenhall, Frances E. 327
Mendes, Sandra Regina 49
Mendoza Jr., Rambaldo 57
Menswar, Kristin M. 243
Meola, Arthur A. 317
Mercado, Marco 520
Mercer, Robert 82
Merchant, Wanda Argatha H. 80
Merideth, Faith E. R. 408
Mero, James H. 309
Merry, Donna 334
Mertens, Boots 321
Mertz, Jack R. 319
Mesen, Robert 114
Meshelle, Carol Rich 487
Metz, Kimberly 239
Metzger, Leah 604
Metzinger, Maureen 615
Meyer, Etta Taylor 574
Meyer, Jeanne 436
Mezak, Connie 571
Micewicz, Jessica A. 428
Michael, Brett P. 472
Michael, Megan 509
Michaels, Gladys 277
Michelus, Maegan 231
Middleton, Myra 146
Middleton, Samantha L. 217
Mieir, Charles E. 583
Miele, Donna J. 497
Mighty, Debra 489
Mihai, Holland 348
Mikkelsen, Madelyn Boyce 239
Milan 248
Milano, Ken 553
Miles, Beverly A. 492
Miles, Christina Blasi 373
Miles, George 302
Miles, Terry L. 11
Millar, Joe C. 361
Miller, Amanda 396
Miller, Amanda Leigh 400
Miller, Barbara H. 316
Miller, Betty J. 448
Miller, Charles Jacob 634
Miller, Chelle Lynne 306
Miller, Cheri 579

Miller, Clark 446
Miller, Dawn 591
Miller, Erica L. 350
Miller, Greg 433
Miller, Harold R. 345
Miller, Julia 581
Miller, Krista 529
Miller, Larry 146
Miller, Lisa 482
Miller, McKenzie 513
Miller, Melissa 241
Miller, Richard 68
Miller, Richard Edward 166
Miller, Rickey Paul 220
Miller, Sarah Colene 121
Miller, Steven P. 54
Miller, Susan L. 46
Miller, Tara 108
Miller, Ted G. 178
Miller, Yael 174
Millett, Eileen A. 450
Milligan, Tiffany 13
Milliken, Megan 128
Millings, Lorraine 138
Millison, Marjorie 609
Mills, Alice J. 471
Mills, Gary 660
Mills-Price, Ann R. 496
Milman, Sheryl 30
Milonas, Minos 108
Milone III, L. J. 202
Milosavljevic, Jennifer L. 279
Minakis, Maria 543
Ming, Murl 142
Minicozzi, R. 27
Minnick, Janet 403
Minter, Herman G. 464
Mintz, Lynn D. 137
Miron, Judy 264
Misiano II, Tony 120
Misner, Charles 331
Misola, Jean 477
Mitchell, Della J. 413
Mitchell, Dorothy J. 354
Mitchell, Evelyn 595
Mitchell, Maria 544
Mitchell, Phyllis M. 83
Mitchell, Ryan 104
Mitchell, Shamekka B. 73
Mize-Jette, Christina 384
Moak, Christina L. 315
Moctezuma, Joseph 634
Moczulski, Melissa 519
Moetzinger, Julie 257
Moffett, Robin Lynn 119
Moghadassi, Cymud 173
Mojado Jr., Miguel 140
Molcsan, Stephen Edward 201
Momary, William 35
Monaco, Tammy 44
Moncada, Erin Walsh 648
Mone, Guy P. 399
Monger, Marion 531
Monk, Sara 31
Monroe, Christian D. 282
Monroe, Everett Jack 215
Monroe, Reid Douglas 163
Montag, Pam 171
Montague, James D. 630
Montal, Kayla 355
Montalbano-Fenske, Gina 374
Montemarano, Michael 526
Montes, Troy D. 76
Montgomery, Melsyne 546
Montgomery, Ray 107
Montgomery, T. M. 27

Montoya, Patti 48
Montrone, Cheryl 467
Moodie, Mindy 248
Moody, Christopher D. 408
Moody, Karen Kenyatta 522
Mooers, Evelyn 441
Moon, Donika 427
Moonier, Carrie 657
Moon Star 514
Moore, Amy E. 427
Moore, Bryan 267
Moore, Erin A. 457
Moore, Frederick Shayne 588
Moore, Helen Sheets 639
Moore, Joyce A. 630
Moore, Juanita E. 186
Moore, Katie 133
Moore, Kirsten 509
Moore, Leona 531
Moore, Orlantha 621
Moore, Robert 124
Moore, Robin 99
Moore, Thelma 52
Moore, Virginia E. 90
Morales, Kim 560
Morales, Monica 567
Morales, Tina 48
Moran, Great Grandpa 214
Moran, Kent 227
Moranda, Robert E. P. 35
Morch, Robert A. 114
Moreno, Helen R. 438
Morey, Joyce 507
Morgan, Cindy 376
Morgan, Jessie Smith 406
Morgan, Jim Lee 639
Morgan, Lorraine 252
Morgan, Marie Ann 254
Morgan, Matthew Laurence 532
Morgan, Paige 22
Morgan, Robert E. 35
Morgan, Shirley Mae 74
Morgan Sr., Phillip L. 90
Morimoto, Mary 230
Moro, Barbara Mercedes 262
Morris, Donna 379
Morris, Elsie D. 75
Morris, Francine M. 392
Morris, Lisa 155
Morris, Matthias 622
Morris, Mona 522
Morris, Teresa 196
Morrison, Jeffrey Howard 507
Morrow, Austin G. 303
Morse, Donald W. 323
Moseley, Clayton G. 386
Moses, Nell 612
Mosher, Suzy 50
Moshier, Dorothy 377
Mosley, Emmye 499
Moss, Jeanne Palmer 283
Mosseri, Ruth 61
Mosteirin, Monica 255
Mosteller, Teresa M. 48
Motl, Mary 149
Mott, Doug 593
Moudy, R. Dean 9
Mousseaux, Theresa 223
Mouton, Nicole 525
Mowell, Frank D. 387
Moy, Angie 276
Moyer, Agnes B. 443
Mracek, Anna 399
Mshar, Karen 247
Mueller, Isabel 647
Mueller, Laura 250

Muldoon, Patricia 120
Muldrew, Minnie G. 621
Mullenix, Rock 107
Mullick, P. E. 118
Mullins, Mark Dwane 523
Mulluk Jr., Aqpik-Robert 328
Mumau, Janet 626
Mumford, Marcy R. 534
Munn, Shelley D. 69
Munoz, Grace 474
Munoz, Moses 596
Munoz, Tony C. 106
Murdoch, Nicole 242
Murdock, Crista 630
Murillo, Alejandro B. 437
Murillo, Dominick 639
Murney, Michele Maszk 153
Murphey, Martha 523
Murphy, Christopher 53
Murphy, Edwin G. 589
Murphy, Katherine 236
Murphy, Lorette 520
murphy, marion 515
Murphy, Norman E. 512
Murphy, Sean 173
Murr, Stewart J. 66
Murray, Amanda S. 370
Murray, Anne Firth 291
Murray, Brian 387
Murray, Tiffany 198
Murrell, Ann 507
Murthy, Anitha 404
Musca, Nancy M. 247
Muszynski, Peg 212
Myers, Brian A. 311
Myers, Dale R. 594
Myers, DeeLola 473
Myers, Lorin 248
Myers, Melanie 142
Myers, Nicole 536
Myers, Regina A. 61
Myszka, Linda 547
N., Eduardo Noriega DelValle 308
Nabhan, Jean 329
Nabieva, Elena 282
Nacoff, Linda M. 148
Nadeau, Leah J. 601
Nadler, Dot Luria 444
Nagel, William J. 55
Nago, Stephanie 185
Nakamura, CariLee Yachiyo 425
Nalis, Will Mae 10
Nandapurkar, Priya 58
Napoleon, Beth 571
Nat, Hilary 498
Nauss Jr., Frank P. 287
Nauton, Fred A. 426
Nauyalis, Nicole 522
Nava, Angel 585
Navarre, Michael 535
Navarro II, Thomas W. 178
Nawoj, Allison 384
Neal, Carrie B. 366
Neary, Margot M. 524
Neary, Mary Hamilton 130
Neave, Merrill 520
Necci, Nicole 251
Neel, Dale 470
Neff, David 473
Neff, Duane R. 470
Neidy, Candice 380
Neiman, Jille Jennifer 465
Nelmes, Lydia 516
Nelson, Audrey M. 261
Nelson, Dan 639
Nelson, Gregg 467

Nelson, Heather 400
Nelson, Helen L. 633
Nelson, Jennifer 586
Nelson, Jennifer E. 488
Nelson, Marilyn 229
Nelson, Patti Jean 36
Nelson, Paul 119
Nelson, Paula 175
Nelson, Peg 14
Nelson, Rebecca Leigh 179
Nelson, Stafford A. 8
Nelson, William R. 185
Nemunis, Grazina 366
Nero, Eugenia A. 447
Neth, Tom 210
Nettles, David E. 377
Neuman, Kathe R. 126
Nevarez, Bette 449
Nevshemal, John 626
Newcomb, Christy 481
Newcomer, Blodwyn L. 464
Newell, Summers McKay 56
Newhouse, Mary A. 530
Newman, Myria 556
Newman, Nora 521
Ng, Amy S. 584
Nguyen, Cathy T. 477
Nguyen, Hach C. 504
Nguyen, Jenny 320
Nguyen, Matthew 146
Nguyen, Michael V. 561
Nhoung, Sokhoeun 105
Nicholas, Lloyd G. 602
Nicholosi, Joseph J. 660
Nichols, Ben 573
Nichols, Betty 457
Nichols, Gail 448
Nichols, Gary B. 576
Nichols, Mitchell Lee 602
Nichols, Tracy 123
Nicholson, Jamie 449
Nicholson, Linda S. 136
Nicholson, Mary Grace 518
Nickel, Richard E. 180
Nickell, Scott 15
Nickelson, Barbara 383
Nickerson, David Martin 309
Niemann, Lindsay 610
Niemeyer, Thomas Charles 67
Nillo, David 456
Nix, Ruth 62
Nixon, Lorette F. 550
Nkhoma, Ella 282
Noble, Hetty F. 424
Nodal, Josie G. 207
Nodes, Jessica 642
Noe, Debbie 490
Nolan, Susan E. 178
Nolen, Betty J. 336
Nolen, Russell D. 84
Noorigian, Helen 627
Norman, Delores 356
Norris, Mike 240
Norris, Shawn Eugene 225
North, Derek Ray 391
Northrop, Linda 235
Norton, Maryclaire 524
Norwood, Marney L. 521
Notarianni, Sofia Mary Ann 106
Nowotarski, Michael John 563
Noyes, Patricia 5
Nuckols, Peggy L. 46
Nulph, Emily J. 444
Nunez, Leah 242
Nunley, Carol Joy 310
Nyers, Amelia 577

Nygren, Brenda 455
Nylen, Brandi 466
Oakes, Pamela 119
Oberst, Anna 291
Obney, Olive 237
Obregon, Arturo 467
O'Brien, Dorothy R. 381
O'Brien, Jennifer 346
O'Brien, Paula 85
O'Brien Sr., William Forrester 206
O'Connell, Peter A. 203
O'Connor, Shawn 166
Odom, Kay 618
Odonnell 480
O'Donnell, James C. 646
O'Donnell-Imran, Michele 606
O'Donohue, John F. 463
Ofori, Kwame 598
Oftelie, Karen 246
Ogbuike, Chinedu Dean 427
Ogilvie, Kim 157
Ogle, Peggy 72
Ohnstad, Glen G. 187
Oho, Teri Ann 53
Oisen, Jessica 486
O'Keefe, Helena 284
Okpaleke, Osita 155
Olden, Gladys 578
Oldham, Mildred 623
Olivares, Stefanie A. 183
Olive, Renee 160
Olmstead, Delores 379
Olsen, Allison June 649
Olsen, Luci L. 521
Olsen, Roy 95
Olson, Cheri 366
Olson, Gloria 267
Olson Sr., Robert Dean 161
Olson, Tacha Renee 36
O'Malley, Pat 219
Ommondson, Lora L. 139
O'Neil, Connie 499
O'Neil, Sydney 170
O'Neill, CoLetta M. 360
O'Neill, Erin 315
O'Neill, Megan 247
Onwuka, Madu 543
Opat, Robert 197
Oram, Charlayne 100
Oranday, Edmundo 593
Orange, George 493
O'Reilly, Nicholas Osgood 597
Orejola, Wilmo C. 225
Orman, Nichole 532
Ormond, Terance 125
Ormsbee, Theresa 660
Orosz, E. L. 173
Orr, Leonard 614
Orsomarso, Marguerite Rocco 559
Ortez, Sandra 166
Orth, Anton P. 98
Ortiz, Jonathan 433
Ortiz, Maria A. 606
Ortiz, Nora 524
Ortiz, Shannon Byrnes 32
Ortman, Herbert M. 208
Osborne, Vincent 114
Osher, Gina 170
Oshetsky, Sandra L. 19
Osmond, Terence 47
Ostrem, Laurie 129
O'Sullivan, Claire P. 327
Oswalt, Brenda K. 334
Otoshi, Yoshiyuki 175
Ott, Ellis Michael 409
Otto, Angie 123

Ottosen, Wendy 119
Ouellette, Shannon 55
Overbeck, Lisa 548
Overfield, Jack 304
Overholser, Shawn D. 195
Owen, Robert James 9
Owens, Jacquelyn F. 355
Owens, Roger 36
Owens, Shelia 45
Owings, Rachael 64
Ownbey, Jenna V. 453
Oxford, Cheryl R. 373
Ozment, Kim J. 613
Pace, J. Patrick 183
Pacheco, Angie 397
Pacheco, Linda 620
Pacheco, Miriam 513
Pack, Edna 460
Pack, Hollie 349
Padilla, Melody 239
Page, Bonnie 378
Page, John R. 371
Page, Talia 169
Paglinawan, Wayne A. 87
Paguia, Sheena 206
Paight, Charlene Skylar 393
Paine, Alan 464
Palardy, Pamela 115
Paliouras, Vicky 61
Palladino, Dorothy 464
Pallone, John W. 575
Palm, Wesley 160
Palmatier, Howard N. 431
Palmer, Christiana 426
Palmer, Hazel M. 469
Palmer, Leonard R. 534
Palmer, Louis D. V. 529
Palmer-Fogarty, Brandey 345
Pandey, Dhirendra Kumar 359
Pannell, Sharen Pinkett 176
Papion, Connie M. 385
Pappas, Banks 442
Pappaterra, Joane L. 395
Papritz, Carew 166
Parent, Cindy 474
Parish, Emma E. 385
Park, Delbert 631
Park, Kathy 564
Parke, Katherine L. 512
Parker, April LaTishe 465
Parker, Brenda 459
Parker, Bryan 323
Parker, Caronda 501
Parker, George C. 292
Parker, Lee A. 152
Parker, Pauline 161
Parker, Rachel I. 220
Parker, Sabrina 91
Parker, Suzanne I. 196
Parkes, Eugene A. 368
Parks, Jay Nelson 398
Parks, LaWanda 154
Parks, Mandie Jo 246
Parmalee, Tanya S. 35
Parnella, Lauri L. 230
Paro, Sharon 29
Parrish, Tommy 184
Parsons, Bonnie 451
Parsons, Eve 288
Partridge, Ruth 190
Parvino, Bonnie R. 363
Pascoe, Clive B. 283
Pasha, Jamilah D. 263
Patchen, Dale R. 376
Pate, Carol S. 208
Patel, Kosha 519

Patki, Shamal 125
Paton, Michelle 515
Patrick, Benita C. 588
Patrick, Deborah 335
Patterson, Christina M. 322
Patterson, Lelia 127
Patterson, Patricia 96
Patterson, Star 346
Patton, Jessica R. 490
Patton, Scott 62
Patty 165
Paul, Cassaundra Hope 346
Paul, Debika 639
Paul, Wanda Anderson 73
Paver, Mary 532
Paxton, Hildred E. 403
Payen, Rosalyn 166
Payenson, Alon 649
Payne, Clarissa J. 645
Payne, Danny 472
Payne, Ray E. 207
Peach, Doris F. 571
Peachey, Alice T. 594
Peak, Valerie 47
Pears, Alfred R. 353
Pearson, Garrett 436
Pearson, Ruth 30
Pearson, Ruth E. 62
Peeke, Ione 389
Peelman, Amy 475
Pegoda, Emily 631
Pekarek, Doreen (Oehlers) 307
Pelloso, David 394
Peltier, Nicole 520
Peluso, Jerry 587
Pena, Melissa J. 538
Penha, Maria 523
Penhall, Sharilyn 176
Pennie, Marsha 479
Pennigar, Kathy M. 571
Pennington Jr., Terry R. 204
Pentaleri, Alan J. 475
Penwell, Shawne 92
Pepe, Franco 359
Pepper, Robert L. 97
Percy, Billie Runbeck 78
Perez, Derenz M. 452
Perez, R. C. 104
Perez, Raquel R. 654
Perhach, Robert E. 111
Perifimos, Mary 562
Perkins, Laura Starr 242
Perkins, Robert E. 14
Perkins, Steven S. 20
Perna, Katherine R. 553
Pernu Jr., Harlan R. 421
Perrault, John Emile 337
Perrine, Scott Michael 79
Perry, Carolyn R. 326
Perry, Charlene A. 344
Perry IV, Randall Scoll 655
Perry, John Louis 326
Perry, William Lewis 118
Persad, Ramsundar 171
Pescador, Guillermo 368
Petersen, Jean E. 352
Peterson, Birgitta 375
Peterson, Sarah S. 214
Peterson, Vellene 38
Petrillo, Sandra 193
Petrone, Donna S. 330
Pettiford, Douglas 296
Pettigrew, Jo Helen 461
Pettingill, Dawnel 491
Pfaff, Verda Fausett 119
Pfeil, Sandi 661

anz III, Henry S. 393
elps, Julie Kay 341
illips, Catherine W. 312
illips, F. Daphne 206
illips, Gerald 283
illips IV, Harry 305
illips, Lori 620
illips, Nathen 517
illips, Trocy 175
ilpitt, Edward T. 315
otikarmbumrung, Elma Diel 583
azza, Karen A. 549
iché, Neal 227
ckering, Pauline 50
ckering, Tiffen B. 199
cone, Arthur 398
el, Jeanette 465
ierce, Diane 388
ierce, Jane A. 383
ierce, Kerri Elizabeth 246
ierce, Patrick L. 33
ierce, Randy 104
ierson, Janice 442
iette, Debbie 404
ikutis, Paul 17
ilchak, Bridget 633
ilkenton, Pauline 181
ina, Sandra Jeanne 10
ina-Sandoval, Ernestine 327
inckard, James R. 289
inckney, Jerry 453
ino, Christina L. 649
inson, Robert T. 71
iryaei, Rohollah 90
ittman, Linda S. 513
Pittman, Rosemary 6
Pitts, Thurayyah Anisha 76
Pizzano, Gina 112
Place, Marjorie E. 130
Plager, Jenny 265
Platis, Angelike 323
Plessen II, Roger 210
Plummer, Dawn Michaelle 368
Poeske, Gin M. 475
Pogue, Gary Dale 109
Polcari, Michael 566
Polford, Cecelia Marie 649
Pollard, Ron 169
Pommier, Sylvia M. 8
Ponce, Angela Lapinid 632
Ponton, Johnnie Mae 339
Pool, C. J. 216
Pope, Allison 299
Pope, Daniel Timothy 49
Popovich, Sharon L. 169
Popovits, Kevin 613
Porchia, Donald C. 329
Porter, John 261
Post, Daniel 275
Postal, Paul R. 185
Poston, Tina M. 96
Potter, Kathryn J. 133
Potter, Linda D. 242
Potton, Sharon 64
Potts, Michelle Ann 524
Poulos, Elijah M. 497
Poureshagh, Edgar 354
Pov, Sovonn 43
Powell, Armand 348
Powell, Chris 226
Powell, Kristiann Louise 537
Powley, Bernice N. 390
Pratt, Nancy J. 153
Pratt, Reuben 183
Pratte, Sara E. 55
Precht, Roxanne L. 119

Prendes, Michelle Marie 519
Present, Sarah 46
Prewitt, Renee 124
Price, Jason Michael 445
Price, Kathleen 616
Price, Leroy 603
Price, Linda Dianna 527
Price, Maureen 547
Price, Maxine 600
Pridgen, Sandra Solomon 55
Prior, Jennifer 442
Prisock, Mary V. 251
Proctor, Candace Elaine 655
Prohaska, Jenny-Rebecca 465
Prosser, Merle H. 243
Proveaux-Cox, Deidra 265
Pruitt, Peggy 122
Pryor, Vicky 117
Przybylowski, Steven 163
Puccio, Lauren V. 236
Puckett, Dema 284
Puckett, Julia 353
Pugh, Bates J. 590
Pugmire, Margaret 158
Pullen, Rhea T. 170
Pulse, C. G. 54
Puopolo, Erica 502
Purcell Sr., Bobby 320
Purkey, Vera L. 102
Purvines, Lynn 567
Putnam, Harold 329
Putney, Michael T. 512
Pyle, Florence 636
Quan, LaTricia M. 251
Querubin, Sam 27
Quezada, Susan Folger 94
Quick, Quentin 162
Quijada Jr., Gil 258
Quinn, Nancy 620
Quintela, Phillip 61
Quintero, Cristina 326
Quintero, Linda 253
Qureshi, Hasan A. 69
Raasch, Todd A. 114
Rabideau, Jamie L. 409
Rabinovich, Allen 274
Rabus, George 448
Rader, Aura Inez 313
Radic, Dragica 441
Radiff, Marilyn L. 542
Radoslovich, Michael 243
Radulescu, Silvia 62
Rae, Dorothy 499
Rafle, Thelma 40
Ragan, Ronald Joel 482
Ragoobeer, Bidjawatie 403
Ragoonanan, Deodath 68
Rainer, Elissa 356
Raines, Ginger 375
Rainey, Cathy A. 308
Rainey, Eleanor 314
Rains, Fern E. 186
Ralli, Susanna 55
Ralston, Dana 399
Ramirez, Hector 642
Ramos, Claudette 417
Rampani, Robert M. 12
Rampton, Kathleen 130
Ramshaw, Maryann 557
Rankin-Smith, Pamela 94
Rapold, Patricia Urroz 160
Rascon, Erika Karla Ochoa 469
Rasey, Nancy C. 252
Rath Jr., Donald L. 419
Rathbun, Leonard F. 247
Raughley, Mary Jo 549

ray, d j 202
Ray, Neil 561
Ray, Vicki L. 43
Raybe, Dorothy 308
Raymond, Jeanette B. 394
Reardon, Mike 548
Reason, Marsha G. 239
Reavis, Vincent Shawn 225
Reay, S. L. 74
Reckard, Derek J. 475
Rector, Mileah J. 147
Reddick-Langford, Lisa 253
Redding, Sharon 656
Reddoch, Mildred Lucas 616
Redman, Angela 484
Redmon, Janet 171
Redmon, Shelia 9
Redmond, Carmelitta J. 508
Redmond, Lucas 518
Reece, Marah 523
Reece, Virginia Maria 49
Reed, Janice 458
Reed, Amber 282
Reed, Deborah S. 576
Reed, Mae C. 231
Reed, Naomi 252
Reed, Sally 202
Rees, Janet 396
Reese, BJ 428
Reeves, Jessica 388
Refior, Everett L. 435
Regalbuto, Dolores M. 483
Reich, James 282
Reich, Theodore R. 13
Reichel, Barbara 292
Reichel, Jody 125
Reid, Cheryl 414
Reid, David W. 491
Reid, Denise 324
Reid, Starlet 657
Reidl, Daniel 594
Reilly, William R. 54
Reindenbach, Rene S. 118
Reisch, Paia 178
Reiss, Andrew S. 471
Reitenauer, Suzanne 179
Rejcek, Adell 368
Rekett, Sharon 59
Rembert, Leslie G. I 617
Rembisz, Elizabeth D. 381
Rennekamp, Eugene E. 577
Renniger, Doris 363
Rensink, Beverly 371
Revill, E. Lucille 107
Rex, Patricia A. 182
Rey-Snyder, Mildred 619
Reynders, Fred N. 335
Reynolds, Madge 612
Reynolds, Minnie 614
Rezvani, Bruce 363
Rhodes, Cynthia E. 488
Rhodes, Hana 275
Rhodes, Robert V. 48
Rhyan, William A. 206
Rhyet 516
Ricci, Frances B. 451
Rice, Ann Blakely 493
Rice, Jason 426
Rice, Keith 209
Rice, Michael J. 549
Richards, Daniel 402
Richardson, Aleta L. 299
Richardson, Joel E. 447
Richardson, Lori 231
Richardson, Becky J. 325
Richardson, Mavis R. 622

Richardson, Melody L. 131
Richardson, Patricia F. E. 124
Richardson, Robbi 116
Richardson, Stormy 203
Richardson, Tiffany 113
Rickert, Elizabeth A. 358
Rickord, Brian L. 441
Riddle, Amanda 462
Riddle, Carol Ann 330
Rideout, Christine E. 306
Rider, Chris 369
Rider, Phyllis J. 205
Ridgeway, Charlie 402
Ridgeway, Kirk 603
Riedy, Lynne 551
Rieken, Max 155
Rigg, John 454
Rihn, Toni A. 209
Riley, Beverley F. 332
Riley, Patricia Ann 223
Riley, Renee 20
Rinard, Nicholas Rezanof 526
Rincon, Linda 231
Rindahl, Mark 524
Ringgold, Julie 415
Rini, Simone 125
Rinkel, Jennifer 475
Rinker, Rebecca 107
Rio, Erika 454
Rising, Colleen 271
Risinger, Kenneth 241
Ritchie, Robert 67
Ritz, Ann E. 642
Rivenbark, Cynthia Atkinson 446
Rivers, Patricia 105
Rivet, Paul E. 25
Rizzuto, Janifer O. 335
Rizzuto, Letitia 618
Roach, Dale 400
Roades, Wilma L. 174
Roark, Sheila B. 59
Robb Jr., Jay 491
Robbins, Andrew 393
Roberts, Amanda C. 459
Roberts, E. Pearl 15
Roberts, Jacqueline D. 461
Roberts, Jesseca B. 393
Roberts, Lorraine 147
Roberts, Myriah C. 524
Roberts, Nathan Alan 533
Roberts, Sue Ellen 163
Roberts, Terry 194
Robertson, Bev 380
Robertson, C. Regan 124
Robertson, Jodi 464
Robertson, Warren A. 218
Robin Kills-A-Hundred 18
Robinson, Belk N. 508
Robinson, Cathy 643
Robinson, Cliff 400
Robinson, David Alan 297
Robinson, Donna M. 438
Robinson, Gladys H. 328
Robinson, Kathy 516
Rocco, Mary E. 245
Rocha, Lisa Marie 608
Rocks, Deborah 432
Rockwood, Martha Margaret 240
Roden, Mary Baker 254
Rodgers, Jill 437
Rodkey, Margaret L. 559
Rodrigues Jr., Joseph O. 305
Rodríguez, Eduardo 588
Rodriguez, Mary H. 598
Rodriguez, Nancy R. 153
Rodriguez, Ruben 227

Rodriguez, Ruth 164
Rodriguez, Tabatha 201
Roe, Brian Michael 657
Roehrman, Terry 187
Roffler, Ilse 442
Rogers, H. 223
Rogers, Julie 647
Rogers, Martha M. 231
Rogers, Mary S. 148
Rogers, Robert 180
Rogers, Teresa 101
Rogers, Wayne 36
Rogneby, Erik 633
Rohe, Tara 70
Rolfe, Howard C. 570
Rollin, Marty 623
Rollison, Rembert G. 181
Rolny, Peter 58
Rondeau, Roberta 81
Roney, Calvin 638
Rook, Heather 303
Root, Ica Lyndsay 288
Rose, Devon Alexandria 548
Rose, Jean 656
Rose, Maryah 609
Rose, Naomi A. 608
Rose, Samantha 174
Rose, Sarah Elizabeth 51
Roseboro, Clifford Duane 639
Ross, Barbara 390
Ross, Cree 572
Ross, Robert W. 169
Ross, Rosetta E. 12
Ross, Teresa Nicole 9
Rotchford, Maria 255
Roth, Dorothy Hubbard 39
Roth, Linda 250
Roth, Stacy Minor 117
Rothlisberg, Allen P. 295
Rothweiler, Nicholas 242
Roubal, Susan 54
Rouleau, Chris 500
Rouse, Shelly L. 56
Roussel, Gary K. 222
Rowe, Christina F. Y. 263
Rowe, Elva P. 328
Royal, Fred 593
Rozum, Shannon 198
Ruble, Rodney Lynn 85
Ruby, Donna 117
Ruckman, Patricia A. 86
Ruddlesden, Dalton Jerry 360
Rudloff, Joseph D. 633
Ruff Sr., Guy F. 503
Ruffin, Sharlene 101
Ruiz, Veronica 182
Ruleman, Kellie 563
Rulka, John S. 332
Rumery, Becky Libby 586
Ruprecht Jr., William Michael 57
Russell, Bojana 451
Russell, J. J. 187
Russell, Lally 66
Russell, Roy 78
Russin, Hannah 424
Russo, Bernadette 452
Rutigliano, Edmond P. 313
Rutkowski, Joseph 633
Ryan, Charlotte M. 228
Ryan, Krista M. 604
Ryan, Sarah 56
Ryan, Susan 179
Ryder Sr., Dana K. 369
Rykert, Katharyn Grace 654
Ryno, Marie F. 610
Rypple, Deborah L. 320
Rythems, Conner 407
Sabessar, Tina 44
Sabine, Lisalynn 242
Sailer, Paula 36
Saincome, Mark 611
Saintil, Claire Judine 310
Salam, Isabel 458
Salas, Albert Marrero 312
Salerno, Paul 42
Sales, Leonides S. 558
Salgado, Laurie 149
Sallee, Opal 540
Sallila, Mae 533
Salmon, Lindsay 525
Salute, Sandra 20
Saly, Catherine 274
Sample, Judith C. 410
Sample, Teresa L. 191
Sampson, Harold 601
Sams, Wayne D. 77
Samuelson, R. L. 184
Sanborn, Denise 439
Sanchez, Anna Lee 582
Sanchez, Jean Ann 489
Sandberg, Sue 51
Sanders, Cynthia Elaine 464
Sanders Jr., Bruce L. 299
Sanders, Melody Music 533
Sanders, Norma Ruth 519
Sanders-Strickland, Maggie 602
Sanderson, Elaine 272
Sandifer, Eryn 324
Sandler, J. 106
Sandoval, Connie 396
Sands, Natalie 139
Sandstrom, Aaron J. 440
Santa, Betty 595
Santillo, Alfred V. 317
Santini, Tara T. 62
Santora, Jessica F. 388
Santos, Sondra R. 207
Santos-Prior, Karmen D. 235
Sargent, Kenneth Gary 523
Sarnataro, Henry T. 417
Satterfield, Christie 400
Saucier, Eric Foley 478
Sauer, Heidi 339
Saulis, Michael J. 251
Saurman, George E. 431
Sautter, Karen 231
Sauvageau, John 391
savage, rex d. 174
Savant, Karen L. 605
Sawelenko, Christina 317
Sayner, Allison 425
Scammell, Janine 341
Scannapieco, Lynn M. 254
Scarbeary, Gary 397
Scatena, Danielle 588
Scauzillo, R. 6
Schad, Perrie 198
Schaefer, Linda M. 244
Schafer, Karen 236
Schatz, Thomas R. 91
Scheuhing, Holly 391
Schiller, Marje 102
Schindel, Dori 465
Schindler, Jake Michael 326
Schism, Gayle 419
Schladweiler, Mary Joyce 545
Schlesselman, Lorraine 241
Schlosser, Patricia 66
Schlosser, Wendy A. T. 215
Schmeidler, Cheryl K. 634
Schmickle, Cindy 644
Schmidt, Carrie 433
Schmidt, Robert F. 7
Schmidt, Tony 5
Schmierer, Tracy 190
Schmitt, Mildred 512
Schmucki, Robert J. 41
Schnitter, Sophie E. 5
Schnoebelen, Sharee Raphael 205
Schoen, Alfred H. 323
Schoen, Elena 309
Schoen, Gordon W. 325
Scholes, Marsha E. 144
Schonberger, Clay 381
Schramm, Mara 543
Schreiber, Stella 196
Schrey, Amanda 710
Schroeder, Arlene K. 342
Schroeder, Deborah 345
Schubert, Mary E. 552
Schuler, Gary A. 452
Schuler, Kourtney 514
Schult, Chris Dowdall 317
Schultz, Chris 395
Schultz, Holly 381
Schultz, Lorraine O. 37
Schultz, Timothy Eric 99
Schulz, Elaine L. 263
Schumaker, David 328
Schutte, Angela 302
Schwab, Julia M. 297
Schwappach, Pat 14
Schwartz, Marcia 613
Schwartz, Sally 224
Schwarz, Barbara 313
Schweikert, Leona 528
Schweinfurth, Dodd C. 505
Schwingel, Jessica 641
Scofield, Ruth 123
Scott, Anita G. 493
Scott, Carolyn Lea 463
Scott, Jessica 457
Scott, Karen 253
Scott, Kendall W. 623
Scott, Mel 624
Scott, Michael 558
Scott, Sarah 108
Scott, Susan 93
Scott, William 17
Scouten, Elisabeth A. 44
Scribner, Sabrina 197
Scruth, Elizabeth 582
Scuccimarri, Melissa 228
Scudder, Robert M. 115
Scuderi, Maria 554
Sealy, Ira Gay 297
Sears, Charles D. 572
Seawright, Victoria Elizabeth 167
Sebastian 180
Sebby, Nyki 244
Seeley, Debra Anne 396
Seely, Colleen 468
Seelye, Bryan 385
Seese, Cheryl Anne 381
Seesholtz, Barbara 636
Segal, Diane 460
Segal, Eloise B. 353
Segall, Jo-Ann 450
Segelke, Ashley 445
Seibert, Kathy 652
Seibold, Jeremy 284
Seidl, Alicia 382
Seime, Judith Townsend 571
Selby, Melanie G. 526
Self, Autumn Dawn 356
Sellers, Kathy 145
Selm, Earleta N. 373
Semenick, Charles 422
Senato, F. R. 182
Senteio, Shannon 52
Senter, Eryn 425
Sentz, Ryan 84
Sepulveda, Thomas Andrew 223
Sequeira, Sher 114
Serio, Helen L. 454
Serrao, Lorrie 128
Servey, Joyce 412
Setlock, Carlta J. 365
Settle, Mary Jane 135
Sexton-Hill, Lou Rinda 605
Seymour, Gayle 323
Seymour, Sara 193
Sha, Jeanne 259
Shahidi, Karen 525
Shannon, Ethel M. 342
Sharer, Holly K. 432
Sharkey, Beth 475
Sharp, Dale L. 503
Sharp, Dawn 577
Sharp, Don 291
Sharp, Etta R. 276
Sharp, Pat 171
Sharp, Sarah 225
Shaul, John B. 468
Shaulis, Bonnie Ruth 196
Shaull, Belva 392
Shaw, Angela 416
Shaw, Apikia 329
Shaw, Fanny Lee Baker 470
Shaw, Marlee Payne 141
Shawk, Justine Bowen 469
Shay, Jennifer 454
Shay, Sarah 202
Sheldon, Jennifer 388
Shellnutt, Meredeth 135
Shelton, Gail L. 403
Shelton, Jeffery R. 348
Shelton, Lawrence M. 235
Shelvey, Madeline 253
Shepard, Angie L. 374
Shephard, Francine 314
Shepherd, Nycol Lyn 599
Shepherd, William O. 172
Sheppard, Julie Ann 311
Sheppard-Wolford, Sali 59
Sheriff, David G. 633
Sherin, Barbara A. 383
Sherman, Robert 51
Sherwin, Helen 104
Sherwood, Bill 371
Shetterly, Frances M. 308
Shields, Teena 213
Shilling, Faye O. 88
Shillito, Ruth V. 89
Shiltz, Mark Andrew 511
Shindler, Denise 401
Shiparski, Laurie 533
Shively, Heather 369
Shoemate, Ruth 220
Shoger, Allison 284
Sholler, Jennifer S. 505
Shook, Jenna 491
Short, Luellen 515
Short, Melissa 608
Shorthouse, Courtney Leanne 378
Shoup, Jessica Lynn 312
Showalter, Alma 15
Shubert, John F. 642
Shuey, Ed 465
Shumate, Casey 430
Siciliano, Melissa L. 619
Sicina, Gloria W. 468
Sides, Barbara 588
Sides, Richard J. 65

ebel, Shellie 5
eck, Mary Ellen 533
egel, Eric 508
ems, Bruce Allen 385
en, Michelle 251
gan, Audra 451
kora, Phil 117
korski, Vernon M. 119
lber, Ben 416
ilva, Heather T. 335
ilva, Julie 259
ilva, Susan 14
ilverman, Ellen 453
imkins, Julia Ottice 164
immons, Janet 304
imon, Jennifer 410
imon, Karla 551
imon, Robert 123
imonian, Jeannine 368
imorangkir, Anneke G. 433
impson, Taryn 480
ingh, Crystal 575
ingh, Roma 116
ingleton, Alice Faye 400
ingleton, Carl 75
ink, Kelly 537
ipkowski, Ted 63
isson, Marilyn 615
itterlet, Carla 294
itzlar, Sherry 111
izer, Rob 197
joberg, Linda A. 548
kinner, Clarence A. 572
kinner, Regenia 56
kriba, Miranda 229
kydell, Sara Lee 168
Slater, Kat 244
Sledge, Lindell 138
Slick, Katherine 561
Slings, Randee K. 195
Sloan, Marianne 610
Sloan, Michelle D. 566
Sloan, Shana C. 63
Slotke, Michelle L. 237
Sly, Joanne Elizabeth 366
Small, Charles H. 404
Smedley, Debbie 573
Smedley, Donna J. 421
Smith, Abbie 469
Smith, Alexis D. 372
Smith, Amanda S. 425
Smith, Angelique Michele 422
Smith, Anna 582
Smith, Annie T. 272
Smith, Aubrey L. 314
Smith, Berniece C. 484
Smith, Billy 627
Smith, Caroline C. 651
Smith, Dana 646
Smith, Danielle 369
Smith, Dara 4
Smith, Deanna 360
Smith, Deatrice A. 478
Smith, Diana L. 352
Smith, Donna J. 572
Smith, Donna Marie 646
Smith, Gary Tom 358
Smith, Ginger 285
Smith, Gwyndolyn 411
Smith, Hazel H. 585
Smith, Jason Andrew 465
Smith, Jean M. 342
Smith, Joseph 655
Smith, Kay 159
Smith, Kelly S. 551
Smith, Laurie L. 558
Smith, Lawrence Wilson 137
Smith, Leslie Corrine 509
Smith, Lillian 250
Smith, Linda J. 252
Smith, Lindsey 530
Smith, Lucile 563
Smith, Marci 233
Smith, Maureen L. 610
Smith, Michael D. 435
Smith, Michelle 239
Smith, Miriam L. 481
Smith, Nicole 615
Smith, Paul L. 70
Smith, Ray 19
Smith, Ruth F. 176
Smith, Samantha 45
Smith, Shannon 199
Smith, Terry 21
Smith, Tiffany Ann 479
Smith, Tim 4
Smith, Timothy L. 187
Smith, Tracy L. 100
Smith, Vaughn Brent 200
Smith, Verna 47
Smith, Zelma K. 69
Smith-Donalds, Ionie 416
Snead, Olivia S. 235
Snethen, Dawna 488
Snow, Dawn 450
Snyder, Cynthia L. 281
Snyder, Mark T. 614
Snyder, Sam Stuart 196
Snyder Sr., Emmett A. 369
Snyer, Kathleen 523
Sobczyk, Arthur 383
Sofield, Ray 186
Sojka, Kristina 239
Solano, Evelyn Alexis 379
Solimine, Sharon L. 23
Soliz, Melissa Ann 242
Solloway, M. Elise 182
Solo, Will 125
Solomon, Amanda 441
Solorio, Daniel 456
Solozabal, Eduardo M. 61
Sonny 160
Sorel, Germaine J. 287
Sorgen, Pauline 58
Sorrows, Steven 12
Sottile, Kathleen C. 247
Soulages, Walter R. 49
Sousa, Tony 191
South, Kristi 536
Souza, Laine 141
Sowder, Keith 526
Spahr, Julie 260
Spain, Karen L. 564
Spalding, Cerelda 319
Spanoghe, Sarah 63
Spargur, Kevin 555
Sparrow, Daphne 323
Spaulding, Zach 118
Spawn, Stacy Lena 189
Spear, Lila M. 517
Spears-Coffey, Chari 366
Spee, Johanna A. 395
Spellman-Rock, Brenda 295
Spells, Paula R. 71
Spence, Tia 95
Spencer, Crystal 319
Spencer, Diane M. 375
Spencer, Janice Carol 381
Spencer, Lori L. 538
Spencer, Lynn 602
Spencer, Pam Jennings 72
Speta, Violet 178
Speyer, David Leon 359
Spieles, Dolores A. 456
Spiler, Norell 248
Spina, Lee Ann 158
Spinelli, Ronald G. 51
Spiro, Sally L. 92
Spivey, Kelly 623
Splitt, Evelyn L. 634
Spoonmore, Tobra 210
Springer, Lucy 126
Springer, Rhonda Jo 98
Springfield, Chance 422
Squyres, Mary E. 605
Srok, Lisa 515
Stacey, Kim 622
Stachowski, Mary 539
Stahl, Cameo Danielle 477
Stahl, Heather Renee 432
Stallmer, Meghan 562
Stallworth, E. Faye 653
Stamper, Bill 162
Stamper, R. C. 50
Stamps, Jamie 426
Stanford, Shannon 89
Stanger, Edith M. 386
Stanke, Anita 479
Stanton, Larry A. 537
Stark, Hanna 476
Stark, Helen Atwood 429
Stark, Walter Lee 73
Starkey, Margaret 147
Starks, Sandra J. 111
Starnater, Darcey 574
Starr-Schmick, Leslie A. 612
Starrett, Alice M. 296
Stata, Evelyn 324
Staton, B. 213
Stauffacher, Robert Forrest 212
Stebbins, Doris E. 578
Steel, Alexander W. 291
Steele, Carol R. 331
Steele, Justin D. 407
Steele, Lucile H. 232
Steen, Debbie 496
Steepleton, Kelly 139
Stefanko, Brad 487
Stefany, Barbara 578
Steffey, Terry 165
Steigerwalt, Debra 209
Stein, Ada 365
Stein, Lourdes P. 144
Steinman, Diana 347
Stengel, Jessica 576
Stenhouse, Mary Livingston 232
Stephens, Mark 596
Stephensen, Randi 122
Stepp, Gina 272
Stevanovich, Judith W. 270
Stevens, Mark Lawrence 134
Steward, Bev 471
Stewart, Callie L. 389
Stewart, Hascal Vaughan 434
Stewart, Jessica 260
Stewart, Losita 550
Stewart, Mattie M. 511
Stewart, Ruby 187
Stewart, Ruth 26
Stiles, Donald C. 376
Still, Paul A. 29
Stillman, Heather J. 412
Stiltner, Megan 483
Stinson, Shelly 11
Stitely, Misty D. 546
Stockman, Lee 612
Stockwell, Carrie 571
Stoers, Lisa Marie 558
Stoicescu, Constantin 315
Stokes, Mary E. 238
Stokesberry, Megan 551
Stokley, Gladys L. 469
Stonaker, Victoria 219
Stone, Charles E. 410
Stone, Cynthia J. 301
Stone, Fiora 503
Stone, Jennifer 318
Stone, Marjorie A. 550
Stone, Troy J. 121
Storie, Diane J. 401
Stork, Richard H. 58
Stott, Fran 655
Stoughton, Jason P. 105, 385
Strathearn, Kristin 610
Stratman, Carol J. 486
Straub, MacKenzie 225
Strazzulla, Nicholas J. 244
Strehle, Carole 314
Stricker, Andrea Mae 259
Strickland, April 389
Strid, Burton L. 580
Stroebel, Loren 482
Strong, Amanda 382
Strong, Anthony P. 423
Strong, Darrell 6
Strong, Johnny 398
Strother, Jeannette L. 316
Stroud, Josie 504
Stuart, Laura 58
Stufflebeam, Thomas 5
Stulgin, Betty 321
Stup, J. Jerry 101
Sturdevant, Clark 339
Sturges, Sherry 208
Stutler, Jane 376
Stuver, Ella 365
Stuver, Jack 477
Sublett, Jean 506
Suelzer, Marianne Leah 600
Sugiura, Sally Anne 170
Suiters, Cloamae 466
Sullivan, Angela 458
Sullivan, Caitlin 470
Sullivan, Donna 497
Sullivan, Mary 527
Sullivan, Timothy P. 31
Sullivan, Wanda 122
Sullman, Wanda Dee 80
Summerall, Vivian C. 175
Summersill, Devonia Renee 426
Sundin, Marvel K. 531
Sung, Sherry 105
Susee, Chris 456
Suter, Suzanne T. 174
Sutherland, Carin A. 482
Sutton Jr., Darrell W. 280
Swager, T. Steven 8
Swagler, Andrew 304
Swaim, Gillian 444
Swanson, Donna L. 256
Swanson Sr., Frederick C. B. 74
Swartz, William 43
Sweatman, Heath 338
Sweaza, Derwood 302
Sweeney, Frank J. 266
Sweeny, J. P. 81
Swenson, Dave 343
Swetland, Christine 436
Swiderski, Mary J. 529
Swieringa, Marian A. 516
Swift, Donald F. 365
Swig, Lura Martin 134
Swiggum, Aaron 434
Swisher, Tracy B. 116

Swope, Donna L. 644
Syal, Harshi 584
Sykes, Delois J. 377
Sykes, Dianne 186
Sykes, Jeffrey 341
Szabo, Eileen E. 473
Szatkowski, Sally L. 56
Tabron, Paul L. 9
Tafoya, Laura 600
Tafoya, Michael Allan 136
Tague, Tiffany Marie 89
Tak, Newton 145
Tamuty, April 287
Tanksley, Dana 408
Tanner, Eulene 359
Tarantino, Patricia 7
Tarkington, Diane 488
Tarnow, Norma Jean 545
Tarvin, Laurie Ann 254
Tashash, Louis G. 252
Tate, Teena 109
Tatum, Betty Jeanne 583
Tawfik, David 379
Taylor, Amber 359
Taylor, Beverly 261
Taylor, Dawn M. 484
Taylor, Donnaclaire 486
Taylor, Kandice Dawn 234
Taylor, Krisinda 511
Taylor, Mary Eva 527
Taylor, Meoshameka L. 596
Taylor, P. J. 44
Taylor, Rosalind E. 173
Taylor, Tanya 114
Taylor, Terry Lee 180
Taylor, Wes 125
Tchinchinian, Maria A. 542
Teague, Faye 580
Teague, Kathy 623
Teague, Roberta I. 20
Teitler, Cloie J. 642
Tekavec, R. E. 124
Temple, Penny 43
Tennison, Chrissy 635
Tensley, John 645
Terry, Doris C. 261
Terry, Frank W. 415
Terry, Steven 67
Texier, Jacqueline Anne 227
Thacker, Nora L. 245
Thai, Khiem Vinh 233
Thayne, Robert D. 44
"The Traveler" 386
Theophilos, Constantina 416
Therian, Jennifer A. 583
Therrien, Stephen 68
Thesing, Colleen 394
Theule, Heidi 481
Thiele, Karen Ely 255
Thielen, Pam 47
Tholl, Paul T. 57
Thoman, Laura A. 545
Thomas, Andrew 474
Thomas, Chanel 377
Thomas, Dawn 258
Thomas, Eleanor Everly 305
Thomas, Esther M. 650
Thomas, Faye 500
Thomas, Jason 334
Thomas, John Edmond 411
Thomas, Lynn 135
Thomas, Natasha 654
Thomas, Orie 156
Thomas, Rebecca M. 77
Thomas, Sarah 72
Thomas, Vaudaline 82
Thomason II, Dillman Sean 383
Thomason, Judy 429
Thommi, Bridget 394
Thompson, Carrie 305
Thompson, Catherine 362
Thompson, Catherine R. 418
Thompson, Dewayne 8
Thompson, James M. 369
Thompson, Nedra 239
Thompson, Sean 7
Thompson, Theresa 45
Thompson, Vivian A. 79
Thomson, Kelly 515
Thornburg, Dorothy 343
Thornes, Robbie J. 225
Thornhill, Nikisha 232
Thornock, Carissa M. 472
Thornton, B. 44
Tibbs, Tom 60
Tice, Alex 320
Tickle, Jason 581
Tienne 111
Tiller, Aaron 634
Tiller, Leona 542
Todd, Penny L. 189
Tokumine, Wade 51
Tolar, Phillip 224
Toles, Jennifer 103
Tolman, Lianne Kinsella 140
Tomlinson, Donna Parks 496
Tompkins, Edgar L. 429
Tompkins, Michelle 611
Tonge, Sylvia 51
Tonnesen, Marilyn Kriney 613
Toole, Amy 317
Toppen, Doris 284
Toranzo, Karen M. 552
Torcasso, Mark Steven 527
Torre, Emily 587
Torres, Anthony 498
Torres, Carlos C. 378
Torres, Patricia I. 28
Toscano, Nicholas 616
Tosun, Sylvia 19
Totdahl, Katie 135
Totsch, Suzanne C. 34
Tovar, Jeffrey 581
Towle, Debra A. 594
Townsend, Kimberly Ann 131
Tracy, Vickie E. 221
Tramel, Taryn 52
Trask, Evelyn E. 589
Traugh, Jessica M. 360
Trauth, Jeanette 641
Traversa, Melissa 514
Trees, Sherry 109
Trehern, Megan Caroline 535
Tremblay, Esi 388
Tremblay, Robin L. 21
Trembone, Allen Christopher 454
Trent, Lucille 541
Trevithick, Eleanor 631
Triant, Diane Speare 579
Trice, Meleah 566
Trimby, Peggy 13
Trimmell, Steven 185
Tringali, Silvio John 74
Trishell, Carmen 635
Troll, Florence N. 588
Trombetta, Gina 325
Tromp, Jaimi Lyn 659
Troso, Matthew 556
Trotter, Thomas B. 198
Troudt, Elizabeth A. 323
Trout, Theresa A. 184
Troxell, Dianna 285
Troxell, Dickie E. 385
Trueay, Steve 194
Truelove, Trisha 26
Trujillo, Vida 61
Trull, Jens R. 417
Trulove, Angella 628
Truncellito, Sandy 37
Tschampel, Kathleen Marie 611
Tschupp, Edward J. 376
Tubosnick, Michael 131
Tucker, Chet 507
Tucker, Kenneth A. 609
Tucker, Sally Daly 201
Tucker, Sean 122
Tuckman, Margery Mulberg 229
Tudor, Jeannie 313
Tuffly, Bart 269
Tuller, Larae 557
Tunuchuk, Sandra 41
Turkington, Mildred 145
Turner, David G. 438
Turner, Jessica S. 274
Turner, Jessie D. 342
Turner, Kim 248
Turner, Marie Eubank 544
Turner, Peggy 121
Turner, Troyce L. 60
Tuttle, John H. 475
Tuttle, Jonathon D. 329
Twigg, Faye 362
Tyler, Tom 47
Tyler-Parker, Sydney 654
Tyrrell, David J. 353
Tyson II, Johnny A. 487
Tyson, Kate 242
Tyson, Wycliffe E. 53
Udo, Uko-Bendi 159
Udosen, Okokon Sam 106
Ulmer, Thomas P. 177
Umsteadt, Danyelle 638
Unanue, Lillian L. 231
Unbehaun, Gabriel 650
Underwood, Anthony 346
Unger, Robert J. M. 47
Ungersma, Dawn 329
Unsworth, Joyce 319
Uphoff Jr., Baron Joseph A. 104
Urash, Mike 515
Utrup, Allison 398
Uzunalich, Narcisa 528
Vachon, Gary 93
Valdez, Felix 630
Valenzuela, Susy 42
Valeu, Mary M. 519
Vallee, Arthur A. 502
Vallis, Akwelle 472
Van Buren, Harry Lee 414
Van Buskirk, Luegenia 254
Van Bysteren, Peter T. 98
Van Dyck, Haley 595
Van Hofwegen, Donna 591
Van Nav, Nicky 143
Van Nostern, Sara 177
Van Rooy, Cammie 490
Van Vreede, Sheree 81
Van Wagner, Gloria A. 458
VanDenbussche, Mary 126
VanderVort, Megan 135
Vanderwood, Deborah M. 592
Vandine, Shirley 661
VanMarter, Rebecca 209
Vannoy, Dennis 47
Vanover, David Matthew 462
Vardin, Jay 284
Varela, James A. 593
Varga, Melissa L. 522
Vargas-Willis, Gloria E. 275
Varrone, Natalie 598
Vasilis, Donna L. 406
Vaughan, Ashley 28
Vaughn, Carrie 302
Vazquez, Nadine 548
Vega Jr., Vladimir 114
Velazco, Julio E. 273
Velazquez, Rebecca 176
Venn, Jennifer 582
Vennebush, Jo Ann 291
Vento, Deanna L. 281
Venturini, Jean-Marie 431
Verlinda, Sharron 165
Vermette, Holly Marie 593
Verrinder, Kerry F. 541
Vestal, Louise 509
Vezzoli, Dante 320
Vick, S. J. 4
Victor, Carmel 462
Vidal, Camiel Renieta 590
Vien, Alicia 274
Vierra, Judith H. 576
Vigil, Veronica 167
Viljoen, Sharon A. 22
Villa, Nichole Leigh 241
Villega, George Michael 494
Villegas, Lorena Yvette 513
Vinal, Evelyn 594
Vincent, Timothy 214
Vinnik, Polina 216
Vinson, Karen 515
Vinson-Akins, La'Tesha 148
Vistica, Jean F. 632
Vitatoe, Wayne E. 214
Vivier, Elme 399
Vochatzer, Gary 301
Voelker, Dan 469
Vogel, -Tana 87
Volkmann, Patricia 82
Vollmar, David 396
Vora, Roohi 181
Vowell, Dawn Marie 632
Voyles, Tiffany Ann 43
Vroegindewey, Adrian C. 573
Vu, Tra 189
Vurture, Frank G. 493
Vyas, Swati 97
Wabschall, G. D. 49
Waddell, Diane Drishell 402
Waddell, LaVohn W. 522
Waddell, Melissa 553
Waddell, Wendy 201
Wade, Ashley 347
Wade, Lanny 524
Wade, Maria W. 188
Wade, Michele 133
Wade, Ruth 121
Wadkins, Pamela 50
Wagner, Edith 459
Wagner, Jill M. 275
Wagner, MaryAnn Blakely 598
Wahidi, Zhenus 92
Wahl, Jessica J. 638
Wakefield, Christine 506
Walding, Kelly L. 619
Walding, Miranda 521
Wale, Maria E. 154
Wales, Mary 233
Walker, Anona Bourassa 294
Walker, Camela 93
Walker, Gladys A. 401
Walker, Gwendolyn Y. 325
Walker, Linda G. 235
Walko, Ann 265
Wall, Jason D. 453

Wallace, Doyle E. 471
Wallace, Frances A. 430
Wallace, Juanita 474
Wallace, Katie Ellen 566
Wallace, Morgan A. 607
Wallach, Bradley Joseph 480
Wallachy, Mary Helen 236
Wallander, Richard A. 113
Wallin, Jeffrey T. 569
Wallmark, Elizabeth 307
Wallow, Terri 118
Walsh, Lynn 611
Walsh, Marcia M. 530
Walters, Lorie 150
Walters, Mitchel 622
Walters, Sharon 30
Walton, Anita H. 468
Walton, Marylee 625
Walton, Nathan 129
Walver, Cheryl S. 460
Wamsley, C. Huston 352
Wance, Madison Leigh 157
Wansor, Betty L. 444
Want, Mary L. 254
Wantz, James 293
Warburton, T. Lynette 185
Ward, Amy Michelle 351
Ward, Cassandra 380
Ward, Christina M. 355
Ward, Deanna 379
Ward, Joseph Allen 457
Ward, Karen 519
Ward, Steven James 201
Wardner, Brant J. 285
Ware, Salena L. 125
Warnecke, Terry 163
Warner, Berniece E. 578
Warner, Carolyn M. 99
Warner, Sharon 3
Warner, Tara 172
Warnock, Dina 644
Warnock, Emma 277
Warren, Mia 447
Wascher, Leisa A. 134
Washington, Cecelia E. 499
Washington, John W. 415
Waters, Ashley 649
Wathen, Lois L. 545
Watkins, Anita J. 483
Watkins, Cindy Anne 376
Watkins, Nell 559
Watson, Drew Von 574
Watson, Laura 127
Watson, Tandy Lenore 8
Watters, Katherine M. 238
Watts, Jennifer 453
Watts, Joshua D. 483
Watts, Katie 241
Watts, Stephen 169
Waugh, Betty M. 351
Waye, Romayne 70
Wear, Mary Ann 70
Weaver, Florence E. 580
Weaver, Onalee Ann Butler 526
Weaver, Vernieca G. 80
Webb, Ellen Kaye 440
Webb, Letha Rose 529
Webb, Mariana C. 532
Webber, Rinda L. 212
Weber, Chris B. 476
Weber, Lauren 543
Webster, Laura N. 597
Wedding, Brian K. 496
Wedemeyer, Herman A. 580
Weed, Dale A. 341
Weeks, Tammy A. 43
Wehde, Irene N. 400
Wehrle, Matt 597
Wehrly, Joe 581
Weiche, Juanita Hall 473
Weigand, Linda J. 615
Wein, Bella 391
Weinberg, Irving 321
Weinberg, PH.D, Kerry 598
Weinberg, Laurence M. 512
Weiner, Kristine 531
Weintraub, Julie Wright 299
Weisenthal, Jeffry 446
Weiss, Edward 452
Weiss, Robert B. 62
Weiss, Ursula 65
Welch, Calvin B. 475
Welch, Gary 306
Welch, John C. 576
Welch, Richard James 179
Weldy, Kathryn Nancy 511
Wellbaum, Mary Ellen 553
Welles, Notie L. 549
Wells, Kathryn 563
Wells, Martha 155
Wells, Miles B. 530
Wells, Rosemary 90
Welsh, Beth 486
Wendling, David 487
Wengland, Thressa J. 117
Wentland, Lindsey 518
Weppener, Barbara S. 278
Wertz, Delores Fore 395
Wessel, Patricia A. 165
West, Bertha 357
West, Bonnie Cantrell 466
West, Bonnie Jean 259
West, Karen L. 241
West, Lisa 547
West, Toni R. 41
Weston, Shirley A. 185
Whaley, Shirley A. 52
Wheeler, G. Egan 161
Wheeler, Janis 570
Whipple, Gail Baldwin 311
Whitaker, Teresa G. 22
White, Colene 296
White, Debbie 159
White, Deborah 327
White, Diana Lee 482
White, Edward J. 366
White II, Alfred C. 490
White, Joanne F. Wisener 287
White, Lillian C. 229
White, Marie R. 247
White, Mary 522
White, MaryAnn 246
White, Shauntay Dunbar 193
Whitehair, Heidi Rouleau 411
Whitehead, Jacky R. 262
Whiteside, Katina 530
Whitlock, Ivy 454
Whitmire, Bonita 302
Whitmire, Jamie 584
Whitmore, Charlotte 330
Whittaker, David L. 472
Whitteker, Katie 140
Whittemore, Nathan 521
Whittington, Shirley R. 166
Whittle, Erma 348
Whitty, Kristine M. 567
Wiatt, A. Roberta 7
Wickl, Nicola 539
Wicklund, Windy 78
Wietecha, Andy 592
Wiggs, Giula S. 290
Wilbraham, Linda 248
Wilbur, Laurel J. 250
Wilbur, T. L. 176
Wilcox, D. 69
Wild, Drew Ian 586
Wilde, Kory 517
Wilder, Cathy Anne Bales 293
Wiles, Wanda 172
Wilhelm, Corinna M. 364
Wilhelmy, Gus 322
Wilkie, Wilma 190
Wilkins, Kelley 239
Wilkinson, Judy L. 588
Wilkinson, Lynn E. 234
Wilkinson, Margaret 526
Willett, Dara 495
Willett, Gracie L. 339
Willey, Jessica 418
Willey, Shirley Jean 170
Williams, Alexandria 31
Williams, Angela 330
Williams, Angelique 262
Williams, Anthony S. 280
Williams, Barbara 378
Williams, Barbarette 500
Williams, Brenda C. 378
Williams, Carole Knaul 573
Williams, Darryl 355
Williams, Debra 595
Williams, Debra Simon 266
Williams, Helen M. 381
Williams II, Edward 587
Williams, James D. 658
Williams, Janet C. 573
Williams, Janeta 331
Williams, Jason 474
Williams, Jeffrey S. 325
Williams, Jessica M. 590
Williams, Joshua 439
Williams, Laura 517
Williams, Lillian H. 151
Williams, Lonnie 239
Williams, Lori D. 136
Williams, Nancy 609
Williams, Patricia A. 41
Williams, Reanne 54
Williams, Renee E. 211
Williams, Sharel 100
Williams, Sheena R. 170
Williams, Stanley 168
Williams, Tiffany Ann 17
Williams, Timothy E. 107
Williams, Willie C. 210
Williamson, H. L. 27
Williamson, Marguerite Pons 517
Willinhart, Elaine 351
Willis, Bill G. 640
Wills, Beth Sudduth 396
Wilson, Bob 448
Wilson, Brenda 385
Wilson, Clyde 343
Wilson, David J. 427
Wilson, Douglas 364
Wilson, Elizabeth Briggs 275
Wilson, Grace L. 457
Wilson, Jamie 477
Wilson, Jessie Dawson 309
Wilson, Karen M. 522
Wilson, Lyda R. 254
Wilson, Michael 425
Wilson, Michele Irene 541
Wilson, Nellie M. 533
Wilson, Regina 26
Wilson, Ruby Zundell 48
Wilson, Terri R. 204
Wilson, V. 22
Wimberly, Juanita 401
Winchester, Dewey R. 379
Winckler, Laura 235
Wind, T. A. 176
Windsor, Lang 532
Winfield, Lisa 512
Winger, Dennis K. 378
Wingo, Vickie K. 21
Winnen, Ken 527
Wirkus, Lydia H. 556
Wise, Alexandria 455
Wise, Bridget 641
Wise, Dorothy A. 626
Wise, Jenny 317
Wiseman, Clifton E. 367
Witham, Helen 441
Withee, Beverly 648
Witherspoon, Debra Lyn 429
Withrow, D. Michael 173
Witt, Kyle 569
Witt, Marty 246
Witte, Kristin 607
Wix, Wyndom 219
Wohlgelernter, Talia 94
Wojciek, Amanda 312
Wojtala, Rick 174
Wold, Carol A. 398
Wolf, Charlotte 635
Wolf, Sheldon 186
Wolf, Susie 55
Wolfe, Heather Dawn 257
Wolfe, Michelle 126
Wolfgang 218
Wolski, Kristina 597
Womble, Leotha 145
Womble, Michelle A. 560
Wong, Jennifer 388
Wonson, Kimberly D. 134
Wood, Darlene 372
Wood, David 478
Wood Jr., Kenneth W. 140
Wood, Kriston B. 230
Wood, Tara 211
Wood, Virchel E. 168
Wood, Yvonne 74
Woodard, Mozelle 564
Wooden, Kathy 143
Woodland, Carole 370
Woodley, Jeffrey 422
Woodley, John 257
Woodruff, Debra L. 322
Woods, Judy 376
Woods, Nina L. 530
Woodson, Donald A. 502
Wooley, Geraldine H. 265
Woolf, Lynda L. 565
Workman, Kristy Ellis 154
Worlow, Derek 439
Worrell, Tyson 114
Worthington, Kary J. 245
Wrede, Lu 237
Wrigglesworth, Sandra 159
Wright, B. Renee 25
Wright, Curtis L. 404
Wright, David 258
Wright, David A. 302
Wright, Earl E. 354
Wright Jr., Robert 193
Wright, Marion H. 532
Wright, Philip M. 168
Wright, Robert D. 54
Wrightsil, Zachary 76
Wring, Bo 389
Wuest, Rebecca 172
Wuesthoff, Nancy Morgan 603
Wunderlich, Kiffany 128
Wurzer, Robin D. 116

Wyatt, H. Winfield 93
Wyatt, Joseph T. 23
Wyatt, Sherry L. 11
Wylie, Malou 531
Yablansky, Barbara Vecchione 580
Yacht, Derk J. Vander 300
Yager, Theda D. 81
Yandell, Norma V. 516
Yang, Linda 529
Yarbrough, Dan 299
Yardley, John Wallace 414
Yaroslawski, Mary Frances 63
Yasparro, Rosemary Muntz 171
Yell, Chester R. 313
Yesaeil, Ramina S. 170
Yinger, Martha L. 243
Yokeley, Sandra 171
Yokley, April Robinson 493
Yolo, Tamara DeAnn 207
Young, April 575
Young, Daniel L. 476
Young, Henry William 497
Young, James D. 371
Young, James Wesley 577
Young, Jennifer 573
Young, Karen Terese 558
Young, Margaret B. 164
Young, Pauline 18
Young, Sabrina 66
Youngblood Jr., William Leddrew 117
Younger-Scott, Bonnie 636
Youngren, Margaret R. 624
Younke, Michael Douglas 617
Yuschock, Jonathan M. 266
Zachery, Kevin M. 150
Zakrzewski, Lisa 137
Zambrano, April Dawn 488
Zamora, Roseann 163
Zaritzky, Aaron 484
Zavala, Peggy 53
Zboran, Lori A. 552
Zeller, Margie Davis 237
Zeller, Richard 61
Zemann, Melissa 141
Zepponi, Frances 393
Zerafa, David A. 590
Zerfas, Terry 221
Ziegler, Karen 540
Ziehms, Shelley 182
Zielinski, Brian 594
Zielke, Pauline Good 50
Zimmerman, Jean 287
Zimmerman Jr., Donald D. 278
Zimmerman, Linda 516
Zimmerman, Rebecca 14
Zimmerman, Susan 71
Zinnante, Bonnie 629
Zissu, Ana 301
Zitting, Shanna 216
Zolcienski, Melanie 249
Zuolenski, Linda 148